Collins
Gage
Canadian
Paperback
Dictionary

 Collins

NELSON EDUCATION

NELSON EDUCATION

Page Design: Artplus Ltd.

Database: TotalGraphics

Library and Archives Canada Cataloguing in Publication

Collins Gage Canadian paperback dictionary.
ISBN 0-17-611781-4

1. English language—Canada—Dictionaries.
2. English language—Dictionaries. 3. Canadianisms (English)—Dictionaries.

PE3235.C54 2006   423
C2006-901163-X

Collins Gage Canadian reference resources combine the strengths of the Collins and Gage reference lines. They contain the most accurate and up-to-date information, prepared in consultation with Canadian educators for Canadian students.

Collins is one of the world's leading reference publishers. The **Collins Word Web** contains 125 million words of Canadian English and grows at over 1.5 million words per month.

Gage represents a 40-year tradition of Canadian dictionary making. Today, Gage is the reference division of **Nelson Education Ltd.**, Canada's foremost educational publisher.

CONTENTS

Collins Gage Canadian Paperback Dictionary

Editorial and Production

Director of Publishing
Bev Buxton

**General Manager, Literacy,
Reference, and International**
Kevin Martindale

**Director of Publishing,
Literacy and Reference**
Joe Banel

Publisher, Reference
David Friend

**Executive Managing Editor,
Development**
Darleen Rotozinski

**Senior Program Manager,
Reference**
Ann Downar

Assistant Editor
Lisa Peterson

Production Coordinator
Cathy Deak

Creative Director
Ken Phipps

Cover Design
Johanna Liburd

Compositor
Zenaida Diores

Editorial Team, Original Edition

Joe Banel
Chelsea Donaldson
Ann Downar
Jan Harkness
T. K. Pratt
Darleen Rotozinski
Debbie Sawczak
Tom Shields
Fraser Sutherland
Carol Waldock

Consulting Editor

T.K. Pratt
Professor Emeritus of English,
University of Prince Edward Island

Reviewers

CANADIAN ENGLISH

by T.K. Pratt

Canadian English is a unique blend of elements shared, partly shared, and original. It is all around us. Take, for example, our names for holidays and other special days of the year. Like the Americans, we celebrate *Groundhog Day* and *Halloween*. Like them we also celebrate *Labour Day* and *Thanksgiving*, but no American would spell the first with a *u*, or hold the second as early as October. Unlike the Americans, but like our linguistic predecessors, the British, we relax on *Boxing Day*. Somewhat like them we recall past sacrifices on *Remembrance Day*, rather than their *Remembrance Sunday* or the *Americans' Veteran's Day* and *Memorial Day*. We are more British than the British themselves with *Victoria Day*, but we certainly have our own national celebration, *Canada Day* (formerly *Dominion Day*). Add to the mix our regional differences: some but not all Canadians have a Civic Holiday in August, recently named *Simcoe Day* in Ontario; only Albertans can take *Family Day* in February; only Québeckers celebrate *Saint-Jean-Baptiste Day*.

This Canadian blend is even more in evidence in our politics. Side by side with terms from the British parliamentary tradition—*back bench, the House, MP, Official Opposition, press gallery, Throne Speech, whip*—are terms uniquely Canadian: *Crown corporation, First Nations, Grits, notwithstanding clause, premier, red Tories, and SIN*. We have a federal system like the US, but only Canadians can now be *federalists*, or disregard *the Senate*, or consider a *lieutenant-governor* above politics. And here too provinces differ with each other, for example calling their legislators *MPP's, MLA's, or MHA's* (*Members of the Provincial Parliament, Legislative Assembly, or House of Assembly*). And only in Québec can they be *MNA's* (*Members of the National Assembly*).

In fact the Canadian blend spreads through a great many aspects of our existence. We use borrowings from native languages to describe the natural environment— *caribou, muskeg, tamarack*—along with more borrowings that teach survival in that environment—*kayak, mackinaw, parka*. Similarly, Canadian French has contributed *portage, prairie, cache, traverse,* and *tuque*. We mingle terms given by Canada to the world—*kerosene, pablum*—with those brought here by the world's immigrants: *chow mein, ravioli, smorgasbord*. With the British we use *taps*, but we avoid their *petrol*. We say *railway* more often than the American *railroad*, and similarly *reserve* not *reservation*, *exclamation mark* not *exclamation point*, *bag of groceries* not *sack*, and *zed* not *zee*. We freely intersperse usages that are wholly Canadian, like *deke, hoser, impaired driving, Mountie*, and *pogey* with well known regionalisms like *outport, poutine, concession road*, and *potlatch*, and with international words that have specially charged overtones in Canada like *Anglophone, bilingualism, Francophone*. We even combine English phrases with French word order: *Lake Huron, Revenue Canada, Theatre Prince Edward Island*.

As with vocabulary (and, in the last example, grammar), so with pronunciation. Canadians abroad are often mistaken for Americans, and that is only to be expected given our shared linguistic history on this continent. But thanks to our stronger British heritage we use (or tolerate) several double pronunciations in, for example, *either, leisure, lieutenant,* and *schedule*. We would immediately identify as British any speaker who rhymed *clerk* with *dark*, but equally we know Americans by their rhyming *lever* with *sever*.

Our spelling system is also a mixed bag, jumbled differently in different parts of the country. Most of us share with the British such spellings as *catalogue* or *cheque*. Yet some Canadians, especially westerners, spell these words the American way, and no Canadian would accept the British *tyre*.

Our best-known preferences within the British model are the *-our* and *-re* words: *colour* and *humour, kilometre* and *theatre*. Even here, however, the chosen spelling can depend on who is writing and what is being written about. Albertans are more likely than British Columbians to be *neighbours*, and an arts complex is more likely than a hockey rink to be a *Centre*.

This Canadian English blend is a natural result of the history of the country. Early English explorers and traders picked up useful words from the native peoples and the French who were here before them. The very name *Canada* is probably based on an Iroquois word transmitted through Canadian French. But it was not until the eighteenth century that English began to be a significant language in the territory. In the Treaty of Utrecht, 1713, France gave up Nova Scotia, and so opened it to English settlers from New England. France's loss of all its North American colonies after the fall of Québec, 1759, meant still more English speakers both in the Maritime provinces and in Québec. Shortly afterward came the American Revolution, 1776-1783, which caused some 50 000 United Empire Loyalists, determined to remain loyal to the king of England, to flee what is now the United States. Again the population of the Maritimes and Québec swelled, but now for the first time Ontario began to get English-speaking settlers as well. A second, stronger wave of Americans—the "Late Loyalists"—arrived in the last decade of the century, moved not so much by loyalty as by hunger for land. They came especially to Ontario, bringing its population to 100 000 by 1812. The American base layer of the Canadian English mixture was thus laid down. When the rest of the country began to be settled, it was anglophone immigrants from Ontario who led the westward movement, carrying their dialect with them.

The Loyalists and their descendants confirmed their allegiance to the crown by defining themselves in the War of 1812 as 'not American', something Canadians have been doing ever since. But the authorities in London now thought it prudent to leaven the number of former republicans with settlers directly from the British Isles. As a result, some two million speakers of English crossed the Atlantic to Canada during the nineteenth century. From a language standpoint, the policy was only a partial success. Not only did the children of these immigrants conform their speech to that of the people already here (just as immigrant children continue to do), but the many Irish and Scottish among them found that speaking like Americans was a convenient way of rebelling against England. Nevertheless, the British overlay in Canadian English comes from these speakers, and especially from their predominant influence in government, education, and publishing.

Our recent linguistic history has been the most eventful of all. Once again there is fear that Canadian English will disappear into general American, this time under the pressure of free trade, media concentration, the Internet, and American-dominated globalization. For example, some Canadian books for children now employ spellings that are totally non-British, the better to assure sales south of the border. For a vocabulary example, the word *chesterfield*, until recently a strong marker of Canadian vocabulary, appears to have collapsed under the weight of the more American *couch*.

Yet the larger view of history shows that this fear of dominance has always been present, and reactions against such Americanization are a prevailing feature of the Canadian dialect. A striking example on this side is that, beyond the introduction of popular and often transient vocabulary, neither radio nor film nor television had the homogenizing effect in the twentieth century that was widely predicted. Similarly, Canadian English will persist in the twenty-first century as long as we have distinctively Canadian things to talk about. There is no lack of these, whether concerning our unique environment, our native peoples, our immigration policies, our blend of multilingualism and bilingualism, our particular mix of federal and provincial politics—or the days of the year when we like to look at our traditions and celebrate who we are.

USING THIS DICTIONARY

The *Collins Gage Canadian Paperback Dictionary* aims to include as many of the most commonly needed words and meanings as possible in a compact format, without sacrificing any of the kinds of information people expect when they look up a word in the dictionary. This is helped by the following:

Grouping of entries sharing a root

The root word or most common word opens the entry, but included are derived words and compounds that build on this root. For example, under the main entry **back**, you will find *backing, back bacon, backlash,* etc., as well as the idioms *back out of, turn one's back on,* etc.

This makes it easy to find related words. For example, you may want to know the adjective that corresponds to the verb *deride*, or the noun that corresponds to the adjective *supreme*. It also spares needless repetition: the meaning and pronunciation of derived words have been omitted (as for *gluttonous* and *gluttony* under **glutton**), where they are obvious from the root word.

Etymologies

Etymologies are given for each main entry. The source of the word has been kept, often with links that show the main changes in form and sense.

Inflections

Any inflected forms that follow a regular pattern (such as *–y* turning to *–ies* or *–ied* in a plural or past form, or a final *–e* being dropped before adding an ending) have not been included. Truly irregular inflections, that is, unpredictable ones (*Do I double the consonant before adding the ending, or not?*), and variants are all listed.

Pronunciation

Pronunciation is given for each main entry, using the International Phonetic Alphabet. See the inside back cover for the pronunciation key.

Arrangement of parts in an entry

For details about how entries are arranged, see the sample on the opposite page. This sample can also be found on the inside of the front cover.

Abbreviations used in this dictionary

Throughout this dictionary you will find that frequently used words have been abbreviated. Here is a list of these abbreviations.

abbrev	abbreviation	obj	objective
adj	adjective	orig	originally
adv	adverb	pl	plural
c	century	poss	possessive
Cdn.	Canadian	pp	past participle
conj	conjunction	ppr	present participle
def.	definition	prep	preposition
esp	especially	pron	pronoun
fem.	feminine	pt	past tense
interj	interjection	sg	singular
masc.	masculine	subj	subjective
n	noun	v	verb

guide word **entry word** **pronunciation** **part of speech** **etymology** **definition number**

9

toast 902

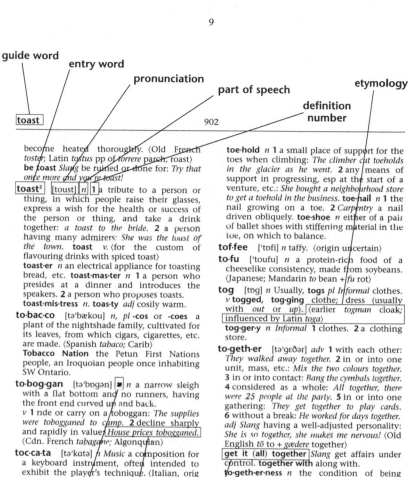

become heated thoroughly. (Old French *toster*; Latin *tostus* pp of *torrere* parch, roast) **be toast** *Slang* be ruined or done for: *Try that once more and you're toast!*

toast² [toust] *n* **1** a tribute to a person or thing, in which people raise their glasses, express a wish for the health or success of the person or thing, and take a drink together: *a toast to the bride.* **2** a person having many admirers: *She was the toast of the town.* **toast** *v.* (for the custom of flavouring drinks with spiced toast)
toast·er *n* an electrical appliance for toasting bread, etc. **toast·mas·ter** *n* **1** a person who presides at a dinner and introduces the speakers. **2** a person who proposes toasts. **toast·mis·tress** *n.* **toas·ty** *adj* cosily warm.

to·bac·co [tə'bækou] *n, pl* -**cos** or -**coes** a plant of the nightshade family, cultivated for its leaves, from which cigars, cigarettes, etc. are made. (Spanish *tabaco*; Carib)
Tobacco Nation the Petun First Nations people, an Iroquoian people once inhabiting SW Ontario.

to·bog·gan [tə'bɒgən] *n* a narrow sleigh with a flat bottom and no runners, having the front end curved up and back.
v **1** ride or carry on a toboggan: *The supplies were tobogganed to camp.* **2** decline sharply and rapidly in value: *House prices tobogganed.* (Cdn. French *tabagane*; Algonquian)

toc·ca·ta [tə'kɑtə] *n Music* a composition for a keyboard instrument, often intended to exhibit the player's technique. (Italian, orig pp of *toccare* touch)

toc·sin ['tɒksən] *n* an alarm sounded on a bell. (French; Provençal *tocasenh; tocar* strike, touch + *senh* bell)

to·day [tə'deɪ] *n* the present day, time, or period: *The photographer of today has many types of film to choose from.*
adv **1** on or during this day: *I have to go to the dentist today.* **2** at the present time or period: *these days: Most Canadian homes today have a refrigerator.* (Old English *tō dæge* on (the) day)

tod·dle ['tɒdəl] *v* walk with short, unsteady steps, as a baby does. **tod·dle** *n.* (origin unknown)
tod·dler *n* a young child, esp one between the ages of one and two or three.

tod·dy ['tɒdi] *n* a usually hot drink made of an alcoholic liquor mixed with water, sugar,

toe·hold *n* **1** a small place of support for the toes when climbing: *The climber cut toeholds in the glacier as he went.* **2** any means of support in progressing, esp at the start of a venture, etc.: *She bought a neighbourhood store to get a toehold in the business.* **toe·nail** *n* **1** the nail growing on a toe. **2** *Carpentry* a nail driven obliquely. **toe·shoe** *n* either of a pair of ballet shoes with stiffening material in the toe, on which to balance.

tof·fee ['tɒfi] *n* taffy. (origin uncertain)

to·fu ['toufu] *n* a protein-rich food of a cheeselike consistency, made from soybeans. (Japanese; Mandarin *to* bean + *fu* rot)

tog [tɒg] *n* Usually, **togs** *pl Informal* clothes. *v* **togged**, **tog·ging** clothe; dress (usually with *out* or *up*). (earlier *togman* cloak; influenced by Latin *toga*)
tog·ger·y *n Informal* **1** clothes. **2** a clothing store.

to·geth·er [tə'gɛðər] *adv* **1** with each other: *They walked away together.* **2** in or into one unit, mass, etc.: *Mix the two colours together.* **3** in or into contact: *Bang the cymbals together.* **4** considered as a whole: *All together, there were 25 people at the party.* **5** in or into one gathering: *They get together to play cards.* **6** without a break: *He worked for days together.* *adj Slang* having a well-adjusted personality: *She is so together, she makes me nervous!* (Old English *tō* to + *gædere* together)
get it (all) together *Slang* get affairs under control. **together with** along with.
to·geth·er·ness *n* the condition of being closely associated or united, esp in family or social activities.

USAGE
A singular subject followed by 'together with—' still takes a singular verb: *My uncle, together with my two cousins, was there to meet me.* Compare this with: *My uncle and my two cousins were there to meet me.*

tog·gle ['tɒgəl] *n* **1** a pin, bolt, etc. put through a loop to keep it in place, to act as a fastening for a coat, etc. **2** *Computers* a function that is activated and deactivated by the same command. **tog·gle** *v.* (perhaps earlier *tog* tug)
toggle switch an electric switch having a projecting lever that is pushed up or down to open or close the circuit.

toil [tɔɪl] *n* hard work: *to succeed after years of*

Canadianism   **example**   **idiom**   **related word**   **feature box** (usage, grammar, confusables, synonyms, spelling, punctuation)

Aa

a or **A** [ei] *n, pl* **a's** or **A's** 1 the first letter of the English alphabet, or any speech sound represented by it. 2 the first person or thing in a series: *A works twice as hard as B.* 3 **A** the highest grade in a rating system: *grade A eggs.* 4 *Music* the sixth tone in the scale of C major. 5 **A** the type of human blood containing antigen A, one of the four main types in the ABO system.

a *indefinite article* 1 a word used before singular nouns when the person or thing referred to is not specific. 2 per; for each: *ten cents a bag.*

a– *prefix* not or without; a form of **an–**. ⟨Greek⟩

aard·vark ['ɑrd,vɑrk] *n* an African burrowing mammal with a very long, flat, sticky tongue with which it catches ants and termites. An aardvark is about 1.5 m long. ⟨Afrikaans; Dutch *aarde* earth + *vark* pig⟩

ab– *prefix* from, away, away from, or off. ⟨Latin *ab-*⟩

a·back [ə'bæk] *adv* **taken aback,** taken by surprise. ⟨Old English *on bæc*⟩

ab·a·cus ['æbəkəs] *n, pl* **-cus·es** or **-ci** [-,saɪ] *or* [-,si] a calculating device consisting of a frame with rows of counters or beads that slide up and down in grooves or on wires. ⟨Greek *abax, abacos*⟩

ab·a·lo·ne [,æbə'louni] *n* any of several species of edible marine snail found mainly along temperate Pacific coasts, with a single flat, ear-shaped shell used for buttons and ornaments. ⟨American Spanish *abulón*⟩

a·ban·don [ə'bændən] *v* 1 give up entirely; relinquish: *to abandon an idea.* 2 leave without intending to return; desert: *to abandon a sinking ship.* 3 yield (oneself) completely (to a feeling, impulse, etc.): *to abandon oneself to grief.*
n complete freedom from restraint: *to celebrate with abandon.* **a·ban·don·ment** *n.* ⟨Old French *a ban doner* give over to another's jurisdiction⟩
a·ban·doned *adj* 1 deserted: *an abandoned homestead.* 2 completely unrestrained.

a·base [ə'beis] *v* make lower in rank or prestige; humiliate; degrade. **a·base·ment** *n.* ⟨Old French *abaissier*; Latin *bassus* low⟩

a·bash [ə'bæʃ] *v* embarrass and confuse; make shy or slightly ashamed. **a·bash·ment** *n.* ⟨Old French *esbaïr* be astonished⟩

a·bate [ə'beit] *v* become less violent, intense, etc. **a·bate·ment** *n.* ⟨Old French *abatre* beat down; Latin *ad-* + *battere*⟩

ab·at·toir [,æbə'twɑr] *or* ['æbə,twɑr] *n* slaughterhouse. ⟨French⟩

ab·bey ['æbi] *n, pl* **-beys** 1 a monastery or convent governed by an **abbot** or **abbess**. 2 a church that was once a monastery or convent. ⟨Latin *abbatia; abbas, -atis* abbot⟩

ab·bre·vi·ate [ə'brivi,eit] *v* 1 make (a word or phrase) shorter so that a part stands for the whole: *We can abbreviate Alberta to AB.* 2 make briefer: *She was asked to abbreviate her speech.* **ab·bre·vi·a·tion** *n.* ⟨Latin *ad-* to + *brevis* short. Compare ABRIDGE.⟩

CONFUSABLES
An **abbreviation** is a shortened form of a word. A **contraction** is a combination of two words, the last of which is an abbreviation: *isn't, it's.*

ab·di·cate ['æbdɪ,keit] *v* give up or renounce (an office or responsibility). **ab·di·ca·tion** *n.* ⟨Latin *ab-* away + *dicare* proclaim⟩

ab·do·men ['æbdəmən] *n* the part of the body containing the stomach, the intestines, and other digestive organs. **ab·dom·i·nal** *adj.* ⟨Latin⟩

ab·duct [æb'dʌkt] *v* carry off (a person) by force or deceit. **ab·duc·tion** *n.* **ab·duc·tor** *n.* ⟨Latin *ab-* away + *ducere* lead⟩

A·beg·weit ['æbəg,weit] *n* ✺ a First Nations name for Prince Edward Island, meaning 'cradle of the waves'. ⟨Mi'kmaq⟩

Ab·e·na·ki [,æbə'næki] *n, pl* **-ki** or **-kis** 1 a member of the First Nations or Native Americans living mainly in southern Québec and Maine. 2 the Algonquian language spoken by the Abenaki. **Ab·e·na·ki** *adj.* Also, **Ab·na·ki.** ⟨Algonquin⟩

ab·er·rant [æ'berənt] *or* ['æbərənt] *adj* deviating from what is regular or normal.
n an aberrant person or thing. **ab·er·rance** *n.* **ab·er·ra·tion** *n.* ⟨Latin *errare* wander⟩

a·bet [ə'bet] *v* encourage or help, esp in doing something wrong. **a·bet·tor** or **a·bet·ter** *n.* ⟨Old French *abeter* arouse⟩

a·bey·ance [ə'beiəns] *n* a state of suspended action: *The whole question is being held in abeyance until a new committee is formed.* ⟨French *abeiance*; Latin *ad-* at + *batare* gape⟩

ab·hor [æb'hɔr] *v* detest; loathe. **ab·hor·rence** *n.* **ab·hor·rent** *adj.* ⟨Latin *ab-* from + *horrere* dread⟩

a·bide [ə'baid] *v* **a·bode** or **a·bid·ed**, **a·bid·ing** 1 put up with; endure; tolerate (usually negative): *She cannot abide stinginess.* 2 stay; remain: *"Though much is taken, much abides."* **a·bid·ing** *adj.* ⟨Old English *ābīdan* stay on⟩
abide by accept and act upon.

a·bil·i·ty [ə'biləti] *n* 1 the power to do a specific thing: *This software gives you the ability to control inventory.* 2 skill or talent: *He has great ability as a writer.* ⟨Latin *habilitas; habilis.* See ABLE.⟩

a·bi·ot·ic ['eibaɪ'ɒtɪk] *adj* to do with the absence of living things.

ab·ject ['æbdʒɛkt] *adj* 1 wretched; miserable:

abject poverty. **2** deserving contempt: *an abject flatterer.* **3** showing humiliation or complete resignation: *an abject apology.* **ab·ject·ly** *adv.* **ab·jec·tion** *n.* ⟨Latin *abjectus; ab-* down + *jacere* throw⟩

ab·jure [æb'dʒur] *v* swear to give up: *to abjure one's religion, to abjure alcohol.* **ab·ju·ra·tion** *n.* ⟨Latin *ab-* away + *jurāre* swear⟩

a·blaze [ə'bleiz] *adv, adj* (never precedes a noun) burning; blazing.

a·ble ['eibəl] *adj* **a·bler, a·blest 1** having power, means, opportunity, etc. (*to*): *able to swim. We are not able to attend.* **2** skilled; competent: *She is an able hockey player.* **a·bly** *adv.* ⟨Latin *habilis,* apt, manageable⟩
a·ble–bod·ied ['eibəl ,bɒdid] *adj* physically fit; strong and healthy.

ab·lu·tion [ə'bluʃən] *n* the act of washing oneself. ⟨Latin *ablutio* a washing off⟩

ab·ne·gate ['æbnɪ,geit] *v* **1** surrender; give up (a right or privilege). **2** deny; recant (a belief or doctrine). **ab·ne·ga·tion** *n.* ⟨Latin *ab-* off, away + *negare* deny⟩

ab·nor·mal [æb'nɔrməl] *adj* deviating from what is normal. **ab·nor·mal·ly** *adv.* **ab·nor·mal·cy** *n.*
ab·nor·mal·i·ty *n* an abnormal thing, event, or condition: *an abnormality of the blood.*

a·board [ə'bɔrd] *adv, prep* **1** on, in, or into a ship, train, bus, aircraft, etc. **2** as part of a group or undertaking: *We've brought two new salespeople aboard.*

a·bode [ə'boud] *n Poetic* a home.

a·bol·ish [ə'bɒlɪʃ] *v* do away with (a law, institution, or custom) completely; put an end to. ⟨French *abolir;* Latin *abolere* destroy⟩
ab·o·li·tion *n* the act of abolishing a specific law or practice, esp slavery or capital punishment. **ab·o·li·tion·ist** *n.*

a·bom·i·na·ble [ə'bɒmənəbəl] *adj* **1** evil, disgusting, or detestable. **2** very bad: *abominable spelling.* **a·bom·i·na·bly** *adv.* ⟨Latin *ab-* off + *ominari* prophesy⟩
abominable snowman a humanlike monster supposed to inhabit the higher parts of the Himalayas. It is called 'yeti' by the local people. **a·bom·i·nate** *v* feel revulsion or hatred toward. **a·bom·i·na·tion** *n* a revolting thing.

ab·o·rig·i·ne [,æbə'rɪdʒəni] *n* **1** Usually, **Aborigine** a member of a dark-skinned people who are the original inhabitants of Australia. **2** one of the earliest known inhabitants of a country. ⟨Latin *ab origine* from the beginning⟩
ab·o·rig·i·nal *adj* **1** existing in a place from the beginning. **2** Often, **Aboriginal** of or to do with the original or earliest known inhabitants of a region; in Canada, to do with the First Nations, Métis, or Inuit.

USAGE
See the note at **Indian.**

a·bort [ə'bɔrt] *v* **1** of a fetus, be or cause to be expelled before it is viable. **2** cut short or cancel: *to abort a space flight.* **a·bor·tion** *n.*

a·bor·tive *adj.* ⟨Latin *abortus; ab-* amiss + *oriri* be born⟩
a·bor·tion·ist *n* a person in favour of, or performing, abortion.

a·bound [ə'baund] *v* be plentiful; be rich (*in*): *Alberta abounds in oil.* ⟨Latin *ab-* off + *undare* flow⟩

a·bout [ə'baut] *prep* **1** to do with: *a book about bridges.* **2** around: *a fence about the garden.* **3** doing: *I must be about my business.* **4** defined or motivated by: *This company is about service and integrity.*
adv **1** nearly: *The buckets and tubs are about full.* **2** all around: *The girl looked about.* **3** stirring; active: *up and about.* **4** in the opposite direction: *Face about!*
⟨Old English *onbūtan* on the outside of⟩
about to going, intending, or ready to: *The plane is about to take off.* **go about** tackle; approach (a task): *I'm not sure how to go about putting in a bathroom.* **how** or **what about** used to make a suggestion: *How about a game of tennis?*
a·bout–face [ə'baut ,feis] *n* a complete change of direction, opinion, etc.: *At the first hint of opposition, the policy committee did an about-face.* **a·bout-face** [ə,baut 'feis] *v.*

a·bove [ə'bʌv] *adv* **1** in a higher place: *The sky is above.* **2** earlier in a piece of writing: *as mentioned above.*
prep **1** in or to a higher place than: *Birds fly above the trees.* **2** more than: *The weight is above a tonne.* **3** too difficult for: *That joke is far above him.* **4** too moral or dignified for: *She is above lying.*
n the **above** what is written above. ⟨OE *abufan*⟩
a·bove·board [ə'bʌv,bɔrd] *or* [ə'bʌv'bɔrd] *adv, adj* without tricks or concealment.

a·brade [ə'breid] *v* wear away by rubbing. ⟨Latin *ab-* off + *radere* scrape⟩
a·bra·sion *n* **1** the act of abrading. **2** a place scraped by rubbing. **a·bra·sive** [ə'breisɪv] *or* [ə'breizɪv] *adj* **1** wearing away by rubbing; causing abrasion: *the abrasive action of water on stone.* **2** of someone's manner, irritating; likely to offend: *an abrasive personality.* **a·bra·sive** *n.* **a·bra·sive·ly** *adv.* **a·bra·sive·ness** *n.*

a·breast [ə'brɛst] *adv, adj* (never precedes a noun) side by side: *marching three abreast.*

a·bridge [ə'brɪdʒ] *v* make shorter, esp something written; condense. **a·bridg·ment** or **a·bridge·ment** *n.* ⟨Old French *abrégier;* Latin *abbreviare.* See ABBREVIATE.⟩

a·broad [ə'brɒd] *adv* **1** outside one's country, esp overseas. **2** out of doors, esp away from one's home: *Fewer enemy patrols were abroad at night.* **3** going around; in circulation: *There is a rumour abroad that the mayor is resigning.*

ab·ro·gate ['æbrə,geit] *v* abolish by legislation. **ab·ro·ga·tion** *n.* **ab·ro·ga·ble** *adj.* ⟨Latin *ab-* away + *rogare* demand⟩

a·brupt [ə'brʌpt] *adj* **1** sudden: *an abrupt end.* **2** very steep: *an abrupt slope.* **3** so short in speech or manner as to appear rude.

a·brupt·ly adv. **a·brupt·ness** n. ⟨Latin abruptus; ab- off + rumpere break⟩

ABS anti-lock braking system.

ab·scess [ˈæbsɛs] n a swollen, painful pus-filled lump on the skin.
v form an abscess. ⟨Latin abscessus; ab(s)-away + cedere go⟩

ab·scis·sa [æbˈsɪsə] n, pl -sas or -sae [-si] or [-saɪ] Mathematics the first number in an ordered pair; the horizontal coordinate, or x-value, in a system of Cartesian coordinates. Compare ORDINATE. ⟨Latin (linea) abscissa (line) cut off; ab- off + scindere cut⟩

ab·scond [æbˈskɒnd] v go away suddenly and secretly, esp with something stolen. ⟨Latin ab(s)- away + condere store⟩

ab·seil [ˈɑpˌzaɪl] or [ˈɑpˌsaɪl] v descend by rope. **ab·seil** n. ⟨German ab down + Seil rope⟩

ab·sent [ˈæbsənt] adj 1 not in the expected place: absent from class. 2 lacking: Trees are completely absent in some parts of the Prairies. 3 preoccupied; faraway: an absent expression. v [æbˈsɛnt] take or keep (oneself) away. **ab·sence** n. ⟨Latin absens, ppr of abesse; ab- away + esse to be⟩
ab·sen·tee [ˌæbsənˈti] n a person who is absent. **absentee ballot** ✱ a system that allows a voter who is away from home to vote in an election. **ab·sen·tee·ism** n the practice or habit of being absent from work. **absentee landlord** a landowner who draws an income from a piece of land but does not live on it. **ab·sent–mind·ed** adj with one's mind on other things. **ab·sent–mind·ed·ly** adv.

ab·sinthe [ˈæbsɪnθ] n a strong, green, somewhat bitter liqueur. Also, **absinth.** ⟨Greek apsinthion wormwood⟩

ab·so·lute [ˈæbsəˌlut] or [ˌæbsəˈlut] adj 1 complete; perfect: absolute silence. 2 not qualified or restricted in any way: absolute monarchy. 3 not compared with or relative to anything else: absolute velocity. ⟨Latin absolutus, pp of absolvere. See ABSOLVE.⟩
absolute alcohol ethyl alcohol that contains not more than one percent by mass of water. **absolute humidity** the amount, in grams, of water vapour present in a unit volume of air. **ab·so·lute·ly** adv 1 completely: absolutely pure. 2 Informal positively or definitely: She is absolutely the finest person I know. "Can I try out your new car?" "Absolutely not!" **absolute temperature** THERMODYNAMIC TEMPERATURE. **absolute value** the value of a real number regardless of any accompanying sign: The absolute value of +5 or –5 is 5. **absolute zero** the lowest temperature possible according to scientific theory, equal to –273.16°C or zero kelvins. **ab·so·lut·ism** n a political or philosophical system in which power, truth, etc. is absolute. **ab·so·lut·ist** adj.

USAGE
In speech, **absolutely** is often used with general emphatic force: She is absolutely the finest person I know; used alone as a reply it is an emphatic 'yes'. In formal writing it is used only with its original meaning of 'completely'.

ab·solve [æbˈzɒlv] or [æbˈsɒlv] v declare (a person) free from sin, guilt, blame, or duty. **ab·so·lu·tion** n. ⟨Latin ab- from + solvere loosen⟩

ab·sorb [æbˈzɔrb] v 1 take in and hold: A sponge absorbs water. 2 process mentally; understand: Her rapid explanation was difficult to absorb. ⟨Latin ab- from + sorbere suck in⟩ **ab·sorbed** adj so interested as to be totally occupied. **ab·sorb·ent** adj able to absorb much. **ab·sorb·en·cy** n. **ab·sorb·ing** adj extremely interesting. **ab·sorp·tion** n 1 the process of absorbing or of being absorbed. 2 great interest (in something).

ab·stain [æbˈstein] v 1 do without something voluntarily: to abstain from smoking, to abstain from alcohol. 2 decline to vote. ⟨Latin ab(s)- off + tenere hold⟩ **ab·stain·er** n one who abstains, esp from alcohol. **ab·sten·tion** [æbˈstɛnʃən] n the act of declining to vote. **ab·sti·nence** [ˈæbstənəns] n voluntary avoidance of sex, certain foods, etc. **ab·sti·nent** adj.

ab·ste·mi·ous [æbˈstimiəs] adj sparing in eating and drinking; moderate. **ab·ste·mi·ous·ly** adv. **ab·ste·mi·ous·ness** n. ⟨Latin ab(s)- off + temetum potent liquor⟩

ab·sti·nence See ABSTAIN.

ab·stract [ˈæbstrækt] adj 1 thought of apart from any particular object or real thing; not concrete: A lump of sugar is concrete; the idea of sweetness is abstract. 2 hard to understand; intricate and highly theoretical. 3 Art representing ideas or feelings by forms which have little resemblance to actual objects. v [æbˈstrækt] take away; remove. n [ˈæbstrækt] a very brief summary. ⟨Latin abstractus; ab(s)- away + trahere draw⟩ **in the abstract** in theory rather than in practice. **ab·stract·ed** adj lost in thought; absent-minded. **ab·stract·ed·ly** adv. **ab·strac·tion** n 1 the idea of a quality thought of apart from any particular object: Bravery and length are abstractions. 2 the state of being lost in thought; absence of mind.

ab·struse [æbˈstrus] adj hard to understand. ⟨Latin abstrusus; ab(s)- away + trudere thrust⟩

ab·surd [æbˈzɜrd] or [æbˈsɜrd] adj plainly not true or sensible; contrary to reason; ridiculous. **ab·surd·ity** n. ⟨Latin absurdus out of tune, senseless⟩ **ab·surd·ist** n a person who believes that life is senseless, ridiculous, etc. **absurdist** adj.

a·bun·dance [əˈbʌndəns] n a quantity that is more than enough. **a·bun·dant** adj. ⟨Latin abundantia, from abundare. See ABOUND.⟩

a·buse [əˈbjuz] v 1 use wrongly; make bad use of: to abuse a privilege. 2 treat badly; mistreat. 3 use harsh, insulting language to. n [əˈbjus] 1 a wrong or bad use: the abuse of alcohol. 2 harsh treatment: child abuse. 3 harsh and insulting language. **a·bus·er** n. **a·bu·sive** [əˈbjusɪv] adj. ⟨Latin abusus; ab- away + uti use⟩

a·but [əˈbʌt] v touch at one end or edge.

a·but·ting *adj.* ⟨Old French *abouter* join end to end; *bout* end⟩

a·but·ment *n* a support for an arch or bridge.

a·bys·mal [ə'bɪzməl] *adj* **1** esp of something negative, immeasurable; very great: *abysmal ignorance.* **2** immeasurably bad: *abysmal taste.* **a·bys·mal·ly** *adv.*

a·byss [ə'bɪs] *n* **1** a very deep crack in the earth. **2** anything bad that is seemingly endless or immeasurable: *the abyss of despair.* ⟨Greek *a-* without + *byssos* bottom⟩ **a·byss·al** *adj* to do with the lowest depths of the ocean. **abyssal zone** *Ecology* the zone along the floor of the deep part of the ocean (3600 m to 6000 m).

a·ca·cia [ə'keiʃə] *n* any of a large genus of flowering trees and shrubs of the pea family. ⟨Greek *akakia*, a thorny Egyptian tree⟩

ac·a·de·mia [,ækə'dimiə] *n* the academic community or academic life. Also, **ac·a·deme** ['ækə,dim]. ⟨Greek *Akadēmeia*, the grove where Plato taught⟩

ac·a·dem·ic [,ækə'dɛmɪk] *adj* **1** to do with schools and their programs of study. **2** concerned with education in the arts and sciences rather than with commercial or technical training. **3** theoretical; with no practical significance: *an academic question.* *n* a person engaged in scholarly pursuits, esp at a college or university. **ac·a·dem·i·cal·ly** *adv.* **academic freedom** the freedom of scholars to investigate and discuss any issue without interference. **academic year** the part of the year during which a school is in regular session. **a·cad·e·my** [ə'kædəmi] *n* **1** a school, often private or specializing in a certain field. **2** a scholarly society.

A·ca·di·a [ə'keidiə] *n* ✱ **1** the areas of French settlement and culture in the Maritime Provinces. **2** formerly, the French colony comprising the Maritime Provinces and adjacent parts of Québec and New England. **A·ca·di·an** *adj.* ⟨Latinized from French *Acadie*⟩

a cap·pel·la [ɑ kə'pɛlə] *Music* without instrumental accompaniment. ⟨Italian = in the manner of chapel (music)⟩

ac·cede [æk'sid] *v* **1** give in or agree (*to*): *accede to popular demand.* **2** come or attain (to an office or dignity): *accede to the throne.* **ac·ces·sion** [æk'sɛʃən] *n.* ⟨Latin *ad-* to + *cedere* come⟩

ac·cel·er·ate [æk'sɛlə,reit] *v* **1** go or cause to go faster or happen sooner: *Rest can accelerate recovery from an illness.* **2** follow an academic stream that completes the usual program in less than the usual time. **ac·cel·er·a·tion** *n.* ⟨Latin *ad-* to + *celer* swift⟩ **ac·cel·er·a·tor** *n* **1** a device for controlling the speed of a machine, esp the pedal controlling the speed of an automobile engine. **2** *Chemistry* any substance that speeds up a chemical reaction. Also, **ac·cel·er·ant.** **3** *Physics* an apparatus for accelerating electrically charged atomic particles.

ac·cent ['æksɛnt] *n* **1** a distinctive manner of pronunciation typical of a given group: *a* Scottish *accent.* **2** force or stress placed on a given syllable in speaking, or a mark (e.g., ') showing this. **3** emphasis: *The accent is on style.* **4** in some languages, a mark over a vowel, indicating its quality. **5** an object providing contrast in a colour scheme: *a beige room with dark green accents.* **6** *Music* emphasis given to a note or chord, or the mark (>) indicating this. *v* ['æksɛnt] *or* [æk'sɛnt] **1** pronounce, write, sing, or play with an accent. **2** emphasize. ⟨Latin *accentus*, lit., song added to (speech); *ad-* to + *cantus* song⟩

ac·cen·tu·ate [æk'sɛntʃu,eit] *v* emphasize: *Her black hair accentuated the whiteness of her skin.*

French words in English sometimes keep their accent marks: *café, outré, attaché, crêpe, tête-à-tête, à la mode.* Words used frequently in English usually drop the accent marks after a time unless the marks are necessary to indicate pronunciation (as in *café, attaché*).

ac·cept [æk'sɛpt] *v* **1** take or receive: *to accept a gift.* **2** say yes to; approve; believe: *to accept an invitation, to accept a hypothesis.* **ac·cept·ance** *n.* **ac·cept·or** *n.* ⟨Latin *ad-* to + *capere* take⟩ **ac·cept·a·ble** *adj* **1** worth accepting: *an acceptable gift.* **2** good enough but not outstanding: *an acceptable performance.* **ac·cept·a·bly** *adv.* **ac·cept·ed** *adj* generally approved: *the accepted behaviour at weddings.*

ac·cess ['æksɛs] *n* **1** the right to approach, enter, or use; admission: *Students have access to the library all day.* **2** a way or means of approach: *A ladder was the only access to the attic.* **3** *Computers* the act or power of retrieving data. *v* **1** *Computers* retrieve (data) from a storage device. **2** *Informal* get access to. ⟨Latin *accessus; accedere.* See ACCEDE.⟩ **ac·ces·si·ble** [æk'sɛsəbəl] *adj* **1** capable of being entered or reached: *The camp is accessible only by boat, plane.* **2** capable of being influenced: *accessible to reason.* **3** easy to understand or appreciate: *Her poetry is accessible to most people.* **ac·ces·si·bil·i·ty** *n.* **access road** ✱ **1** a road built to give entry to a place that is otherwise sealed off, as by dense brush, muskeg, etc. **2** a road leading onto an expressway. **access time** the time it takes to retrieve data on a computer.

ac·ces·sion See ACCEDE.

ac·ces·so·ry [æk'sɛsəri] *n* **1** something added that is decorative or useful but not essential: *a mirror and other bike accessories, colourful accessories for a suit.* **2** *Law* a person who helps an offender without actually taking part in the offence. **ac·ces·so·rize** *v* provide or furnish with accessories: *to accessorize an outfit.*

The pronunciation [ə'sɛsəri] is non-standard.

ac·ci·dent ['æksədənt] *n* **1** something harmful or undesirable that happens unexpectedly and apparently by chance: *a* *car accident.* **2** anything that happens without being planned: *Their meeting was an accident.* ⟨Latin *accidens; ad-* to + *cadere* fall⟩

by accident by chance; not on purpose.

ac·ci·den·tal [ˌæksəˈdɛntəl] *adj* **1** happening unexpectedly or by chance: *an accidental injury.* **2** nonessential. *n Music* a sharp or flat. **ac·ci·den·tal·ly** *adv.* **ac·ci·dent–prone** *adj* tending to have accidents.

CONFUSABLES

Accidental describes some feature or part that is not essential to a certain thing: *Songs are essential to musical comedy, but accidental to Shakespeare's plays.* **Incidental** describes something that may be necessary but is subordinate to other things: *My mother pays my tuition and board at college, but not incidental expenses such as laundry.*

ac·claim [əˈkleim] *v* **1** show public approval of: *The crowd acclaimed the firefighters for their brave rescue. They were acclaimed heroes.* **2** ✶ elect to an office without opposition: *She was acclaimed mayor.*

n enthusiastic public approval: *His third album won wide acclaim.* **ac·cla·ma·tion** *n.* ⟨Latin *ad-* to + *clamare* cry out⟩

by acclamation ✶ without opposition in an election: *Since no candidate opposed him, he was elected by acclamation.*

ac·cli·ma·tize [əˈklaiməˌtaiz] *v* accustom or become accustomed to a new climate or new conditions. **ac·cli·ma·ti·za·tion** *n.*

ac·cliv·i·ty [əˈklivəti] *n* an upward slope. ⟨Latin *ad-* toward + *clivus* rising ground⟩

ac·co·lade [ˈækəˌleid] or [ˈækəˌlɑd] *n* praise; award. ⟨Italian *accollata* an embrace about the neck; Latin *collum* neck⟩

ac·com·mo·date [əˈkɒməˌdeit] *v* **1** have room for: *This bedroom will accommodate two beds.* **2** satisfy the need or request of: *She wanted change for a quarter, but I could not accommodate her.* **3** give lodging to. **4** adapt (oneself): *The eye can accommodate itself to objects at different distances.* **5** accept; make allowance for: *to accommodate our differences.* ⟨Latin *ad-* to + *commodare* make fit⟩

ac·com·mo·dat·ing *adj* obliging; willing to help. **ac·com·mo·da·tion(s)** *n* lodging.

ac·com·pa·ny [əˈkʌmpəni] *v* **-nied, -ny·ing** **1** go somewhere with: *to accompany a friend on a walk.* **2** happen in connection with: *Fire is accompanied by heat.* **3** play music for (a vocalist or solo instrument). **ac·com·pa·ni·ment** *n.* **ac·com·pa·nist** *n.* ⟨Old French *accompagner.* See COMPANION.⟩

ac·com·plice [əˈkɒmplɪs] *n* a person who aids another in committing a crime or mischief. ⟨Latin *com-* together + *plectere* twist⟩

ac·com·plish [əˈkɒmplɪʃ] *v* succeed in fulfilling (a purpose); get done; finish. ⟨French *accomplir;* Latin *ad-* + *complere* fill up⟩ **ac·com·plished** *adj* **1** expert: *an accomplished liar.* **2** skilled in the social arts: *Their very accomplished daughter entertained us.* **ac·com·plish·ment** *n.*

ac·cord [əˈkɔrd] *v* **1** agree or be in harmony (with): *His account of the accident accords with yours.* **2** grant (a right, privilege, request, etc.). *n* **1** agreement; harmony: *The various city groups are now in accord on the parks issue.* **2** an agreement between nations; treaty. ⟨Latin *ad-* to + *chorda* string⟩

of one's own accord voluntarily. **with one accord** unanimously or in unison.

ac·cord·ance *n* **1** agreement; harmony (with): *What she did was in accordance with what she said.* **2** the act or fact of granting: *the accordance of certain rights.* **according as** depending on how or whether. **according to** on the authority or basis of. **ac·cord·ing·ly** *adv* in agreement with that; on that basis: *These are the rules; act accordingly. She cheated; accordingly, her entry was disqualified.*

ac·cor·di·on [əˈkɔrdiən] *n* a portable musical wind instrument with a keyboard and bellows. **ac·cor·di·on·ist** *n.* ⟨Italian *accordare* harmonize, tune (an instrument)⟩

ac·cost [əˈkɒst] *v* **1** confront in a bold or hostile way: *He was accosted by a thief.* **2** greet. **3** of a prostitute, solicit. ⟨Latin *ad-* to + *costa* side, rib⟩

ac·count [əˈkaʊnt] *n* **1** a report or story: *an account of the trial.* **2** an explanation: *a satisfactory account of his absence.* **3** an arrangement for banking money. **4** an ongoing arrangement for purchasing on credit. **5** a client with such an arrangement. **6** accounts, *pl* a record of money received and spent: *keep careful accounts.* **7** worth or importance: *an error of no account.* ⟨Latin *accomptare; ad-* up + *computare* count⟩

account for give a reason for; tell what has happened to. **call (or bring) to account a** demand an explanation from. **b** scold; reprimand. **on account** as part payment. **on account of** because of. **on no account** under no circumstances. **take account of** notice. **take into account** make allowance for. **turn to account** use for one's own profit. **ac·count·a·ble** *adj* responsible: *You are accountable for your actions.* **ac·count·a·bil·i·ty** *n.* **ac·count·an·cy** *n* the profession or position of an accountant. **ac·count·ant** *n* a person trained in **accounting**, the system of recording and analyzing financial data.

ac·cou·tre [əˈkutər] *v* equip; array: *Knights were accoutred in armour.* Also, **ac·cou·ter.** ⟨French *accoutrer*⟩

ac·cou·tre·ments *n pl* clothing and equipment.

ac·cred·it [əˈkrɛdɪt] *v* **1** recognize as coming up to an official standard: *to accredit a college.* **2** consider (a thing) as due (*to*): *The invention of the telephone is accredited to Alexander Graham Bell.* **3** provide with credentials: *to accredit an ambassador as the representative of his, her own country.* **ac·cred·i·ta·tion** *n.* ⟨French *accréditer; à* to + *crédit* credit⟩

ac·cre·tion [əˈkriʃən] *n* **1** growth by accumulation or expansion: *the accretion of political power, the accretion of land by deposits of soil.* **2** the part added. **3** growth of separate things into one. **ac·crete** v. ⟨Latin accretio; ad- to + crescere grow⟩

ac·crue [ə'kru] v come as a growth or result: *Interest accrues on a savings account.* **ac·cru·al** n. ⟨French acreüe; Latin accrescere. See ACCRETION.⟩

ac·cul·tur·ate [ə'kʌltʃə,reit] v adapt or cause to adapt to another culture: *Inuit in some parts of the North have acculturated to southern Canadian society.* **ac·cul·tu·ra·tion** n.

ac·cu·mu·late [ə'kjumjə,leit] v collect little by little: *She accumulated a fortune by hard work. Dust had accumulated while we were away.* **ac·cu·mu·la·ble** adj. **ac·cu·mu·la·tion** n. **ac·cu·mu·la·tor** n. ⟨Latin ad- up + cumulus heap⟩
ac·cu·mu·la·tive adj **1** resulting from or characterized by a process of accumulation. **2** eager to accumulate money or possessions.

ac·cu·rate ['ækjərɪt] adj **1** containing or making no errors: *an accurate report* **2** exact: *accurate measure.* **ac·cu·ra·cy** n. **ac·cu·rate·ly** adv. ⟨Latin accuratus; ad- to + cura care⟩

ac·curs·ed [ə'kɜrsɪd] or [ə'kɜrst] adj **1** damnable; detestable; hateful. **2** under a curse; damned. Also, *literary,* **ac·curst.**

ac·cuse [ə'kjuz] v **1** charge with having done something wrong (with *of*): *He was accused of murder.* **2** find fault with; blame. **ac·cu·sa·tion** n. **ac·cus·er** n. **ac·cus·ing·ly** adv. ⟨Latin accusare; ad- to + causa cause⟩
ac·cu·sa·to·ry [ə'kjuzə,tɔri] adj containing or expressing an accusation: *an accusatory tone.*
the accused n Law the person or persons appearing in court on a criminal charge.

ac·cus·tom [ə'kʌstəm] v make familiar with something (with *to*): *We must accustom the dog to the noise of traffic.*
ac·cus·tomed adj usual; customary: *Move the dining table back to its accustomed place.*
accustomed to used to; in the habit of.

ace [eis] n **1** a playing card, domino, or side of a die with one spot. **2** Sports a point won by a single stroke. **3** an expert at anything.
v Informal **1** achieve a high mark in (an exam, etc.). **2** win (a game) or defeat (an opponent) decisively. ⟨Latin *as* smallest unit⟩
ace in the hole (or **up one's sleeve**) a decisive advantage that is kept hidden until needed.
within an ace of on the very point of: *I came within an ace of quitting.*

–aceae suffix of plants from a family: *Acantheaceae.*

a·cer·bic [ə'sɜrbɪk] adj **1** sour in taste. **2** sharp, bitter, or harsh in tone, mood, or temper: *an acerbic remark, an acerbic writer.* **a·cer·bi·cal·ly** adv. **a·cer·bi·ty** n. ⟨Latin acerbus bitter⟩

ac·e·ta·min·o·phen [ə,setə'mɪnəfɪn] or [ə,sitə'mɪnəfɪn] n a white crystalline compound used to relieve pain and fever. ⟨acet(ic) + amino + phenol⟩

ac·e·tate ['æsə,teit] n **1** a compound, in full **cellulose acetate**, produced by the action of acetic acid and sulphuric acid on cellulose. **2** something made from this, such as a fabric, photographic film, or a transparency for use with an overhead projector.

a·cet·i·fy [ə'sitə,faɪ] or [ə'setə,faɪ] v turn into vinegar or acetic acid. **a·ce·tic** adj. **a·cet·i·fi·ca·tion** n.
a·ce·tic acid a very sour, colourless acid, the main constituent of vinegar. **ac·e·tous** ['æsətəs] adj vinegary; producing vinegar; tart. Also, **ac·e·tose** ['æsə,tous].

ac·e·tone ['æsə,toun] n a colourless, volatile, flammable liquid, used as a solvent. **ac·e·ton·ic** [,æsə'tɒnɪk] adj.

a·cet·y·lene [ə'setə,lin] or [ə'setəlɪn] n a colourless gas that burns with a bright light and a very hot flame.

ac·e·tyl·sal·i·cyl·ic acid [,æsətɪl,sælə'sɪlɪk] or [ə,sitəl,sælə'sɪlɪk] a drug used to relieve pain and fever. *Abbrev* **ASA**

ache [eik] v **1** feel dull, continuous pain. **2** Informal desire intensely: *aching to see you.* n a dull, steady pain. **ach·ing·ly** adv. **ach·y** ['eiki] adj. ⟨Old English acan⟩

a·chieve [ə'tʃiv] v **1** get done; produce; accomplish: *to achieve one's purpose, to achieve an effect.* **2** get by effort or skill: *She achieved distinction in mathematics.* **a·chiev·a·ble** adj. **a·chieve·ment** n. **a·chiev·er** n. ⟨Old French achever; a chief (come) to a head. See CHIEF.⟩

A·chil·les' heel a vulnerable area.
Achilles tendon the tendon joining the heel bone to the muscles of the calf. ⟨after the hero of Homer's *Iliad*⟩

ach·ro·mat·ic [,eikrə'mætɪk] or [,ækrə'mætɪk] adj **1** capable of refracting white light without breaking it up into the colours of the spectrum. **2** with no hue. Black, white, and neutral greys are achromatic colours. **3** Biology containing material that resists ordinary stains: *achromatic cells.* **4** Music with no accidentals or changes of key: *an achromatic scale.* **ach·ro·mat·i·cal·ly** adv. ⟨Greek a- without + chrōma colour⟩

ac·id ['æsɪd] n **1** Chemistry any compound that yields hydrogen ions when dissolved in water and usually reacts with a base to form a salt. The water solution of an acid turns blue litmus paper red. **2** a sour substance. **3** a harsh, biting, or bitter quality or character: *acid in his voice.* **4** Slang LSD.
adj **1** containing an acid: *an acid solution.* **2** sharp to the taste; sour. **3** harsh, biting, or bitter: *acid humour.* **a·cid·ly** adv. **a·cid·ness** n. ⟨Latin acidus sour⟩
acid head or **freak** Slang a habitual user of LSD. **a·cid·ic** [ə'sɪdɪk] adj **1** acid-forming. **2** acid: *Rainfall is growing more acidic in many parts of the world.* **a·cid·i·fy** v **1** change into an acid. **2** make or become sour. **a·cid·i·ty** n **1** the fact of being acid or sour: *the acidity of vinegar.* **2** excessive stomach acid. **acid number** or **acid value** a number indicating the amount of free acid in a substance. **acid rain ✲** rain or snow contaminated by acids formed by industrial pollutants in the atmosphere. **acid rock** rock music dating from the late 1960s, known for its harsh and

distorted electronic sounds and its association with drug culture. **acid test** a decisive test of the real worth of a person or thing. **a·cid–tongued** adj cuttingly sarcastic.

ac·knowl·edge [æk'nɒlədʒ] v **1** admit; recognize: *I acknowledge my own faults. She was acknowledged to be the best player on the team.* **2** indicate that one has received (something) or noticed (someone). **ac·knowl·edg·er** n. **ac·knowl·edg·ment** or **ac·knowl·edge·ment** n. ⟨Middle English *aknowen* admit and *knowleche* knowledge⟩

ac·me ['ækmi] n the highest point; culmination. ⟨Greek *akmē* point⟩

ac·ne ['ækni] n a pimply skin condition. ⟨Latin, misspelling of Greek *akmē* point⟩

ac·o·lyte ['ækə,lait] n **1** a person who helps a priest during certain religious services. **2** attendant. ⟨Greek *akolouthos* follower⟩

a·corn ['eikɔrn] n the nut, or fruit, of an oak tree. ⟨Old English *æcern*⟩

a·cous·tic [ə'kustik] adj **1** to do with the physical properties of sound. **2** of music or instruments, without electronic amplification: *acoustic rock.* **a·cous·ti·cal·ly** adv. ⟨Greek *akoustikós; akouein* hear⟩
acoustic mine an explosive device detonated by sound waves. **a·cous·tics** n **1** the qualities of a room that determine how well sounds can be heard in it (with a plural verb): *The acoustics in here are good.* **2** the scientific study of sound (with a sg verb): *Acoustics is a branch of physics.* **acoustic tile** tile designed to absorb sound, as in a studio, etc.

ac·quaint [ə'kweint] v make familiar: *He gave us a little tour to acquaint us with the neighbourhood.* ⟨Old French *acointer*; Latin *ad*- to + *cognitus*, pp of *cognoscere* know⟩
be acquainted with know: *She is acquainted with my father. I am acquainted with the facts.* **ac·quaint·ance** n a person known to one, but not a close friend. **make someone's acquaintance** get to know someone. **ac·quaint·ance·ship** n.

ac·qui·esce [,ækwi'ɛs] v accept or agree passively, by not objecting. **ac·qui·es·cence** n. **ac·qui·es·cent** adj. ⟨Latin *ad*- to + *quiescere* to rest; *quies* rest⟩

ac·quire [ə'kwair] v get as one's own: *to acquire land, to acquire a skill.* **ac·quir·a·ble** adj. **ac·qui·si·tion** [,ækwə'zɪʃən] n. ⟨Latin *ad*- to + *quaerere* seek⟩
Acquired Immune Deficiency Syndrome a disease of the immune system, caused by a virus transmitted through body fluids. *Abbrev* **AIDS**. **ac·quis·i·tive** [ə'kwɪzətɪv] adj greedy for material wealth: *She valued contentment and simplicity and found him too acquisitive.* **ac·quis·i·tive·ness** n.

ac·quit [ə'kwɪt] v **-quit·ted, -quit·ting 1** declare (a person) not guilty. **2** conduct (oneself): *The soldiers acquitted themselves well in battle.* **ac·quit·tal** n. ⟨Old French *a*- + *quitte* free; Latin *quietus* quiet⟩

a·cre ['eikər] n a non-metric unit for measuring land area, equal to about 4047 m².

a·cre·age ['eikərɪdʒ] n **1** acres collectively or the number of acres. **2** a piece of land measuring an unspecified number of acres: *a small acreage north of town.*

ac·rid ['ækrɪd] adj **1** sharp or bitter in taste or smell; stinging the mouth or nose. **2** sharp or irritating in tone: *an acrid comment.* **ac·rid·ly** adv. **ac·rid·ness** n. ⟨Latin *acer, acris* sharp⟩

ac·ri·mo·ny ['ækrə,mouni] n bitterness or hostility. **ac·ri·mo·ni·ous** adj. **ac·ri·mo·ni·ous·ly** adv. ⟨Latin *acrimonia; acer* sharp⟩

ac·ro·bat ['ækrə,bæt] n a person who performs on a trapeze or tightrope, turns handsprings, etc. **ac·ro·bat·ic** [,ækrə'bætɪk] adj. **ac·ro·bat·i·cal·ly** adv. ⟨Greek *akros* tip (of the toes) + *-batos* going⟩
ac·ro·bat·ics n pl **1** the skilled moves of an acrobat. **2** manoeuvres that are skilful, difficult or intricate. *political acrobatics.*

ac·ro·nym ['ækrə,nɪm] n a word or name formed from the first letters or syllables of other words, such as RADAR (RAdio Detecting And Ranging) or UNESCO (United Nations Educational, Scientific, and Cultural Organization). **ac·ro·nym·ic** adj. ⟨Greek *akros* tip + *onoma* name⟩

ac·ro·pho·bi·a [,ækrə'foubiə] n Psychiatry extreme, irrational fear of high places. **ac·ro·phobe** n. **ac·ro·pho·bic** adj. ⟨Greek *akros* tip + English *-phobia*⟩

a·crop·o·lis [ə'krɒpəlɪs] n the fortified hill in the centre of an ancient Greek city. ⟨Greek *akros* tip + *polis* city⟩

a·cross [ə'krɒs] prep **1** from one side to the other of: *to build a bridge across a river.* **2** on the other side of; beyond: *lands across the sea.* adv from one side to the other: *What is the distance across?*
a·cross–the–board adj affecting all members of a group: *an across-the-board raise in pay.* **across the line** (or **lines**) ✱ in or to the US.

a·cros·tic [ə'krɒstɪk] n a poem or an arrangement of words in which the first (or occasionally last) letters in each line, taken in order, spell a word or phrase. **a·cros·tic** adj. ⟨Greek *akros* tip + *stichos* row⟩

a·cryl·ic [ə'krɪlɪk] adj to do with acrylic acid or its derivatives.
n **1** a paint with an acrylic resin base. **2** a painting made with this paint. **3** a synthetic fibre or fabric made from a derivative of acrylic acid. ⟨Latin *acer* sharp + *olere* smell⟩
acrylic acid an unsaturated organic acid in the form of a colourless, sharp-smelling liquid, used in the manufacture of many synthetic materials.

act [ækt] n **1** something done; a deed: *an act*

of kindness. **2** the process of doing: *He was caught in the act of stealing.* **3** a main division of a play. **4** a law. An **Act of Parliament** is a bill that has been passed by Parliament. **5** one of several performances on a program: *Your act is after the conjurer's.* **6** a display of pretended behaviour meant to deceive: *She didn't really faint; that's just an act.*
v **1** do something: *The firefighters acted promptly and saved the house.* **2** behave: *to act like a fool.* **3** have an effect (on): *Yeast acts on dough and makes it rise.* **4** perform in a play, film, etc. **5** behave insincerely, as if playing a role. **6** serve: *The foam acts as insulation.* ⟨Latin *actum* (a thing) done; *agere* do⟩
act for serve as (someone's) agent or representative. **act of God** a happening beyond a person's control: *Floods, storms, and earthquakes are called acts of God.* **act on** follow; put into practice: *to act on a decision at once.* **act out** represent in actions: *to act out a story.* **act up** **a** behave badly: *They left when their son started acting up.* **b** be troublesome: *The knee I hurt last summer is acting up again.* **clean up one's act** improve one's behaviour. **get into the act** *Informal* take part; get involved. **get one's act together** get organized. **put on an act** behave insincerely, with fake emotion, etc.
act·ing *n* the profession of an actor. *adj* doing another person's duties temporarily: *While the principal was sick, one of the teachers was made acting principal.* **ac·tor** *n* **1** a person who acts on stage, in films, on radio, etc. **2** a participant in anything.
ac·tin·i·um [æk'tɪniəm] *n* a metallic element resembling radium. *Symbol* **Ac** ⟨Greek *aktis* ray⟩
ac·tion ['ækʃən] *n* **1** the process of doing something: *to put a plan into action.* **2** habitual activity, esp with energy or initiative: *a man of action.* **3** the way a thing moves or works: *the action of a pendulum.* **4 actions** *n pl* **a** behaviour: *You will be judged by your actions.* **b** gestures; body movements intended to represent ideas or words: *Do you know the actions to that song?* **5** *Informal* exciting activities: *to go where the action is.* **6** the effect of one thing on another: *the action of a drug.* **7** military combat: *killed in action.* **8** the events forming the story or plot of a play, novel, etc.: *Most of the action takes place in Manitoba.* **9** lawsuit: *to bring an action against someone.* **10** the moving parts of a machine. ⟨Latin *actio; agere* do⟩
take action begin to act, esp in response to some problem.
ac·tive ['æktɪv] *adj* **1** capable of acting or reacting: *an active volcano.* **2** lively or busy: *an active child.* **3** taking initiative; taking positive action **4** in current use: *an active file.* **5** *Grammar* of a verb, in the voice that shows the subject as the doer of the action. **ac·tive·ly** *adv.* ⟨Latin *activus; agere* act⟩
ac·ti·vate *v* **1** make active; switch on. **2** *Physics* make radioactive. **3** *Chemistry* make capable of reacting or of speeding up a reaction. **ac·ti·va·tion** *n.* **ac·tiv·ism** *n* a policy

of direct action in support of one's point of view. **ac·tiv·ist** *n.* **ac·tiv·i·ty** [æk'tɪvəti] *n* **1** the state of being active. **2** action; something engaged in: *the activities of teenagers.* **3** a thing to do or take part in: *not enough activities for the kids.*
ac·tu·al ['æktʃuəl] *adj* **1** real: *What he told us was not a dream but an actual happening.* **2** now existing: *the actual state of affairs.* **ac·tu·al·i·ty** [,æktʃu'æləti] *n.* ⟨Latin *āctuālis; actus* a doing. See ACT.⟩
ac·tu·al·ize *v* make real as opposed to merely possible. **ac·tu·al·i·za·tion** *n.* **ac·tu·al·ly** ['æktʃuəli] *or* ['ækʃəli] *adv* really; in fact: *Are you actually going abroad this summer?*
ac·tu·ar·y ['æktʃu,ɛri] *n* a person whose work involves figuring risks, rates, etc. for insurance companies. **ac·tu·ar·i·al** *adj.* ⟨Latin *actuarius* account keeper, from *actus.* See ACT.⟩
ac·tu·ate ['æktʃu,eit] *v* cause to act: *This pump is actuated by a belt driven by an electric motor. He was actuated by love for his father.* **ac·tu·a·tion** *n.* **ac·tu·a·tor** *n.* ⟨Latin *actuare*, from *actus* a doing. See ACT.⟩
a·cu·i·ty [ə'kjuəti] *n* sharpness; acuteness. ⟨Latin *acuitas; acus* needle⟩
a·cu·men ['ækjəmən] *n* keen insight, as, for example, in business. ⟨Latin *acumen; acuere* sharpen⟩
ac·u·punc·ture ['ækjə,pʌŋktʃər] *n* a method of relieving pain and treating disease by inserting needles into the body at specific points. **ac·u·punc·tur·ist** *n.* ⟨Latin *acus* needle + English *puncture*⟩
ac·u·pres·sure ['ækjə,prɛʃər] *n* a method of treatment using the application of pressure, instead of needles, to the points used in acupuncture.
a·cute [ə'kjut] *adj* **1** keen: *Dogs have an acute sense of smell.* **2** sharp; intense: *acute pain.* **3** severe: *an acute shortage.* **4** of a disease, reaching a crisis quickly. **5** *Geometry* of an angle, less than 90°. **a·cute·ly** *adv.* **a·cute·ness** *n.* ⟨Latin *acutus*, pp of *acuere* sharpen⟩
acute accent a mark (´) indicating vowel quality: é
ad [æd] *n Informal* advertisement.
AD in the year of the Lord; since Jesus Christ was born (for Latin *anno Domini*).
ad·age ['ædɪdʒ] *n* a wise saying that has been much used; proverb. ⟨Latin *adagium*⟩
a·da·gio [ə'dædʒiou] *or* [ə'dɑdʒou] *Music adj, adv* slow or slowly.
n a slow dance or piece of music. ⟨Italian *ad agio* at ease⟩
ad·a·mant ['ædəmənt] *adj* insistent; stubborn or unyielding. **ad·a·mant·ly** *adv.* ⟨Old French *adamaunt* the hardest stone; Greek *a-* not + *damaein* conquer, tame⟩
Adam's apple the lump in the front of the throat of men. ⟨from the story of the forbidden fruit sticking in Adam's throat⟩
a·dapt [ə'dæpt] *v* **1** adjust: *She has adapted well to the new school.* **2** modify for a different use: *to adapt a barn for use as a garage.*

a·dapt·a·ble *adj.* **a·dapt·a·bil·i·ty** *n.* **a·dap·tive** *adj.* ⟨Latin *ad-* to + *aptare* fit⟩

ad·ap·ta·tion *n* **1** the act, fact, or result of adapting: *That movie is an adaptation of the novel.* **2** *Biology* an evolutionary change to suit different conditions: *Wings are adaptations of the upper limbs for flight.*

a·dapt·er or **a·dap·tor** *n* a device for fitting together parts that do not match, changing the function of a machine, etc.: *North American appliances cannot be used in Europe without adapters.*

add [æd] *v* **1** put one thing together with another: *Add another stone to the pile. Add 8 and 2 and you have 10.* **2** say further: *She said goodbye, adding that she had enjoyed her visit.* ⟨Latin *addere; ad-* to + *dare* put⟩
add in include in a total. **add to** increase: *The fine weather added to our pleasure.* **add up a** find the sum of. *Add up these figures.* **b** *Informal* make sense: *Her explanation just didn't add up.* **add up to a** come to a total of: *9 and 7 add up to 16.* **b** have the cumulative effect of: *All his efforts didn't add up to much.*

ad·di·tion *n* **1** the act or fact of adding. **2** something added, often specifically a part added to a building. **ad·di·tion·al** *adj.* **ad·di·tion·al·ly** *adv.* **ad·di·tive** *n* a substance added in small amounts to produce a desirable colour, act as a preservative, increase efficiency, etc. **additive inverse** *Mathematics* the number which, added to a given number, will equal zero. The additive inverse of -2 is $+2$. **add-on** *n* a component added as an accessory or supplement.

ADD or **ADHD** ATTENTION DEFICIT (HYPERACTIVITY) DISORDER.

ad·den·dum [ə'dɛndəm] *n, pl* **-da** [-də] a thing added, or to be added, esp to something written. ⟨Latin⟩

ad·der ['ædər] *n* a small poisonous snake; viper. ⟨Middle English *a nadder* (Old English *næder*), taken as *an adder*⟩

ad·dict ['ædɪkt] *n* **1** a person dependent on a chemical substance, esp a narcotic drug. **2** a person who has given himself or herself up to a habit: *a movie addict.*
v [ə'dɪkt] make into an addict: *One concert has addicted me to jazz.* ⟨Latin *addicere* devote; *ad-* to + *dicere* say⟩
ad·dict·ed *adj* dependent on (a substance); slavishly indulging in (a habit or practice): *addicted to cigars, addicted to TV.* **ad·dic·tion** *n* the condition of being addicted. **ad·dic·tive** *adj* causing addiction.

ad·di·tion, ad·di·tive See ADD.

ad·dle ['ædəl] *v* **1** muddle: *The wine has quite addled them.* **2** of eggs, become rotten. ⟨Old English *adela* liquid filth⟩

ad·dress [ə'drɛs]; *n 1-3 also* ['ædrɛs] *n* **1** the place at which a person, business, etc. may be found: *She no longer lives at this address.* **2** the writing on a letter, package, etc. indicating where it is to be sent: *The address is incomplete.* **3** *Computers.* a code label representing the exact location of data stored in memory. **4** a formal speech. **5** skill: *He handled the matter with great address.*
v **1** direct speech or writing to: *to address Parliament.* **2** use titles or other forms in speaking or writing to: *How do you address a mayor?* **3** write on (a letter, package, etc.) the information that shows where it is to be sent. **4** deal with: *to address the problem at hand.* **5** apply (oneself) in speech (*to* a person or group): *He addressed himself to the chairperson.* **6** apply or devote (oneself): *She addressed herself to completing the report.*
ad·dress·er or **ad·dress·er** *n.* **ad·dress·ee** *n.* ⟨Old French *adrecier*; Latin *ad-* to + *directare* direct⟩

USAGE
When the various parts of a mailing or street address are written on the same line, they are separated by commas: *Reply to Ms. Louise Finney, 48 Pine St., Charlottetown, P.E.I.*

ad·duce [ə'djus] *or* [ə'dus] *v* give as a reason, proof, or example: *to adduce statistics in support of an argument.* **ad·duc·i·ble** *adj.* **ad·duc·tion** *n.* ⟨Latin *ad-* to + *ducere* lead⟩

ad·e·noid ['ædə,nɔɪd] *or* ['ædnɔɪd] *n* Usually, **ad·e·noids** *pl* lymphoid tissue in the upper part of the throat, just behind the nose. ⟨Greek *adenoeidēs; adēn* gland, acorn⟩

a·dept [ə'dɛpt] *adj* expert; thoroughly skilled. **adept** ['ædɛpt] *or* [ə'dɛpt] *n.* **a·dept·ly** *adv.* **a·dept·ness** *n.* ⟨Latin *adeptus*, pp of *adipisci* attain; *apisci* get⟩

ad·e·quate ['ædəkwɪt] *adj* as much or as good, competent, etc. as is needed: *Her wages are adequate to support three people. The old technology is no longer adequate.* **ad·e·qua·cy** *n.* **ad·e·quate·ly** *adv.* **ad·e·quate·ness** *n.* ⟨Latin *adaequātus*, pp of *adaequāre* be equal⟩

à deux [a'dø] *French* **1** for two. **2** intimate.

ad·here [æd'hir] *v* **1** stick: *Mud adheres to your shoes.* **2** hold firmly: *to adhere to a plan.* **ad·her·ence** *n.* ⟨Latin *ad-* to + *haerere* stick⟩
ad·her·ent *n* a faithful supporter. **ad·he·sion** [æd'hiʒən] *n* **1** the act or fact of sticking together. **2** *Physics* the attraction between molecules of different substances. Compare COHESION. **ad·he·sive** [æd'hisɪv], [æd'hizɪv] *or Informal* [ə'dizɪv] *adj* sticky; used for sticking. *n* tape, glue, or other substance for sticking.

ad hoc ['æd 'hɒk] concerned with a particular purpose or case, without general application: *an ad hoc committee. The decision was made ad hoc.* ⟨Latin = for this⟩
ad hockery *Slang* the practice of deciding things case by case instead of by general rule.

ad ho·mi·nem ['æd 'hɒmənəm] attacking a person's character rather than replying to his or her arguments. ⟨Latin = to the man⟩

a·dieu [ə'dju] *or* [ə'du] *n, pl* **a·dieus** or **a·dieux** [ə'djuz] *or* [ə'duz] goodbye; farewell. ⟨Old French *a dieu* to God⟩

ad in·fi·ni·tum ['æd ,ɪnfə'nəitəm] without limit; endlessly. ⟨Latin⟩

ad·i·pose ['ædə,pous] *adj* to do with animal fat; fatty: *adipose tissue.* ⟨Latin *adeps* fat⟩

ad·ja·cent [ə'dʒeisənt] *adj* lying beside or near. **ad·ja·cen·cy** *n.* **ad·ja·cent·ly** *adv.* ⟨Latin *ad-* near + *jacere* lie⟩

ad·jec·tive ['ædʒɪktɪv] *n* any of a class of words that limit or add to the meaning of nouns. *Examples: blue, powerful, wise.* *adj* forming, or serving as, an adjective: *an adjective phrase. Abbrev* **adj** ⟨Latin *adjectivus* added thing; *ad-* to + *jacere* throw⟩ **ad·jec·ti·val** [ˌædʒɪk'taɪvəl] *adj* **1** forming an adjective: *an adjectival suffix.* **2** used as an adjective. *Toy poodle* is an adjectival use of the noun *toy.* **ad·jec·ti·val** *n.* **ad·jec·ti·val·ly** *adv.*

ad·join [ə'dʒɔɪn] *v* be next to: *Canada adjoins the United States.* **ad·join·ing** *adj.* ⟨Latin *ad-* to + *jungere* join⟩

ad·journ [ə'dʒɜrn] *v* **1** break off for a time: *The meeting was adjourned at 10 o'clock.* **2** *Informal* go to another place to do something different: *After the meeting we adjourned to the cafeteria.* **ad·journ·ment** *n.* ⟨Old French *ajorner; jorn* day⟩

ad·ju·di·cate [ə'dʒudəˌkeit] *v* act as judge in a competition or dispute. **ad·ju·di·ca·tion** *n.* **ad·ju·di·ca·tor** *n.* ⟨Latin *ad-* to + *judicare* judge⟩

ad·junct ['ædʒʌŋkt] *n* **1** something added which is useful but not necessary. **2** an assistant of a more important person. **3** *Grammar* a word or phrase that qualifies or modifies another. Adjectives and adverbs are adjuncts. **ad·junct** *adj.* **ad·junct·ive** *adj.* ⟨Latin *adjunctus,* pp of *adjungere.* See ADJOIN.⟩

ad·just [ə'dʒʌst] *v* **1** set so as to suit a particular person, condition, etc.: *to adjust the height of a seat.* **2** alter (machinery or controls) to work as required: *to adjust a TV set.* **3** get used (*to*): *to adjust to city life.* **4** settle satisfactorily: *to adjust a difference of opinion.* **ad·just·a·ble** *adj.* **ad·just·ment** *n.* ⟨French *ajuster* from *juste* right; Latin *justus*⟩ **ad·just·er** or **ad·jus·tor** *n* a person who determines the amount of a claim for an insurance firm.

ad·ju·tant ['ædʒətənt] *n Military* an officer who assists a commanding officer. ⟨Latin *adjutans,* ppr of *adjutare* assist⟩

ad lib ['æd 'lɪb] **1** freely; on the spur of the moment. **2** *Informal* (**libbed, lib·bing**) make (something) up as one goes along. **ad–lib** *adj.* ⟨shortened from Latin *ad libitum* at pleasure⟩

ad·min·is·ter [æd'mɪnɪstər] *v* **1** manage: *The Minister of Defence administers a department of the government.* **2** give: *to administer medication, to administer justice.* ⟨Latin *administrare; ad-* to + *minister* servant⟩ **ad·min·is·trate** *v* manage or direct the affairs of (a business, school, government, etc.). **ad·min·is·tra·tion** *n* **1** the work of administrating. **2** the people who do this work for a particular organization. **ad·min·is·tra·tive** [æd'mɪnɪˌstreitɪv] *adj.* **ad·min·is·tra·tive·ly** *adv.* **ad·min·is·tra·tor** *n.*

ad·mi·ral ['ædmərəl] *n* **1** the commander-in-chief of a fleet. **2** ✹ formerly, the leader of a fishing fleet in Newfoundland and Labrador. **ad·mi·ral·ty** *n* a law or court dealing with affairs of the sea and ships. ⟨earlier *amiral;* Arabic *amir* chief⟩

ad·mire [æd'maɪr] *v* regard with approval; think highly of: *to admire a brave deed.* **ad·mi·ra·tion** [ˌædmə'reiʃən] *n.* **ad·mi·ra·ble** ['ædmərəbəl] *adj.* **ad·mi·ra·bly** *adv.* **ad·mir·er** *n.* ⟨Latin *ad-* at + *mirari* wonder; *mirus* wonderful⟩

ad·mis·si·ble [æd'mɪsəbəl] *adj* eligible; that can be allowed under the rules. **ad·mis·si·bil·i·ty** *n.* **ad·mis·si·bly** *adv.*

ad·mis·sion [æd'mɪʃən] *n* **1** the act of allowing (a person, animal, etc.) to enter. **2** the right to enter or use. **3** the price paid for this. **4** the act of acknowledging or accepting: *Admission of such an embarrassing fact takes a lot of courage.* ⟨Latin *admissio; admittere.* See ADMIT.⟩

ad·mit [æd'mɪt] *v* **1** say that (a damaging fact, etc.) is true: *She admitted her mistake.* **2** accept: *to admit a hypothesis.* **3** let in: *The head waiter refused to admit him without a tie.* **4** permit (usually with *of*): *Her argument admits of no reply.* ⟨Latin *ad-* to + *mittere* let go⟩ **ad·mit·tance** *n* **1** the right to enter. **2** the act of allowing to enter. **3** *Electricity* the ratio of current to voltage. **ad·mit·ted·ly** *adv* it is to be admitted: *Admittedly, I was the one who forgot.*

ad·mix [æd'mɪks] *v* mix in. **ad·mix·ture** *n.* ⟨Latin *admixtus,* pp of *admiscere.* See MIX.⟩

ad·mon·ish [æd'mɒnɪʃ] *v* **1** urge strongly; advise; remind: *The police officer admonished us not to drive too fast.* **2** reprove gently: *The teacher admonished her for her careless work.* **ad·mo·ni·tion** *n.* **ad·mon·i·to·ry** [æd'mɒnəˌtɔri] *adj.* ⟨Latin *ad-* to + *monere* warn⟩

ad nau·se·am ['æd 'nɒziəm] to a disgusting or sickening degree. ⟨Latin = to nausea⟩

a·do [ə'du] *n* bother, fuss, or trouble. ⟨Middle English *at do* to do to do⟩.

a·do·be [ə'doubi] *n* clay mixed with straw or grass and dried in the sun, usually made into bricks. ⟨Spanish; Arabic *al-tub* the brick⟩

ad·o·les·cent [ˌædə'lɛsənt] *n* a person in the stage between childhood and maturity. **ad·o·les·cent** *adj.* **ad·o·les·cence** *n.* ⟨Latin *ad-* to + *olescere* grow up. Related to ADULT.⟩

a·dopt [ə'dɒpt] *v* **1** take or use as one's own: *to adopt someone's idea.* **2** accept formally: *to adopt a policy.* **3** legally take (a child of other parents) and bring up as one's own. **a·dop·tion** *n.* ⟨Latin *ad-* to + *optare* choose⟩ **a·dopt·ee** *n* someone who has been adopted. **a·dop·tive** *adj* related by adoption: *adoptive parents.*

a·dore [ə'dɔr] *v* **1** honour very highly and love deeply. **2** worship. **3** *Informal* like very much. **ad·o·ra·tion** *n.* **a·dor·ing·ly** *adv.* ⟨Latin *ad-* to + *orare* pray⟩ **a·dor·a·ble** *adj* **1** *Informal* lovely; cute. **2** worthy of adoration. **a·dor·a·bly** *adv.*

a·dorn [ə'dɔrn] *v* **1** put ornaments on; decorate. **2** add beauty to. **a·dorn·ment** *n.* ⟨Latin *ad-* to + *ornare* fit out⟩

ADP automatic data processing.

ad·re·nal [ə'drinəl] *adj* to do with the kidney or the ADRENAL GLANDS. ⟨Latin *ad-* near + *renes* kidneys⟩

adrenal gland either of the two ductless glands situated one on top of each kidney. **ad·ren·al·in** [ə'drɛnəlɪn] *n* 1 a hormone secreted by the adrenal glands. **2 Adrenalin** *Trademark* a white, crystalline drug prepared from this hormone, used to stimulate the heart and stop bleeding. **rush of adrenalin** a sudden increase in strength or courage, esp as a result of awareness of danger.

a·drift [ə'drɪft] *adv, adj* (never before a noun) **1** being carried along by the current, without control: *Having lost the paddle, we were adrift on the lake.* **2** without guidance, security, or purpose: *The team was adrift for three weeks while the coach was sick.*

a·droit [ə'drɔɪt] *adj* **1** expert in the use of the hands. **2** resourceful; skilled: *A good teacher is adroit in the use of questions.* **a·droit·ly** *adv.* **a·droit·ness** *n.* ⟨French *à droit* rightly⟩

ad·sorb [æd'zɔrb] *or* [æd'sɔrb] *v* cause (a gas, liquid, or dissolved substance) to adhere in a very thin layer of molecules to the surface of a solid. **ad·sorp·tion** *n.* **ad·sorp·tive** *adj.* ⟨Latin *ad-* to + *sorbere* suck in⟩

ad·u·late ['ædʒə,leit] *v* praise too much; flatter. **ad·u·la·tor** *n.* **ad·u·la·tion** *n.* **ad·u·la·to·ry** *adj.* ⟨Latin *adulari*⟩

a·dult [ə'dʌlt] *or* ['ædʌlt] *adj* **1** fully developed and mature: *An adult frog looks very different from a tadpole.* **2** of, intended for, or appealing to grown-up people: *adult education, adult tastes.* **3** appealing to sexual interests: *adult bookstores.* *n* **1** a full-grown person, animal, or plant. **2** a person who has reached an age of legal responsibility: *In some provinces, one is an adult at 18.* **a·dult·ness** *n.* **a·dult·hood** *n.* ⟨Latin *adultus*, pp of *adolescere* grow up⟩

a·dul·ter·ate [ə'dʌltə,reit] *v* lower the quality of by adding inferior or impure matter: *to adulterate milk with water. His Jungian theory is adulterated with a lot of pop psychology.* **a·dul·ter·a·tion** *n.* ⟨Latin *ad-* to + *alter* other, different⟩

a·dul·ter·y [ə'dʌltəri] *n* sexual unfaithfulness of a husband or wife. **a·dul·ter·er** or **a·dul·ter·ess** *n.* **a·dul·ter·ous** *adj.* ⟨Latin *adulterare* to corrupt. See ADULTERATE.⟩

ad·vance [æd'væns] *v* **1** move forward: *The troops advanced.* **2** make progress: *to advance in knowledge.* **3** help to succeed; promote: *to advance the cause of peace.* **4** put forward: *to advance a new theory.* **5** make earlier: *to advance the time of a meeting.* **6** give ahead of time: *Ask if they'll advance you $50 on next week's pay.* **7** lend (money), esp on security: *to advance a loan.* *adj* given or done ahead of time: *Customers were sent advance notice of the price increase.* *n* **1** the act or fact of advancing. **2** an amount, distance, etc. advanced: *an advance of 30 km. They gave me an advance of $50.* **3 advances,** *pl* actions or words meant to initiate an acquaintance, a reconciliation, a deal, or a campaign of aggression. ⟨Latin *ab-* from + *ante* before⟩

ad·vanced *adj* **1** ahead of most others in progress or development: *advanced ideas, an advanced class in school.* **2** far along in life; very old: *She lived to the advanced age of ninety years.* **advanced credit** or **standing** credit given to a student for courses to be taken at a different institution. **advanced green** at an intersection, a flashing green light for vehicles turning left while oncoming traffic still has a red light. **ad·vance·ment** *n* **1** progress: *the advancement of knowledge through books.* **2** promotion: *There is good opportunity for advancement in this job.* **advance poll ✱** in a general election, an arrangement whereby persons expecting to be absent from their riding on election day may cast their votes at an earlier date. **advance vote ✱** a vote cast in such a poll.

ad·van·tage [æd'væntɪdʒ] *n* **1** a favourable condition, circumstance, or opportunity; benefit: *Good health is a great advantage.* **2** a better position: *He had an advantage over his opponent in that he had more experience.* *v* give an advantage to; help; benefit. ⟨French *avantage.* See ADVANCE.⟩ **have the advantage of** (someone), know someone to whom one is not known: *You have the advantage of me; I don't know you.* **take advantage of a** make good use of for oneself: *She took advantage of the hubbub to slip out of the room.* **b** impose upon (a person's good nature, etc.). **to advantage** so as to produce a good effect or show the merits of: *a painting displayed to advantage.* **to one's advantage** profitable for one: *It would be to your advantage to learn a second language.* **ad·van·ta·geous** [,ædvən'teidʒəs] *adj* favourable; profitable: *His large inheritance put us in a very advantageous position.* **ad·van·ta·geous·ly** *adv.* **ad·van·ta·geous·ness** *n.*

ad·vent ['ædvɛnt] *n* **1** arrival: *the advent of spring.* **2** *Christianity* **Advent a** the birth of Christ. **b** the season of devotion including the four Sundays before Christmas. ⟨Latin *adventus*, pp of *advenīre* arrive⟩

Ad·vent·ist [æd'vɛntɪst] *or* ['ædvəntɪst] *n* a member of a Christian denomination that believes the second coming of Jesus Christ is near at hand. See SEVENTH DAY ADVENTIST.

ad·ven·ti·tious [,ædvɛn'tɪʃəs] *adj* **1** coming from outside; accidental: *The romantic life of the author gives his book an adventitious interest.* **2** *Biology* appearing in an unusual place: *Adventitious roots can grow from leaves.* **ad·ven·ti·tious·ly** *adv.* **ad·ven·ti·tious·ness** *n.* ⟨Latin *adventīcius.* See ADVENT.⟩

ad·ven·ture [æd'vɛntʃər] *n* **1** an undertaking involving unknown risks and danger. **2** an unusual or exciting experience: *It was an adventure to be in a strange city.* *v* take part in daring undertakings: *a summer of adventuring in the wilderness.* **ad·ven·tur·er** *n.* **ad·ven·tur·ous** *adj.* **ad·ven·tur·ous·ly** *adv.* **ad·ven·tur·ous·ness** *n.* **ad·ven·ture·some** *adj.*

⟨Latin *adventura (res)* (thing) about to happen. See ADVENT.⟩

ad·ven·tur·ism *n* the attempting of projects with too little preparation. **ad·ven·tur·ist** *n, adj.*

ad·verb ['ædvɜrb] *n* a word used to extend or limit the meaning of a verb or to qualify an adjective or other adverb. *Soon, here, very, gladly,* and *not* are adverbs. *Abbrev* **adv ad·ver·bi·al** [æd'vɜrbiəl] *adj.* **ad·ver·bi·al·ly** *adv.* ⟨Latin *ad-* to + *verbum* verb⟩

USAGE
In informal use, some common adverbs may occur in the same form as adjectives: *Don't talk so loud. You drive too slow.* It is better to use the *-ly* form in formal English.

ad·verse [æd'vɜrs] *or* ['ædvɜrs] *adj* **1** harmful; unfavourable: *The climate had an adverse effect on his health.* **2** disapproving: *adverse criticism.* **ad·verse·ly** *adv.* **ad·verse·ness** *n.* ⟨Latin *adversus*, pp of *advertere.* See ADVERT.⟩ **ad·ver·sar·y** ['ædvər,sɛri] *n* an enemy; opponent. **ad·ver·sa·ri·al** [,ædvər'sɛriəl] *adj.* **ad·ver·si·ty** [æd'vɜrsəti] *n* hardship; trouble or misfortune.

CONFUSABLES
Adverse is not used with *to*; **averse** is. *He has an adverse opinion of talk shows. He is averse to talk shows.*

ad·vert [æd'vɜrt] *v* refer (*to*): *The speaker adverted to the need for more parks.* ⟨Latin *ad-* to + *vertere* turn⟩

ad·ver·tise ['ædvər,taɪz] *v* **1** give public notice of in a newspaper, on television or radio, etc.: *The meeting was well advertised in the newspaper.* **2** ask (*for*) by public notice: *to advertise for a job.* **3** praise a product, etc. to promote sales: *Many manufacturers advertise in this magazine.* **4** make generally known: *There's no need to advertise your mistakes.* **ad·ver·tis·er** *n.* **ad·ver·tis·ing** *n.* ⟨Old French *avertir*, from Latin. See ADVERT.⟩ **ad·ver·tise·ment** [,ædvər'taɪzmənt] *or, for 2,* [æd'vɜrtɪsmənt] **1** the act or fact of advertising. **2** a public notice in a newspaper, etc. Usually informally shortened to **ad.**

ad·vice [æd'vəɪs] *n* an expressed opinion about what should be done: *Take the doctor's advice.* ⟨Latin *ad-* + *vīsum* thing seen⟩

ad·vise [æd'vaɪz] *v* **1** give advice (to): *I shall act as you advise. Advise him to stay in bed.* **2** inform (often with *of*): *We were advised of the dangers before we began our trip.* **3** recommend: *I advise caution.* **ad·vis·a·ble** *adj* to be recommended; wise. **ad·vis·a·bil·i·ty** *n.* **ad·vis·a·bly** *adv.* **ad·vis·ed·ly** *adv* after careful consideration. **ad·vis·or** *or* **ad·vi·ser** *n* a person who gives advice, esp someone appointed to do so. **ad·vi·so·ry** *adj* with power or intent to advise: *an advisory committee. n* a bulletin or report containing advice or advance information: *a weather advisory.* **under ad·vise·ment** *n* under careful consideration: *The lawyer took our case under advisement and said she would give us an answer in two weeks.*

ad·vo·cate ['ædvə,keit] *v* **1** speak in favour of; recommend: *to advocate increased spending for public transportation.* **2** speak publicly or engage in activism on behalf of a certain group: *to advocate for the homeless. n* ['ædvəkət] **1** a person who pleads or argues for something or defends a certain group: *an advocate for the poor.* **2** a lawyer who pleads in a court of law. **ad·vo·ca·cy** *n.* **ad·vo·ca·tion** *n.* ⟨Latin *ad-* to + *vocāre* call⟩

ad·ware ['ædweir] *n Computers* free software that displays advertisements. ⟨*ad* + *(soft) ware*⟩

adze [ædz] *n* a tool for shaping wood, resembling an axe but with a curved blade. ⟨Old English *adesa*⟩

ae·gis ['idʒɪs] *n* official protection: *under the aegis of the law.* ⟨Greek *aigis* shield⟩

ae·gro·tat ['aɪgrou,tæt] *n* a certificate stating that a student cannot write an examination because of illness. ⟨Latin = he is sick⟩

ae·on ['iən] *or* ['ɪɒn] See EON.

aer·ate ['ereit] *v* **1** expose to air, mix with air, or increase the circulation of air in. **2** charge with a gas. Soda water is water that has been aerated with carbon dioxide. **3** expose to chemical action with oxygen. Blood is aerated in the lungs. **aer·a·tion** *n.* **aer·a·tor** *n.* ⟨Greek *aēr* air⟩

aer·i·al ['ɛriəl] *or, for 2* [ei'iriəl] *adj* **1** of or in the air: *aerial spirits, an aerial ballet.* **2** thin, light, and insubstantial as air. **3** to do with aircraft: *aerial navigation, aerial warfare, an aerial photograph.* **4** *Botany* growing in the air instead of in soil or water: *aerial ferns. n* ['ɛriəl] a radio or television antenna, esp on a vehicle. **aer·i·al·ly** *adv.*⟨Greek *aēr* air⟩ **aer·i·al·ist** *n* an acrobat who performs feats on a trapeze, high wire, etc. **aerial ladder** an extending ladder often used on fire engines.

aero– [ɛrou] *combining form* **1** air or air travel: *aerospace.* **2** gas: *aerosol.* ⟨Greek *aēr* air⟩ **aer·o·bat·ics** [,ɛrou'bætɪks] *n pl* tricks or skilful moves performed with an aircraft in flight. **aer·o·bat·ic** *adj.* **aer·obe** ['ɛroub] *n* a micro-organism, such as a bacterium, that can live only in air. Compare ANAEROBE. **aer·o·bic** [ɛ'roubɪk] *adj* **1** living only in air. **2** of physical activity, improving circulation (and hence aeration of the blood). **aerobics** *n pl* aerobic exercises. **aer·o·dy·nam·ics** [,ɛroudaɪ'næmɪks] *n* the branch of physics that deals with the motion of air and other gases. **aer·o·dy·nam·i·cist** *n.* **aer·o·dy·nam·ic** *adj* **1** designed so as to minimize air resistance. **2** to do with aerodynamics. **aer·o·dy·nam·i·cal·ly** *adv.* **aer·o·gram** *or* **aer·o·gramme** ['ɛrou,græm] *n* a pre-stamped, folding letter form needing no envelope, used for international air mail. **aer·o·nau·tics** [,ɛrə'nɒtɪks] *n* the science of the design, manufacture, and operation of aircraft. **aer·o·nau·ti·cal** *or* **aer·o·naut·ic** *adj.* **aer·o·nau·ti·cal·ly** *adv.* **aer·o·quay** ['ɛrou,ki] *n* an airport building comprising ticket offices, shops, etc. as well as docklike bays at which

aircraft take on and let off passengers.
aer·o·sol ['ɛrə,sɒl] *n* **1** a suspension of fine particles in a gas. **2** an apparatus for dispensing paint, insecticide, etc., under pressure as a mist or foam. **aer·o·space** ['ɛrou,speis] *n* **1** the earth's atmosphere and the space beyond it. **2** the branch of science that deals with the earth's atmosphere and outer space, esp in relation to space travel. **aer·o·space** *adj*.

aes·thete ['ɛsθit] *or* ['isθit] *n* **1** a person who is sensitive to beauty; lover of beauty. **2** a person who pretends to care a great deal about beauty. Also, **es·thete**. ⟨Greek *aisthētēs* one who perceives⟩
aes·the·ti·cian *n* **1** the operator of a beauty parlour. **2** a person skilled in aesthetics.
aes·thet·i·cism [ɛs'θɛtə,sɪzəm] *n* **1** the belief that beauty is the highest standard of value. **2** appreciation of beauty and the arts.
aes·thet·ics [ɛs'θɛtɪks] *n* the study of beauty in art and nature; philosophy of beauty. **aes·thet·ic** *adj*. **aes·thet·i·cal·ly** *adv*.

aes·ti·vate See ESTIVATE.

a·far [ə'fɑr] *adv* far; far away; far off.

af·fa·ble ['æfəbəl] *adj* friendly. **af·fa·bil·i·ty** *n*. **af·fa·bly** *adv*. ⟨Latin *affari; ad-* to + *fari* speak⟩

af·fair [ə'fɛr] *n* **1** something done or to be done; concern: *That's my affair.* **2 affairs** *n pl* matters of interest or concern, esp public matters: *current affairs.* **3** an action, object, etc. referred to in vague terms: *The party last night was a dull affair.* **4** a sexual relationship between people not married to each other. ⟨Old French *à faire (Latin facere)* to do⟩

af·fect¹ [ə'fɛkt] *v* **1** have an effect or influence on: *The small amount of rain last year affected the growth of crops.* **2** touch the heart of: *Their story so affected her that she immediately offered to help.*
n ['æfɛkt] *Psychology* an emotion associated with an object or idea. ⟨Latin *affectus,* pp of *afficere* act upon⟩
af·fect·ing *adj* moving the emotions. **af·fec·tion** *n* warm, friendly feeling; fondness. **af·fec·tion·ate** *adj* expressing affection. **af·fec·tion·ate·ly** *adv*. **af·fec·tive** *adj* of the feelings; emotional. **af·fec·tive·ly** *adv*.

CONFUSABLES
Affect means to influence. Effect means to bring about. As a noun, it means 'result'.

af·fect² [ə'fɛkt] *v* **1** pretend (to have or feel): *He affected ignorance of the fight, but we knew he had seen it.* **2** assume falsely, merely for show: *to affect a British accent.* **af·fect·ed** *adj*. **af·fect·ed·ly** *adv*. ⟨Latin *affectare* strive for⟩
af·fec·ta·tion [,æfɛk'teiʃən] *n* **1** something adopted merely for show: *That pipe is an affectation; he doesn't even smoke.* **2** pretence; false appearance: *an affectation of ignorance.*

af·fi·da·vit [,æfə'deivɪt] *n Law* a written, sworn statement. ⟨Latin = he has stated on oath⟩

af·fil·i·ate [ə'fɪli,eit] *v* connect in close association: *This organization is not affiliated with any political party.*

n [ə'fɪliɪt] a person or organization that is affiliated. **af·fil·i·a·tion** *n*. ⟨Latin *affiliare* adopt; *ad-* to + *filius* son⟩

af·fin·i·ty [ə'fɪnəti] *n* **1** a natural attraction to or liking for a person or thing: *a strong affinity for the sciences.* **2** *Chemistry* an attraction or force between certain particles or substances that causes them to combine chemically. **3** a close relationship or connection, as between ideas, languages, etc. ⟨Latin *affinitas; ad-* on + *finis* boundary⟩

af·firm [ə'fɜrm] *v* **1** declare to be true; assert. **2** encourage or build up: *She affirmed me as an artist.* **af·fir·ma·tion** [,æfər'meiʃən] *n*. ⟨Latin *affirmare; ad-* to + *firmus* strong⟩
af·firm·a·tive *adj* **1** stating that a fact is so. **2** optimistic or encouraging. *n* **1** a word or statement that indicates agreement. **2 the affirmative** the side arguing in favour of a resolution being debated. **af·firm·a·tive·ly** *adv*. **in the affirmative** with a 'yes': *She replied in the affirmative.* **affirmative action** policies designed to increase the representation, in various fields, of groups that have suffered discrimination, such as women or members of racial minorities.

af·fix [ə'fɪks] *v* **1** fix or stick (one thing to or on another): *to affix postage to a letter.* **2** add at the end: *to affix a signature to a document.* **3** attach; assign: *to affix blame.*
n ['æfɪks] a prefix, suffix, or infix. *Un-* and *-ly* are affixes. ⟨Latin *affixāre; ad-* to + *figere* fix⟩
af·fix·a·tion [,æfɪk'seiʃən] *n Linguistics* the process of forming a new word by attaching an affix to a stem.

af·flict [ə'flɪkt] *v* cause great suffering or distress to: *to be afflicted with financial troubles.* **af·flict·ed** *adj*. **af·flic·tion** *n*. ⟨Latin *affligere; ad-* upon + *fligere* dash⟩

af·flu·ent ['æfluənt] *adj* relatively wealthy. *n* a stream flowing into a larger body of water. **af·flu·ence** *n*. ⟨Latin *affluere; ad-* to + *fluere* flow⟩

af·ford [ə'fɔrd] *v* **1** have the money for. **2** manage to give, spare, etc.: *Can you afford the time for this?* **3** risk the consequences of: *We can't afford a fight now.* **4** furnish; yield: *Reading affords pleasure.* **af·ford·a·ble** *adj*. ⟨Old English *geforthian* further, accomplish⟩

af·for·est [ə'fɔrəst] *v* plant (an area) with trees. **af·for·est·a·tion** [ə,fɔrə'steiʃən] *n*.

af·front [ə'frʌnt] *n* a remark or act that openly expresses disrespect: *an affront to decency, an affront to my intelligence.*
v insult openly; offend purposely. ⟨Latin *ad frontem* against the forehead⟩

Af·ghan ['æfgæn] *or* ['æfgən] *n* **1** a native or inhabitant of Afghanistan. **2 afghan** a knitted or crocheted blanket.
adj to do with Afghanistan or its people.

a·fi·cio·na·do [ə,fɪsjə'nɑdou] *n* an enthusiastic fan. **a·fi·cio·na·da** *n*. ⟨Spanish⟩

a·field [ə'fild] *adv, adj* (never before a noun) **1** away from home; away. **2** out of the way; astray.

a·fire [ə'faɪr] *adv, adj* (never precedes a noun) on fire: *afire with patriotism. They set the whole house afire.*

a·flame [ə'fleɪm] *adv, adj* (never precedes a noun) flaming: *aflame with curiosity, a garden aflame with colour.*

a·float [ə'floʊt] *adv, adj* (never precedes a noun) **1** floating. **2** at sea. **3** flooded. **4** in circulation; current: *Rumours of revolt were afloat.* **5** *Informal.* solvent; financially viable: *She took out a loan to keep her business afloat.*

a·flut·ter [ə'flʌtər] *adv, adj* (never precedes a noun) fluttering: *The chickens were aflutter in the yard. Her voice set his heart aflutter.*

AFN ASSEMBLY OF FIRST NATIONS.

a·foot [ə'fʊt] *adv, adj* (never precedes a noun) **1** going on: *Preparations for dinner were afoot in the kitchen.* **2** on foot; walking.

a·fore·men·tioned [ə'fɔr,mɛnʃənd] *adj* spoken of before; mentioned above.

a·fore·said [ə'fɔr,sɛd] *adj* spoken of before.

a·fore·thought [ə'fɔr,θɒt] *adj* thought of beforehand; deliberately planned.

a·foul [ə'faʊl] *adv, adj* (never precedes a noun) in a tangle; in a collision; entangled.
run afoul of a get into difficulties with; come into conflict with: *The gang ran afoul of the police.* **b** crash into or become entangled with: *The canoe ran afoul of the motorboat.*

a·fraid [ə'freɪd] *adj* **1** feeling fear: *afraid of the dark.* **2** sorry (to express polite regret): *I'm afraid I'll have to ask you to leave.* ⟨orig pp of archaic *affray* frighten⟩

a·fresh [ə'frɛʃ] *adv* once more; again.

Af·ri·ca ['æfrəkə] *n* a large continent south of the Mediterranean Sea, bordered by the Atlantic Ocean to the west and the Indian Ocean to the east. **Af·ri·can** *adj, n.* ⟨Latin⟩ **Af·ro** or **af·ro** *n* a hairstyle for very curly hair, leaving it bushy and clipped into a rounded shape. **Afro–** *combining form* **1** of African descent: *Afro-American.* **2** involving Africa and ——: *an Afro-Asian conference.*

aft [æft] *adv, adj* at or toward the stern of a ship or aircraft. ⟨Old English *ætan* from behind⟩

af·ter ['æftər] *prep* **1** next to or behind (in space): *in line one after another.* **2** later in time than: *after supper.* **3** in pursuit of: *Run after him.* **4** about: *Your aunt asked after you.* **5** in view of: *After what she did, who could like her?* **6** in spite of: *After all her suffering, she is still cheerful.* **7** in imitation of: *a fable after the manner of Aesop.* **8** lower in importance than: *A captain is after a general.* **9** for: *named after his cousin.*
adv **1** behind: *to follow after.* **2** later: *three hours after.*
adj later; subsequent: *In after years he regretted the mistakes of his boyhood.*
conj later than the time that: *We'll eat after he goes.* ⟨Old English *æfter* further back, later⟩
after all a in spite of everything: *We decided to go after all.* **b** taking everything into consideration: *After all, does it really matter?*
af·ter·birth *n* the placenta and membranes

expelled from the uterus after childbirth.
af·ter·burn·er *n* in a turbojet aircraft, an extra section in which additional fuel is sprayed into the burning exhaust gases, permitting the aircraft to reach very high speeds. **af·ter·care** *n* care or assistance given to people who have been discharged from hospitals or other facilities. **af·ter·deck** *n* the deck toward or at the stern of a ship. **af·ter–ef·fect** *n* a result or effect that follows some time later. **af·ter·glow** *n* **1** the glow in the sky after sunset. **2** the good feeling that follows a pleasant event. **af·ter·im·age** *n* a visual sensation that persists or recurs after the stimulus is withdrawn. **af·ter·life** *n* **1** life or existence after death. **2** a later part of life. **af·ter·mar·ket** *n* the market for replacement parts, service, etc.: *the aftermarket in the automotive industry.* **af·ter·math** *n* **1** the negative or challenging consequences of some cataclysmic event: *The aftermath of war is hunger and disease.* **2** a crop gathered after the first crop. ⟨*math* (Old English *mæth*) a mowing⟩ **af·ter·noon** *n* **1** the part of the day between noon and evening. **2** a period of gradual decline following the stage of greatest health, success, etc. *adj* of, in, or for the afternoon. **af·ter·pains** *n* pains caused by uterine contractions after childbirth. **af·ter·shave** *n* a usually scented, astringent lotion for applying to the face after shaving. **af·ter·shock** *n* **1** a minor tremor that closely follows an earthquake. **2** an unpleasant event linked to and following a more serious one. **af·ter·taste** *n* **1** a taste, usually bad, that remains after eating or drinking. **2** the feeling, usually negative, that lingers after some experience. **af·ter·thought** *n* **1** a later thought or explanation. **2** something added later and not properly integrated into the whole. **3** a thought that comes too late. **af·ter·ward** or **afterwards** *adv* at a later time. **af·ter·word** *n* a critical commentary at the end of a book. **af·ter·world** *n* in some belief systems, a world entered after death.

a·gain [ə'gɛn] *or* [ə'geɪn] *adv* **1** once more: *Try that again.* **2** *Formal* besides; moreover. **3** *Archaic, poetic* back (to a person or place): *Bring us word again.* ⟨Old English *ongean*⟩
again and again often; frequently. **as much again** twice as much or many. **then again** on the other hand.

a·gainst [ə'gɛnst] *or* [ə'geɪnst] *prep* **1** in an opposite direction to, so as to meet: *to sail against the wind.* **2** in opposition to: *against reason.* **3** so as to be touching or supported by: *leaning against the wall.* **4** in contrast to or with: *The ship appeared against the sky.* **5** from: *A fire is a protection against cold.* **6** in preparation for: *Squirrels store up nuts against the winter.* **7** of an amount, as a deduction from: *The charges were entered against the total.* ⟨Old English *ongean* again + *-st*⟩
over against in contrast or opposition to. **up against it** under pressure and with no options.

a·gar ['eigɑr], ['ɑgər], *or* ['ægər] *n* a preparation containing **a·gar–a·gar,** an extract resembling gelatin, used in making cultures for bacteria, etc. ⟨Malay⟩

ag·ate ['ægɪt] *n* a type of quartz, often polished to make a gemstone. ⟨Greek *achatēs*⟩

a·ga·ve [ə'geivi] *n* any of a genus of tropical American plants with thick, fleshy leaves, important as sources of soap, sisal, and alcoholic drinks. ⟨Greek *agauē* noble⟩

age [eidʒ] *v* **aged, age·ing** or **ag·ing 1** grow old: *He is aging rapidly.* **2** cause to seem or feel old: *Fear and worry aged her.* **3** improve by keeping for a time; mature: *to age wine.*
n **1** a particular time of life in years, months, etc.: *He married at the age of thirty.* **2** the length of time something has existed: *The age of the earth is open to question.* **3** a period in life: *middle age.* **4** the latter part of life: *the wisdom of age.* **5** a period in history: *the space age, the Ice Age.* **6** *Informal* a long, or apparently long, time: *We haven't seen her in ages.* ⟨Old French *aage*; Latin *aetas* age⟩
of age old enough to have full legal rights and responsibilities.

a·ged [eidʒd] *adj* **1** of the age of: *a child aged six.* **2** made flavourful by keeping: *aged cheese.* **3** ['eidʒɪd] having lived a long time: *An aged person. n* **the aged** ['eidʒɪd], *pl* elderly people: *The aged now lead much more active lives.* **age·ism** *n* discrimination on the basis of age, esp against the elderly. **age·ist** *n* or *adj.* **age·less** *adj* never growing or seeming to grow old or older. **age·less·ly** *adv.* **age·less·ness** *n.* **age of consent** the age at which a person can legally agree to marriage, sexual intercourse, medical treatment, etc. without the consent of a parent or guardian. **age–old** *adj* that has existed for ages: *the age-old struggle between good and evil.*

a·gen·cy ['eidʒənsi] *n* **1** action producing an effect; means: *Snow is drifted by the agency of the wind.* **2** a business firm with authority to act for a person or group: *An agency rented my house for me.* **3** its offices. **4** an organization, often governmental, serving the public in some way. ⟨Latin *agens*, ppr of *agere* do⟩
a·gent *n* **1** a person or company with authority to act for another. **2** a person or thing producing a particular effect: *an agent of tragedy.* **3** SECRET AGENT. **4** a travelling sales representative. **5** *Chemistry* a substance causing a reaction. **6** *Computers* BOT². **agent general** *pl* **agents general** or **agent generals** a representative of a Canadian province in another country. *Abbrev* **A.G. a·gen·tive** [ə'dʒɛntɪv] *Grammar adj* to do with a form indicating agency: *the agentive suffixes -er and -or. n* such a form. *Worker* is an agentive. **agent pro·vo·ca·teur** [aʒã prɔvɔka'tœR] *French* a person who incites others to do something that will make them liable to punishment.

a·gen·da [ə'dʒɛndə] *n* **1** a list or plan of things to be done: *the agenda for the next meeting, this afternoon's agenda.* **2** an ulterior motive or objective: *He always has an agenda.* ⟨Latin = things to be done, from *agere* do⟩

ag·glom·er·ate [ə'glɒmə,reit] *v* gather or cluster together.

n [ə'glɒmərɪt] **1** a clustered mass. **2** *Geology* a rock composed of volcanic fragments fused by heat. **ag·glom·er·ate** *adj.* **ag·glom·er·a·tion** *n.* **ag·glom·er·a·tive** *adj.* ⟨Latin *ad-* to + *glomus* mass, ball⟩

ag·gran·dize [ə'grændaɪz] *v* increase in power, wealth, prestige, etc.: *to aggrandize oneself at the expense of other people.* **ag·gran·dize·ment** [ə'grændɪzmənt] *n.* ⟨Latin *ad-* to + *grandis* large⟩

ag·gra·vate ['ægrə,veit] *v* **1** make worse: *Her bad temper was aggravated by her headache.* **2** *Informal* annoy. **ag·gra·vat·ing·ly** *adv.* **ag·gra·va·tion** *n.* ⟨Latin *ad-* to + *gravis* heavy⟩

ag·gre·gate ['ægrəgɪt] *adj* **1** combined into one body or amount: *The aggregate value of all the gifts was $1000.* **2** *Botany* composed of many parts or units: *The raspberry is an aggregate fruit.* **3** *Geology* composed of rock fragments: *Granite is an aggregate rock.*
v ['ægrə,geit] **1** combine into one mass. **2** amount to: *The money collected will aggregate over $3000.* **ag·gre·gate** ['ægrəgɪt] *n.* **ag·gre·gate·ly** *adv.* **ag·gre·ga·tion** *n.* ⟨Latin *ad-* to + *grex, gregis* flock⟩

ag·gres·sive [ə'grɛsɪv] *adj* **1** attacking or tending to attack; starting quarrels: *aggressive behaviour.* **2** pushy: *an aggressive salesperson.* **3** energetic and forceful: *an aggressive political campaign.* ⟨Latin *aggredi; ad-* to + *gradi* to step⟩ **ag·gress** *v* start a quarrel. **ag·gres·sor** *n.* **ag·gres·sion** *n* an attack, esp unprovoked. **ag·gres·sive·ly** *adv.* **ag·gres·siv·i·ty** *n.*

USAGE
Aggressive and **assertive** have undergone recent amelioration, almost merging in some contexts to mean initiative and persistence in ensuring that one's cause, interests, etc. are taken seriously. However, both remain open to negative interpretation, especially **aggressive**.

ag·grieve [ə'griv] *v* **1** offend; injure: *He was aggrieved at the insult.* **2** infringe on the legal rights of (workers, etc.). **ag·grieved** *adj.* ⟨Latin *aggravare.* See AGGRAVATE.⟩

a·ghast [ə'gæst] *adj* (never before a noun) filled with extreme surprise or horror: *They were aghast at the violence of the crime.* ⟨Old English *gæstan* frighten. Related to GHOST.⟩

ag·ile ['ædʒaɪl] *or* ['ædʒəl] *adj* moving swiftly and easily: *A gymnast has to be agile.* **2** able to think quickly. **ag·ile·ly** *adv.* **a·gil·i·ty** [ə'dʒɪləti] *n.* ⟨Latin *agilis; agere* move⟩

ag·i·tate ['ædʒə,teit] *v* **1** stir up; shake: *A gust of wind agitated the leaves.* **2** make nervous, upset, or excited: *She was much agitated by the news of her brother's accident.* **3** keep arguing about a matter to raise awareness and elicit action: *to agitate for a shorter work week.* **ag·i·tat·ed·ly** *adv.* **ag·i·ta·tion** *n.* ⟨Latin *agitare; agere* move⟩
ag·i·ta·tor *n* **1** a person who tries to make people discontented with things as they are. **2** a device for shaking or stirring: *the agitator in a washing machine.*

a·glow [ə'glou] *adv, adj* (never precedes a noun) glowing.

ag·lu or **ag·loo** ['æglu] *n* ✱ a breathing-hole in ice, made by seals. ⟨Inuktitut⟩

ag·nos·tic [æg'nɒstɪk] *n* a person who believes that nothing can be known about the existence of God. **ag·nos·tic** *adj.* **ag·nos·ti·cal·ly** *adv.* **ag·nos·ti·cism** *n.* ⟨Greek *a*- not + *gnōstos* (to be) known⟩

a·go [ə'gou] *adv* in the past; counting back from the present: *a year ago. She went long ago.* ⟨Old English *āgān* gone by⟩

a·gog [ə'gɒg] *adj, adv* (never precedes a noun) greatly excited or amazed. ⟨prob. Old French *en gogues* in happy mood⟩

ag·o·nize ['ægə,naɪz] *v* **1** feel great anguish. **2** struggle intensely. ⟨Greek *agōnizethai* to struggle; *agón* contest⟩ **ag·o·niz·ing** *adj* causing great anguish: *an agonizing decision.* **ag·o·niz·ing·ly** *adv.* **ag·o·ny** *n* great pain or suffering.

ag·o·ra·pho·bi·a [,ægərə'foubiə] or [ə,gɔrə'foubiə] *n* an abnormal fear of open spaces or public places. **ag·o·ra·phobe** *n.* **ag·o·ra·pho·bic** *adj, n.* ⟨Greek *agōra* marketplace + English *phobia*⟩

a·grar·i·an [ə'grɛriən] *adj* **1** to do with land, its use in farming, or its ownership. **2** favouring the interests of farmers. *n* a person who favours a new division of land. **a·grar·i·an·ism** *n.* ⟨Latin *agrarius; ager* field⟩

a·gree [ə'gri] *v* **1** have the same opinion: *I agree with you. She does not agree.* **2** be consistent (*with*): *Her story agrees with theirs.* **3** consent (*to*): *We agreed to their proposal.* **4** *Grammar* be the same in number, case, gender, or person. **a·gree·ment** *n.* ⟨Old French *à gré* to (one's) liking; Latin *ad* to + *gratum* pleasing⟩ **not agree with** of food, cause illness or indigestion in: *Bananas don't agree with me.* **a·gree·a·ble** *adj* **1** pleasant: *an agreeable climate, agreeable manners.* **2** ready to agree: *agreeable to a suggestion.* **3** of a proposed arrangement, satisfactory. **a·gree·a·bil·i·ty** or **a·gree·a·ble·ness** *n.* **a·gree·a·bly** *adv.* **a·greed** *adj* set by common consent: *at the agreed time.*

ag·ri·cul·ture ['ægrə,kʌltʃər] *n* farming; the raising of crops and livestock. **ag·ri·cul·tur·al** *adj.* **ag·ri·cul·tur·al·ly** *adv.* **ag·ri·cul·tur·ist** or **ag·ri·cul·tur·al·ist** *n.* ⟨Latin *ager* field + *cultura* cultivation⟩ **ag·ri·busi·ness** *n* the production and marketing of agricultural products, esp as distinct from small-scale farming.

a·grol·o·gy [ə'grɒlədʒi] *n* the branch of agricultural science that deals with soils. **ag·ro·log·i·cal** *adj.* **a·grol·o·gist** *n.* ⟨Greek *agros* field + English *-logy*⟩ **ag·ro·bi·ol·o·gy** *n* the study of plant nutrition and soil management. **ag·ro·bi·o·log·i·cal** *adj.* **ag·ro·bi·ol·o·gist** *n.* **ag·ro·chem·i·cal** *n* a chemical used to increase the quantity and quality of agricultural products. **a·gron·o·my** *n* the branch of agriculture dealing with crop production. **ag·ro·nom·ic** [,ægrə'nɒmɪk] or

ag·ro·nom·i·cal *adj.* **a·gron·o·mist** *n.* ⟨Greek *agros* land + *nomos* arrangement⟩

a·ground [ə'graund] *adv, adj* (never precedes a noun) on or onto the shore: *The ship ran aground on a reef.*

a·gue ['eigju] *n* **1** a malarial fever with chills and sweating occurring at regular intervals. **2** a fit of shivering; chill. **a·gu·ish** *adj.* ⟨Latin *acuta (febris)* severe (fever)⟩

ah [ɑ] *interj* an exclamation of pain, sorrow, pity, admiration, surprise, joy, contempt, etc.

a·ha [ɑ'hɑ] *interj* an exclamation of triumph, satisfaction, surprise, etc.

a·head [ə'hɛd] *adv* **1** in front: *He stood ahead of me in line.* **2** forward: *Walk ahead ten paces.* **3** in advance: *to phone ahead for reservations.* **4** in or into the lead, as in a race or game: *Our team shot ahead 3 to 1.* **ahead of one's time** having ideas more advanced than everybody else's. **ahead of time** in advance. **be ahead** have gained: *At the end of the day he was ahead $35.* **get ahead** *Informal* succeed in life. **go ahead a** feel free to do what has been suggested or thought of. **b** proceed; move forward.

a·hem [ə'hɛm] *interj* used to represent the sound of clearing the throat. ⟨imitative⟩

a·him·sa [ə'hɪm,sɑ] *n* the principle of non-violence in Hinduism, Buddhism, etc. ⟨Sanskrit *a* not + *hiṁsā* injury⟩

a·hold [ə'hould] *n Informal* a grasp on something: *Get ahold of yourself!*

–aholic *combining form Informal, often facetious* one who is addicted. A *chocaholic* is addicted to chocolate. ⟨modified from (*alc*)*oholic*⟩

a·hoy [ə'hɔi] *interj* a call used by sailors to attract the attention of persons at a distance: *"Ship ahoy!"* ⟨Middle English⟩

Ah·ri·man ['ɑrɪmən] *n* ANGRA MAINYU.

A·hu·ra Maz·da [ə'hʊrə 'mæzdə] in Zoroastrianism, the supreme deity; the wise and good lord of creation; the good spirit of the cosmos. ⟨Avestan = wise lord⟩

AI or **A.I.** **1** *Computers* artificial intelligence. **2** artificial insemination.

aid [eid] *v* help: *The Red Cross aids flood victims.* *n* **1** help; support: *to walk without aid.* **2** a person or thing that helps: *They hired a teacher's aid. He wears a hearing aid.* ⟨Old French *aidier,* from Latin *adjūvāre; ad-* to + *jūvāre* help⟩ **aid station** a medical centre providing immediate medical aid to troops in the field.

aide [eid] *n* **1** AIDE-DE-CAMP. **2** any assistant. ⟨French⟩ **aide–de–camp** ['eid də 'kæmp] or [ɛddə'kɑ̃] *n,* *pl* **aides–de–camp** a military officer who acts as an assistant to a superior. *Abbrev* **ADC,** **A.D.C.,** or **a.d.c.** ⟨French⟩

aide–mé·moire [ɛdme'mwaʀ] *n French* anything that reminds, such as a note.

AIDS [eidz] *n* ACQUIRED IMMUNE DEFICIENCY SYNDROME. **AIDS–related complex** a viral condition that is often a precursor to AIDS.

ai·ki·do [aɪˈkidou] *or* [ˌaɪkiˈdou] *n* a martial art used for self-defence. 〈Japanese *ai* match + *ki* spirit + *do* way〉

ail [eil] *v* **1** be the matter with: *What ails you?* **2** be ill: *She is ailing.* 〈Old English *eglan*〉 **ail·ment** *n* illness.

ai·lan·thus [eiˈlænθəs] *n* any of a genus of trees and shrubs with compound leaves, native to tropical Asia. 〈Amboinan (language of Amboina in the Dutch East Indies) *aylanto* tree of heaven; influenced by Greek *anthos* flower〉

ai·ler·on [ˈeiləˌrɒn] *n* a small, movable section on the wing of an aircraft for controlling side-to-side motion. 〈French *aileron*, diminutive of *aile*; Latin *ala* wing〉

aim [eim] *v* **1** point (a gun, etc.) in order to hit a target. **2** direct (words or acts): *The prime minister's speech was aimed at young people.* **3** *Informal* intend: *I aim to go.* *n* **1** the act of aiming. **2** purpose; intention. **3** the ability to hit a target: *to have good aim.* 〈Old French *esmer*; Latin *aestimare* appraise〉 **take aim** (at) aim a weapon, words, etc. (at). **aim·less** *adj* without any goal or purpose. **aim·less·ly** *adv.* **aim·less·ness** *n.*

ain't [eint] *Informal* **1** am not, are not, or is not. **2** have not or has not.

USAGE
Although **ain't** has been used in English for a very long time, it is unacceptable to most educated speakers.

air [er] *n* **1** the mixture of gases that surrounds the earth. **2** fresh air; ventilation. **3** transportation by aircraft: *We're going to Iqaluit by air.* **4** the general character of anything: *an air of mystery.* **5 airs** *n pl* affected manners. **6** any tune or melody, esp a simple one. **7** *Informal* short for AIR CONDITIONING. *v* **1** let air through: *to air clothes.* **2** make known: *to air an opinion.* **3** *Informal* broadcast or be broadcast: *Her show airs every day.* 〈Greek *aēr*〉 **give air to** state or discuss openly. **in the air a** current: *a rumour in the air.* **b** exerting a vague general effect: *There's love in the air.* **into thin air** without leaving a trace: *to disappear into thin air.* **off the air** not broadcasting. **on the air** broadcasting. **out of thin air** as if by magic: *to appear out of thin air.* **take the air** go outdoors. **up in the air** uncertain. **walking on air** very happy.

air ambulance an aircraft used as an ambulance. **air bag** a large plastic bag in a vehicle, designed to inflate in a collision so as to protect passengers from impact. **air base** headquarters for military aircraft. **air·borne** *adj* carried through the air: *airborne seeds, airborne troops.* **air brake** a brake worked by compressed air. **air·brush** *n* a device that uses compressed air to apply a fine spray of paint, etc. **air·brush** *v.* **air·bus** *n* a passenger aircraft which one may board by paying cash as on a bus or streetcar. **air cadet** a person under military age who is undertaking basic air-command training. **air coach** *esp US* an aircraft operated by an

airline charging low passenger rates. **Air Command ✱** a major organizational element of the Canadian Forces, whose role is to provide combat-ready air defence forces. **air conditioner** an apparatus used to cool and regulate the air in a room, train, etc. **air–con·di·tion** *v.* **air conditioning** *n.* **air–cool** *v* cool something by blowing cool air into it. **air–cooled** *adj.* **air corridor** a route along which aircraft are permitted to fly. **air·craft** *n, pl* **-craft** any machine for travelling in the air. **aircraft carrier** a warship with a large, flat deck used by aircraft for takeoff and landing. **air cushion 1** an inflatable cushion. **2** a layer of air under pressure to lessen the shock of an impact, support a Hovercraft, etc. **air·drop** *v* drop (supplies) from an aircraft. **air·drop** *n.* **air–dry** *v* dry by exposing to air. **air express** a quick means of sending goods by aircraft. **air–express** *v.* **air·fare** *n* the cost of an airplane ticket. **air·field** *n* the landing field of an airport. **air·flow** *n* the motion of air relative to the surface of a moving object. **air·foil** *n* any surface designed to help lift or control an aircraft. **air force** Often, **Air Force** the branch of the armed forces of a nation responsible for military aircraft; in Canada, Air Command of the Canadian Forces. **air freight** freight carried by air. **air–freight** *v.* **air gun 1** a gun worked by compressed air. **2** a handheld instrument for spraying liquids, worked by compressed air. **air·head** *n* **1** *Slang* a silly person. **2** a place captured by invading forces for landing aircraft. Compare BEACHHEAD. **air hole 1** any hole that allows air to pass through. **2** a hole in the ice used for breathing by seals, muskrats, etc. **air·ing** *n* **1** exposure to air. **2** a walk, ride, etc. in the open air. **3** exposure to public discussion, criticism, etc. **air lane** a regular route used by aircraft. **air·less** *adj* **1** without fresh air; stuffy. **2** with no air at all. **air letter** See AEROGRAM. **air·lift** *n* the use of aircraft to transport supplies and troops when land approaches are closed. **air·lift** *v.* **air·line** *n* a company operating a system of air transportation. **air·lin·er** *n* a large passenger aircraft. **air lock** an airtight compartment in which the air pressure can be adjusted, as at the entrance to a submarine. **air mail** mail sent by aircraft. **air·mail** or **air–mail** *v.* **air·man** *n, pl* **-men** a man connected with flying, esp as a pilot, crew member, or ground technician. **air mass** a part of the atmosphere with nearly uniform temperature and humidity. **air mattress** an inflatable rubber casing for use as a mattress. **air mile** NAUTICAL MILE. **air piracy** hijacking. **air pirate** hijacker. **air·plane** *n* a heavier-than-air aircraft driven by engines and supported by upward thrust on fixed wings. **air plant** a plant that grows on other plants and draws nourishment from the air and the rain. **air·play** *n* the fact of being played on radio or television. **air pocket** a downward air current causing a sudden, short drop in the altitude of an aircraft. **air·port** *n* a place where aircraft regularly come and go carrying passengers or freight.

air power 1 the strength of a country in military aircraft. **2** a country with a major air force. Compare SEA POWER. **air pressure 1** the force exerted by air confined in a restricted space. **2** atmospheric pressure. **air quality index** a numerical value given to the air, indicating degree of pollution. **air raid** an attack by aircraft. **air–raid shelter** a place for protection during an air raid. **air rifle** a rifle that is worked by compressed air. **air rights** the right to use the space above a building, road, railway, etc. **air shaft** a passage for letting fresh air into a tunnel, building, etc. **air·ship** n a dirigible. **air·sick** adj feeling nauseated from the motion of an aircraft. **air·sick·ness** n. **air·space** n space in the air, belonging to a particular country: a violation of our airspace. **air·speed** n the speed of an aircraft measured in relation to the movement of the air rather than to the ground. **air–spray** v spray by means of compressed air. **air·stream** n the stream of air created around a moving object. **air·strike** n an attack by missiles or aircraft. **air·strip** n a paved or cleared strip on which planes can land and take off. **air·tight** adj **1** so tight that no air or gas can get in or out. **2** with no weak points open to attack: an airtight explanation. **air time 1** the time when a radio program is scheduled to begin: a few minutes to air time. **2** an amount of broadcasting time: The advertiser paid $75 000 for air time. **air–to–air** adj from one flying aircraft to another. **air–to–surface** adj of a missile, etc., directed from an aircraft toward the surface of the earth. **air–traffic controller** a person who directs aircraft in an airport. **air·waves** n pl the medium by which radio and television signals are transmitted. **air·way** n **1** a route for aircraft. **2** a passage for air, esp for breathing. **3** a specific radio frequency for broadcasting. **air·wor·thy** adj fit for service in the air. **air·wor·thi·ness** n. **air·y** adj **1** like air; light or insubstantial. **2** breezy. **3** light-hearted. **4** haughty; pretentious. **5** reaching high into the air; lofty. **air·i·ly** adv. **air·i·ness** n. **air·y–fair·y** adj Informal very fanciful or idealistic.

aisle [aɪl] n a passage between rows of seats in a hall, theatre, etc. or between shelves of goods in a store. ⟨Latin ala wing; infl. in form by French aile and English isle, in meaning by alley⟩

a·jar[1] [əˈdʒɑr] adv, adj (never precedes a noun) of a door or gate, opened a little way. ⟨Middle English on char on the turn⟩

a·jar[2] [əˈdʒɑr] adv, adj not in harmony. ⟨a- in + jar discord⟩

a·ji·va [əˈdʒivə] n Jainism **1** all that is not JIVA, or living soul. **2** materialism. ⟨Sanskrit⟩

a.k.a. also known as.

a·kim·bo [əˈkɪmbou] adj, adv (never precedes a noun) of the arms, with hands on hips and elbows bent outward. ⟨Middle English in kene bowe at a sharp angle⟩

a·kin [əˈkɪn] adj (never precedes a noun) related; similar: actions akin to stealing. The friends are akin in their love of sports. ⟨for of kin⟩

à la or **a la** [ˈælə] or [ˈɑlə] French [ala] in the manner of; in the style of: bread pudding à la Grandma Martin. ⟨French⟩

> **USAGE**
> **à la, a la.** In formal writing and some advertising (for cosmetics and fashionable clothes), the accent mark is often kept. It is usually dropped in informal writing.

al·a·bas·ter [ˈæləˌbæstər] or [ˌæləˈbæstər] n a smooth, white, translucent variety of gypsum. adj smooth, white, and translucent like alabaster. **al·a·bas·trine** [-ˈbæstrɪn] adj. ⟨Greek alabast(r)os⟩

à la carte [ˌæ lə ˈkɑrt] or [ˌɑ lə ˈkɑrt] French [ala·kaʀt] according to the menu, with each dish priced separately. Compare TABLE D'HÔTE. ⟨French = according to the bill of fare⟩

a·lac·ri·ty [əˈlækrəti] n **1** eagerness; cheerful willingness: She carried out the task with alacrity. **2** liveliness. ⟨Latin alacer brisk⟩

à la mode or **a la mode** [ˌæ lə ˈmoud] or [ˌɑ lə ˈmoud] adv **1** according to fashion. **2** in a certain way. Desserts à la mode are served with ice cream. ⟨French⟩

a·larm [əˈlɑrm] n **1** sudden fear; fright. **2** a warning of approaching danger. **3** a device that gives such a warning: a fire alarm on a wall. **4** the sound made by such a device or by an ALARM CLOCK.
v **1** frighten. **2** warn (someone) of approaching danger.
alarm clock a clock that can be set to ring, buzz, etc. at any desired time. **a·larm·ing** adj frightening. **a·larm·ing·ly** adv. **a·larm·ist** n one who raises alarms without good reason. adj typical of such a person. **a·larm·ism** n.

a·las [əˈlæs] interj an exclamation of sorrow, grief, regret, pity, or dread. ⟨Old French a ah + las miserable; Latin lassus weary⟩

Alaska black diamond ✱ hematite.
Alaska pine ✱ a species of hemlock.

al·ba·core [ˈælbəˌkɔr] n, pl -core or -cores a long-finned, edible fish related to the tuna. ⟨Portuguese albacor; Arabic al-bakūra⟩

al·ba·tross [ˈælbəˌtrɒs] n **1** any of a family of large ocean birds with very long, narrow wings and mostly white plumage. **2** a burden that one is obliged to bear, esp as a consequence of one's actions (from Coleridge's The Rime of the Ancient Mariner; the Mariner shoots an albatross and is forced to wear the dead bird around his neck). ⟨Portuguese alcatraz frigate bird; Arabic al-qadus bucket⟩

al·be·it [ɒlˈbiɪt] conj although; even though. ⟨Middle English al be it although it be⟩

Al·ber·ta [ælˈbɜrtə] n a western province of Canada. Abbrev AB. **Al·ber·tan** n, adj.

al·bi·no [ælˈbaɪnou] n a person, animal, or plant lacking normal pigment as a result of a gene defect. **al·bi·n·ism** [ˈælbəˌnɪzəm] n. **al·bin·is·tic** or **al·bin·ic** [ælˈbɪnɪk] adj. ⟨Portuguese, from Latin albus white⟩

al·bum ['ælbəm] *n* **1** a book with blank pages for holding pictures, stamps, etc. **2** a book like this filled with collected items. **3** a phonograph record. ⟨Latin *albus* white⟩

al·bu·men [æl'bjumən] *or* ['ælbjəmən] *n* **1** the white of an egg. **2** *Botany* the food for a young plant, stored in a seed. ⟨Latin, from *albus* white⟩

al·bu·min [æl'bjumən] *or* ['ælbjəmən] *n* *Chemistry* any of a class of proteins soluble in water and found in the white of eggs and in many other animal and plant tissues. **al·bu·mi·nous** [æl'bjumənəs] *adj.* ⟨French *albumine*, from Latin. See ALBUMEN.⟩
al·bu·mi·nate [æl'bjumə,neit] *n* a compound produced by the action of an acid or alkali on albumin. **al·bu·mi·noid** [æl'bjumə,nɔɪd] *n* any protein, such as gelatin, which is difficult to dissolve in water.

al·che·my ['ælkəmi] *n* medieval chemistry, esp the search for a process to turn base metals into gold. **al·chem·i·cal** *adj.* **al·che·mist** *n.* **al·che·mis·tic** *adj.* ⟨Arabic *al-kīmiyā*; Greek *chymeia* infusion⟩

al·co·hol ['ælkə,hɒl] *n* **1** the liquid in wine, beer, whisky, etc. that intoxicates. **2** any intoxicating liquor. **3** *Chemistry* any of a group of organic compounds that react with organic acids to form esters. ⟨Arabic *al-koḥ'l* powdered antimony⟩
al·co·hol·ic *adj* containing alcohol. *n* a person who is affected with alcoholism. **al·co·hol·ism** *n* **1** addiction to alcohol. **2** the attendant physical symptoms.

al·cool [æl'kul] ✱ WHISKY BLANC. ⟨French⟩

al·cove ['ælkouv] *n* **1** a recessed section of a room. **2** a niche, usually arched, in a wall. ⟨Arabic *al-qubbah* vaulted chamber⟩

al·de·hyde ['ældə,haɪd] *n* a colourless liquid with a suffocating smell, produced by partial oxidation of ordinary alcohol. **al·de·hy·dic** *adj.* ⟨Latin *al(cohol) dehyd(rogenatum)*⟩

al den·te [ɑl 'dɛnteɪ] *or* [æl 'dɛnti] *Italian* [al 'dɛnte] of pasta, etc., cooked so as to be still firm when eaten. ⟨Italian = to the tooth⟩

al·der ['ɒldər] *n* any of a genus of shrubs or trees of the birch family found especially in cool, wet parts of the northern hemisphere. ⟨Old English *alor*⟩

al·der·man ['ɒldərmən] *n, pl* -men an elected member of a municipal council; now usually called a **councillor**. ⟨Old English *(e)aldor* elder + *mann* man⟩

ale [eil] *n* an alcoholic drink brewed from malt, yeast, and hops. ⟨Old English *alu*⟩
ale·house ['eil,hʌus] *n* formerly, a place where ale or beer was sold and drunk.

a·leph–null *or* **a·leph–zero** ['eilɪf] *or* ['ɑlɪf] *n* *Mathematics* the smallest infinite cardinal number. *Symbol* $\aleph_0$ ⟨*aleph* first letter of the Hebrew alphabet⟩

a·lert [ə'lɜrt] *adj* wide-awake; observant and reacting quickly: *He was alert to every sound.* *n* **1** a signal warning of impending danger. **2** a signal to troops to be ready for action.

v **1** warn. **2** draw the attention of (a person): *Alert him to the problem.* **3** call to arms. **a·lert·ly** *adv.* **a·lert·ness** *n.* ⟨Italian *all' erta* on the watch⟩
on the alert on the lookout; watchful.

ale·wife ['eil,waif] *n, pl* -wives a food fish of the herring family found in salt and fresh waters of eastern North America; gaspereau. ⟨origin uncertain⟩

al·ex·an·drine *or* **Al·ex·an·drine** [,ælig'zændrɪn] *or* [,ælig'zændrin] *n* a line of poetry having six iambic feet, with a caesura (pause) after the third foot. *Example:*
He séeks I out míght I y chárms, I to tróu I ble sléep I y mínds. **al·ex·an·drine** *adj.* ⟨from Old French poems on *Alexander* the Great⟩

al·fal·fa [æl'fælfə] *n* a European plant of the pea family, widely cultivated for forage. ⟨Arabic *al-fasfasah* the best kind of fodder⟩

al·fres·co *or* **al fres·co** [æl'freskou] *adv, adj* in the open air; outdoors. ⟨Italian⟩

al·gae ['æld3i] *or* ['æld3aɪ] *n pl, sg* **al·ga** ['ælgə] a large group of mainly aquatic organisms traditionally classified as plants, but lacking true stems, roots, and leaves. **al·gal** ['ælgəl] *adj.* ⟨Latin, pl of *alga* seaweed⟩
al·gi·cide ['æld3ə,saɪd] *n* a seaweed killer.

> **USAGE**
> Although **algae** is technically a plural noun, it is sometimes used with a singular verb in less formal contexts: *Algae growing on the rock has made it slippery.*

al·ge·bra ['æld3əbrə] *n* **1** a generalization of arithmetic in which letters or other symbols are used to represent numbers. **2** any rule-governed system using symbols to represent propositions: *Boolean algebra.* **al·ge·bra·ic** [,æld3ə'breɪk] *adj.* **al·ge·bra·i·cal·ly** *adv.* ⟨Arabic *al-jabr* bone setting; hence, reduction of parts to a whole⟩
algebraic equation a polynomial equation in which a number of terms is equated to zero. **algebraic number** a number that is the root of a polynomial equation whose coefficients are rational numbers.

Al·gon·quin [æl'gɒŋkɪn] *or* [æl'gɒŋkwɪn] *n* **1** a member of a First Nations people living in Ontario and Québec. **2** their language. **Al·gon·quin** *adj.*
Al·gon·qui·an [æl'gɒŋkiən] *or* [æl'gɒŋkwiən] *n* **1** a family of languages spoken by a large number of Aboriginal peoples traditionally occupying much of central and eastern North America. **2** a speaker of any of these languages. **Al·gon·qui·an** *adj.*

al·go·rithm ['ælgə,rɪðəm] *n* any set of rules or step-by-step procedure (orig for solving a problem in mathematics). ⟨*al-Khowarizmi*, 9c Arab mathematician; influenced by Greek *arithmos* number⟩

a·li·as ['eiliəs] *n* an assumed name: *The spy's real name was Leblanc, but he sometimes went by the alias of Martinet.*
adv otherwise called: *Smith alias Jones.* ⟨Latin = at another time⟩

al·i·bi ['ælə,baɪ] *n, pl* **-bis 1** *Law* the plea that an accused person was somewhere else when the offence was committed. **2** *Informal* an excuse. ⟨Latin = elsewhere⟩

al·ien ['eiliən] *n* **1** a person who is neither a citizen nor a legal immigrant in the country where he or she is. **2** a stranger. **3** a supposed being from some other planet.
adj **1** foreign; strange or unfamiliar: *alien ideas.* **2** not characteristic or compatible (with *to*): *Unkindness is alien to her nature.* ⟨Latin *alienus; alius* other⟩
al·ien·a·ble *adj* capable of being transferred to another person: *alienable property.* **al·ien·a·bil·i·ty** *n.* **al·ien·ate** *v* **1** cause to become indifferent or hostile: *His moodiness is alienating his friends.* **2** turn away: *to alienate someone's affections.* **3** cause (a person) to feel as though he or she does not belong in society: *alienated youth.* **4** *Law* take away legally: *Enemy property was alienated during the war.* **al·ien·a·tion** *n.* **al·ien·ist** *n* a psychiatrist who testifies in court.

a·light[1] [ə'laɪt] *v* **a·light·ed** or **a·lit, a·light·ing 1** get down: *to alight from a horse.* **2** of something flying, land. ⟨Old English *līht* LIGHT[2]; orig with reference to taking one's weight off a horse⟩

a·light[2] [ə'laɪt] *adv, adj* (never precedes a noun) **1** lighted up; shining: *a face alight with joy.* **2** on fire: *The candles were still alight.* ⟨Old English *ālīht* illuminated⟩

a·lign [ə'laɪn] *v* **1** bring into line: *to align the wheels of a car.* **2** bring (groups, oneself, etc.) into an alliance with or against another: *They aligned themselves in the cause of anti-racism.* **a·lign·ment** *n.* ⟨French *aligner*; Latin *ad-* on + *linea* line⟩

a·like [ə'laɪk] *adv* in the same or a similar way: *He and his father walk alike.*
adj (never precedes a noun) **1** identical: *No two snowflakes are alike.* **2** similar: *The twins are very much alike.* ⟨Old English *gelīc, onlīc*⟩

al·i·men·ta·ry [,ælə'mɛntəri] *adj* to do with nutrition. ⟨Latin *alimonia* sustenance⟩
alimentary canal the parts of the body through which food passes. **al·i·men·ta·tion** [,æləmɛn'teiʃən] *n* nourishment; nutrition.

al·i·mo·ny ['ælə,mouni] *n* **1** *Law* money paid to support a spouse under a separation agreement. Compare MAINTENANCE. **2** loosely, money paid for the support of a former spouse after divorce. ⟨Latin *alimonia* sustenance; *alere* nourish⟩

al·i·quot ['æləkwət] *or* ['ælə,kwɒt] *adj* able to divide a number or quantity without leaving a remainder: *3 is an aliquot part of 12.* ⟨Latin, from *alius* some + *quot* how many⟩

a·lit [ə'lɪt] *v* a pt and a pp of ALIGHT[1].

a·live [ə'laɪv] *adj* (never precedes the noun except occasionally def. 3) **1** living; not dead. **2** active; operating: *Keep the principles of democracy alive.* **3** vibrant; lively. **4** charged with electricity. ⟨Old English *on līfe*⟩
alive to noticing; alert or sensitive to. **alive with** full of (something living): *The street is*

alive with people. **look alive!** hurry up! be quick!

al·ka·li ['ælkə,laɪ] *n, pl* **-lis** or **-lies 1** *Chemistry* any base that is soluble in water and turns red litmus blue. **2** any salt or mixture of salts that neutralizes acids. **al·ka·line** ['ælkə,laɪn] *or* ['ælkəlɪn] *adj.* **al·ka·lin·i·ty** [,ælkə'lɪnəti] *n.* **al·ka·lize** *v.* Also, **al·ka·lin·ize. al·ka·li·za·tion** *n.* ⟨Arabic *al-qalī* the ashes of saltwort (a plant)⟩
Alkali Dry Belt ✳ on the Prairies, a region of low precipitation with a number of dried-out dugouts having an alkaline cover. **alkali flat** in western Canada, an arid area in which natural water evaporates, leaving large deposits of alkali. **alkali metal** *Chemistry* any one of the univalent metals whose hydroxides are alkalis. **al·ka·lim·e·ter** *n* **1** a device for finding the level of carbon dioxide in carbonates. **2** a device for finding the level of alkalinity in soil, etc. **alkaline–earth metals** calcium, strontium, and barium. Some authorities include beryllium, radium, and magnesium. **alkaline earths** the oxides of the alkaline-earth metals. **al·ka·loid** *n* a substance that resembles an alkali and contains nitrogen. Some alkaloids obtained from plants are drugs, such as cocaine, strychnine, morphine, and quinine. Many alkaloids are very poisonous. **al·ka·loid·al** *adj.*

al·kyd ['ælkɪd] *n* any of several synthetic resins, used especially for paints and other finishes. Also, **alkyd resin.** ⟨*alkyl* + *acid*⟩

all [ɒl] *adj* **1** the whole of: *all Europe.* **2** every one of: *all babies.* **3** the greatest possible: *make all haste.* **4** any: *The prisoner denied all connection with the crime.*
pron the whole number; everything: *All of us are going. All that glitters is not gold.*
n everything one has or is: *She gave her all for her family.*
adv **1** entirely: *The cake is all gone.* **2** each: *The score was even at forty all.* **3** only: *all words and no thought.* ⟨Old English *eall*⟩
above all more important than anything else. **after all** See AFTER. **all at once** suddenly. **all but** almost; nearly: *All but dead from fatigue, he struggled on.* **all in** *Informal* weary; worn out. **all in all 1** taking everything into consideration: *All in all it was an exciting day.* **2** one's ultimate treasure: *You are my all in all.* **all of** no less than: *She weighs all of 5 kg.* **all the more** (or any other comparative), even more: *We must work all the harder now that the holidays are over.* **at all** under any conditions; in any way: *If you can help at all, I'd be grateful.* **for all** (**that**) in spite of: *For all her beauty, she is still boring.* **go all out** use all one's resources: *They decided to go all out and hire a band.* **in all** in total; altogether: *There were 100 families in all.* **not all that** *Informal* not very; not so (followed by an adjective or adverb): *I wasn't all that keen on going.*
all–a·round *adj* all-round. **all–Ca·na·di·an** *adj* **1** representative of Canada or Canadians: *an all-Canadian menu.* **2** composed entirely of Canadians or Canadian elements: *an all-Canadian hockey team.* **all clear** a signal indicating the end of a danger. **all dressed**

Informal of a hamburger, etc. with all the garnishes or toppings. **all get out** *Informal* (to) an extreme degree (preceded by *as* or *like*): *tired as all get out.* **all hail** an exclamation of greeting or welcome. **All·hal·lows** *n* ALL SAINTS' DAY. **Allhallows Eve** October 31, Halloween. **all·heal** *n* valerian. **all–im·por·tant** *adj* essential. **all–in·clu·sive** *adj* including everything. **all–out** *adj* total; thoroughgoing: *an all-out effort.* **all·o·ver** *adj* covering the whole surface: *an allover pattern on fabric.* **all–pow·er·ful** *adj* with power over all people, things, etc. **all–pur·pose** *adj* suitable for a variety of purposes: *all-purpose flour.* **all right 1** yes; agreed. **2** in good health; uninjured: *My arm seems to be all right now.* **3** satisfactory. **4** able to cope: *Are you all right with that?* **all–round** *adj* useful or skilled in many ways. **All Saints' Day** *Christianity* November 1, a day honouring all the saints. **all·spice** *n* a spice with a flavour like a combination of cinnamon, nutmeg, and cloves. **all–star** *adj* involving the best players or performers. **all–star** *n* a member of such a group. **all–ter·rain vehicle** a rugged vehicle designed for off-road travel. *Abbrev* **ATV all–time** *adj Informal* for all time up to the present: *an all-time high in wheat prices.* **all–weath·er** *adj* designed for all kinds of weather: *an all-weather coat.*

Al·lah ['ælə] *or* ['ɑlə] *n* in Islam, the name of the one Supreme Being; God. ⟨Arabic *allah, al-ilāh*⟩

al·lay [ə'leɪ] *v* **1** put at rest; quiet: *to allay fears.* **2** relieve: *Her fever was allayed by the medicine.* ⟨Old English *ālecgan*⟩

al·lege [ə'lɛdʒ] *v* assert without proof: *She alleges that her watch has been stolen.* **al·le·ga·tion** [ˌælə'geɪʃən] *n.* ⟨Latin *allegare* charge, cite; *lex, legis* law⟩ **al·leged** *adj* **1** being so only according to what someone alleges: *the alleged theft.* **2** so-called; improperly designated as such: *His alleged best friend didn't even invite him.* **al·leg·ed·ly** [ə'lɛdʒɪdli] *adv.*

al·le·giance [ə'lidʒəns] *n* loyalty; faithfulness. ⟨Old French *ligeance; lige* liege⟩

al·le·go·ry ['ælə,gɔri] *n* **1** a story with an underlying meaning parallel to but different from the surface meaning. Each major element in an allegory stands for a particular person or thing in real life. **2** a symbol. ⟨Greek *allos* other + *agoreuein* speak⟩ **al·le·gor·i·cal** *adj* explaining something by a story; using allegory. **al·le·gor·i·cal·ly** *adv.* **al·le·go·rize** ['æləgə,raɪz] *v* **1** make into an allegory. **2** treat or interpret as an allegory. **3** use allegories.

SYNONYMS

An **allegory** is a story whose characters are often personifications (*Courtesy, Jealousy*) or types (*Mr. Wordly Wiseman*). A **fable** has as its characters animals or objects that act and talk like humans and so call attention to human weaknesses. A **parable** is a short story of everyday life illustrating a general idea.

---

al·le·gro [ə'lɛgrou] *or* [ə'leigrou] *adv, adj Music* quick; lively. ⟨Italian; Latin *alacer* brisk⟩ **al·le·gret·to** [ˌælə'grɛtou] *adv, adj Music* quick, but not as quick as allegro.

al·lele [ə'lil] *n Genetics* **1** one of two or more genes that occupy the same position on each of a pair of chromosomes. **2** an alternative form of a given gene. Also, **al·le·lo·morph** [ə'lilou,mɔrf] *or* [ə'lɛlou,mɔrf] **al·lel·ic** *adj.* **al·le·lo·mor·phic** *adj.* ⟨Greek *allel-* one another + *morphe* shape⟩

al·le·lu·ia [ˌælə'lujə] *interj* a liturgical form of **hallelujah**, meaning 'praise the Lord'. ⟨Latin, from Hebrew *hallēlūjāh* praise Jehovah⟩

al·ler·gy ['ælərdʒi] *n* **1** an unusual sensitivity to a particular substance, manifested by a rash, puffiness of the eyes, indigestion, etc. **2** *Informal, facetious* a strong dislike: *an allergy to work.* ⟨Greek *allos* different, strange + *ergon* action⟩ **al·ler·gen** ['ælərdʒən] *n* any substance that causes an allergic reaction. **al·ler·gen·ic** *adj.* **al·ler·gic** *adj* **1** of or caused by allergy: *an allergic reaction.* **2** having an allergy: *I'm allergic to cats.* **3** *Informal, facetious* having a strong dislike: *I'm allergic to winter.* **al·ler·gist** *n* a doctor who specializes in the treatment of allergies.

al·le·vi·ate [ə'livi,eit] *v* relieve; lessen: *Heat often alleviates pain.* **al·le·vi·a·tion** *n.* **al·le·vi·a·tive** *adj.* ⟨Latin *alleviare; ad-* up + *levis* light⟩

al·ley[1] ['æli] *n* **1** a narrow back street. **2** a path in a park or garden, bordered by trees. **3** a building equipped with lanes for bowling. ⟨Old French *alee* a going; *aler* go⟩ **(right) up one's alley** closely related to one's work or interests. **alley cat** a cat, usually a mongrel, that lives in back streets. **al·ley·way** *n* ALLEY (defs. 1, 2).

al·ley[2] ['æli] *n* a marble used to shoot at the other marbles in a game. ⟨*alabaster*⟩

al·li·ance See ALLY.

al·li·cin ['ælɪsɪn] *n* an antibacterial substance extracted from garlic. ⟨Latin *allium* garlic⟩

al·li·ga·tor ['ælə,geitər] *n* a reptile with a long, thick body and tail, powerful jaws with sharp teeth, and eyes and nostrils set on top of the skull. ⟨Latin *lacertus* lizard⟩ **alligator clip** a long, narrow, toothed clip used in electrical work.

al·lit·er·a·tion [ə,lɪtə'reiʃən] *n* a repetition of the same initial sound in a group of words or line of poetry. **al·lit·er·ate** [ə'lɪtə,reit] *v.* **al·lit·er·a·tive** [ə'lɪtərətɪv] *or* [ə'lɪtə,reitɪv] *adj.* **al·lit·er·a·tive·ly** *adv.* ⟨Latin *ad-* to + *litera* letter⟩

al·lo·cate ['ælə,keit] *v* **1** assign; designate: *to allocate funds, workers to a project.* **2** distribute; allot: *The money received has not yet been allocated among member organizations.* **al·lo·cat·a·ble** *adj.* **al·lo·ca·tion** [ˌælə'keiʃən] *n.* ⟨Latin *ad-* to, at + *locus* place⟩

al·lo·morph ['ælə,mɔrf] *n* **1** *Chemistry* allotrope. **2** *Linguistics* one of the forms of a morpheme: *The prefix* cor- *in* corrode *is an* allomorph of the morpheme *com-*. **al·lo·mor·phic** *adj.* **al·lo·mor·phism** *n.* ⟨Greek *allos* other + *morphē* form⟩

al·lop·a·thy [ə'lɒpəθi] *n* a method of treating a disease by using remedies to produce effects different from the symptoms. Compare HOMEOPATHY. **al·lo·path·ic** [ˌælə'pæθɪk] *adj.* **al·lo·path·i·cal·ly** *adv.* ⟨Greek *allos* other + *patheia* suffering⟩

al·lo·path ['ælə,pæθ] *n* a doctor who uses this method. Also, **al·lop·a·thist** [ə'lɒpəθɪst] *n.*

al·lo·phone ['ælə,foun] *n* **1** any one of a set of similar speech sounds heard as the same sound by native speakers. In English, the *t* in *top* and the *t* in *stop* are allophones of the phoneme *t*. Since each occurs in a different phonetic environment, allophones cannot be used to distinguish meaning. **2** ✳ esp in Québec, a speaker of a language other than French or English. **al·lo·phon·ic** [-'fɒnik] *adj.* ⟨Greek *allos* other + *phōnē* sound⟩

al·lo·saur ['ælə,sɔr] *n* a large, carnivorous dinosaur whose fossilized remains have been found in North America. ⟨Greek *allos* other + *sauros* lizard⟩

al·lot [ə'lɒt] *v* **-lot·ted, -lot·ting 1** distribute in parts or shares: *The profits have all been allotted.* **2** assign: *The teacher allotted work to each student.* **al·lot·ment** *n.* ⟨Old French *a-* to + *lot* lot⟩

al·lo·trop·ic [ˌælə'trɒpɪk] *adj* *Chemistry* occurring in forms that differ in physical and chemical properties but not in the kind of atoms of which they are composed. **al·lot·ro·py** [ə'lɒtrəpi] *n.* Also, **al·lot·ro·pism.** ⟨Greek *allos* other + *tropos* manner⟩

al·lo·trope ['ælə,troup] *n* an allotropic form.

al·low [ə'laʊ] *v* **1** permit: *not allowed to leave.* **2** let have; give: *His mother allows him $10 a week as spending money.* **3** admit: *to allow a claim.* **4** add or subtract to make up for something: *to allow an extra hour for travelling time.* **5** enable: *This program allows you to do your work faster.* **6** *Informal* say; think: *He allowed that he was going to the dance.* **al·low·a·ble** *adj.* ⟨Old French *alouer;* Latin *allaudare* praise and *allocare* to place⟩

allow for take into account; provide for: *He made the pants large to allow for shrinking.*

al·low·ance *n* **1** an amount of money given out, such as spending money given regularly to a child or money given to an employee to cover job-related expenses: *a travel allowance.* **2** a ration: *a daily sugar allowance.* **3** an amount added or subtracted to make up for something: *a car trade-in allowance of $700.* **4** the act of allowing: *allowance of a claim.*

make allowance(s) (for) **a** take into consideration; allow for: *to make allowance for the weather.* **b** excuse; judge leniently in view of mitigating factors: *They make allowances for him because he is new.*

al·loy ['ælɔɪ] *n* **1** a metal made by mixing: *Brass is an alloy of copper and zinc.* **2** an inferior metal mixed with a more valuable one: *This gold is not pure; there is some alloy in it.* **3** any inferior mixture.

v [ə'lɔɪ] **1** mix with another metal. **2** lower in value by mixing with something inferior. ⟨Old French *alier;* Latin *ad-* to + *ligare* bind⟩

al·lude [ə'lud] *v* refer indirectly *(to):* *Do not ask him about his failure; do not even allude to it.* **al·lu·sion** *n.* **al·lu·sive** *adj.* **al·lu·sive·ly** *adv.* **al·lu·sive·ness** *n.* ⟨Latin *ad-* with + *ludere* play⟩

CONFUSABLES
Allusion means 'indirect reference'.
Illusion means 'false idea or impression'.

al·lure [ə'lur] *v* tempt very strongly. *n* fascination. **al·lure·ment** *n.* **al·lur·ing** *adj.* ⟨Old French *a-* to + *leurre* lure; Germanic.⟩

al·lu·sion See ALLUDE.

al·lu·vi·um [ə'luviəm] *n, pl* **-vi·ums** or **-vi·a** [-viə] the sand, mud, etc. left by flowing water. **al·lu·vi·al** *adj.* ⟨Latin *ad-* up + *luere* wash⟩

alluvial fan a gently sloped, alluvial deposit in the shape of a fan, resulting from a gradual decrease in the speed of a river.

al·ly [ə'laɪ] *v* (often reflexive) join forces for some special purpose: *The nation has allied itself with its neighbours to protect its interests.* *n* ['ælaɪ] one so joined with another. ⟨Old French *alier;* Latin *ad-* to + *ligare* bind⟩

al·li·ance [ə'laɪəns] *n* **1** a union formed by agreement. **2** the nations, persons, etc. who belong to such a union. **3** a relationship. **4 Alliance Party** CANADIAN ALLIANCE. **al·lied** [ə'laɪd] *adj* related: *Dogs are allied to wolves.* **Al·lies** ['ælaɪz] *n pl* **1** the countries that fought against Germany in World War I. **2** the countries that fought against Germany, Italy, and Japan (the **Axis**) in World War II.

al·ma ma·ter or **Al·ma Ma·ter** ['ælmə 'matər], ['ɑlmə 'mɑtər], *or* ['ælmə 'meitər] a person's former school, college, or university. ⟨Latin = bounteous mother⟩

al·ma·nac ['ɒlmə,næk] *or* ['ælmə,næk] *n* a calendar in book form, usually giving information about the weather and other facts. ⟨Arabic *al-manākh*⟩

al·might·y [ɒl'maiti] *adj* **1** having supreme power; all-powerful. **2** *Informal* huge. *n* the **Almighty** God. **al·might·i·ly** *adv.* **al·might·i·ness** *n.*

al·mond ['ɒlmənd], ['ɒmənd], *or* ['æmənd] *n* a small tree native to SW Asia, whose oval-shaped seed is eaten as a nut. ⟨Old French *almande;* Greek *amygdalē*⟩

al·most ['ɒlmoust] *adv* nearly: *It is almost ten o'clock.* ⟨Old English *eal māst*⟩

alms ['ɒmz] *or* ['ɒlmz] *n sg or pl* money or gifts to help the poor. **alms·giv·er** *n.* **alms·giv·ing** *n, adj.* ⟨Old English *ælmysse;* Greek *eleēmosynē* compassion⟩

alms·house *n* a home for people too poor to support themselves.

al·oe ['ælou] *n, pl* **-oes 1** a large genus of plants of the lily family, with fleshy leaves. **2 aloes** a bitter drug made from the dried juice of the leaves of certain plants of this genus (with a sg verb). **al·o·et·ic** *adj.* ⟨Greek⟩

aloe vera ['vɛrə] *or* ['virə] an aloe valued for its medicinal properties.

a·loft [ə'lɒft] *adv, adj* (never precedes a noun) high above the earth, the deck of a ship, etc. ⟨Old Norse *á lopt* in the air⟩

a·lo·ha [ə'louə] *or* [ɑ'louhɑ] *n, interj* **1** hello. **2** goodbye. ⟨Hawaiian⟩

a·lone [ə'loun] *adj* (never precedes a noun) **1** apart from other persons or things: *He was alone in the house.* **2** only: *Money alone is not sufficient.* **3** without equal or rival: *She is alone in the field of cancer research.*
adv **1** apart from other persons or things: *One tree stood alone on the hill.* **2** without help: *I can do it alone.* **3** only; exclusively. **alone·ness** *n.* ⟨Middle English *al one* all (completely) one⟩
leave alone not bother; not alter or meddle with. **leave well enough alone** not alter things that are fine as they are. **let alone a** not bother; not meddle with. **b** not to mention: *This is a hot day for summer, let alone early spring.*

a·long [ə'lɒŋ] *prep* from one end of (something) to the other: *to walk along a street.*
adv **1** further; onward: *Move along.* **2** with one: *He took his dog along.* **3** together (*with*): *We had pop along with the food.* **4** *Informal* there: *I'll be along in a minute.* **5** advanced in a pregnancy: *She is three months along already.* ⟨Old English *andlang*⟩
all along from the very beginning: *She was here all along.* **along the way** on the way or in the process: *He taught me how to sail, but along the way I learned a lot about courage.* **come along a** accompany one: *Want to come along to the store?* **b** stop resisting and co-operate: *Come along now, be decent.* **c** (usually in progressive) make progress: *He's coming along well.* **get along a** manage with at least some success. **b** agree; have play, etc. in harmony. **c** go away; leave. **d** advance, often specifically in age: *She's getting along in years.*

a·long·side [ə,lɒŋ'saɪd] *adv* at the side; close to the side; side by side.
prep [ə'lɒŋ,saɪd] by the side of; beside. **alongside of** *Informal* beside; next to.

a·loof [ə'luf] *adv* at a distance; apart: *One girl stood aloof from all the others.*
adj (never precedes a noun) unsympathetic; reserved or distant in manner. **a·loof·ly** *adv.* **a·loof·ness** *n.* ⟨obsolete *loof* windward⟩

a·loud [ə'laʊd] *adv* **1** loud enough to be heard. **2** in a loud voice; loudly.

Alps [ælps] *n pl* a range of mountains in western Europe. **Al·pine** ['ælpaɪn] *adj.* ⟨Latin *Alpes* the Alps⟩
alp *n* a high mountain. **alpine** *adj* **1** to do with or found in mountainous areas: *alpine flowers.* **2** to do with downhill as opposed to cross-country skiing. **alpine fir** a fir tree found esp in the Rocky Mountains. **al·pin·ist** ['ælpɪnɪst] *n* mountain climber.

al·pac·a [æl'pækə] *n* **1** a domesticated grazing animal of the mountains of Peru and Bolivia, raised mainly for its long, soft, silky wool. **2** a warm, soft cloth made from this wool.

3 glossy, wiry cloth made of wool and cotton, usually black. ⟨Arabic *al* the + Peruvian *paco*⟩

al·pha ['ælfə] *n* **1** the first letter of the Greek alphabet (A, α). **2** the first in a series. **3 Alpha** *Astronomy* the brightest star in a constellation: *Alpha Herculis is the brightest star in the constellation Hercules.*
adj Chemistry denoting the first position in an organic compound that a molecule can attach to. ⟨*alpha* first letter of the Greek alphabet⟩
alpha and omega the beginning and the end; the be-all and end-all. See OMEGA.
alpha decay *Physics* a radioactive process that decreases the atomic number of an atom by two. **al·pha–fe·to·pro·tein** [,ælfə ,fitou'proutin] *n* a serum protein present in a normal fetus and sometimes in large amounts in adults, where it is usually a sign of disease. **al·pha·nu·mer·ic** *adj Computers* consisting of letters of the alphabet and numerals, sometimes with other keyboard characters: *The Canadian postal code is an alphanumeric code.* **alpha particle** *Physics* a positively charged particle consisting of two protons and two neutrons, released in the disintegration of radioactive substances. **alpha wave** a form of electrical activity in the brain, denoting relaxation. Compare BETA WAVE.

al·pha·bet ['ælfə,bɛt] *n* **1** a set of characters representing sounds, used in writing a language. **2** elementary principles. ⟨*alpha* + *beta* first two letters of the Greek alphabet⟩
al·pha·bet·i·cal [,ælfə'bɛtɪkəl] *or* **al·pha·bet·ic** *adj* **1** arranged in the order of the alphabet: *an alphabetical index.* **2** consisting of letters of the alphabet. **al·pha·bet·ize** ['ælfəbə,taɪz] *v* put in alphabetical order. **al·pha·bet·i·za·tion** *n.* **alphabet soup** *Informal* a confusing array of acronyms or initialisms.

al·read·y [ɒl'rɛdi] *adv* **1** by this time: *The house is already full.* **2** so soon: *Must you go already?* **3** *Informal* an expression of impatience, used at the end of a sentence: *Enough whining already!* ⟨for *all ready*⟩

Al·sa·tian [æl'seɪʃən] *n* **1** a breed of large dog; German shepherd. **2** a native of Alsace, a region in northeastern France, or the German dialect spoken there. **Al·sa·tian** *adj.*

al·so ['ɒlsou] *adv* in addition; besides; too. ⟨Old English *ealswā* all so, quite so⟩
al·so–ran *n* **1** a horse or dog that does not finish among the first three in a race. **2** a person who fails to acquire distinction in any field.

al·tar ['ɒltər] *n* **1** a table or stand in the most sacred part of a church, synagogue, or temple. **2** a raised place built of earth or stone on which to make sacrifices to a god. ⟨Latin *altare; altus* high⟩
lead to the altar marry.
altar boy or **girl** *Christianity* a boy or girl who helps a priest during certain religious services; acolyte. **al·tar·piece** *n* reredos; a decorated panel behind and above an altar in a church.

al·taz·i·muth [ɒl'tæzɪməθ] *n* an instrument equipped with a telescope for measuring angles vertically and horizontally, used in astronomy and in surveying. A theodolite is a portable altazimuth. ⟨alt(itude) + azimuth⟩

al·ter ['ɒltər] v 1 change: *Since her trip to Europe, her outlook has altered.* 2 adjust so as to fit the user: *to alter a coat, to alter a curriculum.* **al·ter·a·ble** adj. **al·ter·a·tion** n. **al·ter·a·tive** ['ɒltərətɪv] or ['ɒltə,reitɪv] adj. ⟨Latin alterāre; alter other⟩

al·ter e·go 1 one of two very different sides of one's nature. 2 a very intimate friend. ⟨Latin = other self⟩

al·ter·cate ['ɒltər,keit] v dispute angrily. **al·ter·ca·tion** n. ⟨Latin altercari⟩

al·ter·nate ['ɒltər,neit] v 1 occur or arrange by turns, first one and then the other: *Squares and circles alternate in this row:* □ ○ □ ○ □ ○. 2 switch back and forth: *to alternate between pity and anger.* 3 *Electricity* of a current, reverse direction at regular intervals. adj ['ɒltərnɪt] or [ɒl'tɜrnɪt] 1 every other: *The cleaner comes on alternate days.* 2 placed or occurring by turns: *alternate designs in a pattern.* 3 constituting another choice: *If that doesn't work, try an alternate method.*
n ['ɒltərnɪt] or [ɒl'tɜrnɪt] appointed substitute. **al·ter·nate·ly** adv. **al·ter·na·tion** n. ⟨Latin alternare; alter other⟩

alternate angles two angles formed when two lines are crossed by a third, and being on opposite sides of the third line. **alternating current** an electric current that reverses its direction at regular intervals. *Abbrev* **A.C.**, **a.c.**, or **a-c.** Compare DIRECT CURRENT.
al·ter·na·tive [ɒl'tɜrnətɪv] adj to do with a choice between only two things, or, more loosely, from among more than two things: *an alternative route from Ottawa to Iqaluit.* n 1 such a choice: *We have the alternative of going out, watching a TV movie.* 2 one of the things to be chosen: *She chose the sensible alternative and stayed in school.* **al·ter·na·tive·ly** adv. **alternative conjunction** a conjunction connecting alternative terms. *Examples: either...or, neither...nor.* **alternative school** a school within the public system, but outside the norm in curriculum or method. **al·ter·na·tor** ['ɒltər,neitər] n a generator for producing an alternating electric current, as for the engine of a motor vehicle.

USAGE
Alternative comes from Latin *alter*, meaning 'the second of two'. Some writers, because of the word's origin, confine its meaning to one of two possibilities, but it is commonly used to mean one of several possibilities.

al·though [ɒl'ðou] conj in spite of the fact that; even if; though: *Although I understand your point, I disagree. The clothes, although clean, were faded.* ⟨ME al thogh even though⟩

al·tim·e·ter [æl'tɪmətər] or ['æltɪ,mitər] n any instrument for measuring altitude. ⟨alti(tude) + -meter⟩

al·ti·tude ['æltə,tjud] or ['æltə,tud], ['ɒltə,tjud] or ['ɒltə,tud] n 1 height above sea level: *The altitude of Calgary, Alberta, is 1079 m.* 2 a high

place: *At these altitudes, snow never melts.* 3 *Geometry* the vertical distance from the base of a figure to its highest point. 4 *Astronomy* the angular distance of a star, planet, etc. above the horizon. *Abbrev* **alt** **al·ti·tu·di·nal** adj. ⟨Latin altitudo; altus high⟩
altitude sickness a condition resulting from deficiency of oxygen in the body because of the thinness of the air at high altitudes. It is characterized by sleepiness, headache, muscle weakness, etc., and can be fatal.

al·to ['ɒltou] or ['æltou] n 1 the lowest female singing voice or the highest adult male singing voice. 2 a singer with such a voice, or the part written for it. 3 an instrument with a range lower than that of the soprano, or treble, in a family of instruments. **al·to** adj. *Abbrev* **a.** or **alt** ⟨Italian; Latin altus deep, high⟩
alto clef *Music* a C clef which identifies middle C as being on the third line of the staff.

al·to–cu·mu·lus [,æltou 'kjumjələs] n, pl -li [-laɪ] or [-li] a fleecy cloud formation with rounded heaps of cloud, at heights between 2400 and 6000 m.

al·to·geth·er ['ɒltə'gɛðər] adv 1 completely: *altogether wicked.* 2 considering everything: *Altogether, I'm sorry it happened.* 3 in total: *There were ten of us altogether.*
n **the altogether** *Informal* the nude: *They went swimming in the altogether.* ⟨Middle English altogedere⟩

CONFUSABLES
Do not confuse **altogether** with the phrase **all together**, which means 'together in a group': *We found them all together in the yard.*

al·to–stra·tus [,æltou 'streitəs] or [-'strætəs] n, pl -ti [-taɪ] or [-ti] a bluish grey, sheetlike cloud formation, occurring at heights between 2400 and 6000 m. ⟨Latin altus high + E stratus⟩

al·tru·ism ['ɒltru,ɪzəm] or ['æltru,ɪzəm] n 1 unselfishness. 2 *Philosophy* the belief that the collective good is the responsibility of the individual. **al·tru·ist** n. **al·tru·is·tic** adj. **al·tru·is·ti·cal·ly** adv. ⟨Italian altrui of or for others; Latin alter other⟩

al·um ['æləm] n 1 a white mineral salt used in medicine and dyeing. 2 a colourless crystalline salt containing ammonia, used in baking powder, medicine, etc. ⟨Latin alumen⟩

a·lu·mi·nous [ə'lumənəs] adj of or containing alum or aluminum.

a·lu·mi·num [ə'lumənəm] n a silver-white, very light, metallic element that resists tarnish and is used for making utensils, instruments, etc. *Symbol* **Al** ⟨Latin alumen alum⟩
a·lu·mi·nif·er·ous [ə,lumə'nɪfərəs] adj containing or yielding aluminum. **a·lu·mi·nize** v coat or treat with aluminum. **aluminum foil** TIN FOIL.

a·lum·nus [ə'lʌmnəs] n, pl -ni [-naɪ] a male graduate of a school, college, or university. ⟨Latin alumnus foster child; alere nourish⟩
a·lum·na [ə'lʌmnə] n, pl -nae [-ni] a female graduate of a school, college, or university.

al·ve·o·lus [æl'viələs] or [,ælvi'ouləs] n, pl -li [-laɪ] or [-li] Anatomy 1 a small vacuity, pit, or cell. 2 the socket of a tooth. ⟨Latin alveolus, diminutive of alveus cavity⟩
al·ve·o·lar adj 1 Anatomy of the part of the jaws where the sockets of the teeth are. 2 Phonetics formed by touching the tip of the tongue to the upper alveoli. English t and d are alveolar sounds. **alveolar ridge** the ridge between the upper front teeth and the palate.

al·ways ['ɒlwɪz] or ['ɒlweɪz] adv 1 in every case: Water always has some air in it. 2 all the time: Mother is always cheerful. 3 forever: I'll love you always. 4 in any event: I could always leave at four rather than five. ⟨all + way⟩

a·lys·sum [ə'lɪsəm] n any of a genus of plants of the mustard family, with greyish leaves and fragrant flowers. ⟨Greek alysson plant thought to cure rabies; lyssa madness⟩

Alz·hei·mer's disease ['ɒltshaɪmərz] a degenerative disease of the brain cells, possibly hereditary, leading eventually to severe mental impairment and death. ⟨A. Alzheimer, 19–20c German physician⟩

am [æm] v the first person singular present indicative of BE: I am a student. I am going home tomorrow. ⟨Old English eom⟩

a.m. or **A.M.** 1 before noon (to refer to a particular time before midday, starting with midnight): The appointment is for 10:00 a.m. 2 Informal morning: Come over in the a.m. ⟨for Latin ante meridiem before midday⟩

AM or **A.M.** AMPLITUDE MODULATION.

a·ma·bi·lis fir [ə'mæbəlɪs] a fir tree found esp on Vancouver Island and along the coast of British Columbia. ⟨Latin = lovable⟩

a·mah ['amə] n in India, China, etc., a nanny or maid. ⟨Portuguese ama⟩

a·mal·gam [ə'mælgəm] n 1 an alloy of mercury with some other metal or metals, used especially formerly for dental fillings. 2 any blend. ⟨Greek malagma emollient⟩ **a·mal·ga·mate** v unite; combine; blend: The two companies amalgamated to form one big one. **a·mal·ga·ma·ble** adj. **a·mal·ga·ma·tion** n.

a·man·u·en·sis [ə,mænju'ɛnsɪs] n, pl -ses [-siz] a person who writes down what another says, or copies what another has written. ⟨Latin; from (servus) a manu hand (servant) + -ensis belonging to⟩

am·a·ranth ['æmə,rænθ] n 1 Poetic an imaginary flower that never fades. 2 any of a genus of plants including some well-known garden plants, such as love-lies-bleeding, and many weeds. 3 a dark reddish purple. **am·a·ran·thine** [-θaɪn] or [-θɪn] adj. ⟨Greek a- not + marainein wither; infl. by anthos flower⟩

am·a·ryl·lis [,æmə'rɪlɪs] n a lilylike South African plant with clusters of very large flowers on a thick stalk. ⟨Greek, typical name for a country girl⟩

a·mass [ə'mæs] v heap together; accumulate: The miser amassed a fortune for himself. **a·mass·ment** n. ⟨French amasser; Latin massa kneaded dough⟩

A·ma·ter·a·su [,amate'rasʊ] n in Shintoism, the sun goddess; the most highly revered of the many Japanese deities.

am·a·teur ['æmətʃər], [,æmə'tʃʊr], or [,æmə'tɜr] n 1 a person who undertakes some activity for pleasure, not for money or as a profession. 2 a person who shows little skill or professionalism. **am·a·teur** adj. ⟨French; Latin amator lover⟩
am·a·teur·ish adj not expert; not very skilful. **a·ma·teur·ish·ly** adv. **a·ma·teur·ish·ness** n. **am·a·teur·ism** n.

am·a·to·ry ['æmə,tɔri] adj of love; causing love; to do with making love or with lovers. ⟨Latin amatorius; amare to love⟩

a·maut [ə'mʌut] n ✱ a hood in the back of a parka for an Inuit woman to carry a child. ⟨Inuktitut⟩

a·maze [ə'meɪz] v surprise greatly; strike with sudden wonder. **a·mazed** adj. **a·maz·ed·ly** [ə'meɪzɪdli] adv. **a·maze·ment** n. **a·maz·ing** adj. ⟨Old English āmasian⟩

am·a·zon ['æmə,zɒn] or ['æməzən] n a tall, athletic woman. **am·a·zo·ni·an** [,æmə'zouniən] adj. ⟨the Amazons, in Greek myth, a race of female warriors⟩

am·bas·sa·dor [æm'bæsədər] or [æm'bæsə,dɔr] n 1 the highest diplomatic representative sent by one government to another. 2 a representative of a government at the meetings of an international organization on a special mission: The Canadian ambassador to NATO. 3 any representative of a group who reflects its typical qualities: Visiting Scouts can be ambassadors of good will. **am·bas·sa·do·ri·al** adj. **am·bas·sa·dor·ship** n. ⟨Italian ambasciatore⟩
am·bas·sa·dor–at–large n a representative appointed for a special occasion, but not dealing with a specific country.

am·ber ['æmbər] n a translucent, brownish yellow fossilized resin used for jewellery. adj brownish yellow. ⟨Arabic 'anbar ambergris⟩

am·ber·gris ['æmbər,gris] or ['æmbərgrɪs] n a waxlike greyish substance secreted by sperm whales and used in making perfumes. ⟨French ambre gris grey amber⟩

am·bi·dex·trous [,æmbə'dɛkstrəs] adj 1 able to use both hands equally well. 2 very skilful. 3 deceitful. **am·bi·dex·trous·ly** adv. **am·bi·dex·ter·i·ty** [,æmbədɛk'stɛrəti] n. ⟨Latin ambi- both + dexter right⟩

am·bi·ence ['æmbi,ans], ['ambi,ãs], or ['æmbiəns] French [ã'bjãs] n atmosphere: the formal ambience of an expensive restaurant. Also, **am·bi·ance**. ⟨French; Latin ambiens going around, from ambi- around + ire go⟩
am·bi·ent ['æmbiənt] adj of the surrounding atmosphere: the ambient temperature.

am·big·u·ous [æm'bɪgjuəs] adj 1 with more than one possible meaning. 2 not clear; uncertain: She was left in an ambiguous position by their failure to appear and help her. **am·bi·gu·i·ty** [,æmbə'gjuɑti] n. **am·big·u·ous·ly** adv. ⟨Latin ambi- in two ways + agere drive⟩

am·bit ['æmbɪt] *n* **1** the bounds or limits of a district, estate, etc. **2** sphere of influence; scope. ⟨Latin = it goes around. See AMBIENCE.⟩

am·bi·tion [æm'bɪʃən] *n* **1** a strong desire for fame, honour, or power. **2** something strongly desired; goal: *Her ambition was to be a great actor.* **am·bi·tion·less** *adj.* ⟨Latin *ambitio* a canvassing for votes; *ambire.* See AMBIENCE.⟩ **am·bi·tious** *adj* **1** full of ambition: *an ambitious young woman.* **2** requiring much skill or effort: *an ambitious undertaking.* **am·bi·tious·ly** *adv.* **am·bi·tious·ness** *n.*

am·biv·a·lence [æm'bɪvələns] *n* the state of having simultaneous but conflicting feelings or attitudes, such as love and hate, toward some person or thing. **am·biv·a·lent** *adj.* **am·biv·a·lent·ly** *adv.* ⟨Latin *ambi-* in two ways + *valere* be worth⟩

am·ble ['æmbəl] *n* **1** the gait of a horse when it lifts first the two legs on one side and then the two on the other. **2** a slow, easy walking pace. **am·ble** *v.* ⟨Latin *ambulare* walk⟩

am·bro·sia [æm'brouʒə] *n* **1** *Greek and Roman myth* the food of the gods. **2** anything delicious. **3** a mixture of pollen and nectar eaten by certain bees. **am·bro·sial** *adj.* ⟨Greek; *a-* not + *brotos* mortal⟩

am·bu·lance ['æmbjələns] *n* a vehicle, boat, or aircraft equipped to carry sick or wounded persons. ⟨French *ambulance,* from *(hôpital) ambulant* walking hospital⟩

am·bu·late ['æmbjə,leit] *v* walk or move about. **am·bu·la·tion** *n.* ⟨Latin *ambulare*⟩ **am·bu·la·to·ry** *adj* **1** to do with walking. **2** moving from place to place. *n* a covered place for walking; cloister.

am·bus·cade [,æmbə'skeid] *n, v* ambush. ⟨French *embuscade*; Italian *imboscare*⟩

am·bush ['æmbʊʃ] *n* **1** a surprise attack from some hiding place. **2** the place where attackers are hidden. **3** the act of lying in wait: *to trap enemies by ambush instead of meeting them in open battle.* **am·bush** *v.* ⟨Old French *en* in + *busche* wood, bush⟩

a·me·ba See AMOEBA.

a·mel·io·rate [ə'miliə,reit] *or* [ə'miljə,reit] *v* make or become better: *New housing has ameliorated living conditions in the slums.* **a·mel·io·ra·ble** *adj.* **a·mel·io·ra·tion** *n.* **a·mel·io·ra·tive** [ə'miljərətɪv] *or* [ə'miljə,reitɪv] *adj.* ⟨Latin *ad-* + *melior* better⟩

a·men [ei'mɛn] *or* [ɑ'mɛn] *interj* **1** be it so; may it become true. *Amen* is said after a prayer. **2** *Informal* an expression of approval. ⟨Hebrew = truth, certainty⟩

a·me·na·ble [ə'minəbəl] *or* [ə'mɛnəbəl] *adj* **1** open to suggestion or advice; responsive: *A reasonable person is amenable to persuasion.* **2** answerable: *People living in a country are amenable to its laws.* **3** that can be tested or dealt with according to certain principles (with *to*). **a·me·na·bil·i·ty** *n.* **a·me·na·bly** *adv.* ⟨French *a-* + *mener* lead; Latin *minare* drive⟩

a·mend [ə'mɛnd] *v* **1** change the wording of (a law, bill, motion, etc.). **2** improve or

correct: *to amend one's ways.* **a·mend·a·ble** *adj.* **a·men·da·to·ry** *adj.* **a·mend·ment** *n.* ⟨Old French *amender,* from Latin. See EMEND.⟩ **a·mends** *n pl* a payment for loss; satisfaction for an injury: *$500 in amends.*

make amends atone for what one has done.

a·men·i·ty [ə'minəti] *or* [ə'mɛnəti] *n* **1** (often *pl*) something which makes life easier or more pleasant. **2** a conventional act of politeness. **3** agreeableness: *the amenity of a warm climate.* ⟨Latin *amoenus* pleasant⟩

a·men·or·rhe·a [ei,mɛnə'riə] *n* failure to menstruate; the absence of menstruation. ⟨Greek *a-* not + *men* month + *rhoia* flux, flow⟩

A·men–Ra ['ɑmɛn 'rɑ] *n* the principal god of ancient Egypt.

a·men·tia [ei'mɛnʃə] *n* failure to develop mentally. ⟨Latin = insanity; *a-* not + *mens* mind⟩

A·mer·i·ca [ə'mɛrəkə] *n* **1** the United States. **2** Often, **the Americas** North, Central, and South America; the western hemisphere. **A·mer·i·can** *n, adj.* ⟨*Amerigo* Vespucci, Italian explorer; or *Amerrique,* Spanish name of a Nicaraguan mountain range⟩

American Indian AMERINDIAN. **A·mer·i·can·ism** [ə'mɛrəkə,nɪzəm] *n* **1** devotion to the US. **2** an expression or custom peculiar to or originating in the US. **A·mer·i·can·ize** *v* make or become American in habits or character. **A·mer·i·can·i·za·tion** *n.* **American plan** a system used in hotels where one price covers room, board, and service. Compare EUROPEAN PLAN. **American Sign Language** a language made up of manual and facial gestures, used by much of the North American deaf community; Ameslan. **American speedwell** a low-growing marsh plant, common in Canada, with small blue flowers. Also called **ve·ron·i·ca**. **am·er·i·ci·um** [,æmə'rɪʃiəm] *n* an artificial metallic element. *Symbol* **Am**

Am·er·in·di·an [,æmə'rɪndiən] *Anthropology, Linguistics adj* **1** of or designating a major stock of people, the original inhabitants of the western hemisphere south of the Arctic coastal regions. **2** designating the aboriginal languages of these people, forming numerous distinct language families. **Am·er·in·di·an** *n.* ⟨*Amer(ican)* + *Indian*⟩

am·e·thyst ['æməθɪst] *n* a semiprecious purple variety of quartz. ⟨Greek *a-* not + *methy* wine; thought to prevent intoxication⟩

a·mi·a·ble ['eimiəbəl] *adj* good-natured and friendly. **a·mi·a·bil·i·ty** *n.* **a·mi·a·bly** *adv.* ⟨Old French *amiable,* from Latin. See AMICABLE.⟩

am·i·ca·ble ['æməkəbəl] *adj* peaceable; without hostility: *Instead of fighting, the two nations settled their quarrel in an amicable way.* **am·i·ca·bil·i·ty** *n.* **am·i·ca·bly** *adv.* ⟨Latin *amicabilis; amicus* friend⟩

a·mi·cus cu·ri·ae [ə'mikəs 'kjuri,ai] *or* [ə'məikəs 'kjuri,i] *Law* a disinterested person called in to advise the judge. ⟨Latin = friend of the court⟩

a·mid [ə'mɪd] *prep* in the middle or midst of (not before plural nouns). Also, **a·midst**. ⟨Old English *on middan* in the middle⟩

a·mid·ships [ə'mɪdˌʃɪps] *adv* in or toward the middle of a ship.

am·ide ['æmaɪd] *n Chemistry* a compound in which a metal atom replaces one of the hydrogen atoms of ammonia. **a·mi·do** *adj.* ⟨*am*(*monia*) + -*ide*⟩

am·ine ['æmin] *or* [ə'min] *n Chemistry* a compound formed from ammonia by replacement of one or more of its hydrogen atoms by univalent hydrocarbon radicals. **a·min·ic** [ə'mɪnɪk] *adj.* ⟨*am*(*monia*) + -*ine*⟩

a·mi·no acids [ə'minou] *or* ['æmə,nou] *Chemistry* twenty complex organic acids that combine in various ways to form proteins. **a·mi·no·ben·zo·ic acid** [ə,minoubɛn'zouɪk] *or* [,æmənoubɛn'zouɪk] a substance used to make, among other things, sunscreen lotion.

a·mir [ə'mir] *n* in Muslim countries, a commander, ruler, or prince. Also, **a·meer.** ⟨Arabic = commander. Related to ADMIRAL.⟩

Am·ish ['ɑmɪʃ] *n* **the Amish** *n pl* the members of a strict Mennonite sect, living in southern Ontario and parts of the US. They form part of the group often called Pennsylvania Dutch. **A·mish** *adj.* ⟨after Jacob *Amen*, 17c Mennonite preacher⟩

a·miss [ə'mɪs] *adv* in the wrong way.
adj (never before the noun) improper. ⟨Middle English *a mis* by (way of) fault⟩
take amiss be offended at because of a misunderstanding: *He had not meant to be rude to his mother but she took his answer amiss.*

am·i·ty ['æməti] *n* peace and friendship: *amity between nations.* ⟨Old French *amitié*; Latin *amīcus* friend⟩

am·me·ter See AMPERE.

am·mo ['æmou] *n Informal* ammunition.

am·mo·nia [ə'mounjə] *n* **1** a strong-smelling colourless gas consisting of nitrogen and hydrogen. **2** this gas dissolved in water. **am·mon·ic** [ə'mɒnɪk] *or* [ə'mounɪk] *adj.* ⟨Greek *ammōniakon*; a salt obtained near the shrine of *Ammon* in Libya⟩
am·mo·ni·ac [ə'mouni,æk] *n* a gum resin used for medicines. **am·mo·ni·ate** *v* treat with ammonia. **am·mo·ni·a·tion** *n.* **am·mo·ni·um** *n* a group of nitrogen and hydrogen atoms present in ammonia salts.

am·mu·ni·tion [,æmjə'nɪʃən] *n* **1** bullets, shells, etc. for guns or other weapons. **2** anything that can be shot, hurled, or thrown. **3** a means of attack or defence: *Rational argument is your best ammunition.* ⟨French *amunition*. See MUNITION.⟩

am·ne·sia [æm'niʒə] *n* loss of memory due to injury to the brain. **am·ne·si·ac** [æm'niziæk] *adj*, *n.* Also, **am·ne·sic** [æm'nizɪk]. ⟨Greek *amnēsia*; *a-* not + *mnasthai* remember⟩

am·nes·ty ['æmnɪsti] *n* a general pardon for past offences against a government.
v give amnesty to; pardon. ⟨Greek *amnēstia*. See AMNESIA.⟩

am·ni·on ['æmniən] *or* ['æmni,ɒn] *n*, *pl* -**ni·ons** *or* -**ni·a** [-niə] a membrane lining the sac of fluid that encloses the embryos of reptiles, birds, and mammals. **am·ni·ot·ic** *adj.* ⟨Greek *amnion*, diminutive of *amnos* lamb⟩

am·ni·o·cen·te·sis [,æmniousen'tisɪs] *n* a procedure for obtaining amniotic fluid from around a fetus, used in prenatal diagnosis.

a·moe·ba [ə'mibə] *n*, *pl* -**bas** or -**bae** [-bi] *or* [-baɪ] any of a genus of protozoans found in water or moist soil or living as parasites in humans and animals. Sometimes, **a·me·ba.** **a·moe·bic** or **a·me·bic** *adj.* ⟨Greek *amoibē* change⟩

a·mok See AMUCK. ⟨Malay⟩

a·mong [ə'mʌŋ] *prep* (only before plural nouns) **1** surrounded by: *a house among the trees.* **2** one of: *Canada is among the largest countries in the world.* **3** to each of: *She divided the chores among the three of them.* **4** by, with, or through the whole group of: *unrest among the people.* **5** by the combined action or resources of: *Among us we had $87.* **6** in with: *He fell among thieves.* Also, esp for defs. 1 and 5, **a·mongst.** ⟨Old English *amang*; *on gemang* in a crowd⟩

a·mor·al [ei'mɔrəl] *or* [æ'mɔrəl] *adj* **1** not involving any question of morality; nonmoral. **2** with no sense of right or wrong. **a·mo·ral·i·ty** *n.* **a·mor·al·ly** *adv.*

am·o·rous ['æmərəs] *adj* in love; feeling or expressing romantic love. **am·o·rous·ly** *adv.* **am·o·rous·ness** *n.* ⟨Latin *amor* love⟩

a·mor·phous [ə'mɔrfəs] *adj* **1** shapeless; not organized. **2** of no identifiable type. **3** *Geology* lacking stratification. **4** *Biology* with no definite structure. **5** *Chemistry* not consisting of crystals. **a·mor·phous·ly** *adv.* **a·mor·phous·ness** or **a·mor·phism** *n.* ⟨Greek *a-* without + *morphē* shape⟩

am·or·tize ['æmər,taɪz] *v* **1** pay off (a mortgage, etc.) over time by making regular transfers into a special fund. **2** *Accounting* write off (expenses, debts, etc.) proportionately over a fixed period. **am·or·ti·za·tion** *n.* ⟨Latin *ad* to + *mors, mortis* death⟩

a·mount [ə'maunt] *n* **1** sum; quantity: *the amount of the day's sales.* **2** the full effect, value, or extent: *The sheer amount of the evidence convinced him.* **3** a whole viewed as a quantity: *a great amount of intelligence.*
v **1** add up (*to*): *The loss amounts to ten million dollars.* **2** be equivalent (*to*): *Keeping what belongs to another amounts to stealing.* ⟨Latin *ad* to + *mons, montis* mountain⟩

USAGE
Amount is used with non-countable nouns. Number is used with countable nouns: *an amount of milk, a number of glasses of milk.*

a·mour [ə'mur] *n* a love affair, often specifically a secret or illicit one. ⟨French⟩
a·mour–pro·pre [ɑ'muʀ 'pʀɔpʀ] *n French* self-esteem.

am·pere ['æmpir] *or* ['æmpɛr] *n* an SI unit for measuring the rate of flow of an electric current. *Symbol* **A** ⟨for André *Ampère* 19c French physicist⟩
am·me·ter ['æm,mitər] *n* an instrument for

measuring in amperes the strength of an electric current. **am·per·age** *n* the strength of an electric current in amperes. *Abbrev* **a** or **amp**.

am·per·sand ['æmpər,sænd] *n* the sign &, meaning 'and'. ⟨*and per se and*, (the symbol) & by itself (means) and⟩

am·phet·a·mine [æm'fɛtə,min] *or* [æm'fɛtəmɪn] *n* a drug which has a strong stimulatory effect on the central nervous system, used to treat narcolepsy, epilepsy, etc.

am·phib·i·an [æm'fɪbiən] *n* **1** any of a class of cold-blooded, mostly scaleless vertebrates, such as frogs, whose young at first breathe by means of gills but mature into land-living animals with lungs and legs. **2** an animal or plant adapted to life in water and on land. **3** an aircraft that can take off and land on either land or water. **4** a vehicle for use on either land or water. ⟨Greek *amphi-* both + *bios* life⟩
am·phib·i·an *adj* to do with amphibians. **am·phib·i·ous** *adj* **1** adapted to both land and water. **2** having two distinct natures.

am·phi·brach ['æmfə,bræk] *n Prosody* a measure or foot consisting of one long or strongly stressed syllable between two short or weakly stressed ones. *Example:*
> Behínd shut | the póstern, | the líghts sank | to rést,
> And ínto | the mídnight | we gálloped | abreást.

⟨Greek *amphi-* both (ends) + *brachys* short⟩

am·phi·the·a·tre ['æmfə,θiətər] *n* **1** a circular or oval building with tiers of seats around a central open space; arena. **2** a movie theatre, lecture hall, etc. with ascending rows of seats, esp in a semicircle. **3** a low, level place surrounded by a steep slope. Sometimes, **am·phi·the·a·ter.** ⟨Greek *amphi-* both (sides) + *theatron* theatre⟩

am·pho·ra ['æmfərə] *n, pl* **-rae** [-,ri] *or* [-,raɪ] a tall, two-handled jar used by the ancient Greeks and Romans. ⟨Greek *amphi-* both (sides) + *phoreus* bearer⟩

am·pi·cil·lin [,æmpɪ'sɪlɪn] *or* ['æmpɪ,sɪlɪn] *n* a form of penicillin effective against Gram-positive and Gram-negative bacteria. ⟨*am(ino)* + *p(en)icillin*⟩

am·ple ['æmpəl] *adj* **1** large or extensive: *an ample backyard.* **2** plenty of: *ample food.* **am·ple·ness** *n.* **am·ply** *adv.* ⟨Latin *amplus* large, wide⟩

am·pli·fy ['æmplə,faɪ] *v* **1** make greater, stronger, fuller, etc.; expand: *to amplify a description, to amplify a point in argument.* **2** *Electronics* increase the strength of (an electrical impulse) by means of an amplifier. **am·pli·fi·ca·tion** *n.* ⟨Latin *amplus* large, wide⟩
am·pli·fi·er *n* **1** an electronic device attached to a radio, electric guitar, microphone, etc. for strengthening electrical impulses. **2** any other thing that amplifies.

am·pli·tude ['æmplə,tjud] *or* ['æmplə,tud] *n* **1** width; breadth; size. **2** abundance; fullness. **3** *Physics* the maximum range of vibration from the mean, or zero, position. **4** *Electricity*

the maximum departure from the average cycle of an alternating current. **5** *Astronomy* the distance between a rising or setting star and true east or west, respectively.

amplitude modulation *Radio* a method of transmitting sound signals by changing their strength, or amplitude. Compare FREQUENCY MODULATION. *Abbrev* **AM** or **A.M.**

am·pu·tate ['æmpjə,teit] *v* cut off (a limb) as a surgical procedure: *to amputate a leg.* **am·pu·ta·tion** *n.* ⟨Latin *amputare; ambi-* about + *putare* prune⟩
am·pu·tee [,æmpjə'ti] *n* a person who has had an arm, leg, etc. amputated.

am·rit ['ɑmrit] *n Sikhism* a sweetened water used as a sacred drink and for baptism. Also, **am·rita** [ɑm'ritə]. ⟨Sanskrit *amrta* immortal⟩

a·muck [ə'mʌk] *adv.* ⟨Malay *amok* engaging furiously in battle⟩
run amuck a run about in a murderous frenzy. **b** become uncontrollable. Also, **a·mok.**

am·u·let ['æmjəlɪt] *n* an object worn as a magic charm against evil. ⟨Latin *amuletum*⟩

a·muse [ə'mjuz] *v* **1** cause to laugh or smile; be funny to. **2** keep pleasantly interested: *The new toy amused the children for hours.* **a·mused** *adj.* **a·mus·ing** *adj.* **a·mus·ing·ly** *adv.* ⟨Old French *amuser; a-* + *muser* stare⟩
a·muse·ment *n* **1** the condition, or a means, of being amused: *They often window shop for amusement.* **2** a ride, game, or other activity at a fair, theme park, etc. **amusement park** an outdoor attraction with refreshment stands, rides, games, etc.

am·yl·ase ['æmə,leis] *n* an enzyme in saliva or in plants that helps to change starch into sugar. ⟨Greek *amylon* starch⟩

a·my·o·troph·ic lateral sclerosis [,eimaɪə'trɒfɪk] a disease characterized by the deterioration of nerve cells, resulting in loss of muscle control; Lou Gehrig's disease. ⟨Greek *a-* not + *my-* muscle + *trophe* food⟩

an [ən] the form of the indefinite article **a** occurring before a vowel sound.

An·a·bap·tist [,ænə'bæptɪst] *n* a member of any Protestant sect practising adult rather than infant baptism. ⟨Greek *ana-* back, again + *baptism*⟩

a·nab·o·lism [ə'næbə,lɪzəm] *n* the part of the process of metabolism by which food is changed into living tissue. **an·a·bol·ic** [,ænə'bɒlɪk] *adj.* ⟨Greek *ana-* back, again + *(meta)bolism*⟩
anabolic steroid any of various synthetic androgens used to stimulate the growth of muscle and bone.

a·nach·ro·nism [ə'nækrə,nɪzəm] *n* something occurring out of its proper time, such as an airplane in a movie about medieval times. **a·nach·ro·nis·tic** *adj.* **a·nach·ro·nis·ti·cal·ly** *adv.* ⟨Greek *ana-* backward + *chronos* time⟩

an·a·con·da [,ænə'kɒndə] *n* a very large green snake, a tropical American boa, living in trees and around water. It kills its prey by coiling around it and squeezing until it suffocates. ⟨? Sinhalese *henakandayā*⟩

a·nad·ro·mous [ə'nædrəməs] *adj* going up rivers from the sea to spawn, as salmon do. ⟨Greek *ana-* up, back + *dromos* a running⟩

a·nae·mi·a See ANEMIA.

an·aer·obe ['ænə,roub] *or* [æ'nɛroub] *n* an organism that cannot use, or does not need, free oxygen. Compare AEROBE. **an·aer·o·bic** *adj.* ⟨Greek *an-* without + *aer* air + *bios* life⟩

an·aes·the·sia See ANESTHESIA.

an·a·gram ['ænə,græm] *n* a word or phrase formed by transposing the letters of another. *Example: table—bleat.* **an·a·gram·mat·ic** *adj.* ⟨Greek *ana-* up, back + *gramma* letter⟩

a·nal See ANUS.

An·a·lects ['ænə,lɛkts] *n pl Confucianism* the most revered and influential text containing the sayings and conversations of Confucius. ⟨Greek *analekta; ana-* up + *legein* gather⟩

an·al·ge·si·a [,ænəl'dʒiziə] *n* inability to feel pain even while conscious. ⟨Greek *an-* not + *algeein* feel pain; *algos* pain⟩

an·al·ge·sic *n* a drug or other agent that causes analgesia; painkiller. **an·al·ge·sic** *adj.*

an·a·logue ['ænə,lɒg] *n* **1** something analogous. **2** a measurement in which a constantly fluctuating value is understood as a percentage of another value. *adj* **1** to do with an electronic system in which the signal is linked to a visible change. **2** of a dial, bearing hands rather than digits to indicate an amount. **3** using an ANALOGUE COMPUTER. Compare DIGITAL. Also, **an·a·log.** ⟨Greek *analogia* proportion⟩

a·nal·o·gize *v* **1** make analogies. **2** explain by analogy. **a·nal·o·gous** [ə'næləgəs] *adj.* **a·nal·o·gous·ly** *adv.* **analogue computer** *Computers* a computer that processes data internally in a continuous form (such as voltage). Compare DIGITAL COMPUTER. **a·nal·o·gy** [ə'nælədʒi] *n* **1** a likeness, esp structural or relational, between two things that are otherwise unlike: *to draw an analogy between government and a parent.* **2** a comparison of two such things: *to draw an analogy between government and a parent.* **3** *Biology* correspondence in function but not in structure and origin. **4** *Logic* the inference that things alike in some respects will be alike in others: *It is risky to argue by analogy.* **an·a·log·i·cal** [,ænə'lɒdʒɪkəl] *adj.*

an·a·lyze *or* **an·a·lyse** ['ænə,laɪz] *v* **1** examine carefully and in detail and draw conclusions. **2** separate a thing into its parts and determine the nature, amount, etc. of each. **3** psychoanalyze. **an·a·lyz·er** *or* **an·a·lys·er** *n.* **an·a·lyst** *n.* **a·nal·y·sis** [ə'næləsɪs] *n, pl* -ses [-,siz]. ⟨Greek *ana-* up + *lyein* loose⟩

an·a·lyt·ic [,ænə'lɪtɪk] *adj Linguistics* of a language, using word order and function words instead of inflections to express grammatical relationships: *English is an analytic language.* **an·a·lyt·i·cal** *adj* **1** to do with analysis: *analytical skills.* **2** skilled in analysis; inclined to analyze: *an analytical mind.* **an·a·lyt·i·cal·ly** *adv.* **analytic geometry**

Mathematics the use of algebra and co-ordinates (or calculus) to solve problems.

an·a·pest *or* **an·a·paest** ['ænə,pɛst] *or* ['ænə,pist] *n Prosody* a measure or foot consisting of two short or weakly stressed syllables followed by a long or strongly stressed one. *Example:*
From the cén I tre all róund I to the séa
I am lórd I of the fówl I and the brúte.
an·a·pes·tic *or* **an·a·paes·tic** *adj.* ⟨Greek *ana-* backwards + *paistos* beaten⟩

an·a·phase ['ænə,feiz] *n* the third stage of cell division, in which chromosomes separate.

an·a·phy·lac·tic [,ænəfə'læktɪk] *adj* to do with an extreme sensitivity and acute, potentially fatal reaction to certain allergens. ⟨Greek *ana-* again + *phylaxis* protection⟩

an·ar·chy ['ænərki] *n* **1** a state of political disorder due to the absence of governmental authority. **2** chaos; confusion. **an·ar·chic** [æ'nɑrkɪk] *adj.* ⟨Greek *an-* without + *arkhos* ruler⟩

an·ar·chism ['ænər,kɪzəm] *n* **1** the political theory that government and law are unnecessary and harmful because they prevent individuals from reaching their greatest development. **2** lawlessness or terrorism. **an·ar·chist** *n.* **an·ar·chis·tic** *adj.*

a·nath·e·ma [ə'næθəmə] *n* **1** a solemn curse by church authorities excommunicating a person. **2** a person or thing that is detested and condemned. ⟨Greek *anathema* thing devoted, esp to evil⟩
a·nath·e·ma·tize *v* curse.

a·nat·o·my [ə'nætəmi] *n* **1** the science that deals with the structure of living things. **2** the structure of an animal or plant: *the anatomy of a worm.* **3** the structure of anything. **an·a·tom·i·cal** [,ænə'tɒmɪkəl] *adj.* **an·a·tom·i·cal·ly** *adv.* **a·nat·o·mist** *n.* ⟨Greek *ana-* up + *temnein* cut⟩
anatomically correct of a model, doll, etc., showing accurate anatomical detail.

an·ces·tor ['ænsɛstər] *n* **1** a person from whom one is descended, such as a parent or grandparent. **2** an original model from which others are developed: *The harpsichord is the ancestor of the piano.* ⟨Latin *antecessor* from *ante* before + *cedere* go⟩
an·ces·tral [æn'sɛstrəl] *adj* **1** having to do with one's ancestors: *their ancestral homeland.* **2** inherited from ancestors: *an ancestral trait.* **an·ces·tral·ly** *adv.* **an·ces·try** ['ænsɛstri] *n* descent; parents and other ancestors: *of French ancestry.*

an·chor ['æŋkər] *n* **1** a heavy piece of shaped iron attached to a ship, boat, etc. by a cable and dropped in the water to prevent drifting. **2** anything used to hold something else in place. **3** *Sports* the last person on a team to swim, run, bowl, etc. **4** *Radio and television* the co-ordinator of a broadcast consisting of direct reports from different locations.
v **1** hold in place with an anchor: *to anchor a ship.* **2** fix firmly: *to anchor a tent to the ground. A child's self-esteem is anchored in the*

love of a family. **3** be an anchor for (a team, broadcast, etc.). ⟨Greek *agkyra*⟩
at anchor held by an anchor. **cast anchor** drop the anchor. **ride at anchor** be kept floating in one spot by an anchor. **weigh anchor** take up the anchor.
an·chor·age *n* a place to anchor a ship, or the charge for this.

an·cho·rite [ˈæŋkəˌraɪt] *n* a person who lives alone in a solitary place for religious meditation; hermit. **an·chor·it·ic** [-ˈrɪtɪk] *adj.* ⟨Greek *ana-* back + *chōrein* withdraw⟩

an·cho·vy [ˈæntʃouvi], [ˈæntʃəvi], *or* [ænˈtʃouvi] *n* any of a family of tiny fishes distantly related to the herring. ⟨Spanish *anchova*⟩

an·cient [ˈeinʃənt] *adj* **1** of times long past, esp before the fall of the Roman Empire in A.D. 476. **2** very old: *an ancient cat.*
n **the ancients** *pl* people of ancient times. **an·cient·ness** *n.* ⟨Latin *antianus* former⟩

an·cil·lar·y [ænˈsɪləri] *or* [ˈænsəˌleri] *adj* subordinate; supplementary: *ancillary information.* **an·cil·lar·y** *n.* ⟨Latin *ancilla* handmaid⟩

and [ænd] *conj* **1** as well as: *wet and cold. She sings and dances.* **2** added to; with: *4 and 2 make 6. I like ham and eggs.* **3** next or as a result: *The sun came out and the rain dried up.* **4** whereas: *She's a traveller and he's a homebody.* ⟨Old English⟩

an·dan·te [ɑnˈdɑntei] *adv Music* moderately slowly. ⟨Italian = walking⟩

and·i·ron [ˈændaɪərn] *n* one of a pair of metal supports for wood in a fireplace. ⟨Old French *andier*; ending infl. by *iron*⟩

an·dro·gen [ˈændrədʒən] *n* a male sex hormone such as testosterone. ⟨Greek *andros* man + English *-gen*⟩

an·drog·y·nous [ænˈdrɒdʒənəs] *adj* with both male and female characteristics.
an·drog·y·ny *n.* ⟨Greek *andros* man + *gynē* woman⟩

an·droid [ˈændrɔɪd] *n* a robot shaped like a human. ⟨Greek *andros* man + English *-oid*⟩

an·ec·dote [ˈænɪkˌdout] *n* a short account of some interesting or amusing incident. ⟨Greek *anékdota* unpublished (things)⟩
an·ec·do·tal *adj* consisting of narratives of individual cases rather than statistics or generalizations: *anecdotal evidence.*

a·ne·mi·a [əˈnimiə] *n* an insufficiency of hemoglobin or of red cells in the blood. Also, **a·nae·mi·a. a·ne·mic** *adj.* ⟨Greek *an-* without + *haima* blood⟩

an·e·mom·e·ter [ˌænəˈmɒmətər] *n* an instrument for measuring the force of the wind. ⟨Greek *anemos* wind + English *-meter*⟩

a·nem·o·ne [əˈnɛməni] *n* any of a large genus of small flowers of the buttercup family. The prairie crocus is an anemone. ⟨Greek, wind flower, from *anemos* wind⟩

aneroid barometer a barometer that records the changing pressure of air on the flexible top of an airtight metal box from which some of the air has been pumped out. ⟨Greek *a-* without + *neros* wet⟩

an·es·the·sia [ˌænəsˈθiʒə] *n* an entire or partial loss of sensation, produced by drugs, hypnotism, etc. **General anesthesia** produces complete or partial unconsciousness. **Local anesthesia** affects only a part of the body. ⟨Greek *an-* without + *aisthēsis* sensation⟩
an·es·the·si·ol·o·gist [ˌænəsˌθiziˈɒlədʒɪst] *n* a medical doctor specializing in the use, effects, etc. of anesthetics. Compare ANESTHETIST. **an·es·the·si·ol·o·gy** *n.* **an·es·thet·ic** [ˌænəsˈθɛtɪk] *n* a substance that produces anesthesia. **an·es·the·tist** [əˈnisθətɪst] *or* [əˈnɛsθətɪst] *n* a medical practitioner who administers anesthetics during surgery. Compare ANESTHESIOLOGIST. **an·es·the·tize** *v.*
an·es·the·ti·za·tion *n.* Also, **an·aes·the·sia, an·aes·thet·ic,** etc.

an·eu·rysm *or* **an·eu·rism** [ˈænjəˌrɪzəm] *n* a permanent swelling of an artery due to pressure of the blood on a weak part. ⟨Greek *ana-* up + *eurýs* wide⟩

a·new [əˈnju] *or* [əˈnu] *adv* once more; again. ⟨Old English *of newe*⟩

an·ga·koq *or* **an·ga·kok** [ˈæŋɡəˌkɒk] *n* ✸ an Inuit shaman. ⟨Inuktitut⟩

an·gel [ˈeindʒəl] *n* in certain religions, an immortal spiritual being who is an attendant or messenger of God. ⟨Greek *angelos* messenger⟩
an·gel·ic [ænˈdʒɛlɪk] *adj* like an angel; pure; lovely and good. **an·gel·i·cal·ly** *adv.* **an·gel·fish** *n, pl* **-fish** *or* **-fish·es** a small, tropical freshwater fish. **angel food cake** a very light, spongy white cake containing egg whites but no yolks or fat. **angel hair** threads of spun glass, used to trim a Christmas tree. **angel–hair pasta** very thin spaghetti.

an·ger [ˈæŋɡər] *n* strong displeasure; the feeling of wanting to punish or retaliate against some person or thing that offends.
v cause to feel anger: *The girl's disobedience angered her mother.* ⟨Old Norse *angr* trouble⟩
an·gry *adj* **1** feeling or showing anger: *He was angry with his brother.* **2** stormy: *an angry sky.* **3** inflamed and sore: *She had an angry cut on her arm.* **an·gri·ly** *adv.* **an·gri·ness** *n.*

an·gi·na [ænˈdʒaɪnə] *n* **1** in full, **angina pec·to·ris** [ˈpɛktərɪs] *or* [pɛkˈtɔrɪs] a serious disease of the heart characterized by sharp chest pains and a feeling of suffocation, caused by a sudden decrease in the flow of blood to the heart muscles. **2** any disease of the mouth or throat marked by painful attacks of suffocation. **an·gi·nal** *adj.* ⟨Latin *angina; angere* choke; *pectoris* of the chest⟩

an·gi·o·gram ['ændʒɪəˌɡræm] *n* an X-ray picture of blood vessels. ⟨Greek *angeion* vessel + English -*gram*⟩

an·gi·o·plas·ty ['ændʒɪəˌplæsti] *n* any procedure used to clear or repair a vein. It may involve surgery, laser, or catheters. ⟨Greek *angeion* vessel + *plastia* a forming⟩

an·gi·o·sperm ['ændʒɪouˌspɜrm] *n* any plant producing flowers and having its seeds enclosed in an ovary which becomes the fruit after fertilization. **an·gi·o·sperm·ous** *adj*. ⟨Greek *angeion* vessel + *sperma* seed⟩

an·gle¹ ['æŋɡəl] *n* **1** the space between two lines extending in different directions from the same point, or two surfaces extending from the same line. **2** a corner. **3** *Informal* point of view.
v **1** move or lie on a slant. **2** present (something) from a particular point of view or with a bias; slant. ⟨Latin *angulus*⟩
angle brackets angled parentheses: ⟨⟩. **angle of deviation** the angle made between a ray of light as it enters a prism and the ray that emerges. **angle of incidence** the angle made by a ray of light falling on a surface with a line perpendicular to that surface. **angle of reflection** the angle that a ray of light makes on reflection from a surface with a line perpendicular to that surface. **angle of refraction** the angle made between a ray of light refracted at a surface separating two media and a line perpendicular to the surface. **angle parking** the parking of vehicles at an angle to a curb or line, side by side rather than end to end. **an·gu·lar** *adj* **1** sharp-cornered: *an angular rock.* **2** somewhat thin and bony: *She has a tall, angular body.* **an·gu·lar·i·ty** *n*.

an·gle² ['æŋɡəl] *v* **1** fish with a hook and line. **2** try to get something by using tricks (with *for*): *to angle for an invitation.*
n a means of obtaining an advantage, esp an unfair one: *He always has an angle for getting the better of you.* **an·gler** *n*. ⟨Old English *angul* fish-hook⟩

An·gli·can ['æŋɡləkən] *adj* to do with the Church of England or associated churches like the **Anglican Church of Canada**.
n a member of one of these churches. **An·gli·can·ism** *n*. ⟨Latin *Anglicus* of England⟩

An·gli·cism ['æŋɡləˌsɪzəm] *n* a word, phrase, meaning, or custom used in England or by English-speaking people.
An·gli·cize or **an·gli·cize** *v* make or become English in form, pronunciation, habits, etc. **An·gli·ciz·a·tion** or **an·gli·ciz·a·tion** *n*.

An·glo ['æŋɡlou] *n* **1** a person of English or, loosely, British descent. **2** ✷ Anglophone. ⟨Latin *Angli* the English⟩
Anglo– *combining form* **1** of English descent or English-speaking: *the Anglo-Canadian population.* **2** English or British and ——: *an Anglo-American conference.* **An·glo·phile** *n* **1** a person who greatly admires England, its people, and culture. **2** ✷ a French Canadian who shows particular sympathy with English-speaking Canada. **An·glo·phobe** *n* **1** a person who dislikes England and its

people. **2** ✷ a French Canadian who fears or dislikes English-speaking Canadians. **An·glo·pho·bi·a** *n*. **An·glo·phone** *n* a person whose first or main language is English. **An·glo–Sax·on** ['æŋɡlou 'sæksən] *adj* to do with that part of the vocabulary of English that is derived from Old English, including many everyday words and some commonly considered offensive: *Horse, and hand are Anglo-Saxon words. She cursed him in Anglo-Saxon monosyllables.*

An·go·ra [æŋ'ɡɔrə] *n* Usually, **angora** the hair of the **Angora rabbit**, a breed with long, soft hair that is used for making yarns. **Angora cat** a breed of cat with long, silky hair. **Angora goat** a breed of goat with long, silky, curly white hair that is used for making a cloth called mohair. ⟨*Angora*, Turkey, origin of this cat and goat⟩

An·gra Main·yu ['æŋɡrə 'maɪnju] in Zoroastrianism, the evil spirit of the cosmos. ⟨Avestan = destroying spirit⟩

angst [ɑŋst] *or* [æŋst] *n* a continuous, vague anxiety not consciously related to any specific external thing: *adolescent angst.* ⟨German⟩

ang·strom or **Ång·ström** ['æŋstrəm] *n* a unit for measuring length, equal to one ten-millionth of a millimetre, sometimes used to measure wavelengths of light. *Symbol* Å ⟨for A. J. *Angstrom*, 19c Swedish physicist⟩ **angstrom unit** angstrom. *Abbrev* **AU.**

an·guish ['æŋɡwɪʃ] *n* great pain or grief. *v* cause or feel anguish. **an·guished** *adj* suffering anguish. ⟨Latin *angustia* tightness⟩

an·gu·lar See ANGLE¹.

an·hy·drous ['ænhaɪdrəsʃ] *adj* **1** without water: *an anhydrous region.* **2** *Chemistry* containing no water of crystallization. ⟨Greek *an-* without + *hydōr-* water⟩
an·hy·dride *n* **1** any oxide that unites with water to form an acid or base. **2** any compound formed by the removal of water.

an·i·line ['ænəlɪn], ['ænəˌlin], *or* ['ænəˌlaɪn] *n* a poisonous, oily liquid, obtained from coal tar, used in making dyes, plastics, etc. ⟨*anil*, shrub, source of indigo; Arabic *al* the + *nil* indigo⟩

an·i·ma ['ænəmə] *n* **1** life; soul. **2** *Psychology* the feminine aspect of a man's nature. ⟨Latin = life, breath⟩

an·i·mal [ˌænəməl] *n* **1** any living thing that is not a plant, fungus, moneran, or protist. Compare PLANT, FUNGUS, MONERAN, and PROTIST. **2** any such creature other than a human being. **3** a four-footed creature. **4** a person thought of as being like a brute or beast.
adj **1** characteristic of animals, esp the higher animals other than humans: *animal intelligence.* **2** to do with the physical nature of human beings, as opposed to the spiritual: *animal appetites.* **an·i·mal·i·ty** *n*. ⟨Latin *anima* life, breath⟩
an·i·mal·cule [ˌænə'mælkjul] *n* a tiny animal, such as a protozoan. **animal husbandry** the science of farming with animals. **an·i·mal·ism** **1** preoccupation with physical needs and

desires. **2** the belief that humans are animals without souls. **an·i·mal·ist** *n.* **an·i·mal·is·tic** *adj.* **an·i·mal·ize** *v* **1** dehumanize. **2** change into animal matter: *Food assimilated into the body is animalized.* **an·i·mal·i·za·tion** *n.* **animal kingdom** one of the five basic groups into which all living things are divided: *The animal kingdom includes all living animals, birds, fish, insects, etc.* **animal magnetism** sex appeal. **animal spirits** natural liveliness; healthy cheerfulness.

an·i·mate [ˈænəˌmeit] *v* **1** add liveliness or zest to: *Her stories animated the whole party.* **2** stir up; inspire: *Fierce love animated her efforts.* **3** make into an ANIMATED CARTOON: *to animate a children's story.* **an·i·ma·tion** *n.* **an·i·ma·tor** *n.* *adj* [ˈænəmɪt] living; having life: *Animate nature means all living plants and animals.* ⟨Latin *animare*. See ANIMA.⟩ **an·i·mat·ed** *adj* **1** lively: *an animated discussion.* **2** simulating life: *animated dolls.* **an·i·mat·ed·ly** *adv.* **animated cartoon** a series of drawings arranged to be photographed and shown in rapid succession as a movie.

an·i·ma·teur [ˌænɪməˈtɜr] *n* one who leads a discussion, moderates a panel, etc. ⟨French⟩

an·i·me [ˈænɪˌmei] *n* a Japanese style of animated cartoon, typically action-oriented and featuring characters with large eyes. Also called **Japanimation.**

an·i·mism [ˈænəˌmɪzəm] *n* religion based on a belief that there are living souls in trees, stones, stars, etc. **an·i·mist** *n.* **an·i·mis·tic** *adj.*

an·i·mos·i·ty [ˌænəˈmɒsɪti] *n* active or violent dislike. ⟨Latin *animositas; animosus* spirited⟩

an·i·mus [ˈænəməs] *n* **1** active dislike or enmity; animosity. **2** an animating thought or spirit: *Ambition was his animus.* ⟨Latin = spirit, feeling⟩

an·i·on [ˈænaɪən] *n* **1** a negatively charged ion that moves toward the positive pole in electrolysis. **2** an atom or group of atoms with a negative charge. **an·i·on·ic** *adj.* ⟨Greek *an-* negative prefix + *ion*. See ION.⟩

an·ise [ˈænɪs] *or* [əˈnis] *n* a plant of the parsley family, widely cultivated for its licorice-flavoured seeds. ⟨Greek *anison*⟩ **an·i·seed** [ˈænəˌsid] *n* the seed of anise, used as a flavouring or in medicine. **an·i·sette** [ˌænəˈzɛt] *or* [ˌænəˈsɛt] *n* a liqueur flavoured with aniseed.

A·nish·i·na·be [əˌnɪʃiˈnabei] *n, pl* **A·nish·i·na·beg** **1** a member of a First Nations people living around Lake Superior. **2** their Algonquian language. **Anishinabe** *adj.* Also called **Ojibwa.**

ankh [ɑŋk] *n* an ancient Egyptian symbol of life, a cross with a loop at the top instead of a vertical arm. ⟨Egyptian *'nh* life, soul⟩

an·kle [ˈæŋkəl] *n* the part of the leg between the foot and the calf. ⟨Old English *ancleow*⟩ **an·klet** *n* a band or chain worn around the ankle as an ornament.

an·ky·lo·sis [ˌæŋkəˈloʊsɪs] *n* a fusion of bones as a result of disease or injury. **an·ky·lot·ic** [-ˈlɒtɪk], *adj.* ⟨Greek *ankylos* crooked⟩

an·nals [ˈænəlz] *n pl* **1** a written account of events year by year. **2** any historical record. ⟨Latin *annales libri* annual records; *annus* year⟩

an·neal [əˈnil] *v* toughen (glass, metals, etc.) by heating and then cooling them. ⟨Old English *an-* on + *ælan* burn⟩

an·ne·lid [ˈænəlɪd] *n* any of more than 8000 species of segmented worms, including sea worms, earthworms, and leeches. ⟨Latin *anellus* diminutive of *anus* ring⟩

an·nex [ˈænɛks] *n* a part added to a building, city, piece of land, etc. *v* [əˈnɛks] **1** join or add to existing territory: *England annexed Acadia in 1713.* **2** *Informal* appropriate as one's own, esp without permission. ⟨Latin *ad-* to + *nectere* bind⟩ **an·nex·a·tion** [ˌænəkˈseiʃən] *n* **1** the act or fact of annexing. **2** ✸ political union of Canada with the US. **an·nex·a·tion·ist** *n* **1** one who favours annexation, as of one city, nation, etc. by another. **2** ✸ a person advocating political union with the US.

an·ni·hi·late [əˈnaɪəˌleit] *v* utterly destroy. **an·ni·hi·la·tor** *n.* **an·ni·hi·la·ble** *adj.* **an·ni·hi·la·tion** *n.* ⟨Latin *ad-* to + *nihil* nothing⟩

an·ni·ver·sa·ry [ˌænəˈvɜrsəri] *n* **1** the date on which an event occurred in an earlier year: *the anniversary of our wedding.* **2** a celebration of this. ⟨Latin *annus* year + *vertere* turn⟩

an·no Dom·i·ni [ˈænou ˈdɒməni] *or* [ˈdɒməˌnaɪ] *Latin* in the year of our Lord; any year since the birth of Jesus Christ. *Abbrev* A.D.

an·no·tate [ˈænəˌteit] *v* provide with explanatory notes: *an annotated edition of Shakespeare.* **an·no·ta·tor** *n.* **an·no·ta·tion** *n.* ⟨Latin *ad-* to + *nota* note⟩

an·nounce [əˈnaʊns] *v* **1** give formal or public notice (of): *to announce a wedding in the papers.* **2** make known in a definite, open, matter-of-fact manner: *She announced that she was not going to school.* **an·nounce·ment** *n.* ⟨Latin *ad-* to + *nuntius* messenger⟩ **an·nounc·er** *n.* **1** anyone who announces anything. **2** *Radio and television* a person who introduces programs, reads news, etc.

an·noy [əˈnɔɪ] *v* **1** make mildly angry; bother: *Her teasing annoys him.* **2** harass by means of repeated attacks: *a series of raids designed to annoy the enemy.* **an·noy·ance** *n.* **an·noy·ing** *adj.* **an·noy·ing·ly** *adv.* ⟨Old French *anuier* from Latin *in odio* in hate⟩

an·nu·al [ˈænjuəl] *adj* **1** coming once a year: *Your birthday is an annual event.* **2** for the period of a year: *annual rainfall, an annual salary of $75 000.* **3** *Botany* living only one year or season. Compare BIENNIAL, PERENNIAL. *n* **1** a book, journal, etc. published once a year. **2** a plant that lives one year or season. **an·nu·al·ly** *adv.* ⟨Latin *annus* year⟩

an·nu·i·ty [əˈnjuɪti] *or* [əˈnuɪti] *n* **1** a fund or investment that provides a fixed yearly income during one's lifetime. **2** a payment from it. ⟨Latin *annuitas* from *annus* year⟩

an·nu·i·tant *n* one who receives an annuity.

an·nul [ə'nʌl] *v* **-nulled, -nul·ling** destroy the force of; make legally void: *to annul a marriage, to annul a contract.* **an·nul·ment** *n.* ⟨Latin *ad-* to + *nullum* none⟩

an·nu·lus ['ænjələs] *n, pl* **-li** [-,laɪ] *or* [-li] a ringlike part, band, or space. **an·nu·lar** *adj.* ⟨Latin *anulus* diminutive of *anus* ring⟩

annular eclipse a solar eclipse in which the sun appears as a ring of light surrounding the dark moon.

an·nun·ci·a·tion [ə,nʌnsi'eiʃən] *n* **1** **the Annunciation** *Christianity* the angel Gabriel's announcement to the Virgin Mary that she was to be the mother of Jesus. **2** a painting, etc. of this.

an·ode ['ænoud] *n* **1** the negatively charged electrode of a primary cell. **2** the positive electrode in an electrolytic cell. **3** the positive electrode in a vacuum tube. **an·od·ic** [ə,nɒdɪk] *adj.* ⟨Greek *ana-* up + *hodos* way⟩

an·o·dize ['ænə,daɪz] *v* cover (a light metal) with a protective oxide film by electrolysis.

an·o·dyne ['ænə,daɪn] *n* anything that lessens pain or gives comfort. **an·o·dyne** *adj.* ⟨Greek *an-* without + *odýnē* pain⟩

a·noint [ə'nɔɪnt] *v* **1** put oil on ceremonially as a sign of consecration: *The archbishop anointed the new king.* **2** put oil or ointment on: *to anoint sunburned skin with lotion.* **a·noint·er** *n.* ⟨Latin *in-* on + *unguere* smear⟩

a·nom·a·ly [ə'nɒməli] *n* **1** a departure from a general rule; abnormality. **2** *Astronomy* the angle between an orbiting body, the last point at which it was closest to the sun, and the sun. **a·nom·a·lous** *adj.* **a·nom·a·lous·ly** *adv.* ⟨Greek *an-* not + *homalos* even⟩

a·non [ə'nɒn] *adv Archaic, poetic* **1** soon. **2** at another time; again. ⟨Old English *on āne* in one, at once⟩

ever and anon now and then.

a·non·y·mous [ə'nɒnəməs] *adj* **1** of or by a person whose identity is unknown or not given: *an anonymous letter, the anonymous author of a poem. Abbrev* **anon.** **2** without distinguishing features: *an anonymous face in a crowd.* **3** leaving one's background, connections, etc. undisclosed in order to avoid certain kinds of social obligation. **4** **Anonymous**, part of the title of a support group for addicts which allows members to do this: *Alcoholics Anonymous.* **a·non·y·mous·ly** *adv.* **a·non·ym·i·ty** [,ænə'nɪməti] *n.* ⟨Greek *an-* without + *onyma* name⟩

a·noph·e·les [ə'nɒfə,liz] *n, pl* **-les** any of a genus of mosquitoes which includes all the species that transmit malaria to humans. **a·noph·e·line** [-,laɪn] *adj.* ⟨Greek = harmful⟩

a·no·rak ['ænə,ræk] *n* **1** a waterproof, hooded outer coat of skins, often worn by Inuit when hunting in a kayak; its lower edge can be tightly fastened around the kayak's opening. **2** a long jacket, esp a waterproof one with a belt or drawstring at the waist. ⟨Inuktitut, Greenland dialect⟩

an·o·rex·i·a [,ænə'rɛksiə] *n* chronic loss of appetite. **an·o·rex·ic** *n, adj.*

anorexia ner·vo·sa [nər'vousə] an emotional disorder characterized by a refusal to eat. ⟨Greek *an-* without + *orexis* appetite⟩

an·oth·er [ə'nʌðər] *adj* **1** one more: *Have another glass of milk.* **2** different; not the same: *That is another matter entirely.*
pron **1** one more: *He ate a piece of cake and then asked for another.* **2** a different one: *I don't like this book; give me another.*

an·swer ['ænsər] *n* **1** words said in response to a question or challenge: *I did not hear your answer.* **2** the solution to a problem: *A new car, that's your answer.* **3** anything said or done in return: *A nod was her only answer.* **4** a counterpart, esp something produced in imitation or competition: *This new line of clothing is their answer to designer fashions.*
v **1** reply (to): *Answer me!* **2** pick up (a phone) or open (a door being knocked on). **3** act in response (to): *The brake answers to the slightest touch.* **4** be responsible: *to answer for someone's safety. I answer to nobody.* **5** correspond (to): *This house answers to his description.* **6** of an animal, recognize (a name) as its own (with to): *The dog answers to Lucky.* **7** serve: *Will this answer your purpose?* **an·swer·less** *adj.* ⟨Old English *and-* against + *swerian* swear⟩

answer back reply in a saucy way. **know all the answers a** be extremely well-informed. **b** make a boastful and annoying display of one's knowledge.

an·swer·a·ble *adj* responsible: *The treasurer is answerable to the club for the money entrusted to her.* **answering machine** a machine that receives telephone calls in one's absence and records callers' messages. **answering service** a business that takes the telephone calls of subscribers in their absence and, when they return, reports to them on the calls received.

ant [ænt] *n* any of a large family of mainly wingless insects that live in highly organized groups called colonies. **ant·like** *adj.* ⟨Old English *æmete*⟩

ant·hill or **ant hill** *n* a heap of dirt piled up by ants around the entrance to their underground nest. **ant·sy** *adj Slang* nervous or excited.

ant·ac·id [ænt'æsɪd] *n* a substance that neutralizes acids, particularly stomach acids which cause indigestion. **ant·ac·id** *adj.*

an·tag·o·nize [æn'tægə,naɪz] *v* arouse opposition or hostility in: *Her unkind remarks antagonized people who had been her friends.* ⟨Greek *anti-* against + *agōn* contest⟩
an·tag·o·nism *n* active opposition; hostility. **an·tag·o·nist** *n* opponent, often to a hero. **an·tag·o·nis·tic** *adj.* **an·tag·o·nis·ti·cal·ly** *adv.*

ant·al·ka·li [ænt'ælkə,laɪ] *n* any substance that neutralizes alkalis. **ant·al·ka·line** [-'ælkəlɪn] *or* [-'ælkə,laɪn] *adj.* ⟨*anti-* against + *alkali*. See ALKALI.⟩

ant·arc·tic [æn'tɑrktɪk] *or* [æn'tɑrtɪk] *adj* Often, **Antarctic** to do with the south polar region.
n **the Antarctic** the south polar region. ⟨Greek *anti-* opposite. See ARCTIC.⟩

Antarctic Circle the parallel of latitude at 66°33' south of the equator that marks the boundary of the south polar region.

an·te ['ænti] *n* **1** in the game of poker, a stake that every player must put up. **2** the amount to be paid in advance as one's share in any financial undertaking. **an·te** *v*.
ante up a in poker, put in one's stake. **b** pay one's share. **up the ante** increase the stakes.

ante– *prefix* **1** before; earlier: *antenatal*. **2** in front of: *anteroom*. ⟨Latin⟩

ant·eat·er ['ænt,itər] *n* any of a family of toothless mammals of the tropical forests of South America, having a long, sticky tongue with which it catches ants and termites.

an·te–bel·lum [,ænti 'bɛləm] *adj* **1** before the war. **2** *US* before the American Civil War. ⟨Latin = before the war⟩

an·te·ced·ent [,ænti'sidənt] or ['ænti,sidənt] *n* **1** a previous event. **2** *Grammar* the word, phrase, or clause referred to by a pronoun or relative adverb. In *'the house that Jack built'*, *house* is the antecedent of *that*. **3** *Mathematics* the first term of a ratio; the first or third term in a proportion. **4** *Logic* the condition on which a conclusion depends. **5 antecedents** *pl* **a** background; history: *No one knew the mysterious stranger's antecedents*. **b** ancestors. *adj* previous. ⟨Latin *ante-* before + *cedere* go⟩

an·te·cham·ber ['ænti,tʃeimbər] *n* anteroom.

an·te·date [,ænti'deit] *v* come before in time: *Shakespeare's* Hamlet *antedates* Macbeth *by about six years*. **an·te·date** *n*.

an·te·di·lu·vi·an [,æntidə'luviən] *adj* **1** to do with the period before the Flood. Compare POSTDILUVIAN. **2** very old or old-fashioned. ⟨*ante-* + Latin *diluvium* flood⟩

an·te·lope ['æntə,loup] *n, pl* **-lope** or **-lopes** **1** any of a group of mainly African animals with non-branching horns that are not shed. **2** a similar animal of the North American plains whose horns have a permanent core and an outer layer that is shed yearly. Also called **pronghorn**. ⟨Greek *antholops*⟩

an·te·na·tal [,ænti'neitəl] *adj* occurring in, or having to do with, the time before birth.

an·ten·na [æn'tɛnə] *n, pl* **-nae** [-ni] or [-nei] *for 1*; **-nas** *for 2* **1** one of two feelers on the head of an insect, lobster, etc. **2** *Radio and television* a long wire for sending or receiving electromagnetic waves. ⟨Latin, orig sailyard⟩
an·ten·nule [æn'tɛnjul] *n* a small antenna.

an·te·pe·nul·ti·mate [,æntipə'nʌltəmit] *adj, n* third from the end; last but two. **an·te·pe·nult** [,æntipə'nʌlt] or [,ænti'pinʌlt] *n* the third-last syllable of a word.

an·te·ri·or [æn'tiriər] *adj* **1** toward the front: *The anterior part of a fish's body contains the head and gills*. **2** earlier. Compare POSTERIOR. ⟨Latin, comparative of *ante* before⟩

an·te·room ['ænti,rum] or [-,rʊm] *n* a small room leading to a larger one; waiting room.

an·te·type ['ænti,təip] *n* a person or symbol prefigured in an earlier type: *Noah's Ark is seen as an antetype of the Resurrection*.

an·them ['ænθəm] *n* **1** a song of praise, devotion, or patriotism. Most countries have a **national anthem**. **2** a piece of Christian sacred music, usually with words from the Bible. ⟨Greek *antiphōna* antiphon⟩

an·ther ['ænθər] *n* on a flower, the part of the stamen that bears the pollen. ⟨Greek *anthērós* flowery; *anthos* flower⟩

an·thol·o·gy [æn'θɒlədʒi] *n* a collection of writings in one volume. ⟨Greek *anthologia* bouquet; *anthos* flower + *legein* gather⟩
an·thol·o·gist *n* the compiler of an anthology.

an·thra·cite ['ænθrə,səit] *n* a type of coal that burns with little smoke. **an·thra·cit·ic** [-'sıtık] *adj*. ⟨Greek *anthrakitēs* coal-like⟩

an·thra·co·sis [,ænθrə'kousıs] *n* BLACK LUNG. ⟨Greek *anthrax* coal + English *-osis*⟩

an·thrax ['ænθræks] *n* a bacterial disease of cattle, sheep, etc. that may be transmitted to human beings. ⟨Greek = coal⟩

anthropo– *combining form*. human being, as in *anthropology*. ⟨Greek *anthrōpos*⟩

an·thro·po·cen·tric [,ænθrəpə'sɛntrık] *adj* placing human beings at the centre of the universe; defining all reality with reference to human beings. **an·thro·po·cen·trism** *n*.

an·thro·poid ['ænθrə,pɔid] *adj* humanlike (esp with reference to members of the ape family). **an·thro·poid** *n*.

an·thro·pol·o·gy [,ænθrə'pɒlədʒi] *n* the study of the various physical types, societies, and cultural customs of human beings. **an·thro·po·log·i·cal** [,ænθrəpə'lɒdʒıkəl] *adj*. **an·thro·po·log·i·cal·ly** *adv*. **an·thro·pol·o·gist** *n*.

an·thro·po·mor·phic [,ænθrəpə'mɔrfık] *adj* attributing human form or qualities to gods, animals, etc. **an·thro·po·mor·phi·cal·ly** *adv*. **an·thro·po·mor·phism** *n*. **an·thro·po·mor·phize** *v*. ⟨Greek *anthrōpos* man + *morphē* form⟩
an·thro·po·mor·phous *adj* like a human being in form.

anti ['ænti] *Informal prep* against: *anti everything new*.
n a person opposed to some plan, idea, etc.
adj contrary: *He is anti by nature*. ⟨See ANTI-.⟩

anti– ['ænti] *prefix* **1** against; opposed to: *anti-abortion*. **2** preventing or counteracting: *antirust*. **3** not; the counterpart or opposite of: *antimatter*. Also, **ant-** before vowels and *h*. ⟨Greek = against, opposite⟩

USAGE
Words beginning with **anti-** may be spelled with or without a hyphen. In this dictionary a hyphen is always used before root words that begin with a vowel and before proper nouns and adjectives: **anti-intellectual, anti-Semite**.

an·ti–air·craft ['ænti 'ɛr,kræft] *adj* used in defence against enemy aircraft.

an·ti–at·om ['ænti ,ætəm] *n* an atom of antimatter.

an·ti·bac·te·ri·al [,æntibæk'tiriəl] *adj* that destroys or impedes the growth of bacteria.

an·ti·bal·lis·tic **missile** [,æntibə'lıstık] a

ballistic missile designed to destroy other ballistic missiles in flight.

an·ti·bi·ot·ic [ˌæntibaɪˈɒtɪk] *n* an organic substance used as a drug to destroy or weaken harmful bacteria. Penicillin is an antibiotic. **an·ti·bi·ot·ic** *adj.*

an·ti·bod·y [ˈæntɪˌbɒdi] *n* any of various proteins produced in the blood in reaction to foreign substances called antigens, and providing immunity to diseases.

an·tic [ˈæntɪk] *n* Usually, **antics** *pl* silly or ridiculous acts: *The clown amused us by his antics.* ⟨Italian *antico* old, grotesque⟩

an·ti·choice [ˈæntiˈtʃɔɪs] *adj* (as used by those favouring universal access to abortion) anti-abortion; pro-life.

An·ti·christ [ˈænti̩ˌkraɪst] *n* Christianity the great opponent of Christ, expected by some Christians to set himself up against Christ just before Christ's Second Coming.

an·tic·i·pate [ænˈtɪsəˌpeit] *v* **1** look forward to: *to anticipate a vacation.* **2** take care of ahead of time: *The nurse anticipated all the patient's needs.* **3** do, make, think of, or use (something) before (someone): *to anticipate a later theorist. The ancient Chinese anticipated some modern inventions.* **an·tic·i·pa·tion** *n.* **an·tic·i·pa·to·ry** [ænˈtɪsəpəˌtɔri] *adj.* ⟨Latin *ante-* before + *capere* take⟩

an·ti·cler·i·cal [ˌæntiˈklɛrəkəl] *adj* opposed to the influence of a church. **an·ti·cler·i·cal** *n.* **an·ti·cler·i·cal·ism** *n.*

an·ti·cli·max [ˌæntiˈklaɪmæks] *n* **1** an abrupt descent from the important to the trivial. *Example: "Alas! Alas! what shall I do? I've lost my wife and best hat, too!"* **2** any descent (in importance) contrasting with a previous rise. **3** something disappointingly duller than what events have led one to expect. **an·ti·cli·mac·tic** [ˌæntiklaɪˈmæktɪk] *adj.* **an·ti·cli·mac·ti·cal·ly** *adv.*

an·ti·co·ag·u·lant [ˌæntikouˈægjələnt] *n* a substance that prevents or slows down the clotting of blood. **an·ti·co·ag·u·lant** *adj.*

an·ti·de·pres·sant [ˌæntɪdɪˈprɛsənt] *n* a drug relieving depression. **an·ti·de·pres·sant** *adj.*

an·ti·dote [ˈæntɪˌdout] *or* [ˈæntiˌdout] *n* **1** a medicine that counteracts a poison: *Milk is an antidote for some poisons.* **2** anything that counteracts or relieves: *The flowers served as an antidote to the room's ugliness.* **an·ti·do·tal** *adj.* ⟨Greek *anti-* against + *doton* given⟩

an·ti·freeze [ˈæntiˌfriz] *n* a substance added to a liquid, as to the water in the radiator of a motor vehicle, to lower its freezing point.

an·ti·gen [ˈæntədʒən] *n* any substance that stimulates the production of antibodies. Bacteria and viruses are sources of antigens. **an·ti·gen·ic** [-ˈdʒɛnɪk] *adj.* ⟨*anti*(body) + -*gen*⟩

an·ti·gra·vi·ty [ˌæntiˈgrævəti] *n* Physics a hypothetical force countering gravity. **anti-G suit** [ˌænti ˈdʒi] clothing for pilots and astronauts to aid circulation of the blood, which tends to pool at the extremities

as an effect of rapid acceleration. Also, **G–suit.** ⟨shortened from *anti-gravity*⟩

an·ti·he·ro [ˈæntiˌhirou] *n* a main character in a novel, play, etc. who has none of the qualities expected of a hero. **an·ti·he·ro·ic** *adj.* **an·ti·her·o·ine** [ˌæntiˈhɛrouɪn] *n.*

an·ti·his·ta·mine [ˌæntiˈhɪstəˌmin] *or* [-ˈhɪstəmɪn] *n* any drug used to neutralize histamine. It relieves sneezing, runny nose, itching, etc. due to colds and allergies.

an·ti–in·flam·ma·to·ry [ˌænti ɪnˈflæməˌtɔri] *n* any drug that reduces inflammation. **an·ti–in·flam·ma·to·ry** *adj.*

an·ti–in·fla·tion [ˌænti ɪnˈfleiʃən] *adj* that counteracts inflation. **an·ti–in·fla·tion·ary** *adj.*

an·ti·knock [ˈæntiˈnɒk] *adj* of a fuel additive, serving to reduce engine noise caused by too rapid combustion.

an·ti·lock braking system [ˈæntiˈlɒk] a system that keeps brakes from locking when applied suddenly by automatically engaging and disengaging them many times per second. *Abbrev* **ABS**

an·ti·mat·ter [ˈæntiˌmætər] *n* a hypothetical form of matter composed of ANTIPARTICLES.

an·ti·mis·sile [ˌæntiˈmɪsaɪl] *or* [-ˈmɪsəl] *adj* for use in defence against ballistic missiles, rockets, etc.

an·ti·mo·ny [ˈæntəˌmouni] *n* a crystalline, metallic element that occurs chiefly in combination with other elements. *Symbol* **Sb** ⟨Latin *antimonium*⟩ **an·ti·mon·ic** [ˌæntɪˈmɒnɪk] *adj* to do with antimony, esp pentavalent antimony. **an·ti·mo·nous** [ˈæntəmənəs] *adj* to do with trivalent antimony.

an·ti·nu·cle·ar [ˌæntiˈnjukliər] *or* [ˌæntiˈnukliər] *adj* opposing the use of nuclear energy, whether for military use or as a source of power for use as fuel: *an antinuclear demonstration.* **an·ti–nuke** [-ˈnjuk] *or* [-ˈnuk] *adj* Slang antinuclear. **an·ti–nu·ker** *n.*

an·ti·par·ti·cle [ˈæntiˌpɑrtəkəl] *n* an elementary particle with the same mass as a given particle but with an opposite electric charge. If a particle collides with an antiparticle, both are annihilated.

an·ti·pas·to [ˌæntiˈpæstou] *n* an Italian dish consisting of fish, meats, pickles, etc., served as an appetizer. ⟨Italian⟩

an·tip·a·thy [ænˈtɪpəθi] *n* a strong or fixed dislike. **an·ti·pa·thet·ic** [ˌæntɪpəˈθɛtɪk] *adj.* ⟨Greek *anti-* against + *pathos* feeling⟩

an·ti·per·son·nel [ˌæntiˌpɜrsəˈnɛl] *adj* Military directed against persons rather than against equipment, supplies, etc.

an·ti·per·spi·rant [ˌæntiˈpɜrspərənt] *n* an astringent applied to the skin to check perspiration. **an·ti·per·spi·rant** *adj.*

an·ti·phon [ˈæntəˌfɒn] *n* **1** verses sung or chanted in response in a worship service. **2** anything sung or spoken responsively.

an·ti·pho·nal [æn'tɪfənəl] *adj.* **an·ti·pho·nal·ly** *adv.* ⟨Greek *anti-* opposed to + *phōnē* sound⟩

an·ti·pode ['æntə,poud] *n* anything exactly opposite; direct opposite.

an·tip·o·des [æn'tɪpə,diz] *n pl* **1** two places on directly opposite sides of the earth, such as the North and South Poles. **2** two diametrical opposites: *Forgiveness and revenge are antipodes.* **3 Antipodes** (used by dwellers in the Northern Hemisphere) Australia and New Zealand. **an·tip·o·dal** *adj.* **an·tip·o·de·an** [æn,tɪpə'diən] *adj.* ⟨Greek *anti-* opposite + *podes* feet⟩

an·ti·pro·ton [,ænti'prouton] *n* the antiparticle of the proton, with the same mass, etc. but an opposite electric charge.

an·ti·py·ret·ic [,æntɪpaɪ'rɛtɪk] *adj* checking or preventing fever.

an·ti·quar·i·an [,æntə'kwɛriən] *adj* to do with antiques or rare books or the people who collect them: *an antiquarian bookstore.* **an·ti·quar·i·an** *n.* **an·ti·quar·i·an·ism** *n.*

an·ti·quar·y ['æntə,kwɛri] *n* a student or collector of antiques or rare books.

an·ti·quat·ed ['æntə,kweitɪd] *adj* old or old-fashioned; out-of-date.

an·tique [æn'tik] *adj* **1** of a manufactured object, old. To dealers, 'antique' means over 100 years old. Canada Customs defines it as over 50 years old. **2** exhibiting or selling such objects: *an antique auction.* **3** intended to be reminiscent of such objects: *antique green.* **4** in the style of earlier times; quaintly old-fashioned: *antique manners.*
n **1** an antique object. **2** a typeface in which all lines are of equal thickness.
v **1** finish or refinish, decorate, etc. in an antique style. **2** hunt for or collect antiques. ⟨Latin *antiquus* from *ante* before⟩
an·tiq·ui·ty [æn'tɪkwəti] *n* **1** oldness; great age. **2** times long ago; usually, the period from 5000 B.C. to A.D. 476. **3 antiquities** *pl* things belonging to olden times.

an·ti–Sem·i·tism [,ænti 'sɛmə,tɪzəm] *n* hatred of Jews. **an·ti–Sem·ite** [,ænti 'sɛmait] *or* ['simait] *n.* **an·ti–Se·mit·ic** [,ænti sə'mɪtɪk] *adj.*

an·ti·sep·tic [,æntɪ'sɛptɪk] *adj* **1** preventing infection by killing germs. **2** free from contaminants; sterile. **3** seemingly removed from the realities of ordinary imperfect life.
n a substance that prevents infection by killing germs. Iodine, peroxide, and alcohol are antiseptics. **an·ti·sep·ti·cal·ly** *adv.* ⟨Greek *anti-* against + *septikós* from *sepein* rot⟩

an·ti·se·rum ['æntɪ,sirəm] *n* a serum containing antibodies for a given antigen, used for immunization or treatment.

an·ti·so·cial [,ænti'soufəl] *adj* **1** violating the accepted rules of social interaction: *antisocial behaviour.* **2** unsociable: *They're antisocial and don't like parties.* **an·ti·so·cial·ly** *adv.*

an·tith·e·sis [æn'tɪθəsɪs] *n, pl* **-ses** [-,siz] **1** the direct opposite: *Hate is the antithesis of love.* **2 a** a contrast of ideas, expressed by parallel arrangements of words, clauses, etc. *Example: "To err is human; to forgive, divine."* **b** the

second half of such an arrangement, the first being the thesis. **an·ti·thet·i·cal** [,æntə'θɛtɪkəl] *adj.* **an·ti·thet·i·cal·ly** *adv.* ⟨Greek *anti-* against + *tithenai* set⟩

an·ti·tox·in [,ænti'tɒksɪn] *n* **1** a substance formed in the body to counteract a disease or poison. **2** a serum containing antitoxin.

an·ti·trust [,ænti'trʌst] *adj* opposed to the formation of large corporations that control trade practices: *antitrust laws.*

an·ti·type ['ænti,təip] *n* one of two opposite types or symbols: *The hero and the villain are antitypes.*

an·ti·u·ni·verse [,ænti'junə,vɜrs] *n* a hypothetical universe made up of antimatter.

an·ti·ven·in [,ænti'vɛnɪn] *n* an antitoxin to counteract a venom.

an·ti·vi·ral [,ænti'vairəl] *adj* counteracting or destroying viruses: *an antiviral drug, antiviral software.*

ant·ler ['æntlər] *n* a branched horn of a deer or similar animal. **ant·lered** *adj.* ⟨Old French *antoillier*⟩
antlerless season ✱ an open season in which young deer may be hunted legally.

an·to·nym ['æntə,nɪm] *n* a word that means the opposite of another word: *Right is the antonym of wrong. Abbrev* **ant.** Compare SYNONYM. **an·ton·y·mous** [æn'tɒnəməs] *or* **an·to·nym·ic** *adj.* ⟨Greek *anti-* opposite + *onyma* name⟩

ant·sy See ANT.

an·u·re·sis [,ænju'risɪs] *n* a condition in which elimination of urine is blocked. **an·u·ret·ic** [-'rɛtɪk] *adj.* ⟨Greek *an-* without + *ouresis* urination; *ouron* urine⟩
a·nu·ri·a [ə'njuriə] *n* inability to secrete urine due to kidney failure. **an·u·ric** *adj.*

a·nus ['einəs] *n* the opening at the lower end of the alimentary canal. ⟨Latin, orig = ring⟩
a·nal *adj* **1** to do with or involving the anus. **2** *Psychoanalysis* to do with the second stage in a child's psychosexual maturation, revolving around excretory functions. **3** *Informal* short for **a·nal–re·ten·tive**, obsessively neat, particular, or stingy.

an·vil ['ænvəl] *n* a block on which metals are hammered and shaped. ⟨Old English *anfilt*⟩

anx·ious ['æŋkʃəs] *or* [,æŋʃəs] *adj* **1** uneasy because of thoughts or fears of what might happen. **2** wishing very much: *She is anxious to leave home.* **anx·ious·ly** *adv.* **anx·ious·ness** *n.* **anx·i·e·ty** [æŋ'zaɪəti] *or* [æŋk'saɪəti] *n.* ⟨Latin *anxius* troubled; *angere* choke⟩

an·y ['ɛni] *adj* **1** one (no matter which) out of many: *Any book will do.* **2** (in questions or with words having negative force) **a** some: *Have you any fresh fruit?* **b** even one; even the smallest amount: *She was forbidden to go to any movie.* **3** every: *Any child knows that.*
pron **1** (with words having negative force) **a** some: *I asked him for some paper, but he didn't have any.* **b** even one: *I asked three questions and didn't get an answer to any of them.* **2** no matter which one(s): *Take any that you want.*

adv at all (in questions, with negatives, and in conditional clauses): *If she leans over any farther, she'll fall.* ⟨Old English *ǣnig*⟩

an·y·bod·y ['ɛni,bʌdi] *or* ['ɛni,bɒdi] *pron, n* **1** any person: *Has anybody been here?* **2** any important person: *Is she anybody?* **an·y·how** *adv Informal* **1** in any way whatever: *The answer is wrong anyhow you look at it.* **2** in any case: *It's raining but I'm going anyhow.* **3** carelessly: *He does his work anyhow.* **an·y·more** or **any more** *adv* (in conditional clauses, with negatives, and in questions) now or then, after the time in question: *That book is not available anymore. Did you ever see her anymore after that?* **an·y·one** *pron* any person; anybody. **an·y·place** *adv Informal* anywhere. **an·y·thing** *pron* any thing. *adv* at all: *Is he anything like his brother?* **anything but** not in the least; in no way: *anything but poor.* **like anything** *Informal* with intense effort or enthusiasm: *He ran like anything to escape the bully.* **an·y·time** *adv* at any time: *Feel free to drop in anytime.* **an·y·way** *adv* **1** in any case: *I am coming anyway, no matter what you say.* **2** at least: *It must have been three hours anyway.* Also, *Slang* **an·y·ways. an·y·where** *adv* **1** in, at, or to any place. **2** at any point in some range of quantities: *I guess her age to be anywhere between 30 and 50.* **get anywhere** succeed to any extent: *I'm not getting anywhere with this essay.*

> **CONFUSABLES**
> **Anymore** is an adverb of time: *I never go there anymore.* **Any more** is a phrase in which **any** is a pronoun or adjective: *You can have the rest of this cake, I don't want any more. Do you know if any more people are coming?*

A–OK or **A–O.K.** [,ei ou'kei] *adj, adv Informal* working, functioning, etc. perfectly.

A–1 ['ei 'wʌn] *adj Informal* first-rate; first-class; excellent. Also, **A–one.**

a·or·ta [ei'ɔrtə] *n, pl* **-tas** or **-tae** [-ti] *or* [-taɪ] the main artery that carries blood from the left side of the heart to all parts of the body except the lungs. **a·or·tic** or **a·or·tal** *adj.* ⟨Greek *aortē* that which is hung⟩

a·pace [ə'peis] *adv Poetic* swiftly; quickly.

a·part [ə'pɑrt] *adv* **1** in or into separate parts: *He took the watch apart.* **2** away from each other: *Keep the dogs apart.* **3 a** to one side; aside: *She stood apart from the others.* **b** out of consideration; excluded: *These few criticisms apart, it is a fine essay.* *adj* (never before the noun) distinct; unique: *a world apart.* ⟨Old French *à part* aside⟩ **apart from** except for: *Apart from a little stiffness, she felt no ill effects.*

a·part·heid [ə'pɑrt,heit] *or* [ə'pɑrt,haɪt] *n* formerly, in South Africa, the policy of racial segregation. ⟨Afrikaans = separateness⟩

a·part·ment [ə'pɑrtmənt] *n* a self-contained room or set of rooms to live in. ⟨Italian *appartamento*; *a parte* apart⟩ **apartment block** a series of similar apartment buildings. **apartment building** a building

containing many apartments. Also, especially for a smaller one, **apartment house.**

ap·a·tet·ic [,æpə'tɛtɪk] *adj* of the colouring of an animal, protecting by camouflage. ⟨Greek *apate* deceit⟩

ap·a·thy ['æpəθi] *n* **1** lack of interest or desire: *apathy toward schoolwork.* **2** lack of emotional response. **ap·a·thet·ic** [,æpə'θɛtɪk] *adj.* **ap·a·thet·i·cal·ly** *adv.* ⟨Greek *a-* without + *pathos* feeling⟩

ape [eip] *n* **1** any of the family of tailless primates most resembling humans. **2** a big, clumsy or boorish person. **3** a mimic. *v* imitate; mimic. **ape·like** *adj.* **ap·ish** *adj.* ⟨Old English *apa*⟩ **go ape** *Slang* become very enthusiastic: *to go ape over a new style of music.*

APEC or **A.P.E.C.** Atlantic Provinces Economic Council.

a·per·çu [,æpər'su] *French* [apɛʀ'sy] *n* **1** a brief glimpse. **2** a short summary.

a·per·i·tif [ə,pɛrə'tif] *French* [apeʀi'tif] *n* an alcoholic drink taken before a meal to stimulate the appetite.

ap·er·ture ['æpərtʃər] *or* ['æpər,tʃʊr] *n* an opening or hole; specifically, the opening letting light into a camera, telescope, etc. ⟨Latin *apertura* opening; *aperire* to open⟩

a·pex ['eipɛks] *n, pl* **a·pex·es** or **ap·i·ces** [-,siz] the highest point; peak: *the apex of a triangle.* ⟨Latin⟩

a·pha·sia [ə'feiʒə] *or* [ə'feiziə] *n* a loss of the ability to use or understand words, usually caused by an injury or disease that affects the brain. **a·pha·sic** or **a·pha·si·ac** *adj, n.* ⟨Greek *a-* not + *phasis* utterance⟩

a·phe·li·on [ə'filiən] *n, pl* **-li·ons** or **-li·a** [-liə] the point in the orbit of a heavenly body where it is farthest from the sun. Compare PERIHELION. ⟨Greek *apo-* away from + *hēlios* sun⟩

a·phid ['eifɪd] *or* ['æfɪd] *n* any of a family of tiny insects with a tube-shaped mouth for piercing plants and sucking the juices. ⟨Latin *aphidis*, genitive of *aphis*⟩

aph·o·rism ['æfə,rɪzəm] *n* a terse sentence expressing a general thought; proverb. *Example:* *"Love is blind."* **aph·o·rist** *n.* **aph·o·ris·tic** *adj.* **aph·o·ris·ti·cal·ly** *adv.* **aph·o·rize** *v.* ⟨Greek *aphorismos* definition⟩

a·pho·tic [ei'foutɪk] *or* [ə'fɒtɪk] *adj* **1** growing without light. **2** designating that part of the ocean (below 100 m) reached by insufficient light for photosynthesis to take place. ⟨Greek *a-* without + *phos, photos* light⟩

aph·ro·dis·i·ac [,æfrə'diziæk], [,æfrə'diʒiæk], *or* [,æfrə'dɪziæk] *n* any drug, food, etc. that arouses or increases sexual desire. ⟨Greek *aphrodīsios* of Aphrodite, love goddess⟩

a·pi·an ['eipiən] *adj* to do with bees. ⟨Latin *apis* bee⟩ **a·pi·ar·y** ['eipi,ɛri] *n* a place where bees are kept. **a·pi·a·rist** *n.* **a·pi·cul·ture** ['eipə,kʌltʃər] *n* the raising and care of bees. **a·pi·cul·tur·al** *adj.* **a·pi·cul·tur·ist** *n.*

a·piece [ə'pis] *adv* for each one; each: *These apples are forty cents apiece.*

a·pla·cen·tal [,eiplə'sɛntəl] *adj* bearing live young but having no placenta, as marsupials.

a·plen·ty [ə'plɛnti] *adv Informal* in plenty.

a·plomb [ə'plɒm] *n* self-confidence; poise. 〈French *à plomb* according to the plummet〉

ap·ne·a ['æpniə] *n* a temporary failure to breathe, occasionally lasting long enough to cause unconsciousness. It is a sleep disorder. 〈Greek *a-* without + *pnoie* wind, breath〉

a·poc·a·lypse [ə'pɒkə,lɪps] *n* 1 a revelation, esp a terrifying one about the future. 2 the Apocalypse the book of Revelation at the end of the New Testament. **a·poc·a·lyp·tic** [ə,pɒkə'lɪptɪk] *adj.* **a·poc·a·lyp·ti·cal·ly** *adv.* 〈Greek *apo-* off + *kalyptein* cover〉

A·poc·ry·pha [ə'pɒkrəfə] *n pl* 1 fourteen books found in a Greek Bible of the 3rd century B.C. Eleven are included in the Roman Catholic Bible though none are included in the Jewish or, usually, the Protestant Bibles. 2 apocrypha any writings of doubtful authorship or authority. **a·poc·ry·phal** *adj.* 〈Greek *apo-* away + *kryptein* hide〉

ap·o·gee ['æpə,dʒi] *n* 1 the point where anything in orbit is farthest from the centre of the earth. Compare PERIGEE. 2 the farthest or highest point. **ap·o·ge·an** [,æpə'dʒiən] *adj.* 〈Greek *apo-* away + *gē* or *gaia* earth〉

a·po·lit·i·cal [,eipə'lɪtəkəl] *adj* not concerned with political issues. **a·po·lit·i·cal·ly** *adv.*

ap·o·lo·gi·a [,æpə'loudʒiə] *n* a statement in defence or justification. 〈Greek. See APOLOGY.〉

a·pol·o·gy [ə'pɒlədʒi] *n* 1 words of regret for an offence: *to make an apology.* 2 a systematic defence of an idea, doctrine, etc. 3 an inferior substitute: *This dish is a rather poor apology for Eggs Benedict.* 〈Greek *apologia; apo-* off + *legein* speak〉
a·pol·o·get·ic [ə,pɒlə'dʒɛtɪk] *adj* 1 making an apology: *an apologetic reply.* 2 speaking or acting uncertainly, as if aware of the weakness of one's position: *Don't be apologetic about teaching grammar. n* 1 a systematic defence of a doctrine, etc. 2 apologetics the branch of theology that deals with the rational defence of religious faith. **a·pol·o·get·i·cal·ly** *adv.* **a·pol·o·gist** *n* a person who defends an idea. **a·pol·o·gize** *v* express regret for one's actions.

ap·o·plex·y ['æpə,plɛksi] *n* a cerebrovascular accident; stroke. 〈Greek *apo-* off + *plēssein* strike〉
ap·o·plec·tic [,æpə'plɛktɪk] *adj* 1 to do with apoplexy. 2 intense enough to cause apoplexy: *an apoplectic rage.* **ap·o·plec·ti·cal·ly** *adv.*

ap·o·se·mat·ic [,æpousɪ'mætɪk] *adj* of an animal's colouring, protecting by warning off predators. **ap·o·se·mat·i·cal·ly** *adv.* 〈Greek *apo* away, off + *sema* sign〉

a·pos·ta·sy [ə'pɒstəsi] *n* the act or fact of forsaking one's faith, ideology, or principles. **a·pos·tate** [ə'pɒsteit] *or* [ə'pɒstɪt] *n, adj.* **a·pos·ta·tize** [ə'pɒstə,taɪz] *v.* 〈Greek *apo-* away + *stasia* (from *stanai* stand)〉

a·pos·tle [ə'pɒsəl] *n* 1 Apostle any of the twelve disciples chosen by Jesus to preach the gospel. 2 any early Christian leader or missionary. 3 a leader of any movement. 〈Greek *apo-* off + *stellein* send〉
a·pos·to·late [ə'pɒstəlɪt] *n* 1 the office or work of an apostle. 2 apostles collectively. **ap·o·stol·ic** [,æpə'stɒlɪk] *adj.* **apostolic succession** in some Christian churches, the unbroken line of succession from the Apostles down to present-day priests.

a·pos·tro·phe [ə'pɒstrəfi] *n* 1 a sign (') used: **a** to show the omission of one or more letters as in *o'er* for *over* or *'lectric for electric.* **b** to show the possessive of nouns or indefinite pronouns: *the lions' den, everybody's business.* **c** to form plurals of (especially) lower-case letters, sometimes of numerals or initialisms: *two p's in 'hopped', six MP's.* 2 the addressing of words to an absent person or to a thing as if it could understand. *Example: "Western wind, when wilt thou blow."* **ap·o·stroph·ic** [,æpə'strɒfɪk] *adj.* 〈Greek *apostrephein* get rid of; *apo-* away + *strephein* turn〉

a·poth·e·car·y [ə'pɒθə,keri] *n Archaic* pharmacist; druggist. 〈Latin *apothecarius* warehouseman; Greek *apothēkē* storehouse〉
apothecaries' measure a system of units for measuring volume, traditionally used by pharmacists. **apothecaries' weight** a parallel system for mass.

ap·o·thegm ['æpə,θɛm] *n* a short, forceful saying. *Example: "Beauty is only skin-deep."* Also, **ap·o·phthegm. ap·o·theg·mat·ic** *adj.* 〈Greek *apo-* forth + *phtheggesthai* utter〉

a·poth·e·o·sis [ə,pɒθi'ousɪs] *or* [,æpə'θiəsɪs] *n, pl* **-ses** the raising of a human being to the rank of a god: *The apotheosis of the emperor became a Roman custom.* 2 glorification. 3 a glorified ideal. **a·poth·e·o·size** [ə'pɒθiə,saɪz] *or* [,æpə'θiə,saɪz] *v.* 〈Greek = deification; *theos* god〉

ap·pal or **ap·pall** [ə'pɒl] *v* **-palled, -pall·ing** fill with horror. **ap·pall·ing** *adj.* **ap·pall·ing·ly** *adv.* 〈Old French *apallir* turn pale. See PALE¹.〉

ap·pa·loo·sa [,æpə'lusə] *n* a breed of horse with mottled skin and a skimpy tail. 〈*a Palouse* horse, for the Palouse River area in Washington, where the breed is said to have been developed by the Nez Percé nation〉

ap·pa·ra·tus [,æpə'rætəs] *or* [,æpə'reitəs] *n, pl* **-tus** or **-tus·es** 1 the things necessary for a particular use: *all the apparatus for a chemistry experiment, our digestive apparatus, a climbing apparatus in a gym.* 2 the system which keeps a thing functioning: *the apparatus of corporate affairs.* 〈Latin *ad-* + *paratus* prepared (thing)〉

ap·par·el [ə'pɛrəl] *or* [ə'pærəl] *n* clothing. *v* **-elled** or **-eled, -el·ling** or **-el·ing** *Poetic* clothe. 〈Old French *apareiller* clothe〉

ap·par·ent [ə'pɛrənt] *or* [ə'pærənt] *adj* 1 obvious; plain to see or understand: *The flaw in the fabric was quite apparent. It was apparent that she had lied.* 2 seeming; according to appearances: *the apparent motion of the sun.* **ap·par·ent·ly** *adv.* **ap·par·ent·ness** *n.* 〈Latin *apparens; apparere* appear〉

ap·pa·ri·tion [‚æpə'rɪʃən] *n* **1** a ghost; phantom. **2** any strange sight. ⟨Latin *apparitio* an appearing⟩

ap·peal [ə'pil] *v* **1** make an earnest request (*to* or *for*): *The children appealed to their mother for help.* **2** *Law* ask that (a case) be taken to a higher court to be reviewed. **3** call on some person or resort to some principle to decide a matter in one's favour. **4** be attractive: *Bright colours appeal to young children.* **ap·peal** *n.* **ap·peal·ing** *adj.* **ap·peal·ing·ly** *adv.* ⟨Latin *appellare* accost, address⟩

ap·pear [ə'pir] *v* **1** become visible: *One by one the stars appear.* **2** seem to the eyes or mind: *The apple appeared sound, but was rotten inside. It appears to be true.* **3** be presented to the public: *The movie will appear soon.* **4** present oneself: *to appear on stage, to appear in court.* ⟨Latin *ad-* + *parere* come in sight⟩
ap·pear·ance *n* **1** the act or fact of appearing. **2** the way a person or thing looks. **3** show; pretence. **4 appearances**, *pl* the impression given by something: *to judge by appearances.* **for (the sake of) appearances** so as to give others the right impression. **keep up appearances** pretend that all is well. **make** or **put in an appearance** appear briefly; show up. **to all appearances** as far as one can see.

ap·pease [ə'piz] *v* **1** satisfy (an appetite or desire): *A good dinner appeased his hunger.* **2** make calm or content: *to appease a crying child.* **3** give in to the demands of (a potential enemy): *Hitler was appeased at Munich.* **ap·pease·ment** *n.* **ap·peas·er** *n.* **ap·peas·ing·ly** *adv.* ⟨Old French *apaisier, a-* to + *pais* peace⟩

ap·pel·lant [ə'pɛlənt] *n* a person who appeals a court's decision.
ap·pel·late [ə'pɛlɪt] *adj* hearing appeals: *an appellate judge, appellate court.*

ap·pel·la·tion [‚æpə'leiʃən] *n* a name or title. ⟨Latin *appellatio*, from *appellare*. See APPEAL.⟩

ap·pend [ə'pɛnd] *v* add to a larger thing: *A fee schedule is appended to the application form.* ⟨Latin *ad-* on + *pendere* hang⟩
ap·pend·age *n* **1** something attached. **2** *Biology* any external or subordinate part. Arms, tails, fins, legs, etc. are appendages. **ap·pen·dec·to·my** [‚æpen'dɛktəmi] *n* surgical removal of the appendix. **ap·pen·di·ci·tis** [ə,pɛndə'saitɪs] *n* inflammation of the appendix. **ap·pen·dix** [ə'pɛndɪks] *n, pl* **-dix·es** or **-di·ces 1** an addition at the end of a book, containing supplementary material. **2** an outgrowth of an organ, etc., specifically the **vermiform appendix**, a small tube-shaped sac on the large intestine.

USAGE
The Latin plural **appendices** is more common for def. 1, **appendixes** for def. 2.

ap·per·tain [‚æpər'tein] *v* belong as a part; relate: *Forestry appertains to geography, to botany, and to agriculture.* ⟨Latin *ad-* to + *pertinere* pertain, belong⟩

ap·pe·tite ['æpə,tait] *n* **1** the desire for food. **2** a desire or inclination: *an appetite for good fiction.* ⟨Latin *appetitus; ad-* + *petere* seek⟩

ap·pe·tiz·er ['æpə,taizər] *n* food or drink served, esp before a meal, to stimulate the appetite. **ap·pe·tiz·ing** *adj* arousing the appetite. **ap·pet·iz·ing·ly** *adv.*

ap·plaud [ə'plɒd] *v* **1** clap hands, cheer, etc. in approval. **2** express approval of; praise. **ap·plaud·er** *n.* **ap·plause** [ə'plɒz] *n.* ⟨Latin *ad-* to + *plaudere* clap⟩

ap·ple ['æpəl] *n* the firm, roundish fruit of a tree widely grown in temperate regions. ⟨Old English *æppel*⟩
apple of one's eye a cherished person or thing: *She is the apple of her father's eye.* **upset the apple cart** spoil a situation; disrupt a plan: *The delegates hoped no one would upset the apple cart before the bylaw was signed.*
apple butter a smooth, dark, jamlike spread made from apples. **ap·ple·jack** *n* hard cider; an alcoholic drink made from apples. **apple–pie order** *Informal* perfect condition. **ap·ple–pol·ish·er** *Informal* a person who tries to curry favour with superiors. **ap·ple–pol·ish** *v.* **ap·ple·sauce** *n* **1** apples cut up and cooked with sugar and water until soft. **2** *Informal* nonsense.

ap·pli·ance See APPLY.

applic-, applied See APPLY.

ap·pli·qué ['æplə,kei] *n* **1** the art of attaching pieces of fabric in various shapes and colours onto a larger piece for decoration. **2** any of the pieces of fabric so attached.
v [‚æplə'kei] or ['æplə,kei] **-quéd, -qué·ing.** ⟨French, pp of *appliquer* apply⟩

ap·ply [ə'plai] *v* **1** put on (for some special purpose): *to apply paint to a wall.* **2** put into effect: *She knows the rule but not how to apply it.* **3** fit the circumstances: *The new policy does not apply to this case.* **4** make a formal request: *to apply for a job.* **5** set to work and stick to it (reflexively): *He applied himself to learning French.* **6** designate for a special purpose: *to apply funds to charity.* ⟨Latin *applicare; ad-* on + *plicare* lay⟩
ap·pli·ance *n* a household machine, esp a large one such as a stove or dryer. Smaller appliances include toasters, blenders, etc. **ap·pli·ca·ble** ['æpləkəbəl] *or* [ə'plɪkəbəl] *adj* fitting the particular case: *The rule is not always applicable.* **ap·pli·ca·bil·i·ty** [‚æpləkə'bɪləti] *n.* **ap·pli·cant** ['æpləkənt] *n* a person who applies (for a job, loan, etc.). **ap·pli·ca·tion** *n* **1** the act, fact or way of applying: *the application of a rule, application of paint to a house.* **2** a preparation to be applied: *This application is made with aloes.* **3** a form to be filled out in making an official request: *Submit two copies of your application.* **4** continued effort; close attention: *By application to her work she won promotion.* **5** *Computers* a program designed and written to serve a specific purpose for the user. **ap·pli·ca·tor** *n* a device for applying polish, paint, etc. **ap·plied** *adj* studied with a view to practical use: *applied mathematics.* **applied science** any discipline using scientific theory to solve practical problems, design technology, etc.

ap·point [ə'pɔɪnt] *v* **1** name to a position: *He was appointed chairperson.* **2** decide on; fix: *to appoint a time for the meeting.* **3** furnish: *a well-appointed room.* ⟨Latin *ad-* to + *punctum* point⟩
ap·point·ee [,æpɔɪn'ti] *n* a person appointed to a position. **ap·point·er** *n*. **ap·poin·tive** *adj* filled by appointment rather than election: *Most positions in the Senate are appointive.* **ap·point·ment** *n* **1** the act of naming to a position. **2** a position so filled. **3** an engagement to be somewhere at a certain time. **4 appointments** *pl* furnishings.

ap·por·tion [ə'pɔrʃən] *v* give out in shares: *The mother's property was apportioned among her children.* **ap·por·tion·ment** *n*. ⟨Latin *ad-* to + *portiō* portion⟩

ap·po·site ['æpəzɪt] *adj* appropriate.
ap·po·site·ly *adv*. **ap·po·site·ness** *n*.
ap·po·si·tion *n* **1** *Grammar* the relation of two parts of a sentence when one is added as an explanation to the other and both perform a single syntactic function. In *Joe, my brother, has a new car,* the words *Joe* and *my brother* are in apposition. **2** the act of putting side by side. **ap·pos·i·tive** [ə'pɒzətɪv] *n, adj*. ⟨Latin *appositus* placed near⟩

ap·praise [ə'preɪz] *v* estimate the value, amount, quality, etc. of: *to appraise someone's character, to appraise jewellery.* **ap·prais·al** *n*. **ap·prais·er** *n*. **ap·prais·ing·ly** *adv*. ⟨rare *apprize*, influenced by *praise*. See APPRECIATE.⟩

ap·pre·ci·ate [ə'priʃi,eit] *v* **1** find enjoyable: *Almost everybody appreciates good food.* **2** have an informed opinion of the worth of: *to appreciate art.* **3** be aware of: *A musician can appreciate small differences in sounds.* **4** be grateful for: *I really appreciate your driving me home.* **5** rise in value: *This land will appreciate as soon as the road is built.* **ap·pre·ci·a·to·ry** *adj*. ⟨Latin *appretiare* appraise; *ad-* + *pretium* price⟩
ap·pre·ci·a·ble [ə'priʃəbəl] *adj* enough to be worth noticing: *an appreciable difference.* **ap·pre·ci·a·bly** *adv*. **ap·pre·ci·a·tion** [ə,priʃi'eiʃən] *n* **1** the fact of appreciating. **2** gratitude. **ap·pre·ci·a·tive** [ə'priʃətɪv] *or* [ə'priʃi,eitɪv] *adj* showing appreciation or gratitude; grateful. **ap·pre·ci·a·tive·ly** *adv*. **ap·pre·ci·a·tive·ness** *n*.

ap·pre·hend [,æprɪ'hɛnd] *v* **1** grasp with the mind: *They were able to apprehend her meaning from her gestures.* **2** arrest: *The thief has been apprehended by the police.* ⟨Latin *ad-* upon + *prehendere* seize⟩
ap·pre·hen·si·ble *adj* that can be apprehended. **ap·pre·hen·sion** *n* **1** the act or fact of apprehending. **2** fear; dread. **ap·pre·hen·sive** *adj*. **ap·pre·hen·sive·ly** *adv*. **ap·pre·hen·sive·ness** *n*.

ap·pren·tice [ə'prɛntɪs] *n* **1** a person learning a trade or craft by working under skilled supervision. **2** any beginner; learner. *v* attach (oneself) or take (another) as an apprentice: *He was apprenticed to his uncle.* **ap·pren·tice·ship** *n*. ⟨Old French *aprentis* from *apprendre* learn⟩

ap·prise [ə'praɪz] *v* give notice to; inform (often with *of*): *They were apprised by letter of*
the delay. ⟨French *appris*, pp of *apprendre* learn⟩

ap·proach [ə'proutʃ] *v* **1** come near or nearer (to) in space or time: *We're approaching the town. Winter approaches.* **2** come near or nearer to (in character, quality, amount): *The wind was approaching gale force.* **3** go to speak to or negotiate with: *We approached the principal about rescheduling exams.* **4** adopt a particular method or attitude in dealing with something: *How would you approach this problem?* **ap·proach** *n*. **ap·proach·a·ble** *adj*. **ap·proach·a·bil·i·ty** *n*. ⟨Old French *aprochier* from *proche* near⟩

ap·pro·ba·tion [,æprə'beiʃən] *n* favourable opinion; approval. ⟨Latin *approbatio*. See APPROVE.⟩

ap·pro·pri·ate [ə'proupriɪt] *adj* suitable: *Jeans and a sweater are appropriate clothes for the hike.* *v* [ə'proupri,eit] **1** take for oneself: *Do not appropriate other people's belongings without permission.* **2** set aside for some purpose: *to appropriate funds for roads.* **ap·pro·pri·ate·ly** *adv*. **ap·pro·pri·ate·ness** *n*. **ap·pro·pri·a·tion** *n*. ⟨Latin *ad-* to + *proprius* one's own⟩

ap·prove [ə'pruv] *v* **1** think well (*of*); agree with: *Her family did not approve of her actions. I mentioned your idea; he did not approve.* **2** consent to; ratify: *The Board approved the plan.* **3** express satisfaction with: *Her boss approved her work.* **ap·prov·ing·ly** *adv*. ⟨Latin *approbare* from *ad-* to + *probus* good⟩
ap·prov·al *n* **1** favourable opinion: *He tried to win the teacher's approval.* **2** consent: *She gave her approval to the project.* **on approval** with the option of buying: *We had the car for a day on approval.* **on approved credit** if conditions for a loan are met. *Abbrev* **OAC**

Approve is a general word indicating explicit consent by an authority: *Mom approved our travel plans.* **Sanction** usually suggests public support or philosophical agreement: *Our government does not sanction child labour.* **Ratify** implies official confirmation according to a procedure: *The council ratified the by-laws.*

ap·prox·i·mate [ə'prɒksəmɪt] *adj* not exact but nearly so; roughly calculated: *The approximate number of people expected is 500.* *v* [ə'prɒksə,meit] approach in nature or amount; be close to: *to approximate the truth.* **ap·prox·i·mate·ly** *adv*. **ap·prox·i·ma·tion** *n*. ⟨Latin *ad-* to + *proximus* nearest⟩

ap·pur·te·nance [ə'pɜrtənəns] *n* **1** an accessory; secondary accompaniment. **2** a right or privilege subordinate to another. **3 appurtenances** *pl* equipment. ⟨Anglo-French *apurtenance*. Related to APPERTAIN.⟩

a·près–ski ['æprei 'ski] *French* [aprɛ'ski] *n* a social activity held in the evening after a day of skiing. ⟨French *après* after + *ski*⟩

ap·ri·cot ['æprə,kɒt] *or* ['eiprə,kɒt] *n* a tree cultivated in warmer temperate regions for its round, juicy, pale orange or yellow fruit. ⟨Arabic *al-burquq*; Latin *praecox* early ripe⟩

A·pril ['eiprəl] *n* the fourth month of the year. It has 30 days. ⟨Latin *Aprilis*⟩
April fool any person who gets fooled on **April Fools' Day,** April 1, a day observed by playing tricks and jokes.

a pri·o·ri [ˌei pri'ɔri] *or* [ˌei pri'ɔrai] **1** from cause to effect; from a general rule to a particular case. The opposite is **a posteriori** [pɒs,tiri'ɔrai] or [-ri]. **2** based on preconception rather than on actual observation. **3** not needing experience to verify it. **a·pri·o·ri·ty** *n.* ⟨Latin = from (something) previous⟩

a·pron ['eiprən] *n* **1** a garment worn over the front part of the body to protect one's clothes. **2** a protective structure to prevent the washing away of a surface, such as a sea wall, river bank, etc. **3** a paved area in front of a building. **4** the part of a theatre stage that extends in front of the curtain. ⟨Old French *naperon* diminutive of *nape* napkin⟩ **apron strings 1** ties used to fasten an apron. **2** connections that make one dependent; esp in **cut the apron strings, tied to one's mother's apron strings.**

ap·ro·pos [ˌæprə'pou] *adv* **1** fittingly. **2** incidentally (to introduce some related but new point): *Apropos, what are you doing later? adj* fitting: *an apropos remark.* ⟨French *à propos* to the purpose⟩
apropos of with regard to.

apse [æps] *n* a recess in a church, usually at the east end, with an arched or vaulted roof. **ap·si·dal** *adj.* ⟨Greek *hapsis* loop, arch⟩

apt [æpt] *adj* **1** likely: *A careless person is apt to make mistakes.* **2** suitable: *an apt reply.* **3** quick to learn: *an apt pupil.* **apt·ly** *adv.* **apt·ness** *n.* ⟨Latin *aptus*, pp of *apere* fit⟩
ap·ti·tude ['æptə,tjud] *or* ['æptə,tud] *n* **1** a natural ability: *an aptitude for fixing things.* **2** quickness to learn. **aptitude test** a test taken to find out what sort of work, studies, etc. one is suited for.

apt. apartment.

ap·ter·ous ['æptərəs] *adj Biology* wingless. ⟨Greek *a-* without + *pteron* wing⟩

ap·ti·tude See APT.

aq·ua ['ækwə] *or* ['ɑkwə] *n Chemistry* a liquid solution: *aqua fortis.* Abbrev **aq** ⟨Latin = water⟩ **aq·ua re·gi·a** ['ridʒiə] *n* a mixture of nitric acid and hydrochloric acid that will dissolve gold. ⟨Latin = royal water⟩ **aq·ua vi·tae** ['vitai] *or* ['vəiti] spirits; brandy, whisky, etc. ⟨Latin = water of life⟩

aq·ua·cul·ture ['ækwə,kʌltʃər] *n* the raising of water animals and plants, esp fish, for commercial purposes. Also, **aq·ui·cul·ture.** **aq·ua·cul·tur·ist** *n.*

Aq·ua·lung ['ækwə,lʌŋ] *n Trademark* a diving apparatus consisting of cylinders of compressed air strapped to the diver's back and a watertight mask over eyes and nose.

aq·ua·ma·rine [ˌækwəmə'rin] *or* [ˌɑkwəmə'rin] *n* **1** a transparent, bluish green precious stone. **2** bluish-green. **aq·ua·ma·rine** *adj.*

aq·ua·plane ['ækwə,plein] *n* a wide board on which a person stands as it is towed over the water by a speeding motorboat.
v **1** use one of these. **2** HYDROPLANE.

aq·ua·relle [ˌækwə'rɛl] *n* painting done with ink and transparent water colours. ⟨French⟩

a·quar·i·um [ə'kwɛriəm] *n, pl* **a·quar·i·ums** or **a·quar·i·a** a tank, glass bowl, or pond for living fish, water animals, and water plants. ⟨Latin *aquarium* of water; *aqua* water⟩ **a·quar·ist** [ə'kwɛrɪst] *n* keeper of an aquarium.

a·quat·ic [ə'kwɒtɪk] *or* [ə'kwætɪk] *adj* found or occurring in water: *aquatic plants.*
n **aquatics** *pl* sports that take place in or on water. **a·quat·i·cal·ly** *adv.*

aq·ua·tint ['ækwə,tɪnt] *n* **1** a printmaking process in which the spaces in a design, not the lines, can be etched by acid. **2** an etching so made. **aq·ua·tint** *v.*

aq·ue·duct ['ækwə,dʌkt] *n* an artificial channel or large pipe for bringing water from a distance. ⟨Latin *aqua* water + *ductus*, pp of *ducere* lead⟩

a·que·ous ['ækwiəs] *or* ['eikwiəs] *adj* to do with water.
aqueous humour or **humor** the watery liquid in the eye between the cornea and the lens.

aq·ui·fer ['ækwəfər] *n* an underground layer of porous rock, sand, etc. containing water which can be tapped by wells. **a·quif·er·ous** [ə'kwɪfərəs] *adj.* ⟨Latin *aqua* water + *ferre* carry⟩

aq·ui·line ['ækwə,lain] *or* ['ækwəlin] *adj* **1** of or like an eagle. **2** of a nose, curved or hooked like an eagle's beak. ⟨Latin *aquila* eagle⟩

Ar·ab ['ɛrəb] *or* ['ærəb] *n* a member of a Semitic people widely scattered throughout the Middle East and North Africa. **Ar·ab** *adj.* ⟨Arabic *'arab*⟩
A·ra·bi·an [ə'reibiən] *adj* of or from the Arabian Peninsula. *n* a swift, graceful horse of a breed originating in this region. **Arabian camel** a species of camel with one hump. **Ar·a·bic** ['ɛrəbɪk] *or* ['ærəbɪk] *n* a Semitic language, the main language of Saudi Arabia and other countries. It is written in a nonroman script. **Ar·a·bic** *adj.* **Arabic numerals** the figures 1, 2, 3, 4, 5, 6, 7, 8, 9, 0.

USAGE
Arab applies most commonly to the people or their culture: *the Arab world.* **Arabian** usually applies more to the territory traditionally seen as their home: *Arabian sands.* **Arabic** applies to the language: *Arabic poetry.*

ar·a·besque [ˌɛrə'bɛsk] *or* [ˌærə'bɛsk] *n* **1** *Ballet* a pose in which the dancer stands on one leg with the other extended horizontally behind and the arms stretched out at the sides. **2** an elaborate and fanciful design of flowers, leaves, etc. **3** *Music* **a** an ornamentation of a melody. **b** a short, graceful, often highly ornamented piece. ⟨French, from Italian *arabesco* in Arab style⟩

ar·a·ble ['ɛrəbəl] *or* ['ærəbəl] *adj* fit for growing crops: *There is little arable land on the Canadian Shield.* **ar·a·bil·i·ty** *n.* ⟨Latin *arare* to plough⟩

a·rach·nid [ə'ræknɪd] *n* any of a class of small, air-breathing arthropods, such as scorpions and spiders, with four pairs of walking legs and no antennae or wings. ⟨Greek *arakhnē* spider, web⟩
a·rach·no·pho·bia [ə,rækna'foubiə] *n* an abnormal fear of spiders.

Ar·a·ma·ic [,ɛrə'meiɪk] *or* [,ærə'mciɪk] *n* a Semitic language or group of dialects, including Syriac and the language spoken in Palestine at the time of Christ.

ar·bi·trage ['ɑrbətrɪdʒ] *or* ['ɑrbə,trɑʒ] *n* Business the trading of stocks, bonds, etc. in several markets simultaneously to take advantage of price differences. **ar·bi·trag·eur** [,ɑrbɪtrɑ'ʒɜr] *or* ['ɑrbɪ,trɑʒər] *n*. ⟨French, from *arbitrer;* Latin *arbitrārī*. See ARBITRATE.⟩

ar·bi·trar·y ['ɑrbə,trɛri] *adj* **1** based on a whim: *an arbitrary decision to quit the team.* **2** random: *an arbitrary selection.* **3** decided ad hoc by a judge or tribunal rather than by direct application of a specific law. **4** despotic: *arbitrary rule.* **ar·bi·trar·i·ly** *adv.* **ar·bi·trar·i·ness** *n.*

ar·bi·trate ['ɑrbə,treit] *v* **1** decide (a dispute) as a disinterested party: *to arbitrate between two persons in a quarrel.* **2** submit to this method of settlement: *The two nations agreed to arbitrate their dispute.* **ar·bi·tra·ble** *adj.* **ar·bi·tra·tion** *n.* **ar·bi·tra·tor** *n.* ⟨Latin *arbitrārī* act as arbiter⟩
ar·bi·ter ['ɑrbətər] *n* a person with final authority to decide: *Who made you the arbiter of morality?*

ar·bor ['ɑrbər] See ARBOUR.

ar·bo·re·al [ɑr'bɔriəl] *adj* to do with trees. ⟨Latin *arbor* tree⟩
ar·bo·re·tum [,ɑrbə'ritəm] *n* a place where trees and shrubs are grown. **ar·bo·ri·cul·ture** ['ɑrbərə,kʌltʃər] *or* [ɑr'bɔrə,kʌltʃər] *n* tree farming. **ar·bor·ist** ['ɑrbərɪst] *n* a tree expert.

ar·bor·vi·tae ['ɑrbər'vitaɪ] *or* ['ɑrbər'vəiti] *n, pl* **-vi·tae** *or* **-vi·taes** any evergreen tree of the cypress family found in North America and E Asia. ⟨Latin = tree of life⟩

ar·bour *or* **ar·bor** ['ɑrbər] *n* a shady place formed by trees or by vines growing on latticework. **ar·boured** *adj.* ⟨Anglo-French *erber* from Latin *herbarium; herba* herb. Influenced by Latin *arbor* tree.⟩
Arbour Day *or* **Arbor Day** a day observed in certain Canadian provinces and in some other countries by planting trees. The date varies in different places.

ar·bu·tus [ɑr'bjutəs] *n* **1** any shrub or tree of the heath family, with broad, leathery, evergreen leaves, clusters of flowers, and red, berrylike fruit. **2** See TRAILING ARBUTUS. ⟨Latin⟩

arc [ɑrk] *n* **1** part of the perimeter of a circle or ellipse, or its angular measurement. **2** a curved line. **3** *Electricity* a discharge of electricity seen as a curved stream of brilliant light. **4** *Astronomy* the apparent path of a heavenly body above the horizon (**diurnal arc**) or below the horizon (**nocturnal arc**).
v **arced** [ɑrkt], **arc·ing** ['ɑrkɪŋ] **1** *Electricity*

form an arc. **2** follow a curved path. **arc lamp** a lamp whose light comes from an electric arc. **arc welding** a method of welding in which the heat is produced by an electric arc. ⟨Latin *arcus* bow⟩

ARC [ɑrk] AIDS-RELATED COMPLEX.

ar·cade [ɑr'keid] *n* **1** a wide, covered passage, often with an arched roof. **2** a row of arches supported by columns. **3** a hall with video games in it. ⟨French, from Latin *arca* chest⟩

ar·cane [ɑr'kein] *adj* mysterious; esoteric. ⟨Latin *arcanum* hidden (thing); *arca* chest⟩
ar·ca·num [ɑr'keinəm] *n, pl* **-nums** *or* **-na** [-nə] a secret; mystery.

arch[1] [ɑrtʃ] *n* **1** *Architecture* an upright structure with a curved top, used in bridges, etc. as a support for the weight above it. **2** any curved structure.
v bend or form into an arch. **arched** *adj.* **arch·ing** *adj.* ⟨French *arche;* Latin *arcus* bow⟩
arch·way *n* an entrance with an arch above it.

arch[2] [ɑrtʃ] *adj* **1** chief; principal: *the arch villain of a story.* **2** consciously playful or mischievous: *an arch reply.* **arch·ly** *adv.* **arch·ness** *n.* ⟨See ARCH-.⟩

arch– *prefix* **1** principal: *archbishop.* **2** first; original: *archiblast.* Also, **archi-.** ⟨Greek *arche-; arkhos* chief⟩

archaeo– *combining form* **1** ancient; primitive: *archaebacteria.* **2** to do with archaeology: *archeozoology.* Also, **archae-.** ⟨Greek *archaios* ancient; *arkhē* beginning⟩

ar·chae·ol·o·gy [,ɑrki'ɒlədʒi] *n* the study of the life of ancient times through the remains left by various civilizations. Also, **ar·che·ol·o·gy.** **ar·chae·o·log·i·cal** *adj.* **ar·chae·o·log·i·cal·ly** *adv.* **ar·chae·ol·o·gist** *n.* ⟨Greek *archaios* ancient + English *-logy*⟩

ar·chae·op·ter·yx [,ɑrki'ɒptərɪks] *n* the oldest known fossil bird of the European Upper Jurassic period. Also, **ar·che·op·ter·yx.** ⟨*archaeo-* + Greek *pteryx* wing⟩

Ar·chae·o·zo·ic [,ɑrkiə'zouɪk] *Geology n* the oldest era, starting about 2 billion years ago, during which living things first appeared. **Ar·chae·o·zo·ic** *adj.* Also, **Ar·che·o·zo·ic.** ⟨*archaeo-* + Greek *zōē* life⟩

ar·cha·ic [ɑr'keiɪk] *adj* from an earlier time; no longer in general use. **ar·cha·i·cal·ly** *adv.* ⟨Greek *archaikos* from *arkhē* beginning⟩
ar·cha·ism ['ɑrkei,ɪzəm] *or* ['ɑrki,ɪzəm] *n* a word or expression no longer in general use. *Methinks* is an archaism meaning *it seems to me.*

arch·an·gel ['ɑrk,eindʒəl] *n* the chief angel.

arch·bish·op ['ɑrtʃ,bɪʃəp] *n* a bishop of the highest rank, presiding over a church district called an **archdiocese** [-'daɪəsɪs] *or* [-'daɪə,siz].

arch·duch·y [,ɑrtʃ'dʌtʃi] *n* the territory ruled by an **archduke** or **arch·duch·ess**, nobles of the former ruling house of Austria-Hungary. **arch·du·cal** [,ɑrtʃ'djukəl] *or* [-'dukəl] *adj.*

ar·che·go·ni·um [,ɑrkə'gouniəm] *n, pl* **-ni·a** [-niə] *Botany* the female reproductive organ in ferns, mosses, etc. ⟨Greek *arkhē* beginning + *gonos* seed⟩

arch·en·e·my [,ɑrtʃ'ɛnəmi] *n* **1** one's chief enemy. **2 the Archenemy** Satan.

ar·che·ol·o·gy See ARCHAEOLOGY.

Ar·che·o·zo·ic See ARCHAEOZOIC.

arch·er ['ɑrtʃər] *n* a person who shoots with bow and arrows. **arch·er·y** *n*. ⟨Anglo-French, from Latin *arcus* bow⟩

ar·che·type ['ɑrkə,təip] *n* **1** an original model or pattern. **2** a typical example. **ar·che·typ·al** or **ar·che·typ·i·cal** [,ɑrkə'tɪpəkəl] *adj*. ⟨Greek *arkhe* beginning + *typos* print⟩

Ar·chi·me·des principle [,ɑrkə'midɪz] *Physics* the principle that the apparent loss of weight of a body when immersed in a liquid is equal to the weight of the liquid displaced. **Archimedes' screw** a water-raising device used by the ancients, consisting of a spiral tube around or inside a cylindrical shaft. ⟨*Archimedes*, 3c B.C. Greek mathematician⟩

ar·chi·pel·a·go [,ɑrkə'pɛlə,gou] *n, pl* **-gos** or **-goes** a group of many islands: *the islands of the Canadian Archipelago in the Arctic Ocean*. **ar·chi·pe·lag·ic** [-pə'lædʒɪk] *adj*. ⟨Greek *arkhi-* chief + *pelagos* sea; orig, the Aegean⟩

ar·chi·tec·ture ['ɑrkə,tɛktʃər] *n* **1** the art and science of designing buildings. **2** a particular design or way of building: *Greek architecture, flimsy architecture*. **3** the structure of any system. **ar·chi·tec·tur·al** *adj*. **ar·chi·tec·tur·al·ly** *adv*. ⟨Greek *arkhi-* chief + *tekton* builder⟩ **ar·chi·tect** *n* **1** a professional designer of buildings. **2** the designer, planner, or creator of anything: *architects of modern technology*. **ar·chi·tec·ton·ics** [,ɑrkətɛk'tɒnɪks] *n* **1** the science of architecture. **2** the specifics of any design; structure. **ar·chi·tec·ton·ic** *adj*. **ar·chi·tec·ton·i·cal·ly** *adv*.

ar·chi·trave ['ɑrkə,treiv] *n Architecture* **1** the beam resting on the top of a column. **2** the moulding around a door, arch, etc. ⟨Italian, from Greek *arkhi-* chief + Latin *trabs* beam⟩

ar·chive ['ɑrkaɪv] *n* Usually, **archives** *pl* **1** a place where historical documents are preserved: *the National Archives of Canada*. **2** the documents kept in such a place. *v* **1** store (documents) no longer in regular use. **2** *Computers* save in a reserve file. **ar·chi·val** [ɑr'kaɪvəl] *adj*. ⟨Latin *archivum*; Greek *archeion* government building⟩ **ar·chiv·ist** ['ɑrkɪvɪst] *n* a person in charge of archives.

arc·tic ['ɑrktɪk] or ['ɑrtɪk] *adj* **1** Often, **Arctic** to do with the north polar region. **2** extremely cold; frigid: *arctic temperatures*. *n* **1 the Arctic a** the north polar region. **b** the Arctic Ocean. **2 arctics** *pl* warm, waterproof boots. ⟨Greek *arktos* Bear (constellation)⟩ **arctic char** or **Arctic char** a food fish of the salmon and trout family found throughout the Arctic. **Arctic Circle** the parallel of latitude at 66°33′ N that marks the boundary of the north polar region. **arctic fox** a fox of the arctic regions, grey in summer and white in winter. **arctic grayling ✳** a silver-grey freshwater fish found in northern waters. **arctic ground squirrel ✳** the largest ground squirrel of the Americas. **arctic hare ✳** a large, thickset hare found in arctic Canada. It is pure white in winter, except for its black-tipped ears. **arctic haze** a pollution problem in the far north, in which particles of pollutants suspended in the arctic air increase in concentration during winter. **arctic hysteria ✳** CABIN FEVER. **arctic loon** a loon similar to the common loon but smaller. **Arctic Ocean** the ocean over and around the North Pole. **arctic tern** a tern that breeds in the Arctic and winters in the oceans of the southern hemisphere. **arctic willow** a low-growing willow of the tundra and northern alpine regions.

ar·dent ['ɑrdənt] *adj* **1** very enthusiastic or passionate; zealous. **2** burning; fiery. **ar·den·cy** *n*. **ar·dent·ly** *adv*. **ar·dour** or **ar·dor** *n*. ⟨Latin *ardere* burn⟩

ar·du·ous ['ɑrdjuəs] or ['ɑrdʒuəs] *adj* **1** requiring much effort; difficult: *an arduous lesson*. **2** intense; strenuous: *an arduous effort*. **3** hard to climb; steep: *an arduous hill*. **ar·du·ous·ly** *adv*. **ar·du·ous·ness** *n*. ⟨Latin *arduus* steep⟩

are[1] [ɑr] *v* the plural present indicative of BE: *we are, you are, they are*. ⟨Old English *aron*⟩

are[2] [ɛr] or [ɑr] *n* a measure of area, equal to 100 m². *Symbol* **a** ⟨French, from Latin *area* area⟩

ar·e·a ['ɛriə] *n* **1** the measure of a surface: *The area of this floor is 60 m²*. **2** region: *a mountainous area*. **3** a space devoted to a particular use: *a play area*. **4** field of study or activity: *more development in the area of social skills*. **5** range; scope: *Provincial governments often try to limit the area of federal responsibility*. **ar·e·al** *adj*. **ar·e·al·ly** *adv*. ⟨Latin *area* piece of level ground⟩ **area code** a number designating a given local area within the total region served by a telephone system. **area rug** a rug covering only a small area.

a·re·na [ə'rinə] *n* **1** a building for indoor sports with a large play area surrounded by tiers of seats for spectators. **2** any sphere of public action, esp one involving competition: *the political arena*. ⟨Latin *arena* sand; Roman arenas had sand-covered floors⟩

a·re·o·la [ə'riələ] *n* **-lae** [-,li] or [-,laɪ] or **-las** *Anatomy* the small ring around something, as around a nipple, pimple, etc. Also, **ar·e·ole** ['ɛri,oul]. **a·re·o·lar** *adj*. **a·re·o·la·tion** *n*. ⟨Latin *āreola* diminutive of *ārea* area⟩

a·rête [ə'reit] *n* a sharp, rocky ridge on a mountain, usually above the winter snow line. ⟨French = fish backbone⟩

ar·gent ['ɑrdʒənt] *n Poetic* silver. ⟨Latin *argentum* silver⟩ **ar·gen·tif·er·ous** [-'tɪfərəs] *adj* containing silver.

ar·gon ['ɑrgɒn] *n* an element that is a colourless, odourless, inert gas forming a very small part of the air. *Symbol* **Ar** ⟨Greek *a-* without + *ergon* work⟩

ar·got ['ɑrgou], [ɑr'gou], or ['ɑrgət] *n* the

specialized language, or jargon, of people who share a particular kind of work or way of life, esp one that is more or less secret: *underworld argot*. 〈French〉

ar·gue ['ɑrgju] *v* **1** discuss with someone who disagrees: *to argue a question. He argued with his boss.* **2** give a reasoned presentation: *She argued against the passage of the bill. Columbus argued that the world was round.* **ar·gu·er** *n*. 〈Latin *arguere* make clear〉
ar·gu·a·ble *adj* **1** open to reasonable debate: *an arguable question.* **2** that can be supported by reason: *an arguable defence.* **ar·gu·a·bly** *adv.*
ar·gu·ment *n* **1** a debate or dispute. **2** the reasons given for or against. **3** the act of giving reasons. **4** *Mathematics* independent variable. **5** *Logic* the term in the first two statements of a syllogism but not in the conclusion. **ar·gu·men·ta·tion** *n* the process of arguing or giving reasons. **ar·gu·men·ta·tive** *adj* fond of arguing. **ar·gu·men·ta·tive·ly** *adv.*

ar·hant ['ɑrhənt] *n Buddhism* a title of respect for someone who has attained enlightenment. 〈Sanskrit〉

a·ri·a ['ɑriə], ['æriə], *or* ['ɛriə] *n* a melody for a single voice with instrumental or choral accompaniment. 〈Italian; Latin *aer* air〉

ar·id ['ærɪd] *or* ['ɛrɪd] *adj* **1** dry; barren: *Desert lands are arid.* **2** dull; uninteresting: *an arid, tiresome speech.* **a·rid·i·ty** [ə'rɪdəti] *n*. **ar·id·ly** *adv.* **ar·id·ness** *n*. 〈Latin *āridus* dry〉

a·right [ə'raɪt] *adv Poetic* correctly; rightly.

a·rise [ə'raɪz] *v* **a·rose**, **a·ris·en**, **a·ris·ing 1** get up: *The audience arose as one body.* **2** move upward. **3** appear or begin: *A great wind arose. Many accidents arise through carelessness.* 〈Old English *ārīsan*〉

ar·is·toc·ra·cy [ˌɛrɪ'stɒkrəsi] *or* [ˌærɪ'stɒkrəsi] *n* **1** people of noble rank, title, or birth. **2** any class that is considered superior because of birth, intelligence, culture, or wealth. **3** a government in which a privileged upper class rules. 〈Greek *aristos* best + *kratia* rule〉 **a·ris·to·crat** [ə'rɪstə,kræt], ['ɛrɪstə,kræt], *or* ['ærɪstə,kræt] *n* a member of an aristocracy. **a·ris·to·crat·ic** *adj.* **a·ris·to·crat·i·cal·ly** *adv.*

Ar·is·to·te·li·an [ˌɛrɪstə'tiljən], [ˌærɪstə'tiljən], *or* [ə,rɪstə'tiljən] *adj* to do with the Greek philosopher Aristotle (4c B.C.) or his ideas.

a·rith·me·tic [ə'rɪθmə,tɪk] *n* the branch of mathematics dealing with computation using real numbers.
adj [ˌɛrɪθ'mɛtɪk] *or* [ˌærɪθ'mɛtɪk] to do with arithmetic; involving addition, subtraction, multiplication and division. Also, **a·rith·me·ti·cal. ar·ith·met·i·cal·ly** *adv.* 〈Greek *arithmētikē* from *arithmos* number〉
arithmetic mean the average obtained by dividing the sum of several quantities by the number of quantities. **arithmetic progression** a series in which there is always the same difference between one number and the next. Compare GEOMETRIC PROGRESSION.

ark [ɑrk] *n* **1** in the Bible, the large boat God told Noah to build in order to save himself, his family, and a pair of each kind of animal

from the Flood. **2** Also, **Ark of the Covenant a** the wooden chest or box in which the ancient Hebrews kept the two tablets of stone containing the Ten Commandments. **b** the chest in a synagogue that symbolizes this. 〈Old English *arc* from Latin *arca* chest〉

arm¹ [ɑrm] *n* **1** the upper limb of the human body between the shoulder and the hand. **2** anything like this in shape or use: *the arm of a chair.* **3** authority; power to act: *the strong arm of the law.* **4** a branch of an organization or government. **arm·less** *adj.* 〈Old English *earm*〉
an arm and a leg a large sum of money: *That platter cost an arm and a leg.* **arm in arm** with arms linked: *She walked arm in arm with her sister.* **at arm's length** relating in such a way as to: **a** avoid familiarity: *He was never very friendly and kept everyone at arm's length.* **b** prevent direct influence by any of the parties over the other or others: *The new regulatory body will be at arm's length from both industry and government.* **with open arms** in a warm, friendly way.
arm·band *n* a circlet of cloth worn around the sleeve as a sign of rank, mourning, etc. **arm·chair** *n* a chair with side pieces to support a person's arms or elbows. *adj* **1** guided by theory uninformed by actual experience in the real world: *armchair politicians.* **2** being so vicariously, as by reading, watching TV, etc.: *an armchair explorer.* **arm·ful** *n* as much as one arm or both arms can hold. **arm·hole** *n* a hole for the arm in a garment. **arm·lock** *n Wrestling* a hold which uses the arm and hand to immobilize one's opponent's arm. **arm·pit** *n* the hollow under the arm at the shoulder. **arm·rest** *n* the part of a chair, car door, etc. that supports a person's arm. **arm–twist·ing** *n* strong pressure used to get one's way: *It took some arm-twisting, but we finally got them to help.* **arm wrestling** a contest in which two people with elbows supported on a flat surface clasp hands, each trying to force the other's forearm down flat. **arm–wres·tle** *v.*

arm² [ɑrm] *n* Usually, **arms**, *pl* **1** any instrument used for defence or attack. **2** the symbols used in heraldry. See COAT OF ARMS.
v **1** supply with weapons. **2** prepare for war. **3** provide with a means of defence or attack: *armed with more data.* 〈Latin *arma* weapons〉
bear arms a serve as a soldier. **b** own and use a weapon. **c** own and display a coat of arms. **take up arms a** arm for attack or defence. **b** argue militantly: *I see you've taken up arms against the new cutbacks.* **to arms!** prepare for battle! **under arms** equipped for fighting. **up in arms a** angry; outraged. **b** in revolt.
armed forces the combined military strength of a nation, including sea, land, and air elements. Also called **armed services.**

ar·ma·da [ɑr'mɑdə] *or* [ɑr'mædə] *n* **1** a fleet of warships or warplanes. **2 the Armada** the Spanish fleet sent to attack England in 1588. 〈Spanish; Latin *armata* armed. Compare ARMY.〉

ar·ma·dil·lo [ˌɑrmə'dɪlou] *n* any of a family

of burrowing mammals of tropical America with an armourlike covering of small, jointed, bony plates. 〈Spanish, diminutive of *armado* armed (one)〉

Ar·ma·ged·don [ˌɑrməˈgɛdən] *n* **1** in the Bible, the scene of a great and final conflict between the forces of good and evil. **2** any great and final conflict. 〈Hebrew *har megiddon* a mountain site of great battles〉

ar·ma·ment [ˈɑrməmənt] *n* **1** Sometimes, **armaments** *pl* war equipment and supplies. **2** all the armed forces of a nation. **3** the act or process of preparing for war. **4** the weapons on a naval vessel, tank, aircraft, etc. **5** anything used for protection or defence. 〈Latin *armamentum* from *armare* arm〉

ar·ma·ture [ˈɑrmətʃər] *n* **1** a part of an animal or plant serving for offence or defence: *A turtle's shell is an armature.* **2** wire wound around and around a cable. **3** a piece of soft iron placed in contact with the poles of a magnet to preserve its magnetic power. **4** a revolving part of an electric motor or generator. **5** *Sculpture* a framework which supports the clay used for modelling a figure. 〈Latin *armatura* from *armare* to arm〉

ar·mi·stice [ˈɑrməstɪs] *n* a formal agreement between governments to cease hostilities. 〈Latin *arma* arms + *stitium* a stopping〉

ar·moire [ˌɑrˈmwɑr] *n* a large, usually ornate wardrobe or cupboard. 〈French; Latin *armarium* cabinet〉

ar·mour or **ar·mor** [ˈɑrmər] *n* **1** a covering worn to protect the body in fighting. **2** any protective covering, such as steel or iron plates on a vehicle, ship, etc. **3** the tanks and other armoured vehicles of an army. **4** anything that protects or defends: *An informed public opinion is the best armour against propaganda.*
v protect with armour. **ar·moured** or **ar·mored** *adj.* 〈Old French *armeure*; Latin *armatura*. See ARMATURE.〉
ar·mo·ri·al *adj* to do with coats of arms. **armorial bearings** a COAT OF ARMS. **ar·mour·bear·er** *n* formerly, an attendant who carried the armour of a warrior. **armoured cable** an electric cable with a protective covering of metal. **armoured car** any vehicle with a protective covering of armour plate. **ar·mour·er** *n* a person in charge of firearms. **ar·mour·ies** or **ar·mor·ies** *n pl* **✱** headquarters of the reserve units of the armed forces. **armour plate** metal plating to protect warships, forts, etc. **ar·mour–plat·ed** *adj.* **ar·moury** or **ar·mory** *n* a place where weapons are kept.

ar·my [ˈɑrmi] *n* **1** a large, organized group of people trained and armed for war. **2** Often, **Army** such a group serving as the land forces of a nation. In Canada, the function of an army is served by Mobile Command of the Canadian Forces. **3** a very large number: *an army of reporters.* 〈Old French *armee* from Latin *armata* armed〉
army ant any of various mainly tropical ants that migrate in large groups and devour

other insects and small animals in their path. **army cadet** a person under military age taking basic military training. **army worm** a moth larva that travels over the ground in large numbers, eating the vegetation.

a·ro·ma [əˈroumə] *n* a pleasant, sweet, or savoury smell: *the aroma of a cake in the oven.* **ar·o·mat·ic** [ˌɛrəˈmætɪk] or [ˌærəˈmætɪk] *adj.* **ar·o·mat·i·cal·ly** *adv.* 〈Greek = spice〉

a·rose [əˈrouz] *v* pt of ARISE.

a·round [əˈraʊnd] *prep* **1** in a circle about: *to travel around the world.* **2** closely wrapping: *She had a coat around her shoulders.* **3** on all sides of: *Woods lay around the lake.* **4** *Informal* approximately: *That car cost around $15 000.* **5** somewhere in or near: *He stuck around the house.* **6** on or to the far side of: *around the corner.* **7** beside and past, so as to avoid: *Drive around that pothole.* **8** in such a way as to avoid conflict with: *I'll have to plan the trip around the baby's naptimes.* **9** having as a focus: *discussions around the question of funding.*
adv **1** in a circle. **2** in circumference: *The tree measures 2 m around.* **3** here and there: *We walked around to see the town.* **4** so as to face the other direction or form a different arrangement: *Turn around! I switched them around.* **5** nearby: *He's around somewhere.* **6** on all sides: *A dense fog lay around.* **7** in existence: *That type of wallpaper just isn't around anymore.* **8** through a circuit or cycle: *going around to all the hotels. Wake me when my turn comes around.* **9** for a brief visit: *Bring the kids around sometime.* **10** back to consciousness: *Fresh air should bring him around.* **11** to the desired point of view: *Leave her alone, she'll come around eventually.*
have been around *Informal* be experienced and worldly-wise.

USAGE
Around and round are interchangeable in many of the above senses, but **around** is more usual in Canada.

a·rouse [əˈrauz] *v* **1** awaken **2** excite; stimulate. **a·rous·er** *n.* **a·rous·al** *n.*

ar·peg·gio [ɑrˈpɛdʒiou] *n Music* a sounding of the notes of a chord in rapid succession instead of together. 〈Italian, from *arpa* harp〉

ar·pent [ˈɑrpənt] *French* [ɑrˈpɑ̃] *n* **✱** formerly: **1** an old French measure of land area used in Canada, equal to about 3400 m² or 100 square perches. **2** a measure of length, equal to about 58 m. 〈French〉

ar·rack [ˈɛrək], [ˈærək], or [əˈræk] *n* an alcoholic drink distilled from the sap of the coconut palm or from rice, sugar cane, etc. Also, **a·rak**. 〈Arabic *'araq* liquor, sweet juice〉

ar·raign [əˈrein] *v* **1** *Law* bring before a court to answer a charge: *The gangster was arraigned on a charge of stealing.* **2** find fault with. **ar·raign·er** *n.* **ar·raign·ment** *n.* 〈Anglo-French *arainer* from Latin *rationis* account〉

ar·range [əˈreindʒ] *v* **1** put in the proper order: *arranged by size.* **2** plan or prepare; set (things) up: *to arrange trasnportation for a* *class trip. Can you arrange to meet me at 4:30?* **3** *Music* adapt (a piece) to a given instrument, voice, or style. **ar·rang·er** *n.* **ar·range·ment** *n.* ⟨Old French *a-* to + *rang* rank[1]⟩

ar·rant ['ɛrənt] *or* ['ærənt] *adj* extreme; downright: *an arrant liar.* **ar·rant·ly** *adv.* ⟨variant of *errant*⟩

ar·ray [ə'rei] *n* **1** order: *troops in battle array.* **2** a display of persons or things: *an array of pastries on the table.* **3** clothes: *in bridal array.* **4** *Mathematics* an arrangement of data in rows and columns. **5** *Computers* linked items sharing a common name and kept in consecutive positions in memory. **ar·ray** *v.* **ar·ray·al** *n.* ⟨Old French *a* to + *rei* order⟩

ar·rears [ə'rirz] *n pl* **1** overdue debts. **2** unfinished work. **ar·rear·age** *n.* ⟨Old French *arere* from Latin *ad retro*⟩
in arrears behind in payments, work, etc.

ar·rest [ə'rɛst] *v* **1** take to jail or court. **2** stop; check: *Filling a tooth arrests decay.* **ar·rest** *n.* **ar·rest·er** *n.* ⟨Latin *ad-* to + *restare* stay⟩ **under arrest** being held by the police. **ar·rest·ing** *adj* catching the attention in a desirable way: *arresting eyes.* **ar·rest·ing·ly** *adv.*

ar·rhyth·mi·a [ə'rɪðmiə] *n* irregularity in heart beat. **ar·rhyth·mic** *adj.* ⟨Greek⟩

ar·rive [ə'raiv] *v* **1** reach the end of a journey: *We arrived at noon.* **2** reach (with *at*): *You must arrive at a decision soon.* **3** come; occur: *The time has arrived for you to study.* **ar·riv·al** *n.* ⟨Latin *ad ripam* to the shore⟩ **ar·ri·viste** [,ɑri'vist] *or* [,ɛri'vist] *n* a person who has recently acquired money, power, prestige, etc. by nonstandard methods.

ar·ro·gance ['ɛrəgəns] *or* ['ærəgəns] *n* too great pride; haughtiness. **ar·ro·gant** *adj.* **ar·ro·gant·ly** *adv.* ⟨See ARROGATE.⟩

ar·ro·gate ['ɛrə,geit] *or* ['ærə,geit] *v* **1** take without right: *The despotic king arrogated all power to himself.* **2** attribute without good reason: *People are only too ready to arrogate dishonesty to a politician.* **ar·ro·ga·tion** *n.* ⟨Latin *arrogare* from *ad-* to + *rogare* ask⟩

ar·row ['ɛrou] *or* ['ærou] *n* **1** a slender stick made to be shot from a bow, with a pointed tip and feathers at the tail end. **2** anything like an arrow in shape or speed.
v **1** indicate with an arrow: *The main points are arrowed in the margin.* **2** move swiftly like an arrow: *Jet planes arrowed through the sky.* **ar·row·like** *or* **ar·row·y** *adj.* ⟨Old English *arwe*⟩ **ar·row·head** *n* **1** the head or tip of an arrow. **2** any of a genus of water plants of temperate and tropical America, typically having arrowhead-shaped leaves. **ar·row·root** *n* a plant yielding an easily digestible starch.

ar·roy·o [ə'rɔiou] *n* **1** the dry bed of a stream; gully. **2** a small river. ⟨Spanish⟩

ar·se·nal ['ɑrsənəl] *n* **1** a building for storing or manufacturing weapons and ammunition. **2** a useful collection: *an arsenal of facts.* ⟨Arabic *dar accina'ah* house of manufacturing⟩

ar·se·nic ['ɑrsənɪk] *n* **1** a greyish white element, having a metallic lustre and volatilizing when heated. *Symbol* **As 2** a highly poisonous, tasteless, white compound of arsenic. **ar·se·nic** ['ɑrsənɪk] *or* [ɑr'sɛnɪk] *adj.* ⟨Greek *arsenikon*⟩
ar·se·nate of lead ['ɑrsənɪt] *or* ['ɑrsə,neit] an insecticide derived from arsenic acid.

ar·son ['ɑrsən] *n* the criminal offence of setting fire to property. **ar·son·ist** *n.* ⟨Latin *arsio(nis)* a burning from *ardere* burn⟩

art[1] [ɑrt] *n* **1 a** Also, **fine art** an activity involving imagination, originality, and creative skill, such as drawing, poetry, music, drama, etc. **b** specifically, such an activity whose product is visual, such as painting or sculpture. **2** the product of any such activity: *art hanging on the walls.* **3 arts** *pl* a group of academic studies including literature, history, philosophy, etc. and excluding the sciences. **4** any activity or craft involving skill and imagination: *the household arts of cooking and sewing, the art of making friends.* **5** human skill or effort: *a garden owing more to art than to nature.* **6** Usually, **arts** *pl* cunning; tricks. *adj* to do with art or artists: *an art gallery.* ⟨Latin *ars, artis*⟩
art deco ['dɛkou] a decorative but utilitarian style in furniture, textiles, etc. originating in cubism. **art·ful** *adj* **1** crafty; deceitful: *a swindler's artful tricks.* **2** having or showing creative skill. **art·ful·ly** *adv.* **art·ful·ness** *n.* **ar·ti·san** ['ɑrtəzən] *or* ['ɑrtə,zæn] *n* a person skilled in some craft or trade. **art·ist** *n* **1** a person skilled in any of the arts, often specifically the visual arts or popular music. **2** a person who does work with skill and good taste. **ar·tis·tic** *adj.* **ar·tis·ti·cal·ly** *adv.* **ar·tiste** [ɑr'tist] *n* a performer or a skilful worker in any craft. **art·ist·ry** *n* artistic work or expertise. **art·less** *adj* **1** innocent, natural, or sincere: *Small children ask many artless questions.* **2** crude, uncultured, or clumsy. **art·less·ly** *adv.* **art·less·ness** *n.* **art nou·veau** [ɑrnu'vo] *French* a movement in the arts at the end of the 19th century in which very rounded stylizations of natural forms predominated. **art·sy** *or* **art·y** *adj Informal* having or catering to artistic interests, often in a precious or overdone way. **art·sy–craft·sy** [,ɑrtsi 'kræftsi] *adj Informal* to do with arts or crafts, esp when carried out in a fussy, trendy, or superficial way. **art·work** *n* **1** art (def. 2). **2** graphics in a magazine, book, etc.

art[2] [ɑrt] *v Archaic, poetic* 2nd person singular present indicative, of BE. *Thou art* means *you* (singular) *are.* ⟨Old English *eart*⟩

ar·ter·y ['ɑrtəri] *n* **1** *Anatomy* any of the tubes that carry blood from the heart to all parts of the body. **2** a main road. **ar·te·ri·al** [ɑr'tiriəl] *adj.* ⟨Greek *arteria*⟩ **ar·te·ri·ole** [ɑr'tiri,oul] *n* a small artery. **ar·te·ri·o·scle·ro·sis** [ɑr,tiriousklə'rousɪs] *n* a hardening and thickening of the walls of the arteries. **ar·te·ri·o·scle·rot·ic** [-sklə'rɒtɪk] *adj.*

ar·te·sian well [ɑr'tiʒən] a deep-drilled well, esp one from which water gushes up without being pumped. ⟨French *artésien* of Artois, former province⟩

ar·thri·tis [ɑr'θrəitɪs] *n Medicine* a disease characterized by inflammation of the joints. **ar·thrit·ic** [ɑr'θrɪtɪk] *adj*. 〈Greek *arthron* joint〉

ar·thro·pod ['ɑrθrə,pɒd] *n* any of a large group of invertebrates with segmented body and legs, including insects and crustaceans and making up about three-quarters of all the known species of animals. **ar·throp·o·dal** [ɑr'θrɒpədəl], **ar·throp·o·dan**, **ar·throp·o·dous** *adj*. 〈Greek *arthron* joint + *pous, podos* foot〉

Ar·thu·ri·an [ɑr'θjuriən] *or* [ɑr'θuriən] *adj* to do with the legend of King Arthur and his knights.

ar·ti·choke ['ɑrtə,tʃouk] *n* a plant native to Eurasia, widely cultivated for its large flower heads, which are eaten as a vegetable. 〈Italian *articiocco* from Arabic *al-kharshof*〉

ar·ti·cle ['ɑrtəkəl] *n* **1** a piece of writing forming part of a magazine, newspaper, or website: *an article on jazz*. **2** a clause in a legal document: *Article 3 of the club's constitution deals with fees*. **3** a particular thing; item: *Bread is a main article of food*. **4** one of the words *a, an,* or *the*. *A(n)* is the **indefinite article**; *the* is the **definite article**.
v bind by a contract, esp for training: *The apprentice was articled to serve the master craftsman for seven years*. 〈Latin *articulus* diminutive of *artus* joint〉
Articles of Confederation the constitution adopted by the thirteen original states of the US in 1781, replaced by the present Constitution in 1789. **articles of faith** a formal statement of religious beliefs.

ar·tic·u·late [ɑr'tɪkjəlɪt] *adj* **1** uttered in distinct syllables or words: *A baby does not use articulate speech*. **2** having the power of speech: *Dogs are not articulate*. **3** good at putting thoughts into words: *She is the most articulate of the sisters*. **4** made up of distinct parts. **5** jointed; segmented.
v [ɑr'tɪkjə,leit] **1** speak distinctly. **2** express in words: *He was overcome by a feeling he could not articulate*. **3** fit together by a joint that allows bending: *an articulated streetcar*. **4** form or join distinct parts into a system, sequence, etc.: *an articulated curriculum*. **ar·tic·u·late·ly** *adv*. **ar·tic·u·late·ness** *n*. **ar·tic·u·la·tion** *n*. **ar·tic·u·la·to·ry** *adj*. 〈Latin *articulare* form into joints. See ARTICLE.〉
ar·tic·u·la·tor *n Phonetics*. any part, such as lips, teeth, larynx, or tongue, whose movement results in a speech sound.

ar·ti·fact or **ar·te·fact** ['ɑrtə,fækt] *n* any thing made or any effect caused by human skill or activity, whether intentionally or not. 〈Latin *ars, artis* art + *factus* made〉

ar·ti·fice ['ɑrtəfɪs] *n* **1** a trick: *He will use any artifice to get his way*. **2** trickery; craft: *Her conduct is free from artifice*. 〈Latin *ars, artis* art + *facere* make〉
ar·tif·i·cer *n* a skilled worker; craftsperson.
ar·ti·fi·cial [,ɑrtə'fɪʃəl] *adj* **1** produced by human skill or effort, not nature: *reading by artificial light. Advertising creates an artificial need for things*. **2** manufactured as an express imitation of a natural thing: *artificial flowers*.

3 false; affected: *an artificial tone of voice*. **ar·ti·fi·cial·ly** *adv*. **ar·ti·fi·ci·al·i·ty** [,ɑrtə,fɪʃi'æləti] *n*. **artificial insemination** introduction of semen into a female by means other than sexual intercourse. **artificial intelligence** the ability of some computers to simulate human reasoning. **artificial respiration** the process of restoring a person's breathing by forcing air into and out of his or her lungs.

SYNONYMS
Artificial describes things which are made by human labour, in contrast to those produced in nature: *You can get burned by the artificial light of a sun lamp*. **Synthetic** describes things which are put together by chemical combination: *Nylon is a synthetic fabric*.

ar·til·ler·y [ɑr'tɪləri] *n* **1** mounted guns; cannon. **2** the part of an army that uses these. 〈Old French *artillerie; artiller* equip〉

ar·um ['ɛrəm] *n* any of a genus of plants with small flowers densely clustered on an upright fleshy part (spadix) enclosed by a leafy part called a spathe. 〈Greek *aron*〉

Ar·y·an ['ɛriən], ['æriən], *or* ['ɛrjən] *n* **1** in Nazi use, a person of Nordic descent who is not Jewish, Slav, or Gypsy. **2** a member of any of the peoples speaking Indo-European languages. **3** the hypothetical parent of these languages. **4** any of the people who supposedly spoke it. **Ar·y·an** *adj*. 〈Sanskrit *aryas* noble〉

as [əz] *adv* to the same degree or extent: *just as good, but not nearly as expensive*.
conj **1** to the same degree that: *She went only so far as she was told*. **2** in the same way that: *Behave as I do*. **3** while; when: *He sang as he worked*. **4** because: *As he is highly skilled, they pay him well*. **5** though: *Brave as they were, they began to tremble*. **6** *Informal* that; if; whether: *I don't know as that's such a good idea*.
prep **1** doing the work of: *Who will act as teacher?* **2** like: *They treat me as their own child*.
pron **1** a fact that: *She is very careful, as her work shows*. **2** that: *He likes the same music as I do*. 〈Old English *ealswā*. Compare ALSO.〉
as for in the case of: *We're leaving now; as for the rest, they'll have to come later*. **as good as** almost: *as good as dead*. **as if** as it would be if: *The cat looked as if it had been mistreated*. **as is** in its present condition: *to buy a used car as is*. **as it were** so to speak. **as of** starting or dating from: *As of June, we will be on summer hours*. **as though** as it would be if. **as to a** about: *We have no information as to the cause of the riot*. **b** according to: *sorted as to colour and size*. **as well** also. **as well as** in addition to. **as yet** so far: *Nothing has been done as yet*.

ASAP ['eisæp] as soon as possible.

as·bes·tos [æs'bɛstəs] *or* [æz'bɛstəs] *n* a mineral that does not burn or conduct heat, usually occurring in fibres. **as·bes·tine** [-tin] *adj*. 〈Greek = unquenchable〉
as·bes·to·sis [,æsbɛs'tousɪs] *n* a disease of the lungs caused by inhalation of asbestos fibres.

as·cend [ə'sɛnd] *v* **1** go up; move or incline upward: *smoke ascending into the air*. **2** climb: *an expedition planning to ascend Mt. Everest*.

as·cent *n.* ⟨Latin *ad-* to, up + *scandere* climb⟩ **ascend the throne** become king, queen, etc. **as·cend·an·cy** or **as·cend·ance** *n* dominance; control. **as·cend·ant** *adj* **1** rising. **2** dominant; in control. *n* **1** a position of dominance or of increasing influence. **2** *Astrology* a position just above the eastern horizon at a given time: *Aries is in the ascendant now.* **as·cend·er** *n Printing* the upper, projecting part of a lower-case letter such as b, d, h, or k. Compare DESCENDER. **as·cend·ing** *adj* rising or sloping upwards. **as·cen·sion** *n* **1** the act of ascending; ascent. **2** *Christianity* **Ascension** the bodily passing of Jesus Christ from earth to heaven.

as·cer·tain [ˌæsərˈteɪn] *v* find out; determine. **as·cer·tain·a·ble** *adj.* **as·cer·tain·ment** *n.* ⟨Old French *acertener*. See CERTAIN.⟩

as·cet·ic [əˈsɛtɪk] *adj* avoiding comfort; practising self-denial, esp as a spiritual discipline. **as·cet·ic** *n.* **as·cet·i·cal·ly** *adv.* **as·cet·i·cism** *n.* ⟨Greek *askētikos; askein* exercise⟩

ASCII [ˈæski] *Computers n* American Standard Code for Information Interchange, a common code used to represent characters of data. **ASCII** *adj.*

as·co·my·cete [ˌæskəˈməɪsit] *n* any of a class of fungi that includes yeasts, moulds, truffles, and mildews. **as·co·my·ce·tous** [-məˈsitəs] *adj.* ⟨Greek *askos* bag + *mykētos* fungus⟩

a·scor·bic acid [əˈskɔrbɪk] or [eiˈskɔrbɪk] vitamin C. ⟨*a-* + *scorb(ut)ic*⟩

as·cot [ˈæskət] or [ˈæskɒt] *n* a neck scarf that is worn turned over in a loose single knot at the throat. ⟨*Ascot*, famous English racetrack⟩

as·cribe [əˈskraɪb] *v* **1** assign (*to*) as a source or cause: *The police ascribed the accident to fast driving.* **2** consider as belonging (*to*): *ascribing human characteristics to gods.* **as·crip·tion** *n.* **as·crip·tive** *adj.* ⟨Latin *ad-* to + *scribere* write⟩

a·sep·tic [eiˈsɛptɪk] *adj* free from germs that cause infection. **a·sep·ti·cal·ly** *adv.* **a·sep·sis** *n.*

a·sex·u·al [eiˈsɛkʃuəl] *adj Biology* **1** sexless. **2** independent of sexual processes. **a·sex·u·al·ly** *adv.*

ash¹ [æʃ] *n* **1** (often *pl*) what remains of a thing after it has been thoroughly burned: *Wood ash was mixed with grease for ointment.* **2 ashes** *pl* **a** ruins: *a whole city laid in ashes.* **b** the remains of a dead person: *buried beside the ashes of his forefathers.* ⟨Old English *æsce*⟩ **ash·can** *n* any receptacle, such as a barrel or large can, for holding ashes and other waste. **ash·en** *adj* pale as ashes. **ash·tray** *n* a small receptacle for tobacco ashes. **ash·y** *adj* **1** of or covered with ashes. **2** very pale.

ash² [æʃ] *n* any of a genus of trees of the olive family found in the northern hemisphere, with compound leaves and greyish twigs. **ash·en** *adj.* ⟨Old English *æsc*⟩ **ash–leaf maple ✳** the MANITOBA MAPLE.

a·shamed [əˈʃeimd] *adj* **1** feeling shame: *She was ashamed of her dishonesty.* **2** unwilling because of shame: *I was ashamed to tell them.*

Ash·ke·naz·im [ˌæʃkəˈnæzɪm] or [ˌaʃkəˈnazɪm] *n pl* the Jews of central and eastern Europe, as distinguished from Spanish and Portuguese Jews (Sephardim). **Ash·ke·naz·ic** *adj.* ⟨Hebrew = German from ancient kingdom of *Ashkenaz*⟩

a·shore [əˈʃɔr] *adv, adj* on, to, or toward the shore; on or toward land.

ash·ram [ˈæʃrəm] or [ˈaʃrəm] *n* a place for Hindu religious instruction and retreat. ⟨Sanskrit *āsrama*⟩

A·sia [ˈeiʒə] *n* large continent including the Far East and parts of the Middle East. ⟨Greek⟩ **A·sian** *adj* **1** of, from, or native to Asia. **2** Asiatic. **Asian** *n.* **Asian flu** an acute type of influenza. **A·si·at·ic** [ˌeiʒiˈætɪk] or [ˌeiziˈætɪk] *adj* to do with Asia or its peoples.

a·side [əˈsaɪd] *adv* **1** on or to one side: *Move the table aside* **2** out of one's thoughts: *Put your troubles aside.* **3** in reserve for future use: *The salesperson put the coat aside for me.* **4** notwithstanding; in spite of: *Kidding aside, tell me what you really think of the idea.* *n* words meant not to be heard by someone; esp, in the theatre, an actor's remark that is meant to be heard by the audience but not by the other characters in the play. **aside from** apart from; other than; except for.

as·i·nine [ˈæsəˌnaɪn] *adj* **1** like an ass; stupid; silly. **2** of asses. **as·i·nine·ly** *adv.* **as·i·nin·ity** [ˌæsəˈnɪnəti] *n.* ⟨Latin *asininus; asinus* ass⟩

ask [æsk] *v* **1** try to find out by a question: *If you don't know, ask. Ask why she's calling.* **2** seek the answer to: *Ask questions.* **3** address a question to: *Ask him; he knows.* **4** demand: *to ask too high a price.* **5** invite: *She asked ten guests to the party.* **6** request: *Ask her to sing.* ⟨Old English *āscian*⟩ **ask for a** request: *to ask for a drink.* **b** invite or provoke (trouble): *asking for a fight.* **asking price** the price asked in a sale.

a·skance [əˈskæns] *adv.* ⟨origin uncertain⟩ **look askance a** look with suspicion or disapproval: *They looked askance at my suggestion.* **b** look sideways. Also, **a·skant.**

a·skew [əˈskju] *adv, adj* (never before the noun) to one side: *Your hat is askew.*

ASL AMERICAN SIGN LANGUAGE.

a·sleep [əˈslip] *adj* (never before the noun), *adv* **1** sleeping: *The cat is asleep.* **2** numb: *My foot is asleep.* **3** not alert; inattentive: *asleep on the job.* **4** *Poetic* dead.

a·so·cial [eiˈsouʃəl] *adj* **1** not living in groups. **2** antisocial.

asp [æsp] *n* the Egyptian cobra, a very poisonous snake about 180 cm long. It was sacred to the Egyptians and became a symbol of royalty. ⟨Greek *aspis*⟩

as·par·a·gus [əˈspɛrəgəs] or [əˈspærəgəs] *n* any of a genus of perennial plants of the lily family whose many-branched stems have tiny, scalelike leaves; esp, one species widely cultivated for its edible young shoots. Some other species, usually called **asparagus ferns**, are grown ornamentally. ⟨Greek *asparagos*⟩

a·spar·tame [ˈæspərˌteim] or [əˈspɑrˌteim] *n*

an artificial sweetener many times sweeter than sugar and virtually noncaloric. ⟨aspart(ic acid) + (phenyl)a(lanine) m(ethyl) e(ster)⟩

as·pect ['æspɛkt] *n* **1** one side, part, or view (of a subject): *various aspects of human nature.* **2** appearance: *the wintry aspect of the countryside.* **3** direction in which anything faces; exposure: *This house has a western aspect.* **4** *Grammar* a category of verb form expressing duration, onset, repetition, etc. of an action. **as·pec·tu·al** *adj.* ⟨Latin *aspectus* from *ad-* at + *specere* look⟩

as·pen ['æspən] *n* any of several trees of the willow family whose flattened leaf stalks cause the leaves to flutter in the slightest breeze.

as·per·i·ty [ə'spɛrəti] *n* roughness; harshness; severity. ⟨Latin *asper* rough⟩

as·per·sion [ə'spɜrʒən] *n* **1** a damaging or false comment. **2** a sprinkling with water. ⟨Latin *ad-* to, on + *spargere* sprinkle⟩
cast aspersions on speak damagingly about.

as·phalt ['æsfɒlt] *or, sometimes,* ['æffɒlt] *n* **1** a dark-coloured, almost solid, tarry substance; bitumen. **2** a mixture of this substance with sand or rock, used for pavements, roofs, etc. *v* surface or seal with asphalt. **as·phalt** *adj.* **as·phal·tic** *adj.* ⟨Greek *asphaltos*⟩
asphalt jungle *Informal* a densely built-up city area thought of as breeding violent crime.

as·pho·del ['æsfə,dɛl] *n* **1** any of various European plants of the lily family, with spikes of white or yellow flowers. **2** an immortal flower of Greek legend, said to cover the fields of Elysium. ⟨Greek *asphodelos*⟩

as·phyx·i·a [æs'fɪksiə] *n* suffocation; lack of oxygen and excess of carbon dioxide in the blood. **as·phyx·i·ate** *v.* **as·phyx·i·a·tion** *n.* ⟨Greek *a-* without + *sphyxis* pulse⟩
as·phyx·i·ant *n* a substance causing asphyxiation. **as·phyx·i·ant** *adj.*

as·pic ['æspɪk] *n* a jelly made of meat or fish stock, tomato juice, etc., often set in a mould with seafood, meat, etc. ⟨French⟩

as·pi·dis·tra [,æspə'dɪstrə] *n* any of a genus of plants of the lily family native to E Asia, esp a cultivated species commonly called the cast-iron plant. ⟨Greek *aspis, aspidos* shield + *astra* stars⟩

as·pire [ə'spaɪr] *v* have as an ambition or goal: *She aspires to be team captain.* **aspir·ing** *adj.* ⟨Latin *ad-* toward + *spirare* breathe⟩
as·pir·ant [ə'spaɪrənt] *or* ['æspərənt] *n* a person who seeks a position of honour, advancement, etc. **as·pir·ant** *adj.* **as·pi·rate** ['æspə,reit] *v* **1** *Phonetics* **a** pronounce (a stop) with a following or accompanying puff of air. *P* is aspirated in *pin* but not in *spin* or *nip.* **b** begin (a word or syllable) with an *h* sound, as in *hoot* [hut]. **2** draw into the lungs; breathe in. **3** *Medicine* suction out from a body cavity. *n* ['æspərɪt] an aspirated sound. **as·pi·rate** *adj.* **as·pi·ra·tion** *n* **1** the act or object of aspiring; an earnest desire or ambition. **2** the act or fact of aspirating. **as·pi·ra·tor** *n* **1** a device for dispensing

medicine to be inhaled. **2** any device used to suction things. **as·pi·ra·to·ry** [ə'spaɪrə,tɔri] *adj.*

As·pi·rin ['æspərɪn] *n Trademark* a brand of tablets of acetylsalicylic acid, a drug used to relieve pain. ⟨< *A(cetyl)* + *spir(ea)* + *-in*⟩

ass [æs] *n* **1** donkey. **2** any of several wild animals of Asia and Africa, smaller than the horse but very fast and having long, erect ears, a very short mane, and a long tail with a tuft at the end. **3** a silly or stupid person. ⟨Old English *assa,* via Celtic from L *asinus*⟩

as·sail [ə'seil] *v Poetic* **1** attack: *to assail a fortress.* **2** overwhelm or have a sudden powerful impact on: *The smell of garlic assailed her nostrils.* **as·sail·a·ble** *adj.* **as·sail·ant** *n.* ⟨Latin *ad-* at + *salire* leap⟩

as·sas·sin [ə'sæsɪn] *n* **1** a murderer, esp of a political figure. **2** one who destroys or does serious damage: *character assassins.* **as·sas·si·nate** *v.* **as·sas·si·na·tion** *n.* ⟨Arabic *hashshāshīn* hashish eaters⟩

as·sault [ə'sɒlt] *n* **1** an attack, esp sudden or unprovoked. **2** *Law* a threat or attempt to do physical harm to another. In criminal law, touching another without his or her consent can constitute assault. **as·sault** *v.* **as·sault·er** *n.* ⟨Latin *ad-* at + *saltare* jump⟩
assault and battery *Law* intentionally doing physical harm to a person.

as·say ['æsei] *or* [ə'sei] *n* **1** an analysis of an ore, alloy, etc. to find out the amount of metal in it. **2** any test or trial; examination. **as·say** [ə'sei] *or* ['æsei] *v.* **as·say·er** *n.* ⟨Old French *a(s)sayer* variant of *essayer.* See ESSAY.⟩

as·sem·ble [ə'sɛmbəl] *v* **1** gather; come or bring together: *We will assemble in the gym at noon.* **2** put together the parts of: *to assemble a model plane.* **3** *Computers* convert (anything written in ASSEMBLY LANGUAGE) into machine language. ⟨Latin *assimulare; ad-* + *simul* together⟩
as·sem·blage *n* **1** a group of people or things gathered together. **2** the act or manner of assembling parts. **3** an art form in which diverse objects are put together into a collage or sculpture. **as·sem·bler** *n* **1** *Computers* **a** a program converting assembly language into machine language. **b** ASSEMBLY LANGUAGE. **2** any person or thing that assembles. **as·sem·bly** *n* **1** a group of people gathered together for some purpose; meeting. **2 Assembly ✳** in Québec, the NATIONAL ASSEMBLY. **3** any lawmaking body; esp the lower house or branch of a legislature. **4** the act or fact of assembling. **5** a set of assembled parts forming a unit: *The whole wing assembly fell off.* **assembly language** *Computers* a low-level computer language using words and abbreviations which are then converted into the digital instructions of machine language. **assembly line** a row of workers and machines along which work is passed until the end product is finished. **assembly member** *n* **1** in Prince Edward Island, one of fifteen members of the Legislative Assembly. **2** in the US, a member of a state legislature, esp of a lower house. **Assembly of First Nations ✳** a

political organization made up of representatives of the First Nations.

as·sent [ə'sɛnt] *v* express agreement; agree. **as·sent** *n.* **as·sent·er** *n.* **as·sent·ing** *adj.* ⟨Latin *ad-* along with + *sentire* feel, think⟩

as·sert [ə'sɜrt] *v* 1 state positively; declare. 2 insist on (a right, a claim, etc.): *to assert one's independence.* **as·sert·er** or **as·ser·tor** *n.* **as·ser·tion** *n.* ⟨Latin *ad-* to + *sertus* joined⟩ **assert oneself** insist on one's rights: *You'll never get waited on if you don't assert yourself.* **as·ser·tive** *adj* asserting oneself. **as·ser·tive·ly** *adv.* **as·ser·tive·ness** *n.*

as·sess [ə'sɛs] *v* 1 examine critically and estimate the merit, significance, value, etc. of: *The committee met to assess the idea of establishing a new university.* 2 estimate the value of (property or income) for taxation. 3 fix the amount of (a tax, fine, damages, etc.). 4 put a tax on or call for a contribution from (a person, property, etc.): *Each member will be assessed one dollar to pay for the trip.* **as·sess·a·ble** *adj.* **as·sess·ment** *n.* **as·ses·sor** *n.* ⟨Latin *assessare* fix a tax⟩

as·set ['æsɛt] *n* 1 something valuable: *Her main asset as a politician is her speaking ability.* 2 **assets** *pl* **a** the entire property of a person, company, etc. **b** property that can be used to pay debts. **c** *Accounting* the entries on a balance sheet showing total resources. ⟨Latin *ad-* + *satis* enough⟩

as·sev·er·ate [ə'sɛvə,reit] *v* declare solemnly. **as·sev·er·a·tion** *n.* **as·sev·er·a·tive** *adj.* ⟨Latin *asseverare*; *severus* serious⟩

as·sid·u·ous [ə'sɪdʒuəs] or [ə'sɪdjuəs] *adj* careful and attentive; diligent. **as·si·du·i·ty** [,æsə'dʒuəti] or [,æsə'djuəti] *n.* **as·sid·u·ous·ly** *adv.* **as·sid·u·ous·ness** *n.* ⟨Latin *assidere* sit at⟩

as·sign [ə'saɪn] *v* 1 give as a share, duty, etc.: *to assign homework.* 2 appoint: *to assign soldiers to guard a gate.* 3 fix; set: *to assign a day for the trial.* 4 attribute (*to* a given source or cause): *His breakdown was assigned to stress.* 5 *Law* transfer (property, rights, etc.) *n Law* a person to whom property or a right is assigned. Also, **as·sign·ee.** **as·sign·a·ble** *adj.* **as·sign·er** or (*Law*) **as·sign·or** *n.* **as·sign·ment** *n.* ⟨Latin *ad-* to, for + *signare* to mark⟩

as·sim·i·late [ə'sɪmə,leit] *v* 1 digest and absorb, physically or mentally. 2 adopt or cause to adopt the customs and viewpoint of a majority group: *Not all immigrants to Canada are eager to assimilate.* 3 become similar or alike. **as·sim·i·la·ble** *adj.* **as·sim·i·la·tion** *n.* **as·sim·i·la·tive** *adj.* ⟨Latin *ad-* to + *similis* like⟩ **as·sim·i·la·tion·ism** *n* a policy that seeks to conform cultural minorities to the general population: *Canada subscribes to a cultural mosaic policy rather than assimilationism.* **as·sim·i·la·tion·ist** *adj, n.*

As·sin·i·boine [ə'sɪnə,bɔɪn] See NAKOTA.

as·sist [ə'sɪst] *v* 1 help: *Let me assist you.* 2 have a supporting role in something, such as a ceremony or the scoring of a goal: *to assist at Mass.* *n* 1 an instance of giving help: *With an assist from me, he climbed the fence.* 2 *Sports* the credit given to a player who helps a teammate score a goal, put an opposing player out, etc. **as·sist·ance** *n.* **as·sist·ant** *n.* ⟨Latin *ad-* by + *sistere* take a stand⟩

assistant professor a college or university teacher ranking below an associate professor but above a lecturer.

as·size [ə'saɪz] *n* 1 **assizes** *pl* periodical sessions of a court of law. 2 an inquest or its verdict. ⟨Old French *assise,* pp of *asseeir* sit⟩

as·so·ci·ate [ə'souʃi,eit] or [ə'sousi,eit] *v* 1 connect in thought: *We associate camping with summer.* 2 mix socially (*with*): *She associates only with people interested in sports.* 3 make (oneself or another) a partner or companion: *She has associated herself with the green movement.* *n* [ə'souʃiɪt] or [ə'sousiɪt] 1 a colleague or companion. 2 a member of an association, often without full rights and privileges. *adj* [ə'souʃiɪt] or [ə'sousiɪt] (only before the noun) 1 associated; connected. 2 having partial rights and privileges in an association: *an associate member.* **as·so·ci·a·tor** *n.* ⟨Latin *ad-* to + *socius* companion⟩

associate professor a university or college teacher ranking below a professor but above an assistant professor. **as·so·ci·a·tion** *n* 1 the act or fact of associating. 2 a group of people formally joined together for some purpose. *Abbrev* **assn.** or **Assn., assoc.** or **Assoc.** 3 companionship. 4 *Chemistry* the linking of molecules by weak bonds. 5 *Ecology* a group of related organisms sharing a habitat. **association football** soccer. **as·so·ci·a·tive** [ə'souʃətɪv] or [ə'sousi,eitɪv] *adj* 1 to do with association. 2 *Mathematics* of a property of a given operation whereby any change in the grouping of its elements will not affect the result: *Addition and multiplication are associative. Example: (7 + 3) + 8 = 7 + (3 + 8).*

as·so·nance ['æsənəns] *n* 1 a partial rhyme in which the vowels are alike but the final consonants are not. *Examples: brave—vain, lone—show.* 2 the repetition of similar vowel sounds for effect, as the sounds [i], [u], and [ɜr] in the following example: "She moved near me to soothe my gloomy fear/And murmured fervent verses in my ear." **as·so·nant** *adj.* ⟨Latin *ad-* to, along with + *sonāre* sound⟩

as·sort·ment [ə'sɔrtmənt] *n* a group made up of various kinds; miscellaneous collection: *an assortment of candy.* **as·sort·ed** *adj.*

asst. or **Asst.** assistant.

as·suage [ə'sweidʒ] *v* relieve: *to assuage a guilty conscience, to assuage one's thirst.* **as·suage·ment** *n.* ⟨Latin *ad-* toward + *suavis* sweet⟩

as·sume [ə'sum] or [ə'sjum] *v* 1 take for granted without proof; suppose: *He assumed that the train had arrived on time.* 2 take upon oneself; undertake: *to assume control.* **3** adopt (an attitude, etc.) for effect: *to assume an air of superiority.* **4** pretend: *I assumed ignorance.* ⟨Latin *ad-* to + *sumere* take⟩

as·sumed *adj* false: *under an assumed name.*

as·sum·ing *adj* taking too much for granted.

as·sump·tion *n* **1** the act or fact of assuming or the thing assumed: *an assumption of innocence.* **2** arrogance; unpleasant boldness. **3 the Assumption** *Roman Catholic Church* **a** the bodily taking of the Virgin Mary from earth to heaven after her death. **b** a church festival in honour of this, held on August 15. **as·sump·tive** *adj.*

as·sure [ə'ʃʊr] *v* **1** make sure or certain: *He assured himself that the bridge was safe before crossing it.* **2** tell positively: *The captain assured the passengers that there was no danger.* **3** make safe; secure. **as·sur·er** *n.* **as·sur·ance** *n.* ⟨Latin *ad-* + *securus* safe. Compare SURE.⟩

as·sured [ə'ʃʊrd] *or* [ə'ʃɜrd] *adj* **1** sure; certain. **2** confident; bold. **as·sur·ed·ly** [ə'ʃʊrɪdli] *adv.*

as·ta·tine ['æstə,tin] *or* ['æstətɪn] *n* a radioactive element of the halogen group, produced artificially and also formed naturally by radioactive decay. *Symbol* **At** ⟨Greek *a-* not + *statos* stable⟩

as·ter ['æstər] *n* **1** any of a genus of plants of the composite family with daisylike flowers. **2** *Biology* a star-shaped structure arising around the centrosome during cell division. ⟨Greek *aster* star⟩

as·ter·isk ['æstə,rɪsk] *n* a star-shaped mark (*) used in written material to call attention to a footnote, etc. ⟨Greek *asteriskos* little star⟩

a·stern [ə'stɜrn] *adv* **1** at or toward the rear of a ship or aircraft. **2** backward. **3** behind.

as·ter·oid ['æstə,rɔɪd] *n* any of the many very small planets revolving around the sun between the orbits of Jupiter and Mars. **as·ter·oid** *adj.* ⟨Greek *aster* star + English *-oid*⟩

asth·ma ['æzmə] *or* ['æsmə] *n* a chronic disease that causes coughing and difficulty in breathing. **asth·mat·ic** *adj, n.* ⟨Greek = panting, from *azein* breathe hard⟩

a·stig·ma·tism [ə'stɪgmə,tɪzəm] *n* **1** a defect of the eye that makes it difficult to focus. **2** imperfect or distorted understanding. **as·tig·mat·ic** [,æstɪg'mætɪk] *adj.* ⟨*a-* without + Greek *stigma* point⟩

a·stir [ə'stɜr] *adv, adj* (never precedes a noun) **1** out of bed; up and around: *It was only six o'clock, but already the girls were astir.* **2** in motion.

as·ton·ish [ə'stɒnɪʃ] *v* surprise greatly; amaze. **as·ton·ish·ing** *adj.* **as·ton·ish·ing·ly** *adv.* **as·ton·ish·ment** *n.* ⟨variant of *astoun*; see ASTOUND.⟩

as·tound [ə'staʊnd] *v* surprise very greatly; amaze. **as·tound·ing** *adj.* **as·tound·ing·ly** *adv.* ⟨earlier *astoun,* from Old French *estoner;* related to Latin *tonare* thunder⟩

as·tra·khan or **as·tra·chan** ['æstrəkən] *n* **1** the curly, furlike wool of young lambs from

Astrakhan, a district in SW Asia. **2** a woollen cloth that looks like this.

as·tral ['æstrəl] *adj* **1** to do with the stars. **2** *Biology* having to do with the aster of a dividing cell. ⟨Greek *astron* star⟩

a·stray [ə'streɪ] *adj, adv* (never precedes a noun) off the right path.

a·stride [ə'straɪd] *adj* (never precedes a noun), *adv* **1** with one leg or end part on each side. **2** with legs far apart. *prep* with one leg or end part on each side of.

as·trin·gent [ə'strɪndʒənt] *adj* **1** causing the contraction of soft body tissues: *an astringent lotion.* **2** severe; harsh: *astringent criticism.* **as·trin·gent** *n.* **as·trin·gen·cy** *n.* **as·trin·gent·ly** *adv.* ⟨Latin *ad-* to + *stringere* bind⟩

astro— *combining form* **1** of stars, planets, or other heavenly bodies: *astrophysics.* **2** of outer space: *astronaut.* **3** of the aster of a dividing cell: *astrosphere.* ⟨Greek *astron* star⟩

as·tro·dome ['æstrə,doum] *n* a transparent domed structure for observing the heavens, esp one on an aircraft for navigation.

as·tro·labe ['æstrə,leɪb] *or* ['æstrə,læb] *n* an astronomical instrument formerly used for measuring the altitude of the sun or stars. ⟨Greek *astron* star + *lambanein* take⟩

as·trol·o·gy [ə'strɒlədʒi] *n* a study that interprets an assumed influence of the stars and planets on persons, events, etc. **as·trol·o·ger** *n.* **as·tro·log·i·cal** *adj.*

as·tro·naut ['æstrə,nɒt] *n* a member of the crew of a spacecraft. ⟨*astro-* + (*Argo*)*naut*⟩ **as·tro·nau·tics** *n* the design and operation of space vehicles. **as·tro·nau·tic** *adj.*

as·tron·o·my [ə'strɒnəmi] *n* the science that deals with the sun, moon, stars, and planets. **as·tron·o·mer** *n.* ⟨Greek *astron* star + *nomos* arrangement⟩ **as·tro·nom·i·cal** *adj* **1** to do with astronomy. **2** enormous, like the numbers reported in astronomy. **as·tro·nom·i·cal·ly** *adv.* **astronomical unit** a unit for measuring distance, equal to 149 600 gigametres, which is the mean distance of the earth from the sun. *Abbrev* **AU. astronomical year** the period of the earth's revolution around the sun: 365 days, 5 hours, 48 minutes, 45.51 seconds.

as·tro·phys·ics [,æstrou'fɪzɪks] *n* (with a sg verb) the branch of astronomy that deals with the physical and chemical characteristics of heavenly bodies. **as·tro·phys·i·cal** *adj.*

as·tute [ə'stjut] *or* [ə'stut] *adj* **1** having or showing keen, perceptive intelligence: *an astute remark.* **2** shrewd: *an astute business deal.* **as·tute·ly** *adv.* **as·tute·ness** *n.* ⟨Latin *astutus; astus* cunning⟩

a·sun·der [ə'sʌndər] *adv, adj Poetic* (never precedes a noun) in pieces: *torn asunder.* ⟨Old English *on sundran*⟩

a·sy·lum [ə'saɪləm] *n* **1** formerly, an institution for the care of the mentally ill. **2** refuge; protection: *refugees seeking political asylum in another country.* ⟨Greek *asylon* refuge⟩

a·sym·me·try [ei'sımətri] or [æ'sımətri] n lack of symmetry; imbalance. **a·sym·met·ri·cal** or **a·sym·met·ric** adj.

assymetrical federalism ✱ the unequal distribution of powers to the provinces, esp with reference to extra privileges allegedly enjoyed by Québec.

as·ymp·tote [ˈæsɪm,tout] n Mathematics a straight line that continually approaches a curve, but does not meet it within a finite distance. **as·ymp·tot·ic** [,æsɪmp'tɒtɪk] adj. **as·ymp·tot·i·cal·ly** adv. ⟨Greek a- not + syn- together + ptōtos apt to fall⟩

at [æt] prep 1 in; on; near: at the front door. 2 toward: Look at me. 3 in the position, manner, or condition of: at right angles, at war, moving at a crawl. 4 engaged in: at work. 5 for: two books at a dollar each. 6 with respect to: poor at math. 7 by or because of: I'm amazed at your progress. ⟨Old English æt⟩ **at–home** n an informal reception, usually in the afternoon.

at·a·vism [ˈætə,vɪzəm] n 1 in a plant or animal, the reappearance of a characteristic that has been absent for generations. 2 an individual showing such a characteristic; throwback. ⟨Latin atavus ancestor⟩ **at·a·vis·tic** adj 1 to do with atavism. 2 reverting to something ancient, ancestral, or primitive: atavistic instincts.

a·tax·i·a [ə'tæksiə] n an inability to co-ordinate voluntary muscular movements, as in some nervous disorders. **a·tax·ic** adj. ⟨Greek a- without + taxis order⟩

ate [eit] v pt of EAT.

at·el·ier [,ætə'ljei] n a workshop, esp an artist's studio. ⟨French, orig = pile of (wood) chips; Latin astula chip⟩

a tem·po [ɑ 'tɛmpou] Music in time; at the former speed. ⟨Italian⟩

Ath·a·pas·can [,æθə'pæskən] n 1 a major group of Aboriginal languages of NW Canada, Alaska, and the SW United States, including Chippewayan, Navaho, Dogrib, and others. 2 a member of a nation speaking any of these languages. **Ath·a·pas·can** adj.

a·the·ism [ˈeiθi,ɪzəm] n the belief that there is no God. **a·the·ist** n. **a·the·is·tic** adj. **a·the·is·ti·cal·ly** adv. ⟨Greek a- no + theos god⟩

A·the·ni·an [ə'θiniən] adj of Athens, the capital of Greece, or its people. **A·the·ni·an** n.

ath·er·o·scle·ro·sis [,æθərousklə'rousɪs] n a narrowing and hardening of the arteries due to deposits of cholesterol and fatty acids along the artery walls. **ath·er·o·scle·rot·ic** adj. ⟨Greek ather chaff + skleros hard⟩

ath·lete [ˈæθlit] n a person engaging in competititve sport or in activities requiring physical strength, speed, and skill. **ath·let·ic** [æθ'lɛtɪk] adj. **ath·let·i·cal·ly** adv. **ath·let·icism** n. ⟨Greek athlētēs; athlon contest, prize⟩ **athlete's foot** a contagious skin disease of the feet, caused by a fungus. **ath·let·ics** n (usually pl in use) exercises of strength, speed, and skill; active games and sports. **athletic**

support an elasticized belt and pouch worn by men to support and protect the genitals during athletic activity.

a·thwart [ə'θwɔrt] adv 1 crosswise; across from side to side. 2 so as to prevent passage. prep 1 across. 2 so as to oppose.

at·i·gi [ˈætəgi] or [ə'tigi] n ✱ 1 a hooded, knee-length inner shirt made of summer skins worn with the hair against the body, used in winter esp by Inuit, often for indoor wear. 2 a hooded outer garment of fur or other material; parka. Also, **art·i·gi**. ⟨Inuktitut⟩

At·lan·tic [æt'læntɪk] n the **Atlantic Ocean**, separating the Americas from Europe and Africa. adj 1 in, on, or across this ocean: Atlantic currents, Atlantic air routes. 2 to do with NATO: the Atlantic alliance. ⟨Greek Atlantikos pertaining to Atlas⟩ **Atlantic Provinces** Newfoundland and Labrador, Prince Edward Island, Nova Scotia, and New Brunswick. Compare MARITIME PROVINCES. **Atlantic salmon** a salmon found along the Atlantic coasts of North America and Europe.

at·las [ˈætləs] n 1 a book of maps. The first such books always had at the front a picture of Atlas supporting the world. 2 a book of plates, tables, or charts illustrating a particular subject: a bird atlas. ⟨Atlas, in Greek myth a Titan who rebelled against Zeus and was punished by being made to support the heavens with his head and hands⟩

ATM Computers automated teller machine.

at·man n [ˈɑtmən] Hinduism 1 the soul, capable of reincarnation; the spiritual self. 2 Also, **At·man**, the spiritual principle animating all creation. ⟨Sanskrit atma breath⟩

at·mos·phere [ˈætməs,fir] n 1 the air that surrounds the earth, consisting mainly of nitrogen and oxygen and made up of different layers. 2 the mass of gases that surrounds any heavenly body. 3 air in any given place: a damp atmosphere. 4 mental or moral environment; surrounding influence: an atmosphere of poverty. 5 a pleasant effect produced by the décor of a place: This café has a lot of atmosphere. **at·mos·pher·ic** [,ætməs'fɛrɪk] adj. **at·mos·pher·i·cal·ly** adv. ⟨Greek atmos vapour + sphaira sphere⟩ **atmospheric pressure** the pressure exerted by the air on the surface of the earth. The standard atmospheric pressure is about 101 kilopascals. **at·mos·pheri·cs** n pl interference in the form of crackling or hissing sounds in a radio receiver, caused by electrical disturbance in the atmosphere.

at·oll [ˈætɒl] or [ə'tɒl] n a ring of coral, or the top of a volcano, projecting above the surface of the ocean and forming a pool in the centre called a lagoon. ⟨Maldive (lang. of the Maldive Islands)⟩

at·om [ˈætəm] n 1 the smallest part of an element that has all the properties of the element. The basic particles making up an atom are protons and neutrons (themselves

made up of quarks) constituting its central portion, or nucleus, and electrons orbiting the nucleus. **2** a very small particle, thing, or quantity: *not an atom of strength left*. **a·tom·ic** [ə'tɒmɪk] *adj*. **a·tom·i·cal·ly** *adv*. ⟨Greek *atomos* indivisible; *a-* not + *tomos* cutting⟩
atom bomb or **atomic bomb** a bomb that uses the energy released by the very rapid splitting of atoms to cause an explosion of tremendous force. **atomic age** the era that began in 1945 with the first use of ATOMIC ENERGY. **atomic clock** a highly accurate clock that is run by controlled radio waves. **atomic energy** the energy that exists in atoms, which can be released slowly as in a reactor or suddenly as in a bomb. **atomic mass** the mass of an atom, equal to its ATOMIC WEIGHT times the ATOMIC MASS UNIT, and expressed in atomic mass units. *Abbrev* **at.mass**. **atomic mass unit** a unit of mass equalling one-twelfth of the mass of a neutral atom of carbon-12. *Abbrev* **amu**. **atomic number** *Chemistry, physics* a number used in describing an element, determining its place in the periodic table. The atomic number of an element represents the number of protons in the nucleus of one of its atoms. *Abbrev* **at.no.** **atomic pile** NUCLEAR REACTOR. **atomic power** NUCLEAR POWER. **atomic volume** the ATOMIC WEIGHT of an element divided by its density. **atomic weight** the ratio of the average mass per atom of an element to one-twelfth of the mass of an atom of carbon-12. **at·om·ize** *v* **1** reduce to separate atoms. **2** change (a liquid) into a fine spray. **at·om·i·za·tion** *n*. **at·om·iz·er** ['ætə,maɪzər] *n* a device that does this. **atom smasher** cyclotron.

a·ton·al [ei'tounəl] *adj Music* not having a central or dominant tone, or key. **a·to·nal·i·ty** *n*. **a·ton·al·ly** *adv*.

a·tone [ə'toun] *v* **1** make amends; make up (*for*): *to atone for a crime*. **2** cancel or wipe out (guilt, etc.) by doing so: *to atone guilt, to atone a loss*. ⟨back formation from *atonement*, *at onement* being at one⟩
a·tone·ment 1 the act of atoning, or that which is given in order to atone. **2 the Atonement** *Christianity* the reconciliation of God with sinners through the death of Christ in their place. ⟨*at onement* being at one⟩

a·top [ə'tɒp] *adv* on or at the top. *prep* on the top of.

a·tri·um ['eitriəm] *n*, *pl* **a·tri·a** ['eitriə] **1** the main room of an ancient Roman house. **2** a hall that has skylights or is open to the sky. **3** either of the upper chambers of the heart. **a·tri·al** *adj*. ⟨Latin⟩

a·tro·cious [ə'trouʃəs] *adj* **1** very wicked or cruel; brutal: *atrocious crimes*. **2** *Informal* very bad: *atrocious weather*. **a·tro·cious·ly** *adv*. **a·tro·cious·ness** *n*. **a·troc·i·ty** *n*. ⟨Latin *atrox*, *atrocis* cruel; *ater* dark⟩

at·ro·phy ['ætrəfi] *v* **1** of bodily tissue or an organ, etc., waste away or fail to develop properly. **2** of skills, etc., degenerate through

disuse. **at·ro·phy** *n*. **a·troph·ic** [ə'trɒfɪk] *adj*. ⟨Greek *a-* without + *trophē* nourishment⟩

at·tach [ə'tætʃ] *v* **1** fasten or add (*to*): *attach a boat to the pier by means of a rope, attach a file to an e-mail*. **2** add at the end: *to attach names to a petition*. **3** attribute: *to attach little importance to something*. **4** (usually as pp **attached**) bind by emotional ties: *Don't get too attached to him*. **at·tach·a·ble** *adj*. **at·tach·ment** *n*. ⟨Latin *ad-* to + Old French *tache* a fastening⟩

at·ta·ché [ə'tæʃei] *or* [,ætə'ʃei] *n* a specialist on the staff of an ambassador: *a cultural attaché, a press attaché*. ⟨French⟩
attaché case a briefcase shaped like a small, thin suitcase with a rigid frame and sides.

at·tack [ə'tæk] *v* **1** begin fighting against. **2** criticize vehemently. **3** set to work on with energy: *They attacked their dinner with gusto*. *n* **1** the act of attacking. **2** a sudden onset of illness, discomfort, etc.: *an attack of remorse*. **at·tack·er** *n*. ⟨Italian *attaccare*⟩

SYNONYMS

Attack is the general word, and suggests falling upon someone without warning, often without cause: *Germany attacked Belgium in 1914*. **Assail** is somewhat literary and suggests repeated or persistent onslaughts, while **assault** is a legal term and always suggests actual personal contact: *In a rage he assaulted his neighbour with a knife*.

at·tain [ə'tein] *v* **1** arrive at; reach: *to attain years of discretion*. **2** gain; accomplish. **at·tain·a·ble** *adj*. **at·tain·a·bil·i·ty** *n*. **at·tain·ment** *n*. ⟨Latin *ad-* to + *tangere* touch⟩
attain to succeed in coming to or getting: *to attain to a position of great influence*.

at·tain·der [ə'teindər] *n* formerly, the loss of property and civil rights as the result of being sentenced to death or outlawed. ⟨Old French *ataindre* attain, infl. by English *taindre* taint⟩

at·tar ['ætər] *n* a perfume made from the petals of roses or other flowers. Also, **ot·tar**. ⟨Persian *'aṭar*; Arabic *'uṭur* aroma⟩

at·tempt [ə'tempt] *v* **1** try; try to do: *to attempt a back flip, attempting to score*. **2** try to take, gain, climb, etc.: *to attempt Mt. Everest*. *n* **1** a try; an effort to do something, esp a difficult thing. **2** an attack: *an attempt on the king's life*. ⟨Latin *ad-* toward + *temptare* try⟩

at·tend [ə'tend] *v* **1** be present at: *to attend school*. **2** do something about (with *to*): *Attend to this matter immediately*. **3** look or listen; pay attention: *Attend to the instructions*. **4** wait on; care for; serve (sometimes with *on*): *Nurses attend the sick*. ⟨Latin *ad-* toward + *tendere* stretch⟩
at·tend·ance *n* **1** the act or fact of attending. **2** the number of people attending: *Attendance was low*. **dance attendance on** wait on with excessive attentions. **in attendance** attending.
at·tend·ant *n* **1** a person who waits on another or provides some (usually minor) service. **2** an accompanying thing: *Hatred developed as an attendant on fear*. *adj* **1** waiting

on another to help or serve: *an attendant nurse*. **2** accompanying, esp as a result: *weakness attendant on illness*. **at·tend·ee** *n* a person who is attending (a conference, etc.).

at·ten·tion [ə'tɛnʃən] *n* **1** concentration; careful looking or listening: *undivided attention*. **2** notice: *She called my attention to the error*. **3** thought and action to deal with something: *The matter requires our immediate attention*. **4** courtesy; thoughtfulness: *He showed his mother much attention*. **5 attentions** *pl* acts of courtesy or devotion, esp by someone fond of another. **6** *Military* a standing position taken by a soldier, in which the body is straight, heels together, arms straight down at the sides, and eyes looking forward. The position is taken to prepare for another command: *Stand at attention*.
pay attention watch or listen carefully. **attention deficit (hyperactivity) disorder** a disorder, mainly in children, characterized by an inability to concentrate. *Abbrev* **ADHD**. **at·ten·tive** *adj* **1** paying attention. **2** considerate: *an attentive host*. **at·ten·tive·ly** *adv*. **at·ten·tive·ness** *n*.

at·ten·u·ate [ə'tɛnju,eɪt] *v* make or become thinner or weaker. **at·ten·u·a·tion** *n*. **at·ten·u·a·tor** *n*. ⟨Latin *ad-* + *tenuis* thin⟩

at·test [ə'tɛst] *v* **1** give proof of: *The child's good health attests her parents' care*. **2** declare to be true or genuine. **3** bear witness; testify: *The expert attested to the genuineness of the signature*. **at·test·er** or **at·test·or** *n*. **at·tes·ta·tion** *n*. ⟨Latin *ad-* to + *testis* witness⟩

at·tic ['ætɪk] *n* a small room or space in a house just below the roof and above the other rooms. ⟨*Attica*, Greece, where such architecture was common⟩
At·ti·cism ['ætɪ,sɪzəm] simple elegance of expression. **Attic salt** or **wit** incisive wit.

At·tik·a·mek [ə'tɪkə,mɛk] *n, pl* **-mek 1** a member of a First Nations people living in the St. Maurice River area in SW Québec. **2** their dialect of Cree. **At·tik·a·mek** *adj*.

at·tire [ə'taɪr] *v* clothe, esp in rich or formal clothes: *She was attired in full uniform*. *n* clothes. ⟨Old French *atirer* arrange; *tire* row⟩

at·ti·tude ['ætə,tjud] *or* ['ætə,tud] *n* **1** a way of thinking or feeling: *one's attitude toward school*. **2** a pose suggesting an intention, emotion, etc: *standing in a defensive attitude*. **3** *Informal* **a** a spirit of antagonism or defiance: *There's a kid with an attitude!* **b** (as non-countable noun) *Slang* feistiness; style or flair: *a coffee shop with attitude*. **at·ti·tu·di·nal** *adj*. ⟨Latin *aptitudo*. Doublet of APTITUDE.⟩
strike an attitude pose for effect.

attn. attention.

at·tor·ney [ə'tɜrni] *n* **1** a person with legal power to act for another. **2** *esp US* lawyer. *Abbrev* **atty.** ⟨Old French *atourner* appoint; *tourner* turn⟩
attorney general (or **A- G-**), *pl* **attorneys general** or **attorney generals 1** a chief law officer. **2 Attorney General ✻ a** the chief law

officer of Canada, head of the Department of Justice and a Cabinet member. **b** the chief law officer of a province. Compare SOLICITOR GENERAL. Also, **attorney–general**.

at·tract [ə'trækt] *v* **1** draw to oneself or itself: *A magnet attracts iron*. **2** appeal to: *Bright colours attract children*. **at·trac·tion** *n*. **at·trac·tive** *adj*. **at·trac·tive·ly** *adv*. **at·trac·tive·ness** *n*. ⟨Latin *ad-* toward + *trahere* draw⟩

at·trib·ute [ə'trɪbjut] *v* **1** consider (a certain quality) as belonging: *to attribute intelligence to a dog*. **2** assign to a particular cause or source: *to attribute success to hard work. This poem has been attributed to Emily Dickinson*.
n ['ætrə,bjut] **1** a characteristic: *Prudence should be an attribute of a judge*. **2** an object linked with a person, rank, or office as a symbol: *The eagle was the attribute of Jupiter*. **at·trib·ut·a·ble** *adj*. **at·tri·bu·tion** *n*. ⟨Latin *ad-* to + *tribuere* assign, orig by tribe; *tribus* tribe⟩ **at·trib·u·tive** [ə'trɪbjətɪv] *adj Grammar* of an adjective, adjacent to the noun it modifies, as *general* in *general store* and *governor general*, unlike a predicate adjective which is separated from its noun by a linking verb. **at·trib·u·tive** *n*. **at·trib·u·tive·ly** *adv*.

at·tri·tion [ə'trɪʃən] *n* **1** a gradual wearing down or wearing away. **2** a gradual reduction in staff due to natural events such as retirement rather than to dismissals or layoffs. ⟨Latin *attritio; ad-* against + *terere* rub⟩

at·tune [ə'tjun] *or* [ə'tun] *v* **1** bring into harmony (with *to*): *He could not attune his ears to the sounds of the big city*. **2** make sensitive or responsive: *Her years in politics had attuned the minister to subtle shifts in public opinion*. **at·tune·ment** *n*.

ATV ALL-TERRAIN VEHICLE.

a·twit·ter [ə'twɪtər] *adj, adv* (never before a noun) twittering, often from excitement.

a·typ·i·cal [eɪ'tɪpəkəl] *adj* not typical; irregular; abnormal. **a·typ·i·cal·ly** *adv*.

au·bade [ou'bɑd] *or* [ou'bæd] *n* a musical composition, lyric poem, etc. appropriate to the morning. ⟨French, from *aube* dawn⟩

au·berge [ou'bɛrʒ] *n* inn. ⟨French⟩

au·ber·gine ['oubər,ʒin] *or* ['oubər,dʒin] *n* eggplant. ⟨French, from Arabic *al badhinjan*⟩

au·burn ['ɒbərn] *n, adj* reddish brown. ⟨Latin *alburnus* whitish, from *albus* white; confused with Middle English *brun* brown⟩

au cou·rant [oku'Rã] *French* up-to-date on the events and topics of the day.

auc·tion ['ɒkʃən] *n* a sale in which each item is sold to the person who offers most for it. *v* (often with *off*) sell at an auction. ⟨Latin *auctio(nis); augere* increase⟩
auction bridge a card game for four people playing in two opposing pairs. Any tricks made in excess of a bid may be counted toward a game. Compare CONTRACT BRIDGE. **auc·tion·eer** [,ɒkʃə'nir] *n* a person who conducts an auction. **auc·tion·eer** *v*.

auc·to·ri·al [ɒk'tɔriəl] *adj* See AUTHOR.

au·da·cious [ɒ'deɪʃəs] *adj* **1** daring; bold.

2 brazen; rude. **au·da·cious·ly** *adv.* **au·dac·i·ty** [ɒ'dæsəti] *n.* ⟨Latin *audax; audere* dare⟩

au·di·ble ['ɒdəbəl] *adj* loud enough to be heard.
n a change of plan ordered by a quarterback at the line of scrimmage. **au·di·bil·i·ty** *n.* **au·di·bly** *adv.* ⟨Latin *audibilis; audire* hear⟩

au·di·ence ['ɒdiəns] *n* 1 the people gathered to hear a performance: *The audience cheered.* 2 the people reached by radio or television broadcasts, books, etc.: *This book is intended for a juvenile audience.* 3 a chance to be heard: *Explain your plan; the committee will give you an audience.* 4 a formal interview with a person of high rank: *an audience with the queen.* ⟨Latin *audientia* hearing; *audire* hear⟩

au·di·o ['ɒdiou] *adj* to do with sound reproduction: *audio equipment.* **au·di·o** *n.* **audio–** *combining form* sound or hearing: *audiovisual.* **audio frequency** a frequency corresponding to audible sound vibrations. *Abbrev* **AF, A.F.,** or **a.f. au·di·ol·o·gy** *n* the medical science dealing with hearing. **au·di·o·log·i·cal** *adj.* **au·di·ol·o·gist** *n.* **au·di·o·phile** ['ɒdiə,faɪl] *n* a person greatly interested in the high-fidelity reproduction of sound. **au·di·o–vid·e·o** *adj* to do with the transmission or reception of both sounds and images. **au·di·o·vis·u·al** *adj* to do with the use of both hearing and sight: *audiovisual aids such as films. Abbrev* **AV** or **A.V.**

au·dit ['ɒdɪt] *v* 1 examine (business accounts) officially. 2 attend (a class) as a listener, without getting credit for the course. **au·dit** *n.* **au·di·tor** *n.*
Auditor General *pl* **Auditors General** or **Auditor Generals** ✱ an officer appointed to audit the accounts of a federal or provincial government. **au·di·tion** *n* a demonstration of a performer's skills with a view to selection for a role, a course of study, etc. *v* hold or give an audition. **au·di·to·ri·um** *n, pl* **-to·ri·ums** or **-to·ri·a** a large room or hall designed for lectures, concerts, etc. **au·di·to·ry** *adj* to do with hearing. **au·di·to·ri·ly** *adv.*

au·ger ['ɒgər] *n* 1 a type of drill. 2 a device with a spiral channel inside a tube, used for moving bulk substances such as grain. ⟨Middle English *nauger;* Old English *nafugār*⟩

CONFUSABLES
Auger means *drill*; augur means *predict* or *be a sign of*.

aught [ɒt] *n Formal, poetic* anything: *You may resign your job for aught I care.* ⟨Old English *āwiht; ā* ever + *wiht* a thing⟩

aug·ment [ɒg'mɛnt] *v* 1 increase; enlarge by adding to. 2 *Music* **a** raise by a half step. **b** change (a melody) by increasing the time value of the notes. **aug·men·ta·ble** *adj.* **aug·men·ta·tion** *n.* **aug·ment·ed** *adj.* ⟨Latin *augmentare* from *augere* increase⟩

au gra·tin [ou'grætən] or [ou'grɒtən] *French* [ogʀa'tɛ̃] cooked with crumbs or cheese on top. ⟨lit., with grated (cheese)⟩

au·gur ['ɒgər] *n* a prophet; fortuneteller.

v 1 predict. 2 be a sign of. **au·gu·ry** *n.* ⟨Latin *augur; augere* increase (crops)⟩
augur ill (or **well**) be a bad (or good) sign.

Au·gust ['ɒgəst] *n* the eighth month of the year. It has 31 days. ⟨*Augustus* Cæsar (63 B.C.-A.D. 14), Roman emperor⟩

au·gust [ɒ'gʌst] *or* ['ɒgʌst] *adj* inspiring reverence and admiration; majestic; imposing. **au·gust·ly** *adv.* **au·gust·ness** *n.* ⟨Latin; related to *augere* increase⟩

auk [ɒk] *n* any of various swimming and diving sea birds found along northern coasts. The **great auk,** a flightless bird, has been extinct for over a century. ⟨Old Norse *álka*⟩

au lait [o'le] *French* [o'lɛ] with milk.

auld lang syne ['ɒld 'læŋ 'saɪn] *or* ['zaɪn] *Scottish* old times; long ago.

au na·tu·rel ['ou ,nætʃə'rɛl] *French* [onaty'ʀɛl] 1 in the nude. 2 in a natural, lifelike way. 3 in the simplest manner.

aunt [ænt] *Atlantic Canada* [ɒnt] *n* 1 the sister of one's father or mother. 2 one's uncle's wife. ⟨Latin *amita* father's sister⟩

au pair [ou 'pɛr] a person, esp a young woman, who works in another country as a housekeeper, nanny, etc., usually temporarily in order to learn the language of the country. ⟨French = on equal terms (with host family)⟩

au·ra ['ɒrə] *n, pl* **au·ras** or **au·rae** ['ɒri] *or* ['ɒraɪ] 1 something supposed to come from a person or thing and surround him, her, or it as an atmosphere: *an aura of holiness.* 2 a delicate fragrance arising, as from flowers. 3 *Medicine* a peculiar sensation that usually announces the onset of a seizure. ⟨Greek⟩

au·ral ['ɒrəl] *adj* to do with the ear or hearing. **au·ral·ly** *adv.* ⟨Latin *auris* ear⟩

au·re·ole ['ɒri,oul] *n* 1 a halo. 2 *Astronomy* a ring of light surrounding the sun. ⟨Latin *aureola* golden; *aurum* gold⟩

au re·voir [ɒr'vwaʀ] *French* goodbye; till we see each other again.

au·ri·cle ['ɒrəkəl] *n* 1 the outer part of the ear. 2 either atrium of the heart. 3 an earlike part. ⟨Latin *auricula,* diminutive of *auris* ear⟩

au·rif·er·ous [ɒ'rɪfərəs] *adj* yielding gold. ⟨Latin *aurum* gold + *ferre* bear⟩

au·ro·ra [ə'rɒrə] *or* [ɔ'rɒrə] *n* 1 streams or bands of light appearing in the sky at night at high latitudes, called **aurora aus·tral·is** [ɒ'strælɪs] in the southern hemisphere and **aurora bo·re·al·is** [,bɒri'ælɪs] *or* [,bɒri'eɪlɪs] in the northern hemisphere. 2 dawn. **au·ro·ral** *adj.* ⟨Latin⟩
aurora trout an endangered, nonspotted subspecies of the brook trout found only in certain lakes of northern Ontario.

aus·cul·tate ['ɒskəl,teit] *v Medicine* listen to (sounds within the human body), usually with a stethoscope, to determine the condition of the heart, lungs, etc. **aus·cul·ta·tion** *n.* ⟨Latin *auscultare* listen⟩

aus·pice ['ɒspɪs] *n*
under the auspices of hosted, administered,

or sponsored by: *The fair was held under the auspices of the Home and School Association.*
aus·pi·cious [ɒ'spɪʃəs] *adj* indicating or under a good omen; favourable or fortunate. 〈Latin *auspicium; avis* bird + *specere* look; from divination by observing birds' flight〉
Aus·sie ['ɒzi] *adj, n Slang* Australian.

aus·tere [ɒ'stir] *adj* **1** harsh; stern: *a silent, austere man.* **2** strict in moral discipline: *The Puritans were austere.* **3** severely simple: *the austere beauty of plain columns.* **4** thrifty; frugal. **aus·tere·ly** *adv.* **aus·ter·i·ty** [ɒ'stɛrəti] *n.* 〈Greek *austēros*〉

aus·tral ['ɒstrəl] *adj* **1** southern. **2 Austral** to do with Australia. 〈Latin *auster* south wind〉
Aus·tral·a·sia [,ɒstrə'leɪʒə] *n* the islands of the SW Pacific Ocean. **Aus·tral·a·sian** *adj, n.*
Aus·tra·lo·pith·e·cine [,ɒstrələu'pɪθə,sin] *n* any of the primates of the genus *Australopithecus,* now extinct but believed to have lived in southern Africa in the Pleistocene epoch. **Aus·tro·ne·sia** [,ɒstrə'niʒə] *n* the islands of the central and S Pacific. **Aus·tro·ne·sian** *adj, n.*

au·tarch ['ɒtɑrk] *n* an absolute ruler; autocrat. **au·tar·chic** *adj.* **au·tar·chy** *n.* 〈Greek *autos* self + *archein* rule〉

au·tar·ky ['ɒtɑrki] *n* self-sufficiency, esp economic self-sufficiency of a nation. **au·tar·kic** *adj.* 〈Greek *auto-* self + *arkein* suffice〉

au·then·tic [ɒ'θɛntɪk] *adj* **1** genuine: *an authentic signature.* **2** reliable; credible. **3** of a document, properly executed and therefore legally valid. **au·then·ti·cal·ly** *adv.* **au·then·tic·i·ty** [,ɒθɛn'tɪsəti] *n.* 〈Greek *authentikos; auto-* oneself + *hentēs* doer〉 **au·then·ti·cate** *v* show to be valid or genuine. **au·then·ti·ca·tor** *n.* **au·then·ti·ca·tion** *n.*

au·thor ['ɒθər] *n* **1** a published writer. **2** an author's works: *Do read this author.* **3** a person who creates or begins anything.
v be the author of; write: *She has authored several plays.* **au·tho·ri·al** or **auc·to·ri·al** *adj.* **au·thor·ship** *n.* 〈Latin *auctor*〉

au·thor·i·ty [ə'θɔrəti] *n* **1** the right to demand obedience and the power to enforce it: *Parents have authority over their children.* **2** a person who has such power or right. **3 the authorities a** government officials. **b** any administration. **4** a government body that runs some activity on behalf of the public: *the St. Lawrence Seaway Authority.* **5** a reliable source of correct information: *A good dictionary is an authority on the meanings of words. She is an authority on Canadian history.* 〈Latin *auctoritas; auctor* author〉
au·thor·i·tar·i·an *adj* insisting on authority; valuing obedience over individual freedom. **au·thor·i·tar·i·an** *n.* **au·thor·i·tar·i·an·ism** *n.*
au·thor·i·ta·tive [ə'θɔrə,teitɪv] *adj* **1** having authority; constituting or proceeding from an authority: *Authoritative orders came from the general.* **2** commanding: *to speak in authoritative tones.* **au·thor·i·ta·tive·ly** *adv.* **au·thor·i·ta·tive·ness** *n.*
au·thor·ize ['ɒθə,raɪz] *v* **1** give authority to:

The prime minister authorized her to set up a committee. **2** of an authority, approve or consent to: *These expenditures were never authorized by Parliament.* **au·thor·i·za·tion** *n.*
Authorized Version the English translation of the Bible authorized by King James in 1611.

au·tism ['ɒtɪzəm] *n* a cognitive, emotional, and behavioural disorder characterized by difficulty in understanding and responding to what one sees and hears. **au·tis·tic** *adj.* 〈Greek *autos* self; orig seen as self-absorption〉

au·to ['ɒtou] *n* (esp in industry and commerce) automobile.
au·to·mak·er *n* an automobile manufacturer.

auto– *combining form* **1** by, for, or of oneself: *autobiography.* **2** independent(ly); an *automobile* is a self-propelled vehicle. 〈Greek〉
au·to·an·ti·bod·y [,ɒtou'æntɪ,bɒdi] *n* an antibody that fights against the system it is supposed to protect.

au·to·bi·og·ra·phy [,ɒtəbaɪ'ɒgrəfi] *n* the story of a person's life written by that person. **au·to·bi·o·graph·i·cal** or **au·to·bi·o·graph·ic** *adj.* **au·to·bi·o·graph·i·cal·ly** *adv.*

au·to·bog·gan ['ɒtə,bɒgən] *n ✸* a motorized sled. 〈*auto-* + (*to*)*boggan*〉

au·toch·thon [ɒ'tɒkθən] *n* **1** an aboriginal inhabitant. **2** an indigenous plant or animal. **au·toch·tho·nous** *adj.* **au·toch·tho·nous·ly** *adv.* 〈Greek *auto-* self + *chthōn* earth, soil〉

au·to·clave ['ɒtə,kleiv] *n* a pressurized vessel used for sterilizing, cooking, etc. by steam. **au·to·clave** *v.* 〈*auto-* + Latin *clavis* key〉

au·toc·ra·cy [ɒ'tɒkrəsi] *n* government by an absolute ruler. 〈Greek *autos* self + *kratia* rule〉
au·to·crat ['ɒtə,kræt] *n* **1** a ruler with absolute power. **2** a person who uses authority in a very controlling way. **au·to·crat·ic** *adj.* **au·to·crat·i·cal·ly** *adv.*

au·to–da–fé [,ɒtou də 'fei] or [,ʌutou-] *n, pl* **au·tos–da–fé 1** the public ceremony that accompanied the passing of sentence by the Spanish Inquisition. **2** the burning of a heretic. 〈Portuguese = act of the faith〉

au·to·di·dact [,ɒtou'daɪdækt] *n* a self-educated person. **au·to·di·dac·tic** *adj.*

au·to·e·rot·i·cism [,ɒtoui'rɒtə,sɪzəm] *n* sexual self-stimulation; masturbation. Also, **au·to·e·rot·ism** [,ɒtou'ɛrə,tɪzəm].

au·to·graft ['ɒtə,græft] *n* a graft, such as a skin graft, taken from the patient's own body.

au·to·graph ['ɒtə,græf] *n* **1** a person's signature, esp given as a memento. **2** something written in a person's own handwriting. **au·to·graph** *v.* **au·to·graph·ic** *adj.* **au·to·graph·i·cal·ly** *adv.* 〈Greek *autos* self + *graphein* write〉

Au·to·harp ['ɒtou,hɑrp] *n Trademark* a zither with dampers that suppress all but the strings included in a desired chord.

au·to·hyp·no·sis [,ɒtouhɪp'nousɪs] *n* self-induced hypnosis. **au·to·hyp·not·ic** *adj.*

au·to·im·mune [,ɒtouɪ'mjun] *adj* to do with or characterized by the development of antibodies hostile to the organism's own cells. **au·to·im·mu·ni·ty** *n.*

au·to·in·fec·tion [ˌɒtouɪnˈfɛkʃən] *n* infection due to agents already present in the organism.

au·to·in·tox·i·ca·tion [ˌɒtouɪn,tɒksəˈkeɪʃən] *n* poisoning by toxic substances produced within the body.

au·to·load·ing [ˈɒtou,loudɪŋ] *adj* self-loading; of a firearm, semi-automatic.

au·tol·y·sis [ɒˈtɒləsɪs] *n* a process by which enzymes destroy the cells and tissues of which they are a part, as in the decay of a dead organism. **au·to·lyse** *v.* **au·to·lyt·ic** [ˌɒtəˈlɪtɪk] *adj.* ⟨*auto-* + Greek *lysis* a loosening⟩

au·to·mat·ic [ˌɒtəˈmætɪk] *adj* **1** made or done without thought or attention, as from force of habit, etc.: *Her automatic reply to questions from reporters was, "No comment."* **2** mainly or entirely involuntary; reflex: *Breathing is automatic.* **3** of a mechanism, machine, etc., made or set to move or act by itself: *automatic transmission.* **4** as a necessary consequence: *Any violation of the rules means automatic disqualification.*
n **1** an automobile equipped with an automatic transmission. **2** an automatic firearm. **3** any other automatic machine. **au·to·mat·i·cal·ly** *adv.* **au·to·mat·ic·i·ty** *n.* ⟨Greek *automatos* self-acting⟩ **au·to·mate** *v* convert to automatic operation; cause or design to be done by machine. **au·to·ma·tion** *n.* **automated teller machine** a machine that allows the user to carry out banking functions electronically, without the aid of a human teller. *Abbrev* **ATM. automatic pilot** a program designed to keep an aircraft, missile, etc. on a given course without human assistance. **au·tom·a·tism** [ɒˈtɒmə,tɪzəm] *n* **1** the quality or fact of being automatic. **2** *Psychology* **a** an action not controlled by the conscious mind. **b** an action not subject to outside stimuli. **3** *Philosophy* the belief that the living body is a machine controlled by the laws of physics rather than by the conscious mind. **au·tom·a·tist** *n.* **au·tom·a·ton** *n, pl* **-ta** [-tə] **1** robot. **2** a person or animal that seems to act like a machine or robot.

au·to·mo·bile [ˈɒtəmə,bil] *n* a vehicle with its own engine, esp a passenger vehicle; car. ⟨French⟩ **au·to·mo·tive** [ˌɒtəˈmoutɪv] *adj* **1** to do with cars, trucks, and other self-propelled vehicles. **2** self-propelling.

au·ton·o·mous [ɒˈtɒnəməs] *adj* **1** self-governing. **2** *Biology* **a** independent from other parts. **b** producing its own food. **au·ton·o·mous·ly** *adv.* **au·ton·o·my** *n.* ⟨Greek *auto-* of oneself + *nomos* law⟩
autonomic nervous system [ˌɒtəˈnɒmɪk] *Physiology* the nervous system of vertebrates, which controls digestive, reproductive, respiratory, and other involuntary functions.

au·to·pho·bia [ˌɒtəˈfoubiə] *n* an abnormal fear of being alone.

au·to·pi·lot [ˈɒtou,paɪlət] *n* AUTOMATIC PILOT.

au·top·sy [ˈɒtɒpsi] *or* [ˈɒtəpsi] *n* **1** the dissection of a dead body to find the cause of death. Compare BIOPSY. **2** the critical examination of something that has ended or failed: *an autopsy of the Meech Lake Accord.* ⟨Greek *auto-* for oneself + *opsis* a seeing⟩

au·to·tox·in [ˈɒtou,tɒksɪn] *n* a toxic substance generated within the organism poisoned by it.

au·to·troph [ˈɒtə,trɒf] *n* an organism that manufactures its own food from inorganic substances, such as a plant by photosynthesis. **au·to·troph·ic** *adj.* **au·to·troph·i·cal·ly** *adv.* ⟨Greek *auto-* self + *trophe* food⟩

au·tumn [ˈɒtəm] *n* **1** the season of the year between summer and winter; fall. **2** a time of maturity and the beginning of decay. **au·tum·nal** *adj.* ⟨Latin *autumnus*⟩
autumnal equinox the equinox occurring about September 22.

USAGE
Autumn is not as common in Canadian English as **fall**, and is slightly more literary, often conveying a picturesque connotation or a metaphorical meaning.

aux. auxiliary.

aux·il·i·a·ry [ɒgˈzɪləri] *or* [ɒgˈzɪljəri] *adj* **1** supplementary or additional: *an auxiliary power supply.* **2** supporting: *Intellect and imagination should be auxiliary to each other.*
n **1** a supplementary or supporting person, group, or thing; often, specifically, a group of volunteers: *a gift shop staffed by the Hospital Auxiliary.* **2** AUXILIARY VERB. **3 auxiliaries** *pl* foreign or allied troops that help the army of a nation at war. ⟨Latin *auxilium* aid⟩
auxiliary verb a verb used to form the tenses, moods, aspects, or voices of other verbs, such as *be, do, have, shall,* and *will. Examples:* I *am* going; he *will* go; they *are* lost; they *have* lost.

AV audiovisual.

a·vail [əˈveil] *v* be of use or value (to): *Money will not avail you after you are dead.*
n use; advantage (esp with a negative): *He tried again and again, but to no avail.* ⟨Latin *ad-* to + *valere* be worth⟩
avail oneself of make use of: *While in Québec, I availed myself of the chance to speak French.*
a·vail·a·ble *adj* **1** ready or handy to be used: *an available water supply.* **2** that can be obtained: *There are no more tickets available.* **3** willing or free to do something: *She will be available to help on Monday.* **a·vail·a·bil·i·ty** *n.* **a·vail·a·bly** *adv.*

av·a·lanche [ˈævə,læntʃ] *n* **1** a large mass of snow and ice, or dirt and rocks, sliding or falling down a mountainside. **2** anything like an avalanche: *an avalanche of junk mail.* ⟨Swiss French *lavenche* influenced by French *avaler* go down; Latin *ad vallem* to the valley⟩

a·vant–garde [ˌævɑ̃ˈgɑrd] French [avɑ̃ˈgaʀd] *n* the people who develop new and experimental ideas, esp in the arts. **a·vant–garde** *adj.* **a·vant–gard·ism** *n.*

a·vant–gard·ist *n, adj.* ⟨French, lit. = advance guard (of an army)⟩

av·a·rice ['ævərɪs] *n* an extreme desire to acquire and keep money or property; greed. **av·a·ri·cious** *adj.* **av·ar·i·cious·ly** *adv.* ⟨Latin *avaritia; avarus* greedy⟩

a·vast [ə'væst] *interj Nautical* a command to stop. ⟨perhaps from Dutch *houd vast* hold fast⟩

av·a·tar ['ævə,tɑr] *n* **1** *Hinduism* the descent of a god to earth in bodily form; incarnation. **2** a fictitious identity as, for example, adopted in a CHAT ROOM to ensure the user's privacy or to deceive others. ⟨Sanskrit *avatāra* descent⟩

ave. or **Ave.** Avenue.

a·venge [ə'vɛndʒ] *v* **1** inflict punishment in return for: *to avenge an insult.* **2** take vengeance on behalf of (oneself or another): *The clan avenged their slain chief.* **3** get revenge (in the passive): *She swore to be avenged.* **a·veng·er** *n.* ⟨Old French *avengier;* Latin *ad-* + *vindicare* punish⟩

av·ens ['ævɪnz] *n* **1** any of several perennial plants of the rose family found in temperate and arctic regions, including several common Canadian wildflowers. **2** See MOUNTAIN AVENS. ⟨Old French *avence*⟩

av·e·nue ['ævə,nju] *n* **1** a wide or main street. **2** a road or walk bordered by trees. **3** a way of approach: *avenues to fame.* ⟨French, fem. pp of *avenir;* Latin *ad-* to + *venire* come⟩

a·ver [ə'vɜr] *v* **a·verred, a·ver·ring** state to be true. **a·ver·ment** *n.* ⟨Latin *ad-* + *verus* true⟩

av·er·age ['ævrɪdʒ] *n* **1** the quantity found by dividing the sum of several quantities by the number of those quantities: *The average of 3, 5, and 10 is 6.* **2** the usual quality or amount: *His work was far above the average.* *v* **1** find the average of. **2** amount to as an average: *The cost for lunch at the cafeteria averages about six dollars a day.* **3** do, get, yield, etc. as an average: *He averages six hours of work a day.* **4** *Finance* buy or sell set amounts of stock at varying prices in order to get a better average cost (with *up* or *down*). *Abbrev* **avg.** **av·er·age** *adj.* ⟨Arabic *'awāriya* damage from sea water, with reference to the equal distribution of resulting losses⟩ **on (the) average** as an average amount: *She worked 35 hours a week on average.* **average out** come to an average: *The expenses averaged out to $250 a month.*

a·verse [ə'vɜrs] *adj* **1** opposed; having an active distaste (with *to*): *He was averse to fighting.* **2** *Botany* not facing the principal stem. **a·verse·ly** *adv.* **a·verse·ness** *n.* ⟨Latin *aversus,* pp of *avertere.* See AVERT.⟩

a·ver·sion *n* **1** the fact of being averse; strong dislike or opposition: *an aversion to work.* **2** the act or fact of averting. **aversion therapy** a method of treating addicts or obsessives by repeatedly associating very unpleasant experiences with indulgence of the habit. Also called **aversive conditioning.**

a·vert [ə'vɜrt] *v* **1** prevent; avoid: *He averted the accident by a quick turn of the wheel.* **2** turn away; turn aside: *She averted her eyes from the wreck.* ⟨Latin *ab-* away from + *vertere* turn⟩

A·ves·ta [ə'vɛstə] *n* the sacred writings of the ancient Zoroastrian religion. **A·ves·tan** *n* the language, closely related to Old Persian, of the Avesta. **A·ves·tan** *adj.*

avg. average.

a·vi·an ['eiviən] *adj* to do with birds. ⟨Latin *avis* bird⟩ **a·vi·ar·y** ['eivi,ɛri] *n* an enclosure or large cage in which to keep birds. **a·vi·cul·ture** *n* the rearing or keeping of birds. **a·vi·cul·tur·ist** *n.* **a·vi·fau·na** *n* the birds of a particular region, environment, or time.

a·vi·a·tion [,eivi'eiʃən] *n* the design, manufacture, and operation of aircraft, esp airplanes. ⟨Latin *avis* bird⟩ **a·vi·a·tor** *n* a pilot. **a·vi·on·ics** *n pl* (with sg verb) electronics as used in aircraft and rockets. **a·vi·on·ic** *adj.*

av·id ['ævɪd] *adj* **1** enthusiastic: *an avid reader.* **2** eager; greedy: *avid for gold.* **a·vid·i·ty** *n.* **av·id·ly** *adv.* ⟨Latin *avidus; avere* crave⟩

a·vi·ta·min·o·sis [,ei,vəitəmə'nousɪs] *n* any disorder resulting from vitamin deficiency.

av·o·ca·do [,ævə'kɑdou] or [-'kɒdou] *n* the fruit of a tropical American tree of the laurel family, having a dark green skin, soft, edible greenish yellow pulp, and a very large stone. Also called **alligator pear.** ⟨Spanish, var. of *aguacate;* Aztec *ahuacatl*⟩

av·o·ca·tion [,ævə'keiʃən] *n* an activity or interest outside one's regular business; hobby: *She is a lawyer, but writing stories is her avocation.* ⟨Latin *ab-* away + *vocare* to call⟩

av·o·cet ['ævə,sɛt] *n* any of several web-footed wading birds of temperate and tropical regions, with a long, slender bill that curves upward. Also, **av·o·set.** ⟨Italian *avosetta*⟩

A·vo·gad·ro's law [,ɑvə'gɑdrouz] *Physics* the law stating that equal volumes of different gases, under like conditions of pressure and temperature, contain the same number of molecules. ⟨Count Amedeo Avogadro (1776-1856), Italian physicist⟩ **Avogadro's number** or **constant** the number of molecules in one MOLE of any substance.

a·void [ə'vɔɪd] *v* **1** keep (away) from: *We avoided large cities on our trip. I couldn't avoid telling the truth.* **2** prevent the need for or the occurrence of: *Avoid spills in the lab.* **a·void·a·ble** *adj.* **a·void·ance** *n.* ⟨Old French *esvuidier* empty; Latin *ex-* out + *vocitare* empty⟩

av·oir·du·pois [ə'vwardjʊ,pwɑ] or ['ævərdə,pɔɪz] *n* **1** avoirdupois weight, the system of weighing in Canada before the change to the SI, or metric system. One pound avoirdupois is equal to about 0.454 kg. Compare APOTHECARIES' WEIGHT. **2** *Informal* a person's mass or weight. ⟨Old French *aveir de peis* goods of weight⟩

a·vow [ə'vaʊ] *v* declare frankly or openly: *He avowed that he could not sing.* **a·vow·al** *n.* ⟨Old French *avouer;* Latin *advocare.* Compare AVOUCH.⟩

a·vowed *adj* admitted: *That was her avowed intention all along.* **a·vow·ed·ly** [ə'vaʊɪdli] *adv.*

a·vun·cu·lar [ə'vʌŋkjələr] *adj* of or like an uncle. ⟨Latin *avunculus* uncle; from *avus* grandfather⟩

aw [ɒ] *interj* an exclamation of mild protest, resignation, pity, or embarrassment.

a·wait [ə'weit] *v* **1** wait for; look forward to: *to await someone's arrival.* **2** be ready for; be in store for: *A surprise awaited them at home.* ⟨Old French *a-* for + *waitier.* See WAIT.⟩

a·wake [ə'weik] *v* **a·woke, a·wok·en, a·wak·ing** **1** cease or cause to cease sleeping: *We awoke from a sound sleep.* **2** make or become active: *The song awoke old memories.* Also, **a·wak·en.** *adj* (not before the noun except occasionally for def. 2) **1** not asleep: *She is always awake early.* **2** alert: *awake to danger.* **a·wak·en·ing** *n.* ⟨Old English *āwacian*⟩

a·ward [ə'wɔrd] *v* **1** give in consideration of merit: *to award a medal.* **2** rule by law in someone's favour: *to award damages of $5000.* **a·ward** *n.* **a·ward·ee** *n.* **a·ward·er** *n.* ⟨Old French *esguarder* observe, decide⟩

a·ware [ə'wɛr] *adj* **1** knowing; realizing; conscious (*of* or *that*): *too sleepy to be aware of the cold.* **2** alert and well-informed: *an aware teen.* **a·ware·ness** *n.* ⟨Old English *gewær*⟩

a·wash [ə'wɒʃ] *adj, adv* (never before the noun) **1** floating. **2** flooded.

a·way [ə'wei] *adv* **1** to or at a distance: *away from home. Get away from the fire.* **2** in another direction: *turn away.* **3** out of one's possession or use: *He gave his boat away.* **4** somewhere else, esp in a storage place: *to stash candy away.* **5** out of existence: *The sound faded away.* **6** continuously and with concentration: *working away at her project.* **7** off (so as to launch an action): *Away we go!* *adj* **1** at a distance. **2** absent: *Who is away today?* **3** hosted by the other team: *an away game.* ⟨Old English *onweg*⟩
away back *Informal* far back in space or time.
away with a go or take away: *Away with you now!* **b** a general expression of denunciation: *Away with taxes!* **do away with a** put an end to; get rid of. **b** kill. **from away ✱** in the Atlantic Provinces, from outside the province or region.

awe [ɒ] *n* **1** wonder and reverence inspired by something sacred or magnificent: *I gazed in awe at the mountains towering above me.* **2** respect or fear: *They were in awe of the old woman's disapproval.*
v fill with awe. ⟨Old Norse *agi*⟩
awe·some *adj* **1** causing awe: *an awesome sight.* Also, **awe–in·spir·ing.** **2** *Slang* a generalized term of approval: *awesome desserts.* **awe·some·ly** *adv.* **awe·some·ness** *n.* **awe–struck** *adj* filled with awe.

aw·ful ['ɒfəl] *adj* **1** dreadful; terrible: *an awful storm.* **2** *Informal* very bad, ugly, etc.: *an awful mess.* **3** deserving great respect and reverence; awesome: *the awful power of God.* **4** *Slang* very: *She's awful mad.* **aw·ful·ness** *n.* **aw·ful·ly** ['ɒfli] *or* ['ɒfəli] *adv.* ⟨awe + -ful⟩

a·while [ə'wail] *adv* for a short time.

awk·ward ['ɒkwərd] *adj* **1** clumsy: *The seal is awkward on land, but graceful in the water.* **2** not well suited to use: *The handle has an awkward shape.* **3** embarrassing; embarrassed: *an awkward question. I feel rather awkward about it.* **awk·ward·ly** *adv.* **awk·ward·ness** *n.* ⟨obsolete *awk* perversely + -*ward*⟩

awl [ɒl] *n* a pointed tool used for making holes in leather or wood. ⟨Old English *al*⟩

awn [ɒn] *n* one of the bristly hairs extending from the spikelets of some cereal grains. **awn·less** *adj.* ⟨Old Norse *ögn* chaff⟩

awn·ing ['ɒnɪŋ] *n* a rooflike structure of metal, canvas, etc. spread over a frame and attached over a door, window, etc. as protection from the sun or rain. ⟨origin uncertain⟩

a·woke See AWAKE.

A.W.O.L., a.w.o.l., or **AWOL** ['eiwɒl] absent without leave.

a·wry [ə'rai] *adv, adj* (never precedes a noun) **1** with a twist or turn to one side: *Her hat was blown awry by the wind.* **2** wrong: *Our plans have gone awry.* ⟨wry⟩

axe [æks] *n* a tool for chopping and splitting wood, etc., consisting of a sharp-edged, heavy metal head on a long wooden handle. *v* **1** chop with an axe. **2** *Informal* remove: *Several budget items were axed due to lack of funds.* Rarely, **ax. axe·like** *adj.* ⟨Old English *æx*⟩ **get the axe** *Informal.* **a** be dismissed from a job. **b** be removed, ended, etc. **have an axe to grind a** have a special, usually selfish and covert, agenda. **b** have a grievance to settle.

ax·el ['æksəl] *n* Figure skating a jump in which the skater takes off from one foot, makes one and a half turns in the air, and lands on the other foot. (< *Axel* Paulson, Norwegian skater)

ax·es¹ ['æksəz] *n* pl of AXE.

ax·es² ['æksiz] *n* pl of AXIS.

ax·il ['æksɪl] *n* Botany the angle between the upper side of a leaf or stem and the supporting stem or branch. **ax·il·lar·y** ['æksə,lɛri] *adj.* ⟨Latin *axilla* armpit⟩

ax·i·ol·o·gy [,æksi'ɒlədʒi] *n* the branch of philosophy dealing with moral and aesthetic values. **ax·i·o·log·i·cal** *adj.* **ax·i·o·log·i·cal·ly** *adv.* **ax·i·ol·o·gist** *n.* ⟨Greek *axios* worthy + English -*logy*⟩

ax·i·om ['æksiəm] *n* **1** a self-evident truth: *It is an axiom that if equals are added to equals the results will be equal.* **2** an established principle. **ax·i·o·mat·ic** *adj.* ⟨Greek *axiōma; axios* worthy⟩

ax·is ['æksɪs] *n, pl* **ax·es** [-siz] **1** a line that passes through an object and around which the object turns or seems to turn. The earth's axis is an imaginary line through the North and South Poles. **2** a numbered line for positioning coordinates, as on a graph. **3** a principal line or linear structure around which parts are regularly arranged. **4 a** an alignment; relationship thought of as a line joining entities. **b the Axis** specifically, in World War II, Germany, Italy, Japan, and their allies. **ax·i·al** *adj.* **ax·i·al·ly** *adv.* ⟨Latin⟩

axial flow the flow of air along the longitudinal axis of a jet engine.

ax·le ['æksəl] *n* a bar on or with which a single wheel or set of wheels turns. ⟨Old English *eaxl* shoulder, crossbar; influenced by Old Norse *öxul* axle⟩
ax·le·tree *n* a crossbar joining two wheels.

ax·o·lotl ['æksə,lɒtəl] *n* any of several species of salamander, found in certain lakes of Mexico and the W United States, that ordinarily never lose their gills but otherwise live and breed like other salamanders. ⟨Nahuatl = servant of water⟩

ax·on ['æksɒn] *n* the part of a nerve cell that carries impulses away from the cell body. Also, **axone**. **ax·on·al** ['æksənəl] *adj.* ⟨Greek *axōn* axis⟩

a·yah ['ɑjə] *n* a maid or nurse in India and related cultures. ⟨Hindi *āya;* Portuguese *aia* governess⟩

a·ya·tol·lah [,ɑjə'toulə] *n* 1 a title of respect given to the most eminent scholars in Shiite Islamic theology and law. 2 *Informal* a person having or aspiring to great authority: *the ayatollahs of the media.* ⟨Persian *ayat* sacred mark or sign + *ollah* God⟩

aye¹ or **ay** [ei] *adv* always; ever. ⟨Old Norse *ei*⟩

aye² or **ay** [aɪ] *adv* yes: *Aye, aye, captain.*
n an affirmative answer, vote, or voter: *The ayes were in the majority.* ⟨origin uncertain⟩

ay·ur·ve·da [,ɑjʊr'veidə] *n* traditional Hindu herbal medicine dating from the 1st century A.D. ⟨Sanskrit *ayur* life + *veda* knowledge⟩

a·zal·ea [ə'zeiljə] *n* any of various species and cultivated varieties of rhododendron, esp those with deciduous leaves. ⟨Greek *azaleos* dry; *azein* parch⟩

a·zan [ɑ'zɑn] *or* [ə'zæn] *n* the Muslim call to public prayer, proclaimed five times a day by the muezzin, or crier, from the minaret of a mosque. ⟨Arabic *adhān* invitation⟩

az·i·muth ['æzəməθ] *n Astronomy* the angular distance east or west from a point due north: *A star due northeast from the observer has an azimuth of 45°E.* *Abbrev* **az. az·i·muth·al** *adj.* ⟨Arabic *as-sumūt* the ways⟩

a·zo·ic [ei'zouɪk] *adj* lifeless; showing no evidence of life. ⟨Greek *a-* no + *zōē* life⟩

Az·tec ['æztɛk] *n* 1 a member of the Indian people that ruled Mexico before its conquest by the Spaniards in 1519. 2 the language of this people. **Az·tec** *adj.*

az·ure ['æʒʊr], ['æʒər], *or* ['eiʒər] *adj* blue; sky blue. ⟨Old French *l'azur*, from Persian *lajward* lapis lazuli⟩
az·u·rite *n* a blue copper ore; a basic carbonate of copper.

Bb

b or **B** [bi] *n, pl* **b's** or **B's 1** the second letter of the English alphabet, or any speech sound represented by it. **2** the second person or thing in a series: *Part B.* **3 B** the second-highest grade in a rating system: *a B movie.* **4** *Music* the seventh tone in the scale of C major. **5 B** the type of human blood containing antigen B, one of the four main types in the ABO system. **6 B** a symbol used on pencils indicating degree of softness.
plan B a course of action to fall back on if the preferred plan fails.

baa [bæ] *or* [bɑ] *n, v* bleat. ⟨imitative⟩

bab·ble ['bæbəl] *v* **1** make indistinct sounds like a baby. **2** talk foolishly or too much. **3** make a soft flowing noise. **bab·ble** *n.* **bab·bler** *n.* ⟨Middle English *babel*; imitative⟩

babe [beib] *n* **1** *Poetic* a baby. **2** an innocent or inexperienced person. ⟨Middle English⟩
babe in arms a very young baby. **babe in the wood** (or **woods**) a naive, childlike person.

ba·bel ['bæbəl] *or* ['beibəl] *n* a confusion of many different sounds. ⟨*Babel*, biblical tower where God confused builders' languages⟩

ba·biche [bæ'biʃ] *n* ✷ rawhide thongs or lacings used to make snowshoes. ⟨Cdn. French, from Algonquian⟩

ba·boon [bə'bun] *n* **1** any of various large, fierce monkeys having a doglike face. **2** a boorish or foolish person. **ba·boon·er·y** *n.* **ba·boon·ish** *adj.* ⟨Old French *babouin* stupid person⟩

ba·bush·ka or **ba·boush·ka** [bə'buʃkə] *n* **1** a kerchief knotted under the chin. **2** term of affection for an elderly woman. ⟨Russian = grandmother; *baba* old woman⟩

ba·by ['beibi] *n* **1** a very young child or animal. **2** the youngest of a family or group. **3** a childish person. **4** *Slang* a project that is held dear or is a source of pride. **5** *Slang* general term of appreciation or endearment: *This baby here is our best sedan. Baby, I love you.* *adj* **1** of, for, or suited to a baby: *baby shoes, a baby face.* **2** small of its kind: *my baby finger.* *v* **1** treat as a baby: *to baby a sick child.* **2** handle very carefully: *to baby a new car.* **ba·by·hood** *n.* ⟨Middle English *babe*⟩
throw the baby out with the bathwater lose the good in one's zeal to get rid of the bad.
baby beef the meat of a young beef animal. **baby blue** pale blue. **baby blues** *n pl Informal* mild depression following childbirth. **baby bonus** ✷ *Informal* the FAMILY ALLOWANCE. **baby boom** the marked increase in the birth rate (1945-1965) following World War II. **baby boomer** *n.* **baby carriage** or (*Informal*) **buggy** a light carriage used for wheeling a baby. **baby dolls** a woman's pyjamas consisting of a short, sheer top worn with matching bikini panties. **baby grand** a small GRAND PIANO. **ba·by·ish** *adj* very immature; silly. **baby's breath** or **babies'-breath** any of various

plants of the pink family, with many tiny white or pink flowers on delicate stems. **ba·by·sit** *v* **-sat, -sit·ting** take care of (a child) during the temporary absence of the parents. **ba·by·sit·ter** *n.* **baby tooth** one of the first set of teeth of a child or young animal.

bac·ca·lao [,bækə'leiou] ✷ **1** dried, salted cod. **2 baccalao bird** in coastal Labrador and NE Newfoundland, any of several birds of the family Alcidae. ⟨Portuguese *bacalhau*⟩

bac·ca·lau·re·ate [,bækə'lɔriit] *n* **1** a bachelor's degree. **2** a speech delivered to a graduating class. ⟨Latin *baccalaureus* bachelor⟩

bac·ca·rat [,bækə'rɑ] *or* ['bækə,rɑ] *n* a card game played for money. ⟨French⟩

bac·cha·na·li·a [,bækə'neiliə] *n pl* a wild party. **bac·cha·na·li·an** *adj, n.* ⟨Latin, name of a festival in honour of *Bacchus* god of wine⟩

bach·e·lor ['bætʃələr] *n* **1** an unmarried man. **2** a holder of the first degree offered by a university or college. **bach·e·lor·hood** *n.* ⟨Latin *baccalarius* young man⟩
bach ['bætʃ] *v Informal* live on one's own, esp temporarily (often with *it*): *She's baching it while her parents are away.* **bachelor apartment** or **suite** a small apartment with the living room doubling as the only bedroom. **bach·e·lor·ette** *n* ✷ a very small apartment consisting of one room, with kitchen and lounge facilities, and a separate bathroom.

ba·cil·lus [bə'siləs] *n, pl* **-li** [-lai] *or* [-li] **1** any of a genus of rod-shaped aerobic bacteria. **2** loosely, any bacterium. **ba·cil·lar** [bə'silər] *or* ['bæsələr] *adj.* ⟨Latin = little rod⟩
ba·cil·li·form *adj* rod-shaped.

back [bæk] *n* **1** the part of a person's body opposite the chest and abdomen. **2** the upper part of an animal's body from the neck to the end of the backbone. **3** SPINE (def. 1). **4** the side opposite the front: *the back of the head.* **5** the side not meant to be displayed: *the back of a rug.* **6** the part toward the far end: *the back of the garden.* **7** *Sports* a player whose position is behind the front line.
adj **1** opposite or behind the front: *the back seat of a car.* **2** directed backward: *a back flip.* **3** past: *back issues of a magazine.* **4** in distant or frontier regions: *back country.*
v **1** support or favour: *to back someone's plan.* **2** support financially: *The show is backed by a group of local businesses.* **3** move or cause to move backward: *to back a car into a driveway.* **4** bet on: *to back a horse.* **5** have the back facing toward (with *on* or *onto*): *Our house backs onto a park.* **6** be at the back of: *A forest backed the farm.* **7** coat, line, or reinforce the back of: *a photo backed with cardboard.* **8** *Meteorology* of the wind, switch direction.
adv **1** to or toward the rear: *Please step back.* **2** in or into the original place or condition: *Put the books back.* **3** in or toward the past: *some years back.* **4** in return: *to pay back a favour.* **5** in check: *Hold back your temper.* **back·less** *adj.* ⟨Old English *bæc*⟩
back and fill a trim a boat's sails so as to keep with the current. **b** of cars, etc., go forward and backward alternately in order to get out

of mud or snow or make a difficult turn. **c** keep changing one's mind. **back and forth** first one way, then the other: *to pace back and forth*. **back down** give up a challenge. **back into** *Informal* get by accident: *He backed into a place on the team when our goalie fell ill*. **back of** or **in back of** *Informal* behind: *The shed is back of the house*. **back off** a move backward in retreat. **b** become less aggressive, insistent, etc. **back out (of)** *Informal* **a** withdraw from (an undertaking). **b** break (a promise). **back to back** **1** with backs facing each other. **2** consecutively. **back–to–back** *adj*. **back up a** move backward. **b** support. **c** *Computers* save a copy of: *Back your files up*. **d** clog; jam: *Traffic was backed up*. **behind someone's back** secretly. **(flat) on one's back** bedridden. **get off someone's back** *Informal* stop criticizing someone. **get** (or **put**) **one's** (or **someone's**) **back up** *Informal* make or become angry and stubborn: *Now, don't get your back up*. **go back on** *Informal* not be faithful to (one's promises, etc.). **on someone's back** *Informal* continually criticizing a person. **put one's back into** work hard at. **turn one's back on** reject or ignore. **with one's back to the wall** in a desperate situation with no options.

back·ache *n* a continuous pain in the back. **back bacon** ✱ bacon cut from the loin, having little fat and a hamlike flavour. **back bench** Usually, **back benches** *pl* in a legislature, the seats of members who are not part of the cabinet nor leading members of an opposition party. **back·bench** or **back–bench** *adj*. **back·bench·er** *n*. **back·bite** *v* **-bit**, **-bit·ten** or **-bit**, **-bit·ing** say spiteful things about (an absent person). **back·bit·er** *n*. **back·board** *n* a board that forms the back or support of something. **back·bone** *n* **1** SPINAL COLUMN. **2** the chief support: *She is the backbone of the organization*. **3** strength of character: *A coward lacks backbone*. **back·break·ing** *adj* physically very tiring. **back burner** a heating element at the back of a stove. **on the back burner** *Informal* in abeyance. **back·chat** *n* *Informal* disrespectful retorts. **back·check** *v* **1** examine (completed work) to verify its accuracy. **2** *Hockey* skate back toward one's own goal to cover an opponent's rush. **back concessions** ✱ *Ontario and Québec* rural areas as opposed to urban centres. **back country** a region away from any centre of population. **back–coun·try** *adj*. **back·cross** *v* *Horticulture* cross (a hybrid) with its parent. **back·date** *v* put a date on (something) earlier than the actual date. **back·door** *adj* **1** underhand. **2** of or near a back door to a building: *the backdoor stairway*. **back·drop** *n* **1** the curtain at the back of a stage. **2** the background to anything. **back East** ✱ in or to eastern Canada. **back·er** *n* a sponsor. **back·fill** *v* refill (an excavation) with soil or other material. **back·fire** *v* **1** of an engine or gun, have gases or charges explode too soon or the wrong way. **2** *Informal* of a plan, have unexpected, unfavourable results for the planner. *n* **1** the fact of backfiring. **2** a fire set to check a fire by burning off the area in front of it. **back**

formation a word formed from another word of which it appears to be the root. *Example: burgle* from *burglar*. **back forty** ✱ the part of a farm farthest from the house. **back·gam·mon** ['bæk͵gæmən] *or* [͵bæk'gæmən] *n* a board game for two played with pieces moved according to the throw of dice. **back·ground** *n* **1** the part of a scene farthest from the viewer: *a lake scene with mountains in the background*. **2** a surface against which things are seen: *fabric with pink flowers on a white background*. **3** conditions preceding or surrounding an event that help to explain it: *the background to World War I*. **4** one's past experience. **5** the accompanying music or sound effects in a play, film, etc. **in the background** not prominent. **back·hand** *n* a stroke made with the back of the hand turned forward, esp in racquet sports. **back·hand·ed** *adj* **1** done or made with the back of the hand turned forward. **2** awkward. **3** ambiguous: *a backhanded compliment*. **back·hoe** *n* a large digging machine. **back·ing** *n* help or support, esp financial or political. **back·lash** *n* a sudden hostile reaction to an earlier action or popular trend. **back·light** *v* **-lit**, **-light·ing** light from behind. **back·list** *n* previous publications that are still in print. **back·log** *n* an accumulation of tasks, orders, etc. that have not yet been fulfilled: *The company hired extra staff to help clear the backlog of orders*. **back nine** *Golf* the last nine holes (10 through 18). **back number a** an old issue of a magazine or newspaper. **b** an outdated person or an obsolete thing. **back order** an order for goods not currently in stock. **back–or·der** *v*. **back·pack** *n* a lightweight bag strapped onto a person's back for carrying things. *v* carry in a backpack. **back·pack·er** *n*. **back·pack·ing** *n*. **back·ped·al** *v* **-alled** or **-aled**, **-al·ling** or **-al·ing** **1** move the pedals of a bicycle backward. **2** retreat from an opinion, promise, etc. **back·rest** *n* anything that supports the back. **back road** a little-used rural road. **back·room** *adj* working behind the scenes. **back–scratch·er** *n* **1** a device for scratching the back. **2** *Informal* a person who tries to gain advancement by flattering a superior. **back·scratch·ing** *n*. **back seat 1** a seat at or in the back. **2** *Informal* a less powerful position. **back–seat driver 1** a passenger in an automobile who criticizes and advises the driver. **2** a person who offers criticism and advice without assuming any responsibility. **back·side** *n* **1** the back. **2** the buttocks. **back·slap** *v* **-slapped**, **-slap·ping** slap on the back in an overly friendly way. **back·slap·per** *n*. **back·slide** *v* **-slid**, **-slid** or **-slid·den**, **-slid·ing** slide back into wrongdoing; lose one's zeal, esp for religion. **back·slid·er** *n*. **back·space** *v* use the keyboard to move the cursor on a computer screen backward. **back·spin** *n* a reverse spin given to a ball, hoop, etc., causing it to rebound from a surface at a different angle from the angle at which it hit. **back·split** *n* a SPLIT-LEVEL home in which the back is divided into two floors, one higher than the front and one lower.

back–stab·ber *n* *Informal* one who secretly harms a supposed friend. **back·stage** *adv, adj* **1** in the dressing rooms of a theatre. **2** toward the rear of a stage. **3** not known to the general public. **back·stairs** *adj* secret or underhand: *backstairs political bargaining.* Also, **back·stair.** **back stairs 1** stairs in the back part of a house; formerly, those used mainly by servants. **2** a secret or underhanded method. **back·stitch** *n* a stitching method in which the thread doubles back each time on the preceding stitch. **back·stitch** *v.* **back·stop** *n* **1** *Sports* a fence or screen used to keep the ball from going too far. **2** *Baseball* a catcher. **3** any person or thing that acts as a support. **back·stretch** *n* **1** the part of a racetrack farthest from the winning post. Compare HOME STRETCH. **2** the stables, bunkhouses, etc., near a racetrack. **back·stroke** *n* **1** a swimming stroke made lying on one's back. **2** a backhanded stroke. **back·swing** *n* *Golf, tennis, etc.* a raising of the club or racquet up and behind the player's hand to give momentum to a following forward stroke. **back·talk** *n* *Informal* disrespectful retorts. **back·track** *v* **1** go back over a course or path. **2** withdraw from a position: *He backtracked on the claim he made last week.* **back·up** *n* **1** a person, group, or thing that serves as a support or substitute. **2** an accumulation due to delay, obstruction, etc.: *a backup of traffic.* **3** *Computers* a copy of programs or data saved separately in case the originals are destroyed or lost. **back·ward** *adv* **1** toward the back: *She glanced backward.* **2** with the back foremost: *trying to walk backward.* **3** opposite to the usual way: *to read backward.* **4** from better to worse: *Economic conditions went backward.* Also, **backwards.** *adj* **1** directed toward the back: *a backward look.* **2** done in reverse order. **3** slow in development: *a backward child.* **back·ward·ness** *n.* **bend** (or **lean** or **fall**) **over backwards** be very accommodating. **back·wash** *n* the water thrown back by the passing of a ship, etc. **back·wash** *v.* **back·wa·ter** *n* **1** a stretch of still water close to the bank of a river. **2** a place thought of as backward: *a cultural backwater.* **back·woods** *n pl* uncleared forests or wild areas far away from towns. *adj* rustic; crude; rough. **back·woods·man** *n.* **back·yard** *n* a yard behind a house. **in one's own backyard** in one's own domain: *We have a lot of talented people right here in our own backyard.* **not in my backyard** an expression of protest against something considered unpleasant coming into one's neighbourhood. Often abbreviated to NIMBY ['nɪmbi].

ba·con ['beikən] *n* salted and smoked meat from the back and sides of a pig. ⟨Old French⟩ **bring home the bacon** *Informal* **a** succeed. **b** be the breadwinner; earn an income.

bac·te·ri·a [bæk'tiriə] *n pl, sg* **-te·ri·um** a group of one-celled micro-organisms found wherever there is life, in soil, water, and air, and within other organisms. **bac·te·ri·al** *adj.* ⟨Greek *baktērion*, diminutive of *baktron* stick⟩

bac·te·ri·cide [bæk'tirə,saɪd] *n* a substance that kills bacteria. **bac·te·ri·ol·o·gy** *n* the science dealing with bacteria. **bac·te·ri·o·log·i·cal** *adj.* **bac·te·ri·ol·o·gist** *n.*

bad [bæd] *adj* **worse, worst 1** poor in quality or skill: *bad poetry, bad light.* **2** unpleasant or distressing: *bad news.* **3** severe: *a bad storm.* **4** evil: *a bad influence.* **5** naughty: *Don't be a bad girl!* **6** harmful: *Sugar is bad for your teeth.* **7** sorry: *I feel bad about your loss.* **8** not valid: *a bad cheque.* **9** defective: *a bad disk, bad grammar.* **10** rotten; spoiled: *bad meat.* **11** sick; suffering: *The patient is very bad today.* *adv* *Slang* badly: *It hurts bad.* **bad·ness** *n.* ⟨Middle English *badde*⟩
go bad **a** become spoiled or rotten: *The leftovers went bad.* **b** develop a bad moral character. **in bad** *Informal* in disfavour (*with* someone): *I'm in bad with my sister.* **not bad** acceptable. **not half bad** better than average. **not so bad** better than expected or assumed. **to the bad** in debt or having lost: *We are now several hundred dollars to the bad.*
bad blood an unfriendly feeling: *The bad blood between them grew to a feud.* **bad·die** *n* *Informal* a villain in a story or film, etc. **bad egg** a bad person. **bad·lands** *n* a barren region of rock formations caused by erosion, as in Saskatchewan and Alberta. **bad·ly** *adv* **1** in a bad manner. **2** greatly: *Rain is badly needed.* **bad–mouth** *v* speak badly of: *to bad-mouth an opponent.* **bad–tem·pered** *adj* **1** angry; cross: *a bad-tempered remark.* **2** of a horse or other animal, hard to manage.

bade See BID.

badge [bædʒ] *n* **1** a pin, cloth logo, name tag, etc. worn on one's clothing as a sign of affiliation or rank, reward for achievement, etc. **2** any identifying symbol or sign: *The traditional badge of office of a mayor is a chain.* ⟨Middle English *bage*⟩

badg·er ['bædʒər] *n* any of various nocturnal burrowing animals of the weasel family with a heavy body and sharp claws. ⟨possibly from *badge*, for white spot on its head⟩ *v* annoy or harass by persistent questioning, nagging, coaxing, etc.: *badgered by pushy salespeople. The lawyer is badgering the witness.*

bad·min·ton ['bædmɪntən] *n* a game in which players use light racquets to volley a shuttlecock over a high net. ⟨name of the Duke of Beaufort's estate⟩

baf·fle ['bæfəl] *v* be too hard for (a person) to solve or understand: *This puzzle baffles me.* *n* a wall, screen, or similar device controlling the flow of air, water, etc. by hindering its movement or changing its course. **baf·fler** *n.* **baf·fle·ment** *n.* **baf·fling** *adj.* ⟨origin uncertain⟩ **baf·fle·gab** ['bæfəl,gæb] *n* meaningless or incomprehensible talk designed to impress, confuse, or equivocate.

bag [bæg] *n* **1** a nonrigid container made of paper, leather, etc. that can close at the top. **2** a suitcase or purse. **3** a loose bulge: *bags under one's eyes.* **4** the game caught by a hunter in one trip. **5** *Baseball* a base. **6** *Informal* one's particular interest, area of skill, etc.: *Math was never his bag.*
v **bagged, bag·ging 1** put into a bag: *to bag groceries.* **2** swell or bulge: *His pants bag at the knees.* **3** kill or catch in a hunt. **4** *Informal* get; take; steal. ⟨Old Norse *baggi* pack⟩
bag and baggage with all one's belongings. **in the bag** *Informal* certain to succeed or be obtained: *That contract is in the bag.* **leave someone holding the bag** *Informal* leave a person to take all the responsibility or blame. **bag·ful** *n* **1** the amount held by a bag. **2** *Informal* a lot. **bagged** *adj Slang* **1** exhausted. **2** drunk. **bag·gy** *adj* of clothing: **1** loose; oversized. **2** bulging limply. **bag lady** a homeless woman carrying all her possessions in shopping bags.

ba·gel [ˈbeigəl] *n* a doughnut-shaped bread roll of yeast dough, simmered in water and then baked. ⟨Yiddish *beigel* ring⟩

bag·gage [ˈbægɪdʒ] *n* **1** suitcases, bags, etc. taken on a trip; luggage. **2** the equipment accompanying an army. **3** Sometimes, **excess baggage**, anything that burdens or hinders; often, learned negative behaviours, grudges, emotional wounds, etc. ⟨Old French *bagage*⟩
baggage car a railway car for passengers' baggage.

USAGE

Baggage (def. 1) and **luggage** are synonymous in Canadian English, but **luggage** is limited to suitcases and other bags carried by hand, whereas **baggage** may include boxes and crates, or large items shipped separately. Only **luggage** is used for suitcases, etc. when they are empty: *She bought a new set of luggage.*

bag·gat·a·way [bəˈgætəˌwei] *n* ✳ formerly, a game of the First Nations of eastern Canada, from which lacrosse developed. Also, **bag·gat·i·way.** ⟨Algonquian⟩

bag·pipe [ˈbægˌpəip] *n* Usually, **bagpipes** *pl* a musical wind instrument in which the sound is produced by pipes supplied with air from a bag held under the arm and inflated by blowing through a mouthpiece.

ba·guette [bæˈgɛt] *n* **1** a long, narrow loaf of bread. **2** a gem cut in a narrow oblong shape. ⟨French; Italian *bacchetta* small stick⟩

bah [bɑ] *interj* an exclamation of contempt.

Ba·hai [bəˈhaɪ] *or* [ˈbɑhaɪ] *n* **1** a follower of 19c prophet **Ba·ha Ul·lah** [bɑˌhɑ ʊˈlɑ], born Mirza Hussein Ali Nuri in Persia, who taught the basic unity of all faiths. **2** the religion of Bahais. **Ba·hai** *adj*. **Ba·haism** *n*. ⟨Persian⟩

bail[1] [beil] *n* money that must be given as security to set an arrested person free until he or she is due to appear for trial.
v obtain the freedom of by paying bail. ⟨French *baillier* deliver; Latin *bajulare* carry⟩
bail out a pay the bail for. **b** help out of a

difficulty, esp financially. **bail·out** *n.* **go** (or **stand**) **bail for a** pay bail for. **b** vouch for; guarantee: *I'll go bail for their good behaviour on the trip.* **jump bail** disobey court orders by not appearing at one's trial. **out on bail** released from jail while awaiting trial.

bail[2] [beil] *n* a scoop used to throw water out of a boat. **bail** *v.* ⟨Latin *bajulus* carrier⟩
bail out a make an emergency jump with a parachute from an aircraft. **b** throw water out of (a boat) with a container. **bail·out** *n.*

bail·iff [ˈbeilɪf] *n* **1** an official in charge of writs, processes, arrests, etc. **2** a court officer in charge of prisoners appearing for trial. **3** the overseer of an estate. **4** a creditor's agent who seizes goods in lieu of payment. ⟨Old French *baillif;* Latin *bajulus* carrier⟩

bail·i·wick [ˈbeiləˌwɪk] *n* **1** the jurisdiction of a sheriff or bailiff. **2** the place, field of activity, etc. that a person is identified with: *She is a big name in her own bailiwick.* ⟨Middle English *bailie* Scottish town official + *wick* office⟩

Bai·ram [baɪˈrɑm] *n* either of two Muslim festivals, the **lesser Bairam,** following immediately after Ramadan, or the **greater Bairam,** occurring 70 days later. ⟨Turkish⟩

bairn [bɛrn] *n Scottish* child. ⟨Old English *bearn,* from *beran* to bear⟩

Bai·sak·hi Day [bəiˈsɑki] a Sikh festival in April commemorating the establishment by Guru Gobind Singh, of the Khalsa, or community of baptized Sikhs.

bait [beit] *n* **1** anything, esp food, used to attract animals so as to catch them. **2** anything used to lure or attract.
v **1** put bait on or in (a hook, trap, etc.). **2** lure or attract. **3** set dogs to attack (a chained animal): *Bears and bulls were formerly baited as sport.* **4** torment with unkind remarks. **bait·er** *n.* ⟨Old Norse *beita* cause to bite, and *beita* food⟩
bait–and–switch *n* fraudulent sales technique in which the customer is first lured by the promise of something cheaper which may not actually exist.

baize [beiz] *n* a thick green cloth with a nap, used especially for pool table covers. ⟨French *baies,* pl, chestnut-coloured. See BAY[s].⟩

bake [beik] *v* **1** cook (food) by dry heat. **2** dry or harden by heat: *to bake bricks.* **3** make or become very warm: *lie in the sun and bake.* **bak·er** *n.* **bak·ing** *n.* ⟨Old English *bacan*⟩
bake·ap·ple *n* ✳ *esp Atlantic Provinces* a creeping plant of the rose family that grows in swampy areas, with edible berries like small raspberries; cloudberry. **baked beans** dried beans baked for a long time with tomato sauce and spices. **bake–off** *n* a baking contest. **baker's dozen** thirteen. **bak·er·y** *n* a place where bread, pies, cakes, etc. are made or sold. Also, **bake shop. bake sale** a sale of homemade baked goods to raise money. **bake·ware** *n* pans, casserole dishes, etc. for baking. **baking powder** a mixture of baking soda, starch, and an acid compound

such as cream of tartar, used as a leavening agent. **baking soda** SODIUM BICARBONATE.

bak·la·va or **bac·la·va** ['bɑklə,va] or [,bɑklə'va] *n* a flaky Greek pastry made with nuts and honey. ⟨Turkish⟩

bak·sheesh or **bak·shish** ['bʌkʃiʃ], ['bakʃiʃ], or ['bækʃiʃ] *n* in Egypt, Turkey, India, etc., money given as a tip. Also, **back·sheesh, back·shish.** ⟨Persian = gift; *bakhshidan* give⟩

bal·a·clav·a [,bælə'klavə] or [,bælə'klævə] *n* a type of knitted headgear covering all of the head and neck except the eyes. Also, **balaclava helmet.** ⟨after Crimean War battle site⟩

bal·ance ['bæləns] *n* **1** a weighing device consisting of a horizontal bar freely suspended by its centre with a shallow pan hanging from each end. **2** the condition of having equal mass on each side. **3** good proportion in design, etc.: *a balance of colours.* **4** a contrasting element that offsets another of similar weight: *His humour serves as a balance for his strictness.* **5** steady condition, whether bodily, mental, or emotional: *She lost her balance and fell.* **6** *Accounting* equality of debit and credit. **7** the part left over: *They were dismissed for the balance of the term.* **bal·ance** *v.* **bal·anced** *adj.* **bal·anc·er** *n.* ⟨Latin *bilanx* two-scaled⟩ **in the balance** a undecided. b at stake. **on balance** overall; all things considered. **balance beam** a long, narrow piece of wood on supports, on which gymnasts perform. **balanced diet** a diet with optimal amounts of food from all four food groups. **balance of nature** *Ecology* interaction of different species and their habitat so that populations remain steady and the habitat unharmed. **balance of payments** a calculation of the credits and debits of an organization or country with respect to debtors and creditors. **balance of power 1** an even distribution of power. **2** the power of a small group to give control to a large group by joining forces with it. **balance of trade** the difference in value between the imports and the exports of a country. **balance sheet** a written statement showing the profits and losses, the assets and liabilities, and the net worth of a business.

bal·co·ny ['bælkəni] *n* **1** a projecting platform on the outside of a building. **2** in a theatre or hall, a projecting upper floor with seats for an audience. **bal·co·nied** *adj.* ⟨Italian *balcone; balco* scaffold⟩

bald [bɒld] *adj* **1** wholly or partly without hair on the head. **2** without natural covering such as trees: *bald prairie.* **3** bare; plain; unadorned: *bald facts.* **4** of tires, having little or no tread left. **bald·ly** *adv.* **bald·ness** *n.* ⟨Middle English *balled* from *ball* white spot⟩ **bald cypress** a large coniferous tree of the same family as the redwood. It is named for the fact that, unlike most conifers, it loses its leaves each fall. **bald eagle** a large North American eagle having plumage that is mainly dark brown, with pure white on the head, neck, and tail. **bald–faced** *adj* brazen; bold: *a bald-faced lie.* **bald·head·ed** *adj* **1** with

little or no hair on the head. **2** ✱ devoid of trees or brush: *baldheaded prairie.* **bald·ing** *adj* becoming bald. **bal·dy** *n Informal* someone who is bald.

bal·der·dash ['bɒldər,dæʃ] *n* nonsense. ⟨16c slang for absurd mixture, e.g., milk and beer⟩

bale [beil] *n* a large, compact rectangular bundle of material, such as hay or newspapers, securely wrapped. **bale** *v.* ⟨Middle English⟩ **bal·er** *n* a machine that compresses and bundles such things as hay, paper, etc..

ba·leen [bei'lin] or [bə'lin] *n* an elastic horny substance that grows in large fringed sheets from the roof of the mouth of certain whales. It traps the plankton taken into the whale's mouth with water. ⟨Greek *phalaina* whale⟩ **baleen whale** any of a suborder of whales including right whales, rorquals, and blue whales, all lacking teeth but having baleen.

bale·ful ['beilfəl] *adj* evil; threatening or malevolent. **bale·ful·ly** *adv.* ⟨archaic *bale;* Old English *bealu*⟩

balk [bɒk] or [bɒlk] *v* **1** stop short and refuse to go on. **2** *Sports* **a** make an incomplete or misleading move. **b** *Baseball* cause (a runner on third base) to score by illegally faking a pitch. **3** draw back in fear or distaste: *The child balked at the rice pudding.* **balk** *n.* ⟨Old English *balca* ridge⟩ **balk·y** *adj* balking or likely to balk: *a balky horse.* **balk·i·ly** *adv.* **balk·i·ness** *n.*

bal·kan·ize ['bɒlkə,naɪz] *v* divide (a country or territory) into small independent units, as the countries of the Balkan Peninsula were divided after World War I. **bal·kan·i·za·tion** *n.*

ball¹ [bɒl] *n* **1** a round or oval object that is thrown, kicked, etc., in various games. **2** the game of baseball. **3** *Baseball* a ball pitched too high, too low, or not over the plate and not struck at by the batter. **4** anything round like a ball: *a ball of string.* **5** the roots of a live plant, collected in a bundle.
v make or form into a ball. ⟨Old Norse *böllr*⟩ **ball up 1** form a compact ball. **2** *Slang* mess up or confuse: *They balled it up so badly we had to start over.* **get** (or **keep**) **the ball rolling** get an activity started or keep it going. **on the ball** *Informal* mentally alert. **play ball a** begin or resume a ball game. **b** co-operate: *If everyone will play ball, we can get the job done quickly.* **the whole ball of wax** *Informal* the entire situation or collection.
ball and chain 1 a heavy metal ball attached by a short chain to the leg of a prisoner. **2** *Informal* anything that restricts freedom. **ball–and–sock·et joint** a flexible joint formed by a ball or knob fitting in a socket. **ball bearing 1** a bearing in which the shaft turns upon a number of freely moving metal balls contained in a grooved ring around the shaft. **2** any of the metal balls so used. **ball boy** (or **girl**) *Sports* a person who collects loose balls during a game, has charge of extra balls for drills, etc. **ball cock** or **ball valve** a device regulating the supply of water in a tank, cistern, etc. by means of a buoyant ball attached to a valve. **ball·game** *n* a baseball

game. **a whole new** (or **other**) **ball game**
Informal a totally different situation. **ball
hockey** a hockeylike game played with
hockey sticks and a tennis ball, usually on
pavement. **ball joint** a BALL-AND-SOCKET JOINT
transferring motion from the tie rods to the
wheels of a motor vehicle. **ball lightning**
lightning in the form of a red-orange ball
that moves quickly before disintegrating.
ball·park *n* a stadium for playing baseball or
football. **in the ballpark** *Informal* **a** of an
estimate, fairly close. **b** meeting minimum
requirements. **ballpark figure** *Informal* a
rough estimate. **ball–peen hammer** ['bɒl
‚pin] a hammer with one end of the head
rounded like a ball, for shaping metal, etc.
ball·play·er *n* **1** a baseball player. **2** a member
of any team. **ball·point** (**pen**) *n* a pen with a
small metal ball in place of a nib.

ball² [bɒl] *n* **1** a large, formal party with
dancing. **2** *Informal* a lot of fun: *We had a ball
on the water slide.* ⟨Latin *ballare* to dance⟩
ball·room *n* a large hall for dancing.
ballroom dancing formal dancing in couples,
with waltzes, tangos, etc.

bal·lad ['bæləd] *n* **1** a simple song or poem
telling a story. **2** a popular love song, usually
slow. **bal·lad·eer** *n*. **bal·lad·ry** *n*. ⟨Old French
balade dancing song⟩

bal·last ['bæləst] *n* **1** weight carried in a ship,
dirigible, etc. to steady it. **2** anything that
steadies a person or thing. **3** the crushed rock
used for the bed of a road or train track.
bal·last *v*. ⟨Old Norse; *last* load⟩
ballast tube in fluorescent lighting, etc., a
device to keep the electric current constant.

bal·let [bæ'lei] *or* ['bælei] *n* an artistic dance
that usually tells a story or expresses a mood,
performed on stage by a soloist or a group.
bal·let·ic [bæ'lɛtɪk] *adj*. **bal·let·i·cal·ly** *adv*.
⟨French, diminutive of *bal* dance. See BALL².⟩
bal·le·ri·na [‚bælə'rinə] *n* a female ballet
dancer. **bal·let·o·mane** [bæ'lɛtə‚mein] *n* a
ballet enthusiast. **bal·let·o·ma·nia** *n*.

bal·lis·tics [bə'lɪstɪks] *n* **1** the properties of a
bullet, etc., that affect its trajectory. **2** the
science dealing with the motion of
projectiles. ⟨Greek *ballein* throw⟩
bal·lis·tic *adj* **1** to do with the motion of
projectiles. **2** of exercises, composed of jerky
movements. **bal·lis·ti·cal·ly** *adv*. **go ballistic**
Slang become suddenly extremely angry or
excited. **ballistic missile** a projectile launched
by a rocket, used especially as a long-range
weapon of offence.

bal·loon [bə'lun] *n* **1** an airtight rubber bag
filled with air or a gas lighter than air and
used as a toy or decoration. **2** a large cloth
bag held aloft by hot air inside it. **3** in
cartoons, an outlined space containing the
words of a speaker.
v swell out like a balloon. **bal·loon·ist** *n*.
bal·loon·like *adj*. ⟨Italian *ballone*, from *balla*
ball⟩

bal·lot ['bælət] *n* **1** a piece of paper or other
object used in voting. **2** the total number of
votes cast. **3** vote; voting process: *The ballot

went in her favour. **4** the list of candidates in
an election: *too late to get on the ballot.*
v vote or decide using ballots. ⟨Italian *ballota*
little ball (dropped in ballot box)⟩
ballot box the box into which voters put
their ballots.

bal·ly·hoo ['bæli‚hu] *n Informal* **1** sensational
advertising; hype. **2** an uproar or outcry.
v ['bæli‚hu] *or* [‚bæli'hu] make exaggerated
claims about. **bal·ly·hoo·er** *n*. ⟨origin uncertain⟩

balm [bɒm] *or* [bɑm] *n* **1** any of various
fragrant, oily, resinous substances obtained
from tropical trees, used to relieve pain or to
heal. **2** anything that soothes or comforts:
Kind words are a balm for wounded feelings.
3 any of various plants of the mint family
used as flavouring and in making perfume.
⟨Old French *basme*; Greek *balsamon* balsam⟩
balm of Gil·e·ad a small evergreen tree, or the
fragrant ointment made from its resin.

balm·y¹ ['bɒmi] *or* ['bɑmi] *adj* **1** soft; mild;
soothing: *balmy breezes.* **2** fragrant. ⟨*balm*⟩

balm·y² ['bɒmi] *or* ['bɑmi] *adj Informal* silly;
crazy. ⟨var. of *barmy*⟩

ba·lo·ney [bə'louni] *n Informal* **1** nonsense.
2 bologna. ⟨altered from *bologna*⟩

bal·sa ['bɒlsə] *n* **1** a tropical tree with very
light wood. **2** a raft, esp one consisting of
two or more floats. ⟨Spanish = raft⟩

bal·sam ['bɒlsəm] *n* **1** any of various
fragrant, resinous substances containing
benzoic acid, used in medicine and perfume.
2 any of various turpentines. **3** a tree that
yields balsam, esp the BALSAM FIR. **bal·sam·ic**
[bɒl'sæmɪk] *adj*. ⟨Greek *balsamon*⟩
balsam fir a fir with shiny, dark green
needles. **balsam poplar** a poplar with resin-
coated buds that have a strong balsam
odour; tacamahac.

bal·us·ter ['bæləstər] *n* one of a set of posts
supporting a railing, as along the edge of a
staircase. ⟨Greek *balaustion* pomegranate
blossom, for the orig shape⟩
bal·us·trade ['bælə‚streid] *or* [‚bælə'streid] *n*
an ornamental railing together with its
supporting balusters.

bam·bi·no [bæm'binou] *n, pl* **-nos** or **-ni** [-ni]
Italian **1** a baby; little child. **2** an image of the
infant Jesus. ⟨diminutive of *bambo* silly⟩

bam·boo [bæm'bu] *n* any of a family of
treelike tropical grasses with hollow, jointed
stems. ⟨Dutch *bamboes*, probably from Malay⟩
Bamboo Curtain an imaginary wall between
China and non-communist nations.

bam·boo·zle [bæm'buzəl] *v Informal* **1** trick;
defraud. **2** perplex; confuse. **bam·boo·zler** *n*.
bam·booz·le·ment *n*. ⟨origin uncertain⟩

ban¹ [bæn] *v* **banned, ban·ning** **1** prohibit;
forbid by law: *Swimming is banned in this lake.*
2 pronounce a curse on. **ban** *n*. ⟨Old English
bannan summon⟩

ban² [bæn] *n* **1** a public proclamation. **2** in
medieval times, the summoning of the king's
vassals for war. ⟨*ban¹*, fused with Old French
ban proclamation⟩

ba·nal [bə'næl] *or* [bə'nɑl] *adj* commonplace; trite or trivial: *banal remarks about the weather.* **ba·nal·i·ty** *n.* **ba·nal·ly** *adv.* ⟨related to *ban²* in sense 'open to the public'⟩

ba·na·na [bə'nænə] *n* 1 the long, curved fruit of any of a genus of tropical plants, with sweet, whitish pulp and a thick, yellow skin. 2 a person with reference to rank: *He's the top banana.* ⟨Portuguese or Spanish⟩
banana belt *Informal, often facetious* a region with a mild climate: *the banana belt of southwestern BC.* **banana oil** 1 a clear liquid smelling like bananas, used as a solvent and in flavourings. 2 *Slang* flattery. **banana republic** a small country dependent on a single crop. **bananas** *Slang* crazy; wild: *The fans went bananas when she came on stage.*

band¹ [bænd] *n* 1 a group moving or acting together: *a band of robbers.* 2 a group of musicians who play popular music together. 3 ✹ a group of First Nations people of a particular reserve or region, recognized by the Federal Government as an administrative unit under the Indian Act.
v join together in a group. ⟨Latin *banda*⟩
band council ✹ a group of First Nations people chosen to govern their band. **band·lead·er** *n* the chief player in a band of musicians. **band leader** an important person in a First Nations band. **band·mas·ter** *n* the conductor of a band of musicians. **band·shell** *n* an outdoor platform for musical concerts that has a shell-shaped rear wall. **band·stand** *n* 1 an outdoor platform, usually roofed, for band concerts. 2 a similar platform indoors. **band·wag·on** *n* a wagon carrying a musical band in a parade. **jump** (or **climb**, or **get**) **on the bandwagon** join a popular trend.

band² [bænd] *n* 1 a thin strip of material for binding, trimming, etc.: *a narrow band of lace, an elastic band.* 2 a stripe: *a white cup with a gold band near the rim.* 3 **bands** *pl* two strips hanging from the front of a collar in certain academic, clerical, or legal costumes. 4 a particular range of wavelengths of sound or light. 5 a plain finger ring: *a wedding band.* 6 anything that ties, binds, or unites: *the bands of love.* Compare BOND.
v 1 put a band on. 2 mark with stripes. ⟨French *bande*⟩
band·age *n* a strip of cloth used to bind up a wound, injured limb, etc. **band·age** *v.* **Band–Aid** *n Trademark* for minor wounds, a thin gauze pad attached to a strip of adhesive tape. **band·aid** *n* a temporary solution or stopgap. **band saw** a saw in the form of an endless steel belt. **band·width** *n* 1 *Radio, telecommunications* the range of frequencies necessary to send a certain signal. 2 *Computers* a measure of the connection between computers in terms of the maximum volume of data traffic it allows, expressed in bits per second.

ban·dan·a or **ban·dan·na** [bæn'dænə] *n* a large, colourful handkerchief. ⟨prob. Hindi *bandhnu* to tie for tie-dyeing⟩

ban·di·coot ['bændə,kut] *n* any of about 20 species of marsupial resembling kangaroos. ⟨Telugu *pandikokku* pig-rat⟩

ban·dit ['bændɪt] *n, pl* **ban·dits** or **ban·dit·ti** [bæn'dɪti] 1 a highwayman; robber. 2 anyone who steals, cheats, or defrauds. **ban·dit·ry** *n.* ⟨Italian *bandito,* pp of *bandire* banish⟩

ban·do·lier or **ban·do·leer** [,bændə'lir] *n* a belt worn over one shoulder, with loops to hold cartridges, etc. ⟨Spanish *bandolera*⟩

ban·dy¹ ['bændi] *v* 1 throw back and forth. 2 give and take; exchange: *To bandy words with a foolish person is a waste of time.* ⟨French *bander*⟩

ban·dy² ['bændi] *adj* bent or curved outward: *bandy legs.* ⟨French *bandé* bent⟩
ban·dy–leg·ged ['bændi ,lɛgɪd] or [,lɛgd] *adj.*

bane [bein] *n* 1 a cause of death, ruin, or harm: *Wild animals were the bane of the frontier village.* 2 (in compounds) poison: *ratsbane.* **bane·ful** *adj.* ⟨Old English *bana* murderer⟩

bang¹ [bæŋ] *n* 1 a sudden, loud noise. 2 a violent or noisy impact. 3 vigour, impetus: *to start a campaign off with a bang.* 4 *Slang* thrill: *They really got a bang out of the incident.*
v 1 make a sudden loud noise. 2 hit violently or sharply. 3 shut with a noise: *She banged the door as she went out.*
adv 1 violently and noisily: *The car went bang into a tree.* 2 precisely; squarely: *It ended bang at ten.* ⟨possibly Old Norse *banga* to hammer⟩
bang around *Informal* handle roughly. **bang on** *Informal* exactly right or on target: *Your answer is bang on.* **bang up** *Informal* damage or injure by violence: *The thugs banged up all the cars on the street.* (**more**) **bang for your buck** (greater) effect relative to the cost in effort, time, or money.
bang–up ['bæŋ,ʌp] *adj Slang* excellent: *a bang-up job.*

bang² [bæŋ] *n* Usually, **bangs** *pl* a trimmed fringe of hair falling on the forehead. ⟨short for *bangtail,* racehorse with clipped tail⟩

ban·gle ['bæŋgəl] *n* a rigid bracelet. ⟨Hindi *bangli* glass bracelet⟩

ban·ish ['bænɪʃ] *v* 1 cause to leave one's country, town, etc. as a punishment; exile. 2 get rid of; drive away: *to banish the blues.* **ban·ish·ment** *n.* ⟨Latin *bannire* ban⟩

SYNONYMS
Banish (def. 1) implies punishment by some authority: *Napoleon was banished to Elba.* **Exile** is broader; its agent may be the force of circumstances, fear of violence, etc.: *Famine has exiled many people.* **Deport** means to banish a person from a country of which he or she is not a citizen: *We deport immigrants who enter Canada illegally.*

ban·is·ter ['bænɪstər] *n* Often, **banisters** *pl* the railing of a staircase together with the balusters. Also, **ban·nis·ter.** ⟨var. of *baluster*⟩

ban·jo ['bændʒou] *n, pl* **-jos** or **-joes** a stringed musical instrument with a small round body and a long neck, played by plucking. **ban·jo·ist** *n.* ⟨Spanish *bandore;* Greek *pandoura,* three-stringed instrument⟩

bank¹ [bæŋk] *n* **1** a long pile or heap: *a bank of snow.* **2** the ground bordering a river. **3** a shallow place in an ocean; shoal: *the fishing banks of Newfoundland.* **4** a slope: *the bank of a corner on a race track.* **5** the tilting of an airplane to make a turn.
v **1** border with a bank or ridge. **2** form into a bank; pile up: *Clouds are banking along the horizon.* **3** slope. **4** tilt (an airplane) to make a turn. **5** lessen the draft and cover (a fire) with ashes or fresh fuel to slow the burning. **6** *Basketball* score by bouncing (the ball) off the backboard into the basket. **7** *Billiards* hit (a ball) so as to make it bounce back off the bank, or cushion. ⟨Old Norse⟩ **bank barn** ✴ esp in Ontario, a two-storey barn built into a hill so as to permit entry to the bottom level from one side and to the top level from the other. **bank·er** *n* ✴ a fisher or fishing vessel on the GRAND BANKS.

bank² [bæŋk] *n* **1** an institution dealing with money. **2** a container for saving small sums at home: *a piggy bank.* **3** in some games, the funds kept by the dealer for players' use. **4** a supply of anything, continually drawn on and replenished: *a blood bank, a food bank.* **5** *Computers* a section of memory.
v **1** put or keep (money) in a bank: *to bank one's savings.* **2** transact business with a bank: *He banks at this branch.* **bank·ing** *n*. ⟨Italian *banca* bench, money changers' table⟩ **bank on** depend on; be sure of. **bank·a·ble** *adj* **1** acceptable to a bank. **2** likely to be profitable. **3** that can be counted on. **bank account** an arrangement for keeping one's money in a bank until it is needed: *to open a bank account.* **bank·book** *n* a book containing a record of a person's account. **bank card** a card with a magnetic strip, allowing the holder to use a BANK MACHINE and to make purchases by instantaneous debit to his or her account. **bank draft** a cheque drawn by a bank on another bank. **bank·er** *n* **1** a person or company that manages a bank. **2** *Informal* any person who lends or advances money in order to make a profit: *a banker in a loan shark operation.* **bank machine** a machine allowing users to carry out bank transactions electronically, without the aid of a human teller. **bank note** a piece of paper currency. **Bank of Canada** an agent of the Government of Canada that issues all Canadian bank notes and executes national monetary policy. **bank rate** the standard rate of discount for a specified type of note, security, etc., set by a central bank. **bank·roll** *Informal n* the amount of money a person has in hand. *v* finance: *Several businesses bankrolled the theatre festival.* **bank·rupt** ['bæŋk,rʌpt] *adj* **1** legally declared unable to pay one's debts; at the end of one's financial resources. **2** completely lacking in some way: *bankrupt of ideas.* *n* a bankrupt person: *moral bankrupt.* *v* make bankrupt. **bank·rupt·cy** ['bæŋkrəpsi] *n*. ⟨Latin *rupta* fem. pp of *rumpere* break⟩

bank³ [bæŋk] *n* a row, tier, or close arrangement of things, as of switches on a panel, keys on a keyboard, etc.
v arrange in rows. ⟨Germanic; akin to BENCH⟩

ban·ner ['bænər] *n* **1** flag. **2** a slogan, advertisement, greeting, etc., on a long piece of cloth or paper, or displayed on a computer screen. **3** a large newspaper headline, usually extending across an entire page.
adj outstanding; worth celebrating: *This has been a banner year in sports at our school.* ⟨Old French *ban(i)ere*⟩

ban·nock ['bænək] *n* **1** a flat cake like a tea biscuit, usually unleavened, made from oatmeal or barley flour and baked or fried. **2** ✴ a similar cake made from wheat flour, sometimes leavened with baking powder, and often cooked over an open fire on the end of a stick. ⟨Old English *bannuc* bit, piece⟩

banns [bænz] *n pl* a public notice, given three times in church, that two people are to be married. ⟨*bann*, var. of *ban²*⟩

ban·quet ['bæŋkwɪt] *n* **1** a formal dinner with speeches. **2** any feast. ⟨Italian *banchetto*, diminutive of *banco* bench⟩

ban·shee ['bænˌʃi] *or* [ˌbæn'ʃi] *n* a spirit whose wails are supposed to presage a death. ⟨Irish *bean sidhe* woman of the fairies⟩

ban·tam ['bæntəm] *n* **1** Often, **Bantam** any of several breeds of dwarf ornamental fowl. **2** a small, aggressive person. **3** *Sports* **a** a class for players under 15. **b** Also, **ban·tam·weight**, a boxer who weighs between 51 and 54 kg.
adj small and light. ⟨probably from *Bantam*, city in Java⟩

ban·ter ['bæntər] *n* playful teasing; joking. **ban·ter** *v*. ⟨origin unknown⟩

ba·o·bab ['beiouˌbæb] *or* ['baouˌbæb] *n* a tall, tropical African tree with a very thick trunk. ⟨origin uncertain⟩

bap·tize ['bæptaɪz] *or* [bæp'taɪz] *v* **1** dip (a person) in water or sprinkle with water as a sign of cleansing from sin and of admission into a faith community. **2** name (a person) at baptism; christen. **3** purify, initiate, immerse, or name. **bap·tism** *n*. **bap·tis·mal** *adj*. **bap·tiz·er** *n*. ⟨Greek *baptizein; baptein* dip⟩ **baptism of fire 1** the first time a soldier is under fire. **2** a severe trial or test. **Bap·tist** *n* a member of a Christian church teaching that baptism should be given to adults only, by full immersion. **bap·tist·ry** ['bæptɪstri] *n* a tank, room, etc. where baptism is performed. Also, **bap·tis·ter·y** [bæp'tɪstəri].

bar¹ [bar] *n* **1** a long, evenly shaped piece of some solid: *a bar of soap.* **2** a rod put across a door, window, etc. to fasten it. **3** a hindrance or barrier: *Arrogance is a bar to making friends.* **4** a band of colour. **5** *Music* a unit of rhythm, represented on a staff. **6 a** a counter at which alcoholic drinks are served. **b** an establishment with such a counter. **c** a counter, kiosk, or other small place where specific goods or services are sold: *a snack bar.* **7 the bar a** the profession or community of lawyers: *Judges are chosen from the bar.* **b** the railing that separates the bench and the lawyers' seats from the rest of a courtroom.

8 a law court, or anything like this: *the bar of public opinion.* **9** *Archaic, poetic* the mouth of a harbour.
v **1** fasten or shut with a bar: *to bar a door.* **2** block: *The exit is barred by chairs.* **3** forbid. **4** mark with bands of colour. ⟨Latin *barra* thick ends of bushes; Celtic⟩
bar none with no exception. **cross the bar** die. **bar·bell** *n* a long bar with weights at each end, used for lifting exercises. **bar code** a set of lines printed on a package, encoding price and inventory data, to be electronically scanned into a computer by a **bar–code reader. bar·fly** *n* a person who spends much time in bars or taverns. **bar graph** a chart showing different quantities by means of vertical or horizontal bars of proportional lengths. **bar·hop** *v* **-hopped, -hop·ping** go from bar to bar, drinking at each. **bar·keep·er** *n* bartender. **bar line** *Music* the vertical line between two measures on a staff. **bar·maid** *n* a woman who works in a bar, serving customers. **bar·man** *n, pl* **-men** a male barkeeper. **barred owl** a fairly large owl with a striped breast. **bar·ring** *prep* assuming the absence of: *Barring accidents, we should reach Iqaluit at noon.* **bar·room** *n* a room with a bar for the sale of alcoholic drinks. **bar·tend·er** *n* a person who mixes or serves alcoholic drinks.

bar² [bɑr] *n* a unit of pressure equal to 100 kilopascals. *Symbol* **bar** ⟨Greek *baros* weight⟩

ba·ra·chois [ˌbɛrəˈʃwɑ] *or* [ˈbɛrəˌʃwɑ] *French* [baʀaˈʃwɑ] *n* ✳ a strip of sand or gravel rising above the surface of adjacent water, often cutting it off from a larger body of water. ⟨Cdn. French = sandbar at river mouth⟩

barb [bɑrb] *n* **1** a point projecting backward from a main point, as on an arrowhead or spear. **2** *Zoology* one of the hairlike branches on the shaft of a bird's feather. Also, **bar·bule**. **3** barbel. **4** anything sharp and wounding, esp a mean-spirited remark.
v furnish with a barb. ⟨Latin *barba* beard⟩
barbed *adj* **1** having a barb or barbs. **2** sharp and wounding: *barbed criticism.* **barbed wire** twisted wire with sharp points fixed to it, used for fences, etc. to deter climbers. Also, **barb·wire. bar·bel** [ˈbɑrbəl] *n* **1** a long, thin, whiskerlike growth near the mouth of a fish. **2** any of several large European freshwater fishes having such growths.

bar·bar·i·an [bɑrˈbɛriən] *or* [bɑrˈbæriən] *n* **1 a** in antiquity, a member of any people outside the Greek or Roman Empire. **b** a member of any people considered uncivilized. **2** a person with unacceptable manners or without sympathy for the arts; boor. **3** a brutal person. **bar·bar·i·an** *adj.* ⟨Greek *barbaros* foreign; imitative of stammering⟩
bar·bar·ic [bɑrˈbɛrɪk] *or* [bɑrˈbærɪk] *adj* **1** typical of barbarians; unrefined. **2** crudely rich or lavish: *barbaric splendour.* **3** barbarous. **bar·bar·i·cal·ly** *adv.* **bar·ba·rism** [ˈbɑrbəˌrɪzəm] *n* **1** the condition of being barbarous or barbaric. **2** a custom, expression, or object that offends against accepted standards of

taste, grammar, etc. **3** brutality or a brutal act. **bar·bar·i·ty** *n* **1** brutal cruelty. **2** barbaric manner or style. **bar·ba·rize** *v* make barbarian. **bar·ba·ri·za·tion** *n.* **bar·ba·rous** *adj* **1** cruelly brutal: *the barbarous treatment of prisoners at that time.* **2** uncivilized. **bar·ba·rous·ly** *adv.* **bar·ba·rous·ness** *n.*

bar·be·cue [ˈbɑrbɪˌkju] *n* **1** an outdoor grill for cooking meat, etc. **2** food prepared on a barbecue or in a highly seasoned tomato sauce. *v* **1** roast over an outdoor grill or open fire. **2** cook in a highly seasoned tomato sauce. ⟨Haitian *barboka* framework of sticks⟩

bar·ber [ˈbɑrbər] *n* a person whose business is cutting hair and beards. **bar·ber** *v.* ⟨Latin *barba* beard⟩
barber pole a pole placed outside a barber's shop to signify the trade, with spiral red and white stripes. **bar·ber·shop** *n* a barber's place of business. *adj* typical of a BARBERSHOP QUARTET: *barbershop harmony.* **barbershop quartet** or **quartette** a quartet that sings popular sentimental songs, usually in close harmony.

bar·bi·can [ˈbɑrbəˌkæn] *or* [ˈbɑrbəkən] *n* a tower for defence built over an entry into a medieval city or castle. ⟨Latin *barbacana*⟩

bar·bi·tu·rate [bɑrˈbɪtʃərɪt] *or* [bɑrˈbɪtʃəˌreit] *n* any of several sedative or hypnotic drugs derived from **barbituric acid** [ˌbɑrbəˈtʃʊrɪk]. ⟨*Usnea barbata*, a lichen, from L *barba* beard⟩

bard [bɑrd] *n* **1** a poet and singer of long ago. **2** *Poetic* a poet. ⟨Irish and Scots Gaelic⟩
Bard of Avon Shakespeare.

bare [bɛr] *adj* **1** unclothed; with no covering: *bare feet.* **2** not concealed or disguised: *bare emotion.* **3** not furnished; empty: *bare rooms.* **4** plain; simple: *bare facts.* **5** only that and no more: *a bare five percent.*
v uncover; reveal: *to bare one's feelings, to bare one's teeth.* **bare·ness** *n.* ⟨Old English *bær*⟩
lay bare uncover: *The plot was laid bare.* **with one's bare hands** without weapons or tools.
bare·faced *adj* **1** shameless: *a barefaced lie.* **2** forthright. **3** with the face uncovered. **bare·fac·ed·ly** [-ˌfeisɪdli] *adv.* **bare·fac·ed·ness** *n.* **bare·foot** *adj, adv* without shoes or socks on. **bare·hand·ed** *adj, adv* **1** without tools or weapons: *He fought the lion barehanded.* **2** wearing nothing on the hands. **bare·head·ed** *adj, adv* wearing nothing on the head. **bare·knuck·le** *adj* **1** without boxing gloves. **2** in which any tactic is admissible: *a bareknuckle argument.* **bare·leg·ged** [ˈbɛrˌlɛgɪd] *or* [ˈbɛrˌlɛgd] *adj, adv* without stockings. **bare·ly** *adv* **1** only just; hardly: *barely enough money to live on.* **2** sparsely or austerely: *a barely furnished room.* **3** forthrightly; plainly: *She put the question rather barely.*

barf [bɑrf] *v Slang* vomit. ⟨possibly imitative⟩

bar·gain [ˈbɑrgən] n 1 an agreement to trade or exchange goods, money, services, etc. 2 something offered or bought at a low price. 3 any advantageous deal.
v 1 try to get good terms; negotiate. 2 trade; offer or give in a negotiation: *They have bargained away our future.* 3 make a deal. **bar·gain·er** n. ⟨Old French *bargaigne*⟩
bargain for (or **on**) be ready for; expect: *The rain wasn't so bad, but hail was more than we bargained for.* **into the bargain** besides; also: *It's late and I'm tired into the bargain.* **strike a bargain** make a deal.
bargain basement a store basement where goods are sold cheaply. **bargain counter** in a store, a small area with low-priced goods. **bargaining chip** a helpful factor in negotiation.

barge [bɑrdʒ] n 1 a large, flat-bottomed boat for carrying freight. 2 a large boat furnished and decorated for use on a special occasion. 3 any big, old boat.
v 1 go aggressively or rudely: *Everyone turned as she barged into the room.* 2 move heavily or clumsily like a barge. 3 transport by barge. ⟨Greek *baris* boat used on the Nile⟩
barge in intrude: *He's forever barging in where he's not wanted.*
barge·pole n the long stick used to steer a barge. **not touch something with a bargepole** avoid all involvement with: *I wouldn't touch that topic with a bargepole.*

bar·goon [bɑrˈgun] n ✻ *Slang* bargain.

bar·i·tone [ˈbɛrəˌtoun] or [ˈbærəˌtoun] n 1 a male voice between tenor and bass. 2 *Music* a brass B-flat band instrument. **bar·i·tone** adj. ⟨Greek *barys* deep + *tonos* pitch⟩

bar·i·um [ˈbɛriəm] or [ˈbæriəm] n a soft metallic element. *Symbol* **Ba** ⟨Greek *barytēs* weight⟩

bark[1] [bɑrk] n *Botany* the tough outer covering of woody plants.
v 1 scrape the skin from by accident: *I fell and barked my shins.* 2 strip bark from. 3 treat or tan with bark. ⟨Old Norse *börkr*⟩

bark[2] [bɑrk] n 1 the short, sharp sound that a dog makes. 2 a sound like this.
v 1 make this sound. 2 speak sharply: *The officer barked out the orders.* 3 call or shout to attract people into a circus tent, market stall, etc. 4 cough. **bark·er** n. ⟨Old English *beorcan*⟩ **bark at the moon** make a fuss to no effect. **bark up the wrong tree** go after something by mistake or use wrong means to get at. **bark·ing** adj *Informal* crazy.

bark[3] See BARQUE.

bar·ley [ˈbɑrli] n any of various cereal grasses, widely cultivated as grain and forage. ⟨Old English *bærlic*⟩

bar mitz·vah [ˈbɑr ˈmɪtsvə] *Judaism* 1 a ceremony formally admitting a boy into the religious community, usually held when the boy is thirteen years old. Compare BAT MITZVAH. 2 a boy of thirteen years, the age of religious responsibility. Also, **Bar Mitzvah**. ⟨Hebrew = son of the commandment⟩

barm·y [ˈbɑrmi] adj 1 fermenting; foaming. 2 *Informal* crazy. ⟨*barm* foam on fermenting liquor⟩

barn [bɑrn] n 1 a building for storing hay, grain, farm machinery, etc. and for sheltering livestock. 2 any large, rather plain building (often in names of self-serve, warehouse-style stores). 3 *Nuclear physics* a unit of area equal to 10^{-24} m². **barn·like** adj. ⟨Old English *bern; bere* barley + *ærn* storage⟩
barn burner *Informal* something or someone spectacular. **barn dance** a rural community dance held in a barn. **barn owl** a common owl which lives in barns and eats mice. **barn raising** a gathering of neighbours to build a barn. **barn·storm** v tour (small towns and country districts) performing plays or shows, making speeches, giving exhibitions, etc. **barn·storm·er** n. **barn·yard** n the yard around a barn for livestock, etc. adj 1 to do with a barnyard: *barnyard animals.* 2 fit for a barnyard; crude; lewd: *barnyard humour.*

bar·na·cle [ˈbɑrnəkəl] n 1 any of a large group of marine crustaceans that spend their entire adult life attached to some underwater object like a rock or ship bottom or to a larger sea creature like a whale. 2 *Informal* any person or thing that will not go away. ⟨Old French *bernaque*⟩

ba·rom·e·ter [bəˈrɒmətər] n 1 an instrument measuring atmospheric pressure. 2 anything that indicates changes or trends: *Newspapers are often barometers of public opinion.* **bar·o·met·ric** [ˌbɛrəˈmɛtrɪk] or [ˌbærəˈmɛtrɪk] adj. **bar·o·met·ric·al·ly** adv. ⟨Greek *baros* weight + *metron* measure⟩
barometric pressure pressure exerted by the atmosphere as measured by a barometer. It is expressed in kilopascals.

bar·on [ˈbɛrən] or [ˈbærən] n 1 a nobleman of relatively low rank. 2 a powerful merchant or financier: *a railway baron.* 3 a large cut of meat: *a baron of beef.* ⟨Old High German *baro* man, fighter⟩
bar·on·ess n 1 a noblewoman holding a rank equal to that of a baron. 2 the wife or widow of a baron. **bar·on·et** [ˌbɛrəˈnɛt] or [ˈbɛrənɪt] n in Britain, a man ranking below a baron and above a knight. **ba·ro·ni·al** [bəˈrouniəl] adj 1 of a baron. 2 suitable for a baron; splendid; stately. **bar·o·ny** [ˈbɛrəni] or [ˈbærəni] n 1 the domain of a baron. 2 a vast region or enterprise under private ownership or control.

ba·roque [bəˈrouk] or [bəˈrɒk] adj 1 Often, **Baroque**, to do with a style of art, music, architecture, etc. that flourished in Europe in the 1600s, characterized by elaborate ornamentation. 2 overly ornate or intricate. ⟨French; Portuguese *barroco* irregular⟩

barque [bɑrk] n 1 *Poetic* any boat or ship. 2 a sailing ship with three masts, the first two square-rigged, the other fore-and-aft-rigged. Also, **bark**. ⟨French; Italian *barca*⟩

bar·rack [ˈbɛrək] or [ˈbærək] n Usually, **barracks** sg or pl 1 a building or buildings for members of the armed forces to live in. 2 ✻ a building housing a local unit of the Royal

Canadian Mounted Police. **3** ✷ *Informal* a training centre of the Royal Canadian Mounted Police. **4** a large, plain building housing many people. ⟨Italian *baracca*⟩

bar·ra·cu·da [ˌbɛrəˈkudə] *or* [ˌbærəˈkudə] *n, pl* **-da** or **-das** any of several pikelike fishes of warm seas, with razor-sharp teeth. ⟨Spanish, from West Indian name⟩

bar·rage [bəˈrɑʒ] *n* **1** a barrier of artillery fire. **2** any heavy onslaught or attack: *a barrage of criticism.* **3** [ˈbɑrɪdʒ] an artificial barrier in a river; dam.
v [bəˈrɑʒ] subject to a barrage. ⟨French, from *barrer* to bar⟩

barre [bɑr] *n* the supporting rail that ballet dancers use for exercises. ⟨French⟩

bar·rel [ˈbɛrəl] *or* [ˈbærəl] *n* **1** a large container shaped like a cylinder with bulging sides, usually made of boards held together by hoops. **2** a unit of volume of oil equal to about 159 L. **3** the metal tube of a firearm, through which the bullet travels. **4** *Informal* a large quantity or number: *a barrel of fun, a barrel of laughs.*
v **-relled** or **-reled**, **-rel·ling** or **-rel·ing** **1** *Informal* roll fast or wildly: *barrelling along the highway at 130 km/h.* **2** put into barrels. ⟨French *baril*, prob. from Latin *barra* stave⟩
have over a barrel have (someone) in a situation that renders him or her powerless.
bar·rel–chest·ed *adj* having a large, rounded rib cage. **bar·rel·house** *n Music* a type of jazz known for its roughness and hard rhythms, so called from its origin in saloons with barrels stacked along the walls. **barrel organ** a large music box played by turning a crank. **barrel roll** an airplane stunt in which the plane describes a spiral while turning over. **barrel vault** *Architecture* a vault in the shape of a half-barrel.

bar·ren [ˈbɛrən] *or* [ˈbærən] *adj* **1** not producing anything: *A sandy desert is barren.* **2** unable to bear offspring. **3** empty and dull. **4** completely lacking; without (with *of*): *barren of imagination.*
n ✷ Usually, **barrens** *pl* **a** a wasteland. **b the Barrens** the BARREN GROUND. **bar·ren·ness** *n*. ⟨Old French *baraine*⟩
Barren Ground(s) ✷ the treeless, thinly populated region between Hudson Bay on the east and Great Slave and Great Bear Lakes on the west. Also, **Barren Lands.**

bar·rette [bəˈrɛt] *n* a hairpin with a clasp. ⟨French, diminutive of *barre* bar⟩

bar·ri·cade [ˈbɛrəˌkeid] *or* [ˈbærəˌkeid] *n* **1** a rough, hastily-built barrier for defence. **2** any barrier or obstruction. **3** ✷ large blocks of ice remaining frozen to a shore or river bank after the spring breakup. **bar·ri·cade** *v.* ⟨Provençal *barrica* cask; casks were so used⟩

bar·ri·er [ˈbɛriər] *or* [ˈbæriər] *n* **1** something that stands in the way, stopping progress or preventing approach. **2** something that separates people or things. **3** *Horse racing* starting gate. ⟨Latin *barraria; barra.* See BAR[1].⟩

barrier reef a long line of rocks or coral reef not far from the mainland.

bar·ris·ter [ˈbɛrɪstər] *or* [ˈbærɪstər] *n* a lawyer who pleads in court. Compare SOLICITOR. ⟨*bar* + *-ster*⟩

bar·row[1] [ˈbɛrou] *or* [ˈbærou] *n* **1** a frame with two short handles at each end, used for carrying a load. **2** wheelbarrow. **3** handcart. ⟨Old English *bearwe.* Related to BEAR[1].⟩

bar·row[2] [ˈbɛrou] *or* [ˈbærou] *n* a mound of earth or stones over an ancient or prehistoric grave. ⟨Old English *beorg*⟩

bar·ter [ˈbɑrtər] *v* **1** trade goods or services without using money. **2** exchange (*for*): *She bartered her boat for a car.* **3** trade without an equal return (with *away*): *In his eagerness to make a fortune, he bartered away his freedom.*
n **1** the act of bartering. **2** something bartered. **bar·ter·er** *n* ⟨Old French *barater* to exchange⟩

CONFUSABLES
Barter means to trade goods without money changing hands. To negotiate for a better price is not to **barter** but to **bargain.**

bar·y·on [ˈbɛriˌɒn] *or* [ˈbæriˌɒn] *n Physics* any of a class of elementary particles, including protons, neutrons and hyperons, having a spin of 1/2 and, generally, a mass greater than that of the mesons. ⟨Greek *barys* heavy⟩

bas·al See BASE[1].

ba·salt [ˈbeisɒlt], [ˈbæsɒlt], *or* [bəˈsɒlt] *n* a hard, dark-coloured volcanic rock. **ba·sal·tic** *adj.* ⟨Latin *basaltes;* Greek *basanos* touchstone⟩

base[1] [beis] *n* **1** the bottom or lowest part of something: *the base of a tree.* **2** a support, holder, etc. at the bottom: *The machine rests on a steel base.* **3** the essential element, to which other things are added: *a sauce with a cream base.* **4** *Chemistry* a compound that reacts with an acid to form a salt. **5** an undercoat of paint. **6 a** *Baseball* any of the four corners of the diamond. **b** a starting place or goal in various other games. **7** a starting point and supply post for a military force, survey, etc. **8** a place where units of the armed forces are permanently stationed: *There is a large base at Gagetown, New Brunswick.* **9** the number that is a starting point for a system of numeration. **10** *Geometry* a line or surface forming that part of a geometrical figure on which it is supposed to stand. **11** *Biology* the part of an organ nearest its point of attachment.
v **1** make or form a base or foundation for (often as pp in compounds): *oil-based paints.* **2** establish; found (*on* or *upon*): *Their large business was based on good service.* **3** station or locate at a base: *based in Ottawa.*
adj serving as a starting point: *base line, base pay.* ⟨Greek *basis* base; lit., a step⟩
cover all the bases a examine all angles of something. **b** ensure success or security by dealing with all vulnerable points. **get to first base** make the first step successfully. **off base** *Informal* not right or sensible: *Your idea is off base.* **touch base** (or **bases**), make contact (*with* someone) for an update.

bas·al ['beisəl] *or* ['beizəl] *adj* **1** to do with a base or starting point. **2** fundamental; basic. **bas·al·ly** *adv.* **basal metabolism** the minimum energy used for the vital life processes of an individual at rest. **basal reader** a beginning reader with limited vocabulary and structures and a formulaic approach. **base·ball** *n* **1** a game played with bat and ball by two teams of nine players each, on a field with four bases. **2** the ball used in this game. **base·board** *n* a length of wood trim at the base of a wall. **baseboard heating** indoor heating by means of small radiators near the floor. **base hit** *Baseball* a hit that lets the batter get at least to first base without the help of an error. **base·less** *adj* without good foundation: *baseless rumours*. **base line 1** a line used as a starting point for measuring or calculating, esp in land surveys, etc. **2** Often, **baseline** a basic standard of value against which things are measured or compared. **3** *Baseball* a line inside which a runner must stay when running between bases. **4** *Tennis, basketball* a line marking the limit of play at either end of the court. **base·man** *n, pl* **-men** *Baseball* a player guarding one of the bases. **base·ment** *n* the lowest storey of a building, partly or wholly underground. **base pay** basic wages for any job, not counting bonuses, overtime, etc.

CONFUSABLES
Base is chiefly used literally, and applies to the bottom and supporting part of objects: *the base of a statue*. Basis is used figuratively and applies to whatever supports an argument, belief, etc.: *His opinion has no basis in fact.*

base² [beis] *adj* **1** morally low; selfish or cowardly. **2** fit only for an inferior person or thing: *No needful service is to be looked on as base*. **3** *Archaic* of humble birth or origin. **4** debased; counterfeit: *base coin*. **base·ly** *adv.* **base·ness** *n.* ⟨Latin *bassus* low⟩
base·born *adj Archaic* **1** born of slaves or other humble parents, or of an unmarried mother. **2** dishonourable; contemptible. **base metal** any of the non-precious metals, such as lead, zinc, iron, etc.

ba·ses¹ ['beisiz] *n* pl of BASIS.

bas·es² ['beisɪz] *n* pl of BASE¹.

bash [bæʃ] *v Informal* strike violently: *They bashed down the door.*
n **1** *Informal* a smashing blow: *a bash on the head*. **2** *Slang* a big party: *They're giving her a retirement bash*. **3** *Slang* an attempt: *Let me have a bash at it*. **bash·er** *n.* ⟨imitative⟩

bash·ful ['bæʃfəl] *adj* uneasy and awkward in the presence of strangers. **bash·ful·ly** *adv.* **bash·ful·ness** *n.* ⟨*bash* var. of *abash* + *-ful*⟩

ba·sic ['beisɪk] *adj* **1** fundamental; essential: *basic beliefs*. **2** beginning or introductory; elementary: *a basic course in drawing*. **3** standard minimum, excluding extras: *a basic salary of $38 000*. **4** *Chemistry* of, being, or containing a base. **5** *Geology* of igneous rocks, containing a small proportion of silica. *n* Usually, **basics** *pl* essential or elementary

facts, principles, etc.: *the basics of flying*.
BASIC *acronym for* Beginner's All-purpose Symbolic Instruction Code, a programming language using ordinary words. **ba·si·cal·ly** *adv* **1** fundamentally. **2** *Informal* in short.

bas·il ['bæzəl] *or* ['beizəl] *n* a herb of the mint family with strongly aromatic leaves used in cookery. ⟨Greek *basileus* king⟩

ba·sil·i·ca [bə'sɪləkə] *n* **1** a long room with a raised platform at one end and wide side aisles separated from the main area by a row of columns. **2** any early Christian church built in this form. **3** a Roman Catholic church with certain rights and privileges. ⟨Greek *basilikē* royal; *basileus* king⟩

bas·i·lisk ['bæzə,lɪsk] *or* ['bæsə,lɪsk] *n* **1** any of various tropical American lizards related to the iguanas, noted for their ability to run on their hind legs in an almost upright position. **2** a lizardlike reptile of classical legend whose breath and gaze were fatal. ⟨Greek *basiliskos*, diminutive of *basileus* king⟩

ba·sin ['beisən] *n* **1** a wide, shallow bowl used esp for liquids. **2** a bathroom sink. **3** all the land drained by a river and its tributaries: *the St. Lawrence basin*. **4** a relatively shallow depression in land, usually containing water. ⟨Latin *baccinum*, from *bacca* water vessel; Celtic⟩

ba·sis ['beisɪs] *n, pl* **-ses** [-siz] **1** the basic or main part; foundation. **2** a fundamental idea or set of ideas. **3** a way of operating or proceeding: *to pay on a monthly basis, to deal with someone on a first-name basis*. ⟨Greek⟩
basis point (in interest rates, exchange rates, etc.) one-hundredth of one percent.

USAGE
The use of **basis** in sense 3 above is often wordy and replaceable by a simple adverb: *monthly* rather than *on a monthly basis*, *amicably* rather than *on an amicable basis.*

bask [bæsk] *v* **1** warm oneself pleasantly: *The cat was basking before the fire*. **2** take great pleasure: *He basked in the praise of his friends*. ⟨Old Norse *bathask* bathe oneself⟩

bas·ket ['bæskɪt] *n* **1** a rigid or semirigid container made of twigs, fibres, etc. woven together. **2** anything resembling a basket. **3** *Basketball* **a** a net hung on a metal rim and open at the bottom, used as the goal. **b** a score made by tossing the ball through the basket. **bas·ket·like** *adj.* **bas·ket·ry** *n.* ⟨Middle English⟩ **bas·ket·ball** *n* **1** a game between two teams, usually of five players each, who try to score by sinking a large round ball in the opposing team's basket. **2** the ball used in this game. **basket case** *Informal* a person completely incapacitated by mental or emotional breakdown. ⟨orig in WWI, a soldier who had lost all limbs⟩ **basket hilt** on some swords, a hilt with a basket-shaped guard for the hand. **Basket Maker** a member of any of several native peoples of the SW United States up to the sixth century A.D., characterized by skill in basket-making. **basket weave 1** a weave in cloth that looks like the weave in a basket. **2**

a place where several highways cross over and under one another; also, **bas·ket·weave**. **bas·ket·work** *n* any basketlike weaving.

bas·ma·ti rice [bɑs'mɑti] a type of faintly aromatic rice with long grains. ⟨Hindi⟩

bas–re·lief [ˌbɑ rɪ'lif] *or* [ˌbæs rɪ'lif] *n* relief sculpture in which the modelled forms stand out only slightly from the background. ⟨French, from Italian *basso-rilievo* low relief⟩

bass[1] [beis] *n* **1** the lowest adult male singing voice. **2** a singer with such a voice, or the part written for it. **3** an instrument with the lowest range in a family of musical instruments, esp a DOUBLE BASS. **4** the lower half of the whole musical range in sound reproduction. Compare TREBLE. **bass** *adj.* ⟨Italian *basso*⟩
bass clef *Music* a symbol (𝄢) showing that the pitch of the notes on a staff is below middle C. **bass drum** a large double-headed drum that produces a deep sound. **bass·ist** *n* a person who plays a DOUBLE BASS. **basso pro·fun·do** [prə'fʌndou] *Italian* [pro'fundo] the lowest bass voice.

bass[2] [bæs] *n, pl* **bass** *or* **bass·es 1** any of various perchlike marine fishes, highly valued as food and game fishes. **2** any of several large freshwater game fishes of the sunfish family. ⟨var. of *barse* perch; Old English *bears*⟩

bas·si·net [ˌbæsə'nɛt] *or* ['bæsə,nɛt] *n* a baby's basketlike cradle, usually with a hood and set on a stand. ⟨French, diminutive of *bassin* basin⟩

bas·soon [bə'sun] *n* a deep-toned wind instrument with a double reed, having a long wooden body with a tube attached at the side leading to a curved metal mouthpiece. **bas·soon·ist** *n*. ⟨Italian *bassone; basso* bass⟩

bas·tard ['bæstərd] *n* **1** a child born of parents not legally married. **2** anything inferior or not genuine. **3** *Slang* a cruel, treacherous or very unpleasant person. *adj* **1** born of parents not legally married. **2** inferior; not genuine. **3** irregular or unusual in shape, size, style, etc. **bas·tard·y** *n*. ⟨Old French, orig, mule; *bast* packsaddle⟩ **bas·tard·ize** *v* degrade by mixing with inferior elements. **bas·tar·di·za·tion** *n*.

baste[1] [beist] *v* drip or pour melted fat or butter on (roasting meat). **bast·er** *n*. ⟨Old French *basser* moisten. Related to BASIN.⟩

baste[2] [beist] *v* sew with long, loose stitches to hold in place temporarily. **bast·ing** *n*. ⟨Old French *bastir;* Germanic⟩

bas·tion ['bæstʃən] *or* ['bæstiən] *n* **1** a projecting part of a fortification made so that the defenders can fire from as many angles as possible. **2** someone or something that acts as a strong defence: *a bastion of freedom.* ⟨Italian *bastione; bastire* build⟩

bat[1] [bæt] *n* **1** *Sports* **a** a specially shaped stick used for hitting the ball as in baseball or cricket. **b** a turn at hitting the ball: *It's her bat next.* **2** *Informal* a squash racquet, table tennis paddle, etc. **3** *Informal* a stroke or blow.

4 *Slang* a drinking spree or binge.
v **bat·ted, bat·ting 1** hit with or as if with a bat. **2** use a bat: *She's batting well this season.* **3** have a turn at bat: *Who'll bat first?* **4** (often metaphorical) have a given BATTING AVERAGE: *Any player who bats over 400 is valuable.* **bat·ter** *n*. ⟨Old French *batte* club; *battre* strike⟩
at bat in position to bat. **bat around a** *Baseball* go right through the batting order in one inning. **b** *Slang* go here and there with no definite purpose: *batting around town* **c** *Slang* discuss (a topic) freely and informally. **go to bat for** *Informal* speak on behalf of. **(right) off the bat** *Informal* immediately.
bat·boy or **bat·girl** *n* a boy or girl who looks after the bats in a baseball game. **bats·man** *n, pl* **-men** *Cricket* a player who is batting. **batting average 1** *Baseball* a player's ratio of base hits to the number of times at bat. **2** any index of performance: *Two promotions in two years is a pretty good batting average.* **batting cage** *Baseball* a screened enclosure for batting practice.

bat[2] [bæt] *n* any of a large order of flying mammals with membranes between the forelimbs, enabling them to fly, and a radarlike sense organ by which they navigate in the dark. **bat·like** *adj.* ⟨alteration of Middle English *bakke*⟩
blind as a bat totally blind. Also, **bat–blind. have bats in the belfry** be or seem crazy.

bat[3] [bæt] *v* **bat·ted, bat·ting** flutter (the eyelashes); blink. ⟨Middle English *baten*⟩
not bat an eye be not at all surprised.

batch[1] [bætʃ] *n* **1** a quantity of cookies, bread, etc., baked at once. **2** a number of persons or things dealt with together: *a batch of essays to mark.* **3** *Computers* a set of instructions, etc. for a computer to perform in one run. ⟨Middle English *bacche*⟩
batch file *Computers* in some computers, a file containing commands to the operating system. **batch processing** *Computers* a method of processing in which records are first collected into batches.

batch[2] [bætʃ] See BACH (BACHELOR).

bate [beit] *v* abate; lessen. ⟨var. of *abate*⟩
with bated breath holding the breath in suspense: *to listen with bated breath.*

ba·teau or **bat·teau** [bæ'tou] *n, pl* **-teaux** [-'touz] ❋ a light, flat-bottomed riverboat propelled by oars, poles, or sails, formerly used esp on the upper St. Lawrence. ⟨Cdn. French⟩

bath [bæθ] *n, pl* **baths** [bæðz] **1** a washing of the body. **2** the water, etc. for this: *to draw a bath.* **3** a tub, room, etc. for bathing in: *In ancient Rome, baths were often elaborate public buildings.* **4** a liquid, such as photographic solution or dye, for washing or dipping something. **5** the container holding it.
v **bathed, bath·ing 1** give a bath to. **2** take a bath. ⟨Old English *bæth*⟩
take a bath *Informal* lose a lot of money.
bath·house a house or building fitted up for taking baths. **bath·mat** *n* a small mat to stand on when stepping out of the bath or shower. **bath·robe** *n* a loose garment worn to and

from a bath or when resting. **bath·room** n
1 a room equipped for taking baths, usually
with washbasin, toilet, and bathtub. **2** any
room with a toilet or toilets. **go to the
bathroom a** use a toilet. **b** Informal urinate or
defecate. **bath·tub** n a tub to bathe in.
bath·wa·ter n the water one bathes in.

bathe [beið] v **bathed, bath·ing 1** take a
bath. **2** give a bath to. **3** wash or soak in any
liquid: The doctor told me to bathe the wound in
this solution. **4** go swimming. **5** surround;
cover: The valley is bathed in sunlight. **bath·er** n.
⟨Old English bathian⟩
bathing cap a tight-fitting rubber cap worn
to protect the hair while swimming. **bathing
suit** a garment worn for swimming.

ba·thos ['beiθɒs] or ['beiθous] n **1** dullness or
triteness in speech or writing, esp
immediately after more elevated expression.
Example: The exile came back to his home,
crippled, unfriended, and hatless. **2** strained or
insincere pathos. **ba·thet·ic** [bə'θɛtɪk] adj.
⟨Greek bathos depth, lowness⟩

ba·tik [bə'tik] or ['bɑtik] n **1** the art and
method of making designs on cloth by
dyeing only part at a time, the rest being
covered by a wax coating which is later
removed. **2** cloth dyed in this way. ⟨Malay⟩

bat mitz·vah ['bɑt 'mɪtsvə] Judaism a girl
assuming religious responsibility, usually at
the age of twelve. Also, **bas** or **bath mitzvah**.
⟨Hebrew = daughter of the commandment⟩

ba·ton [bə'tɒn] n **1** a stick used by the leader
of an orchestra, chorus, etc. to indicate the
beat and direct the performance. **2** a stick
passed from runner to runner in a relay race.
3 a light, hollow metal rod twirled by a drum
major or majorette as a showy display. **4** a
staff or stick carried as a symbol of office or
authority. ⟨French = stick⟩
ba·ton·nier [ˌbætɒn'jei] French [batɔn'je] n
✱ an official of the Québec Bar Association.

batt [bæt] n **1** COTTON BATTING. **2** a thick sheet
of cotton batting, fibreglass, or other pressed
fibre.
bat·ting n layers of pressed cotton, wool, or
other fibre, used for lining quilts, packing, etc.

bat·tal·ion [bə'tæljən] n **1** a formation of
four companies within an infantry regiment.
2 any large group organized to act together: a
battalion of volunteers. Abbrev **Bn** ⟨Italian
bataglione; battaglia battle. See BATTLE.⟩

bat·ten ['bætən] n **1** a long, thick board used
for flooring. **2** a thin strip of wood used to
reinforce, seal a joint, hold a tarpaulin in
place, etc. **3** Theatre **a** a wooden or metal bar
from which to hang lights, scenery, etc. **b** the
lights hung from such a bar.
v fasten or strengthen with battens. ⟨baton⟩
batten down the hatches a prepare for a
storm at sea by covering all entranceways to
the lower decks with boards. **b** prepare for
any other emergency.

bat·ter¹ ['bætər] v **1** beat with repeated
blows: Violent storms battered the coast.
2 damage by hard use: battered to pieces.

3 abuse physically: battered wives. ⟨Old
French batre beat⟩
battering ram 1 a heavy beam of wood with
a metal ram's head on the end, used in
ancient and medieval warfare to batter down
walls, gates, etc. **2** any object similarly used.

bat·ter² ['bætər] n a thick liquid mixture of
flour, milk, eggs, etc. that becomes solid
when cooked. Cakes, pancakes, etc. are made
from batter. ⟨Old French bature beating⟩

bat·ter³ See BAT¹.

bat·ter·y ['bætəri] n **1 a** a container holding
materials that produce electricity by
chemical action; a single electric cell. **b** a set
of two or more such cells in one unit: a car
battery. **2** a set of guns or other weapons for
combined action. **3** a formation of several
troops in an artillery regiment. **4** any set of
connected or similar things or people: a
battery of tests, a battery of lawyers. **5** Baseball
the pitcher and catcher together. **6** Law
assault causing actual bodily harm. ⟨French
batterie from battre beat; Latin battuere⟩

bat·tle ['bætəl] n **1** a single confrontation
between opposing armed forces. **2** fighting or
war: wounds received in battle. **3** any fight or
contest: a battle of words.
v fight; struggle or contend (with): battling
cancer. ⟨Latin battalia; battuere beat⟩
do (or **give**) **battle** fight. **half the battle** a big
and difficult first step in a challenging process:
Admitting you have a problem is half the battle.
bat·tle–axe n a type of axe used as a weapon
of war. Sometimes, **battle–ax. battle cry 1** the
shout of soldiers in battle. **2** a motto or
slogan in any struggle. **battle dress** a two-
piece uniform consisting of pants and a
short, loose jacket. **battle fatigue** a neurosis
of soldiers caused by the prolonged anxiety
and emotional strain of combat. **bat·tle·field**
or **bat·tle·ground** n **1** the place where a battle
is fought or has been fought. **2** any area of
struggle. **bat·tle·front** n **1** the place where
actual fighting between two armies is taking
place. **2** the position of direct confrontation
in any struggle. **bat·tle·ment** n a wall for
defence at the top of a tower or wall, with
indentations through which the defenders
can shoot. **bat·tle·ment·ed** adj. **battle royal**
1 a fight in which many people take part;
riot. **2** a prolonged and intense argument.
bat·tle·ship n the largest, most powerful, and
most heavily armoured type of warship.
battle stations 1 the positions taken by parts
of an army, navy, etc. ready for battle. **2** a
state of readiness for any conflict.

bau·ble ['bɒbəl] n a showy trifle having no
real value. ⟨Old French babel, baubel toy⟩

baud [bɒd] n, pl **baud** or **bauds 1** a unit of
speed in sending messages by telegraph.
2 Computers a unit of speed of a computer
system, calculated in bits of data transmitted
per second. ⟨J.M.E. Baudot, 19c French
engineer⟩

baux·ite ['bɒksəit] n a claylike mineral and
an ore of aluminum. ⟨from Les Baux, France⟩

bawd [bɒd] *n* a woman who runs or works in a brothel. ⟨Old French *bald* bold; Germanic⟩ **bawd·y** *adj* humorously and exuberantly lewd or indecent: *bawdy songs.* **bawd·i·ly** *adv.* **bawd·i·ness** *n.* **bawd·y–house** *n* brothel.

bawl [bɒl] *v* 1 call out noisily: *The sergeant bawled a command.* 2 *Informal* weep loudly. **bawl** *n.* **bawl·er** *n.* ⟨Latin *baulare* bark⟩
bawl out *Informal* scold severely: *We got bawled out for leaving our bikes in the driveway.*

bay¹ [bei] *n* 1 a part of a sea or lake extending into the land. **2 the Bay ✱** *Informal* **a** the Hudson's Bay Company. **b** formerly, Hudson Bay. ⟨Latin *baia*⟩
bay ice ✱ ice of recent formation in bays and sheltered places. **Bay Street ✱** the financial interests of Toronto, Canada's main centre of finance. ⟨street with many financial houses⟩

bay² [bei] *n* 1 a section of wall set off by columns, pillars, etc., forming a slight recess. **2** BAY WINDOW. **3** a compartment, alcove, platform, or other area for a specified purpose: *an unloading bay, a sick bay.* ⟨Old French *baie* opening; Latin *batare* gape⟩
bay window 1 a window projecting out from a wall, making extra space in a room. **2** *Informal* a large belly.

bay³ [bei] *n* 1 a long howl or bark, esp of a hound. **2** the position of a hunted animal when escape is impossible and it must face its pursuers: *The stag stood at bay on the edge of the cliff.* **3** the position of the pursuers being kept off: *holding the hounds at bay.*
v utter a howl or prolonged barks. ⟨Old French *(a)bayer* bark⟩

bay⁴ [bei] *n* laurel, a Mediterranean shrub or tree whose leaves are used as seasoning. ⟨Old French *baie;* Latin *baca* berry⟩
bay·ber·ry *n* 1 a shrub of the wax-myrtle family with clusters of round nuts. **2** a tree of the myrtle family whose leaves yield an aromatic oil.

bay⁵ [bei] *adj* reddish brown: *a bay mare.* ⟨Old French *bai;* Latin *badius*⟩

bay·o·net [ˌbeiəˈnɛt] *or* [ˈbeiənɪt] *n* a heavy, daggerlike blade made to be attached to the end of a rifle.
v **-net·ed, -net·ing** stab with a bayonet. ⟨French *baïonnette;* from *Bayonne,* France⟩

bay·ou [ˈbaɪju] *or* [baɪˈju] *n esp S US* a marshy inlet or outlet of a lake, river, or gulf. ⟨Choctaw *bayuk* small stream⟩

ba·zaar [bəˈzɑr] *n* 1 esp in the Middle East and the Indian subcontinent, a market. **2** a sale of donated items, often to raise money for charity. ⟨Persian *bazar*⟩

ba·zoo·ka [bəˈzukə] *n* a rocket gun for use against tanks. ⟨trombonelike instrument which it resembled, created and named by Bob Burns, 20c American humorist⟩

BB [ˈbibi] *n, pl* **BB's** a standard size of shot, approximately 0.45 cm in diameter.
BB gun AIR RIFLE. Also, **bee–bee gun.**

BC before Christ (in dates, counting back from the birth of Christ).

BCE before the Christian (or Common) Era (to indicate years BC).

be [bi] *v present indicative sg* **am, are, is** *pl* **are** *past indicative* **was, were, was** *pl* **were** *pp* **been** *ppr* **be·ing** 1 have reality; exist: *The days of the pioneers are no more.* **2** happen: *Graduation was last month.* **3** have a particular place or position: *The food is on the table.* **4** represent: *Let "x" be the unknown quantity.* **5** belong to a particular category: *The new baby is a boy. Elephants and mice are mammals.* **6** have a particular quality or condition: *I am sad. The book is red.* **7** Be is also used as an auxiliary verb with: **a** the present participle of another verb to form a progressive: *I am asking. They were asking.* **b** the past participle of another verb to form the passive: *I was asked. You will be asked.* **c** the past participle of some intransitive verbs to form an archaic or poetic perfect tense: *The sun is risen.* **8** Be is also used with an infinitive to express expectation, duty, or possibility: *She is to arrive here at nine. No shelter was to be seen. You are to tell no one.* ⟨Old English *bēon*⟩
be off leave.
be–all and end–all the person or thing of ultimate importance. ⟨coined by Shakespeare in *Macbeth*⟩

be– *prefix* 1 thoroughly: *bespatter.* **2** at; on; about, etc. (making an intransitive verb transitive): *bewail = wail about.* **3** make; cause to seem: *belittle.* **4** provide with: *bespangle.* ⟨Old English⟩

beach [bitʃ] *n* the almost flat shore of sand or small stones beside a lake or ocean, over which the water washes when high.
v run or drive up on shore: *We beached the boat in a little inlet.* ⟨origin uncertain⟩
beach ball a large, inflated ball for use on the beach or in water. **beach·comb·er** *n* 1 a vagrant on beaches, esp in islands of the S Pacific. **2** a long wave rolling in from the ocean. **3 ✱** *British Columbia* a person who salvages logs broken loose from log booms. **beach·comb** *v.* **beach·head** *n* 1 the first position established by an invading army on an enemy shore. **2** a position from which to launch any campaign. **beach umbrella** a large shade umbrella stuck into the sand by its pointed handle. **beach·wear** *n* clothing, such as bathing suits, for wearing at a beach.

bea·con [ˈbikən] *n* 1 a signal fire or guiding light. **2** a marker, light, or radio station that guides pilots through fogs, etc. **3** any thing that guides or inspires. ⟨Old English *bēacn*⟩

bead [bid] *n* 1 a small bit of glass, metal, etc. with a hole through it so that it can be strung on a thread with others. **2 beads** *pl* **a** a string of beads used as a necklace. **b** a rosary; string of beads for keeping count of recited prayers. **3** any small, round object; a drop or bubble: *beads of sweat.* **4** a small metal knob at the end of a gun barrel, used in aiming. **5** a narrow semicircular moulding. **6** the froth on beer or a carbonated drink.
v 1 supply, trim, or cover with beads: *a beaded vest. Her forehead was beaded with*

sweat. **2** form into beads or drops: *Water will bead on an oily surface.* **bead·like** *adj.* ⟨Old English *bedu* prayer. See def. 2b.⟩

draw a bead on aim at. **tell** (or **count,** or **say) one's beads** say prayers using a rosary.

bead·ing *n* **1** trim made of beads threaded into designs. **2** a pattern of small, round bumps on wood, silver, etc. Also, **bead·work. bead·y** *adj* small, round, and shiny: *beady eyes.*

bea·gle ['bigəl] *n* a breed of small hunting dog with smooth hair, short legs, and droopy ears. ⟨perhaps Old French *begueule* wide throat⟩

beak [bik] *n* **1** a bird's bill, esp one that is big, strong, or hooked. **2** a similar part in other animals, such as some turtles. **3** the projecting bow of an ancient warship. **4** *Slang* the nose, esp if large or hooked. **beak·like** *adj.* ⟨Latin *beccus;* Celtic⟩

beak·er ['bikər] *n* **1** a tall, glass or metal cup with a lip for pouring and no handle, used in laboratories. **2** a baby's cup with a lid that has a spout. ⟨Old Norse *bikarr;* Latin *bacarium*⟩

beam [bim] *n* **1** a long, thick piece of timber, metal, etc., used in building as a main horizontal support. **2** a ray of light. **3** a stream of nuclear particles, electromagnetic radiation, etc.: *a laser beam.* **4** a radio signal directed to guide aircraft, ships, etc. **5** the crossbar of a balance, with pans hung from the ends. **6** the greatest width of a ship, or, metaphorically, of a person. **7** *Gymnastics* BALANCE BEAM.

v **1** send out rays of light; shine. **2** smile brightly. **3** direct (a broadcast, light source, etc.): *to beam programs into the Yukon.* ⟨Old English *bēam*⟩

on the beam a at right angles to a ship's keel. **b** of an aircraft, on the right course. **c** *Informal* on the right track. **d** sharp and alert.

beam–ends *n pl* the ends of a ship's beams. **on her beam–ends** of a ship, almost capsizing. **on one's beam–ends** in dire straits.

bean [bin] *n* **1** any of a number of plants of the pea family. **2** the dried mature seed of such a plant: *baked beans.* **3** the pod of a bean plant, used as a vegetable: *green beans.* **4** any of various other seeds or fruits resembling a bean: *coffee beans.* **5** *Slang* the head. **6 beans** *pl Slang* (with negatives) the slightest bit: *not worth beans. I don't know beans about cars.*

v Slang hit (someone) on the head, esp with a thrown object: *The pitcher beaned one batter twice.* **bean·like** *adj.* ⟨Old English *bēan*⟩ **full of beans** *Informal* lively; high-spirited. **spill the beans** tell a secret.

bean·bag *n* a small cloth bag loosely filled with dry beans, tossed in play. **beanbag chair** a big, soft chair, usually made of vinyl and stuffed with polystyrene beads. **bean curd** tofu. **bean·er·y** *n* a cheap restaurant. **bean·ie** *n* a cap with no visor and a little button at the top. **bean·pole** *n* **1** a pole for bean vines to climb on. **2** *Informal* a tall, thin person. **bean sprouts** *n pl* the sprouts of any of various bean seeds, used as a vegetable. **bean·stalk** *n* the stem of a bean plant.

bear¹ [bɛr] *v* **bore, borne 1** support: *The ice*

will bear your weight. **2** stand; endure: *I can't bear the pain.* **3** produce; yield: *This tree bears apples.* **4** (**born** in the passive) give birth to: *She had borne four boys. He was born in June.* **5** *Poetic* carry; transport: *A voice was borne upon the wind.* **6** take upon oneself: *to bear the cost.* **7** go in a certain direction: *The ship bore north.* **8** behave: *He bore himself with great dignity.* **9** bring forward; give: *to bear a hand, to bear witness to what happened.* **10** hold in mind: *to bear a grudge.* **11** have; hold. **bear·er** *n.* ⟨Old English *beran*⟩

bear a hand help. **bear down a** of a woman in childbirth, use effort to expel the baby. **b** exert pressure. **c** esp of something menacing, approach steadily (with *on*). **d** try hard; apply oneself. **bear out** demonstrate; prove. **bear up a** keep one's courage; not lose hope. **b** cope: *How is she bearing up?* **bear with** be patient with. **bring to bear** cause to have an influence (*on*).

bear·a·ble *adj* endurable: *The pain was severe but bearable.* **bear·a·ble·ness** *n.* **bear·a·bly** *adv.*

bear·ing *n* **1** general manner, posture, etc: *a military bearing.* **2** relevance: *Her question has no bearing on the problem.* **3** a part of a machine on which another part turns or slides. **4 bearings** *pl* **a** position in relation to other things: *The pilot radioed her bearings.* **b** sense of orientation: *to lose one's bearings.*

bear² [bɛr] *n* **1** any of a family of large, heavily built mammals found mainly in the temperate parts of the northern hemisphere, having shaggy hair, small rounded ears, and large paws with powerful claws. **2** a gruff, surly person. **3 a** a person who anticipates a decline in stocks. Compare BULL¹ (def. 2). **b** a person who is pessimistic about anything. *adj* to do with a stock market in which prices are declining. **bear·like** *adj.* ⟨Old English *bera*⟩

a bear for punishment one who easily accepts and even enjoys challenges.

bear·bait·ing *n* **1** a sport that was popular for several hundred years, in which dogs were set to torment a chained bear. **2** the unfair attacking of someone by a group. **bear·cat** *n* **1** PANDA. **2** a strong, aggressive person. **bear garden 1** formerly, a place for bearbaiting. **2** any noisy or unruly place. **bear·hug** *n* an embrace, often by a bigger person hugging tightly. **bear·ish** *adj* **1** like a bear; surly. **2** to do with or expecting a decline in the stock market. Compare BULLISH. **3** pessimistic. **bear·pit session ✴** a frank gathering of political party members at a convention, when members of Parliament or a legislature must defend their policies. **bear·skin** *n* **1** the skin of a bear with the fur on it. **2** a tall black fur cap worn by members of certain regiments.

beard [bird] *n* **1** the hair that grows on a man's chin, cheeks, and upper throat. **2** a tuft or growth of hair or bristles on the face or chin of any of certain animals or birds. **3** a tuft or crest of hairs or bristles on a plant. *v* **1** face boldly; defy. **2** grasp by the beard. **beard·ed** *adj.* **beard·like** *adj.* ⟨Old English⟩ **bearded seal ✴** a very large seal found along the arctic coasts of the world, distinguished esp by its long, whiskerlike bristles. **beard·less** *adj* **1** having no beard. **2** too young to have a beard: *a beardless youth.* **3** young and inexperienced.

Bear·lake ['bɛr,leik] *n, pl* **-lake 1** a member of a First Nations people living around the SW end of Great Bear Lake in the Northwest Territories. **2** their Athapascan language. **Bear·lake** *adj.*

beast [bist] *n* **1** any animal except a human being. **2** any four-footed animal. **3** a coarse or brutal person. ⟨Latin *besta*⟩ **beast·ly** *adj* **1** like a beast; brutal; coarse; vile. **2** *Informal* very unpleasant: *a beastly headache.* *adv Informal* very unpleasantly: *It was beastly cold.* **beast·li·ness** *n.* **beast of burden** an animal used for carrying loads. **beast of prey** any animal that kills other animals for food.

beat [bit] *v* **beat, beat·en** or **beat, beat·ing** **1** strike again and again: *The cruel man beat his horse.* **2** throb: *Her heart beat fast with joy.* **3** force by blows: *He beat the savage dog off.* **4** make a sound by being struck: *The drums beat loudly.* **5** mark (time) by striking a drum, tapping fingers, waving a baton, etc.: *to beat a tattoo.* **6** defeat: *Their team beat ours easily.* **7** surpass: *Nothing beats real butter.* **8** do or arrive before: *They beat us to the theatre.* **9** *Informal* baffle: *This problem beats me.* **10** shape with a hammer: *to beat gold into thin strips.* **11** stir quickly: *to beat eggs.* **12** go through (woods or underbrush) in a hunt: *The men beat the woods in search of the child.* *n* **1** one of a series of strokes, or its sound. **2** throb: *the beat of the heart.* **3** *Music* **a** a unit of time; accent: *three beats to a bar.* **b** a stroke of the hand, baton, etc. showing this. **c** rhythm: *music with a fast beat.* **4** the regular circuit or route of a police officer or sentry. **5** *Informal* one's regular sphere of activity, knowledge, etc.: *That sort of thing is off my beat.* **6** *Informal* something that excels: *I've never seen the beat of that.* *adj* **1** *Informal* worn out; exhausted. **2** *Slang* of or typical of beatniks: *the beat generation of the 50s.* ⟨Old English *bēatan*⟩ **beat about** search around: *She beat about in vain for a fitting answer.* **beat a retreat** a run away. **b** sound a retreat on a drum. **beat around** (or **about**) **the bush** avoid coming to the point: *Stop beating around the bush and tell me what you want.* **beat back** force to retreat. **beat down a** force to set a lower price by negotiation. **b** of the sun, shine intensely. **c** subdue. **beat it** *Slang* go away; scram. **beat off a** drive off by blows. **b** drive away; repel: *We beat off our fear by singing to each other.* **beat out** *Informal* outdo; surpass. **beat someone to it** be first to do something. **beat the rap** *Slang* escape a charge without penalty. **beat up** *Informal* **1** thrash severely. **2** scold; punish with shame and guilt.

beat·en *adj* **1** shaped by blows of a hammer: *beaten silver.* **2** much walked on or travelled: *a beaten path.* **3** discouraged by defeat: *They were a beaten lot.* **off the beaten path** or **track a** in an out-of-the-way or remote place.

b unconventional; original. **beat·er** *n* **1** a utensil for beating eggs, cream, etc.: *an electric beater.* **2** ✻ a young harp seal. **3** a person hired to rouse game during a hunt. **beat·ing** *n* **1** a series of violent blows. **2** hard use. **3** defeat: *The team took a beating last night.* **beat·nik** ['bitnɪk] *n* a person who adopts a mode of life calculated to show indifference to or contempt for conventions. ⟨*beat* + Yiddish *-nik*⟩ **beat–up** *adj Slang* **1** in very bad condition; worn out. **2** exhausted.

be·at·i·fy [bi'ætə,faɪ] *v* **1** make supremely happy; bless. **2** *Roman Catholic Church* declare (a person) by papal decree to be among the blessed in heaven. **be·at·i·fi·ca·tion** *n.* ⟨Latin *beatus* happy + *facere* make⟩ **be·a·tif·ic** [,biə'tɪfɪk] *adj* blissful: *beatific smile.* **be·a·tif·i·cal·ly** *adv.* **be·at·i·tude** [bi'ætə,tjud] *or* [bi'ætə,tud] *n* **1** bliss. **2** a blessing.

beat·nik See BEAT.

beau [bou] *n, pl* **beaus** or **beaux** [bouz] **1** suitor; lover. **2** a man who pays much attention to the stylishness of his clothes. ⟨French = handsome; Latin *bellus*⟩ **beaux–arts** ['bo'zaʀ] *n pl French* fine arts; painting, sculpture, music, etc.

Beau·fort scale ['boufərt] a scale of wind velocities, using code numbers from 0 to 17. ⟨Admiral Sir Francis *Beaufort*, who devised the scale in 1805⟩

beau·ty ['bjuti] *n* **1** a quality that gives great pleasure to the senses and to the mind. **2** a person or thing showing this quality, esp a beautiful woman. **3** *Informal* a notable example of its kind: *That catch was a beauty!* Often shortened to **beaut. beau·ti·ful** *adj.* **beau·ti·ful·ly** *adv.* ⟨Old French *beauté; beau* beautiful. See BEAU.⟩ **beau·te·ous** ['bjutiəs] *adj Poetic* beautiful. **beau·ti·cian** *n* a specialist in the use of cosmetics. **beau·ti·fy** *v* make or become (more) beautiful. **beau·ti·fi·ca·tion** *n.* **beauty salon** or **shop** a place that provides services such as hairdressing, manicuring, etc. Also, **beauty parlour** or **parlor. beauty sleep** *Informal* **1** any short nap. **2** the hours of sleep taken before midnight, supposed to be those that are most beneficial. **beauty spot 1** a small, black patch formerly worn on the face to show off the whiteness of the skin by contrast. **2** a mole or small mark on the skin. Also, **beauty mark. 3** a place of remarkable natural beauty.

SYNONYMS
Beautiful suggests delighting the senses as well as the mind or spirit: *a beautiful painting.* **Lovely** emphasizes emotional appeal: *her lovely smile, a lovely gift.* **Handsome** = pleasing to look at because well proportioned, well formed, etc.: *a handsome oak table.*

bea·ver¹ ['bivər] *n pl* **-vers** or (def. 1) **-ver 1** a large rodent that lives in and around water, having a thickset body, a broad, flat, scaly tail, webbed hind feet, and chisel-like front teeth. The North American beaver (*Castor canadensis*) has been an emblem of Canada

for over two hundred years. **2** the fur of a beaver. **3** a man's high silk hat, formerly made of this fur. **4** *Informal* a hard worker.
v Informal work hard or energetically (often with *away*): *He has been beavering away all day.* ⟨Old English *beofor*⟩
beaver fever ✱ a parasitic infection from drinking impure water; giardiasis. **Beaver Tail** ✱ *Trademark* an elliptical piece of dough deep-fried and served with any of various sweet toppings or coatings.
bea·ver² ['bivər] *n* **1** a movable piece of armour protecting the chin and mouth. **2** the movable front part of a helmet; visor. ⟨Old French *bavière* orig, bib; *bave* saliva⟩
Beaver ['bivər] See DUNNE-ZA.
be·bop ['bi,bɒp] *n Music* a style of jazz that evolved in the 1940s. ⟨imitative⟩
be·calm [bɪ'kɒm] *or* [bɪ'kɑm] *v* **1** keep (a ship, etc.) from moving because of lack of wind (usually in the passive): *We were becalmed for several hours.* **2** soothe.
be·came [bɪ'keim] *v* pt of BECOME.
be·cause [bɪ'kʌz] *or* [bɪ'kɒz] *conj* for the reason that; since: *We play ball because we enjoy it.* ⟨Middle English *bi cause* by cause⟩
because of due to; on account of: *She did not go because of the rain.*

USAGE
Because introduces a subordinate clause that gives a reason: *We hurried because we were late.* **As** is often used instead when the subordinate clause is 'old' information; it may also express a less definite causal relation. **Since** has a similar function but may be ambiguous since it can refer to time as well as cause: *Since she left, he has quit working.*

beck [bɛk] *n.* ⟨*beck, v* shortened from *beckon*⟩
at someone's beck and call ready or obliged to do whatever someone orders or wants.
beck·on ['bɛkən] *v* **1** signal to come by a motion of the head or hand. **2** entice; be attractive (to): *Adventure beckons; let us be off!* ⟨Old English *bēcnan*. Related to BEACON.⟩
be·come [bɪ'kʌm] *v* **-came, -come, -com·ing** **1** come to be: *to become wiser.* **2** be suitable for: *The rude comment did not become his position as chair.* **3** look good on: *That dress becomes her.* ⟨Old English *becuman*⟩
become of happen to: *What will become of her?*
be·com·ing *adj* **1** suitable: *becoming conduct.* **2** that looks good on the person wearing it: *a becoming dress.* **be·com·ing·ly** *adv.*
bec·que·rel [,bɛkə'rɛl] *n* an SI unit for measuring the rate of disintegration of the atoms of radioactive elements. One becquerel equals one disintegration per second. *Symbol* **Bq** ⟨A.H. *Becquerel*, 19c French physicist⟩
bed [bɛd] *n* **1 a** a piece of furniture to sleep or rest on. **b** sometimes, only the frame, or only the sheets and blankets: *an unmade bed.* **c** bedtime: *before bed.* **2** any place where

people or animals rest or sleep. **3** a flat base in which anything is laid: *They set the patio stones in a bed of concrete.* **4** the ground under a body of water: *the bed of a river.* **5** an area for planting in a garden: *a bed of pansies.* **6** *Geology* a layer or stratum: *a bed of coal.*
v **bed·ded, bed·ding** **1** settle in a sleeping place (with *down*): *to bed a horse down with straw. He bedded down on a couch.* **2** fix in a flat base. **3** *Informal* have sexual intercourse with. ⟨Old English *bedd*⟩
bed and board sleeping accommodation and meals. **get up on the wrong side of the bed** be irritable or bad-tempered. **go to bed with** *Informal* have sexual intercourse with. **put to bed a** make (a child or invalid) go to bed. **b** prepare (an edition of a newspaper, etc.) for printing. **take to one's bed** stay in bed because of sickness or weakness.
bed and breakfast an establishment offering overnight lodging and breakfast the next morning. **bed–and–breakfast** *adj.* **bed·board** *n* a board or sheet of wood placed under a mattress to give firm support. **bed·bug** *n* a small bug that hides in folds of mattresses, etc. and feeds on the blood of humans. **bed·cham·ber** *n Poetic or archaic* bedroom. **bed·cov·er** *n* a blanket or top cover for a bed. **bed·ding** *n* **1** sheets, blankets, etc. Also, **bed·clothes** or **bed linen**. **2** material for beds: *Straw is used as bedding for cows and horses.* **bedding plant** a plant ready to be transplanted into a flower bed. **bed·fel·low** *n* **1** the person with whom one shares a bed. **2** a close associate in some cause: *strange bedfellows.* **bed·frame** *n* the structure that supports the springs and mattress of a bed. **bed of roses** a situation of ease and comfort (usually in the negative): *Life isn't a bed of roses.* **bed·pan** *n* **1** a pan used as a toilet by sick people in bed. **2** formerly, a pan filled with hot coals for warming a bed. **bed·post** *n* an upright support at a corner of a bed. **bed rest** a period of resting in bed, as after illness, surgery, etc. **bed·rid·den** *adj* confined to bed for a long time because of sickness or weakness. **bed·rock** *n* **1** the solid rock beneath the soil and looser rocks. **2** a firm foundation. **3** the lowest level. **bed·roll** *n* bedding that can be rolled up and tied to a saddle, etc. **bed·room** *n* a room to sleep in. *adj* **1** to do with a bedroom: *bedroom furniture.* **2** *Informal* to do with or suggestive of sex: *bedroom eyes.* **bedroom suburb** or **community** a suburb inhabited by people who work outside that area and only return there in the evening. **bed·sheet** *n* any sheet used on a bed. **bed·side** *n* the side of a bed. *adj* to do with attending the sick: *She has a good bedside manner.* **bed–sit·ting room** a room doubling as living and sleeping area. **bed sofa** a sofa that can open out into a bed. **bed·sore** *n* a sore caused by lying too long in the same position. **bed·spread** *n* a decorative cover spread over other bedding. **bed·stead** *n* bedframe. **bed·spring** *n* a set of springs in a

frame, supporting a mattress. **bed·time** *n* the time for going to bed. **bed–wet·ting** *n* a lack of bladder control at night, during sleep. **bed-wet·ter** *n*.

be·dev·il [bɪ'dɛvəl] *v* **-illed** or **-iled**, **-il·ling** or **-il·ing** 1 torment. 2 confuse completely. 3 put under a spell. **be·dev·il·ment** *n*.

bed·lam ['bɛdləm] *n* uproar; confusion: *When the home team won, there was bedlam in the arena.* 〈*Bedlam,* traditional popular name for a mental hospital in London, England; from a variant of *Bethlehem*〉

bed·lam·er ['bɛdləmər] *n* ✹ a young seal, esp a harp seal. 〈prob. corruption of French *bête de la mer* sea beast〉

be·drag·gle [bɪ'drægəl] *v* make wet, dirty or untidy with or as if with rain, mud, etc. **be·drag·gled** *adj.* 〈*be-* + *drag* + *-le*〉

bee[1] [bi] *n* any of about 20 000 species making up a superfamily of flying insects that feed their young with a mixture of pollen and honey stored in their nests. 〈Old English *bēo*〉 **have a bee in one's bonnet** *Informal* **a** be preoccupied with one thing. **b** be slightly crazy. **the bee's knees** *Slang* the best there is. **bee·balm** *n* a plant of the mint family with clusters of bright red flowers. **bee·hive** *n* 1 a home for bees. 2 a busy place. **bee·keep·ing** *n* the art of managing colonies of honeybees in order to harvest their honey and wax. **bee·keep·er** *n*. **bee·line** *n* a straight path to a place. **make a beeline for** *Informal* hurry straight toward· *The startled calf made a beeline for its mother.* **bees·wax** *n* a pleasant-smelling wax secreted by worker bees and processed into candles, furniture polish, modelling wax, etc. **none of one's beeswax** *Slang* none of one's concern: *What I do with my money is none of your beeswax.*

bee[2] [bi] *n* a gathering for work or competition: *a spelling bee, a quilting bee.* 〈prob. dialect *been* help from neighbours; Old English *bēn* prayer. Related to BOON.〉

beech [bitʃ] *n* any of a genus of trees of North America and Europe, bearing sweet, edible nuts. **beech·nut** *n*. **beech·wood** *n*. 〈Old English *bēce*〉

beef [bif] *n* 1 the meat from a steer, cow, or bull. 2 *pl* **beeves** a steer, cow, or bull fattened for food, or such animals collectively: *fifty beeves for slaughter. He raises beef.* 3 *Informal* muscle; brawn: *This'll put some beef on you.* 4 *pl* **beefs** *Slang* complaint. *v* 1 *Informal* strengthen (with *up*): *Beef up your essay with a few examples.* 2 *Slang* complain. 〈Old French *boef*; Latin *bos, bovis* ox〉 **beef·a·lo** ['bifə,lou] *n* a cross between bison and cattle, raised for meat. **beef bouillon** a clear beef broth. **beef·cake** *n* *Slang* muscular, attractive men displayed in photographs. Compare CHEESECAKE. **beef·eat·er** *n* 1 a warder and guide of the Tower of London. 2 one who eats beef. **beef extract** an extract of beef or beef juices, for use in making broth, gravy, sauce, etc. **beef·steak** *n* a slice of beef for

broiling or frying. **beefsteak tomato** a very large tomato. **beef tea** a strong beef broth. **beef Wellington** a dish of beef covered in liver pâté and pastry and then baked. **beef·y** *adj* 1 like beef: *a beefy taste.* 2 strong; muscular. 3 heavy; solid. **beef·i·ness** *n*.

been [bin] *or* [bɪn] *v* pp of BE.

beep [bip] *n* any short, high-pitched sound: *the beep of a car horn.* **beep** *v*. 〈imitative〉 **beep·er** *n* a small radio-controlled device that emits a beep to tell the wearer to return a phone call, take medication, etc.

beer [bir] *n* 1 an alcoholic, fermented drink made from malt and, usually, hops. 2 a nonalcoholic carbonated drink made from roots or other parts of certain plants: *root beer.* **beer·y** *adj.* 〈Old English *bēor*〉 **beer and skittles** *Informal* pleasures and material comforts: *Life is not all beer and skittles.* **beer–bel·ly** *n* a protruding abdomen due to excessive beer drinking. **beer·fest** *n* *Informal* a celebration at which much beer is drunk. **beer garden** a patio outside a café, pub, etc., where beer is sold and drunk. **beer mat** a COASTER, often of cardboard, used in a bar or pub. **beer parlour** or **parlor** ✹ a pub, tavern, or bar offering beer.

beet [bit] *n* a plant of the goosefoot family, widely cultivated for its sweet, thick, roundish root and edible leaves. 〈Latin *beta*〉 **beet·root** *n* Brit beet.

bee·tle ['bitəl] *n* any of an order of insects with four wings, the front pair of which are modified into hard coverings. *v Informal* move quickly; scurry: *beetling down the road.* 〈Old English *bitela*; *bitan* bite〉

bee·tle–browed ['bitəl ,braʊd] *adj* 1 having projecting eyebrows. 2 scowling; sullen. 〈Middle English *bitel* biting + *brow*〉

beeves [bivz] *n* pl of BEEF (def. 2).

be·fall [bɪ'fɔl] *v* **-fell**, **-fall·en**, **-fall·ing** happen (to): *Be careful that no harm befalls you.* 〈Old English *befeallan*〉

be·fit [bɪ'fɪt] *v* **-fit·ted**, **-fit·ting** be suitable or proper for: *clothes that befit the occasion.*

be·fog [bɪ'fɒg] *v* **-fogged**, **-fog·ging** 1 fill, surround, or cover with fog. 2 confuse.

be·fore [bɪ'fɔr] *prep* 1 earlier than: *Come before noon.* 2 rather than: *We would choose death before dishonour.* 3 in the presence of: *to stand before the king.* 4 in front of; ahead of: *The guide went before them. The worst is still before us.* 5 under consideration by: *The matter is before the Committee.* *adv* 1 earlier: *Come at five o'clock, not before.* 2 until now or then: *I didn't know that before.* 3 in front; ahead: *He went before to see if the road was safe.* *conj* 1 previously to the time when: *Before she goes, I would like to talk to her.* 2 rather than: *I'll give up the trip before I'll go with them.* 〈Old English *beforan*〉

be·fore·hand *adv, adj* (never precedes a noun) 1 ahead of time; in advance: *Get everything ready beforehand.* 2 showing forethought: *That was very beforehand of you.*

be·friend [bɪ'frɛnd] *v* become a friend to; help: *to befriend new neighbours.*

be·fud·dle [bɪ'fʌdəl] *v* confuse, often with alcoholic drink. **be·fud·dle·ment** *n.*

beg [bɛg] *v* **begged, beg·ging 1** ask for money, esp from strangers in public places. **2** ask earnestly or humbly: *He begged his mother to forgive him.* **3** ask formally and courteously: *I beg your indulgence, gentlemen.* ⟨Middle English *beggen*⟩
beg off ask to be excused from (an obligation or engagement): *She asked me to go along, but I begged off. I'll have to beg off dinner tonight.*
beg the question a take for granted the very thing argued about: *Arguing about how often you can use the car begs the question whether you can borrow it at all.* **b** unintentionally raise another, more basic issue. **c** evade the issue. **go begging** find no acceptance: *The architect's suggestion went begging.* **I beg your pardon** a polite formula of apology.
beg·gar *n* **1** a person who makes a living by begging. **2** any very poor person. **3** *Slang* fellow: *That dog's a friendly little beggar.* *v* **1** bring to poverty: *Your reckless spending will beggar your parents.* **2** make to seem inadequate: *The grandeur of Niagara Falls beggars description.* **beg·gar·ly** *adj.* **beg·gar·li·ness** *n.*

SYNONYMS
Beg = ask earnestly or humbly: *He begged for more time.* **Plead** adds the idea of persistence. **Implore** and **beseech**, more formal and somewhat archaic respectively, can only be used with an infinitive complement. **Implore** emphasizes earnestness or urgency; **beseech** humility and reverence: *We implore you not to ruin your life by doing anything so foolish. The mother besought the queen to pardon her son.*

be·get [bɪ'gɛt] *v* **be·got** or (*archaic*) **be·gat**, **be·got·ten** or **be·got**, **be·get·ting 1** become the father of. **2** cause to be; produce: *Hate begets hate.* **be·get·ter** *n.* ⟨Old English *begitan* influenced by *gete(n)* get⟩

be·gin [bɪ'gɪn] *v* **be·gan, be·gun, be·gin·ning 1** start: *She began to speak.* **2** come or bring into being: *The club began two years ago.* **be·gin·ning** *n, adj.* ⟨Old English *beginnan*⟩
be·gin·ner *n* **1** a person without experience in something. **2** one who begins anything. **beginner's luck** invoked to account for a surprisingly good performance by a beginner.

be·gone [bɪ'gɒn] *interj Poetic* go away!

be·go·ni·a [bɪ'goʊnjə] *or* [bɪ'goʊniə] *n* any of a large genus of flowering plants grown for their showy, waxy flowers. ⟨Michel *Bégon* (1638-1710), French colonial governor⟩

be·grudge [bɪ'grʌdʒ] *v* **1** be reluctant or too stingy to give: *to begrudge food to a dog.* **2** resent (someone) because of (something they have or enjoy): *They begrudge us our new house.*

be·guile [bɪ'gaɪl] *v* **1** lure by deception: *His pleasant ways beguiled me into thinking he was my friend.* **2** entertain or charm. **3** pass (time) pleasantly. **4** cheat cunningly (with *of*): *They beguiled him of his money.* **be·guil·ing** *adj.*

be·half [bɪ'hæf] *n.* ⟨Middle English *behalve*⟩ **on** (or **in**) **behalf of a** as a representative of: *on behalf of a client.* **b** in the interests of.

be·have [bɪ'heɪv] *v* **1** conduct (oneself): *to behave badly.* **2** *Informal* act acceptably: *Did you behave today? You'd better behave yourself!* **3** act: *Water behaves in different ways when it is heated and when it is frozen.* **be·hav·iour** or **be·hav·ior** *n.* ⟨*be-* + *have*⟩
be·hav·iour·al or **be·hav·ior·al** *adj* **1** to do with behaviour in general. **2** observing and analyzing human behaviour: *behavioural sciences.* **be·hav·iour·ism** or **be·hav·ior·ism** *n* **1** the theory that the observable behaviour of people and animals, as opposed to their thought processes, moral development, etc., is the proper subject of psychology. **2** the theory that all voluntary behaviour is a result of conditioning. **be·hav·iour·ist** *n.* **be·hav·iour·is·tic** *adj.* **behaviour modification** *Psychology* simple conditioning in which desirable behaviour is rewarded and undesirable behaviour punished. **behaviour therapy** treatment using such methods.

be·head [bɪ'hɛd] *v* cut off the head of.

be·he·moth [bɪ'himəθ] *or* ['biəməθ] *n* any huge, powerful thing. ⟨Hebrew *b'hēmōth, pl* beasts; a huge unknown biblical animal⟩

be·hest [bɪ'hɛst] *n* a command; order. ⟨Old English *behǽs* promise⟩

be·hind [bɪ'haɪnd] *prep* **1** at the back of: *behind the sofa.* **2** hidden by: *Treachery lurked behind her smooth manner.* **3** less advanced than: *behind the others in math.* **4** supporting: *Her friends are behind her.* **5** in (someone's) past; over for: *Our problems are behind us.* **6** at the source of; causing: *Who is behind all this? adv* **1** at the back: *Your hem hangs down behind.* **2** farther back; less advanced: *The other hikers are still far behind. She is behind in music.* **3** late: *The plane is an hour behind.* *n Informal* buttocks. ⟨Old English *be-* by + *hindan* from behind⟩
be·hind·hand *adj* (never before a noun), *adv* **1** late or slow. **2** in debt; in arrears.

be·hold [bɪ'hoʊld] *Archaic or poetic v* **be·held, be·hold·ing** see; look at. *interj* look! see! **be·hold·er** *n.* ⟨Old English *behealdan*⟩

be·hold·en [bɪ'hoʊldən] *adj* indebted or obliged: *I am much beholden to you.*

be·hoove [bɪ'huv] *v* be necessary or proper for: *It behooves us to answer the challenge.* ⟨Old English *behōfian* need⟩

beige [beɪʒ] *n, adj* very light, greyish brown; a neutral colour. ⟨French⟩

be·ing ['biɪŋ] *n* **1** a living creature: *human beings.* **2** existence: *A new era came into being.* **3** self: *Her whole being yearned for home.* **being as** (or **that**) *Informal* since; in view of the fact that. **for the time being** for now: *Leave that for the time being and do it later.*

be·jew·el [bɪ'dʒuəl] *v* **-elled** or **-eled, -el·ling** or **-el·ing** adorn with jewels, or as if with jewels: *The sky is bejewelled with stars.*

bel [bɛl] *n* a unit for comparing levels of power or loudness. ⟨after Alexander Graham Bell (1847-1922), Scottish inventor⟩

be·la·bour or **be·la·bor** [bɪˈleibər] *v* **1** insist on or develop more than necessary: *to belabour a point in an argument.* **2** abuse or ridicule: *belaboured by the press.* **3** beat.

be·lat·ed [bɪˈleitɪd] *adj* happening or coming late: *a belated birthday card.* **be·lat·ed·ly** *adv.* **be·lat·ed·ness** *n.*

be·lay [bɪˈlei] *v* **1** fasten (a line or rope) by winding it around a cleat, piton, etc. **2** secure (a climber) at the end of a rope. **3** *Nautical, Informal* stop (usually imperative): *Belay there!* *n* an object, such as a projecting piece of rock, used to secure a rope in mountaineering. ⟨Old English *belecgan*⟩
belaying pin a removable pin for fastening rigging lines.

belch [bɛltʃ] *v* **1** expel gas from the stomach through the mouth; burp. **2** throw out with force: *The volcano belched smoke.* **belch** *n.* **belch·er** *n.* ⟨Old English *bealcian*⟩

be·lea·guer [bɪˈligər] *v* **1** beset; trouble continuously: *beleaguered by debts.* **2** besiege: *a beleaguered city.* ⟨Dutch *belegeren; leger* camp⟩

bel·fry [ˈbɛlfri] *n* a tower, or a room in a tower, containing a bell or bells. ⟨Old French *berfrei*⟩

be·lie [bɪˈlai] *v* **-lied, -ly·ing 1** give a false idea of: *Her frown belied her usual good nature.* **2** contradict: *Your actions belie your words.* **be·li·er** *n.* ⟨Old English *beléogan*⟩

be·lieve [bɪˈliv] *v* **1** accept as true: *I don't believe her story.* **2** think that (another person) tells the truth: *I don't believe her.* **3** suppose; think: *I believe they're out today.* **4** have religious faith: *He used to be very devout but no longer believes.* **be·liev·a·ble** *adj.* **be·liev·a·bly** *adv.* **be·liev·a·bil·i·ty** *n.* **be·liev·er** *n.* ⟨Old English *belefan*⟩
believe in a have faith or confidence in: *I believe in you.* **b** accept as real: *Do you believe in ghosts?* **c** approve of: *She doesn't believe in protecting kids from harsh truth.*

be·lief [bɪˈlif] *n* **1** the act or fact of believing or trusting: *statements unworthy of belief.* **2** the thing believed: *That violates her Jewish beliefs. It's my belief we're in for a cold winter.*

be·lit·tle [bɪˈlɪtəl] *v* put down; cause to seem unimportant: *Jealous people belittled the explorer's great discoveries.* **be·lit·tling** *adj.*

bell [bɛl] *n* **1** a hollow device usually shaped like a cup with a flared opening, that rings when struck. **2** on shipboard, the stroke of a bell to indicate each half hour counted from 12:00, 4:00, or 8:00. **3** Usually, **bells** *pl* a percussion instrument consisting of a series of metal tubes that make ringing tones when struck. **4** anything shaped like a bell, such as the opening of a trumpet.
v **1** put a bell on. **2** swell out like a bell. **bell–like** *adj.* ⟨Old English *belle*⟩

bells and whistles fancy optional features. **bell the cat** do a dangerous job for the common good. **ring a bell** seem familiar: *That name rings a bell.* **with bells on** with whole-hearted enthusiasm.
bell–bot·toms *n pl* pants with legs that flare out at the bottom. **bell–bot·tom** *adj.* **bell·boy** *n* a man or boy whose work is carrying baggage and doing errands for the guests of a hotel or club. Also, **bell·hop. bell buoy** a buoy with a bell rung by the movement of the waves. **bell curve** the standard variation on a statistical graph, forming a bell-like shape. **bell jar** a glass, bell-shaped cover or container used esp in scientific experiments requiring reduced air pressure. **bell pepper** a sweet pepper used as a vegetable. **bell tower** a tower built to house a bell or bells, often as part of a larger building, such as a church.

Bel·la Bel·la [ˈbɛlə ˈbɛlə] See HEILTSUK.

Bel·la Coo·la [ˈbɛlə ˈkulə] See NUXALK.

bel·la·don·na [ˌbɛləˈdɒnə] *n* a very poisonous European plant of the nightshade family; deadly nightshade. ⟨Italian = fair lady⟩
belladonna lily an amaryllis of S Africa.

belle [bɛl] *n* **1** a beautiful woman or girl. **2** the prettiest or most admired woman or girl: *the belle of the ball.* ⟨French *belle*, fem. of *beau*. See BEAU.⟩

belles–let·tres [bɛl ˈlɛtrə] *French* [ˈbɛl ˈlɛtʀ] *n pl* literature valued for its enduring artistic appeal. **bel·let·rist** [ˌbɛlˈlɛtrɪst] *n.* ⟨French⟩

bel·li·cose [ˈbɛləˌkous] *adj* warlike; fond of fighting. **bel·li·cos·i·ty** [ˌbɛləˈkɒsəti] *n.* ⟨Latin *bellicosus; bellum* war⟩

bel·lig·er·ent [bəˈlɪdʒərənt] *adj* **1** taking an aggressively hostile attitude. **2** at war.
n **1** a person engaged in a fight. **2** a nation at war. **bel·lig·er·ence** *n.* ⟨Latin *belligerans; bellum* war + *gerere* wage⟩

bel·low [ˈbɛlou] *v* **1** roar as a bull does. **2** shout or yell with a deep tone. **bel·low** *n.* **bel·low·er** *n.* ⟨Middle English *belwe*⟩

bel·lows [ˈbɛlouz] *n pl or sg* **1** a device with many folds that allow it to expand with the intake of air and then squeeze it out, used to blow on a fire or sound an accordion, organ, etc. **2** in certain cameras, the folding part behind the lens. ⟨Old English *belgas*, pl of *belg* bag, belly⟩

bell·weth·er [ˈbɛlˌwɛðər] *n* **1** a male sheep that wears a bell and leads the flock. **2** any leader or trendsetter: *Our riding is the political bellwether for the rest of the province.*

bel·ly [ˈbɛli] *n* **1** the lower part of the human body, containing the stomach and intestines. **2** the underpart of an animal's body. **3** the bulging part of anything. **4** the space deep inside anything: *the belly of the cargo plane.* **5** *Archaic* the womb.
v swell out; bulge: *The sails bellied in the wind.* ⟨Old English *belg, belig* bag⟩
bel·ly·ache *Informal n* **1** a pain in the abdomen.

2 a complaint. *v* complain, esp over trifles.
bel·ly·ach·er *n*. belly button *Informal* navel.
belly dance a Middle Eastern dance
performed by a woman with naked
abdomen. **bel·ly–dance** *v*. **bel·ly–danc·er** *n*.
bel·ly·flop *v* -**flopped, -flop·ping** *Slang v* dive
and strike the water with the abdomen.
bel·ly·flop *n*. **bel·ly·ful** *n Informal* more than
one wants or can stand. **belly laugh** a deep,
hearty laugh. **bel·ly–up** *adv* on one's back:
dead fish floating belly-up. **go belly–up** *Informal*
of an organization, business, etc., fail; fold.

be·long [bɪˈlɒŋ] *v* 1 have its proper place:
That book belongs on this shelf. 2 be accepted
or included by a group: *Everyone needs to
belong.* ⟨Old English *gelang* belonging to⟩
belong to a be the property of. **b** be a part of;
be connected with. **c** be a member of (an
organization). **d** be the duty or concern of:
This responsibility belongs to the club secretary.
belongings *n pl* personal possessions.

be·lov·ed [bɪˈlʌvɪd] *or* [bɪˈlʌvd] *adj* dear.
n a person who is loved; darling.

be·low [bɪˈlou] *adv* 1 in or to a lower place:
*From the top of the hill she looked down on the
road below.* 2 on or to a lower floor or deck:
The sailor went below. 3 farther on in a piece
of writing: *E-mail addresses are listed below.*
4 less than zero on a scale of temperature: *It
was four below last night.*
prep 1 lower or less than; under: *below the
third floor, a price below $10 000.* 2 unworthy
of: *He said it would be below him to argue the
point.* ⟨Middle English *biloghe* by low⟩

belt [bɛlt] *n* 1 a strip of leather, cloth, etc.
worn around the body. 2 any broad strip or
band: *a belt of trees.* 3 a region having
distinctive characteristics: *the wheat belt.* 4 an
endless band that transfers motion: *a fan
belt.* 5 *Slang* a sharp blow: *a belt on the chin.*
6 *Slang* a hasty or greedy drink, esp of liquor:
a belt of whisky. 7 *Slang* a jolt of excitement.
v 1 provide or fasten with a belt. 2 beat with
a belt. 3 *Slang* hit suddenly and hard: *He
belted his opponent.* 4 *Slang* drink hurriedly or
greedily (usually with *down*): *to belt down a
couple of drinks.* 5 *Slang* sing loudly (with *out*):
belting out old love songs. **belt·ed** *adj.*
⟨probably Latin *balteus* girdle⟩
below the belt unfair or unfairly: *That remark
was below the belt.* **tighten one's belt** spend
less. **under one's belt a** in one's stomach: *a
good dinner under his belt.* **b** to one's credit: *six
years' training under her belt.*
belt line a railway, bus line, etc. taking a
more or less circular route, e.g., around a city.

be·lu·ga [bəˈlugə] *n* 1 a white toothed whale
found in the Arctic and as far south as the
Gulf of St. Lawrence. Also called **white
whale.** 2 a very large, white sturgeon of the
Black and Caspian Seas and the Sea of Azov.
⟨Russian *bielo-* white⟩

be·moan [bɪˈmoun] *v* 1 moan or complain
about. 2 mourn.

be·muse [bɪˈmjuz] *v* 1 bewilder; confuse; daze.
2 absorb in thought (usually passive).
be·mused *adj.* **be·muse·ment** *n*.

bench [bɛntʃ] *n* 1 a long seat, often backless,
usually of wood, stone, or plastic. 2 an
artisan's worktable. 3 **the bench a** a judge or
panel of judges presiding in a court of law.
b the office of judge: *The lawyer was appointed
to the bench.* **c** a court of law. 4 *Sports* **a** the
place where team members sit while waiting
to play. **b** these players collectively.
v take (a player) out of a game. ⟨Old English
benc⟩
bench·er [ˈbɛntʃər] *n* 1 a person who sits on
a bench, esp a judge, magistrate, etc. 2 in
Canada, one of the elected officials of a
provincial law society. **bench·mark** or **bench
mark** *n* 1 *Surveying* a reference mark made on
a permanent object of known position and
elevation. 2 any point of reference for
evaluating other things: *This ruling will serve
as a benchmark for future cases.* 3 *Computers* a
test to measure the performance of hardware
or software. **bench penalty** or **bench minor** *
Hockey a two-minute penalty against a team,
served by a player designated by the team's
coach or manager. **bench press** a manner of
lifting weights with the arms while lying flat
on one's back on a bench, with one's feet on
the floor. **bench–press** *v*.

bend [bɛnd] *v* **bent, bend·ing** 1 make, be, or
become curved or crooked: *The lynx's weight
bent the branch.* 2 stoop: *She bent to pick up a
leaf.* 3 submit or force to submit: *"I will bend
you or break you!" cried the villain, but the hero
would not bend.* 4 direct (one's mind, effort,
steps, etc.): *bent for home. He bent his mind to
the task.* 5 fasten (a sail, rope, etc.).
n 1 the act or result of bending: *a bend in the
road.* 2 *Nautical* a type of knot. 3 **the bends**
Informal DECOMPRESSION SICKNESS. **bend·a·ble** *adj.*
bend·y *adj.* ⟨Old English *bendan* bind, band⟩
around (or **round**) **the bend** *Slang* crazy.
bend over backward(s) go to great lengths to
oblige someone.
bend·er *n* 1 *Slang* a drinking spree. 2 a
person or thing that bends.

be·neath [bɪˈniθ] *adv* below; underneath: *He
dozed in the hammock, his dog lying beneath.*
prep 1 under; below: *beneath the tree.*
2 unworthy of; worthy not even of: *a traitor
beneath contempt. Shoplifting is beneath her.*
⟨Old English *be-* by + *neothan* below⟩

Ben·e·dic·tine [ˌbɛnəˈdɪktin] *or* [ˌbɛnəˈdɪktɪn]
adj of Saint Benedict (480?-543?) or the order
of monks he founded.
n 1 *Roman Catholic Church* a monk or nun of
this order. 2 a liqueur originally made by
such monks. ⟨French *bénédictin*⟩

ben·e·dic·tion [ˌbɛnəˈdɪkʃən] *n* 1 a prayer of
blessing at the end of a religious service.
2 blessing. 3 *Roman Catholic Church* a special
service at which the Host is displayed for the
blessing of the congregation. **be·ne·dic·to·ry**
adj. ⟨Latin *benedicere* bless⟩

ben·e·fac·tor [ˈbɛnəˌfæktər] *n* a person who
helps someone through gifts or kind acts: *We
thanked our benefactors for all they had given
us.* **ben·e·fac·tion** *n*. **ben·e·fac·tress** *n*. ⟨Latin
bene well + *facere* do⟩

ben·e·fice ['bɛnəfɪs] *n* **1** a permanent position created by church authority. **2** the money earned from it. ⟨Latin *beneficus,* from *benefacere.* See BENEFACTOR.⟩

be·nef·i·cence [bə'nɛfəsəns] *n* **1** kindness. **2** a donation or charitable act. **be·nef·i·cent** *adj* **1** kind; doing good. **2** having good results.

ben·e·fi·cial [,bɛnə'fɪʃəl] *adj* helpful; favourable; producing good: *Moisture and light are beneficial to plants.* **ben·e·fi·cial·ly** *adv.* **ben·e·fi·ci·ar·y** [,bɛnə'fɪʃəri] *or* [,bɛnə'fɪʃi,ɛri] *n* **1** a person who receives benefit: *All the children are beneficiaries of the new playground.* **2** the person who gets the money or property from an insurance policy, trust fund, will, etc. **3** one who holds a BENEFICE (def. 1).

ben·e·fit ['bɛnəfɪt] *n* **1** help; advantage or profit; good effect, or any source of these. **2 benefits** *pl* payments received from an insurance plan administered by government or an employer: *dental benefits, unemployment benefits.* **3** a performance by professionals to raise money for a charitable cause. **4** *Archaic* an act of kindness; a favour.
v **1** be good for: *Rest benefits a sick person.* **2** receive good; profit: *She benefited from the medicine.* ⟨Latin *benefactum.* See BENEFACTOR.⟩ **benefit of clergy** the approval, services, or rites of the church. **give someone the benefit of the doubt** decide in someone's favour without proof of merit or innocence.

be·nev·o·lence [bə'nɛvələns] *n* **1** good will; kindness or kindly feeling. **2** a generous gift or kind act. **be·nev·o·lent** *adj.* ⟨Latin *bene* well + *volere* wish⟩

be·night·ed [bɪ'nəɪtɪd] *adj* in darkness, esp the darkness of ignorance.

be·nign [bɪ'naɪn] *adj* **1** gentle; harmless or innocent: *a benign old lady.* **2** favourable; mild: *a benign climate.* **3** *Medicine* **a** doing no permanent harm: *benign leukemia.* **b** not cancerous: *benign tumours.* **be·nign·ly** *adv.* ⟨Latin *benignus* good-natured⟩

Ben·nett buggy ['bɛnət] ✱ during the Depression of the 1930s, a car drawn by horses because the owner could not afford gas, oil, or a licence for it. ⟨R.B. *Bennett,* then prime minister of Canada, whose government was blamed⟩

ben·ny ['bɛni] *n Slang* an amphetamine tablet taken as a stimulant. ⟨*Benzedrine*⟩

bent [bɛnt] *adj* **1** not straight; crooked. **2** determined: *bent on staying.* **3** bound (for): *bent toward Jerusalem.* **4** *Slang* dishonest.
n an inclination: *a bent for drawing.*
bent out of shape *Slang* angry; resentful.
bent·wood *n* wood bent into various shapes by steam and pressure.

ben·zene [bɛn'zin] *or* ['bɛnzin] *n* a colourless, flammable liquid hydrocarbon used in the manufacture of many chemical products, including detergent, insecticides, and motor fuel. ⟨*benzoin* a resin; Arabic *luban jawi* incense of Java⟩
benzene ring the hexagonal molecular structure of benzene and its compounds, in which six carbon atoms are bonded to each other and to six hydrogen atoms. **ben·zo·ate of soda** ['bɛnzout] *or* ['bɛnzou,eit] a common food preservative.

Be·o·thuk [bi'ɒθək] *or* [bi'ɒtək] *n, pl* **-thuk** or **-thuks 1** a member of a First Nations people of Newfoundland, extinct by 1829. **2** their language. **Be·o·thuk** *adj.* Also, **Be·o·thic.**

be·queath [bɪ'kwiθ] *or* [bɪ'kwið] *v* **1** give or leave (property, etc.) by a will. **2** hand down to posterity: *One age bequeaths its values to the next.* **be·quest** [bɪ'kwɛst] *n.* ⟨Old English *be-* to, for + *cwethan* say; Middle English *biqueste*⟩

be·rate [bɪ'reit] *v* scold sharply.

be·reave [bɪ'riv] *v* **be·reaved** or **be·reft, be·reav·ing 1** deprive *(of)* ruthlessly; rob: *to bereave someone of hope.* **2** take away from by death: *bereaved of their mother at an early age.* **3** leave desolate. **be·reave·ment** *n.* ⟨Old English *be-* away + *rēafian* rob⟩
be·reaved *adj* suffering the loss of a loved one by death. **the bereaved** *n.* **be·reft** [bɪ'rɛft] *adj* cruelly deprived; dispossessed.

be·ret [bə'rei] *n* a soft, round cap of wool or felt. ⟨French *béret;* Latin *birretum.* See BIRETTA.⟩

ber·ga·mot ['bɜrgə,mɒt] *n* **1** a small citrus tree bearing fruit whose rind yields a fragrant essential oil used in perfumes. **2** any of several plants of the mint family yielding an oil with a similar fragrance. ⟨*Bergamo,* Italy⟩

ber·i·ber·i ['bɛri,bɛri] *n* a disease caused by a lack of thiamine, affecting the heart or nervous system. ⟨Sinhala (language of Sri Lanka), reduplication of *beri* weakness⟩

ber·ke·li·um ['bɜr'kiliəm] *n* an artificial metallic element. *Symbol* **Bk** ⟨*Berkeley,* California, where it was first produced⟩

berm [bɜrm] *n* **1** a high ridge of earth functioning as a protective barrier, a base or covering for a pipeline, etc. **2** a narrow strip of grass beside a road. **3** a narrow ledge or path between a moat and a rampart in a fortification. ⟨Dutch *berm*⟩

Ber·mu·da shorts [bər'mjudə] short tailored pants that reach to just above the knee. **Bermuda Triangle** a region of the Atlantic bounded by Florida, Bermuda, and Puerto Rico, in which ships and planes are said to have mysteriously disappeared.

ber·ry ['bɛri] *n* **1** any small, juicy fruit with many seeds instead of a single pit, such as a currant or strawberry. **2** *Botany* a simple fruit with two or more seeds in the pulp and a skin or rind, such as a grape or banana. **3** the dry seed or fruit of certain other kinds of plants. **4** an egg of a lobster or fish.
v **1** gather or pick berries. **2** bear or produce berries: *a berrying shrub.* ⟨Old English *berie*⟩

ber·serk [bər'zɜrk] *adj* frenzied. ⟨Icelandic *berserkr* wild warrior; *ber-* bear + *serkr* shirt⟩ **ber·serk·er** *n* **1** a fierce Norse warrior. **2** one who behaves violently or wildly.

berth [bɜrθ] *n* **1** a place to sleep on a train, ship, or aircraft. **2** a place for a ship at anchor, parked transport vehicle, etc.

3 *Sports* a place or standing: *to win a berth in the finals.* **4** a position; job, esp somewhat prestigious. **5 ✳** an area in which a company or individual has the right to fell trees.
v **1** put into a berth; provide with a berth. **2** have or occupy a berth. ⟨perhaps from *bear¹*⟩ **give something a wide berth** keep well away from: *I gave the growling dog a wide berth.*

ber·yl [ˈbɛrəl] *n* a very hard mineral, usually green or greenish blue. ⟨Greek *bēryllos*⟩
be·ryl·li·um [bəˈrɪliəm] *n* a hard, strong, metallic element. *Symbol* **Be** ⟨*beryl*⟩

be·seech [bɪˈsitʃ] *v* **be·sought** or **be·seeched, be·seech·ing** ask earnestly; beg. ⟨Middle English *be-* thoroughly + *sechen* seek⟩

be·set [bɪˈsɛt] *v* **-set, -set·ting 1** attack on all sides: *beset by mosquitoes.* **2** trouble or hinder continually: *a task beset with many difficulties.* ⟨Old English *be-* around + *settan* set⟩
be·set·ting sin a habitual weakness.

be·side [bɪˈsaɪd] *prep* **1** by the side of; next to: *Grass grows beside the brook.* **2** compared with: *He seems dull beside his sister.* ⟨Old English *be sidan* by side⟩
beside oneself extremely excited or upset: *beside oneself with fear, beside oneself with joy.* **beside the point** irrelevant.

be·sides [bɪˈsaɪdz] *adv* **1** also; in addition: *He didn't want to quarrel; besides, he wasn't completely sure he was right.* **2** otherwise; else: *She is ignorant of politics, whatever she may know besides.*
prep **1** in addition to: *The picnic was attended by others besides our own family.* **2** except; other than: *We spoke to no one besides you.*

be·siege [bɪˈsidʒ] *v* **1** surround and try to capture: *to besiege a city.* **2** overwhelm with attention, requests, questions, etc.: *The returning astronauts were besieged by reporters.*

be·smirch [bɪˈsmɜrtʃ] *v* **1** make dirty; stain. **2** dishonour: *to besmirch a good reputation.*

be·sot [bɪˈsɒt] *v* **-sot·ted, -sot·ting** make foolish, as with drunkenness, infatuation, etc.

be·sought [bɪˈsɒt] *v* a pt and pp of BESEECH.

be·speak [bɪˈspik] *v* **-spoke, -spo·ken, -speak·ing 1** reserve; speak for: *to bespeak tickets to a play.* **2** indicate: *A neat appearance bespeaks care.* **3** foreshadow: *Their early successes bespeak a great future.*

be·spec·ta·cled [bɪˈspɛktəkəld] *adj* wearing glasses.

best [bɛst] *adj* (superlative of GOOD) **1** most valuable, excellent, beneficial, etc.: *the best players, the best thing to do.* **2** largest: *We spent the best part of the day just getting organized.* **3** *Informal* (used esp by children) favourite; preferred: *my best colour.*
adv (superlative of WELL) **1** most excellently: *Who reads best?* **2** in the highest degree: *I like this book best.*
n **1** the person, thing, quality, etc. that is best: *Of all our trips, this one has been the best.* **2** utmost: *I did my best to finish on time.*
v Informal defeat: *Our team was bested in the final game.* ⟨Old English *betst*⟩

(all) for the best advantageous in the end: *At first we were unhappy about the change, but it turned out to be all for the best.* **as best one can** *Informal* as well as possible. **at best** even given the most favourable circumstances or interpretation: *Summer is at best very short. It was a sad effort at best.* **at one's** (or **its**) **best** showing all the best qualities of: *This article is journalism at its best. I'm at my best in the evening.* **get the best of** defeat or outwit. **had best** ought to: *We had best postpone the party.* **make the best of** do as well as possible with: *We'll just have to make the best of a bad job.* **Sunday best** (one's) best clothes. **with the best** as well as anyone: *She can swim with the best.*
best friend most intimate friend. **best man** the bridegroom's chief attendant at a wedding. **best·sell·er** or **best seller** *n* any product, esp a book, that sells very well.

bes·tial [ˈbistʃəl], [ˈbɛstʃəl], or [ˈbɛstiəl] *adj* **1** beastly; brutal. **2** of beasts. **bes·tial·ly** *adv*. **bes·ti·al·ize** *v*. ⟨Latin *bestia* beast⟩
bes·ti·al·i·ty *n* **1** bestial character or conduct. **2** sexual acts between a person and an animal. **bes·ti·ar·y** [ˈbɛstʃiˌɛri] or [ˈbɪstʃiˌɛri] *n* a medieval collection of allegorical descriptions of real or mythical animals.

be·stir [bɪˈstɜr] *v* **-stirred, -stir·ring** stir up; rouse; exert: *to bestir oneself to action.*

be·stow [bɪˈstoʊ] *v* **1** give as a gift (with *on* or *upon*): *to bestow a privilege on someone.* **2** make use of; apply: *We bestowed a great deal of thought on the plan.* **be·stow·al** *n*. ⟨Middle English *bistowe(n)*⟩

bet [bɛt] *n* **1** an agreement between two people that the one proved wrong about the outcome of an event or inquiry will give a particular thing or sum to the one proved right. **2** the thing or sum of money so risked. **3** a thing to bet on: *That horse is a good bet.*
v **bet** or **bet·ted, bet·ting 1** promise (money or something else) to (a person) if that person is proved right about the outcome of an event: *I bet you two cents I won't pass this test.* **2** make a bet: *Did you bet on the race?* **3** *Informal* be very sure: *I bet this will be fun.* **bet·ter** or **bet·tor** *n*. ⟨origin uncertain⟩
you bet *Informal* certainly: *"Are you going to the game?" "You bet!"*

be·ta [ˈbeɪtə] or [ˈbitə] *n* **1** the second letter of the Greek alphabet (B, β). **2** the second in any series. **3 Beta** *Astronomy* the second brightest star in a constellation.
beta blocker a drug used to control high blood pressure by blocking the stimulation of the neural receptors that speed heart rate. **beta decay** radioactive decay of a substance, resulting in a new substance and the emission of an electron or positron (**beta particle**) by a nucleus. **beta endorphin** a chemical substance in the brain which acts as a pain reliever.

be·take [bɪˈteik] *v* **-took, -tak·en, -tak·ing** (used reflexively) go: *He betook himself to the mountains.*

be·tel [ˈbitəl] *n* a climbing pepper plant of tropical Asia. ⟨Portuguese; Malayalam *vettila*⟩

betel nut the mildly narcotic seed of the tropical Asian **betel palm**, boiled and dried for chewing with betel leaves.

bête noire ['bɛt 'nwɑr] the thing or person one dreads or hates. ⟨French = black beast⟩

be·think [bɪ'θɪŋk] v -**thought, -think·ing** cause (oneself) to reflect or remember (with of). ⟨Old English bethencan⟩

be·tide [bɪ'taɪd] v **woe betide** a severe warning to: Woe betide anyone who touches my pie. ⟨Middle English be- + tiden happen⟩

be·to·ken [bɪ'toukən] v **1** be a sign of: His smile betokened an inner peace. **2** foreshadow.

be·took [bɪ'tʊk] v pt of BETAKE.

be·tray [bɪ'treɪ] v **1** deliver into the enemy's hands by treachery: The traitor betrayed her country. **2** be unfaithful to: to betray one's principles. He betrayed his friends. **3** mislead; deceive. **4** give away (a secret); reveal: His mistakes betrayed his lack of education. **be·tray·er** n. **be·tray·al** n. ⟨Middle English be- + traie(n) betray; Latin tradere hand over⟩

be·troth [bɪ'trouð] or [bɪ'trɒθ] v promise in marriage. **be·troth·al** n. **be·trothed** adj, n. ⟨Old English trēowth pledge⟩

bet·ter ['bɛtər] adj (comparative of GOOD) **1** more valuable, excellent, beneficial, etc.: better facilities, a better thing to do. **2** less sick: The child is better today. **3** larger: Four days is the better part of a week.
adv (comparative of WELL) **1** more excellently: He'll do better next time. **2** in a higher degree: I like her better than I like her brother.
n **1** a person or thing that is better: the better of the two routes. **2** Usually, **betters** pl one's superiors in rank or merit.
v **1** make or become better: to better one's skill. **2** do better than: They were unable to better our record. ⟨Old English betera⟩
better off a in a better condition: The theatre was noisy; we would have been better off with a video at home. **b** having more money. **for the better** bringing improvement: Her illness took a turn for the better. **get** or **have the better of** defeat; outwit. **had better** would be wise to: You had better be there on time. **think better of** think over and change one's mind: I was going to speak, but thought better of it and kept quiet.
better half Informal a female spouse.
bet·ter·ment n **1** improvement: Doctors work for the betterment of their patients' health. **2** (usually pl) Law an improvement of real estate property.

be·tween [bɪ'twin] prep **1** in or into the space or time separating: Many cities lie between Fredericton and Edmonton. There are no holidays between now and the end of school. **2** involving: war between two nations. **3** by the joint effort, ownership, contribution, etc. of: Between us we had $57. **4** in or into portions for: The estate was divided between the two children. **5** restricted to: Keep the matter between us.
adv in or into an intermediate space or time: We could no longer see the moon; a cloud had come between. ⟨Old English betwēonum⟩
between the devil and the deep blue sea See DEVIL. **between you and me** as a personal confidence: Between you and me, he has no hope of winning. **in between** in the middle (of): Fold the blanket and pack the mirror in between.

be·twixt [bɪ'twɪkst] prep, adv Poetic between. **betwixt and between** neither one nor the other. ⟨Old English betweox⟩

bev·el ['bɛvəl] n a sloped edge, as on plate glass, moulding, tabletops, etc.
v -**elled** or -**eled, -el·ling** or -**el·ing 1** cut at an angle other than a right angle. **2** slope. ⟨origin uncertain⟩

bev·er·age ['bɛvərɪdʒ] n a liquid served for drinking: milk, juice, pop, and other beverages. ⟨Old French bevre to drink; Latin bibere⟩
beverage room ⚹ BEER PARLOUR.

bev·y ['bɛvi] n a group: a bevy of girls. ⟨perhaps Anglo-French bevée drinking group⟩

be·wail [bɪ'weɪl] v mourn; complain about: to bewail one's fate.

be·ware [bɪ'wɛr] v (infinitive or imperative only) **1** watch out (for): Beware (of) thieves. **2** be careful: Beware lest you make him angry. She told us to beware how we approach them. ⟨be + archaic ware wary⟩

be·wil·der [bɪ'wɪldər] v confuse totally; make unable to cope or understand: bewildered by the huge crowds. **be·wil·der·ment** n. ⟨be- + Old English wilder lead astray⟩

be·witch [bɪ'wɪtʃ] v **1** put under a spell. **2** delight; fascinate. **be·witch·ed** adj. **be·witch·ing** adj. **be·witch·ment** n.

be·yond [bi'jɒnd] prep **1** on or to the farther side of: beyond the sea. **2** later than: beyond the set time. **3** out of the reach of: beyond help. **4** more than: I did nothing beyond what you asked. **5** surpassing: beyond description.
adv **1** farther away in space or time: till midnight and beyond. Beyond were the hills. **2** in addition: The farmer had ten cows, and a flock of sheep beyond. ⟨Old English begeondan⟩
the (great) beyond life after death.

Bha·ga·vad Gi·ta ['bʌgəvəd 'gitə] Hinduism a philosophical dialogue embodied in the Mahabharata, an ancient Sanskrit epic. ⟨Sanskrit = Song of the Blessed One⟩

bhak·ti ['bʌkti] or ['bɑkti] n Hinduism devotion to a particular god. ⟨Sanskrit = a share⟩

bhik·ku ['bɪku] *n Buddhism* a fully ordained monk. ⟨Sanskrit *bhiksu*⟩
bhik·ku·ni [bɪ'kuni] *n* a fully ordained nun.

bi– *prefix* **1** every two: *bimonthly*. **2** doubly; in two ways: *biconcave*. **3** joining or involving two: *bilateral, bilingual*. **4** *Chemistry* **a** a chemical with twice as much of a given element: *sodium bicarbonate*. **b** in an organic compound, containing two radicals of similar type: *biphenyl*. ⟨Latin⟩

bi·an·nu·al [baɪ'ænjuəl] *adj* occurring twice a year: *biannual dental checkups*. **bi·an·nu·al·ly** *adv*. See also BIENNIAL.

bi·as ['baɪəs] *n* **1** a slanting or oblique line. **2** an inclination or preference that interferes with fair judgment: *The article showed a bias in favour of the union*. **3** *Statistics* distortion due to neglect of some factor.
v **bi·ased** or **bi·assed, bi·as·ing** or **bi·as·sing** cause to have a bias: *Several bad experiences biased her against teenage drivers*. ⟨French *biais* slant; Latin *biaxius* having a double axis⟩
bias ply tire a car tire with rubber ribs in a pattern of crossed diagonal lines. Compare RADIAL TIRE. **bi·ased** or **bi·assed** *adj* having or showing BIAS (def. 2): *a biassed judge*.

bi·ath·lon [baɪ'æθlɒn] *n* an Olympic event in which skiers with rifles race along a 20 km cross-country course, shooting at four targets on the way. **bi·ath·lete** *n*. ⟨*bi-* + Greek *athlon* contest⟩

bi·ax·i·al [baɪ'æksiəl] *adj* having two axes.

bib [bɪb] *n* **1** a cloth worn under the chin, esp by very young children to protect their clothing during meals. **2** the part of an apron or overalls extending above the waist in front. ⟨Middle English = drink; Latin *bibere*⟩
bib and tucker *Informal* clothes: *Put on your best bib and tucker, we're going out to dinner*.

Bi·ble ['baɪbəl] *n* **1** the sacred writings of the Christian faith, comprising the Old and New Testaments. **2** the sacred writings of Judaism, identical with the Old Testament of the Christian Bible. **3** the sacred writings of any religion. **4 bible** a book whose authority in some field is undisputed: *The Canada Year Book is the geographer's bible*. **bib·li·cal** or **Bib·li·cal** ['bɪbləkəl] *adj*. **bib·li·cal·ly** or **Bib·li·cal·ly** *adv*. ⟨Greek *biblia*, pl diminutive of *biblos* book⟩
Bible Belt an area where Christian fundamentalism predominates.

bib·li·og·ra·phy [ˌbɪbli'ɒgrəfi] *n* **1** a list of the sources used by an author in a certain work. **2** a list of books, articles, etc. about a certain subject or by a certain author. **3** the work of a bibliographer. **bib·li·o·graph·i·cal** or **bib·li·o·graph·ic** *adj*. **bib·li·o·graph·i·cal·ly** *adv*.
bib·li·og·ra·pher *n* **1** someone who compiles a bibliography. **2** a person who studies the authorship, edition, etc. of publications or manuscripts.

bib·li·o·phile ['bɪbliəˌfaɪl] *n* a lover or collector of books. **bib·li·o·phil·ic** [-'fɪlɪk] *adj*.
bib·li·o·phobe [-ˌfoub] *n* a person who hates or fears books. **bib·li·o·pho·bic** *adj*.

bi·cam·er·al [bəɪ'kæmərəl] *adj* **1** consisting of two legislative bodies: *The federal Parliament is bicameral; it has both a Senate and a House of Commons*. **2** made up of two parts or halves that work together: *the bicameral mind*. ⟨*bi-* + Latin *camera* chamber⟩

bicarbonate of soda SODIUM BICARBONATE.

bi·cen·ten·ar·y [ˌbaɪsən'tɛnəri] *or* [ˌbaɪsən'tinəri] *adj* to do with a period of 200 years.
n **1** a period of 200 years. **2** a 200th anniversary or its celebration.
bi·cen·ten·ni·al *adj* **1** to do with a period of 200 years. **2** occurring every 200 years.
n a 200th anniversary or its celebration.

bi·ceps ['baɪsɛps] *n sg or pl* any muscle having two points of origin, esp the large muscle at the front of the upper arm. ⟨Latin *biceps* two-headed; *bi-* two + *caput* head⟩

bick·er ['bɪkər] *v* engage in a petty quarrel. **bick·er** *n*. **bick·er·er** *n*. ⟨Middle English *bikeren*⟩

bi·cul·tur·al [baɪ'kʌltʃərəl] *adj* **1** having or involving two distinct cultures. **2** ✹ to do with the coexistence of English and French cultures in Canada.
bi·cul·tur·al·ism *n* **1** the condition of being bicultural. **2** a policy that promotes this.

bi·cus·pid [baɪ'kʌspɪd] *n* a double-pointed tooth. An adult human has eight bicuspids. **bi·cus·pid** or **bi·cus·pid·ate** *adj*. ⟨*bi-* + Latin *cuspis* point⟩
bicuspid valve *Anatomy* in the heart, the valve between the left ventricle and the left atrium.

bi·cy·cle ['baɪsəkəl] *n* a vehicle propelled by pedals and consisting of a metal frame with two wheels set one behind the other, handles for steering, and a seat. **bi·cy·cle** *v*. **bi·cy·cler** or **bi·cy·clist** *n*. ⟨*bi-* + Greek *kyklos* wheel⟩

bid [bɪd] *v* **bade** or **bid, bid·den** or **bid, bid·ding** for defs. 1, 2; **bid, bid·ding** for defs. 3, 4. **1** command: *Do as I bid you*. **2** say as a wish or greeting: *to bid someone goodbye*. **3** offer (a price) competitively: *Both companies will bid for the contract*. **4** *Card games* state what one proposes to make or win. **bid·der** *n*.
n **1** an act of bidding or the amount bid: *Are you going to make a bid on that table?* **2** an attempt to secure, achieve, etc.: *She made a bid for our sympathy*. ⟨Old English *biddan* ask; meaning influenced by *bēodan* offer⟩
bid fair seem likely: *The plan bids fair to succeed*. **bid in** at an auction, overbid on behalf of the owner in an effort to keep the article unsold. **bid up** raise the price of something by bidding more.
bid·da·ble *adj* **1** obedient; docile. **2** *Card games* suitable to bid on. **bid·ding** *n* **1** a request or command. **2** the making of bids. **do someone's bidding** obey someone.

bid·dy¹ ['bɪdi] *n* hen. ⟨*chickabiddee* a traditional call to poultry⟩

bid·dy² ['bɪdi] *n* a talkative old woman. ⟨Anglo-Irish *Biddy*, diminutive of *Bridget*⟩

bide [baɪd] *v* **bid·ed, bid·ed, bid·ing**. ⟨Old English *bīdan*⟩
bide one's time wait for a good chance: *If you bide your time, you'll get a bargain*.

bi·det [bɪ'dei] *or* ['bidei] *n* a bathroom fixture similar to a toilet, for bathing the genitals and anal area. ⟨French = small horse⟩

bi·di·rec·tion·al [ˌbaɪdə'rɛkʃənəl] *adj* **1** that works in two directions at once: *a bidirectional antenna.* **2** *Computers* printing first from left to right, then from right to left.

bi·en·ni·al [baɪ'eniəl] *n* a plant that lives two years, usually producing flowers and seeds the second year. Compare ANNUAL, PERENNIAL. *adj* **1** of such plants. **2** occurring every two years: *a biennial conference.* **bi·en·ni·al·ly** *adv.* ⟨Latin *biennium; bi-* two + *annus* year⟩

CONFUSABLES

Biennial and biannual ultimately come from identical Latin roots, but the former means 'happening every two years' and the latter 'happening twice a year'.

---

bier [bir] *n* a movable stand for a coffin or dead body. ⟨Old English *bēr; beran* bear[1]⟩

biff [bɪf] *n, v Slang* hit; slap. ⟨imitative⟩

biff·y ['bɪfi] *n* ✱ *Slang* a toilet, bathroom, or outhouse. ⟨origin uncertain⟩

bi·fo·cal [baɪ'foukəl] *or* ['baɪˌfoukəl] *adj* with two foci.
n **bifocals** *pl* eyeglasses with bifocal lenses, for distance and close-up vision.

bi·fur·cate ['baɪfərˌkeit] *or* [ˌbaɪ'fɜrkeit] *v* divide into two parts or branches.
bi·fur·cate ['baɪfərkɪt] *or* [ˌbaɪ'fɜrkɪt] *adj.* **bi·fur·ca·tion** *n.* ⟨*bi-* + Latin *furca* fork⟩

big [bɪg] *adj* **big·ger, big·gest 1** large: *a big car.* **2** grown up: *I want to be a pilot when I'm big.* **3** loud, full, etc.: *a big voice.* **4** *Informal* important: *big news.* **5** generous: *a big heart.* **6** *Informal* popular: *E-mail is big these days.* **7** of a sibling, older: *my big sister.* **8** boastful: *big talk.*
adv **1** *Informal* boastfully: *He talks big.* **2** *Slang* in a big way; boldly, fully, grandly, etc.: *to sing big. Think big.* **big·ness** *n.* ⟨Middle English⟩ **be big on** have a strong interest in or liking for: *She's big on Kantian philosophy.* **big with child** in an advanced state of pregnancy. **in a big way** very much.
big band a jazz or dance band of 15 to 20 musicians. **big-band** *adj.* **big bang theory** the theory that the universe began with an enormous explosion. Compare STEADY-STATE THEORY. **Big Brother** a dictator or government whose subjects are kept constantly under secret observation. ⟨dictator in George Orwell's novel *1984*⟩ **big cheese** an important person. **big deal** *Slang* something important (often ironic). **Big Dipper** the seven principal stars in the constellation Ursa Major. Compare LITTLE DIPPER. **Big·foot** *n* the Sasquatch of the Coast Range. **big game** large animals sought by hunters. **big·gie** *n Slang* a big person or thing. **big·gish** *adj* quite big. **big gun** *Informal* an important or powerful person. **big hair** *Slang* a high, wide, or puffy hairdo. **big–heart·ed** *adj* generous. **big·horn** *n* a wild mountain sheep found mainly in the Rocky Mountains, with huge horns that curl back. **big house, the** *Slang* prison. **big league**

1 MAJOR LEAGUE. **2** Often, **big leagues** *pl* the group, place, etc. recognized as the best or most influential within its sphere: *The star of the new musical is from the big leagues.* **big–leagu·er** *n.* **big–league** *adj.* **big·mouth** *n* someone who talks a lot, esp to spread gossip. **big name** *Informal* a celebrity. **big noise** *Slang* an important person. **big shot** *Slang* an important person. **big·shot** *adj.* **big–tick·et** *adj Informal* costing a lot: *big-ticket items such as cars.* **big time** *Slang* **1** the top level of advancement or achievement. **2** in an extreme way or to an extreme degree: *He was sued and lost big time.* **big·time** *adj.* **big–tim·er** *n.* **big top** the main tent at a circus. **big wheel** *Informal* an important person. **big·wig** *n Informal* an important person.

big·a·my ['bɪgəmi] *n* the criminal offence of marrying someone while still legally married to someone else. **big·a·mist** *n.* **big·a·mous** *adj.* ⟨*bi-* twice + Greek *gamos* married⟩

bight [bəit] *n* **1** a long inward curve in a coastline. **2** a loop of rope. ⟨Old English *byht*⟩

big·ot ['bɪgət] *n* an intolerant, prejudiced person. **big·ot·ed** *adj.* **big·ot·ry** *n.* ⟨French⟩

bi·jou ['biʒu] *or* [bi'ʒu] *n, pl* **-joux** [-ʒuz] **1** a jewel. **2** something small and fine. ⟨French⟩

bike [baik] *n* a bicycle or motorcycle. **bike** *v.* ⟨shortened from *bicycle*⟩
bik·er *n* **1** cyclist. **2** a motorcyclist, esp one who wears leather and belongs to a club.

bi·ki·ni [bɪ'kini] *n* **1** a very brief, two-piece swimsuit for women and girls. **2** a pair of brief, tight underpants or men's swimming trunks. ⟨*Bikini*, an atoll in the Marshall Islands in the W Pacific Ocean⟩

bi·lat·er·al [baɪ'lætərəl] *adj* **1** of or having two sides: *bilateral symmetry.* **2** involving two sides or parties equally: *a bilateral treaty.* **bi·lat·er·al·ly** *adv.* **bi·lat·er·al·ism** *n.*

bile [baɪl] *n* **1** a bitter liquid secreted by the liver and stored in the gall bladder. It is discharged into the small intestine, where it aids digestion. **2** ill humour. ⟨Latin *bilis*⟩
bil·ious ['bɪljəs] *adj* **1** of bile. **2** caused by trouble with the bile or the liver: *a bilious attack.* **3** bad-tempered. **4** disgusting: *bilious green.* **bil·ious·ness** *n.* **bi·li·ru·bin** [ˌbɪlə'rubən] *n* a reddish yellow pigment in bile, blood, and urine.

bilge [bɪldʒ] *n* **1** the lowest part of a ship's hold. **2** BILGE WATER. **3** *Informal* nonsense. **bil·gy** *adj.* ⟨origin uncertain⟩
bilge water the dirty water that collects by seeping or leaking into the bottom of a ship.

bi·lin·gual [baɪ'lɪŋgwəl] *or* [baɪ'lɪŋgjuəl] *adj* **1** able to speak two languages. **2** of, using, or expressed in two languages: *a bilingual dictionary.* **3** ✱ **a** able to speak both English and French. **b** of, using, or expressed in both English and French: *a bilingual school.*
n a bilingual person. **bi·lin·gual·ize** *v.* **bi·lin·gual·ly** *adv.* ⟨Latin *bi-* two + *lingua* language⟩
bilingual district ✱ a region, established under the federal Official Languages Act, in which

all federal services must be provided in both English and French. **bi·lin·gual·ism** *n* **1 a** the ability to speak two languages. **b ⁕** the ability to speak English and French. **2 a** a policy of promoting two languages equally. **b ⁕** the policy of according equal status to English and French throughout Canada.

bil·ious See BILE.

bilk [bɪlk] *v* **1** defraud. **2** elude. **3** avoid paying. **bilk** or **bilk·er** *n*. ⟨origin uncertain⟩

bill[1] [bɪl] *n* **1** a statement of money owed or paid for goods or services. **2** a piece of paper money: *a five-dollar bill.* **3** an advertisement, notice, etc. posted in a public place. **4** a proposed law presented to a lawmaking body. *v* **1** send a statement of charges to: *The store will bill us.* **2** advertise: *It was billed as the greatest show on earth.* ⟨Middle English *bille*; Latin *bulla* document, seal, bull[2]⟩
fill the bill *Informal* satisfy requirements fully.
foot the bill *Informal* pay, usually on behalf of others.
bill·board *n* a large board, usually outdoors, on which advertisements are displayed.
bill·fold *n* a folding wallet. **bill·ing** *n* **1** on a playbill or similar advertisement: **a** a list of the performers, acts, etc. **b** the position in such a list: *star billing.* **2** a list or total of amounts billed: *Quarterly billings were low.* **bill of exchange** a written instruction to pay a certain sum to a specified person. **bill of fare** a menu. **bill of goods** a shipment of merchandise. **sell someone a bill of goods** *Slang* mislead. **bill of health** a certificate stating whether or not there are infectious diseases on a ship or in the port which it is leaving. **clean bill of health a** a bill of health showing absence of infectious diseases. **b** *Informal* a clean record or favourable report after previous problems. **bill of lading** a receipt given by a shipping company, etc. showing a list of goods delivered to it for transportation. *Abbrev* **b.l.** or **B/L. bill of rights 1** a statement of the fundamental rights of the people of a nation. **2 Bill of Rights** in Canada, a statement of human rights and fundamental freedoms enacted by Parliament in 1960, since 1982 largely superseded by the Canadian Charter of Rights and Freedoms. **bill of sale** a written statement transferring ownership from a seller to a buyer. **Bill 101 ⁕** a law enacted in 1971 in Québec to protect the French language by giving it preferred status.

bill[2] [bɪl] *n* the horny part of the jaws of a bird; beak.
v of birds, touch bills. ⟨Old English *bile*⟩
bill and coo caress and talk as lovers do.

bil·let [ˈbɪlɪt] *n* a place, esp a private home, where an individual member of a visiting group is assigned to be lodged: *The team will require twenty billets.*
v provide a billet or billets for. ⟨Middle English *billette*, diminutive of *bille* bill[1]⟩

bil·liards [ˈbɪljərdz] *n* a game played with two white balls and a red one on a special table, with a long stick called a cue to hit the balls. ⟨French *billard(s)*; *bille* log⟩

bil·lion [ˈbɪljən] *n, adj* **1** in Canada and the US, a thousand million. **2** in some countries, a million million. ⟨*bi-* two (i.e., to the second power) + (*mi*)*llion*⟩
bil·lion·aire [ˈbɪljə,nɛr] or [ˌbɪljəˈnɛr] *n* a person whose wealth adds up to at least a billion dollars, pounds, etc. **bil·lionth** *adj, n* one, or being one, of a billion equal parts.

bil·low [ˈbɪlou] *n* **1** a great wave: *sea billows, billows of smoke.* **2** a bulge or act of bulging. *v* **1** rise or roll, as big waves. **2** bulge or cause to bulge out, esp from the action of the wind: *skirts billowing in the wind.* **bil·low·y** *adj.* **bil·low·i·ness** *n.* ⟨Old Norse *bylgja*⟩

bil·ly [ˈbɪli] *n* a club, esp one carried by a police officer. ⟨diminutive of French *bille* log⟩

bil·ly·can [ˈbɪli,kæn] *n* a metal pot to boil water in, esp over a campfire. Also, **bil·ly.** ⟨native Australian *billa* water + E *can*⟩

billy goat a male goat. ⟨pet name *Billy*⟩

bim·bo [ˈbɪmbou] *n Slang* a foolish, superficial person. ⟨Italian = child⟩

bi·met·al [ˈbaɪmɛtəl] *n* an alloy of two different metals. **bi·me·tal·lic** [ˌbaɪməˈtælɪk] *adj.* **bi·met·al·lism** [baɪˈmɛtəlɪzəm] *n* use of gold and silver together, at a fixed ratio, as the standard of value for a nation's currency.

bi·month·ly [baɪˈmʌnθli] *adj* **1** happening, published, etc. once every two months. **2** loosely, happening twice a month. *n* a bimonthly periodical. **bi·month·ly** *adv.*

> **USAGE**
> Strictly speaking, **bimonthly, biweekly,** and **biannual** mean 'every two months', etc. but are sometimes used loosely to mean 'twice a month', etc. To avoid confusion, it is better to use **semi-monthly** or **twice a month** for one meaning and **every two months** for the other. See also the note at BIENNIAL.

bin [bɪn] *n* a large box or boxlike enclosure for storage. ⟨Old English *binn*⟩

bi·na·ry [ˈbaɪnəri] *adj* **1** to do with two; dual. **2** *Mathematics, computers* using BINARY DIGITS. *n* **1** something composed of two parts or things. **2** *Mathematics, computers* a number expressed in BINARY NOTATION. **3** BINARY STAR. ⟨Latin *binarius; bini* two at a time⟩
binary digit either of the digits 0 or 1, serving as the basic unit of information in a digital computing system. Also called **bit.** The two digits represent the *off* and *on* states, respectively, of an electric circuit. **binary notation** a system of notation used in computing, using BINARY DIGITS. **binary scale** *Mathematics* a numerical system having a base of 2 rather than 10. Also, **binary (number) system. binary star** a pair of stars that revolve around a common centre of gravity, often appearing as a single object.

bind [baɪnd] *v* **bound, bind·ing 1** tie; fasten. **2** stick together. **3** hold by force; restrain. **4** hold by a promise, love, duty, law, etc.: *in duty bound to help.* **5** dress with bandages:

to bind up a wound. **6** fasten (pages) into a cover to form a book. **7** chafe; be too tight. *n Informal* a very inconvenient situation: *It'll put me in a real bind if he doesn't pay me back today.* ⟨Old English *bindan*⟩ **bind hand and foot a** tie up thoroughly. **b** restrict excessively, as by a rule or contract. **bind·er** *n* **1** a cover for holding loose sheets of paper together. **2** a machine that cuts stalks of grain and ties them in bundles. **3** a person who binds books. **4** anything that holds things together. **5** a substance that makes other things cohere. **binder twine** ✱ strong, coarse string of the kind used for binding grain into sheaves. **bind·er·y** *n* a place where books are bound. **bind·ing** *n* **1** the covering of a book. **2** a fabric strip protecting or ornamenting an edge. **3** the foot fastening on a ski. *adj* **1** that binds. **2** that must be fulfilled or upheld: *a binding contract.* **bind·weed** *n* any of various plants that twine around other plants or a support.

binge [bɪndʒ] *n Slang* **1** a session of heavy drinking. **2** a bout of indulgence in anything. *v* have a binge (with *on*): *to binge on doughnuts.* ⟨dialect *binge* to soak⟩ **binge eating** an eating disorder characterized by alternate bouts of overeating and purging; bulimia.

bin·go [ˈbɪŋgou] *n* a game of chance in which each player has a card with randomly numbered squares, which he or she covers with markers as the numbers are drawn and called out by a caller until an unbroken line of numbers is covered. *interj* **1** word called out by a winner in this game. **2** correct! exactly! ⟨origin uncertain⟩

bin·oc·u·lars [bəˈnɒkjələrz] *pln* two small telescopes joined as a unit for use with both eyes. ⟨Latin *bini* two at a time + *oculi* eyes⟩

bi·no·mi·al [baɪˈnoumiəl] *adj* consisting of two terms. *n* **1** *Algebra* an expression consisting of two terms connected by a plus or minus sign. **2** *Biology* the two-part name (genus and species) identifying a plant or animal according to an international system of classification. *Example: Castor canadensis* for the North American beaver. Also, **bi·no·min·al** [baɪˈnɒmənəl]. ⟨*bi-* + Latin *nomen* name⟩ **binomial theorem** *Mathematics* an algebraic system, invented by Sir Isaac Newton, for raising a binomial to any power.

bio [ˈbaɪou] *n Informal* biography, esp one in capsule form.

bio– *combining form* **1** life; living things: *biology.* **2** biological: *biochemistry = biological chemistry.* ⟨Greek *bios* life⟩

bi·o·chem·is·try [ˌbaɪouˈkɛmɪstri] *n* the chemistry of living things; biological chemistry. **bi·o·chem·i·cal** *adj.* **bi·o·chem·ist** *n.*

bi·o·de·grad·a·ble [ˌbaɪoudɪˈgreɪdəbəl] *adj* able to be broken down, or decomposed, by a natural process such as the action of bacteria. **bi·o·de·grad·a·bil·i·ty** *n.* **bi·o·de·grade** *v.*

bi·o·en·gi·neer·ing [ˌbaɪou,ɛndʒəˈnɪrɪŋ] *n*

the science dealing with the relationship of engineering with living matter, such as in the development of pacemakers, etc.

bi·o·eth·ics [ˌbaɪouˈɛθɪks] *n* the study of the ethical problems arising from research or involving humans or live animals, or from the application of new medical advances. **bi·o·eth·i·cal** *adj.* **bi·o·eth·i·cist** *n.*

bi·o·feed·back [ˌbaɪouˈfid,bæk] *n* the control of normally involuntary or unconscious body processes, such as heartbeat, through mental concentration.

bi·o·gen·e·sis [ˌbaɪouˈdʒɛnəsɪs] *n* **1** the theory that living things can be produced only by other living things. **2** the production of living things from other living things.

bi·og·ra·phy [baɪˈɒgrəfi] *n* the written story of a person's life. **bi·og·ra·pher** *n.* **bi·o·graph·i·cal** [ˌbaɪəˈgræfɪkəl] *adj.* Also, **bi·o·graph·ic. bi·o·graph·i·cal·ly** *adv.*

bi·o·haz·ard [ˈbaɪou,hæzərd] *n* anything that harms plant or animal life.

bi·ol·o·gy [baɪˈɒlədʒi] *n* **1** the science of living matter in all its forms. **2** the plant and animal life of a particular region. **3** the facts about a particular type of plant or animal: *feline biology.* **bi·o·log·i·cal** [ˌbaɪəˈlɒdʒɪkəl] *adj.* **bi·o·log·i·cal·ly** *adv.* **bi·ol·o·gist** [baɪˈɒlədʒɪst] *n.* **biological accumulation** or **bi·o·ac·cum·u·la·tion** the process by which poisonous substances collect in living matter. **biological clock** a mechanism in living things that is responsible for the timing of various functions, esp those synchronized to the cycle of day and night and those related to childbearing. **biological control** or **biocontrol** control of pests by natural means, such as predators, rather than by chemical substances. **biological warfare** war in which disease-producing micro-organisms are used as a weapon.

bi·o·lu·min·es·cence [ˌbaɪou,lumɪˈnɛsəns] *n* the ability of certain organisms, such as fireflies, to change chemical energy in the body into light. **bi·o·lu·min·es·cent** *adj.*

bi·o·mass [ˈbaɪou,mæs] *n* **1** the total amount or mass of living organisms in the world or in a given area: *the biomass of plankton.* **2** organic waste or remains.

bi·ome [ˈbaɪoum] *n* an extensive ecological community, esp one dominant type of vegetation: *the tundra biome.* ⟨*bio-* + Greek *-oma* mass⟩

bi·o·me·chan·ics [ˌbaɪouməˈkænɪks] *n* the science that deals with the effects of forces, esp gravity, on a living organism.

bi·on·ic [baɪˈɒnɪk] *adj* to do with an artificial body part or a device that strengthens or replaces a natural body function, esp one that operates electronically: *a bionic arm.* **bi·on·i·cal·ly** *adv.* **bi·on·ics** *n pl or sg.*

bi·o·phys·ics [ˌbaɪouˈfɪzɪks] *n* (with a sg verb) the science dealing with the application of the principles of physics to biology. **bi·o·phys·i·cal** *adj.* **bi·o·phys·i·cist** *n.*

bi·o·pic ['baɪou,pɪk] *n Informal* a biographical film. ⟨*bio*(*graphy*) + *pic*(*ture*)⟩

bi·op·sy ['baɪɒpsi] *n* an examination of tissue taken from a living person or animal as an aid to medical diagnosis. Compare AUTOPSY. ⟨*πbio*- + Greek *opsis* a viewing⟩

bi·o·rhythm ['baɪou,rɪðəm] *n* a hypothetical cycle of bodily or mental functions.

bi·o·sphere ['baɪə,sfir] *n* the parts of the earth and its atmosphere inhabited by living things.

bi·o·ta [baɪ'outə] *n* all the living organisms of a given place or time. ⟨Greek *biōte; bios* life⟩

bi·o·tech·nol·o·gy [,baɪoutɛk'nɒlədʒi] *n* 1 the use or genetic manipulation of living organisms for industrial ends. 2 the science dealing with this. **bi·o·tech·no·log·ic·al** *adj.* **bi·o·tech·nol·o·gist** *n.*

bi·o·ter·ror ['baɪou,tɛrər] *n* 1 Also, **bioterrorism**, the use of disease to create terror in a population. 2 the terror so caused: *a nation in the grip of bioterror.*

bi·ot·ic [baɪ'ɒtɪk] *adj* to do with life or living things. ⟨Greek *biōtikos; bios* life⟩

bi·par·ti·san [baɪ'pɑrtəzən] *or* [baɪ'pɑrtə,zæn] *adj* of or representing two political parties. **bi·par·ti·san·ship** *n.*

bi·par·tite [baɪ'pɑrtaɪt] *adj* consisting of two parts.

bi·ped ['baɪpɛd] *n* a two-footed animal. **bi·ped** or **bi·ped·al** *adj.* ⟨*bi*- + Latin *pedis* foot⟩

bi·plane ['baɪpleɪn] *n* an airplane having two sets of wings, one above the other.

bi·po·lar [baɪ'poulər] *adj* 1 having two contrary extremes. 2 to do with both polar regions. 3 having BIPOLAR AFFECTIVE DISORDER. **bi·po·lar·i·ty** [,baɪpə'lɛrəti] *or* [-'læræti] *n.* **bipolar affective disorder** a mental illness in which periods of depression and manic behaviour succeed each other. Also called **manic–depressive disorder.**

birch [bɜrtʃ] *n* 1 any of a genus of trees and shrubs of the northern hemisphere having strong, hard, light-coloured wood used for furniture and whitish bark that peels off in thin layers. 2 a supple birch stick for flogging. *v* whip with a birch. ⟨Old English *bierce*⟩ **birch·bark** *n* the bark of a birch, esp the white, or paper, birch, traditionally used by First Nations peoples of the eastern woodlands to make canoes.

bird [bɜrd] *n* 1 any of a class of warm-blooded, egg-laying, feathered vertebrates with forelimbs modified into wings. 2 shuttlecock. 3 *Informal* person: *He's a strange bird.* 4 *Slang* a rude noise made by vibrating the lips. 5 *Slang* BALLISTIC MISSILE. *v* engage in birdwatching. **bird·er** *n.* **bird·like** *adj.* ⟨Old English *bridd*, bird⟩ **a little bird told me** formula for concealing the source of a rumour. **bird in the hand** something certain because one already has it. **birds of a feather** people with similar ideas or interests. **eat like a bird** have a very small appetite. **for the birds** *Informal* not worth doing or having: *I think housecleaning is for the birds.* **have a bird** *Slang* overreact; have a fit. **kill two birds with one stone** get two things done by one action. **the birds and the bees** *Informal* the basic facts of sexual reproduction and development.

bird·bath *n* a shallow basin of water on a pedestal, for birds to bathe in or drink from. **bird·brain** *n Slang* a stupid or scatterbrained person. **bird·brained** *adj.* **bird call** 1 the sound that a bird makes. 2 an instrument for imitating it. **bird dog** *n* 1 any of several breeds of dog trained to locate game birds and bring them to the hunter. 2 *Informal* a talent scout. **bird·house** *n* 1 a small roofed box for wild birds to nest in. 2 an aviary. **bird·ie** *n* 1 *Informal* a little bird. 2 *Golf* a score of one stroke less than par for any hole. *v* **bird·ied, bird·ie·ing** score one less than par on (any hole). **bird of paradise** 1 any of about 40 species of songbird of New Guinea, the male of many species having vividly coloured plumes. 2 an African plant of the banana family, whose flowers form a crest like that of a bird of paradise. **bird of passage** 1 a bird that migrates from one region to another as the seasons change. 2 *Informal* a drifter. **bird of prey** any bird that kills other birds or animals for food. **bird·seed** *n* a mixture of seeds fed to birds. **bird's–eye view** 1 a view from above: *a bird's-eye view of the town from that hill.* 2 a general survey or outline. **bird·song** *n* the musical sounds made by birds. **bird·watch** *v* observe and study wild birds in their natural habitat. **bird·watch·er** *n.* **bird·watch·ing** *n.*

bi·ret·ta [bə'rɛtə] *n* a stiff, square ceremonial cap worn by Roman Catholic priests. Also, **be·ret·ta.** ⟨Latin *birretum* cap⟩

birl [bɜrl] *v* 1 rotate (a log) in the water by moving the feet while standing on it. 2 spin rapidly. **birl·er** *n.* ⟨Scottish *birr* momentum, vigour, influenced by *whirl*⟩ **birl·ing** *n* a game in which two people see who can stay on a log which both are birling.

birth [bɜrθ] *n* 1 the process or fact of being born; emergence from the womb: *the birth of a child.* 2 any beginning: *the birth of a nation.* 3 heredity: *a musician by birth.* 4 parentage: *She is of Spanish birth.* *v* give birth to. ⟨ probably Old Norse *burthr*⟩ **give birth (to) a** bear (young, a child, etc.); bring forth from the womb. **b** be the author or source of: *Injustice gave birth to revolution.* **birth control** the use of any method of contraception. **birth–con·trol** *adj.* **birth·day** *n* the day on which a person is born or a thing begins, or its anniversary. **birthday suit** one's bare skin. **birth defect** an abnormality present at birth. **birthing room** a room set up for the act of birth, often a homelike room in a hospital. **birth·mark** *n* a congenital mark on the skin. **birth mother** biological (as opposed to adoptive) mother. **birth name** the surname that a woman used before marriage; maiden name. **birth·place** *n* the place of birth or origin. **birth rate** the ratio of births per year to the total population or to some other stated number. **birth·right** *n* **1** the special rights of a firstborn child. **2** a right enjoyed by a person because of any other circumstance of birth, or simply by virtue of being a human being. **birth·stone** *n* a gem associated with a certain month of the year.

bis·cot·ti [bɪs'kɒti] *Italian* [bis'kɔtti] *n pl* hard, thick, oblong cookies with almonds or other nuts, eaten with coffee.

bis·cuit ['bɪskɪt] *n* **1** a type of bread baked in small, soft cakes. **2** a cracker or crisp wafer. **3** pottery or china that has been fired (baked) once but not yet glazed. ⟨French *bis* twice + *cuit*, pp of *cuire* cook⟩

bi·sect [bəi'sɛkt] *v Mathematics* divide into two equal parts. **bi·sec·tion** *n*. **bi·sec·tor** *n*. ⟨*bi-* + Latin *sectus*, pp of *secare* cut⟩

bi·sex·u·al [bai'sɛkʃuəl] *adj* **1** sexually attracted to members of both sexes. **2** to do with both sexes. **3** having male and female reproductive organs in a single individual. **bi·sex·u·al·ism** *n*. **bi·sex·u·al·i·ty** *n*.

bish·op ['bɪʃəp] *n* **1** in some Christian churches, a high ranking member of the clergy. **2** *Chess* one of two pieces that may be moved diagonally. ⟨Greek *episkopos; epi-* over + *skopos* watcher⟩

bis·muth ['bɪzməθ] *n* a metallic element. Some compounds are used in medicine and in alloys. *Symbol* **Bi** ⟨Greek⟩

bi·son ['baɪzən] *or* ['bəisən] *n, pl* **-son** either of two species making up a genus of bovine animals. The North American bison is commonly called a buffalo; the European bison is called a wisent. ⟨Latin⟩

bisque¹ [bisk] *or* [bɪsk] *n* a thick, creamy soup made of strained tomatoes, asparagus, etc. or from shellfish, birds, or rabbit. ⟨French⟩

bisque² [bisk] *or* [bɪsk] *n* **1** BISCUIT (def. 3) purposely left unglazed, used esp in figurines, dolls, etc. **2** its beige colour. ⟨shortened from *biscuit*⟩

bis·tro ['bistrou] *n* a small restaurant, wine bar, or café. ⟨French⟩

bit¹ [bɪt] *n* **1** the part of a bridle that goes in a horse's mouth. **2** anything that curbs or restrains. **3** the cutting part of a drill. **4** the part of a key that goes into a lock. *v* **bit·ted, bit·ting 1** restrain with a bit. **2** make the bit on (a key). ⟨Old English *bite*⟩ **take the bit in one's teeth a** of a horse, resist control by biting on the bit so that it cannot be pulled against the soft part of the mouth. **b** act on one's own, esp irresponsibly: *The young soldier took the bit in his teeth and charged, despite the order to wait.*

bit² [bɪt] *n* **1** a small piece or amount: *a bit of cake.* **2** a small degree or extent: *I'm a bit tired.* **3** a part: *I liked the funny bits.* **4** a short time: *Stay a bit.* **5** *Informal* a given set of behaviours, attitudes, etc.: *the whole do-it-yourself bit.* ⟨Old English *bita*⟩ **bit by bit** gradually; piecemeal. **do one's bit**

do one's share. **every bit** in every way; totally. **two bits** a quarter; 25 cents.

bit part a small role in a play or film, with a few spoken lines.

bit³ [bɪt] *n Computers* the basic unit of information in a computer, expressed as either 0 or 1 in binary notation. ⟨*b(inary) (dig)it*⟩

bits per second *Computers* a measure of the speed of data transmission. *Abbrev* **bps**

bitch [bɪtʃ] *n* **1** a female dog, wolf, fox, etc. **2** *Slang* an unpleasant or difficult person or thing. **3** *Slang* a complaint. *v Slang* grumble: *He's always bitching about something.* ⟨Old English *bicce*⟩ **bitch·y** *adj Slang* ill-tempered or malicious.

bite [bəit] *v* **bit, bit·ten** *or* **bit, bit·ing 1** seize, cut into, or cut off with the teeth: *to bite into an apple. I bit my tongue.* **2** wound with fangs or a sting: *A mosquito bit me.* **3** nip; snap: *a dog biting at fleas.* **4** cause a sharp, stinging pain (to): *The wind bit our faces.* **5** take a tight hold on; grip: *The wheels bite the rails.* **6** *Informal* cheat; take in.
n **1** a piece bitten off; mouthful. **2** a light meal: *We usually have a bite before going to bed.* **3** the act, result, or site of biting. **4** a sharp, stinging or cutting quality: *the bite of a cold wind, the bite of sarcasm.* **5** a tight hold or grip: *the bite of train wheels on the rails.* **6** *Dentistry* the way in which the upper and lower teeth meet when the mouth is closed. **bit·er** *n.* **bit·ing** *adj.* ⟨Old English *bitan*⟩ **bite back** hold back (words, cries, etc.). **bite me** *Slang* an expression of contempt for challengers. **bite off more than one can chew** attempt more than one can accomplish. **bite one's tongue** keep from speaking. **bite someone's head off** react in an unduly hostile way. **bite the bullet** brace oneself to accept something stoically. **bite the dust** *Informal* die or be defeated. **bite the hand that feeds one** show ingratitude. **bitten by the (travel, gardening,** etc.) **bug** See BUG. **once bitten, twice shy** reluctant to try something because of previous negative experience. **put the bite on** *Informal* demand money from, as a bribe or loan. **take a bite out of** *Informal* reduce significantly.

bite–size *or* **bite–sized** small enough to be taken in one mouthful: *bite-size pieces of fruit.*

bit·ter ['bɪtər] *adj* **1** having a sharp, unpleasant taste. **2** causing or expressing pain or grief: *a bitter defeat, bitter wounds, a bitter cry.* **3** full of resentment or cynicism: *bitter hatred. She is bitter about her loss.* **4** of weather, very cold or severe: *a bitter wind.* *adv* extremely (cold). *n Brit* a somewhat bitter-tasting draft beer strongly flavoured with hops. **bit·ter·ly** *adv.* **bit·ter·ness** *n.* ⟨Old English *biter.* Related to BITE.⟩ **to the bitter end a** until the very end. **b** to death. **bit·ter–end·er** *n* one who refuses to give in even when all is lost; a die-hard. **bit·ters** *n pl* an alcohol-based liquid, flavoured with some bitter plant, used as an ingredient in drinks or as an aid to digestion.

bit·ter·sweet ['bɪtər,swit] *adj* bitter and sweet at the same time: *bittersweet chocolate, bittersweet memories.*

bit·tern ['bɪtərn] *n* any of a small subfamily of wading birds of the same family as herons, having a booming call. ⟨Old French *butor*⟩

bi·tu·men [bə'tjumən], [bə'tumən], *or* ['bɪtʃəmən] *n* a heavy, almost solid form of petroleum occurring in natural deposits, as in the Athabasca tar sands; pitch or asphalt. **bi·tum·i·noid** *adj.* **bi·tu·mi·nous** *adj.*

bituminous coal a plentiful form of soft coal.

bi·va·lent [baɪ'veɪlənt] *or* ['bɪvələnt] *adj* **1** *Chemistry* having a valence of two or having two valences. **2** *Biology* formed from two equal chromosomes.

n Biology such a chromosome. **bi·va·lence** *n.* ⟨*bi-* + Latin *valens*, ppr of *valere* be worth⟩

bi·valve ['baɪvælv] *n* any of a class of molluscs having gills and a shell consisting of two hinged sections, called valves.

adj **1** to do with this class of molluscs. **2** of a seed, having two similar parts.

biv·ou·ac ['bɪvu,æk] *n* a temporary camp made by soldiers, etc.

v **-acked, -ack·ing** erect or stay in such a camp. ⟨French; German *Beiwacht* extra guards⟩

bi·week·ly [baɪ'wikli] *adj* **1** happening once every two weeks. **2** loosely, happening twice a week.

n a biweekly newspaper or magazine. **bi·week·ly** *adv.* See also note at BIMONTHLY.

biz [bɪz] *n Slang* business: *show biz.*

bi·zarre [bə'zɑr] *adj* very odd or strange; grotesque. **bi·zarre·ly** *adv.* **bi·zarre·ness** *n.* ⟨French; Basque *bezar* beard⟩

blab [blæb] *v Slang* **blabbed, blab·bing** tell (secrets); talk too much.

n **1** chatter. **2** a person who blabs. **blab·ber** *n.* ⟨Middle English *blabbe*⟩

blab·ber *v, n Slang* chatter. **blab·ber·mouth** *n Slang* a person who reveals secrets.

black [blæk] *adj* **1** of the colour of coal or soot. **2** without any light: *The room was black as night.* **3** Also, **Black** to do with any people of African or Australian Aboriginal descent: *a black Trinidadian.* **4** of coffee, without cream or milk. **5** calamitous: *It was a black day when the stocks fell.* **6** joking about tragic things: *black humour.* **7** angry: *a black look.*

n **1** black mourning clothes. **2** Also, **Black** of African or Australian Aboriginal descent. **black·ly** *adv.* **black·ness** *n.* ⟨Old English *blæc*⟩

black and blue severely bruised. **black out a** temporarily lose consciousness, vision, or memory. **b** darken completely. **c** suppress local broadcasting of (a sports event) in order to encourage attendance. **d** cause a BLACKOUT (def. 1) in: *The storm has blacked out some parts of the city.* **in the black** showing a profit, or no loss.

black and white *n* **1** print or writing: *I asked him to give me the promise in black and white.* **2** a colour scheme representing everything in black, white, and shades of grey. **3 a** morally

unambiguous: *Some issues are not black and white.* **b** a worldview that allows for no moral ambiguity: *He sees everything in black and white.* **black–and–white** *adj.* **black art** BLACK MAGIC. **black·ball** *v* vote against a person or thing ⟨from the practice of placing a black ball in the ballot box⟩. **black bear** a North American bear found in forest regions and swamp areas from Mexico north to the edge of the tundra. **black belt** the highest level of skill recognized in judo or karate, symbolized by a black sash. **black·ber·ry** *n* the edible fruit of various bushes and vines of the rose family. *v* gather blackberries. **black·bird** *n* any of several mainly black species of songbird. Among the species found in Canada are the red–winged blackbird and the common grackle. **black blizzard ✱** a prairie dust storm. **black·board** *n* a black chalkboard. **black body** a surface or body that can absorb all the radiation that falls on it. **black book 1** a book containing the names of people to be criticized or punished. **2 little black book** one's book of names, addresses, etc. of available romantic partners. **be in someone's black book(s)** be in disfavour with someone. **black box 1** a self-contained electronic or automatic device to record data, control or monitor a complex mechanical process, etc. **2** any sophisticated but poorly explained mechanism governing behaviour. **black bread** heavy, coarse, dark rye bread. **black·cod** *n* ✱ an important commercial food fish of the N Pacific coasts. Also called **sa·ble·fish. black·damp** *n* in some mines, suffocating air with high levels of carbon dioxide and nitrogen. **Black Death** a violent outbreak of the bubonic plague in Europe and Asia in the 1300s. **black diamond 1** an opaque, dark type of diamond found chiefly in Brazil. **2 black diamonds** *pl* coal. **black·en** *v* **1** make or become black. **2** damage the reputation of. **Black English** a variety of English spoken by Blacks, esp in the US. **black eye 1** a bruise around an eye. **2** *Informal* **a** a severe blow: *The insult gave her pride a black eye.* **b** a cause of disgrace, discredit, or disfigurement: *Substandard housing is a black eye to the whole community.* **black–eyed Su·san** either of two North American wildflowers whose blooms have yellow ray flowers around a cluster of dark brown disk flowers. **black·face** *n* formerly, the make-up for an actor caricaturing a Black, esp for a minstrel show. **black fly** *n* any of many species of small fly having mouth parts adapted for sucking blood. **Black·foot** See SIKSIKA. **Black Forest cake** a rich chocolate cake layered with cherries and whipped cream. **Black Forest ham** a type of smoked ham. **black frost** weather cold enough to turn plants black. **black gold** oil. **black·guard** ['blægərd] *n* a scoundrel.

black·guard·ly *adj, adv.* **black·head** *n* a small, black-tipped lump of dead cells and oil plugging a pore of the skin. **black hole 1** a region in space, produced by the collapse of a star, with such a strong gravitational field that anything caught in it, including light, can never escape. **2** any horrible place of confinement, named for a small cell where many prisoners were supposedly kept in Calcutta in 1756. **black ice** ✱ thin ice appearing black on the surface of a road, making driving conditions dangerous. **black·ing** *n* a black polish used on shoes, stoves, etc. **blackish** *adj* somewhat black. **black·jack** *n* **1 a** a card game in which players try to get a count of twenty-one. **b** a count of twenty-one with only two cards, namely an ace and a ten or any face card. **2** a club with a flexible handle. **3** the black flag of a pirate. *v* **1** hit with a blackjack. **2** coerce. **black list** or **black·list** a list of names of people believed to deserve punishment, blame, suspicion, etc. **black·list** *v*. **black lung** anthracosis, a disease caused by prolonged breathing of coal dust. **black magic** evil magic. Compare WHITE MAGIC. **black·mail** *n* **1** the extortion of money, etc. by threats. **2** manipulation of a person using unfair pressure, moral intimidation, etc.: *emotional blackmail.* **3** the money or other advantage so obtained. **black·mail** *v*. **black·mail·er** *n*. **Black Ma·ri·a** [məˈraɪə] **1** *Slang* a police patrol wagon or prison van. **2** hearse. **black mark** disgrace or discredit. **black market** the trade in smuggled or stolen goods. **black–mark·et** *v*. **black mar·ke·teer** *n*. **black·out** *n* **1** a power failure. **2** total darkening of an area as protection against an air raid. **3** a temporary loss of consciousness, memory, or vision due to lack of circulation of blood in the brain. **4** the suppression of information for security purposes: *news blackouts during the war.* **5** suppression of a sportscast in a local area in order to encourage attendance. **black pepper** a hot-tasting seasoning made from the ground dried berries of the pepper vine. Compare WHITE PEPPER. **black raspberry** a species of raspberry bush bearing purple-black fruit. **Black Rod 1** ✱ the chief usher of the Senate. **2** in the UK, the chief usher in the House of Lords, whose symbol of authority is a black rod. **black rot** any of several plant diseases caused by bacteria or fungi and producing dark brown discoloration and decay. **black sheep** a permanently disgraced family member. **black·smith** *n* a person who makes and repairs things of iron. **black spruce** a spruce with dark green needles, found throughout N Canada up to the edge of the tundra. **black·strap molasses** a thick, dark molasses from cane sugar. **black·tailed deer** a deer of NW North America whose tail is black on top. Also called **black·tail**. **black tea** tea leaves that have been allowed to ferment in the air for some time before being dried in ovens. **black tie 1** a black tie, esp a black bow tie, for formal wear with a dinner jacket or tuxedo. **2** a dinner jacket or tuxedo, as opposed to full evening dress or tails. Compare WHITE TIE.

black·top *n* asphalt and crushed rock, mixed for use as pavement. *v* **-topped, -top·ping** pave with blacktop. **black walnut** a North American walnut tree. **black widow** any of a genus of poisonous black spiders.

blad·der [ˈblædər] *n* **1** a soft, thin bag of membrane in the body of an animal, which holds urine until it is discharged. **2** any similar bag for liquid or air in a plant or animal body: *the swim bladder of a fish.* **3** a strong rubber bag made to hold liquid or air. ⟨Old English *blædre*⟩

blade [bleid] *n* **1** the cutting part of a tool or weapon. **2** a sword or swordsman. **3** a dashing young man. **4** a leaf of grass. **5** *Botany* the flat, wide part of a leaf as distinguished from the stalk. **6** a flat, wide part of anything: *the blade of a paddle, the shoulder blade.* **7** the sharpened metal part of a skate, which makes contact with the ice. *v* **blad·ed, blad·ing** *Informal* to go inline skating. **blade·like** *adj*. ⟨Old English *blæd*⟩

blah [blɑ] *adj* **1** dull and mediocre: *a blah speech.* **2** rather low-spirited and lethargic. *n Slang* **1** a meaningless syllable repeated in imitation of tiresome talk: *They said they were sorry but it was company policy, and blah blah blah.* **2 the blahs** *pl* low spirits and lethargy: *the February blahs.* ⟨imitative⟩

blame [bleim] *v* **1** hold responsible (*for* something bad): *We blame the fog for our accident.* **2** find fault with: *I can't blame you for being upset, under the circumstances.* *n* **1** the responsibility for something bad. **2** criticism. ⟨Old French *blasmer* from Greek *blasphēmeein*; blas- slanderous + *phēmē* word⟩ **be to blame** deserve the blame: *Who is to blame for this?* **blame on** attribute (some unfortunate fact or event) to: *The accident was blamed on the icy road.* **blamed** *adj Informal* darned; confounded: *Where did I put the blamed thing?* **blame·less** innocent; irreproachable. **blame·wor·thy** *adj* deserving blame.

blanch [blæntʃ] *v* **1** turn white: *to blanch with fear.* **2** loosen the skins of (raw vegetables, nuts, etc.) by plunging them first in boiling water and then in cold water. **3** boil (vegetables, meat, etc.) briefly to prepare for freezing, remove a bitter taste, etc. **4** keep (growing celery, etc.) from becoming green by covering so as to exclude sunlight. ⟨Old French *blanchir; blanc* white⟩

bland [blænd] *adj* **1** not spicy; with no strong or exotic flavours: *a bland diet.* **2** agreeable; polite, esp in an ingratiating way. **3** without character; dull. **bland·ly** *adv.* **bland·ness** *n.* ⟨Latin *blandus* soft⟩

blan·dish ['blændɪʃ] *v* coax by flattering. **blan·dish·ment** *n.* ⟨Old French *blandiss-*, stem of *blandir;* Latin *blandiri* flatter⟩

blank [blæŋk] *adj* **1** empty; without images, printing, recording, etc.: *blank paper, a blank tape.* **2** with spaces to be filled in: *a blank form.* **3** of a gun cartridge, containing powder but no bullet. **4** with no understanding or expression: *a blank stare.* **5** absolute; utter: *blank dismay.* **6** direct: *a blank refusal.*
n **1** a space left to be filled in later: *Leave a blank after each name.* **2** something without the usual contents, markings, etc.: *Her mind was a complete blank for several hours after the accident.* **3** a blank cartridge. **4** a space (often read aloud as 'blank') replacing a taboo word.
v **1** keep (an opponent) from scoring in a game. **2** cause to become blank; replace with a blank (often with *out*). **blank·ly** *adv.* **blank·ness** *n.* ⟨French *blanc* white⟩
blank out a become confused or distracted: *I blanked out and couldn't remember their names.* **b** cancel, erase or make invisible. **draw a blank** fail completely, often in remembering or finding something.
blank cheque 1 a signed cheque that allows the bearer to fill in the amount. **2** *Informal* freedom to do as one pleases. **blankety–blank** a facetious substitute for a taboo word. **blank verse** unrhymed iambic pentameter: *The plays of Shakespeare are written in blank verse.*

blan·ket ['blæŋkɪt] *n* **1** a cover, usually of soft fabric, to keep people or animals warm. **2** anything like a blanket: *A blanket of snow covered the ground.*
adj covering all instances or cases: *a blanket insurance policy. Don't make blanket statements.*
v **1** cover with or like a blanket: *Fallen leaves blanketed the lawn.* **2** stifle or suppress: *They have blanketed all debate on the issue.* ⟨Old French *blankete; blanc* white. Related to BLANK.⟩
blanket stitch a stitch used for edging thick fabric such as blankets.

blare [blɛr] *v* **1** make a loud, harsh sound: *Trumpets blared.* **2** utter harshly or loudly.
n a loud, harsh sound: *the blare of car horns.* ⟨Middle Dutch *blaren*⟩

blar·ney ['blɑrni] *n* flattering talk. **blar·ney** *v.* **kiss the Blarney Stone** get skill in flattering and coaxing people. ⟨a stone in the wall of Blarney Castle, Ireland, said to give skill in flattery to anyone who kisses it⟩

bla·sé [blɑ'zei] *adj* **1** bored; world-weary. **2** unmoved by something, esp because of overexposure: *With our youngest child we were pretty blasé about all the milestones.* ⟨French, pp of *blaser* exhaust with pleasure⟩

blas·pheme [blæs'fim] *or* ['blæsfim] *v* **1** speak about (God or sacred things) with contempt. **2** utter profanities or curses. **blas·phem·er** *n.* **blas·phe·mous** ['blæsfəməs] *adj.* **blas·phe·my** *n.* ⟨Greek *blasphēmeein; blas* slanderous + *phēmē* word⟩

blast [blæst] *n* **1** a sudden rush of air: *the icy blasts of winter.* **2** the blowing of a horn. **3** a current of air used in smelting, etc. A furnace is **in blast** when in operation; it is **out of blast** when stopped. **4** an explosion. **5** *Slang* an outburst of anger, severe criticism, etc. **6** *Slang* **a** a big, wild party. **b** a lot of fun: *That new game is a blast!*
v **1** blow up or clear with an explosive: *They blasted a hole in the rock.* **2** wither; ruin: *The intense heat blasted the vines. His conviction for fraud blasted his reputation.* **3** criticize angrily.
interj an exclamation of frustration, anger, etc. **blast·er** *n.* ⟨Old English *blæst*⟩
(at) full blast at full volume or speed: *playing the stereo full blast.* **blast from the past** *Informal* something highly reminiscent of former times, esp in a nostalgic way. **blast off** of rockets, missiles, etc., take off.
blast·ed *adj* **1** withered; ruined. **2** *Informal* a generalized term of impatience or anger: *This blasted pen won't write.* **blast furnace** a furnace for smelting ore in which a strong current of air produces intense heat. **blast·off** or **blast–off** *n* the process or moment of launching a rocket, spacecraft, etc.

blas·tu·la ['blæstʃələ] *n, pl* **-lae** [-li] *or* [-ˌlaɪ] *Zoology* the embryo of an animal. **blas·tu·lar** *adj.* ⟨Latin; Greek *blastos* sprout, germ⟩

bla·tant ['bleitənt] *adj* offensively obvious: *blatant stupidity.* **bla·tan·cy** *n.* **bla·tant·ly** *adv.* ⟨coined by Spenser from Latin *blatire* babble⟩

blath·er ['blæðər] *n* foolish talk. **blath·er** *v.* **blath·er·er** *n.* ⟨Old Norse *blathr*⟩
blath·er·skite *n Informal* a blatherer. ⟨*blather* + Scottish *skate* a term of contempt⟩

blaze¹ [bleiz] *n* **1** a bright flame or fire. **2** a glow of brightness: *the blaze of the noon sun.* **3** a violent outburst: *a blaze of temper.* **blaze** *v.* ⟨Old English *blæse*⟩
blaze away a fire a gun, etc. **b** talk rapidly and excitedly. **go to blazes** *Informal* go to hell.

blaze² [bleiz] *n* **1** a mark made on a tree with paint or by chipping off a piece of bark. **2** a white mark on an animal's forehead.
v **1** make a blaze on (a tree or trees). **2** mark (a trail) in this way. ⟨Low German *bläse*⟩

blaz·er ['bleizər] *n* a jacket cut like a suit coat.

bla·zon ['bleizən] *v* **1** *Poetic* make known. **2 a** decorate; adorn. **b** display, esp colourfully. **3** describe or paint (a coat of arms).
n **1** coat of arms. **2** a bright or colourful display. **bla·zon·ment** *n.* ⟨Old French *blason* shield⟩

bleach [blitʃ] *v* whiten by exposing to sunlight or chemicals: *We bleached the stains out of the shirt.*
n a chemical whitener. ⟨Old English *blǣcean; blǣce* pale. Related to BLEAK.⟩
bleach·ers *n pl* the rows of tiered seats around a playing field or indoor court, for spectators.

bleak [blik] *adj* **1** bare or colourless: *bleak mountain peaks, a bleak landscape.* **2** chilly; cold: *a bleak wind.* **3** dreary; dismal: *the future looked bleak.* **bleak·ly** *adv.* **bleak·ness** *n.* ⟨Middle English *bleke* pale; Scandinavian⟩

blear [blir] *v* make dim or blurry. **blear·y** or **blear** *adj.* ⟨Middle English *blere(n)*⟩

bleat [blit] *v* **1** make the characteristic cry of a sheep, goat, or calf. **2** complain, esp feebly or with a whine. **3** babble. **bleat** *n.* **bleat·er** *n.* ⟨Old English *blætan*⟩

bleb [blɛb] *n* **1** a blister. **2** a bubble. ⟨variant of *blob*⟩

bleed [blid] *v* **bled, bleed·ing 1** lose blood. **2** take blood from: *Doctors used to bleed sick people.* **3** feel pity, sorrow, or grief. **4** *Informal* extort money from. **5** of a dark colour, show through a top coat of lighter colour. **6** run, as colours in wet cloth. **7** *Printing* extend to the edge of (a page), leaving no margin. **8** empty (a container) of fluid. ⟨Old English *bledan; blod* blood⟩
bleed white take all the resources of. **one's heart bleeds** (often ironic) one feels pity.
bleeding heart 1 a perennial herb with drooping, heart-shaped flowers. **2** *Informal* a person who allows feelings of pity to override sound judgment. **bleeding station** a lab taking blood samples for analysis elsewhere.

bleep [blip] *v* **1** esp of electronic equipment, emit a short, high-pitched sound. **2** *Radio and television* censor (a word, etc.) in a broadcast by substituting a bleep (often with *out*). **bleep** *n.* ⟨imitative⟩

blem·ish ['blɛmɪʃ] *n* **1** a stain; spot; scar. **2** a defect; fault: *A quick temper was the only blemish in her character.*
v stain, spot, or mar. ⟨Old French *blemiss-*, stem of *blemir* make livid⟩

blend [blɛnd] *v* **1** mix together thoroughly: *Oil and water will not blend.* **2** make by mixing several kinds together: *to blend tea.* **3** make a gradual transition: *The colours of the rainbow blend into one another.* **4** harmonize.
n **1** the act or product of blending: *a blend of several coffees.* **2** *Linguistics* a word made by fusing two others, often with a syllable in common. *Blotch* is a blend of *blot* and *botch.* **3** a sequence of consonants beginning or ending a single syllable, as the *bl* in *blue* or the *st* in *fast.* ⟨Old Norse *blanda*⟩
blended family a family including children of one or more previous marriages. **blend·er** *n* a small household appliance for mixing ingredients, usually into a liquid.

blen·ny ['blɛni] *n, pl* **-ny** or **-nies** any of a family of small, scaleless, bottom-living fishes of coastal waters, with a big head and tapering body. ⟨Greek *blennos; blenna* slime⟩

bless [blɛs] *v* **blessed** or (*Poetic*) **blest, bless·ing 1** make holy or sacred: *to bless a church.* **2** ask God's favour for: *Bless these little children.* **3** feel or express gratitude to: *They blessed her for her kindness.* **4** favour with prosperity or any good gift: *I am blessed with good health. May this country always be blessed.*

5 praise: *Bless the Lord, O my soul.* ⟨Old English *blētsian*⟩
bless my soul! an expression of surprise or pleasure. **bless you!** exclamation in response to another's sneeze.
bless·ed ['blɛsɪd] *or* [blɛst] *adj* **1** holy; sacred. **2** fortunate; happy; favoured by God. **3** ['blɛsɪd] *Informal* a generalized term of annoyance: *Where has that blessed thing got to?* **bless·ed·ness** *n.* **bless·ing** *n* **1** grace said before meals. **2** any other prayer asking God's favour. **3** approval and good wishes: *She left home with her parents' blessing.* **4** any asset or benefit: *Freedom is a great blessing.*

blew [blu] *v* pt of BLOW².

blight [blaɪt] *n* **1** any of several plant diseases causing parts to wither and die. **2** anything that destroys or prevents growth: *the blight of high unemployment.* **blight** *v.* ⟨origin uncertain⟩

blimp [blɪmp] *n* **1** a small, non-rigid dirigible airship. **2** *Informal* anything plump and rounded. **blimp·ish** *adj.* ⟨apparently, Type *B limp*, common type of dirigible in WWI⟩

blind [blaɪnd] *adj* **1** physically unable to see. **2** not guided by judgment or reason: *blind faith.* **3** unable or unwilling to understand or perceive (with *to*): *blind to the beauty of one's environment.* **4** hard to see; hidden: *a blind curve on a highway.* **5** *Slang* drunk.
adv **1** without being able to see properly: *driving blind.* **2** using only instruments: *to fly blind.* **3** extremely (drunk). **4** in a test or experiment, performed without knowing relevant information, so as to be unbiased.
v make blind: *blinded by the bright lights. Her prejudice blinds her.*
n **1** an opaque screen in front of a window, used to shut out light or heat. **2** any thing or person used to conceal an action or purpose. **3** a hiding place for a photographer or hunter. **blind·ly** *adv.* **blind·ness** *n.* ⟨Old English⟩
turn a blind eye (**to**) refuse to see or take notice of.
blind alley 1 a passageway closed at one end. **2** anything that offers no opportunity for progress. **blind date** a social date between two people who have not met. **blind·er** *n* a leather flap designed to keep a horse from seeing to the side; blinker. **wear blinders** be blinded by prejudice. **blind·fold** *v* **1** cover the eyes to prevent seeing: *The robbers blindfolded, gagged, and bound their victim.* **2** prevent (someone) from understanding. *adj, adv* **1** with the eyes covered: *He said he could walk the line blindfold.* **2** reckless(ly). **blind·fold** *n.* **blind·side** *v* **1** attack (someone) while unseen. **2** criticize (someone who has poor or no defence). **3** *Football* tackle (an opponent) from the side on which he or she is not looking. **blind spot 1** a round spot on the retina that is not sensitive to light. **2** an issue on which a person does not know that he or she is prejudiced or poorly informed. **blind trust** an arrangement whereby stocks, bonds, etc. held by an MP, etc. are traded on

his or her behalf so that he or she cannot be caught in a conflict of interest.

blink [blɪŋk] *v* **1** close the eyes and open them again quickly; wink: *We blink every few seconds.* **2** flicker; flash: *A little lantern blinked in the night.*
n **1** the act of blinking. **2** a flash or glimpse. **3** esp in the Far North, a reflection of sunlight on cloud caused by distant ice or snow. ⟨Middle English *blenken*⟩
blink at ignore: *She blinks at all his faults.* **on the blink** *Informal* not working; out of order. **blink·er** *n* **1** blinder. **2** a flashing signal light. *v* **1** put blinders on. **2** constrict the vision, thinking, etc. of: *blinkered by prejudice.*

blintz [blɪnts] *n* a rolled crepe filled with cheese, fruit, etc. ⟨Yiddish; Ukrainian *blynci*⟩

blip [blɪp] *n* **1** an image on a radar screen, in the form of a small dot of light. **2** a short, high-pitched, light or crisp sound.
v **blipped, blip·ping** show or emit a blip.

bliss [blɪs] *n* **1** great happiness. **2** the joy experienced by those in heaven; blessedness. *v Slang* feel or cause to feel intense euphoria, orig from drugs (with *out*): *I blissed out when she kissed me.* **bliss·ful** *adj.* **bliss·ful·ly** *adv.* ⟨Old English *blīths; blīthe* blithe⟩

blis·ter [ˈblɪstər] *n* **1** a little baglike swelling of the skin, filled with fluid, often caused by a burn or by abrasion. **2** a swelling on a leaf due to disease, on a painted surface, etc. **3** a bubblelike shell of transparent plastic used to package a piece of merchandise.
v **1** get or cause to get a blister or blisters. **2** criticize or insult severely. **blis·ter·ing** *adj.* **blis·ter·y** *adj.* ⟨Old Norse *blastr* swelling⟩

blithe [blaɪð] *or* [blaɪθ] *adj* **1** happy; carefree; light-hearted. Also, *(Poetic)* **blithe·some.** **2** airy; casual; thoughtless: *blithe indifference.* **blithe·ly** *adv.* ⟨Old English *blīthe*⟩

blith·er·ing [ˈblɪðərɪŋ] *adv* talking nonsense: *a blithering idiot.* ⟨var. of *blathering*⟩

blitz [blɪts] *n* **1** blitzkrieg. **2** any sudden, violent attack. **3** a short-term, concentrated campaign: *a canvassing blitz for charity.*
v carry out or subject to a blitz. ⟨German = lightning⟩
blitz·krieg [ˈblɪts,krig] *n* offensive military action designed to crush the enemy quickly.

bliz·zard [ˈblɪzərd] *n* **1** a violent, blinding snowstorm. **2** *Informal* an overwhelming number or amount: *a blizzard of angry letters.* *v Informal* blow a blizzard: *It's blizzarding out there.* **bliz·zard·y** *adj.* ⟨origin uncertain⟩

bloat [blout] *v* **1** swell up: *His face was bruised and bloated after the fight.* **2** preserve (herring) by salting and smoking.
n **1** a swelling of the stomach of cattle, sheep, etc. caused by excess gas. **2** *Informal* needless expansion of staff, budget, etc. **bloat·ed** *adj.* ⟨Old Norse *blautr* soft, pulpy⟩
bloat·er *n* **1** a salted, smoked herring. **2** a small Great Lakes cisco trout.

blob [blɒb] *n* **1** a soft lump: *Blobs of wax covered the candlestick.* **2** a splash or irregular patch of colour. **3** anything seen indistinctly.

v **blobbed, blob·bing** *v* mark or apply with blobs. ⟨Middle English *blobe* a bubble⟩

bloc [blɒk] *n* a group of people, companies, parties, nations, etc. aligned politically or economically. ⟨French = block⟩
Bloc Québécois [ˈblʌk ˌkeibɛˈkwɑ] ※ a federal political party championing Québec's interests, including sovereignty.

block [blɒk] *n* **1** a usually solid piece of hard material with rectangular sides. **2** a child's building toy in the shape of a brick. **3** a small area in a city or town, bounded by four streets. **4** the length of one side of such an area: *Walk one block east.* **5** a group of things of the same kind: *a block of seats in a theatre.* **6** a building containing a number of units: *an apartment block.* **7** *Slang* head. **8** anything that prevents progress: *writer's block.* **9** *Sports* the hindering of an opponent's play. **10** a psychological inability to accept or deal with something: *a mental block.*
v **1** prevent passage by: **a** filling or clogging (often with *up*): *roads blocked with snow.* **b** erecting a barrier (often with *off*): *to block off a street.* **2** hinder: *to block a plan.* **3** *Sports* hinder the play of (an opponent). **4** plan roughly; outline (usually with *in* or *out*): *to block in a sketch.* ⟨Old French *bloc*⟩
chip off the old block resembling one's parent. **on the block** for sale at an auction. **block·ade** *n* **1** in war, the closing off of a harbour, city, etc. by the enemy to keep supplies from getting through. **2** any barrier erected to prevent passage. **block·ade** *v.* **run the blockade** try to get through a blockade. **blockade runner. block·age** *n* the fact or cause of being blocked: *We cleared the blockage from the pipe.* **block and tackle** an arrangement of pulleys and ropes used to lift or move heavy objects. **block·bust·er** *n Informal* **1** a book, movie, etc. that is very popular or has a very strong impact: *The new musical is a blockbuster.* **2** an aerial bomb that weighs two or more tonnes, capable of destroying a large area. **block·er** *n* **1** *Sports* a player who hinders an opponent's play. **2** a drug that inhibits a chemical process in the body: *beta blocker.* **block·head** *n* a stupid person. **block heater** an electrical device for keeping the engine block of a motor vehicle slightly warm. **block·house** *n* **1** a military fortification built of heavy timbers or concrete. **2** a heavily reinforced building used as a control centre: *The launching of space vehicles is controlled from a blockhouse.* **block·ish** *adj* stupid. **block letter** a capital letter, usually hand printed. **Block Parent** a designated adult to whose home, identified by a special logo in the window, neighbourhood children may go when in need of help. **block party** a party by or for all the residents of a street block, often with the street closed to traffic. **block print** a print made from an engraved block.

blog [blɒg] *n Computers* in full, **weblog** a website where users can post a journal entry of their thoughts.
v make such an entry. **blog·ger** *n.* **blog·ging** *n.*

bloke [blouk] *n Informal* fellow; chap.

blond [blɒnd] *adj* **1** light-coloured: *blond hair, blond furniture.* **2** fair-haired.
n a blond person, esp a man or boy. **blonde** [blɒnd] *n, adj.* **blond·ness** *n.* ⟨French⟩

blood [blʌd] *n* **1** the red liquid in the veins and arteries of vertebrates. **2** a corresponding liquid in other animals: *The blood of most insects is yellow.* **3** family; heritage; birth: *of French blood.* **4** bloodshed; violence: *too much blood in that movie.* **5** high lineage, esp royal lineage: *a prince of the blood.* **6 Blood** See KAINAI. **7** individuals seen as the energizing force of a group: *What this company needs is new blood.*
v **1** give the first experience of blood to: *to blood a hunting dog, to blood raw troops in a battle.* **2** initiate. ⟨Old English *blōd*⟩
bad blood animosity. **blood is thicker than water** the ties that bind families are stronger than those that link friends. **draw first blood** hit or score first. **have someone's blood on one's hands** or **head** be guilty of someone's murder. **in cold blood** purposely and without emotion. **in one's blood** natural for one; inborn: *Love of the sea is in my blood.* **make one's blood boil** make one very angry. **make one's blood run cold** terrify one.
blood bank a place where blood is stored for transfusions. **blood·bath** *n* massacre; savage or widespread killing. **blood brother 1** a brother by birth. **2** a person who goes through a ceremony of mixing some of his blood with another person's. **blood brotherhood. blood count** a count of the number of red and white corpuscles or platelets in a sample of a person's blood. **blood·cur·dling** *adj* horrible; terrifying. **blood donor** a person who donates blood for transfusions. **blood group** any of four main groups into which human blood is classified: A, B, AB, and O. **blood·hound** *n* **1** a breed of large dog with a keen sense of smell. **2** *Informal* detective. **blood·less** *adj* **1** without blood; pale. **2** without bloodshed: *a bloodless revolution.* **3** without energy or emotion. **4** inhumane; cruel. **blood·let·ting** *n* **1** taking blood from a vein as a treatment for disease. **2** bloodshed. **blood·line** *n* a line of direct descent; pedigree. **blood·mo·bile** ['blʌdmə,bil] *n* a van equipped for taking blood from donors. **blood money 1** money paid to have someone murdered. **2** formerly, money paid to compensate the next of kin of a murdered person. **3** money gained at the cost of another's welfare. **blood poisoning** invasion of the bloodstream by infection. **blood pressure** the pressure of the blood against the inner walls of the blood vessels. **blood–red** *adj* **1** having the colour of blood, a deep, full red. **2** made red with blood: *a blood-red sword.* **blood relation** or **relative** a person related by birth. **blood·shed** *n* the killing of people. **blood·shot** *adj* of the eyes, having the whites tinged with blood because tiny blood vessels have burst. **blood sport** any sport, such as fox hunting, that involves the killing of animals. **blood·stain** *n* a mark

or stain left by blood. **blood·stained** *adj* **1** stained with blood. **2** guilty of murder or bloodshed. **blood·stone** *n* a dark green semiprecious stone with flecks of bright red in it. **blood·stream** *n* **1** the blood flowing in the body. **2** that which keeps something alive: *the bloodstream of our economy.* **blood·suck·er** *n* leech. **blood·suck·ing** *adj.* **blood sugar** the level of glucose in the blood. **blood test** an analysis of a sample of blood. **blood·thirst·y** *adj* eager to kill; murderous. **blood transfusion** an injection of blood from one person or animal into another. **blood type** BLOOD GROUP. **blood vessel** any tube in the body through which the blood circulates. **blood·y** *adj* **1** bleeding: *a bloody nose.* **2** covered or stained with blood: *a bloody sword.* **3** with much bloodshed: *a bloody battle.* **4** eager for bloodshed; murderous. **5** like blood; blood-red. **6** *Slang* a generalized term of irritation or anger: *He's a bloody fool. adv Slang* an intensive, expressing irritation or anger: *You know bloody well why. v* **1** cause to bleed: *My nose was bloodied in the fight.* **2** stain with blood. **blood·y–mind·ed** *adj* obstinate; contrary. **bloody murder** *Informal* loudly and insistently: *scream bloody murder.*

bloom [blum] *n* **1** a flower; blossom. **2** the condition or time of greatest vigour, beauty, etc.: *in the bloom of youth.* **3** a healthy glow. **4** the powdery or downy coating on some fruits and leaves, as on plums or spruce needles. **5** *Ecology* the sudden appearance of large clumps of algae on the surface of water. *v* **1** open into flowers: *Many plants bloom in the spring.* **2** glow with health and beauty. **3** reach the peak of one's development: *She bloomed in her 40s.* ⟨Old Norse *blóm*⟩
bloom·er *n* **1** something that blooms. **2** a person with regard to how or when he or she develops: *She's a late bloomer.* **bloom·ing** *adj* **1** bearing flowers. **2** flourishing.

bloom·ers ['blumərz] *n pl* **1** loose shorts, gathered above the knee, formerly worn by women and girls for athletics. **2** underpants made like this, but shorter. ⟨from a magazine published by A. J. *Bloomer*, 1851⟩

bloop·er ['blupər] *n Slang* an embarrassing mistake.

blos·som ['blɒsəm] *n* **1** a flower, esp of a tree or other plant that produces fruit: *apple blossoms.* **2** the condition or time of flowering: *a cherry tree in blossom.*
v **1** have flowers. **2** open out; develop: *Her talent blossomed under her mom's guidance.* **blos·som·y** *adj.* ⟨Old English *blōstma*⟩

blot [blɒt] *n* **1** a spot or stain: *an ink blot.* **2** a blemish; disgrace.
v **blot·ted, blot·ting** **1** make blots (on). **2** formerly, dry (ink, etc.) by pressing with absorbent material: *She blotted her signature before folding the letter.* **3** erase: *I've blotted it from my mind.* ⟨Middle English⟩

blot one's copybook spoil one's record or reputation. **blot out a** darken or cover: *Clouds blot out the sun.* **b** wipe out. **blot·ter** *n* **1** a piece of BLOTTING PAPER. **2** a notebook or pad for recording events or transactions: *A police blotter is a record of arrests.* **3** anything that soaks up or absorbs: *She has a blotter of a mind; she remembers everything.* **blotting paper** a soft paper formerly used to soak up excess ink when writing. **blotch** *n* a large stain or irregular patch of colour. **blotch** *v.* **blotch·y** *adj.* **blot·to** *adj Slang* very drunk.

blouse ['blaʊz] *or* [blʌus] *n* **1** a light garment for the upper body, worn by women and girls. **2** any loosely fitted garment for the upper body. Sailors wear blouses. **3** the upper part of a battle dress uniform. **blouse·like** *adj.* ⟨Provençal *(lano) blouso* short (wool)⟩
blous·on [blu'zɒn] *or* ['bluzɒn] *French* [blu'zɔ̃] *n* a garment with a top styled loosely like a blouse. ⟨French⟩

blow¹ [bloʊ] *n* **1** a hard hit; stroke. **2** a sudden misfortune, or its impact: *His death was a great blow to us.* ⟨Middle English *blaw*⟩
at one blow by one act or effort. **come to blows** start fighting. **without striking a blow** with no effort; without even trying. **blow–by–blow** *adj* of a report, etc., very detailed: *We had to listen to a blow-by-blow account of the game.*

SYNONYMS
Blow, both figuratively and literally, emphasizes force: *a heavy blow on the head.* **Stroke** emphasizes technique: *with one stroke of his sword, a bold stroke against convention.*

blow² [bloʊ] *v* **blew, blown, blow·ing 1** send forth (a current of air): *The fan blew fresh air into the room. She blew on the soup to cool it.* **2** of air, move in a current: *A wind is blowing from the east.* **3** move or be moved by wind: *The wind blew the curtains. His hat blew away.* **4** shape by means of blown air: *to blow bubbles, to blow glass.* **5** (of trumpets, horns, etc.) sound: *to blow a trumpet. The horn blew for dinner.* **6** clear or empty by blowing air through: *to blow one's nose, to blow eggs.* **7** explode: *The thieves blew the safe.* **8** *Informal* boast; brag. **9** *Slang* spend or use up (money, time, etc.) wastefully. **10** burn out (a fuse, etc.): *A short circuit blew the fuse. The engine blew.* **11** *Slang* handle badly; wreck: *You blew it.* **12** *Slang* leave: *She blew town.*
n **1** the act or fact of blowing or being blown: *a blow of the whistle.* **2** a gale; storm. ⟨Old English *blāwan*⟩
blow hot and cold change from a favourable opinion to an unfavourable one. **blow in** *Informal* visit unexpectedly. **blow off 1** get rid of noisily or explosively. **2** *Slang* reject the advances of (a person). **blow one's cool** *Slang* lose one's composure. **blow one's own horn** brag about one's accomplishments. **blow one's top** (or **stack**, or **cork**, etc.) *Slang* become very angry. **blow out a** extinguish with a current of air: *Blow out the candle.* **b** of bad weather, disperse (itself): *The storm blew itself out.* **blow over a** of bad weather, pass by

or over: *The storm has blown over.* **b** of some scandal, etc., be forgotten. **blow someone away** *Informal* **a** kill, usually by shooting. **b** overwhelm with admiration, surprise, etc. **blow someone's cover** reveal someone's hidden plan or identity. **blow someone's mind** surprise greatly. **blow the whistle (on)** reveal someone's guilty secret. **blow up a** explode. **b** fill with air. **c** *Informal* become very angry. **d** enlarge (a photograph). **e** exaggerate.
blow dry·er or **blow–dry·er** *n* a hand-held electrical apparatus for drying and styling the hair by means of a strong current of hot air. **blow–dry** *v.* **blow·er** *n* a machine for forcing air into a building, furnace, mine, etc. **blow·fish** PUFFER (def. 1). **blow·fly** *n* any of several species of large fly that makes a loud buzzing sound in flight. **blow·gun** *n* weapon consisting of a tube through which one blows arrows or darts. **blow·hard** *n Slang* braggart. **blow·hole** *n* **1** a hole for breathing in the top of the head of a whale. **2** a hole in the ice where whales, seals, etc. come to breathe. **blow·off** *n* **1** an explosive output of steam or water. **2** a blowing away of topsoil by wind. **3** *Slang* a self-important person. **blow·out** *n* **1** the bursting of a tire. **2** the sudden, uncontrolled eruption of an oil or gas well. **3** *Slang* a big party or other celebration. **blow·torch** *n* a small torch that shoots out a hot flame for welding or cutting metal. **blow·up** *n* **1** explosion. **2** *Informal* **a** an outburst of anger. **b** a quarrel. **3** *Informal* an enlarged photograph. **blow·y** *adj* windy.

BLT a bacon, lettuce, and tomato sandwich.

blub·ber ['blʌbər] *n* **1** the fat of whales and some other sea animals. **2** unwanted fat on a human being. **3** a noisy weeping.
v **1** weep noisily. **2** utter while crying and sobbing: *The child blubbered an apology.* **blub·ber·y** *adj.* ⟨probably imitative⟩

bludg·eon ['blʌdʒən] *n* a short, heavy club. *v* **1** strike with a club. **2** bully; threaten. **bludg·eon·er** *n.* ⟨origin unknown⟩

blue [blu] *n* **1** the colour of the clear sky in daylight. **2 the blues** *pl Informal* low spirits. **3 blues** *pl* (with a sg verb) *Music* a style of jazz characterized by a melancholy sound. **blues·y** *adj.* **4 the blue a** the sky: *high up in the blue.* **b** the far distance. **c** the sea.
adj **1** of or having the colour of the clear sky in daylight. **2** of animals or plants, bluish (in compounds): *blue spruce, bluefish.* **3** of the skin, ashen: *blue with cold.* **4** sad; gloomy: *I was feeling blue.* **5** *Informal* indecent: *a blue joke.* **6 ❋** to do with the Conservative Party.
v **blued, blu·ing** or **blue·ing** use bluing on. **blue·ness** *n.* **blu·ish** or **blueish** *adj.* ⟨Old French *bleu*; Germanic⟩
into the blue far away; out of reach or sight: *The airplane took off and swiftly vanished into the blue.* **once in a blue moon** very rarely. **out of the blue** completely unexpected(ly): *Suddenly, out of the blue, she announced that she was quitting.* **sing** or **cry the blues** be sad or dissatisfied.

blue·back *n* ✹ a three-year-old COHO SALMON. **blue·bell** *n* a common wildflower with blue, bell-shaped flowers. **blue·ber·ry** *n* the small, sweet, dark blue berry of any of several shrubs of the heath family. **blue·bird** *n* any of a small genus of North American songbirds, the males all having mainly bright blue plumage. **blue blood** 1 aristocratic descent. 2 **blueblood** aristocrat. **blue–blood·ed** *adj.* **blue book** 1 a book that lists socially prominent people. 2 **Blue Book a** ✹ an official statement of public accounts, published annually by the Government of Canada. **b** any of various other official government publications. **blue·bot·tle** *n* any of several species of blowfly. **blue box** ✹ a large blue plastic box used in some municipalities for the collection of recyclable household waste. **blue cheese** any cheese veined with mould. **blue–chip** *adj* 1 to do with any relatively low-yield, high-security stock. 2 *Informal* reliable. **blue–col·lar** *adj* to do with industrial or manual workers as a group. Compare WHITE-COLLAR, PINK-COLLAR. **blue devils** 1 low spirits. 2 DELIRIUM TREMENS. **blue flag** any of several blue-flowered wild irises. **blue fox** a rare colour phase of the ARCTIC FOX. **blue·gill** *n* a bluish-coloured freshwater sunfish. **blue goose** ✹ the SNOW GOOSE in its 'blue' colour phase, with mainly bluish grey upper parts and wings. **blue·grass** *n* 1 any of several grasses with bluish green stems. 2 a type of country music with fast rhythms and bluesy harmony. **blue jay** *n* a jay found in southern Canada and the US, with a crest on the head and a blue upper body and head. Also, **blue·jay**. **blue jeans** jeans made of blue denim. **blue–jeaned** *adj.* **blue laws** any very strict and puritanical laws. **blue·line** *n* either of the two blue lines drawn midway between the centre of a hockey rink and each goal. **blue mould** a fungus with bluish spores, found on bread and some cheeses. **blue murder** *Informal* euphemism for BLOODY MURDER. **Blue·nose** *n Informal* 1 ✹ a Nova Scotian. 2 ✹ a famous racing schooner built in Nova Scotia and launched in 1921. **Bluenose II** was its successor. 3 **bluenose** a prudish or puritanical person. **blue note** *Music* a minor third or seventh, as used in some jazz. **blue–pen·cil** *v* -**cilled** or -**ciled**, -**cil·ling** or -**cil·ing** change or cross out, esp by using a pencil with blue lead, such as editors often use. **blue·print** *n* 1 a photographic copy of an original drawing of a building plan, map, etc., usually showing white lines on a blue background. 2 a detailed plan for any enterprise. *v* 1 make a blueprint of. 2 make or explain (a plan) in detail. **blue ribbon** first prize; highest honour. **blue–rib·bon** *adj.* **blue spruce** a spruce tree having bluish green needles, commonly used as an ornamental tree throughout North America. **blue streak** *Informal* anything very fast. **talk a blue streak** *Informal* speak rapidly and excitedly and at length. **blue violet** a small wildflower with pale purple flowers. It is the provincial flower of New Brunswick. **blue vitriol** hydrous

COPPER SULPHATE. **blue whale** a greyish blue baleen whale, the largest animal that has ever existed on earth. **blu·ing** or **blue·ing** *n* a blue liquid or powder added to rinsewater in order to keep whites from turning yellow.

bluff¹ [blʌf] *n* 1 a high, steep cliff. 2 ✹ a clump of trees standing on the flat prairie. *adj* 1 frank and rough in a good-natured way. 2 of a cliff, ship's bow, etc., rising steeply with a broad front. **bluff·ly** *adv.* **bluff·ness** *n.* ⟨probably Dutch *blaf* broad flat face⟩

bluff² [blʌf] *n* 1 a show of confidence used to deceive or mislead. 2 a threat that cannot be carried out. **bluff** *v.* **bluff·er** *n.* ⟨perhaps Dutch *bluffen*, baffle, mislead; brag⟩ **call someone's bluff** challenge a bluff.

blun·der ['blʌndər] *n* a stupid mistake. *v* 1 make a stupid mistake. 2 act clumsily. **blun·der·er** *n.* ⟨Middle English *blondre(n)*⟩ **blunder on** or **across** discover by chance.

blun·der·buss ['blʌndər,bʌs] *n* 1 formerly, a short gun with a wide muzzle. 2 a person who blunders. ⟨Dutch *donderbus* thunder gun⟩

blunt [blʌnt] *adj* 1 without a sharp point or edge. 2 plain-spoken; frank, often excessively so. 3 slow to perceive or understand. *v* make or become blunt. **blunt·ly** *adv.* **blunt·ness** *n* ⟨Middle English⟩

SYNONYMS
Blunt emphasizes tactlessness and potential offensiveness: *He thinks that blunt speech proves he is honest.* **Bluff** suggests frank or rough speech or manner combined with heartiness and warmth: *Everyone likes the bluff police officer on the beat.* **Curt** = rudely brief: *A curt nod was his only response to her greeting.*

blur [blɜr] *v* **blurred**, **blur·ring** 1 make or become unclear in form or outline: *Mist blurred the hills.* 2 make or become unable to form clear images: *blurred vision.* 3 smear (ink or paint). **blur** *n.* **blur·ry** *adj.* **blur·ri·ness** *n.* ⟨possibly a variant of *blear*⟩

blurb [blɜrb] *n Informal* words of praise, forming part of promotional material, esp on the cover of a book. ⟨supposedly coined in 1907 by US humorist Gelett Burgess⟩

blurt [blɜrt] *v* say suddenly or without thinking (often with *out*): *In his anger he blurted out the secret.* ⟨imitative⟩

blush [blʌʃ] *n* 1 a reddening of the skin due to embarrassment or excitement. 2 a rosy colour. 3 a red or pink cosmetic for the face; also, **blush·er**. ⟨Old English *blyscan*⟩ **at first blush** on first consideration. **blush wine** rosé; pink wine.

blus·ter ['blʌstər] *v* 1 storm or blow violently: *The wind blustered around the house.* 2 talk noisily and boastfully or threateningly: *He blusters a lot but he's really a coward.* **blus·ter** *n.* **blus·ter·er** *n.* **blus·ter·y** *adj.* ⟨Low German *blüstern* blow violently⟩

Blvd. (in street names) boulevard.

BNA Act or **B.N.A. Act** BRITISH NORTH AMERICA ACT.

bo·a ['bouə] *n* **1** any of various non-poisonous tropical snakes that kill their prey by squeezing until it suffocates. **2** a woman's long scarf made of fur or feathers. ⟨Latin⟩
boa constrictor a large tropical American boa averaging about 340 cm in length.

boar [bɔr] *n* **1** an uncastrated male of the domestic pig. **2** wild pig. ⟨Old English *bār*⟩

board [bɔrd] *n* **1** a long, flat, trimmed piece of lumber. **2 a** a flat piece of material for a special purpose (often in compounds): *an ironing board, a scoreboard, a snowboard.* **b** specifically, a chalkboard. **3 the boards** *pl* **a** the stage of a theatre. **b** *Hockey* the wooden barrier surrounding the ice. **c** *Basketball* the backboard. **4** *Poetic* a dining table. **5** meals provided for pay. **6** a group of people managing something: *a board of health.*
v **1** cover with boards (usually with *up*): *to board up a broken window.* **2 a** provide with room and meals, for pay: *They boarded him at his uncle's house for a while.* **b** get room and meals, for pay: *She boards at our house.* **3** get on (a ship, train, etc.). **4** *Hockey* BOARD-CHECK. **5** *Informal* use a snowboard, surfboard, etc. **board·ing** *n.* ⟨Old English *bord*⟩
across the board affecting every person or thing equally: *Prices have increased across the board again.* **go by the board** be given up or neglected. **on board** on a ship, train, etc. **tread the boards** act in the theatre.
board check *Hockey* the act of bodychecking an opposing player into the boards of a rink. **board–check** *v.* **board·er** *n* **1** a person who pays for room and meals at another's house. **2** a resident pupil at a BOARDING SCHOOL. **board foot** a unit of volume for measuring logs and lumber equal to 144 cubic inches (about 2360 cm³). *Abbrev* **bd.ft. board game** any game played by moving pieces on a marked board. **boarding house** a house where room and meals are provided for pay. **boarding school** a school that provides lodging and food during the school term for some or all of its students. **board measure** a system for measuring logs and lumber. The unit is the BOARD FOOT. **board of control** the executive branch of the governing council of certain large cities. **board of education** a group of people, usually elected, who manage the schools in an area. **board of health** the department of a local government in charge of public health. **board·room** *n* a room used for meetings by a board of directors. **board·walk** *n* a walkway made of boards, usually along a waterfront.

boast [boust] *v* **1** speak highly of one's plans, achievements, abilities, or possessions. **2** have and be proud of: *Our town boasts many fine parks.*
n a high claim about one's plans, abilities, achievements, etc. **boast·er** *n.* **boast·ful** *adj.* ⟨Middle English *boste(n)*⟩

boat [bout] *n* a small, open vessel for travel on water. **boat** *v.* ⟨Old English *bāt*⟩
burn one's boats cut off all chance of retreat.

in the same boat in the same (unfortunate) position: *We're all in the same boat, so stop griping.* **miss the boat 1** miss an opportunity. **2** be on the wrong track. **rock the boat** *Informal* disturb the status quo.
boat·er *n* **1** one who sails a boat. **2** a straw hat with a brim and a flat top. **boat·hook** *n* a pole with a metal hook at one end, used to pull or push a boat, raft, etc. **boat·house** *n* a shelter built over the water next to the shore, for storing boats. **boat·ing** *n* rowing; sailing. **boat·load** *n* as much or as many as a boat can carry. **boat·man** *n, pl* **-men 1** a man who rents out boats or takes care of them. **2** a man whose work is rowing or sailing small boats or who is skilled in their use. **3** any of various insects that crawl on water. **boat neck** a wide, shallow, scooped neckline. **boat people** refugees who have escaped by boat, esp those who fled Vietnam in the 70s. **boat song ✹** a song used by the VOYAGEURS to help them maintain a steady rhythm in paddling. Also, **paddling song. boat·swain** ['bousən] *less often*, ['bout,swein] *n* BOSUN.

bob¹ [bɒb] *v* **bobbed, bob·bing 1** move up and down with short, quick motions: *The bird bobbed its head up and down. The little boat bobbed on the waves.* **2** curtsy quickly. **3** try to catch with the teeth something floating or hanging: *bob for apples.* **bob** *n.* ⟨Middle English⟩

bob² [bɒb] *n* **1** a short haircut. **2** a weight on the end of a pendulum or plumb line. **3** a float for a fishing line.
v **bobbed, bob·bing 1** cut (hair) short. **2** fish with a bob. **bob·ber** *n.* ⟨Middle English *bobbe* bunch⟩
bob·by pin ['bɒbi] a thin, flat wire clip for the hair. **bob·tail** *n* **1** a tail cut short. **2** an animal with such a tail.

bob·bin ['bɒbən] *n* a reel or spool for holding thread, yarn, wire, etc. ⟨French *bobine*⟩

bob·cat ['bɒb,kæt] *n* a lynx found mostly in the US, related to the Canada lynx but smaller, spotted, and with no ear tufts.

bob·o·link ['bɒbə,lɪŋk] *n* a New World songbird of the same family as the orioles and meadowlarks. ⟨imitative⟩

bob·sled ['bɒb,slɛd] *n* a long sled with two sets of runners, a steering wheel, and brakes. *v* **-sled·ded, -sled·ding** ride on a bobsled.

boc·cie, boc·ce, or **boc·ci** ['bɒtʃi] an Italian bowling game played on a boarded court of sand, or sometimes on grass, with wooden balls. ⟨Italian = wooden balls⟩

bode [boud] *v* be a sign of; indicate beforehand: *Dark clouds boded rain.* ⟨Old English *bodian; boda* messenger⟩
bode ill (or **well**) be a bad (or good) sign.

bo·de·ga [bou'deigə] *n* a small Spanish grocery store or wine store. ⟨Spanish⟩

Bod·hi·satt·va [,boudi'sʌtvə] *n Buddhism* one who has attained enlightenment yet remains in the world to save others. ⟨Sanskrit⟩

bod·ice ['bɒdɪs] *n* **1** the part of a dress from the shoulders to the waist. **2** formerly, an outer garment for women and girls, worn over a blouse and laced up the front. ⟨*body*⟩

bod·y ['bɒdi] *n* **1** the whole material part of a human being, as distinct from the spiritual part, or of an animal: *This girl has a strong, healthy body.* **2** the main part, or torso, of a human being or animal, excluding the head and limbs. **3** the main part of anything: *the body of an essay, a car body.* **4** a group or quantity thought of as a unit: *the student body of a school, a body of water.* **5** *Informal* a person: *She's a good-natured body.* **6** substance; substantial quality: *soup with a lot of body.* **7** any object with physical reality: *planets and other celestial bodies.* **8** of flavours and tones, mellowness or richness: *a red wine with body.* **bod·i·less** *adj.* ⟨Old English *bodig*⟩
keep body and soul together stay alive. **over my dead body** never with my consent.
bod [bɒd] *n Informal* body. **–bodied** *combining form* having a body of a certain kind: *a full-bodied wine, able-bodied helpers.* **bod·i·ly** *adj* of or in the body: *assault causing bodily harm. adv* **1** in person: *The person we had thought dead walked bodily into the room.* **2** as one body: *The audience rose bodily.* **3** by taking hold of the body: *She carried the kicking child bodily from the room.* **body bag** a large rubber bag fastened with a zipper, used for carrying a dead body. **body blow 1** *Boxing* a blow hitting between the bust and the navel. **2** a serious setback. **bod·y·build·ing** *n* development of the muscles through weightlifting and other strenuous exercises. **bod·y·build·er** *n.* **bod·y·check** *n Hockey, lacrosse, etc.* a defensive play using body contact to stop an opponent's progress. Also, **body check. bod·y·check** *v.* **bod·y·guard** *n* a person or persons who protect someone when he or she is out in public. **body language** gestures and position of the body, conveying one's mental attitude. **body politic** the people of a politically organized society. **body rub** full-body massage, usually erotic. **body shirt** or **bod·y·shirt** *n* a women's fitted shirt or blouse that ends in a brief pantie. **body shop** a garage specializing in **bodywork** repairs to the body of a vehicle. **body snatcher** a person who steals bodies from graves. **body stocking** a tight, stretchy, one-piece garment for gymnasts, dancers, etc., covering the whole body, sometimes excluding the legs. **body suit** a BODY SHIRT or BODY STOCKING. Also, **bod·y·suit. bod·y·surf** *v* ride waves with no surfboard. **bod·y·surf·er** *n.*

Boer [bur] *n* a South African resident of Dutch background. ⟨Dutch = farmer⟩
Boer War the war between Great Britain and the Boers of South Africa, from 1899 to 1902.

bog [bɒg] *n* an area of soft, wet, spongy ground; swamp.
v sink or get stuck in a bog. **bog·gy** *adj.* **bog·gi·ness** *n.* ⟨Irish or Scots Gaelic = soft⟩
bog down get stuck or cause to get stuck as if in mud: *Don't get bogged down in the details.*

bo·gey¹ ['bougi] *n, pl* **-geys** *Golf* one stroke over par.

v play (a hole) in one stroke over par. ⟨Colonel *Bogey*, imaginary partner⟩

bo·gey² or **bo·gy** ['bugi] *or* ['bougi] *n, pl* **-geys 1** an evil spirit. **2** a personal source of trouble or fear: *His bogey was spelling.* Also, **bog·ie, bog·le.** ⟨obsolete *bog* bugbear⟩
bo·gey·man *n* a scary imaginary being mentioned, esp formerly, to frighten children into obedience.

bog·gle ['bɒgəl] *v* **1** overwhelm or become overwhelmed: *The sheer number of stars boggles the mind. Her mind boggled at the idea of such a huge project.* **2** balk at something overwhelming. **bog·gle** *n.* **bog·gler** *n.* **bog·gling·ly** *adv.* ⟨perhaps Scottish *bogle*⟩

bo·gus ['bougəs] *adj* sham; empty, false, or counterfeit. ⟨origin unknown⟩

bo·he·mi·an [bou'himiən] *n* an artist who leads a free-and-easy, unconventional life. **bo·he·mi·an** *adj.* **bohemianism** *n.*

boil¹ [bɔil] *v* **1 a** of heated liquids, bubble up and give off gas or vapour: *Water boils when heated to about 100°C.* **b** reach BOILING POINT: *Water boils faster at high altitudes.* **2** cook in boiling water or other liquid: *to boil eggs.* **3** be stirred up, esp by anger: *She is still boiling over the incident.* **4** be or feel very hot. **5** of liquids, move violently. **boil** *n.* ⟨Old French *boillir*; L *bullire* to bubble⟩
boil down a reduce through evaporation by boiling: *Boil the sauce down.* **b** reduce by getting rid of unimportant parts: *I boiled down my notes to a list of the main facts.* **c** be essentially equivalent (*to*): *Plain jealousy, that's what it boils down to.* **boil over a** boil and overflow. **b** show great excitement or anger.
boil·er ['bɔilər] *n* **1** any container to heat liquids in. **2** a tank for holding hot water, esp to make steam to heat buildings or drive engines. **boil·er·mak·er** *n* **1** a person who makes or repairs boilers. **2** *Informal* a drink of whisky followed by beer. **boiling point 1** the temperature at which a liquid boils. The boiling point of water at sea level is 100°C. **2** the point at which matters come to a head or one loses one's temper.

SYNONYMS
Boil suggests violence of anger or intensity of excitement: *She boiled at their insults.* **Simmer** suggests less intensity, or some restraint, often implying imminent explosion: *Simmering with indignation, he turned and stalked away.*
Seethe emphasizes the restlessness or disquiet caused by strong emotion, so that the feelings or thoughts are imagined as churning and foaming: *The people seethed with discontent.*

boil² [bɔil] *n* an abscess in the skin and the tissues just beneath it, consisting of pus around a hard core. ⟨Old English *bȳl(e)*⟩

bois·ter·ous ['bɔistərəs] *adj* noisy or active or rough, but in a cheerful way: *a boisterous game.* **bois·ter·ous·ly** *adv.* **bois·ter·ous·ness** *n.* ⟨Middle English *boistrous*, earlier *boistous*⟩

bok choy ['bɒk 'tʃɔi] CHINESE CABBAGE.

bold [bould] *adj* **1** fearless; daring: *a bold explorer.*

2 so free, familiar, or assertive as to be rude: *The bold child made faces at everyone.* 3 striking; clear: *trees in bold outline against the sky.* 4 of type, heavier than normal. **bold·ly** *adv.* **bold·ness** *n.* ⟨Old English *bald*⟩ **make (so) bold (as)** take the liberty (*to*); dare: *May I make so bold as to ask for a ride home?* **bold·face** *n Printing* a heavy type that stands out clearly. **This sentence is in boldface.** **bold·face** *adj.* **bold·faced** *adj* presumptuous.

bole [boul] *n* the trunk of a tree. ⟨Old Norse *bolr*⟩

bo·le·ro [bə'lɛrou] *n* 1 a lively Spanish dance in 3/4 time. 2 a short, loose jacket worn open at the front. ⟨Spanish⟩

boll [boul] *n* a rounded seed pod, esp that of cotton or flax. ⟨variant of *bowl*⟩
boll weevil a serious pest of cotton plants.

bo·lo·gna [bə'louni] *n* a large sausage made of beef, veal, and pork. ⟨*Bologna*, city in Italy⟩

bolo tie a tie made of thin cord, its ends kept together by an ornament which slides along them. ⟨altered from *bola* weapon consisting of stone or metal balls tied to cords⟩

Bol·she·vik ['boulʃə,vɪk] *or* ['bɒlʃə,vɪk] *n, pl* **-viks** *or* **-vi·ki** [-'viki] 1 a member of the radical wing of the Russian Social Democratic Party which took power in 1917. 2 a Communist. 3 Often, **bolshevik** any left-wing radical with revolutionary tendencies. **Bol·she·vik** *or* **bol·she·vik** *adj.* **Bol·she·vism** *or* **bol·she·vism** *n.* **Bol·she·vis·tic** *adj.* ⟨Russian, from *bolshe* greater; it was at one time the majority wing⟩

bol·ster ['boulstər] *n* a long, firm, cylindrical pillow for a bed.
v support; reinforce: (often with *up*): *to bolster an argument with statistics.* ⟨Old English⟩

bolt [boult] *n* 1 a sort of metal pin made to hold parts together, having a head at one end and a thread with a nut on the other. 2 a sliding fastener for a door, gate, etc. 3 the part of a lock moved by a key. 4 a sliding bar that opens and closes the breech of a rifle. 5 a short arrow with a thick head, shot from a crossbow. 6 a discharge of lightning. 7 a dash; sprint. 8 a roll of cloth or wallpaper. *v* 1 fasten with a bolt. 2 a dash; sprint. b run away. 3 swallow (food) too fast or without chewing. ⟨Old English *bolt* arrow⟩
bolt from the blue a completely unexpected event. **bolt upright** stiffly erect: *Awakened by a noise, she sat bolt upright in bed.* **shoot one's bolt** exhaust one's abilities, resources, etc. on an effort.

bo·lus ['boulǝs] *n* 1 a small, rounded mass, esp of medicine. 2 any small, rounded mass. ⟨Greek *bōlos* lump⟩

bomb [bɒm] *n* 1 a container filled with an explosive, set off by a timed mechanism, a fuse, or contact. 2 a spray container filled with liquid under pressure, such as paint, insecticide, etc. 3 Also, **bomb·shell** a totally unexpected event or piece of news. 4 *Slang* a miserable failure; flop. 5 **the bomb** nuclear weapons: *Many nations now have the bomb.*

v 1 attack or damage with a bomb or bombs, often from aircraft. 2 *Slang* fail miserably: *All his jokes bombed.* 3 *Computers* fail suddenly; crash. 4 *Slang* speed: *bombing down the highway.* ⟨Greek *bombos* BOOM[1]⟩
drop a bomb(shell) make a totally unexpected announcement.
bom·bard *v* 1 attack with heavy fire from big guns. 2 keep attacking vigorously: *The lawyer bombarded the witness with questions.* **bom·bard·ment** *n.* **bom·bar·dier** [,bɒmbǝ'dir] *or* ['bɒmbǝ,dir] *n* the person in a bomber who releases the bombs. *Abbrev* **Bdr** *or* **Bdr.** **bombed** *adj Slang* very drunk. **bomb·er** *n* 1 a warplane used to drop bombs. 2 a person who throws or drops bombs. **bomber jacket** a short jacket ending in an elasticized waist. **bomb·proof** *adj* safe from bombs and shells. **bomb·shell** *n* 1 a bomb. 2 a totally unexpected and often disturbing event or piece of news. **bomb shelter** an underground or highly fortified shelter from bombs.

Bom·bar·dier [,bɒmbǝ'dir] *or* [bɒm'bardjei] *n* ✸ *Trademark* a large covered vehicle for travelling over snow and ice, equipped with tracked wheels at the rear and runners at the front. ⟨Armand *Bombardier* (1908-1964), its inventor and manufacturer⟩

bom·bast ['bɒmbæst] *n* pompous language. **bom·bas·tic** *adj.* **bom·bas·ti·cal·ly** *adv.* ⟨Greek *bambax* cotton; *bombyx* silkworm, silk⟩

bombe [bɒm], [bɒmb], *or* [b3b] *n* a dessert made with eggs and sugar encased in ice cream, usually of a round shape. ⟨French⟩

bo·na fi·de ['bounǝ 'faɪd], ['bounǝ 'faɪdi], *or* ['bounǝ 'fidei] in good faith; genuine. ⟨Latin⟩

bo·nan·za [bǝ'nænzǝ] *n* 1 a rich mass of ore in a mine. 2 any rich source of profit. ⟨Spanish *bonanza* prosperity; Latin *bonus* good⟩

bon ap·pé·tit [,bɔnape'ti] good appetite, a wish for someone about to eat.

bon·bon ['bɒn,bɒn] *n* a candy, esp a fancy one. ⟨French, reduplication of *bon* good⟩

bond [bɒnd] *n* 1 anything that constrains or unites: *bonds of duty*, *a bond of affection between sisters.* 2 a certificate of debt issued by a government or company, promising to pay back the money borrowed plus interest. 3 a *Law* a written agreement that a person will pay a certain sum of money if he or she does not perform duties properly. b the sum of money. c any binding agreement. 4 BOND PAPER. 5 the fact or manner of sticking together, as of mixed substances, atoms in a molecule, etc. 6 **bonds**, *pl* a chains; shackles. b imprisonment.
v 1 issue bonds on the strength of (assets); mortgage. 2 a take out an insurance policy covering any losses caused by (an employee). b obligate by a bond (def. 3a). 3 stick or join firmly together: *This glue bonds instantly.* 4 develop strong emotional ties: *The child quickly bonded with her adoptive parents.* **bond·a·ble** *adj.* **bond·er** *n.* ⟨variant of BAND[2]⟩
in bond of goods, held in a warehouse until taxes are paid.

bond·age ['bɒndɪdʒ] *n* **1** slavery or oppression of any kind. **2** the status of a feudal serf. **3** sexual activity involving the use of physical restraints. **bond·hold·er** *n* a person who owns bonds issued by a government or company. **bond·ing** *n* the development of emotional ties: *Bonding between mother and child begins in the first few minutes after birth.* **bond paper** a good quality paper, originally used for documents. **bond·ser·vant** *n* **1** an unpaid servant. **2** slave.

SYNONYMS
Bond (n def. 1), when used of a connection between people, suggests unity, intimacy, and emotional strength: *bonds of affection.*
Tie is often used of less voluntary connections, or their outward manifestation: *He broke all ties with his old friends.*

bone [boun] *n* **1 a** one of the parts of the skeleton of a vertebrate. **b** the material of which these are made, or its colour. **2 bones** *pl* **a** *Slang* dice. **b** wooden clappers used to keep time to music. **c** a skeleton. **3** a small thing given to placate someone.
v take bones out of: *to bone fish.* **bone·less** *adj.* **bone·like** *adj.* ⟨Old English *bān*⟩ **bone of contention** the subject of a dispute. **bone up on** study intensively to prepare for some challenge: *You'd better bone up on your French for your Québec trip.* **feel in one's bones** be sure without knowing why. **have a bone to pick** have cause for complaint. **make no bones** show no hesitation. **near the bone** approaching the bounds of acceptability or decency: *His jokes were very near the bone.* **bone china** a very white and translucent type of china. **bone–dry** *adj* very dry. **bone·head** *n Informal* a stupid person. **bone–head·ed** *adj.* **bone meal** ground bones, used as fertilizer and as food for animals. **bon·er** *n Slang* a foolish mistake or bad joke. **bone–weary** *adj* very tired. **bone·yard** *n* **1** a graveyard. **2** *Informal* a place where things are lost or abandoned forever. **bon·fire** *n* a large fire built outdoors. ⟨Middle English *bonefire* bone fire⟩ **bon·y** *adj* **1** having big, protruding bones. **2** skinny. **3** like bone or full of bones. **4** of a fish, having bone instead of cartilage.

bon·go ['bɒŋgou] *n, pl* **-gos** or **-goes** one of a pair of small connected drums beaten with the hands. ⟨American Spanish⟩

bon·ho·mie [ˌbɒnə'mi] *n* amiable nature or atmosphere. ⟨French; *bonhomme* good fellow⟩

Bon·homme [bɒ'nɒm] or [bʌn'ʌm] *French* [bɔ'nɔm] *n* ✱ a giant snowman, traditional character of the winter carnival in Québec City. ⟨Cdn. French. See BONHOMIE.⟩

bonk [bɒŋk] *Slang n* **1** a hit, esp on the head. **2** its sound. **bonk** *v.* ⟨imitative⟩ **bonk·ers** ['bɒŋkərz] *adj Slang* crazy.

bon mot [bɒn 'mou] *pl* **bons mots** [bɒn 'mouz] *French* [bɔ'mo] a witty saying.

bon·net ['bɒnɪt] *n* **1** a head covering usually tied under the chin. **2** a round, soft, brimless cap worn by men and boys in Scotland. **3** See WAR BONNET. **4** a metal cover over a machine, chimney, etc. ⟨Old French *bonet,* originally fabric for hats⟩

bon·nie or **bon·ny** ['bɒni] *adj* **1** handsome or healthy-looking. **2** fine; excellent. ⟨Middle English *bonie;* Old French *bon, bonne* good⟩

bon·sai ['bɒnsaɪ] or ['bounsaɪ] *n* a potted tree or shrub, dwarfed by pruning branches and roots. ⟨Japanese *bon* basin + *sai* plant⟩

bon·spiel ['bɒnˌspil] *n Curling* a tournament. ⟨Scots; Dutch *bond* league + *spel* game⟩

bo·nus ['bounəs] *n* something extra given: *The boss gave us all a summer bonus.* ⟨Latin = good⟩

bon vi·vant ['bɔ̃ vi'vɑ̃] *pl* **bons vi·vants** ['bɔ̃vi'vɑ̃] *French* a person who is fond of good food and luxury.

bon vo·yage ['bɔ̃ vwa'jaʒ] *French* goodbye; a farewell for someone going on a trip.

boo [bu] *n, interj* a sound made: **1** to show dislike or contempt. **2** to frighten. **boo** *v.*

boob [bub] *n Slang* **1** a stupid person; fool; dunce. **2** a silly mistake; booboo: *I made a real boob on the exam.* **boob** *v.* ⟨booby⟩ **boo-boo** *n Slang* **1** a silly mistake. **2** (child's word) a minor cut or scrape. **boob tube** *Slang* television. **boo·by** *n* **1** a stupid person; fool. **2** a large tropical sea bird. ⟨probably Spanish *bobo;* Latin *balbus* stammering⟩ **booby prize** a prize for the person who does worst in a game or contest. **booby trap 1** a trick or trap set up for some unsuspecting person. **2** a bomb arranged to explode when a certain object is touched. **boo·by–trap** *v* **-trapped,** **-trap·ping** fit with a booby trap: *Look out! That doorway may be booby-trapped!*

boo·dle ['budəl] *n Slang* money or loot from bribery or robbery. ⟨Dutch *boedel* goods⟩

boo·gie ['bugi] *Informal n* rock and roll. *v* **1** dance to rock and roll music. **2** *Slang* go; move: *Let's boogie on down to the drugstore.* ⟨origin uncertain⟩ **boo·gie–woo·gie** ['bugi 'wugi] or ['bugi 'wugi] *n Music* a style of jazz usually played on the piano, in which a rhythmic, repeating harmonic progression accompanies a melody that is often improvised.

boo·hoo ['bu'hu] *Informal n* the sound of loud weeping. **boo·hoo** *v.* ⟨imitative⟩

book [bʊk] *n* **1 a** a bound set of written or printed pages, usually with attached front and back covers. **b** the content of an existing or planned work of this kind: *Her book is not published yet. Everyone has one good book in them.* **2** a set of blank sheets bound along one edge, for taking notes, drawing, keeping records, etc. **3** a main division of a large literary work: *the books of the Bible.* **4** a series of like things fastened together like a book: *a book of tickets, a book of matches.* **5** LIBRETTO. **6** a record of bets. **7** in some card games, a number of cards or tricks forming a set. **8 books** *pl* **a** the financial records of a business. **b** academic studies.
v **1** *Informal* record a charge against (a person) at a police station: *booked for theft.*

2 reserve; engage: *to book theatre tickets, to book a band.* **book·ing** *n.* ⟨Old English *bōc*⟩ **a closed book** a person or matter shrouded in secrecy. **an open book** a person or matter that is easy to know and understand. **bring to book a** demand an explanation from. **b** rebuke. **by the book** strictly according to the rules. **close the book(s)** bring (an affair) to a close or stop keeping track of it: *Let's just close the book on the whole sorry mess.* **every trick in the book** *Informal* all possible stratagems. **in one's book** *Informal* in one's opinion. **in someone's good** (or **bad**) **books** in favour (or disfavour) with someone. **one for the book** an item worth noting. **on the books** on the official record. **read someone like a book** accurately guess someone's thoughts or feelings. **throw the book at a** *Slang* punish as severely as the law allows. **b** *Informal* marshal every argument against. **book·bind·ing** *n* the craft of binding books. **book·bind·er** *n.* **book·bind·er·y** *n.* **book·case** *n* a piece of furniture with shelves for holding books. **book club** a business organization that regularly mails selected books to subscribers. **book·end** *n* a support placed at the end of a row of books to hold them upright. **book·ie** *n Informal* BOOKMAKER. **book·ish** *adj* **1** fond of reading or studying. **2** learned; pedantic: *bookish diction.* **book·ish·ly** *adv.* **book·ish·ness** *n.* **book·keep·ing** *n* the process of recording the financial transactions of a business. **book·keep·er** *n.* **book learning** knowledge learned from books, not from real life. **book–learn·ed** [ˈbʊk ˌlɜrnɪd] *adj.* **book·let** *n* a thin book stapled together. **book·mak·er** *n* a person who makes a business of taking bets on races, etc. **book·mak·ing** *n.* **book·mark** *n* **1** something put between the pages of a book to mark the place. **2** *Computers* a record of the location of a piece of data in a Web home page, allowing instant return to it. **book·mo·bile** *n* a large van that serves as a travelling branch of a public library. **Book of Mormon** the sacred book of the Mormon religion. **book·plate** *n* a label for pasting in books, bearing the owner's name or emblem. **book·rack** *n* **1** a rack for holding an open book. **book·rest** *n* a stand for holding an open book. **book review** an article written about a book, discussing its merits, faults, etc. **book·sell·er** *n* a person or store selling books. **book·shelf** *n* a shelf for books. **book·stall** [ˈbʊkˌstɒl] *n* a booth where books are sold, often outdoors. **book·stand** *n* **1** a stand for an open book. **2** a stand displaying books for sale. **3** a booth where books are sold. **book·store** or **book·shop** *n* a store where books are sold. **book value 1** the value of anything as recorded in the owner's account books or a standard, authoritative list of prices. **2** the capital worth of a business. **book·worm** *n* **1** any of various insects which feed on the bindings or pages of books. **2** a person who loves reading.

boom[1] [bum] *n* **1** a deep, loud, hollow sound. **2** a sudden activity or increase, as in business or population. **boom** *v.* ⟨imitative⟩ **boom·box** *n Slang* a powerful portable stereo. **boom·er** *n Informal* a person born during the BABY BOOM. **boom·let** *n* a small boom (def. 2). **boom town** a town that has grown up quickly as a result of economic activity.

boom[2] [bum] *n* **1** the horizontal arm of a derrick, crane, etc. **2** a movable overhead pole in a recording studio, carrying microphones, lights, etc. **3** a long pole used to extend the bottom of a sail. **4** *Logging* **a** a floating line of linked timbers used to keep logs from floating away or to block the passage of boats. **b** timbers lashed together into a large raft. ⟨Dutch *boom* tree⟩ **booming ground** ❋ the part of a river, lake, or ocean where booms of logs are held.

boom·er·ang [ˈbumǝˌræŋ] *n* **1** a narrow, flat, curved piece of wood used as a throwing weapon by aboriginal peoples of Australia. **2** anything that returns to, or backfires on, its originator. **boom·er·ang** *v.* ⟨from a native language of New South Wales⟩

boon[1] [bun] *n* a blessing; favour. ⟨Old Norse *bón* petition⟩

boon[2] [bun] *adj, only in* **boon companion** a close friend.⟨Old French *bon* good⟩

boon·docks [ˈbundɒks] *n pl Informal* rough backwoods. ⟨Tagalog *bundók* mountain⟩ **boon·ies** [ˈbuniz] *n pl Slang* boondocks.

boon·dog·gle [ˈbunˌdɒgǝl] *v Informal* do trivial or pointless work. *n* **1** *Informal* trivial or pointless work, often at public expense. **2** ❋ a device used to take up the slack in a chin strap, such as a large bead. **boon·dog·gler** *n.* ⟨origin uncertain⟩

boor [bur] *n* someone rude, uncultured, or insensitive. **boor·ish** *adj.* ⟨Dutch *boer* farmer⟩

boost [bust] *n Informal* **1** a push that helps a person up or over: *a boost over the fence.* **2 a** anything that helps someone advance. **b** encouragement: *Their visit gave the sick lady a boost.* **3** increase: *a boost in salary.* **4** a promotion of an idea, product, etc. **5** a start given to a motor vehicle by using BOOSTER CABLES. **boost** *v.* ⟨blend of *boom* and *hoist*⟩ **boost·er** *n* **1** a person or thing that boosts, esp an auxiliary device for increasing force, power, voltage, etc. **2** the first stage of a multistage rocket. **3** Also, **booster shot** a supplementary injection to reinforce an earlier inoculation. **booster cables** or **jumper cables** a pair of insulated cables for connecting the terminals of two batteries to enable a transfer of energy.

boot[1] [but] *n* **1** a covering for the foot and lower leg. **2** *Informal* a kick. **3** *Computers* the start-up of a computer or program. **4** **the boot** *Slang* a rude or abrupt dismissal. *v Informal* kick. ⟨Old French *bote*⟩ **bet your boots** *Informal* depend on it: *You can bet your boots that our team will win.* **boot out** *Slang* dismiss or eject abruptly. **boot up** *Computers* cause the operating system of a computer to start itself. **die with one's boots on** die fighting or working. **have one's heart**

in one's boots be in low spirits. **lick someone's boots** flatter someone. **too big for one's boots** *Informal* conceited. **wipe one's boots on** treat in an insulting way.

boot·black *n* a person whose work is shining shoes and boots. **boot camp** an initial training camp for military recruits. **boot·ee** ['buti] *or* [bu'ti] *n* **1** a baby's soft shoe. Also, **boot·ie** ['buti]. **2** a woman's short boot. **boot·jack** *n* a device to help in pulling off one's boots. **boot·leg** *v* **-legged, -leg·ging** sell, transport, or make illegally. ⟨from the practice of smuggling liquor in boot legs⟩ **boot·leg** *n Informal* alcoholic liquor made, sold, or transported unlawfully. **boot·leg** *adj.* **boot·leg·ger** *n.* **boot·lick** *v Informal* fawn on (a person) to gain favour. **boot·lick·er** *n.* **boot·strap** *n* **1** a strap used for pulling a boot on. **2** *Computers* a short routine that instructs the computer to take in other routines or information. **by one's own bootstraps** without any help from others: *He raised himself to his present position by his own bootstraps.* **boot tree** a device shaped like a foot and put into a boot to keep it in shape.

boot² [but] *n, v Archaic* profit; benefit. **boot·less** *adj.* ⟨Old English *bōt* advantage⟩
to boot in addition: *She gave me her knife for my book and fifty cents to boot.*

booth [buθ] *n, pl* **booths** [buðz] *or* [buθs] a small structure or partly enclosed space that contains a public telephone, a private table in a restaurant, goods on display at a market or fair, etc. A booth also gives a voter privacy for marking the ballot. ⟨Middle English *bothe*⟩

boo·ty ['buti] *n* **1** things seized by violence or robbery: *pirates' booty.* **2** any valuable prize. ⟨*boot²*⟩

booze [buz] *Informal n* any alcoholic drink. *v* drink heavily. **booz·er** *n.* **booz·y** *adj.* ⟨probably Middle Dutch *busen* drink to excess⟩

bop¹ [bɒp] *Slang v* **bopped, bop·ping** hit; strike. **bop** *n.* ⟨imitative⟩

bop² [bɒp] *v* **bopped, bopping** go about in a cheerful way: *She's been bopping around town all morning.* **bop** *n.* ⟨*bebop*, style of jazz⟩

bo·rax ['bɔræks] *n* a white, crystalline powder used as an antiseptic, detergent booster, etc. ⟨Persian *bōrah*⟩

bor·del·lo [bɔr'dɛlou] *n* brothel. ⟨Italian; Latin *bordellus* little cottage⟩

bor·der ['bɔrdər] *n* **1** an edge or outer part: *a plate with a fluted border.* **2** the line separating two countries, provinces, etc. **3 the border** the border between Canada and the US. *v* **1** decorate or be around the edge of. **2** touch at the border; be adjacent (with *on*). **3** approach in character (with *on*): *The accusations in this article border on libel.* ⟨Old French *bordure; bord* side⟩
bor·der·land *n* **1** the land next to a border. **2** an uncertain territory or condition: *the borderland between sleep and waking.* **bor·der·line** *n* a boundary; dividing line. *adj* of uncertain status; esp, verging on the

unacceptable or abnormal. **border town** a town near a political border.

bore¹ [bɔr] *v* **bored, bor·ing** drill (a hole). *n* **1** a hole made by a revolving tool. **2** the hollow space inside a tube, or gun barrel: *He cleaned the bore of his gun.* **3** the diameter of a tube. ⟨Old English *borian*⟩
bor·er *n* **1** a tool for boring holes. **2** an insect or worm that bores into wood, fruit, etc.

bore² [bɔr] *v* **bored, bor·ing** make weary by being dull or tiresome. *n* a tiresome person or thing. **bored** *adj.* **bore·dom** *n.* **bor·ing** *adj.* ⟨origin unknown⟩

bore³ [bɔr] *v* pt of BEAR¹.

bore⁴ [bɔr] *n* a sudden tidal wave that rushes up a channel. ⟨Old Norse *bára* wave⟩

bo·re·al ['bɔriəl] *adj* northern. ⟨Greek *Boreas* the north wind⟩
boreal forest the vast primeval forest almost completely encircling the northern part of the globe and stretching, in Canada, from the tundra down to the mountains and prairies, the Great Lakes, and the Gaspé.

bo·ric See BORON.

born [bɔrn] *adj* **1** brought into life or being. **2** by nature: *a born athlete.*
in all my born days in my whole life. **was not born yesterday** is not gullible or naive: *You can't fool me—I wasn't born yesterday.*
born–again *adj* **1** with new spiritual life from God: *born-again Christian.* **2** fundamentalist. **3** *Informal* zealous; committed.

borne [bɔrn] *v* a pp of BEAR¹.

bo·ron ['bɔrɒn] *n* a non-metallic element found in borax. *Symbol* **B** ⟨blend of *bor(ax)* and (*carb*)*on*⟩
bo·ric *adj* of or containing boron. Also, **bor·ac·ic** [bə'ræsɪk]. **boric acid** a white, crystalline substance used as an antiseptic, as a food preservative, etc.

bor·ough ['bʌrou] *n* **1** ✻ formerly in Ontario, an urban community constituting a township but not a city. **2** in the US and UK, various other kinds of urban political entity. ⟨Old English *burg* politically important town⟩

bor·row ['bɔrou] *v* **1** get (something) from another person with the understanding that it is to be returned. **2** take and use as one's own: *Rome borrowed many ideas from Greece.* **3** take (a word or expression) from another language to use like a native word. The word *mukluk* was borrowed from Inuktitut. **bor·row·er** *n.* **bor·row·ing** *n.* ⟨Old English *borgian; borg* pledge, surety⟩
borrow trouble worry about something before there is reason to. **on borrowed time** beyond the time one can legitimately expect.

borsch [bɔrʃ] *n* a soup made from meat stock and beets. Also, **borscht** [bɔrʃt]. ⟨Russian *borshch*⟩

bor·zoi ['bɔrzɔɪ] *n* a breed of tall, swift dog with long, silky hair. ⟨Russian *borzoy* swift⟩

bo's'n ['bousən] *n* boatswain.

bos·om ['buzəm] *or* ['buzəm] *n* **1** the human chest, esp the female breasts. **2** the inmost part: *the bosom of her family*. ⟨Old English *bōsm*⟩

bos·om·y *adj* having large breasts.

bo·son ['boʊsɒn] *n* any elementary particle of a class that includes mesons and the photon, whose spin is zero or an integral number. ⟨S.N. *Bose* (1858-1937), Indian physicist⟩

boss¹ [bɒs] *Informal n* a person who directs workers.
adj Slang excellent. **boss** *v*. ⟨Dutch *baas*⟩
boss·y *adj* fond of telling others what to do.
boss around give orders to without authority.

boss² [bɒs] *n* **1** an ornamentation rising above a flat surface. **2** an enlarged part of a machine shaft. **3** *Geology* a protruding dome of igneous rock. ⟨Middle English *boce*⟩

Boston ['bɒstən] *n* US city name used in compounds.
Boston cream the creamy whipped filling of **Boston cream pie** (actually a layer cake) and **Boston cream doughnuts. Boston fern** a variety of sword fern with long, drooping fronds. **Boston lettuce** a variety of head lettuce with loose, soft leaves. **Boston Tea Party** a raid on British ships in Boston harbour in 1773, protesting unfair taxes.

bo·sun ['boʊsən] *n* a ship's officer in charge of the deck crew, the anchors, ropes, rigging, etc. Also, **boat·swain** or **bo's'n.**

bot [bɒt] *n Computers* (often in compounds) a short automatic program operating over a network, triggered by a certain type of input: *searchbot, infobot*. Also called an **a·gent.**

bot·a·ny ['bɒtəni] *n* **1** the science of plants. **2** the scientific facts about plants of a certain region or type: *the botany of the Canadian Shield, the botany of roses*. **bo·tan·i·cal** *adj*. **bot·a·nist** *n*. ⟨Greek *botanē* plant⟩
botanical garden a place where plants are grown and studied, open to the public.

botch [bɒtʃ] *v* spoil by poor work or lack of skill: *The contractor botched our deck*. **botch** *n*. **botch·er** *n*. ⟨Middle English *bocchen*⟩

both [boʊθ] *adj* two, when only two are being considered: *Both houses are white.*
pron the two together: *Both belong to him.*
adv, conj together; alike: *She can both sing and dance. I like baseball and hockey both.* ⟨Middle English; Old Norse *báthir*⟩

both·er ['bɒðər] *v* **1** concern oneself: *Don't bother about my breakfast; I'll do it.* **2** make uncomfortable, anxious, or annoyed: *The heat bothers me.* **3** disturb: *Don't bother me now.*
n **1** worry; fuss; trouble. **2** a cause of this.
interj a word used to express annoyance: *Oh, bother! I forgot the sugar.* ⟨altered from *pother*⟩
both·er·a·tion *n, interj Informal* bother.
both·er·some *adj* causing worry or fuss.

bot·tle ['bɒtəl] *n* **1 a** a container for liquids, with a narrow neck and a lid or cap. **b** such a container whose cap includes a nipple, used to feed a baby. **2 the bottle** alcohol.
v **1** put into bottles: *to bottle milk.* **2** hold in (often with *up*): *to bottle up one's anger.*
bot·tle·like *adj*. **bot·tler** *n*. **bot·tle·ful** *n*. ⟨Latin *butticula*, diminutive of *butta* barrel⟩

hit the bottle *Slang* drink too much alcohol.
bot·tle·brush *n* a long, narrow brush for washing the inside of bottles. **bot·tle·neck** *n* **1** a narrowing in a passageway or street. **2** a delay due to volume of traffic or work.

bot·tom ['bɒtəm] *n* **1** the lowest part or position: *at the bottom of the class. Look in the bottom of the cupboard.* **2** underside: *the bottom of a shelf.* **3 bottoms** *pl* the pants of a suit of pyjamas, etc. **4** the buttocks. **5** the land under a body of water. **6** *Baseball* the second half of an inning. **7** the far end: *the bottom of the garden.* **8** endurance.
adj at or of the bottom; lowest: *bottom prices.*
bot·tom·most *adj*. ⟨Old English *botm*⟩
at bottom fundamentally: *At bottom, she's a kind person.* **be at the bottom of** be the cause or source of. **bet one's bottom dollar** *Slang* be absolutely certain. **bottom out** reach a low point and level off: *It seems the stock market has bottomed out.* **bottoms up!** *Informal* drink up! **get to the bottom of** discover the underlying cause of.
bot·tom·less *adj* **1** without a bottom. **2** extremely deep. **3** endless or inexhaustible.
bottom line 1 the final line of a financial statement, showing profit and loss. **2** the fundamental point or principle.

bot·u·lism ['bɒtʃə,lɪzəm] *n* acute FOOD POISONING caused by poorly preserved food. ⟨Latin *botulus* sausage, orig assumed source⟩

bou·doir ['budwɑr] *or* [bu'dwɑr] *n* a lady's private dressing room or sitting room. ⟨French, from *bouder* sulk⟩

bouf·fant [bu'fɒnt] *French* [bu'fɑ̃] *adj* puffy: *bouffant sleeves, a bouffant hairdo.* ⟨French⟩

bou·gain·vil·le·a [,bugən'vɪliə] *n* any of several tropical climbing shrubs with large, brilliant red leaves. ⟨L.A. de *Bougainville*, 18c French navigator and explorer⟩

bough [baʊ] *n* one of the main branches of a tree. ⟨Old English *bōg* bough, shoulder⟩

bought [bɒt] *v* pt and pp of BUY.
bought·en *adj Dialect* bought from a store; not homemade: *Is that a boughten dress?*

bouil·la·baisse [,buljə'beis] *French* [buja'bɛs] *n* a fish chowder seasoned with wine, herbs, etc. ⟨Provençal *boui* boil + *abaisso* go down⟩

bouil·lon ['buljən] *or* ['buljɒn] *French* [bu'jɔ̃] *n* **1** a clear broth of meat, fish, or vegetables. **2** a medium for bacteria culture. ⟨French *bouillir* boil; Latin *bullire*⟩

boul·der ['boʊldər] *n* a large rock rounded or worn by the action of water or weather. ⟨*boulderstone*, Middle English; Scandinavian⟩

boul·e·vard ['bulə,vɑrd] *n* **1** a broad street. **2** the strip of grass between a sidewalk and a curb. **3** a centre strip dividing a road. *Abbrev* **blvd.** ⟨French, orig a passageway along a rampart. Related to BULWARK.⟩

bounce [baʊns] *v* **1** spring or cause to spring into the air after striking a surface. **2** spring back after being stretched. **3** come or go energetically: *He bounced out of the room.* **4** *Slang* throw out (a disorderly person).

5 *Informal* of a cheque, be returned by a bank because there are insufficient funds in the account on which it is drawn. **6** of an undeliverable e-mail, return to its sender.
n **1** ability to bounce: *This ball has lots of bounce.* **2** *Informal* energy; high spirits: *full of bounce.* **3 the bounce** *Slang* rude or abrupt dismissal or ejection: *They gave him the bounce.* **boun·cy** *adj.* ⟨Middle English *bunse(n)*⟩
bounce back recover quickly.
bounc·er *n* a person employed by a nightclub, etc. to calm or remove disorderly people.
bounc·ing *adj* of babies, strong and vigorous.

bound¹ [baʊnd] *adj* **1** under some obligation: *bound by law to keep the peace.* **2** certain: *It's bound to rain.* **3** (in compounds) confined to or immobilized by: *snowbound for three days.* **4** *Informal* determined: *She was bound to go.* **5** of a book or a set of pages, joined at one edge and having covers.
v pt and pp of BIND.
bound up in or **with a** closely connected with. **b** emotionally involved with.
bound·en *adj* (only in *bounden duty*) required.

bound² [baʊnd] *v, n* **1** leap. **2** bounce. ⟨French *bondir*⟩

bound³ [baʊnd] *n* **bounds** *pl* a boundary or limit: *the farthest bounds of the estate.*
v **1** be or form the boundary of: *A poplar bluff bounds the property to the north.* **2** border (*on*): *Canada bounds on the United States.* ⟨Old French *bodne;* Latin *butina*⟩
out of bounds beyond the established limits.
bound·a·ry *n* a line, real or imaginary, marking off an area or territory: *the boundary between Manitoba and Nunavut.* **bound·less** *adj* unlimited, or seemingly so; enormous: *boundless love, the boundless ocean.* **bound·less·ly** *adv.*

bound⁴ [baʊnd] *adj* going; on the way (often in compounds): *westbound, bound for home.* ⟨Old Norse *búinn,* pp of *búa* get ready⟩

boun·ty ['baʊnti] *n* **1** generosity. **2** a reward for catching or killing. **3** *Poetic* a generous gift: *God's bounties.* ⟨Latin *bonitas* goodness⟩
boun·ti·ful or (*Poetic*) **boun·te·ous** *adj* **1** full of good things: *a bountiful land.* **2** abundant: *a bountiful harvest.* **3** generous. **boun·ti·ful·ly** *adv.*
bounty hunter a person who makes a living by hunting animals (or, formerly, outlaws) for their bounty. **bounty hunting.**

bou·quet [bu'kei] or [bou'kei] *n* **1** a bunch of flowers. **2** [bu'kei] fragrance, esp of wine. ⟨French *bouquet* little wood; *bosc* wood⟩

bour·bon ['bɜrbən] *n* whisky made from a grain mash, over half corn. ⟨*Bourbon* County, Kentucky, where it was originally made⟩

bour·geois [bur'ʒwɑ] or ['burʒwɑ] *French* [buʀ'ʒwɑ] *n, pl* **-geois,** *fem* **-geoise** [-ʒwɑz] a person of the middle class, or with typical middle-class values. **bour·geois(e)** *adj.* ⟨Latin *burgensis; burgus* fort⟩
bour·geoi·sie [,burʒwɑ'zi] *n* the middle class.

bout [baʊt] *n* **1** a match or contest. **2** a period, esp of illness, hardship, or effort: *a long bout of the flu.* ⟨variant of *bought* a bending. Rel. to BOW¹.⟩

bou·tique [bu'tik] *n* a small shop or a department in a large store that specializes in fashionable clothes, in gifts, etc. ⟨French⟩

bou·ton·niere or **bou·ton·nière** [,butə'nir] or [,butə'njɛr] *French* [butɔ'njɛr] *n* a flower worn in a buttonhole. ⟨French = buttonhole⟩

bo·vine ['bouvaɪn] *adj* **1** to do with a group of mammals that includes buffalo, bison, domestic cattle, etc. **2** slow and rather stupid or insensitive. ⟨Latin *bos, bovis* ox, cow⟩

bow¹ [baʊ] *v* **1** bend (the head or body) in greeting, respect, etc. **2** submit: *We must bow to necessity.* **3** cause to stoop: *bowed by old age.*
bow *n.* ⟨Old English *būgan*⟩
bow and scrape be slavishly polite. **bow down a** weigh down: *bowed down with care.* **b** worship. **bow out** withdraw gracefully: *to bow out of a tournament.* **make one's bow a** make an entrance. **b** make a debut as a performer. **c** retire from public notice. **take a bow** accept praise, applause, etc.

bow² [bou] *n* **1** a weapon for shooting arrows. **2** a looped knot: *a bow of ribbon.* **3** a slender rod strung with horsehair, for playing a violin, etc. **4** a curve; bend.
v **1** curve; bend. **2** use a bow on (a violin, etc.). ⟨Old English *boga*⟩
bow·fin *n* a voracious freshwater fish with a very long dorsal fin. Also called **dog·fish, mud·fish. bow·head** *n* a right whale having a huge mouth, with the lower lip curving upward on each side. **bow·knot** *n* a slipknot of the kind made in tying laces. **bow·leg** *n* a leg that curves outward at or below the knee. **bow·leg·ged** [-,lɛgɪd] or [-,lɛgd] *adj.* **bow·man** *n, pl* **-men** an archer. **bow·string** *n* a strong cord stretched between the ends of a BOW (def. 1). **bow tie** a necktie worn in a small bowknot. **bow window** a curved BAY WINDOW.

bow³ [baʊ] *n* the forward part of a ship, boat, or aircraft. ⟨probably Low German or Scandinavian. Akin to BOUGH.⟩
on the port (or starboard) bow contained in the right angle to the left (or right) of the point immediately ahead. **bow·line** ['boulən] or ['bou,laɪn] *n* **1** a knot used in making a fixed loop; also, **bowline knot.** **2** the rope tied to the edge of a square sail nearest the wind. **bow·sprit** ['baʊ,sprɪt] or ['bou,sprɪt] *n* a pole projecting forward from a ship's bow.

bowd·ler·ize ['baʊdlə,raɪz] or ['boudlə,raɪz] *v* purge of improper words. **bowd·ler·ism** *n.* **bowd·ler·i·za·tion** *n.* ⟨T. *Bowdler* (1754-1825), publisher of expurgated text of Shakespeare⟩

bow·el ['baʊəl] *n* **1** Usually, **bowels** *pl* intestines. **2 bowels** *pl* the inner part: *Miners dig for coal in the bowels of the earth.* ⟨Old French *boel;* Latin *botellus* little sausage⟩
move one's bowels defecate.
bowel movement 1 the expulsion of waste matter from the large intestine. **2** feces.

bow·er¹ ['baʊər] *n* **1** a shelter of leafy branches. **2** a summerhouse or arbour. **bow·er·y** *adj.* ⟨Old English *būr* dwelling⟩

bow·er² [ˈbaʊər] *n* the high card in certain card games. The **right bower** is a jack of the suit that is trump; the **left bower** the jack of the suit of the same colour. The **best bower** is the joker. ⟨German *Bauer* jack; lit., peasant⟩

bowl¹ [boul] *n* **1** a concave rounded dish. **2** a rounded, concave part, as of a spoon or pipe. **bowl·ful** *n*. ⟨Old English *bolla*⟩

bowl² [boul] *v* **1** *Bowling* **a** take part in a game of bowling. **b** roll the ball at the pins. **2** move or roll rapidly and smoothly: *bowling along at a good speed.* **3** *Cricket* **a** send (the ball) by an overarm throw. **b** dismiss (a batsman). *n* **1** *Bowling* the act of rolling the ball at the pins. **2 bowls** *pl* (usually with sg verb) **a** lawn bowling. **b** skittles; tenpins. **bowl·er** *n*. ⟨Middle English *boule*; Latin *bulla* ball, bubble⟩ **bowl down** knock down. **bowl over a** knock over. **b** *Informal* overwhelm; surprise.

bowl·ing *n* **1** an indoor game in which heavy balls are rolled down a lane at bottle-shaped pins. **2** LAWN BOWLING. **bowling alley** an establishment having a number of lanes for bowling. **bowling green** a smooth stretch of grass for lawn bowling.

box¹ [bɒks] *n* **1** a rectangular container, usually with a lid. **2** a rectangle. **3** a partly enclosed area in a theatre, etc., for a small group of patrons. **4** an enclosed space in a courtroom, as for a jury, witness, or prisoner. **5** a small shelter: *a sentry box.* **6** *Baseball* **a** the place where the pitcher stands. **b** the place where the batter stands. **7** ✹ an enclosed area for playing lacrosse. **8** a compartment for a horse in a stable. **9** a receptacle in a post office from which a subscriber collects mail. *v* pack in a box. **box·like** *adj.* **box·y** *adj.* ⟨specialization of meaning of *box³*⟩ **box in a** put into a difficult situation with no way out. **b** surround or hem in: *Other cars in the parking lot had boxed ours in.* **box the compass a** name the points of a compass in order. **b** go all the way around and end up where one started. **in a box** in a difficult situation from which there is no escape.

box·board *n* a stiff cardboard used to make small boxes. **box·car** *n* a railway freight car enclosed on all sides. **Boxing Day** December 26, a legal holiday in all provinces except Québec. **box lacrosse** ✹ a form of lacrosse played on an enclosed playing area about the size of a hockey rink. **box lunch** a lunch for one person, packed in a box. **box office 1** the place where tickets are sold in a theatre, hall, etc. **2** the power to attract ticket buyers: *Action films are good box office.* **box pleat** a double pleat. **box social** ✹ formerly, a social gathering where boxes of sandwiches are auctioned to male bidders, each buyer having the privilege of eating and dancing with the woman who prepared the box. **box spring** a bedspring set in a wooden frame.

box² [bɒks] *n* a blow with the open hand or the fist, esp on the side of the head. *v* **1** strike such a blow. **2** fight with the fists. In the sport of boxing, contestants wear padded gloves. **box·ing** *n*. ⟨origin uncertain⟩

box·er *n* **1** a person who engages in the sport of boxing. **2** a breed of medium-sized dog with a deep chest and a short, square muzzle. **3 Boxer** formerly in China, a member of a group opposed to foreigners and Christianity. **boxer shorts** loose shorts with an elastic waistband, often worn as underwear. **boxing gloves** the padded gloves worn when boxing.

box³ [bɒks] *n* any of a genus of evergreen shrubs and small trees, often used for hedges. ⟨Greek *pyxos* a box made from this wood⟩ **box·wood** *n* **1** the hard, fine-grained, durable wood of a BOX³. **2** a box tree or shrub.

boy [bɔɪ] *n* **1** a male child. **2** a son. **3** a boy or man hired to run errands, etc. **4** *Informal* any man: *He's a local boy.* *interj Informal* a general exclamation: *Boy, it's hot!* **boy·hood** *n*. **boy·ish** *adj.* ⟨Middle English⟩ **boy·friend** *n* **1** a male romantic partner. **2** a boy who is one's friend.

boy·cott [ˈbɔɪˌkɒt] *v* combine against and have nothing to do with (a person, business, nation, etc.). **bo·ycott** *n*. **boy·cot·ter** *n*. ⟨Captain *Boycott*, 19c English land agent in Ireland who was so treated⟩

boy·sen·ber·ry [ˈbɔɪzənˌbɛri] *n* a purple berry, probably a cross of loganberry, raspberry, and blackberry. ⟨R. *Boysen,* US botanist who developed it⟩

BP 1 *Geology* before the present. **2** Usually **B/P**, blood pressure.

bpi *Computers* bits per inch.

bps *Computers* bits per second.

bra [brɑ] *n* brassiere. **bra·less** *adj.*

brace [breis] *n* **1** something that holds parts in place. **2** a pair (of ducks or rabbits). **3** a handle for a drill. **4** either of these signs { } enclosing items to be considered together. **5 braces** *pl* a pair of elasticized straps to hold up pants. **6 braces** *pl* wires attached to teeth in order to straighten them. **7** a device to strengthen or support a weak or deformed part of the body: *leg braces.* *v* **1** give strength or firmness to. **2** enliven; invigorate. **brac·ing** *adj.* ⟨Old French *bracier* embrace; Greek *brakhion* upper arm⟩ **brace oneself** prepare mentally for an ordeal. **brace and bit** a tool for drilling, consisting of a bit fitted into a cranklike handle.

brace·let [ˈbreislɪt] *n* **1** an ornamental band worn around the wrist or arm. **2** *Informal* handcuff. **brace·let·ed** *adj.* ⟨Old French *bracelet*; Greek *brakhion* upper arm⟩

brack·en [ˈbrækən] *n* a fern found in many parts of the world, with large, triangular fronds and creeping underground stems. ⟨Middle English *braken*; Scandinavian⟩

brack·et [ˈbrækɪt] *n* **1** a flat-topped piece of stone, metal, wood, etc., projecting from a wall to support a shelf, statue, etc. **2** a special fixture on a wall to support a thing that hooks or slides into it. **3** any of the signs [ ] or ( ) or { }, used to enclose words, figures, etc. **4** a grouping according to age, income, etc.: *a middle-income bracket.*

v **1** enclose within brackets. **2** support with brackets. **3** consider or think of together; group: *She is usually bracketed with the avant-garde in music.* ⟨Latin *bracae* breeches; confused with *brachia* arms⟩

brack·ish [ˈbrækɪʃ] *adj* **1** of water, slightly salty. **2** distasteful. **brack·ish·ness** *n.* ⟨dialect *brack* salty; Middle Low German *brac*⟩

bract [brækt] *n* a small leaf at the base of a flower or flower stalk. **bract·let** *n.* ⟨Latin *bractea* thin metal plate⟩

brag [bræg] *v* **bragged, brag·ging** speak too highly or proudly of oneself, one's family, achievements, etc. **brag** *n.* **brag·ger** *n.* ⟨Middle English⟩
brag·gart *n* one who habitually brags.

Brah·ma [ˈbrɑmə] *n Hinduism* the highest god and creator of all things. ⟨Sanskrit⟩
Brah·man *n, pl* **-mans 1** *Classical Hinduism* the eternal, supreme reality that is the basis of the universe. **2** a member of the highest Hindu caste, the priestly caste. **3** any of several breeds of humpbacked cattle. **Brah·man·ic** [brɑˈmænɪk] *adj.* **Brah·man·ism** *n.* **Brah·min** *n* **1** BRAHMAN. **2** an upper-class highbrow intellectual. **Brah·min·ism** *n.*

braid [breid] *n* **1** a length of hair made up of three or more interwoven strands. **2** ribbon or cord consisting of interwoven strands, used as trim. Also, **braid·ing. braid** *v.* **braid·ed** *adj.* ⟨Old English *bregdan*⟩

braille or **Braille** [breil] *n* a writing system for blind people in which the letters are represented by specially arranged groups of up to six raised dots that are read by touch. ⟨Louis *Braille*, 19c French teacher of the blind⟩

brain [brein] *n* **1** the mass of nerve tissue enclosed in the skull of vertebrates, the organism's control centre. **2** mind; intellect: *She has a good brain.* **3** *Slang* a very intelligent person. **4** Usually, **brains** *pl* a intelligence: *She has more brains than anyone else I know.* **b** the main planner: *He is the brains of the firm.*
v **1** kill by smashing the skull of: *The trapper brained the injured wolf with a large stone.* **2** hit hard on the head. ⟨Old English *brægen*⟩
beat (or **rack**, or **cudgel**) **one's brain(s)** try hard to think of something. **have on the brain** *Informal* to be preoccupied with or fanatical about: *He has cars on the brain.* **pick someone's brains** get ideas from someone.
brain cell a nerve cell in the brain. **brain·child** *n, pl* **-chil·dren** an original product of a person's thought or imagination. **brain coral** a large coral whose surface looks like a brain. **brain dead** lacking all brain function. **brain death. brain drain** a departure of the most highly skilled or educated people from a region because of better opportunities elsewhere. **brain·less** *adj* foolish. **brain power** intellect thought of as a force to be used. **brain stem** the base of the human brain, connected to the spinal cord. **brain·storm** *n* **1** *Informal* a sudden inspired idea. **2** a sudden, but temporary, mental disturbance. *v* try to solve a problem in a group by having the members suggest every solution they can

think of. **brain·teas·er** *n* a difficult puzzle. **brain trust** or **brains trust** a group of expert advisers. **brain·wash·ing** *n* **1** forced indoctrination. **2** *Informal* persuasion by long or intensive exposure to propaganda. **brain·wash** *v.* **brain·wave** *n* **1** a rhythmic increase and decrease of voltage between parts of the brain, creating an electric current. **2** *Informal* a sudden inspiration or bright idea. **brain·work** *n* work requiring the use of the mind primarily, as opposed to manual work. **brain·y** *adj Informal* intelligent.

braise [breiz] *v* brown (meat) quickly and then cook it slowly in a covered pan with very little liquid. ⟨French *braise* hot charcoal⟩

brake [breik] *n* **1** a device which reduces or stops the motion of a wheel by pressing on it. **2** anything that stops or holds back. *v* apply brakes. ⟨Middle Dutch *braeke*⟩
brake drum on a wheel or axle, a metal cylinder against which a brake shoe or band is pressed in braking. **brake light** a light at the rear of a vehicle that comes on whenever the brakes are applied, to warn drivers behind. **brake lining** a pad of mineral or metal attached to a brake band to provide friction. **brake·man** *n, pl* **-men 1** an assistant to the conductor or engineer of a railway train. **2** the rear person on a bobsled team, who applies the brake. **brake shoe** a shaped block which presses against a wheel, drum, or other surface in motion to provide friction when the brakes are applied.

bram·ble [ˈbræmbəl] *n* **1** any of a genus of mostly prickly shrubs of the rose family. **2** any rough, prickly shrub. **bram·bly** *adj.* ⟨Old English *bræmbel*; *brōm* broom⟩

bran [bræn] *n* the husk of the grains of wheat, rye, etc. **bran·ny** *adj.* ⟨Old French⟩

branch [bræntʃ] *n* **1** a subdivision of the stem of a plant. **2** any division or part of a main body or source: *a branch of a river, a branch of a family, a branch of mathematics.* **3** a local office: *The head office is in Moncton, but we have branches in several other cities.* **4** *Computers* an instruction to choose the next task from a set of alternatives. *v* divide into branches. ⟨Old French *branche*; Latin *branca* paw⟩
branch off go off in another direction from a main route: *Their street branches off the main road.* **branch out 1** subdivide into branches. **2** venture into different areas of activity: *Her firm is branching out into family law.* **branch·let** *n* a small branch. **branch plant** a business controlled by a company with its headquarters elsewhere. **branch–plant** *adj* characterized by branch plants and hence by remote decision-making: *branch-plant economy.*

SYNONYMS
Branch is the general word referring to any of the woody outgrowths of a tree or shrub.
Bough applies to any branch, but is slightly poetic: *Cedar boughs decorated the hallway.*
Limb refers to a large branch: *The wind broke a whole limb from the tree.*

brand ['brænd] *n* **1** a line of product made by a particular company: *a popular brand of coffee.* **2** BRAND NAME or trademark. **3** a mark in the skin of cattle to show who owns them, made by burning the skin with a hot iron. **4** BRANDING IRON. **5** a mark of disgrace. **6** a burning piece of wood.
v **1** mark by burning the skin with a hot iron. **2** call by a term of disgrace: *He has been branded a traitor.* **brand·er** *n.* ⟨Old English⟩
branding iron an iron stamp for burning an identification mark on hide, wood, etc.
brand name 1 a name given to a product by its manufacturer to distinguish it from those of competitors. **2** a famous name of this kind, or a product with that name. **brand–name** *adj.* **brand–new** *adj* completely new.

bran·dish ['brændɪʃ] *v* wave threateningly: *The knight brandished a sword at his enemy.* ⟨Old French *brandir;* *brand* sword⟩

bran·dy ['brændi] *n* a strong alcoholic liquor distilled from wine. **bran·died** *adj.* ⟨Dutch *brandewijn* burnt (i.e., distilled) wine⟩

brant [brænt] *n, pl* **brants** or **brant** a small wild goose that breeds in the Arctic tundra. ⟨origin uncertain⟩

brash [bræʃ] *adj* **1** loud, forward, and showing rather poor taste. **2** impetuous; rash. **3** impudent. ⟨origin uncertain⟩

brass [bræs] *n* **1** a yellow metal, an alloy of copper and zinc. **2 a** BRASS INSTRUMENT. **b** such instruments collectively in an orchestra. **3** *Informal* nerve; audacity. **4** high-ranking officials. **brass·y** *adj.* ⟨Old English *bræs*⟩
brass band a group of musicians on brass wind instruments. **brass·bound** *adj* **1** keeping strictly to rules. **2** bound with brass: *a brassbound box.* **brass hat** *Slang* a high-ranking military officer. **bras·sie** *n Golf* the number 2 wood golf club. **brass instrument** a musical wind instrument usually made of brass, such as a trumpet, tuba, horn, etc. **brass knuckles** a metal bar that fits across the knuckles, used in street fighting. **brass ring** the highest prize. ⟨from a brass ring hanging above carousel riders; anyone grabbing it got a free ride⟩ **brass tacks** *Informal* the basic facts of a matter: *Let's get down to brass tacks.* ⟨Cockney rhyming slang for *facts*⟩ **brass·ware** *n* things made of brass. **bra·zen** *adj* **1** shameless. **2** made of brass; like brass. **3** loud and harsh. **bra·zen·ly** *adv.* **brazen out** act as if one felt no embarrassment about: *He was there without an invitation, but brazened it out and had a good time.* **bra·zier** ['breiʒər] *or* ['breiziər] *n* a person who works with brass. Also, **bra·sier.**

bras·siere or **bras·sière** [brə'zir] *n* a woman's undergarment worn to support the breasts; bra. ⟨French *brassière* bodice; *bras* arm⟩

bras·se·rie [,bræsə'ri] *or* ['bræsəri] *n* a bar or small restaurant serving alcoholic drinks, esp beer. ⟨French *brasser* brew⟩

brat [bræt] *n* a spoiled or irritating child. **brat·ty** *adj.* **brat·ti·ness** *n.* ⟨origin uncertain⟩

brat·wurst ['bræt,wɜrst] *German* ['brɑt,vʊrst] *n* a highly-seasoned veal and pork sausage. ⟨Old High German *brato* lean meat + *wurst* sausage⟩

brave [breiv] *adj* **1** having the strength of mind to control fear. **2** handsome; fine.
n traditionally, a First Nations warrior.
v **1** meet bravely: *to brave danger.* **2** dare; defy: *She braved the odds.* **brave·ly** *adv.* **brav·er·y** *n.* ⟨Italian *bravo;* Latin *barbarus* barbarous⟩
bra·va·do [brə'vɑdou] *n* a great show of boldness without much real courage. **bra·vo** ['brɑvou] *or* [brɑ'vou] *interj* well done! **bra·vu·ra** [brə'vjurə] *n* a display of skill or daring. **bra·vu·ra** *adj.*

brawl [brɒl] *n* a noisy fight. **brawl** *v.* **brawl·er** *n.* ⟨Middle English *brallen*⟩

brawn [brɒn] *n* muscles; muscular strength. **brawn·y** *adj.* ⟨Old French *braon*⟩

bray [brei] *n* the loud, harsh sound made by a donkey. **bray** *v.* ⟨Old French *braire*⟩

bra·zen See BRASS.

bra·zier[1] See BRASS.

bra·zier[2] ['breiʒər] *or* ['breiziər] *n* a metal container to hold burning charcoal or coal. Also, **bra·sier.** ⟨French *brasier;* *braise* hot coals⟩

Brazil nut [brə'zɪl] a large, triangular, edible nut of a tropical South American tree.

breach [britʃ] *n* **1** a gap broken in something solid. **2** the breaking of a law, promise, duty, etc., or of friendly relations. **3** a whale's leap clear of the sea.
v **1** break through: *The attack breached the wall.* **2** of whales, rise or leap clear of the sea. ⟨Middle English *breche;* Old French⟩
breach of faith the breaking of a promise. **breach of promise** the breaking of a promise to marry. **breach of trust** improper behaviour by a trustee of property.

bread [bred] *n* **1** a food made of flour or meal mixed with milk or water and, usually, yeast. **2** food; livelihood. **3** *Slang* money.
v coat with breadcrumbs before cooking. **bread·less** *adj.* ⟨Old English *brēad*⟩
break bread a share a meal. **b** administer or take Communion. **cast one's bread upon the waters** do good with little or no prospect of reward. **know which side one's bread is buttered on** know what is to one's advantage. **take the bread out of someone's mouth a** take away a person's livelihood. **b** take from a person what he or she is just about to enjoy. **bread and butter 1** bread spread with butter. **2** *Informal* necessities; a living. **bread·bas·ket** *n* **1** a basket for bread. **2** a region that is a chief source of grain: *The Prairies are Canada's breadbasket.* **3** *Slang* stomach. **bread·board** *n* **1** a board on which to slice bread. **2** a board on which electrical circuits are laid out experimentally. **bread·box** *n* a box in which to keep bread. **bread·crumb** *n* a crumb of bread. *v* coat with breadcrumbs for cooking. **bread·fruit** *n* a large, starchy tropical fruit that tastes somewhat like bread when baked. **bread line** a lineup for food issued as charity or relief. **bread stick** dough baked in the form of a stick. **bread·win·ner** *n* the main wage-earner of a family.

breadth [brɛdθ] or [brɛtθ] n **1** how broad a thing is: *the breadth of his back.* **2** freedom from narrowness: *She is known for her breadth of mind.* **3** great extent or scope. ⟨Old English *brǣdu; brād* broad⟩

break [breik] v **broke** or (*archaic*) **brake, bro·ken** or (*archaic*) **broke, break·ing** v **1** come or cause to come apart in pieces: *How did you break the plate? It broke when it fell on the floor.* **2** destroy the evenness, wholeness, etc. of: *to break a five-dollar bill.* **3** make inoperative: *She broke her watch by winding it too tightly.* **4** fracture the bone of: *to break one's arm.* **5** fail to keep: *to break a law.* **6** escape from: *to break jail.* **7** force open: *to break a safe.* **8** force one's way (in or out). **9** of a gathering storm, begin. **10** end: *Her fever has broken. We broke our fast after 30 hours.* **11** decrease the force or impact of: *The bushes broke his fall.* **12** give way: *Eventually their nerve broke.* **13** train to obey; tame: *to break a colt.* **14** ruin the health, morale, finances, etc. of. **15** exceed: *to break all records.* **16** wean away from a habit: *She's trying to break herself of nail biting.* **17** interrupt (a journey, work, etc.): *Let's break for lunch.* **18** solve: *to break a code.* **19** of important news, tell or be told: *The story broke at last. Break it to her gently.* n **1** the act, site, or result of breaking. **2** a pause for rest. **3** *Informal* relief from hardship. **4** *Informal* a good opportunity. **5** a gap or opening: *a break in traffic.* **6** a series of successful shots in snooker or billiards. **break·a·ble** adj. **break·age** n. ⟨Old English *brecan*⟩

break a leg! an ironic good luck wish to an actor. **break away** leave or escape, esp suddenly or with effort. **break down** a stop functioning. **b** collapse; yield. **c** start to cry. **d** separate into components. **break even** finish without having lost or gained anything. **break in** a enter illegally or by force: *The thieves broke in through the cellar.* **b** interrupt. **c** train (a beginner). **d** accustom (anything new) to use. **break in on** disturb; disrupt. **break into** a enter illegally or by force: *Our house was broken into.* **b** begin suddenly: *She broke into song.* **c** interrupt: *to break into a conversation.* **d** enter (a profession or field), esp with some difficulty: *to break into the advertising business.* **break off** a stop suddenly. **b** end (a relationship). **break out** a begin suddenly: *War broke out.* **b** have an eruption on the skin: *to break out in measles.* **c** escape. **break trail** ✹ move ahead, making a way through deep snow. **break up** a scatter: *The fog is breaking up.* **b** stop; end: *The meeting broke up early.* **c** disturb greatly: *He's very broken up by the news.* **d** break into pieces: *to break up the soil.* **e** end a partnership or other relationship. **f** *Informal* laugh or cause to laugh uncontrollably. **g** stop (a fight). **break wind** release gas from the intestines. **break with** dissociate oneself from: *She decided to break with her bourgeois upbringing and pursue a radical lifestyle.* **get all the breaks** *Informal* have a lot of good luck. **give someone a break** *Informal* stop criticizing or nagging. **make a**

break for it make a sudden attempt to escape or run for shelter. **break and enter** (or **entry**) an instance of BREAKING AND ENTERING. **break·a·way** n **1** the start of a race: *Three horses got well ahead of the others at the breakaway.* **2** *Hockey, lacrosse* the sudden launch of an attack on goal while defensive players are out of position. **3** the act of separating from a group. **4** *Slang* a stage property made so that it breaks easily. **break dancing** a style of acrobatic solo dancing to rock music in which dancers often spin on their backs. **break–dance** v. **break dancer** n. **break·down** n **1** a loss of health, vigour, or the ability to function: *a mental breakdown, the breakdown of a car, the breakdown of society.* **2** an analysis; a separation into components. **3** a noisy, lively country dance. **break·er** n a wave that breaks into foam on the shore. **break·fast** ['brɛkfəst] n the first meal of the day. **break–in** n a burglary. **breaking and entering** *Law* entry by force or guile with the object of committing a crime. **breaking point** the point at which anything breaks under strain. **break·neck** adj likely to cause a broken neck: *breakneck speed.* **break of day** dawn. **break·out** n **1** an eruption of the skin into pimples or a rash. **2** an escape. **break·through** n any significant advance, esp one that solves a long-standing problem. **break–up** or **break·up** n **1** the end of a relationship. **2** ✹ the breaking of the ice on a river or lake in spring: *We stood on the bridge and watched the break-up.* **break·wa·ter** n a barrier built near the shore to break the force of waves.

bream [brim] n, pl **bream** or **breams** any of several European freshwater fishes of the minnow family. ⟨Old French *bre(s)me*⟩

breast [brɛst] n **1** either of the two milk-producing glands on the chest of the human female. **2** the human chest or the analogous part in animals. **3** the heart or feelings. v advance against: *The experienced swimmer breasted the waves.* ⟨Old English *brēost*⟩ **beat one's breast** express grief, guilt, etc., dramatically in public. **make a clean breast of** (**it**) confess fully. **breast·bone** n the thin, flat bone in the chest, to which the ribs are attached. **breast–feed** v **–fed, –feed·ing** feed (a baby) by letting it suck at the breast. **breast·plate** n a piece of armour for the chest. **breast stroke** or **breast·stroke** n *Swimming* a stroke performed by extending both arms forward from the breast and then sweeping them out to the sides and back.

breath [brɛθ] n **1** air drawn into and forced out of the lungs. **2** an instance of breathing in or out. **3** the ability to breathe easily: *Running makes you lose your breath.* **4** a short rest. ⟨Old English *brǣth* odour, steam⟩ **catch one's breath** a gasp. **b** rest briefly. **hold one's breath** stop breathing voluntarily. **in the same breath** at the same time. **out of breath** breathing very hard as a result of exertion. **save one's breath** avoid useless speaking, esp to persuade: *You can save your*

breath; he'll never listen. **take one's breath away** leave one breathless with awe, surprise, etc. **under one's breath** in a whisper. **waste one's breath** waste energy in speaking.
Breath·a·lys·er ['brɛθə,laɪzər] *n Trademark* a device for measuring the alcohol in a person's blood by a test of the breath. Also, *US,* **Breath·a·ly·zer**. **breath·less** *adj* **1** out of breath. **2** holding one's breath from awe, suspense, excitement, etc.: *The mountain scenery left me breathless.* **breath·tak·ing** *adj* so exciting or amazing as to leave one breathless. **breath·y** *adj* full of the audible sound of breathing.

breathe [bri ð] *v* **1 a** draw (air) into the lungs and force it out. **b** draw in or send out with the breath: *I breathed the fresh pine fragrance. The dragon breathed fire and smoke.* **2** stop and rest briefly: *I need a moment to breathe.* **3** say softly: *"Don't move until I give the signal," she breathed.* **4** be alive. **5** inject (a quality): *to breathe new life into the team.* **6** of a material, be porous enough to let air through. **7** blow lightly. **8** exude; display naturally and clearly: *His whole manner breathes confidence.* **breath·a·ble** *adj.* ⟨Middle English *brethen*⟩
breathe again (or **freely** or **easily**) feel relieved. **breathe down someone's neck** pursue or watch a person closely. **breathe one's last** die. **not breathe a word of** keep secret.
breath·er *n* a brief rest. **breathing space** an opportunity to rest.

breech [britʃ] *n* **1** in a firearm, the opening where the shells are inserted. **2** the buttocks. **breech·less** *adj.* ⟨Old English *brēc,* pl of *brōc* breech⟩
breech birth a birth in which the baby's feet are presented first. **breech·cloth** *n* garment consisting of a length of cloth or leather passed between the legs and fastened around the waist. **breech·es** ['britʃiz] *or* ['britʃiz] *n pl* **1** short pants fastened at the knees. **2** *Informal* pants. **too big for one's breeches** (or **britches**) conceited. **breech·load·er** *n* a gun loaded from behind the barrel. **breech·load·ing** *adj.*

breed [brid] *v* **bred, breed·ing 1** produce young: *Rabbits breed rapidly.* **2** develop certain types by selective mating: *She breeds horses for racing.* **3** cause: *Carelessness breeds accidents.* **4** (passive only) raise; train in social and moral behaviour: *born and bred in the city. I wasn't bred to give up easily.* **5** *Physics* produce (fissionable material) by nuclear reaction.
n a distinctive type of a given species of plant or animal. **breed·ing** *n.* ⟨Old English *brēdan*⟩
breed·er *n* a person who breeds animals or plants: *a dog breeder.* **breeding ground** a place where something grows easily: *Colonialism made Africa a breeding ground of nationalism.*

breeze [briz] *n* **1** light wind. **2** *Meteorology* any air current blowing at 6 to 49 km/h. **3** *Informal* a very easy task.
v come or go briskly and cheerily: *He breezed into the room.* ⟨Portuguese *briza* NE wind⟩
breeze through do easily: *She breezed through her exams.* **in a breeze** *Informal* easily; with little effort. **shoot the breeze** *Slang* chat.

breeze·way *n* a roofed passageway between buildings. **breez·y** *adj* **1** with light wind. **2** brisk; lively; cheery: *a breezy, joking manner.*

breth·ren ['brɛðrən] *n pl* **1** *Archaic* brothers. **2** the fellow members of a church, society, or religious order.

brev·i·ty See BREVITY.

brew [bru] *v* **1** make (beer, tea, potion, etc.) by steeping, boiling, fermenting, etc. **2** plot: *brewing some mischief.* **3** begin to form: *A storm is brewing.*
n **1** a drink made by brewing. **2** the quantity brewed at one time. **3** *Slang* (a glass or bottle of) beer. **brew·er** *n.* ⟨Old English *brēowan*⟩
brew·er *n* a maker or manufacturer of beer or ale. **brewer's yeast** a selected strain of yeast used in brewing beer. **brew·er·y** *n* a place where beer, ale, etc., are brewed.

brewis [bruz] *or* ['bruɪs] *n ✱* in Newfoundland and Labrador, a stew prepared by boiling hardtack with codfish, pork fat, and vegetables. Also, **brose.** ⟨variant of dialect *brose* soaked bread⟩

bribe [braɪb] *n* **1** money offered to a person to act dishonestly. **2** a reward for doing something one does not want to do: *a bribe to do well in school.* **bribe** *v.* **brib·a·ble** *adj.* **brib·er·y** *n.* ⟨Old French *bribe* bit of bread⟩

bric–a–brac or **bric·à·brac** ['brik ə ,bræk] *n* knick-knacks collectively. ⟨French⟩

brick [brik] *n* **1 a** a block of baked clay or similar material, used in building. **b** such blocks collectively. **2** anything shaped like a brick: *a brick of ice cream.* **3** *Informal* someone dependable.
v close or fill with bricks (with *in* or *up*): *The doorway was bricked up.* ⟨Middle Dutch *bricke*⟩
hit the bricks *Slang* go on strike. **make bricks without straw** do anything without the wherewithal. **one brick short of a load** a little crazy or simple.
brick·bat *n* **1** a piece of broken brick used as a weapon. **2** *Informal* an insult. **brick·lay·er** *n* a person whose work is building with bricks. **brick·lay·ing** *n.* **brick–red** *adj* brownish red. **brick·yard** *n* a place where bricks are made.

bri·co·lage [,brikou'laʒ] *n* **1** the art of making things from found materials. **2** anything made in this way. ⟨French⟩

bride [braɪd] *n* a woman just married or soon to be married. **brid·al** *adj.* ⟨Old English *brȳd*⟩
bride·groom *n* a man just married or about to be married. **brides·maid** *n* a woman who attends the bride at a wedding.

bridge¹ [bridʒ] *n* **1** a structure built over a river, road, etc., to allow passage across. **2** the platform above a ship's deck. **3** the upper part of the nose. **4** a partial denture fitted between natural teeth. **5** a piece of wood on a violin, guitar, etc., over which the strings are stretched. **6** *Music* a connecting passage. **7** *Billiards* a long stick with a frame at the end used to support a cue for a difficult shot, or a similar support formed by the hand.
v **1** build or be a bridge over. **2** make a way over: *Politeness will bridge many difficulties.*

bridge·a·ble *adj.* ⟨Old English *brycg*⟩
burn one's bridges cut off all chance of retreat.
bridge·head *n* **1** a position held within enemy territory, used as a starting point for further attack. **2** any position from which to advance. **bridge·work** *n* false teeth in a mounting fastened to adjacent natural teeth.

bridge² [brɪdʒ] *n* a card game based on whist, for two teams of two players each. ⟨origin uncertain⟩
bridge table a small table with legs that fold under the top, used for playing cards, etc.

bri·dle *n* **1** a harness for a horse's head. **2** a restraint. **3 ✷** the toe loop on a snowshoe.
v **1** control: *Bridle your temper.* **2** react indignantly by raising the chin. ⟨Old English *brigdels; bregdan* to braid⟩
bridle path a path for people on horseback.

brief [brif] *adj* **1** short: *a brief visit, brief shorts, a brief announcement.* **2** curt.
n **1** a short article. **2** a formal statement of opinion: *She submitted a brief to the Royal Commission on Taxation.* **3** a lawyer's record of all the facts concerning a case in court. **4 briefs** *pl* close-fitting underpants.
v **1** prepare (someone) with background information and instructions. **2** retain as a lawyer or counsel. **brief·ing** *n.* **brief·ly** *adv.* ⟨Old French *bref;* Latin *brevis* short⟩
hold a brief for support; defend. **in brief** in a few words.
brev·i·ty *n* shortness. **brief·case** *n* a flat case for carrying loose papers, books, etc.

bri·er¹ [ˈbraɪər] *n* a prickly bush, esp the wild rose. Also, **bri·ar.** ⟨Old English *brēr*⟩

bri·er² [ˈbraɪər] *n* **1** an evergreen shrub of the heath family with a hard, woody root used to make tobacco pipes. **2** a pipe made of this. Also, **briar.** ⟨French *bruyère* heath⟩

Bri·er [ˈbraɪər] *n* **✷** the Canadian national curling championship.

brig [brɪg] *n* **1** a square-rigged ship with two masts. **2** a military prison, esp on a ship. ⟨short for *brigantine*⟩

bri·gade [brɪˈgeid] *n* **1** a part of an army, usually two or more regiments. **2** any group of people organized for a particular purpose: *The fire brigade put out the fire.* **3 ✷** formerly, a fleet of canoes, bateaux, Red River carts, dog sleds, etc., carrying goods to and from inland trading posts. ⟨Italian *brigata,* from *brigare.* See BRIGANTINE.⟩
brig·a·dier–gen·er·al [ˌbrɪgəˈdir] *n* an officer in the armed forces, ranking next above a colonel and below a major-general.

brig·and [ˈbrɪgənd] *n* a highway robber; bandit. ⟨Italian *brigante* fighter. See BRIGANTINE.⟩

brig·an·tine [ˈbrɪgənˌtin] *n* a two-masted ship with foremast square-rigged and mainmast fore-and-aft-rigged. ⟨Italian *brigantino,* from *brigare* to fight; *briga* a fight⟩

bright [braɪt] *adj* **1** of light, intense. **2** giving or having much light. **3** vivid: *bright colours.* **4** intelligent: *a bright student.* **5** cheerful: *a bright smile.* **bright·en** *v.* **bright·ly** *adv.*

bright·ness *n.* ⟨Old English *briht, beorht*⟩
bright–eyed and bushy–tailed *Informal* alert and full of energy.

Bright is the general word, applying to anything giving out or reflecting light: *She wore earrings and a bracelet of bright silver.* **Radiant** suggests a warm light from deep within: *The bride's radiant face spoke her joy.* **Brilliant** emphasizes the intensity of light and sometimes suggests sparkling: *The surface of the lake was brilliant in the sunlight.*

bril·liant [ˈbrɪljənt] *adj* very bright: *brilliant red, a brilliant scientist, a brilliant future.*
n a diamond or other gem cut to enhance its sparkle. **bril·liance** *n.* **bril·liant·ly** *adv.* ⟨French *briller* shine; perhaps Latin *beryllus* beryl⟩
bril·lian·tine *n* an oily preparation used to make the hair glossy.

brim [brɪm] *n* **1** the edge of a container. **2** the projecting edge of a hat.
v **brimmed, brim·ming** be nearly overflowing: *brimming with excitement.* **brim·less** *adj.* **brim·ful** *adj.* ⟨Middle English *brimme*⟩

brim·stone [ˈbrɪmˌstoun] *n* sulphur. ⟨Middle English *brinston; brinnen* burn + *ston* stone⟩

brin·dled [ˈbrɪndəld] *adj* tawny with darker spots. Also, **brin·dle.** ⟨Middle English *brended.* Probably related to BRAND.⟩

brine [braɪn] *n* very salty water: *onions pickled in brine.* **brin·y** *adj.* ⟨Old English *brÿne*⟩
brine shrimp a small saltwater shrimp used as tropical fish food. **the briny** *Slang* the sea.

bring [brɪŋ] *v* **brought, bring·ing 1** carry or take with oneself: *I didn't bring enough money.* **2** cause: *War brings misery.* **bring·er** *n.* ⟨Old English *bringan*⟩
bring about cause. **bring around a** restore to consciousness. **b** convince. **c** influence (a person) to be in a better mood. **bring down** officially propose (a budget, legislation, etc.). **bring forth** produce; reveal. **bring forward** *Accounting* carry over from one page to another. **bring home to** make realize: *The accident brought home to us how very fragile life is.* **bring in a** introduce. **b** report officially: *to bring in a verdict.* **bring off** carry out successfully. **bring on** cause the onset of: *I think my cold was brought on by lack of sleep.* **bring oneself** overcome one's reluctance (*to* do something) **bring out a** reveal; show: *His paintings bring out the loneliness of the North.* **b** offer to the public: *She's brought out a new book of poems.* **bring to** restore to consciousness: *We tried to bring him to by loosening his clothing.* **bring to nothing** ruin. **bring up a** care for and train in childhood. **b** raise for discussion. **c** vomit.

brink [brɪŋk] *n* the edge of a cliff, deep pit, steep bank, etc. ⟨Middle English⟩
on the brink of very near.
brink·man·ship *n* **1** the practice of taking a given foreign policy to the brink of war before yielding. **2** the practice in any situation of giving in only at the last moment. Also, **brinks·man·ship.**

bri·quette or **bri·quet** [brɪ'kɛt] *n* a block of compressed charcoal, coal dust, etc. used for fuel. ⟨French *briquette; brique* brick⟩

bris [brɪs] *n Judaism* a ceremony held when a boy is eight days old, during which he is circumcised. ⟨Yiddish; Hebrew *berit*⟩

brisk [brɪsk] *adj* **1** quick and energetic: *a brisk walk.* **2** keen; sharp: *brisk weather.* **brisk·ly** *adv.* **brisk·ness** *n.* ⟨perhaps related to *brusque*⟩

bris·ket ['brɪskɪt] *n* the breast, or breast meat, of an animal. ⟨Old French *bruschet*⟩

bris·tle [brɪsəl] *n* **1** any short, stiff hair of an animal or plant. **2** a substitute for this, in a brush: *My toothbrush has nylon bristles.*
v **1** of hair, stand or cause to stand on end: *The angry dog's hair bristled.* **2** show that one is aroused and ready to fight: *The whole country bristled with indignation.* **3** be thick (with); be thickly set: *Our path bristled with difficulties.* **bris·tly** *adj.* ⟨Old English *byrst*⟩

bris·tol·board ['brɪstəl] *n* a smooth, sturdy cardboard. ⟨Bristol, city in England⟩

Brit·ain ['brɪtən] *n* Great Britain or the United Kingdom. ⟨Old English *Brittas* Britons; Celtic⟩ **Brit·i·cism** ['brɪtə,sɪzəm] *n* an expression or custom used esp by the British. **Brit·ish** ['brɪtɪʃ] *adj* to do with the United Kingdom or its people. *n* **the British** *pl* the people of the United Kingdom. **British Co·lum·bi·a** the westernmost province of Canada. *Abbrev* **BC.** **British Co·lum·bi·an** *n, adj.* **British Isles** Great Britain, Ireland, and the Isle of Man. **British North America Act** (since 1981 called **Constitution Act, 1867**) the Act of Parliament that in 1867 created the Government of Canada, uniting Ontario, Québec, Nova Scotia, and New Brunswick. The other six provinces joined later. *Abbrev* **BNA Act** or **B.N.A. Act. British subject 1** a citizen of the United Kingdom. **2** a citizen of any country, such as Canada, of which the British monarch is the official head of state. **British thermal unit** a non-metric unit of heat; the amount of heat needed to raise the temperature of one pound of water one Fahrenheit degree (about 1.06 kJ). *Abbrev* **B.T.U. Brit·on** *n* **1** a native or inhabitant of Great Britain. **2** a member of a Celtic people who lived there before the Roman conquest.

brit·ches ['brɪtʃɪz] *n pl Informal* breeches.

brit·tle ['brɪtəl] *adj* rigid but easily broken: *Thin glass is brittle.*
n flat, hard candy made with sugar and nuts: *peanut brittle.* **brit·tle·ness** *n.* ⟨Middle English *britel;* Old English *brēotan* break⟩

broach [broutʃ] *v* **1** open a container, originally by making a hole: *to broach a barrel of cider.* **2** raise (a subject, esp a delicate one). ⟨Latin *broccus* projecting⟩

broad [brɔd] *adj* **1** large across; wide: *a broad road.* **2** extensive; varied: *broad experience.* **3** liberal in outlook: *broad ideas.* **4** general: *a broad outline.* **5** not subtle: *a broad hint.* **broad·en** *v.* **broad·ly** *adv.* ⟨Old English *brād*⟩ **broad·band** *adj Radio* operating over a wide range of frequencies. **broad–base(d)** *adj*

depending on a wide range of items: *a broad-based economy.* **broad bean** a large, flat, edible bean. **broad·cast** *v* **-cast** or **-cast·ed,** **-cast·ing 1** transmit (programs, etc.) by radio or television. **2** scatter widely: *to broadcast seed.* **3** make widely known: *to broadcast a rumour. n* a radio or television program. **broad·cast·er** *n.* **broad·cloth** *n* a fine, closely woven cloth, originally wider than 74 cm. **broad gauge** a width of railway track greater than the standard 144 cm. **broad–gauge** or **broad–gauged** *adj.* **broad·leaf** *n* a type of tobacco with wide leaves, used for cigars. **broad·loom** *n* carpeting made on a wide loom, cut from the roll to fit a floor exactly. *v* fit with such carpet. **broad–mind·ed** *adj* willing to entertain different points of view. **broad·sheet** *n* a large sheet of paper printed on one side as a newsletter, advertisement, etc. **broad·side** *n* **1** the firing of all the guns from one side of a ship. **2** a violent attack in words. *adv* with the side turned toward an object: *to hit another vehicle broadside.* **3** a large sheet of paper printed on one side only. **4** a newspaper with a large format that takes a somewhat less sensationalist approach to news. Compare TABLOID. *v* hit broadside. **broad–spec·trum** *adj* with a wide range of application: *a broad-spectrum drug.* **broad·sword** *n* a sword with a wide blade.

bro·cade [brou'keid] *n* a heavy cloth woven with a raised design. ⟨Spanish *brocado,* pp of *brocar* embroider⟩

broc·co·li ['brɒkəli] *n* a type of cabbage with dense clusters of green flower heads. ⟨Italian *broccoli* sprouts; Latin *broccus* project⟩ **broc·co·flow·er** *n* a cross between broccoli and cauliflower. ⟨*brocco*(li) + (*cauli*)*flower*⟩

bro·chette [brou'ʃɛt] *n* meat and vegetables broiled on a skewer. ⟨French *broche* pin, spit⟩

bro·chure [brou'ʃʊr] *n* a booklet or folding flyer. ⟨French, from *brocher* stitch⟩

brogue [broug] *n* an Irish accent in the speaking of English. ⟨probably Irish *barróg* defect of speech⟩

broil [brɔɪl] *v* cook by placing on a rack directly over or under a flame; grill. ⟨Old French *bruillir* burn⟩ **broil·er** ['brɔɪlər] *n* **1** a person or thing that broils, esp a compartment or element in an oven. **2** a pan or rack for broiling food. **3** a young chicken suitable for broiling.

broke [brouk] *v* pt of BREAK.
adj Informal without money.
go for broke *Informal* stake everything on a risky venture.
bro·ken ['broukən] *v* pp of BREAK.
adj **1** not whole: *a broken cup.* **2** not in working order: *a broken toaster.* **3** weakened in strength, spirit, etc.: *He was a broken man after his loss.* **4** rough: *broken ground.* **5** violated: *a broken promise.* **6** imperfectly spoken: *broken French.* **7** interrupted: *broken sleep.* **bro·ken·ly** *adv.* **bro·ken·ness** *n.*
bro·ken–down *adj* in a very bad state of repair. **bro·ken–heart·ed** *adj* crushed by

sorrow or grief. **broken home** a family in which the parents are divorced.

bro·ker ['broukər] *n* a person who acts as an agent in arranging contracts, sales, etc., in return for a fee. **bro·ker** *v*. ⟨Anglo-French *brocour* tapster, wineseller. Related to BROACH.⟩ **bro·ker·age** *n* the business or fee of a broker.

bro·mine ['broumin] *n* a non-metallic element that evaporates quickly, giving off an irritating vapour. *Symbol* **Br** ⟨Greek *bromos* stench⟩ **bro·mide** ['broumaɪd] *or* ['broumɪd] *n* **1** a compound of bromine. **2** potassium bromide, a drug used to induce sleep. **3** a trite remark. **bro·mid·ic** [brou'mɪdɪk] *adj*.

bron·chi ['brɒŋkaɪ] *or* ['brɒŋki] *n pl*, *sg* **bron·chus 1** the two main branches of the windpipe. **2** the smaller tubes in the lungs. ⟨Greek *bronchos* windpipe⟩ **bron·chi·a** *n pl* the bronchi, esp the smaller tubes. **bron·chi·al** *adj*. **bronchial pneumonia** inflammation and congestion of the bronchial tubes. **bron·chi·ole** *n* any of the smallest bronchia. **bron·chi·tis** [brɒŋ'kaɪtɪs] *n* inflammation of the lining of the bronchi. **bron·chit·ic** [brɒŋ'kɪtɪk] *adj*. **bron·cho·di·la·tor** *n* [ˌbrɒŋkou'daɪleɪtər] any medication that serves to dilate the bronchi, usually for the relief of asthma.

bron·co ['brɒŋkou] *n* a western pony, often wild or only half tamed. Also, **bron·cho**. ⟨Spanish = rough, rude⟩ **bron·co·bust·er** *n Slang* in the West, one who breaks in wild horses. **bron·co·bust·ing** *n*.

bron·to·sau·rus [ˌbrɒntə'sɔrəs] *n* any of a genus of giant, plant-eating dinosaurs with a long neck and tail and small head. Also, **bron·to·saur** ['brɒntəˌsɔr]. The brontosaurus is more correctly known as *apatosaurus*. ⟨Greek *brontē* thunder + *sauros* lizard⟩

bronze [brɒnz] *n* **1** a brownish metal, an alloy of copper and tin. **2** a statue, medal, etc., made of bronze: *She won a bronze in the swimming competition.* *v* **1** tan: *bronzed from the sun.* **2** cover with bronze: *They had her baby shoes bronzed.* **bronze** *adj*. **bronz·y** *adj*. ⟨Italian *bronzo*⟩ **Bronze Age** the period in human culture following the Stone Age, characterized by the use of bronze tools, weapons, etc.

brooch [broutʃ] *n* an ornamental pin with its point secured by a clasp. ⟨variant of *broach*⟩

brood [brud] *n* **1** the young birds hatched at one time. **2** all the offspring of one mother. *v* **1** sit on (eggs) in order to hatch them. **2** worry; reflect gloomily: *She broods a lot these days.* ⟨Old English *brōd*⟩ **brood on** or **over** a keep thinking about. **b** hover over; hang close over. **brood·er** *n* **1** an incubator for chicks. **2** a hen brooding or ready to brood eggs. **brood·mare** *n* a mare kept for breeding. **brood·y** *adj* **1** inclined to moody reflection. **2** of hens, ready to brood eggs. **3** wanting to have a baby. **brood·i·ly** *adv*. **brood·i·ness** *n*.

brook[1] [brʊk] *n* a small, natural freshwater stream; creek. ⟨Old English *brōc*⟩ **brook trout** a freshwater food and game fish of North America.

brook[2] [brʊk] *v* put up with: *Her pride would not brook such insults.* ⟨Old English *brūcan* use⟩

broom [brum] *n* **1** a long-handled brush for sweeping. **2** a shrub of the pea family. ⟨Old English *brōm*⟩ **broom·ball** *n* ✹ a hockeylike game using corn brooms and a volleyball. **broom·stick** *n* the handle of a broom.

broth [brɒθ] *n* **1** a thin soup made from water in which meat or fish or vegetables have been boiled. **2** a medium in which cultures of bacteria are grown. ⟨Old English⟩

broth·el ['brɒθəl] *n* an establishment where prostitutes can be hired. ⟨Old English *brēothan* go to ruin⟩

broth·er ['brʌðər] *n*, *pl* **broth·ers** or (*Poetic or archaic*) **breth·ren 1** a son of the same parents; sometimes, only of the same mother or father (a **half brother**). **2** a male friend or colleague. **3** a monk or male member of any faith community. **4** an informal term of address for a man: *Watch your step, brother.* *adj* being in the same profession: *brother officers.* *interj Informal* an emphatic exclamation, often of annoyance: *Oh, brother!* **broth·er·less** *adj*. **broth·er·like** *adj*. **broth·er·ly** *adj*. ⟨Old English⟩ **broth·er·hood** *n* **1** the relationship between brothers. **2** an association of men with some common aim, belief, etc.: *the brotherhood of engineers.* **broth·er–in–law** *n*, *pl* **broth·ers–in–law 1** one's spouse's brother. **2** the husband of one's own or of one's spouse's sister.

brought [brɒt] *v* pt and pp of BRING.

brou·ha·ha ['bruhɑˌhɑ] *or* [bru'hɑhɑ] *n* an uproar or commotion. ⟨French; imitative⟩

brow [braʊ] *n* **1** the forehead. **2** the eyebrow, or the ridge on which it grows. **3** the crest of a hill. ⟨Old English *brū*⟩ **brow·beat** *v* -beat, -beat·en, -beat·ing bully; intimidate. **brow·beat·er** *n*.

brown [braʊn] *n* the colour of coffee. *v* make or become brown: *Brown the onions in oil.* **brown** *adj*. **brown·ish** *adj*. **brown·ness** *n*. ⟨Old English *brūn*⟩ **browned off** *Slang* annoyed. **brown algae** phylum of marine algae having brown pigment as well as chlorophyll. **brown–bag** *v* -bagged, -bag·ging Usually, **brown–bag** is *Informal* carry lunch to work or school, usually in a brown paper bag. **brown bear** the largest and most widespread species of bear, found throughout the northern parts of the world. The grizzly is a subspecies. **brown belt** a degree just below the highest in judo, karate, or other martial art. Compare BLACK BELT. **brown betty** a baked dessert made of apples, sugar, and spices with crumbs on top. **brown·ie** *n* **1** a small square of a rich, dense chocolate cake. **2** a helpful elf or fairy. **brownie points** *Informal* credit earned for good behaviour. **brown·out** *n* a power cut; partial BLACKOUT (def. 1). **brown rot** a fungal disease of some fruits. **Brown Shirt** or **Brownshirt** one of Hitler's force of storm troopers (1923 to 1934). **brown·stone** n 1 a reddish brown sandstone used in building. 2 a building made of this. **brown study** a pensive state. **brown sugar** sugar with the brown colour of the molasses still in it or added to it.

browse [brauz] v 1 pass the time looking casually at a book or books, at articles for sale in a store, etc. 2 *Computers* search casually for material of interest on the WORLD WIDE WEB. 3 feed on growing plants: *The deer browsed on young shoots and leaves.* n 1 the act of browsing. 2 tender shoots, leaves, and twigs of trees and shrubs used as food by animals. ⟨French *broust* a bud, shoot⟩ **brows·er** n *Computers* a piece of software which enables the user to browse on the WORLD WIDE WEB.

bru·in ['bruən] n *Poetic* a bear, esp a brown bear. ⟨Middle Dutch *bruin* brown⟩

bruise [bruz] n 1 a an injury that breaks blood vessels without breaking the skin. b the resulting discoloured area. 2 an injury to the outside of a fruit, vegetable, plant, etc. 3 an emotional injury: *His insult was a bruise to her pride.* **bruise** v. ⟨fusion of Old English *brȳsan* crush and Old French *bruisier* break⟩ **bruis·er** n *Informal* 1 PRIZE FIGHTER. 2 a bully.

bruit [brut] v spread (a rumour): *Rumours of the princess's engagement were bruited about.* ⟨Old French *bruit* noise, rumour; *bruire* roar⟩

brunch [brʌntʃ] n a meal, taken in the late morning, that combines breakfast and lunch. ⟨br(eakfast) + (l)unch⟩

bru·nette [bru'nɛt] n a woman or girl with dark hair. ⟨French⟩

brunt [brʌnt] n the main force or violence; hardest part: *to bear the brunt of an attack.* ⟨Middle English = a blow; origin uncertain⟩

brush¹ [brʌʃ] n 1 a tool for cleaning, painting, etc., made of bristles, hair, or wires set into a stiff back or a handle. 2 a stroke of a brush. 3 a light touch in passing. 4 an encounter: *a brush with the law.* 5 a fox's tail. 6 a piece of carbon, copper, etc. used to conduct electricity. 7 *Informal* brushoff. v 1 use a brush on. 2 remove with a light sweeping motion: *to brush away tears.* 3 touch lightly in passing. **brush·like** adj. ⟨Old French *broisse*⟩ **brush aside** (or **away**) refuse to consider. **brush off** *Informal* refuse (a request, person, etc.) in a curt way: *He brushed us off when we asked for his autograph.* **brush up** (**on**) review: *I have to brush up on my geometry for the test.* **brush·cut** n a very short haircut in which the hair stands up from the scalp. **brushed** adj of cloth or leather, rubbed with a brush so as to raise the nap. **brush·off** n *Informal* a curt or offhand dismissal. **brush·stroke** n one movement of a brush, esp a paintbrush. **brush·work** n an artist's technique in applying paint with a brush.

brush² [brʌʃ] n 1 shrubs, bushes, and small trees growing thickly together. 2 branches broken or cut off. ⟨Old French *broche*⟩ **brush wolf** ✻ coyote. **brush·wood** n BRUSH². **brush·y** adj covered with bushes, shrubs, etc.

brusque [brʌsk] or [brusk] adj abrupt in manner. **brusque·ly** adv. **brusque·ness** n. ⟨French; Gaulish *brucus*, Latin *ruscum* broom⟩

Brussels sprouts ['brʌsəlz] a variety of cabbage that bears many small green heads, like tiny cabbages, along its tall, thick stem.

brute [brut] n 1 an animal without power to reason. 2 a cruel, coarse, or sensual person. adj 1 without thought or feeling. 2 cruel, coarse, or sensual. ⟨Latin *brutus* heavy, dull⟩ **bru·tal** adj 1 savagely cruel. 2 hard to bear: *a brutal winter, brutal facts.* **brut·al·ly** adv. **bru·tal·i·ty** n. **bru·tal·ize** v 1 make brutal: *War brutalizes people.* 2 treat brutally: *Police officers may not brutalize suspects.* **bru·tal·i·za·tion** n. **brut·ish** adj coarse; savage.

bsmt. basement.

B.T.U. or **BTU** BRITISH THERMAL UNIT(S).

BTW by the way.

bub·ble ['bʌbəl] n 1 a thin round film of liquid enclosing gas: *soap bubbles.* 2 a pocket of air or gas in a liquid or solid, as in ice, glass, paint, etc. 3 something clear and shaped like a bubble. 4 anything short-lived. v 1 have, form, or flow with bubbles. 2 talk animatedly. ⟨Middle English *bobel*⟩ **bubble over a** overflow. b be so full of joy, enthusiasm, etc. that it must be expressed. **bubble and squeak** cooked cabbage and potato mashed together and fried. **bubble bath** 1 a bath with many bubbles formed by adding a special liquid. 2 the liquid. **bubble gum** chewing gum that can be blown up into bubbles. **bubble pack** 1 a packaging method in which the objects are sealed in a clear, rigid plastic covering. Also, **blister pack.** 2 a cushiony packing material consisting of two layers of plastic, the space between them being entirely filled with small bubbles. **bub·bly** adj enthusiastic or high-spirited: *a bubbly personality.* n *Informal* champagne.

bubonic plague a dangerous infectious disease accompanied by fever, chills, and swelling of the lymph glands, carried to human beings by fleas from rats or squirrels. ⟨Greek *boubon* groin (site of swellings)⟩

buc·ca·neer [ˌbʌkə'nir] n a pirate. ⟨Tupi *boucan* frame for curing meat, as used by the French in Haïti⟩

buck¹ [bʌk] n 1 the adult male of deer, rabbits, and similar animals. 2 *Informal* a bold, lively, dashing young man. adj male. ⟨Old English *buc*⟩ **buck·saw** n a two-handed saw for wood, set in a light H-shaped frame. **buck·shot** n a coarse lead shot for shooting large game such as deer. **buck·skin** n 1 a tough, coarse, greyish yellow leather made from the skin of a male deer. 2 **buckskins** pl clothing made from this. **buck·tooth** n, pl **-teeth** a front tooth that sticks out. **buck·toothed** adj.

buck² [bʌk] v 1 of horses, throw or attempt to

throw a rider by jumping up with arched back and coming down with front legs stiff. **2** *Informal* fight against: *bucking the system.* **3** *Informal* of a car, motor, etc., run unevenly; backfire. **4** *Football* charge into (the opposing line) with the ball. **buck** *n.* ⟨special use of *buck¹*⟩ **buck up** cheer up.

buck³ [bʌk] *n* formerly, a marker placed before a player in poker to show that he or she had to deal. ⟨origin uncertain⟩ **pass the buck** *Informal* shift responsibility or blame. **buck·pas·ser** *n.* **buck·pas·sing** *n.*

buck⁴ [bʌk] *n Slang* dollar. ⟨origin uncertain⟩ **a fast** (or **quick**) **buck** money made easily and usually dishonestly. **buck·a·roo** *n Slang* dollar.

buck·et ['bʌkɪt] *n* **1** a deep container for water, sand, etc. with a handle; pail. **2** the scoop of a backhoe or any other bucketlike thing. **3** *Slang* an old car, boat, etc. *v* **1** lift or carry in a bucket. **2** ride (a horse) hard. **3** *Informal* move along fast and roughly. **buck·et·ful** *n.* ⟨Anglo-French *buket*⟩ **kick the bucket** *Slang* die. **bucket brigade** a line of people passing buckets of water from hand to hand to put out a fire. **bucket seat** a low-slung, concave seat, esp in a sports car or small plane.

buck·le¹ ['bʌkəl] *n* **1** a device used to fasten the loose end of a belt. **2** a metal ornament resembling this, esp one for a shoe. *v* fasten together with a buckle. ⟨Latin *buccula* cheek strap on helmet; *bucca* cheek⟩ **buckle down** (**to**) begin to work hard (at): *You'd better buckle down to your homework.* **buck·ler** *n* a small, round shield.

buck·le² ['bʌkəl] *v* bend or fold under heavy stress: *The heavy snowfall caused the roof to buckle.* **buck·le** *n.* ⟨French *boucler* bulge⟩

buck·wheat ['bʌk,wit] *n* **1** any of a genus of Eurasian annuals, two species of which have been cultivated in North America for their edible seeds. **2 wild buckwheat** a common Canadian weed, originally native to Europe. Also called **black bindweed**. ⟨Old English *bōc* beech + *wheat*; seeds are beechnut-shaped⟩

bu·col·ic [bju'kɒlɪk] *adj* peaceful and rustic or rural; pastoral. *n* **1** a pastoral poem. **2** a rustic person. **bu·col·i·cal·ly** *adv.* ⟨Greek *boukolos* shepherd⟩

bud [bʌd] *n* **1** on a plant, a small swelling that will develop into a flower, leaf, or branch. **2** anything not yet developed. *v* **bud·ded, bud·ding 1** put forth buds: *The rosebush has budded.* **2** begin to grow or develop. **bud·like** *adj.* ⟨Middle English *budde*⟩ **in bud** budding: *The pear tree is in bud.* **nip in the bud** stop at the very beginning. **bud·ding** *adj* potential; developing: *budding physicists. n* a type of asexual reproduction in which the new individual forms as an outgrowth on the parent.

Bud·dha ['budə] *or* ['budə] *n* the title of Siddhartha Gautama (563?–483? B.C.), Indian philosopher, religious teacher, and founder of Buddhism. ⟨Sanskrit = enlightened one⟩

Bud·dhism *n* the religion based on the teachings of Buddha. **Bud·dhist** *adj, n.*

bud·dy ['bʌdi] *n Informal* a good friend; pal. ⟨origin uncertain⟩ **bud·dy–bud·dy** *adj Slang* friendly in a way that is too effusive or familiar. **buddy system** an arrangement for work, play, etc. whereby each person is paired with a partner for safety.

budge [bʌdʒ] *v* move at all: *She won't budge. I can't budge this rock.* ⟨French *bouger* stir⟩

budg·er·i·gar ['bʌdʒərɪ,gɑr] *n* (usually shortened to **budgie**) a small, long-tailed parrot native to Australia, but popular in many countries as a cage bird. ⟨native Australian *budgeri* good + *gar* cockatoo⟩

budg·et ['bʌdʒɪt] *n* an estimate, for a given period, of the amounts to be spent on various things by a government, business, family, etc. **budg·et** *v.* **budg·et·ar·y** *adj.* ⟨Old French *bougette*; *bouge* leather bag⟩

buff¹ [bʌf] *n* **1** a strong, soft, dull yellow leather with a fuzzy nap, made from buffalo hide. **2** a dull yellow. *v* polish by rubbing. **buff** *adj.* ⟨French *buffle* = buffalo. See BUFFALO.⟩ **in the buff** nude.

buff² [bʌf] *n Informal* fan; enthusiast: *a hockey buff, a theatre buff.* ⟨origin uncertain⟩

buf·fa·lo ['bʌfə,lou] *n, pl* **-loes**, **-los**, or **-lo 1** the North American bison, a large bovine of the plains with a prominent shoulder hump, short curved horns, and shaggy brown hair. **2** any of several large hoofed, long-horned mammals of Africa and Asia. *v* **1** *Slang* stymie; stump; baffle: *We were all buffaloed by the last question on the exam.* **2** *Slang* intimidate or overawe. ⟨Italian *bufalo;* Greek *boubalos* wild ox⟩ **buffalo grass** a short grass of the plains, valued for winter pasture. **buffalo jump ✽** a place where the First Nations of the Plains killed buffalo by stampeding them over a cliff. **buffalo robe** a warm wrap of buffalo hide.

buff·er ['bʌfər] *n* **1** anything helping to soften a shock or neutralize opposing forces: *Mother was a buffer between my sister's anger and me.* **2** any substance in a solution that neutralizes acid or alkali. **3** *Computers* a repository for data being stored temporarily. **buffer** *v.* ⟨Old French *buffe* a blow⟩ **buffer state** a small country between two larger rival countries, thought of as lessening the danger of open conflict between them. **buffer zone** a neutral area separating two enemy territories; NO-MAN'S-LAND (def. 1).

buf·fet¹ ['bʌfɪt] *n* a hard blow. **buf·fet** *v.* ⟨Old French *buffet*, diminutive of *buffe* blow⟩

buf·fet² [bə'fei] *or* [bu'fei] *n* **1** a low cabinet with a flat top, for dishes, table linen, etc. **2** a meal at which guests serve themselves from food laid out. ⟨French⟩

buf·foon [bə'fun] *n* clown; clownish person. **buf·foon** *v.* **buf·foon·ish** *adj.* **buf·foon·er·y** *n.* ⟨Italian *buffone; buffa* jest⟩

bug [bʌg] *n* **1** any of an order of sucking

insects with wings that overlap on the body when at rest. **2** any insect or insectlike creature. **3** *Informal* a disease bacterium or virus: *the flu bug.* **4** *Informal* a defect: *a bug in the software.* **5** *Informal* enthusiast: *a camera bug.* **6** *Informal* a tiny hidden microphone.
v **bugged, bug·ging 1** *Informal* annoy; irritate: *Her constant grumbling bugs me.* **2** *Informal* fit with a tiny concealed microphone. **3** of eyes, be so wide open from astonishment, fear, etc., as to seem to protrude like a bug's: *Their eyes bugged at the unbelievable sight.* ⟨perhaps from obsolete Welsh *bwg* ghost⟩
bitten or **stung by the — bug** obsessed or fascinated by. **bug off** *Slang* go away.
bug·a·boo ['bʌgə,bu] *n* something, usually imaginary, that frightens: *ogres, ghosts, and other bugaboos.* **bug·bear** *n* **1** bugaboo. **2** a cause of difficulties; a snag. **bug–eyed** *adj Slang* staring, esp with wonder or excitement. **bug·gy** *adj* **1** swarming with bugs. **2** *Slang* crazy. Also, **bug·house.**

bug·ger ['bʌgər] *n* **1** *Slang* **a** an annoying or frustrating person or thing. **b** a humorous term for any person or thing. **2** a person who commits BUGGERY.
v engage in buggery (with). ⟨Old French *bougre*; Latin *Bulgarus* Bulgarian, heretic⟩
bugger all *Slang* nothing. **bugger around** *Slang* fool around; waste time. **bugger up** *Slang* foul up; make a mess of.
bug·ger·y *n* anal sexual intercourse.

USAGE
The slang senses of **bugger** and related idioms may be offensive to some people.

bug·gy¹ ['bʌgi] *n* **1** a four-wheeled horse-drawn carriage. **2** a cart used by shoppers in a store. **3** BABY CARRIAGE. **4** *Informal* an old car. ⟨origin uncertain⟩

bug·gy² ['bʌgi] *adj* See BUG.

bu·gle ['bjugəl] *n* a wind instrument like a small trumpet, made of brass or copper, and sometimes having keys, or valves. **bu·gle** *v.* **bu·gler** *n.* ⟨Latin *buculus* diminutive of *bos* ox; reference to early hunting horns⟩

build [bɪld] *v* **built, build·ing 1** make by putting materials or parts together: *to build a house, to build a model ship.* **2** develop or form gradually: *to build a business.* **3** gradually intensify or increase: *The tension between the factions has been building.*
n **1** style or manner of construction. **2** body type: *a man of heavy build.* **build·er** *n.* ⟨Old English *byldan; bold* dwelling⟩
build in include in a structure during the process of building. **build up a** develop over time: *to build up a reputation.* **b** accumulate: *Ice had built up on the driveway.* **c** fill (an area) with houses, etc. **d** advertise; promote. **e** encourage; foster the self-esteem of.
build·ing *n* **1** a permanent structure with walls and roof. **2** the trade or industry of builders. **building starts** all instances, over a certain period, of a developer starting a building project; a statistic used as an index of the economy. **build·up** or **build–up** *n*

1 accumulation. **2** promotion; hype. **built–in** *adj* included in a larger structure during the process of building or development: *a built-in closet, built-in checks and balances.*

Buk·wus ['bʊkwʊs] *n* In Kwakwaka'waka (Kwakiutl) myth, a gnomelike creature, chief of ghosts, who tries to lure people into his invisible world to eat spirit food like slugs. ⟨Kwakwaka'waka⟩

bulb [bʌlb] *n* **1** the underground bud produced by certain plants, such as onions, lilies, and tulips, from which a new plant can grow. **2** LIGHT BULB. **3** the rounded end of any object: *the bulb of a thermometer.* **bulb·like** *adj.* ⟨Greek *bolbos* onion⟩
bul·bif·er·ous *adj* producing bulbs (def. 1). **bulb·ous** *adj* **1** shaped like a bulb: *a bulbous nose.* **2** producing or growing from bulbs.

bulge [bʌldʒ] *v* swell out: *Her pockets bulged with apples and candy.*
n **1** an outward swelling. **2** a temporary increase: *The graph shows a bulge in the birth rate.* **bulg·y** *adj.* **bul·gi·ness** *n.* ⟨Latin *bulga* bag⟩

bul·gur ['bʌlgər] or ['bʌlgʊr] *n* a Middle Eastern food made from cracked wheat. Also, **bul·ghur.** ⟨Turkish⟩

bu·lim·i·a [bə'limiə] *n* an eating disorder characterized by alternate bouts of bingeing and purging or self-induced vomiting. In full, **bulimia nervosa. bu·lim·ic** *adj.*

bulk [bʌlk] *n* **1** mass; size, esp large or unwieldy size: *an elephant of great bulk.* **2** the largest part: *The ocean forms the bulk of the earth's surface.* **3** a ship's cargo or hold.
adj bought or sold in bulk: *bulk food.*
v **1** (usually with *large*) be big or important. **2** grow or cause to swell. **bulk·y** *adj.* **bulk·i·ly** *adv.* **bulk·i·ness** *n.* ⟨Old Icelandic *bulki* heap⟩
in bulk a loose in bins, not packaged. **b** in large quantities.

bulk·head *n* **1** one of the partitions dividing a ship, aircraft, etc. into compartments. **2** any partition built to hold back water, earth, rocks, air, etc.

bull¹ [bʊl] *n* **1** the adult male of cattle, moose, buffalo, elephants, and certain other animals. **2** a person who expects a rise in prices in the stock market. Compare BEAR. **3** *Slang* false, glib, or meaningless talk.
v **1** *Slang* talk bull: *She'll bull her way through the oral exam.* **2** try to raise prices of (stocks) or in (the stock market). **3** powerfully push or drive through something: *to bull one's way through a crowd.* ⟨Old Norse *boli*⟩
shoot the bull *Slang* talk idly. **take the bull by the horns** act bravely and with initiative.
bull·dog *n* a breed of strong, short-haired, heavily built dog, tenacious and courageous. *v* **-dogged, -dog·ging** in the western parts of Canada and the US, throw (a steer, etc.) to the ground by grasping its horns and twisting its neck. **bulldog edition** the first edition of a morning newspaper, which is sent to other places. **bull·doze** *v* **1** move, clear, etc. with a bulldozer. **2** *Informal* coerce (someone) or force through by manipulation or threats. **bull·doz·er** *n* a powerful tractor that moves

dirt, etc., by means of a wide steel blade attached to the front. **bull·fight** *n* a public performance in which a person confronts and arouses a bull in an arena, performs a series of skilful manoeuvres to avoid its horns as it charges, and eventually kills it. **bull·fight·er** *n*. **bull·fight·ing** *n*. **bull·finch** *n* a small, plump finch of Europe and Asia. The male has a pinkish breast. **bull·frog** *n* any of a genus of large frogs of North America, Africa, and India, the males having a loud, deep call. **bull·head·ed** *adj* stupidly stubborn. **bull·horn** *n* a megaphone with an electric amplifier. **bull·ish** *adj* 1 expecting a rise in stock prices. 2 generally optimistic. **bull·ock** *n* a castrated bull. **bull·pen** or **bull pen** *Baseball* **a** a place outside the playing area, where pitchers warm up during a game. **b** the pitchers. **bull·ring** or **bull ring** an arena for bullfights. **bull's-eye** *n* the centre of a target. **bull thistle** the common thistle, with purple brushlike flowers and spiny leaves.

bull² [bʊl] *n Roman Catholic Church* a formal announcement from the Pope. ⟨Latin *bulla* document, seal; orig. amulet, bubble⟩

bul·let [ˈbʊlɪt] *n* 1 a piece of lead or other metal designed to be shot from a rifle, pistol, or other small firearm. 2 *Printing* a small dot drawing attention to an item in a list. ⟨French *boulette* diminutive of *boule* ball⟩ **bul·let·proof** *adj* not letting bullets through: *a bulletproof vest.* **bul·let·proof** *v.*

bul·le·tin [ˈbʊlətɪn] *n* 1 a short statement of news. 2 a periodical publication of some organization. 3 in some churches, a leaflet giving the order of service, notices, etc. ⟨Italian *bulletino*, diminutive of *bulla* bull²⟩ **bulletin board** 1 a board used for posting notices. 2 *Computers* in full, **bul·le·tin–board system** a system allowing networked users to post notices or messages, download and upload data or programs, etc. *Abbrev* **BBS**

bul·lion [ˈbʊljən] *n* gold or silver in bulk format. ⟨Anglo-French *bullion; bouillir* boil⟩

bul·ly [ˈbʊli] *n* a person who frightens, hurts, or teases weaker people. **bul·ly** *v.* ⟨perhaps Middle Dutch *boele*⟩ **bully for** congratulations to (often ironic): *He got my job, did he? Well, bully for him.* **bul·ly·rag** *v* **-ragged, -rag·ging** tease; abuse.

bully beef canned or pickled beef. ⟨perhaps French *bouilli* boiled beef; *bouillir* boil⟩

bul·rush [ˈbʊl,rʌʃ] *n* any of a genus of tall marsh plants of North America and Eurasia, with very long, flat leaves and fuzzy brown flower spikes; cattail. ⟨Middle English *bule* bull + Old English *rysc* rush⟩

bul·wark [ˈbʊlwərk] *n* 1 a wall for defence. 2 any defence: *Her common sense was our bulwark during the crisis.* 3 a breakwater. 4 Usually, **bulwarks** *pl* the part of a ship's side extending above the deck. ⟨Middle English *bole* tree trunk + *werk* work, structure⟩

bum¹ [bʌm] *Informal n* 1 a lazy or otherwise dishonourable person. 2 a tramp; vagrant. 3 an enthusiast so devoted to a hobby as to neglect ordinary responsibilities: *a ski bum.* *v* **bummed, bum·ming** 1 be idle. 2 get by begging: *She tried to bum a ride.* *adj* **bum·mer, bum·mest** 1 of low quality. 2 injured or lame: *a bum knee.* 3 false or unfair: *a bum rap.* ⟨Scottish dialect (special use of *bum²*); partly German *Bummler* loafer⟩ **bummed (out)** *Slang* disappointed; upset. **on the bum a** living as a tramp: *He spent two years on the bum.* **b** *Informal* out of order: *Our toaster is on the bum.* **the bum's rush** *Informal* forcible ejection (of a person from a place). **bum·mer** *n Slang* a bad or depressing fact or experience: *It's a bummer that you're leaving.*

bum² [bʌm] *n Informal* buttocks; bottom. ⟨Middle English *bom; botem* bottom⟩

bum·ble [ˈbʌmbəl] *n* an awkward mistake. *v* act in a bungling or awkward way; botch. **bum·bling** *n, adj.* ⟨perhaps *b(ungle)* + *(st)umble*⟩

bum·ble·bee [ˈbʌmbəl,bi] *n* any of a family of large, fuzzy bees, usually with yellow stripes. ⟨Middle English *bumme, bumbe* buzz + *bee*⟩

bump [bʌmp] *v* 1 push or strike (against something hard): *to bump one's head.* 2 *Slang* remove from a reserved position: *The local performer was bumped from the program in favour of a bigger star.* *n* 1 a knock or jolt. 2 a swelling caused by a blow. 3 a hard raised spot: *a bump on a road.* **bump·y** *adj.* **bump·i·ly** *adv.* **bump·i·ness** *n.* ⟨perhaps Scandinavian, imitative⟩ **bump into a** strike accidentally. **b** *Informal* meet by chance. **bump off** *Slang* kill. **bump up** *Informal* raise (a salary, fee, grade, etc.). **bump·er** *n* the bar across each end of a vehicle, protecting it from damage if bumped. *adj* unusually large: *a bumper crop of wheat.* **bumper–to–bumper** *adj* of traffic, congested; moving very slowly. **bumper sticker** a sticker for a bumper, with a slogan on it. **bump·tious** *adj* conceited; unpleasantly assertive.

bump·kin [ˈbʌmpkɪn] *n* a backward country person. ⟨Middle Dutch *bommekyn* little barrel⟩

bun [bʌn] *n* 1 a small loaf of yeast dough, separately baked. 2 hair coiled into a knot shape. ⟨Middle English *bunne*⟩

bunch [bʌntʃ] *n* 1 any group: *They are a friendly bunch.* 2 a number of things of one kind fastened together or growing together: *a bunch of grapes, a bunch of keys.* 3 *Informal* a large quantity; mass: *a whole bunch of paint.* *v* come or bring together in a mass or cluster (often with *up*). **bunch·y** *adj.* ⟨Middle English *bunche*⟩

bun·dle [ˈbʌndəl] *n* 1 a number of things tied or wrapped up together. 2 *Informal* a lot of money: *She made a bundle on that deal.* 3 *Botany, Anatomy* a collection of fibres. *v* 1 wrap or tie together. 2 send or go away in a hurry (usually with *off*): *They bundled her off to the hospital.* ⟨Middle English *bundel.* Related to BIND.⟩ **be a bundle of nerves** be extremely nervous. **bundle of joy** a new baby. **bundle up** dress warmly: *It's cold; bundle up when you go out.*

bundle buggy a shopping cart, esp one owned by the user.

bung [bʌŋ] *n* a stopper for a **bunghole**, the hole in a barrel.
v (usually with *up*) **1** close (a hole) with a stopper. **2** clog; plug. **3** *Slang* mess up; wreck. ⟨probably Middle Dutch *bonghe*⟩

bun·ga·low ['bʌŋɡə,lou] *n* a one-storey house. ⟨Hindi *bangla* of Bengal⟩

Bun·gee ['bʌŋɡi] *n* **1** a lingua franca spoken in the 1800s in the Red River area in Manitoba. **2** an Ojibwa or Salteaux.

bun·gee ['bʌndʒi] *n* an elastic cable with strong hooks on the ends, for securing loads, etc. Also, **bungee cord.** ⟨origin uncertain⟩
bungee jumping the sport of leaping off a high place with an elasticized cable tied to one's ankles.

bun·gle ['bʌŋɡəl] *v* spoil through clumsiness. **bun·gle** *n.* **bun·gler** *n.* ⟨origin uncertain⟩

bun·ion ['bʌnjən] *n* an enlargement of the joint of the big toe due to various causes. ⟨perhaps from obsolete *bunny* a swelling⟩

bunk[1] [bʌŋk] *n* a bed, usually one of two built one above the other.
v Informal spend the night; sleep: *It was too late to go home so they bunked at our house.* ⟨perhaps back-formed from *bunker*⟩
bunk bed one of a set of beds built one above the other. **bunk·house** *n* a building equipped with bunks for sleeping.

bunk[2] [bʌŋk] *n Informal* foolish or insincere talk. Also, **bunk·um, bunc·ombe** ['bʌŋkəm]. ⟨pointless speeches by a US congressman on behalf of *Buncombe,* his constituency⟩

bunk·er ['bʌŋkər] *n* **1** a sandy hollow on a golf course. **2** a steel-and-concrete fortification built partly or wholly underground. **3** a place to store fuel on a ship. ⟨Scottish, orig = bench⟩
bunker fuel or **oil** a thick, heavy oil for use as fuel, esp for ships.

bun·ny ['bʌni] *n* a pet name for a rabbit. ⟨origin uncertain⟩

Bun·sen burner ['bʌnsən] a gas burner with a hot blue flame, used in laboratories. ⟨Robert *Bunsen,* 19c German chemist⟩

bunt [bʌnt] *v Baseball* hit (a ball) lightly so that it falls to the ground and rolls only a short distance. **bunt** *n.* **bunt·er** *n.* ⟨*butt*[3]⟩

bun·ting[1] ['bʌntɪŋ] *n* **1** long pieces of cloth used to decorate buildings and streets on special occasions. **2** Often, **bunting bag** a baby's winter garment like a bag with a hood. ⟨perhaps Middle English *bonten* sift, since the cloth was used for sifting⟩

bun·ting[2] ['bʌntɪŋ] *n* any of numerous New and Old World finches, such as the **indigo bunting** and **snow bunting.** ⟨origin uncertain⟩

buoy [bɔɪ] *or* ['bui] *n* **1** a floating object, warning of hidden rocks or shallows or marking off a swimming area. **2** a belt, ring, etc. used to keep a person afloat.
v (often with *up*) **1** keep afloat. **2** encourage or cheer: *buoyed by hope.* ⟨Old French *boie*⟩
buoy·an·cy *n* **1** the power to float or (of

water) to keep things afloat. **2** a tendency to rise. **3** the ability to stay cheerful during bad times, or to recover quickly from low spirits. **4** a body's loss in weight when immersed in liquid. **buoy·ant** *adj.* **buoy·ant·ly** *adv.*

bur·ble ['bɜrbəl] *v* **1** make a bubbling or gentle flowing noise. **2** speak in a confused, excited way. **bur·bler** *n.* ⟨probably imitative⟩

bur·bot ['bɜrbət] *n, pl* **-bot** or **-bots** a freshwater food fish related to the cod. ⟨French *bourbotte; bourbe* mud⟩

burbs [bɜrbz] *n pl Informal* the suburbs.

bur·den ['bɜrdən] *n* **1** a heavy load of things to carry, responsibility, worry, etc. **2** anything difficult to bear. **3** the main content of a message. **bur·den** *v.* **bur·den·some** *adj.* ⟨Old English *byrthen.* Related to BEAR[1].⟩
burden of proof the obligation to prove one's statements.

bur·dock ['bɜrdɒk] *n* any of a genus of weedy herbs of the composite family, having broad leaves and prickly fruits. ⟨*burr* + *dock*[4]⟩

bu·reau ['bjʊrou] *n, pl* **-reaus** or **-reaux** [-rouz] **1** a CHEST OF DRAWERS. **2** a large desk with drawers. **3** an office or agency: *a travel bureau.* **4** a branch of a government department. ⟨French = desk, orig, cloth-covered; *bure* woollen fabric⟩
bu·reauc·ra·cy [bjʊ'rɒkrəsi] *n* **1** excessive concentration of power in administrative offices. **2** excessive insistence on rigid official routine. **3** the officials of a (usually large) administration. **bu·reau·crat** ['bjʊrou,kræt] *n* a member, esp an officious one, of any large administration. **bu·reau·crat·ic** *adj.* **bu·reau·ra·tese** [bjʊ,rɒkrə'tiz] *n Informal* the jargon-filled language used by bureaucrats. **bu·reauc·ra·tize** *v.* **bu·reauc·ra·ti·za·tion** *n.*

burg or **burgh** [bɜrg] *n Informal* a town or city. ⟨var. of *borough*⟩
bur·gess ['bɜrdʒɪs] *n* ✸ in Saskatchewan, a property owner with the right to vote on money by-laws. **burgh·er** ['bɜrgər] *n* a decent, ordinary citizen of a town.

bur·geon ['bɜrdʒən] *v* **1** sprout: *burgeoning leaves.* **2** flourish; grow: *burgeoning talent, a burgeoning population.* ⟨Old French *burjon*⟩

bur·ger ['bɜrgər] *n Informal* HAMBURGER (def. 2). **–burger** *combining form* **1** a fried or grilled piece of —— in a split bun: *fishburger.* **2** a HAMBURGER (def. 2) with——: *cheeseburger.*

bur·glar ['bɜrglər] *n* one who breaks into a building to steal. **bur·glar·ize** or (*Informal*) **bur·gle** *v.* **bur·glar·y** *n.* ⟨Anglo-Latin *burglator,* perhaps from Old English *burgbryce*⟩
bur·glar·proof *adj* impossible to break into.

bur·gun·dy ['bɜrgəndi] *n* **1** a dark purplish red. **2** wine, esp red, from Burgundy, a region of France. **bur·gun·dy** *adj.*

bur·i·al See BURY.

burl [bɜrl] *n* a knot in wool, cloth, or wood. *v* remove knots from. ⟨Latin *burra*⟩

bur·lap ['bɜrlæp] *n* coarse, heavy woven fabric used mainly for sacks. ⟨Middle English *borel* coarse cloth + *lappa* garment flap⟩

bur·lesque [bər'lesk] *n* **1** a drama or literary composition in which a serious subject is treated ridiculously or with mock seriousness: *a burlesque of the classical detective story.* **2** any mockery: *That debate was a burlesque of parliamentary democracy.* **3** a show featuring broad or bawdy humour, striptease, etc.
v imitate in a mocking way. **bur·lesque** *adj.* ⟨French, from Italian *burlesco; burla* jest⟩

bur·ly ['bərli] *adj* **1** big and sturdy; husky. **2** bluff; rough. ⟨Old English *borlice* excellently⟩

burn¹ [bərn] *v* **burned** or **burnt**, **burn·ing** **1** be on fire or set on fire: *The campfire burned all night.* **2** be or cause to be consumed, injured, or damaged by fire, acid, radiation, etc.: *The back of her neck is burned from the sun.* **3** produce (a hole, carving, etc.) by any of these means. **4** use as fuel: *This stove burns wood or coal.* **5** give light: *Lamps burned in every room.* **6** be full of intense emotion: *burning with anger.* **7** cheat; disappoint: *I got burned in that deal.*
n **1** an injury or mark caused by fire, heat, acid, electricity, or radiation: *cigarette burns on the floor.* **2** the process of burning. **burn·a·ble** *adj.* ⟨Old English *beornan, bærnan*⟩ **burn down a** burn to the ground. **b** burn less strongly as fuel gets low. **burn one's boats** or **bridges** cut off all one's means of retreat. **burn out a** destroy the inside or contents of by burning. **b** cease to burn or shine: *This bulb has burned out. The campfire had burned out and we were in darkness.* **c** ruin through long or improper use or excessive heat: *to burn out a motor.* **d** bring or come to a state of physical or emotional exhaustion: *She burned herself out with overwork.* **burn up a** burn completely· *By the time the police got there, the papers were burned up.* **b** *Informal* make angry: *Her smugness really burns me up.* **c** (also **burn off**) use up (calories, fat, energy) through activity. **do a slow burn** seethe with suppressed anger. **have (money, etc.) to burn** have enough money, etc. to waste.
burn·er *n* **1** the part of a stove, furnace, etc., where the flame or heat is produced. **2** any apparatus that works by burning: *a Bunsen burner.* **on the back burner** *Informal* in or into a state of temporary inactivity: *We've put that issue on the back burner for now.* **burn·ing** *adj* **1** glowing hot. **2** vital; urgent: *burning issues.*
burning bush any of various North American bushes with red fruit or leaves. **burn·out** *n* **1** a failure due to burning or extreme heat. **2** shutdown of a jet or rocket engine due to lack of fuel. **3** exhaustion through overwork. **burnt offering 1** the burning of an animal, harvest fruits, etc., as a religious sacrifice. **2** anything offered in sacrifice or atonement. **burnt sienna** a dark brown colour. **burnt umber** a reddish brown colour.

USAGE
The past tense and past participle of **burn** are either **burned** or **burnt**. Many people keep **burned** for the verb and use **burnt** when the participle is adjectival: *partially burnt papers. They hastily burned all the letters.*

burn² [bərn] *n Scottish* a small stream; creek.

bur·nish ['bərnɪʃ] *v, n* polish. ⟨Old French *burniss-*, stem of *burnir* make brown, polish⟩

burp [bərp] *Informal v* **1** belch. **2** cause to belch: *to burp a baby.* **burp** *n.* ⟨imitative⟩

burr¹ or **bur** [bər] *n* **1** the prickly, clinging seedcase or flower of various plants. **2** any clingy thing or person. **3** a rough edge left on metal, wood, etc., by cutting or drilling. **4** any small cutting tool with a rough head, such as a dentist's drill. **bur·ry** *adj.* ⟨probably Scandinavian⟩

burr² [bər] *n* **1** a pronunciation in which *r* sounds are trilled: *a Scottish burr.* **2** a whirring sound. **burr** *v.* **bur·ry** *adj.* ⟨imitative⟩

bur·ri·to [bə'ritou] *n* a Mexican dish consisting of a wheat tortilla rolled around a filling of ground beef, beans, etc.

bur·ro ['bərou] *n* a small donkey, esp one used as a beast of burden in Latin America and the SW United States. ⟨Spanish, from *burrico* small horse; Latin *burricus*⟩

bur·row ['bərou] *n* a hole dug in the ground by an animal for refuge: *a rabbit's burrow.*
v **1** dig or otherwise create such a hole or cavelike refuge: *She burrowed under the warm blankets.* **2** dig or root around: *He burrowed in his pockets for a dime.* ⟨related to Old English *beorg* burial place; *byrgen* grave⟩

bur·sa ['bərsə] *n, pl* **-sae** [-si] *or* [-saɪ] *or* **-sas** a pouch in the body, esp one located between joints and containing a lubricating fluid. ⟨Latin; Greek *byrsa* wineskin. Compare PURSE.⟩ **bur·si·tis** [bər'saɪtɪs] *n* inflammation of a bursa, usually in the shoulder or the hip.

bur·sar ['bərsər] *n* a treasurer, esp of a university or college. ⟨Latin *bursa* purse⟩ **bur·sa·ry** *n* a grant of money to a student at a college or university.

burst [bərst] *v* **burst**, **burst·ing** **1** fly apart or break open suddenly and with force: *The balloon burst.* **2** be full to the breaking point: *bursting with grain, bursting with enthusiasm.* **3** come, start, etc., suddenly and with energy: *to burst into tears, to burst into a room.*
n a sudden energetic outbreak or display: *a burst of laughter, a burst of speed, a burst of artillery fire.* ⟨Old English *berstan*⟩

bur·y ['beri] *or* ['bəri] *v* **1** put (a dead body) in the earth, a tomb, the sea, etc., usually with a ceremony. **2** cover with earth or something else: *buried treasure.* **3** hide: *buried talent. He buried his face in his hands.* **4** engross: *She buried herself in her work.* **5** repress, ignore, or put aside. **bur·i·al** *n.* ⟨Old English *byrgan*⟩ **burial ground** a graveyard or cemetery.

bus [bʌs] *n, pl* **bus·es** or **bus·ses** **1** a large motor vehicle for passengers. **2** *Computers* a hardware pathway for transfer of data.
v **1** carry or travel by bus: *She buses to work.* **2** serve as BUS BOY. **bus·load** *n.* ⟨*omnibus*⟩ **miss the bus** *Informal* lose an opportunity. **bus·bar** *n* an electrical conductor to which several circuits are connected. **bus boy** a waiter's assistant who clears tables, etc.

busman's holiday a holiday spent in activity similar to one's usual work, as a bus trip taken by a driver on his or her day off. **bus shelter** a structure in which to wait for a bus.

bus·by ['bʌzbi] *n* **1** a tall fur hat worn by hussar regiments. **2** BEARSKIN (def. 2). ⟨origin uncertain⟩

bush [buʃ] *n* **1** any woody plant with many branches starting from the ground. **2** forest, esp the vast forested wilderness. **3 ✱** a treed area on a farm: *They have a sugar bush.*
v spread out like a bush (often with *out*).
adj Informal unpolished; backward; suited to a BUSH LEAGUE: *The golfers, the course, and the play were all bush.* ⟨Old Norse *buskr*⟩
beat around (or **about**) **the bush** take a long time getting to the point.
bush baby any of several species of small, nocturnal primates of the African forests. **bush bean** a plant bearing green beans, which grows like a bush instead of a vine. **bush·craft** *n* knowledge of how to keep alive in the bush. **bushed** *adj* **1** lost in the bush. **2** *Informal* ✱ mentally unbalanced as a result of isolation in the wilderness. **3** *Informal* exhausted. **bush league** *Informal* **1** *Baseball* a minor league. **2** any second-rate or backward group in any field. **bush–league** *adj.* **bush–leag·uer** *n.* **bush line** ✱ an airline that transports freight and passengers in the Far North. **bush lot** ✱ part of a farm where the trees have been left standing to provide firewood, fence posts, etc. **bush·man** *n, pl* **-men 1** *Australian* an outback dweller or settler in the bush. **2** a person who knows much about living in the woods; woodsman. **bush partridge** ✱ spruce grouse. **bush pilot** ✱ an aviator who does most of his or her flying in the Far North. **bush·whack** *v* **1** make one's way through the bush. **2** live or work in the bush. **3** ambush or raid in the bush. **bush·whack·er** *n.* **bush·work·er** *n* ✱ a person who works in the bush, esp a logger. **bush·y** *adj* **1** growing thickly like a bush: *a bushy beard.* **2** overgrown with bushes.

bush·el ['buʃəl] *n* a non-metric unit of volume for grain and other produce, equal to about 0.036 m³. ⟨Old French *boissiel; boisse* a measure⟩
bushel basket a basket holding one bushel.

bush·ing ['buʃɪŋ] *n* a metal lining used to protect machine parts, reduce a pipe's bore, or insulate wire. ⟨Middle Dutch *busse* box⟩

busi·ness ['bɪznɪs] *n* **1** buying and selling and related fields of activity. **2** a commercial enterprise: *a plumbing business.* **3** customers: *This store gets a lot of business.* **4** work: *Business before pleasure.* **5** a matter or affair: *His dismissal was a sad business.* ⟨*busy*⟩
about one's business doing one's work. **in business 1** running a commercial enterprise. **2** *Informal* all set; ready to start: *Once our new computers arrive, we'll be in business.* **like nobody's business** *Informal* very fast, hard, etc. **mean business** *Informal* be serious. **mind one's own business** avoid meddling. **on business** engaged in a business errand.

business card a calling card for use in business, printed with one's name, position, business address and telephone number, etc. **business end** *Informal* the part that does the work: *The business end of a pen is its point.* **busi·ness·like** *adj* matter-of-fact; methodical, efficient, professional, etc. **busi·ness·per·son** *n* **1** a person in business. **2** a person with the skills, personality, etc. needed to succeed in business. **busi·ness·man**, **busi·ness·wom·an** *n.*

busk·er ['bʌskər] *n* a street musician or other street entertainer. **busk** *v.* **bus·king** *n.* ⟨dialect⟩

buss [bʌs] *v, n Informal* kiss. ⟨German dialect *bus*; Welsh, Gaelic *bus* kiss, lip⟩

bust¹ [bʌst] *n* **1** a sculpture of a person's head, shoulders, and chest. **2** the breasts of a woman. **3** the measurement around a woman's body at the breasts: *a 92 cm bust.* ⟨Latin *bustum* funeral monument⟩
bus·tier ['bustjei] *n* a tight-fitting, sleeveless and often strapless bodice.

bust² [bʌst] *v* **1** *Slang or dialect* burst. **2** *Slang* make bankrupt. **3** *Informal* punch; hit: *to bust someone on the nose.* **4** *Slang* **a** arrest. **b** raid. **5** *Slang* reduce to a lower rank: *He was busted to private.* **6** *Slang* break: *Don't bust my watch.* *n* **1** *Slang* a failure; flop. **2** *Informal* a punch. **3** *Informal* spree. **4** *Slang* a raid or arrest. ⟨var. of *burst*⟩
go bust *Informal* become bankrupt. **—— or bust** *Slang* used, esp by hitchhikers, to announce destination: *Sudbury or bust.* **–buster** *combining form, often in trademarks* a person or thing that gets rid of —: *ghostbuster.* **bust–up** *n Slang* a quarrel or fight.

bust·er ['bʌstər] *n Slang* rude form of address for a man or boy: *Watch it, buster!*

bus·tle¹ ['bʌsəl] *v* **1** hurry around busily. **2** make (others) hurry. **bus·tle** *n.* ⟨perhaps imitative⟩

bus·tle² ['bʌsəl] *n* a pad or framework used in the late 19c to puff out the upper back part of a woman's skirts. ⟨possibly special use of *bustle¹*⟩

bus·y ['bɪzi] *adj* **1** active or full of activity: *a busy child, busy days.* **2** occupied; engaged: *Don't bother me now; I'm busy.* **3** in use: *I tried to phone her but her line was busy.* **4** *Informal* cluttered; ornate: *a busy wallpaper pattern.* *v* make or keep busy: *The stagehands busied themselves in setting up the stage.* **bus·i·ly** *adv.* **bus·y·ness** *n.* ⟨Old English *bisig*⟩
bus·y·bod·y ['bɪzi,bɒdi] *or* ['bɪzi,bʌdi] *n* a meddler. **bus·y·work** *n* work meant only to make one feel or appear busy.

but [bʌt] *conj* **1** however; yet; still: *It rained, but I went anyway.* **2** on the contrary; rather: *She is not snobbish but shy.* **3** unless: *It never rains but it pours.*
prep except; other than: *everyone but me.*
adv Poetic only: *He is but a boy.*
n objection: *No buts!* ⟨Old English *būtan* without, unless; *be-* + *ūtan* outside⟩
all but nearly; almost: *The work is all but finished.* **but for** without; apart from: *I would've died but for your quick thinking.*

bu·tane ['bjutein] or [bju'tein] n a colourless, flammable gas used as fuel. ⟨Latin butyrum butter; Greek boutyron⟩

butch·er ['butʃər] n 1 a person whose work is cutting up meat to be sold for food. 2 a brutal killer or murderer. 3 Informal a person who bungles something. **butch·er** v. ⟨Old French bocher; boc he-goat, buck¹⟩

butcher block 1 a hardwood block or surface made of narrow strips of wood, on which to cut meat. 2 material imitating this, used for countertops. **butcher shop** a butcher's place of business. **butch·er·y** n 1 wholesale killing. 2 a slaughterhouse. 3 something botched or spoiled, or the act of botching or spoiling.

but·ler ['bʌtlər] n 1 the chief male servant of a household. 2 a male servant in charge of wines and liquors. ⟨Old French bouteillier; bouteille bottle⟩

butt¹ [bʌt] n 1 the thicker end of anything: The butt of a gun. 2 the end that is left over: a cigar butt. 3 Slang buttocks. 4 Slang an (unsmoked) cigarette. 5 Also, **butt joint** a joint where two boards or beams meet end to end. v **butt out** a extinguish (a cigarette or cigar) by pressing the lit end against something. b Informal quit smoking. ⟨Middle English but, bott (related to buttocks) and Old French bout end⟩

butt weld a butt joint that has been welded.

butt² [bʌt] n 1 target. 2 an object of ridicule: He was the butt of their jokes. 3 on a rifle, archery, or artillery range, a mound of earth, bale of straw, etc. behind the target. 4 **the butts** shooting range. ⟨French but goal⟩

butt³ [bʌt] v 1 ram with the head. 2 jut: My bedroom butts out over the garage. n a push or blow with the head. ⟨Old French bouter thrust⟩

butt in Informal a meddle; interfere. b enter a lineup elsewhere than at the end.

butt out! Slang mind your own business!

butte [bjut] n ❉ a steep, often flat-topped hill standing alone, as in S Alberta. ⟨French⟩

but·ter ['bʌtər] n 1 the yellow fat obtained by churning milk. 2 something like butter in consistency: peanut butter. 3 Informal flattery. v put butter on. **but·ter·less** adj. ⟨Greek boutyron⟩

butter up flatter.

but·ter·ball n Informal a plump person. **but·ter·cup** n any of a number of wildflowers with yellow flowers. **but·ter·fat** n the fatty content of milk from which butter is made. **but·ter·fin·gers** n Informal a person who drops things. **but·ter·fin·gered** adj. **but·ter·fly** n 1 any of a large group of insects with four large, often colourful wings. Compare MOTH. 2 a flighty person. 3 a swimming stroke in which the outstretched arms move in a circular motion together while the legs kick up and down. 4 the butterfly-shaped metal clasp securing the post of an earring in a pierced ear. 5 WING NUT (def. 1). 6 **butterflies** pl a queasy feeling caused by anxiety: I get butterflies in my stomach just thinking about it. ⟨Old English buterflēoge⟩ **but·ter·milk** n 1 the

liquid left after butter is churned from cream. 2 milk deliberately soured by adding certain bacteria. **but·ter·nut** n a North American tree of the walnut family, or its oily, edible nut. **butternut squash** a type of squash with orange skin and pulp. **but·ter·scotch** n candy or syrup made from brown sugar and butter. **butter tart** ❉ a rich, sweet tart with a filling made from butter, brown sugar, corn syrup, raisins, spices, etc. **but·ter·y** adj 1 like butter; yellow or smooth. 2 with a lot of butter in it or on it. n pantry.

but·tocks ['bʌtəks] n pl the fleshy part of the body where the legs join the back; rump. ⟨Old English buttuc end, small piece of land⟩

but·ton ['bʌtən] n 1 a knob or disk serving to hold parts together when passed through a slit or loop. 2 a knob or disk that is pushed or turned to open or close an electric circuit: an elevator button. 3 a badge with a slogan, etc., printed on it and a pin at the back for attaching to clothing: The publisher was giving away buttons to promote the new book. 4 anything like a button. v fasten with buttons. **but·ton·less** adj. ⟨Old French boton; bouter. See BUTT³.⟩

button up Informal a stop talking. b finish arranging: button up the details. **on the button** Informal exactly: five o'clock on the button. **push someone's buttons** use one's knowledge of a person's vulnerable points to manipulate him or her into reacting a certain way.

but·ton–down adj 1 of a shirt collar, fastening with buttons to the body of the shirt. 2 staid; conventional or uptight. **but·ton·hole** n the slit through which a button is passed. v 1 make buttonholes in. 2 accost and force to listen, as if by holding by the buttonhole: She buttonholed me as I tried to sneak out of the room. **but·ton·hol·er** n.

but·tress ['bʌtrɪs] n 1 a structure built against a wall to strengthen or support it. 2 any support; prop: The experience was a buttress to his faith. **but·tress** v. ⟨Old French bouterez (pl); bouter. See BUTT³.⟩

bux·om ['bʌksəm] adj of a woman, plump and full-bosomed. **bux·om·ness** n. ⟨Middle English buhsum; Old English būgan bend⟩

buy [baɪ] v **bought, buy·ing** 1 get in exchange for money, or sometimes for goods or favours: I bought a pencil for 20 cents. You can't buy my love. 2 shop: I won't buy there again. 3 bribe: Two members of the jury had been bought. 4 Informal accept (an idea): If you say it's true, I'll buy it. n Informal something bought, esp at a bargain: a good buy. **buy·a·ble** adj. ⟨Old English bycgan⟩

buy into a obtain an interest in by purchase: She bought into the new company. b commit oneself to (a principle, philosophy, etc.). **buy off** get rid of or placate by paying money to. **buy out** a buy all the shares, rights, etc., of. b buy all there is of. **buy time** stall or delay in hopes of gaining an advantage. **buy up** buy all one can of or all there is of.

buy·back n 1 the repurchase of something

one has sold. **2** a purchase made as a condition of sale, as when a supplier agrees to buy its customer's product. **3** purchase by a company of its own shares, to reduce the number of shares available. **buy·er** *n* **1** a person who buys. **2** a person whose work is buying goods, esp for a retail store. **buyer's market** a situation in which the buyer has the advantage because goods are plentiful and prices low. Compare SELLER'S MARKET. **buy·out** *n* the purchase of a whole company, as by its employees.

buzz [bʌz]*n* **1** a humming sound made by flying insects, and also by some machines. **2** the indistinct sound of people talking. **3** *Informal* a telephone call: *Give me a buzz tonight.* **4** a state of high excitement or activity. **5** *Slang* a haircut, esp a short one. **6** *Slang* a slight rush; euphoria. **7** *Slang* news; gossip: *What's the buzz about me?* *v* **1** hum or make an indistinct murmuring sound. **2** approach quickly and pass closely with an aircraft or small boat **3** signal by pressing a buzzer. **4** *Informal* to telephone: *I'll buzz you when I find out.* **5** *Slang* give a haircut to, esp a short one. ⟨imitative⟩ **buzz around** move around busily. **buzz off** *Slang* go away. **buzz·er** *n* something that buzzes, esp an electric device. **buzz saw** a circular saw. **buzz·word** a fashionable piece of jargon.

buz·zard [ˈbʌzərd] *n* **1** any of several species of vulture of the western hemisphere, esp the turkey vulture, or turkey buzzard. **2** a mean, greedy person. ⟨Old French *busart*; Latin *buteo* hawk⟩

B/W or **B&W** of images, movies, etc. black and white, as distinct from coloured.

by [baɪ] *prep* **1** beside or near: *The garden is by the house.* **2** along or on (a route): *to go by the bridge.* **3** through the action or means of: *He was captured by police. They keep in touch by e-mail.* **4** in units of: *Eggs are sold by the dozen. I took the steps two by two.* **5** according to: *Play by the rules.* **6** during: *by day.* **7** not later than: *by now.* **8** combined with in dimensions or multiplication: *5 m by 8 m.* *adv* **1** at hand: *close by.* **2** past: *days gone by.* ⟨Old English *bī*⟩

by and by after a while; soon: *You will feel stronger by and by.* **by and large** on the whole; in general: *It has some faults, but by and large it is a good book.* **by oneself** alone. **by the way** (or **by the by**) incidentally: *By the way, what time is it?* **by–** *combining form* **1** secondary; less important: *by-product.* **2** nearby: *bystander.* **by–and–by** [ˈbaɪ ən ˈbaɪ] *n* the future. **by–e·lec·tion** *n* an election held in one riding because of the death or resignation of its elected representative. **by·gone** [ˈbaɪˌɡɒn] *adj* past; former: *The Romans lived in bygone days.* *n* something in the past. **let bygones be bygones** let past offences be forgotten. **by–law** or **by·law** *n* **1** a local law. **2** a secondary regulation. **by–line** *n* a line at the beginning of an article identifying the writer. **by·pass** [ˈbaɪˌpæs] *n* **1** a road around, esp around a city. **2** a section of blood vessel grafted onto a blocked one, usually a coronary artery, to carry blood around the obstruction. **3** *Electricity* a shunt. *v* skip over or go around; not bother with. **by–prod·uct** *n* **1** something produced in making something else: *Kerosene is a by-product of petroleum refining.* **2** a side effect. **by·road** or **by–road** *n* a side road. **by·stand·er** *n* a person who stands near or looks on but does not take part. **by·way** or **by–way** *n* **1** a side path; a way that is little used. **2** a less important area of activity. **by·word** [ˈbaɪˌwɜrd] *n* **1** a common saying. **2** a person or thing commonly taken as typifying a certain characteristic, esp an unfavourable one: *They had become a byword for unhospitality throughout the region.*

bye¹ [baɪ] *n* **1** *Sports* the position of the odd player or team that does not play in a round involving pairs. **2** *Golf* the holes not played after one player has won. **by the bye** incidentally.

bye² or **'bye** [baɪ] *interj Informal* goodbye. Also, **bye–bye**.

BYOB bring your own bottle (or beer).

byte [baɪt] *n Computers* a sequence of eight binary digits (bits) processed as a single unit of information. ⟨perhaps a variant of *bite*⟩

Cc

c or **C** [si] *n, pl* **c's** or **C's** 1 the third letter of the English alphabet, or any speech sound represented by it. 2 the third person or thing in a series. 3 a person or thing considered as belonging to the third best group: *grade C eggs.* 4 *Music* the first tone in the scale of C major. 5 the Roman numeral for 100.

c 1 centi- (an SI prefix). 2 cent(s). 3 approximately (for Latin *circa*). Also, **ca.** 4 century. 5 *Sports* catcher. 6 copyright.

C 1 Celsius. 2 carbon. 3 *Mathematics* constant. 4 coulomb.

C14 CARBON-14.

ca approximately (for Latin *circa*). Also, **c.**

C.A. 1 Chartered Accountant. 2 Consular Agent. 3 Central America. 4 Court of Appeal.

cab [kæb] *n* 1 taxi; a car or, formerly, horse-drawn carriage for hire with a driver. 2 the part of a truck, locomotive, etc., where the driver sits. ⟨shortened from *cabriolet*⟩ **cab·by** or **cab·bie** *n Informal* cab driver.

ca·bal [kə'bæl] *n* a small group of people working or plotting in secret. ⟨from CABALA; Hebrew *qabbalah*⟩ **cab·a·la** ['kɑbələ], ['kæbələ], *or* [kə'bɑlə] *n* 1 a secret form of rabbinical Jewish mysticism. 2 any mystical belief or secret doctrine. **cab·a·lism** *n.* **cab·a·lis·tic** *adj.*

ca·ba·ña [kə'bɑnə], [kɔ'bɑnjə], *or* [kə'bænə] *n* 1 a shelter on the beach for changing or shade. 2 bathhouse. ⟨Spanish; Latin *capanna*⟩

cab·a·ret [,kæbə'rei] *or* ['kæbə,rei] *n* 1 a restaurant with singing and dancing as entertainment. 2 the entertainment provided there. ⟨French = tavern⟩

cab·bage ['kæbɪdʒ] *n* a cultivated plant with large, round leaves, used as a vegetable. ⟨French *caboche;* Latin *caput* head⟩ **cab·bage·town** *n* ✶ a run-down urban area; slum. ⟨*Cabbagetown* formerly such an area in E Toronto, so-called from inhabitants' diet⟩

cab·in ['kæbən] *n* 1 a small, roughly built and simply equipped house, often for holiday use: *a hunting cabin in the woods.* 2 a small, rough bunkhouse assigned to a group of participants at a CAMP (def. 2). 3 a room for passengers on a boat or aircraft. ⟨French *cabane;* Latin *capanna*⟩ **cabin boy** a boy who serves officers and passengers on a ship. **cabin class** a class of accommodation on a ship, above tourist and below first class. **cabin cruiser** a motorboat with a cabin. **cabin fever** ✶ 1 depression or hysteria due to prolonged isolation, as in the northern wilderness. 2 *Informal* restlessness due to long confinement indoors.

cab·i·net ['kæbənɪt] *n* 1 a piece of furniture with doors and shelves, or with drawers: *a china cabinet.* 2 **Cabinet** any body of executive advisers to a head of government, representing different departments. 3 any body of advisers to a head of state. ⟨diminutive of *cabin*⟩ **cab·i·net·mak·er** *n* a person skilled in making fine wooden furniture. **cab·i·net·mak·ing** *n.*

ca·ble ['keibəl] *n* 1 a strong, thick rope, usually made of wires twisted together. 2 an insulated bundle of wires made to carry an electric current. 3 CABLE TELEVISION. ⟨Latin *capulum* halter⟩ **cable car** a car pulled, often up a steep hill, by a moving cable. **cable television** (or **TV**) a system by which signals are picked up by a central antenna and sent by cable to the sets of subscribers.

ca·boo·dle [kə'budəl] *n.* **the whole (kit and) caboodle** the whole lot; everyone or everything. ⟨*ca-* intensifying prefix (German *ge-*) + Dutch *boedel* property⟩

ca·boose [kə'bus] *n* 1 a car on a freight train where the crew can live, usually the last car. 2 ✶ esp in the North, a cabin, or a loggers' bunkhouse, cookhouse, etc., pulled along on runners. ⟨Dutch *kabuis* hut, cabin⟩

cab·ri·o·let [,kæbriə'lei] *n* 1 a small car with a folding top. 2 formerly, a light, one-horse, two-wheeled carriage, often with folding top. ⟨French *cabrioler* leap, for bouncing motion⟩

ca·ca·o [kə'keiou] *or* [kə'kaou] *n* a tropical tree that produces **cacao beans,** from which chocolate is made. ⟨Mexican *caca-uatl*⟩

cac·cia·to·re [,kɑtʃə'tɔri] *Italian* [,katʃa'tɔre] *adj* cooked in a casserole with tomatoes, onions, and spices: *chicken cacciatore.* ⟨Italian = hunter; *cacciare* hunt⟩

cache [kæʃ] *n* 1 a hiding place, or the things hidden in it. 2 ✶ **a** a place to store food, furs, etc., away from animals and the elements. **b** a supply of goods so stored. 3 *Computers* a dedicated, quick-access data storage, either a section of the main memory or supplied by a special chip. *v* 1 hide or conceal. 2 ✶ deposit in a cache. ⟨French *cacher* hide⟩

ca·chet [kæ'ʃei] *n* 1 a prestigious aura or distinguishing mark of quality. 2 an official seal or stamp, as of a king. ⟨French⟩

cack·le ['kækəl] *v* 1 of a hen, make a shrill, intermittent cry. 2 laugh with harsh or intermittent sounds. 3 chatter. **cack·le** *n.* ⟨Middle English *cakelen;* imitative⟩

ca·coph·o·ny [kə'kɒfəni] *n* a harsh, clashing noise or mixture of noises. **ca·coph·o·nous** *adj.* ⟨Greek *kakos* bad + *phōnē* sound⟩

cac·tus ['kæktəs] *n, pl* **-tus·es** *or* **-ti** [-tai] *or* [-ti] any of a family of desert plants having fleshy stems with spines. ⟨Greek *kaktos*⟩

cad [kæd] *n* a man who behaves very dishonourably. **cad·dish** *adj.* ⟨*caddie*⟩

CAD COMPUTER-AIDED DESIGN.

ca·dav·er [kə'dævər] *n* a corpse, esp a human body intended for dissection. ⟨Latin⟩ **ca·dav·er·ous** *adj* pale and ghastly.

Cad·bo·ro·sau·rus [,kædbərə'sɔrəs] *n* ✶ a sea serpent supposed to frequent the waters off Victoria, BC. ⟨*Cadboro* Bay⟩

cad·die or **cad·dy** ['kædi] *n Golf* **1** a person who helps a golfer by carrying the clubs, finding the ball, etc. **2** a small two-wheeled trolley for carrying golf clubs.
v **-died, -dy·ing** serve as a caddie. ⟨French *cadet*. See CADET.⟩

cad·dis fly ['kædɪs] any of an order of aquatic insects with two pairs of membranous wings and jointed antennae. ⟨origin uncertain⟩
caddis worm its omnivorous larva, which builds a protective case of silk and bits of sand and debris.

cad·dy[1] ['kædi] *n* a small box or canister: *a tea caddy.* ⟨Malay *kati* a small weight⟩

cad·dy[2] See CADDIE.

ca·dence ['keidəns] *n* **1** rhythm: *the steady cadence of a march.* **2** a rising and falling sound: *She speaks with a pleasant cadence.* **3** falling intonation at the end of a sentence. **4** *Music* a series of chords resolving a passage. ⟨Latin *cadentia*⟩

ca·den·za [kə'dɛnzə] *n Music* a showy solo passage. ⟨Italian⟩

ca·det [kə'dɛt] *n* a young person training to be an officer in the armed forces or the police force. ⟨French, from Gascon *capdel;* Latin *capitellum* diminutive of *caput* head⟩

cadge [kædʒ] *v* **1** *Dialect* peddle. **2** *Informal* beg. **cadg·er** *n*. ⟨origin uncertain⟩

cad·mi·um ['kædmiəm] *n* a ductile metallic element used in plating to prevent rust. *Symbol* **Cd** ⟨Greek *kadmeia* zinc ore⟩

ca·dre ['kɑdrei] or ['kædrei] *n* a group of people forming the core of an organization. ⟨French; Latin *quadrum* square⟩

Caesarean section [sə'zɛriən] delivery of a baby by cutting through the wall of the abdomen and uterus of the mother. Also called **C–section**. ⟨from the belief that Julius Caesar was born in this way⟩

Caesar salad ['sizər] a salad of greens, cheese, croutons, etc.

cae·su·ra [sɪ'zjʊrə] or [sɪ'ʒʊrə] *n* a pause in a line of verse or in music. Also, **ce·su·ra**. ⟨Latin = cutting; *caedere* cut⟩

CAF or **C.A.F.** Canadian Armed Forces.

ca·fé [kæ'fei] or [kə'fei] *n* **1** a small restaurant serving light meals. **2** *French* coffee. ⟨French⟩
ca·fé au lait [kæ'fei ou 'lei] *French* [kafeo'lɛ] coffee made partly with hot milk. **café curtains** short curtains for the lower half of a window. **caf·e·te·ri·a** [,kæfə'tiriə] *n* a casual buffet-style restaurant in an institution.
caf·feine or **caf·fein** [kæ'fin] *n* a stimulant in coffee and tea. **caf·fein·at·ed** *adj.*

caf·tan ['kæftən] *n* a loose, long-sleeved, ankle-length garment worn in some eastern cultures. Also, **kaf·tan**. ⟨Turkish *qaftan*⟩

cage [keidʒ] *n* **1** a box with walls of mesh or bars, for confining an animal. **2** anything shaped or used like a cage: *an elevator cage.* **3** a prison. **4** *Hockey* the network structure forming the goal. **5** *Baseball* a screen used to stop balls during batting practice.
v put or keep in a cage. ⟨Latin *cavea* cell⟩
rattle someone's cage provoke someone.
cage·ling *n* a bird kept in a cage. **ca·gey** or **ca·gy** *adj* **-gi·er, -gi·est** shrewdly cautious; guarded. **ca·gi·ly** *adv.* **ca·gi·ness** *n.*

ca·hoots [kə'huts] *n Slang*
in cahoots in partnership for a wrongful purpose; conspiring. ⟨origin uncertain⟩

cairn [kɛrn] *n* a pile of stones heaped up as a memorial, tomb, or landmark. ⟨Scots Gaelic *carn* heap of stones⟩

caisse pop·u·laire ['kɛs pɒpjə'lɛr] *French* [,kɛspɒpy'lɛʀ] ✲ esp in Québec, credit union. Often, **caisse**. ⟨Cdn. French⟩

cais·son ['keisɒn] or ['keisən] *n* **1** a watertight chamber for doing construction work under water. **2** a box for ammunition. ⟨French *caisson; caisse* chest, Latin *capsa* box⟩

ca·jole [kə'dʒoul] *v* persuade by flattery. ⟨French *cajoler*⟩ **ca·jol·ing·ly** *adv.* **ca·jol·er·y** *n.*

Ca·jun ['keidʒən] *n* **1** a native or inhabitant of a French-speaking area of Louisiana. **2** the French dialect of these people.
adj **1** to do with Cajuns. **2** with hot spices used by the Cajuns. ⟨corruption of *Acadian*⟩

cake [keik] *n* **1** a baked mixture of flour, sugar, eggs, etc.: *a fruit cake.* **2** any small, flat mass of food fried on both sides: *a fish cake.* **3** a hard, shaped mass: *a cake of soap.*
v **1** harden into cakelike masses: *caked mud.* **2** cover with such masses. ⟨Old Norse *kaka*⟩
piece of cake an easy task. **take the cake** *Informal* **a** win first prize. **b** be the strangest, worst, most amazing, etc. thing yet.
cake·walk *n* **1** a folk event in which people perform a promenade to music, with a prize of a cake for the best steps. **2** *Informal* an easy task or victory: *The election was a cakewalk.*

ca·la·ma·ri or **ca·la·ma·ry** [,kɑlə'mɑri] or [,kælə'mɑri] *n* the meat of a giant squid served as food. ⟨Latin *calamarius*⟩

cal·a·mine ['kælə,main] or ['kæləmɪn] *n* a pink powder consisting of zinc oxide and ferric oxide, used in skin ointments. ⟨Latin *calamina*, from *cadmia*. See CADMIUM.⟩

ca·lam·i·ty [kə'læməti] *n* serious trouble; misery, or the cause of this. **ca·lam·i·tous** *adj.* ⟨Latin *calamitas*⟩

cal·ci·um ['kælsiəm] *n* a soft metallic element found in limestone, milk, bone, etc. *Symbol* **Ca** ⟨Latin *calx, calcis* lime⟩
cal·ci·fy *v* make or become hard by the deposit of lime. **cal·ci·fi·ca·tion** *n*. **calcium car·bo·nate** ['kɑrbə,neit] a mineral occurring in rocks as marble and limestone, in animals as bones, shells, teeth, etc., and to some extent in plants. Also called **cal·cite**. **calcium chlo·ride** ['klɔraid] an absorbent compound of calcium and chlorine, used as a refrigerant, preservative, and drying agent. **calcium hy·drox·ide** [hai'drɒksaid] SLAKED LIME. **calcium oxide** quicklime. **calcium phos·phate** a compound of calcium and phosphoric acid, used in medicine, enamels, etc.

cal·cu·late ['kælkjə,leit] *v* **1** find out through

arithmetic or any other form of logic. **2** *Informal* plan; design: *That remark was calculated to hurt my feelings.* **cal·cu·la·ble** *adj.* **cal·cu·la·tion** *n.* ⟨Latin *calculus* pebble used in counting; diminutive of *calx* stone⟩

calculate on *Informal* **a** expect: *We calculated on ten guests, but only two arrived.* **b** rely on. **cal·cu·lat·ed** *adj* deliberate. **cal·cu·lat·ing** *adj* shrewd; scheming. **cal·cu·la·tor** *n* a machine that performs mathematical calculations. **cal·cu·lus** *n, pl* **-lus·es** or **-li** [-ˌlaɪ] *or* [-ˌli] **1** *Mathematics* a method of reasoning using a highly specialized system of notation. See also DIFFERENTIAL CALCULUS, INTEGRAL CALCULUS. **2** *Medicine* a stone or hard mass formed in the body, as in the kidney or gall bladder. **3** a hard coating on the teeth formed by bacterial action on saliva and food particles; tartar.

ca·lèche [kəˈlɛʃ] *n* ✿ a light, two-wheeled, one-horse carriage with a seat in front for the driver and, usually, a folding top. ⟨French⟩

cal·en·dar [ˈkæləndər] *n* **1** a series of charts showing the months and weeks of the year. **2** a long-term schedule: *The court calendar is full.* **3** a list, esp of the programs, courses, and faculty of a university or college. ⟨Latin *calendarium* account book; *calendae* calends (day bills were due)⟩

calendar day the 24 hours from one midnight to the next midnight. **calendar month** one of the 12 named parts into which a year is divided. **calendar year** a period of 365 (or in leap year, 366) days that begins January 1 and ends December 31.

calf¹ [kæf] *n, pl* **calves 1** the young of the domestic cow, buffalo, elephant, whale, etc. **2** a small mass of ice that has broken off a glacier, iceberg, etc. ⟨Old English⟩

kill the fatted calf prepare a feast to celebrate something or welcome someone.

calf love PUPPY LOVE. **calf·skin** *n* leather made from the skin of a calf. **calve** [kæv] *v* give birth to a calf.

calf² [kæf] *n, pl* **calves** the fleshy back part of the human lower leg. ⟨Old Norse *kálfi*⟩

cal·i·bre [ˈkæləbər] *n* **1** diameter, esp inside diameter of a gun or tube. **2** quality or worth: *How can we improve the calibre of our product?* Also, **cal·i·ber**. ⟨French; Arabic *qalib* mould⟩

cal·i·brate *v* **1** check or adjust the accuracy of (a scale or other measuring instrument). **2** measure. **cal·i·bra·tor** *n.* **cal·i·bra·tion** *n.*

cal·i·co [ˈkæləˌkou] *n, pl* **-coes** or **-cos** a cotton cloth printed with coloured patterns. *adj* **1** made of calico. **2** spotted in colours: *a calico cat.* ⟨*Calicut*, India⟩

cal·i·for·ni·um [ˌkæləˈfɔrniəm] *n* a highly radioactive artificial element. *Symbol* **Cf** ⟨*California*, where it was first produced⟩

ca·liph [ˈkeilɪf] *or* [ˈkælɪf] *n* a traditional title of the leader of the Muslim community. ⟨Arabic *khalifah* successor, vicar⟩

cal·is·then·ics or **cal·lis·then·ics** [ˌkælɪsˈθɛnɪks] *n* exercises using no equipment, designed to develop a strong and graceful body.

cal·is·then·ic or **cal·lis·then·ic** *adj.* ⟨Greek *kallos* beauty + *sthenos* strength⟩

call [kɒl] *v* **1** speak or say loudly (often used with *out*): *I called out all the names.* **2** say or shout the name of as a signal to come or to listen: *Call the boys; dinner's ready.* **3** summon; command: *Duty calls.* **4** telephone. **5** make a short visit. **6** give a name or label to: *They called the dog Rover.* **7** think of as; consider: *Everyone called the party a success.* **8** issue orders for: *to call a meeting, to call a truce.* **9** of a bird or animal, utter its characteristic sound. **10** stop or cancel (a game) on account of rain, etc. **11** demand payment of (a loan). *n* **1** the act or sound of calling. **2** claim; demand: *A mother has many calls on her time.* **3** occasion; need: *There's no call for that kind of behaviour.* **4** a brief visit: *to pay a call on her.* ⟨Old English *ceallian*⟩

be called away leave to attend to some matter. **call attention to** bring to people's notice. **call back a** ask a person to return: *He headed for the door but I called him back.* **b** telephone (someone who has called earlier). **c** visit or telephone again: *She's not here; call back tomorrow.* **call down** rebuke; scold. **call for a** go and get: *Call for the pictures any time after three.* **b** require: *The recipe calls for two eggs. This situation calls for tact.* **c** predict: *The forecast calls for showers.* **d** ask for: *to call for the waiter.* **call forth** bring into action or being: *a story that calls forth strong emotions.* **call in** summon for consultation: *to call in a specialist.* **b** collect (debt): *to call in a mortgage.* **call into being** or **existence** create. **call into question** raise doubts about. **call it a day** *Informal* quit. **call off a** order back: *Call off your dog.* **b** cancel: *We called off our trip.* **c** read aloud from a list: *Names were called off alphabetically.* **call of nature** *Informal* the need to relieve oneself. **call on a** visit. **b** appeal to: *We call on all people everywhere to fight against racism.* **call out a** summon into service or action: *to call out troops.* **b** order (workers) to strike. **c** elicit; bring into play. **d** shout. **call someone's bluff** See BLUFF. **call to order** make (an assembly) attentive and ready to proceed. **call up a** bring to mind. **b** telephone. **c** conscript. **on call** available at any time: *The doctor is on call all night.* **within call** near enough to hear a call.

call·a·ble *adj* of a loan, payable on demand. **call·back** *n Informal* **1** a recalling of workers previously laid off, successful auditioners, etc. **2** a follow-up call to a client: *The sales representative spent the whole day on callbacks.* **call·er** *n* **1** a person who makes a short visit. **2** a person who calls out the steps at a square dance. **call girl** a prostitute with whom appointments may be made by telephone. **call·ing** *n* **1** occupation; profession. **2** a spiritual or divine summons. **calling card 1** formerly, a small card left by a visitor with his or her name on it. **2** an identifying sign or trace. **call letters** the letters identifying a radio or television station. Also, **call sign. call number** a series of letters and numbers by which a library book is classified. **call–up** *n* a summoning to military duty.

cal·li·bo·gus [ˌkælə'bougəs] *or* ['kælə,bougəs] ✱ *Atlantic n* a drink made of rum, molasses, and spruce beer. ⟨origin unknown⟩

cal·lig·ra·phy [kə'lɪgrəfi] *n* 1 the art of beautiful handwriting. 2 handwriting. **cal·lig·ra·pher** *n.* **cal·li·graph·ic** [ˌkælə'græfɪk] *adj.* ⟨Greek *kallos* beauty + *graphein* write⟩

cal·li·o·pe [kə'laɪəpi] *n* a musical instrument having a series of steam whistles played by a keyboard. ⟨Greek *kallos* beauty + *ops* voice⟩

cal·li·per or **cal·i·per** ['kæləpər] *n* 1 Usually, **callipers** *pl* an instrument consisting of a pair of hinged legs, used to measure diameter or thickness. 2 the part of a brake that provides friction. ⟨variant of *calibre*⟩

cal·low ['kælou] *adj* young and inexperienced. **cal·low·ness** *n.* ⟨Old English *calu* bald (=unfeathered)⟩

cal·lus ['kæləs] *n* 1 a hard, thickened place on the skin. 2 a new growth uniting the ends of a broken bone. 3 a substance that grows over the wounds of plants. ⟨Latin⟩ **cal·lous** *adj* 1 of skin, thickened and hardened. 2 unfeeling; insensitive: *Only a callous person can be unmoved by such suffering.* **cal·lous·ly** *adv.* **cal·lous·ness** *n.*

calm [kɒm] *adj* 1 not stormy or windy; still. 2 not excited. **calm** *n, v.* **calm·ly** *adv.* **calm·ness** *n.* ⟨Greek *kauma* heat of the day; hence, time for rest⟩

SYNONYMS
Calm = showing no sign of excitement: *His calm behaviour quieted the frightened child.*
Composed = calm as the result of having command over one's thoughts and feelings: *She was quiet and composed at the funeral.*
Collected emphasizes presence of mind and lack of confusion: *The leader of the rescue party looked grim but collected.*

cal·o·rie ['kæləri] *n* 1 a non-metric unit of heat. 2 a unit of energy produced by food as it is metabolized: *Thirty grams of sugar produce about 100 calories.* **ca·loric** [kə'lɔrɪk] *adj.* ⟨Latin *calor* heat⟩

calque [kælk] *n Linguistics* a borrowing from another language by translating each part of a compound word. ⟨French *calquer* to trace⟩

cal·u·met ['kæljə,met] *n* ✱ an ornamented sacred tobacco pipe traditionally smoked in ceremonies among the First Nations of the plains and eastern woodlands. ⟨Greek *kalamos* reed⟩

cal·um·ny ['kæləmni] *n* a false and injurious statement. **ca·lum·ni·ous** *adj.* ⟨Latin *calumnia* false accusation⟩ **ca·lum·ni·ate** *v* make such statements about. **ca·lum·ni·a·tion** *n.* **ca·lum·ni·a·tor** *n.*

calve See CALF[1].

Cal·vin·ism ['kælvə,nɪzəm] *n* the teachings of John Calvin, a 16c French leader of the Protestant Reformation. **Cal·vin·ist** *n, adj.* **Cal·vin·is·tic** *adj.*

ca·lyp·so [kə'lɪpsou] *n* 1 a syncopated style of music originating in Trinidad and often featuring songs with satirical or humorous lyrics. 2 a Canadian wild orchid. Also called **fairy slipper.** ⟨perhaps from *Calypso,* sea nymph in Homer's *Odyssey*⟩

ca·lyx ['keilɪks] *or* ['kælɪks] *n, pl* **ca·lyx·es** or **cal·y·ces** ['kæləsiz] *or* ['keiləsiz] *Botany* the outer leaves surrounding the unopened bud of a flower. ⟨Greek *kalyx* covering⟩

cam [kæm] *n* a projection on a wheel or shaft that changes circular motion into irregular circular motion or back-and-forth motion. ⟨Dutch *kam* cog, comb⟩

ca·ma·ra·de·rie [ˌkɑmə'rɑdəri] *or* [ˌkæmə'rædəri] *n* the light-hearted, friendly conversation and fellowship of comrades. ⟨French⟩

cam·as or **cam·ass** ['kæməs] *n* any of a genus of plants of the lily family native to W North America. The bulb was formerly a staple food of the NW First Nations peoples. ⟨Chinook *quamash* bulb⟩

cam·ber ['kæmbər] *n* the slight arch of a surface such as that of a ship's deck, a road, or a piece of timber. **cam·bered** *adj.* ⟨French *cambre* bent; Latin *camur*⟩

cam·bi·um ['kæmbiəm] *n* the soft, growing tissue between the inner bark and the wood of trees and shrubs, from which new bark and wood grow. **cam·bi·al** *adj.* ⟨Latin *cambium* exchange⟩

Cam·bri·an ['kæmbriən] *or* ['keimbriən] *n Geology* the first period of the Paleozoic era. It began about 600 million years ago. **Cam·bri·an** *adj.* ⟨*Cambria* variant of Latin *Cumbria* Wales; Welsh *Cymru*⟩

cam·cord·er ['kæm,kɔrdər] *n* a hand-held combination of a TV camera and a video recorder. ⟨*cam(era)* + *(re)corder*⟩

came [keim] *v* pt of COME.

cam·el ['kæməl] *n* either of two species of desert mammals with one or two humps on the back. See also ARABIAN CAMEL and BACTRIAN CAMEL. ⟨Greek *kamēlos;* of Semitic origin⟩ **camel hair** a soft, fuzzy cloth, usually light yellowish brown, made from, containing, or imitating camel hair. **camel–hair** *adj.*

ca·mel·lia [kə'miljə] *n* any of several E Asian evergreen shrubs and trees with large, waxy, roselike flowers. ⟨G. J. *Kamel* or *Camellus,* 17c missionary to the Philippines⟩

cam·e·o ['kæmi,ou] *n* 1 a gemstone having layers of different colours, carved with a raised image in one colour on a background of another colour. 2 an appearance by a famous actor in a minor role. 3 a short literary sketch. ⟨Italian *cammeo*⟩

cam·er·a ['kæmərə] *n* an apparatus for taking photographs, videotapes, or movies, consisting of a lightproof chamber in which the image is formed on exposed film or plates by means of a lens. ⟨Latin = (chamber)⟩ **in camera a** in a judge's private office. **b** with the press and public excluded. **c** privately. **on** or **off camera** *Film* placed so as to fall in

or outside the field of vision of the camera.
cam·er·a·man *n*, *pl* **-men** a man who operates a camera, esp a movie or television camera.
cam·er·a–read·y *adj* ready to be photographed for printing: *camera-ready copy.*

cam·i·sole ['kæmə,soul] *n* a waist-length, sleeveless undergarment worn by women and girls. ⟨Spanish *camisa* shirt⟩

cam·o·mile ['kæmə,maɪl] *or* ['kæmə,mɪl] *n* any of a genus of aromatic herbs of the composite family. Also, **cham·o·mile**. ⟨Greek *chamaimēlon* earth apple⟩

cam·ou·flage ['kæmə,flɑʒ] *n* **1** an outward appearance that makes a person, animal, or thing blend in with its natural surroundings. **2** something producing this effect, used to conceal something or someone: *A camouflage of earth and branches effectively hid the guns.* **cam·ou·flage** *v.* ⟨French; *camoufler* disguise⟩

camp [kæmp] *n* **1** a temporary shelter, tent, trailer, etc. or the ground on which it stands: *Her camp was beside the river.* **2 a** a temporary community of people living in cabins, tents, etc., usually with a structured program of activities, for recreation or for training of some kind: *wilderness camp, hockey camp.* **b** a day program for children or youth during school holidays. **3** a group promoting a particular idea or agenda: *the liberal camp.* **4** humour based on exaggeration of a particular style, often with vulgar elements. **camp** *v*, *adj*. ⟨French; Latin *campus* field⟩
break camp pack up tents and equipment and leave. **camp it up** *Informal* act in a camp way. **camp out** live in a tent or other temporary shelter, or without the usual conveniences. **make camp** set up a camp.
camp·craft *n* the skills needed to be a successful outdoor camper. **cam·per** *n* **1** a person who camps or attends a camp. **2** a vehicle equipped for camping. **camp·fire** *n* **1** a fire in a camp, for warmth or cooking. **2** a social gathering for soldiers, scouts, etc. **camp·ground** *n* a place with marked sites for tents, trailers, etc. and conveniences for campers. **camp·ing** *n* the practice of living outdoors in a temporary shelter, esp for recreation. **camp meeting** a religious gathering held outdoors under a large tent, often for days. **camp·site** *n* **1** a marked place for a tent or trailer in a campground. **2** any place where someone camps or has camped. **camp·y** *adj* making use of camp (def. 4).

cam·paign [kæm'pein] *n* **1** a series of linked military operations. **2** any prolonged, planned effort to win or achieve something: *a fundraising campaign, an election campaign.* **cam·paign** *v.* ⟨French *campagne* open country; Latin *campus* field⟩
on the campaign trail travelling to different communities as part of an election campaign.

cam·phor ['kæmfər] *n* a white, bitter, crystalline compound with a strong odour, used in medicine and in the manufacture of film and lacquers. **cam·phor·at·ed** *adj*. ⟨Latin *camphora;* Malay *kāpūr*⟩

cam·pus ['kæmpəs] *n* the grounds and buildings of a university, college, or school. ⟨Latin = field, plain⟩

can[1] [kæn] *v pres sg and pl (all persons)* **can**, *pt* **could** (auxiliary followed by an infinitive without *to*) **1 a** be able to: *I can swim.* **b** does or will in some cases: *This approach can be problematic.* **2** have the right to, by custom, agreement, permission, or law: *You can cross the street here.* ⟨Old English *can(n)* know, know how, can⟩

USAGE

In formal English many people make a point of distinguishing between **may**, meaning 'be allowed to', and **can**, meaning 'be able to': *You may go now. She can walk with crutches.*

can[2] [kæn] *n* **1** a small metal container in which foods are preserved. **2** a container, usually tall, cylindrical, and with a lid: *a garbage can.* **3** *Slang* toilet. **4** *Slang* jail.
v **canned**, **can·ning** **1** preserve by putting in airtight cans or jars: *to can fruit.* **2** *Slang* dismiss from a job, remove from a budget or schedule, etc. **3** *Slang* stop: *Can that racket!* **4** *Slang* prerecord as accompaniment to a live performance: *canned laughter.* **canned** *adj*. **can·ning** *n*. ⟨Old English *canne* vessel⟩
can of worms *Informal* a very complicated issue or situation. **in the can** *Slang* of movie film, finished and ready to show.
can·ner·y *n* a factory where food is canned.

Can·a·da ['kænədə] *n* a country occupying the northern part of North America except Alaska. **Ca·na·di·an** [kə'neidiən] *n*, *adj*. **Ca·na·di·an·ness** *n*. ⟨word for 'village' in an extinct Iroquoian language⟩
Canada Act the Act of 1791 that divided the province of Québec into Upper and Lower Canada. **Canada Council** a body founded by Parliament in 1957 to administer funds in support of the arts. **Canada Day** July 1st, Canada's national holiday. **Canada goose** a large, wild goose of North America. **Canada jay** a jay common throughout Canada and the northern US; grey jay. **Ca·na·darm** *n* an extension, built in Canada, of a spacecraft, allowing astronauts to manipulate objects in space. **Ca·na·di·a·na** *n* things relating to Canada and its culture and history, esp early Canadian furniture, textiles, books, etc. **Canadian Alliance** a federal political party that merged with the Progressive Conservative party to form the Conservative Party of Canada. See also REFORM PARTY. **Canadian Charter of Rights and Freedoms** See CHARTER OF RIGHTS AND FREEDOMS. **Ca·na·di·an·ism** *n* **1** an expression or custom originating in or peculiar to Canada. **2** devotion to Canada, its culture or national character, traditions, etc. **Ca·na·di·an·ize** *v* **1** make Canadian in character or custom. **2** bring under Canadian control or ownership. **Ca·na·di·an·i·za·tion** *n*. **Canadian Radio–television and Telecommunications Commission** a federal government body regulating the broadcasting and communications industry

in Canada. *Abbrev* **CRTC**. **Canadian Shield** a region of ancient rock, chiefly Precambrian granite, encircling Hudson Bay and covering nearly half the mainland of Canada.

ca·nal [kə'næl] *n* **1** a waterway dug across land. **2** a passage or series of connected passages in the body or in a plant: *the alimentary canal, the birth canal.* ⟨Latin *canalis* trench, pipe⟩

can·a·pé [ˌkænə'peɪ] *or* ['kænəpi] *n* a cracker or thin piece of toast spread with a seasoned mixture of fish, cheese, etc., as an appetizer. ⟨French. Related to CANOPY.⟩

ca·nard [kə'nɑrd] *n* a false rumour. ⟨French, literally, duck⟩

ca·nar·y [kə'nɛri] *n* **1** a small yellow finch native to the Canary Islands, popular as a cage bird. **2** light yellow. **3** *Slang* informer; tattletale. ⟨*Canary* Islands⟩

ca·nas·ta [kə'næstə] *n* a card game played with two decks, in which players try to get sets of seven or more cards. ⟨Spanish = basket⟩

can·can ['kæn,kæn] *n* a dance with much high kicking, performed by women in a chorus line and originating in 19c Paris. ⟨French⟩

can·cel ['kænsəl] *v* **-celled** *or* **-celed, -cel·ling** *or* **-cel·ing 1** call off (a planned event) or stop (something in progress): *The game has been cancelled. Cancel that book order.* **2** mark something so that it cannot be used again: *to cancel a postage stamp.* **3** wipe out; annul: *The debt was cancelled.* **4** balance or match with an opposite effect; neutralize (often with *out*): *Your 20 points cancel out 20 of mine.* **can·cel·la·tion** *n.* ⟨Latin *cancellare* cross out with latticed lines; *cancelli* crossbars⟩

can·cer ['kænsər] *n* **1** a disease characterized by an uncontrolled growth of body cells, destroying healthy tissue. **2** any harmful or evil thing that tends to spread: *the cancer of hatred.* **can·cer·ous** *adj.* ⟨Latin = crab, tumour⟩

Can·con ['kæn,kɒn] *n* ✷ *Informal* Canadian content, esp as required under certain regulations for radio and television stations.

Can·cult ['kæn,kʌlt] *n* ✷ *Informal* Canadian culture.

can·de·la [kæn'dɛlə] *or* [kæn'dilə] *n* an SI unit measuring intensity of light shining in one direction from a glowing object. *Symbol* **cd** ⟨Latin = candle⟩

can·de·la·bra See CANDLE.

can·did ['kændɪd] *adj* **1** frank; honest: *candid criticism.* **2** fair; impartial: *a candid decision.* **3** of a photograph: **a** not posed. **b** taken without the subject's knowledge. **can·did·ly** *adv.* **can·dour** *or* **can·dor** *n.* ⟨Latin *candidus* white⟩ **candid camera** a camera for photographing people without their knowledge. **on candid camera** being photographed unawares.

can·di·date ['kændə,deɪt] *or* ['kændədɪt] *n* **1** a person seeking, or proposed for, a certain honour or position: *There were two candidates for the award.* **2** a person taking an examination. **3** a person who seems to have a particular fate in store: *a likely candidate*

for prison. **can·di·da·cy** *n.* ⟨Latin *candidatus* clothed in a white toga; *candidus* white⟩

can·dle ['kændəl] *n* **1** a stick of wax or tallow with a wick in it, burned to give light. **2** anything shaped or used like a candle. *v* **1** test eggs by holding them in front of a light. **2** ✷ of ice, form into CANDLE ICE. ⟨Latin *candela; candere* shine⟩
burn the candle at both ends try to do more than one has energy or time for. **not hold a candle to** be far inferior to: *The cake from the bakery couldn't hold a candle to yours.*
can·de·la·brum [ˌkændə'læbrəm] *n, pl* **-bra** [-brə] *or* **-brums** Often, **candelabra** *used as sg* an ornamental candlestick with several branches for holding candles, or an electric light in imitation of this. **can·dle·fish** ✷ oolichan. **can·dle·hold·er** *or* **can·dle·stick** *n* a holder for a candle, to make it stand upright. **candle hour** a unit of light equal to the energy derived in one hour from a source of light with the intensity of one CANDELA. **candle ice** *or* **candled ice** ✷ ice on a river, lake, etc., that has deteriorated into masses of candlelike shapes, usually shortly before breakup. **can·dle·light** *n* light from a candle. **can·dle·lit** *adj.* **can·dle·pow·er** the intensity of light given by a standard candle, measured in candelas. **can·dle·wick** *n* a soft twisted cotton thread similar to that used for wicks. *adj* having a pattern made with such threads: *a candlewick bedspread.*

can·dour *or* **can·dor** See CANDID.

CANDU *or* **Candu** ['kæn'du] *n* ✷ a nuclear reactor made in Canada. ⟨*Can(ada)* + *d*euterium + *u*ranium⟩

C and W COUNTRY AND WESTERN.

can·dy ['kændi] *n* a confection made with sugar, flavouring, and other ingredients. *v* **1** cook or soak in sugar, or glaze with sugar. **2** of honey, syrup, etc., crystallize. **can·died** *adj.* ⟨French *(sucre) candi*; Persian *quand* sugar⟩ **candy apple** an apple on a stick, dipped in taffy or in a red candy glaze. **candy bar** *esp* US CHOCOLATE BAR. **candy cane** a stick of peppermint candy shaped like a cane and typically eaten at Christmastime. **candy floss** spun sugar candy; COTTON CANDY. **candy stripe** a narrow stripe of two alternating colours, generally red and white. **can·dy·strip·er** *n* a hospital volunteer (with reference to the former striped uniform).

cane [keɪn] *n* **1** a walking stick, usually with a curved end. **2** a hollow, jointed stem, as of a reed or bamboo. **3** a long, slender stem of a woody plant such as raspberry. *v* **1** make or repair with strips of rattan, bamboo, etc.: *to cane a chair seat.* **2** beat with or as if with a stick or rod. ⟨Greek *kanna* reed⟩ **cane sugar** sugar made from SUGAR CANE.

ca·nine ['keɪnaɪn] *adj* to do with dogs. *n* **1** dog. **2** in full, **canine tooth** one of the four pointed teeth next to the incisors; cuspid. ⟨Latin *canis* dog⟩

can·is·ter ['kænɪstər] *n* **1** a small storage box or can with a lid, esp for dry foods. **2** the main boxlike part of some vacuum cleaners, containing the motor and dirt bag. ⟨Greek *kanastron* basket⟩

can·ker ['kæŋkər] *n* **1** a spreading sore, esp one in the mouth. **2** a disease of plants that causes slow decay. **3** anything that destroys by a gradual eating away. ⟨Latin *cancer* crab, tumour, gangrene⟩

Can·Lit ['kæn'lɪt] *n* ✹ *Informal* Canadian Literature.

can·na·bis ['kænəbɪs] *n* **1** the dried flowering tops of the female hemp plant. Compare MARIJUANA, HASHISH. **2** hemp. ⟨Greek *kánnabis*⟩

can·nel·lo·ni [ˌkænə'louni] *n pl* large noodles stuffed with meat or cheese and baked in a tomato sauce. ⟨Italian *cannello* tube⟩

can·ni·bal ['kænəbəl] *n* **1** any person who eats human flesh. **2** an animal or fish that eats others of its own kind. **can·ni·bal·ism** *n*. **can·ni·bal·is·tic** *adj*. ⟨Spanish *Canibal,* from *Caribe* Carib⟩
can·ni·bal·ize *v* use the parts of (an old piece of equipment) to assemble or repair another.

can·non ['kænən] *n, pl* **-non** or **-nons 1** a big gun fixed to the ground or mounted on a carriage. **2** any analogous piece of equipment for shooting something.
v **1** fire at with a cannon. **2** make a loud noise like a cannon. **3** collide with a rush: *to cannon against a tree.* ⟨French *canon*⟩
can·non·ade *n* **1** a continuous firing of cannon. **2** a vehement verbal assault: *a political cannonade.* **cannon·ball** *n* **1** a large metal ball fired from a cannon. **2** in tennis, a driving serve. **3** a jump into water with the body in a curled-up position. *v* **1** perform a cannonball jump or serve. **2** move with speed and force. Also, for *n,* **cannon ball.**
cannon bone in hoofed animals, the long bone between the hock and the fetlock.
cannon fodder military personnel considered expendable in war. **can·non·ry** *n* heavy artillery.

can·not [kə'nɒt] *or* ['kænɒt] *v* can not.

can·ny ['kæni] *adj* **-ni·er, -ni·est 1** shrewd, esp in business. **2** thrifty. **3** *esp Scottish* a fortunate or lucky. **b** nice, good, pleasant, etc. **can·ni·ly** *adv*. **can·ni·ness** *n*. ⟨*can*[1]⟩

ca·noe [kə'nu] *n* a light, narrow boat moved by paddles. **ca·noe** *v*. **ca·noe·ist** *n*. ⟨Haitian *canoa;* Arawakan⟩

Ca·no·la [kə'noulə] *n Trademark* ✹ **1** any of several varieties of the rape plant with low amounts of erucic acid and glucosinolate. **2** a livestock meal prepared from its seed. ⟨Can(ada) + -ola; Latin *oleum* oil⟩

can·on ['kænən] *n* **1** a law of a church. **2** a common rule of judgment: *the canons of good taste.* **3** an official list of divinely inspired writings. **4** a list of the works of an author: *the Shakespearean canon.* **5** the list of saints. **6** any official list. **7** *Music* a round or fugue. **8** a clergy member belonging to a cathedral or to any of certain Roman Catholic orders.
ca·non·i·cal [kə'nɒnəkəl] *adj*. ⟨Greek *kanōn*⟩
can·on·ize *v* **1** declare (a dead person) a saint.

2 declare (writings) to be divinely inspired. **can·on·i·za·tion** *n*. **canon law** church law.

can·o·py ['kænəpi] *n* **1** a covering fixed over a bed, entrance, etc. **2** any rooflike covering: *the canopy of the forest.* ⟨Greek *kōnōpeion* couch with mosquito net curtains; *kōnōps* gnat⟩

cant [kænt] *n* **1** glib talk. **2** the peculiar language of a special group, including words incomprehensible to outsiders: *thieves' cant.* **cant** *adj*. ⟨Latin *cantus* song⟩

can·ta·loupe *or* **can·ta·loup** ['kæntəˌloup] *n* a variety of muskmelon with orange flesh. ⟨Italian *Cantalupo,* where first cultivated⟩

can·tan·ker·ous [kæn'tæŋkərəs] *adj* cranky; ill-tempered; crabby. **can·tan·ker·ous·ly** *adv*. **can·tan·ker·ous·ness** *n*. ⟨Middle English *contecker* contentious person⟩

can·ta·ta [kən'tɑtə] *or* [kən'tætə] *n* a musical composition telling a story, sung by a chorus and soloists. ⟨Italian = that which is sung⟩

can·teen [kæn'tin] *n* **1** a small, usually round, flat container for carrying water or other drinks. **2** a snack bar or cafeteria in an institution; tuck shop. **3** a set of cutlery in a box or case. ⟨Italian *cantina* cellar⟩

can·ter ['kæntər] *n* a horse's gait faster than a trot but slower than a gallop. **can·ter** *v*. ⟨the pace of pilgrims riding to *Canterbury*⟩

can·ti·cle ['kæntəkəl] *n Poetic* a song, esp one with words from the Bible. ⟨Latin *canticulum* little song; *cantus* song⟩

can·ti·lev·er ['kæntəˌlivər] *or* [-ˌlɛvər] *n* a large, projecting bracket fastened at one end, supporting a balcony, bridge, etc.
v extend outward on or like a cantilever: *The artist's studio cantilevers out over a sheer cliff.* ⟨origin uncertain⟩
cantilever bridge a bridge made of two cantilevers whose projecting ends meet.

can·to ['kæntou] *n* one of the main divisions of a long poem. ⟨Italian; Latin *cantus* song⟩

can·ton ['kæntən] *or* ['kæntɒn]; *French,* [kɑ̃'tɔ̃] *n* **1** any of the 22 divisions of Switzerland. **2** ✹ *Québec* a municipal unit much like a township. **3** *Heraldry* a rectangular section in the upper corner of a shield or flag. ⟨French⟩
Can·ton·ese [ˌkæntə'niz] *n, pl* **-ese 1** a native or inhabitant of Canton, a city in S China. **2** the language spoken in and around Canton, in Hong Kong, etc. **Can·ton·ese** *adj*.

can·tor ['kæntər] *or* ['kæntɔr] *n* **1** a singer who leads a church choir. **2** liturgical soloist in a synagogue. ⟨Latin = singer; *canere* sing⟩

Ca·nuck [kə'nʌk] *n, adj* ✹ *Informal* Canadian. ⟨origin uncertain⟩

can·vas ['kænvəs] *n* **1** a strong cotton cloth used to make tents, sails, clothing, etc. **2** a sail. **3** a picture painted on canvas: *She's got seven canvases ready for the show.* ⟨Old French *canevas;* Latin *cannabis* hemp⟩
under canvas a in tents. **b** with sails spread: *The boat left the harbour under canvas.*
can·vas·back *n* a North American diving duck.

can·vass ['kænvəs] *v* **1** call or visit residents

of (a street, area, etc.) to ask for donations, votes, opinions, etc. **2** examine: *canvassing the newspapers for job ads.* **3** discuss fully. **can·vass** *n.* **can·vass·er** *n.* ⟨*canvas* orig toss (someone) in a sheet; later, shake out, discuss⟩

can·yon [ˈkænjən] *n* a narrow valley, usually with a stream at the bottom. Also, **ca·ñon.** ⟨Spanish *cañón* tube; Latin *canna* cane⟩

cap [kæp] *n* **1** a close-fitting head covering, usually with little or no brim. **2** a lid; cover for the top or end: *a bottle cap.* **3** a part like a cap, as the top of a mushroom. **4** the highest part. **5** an imposed maximum: *a cap on class size.* **6** a small quantity of explosive forming one of a series of dots on a paper strip. *v* **capped, cap·ping 1** put a cap on. **2** cover the top or end of. **3** be or put the finishing touch to. **4** match with something good or better: *I bet you can't cap that one.* **cap·ful** *n.* **cap·less** *adj.* ⟨Latin *cappa*⟩. **cap in hand** humbly; penitently. **cap gun** a toy gun that discharges caps (def. 6). **cap·stone** *n* **1** the top stone of a wall or other structure. **2** a finishing touch; climax.

ca·pa·ble [ˈkeipəbəl] *adj* fit; able to do a good job: *a capable teacher.* **ca·pa·bil·i·ty** *n.* **ca·pa·ble·ness** *n.* **ca·pa·bly** *adv.* ⟨Latin *capabilis*⟩ **capable of a** having ability, power, or fitness for: *capable of great things, capable of going 1500 km/h.* **b** open to: *a statement capable of many interpretations.*

SYNONYMS

Capable emphasizes dependability and efficiency, while **able** emphasizes skill, expertise, or natural talent. **Competent** suggests meeting or exceeding minimum standards of performance.

---

ca·pac·i·tor [kəˈpæsətər] *n* CONDENSER (def. 1). **ca·pa·ci·tance** *n* the ability of a capacitor to collect and store a charge of electricity.

ca·pac·i·ty [kəˈpæsəti] *n* **1** ability to hold or contain: *The theatre has a capacity of 500.* **2** ability: *a great capacity for learning.* **3** role; position: *He was acting in his capacity as guardian.* ⟨Latin *capacitas; capere* take⟩ **ca·pa·cious** [kəˈpeiʃəs] *adj* roomy; able to hold much: *capacious closets.* **ca·pa·cious·ness** *n.*

cape¹ [keip] *n* a sleeveless outer garment that falls loosely from the shoulders. ⟨French; Latin *cappa.* Related to CAP.⟩

cape² [keip] *n* a point of land extending into the water. ⟨French *cap;* Latin *caput* head⟩ **Cape Breton Island** a large island to the northeast of Nova Scotia.

ca·per¹ [ˈkeipər] *v* jump around playfully. *n* **1** a playful jump. **2** a playful or dishonest trick or scheme. ⟨shortened from *capriole*⟩ **cut a caper** or **cut capers** behave in a frolicsome, playful way.

ca·per² [ˈkeipər] *n* **1** the edible flower bud of a prickly Mediterranean shrub. **2** this shrub. ⟨Middle English *capres;* Greek *kapparis*⟩

cap·il·lar·y [kəˈpɪləri] *or* [ˈkæpəˌlɛri] *n* **1** one of the very tiny blood vessels connecting the smallest arteries with the smallest veins.

2 any very slender tube. *adj* of or like a capillary. ⟨Latin *capillus* hair⟩

cap·i·ta See PER CAPITA.

cap·i·tal [ˈkæpətəl] *n* **1 a** a city which is a centre of government. **b** a chief centre for some industry, activity, etc.: *the sugar capital of the Caribbean.* **2** an upper-case letter, as A, B, C, etc. **3 a** money or property with which a company carries on business. **b** money that is or can be invested. **c** the people who dispose of it, as a class. **d** *Accounting* the net worth of a business after deduction of taxes and other liabilities. **4** the top part of a column or pillar. *adj* **1** being or having to do with capital or a capital. **2** leading; major. **3** of an offence, punishable by death. **cap·i·tal·ly** *adv.* ⟨Latin *capitalis; caput* head⟩ **make capital (out) of** take advantage of: *He made capital of his mother's fame to get the job.* **capital expenditure** the money spent by a business on building and equipment, not on operating expenses. **capital gain** profits from the sale of assets. **capital goods** *Economics* goods, such as machinery, that can be used to produce other goods. Compare CONSUMER GOODS. **cap·i·tal–in·ten·sive** *adj* requiring the investment of a lot of money. Compare LABOUR-INTENSIVE. **cap·i·tal·ism** *n* an economic system in which the means of production are privately owned. Compare COMMUNISM and SOCIALISM. **cap·i·tal·ist** *n* **1** an adherent of this system. **2** a wealthy, powerful person in such a system. **cap·i·tal·ist** *adj.* **cap·i·tal·is·tic** *adj.* **cap·i·tal·ize** *v* **1** write with an upper-case initial letter. **2** turn into capital. **3** take advantage (with *on*): *We capitalized on the hot weather by selling cold pop.* **cap·i·tal·i·za·tion** *n.* **capital letter** upper-case letter. **capital punishment** the death penalty for a crime.

ca·pit·u·late [kəˈpɪtʃəˌleit] *v* surrender; stop resisting. **ca·pit·u·la·tion** *n.* ⟨Latin *capitulare* draw up under separate heads; *caput* head⟩

cap·let [ˈkæplɪt] *n* an oblong, coated pill.

cap·lin or **cape·lin** [ˈkæplɪn] *or* [ˈkeiplɪn] *n* a small fish of the smelt family found in N Atlantic and Pacific coastal waters.

Cap'n [kæpn] *or* [kæpm] *n* Captain.

ca·po [ˈkeipou] *n* a device fastened over the strings of a guitar to change key. ⟨Italian = chief, head⟩

ca·pon [ˈkeipɒn] *or* [ˈkeipən] *n* a rooster that has been castrated to improve the flesh for eating. ⟨Latin *capo, caponis*⟩

cap·puc·ci·no [ˌkæpəˈtʃinou] *n* coffee, esp espresso, served with hot milk or cream, and often flavoured with cinnamon, chocolate, liqueur, etc. ⟨Italian = Capuchin; it is light brown like a Capuchin's habit⟩

ca·price [kəˈpris] *n* **1** a sudden arbitrary change of mind; whim. **2** a tendency to act on such whims: *Her withdrawal of the research grant was pure caprice.* **ca·pri·cious** [kəˈprɪʃəs] *or* [kəˈpriʃəs] *adj.* **ca·pri·cious·ly** *adv.* **ca·pri·cious·ness** *n.* ⟨French; Italian *capriccio*⟩

cap·si·cum [ˈkæpsəkəm] *n* any of a genus of

small, tropical shrubs of the nightshade family bearing peppers. ⟨Latin *capsa* box⟩

cap·size ['kæpsaɪz] *or* [kæp'saɪz] *v* of a boat, turn bottom up; overturn. ⟨origin unknown⟩

cap·stan ['kæpstən] *n* a machine for lifting or pulling, like a winch set on end. A ship's anchor is hoisted by means of a capstan. ⟨Latin *capistrum* halter; *capere* take⟩

cap·sule ['kæpsəl] *or* ['kæpsjul] *n* **1** a small soluble container enclosing a dose of medicine. **2** the enclosed front section of a rocket, carrying the instruments, astronauts, etc. **3** a concise summary. **4** *Botany* a dry seedcase that opens when ripe. **cap·su·lar** *adj*.

cap·tain ['kæptən] *n* **1** the commander of a ship or commercial flight crew. **2** the leader of a sports team. **3** any leader. **4** *Canadian Forces* an officer ranking above a lieutenant and below a major. *Abbrev* **Capt. b** in Maritime Command, the equivalent of a colonel. *Abbrev* **Capt.(N) 5** a police or fire department officer ranking next above a lieutenant. **cap·tain** *v*. **cap·tain·cy** *n*. ⟨Latin *capitaneus* chief; *caput* head⟩

cap·tion ['kæpʃən] *n* **1** text accompanying a picture. **2** a subtitle in a film. **cap·tion** *v*. ⟨Latin *captio* a taking; *capere* take⟩

cap·tious ['kæpʃəs] *adj* **1** hard to please. **2** made only to pick a quarrel: *captious arguments*. **cap·tious·ly** *adv*. **cap·tious·ness** *n*. ⟨Latin *captiosus; capere* take⟩

cap·tive ['kæptɪv] *n* a person or animal taken and held by force, skill, or trickery. *adj* **1** taken or caught and kept under control: *a captive balloon, captive soldiers*. **2** having no choice: *a captive audience, a captive market*. **cap·tiv·i·ty** *n*. ⟨Latin *captivus; capere* take⟩

cap·ti·vate *v* hold the attention of: *captivated by the adventure story*. **cap·ti·vat·ing·ly** *adv*. **cap·ti·va·tion** *n*. **cap·tor** *n* one who takes or holds a prisoner. **cap·ture** ['kæptʃər] *v* **1** take by force, skill, or trickery. **2** attract and hold: *The tinkling bell captured the baby's attention*. **3** succeed in preserving or portraying: *The artist was able to capture the mood of a rainy fall day*. **cap·ture** *n*.

cap·u·chin ['kæpjuˌʃɪn] *or* ['kæpjuˌtʃɪn] *n* **1** any of a genus of South American monkeys typically having a thick, cowl-like crown of hair. **2 Capuchin** a friar of a branch of the Franciscan order distinguished by a long, pointed hood or cowl. ⟨Italian *cappuccio* hood⟩

cap·y·ba·ra [ˌkæpə'barə] *n* a semiaquatic rodent of tropical America. ⟨native name⟩

car [kar] *n* **1** a relatively small passenger vehicle with its own engine, used on roads. **2** a vehicle that runs on rails, such as a railway car or a streetcar, or that is pulled by a cable. **3** the closed platform of an elevator. **car·ful** *n*. ⟨Latin *carrus* two-wheeled cart⟩ **car·fare** *n* the money that must be paid for using public transit. **car·jack·ing** *n Informal* theft of a car by using force or threats against the driver. **car·jack** *v*. **car·load** *n* the number or amount that a car can carry. **car pool** an arrangement by which members of a group

take turns using their own cars to transport the group. **car·pool** *v*. **car·port** *n* a roofed shelter attached to a house, for one or more cars. **car seat 1** the seat of a car. **2** a portable safety seat for a child's use in a car, held in place by the car's seat belt. **car–sick** *adj* nauseated by the motion of a car, train, etc. **car–sick·ness** *n*. **car·wash** *n* a place where cars and other light vehicles are washed, usually by machine.

car·a·cal ['kærəˌkæl] *or* ['kɛrəˌkæl] *n* a small wildcat of African and Asian desert regions. Also called **Persian lynx, desert lynx**.

ca·rafe [kə'ræf] *n* a tall, slim jug to hold wine, water, etc. at table. An insulated variety holds hot drinks. ⟨Arabic *gharrâf*⟩

car·a·ga·na [ˌkɛrə'gænə] *or* [ˌkærə'gænə] *n* any of a genus of shrubs or small trees of the legume family, suited to dry climates and popular as windbreaks on the Prairies. ⟨Tatar⟩

car·a·mel ['kɛrəməl], ['kærəməl], *or* ['karməl] *n* **1** sugar browned over heat. **2** a chewy candy flavoured with this. **car·a·mel·ize** *v*. **car·a·me·li·za·tion** *n*. ⟨Spanish *caramelo*⟩

car·a·pace ['kɛrəˌpeɪs] *or* ['kærəˌpeɪs] *n* the shell on the back of a turtle, lobster, etc. ⟨Spanish *carapacho*⟩

car·at ['kɛrət] *or* ['kærət] *n* **1** a unit of mass for precious stones, equal to 200 mg. **2** See KARAT. ⟨Greek *keration* small horn-shaped bean used as a weight; *keras* horn⟩

car·a·van ['kɛrəˌvæn] *or* ['kærəˌvæn] *n* **1** a group of vehicles or beasts of burden carrying people who are travelling together. **2** a large covered wagon. **car·a·van, -vanned, -van·ning** *v*. ⟨French *caravane;* Persian *karwan*⟩

car·a·way ['kɛrəˌweɪ] *or* ['kærəˌweɪ] *n* a herb of the parsley family with a fragrant fruit usually called **caraway seed**. ⟨Arabic *karawya*⟩

car·bide, car·bo·hy·drate See CARBON.

car·bine ['karbaɪn] *or* ['karbɪn] *n* a short, light rifle. ⟨French *carabine*⟩

carbolic acid [kar'bɒlɪk] a poisonous, corrosive compound present in tar, used as a disinfectant and antiseptic; phenol.

car·bon ['karbən] *n* a very common non-metallic element found in combination with other elements in all plants and animals. *Symbol* **C**. **car·bon** *adj*. **car·bo·na·ceous** *adj*. ⟨Latin *carbo* coal⟩ **car·bide** *n* a compound of carbon with a metal. **car·bo·hy·drate** [ˌkarbə'haɪdreɪt] *n* any of a group of compounds composed of carbon, hydrogen, and oxygen that take part in the chemical processes in living plants and animals. Sugar and starch are carbohydrates. **car·bon–12** the most common isotope of carbon, used for determining the atomic mass of chemical elements. **car·bon–13** a stable isotope of carbon, used as a tracer in cancer research. **car·bon–14** a radioactive isotope of carbon, used in CARBON DATING. *Abbrev* **C14 carbon arc** a curved stream of light formed when a strong electric current jumps from one carbon electrode to another.

car·bon·ate *n* ['kɑrbənɪt] *or* ['kɑrbə,neɪt] a salt or ester of CARBONIC ACID. *v* ['kɑrbə,neɪt] **1** charge (liquid) with carbon dioxide to make it fizzy. **2** burn to carbon. **car·bon·a·tion** *n*.

carbon black a smooth, black powdered pigment consisting of pure carbon formed by deposits from burning gas, oil, etc. **carbon copy 1** a copy made with CARBON PAPER. **2** a copy of an e-mail sent simultaneously to another person. **3** any seemingly exact copy: *His ideas are a carbon copy of his dad's.* **carbon–copy** *v* send a carbon copy to. **carbon cycle 1** *Physics* the process whereby nuclear changes in the interior of stars gradually transform hydrogen to helium by liberating atomic energy. **2** *Biology* the circulation of carbon in nature. **car·bon–date** *v* measure the age of any carbonaceous material by checking the extent to which the carbon-14 in it has disintegrated. **carbon-dating** *n*. **carbon dioxide** a colourless, odourless gas present in the atmosphere, breathed out by animals and absorbed by plants. **car·bon·ic acid** the acid formed when carbon dioxide is dissolved in water. **Car·bon·if·er·ous** *n Geology* a period beginning about 360 million years ago, in the Paleozoic era, when the warm, moist climate produced a rank growth of tree ferns, etc, whose remains form the great coal beds. *adj* **1** of this period. **2 carboniferous** yielding coal. **carbon monoxide** a colourless, odourless, poisonous gas formed when carbon burns with an insufficient supply of air. It is found in car exhaust. **carbon paper** a thin paper with carbon or some other inky substance on one surface, placed between sheets of regular paper to make copies of whatever is written or typed on top. **Car·bo·run·dum** *n* an extremely hard compound of carbon and silicon, used for grinding, polishing, etc.

car·bun·cle ['kɑrbʌŋkəl] *n* **1** a severe boil. **2** *Archaic* a deep red jewel not cut in facets. ⟨Latin *carbunculus; carbo* coal⟩

car·bu·re·tor *or* **car·bu·ret·tor** ['kɑrbə,reɪtər] *n* a device for sending air through liquid fuel so as to produce an explosive mixture. **car·bu·re·tion** *n*. ⟨*carbon*⟩

car·cass ['kɑrkəs] *n* **1** the body of a dead animal. **2** the shell or framework of a thing that no longer functions. ⟨Italian *carcassa*⟩

car·cin·o·gen [kɑr'sɪnədʒən] *n* any substance that potentially causes cancer. **car·cin·o·gen·ic** [,kɑrsɪnə'dʒɛnɪk] *adj*. **car·cin·o·gen·e·sis** *n*. ⟨Greek *karkinōma* ulcer + *-gen*⟩ **car·ci·no·ma** [,kɑrsə'noumə] *n*, *pl* **-mas** *or* **-ma·ta** [-mətə] a cancerous growth; tumour. **car·ci·no·ma·tous** *adj*.

card¹ [kɑrd] *n* **1** a small, rectangular piece of stiff paper, cardboard, or thin plastic: *business card, credit card, score card.* **2** PLAYING CARD. **3 cards** *pl* any of various games played with a set of playing cards or other marked cards. **4** a piece of paper, usually folded and printed with a graphic and message, sent or given to acknowledge a special occasion such as a birthday. **5** POSTCARD. **6** *Informal* an amusing person. **7** *Computers* a circuit board giving specific capabilities: *graphics card, sound card.* Also called **expansion card, adapter, board.** ⟨French *carte;* Greek *chartēs* papyrus leaf⟩

card up one's sleeve a plan in reserve. **hold all the cards** have complete control. **(not) in** or **on the cards** sure (not) to happen. **play one's cards well** (or **right,** etc.) act cleverly. **put (all) one's cards on the table** be perfectly frank about one's plans, resources, etc. **show one's cards** reveal one's plans.

card·board *n* fairly thick, stiff paper, used to make cards, boxes, etc. *adj* **1** made of cardboard. **2** unrealistic or poorly developed: *cardboard characters in a novel.* **card–car·ry·ing** *adj* being a firm adherent of some ideology: *a card-carrying anarchist.* **card catalogue** or **card index** a reference catalogue of cards individually listing books and other items in a library. **card file** a set of cards arranged systematically and containing information. **card·hold·er** *n* the bearer of a credit card or other card giving special rights. **card·sharp(er)** *n* a cheater at cards. **card table** a small, square folding table used for card games.

card² [kɑrd] *n* **1** a toothed tool for combing fibres to be spun. **2** a machine, or part of one, that performs the same function. **card** *v*. ⟨Latin *carere* to card; infl. by *carduus* thistle⟩

car·da·mom or **car·da·mum** ['kɑrdəməm] *n* a spice of the ginger family. Also, **car·da·mon** [-mən]. ⟨Greek *kardamōmon*⟩

car·di·ac ['kɑrdi,æk] *adj* to do with the heart: *cardiac symptoms.* ⟨Greek *kardia* heart⟩ **cardiac arrest** heart failure. **car·di·o·gram** *n* a graphic record of the action of the heart. **car·di·o·graph** *n* an instrument that records the action of the heart. **car·di·og·ra·phy** *n*. **car·di·oid** *n Mathematics* the heart-shaped path traced by a point on a circle which is rolling around an equal-sized fixed circle. **car·di·ol·o·gy** *n* the branch of medicine dealing with heart diseases. **car·di·ol·o·gist** *n*. **car·di·o·pul·mon·a·ry** [,kɑrdiou'pʌlmə,nɛri] *adj* of the heart and lungs and their interaction. **cardiopulmonary resuscitation** a lifesaving technique that combines mouth-to-mouth respiration with rhythmic pressure on the heart. *Abbrev* **CPR. car·di·o·vas·cu·lar** *adj* of the heart and blood vessels together.

car·di·gan ['kɑrdəgən] *n* a sweater that opens down the front. ⟨Earl of *Cardigan*⟩

car·di·nal ['kɑrdənəl] *adj* **1** main; principal: *Her idea was of cardinal importance to the plan.* **2** bright red.
n **1** *Roman Catholic Church* one of the high officials second to the Pope, distinguished by their red robes. **2** a North American songbird, the male having bright red plumage. ⟨Latin *cardinalis* chief; *cardo* hinge⟩ **cardinal number** any of the numbers such as one, fifteen, eight hundred, etc., that show quantity and are used in simple counting. Compare ORDINAL NUMBER. **cardinal points** the four main directions of the compass; north, south, east, and west. **cardinal virtues** justice, prudence, temperance, and fortitude.

care [kɛr] *n* **1** watchful keeping: *The child was left in his sister's care.* **2** the supplying of food, shelter, protection, medical treatment, emotional support, and whatever else is needed for well-being. **3** serious attention to what one is doing: *Handle with care.* **4** worry or a cause of worry: *Few people are completely free from care.*
v **1** be concerned or interested: *We care about conservation.* **2** wish: *They said they didn't care to come.* **3** to object; mind (usually in negative or interrogative): *Will he care if I borrow his sweater?* **car·er** *n.* ⟨Old English *caru*⟩
care for a like: *She doesn't care for him.* **b** want: *I don't care for any dessert.* **c** look after: *The nurse will care for him.* **couldn't care less** be totally unconcerned. Often, **could care less. have a care** be careful. **(in) care of** at the address or in the charge of: *Send it care of her father. Symbol* **c/o. take care a** be careful. **b** *Informal* an expression of farewell. **take care of a** attend to: *The waiter will take care of your order.* **b** look after: *He has to take care of his little sister.* **c** be careful with: *Take care of your money.* **d** deal with conclusively: *That takes care of that little problem.*
care·ful *adj* **1** giving thought and attention to what one is doing. **2** avoiding risk. **care·ful·ly** *adv.* **care·ful·ness** *n.* **care·free** *adj* with nothing to worry about. **care·giv·er** *n* anyone who looks after another, whether paid or not. **care·less** *adj* **1** sloppy; giving little thought to what one is doing. **2** not caring; indifferent: *careless of the needs of others.* **care·less·ly** *adv.* **care·less·ness** *n.* **care·tak·er** *n* **1** janitor. **2** (*adjl*) of a provisional government or management, functioning at a basic level pending accession of a new administration. **care·worn** *adj* affected by continuous worry.

SYNONYMS

Careful = giving serious attention to what one is doing, especially to details: *She is careful to tell the truth at all times.* **Cautious** = aware of possible dangers and guarding against them by taking no chances: *He is cautious about making promises.* **Wary** has a similar meaning but suggests a degree of suspicion: *She is wary of people who suddenly become very friendly.*

ca·reen [kə'rin] *v* **1** rush along with a bobbing or side-to-side movement: *The server careened among the tables, balancing a heavy tray on one hand.* **2** lean to one side: *The ship careened in the strong wind.* ⟨Latin *carina* keel⟩

ca·reer [kə'rir] *n* **1** a way of making a living, esp when pursued with some care and commitment: *a career in law.* **2** one's general course of action or progress through life.
v rush along wildly: *The runaway horse careered through the streets.*
adj seriously following a given profession: *a career diplomat.* ⟨French *carrière* race course; Latin *carrus* wagon⟩
ca·reer·ist *n* a person interested only in his or her own professional advancement, often at the expense of other people. **ca·reer·ism** *n.*

ca·ress [kə'rɛs] *n* a gentle, loving touch. **ca·ress** *v.* ⟨French *caresse;* Latin *carus* dear⟩

car·et ['kɛrət] *or* ['kærət] *n* a proofreader's mark (ʌ) showing where something should be inserted. ⟨Latin *caret* it is lacking⟩

car·go ['kargou] *n, pl* **-goes** *or* **-gos** a load of goods: *The ship unloaded its cargo of wheat.* ⟨Spanish; Latin *carrus* wagon⟩

Car·ib·be·an [ˌkɛrə'biən], [ˌkærə'biən], *or* [kə'rɪbiən] *adj* to do with the Caribbean Sea, north of South America, or the islands in it.

car·i·bou ['kɛrə,bu] *or* ['kærə,bu] *n, pl* **-bou** *or* **-bous** any of several subspecies of reindeer found in northern North America, of which the most widely spread are the **barren–ground caribou** and the **woodland caribou.** ⟨Algonquian *xalibu* pawer, from its habit of pawing snow in search of grass⟩
caribou bird ⚹ CANADA JAY. **Caribou Inuit** a member of a group of Inuit living in the Barren Ground west of Hudson Bay.

car·i·ca·ture ['kɛrəkətʃər] *or* ['kærəkətʃər] *n* **1** a cartoon, description, etc. that deliberately exaggerates the peculiarities of a subject. **2** a very poor imitation or rendition. **3** a very stereotyped character in a book, movie, etc. **car·i·ca·ture** *v.* **car·i·ca·tur·ist** *n.* ⟨Italian *caricatura; caricare* overload, exaggerate⟩

car·ies ['kɛriz] *or* ['kɛri,iz] *n* decay, esp of a tooth. ⟨Latin⟩

car·il·lon ['kɛrə,lɒn], ['kærə,lɒn], *or* [kə'rɪljən] *n* **1** a set of large bells arranged for playing melodies: *There is a carillon in the Peace Tower in Ottawa.* **2** an instrument simulating its sound. **car·il·lon·neur** [-'nər] *n.* ⟨French⟩

car·i·o·ca [ˌkɛri'oukə] *or* [ˌkær-] *n* a dance of South America. ⟨Brazilian Portuguese⟩

car·i·ole *or* **car·ri·ole** ['kɛrI,oul] *or* ['kær-] *n* **1** ⚹ **a** a light, open horse-drawn sleigh. **b** a dogsled for carrying freight or a single person lying down. **2** a small, one-horse carriage or covered cart. ⟨French; Latin *carrus* wagon⟩

car·mine ['karmaɪn] *or* ['karmən] *n, adj* deep red. ⟨Latin *carminium;* Arabic *qirmiz* the kermes insect + Latin *minium* red lead⟩

car·nage ['karnɪdʒ] *n* great slaughter or destruction. ⟨Latin *caro, carnis* flesh⟩

car·nal ['karnəl] *adj* **1** of purely physical pleasures or lusts; fleshly: *carnal vices such as gluttony.* **2** worldly; unspiritual. **car·nal·i·ty** *n.* **car·nal·ly** *adv.* ⟨Latin *caro, carnis* flesh⟩
carnal knowledge of sexual intimacy with.

car·na·tion [kar'neiʃən] *n* any of numerous cultivated varieties of pink with large, many-petalled flowers. ⟨Italian *carnagione* flesh tint⟩

car·ni·val ['karnəvəl] *n* **1** a fair or travelling show with rides, games, sideshows, etc. **2** an organized program of events around a certain sport, theme, etc.: *a water carnival.* **3** general merrymaking. **4** in some traditional Roman Catholic cultures, a time of merrymaking just before Lent. ⟨Latin *carnem levare* the putting away of meat (before Lent)⟩

car·ni·vore ['karnə,vɔr] *n* any animal that feeds chiefly on flesh. ⟨Latin *caro, carnis* flesh + *vorare* devour⟩

car·niv·o·rous *adj* **1** feeding on flesh. **2** of a plant, able to use animal substance as food.

car·ob ['kɛrəb] *or* ['kærəb] *n* an evergreen of the pea family with edible pods whose sweet flesh is used to make a substitute for chocolate. ⟨Arabic *kharrub* bean pod⟩

car·ol ['kɛrəl] *or* ['kærəl] *n* a song or hymn of joy, esp a seasonal one: *Christmas carols.* **car·ol, -olled** or **-oled, -ol·ling** or **-ol·ing** *v.* **car·ol·ler** or **car·ol·er** *n.* ⟨Greek *choraulēs; choros* dance + *aulos* flute⟩

car·om ['kɛrəm] *or* ['kærəm] *n* **1** *Billiards* a shot in which the ball struck with the cue hits two balls, one after the other. **2** a ricochet. **car·om** *v.* ⟨Spanish *carambola*⟩

car·o·tene ['kɛrə,tin] *or* ['kærə,tin] *n* a reddish pigment found in carrots, converted by the body into vitamin A. Also, **car·o·tin.** ⟨Latin *carota* carrot⟩

ca·rot·id [kə'rɒtɪd] *n* either of two large arteries, one on each side of the neck, that carry blood to the head. **ca·rot·id** *adj.* ⟨Greek *karōtides; karos* stupor (caused by compression of carotids)⟩

ca·rouse [kə'raʊz] *v* drink and feast noisily; party. **ca·rous·al** *n.* **ca·rouse** *n.* **ca·rous·er** *n.* ⟨German *gar aus(trinken)* (drink) all up⟩

car·ou·sel or **car·rou·sel** ['kɛrə,sɛl] *or* ['kær-], [,kɛrə'sɛl] *or* [,kær-] *n* **1** a merry-go-round. **2** at an airport, a revolving platform for baggage. **3** the rotating slide holder on a projector. ⟨Italian *carosello;* Latin *carrus* cart⟩

carp¹ [kɑrp] *v* find fault; complain. **carp·er** *n.* **carp·ing·ly** *adv.* ⟨Old Norse *karpa* wrangle⟩

carp² [kɑrp] *n, pl* **carp** or **carps** a freshwater food fish of the minnow family. ⟨Latin *carpa*⟩

car·pal ['kɑrpəl] *adj* to do with the **carpus,** the bones of the wrist. ⟨Greek *karpos* wrist⟩

carpal tunnel syndrome pain or numbness in the hand and wrist due to highly repetitive movements as in keyboarding.

car·pe di·em ['kɑrpei 'diəm] *Latin* make the most of the present. ⟨literally, seize the day⟩

car·pel ['kɑrpəl] *n* the central part of a flower, containing the ovules, which develop into seeds. ⟨Greek *karpos* fruit⟩

car·pen·ter ['kɑrpəntər] *n* a person skilled in the trade or art of building wooden structures. **car·pen·ter** *v.* **car·pen·try** *n.* ⟨Latin *carpentarius; carpentum* wagon⟩

carpenter ant any of several large ants which eat complex burrows in wood.

car·pet ['kɑrpɪt] *n* **1** a thick, heavy, woven covering for floors and stairs. **2** anything like a carpet: *a carpet of grass.* **car·pet** *v.* ⟨Latin *carpeta* thick cloth; *carpere* to card (wool)⟩ **on the carpet a** being considered or discussed. **b** *Informal* being scolded or rebuked.

car·pet–bomb *v* bomb (a wide area) with many bombs. **car·pet–bomb·ing** *n.* **car·pet·ing** *n* carpets in general or carpet material.

car·ra·geen or **car·ra·gheen** ['kɛrə,gin] *or* ['kærə,gin] *n* an edible seaweed yielding an emulsifying agent used in pharmaceuticals,

cosmetics, some foods, etc. Also, **car·a·geen.** ⟨*Carragheen,* Ireland, where it is abundant⟩

car·ra·geen·an *n* a derivative of carrageen used as an emulsifier. Also, **car·a·geen·an.**

car·rel ['kɛrəl] *or* ['kærəl] *n* an enclosed space for individual study in a library. Sometimes, **car·rell.** ⟨Middle English *carole* ring⟩

car·riage ['kɛrɪdʒ] *or* ['kærɪdʒ] *n* **1** a horse-drawn vehicle on four wheels. **2** a wheeled, padded cart to push a baby in. **3** any other wheeled vehicle. **4** posture and bearing: *She has a queenly carriage.* **5** the act, fact, or cost of carrying. **6** a part that supports something as it moves: *a gun carriage.* ⟨Old French *cariage; carier* carry. See CARRY.⟩

carriage bolt a bolt whose round shaft has a square part just under the head. **carriage trade** wealthy clientele.

car·ri·er ['kɛriər] *or* ['kæriər] *n* **1** a person, company, or thing that carries or transports people or things. **2** a person or animal that carries a disease. **3** *Genetics* an individual carrying a given mutant allele paired with a normal one. **4 Carrier** See WET'SUWET'EN.

car·ri·on ['kɛriən] *or* ['kæriən] *n* **1** dead and decaying flesh. **2** rottenness; filth. **car·ri·on** *adj.* ⟨Old French *carogne;* Latin *caro* flesh⟩

car·rot ['kɛrət] *or* ['kærət] *n* **1** a cultivated herb of the parsley family with a long, tapered orange root used as a vegetable. **2** a promise of reward, used as an incentive. **car·rot·y** *adj.* ⟨Greek *karōton*⟩

car·ry ['kɛri] *or* ['kæri] *v* **1 a** hold and take from one place to another. **b** have on one's person: *to carry identification.* **2** bear the weight of: *Pillars carry the roof.* **3** hold (one's body, head, etc.) in a certain way. **4** be or get passed by a decision-making body: *The motion to adjourn was carried. The amendment carried.* **5** win: *The NDP carried nine ridings.* **6** extend: *to carry a road into the mountains.* **7** cover a (given) distance: *Her voice carries to the back of the room.* **8** stock: *This store carries men's wear.* **9** print: *The paper carried an article on child poverty.* **10** have as an attribute or result: *Her opinions carry great weight around here.* **11** sing (a tune) with correct pitch. **12** be pregnant with. **13** *Arithmetic* in adding, transfer (a value) to the next column on the left. **14** drink (alcohol) without showing the effect: *He can't carry his liquor.* **15** host (a disease germ) and pass it to others without having symptoms oneself. ⟨Old French *carier;* Latin *carricare* from *carrus* cart⟩ **carried away** affected so strongly by emotion that it interferes with one's reason. **carry everything before one** have uninterrupted success. **carry forward a** proceed with. **b** in bookkeeping, re-enter in a later column of an accounting record. **carry off a** win (a prize, honour, etc.). **b** do successfully: *It was her first speech, but she carried it off all right.* **c** take away by force. **carry on a** manage or conduct over time: *to carry on a business, to carry on a* *relationship.* **b** continue or resume: *Carry on from where you left off.* **c** *Informal* act wildly, comically, or foolishly. **d** talk at length: *What's he carrying on about now?* **carry out** do; perform. **carry over a** extend or renew beyond the original period. **b** keep until later. **c** transfer. **carry the ball** *Informal* be the chief participant in an activity. **carry the day** be victorious. **carry through a** bring (a task) to completion. **b** bring through trouble. **car·ry·all** *n* a large bag or basket. **carrying charge** interest charged on money owing. **car·ry·ing–on** *n* fuss. **car·ry·ings–on** *n* indiscreet behaviour. **carrying place ＊** a portage. **car·ry–on** *adj* of a piece of luggage, small enough to go under an airplane seat.

cart [kɑrt] *n* any of various small, wheeled vehicles for carrying loads, moved by hand. *v* **1** *Informal* **a** carry in an inconvenient or inelegant way: *carting that thing all over town. The demonstrators were carted off by the police.* **b** traipse. **2** carry by cart. ⟨Old Norse *kartr*⟩ **put** (or **have**) **the cart before the horse** switch the proper or natural order of things. **cart·age** *n* the cost of carting. **cart·load** *n* as much as a cart can carry. **cart·wheel** *n* **1** the wheel of a cart. **2** a sideways handspring. **cart·wheel** *v.* **do cartwheels** (usually ironic) be demonstratively joyful.

carte [kɑrt] *French n* BILL OF FARE. ⟨card⟩ **à la carte** as individual menu items. **carte blanche** [ˈkɑrt ˈblɑʃ] *French* [kaRtˈblɑʃ] freedom to do whatever one pleases. **carte du jour** [ˌkɑrt du ˈʒur] *French* [kaRtdyˈʒuR] the menu for a particular day.

car·tel [kɑrˈtɛl] *n* **1** a league of independent businesses formed to control production and marketing of goods. **2** an alliance of political groups for a common cause. ⟨Italian *cartello* little card[1] (with written challenge to a duel)⟩

Car·te·sian coordinates *Geometry* an ordered pair (or triple) of numbers by which one can plot, from a given starting point, the location of any point in space.

car·ti·lage [ˈkɑrtəlɪdʒ] *n* a tough, elastic tissue found in adults at the ends of the long bones, between the bones of the spine, in the nose, etc. ⟨Latin *cartilago*⟩ **car·ti·lag·i·nous** [ˌkɑrtəˈlædʒənəs] *adj* **1** of or like cartilage. **2** of fish, such as sharks, with a skeleton made of cartilage rather than bone.

car·tog·ra·phy [kɑrˈtɒgrəfi] *n* the making of maps or charts. **car·tog·ra·pher** *n.* ⟨Latin *carta* chart, map + English *-graphy*⟩

car·ton [ˈkɑrtən] *n* a boxlike container made of cardboard, often waxed. ⟨French = cardboard; Latin *charta* card⟩

car·toon [kɑrˈtun] *n* **1** a humorous drawing, usually in an exaggerated style. **2** ANIMATED CARTOON. **3** COMIC STRIP. **4** CARICATURE (def. 3). **car·toon·ist** *n.* ⟨*carton*; drawn on cardboard⟩

car·tridge [ˈkɑrtrɪdʒ] *n* **1** a tube containing a charge of explosive and, usually, shot or a bullet, for a firearm. **2** a sealed, replaceable container of toner for a printer, film for a camera, etc. ⟨French *cartouche* roll of paper⟩

carve [kɑrv] *v* **1** cut; make by cutting: *to carve a roast of meat, to carve a statue from marble.* **2** make by planned effort over time (often with *out*): *She is carving a niche for herself in that company.* ⟨Old English *ceorfan*⟩ **carv·er** *n* **1** a person who carves. **2** CARVING KNIFE. **carv·ing** *n* a piece of carved work: *wood carvings.* **carving fork** a large, long-handled fork to hold meat for carving. **carving knife** a large, sharp knife for carving meat. **carving set** a carving knife, carving fork, and a long steel for sharpening the knife.

Cas·a·no·va [ˌkæsəˈnouvə] *n* a man who has many romantic affairs. ⟨Giovanni J. *Casanova*, 18c Italian adventurer known for his *Memoirs*⟩

cas·cade [kæˈskeɪd] *n* **1** a small waterfall. **2** anything like a waterfall: *cascades of ruffles.* **3** a rapid series of events, each triggering the next. **cas·cade** *v.* ⟨*cascata*; Latin *cadere* fall⟩

case[1] [keɪs] *n* **1** an example: *a case of poor work.* **2** a situation: *worst-case scenario.* **3** a matter submitted to a court of law. **4** the facts making up an argument: *the case for gun control.* **5** a patient; person in need of social services. **6** *Grammar* in many languages, a form of a noun or adjective that shows its relation to other words in a sentence, for example, whether it is the doer, receiver, or means of an action. **7** *Slang* a peculiar person. ⟨Latin *casus* a fall, chance; *cadere* fall⟩ **be the case** be true. **get on** (or **off**) **someone's case** begin (or stop) nagging someone. **in any case a** under any circumstances: *In any case, let's prepare for the worst.* **b** nevertheless. **c** at least. **in case a** if. **b** so as to be prepared (if): *Keep this form in case they ask you for it later. Take your swimsuit just in case.* **in case of** if there should be: *In case of fire, do not use the elevators.* **in no case** under no circumstances. **case·hard·en** *v* **1** harden (iron or steel) on the surface. **2** make insensitive by long exposure. **case history** all the facts about a person that may be useful in deciding what treatment, services, etc. are needed. **case law** law based on previous judicial decisions. **case·load** *n* the number of cases handled by a court, a social worker, etc. in a given time. **case study 1** a research method in which a single case is studied intensively. **2** an apt example: *That firm was a case study in poor management.* **case·work** *n* thorough study of a person or persons and their situation by a social worker. **case·work·er** *n.*

Case and **instance** both mean 'example', but **case** usually applies to a whole situation exhibiting typical features: *The accident was a case of reckless driving.* **Instance** is usually more focussed and refers to a single fact or event exactly fitting a set of criteria: *Police noted six instances of running a red light.*

case[2] [keɪs] *n* **1** a strong, heavy box. **2** the cover or container designed for something: *a violin case.* *v* **1** put in a case. **2** *Informal* examine with a view to committing a crime: *The thieves cased the bank.* ⟨Latin *capsa* box; *capere* hold⟩

case·ment *n* a window opening on vertical hinges. **cas·ing** *n* **1** a snugly-fitting protective cover for something. **2** a cleaned intestine of an animal, enclosing sausage. **3** a pipe lining a well. **4** a frame: *the casing for a window.*

ca·sein ['keisin] *or* ['keisiɪn] *n* the protein, found esp in milk, which is the main ingredient of cheese. ⟨Latin *caseus* cheese⟩

cash [kæʃ] *n* **1** money in the form of coins and bills. **2** ready money on which cheques can be drawn, not credit or investments. *v* exchange for ready money: *I'll have to cash a cheque.* **cash·less** *adj.* **cash·a·ble** *adj.* ⟨Latin *capsa* box, coffer⟩
cash in on *Informal* **a** make a large profit from. **b** take advantage of. **cash in one's chips a** exchange poker chips, etc. for cash. **b** *Slang* die. **c** *Slang* retire.
cash–and–car·ry *adj* with payment by cash and no delivery service. **cash bar** a bar at a party where one pays for one's own drinks. **cash·book** *n* a record of money received and paid out. **cash cow** *Slang* a ready source of income. **cash crop** a crop grown for sale, not for consumption on the farm. **cash flow 1** the movement of funds in and out of a business, household, etc. **2** the balance between expenditures and income: *plenty of assets, but a negative cash flow.* **cash·ier** *n* **1** a person who has charge of money in a bank or business. **2** a person who takes money for goods at a store checkout. **cash on delivery** payment when goods are delivered. *Abbrev* **C.O.D.** or **c.o.d. cash register** a machine that records and shows the amount of a sale.

cash·ew ['kæʃu] *or* [kə'ʃu] *n* a kidney-shaped nut that grows on a species of evergreen tree of tropical and subtropical America. ⟨Brazilian Portuguese *acajú*; Tupi-Guarani⟩

cash·mere ['kæʃmir] *n* cloth made from the soft undercoat of a breed of goats raised esp in Kashmir and Tibet. ⟨*Kashmir*⟩

ca·si·no [kə'sinou] *n* a place for gambling, often with other entertainment also. ⟨Italian, diminutive of *casa* house; Latin *casa*⟩

cask [kæsk] *n* a container like a barrel, often smaller. ⟨Spanish *casco* skull, cask of wine⟩

cas·ket ['kæskɪt] *n, v* **1** coffin. **2** a small box for jewellery, etc. ⟨origin uncertain⟩

cas·sa·va [kə'savə] *or* [kə'sævə] *n* any of several tropical plants of the spurge family grown for their large, starchy edible roots. ⟨French *cassave*; Haitian *cacábi*⟩

cas·se·role ['kæsə,roul] *n* **1** an oven dish in which food can be both cooked and served. **2** a mixed dish so cooked, constituting a whole entree: *a chicken-and-rice casserole.* ⟨French, from *casse* pan; Greek *kyathos* cup⟩

cas·sette [kə'sɛt] *n* a sealed plastic case containing magnetic tape or film on reels or spools. ⟨French = little case⟩

cas·sia ['kæʃə] *or* ['kæsiə] *n* **1** a spice similar to cinnamon. **2** any of a genus of mainly tropical plants of the pea family, esp any yielding senna, a mild laxative. ⟨Old English; Hebrew *q'tsi'ah*⟩

cas·sock ['kæsək] *n* a long outer garment, usually black, worn by a member of the clergy. **cas·socked** *adj.* ⟨Italian *casacca*⟩

cas·so·war·y ['kæsə,wɛri] *n* any of three species of large, flightless birds of N Australia and nearby islands. ⟨Malay *kasuari*⟩

cast [kæst] *v* **cast, cast·ing 1** throw or toss; specifically: **a** dice or **b** the end of a fishing line (into water). **2** direct; turn: *She cast a glance in my direction.* **3** shed: *The snake cast its skin.* **4** shape by pouring into a mould to harden. **5 a** assign the various parts of (a play). **b** assign a part to (an actor).
n **1** the act or distance of throwing. **2** a mould or something that is made in it. **3** a plaster sheath for a body part, used to keep a broken bone in place while it is mending. **4** the actors in a play, movie, etc. **5** shape, kind, or appearance: *His face had a gloomy cast.* **6** tint: *a white dress with a pink cast.*
adj made by casting in a mould: *cast iron.* ⟨Old Norse *kasta* throw⟩
cast a ballot vote. **cast about** look around uncertainly. **cast aside** reject. **cast aspersions on** discredit. **cast away a** reject. **b** shipwreck or maroon. **cast·a·way** *n.* **cast back** return in memory or speech. **cast down a** turn (one's eyes, face, etc.) downward. **b** discourage. **cast lots** use lots to decide something: *We cast lots for first try on the raft.* **cast off a** untie a boat from its moorings. **b** *Knitting* make the last row of stitches. **cast on** *Knitting* make the first row of stitches. **cast out** banish; expel. **the die is cast** the future is decided.
cast·a·way *n* a shipwrecked person. **cast·er** or **cast·or** *n* a small swivelling wheel in the base of a piece of furniture, letting it roll. **cast iron** an alloy of iron, carbon, and silicon, poured into moulds to harden. **cast–i·ron** *adj* **1** made of this. **2** strong; firm: *a cast-iron will, a cast-iron alibi. He has a cast-iron stomach and can eat anything.* **cast–iron plant** an aspidistra often grown as a house plant. **cast·off** *adj* thrown away; abandoned. **cast·off** *n.*

cas·ta·net [,kæstə'nɛt] *n* a small rhythm instrument consisting of two parts held in the hand and clicked together. ⟨Spanish *castaneta*; Latin *castanea*⟩

caste [kæst] *n* **1** any of the hereditary social classes recognized in Hinduism. **2** (usually ironic) any of the classes in a highly stratified society. **3** *Zoology* any of the forms of a social insect differentiated by function.
lose caste lose social status. ⟨Portuguese *casta* race; Latin *castus* pure⟩

cas·ti·gate ['kæstə,geit] *v* criticize or punish severely. **cas·ti·ga·tion** *n.* **cas·ti·ga·tor** *n.* ⟨Latin *castigare*; *castus* pure⟩

cas·tle ['kæsəl] *n* **1** a building with thick walls and other defences against attack. **2** a large and imposing residence. **3** *Chess* rook. *v Chess* move the castle next to the king and then the king to the other side of the castle in the same turn. ⟨Latin *castellum* diminutive of *castrum* fort⟩
castle in the air or **in Spain** lovely daydream.

castor oil a yellow oil obtained from castor

beans, the seeds of the CASTOR-OIL PLANT, used as a cathartic, lubricant, etc.

cas·tor–oil plant a tall, tropical herb of the spurge family.

cas·trate ['kæstreit] *v.* **1** remove the testicles of; geld. **2** take away the strength or vitality of. **cas·tra·tion** *n.* ⟨Latin *castrare*⟩

cas·u·al ['kæʒuəl] *adj* **1** informal: *casual dress.* **2** having or showing no concern or interest: *a casual glance.* **3** happening by chance: *a casual meeting.* **4** not regular: *casual work.* **cas·u·al·ly** *adv.* **cas·u·al·ness** *n.* ⟨Latin *casualis; casus* chance⟩

cas·u·al·ty ['kæʒuəlti] *or* ['kæʒəlti] *n* **1** a person injured or killed in an accident or disaster, captured by the enemy in war, etc. **2** anything lost, harmed, or destroyed, usually by accident. **3** the accident itself.

cas·u·ist ['kæʒuɪst] *n* a person who reasons cleverly but falsely, esp on moral issues. **cas·u·is·tic** *adj.* **cas·u·is·ti·cal·ly** *adv.* **cas·u·ist·ry** *n.* ⟨Latin *casus* case⟩

cat [kæt] *n* **1** a small domestic mammal of the cat family. **2** any of a family of meat-eating mammals that have retractable claws. **3** *Informal* a spiteful woman. **4** *Slang* person. ⟨Old English *catt(e)*; Latin *catta*⟩ **let the cat out of the bag** tell a secret. **rain cats and dogs** rain very hard.

cat·bird *n* a songbird with a call like the mewing of a cat. **catbird seat** a position of advantage or power. **cat burglar** a burglar who excels in stealth or enters by skilful climbing. **cat·call** *n* a shrill cry or whistle of disapproval from someone in an audience. **cat·call** *v.* **cat·fish** *n, pl* **-fish** or **-fish·es** any of an order of mostly freshwater fishes with long, whiskerlike barbels around the mouth. **cat·gut** *n* very tough cord made from the dried and twisted intestines of animals, or an imitation of this, for stringing racquets and certain musical instruments. **cat·kin** *n* the fluffy spike of the flowers of willows, poplars, birches, etc. **cat·like** *adj* like a cat; especially, stealthy or nimble. **cat·nap** *n* a short nap or doze. **cat·nap, -napped, -nap·ping** *v.* **cat·nip** *n* a plant of the mint family with scented leaves that cats like. **cat–o'–nine–tails** *n* a whip consisting of usually nine pieces of knotted cord. **cat's cradle 1** a game in which a loop of string, stretched over the fingers in an intricate pattern, is passed from one player to another, each forming a new pattern. **2** something mixed up. **cat's–eye** *n* **1** a gem showing changes of colour suggesting a cat's eye. **2** one of a row of small reflectors on a road or curb acting as guides by catching the headlights of approaching vehicles. **3** a type of playing marble containing a green or blue swirl in the middle. **cat's–paw** or **cats·paw** *n* **1** a person used by another to do something hard or dangerous. **2** a light breeze ruffling a stretch of water. **cat·tail** or **cat–tail** *n* any of a genus of marsh plants with flowers that form long, brown spikes. **cat·ty** *adj* **1** mean; spiteful. **2** of or like cats. **cat·ti·ly** *adv.*

cat·ti·ness *n.* **cat·walk** *n* a high, narrow place to walk.

ca·tab·o·lism [kə'tæbə,lɪzəm] *n Biology* the process of breaking down living tissues into simpler substances or waste, releasing energy. **ca·ta·bol·ic** [,kætə'bɒlɪk] *adj.* **ca·tab·o·lize** *v.* ⟨Latin *cata-* down + (*meta*)*bolism*⟩

cat·a·clysm ['kætə,klɪzəm] *n* **1** any sudden, violent change in the earth such as a flood or earthquake. **2** a violent change: *the cataclysm of World War II.* **cat·a·clys·mic** *adj.* ⟨Greek *kataklysmos* flood; *kata-* down + *klyzein* wash⟩

cat·a·comb ['kætə,koum] *n* (usually *pl*) an underground gallery forming a burial place. ⟨Greek *kata-* down + *tymbos* among tombs⟩

cat·a·logue ['kætə,lɒg] *n* **1** a list of items in a collection. **2** a book printed for customers by a store or company, with pictures and prices of the items it sells. **3** a book issued by a university or college listing rules, courses, etc.; calendar. **4** any list; series: *a catalogue of lies.* **cat·a·logue** *v.* Also, *esp U.S.,* **cat·a·log. cat·a·logu·er** *n.* **cat·a·logu·ist** *n.* ⟨Greek *katadown + legein* count⟩

ca·tal·y·sis [kə'tæləsɪs] *n, pl* **-ses** [-,siz] *Chemistry* acceleration of a reaction by the presence of a substance not permanently affected. **cat·a·lyse** *v.* ['kætə,laɪz] **cat·a·lyst** *n.* **cat·a·lyt·ic** [,kætə'lɪtɪk] *adj.* ⟨Greek *kata-* down + *lysis* a loosening⟩ **catalytic converter** a device in the exhaust system of a vehicle, designed to control, by a chemical reaction, the emission of pollution.

cat·a·ma·ran [,kætəmə'ræn] *n* **1** a boat with two hulls or floats joined side by side by a frame. Compare TRIMARAN. **2 ⁂** a platform on two runners, used for hauling lumber, etc. ⟨Tamil *kattamaram* tied tree⟩

cat·a·mount ['kætə,maunt] *n* any of various wildcats such as the cougar or lynx. ⟨short for *catamountain* cat of (the) mountain⟩

cat·a·pult ['kætə,pʌlt] *n* **1** an ancient war machine for shooting stones, arrows, etc. **2** a device for launching an aircraft from a ship's deck. **3** slingshot. **cat·a·pult** *v.* ⟨Greek *kata-* down + *pallein* hurl⟩

cat·a·ract ['kætə,rækt] *n* **1** a large, steep waterfall. **2** a violent rush of water; flood. **3** an opaque condition that develops in the lens of the eye. ⟨Greek *katarrhaktēs; kata-* down + *arassein* dash⟩

ca·tarrh [kə'tɑr] *n* inflammation of a mucous membrane, usually of the nose or throat, as in a head cold. **ca·tarrh·ous** or **ca·tarrh·al** *adj.* ⟨Greek *kata-* down + *rheein* flow⟩

ca·tas·tro·phe [kə'tæstrəfi] *n* **1** a very great misfortune. **2** *Geology* a sudden, violent change such as an earthquake. **cat·a·stroph·ic** [,kætə'strɒfɪk] *adj.* **cat·a·stroph·i·cal·ly** *adv.* ⟨Greek *kata-* down + *strephein* turn⟩

cat·a·to·nia [,kætə'touniə] *n* a condition, especially symptomatic of schizophrenia, of stupor and rigidity, often alternating with psychotic excitement. **cat·a·ton·ic** [-'tɒnɪk] *adj.* ⟨Greek *kata-* down + *tonos* tension⟩

catch [kætʃ] *v* **caught, catch·ing 1** seize and hold (something moving): *She caught the child just as he reached the street.* **2** capture: *caught in a trap.* **3** become or cause to become hooked, pinched, or tangled: *My skirt caught on that nail.* **4** become affected by: *to catch the spirit, to catch a cold.* **5** hit suddenly and by surprise: *caught in the rain.* **6** discover; detect (secret action or the one doing it): *My mother caught me hiding her present.* **7** take or get suddenly or briefly: *I caught a glimpse of her. We caught the last few minutes of the show.* **8** meet and board: *to catch a bus.* **9** hear, see, understand, etc., by an effort: *Did you catch what he said?* **10** check suddenly: *She caught her breath.* **11** *Baseball* act as catcher. *n* **1** the act of catching, or the thing or amount caught. **2** a game of throwing and catching a ball: *They're outside playing catch.* **3** something that holds something else in place: *We can't fasten the windows because the catch is broken.* **4** *Informal* a person well worth marrying, hiring, etc. **5** a trick or hidden problem: *That's too good a deal—there must be a catch.* **6** a short stopping of the voice or breath: *a catch in his voice.* ⟨Old French *cachier*; Latin *captiare*, from *capere* take⟩

catch alight CATCH FIRE. **catch as catch can a** grab or wrestle in any way. **b** take whatever chances one gets. **catch at** try to grab: *She caught at the rope as it swung by her.* **catch fire a** start burning. **b** become enthusiastic. **catch in the act** or **catch red–handed** find someone in the process of doing something wrong. **catch it** *Informal* be scolded or punished: *I'll catch it if I'm late again.* **catch on** *Informal* **a** get the idea: *to catch on to a joke.* **b** become popular: *The song never caught on.* **catch out** discover doing wrong, esp habitually: *He always cheated, but they never did catch him out.* **catch sight of** notice: *The dog suddenly caught sight of the cat.* **catch someone's eye** attract and hold someone's gaze or attention. **catch up a** come up even (*with* or *to* a person or thing going the same way): *He ran hard, trying to catch up with his sister.* **b** pick up suddenly and lift: *He caught the child up in his arms.* **c** become too much for (with *with*): *Her late nights were beginning to catch up with her.* **d** bring or get up to date; make up for lost time: *to catch up on the news, to catch up on one's sleep.* **caught up a** involved unwillingly: *caught up in a scandal.* **b** deeply engrossed: *all caught up in his new boat.*

catch–all *n* **1** a container for odds and ends. **2** a term, category, etc., used to cover various unspecified possibilities: *The word 'etc.' is a catch-all.* **catch–all** *adj.* **catch–as–catch–can** *n* **1** a situation in which one must take what chances one gets. **2** a style of wrestling permitting use of the legs and feet. **catch basin 1** a grate at the entrance of a sewer, blocking matter that could hinder sewage flow. **2** a reservoir to catch and hold surface drainage over large areas. **catch·er** *n Baseball* the player who squats behind the batter to catch balls pitched or thrown. **catch·ing** *adj* contagious. **catch·ment** *n* a reservoir for catching drainage. **catchment (area) 1** the area drained by a river system. **2** the area served by a social institution. **catch–22** *n* a choice where one loses or fails either way (from the title of a novel by Joseph Heller). **catch·word** *n* an expression that has become representative of a party, point of view, etc.: *"Canada first" was the catchword of a 19th century movement for cultural independence.* **catch·y** *adj* pleasing and easy to remember: *catchy tunes.* **catch·i·ness** *n*.

cat·e·chism [ˈkætəˌkɪzəm] *n* **1** a set of questions and answers used for teaching a system of belief. **2** any systematic series of questions. **cat·e·chis·mal** *adj.* ⟨Greek *katēchein; kata-* thoroughly + *echein* to sound⟩ **cat·e·chize** *v* **1** teach a system of belief by a set of questions and answers. **2** question closely and at length. **cat·e·che·sis** [ˌkætəˈkisɪs] *n, pl* **-ses** [-siz] the process of teaching by a catechism. **cat·e·chet·i·cal** [ˌkætəˈkɛtəkəl] or **cat·e·chet·ic** *adj.* **cat·e·chu·men** [-ˈkjumən] *n* a person receiving rigorous teaching in any system of belief.

cat·e·go·ry [ˈkætəˌɡɔri] *n* **1** a group in a system of classification. **2** in various systems of philosophy, any of certain basic concepts into which all existing things can be resolved. ⟨Greek *kata-* down + *agoreuein* speak⟩ **cat·e·gor·ize** *v* assign to a category or set of categories. **cat·e·gor·i·za·tion** *n.* **cat·e·gor·i·cal** [ˌkætəˈɡɔrəkəl] *adj* positive; absolute; without qualification. **cat·e·gor·i·cal·ly** *adv.* **categorical imperative** the doctrine of philosopher Immanuel Kant that one should do only what would be good if everyone did it.

cat·e·nar·y [ˈkætəˌnɛri] or [kəˈtinəri] *n Mathematics* the curve formed by a chain hanging freely from two points. **cat·e·nar·y** *adj.* ⟨Latin *catena* chain⟩

ca·ter [ˈkeitər] *v* **1** provide food or supplies for special events: *Who catered for the wedding?* **2** serve the needs or interests of (with *to*): *a TV station catering to teens.* **3** indulge the desires or weaknesses of. ⟨Old French *acater* buy⟩ **ca·ter·er** *n* a person or group whose business is to provide food, etc. for special events.

cat·er·pil·lar [ˈkætərˌpɪlər] or [ˈkætəˌpɪlər] *n* the wormlike larva of a butterfly or moth. ⟨Old French *chatepelose* hairy cat⟩ **Cat·er·pil·lar** *n Trademark* a brand of tractor with cogged wheels in a moving belt, for use on rough ground.

cat·er·waul [ˈkætərˌwɒl] *v* **1** howl like a cat; screech. **2** quarrel noisily. **cat·er·waul** *n.* ⟨Middle English *caterwrawe; wrawe* wail, howl⟩

ca·thar·sis [kəˈθɑrsɪs] *n* **1** a purging of the digestive system. **2** release or expression of deep emotion, with a cleansing effect. ⟨Greek *katharsis; katharos* clean⟩ **ca·thar·tic** *n* **1** a strong laxative. **2** anything serving to cleanse the psyche by releasing deep emotion. **ca·thar·tic** *adj.*

ca·the·dral [kəˈθidrəl] *n* the official church of a bishop, or any large, important church. **ca·the·dral** *adj.* ⟨Greek *kathedra* seat⟩

cath·e·ter ['kæθətər] *n* a slender tube to be inserted into a passage or cavity of the body to carry fluid in or out. **cath·e·ter·ize** *v.* ⟨Greek *kathetēr; kata-* down + *hienai* send⟩

cath·ode ['kæθoud] *n* **1** the positively charged electrode of a primary cell or storage battery. **2** the negative electrode of an electrolytic cell. **3** *Electronics* the electrode that is the main source of electrons in a vacuum tube. **ca·thod·ic** [kə'θɒdɪk] *adj.* ⟨Greek *kathodos; kata-* down + *hodos* way⟩
cathode–ray tube a vacuum tube producing images on a fluorescent screen by means of a high-speed stream of electrons (**cathode ray**) emitted by a heated cathode.

cath·o·lic ['kæθəlɪk] *or* ['kæθlɪk] *adj* **1** broad or general; universal. **2** broad-minded. **3** of the whole Christian church. **cath·o·li·cal·ly** *adv.* **cath·o·lic·i·ty** [ˌkæθə'lɪsəti] *n.* ⟨Greek *katholikos; kata-* in respect to + *holos* whole⟩
Cath·o·lic *n* **1** a member of the Christian church whose earthly leader is the Pope. **2** a member of any Christian church claiming continuity with the ancient undivided church. **Cath·o·lic** *adj.* **Ca·thol·i·cism** [kə'θɒləsɪzəm] *n.* **Cath·o·lic·i·ty** *n.*

cat·i·on ['kætaɪən] *n* a positively-charged ion. **cat·i·on·ic** *adj.* ⟨Greek *kata-* down + ION⟩

CAT scan [kæt] **1** *Medicine* an examination of the brain for diagnosis using COMPUTERIZED AXIAL TOMOGRAPHY. **2** the X-ray picture thus obtained. **CAT scanner.**

cat·tle ['kætəl] *n* domesticated bovine animals; cows, bulls, steers, or oxen. ⟨Old French *catel;* Latin *capitale* property⟩

cat–train ['kæt ˌtreɪn] *n* ❉ in the North, a series of sleds pulled by a Caterpillar tractor.

cau·cus ['kɒkəs] *n* **1** in Canada, members of Parliament of one party who meet to discuss policy, plan strategy, etc. **2** a similar body in other countries. **3** a committee within an organization or political party, whose function is to determine policy. ⟨probably from Algonquian; compare Virginian *caucauasu* counsellor⟩

Caugh·na·waugh·a See KAHNAWAKE.

caught [kɒt] *v* pt and pp of CATCH.

caul [kɒl] *n* a portion of the membrane that encloses a child in the womb, sometimes found clinging to the head at birth. ⟨perhaps Old French *cale* little cap⟩

caul·dron or **cal·dron** ['kɒldrən] *n* a large pot or kettle. ⟨Latin *caldaria; calidus* warm⟩

cau·li·flow·er ['kɒli,flaʊər] *n* a variety of cabbage whose tightly set flower cluster forms a solid white head. ⟨Latin *cauliflora; caulis* cabbage + *flos, floris* flower⟩
cauliflower ear an ear misshapen by injuries received in boxing, etc.

caulk [kɒk] *v* fill up (a seam, crack, or joint) to make it watertight or airtight. Also, **calk.** **caulk·er** *n.* ⟨Latin *calcare* tread, press in⟩
caulk·ing *n* a soft, puttylike compound used for this.

cause [kɒz] *n* **1** whatever produces an effect. **2** a good reason: *She was angry without cause.* **3** a goal or movement to which people give their support: *the cause of world peace.* **4** *Law* case: *Who will plead my cause?*
v bring about; make happen or do: *Smoking causes cancer. Her questions caused us to think.* **cause·less** *adj.* **cause·less·ly** *adv.* ⟨Latin *causa*⟩
make common cause with join forces with.
caus·al *adj* **1** to do with a cause, or with cause and effect. **2** *Grammar* expressing cause: *a causal conjunction.* **caus·al·ly** *adv.* **cau·sal·i·ty** *n* **1** the relationship between cause and effect. **2** the principle that nothing exists without a cause. **cau·sa·tion** *n* the act or fact of causing. **caus·a·tive** *adj* **1** being a cause; creating an effect. **2** *Grammar* expressing causation. In *enrich, en-* is a causative prefix. **caus·a·tive·ly** *adv.* **cause cé·lè·bre** ['kouz seɪ'lɛbrə] *or* ['kɒz sə'lɛb] *French* [kozse'lɛbʀ] *French* **1** *Law* a famous case. **2** a notorious incident.

cause·way ['kɒz,weɪ] *n* a raised road or path built across water. ⟨Middle English *cauci* (infl. by *way*); Latin *calciata* paved, *calx* limestone⟩

caus·tic ['kɒstɪk] *n* a substance that burns or eats away by chemical action.
adj **1** corrosive. **2** sarcastic; biting: *caustic wit.* **caus·ti·cal·ly** *adv.* ⟨Greek *kaustikos*⟩
caustic soda an alkaline compound used in bleaching and in making soap, paper, etc.; sodium hydroxide.

cau·ter·ize ['kɒtə,raɪz] *v* destroy (defective tissue) or seal (a wound) by burning. **cau·ter·i·za·tion** *n.* ⟨Greek *kauter* branding iron⟩

cau·tion ['kɒʃən] *n* **1** the practice of taking care to be safe, or of not taking chances: *Use caution in crossing streets.* **2** a warning. **3** *Law* a formal warning to an accused person that anything he or she says may be used as evidence. **4** *Informal* a funny or remarkable person or thing.
v warn. ⟨Latin *cautio; cavere* beware⟩
cau·tion·ar·y *adj* warning. **cau·tious** *adj* using caution. **cau·tious·ly** *adv.* **cau·tious·ness** *n.*

cav·al·cade [ˌkævəl,keɪd] *or* [ˌkævəl'keɪd] *n* **1** a procession of people on horses or in cars or carriages. **2** a series of scenes or events: *a cavalcade of sports.* ⟨Italian *cavalcare* ride horseback; Latin *caballus* horse⟩

cav·a·lier [ˌkævə'lɪr] *n* **1** a gentleman or knight. **2 Cavalier** a supporter of Charles I in his struggle with Parliament (1641-1649).
adj too casual; offhand: *a cavalier disregard for danger.* **cav·a·lier·ly** *adv.* **cav·a·lier·ness** *n.* ⟨French = knight; Latin *caballus* horse⟩

cav·al·ry ['kævəlri] *n* troops trained to fight in armoured vehicles or, formerly, on horseback. **cav·al·ry·man** *n, pl* -**men.** ⟨French *cavalerie* knighthood;. Latin *caballus* horse⟩

cave [keɪv] *n* a hollow space underground, often opening out on the side of a hill or cliff.
v **1** *Informal* CAVE IN. **2** engage in CAVING. **cave·like** *adj.* **cav·er** *n.* ⟨Latin *cava* hollow⟩

cave in a collapse: *The roof caved in under the snow's weight.* **b** *Informal* give in. **cave–in** *n.*

cave dweller a prehistoric person who lived in a cave. **cave·man** *n* CAVE DWELLER. **cav·ern** ['kævərn] *n* a large cave. **cav·ern·ous** *adj* large, dark, hollow, echoing, etc.: *cavernous hallways.* **cav·ern·ous·ly** *adv.* **cav·ing** *n* the sport of exploring caves.

ca·ve·at ['kævi,æt] *or* ['keivi,æt] *n* **1** a warning. **2** *Law* a notice to a legal authority not to do something until the person giving notice can be heard. 〈Latin *caveat* let (him) beware〉

caveat emp·tor ['ɛmptɔr] *Latin* let the buyer beware; you buy at your own risk.

cav·i·ar ['kævi,ɑr] *n* the salted eggs of sturgeon or other fish. 〈Turkish *khaviar*〉

cav·il ['kævəl] *v* **-illed** or **-iled, -il·ling** or **-il·ing** make trivial criticisms or objections. **cav·il** *n.* **cav·il·ler** or **cav·il·er** *n.* 〈Latin *cavillari* jeer〉

cav·i·ty ['kævəti] *n* **1** a hole; hollow place. **2** an enclosed space inside the body: *the abdominal cavity.* **3** a hole in a tooth, caused by decay. 〈Latin *cavitas; cavus* hollow〉

ca·vort [kə'vɔrt] *v* *Informal* frolic; jump around in a frisky way: *colts cavorting in the pasture.* 〈origin uncertain〉

cay·enne [kaɪ'ɛn] *or* [kei'ɛn] *n* RED PEPPER (def. 1). 〈*Cayenne* in French Guiana〉

cay·man ['keimən] *n* a large alligator of tropical America. Also, **cai·man.** 〈Carib *caiman*〉

Ca·yu·ga [kə'jugə] *n* **1** a member of a First Nations or Native American people living in New York State and Ontario. **2** their Iroquoian language. **Cayuga** *adj.* Also called **Kayonkwe'haka.**

CB CITIZENS' BAND.

CBC the Canadian Broadcasting Corporation.

cc 1 cubic centimetres, now usually written cm³. **2** CARBON COPY.

CCF or **C.C.F.** Co-operative Commonwealth Federation, a Canadian political party which was established in 1932 and joined with the Canadian Labour Congress in 1961 to form the New Democratic Party.

cd candela.

CD 1 COMPACT DISC. **2** Often, **C.D.** CIVIL DEFENCE.

Cdn. Canadian.

CD–ROM ['si di 'rɒm] *Computers* **1** a CD that contains data or software. A user can store data once on a **CD-R** (-recordable), or more than once on a **CD-RW** (-rewritable). **2** loosely, the drive that reads it. 〈*compact disc – read-only memory*〉

CE 1 COMMON ERA or CHRISTIAN ERA (to indicate years after the birth of Christ). **2** CIVIL ENGINEER.

cease [sis] *v* stop; end: *The music ceased suddenly. The company has ceased operations.* **ces·sa·tion** [sɛ'seiʃən] *n.* 〈Latin *cessare*〉

cease–fire *n* a formal, usually temporary cessation of combat between armed forces. **cease·less** *adj* unending: *the ceaseless noise of traffic.* **cease·less·ly** *adv.* **cease·less·ness** *n.*

ce·dar ['sidər] *n* **1** any of a genus of evergreen trees of the pine family with short, sharp needles. **2** any of various other conifers including arborvitae and junipers. 〈Greek *kedros*〉

cede [sid] *v* hand over; surrender or yield: *In 1763 France ceded Canada to Britain. We had to cede the point to the other team.* **ces·sion** ['sɛʃən] *n.* 〈Latin *cedere*〉

ce·dil·la [sə'dɪlə] *n* a mark written under a *c* (ç) before *a, o,* or *u* to show that it has the sound of *s,* as in *façade.* 〈Spanish, diminutive of *ceda;* Greek *zeta* zed〉

CEGEP [sei'ʒɛp] *French* ✱ Collège d'enseignement général et professionel (vocational and liberal arts college).

ceil·ing ['silɪŋ] *n* **1** the inside top covering of a room. **2** the distance between the earth and the lowest clouds. **3** an imposed upper limit: *a ceiling on rent.* 〈perhaps from French *ciel,* Latin *caelum*〉

hit the ceiling *Slang* react with a burst of anger: *When she saw the bill she hit the ceiling.*

cel·e·brate ['sɛlə,breit] *v* **1** mark (a special time) with ceremonies and festivities: *to celebrate Thanksgiving.* **2** perform publicly with the proper rites: *The priest celebrated Mass.* **3** express joy; make merry: *The people celebrated in the streets when the war ended.* **4** dwell on in an appreciative way; honour: *to celebrate nature.* **cel·e·bra·tion** *n.* **cel·e·bra·to·ry** ['sɛləbrə,tɔri] *adj.* 〈Latin *celebrare*〉 **cel·e·brant** *n* **1** a person who performs a rite or ceremony. **2** merrymaker. **cel·e·brat·ed** *adj* famous; much talked about: *a celebrated author.* **ce·leb·ri·ty** *n* **1** a famous person. **2** fame.

cel·er·y ['sɛləri] *or* ['sɛlri] *n* a biennial herb of the carrot family with long, crisp, pale green stalks. 〈French *céleri;* Greek *selinon* parsley〉 **ce·ler·i·ac** [sə'lɛri,æk] *n* a variety of celery cultivated for its edible root. **celery salt** salt mixed with ground celery seed.

ce·les·tial [sə'lɛstʃəl] *adj* **1** to do with the sky or heaven. **2** very beautiful: *a celestial voice.* **3 Celestial** of the former Chinese empire or its people. **ce·les·tial·ly** *adv.* 〈Latin *caelestis* heavenly; *caelum* heaven〉

celestial equator *Astronomy* the imaginary great circle representing the intersection of the plane of the earth's equator with the CELESTIAL SPHERE. **celestial sphere** *Astronomy* the imaginary sphere that apparently encloses the universe, of a size approaching infinity.

celiac disease ['sili,æk] a chronic intestinal disorder usually of childhood, resulting in diarrhea, swelling of the abdomen, etc.

cel·i·bate ['sɛləbɪt] *adj* abstaining from sexual intercourse and marriage, often having taken a vow to do so. **cel·i·bate** *n.* **cel·i·ba·cy** *n.* 〈*caelibatus; caelebs* unmarried〉

cell [sɛl] *n* **1** *Biology* the smallest structural unit of living matter that can function independently. **2** a small room in a prison, convent, or monastery. **3** any of a series of small compartments: *the cells of a honeycomb, the cells in a table or spreadsheet.* **4** a device producing electricity, consisting of one positive and one negative electrode immersed in an electrolyte. **5** Often, **cell group** a small group acting as the basic unit of an organization, revolutionary movement, etc. **cel·lu·lar** *adj.* ⟨Latin *cella* small room⟩ **cell block** a single prison building containing cells. **cell·mate** *n* one who shares a prison cell. **cellphone** or **cellular telephone** a telephone using radio frequencies to send the signal across small areas called cells. Satellite dishes convey it from cell to cell.

cel·lar ['sɛlər] *n* **1** an underground room for storing food, wine, etc. **2** a supply of wines. ⟨Latin *cellarium; cella* small room⟩

cel·lo ['tʃɛlou] *n* the second largest instrument of the modern violin family. **cel·list** *n*. ⟨shortened from *violoncello*⟩

cel·lo·phane ['sɛlə,fein] *n* a transparent film made from cellulose and used especially for packaging. ⟨*cellulose* + Greek *phanein* appear⟩

cel·lu·lite ['sɛljə,lait] *n* adipose deposits on the hips or buttocks. ⟨French; Latin *cellula* small cell⟩

cel·lu·loid *n* **1** a transparent plastic made from cellulose treated with nitric and sulphuric acids. **2** movie film or movies collectively. **cel·lu·lose** *n* the chief constituent of plant cell walls and fibres, used extensively in the manufacture of paper, plastics, textiles, etc. **cel·lu·lo·sic** *adj.*

Celsius ['sɛlsiəs] *or* ['sɛlʃəs] *adj* to do with a temperature scale in which 0 degrees is the temperature at which water freezes and 100 degrees the temperature at which it boils, under normal atmospheric pressure. *Symbol* **C** ⟨Anders *Celsius*, 18c Swedish astronomer⟩

Celt [kɛlt] *or* [sɛlt] *n* a member of an ancient people of W Europe and the British Isles, including the Britons and Gauls. **Celt·ic** ['kɛltɪk] *or* ['sɛltɪk] *adj.* ⟨Latin; Greek *Keltoi*⟩ **Celtic cross** a cross with a circle or circles intersecting the four arms.

ce·ment [sə'mɛnt] *n* **1** a fine, grey powder made by burning clay and limestone. When mixed with water and sand, gravel, or crushed stone, it forms concrete. **2** any soft substance that hardens to make things stick together: *rubber cement*. **3** anything that unites. **4** filling for dental cavities. *v* **1** fasten together with cement. **2** spread concrete for: *to cement a sidewalk*. **3** make into a firm union: *to cement a friendship*. ⟨Latin *caementum* stone chips; *caedere* cut⟩

cem·e·ter·y ['sɛmə,tɛri] *n* a burial ground; graveyard. ⟨Greek *koimētērion; koimaein* lull to sleep⟩

cen·o·taph ['sɛnə,tæf] *n* a monument in memory of many dead, such as soldiers killed in a war, who are buried elsewhere. ⟨Greek *kenotaphion; kenos* empty + *taphos* tomb⟩

Ce·no·zo·ic [,sinə'zouɪk] *or* [,sɛnə'zouɪk] *n* the most recent geological era, extending from about 66 million years ago to the present. **Ce·no·zo·ic** *adj.* ⟨Greek *kainos* recent + *zoē* life⟩

cen·ser ['sɛnsər] *n* a container in which incense is burned. ⟨Old French *(en)censier;* Latin *incensum* incense⟩

cens et rentes [sɑ̃ze'rɑ̃t] *French* ✴ formerly, in New France and Lower Canada, payment in cash (*cens*) and kind (*rentes*) to a seigneur in recognition of his rights.

cens·i·taire [sɑ̃zi'tɛr] *French* ✴ *n* formerly, in French Canada, a habitant qualified to vote.

cen·sor ['sɛnsər] *n* **1** a person authorized to change books, letters, motion pictures, etc., to ensure they contain nothing obscene, libellous, politically incorrect or dangerous, etc. **2** in ancient Rome, a magistrate who took the census and supervised the conduct of citizens. **3** a person who likes to judge or find fault. **cen·sor** *v.* **cen·sor·ship** *n.* ⟨Latin, from *censere* appraise⟩ **cen·so·ri·ous** [sɛn'sɔriəs] *adj* too apt to find fault. **cen·so·ri·ous·ly** *adv.* **cen·so·ri·ous·ness** *n.*

cen·sure ['sɛnʃər] *n* public official criticism or a statement of disapproval, often as a form of discipline. **cen·sur·a·ble** *adj.* **cen·sure** *v.* **cen·sur·er** *n.* ⟨Latin *censura; censere* appraise⟩

cen·sus ['sɛnsəs] *n* an official count of a population. ⟨Latin, from *censere* appraise⟩

cent [sɛnt] *n* **1** a unit of money in Canada, equal to one hundredth of a dollar. **2** a corresponding unit in other countries. See Appendix. *Symbol* ¢ ⟨Latin *centum* hundred⟩

cen·taur ['sɛntɔr] *n* Greek myth one of a race of creatures that had the head, arms, and chest of a man, and the body and legs of a horse. ⟨Greek *kentauros*⟩

cen·ten·ar·y [sɛn'tɛnəri] *or* [sɛn'tinəri] *n* a 100th anniversary. **cen·ten·ar·y** *adj.* ⟨Latin *centenarius; centum* hundred⟩ **cen·te·nar·i·an** [sɛntə'nɛriən] *n* a person who is 100 years old or more. **cen·ten·ni·al** [-'tɛnjəl] *adj* of or for 100 years or a 100th anniversary: *a centennial exhibition. n* a 100th anniversary.

centi– *prefix* **1** SI *prefix* one hundredth. *Symbol* **c** **2** one hundred, as in *centipede*. ⟨Latin *centum* hundred⟩ **cen·ti·are** ['sɛnti,ɛr] *n* one hundredth of an are; one square metre. **cen·ti·grade** *adj* **1** divided into 100 degrees. **2** Centigrade Celsius. **cen·ti·me·tre** *n* an SI unit of length, equal to one hundredth of a metre, or ten millimetres. *Symbol* **cm** Also, **cen·ti·me·ter.** **cen·ti·me·tre–gram–sec·ond** *adj* to do with a system of measurement whose basic units of length, mass, and time are the centimetre, gram, and second respectively. *Abbrev* **cgs.** **cen·ti·pede** *n* any of a class of arthropods having a long body with many segments and one pair of legs to each segment.

cen·tre ['sɛntər] *n* **1** a point within a circle or sphere, equally distant from all parts of the circumference or surface. **2** the middle part or place: *the centre of a room*. **3** a person or thing that is most important; focus: *She was the centre of attention*. **4** a place of major influence or activity: *an economic centre*. **5** an institution offering facilities of a given kind: *a health centre, a shopping centre*. **6 a** a moderate political position. **b** all the people and parties having moderate political views. **7** *Sports* a player in the middle position of a forward line. **8** a mass of nerve cells acting together: *the respiratory centre.* *v* **1** place in or at the centre. **2** focus: *The story centres on her early childhood.* **3** establish the centre of: *The company is centred in Regina.* **4** (reflexively) achieve personal spiritual focus, balanced perspective, etc. Also, **cen·ter.** **cen·tral** *adj.* **cen·tral·i·ty** *n.* **cen·tral·ly** *adv.* ⟨Greek *kentron* sharp point⟩ **cen·tral·ism** *n* a policy of concentrating power in a central agency, esp a government. **cen·tral·ist** *n, adj.* **cen·tral·ize** *v* bring under central control. **cen·tral·i·za·tion** *n.* **central nervous system** the brain and spinal cord. Compare PERIPHERAL NERVOUS SYSTEM. **Central Powers** in World War I, Germany, Austria-Hungary; often also their allies Turkey and Bulgaria. **central processing unit** *Computers* the part of a computer that controls its operations. *Abbrev* **CPU.** **cen·tre·board** *n* a sailboat's movable keel. **–cen·tred** *combining form* having a given thing as its defining focus: *a student-centred curriculum.* **centre field** *Baseball* the area of the outfield behind second base. **centre fielder.** **cen·tre·fold** *n* a picture covering the two facing pages at the centre of a magazine. **centre ice** *Hockey* **1** the centre of the ice surface from which play begins at the start of each period. **2** the area of ice surface between the bluelines. **centre line** *Hockey* a red line passing through CENTRE ICE at an equal distance from each of the bluelines. **centre of gravity** the point in a body around which its mass is evenly balanced. **centre of mass** a point in a body which moves as though it bore the entire mass of the body. **cen·tre·piece** *n* **1** an ornament for the centre of a table. **2** the main item in a display. **cen·trist** *n* a political moderate. **cen·trism** *n.*

cen·trif·u·gal [sɛn'trɪfjəgəl] *or* [,sɛntrə'fjugəl] *adj* **1** moving away from a centre. **2** making use of CENTRIFUGAL FORCE. **cen·trif·u·gal·ly** *adv.* ⟨Latin *centrum* centre + *fugere* flee⟩ **centrifugal force** the inertia of a revolving body that tends to move it away from the centre around which it revolves. **cen·tri·fuge** *n* a machine for removing solids from a fluid by means of centrifugal force. *v* spin in a centrifuge.

cen·trip·e·tal [sɛn'trɪpətəl] *adj* **1** moving toward a centre. **2** making use of CENTRIPETAL FORCE. **cen·trip·e·tal·ly** *adv.* ⟨Latin *centrum* centre + *petere* seek⟩ **centripetal force** a force, such as gravity, that tends to move things toward the centre around which they are turning.

cen·tu·ry ['sɛntʃəri] *n* **1** each full 100 years

counted from a starting point in a calendar system, such as the birth of Christ: *The sixth century is from A.D. 501 to 600.* **2** any period of 100 years: *From 1824 to 1924 is a century.* **3** a group of 100. ⟨Latin *centum* hundred⟩ **cen·tu·ri·on** [sɛn'tʃʊriən] *or* [sɛn'tjuriən] *n* in the ancient Roman army, a commander of a group of about 100 soldiers.

CEO CHIEF EXECUTIVE OFFICER.

ce·phal·ic [sə'fælɪk] *adj* to do with the head. ⟨Greek *kephalē* head⟩ **ceph·a·lo·pod** ['sɛfələ,pɒd] *n* any of a class of molluscs, including squids and octopuses, with tentacles around the mouth.

ce·ram·ic [sə'ræmɪk] *adj* made of baked clay. *n* **1** ceramics the art of making articles from baked clay (with a singular verb). **2** an article of baked clay. **cer·a·mist** ['sɛrəmɪst] *or* [sə'ræmɪst] *n.* Also, **cer·a·mi·cist** [sə'ræməsɪst]. ⟨Greek *keramos* potter's clay⟩

ce·re·al ['siriəl] *n* **1** food, esp breakfast food, made from grain. **2** any grass that produces a grain used as food. **ce·re·al** *adj.* ⟨Latin *Ceres* goddess of agriculture⟩

cer·e·bel·lum [,sɛrə'bɛləm] *n, pl* **-lums** *or* **-la** a major division of the brain situated below the cerebrum, responsible for co-ordination and physical balance. **cer·e·bel·lar** *adj.* ⟨Latin, diminutive of *cerebrum* brain⟩ **ce·re·bral** *adj* **1** of the brain: *a cerebral hemorrhage.* **2** intellectual: *She likes cerebral games like chess.* **cerebral hemisphere** either of the two halves of the CORTEX (def. 3b). **cerebral palsy** a disorder characterized by impaired muscle function, due to brain damage, usually before or during birth. **cer·e·brate** ['sɛrə,breit] *v* think. **cer·e·bra·tion** *n.* **ce·re·bro–** *combining form* of the brain: *cerebrovascular.* **ce·re·brum** [sə'ribrəm] *or* ['sɛrəbrəm] *n, pl* **-brums** *or* **-bra** the part of the brain that is responsible for cognitive activities and fine motor function.

cer·e·mo·ny ['sɛrə,mouni] *n* **1** a fixed set of actions or words for special occasions such as weddings, etc. **2** very formal, polite conduct: *The usher showed us in with a great deal of ceremony.* **3** formal character: *the ceremony of court life.* **4** long, complex procedure: *Getting this permit is such a ceremony!* ⟨Latin *caerimonia*⟩ **stand on ceremony** insist on formal conduct. **cer·e·mo·ni·al** *adj* of or for a ceremony: *ceremonial attire.* **cer·e·mo·ni·al·ly** *adv.* **cer·e·mo·ni·ous** *adj* very formal, often ostentatiously so: *The waiter served us with ceremonious politeness.* **cer·e·mo·ni·ous·ly** *adv.*

ce·rise [sə'riz] *or* [sə'ris] *n, adj* bright pinkish red. ⟨French = cherry; Greek *kerasos*⟩

ce·ri·um ['siriəm] *n* a greyish metallic element. *Symbol* **Ce** ⟨Latin, from *Ceres* name of an asteroid⟩

cer·tain ['sɜrtən] *adj* 1 established beyond doubt; reliable: *It is certain that 2 and 3 do not add up to 6.* 2 sure (*to*): *She is certain to see it.* 3 specific; definite; known, but not named: *a certain percentage of the profit. A certain person told us.* 4 confident; positive: *Are you certain this is safe?* 5 of a particular but unspecified or unknown amount or character: *To a certain extent we're all at fault. She has a certain charm.* *pron* Formal a definite but unspecified number: *Certain of the students will be asked to give an oral report.* **cer·tain·ty** *n.* **cer·ti·tude** *n.* ⟨Old French; Latin *certus* sure⟩
for certain definitely: *It will rain for certain.*
cer·tain·ly *adv* 1 surely; definitely. 2 yes; of course: *"May I borrow this CD?" "Certainly."* 3 *Informal* very: *I'm certainly glad you came.* 4 confidently; positively.

cer·ti·fy ['sɜrtə,faɪ] *v* 1 declare to be true or to have met certain criteria, usually by issuing a certificate: *The doctor certified that the cause of death was a heart attack.* 2 legally declare (a person) insane. 3 of a bank, guarantee in writing on the face of (a cheque) that the funds to cover it have already been set aside from the drawer's account. **cer·ti·fi·a·ble** *adj.* **cer·ti·fi·a·bly** *adv.* **cer·ti·fi·ca·tion** *n.* **cer·ti·fied** *adj.* ⟨Latin *certificare*; *certus* sure + *facere* make⟩
cer·tif·i·cate *n* a written statement declaring something to be true or genuine or to have met certain criteria: *a birth certificate.* **certificate of deposit** a document given by a bank to confirm receipt of money to be held for a time as an interest-gaining deposit. **certificate of fran·ci·sa·tion** or **fran·ci·sa·tion** [,frænsə'zeɪʃən] *or* [,frænsəsə'zeɪʃən] ✱ a document required to operate a business in Québec, certifying that French is the main language used in the business. **certified cheque** a cheque which a bank guarantees to be good because funds have already been set aside to cover it.

ce·ru·le·an [sə'ruliən] *adj, n* Poetic sky blue. ⟨Latin *caeruleus* dark blue⟩

cer·vix ['sɜrvɪks] *n, pl* **-vix·es** or **-vi·ces** [,siz] 1 the narrow opening of the uterus. 2 the neck, esp the back of the neck. **cer·vi·cal** *adj.* ⟨Latin⟩
cervical cap a contraceptive device shaped like a flexible cap and fitted over the opening of the uterus. **cervical smear** cells scraped from the cervix to be tested for malignancy. Also called **Pap test.**

ce·si·um or **cae·si·um** ['siziəm] *n* a silvery metallic element. *Symbol* **Cs** ⟨Latin *caesius* bluish grey⟩

ces·sa·tion See CEASE.

ces·sion See CEDE.

cess·pool ['sɛs,pul] *n* 1 a pit or underground tank for grey water and sewage. 2 any filthy place. ⟨origin uncertain⟩

ce·ta·cean [sə'teɪʃən] *n* any of an order of marine fishlike mammals, such as whales and dolphins. **ce·ta·cean** *adj.* **ce·ta·ceous** *adj.* ⟨Greek *kētos* whale⟩

cf. compare (for Latin *confer*).

CFB Canadian Forces Base.

CFC (*pl* **CFCs**) chlorofluorocarbon.

CFL or **C.F.L.** Canadian Football League.

cgs centimetre-gram-second.

cha–cha ['tʃɑ ,tʃɑ] *n* a Latin American ballroom dance with a fast, strong rhythm. **cha–cha** *v.* Also, **cha–cha–cha.** ⟨imitative⟩

chad [tʃʌd] *n* a piece of waste material caused by the punching of a card or ballot. ⟨origin unknown⟩

cha·dor ['tʃʌdər] *n* a large piece of cloth used as a cloak and veil by some Muslim women. ⟨Persian *chaddar, chadur* veil, sheet⟩

chafe [tʃeɪf] *v* 1 make (a place on the skin) sore by rubbing: *The rough collar chafed my neck.* 2 annoy or become annoyed: *He chafed under their teasing. They chafed at the long delay.* 3 rub to make warm: *She chafed her cold hands.* **chafe** *n.*⟨Old French *chaufer* to warm; Latin *calefacere*, from *calere* be warm⟩

chaff[1] [tʃæf] *n* 1 husks of grain. 2 worthless stuff. ⟨Old English *ceaf*⟩

chaff[2] [tʃæf] *v* make fun of (someone) in a good-natured way; tease. ⟨origin uncertain⟩

cha·grin [ʃə'grɪn] *n* a feeling of grave disappointment or embarrassment. **cha·grin** *v.* ⟨Middle French *chagrin* sad⟩

chain [tʃeɪn] *n* 1 a flexible series of connected links: *a gold chain.* 2 any connected series: *a mountain chain, chain of events.* 3 anything that binds or restrains. 4 a group of stores, restaurants, etc. with the same name, operated by one company. **chain** *v.* ⟨Old French *chaeine*; Latin *catena*⟩
chained to unable to leave: *chained to the house, chained to one's job.*
chain gang in S United States, a gang of convicts, etc. chained together while at work outdoors. **chain letter** a letter that each recipient is asked to copy and send to several others in order to get some supposed benefit. **chain–link** *adj* of a fence, made of interwoven steel links. **chain mail** flexible armour made of many tiny metal rings linked together. **chain reaction** 1 *Chemistry, physics* a process that continues automatically once started, consisting of a series of reactions, the product or effect of each causing the next. 2 any series of events, each caused by the preceding one. **chain reference** one of a system of cross-references in a text, each one leading to a new, related one. **chain–ref·er·ence** *adj, v.* **chain saw** a portable power saw whose teeth are linked together in an endless chain. **chain–smoke** *v* smoke cigarettes one after another. **chain–smok·er** *n.* **chain stitch** a crochet or embroidery stitch in which each stitch makes a loop through which the next stitch is taken. **chain–stitch** *v.* **chain store** a group of stores operated by a single company, or one store of such a group.

chair [tʃɛr] *n* 1 a separate seat for one person. 2 the position of department head in a university, the leader of a meeting, etc: *the chair of Physics.* 3 Often, **chair·per·son,**

chair·man, or **chair·wom·an** the holder of this position.
v act as chairperson of: *to chair a meeting.* ⟨Old French *chaiere;* Greek *kathedra* seat⟩
take the chair preside at a meeting.
chair lift or **chairlift** *n* an apparatus for conveying people up a slope, consisting of chairs suspended from an endless cable.

> **USAGE**
> The word **chairman** may be used for either a man or a woman. **Chairperson** is also widely used, so that the term **chairwoman** is less frequently needed. Of the three terms, only **chairman** is used as a form of address: *Mr. Chairman, Madam Chairman.*

chaise [ʃeiz] *or* [ʃɛz] *n* **1** formerly, any of several kinds of light carriage. **2** CHAISE LONGUE. ⟨French, variant of *chaire*. See CHAIR.⟩
chaise longue ['ʃeiz 'lɒŋ] *French* [ʃɛz'lɔ̃g] a chair with a long seat, in which one person can sit with outstretched legs. **chaise lounge** ['ʃeiz 'laʊndʒ] CHAISE LONGUE. ⟨misreading of *longue*, influenced by *lounge*⟩

chak·ra ['tʃɑkrə], ['tʃʌkrə], *or* ['tʃækrə] *n Yoga* any of the six or seven concentration points of psychic power in the body. ⟨Sanskrit⟩

chal·ced·o·ny [kæl'sɛdəni] *or* ['kælsə‚douni] *n* a variety of quartz that occurs in various colours and forms. ⟨Greek *chalkēdōn*⟩

cha·let [ʃæ'lei] *n* **1** a herder's hut or cabin in the Alps. **2** a Swiss house with a steep roof and wide, overhanging eaves. **3** any house of similar design, esp a cottage or a ski lodge. ⟨Swiss French⟩

chal·ice ['tʃælɪs] *n* a cup, esp one used in a Communion service. ⟨Latin *calix* cup⟩

chalk [tʃɒk] *n* **1** a soft limestone, made up mostly of tiny fossil sea shells. **2** a substance like this, esp in the form of a crayon. ⟨Latin *calx, calcis* lime⟩
chalk up a write down, esp with chalk. **b** score; earn: *to chalk up a goal.* **c** attribute: *Chalk it up to simple human error.*
chalk·board *n* a board with a specially prepared dark surface for writing or drawing on with chalk. **chalk·y** *adj* **1** of or containing chalk. **2** like chalk in colour or texture; white: *The clown's face was chalky.* **chalk·i·ness** *n.*

chal·lah ['xɑlə] *or* ['xɑlə] *n* the loaf of rich white bread traditionally eaten on the Jewish Sabbath. ⟨Hebrew *chala* loaf of bread⟩

chal·lenge ['tʃæləndʒ] *v* **1** call to engage in a fight or contest. **2** stop (a person) to ask his or her name or purpose: *When she tried to enter, the guard challenged her.* **3** question; dispute (something): *to challenge a statement.* **4** resist the authority of; defy. **5** require or get serious effort from: *Good teachers know how to challenge their students.* **chal·lenge** *n.* **chal·leng·er** *n.* ⟨Old French *chalonge*; Latin *calumnia* false accusation⟩

cham·ber ['tʃeimbər] *n* **1** *Archaic, poetic* a room in a house, esp a bedroom. **2** a hall where a governing body meets. **3** a legislative or judicial body: *The Canadian Parliament has* two *chambers, the Senate and the House of Commons.* **4** chambers *pl* **a** a set of rooms to live in or use as offices. **b** the office of a judge or lawyer. **5** an enclosed space; compartment, as in the human heart, a revolver, etc. ⟨Old French *chambre*, Latin *camera;* Greek *kamaru* vaulted room⟩
cham·ber·lain ['tʃeimbərlən] *n* the steward of a noble household. **cham·ber·maid** *n* a maid who makes beds, cleans rooms, etc., now esp in hotels. **chamber music** orchestral music suited to a room or small hall. **chamber orchestra**. **Chamber of Commerce** an organization of local business people. **chamber pot** formerly, in a bedroom, a pot in which to relieve oneself during the night.

cham·bray ['ʃæmbrei] *n* a fine cloth combining coloured warp threads with white filling threads. ⟨*Cambrai*, France⟩

cha·me·le·on [kə'miljən] *n* **1** any of a family of lizards whose skin changes colour to match their environment, as camouflage. **2** *Informal* a changeable or fickle person or thing. ⟨Greek *chamai* dwarf + *leōn* lion⟩

cham·ois [ʃæm'wɑ] *or* ['ʃæmwɑ] *n, pl* **-ois** **1** a mountain goat of Europe and SW Asia. **2** ['ʃæmi] a very soft, brownish yellow suede leather orig made from its hide, often used for polishing.
v ['ʃæmi] **-oised, -ois·ing** ['ʃæmid], ['ʃæmiɪŋ] wipe or polish with a chamois. ⟨French; Latin *camox*⟩

champ¹ [tʃæmp] *v* **1** bite and chew noisily. **2** bite on impatiently. ⟨related to CHOP²⟩
champ (at) the bit be very impatient.

champ² [tʃæmp] *n Informal* champion.

cham·pagne [ʃæm'pein] *n* a sparkling wine first made in Champagne, France.

cham·pi·on ['tʃæmpiən] *n* **1** whatever wins first place in a game or contest: *the swimming champion of the world.* **2** a person who fights or speaks for another: *a champion of the poor.*
v fight or speak on behalf of. **cham·pi·on·ship** *n.* ⟨Latin *campio; campus* field (of battle)⟩

chance [tʃæns] *n* **1** opportunity: *a chance to make some money.* **2** probability: *There's a good chance she'll arrive in time for dinner.* **3** fate; an unplanned event: *Chance led to the finding of the diamond mine.* **4** a risk.
adj not planned: *a chance meeting.*
v **1** *Poetic* happen. **2** risk: *I wouldn't chance a canoe ride without a life jacket.* ⟨Old French *cheance;* Latin *cadentia*, from *cadere* fall⟩
by chance a accidentally: *The meeting came about by chance.* **b** by some turn of events: *If by chance the weather clears, we can go.* **chance it** *Informal* take a risk. **on the (off) chance** depending on the (unlikely) possibility: *She went to the theatre on the off chance of getting a returned ticket.* **stand a chance** have reasonable hopes: *Our team still stands a chance of winning.* **(the) chances are (that)** it is likely (that).
chanc·y *adj Informal* risky; uncertain.

chan·cel ['tʃænsəl] *n* the space around the altar of a church. ⟨Latin *cancelli* a grating⟩

chan·cel·lor *n* **1** a high official at court or in an embassy. **2** the prime minister or other very high official of some European countries. **3** the chief judge of a chancery. **4** the honorary head of a university. **chan·cel·ler·y** or **chan·cel·lor·ship** *n*. **chan·cer·y** *n* a court dealing with cases outside the scope of common law or statute law. **in chancery a** in such a court. **b** in a helpless position.

chan·cre ['ʃæŋkər] *n* a hard, reddish sore, the first symptom of syphilis. **chanc·rous** *adj.* ⟨French; Latin *cancer*⟩

chan·de·lier [ˌʃændə'lir] *n* a hanging light fixture with many branches or tiers. ⟨Old French; Latin *candela* candle, *candere* shine⟩

chan·dler ['tʃændlər] *n* **1** a maker or seller of candles. **2** a dealer in supplies of a given kind: *a ship chandler.* ⟨Anglo-French *chandeler.* See CHANDELIER.⟩

change [tʃeindʒ] *v* **1** make or become different. **2** of the male voice in adolescence, lower in pitch. **3** get rid of one thing in favour of something else: *We are changing to a new format.* **4** pass or cause to pass from one position or state to another: *The wind changed to the east. A witch changed him into a toad.* **5** exchange: *I changed seats with my sister.* **6** get or give small units of money that equal (a larger unit): *to change a five-dollar bill.* **7** put fresh or different clothes, diapers, or other coverings on: *to change the bed, to change into a swimsuit.* **8** transfer from one bus, plane, etc., to another: *It's not a direct flight; you have to change in Ottawa.* *n* **1** the act or fact of changing, or the resulting condition. **2** variety. **3** a fresh set: *a change of clothes.* **4** smaller units of money given in place of a larger unit or returned as a balance of money when the sum paid is larger than the sum due. **5** coins. **6 changes** *pl* the different patterns in which a set of bells can be rung. **change·a·ble** *adj.* **change·a·bil·i·ty** *n.* **change·less** *adj.* **chang·er** *n.* ⟨Old French *changer;* Latin *cambiare*⟩ **and change** formula for indicating one has rounded off a price or quantity: *You can get that for 50 dollars and change.* **change around** rearrange or reverse. **change for the better** improve. **change hands** See HAND. **change off** take turns: *We changed off hoeing and raking to make the job easier.* **change one's tune** See TUNE. **change over a** switch places or tasks. **b** adopt a new system or method: *Canada changed over to the metric system years ago.* **change places with** have someone else's lifestyle or job. **ring the changes** do or express something in many different ways. **change·ling** *n* a child apparently left in place of another. **change of heart** a profound change of attitude. **change of life** menopause. **change of venue** a change of the place of a trial. **change·o·ver** or **change–over** *n* **1** a conversion to a different system, method, etc. **2** transfer of ownership. **change table** a table on which to change a baby's diaper.

chan·nel ['tʃænəl] *n* **1** the bed of a stream, river, etc. **2** a body of water joining two larger ones: *the English Channel.* **3** a groove for something to slide in. **4** a means of communication: *secret channels.* **5** an outlet; way to use talent or energy, vent emotion, etc.: *a channel for her enthusiasm.* **6** a narrow band of radio or television frequencies for one-way transmission. *v* **-nelled** or **-neled, -nel·ling** or **-nel·ing 1** convey through a channel. **2** form a channel in. **3** direct into a particular course: *to channel one's energies into politics.* ⟨Old French *chanel;* Latin *canalis*⟩

chant [tʃænt] *v* **1** sing with several syllables or words on one tone. **2** talk in a rhythmic, monotonous way. **chant** *n.* ⟨Old French *chanter* sing; Latin *cantare*⟩ **chan·ter** *n* **1** the chief singer in a choir. **2** the singer of a liturgy. **3** on a bagpipe, the pipe on which the melody is played.

chan·teuse [ʃɑ̃'tøz] *n French* a female singer.

chan·ti·cleer ['tʃæntə,klir] *n Poetic* rooster. ⟨Old French *chanter* sing + *cler* clear; name of the cock in medieval tale *Reynard the Fox*⟩

Cha·nu·kah or **Cha·nuk·kah** See HANUKKAH.

cha·os ['keiɒs] *n* **1** total confusion. **2** the formless matter thought to have existed before the universe began. **cha·ot·ic** *adj.* **cha·ot·i·cal·ly** *adv.* ⟨Greek⟩

chap¹ [tʃæp] *v* **chapped, chap·ping** of skin, crack open from dryness or cold. ⟨Middle English *chappe(n)* cut⟩

chap² [tʃæp] *n Informal* a fellow; man; boy. ⟨a shortened form of archaic *chapman* pedlar⟩

chap·ar·ral [ˌʃæpə'ræl] or [ˌtʃæpə'ræl] *n* in the SW United States, a thicket of low shrubs, etc., esp dwarf evergreen oaks. ⟨Spanish *chuparro* evergreen oak⟩

cha·pa·ti [tʃə'pɑti] *n* a flat East Indian bread cooked on a griddle. ⟨Hindi *capati* flat⟩

chap·el ['tʃæpəl] *n* **1** a small church. **2** a small place for worship in a larger building such as a church, airport, hospital, etc. ⟨Latin *cappella*⟩

chap·er·one or **chap·er·on** ['ʃæpə,roun] or [ˌʃæpə'roun] *n* **1** an adult who accompanies a young person for supervision. **2** formerly, a married or older woman accompanying an unmarried woman in public. **chap·er·one** *v.* **chap·er·on·age** ['ʃæpərənədʒ] *n.* ⟨French = hood, protector; *chape* cape, Latin *cappa*⟩

chap·lain ['tʃæplən] *n* a member of the clergy serving an institution such as a prison, university, hospital, army, etc. **chap·lain·cy** *n.* ⟨Latin *capellanus.* See CHAPEL.⟩

chap·let ['tʃæplɪt] *n* **1** a wreath worn on the head. **2** *Roman Catholic Church* **a** a short rosary. **b** the prayers said with it. ⟨Old French, diminutive of *chapel* headdress⟩

chap·ter ['tʃæptər] *n* **1** a main division of a book or story. **2** anything viewed as part of a story: *The development of television is an interesting chapter in modern science.* **3** a local branch of an organization. **4** a group of clergy or monks. ⟨Old French *chapitre;* Latin *capitulum,* diminutive of *caput* head⟩

chapter and verse 1 the exact reference for a passage of Scripture. **2** precise authority: *He cited chapter and verse for his opinions.*

char[1] [tʃɑr] *v* **charred, char·ring 1** burn to charcoal. **2** burn slightly. ⟨*charcoal*⟩
char·broil or **char–broil** *v* cook on a rack over burning charcoal.

char[2] [tʃɑr] *n, pl* **char** any of a genus of mostly freshwater fish of the salmon or trout family. The **arctic char** is common in Canada. ⟨origin uncertain⟩

char·ac·ter ['kerɪktər] *or* ['kærɪktər] *n* **1** a person or animal in a story or play: *The main character is a miner.* **2** *Informal* a remarkable person: *I hear she's quite a character.* **3** the combination of qualities that distinguishes a thing: *The soil here is of a claylike character.* **4** the combined moral qualities of a person or group: *a person of shallow character.* **5** moral firmness: *It takes character to endure hardship for very long.* **6** reputation. **7** role; capacity: *in her character as committee chair.* **8** a letter, number, or other symbol, or a meaningful space in a series of these; any symbol that can be stored and processed by a computer. **char·ac·ter·less** *adj.* ⟨Greek *charaktēr* stamped mark; *charassein* engrave⟩
in character a *Theatre* true to the character being played: *The actor remained in character throughout the play.* **b** consistent with a person's known character: *Her cutting remarks were entirely in character.* **out of character** not as expected, given the person's character or the role being played.
character actor an actor who can play a variety of roles, esp those with pronounced or unusual characteristics. **character role**.
char·ac·ter·is·tic *adj* distinctive; typical: *Bananas have a characteristic smell. n* quality or feature: *A skunk's odour is its most obvious characteristic.* **char·ac·ter·is·ti·cal·ly** *adv.*
char·ac·ter·ize *v* **1** describe the character of. **2** be a distinctive feature of: *A giraffe is characterized by a long neck.* **char·ac·ter·i·za·tion** *n.*
character sketch a brief description of a person's qualities.

Character applies to moral qualities that can be consciously developed, such as courage, generosity, etc. **Personality** applies to the combination of qualities that make an individual unique, including natural strengths and weaknesses, mannerisms, preferences, abilities, and so on. **Temperament** is narrower and refers to emotional qualities that predispose a person to react in typical ways or choose typical kinds of activity, etc.

cha·rade [ʃə'reɪd] *n* **1** a word or idea represented by a pantomime. **2 charades** *pl* a game in which a word, title, proverb, etc. is acted out by one person or team while others try to guess what it is. **3** a very obvious pretence. ⟨Provençal *charrada; charra* chatter⟩

char·coal ['tʃɑr,koul] *n* **1** a form of carbon made by partly burning wood or bones in a place from which the air is shut out. **2** a very dark grey. ⟨Middle English *charcole*⟩

chard [tʃɑrd] *n* a variety of white beet; Swiss chard. ⟨Latin *carduus* thistle, artichoke⟩

charge [tʃɑrdʒ] *v* **1** ask (someone) as a price: *He charged us $45 to repair the radio.* **2** require payment (*for*): *They charge for hot water in the cafeteria.* **3** record, or have recorded, as a debt to be paid later: *This store will charge purchases. Can I charge this to my account?* **4** load; fill: *an atmosphere charged with emotion.* **5** restore the active materials of (a storage battery). **6** give responsibility to: *The law charges the police with keeping order.* **7** accuse, esp in a court of law: *to be charged with speeding.* **8** of a judge, instruct (the jury). **9** attack; rush at: *The soldiers charged the enemy.* **10** *Hockey* try to stop (an opponent) illegally by taking more than two steps toward him or her in an attack. *n* **1** a price asked for or placed on something. **2** a debt: *Will that be cash or charge?* **3** that with which a thing is filled or loaded. **4** an amount of electricity. **5** responsibility. **6** care or management. **7** a person in another's care: *She fed her young charges.* **8** instruction or order: *a judge's charge to a jury.* **9** accusation. **10** an attack; forceful rush. **11** *Informal* thrill; fun: *I get a real charge out of that game!*
charge·a·ble ['tʃɑrdʒəbəl] *adj.* ⟨Old French *charger*; Latin *carricare* load, *carrus* wagon⟩
charge out a check (books) out of a library. **b** check out of a hotel, etc. **charge up** record as a credit: *charge it up to experience.* **in charge** in command. **in charge of** responsible for: *in charge of the class.* **in the charge of** in the custody of: *placed in the charge of an officer.* **take charge** assume control.
charge account an arrangement for buying goods or services on credit. **charge card** CREDIT CARD. **char·gé d'af·faires** [ʃɑr,ʒei də'fer] *pl* **char·gés d'af·faires** an official taking the place of an ambassador or other diplomat. **charg·er** *n* **1** a warhorse. **2** a person or thing that charges: *a battery charger.*

char·i·ot ['tʃæriət] *or* ['tʃeriət] *n* in ancient times, a two-wheeled horse-drawn vehicle. **char·i·ot·eer** *n.* ⟨Old French *chariot* from *char*; Latin *carrus* cart⟩

cha·ris·ma [kə'rɪzmə] *n, pl* **-ma·ta** [-mətə] great personal power to attract and hold a following. **char·is·mat·ic** [,kerɪz'mætɪk] *or* [,kæriz-] *adj.* ⟨Greek⟩

char·i·ty ['tʃærəti] *or* ['tʃeɪrəti] *n* **1** help offered free of charge to those in need. **2** an organization helping the poor or suffering. **3** kindness; love for others. ⟨Latin *caritas*⟩
char·i·ta·ble *adj* **1** kind; esp, thinking the best of someone. **2** of or for a charity (def. 2). **char·i·ta·ble·ness** *n.* **char·i·ta·bly** *adv.*

char·la·tan ['ʃɑrlətən] *n* a person pretending to have more knowledge or skill than he or she has. **char·la·tan·ism** or **char·la·tan·ry** *n.* ⟨Italian *ciarlatano*; Mongolian *dzar* tell lies⟩

char·ley horse ['tʃɑrli] *Informal* a painful muscle cramp, esp of the leg or arm, caused by strain. ⟨19c baseball slang, likely referring to a lame racehorse⟩

charm [tʃɑrm] *n* **1** the power of delighting or fascinating: *the charm of novelty.* **2** a very pleasing feature: *One of her many charms.* **3** a small ornament worn on a chain. **4** a word, verse, etc. supposed to have magic power, esp to protect. **5** *Physics* a theoretical property by which one class of quarks may be distinguished from the several others thought to exist. **charm** *v.* **charmed** *adj.* **charm·less** *adj.* **charm·er** *n.* ⟨Old French *charme;* Latin *carmen* song, enchantment⟩ **charm·ing** *adj* (often ironic) delightful, engaging, endearing, etc. **charm·ing·ly** *adv.*

chart [tʃɑrt] *n* **1** information presented in the form of a diagram, table, or list. **2** Usually, **charts** *pl Informal* a list of the best-selling recordings: *no. 3 in the charts.* **3** a map, esp one for use in sailing or aviation. *v* **1** make a chart of: *to chart inflation, to chart a coastline.* **2** plan in detail. **chart·less** *adj.* ⟨Latin *charta;* Greek *chartēs* leaf of paper⟩

char·ter ['tʃɑrtər] *n* **1** a written grant by a government giving the right of organization and specifying the form of organization. **2** a document setting forth the fundamental principles governing a group: *the Canadian Charter of Rights and Freedoms.* **3** the hiring of a bus, ship, aircraft, etc., together with a driver or pilot, for temporary private use. **char·ter** *v.* **char·ter·less** *adj.* ⟨Old French *chartre;* Latin *chartula,* diminutive of *charta.* See CHART.⟩
chartered accountant a member of an accountants' institute chartered by the Crown. *Abbrev* **C.A. chartered bank** in Canada, any bank chartered by Parliament. **charter member** one of the founding members of a group. **Charter of Rights and Freedoms ✻** principles enshrined in the Constitution Act, 1982, guaranteeing basic human freedoms and rights. **charter school ✻** a school funded by and holding a charter directly from the government, independent of the local school board.

char·treuse [ʃɑr'truz] *or* [ʃɑr'trʊz] *French* [ʃaʀ'tʀøz] *n* **1** a greenish liqueur first made by Carthusian monks. **2** a light, yellowish green. ⟨French = Carthusian⟩

char·y ['tʃɛri] *adj* **1** wary: *chary of strangers. A cat is chary of wetting its paws.* **2** sparing; stingy: *chary of praise for others.* **char·i·ly** *adv.* **char·i·ness** *n.* ⟨Old English *cearig; caru* care⟩

chase [tʃeis] *v* **1** hurry after in order to catch or kill. **2** rush at (a person or thing) and force to go: *to chase a cat out of the garden.* **3** engrave. *n* **1** the act of going after in order to catch or kill: *They were caught after a chase.* **2** hunting as a sport: *fond of the chase.* **3** a hunted animal: *The hunter brought down his chase.* **chased** *adj.* ⟨Old French *chacier;* Latin *captiare*⟩ **chase after** pursue. **chase around** *Informal* rush here and there (in): *chasing around town.* **chase away** get rid of: *chase away the blues.* **chase up** (or **down**) look for and find or get: *to chase up a few more chairs.* **give chase** chase a person or thing.
chas·er *n* a mild drink after strong liquor.

chasm ['kæzəm] *n* **1** a deep opening in the earth. **2** a great difference of feeling or interest: *The chasm between her and her parents widened daily.* **chas·mic** *adj.* ⟨Greek *chasma*⟩

chas·sis ['ʃæsi] *or* ['tʃæsi] *n, pl* **chas·sis** [-iz] **1** the frame that supports the body of a car, the working parts of a radio, etc. **2** *Slang* a person's body, esp a woman's. ⟨Old French *châsse* frame or sash⟩

chaste [tʃeist] *adj* **1** virginal. **2** abstaining from sexual activity outside of marriage. **3** modest in behaviour. **4** simple and plain in style. **chaste·ly** *adv.* **chaste·ness** *n.* **chas·ti·ty** *n.* ⟨Latin *castus* pure⟩
chas·ten ['tʃeisən] *v* **1** subdue, humble, make more restrained, etc.: *The experience chastened them.* **2** discipline with a view to improving. **chas·tise** [tʃæs'taiz] *v* **1** punish. **2** rebuke severely: *The coach chastised the players for being late.* **chas·tise·ment** *n.* **chas·tis·er** *n.*

chas·u·ble ['tʃæzəbəl] *or* ['tʃæzjəbəl] *n* a sleeveless outer garment worn by a Christian priest. ⟨Latin *casubula*⟩

châ·teau or **cha·teau** [ʃæ'tou] *or* [ʃə'tou] *French* [ʃa'to] *n, pl* **-teaux** [-'touz] *French* [-'to] **1** a castle or a large country house. **2** a building resembling such a house, such as a grand hotel. **3** formerly, in French Canada: **a** the residence of a governor or a seigneur. **b Château** the Château St. Louis in Québec City, residence of the Governor of Québec. ⟨French = castle; Latin *castellum*⟩
chat·e·laine [,ʃætə'lein] *or* ['ʃætə,lein] *n* the mistress of a château or of any large, wealthy household.

chat·tel ['tʃætəl] **1** *n* a movable possession; a piece of property that is not real estate. **2** a slave, or someone who seems to be one. ⟨Old French *chatel;* Latin *capitalis*⟩

chat·ter ['tʃætər] *v* **1** talk constantly, rapidly, and foolishly. **2** make rapid, indistinct sounds: *Monkeys chatter.* **3** of teeth, rattle together from cold, fear, etc. **chat·ter** *n.* **chat·ter·er** *n.* ⟨imitative⟩
chat *n* **1** an easy, familiar talk. **2** a conversation over the Internet, as among participants in a CHAT ROOM. **chat, chat·ted, chat·ting** *v.* **chat·ty** *adj.* **chat·ti·ly** *adv.* **chat·ti·ness** *n.* **chat up** *Informal* talk with in a flirtatious or flattering way. **chat group** a group of computer users who regularly participate in a particular CHAT ROOM. **chat room** (or **line** or **site**) an Internet site where users can converse online in real time by typing on their computer keyboards. **chat·ter·box** *n* a habitual chatterer.

chauf·feur [ʃou'fər] *or* ['ʃoufər] *n* a person whose work is driving a car for its owner. **chauf·feur** *v.* ⟨French *chauffeur* stoker, from the days of steam automobiles⟩

chau·vin·ism ['ʃouvə,nizəm] *n* a strong, irrational belief in the natural superiority of one's own sex, nation, class, etc. **chau·vin·ist** *n, adj.* **chau·vin·is·tic** *adj.* ⟨Nicolas *Chauvin,* over-enthusiastic French patriot⟩

chaw [tʃɒ] *interj* ✻ (to a dog team) left!

cheap [tʃip] *adj* **1** costing little money or

effort: *cheap rent, a cheap victory.* **2** of low quality or value: *cheap entertainment, cheap pants.* **3** of little account: *Life was cheap back then.* **4** stingy: *too cheap to leave a tip.* **5** low; not noble or classy: *a cheap thing to do.* **cheap·ly** or **cheap** *adv.* **cheap·ness** *n.* ⟨short for *good cheap* good bargain; Old English *cēap* price, bargain⟩
feel cheap feel inferior and ashamed. **hold cheap** value little. **on the cheap** at low cost. **cheap·en** *v* **1** lower the price or value of. **2** lower the reputation of: *He cheapened himself by his slovenly manners.* **cheap·jack** *n* a person who deals in cheap or worthless goods. *adj* worthless; inferior. **cheap·skate** *n Slang* a stingy person.

SYNONYMS

Cheap means 'low in price', but often expresses a negative attitude, implying little value for little money: *I won't buy cheap shoes.* **Inexpensive** usually expresses a more neutral attitude or may suggest a 'sensible' purchase: *furniture that is inexpensive but sturdy.*

cheat [tʃit] *v* **1** trick or deceive (someone) in order to gain unfairly: *to cheat at cards. They cheated him out of his life savings.* **2** deprive of something unfairly: *She was cheated of her childhood.* **3** be sexually unfaithful (with *on*). **4** escape by clever means: *to cheat death.*
n **1** a person who uses trickery for unfair gain. **2** a swindle; trick. **cheat·er** *n.* ⟨variant of *escheat;* Latin *ex-* out + *cadere* fall⟩
cheat sheet *Slang* a hidden slip of paper with answers on it, used to cheat in a test or examination.

check [tʃek] *v* **1** stop (something), usually with a preventive effect: *They checked their steps when they heard the growl. The bushes checked her fall.* **2** hold back; restrain: *to check one's anger.* **3** *Hockey* impede the progress of (the puck-carrier), using the stick or the body. **4 a** investigate; find out: *Check whether the doors are locked.* **b** examine to prove true or right: *Check your answers.* **c** verify the status of (often with *on* or *up on*): *to check on the kids. Check the cake in the oven.* **5** (often with *off*) mark with a CHECK MARK. **6** leave for safekeeping: *to check one's coat.* **7** hand over (baggage) to be sent to a destination. **8** mark in a pattern of squares. **9** *Chess* put (an opponent's king) in a position of danger.
n **1** an act, process, or means of checking: *Do a thorough check of the brakes.* **2** anything that stops or restrains something else: *This should act as a check on expenditures.* **3** CHECK MARK. **4** a ticket allowing one to reclaim a checked bag, garment, etc. **5** the bill for food bought in a restaurant. **6** a pattern of squares of alternating colours, or a fabric, wallpaper, etc. with such a pattern. **7** *US* cheque.
interj **1** *Chess* a warning of immediate danger to an opponent's king. **2** *Informal* OK. ⟨Old French *eschec* check (chess); Persian *shāh* king⟩
check in a arrive and register at a hotel, airline counter, etc. **b** visit briefly to see how things are going. **check on** check (*v* def. 4c) **check out a** leave and pay for a room in a

hotel. **b** in a store, have one's purchases totalled at the cash desk and pay for them. **c** *Slang* die. **d** verify: *to check out a statement.* **e** inspect: *to check out a plane before takeoff.* **f** appear to be satisfactory on investigation: *Well, her story about the fire checks out.* **g** borrow from a library: *to check out a book.* **h** *Slang* take a look at: *Hey, check out his new bike!* **check over** inspect; examine. **check up (on)** verify that all is in order with, esp when one has reason to suspect. **check·up** *n.* **in check a** held back. **b** *Chess* of a king, in immediate danger from an opponent.
checked *adj* marked in a pattern of squares. **check·er** *n* **1** a person who checks: *a fact checker.* **2** one of the pieces used in the game of CHECKERS. **check·ered** *adj.* **check·er·board** *n* a square board marked in a pattern of 64 squares of two alternating colours and used in playing checkers or chess. **check·ers** *n* a game for two, played on a checkerboard with twelve coloured discs each. **check·list** *n* a list of criteria, needed items, etc., that are checked off as each is satisfied or dealt with. **check mark** a mark (√) showing that a thing is correct or has been counted, verified, etc. **check·mate** *v* **1** *Chess* put (an opponent's king) in check with no recourse, and so win the game. **2** foil or outmanoeuvre; defeat. **check·mate** *n, interj.* **check·out** *n* **1** in a supermarket, the counter where purchases are totalled and paid for. **2** Often, **checkout time** in a hotel or motel, the time by which one must leave and pay. **check·point** *n* one of a series of points along a route where some type of check is made. **check·up** *n* a thorough examination.

chee·cha·ko [tʃiˈtʃɑkou] or [tʃiˈtʃækou] *n* ✱ *West Coast* newcomer; greenhorn. ⟨Chinook jargon; Chinook *t'shi* new + *chakho* come⟩

cheek [tʃik] *n* **1** the side of the face below either eye. **2** *Slang* buttock. **3** impudence. **4** anything like a cheek in form or position. **cheek·y** *adj.* **cheek·i·ly** *adv.* **cheek·i·ness** *n.* ⟨Old English *cēce*⟩
cheek by jowl side by side and close together. **turn the other cheek** not repay a wrong. **cheek·bone** *n* a bone just below either eye.

cheep [tʃip] *v* make a short, high-pitched sound like a young bird. **cheep** *n.* ⟨imitative⟩

cheer [tʃir] *n* **1** gladness; light-heartedness; joy: *good cheer.* **2** encouragement or comfort: *The flowers brought cheer to the sick girl.* **3** a shout or chant of encouragement, approval, praise, etc. **cheer** *v.* **cheer·er** *n.* **cheer·less** *adj.* **cheer·less·ly** *adv.* ⟨Old French *chere;* Latin *cara* face, Greek *kara*⟩
cheer on urge on with cheers. **cheer up** make or become happier.
cheer·ful *adj* **1** in good spirits; happy; content. **2** cheery (def. 2): *a cheerful kitchen.* **3** willing: *cheerful efforts.* **cheer·ful·ly** *adv.* **cheer·ful·ness** *n.* **cheer·i·o** *interj Informal* goodbye. **cheer·lead·er** *n* **1** one who leads the organized cheering of a crowd at a sporting event. **2** someone who rallies others to a cause. **cheer·lead·ing** *n.* **cheers** *interj* **1** a toast

before drinking. 2 *Informal* goodbye; often as a closing formula in a letter. **cheer·y** *adj.* 1 briskly light-hearted and animated. 2 bright and warm. **cheer·i·ly** *adv.* **cheer·i·ness** *n.*

cheese [tʃiz] *n* a solid food made from the curds of milk. **cheese·like** *adj.* ⟨Latin *caseus*⟩ **cheese off** *Slang* annoy; anger. **say cheese** *Informal* smile for a photograph. **cheese·burg·er** hamburger with a slice of cheese. **cheese·cake** *n* 1 a rich dessert made of cheese, eggs, etc., often in a crumb crust. 2 *Slang* photographs of alluring women. Compare BEEFCAKE. **cheese·cloth** *n* a loosely woven cloth used orig for wrapping cheese. **cheese·par·ing** *n* a worthless thing. *adj* stingy. **chees·y** *adj* 1 like cheese. 2 *Slang* **a** not well made; inferior. **b** tacky; hokey; corny. **chees·i·ness** *n.*

chee·tah [ˈtʃitə] *n* a long-legged animal of the cat family, thought to be the fastest mammal on earth. ⟨Hindi *chita*⟩

chef [ʃɛf] *n* 1 a head cook. 2 any cook. ⟨French *chef (de cuisine)* head of the kitchen⟩ **chef–d'oeu·vre** [ʃeˈdœvʀ] *n*, *pl* **chefs–d·oeuvre** [ʃeˈdœvʀə] *French* masterpiece.

chem·i·cal [ˈkɛməkəl] *n* 1 any complex substance produced in a laboratory or in the body from basic raw materials or elementary susbtances. Paints, insecticides, and drugs are examples; so are neurotransmitters and enzymes. 2 a psychoactive drug or alcohol. *adj* 1 to do with or making use of any of these substances: *a chemical toilet, the chemical industry.* 2 to do with chemistry. **chem·i·cal·ly** *adv.* ⟨Latin *chimicus; alchimicus* of alchemy. See ALCHEMY.⟩ **chemical abuse** the habitual overuse of a drug or alcohol. **chemical change** a change in which one substance is converted into one or more substances with different properties. **chemical engineering** the science or profession applying chemistry to industrial purposes. **chemical engineer. chemical warfare** the use of chemicals other than explosives as weapons. **chem·i·lu·mi·nes·cence** [ˌkɛmə,lumə'nɛsəns] *n* luminescence resulting from chemical action and not involving heat. **chem·is·try** [ˈkɛmɪstri] *n* 1 the science dealing with elementary substances and the laws of their interaction. 2 chemical processes, properties, etc.: *Her body chemistry predisposes her to acne.* 3 qualities of personality in interaction: *The addition of new members altered the chemistry of the group.* 4 human activity viewed as a chemical phenomenon: *the chemistry of love.* **chem·ist** *n.* **che·mo·ther·a·py** [ˌkimou'θɛrəpi] *n* the treatment or control of disease, esp cancer, by means of chemical agents.

che·mise [ʃəˈmiz] *n* 1 a loose, shirtlike undergarment for women or girls. 2 a loose, straight-cut dress. ⟨French; Latin *camisia*⟩

che·nille [ʃəˈnil] *n* a fabric made with rows of tufted cord forming a soft, piled surface. ⟨French = caterpillar; from its furry look⟩

cheque [tʃɛk] *n* a written order to a bank to take money from the account of the signer

and pay it to the party named: *Make the cheque out to the Auto Repair Shop.* **cheque·book** *n* a book of blank cheques. **chequing account** an account on which cheques can be drawn.

cher·ish [ˈtʃɛrɪʃ] *v* 1 hold dear; treasure. 2 care for tenderly. 3 keep in mind: *She cherished the hope that her son was still alive.* ⟨Old French *cherir; cher* dear; Latin *carus*⟩

che·root [ʃəˈrut] *n* a cigar cut off square at both ends. ⟨Tamil *shuruttu* roll⟩

cher·ry [ˈtʃɛri] *n* 1 a small, round, edible fruit with a stone in the centre, produced by trees and shrubs in the rose family. 2 bright red. **cherry** *adj.* ⟨Greek *kerasos*⟩ **cherries jubilee** cherries flambéd in brandy. **cherry bomb** a round, red firecracker. **cherry picker** *Informal* a type of crane with a box on the end in which a person can stand to carry out operations high above ground. **cherry tomato** a miniature tomato.

cher·ub [ˈtʃɛrəb] *n* 1 *pl* **cher·u·bim** a winged celestial being representing divine justice. 2 *pl* **cher·ubs** a beautiful or good child. **che·ru·bic** [tʃəˈrubɪk] *adj.* **che·ru·bi·cal·ly** *adv.* ⟨Hebrew *kerūb*⟩

cher·vil [ˈtʃɜrvəl] *n* an aromatic Eurasian herb related to parsley. ⟨Greek *chairephyllon; chairein* rejoice + *phyllon* leaf⟩

chess [tʃɛs] *n* a game played on a checkered board with 64 squares by two people, each having 16 pieces, whose object is to capture pieces until the king is in a position of no escape without being captured. ⟨Old French *esches*, pl of *eschec*. See CHECK.⟩ **chess·board** *n* a board marked in a pattern of 64 squares of alternating colours. **chess·man** [ˈtʃɛs,man] *n*, *pl* **-men** one of the 16 pieces used in chess.

chest [tʃɛst] *n* 1 the part of the body of a person or animal enclosed by the ribs. 2 the measurement around a person's body at the widest part of the chest: *He has a 100 cm chest.* 3 a large, sturdy box with a lid, used for storage: *linen chest, tool chest.* 4 a small cabinet: *medicine chest.* ⟨Greek *kistē* box⟩ **get something off one's chest** relieve one's mind by talking about some problem. **chest of drawers** a piece of furniture with several drawers for keeping clothes, etc. **chest wader** a waterproof garment like overalls, used for wading through swamps. **chest·y** *adj Informal* full-breasted.

ches·ter·field [ˈtʃɛstər,fild] *n* ✱ sofa; couch. ⟨19c Earl of *Chesterfield*⟩

chest·nut [ˈtʃɛsnʌt] *or* [-nət] *n* 1 any of a genus of trees of the beech family native to north temperate regions and producing burrlike fruits containing two or three edible nuts. 2 dark reddish brown. 3 a brown horse. 4 *Informal* a stale joke or story. ⟨Greek *kastanea* + NUT⟩

chev·re [ˈʃɛvrə] *French* [ʃɛvʀ] *n* goat's-milk cheese. ⟨French *chèvre* goat⟩

chev·ron [ˈʃɛvrɒn] *or* [ˈʃɛvrən] *n* a V-shaped mark. ⟨Old French = rafter; *chèvre* goat⟩

chew [tʃu] *v* crush with the teeth. **chew·a·ble** *adj.* ⟨Old English *cēowan*⟩ **chew out** *Slang* reprimand. **chew over** *Informal* consider or discuss at length. **chew the fat** *Slang* converse idly. **chew up a** chew to a pulp. **b** crush or mangle as if with teeth: *The wheels of the car chewed up the lawn.* **chewing gum** a flavoured gummy preparation for chewing. **chewing tobacco** tobacco for chewing rather than smoking. **chew·y** *adj* soft and sticky and requiring much chewing.

chez [ʃei] *French* at the home of.

ch'i [tʃi] *n Chinese philosophy* the life force that dwells in the body and breath.

chi·a·ro·scu·ro [ki,ɑrə'skjurou] *n* **1** the effect or treatment of light and shade in a picture. **2** a style of painting, drawing, etc. using only light and shade; monochrome. **3** contrast, as of joy and sadness, etc. in a story or piece of music. ⟨Italian *chiaro* light + *oscuro* dark⟩

chic [ʃik] *n* fashionable style. **chic** *adj.* **chic·ly** *adv.* ⟨French⟩

chi·can·er·y [ʃɪ'keinəri] *n* clever, dishonest argument. **chi·cane** *v.* ⟨French *chicaner*⟩

chi–chi ['ʃi ʃi] *adj Informal* stylish, esp in an affected way: *chi-chi boutiques.* ⟨French⟩

chick [tʃɪk] *n* **1** a baby chicken. **2** any baby bird. **3** child. ⟨*chicken*⟩ **chick pea** the edible seed of a plant resembling the garden pea, but yellow and bigger. **chick·weed** *n* any of several plants, some of which are attractive to birds.

chick·a·dee ['tʃɪkə,di] *n* any of several songbirds of the titmouse family, with a patch on the head. ⟨imitative of its song⟩

chick·en ['tʃɪkən] *n* **1** a common domestic fowl bred for its eggs or flesh. **2** ✿ *Informal* PRAIRIE CHICKEN. **3** *Slang* coward. **chick·en** *adj.* ⟨Old English *cicen*⟩ **chicken out** *Slang* withdraw because of lack of courage. **count one's chickens before they are hatched** reckon on future good fortune which may not materialize. **play chicken** engage in a risky contest, hoping that the other person will back down first. **chick·en·burg·er** *n* a burger made with chicken. **chicken feed 1** food for chickens. **2** *Slang* an insignificant amount of money. **chicken hawk** any of various hawks that raid poultry yards. **chick·en–heart·ed** *adj* cowardly. **chicken pox** a contagious childhood disease marked by pus-filled skin eruptions. **chicken wire** a light wire netting of six-sided mesh.

chic·le ['tʃɪkəl] *n* a tasteless gum prepared from the milky juice of the sapodilla tree and used to make chewing gum. ⟨Nahuatl *chietli*⟩

chic·o·ry ['tʃɪkəri] *n* a European perennial herb whose leaves are used in salads and whose roots are used as a coffee substitute; a common weed in Canada. ⟨Greek *kichōrion*⟩

chide [tʃaid] *v* **chid·ed** or **chid; chid·ed, chid,** or **chid·den; chid·ing** reproach; scold: *She chided her son for getting his sweater dirty.* **chid·ing·ly** *adv.* ⟨Old English *cīdan*⟩

chief [tʃif] *n* **1** the leader of any group; head.

2 a the head of a First Nations band. **b** the head of a tribe or clan. *adj* **1** in authority: *the chief engineer.* **2** most important: *the chief attraction.* ⟨Old French; Latin *caput* head⟩ **in chief a** in the highest position (often in compounds: *editor-in-chief*). **b** chiefly. **chief·dom** *n* the position or territory of a chief. **chief executive officer** the head of the executive branch of a government or large corporation. *Abbrev* **CEO chief justice 1** in Canada, the senior judge of a supreme court. **2** in the US: **a** a similar official. **b** a judge who presides over a court made up of a group of judges. **chief·ly** *adv* mainly; mostly: *I came chiefly out of curiosity.* **chief of staff** the principal adviser to the commander of a military organization or to the head of a government. **Chief of the Defence Staff ✿** Canada's highest-ranking military officer. **chief·tain** *n* the chief of a tribe or clan.

chif·fon [ʃə'fɒn] *n* a very thin, delicate fabric. ⟨French = rag⟩

chi·hua·hua [tʃə'wɑwɑ] *n* an ancient breed of tiny dog orig developed in Mexico, having large, protruding eyes and short hair. ⟨*Chihuahua,* a state and city in N Mexico⟩

chil·blain ['tʃɪl,blein] *n* Usually, **chilblains** *pl* itchy redness on the hands or feet, caused by cold. **chil·blained** *adj.* ⟨*chill* + *blain* a sore⟩

Chil·cot·in See Tsɪʟнǫот'ɪɴ.

child [tʃaild] *n, pl* **chil·dren 1** a boy or girl, esp one up to the early teens. **2** son or daughter. **3** descendant. **4** a person regarded as belonging to a particular environment: *a child of the nuclear age.* **child·less** *adj.* **child·less·ness** *n.* ⟨Old English *cild*⟩ **with child** pregnant. **child·bear·ing** *n* the process of conceiving and giving birth to children. **child·bear·ing** *adj.* **child·bed** *n* the condition of a woman giving birth. **child·birth** *n* the process of giving birth to a child. **child·hood** *n* **1** the condition of being a child: *the carefree days of childhood.* **2** an early stage of anything. **child·ish** *adj* **1** of a child: *childish dreams.* **2** being, or engaging in, behaviour unsuitable for a grown person: *It was childish of her to make a fuss.* **child·ish·ly** *adv.* **child·ish·ness** *n.* **child labour** or **labor** work done by children in factories, business, etc. **child·like** *adj* natural, trusting, innocent, curious, etc. as a child is. **child·like·ness** *n.* **child·proof** *adj* so arranged as to prevent damage by or to a young child: *Is your home childproof?* **child·proof** *v.* **child's play** something usually very easy to do.

> **CONFUSABLES**
>
> **Childish** means 'immature like a child', and has negative connotations when applied to an adult: *a childish attitude.* **Childlike** means 'innocent like a child', and has no negative connotations when applied to an adult: *She had a childlike respect for her parents.*

chil·i ['tʃɪli] *n, pl* chil·ies 1 the small, hot-tasting fruit of any of several varieties of PEPPER (def. 2), often ground to powder. 2 kidney beans cooked with chilies and tomatoes and, usually, beef. Also, chil·li. ⟨Mexican *chilli*⟩ chil·i con car·ne chili (def. 2) with beef in it. chili dog a hot dog with chili (def. 2) on it. chili sauce a sauce made of chilies, tomatoes, and spices.

Chil·kat ['tʃɪlkæt] *n, pl* -kat or kats a member of a Native American people living mainly in SE Alaska and noted for making coloured, D-shaped blankets from mountain-goat wool and cedar bark. Chil·kat *adj.*

chill [tʃɪl] *n* 1 a moderate but unpleasant coldness: *a chill in the air.* 2 a mild cold: *I've caught a chill.* 3 unfriendliness: *a chill in his voice.* 4 a check on enthusiasm; depressing influence. 5 a sudden feeling of fear or dread, or the shiver that accompanies it. 6 chills *pl* a a thrill of fear or, less often, pleasure. b a bout of shivering due to illness. *v* 1 cool or refrigerate. 2 affect with a chill. 3 *Slang* relax (often with *out*): *just chilling on the porch. Chill out, it's only a spider!* chill *adj.* chill·ing *adj.* chill·y *adj.* chill·i·ness *n.* ⟨Old English *ciele*⟩ chill·er *n* 1 *Informal* a horror story or film. 2 a person or thing that chills or gives chills.

CONFUSABLES
Chilly means 'unpleasantly cool': *a chilly room.* Chill is more literary and not only implies greater coolness but, especially when used metaphorically, unpleasantness: *a chill wind, a chill atmosphere.* Chilling means 'frightening' and has a sinister connotation.

chime [tʃaɪm] *n* 1 Usually, chimes *pl* a set of bells or metal tubes tuned to a musical scale, played by hammers or simple machinery. 2 the musical sound made by a bell, or a sound like this: *the chime of the old clock, chimes of laughter.* chime *v.* chim·er *n.* ⟨Middle English *chymbe*; Greek *kymbalon*⟩ chime in *Informal.* interrupt or join others in speaking. b be in harmony; agree: *Her ideas chimed in with mine.*

chi·me·ra [kə'mirə] *or* [kaɪ'mirə] *n* 1 Chimera *Greek myth* a female monster with a lion's head, goat's body, and serpent's tail, supposed to breathe out fire. 2 a horrible or bizarre creature of the imagination. 3 an absurd idea: *The idea of changing lead to gold was a chimera.* 4 *Biology* an individual composed of cells from two zygotes. Also, chi·mae·ra. chi·mer·ic [-'mɛrɪk] *or* chi·mer·i·cal *adj.* chi·mer·i·cal·ly *adv.* ⟨Greek *chimaira*⟩

chim·ney ['tʃɪmni] *n* 1 an upright structure creating a passageway to bring draft to a fire and carry away smoke. 2 the part of this that rises above a roof. 3 a glass tube around the flame of a lamp. 4 a crack or opening in rock, in a volcano, etc. chim·ney·less *adj.* ⟨Latin *caminata; caminus* oven, Greek *kaminos*⟩ chimney piece mantelpiece. chimney sweep a person whose work is cleaning chimneys.

chi·mo ['tʃimou] *or* ['tʃaɪmou] *interj* ✱ *North* a call or exclamation of greeting. ⟨Inuktitut⟩

chim·pan·zee [,tʃɪmpæn'zi] *or* [tʃɪm'pænzi] *n* an anthropoid ape of Africa, smaller than a gorilla. Often shortened to chimp. ⟨Bantu⟩

chin [tʃɪn] *n* the lower jaw, esp the front part, below the mouth. *v* chinned, chin·ning *Informal* chat; gossip. chin·less *adj.* ⟨Old English *cinn*⟩ chin oneself do a chin-up or chin-ups. keep one's chin up bear hardship bravely. take it on the chin *Informal* a suffer severe hardship. b endure stoically. chin–up *n* the exercise of hanging by the hands from a bar and pulling oneself up until one's chin is level with the bar.

chi·na ['tʃaɪnə] *n* 1 a fine white ceramic made of pure clay. 2 dishes or ornaments, etc. of this. chi·na *adj.* ⟨short for earlier *china-ware* ware from China⟩ Chi·na·town *n* a section of a city inhabited mainly by Chinese people and having many Chinese stores and restaurants. chi·na·ware *n* dishes, vases, etc. Chinese cabbage any of several edible plants native to Asia, tasting like cabbage. Chinese checkers a game played by two to six people using small marbles on a pitted board patterned as a six-pointed star. Chinese lantern 1 a lantern of thin, coloured paper that can be folded up accordion-style. 2 Often, Chinese lantern plant a perennial plant with a thin, hollow red fruit casing.

chinch [tʃɪntʃ] *n* Usually, chinch bug a small insect that sucks the juice of grain plants. ⟨Spanish *chinche*; L *cimex* bug⟩

chin·chil·la [tʃɪn'tʃɪlə] *n* a small rodent widely bred in captivity for its soft, grey fur. ⟨Spanish⟩

chink¹ [tʃɪŋk] *n* a narrow opening: *the chinks between the logs of the cabin.* *v* 1 fill up the chinks in: *chinked with mud.* 2 make chinks in. ⟨Old English *cinu* fissure⟩

chink² [tʃɪŋk] *n* the short ringing sound of coins hitting together. chink *v.* ⟨imitative⟩

chi·no ['tʃinou] *or* ['ʃinou] *n* 1 twilled cotton fabric used especially for sportswear. 2 chinos *pl* pants made of this. ⟨origin unknown⟩

chi·nook [ʃə'nʊk] ✱ *n* a warm, usually dry, winter wind that blows from the west across the Rocky Mountains, sometimes extending into Saskatchewan. chi·nook *v.* chinook arch ✱ an arch of blue sky above the western horizon, often seen just before or during a chinook. chinook salmon a spring salmon, esp a large one.

Chi·nook [ʃə'nʊk] *or* [tʃə'nuk] *n, pl* -nook or -nooks 1 a member of an American Indian people who lived along the Columbia River in the NW United States. 2 the Chinookan language of the Chinook and other peoples of the region. 3 CHINOOK JARGON. Chi·nook *adj.* Chi·nook·an *n* a family of languages spoken by aboriginal peoples of the N Pacific coast of North America. Chi·nook·an *adj.* Chinook jargon ✱ a trade language of the Pacific coast of North America based on Chinook, with Nootka, Salishan, English, and French words.

chintz [tʃɪnts] *n* a glazed cotton fabric, usually in colourful prints. ⟨orig pl, from Hindi *chint*, Sanskrit *citra* variegated⟩ **chintz·y** *adj* **1** like chintz. **2** *Informal* cheap; tacky: *chintzy furniture, chintzy behaviour.*

chip [tʃɪp] *n* **1** a small piece cut or broken off. **2** the dent left: *This plate has a small chip.* **3** a small or thin piece of food: *banana chips.* **4** POTATO CHIP (def. 1): *We ate a whole bag of chips.* **5** FRENCH FRY: *fish and chips.* **6** *Games* a disc used as a counter. **7** *Electronics* **a** a tiny wafer of semiconductor material used in an integrated circuit. **b** INTEGRATED CIRCUIT. **8** a piece of dried dung, used for fuel in some regions: *buffalo chips.* **9** CHIP SHOT. *v* **chipped, chip·ping 1** cut or break small pieces from: *to chip a plate, to chip paint. He chipped away at the block of wood.* **2** become chipped: *China chips easily.* **3** *Golf* make a CHIP SHOT. ⟨Old English *(for)cippian*⟩ **chip in** *Informal* **a** join with others in giving (money or help). **b** put in (a remark) when others are talking. **cash in one's chips** a *Poker* redeem one's chips for cash. **b** *Slang* quit or retire. **c** *Slang* die. **chip off the old block** *Informal* a person very much like his or her parent. **chip on one's shoulder a** a permanent sense of injury. **b** a readiness to fight. **when the chips are down** in a crisis. **chip·board** *n* a building material made of wood chips and fibres pressed together. **chip shot** *Golf* a short, lofted shot used to get the ball onto the green. **chip·py** *adj* ✱ *Informal* **1** short-tempered; aggressive: *He was known as a chippy player.* **2** with much rough play or fighting: *a chippy hockey game.*

Chip·e·wy·an [ˌtʃɪpə'waɪən] *n, pl* **-an** or **-ans 1** a member of a traditionally nomadic First Nations people of northern Manitoba and Saskatchewan and the Northwest Territories. The Chipewyan are one of the Dene. **2** their Athapascan language. **Chip·e·wy·an** *adj*. Also, **Chip·e·way·an.**

chip·munk ['tʃɪpmʌŋk] *n* any of several small North American animals of the squirrel family that live mainly on the ground, with black stripes along the back. ⟨Algonquian⟩

chip·per ['tʃɪpər] *adj Informal* lively and cheerful. ⟨origin uncertain⟩

Chip·pe·wa ['tʃɪpə,wɒ],   ['tʃɪpəwə],   *or* ['tʃɪpə,weɪ] *n, pl* **-wa** or **-was** Ojibwa.

chiromancy ['kaɪrə,mænsi] *n* palmistry; the art of palm-reading. ⟨Greek *cheir* hand + *manteia* divination⟩

chi·rop·o·dy [kə'rɒpədi] *n* the health science concerned with the feet. Increasingly called **podiatry. chi·rop·o·dist** *n*. ⟨Greek *cheir* hand + *pous, podos* foot; orig treatment of both⟩

chi·ro·prac·tic [ˌkaɪrə'præktɪk] *n* treatment of disorders by manipulation of the bones, esp those of the spine. **chi·ro·prac·tic** *adj*. **chi·ro·prac·tor** ['kaɪrə,præktər] *n*. ⟨Greek *cheir* hand + *praktikos* of practice⟩

chirp [tʃɜrp] *v* make a short, high-pitched

sound like that of certain birds and insects. **chirp** *n*. **chirp·er** *n*. ⟨probably imitative; Middle English *chirken*⟩

chirp·y *adj* **1** disposed to chirp. **2** lively and cheerful. **chirp·i·ly** *adv*. **chirp·i·ness** *n*. **chir·rup** ['tʃɪrəp] *or* ['tʃɜrəp] *v* **-rupped** or **-ruped, -rup·ping** or **-rup·ing** chirp again and again: *He chirrupped to his horse to make it go faster.* **chir·rup** *n*. **chir·rup·y** *adj*.

chis·el ['tʃɪzəl] *n* a slender cutting tool with a sharp edge, for shaping wood, stone, or metal by hammering on the top. *v* **-elled** or **-eled, -el·ling** or **-el·ing 1** shape with a chisel. **2** *Slang* swindle. **chis·el·ler** or **chis·el·er** *n*. ⟨Latin *caesellum; caedere* cut⟩ **chis·elled** or **chis·eled** *adj* **1** shaped with a chisel. **2** having clear, sharp outlines, as if cut with a chisel: *chiselled features.*

chi–square test ['kaɪ ˌskwɛr] *n Statistics* a test of the validity of a specific frequency distribution.

chit[1] [tʃɪt] *n* **1** child. **2** a saucy, forward girl. ⟨related to KITTEN; dialect for 'kitten'⟩

chit[2] [tʃɪt] *n* a note or slip of paper, esp a promissory note, voucher, etc. ⟨Hindi *chitthi* letter; Sanskrit *chitra* spot, mark⟩

chit·chat ['tʃɪt,tʃæt] *n* friendly chat; light talk. **chit·chat, -chat·ted, -chat·ting** *v*. ⟨*chat*⟩

chi·tin ['kəɪtən] *n* horny substance forming the hard outer covering of beetles, lobsters, etc. **chi·tin·ous** *adj*. ⟨Greek *chiton* tunic⟩

chit·ter ['tʃɪtər] *v* twitter. ⟨imitative⟩

chit·ter·lings ['tʃɪtərlɪŋz] *n pl* the small intestines of pigs, cooked as food. ⟨Middle English; origin uncertain⟩

chiv·al·ry ['ʃɪvəlri] *n* **1** the knightly culture and social system of the Middle Ages, with its honourable ideals of bravery, generosity, justice, courtesy, etc. **2** courteous behaviour, esp the courtesies expected of a gentleman toward women. ⟨Old French *chevalerie* knighthood; Latin *caballerius* horseman, *caballus* horse⟩ **chiv·al·ric** ['ʃɪvəlrɪk] *or* [ʃə'vælrɪk] *adj* to do with the system of chivalry. **chiv·al·rous** *adj* gentlemanly; brave, courteous to women, etc. **chiv·al·rous·ly** *adv*. **chiv·al·rous·ness** *n*.

chive [tʃaɪv] *n* Usually, **chives** *pl* a plant closely related to the onion. Its green shoots are used in salads, etc. ⟨Latin *caepa* onion⟩

chiv·vy or **chiv·y** ['tʃɪvi] *v* **1** harass; nag: *chivvied into going.* **2** get by chivvying: *He chivvied a dollar out of me.* ⟨origin uncertain⟩

chla·myd·ia [klə'mɪdiə] *n, pl* **-diae** [-di,i] **1** a venereal disease of the genito-urinary tract which can lead to sterility. **2** any of a genus of parasitic, disease-causing bacteria. ⟨Greek *chlamys* cloak⟩

chlo·rine [klɔ'rin] *or* ['klɔrin] *n* a poisonous, greenish yellow element that is a gas at normal temperatures. *Symbol* **Cl** ⟨Greek *chlōros* green⟩ **chlo·ride** *n* any compound of chlorine and another element or radical. **chlo·rin·ate** bleach or disinfect with chlorine. **chlo·rin·a·tion** *n*.

chloro– or **chlor–** *combining form* **1** green: *chlorophyl.* **2** chlorine. **chlo·ro·fluo·ro·car·bon** [ˌklɔrouˌflɔrə'karbən] *n* any of several compounds of carbon formerly much used in refrigerators, aerosol cans, etc. with a damaging effect on the ozone layer of the earth's atmosphere. *Abbrev* **CFC**, *pl* **CFCs**. **chlo·ro·form** *n* a colourless, sweet-smelling liquid used as an anesthetic. *v* anesthetize with chloroform. **chlo·ro·phyl** or **chlo·ro·phyll** ['klɔrə,fɪl] *n Botany* the green colouring matter of plants.

chock [tʃɒk] *n* **1** a block; wedge. **2** on a boat, a heavy piece of metal or wood for a rope to pass through. *adv* as close or tight as can be: *chock up against the wall.* ⟨Norman French *choque* log⟩ **chock–a–block** *adj* very crowded. **chock–full** or **chuck–full** *adj* as full as can be.

choc·o·late ['tʃɒklɪt] *n* **1** the roasted seeds of the cacao tree. **2** candy, or a piece of candy, made from this. **3** a drink made of chocolate, milk or water, and sugar. **4** rich dark brown. **choc·o·late** *adj*. **choc·o·lat·ey** or **choc·o·lat·y** *adj*. ⟨Aztec *chocolatl*⟩ **chocolate bar** a bar of chocolate, or of a mixture of things such as candy, raisins, nuts, etc. coated with chocolate. **choc·o·la·tier** [ˌtʃɒklə'tir] *n* a maker of fine chocolates.

choice [tʃɔɪs] *n* **1** the act of choosing: *Leave the choice to her.* **2** the right or opportunity to choose: *I have no choice.* **3** the person or thing chosen: *My choice was cabbage rolls.* **4** a quantity and variety to choose from: *a wide choice of vegetables.* *adj* of fine quality: *a choice steak.* **choice·ness** *n*. ⟨Middle English *chois*; Old French *choisir*⟩ **of choice** preferred: *the treatment of choice.*

choir [kwaɪr] *n* a large, organized group of singers. **cho·ral** ['kɔrəl] *adj.* See also CHORUS. ⟨Old French *cuer;* Latin *chorus*⟩ **choir·boy, choir·girl** *n* a boy (girl) who sings in a choir. **choir loft** in a church, a balcony for a choir. **choir·mas·ter** *n* the director of a choir. **chor·is·ter** ['kɔrɪstər] *n* a singer in a choir, esp a child.

choke [tʃouk] *v* **1** make or be unable to breathe or swallow because of constriction or obstruction of the windpipe. **2** clog (often with *up*): *streets choked with traffic.* **3** reduce or cut off the supply of air to (a gas engine, fire, etc.). **4** overcome and stop the growth of: *to choke a rebellion. Weeds choked the flowers.* *n* **1** the act or sound of choking. **2** a valve that reduces or cuts off a supply of air. ⟨Old English *ācēocian*⟩

choke back suppress (tears, laughter, etc.). **choke down** swallow with difficulty: *She managed to choke down the dry bread.* **choke off** stop the flow of: *The beavers choked off our water supply.* **choke on** find hard to accept, utter, or swallow: *to choke on an apology.* **choke up** be or cause to be near tears. **choke collar** or **chain** a collar for a dog, which tightens when the dog pulls on it. **chok·er** *n* **1** a necklace or ornamental band fitting closely around the neck. **2** ✷ *Logging* a cable and hook used to haul logs. **cho·ky** *adj Informal* **1** inclined to choke, esp with emotion. **2** suffocating: *a choky collar.*

cho·lent ['tʃoulənt] *or* ['tʃʌlənt] *n* a Jewish dish consisting of beef, potatoes, beans, etc., stewed for a long time and prepared overnight for the Sabbath. ⟨Yiddish⟩

chol·era ['kɒlərə] *n* an acute, infectious disease of the stomach and intestines, usually contracted by drinking impure water. ⟨Greek, from *cholē* bile⟩ **chol·er·ic** *adj* easily made angry; irritable.

cho·les·ter·ol [kə'lɛstə,rɒl] *or* [kə'lɛstərəl] *n* a crystalline fatty alcohol produced by all vertebrates and concentrated in the nervous system. Improperly absorbed cholesterol can lead to hardening of the arteries, impeding circulation. ⟨Greek *cholē* bile + *stereos* solid⟩

chomp [tʃɒmp] *v* **1** chew noisily: *to chomp one's food.* **2** bite down: *He chomped on his cigar.* ⟨variation of CHAMP[1]⟩

choose [tʃuz] *v* **chose, cho·sen, choos·ing** **1** decide to take, pursue, do, etc. (one thing rather than another); pick: *I chose the kosher meal.* **2** want and decide (with an infinitive): *She did not choose to go.* **cannot choose but** must: *Since he had received both first prizes, he could not choose but be satisfied.* **choos·er** *n.* ⟨Old English *cēosan*⟩ **choos·y** *adj Informal* picky; fussy. **choos·i·ness** *n.*

chop[1] [tʃɒp] *v* **chopped, chop·ping** *v* **1** cut by hitting with something sharp: *to chop wood.* **2** cut into small pieces (sometimes with *up*): *to chop onions.* **3** get rid of or reduce: *The government has chopped welfare payments.* **4** make, or hit with, a quick, sharp stroke. *n* **1** a cutting stroke. **2** a slice of meat from the rib, loin, or shoulder. **3** a short, irregular, broken motion of waves. **4** a short, sharp downward stroke. ⟨Middle English⟩ **chop down** fell by chopping. **get the chop** *Informal* be reduced, eliminated, fired, etc. **chop·per** *n* **1** a tool or machine for chopping. **2** *Informal* helicopter. **3 choppers** *pl Slang* teeth. *v* fly or carry by helicopter. **chopping block** a large wooden slab on which to cut meat, vegetables, etc. **on the chopping block** of budget items, etc., about to be eliminated.

chop·py *adj* **1** jerky: *a choppy ride.* **2** moving in short, irregular, broken waves: *The lake is choppy today.* **chop·pi·ness** *n.*

chop² [tʃɒp] *n* **1** the jaw. **2 chops** *pl* the cheeks or jaws, esp an animal's jaws: *The cat is licking the milk off its chops.* ⟨*chop¹*⟩ **lick one's chops** *Informal* relish the prospect of something good to come.

chop³ [tʃɒp] *v* **chopped, chop·ping** switch suddenly, esp in **chop and change** make frequent changes. ⟨obsolete *chap* buy and sell, exchange⟩

chop·sticks [ˈtʃɒp,stɪk] *n pl* a pair of small, shaped sticks used especially in Oriental cultures to raise food to the mouth. ⟨Chinese Pidgin English *chop* quick + English *stick¹*⟩

chop su·ey [ˈtʃɒp ˈsui] a Chinese-American dish consisting of meat and vegetables cooked together in their own juices. ⟨Cantonese *tsa-sui* odds and ends⟩

cho·ral, cho·rale See CHORUS.

chord¹ [kɔrd] *n Music* a combination of two or more notes sounded together in harmony. ⟨variant of *cord*, variant of *accord*, n⟩

chord² [kɔrd] *n* **1** *Geometry* a straight line or segment between two points on a curve. **2** a feeling, esp an emotional response: *to touch a sympathetic chord.* ⟨Greek *chordē* string⟩

chor·date [ˈkɔrdeit] *n* any of a phylum of animals that includes all animals having an internal skeleton and a central nervous system located along the back. **chor·date** *adj.*

chore [tʃɔr] *n* **1** a minor task, esp a domestic one that must be done daily: *Feeding the chickens was her chore on the farm.* **2** a disagreeable task: *Reading his letters is such a chore.* ⟨Old English *cerr* turn, business⟩

cho·re·o·graph [ˈkɔriə,græf] *v* **1** arrange or compose (a ballet or other dance or dancelike movements) for the stage. **2** arrange or plan (anything complex). **cho·re·og·ra·pher** *n.* **cho·re·o·graph·ic** *adj.* **cho·re·og·ra·phy** *n.* ⟨Greek *choreia* dance + *graphein* write⟩

cho·ri·on [ˈkɔri,ɒn] *n* **1** the outermost membrane enveloping the fetus of a higher vertebrate. **2** the eggshell of an insect or other invertebrate. ⟨Greek⟩

chor·is·ter See CHOIR.

chor·tle [ˈtʃɔrtəl] *v* laugh noisily or with snorts. **chor·tle** *n.* **chor·tler** *n.* ⟨blend of *chuckle* and *snort*; coined by Lewis Carroll⟩

cho·rus [ˈkɔrəs] *n* **1** a large group of singers; choir. **2** a musical composition to be sung by a chorus. **3** the part of a song repeated after each stanza; refrain. **4** an utterance by many at the same time: *a chorus of no's.* **5** a group of singers and dancers. **6** *Classical Drama* an actor or group of actors who comment on the action of a play.
v sing or speak all at the same time: *The birds were chorusing around me.* ⟨Greek *choros* dance, band of dancers⟩
in chorus all together at the same time.
cho·ral *adj* to do with a chorus or choir.
choral speaking the recitation of poetry, etc.

by a group together. **cho·rale** [kəˈræl] *or* [kɔˈræl] *n* **1** a group of singers; a choir. **2** a slow, stately hymn tune, esp one arranged for choir or orchestra. **chorus boy** or **chorus girl** a person who sings and dances in a chorus of a musical comedy or revue. **chorus line** a chorus for a musical comedy or revue, singing and dancing in a line.

SYNONYMS

Chorus and **chorale** are both synonyms of **choir**. **Chorus** often refers to a subgroup of a choir chosen to sing only certain selections: *The children's chorus joins the adult choir on this song.* A **chorale** typically sings religious music.

---

chose [tʃouz] *v* pt of CHOOSE.

chow [tʃaʊ] *n Slang* food.
chow down (on) *Slang* eat heartily. ⟨Chinese Pidgin English *chow-chow* mixed preserve⟩

chow·der [ˈtʃaʊdər] *n* a thick soup or stew, often made of seafood or corn in a milk base. ⟨French *chaudière* pot; Latin *calidus* hot⟩

chow mein [ˈtʃaʊ ˈmein] a Chinese-American dish consisting of onions, celery, meat, etc. served over fried noodles. ⟨Cantonese *ch'ao mien* fried flour⟩

chrism [ˈkrɪzəm] *n* **1** the consecrated oil used for ritual anointing in some Christian churches. **2** such an anointing. **chris·mal** *adj.* ⟨Greek *chrisma; chriein* anoint⟩

Christ [kraist] *n* Jesus of Nazareth, regarded by Christians as the true Messiah. ⟨Greek *Christos* anointed one⟩
chris·ten [ˈkrɪsən] *v* **1** baptize. **2** name. **3** *Informal* make the first use of. **chris·ten·ing** *n.* **Chris·ten·dom** *n* **1** countries whose people are traditionally or predominantly Christian. **2** all Christians. **Chris·tian** *n* a person who believes, follows, or belongs to a religion based on the teachings of Jesus Christ. **Chris·tian** *adj.* **Chris·tian·like** *adj.* **Chris·tian·ly** *adj, adv.* **Christian Era** COMMON ERA. **Chris·ti·an·i·ty** [,krɪstʃiˈænəti] *or* [,krɪstiˈænəti] *n* a religion based on the teachings of Jesus Christ. **Chris·tian·ize** *v.* **Chris·tian·i·za·tion** *n.* **Christian name** given name; first name. **Christian Science** a religion based on the belief that pain and disease are directly caused by a sinful mind and that physical healing is possible through spiritual healing. **Christ·like** *adj* like Jesus Christ. **Christ·mas** [ˈkrɪsməs] *n* **1** the Christian festival held in December, commemorating Christ's birth. **2** the season around Christmas, lasting until New Year's. Also, **Christ·mas·time** or ⟨*Poetic, Archaic*⟩ **Christ·mas·tide**. **Christmas cake** a rich, moist cake traditionally served at Christmas, containing candied fruit, nuts, dates, rum, etc. **Christmas Day** December 25. **Christmas Eve** December 24. **Christmas stocking** a large, decorative, sock-shaped bag hung up at Christmas to be filled with small gifts. **Christmas tree 1** an evergreen tree hung with ornaments and lights at Christmas, indoors or outdoors. **2 ✹** a Christmas party, esp one given for children by a church or charity. **3** in

oil drilling, a complex arrangement of pipes, valves, etc. to control flow.

chro·mat·ic [krou'mætɪk] *adj* 1 to do with colour. 2 *Music* to do with a CHROMATIC SCALE. **chro·mat·i·cal·ly** *adv.* ⟨Greek *chrōma* colour⟩ **chro·matics** *n* (with sg verb) the science of colour. **chromatic scale** *Music* a scale dividing the octave into 12 semitones. **chro·ma·tin** ['kroumətɪn] *n* the substance, consisting of DNA and proteins and forming a spongy network of chromosomes, in the nucleus of a plant or animal cell in a resting stage. **chro·ma·tog·ra·phy** [ˌkroumə'tɒgrəfi] *n* the separation of a mixture of liquids or gases by passing it through an adsorbent, such as clay. **chro·mat·o·graph·ic** [krəˌmætə'græfɪk] *adj.* **chro·mi·um** ['kroumiəm] *n* a shiny, brittle metallic element that resists rust. *Symbol* **Cr** Also, **chrome. chro·mo·some** ['kromə,soum] *n Genetics* any of the long, thin strands of protein and DNA carrying genes, the coded information for heredity. **chro·mo·so·mal** *adj.*

chron·ic ['krɒnɪk] *adj* 1 of a disease, lasting a long time or often recurring. 2 to do with such disease: *chronic care.* 3 habitual: *chronic lying.* **chron·i·cal·ly** *adv.* ⟨Greek *chronos* time⟩ **chronic fatigue syndrome** a disorder mainly characterized by extreme long-term tiredness. **chron·i·cle** *n* a record of events in the order of occurrence. **chron·i·cle** *v.* **chron·i·cler** *n.* **chron·o·log·i·cal** [ˌkrɒnə'lɒdʒəkəl] *adj* based on the order of actual occurrence in time. **chron·o·log·i·cal·ly** *adv.* **chro·nol·o·gy** *n* 1 a chart, list, etc. giving the exact dates of events arranged in the order in which they occurred. 2 the science of measuring time and dating events. **chro·nom·e·ter** [krə'nɒmətər] *n* an extremely accurate clock. **chron·o·met·ric** *adj.*

chrys·a·lis ['krɪsəlɪs] *n, pl* **chrys·a·lis·es** or **chry·sal·i·des** [krə'sælə,diz] 1 the pupa of a butterfly. 2 a stage of development or change. **chrys·a·lid** *n, adj.* ⟨Greek *chrysallis* golden sheath; *chrysos* gold⟩

chry·san·the·mum [krə'sænθəməm] *n* any of various plants of the composite family with flowers that bloom in late summer and fall. ⟨Greek *chrysos* gold + *anthemon* flower⟩

chub [tʃʌb] *n, pl* **chub** or **chubs** any of various freshwater game fishes of the minnow family. ⟨Middle English *chubbe*⟩

chub·by ['tʃʌbi] *adj* round and plump: *chubby cheeks.* **chub·bi·ness** *n.*

chuck¹ [tʃʌk] *v* 1 tap, esp under the chin. 2 *Informal* toss. 3 *Informal* give up or quit. 4 *Slang* vomit (with *up*). *n* 1 a light tap under the chin. 2 a toss. 3 *West* food; provisions. ⟨probably imitative⟩ **chuck·wag·on** *n* in W Canada and the US, a wagon carrying food and cooking equipment for cowboys, harvest hands, etc.

chuck² [tʃʌk] *n* 1 a device for holding something in a machine. 2 a cut of beef between the neck and shoulder. **chuck** *adj.* ⟨variant of *chock*⟩

chuck³ [tʃʌk] *n* ✱ *West Coast* a large body of water, formerly especially a river but now usually the ocean. ⟨Chinook jargon⟩

chuck·le ['tʃʌkəl] *v* laugh quietly. **chuck·le** *n.* **chuck·ler** *n.* ⟨obsolete *chuck* cluck; imitative⟩

chuff [tʃʌf] *n or v* chug. ⟨imitative⟩

chug [tʃʌg] *n* a short, loud, explosive sound: *the chug of an engine.* *v* **chugged, chug·ging** 1 make short, loud, explosive sounds. 2 go or move with such sounds. 3 *Informal* of work, etc., proceed at a steady pace: *"How are you doing with that essay?" "Oh, it's chugging along."* ⟨imitative⟩

chug–a–lug ['tʃʌg ə 'lʌg] *Slang adv* all in one gulp, or steadily in large gulps. **chug–a–lug, –lugged, –lug·ging** *v.* ⟨imitative⟩

chum¹ [tʃʌm] *Informal n* a close friend. *v* **chummed, chum·ming** be friends. ⟨perhaps shortened from *chamber mate*⟩ **chum·my** *adj* too cosy or familiar in manner. **chum·mi·ly** *adv.* **chum·mi·ness** *n.*

chum² [tʃʌm] *n* bait for fish, esp bait consisting of other fish chopped up and scattered on the water. ⟨origin unknown⟩

chum³ [tʃʌm] *n* ✱ a Pacific salmon found esp along the coast of British Columbia and Alaska. ⟨Chinook jargon *tzum* spotted⟩

chump [tʃʌmp] *n Informal* a foolish or boorish person. ⟨origin uncertain⟩

chunk [tʃʌŋk] *n* 1 a thick piece or lump: *chunks of ice.* 2 a considerable amount or part: *a good chunk of time.* ⟨variant of *chuck²*⟩ **chunk·y** *adj Informal* 1 short and thick. 2 of stocky build. 3 containing chunks: *chunky soup.* **chunk·i·ly** *adv.* **chunk·i·ness** *n.*

church [tʃʌrtʃ] *n* 1 a building for public religious services, esp Christian. 2 **the church** all Christians. 3 a group of people, esp Christian, with similar religious beliefs and meeting in local congregations united under one authority; denomination: *the Pentecostal Church, the Baptist Church.* 4 Christian clergy or religious authorities. **church·like** *adj.* ⟨Greek *kyriakon (doma)* (house) of the Lord; *kyrios* lord⟩ **church·go·er** *n* a person who goes to church regularly. **church·go·ing** *n, adj.* **Church of Christ, Scientist** the official name of the CHRISTIAN SCIENCE church. **Church of Jesus Christ of Latter–day Saints** the official name of the MORMON church. **church·ward·en** *n* 1 *Anglican Church* a lay official who manages the business matters of a church. 2 a clay tobacco pipe with a long stem. **church·yard** *n* the ground immediately surrounding and belonging to a church.

churl [tʃʌrl] *n* a rude, surly person. **churl·ish** *adj.* **churl·ish·ly** *adv.* **churl·ish·ness** *n.* ⟨Old English *ceorl* freeman (of low rank)⟩

churn [tʃʌrn] *n* 1 a container in which butter is made from cream or milk by beating and shaking. 2 a violent stirring. **churn** *v.* **churn·er** *n.* ⟨Old English *cyrn*⟩ **churn out** produce quickly in large quantities.

chute¹ [ʃut] *n* 1 an inclined trough used to carry things, such as mail or garbage, to a lower level. **2** waterfall. **3** a steep slope. **4** a narrow passage or stall for an animal about to race or perform, or for one that is being branded, disinfected, etc. **chute** *v.* ⟨apparent blend of French *chute* fall and English *shoot*⟩

chute² [ʃut] *n, v Informal* parachute.

chut·ney ['tʃʌtni] *n* a spicy sauce or relish made of fruits or vegetables. ⟨Hindi *chatni*⟩

chutz·pah ['xʊtspə] *or* ['hʊtspə] *n Slang* bold self-confidence; nerve; gall. Also, **hutz·pah**. ⟨Yiddish *khutspe*⟩

chyme [kaɪm] *n* the thick semiliquid mass produced in the stomach in the first stage of digestion. ⟨Greek *chymos; cheein* pour⟩

ciao [tʃaʊ] *interj Informal* hello or goodbye. ⟨Italian⟩

ci·ca·da [sə'keidə] *or* [sə'kɑdə] *n, pl* **-das, -dae** [-di] *or* [-daɪ] any of a family of medium- to large-sized insects noted for the loud buzzing sound made by the male. ⟨Latin⟩

cic·a·trix ['sɪkətrɪks] *or* [sɪ'keitrɪks] *n, pl* **cic·a·tri·ces** [ˌsɪkə'traisiz] *Medicine, Biology* the scar left by a healed wound, by a fallen leaf, fruit or branch, etc. Also, **cic·a·trice** [-trɪs]. **cic·a·tri·cial** [-trɪʃəl] *adj.* **cic·a·trize** *v.* ⟨Latin⟩

CIDA Canadian International Development Agency.

–cide *combining form* killing: *regicide* = the killing of a king. ⟨Latin *-cidium* act of killing; *caedere* kill⟩

ci·der ['saidər] *n* the juice pressed out of apples. **Sweet cider** is the unfermented juice; **hard cider** is fermented. ⟨Old French *sidre*, via Latin and Greek; Hebrew *shēkār* liquor⟩

CIE. or **cie.** company (for French *compagnie*).

ci·gar [sə'gɑr] *n* a thick, tight roll of dried tobacco leaves for smoking. ⟨Spanish *cigarro*⟩ **cig·a·rette** [ˌsɪgə'rɛt] *or* ['sɪgəˌrɛt] *n* a small roll of finely cut tobacco (or marijuana, etc.), wrapped in thin paper for smoking. **cig·a·ril·lo** [ˌsɪgə'rɪlou] *or* [ˌsɪgə'rijou] *n* a thin cigar.

cil·i·a ['sɪliə] *n pl, sg* **cil·i·um** ['sɪliəm] **1** *Biology* tiny, hairlike projections on the surface of some types of cell. **2** eyelashes. **cil·i·ate** *adj, n.* ⟨Latin⟩

C. in C. commander-in-chief.

cinch [sɪntʃ] *n* **1** a strong band for fastening a saddle or pack on a horse. **2** *Informal* a very sure or easy thing. **cinch** *v.* ⟨Spanish *cincha*, Latin *cincta* girdle; *cingere* bind⟩ **cinch·y** *adj Informal* very easy.

cin·der ['sɪndər] *n* **1** a piece of burned wood or coal. **2 cinders** *pl* ashes. **3** slag. **4** a lava fragment ejected from a volcano. ⟨Old English *sinder*⟩ **cinder track** a race track surfaced with cinders.

cin·e·ma ['sɪnəmə] *n* **1** a movie theatre. **2 the cinema** movies as an art form. **cin·e·mat·ic** *adj.* **cin·e·mat·i·cal·ly** *adv.* ⟨short for *cinematography*; Greek *kīnēma* motion + English *-graphy*⟩ **cin·e·ma·tog·ra·phy** *n* the art and science of

filming motion pictures; movie photography. **cin·e·ma·tog·ra·pher** *n.* **ci·né·ma vé·ri·té** [sinema veri'te] *French* a film style that aims for realism by filming spontaneous action. **ci·ne·phile** ['sɪnəˌfaɪl] *n* a lover of the cinema.

cin·na·bar ['sɪnəˌbɑr] *n* a reddish mineral and chief source of mercury; native mercuric sulphide. ⟨Greek *kinnabari*; Persian *šängärf*⟩

cin·na·mon ['sɪnəmən] *n* a reddish brown, fragrant spice that is the dried inner bark of a tropical evergreen tree. ⟨Greek *kinnamon*; of Semitic origin⟩ **cinnamon bear** a reddish brown variety of the North American black bear.

cin·quain ['sɪŋkein] *n* **1** a five-line stanza. **2** a five-line poem, usually unrhymed, the lines having 2, 4, 6, 8, and 2 syllables or 1, 2, 3, 4, and 1 words, respectively. ⟨French *cinq* five, on the analogy of *quatrain*⟩

cinque·foil ['sɪŋkˌfɔil] *n* **1** any of a genus of plants of the rose family, having flowers with five roundish petals. **2** *Architecture* an ornament made up of five arcs joined in a circle. ⟨Latin *quinque* five + *folium* leaf⟩

ci·paille [sɪ'paɪ] *French* [sɪ'paj] *n* ✱ a pie with layers of various meats (pork, chicken, veal, game) alternating with pastry. ⟨French⟩

ci·pher ['saifər] *n* **1** a written secret code. **2** a coded message. **3** zero; 0. **4** a person or thing of no importance. **5** any Arabic numeral. **6** a monogram.
v **1** express (a message or information) in cipher. **2** *Archaic* do arithmetic; work out (a problem) by arithmetic. Also, **cy·pher**. ⟨Latin *ciphra*; Arabic *sifr* empty.⟩

cir·ca ['sɜrkə] *prep, adv* about: *Muhammad was born circa* A.D. *570. Abbrev* **c, c.**, or **ca.** ⟨Latin⟩

cir·ca·di·an [sər'keidiən] *adj* to do with biological processes having a 24-hour cycle. ⟨Latin *circa* about + *dies* day⟩

cir·cle ['sɜrkəl] *n* **1** a continuously curving line, every point of which is equally distant from a fixed point called the centre. **2** a ring; a number of things arranged so as to form a circle: *sitting in a circle.* **3** group of people held together by the same interests: *a circle of friends.* **4** a sphere of influence, action, etc. **5** cycle; any path or any progression of ideas, events, etc., which ends up where it started.
v **1** move in a circle around: *The moon circles the earth.* **2** draw a circle around: *Circle the best answer.* ⟨Latin *circulus* diminutive of *circus* ring⟩
come full circle pass through various stages and end up at the starting point again.
cir·clet *n* a band worn for ornament around the head, neck, arm, or finger. **cir·cu·lar** *adj* **1** being or forming a circle; specifically, of an argument, depending on the proposition it is supposed to prove. **2** circuitous. *n* a letter, notice, etc. sent to each member of a group. **cir·cu·lar·i·ty** *n.* **cir·cu·lar·ly** *adv.* **circular saw** a saw blade in the form of a thin steel disk with a toothed edge, rotated at high speed by an electric motor. **cir·cu·late** *v* move or pass around, freely or in a circuit: *The hot water is*

circulated through a system of pipes. The gossip circulated rapidly. **circulating library** lending library. **cir·cu·la·tion** [ˌsɜrkjəˈleiʃən] n **1** the act or process of circulating: the circulation of air in a room. **2** specifically, the circular movement of the blood in the human body: Poor circulation leads to cold feet and hands. **3** the number of copies of a newspaper or periodical that are sent out at a certain time: The magazine has a circulation of 50 000. **cir·cu·la·to·ry** [ˈsɜrkjələˌtɔri] adj.

cir·cuit [ˈsɜrkɪt] n **1** a complete journey, esp one that is more or less circular or goes around something: It takes a year for the earth to make its circuit of the sun. **2** the complete path, or its connected components, followed by an electric current. **3** a set of venues, communities, or events visited in turn by a show, athlete, speaker, or other travelling phenomenon.
v go around in a circuit. **cir·cuit·al** adj. ⟨Latin circuitus; circum around + itus a going⟩
circuit board a board of insulating material on which electronic components are mounted and connected. **circuit breaker** a switch taking the place of a fuse, automatically opening or interrupting an electric circuit if the current gets too strong. **cir·cu·i·tous** [sərˈkjuətəs] adj roundabout: To avoid left turns he took a circuitous route home. **cir·cu·i·tous·ly** adv. **cir·cu·i·tous·ness** or **cir·cu·i·ty** n. **circuit rider** formerly, a Methodist minister who rode from place to place over a circuit to preach. **cir·cuit·ry** n the parts of an electric circuit.

cir·cu·lar, cir·cu·late See CIRCLE.

circum– combining form around; in a circle: circumpolar, circumnavigate. ⟨Latin⟩

cir·cum·bo·re·al [ˌsɜrkəmˈbɔriəl] adj to do with animals and plants of the northern regions of North America and Eurasia.

cir·cum·cen·tre [ˈsɜrkəmˌsɛntər] n the centre of a circle drawn around another figure.

cir·cum·cise [ˈsɜrkəmˌsaiz] v **1** cut off the foreskin of a male as part of a religious practice, or as a medical procedure. **2** cut off the clitoris or labia, traditionally practised by some peoples. **cir·cum·ci·sion** [ˌsɜrkəmˈsɪʒən] or [ˈsɜrkəmˌsɪʒən] n. ⟨Latin circum- + cisus pp of caedere cut⟩

cir·cum·fer·ence [sərˈkʌmfərəns] n **1** the boundary line of a circle or of any figure enclosed by a curve. **2** the distance around a circle or any object with a curved edge. ⟨Latin circum- + ferre bear⟩

cir·cum·flex [ˈsɜrkəmˌflɛks] n an accent (^) used especially over vowels in some languages to indicate their quality. **cir·cum·flex** adj.

cir·cum·lo·cu·tion [ˌsɜrkəmləˈkjuʃən] n a roundabout expression, as the wife of your father's brother for your aunt.

cir·cum·nav·i·gate [ˌsɜrkəmˈnævəˌgeit] v sail completely around. **cir·cum·nav·i·ga·tion** n.

cir·cum·po·lar [ˌsɜrkəmˈpoulər] adj around the North or South Pole.

cir·cum·scribe [ˌsɜrkəmˈskraib] v **1** draw a line around; mark the boundaries of. **2** limit; restrict. **3** Geometry **a** draw (a figure) around another figure so as to touch as many points as possible. **b** of a figure, be so drawn around (another). **cir·cum·scrib·ed** adj.

cir·cum·spect [ˈsɜrkəmˌspɛkt] adj careful; prudent. **cir·cum·spect·ly** adv. **cir·cum·spec·tion** or **cir·cum·spect·ness** n. ⟨Latin circum- + spectus pp of specere look⟩

cir·cum·stance [ˈsɜrkəmˌstæns] n **1** any or all of the conditions contributing to an event: to consider all the circumstances, a victim of circumstance. **2** a happening: an unfortunate circumstance. **3** circumstances pl financial situation: in easy circumstances.
under no circumstances never. **under the circumstances** in view of the situation. **cir·cum·stan·tial** adj **1** of evidence, consisting of events or facts that make certain conclusions obvious. **2** incidental. **3** detailed: a circumstantial report. **cir·cum·stan·ti·al·i·ty** n.

cir·cum·vent [ˌsɜrkəmˈvɛnt] v **1** evade or defeat by cleverness: to circumvent the law. **2** avoid by going around: to circumvent traffic. **cir·cum·ven·tion** n. **cir·cum·ven·tive** adj.

cir·cus [ˈsɜrkəs] n **1** a travelling show of clowns, acrobats, magicians, freaks of nature, etc., often with trained animals. **2** Informal a lively but chaotic time or place. **3** in ancient Rome, an oval or oval stadium. ⟨Latin = ring⟩

cirque [sɜrk] n Geology a steep-sided hollow, often containing a small lake or glacier. ⟨French; Latin circus ring⟩

cir·rho·sis [səˈrousɪs] n a chronic progressive disease of the liver, with excessive formation of connective tissue. **cir·rhot·ic** [səˈrɒtɪk] adj. ⟨Greek kirrhos orange yellow⟩

cir·rus [ˈsɪrəs] n, pl **cir·ri** [ˈsɪrai] or [ˈsɪri] **1** a very high, wispy cloud formation. **2** the tendril of a plant. **3** an antenna or other thin appendage of an insect. ⟨Latin cirrus curl⟩
cir·ro– combining form a cloud formation with features of both cirrus and some other kind of cloud: cirrostratus, cirrocumulus.

CIS COMMONWEALTH OF INDEPENDENT STATES.

cis·al·pine [sɪsˈælpain] or [sɪsˈælpin] adj on the southern side of the Alps.

cis·at·lan·tic [ˌsɪsætˈlæntɪk] adj on this side of the Atlantic Ocean.

cis·co [ˈsɪskou] n, pl **-coes** or **-cos** any of various whitefishes found in lakes throughout Canada and the NE United States. ⟨Cdn. French ciscoette; perhaps Algonquian⟩

Cis·ter·cian [sɪˈstɜrʃən] n Roman Catholic Church a monk or nun of a very strict order founded as an offshoot of the Benedictines. ⟨Latin Cistercium Citeaux, founding site⟩

cis·tern [ˈsɪstərn] n **1** a large tank or artificial reservoir for storing water. **2** the water tank forming part of a toilet. **3** Anatomy a cavity holding fluid. ⟨Latin cisterna; cista box⟩

cit·a·del [ˈsɪtədəl] or [ˈsɪtəˌdɛl] n **1** a fortress commanding a city. **2** any strong, safe place; refuge. ⟨Italian cittadella; città city⟩

cite [sait] v **1** quote or refer to as an example

or authority: *The lawyer cited a similar case.*
2 mention publicly in recognition of some
outstanding service. **3** summon to appear
before a court of law. **cite·a·ble** or **cit·a·ble** *adj.*
ci·ta·tion *n.* ⟨Latin *citare* summon⟩

cit·i·zen [ˈsɪtəzən] *or* [ˈsɪtəsən] *n* **1** a person
who is a member of a nation or state,
entitled to protection and other rights. **2** a
civilian, as opposed to a member of the armed
forces or police. **3** an inhabitant of a city or
town. **cit·i·zen·ship** *n.* ⟨Anglo-French *citisein;*
Old French *cite* city⟩
cit·i·zen·ry *n* citizens as a group. **citizen's
arrest** an arrest of a suspected criminal made
by an ordinary person. **citizens' band** a range
of radio frequencies reserved for two-way
communication by the public. *Abbrev* **CB**

cit·ric [ˈsɪtrɪk] *adj* of or from citrus fruits.
⟨Latin *citrus*⟩
citric acid a sour-tasting acid in such fruits as
lemons, limes, etc. **cit·ron** [ˈsɪtrən] *n* a pale
yellow citrus fruit like a lemon but larger, less
acid, and with a thicker rind. **cit·ron·el·la** *n*
an oil with a lemony smell, used to make
soap, etc., and for keeping mosquitoes away.
cit·rus *n* any of a genus of trees or shrubs of
the rue family, bearing **citrus fruit** such as
oranges or limes. **cit·rous** *adj.*

cit·y [ˈsɪti] *n* **1** a large and important urban
community. **2** in Canada, an incorporated
community with fixed boundaries and a
certain minimum population, granted status
by its provincial government. **3** a city's
government: *The city passed a new by-law.* ⟨Old
French *cite;* Latin *civitas,* from *civis* citizen⟩
cit·i·fy *v Informal* cause to conform to an urban
way of life. **cit·i·fi·ca·tion** *n.* **cit·i·fied** *adj.* **city
council** the administrative body of a city. **city
councillor. city hall 1** the headquarters of the
government of a city. **2** this government
itself. **3** petty bureaucracy: *to fight city hall.*
cit·y·scape *n* visual aspects of a city. **city
slicker** *Slang* a city dweller looked on with
scorn or suspicion by rural people. **city–state**
n an independent state consisting of a city
and the territories depending on it, as in
ancient Greece and Renaissance Italy.
ci·ty·wide *adj, adv* throughout a city.

civ·et [ˈsɪvɪt] *n* a fatty, yellowish, musky fluid
secreted by the CIVET CAT, used as a fixative in
perfumes. ⟨French *civette;* Arabic *zabad*⟩
civet cat any of various catlike mammals
having anal glands that secrete civet.

civ·ic [ˈsɪvɪk] *adj* **1** to do with a city. **2** to do
with citizenship: *civic duties, civic pride.*
civ·i·cal·ly *adv.* ⟨Latin *civicus; civis* citizen⟩
civic centre 1 COMMUNITY CENTRE. **2** the offices
of a municipal government. **civ·ic–mind·ed**
adj taking one's civic duty seriously. **civ·ics** *n*
the study of the duties, rights, and privileges
of citizens.

civ·il [ˈsɪvəl] *adj* **1** minimally polite: *a civil
conversation.* **2** to do with citizens: *civil rights,
civil liberties.* **3** to do with the government of
a state. **4** to do with the private rights and
transactions of individuals, or with related
offences: *civil law as opposed to criminal law.* **5**

not connected with the armed forces or the
church: *a civil marriage.* **ci·vil·i·ty** *n.* **civ·il·ly** *adv.*
⟨Latin *civilis; civis* citizen⟩
civil defence a program of action for civilian
volunteers to cope with a general emergency,
such as enemy attack. **civil disobedience**
principled refusal to obey the law, as a
protest or act of conscience. **civil engineering**
the planning of the construction of bridges,
roads, harbours, etc. **civil engineer. ci·vil·ian** *n*
a person not in the armed forces or police.
ci·vil·ian *adj.* **civil law** the body of law that
protects private rights. Compare CRIMINAL
LAW. **civil liberty** the right of a person to do,
think, and say what he or she pleases as long
as he or she does not harm anyone or break
established laws. **civil marriage** a marriage
performed by a government official rather
than by a member of the clergy. **civil rights**
the constitutional rights of all citizens, such
as the right to vote and to be treated equally
under the law. **civil servant** a government
employee, as opposed to an elected official.
civil service civil servants collectively, or
their work. **civil war 1** a war between two
groups of citizens of one nation. **2 Civil War
a** in the US, the war between the northern
and southern states, 1861-1865. **b** in
England, the war between the king and
Parliament, 1642-1646 and 1648-1652. **civ·ies**
See CIVVIES.

civ·i·lize [ˈsɪvəˌlaɪz] *v* **1** change (a so-called
primitive social system) to a much more
complex one that includes knowledge of the
arts and sciences. **2** improve (someone) in
culture and good manners. **civ·i·lized** *adj.*
civ·i·li·za·tion *n* **1** an advanced stage of social
organization. **2** the total culture of a people
at a given time: *Aztec civilization, 19th-century
Canadian civilization.* **3** modern or urban
comforts and amenities: *After the ten-day
canoe trip, it was nice to get back to civilization.*

clack [klæk] *v* make or cause to make a short,
sharp, loud sound: *high heels clacking on tile
floors.* **clack** *n.* **clack·er** *n.* ⟨imitative⟩

clad¹ [klæd] *v* a pt and a pp of CLOTHE.

clad² [klæd] *v* **clad, clad·ding** cover with a
protective layer or coating: *Aluminum pots are
sometimes clad with copper for better heat
distribution.* **clad·ding** *n.* ⟨Old English *clæthan*
clothe, now obsolete in that sense⟩

claim [kleɪm] *v* **1** say that one has and that
others must recognize (a right, possession,
title, etc.): *to claim a tract of land.* **2** identify
as one's own and retrieve: *to claim one's
baggage.* **3** declare as a fact despite potential
opposition: *She claimed he had already gone.*
4 call for: *Business claims her attention.*
n **1** the act of claiming, or the thing claimed;
a demand or assertion. **2** a right or title to
something. **3** a piece of public land marked
out for possession by a settler or prospector.
claim·a·ble *adj.* ⟨Old French *clamer;* Latin
clamare call, proclaim⟩
jump a claim illegally seize a piece of land
staked for mining by another. **lay claim to**
CLAIM (defs 1, 2). **put in a** (or **one's**) **claim for**

ask for as one's right: *I'm putting in my claim right now for a share of the saskatoons we picked.* **stake a claim** a claim an area of land for mining rights by setting stakes to mark its boundaries. **b** claim anything, esp space, as one's own: *The house has four bedrooms; the kids have already staked their claims.*
claim·ant *n* one who makes a claim.

SYNONYMS
Claim conveys an assumption of right in the face of potential contest: *Governments protect us and in return claim our allegiance.* **Demand**, by contrast, may convey selfish whim, but always suggests insistence and often urgency: *She demands attention all day long.* **Require** implies force or necessity: *The principal requires the co-operation of all students.*

clair·voy·ant [klɛr'vɔiənt] *adj* **1** able to see things that are out of sight or in the future. **2** having exceptional insight. **clair·voy·ant** *n*. **clair·voy·ant·ly** *adv.* **clair·voy·ance** *n.* ⟨French *clair* clear + *voyant*, ppr of *voir* see⟩

clam [klæm] *n* **1** any of various molluscs with a shell closed by a muscle at each end and having a powerful, muscular foot for burrowing into sand or mud. **2** *Informal* a person who speaks very little.
v **clammed, clam·ming** dig for clams. **clam·like** *adj.* ⟨Old English *clamm* fetter⟩
clam up *Informal* refuse to speak.
clam·bake ['klæm,beik] *n* **1** a picnic where clams are baked or steamed. **2** *Informal* any large, noisy social gathering. **clam·shell** *n* **1** the shell of a clam. **2** a bucket hinged like a clamshell and attached to a heavy machine used in dredging and loading.
clam·ber ['klæmbər] *v* climb using hands and feet; climb awkwardly or with difficulty. **clam·ber** *n.* ⟨Middle English *clambre(n)*⟩
clam·my ['klæmi] *adj* unpleasantly cold and damp. **clam·mi·ness** *n.* **clam·mi·ly** *adv.* ⟨Old English *clæman* smear; *clām* clay⟩
clam·our or **clam·or** ['klæmər] *n* **1** a loud, continual uproar. **2** a loud complaint or demand. **clam·our** or **clam·or** *v.* **clam·our·er** or **clam·or·er** *n.* **clam·or·ous** *adj.* ⟨Latin *clamor*⟩
clamp [klæmp] *n* **1** a device for holding or pressing things firmly together. **2** a wrestling hold, posture, etc. that immobilizes: *She saw by the clamp of his jaw that he meant it.*
v **1** hold firmly in a clamp. **2** impose: *to clamp a tax on imports.* ⟨Middle Dutch *klampe*⟩
clamp down on *Informal* take strict measures against: *The police clamped down on speeding.* **clamp·down** *n.*
clan [klæn] *n* **1** a group of related families functioning as a unit of social organization. **2** any extended family: *We're hosting the clan for Thanksgiving.* ⟨Scots Gaelic *clann* family⟩
clan·nish *adj* **1** not liking outsiders. **2** like a clan. **clan·nish·ness** *n.* **clans·man** *n, pl* **-men** a member of a clan. **clans·wom·an** *n, pl* **-wom·en.**
clan·des·tine [klæn'dɛstən] *adj* secret; kept hidden. ⟨Latin *clandestinus; clam* secretly⟩

clang [klæŋ] *n* a loud, harsh, resonant sound like metal striking metal: *the clang of the fire alarm.* **clang** *v.* ⟨imitative⟩
clang·er *n Informal* a bad or blatant mistake.
clan·gour or **clang·or** ['klæŋər] *or* ['klæŋgər] *n* continued clanging: *the clangour of bells.* **clan·gor·ous** *adj.* ⟨Latin *clangor; clangere* clang⟩
clank [klæŋk] *n* a harsh, grating or striking sound of metal, like the rattle of a heavy chain. **clank** *v.* ⟨imitative⟩
clap [klæp] *n* **1** a sudden, sharp, loud noise, as of the hands being struck together. **2** a hit or blow; slap: *a clap on the shoulder.* **clap, clapped, clap·ping** *v.* ⟨Old English *clæppan*⟩
clap eyes on *Informal* see.
clap·board ['klæp,bɔrd] *or* ['klæbərd] *n* one of a series of thin boards used overlappingly to cover the outer walls of buildings. **clap·per** *n* the movable part inside a bell that strikes the outer part. **clap·trap** ['klæp,træp] *n* empty talk aimed at getting attention. **clap·trap** *adj.*
clar·et ['klɛrət], ['klærət], *or* [klɑ'rei] *n* dry, red table wine, orig made in Bordeaux, France. ⟨Old French *claret* light-coloured⟩
clar·i·fy ['klɛrə,faɪ] *or* ['klærə,faɪ] *v* **1** remove impurities or solid particles from. **2** explain: *Clarify your statement for the public.* **3** make transparent. **clar·i·fi·ca·tion** *n.* **clar·i·fied** *adj.* ⟨Latin *clarificare; clarus* clear + *facere* make⟩
clar·i·net [,klɛrə'nɛt] *or* [,klærə'nɛt] *n* a wind instrument consisting of a straight tube with a flared end and holes opened and closed by keys. **clar·i·net·tist** or **clar·i·net·ist** *n.* ⟨Italian *clarinetto; clarino* trumpet; Latin *clarus* clear⟩
clar·i·on ['klɛriən] *or* ['klæriən] *adj Poetic* clear. *n* an ancient trumpet with clear tones. ⟨Latin *clarionis; clarus* clear⟩
clar·i·ty ['klɛrəti] *or* ['klærəti] See CLEAR.
clash [klæʃ] *v* **1** make or cause to make a loud, harsh, discordant sound. **2** come into or be in conflict: *The two armies clashed.* **3** of colours, fail to harmonize. **clash** *n.* ⟨imitative⟩
clasp [klæsp] *n* **1** a device to fasten two parts together: *a belt with a gold clasp.* **2** a close grip with the arms or hands. **clasp** *v.* ⟨Middle English *claspe(n)*⟩
clasp knife a jack-knife, esp one with a clasp to hold each blade open.
class [klæs] *n* **1** a group of persons or things alike in some way. **2** a group of students taught together, or the time during which they are taught. **3** social rank, or a system of social ranks: *the middle class. Class can get in the way of relationships.* **4** quality: *first class.* **5** elegant or honourable character. **6** *Biology* a major category in the classification of plants and animals, more specific than phylum (or division) and more general than order.
adj Informal of excellent quality; showing elegance and style: *a class act.*
v put in a class or group. ⟨Latin *classis*⟩
in a class by itself (or **oneself**) superior to all others; unique.
class action a legal action brought on behalf of all the injured parties in a situation.
class–con·scious *adj* very aware of people's

status as members of a particular social class. **class–con·scious·ness** *n.* **clas·si·fied** *adj* **1** of government documents, placed in any of three categories including secret, confidential, and restricted. **2** *Informal* secret. **classified advertisement** or **ad** a short notice appearing in a newspaper or periodical under one of a set of thematic headings. **classifieds** *n pl.* **clas·si·fy** *v* arrange in classes or groups. **clas·si·fi·a·ble** *adj.* **clas·si·fi·ca·tion** *n.* **class·ism** *n* discrimination on the basis of social class. **class·ist** *n, adj.* **class·less** *adj* not divided into ranked social classes: *a classless society.* **class·mate** *n* a member of the same class in school. **class·room** *n* a room where classes meet in school. **class struggle** conflict between social classes. **class·y** *adj Informal* of high class or quality; elegant or honourable.

clas·sic ['klæsɪk] *adj* **1** outstanding and therefore established as a standard: *a classic example of dramatic irony.* **2** elegantly simple in a way that has enduring appeal: *the classic lines of the new bridge.* **3** CLASSICAL.
n **1** any classic thing, esp a work of art of enduring appeal: The Tin Flute *is a classic.* **2 the classics** the literature of ancient Greece and Rome. ⟨Latin *classicus; classis* class⟩
clas·si·cal *adj* **1** to do with ancient Greece and Rome or with the arts, literature, and educational ideals that flourished at that time: *classical studies.* **2** orthodox, but not up to date: *classical physics.* **3 a** to do with the European tradition of written music, esp of the last 300 years or so: *She prefers classical music to pop.* **b Classical** designating such music by late 18c composers such as Mozart. **clas·si·cal·ly** *adv.* **classical college ✵** in French Canada, a combined high school and college offering a program mainly in the classics and liberal arts, feeding into a degree program at an affiliated university. **clas·si·cism** *n* **1** the principles of classical art, literature, or education. **2** a Greek or Latin expression borrowed by another language. **clas·si·cist** *n.*

clat·ter ['klætər] *n* a loud rattling noise: *the clatter of dishes.* **clat·ter** *v.* **clat·ter·er** *n.* ⟨Old English *clatrian*⟩

clause [klɒz] *n* **1** *Grammar* the unit formed by a subject and its predicate. In *He came before we left,* He came *is a* **main clause,** *and* before we left *is a* **subordinate clause.** **2** a provision of a written agreement: *a no-fault clause in a contract.* **claus·al** *adj.* ⟨Latin *clausula* close of a period; *claudere* close⟩

claus·tro·pho·bi·a [ˌklɒstrə'foubiə] *n* abnormal fear of enclosed spaces. **claus·tro·pho·bic** *adj, n.* **claus·tro·pho·bi·cal·ly** *adv.* ⟨Latin *claustrum* closed place + E *-phobia* fear⟩

cla·ve ['klɑvei] *n* either of a pair of wooden rhythm sticks used especially in Latin music. ⟨Spanish; Latin *clavis* key⟩

clav·i·chord ['klævəˌkɔrd] *n* an early type of piano. ⟨Latin *clavis* key + *chorda* string⟩

clav·i·cle ['klævəkəl] *n* the collarbone. ⟨Latin *clavicula* bolt; *clavis* key⟩

claw [klɒ] *n* **1** a sharp, hooked nail on each toe of a bird and of some animals. **2** one of the pincers of a lobster, crab, etc.
v scratch, tear, seize, or pull with claws or fingernails. ⟨Old English *clawu*⟩
claw back of a government, take back by way of taxation, deductions, or fees money given in grants, subsidies, etc. **claw·back** *n.*
claw hammer a hammer with one end of the head curved and split like claws.

clay [klei] *n* **1** a stiff, sticky, mouldable earth. **2** *Poetic* **a** earth. **b** the human body. **clay·ey** *adj.* ⟨Old English *clæg*⟩
clay·ma·tion *n* film animation in which the images are of sculpted clay. **clay·pan** *n* a layer of clay in the soil that holds water. **clay pigeon** a saucerlike clay disk thrown in the air as a flying target for skeet shooting.

clean [klin] *adj* **1** free of dirt or litter: *clean clothes.* **2** tidy: *Is your room clean?* **3** free of guilt: *a clean heart.* **4** not obscene: *clean jokes.* **5** even or smooth; clear: *a clean cut, a clean jump.* **6** honest and fair: *a clean player.* **7** free of corrections: *a clean copy.* **8** blank: *I need a clean page.* **9** not using drugs: *The athlete was found to be clean.* **10** pure or acceptable under some ceremonial or dietary law.
adv **1** *Informal* completely: *I clean forgot.* **2** in a clean manner: *She jumped clean across.*
v **1** make clean. **2** prepare (fish, chicken, etc.) for cooking by removing entrails, feathers, scales, etc. **clean·ly** *adv.* **clean·ness** *n.* ⟨Old English *clæne*⟩
clean out a make clean by emptying: *Clean out your desk.* **b** empty; use up: *They cleaned out a whole box of cookies.* **c** *Slang* take or use all the money of. **clean up a** make thoroughly clean. **b** wash or groom oneself. **c** put things away or in order: *Clean up when you're done.* **d** *Informal* finish. **e** *Slang* make a lot of money or win by a wide margin. **clean–up** *n.* **come clean** confess the truth.
clean and jerk a weightlifting technique in which the barbell is raised to the shoulders in one movement, and then above the head. **clean–cut** *adj* **1** having clear, sharp outlines. **2** having a neat and wholesome appearance. **clean·er** *n* **1** a person whose work is cleaning buildings, windows, etc. **2** any substance or device that cleans. **3** DRY CLEANER. **take someone to the cleaners** *Slang* take all of his or her money. **clean·ly** ['klɛnli] *adj* habitually keeping oneself and one's quarters clean. **clean·li·ness** *n.* **cleanse** [klɛnz] *v* make thoroughly clean or pure. **cleans·er** *n* a substance that cleans and disinfects, such as a household cleaning product. **clean–shav·en** [-'ʃeivən] *or* [-ˌʃeivən] *adj* with the face shaved. **clean–up** *n* an act of cleaning up.

SYNONYMS
Clean is the general word meaning 'to remove dirt, litter, or clutter', especially from objects or spaces: *The men cleaned the streets.* **Cleanse** is used either metaphorically, or scientifically to refer to removal of bacteria, pollutants, etc. by chemical means: *to cleanse the air, to cleanse wounds, to cleanse one's mind of unwholesome thoughts.*

clear [klir] *adj* 1 not cloudy, misty, or hazy.
2 transparent. 3 distinct: *clear outlines, a clear
idea.* 4 not cluttered or obstructed: *a clear
view, a clear path.* 5 free of blemishes: *clear
skin.* 6 easy to see or understand: *a clear
explanation. It's clear that we will win.* 7 keen;
perceiving things distinctly: *clear eyesight.*
8 not touching: *The ship was clear of the
iceberg.* 9 not guilty.
v 1 make or become clear: *Clear the way. The
sky cleared.* 2 get by or over without
touching: *The horse cleared the fence.* 3 prove
innocent. 4 make as profit: *We cleared $90 on
the used book sale.* 5 get or give permission
for: *Did you clear that idea with the principal?*
6 settle (a debt or misunderstanding). 7 leave
or get through, having satisfied authorities:
to clear customs, to clear port. 8 process or be
processed: *Has the cheque cleared yet?*
adv completely: *The bullet went clear through
the door.* **clear·ly** *adv.* **clar·i·ty** or **clear·ness** *n.*
⟨Middle English *cler*; Latin *clarus*⟩
clear off a remove (things) from (a surface):
Clear off the table. Clear those papers off.
b leave: *She cleared off as soon as she heard
what was involved.* **clear out** a make clear by
taking out. **b** *Informal* leave: *Everyone had
cleared out by four o'clock.* **clear up** a explain
or solve. **b** become clear after rain or a storm.
c cure or be cured: *Her rash cleared up.*
d finish or put in order. **e** make or become
clear. **in the clear** a innocent. **b** free of debt or
other burdens or constraints. **make clear** state
definitely: *She made clear she was not coming.*
clear·ance *n* 1 the distance between objects
that allows free movement: *The underpass has
a clearance of 4 m.* 2 official permission to go
ahead: *The pilot waited for clearance from the
control tower.* 3 Also, **clearance sale** a sale held
to clear out old stock. **clear–cut** [ˈklir ˈkʌt]
adj definite: *clear-cut ideas.* *v* [ˈklir ˌkʌt] cut
down and remove all the trees in (an area).
clear·cut·ting *n.* **clear–head·ed** *adj* thinking
clearly. **clear·ing** *n* an open space of cleared
land in a forest. **clearing house** a place where
banks settle their accounts, or where goods
of some kind are collected and distributed.

cleat [klit] *n* 1 one of several studs on the
sole of a shoe or boot to prevent slipping. 2 a
strip of wood, metal, etc. fastened across a
surface for sure footing. 3 one of the raised
bars across the track of a vehicle that travels
over snow. 4 a piece of wood, metal, etc.
fixed to a flagpole, gunwale of a boat, etc.,
for securing a rope by winding it around.
v 1 fasten with a cleat. 2 furnish with cleats.
⟨Middle English *cleete*⟩

cleave[1] [kliv] *v* **cleft, clove**, or **cleaved; cleft,
cleaved**, or **clo·ven; cleav·ing** cut or split
open; divide; pierce. ⟨Old English *clēofan*⟩
cleav·age *n* 1 the site of a split or division,
esp that between a woman's breasts as
revealed by a low neckline. 2 *Biology* cell
division, esp in the development of an
embryo from a fertilized egg. 3 *Chemistry* the
breaking up of molecules into simpler ones.
4 *Mineralogy* the tendency of a crystallized
substance to split along definite planes.

cleav·er *n* a butcher's cutting tool with a
heavy, broad blade and a short handle.

cleave[2] [kliv] *v* **cleaved, cleav·ing** hold fast
(*to*); be faithful (*to*): *to cleave to an idea.* ⟨Old
English *cleofian*⟩

clef [klɛf] *n Music* 1 a symbol indicating the
pitch of the notes on a staff. 2 the range of
pitch indicated by the symbol. See BASS CLEF,
TREBLE CLEF. ⟨French; Latin *clavis* key⟩

cleft [klɛft] *v* a pt and a pp of CLEAVE[1].
n an opening made by splitting; crack.
adj split; divided. ⟨Old English *(ge)clyft*⟩
cleft palate failure of the two halves of the
palate to join, leaving a narrow opening
running lengthwise in the roof of the mouth.

clem·a·tis [kləˈmætəs] or [ˈklɛmətɪs] *n* any of
a genus of mainly climbing shrubs of the
buttercup family. ⟨Greek *klēma* vine branch⟩

clem·ent [ˈklɛmənt] *adj* 1 of weather, clear and
mild. 2 merciful; lenient. **clem·en·cy** *n.* ⟨Latin
clemens⟩

clem·ent·ine [ˈklɛmənˌtaɪn] or [ˈklɛmənˌtin]
n a small, tangerinelike type of orange.

clench [klɛntʃ] *v* 1 close tightly together: *to
clench one's fists.* 2 grasp firmly: *The officer
clenched the prisoner's arm.* **clench** *n.* ⟨Old
English *(be)clencan* hold fast⟩

clere·sto·rey [ˈklirˌstɔri] *n* 1 *Architecture* the
upper part of a church wall, with windows in
it above the roofs of the side aisles. 2 any
similar structure. ⟨*clere* clear + *storey*⟩

cler·gy [ˈklɜrdʒi] *n* a body of people ordained
to perform religious services. Compare LAITY.
⟨Old French *clergie*; Greek *klēros* clergy⟩
cler·gy·man *n, pl* -men a male member of the
clergy. **Clergy Reserves** ✳ the lands set aside
in Lower and Upper Canada in 1791 for the
support of a Protestant clergy.

cler·ic [ˈklɛrɪk] *n* a member of the clergy.
⟨Greek *klērikos; klēros* clergy⟩
cler·i·cal *adj* 1 of or for an office clerk: *a
clerical job.* 2 to do with the clergy: *clerical
robes.* **clerical collar** a stiff white collar fastened
at the back, worn by some Christian clergy.
cler·i·cal·ism *n* political influence of the clergy.
cler·i·cal·ist *n, adj.*

clerk [klɜrk] *n* 1 a salesperson in a store. 2 an
office worker in charge of files and records, a
receptionist, or a bookkeeper. 3 an official
who takes care of regular business in a
legislature or law court. 4 a hotel employee
who registers guests, assigns rooms, etc.
v work as a clerk. ⟨See CLERIC.⟩

clev·er [ˈklɛvər] *adj* 1 bright; having a quick
mind. 2 skilful. 3 annoyingly witty or slick:
clever remarks, clever effects. **clev·er·ly** *adv.*
clev·er·ness *n.* ⟨Middle English *cliver*⟩

SYNONYMS
Clever conveys general quickness of mind,
especially where learning or strategy is
involved: *He had no training, but was clever
enough to become the top salesperson.*
Ingenious focusses on being inventive or
quick to see possiblities: *Some ingenious person
designed the first electric can opener.*

cli·ché [kliˈʃei] *n* a timeworn expression or idea. ⟨French, pp of *clicher* to stereotype⟩

click [klɪk] *n* **1** a light, short, sharp sound, as of a key turning in a lock. **2** *Computers* an act of pressing and releasing a button on a mouse in order to select something.
v **1** make or cause to make a click. **2** *Informal* get along well: *We clicked from the start.* **3** *Informal* suddenly make sense: *Then it clicked: she had seen him before.* **4** *Computers* press and release a mouse button. ⟨imitative⟩
click·er *n* a remote control that is part of an interactive system used in classrooms to record, tally, and display students' responses to questions.

cli·ent [ˈklaɪənt] *n* **1** someone receiving the services of a professional. **2** customer. ⟨Latin *cliens* (related to *clinare* lean)⟩
cli·en·tele [ˌklaɪənˈtɛl] *or* [ˌkliɑnˈtɛl] *n* **1** clients collectively. **2** personal followers.

cliff [klɪf] *n* a steep, long drop from high land to lower land. **cliff·like** *adj.* ⟨Old English *clif*⟩
cliff·hang·er *n Informal* **1** a break in a story at a point of high suspense. **2** an election or other contest whose outcome is in doubt till the very end.

cli·mac·ter·ic, cli·mac·tic See CLIMAX.

cli·mate [ˈklaɪmɪt] *n* **1** the weather patterns in a place over a period of years. **2** a place with reference to its climate: *She was advised to move to a drier climate.* **3** prevailing state or trend: *the climate of public opinion.* **4** moral environment: *a climate of love and acceptance.* **cli·mat·ic** [klaɪˈmætɪk] *adj.* **cli·mat·i·cal·ly** *adv.* ⟨Greek *klima* slope (of earth); *klinein* incline⟩
cli·ma·tol·o·gy *n* the science that deals with climate. **cli·ma·to·log·i·cal** *adj.* **cli·ma·tol·o·gist** *n.*

cli·max [ˈklaɪmæks] *n* **1** the highest point; most exciting or suspenseful part. **2** orgasm. **cli·max** *v.* **cli·mac·tic** *adj.* **cli·mac·ti·cal·ly** *adv.* ⟨Greek *klimax* ladder⟩
cli·mac·ter·ic [klaɪˈmæktərɪk] *or* [ˌklaɪmækˈtɛrɪk] *n* **1** crucial time; turning point. **2** menopause. **cli·mac·ter·ic** *adj.* **climax community** *Ecology* the last community of plants or animals to develop in a particular area.

climb [klaɪm] *v* **1** go up, esp by using the hands or feet or both: *to climb a ladder.* **2** rise in rank with steady effort: *to climb to a position as manager.* **3** of a vine, grow upward by sticking to a surface. **4** slope upward: *The road climbs for 30 m.* **5** increase: *Gas prices are still climbing.* **6** get in or out with effort: *The heavy woman climbed out of the car.* **climb** *n.* **climb·er** *n.* ⟨Old English *climban*⟩

SYNONYMS
Climb emphasizes effort: *This car will never climb that hill.* **Ascend** is more formal, and suggests going straight up: *She ascended the steps like a princess.*

clime [klaɪm] *n Poetic* a country or region with reference to its climate. ⟨*climate*⟩

clinch [klɪntʃ] *v* **1** fasten (a driven nail) firmly by bending its projecting end. **2** secure; make certain: *A deposit of five dollars clinched the*

bargain. **3** *Boxing, wrestling* grapple. **4** *Slang* embrace. **clinch** *n.* ⟨variant of *clench*⟩
clinch·er *n* **1** a tool for clinching nails. **2** *Informal* a decisive event, argument, etc.

cline [klaɪn] *n* **1** any gradual progression; continuum. **2** *Biology* gradual change in an organism or in a characteristic of a species. **cli·nal** *adj.* ⟨Greek *klinein* lean⟩

cling [klɪŋ] *v* **clung, cling·ing** **1** hold firmly (to). **2** stick: *The static electricity made my skirt cling to my legs.* **3** hang around, looking for attention. **cling** *n.* **cling·ing** *adj.* **cling·y** *adj.* ⟨Old English *clingan*⟩
cling·stone *n* a peach whose flesh clings to the stone.

clin·ic [ˈklɪnɪk] *n* **1** a part of a hospital where out-patients are treated. **2** a centre where a group of doctors work together. **3** a session held to provide a special service, instruction, etc.: *a blood donor clinic, a soccer clinic.* **4** a practical class in medicine, where students watch doctors examine and treat patients. ⟨Greek *klinikos* of a bed; *klinē* bed⟩
clin·i·cal *adj* **1** to do with a clinic. **2** to do with actual diagnosis and treatment rather than research or general theory: *clinical psychology.* **3** detached; analytical: *He looked the applicant over with a clinical eye.* **4** sterile: *The kitchen seemed clinical.* *n* CLINIC (def. 4). **clin·i·cal·ly** *adv.* **cli·ni·cian** [kləˈnɪʃən] *n.*

clink¹ [klɪŋk] *n* a light, short ringing sound like that of glasses hitting together. **clink** *v.* ⟨imitative⟩

clink² [klɪŋk] *n Slang* prison. ⟨*Clink* Street in London, site of a former prison⟩

clip¹ [klɪp] *v* **clipped, clip·ping** **1** cut; cut out. **2** cut or trim the fur of: *Our dog is clipped every summer.* **3** damage (a coin) by shaving off the edge. **4** *Informal* move fast. **5** *Informal* hit or punch sharply. **6** *Slang* overcharge; cheat. **clip** *n.* ⟨Old Norse *klippa*⟩
clip–clop *n* the sound of a horse trotting. **clip–clop** *v.* **clip·per** *n* **1** Often, **clippers** *pl* a tool for cutting, esp for hair or plants. **2** a fast sailing ship. **clip·ping** *n* a piece cut from or out of something, esp an article cut out of a newspaper or magazine. **clipping service** a company that monitors newspapers and magazines for mention of its clients and sends the client relevant clippings.

clip² [klɪp] *n* **1** a fastener with two parts that squeeze together: *a paper clip.* **2** of certain firearms: **a** a metal holder for cartridges. **b** the rounds it holds.
v **clipped, clip·ping** **1** fasten with a clip. **2** *Football* tackle (a player without the ball) from behind. ⟨Old English *clyppan* embrace⟩
clip·board *n* **1** a board with a spring clip at one end for holding papers. **2** *Computers* an area of memory for storing data temporarily. **clip–on** *adj* attaching by means of a clip.

clique [klik] *or* [klɪk] *n* a small, exclusive group of people within a larger group. **cliqu·ey** *or* **cliqu·y** *adj.* **cliqu·ish** *adj.* **cliqu·ish·ly** *adv.* **cliqu·ish·ness** *n.* ⟨French, from *cliquer* click⟩

clit·o·ris ['klɪtərɪs] *n* a small erectile organ at the front of the vulva, part of the female genitals. **clit·o·ral** *adj.* ⟨Greek *kleitoris*⟩ **clit·or·i·dec·to·my** *n* **1** surgical removal of the clitoris. **2** female circumcision.

clo·a·ca [klou'eikə] *n, pl* **-cae** [-si] *or* [-saɪ], [-ki] *or* [-kaɪ] **1** sewer or privy. **2** a cavity in the body of birds, reptiles, etc. into which the intestinal, urinary, and generative canals open. ⟨Latin, probably from *cluere* purge⟩

cloak [klouk] *n* **1** a loose outer garment. **2** anything that hides or conceals. **cloak** *v.* ⟨Old Irish *cloc* bell; for its flared shape⟩ **cloak–and–dag·ger** *adj* to do with spies, intrigue, and adventure. **cloak·room** *n* a room where coats, hats, etc. can be left for a time.

clob·ber ['klɒbər] *v Slang* **1** strike violently. **2** defeat severely. **3** attack verbally: *They were clobbered by the press.* ⟨origin unknown⟩

cloche [klouʃ] *n* a bell-shaped glass cover to protect tender plants. ⟨French = bell; ultimately Old Irish *cloc*⟩

clock [klɒk] *n* **1** an instrument that measures and indicates time. **2** anything like a clock in form or function. **3** *Computers* an electronic circuit synchronizing the internal operations of system components. *v* record the time of: *The coach clocked the three girls on the 50 m dash.* ⟨Middle Dutch *clocke*; Latin *clocca*. Related to CLOAK.⟩ **against the clock** under strong pressure from a deadline. **around the clock** all day and all night. **put** or **turn the clock back** return to an older way of doing things. **clock radio** a radio with a built-in clock that can be set to turn it on at a certain time. **clock speed** *Computers* the rate, measured in megahertz, at which a component's clock produces its signals. **clock·wise** *adv, adj* in the direction in which the hands of a clock rotate. **clock·work** *n* **1** the machinery that runs a clock. **2** any complex mechanism. **like clockwork** very smoothly or regularly.

clod [klɒd] *n* **1** a lump of earth. **2** a rude, mean, or stupid person. ⟨Old English⟩ **clod·hop·per** *n* **1** a large, heavy shoe or boot. **2** a boor.

clog [klɒg] *v* **clogged, clog·ging** fill up so as to block, jam, or slow: *Hair clogged the drain. Sand clogged the reel of the fishing rod.* *n* **1** something that hinders. **2** a shoe or sandal with a wooden sole. ⟨Middle English *clogge* block⟩

cloi·son·né [ˌklɔɪzə'nei] *French* [klwazɔ'ne] *n* enamelware in which the different colours are separated by thin metal strips set on edge. ⟨French = partitioned; *cloison* partition⟩

clois·ter ['klɔɪstər]*n* **1** a covered walk along the wall of a building. **2** a monastery or convent. **3** any place of quiet or isolation. *v* shut away in a cloister or other quiet place. **clois·tered** *adj.* ⟨Latin *claustrum* closed place⟩

clone [kloun] *n* **1** an organism produced from part of a single individual, to which it is genetically identical, by means of cuttings, fission, or the development of an unfertilized ovum. **2** any apparently identical copy. **3** *Computers* hardware or software emulating that produced by another company. **clone** *v.* **clon·ing** *n.* ⟨Greek *klon* twig⟩

clop [klɒp] *v* **clopped, clop·ping** make a hollow, hard sound like a horse's hoof on a paved road. **clop** *v.* ⟨imitative⟩

close¹ [klouz] *v* **1** shut; cover with a lid or bring parts together so there is no longer an opening. **2** end: *to close a meeting.* **3** stop activity (in): *The shop is closed.* **4** complete (a sale); be completed: *The house sale will close on the 15th.* **5** begin to grapple. **6** *Electricity* unite the parts of (a circuit) so current will flow. **7** *Computers* terminate the readiness of (a file, application, window, etc.) for use. **clos·a·ble** *adj.* **close** *n.* ⟨Old French *clos-*, stem of *clore* close; Latin *claudere*⟩ **close down** close completely or permanently. **close in** approach from all sides. **close in on** surround closely. **close on** catch up to. **close out a** sell to get rid of: *to close out old stock.* **b** go out of business: *They are closing out next month.* **close up a** block. **b** bring or come nearer together. **c** of a wound, heal. **closed** *adj* **1** restricted to certain people or limited by other conditions: *a closed meeting.* **2** not open to new ideas: *a closed mind.* **3** not open to further discussion: *a closed question.* **4** *Mathematics* **a** of a curve, endless. **b** of a set, yielding another member of the same set whenever an operation is performed on any of its members. **closed–cap·tioned** *adj* of a television program, having subtitles for the deaf which can be seen only by using a special device. **closed captioning. closed–cir·cuit** *adj* to do with television broadcasting received only by a certain television set or series of sets, as in a chain of theatres, a school, etc. **closed–door** *adj* of a meeting, secret. **closed–end** *adj* to do with investment trusts having a fixed capitalization of shares which are traded on the free market and need not be redeemed on the holder's demand. **closed season** any part of the year when hunting or fishing is restricted. **closed shop** a factory or business that employs only members of labour unions. Compare OPEN SHOP, PREFERENTIAL SHOP. **closed syllable** a syllable that ends in a consonant sound. **clos·ing** *n* the final settlement between buyer and seller. *adj* final: *closing price, closing words.* **in closing** formula introducing a final point or remark. **clo·sure** *n* **1** the act, fact, or means of closing. **2** in a legislature, an end imposed on a debate so as to hold an immediate vote on the issue. **3** psychological resolution.

close² [klous] *adj* **1** near; a short distance from something: *close to home, close to death.* **2** dense or tight: *close quarters, a close weave.* **3** intimate: *my closest friends.* **4** exact: *a close translation.* **5** stuffy: *With the windows shut, the room soon became hot and close.* **6** with full concentration: *Pay close attention.* **7** not fond of talking; secretive. **8** stingy. **9** with competitors well matched: *a close contest.* **close·ly** *adv.* **close·ness** *n.* ⟨Latin *clausum* closed place; *claudere* close⟩

close to the wind a *Sailing* facing into the wind. **b** *Informal* just barely within the rules. **come close to a** almost do: *I came close to drowning.* **b** almost amount to: *That comes close to fraud.* **close up** close to one's face. **close call** or **close shave** *Informal* a narrow escape from disaster. **close–fist·ed** *adj* stingy. **close–fist·ed·ness** *n.* **close–fit·ting** *adj* fitting tightly. **close–grained** *adj* of wood, having a dense grain, as, for example, mahogany. **close–hauled** *adj* having sails set as nearly as possible in the direction from which the wind is blowing. **close–knit** *adj* firmly united by affection or common interests: *a close-knit family.* **close–mouthed** [-'maʊðd] *or* [-'mʌuθt] or **close–lipped** *adj* secretive. **close quarters** a cramped place: *living in very close quarters.* **at close quarters** very close up: *I had never seen a bear at close quarters before.* **close–up** *n* **1** a photo taken at close range. **2** a close view.

clos·et ['klɒzɪt] *n* a small room for storing clothes or household supplies.
adj private or secret: *a closet drinker.*
v shut up in a private room for a secret talk: *She is closeted with her personal advisers.* ⟨Old French, diminutive of *clos.* See CLOSE[1].⟩
(come) out of the closet (make oneself) known to others after having been in a state of secrecy or concealment: *More separatists were coming out of the closet.*

clot [klɒt] *n* a semisolid lump: *A clot of blood blocked the artery.* **clot, clot·ted, clot·ting** *v.* ⟨Old English *clott*⟩

cloth [klɒθ] *n, pl* **cloths** [klɒðz] *or* [klɒθs] **1** a material made by weaving together fibres of wool, cotton, synthetics, etc. **2 the cloth** the clergy. ⟨Old English *clāth*⟩
cloth·bound *adj* of a book, having hard covers faced with cloth.

clothe [kloʊð] *v* **clothed** or **clad, cloth·ing** put clothes on.
n **clothes** [kloʊðz] *or* [klouz] *pl* coverings for the body. ⟨Old English *clāthian; clāth*⟩
clothes·horse *n* **1** a frame to hang clothes on for drying or airing. **2** *Informal* a person who is always well and fashionably dressed. **clothes·line** *n* a rope or wire to hang clothes on for drying or airing. **clothes·peg** *n* **1** a peg for hanging clothes on. **2** clothespin, esp if peglike. **clothes·pin** *n* a clip to hold clothes on a clothesline. **clothes·press** *n* a chest or closet to keep clothes in. **clothes tree** **1** a pole with branches to hang coats and hats on. **2** a similar device to dry clothes on. **cloth·ier** ['kloʊðjər] *n* a seller or maker of clothing. **cloth·ing** *n* clothes.

SYNONYMS

Clothe is slightly more poetic than **dress** and often metaphorical. It is used most commonly in the passive (*The woods were clothed in red and orange*); as an active verb, it needs an object and an adverb or phrase telling how or with what: *He clothed himself in an old tweed suit.* **Dress** can be used with or without an object or modifier; without them it implies putting on whatever clothes are needed: *She dressed hurriedly. He was dressed in blue.*

---

cloud [klaʊd] *n* **1** a mass in the sky, made up of tiny drops of water or ice particles. **2** a mass of smoke or dust. **3** anything that darkens, obscures, or dims.
v **1** develop clouds: *The sky clouded.* **2** make or become less bright or transparent: *The suspended sand clouds the water. That detergent has clouded my silver.* **3** make or become gloomy: *His face clouded.* **4** confuse: *It only clouds the issue.* **cloud·less** *adj.* **cloud·like** *adj.* **cloud·y** *adj.* ⟨Old English *clūd*⟩
in the clouds a up in the sky. **b** unrealistic. **c** daydreaming. **under a cloud a** in disgrace; under suspicion. **b** sad or in trouble.
cloud·ber·ry *n* **1** ✱ a plant of the rose family found in northern latitudes, with white flowers and edible berries. **2** ✱ bakeapple. **cloud·burst** *n* a short, very heavy rainfall. **cloud·let** *n* a little cloud. **on cloud nine** very happy. **cloud seeding** the scattering of carbon dioxide or other chemicals in clouds to produce rain.

clove[1] [kloʊv] *n* the strongly fragrant, dried flower bud of a tropical tree of the myrtle family. ⟨Latin *clavus* nail⟩

clove[2] [kloʊv] *n* a small, separable section of a bulb: *a clove of garlic.* ⟨Old English *clufu*⟩

clove[3] [kloʊv] *v* a pt of CLEAVE[1].

clove hitch a knot used in tying a rope around a pole, spar, etc.

clo·ven ['kloʊvən] *v* a pp of CLEAVE[1]. *adj* split; divided.
cloven hoof (or **foot**) a hoof divided into two parts. **clo·ven–hoofed** or **clo·ven–foot·ed** *adj* **1** having cloven hoofs. **2** devilish.

clo·ver ['kloʊvər] *n* any of a genus of low herbs of the pea family with leaves consisting of three leaflets. ⟨Old English *clāfre*⟩
in clover *Informal* enjoying a life of ease.
clo·ver·leaf *n* a series of access ramps at the intersection of two highways.

clown [klaʊn] *n* **1** a person whose work is to entertain by jokes and antics. **2** anyone who is always trying to be funny: *the class clown.* **3** an ill-mannered or awkward person.
v act like a clown; act silly: *We were clowning around on the stage.* **clown·er·y** *n.* **clown·ish** *adj.* ⟨perhaps Norse; compare Icelandic *klumni* clumsy one⟩

cloy [klɔɪ] *v* cause disgust by an excess of something orig pleasurable: *cloyed with sweets. Her constant helpfulness soon begins to cloy.* **cloy·ing·ly** *adv.* ⟨Old French *encloyer* drive a nail in; *clou* nail⟩

cloze test [klouz] a reading comprehension test in which certain words of a text are replaced by blanks for which the reader must resupply a suitable word. ⟨altered from *close*[1]⟩

club [klʌb] *n* **1** a thick, heavy stick used as a weapon. **2** any of the specially shaped sticks used in golf to hit the ball. **3** an organized group of people joined for recreational or social activity: *a chess club, a singles' club.* **4** a sports team. **5** building or rooms used by a club. **6** nightclub. **7** a playing card with one or more black designs on it like this: ♣

v **clubbed, club·bing 1** beat with a club. **2** join for a common purpose (usually with *together*). ⟨Middle English; Old Norse *klubba*⟩ **club·ba·ble** *adj* sociable. **club·by** *adj Informal* **1** sociable. **2** having an atmosphere like that of a social club. **club car** a luxurious railway passenger car. **club·foot** *n, pl* **-feet** deformity in which the foot is misshapen and twisted, often resembling a club. **club·foot·ed** *adj*. **club·house** *n* **1** the building used by a club. **2** part of a racetrack grandstand containing a restaurant. **club sandwich** a thick sandwich consisting of at least three layers of bread and filled with meat (esp chicken), lettuce, tomato, etc. **club soda** SODA WATER.

cluck [klʌk] *n* **1** the sound made by a hen calling her chickens. **2** a sound like this. **3** *Slang* a stupid person. **cluck** *v*. ⟨imitative⟩

clue [klu] *n* **1** anything that helps to solve a mystery or puzzle. **2** *Informal* the least idea. *v* **1** indicate something to by means of a clue. **2** *Informal* tell (usually with *in*): *Clue me in.* ⟨Old English *cliewen* ball of string⟩ **clue·less** *adj Informal* **1** knowing nothing: *clueless about wine.* **2** generally incompetent.

clump [klʌmp] *n* **1** a cluster: *a clump of trees.* **2** a lump: *a clump of earth.* **3** the sound of heavy, clumsy walking. **clump** *v*. **clump·y** *adj*. ⟨Old English *clympre* lump of metal⟩

clumsy [ˈklʌmzi] *adj* **1** not graceful or skilful: *clumsy dancers, a clumsy apology.* **2** not easy to use: *a clumsy piece of equipment.* **clum·si·ly** *adv*. **clum·si·ness** *n*. ⟨*clumse* be numb with cold, probably Scandinavian⟩

clung [klʌŋ] *v* pt and pp of CLING.

clunk [klʌŋk] *n* **1** a dull falling or banging sound; thump. **2** a dull or stupid person. *v* move or strike with such a sound: *clunk a person on the head.* ⟨imitative⟩ **clunk·er** *n Slang* **1** an old, run-down machine, esp a car. **2** something unsuccessful, worthless, etc. **3** a stupid mistake. **clunk·y** *adj Informal* **1** making a thumping sound: *clunky footsteps.* **2** bulky and heavy: *clunky shoes, clunky furniture.* **3** dull, unskilful, etc.: *clunky writing.* **clunk·i·ly** *adv*. **clunk·i·ness** *n*.

clus·ter [ˈklʌstər] *n* **1** a tight bunch of things of the same kind: *a cluster of curls.* **2** a group of stars relatively close to each other. **clus·ter** *v*. ⟨Old English⟩

clutch[1] [klʌtʃ] *n* **1** a tight grasp: *The eagle loosened its clutch and the rabbit escaped.* **2** Usually, **clutches** *pl* control; power: *in the clutches of terrorists.* **3** a device for engaging and disengaging two working parts of a machine: *the clutch in a car.* *v* grasp tightly. ⟨Old English *clyccan* clench⟩ **clutch at** try eagerly to grasp: *She clutched at the branch, but missed it and fell.* **clutch purse** a woman's handbag that is carried under the arm.

clutch[2] [klʌtʃ] *n* **1** a nest of eggs. **2** a brood of chickens. **3** a small group: *There was a clutch of journalists covering the story.* ⟨variant of earlier *cletch*; Old Norse *klekja* hatch⟩

clut·ter [ˈklʌtər] *n* **1** many things in a relatively small space, esp if untidy or unnecessary. **2** clatter. **clut·ter** *v*. ⟨*clot*⟩

cm centimetre(s). The symbol for cubic centimetre is **cm³**.

CNE Canadian National Exhibition.

co– *prefix* **1** with; together: *co-operate.* **2** joint; fellow: *co-author.* **3** equally: *co-extensive.* **4** *Mathematics* complement of: *cosine.* ⟨Latin, variant of *com-* with⟩

c/o (in postal addresses) in care of.

Co. or **co. 1** company. **2** county.

coach [koutʃ] *n* **1** a bus, esp one that travels between cities. **2** a passenger car of a railway train. **3** an inexpensive class in air or rail travel. **4** a person who trains an athlete or team: *a hockey coach.* **5** any of various kinds of private tutors or special instructors giving extra help, formally or informally, in a given subject: *an acting coach, a math coach.* **6** formerly, a large horse-drawn carriage, esp a stagecoach. *v* work as a coach in or for; help or advise as a coach would: *He coaches baseball. She coached me in how to ask for a date.* ⟨Middle French *coche*; possibly Magyar *kocsi*, from *Kocs*, Hungary where coaches were first made⟩ **coach–and–four** *n* formerly, a coach pulled by four horses. **coach·man** *n, pl* **-men** driver of a coach.

co·ag·u·late [kouˈægjəˌleit] *v* thicken; clot: *Blood coagulates in air.* **co·ag·u·la·tion** *n*. ⟨Latin *co-* together + *agere* drive⟩ **co·ag·u·lant** *n* a substance that causes or speeds coagulation.

coal [koul] *n* **1** a combustible sedimentary rock, black and containing carbon, used as a fuel. It is formed over long periods from partial decomposition of vegetable matter away from air and under varying degrees of pressure. **2** a piece of burning or charred coal, wood, etc.; ember. ⟨Old English *col*⟩ **carry coals to Newcastle a** waste one's time. **b** bring something to a place where it is not needed (as coal to Newcastle, where it was plentiful). **haul** (or **rake**, or **drag**) **over the coals** scold. **heap coals of fire on someone's head** make a person sorry by returning good for evil.

coal car a railway car used for carrying coal. **coal·er** *n* a ship, railway car, etc. used for carrying coal. **coal·field** or **coal field** *n* an area where beds of coal are found. **coal gas 1** a gas made by distilling coal, formerly used for heating and lighting. **2** the toxic gas given off by burning coal. **coal·i·fi·ca·tion** *n* the natural process by which plant material is changed into coal. **coal oil 1** kerosene. **2** petroleum. **coal tar** a black, heavy, sticky liquid obtained by distilling coal. **coal·y** *adj* like coal; esp, black.

co·a·lesce [ˌkouəˈlɛs] *v* **1** grow together. **2** unite into one body, mass, party, etc.; join. **co·a·les·cence** *n*. **co·a·les·cent** *adj*. ⟨Latin *co-* together + *alescere* grow⟩

co·a·li·tion [ˌkouəˈlɪʃən] *n* **1** a formal arrangement by which political parties or leaders agree to work together for a period of time or for a special purpose. **2** any union. **co·a·li·tion·ist** *n.* ⟨Latin *coalitio*, from *coalescere*. See COALESCE.⟩

coarse [kɔrs] *adj* **1** made up of fairly large parts: *coarse sand*. **2** heavy and rough in appearance or texture: *Burlap is coarse fabric.* **3** intended for rough work: *a coarse file.* **4** of low quality: *coarse food.* **5** rude; rough: *coarse language.* **coarse·ly** *adv.* **coarse·ness** *n.* **coars·en** *v.* ⟨*course*, in sense of 'ordinariness'⟩ **coarse–grained** *adj* **1** having a coarse texture. **2** rough; crude.

SYNONYMS
Coarse emphasizes roughness and crudeness: *The soldier's coarse language was fit only for the barracks.* **Vulgar** suggests being disgusting or indecent, or deliberate and offensively rude: *He is so vulgar that no one at school likes him.*

coast [koust] *n* **1** the land along the edge of the sea. **2 the Coast** in Canada and the US, the region along the Pacific Ocean.
v **1** sail from port to port of a coast. **2** ride or slide along by gravity or momentum, using no power. **3** advance without effort: *to coast through school.* **coast·al** *adj.* ⟨Latin *costa* side⟩
the coast is clear the danger is gone.
coast·er *n* **1** a little mat on which a glass or bottle may be placed to protect the surface underneath. **2** a person who or thing that coasts. **3** ROLLER COASTER. **coaster brake** a brake on the rear wheel of a bicycle, worked by pushing back on the pedals. **coast guard 1** a government service responsible mainly for search-and-rescue operations at sea. **2** a coastal patrol whose work is preventing smuggling and protecting lives and property along the coast. **coast·line** *n* the outline of a coast: *the sandy coastline of Prince Edward Island.* **Coast Salish 1** a member of a First Nations people, among them the Nanaimo and Sechelt bands, living in SW British Columbia including Vancouver Island. **2** their Salishan language. **coast–to–coast** *adj, adv* across a continent or island; in Canada, nationwide.

coat [kout] *n* **1** an outer garment with long sleeves. **2** any outer covering: *a dog's coat of hair, a coat of paint.*
v cover with a layer: *coated with dust.* **coat·ing** *n.* **coat·less** *adj.* ⟨Old French *cote*⟩
coat check in a theatre or similar public place, a room where patrons may leave their coats, hats, etc. in the care of staff. **coat·hanger** a shaped piece of wire, plastic, or wood on which to hang clothes, which is in turn hung on a rod or peg by means of a hook at the top. **coat of arms** a design, often shaped like a shield, containing symbols of the things which distinguish a particular noble family, a government, city, etc. **coat·tail** *n* **1** the back part of a coat below the waist. **2 coattails** *pl* the skirt of a formal coat. **(ride) on someone's coattails** (advance in career or popularity) by associating with a more successful or more popular person.

co–au·thor [kou ˈɒθər] *n* a joint author. **co–au·thor** *v.*

coax [kouks] *v* persuade by pleasant ways or talk. **coax·er** *n.* ⟨obsolete *cokes* a fool⟩

co·ax·i·al [koˈæksiəl] *adj* **1** having a common axis. **2** of or having to do with a **coaxial cable**, a cable enclosing two or more conductors that carry telecommunications signals.

cob [kɒb] *n* **1** the centre part of an ear of corn. **2** a strong riding horse with short legs. **3** a male swan. ⟨Middle English *cob, cobbe*⟩

co·balt [ˈkoubɒlt] *n* **1** a metallic element similar to nickel and iron and occurring with them, used in alloys and for making pigment. *Symbol* **Co 2** COBALT BLUE. ⟨German *kobalt*, variant of *kobold* goblin⟩
cobalt blue a bright blue pigment made from a mixture of cobalt and aluminum oxides. **cobalt–60** a radioactive form of cobalt used in industry and medicine.

cob·ble [ˈkɒbəl] *v* **1** mend or make (footwear) by hand. **2** assemble clumsily: *A program was quickly cobbled together.* ⟨perhaps akin to COB⟩
cob·bler *n* **1** shoemaker. **2** a clumsy worker. **3** a fruit pie with a crumb crust only on top. **4** an iced drink made of wine, fruit juice, etc.

cob·ble·stone [ˈkɒbəlˌstoun] *n* a rounded stone formerly much used in paving. Also, **cob·ble.** ⟨Middle English *cobel ston*⟩

co·bra [ˈkoubrə] *n* any of several very poisonous snakes that can spread out their upper ribs, causing the skin just below the head to expand into a hoodlike shape. ⟨Portuguese; Latin *colubra* snake⟩

cob·web [ˈkɒbˌwɛb] *n* **1** a spider's web or the stuff it is made of. **2 cobwebs** *pl Informal* lack of alertness due to inactivity. **cob·web·by** *adj.* ⟨Old English *(ātor)coppe* spider + *web*⟩

co·ca [ˈkoukə] *n* any of several shrubs of South America, esp one species whose leaves are a source of cocaine and other alkaloids. ⟨Quechuan *cuca*⟩
co·caine [kouˈkein] *or* [ˈkoukein] *n* a drug obtained from coca leaves, used to deaden pain and illegally as a stimulant. **co·cain·ism** *n* addiction to cocaine.

coc·cyx [ˈkɒksɪks] *n, pl* **coc·cy·ges** [kɒkˈsaɪdʒiz] in humans and tailless apes, a small triangular bone at the base of the spinal column. ⟨Greek *kokkyx* orig cuckoo; shaped like cuckoo's bill⟩

coch·i·neal [ˌkɒtʃəˈnil] *or* [ˈkɒtʃəˌnil] *n* a bright red dye. ⟨Spanish *cocinilla*; Latin *coccinus* scarlet, from Greek *kokkos* oak gall⟩
cochineal insect any of various scale insects with red body fluid once used to make dye.

coch·le·a [ˈkɒkliə] *n, pl* **-le·ae** [-li,i] *or* [-li,aɪ] *Anatomy* a spiral-shaped cavity of the inner ear. **coch·le·ar** *adj.* ⟨Greek *kochlias* snail⟩

cock¹ [kɒk] *n* **1** an adult male of various birds; esp, a rooster. **2** the hammer of a gun. **3** the state of a gun when this is raised, ready for firing. **4** an upward turn or tilt of the eye, ear, head, etc. **5** a tap or valve. **6** *Curling* the part of the rink aimed at.
v **1** pull back the hammer of (a gun), ready to

fire. **2** tilt upward and to one side: *The dog cocked its ears.* ⟨Old English *cocc*⟩

cock of the walk an arrogant, powerful person in a group.

cock–a–doo·dle–doo ['kɒkə'dudəl'du] *n* a rooster's cry. **cock·a·leek·ie** [,kɒkə'liki] *n* a Scottish soup of chicken broth with leeks. **cock–and–bull story** an absurd, incredible story. **cock·crow** *n* dawn, when roosters crow. **cock·er·el** *n* a young rooster. **cock–eyed** *adj* **1** cross-eyed. **2** *Informal* tilted or twisted to one side. **3** *Informal* foolish; silly. **cock·fight** *n* a fight between roosters. **cock·fight·ing** *n* the setting of roosters or gamecocks to fight each other for the entertainment of spectators. Cockfighting is illegal in Canada. **cock·pit** *n* **1** a place where the pilot sits in an aircraft, or the driver's seat in a racing car. **2** an enclosed place for cockfights. **cocks·comb** *n* **1** the red fleshy crest on a rooster's head. **2** COXCOMB (def. 1). **cock·sure** *adj* **1** arrogantly confident. **2** quite certain: *He hesitated, not being cocksure of his position.* **cock·y** *adj* conceited; too self-confident. **cock·i·ly** *adv.* **cock·i·ness** *n.*

cock² [kɒk] *n* a small pile of hay, rounded on top. **cock** *v.* ⟨Middle English⟩

cock·ade [kɒ'keɪd] *n* a knot of ribbon worn on a hat as a badge. ⟨French *cocarde; coq* cock⟩

cock·a·ma·mie ['kɒkə,meimi] *adj* **1** of poor quality; cheap. **2** foolish; absurd. ⟨*cock-a-nee-nee* cheap molasses candy in 19c New York⟩

cock·a·tiel ['kɒkə,til] *or* [,kɒkə'til] *n* a small Australian parrot with a crest and a long tail. ⟨Dutch *kaketielje* from *kaketoe*. See COCKATOO.⟩

cock·a·too ['kɒkə,tu] *or* [,kɒkə'tu] *n* any of various large parrots with mainly white plumage and a crest. ⟨Dutch *kaketoe;* Malay *kakatua*⟩

cock·a·trice ['kɒkətrɪs] *n* a fabled serpent hatched from a cock's egg, whose look was supposed to cause death. ⟨Old French *cocatris,* Latin *calcatrix* trampler; infl. by *cock*⟩

cock·le ['kɒkəl] *n* any of various saltwater clams, esp an edible European species. ⟨Greek *konchylion; konchē* conch⟩ **warm the cockles of one's heart** *Facetious* be very heartwarming or gratifying.

cock·le·shell *n* **1** the shell of a cockle or of any similar mollusc. **2** a small, shallow boat.

Cock·ney or **cock·ney** ['kɒkni] *n* a native or inhabitant of the East End of London, England, who speaks a particular dialect of English. ⟨Middle English *cokeney* cock's egg, pampered child, city fellow⟩

cock·roach ['kɒk,routʃ] *n* any of an order of insects, most of which are active at night, having long feelers and a long, flat, shiny body. ⟨Spanish *cucaracha*⟩

cock·tail ['kɒk,teil] *n* **1** an iced drink made from spirits or liqueur mixed with fruit or vegetable juices, often with a garnish. **2** an appetizer. **3** mixed diced fruit. **4** any mixture, as of chemicals, etc. (also often figurative). **cocktail lounge** a room in a hotel, restaurant, etc. where alcohol is served.

co·coa ['koukou] *n* **1** a brown powder made from chocolate. **2** a hot, sweet drink made from this powder. ⟨variant of *cacao*⟩ **cocoa bean** the seed of the cacao. **cocoa butter** a fat obtained from chocolate liquor, used in making soap, cosmetics, candy, etc.

co·co·nut ['koukə,nʌt] *n* the fruit of the coconut palm, having edible white meat in a hard, brown shell and sweet, whitish liquid (**coconut milk**) in its hollow centre.

co·coon [kə'kun] *n* **1** a covering prepared by an insect larva to protect itself while it is becoming an adult. **2** any environment or structure that similarly protects or isolates. **co·coon** *v.* ⟨French *cocon; coque* shell⟩ **co·coon·ing** *n* the practice of conducting business in or from one's own home and relying on videos, takeout food, etc. instead of going out for recreation. **co·coon·er** *n.*

cod [kɒd] *n, pl* **cod** or **cods** **1** an important food fish of the N Atlantic Ocean. Also, **codfish. 2** any member of a family of fish including the cods, haddock, hakes, and pollocks. ⟨Middle English; origin uncertain⟩ **cod·der** *n ✶ Maritimes* **1** a boat used for cod fishing. **2** a cod fisher. **cod·head** *n ✶ Slang* a Newfoundlander. **cod–liv·er oil** oil extracted from the liver of cod, rich in nutrients.

C.O.D. CASH ON DELIVERY.

co·da ['koudə] *n* **1** *Music* a separate passage at the end of a composition, designed to bring it to a satisfactory close. **2** *Ballet* the concluding section of a *pas de deux.* ⟨Italian; Latin *cauda* tail⟩

cod·dle ['kɒdəl] *v* **1** indulge or overprotect: *coddle sick children.* **2** cook in water without boiling: *coddle an egg.* **cod·dler** *n.* ⟨variant of *caudle* gruel; Latin *calidus* hot⟩

code [koud] *n* **1 a** a system of secret writing. **b** alternative vocabulary; often, specifically, jargon or a euphemism. **2** any symbolic system of communication, including ordinary language, flag semaphore, Morse, etc. **3** one of a finite series of identifying tags, esp a machine-readable one: *bar code, postal code.* **4** *Computers* a program, or the set of symbols used to write it. **5** a set of rules or standards: *a moral code, a legal code, a building code. v* **1** express or conceal in code. **2** *Computers* program. **co·der** *n.* ⟨See CODEX.⟩ **code word** euphemism. **cod·i·fy** ['koudə,faɪ] *or* ['kɒdə,faɪ] *v* set down and arrange (laws, procedures) systematically. **cod·i·fi·ca·tion** *n.* **cod·i·fi·er** *n.*

co·de·fen·dant [,koudi'fɛndənt] *n* a joint defendant in a legal case.

co·deine ['koudin] *n* a drug obtained from opium, used to relieve pain and cause sleep. ⟨Greek *kōdeia* poppy head⟩

co·dex ['koudɛks] *n, pl* **co·di·ces** ['koudə,siz] *or* ['kɒdə,siz] a manuscript or volume of manuscripts. ⟨Latin *codex,* variant of *caudex* tree trunk, block, book⟩

codg·er ['kɒdʒər] *n Informal* a peculiar old person. ⟨origin uncertain⟩

cod·i·cil ['kɒdə,sɪl] *or* ['kɒdəsəl] *n* **1** *Law*

something added to a will to change it or explain it. **2** any additional statement. ⟨Latin *codicullus*, diminutive of *codex*. See CODEX.⟩

co–di·rect [ˈkou dəˈrɛkt] *v* direct (a film, etc.) jointly. **co–di·rec·tor** *n*.

cod·piece [ˈkɒd‚pis] *n* in the 15c and 16c in Europe, a pouch or flap attached to the front of men's breeches to cover the genitals. ⟨Old English *codd* bag, husk, scrotum + *piece*⟩

co–ed [ˈkou ˈɛd] *n Informal esp formerly*, a female student at a co-educational school, college, or university. **co–ed** *adj*.
co–ed·u·ca·tion *n* the education of students of both sexes together. **co–ed·u·ca·tion·al** *adj*.

co–ed·it [ˈkou ˈɛdɪt] *v* edit jointly. **co–ed·it·or** *n*.

co·ef·fi·cient [‚kouəˈfɪʃənt] *n* **1** *Mathematics* a number or symbol put before another as a multiplier. In 3*x*, 3 is the coefficient of *x*; in *axy*, *a* is the coefficient of *xy*. **2** *Physics* a ratio used as a multiplier to calculate the behaviour of a substance under different conditions of heat, light, etc.: *coefficient of expansion*.

coe·la·canth [ˈsilə‚kænθ] *n* any of an order of fishes with rounded scales and limblike pectoral fins. ⟨Greek *koilos* hollow + *akantha* thorn, spine⟩

coe·len·ter·ate [sɪˈlɛntərɪt] *or* [-‚reit] *n* any of a phylum of mostly marine invertebrates, such as a jellyfish or hydra, having a saclike body with one opening. Also called **cni·dar·i·an**. ⟨Greek *koilos* hollow + *enteron* intestine⟩

coe·li·ac [ˈsili‚æk] *adj* See CELIAC DISEASE.

coerce [kouˈɜrs] *v* use force or manipulation to compel. **co·erc·er** *n*. **co·er·cion** *n*. **co·er·cive** *adj*. ⟨Latin *co-* together + *arcere* restrain⟩

co–e·val [kou ˈivəl] *adj* **1** of the same age or duration. **2** contemporary. **co·e·val·ly** *adv*.

co–ex·ec·u·tor [‚kou ɛgˈzɛkjətər] *n* a joint executor of a will.

co–ex·ist [‚kou ɛgˈzɪst] *v* **1** exist at the same time and place: *Orange trees have co-existing fruit and flowers*. **2** live together peacefully. **co–ex·ist·ence** *n*. **co–ex·ist·ent** *adj*.

co–ex·ten·sive [‚kou ɛkˈstɛnsɪv] *adj* covering the same space or time. **co–ex·ten·sive·ly** *adv*.

cof·fee [ˈkɒfi] *n* **1** a dark brown drink or flavouring made from the roasted beans, or seeds, of any of a genus of tropical evergreen shrubs. **2** the roasted, usually ground, beans. ⟨Turkish *qahveh*; Arabic *qahwa*⟩
coffee break a pause for refreshment. **cof·fee·cake** *n* a breadlike cake or sweet bun eaten with coffee. **coffee house** a casual restaurant serving coffee and other light refreshments. **coffee table** a low table usually placed in front of a chesterfield and used for serving coffee, etc. **coffee–table book** a large, lavishly illustrated book designed mainly for display, as on a coffee table.

cof·fer [ˈkɒfər] *n* **1** a box, chest, or trunk, esp one holding money or treasure. **2 coffers** *pl* treasury; funds. **3** an ornamental panel in a ceiling, etc. **4** a lock in a canal. **cof·fered** *adj*. ⟨Old French *cofre*; Greek *kophinos* basket⟩
cof·fer·dam *n* **1** a watertight enclosure built

in a shallow river or lake and pumped dry to permit construction of a bridge, etc. **2** a space between compartments of a ship's hold.

cof·fin [ˈkɒfən] *n* a box into which a dead body is put to be buried or cremated. ⟨Old French *cofin*; Greek *kophinos* basket⟩

cog [kɒg] *n* **1** one of a series of teeth on the edge of a wheel that transfer motion by interlocking with the teeth of a similar wheel. **2** such a wheel. Also, **cog·wheel**. **3** a person playing a small but critical part in a large, complex organization. ⟨Middle English *cogge*⟩ **slip a cog** *Informal* make a mistake.
cog railway a railway on a steep slope, with traction provided by a centre rail whose cog engages with a cog on the car's engine.

co·gen·er·a·tion [‚koudʒɛnəˈreɪʃən] *n* the production of heat or electricity from steam not fully used up in an industrial process.

co·gent [ˈkoudʒənt] *adj* of reasoning, sound and convincing: *cogent arguments*. **co·gen·cy** *n*. **co·gent·ly** *adv*. ⟨Latin *cogens* ppr of *cogere; co-* together + *agere* drive⟩

cog·i·tate [ˈkɒdʒə‚teit] *v* think carefully and deeply; reflect. **cog·i·ta·tion** *n*. **cog·i·ta·tive** *adj*. ⟨Latin *co-* (intensive) + *agitare* consider⟩

co·gnac [ˈkɒnjæk] *or* [ˈkounjæk] *French* [kɔˈnjak] *n* a fine brandy orig produced in W France. ⟨*Cognac* town, region in France⟩

cog·nate [ˈkɒgneit] *adj* **1** related by family or origin. **2** of languages or words, having a common source in another language. **3** of similar nature or quality.
n **1** a cognate word or thing. **2** a matrilineal relative. ⟨Latin *co-* together + *gnatus* born⟩

cog·ni·tion [kɒgˈnɪʃən] *n* **1** mental process of acquiring knowledge. **2** the knowledge or understanding acquired. **cog·ni·tive** *adj*. ⟨Latin *cognitio* from *cognoscere; co-* (intensive) + *gnoscere* know⟩

cog·ni·zance [ˈkɒgnəzəns] *n* **1** knowledge; awareness. **2** jurisdiction; are of responsibility. **3** [ˈkɒnəzəns] *Law* **a** knowledge upon which a judge is bound to act without having it proved in evidence. **b** the power to deal with something judicially. **c** official notice. **take cognizance of** notice. **cog·ni·zant** *adj* aware; attentive; taking notice (*of*). **co·gno·scen·ti** [‚kɒnjouˈʃɛnti] *or* [‚kɒgnəˈʃɛnti] *n pl*, *sg* **co·gno·scen·te** [-tei] *or* [-ti] people having or claiming expert knowledge in a given field, as in art, literature, or politics.

co·hab·it [kouˈhæbɪt] *v* **1** live together as husband and wife. **2** live in the same place or territory. **co·hab·it·ant** *n*. **co·hab·i·ta·tion** *n*. ⟨Latin *co-* with + *habitare* dwell⟩

co–heir [ˈkou ˈɛr] *n* a joint heir.

co·here [kouˈhir] *v* **1** of a mixture, group or anything with elements or members, hold together as a unit: *Egg helps meatballs cohere better. This paragraph does not cohere.* **2** *Physics* be united by the action of molecular forces. ⟨Latin *co-* together + *haerere* stick⟩
co·her·ent *adj* logically connected. **co·her·ence** *n*. **co·he·sion** *n* **1** tendency to hold together: *Sand has more cohesion when wet.* **2** unity.

3 *Physics* an attraction between molecules of the same kind. Compare ADHESION (def. 2). **4** *Botany* a union of parts. **co·he·sive** [kou'hisɪv] *or* [kou'hizɪv] *adj.* **co·he·sive·ly** *adv.* **co·he·sive·ness** *n.*

co·ho ['kouhou] *n, pl* **-hoes** *or* **-ho** ✱ a Pacific salmon found along the west coast from S California to Alaska, very highly valued as a food fish. Also, **co·hoe**. ⟨origin uncertain⟩

co·hort ['kouhɔrt] *n* **1** in ancient Rome, a part of a legion. **2** a group or band, esp of soldiers. **3** *Informal* companion; associate. **4** *Statistics* an age group or similarly well-defined group. ⟨Latin *cohors* court, enclosure⟩

co–host ['kou 'houst] *v* host (a television show, event, etc.) jointly. **co–host** *n.*

coif [kɔɪf] *n* **1** a cap that fits closely around the head. **2** [kwɑf] coiffure.
v [kwɑf] style (the hair). ⟨Old French *coife*⟩
coif·feur [kwa'fɜr] *French* [kwa'fœʀ] *n* a male hairstylist. **coif·feuse** [-'fʊz] *or* [-'fjuz] *French* [kwa'føz] *n* a female hairdresser. **coif·fure** [kwa'fjʊr] *French* [kwa'fyʀ] *n* **1** a hairstyle. **2** a covering for the hair or head.

coil [kɔɪl] *v* wind around and around to form a spiral or tube: *to coil a rope. The snake coiled around a branch.* **coil** *n.* **coil·er** *n.* ⟨Old French *coillir*; Latin *colligere*. See COLLECT.⟩

coin [kɔɪn] *n* **1** a piece of metal stamped by a government for use as money. **2** currency; coins collectively.
v **1** make (metal money). **2** make up; invent (a word): *Lewis Carroll coined the word 'chortle'.* **coin·er** *n.* ⟨Latin *cuneus* wedge⟩
coin money *Informal* get rich: *He's coining money in the oil industry.* **pay someone back in his or her own coin** treat someone as he or she treated oneself or others. **the other side of the coin** the opposite view or aspect.

coin·age *n* **1** coins or a system of coins. **2** a recently invented word. **coin–op·er·at·ed** *adj* worked by the insertion of a coin or coins: *a coin-operated washing machine.*

co·in·cide [ˌkouɪn'saɪd] *v* **1** occupy the same place in space: *If these triangles Δ Δ were placed one over the other, they would coincide.* **2** occur simultaneously by chance: *My visit coincided with the local elections.* **3** agree or correspond exactly: *Her opinion coincides with mine.* **co·in·ci·dent** *adj.* ⟨Latin *co-* together + *in* upon + *cadere* fall⟩
co·in·ci·dence [kou'ɪnsədəns] *n* **1** the chance occurrence of two things together in such a way as to seem remarkable, fitting, etc. **2** an exact correspondence or agreement. **co·in·ci·den·tal** *adj* involving or resulting from coincidence (def. 1). **co·in·ci·den·tal·ly** *adv.*

co·i·tus ['kouɪtəs], ['kɔɪtəs], *or* [kou'əitəs] *n* sexual intercourse. ⟨Latin *coitio*, from *coire*; *co-* together + *ire* go⟩

coke¹ [kouk] *n* **1** a fuel made from coal that burns with much heat and little smoke. **2** the solid waste left from refining petroleum.
v make into coke. ⟨? variant of *colk* core⟩

coke² [kouk] *n Slang* cocaine.
v use, or drug with, cocaine (with *out* or *up*).

col [kɒl] *n* **1** a gap or depression in a range of mountains or hills, usually forming a pass. **2** *Meteorology* the point of lowest pressure between anticyclones. ⟨Latin *collum* neck⟩

co·la ['koulə] *n* **1** any of various carbonated drinks flavoured with kola nuts. **2** See KOLA.

col·an·der ['kɒləndər] *or* ['kʌləndər] *n* a dish with many small holes for draining liquid from foods. ⟨Latin *colare* strain⟩

cold [kould] *adj* **1** much less warm than the body. **2** feeling too little warmth: *Get a jacket if you're cold.* **3** relatively low in temperature: *This coffee is cold.* **4** indifferent or unfriendly: *a cold greeting.* **5** sexually unresponsive. **6** not influenced by emotion: *cold logic.* **7** not primed or prepared by previous activity or interaction: *a cold engine, to start cold.* **8** of a scent, weak; old. **9** unconscious.
n **1** the lack of heat: *the cold of winter.* **2** a common viral infection producing a stuffy or runny nose. **3** the sensation of not being warm enough. **cold·ly** *adv.* **cold·ness** *n.* ⟨Old English *cald*⟩
catch *or* **take cold** become sick with a cold. **cold comfort** poor consolation. **come in from the cold** return or be restored to one's usual status in a group. **give someone the cold shoulder** *or* **turn a cold shoulder** treat with deliberate unfriendliness or indifference; consciously neglect. **cold–shoul·der** *v.* **in cold blood** See BLOOD. **leave one cold** arouse no interest in one. **out cold** unconscious. **(out) in the cold** all alone; neglected; ignored. **throw** *or* **pour cold water on** actively discourage: *He threw cold water on our plans.*
cold–blood·ed *adj* **1** having blood whose temperature varies with that of the surroundings. **2** characterized by a lack of consideration, pity, or kindness. **cold cash** ready money, as distinct from credit. **cold cream** an oil-based salve for softening or cleansing the skin. **cold cuts** cooked or cured meats, sliced and served cold. **cold feet** sudden fear or reluctance. **cold fish** a person with little personal warmth. **cold frame** a low box used to protect delicate plants from cold while allowing exposure to sunlight. **cold front** *Meteorology* the front edge of a cold air mass advancing into and replacing a warm one. **cold–heart·ed** *adj* lacking in feeling. **cold pack 1** something cold put on the body for therapeutic purposes. **2** a method of canning fruits or vegetables in which they are heated only after being placed in the container. **cold–pack** *v.* **cold snap** a sudden spell of cold weather. **cold sore** a sore on or near the lips consisting of a group of small blisters that break and form a crust before healing. It is a form of herpes simplex. **cold sweat** perspiration caused by fear, nervousness, pain, or shock and accompanied by a chilly feeling: *She broke out in a cold sweat just thinking about her narrow escape.* **cold turkey** *Slang* **1** sudden total withdrawal from a drug to which one is addicted: *One way to quit smoking is cold turkey.* **2** without preparation or preliminaries: *He approached the manager cold turkey and asked*

for a raise. **3** bluntly: *talk cold turkey to a person.* **cold war** a prolonged contest for supremacy using diplomatic, economic, and psychological rather than military means.

co·lec·to·my [kə'lɛktəmi] *n* See COLON.

cole·slaw ['koul,slɒ] *n* a salad made of shredded raw cabbage. ⟨Dutch *kool sla* cabbage salad⟩

col·ic ['kɒlɪk] *n* a condition in young babies characterized by constant crying due to various physical complaints. **col·ick·y** *adj* ⟨Greek *kolikos* of the colon⟩

co·li·form, co·li·tis See COLON.

col·i·se·um [,kɒlə'siəm] *n* **1** a large building or stadium for public events. **2 Coliseum.** See COLOSSAL. ⟨See COLOSSAL.⟩

col·lab·o·rate [kə'læbə,reit] *v* **1** work (*on* a project) together: *writers collaborating on a book.* **2** co-operate with an enemy as a traitor. **col·lab·o·ra·tion** *n.* **col·lab·o·ra·tive** [kə'læbərətɪv] *or* [kə'læbə,reitɪv] *adj.* **col·lab·o·ra·tor** *n.* ⟨Latin *com-* with + *laborare* work⟩

col·lage [kə'lɑʒ] *n* **1** an artistic arrangement of different items pasted on a background. **2** anything made of odd parts or pieces. ⟨French, from *coller* to glue; Greek *kolla* glue⟩

col·la·gen ['kɒlədʒən] *n* any of a group of fibrous proteins found in connective tissue such as skin, ligaments, etc. **col·la·gen·ic** *adj.* ⟨Greek *kolla* glue + -GEN⟩

col·lapse [kə'læps] *v* **1** fall suddenly down or in as a result of outside pressure or loss of support. **2** fail; break down: *His business collapsed and with it his health.* **3** fold or push together: *to collapse a telescope.* **col·lapse** *n.* ⟨Latin *collapsus,* pp of *collabi; com-* + *labi* fall⟩ **col·laps·i·ble** *adj* made so it can be folded or pushed into a smaller format.

col·lar ['kɒlər] *n* **1** a strip of cloth attached to the neckline of a garment. **2** a band for the neck of a pet. **3** a piece of jewellery resembling a collar. **4** a thick, padded oval ring forming part of the harness of a draft animal, to fit around the neck: *A horse's collar bears the weight of the load.* **5** a ring, flange, etc. around a pipe or shaft. **6** *Informal* an arrest. **col·lar** *v.* **col·lar·less** *adj.* **col·lar·like** *adj.* ⟨Middle English; Latin *collum* neck⟩

col·lar·bone *n* the bone connecting the breastbone and the shoulder blade.

col·lard ['kɒlərd] *n* **1** a variety of kale. **2 collards** or **collard greens** *pl* its leaves, eaten as a vegetable. ⟨altered from *colewort*⟩

col·late ['kouleit] *or* [kə'leit] *v* **1** assemble and compare (data from different sources). **2** put together in proper order: *to collate the pages of a report.* **col·la·tor** *n.* ⟨Latin *collatus,* pp of *conferre; com-* together + *ferre* bring⟩

col·la·tion *n* a light meal.

col·lat·er·al [kə'lætərəl] *n* **1** assets pledged as security for a loan. **2** a collateral relative. *adj* **1** parallel; side by side. **2** related but secondary. **3** descended in a different line from the same ancestors. **4** corresponding in rank, importance, or time.

col·lat·er·al·ly *adv.* **col·lat·er·al·ize** *v.* ⟨Latin *com-* together + *lateralis* lateral⟩

collateral damage a wartime euphemism for civilian casualties and property damage near a military installation under attack.

col·league ['kɒlig] *n* an associate; a fellow worker. ⟨Latin *com-* together + *legare* send or choose as deputy⟩

col·lect [kə'lɛkt] *v* **1** gather (things): *Collect the assignments.* **2** accumulate: *Drifting snow collects behind snow fences.* **3** gather and save as a hobby: *to collect stamps.* **4** pick up: *I've come to collect my daughter.* **5** ask and receive payment for (dues, bills, taxes, etc.) *adj, adv* with charges to be paid by the recipient: *a collect telegram. Phone collect.* *n* ['kɒlɛkt] a short prayer used in certain Christian church services. ⟨Latin *collectus,* pp of *colligere; com-* + *legere* gather⟩

col·lect·a·ble or **col·lect·i·ble** *adj* that may be collected; suitable for collection. *n* anything having a current attraction for collectors: *a shelf full of toy cars and other collectables.*

col·lect·ed *adj* **1** gathered together in a set or volume: *the author's collected works.* **2** calm; not confused. **col·lec·tion** *n* **1** the act of collecting. **2** a group of things together in one place or belonging to one owner: *a collection of books.* **3** a group of things gathered and saved as a hobby: *a bottle cap collection.* **4** money collected, as in a church or for charity. **5** accumulation; heap: *a little collection of dust.* **col·lec·tive** *adj* **1** of a group: *collective effort.* **2** run co-operatively by a group: *a collective farm.* *n* **1** COLLECTIVE NOUN. **2** a collective business operation or the group that runs it. **col·lec·tive·ly** *adv.* **collective bargaining** negotiation between workers organized as a group and their employer.

collective noun a noun, such as *crowd, team, choir,* etc. that is singular in form but refers to a group. **col·lec·tiv·ism** *n* control of the distribution of wealth by the people or state. **col·lec·tiv·ist** *n, adj.* **col·lec·tiv·is·tic** *adj.* **col·lec·tiv·i·ty** *n* **1** the fact of being collective. **2** a group acting as a unit. **col·lec·ti·vize** *v* cause to be run as a COLLECTIVE (*n* def. 2). **col·lec·ti·vi·za·tion** *n.* **col·lec·tor** *n* **1** a person who collects things as a hobby: *a coin collector.* **2** a person hired to collect debts. **collector's item** something worth adding to a collection.

USAGE

A **collective noun** is used with a singular verb when it refers to a group as a whole: *The committee was silent.* It may be used with a plural verb when the individuals in the group are thought of as acting separately: *The committee were asked to prepare separate reports for the presentation.*

col·lege ['kɒlɪdʒ] *n* **1** an institution that offers vocational training or instruction or pre-university courses: *the Victoria College of Art, a community college.* **2** *esp US Informal* university. **3** a major academic division of a university, offering programs of a certain kind, often professional; faculty: *a college of* *engineering.* **4** a social and administrative unit within a university, often corresponding to a former independent institution or a separate campus, or specializing in certain studies. **5** an association supervising the members of a profession: *the College of Physicians.* **6** any official group having certain powers and duties: *the electoral college in the US.* ⟨Latin *collegium.* See COLLEAGUE.⟩

College of Cardinals in the Roman Catholic Church, the body that elects and advises the Pope. **col·le·gi·al** [kə'lidʒəl] *adj* **1** to do with a college (defs. 5, 6). **2** sharing power equally among colleagues. **col·le·giate** [kə'lidʒɪt] *n* **✻ 1** a COLLEGIATE INSTITUTE. **2** *Informal* any large high school. *adj* **1 ✻** of or like a high school or its students. **2** of or like a college or its students. **collegiate institute ✻** in some provinces, a secondary school exceeding the requirements of a high school; formerly, in Ontario, one offering grade thirteen.

col·lide [kə'laɪd] *v* **1** come violently into contact: *Two large ships collided in the harbour.* **2** clash; conflict. **col·li·sion** [kə'lɪʒən] *n.* ⟨Latin *com-* together + *laedere,* orig strike⟩

collision course a course that will inevitably lead to serious conflict or other disaster.

col·lie ['kɒli] *or* ['kouli] *n* a breed of large, thick-haired dog having a long, pointed nose and a bushy tail. ⟨origin uncertain⟩

col·lier ['kɒljər] *n* **1** a ship carrying coal. **2** a coal miner. ⟨Middle English *colier; col* coal⟩ **col·lier·y** *n* a coal mine and its buildings.

col·lin·e·ar [kə'lɪniər] *adj Geometry* lying in the same straight line: *collinear points.*

col·li·sion See COLLIDE.

col·lo·cate ['kɒlə,keit] *v* **1** place together or arrange. **2** of certain words, routinely occur together. **col·lo·ca·tion** *n.* ⟨Latin *com-* together + *locare* place⟩

col·loid ['kɒlɔɪd] *n* **1** a substance made up of tiny particles that will remain suspended in a different medium without dissolving. **2** such a substance together with the medium in which it is suspended. Fog is a colloid. **col·loi·dal** *adj.* ⟨Greek *kolla* glue⟩

col·lo·qui·al [kə'loukwiəl] *adj* standard, but used only in everyday speech rather than in formal speech or writing. Compare INFORMAL. **col·lo·qui·al·ly** *adv.* ⟨Latin *com-* together + *loqui* speak⟩ **col·lo·qui·al·ism** *n* a colloquial expression or construction. **col·lo·qui·um** *n, pl* **-qui·ums** *or* **-qui·a** a scholarly conference. **col·lo·quy** *n* ['kɒləkwi] **1** a conversation; conference. **2** a written dialogue: *Erasmus' Colloquies.*

col·lude [kə'lud] *v* act together secretly; conspire. **col·lu·sion** *n.* ⟨Latin *com-* with + *ludere* play⟩

co·logne [kə'loun] *n* a fragrant liquid for use on the body, not as strong as perfume. ⟨French; *Cologne,* Germany, where first made⟩

co·lon[1] ['koulən] *n* a punctuation mark (:) used to show that a list, explanation, long quote, etc. follows. ⟨Greek *kōlon* limb, clause⟩

co·lon[2] ['koulən] *n, pl* **co·lons** or **co·la** ['koulə] the main part of the large intestine, from the caecum to the rectum. **co·lon·ic** [kə'lɒnɪk] *adj.* ⟨Greek *kolon*⟩ **co·lec·to·my** [kə'lɛktəmi] *n* surgical removal of the colon. **co·li·form** ['koulə,fɔrm] *or* ['kɒlə,fɔrm] *adj* to do with bacteria found in the colon of vertebrates, excreted in the feces and potentially contaminating water, etc. **co·li·tis** [kə'laɪtɪs] *n* inflammation of the colon, often causing severe pain. **co·los·to·my** [kə'lɒstəmi] *n* the making of an artificial opening in the colon. **co·lot·o·my** [kə'lɒtəmi] *n* a surgical incision into the colon.

colo·nel ['kɜrnəl] *n* a military officer above a lieutenant-colonel and below a brigadier-general. *Abbrev* **Col. colo·nel·cy** *n.* ⟨French *coronel, colonel,* Italian *colonnello* leader of a regiment (*colonna*); Latin *columna* column⟩

co·lo·ni·al, co·lo·niz·er, etc. See COLONY.

col·on·nade [,kɒlə'neid] *n Architecture* a row of columns equally spaced. **col·on·nad·ed** *adj.* ⟨Italian *colonnata,* from *colonna.* See COLONEL.⟩

col·o·ny ['kɒləni] *n* **1** a group of people who settle in another land claimed by their own government, under whose authority they remain. **2** a territory distant from the country that governs it. **3** a group of people of the same ethnicity, culture, profession, religion, etc. living together: *a nudist colony. There are several Doukhobor colonies in British Columbia.* **4** *Biology* a group of animals or plants of one kind living together. **5** *Bacteriology* a mass of bacteria arising from a single cell, living on or in a solid medium. **6 the Colonies a** the thirteen British colonies that became the United States. **b** the colonies, as opposed to sovereign nations, in the Commonwealth. ⟨Latin *colonus* cultivator; *colere* cultivate⟩ **co·lo·ni·al** [kə'louniəl] *adj* **1** to do with a colony. **2** Often, **Colonial** to do with the thirteen colonies that became the United States: *colonial furniture.* **co·lo·ni·al·ism** *n* the practice of a nation claiming and ruling over others as its colonies. **co·lo·ni·al·ist** *n, adj.* **col·o·nist** *n* a person who helps found or settles in a colony. **col·o·nize** *v* establish a colony in: *France colonized parts of Canada.* **col·o·ni·za·tion** *n.* **col·o·niz·er** *n.*

color, col·or·ant, col·or·a·tion See COLOUR.

col·o·ra·tu·ra [,kʌlərə'turə] *or* [,kɒlərə'turə] *n Music* ornamental passages such as trills, runs, etc. ⟨Italian = colouring⟩

co·los·sal [kə'lɒsəl] *adj* **1** huge; gigantic. **2** remarkable; outstanding: *colossal talent.* **co·los·sal·ly** *adv.* ⟨Greek *kolossos* huge statue⟩ **Col·os·se·um** *n* in Rome, a large, outdoor theatre formerly used for games and contests. **co·los·sus** *n, pl* **-los·sus·es** or **-los·si** [-'lɒsaɪ] *or* [-'lɒsi] **1** a huge statue. **2** anything huge.

co·los·to·my, co·lot·o·my See COLON.

co·los·trum [kə'lɒstrəm] *n* the thin milk secreted by a mammal for the first few days after the birth of young. ⟨Latin⟩

col·our or **col·or** ['kʌlər] *n* **1** the sensation

produced by the effects of light waves of different lengths striking the eye. **2** any colour other than black, white, or grey; hue. **3** paint, dye, or pigment: *oil colours*. **4** the natural, healthy colour of a person's face. **5** the colour of one's skin due to pigment. **6** redness of skin due to blushing: *The colour rushed to her face*. **7** vividness, detail, or distinctive character; that which evokes an emotional response: *to add colour to a story*. **8** outward appearance: *a colour of truth*. **9 the colours** the flag of a nation, regiment, etc. **10** *Physics* a theoretical property of quarks, governing their interaction. *v* **1** give colour or a new colour to; acquire colour. **2** blush. **3** present so as to mislead: *The general coloured his report of the battle to make his mistakes seem the fault of his officers.* **4** draw or colour pictures with crayons, markers, etc., as a pastime: *The child would sit and colour for hours.* ⟨Latin *color*⟩ **give** (or **lend**) **colour to** make plausible. **in colour** with all the real colours shown. **lose colour** become pale. **of colour** having skin of a colour other than white: *people of colour*. **one's** (**true**) **colours** one's real character, plans, or opinions. **with flying colours** with great success; triumphantly: *She passed the exam with flying colours.* **col·or·ant** *n* a colouring agent, such as a dye. **col·or·a·tion** *n* way in which something is coloured: *The coloration of some animals is like that of their surroundings.* **colour bar** denial of rights, privileges, and opportunities on the grounds of skin colour. **col·our–blind** *adj* **1** unable to see colour or tell certain colours apart. **2** *Informal* not racist. **colour blindness**. **col·our–code** *v* use colours as a means of identifying: *The wires in the electrical system are colour-coded.* **col·oured** *adj* **1** not black, white, grey, or clear: *coloured shirts*. **2 a** *Offensive* BLACK (def. 3). **b** *South African* of racially mixed descent. **3** biassed: *The paper published a coloured account of the political convention.* **4 ✱** of leaves, having turned colour in the fall. **col·our·fast** *adj* resistant to change of colour by fading or washing. **colour filter** a coloured medium, such as gelatin, through which light is directed, for stage effects or photography, etc. **col·our·ful** *adj* **1** abounding in colour. **2** picturesque, vivid, or full of character. **col·our·ful·ly** *adv.* **col·our·ful·ness** *n.* **colour guard** the honour guard of a military unit that carries the flag during ceremonies. **col·our·ing** *n* **1** the colour or colour pattern that a person or thing shows. **2 a** substance used to colour; pigment. **3** false appearance: *a colouring of truth.* **colouring book** a book containing outline drawings for children to colour. **colouring matter** a substance used to colour; pigment. **col·our·less** *adj* **1** without colour. **2** uninteresting; without character. **col·our·less·ly** *adv.* **col·our·less·ness** *n.* **colour phase 1** a seasonal change in the colouring of an animal. **2** an individual or group of individual animals with different colouring

from the rest of the same species: *The panther is a black colour phase of the leopard.*

colt [koult] *n* **1** a young horse, donkey, etc., esp a male under four or five years old. **2** a young, inexperienced, or playful person. **colt·ish** *adj.* **colt·ish·ly** *adv.* ⟨Old English⟩

col·umn ['kɒləm] *n* **1** *Architecture* a tall, slender, upright structure; pillar. **2** a line of soldiers, vehicles, things, etc.: *a long column of cars, a column of ants. Add up this column of figures.* **3** a narrow division of a page reading from top to bottom. **4** a regular part of a newspaper or periodical devoted to a special subject or contributed by a certain writer. **5** anything long, slender and giving vertical support like a column: *the spinal column.* **co·lum·nar** [kə'lʌmnər] *adj.* ⟨Latin *columna*⟩ **col·um·nist** ['kɒləmnɪst] *n* the writer of a COLUMN (def. 4).

co·ma ['koumə] *n* a long unconsciousness caused by disease, injury, etc. ⟨Greek *kōma*⟩ **co·ma·tose** ['koumə,tous] *or* ['kɒmə,tous] *adj* **1** in a coma. **2** sound asleep. **3** completely unresponsive or unaware of surroundings.

comb [koum] *n* **1** a strip of metal, plastic, etc. with teeth, used to arrange the hair. **2** anything shaped or used like a comb. **3** the crest on the top of the head in some fowls. **4** the top of a wave rolling over or breaking. *v* **1** arrange with a comb. **2** search through: *to comb the city for a lost dog.* ⟨Old English⟩

com·bat [kəm'bæt] *v* **-bat·ted** *or* **-bat·ed**, **-bat·ting** *or* **-bat·ing** fight; fight against: *Doctors combat disease.* *n* ['kɒmbæt] **1** fighting between armed forces; battle. **2** any fight or struggle. ⟨Latin *com-* (intensive) + *battuere* beat⟩ **com·bat·ant** [kəm'bætənt] *or* ['kɒmbətənt] *n* a fighter, esp a soldier who takes part in the action. **com·bat·ant** *adj.* **combat fatigue** a state of mental exhaustion that sometimes occurs among soldiers in the front lines. **com·bat·ive** [kəm'bætɪv] *or* ['kɒmbətɪv] *adj* quick to get into a fight; fond of fighting. **com·bat·ive·ly** *adv.* **com·bat·ive·ness** *n.*

com·bine [kəm'baɪn] *v* **1** put or go together; mix; unite: *to combine eggs and milk. The decor combined boldness with taste.* **2** *Chemistry* unite into a compound. **3** cut and thresh (grain) with a combine. *n* ['kɒmbaɪn] **1** a machine that cuts and threshes grain in one operation. **2** a group of people joined for commercial or political advantage: *The companies formed a combine to keep prices up.* **com·bin·a·ble** *adj.* **com·bined** *adj.* ⟨Latin *com-* together + *bini* two by two⟩ **com·bi·na·tion** [,kɒmbə'neɪʃən] *n* **1** the act or fact of combining. **2** a mix; union: *The drink is a combination of juice and pop.* **3** a series of numbers or letters used to open a COMBINATION LOCK. **4** a one-piece, full-body undergarment. **5** *Mathematics* the arrangement of individual members of a set into groups of a given size, without regard to order. Six combinations of *a*, *b*, and *c*, taken two at a time, are possible: *ab*, *ac*, *ba*, *bc*, *ca*, and *cb*. **com·bi·na·tion·al** *adj*. **combination lock** a lock opened only by a preselected sequence of numbers or letters. **combination square** a carpenter's measuring instrument which is a combination of a TRY SQUARE and a SPIRIT LEVEL. **combining form** a form of a word used for combining with other word elements, such as *socio-* in *socioeconomic*. **com·bo** *n* **1** a combination, esp of items on a menu. **2** *Informal* a small jazz band.

com·bus·tion [kəm'bʌstʃən] *n* **1** the act or process of burning: *the combustion of gases.* **2** oxidation, either rapid and accompanied by high temperature and light, or slow. The cells of the body transform food into energy by combustion. **com·bust** *v.* **com·bust·ive** *adj.* ⟨Latin *combustio,* from *comburere; co-urere* burn together and *amburere* burn on both sides⟩ **com·bus·ti·ble** *adj* **1** easily burned: *Gasoline is highly combustible.* **2** easily excited; fiery. *n* a combustible substance. **com·bus·ti·bil·i·ty** *n.*

come [kʌm] *v* **came, come, com·ing 1** move toward the speaker: *Come this way.* **2** arrive; reach a place: *I came home yesterday.* **3** appear: *Light comes and goes.* **4** progress (often with *along*): *How is your project coming?* **5** hold or attain a certain position or rank in a series: *She came second in the high jump.* **6** originate: *Milk comes from cows.* **7** become: *His dream came true. My shoelace came undone.* **8** be the result: *That's what comes of meddling.* **9** occur to the mind: *The solution has just come to me.* **10** be available: *This dress comes in white and yellow.* **11** add up (*to*): *The bill comes to $100.* **12** *Informal* reach sexual orgasm. *interj* an exclamation of impatience or disbelief: *Oh, come now!* ⟨Old English *cuman*⟩ **as good** (or **strong, rich,** etc.) **as they come** one of the best (strongest, richest, etc.). **come about** take place; happen: *How did that come about?* **come across a** meet or find by chance. **b** be communicated effectively: *The actor's portrayal of terror didn't come across.* **c** *Informal* (with *as*) give the impression of being: *He comes across as a tough guy.* **d** meet a demand or need: *She came across with a $100 donation.* **come again** *Informal* (with rising intonation) repeat what you have just said. **come along a** arrive by chance. **b** accompany one: *I'm going out; want to come along?* **c** make progress. **come around a** agree or join in at last: *Stop coaxing her; she'll come around.* **b** return to consciousness. **come at** rush or lunge at. **come back a** retort. **b** return to prominence. **come·back** *n.* **come between** cause unfriendly feeling between: *The friends vowed not to let anything come between them.* **come by a** acquire: *How did you come by that black eye?* **b** come to visit. **come down a** lose position, money, rank, etc.: *He's certainly come down in the last year.* **come·down** *n.* **b** be passed down: *Many fables have come down through the ages.* **c** *Informal* get sick (*with*): *I came down with the flu.* **come down on** *Informal* scold. **come forward** volunteer. **come from a** be descended from: *She comes from a large family.* **b** be a native or (former) resident of: *They come from Regina.* **come in a** enter: *Please come in.* **b** begin to be used: *Steamboats came in soon after the steam engine was invented.* **c** win a certain place in a competition: *She came in third.* **come in for** *Informal* get: *He came in for a lot of criticism on his handling of the deal.* **come into** acquire by inheritance or luck. **come off a** happen: *When is the final game going to come off?* **b** become detached: *The label came off.* **c** *Informal* succeed: *Her plan never came off.* **come off it!** *Slang* You can't be serious! **come on a** *Informal* approach people in a given way: *He comes on too strong.* **b** progress: *Our garden is coming on fine.* **c** approach; begin: *Winter is coming on. I feel a sneeze coming on.* **d** meet or find by chance. *I came on a strange sight while walking by the river.* **e** appear on stage or screen, or be heard on radio: *My favourite show comes on at 4.* **f** *Informal* (with *to*) make sexual overtures: *Stop coming on to me, I'm old enough to be your father.* **come on!** *Informal* **a** hurry: *Come on! We're late!* **b** an expression of impatience or disbelief: *Oh, come on! It's only a little thing. Two hundred dollars for that watch? Come on!* **c** please! **come out a** be made public: *The details of the scandal never came out.* **b** be offered to the public: *A new model came out last year.* **c** end up: *How did your pictures come out?* **d** state one's opinion publicly: *She came out strongly in favour of the expressway.* **e** reveal the truth about oneself, esp one's homosexual orientation. **come out for** support; endorse. **come out with a** *Informal* say openly: *That child comes out with the strangest questions.* **b** offer to the public: *The publisher has come out with a new edition.* **come over a** happen to and strongly affect: *A strange feeling came over me.* **b** *Informal* visit: *When are you coming over?* **come through a** endure (hardship) successfully: *He's come through a lot.* **b** *Slang* do what is promised or required. **c** be released by an administration: *We can't leave till our visas come through.* **d** wear or show through. **come to** return to consciousness. **come up a** arise: *The issue is sure to come up in class.* **b** advance in status: *That actor has come up in the world.* **c** (often with *to*) approach or accost someone: *She came up to us with a big smile on her face.* **come upon** meet or find by chance. **come up with a** supply: *He couldn't come up with the money.* **b** invent; produce: *She comes up with some weird ideas.* **have coming to one** deserve. **see coming** anticipate.

come·back *n* **1** a return to prominence. **2** a clever retort. **come·down** *n* a loss of position, rank, money, etc. **come–hither** *adj Informal* enticing; flirtatious: *a come-hither look.* **come–on** *n Informal* **1** something offered to attract; gimmick: *The offer of a free sample is just a come-on.* **2** something said or done as a sexual overture. **comer** *n Informal* one who shows promise. **come·up·pance** *n Informal* whatever penalty one deserves. **com·ing** *n* an approach or arrival. *adj* **1** now approaching; next: *this coming spring.* **2** *Informal* on the way to success, importance, or fame.

com·e·dy ['kɒmədi] *n* **1** an amusing play or show with a happy ending. **2** the branch of drama concerned with such plays. **3** the funny element of literature, or of life in general; humour: *His impressions of the boss injected a bit of comedy into the meeting.* **4** any literary work with comic themes or devices. **co·me·dic** [kə'midɪk] *adj.* ⟨Greek *kōmōidia kōmos* merrymaking + *oide* song⟩ **co·me·di·an** [kə'midiən] *n* **1** an entertainer who tells jokes and funny stories. **2** anyone who amuses others with funny talk and actions. **3** an actor specializing in comic roles. **co·me·di·enne** [kə,midi'ɛn] *n* a female comedian. **comedy of manners** a play or story ridiculing high-society behaviour. **com·ic** ['kɒmɪk] *adj* **1** of comedy: *a comic actor.* **2** amusing. *n* **1** comedian. **2** *Informal* COMIC BOOK or COMIC STRIP. **3** comics *pl* the page or section of a newspaper containing COMIC STRIPS. **4** the amusing or funny side of literature, life, etc. **com·i·cal** *adj* **1** funny. **2** *Informal* strange; odd. **com·i·cal·ly** *adv.* **com·i·cal·ness** *n.* **comic book** a magazine containing stories told in comic strips. **comic relief** any episode introduced in a serious work to relieve tension. **comic strip** a series of drawings that tell a joke or story.

come·ly ['kʌmli] *adj* **1** pretty: *She has a comely face.* **2** fitting; proper. **come·li·ness** *n.* ⟨Old English *cȳmlic*⟩

co·mes·ti·ble [kə'mɛstəbəl] *n* something to eat. *adj* eatable. ⟨Latin *comesus,* pp of *comedere; com-* (intensive) + *edere* eat⟩

com·et ['kɒmɪt] *n Astronomy* a starlike object that travels in an oval orbit around the sun, consisting of a nucleus of frozen gases, ice, and dust surrounded by a hazy cloud and often having a long, shining tail. ⟨Greek *komētēs* wearing long hair; *komē* hair⟩

com·fort ['kʌmfərt] *v* **1** ease the sorrow or disappointment of (someone): *to comfort a crying child.* **2** give ease to: *This will comfort your sore back.*
n **1** anything that makes trouble or sorrow easier to bear. **2** freedom from pain and hardship; ease; a feeling of being well and contented. **com·fort·ing** *adj.* **com·fort·less** *adj.* ⟨Latin *confortare; com-* together + *fortis* strong⟩
com·fort·a·ble *adj* **1** causing or experiencing no pain, hardship, or awkwardness: *a very comfortable bed, a comfortable life. They sat together in comfortable silence.* **2** *Informal* enough for one's needs: *a comfortable income.* **com·fort·a·ble·ness** *n.* **com·fort·a·bly** *adv.* **com·fort·er** *n* **1** one that comforts. **2** a padded or quilted covering for a bed. **comfort station** a public washroom, esp in a park or

campground, or on a highway. **com·fy** *adj Informal* comfortable: *I prefer this chair, because it is soft and comfy.*

Comfort = lessen sorrow by giving the person hope, sympathy, etc.: *They comforted the mother of the burned child.* **Console** = make trouble easier to bear by offering something to compensate or distract: *The police consoled the lost child with treats till his father arrived.*

com·ic See COMEDY.

com·i·ty ['kɒməti] *n* courtesy; civility. ⟨Latin *comitas; comis* friendly⟩
comity of nations respect shown by one nation for the laws and customs of another.

com·ma ['kɒmə] *n* a punctuation mark (,) used to show a slight separation of elements in a sentence. ⟨Greek *komma* piece cut off⟩
comma splice or **fault** *Grammar* the joining of two main clauses by a comma rather than a co-ordinate conjunction. *Example: He said he would come, however, he broke his promise.*

com·mand [kə'mænd] *v* **1** give an order to: *The captain commanded the troops to fire.* **2** have authority over: *The captain commands the ship.* **3** have ready for use: *She commands enough political knowledge to answer almost any question on current affairs.* **4** ask for and get: *to command respect, to command a high price.* **5** control or overlook by virtue of height: *The hilltop commands the surrounding plain.*
n **1** an order: *to obey a command.* **2** authority: *under my command.* **3** the troops, ships, etc. under an officer's authority: *The captain knew every soldier in her command.* **4 Command ✹** any of the main tactical formations of the Canadian Forces: *Maritime Command is the navy.* **5** skill in using: *a good command of the language.* **6** a royal invitation. **7** *Computers* an instruction to an operating system. ⟨Latin *com-* with + *mandare* commit, command⟩
at one's command available for one's use. **in command** in charge; in authority.
com·man·dant [,kɒmən'dænt] *or* [-'dɑnt] *n* the officer in command of a military base, camp, etc. **com·man·deer** [,kɒmən'dir] *v* **1** seize (private property) for military or public use. **2** take by force. **com·mand·er** [kə'mændər] *n* **1** a person who commands. **2** *Canadian Forces* in Maritime Command, the equivalent of a lieutenant-colonel. *Abbrev* **Cdr. com·mand·er–in–chief** *n, pl* **com·mand·ers–in–chief** a person who has complete command of the armed forces in a war, a garrison, etc. *Abbrev* **C. in C.** **com·mand·ing** *adj* **1** of an officer, in command. **2** authoritative: *to speak in a commanding voice.* **3** giving control: *a commanding position.* **com·mand·ing·ly** *adv.* **com·mand·ment** *n* **1** an order. **2** a biblical law, esp one of the ten that God gave Moses. **command module** the main section of a spacecraft, designed to carry the crew and equipment. **com·man·do** *n, pl* **-dos** or **-does** a soldier who makes brief, daring raids in enemy territory and does close-range fighting. **command performance** a stage

performance, etc. given before royalty by request or order. **command post** the centre of operations of a military commander.

comma splice See COMMA.

com·mem·o·rate [kə'mɛmə,reit] v preserve or honour the memory of: *a coin commemorating the end of World War II*. **com·mem·o·ra·tion** n. **com·mem·o·ra·tive** adj. ⟨Latin com- together + memorare remind⟩

com·mence [kə'mɛns] v begin; start. **com·menc·er** n. ⟨Old French comencer; Latin com- together + initiare begin. See INITIAL.⟩ **com·mence·ment** n **1** a start. **2** graduation day. **3** the ceremonies held on this day.

com·mend [kə'mɛnd] v **1** praise; speak well of. **2** hand over for safekeeping: *to commend a child to someone's care*. **com·men·da·tion** [,kɒmɛn'deiʃən] n. **com·mend·a·to·ry** adj. ⟨Latin com- (intensive) + mandare commit⟩ **com·mend·a·ble** adj good; praiseworthy. **com·mend·a·bly** adv.

com·men·su·ra·ble [kə'mɛnʃərəbəl] or [kə'mɛnsərəbəl] adj **1** corresponding in size, amount, or degree: *He was a big man, very tall and of commensurable mass*. **2** measurable by the same set of units: *Distance and mass are not commensurable*. **com·men·su·ra·bil·i·ty** n. **com·men·su·ra·bly** adv. **com·men·su·rate** [kə'mɛnʃərɪt] or [kə'mɛnsərɪt] adj **1** in the proper proportion: *The pay is commensurate with the work*. **2** of the same size, extent, etc. **3** commensurable. **com·men·su·rate·ly** adv. **com·men·su·rate·ness** n.

com·ment ['kɒmɛnt] n **1** a short statement of explanation or opinion on something. **2** any remark. **3** talk; gossip: *There was a lot of neighbourly comment on his comings and goings*. **com·ment** v. ⟨Latin commentus, pp of comminisci; com- with + minisci think⟩ **com·men·tar·y** n **1** ongoing explanation or interpretation: *Newspapers provide commentary on current events*. **2** a book, article, speech, collection of notes, etc. interpreting and explaining: *a two-volume Bible commentary*. **3** a live description of a sporting event, public ceremony, etc., esp over television or radio. **4** anything that explains or illustrates: *The way I dress is often a commentary on my mood*. **com·men·tate** v provide commentary. **com·men·ta·tor** n.

com·merce ['kɒmərs] n **1** business; trade; buying and selling. **2** interaction between people: *After such conduct, there can be no more commerce between us*. ⟨Latin commercium; com- with + merx, mercis wares⟩ **com·mer·cial** adj **1** to do with commerce: *commercial law*. **2** done for profit, usually at the expense of artistic merit or true spiritual meaning: *Her recent films are very commercial. Christmas has become so commercial now*. **3** supported by advertising: *commercial radio*. n an advertisement on radio or television. **com·mer·cial·ly** adv. **commercial art** the profession of producing illustrations for advertising, books, etc. **commercial artist**. **com·mer·cial·ism** n the methods and attitudes that drive commerce, esp a concern for profit: *Commercialism has almost ruined him as an artist*. **com·mer·cial·ist** n. **com·mer·cial·ize** v. **com·mer·cial·i·za·tion** n.

com·mie or **Com·mie** ['kɒmi] n Slang a communist, or anyone with leftist leanings.

com·mis·er·ate [kə'mɪzə,reit] v sympathize (with). **com·mis·er·a·tion** n. ⟨Latin com- with miser wretched⟩

com·mis·sar ['kɒmə,sɑr] n in the former Soviet Union: **1** the head of a government department. **2** an official representing the Communist Party in the army, etc. ⟨Russian kommisa; Latin commissarius from commissus, pp of committere entrust. See COMMIT.⟩ **com·mis·sar·i·at** [,kɒmə'sɛriət] n the part of an army that provides daily supplies for soldiers. **com·mis·sar·y** n **1** a store in a mining, lumber, or military camp. **2** a cafeteria in a film studio. **3** deputy; representative.

com·mis·sion [kə'mɪʃən] n **1** pay based on a percentage of the amount of business done: *She gets a commission of 15 percent on all the sales she makes*. **2** a request for a work of art to be made to order. **3** a special task for which authority is given. **4** a group of people given authority for a particular purpose; often, specifically, a government agency. **5** the rank of an officer in the armed forces. **6** a document giving certain powers and duties. **7** the act or fact of committing: *People are punished for the commission of crimes*. v **1** give a commission to. **2** pay for (artwork) to be done: *to commission a painting*. **3** equip and put into service. ⟨Latin commissio, from committere. See COMMIT.⟩ **in** (or **out of**) **commission** ready (or not ready) for service or use. **com·mis·sioned** adj having a commission: *a commissioned officer*. **com·mis·sion·er** n **1** a member of a COMMISSION (def. 4). **2** an official in charge of a department: *a commissioner of public health*. **3 Commissioner ✱ a** the highest ranking officer of the RCMP. **b** the chief executive officer of a Territory.

com·mit [kə'mɪt] v **-mit·ted, -mit·ting 1** hand over for safekeeping: *He committed himself to the doctor's care*. **2** involve or engage (oneself); pledge one's time, support, etc., often by making a definite statement: *The mayor did not commit herself on the issue of housing. This organization needs volunteers who will commit long-term*. **3** bind; oblige: *His promises have committed him to cutting taxes*. **4** do (a wrong thing): *to commit a crime*. **5** officially put (a mentally ill person) into institutional care. **6** deliver for disposal, etc.: *I committed my manuscript to the fire*. **com·mit·ta·ble** adj. ⟨Latin com- with + mittere send, put⟩ **commit to memory** learn by heart. **commit to paper** or **writing** write down. **com·mit·ment** n **1** a promise; pledge. **2** the thing to which one has committed oneself: *My school commitments take up much of my time*. **3** dedication: *Becoming a skilled musician takes commitment*. **com·mit·tal** n **1** an act of committing. **2** the act of burying a dead person, or the rites accompanying this. **com·mit·tee** [kə'mɪti] *n* a group of people appointed or elected to consider certain matters on behalf of a larger body and report back. **in committee** under consideration by a committee: *The bill is still in committee.* **committee of the whole** a committee made up of all the members present of a club, legislature, etc.

> **SYNONYMS**
>
> **Commit** = hand over to the care of, and suggests merely relinquishing control: *The court committed the financial affairs of the orphan to a guardian.* **Entrust**, as its root suggests, emphasizes trust in the recipient: *I entrusted my door key to my neighbour.* **Consign** is often used of a formal transfer of property (*He consigned his share of the bonds to his sister*) but it can also mean permanently handing over to an undesirable condition or fate: *consigned to the wrecker's ball.*

com·mode [kə'moud] *n* **1** chest of drawers. **2** washstand. **3** a special chair housing a chamber pot. **4** toilet. ⟨Latin *commodus* convenient; *com-* with + *modus* measure⟩ **com·mo·di·ous** [kə'moudiəs] *adj* roomy. **com·mo·di·ous·ly** *adv.* **com·mo·di·ous·ness** *n.*

com·mod·i·ty [kə'mɒdəti] *n* **1** anything that is bought and sold: *Groceries are commodities.* **2** a useful thing. ⟨Latin *commoditas*, fitness, adaptation; *commodus.* See COMMODE.⟩

com·mo·dore ['kɒmə,dɔr] *n* **1** *Canadian Forces* in Maritime Command, the equivalent of a brigadier-general. *Abbrev* **Cmdre.** **2** the chief officer of a merchant fleet, yacht club, etc. (earlier *commandore*; probably French *commandeur* commander⟩

com·mon ['kɒmən] *adj* **1** shared by all, or by all those in question: *common knowledge, the common good. Our friendship is based on common interests.* **2** recognized by all; familiar; ordinary; everyday: *common table salt, common courtesy. The common name for Equus caballus is horse.* **3** usual; typical: *Snow is common in cold countries.* **4** not part of the nobility: *the common people.* **5** low; coarse or vulgar. *n* **1 the Commons** the HOUSE OF COMMONS. **2** Also, **com·mons** *pl* land for the use of all the people of a town, village, etc. **com·mon·ly** *adv.* **com·mon·ness** *n* ⟨Latin *communis*⟩ **in common** equally with others; jointly. **com·mon·al·i·ty** *n* the fact of being shared: *a commonality of purpose.* **common cold** COLD (*n* 2). **common denominator 1** *Mathematics* a denominator that is a COMMON MULTIPLE of the denominators of a group of fractions. **2** a quality, interest, etc. shared by all in a group. **com·mon·er** *n* one of the common people; a person who is not a noble. **Common Era** the time since the birth of Christ. Also, **Christian Era.** The label C.E. or A.D. is used for dates in this era. **common fraction** *Mathematics* a fraction in which both numerator and denominator are whole numbers. **common gender** *Grammar* a classification consisting of nouns that may be replaced by either *he* or *she* (e.g., *friend, teacher*) or, sometimes, by *it*

(*baby, dog*). **common law** the body of law based on custom and usage, as distinguished from civil and canon law and law created by statute. **common–law marriage** a marriage not solemnized by any ceremony, but legally recognized for most purposes. **com·mon–law** *adj, adv.* **Common Market** the EUROPEAN ECONOMIC COMMUNITY, former name of the EUROPEAN UNION. **common multiple** *Mathematics* a number that can be divided by two or more others without a remainder. A common multiple of 3 and 6 is 12. **common noun** *Grammar* any noun that is not a PROPER NOUN. **com·mon·place** *n* **1** an ordinary or everyday thing: *Sixty years ago radio was a novelty; today it is a commonplace.* **2** an ordinary or obvious remark. *adj* not new or interesting: *We found the movie altogether commonplace.* **common(s)** room a room in a school, college, etc. where students or staff can socialize and relax. **common sense** ordinary good judgment. **com·mon–sense** *adj.* **com·mon·sen·si·cal** *adj.* **common stock** company stock without a definite dividend rate. Compare PREFERRED STOCK.

com·mon·wealth *n* **1 the Commonwealth** or **Commonwealth of Nations** an association of countries formerly under British rule, all of whose members, including the UK, have equal status. **2** the people of a nation. **3** any democratic state; republic. **Commonwealth of Independent States** an association made up of Armenia, Belarus, Kazakhstan, Kyrgyzstan, Moldova, Russia, Turkmenistan, Tajikistan, Ukraine, and Uzbekistan, formerly all part of the Soviet Union.

com·mo·tion [kə'mouʃən] *n* confusion; noise; violent movement. ⟨Latin *commotio* from *commovere; com-* with + *movere* move⟩

com·mune¹ [kə'mjun] *v* **1** have intimate conversation. **2** have thoughts in a spiritual relationship (*with*): *to commune with nature.* **3** receive Holy Communion. **com·mun·ion** *n.* ⟨Old French *communer; comun.* See COMMON.⟩ **com·mu·ni·ca·ble** [kə'mjunəkəbəl] *adj* that can be communicated or passed on to others: *communicable diseases. Ideas are communicable by words.* **com·mu·ni·cant** *n* **1** a person who receives Holy Communion. **2** a person who is in regular fellowship at a church. **3** a person who gives information. **com·mu·ni·cate** *v* **1** send and receive (messages). **2** of rooms or passages, be connected: *The den communicates with the master bedroom.* **com·mu·ni·ca·tor** *n.* **com·mu·ni·ca·tion** *n.* **communications satellite** an artificial satellite that receives radio and television signals from earth and transmits them back to other earthly points. **com·mu·ni·ca·tive** [kə'mjunɪkətɪv] *or* [-,keitɪv] *adj* open; willing to talk or give information. **com·mu·ni·ca·tive·ness** *n.* **Communion** *n* *Christianity* the commemoration of Christ's Last Supper, in which bread and wine embody symbolically or substantially the body and blood of Christ. **com·mu·ni·qué** [kə,mjunə'kei] *or* [kə'mjunə,kei] *n* an official bulletin or statement.

com·mune[2] ['kɒmjun] n 1 a community of people sharing property and responsibilities. 2 the smallest division for local government in France, Belgium, Switzerland, and Italy. ⟨French commune; Latin communis⟩ com·mu·nal [kə'mjunəl] adj 1 owned jointly by all. 2 of a community or commune. com·mu·nal·ly adv. com·mu·nal·ism n. com·mu·nism ['kɒmjə,nɪzəm] n the political and economic system in which the state controls all property. Compare SOCIALISM, CAPITALISM. com·mu·nist n, adj. com·mu·nis·tic adj. Communist Party a political party devoted to the establishment of communism, esp as derived from Marxism. com·mu·nize v. com·mu·ni·za·tion n.

com·mu·ni·ty [kə'mjunəti] n 1 a group of people living in the same area under the same local government: a farming community. 2 a neighbourhood. 3 a group of people sharing living quarters and activities: a community of monks. 4 any group of people, nations, etc. with a common bond: Edmonton's Italian community, the worldwide community of artists. 5 Ecology a group of animals and plants living in a region. 6 sharedness; the fact of being common: Community of interests helps people work together. ⟨Latin communitas; communis. See COMMON.⟩
community centre 1 a hall used for public meetings, etc. in a community. 2 ✱ an arena run by the community, with facilities for sports and public entertainment. community chest a fund of voluntary contributions supporting various charitable organizations. community college an institution for post-secondary and adult education, esp for training in particular occupations and skills.

com·mute [kə'mjut] v 1 regularly travel a considerable distance, to work, school, etc. and back. 2 change (a penalty) to an easier one: Her death sentence was commuted to life in prison. 3 Electricity reverse the direction of (a current) using a commutator.
n Informal a journey made by a commuter. com·mu·ta·tion n. com·mut·er n. ⟨Latin com- (intensive) + mutare change⟩
com·mu·tate v Electricity reverse the direction of (current). com·mu·ta·tive [kə'mjutətɪv] or ['kɒmjə,teitɪv] adj 1 to do with substitution or exchange. 2 Mathematics of or having to do with an operation in which the order of the elements does not affect the result. com·mu·ta·tor n 1 a device for doing this. 2 a revolving part in a dynamo or motor, carrying the current to or from the brushes.

com·pact[1] ['kɒmpækt] or [kəm'pækt] adj 1 firmly packed together: The leaves of the cabbage are folded into a compact head. 2 using few words: a compact writing style. 3 having the parts neatly arranged in a small space: a compact portable TV set.
n ['kɒmpækt] 1 the second smallest of the basic car sizes. Compare SUBCOMPACT and STANDARD. 2 a small case for carrying face powder or other make-up.
v [kəm'pækt] 1 pack firmly together.

2 condense. com·pact·ly adv. com·pact·ness n. ⟨Latin compactus pp of compingere; com- together + pangere fasten⟩
compact disc a disc on which data has been digitally encoded so as to be readable by a laser beam in a special player. com·pact·or [kəm'pæktər] or ['kɒmpæktər] n a device that crushes garbage.
com·pact[2] ['kɒmpækt] n an agreement or contract. ⟨Latin compactum; com- (intensive) + pacisci to contract⟩

com·pan·ion [kəm'pænjən] n 1 a person or animal who spends time with another or shares in what another is doing. 2 any thing that matches or goes with another in a set. 3 a paid live-in helper. 4 Companion a in certain orders of knighthood, a member of lowest rank. b ✱ a member of the highest rank of the Order of Canada. com·pan·ion·less adj. com·pan·ion·ship n. ⟨Latin companio; com- together + panis bread⟩
com·pan·ion·a·ble adj pleasantly sociable. com·pan·ion·a·bly adv. com·pan·ion·way n a stairway leading from one deck to another on a ship. com·pa·ny ['kʌmpəni] n 1 a group of people travelling or working together: a company of actors. 2 specifically, a commercial organization. 3 (in compounds) owned and supplied by such a company for work-related use by employees: a company car, company day care. 4 partners not named in the title of a firm: Ruja & Co., Printers. 5 people gathered for social purposes: He's quite shy in company. 6 the fact of being together with someone: I enjoy her company. 7 Informal guests: Company is coming. keep company carry on courtship. keep someone company stay with for companionship. part company separate. company town a town built by a company for its workers, to whom it provides services, etc., often including a company store stocked and run by the company.

com·pare [kəm'pɛr] v 1 examine (two or more things) to see similarities and differences (often with with). 2 think, speak, or write of as similar: to compare life to a river. com·par·i·son n. ⟨Latin comparare; com- with + par equal⟩
in comparison to compared to: Even a large lake is small in comparison to an ocean. not to be compared with a very different from. b not nearly as good as.
com·pa·ra·ble ['kɒmpərəbəl], [kəm'pɛrəbəl], or [kəm'pærəbəl] adj 1 able to be compared. 2 similar: of comparable quality and price. com·pa·ra·bly adv. com·par·a·tive [kəm'pɛrətɪv] or [kəm'pærətɪv] adj 1 involving comparison: the comparative method of study. 2 measured by comparison with something else; relative: Screens give us comparative freedom from flies. 3 Grammar to do with the second degree of comparison of an adjective or adverb. Worse is the comparative form of bad. n Grammar a comparative form. com·par·a·tive·ly adv. com·par·i·son n 1 the act or process of comparing. 2 likeness; similarity: There is no comparison between these two cameras; one is excellent and one is a piece of junk. 3 Grammar

a change in an adjective or adverb to show difference of degree. The three degrees of comparison are positive, comparative, and superlative. *Examples: good, better, best; useful, more useful, most useful.* **com·par·i·son–shop** *v* compare the price and quality of the same item in different stores.

com·part·ment [kəm'pɑrtmənt] *n* any of two or more separate divisions of anything. ⟨Italian *compartimento* < *compartire* divide⟩ **com·part·men·tal·ize** [ˌkɒmpɑrt'mɛntəˌlaɪz] *or* [kəmˌpɑrt'mɛntəˌlaɪz] *v* divide into separate compartments. **com·part·men·tal·i·za·tion** *n*.

com·pass ['kʌmpəs] *n* **1** an instrument for showing direction, consisting of a magnetized pivoting needle which points to the North Magnetic Pole. **2** an instrument for drawing circles. **3** perimeter; boundary: *Stay within the compass of the park.* **4** range; scope: *Such questions are outside the compass of this study.* *v* **1** make a circuit of: *The astronaut compassed the earth many times.* **2** encircle; surround: *a farmhouse compassed by trees.* ⟨Latin *compassare* measure, pace off; *com-* with + *passus* step⟩

com·pas·sion [kəm'pæʃən] *n* kindness based on sympathy with those in need or pain. **com·pas·sion·ate** *adj.* **com·pas·sion·ate·ly** *adv.* ⟨Latin *compassio,* from *compati; com-* with + *pati* suffer⟩

com·pat·i·ble [kəm'pætəbəl] *adj* **1** able to exist together in harmony: *My two sisters don't seem to be compatible.* **2** *Computers* of pieces of software or hardware, able to be used together. **com·pat·i·bly** *adv.* **com·pat·i·bil·i·ty** *n.* ⟨Latin *compatibilis; compati.* See COMPASSION.⟩

com·pa·tri·ot [kəm'peɪtriət] *or* [kəm'pætriət] *n* a person from or in the same country as oneself. ⟨Latin *com-* with + *patriota;* Greek *patria* clan, from *patēr* father⟩

com·pel [kəm'pɛl] *v* **-pelled, -pel·ling** force or oblige: *The cold finally compelled him to go inside. Her tone of voice compelled obedience.* ⟨Latin *com-* (intensive) + *pellere* drive⟩ **com·pel·ling** *adj* so fascinating, attractive, etc. as to force interest or appreciation: *compelling stories.* **com·pel·ling·ly** *adv.* **com·pul·sion** [kəm'pʌlʃən] *n* **1** the act of compelling or fact of being compelled: *She claimed that she had signed the confession under compulsion.* **2** *Psychology* an irresistible, irrational desire to act in a certain way. A compulsion may be a form of mental illness. **com·pul·sive** *adj.* **com·pul·sive·ly** *adv.* **com·pul·so·ry** *adj* required; obligatory: *Some form of schooling is compulsory for children.* **com·pul·so·ri·ly** *adv.*

▌CONFUSABLES

Compel = force a particular response in another: *It is impossible to compel people to love their neighbours.* **Impel** = drive to act by strong inner desire or need: *Impelled by hunger, she turned to begging.*

com·pen·di·um [kəm'pɛndiəm] *n, pl* **-di·ums** *or* **-di·a** [-diə] a collection or summary of much information in a little space. **com·pen·di·ous** *adj.* **com·pen·di·ous·ly** *adv.*

⟨Latin *compendium* a saving, shortening; *com-* together + *pendere* weigh⟩

com·pen·sate ['kɒmpən,seɪt] *v* **1** reimburse or pay (for): *Here is a cheque to compensate your loss.* **2** balance by equal weight, power, etc. (usually with *for*): *His good positional play compensates for his lack of speed.* **3** *Mechanics* counterbalance. **4** make amends; atone. **5** *Psychology* attempt to make up for a defect by increasing achievement in some other field. **6** *Biology* reduce the effect of an organic defect by increased activity of another organ or part. **com·pen·sa·tion** *n.* **com·pen·sa·to·ry** [kəm'pɛnsə,tɔri] *adj.* ⟨Latin *com-* with + *pensare* weigh, from *pendere*⟩

com·pete [kəm'pit] *v* **1** try hard to obtain something wanted by others also (with *for*). **2** take part (*in* a contest). **com·pet·i·tor** [kəm'pɛtətər] *n.* ⟨Latin *com-* together + *petere* seek⟩ **com·pe·ti·tion** [ˌkɒmpə'tɪʃən] *n* **1** effort to obtain something wanted by others also. **2** a contest. **3** significant opposition: *They're no competition for our team.* **4** a rival or rivals, esp in business: *We must outsell the competition.* **in competition with** competing against: *She was in competition with five other dancers.* **com·pet·i·tive** [kəm'pɛtətɪv] *adj* **1** to do with or involving competition: *competitive entrance exams for a school.* **2** characterized by a strong drive to win or be the best. **com·pet·i·tive·ly** *adv.* **com·pet·i·tive·ness** *n.*

com·pe·tent ['kɒmpətənt] *adj* **1** adequate for the job; able: *a competent cook.* **2** *Law* legally qualified: *a witness competent to testify.* **com·pe·tent·ly** *adv.* ⟨Latin *competens,* ppr of *competere.* See COMPETE.⟩ **com·pe·tence** or **competency** *n* **1** the fact or state of being competent. **2** a particular skill: *one of her many competences.* **3** enough money to provide a comfortable living.

com·pile [kəm'paɪl] *v* **1** collect in one list, set, or account. **2** make (a book, report, etc.) out of various items or materials. **3** *Computers* translate into MACHINE LANGUAGE for a computer. **com·pi·la·tion** [ˌkɒmpə'leɪʃən] *n.* **com·pi·ler** *n.* ⟨Latin *com-* together + *pilare* press⟩

com·pla·cent [kəm'pleɪsənt] *adj* **1** pleased with oneself: *a complacent smile.* **2** too pleased with oneself to bother trying to improve or watch for pitfalls. **com·pla·cen·cy** or **com·pla·cence** *n.* **com·pla·cent·ly** *adv.* ⟨Latin *complacens,* ppr of *complacere; com-* with + *placere* please⟩

com·plain [kəm'pleɪn] *v* **1** talk about one's pains, troubles, or about anything one does not like. **2** make a formal accusation: *She complained to the police about her neighbour's dog.* **com·plain·er** *n.* **com·plain·ing·ly** *adv.* ⟨Old French *complaindre;* Latin *com-* (intensive) + *plangere* lament⟩ **com·plain·ant** *n* a person who complains, esp one who sues another. **com·plaint** *n* **1** the act of complaining or the thing complained about. **2** an illness: *Indigestion is a common complaint.*

com·ple·ment [ˈkɒmpləmənt] *n* **1** anything that completes, balances, or matches some other thing. **2** the necessary quantity or number: *The ship now had its full complement of sailors.* **3** *Grammar* a word or group of words used after a verb to complete the predicate. **4** *Mathematics* either of a pair of COMPLEMENTARY ANGLES. **5** *Music* either of two intervals which together make up an octave. **6** a substance in normal blood serum and protoplasm which combines with antibodies to destroy bacteria and other foreign bodies. **com·ple·ment** [ˈkɒmpləˌmɛnt] *v.* ⟨Latin *complementum*, from *complere*. See COMPLETE.⟩
com·ple·men·ta·ry [ˌkɒmpləˈmɛntəri] *adj* forming a complement; complementing each other. **com·ple·men·ta·ri·ty** *n.* **complementary angles** two angles which together total 90°. **complementary colours 1** any two colours of the spectrum which together produce white light, such as red and blue-green. **2** any two pigments which produce black, such as red and green.

SYNONYMS

To **complement** is to complete by supplying something necessary to make a whole: *The information from the Internet complemented what he had gleaned from print sources.*
To **supplement** is to add something extra to make better, bigger, richer, etc.: *Extra-curricular activities supplement one's education.*

---

com·plete [kəmˈplit] *adj* **1** with all its parts: *a complete set of dishes.* **2** total; utter: *complete surprise.* **3** finished; done: *My work is complete.* **com·plete·ly** *adv.* **com·plete·ness** *n.* ⟨Latin *completus*, pp of *complere; com-* + *plere* fill⟩
com·plete *v* **1** make complete: *to complete a set.* **2** do; finish: *to complete a task.* **com·ple·tion** *n.*
com·plex [ˈkɒmplɛks] *or* [kɒmˈplɛks] *adj* **1** not simple; involved: *pages of long, complex instructions.* **2** made up of a number of parts. **3** formed by the union of simpler substances: *complex carbohydrate.*
n [ˈkɒmplɛks] **1** a whole made up of a set of interconnected things: *the complex of ideas that make up a theory.* **2** a group of related units such as buildings or roads. **3** *Psychology* a system of related beliefs, feelings, memories, etc., usually subconscious, which strongly affect a person's behaviour in certain ways. **4** *Informal* an exaggerated preoccupation: *a complex about fresh air.* **com·plex·i·ty** *n.* ⟨Latin *complexus*, from *com-* together + *plectere* twine⟩
complex number the sum of a real number and an imaginary one. **complex sentence** *Grammar* a sentence with a main clause and one or more subordinate clauses. Compare COMPOUND SENTENCE.
com·plex·ion [kəmˈplɛkʃən] *n* **1** the general appearance of the skin, particularly of the face. **2** the general appearance or character of anything. ⟨Latin *complexio* constitution, combination, from *complexus*. See COMPLEX.⟩
com·pli·cate [ˈkɒmpləˌkeit] *v* **1** make hard to understand, sort out, handle, etc. by adding factors: *Don't complicate the issue. A breech position complicates delivery of a baby.* **2** make

worse: *a headache complicated by eye trouble.* **com·pli·cat·ed** *adj.* **com·pli·ca·tion** *n.* ⟨Latin *com-* together + *plicare* fold⟩
com·plic·i·ty [kəmˈplɪsəti] *n* partnership in wrongdoing: *Knowingly receiving stolen goods is complicity in theft.* ⟨Latin *complicis* interwoven from *complicare*. See COMPLICATE.⟩
com·pli·ment [ˈkɒmpləmənt] *n* **1** something good said about a person. **2 compliments** *pl* greetings: *Give her my compliments when you visit.* **3** an act of courtesy or recognition: *The town paid the artist the compliment of hosting her exhibit.* **com·pli·ment** [ˈkɒmpləˌmɛnt] *v.* ⟨Spanish *cumplimiento* fulfilment of courtesy, from *cumplir* fulfil; Latin *complere* fill up⟩
with compliments free of charge. **(with the) compliments of** (as) a gift from: *The shampoo and soap are compliments of the hotel. Take this copy with my compliments.*
com·pli·men·ta·ry [ˌkɒmpləˈmɛntəri] *adj* **1** giving or implying a compliment. **2** given free: *a complimentary ticket.*

CONFUSABLES

To **compliment** is to say something in praise: *She complimented him on his skill.*
To **complement** is to complete or balance: *Her inventiveness complements his industry.*

---

com·ply [kəmˈplaɪ] *v* act in agreement (with): *to comply with a doctor's orders.* ⟨Italian *complire*. See COMPLIMENT.⟩
com·pli·ance [kəmˈplaɪəns] *n* **1** the act of complying. **2** a tendency to yield to others. **in compliance with** in accordance with. **com·pli·ant** *adj.* **com·pli·ant·ly** *adv.*
com·po·nent [kəmˈpoʊnənt] *n* **1** a unit or element forming part of a whole or system. **2** *Physics* one of a set of vectors whose sum is a given vector.
adj **1** forming a part: *Blade and handle are the component parts of a knife.* **2** made up of separate units: *a component stereo system.* ⟨Latin *com-* together + *ponere* put⟩
com·port [kəmˈpɔrt] *v Formal, poetic* **1** (reflexively) behave: *She comported herself with dignity.* **2** agree or suit (with): *His silliness at the meeting did not comport with what we had heard of him.* **com·port·ment** *n.* ⟨Latin *com-* together + *portare* carry⟩
com·pose [kəmˈpoʊz] *v* **1** (usually passive) form the substance of: *The ocean is composed of salt water.* **2** create, esp in music or words: *to compose a symphony, to compose a poem.* **3** make (oneself, one's mind, etc.) calm and quiet. **4** arrange the elements of (a photo, piece of art) in an effective way: *He composes his photographs carefully.* **5** settle: *to compose differences.* **com·pos·er** *n.* ⟨Old French *composer; com-* together + *poser*. See POSE.⟩
com·posed *adj* calm and self-controlled. **com·pos·ed·ly** [-ˈpoʊzɪdli] *adv.* **com·po·sure** *n.* **com·pos·ite** [ˈkɒmpəzɪt] *or* [kəmˈpɒzɪt] *adj* **1** made up of various parts. **2** designating a very large family of plants with flower heads made up of many tiny flowers bunched together. **com·pos·ite** *n.* **com·pos·ite·ly** *adv.* **composite number** [ˈkɒmpəzɪt] *Mathematics*

a number that can be exactly divided by some number other than itself or 1. Compare PRIME NUMBER. **composite school ✱** a secondary school that offers academic, commercial, and industrial programs. **com·po·si·tion** *n* **1** the make-up of anything: *the composition of soil.* **2** a piece of writing or music. **3** the way in which parts of a picture are arranged. **4** mixture. **com·po·si·tion·al** *adj.* **com·pos men·tis** ['kɒmpoʊs 'mɛntɪs] *Latin* of sound mind; sane. The opposite is **non compos mentis**. **com·post** ['kɒmpoʊst] *n* a mixture of decayed plant matter used to fertilize soil. *v* **1** convert into compost. **2** fertilize with compost.

com·pound[1] ['kɒmpaʊnd] *n* **1** a word made by joining together two or more separate words. **2** *Chemistry* a substance formed by the combination of two or more elements. Compare MIXTURE (def. 2). **3** a combination: *Her success in business was due to a compound of common sense and long experience.*
adj having more than one distinct part: *a compound leaf.*
v [kɒm'paʊnd] **1** add a new element to: *The weekend visitors compounded the space problem at our house.* **2** combine. **3** calculate (interest) on a sum of money: *The interest is compounded semi-annually.* **4** *Law* accept payment not to prosecute (an offence). **com·pound·a·ble** *adj.* ⟨Latin *com-* together + *ponere* put⟩
compound eye *Biology* an eye made up of many similar sections, each of which forms a part of the image. **compound flower** *Botany* a flower head made up of many very tiny flowers. **compound fracture** a fracture in which the broken bone sticks out through the flesh. Compare SIMPLE FRACTURE. **compound interest** interest paid on both the original sum and on accumulated unpaid interest. Compare SIMPLE INTEREST. **compound leaf** a leaf made up of two or more leaflets on a stalk. **compound microscope** a microscope with multiple lenses. **compound sentence** *Grammar* a sentence made up of two independent clauses. Compare COMPLEX SENTENCE.

com·pound[2] ['kɒmpaʊnd] *n* an enclosed yard with buildings in it. ⟨probably Malay *kampong*⟩

com·pre·hend [ˌkɒmprɪ'hɛnd] *v* **1** fully understand. **2** contain; include in one thing. **com·pre·hend·ing·ly** *adv.* **com·pre·hen·sion** *n.* ⟨Latin *com-* (intensive) + *prehendere* seize⟩
com·pre·hen·si·ble *adj* understandable. **com·pre·hen·si·bly** *adv.* **com·pre·hen·si·bil·i·ty** *n.* **com·pre·hen·sive** *adj* **1** covering a great deal. **2** of insurance, giving protection against a variety of risks. **com·pre·hen·sive·ly** *adv.* **com·pre·hen·sive·ness** *n.*

SYNONYMS
Comprehend suggests taking in an idea and making sense of it: *I comprehend your argument.* **Apprehend** suggests recognizing or receiving information, whether or not one fully understands it: *He dimly apprehended what the foreign sailors were talking about.*

com·press [kəm'prɛs] *v* **1** reduce the size or volume of by pressure, or as if by pressure: *compressed gas. He compressed his speech into a few lines.* **2** squeeze together: *We could see he was angry by the way he compressed his lips.* **3** flatten; cause to appear flat.
n ['kɒmprɛs] a cloth pad applied to the body to stop bleeding, alter temperature, etc. **com·press·i·ble** *adj.* **com·press·i·bil·i·ty** *n.* ⟨Latin *compressare,* frequentative of *comprimere; com-* together + *premere* press⟩
compressed air air put under extra pressure so that it exerts great force when released. **com·pres·sion** *n* **1** the process or result of compressing. **2** specifically, reduction in the volume of a gas in an engine by application of pressure: *A car with worn piston rings will have poor compression.* **com·pres·sor** *n* **1** one that compresses, esp a machine for compressing air. **2** *Anatomy* a muscle that compresses a part of the body.

com·prise [kəm'praɪz] *v* consist of: *Atlantic Canada comprises four provinces.* ⟨Old French *compris,* pp of *comprendre.* See COMPREHEND.⟩

CONFUSABLES
Comprise is often confused with **compose**. A whole *comprises* its parts or *is composed of* its parts. Avoid the construction 'is comprised of'.

com·pro·mise ['kɒmprəˌmaɪz] *v* **1** settle a dispute by agreeing that each side will give up certain demands. **2** sacrifice or risk unwisely: *to compromise one's integrity, to compromise the safety of employees.*
n **1** the act or process of compromising: *Compromise is impossible.* **2** the agreement so reached: *under the terms of the compromise.* **3** anything partway between two opposites. ⟨Latin *compromissus,* pp of *compromittere; com-* together + *promittere* promise⟩

comp·trol·ler [kən'troʊlər] See CONTROLLER.
com·pul·sion, com·pul·sive, com·pul·so·ry See COMPEL.

com·punc·tion [kəm'pʌŋkʃən] *n* the pricking of conscience; remorse or regret: *She had no compunctions about declining the offer.* **com·punc·tious** *adj.* ⟨Latin *compunctio* from *compungere; com-* (intensive) + *pungere* prick⟩

com·pute [kəm'pjut] *v* **1** calculate. **2** use a computer. **com·put·a·ble** *adj.* ⟨Latin *com-* up + *putare* reckon. Compare COUNT[1].⟩
com·pu·ta·tion *n* calculation. **com·put·er** *n* an electronic machine that can store data and perform operations at high speed. See also ANALOG COMPUTER, DIGITAL COMPUTER. **computer–aided** or **computer–assisted design** *Computers* the use of computers to assist in designing buildings, machines, etc. *Abbrev* **CAD. com·put·er·ese** [kəmˌpjutə'riz] *n* the jargon of computer programming and information technology. **computer graphics** the use of a computer to create images. **com·put·er·ize** *v* produce or do by means of a computer: *computerized bookkeeping.* **com·put·er·i·za·tion** *n.* **computerized axial tomography** a method of imaging the soft tissues of the body by using a computer to

combine photographs of separate planes (tomograms), all of them having a common axis. Usually abbreviated to **CAT**. **computer literacy** familiarity with computers. **computer literate**. **computer science** the science dealing with the design, construction and maintenance of computer hardware and software. **computer terminal** a keyboard and screen connected to a computer.

com·rade ['kɒmræd] *or* ['kɒmrəd] *n* **1** friend; companion or partner. **2** a fellow member of a political party (esp Communist) or other organization engaged in a cause. **com·rade·ly** *adj*. **com·rade·ship** *n*. ⟨Spanish *camarada* room-mate; Latin *camera* room⟩

con¹ [kɒn] *v* **conned, con·ning** *Slang* trick; swindle: *He was conned into buying a swamp*. **con** *n*. ⟨short for CONFIDENCE GAME⟩
con artist or **con man** *Slang* a skilled swindler.

con² [kɒn] *adv* against: *The two debating teams argued the question pro and con*.
n a reason against: *to argue the pros and cons of a question*. ⟨short for Latin *contra* against⟩

con³ [kɒn] *n Slang* a convict.

con⁴ [kɒn] *v* **conned, con·ning** direct the steering of: *to con a ship between rocks*.
n **1** the act or process of conning. **2** the post from which it is done. ⟨variant of *cond;* Old French *conduire*, Latin *conducere* guide, lead⟩
con·ning tower 1 a small tower on a submarine, used as an entrance and a place for observation. **2** on a warship, an armoured control station on the deck. **3** any similar structure for observation or supervision.

con·cat·e·nate [kən'kætə,neit] *v* link or be linked together. **con·cat·e·na·tion** *n*. ⟨Latin *com-* together + *catena* chain⟩

con·cave [kɒn'keiv] *or* ['kɒnkeiv] *adj* hollow and curved like the inside of a sphere. **con·cave·ly** *adv*. **con·cav·i·ty** [kɒn'kævəti] *n*. ⟨Latin *com-* (intensive) + *cavus* hollow⟩

con·ceal [kən'sil] *v* hide, mask, or keep secret. **con·ceal·er** *n*. **con·ceal·ment** *n*. ⟨Latin *com-* (intensive) + *celare* hide⟩

con·cede [kən'sid] *v* **1** admit: *We conceded that she was right*. **2** give (what is asked or claimed): *He conceded us the right to walk through his land*. **3** acknowledge defeat (in). ⟨Latin *com-* together + *cedere* yield⟩

con·ceit [kən'sit] *n* **1** too high an opinion of oneself. **2** a fanciful notion or complicated metaphor. **con·ceit·ed** *adj*. **con·ceit·ed·ly** *adv*. ⟨*conceive*, on analogy with *deceit*⟩

con·ceive [kən'siv] *v* **1** think up; devise: *to conceive a plan*. **2** develop (an impression, feeling, etc.): *He conceived a strong dislike for her*. **3** imagine (often used with *of*): *It's hard to conceive of such things*. **4** become pregnant. **5** put in words: *The warning was conceived in plain language*. **con·ceiv·er** *n*. **con·cep·tion** *n*. ⟨Old French *conceveir*, Latin *concipere* take in; *com-* (intensive) + *capere* take⟩
con·ceiv·a·ble *adj* imaginable; plausible. **con·ceiv·a·ble·ness** *n*. **con·ceiv·a·bly** *adv*.

con·cen·trate ['kɒnsən,treit] *v* **1** pay close attention; think hard. **2** focus: *to concentrate our efforts. A convex lens concentrates light rays.* **3** increase the proportion of a substance in (a solution or mixture): *We concentrated the solution by boiling off some of the water.*
n something that has been concentrated: *lemon juice concentrate*. **con·cen·trat·ed** *adj*. **con·cen·tra·tion** *n*. ⟨*con-* together + Latin *centrum* centre⟩
concentration camp a prison camp for political enemies.

con·cen·tric [kən'sɛntrɪk] *adj* having the same centre: *concentric circles*. Compare ECCENTRIC (def. 2). **con·cen·tri·cal·ly** *adv*. **con·cen·tri·ci·ty** [,kɒnsɛn'trɪsəti] *n*.

con·cept ['kɒnsɛpt] *n* **1** a general notion or idea; abstract category: *the concept of equality*. **2** a plan or design. **con·cep·tu·al** [kən'sɛptʃuəl] *adj*. **con·cep·tu·al·ly** *adv*. ⟨Latin *conceptus*, pp of *concipere*. See CONCEIVE.⟩
con·cep·tion *n* **1** a way of thinking about something: *Her conception of the problem is different from mine*. **2** the act of conceiving. **con·cep·tu·al·ize** [kən'sɛptʃuə,laɪz] *v* form an idea of. **con·cep·tu·al·i·za·tion** *n*.

con·cern [kən'sɜrn] *v* **1** have to do with: *The letter concerns your recent proposal*. **2** involve the interests of: *This is a private matter and doesn't concern you*. **3** trouble; worry: *Don't concern her with the details of the accident*.
n **1** whatever involves a person or his or her interests: *It is none of my concern*. **2** worry; a troubled state of mind: *His tone betrayed his concern*. **3** interest; care: *I have concerns about the environment*. **4** a business; company: *He is CEO in a big manufacturing concern*. **con·cerned** *adj*. ⟨Latin *concernere* relate to, mingle with⟩
as concerns about; with regard to. **concern oneself a** occupy one's time and attention (with): *She will concern herself with the water sports program*. **b** worry: *Don't concern yourself; I have everything under control*. **of concern** of importance; of interest: *a matter of concern to all taxpayers*.
con·cern·ing *prep* having to do with; about: *I have questions concerning the accident*.

con·cert ['kɒnsərt] *n* **1** a fairly long musical performance. **2** agreement; harmony; union. *v* [kən'sɜrt] (usually as participial adjective) arrange by agreement. ⟨Italian *concerto*; Latin *com-* with + *certare* strive⟩
in concert a performing publicly: *Hear him in concert at the Opera House!* **b** all together; in harmony or agreement.
con·cert·ed *adj* planned and carried out by all: *a concerted effort*. **con·cert·ed·ly** *adv*. **concert grand** a grand piano for use with an orchestra. **con·cer·ti·na** [,kɒnsər'tinə] *n* a small musical instrument resembling an accordion. **con·cert·mas·ter** *n* the leader, usually the first violinist, of an orchestra. **con·cer·to** [kən'tʃɛrtou] *n, pl* **-tos** or (*Italian*) **-ti** [-ti] a musical composition usually in three movements and written for one or more solo instruments accompanied by an orchestra. **concert pitch 1** *Music* standard pitch of orchestral instruments, in which A

above middle C = 440 hZ. **2** the height of fitness, readiness, co-ordination, etc.: *Our Olympic team is at concert pitch.*

con·ces·sion¹ [kən'sɛʃən] *n* **1** the act of conceding or the thing conceded: *As a small concession, Dad let me stay up an hour longer.* **2** space leased to an individual or company for special use on private or public property, such as a refreshment stand or souvenir shop on a beach, in a park, etc. **3** land, rights, etc. granted by a government. **con·ces·sion·ar·y** *adj.* ⟨Latin *concessio*, from *concedere.* See CONCEDE.⟩ **con·ces·sion·aire** [kən,sɛʃə'nɛr] *n* a person, business, etc., to whom a concession has been granted. **con·ces·sive** *adj* **1** yielding. **2** *Grammar* expressing concession. *Though* and *although* introduce concessive clauses.

con·ces·sion² [kən'sɛʃən] *n* ✹ **1** mainly in Ontario and Québec, a subdivision of land in a township survey. **2** in full, **concession road** esp in Ontario, a rural road between concessions, usually 2 km apart and running north and south. **3 concessions** *pl* rural or bush districts. ⟨Cdn. French⟩

conch [kɒntʃ] *or* [kɒŋk] *n, pl* **conch·es** ['kɒntʃɪz] *or* **conchs** [kɒŋks] any of various large marine snails, or its shell. ⟨Greek *konchē*⟩

con·ci·erge [kɒn'sjɛrʒ] *or* [,kɒnsi'ɛrʒ] *French* [kɔ'sjɛrʒ] *n* **1** a doorkeeper, as in a hotel or a condominium building. **2** janitor. ⟨French⟩

con·cil·i·ate [kən'sɪliˌeit] *v* **1** win over: *She conciliated her angry little sister by taking her to the zoo.* **2** gain or regain (good will, regard, etc.) by friendly acts. **3** reconcile (ideas, etc.); bring into harmony. **con·cil·i·a·tion** *n.* **con·cil·i·a·to·ry** *adj.* ⟨Latin *conciliare; concilium.* See COUNCIL.⟩

con·cise [kən'səis] *adj* expressing much in a few words. **con·cise·ly** *adv.* **con·cise·ness** or **con·ci·sion** *n.* ⟨Latin *concisus,* pp of *concidere; com-* (intensive) + *caedere* cut⟩

con·clave ['kɒnkleiv] *n* **1** a private meeting. **2** a large professional gathering. **3** *Roman Catholic Church* **a** a meeting of cardinals to elect a pope. **b** the cardinals. ⟨Latin *conclave* lockable room; *com-* with + *clavis* key⟩

con·clude [kən'klud] *v* **1** end. **2** settle; arrive at by negotiation: *The two countries concluded a trade agreement.* **3** find by reasoning: *From the clues we found, we concluded that the thief must have left in a hurry.* **4** decide; resolve: *I concluded not to go.* **con·clu·sion** *n.* ⟨Latin *com-* (intensive) + *claudere* close⟩

in conclusion finally; lastly; to conclude.

con·clu·sive *adj* convincing; proving the point: *conclusive evidence.* **con·clu·sive·ly** *adv.* **con·clu·sive·ness** *n.*

con·coct [kən'kɒkt] *v* **1** prepare by mixing ingredients: *to concoct a dessert.* **2** invent or devise, esp something complicated: *to concoct a plan or a clever story.* **con·coc·tion** *n.* ⟨Latin *com-* together + *coquere* cook⟩

con·com·i·tant [kən'kɒmətənt] *adj* happening or existing along with; accompanying: *a concomitant result.* **con·com·i·tant** *n.*

con·com·i·tant·ly *adv.* **con·com·i·tance** *n.* ⟨Latin *com-* (intensive) + *comitari* accompany⟩

con·cord ['kɒnkɔrd] *n* **1** harmony; agreement. **2** *Music* a harmonious combination of tones. **3** treaty. **4** *Grammar* agreement in person, number, gender, tense, etc. ⟨Latin *com-* together + *cor, cordis* heart⟩ **con·cord·ance** [kən'kɔrdəns] *n* **1** a list of the main words or all the words used in a particular body of writing, identifying the passages in which they occur: *a concordance of Shakespeare.* **2** harmony. **con·cord·ant** *adj* **1** agreeing. **2** harmonious: *concordant tones.* **con·cord·ant·ly** *adv.* **con·cor·dat** [kən'kɔrdæt] *n* a formal agreement, esp between a religious body and a government.

con·course ['kɒnkɔrs] *n* **1** a running or flowing together: *The fort stood at the concourse of two rivers.* **2** a large open area where crowds gather or wait: *the main concourse of a train station.* **3** a crowd. ⟨Latin *concursus; com-* together + *currere* run⟩

con·crete ['kɒnkrit] *or* [kɒn'krit] *adj* **1** having material reality: *concrete objects.* **2** making reference to concrete things as opposed to abstract ideas: *a concrete style. Explain it in concrete terms.* **3** specific; definite. **4** *Grammar* of a noun, naming a material thing and not a quality. **5** hard, solid, or firm like concrete. *n* a mixture of crushed stone, sand, cement, and water that hardens as it dries, used for sidewalks, etc. *v* cover with concrete. **con·crete·ly** *adv.* **con·crete·ness** *n.* ⟨Latin *concretus,* pp of *concrescere; com-* together + *crescere* grow⟩

concrete music electronically distorted music.

concrete poetry poetry arranged so as to reflect visually the meaning of the poem. **con·cre·tion** *n* a solidified mass.

con·cu·bine ['kɒŋkjəˌbɑɪn] *n* **1** in certain polygamous societies, a wife with inferior social and legal status, esp of a king or other high-ranking man. **2** a woman living or having an ongoing sexual relationship with a man without being legally married to him. ⟨Latin *concubina; com-* with + *cubare* lie⟩

con·cu·pis·cent [kən'kjupəsənt] *adj* **1** greedy. **2** lustful. **con·cu·pis·cence** *n.* ⟨Latin *concupiscere; com-* (intensive) + *cupere* desire⟩

con·cur [kən'kɜr] *v* **-curred, -cur·ring 1** agree. **2** happen at the same time. **3** work together; have a combined effect: *The events of the week concurred to make the holiday a great one.* **con·cur·rence** *n.* ⟨Latin *com-* with + *currere* run⟩ **con·cur·rent** *adj* **1** happening at the same time. **2** consistent; in agreement: *This action is not concurrent with your former statements.* **3** meeting in a point. **con·cur·rent·ly** *adv.*

con·cuss [kən'kʌs] *v* **1** shake violently by or as if by a blow. **2** *Medicine* injure (the brain) by a blow or violent shaking. **con·cus·sion** *n.* ⟨Latin *concussio* from *concutere* shake hard; *com-* (intensive) + *quatere* shake⟩

con·demn [kən'dɛm] *v* **1** express strong disapproval of: *We condemn racism.* **2** assign to an unpleasant fate: *Poverty condemned them* to a life of frustration. **3** declare unfit for use: *a condemned house.* **4** damn. **con·dem·na·ble** [kən'dɛmnəbəl] *adj.* **con·dem·na·tion** *n.* **con·dem·na·to·ry** *adj.* ⟨Latin *com-* (intensive) + *damnare* cause loss to; *damnum* loss⟩

con·dense [kən'dɛns] *v* **1** make or become denser or stronger; concentrate. **2** change from a gas to a liquid: *Water vapour in the air condenses as dew.* **3** shorten or make more compact by reducing to essentials: *to condense a paragraph into one line.* **con·den·sa·ble** *adj.* **con·den·sa·tion** *n.* ⟨Latin *condensare; com-* together + *densus* thick⟩ **con·den·sate** ['kɒndən,seit] *or* [kən'dɛnseit] *n* a product of condensation. **condensed milk** sweetened evaporated milk. **con·dens·er** *n* **1** a device for receiving and holding a charge of electricity; capacitor. **2** an apparatus for changing gas to liquid.

con·de·scend [,kɒndɪ'sɛnd] *v* **1** come down to the level of one's inferiors in rank: *The king condescended to eat with the beggars.* **2** grant a favour in a patronizing way. **3** lower oneself: *She would not condescend to taking a bribe.* **con·de·scend·ing** *adj.* **con·de·scend·ing·ly** *adv.* **con·de·scen·sion** *n.* ⟨Latin *com-* (intensive) + *descendere* descend⟩

con·di·ment ['kɒndəmənt] *n* anything, such as mustard, used on food to give flavour. ⟨Latin *condimentum; condire* to spice⟩

con·di·tion [kən'dɪʃən] *n* **1** the state in which a person or thing is: *in critical condition.* **2** specifically, a state of physical fitness: *to keep in condition.* **3** an ailment or disorder: *She has a heart condition.* **4 conditions** *pl* circumstances that affect an activity or situation: *poor driving conditions.* **5** anything on which something else depends: *Proper certification is a condition of employment here.* **6** social rank: *People of humble condition.* *v* **1** put in good condition: *to condition your muscles.* **2** shape behaviour through repeated exposure to particular conditions: *This dog has been conditioned to expect food when it obeys a command.* ⟨Latin *condicio* agreement, from *condicere; com-* together + *dicere* say⟩ **on condition that** only if: *I'll go on condition that you will too.* **on no condition** never: *On no condition will I lie for you.* **con·di·tion·al** *adj* depending on something else. **con·di·tion·al·ly** *adv.* **con·di·tion·al·i·ty** *n.* **con·di·tioned** *adj* **1** *Psychology* learned by repeated exposure to particular conditions: *a conditioned response.* **2** subject to certain conditions. **con·di·tion·er** *n* a lotion used to improve the condition of the hair, skin, etc.

con·do ['kɒndou] *n Informal* condominium.

con·dole [kən'doul] *v* express sympathy: *The widow's close friends condoled with her.* **con·do·lence** [kən'doulⱥns] *or* ['kɒndələns] *n.* ⟨Latin *com-* with + *dolere* grieve, suffer⟩

con·dom ['kɒndəm] *n* a sheath worn over the penis during intercourse to prevent infection or conception. ⟨origin unknown⟩

con·do·min·i·um [,kɒndə'mɪniəm] *or* [-'mɪnjəm] *n* **1** one of a set of individually owned apartments or townhouses on land that is jointly owned. **2** a building containing such apartments. Often shortened to **condo**. ⟨Latin *com-* with + *dominium* lordship⟩

con·done [kən'doun] *v* **1** accept or approve of (a behaviour regarded by others as wrong). **2** ignore or overlook (an offence): *His parents always condoned his temper tantrums.* ⟨Latin *com-* (intensive) + *donare* give⟩

con·dor ['kɒndɔr] *n* either of two large New World vultures. ⟨Spanish; Peruvian *cuntur*⟩

con·duce [kən'djus] *or* [kən'dus] *v* be favourable (*to*): *Darkness and quiet conduce to sleep.* **con·du·cive** *adj.* ⟨Latin *com-* together + *ducere* lead⟩

con·duct ['kɒndʌkt] *n* **1** behaviour; way of acting. **2** an act of leading or escorting: *Give the messenger safe conduct to the king.* *v* [kən'dʌkt] **1** act or behave in a certain way (reflexively): *She conducted herself in an honourable way.* **2** direct (an orchestra, choir, etc.). **3** guide; escort: *The usher conducted her to a seat.* **4** transmit (heat, electricity, etc.). ⟨Latin *conductus* pp of *conducere*. See CONDUCE.⟩ **con·duct·ance** *n* the ease with which a substance permits the passage of electricity. **con·duc·tion** *n* **1** *Physics* the transmission of heat, electricity, etc., by a transfer of energy from one particle to another. **2** *Physiology* transmission of sound waves, heat, or neural impulses by a nerve or nerves. **con·duc·tive** *adj.* **con·duc·tiv·i·ty** *n.* **con·duc·tor** *n* **1** the director of an orchestra, choir, etc. **2** the person on a railway train who collects tickets or fares from passengers, helps them board, etc. **3** anything that transmits heat, electricity, light, sound, etc. **con·duit** ['kɒndwɪt], ['kɒndjuɪt], *or* ['kɒnduɪt] *n* a channel, pipe, tube, etc. carrying liquids or cables.

SYNONYMS

Conduct, the more formal word, usually suggests reference to general standards of morality, ethics, or propriety. **Behaviour** often applies to a person's manners, degree of self-control in public, and similar practical aspects of the way people act. It is also routinely used of animals in the same way.

cone [koun] *n* **1** *Geometry* a solid that has a circular base and tapers to a point. **2** anything with a similar shape: *an ice-cream cone.* **3** *Botany* a cluster of overlapping woody scales that contain the seeds of a pine tree. **4** any of the cone-shaped cells in the retina of the eye that are sensitive to light and colour. **cone·less** *adj.* ⟨Greek *kōnos*⟩ **con·ic** ['kɒnɪk] *adj* to do with a cone. **con·i·cal** *adj* cone-shaped: *a wizard's conical hat.* **con·i·cal·ly** *adv.* **conic projection** a map based on an image of the earth's surface as a cone which is unrolled to a plane surface. **conics** *n Geometry* (with sg verb) the branch of geometry dealing with **conic sections**, that is, circles, ellipses, parabolas, and hyperbolas. **con·i·fer** ['kɒnəfər] *n* any tree or shrub with needle-shaped, evergreen leaves and bearing seeds in cones. **co·nif·er·ous** [kə'nɪfərəs] *adj.*

con·fab·u·late [kən'fæbjə,leit] *v* talk together informally and intimately. Often informally shortened to **con·fab** (**-fabbed, -fab·bing**). **con·fab·u·la·tion** or **con·fab** ['kɒnfæb] *Informal n.* ⟨Latin *com-* together + *fabula* fable⟩

con·fec·tion [kən'fɛkʃən] *n* **1** a piece of (esp handmade) candy, fancy pastry, etc. **2** anything very elaborate. ⟨Latin *confectio*, from *conficere*; *com-* with + *facere* make⟩ **con·fec·tion·er** *n* a person whose business is making or selling confections. **con·fec·tion·er·y** [kən'fɛkʃə,nɛri] or [kən'fɛkʃənəri] *n* **1** candies, sweets, etc. collectively. **2** a candy shop.

con·fed·er·ate [kən'fɛdərɪt] *adj* **1** joined as allies or accomplices. **2 Confederate** to do with the CONFEDERATE STATES OF AMERICA. *n* an ally or accomplice. *v* [kən'fɛdə,reit] enter a union or alliance: *Newfoundland confederated with Canada in 1949.* ⟨Latin *com-* together + *foederis* league⟩ **con·fed·er·a·cy** [kən'fɛdərəsi] *n* **1** a union or league of allied individuals, states, nations, etc. **2 Confederacy** in full, the **Confederate States of America** the 11 southern states that seceded from the US in 1860-1861 and whose secession lasted until the end of the Civil War, 1865. **con·fed·er·a·tion** [kən,fɛdə'reiʃən] *n* **1** the act of joining together in a league. **2** a league. **3 Confederation ✹** the original union of Ontario, Québec, Nova Scotia, and New Brunswick in 1867. **4 the Confederation ✹** Canada at any time since, regarded as a league of provinces.

con·fer [kən'fɜr] *v* **-ferred, -fer·ring 1** consult together. **2** award (with *on*); bestow: *The general conferred a medal on the brave soldier.* ⟨Latin *com-* together + *ferre* bring⟩ **con·fer·ee** [,kɒnfə'ri] *n* **1** a person who takes part in a conference. **2** a person on whom something is conferred. **con·fer·ence** *n* **1** a meeting of interested people to discuss a particular subject. **2** an association of local churches, schools, teams, etc. **conference call** a telephone call involving three or more people. **con·fer·ral** or **con·fer·ment** *n* an act of conferring; bestowal.

con·fess [kən'fɛs] *v* **1** admit (a misdeed or embarrassing truth): *I confess I've forgotten your name.* **2** *Christianity* tell (one's sins), esp to a priest. **3** of a priest, hear (a person) tell his or her sins. **4** state (one's faith or beliefs) openly. ⟨Latin *confessare*, from *confiteri*; *com-* (intensive) + *fateri* admit⟩ **con·fessed** *adj* openly acknowledged to be so: *He's a confessed anarchist.* **con·fess·ed·ly** [kən'fɛsɪdli] *adv.* **con·fes·sion** *n.* **con·fes·sion·al** *n* a small booth inside a church where a priest hears confessions. **con·fes·sor** *n* a priest who hears confessions.

con·fet·ti [kən'fɛti] *n* bits of coloured paper (formerly, candies) thrown at weddings, etc. ⟨Italian = sweetmeats, confections⟩

con·fide [kən'faɪd] *v* tell as a secret. ⟨Latin *com-* (intensive) + *fidere* trust⟩ **confide in a** entrust a secret to: *She confides in her sister.* **b** trust: *to confide in God.* **con·fi·dant(e)** ['kɒnfə,dɑnt] or ['kɒnfə,dænt], [,kɒnfə'dɑnt] or [,kɒnfə'dænt] *n* a person (**confidante** for a female) entrusted with one's private affairs, etc. **con·fi·dence** ['kɒnfədəns] *n* **1** a firm belief. **2** boldness. **3** something told as a secret. **con·fi·dent** *adj.* **con·fi·dent·ly** *adv.* **in confidence** as a secret. **confidence game** an operation in which a swindler defrauds a victim after gaining his or her confidence. **confidence man** swindler using a CONFIDENCE GAME. **con·fi·den·tial** [,kɒnfə'dɛnʃəl] *adj* **1** secret; private; not for others to know: *a confidential report.* **2** showing intimacy: *She spoke in a confidential tone of voice.* **3** trusted with private affairs: *a confidential secretary.* **con·fi·den·tial·ly** *adv.* **con·fi·den·ti·al·i·ty** *n.*

con·fig·u·ra·tion [kən,fɪgjə'reiʃən] or [kən,fɪgə'reiʃən] *n* **1** the relative position of parts in a whole or in a system: *Geographers study the configuration of the earth's surface.* **2** *Computers* a particular way in which a system or application is set up according to various options. **con·fig·ure** *v.* ⟨Latin *com-* together + *figura* form⟩

con·fine [kən'faɪn] *v* **1** keep within limits: *The event is confined to children under age 7.* **2** keep indoors or in a certain place: *confined to one's bed.* **3** imprison. *n* Usually, **confines** ['kɒnfaɪnz] *pl* boundary; limits: *These people have never been beyond the confines of their own valley.* **con·fined** *adj.* ⟨Latin *com-* together + *finis* end, border⟩ **con·fine·ment** *n* **1** imprisonment. **2** the time, esp formerly, spent in bed by a mother during and immediately after childbirth.

con·firm [kən'fɜrm] *v* **1** approve; ratify: *The treaty has not been confirmed by Parliament.* **2** make certain of the truth or justice of: *to confirm a rumour. Her fears were confirmed.* **3** administer the rite of confirmation to. ⟨Latin *com-* (intensive) + *firmus* firm⟩ **con·fir·ma·tion** *n* **1** the act of confirming. **2** proof: *The lab has sent confirmation of the diagnosis.* **3** assurance (i.e., that one's plans have not been changed): *The airline requires confirmation of your reservation.* **4** *Christianity* a rite in which a baptized person declares his or her faith and is admitted to full church membership. **5** *Judaism* a ceremony in which a young person reaffirms his or her faith. **con·firm·a·to·ry** *adj* confirming. **con·firmed** *adj* **1** firmly established: *a confirmed fact.* **2** habitual; permanent: *a confirmed bachelor.* **3** having received the rite of confirmation.

SYNONYMS
Confirm = make certain that something is true or correct, by facts or a statement that cannot be doubted: *The mayor confirmed the report that she had resigned.* **Corroborate** = support by a statement or new evidence, but not necessarily conclusively: *Finding the weapon corroborates the police theory.*

con·fis·cate ['kɒnfə,skeit] *v* seize by authority: *The customs officer confiscated the smuggled cigarettes.* **con·fis·ca·tion** *n.* ⟨Latin *confiscare*, orig lay away in a chest; *com-* (intensive) + *fiscus* chest, public treasury⟩ **con·fis·ca·ble** able to be confiscated.

con·fla·gra·tion [ˌkɒnfləˈgreiʃən] *n* a great, destructive fire. ⟨Latin *com-* (intensive) + *flagrare* burn⟩

con·flate [kənˈfleit] *v* merge; combine into one. **con·fla·tion** *n*. ⟨Latin *conflatus* pp of *conflare* fuse together⟩

con·flict [ˈkɒnflɪkt] *n* **1** a fight or struggle. **2** direct opposition, as of different ideas, plans, demands, etc.: *I have a conflict in my schedule; your party is the day of my aunt's visit.*
v [kənˈflɪkt] produce or be in conflict: *His idea conflicts with my findings.* ⟨Latin *conflictus*, pp of *confligere; com-* together + *fligere* strike⟩
conflict of interest opposition between the private interests and public responsibilities of a person in a position of trust.

con·flu·ent [ˈkɒnfluənt] *adj* flowing or running together: *confluent rivers.*
n a stream joining another of similar size. **con·flu·ence** *n*. ⟨Latin *com-* with + *fluere* flow⟩

con·form [kənˈfɔrm] *v* **1** follow a rule; adapt to or accept the normal standards in business, conduct, worship, etc.: *The book conforms to Ministry guidelines.* **2** be or make similar in form or character: *The path conforms to the shoreline. I refuse to conform to the prevailing worldview.* **con·form·i·ty** *n*. ⟨Latin *com-* with + *formare* shape⟩
con·form·a·ble *adj* **1** similar. **2** in agreement. **3** obedient: *The boy was usually conformable to his father's wishes.* **con·form·a·bly** *adv*. **con·form·ance** *n* compliance. **con·form·ism** *n* the policy of conforming to prevailing values, fashions, etc. **con·form·ist** *n, adj*.

con·found [kənˈfaʊnd] *v* *Formal, poetic* **1** throw into confusion. **2** be unable to tell apart: *He confounds 'deprecate' and 'depreciate'.* ⟨Latin *com-* together + *fundere* pour⟩
con·found·ed [kɒnˈfaʊndɪd] *or* [kənˈfaʊndɪd] *adj* (as a mild oath) damned: *That confounded cat stayed out all night.* **con·found·ed·ly** *adv*.

con·front [kənˈfrʌnt] *v* **1** meet face to face. **2** force to recognize something; challenge: *We confronted the thief with the evidence.* ⟨Latin *com-* together + *frons, frontis* forehead⟩
con·fron·ta·tion *n* open conflict: *She doesn't believe in confrontation, and tries to talk things out reasonably.* **con·fron·ta·tion·al** *adj*. **con·fron·ta·tion·ist** *n*.

Con·fu·cius [kənˈfjuʃəs] *n* ancient Chinese teacher (? 551-478 B.C.) of a philosophical and ethical system based on a belief in the natural goodness of all human beings. **Con·fu·cian** *adj, n*. **Con·fu·cian·ism** *n*.
⟨Latinization of *Kung Fu-tse* Kung the master⟩

con·fuse [kənˈfjuz] *v* **1** mix up; throw into disorder. **2** bewilder. **3** be unable to tell apart: *Even the twins' sister sometimes confused them.* **4** make unclear: *You're only confusing the issue.* **5** make ashamed and ill at ease: *Confused by her blunder, she was unable to speak for a few moments.* **con·tus·a·ble** *adj*. **con·fused** *adj*. **con·fus·ed·ly** [kənˈfjuzɪdli] *or* [kənˈfjuzdli] *adv*. **con·fus·ing** *adj*. **con·fu·sion** *n*. ⟨Latin *confusus*, pp of *confundere*. See CONFOUND.⟩
covered in *or* **with confusion** embarrassed.

con·geal [kənˈdʒil] *v* harden or thicken; jell: *congealed blood.* **con·gel·a·tion** [ˌkɒndʒəˈleiʃən] *or* **con·geal·ment** *n*. ⟨Latin *com-* (intensive) + *gelare* freeze⟩

con·ge·ni·al [kənˈdʒinjəl] *or* [kənˈdʒiniəl] *adj* **1** having similar tastes; getting along well together: *congenial companions.* **2** agreeable or pleasant because suited to one's tastes or interests: *congenial work.* **con·gen·ial·ly** *adv*. **con·ge·ni·al·i·ty** *n*. ⟨Latin *com-* together + *genialis; genius* spirit⟩

con·gen·i·tal [kənˈdʒɛnətəl] *adj* **1** existing at birth: *congenital deafness.* **2** being so by nature: *a congenital liar.* **con·gen·i·tal·ly** *adv*. ⟨Latin *com-* with + *genitus* born⟩

con·ger eel [ˈkɒŋgər] *n* a large, scaleless marine eel. Also called **con·ger**. ⟨Old French *congre;* Greek *gongros*⟩

con·gest [kənˈdʒɛst] *v* **1** fill too full; clog: *Rush-hour traffic congested the streets.* **2** cause too much blood or other fluid to gather in (a part of the body): *A head cold will congest the nasal passages.* **con·ges·tion** *n*. ⟨Latin *congestus* pp of *congerere; com-* together + *gerere* carry⟩
con·ges·tive *adj* accompanied by, produced by, or causing congestion. **congestive heart failure** ongoing failure of the heart to pump sufficient blood from the ventricles, so that certain veins and organs are congested with blood while others have an inadaquate supply.

con·glom·er·ate [kənˈglɒmərɪt] *adj* made up of miscellaneous materials.
n **1** *Geology* a sedimentary rock composed of boulders, pebbles, etc. held together by a natural cementing material. **2** a corporation consisting of several different companies.
v [kənˈglɒməˌreit] accumulate into a mass or cluster. **con·glom·er·a·tion** *n*. ⟨Latin *com-* together + *glomeris* ball⟩

con·grat·u·late [kənˈgrætʃəˌleit] *v* express pleasure to (someone) at his or her good fortune. **con·grat·u·la·tion** *n*. **con·grat·u·la·to·ry** *adj*. ⟨Latin *com-* with + *gratulari* show joy⟩
con·grat·u·la·tions *n pl, interj* an expression of pleasure at another's happiness or success: *Congratulations on winning the tournament! I think congratulations are in order.*

con·gre·gate [ˈkɒŋgrəˌgeit] *v* come together into a group. ⟨Latin *congregare; com-* together + *gregis* flock⟩
con·gre·ga·tion *n* **1** a gathering of people or things; often specifically a group gathered, or gathering regularly, for worship. **2** the act of congregating. **3** *Roman Catholic Church* **a** a religious community; order. **b** a committee made up of clergy. **con·gre·ga·tion·al·ism** *n* **1** a system of church government in which each local congregation is autonomous. **2 Congregationalism** a Protestant movement embracing this system. **con·gre·ga·tion·al** *adj*. **Congregational** *adj*.

con·gress [ˈkɒŋgrɪs] *or* [ˈkɒŋgrɛs] *n* **1** a formal meeting of delegates from interested groups: *an international congress on child poverty, the Canadian Labour Congress.* **2** the lawmaking body of a republic. **3 Congress** in the US, the national lawmaking body, consisting of the Senate and House of Representatives. **4** any coming together. **con·gres·sion·al** *adj.* **con·gres·sion·al·ly** *adv.* ⟨Latin *congressus; com-* together + *gradi* go⟩

con·gress·man or **Congressman** *n, pl* **-men** in the US, a member of Congress or of the House of Representatives. **con·gress·wom·an** or **Congresswoman** *n, pl* **-wom·en.**

con·gru·ent ['kɒŋgruənt] *or* [kən'gruənt] *adj* **1** in agreement: *That decision was not congruent with our policy.* **2** *Geometry* exactly coinciding; of identical size and shape: *congruent triangles.* **con·gru·ence** *n.* **con·gru·ent·ly** *adv.* **con·gru·i·ty** [kən'gruəti] *n.* ⟨Latin *congruere* agree⟩

con·gru·ous *adj* fitting. **con·gru·ous·ly** *adv.* **con·gru·ous·ness** *n.*

Con·i·bear trap ['kouni,bɛr] ✳ a steel trap that instantly kills animals as large as beaver. ⟨F. *Conibear,* Canadian trapping expert⟩

con·ic, con·i·fer See CONE.

con·jec·ture [kən'dʒɛktʃər] *n* **1** guessing. **2** opinions, or a specific opinion, so formed: *Her theory is mostly conjecture.* **con·jec·ture** *v.* **con·jec·tur·a·ble** *adj.* **con·jec·tur·al** *adj.* ⟨Latin *conjectura* from *com-* together + *jacere* throw⟩

con·join [kən'dʒɔɪn] *v Formal, poetic* join together. ⟨Old French *conjoindre;* Latin *com-* together + *jungere* join⟩

con·ju·gal ['kɒndʒəgəl] *adj* to do with the relationship between spouses: *conjugal bliss.* ⟨Latin *com-* with + *jugum* yoke⟩

con·ju·gate ['kɒndʒə,geit] *v* **1** *Grammar* make or list the various forms of (a verb) according to a systematic arrangement. **2** join together. *adj* ['kɒndʒəgɪt] *or* ['kɒndʒə,geit] **1** joined together; coupled. **2** *Grammar* derived from the same root. **3** *Chemistry* of acids and bases, related by the presence or absence of a proton. **con·ju·gate** *n.* **con·ju·ga·tion** *n.* ⟨Latin *com-* with + *jugum* yoke⟩

con·junct ['kɒndʒʌŋkt] *or* [kən'dʒʌŋkt] *adj* joined together. **con·junct** ['kɒndʒʌŋkt] *n.* ⟨Latin *conjunctus* pp of *conjungere.* See CONJOIN.⟩

con·junc·tion *n* **1** combination: *An illness in conjunction with the hot weather has left him weak.* **2** *Grammar* a word expressing a connection between similar grammatical units. *And, but,* and *or* are **co–ordinating conjunctions**; *if, because, while,* etc., are **subordinating conjunctions**; *either...or, neither...nor,* and *both...and* are pairs of **correlative conjunctions**. *Abbrev* **conj**. **3** *Astronomy* the apparent nearness of two or more heavenly bodies. **con·junc·tive** *adj.*

Conjunctive adverbs are words which may connect independent clauses or sentences. The most common are: *also, anyhow, anyway, besides, however, indeed, likewise, nevertheless, then, therefore.* If one of these is used to introduce a clause, it is normally preceded by a semicolon or period: *He is very conceited; however, he's so charming that we all overlook it.* Failure to do so produces a comma splice or a run-on sentence.

con·junc·ti·va [,kɒndʒʌŋk'taɪvə] *or* [kən'dʒʌŋktɪvə] *n, pl* **-vas, -vae** [-vi] *or* [-vaɪ] *Anatomy* the mucous membrane covering the front of the eyeball and inner surface of the eyelids. **con·junc·ti·val** *adj.* ⟨Latin *(membrana) conjunctiva* connecting membrane⟩

con·junc·ti·vi·tis [kən,dʒʌŋktə'vəitɪs] *n* an inflammation of the conjunctiva.

con·jure ['kɒndʒər] *or* ['kʌndʒər] *v* **1** cause to appear by magic (often with *up*): *The wizard conjured a dragon.* **2** do magic or sorcery. **3** cause to appear in the mind; evoke (with *up*): *The song conjured up many memories.* **con·ju·ra·tion** *n.* ⟨Latin *conjurare* make a pact (i.e., with a spirit); *com-* with + *jurare* swear⟩

a name (or word) to conjure with one that has great importance: *Since her last novel, hers is a name to conjure with. 'E-commerce' has become a word to conjure with.*

con·jur·er or **con·jur·or** *n* **1** sorcerer; wizard. **2** a magician or juggler.

conk [kɒŋk] *Slang n* **1** a hit, esp on the head. **2** the head. **conk** *v.* ⟨possibly *conch*⟩

conk out *Slang* **a** of a car, machine, etc., break down suddenly. **b** collapse; fall asleep or unconscious: *I'm so tired, I'm about ready to conk out.* **c** die.

con·ker ['kɒŋkər] *n* **1 conkers** a game played by children with horse chestnuts on strings. **2** a chestnut used in this game.

con·nect [kə'nɛkt] *v* **1** join; link: *to connect water pipes. This passage connects the kitchen to the dining room.* **2** associate; relate: *We usually connect spring with rain and flowers.* **3** of an airline flight, bus run, etc., be scheduled so as to allow passengers to change to another without delay. **4** link to an electrical power supply: *Do not clean the toaster while it is still connected.* **5** *Informal* achieve good rapport or meaningful contact: *She spoke to us, but did not really connect.* **con·nect·er** or **con·nec·tor** *n.* ⟨Latin *com-* with + *nectere* tie⟩

con·nect·ed *adj* **1** joined; linked; associated. **2** having ties with other people, esp influential ones: *She is well connected.* **con·nec·tion** *n* **1** the act of connecting or fact of being connected. **2** a thing that connects, or the point at which things are connected: *a loose connection.* **3 connections** people, esp influential ones, with whom one is associated in business dealings, etc. **in connection with** relating to. **in this** (or **that**) **connection** with regard to this (or that). **con·nec·tive** *adj* serving to connect. *n* **1** a thing that connects. **2** *Grammar* a word used to connect other words, phrases, and clauses.

con·ning tower See CON⁴.

con·nip·tion [kə'nɪpʃən] *n Informal* Often, **conniptions** *pl* or **conniption fit** a fit of rage, hysteria, etc.; tantrum. ⟨pseudo-Latin coining⟩

con·nive [kə'naɪv] *v* **1** close one's eyes to wrongdoing: *The mayor was accused of conniving at the misuse of funds.* **2** conspire (with): *The general connived with the enemies of his country.* **con·niv·ance** *n.* **con·niv·er** *n.* ⟨Latin *connivere* shut the eyes, wink⟩

con·nois·seur [ˌkɒnəˈsɜr] n a person having thorough knowledge and able to make fine distinctions in art and matters of taste: *a connoisseur of wines.* **con·nois·seur·ship** n. ⟨French earlier *connoisseur;* Latin *cognoscere* from *com-* (intensive) + *gnoscere* recognize⟩

con·note [kəˈnout] v of a word, have certain emotional overtones or associations: *Portly* and *obese* both mean 'fat', but *portly* connotes dignity, *obese* the opposite. Compare DENOTE. **con·no·ta·tion** n. **con·no·ta·tive** [ˈkɒnəˌteitɪv] or [kəˈnoutətɪv] adj. **con·no·ta·tive·ly** adv. ⟨Latin *com-* with + *notare* to note⟩

con·nu·bi·al [kəˈnjubiəl] or [kəˈnubiəl] adj to do with marriage. **con·nu·bi·al·ly** adv. ⟨Latin *connubium* marriage; *com-* + *nubere* marry⟩

con·quer [ˈkɒŋkər] v 1 win or get control of by defeating in a struggle: *to conquer a people or a country.* 2 get the better of; overcome: *to conquer fears.* **con·quer·a·ble** adj. **con·quer·or** [ˈkɒŋkərər] n. ⟨Latin *conquaerere; com-* (intensive) + *quaerere* seek⟩

con·quest [ˈkɒŋkwɛst] or [ˈkɒnkwɛst] n 1 the act of conquering or the thing conquered. 2 a person whose love or favour has been won. 3 **the Conquest ❉** the British takeover of French lands in North America in 1763.

con·quis·ta·dor [kɒnˈkistəˌdɔr] or [kənˈkwistəˌdɔr] n, pl **-dors** or (*Spanish*) **-dores** [-ˈdɔriz] or [-ˈdɔreis] any of the Spanish conquerors who came to America in the 1500s to look for gold. ⟨Spanish = conqueror⟩

con·san·guin·e·ous [ˌkɒnsæŋˈgwiniəs] adj descended from the same parent or ancestor. **con·san·guin·e·ous·ly** adv. **con·san·guin·i·ty** n. ⟨Latin *com-* together + *sanguinis* blood⟩

con·science [ˈkɒnʃəns] n the sense of moral right and wrong with respect to one's own conduct: *Her conscience prompted her to return the book she had stolen.* **con·science·less** adj. ⟨Latin *com-* with + *scientia* knowledge⟩ **in (all) conscience** honourably; fairly. **on one's conscience** making one feel guilty. **conscience money** money given voluntarily by a person to relieve a guilty conscience. **con·science–strick·en** adj suffering from a feeling of having done wrong. **con·sci·en·tious** [ˌkɒnʃiˈɛnʃəs] adj 1 careful to do what one knows is right. 2 done carefully. 3 done for the right reasons or for reasons of conscience. **con·sci·en·tious·ly** adv. **con·sci·en·tious·ness** n. **conscientious objector** a person whose beliefs keep him or her from being a combatant in time of war. **con·scion·a·ble** [ˈkɒnʃənəbəl] adj acceptable to conscience. **con·scion·a·bly** adv.

con·scious [ˈkɒnʃəs] adj 1 aware: *conscious of a sharp pain.* 2 capable of thought, will, or feeling: *a conscious animal.* 3 awake: *After about five minutes he became conscious again.* 4 deliberate: *a conscious effort.* 5 attentive to; preoccupied with (in compounds): *clothes-conscious.* **con·scious·ly** adv. ⟨Latin *conscius* from *conscire; com-* (intensive) + *scire* know⟩ **con·scious·ness** [ˈkɒnʃəsnɪs] n 1 the state or fact of being conscious. 2 all the thoughts of a person or group: *the moral consciousness of our generation.* **con·scious·ness–rais·ing** n the

process of making people aware of an issue in order to bring about change.

con·script [kənˈskrɪpt] v 1 force by law to enlist in the armed forces. 2 take for state use: *The dictator conscripted both capital and labour.* 3 *Informal* obtain the grudging help or participation of: *We conscripted him to do the dishes.* **con·scrip·tion** n. ⟨Latin *conscriptus* pp of *conscribere; com-* (intensive) + *scribere* write⟩ **con·script** [ˈkɒnskrɪpt] adj conscripted. n a conscripted person.

con·se·crate [ˈkɒnsəˌkreit] v 1 set apart as sacred: *A church is consecrated to God.* 2 ordain (someone) to sacred office. 3 make an object of cherished regard: *Time has consecrated these customs.* 4 dedicate: *He has consecrated his life to music.* **con·se·crat·ed** adj. **con·se·cra·tion** n. ⟨Latin *com-* (intensive) + *sacer* sacred⟩

con·sec·u·tive [kənˈsɛkjətɪv] adj 1 following one after another without interruption: *for six consecutive days.* 2 characterized by logical order: *consecutive thought.* **con·sec·u·tive·ly** adv. **con·sec·u·tive·ness** n. ⟨Latin *consecutus* pp of *consequi; com-* (intensive) + *sequi* follow⟩

con·sen·sus [kənˈsɛnsəs] n 1 general agreement. 2 generally shared decision-making: *to govern by consensus.* **con·sen·su·al** adj. ⟨Latin *consensus; consentire.* See CONSENT.⟩

con·sent [kənˈsɛnt] v give permission: *My mother did not consent to my leaving school.* **con·sent** n. ⟨Latin *com-* together + *sentire* feel, think⟩

SYNONYMS

Consent = give permission, either willingly because one agrees, or by giving in to the wishes of others: *She consented to run for president.* **Assent** = express one's agreement with something put forward for consideration: *He assented to the suggested change in plans.*

con·se·quent [ˈkɒnsəkwənt] or [ˈkɒnsəˌkwɛnt] adj 1 following as a result: *His illness and consequent absence put him behind in his work.* 2 following a logical sequence: *the consequent development of an idea.* n 1 anything that follows something else. 2 *Mathematics* the second term of a ratio. 3 *Logic* the second term, or conclusion, of a conditional proposition. ⟨Latin *consequens* ppr of *consequi.* See CONSECUTIVE.⟩ **consequent on** or **upon** a resulting from. b logically following from. **con·se·quence** n 1 a result of some previous occurrence. 2 a logical result. 3 importance: *of no consequence.* 4 the fact of following as a result: *My mom, and by consequence my dad, said no to the scheme.* **in consequence** as a result (*of*). **take the consequences** accept undesirable results of one's acts. **con·se·quen·tial** [ˌkɒnsəˈkwɛnʃəl] adj 1 important. 2 following as a natural or logical result. 3 self-important or pompous. **con·se·quen·tial·ly** adv. **con·se·quen·ti·al·i·ty** n. **con·se·quent·ly** adv 1 as a result; therefore. 2 in a consequent manner.

con·serve [kənˈsɜrv] v 1 keep from being used up or wasted: *to conserve energy.* 2 keep (the natural environment) from harm or decay. **3** preserve (fruit) with sugar. *n* ['kɒnsɜrv] *or* [kən'sɜrv] jam or preserved fruit. **con·serv·a·ble** *adj.* **con·ser·va·tion** *n.* **con·serv·er** *n.* ⟨Latin *com-* (intensive) + *servare* preserve⟩

conservation area an area kept under official protection and care as a park. **con·ser·va·tion·ist** *n* an activist for conservation of the natural environment. **conservation of energy** *Physics* the principle that the total amount of energy in the universe does not vary. **conservation of mass** (or **matter**) *Physics* the principle that the total mass of any closed system remains unchanged by reactions within the system. **conservation of volume** the principle that a volume of liquid is not affected by the shape of its container. **con·serv·a·tism** *n* conservative attitudes or policies. **con·serv·a·tive** *adj* **1** opposed to change; inclined to keep things as they are or were in the past. **2** Often, **Con·serv·a·tive** to do with a political party that opposes change in social and national institutions and generally advocates a minimum of state intervention in the economy. **b ✻** short for PROGRESSIVE CONSERVATIVE. **c** to do with a branch of Judaism more flexibly interpreting law than Orthodox Judaism. **3** cautious: *conservative estimates.* **4** free from fads; restrained: *a conservative style.* **con·serv·a·tive,** **Con·serv·a·tive** *n.* **con·serv·a·tive·ly** *adv.* **con·serv·a·tive·ness** *n.* **Conservative Party** one of the principal political parties of Canada. **con·serv·a·to·ry** *n* **1** a glass-enclosed room for growing plants. **2** a music school.

con·sid·er [kən'sɪdər] *v* **1** think about in order to decide: *I'd like to consider the matter.* **2** think of as: *We consider E.J. Pratt a great Canadian poet.* **3** allow for: *This watch runs very well, if you consider how old it is.* **4** be thoughtful of (others and their feelings). **5** entertain as a possible course of action: *Would you consider eloping?* **6** observe intently; regard. ⟨Latin *considerare* orig examine the stars; *com-* (intensive) + *sidus* star⟩ **con·sid·er·a·ble** *adj* **1** fairly big: *a considerable sum.* **2** worthy of regard: *a very considerable poet.* **con·sid·er·a·bly** *adv.* **con·sid·er·ate** *adj* thoughtful of others and their feelings. **con·sid·er·ate·ly** *adv.* **con·sid·er·ate·ness** *n.* **con·sid·er·a·tion** *n* **1** the act of considering. **2** something to be considered in a decision: *Price is a consideration in buying anything.* **3** money or other payment: *for a small consideration.* **4** thoughtfulness for others. **5** importance. **in consideration of a** in view of: *In consideration of our son's poor health, we moved to a milder climate.* **b** in return for: *a gift in consideration of your helpfulness.* **on no consideration** not at all; never. **take into consideration** allow for; take into account. **under consideration** being thought about. **con·sid·ered** *adj* **1** carefully thought out. **2** respected. **con·sid·er·ing** *prep* taking into account: *Considering her age, she reads well. adv Informal* taking all things into account: *He does very well, considering.*

con·sign [kən'saɪn] *v* **1** hand over; deliver or commit (often permanently and undesirably): *This writer's works will be consigned to oblivion.* **2** send: *The order will be consigned by express.* **con·sign·a·ble** *adj.* **con·sig·na·tion** *n.* ⟨Latin *com-* with + *signum* seal⟩ **con·sign·ee** [,kɒnsaɪ'ni] *or* [kən'saɪni] *n* the person to whom goods are consigned. **con·sign·ment** *n* a shipment sent to a person for safekeeping or sale. **on consignment** of goods, sent to a retailer on an arrangement whereby the retailer only pays for the goods after having sold them. **con·sign·or** or **con·sign·er** [kən'saɪnər] *or* [,kɒnsaɪ'nɔr] *n.*

con·sist [kən'sɪst] *v* **1** be made up (*of*): *A year consists of twelve months.* **2** have its existence or definition (*in*): *For me, happiness consists in being left alone.* *n* ✻ **1** the way in which a train is made up. **2** the bill of goods being carried in a train. ⟨Latin *com-* together + *sistere* stand⟩ **con·sist·en·cy** [kən'sɪstənsi] *n* **1** degree of firmness or thickness: *Icing for a cake must be of the right consistency to spread easily without dripping.* **2** the fact or quality of being consistent: *consistency of purpose. There is little consistency between the reports.* **con·sist·ent** *adj* **1** keeping to the same principles, policy, etc. over time. **2** in agreement or harmony: *Speeding is not consistent with safety.* **3** of uniformly good quality. **4** *Mathematics* of two or more equations or inequalities, having at least one common solution. **con·sist·ent·ly** *adv.*

con·sole[1] [kən'soul] *v* comfort. **con·sol·a·ble** *adj.* **con·so·la·tion** *n.* **con·sol·er** *n.* **con·sol·ing·ly** *adv.* ⟨Latin *com-* (intensive) + *solari* soothe⟩ **con·so·la·tion match** a match between losers of an earlier round in a tournament. **consolation prize** a prize given to a person or team that has not won but has done well.

con·sole[2] ['kɒnsoul] *n* **1** the desklike part of an organ, containing the keyboard, stops, and pedals. **2** a control panel with switches, buttons, dials, etc. **3** a cabinet for a stereo system, television set, etc. ⟨French⟩

con·sol·i·date [kən'sɒlə,deit] *v* **1** unite; combine or merge: *The two territories were consolidated into one administrative district.* **2** make secure: *The army spent a day consolidating its gains by digging trenches.* **con·sol·i·dat·ed** *adj.* **con·sol·i·da·tion** *n.* ⟨Latin *com-* (intensive) + *solidus* solid⟩

con·som·mé ['kɒnsə,mei] *or* [,kɒnsə'mei] *n* clear soup made from meat, which gels when cooled. ⟨French. See CONSUMMATE.⟩

con·so·nant ['kɒnsənənt] *n* a speech sound formed by partly blocking the breath or by stopping it and then releasing it. *adj* **1** in agreement or harmony. **2** *Music* of tones or chords, harmonious. **con·so·nan·tal** [,kɒnsə'næntəl] *adj.* **con·so·nant·ly** *adv.* ⟨Latin *com-* together + *sonare* sound⟩ **con·so·nance** *n* **1** harmony; agreement. **2** *Music* harmony of sounds; a harmonious chord. Compare DISSONANCE. **3** a partial rhyme in which the consonants are alike but not the vowels. *Examples: lame/loam, seed/side.*

con·sort ['kɒnsɔrt] *n* **1** a spouse, esp of a monarch. **2** an associate; companion. *v* [kən'sɔrt] **1** keep company: *to consort with fools.* **2** agree; fit. ⟨Latin *com-* with + *sortis* lot⟩

con·sor·ti·um [kən'sɔrʃəm] *or* [kən'sɔrtiəm] *n, pl* **-ti·a** [-ʃə] *or* [-tiə] **1** an alliance of companies for a specific business venture. **2** a partnership; association.

con·spec·tus [kən'spɛktəs] *n* **1** a general view. **2** a short summary. ⟨Latin *conspectus* pp of *conspicere; com-* + *specere* look at⟩

con·spic·u·ous [kən'spɪkjuəs] *adj* **1** easily seen: *A traffic sign should be conspicuous.* **2** attracting attention: *conspicuous lack of tact, conspicuous by her absence.* **con·spic·u·ous·ly** *adv.* **con·spic·u·ous·ness** *n.* ⟨Latin *conspicuus* visible; *conspicere.* See CONSPECTUS.⟩
conspicuous consumption lavish spending intended to impress others.

con·spire [kən'spaɪr] *v* **1** plan secretly with others, usually to do something wrong. **2** act together, as if by design: *The rain, the cold, and the mosquitoes conspired to ruin the day.* **con·spir·a·cy** [kən'spɪrəsi] *n.* **con·spir·a·tor** [kən'spɪrətər] *n.* **con·spir·a·to·ri·al** *adj.* ⟨Latin *com-* together + *spirare* breathe⟩

con·sta·ble ['kɒnstəbəl] *n* a police officer of low rank. ⟨Latin *comes stabuli* count of the stable; later, chief household officer⟩
con·stab·u·lar·y [kən'stæbjə,lɛri] *n* constables collectively.

con·stant ['kɒnstənt] *adj* **1** always the same: *Walk due north, keeping your direction constant.* **2** never stopping: *three days of constant rain.* **3** faithful; steadfast: *a constant friend.* **4** *Mathematics, physics* retaining the same value: *a constant force.* *n* anything that never changes. **con·stan·cy** *n.* **con·stant·ly** *adv.* ⟨Latin *constans* ppr of *constare* stand firm; *com-* (intensive) + *stare* stand⟩

con·stel·la·tion [,kɒnstə'leiʃən] *n* **1** any of the groups of stars traditionally thought of as forming outlines of human or animal figures or other objects: *the constellation Ursa Major.* **2** an impressive gathering, as of important, gifted, or beautiful people: *a constellation of heads of state.* **3** any cluster. ⟨Latin *com-* together + *stella* star⟩
con·stel·late *v* cluster together.

con·ster·na·tion [,kɒnstər'neiʃən] *n* great dismay: *To our consternation the train rushed on toward the burning bridge.* **con·ster·nate** *v.* ⟨Latin *consternare* terrify, variant of *consternere* lay low; *com-* (intensive) + *sternere* strew⟩

con·sti·pa·tion [,kɒnstə'peiʃən] *n* a condition in which it is difficult to discharge solid waste from the body. **con·sti·pate** *v.* **con·sti·pat·ed** *adj.* ⟨Latin *com-* together + *stipare* press⟩

con·sti·tute ['kɒnstə,tjut] *or* ['kɒnstə,tut] *v* **1** make up: *the provinces and territories that constitute Canada.* **2** be equivalent to: *Failure to pay constitutes a debt.* **3** establish officially by law, vote, appointment, etc.: *issued by a duly constituted authority.* ⟨Latin *constitutus* pp of *constituere; com-* (intensive) + *statuere* set up⟩

con·stit·u·en·cy *n* **1** riding; a district represented by a single member in a legislature, council, etc. **2** the body of voters in such a district. **con·stit·u·ent** [kən'stɪtʃuənt] *adj* **1** helping to make up a whole: *Flour is a constituent part of bread.* **2** appointing; electing. *n* **1** a part or ingredient. **2** any of the voters represented by an elected official. **con·sti·tu·tion** *n* **1** a person's physical or mental nature. **2** the set of fundamental principles according to which a group is governed: *Our club has a written constitution.* **3 the Constitution** the written set of fundamental principles by which Canada is governed. **4** the act, fact, or manner of constituting a thing. **Constitution Act 1867** since 1981, the name of the BRITISH NORTH AMERICA ACT. **con·sti·tu·tion·al** *adj* **1** to do with a constitution: *Canada's ongoing constitutional debate.* **2** in accord with a constitution: *constitutional rights. Such a law would not be constitutional.* **3** to do with one's basic make-up: *a constitutional weakness. n* a walk taken for the good of one's health. **con·sti·tu·tion·al·ly** *adv.* **con·sti·tu·tion·al·i·ty** *n.* **constitutional monarchy** a monarchy in which the ruler has only the powers given by the constitution and laws of the nation. **con·sti·tu·tive** *adj* having power to establish or enact. **con·sti·tu·tive of** constituting.

con·strain [kən'strein] *v* **1** force physically or morally: *She was constrained to accept her employer's decision or leave her job.* **2** place under certain limits: *art constrained by social convention.* **3** confine; restrain. **con·straint** *n.* ⟨Old French *constreindre,* Latin *constringere; com-* together + *stringere* pull tightly⟩
con·strained *adj* forced and stiff; unnatural: *a constrained smile.* **con·strain·ed·ly** *adv.*

con·strict [kən'strɪkt] *v* draw together; squeeze: *A tourniquet constricts blood vessels so as to stop the bleeding.* **con·stric·tive** *adj.* ⟨Latin *constrictus* pp of *constringere.* See CONSTRAIN.⟩
con·stric·tion *n* **1** the act of constricting or a thing that constricts. **2** a feeling of tightness: *a constriction in my chest.* **3** a constricted part. **con·stric·tor** *n* **1** any snake that kills its prey by squeezing it. **2** *Anatomy* a muscle that constricts some part of the body.

con·struct [kən'strʌkt] *v* **1** put together; build. **2** *Mathematics* draw (a figure) so as to fulfil given conditions. *n* ['kɒnstrʌkt] **1** an idea consciously or unconsciously developed to integrate a variety of facts or perceptions. **2** anything built or put together systematically. **con·struc·tor** *n.* ⟨Latin *constructus* pp of *construere; com-* together + *struere* pile⟩
con·struc·tion *n* **1** something constructed. **2** the act, fact, or manner of constructing. **3** specifically, road building or road repairs. **4** interpretation; a way of construing words or actions: *He put an unfair construction on what I said.* **5** *Grammar* an arrangement of words in a clause or phrase. **con·struc·tion·ist** *n* one who adheres to a particular interpretation of laws, a constitution, etc.: *This judge is a strict constructionist.* **construction paper** a

thick, coloured paper used for arts and crafts.
con·struc·tive *adj* helpful: *constructive criticism.*
con·struc·tive·ly *adv.* **con·struc·tiv·ism** *n* an art movement originating in the former Soviet Union in the 1920s, characterized by the abstract arrangement of planes and masses, using industrial materials such as glass and plastic. **con·struc·tiv·ist** *n, adj.*

con·strue [kən'stru] *v* interpret: *Different lawyers may construe the same law differently. Her inability to hold a job was construed as indifference.* **con·stru·a·ble** *adj.* **con·struc·tion** *n.* ⟨Latin *construere.* See CONSTRUCT.⟩

con·sul ['kɒnsəl] *n* an official appointed by a country to look after its interests and assist its citizens in a foreign city. **con·su·lar** ['kɒnsjələr] *or* [-sələr] *adj.* **con·sul·ship** *n.* ⟨Latin⟩ **con·su·late** ['kɒnsəlɪt] *or* ['kɒnsjəlɪt] *n* the official residence or offices of a consul. **consul general** *pl* **consuls general** a consul of the highest rank.

con·sult [kən'sʌlt] *v* **1** seek information from: *to consult a dictionary.* **2** talk something over with a knowledgeable person: *to consult with one's lawyer.* **con·sul·ta·tion** *n.* **con·sult·a·tive** [kən'sʌltətɪv] *or* ['kɒnsəl,teɪtɪv] *adj.* ⟨Latin *consultare; consulere* take counsel, consult⟩ **con·sult·ant** *n* a professional hired to give informed advice: *a financial consultant.* **con·sul·tan·cy** *n.* **con·sult·ing** *adj* whose job is to give informed advice when asked: *a consulting editor.* **consulting room** the room in which a doctor or other professional sees clients.

SYNONYMS

One **consults** with another who is in a position to give wise advice: *He consulted with his stockbroker before investing.* **Confer** implies mutual exchange of ideas or information: *The manager conferred with her staff.*

---

con·sume [kən'sum] *or* [kən'sjum] *v* **1** eat or drink up. **2** use up: *A student consumes much time in studying.* **3** destroy; burn up. **4** absorb the attention of, to the exclusion of all else: *Model trains consume him.* **5** purchase (goods) for one's own consumption. **con·sum·er** *n.* ⟨Latin *com-* (intensive) + *sumere* take up⟩ **consumed with** completely absorbed by: *consumed with envy.*
con·sum·a·ble *adj* intended to be used up: *consumable supplies such as paper and glue.*
con·sum·a·ble *n.* **con·sum·er–friend·ly** *adj* easy for the consumer to use. **consumer goods** *Economics* goods that people use or consume to satisfy basic needs: *Food and clothing are two kinds of consumer goods.* Compare CAPITAL GOODS. **con·sum·er·ism** *n* **1** the theory that a continued increase in the consumption of goods is economically desirable for a society. **2** the setting of policy according to the interests of consumers. **3** a lifestyle in which buying and consuming goods is the prime interest. **consumer price index** a measure of the change in the cost of living in terms of increase or decrease in the price of selected goods. **con·sump·tion** [kən'sʌmpʃən] *n* **1** the act of consuming or the amount consumed. **2** *Obsolete* tuberculosis of the lungs.

con·sum·mate ['kɒnsə,meɪt] *v* **1** complete (marriage) by sexual intercourse. **2** fulfil: *to consummate a lifelong ambition.*
adj [kən'sʌmɪt] *or* ['kɒnsəmɪt] of the highest degree: *consummate skill, a consummate artist.* **con·sum·mate·ly** *adv.* **con·sum·ma·tion** *n.* ⟨Latin *consummare* bring to a peak; *com-* (intensive) + *summa* highest degree⟩

con·sump·tion, con·sump·tive See CONSUME.

con·tact ['kɒntækt] *n* **1** the condition of touching: *in contact with the skin.* **2** the state of being in communication: *to keep in contact with friends.* **3** a person with whom one can get in touch: *a useful contact.* **4** *Electricity* the connection between two conductors, through which a current passes. **5** **contacts** *pl Informal* contact lenses. **6** an anonymous liaison in a covert operation. **7** *Medicine* exposure to a contagious disease, or a person so exposed.
v **1** reach in order to communicate with: *Contact your doctor.* **2** touch. ⟨Latin *contactus* pp of *contingere; com-* with + *tangere* touch⟩
make contact (with) a manage to reach someone and communicate. **b** touch.
contact lens a lens worn directly over the pupil of the eye to correct defective vision.

con·ta·gion [kən'teɪdʒən] *n* **1** the spreading of disease by contact. **2** a spreading influence, esp one that is unpleasant: *A contagion of fear swept through the crowd.* ⟨Latin *contagio* a touching; *contingere.* See CONTACT.⟩
con·ta·gious *adj* **1** of a disease, communicable by direct contact. Compare INFECTIOUS. **2** carrying a communicable disease: *She is no longer contagious.* **3** easily spreading from one person to another: *Yawning is contagious.* **con·ta·gious·ly** *adv.*

con·tain [kən'teɪn] *v* **1** hold or be capable of holding within itself: *a jug containing one litre.* **2** control; keep within limits: *to contain one's anger, to use force to contain a rebellion.* **con·tain·a·ble** *adj.* **con·tain·ment** *n.* ⟨Latin *continere; com-* together + *tenere* hold⟩
con·tain·er *n* **1** something that contains, esp a box, jar, etc., used for storage or transport. **2** a very large, boxlike, standard-sized receptacle for cargo. **container car** a railway flatcar designed to carry CONTAINERS (def. 2). **container ship** a ship designed for the same purpose.

con·tam·i·nate [kən'tæmə,neɪt] *v* make impure by contact: *Flies can contaminate food.* **con·tam·i·na·tion** *n.* **con·tam·i·na·tive** *adj.* **con·tam·i·na·tor** *n.* ⟨Latin *contaminare; com-* with + *tag-*, root of *tangere* touch⟩
con·tam·i·nant *n* a thing that contaminates.

contd. continued.

con·tem·plate ['kɒntəm,pleɪt] *v* **1** think about for a long time. **2** look at for a long time. **3** consider as a possible course of action: *She contemplated going to Asia after graduation.* **con·tem·pla·tion** *n.* ⟨Latin *contemplari* survey; *com-* with + *templum* restricted area marked off for the taking of auguries⟩
con·tem·pla·tive [kən'templətɪv] *or* ['kɒntəm,pleɪtɪv] *adj* **1** thoughtful. **2** devoted to meditation and prayer. **con·tem·pla·tive·ly** *adv.*

con·tem·po·rar·y [kən'tɛmpə‚rɛri] *adj* **1** of today or of the era in question; current: *contemporary values*. **2** belonging to the same time period.
n a person belonging to the same time period: *Shakespeare and Ben Jonson were contemporaries*. **con·tem·po·ra·ne·i·ty** [kən‚tɛmpərə'niəti] *or* [-'neiəti] *n.* **con·tem·po·ra·ne·ous** *adj.* ⟨Latin *com-* together + *temporarius* of time⟩

con·tempt [kən'tɛmpt] *n* **1** the feeling that someone or something is worthless: *to feel contempt for a liar*. **2** *Law* disrespect for the decisions of a court. A person can be jailed for **contempt of court**. ⟨Latin *contemptus* from *contemnere; com* (intensive) + *temnere* disdain⟩ **con·tempt·i·ble** *adj* worthy of contempt: *a contemptible, cowardly act*. **con·tempt·i·bly** *adv.* **con·temp·tu·ous** *adj* showing contempt: *a contemptuous look*. **con·temp·tu·ous·ly** *adv.* **beneath contempt** worse than contemptible. **hold in contempt** feel contempt for; scorn; despise: *A traitor is held in contempt.*

con·tend [kən'tɛnd] *v* **1** struggle. **2** compete. **3** argue; maintain as fact despite opposition: *Columbus contended that the earth was round.* ⟨Latin *com-* (intensive) + *tendere* stretch⟩ **con·tend·er** *n* **1** a competitor, esp one to be taken seriously or whose chances are good. **2** one aspiring or hoping to achieve something. **con·ten·tion** *n* **1** a statement for which one has argued: *Columbus's contention that the earth was round proved to be true.* **2** argument; strife. **3** a struggle or contest. **con·ten·tious** *adj* **1** quarrelsome; habitually argumentative. **2** characterized by contention: *a contentious election.* **con·ten·tious·ly** *adv.*

con·tent¹ ['kɒntɛnt] *n* **1** Usually, **contents** *pl* what is contained in anything. **2** the ideas, artistic material, and so on contained in a book, speech, word, radio show, course, etc. ⟨Latin *contentum* pp of *continere*. See CONTAIN.⟩

con·tent² [kən'tɛnt] *v* **1** satisfy; please: *Nothing contents her; she is always complaining.* **2** limit (oneself) to (with *with*): *He contented himself with writing a letter to the editor.*
adj satisfied: *content with the outcome.*
n the feeling of being content; satisfaction. **con·tent·ed** *adj.* **con·tent·ed·ly** *adv.* ⟨Latin *contentus* satisfied, filled, pp of *continere*. See CONTAIN.⟩
to one's heart's content as much or as long as one wants: *When exams are over you'll be able to play tennis to your heart's content.* **con·tent·ment** *n* the fact of being content or satisfied, esp with one's lot in life.

con·ten·tion, con·ten·tious See CONTEND.

con·test ['kɒntɛst] *n* **1** a competition. **2** a struggle or argument.
v [kən'tɛst] **1** try to win. **2** struggle (for): *The soldiers contested every spot of ground.* **3** argue against; dispute: *to contest an insurance claim.* **con·test·a·ble** *adj.* ⟨Latin *contestari* call to witness; *com-* (intensive) + *testis* witness⟩ **con·test·ant** [kən'tɛstənt] *n* one who takes part in a competition.

con·text ['kɒntɛkst] *n* **1** the text in which a word, statement, etc. occurs and which helps determine its meaning: *to take a statement out of context.* **2** environment: *in today's political context.* **con·tex·tu·al** *adj.* **con·tex·tu·al·ly** *adv.* ⟨Latin *contextus* pp of *contexere; com-* together + *texere* weave⟩
con·tex·tu·al·ize *v* make more meaningful by adapting to a particular (cultural) context. **con·tex·tu·al·i·za·tion** *n.*

con·tig·u·ous [kən'tɪgjuəs] *adj* adjoining. **con·ti·gu·i·ty** [‚kɒntɪ'gjuti] *n.* ⟨Latin *contiguus; com-* with + *tag-*, root of *tangere* touch⟩

con·ti·nent¹ ['kɒntənənt] *n* any of the seven great masses of land on the earth, which include Asia, Africa, North America, South America, Europe, Australia, and Antarctica. ⟨Latin *continens*, short for *terra continens* land held together. See CONTINENT².⟩
con·ti·nen·tal *adj* **1** to do with a continent. **2 Continental** to do with mainland Europe or its cultures, etc. (as opposed to Britain). **Continental breakfast** a breakfast of muffins, rolls, etc. with coffee or tea and, sometimes, cheese, cold cuts, or spreads. **Continental Divide** a ridge in the Rockies which separates streams flowing toward the Pacific Ocean from those flowing toward the Atlantic or Arctic Oceans; Great Divide. **continental drift** *Geology* the theory that the continents move gradually over the surface of the earth. See also PLATE TECTONICS. **con·ti·nen·tal·ism** *n* ✱ a policy advocating union of the countries of a continent, esp the union of Canada and the US. **con·ti·nen·tal·ist** *n, adj.* **continental shelf** the submerged shelf of land that borders most continents.

con·ti·nent² ['kɒntənənt] *adj* **1** able to control one's bladder and bowel movements. **2** exercising self-control, esp sexually. **con·ti·nence** *n.* **con·ti·nent·ly** *adv.* ⟨Latin *continens* ppr of *continere*. See CONTAIN.⟩

con·tin·gent [kən'tɪndʒənt] *adj* **1** depending on something not certain: *contingent upon the weather.* **2** unexpected or accidental.
n a group coming or sent from a given place: *Canada is sending a contingent of peacekeepers to the region.* **con·tin·gent·ly** *adv.* ⟨Latin *contingere*. See CONTACT.⟩
con·tin·gen·cy *n* **1** the fact of being contingent. **2** a contingent thing or event, esp an unexpected emergency. **3** a thing that may accompany or arise from something else: *the contingencies of foreign travel.*

con·tin·ue [kən'tɪnju] *v* **1** carry on; keep being or doing: *Continue playing. It continued to rain. He has continued faithful to the end.* **2** begin again after stopping: *He ate lunch and then continued work.* **3** last: *Her reign continued for twenty years.* **4** extend in space: *to continue a road.* **5** cause to stay: *to continue a person in office.* **6** *Law* adjourn or postpone. ⟨Latin *continuare; continere*. See CONTAIN.⟩
con·tin·u·al *adj* happening again and again: *continual interference.* **con·tin·u·al·ly** *adv.* **con·tin·u·ance** *n Law* an adjournment or postponement. **con·tin·u·a·tion** *n* **1** the act or fact of continuing. **2** anything by which a thing is continued; an added part: *The next*

issue will carry a continuation of the story.
con·ti·nu·i·ty [ˌkɒntə'njuəti] *or* [ˌkɒntə'nuəti] *n* **1** the quality of being a connected whole: *The story lacks continuity.* **2** a detailed plan of the sequence of scenes in a film, comic strip, etc. **3** *Radio, television* comments connecting parts of a program. **con·tin·u·ous** *adj* without a break: *continuous rain.* **con·tin·u·ous·ly** *adv.* **con·tin·u·um** [kən'tɪnjuəm] *n, pl* **-tin·u·ums** or **-tin·u·a** [-'tɪnjuə] an unbroken whole or series; a gradual progression.

CONFUSABLES
Continual in most instances implies repetition with breaks in between: *Dancing requires continual practice.* **Continuous** means 'without interruption' and can apply to time or space: *a continuous procession of cars.*

con·tort [kən'tɔrt] *v* twist or bend out of the usual shape: *to contort one's face.* **con·tor·tion** *n.* ⟨Latin *contortus* pp of *contorquere; com-* (intensive) + *torquere* twist⟩
con·tor·tion·ist *n* a person who can twist or bend his or her body into odd positions.
con·tour ['kɒntur] *n* **1** the outline of a figure, land mass, body of water, etc. **2** Also, **contour line**, a line representing this, esp one on a map showing the outlines of hills, valleys, etc. at regular intervals above or below sea level. *adj* showing, following, or fitting the contours of something.
v shape to fit the contour of something: *bucket seats contoured to fit the body.* ⟨Latin *com-* with + *tornus* turning lathe; Greek *tornos*⟩
contour map a map showing elevation by means of a series of CONTOUR LINES.
con·tra ['kɒntrə] *n* an armed rebel in Latin America. ⟨Spanish *contrarrevolucionario*⟩
contra– *prefix* **1** in opposition; against: *contradistinction = distinction by opposition or contrast.* **2** *Music* lower in pitch: *contralto.* ⟨Latin *contra* against, adv, prep.⟩
con·tra·band ['kɒntrə,bænd] *n* **1** goods that may not legally be imported or exported: *The plumage of endangered species of birds, such as the ostrich or egret, is contraband in Canada.* **2** smuggled goods. ⟨Italian *contrabando;* Latin *contra-* against + *bandum* ban⟩
con·tra·cep·tion [ˌkɒntrə'sepʃən] *n* the intentional prevention of conception. ⟨CONTRA- + (con)ception⟩
con·tra·cep·tive *n* a substance or device for preventing pregnancy.
con·tract [kən'trækt] *v* **1** make or become narrower or shorter: *Rubber stretches and then contracts again.* **2** *Grammar* shorten (a word, etc.) by omitting some letters or sounds. **3** form: *to contract a bad habit.* **4** catch (a disease): *She contracted malaria.* **5** *Anatomy* draw together (muscle fibre) to move a part of the body. **6** ['kɒntrækt] *or* [kən'trækt] enter into a legal agreement (with): *Her company has contracted to build the library.*
n ['kɒntrækt] an agreement, esp a written legal agreement. **con·tract·i·ble** *adj.* ⟨Latin *contractus* from *contrahere; com-* together + *trahere* draw⟩

contract out subcontract.
contract bridge a version of bridge in which the highest bidder can score only as many points as he or she orig bid. **con·trac·tile** [kən'træktaɪl] *or* [kən'træktəl] *adj* capable of contracting: *Muscle is contractile tissue.* **con·trac·til·i·ty** *n.* **con·trac·tion** *n* **1** the act or fact of contracting. **2** a contracted form of a word or words, such as *ne'er* or *wouldn't.* **3** a single episode of contracting the muscles of the uterus during childbirth. **con·trac·tor** ['kɒntræktər] *or* [kən'træktər] *n* a person who agrees to do a piece of work for a certain price. **con·trac·tu·al** [kən'træktʃuəl] *adj* to do with a contract. **con·trac·tu·al·ly** *adv.*
con·tra·dict [ˌkɒntrə'dɪkt] *v* express the opposite of (a statement). **con·tra·dic·tion** *n.* **con·tra·dic·to·ry** *adj.* ⟨Latin *contradictus* pp of *contradicere; contra* against + *dicere* say⟩
con·tra·dis·tinc·tion [ˌkɒntrədɪ'stɪŋkʃən] *n* a distinction made by opposition or contrast.
con·tra–in·di·cate [ˌkɒntrə 'ɪndə,keit] *v* *Medicine* make or declare unsafe or unwise (usually in the passive): *This medication is contra-indicated for asthmatics.*
con·tral·to [kən'træltou] *n* the lowest female singing voice. ⟨contra- + alto⟩
con·trap·tion [kən'træpʃən] *n* *Informal,* jocular device; gadget. ⟨possibly from *contrive*⟩
con·tra·pun·tal See COUNTERPOINT.
con·tra·ry ['kɒntreri] *adj* **1** opposed; being or meaning the opposite: *contrary to popular opinion.* **2** [kən'treri] stubborn; perverse.
n **1** the opposite: *What she has just told us is the contrary of what we heard yesterday.* **2** *Logic* either of two propositions so linked that only one may be true although both may be false. **con·tra·ri·ly** *adv.* **con·tra·ri·ness** *n.* ⟨Latin *contrarius; contra* against⟩
on the contrary exactly opposite to that: *He didn't go straight home; on the contrary, he stopped at three different stores.* **to the contrary** with the opposite effect or meaning.
con·tra·ri·wise ['kɒntreri,waɪz] *adv* **1** in the opposite way or direction. **2** on the contrary.
con·trast ['kɒntræst] *n* a great difference; opposition in character: *the contrast between black and white.*
v [kən'træst] **1** compare (two things) so as to show their differences: *to contrast the climate of the Mackenzie Valley and that of the Ottawa Valley.* **2** form a contrast (with): *The stiff language of her speeches contrasts oddly with the naturalness of her letters.* **con·trast·a·ble** *adj.* **con·trast·ing·ly** *adv.* **con·trast·ive** *adj.* ⟨Latin *contrastare; contra-* against + *stare* stand⟩
con·tra·vene [ˌkɒntrə'vin] *v* **1** conflict with; oppose. **2** violate; infringe: *to contravene a law.* **con·tra·ven·er** *n.* **con·tra·ven·tion** *n.* ⟨Latin *contra-* against + *venire* come⟩
con·tre·temps ['kɒntrə,tã] *n, pl* **-temps** [-,tãz] *French* [kɔ̃trəˈtã] **1** an unfortunate accident. **2** a disagreement; quarrel. ⟨Old French *contrestant* ppr of *contrester* oppose⟩
con·trib·ute [kən'trɪbjut] *v* **1** give (money, help, etc.) along with others. **2** help to bring

about (with *to*): *Poor nutrition contributed to the child's illness.* **3** write for a newspaper or magazine. **con·tri·bu·tion** *n*. **con·trib·ut·ing** *adj*. **con·trib·u·tor** *n*. **con·trib·u·to·ry** *n*. ⟨Latin *com-* with + *tribuere* bestow, assign, orig divide among the tribes; *tribus* tribe⟩

con·trite ['kɒntrəit] *or* [kən'trəit] *adj* feeling or showing deep regret and sorrow: *contrite words.* **con·trite·ly** *adv*. **con·tri·tion** *n*. ⟨Latin *contritus* pp of *conterere* crush; *com-* (intensive) + *terere* rub, grind⟩

con·trive [kən'traɪv] *v* **1** invent: *to contrive a new kind of engine.* **2** plot: *to contrive a robbery.* **3** manage: *I will contrive to be there by ten o'clock.* ⟨Old French *controver; trover* find⟩ **con·triv·ance** *n* **1** the act or fact of contriving. **2** device; invention. **con·trived** *adj* seeming artificial or unnatural; lame.

con·trol [kən'troul] *n* **1** power over things or people; the ability or authority to make them act in certain ways. **2** restraint: *great control in not losing one's temper.* **3** the act, fact, or means of regulating or checking: *birth control. The new bank policy is a control against inflation.* **4** a device that regulates the working of a machine: *The control for our furnace is in the front hall.* **5** **controls** *pl* the instruments and devices by which a car, aircraft, etc., is operated. **6** a standard of comparison for testing results of a scientific experiment.
v **-trolled, -trol·ling** have or exercise control over; direct, operate, restrain, or regulate. **con·trol·la·ble** *adj*. **con·trolled** *adj*. ⟨French *contrôle*, Old French *contrerolle* register; *contre* against + *rolle* roll⟩ **controlled substance** a drug whose sale and possession is illegal or restricted. **con·trol·ler** *n* **1** a manager who oversees financial affairs. Also, **comp·trol·ler** [kən'troulər]. **2** a person who directs or regulates: *air traffic controller.* **3** *Computers* a device that controls one or more peripheral devices and connects them to a computer. **con·trol·ler·ship** *n*. **control panel** a panel containing all the instruments necessary for the operation of a complex machine. **control room** a room containing all the instruments necessary to control a complex operation, such as the launching of a rocket. **control tower** at an airfield, the building from which takeoff and landing of aircraft is controlled.

con·tro·ver·sy ['kɒntrə,vɜrsi] *n* argument, esp long, significant, or involving many people: *Her new movie has generated a lot of controversy.* ⟨Latin *contro-* against + *versus* pp of *vertere* turn⟩ **con·tro·ver·sial** [,kɒntrə'vɜrʃəl] *or* [-'vɜrsiəl] *adj* **1** of, open to, or arousing controversy: *a controversial question.* **2** fond of controversy. **con·tro·ver·sial·ly** *adv*. **con·tro·ver·sial·ist** *n*. **con·tro·vert** [,kɒntrə'vɜrt] *or* ['kɒntrə,vɜrt] *v* **1** dispute; oppose: *The statement of the last witness controverts previous evidence.* **2** debate. **con·tro·vert·i·ble** *adj* debatable.

con·tu·ma·cy ['kɒntʃəməsi] *or* ['kɒntəməsi] *n*

obstinate disobedience. **con·tu·ma·cious** *adj*. ⟨Latin *contumax* insolent; *tumere* swell up⟩

con·tu·sion [kən'tjuʒən] *or* [kən'tuʒən] *n* a bruise. ⟨Latin *contusus* pp of *contundere; com-* (intensive) + *tundere* pound⟩

co·nun·drum [kə'nʌndrəm] *n* **1** a riddle. **2** any puzzling problem. ⟨origin unknown⟩

con·ur·ba·tion [,kɒnər'beiʃən] *n* a number of urban communities so close together that they can be regarded as one large community. ⟨*con-* together + *urb(an)*⟩

con·va·lesce [,kɒnvə'lɛs] *v* regain strength after illness or injury. **con·va·les·cence** *n*. **con·va·les·cent** *adj, n*. ⟨Latin *com-* (intensive) + *valescere* grow strong; *valere* be strong⟩

con·vec·tion [kən'vɛkʃən] *n* *Physics* the transfer of heat by the circulation of heated particles of a gas or liquid. **con·vec·tion·al** *adj*. ⟨Latin *convectio* from *convehere; com-* together + *vehere* carry⟩ **convection oven** a small, portable oven in which a fan circulates the hot air to keep the temperature even.

con·vene [kən'vin] *v* come or call together for a meeting: *Parliament convenes in Ottawa.* **con·ven·or** *or* **con·ven·er** *n*. ⟨Latin *com-* together + *venire* come⟩

con·ven·tion [kən'vɛnʃən] *n* **1** a formal gathering; meeting: *a convention of a political party to elect a leader.* **2** a formal agreement. A convention between nations is less formal than a treaty. **3** a custom approved by general agreement: *Using the right hand to shake hands is a convention.* **4** such customs collectively or the means by which they are established. **con·ven·tion·al** *adj* **1** existing by convention; customary. **2** ordinary or traditional. **3** of weapons, etc., not nuclear or biological. **con·ven·tion·al·ly** *adv*. **con·ven·tion·al·i·ty** *n*. **con·ven·tion·al·ism** *n* **1** a tendency to follow convention. **2** something conventional. **con·ven·tion·al·ist** *n*. **con·ven·tion·al·ize** *v*. **conventional wisdom** common popular belief. **con·ven·tion·eer** *n* attendee at a convention.

con·ven·ient [kən'vinjənt] *adj* **1** saving trouble: *a convenient tool.* **2** not troublesome; easy to do: *Would it be convenient for you to deliver it today?* **3** within easy reach; handy: *convenient to mall and library.* **con·ven·ient·ly** *adv*. ⟨Latin *conveniens* ppr of *convenire* meet, agree, be suitable. See CONVENE.⟩

con·ven·ience *n* **1** the fact or quality of being convenient: *the convenience of frozen foods.* **2** anything easy to use or making life easier. **3** Often, **conveniences** *pl* washroom. **at one's convenience** so as to suit one. **at one's earliest convenience** as soon as one can conveniently do so. **marriage of convenience** a marriage undertaken only to gain citizenship or other benefit. **convenience store** a small store open every day until late evening or 24 hours a day, selling basic food and household items.

con·vent ['kɒnvɛnt] *or* ['kɒnvənt] *n* **1** a community of nuns. **2** the buildings in which they live. ⟨Latin *conventus* assembly; *convenire*. See CONVENE.⟩

con·ven·tion See CONVENE.

con·verge [kən'vɜrdʒ] *v* **1** meet or tend to meet in a point: *The two roads converge just before the bridge.* **2** come together: *Tourists converge on this resort town every summer.* **3** become more alike. Compare DIVERGE. **con·ver·gence** *n.* **con·ver·gent** *adj.* ⟨Latin *com-* together + *vergere* incline⟩

con·verse¹ [kən'vɜrs] *v* talk informally together. **con·vers·er** *n.* **con·ver·sa·tion** *n.* **con·ver·sa·tion·al** *adj.* **con·ver·sa·tion·al·ly** *adv.* ⟨Latin *conversari* live with; *com-* with + *versari* live, be busy⟩
make conversation talk with someone fairly superficially in order to be polite.
con·ver·sant [kən'vɜrsənt] *adj* familiar by use or study: *conversant with modern cinema.* **con·ver·sa·tion·al·ist** *n* **1** a person with reference to his or her skill in making conversation. **2** a participant in a conversation. **conversation piece** an object which attracts comment by its unusual nature. **con·verse** ['kɒnvɜrs] *n* *Formal* contact; intercourse; exchange.

con·verse² ['kɒnvɜrs] *adj* **1** opposite; contrary. **2** reversed in order. **con·verse** *n.* **con·verse·ly** [kən'vɜrsli] *adv.* ⟨Latin *conversus* pp of *convertere.* See CONVERT.⟩

con·vert [kən'vɜrt] *v* **1** change: *to convert pulp into paper.* **2** change or cause to change from one religion, political party, etc., to another. **3** take and use unlawfully: *to convert public monies for one's own use.* **4** *Football* kick for an extra point after a touchdown.
n ['kɒnvɜrt] **1** a person who has been converted. **2** ✱ *Football* an extra point kicked after a touchdown. **con·ver·sion** *n.* **con·vert·i·ble** *adj.* **con·vert·i·bil·i·ty** *n.* ⟨Latin *com-* (intensive) + *vertere* turn⟩
con·vert·er *n* **1** a device for changing electrical current from alternating to direct. **2** a device for adapting a television set to receive more channels. **con·vert·i·ble** *n* a car with a roof that may be folded down.

con·vex [kɒn'vɛks] *or* ['kɒnvɛks] *adj* curved out, like the outside of a sphere. **con·vex·ly** *adv.* **con·vex·i·ty** *n.* ⟨Latin *convexus* vaulted⟩

con·vey [kən'vei] *v* **1** carry from one place or person to another: *to convey passengers, to convey a message. A wire conveys electric current.* **2** communicate: *Her words convey nothing at all.* **3** *Law* transfer ownership of (property) from one person to another. ⟨Old French *conveier;* Latin *com-* with + *via* road⟩
con·vey·ance *n* **1** the act or fact of conveying. **2** a vehicle. **con·vey·anc·er** *n* a lawyer who prepares contracts, deeds, etc., for transfer of property. **con·vey·anc·ing** *n.* **con·vey·or** *n* **1** a person or thing that conveys. **2** Usually, **conveyor belt** a moving endless belt on which things are carried.

con·vict [kən'vɪkt] *v* declare guilty: *The jury convicted the prisoner of murder.*
n ['kɒnvɪkt] a person found guilty of, or serving a prison sentence for, a crime. ⟨Latin *convictus* pp of *convincere.* See CONVINCE.⟩
con·vic·tion *n* **1** the act or fact of convicting. **2** the appearance or state of being convinced:

She spoke with conviction. **3** a firm belief: *Stand by your convictions.*

con·vince [kən'vɪns] *v* persuade by argument. **con·vin·ci·ble** *adj.* **con·vinc·ing** *adj.* ⟨Latin *com-* (intensive) + *vincere* overcome⟩

> **USAGE**
> **Convince,** in formal English, is always followed by *of* plus a noun or by a *that*-clause: *He convinced me of his innocence. You will soon be convinced that I am right.* The construction *convince someone to do something* is informal.

con·viv·i·al [kən'vɪviəl] *adj* **1** fond of eating and drinking with friends. **2** festive. **con·viv·i·al·i·ty** *n.* **con·viv·i·al·ly** *adv.* ⟨Latin *convivium* feast; *com-* with + *vivere* live⟩

con·vo·ca·tion [ˌkɒnvə'keiʃən] *n* **1** at some universities, a ceremony at which degrees are conferred. **2** at other universities, the officials and graduates as a legislative, advisory, or electoral body. **3** a group gathered in answer to a formal summons. **con·vo·ca·tion·al** *adj.*

con·vo·lut·ed [ˌkɒnvə'lut] *adj* **1** complicated and unclear: *a convoluted style, a convoluted theory.* **2** coiled; twisted. ⟨Latin *convolutus* pp of *convolvere; com-* together + *volvere* roll⟩
con·vo·lu·tion *n* **1** convoluted character; convolutedness. **2** a coil; twist. **3** *Anatomy* an irregular fold on the surface of the brain.

con·voy ['kɒnvɔi] *n* **1** a ship, fleet, vehicle, guard, etc. accompanying a person or group for protection. **2** the protection of an escort: *The gold was moved under convoy of armed guards.* **3** the ship, supplies, etc., together with the protecting escort. **con·voy** *v.* ⟨Old French *convoier, conveier.* See CONVEY.⟩

con·vulse [kən'vʌls] *v* **1** shake or cause to shake violently: *An earthquake convulsed the island.* **2** throw into a fit of laughter: *The clown convulsed the audience.* ⟨Latin *convulsus* pp of *convellere; com-* (intensive) + *vellere* tear⟩
con·vul·sion *n* **1** Often, **convulsions** *pl* violent movement due to muscle spasm. **2** a fit of laughter. **3** the act or fact of convulsing. **con·vul·sive** *adj* sudden, violent, etc., like a convulsion: *The dog made convulsive efforts to free itself from the chain.* **con·vul·sive·ly** *adv.*

co·ny *or* **co·ney** ['kouni] *n* **1** rabbit. **2** pika. **3** a fish of the grouper family, native to tropical Atlantic waters. ⟨Middle English *coni;* Latin *cuniculus* rabbit⟩

cook [kʊk] *v* **1** prepare (food) for eating by applying heat, as in boiling, frying, baking, etc. **2** *Informal* be very hot: *I am just cooking in this coat!* **3** *Informal* tamper with (accounts, etc.): *cooking the company's books.*
n a person who cooks food. ⟨Old English *cōc;* Latin *coquus*⟩
cook someone's goose See GOOSE.
cook up *Informal* **a** cook (food). **b** prepare falsely: *to cook up a story.* **what's cooking?** *Slang* what's happening?
cook·book *n* book of recipes. **cook·er** *n* an apparatus to cook food in. **cook·er·y** *n* **1** the art of cooking food. **2** ✱ a cookhouse. **cook·house** *n* a building for preparing meals, esp in a large camp. **cook–off** *n* a cooking

competition. **cook·out** *n* a social event consisting of cooking and eating a meal outdoors. **cook·stove** *n* a stove for cooking. **cook·ware** *n* pots, pans, etc.

cook·ie ['kʊki] *n* **1** a small, sweet, crisp cake. **2** *Computers* a small amount of data sent to a client computer by a server and stored there to facilitate future transactions. It is client-specific. ⟨Dutch *koekje* little cake⟩ **smart cookie** *Slang* a clever person.

cool [kul] *adj* **1** somewhat cold. **2** giving a cool feeling: *cool clothes.* **3** not excited; calm. **4** showing little enthusiasm or friendliness. **5** *Slang* excellent. **6** of colours such as blue and green, calming; suggesting coolness. **7** without exaggeration or qualification: *a cool million.* **8** *Informal* mellow; restrained in a sophisticated way.
n **1** a cool place or time: *the cool of the evening.* **2** *Slang* self-control: *Keep your cool.* **cool** *v.*
cool·ly *adv.* **cool·ness** *n.* ⟨Old English *cōl*⟩
cool down or **off** make or become cooler. **cool it** *Slang* calm down. **cool one's heels** be kept waiting for a long time. **stay** or **keep cool** *Slang* keep calm.
cool·ant *n* a substance that cools, esp in machinery. **cool·er** *n* **1** an apparatus that keeps food and drink cool. **2** *Slang* a jail. **3** a drink containing a small amount of wine or other alcohol. **cool·ish** *adj* somewhat cool.

coo·lie ['kuli] *n* an unskilled labourer in parts of Asia, esp a porter. ⟨probably Tamil *kuli* hire, hired servant⟩

coon [kun] *n Informal* raccoon.
coon·skin *n* the skin of a raccoon, used in making caps, coats, etc.

coop [kup] *n* **1** a small cage for chickens. **2** *Slang* jail.
v confine, esp in a very small space (usually with *up*): *cooped up indoors.* ⟨Middle English *cupe* basket; Latin *cupa* cask⟩
fly the coop *Slang* escape.

co–op·er·ate [kou 'ɒpə,reit] *v* work together. **co–op·er·a·tor** *n.* **co–op·er·a·tion** *n.* ⟨Latin *co-* together + *operari* to work⟩
co–op ['kou ,ɒp] *n, adj Informal* co-operative. **co–op·er·a·tive** or **co·op·er·a·tive** [kou'ɒpərətɪv] or [-'ɒpə,reitɪv] *adj* **1** wanting or willing to work together with others. **2** to do with a co-operative. (See *n.*) **3** to do with a program in which students work at jobs related to their studies for academic credit instead of pay.
n an enterprise jointly owned and operated by those who use its services or product. **co–op·er·a·tive·ly** *adv.* **co–op·er·a·tive·ness** *n.*
Co–operative Commonwealth Federation a Canadian political party, the CCF, founded in 1932. See also NEW DEMOCRATIC PARTY. **co–operative federalism** a system in which constituent members of a federation, such as provinces in Canada, can vote to accept or reject a federal suggestion.

co–opt [kou 'ɒpt] *v* **1** manage to bring into one's own system, culture, side in a dispute, etc.; take over. **2** of a committee, etc., add (a new member) by group decision. **co–op·tion** *n.* ⟨Latin *co-* with + *optare* to choose⟩

co–or·di·nate or **co·or·di·nate** [kou'ɔrdə,neit] *v* **1** arrange (various elements) in proper order or relation for smooth operation; orchestrate: *to co-ordinate one's arm and leg movements in swimming, to co-ordinate speakers and facilities for a conference.* **2** bring together things of equal importance or rank. **3** *Chemistry* unite in a co-ordinate bond.
adj [kou 'ɔrdənɪt] **1** equal in importance or rank. **2** matching. **3** *Chemistry* of a bond in which one atom shares two electrons with another.
n [kou 'ɔrdənɪt] **1** **co–ordinates** *pl* a matching items of clothing, luggage, furniture, etc. **b** a pair of references, such as latitude and longitude, which fixes a position on a map. **2** *Mathematics* Usually, **coordinate**, any of two or more magnitudes that define the position of a point, line, or plane by reference to a system of lines, etc. **co–or·di·nate·ly** *adv.* **co–or·di·na·tion** or **co·or·di·na·tion** *n.* **co–or·di·na·tive** *adj.* **co–or·di·na·tor** *n.* ⟨*co-* with + Latin *ordinare* regulate; *ordo* rank, order⟩
coordinate geometry the use of algebra and coordinates to solve problems. **co–ordinating conjunction** *Grammar* a conjunction used to join clauses of equal importance.

coot [kut] *n* **1** any of a genus of marsh birds of the rail family, resembling ducks but with toes having scalloplike lobes of skin along the sides. **2** *Informal* a foolish or simple person. ⟨perhaps Dutch *koet*⟩

coot·ie ['kuti] *n Slang* louse. ⟨Malay *kutu* tick⟩

cop [kɒp] *n Slang* a police officer.
v **copped, cop·ping** **1** *Slang* steal. **2** capture; seize; nab. ⟨Old English *coppian*⟩
cop a plea plead guilty to one charge in order to avoid a more serious one.
cop out *Slang* **a** evade an issue. **b** confess to a crime by implicating others. **cop–out** *n.*

co·pa·cet·ic [,koupə'setɪk] *adj Slang* satisfactory. ⟨origin unknown⟩

cope [koup] *v* deal successfully (*with* things): *He said he just couldn't cope any more.* ⟨Old French *coper* strike; *coup.* See COUP.⟩

Co·per·ni·can [kə'pɜrnəkən] *adj* to do with the system of astronomy first articulated by Nikolaus Copernicus (1473-1543), a Polish astronomer, in which the earth revolves on its axis and the planets orbit around the sun.

cop·i·er See COPY.

co–pi·lot ['kou ,paɪlət] *n* the assistant or second pilot in an aircraft.

cop·ing ['koupɪŋ] *n* the top layer of a brick or stone wall. ⟨Latin *cappa* hood; *caput* head⟩ **cope·stone** *n* **1** the top stone of a wall **2** a finishing touch. **coping saw** a saw with a narrow blade set in a U-shaped frame, used to cut curves in wood. Compare FRET SAW.

co·pi·ous ['koupiəs] *adj* **1** plentiful: *copious rainfall.* **2** containing or providing much. **co·pi·ous·ly** *adv.* **co·pi·ous·ness** *n.* ⟨Latin *copis* well-supplied; *co-* with + *ops* resources⟩

co·pla·nar [kou'pleinər] *adj Mathematics* (of points, lines, figures) lying in the same plane.

cop·per¹ [ˈkɒpər] *n* **1** a reddish brown metallic element, easily shaped and resistant to rust. *Symbol* **Cu 2** a copper or bronze coin, esp a penny. **cop·per·y** *adj.* ⟨Latin *cuprum; aes Cyprium* metal of Cyprus⟩

cop·per·head *n* a poisonous snake of the eastern and central US having a copper-coloured head. **Copper Inuit** a group of Inuit living along the Arctic coast near the Coppermine River. **cop·per·plate** *n* **1** a thin piece of copper on which a design, writing, etc. is engraved. **2** a style of elegant handwriting. **cop·per·smith** *n* a person who makes things out of copper. **copper sulphate** or **sulfate** a sulphate of copper used chiefly in dyeing, electroplating, and as a fungicide.

cop·per² [ˈkɒpər] *n Slang* a police officer. ⟨*cop*⟩

cop·ra [ˈkɒprə] *or* [ˈkouprə] *n* the dried meat of ripe coconuts. ⟨Malayalam *koppara*⟩

copse [kɒps] *n* a thicket of small trees, bushes, shrubs, etc. ⟨Old French *copeiz* cutover forest; *couper* cut⟩

Copt [kɒpt] *n* **1** a native of Egypt descended from the ancient Egyptians. **2** a member of the Coptic Church. ⟨Arabic *Quft, Qubt*⟩ **Cop·tic** *adj* to do with the Copts. *n* the language formerly spoken by the Copts. **Coptic Church** the national Christian church of Egypt and of Ethiopia.

cop·u·la [ˈkɒpjələ] *n, pl* **-las** or **-lae** [-ˌli] *or* [-ˌlaɪ] **1** *Logic* the word or words connecting the subject and predicate in a proposition. In *the sky is blue, is* is the copula, *sky* is the subject, and *blue* is the predicate. **2** *Grammar* any of the verbs that perform this function, such as *be, become, seem,* etc. **3** anything serving to connect or link. **cop·u·lar** *adj.* ⟨Latin = bond⟩ **cop·u·late** *v* of humans or animals, be united sexually. **cop·u·la·tion** *n.* **cop·u·la·tive** *adj* **1** serving to connect. **2** *Grammar* serving to connect words or clauses of equal rank.

cop·y [ˈkɒpi] *n* **1** anything made to be just like another. **2** one of a number of books, pictures, etc., made at one printing: *The store has 10 copies of her novel in stock.* **3** text to be set in type for a newspaper, magazine, etc. **4** *Journalism Informal* source of material for an article: *She's always good copy.* *v* **1** make a copy of: *Copy this page.* **2** imitate. **3** steal ideas from (someone) and pass them off as one's own; plagiarize. ⟨Old French *copier;* Latin *copia* plenty. See COPIOUS.⟩ **cop·i·er** *n* **1** a machine that makes copies, esp of text or images. **2** a person who copies; imitator. **cop·y·book** *n Archaic* a book with models of handwriting to be copied in learning to write. *adj* conventional; ordinary: *a copybook speech.* **a blot on one's copybook** a serious error. **co·py·cat** *n* one who irritatingly imitates others in dress, behaviour, etc. **copy editor** a person who edits texts for grammar, style, etc. as opposed to content. **cop·y–ed·it** *v.* **copy–pro·tect** *Computers* program (software) so as to prevent unauthorized creation of usable copies. **copy protection. cop·y·read·er** *n* a person who reads and edits copy for a newspaper. **cop·y·right** *n* the exclusive right to copy, print, or publish a work, granted by law to an author, composer, artist, etc. for a certain number of years. *v* protect by getting a copyright: *Books, songs, plays, etc., are usually copyrighted. adj* protected in this way: *You can't reprint copyright material.* **cop·y·writ·er** *n* a person whose job is writing advertisements and other publicity material.

SYNONYMS

Copy can mean 'follow a model as closely as possible': *She copied the picture on the wall.* **Imitate** suggests doing something in the same style as that used in a model: *Sometimes a teacher asks a class to imitate a piece written by a great author.*

co·quette [kouˈkɛt] *n* a woman who is a flirt. **co·quet·ry** [ˈkoukətri] *n.* **co·quet·tish** *adj.* ⟨French, fem. diminutive of *coq* rooster⟩

cor·a·cle [ˈkɔrəkəl] *n* a small, light, bowl-shaped boat, orig covered with hide. ⟨Welsh *corwgl; corwg* round body or vessel⟩

cor·al [ˈkɔrəl] *n* any of various marine polyps living in colonies and having a stony or leathery external or internal skeleton. ⟨Greek *koral(l)ion*⟩ **coral reef** a reef consisting mainly of coral produced over centuries.

cor·bel [ˈkɔrbəl] *n Architecture* a bracket of stone, wood, etc., on a wall, supporting a ledge above it. **cor·beled** *adj.* ⟨Old French, diminutive of *corp* raven; Latin *corvus*⟩

cord [kɔrd] *n* **1** strong string made of several strands or fibres twisted together. **2** an insulated cable used to connect an electrical appliance to a source of power. **3** *Anatomy* a structure that resembles a cord: *spinal cord, vocal cords.* **4** anything that binds like a cord: *cords of affection.* **5 a** corduroy. **b** cords *pl* corduroy pants. **6** a unit for measuring cut firewood. A **standard cord** measures 8 feet long by 4 feet high by 4 feet deep (about 2.4 m × 1.2 m × 1.2 m). A **face cord** is only 12 to 18 inches (about 30 to 45 cm) deep. ⟨Old French *corde;* Greek *chordē* gut⟩ **cord·age** *n* **1** cords; ropes. **2** the quantity of wood as measured in cords. **cord·less** *adj* of electrical devices, battery-operated and not needing to be plugged into an outlet: *cordless telephone.* **cord·wood** *n* wood measured in cords and suitable for use as firewood.

cor·di·al [ˈkɔrdiəl] *or* [ˈkɔrdʒəl] *adj* **1** friendly: *a very cordial welcome.* **2** heartfelt; sincere: *a cordial dislike.* *n* **1** a drink or medicine meant to strengthen or stimulate. **2** fruit liqueur. **cor·di·al·i·ty** *n.* **cor·di·al·ly** *adv.* ⟨Latin *cordialis; cor* heart⟩

cor·dil·le·ra [kɔrˈdɪlərə] *or* [ˌkɔrdəˈlɛrə] *n* **1** a long mountain range, esp the main mountain system of a given continent. **2 the Cordilleras** the mountain system of N and S America, extending from Alaska to Cape Horn. **Cor·dil·le·ran** *adj.* ⟨Spanish. See CORD.⟩

cor·don [ˈkɔrdən] *n* **1** a line of soldiers, police, ships, etc., around an area to guard it. **2** a rope having the same function. **3** a cord,

braid, or ribbon worn as a badge of honour.
v put a protective line or barrier around (with *off*): *The area around the famous painting was cordoned off.* ⟨French, from *corde* cord⟩

cor·don bleu ['kɔrdɔ̃ 'blʊ] *French* [kɔrdɔ̃'blø] **1** a high honour. **2** a chef skilled in fine French cuisine. **3** this type of cuisine. ⟨French = blue ribbon; the highest order of French knights wore it as a badge⟩

cor·du·roy ['kɔrdə,rɔɪ] **1** cloth with a thick, velvetlike pile in ridges. **2 corduroys** *pl* corduroy pants. ⟨*cord* + obsolete *duroy,* a woollen cloth⟩
corduroy bridge ✱ a bridge with a surface of logs laid crosswise. **corduroy road** ✱ a road similarly surfaced, usually across wet land.

core [kɔr] *n* **1** the central part of some fruits, such as apples, containing the seeds. **2** the central or essential part of anything. **3** the central part of the earth, beginning at a depth of about 2880 km and having a radius of about 3400 km. **4** *Electricity* the centre of an electromagnet, induction coil, etc. **5** the area in the centre of a nuclear reactor where the reaction takes place.
v take out the core of: *to core apples.* **cor·er** *n.* ⟨Middle English; origin uncertain⟩

co·ri·an·der [,kɔri'ændər] *or* ['kɔri,ændər] *n* a herb of the parsley family, with tiny, seedlike fruits. ⟨Greek *koriandron*⟩

Co·ri·o·lis force [,kɔri'oulɪs] the force, resulting from Earth's rotation, that causes a moving body on or above the earth's surface to drift from its course, to the right north of the equator and to the left south of it. ⟨G.G. de *Coriolis* 19c French mathematician⟩

cork [kɔrk] *n* **1** the bark of the CORK OAK, used to make bottle stoppers, notice boards, etc. **2** a bottle stopper made of this or of a synthetic material. **3** the layers of dead tissue in the outer bark of a woody plant.
v stop up with a cork. **cork·y** *adj.* ⟨Latin *quercus* oak⟩
blow one's cork *Informal* explode with rage. **cork·board** *n* **1** material in sheets, made of small bits of cork pressed together. **2** a notice board made of this. **corked** *adj* **1** of wine, having the flavour adversely affected by the cork having too much tannin in it. **2** *Slang* drunk. **cork oak** a Mediterranean evergreen oak, the source of cork. **cork·screw** *n* a tool with a screw, or spiral, for pulling corks out of bottles. *v* spiral or zigzag.

corm [kɔrm] *n* *Botany* a fleshy, bulblike underground stem such as that of the gladiolus, with leaves and buds on the upper surface and roots on the lower. ⟨Greek *kormos* stripped tree trunk; *keirein* shear⟩

cor·mo·rant ['kɔrmərənt] *n* any of a family of large mainly black sea birds having an often brightly-coloured pouch of skin under the mouth. ⟨Old French *cormaran; corp* raven (Latin *corvus*) + *marenc* marine (Latin *mare*)⟩

corn¹ [kɔrn] *n* **1** a tall cereal plant whose kernels grow in rows along a thick, woody axis called a cob. **2** any small, hard seed, esp of cereal plants. **3** *Slang* anything trite or sentimental.
v preserve (meat) with salt. ⟨Old English⟩
corn·ball *Slang adj* corny: *cornball humour. n* an unsophisticated person. **corn bread** a bread made of cornmeal instead of flour. **corn broom** a broom made of corn straw. **corn chip** a chip similar to a potato chip, but made out of cornflour. **corn·cob** *n* **1** the central part of an ear of corn. **2** a tobacco pipe with a bowl hollowed out of a piece of dried corncob. **corn·crib** *n* a bin for storing unshelled corn. **corn dog** *Informal* a wiener dipped in cornmeal batter and deep fried, usually on a stick. **corned** *adj* preserved with salt: *corned beef.* **corn·fed** *adj* **1** of an animal, fed on corn or other grain. **2** *Informal* robust, plump, and rustic: *a cornfed country lass.* **corn·field** *n* a field of growing corn. **corn·flour** *n* flour made from corn rather than wheat. **corn·flow·er** *n* an annual plant with bright blue, pink, or white flowers. **corn·husk** *n* the husk of an ear of corn. **corn·meal** *n* meal made from ground corn. **corn pone** in the S United States, a flat loaf of cornmeal shaped by hand. **corn roast** a picnic at which corn is eaten off the cob. **corn silk** the long, glossy threads that grow from the tip of an ear of corn. **corn smut** a disease of corn characterized by black nodes. **corn snow** snow consisting of granular particles suggesting cornmeal. **corn·stalk** *n* the stalk of a corn plant. **corn·starch** *n* a starchy flour made from corn, used to thicken puddings, sauces, etc. **corn syrup** syrup made from corn. **corn·y** *adj Informal* sentimental, trite, or unsophisticated: *corny jokes.*

corn² [kɔrn] *n* a painful calluslike formation, usually on a toe. ⟨Latin *cornu* horn⟩

cor·ne·a ['kɔrniə] *n* the transparent part of the outer coat of the eyeball. **cor·ne·al** *adj.* ⟨Latin *cornea (tela)* horny (web). See CORN².⟩

cor·ner ['kɔrnər] *n* **1** the place where lines or surfaces meet: *A diagonal joins two opposite corners of a rectangle.* **2** the place where two streets meet. **3** an awkward situation from which there is no escape: *a tight corner.* **4** a monopoly: *a corner on truth.*
v **1** force into a corner. **2** *Business* buy up all that can be had of (something) to raise its price: *Speculators have tried to corner wheat.* **3** of an automobile, round corners at fairly high speed: *It corners well.* ⟨Old French *cornere;* Latin *cornu* horn; pointed tip⟩
cut corners save money, effort, etc., at the expense of quality. **(just) around the corner** imminent. **turn the corner** pass the worst or most critical point.
cor·ner·back *n Football* a defensive back who covers offensive plays directed toward the sidelines. **cor·nered** *adj* without hope of escape: *A cornered animal will fight.* **corner kick** *Soccer* a free kick from the corner of the field by an offensive player after a defensive player has allowed the ball past his or her own goal line. **cor·ner·stone** *n* **1** a stone at the corner of two walls joined by it. **2** such a stone, often with an inscription, laid into the

corner of a building as its formal beginning. **3** a main part on which something else rests: *Clear thinking is the cornerstone of good writing.*

cor·net [kɔr'nɛt] *n* **1** a valved brass wind instrument resembling a trumpet. **2** ['kɔrnɪt] *or* [kɔr'nɛt] a cone-shaped pastry holding a filling such as whipped cream. ⟨Old French, diminutive of *corne*; Latin *cornu* horn⟩ **cor·net·tist** or **cor·net·ist** *n* a person who plays the cornet.

cor·nice ['kɔrnɪs] *n* **1** *Architecture* a moulded, projecting part of a roof or storey supported on columns. **2** an ornamental moulding around the top of a wall, decorating the top of a window, etc. ⟨French; Greek *korōnis* copestone, something bent⟩

cor·nu·co·pi·a [,kɔrnjə'koupiə] *n* **1** a curved horn overflowing with fruits and flowers, symbolizing prosperity. **2** an abundance. ⟨Latin *cornu copiae* horn of plenty⟩

corn·y See CORN[1].

co·rol·la [kə'roulə] *n* the petals of a flower. **cor·ol·late** *adj.* ⟨Latin = garland⟩

cor·ol·lar·y [kə'rɒləri] *or* ['kɔrə,lɛri] *n* **1** a thing proved incidentally in proving another thing. **2** a logical conclusion. **3** a natural consequence: *He believes his good health is a corollary of his simple way of life.* ⟨Latin *corollarium* gift; *corolla* garland⟩

co·ro·na [kə'rounə] *n, pl* **-nas** or **-nae** [-ni] *or* [naɪ] **1** *Meteorology* a ring of light visible around the moon or other luminous body seen through a cloud of water droplets or dust particles. Compare HALO (def. 1). **2** *Astronomy* a layer of gases forming the outer part of the sun's atmosphere. **3** *Botany* the trumpet-shaped inner part of the corolla of some flowers, such as the daffodil. **4** a cigar. **5** *Architecture* the top part of a cornice. ⟨Latin *corona* crown⟩ **cor·o·nar·y** ['kɔrə,nɛri] *adj Anatomy* of either or both of the arteries branching from the aorta and supplying blood to the muscular tissue of the heart. *n* in full, **coronary thrombosis** the blocking of a coronary artery by a clot. Compare MYOCARDIAL INFARCTION. **cor·o·nar·y care unit** a hospital facility dealing specifically with the intensive care of heart disease patients. **cor·o·na·tion** *n* the ceremony of crowning a monarch. **cor·o·ner** *n* an officer appointed by a provincial government to investigate the cause of a sudden death. **cor·o·net** ['kɔrə,nɛt], ['kɔrənɪt], *or* [,kɔrə'nɛt] *n* **1** a small crown. **2** a circle of gold, jewels, or flowers worn around the head as an ornament.

cor·po·ra ['kɔrpərə] *n* pl of CORPUS.

cor·po·ral[1] ['kɔrpərəl] *n* **1** in the armed forces, a non-commissioned officer ranking next above a private. **2** ✹ in the RCMP, a non-commissioned officer ranking above a first constable. *Abbrev* **Corp., Cpl.** or **Cpl** **cor·po·ral·cy** *n.* ⟨French, from Italian *caporale*, *capo* head; Latin *caput*⟩

cor·po·ral[2] ['kɔrpərəl] *adj* to do with the body. ⟨Latin *corporalis; corpus* body⟩

cor·po·ral·i·ty *n* the state of having a body; physical existence. **corporal punishment** physical punishment. **cor·po·rate** ['kɔrpərɪt] *adj* **1** being or relating to a corporation: *corporate finance.* **2** of any group as a whole; united: *corporate worship.* **cor·po·rate·ly** *adv.* **cor·po·ra·tion** *n* a group of people, such as a business, service organization, city council, etc., with legal authority to act as one person. **cor·po·re·al** [kɔr'pɔriəl] *adj* **1** of or for the body: *Food is corporeal nourishment.* **2** material; having physical reality: *Land is a corporeal thing.* **cor·po·re·al·ly** *adv.* **cor·po·re·al·i·ty** *n.*

corps [kɔr] *n, pl* **corps** [kɔrz] **1** a military formation of more than one division. **2** a branch of the armed forces that provides a special service: *the Signal Corps.* **3** any group organized for working together: *a corps of volunteers.* ⟨French = body; Latin *corpus*⟩ **corps de bal·let** ['kɔr də bæ'lei] *French* [kɔrdba'le] in a ballet company, all the dancers not classed as soloists.

corpse [kɔrps] *n* **1** a dead body, esp of a human being. **2** anything that was once lively but is now defunct. ⟨Middle English; Latin *corpus* body⟩

cor·pu·lent ['kɔrpjələnt] *adj* fat; portly. **cor·pu·lence** *n.* **cor·pu·lent·ly** *adv.* ⟨Latin *corpulentus; corpus* body⟩

cor·pus ['kɔrpəs] *n, pl* **-po·ra** [-pərə] **1** a complete collection of writings on some subject. **2** any body of work, data, etc. ⟨Latin *corpus* body⟩ **cor·pus cal·lo·sum** [kə'lousəm] *pl* **cor·po·ra cal·lo·sa** a bundle of nerves in the brain that connects the left and right hemispheres. **cor·pus·cle** ['kɔrpʌsəl] *or* ['kɔrpəsəl] *n* a red or white blood cell. **cor·pus·cu·lar** *adj.* ⟨Latin *corpusculum* diminutive of *corpus* body⟩

cor·ral [kə'ræl] *n* **1** an enclosed space for keeping horses, cattle, etc. **2** a circular camp formed by wagons, carts, etc., for defence against attack. **3** an enclosure in which to trap game, fish, etc. *v* **-ralled, -ral·ling 1** herd into or keep in a corral. **2** capture. **3** form (wagons) into a circular camp. **4** *Slang* persuade to join or participate: *Our club has corralled several new members.* ⟨Spanish, from *corro* ring⟩

cor·rect [kə'rɛkt] *adj* **1** right; free of error: *the correct answer.* **2** meeting social standards of taste or conduct: *correct manners.* *v* **1** remove mistakes from: *Correct any wrong spellings.* **2** adjust to some standard: *to correct the reading of a barometer.* **3** indicate errors in: *to correct test papers.* **4** discipline: *to correct a child.* **5** remedy: *to correct a bad habit.* **cor·rec·tion** *n.* **cor·rect·ly** *adv.* **cor·rect·ness** *n.* **cor·rec·tor** *n.* ⟨Latin *correctus* pp of *corrigere* straighten; *com-* + *regere* direct⟩ **cor·rec·tion·al** *adj* **1** to do with correction. **2** to do with a prison system. **correctional centre** prison. **correctional officer** a prison warden. **correction line** ✹ *Prairies* a surveyor's line running north and south every six miles (about 10 km) to mark municipalities and townships. **cor·rec·tive** *adj* remedial; tending to correct: *corrective exercises to improve posture.* **cor·rec·tive** *n.* **cor·rec·tive·ly** *adv.*

SYNONYMS

Correct, the most general word, suggests only the absence of mistakes or errors: *They gave correct answers to the questions.* **Accurate** emphasizes the careful effort to make something agree exactly with facts: *an accurate account, accurate measurement.*

cor·re·late ['kɔrə,leit] *v* have or show a certain relationship or correspondence: *to correlate user responses with age and income. Our results correlate closely with earlier findings.* *n* ['kɔrəlɪt] either of two related things. **cor·re·la·tion** *n.* ⟨*com-* together + *relate*⟩ **cor·rel·a·tive** [kə'rɛlətɪv] *adj* interdependent. **cor·rel·a·tive·ly** *adv.* **correlative conjunction** either of two conjunctions used together, such as *either...or* or *both...and.*

cor·re·spond [,kɔrə'spɒnd] *v* **1** agree: *Her manner corresponded with what they expected of her.* **2** be similar in terms of function, value, effect, etc. in its own context: *The human arm corresponds to a bird's wing.* **3** exchange letters; write to each other. **cor·re·spond·ing** *adj.* **cor·re·spond·ing·ly** *adv.* ⟨Latin *com-* together, with + *respondere* answer⟩ **cor·re·spond·ence** *n* **1** an act or example of corresponding. **2** *Mathematics* a matching of the members of one set with the members of a second set. **correspondence course** a set of lessons on a certain subject issued by a **correspondence school**, to be completed by the student at home and sent in by mail. **cor·re·spond·ent** *n* **1** a person who exchanges letters with another. **2** a person employed by a newspaper, television network, etc., to send news from a distant place. A **foreign correspondent** gathers news in another country. **3** any corresponding person or thing. **corresponding angles** *Geometry* pairs of angles made on the same side of two or more lines intersected by another line.

cor·ri·dor ['kɔrə,dɔr] *or* ['kɔrədər] *n* **1** a long hallway. **2** anything like this, esp: **a** a strip of land connecting two parts of a country. **b** an urban neighbourhood or a continuous region of settlement concentrated along a major route. **c** the major route itself. ⟨Provençal *corredor*; *correr* run, Latin *currere*⟩

cor·ri·gen·dum [,kɔrə'dʒɛndəm] *n, pl* **-da** [-də] an error to be corrected in a book, manuscript, etc., often one of a list printed in a book. ⟨Latin *corrigendum* (thing) to be corrected; *corrigere.* See CORRECT.⟩

cor·ri·gi·ble ['kɔrədʒəbəl] *adj* able or willing to be corrected. **cor·ri·gi·bil·i·ty** *n.* **cor·ri·gi·bly** *adv.* ⟨Latin *corrigibilis; corrigere.* See CORRECT.⟩

cor·rob·o·rate [kə'rɒbə,reit] *v* confirm; be or provide support for: *Witnesses corroborated the police officer's statement.* **cor·rob·o·ra·tion** *n.* **cor·rob·o·ra·tive** [kə'rɒbərətɪv] *or* [-'rɒbə,reitɪv] *adj.* **cor·rob·o·ra·tive·ly** *adv.* **cor·rob·o·ra·tor** *n.* ⟨Latin *corroborare* strengthen; *com-* + *robur* oak⟩

cor·rode [kə'roud] *v* **1** wear away gradually, esp through chemical action: *Rust had*

corroded the iron railings. **2** deteriorate or cause to deteriorate gradually: *natural kindness corroded by rising ambition.* **cor·rod·i·ble** *adj.* **cor·rod·i·bil·i·ty** *n.* **cor·ro·sion** *n.* ⟨Latin *com-* + *rodere* gnaw⟩ **cor·ro·sive** *adj* **1** causing corrosion. **2** having a gradual destructive effect. *n* a substance causing corrosion, such as an acid.

cor·ru·gate ['kɔrə,geit] *v* form a series of parallel, wavelike ridges in. **cor·ru·ga·tion** *n.* ⟨Latin *com-* (intensive) + *ruga* wrinkle⟩ **corrugated cardboard** cardboard consisting of two sheets of strong paper with another sheet between them bent into a row of wavelike ridges. **corrugated iron** sheet iron or steel, shaped into curved ridges.

cor·rupt [kə'rʌpt] *adj* **1** dishonest: *a corrupt judge.* **2** sinful; morally degenerate. **3** of a text, debased by alterations, etc. **4** decayed or decaying. **cor·rupt** *v.* **cor·rupt·er** *or* **cor·rupt·or** *n.* **cor·rup·tion** *n.* **cor·rupt·ly** *adv.* ⟨Latin *corruptus* pp of *corrumpere; com-* + *rumpere* break⟩ **cor·rupt·i·ble** *adj* **1** that can be corrupted. **2** perishable; deteriorating over time.

cor·sage [kɔr'saʒ] *or* [kɔr'sɑdʒ] *n* a flower to be worn on a woman's dress, wrist, etc. ⟨French; Old French *cors* body; Latin *corpus*⟩

cor·sair ['kɔrsɛr] *n* **1** a privateer. **2** pirate. ⟨French; Latin *cursarius* runner, *cursus* a run⟩

cor·set ['kɔrsɪt] *n* **1** a stiffened undergarment, worn esp formerly by women to support the torso. **2** a similar garment worn by men or women because of weakness or deformity. **cor·set** *v.* ⟨French, diminutive of Old French *cors.* See CORPSE.⟩

cor·tege *or* **cor·tège** [kɔr'tɛʒ] *or* [kɔr'teiʒ] *n* **1** a procession: *a funeral cortege.* **2** a group of followers, attendants, etc.; retinue. ⟨French; Italian *corteggio* from *corte* court⟩

cor·tex ['kɔrtɛks] *n, pl* **-ti·ces** [-tə,siz] **1** *Botany* a layer of tissue between the epidermis and the vascular tissue of a stem or root. **2** the bark or rind of a plant, used as medicine. **3** *Anatomy* **a** the outer part of an internal organ such as the kidneys. **b** specifically, the thin layer of grey matter covering the cerebrum in the brain: *the cerebral cortex.* **cor·ti·cal** ['kɔrtəkəl] *adj.* ⟨Latin *cortex* bark⟩ **cor·ti·co·ster·oid** [,kɔrtɪkou'stɛrɔid] *n* any of a group of steroid hormones produced by the adrenal cortex or made synthetically. **cor·ti·sone** *n* one of these hormones, used in the treatment of various diseases including arthritis and cortisone.

co·run·dum [kə'rʌndəm] *n* an extremely hard mineral, aluminum oxide. ⟨Tamil *kurundam*; compare Sanskrit *kuruvinda* ruby⟩

cor·us·cate ['kɔrə,skeit] *v* give off flashes of light; sparkle. **co·rus·cant** [kə'rʌskənt] *adj.* **cor·us·ca·tion** *n.* ⟨Latin *coruscus* flashing⟩

cor·vette *or* **cor·vet** [kɔr'vɛt] *n* **1** formerly, a warship equipped with sails and only one tier of guns. **2** a small, fast warship for use in antisubmarine and convoy work. ⟨Dutch *korf*, a ship; Latin *corbis* basket⟩

co·se·cant [kou'sikənt] *n Trigonometry* in a right triangle, the ratio of the length of the hypotenuse to the length of the opposite side. *Abbrev* **cosec** ⟨*co-* + *secant*⟩

co·sign ['kousaɪn] *or* [kou'saɪn] *v* sign along with another. **co·sign·er** *n.*

co·sig·na·to·ry [kou'sɪgnə,tɔri] *adj* signing along with another. *n* a person who signs something along with another.

co·sine ['kousaɪn] *n Trigonometry* in a right triangle, the ratio of the length of the adjacent side to the length of the hypotenuse. *Abbrev* **cos** ⟨Latin *co. sinus* short for *complementi sinus* sine of the complement⟩

cos·met·ic [kɒz'mɛtɪk] *n* a preparation for beautifying the skin, hair, nails, etc. *adj* **1** to do with cosmetics. **2** intended to improve something superficially: *cosmetic repainting of an old car.* **cos·met·i·cal·ly** *adv.* ⟨Greek *kosmētikos* of order, adornment; *kosmos* order⟩

cos·me·ti·cian [,kɒzmə'tɪʃən] *n* an expert in the use of make-up. **cosmetic surgery** surgery performed to improve a person's appearance. **cos·me·tol·o·gist** *n* beautician. **cos·me·tol·o·gy** *n.*

cos·mic See COSMOS.

cos·mo·pol·i·tan [,kɒzmə'pɒlətən] *adj* **1** made up of elements or people from many parts of the world: *a cosmopolitan city.* **2** familiar with many parts of the world. **3** sophisticated. **4** of animals or plants, found in most parts of the world. **cos·mo·pol·i·tan** *or* **cos·mop·o·lite** [-'mɒpə,laɪt] *n.* **cos·mo·pol·i·tan·ism** *n.* ⟨Greek *kosmos* world + *politēs* citizen; *polis* city⟩

cos·mos ['kɒzmɒs], ['kɒzmous], *or* ['kɒzməs] *n* **1** the universe thought of as an orderly system. **2** any complete system that is orderly and harmonious. **3** order; the opposite of chaos. **4** any of a genus of flowering plants of the composite family. ⟨Greek *kosmos* order, world⟩

cos·mic ['kɒzmɪk] *adj* **1** of or belonging to the universe. **2** of the universe apart from the earth. **3** vast. **cos·mi·cal·ly** *adv.* **cosmic dust** fine particles of matter from outer space. **cosmic noise** radio waves from the Milky Way. **cosmic rays** streams of electrically charged particles that travel through space at near light speed. **cos·mog·o·ny** [kɒz'mɒgəni] *n* any theory of the origin of the universe. **cos·mo·gon·ic** [,kɒzmə'gɒnɪk] or **cos·mog·o·nal** *adj.* **cos·mog·o·nist** *n.* **cos·mog·ra·phy** *n* the science that tries to map the structure of the universe. Cosmography includes astronomy, geography, and geology. **cos·mol·o·gy** *n* a description of the universe as an ordered whole. **cos·mo·log·i·cal** *adj.* **cos·mol·o·gist** *n.* **cos·mo·naut** *n* a Russian astronaut.

co·spon·sor [kou'spɒnsər] *n* one who sponsors jointly with another. **co·spon·sor** *v.*

cos·set ['kɒsɪt] *v* make a pet of; pamper. ⟨Old English *coss* a kiss⟩

cost [kɒst] *n* **1** the price paid: *The cost of these gloves was $18.* **2** the spending of time, effort, etc.; loss of life, honour, or other valuable thing in order to gain something:

We won, but at great cost to ourselves. **3 costs** *pl* the expenses of a lawsuit. **4** a price with no mark-up for profit: *He's selling it at cost.* *v* **cost, cost·ing 1** require the spending of; have as a price: *Our new car cost $23 000. The school play cost much time and effort.* **2** cause someone loss or sacrifice (of): *That accident cost him his job.* **3** **costed, cost·ing** estimate the cost of: *The contractor is costing a new project.* ⟨Old French *coster*, Latin *constare; com-* with + *stare* stand⟩

at all costs *or* **at any cost** no matter what must be done or sacrificed: *I had to catch the next boat at all costs, or lose all hope of escape.* **cost–ef·fec·tive** *adj* bringing good results for relatively low expense. **cost–ef·fec·tive·ness** *n.* **cost·ly** *adj* **1** of great value: *costly jewels.* **2** costing much: *costly mistakes.* **cost·li·ness** *n.* **cost of living** the average price of necessities such as food, rent, etc., within a given period. **cost of living index** CONSUMER PRICE INDEX. **cost price** cost (*n* def. 4).

co–star ['kou ,star] *n* an actor of equal prominence with another playing a leading role in a movie, play, etc. *v* **–starred, –star·ring** act or feature as co-star.

cos·tume ['kɒstjum] *n* **1** the typical dress of a particular time, place, kind of person, etc. **2** an outfit imitating this or intended to represent an animal or other thing, worn for a party, Halloween, a role in a play, etc.: *a pirate costume, a tiger costume.* **cos·tumed** *adj.* ⟨French; Latin *consuetumen* custom⟩ **costume jewellery** rings, bracelets, etc. made without precious stones.

co·sy *or* **co·zy** ['kouzi] *adj* **1** warm and snug or comfortable: *a cosy corner by the fire.* **2** familiar or intimate. **co·si·ly** *adv.* **co·si·ness** *n.* *n* a cover for a teapot, to keep the tea warm. **cosy** *v.* ⟨Scandinavian; origin uncertain⟩ **cosy up to** *Informal* ingratiate oneself with.

cot [kɒt] *n* a light, narrow, often collapsible bed. ⟨Hindi *khāt*⟩

co·tan·gent [kou'tændʒənt] *n Trigonometry* in a right triangle, the ratio of the length of the adjacent side (not the hypotenuse) to the length of the opposite side. *Abbrev* **cot** ⟨Latin *co. tangens* short for *complementi tangens* tangent of the complement⟩

cote [kout] *n* a shelter for small animals, birds, etc.: *a dovecote.* ⟨Old English⟩

co·teau [kə'tou] *n* ✳ **1** a small hill. **2** a line of hills or ridges. ⟨Cdn. French⟩

co·ten·ant [kou'tenənt] *n* one of two or more tenants of the same place.

co·te·rie ['koutəri] *or* [,koutə'ri] *n* a set or circle of acquaintances. ⟨French, orig an association for tenants of one farm owner; Old French *cote* hut⟩

co·ter·mi·nous [kou'tɜrmənəs] *adj* **1** sharing a boundary. **2** having the same boundaries. ⟨Latin *com-* with + *terminus* boundary⟩

co·til·lion [kou'tɪljən] *n* **1** a dance with frequent changing of partners, led by one couple. **2** a society ball. ⟨French *cotillon* orig petticoat, diminutive of *cotte* coat⟩

cot·tage ['kɒtɪdʒ] *n* **1** a small house for holiday use, by a lake or in the woods, etc. **2** a small rural home. **cot·tag·er** *n*. ⟨Old English *cot* small house or shelter⟩
cottage cheese a soft, white cheese made from the curds of sour skim milk. **cottage country** a region where many people have cottages for holiday use. **cottage industry** industry in which workers make products at home for sale.

cotter pin a metal strip, flat on one side and round on the other, bent double and inserted into a slot to hold small parts together.

cot·ton ['kɒtən] *n* **1** soft white fibres from the seed pods of plants of the mallow family (genus *Gossypium*). **2** any of these plants, or such plants collectively as a crop. **3** thread or cloth made from the fibres.
v Informal **1** agree; get along. **2** take a liking (to): *I cottoned to her at once.* **cot·ton·y** *adj.* ⟨Old French *coton*; Arabic *qutn*⟩
cotton on (to) *Informal* understand: *He still hasn't cottoned on to the joke.* **cotton up to** *Informal* flatter.
cotton batting (or **wool**) fluffy cotton fibre used to pad quilt, dress wounds, etc. **cotton candy** a fluffy, fibrous candy made of spun melted sugar. **cotton gin** a machine for separating cotton fibres from the seeds. **cotton grass** any of a genus of sedges with spikes of flowers resembling tufts of cotton. **cot·ton·seed** *n* the seed of cotton, used for fertilizer, cattle food, etc. **cottonseed oil** oil pressed from cottonseed, used for cooking, making soap, etc. **cot·ton·tail** *n* any of several species of the common wild rabbit of North America, having a fluffy tail with a white underside.

cot·y·le·don [,kɒtə'lidən] *n* the first leaf that grows from a seed. **cot·y·le·don·ous** *adj.* ⟨Greek *kotylēdōn* cuplike hollow; *kotylē* small vessel⟩

couch [kaʊtʃ] *n* **1** chesterfield; sofa. **2** any place to sleep or rest.
v put in words: *foolish ideas couched in elegant language.* ⟨Old French *coucher* lay in a place, Latin *collocare*; *com-* (intensive) + *locus* place⟩
cou·chette [ku'ʃɛt] *n* a berth on a train, containing a seat that folds out into a bed. **couch grass** [kutʃ] a common weed in North America, with long, underground stems by which it spreads; quack grass. **couch potato** *Informal* a sedentary person who watches television a lot.

cou·gar ['kugər] *n* a large animal of the cat family, with a black-tipped tail; mountain lion. ⟨French *couguar*; Tupi-Guarani *guaçu ara*⟩

cough [kɒf] *v* force air suddenly from the lungs with a short, harsh noise. **cough** *n*. ⟨Middle English *coghen*⟩
cough up expel from the throat or lungs by coughing. **b** *Slang* give; pay (what is due). **cough drop** a small medicated candy that relieves coughs, hoarseness, etc.

could [kʊd] *v* pt of CAN. ⟨Old English *cūthe*, altered by analogy with *should*, *would*⟩
could·n't could not.

cou·lee ['kuli] *n* **1** ✳ a deep, narrow ravine, usually dry in summer. **2** a stream of lava. ⟨French *coulée*, fem pp of *couler* flow⟩

cou·lomb ['kulɒm] *or* [ku'lɒm] *n* an SI unit measuring the quantity of electricity flowing past a given section of a circuit within a given time. *Symbol* **C** ⟨Charles A. de *Coulomb* (1736-1806), French physicist⟩

coun·cil ['kaʊnsəl] *n* **1** a group of people called together to make decisions or give advice: *council of war.* **2** a session of such a group. **3** small group of people elected to lead a municipal government, church, etc. ⟨Latin *concilium*; *com-* together + *calare* call⟩
in council deliberating together: *The family is in council planning a vacation.*
coun·cil·lor or **coun·cil·or** *n* **1** elected member of a council. **2** in Prince Edward Island, a member of the Legislative Assembly. **Council of the Northwest Territories** the legislative body of the Northwest Territories. **Council of Trent** the council of the Roman Catholic Church held in Trent, Italy, from time to time between 1545 and 1563. It formulated many of the present Catholic doctrines.

CONFUSABLES

Council is a noun and refers to a group of people: *They called together a council of the town's industrial leaders.* **Counsel** means 'advice' (noun) or 'advise' (verb): *She gave us wise counsel. I cannot counsel you on that.* It can also refer to a lawyer or lawyers representing someone: *Each side tried to hire him as its counsel.*

---

coun·sel ['kaʊnsəl] *n* **1** advice: *good counsel.* **2** the act of talking things over to get or give advice. **3** a lawyer or group of lawyers in court: *counsel for the defence.*
v **-selled** or **-seled**, **-sel·ling** or **-sel·ing** give advice to, often in a professional capacity: *He counsels high school students.* **2** recommend: *She counsels immediate action.* ⟨Latin *consulere* consult, convoke; *com-* together + *sel-* take⟩
hold or **take counsel** talk things over. **keep one's** (**own**) **counsel** keep quiet about one's ideas and plans.
coun·sel·lor or **coun·sel·or** *n* **1** a person who gives advice, often in a professional capacity: *an investment counsellor, a marriage counsellor.* **2** a supervisor at a children's camp. **3** *Mormon Church* an adviser to the leader.

count[1] [kaʊnt] *v* **1** name numbers in order. **2** find how many, by assigning numbers in order to things: *Count the books.* **3 a** include in counting: *Let's not count that game; it was a warm-up.* **b** qualify to be so included: *That last goal doesn't count.* **4** have significance: *Doing your best is what counts.* **5** rely (*on*): *Can I count on you to help?* **6** consider: *Count yourself lucky.* **7** *Music* keep track of (beats): *Count four measures before coming in.*
n **1** the act of counting: *a careful count.* **2** the total number of things counted: *a low blood count.* **3** *Law* a separate charge: *three counts of theft.* **4** ability to keep track in counting: *I've lost count.* **count·a·ble** *adj.* ⟨Old French *conter*, Latin *computare*; *com-* up + *putare* reckon⟩

count for be worth. **count in** *Informal* include: *Count me in.* **count off** divide into equal groups by counting: *The campers were counted off in fours.* **count out** not include in a plan: *If you go skiing, count me out.*

count·down *n* **1** the time just before a special event, such as a rocket launch, when people keep track of the time left. **2** the act of counting minutes, seconds, etc. backward to the moment in question, represented by zero.

count·less *adj* too many to count: *the countless stars.* **count noun** a word denoting a thing which can have a plural. *Bottle* is a count noun; *milk* is not.

count² [kaʊnt] *n* a European nobleman of similar rank to a British earl. **count·ess** ['kaʊntɪs] *n.* ⟨Old French *conte*, Latin *comitis* companion⟩

coun·te·nance ['kaʊntənəns] *n* **1** *Poetic* face or facial expression: *a sad countenance.* **2** approval: *He gave countenance to our plan.* *v* tolerate: *A tyrant countenances no opposition.* ⟨Old French *contenance* from Latin *continentia* demeanour, self-control; *continere* contain⟩ **keep one's countenance a** stay calm. **b** keep from smiling or showing other feelings by one's face. **lose countenance a** get excited. **b** be embarrassed. **put out of countenance** embarrass and confuse.

count·er¹ ['kaʊntər] *n* **1** a disc or other object used for counting. **2** a fixture in a store, restaurant, etc., with a long, flat top surface over which people are served or pay for things: *a lunch counter.* **3** a similar fixture in a kitchen or bathroom, usually including a sink. ⟨Anglo-French *counteour* from *conter.* See COUNT¹.⟩ **over the counter** without a prescription: *Patent medicines can be sold over the counter.* **under the counter** secretly, often illegally. **counter cheque** a blank non-personalized cheque for use in a bank or store.

coun·ter² ['kaʊntər] *adv, adj* in the opposite direction opposite: *counter to common sense.* *v* **1** oppose; act against: *to counter a bad influence.* **2** answer (a blow or move) with another in return. *n* **1** the opposite thing. **2** a move to answer another. ⟨Latin *contra* against⟩

counter– *combining form* **1** against: *counteract.* **2** in return: *counterattack.* **3** corresponding: *counterpart.*

> **USAGE**
> As with many combining forms, use of a hyphen is debatable with **counter**. This dictionary uses a hyphen before a following 'r' and in long compounds where primary stress falls on the second element.

coun·ter·act [,kaʊntər'ækt] *v* act against; neutralize or hinder the action or effect of. **coun·ter·ac·tion** *n.* **coun·ter·ac·tive** *adj, n.*

coun·ter·at·tack [kaʊntərə,tæk] *n* an attack in response to an attack. **coun·ter·at·tack** *v.*

coun·ter·bal·ance ['kaʊntər,bæləns] *n* **1** a mass balancing another mass. **2** an influence, power, etc. balancing another. **3** the fact of balancing in this way: *in counterbalance to the other.* **coun·ter·bal·ance** [,kaʊntər'bæləns] *v.*

coun·ter·charge ['kaʊntər,tʃɑrdʒ] *n* a charge or accusation made to oppose one made by another. **coun·ter·charge** *v.*

coun·ter·check ['kaʊntər,tʃɛk] *n* **1** obstacle; something that opposes. **2** a check made upon a check. **coun·ter·check** *v.*

coun·ter·claim ['kaʊntər,kleim] *n* a claim made in response or opposition to another. **coun·ter·claim** *v.* **coun·ter·claim·ant** *n.*

coun·ter·clock·wise [,kaʊntər'klɒk,waɪz] *adv, adj* in the direction opposite to that in which the hands of a clock move.

coun·ter·cul·ture ['kaʊntər,kʌltʃər] *n* a movement that actively rejects the values of the prevailing culture in favour of other ones. **coun·ter·cul·tur·al** *adj.*

coun·ter–es·pi·o·nage [,kaʊntər 'ɛspiə,nɑʒ] *or* [-'ɛspiənɪdʒ] *n* measures taken to confuse enemy espionage.

coun·ter·feit ['kaʊntərfɪt] *v* **1** copy (money, handwriting, etc.) in order to defraud. **2** be deceptively similar to. **3** fake: *to counterfeit a grief she did not feel.* **coun·ter·feit** *n, adj.* **coun·ter·feit·er** *n.* ⟨Old French *contrefait* pp of *contrefaire; contre-* against + *faire* make⟩

coun·ter·foil ['kaʊntər,fɔɪl] *n* a copy or stub of a cheque, receipt, etc., kept as a record. ⟨*counter-* + *foil* leaf⟩

coun·ter·in·sur·gen·cy [,kaʊntərɪn'sɜrdʒənsi] *n* counterattack against rebel forces.

coun·ter–in·tel·li·gence [,kaʊntər ɪn'tɛlədʒəns] *n* a government or military department whose work is to track down and prevent espionage, sabotage, etc.

coun·ter–in·tu·i·tive [,kaʊntər ɪn'tuətɪv] *adj* against natural intuition.

coun·ter·mand [,kaʊntər'mænd] *or* ['kaʊntər,mænd] *v* cancel (a command, etc.). **coun·ter·mand** ['kaʊntər,mænd] *n.* ⟨Latin *contra-* against + *mandare* order⟩

coun·ter·meas·ure ['kaʊntər,mɛʒər] *n* a measure or move taken to oppose another.

coun·ter·of·fer ['kaʊntər,ɒfər] *n* an offer made in response to an unacceptable offer.

coun·ter·pane ['kaʊntər,pein] *n* bedspread. ⟨Old French *contrepoint*, Latin *culcita puncta* quilt, stitched mattress; influenced by Middle English *pane* piece of cloth⟩

coun·ter·part ['kaʊntər,pɑrt] *n* **1** a person or thing that corresponds to another: *The federal energy minister is holding talks with his provincial counterparts.* **2** a person or thing that complements or completes another: *Night is the counterpart of day.* **3** a copy, esp of a legal document.

coun·ter·point ['kaʊntər,pɔɪnt] *n* **1** *Music* **a** a different melody added to another as an accompaniment. **b** the art of combining melodies to form a harmonious unit. **2** an element, theme, etc., that contrasts with or complements another.

v be or add a counterpoint to. **con·tra·pun·tal** *adj.* ⟨French *contrepoint*⟩

coun·ter–pro·duc·tive [ˌkaʊntər prəˈdʌktɪv] *adj* hindering the achievement of its own goal: *It's counter-productive to spend too many hours on this at one sitting.*

coun·ter·pro·po·sal [ˈkaʊntərprəˌpouzəl] *n* a proposal in response to an unacceptable proposal.

coun·ter–ref·or·ma·tion [ˌkaʊntər ˌrɛfərˈmeiʃən] *n* a reform movement opposed to a previous reform movement. .

coun·ter–rev·o·lu·tion [ˌkaʊntər ˌrɛvəˈluʃən] *n* a revolution against a government established through a previous revolution. **coun·ter–rev·o·lu·tion·ary** *n, adj.*

coun·ter·sign [ˈkaʊntərˌsaɪn] *n* 1 a password given in answer to a sentinel's challenge. 2 a secret signal given in answer to another. 3 a signature added to confirm a signature. *v* sign (a thing already signed by another) to confirm it. **coun·ter·sig·na·ture** [-ˈsɪgnətʃər] *n.* ⟨French *contresigne*⟩

coun·ter·sink [ˈkaʊntərˌsɪŋk] *v* **-sunk, -sink·ing** sink the head of (a screw, bolt, etc.) in such a hole so that it is below or flush with the surface.

coun·ter·ten·or [ˈkaʊntərˌtɛnər] *n* the highest adult male singing voice, above tenor.

coun·ter·vail [ˈkaʊntərˌveɪl] *or* [ˌkaʊntərˈveɪl] *v* 1 counteract. 2 compensate for. ⟨French *contrevaloir;* Latin *contra valere* count against⟩

coun·ter·weight [ˈkaʊntərˌweɪt] *n* a mass that balances another mass.

count·ess See COUNT².

coun·try [ˈkʌntri] *n* 1 a nation with a recognized government and territory. 2 the territory of such a nation. 3 rural area: *We live out in the country.* 4 a region characterized by a particular geography, population, etc.: *the hill country, cottage country.* 5 COUNTRY MUSIC. ⟨Old French *contree,* Latin *contrata* region lying opposite; *contra* against⟩ **coun·tri·fy** *v* make typical of a rural way of life: *I don't like their decorating style; it's too countrified.* **country and western** COUNTRY MUSIC. **country club** a club near a city, with a golf course and often other outdoor sports facilities. **country cousin** 1 a person from the country who finds the city confusing or exciting. 2 the less sophisticated version or counterpart (*of*). **coun·try·man** *n, pl* **-men** a man of one's own country. **coun·try·wom·an** *n, pl* **-wom·en. country mile** a long distance. **country music** a style of music developed from the traditional folk music of white people in the S United States, typically with simple rhythm and harmony, and sentimental lyrics. **coun·try·side** *n* 1 a rural area, esp with reference to its natural beauty, tranquillity, etc. 2 the people of a country: *The whole countryside was up in arms.* **coun·try–wide** *adj, adv* nationwide.

coun·ty [ˈkaʊnti] *n* an administrative division of a country, province, state, etc.

The county form of municipal government is used in Nova Scotia, New Brunswick, Québec, Ontario, and Alberta. ⟨Old French *conte.* See COUNT².⟩

county seat a town or city where the county government is located.

coup [ku] *n, pl* **coups** [kuz] 1 a brilliant or masterly act, esp an unexpected one. 2 a stroke or blow. 3 COUP D'ÉTAT. ⟨French; Greek *kolaphos*⟩ **coup de grâce** [ˈku də ˈgrɑs] *French* [kudˈgʀɑs] 1 an act that gives a merciful death to a suffering animal or person. 2 a finishing stroke: *The runner's final sprint gave the coup de grâce to his opponents.* **coup de main** [ˈku də ˈmɛ̃] *French* [kudˈmɛ̃] a sudden attack. **coup d'é·tat** [ˈku deiˈta] *French* [kudeˈta] the sudden, violent overthrow of a government. **coup de thé·â·tre** [ˈku də teiˈatrə] *French* [kudteˈatʀ] 1 a pivotal event in a dramatic work. 2 an act or event designed to create sensation.

coupe [kup] *n* a two-door non-convertible car. ⟨*coupé*⟩

cou·ple [ˈkʌpəl] *n* 1 two people who are romantically involved, married, paired for a dance, game, etc. 2 any pair. 3 *Informal* a few (with *of*): *a couple of days.* 4 *Mechanics* two balanced forces creating rotation. *v* 1 connect one thing to another. 2 join together in a pair or pairs. 3 copulate. ⟨Old French *cople;* Latin *copula* bond⟩ **cou·pler** *or* **cou·pling** *n* a device or part used to join two things. **cou·plet** *n* two successive lines of verse with the same number of metrical feet, usually rhyming.

Couple always refers to two in number: *A couple of months went by before the subscription expired.* **Few** may refer specifically to three, or not many more than three: *A few players did not like their hot-tempered coach.* **Several** usually refers to more than a few, but not many (for example, from four to seven): *The girl chose several books from the library.*

cou·pon [ˈkupɒn] *or, often,* [ˈkjupɒn] *n* 1 a marked piece of paper that entitles the holder to get something: *a coupon for 50¢ off a pizza.* 2 a statement of interest due on a bond, which can be presented for payment. ⟨French, from *couper* cut⟩

cour·age [ˈkɜrɪdʒ] *n* the inner strength to do what is right or necessary in spite of fear. **cou·ra·geous** [kəˈreidʒəs] *adj.* **cou·ra·geous·ly** *adv.* **cou·ra·geous·ness** *n.* ⟨Old French *curage,* from *cuer* heart; Latin *cor*⟩ **have the courage of one's convictions** act or speak as one believes one should.

Courage applies to moral firmness that enables a person to face danger, pain, etc.: *Although blinded by the explosion, she faced the future with courage.* **Bravery** applies especially to courage shown by bold action in the presence of danger: *The Commandos are famous for their bravery.*

cou·reur de bois [ku'rɜr də 'bwɑ] *French* [kuʀœʀdə'bwa] *pl* **coureurs de bois** (same pronunciation) ✽ formerly, in the North and Northwest, a French or Métis fur trader or woodsman. ⟨Cdn. French = forest runner⟩

cour·i·er ['kɜriər] *or* ['kʊriər] *n* **1** an agency or individual whose business is to deliver letters and parcels rapidly. **2** any messenger or delivery person. ⟨Latin *currere* run⟩

course [kɔrs] *n* **1** studies that make up a curriculum: *a two-year hairdressing course.* **2** a part of a meal served at one time: *the first course.* **3** an area marked out for a game or sport: *a racecourse, a golf course.* **4** an onward movement: *the course of events.* **5** a direction or route taken: *a ship's course.* **6** a line of action: *The sensible course was to go home.* **7** a channel, path or track: *a watercourse.* **8** a series of similar things: *a course of lectures.* **9** a layer or row of bricks, shingles, etc.
v **1** run; move along swiftly: *blood coursing through one's veins.* **2** hunt with hounds. ⟨French *cours, course,* Latin *cursus; currere* run⟩
a matter of course the normal pattern of events or way of proceeding. **in due course** at the proper time. **of course a** as might be expected: *Of course it will rain on the weekend.* **b** an emphatic 'yes'. **off course** straying from the right direction. **on course** going in the planned direction. **run** (or **take**) **its course** come to the end of its natural development.
cours·er 1 warhorse. **2** a hunting hound.

court [kɔrt] *n* **1 a** a place where legal cases are heard and justice is administered, or the judges who administer it. **b** a session in this place. **2** a large enclosed space indoors or outdoors: *a food court in a mall.* **3** a short, wide street that ends in a circle. **4** a place marked off for games: *tennis court.* **5** the residence, family, and attendants of a sovereign. **6** a formal assembly held by a sovereign. **7** attention, often romantic, paid to get someone's favour. **8** ✽ a single act in a skating program.
v **1** try to get the favour of. **2** woo; keep company with (a person one hopes to marry). **3** invite; act so as to get: *courting death.* ⟨Old French *cort;* Latin *cohors* enclosure, retinue⟩
hold court a of a sovereign, hold a formal assembly. **b** receive people in a lordly way. **out of court a** without legal proceedings: *to settle out of court.* **b** not meriting a hearing in court. **pay court to** court (*v* defs.1, 2).
cour·te·san *or* **cour·te·zan** ['kɔrtə,zæn] *or* [-zən] *n* a prostitute whose clients are nobles. **court·house** *n* a building where a law court meets. **cour·ti·er** ['kɔrtiər] *n* **1** a person often present at the court of a king, queen, etc. **2** a person who tries to win another's favour by flattery. **court·ly** *adj* polite; elegant: *courtly manners.* **court·li·ness** *n.* **court–mar·tial** ['marʃəl] *n, pl* **courts–mar·tial** a court trying armed forces personnel accused of breaking military law. *v* **-tialled** or **-tialed, -tial·ling** or **-tial·ing** try in such a court. **court·room** *n* a room where a law court meets. **court·ship** *n* wooing. **court shoe** a shoe for playing court

games such as tennis. **court·yard** *n* a space enclosed by walls in or near a large building.

court·e·sy ['kɜrtəsi] *n* **1** polite or gracious behaviour. **2** Usually, **courtesies** *pl* a polite, often conventional act or remark: *to exchange the usual courtesies.* **cour·te·ous** ['kɜrtiəs] *adj.* **cour·te·ous·ly** *adv.* **cour·te·ous·ness** *n.* ⟨Old French *cortesie* from *cort.* See COURT.⟩
by courtesy as a favour. **by courtesy of** or **through the courtesy of** with the gracious consent of. **courtesy of** free of charge by: *Coffee is provided courtesy of the hotel.*
courtesy car a car lent free of charge by a garage or insurance company while one's own is being repaired.

cous·cous ['kuskus] *n* a North African food made from steamed, coarsely ground wheat. ⟨French, Berber *kuskus; kaskasa* grind, pound⟩

cous·in ['kʌzən] *n* **1** the son or daughter of one's uncle or aunt. **First cousins** share two grandparents, **second cousins** two great-grandparents; etc. A parent's or child's first cousin is one's **first cousin once removed. 2** a distant relative. **3** any person or thing thought of as related to another by similarity: *Swim? He's first cousin to a beaver.* ⟨Old French *cosin;* Latin *consobrinus* mother's sister's child⟩

couth [kuθ] *Facetious adj* sophisticated. *n* sophistication; refinement: *His writing style is colourful but lacks couth.* ⟨back formation from *uncouth*⟩

cou·tu·ri·er [ku'turi,ei] *or* [ku'turiər] *French* [kutyʀ'je] *n* a male fashion designer. ⟨French; Latin *consuere; com-* together + *suere* sew⟩
cou·tu·ri·ère [ku,turi'ɛr] *French* [kuty'ʀjɛr] *n* a female fashion designer.

co·va·lence [kou'veiləns] *n Chemistry* **1** bond in which two atoms share a pair of electrons. **2** ability to form such a bond. **3** the total of the pairs of electrons which one atom of a given element can share with surrounding atoms. Also, **co·va·len·cy. co·va·lent** *adj.*

cove [kouv] *n* **1** a small, sheltered bay. **2** an alcove. ⟨Old English *cofa* chamber⟩

cov·en ['kʌvən] *n* a gathering of witches, traditionally thirteen. ⟨Old French *covin;* Latin *convenire.* See CONVENE.⟩

cov·e·nant ['kʌvənənt] *n* **1** a solemn pledge or agreement. **2** in the Bible, the promises of God to people. **3** a legal contract.
v solemnly agree (to do certain things).
cov·e·nant·al [,kʌvə'næntəl] *adj.* ⟨Old French, from *covenir,* Latin *convenire.* See CONVENE.⟩
cov·e·nan·tor *n Law* a person who makes a covenant and assumes its obligations.

cov·er ['kʌvər] *v* **1** put something over to protect, hide, etc. **2** lie all over the surface of: *Snow covered the ground.* **3** extend or travel over: *a farm covering 300 hectares. We covered 16 km the first day.* **4** deal with: *The review covered everything in the unit.* **5** protect, screen, or shelter: *to cover someone's retreat.* **6** insure: *The house is covered but not the contents.* **7** provide or make up for: *This should cover all your expenses.* **8** *Journalism* act as reporter or photographer of (an event or

subject): *She covers sports.* **9** *Sports* **a** watch and try to thwart (an opposing player). **b** support (a teammate) in play. **10** *Informal* act as a substitute: *He is covering for the manager while she's away.* **11** shield (a guilty or incompetent person) from discovery (with *for*): *I can't keep covering for you.*
n **1** anything that covers: *a book cover.* **2** a blanket on a bed. **3** shelter: *to take cover.* **4** a false identity or other strategem intended to hide; front: *Her office job was just a cover for her activities as a spy.* **5** a table setting for one person. **6** COVER CHARGE. **7** *Philately* an envelope or wrapper with a stamp on it. **cov·er·er** *n*. **cov·er·less** *adj.* ⟨Old French *covrir*, Latin *cooperire; co-* up + *operire* cover⟩
blow someone's cover expose someone's false identity. **break cover** come out of hiding, esp suddenly. **cover up** conceal (error or wrongdoing). **cover up** *n*. **take cover** find a shelter from attack. **under cover** hidden; secret; disguised. **under cover of** hidden by: *They left under cover of darkness.*
cov·er·age *n* the act, scope, or manner of covering, esp of reporting news or of protecting by insurance. **cov·er·alls** *n pl* an outer garment that includes shirt and pants in a single unit. **cover charge** a charge per head in some nightclubs, restaurants, etc., for service in addition to the charge for food or drink. **covered bridge** a bridge with a roof over the roadway. **covered wagon** formerly, a large wagon with a removable canvas cover, used by pioneers. **covering** (or **cover**) **letter** a letter sent with other material, outlining or explaining it. **cov·er·let** *n* a bedspread. **cov·er·slip** *n* a piece of thin glass for covering a preparation on a microscopic slide. **cover story 1** a magazine article dealing with what is shown on the front cover. **2** a false alibi. **cov·er-up** *n* **1** the act of concealing error or wrongdoing. **2** a garment covering another such as a swimsuit: *a beach cover-up.*
cov·ert [ˈkʌvərt] *or* [ˈkouvərt] *adj* secret; hidden; disguised: *covert glances.*
n **1** a shelter. **2** a thicket in which animals hide. **cov·ert·ly** *adv.* **cov·ert·ness** *n*. ⟨Old French *covert* pp of *covrir*. See COVER.⟩
cov·et [ˈkʌvɪt] *v* desire eagerly (a thing that belongs to another). **cov·et·er** *n*. **cov·et·ous** *adj.* **cov·et·ous·ly** *adv.* **cov·et·ous·ness** *n*. ⟨Old French *coveitier*; Latin *cupere* desire⟩
cov·ey [ˈkʌvi] *n* **1** a small flock of partridges, quail; etc. **2** any small group of people: *surrounded by a covey of reporters.* ⟨Old French *covée* from *cover* incubate; Latin *cubare* lie⟩
cow¹ [kaʊ] *n* **1** the full-grown female of any bovine animal, esp of domestic cattle. **2** the female of various other large mammals: *an elephant cow, a cow moose.* ⟨Old English *cū*⟩ **cow·bell** *n* a bell hung around a cow's neck for ease in locating the cow. **cow·bird** *n* a small North American blackbird. **cow·boy** *n* esp in W Canada and the US, a rider who looks after cattle on a ranch and on the range. **cow·catch·er** *n* a metal apron at the front of a locomotive, designed to roll to one

side any obstruction on the tracks. **cow·girl** *n* a woman who looks after cattle on a ranch. **cow·hand** *n* a cowboy or cowgirl. **cow·herd** *n* a person who looks after cattle at pasture. **cow·hide** *n* **1** the hide of a cow. **2** a whip made of braided leather. **cow·lick** *n Informal* a lock of hair that will not lie flat, usually just above the forehead. **cow parsnip ✻** any of several plants of the parsley family. **cow·poke** *n Informal* cowhand. **cow·shed** a building in which cows are kept for shelter or during milking. **cow·pox** *n* a disease of cows; infected cows are the source of the smallpox vaccine. **cow·punch·er** *n* ✻ *Informal* cowhand. **cow·slip** *n* any of various North American plants from the primrose family. **cow·town** *n* in W Canada and US, a town largely dependent on the cattle business.
cow² [kaʊ] *v* make afraid; frighten: *cowed by threats.* ⟨possibly Old Norse *kúga*⟩
cow·ard [ˈkaʊərd] *n* a person who lacks courage; one who runs from danger or pain or attacks the weak. **cow·ard·ice** [ˈkaʊərdɪs] *n*. **cow·ard·li·ness** *n*. **cow·ard·ly** *adj, adv.* ⟨Old French *coart* from *coe* tail, Latin *coda, cauda*⟩
cow·er [ˈkaʊər] *v* crouch or flinch in fear or shame. ⟨Middle English *couren;* Scandinavian⟩
Cow·i·chan [ˈkaʊɪtʃən] *n* a member of a Salishan First Nations people living mainly on Vancouver Island and noted for making **Cowichan sweaters**, heavy wool sweaters with symbolic designs knitted into them, orig black and white but now sometimes multicoloured. **Cow·i·chan** *adj.*
cowl [kaʊl] *n* **1** a cloak with a hood, as that worn by some monks. **2** such a hood, or anything shaped like it. **3** any of various covers, such as a chimney top designed to increase draft, or a metal engine cover. ⟨Old English *cūle, cug(e)le;* Latin *cucullus* hood⟩
cowl neck a wide neck on a woman's garment, consisting of loose folds of fabric vaguely resembling a lowered hood.
co–work·er [ˈkou ˌwɜrkər] *or* [ˌkou ˈwɜrkər] *n* fellow worker.
cow·rie or **cow·ry** [ˈkaʊri] *n* a mollusc with a glossy yellow shell formerly used as money in some societies. ⟨Hindi *kauri*⟩
cox [kɒks] *n* coxswain.
v act as a coxswain (for).
cox·comb [ˈkɒksˌkoum] *n* a vain man; a conceited dandy. ⟨variant of *cock's comb*⟩
cox·swain [ˈkɒksən] *or* [-ˌswein] *n* a person who steers a racing boat and is in charge of its crew. ⟨*cock* cockboat + *swain*⟩
coy [kɔi] *adj* **1** shy; modest. **2** pretending to be shy: *a coy smile.* **coy·ly** *adv.* **coy·ness** *n*. ⟨Old French *coi;* Latin *quietus* at rest⟩
coy·o·te [kaɪˈouti], [ˈkaɪout], *or* [ˈkaɪut] *n, pl* **-otes** or **-ote** a wild doglike animal of North America. ⟨Mexican Spanish; Nahuatl *koyotl*⟩
coy·pu [ˈkɔipu] *n, pl* **-pus** or **-pu** a large beaverlike water rodent of South America. ⟨Spanish *coipu;* Araucanian (S American Indian language) *koypu*⟩

coz·en ['kʌzən] v **1** cheat (usually with *out of* or *of*): *He was cozened out of his inheritance.* **2** deceive: *They cozened her into signing.* **coz·en·er** n. **coz·en·age** n. ⟨origin unknown⟩

co·zy ['kouzi] See COSY.

cp 1 candlepower. **2** chemically pure.

C.P. 1 Communist Party. **2** ✹ *French* Conseil or Conseiller privé (Privy Council or Councillor). **3** *French* case postale (post office box).

cpi *Computers* characters per inch.

CPR 1 cardiopulmonary resuscitation. **2** Canadian Pacific Railway.

cps 1 cycles per second; Hz. **2** *Computers* characters per second.

C.R. ✹ *French* Conseiller de la reine (Queen's Counsel).

crab[1] [kræb] n **1** any ten-legged crustacean whose first pair of legs are pincers. **2** the flesh of a crab. v **crabbed, crab·bing** catch crabs. **crab·ber** n. ⟨Old English *crabba*⟩
catch a crab make a faulty stroke in rowing. **crab·meat** n the flesh of a crab, eaten as food. **crab·wise** adv, adj moving sideways like a crab: *The car slid crabwise into the fence.*

crab[2] [kræb] n a cross, sour, person; one who is always complaining or finding fault. v **crabbed, crab·bing 1** find fault; complain: *Stop crabbing about the weather.* **2** *Informal* spoil: *His lack of enthusiasm crabbed the deal.* ⟨origin uncertain⟩
crab apple the fruit of any of several small trees of the rose family, used especially for jellies and preserves. **crab·bed** ['kræbɪd] *or* [kræbd] adj **1** ill-tempered. **2** of handwriting, hard to read because cramped and irregular. **crab·by** adj *Informal* cross or ill-tempered. **crab·bi·ly** adv. **crab·bi·ness** n. **crab·grass** n or **crab grass** any of various coarse grasses that spread rapidly. **crab louse** (*pl* **lice**) a louse that infests the pubic area. **crabs** n pl crab lice.

crack[1] [kræk] n **1** a break or narrow opening in a surface: *a crack in a cup.* **2** a narrow space: *cracks between the floorboards.* **3** a sudden, sharp noise, or a blow struck with such a noise: *the crack of a whip.* **4** *Slang* a try: *Let me take a crack at opening the jar.* **5** *Slang* a witty remark. **6** *Slang* a nasty remark. *adj Informal* expert: *a crack shot.*
v **1** break without separating into parts. **2** break with a sudden, sharp noise: *The tree cracked and fell.* **3** make or cause to make a sudden, sharp noise: *to crack a whip.* **4** of the voice, change suddenly in pitch or quality. **5** *Informal* give way or cause to give way: *Not even torture could crack him.* **6** break into: *to crack a safe.* **7** solve; figure out: *to crack a code.* **8** *Chemistry* separate (petroleum, coal tar, etc.) into various substances using heat and pressure to lighten the hydrocarbons. ⟨Old English *cracian*, v, Middle English *crak*, n⟩
crack a bottle *Informal* open a new bottle and begin drinking its contents. **crack a joke** tell a joke. **crack a smile** *Informal* smile reluctantly. **crack down (on)** take stern disciplinary measures (against). **crack·down** n. **crack open**

1 open (a door, window, etc.) slightly. **2** *Informal* open (something packaged) for the first time. **crack up** *Informal* **a** crash or smash. **b** suffer a mental collapse. **c** respond or cause to respond with a fit of laughter: *This show always cracks her up.* **crack–up** n. **fall through** (or **between**) **the cracks** be overlooked in a bureaucratic system. **get cracking** *Informal* get started quickly. **not what it's cracked up to be** not satisfying expectations generated by popular claims, advertising, etc.
crack–brained adj of an idea, plan, etc., crazy. **crack·down** n swift, stern disciplinary action: *a crackdown on speeders.* **cracked** adj **1** broken but without falling apart. **2** of the voice, not clear but splitting into discordant tones. **3** *Informal* crazy. **crack·er** n **1** a thin, crisp biscuit, not sweet. **2** a small paper roll used on festive occasions which explodes when it is pulled at both ends, revealing a message, trinket, etc. inside. **crack·er·jack** adj *Slang* of superior ability or quality. **crack·ers** adj *Slang* (not used before the noun) crazy. **crack·le** v **1** make repeated light, sharp sounds, as of a fire or of cellophane being crumpled. **2** of china, acquire many minute cracks in the glaze. **crack·le** n. **crack·ly** adj. **crack·ling** adj. **cracklings** n pl the crisp remains of rendered animal fat, esp from pork. **crack of dawn** the first appearance of the sun over the horizon. **crack·pot** *Slang* n a very eccentric person. **crack·pot** adj. **crack–up** n **1** a crash. **2** *Informal* a mental collapse.

crack[2] n *Slang* a very addictive, crystalline form of cocaine. ⟨origin uncertain⟩
crack·head n a crack addict. **crack house** a place where crack is bought and sold.

cra·dle ['kreidəl] n **1** a baby's little boxlike bed, on rockers or swinging in a frame. **2** babyhood: *I was taught that from the cradle.* **3** the place where a thing begins: *the cradle of civilization.* **4** a frame to support a ship, aircraft, etc., for building or repairs. **5** the part of a telephone that holds the receiver. v hold as in a cradle: *She cradled the child in her arms.* **cra·dle·like** adj. ⟨Old English *cradol*⟩
from (**the**) **cradle to** (**the**) **grave** from birth until death. **cradle–to–grave** adj. **rob the cradle** choose a much younger person as a romantic companion. **cra·dle–rob·ber** n.
cra·dle·board n ✹ a First Nations peoples' device for carrying a baby, consisting of a thin, rectangular board with a bag attached. **cradle song** or **cra·dle·song** n lullaby.

craft [kræft] n **1** a particular artistic skill, esp in handwork, such as knitting or pottery. **2** an article of handwork: *She sells her crafts at the fall fair.* **3** a skilled trade in which aesthetics are important: *Carpentry is a craft.* **4** skill in deceiving others: *He used craft to get all their money.* **5** pl **craft** a boat, ship, aircraft, or spacecraft. v make skilfully or by hand. ⟨Old English *cræft*⟩
craft·er n a person who engages in a craft (def. 1) either as a hobby or for a living. **crafts·man** n, pl **-men** a man highly skilled in

the techniques of a craft. **crafts·man·like** *adj.* **crafts·man·ship** *n.* **crafts·peo·ple** *pl* people who engage in a craft. **crafts·wom·an** *n, pl* **crafts·wom·en.** **craft union** a labour union made up of people in the same craft. **craft·y** *adj* skilful in deceiving others: *a crafty thief.* **craft·i·ly** *adv.* **craft·i·ness** *n.*

crag [krægl] *n* a steep, rugged rock or cliff; a projecting rock. **cragged** *adj.* ⟨Celtic; compare Welsh *craig*⟩
crag·gy *adj* **1** with many crags; rocky: *a craggy hillside.* **2** suggesting the hardness and angularity of a crag; rugged: *a craggy face.* **crag·gi·ly** *adv.* **crag·gi·ness** *n.*

cram ['kræm] *v* **crammed, cram·ming 1** force into a small space; stuff: *She crammed her clothes quickly into the bag.* **2** fill too full: *The hall was crammed with people.* **3** eat or feed too fast or too much. **4** *Informal* try to learn or study a great amount in a short time: *He's cramming for his history exam.*
n a crammed or crowded condition; crush. **cram·mer** *n.* ⟨Old English *crammian; crimman* insert⟩

cramp[1] [kræmp] *n* **1** a painful, involuntary muscle contraction. **2** a temporary paralysis as a result of overexercising: *writer's cramp.* **3 cramps** *pl* sharp, continuous pains in the abdomen.
v make or become painfully stiff (sometimes with *up*): *cramped from sitting in one position for too long.* ⟨Frankish⟩

cramp[2] [kræmp] *n* **1** a clamp. **2** something that confines or hinders.
v **1** fasten together with a cramp. **2** confine in a small space; restrict. ⟨Middle Dutch⟩
cramp one's style *Slang* restrict one's natural behaviour.
cramped *adj* crowded or confining: *living in cramped quarters.* **cram·pon** *n* **1** a strong iron bar with hooks, used to lift heavy things. **2** a spiked plate fastened to the sole of a shoe or boot for traction on ice or when climbing.

cran·ber·ry ['kræn,bɛri] *n* a sour, dark red berry produced by plants of the heath family. ⟨Low German *kraanbere*⟩
cranberry bog a marsh where they grow.

crane [krein] *n* **1** a machine with a long, swinging arm, for lifting and moving heavy weights. **2** any of several devices consisting of a horizontal arm swinging on a vertical axis, such as a boom for a television camera. **3** any of a family of tall grey, brown, or white wading birds with a long bill. **4** a heron.
v stretch (the neck) as a crane does: *He craned his neck to see over the crowd.* **crane·like** *adj.* ⟨Old English *cran*⟩
crane fly any of a family of flies having a long, slender body and very long legs.

cra·ni·um ['kreiniəm] *n, pl* **-ni·ums, -ni·a** [-niə] **1** the skull of a vertebrate. **2** the part of the skull enclosing the brain. **cra·ni·al** *adj.* **cra·ni·al·ly** *adv.* ⟨Greek *kranion*⟩
cra·ni·ot·o·my [,kreini'ɒtəmi] *n* a surgical operation that involves opening the skull.

crank [kræŋk] *n* **1** a machine part joined at right angles to a shaft and turned in order to transmit motion. **2** *Informal* a person with odd whims or notions. **3** *Informal* a grouch.
v **1** work by means of a crank: *to crank a window open.* **2** twist; wind. **3** *Slang* hit hard: *to crank a shot into the net.* ⟨Old English *cranc*⟩
crank up *Informal* increase: *crank up the heat.* **turn someone's crank** *Slang* be or do just the thing that excites someone.
crank call an annoying phone call made as a practical joke. **crank·case** *n* a metal case forming the base of an internal-combustion engine and enclosing, among other things, the crankshaft. **crank·shaft** *n* a shaft turned by a crank. **crank·y** *adj* cross; ill-natured. **crank·i·ly** *adv.* **crank·i·ness** *n.*

cran·ny ['kræni] *n* a small, narrow opening. ⟨French *cran* fissure; Latin *crena* notch⟩

crap [kræp] *n Slang* **1** nonsense. **2** garbage, dirt, or excrement. **crap·py** *adj.* ⟨Old French *crape* scale, ordure; Latin *crappa* chaff⟩

crap·pie ['kræpi] *n* either of two small, edible freshwater fishes of the sunfish family. ⟨Cdn. French *crapet*⟩

craps [kræps] *n* **1** a gambling game played with two dice. **2** a first throw at craps, with a low total. ⟨French *craps* the game of hazard; English *crabs* lowest throw in hazard⟩
shoot craps play craps. **crap·shoot·er** *n.*

crap·u·lent ['kræpjələnt] *adj* sick from too much eating or drinking. **crap·u·lence** *n.* ⟨Latin *crapulentus; crapula* drunkenness⟩
crap·u·lous *adj* **1** habitually given to overeating or over-drinking. **2** sick from overeating or over-drinking.

crash ['kræʃ] *n* **1** a sudden, very loud, harsh noise: *a crash of thunder.* **2** a fall or collision with a violent impact: *an airplane crash.* **3** a sudden severe decline: *a stock market crash.* **4** *Computers* system failure.
v **1** make a sudden, very loud, harsh noise; move noisily and violently: *crashing through the forest.* **2** collide or fall with a violent impact. **3** decline sharply and suddenly. **4** *Computers* of a system, fail due to some error. **5** *Informal* attend without an invitation: *to crash a party.* **6** *Informal* go to sleep, esp after intense or prolonged activity. **7** *Slang* descend quickly from a drug-induced high. **crash·er** *n.* ⟨blend of obsolete *craze* shatter and *mash*⟩
crash course a short, very intensive course of instruction. **crash helmet** padded safety helmet worn by car racers, motorocyclists, etc. **crash·ing** *adj* complete: *a crashing bore.* **crash–land** *v* of an aircraft, make a forced landing, usually with damage to the aircraft. **crash landing.**

crass [kræs] *adj* **1** rude, tasteless, or vulgar. **2** blatant; gross. **crass·ly** *adv.* **crass·ness** *n.* ⟨Latin *crassus* thick⟩

crate [kreit] *n* **1** a large, strong box used to pack furniture, fruit, etc., for shipping or storage. **2** *Slang* an old, worn-out vehicle.
v pack in a crate. ⟨Latin *cratis* wickerwork⟩

cra·ter ['kreitər] *n* **1** a depression around the opening at the top of a volcano. **2** any such bowl-shaped hole: *craters made by exploding shells.* ⟨Greek *kratēr* bowl; *kra-* mix⟩

crave [kreiv] *v* **1** long for; have an intense, often irrational desire for: *to crave friendship, to crave certain foods during pregnancy.* **2** ask earnestly; beg: *to crave a favour.* **crav·ing** *n.* ⟨Old English *crafian* demand⟩

SYNONYMS

Craving = a desire so strong it amounts to a need: *a craving for salt.* **Desire** applies to any strong wish, good or bad, for something a person thinks or hopes he or she can get: *Her desire is to travel.* **Longing** applies to any earnest desire, often for something that seems beyond reach: *His longing for a powerful motorcycle is pathetic.*

cra·ven [ˈkreivən] *adj* cowardly: *a craven act.* *n* a coward. **cra·ven·ly** *adv.* **cra·ven·ness** *n.* ⟨Middle English *cravant*⟩

craw [krɒ] *n* **1** the crop of a bird or insect. **2** the stomach of any animal. ⟨Middle English *crawe*⟩
stick in one's craw be hard to accept or utter.

crawl [krɒl] *v* **1** move with the body close to the ground. **2** move on hands and knees. **3** move slowly: *Traffic crawled on the icy roads.* **4** swarm with crawling things: *The ground was crawling with ants.* **5** of skin or flesh, feel as if covered with crawling things: *My flesh crawled at the grisly sight.* **6** behave abjectly. **7** swim with alternate overarm strokes. *n* **1** a slow pace. **2** a fast way of swimming using alternate overarm strokes. **crawl·er** *n.* ⟨perhaps from Old Norse *krafla*⟩
crawl space a low, often narrow space in a building, giving access to wiring, pipes, etc., esp under a house with no basement. **crawl·y** *adj* **1** crawling: *all sorts of crawly insects.* **2** feeling as if things are crawling on one's skin.

cray·fish [ˈkreiˌfɪʃ] *n, pl* **-fish** or **-fish·es** any of various freshwater crustaceans resembling small lobsters. ⟨Old French *crevice* crab, infl. by English *fish*⟩

cray·on [ˈkreiɒn] *or* [ˈkreiən] *n* a stick or pencil of coloured wax, chalk, charcoal, oil pastel, etc. for drawing. **cray·on** *v.* ⟨French, from *craie* chalk; Latin *creta*⟩

craze [kreiz] *n* something everybody is very much interested in for a short time; fad. *v* make crazy: *She was nearly crazed with the pain.* ⟨Middle English *crase(n)* break⟩
cra·zy *adj* **1** *Informal* insane. **2** irrational or wild: *crazy with fear.* **3** *Informal* ridiculous; foolish: *a crazy idea.* **4** *Informal* extremely enthusiastic (*about*) or eager (*for*). **5** *Informal* unusual; whimsical: *crazy jewellery.* *n Informal* an insane or eccentric person. **cra·zi·ly** *adv.* **cra·zi·ness** *n.* **like crazy** *Informal* wildly or to an extreme degree: *laughing like crazy.* **crazy paving** paving with slabs arranged in an irregular pattern. **crazy quilt 1** a patchwork quilt with no definite pattern. **2** anything similarly irregular. **crazy–quilt** *adj.*

creak [krik] *v* make a prolonged, harsh, squeaking or croaking noise: *creaking hinges.*

creak *n.* **creak·y** *adj.* ⟨Middle English *creken*; apparently imitative⟩

cream [krim] *n* **1** the yellowish part of milk that contains fat. **2** an oily preparation to soften or treat skin. **3** food or drink made with cream or having a smooth texture, rich flavour, etc. like cream: *ice cream, cream of mushroom soup.* **4** yellowish white. **5** the best part: *the cream of the crop.* *adj* containing cream: *cream soup.* *v* **1** beat into a smooth mixture like cream: *to cream butter and sugar together.* **2** put cream into; prepare with cream. **3** take the cream from. **4** *Slang* defeat, beat, or hit soundly. **cream·y** *adj.* ⟨Old French *cresme* blend of Latin *crama* cream + *chrisma* ointment; Greek⟩
the cream rises to the top the best person or idea will succeed.
cream cheese a white mild cheese soft enough to spread. **cream·er** *n* **1** a small cream pitcher. **2** a liquid or powder used in coffee as a substitute for cream. **3** a machine for separating cream from milk. **cream·er·y** *n* a place where butter and cheese are made for sale. **cream of tar·tar** a powder used in cooking and medicine; potassium bitartrate. **cream puff** a light pastry filled with cream or custard. **cream soda** vanilla-flavoured pop.

crease [kris] *n* **1** a fold, esp a deep or marked one. **2** *Hockey, lacrosse* the small area marked off in front of each goal. *v* **1** make a crease in. **2** acquire creases. **creas·er** *n.* **crease·less** *adj.* ⟨origin unknown⟩

cre·ate [kriˈeit] *v* **1** make a thing that never existed before, using skill, intelligence, or power. **2** bring about: *to create a disturbance.* **cre·a·tion** *n.* ⟨Latin *creare*⟩
Creation the creating of the universe by God. **cre·a·tion·ism** *n* the theory that the universe and everything in it were specially created by God and are not the result of accident or evolution. **cre·a·tion·ist** *n.* **cre·a·tion·is·tic** *adj.* **creation science** the use of scientific analysis to support the biblical account of creation by God. **creation scientist. cre·a·tive** *adj* **1** of or having the power to create. **2** imaginative: *creative writing.* **3** showing resourcefulness, originality, etc.: *creative solutions to your business problems.* **4** (euphemistic) ingenious but dishonest or wrong: *creative accounting.* **cre·a·tive·ly** *adv.* **cre·a·tiv·i·ty** or **cre·a·tive·ness** *n.* **cre·a·tor** *n* **1** one who creates. **2 the Creator** God. **crea·ture** [ˈkritʃər] *n* **1** a living being; animal. **2** any created thing. **3** a person who is completely under the influence of another. **4 the creature** *Informal* whisky. **creature comforts** the things that give bodily comfort.

crèche [krɛʃ] *or* [kreiʃ] *n* a nursery or day care. ⟨French⟩

cre·dence [ˈkridəns] *n* **1** belief: *Never give credence to gossip.* **2** credibility; plausibility. ⟨Med.Latin *credentia* < Latin *credere* believe⟩
letter of credence letter of recommendation. **cre·den·tials** [krəˈdɛnʃəl] *n pl* educational or professional background, letters of reference, or any other things that commend a person to potential employers, etc. **cre·den·tialed** *adj.*

cre·den·za [krə'dɛnzə] *n* **1** a piece of office furniture like a low cupboard with doors. **2** a sideboard or buffet. ⟨Italian⟩

cred·i·ble ['krɛdəbəl] *adj* believable; inviting belief or trust. **cred·i·bil·i·ty** *n*. **cred·i·bly** *adv*. ⟨Latin *credibilis; credere* believe⟩

CONFUSABLES

Credible = believable: *Her story is too full of coincidences to be credible.* **Credulous** = too ready to believe: *I was credulous enough to think I would really be given the job.*

cred·it ['krɛdɪt] *n* **1** belief in the truth or worth of something: *They placed little credit in his story.* **2** the amount of money a person has in an account: *He had a credit of $5000.* **3** *Accounting* an entry of money paid into an account. **4** money loaned, or whose payment has been deferred: *Long-term credit is available.* **5** reputation with regard to payment of debts: *Your credit is good.* **6** recognition: *The person who does the work should get the credit.* **7** a source of honour or praise: *Her latest novel is a credit to her.* **8** a notice in a book, film, etc., usually one of a list, acknowledging a contribution of skill, material, capital, etc.: *He was promised a credit for his contribution to the documentary.* **9** an entry on a student's record showing that a course of study has been satisfactorily completed.
v **1** believe. **2** pay into (an account): *We've credited $30 to your account. Your account has been credited $30.* **3** attribute something to: *He credited her with the original idea.* **4** give a credit to. ⟨Latin *creditum* a loan; *credere* trust, entrust⟩

do credit to bring honour or recognition to. **give credit to** trust; believe. **give someone credit for** believe or recognize that a person has: *Give him credit for some intelligence.* **on credit** with payment deferred: *She bought her car on credit.* **to one's credit** in one's favour: *To her credit, she refused to leave.*

cred·it·a·ble *adj* bringing credit or honour: *a creditable record of attendance.* **cred·it·a·bly** *adv*. **credit bureau** an agency that collects data on the credit ratings of individuals or companies. **credit card** a card entitling its holder to charge the cost of goods or services to an account. **credit line 1** mention of one's name among the credits for a film, etc. **2** LINE OF CREDIT. **cred·i·tor** *n* a person to whom money, goods, or services are owed. **credit rating** the financial standing of a person or company according to a standard scale. **credit union** a co-operative association that makes loans to its members at low rates of interest.

cre·do ['kreidou] *or* ['kridou] *n* **1** creed; one's guiding principle. **2** Also, **Credo** *Christianity* any of various historic summaries of belief or their musical settings. ⟨Latin = I believe⟩

cred·u·lous ['krɛdʒələs] *adj* too ready to believe. **cre·du·li·ty** [krə'djuləti] *or* [krə'duləti] *n*. **cred·u·lous·ly** *adv*. **cred·u·lous·ness** *n*. ⟨Latin *credulus; credere* believe⟩

Cree [kri] *n, pl* **Cree** or **Crees 1** a member of a First Nations people living mainly in central Canada and the Prairie Provinces. The Cree may be divided regionally into three groups with distinct culture and dialect, namely, the **Plains Cree** (central Saskatchewan, Alberta), the **Woodland Cree** (northern Saskatchewan, Manitoba), and the **Swampy Cree** (lowlands around Hudson and James Bays). These regional groups are divided into local groups, each with its own Aboriginal name. **2** any of the dialects of the Algonquian language of the Cree. **Cree** *adj*. **Cree Syllabics** a writing system used by the Cree, in which each symbol stands for a particular consonant-vowel combination.

creed [krid] *n* **1** a formal statement of the essential points of religious belief. **2** any set of basic guiding principles: *It was her creed that work should come before play.* **3 the Creed** *Christianity* the Apostles' Creed or the Nicene Creed. ⟨Old English *crēda*. See CREDO.⟩

creek [krik] *or, often,* [krɪk] *n* **1** a small freshwater stream. **2** a narrow bay running some distance inland. ⟨Middle English *creke*⟩ **up the** (or a) **creek** *Slang* in serious difficulty.

creel [kril] *n* **1** a basket for holding a catch of fish. **2** a basketlike trap for fish, lobsters, etc. ⟨Middle English *crele*⟩

creep [krip] *v* **crept, creep·ing 1** crawl: *The cat crept along the branch.* **2** move slowly. **3** grow by sending out rootlets or clinging tendrils: *creeping vines.* **4** usually of something bad, advance by imperceptible degrees: *creeping materialism.* **5** slip out of place a little at a time: *The hall rug creeps.* **6** shiver; shudder: *I could feel my flesh creep, and my hair stood on end.*
n **1** a creeping movement. **2** *Geology* slow movement of soil down a slope, due to frost, gravity, or ground water: *continental creep.* **3 the creeps** *Informal* a feeling of horror or digust, as of things creeping over one's skin. **4** *Informal* a person who gives one the creeps. ⟨Old English *crēopan*⟩

creep up (on) approach slowly and silently: *Night was creeping up on the forest.*

creep·er *n* **1** any creeping plant. **2** any of a family of small birds that climb along tree branches, looking for insects. **3** a piece of material attached to a ski bottom for traction when climbing uphill. **creep·y** *adj Informal* having or causing THE CREEPS. **creep·i·ly** *adv*. **creep·i·ness** *n*. **creep·y–crawl·y** *adj Informal* **1** having or causing THE CREEPS. **2** of insects or other small creatures, creeping. *n, pl* **creep·y–crawl·ies 1** a small insect or other creature that creeps, esp when regarded with horror. **2 the creepy–crawlies** *pl* THE CREEPS.

cre·mate [krɪ'meit] *or* ['krimeit] *v* burn (a dead body) to ashes. **cre·ma·tion** *n*. **cre·ma·tor** *n*. ⟨Latin *cremare* burn⟩
cre·ma·to·ri·um [,krimə'tɔriəm] *or* [,krɛmə'tɔriəm] *n, pl* **-ri·ums** or **-ria** [-riə] a building with a furnace for cremating.

crème [krɛm] *French* [kʁɛm] *n* (in borrowed compounds) cream.
crème brûlée [bru'lei] *French* [bʁy'le] *n* a caramel custard with a skin of burnt sugar.

crème de ca·ca·o [kə'keiou], [kə'kaʊ] *or* ['kou,kou] *French* [ka'kao] chocolate liqueur.
crème de la crème *French* the very best; choicest. **crème de menthe** [mɑnt] *or* [mɛnθ] *French* [mãt] mint liqueur.

cre·nel ['krɛnəl] *n* an arrow-slit or loophole in the top of a battlement. **cren·el·lat·ed** or **cren·el·at·ed** *adj*. **cren·el·la·tion** *n*. ⟨French = notch; Latin *crena*⟩

Cre·ole ['krioul] *or* ['kreioul] *n* **1** one of the descendants of the original French settlers of Louisiana who have preserved their culture. **2** a black or a person of mixed black and French or Spanish ancestry born in Spanish America or the West Indies. **3** the dialect of French spoken by many blacks in Louisiana. **4** the majority language of Haiti, based on French and incorporating other languages. **5** creole a language that is based on two or more other languages and is the mother tongue of a community of speakers. Compare PIDGIN.
adj **1** to do with Creoles. **2 creole** to do with a creole. **3** cooked in a sauce made of stewed tomatoes, peppers, etc. ⟨French; Portuguese *crioulo* from *criar*, Latin *creare* create⟩

cre·o·sote ['kriə,sout] *n* an oily liquid with a strong odour, obtained from wood tar or coal tar and used to preserve wood. ⟨Greek *kreo-*flesh + *sōtēr* saviour; orig meat preservative⟩

crepe or **crêpe** [kreip] *French* [kʀɛp] *n* **1** a woven cloth with a crinkled surface. **2** a black strip of this, worn as a sign of mourning. **3** Usually, **crêpe** a large, very thin pancake typically served folded or rolled up and with a filling. **cre·pey** *adj*. ⟨French *crêpe*; Latin *crispa* curled⟩
crepe de Chine [ʃin] a soft, thin, silk crepe.
crepe paper thin, crinkled, stretchy paper used for making party streamers, etc.

crep·i·tate ['krɛpə,teit] *v* crackle; rattle. **crep·i·tant** *adj*. **crep·i·ta·tion** *n*. ⟨Latin *crepitare*⟩

crept [krɛpt] *v* pt and pp of CREEP.

cre·pus·cu·lar [krɪ'pʌskjələr] *adj* **1** of or resembling twilight; dusky; dim. **2** of certain birds, insects, etc., active by twilight. ⟨Latin *crepusculum* twilight⟩

Cres. Crescent (in street names).

cre·scen·do [krə'ʃɛndou] *n* **1** *Music* a gradual increase in loudness. **2** any gradual increase in force, loudness, etc.: *a crescendo of cheers.* **3** the peak of such an increase: *Complaints reached a crescendo.* **cre·scen·do** *adj, adv, v. Abbrev* **cres.** or **cresc.** ⟨Italian, ppr of *crescere* increase; Latin⟩

cres·cent ['krɛsənt] *n* **1** the shape of the moon as seen from the earth in its first or last quarter. **2** anything having this shape.
adj **1** having this shape. **2** of the moon, waxing. **cres·cent·like** *adj*. ⟨Latin *crescens* ppr of *crescere* grow⟩

cress [krɛs] *n* any of various plants of the mustard family having crisp, peppery-tasting leaves used in salads, etc. ⟨Old English *cresse*⟩

crest [krɛst] *n* **1** a tuft of hair or feathers or growth of skin on the head of a bird or animal. **2** a decoration, plumes, etc., on the top of a helmet. **3** a decoration at the top of a COAT OF ARMS. **4** an emblem, often shaped like a shield, worn by members of a team, regiment, university, etc. **5** the top part of a hill or wave. **6** among peoples of the First Nations on the West Coast: **a** the symbol of a clan or similar social group. **b** the clan or group it identifies.
v **1** of waves, form a crest. **2** of a river, etc., reach its highest level. **3** serve as a crest to. **4** reach the crest of (a hill, etc.). **crest·ed** *adj*. **crest·like** *adj*. ⟨Latin *crista* tuft⟩
crest·fall·en *adj* dejected; discouraged.

Cre·ta·ceous [krɪ'teiʃəs] *n* *Geology* the last period of the Mesozoic era, starting about 144 million years ago, when most of the chalk deposits were made.
adj **1** *Geology* of this period. **2 cretaceous** to do with chalk. ⟨Latin *creta* chalk; *Creta* Crete⟩

cre·tin ['kretən] *or* ['kritən] *n* a person who is severely mentally retarded, esp as a result of congenital thyroid failure having stunted physical and mental development. **cre·tin·ism** *n*. ⟨Old French *chrestien;* Latin *Christianus* Christian, later 'fellow' then 'poor fellow'⟩

cre·ton ['kretən] *French* [kʀɛ'tɔ̃] *n* ✻ a pâté of pork, fat, and spices. ⟨Cdn. French⟩

cre·tonne [krɪ'tɒn] *or* [kri'tɒn] *n* a strong cotton cloth with coloured prints. ⟨French, probably from *Creton*, village in Normandy⟩

Creutz·feldt–Ja·kob disease ['krɔɪts,fɛlt 'jakɔp] *or* ['jakəb] a disease of the nervous system characterized by dementia, blindness, and uncontrolled body movements. ⟨H.G. *Creutzfeldt* and A. *Jakob*, 20c German physicians⟩

cre·vasse [krə'væs] *n* a deep crack in rock or in the ice of a glacier. ⟨Old French *crevace;* Latin *crepacia* from *crepare* to crack⟩

crev·ice ['krɛvɪs] *n* a narrow split or crack. ⟨Middle English *crevace*. See CREVASSE.⟩

crew [kru] *n* **1** the people who work on a ship, aircraft, etc. **2** any group of people who work together: *a camera crew.* **3** *Informal* a group: *The whole crew came for dinner.*
v **1** provide a crew for. **2** work as member of a crew. ⟨Middle French *creüe* reinforcement; *creistre*, Latin *crescere* grow⟩
crew cut a close-cropped haircut for men.
crew·man *n, pl* **-men** a member of a crew.
crew neck a plain round neckline on a T-shirt, sweatshirt, etc.

crew·el ['kruəl] *n* a loosely twisted woollen yarn used for embroidery. ⟨origin uncertain⟩
crew·el·work *n* embroidery using crewel.

crib [krɪb] *n* **1** a baby's small bed with high barred sides. **2** a large bin or racklike structure holding feed for farm animals. **3** a barn stall. **4 a** in cribbage, the cards discarded from each hand for later scoring. **b** *Informal* cribbage. **5** a supporting framework of logs or timbers, used in building. **6** *Informal* **a** CHEAT SHEET. **b** plagiarism or plagiarized material. **7** ✻ a raft of logs to be floated downstream.

v **cribbed, crib·bing** plagiarize or use a CHEAT SHEET. **crib·ber** *n.* ⟨Old English *cribb*⟩

crib death SUDDEN INFANT DEATH SYNDROME.

crib·bage [ˈkrɪbɪdʒ] *n* a card game where the players keep score on a **cribbage board** with movable pegs. ⟨Old English *cribb* stall⟩

crick¹ [krɪk] *n* a sudden muscular cramp: *a crick in the neck.* **crick** *v.* ⟨origin uncertain⟩

crick² [krɪk] *n Dialect* CREEK (def. 1).

crick·et¹ [ˈkrɪkɪt] *n* any of a large family of insects resembling grasshoppers. ⟨Old French *criquet*; imitative⟩

crick·et² [ˈkrɪkɪt] *n* an outdoor game played by two teams with ball, bats, and wickets. **crick·et·er** *n.* ⟨Old French *criquet* goalpost⟩

cri·er [ˈkraɪər] *n* formerly, an official who shouted out public announcements.

crime [kraɪm] *n* **1** an act that is against the law. **2** such acts collectively. **3** a wrong act: *crimes against taste.* ⟨Latin *crimen*⟩

crim·i·nal [ˈkrɪmənəl] *n* a person guilty of a crime. **crim·i·nal** *adj.* **crim·i·nal·ly** *adv.* **criminally insane** driven by insanity to commit crimes. **Criminal Code** in Canada, the list of crimes. **crim·i·nal·ize** *v* make (something) a crime. **criminal law** the branch of law that deals with crimes and is limited to the Criminal Code. Compare CIVIL LAW. **criminal lawyer**. **crim·i·nol·o·gy** *n* the scientific study of the behaviour and treatment of criminals. **crim·i·no·log·i·cal** *adj.* **crim·i·nol·o·gist** *n.*

crimp [krɪmp] *v* **1** press into small, narrow folds: *to crimp hair.* **2** pinch, fold, or bend into shape. **3** hinder; cramp. **crimp** *n.* **crimp·er** *n.* ⟨Old English *(ge)crympan*⟩

put a crimp in *Informal* interfere with; hinder.

crim·son [ˈkrɪmzən] *n, adj* deep red. ⟨Arabic *qirmiz* the kermes insect, source of red dye⟩

cringe [krɪndʒ] *v* **1** shrink from danger or pain. **2** bow or behave in an abject way: *The beggar cringed as he held out his hand.* **cringe** *n.* **cring·ing** *adj.* ⟨Old English *cringan* give way⟩

crin·kle [ˈkrɪŋkəl] *v* **1** become or cause to be full of small wrinkles. **2** rustle or crackle, as paper being crumpled. **crin·kle** *n.* **crin·kly** *adj.* ⟨Old English *crincan* bend⟩

crin·o·line [ˈkrɪnəlɪn] *or* [ˈkrɪnəˌlɪn] *n* a petticoat of stiff cloth to hold out a full skirt. ⟨Latin *crinis* hair + *linum* thread⟩

crip·ple [ˈkrɪpəl] *n* a person or animal that is disabled in a way that hinders movement. *v* **1** make a cripple of. **2** damage; disable; weaken: *The ship was crippled by the storm.* ⟨Old English *crypel*⟩

USAGE
The noun **cripple** has become an offensive term, while the verb is now almost completely confined to metaphorical use: *crippling debt.* **Disable** is preferred in the context of physical or mental conditions of human beings: *He was disabled by a mining accident.*

cri·sis [ˈkraɪsɪs] *n, pl* **-ses** [-siz] **1** a state of urgent need or grave danger: *Kidnappings by the FLQ produced a crisis in Canada in October*

1970. **2** a decisive or pivotal event. **3** the turning point in an illness. ⟨Greek *krisis; krinein* decide⟩

crisp [krɪsp] *adj* **1** firm and brittle or crunchy: *a crisp cookie.* **2** sharp and clear: *a crisp fall day, crisp outlines.* **3** brisk; energetic: *crisp repartee.* **4** neat, trim, businesslike, etc. *n* **1** something crisp, such as a thin cookie. **2** *Brit* a potato chip. **3** a dessert with a crumb topping: *apple crisp.* **crisp** *v.* **crisp·ly** *adv.* **crisp·ness** *n.* **crisp·y** *adj.* ⟨Latin *crispus* curled⟩

burnt to a crisp completely burnt.

crisp·er *n* a compartment in a refrigerator for storing fresh produce.

criss·cross [ˈkrɪsˌkrɒs] *adj, adv* in or with a series of crossing lines: *a crisscross pattern of stripes, sticks laid crisscross on a fire.* *v* **1** mark with crossed lines. **2** come and go across: *Buses crisscross the city.* **3** lie across (one another): *In New York, streets and avenues crisscross.* **criss·cross** *n.* ⟨*Christ's cross*⟩

cri·te·ri·on [kraɪˈtɪriən] *n* **-te·ri·a** a standard for making a judgment; qualification that must be met: *Wealth is only one criterion of success.* ⟨Greek *kritērion; krinein* judge, decide⟩

USAGE
Criterion is one of several common nouns borrowed from Greek and ending in *-on* whose singular and plural are regularly confused. **Criterion** is singular, **criteria** is plural. Another such word is **phenomenon**.

crit·ic [ˈkrɪtɪk] *n* **1** a person who reviews and makes judgments about books, music, films, etc. **2** a person who analyzes anything for its merits and faults. **3** a person who finds fault. **crit·i·cism** [ˈkrɪtəˌsɪzəm] *n.* **crit·i·cize** [ˈkrɪtəˌsaɪz] *v.* ⟨Greek *kritikos; krinein* to judge⟩

crit·i·cal *adj* **1** inclined to find fault: *a critical disposition.* **2** involving careful analysis and judgment: *critical thinking.* **3** key; important; determining the outcome of something: *a critical moment. Speed is critical in such cases.* **4** characterized by urgent need or grave danger: *The situation is critical. The patient is in critical condition.* **crit·i·cal·ly** *adv.* **critical mass** *n* **1** the smallest amount needed to affect an outcome: *a critical mass of voter support.* **2** the minimum quantity of fissile material required for a nuclear reaction. **cri·tique** [krɪˈtik] *n* **1** a critical review. **2** a criticism; a critical comment. **cri·tique** *v.*

crit·ter [ˈkrɪtər] *n Dialect, informal* creature.

croak [krouk] *n* a deep, hoarse sound made by a bullfrog, crow, raven, etc. *v* **1** make such a sound. **2** speak gloomily. **3** *Slang* die. **croak·er** *n.* **croak·y** *adj.* ⟨Old English *crācian*⟩

cro·chet [krouˈʃei] *or* [ˈkrouʃei] *n* a lacy needlework done with a hooked needle (**crochet hook**). **cro·chet, -cheted** [-ˈʃeid], **-chet·ing** [-ˈʃeiɪŋ] *v.* **cro·chet·er** [-ˈʃeiər] *n.* ⟨French, diminutive of *croc* hook⟩

crock [krɒk] *n* **1** an earthenware pot. **2** *Slang* a decrepit vehicle. **3** *Slang* piece of nonsense. ⟨Old English *crocc(a)*⟩

crocked *adj Slang* drunk. **crock·er·y** *n* china or earthenware articles.

croc·o·dile ['krɒkə,daɪl] *n* any of a family of large, aquatic reptiles related to the alligator. **croc·o·dil·i·an** [,krɒkə'dɪliən] *adj.* ⟨Greek *krokodilos; krokē* pebble + *drilos* worm⟩ **crocodile tears** insincere sorrow.

cro·cus ['kroukəs] *n, pl* **cro·cus·es** or **cro·ci** [-saɪ] *or* [-si] **1** any of a large genus of small plants of the iris family. **2** ✷ **prairie crocus** a species of anemone, with a purple or white flower. It is the floral emblem of Manitoba. ⟨Greek *krokos;* Semitic⟩

Crohn's disease [krounz] a chronic inflammation of the lower bowel. ⟨B.B. *Crohn* , 20c US physician⟩

crois·sant [krə'sɒnt] *French* [kʀwa'sɑ̃] *n* a small, flaky roll of bread, often sweet, shaped like a crescent. ⟨French. See CRESCENT.⟩

cro·ki·nole ['kroukə,noul] *n* ✷ a table game in which each player tries to flick disks into or near a hole at the centre of a round board. ⟨French *croquignole* a flick, fillip⟩

crom·lech ['krɒmlək] *n* a circle of upright stones erected in prehistoric times. ⟨Welsh *crom* bent + *llech* flat stone⟩

crone [kroun] *n* a wrinkled, old woman. ⟨Old French *carogne* carcass, hag⟩

cro·ny ['krouni] *n* any friend or associate of a bad person. ⟨origin uncertain⟩

crook [krʊk] *n* **1** *Informal* a thief or swindler. **2** the place where something bends to form a hook or L-shape: *the crook of a hockey stick.* *v* **crooked** [krʊkt], **crook·ing** *v* bend; hook: *She beckoned by crooking her finger at us.* ⟨Middle English *crōc;* Old Norse *krókr*⟩ **crook·ed** ['krʊkɪd] **1** bent: *a crooked piece of lumber.* **2** slanted: *The picture on the wall is crooked.* **3** dishonest: *a crooked politician.* **crook·ed·ly** *adv.* **crook·ed·ness** *n.* **crooked canoe** [krʊkt] ✷ a canoe designed by the Eastern James Bay Cree, having a keel which forms an arc. **crooked knife** ['krʊkɪd] ✷ a woodworking knife with a blade that ends in a hook, used widely in the North, esp by Aboriginal people.

croon [krun] *v* sing tenderly or with exaggerated emotion. **croon** *n.* **croon·er** *n.* ⟨Middle Dutch *kronen* murmur⟩

crop [krɒp] *n* **1** a plant grown in quantity, for home use or for sale: *Wheat is the main crop of the Prairies.* **2** anything like a crop; a newly produced group: *a crop of new books, a crop of graduates.* **3** a short haircut. **4** an act of clipping short. **5** the baglike organ in an animal's body, preparing food for digestion. **6** a short riding whip with a loop for a lash. *v* **cropped, crop·ping 1** cut off short: *Sheep crop grass.* **2** cultivate or harvest (a crop). **3** bear a crop. ⟨Old English *cropp*⟩ **crop out** appear above a surface: *Great ridges of rock cropped out all over the hillside.* **crop up** appear or occur unexpectedly: *All sorts of difficulties cropped up.* **crop–dust·ing** *n* the practice of spraying pesticides from a plane over growing crops.

crop-dust·er *n.* **crop·land** *n* land under cultivation for crops. **crop·per** *n* **1** a person who raises a crop, esp a SHARECROPPER. **2** a plant grown as a crop: *The soybean is a hardy cropper.* **come a cropper** *Informal* a fall heavily. **b** fail; come to grief. **crop rotation** use of the same ground in successive seasons for different crops with varying nutritional requirements so as not to deplete the soil.

cro·quet [krou'kei] *n* an outdoor game played by driving wooden balls through small wire arches by means of mallets. ⟨French, variant of *crochet.* See CROCHET.⟩

cro·quette [krou'kɛt] *n* a small ball or stick of chopped cooked meat, fish, vegetable, etc., coated with crumbs and fried. ⟨French, from *croquer* crunch⟩

cro·sier or **cro·zier** ['krouʒər] *n* **1** an ornamental staff carried ceremonially by or before a bishop, abbot, or abbess. **2** *Botany* the curled top of a young fern. ⟨Old French *crossier* crook bearer; Latin *croccia* crook⟩

cross [krɒs] *n* **1** an upright post with a beam across it near the top, on which the ancient Romans executed those condemned by law. **2 the Cross a** the cross on which Jesus died, seen as an emblem of Christianity. **b** the suffering and death of Jesus. **3** any object or mark shaped like a cross or X. **4** a burden that must be endured. **5** the act or result of mating different varieties, breeds, or species of animals or plants with each other: *Our dog is a cross between a chihuahua and a fox terrier.* **6** a combination of two things, or something intermediate between them: *Documentary drama is a cross between theatre and journalism.* *v* **1** go or lie across: *to cross a bridge. Main Street crosses Lansdowne Avenue.* **2** cancel by drawing a line through (with *off* or *out*): *Cross my name off your list.* **3** draw a line across: *Cross your t's.* **4** put one thing across (another); form a cross with: *He crossed his arms. Don't cross those wires.* **5** trace the form of a cross on (a person or thing) as an act of Christian devotion: *to cross oneself.* **6** oppose or hinder: *If anyone crosses her, she gets very angry.* **7** cause (two different breeds) to mate in order to produce a new kind: *Canadian breeders have crossed cattle with buffalo to produce the cattalo.* *adj* **1** in a bad temper. **2** moving or lying across: *a cross timber, cross traffic.* **cross·ly** *adv.* **cross·ness** *n.* ⟨Old English *cros;* Latin *crux*⟩ **at cross purposes** in conflict or opposition. **cross one's fingers a** put one finger over another in a superstitious gesture intended to keep trouble away or allow one to lie with impunity. **b** hope for the best. **cross one's heart** make the sign of the cross over one's heart when swearing that something is true. **cross one's mind** occur (briefly) to one. **cross someone's path** or **cross paths (with)** meet (a person). **cross swords** engage in controversy. **cross the floor** of a member of a legislature, defect from one's party by moving to a seat in another section of the chamber. **get one's wires crossed** miscommunicate.

cross·bar *n* a bar lying across. **cross·beam** *n* a beam lying crosswise, esp one that extends from wall to wall of a building. **cross·bill** *n* any of a small genus of finches having a strong bill whose points cross each other. **cross·bones** *n pl* two long bones laid crosswise. Poisonous substances are marked with a skull and crossbones. **cross·bow** *n* a medieval weapon consisting of a bow held horizontally, with a grooved piece across the middle of it to direct an arrow. **cross·breed** *v* **-bred, -breed·ing** breed (different varieties or species of animals or plants) together. *n* an individual produced in this way. **cross·bred** *adj*. **cross–check** *v* **1** check against another source. **2** *Hockey, lacrosse* give (an opponent) an illegal check by holding one's stick in both hands and thrusting it in front of the opponent. **cross–check** *n*. **cross–coun·try** *adj* **1** across open country instead of by road. *a cross-country race*. **2** that crosses a country: *a cross-country flight*. **3** to do with skiing over more or less flat country as opposed to down slopes. **cross–cul·tu·ral** ['krɒs 'kʌltʃərəl] *adj* to do with interchange between different cultures: *a cross-cultural study*. **cross·cur·rent** *n* **1** a current of air blowing across another. **2** a contradictory trend: *the crosscurrents of political thought*. **cross·cut** *adj* that has been cut across, esp across the grain. *n* **1** a cut, course, or path across. **2** a section of a film that shows contrasting scenes by turns. **cross·cut, -cut, -cut·ting** *v*. **crosscut saw** a special saw for cutting wood across the grain. **cross–dressing** *adj, n* wearing the clothes of the opposite sex so as to appear to be a member of that sex. **cross–dresser** *n*. **cross–ex·am·ine** *v* **1** of a lawyer in court, question (a witness) who has testified for the opposing side. **2** question long and closely. **cross–ex·am·i·na·tion** *n*. **cross–ex·am·in·er** *n*. **cross–eyed** *adj* having one eye or both eyes turned in toward the nose. **cross–eye** *n*. **cross–fer·ti·lize** *v Biology* fertilize (one flower or species) by another. **cross–fer·ti·li·za·tion** *n*. **cross–fer·tile** *adj* productive if cross-fertilized. **cross·fire** *n* **1** gunfire coming from opposite directions. **2** mutual verbal attack by opposing parties. **cross–grained** *adj* **1** of wood, having an irregular grain. **2** contrary; unco-operative. **cross·hairs** *n pl* **1** two fine strands forming a cross in the focal plane of an optical instrument, for accurately defining the line of sight. **2 crosshair** *sg* in some computer applications, a cross-shaped cursor for making a box on the screen. **cross·hatch** *v* mark with crossed sets of parallel lines. **cross·hatch·ing** *n*. **cross–in·dex** *v* in an index, refer the reader to another place in the same index. **cross·ing** *n* **1** a place where things cross each other. **2** a place at which a street, river, etc., may be crossed. **crossing guard** a person who escorts children across busy streets. **cross–leg·ged** ['krɒs ˌlɛgɪd] *or* [-ˌlɛgd] *adj, adv* **1** with ankles crossed and the knees bent and spread apart: *We sat cross-legged on the floor*. **2** with one leg crossed over the other. **cross·patch** *n Informal* a bad-tempered

person. **cross·piece** *n* a piece lying crosswise. **cross–pol·li·nate** *v* put pollen from the anther of (one flower) onto the stigma of another. **cross–pol·li·na·tion** *n*. **cross–ques·tion** *v* question closely; cross-examine. **cross·rail** *n* a piece of wood, metal, etc., lying crosswise. **cross–re·fer, -ferred, -fer·ring** *v* link by a CROSS-REFERENCE: *The entry 'killer whale' is cross-referred with 'orca'*. **cross–ref·er·ence** *n* a reference in one part of a book to another part for more information. *v* provide (a work) with cross-references. **cross·road** ['krɒs,roud] *n* **1** a road that crosses another. **2 crossroads a** a place where roads cross (with sg or plural verb): *Wait for me at the crossroads*. **b** a point at which a decision must be made (with sg verb): *The country is at an economic crossroads*. **cross section 1** the surface that is exposed if a thing is sliced at right angles to its axis at a certain point. **2** a drawing of this: *a labelled cross section of a volcano*. **3** a representative sample: *a cross section of the community*. **cross–stitch** *n* in embroidery, one stitch crossed over another, forming an X. **cross–stitch** *v*. **cross street** a street connecting main streets. **cross·town** *adj, adv* (going) across a town or city: *a crosstown bus*. **cross·walk** *n* a marked street crossing. **cross·wind** *n* a wind blowing from the side, across the path of a ship or aircraft. **cross·wise** *adv* **1** across. **2** in the form of a cross. **cross·word puzzle** a puzzle with numbered clues for words to be written letter by letter, horizontally and vertically, in blank squares so as to intersect.

crotch [krɒtʃ] *n* **1** a forked part, as where a tree divides into branches. **2** the place where the human body divides into its two legs; the pubic area. **3** the corresponding part of pants or a similar garment. ⟨variant of *crutch*⟩

crotch·et·y ['krɒtʃəti] *adj* **1** cranky. **2** full of odd notions or whims. **crotch·et·i·ness** *n*. ⟨Old French *crochet* hook⟩

crouch [krʌutʃ] *v* stoop low with legs bent. **crouch** *n*. ⟨Old French *crochir; croc* hook⟩

croup[1] [krup] *n* an inflammation of the throat characterized by a hoarse cough and difficult breathing. **croup·y** *adj*. ⟨possibly a blend of *croak* and *whoop*⟩

croup[2] [krup] *n* the rump of a horse. ⟨Old French *croupe*⟩

crou·pi·er ['krupiər] *n* the attendant in charge of the money at a gambling table. ⟨French, orig one riding behind; see CROUP[2].⟩

crou·ton ['krutɒn] *n* a small piece of toasted or fried bread used to garnish soup or salad. ⟨French *croûton; croûte* crust, Latin *crusta*⟩

crow[1] [krou] *v* **1** make the characteristic cry of a rooster. **2** of a baby, make happy, high-pitched sounds. **3** express glad triumph: *The winning team crowed over its victory*. **crow** *n*. ⟨Old English *crāwan*; imitative⟩

crow[2] [krou] *n* any of various large, glossy black birds somewhat smaller than most ravens. ⟨Old English *crāwe*⟩

as the crow flies in a straight line: *It's about 5 km away as the crow flies, but nearly 10 km* *by road.* **eat crow** *Informal* make a humiliating admission or concession.

crow·bar *n* a strong metal bar with a bent forked end, used as a lever. **crow's–feet** *n pl* wrinkles at the outer corners of the eyes. **crow's–nest** or **crows–nest** *n* small lookout platform near the top of a ship's mast.

crowd [kraʊd] *n* **1** a large number of people together. **2** ordinary people of average tastes and intelligence: *films appealing to the crowd.* **3** a large number of things together. *v* **1** collect in large numbers. **2** fill too full with people or things: *to crowd a bus.* **3** push into too little space. **4** *Slang* pressure; harass. **crowd·ed** *adj.* ⟨Old English *crūdan* press⟩ **crowd out** exclude because of lack of space.

crown [ˈkraʊn] *n* **1** a head covering of precious metal and gems, worn by a monarch. **2 the Crown** the office and authority of a monarch. **3** a garland awarded to a winner. **4** the highest part: *the crown of the head, the crown of a tree.* **5** the part of a tooth outside the gum, or an artificial substitute for this. **6** a coin or unit of money in various countries. **7** *Botany* the top of a root and beginning of the stem. *v* **1** make (someone) a monarch; put a crown on the head of. **2** honour. **3** be on top of: *A fort crowns the hill.* **4** add the finishing touch (to): *a crowning achievement.* **5** *Checkers* make a king of (a piece that has moved across the board). **6** *Informal* hit on the head. ⟨Anglo-French *coroune;* Latin *corona*⟩ **Crown attorney** ✱ a lawyer who represents the government in a trial. **crown colony** a colony under the power and authority of the British government. **Crown corporation** ✱ a legal agency through which the Government of Canada or a provincial government carries on its activities. **crown fire** ✱ a forest fire that spreads from treetop to treetop. **crown jewels** jewels that are a traditional part of the regalia of a royal family. **crown land 1** in Canada, public land. **2** land that is owned personally by a monarch. **crown prince** the eldest living son of a king, queen, etc. **crown princess 1** the wife of a crown prince. **2** a woman who is heir apparent to a kingdom. **crown vetch** a plant of the legume family. Also called **ax·seed.**

CRTC Canadian Radio-television and Telecommunications Commission.

cru·cial [ˈkruʃəl] *adj* very important; critical; key. **cru·cial·ly** *adv.* ⟨Latin *crucialis; crux* cross; with reference to the fork of a road⟩

cru·ci·ble [ˈkrusəbəl] *n* a container in which metals, ores, etc., are melted and purified. ⟨Latin *crucibulum* orig night lamp⟩

cru·ci·fix [ˈkrusə,fɪks] *n* **1** a cross with a figure of the crucified Christ on it. **2** a cross. ⟨Latin *cruci fixus* fixed to a cross; *crux* cross + *fixus* pp of *figere* fasten⟩ **cru·ci·fix·ion** *n* **1** the act of crucifying. **2 the Crucifixion** the crucifying of Jesus. **cru·ci·form** [ˈkrusə,fɔrm] *adj* shaped like a cross. **cru·ci·fy** *v* **1** put to death by fastening the hands and feet to a cross. **2** treat cruelly; torture.

3 punish for the wrongs of someone else: *The newspapers crucified the mayor for a mistake made by her assistant.* **cru·ci·fi·er** *n.*

crude [krud] *adj* **1** in a natural or raw state; unprocessed: *crude rubber, crude statistics.* **2** not skilfully done or made: *a crude shack, a crude attempt.* **3** rude or vulgar: *crude remarks.* *n* CRUDE OIL. **crude·ly** *adv.* **crude·ness** *n.* **cru·di·ty** *n.* ⟨Latin *crudus* raw⟩ **crude oil** unrefined petroleum. **cru·di·tés** [ˌkrudiˈtei] *French* [kʀydiˈte] *n pl* small pieces of raw vegetable eaten as a snack.

cru·el [ˈkruəl] *adj* **1** fond of causing pain to others: *a cruel lord.* **2** causing much pain and suffering: *a cruel war.* **cru·el·ly** *adv.* **cru·el·ty** *n.* ⟨Old French; Latin *crudelis* rough⟩

cru·et [ˈkruɪt] *n* a set of bottles to hold oil, vinegar, etc., for the table. ⟨Old French *cruet,* diminutive of *cruie* pot⟩

cruise [kruz] *v* **1** travel from place to place at a steady, unhurried speed, often with no particular destination: *cruising the Caribbean. The taxi cruised along in search of passengers.* **2** travel in an aircraft or car at the speed of maximum mechanical efficiency. **3** *Logging* ✱ examine (a tract of forest) to estimate the value of the timber. *n* **1** a journey for pleasure by ship. **2** the act of cruising. **3** CRUISE MISSILE. ⟨Dutch *kruisen* sail crosswise; *kruis* cross, Latin *crux*⟩ **cruise control** in a vehicle, a device to keep the speed constant. **cruise missile** a guided missile that travels at low altitudes to escape detection by radar. **cruis·er** *n* **1** a warship. **2** a police patrol car.

crul·ler [ˈkrʌlər], [ˈkrulər], or [ˈkrʊlər] *n* a doughnut made of strands of dough twisted together. Also, **krul·ler.** ⟨Dutch *krullen* curl⟩

crumb [krʌm] *n* **1** a very small piece of cake, bread, etc. **2** a little bit: *a crumb of comfort.* **3** the soft, inside part of bread. **4** *Informal* a worthless person. ⟨Old English *cruma*⟩ **crum·ble** *v* **1** break into small pieces: *The cookie crumbled in my hand.* **2** fall apart by losing small pieces over time: *a crumbling old wall.* **3** gradually decay or disintegrate: *a crumbling economy. n* a baked fruit dessert with a crisp crumb topping: *peach crumble.* **crum·bly** *adj* tending to crumble. **crumb·y** *adj* **1** full of crumbs. **2** *Slang* crummy.

crum·my [ˈkrʌmi] *Slang adj* generalized term of disapproval: *a crummy way to treat people, a crummy piece of work. n Logging* ✱ an old truck taking loggers to and from the work site. **crum·mi·ness** *n.* ⟨*crumby*⟩

crum·pet [ˈkrʌmpɪt] *n* something like a very thick pancake, usually toasted, buttered, and eaten hot. ⟨Old English *crompeht*⟩

crum·ple [ˈkrʌmpəl] *v* **1** crush together so as to badly wrinkle: *to crumple a piece of paper.* **2** collapse: *The boxer crumpled to the floor. n* a wrinkle. ⟨Old English *crump* bent⟩

crunch [krʌntʃ] *v* **1** crush noisily with the teeth. **2** produce a noise like that of teeth crushing something hard: *The hard snow crunched under our feet.*

n **1** the act or noise of crunching. **2** *Informal* crisis or shortage: *the oil crunch.* **crunch·y** *adj.* ⟨earlier *cra(u)nch*; influenced by *crush, munch*⟩

crun·nick ['krʌnɪk] *n* ✻ *Maritimes* a twisted, dry piece of firewood. ⟨Old Irish *crann* tree⟩

cru·sade [kru'seid] *n* **1 Crusade** any of the medieval Christian military expeditions made to recover the Holy Land from the Muslims. **2** any war or campaign having a religious purpose. **3** a vigorous campaign against a public evil or promoting some cause: *the crusade against poverty.* **cru·sade** *v.* **cru·sad·er** *n.* ⟨Spanish *cruzada; cruz* cross, Latin *crux*⟩

crush [krʌʃ] *v* **1** squeeze together violently so as to break or bruise. **2** wrinkle or flatten by pressure. **3** break into pieces by grinding. **4** subdue with force; oppress: *to crush a people, to crush a rebellion.* **5** overwhelm with hurt or disappointment.
n **1** a crushing or being crushed. **2** a mass of people, vehicles, etc. crowded close together. **3** *Slang* a sudden, strong and often short-lived romantic attraction. **crush·a·ble** *adj.* **crush·er** *n.* ⟨Middle English *cruschen*⟩

crust [krʌst] *n* **1** the firm, outside part of bread, rolls, etc. **2** a hard, dry piece of bread. **3** the baked outer part of a pie, pizza, or similar dish. **4** any hard outside covering: *The snow had a crust that was thick enough to walk on.* **5** the outer layer of the earth, about 30-50 km thick.
v cover or become covered with a crust. **crust·like** *adj.* ⟨Latin *crusta* rind⟩

crus·ta·cean [krʌ'steiʃən] *n* any of a large class of arthropods with hard shells and two pairs of antennae. **crus·ta·ceous** *adj.* **crust·y** *adj* **1** having a crust: *crusty bread.* **2** bad-tempered or harsh in manner, speech, etc. **crust·i·ly** *adv.* **crust·i·ness** *n.*

crutch [krʌtʃ] *n* **1** a support to help a lame person walk, fitting under the armpit and grasped by a handle partway down. **2** any thing that serves as a prop or support: *She is such a poor manager that she has to use her assistant as a crutch.* ⟨Old English *crycc*⟩

crux [krʌks] *n* the essential or crucial part or point: *the crux of the matter.* ⟨Latin = cross⟩

cry [kraɪ] *v* **cried, cry·ing** **1** weep. **2** make a sound that shows pain, fear, etc. **3** shout. **4** of an animal, make its usual noise. **cry** *n.* ⟨Old French *crier*; Latin *quiritare*, orig beg the aid of the *Quirites* or Roman citizens⟩
a far cry a long way or very different *(from).* **cry down** make little of; denigrate. **cry off** break an agreement. **cry one's eyes** or **heart out** shed many tears. **cry out** a call loudly. **b** complain. **cry (out) for** a ask earnestly for; beg for. **b** need very much. **cry up** praise. **in full cry** in close pursuit.
cry·ba·by *n* one who cries too easily, sulks over defeats, complains a lot, etc. **cry·ing** *adj* demanding attention; very bad: *a crying evil.* **crying shame** an appalling state of affairs.

cry·o·gen·ics [ˌkraɪə'dʒɛnɪk] *n* (sg verb) the branch of physics dealing with very low temperatures. **cry·o·gen·ic** *adj.*

cry·on·ics *n* the rapid freezing of a body immediately after death, in an attempt to preserve it. **cry·on·ic** *adj.* ⟨Greek *kryos* frost⟩

crypt [krɪpt] *n* an underground room, often one used as a burial place. ⟨Greek *kryptē* vault; *kryptos* hidden⟩
cryp·tic *adj* **1** with a hidden meaning; secret; mysterious: *a cryptic message, a cryptic smile.* **2** *Zoology* serving to camouflage. **cryp·ti·cal·ly** *adv.* **cryptic crossword** a crossword for which each clue is a riddle involving wordplay. **cryp·to·gram** *n* a coded message.

crys·tal ['krɪstəl] *n* **1** a variety of quartz, or a piece of this, esp one used to control the frequency of a radio-frequency oscillator, for precision. **2** glass of high quality, having great brilliance. **3** the clear cover on the face of a watch. **4** a regularly shaped mass with angles and flat surfaces, into which a substance solidifies: *crystals of snow.* **crys·tal** *adj.* ⟨Greek *krystallos* clear ice; *kryos* frost⟩
crystal ball a glass ball used in CRYSTAL GAZING. **crys·tal–clear** *adj* **1** perfectly transparent. **2** very easy to understand. **crystal gazing** **1** the practice of staring into a crystal ball supposed to induce visions of remote events, secret truths, etc. **2** *Informal* speculation about the future. **crystal gazer. crys·tal·line** ['krɪstə,laɪn], [-,lɪn], *or* [-lɪn] *adj* consisting of or having to do with crystals. **crys·tal·lize** *v* **1** form into crystals: *Water crystallizes to form snow.* **2** take on definite form or content: *His vague ideas crystallized into a clear plan.* **3** coat with sugar. **crys·tal·li·za·tion** *n.*

CSIS Canadian Security and Intelligence Service, the Canadian secret service.

CT scan CAT SCAN. **CT scanner.**

cu. cubic.

cub [kʌb] *n* **1** a young bear, lion, etc. **2** a young person or novice. ⟨origin uncertain⟩

cub·by·hole ['kʌbi,houl] *n* a small, enclosed space. ⟨UK dialect *cub* shed, coop + *hole*⟩

cube [kjub] *n* **1** a solid with six congruent square sides. **2** *Mathematics* the product when a number is used three times as a factor. The cube of 3 is 27. **3** anything shaped vaguely like a cube: *an ice cube.* **cube** *v.* **cube·like** *adj.* ⟨Latin *cubus*; Greek *kybos* cube, die⟩
cube root *Mathematics* a number which is the factor of a cube: *The cube root of 125 is 5.* **cu·bic** *adj* **1** cube-shaped. **2** of units of CUBIC MEASURE: *a cubic centimetre.* **cubic measure** a system of units measuring volume. **cub·ism** *n* *Art* a style in which objects are represented by means of geometric shapes, including cubes. **cub·ist** *n, adj.* **cu·boid** *n* a solid having six flat sides, each one a rectangle: *A brick is a cuboid.* **cu·boid** *adj.*

cu·bi·cle [kjubəkəl] *n* a compartment, small room, stall, etc., as in a public washroom. ⟨Latin *cubiculum* bedroom; *cubare* lie⟩

cu·bit ['kjubɪt] *n* an ancient unit of length based on the distance from the elbow to the tip of the middle finger. ⟨Latin *cubitum*⟩

cuck·old ['kʌkəld] *n* a man whose wife has been unfaithful.

v make a cuckold of. **cuck·old·ry** *n.* ⟨Old French *cucuault, coucou* cuckoo; from its habit of laying its eggs in another bird's nest⟩

cuck·oo ['kuku] *or, sometimes,* ['kʊku] *n* any of a family of birds that lay their eggs in the nests of other birds.
adj ['kuku] *Slang* foolish or crazy. ⟨imitative⟩
cuckoo clock a clock with a toy bird that pops out of a little door at regular intervals.
cuckoo spit a frothy substance produced on plants by the young of certain insects.

cu·cum·ber ['kjukʌmbər] *n* the long, fleshy fruit of a vine of the gourd family. ⟨Old French *cocombre;* Latin *cucumis*⟩
cool as a cucumber calm and unruffled.

cud [kʌd] *n* food brought up into the mouth from the first and second stomachs of ruminants to be chewed before being swallowed again. ⟨Old English *cudu, cwidu*⟩
chew the cud ponder something.

cud·dle ['kʌdəl] *v* 1 hold close to oneself in a tender or affectionate way. 2 lie close and snug: *The puppies cuddled together in their box.* **cud·dle** *n.* **cud·dly** *adj.* ⟨origin uncertain⟩

cudg·el ['kʌdʒəl] *n* a club; a stick used as a weapon. **cudgel, -elled** or **-eled, -el·ling** or **-el·ing** *v.* ⟨Old English *cycgel*⟩
cudgel one's brains think very hard. **take up the cudgels for** defend strongly.

cue¹ [kju] *n* 1 a hint as to what to do. 2 an action or speech on or behind the stage which is the signal for an actor, singer, musician, etc., to enter or begin.
cue, cued, cue·ing or **cu·ing** *v.* ⟨probably French *queue* tail, end; with reference to the end of a preceding actor's speech⟩
cue in introduce (music, sound effects, etc.) at the right point. **on cue** at just the right moment, as if in response to a signal. **take one's cue from** be guided by.
cue card a card showing the words to be spoken or sung by a television performer, held up off-camera for him or her to read.

cue² [kju] *n Billiards, etc.* a long, tapering stick used for striking the ball. ⟨variant of *queue*⟩
cue ball *Billiards, etc.* the ball, usually white, which is struck by the cue.

cuff¹ [kʌf] *n* 1 the part of a sleeve or glove that goes around the wrist. 2 a turned-up fold or stretchy band around the bottom of a pant leg. 3 handcuff. 4 the part of a blood pressure instrument that wraps round the arm. ⟨Middle English *cuffe* glove⟩
off the cuff without preparation. **on the cuff** on credit.
cuff link a device for linking together the open ends of some shirt cuffs.

cuff² [kʌf] *v, n* hit with the hand or paw. ⟨origin uncertain⟩

cui·rass [kwɪ'ræs] *n* a piece of body armour for the torso. ⟨Old French *cuirasse; cuir* leather⟩

cui·sine [kwɪ'zin] *n* a style of cooking or preparing food: *French cuisine.* ⟨French; Latin *cocina,* variant of *coquina* from *coquus* a cook⟩

cuisse [kwɪs] *n* a piece of armour for the thigh. ⟨French = thigh; Latin *coxa* hip⟩

cuke [kjuk] *n Informal* cucumber.

cul–de–sac ['kʌl də ˌsæk] *or* ['kʊl də ˌsæk] *French* [kyd'sak] *n* a street open at only one end. ⟨French = bottom of a bag⟩

cu·li·nar·y ['kʌlə.nɛri] *or* ['kjulə.nɛri] *adj* to do with cooking or the kitchen: *culinary skill.* ⟨Latin *culina* kitchen⟩

cull [kʌl] *v* 1 select, either to keep or get rid of: *to cull names from a list.* 2 make selections from: *She culled her flower bed for the choicest blooms.* 3 thin by selecting certain members of for elimination: *to cull a herd of deer.*
n an inferior thing picked out from a group.
cull·er *n.* ⟨Old French *cuillir;* Latin *colligere.* See COLLECT.⟩

cul·mi·nate ['kʌlmə.neit] *v* 1 rise to: *a long staircase that culminated in a lookout platform.* 2 reach its climax or end: *The dramatic action culminates in a murder.* **cul·mi·na·tion** *n.* ⟨Latin *culmen* top⟩

cu·lottes [ku'lɒts], [kə'lɒts], *or* ['kulɒts] *n pl* a garment that looks like a skirt but is actually divided into two legs. ⟨French⟩

cul·pa·ble ['kʌlpəbəl] *adj* deserving blame; guilty. **cul·pa·bil·i·ty** *n.* **cul·pa·bly** *adv.* ⟨Latin *culpa* fault⟩

cul·prit ['kʌlprɪt] *n* 1 a person guilty of a fault or a crime. 2 someone or something that is the cause of trouble: *When her tire went flat, she found the nail that was the culprit.* ⟨Anglo-French abbreviation *cul. prit.,* for *culpable* and *prist* ready (for trial)⟩

cult [kʌlt] *n* 1 a system of religious worship. 2 an unorthodox religious group under the domination of a leader, given to extreme practices. 3 great admiration for or devotion to a person or thing: *the cult of fashion.*
adj 1 greatly admired by a small group: *a cult film, a cult novel.* 2 being such a group: *a cult following.* **cult·ic** *adj.* **cult·ish** *adj.* **cult·ism** *n.* **cult·ist** *n.* ⟨Latin *cultus* worship⟩

cul·ti·vate ['kʌltə.veit] *v* 1 prepare and use (land) to raise crops. 2 grow (plants) by care and effort. 3 loosen (soil) to kill weeds and let in more air and water. 4 develop by care and effort: *to cultivate a skill, to cultivate a friendship.* **cul·ti·va·ble** *adj.* **cul·ti·vat·ed** *adj.* **cul·ti·va·tion** *n.* ⟨Latin *cultivare*⟩
under cultivation of land, cultivated; farmed.
cul·ti·gen *n* a cultivated plant of unknown origin and having no wild counterpart, such as the cabbage. **cul·ti·var** *n* a variety of plant produced from a known natural species by cultivation. **cul·ti·va·tor** *n* a tool used to loosen the soil and destroy weeds.

cul·ture ['kʌltʃər] *n* 1 the customs, values, arts, and other forms of human endeavour characteristic of a particular community: *Canadian culture.* 2 refinement of manners, interests, etc. 3 conventional behaviour as opposed to instinct or idiosyncrasy. 4 the commercial raising of bees, fish, silkworms, etc. 5 *Biology* **a** the growth of living micro-organisms in a special medium. **b** a

colony of micro-organisms grown in this way.
v 1 educate culturally, esp in the arts. 2 *Biology* grow (bacteria, etc.) in a special medium. **cul·tur·al** *adj.*　**cul·tur·al·ly** *adv.* **cul·tured** *adj.* ⟨Latin *cultura* a tending; *colere* cultivate⟩
cultured pearl a natural pearl artificially cultivated by introducing a foreign body into an oyster. **culture shock** the confusion, sense of alienation, etc. that results from sudden exposure to a culture that differs markedly from one's own. **culture vulture** *Slang* a person with great interest in artistic and intellectual matters, esp a pretentious one.

cul·vert [ˈkʌlvərt] *n* a pipe or channel to conduct water under a road, railway, etc. ⟨origin uncertain⟩

cum [kʌm] *or* [kʊm] *prep* combined with: *an antique-cum-junk shop.* ⟨Latin = with⟩
cum lau·de [ˈlaʊdei] *Latin* (with *graduate*) with praise or honour.

cum·ber·some [ˈkʌmbərsəm] *adj* clumsy; unwieldy; burdensome: *cumbersome winter boots, a cumbersome bureaucracy.* ⟨obs. *cumber*, Old French *combrer* impede; Celtic⟩

cum·in or **cum·min** [ˈkʌmən] *n* a herb of the parsley family cultivated for its aromatic seeds, used as a spice. ⟨Greek *kyminon*⟩

cum·mer·bund [ˈkʌmərˌbʌnd] *n* a broad sash worn around the waist, now esp with a tuxedo. Also, **kum·mer·bund**. ⟨Persian *kumar* waist, loins + *band* band, bandage⟩

cu·mu·la·tive [ˈkjumjələtɪv] *adj* 1 increasing by continued additions. 2 incorporating all that went before. **cu·mu·la·tive·ly** *adv.* ⟨Latin *cumulare; cumulus* heap⟩
cu·mu·lo– [ˌkjumjəlou] *combining form* a cloud formation with features of both cumulus and some other kind of cloud: *cumulonimbus,　cumulostratus.* **cu·mu·lus** [ˈkjumjələs] *n, pl* **-li** [-ˌlaɪ] *or* [-ˌli] a cloud formation of rounded heaps with a flat base.

cu·ne·i·form [ˈkjuniɪˌfɔrm], [ˈkjunɪˌfɔrm], *or* [kjuˈniɪˌfɔrm] *n* the wedge-shaped characters used in the writing of ancient Babylonia, Assyria, Persia, etc. **cu·ne·i·form** *adj.* ⟨Latin *cuneus* wedge⟩

cun·ni·lin·gus [ˌkʌnəˈlɪŋgəs] *n* stimulation of the female genitals by licking. ⟨Latin *cunnus* vulva + *lingere* lick⟩

cun·ning [ˈkʌnɪŋ] *adj* 1 clever in a tricky or manipulative way: *a cunning rogue, a cunning plot.* 2 skilful: *cunning hands.* **cun·ning** *n.* **cun·ning·ly** *adv.* ⟨Old English, from *cunnan* know (how)⟩

SYNONYMS
Cunning emphasizes intelligence and an understanding of how to use what one knows to manipulate an outcome: *a cunning strategist.* **Crafty** emphasizes the use of trickery and suggests ingenuity and artfulness in deceiving people: *a crafty con artist.*

cup [kʌp] *n* 1 a small container to drink from, usually having a D-shaped handle on the side. 2 a unit of volume equal to 250 mL. 3 a trophy in the shape of a two-handled cup or a goblet. 4 any dish served in a cup: *a mixed fruit cup.* 5 *Christianity* the Communion chalice or the wine in it. 6 that which one must experience or endure: *The defeat was a bitter cup for her.* 7 either of the breast supports of a bra, or its size: *a C cup.* 8 anything like a cup in shape or function.
v **cupped, cup·ping** curve (one's hands, a leaf, etc.) into a shape like that of a cup. **cup·ful** *n.* **cup·like** *adj.* ⟨Latin *cuppa; cupa* tub⟩
in one's cups drunk. **one's cup of tea** *Informal* the thing that pleases one.
cup·bear·er *n* formerly, in royal households, a noble who tasted the wine before his master or mistress. **cup·board** [ˈkʌbərd] *n* a closet with shelves for dishes, food, etc. **cupboard love** insincere love motivated by material gain. **cup·cake** *n* a small cake baked in a cup-shaped container.

Cu·pid [ˈkjupɪd] *n* 1 *Roman myth* the god of sexual love, corresponding to the Greek god Eros. 2 **cupid** a figure of a naked winged boy used as a symbol of sexual love. ⟨Latin *cupidus* desirous; *cupere* long for⟩
cu·pid·i·ty [kjuˈpɪdəti] *n* greed.

cu·po·la [ˈkjupələ] *n* 1 a domed roof. 2 a dome or other small structure on a roof. ⟨Italian; Latin *cupula*, diminutive of *cupa* tub⟩

cu·pre·ous [ˈkjupriəs] *adj* of or containing copper. ⟨Latin *cuprum* copper⟩
cu·pric *adj* of or containing divalent copper. **cupric sulphate** or **sulfate** BLUE VITRIOL.

cur [kɜr] *n* 1 a worthless dog; mongrel. 2 an ill-mannered, despicable person. **cur·rish** *adj.* ⟨Middle English *curre*⟩

cur·a·ble, cur·a·tive See CURE.

cu·ra·re [kjuˈrɑri] *or* [kuˈrɑri] *n* a poisonous extract of certain tropical American plants, which causes paralysis of the muscles. It is used medicinally as a muscle relaxant and traditionally by S American Indians to poison arrows. Also, **cu·ra·ri.** ⟨Tupi⟩

cu·rate [ˈkjʊrɪt] *n* a member of the clergy assisting a pastor, rector, or vicar. **cu·ra·cy** *n.* ⟨Latin *curatus; curare* care for, *cura* care⟩
cu·ra·tor [kjəˈreitər] *or* [ˈkjʊreitər] *n* 1 a person in charge of all or part of a museum, library, etc. 2 the guardian of a minor.

curb [kɜrb] *n* 1 a raised stone or concrete border along the edge of a road, driveway, etc. 2 a chain or strap fastened to a horse's bit and passing under its lower jaw. 3 anything that checks or restrains.
v 1 restrain; hold in check. 2 cause (a driver) to pull over to the curb. 3 lead (a dog) to the curb or other place to defecate. ⟨Old French *courbe;* Latin *curvus* bent⟩
curb roof a roof having two slopes on each side. **curb·stone** *n* a stone forming a curb.

curd [kɜrd] *n* 1 Often, **curds** *pl* the thick part of milk that separates from the watery part in souring. 2 any food that resembles this: *bean curd.* **curd·y** *adj.* ⟨Middle English *curd*⟩

cur·dle *v* form into curds; thicken or sour. **curdle the blood of** terrify; horrify.

cure [kjʊr] *v* **1** bring back to a healthy state. **2** get rid of (some undesirable condition): *to cure a cold, to cure a bad habit.* **3** preserve: *to cure fish by drying and salting.* — *n* **1** a successful treatment for a disease. **2** anything that permanently ends a problem: *a cure for unemployment.* **3** the fact or process of curing or of being cured. **cur·a·ble** *adj.* **cur·a·bil·i·ty** *n.* **cur·a·bly** *adv.* **cure·less** *adj.* **cur·er** *n.* ⟨Latin *curare* care for; *cura* care⟩ **cur·a·tive** *adj* helping to cure. **cur·a·tive** *n.* **cure–all** *n* a remedy for all diseases or evils.

cu·ré [kjʊ'rei] *French* [ky'ʀe] *n* a parish priest. ⟨French; Latin *curatus*. See CURATE.⟩

cur·et·tage [kjʊ'rɛtɪdʒ] *or* [ˌkjʊrə'tɑʒ] *n* a scraping or cleaning of tissues in a body cavity. ⟨French *curetage*⟩ **cu·rette** [kjʊ'rɛt] *n* a scoop for performing curettage. Also, **cu·ret.**

cur·few ['kɜrfju] *n* **1** a time set by parents or other caregivers at which children must be indoors or in bed. **2** a government regulation forbidding people to be on the streets after a certain hour. **3** esp formerly, a signal, such as a bell ringing, announcing this time every evening. ⟨Anglo-French *coeverfu; covrir* cover + *feu* fire; a time to put out all lights⟩

Curia ['kjʊriə] *n Roman Catholic Church* a group of high officials who assist the Pope in church government. ⟨Latin = court; *cura* care⟩

cu·rie ['kjʊri] *or* [kjʊ'ri] *n* a unit of radioactivity. *Symbol* **Ci** ⟨Marie *Curie*, 20c French scientist, born in Poland⟩

cu·ri·ous ['kjʊriəs] *adj* **1** eager to know: *a curious child.* **2** strange; unusual: *a curious old hat.* **cu·ri·os·i·ty** [ˌkjʊri'ɒsəti] *n.* **cu·ri·ous·ly** *adv.* ⟨Latin *curiosus* inquisitive; *cura* care⟩ **cu·ri·o** ['kjʊri,ou] *n* an object valued as a curiosity; exotic souvenir, antique, or relic.

cu·ri·um ['kjʊriəm] *n* a radioactive artificial element. *Symbol* **Cm** ⟨Marie *Curie*, 20c French scientist, born in Poland⟩

curl [kɜrl] *v* **1** twist or grow into a coil or roll (often with *up*): *to curl one's hair. My hair curls naturally. The birchbark curled up as it burned.* **2** move in curves or coils: *smoke curling from the chimney.* **3** of one's lips, twist or curve in scorn. **4** play the game of curling. — *n* **1** a curled lock of hair. **2** anything with a curled shape. **3** the fact of being curled: *Her hair has lost its curl.* **curl·y** *adj.* ⟨Middle English *crul* curly⟩ **curl up a** take a comfortable or defensive position with the legs drawn up. **b** *Informal* collapse or give up. **curl·er** *n* **1** a device on which hair is twisted to make it curl. **2** one who plays the game of CURLING. **curl·i·cue** ['kɜrlɪ,kju] *n* a fancy curly mark or design. **curl·ing** *n* a game played on ice, in which heavy round stones are slid toward a target at the end of the rink. **curling iron** an electrical appliance for curling hair, consisting of a rod which is heated and around which hair is wound. **curl·pa·per** *n* a

piece of paper around which a lock of hair is rolled up tightly to curl it. **curl–up** *n* a modified sit-up in which only the head, neck, and shoulders are raised, with knees bent.

cur·lew ['kɜrlu] *or* ['kɜrlju] *n* any of a genus of wading birds of temperate and subarctic regions with a long, thin, downward-curving bill. ⟨Old French *courlieu;* imitative of its cry⟩

cur·mudg·eon [kər'mʌdʒən] *n* a grouchy old man. **cur·mudg·eon·ly** *adj.* ⟨origin unknown⟩

cur·rant ['kɜrənt] *n* **1** a small, seedless raisin. **2** a small, tart, edible berry, red, black, or white, that grows on any of several shrubs of the saxifrage family. ⟨Middle English *(raysons of) Coraunte* raisins of Corinth⟩

cur·ren·cy ['kɜrənsi] *n* **1** the money used in a country: *Canadian currency.* **2** circulation: *The town gossips gave the rumour currency.* **3** the fact of being current: *The word fire-reels has now passed out of currency.* **4** anything which, in a given community, is regularly exchanged or confers power, acceptance, etc.: *Knowledge is the currency of academia.*

cur·rent ['kɜrənt] *n* **1** a flow or stream of water or air in one direction: *Stay near the shore so you don't get caught in the current.* **2** a flow of electricity along a wire, etc. **3** a general trend: *the current of public opinion.* . — *adj* **1** of or at the present time: *current styles.* **2** generally used or accepted: *A few slang terms of the seventies are still current.* **cur·rent·ly** *adv.* ⟨Latin *currens* ppr of *currere* run⟩

cur·ric·u·lum [kə'rɪkjələm] *n, pl* **-lums** or **-la** [-lə] **1** the studies offered in a school, college, etc.: *the university curriculum.* **2** the prescribed content of any one course of study: *the English curriculum.* **cur·ric·u·lar** *adj.* ⟨Latin = race course; *currere* run⟩ **curriculum vi·tae** ['vitaɪ] *pl* **curricula vitae** a summary of one's life, detailing education, work experience, etc., used especially to accompany job applications. *Abbrev* **c.v.** ⟨Latin = course of life⟩

SYNONYMS

In Canadian usage, **curriculum vitae** is mainly restricted to academic and professional situations. **Résumé** is the more common term.

cur·ry¹ ['kɜri] *v* **1** rub and clean (a horse, etc.). **2** prepare (tanned leather) for use by soaking, scraping, etc. ⟨Old French *correier* put in order; *con-* (intensive) + *reier* arrange⟩ **curry favour with someone** seek a person's favour by flattery, constant attentions, etc. **cur·ry·comb** *n* a brush with metal teeth for rubbing and cleaning a horse.

cur·ry² ['kɜri] *n* a spicy dish prepared with a sauce seasoned with cayenne, ginger, coriander, etc. **cur·ry** *v.* ⟨Tamil *kari*⟩ **curry powder** a finely ground mixture of spices used especially to make curries.

curse [kɜrs] *v* **cursed** or *(Poetic)* **curst, curs·ing** **1** call on a supernatural being to bring evil to; wish evil upon: *to curse one's enemies.* **2** bring evil or harm to: *cursed with poverty.*

3 use blasphemous, obscene, or violent speech to vent anger, etc.: *to curse one's bad luck. He cursed when he hit his thumb with the hammer.* *n* **1** the words said in cursing. **2** the harm or evil that comes as a result. **3** a source of harm or evil: *Greed is the curse of our society.* **4** a blasphemous or obscene utterance said in anger. **5 the curse** *Slang* menstruation. **6** a sentence of excommunication. **curs·er** *n.* ⟨Old English *cūrs, cursian*⟩ **be cursed with** suffer from: *cursed with a weak stomach.*
curs·ed ['kɜrsɪd] *or* [kɜrst] *adj* under a curse; wretched.

cur·sive ['kɜrsɪv] *adj* to do with writing in which the letters are joined together: *cursive script.* **cur·sive·ly** *adv.* ⟨Latin *cursivus* running⟩
cur·sor ['kɜrsər] *n Computers* a mark on the screen indicating where the next character will be placed or the next function carried out. **cur·so·ry** ['kɜrsəri] *adj* hasty; without attention to details: *Even a cursory reading of the letter showed many errors.* **cur·so·ri·ly** *adv.* **cur·so·ri·ness** *n.*

curt [kɜrt] *adj* speaking or spoken so briefly as to be rude. **curt·ly** *adv.* **curt·ness** *n.* ⟨Latin *curtus* cut short⟩

cur·tail [kər'teil] *v* cut short; cut off part of. **cur·tail·ment** *n.* ⟨Old French *curtald;* Latin *curtus;* influenced by *tail;* orig of docked tail⟩

cur·tain ['kɜrtən] *n* **1** a piece of cloth hung over a window for privacy, decoration, or shade. **2** *Theatre* a movable hanging screen that separates the stage from the part where the audience sits. **3** anything that hides or screens: *a curtain of fog.* **4 curtains** *pl Slang* death or an end: *"It's curtains for all of you,"* he snarled. **cur·tain** *v.* **cur·tain·less** *adj.* ⟨Old French *curtine;* Latin *cortina*⟩
bring (or ring) down or **lower the curtain on** bring to an end. **curtain off** separate or close by a curtain. **raise the curtain on a** reveal. **b** mark the beginning of. **ring up the curtain a** open a theatre curtain. **b** start something.
curtain call 1 the return of an actor or other performer to the stage to acknowledge the audience's applause. **2** a final act in the career of a public figure. **curtain raiser 1** *Theatre* a short play preceding the main production. **2** a little event introducing a bigger one: *The plant slowdown was the curtain raiser to a full strike.* **curtain wall** a wall supporting no load.

curt·sy ['kɜrtsi] *n* a bow of respect by women, made by bending the knees and lowering the body. **curt·sy** *v.* ⟨*courtesy*⟩

curve [kɜrv] *n* **1** a line with no straight part. **2** a rounded bend, as in a road. **3** the degree to which a thing curves. **4** a line on a graph, representing statistical data: *the cost-of-living curve.* **5** *Baseball* CURVEBALL.
v bend so as to form a curve. **curved** *adj.* ⟨Latin *curvus* bending⟩
learning curve a drop in performance level or efficiency while one learns a new method, task, piece of hardware, etc. **throw someone a curve** do or say something for which another is not prepared.

cur·va·ceous [kər'veiʃəs] *adj Informal* of a girl or woman, having a full figure. **cur·va·ture** ['kɜrvətʃər] *n* the fact, condition, or degree of curving: *a curvature of the spine, the curvature of the earth's surface.* **curve·ball** *n Baseball* a ball pitched so as to curve away from the batter at the last moment. **curv·y** *adj* **1** *Informal* curvaceous. **2** curving.

cush·ion ['kʊʃən] *n* **1** a soft pad used to sit, lie, or kneel on. **2** anything used or shaped like a cushion, such as a layer of forced air supporting a Hovercraft, etc. **3** anything that makes for greater comfort or lessens the effect of adversity: *a cushion of savings against sickness.* **4 ✱** the enclosed ice surface on which hockey is played. **5** the elastic lining of the sides of a billiard table.
v **1** protect: *Her family's wealth had always cushioned her against failure.* **2** ease the effect of: *The presence of caring friends cushioned her grief.* **cush·ion·like** *adj.* ⟨Old French *coussin;* probably Latin *coxinum* from *coxa* hip⟩

cush·y ['kʊʃi] *adj Slang* luxuriously easy and comfortable: *a cushy job, a cushy life.* **cush·i·ness** *n.* ⟨Hindi *khush* pleasant⟩

CUSO formerly, Canadian Universities Service Overseas, an organization sending youth to work in the developing world.

cusp [kʌsp] *n* **1** a pointed end; point: *A crescent has two cusps.* **2** a point or bump on the crown of a tooth. ⟨Latin *cuspis*⟩
on the cusp of about to experience: *on the cusp of fame.*
cus·pid *n* a tooth with one cusp; a canine.

cuss [kʌs] *Informal n* **1** a curse. **2** an odd or troublesome person or animal.
v curse. **cus·ser** *n.* ⟨variant of *curse*⟩
cuss out scold vehemently and at length.
cuss·ed ['kʌsɪd] *adj Informal* **1** stubborn. **2** cursed. **cuss·ed·ly** *adv.* **cuss·ed·ness** *n.*

cus·tard ['kʌstərd] *n* creamy pudding or sauce made of eggs and milk, usually sweetened. ⟨variant of *crustade,* French; Provençal *croustado* tart⟩
custard apple any of various shrubs or small trees of tropical America whose fruit has a sweet, very soft reddish yellow pulp.

cus·to·dy ['kʌstədi] *n* **1** charge; care: *Parents have custody of their children.* **2** confinement in jail. **cus·to·di·al** *adj.* ⟨Latin *custodia; custos* guardian⟩
cus·to·di·an *n* **1** caretaker; janitor. **2** keeper; guardian: *Voters are custodians of democracy.* **cus·to·di·an·ship** *n.*

cus·tom ['kʌstəm] *n* **1** the accepted way of acting; tradition. **2** a personal habit. **3** the regular business given by a customer. **4 customs** *pl* **a** a duty paid to the government on imports. **b** the government department collecting this duty, or its station at a border. *adj* made or done to order: *custom fenders.* ⟨Old French *custume;* Latin *consuetumen*⟩
cus·tom·ar·y *adj* according to custom; usual; habitual. **cus·tom·ar·i·ly** *adv.* **cus·tom–built** *adj* built according to the specifications of an individual customer: *a custom-built kitchen.*

cus·tom·er *n* **1** a person who buys. **2** *Informal* a person: *a rough customer.* **cus·tom·ize** *v* make according to individual requirements: *to customize a van.* **cus·tom–made** *adj* made according to the specifications of an individual customer. **customs officer** a government official who examines imported goods and charges any taxes due. **customs union** a group of nations agreeing to impose no duty on each other's goods, but only on those of other nations.

cut [kʌt] *v* **cut, cut·ting 1** open, remove part of, or divide, using something sharp: *to cut meat, timber, grass, one's nails, etc. He cut a hole through the wall with an axe.* **2** make or shape by cutting: *to cut stars out of gold foil, to cut a slice from a loaf, to cut one's initials into a tree, to cut a diamond.* **3** injure with something sharp: *I cut my finger on the broken glass.* **4** cut things, or be cut: *This blade cuts well. Bread cuts more easily when cool.* **5** reduce: *to cut expenses. Cut your speech to a half hour.* **6** edit; shorten or remove in editing: *I would cut that paragraph.* **7** divide. **8** dilute: *whisky cut with water.* **9** go by a more direct way: *We cut across the field to save time.* **10** change direction abruptly: *cut to the right.* **11** hurt as if with something sharp: *The cold wind cut me to the bone. Their words cut her deeply.* **12** *Informal* snub; refuse to recognize socially: *They all cut the kid who lied.* **13** *Informal* skip (a class, etc.) without permission. **14** dissolve: *Gasoline will cut grease.* **15** *Film* **a** switch suddenly to another scene. **b** stop filming briefly. **16** make (a record).
n **1** the act, amount, or manner of cutting. **2** a wound, notch, hole, channel, etc. made by cutting. **3** the style in which a thing is cut. **4** a sharp blow or stroke. **5** *Informal* a share: *Each partner has a cut of the profits.* **6** a block or plate with an engraving on it, or the print made from this. **7** one of the sections of a recording. **8** ✷ a natural gully or ravine. ⟨Middle English *cutten*⟩
a cut above *Informal* superior to: *He's a cut above the average politician.* **cut a figure a** look good. **b** invite attention by one's looks or actions. **cut and dried a** fully arranged in advance. **b** predictable. **cut and paste a** cut shapes out of paper, cloth, etc. and stick them on a surface. **b** edit by manually cutting out pieces of text and pasting them elsewhere in a document. **c** *Computers* shift a block of text, piece of art, etc. by deleting it (into a special part of memory) and then reinserting it elsewhere. **cut–and–paste** *adj, n.* **cut and run** leave hastily. **cut and thrust 1** hand-to-hand fighting, esp with swords. **2** vigorous, lively interchange: *the cut and thrust of debate.* **cut back a** reduce output, expenses, etc. **b** go back suddenly. **c** prune or trim (a plant). **cut·back** *n.* **cut both ways a** apply to both sides in a conflict. **b** have good and bad effects. **cut corners a** find or use a quicker method. **b** do a job carelessly. **cut down a** reduce. **b** belittle; criticize harshly or scornfully. **c** kill. **cut down to size** *Informal* humiliate. **cut in a** interrupt.

b interrupt a dancing couple to take the place of one of them. **c** break suddenly into a line of moving traffic, waiting people, etc. **d** insert by splicing. **e** work (butter, etc.) in with other ingredients using a knife. **cut it** be satisfactory: *Her work just doesn't cut it.* **cut it fine** leave oneself very little margin for error; do something very risky. **cut it out** *Informal* stop whatever one is doing. **cut loose** *Informal* speak or act in an uncontrolled way. **cut no ice (with)** *Informal* fail to impress. **cut off a** stop, block, or shut off. **b** break; interrupt. **c** isolate. **d** disinherit. **e** force (another driver) to brake by suddenly moving right in front of his or her vehicle. **cut one's teeth on** become familiar with when very young. **cut out a** leave out; take out. **b** stop doing, using, making, etc.: *to cut out caffeine.* **c** of any machine, suddenly stop working, often briefly or intermittently. **d** make by cutting: *to cut out paper dolls.* **e** move out of one's assigned or expected position. **f** depart unexpectedly. **cut out for** suited to: *She's not cut out for a musical career.* **cut short** See SHORT. **cut someone some slack** allow someone leeway in behaviour. **cut the mustard** *Informal* satisfy requirements. **cut up a** cut into small pieces. **b** *Informal* show off or clown. **c** criticize severely. **d** *Informal* cause emotional pain to. **cut up rough a** become physically violent. **b** make difficulties; misbehave badly. **make the cut** be selected from a list of candidates.

cut·a·way *n* **1** a coat having the lower part cut back in a curve. **2** a model or diagram with part of the outer surface cut away to show the interior. **cut·a·way** *adj.* **cut·back** *n* **1** a reduction in output, expenditure, etc. **2** a flashback in a novel, movie, etc. **cut glass** glass shaped or decorated by grinding and polishing. **cut·off** *n* **1** the limit set for an activity, process, etc. **2** an exit ramp from a highway: **3 cutoffs** *pl* pants that have been cut to serve as shorts, without hemming. **cut·out** *n* a shape that has been cut out or is to be cut out. **cut–rate** *adj* to do with a price below the usual: *cut-rate men's wear.* **cut·ter** *n* **1** a person whose work is cutting cloth to be made up into clothes. **2** a small, light sleigh, usually pulled by one horse. **3** a sled pulled by a snowmobile. **4** a small sailboat. **cut·throat** *n* murderer. *adj* **1** murderous. **2** fierce and relentless: *cutthroat competition.* **cutthroat trout** ✷ a large trout found mainly in the Rocky Mountain region. **cut·ting** *n* **1** a small shoot cut from a plant. **2** a newspaper or magazine clipping. **3** a place or way cut through high ground for a road, track, etc. **4** ✷ a stand of timber. *adj* **1** sharp: *the cutting edge of a knife.* **2** sarcastic: *a cutting remark.* **3** cold and piercing: *a cutting wind.* **cutting edge 1** the forefront, esp in reference to technological advance: *on the cutting edge of computer technology.* **2** the most effective part: *Our excellent sales force is the cutting edge of this company.* **cutting–edge** *adj.* **cut–up** *n* *Informal* a person who shows off or behaves like a clown. **cut·worm** *n* the larva of any of various moths that feeds on young plant stems, cutting them off near ground level.

cute [kjut] *adj Informal* **1** pleasing in a delicate, endearing, or touching way: *a cute puppy.* **2** good-looking; attractive: *cute guys, a cute dress.* **3** clever: *a cute trick.* **4** consciously stylish or mannered: *cute dialogue.* **cute·ly** *adv.* **cute·ness** *n.* ⟨variant of *acute*⟩
cute·sy *adj Informal* cute in an affected way.
cu·tie *n Informal* a cute person.

cu·ti·cle ['kjutəkəl] *n* **1** the strip of hard or dead skin at the base and sides of a nail. **2** in vertebrates, the outer layer of skin. **3** *Botany* a very thin membrane. **4** *Zoology* the hard, dead, outer tissue of many invertebrates, secreted by the epidermis. ⟨Latin *cuticula* diminutive of *cutis* skin⟩

cut·lass ['kʌtləs] *n* a short, heavy, slightly curved sword with a single-edged blade. ⟨French *coutelas;* Latin *culter* knife⟩

cut·ler·y ['kʌtləri] *n* **1** knives, forks, and spoons for table use. **2** knives, scissors, and other cutting instruments. ⟨Latin *culter* knife⟩

cut·let ['kʌtlɪt] *n* a slice of meat from the leg or ribs: *a veal cutlet.* ⟨French *côtelette* from *côte;* Latin *costa* rib⟩

cut·tle·fish ['kʌtəl,fɪʃ] *n* any of various marine molluscs having a thick, calcified internal shell and ten sucker-bearing arms. ⟨Old English *cudele*⟩

cu·vée [ku'vei] *French* [ky've] *n* a mixture of wines, esp of champagnes.

cu·vette [kju'vɛt] *n* **1** a narrow glass tube used in laboratories. **2** a jewel with a bas-relief design. ⟨French = basin⟩

C.V. CURRICULUM VITAE.

cy·an [saɪ'æn] *n, adj* greenish blue. ⟨Greek *kyanos* blue substance⟩
cy·a·nide ['saɪə,naɪd] *or* ['saɪənɪd] *n* a salt of hydrocyanic acid, esp potassium cyanide, a powerful poison.

cy·ber– *combining form* **1** of or for computers: *cyberphobia.* **2** in cyberspace: *cyberart.* ⟨Greek *kybernetes* pilot; *kybernan* steer⟩
cy·ber·ca·fé *n* **1** coffee shop with computers for customer use. **2** CHAT ROOM. **cy·ber·net·ics** *n* the study of communication and control mechanisms in organisms and in machines. **cy·ber·net·ic** *adj.* **cy·ber·pho·bia** *n* the fear of computers. **cy·ber·phobe** *n.* **cy·ber·pho·bic** *adj.* **cy·ber·punk** *n* a person who uses the Internet to commit petty crime, intimidate, hack, etc. **cy·ber·sex** *n* explicitly sexual conversation conducted online. **cy·ber·space** *n* major computer networks thought of as a 'universe' in which things may exist which have no existence in the tangible world. **cy·ber·squat** *v* register an address on the Internet that includes the name of a well-known person or business, with the intention of selling it back to its owner. **cy·ber·squat·ting** *n.* **cy·borg** *n* a person or animal whose bodily functions are regulated or extended by machine.

cy·cla·mate ['saɪklə,meit] *n* any of a group of salts of sodium or calcium formerly used as substitutes for sugar.

cyc·la·men ['saɪkləmən] *or* ['sɪkləmən] *n* any of a genus of plants of the primrose family with showy flowers whose five petals bend backward. ⟨Greek *kyklaminos*⟩

cy·cle ['saɪkəl] *n* **1** a complete process of development or action that repeats itself: *the life cycle of an organism, the cycle of the seasons.* **2** a complete set or series, esp all the stories, poems, etc., on some topic: *the Arthurian cycle.* **3** a bicycle, tricycle, unicycle, or motorcycle. **4** *Physics* one complete or double reversal of an alternating electric current or one complete sound vibration. Frequency is measured in **cycles per second.** **5** *Astronomy* one full revolution in orbit.
v **1** occur again and again in the same order. **2** ride a bicycle. ⟨Greek *kyklos* wheel⟩
cy·clic ['sɪklɪk] *or* ['saɪklɪk] *or* **cy·cli·cal** *adj* **1** of or occurring in a cycle. **2** *Chemistry* with atoms arranged in a ring. **cy·cli·cal·ly** *adv.* **cy·clic·i·ty** *n.* **cy·clist** *n* a bicycle rider.

cy·clone ['saɪkloun] *n* **1** a severe windstorm with winds spiralling toward a centre of low pressure; a hurricane, typhoon, or tornado. **2** any similar movement of air, as in a furnace, centrifuge, or other machine. **cy·clon·ic** [saɪ'klɒnɪk] *adj.* **cy·clon·i·cal·ly** *adv.*
cy·clo·ram·a [,saɪklə'ræmə] *n* **1** a large mural on the wall of a circular room. **2** *Theatre* a wide, curved screen providing a background. ⟨*cycle* + Greek *horama* spectacle⟩

cy·clo·tron ['saɪklə,trɒn] *n* a particle accelerator in which charged particles are accelerated in a spiral. ⟨*cycle* + (*elec*)*tron*⟩

cyg·net ['sɪgnɪt] *n* a young swan. ⟨Latin *cygnus;* Greek *kyknos*⟩

cyl·in·der ['sɪləndər] *n* **1** a solid bounded by two equal, parallel circles and a curved surface. **2** any long, round object with flat or open ends. **3** the part of a revolver that has chambers for the cartridges. **4** the piston chamber of an engine. **cy·lin·dri·cal** [sə'lɪndrəkəl] *adj.* **cy·lin·dri·cal·ly** *adv.* ⟨Greek *kylindros; kylindein* to roll⟩

cym·bal ['sɪmbəl] *n* one of a pair of slightly concave metal plates, usually brass, used as a percussion musical instrument. **cym·bal·ist** *n.* ⟨Greek *kymbalon; kymbē* hollow of a vessel⟩

cyn·ic ['sɪnɪk] *n* **1** a person who believes that people are insincere and act out of selfish motives. **2** a sneering, sarcastic person. **3 Cynic** in ancient Greece, a member of a group of philosophers who taught that self-control is the essence of virtue. **cyn·i·cal** *adj.* **cyn·i·cal·ly** *adv.* **cyn·i·cism** ['sɪnə,sɪzəm] *n.* ⟨Greek *kynikos* doglike; *kyōn* dog⟩

SYNONYMS
Cynical suggests basic distrust of people's sincerity and motives: *She has no friends because she is so cynical about friendship.*
Pessimistic suggests the assumption that despite people's good intentions, things will not turn out well: *He has a very pessimistic attitude toward his work.*

cy·press ['sɑiprəs] *n* any of a genus of evergreen trees of the US, S Europe, and Asia, having small, scalelike leaves and round, upright cones. None are native to Canada. *adj* designating the family of conifers that includes the cypresses, junipers, and arborvitae. ⟨Greek *kyparissos*⟩

Cy·ril·lic [sɪ'rɪlɪk] *adj* to do with the Slavic alphabet used for Russian and certain other languages. **Cy·ril·lic** *n*. ⟨St. *Cyril*, 9c apostle to the Slavs, traditionally credited with it⟩

cyst [sɪst] *n* an abnormal, saclike growth in animals or plants that usually contains fluid and has no opening to the outside. **cyst·ic** *adj*. ⟨Greek *kystis* pouch, bladder⟩ **cys·tec·to·my** *n* **1** surgical removal of a cyst. **2** surgical removal of the gall bladder or part of the bladder. **cystic fibrosis** [faɪ'brousɪs] a congenital disease that causes respiratory infection and malfunction of the pancreas. **cys·ti·tis** *n* inflammation of the bladder.

–cyte *combining form* cell: *leucocyte* = *a white (blood) cell*. ⟨Greek *kytos* hollow thing⟩

cy·tol·o·gy [səi'tɒlədʒi] *n* the branch of biology that deals with animal and plant cells. **cy·to·log·ic·al** *adj*. **cy·tol·o·gist** *n*. ⟨Greek *kytos* receptacle, cell + English -*logy*⟩ **cy·to·plasm** ['səitə‚plæzəm] *n* *Biology* the protoplasm or living substance of a cell, exclusive of the nucleus. **cy·to·plas·mic** *adj*.

czar or **tsar** [zɑr] *n* **1** the title of the former Russian emperors. **2** autocrat. **czar·dom** or **tsar·dom** *n*. **czar·ism** or **tsar·ism** *n*. **czar·ist** or **tsar·ist** *n, adj*. ⟨Russian; Latin *Caesar* Caesar⟩ **czar·e·vitch** or **tsar·e·vitch** ['zɑrə‚vitʃ] *n* the eldest son of a Russian czar. **cza·rev·na** or **tsa·rev·na** [zɑ'rɛvnə] *n* **1** the daughter of a Russian czar. **2** the wife of a czarevitch. **cza·ri·na** or **tsa·ri·na** [zɑ'rinə] *n* the wife of a czar; a Russian empress.

Dd

d or **D** [di] *n, pl* **d's** or **D's 1** the fourth letter of the English alphabet, or any speech sound represented by it. **2** the fourth person or thing in a series: *Do part d of question 7.* **3 D** a grade indicating quality or performance that is below average. **4** *Music* the second tone in the scale of C major. **5 D** the Roman numeral for 500.

d 1 day. **2** deci- (an SI prefix). **3** diameter.

d. 1 died. **2** daughter. **3** departs; departure.

dab [dæb] *v* **dabbed, dab·bing 1** pat with something soft or moist (with *at*): *He dabbed at the spot with his napkin.* **2** apply with light strokes: *to dab ointment on a wound.* *n* the act of dabbing or a quantity applied by dabbing: *a dab of butter.* ⟨Middle English⟩ **dab·ber** *n* a marker for making large dots.

dab·ble ['dæbəl] *v* **1** dip (hands, feet, etc.) in and out of water. **2** work (*at*) in a superficial way: *to dabble at painting.* **dab·bler** *n*. ⟨Flemish *dabbelen*⟩

dace [deis] *n, pl* **dace** or **daces** any of several small freshwater fishes of North America, such as the **pearl dace** common in Canadian waters. ⟨Old French *dars* dart; Latin *darsus*⟩

dachs·hund ['dæʃ,hʊnd], ['dɑks,hʊnd], *or* ['dæks,hʊnt] *German* ['daxs,hʊnt] *n* a breed of small dog with a long body and very short legs. ⟨German *Dachs* badger + *Hund* dog⟩

dac·tyl ['dæktəl] *n* **1** a metrical foot made up of one strongly stressed syllable followed by two weakly stressed ones. *Example:* "Táke hĕr ŭp téndĕrlў." **2** *Zoology* a finger or toe. **dac·tyl·ic** [dæk'tɪlɪk] *adj*. ⟨Greek *daktylos* finger⟩

dad [dæd] *n Informal* father. Also, **dad·dy**. **dad·dy–long·legs** ['dædi 'lɒŋ,lɛgz] *n sg or pl* any of an order of spiderlike arachnids with a round, unsegmented body and four pairs of very long, thin legs.

Da·da·ism or **da·da·ism** [dɑdə,ɪzəm] *n* a style in art and literature developed during World War I and characterized by the use of unconventional materials and techniques and by witty satire of and revolt against existing forms and standards. Also, **Da·da** or **da·da** ['dɑdɑ] *or* ['dɑdə]. **Da·da·ist** or **da·da·ist** *n, adj*. **Da·da·ist·ic** or **da·da·ist·ic** *adj*. ⟨French *dada* horse, hobbyhorse (a child's word)⟩

dae·mon ['dimən] *n* **1** an attendant or guardian spirit. **2** *Greek myth* a supernatural being halfway between a god and a human. ⟨Greek *daimon*⟩

daf·fo·dil ['dæfə,dɪl] *n* any of various plants of the amaryllis family with a trumpetlike corona growing out from the centre of its petals. ⟨variant of *affodill;* Greek *asphodelos*⟩

daff·y ['dæfi] *adj Informal* crazy or silly. **daf·fi·ness** *n*. ⟨Middle English *daffe* fool⟩

daft [dæft] *adj* crazy or silly. **daft·ly** *adv*. **daft·ness** *n*. ⟨Old English *(ge)dæfte* gentle⟩

dag·ger ['dægər] *n* **1** a small weapon with a short, pointed blade. **2** *Printing* a sign (†) referring the reader to a footnote. ⟨probably from obsolete *dag* stab⟩ **look daggers at** look at with hatred or anger.

dahl [dɑl] *n* lentils or other legumes used in Indian cooking. ⟨Hindi *daal* split pulse⟩

dahl·ia ['deiljə] *or* ['dɑljə] *n* any of a genus of plants of the composite family native to Mexico and Central America, grown for their large, showy flower heads that bloom in late summer and fall. ⟨A. *Dahl,* Swedish botanist⟩

dai·ly ['deili] *adj* done, happening, coming, etc. every day: *a daily paper, a daily visit.* *n* **1** a newspaper appearing every day. **2 dailies** *pl Film* prints of the first shot of a scene; rushes. *adv* every day; day by day. **daily bread** livelihood; basic material needs.

dai·mio ['daimjou] *n* in Japan, one of the great feudal nobles who were vassals of the emperor. Also, **daim·yo**. ⟨Japanese; Mandarin *dai* great + *mio* name⟩

dain·ty ['deinti] *adj* **1** beautiful in a delicate way: *a dainty flower.* **2** too refined or delicate in manners. **3** good to eat: *a dainty morsel.* *n* something very good to eat. **dain·ti·ly** *adv*. **dain·ti·ness** *n*. ⟨Old French *deinte;* Latin *dignitas* worthiness⟩

dai·qui·ri ['dækəri] *or* ['dɑikəri] *n* a cocktail made from rum, lime juice, and sugar. ⟨*Daiquiri* Cuba⟩

dair·y ['dɛri] *n* **1** a place where milk and milk products, such as butter and cheese, are processed. **2** milk and milk products: *I don't eat dairy.* **dair·y** *adj*. ⟨Middle English *deierie*⟩ **dairy farm** a farm where cows are raised for milk. **dairy farmer. dairy farming.**

da·is ['deiɪs] *or* ['daiəs] *n* a raised platform at one end of a large room. ⟨Old French *deis;* Latin *discus* quoit, dish, Greek *diskos*⟩

dai·sy ['deizi] *n* any of several plants of the composite family, esp the **ox–eye daisy, Shasta daisy, English daisy,** or **Michaelmas daisy. dai·sy·like** *adj*. ⟨Old English *dæges ēage* day's eye⟩ **pushing up (the) daisies** *Slang* dead and buried. **daisy chain 1** a string of daisies linked together. **2** any chain of linked objects or events. **daisy wheel** formerly in some printers or electric typewriters, a part consisting of a rotatable hub with spokes ending in pieces of type that strike the paper.

Da·ko·ta [də'koutə] *n, pl* **-tas** or **-ta 1** a member of a Native American people of the plains of southern Canada and the N United States. **2** the Siouan language of the Dakotas and Assiniboines. **Da·ko·ta** *adj*. ⟨Dakota *dakota* allies; *da* think of as + *koda* friend⟩

Da·lai La·ma ['dɑlai 'lɑmə] *or* [dɑ'lai 'lɑmə] the chief priest of the religion of Lamaism in Tibet and Mongolia and the political leader of Tibet. ⟨Mongolian *dalai* ocean; see LAMA.⟩

dale [deil] *n Poetic* valley. ⟨Old English *dæl*⟩

Dall sheep [dɒl] a white North American

sheep of the northern Rocky Mountain region. Also, **Dall's sheep.** ⟨W.H. *Dall* (1845-1927), US naturalist⟩

dal·ly ['dæli] *v* **1** loiter; waste time. **2** play or toy: *to dally with an idea*. **3** flirt. **dal·li·ance** *n*. ⟨Old French *dalier* chat⟩

Dal·ma·tian [dæl'meiʃən] *n* a breed of dog, usually white with black spots. ⟨*Dalmatia*, region of former Yugoslavia⟩

dam¹ [dæm] *n* **1** a structure built to hold back flowing water. **2** such a structure built by beavers, with a lodge inside. **3** anything resembling a dam. **4** ✱ on the Prairies, a reservoir of water from the spring thaw and from rainfall, used for watering cattle.
v **dammed, dam·ming 1** block with a dam: *Beavers had dammed the stream*. **2** hold back: *to dam the flow of tears*. ⟨Middle English⟩

dam² [dæm] *n* the female parent of a four-footed animal. ⟨variant of *dame*⟩

dam·age ['dæmɪdʒ] *n* **1** injury that lessens value, beauty, or usefulness. **2 damages** *pl* money paid to make up for harm done. **3** *Slang* cost: *What's the damage?* **dam·age** *v*. **dam·age·a·ble** *adj*. **dam·ag·ing** *adj*. ⟨Old French, from *dam*, Latin *damnum* loss, hurt⟩

dam·ask ['dæməsk] *n* **1** reversible fabric with woven designs. **2** metal with inlaid gold or silver or with a wavy design. **3** a rose colour. **dam·ask** *adj*. ⟨*Damascus*⟩
damask rose a fragrant pink rose.

dame [deim] *n* **1 Dame** in the UK, the title of a woman who belongs to an order of knighthood, or of the wife or widow of a knight or baronet. **2** an elderly or dignified woman. **3** *Slang* any woman. **dame·hood** *n*. ⟨Old French; Latin *domina* mistress⟩

damn [dæm] *v* **1** declare to be bad: *The throne speech was damned by the press*. **2** ruin. **3** swear at. **4** condemn to hell. **5** prove the guilt of (a person): *damning evidence*.
adj, adv Slang damned: *It's a damn shame*.
interj Slang an exclamation of anger.
n Slang the least amount: *not worth a damn*. **dam·na·tion** [dæm'neiʃən] *n, interj*. ⟨Old French *damner*, Latin *damnare; damnum* loss⟩
damn with faint praise praise with so little enthusiasm as to condemn.
dam·mit *interj Slang* damn it. **dam·na·ble** *adj* abominable. **dam·na·bly** *adv*. **dam·na·to·ry** *adj* condemning. **damned** [dæmd] *adj* **1** doomed to hell. **2** *Slang* detestable or abominable: *That's a damned lie!* **3** *Slang* extraordinary (in the superlative): *It was the damnedest thing I ever saw*. *n pl* **the damned** those condemned to hell. *adv Slang* very: *He should be damned glad to get the work*. **do one's damnedest** *Informal* do one's best or utmost.

damp [dæmp] *adj* slightly wet; moist.
n **1** moisture: *the damp in the morning air*. **2** foul or explosive fumes collecting in a mine or emanating from a fire, etc.
v **1** slow down (a fire) by decreasing the air supply (usually with *down*). **2** *Music* stop the vibrations of (a string, etc.). **damp·ly** *adv*. **damp·ness** *n*. ⟨Middle Dutch = vapour⟩

damp·en *v* **1** moisten. **2** deaden; depress; discourage. **damp·er** *n* **1** a source of low spirits or discouragement. **2** a movable plate to control the draft in a fireplace, woodstove, etc. **3** *Music* **a** a device to check vibration and reduce volume. **b** a mute for a horn, etc. **put a damper on** a depress; cause low spirits in. **b** squelch: *Not to put a damper on your suggestion, but is it realistic?*

dam·sel ['dæmzəl] *n Poetic* a young girl. ⟨Middle English *dameisele;* Old French⟩
damsel fly an insect like a small dragonfly.

dance [dæns] *v* **1** move in rhythm, usually to music. **2** bob up and down.
n **1** rhythmic movement, usually to music. **2** a set of special steps used for this: *The waltz is her favourite dance*. **3** a party where people dance. **4** the art of dancing. **5 the dance** ballet. **6** any graceful or lively movement. **danc·er** *n*. ⟨Old French *danser;* Germanic⟩
dance attendance on wait on attentively.
lead someone a dance lure someone into a vain pursuit.
danc·er·cise ['dænsər,saiz] *n* exercise through dancing.

D and C dilatation (of the cervix) and curettage (of the uterus), a procedure used to diagnose and treat uterine disorders.

dan·de·li·on ['dændi,laiən] *n* any of a genus of plants of the composite family, with a single, bright yellow head. The common dandelion is a weed throughout Canada and is also grown for its edible leaves and flowers. ⟨French *dent de lion* lion's tooth⟩

dan·der ['dændər] *n* **1** fragments of skin, hair, etc.: *I'm allergic to cat dander*. **2** *Informal* temper; anger. ⟨origin uncertain⟩
get one's dander up get angry.

dan·dle ['dændəl] *v* move (a child, etc.) up and down on one's knee or in one's arms. ⟨perhaps earlier Italian *dondolare* swing⟩

dan·druff ['dændrəf] *n* small, whitish scales that flake off the scalp. ⟨*dander* + earlier *hurf* scab; Old Norse *hrufa*⟩

dan·dy ['dændi] *n* **1** a man who cares too much for clothes. **2** *Slang* anything that is excellent or pleasing. **dan·dy** *adj*. ⟨orig Scottish, perhaps *Dandy*, a variant of *Andrew*⟩
dan·di·fy *v* make trim or smart like a dandy.

dan·ger ['deindʒər] *n* **1** the possibility of harm: *Life is full of danger*. **2** anything that may cause harm: *Hidden rocks are a danger to ships*. **dan·ger·ous** *adj*. ⟨Old French *dangier;* Latin *dominium* sovereignty, *dominus* master⟩
in danger of liable to undergo (something bad): *The old bridge is in danger of collapsing*.

dan·gle ['dæŋgəl] *v* **1** hang loosely: *The curtain cord dangles*. **2** hold (something) so that it swings loosely: *The nurse dangled the* toys in front of the baby. **3** hold before a person as a temptation or inducement: to dangle false hopes. ⟨Scandinavian⟩

dangling participle a participle which, by its position before a clause, becomes attached to the subject of that clause when it is actually intended to modify something else. Also called **unattached participle.**

GRAMMAR

The **dangling participle** can have ambiguous and ludicrous effects. In Swimming in the pond, the car was out of our sight, the participle swimming becomes attached to the subject car, making nonsense. Such a sentence can be improved in at least two ways. The main clause can be rewritten with a new subject: Swimming in the pond, we could not see the car. Or, the participial phrase can be replaced by a subordinate clause: When we were swimming in the pond, the car was out of our sight.

Dan·ish ['deɪnɪʃ] adj to do with the country Denmark, its people, or their language. n **1** the official language of Denmark. **2** a rich yeast pastry, iced and often filled. ⟨Old English Denisc⟩

dank [dæŋk] adj unpleasantly damp, often with a mildewy smell. ⟨Middle English⟩

dap·per ['dæpər] adj **1** neat; trim. **2** small and quick. **dap·per·ly** adv. **dap·per·ness** n. ⟨Middle Dutch dapper agile, strong⟩

dap·ple ['dæpəl] v mark or become marked with spots or patches of colours. n **1** a spotted appearance. **2** an animal with a spotted or mottled skin. **dap·pled** adj. ⟨Scandinavian⟩

dap·ple–grey adj grey with spots of darker grey. Also, **dapple–gray.**

dare [dɛr] v **dared** or (archaic) **durst, dared, dar·ing 1** be bold enough to: He doesn't dare dive from the bridge. **2** face bravely: The explorers dared the dangers of the Arctic. **3** challenge: I dare you to tell her the truth. n a challenge. **dar·er** n. ⟨Old English dearr⟩

I dare say probably; I guess: I dare say she'll be there by now.

dare·dev·il n **1** a recklessly adventurous person. **2** a stuntman or stuntwoman. **dare·dev·il** adj. **dar·ing** adj bold in taking risks. **dar·ing** n. **dar·ing·ly** adv. **dar·ing·ness** n.

USAGE

Dare can be used without do in negatives and questions: How dare you? How dare he? I dare not try it. It can also be followed by an infinitive without to: If you dare go in, I'll go in with you. He wouldn't dare drive that fast.

dark [dɑrk] adj **1** without light: the dark side of the moon. **2** not light-complexioned: tall, dark, and handsome. **3** closer in colour to black than white: dark green. **4** secret, hidden, or mysterious: dark sayings. He kept his past dark. **5** evil; wicked: a dark deed. **6** gloomy: the dark side of life. **7** unenlightened: a culturally dark age. **8** angry: She gave him a dark look. **9** sounding far back in the mouth. n **1 the dark** absence of light; dark places:

He's afraid of the dark. **2** nightfall: We're not allowed out after dark. **dark·en** v. **dark·ish** adj. **dark·ly** adv. **dark·ness** n. ⟨Old English deorc⟩

in the dark not knowing or understanding: I'm still in the dark about what I'm supposed to do on the project. **keep dark** keep silent. **not darken the door of** never visit.

Dark Ages the early Middle Ages, from the 400s to the 900s, so named from the idea that it was a time of economic and intellectual poverty in Europe. **Dark Continent** formerly, Africa, because little known to Europeans. **dark horse** a little-known but suddenly very promising or successful participant in any field. **dark·room** n a room for developing photographs, having only light of a colour that will not affect photographic materials.

dar·ling ['dɑrlɪŋ] n **1** a term of endearment. **2** a person much loved or favoured: She's the darling of the jet set. adj **1** much loved. **2** Informal attractive in an endearing way; charming: a darling little shop. ⟨Old English dēorling; dēore dear⟩

darn¹ [dɑrn] v mend by weaving rows of thread or yarn across (a hole or tear). n a place mended by darning. ⟨dialect French darner mend, darne piece; Breton darn⟩

darning needle a long needle with an eye large enough to take heavy thread or yarn.

darn² [dɑrn] interj, adj, adv, v Informal a mild form of **damn** or **damned,** used to express annoyance: Darn! The door's locked. ⟨damn; influenced by tarnal, informal for eternal⟩ **darned** [dɑrnd] adj, adv Informal damned.

dart [dɑrt] n **1** a small, pointed weapon, often with feathers on the back end, for throwing or shooting from a tube or gun. **2 darts** an indoor game in which players throw darts at a round board (with sg verb). **3** a sudden quick movement **4** a tapered fold in a garment to shape it. v move or send suddenly and quickly: He darted across the street. She darted an angry glance at her sister. ⟨Middle English⟩

Dar·win·i·an [dɑr'wɪniən] adj to do with Charles Darwin, 19c English scientist, or his theory of evolution, the theory that through natural selection the life forms that survive are those which have better adapted to their environment. **Dar·win·ism** n.

dash [dæʃ] v **1** move with great speed; rush: They dashed by in a new car. **2** strike violently against something: The waves dashed the boat against the rock. **3** ruin: dashed hopes. **4** splash: We dashed water in her face to bring her around. **5** discourage. **6** euphemism for **damn.** n **1** an act of dashing; a splash, rush, or smash. **2** a small amount. **3** a short race: the hundred-metre dash. **4** a mark (—) showing a break in a sentence. **5** Telegraphy a long sound or signal representing a letter or part of a letter. Compare DOT. **6** pizzazz; style; spirit. **7** dashboard. ⟨Middle English daschen⟩ **cut a dash** dress showily. **dash off a** write, do, etc. quickly: He dashed off a short letter. **b** rush away.

dash·board n a panel with controls and

gauges in the front of a car, aircraft, etc.
dashed *adj, adv* damned. **dash·ing** *adj* full of pizzazz, style, spirit, etc.

das·tard ['dæstərd] *n* a mean and devious coward. **das·tard·ly** *adj*. ⟨Middle English *dazed* + *-ard* as in *drunkard*; orig, a stupid person⟩

DAT DIGITAL AUDIO TAPE.

da·ta ['dætə] *or* ['deitə] *n* pl of **datum 1** facts in a form suitable for processing: *All the data indicate the beginning of an economic boom.* **2** *Computers* values, characters, or symbols on which a computer carries out operations.
data bank a body of information available for processing in a computer. **da·ta·base** *n* *Computers* **1** information stored in the form of records that conform to a certain template, esp using a program that makes it easy to extract, compare, and correlate different parts of the information. **2** such a program. **data entry** the process of keying data into a computer. **data processing** operations performed on data, esp by a computer. **da·ta–pro·cess·ing** *adj*. **data processor. data warehouse** a large electronic collection of information of different kinds, accessible to all those on a local computer network.

USAGE

Data is the plural of the seldom-used singular **datum**. Since its meaning is often collective, referring to a group of facts as a whole, **data** is routinely used with a singular verb in informal English: *The data is saved in this file.* Formal English continues to regard **data** as a plural: *Our data do not support this conclusion.*

---

date[1] [deit] *n* **1** the day, month, or year when something happens. **2** the number of a day of the month: *Today's date is the 15th.* **3** a social engagement, usually with a romantic partner: *She has a date with him tonight.* **4** *Informal* the person with whom one has such an engagement: *Who's your date for the dance?* **5 dates** *pl* the years of a person's birth and death.
v **1** mark with a date. **2** find out the date of: *to date a fossil.* **3** belong to or originate in a certain period of time: (with *from* or *back to*): *That house dates from the late 1700s. This custom dates back to the Middle Ages.* **4** cause to seem old-fashioned: *That expression dates you—it's passé.* **5** go out on dates (def. 3): *They've been dating for months.* **6** become out of date. ⟨Latin *data* pp fem of *dare* give⟩
bring up to date a revise to reflect current information. **b** give the latest news to. **out of date** old-fashioned. **to date** till now: *There has been no reply to date.* **up to date a** using current methods, fashions, etc. **b** having current information. **up–to–date** *adj*.
dat·ed *adj* out of date. **dat·ed·ness** *n*. **date line** an imaginary line agreed upon as the place where each calendar day first begins. It runs north and south through the Pacific. **date rape** rape by someone with whom the victim is on a date. **date stamp** a rubber stamp for recording dates. **date–stamp** *v*.

date[2] [deit] *n* the sweet, fleshy oval fruit of

the **date palm**, a tall tropical palm tree. ⟨Middle English; Greek *daktylos* date, finger⟩

daub [dɒb] *v* **1** apply (plaster, mud, etc.) to (a surface) in blobs. **2** paint unskilfully.
n **1** a substance applied by daubing. **2** a smear; blob. **3** a painting showing little skill. **daub·er** *n*. ⟨Old French *dauber*, Latin *dealbare*; *de-* + *albus* white⟩

daugh·ter ['dɒtər] *n* **1** someone's female child or descendant. **2** a female thought of as being produced or formed by something: *a daughter of France.*
adj **1** of, being, or like a daughter. **2** resulting from a primary division, segmentation, or replication: *a daughter cell.* **daugh·ter·ly** *adj*. ⟨Old English *dohtor*⟩
daugh·ter–in–law *n, pl* **daugh·ters–in–law** the wife of one's son.

daunt [dɒnt] *v* intimidate or discourage. ⟨Old French *danter*, Latin *domitare; domare* tame⟩
nothing daunted not discouraged.
daunt·less *adj* not easily daunted.

dav·en·port ['dævən,pɔrt] *n* a large sofa; chesterfield. ⟨origin uncertain⟩

Davy Jones's locker the sea, esp as the grave of those lost or buried at sea.

daw·dle ['dɒdəl] *v* waste time; loiter. **dawd·ler** *n*. ⟨origin uncertain⟩

dawn [dɒn] *n* **1** the beginning of day. **2** any beginning: *before the dawn of history.*
v **1** grow light: *The day dawned.* **2** grow clear to the eye or mind: *It dawned on me that she was expecting a gift.* **3** begin: *A new era is dawning.* ⟨probably Old Norse⟩

day [dei] *n* **1** the time between sunrise and sunset, or the light of the sun during this time. **2** a period of 24 hours, esp from midnight to midnight. **3** *Astronomy* the time needed by any celestial body to turn once on its axis: *The Martian day is longer than Earth's.* **4** the part of a day devoted to work: *a seven-hour day.* **5** a certain period of time: *in olden days, the present day.* **6 days** *pl* a lifetime: *to spend one's days in comfort.* **7** a time of power, vitality, influence, activity, etc.: *He has had his day.* **8** the contest of a particular day: *We won the day.* ⟨Old English *dæg*⟩
call it a day *Informal* stop work. **day after day** every day for many days. **day and night** constantly. **day by day** one day at a time. **day in, day out** every day. **don't quit your day job** *Informal* you will never make any money at that. **from day to day** one day at a time. **have one's day in court** have a chance to give one's side of a story. **in this day and age** nowadays. **one of these days** at some indefinite future time. **pass the time of day** take part in small talk. **(right) from day one** from the very beginning. **the time of day a** the time. **b** social recognition.
day bed or **day·bed** *n* a bed with a support of some kind along one side and both ends so that it can serve as a sofa. **day book 1** a book in which each day's business or plans are recorded. **2** diary. **day·break** *n* dawn. **day camp** a summer camp for children where

they have daytime activities but return home for the night. **day·care** *n* **1** Often, **day care,** care for preschool children, the elderly or disabled, or pets, provided by the day outside the home. **2** a facility offering such a service. **day·care** *adj.* **day coach** a railway passenger car that is not a dining car or sleeping car. **day·dream** *n* a pleasant fantasy. *v* **-dreamed** or **-dreamt, -dream·ing. day·dream·er** *n.* **day labourer** or **laborer** an unskilled worker paid by the day. **day·light** *n* **1** the light of the sun in daytime. **2** dawn. **3** open space; a gap. **scare** (or **beat, knock, etc.**) **the daylights out of** *Slang* scare (or beat, etc.) someone severely. **see daylight** *Informal* **a** understand. **b** approach the end of a tiresome job. **daylight–saving time** time that is one hour in advance of standard time, effective in the spring and summer. Compare STANDARD TIME. **day·lin·er** *n* an express train connecting two cities, or a city and its suburbs, during the day. **day·long** *adj, adv* through the whole day. **Day of Atonement** YOM KIPPUR. **Day of Judgment** in some faiths, the day of God's final judgment of humanity at the end of the world. **day of reckoning** See RECKONING. **day school** a private school for students who live at home. **day·spring** *n Poetic* daybreak. **day·star** *n* MORNING STAR. **day student** a non-boarding student at a boarding school. **day·time** *n* the time when it is day. **day–to–day** *adj* regular; ordinary: *Civil servants perform the day-to-day work of government.* **day trip** a leisure trip lasting no longer than a day. **day–trip·per** *n.*

daze [deiz] *v* **1** confuse; stun: *dazed by a fall.* **2** dazzle. **daze** *n.* **daz·ed·ly** ['deizɪdli] *adv.* ⟨Middle English *dasen*; Old Norse⟩

daz·zle ['dæzəl] *v* **1** overpower (the eyes) with bright or quick-moving lights. **2** overwhelm by skill, beauty, speed, energy, etc.: *The young pianist's performance dazzled the critics.* **daz·zle** *n.* **daz·zler** *n.* **daz·zling** *adj.* ⟨*daze*⟩

db decibel.

DC, D.C., or **d.c.** DIRECT CURRENT.

D.C. 1 *Music* return to beginning (for Italian *da capo*). **2** District of Columbia.

D–day [di ‚dei] *n* **1** the day when the Allies landed in France in World War II; June 6, 1944. **2** the day on which any planned operation is to start. ⟨*D*, first letter of *day*⟩

DDT ['di'di'ti] *n* a powerful and long-lasting poison formerly much used as an insecticide. ⟨*di*chloro - *di*phenyl - trichloroethane⟩

de– *prefix* **1** do the opposite of, as in *decamp, decentralize, demobilize.* **2** down, as in *depress, descend.* **3** away; off, as in *deport, detract, derail.* **4** entirely; completely, as in *despoil.* **5** remove, as in *devein, declaw.* ⟨Latin⟩

de·ac·ces·sion or **de·ac·ces·sion** [‚diæk'sɛʃən] *v* sell off (an item) from the collection in a gallery, museum, or library.

dea·con ['dikən] *n Christianity* a church officer who helps the minister in duties other than preaching. **dea·con·ess** ['dikənɪs] or ['dikə‚nɛs] *n.* ⟨Greek *diakonos* servant⟩

de·ac·ti·vate [di'æktə‚veit] *v* make inactive. **de·ac·ti·va·tion** *n.* **de·ac·ti·va·tor** *n.*

dead [dɛd] *adj* **1** no longer living. **2** like death: *in a dead faint.* **3** dull, stagnant, quiet, etc. **4** insensitive: *dead to all human emotion.* **5** without force, expression, or feeling: *a dead handshake.* **6** no longer active, functioning, relevant, etc.: *a dead issue, a dead volcano, dead languages.* **7** *Informal* extremely tired. **8** complete: *a dead giveaway, dead silence.* **9** precise: *dead centre.* **10** not connected to a power source: *a dead circuit. The line is dead.* *n* **1 the dead** *pl* those who are dead: *in honour of the dead.* **2** the time of greatest darkness, quiet, cold, etc.: *the dead of night.* *adv* **1** totally; very: *dead wrong.* **2** directly: *dead ahead.* **dead·ness** *n.* ⟨Old English *dēad*⟩ **dead in the water** *Slang* **1** done for; doomed. **2** totally inactive. **dead set against** firmly opposed to. **dead to the world** fast asleep. **over my dead body** only with my most strenuous opposition. **play dead** lie still, trying to appear dead. **would not be caught dead** be unwilling to be, do, etc. under any circumstances.

dead air 1 air trapped between two walls for insulation. **2** *Radio, television* a period of no broadcasting. **dead·beat** *n Informal* one who avoids paying or doing his or her share. **dead·bolt** *n* a lock with a bolt moved by a key. **dead centre 1** the stationary centre of a revolving object. **2** the exact centre. **dead duck** *Informal* **1** a doomed person. **2** a person or thing that has lost all force or influence. **dead·en** *v* **1** lessen the intensity, sharpness, etc. of. **2** make insensitive to: *Life in the army deadened them to cruelty.* **dead end 1** a street closed at one end. **2** a point beyond which progress is impossible: *Negotiations have reached a dead end.* **dead–end** *adj.* **dead·fall** *n* **1** a mass of fallen trees and underbrush. **2** a dead tree blown to the ground. **3** a trap that works by dropping a heavy weight on the animal. **dead·head** *n* **1** *Informal* one who rides a bus, sees a game, etc. without paying. **2** *Slang* a stupid or dull person. **3** *Informal* a train, bus, etc. travelling without passengers or freight. **4 ✺** a log or fallen tree submerged in a lake, etc. **dead heat** a race that ends in a tie. **dead letter** a letter that cannot be delivered or returned because the address is wrong, impossible to read, or incomplete. **dead·line** *n* a time limit. **dead load 1** the constant load carried by a bridge, etc., due to the weight of the supported structures, permanent attachments, etc. **2** the mass of a vehicle without cargo. **dead·lock** *n* a position in which it is impossible to act because of disagreement: *Employers and strikers were at a deadlock.* **dead·lock** *v.* **dead·ly** *adj* **1** fatal: *a deadly wound.* **2** like death: *deadly paleness.* **3** filled with hate that lasts till death: *deadly enemies.* **4** causing spiritual death: *deadly sins.* **5** dull: *The party was a deadly affair.* **6** very accurate: *a deadly aim.* **dead·ly** *adv.* **dead·li·ness** *n.* **dead·pan** *adj, adv* with no expression in the face or voice. *n* **1** a deadpan face or manner. **2** one who assumes such a face or manner. **dead·pan, -panned, -pan·ning** *v.* **dead reckoning** the calculation of a ship's position without observation of the sun, stars, etc., by using a compass and studying the record of the voyage. **dead weight 1** the heavy weight of anything inert. **2** a very great burden. **3** DEAD LOAD. **dead·wood** *n* **1** dead branches or trees. **2** useless people or things.

deaf [dɛf] *adj* **1** unable to hear. **2** unwilling to hear: *deaf to all pleas for mercy.* **deaf·ly** *adv.* **deaf·ness** *n.* ⟨Old English *dēaf*⟩ **deaf·en** *v* **1** make deaf. **2** stun with noise. **deaf·en·ing** *adj.*

deal [dil] *v* **dealt, deal·ing 1** have to do (*with*): *This book deals with art history.* **2** take positive, effective action (*with*): *I will deal with the problem at once.* **3** conduct oneself: *Deal fairly with everyone.* **4** do business: *A butcher deals in meat.* **5** (often with *out*) distribute, esp playing cards. **6** sell (illegal drugs).
n **1** a business arrangement; a bargain or contract. **2** *Informal* arrangement: *What's the deal here?* **3** kind of treatment: *a rough deal.* **4** *Cards* **a** the act of dealing cards. **b** one's turn to deal. **c** the cards dealt to a player. **5** a quantity: *a deal of trouble.* ⟨Old English *dǣlan*⟩ **a good deal** or **a great deal** a lot; much: *a great deal of money, a great deal better.* **a square deal** fair treatment or a fair transaction. **big deal** *Slang* an expression of disparagement. **make a big deal (out) of** *Informal* attach too much importance to.
deal·er *n* **1** a person or company that buys and sells: *a car dealer.* **2** *Cards* the one who distributes the cards to players. **3** a person who acts in a particular way: *a plain dealer.* **deal·er·ship** *n* the business of a DEALER (def. 1). **deal·ing** *n* **1** a way of doing business or conducting oneself: *fair dealing.* **2 dealings** *pl* **a** business relations. **b** conduct.

dean [din] *n* **1** at a university or college: **a** the head of a faculty. **b** a faculty member who supervises the behaviour or studies of students. **2** a high Christian church official. **3** the most illustrious member of a given profession, etc.: *Robertson Davies, the dean of Canadian novelists.* **dean·ship** *n.* ⟨Old French *deien*, Latin *decanus* master of ten; *decem* ten⟩

dear [dir] *adj* **1** much loved or cherished; precious. **2** highly esteemed (often in polite address or at the beginning of letters): *Dear Sir.* **3** high-priced; expensive.
adv at a high price or great cost: *to pay dear.*
n (esp as term of address) dear one.
interj exclamation of surprise, trouble, etc. **dear·ly** *adv.* **dear·ness** *n.* ⟨Old English *dēore*⟩ **dear knows** *Informal* no one knows: *Dear knows when he'll come.* **dear me** exclamation of surprise, trouble, etc. **hold dear** value highly. **dear·ie** or **dear·y** *n Informal* dear one. **Dear John letter** *Informal* a letter written to a man by a woman to end a romantic involvement.

dearth [dɜrθ] *n* a scarcity; lack. ⟨Middle English *derthe; dere* hard, grievous⟩

death [dɛθ] *n* **1** the act or fact of dying, or the state of being dead. **2** any ending that is like dying: *the death of all our hopes.* **3** a cause of dying: *He'll be your death.* **4** bloodshed. **death·like** *adj.* ⟨Old English *dēath*⟩
as death as one would be if dead: *pale as death.* **at death's door** almost dead. **be death on** be strongly opposed to: *He's death on all drugs.* **catch one's death (of cold)** get so cold as to become gravely ill. **do to death a** kill; murder. **b** do or say (a thing) too often. **like death (warmed over)** *Informal* very pale, ill, etc. **put to death** execute. **to death a** so as to kill: *to beat someone to death.* **b** beyond endurance: *bored to death.* **to the death** until one, or someone, dies: *a fight to the death.*
death·bed *n* the bed on which one dies. **on one's deathbed** in the last hours of life. **death·bed** *adj.* **death·blow** *n* **1** a fatal blow. **2** anything that puts an end to something. **death camp** a concentration camp where many people are killed. **death cap** a very poisonous mushroom. **death duty** or **tax** inheritance tax. **death knell 1** the tolling of a bell to announce a death. **2** anything that signals the end or ruin of something else. **death·less** *adj* lasting forever. **death·ly** *adj* suggesting or causing death: *deathly tones, a deathly cold. adv* to a fatal degree; extremely: *deathly ill.* **death penalty** punishment by death. **death rate** the proportion of the number of deaths per year to the total population. **death rattle** a rattling sound coming from the throat of a dying person. **death row** a section of a prison housing those to be executed. **death squad** a force hired by an oppressive political regime to liquidate its opponents. **death·trap** *n* an unsafe building or any very dangerous place. **death warrant 1** an official order for a person's death. **2** anything that signals the end or ruin of something else: *CDs were the death warrant for vinyl records.* **sign the death warrant of** cause the end or ruin of. **death·watch** *n* a watch kept over a dying or dead person. **death wish** a suicidal tendency.

de·ba·cle [dɪ'bakəl] *French* [de'bakl] *n* **1** a disaster; fiasco. **2** overthrow; downfall. ⟨French, from *débâcler* free; *dé-* un- + *bâcler* to bar⟩

de·bar [dɪ'bar] or [dɪ'bɑr] *v* **-barred, -bar·ring** shut out; exclude. **de·bar·ment** *n.* ⟨Latin *debarrare; de-* from + *barrare* bar⟩

de·base [dɪ'beis] *v* lower the character or value of: *debased currency, to debase oneself by mean acts.* **de·base·ment** *n.* ⟨*de-* down + *abase*⟩

de·bate [dɪ'beit] *v* **1** discuss reasons for and against (something), esp formally and publicly; specifically, discuss a motion to be voted on in Parliament or another decision-making body. **2** argue against (someone). **3** think over the pros and cons of. **de·bate** *n.* **de·bat·er** *n.* ⟨Latin *debattere; de-* (intensive) + *battuere* beat⟩
de·bat·a·ble *adj* open to debate; questionable.

de·bauch [dɪ'bɒtʃ] v **1** corrupt the morals or judgment of: *debauched by bad companions, a mind debauched by prejudice.* **2** degrade by wild living, drunkenness, etc. **de·bauch** n. **de·bauch·er·y** n. **de·bauch·ment** n. ⟨French *débaucher* entice from duty⟩

de·ben·ture [dɪ'bɛntʃər] n **1** a bond, usually one issued by a corporation rather than a government. **2** a written acknowledgment of a debt. ⟨Latin *debentur* are owed; *debere* owe⟩

de·bil·i·tate [dɪ'bɪlə,teit] v enfeeble; weaken: *debilitated by the hot weather.* **de·bil·i·ta·tion** n. ⟨Latin *debilitare; debilis* weak⟩ **de·bil·i·ty** n weakness.

deb·it ['dɛbɪt] n **1** *Accounting* an entry of an amount owed in an account. **2** the money or sum owed. **3** a liability.
v charge with or as a debt: *Debit her account $90.* ⟨Latin *debitum* pp of *debere* owe⟩
debit card a BANK CARD used to pay for goods or services by instantly debiting an account electronically.

deb·o·nair [ˌdɛbə'nɛr] adj **1** Usually of a man, elegant and refined. **2** light-hearted; cheery. ⟨Old French *de bon aire* of good disposition⟩

de·bone [di'boun] v remove the bones from (meat or fish), esp by machine.

de·brief [di'brif] v question (a combat pilot, intelligence agent, delegate, etc.) on return from a mission. **de·brief·ing** n.

de·bris or **dé·bris** [də'bri] or [dei'bri] n scattered fragments: *debris from an explosion.* ⟨French; Old French *de-* away + *brisier* break⟩

debt [dɛt] n **1** something owed to another. **2** the fact or condition of owing something. **debt·or** n. ⟨Old French *dette;* Latin. See DEBIT.⟩ **in someone's debt** obligated to repay or to show gratitude to someone.

de·bug [di'bʌg] v **-bugged, -bug·ging 1** find and fix errors or weaknesses in (a computer program, plan, or design). **2** remove hidden microphones in (a room, etc.).

de·bunk [dɪ'bʌŋk] v expose as false: *to debunk a theory.* **de·bunk·er** n.

de·but or **dé·but** [dei'bju] or ['deibju] n **1** a first public appearance: *an actor's debut.* **2** the start of a career or involvement. **de·but** or **dé·but, -buted** ['bjud], **-buting** ['bjuɪŋ] v. ⟨French, from *débuter* make a first stroke; *de-* from + *but* mark (in game or sport)⟩
deb·u·tante or **dé·bu·tante** ['dɛbjə,tɑnt] or [ˌdeibju'tɑnt] *French* [deby'tɑ̃t] n a young woman entering high society.

deca– *SI prefix* ten. *Symbol* da ⟨Greek *deka*⟩ **dec·a·gon** ['dɛkə,gɒn] n a figure with ten sides. **dec·a·gram** ['dɛkə,græm] n a unit of mass equal to ten grams. **dec·a·he·dron** [-'hidrən] n, pl **-drons, -dra** [-drə] a solid with ten faces.

dec·ade ['dɛkeid] n **1** a period of ten years. **2** a group of ten. ⟨French; Greek *deka* ten⟩

de·ca·dent ['dɛkədənt] adj **1** in a state of moral decline or decay. **2** *Informal* appealing to the self-indulgent or hedonistic: *a decadent*

chocolate cake. **de·ca·dence** n. ⟨Latin *de-* down + *cadere* fall⟩

de·caf·fein·ate [di'kæfə,neit] v remove the caffeine from: *decaffeinated coffee.*

dec·a·gon, dec·a·gram, dec·a·he·dron See DECA-.

de·cal·ci·fy [di'kælsə,fai] v remove calcium or lime deposits from. **de·cal·ci·fi·ca·tion** n.

de·cal ['dikæl], ['dɛkəl], or [dɪ'kæl] n a design or picture on special paper or film that sticks to glass, metal, etc. In full, **de·cal·co·ma·ni·a** [dɪ,kælkə'meiniə]. ⟨French *décalcomanie; décalquer* transfer a tracing + *manie* mania⟩

de·camp [di'kæmp] v depart quickly or secretly. **de·camp·ment** n.

de·cant [dɪ'kænt] v pour off (a liquid) gently so as not to stir the sediment. **de·can·ta·tion** n. ⟨Latin *de-* from + *canthus* lip (of container); Greek *kanthos* corner of the eye⟩
de·cant·er n a glass bottle with a stopper, used for serving wine or liquor.

de·cap·i·tate [dɪ'kæpə,teit] v cut off the head of. **de·cap·i·ta·tion** n. ⟨Latin *de-* away + *caput, capitis* head⟩

dec·a·pod ['dɛkə,pɒd] n **1** any of an order of crustaceans having five pairs of appendages with at least one pair modified into pincers. **2** any of an order of molluscs with ten arms. **de·cap·o·dal** adj. ⟨*deca-* + Greek *podos* foot⟩

de·cath·lon [dɪ'kæθlɒn] n an athletic contest consisting of ten separate events that include running, jumping, and various kinds of throwing. **de·cath·lete** [dɪ'kæθlit] n. ⟨*deca-* + Greek *athlon* contest⟩

de·cay [dɪ'kei] v **1** rot or cause to rot. *The fruit began to decay.* **2** grow less in strength, beauty, goodness, etc. **3** of radioactive substances, undergo transformation through the disintegration of nuclei. **de·cay** n. ⟨Old French *de-* down + *cair;* Latin *cadere* fall⟩

de·cease [dɪ'sis] n death.
v die. ⟨Latin *decessus* pp of *decedere; de-* away + *cedere* go⟩
de·ceased adj dead. n **the deceased** the person or people who have died.

de·ceive [dɪ'siv] v trick into believing something false; mislead; lie to. **de·ceiv·er** n. **de·ceiv·ing** adj. ⟨Old French *deceveir,* Latin *decipere; de-* away + *capere* take⟩
de·ceit [dɪ'sit] n the act or habit of making people believe what is false. **de·ceit·ful** adj.

CONFUSABLES

Deceit suggests a character trait, a habit of trying to mislead others by covering up or twisting the truth: *a heart full of deceit. She used deceit to get her way.* **Deception** applies to the act or fact of giving a false or wrong idea, but does not always imply a malevolent purpose: *Magic tricks depend on deception.*

de·cel·er·ate [di'sɛlə,reit] v slow down. **de·cel·er·a·tion** n. **de·cel·er·a·tor** n. ⟨*de-* + *(ac)celerate*⟩

December [dɪ'sɛmbər] n the twelfth and last

month of the year. It has 31 days. ⟨Latin; *decem* ten, for original calendar⟩

de·cent ['disənt] *adj* **1** proper and right: *the decent thing to do.* **2** not vulgar, immodest, or obscene: *decent language.* **3** conforming to standards of honesty, civility, morality, etc.: *decent people.* **4** meeting at least minimum standards: *a decent wage, a decent meal.* **de·cen·cy** *n.* **de·cent·ly** *adv.* ⟨Latin *decens* becoming, fitting, ppr of *decere*⟩

de·cen·tral·ize [di'sɛntrə,laɪz] *v* spread or distribute (responsibility, power, etc.) among several agents, departments, etc. **de·cen·tral·i·za·tion** *n.* **de·cen·tral·i·zed** *adj.*

de·cep·tive [dɪ'sɛptɪv] *adj* **1** tending to deceive; misleading: *a deceptive calm before the storm.* **2** meant to deceive; deceitful; false. **de·cep·tion** *n.* **de·cep·tive·ly** *adv.* **de·cep·tive·ness** *n.*

deci– *SI prefix* one tenth. *Symbol* **d** ⟨French *déci-*; Latin *decimus* tenth, *decem* ten⟩
dec·i·bel ['dɛsə,bɛl] *or* ['dɛsəbəl] *n* a unit for expressing loudness. **dec·i·me·tre** *n* an SI unit of length, equal to one tenth of a metre. Also, **dec·i·me·ter.** *Symbol* **dm**

de·cide [dɪ'saɪd] *v* **1** make up or cause to make up one's mind: *We decided to stay home. Your comments have decided me against the proposal.* **2** settle (a question, dispute, etc.) by giving victory to one side. ⟨Latin *decidere* cut off; *de-* away + *caedere* cut⟩
de·cid·ed *adj* **1** clear; definite: *a decided difference.* **2** firm; determined: *very decided opinions.* **de·cid·ed·ness** *n.* **de·cid·ed·ly** *adv.* **de·ci·sion** *n.* decision–making *n, adj.* **de·ci·sive** [dɪ'saɪsɪv] *adj* **1** settling something beyond question. **2** critical: *a decisive moment in her life.* **de·ci·sive·ly** *adv.* **de·ci·sive·ness** *n.*

CONFUSABLES

There is a distinction between **decided**, meaning 'definite or unquestionable', and **decisive**, meaning 'having or giving a clear result': *His height gave him a decided advantage. In World War II the Battle of El Alamein was a decisive victory.*

---

de·cid·u·ous [dɪ'sɪdʒuəs] *adj* **1** falling off in a certain season or stage of growth: *deciduous leaves, deciduous horns.* **2** of trees, shrubs, etc., shedding leaves annually: *maples, oaks, and other deciduous trees.* **de·cid·u·ous·ly** *adv.* ⟨Latin *decidere; de-* + *cadere* fall⟩

dec·i·mal ['dɛsəməl] *adj* to do with or based on the number 10.
n **1** a numeral having a decimal point: *The numerals 23.6, 3.09, and 0.728 are decimals.* **2** DECIMAL POINT: *Put the decimal between the units and the tenths.* ⟨Latin *decimus* tenth⟩
decimal fraction 1 DECIMAL NUMBER. **2** a decimal number less than one. **dec·i·mal·ize** *v* change (a number, currency, etc.) to a decimal form or system. **dec·i·mal·i·za·tion** *n.* **dec·i·mal·ly** *adv* **1** according to a decimal system. **2** by tens. **decimal number** a number that includes a fraction whose denominator is 10, 100, 1000, etc., written with a decimal point. *Examples:* 0.2, 9.93, 4.1. **decimal point**

the period between the units and the tenths of a decimal fraction. **decimal system** a system of numeration based on units of ten. **dec·i·mate** *v* destroy much of: *Pollution had decimated the species.* **dec·i·ma·tion** *n.*

de·ci·pher [dɪ'saɪfər] *v* **1** make out; figure out: *to decipher poor handwriting, to decipher a mystery.* **2** change (something in code) to ordinary language. **de·ci·pher·a·ble** *adj.*

de·ci·sion, de·ci·sive See DECIDE.

deck [dɛk] *n* **1** a floor extending from side to side of a ship. **2** a wooden platform against an outside wall of a house, usually raised with steps to the ground. **3** a set of playing cards.
v **1** decorate: *The hall was decked with flags.* **2** *Slang* knock down: *He decked his opponent.* ⟨Middle Dutch *dek* roof⟩
below deck(s) downstairs on a ship. **clear the deck(s)** prepare for action by removing all unnecessary objects. **deck out** adorn; dress up: *She was decked out in lace.* **hit the deck** *Slang* **a** drop to the ground. **b** prepare for action. **c** get out of bed. **on deck a** out on a ship's main deck. **b** *Informal* ready for work, etc. **c** next in line, esp at bat in baseball. **stack the deck a** arrange a pack of cards dishonestly. **b** arrange things unfairly in advance.
deck chair a light folding chair for outdoor use. **deck hand** an ordinary sailor.

de·claim [dɪ'kleɪm] *v* speak or say loudly and with emotion; write in a corresponding manner. **dec·la·ma·tion** [,dɛklə'meɪʃən] *n.* **de·clam·a·to·ry** [dɪ'klæmə,tɔri] *adj.* ⟨Latin *de-* (intensive) + *clamare* cry⟩

de·clare [dɪ'klɛr] *v* **1** announce publicly and formally. **2** say firmly: *She declared she would solve the problem if it took her all night.* **3** acknowledge possession of (income, assets, goods, etc.) for income tax, customs charges, etc. **dec·la·ra·tion** [,dɛklə'reɪʃən] *n.* ⟨Latin *de-* (intensive) + *clarare* make clear; *clarus* clear⟩
declare oneself a make one's opinion known. **b** show one's true self.
de·clar·a·tive *adj* **1** expressing a statement as opposed to a command or question. **2** firm in tone. **de·clar·a·tive·ly** *adv.*

dé·clas·sé [,deiklæ'sei] *French* [dekla'se] *adj* reduced in rank or status. ⟨French⟩

de·cline [dɪ'klaɪn] *v* **1** refuse, esp politely: *She declined my offer of help.* **2** lose strength, status, value, etc.: *a declining empire, declining stocks.* **3** of the sun, go down. **4** slope downward. **5** *Grammar* in some languages, list the various forms of (a noun, pronoun, or adjective) reflecting case, gender, and number. **de·cline** *n.* ⟨Latin *de-* from + *clinare* bend⟩
declining years advanced age; old age.
de·clen·sion [dɪ'klɛnʃən] *n* **1** *Grammar* **a** in some languages, the set of different forms of a noun, pronoun, or adjective, reflecting case, gender, and number. **b** the act of listing these. **c** the class to which a noun, etc. belongs according to how it is declined. **2** an act or instance of declining. **dec·li·na·tion** [,dɛklə'neɪʃən] *n* **1** a downward slope. **2** a polite refusal. **3** the deviation of a compass

needle from true north or south. **4** *Astronomy* the angular distance of a star, planet, etc. from the celestial equator.

de·cliv·i·ty [dɪ'klɪvəti] *n* a downward slope. ⟨Latin *de*- down + *clivus* slope⟩
de·cliv·i·tous *adj* rather steep.

de·code [di'koud] *v* translate (coded text or speech) into ordinary language.
de·cod·er *n* **1** a machine that unscrambles television signals. **2** *Computers* a circuit that produces a single output from certain inputs.

dé·colle·té [ˌdeikɒlə'tei] *French* [dekɔl'te] *adj* of a dress, blouse, etc., having a revealingly low neckline. **dé·colle·tage** [-'tɑʒ] *n*. ⟨French, pp of *décolleter* bare the neck of; *col* neck⟩

de·col·or·ize [di'kʌlə,raɪz] *v* remove colour from, as by bleaching. **de·col·or·iz·a·tion** *n*.
de·col·or·ant [di'kʌlərənt] *n* a substance that decolorizes. *adj* able to decolorize.

de·com·pose [ˌdikəm'pouz] *v* **1** of organic things, break down into basic constituents by rotting; decay; disintegrate. **2** separate into parts: *A prism decomposes white light into colours.* **de·com·po·si·tion** *n*. **de·com·posed** *adj*.

de·com·press [ˌdikəm'prɛs] *v* **1** release from pressure. **2** gradually readjust (a diver, etc.) to normal air pressure in a DECOMPRESSION CHAMBER. **de·com·pres·sion** *n*.
decompression chamber in a submarine, etc., an airtight compartment used for the readjustment from abnormal to normal air pressure. **decompression sickness** pain and difficulty in breathing due to too rapid return to normal atmospheric pressure; the bends.

de·con·ges·tant [ˌdikən'dʒɛstənt] *n* a drug used to relieve congestion of the mucous membranes in the nose and sinuses.

de·con·struc·tion [ˌdikən'strʌkʃən] *n* a method of literary criticism based on the idea (**deconstructionism**) that textual meaning is never absolute, nor completely coherent, but is informed by and dependent on other texts and its own unstated, often conflicting, assumptions. **de·con·struc·tion·ist** *adj, n*.
de·con·struct *v* **1** analyze (a text) according to this method. **2** take apart.

de·con·tam·i·nate [ˌdikən'tæmə,neit] *v* rid of any sort of contamination such as toxins, radioactivity, etc. **de·con·tam·i·na·tion** *n*.

dec·o·rate ['dɛkə,reit] *v* **1** add things to in order to beautify or as part of a celebration: *to decorate a room with flowers.* **2** paint, paper, carpet, etc. (a room or rooms). **3** plan, often professionally, colour schemes and furnishing styles for (a building's interior). **4** award a medal, ribbon, etc., to (a person) for valour. **dec·o·ra·tion** *n*. ⟨Latin *decorare; decus, decoris* adornment⟩
dé·cor or **de·cor** [dei'kɔr] *n* colour scheme and style and arrangement of furnishings in a room. **dec·o·ra·tive** ['dɛkərətɪv] *adj* **1** having the purpose or effect of decorating: *decorative rugs.* **2** to do with decorating: *decorative skill.* **dec·o·ra·tive·ly** *adv*. **dec·o·ra·tive·ness** *n*. **dec·o·ra·tor** *n* one whose work is decorating

interiors of buildings. *adj* designed or preferred by decorators: *decorator colours.*

de·co·rum [dɪ'kɔrəm] *n* propreness, modesty, and orderliness of dress, speech, behaviour, etc. **dec·o·rous** ['dɛkərəs] *adj*. **dec·o·rous·ly** *adv*. ⟨Latin = seemly⟩

de·cou·page or **dé·cou·page** [ˌdeiku'pɑʒ] *n* the artistic technique of gluing down paper cutouts on a surface and then coating the surface with a finish such as varnish. ⟨French, from *découper* cut out⟩

de·coy ['dikɔi] *n* **1** an artificial bird or animal, or a live trained one, used to lure others of its kind into a trap. **2** any person or thing used to lead or tempt into danger or to distract.
v [dɪ'kɔi] *or* ['dikɔi] **1** lure wild birds, animals, etc. into a trap or within gunshot. **2** lead or tempt into danger. **3 ✹** DEKE. ⟨Middle Dutch *de kooi* the cage⟩

de·crease [dɪ'kris] *v* become or make less: *to decrease one's speed. The wind decreased as the day wore on.* **de·crease** ['dikris] *or* [dɪ'kris] *n*. **de·creas·ing·ly** *adv*. ⟨Old French *descreistre*, Latin *decrescere; de*- down + *crescere* grow⟩
on the decrease decreasing.

de·cree [dɪ'kri] *n* a decision or order made by a government, court, church, etc.
v order in this way: *The government decreed that the election would take place July 8.* ⟨Latin *decretum* pp of *decernere*. See DISCERN.⟩

de·crep·it [dɪ'krɛpɪt] *adj* of people or things, broken down or weakened by age. **de·crep·i·tude** [dɪ'krɛpə,tjud] *or* [-,tud] *n*. ⟨Latin *decrepitus; de*- + *crepare* creak⟩

de·cre·scen·do [ˌdikrə'ʃɛndou] *or* [ˌdei-] *n Music* a gradual decrease in force or loudness. **de·cre·scen·do** *adj, adv, v*. ⟨Italian⟩

de·crim·i·nal·ize [di'krɪmənə,laɪz] *v* remove (an act) from the category of criminal offence; legalize. **de·crim·i·nal·i·za·tion** *n*.

de·cry [dɪ'kraɪ] *v* condemn; speak out against: *He decried gambling in all its forms.* ⟨French *de*- away, apart + *crier* cry⟩

de·crypt [di'krɪpt] *v* convert (a coded message) into readable form. **de·cryp·tion** *n*.

ded·i·cate ['dɛdə,keit] *v* **1** set apart for a particular purpose, often a sacred or solemn one: *to dedicate a new altar.* **2** give wholly to some person or purpose: *to dedicate one's life to the service of humanity.* **3** address (an artistic work) to someone as a mark of respect, affection, etc. **4** open (a bridge, institution, etc.) with a special ceremony. ⟨Latin *de*- (intensive) + *dicare* proclaim⟩
ded·i·cat·ed *adj* **1** wholly committed. **2** for a specific purpose or performing one function only. **ded·i·ca·tion** *n* **1** the act of dedicating. **2** commitment (to a task, etc.).

de·duce [dɪ'djus] *or* [dɪ'dus] *v* conclude from a general principle, or by applying such principles to evidence: *By examining the body he deduced the cause of death.* **de·duc·i·ble** *adj*. ⟨Latin *de*- down + *ducere* lead⟩
de·duct *v* subtract. **de·duct·i·ble** *adj* that can be deducted: *deductible from your income.*

n an amount to be paid by the insured whenever a claim is made: *I had to pay the $500 deductible.* **de·duc·tion** *n* **1** the act of deducting or the amount deducted. **2** the process of deducing, or the conclusion reached in this way. Compare INDUCTION. **de·duc·tive** *adj* of or using deduction; reaching a conclusion by applying a general principle to a particular case. **de·duct·ive·ly** *adv.*

deed [did] *n* **1** an act; something done. **2** a brave, skilful, or unusual act. **3** a document showing ownership or containing a contract. *v* transfer by giving a deed. ⟨Old English *dæd*⟩

dee·jay ['di,dʒei] *n Informal* DISC JOCKEY. ⟨abbreviation of *d*isc *j*ockey⟩

deem [dim] *v* think of as; consider: *The lawyer deemed it unwise to take the case to court.* ⟨Old English *dēman; dōm* judgment⟩

de–em·pha·size [di 'ɛmfə,saɪz] *v* reduce emphasis on: *They agreed to de-emphasize the contentious points.*

deep [dip] *adj* **1** going far down or back: *a deep well, a deep recess.* **2** far on or in: *deep in the forest, deep in the night.* **3** measured from surface to bottom or from front to back: *a tank 2 m deep, a lot 40 m deep.* **4** low in pitch: *a deep voice.* **5** dark and strong: *deep red.* **6** intense: *deep sorrow.* **7** inner; interior: *deep feelings.* **8** showing or needing great thought, intellect, study, etc.: *This book is too deep for me.* **9** involved: *deep in thought.* **10** great: *deep trouble, a deep drink from the refreshing stream.* **11** closely kept: *a deep secret.*
n **1** a deep place. **2** the deepest part: *the deep of winter.* **3 the deep** the sea.
adv **1** far down, back, on, or in: *deep into the night.* **2** deeply: *Drink deep.* **deep·en** *v.* **deep·ly** *adv.* **deep·ness** *n.* **depth** [dɛpθ] *n.* ⟨Old English *dēop*⟩
deep down in one's inmost feelings. **go deep a** *Sports* go far into the outfield or into the opposing team's zone. **b** *Informal* venture far into a dangerous or difficult undertaking. **go off the deep end a** lose one's mind. **b** go beyond reasonable limits. **in deep water** in difficulty. **in (too) deep** involved in a dangerous situation.
deep–dish *adj* baked in a container with high sides; thick: *deep-dish pizza.* **deep–freeze** ['dip 'friz] *or* [-,friz] *v* **-froze, -fro·zen, -freez·ing 1** freeze (food) rapidly or keep frozen for the long term. **2** keep as if frozen: *to deep-freeze a plan. n* ['dip ,friz] **1** a freezer for long-term storage. **2** the state of being deep-frozen: *The government kept the report in deep-freeze.* **deep–freez·er** *n.* **deep–fry** *v* **-fried, -frying** fry in deep fat or oil. **deep–fry·er** *n.* **deep–laid** *adj* planned secretly and carefully. **deep–root·ed** *adj* firmly entrenched: *deep-rooted traditions.* **deep–sea** *adj* of or in the deep parts of the sea: *deep-sea diving.* **deep–seat·ed** *adj* **1** of which, or of the cause of which, one is barely conscious: *deep-seated anxiety.* **2** firmly fixed: *The disease was too deep-seated to be cured.* **deep–set** *adj* **1** set deeply. **2** firmly fixed. **deep–six** *or* **give something the deep six** *Slang v* reject

categorically or defeat decisively. **deep South** *or* **Deep South** in the US, the region including Georgia, Alabama, Mississippi, Louisiana, and part of South Carolina. **deep space** space beyond the earth's atmosphere; outer space. **depths** *pl* **a** most profound degree: *the depths of despair.* **b** low moral condition: *to sink to such depths.* **in depth** thoroughly; in detail: *to study a subject in depth.* **in–depth** *adj.* **out of one's depth a** in water so deep that one cannot touch bottom. **b** in a situation one cannot cope with. **depth charge** an explosive charge set to explode at a certain depth under water. **depth perception** the ability to judge how far away distant objects are from oneself and from one another.

deer [dir] *n, pl* **deer 1** a cud-chewing animal, generally wild, that has split hoofs. The males (and, in some species, females) have solid, bony, deciduous antlers. **2 ✹** *North* caribou. ⟨Old English *dēor* animal⟩
deer·fly *or* **deer fly** any of a genus of small horseflies. **deer mouse** any of several mice, brown with white underparts and feet. **deer·skin** *n* the hide of a deer. **deerskins** *pl* clothing made from this. **deer·stalk·er** ['dir,stɔkər] *n* a cap with earflaps, originally worn by hunters.

de·face [dɪ'feis] *v* spoil the appearance of; mar. **de·fac·er** *n.* **de·face·ment** *n.*

de fac·to [dɪ 'fæktou] *or* [dei 'fæktou] **1** in fact. **2** real, whether legal, official, etc. or not: *a de facto government.* ⟨Latin = from the fact⟩

de·fame [dɪ'feim] *v* attack the reputation of; slander; libel. **def·a·ma·tion** [,dɛfə'meiʃən] *n.* **de·fam·a·to·ry** [dɪ'fæmə,tɔri] *adj.* **de·fam·er** *n.* ⟨Latin *diffamare; de-* down, from (confused with *dis-*) + *fama* rumour⟩

de·fault [dɪ'fɔlt] *n* **1** a failure to decide or act. **2** failure to appear at a contest. **3** *Law* a failure to appear in court at the time set for a legal proceeding. **4** *esp Computers* an action, value, or status adopted automatically in the absence of explicit instructions.
v **1** fail to choose, act, appear, pay, etc. when due. **2** lose (a match, case, etc.) by such a failure. **3** go or revert (*to* a given condition or value) in the absence of explicit instructions. **de·fault** *adj.* ⟨Old French *defaute* from *defaillir; faillir* fail⟩
in default of in view of the absence of.

de·feat [dɪ'fit] *v* **1** win a victory over: *to defeat an opposing team.* **2** prevent the success of: *to defeat a bill in Parliament.* **3** *Law* annul. **de·feat** *n.* ⟨Old French *de(s)fait* pp of *desfaire,* Latin *diffacere; dis-* un- + *facere* do⟩
de·feat·ist *n* one who expects or readily accepts defeat. **de·feat·ist** *adj.* **de·feat·ism** *n.*

def·e·cate ['dɛfə,keit] *v* have a movement of the bowels. **def·e·ca·tion** *n.* ⟨Latin *de-* from + *faeces* dregs, solid excrement⟩

de·fect ['difɛkt] *or* [dɪ'fɛkt] *n* imperfection; fault; lack or incompleteness.
v [dɪ'fɛkt] forsake one's own country, group, etc. for another opposed to it in political or

social doctrine. **de·fect·or** *n.* ⟨L *defectus* want; *deficere* fail. See DEFICIENT.⟩

de·fec·tion *n* **1** the act of defecting. **2** failure.

de·fec·tive *adj* noticeably weak or faulty: *Her hearing is defective.*

de·fend [dɪ'fɛnd] *v* **1** guard from harm; fight for when attacked. **2** *Sports* try to keep an opponent from reaching or getting: *to defend a goal, to defend a title.* **3** justify against a challenge: *to defend one's behaviour.* **4** *Law* act as counsel for in a court of law: *A well-known lawyer is defending him.* **de·fen·da·ble** *adj.* **de·fend·er** *n.* ⟨Latin *defendere*⟩

de·fence or **defense** [dɪ'fɛns] *n* **1** the act of defending; often, specifically, of defending a nation against armed attack. **2** anything that defends: *a defence against cold weather.* **3** ['difɛns] *Sports* **a** the players defending a goal. **b** their play. **4** *Law* **a** the defendant and his or her counsel. **b** their case. **de·fence·less** or **defenseless** *adj.* **de·fence·man** or **defenseman** *n, pl* **-men** *Sports* a player who tries to keep opponents from approaching the goal. **defence mechanism 1** any self-protective reaction by an organism. **2** *Psychology* an unconscious adjustment of behaviour or attitude so as to shut out unpleasant feelings. **de·fend·ant** *n* a person against whom an action or criminal charge is brought in a court of law. **de·fen·si·ble** *adj* **1** justifiable. **2** easily defended from attack. **de·fen·sive** *adj* **1** of or for defence: *a defensive posture, defensive strategy.* **2** too ready to justify or explain; assuming that one is under attack: *a defensive attitude. n* **1** a position or attitude of defence. **2** anything that defends. **de·fen·sive·ly** *adv.* **de·fen·sive·ness** *n.* **on the defensive** with a defensive attitude or in a defensive position.

de·fer¹ [dɪ'fɜr] *v* **-ferred, -fer·ring** put off; postpone. **de·fer·ment** *n.* **de·fer·ra·ble** *adj.* **de·fer·ral** *n.* **de·fer·rer** *n.* ⟨Latin. See DIFFER.⟩

de·fer² [dɪ'fɜr] *v* **-ferred, -fer·ring** submit to another's judgment or wishes out of respect or courtesy: *He deferred to his sister's wishes.* ⟨Latin *de-* down + *ferre* carry⟩

def·er·ence ['dɛfərəns] *n* **1** the act of deferring to another. **2** respect. **def·er·en·tial** *adj.*

de·fi·ance See DEFY.

de·fib·ril·late [di'fɪbrə,leɪt] *v* stop FIBRILLATION of (the heart muscle) by applying electric shock. **de·fib·ril·la·tion** *n.* **de·fib·ril·la·tor** *n.*

de·fi·cient [dɪ'fɪʃənt] *adj* **1** incomplete or not good enough. **2** having too little of (with *in*): *Her diet is deficient in protein.* **de·fi·cien·cy** *n.* **de·fi·cient·ly** *adv.* ⟨Latin *deficere* fail; *de-* away + *facere* make, do⟩

def·i·cit ['dɛfəsɪt] *n* the amount by which a sum of money (or other resource) falls short, or by which liabilities exceed assets: *Since the club owed $150 and had only $100, there was a deficit of $50. adj Economics* conducted with borrowed funds: *deficit spending.*

de·file¹ [dɪ'faɪl] *v* **1** make disgusting or unclean in any way: *to defile one's reputation, a mind defiled by pornography.* **2** make ceremonially unacceptable: *To strict Brahmins,*

food is defiled if touched with the left hand. **de·file·ment** *n.* ⟨Middle English *defoul* infl. by obsolete *file,* Old English *fylan; fūl* foul⟩

de·file² [dɪ'faɪl] *or* ['difaɪl] *n* **1** a steep and narrow valley. **2** a march in a long line. ⟨French *défilé* pp of *défiler* march by files⟩

de·fine [dɪ'faɪn] *v* **1** give the meaning of; explain. **2** make clear or distinct: *Use black lines to better define the shape.* **3** fix; set the limits of. **4** be a distinguishing feature of: *success defined by perseverence.* **de·fin·a·ble** *adj.* ⟨Latin *definire* to limit; *finis* boundary⟩

def·i·nite ['dɛfənɪt] *adj* **1** clear and exact in meaning: *She wouldn't give a definite answer.* **2** with express limits; specific: *a definite sum.* **3** sure; certain: *Is her participation definite?* **def·i·nite·ly** *adv.* **def·i·nite·ness** *n.* **definite article** *Grammar* the word *the* in English; its counterpart in another language. **def·i·ni·tion** [,dɛfə'nɪʃən] *n* **1** the meaning of a term, or the act of explaining it. **2** clarity and distinctness, or ability to make clear and distinct: *an image or lens with high definition.* **de·fin·i·tive** [dɪ'fɪnətɪv] *adj* **1** conclusive; final. **2** authoritative: *the definitive work on marine biology.* **3** defining; distinguishing: *definitive features.* **de·fin·i·tive·ly** *adv.* **de·fin·i·tive·ness** *n.*

de·flate [dɪ'fleɪt] *v* **1** let air or gas out of (a balloon, tire, etc.). **2** reduce; reduce the value of: *to deflate prices or currency.* **3** destroy the pride or confidence of: *deflated by their scornful laughter.* **de·fla·tion** *n.* **de·flat·or** *n.* **de·fla·tion·ar·y** *adj.* ⟨Latin *deflatus* pp of *deflare; de-* off + *flare* blow⟩

de·flect [dɪ'flɛkt] *v* **1** bend or turn aside from a course. **2** move from a neutral or normal position. **de·flec·tion** *n.* **de·flec·tive** *adj.* **de·flec·tor** *n.* ⟨Latin *de-* away + *flectere* bend⟩

de·flow·er [di'flaʊər] *v* spoil the innocence or beauty of. **de·flow·er·er** *n.* **de·flow·er·ing** *n.*

de·fog [di'fɒg] *v* **-fogged, -fog·ging** remove condensation from (a car window, etc.). **de·fog·ger** *n.*

de·fo·li·ate [di'foʊli,eɪt] *v* remove the leaves from (a plant), esp by chemical means. **de·fo·li·ant** *n.* **de·fo·li·a·tion** *n.* **de·fo·li·a·tor** *n.*

de·for·est [di'fɔrɪst] *v* clear (land) of trees. **de·for·est·a·tion** *n.*

de·form [dɪ'fɔrm] *v* **1** spoil the form or shape of; cause to develop the wrong way: *Shoes that are tight deform the feet.* **2** make ugly; distort or disfigure: *a face deformed by rage.* **3** become altered in form or shape. **4** *Physics* change the shape of by stress. **de·for·ma·tion** [,difɔr'meɪʃən] *or* [,dɛfər'meɪʃən] *n.* **de·formed** *adj.* **de·form·i·ty** *n.*

de·fraud [dɪ'frɒd] *v* take money, rights, etc., away from by fraud; cheat. **de·fraud·er** *n*.

de·fray [dɪ'freɪ] *v* pay (costs or expenses): *Park expenses are defrayed by the taxpayers.* **de·fray·al** *n*. ⟨French *défrayer*; *de-* + *frai* cost⟩

de·frock [di'frɒk] *v* unfrock.

de·frost [di'frɒst] *v* **1** remove frost or ice from. **2** thaw out (frozen food).
n a defroster in a car, or its action.
de·frost·er *n* a device that melts frost and ice on car windshields.

deft [dɛft] *adj* nimble, skilful, and efficient: *deft fingers.* **deft·ly** *adv.* **deft·ness** *n*. ⟨*daft*⟩

de·funct [dɪ'fʌŋkt] *adj* dead; extinct. ⟨Latin *defunctus* pp of *defungi* finish; *de-* (intensive) + *fungi* perform⟩

de·fuse [dɪ'fjuz] *v* **1** remove or neutralize a potential source of trouble: *to defuse a tense situation.* **2** [di'fjuz] remove the fuse from (a bomb, etc.).

de·fy [dɪ'faɪ] *v* **1** resist or disobey boldly. **2** challenge (*to* do something). **de·fi·ance** *n*. **de·fi·ant** *adj.* **de·fi·ant·ly** *adv.* ⟨Old French *de(s)fier*; Latin *dis-* away + *fidus* faithful⟩
in defiance of in open opposition to: *She took the car in defiance of her father's wishes.*

de·gen·er·ate [dɪ'dʒɛnə,reɪt] *v* **1** decline in physical, mental, or moral qualities; become gradually worse or weaker. **2** *Biology* **a** of an organism, revert to simpler structure. **b** of a part in an organism, become nonfunctional. *adj* [dɪ'dʒɛnərɪt] that has degenerated, esp morally. **de·gen·er·a·cy** *n*. **de·gen·er·ate** *n*. **de·gen·er·a·tion** *n*. ⟨Latin *degenerare*; *de-* down + *genus* race, kind⟩
de·gen·er·a·tive [dɪ'dʒɛnərətɪv] *adj* causing or characterized by degeneration; specifically, of diseases, characterized by the degeneration of tissues or organs. **de·gen·er·a·tive·ly** *adv.*

de·grade [dɪ'greɪd] *v* **1** lower the dignity or value of; dishonour: *Don't degrade yourself by stealing.* **2** *Geology* erode. **3** *Chemistry* reduce the molecule of (a compound) into others having simpler structure. **de·grad·a·ble** *adj.* **deg·ra·da·tion** [,dɛgrə-] *n*. **de·grad·ing** *adj.* ⟨Latin *de-* down + *gradus* step, grade⟩

de·gree [dɪ'gri] *n* **1** the amount, intensity, or extent of an action or condition: *To what degree is she interested?* **2** a step on a scale or stage in a gradual process: *a first-degree burn, second-degree murder,* the superlative degree of an adjective. *Her skill improved by slow degrees.* **3** a unit of temperature. *Symbol* ° **4** a unit for measuring angles. *Symbol* ° **5** a position on the earth's surface as measured by lines of latitude or longitude. **6** rank: *a lady of high degree.* **7** a title awarded by a university or college to a student whose work fulfils certain requirements: *an M.A. degree.* ⟨Old French *degre*; Latin *degradus*. See DEGRADE.⟩
by degrees gradually. **to a degree** somewhat; rather.
degree Celsius a unit of temperature used with the SI. *Symbol* °C **degree–day** *n* a unit representing one degree of deviation in the

mean outdoor temperature for one day. It is used to determine fuel requirements.

USAGE
Academic degrees are separated from a name by a comma: *Helen Kossos, M.A.; Chris Lee, B.Sc.* When the granting institution or year is mentioned, the form is as follows:
Georgia Smith, B.A. (Prince Edward Island), M.A. (McGill), Ph.D. (Manitoba); Parmeshwar Jha, B.A. '01, M.A. '04.

de·hisce [di'hɪs] *v* of a mature fruit, burst open along a definite line, discharging seeds or pollen. **de·his·cent** *adj.* ⟨Latin *dehiscere*; *de-* down + *hiare* gape⟩

de·hu·man·ize [di'hjumə,naɪz] *v* deprive of human qualities, interest, sympathy, etc. **de·hu·man·i·za·tion** *n*.

de·hu·mid·i·fy [,dihju'mɪdə,faɪ] *v* remove moisture from (the air). **de·hu·mid·i·fi·ca·tion** *n*. **de·hu·mid·i·fi·er** *n*.

de·hy·drate [di'haɪdreɪt] *v* remove or lose water or moisture. **de·hy·dra·tion** *n*.

de–ice [di'aɪs] *v* remove ice from (an aircraft, etc.). **de–ic·er** *n*.

de·i·fy ['diə,faɪ] *v* regard or treat as a god. **de·i·fi·ca·tion** *n*. ⟨Old French *deifier*, Latin *deificare*; *deus* god + *facere* make⟩

deign [deɪn] *v* condescend: *So conceited a man would never deign to notice us.* ⟨Old French *deignier*, Latin *dignari*; *dignus* worthy⟩

de·i·on·ize [di'aɪə,naɪz] *v* purify (water) by removing salt ions. **de·i·on·i·za·tion** *n*.

de·i·ty ['diɪti] *n* **1** a god or goddess. **2** the fact or state of being a god. **3 the Deity** God. ⟨Latin *deitas*; *deus* god⟩
de·ism ['diɪzəm] *n* **1** a belief in a god that does not influence human lives or events in the universe. **2** a belief in a god apart from any particular religion. **de·ist** *n*. **de·ist·ic** *adj.*

dé·jà vu [,deiʒa 'vu] *French* [deʒa'vy] **1** the feeling that one has already experienced what is in fact a new situation. **2** a condition of being rather tiresomely reminded (by current events, etc.) of something in the past. ⟨French = already seen⟩

de·ject [dɪ'dʒɛkt] *v* lower the spirits of; discourage. **de·ject·ed** *adj.* **de·jec·tion** *n*. ⟨Latin *de-* down + *jacere* throw⟩

deke [dik] *v Hockey* ✱ *Slang n* a move, such as a fake shot, intended to draw a defending player out of position. **deke** *v.* ⟨*decoy*⟩

de·lay [dɪ'leɪ] *v* **1** make late or hinder the progress of: *to delay completion of a project. An accident delayed the train for two hours.* **2** go slowly or hesitate: *Don't delay; they're waiting.* **3** put off till a later time; postpone.
n **1** the act of delaying. **2** the time occupied in delay: *a delay of three hours.* ⟨Old French *delaier* postpone; *de-* away + *laier* leave, let⟩

de·lec·ta·ble [dɪ'lɛktəbəl] *adj* very enjoyable, esp to taste. **de·lec·ta·bly** *adv.* ⟨Latin *delectabilis*; *delectare*. See DELIGHT.⟩
de·lec·ta·bles *n pl* delicious things to eat. **de·lec·ta·tion** [,dilɛk'teiʃən] *n* enjoyment.

del·e·gate ['dɛlə,geit] *v* **1** appoint (a person) as a representative or deputy. **2** give (one's authority, a task) to another as deputy.
n ['dɛləgɪt] a person appointed to represent or act on behalf of others, often specifically in an assembly or at a conference. ⟨Latin *de-* (intensive) + *legare* to commission⟩
del·e·ga·tion *n* **1** the act of delegating: *the delegation of authority.* **2** a group of delegates from one place, body, etc.

de·lete [dɪ'lit] *v* strike out or take out; wipe out (text, images, memory, etc.). **de·le·tion** *n.* ⟨Latin *deletus* pp of *delere* destroy⟩

del·e·te·ri·ous [,dɛlə'tiriəs] *adj* harmful. ⟨Greek *dēlētērios; dēleesthai* to hurt⟩

delft [dɛlft] *n* earthenware with an opaque white glaze and decorated in blue. Also, **delft·ware.** ⟨*Delft*, city in SW Netherlands⟩

del·i ['dɛli] *n* DELICATESSEN (def. 1).
adj of the kind sold in a deli: *deli meats.*

de·lib·er·ate [dɪ'lɪbərɪt] *adj* **1** made or done on purpose: *Her excuse was a deliberate lie.* **2** slow and careful: *She's very deliberate and takes a long time to make up her mind.* **3** slow, but firm and purposeful: *deliberate steps.*
v [dɪ'lɪbə,reit] think over or discuss with a view to decision-making. **de·lib·er·ate·ly** *adv.* **de·lib·er·ate·ness** *n.* **de·lib·er·a·tion** *n.* **de·lib·er·a·tive** *adj.* ⟨Latin *de-* (intensive) + *librare* weigh⟩

del·i·cate ['dɛləkɪt] *adj* **1** fine in structure: *delicate features.* **2** easily crushed, broken, hurt, or made ill: *a delicate flower, a delicate child, delicate feelings.* **3** requiring skill and careful handling: *a delicate situation.* **4** tactful; refined in speech or manner: *a delicate way of putting it.* **5** of a colour, pale: *a delicate shade of green.* **6** very sensitive: *delicate instruments.* **7** light and pleasant to taste or smell: *delicate foods.* **del·i·ca·cy** ['dɛləkəsi] *n.* **del·i·cate·ly** *adv.* **del·i·cate·ness** *n.* ⟨Latin *delicatus* pampered⟩

del·i·ca·tes·sen [,dɛlıkə'tɛsən] *n* **1** a store that sells fine prepared foods. **2** the foods sold at such a store. ⟨German *Delikatessen* pl of *Delikatesse* delicacy; French *délicatesse*⟩

de·li·cious [dɪ'lɪʃəs] *adj* **1** very pleasing, esp to taste or smell. **2 Delicious** a sweet variety of apple. **de·li·cious·ly** *adv.* **de·li·cious·ness** *n.* ⟨Latin *deliciosus; delicae* delight. See DELIGHT.⟩

de·light [dɪ'lait] *n* **1** great enjoyment or pleasure. **2** a source of this.
v **1** please greatly. **2** find great pleasure (*in*): *Kids delight in surprises.* **de·light·ed** *adj.* ⟨Old French *delitier*, Latin *delectare*, from *delicere; de-* (intensive) + *lacere* entice⟩
de·light·ful *adj* very pleasing; giving delight. **de·light·ful·ly** *adv.* **de·light·ful·ness** *n.*

de·lim·it [dɪ'lɪmɪt] *v* fix or constitute the limits of. **de·lim·i·ta·tion** *n.* **de·lim·i·ta·tive** *adj.* **de·lim·it·er** *n* Computers a boundary marker that sets off commands, etc.

de·lin·e·ate [dɪ'lɪni,eit] *v* **1** trace or bring out the outline of. **2** draw; sketch. **3** describe carefully in words. **de·lin·e·a·tion** *n.* ⟨Latin *de-* (intensive) + *linea* line⟩

de·lin·quent [dɪ'lɪŋkwənt] *adj* **1** failing to do what is required by law or duty. **2** due and unpaid: *delinquent taxes.*
n a delinquent person: *a juvenile delinquent.* **de·lin·quen·cy** *n.* **de·lin·quent·ly** *adv.* ⟨Latin *delinquere* fail; *de-* down + *linquere* leave⟩

de·lir·i·um [dɪ'liriəm] *n, pl* -**lir·i·ums,** -**lir·i·a** [-'liriə]. **1** a temporary disorder of the mind characterized by excitement, irrational talk, and hallucinations. **2** any wild, irrational excitement. **de·lir·i·ous** *adj.* **de·lir·i·ous·ly** *adv.* **de·lir·i·ous·ness** *n.* ⟨Latin, from *delirare* rave, be crazy; *de lira (ire)* (go) out of the furrow⟩
delirium tre·mens ['trɛmənz] delirium characterized by violent trembling, usually caused by prolonged excessive consumption of alcohol. Shortened informally to **d.t.'s.**

de·liv·er [dɪ'lɪvər] *v* **1** bring to the proper destination(s) or recipient(s): *to deliver mail.* **2** give (a speech, judgment, etc.). **3** strike; throw: *to deliver a blow.* **4** rescue; save from evil or trouble: *Deliver us from evil.* **5** give birth or help give birth (to). **6** give up; hand over. **7** *Informal* do or give what is expected or promised. **de·liv·er·er** *n.* **de·liv·er·y** *n.* ⟨Old French *delivrer*, Latin *deliberare; de-* (intensive) + *liber* free⟩
be delivered of *Poetic, archaic* give birth to. **deliver oneself of** *Formal* **a** utter; give: *He delivered himself of a long moan.* **b** unburden (feelings, etc.).
de·liv·er·a·ble *adj* **1** promised under contract. **2** that can or is to be delivered. *n* **1** a piece of work promised under contract. **2** an item to be delivered. **de·liv·er·ance** *n* a rescue.

dell [dɛl] *n* a small, sheltered glen or valley, usually with trees in it. ⟨Old English⟩

Delphic ['dɛlfɪk] *adj* obscure or ambiguous, like the answers of Apollo's oracle at Delphi.

del·phin·i·um [dɛl'fɪniəm] *n* any of a genus of herbs of the buttercup family, cultivated for their tall spikes of flowers. ⟨Greek *delphin* dolphin; from the shape of its nectar gland⟩

del·ta ['dɛltə] *n* **1** a deposit of earth and sand, usually three-sided, that collects at the mouths of some rivers. **2** the fourth letter of the Greek alphabet (δ,Δ). **3** any triangular area or figure. **del·ta·ic** [dɛl'teiɪk] *adj.* ⟨Greek⟩
delta wave or **rhythm** a type of brain wave associated with a state of deep sleep or brain disease. **del·ta·wing** *adj* of an aircraft, having triangular wings.

de·lude [dɪ'lud] *v* grossly mislead or deceive (esp oneself): *He deluded himself into thinking he could pass his exams without studying.* **de·lud·ed** *adj.* ⟨Latin *de-* (to the detriment of) + *ludere* play⟩
de·lu·sion *n* **1** the act of deluding or state of being deluded. **2** a false belief. **3** *Psychiatry* a false and totally irrational fixed belief due to mental illness: *She suffers from the delusion that her food is being poisoned.* **de·lu·sion·al** *adj.*

del·uge ['dɛljudʒ] *n* **1** a great flood or heavy fall of rain. **2** an overwhelming amount: *a deluge of work.* **3 the Deluge** in the Bible, the great flood in the days of Noah.

v 1 flood. 2 overwhelm as if by a flood: *The movie star was deluged with interview requests.* ⟨Old French; Latin *diluvium* from *diluere; dis-* away + *luere* wash⟩

de·luxe [dəˈlʌks] *French* [dəˈlyks] *adj* of the finest or most luxurious quality. Also, after the noun, **de luxe**. ⟨French⟩

delve [dɛlv] *v* 1 search thoroughly: *delving for information.* 2 *Archaic, poetic, or dialect* dig. **delv·er** *n.* ⟨Old English *delfan*⟩

dem·a·gogue [ˈdɛmə.gɒg] *n* a popular leader who stirs up the people by appealing to their emotions or prejudices. **dem·a·gog·ic** [-ˈgɒdʒɪk] *or* [-ˈgɒgɪk] *adj.* **dem·a·gogu·er·y** [ˌdɛməˈgɒgəri] *or* [ˈdɛmə.gɒgəri] *n.* ⟨Greek *dēmos* people + *agōgos* leader; *agein* lead⟩

de·mand [dɪˈmænd] *v* 1 ask with authority, insistence, or urgency: *to demand a trial. "Where is it?" she demanded.* 2 need; take; call for: *Training a dog demands patience. n* 1 an insistent request. 2 a claim; call: *With two jobs to look after, he has many demands on his time.* 3 a desire or need: *The supply of oil was greater than the demand.* **de·mand·er** *n.* ⟨Latin *de-* from + *mandare* to order⟩
in demand wanted by many. **on demand** as and when asked: *a loan payable on demand.*
de·mand·ing *adj* making many demands or taking much time, effort, concentration, etc.: *a demanding job, a demanding child.* **demand–pull inflation** inflation in which prices rise due to an excess demand for goods.

de·mar·ca·tion [ˌdimɑrˈkeɪʃən] *n* 1 the act of setting limits. 2 a distinction. 3 a boundary. **de·mar·cate** [ˈdimɑr.keit] *or* [dɪˈmɑrkeit] *v.* **de·mar·ca·tor** *n.* ⟨Spanish *demarcación; de-* off + *marcar* mark⟩

de·mean [dɪˈmin] *v* lower in dignity or status; humiliate: *I felt demeaned by their remarks.* **de·mean·ing** *adj.* ⟨*de-* down + *mean²*; formed after *debase*⟩

de·mean·our *or* **de·mean·or** [dɪˈminər] *n* the way a person looks and acts: *a man of serious demeanour.* ⟨Middle English *demenen* behave; Old French *demener*⟩

de·ment·ed [dɪˈmɛntɪd] *adj* insane; crazy. **de·ment·ed·ly** *adv.* ⟨Latin *de-* out of + *mentis* mind⟩
de·men·tia [dɪˈmɛnʃə] *n* partial or complete deterioration of rational powers.

de·mer·it [dɪˈmɛrɪt] *n* 1 a mark against a person's record. 2 a fault or unfavourable feature: *Your plan has a single demerit: cost.*

dem·i·god [ˈdɛmi.gɒd] *n* 1 *Myth* a the offspring of a god or goddess and a human being: *Hercules was a demigod.* b a minor or lesser god. 2 a person so outstanding in some way as to seem godlike: *The famous hockey player was a demigod to his young fans.* **dem·i·god·dess** *n.* ⟨French *demi,* Latin *dimidius* half; *dis-* apart + *medius* middle⟩

de·mil·i·tar·ize [diˈmɪlətə.raɪz] *v* 1 free (an area) from military control by removing forces. 2 take away the military power of. **de·mil·i·ta·ri·za·tion** *n.*

dem·i·monde [ˈdɛmi.mɒnd] *n* a social group seen as not quite respectable, such as street people, prostitutes, etc. ⟨French = half-world⟩

de·mise [dɪˈmaɪz] *n* 1 death. 2 *Law* the transfer of an estate by a will or lease. **de·mise** *v.* ⟨AngloFrench pp of *desmettre* put away; *des-* away + *mettre* put, Latin *mittere*⟩

dem·i·tasse [ˈdɛmi.tæs] *n* 1 a small cup for serving strong, black coffee. 2 a serving of such coffee in it. ⟨French = half-cup⟩

dem·o [ˈdɛmou] *n Informal* 1 a demonstration showing how to use a product. 2 in full, **demonstrator,** a product used for demonstrations or for trial by customers, and therefore not for sale or sold more cheaply.

de·mo·bi·lize [diˈmoubə.laɪz] *v* disband (an armed force). **de·mo·bi·li·za·tion** *n.*

de·moc·ra·cy [dɪˈmɒkrəsi] *n* 1 a government where the people rule either by direct vote or through freely-elected representatives. 2 any administration, as in business, etc., stressing participation and consensus in decision-making. 3 treatment of others as one's equals. ⟨Greek *dēmos* people + *kratos* rule⟩
dem·o·crat [ˈdɛmə.kræt] *n* 1 a person who believes in democracy. 2 **Democrat** *US* a member of the Democratic Party. 3 *Politics* typically, a person with more liberal political views. **dem·o·crat·ic** *adj.* **dem·o·crat·i·cal·ly** *adv.* **de·moc·ra·tize** *v.* **de·moc·ra·ti·za·tion** *n.*

de·mod·u·la·tion [di.mɒdʒəˈleɪʃən] *n Electronics* the process of separating the output signal from a modulated carrier wave.

de·mog·ra·phy [dɪˈmɒgrəfi] *n* 1 the science dealing with statistics intended to give a profile of a given population, such as the age, socioeconomic status, ethnicity, etc. of its members. 2 such statistics or such a profile for a given population; demographics. **de·mog·ra·pher** *n.* ⟨Greek *demos* people + *-graphy*⟩
de·mo·graph·ic *adj* to do with demography. *n* a demographic feature, or set of features, shared by a population. **de·mo·graph·ics** *n* the statistical data profiling a population as to age, socioeconomic status, ethnicity, etc.

de·mol·ish [dɪˈmɒlɪʃ] *v* pull or tear down; completely destroy. ⟨French *démolir,* Latin *demoliri; de-* down + *moles* mass⟩
dem·o·li·tion [ˌdɛməˈlɪʃən] *or* [ˌdi-] *n* 1 the act of demolishing, esp by explosives. 2 **demolitions** *pl* explosives for this purpose. **demolition derby** a contest in which old cars are smashed up with another old car.

de·mon [ˈdimən] *n* 1 an evil spirit; devil. 2 a very wicked or cruel person. 3 an evil influence: *the demon alcohol.* 4 a person with great energy, skill, or enthusiasm: *a demon for work, a speed demon.* 5 Usually, **dae·mon** an attendant or guardian spirit. ⟨Greek *daimōn* divinity, spirit⟩
de·mo·ni·ac [dɪˈmouni.æk] *or* [dɪˈmɒni.æk] *adj* 1 possessed by an evil spirit. 2 Usually, **de·mo·ni·a·cal** [ˌdiməˈnaɪəkəl] as if possessed by an evil spirit; frenzied or wild; fiendish. **de·mo·ni·a·cal·ly** *adv.* **de·mon·ic** [dɪˈmɒnɪk] *adj*

of or caused by evil spirits. **de·mon·ic·al·ly** *adv.*
de·mon·ism *n* the worship of demons.
de·mon·ize *v* **1** subject to demonic activity or influence. **2** regard or characterize as evil.
de·mon·i·za·tion *n.* **de·mon·ol·o·gy** *n* the study of demons; doctrine about demons.

de·mon·e·tize [di'mɒnə,taɪz] *or* [-'mʌnə,taɪz] *v* **1** deprive of its standard value as money. **2** withdraw from circulation as money. **de·mon·e·ti·za·tion** *n.*

dem·on·strate ['dɛmən,streit] *v* **1** show how to do or use (something). **2** show clearly and openly: *She demonstrates her love with a lot of kisses and hugs.* **3** establish the truth of; prove. **4** publicly show feeling about an issue by marching, carrying signs, etc.: *An angry crowd demonstrated in front of the town hall.* **dem·on·stra·tion** *n.* ⟨Latin *de-* (intensive) + *monstrare* show⟩
de·mon·stra·ble [dɪ'mɒnstrəbəl] *or* ['dɛmən-] *adj* that can be proved. **de·mon·stra·bly** *adv* obviously; openly; in a way that can be seen or proved. **de·mon·stra·tive** [dɪ'mɒnstrətɪv] *adj* **1** expressing one's affections openly: *The girl's demonstrative greeting embarrassed her shy brother.* **2** showing or proving (with *of*). **3** of or being any of the adjectives or pronouns *this, that, these,* and *those.* *n* a demonstrative adjective or pronoun. **de·mon·stra·tive·ly** *adv.* **dem·on·stra·tor** *n* **1** one who demonstrates a product or process for an audience. **2** one who takes part in a public demonstration. **3** DEMO (def. 2).

de·mor·al·ize [dɪ'mɔrə,laɪz] *v* weaken the morale, spirit, courage, hope, etc., of: *Lack of food demoralized the crew.* **de·mor·al·i·za·tion** *n.* **de·mor·a·liz·ing** *adj.*

de·mote [dɪ'mout] *v* put back to a lower rank. **de·mo·tion** *n.* ⟨*de-* + (pro)*mote*⟩

de·mur [dɪ'mɜr] *v* **-murred, -mur·ring** object; protest: *She demurred at working overtime.*
de·mur *n.* **de·mur·ral** *n.* ⟨Old French *demurer*, Latin *demorari; de-* (intensive) + *morari* delay⟩
de·mur·rer *n* **1** a person who objects. **2** *Law* an objection by one party that it does not have to respond to a suit.

de·mure [dɪ'mjur] *adj* **1** quiet and modest: *a demure young lady.* **2** artificially proper; coy: *the demure smile of a flirt.* **de·mure·ly** *adv.* **de·mure·ness** *n.* ⟨obsolete *mure*; Old French *meür* mature, Latin *maturus*⟩

de·mys·ti·fy [di'mɪstə,faɪ] *v* take away the mysterious quality of. **de·mys·ti·fi·ca·tion** *n.*

de·my·thol·o·gize [,dimɪ'θɒlə,dʒaɪz] *v* **1** take away allegedly mythological elements of (the Bible, etc.) to arrive at a more rationalistic interpretation. **2** take away the mythical or mystical quality of: *demythologizing Hollywood.*

den [dɛn] *n* **1** the cavelike home of a wild animal: *a bear's den.* **2** a small room in a home where one can read, etc., in privacy. **3** the headquarters, hideout, etc. of an underground operation. ⟨Old English *denn*⟩

de·na·tion·al·ize [di'næʃənə,laɪz] *v* return (an industry) from government to private ownership or control. **de·na·tion·al·i·za·tion** *n.*

de·na·ture [di'neitʃər] *v* **1** change the basic nature of. **2** make (alcohol, food, etc.) unfit for consumption without destroying its usefulness for other purposes. **3** change the properties and structure of (a protein). **4** add an isotope to (fissionable material) to stop it from being used to make nuclear weapons. **de·na·tur·ant** *n.* **de·na·tur·a·tion** *n.*

den·drite ['dɛndraɪt] *n* **1** *Geology* a stone or mineral with branching, treelike markings. **2** such a marking. **3** *Anatomy* the branching part at the receiving end of a nerve cell. **den·drit·ic** [-'drɪtɪk] *adj.* ⟨Greek *dendron* tree⟩

De·ne ['dɛnei] *or* ['dɛni] *n* the Athapascan First Nations of the Northwest Territories. **De·ne** *adj.* ⟨Athapascan = people⟩
Dene Nation ✲ the organization officially representing the Dene. **De·nen·deh** ['dɛnɛn'dɛ] *n* a name given by the Dene for the part of the former Northwest Territories remaining after the creation of Nunavut. **De·ne-Thah** ['dɛnei'ta] *n* **1** a member of a First Nations people living between the Rockies and the Great Slave Lake. **2** their Athapaskan language. **Dene-Thah** *adj.* Also called **Slavey, Slave.**

den·gue ['dɛŋgei] *or* ['dɛŋgi] *n* an infectious tropical fever with severe pain in the joints and muscles. ⟨Spanish; Swahili *kidinga*⟩

de·ni·al See DENY.

den·ier ['dɛnjər] *or* [də'nir] *n* a unit of mass for measuring the fineness of silk, rayon, or nylon yarn. ⟨French from Latin. See DENARIUS.⟩

den·i·grate ['dɛnə,greit] *v* put down; speak ill of; defame. **den·i·gra·tion** *n.* **den·i·grat·or** *n.* **den·i·gra·to·ry** *adj.* ⟨Latin *de-* (intensive) + *nigrare* blacken; *niger* black⟩

den·im ['dɛnəm] *n* **1** a heavy, usually indigo cotton cloth with a diagonal weave, used for jeans and other casual or work clothes. **2 denims** *pl* pants made of denim. ⟨short for French *serge de Nîmes* serge of Nîmes⟩

den·i·zen ['dɛnəzən] *n* **1** one who lives in or frequents a place: *Fish are denizens of the sea.* **2** a foreign word, species, etc. that has been naturalized: *The common English sparrow is a denizen of North America, brought from Europe about 1850.* ⟨AngloFrench *denzein; denz* in⟩

de·nom·i·nate [dɪ'nɒmə,neit] *v* to name. *adj* [dɪ'nɒmənɪt] *or* [-,neit] representing a quantity in terms of a unit of measurement. The *7* in *7 m* is a denominate number. ⟨Latin *de-* (intensive) + *nomen* name⟩
de·nom·i·na·tion [dɪ,nɒmə'neiʃən] *n* **1** name. **2** a division of a religious community usually made up of a number of local congregations who share similar beliefs, rites, and systems of government: *the Presbyterian denomination.* **3** number of units represented by a coin, stamp, voucher, etc.: *The lowest denomination of Canadian coin is the penny; the highest is the toonie.* **de·nom·i·na·tion·al** *adj.* to do with a denomination (def. 2). **de·nom·i·na·tion·al·ism** *n* preference for a particular denomination. **de·nom·i·na·tor** *n* *Mathematics* the number below the line in a fraction.

de·note [dɪ'nout] v 1 of a word, mean, esp apart from its acquired emotional nuances or its associations. Compare CONNOTE. 2 be a sign or symbol of: *The sign × denotes multiplication. A fever usually denotes sickness.* **de·no·ta·tion** n. **de·no·ta·tive** [dɪ'noutətɪv] *or* ['dinou,teitɪv] *adj.* ⟨Latin *de-* down + *nota* mark⟩

de·noue·ment *or* **dé·noue·ment** [,deinu'mɑ̃] n the resolution of the plot at the end of a story. ⟨French, from *dénouer* untie; Latin *de* down from + *nodare* tie⟩

de·nounce [dɪ'naʊns] v 1 express strong disapproval of; condemn publicly. 2 inform against; accuse: *He denounced his own sister to the secret police.* **de·nounc·er** n. **de·nun·ci·a·tion** [dɪ,nʌnsi'eiʃən] n. ⟨Latin *de-* (intensive) + *nuntius* messenger⟩

dense [dɛns] *adj* 1 closely packed together; thick: *a dense forest, dense fog.* 2 profound; intense: *dense ignorance.* 3 dull; slow-witted. **dense·ly** *adv.* **dense·ness** n. ⟨Latin *densus*⟩ **den·si·ty** ['dɛnsəti] n 1 the fact or condition of being dense. 2 the quantity of anything per unit of area: *population density.* 3 *Physics* the quantity of matter per unit of volume. 4 *Electricity* the quantity of electricity per unit of area on a charged surface. 5 *Computers* the quantity of data that may be stored per unit of space on auxiliary storage (disk, tape, etc.).

dent [dɛnt] n 1 a hollow made by a blow or pressure: *Bullets had made dents in the soldier's steel helmet.* 2 *Informal* a noticeable effect, esp one that lessens or weakens: *The new TV set sure put a dent in our bank account.* **dent** v. ⟨Middle English *dente*, variant of *dint*⟩

den·tal ['dɛntəl] *adj* to do with the teeth. **dent·al·ly** *adv.* ⟨Latin *dens, dentis* tooth⟩ **dental floss** a special thread used to remove plaque and food particles from between the teeth. **dental hygienist** a licensed technician who helps a dentist by checking and cleaning clients' teeth, taking X-rays, etc. **den·tate** *adj* having teeth or regular toothlike projections. **den·tine** ['dɛntɪn], ['dɛntin], *or* [dɛn'tin] n the hard, bony material beneath the enamel, forming the main part of a tooth. **den·tist** n a person qualified to practise the prevention and treatment of diseases of the teeth and gums. **den·tist·ry** n the profession of a dentist. **den·ti·tion** n 1 the growth of teeth. 2 the kind, number, and arrangement of teeth: *Dogs and wolves have similar dentition.* **den·ture** n Usually, **dentures** pl false teeth set in a plate to fit over the gum. **den·tur·ist** n a person trained to make and fit dentures.

de·nu·cle·ar·ize [di'njuklia,raɪz] *or* [di'nu-] v make (a place) free of nuclear weapons. **de·nu·cle·ar·i·za·tion** n.

de·nude [dɪ'njud] *or* [dɪ'nud] v 1 make bare: *trees denuded of leaves.* 2 *Geology* expose (rock) by removing what lies above, esp by erosion. **de·nu·da·tion** n. ⟨Latin *de-* (intensive) + *nudus* bare⟩

de·nun·ci·a·tion See DENOUNCE.

de·ny [dɪ'naɪ] v 1 declare (something) is not true. 2 refuse (someone something): *to deny a favour.* 3 refuse to acknowledge; repudiate or reject. **de·ni·al** [dɪ'naɪəl] n. ⟨French *dénier*, Latin *denegare; de-* intensive + *negare* say no⟩ **deny oneself** do without what one wants for the sake of others or of some cause.

de·o·dor·ant [di'oudərənt] n a preparation applied to the body to destroy or mask odour. **de·o·dor·ant** *adj.* **de·o·dor·ize** v. **de·o·dor·iz·er** n a substance or device used to destroy or mask odours indoors.

de·on·tol·o·gy [,diɒn'tɒlədʒi] n the branch of ethics that deals with moral duty and right action based on principle rather than on results. **de·on·to·log·i·cal** *adj.* ⟨Greek *deon* that which is binding; *dein* bind⟩

de·ox·y·ri·bo·nu·cle·ic acid [di,ɒksə,raɪbounju'kliɪk] *or* [-nu'kliɪk] DNA, an essential component of all living matter. ⟨< *de-* + *oxy(gen)* + *ribonucleic acid*⟩

de·part [dɪ'pɑrt] v 1 leave: *The train departs at 6:15.* 2 set out; start: *to depart on a journey.* 3 make a change (*from*): *to depart from one's usual way of doing things.* 4 die. **de·par·ture** n. ⟨Latin *departire* divide; *de-* away + *partis* part⟩ **depart this life** *Poetic, formal* die. **point of departure** starting point for discussion, etc. **de·part·ed** *adj* dead. **the de·part·ed** n a dead person or persons.

de·part·ment [dɪ'pɑrtmənt] n 1 a distinct part of a larger unit such as a government, business, store, school, etc.: *the department of external affairs of the federal government, the English department of a university.* 2 a field of activity: *Cooking meals is not my department.* **de·part·men·tal** [dɪpɑrt'mɛntəl] *or* [,dipɑrt-] *adj.* **de·part·men·tal·ize** v. ⟨See DEPART.⟩ **department store** a store organized into departments selling different kinds of goods.

de·pend [dɪ'pɛnd] v 1 rely; trust (with *on*): *You can depend on my help.* 2 require support or help (with *on*): *Children depend on their parents.* 3 flow from; be determined by (with *on*): *Success will depend partly on the weather.* ⟨Latin *dependere; de-* from + *pendere* hang⟩ **that depends** *or* **it depends** the answer will be determined by certain conditions not yet known or specified. **de·pend·a·ble** *adj* reliable. **de·pend·a·bil·i·ty** n. **de·pend·a·bly** *adv.* **de·pend·ant** n a person who requires the support or help of another: *His younger sister lives with us as a dependant.* *adj* dependent. **de·pend·ence** *or* **dependance** n. **de·pend·en·cy** *or* **dependancy** n 1 a country or territory controlled by another: 2 addiction, as to drugs, alcohol, etc. **de·pend·ent** *adj* 1 relying on another for support or help. 2 controlled by something or someone else: *emotionally dependent, a dependent variable in an equation.* 3 addicted (with *on*). 4 *Grammar* subordinate: *dependent clause.* n dependant.

USAGE
Although some writers use the two forms interchangeably, most use **dependant** for the noun and **dependent** for the adjective.

de·per·son·al·ize [di'pɜrsənə,laɪz] v 1 take away the personal elements or qualities of: *Institutions often depersonalize care.* 2 reify (a person). **de·per·son·al·i·za·tion** n.

de·pict [dɪ'pɪkt] v create a visual or verbal image of: *a carved frieze depicting a battle scene, a novel depicting life on the Prairies in the Depression.* **de·pic·tion** n. ⟨Latin *depictus* pp of *depingere*; *de-* + *pingere* paint⟩

dep·i·late ['dɛpə,leɪt] v remove hair from. **dep·i·la·tion** n. **dep·i·la·tor** n. ⟨Latin *de-* from + *pilus* hair⟩
de·pil·a·to·ry [dɪ'pɪlə,tɔri] adj removing hair. n a substance that removes hair.

de·plane [di'pleɪn] v leave an airplane: *We deplaned at Central Airport.*

de·plete [dɪ'plit] v empty; use up: *to deplete one's funds.* **de·ple·tion** n. ⟨Latin *depletus* pp of *deplere* empty, *de-* + *-plere* fill⟩

de·plore [dɪ'plɔr] v 1 heartily disapprove of: *I deplore your behaviour at the party.* 2 be sorry about. **de·plor·a·ble** adj. ⟨Latin *de-* (intensive) + *plorare* weep⟩

de·ploy [dɪ'plɔɪ] v 1 of troops, etc., spread into a long battle line. 2 distribute (people or resources) in convenient positions for action. 3 use: *to deploy one's talents to the best advantage.* 4 of a device, come into action: *My parachute deployed instantly.* **de·ploy·ment** n. ⟨French *dé-* + *ployer*; Latin *plicare* fold⟩

de·pop·u·late [di'pɒpjə,leɪt] v deprive of inhabitants. **de·pop·u·la·tion** n.

de·port [dɪ'pɔrt] v 1 expel from a country. 2 behave (*oneself*) in a given manner: *Boys, deport yourselves like gentlemen, please.* ⟨Latin *de-* away + *portare* carry⟩
de·por·ta·tion n expulsion from a country. **de·por·tee** [,dipɔr'ti] or [dɪpɔr'ti] n a person who is or has been deported. **de·port·ment** n 1 behaviour. 2 graceful or elegant bearing: *lessons in deportment for young princesses.*

de·pose [dɪ'pouz] v 1 put out of office: *The queen was deposed by the revolution.* 2 Law declare under oath, esp prior to appearing in court: *She deposed that she had seen the prisoner on the day of the murder.* **dep·o·si·tion** [,dɛpə'zɪʃən] or [,dipə'zɪʃən] n. ⟨Old French *deposer*; *de-* down + *poser* put⟩

de·pos·it [dɪ'pɒzɪt] v 1 lay or set down: *The flood deposited a layer of mud in the streets.* 2 put in a place for safekeeping: *People deposit money in banks.* 3 a pay (part of a price) in advance. b pay (a sum), to be refunded only when one returns a rented item or performs to a minimum standard in a contest.
n an item, substance, or sum deposited: *iron deposits in the ground, a deposit of mud, to pay a deposit of ten percent.* **de·pos·i·tor** n. ⟨Latin *depositus* pp of *deponere*; *de-* away + *ponere* put⟩
on deposit in a bank.
dep·o·si·tion [,dɛpə'zɪʃən] or [,di-] n 1 the act of deposing. 2 testimony given in deposing. 3 the process of depositing: *the deposition of sediment at the river mouth.* 4 deposit. **de·pos·i·to·ry** [dɪ'pɒzə,tɔri] n 1 a place where a thing is put for safekeeping 2 trustee.

dep·ot ['dipou] or ['dɛpou] n 1 a bus or railway station. 2 storehouse or warehouse. 3 a military recruitment and distribution centre. ⟨French *dépôt*; Latin. See DEPOSIT.⟩

de·prave [dɪ'preɪv] v thoroughly corrupt or pervert morally. **de·praved** adj. **de·prav·i·ty** [dɪ'prævəti] n. ⟨Latin *de-* + *pravus* crooked⟩

dep·re·cate ['dɛprə,keit] v 1 express strong disapproval of; speak or plead against: *Lovers of peace deprecate war.* 2 loosely, put down; belittle. **dep·re·cat·ing·ly** adv. **dep·re·ca·tion** n. **dep·re·ca·to·ry** ['dɛprəkə,tɔri] adj. ⟨Latin *deprecari* avert by prayer; *de-* + *precari* pray⟩

CONFUSABLES
Deprecate is sometimes used to mean 'disparage'. Apart from the very common expression *self-deprecating*, which has become standard, this sense is properly expressed by **depreciate**: *Don't depreciate her sincere efforts. I must deprecate this course of action.*

de·pre·ci·ate [dɪ'priʃi,eit] v 1 lessen in value: *Certain goods depreciate over time.* 2 speak slightingly of; put down: *She depreciates the value of exercise.* **de·pre·ci·a·tion** n. ⟨Latin *depretiare*; *de-* + *pretium* price⟩
de·pre·ci·a·ble adj losing value over time. **de·pre·ci·a·to·ry** adj disparaging; belittling.

dep·re·da·tion [,dɛprə'deiʃən] n the act of plundering; robbery. ⟨Latin *depraedare* pillage; *de-* + *praeda* booty⟩

de·press [dɪ'prɛs] v 1 make sad or gloomy: *depressed by the bad news from home.* 2 press or push down: *to depress a key on a keyboard.* 3 lower in value or amount. 4 reduce the activity of; slow down: *Some drugs depress the action of the heart.* **de·press·ing** adj. ⟨Latin *depressus* pp of *deprimere*; *de-* + *premere* press⟩
de·pres·sant adj decreasing the rate of vital activities. n a sedative or tranquillizer. **de·pressed** adj 1 gloomy; glum. 2 Psychiatry affected by DEPRESSION (def. 2). 3 of an area, socioeconomically disadvantaged. 4 of the economy, very slow and characterized by high unemployment. 5 lowered in value or amount. 6 pressed or flattened down. **de·pres·sion** n 1 low spirits. 2 Psychiatry a clinical condition characterized by listlessness, lack of concentration, insomnia, and other symptoms. 3 the act of depressing. 4 a low place: *Depressions in the lawn were full of water after the rain.* 5 a a period of very low economic activity and high unemployment. b the Depression a severe instance of this in the 1930s worldwide. 6 Meteorology an area of low barometric pressure. **de·press·ive** adj tending toward depression. n Psychiatry a person who suffers from clinical depression. **de·press·or** n an instrument for pressing down: *a tongue depressor.*

de·prive [dɪ'praɪv] v 1 take away a rightful possession: *to deprive people of their freedom.* 2 keep from having or doing: *Worry deprived her of sleep.* **dep·ri·va·tion** [,dɛprə'veiʃən] n. ⟨Old French *depriver*; *priver* deprive, Latin *privare*⟩
de·prived adj lacking the income, comforts,

experiences, love, etc. necessary for a full and healthy life: *a deprived childhood.*

de·pro·gram [di'prougræm] *v* **-grammed, -gram·ming** teach (someone) to cast off beliefs inculcated by brainwashing.

dept. **1** department. **2** deputy.

depth See DEEP.

de·pute [dɪ'pjut] *v* **1** appoint (someone) to act in one's place. **2** delegate (responsibility, authority, etc.) to another. ⟨Latin *deputare* assign, consider as; *de-* + *putare* think, count⟩ **dep·u·ta·tion** [,dɛpjə'teiʃən] *n* **1** the act of deputing. **2** a group of people appointed to act for others. **dep·u·tize** *v* **1** appoint as deputy. **2** act as deputy. **dep·u·ti·za·tion** *n*. **dep·u·ty** ['dɛpjəti] *n* **1** a person appointed to act in another's place. **2** a representative in certain assemblies, as in Québec's National Assembly. **deputy minister** in Canada, a senior civil servant who acts as assistant to, or representative of, a Cabinet minister.

de·rail [di'reil] *or* [dɪ'reil] *v* **1** run or cause to run off the rails (of a railway). **2** disrupt or frustrate (a plan, process, organization, etc.). **de·rail·ment** *n*.

de·rail·leur [dɪ'reilər] *n* a spring-driven mechanism on a bicycle that changes gears. ⟨French *dérailleur* derailer⟩

de·range [dɪ'reindʒ] *v* **1** disturb or confuse; throw off. **2** make insane. **de·range·ment** *n*. ⟨French *déranger; dé-* away + *ranger* arrange⟩

der·by ['dɑrbi] *n* **1 Derby** *esp Brit.* ['dɑrbi] **a** a famous horse race in England. **b** any annual horse race of similar importance: *the Kentucky Derby.* **2** any contest: *a fishing derby.* **3** a man's stiff hat with a rounded crown and narrow brim. ⟨Earl of *Derby*, founder of the original race in UK⟩

de·reg·u·late [di'rɛgjə,leit] *v* remove restrictions from: *to deregulate air fares.* **de·reg·u·la·tion** *n*.

der·e·lict ['dɛrə,lɪkt] *adj* **1** abandoned: *a derelict ship.* **2** failing in one's duty.
n **1** a ship abandoned at sea. **2** a homeless outcast. **der·e·lic·tion** *n*. ⟨Latin *derelictus* pp of *derelinquere* abandon. See RELINQUISH.⟩

de·ride [dɪ'raɪd] *v* make fun of; ridicule with contempt. **de·ri·sion** *n*. **de·ri·sive** [dɪ'raɪsɪv] *or* [dɪ'rɪzɪv] *adj*. ⟨Latin *de-* down + *ridere* laugh⟩ **de·ri·so·ry** [-'rɔɪsəri] *or* [-'raɪzəri] *adj* **1** derisive. **2** laughable; ridiculous; contemptible.

de ri·gueur [də Ri'gœR] *French* required by etiquette or custom; obligatory.

de·rive [dɪ'raɪv] *v* **1** obtain from a particular source: *to derive pleasure from music, to derive gasoline from petroleum.* **2** specifically, make (a word) by adding affixes to another word. **3** come from, or trace to, a source: *Our word table derives from Latin tabula.* **4** *Chemistry* obtain (one compound) from another by replacing one of the elements. **de·riv·a·ble** *adj*. **der·i·va·tion** *n*. **der·i·va·tion·al** *adj*. ⟨Latin *derivare* draw off; *de-* from + *rivus* stream⟩ **de·riv·a·tive** *adj* of artistic work, lacking in originality. *n* **1** a derived word or substance.

2 *Mathematics* the rate of change of one quantity relative to another.

der·mis ['dɜrmɪs] *n* **1** the sensitive layer of skin beneath the epidermis. **2** the skin. ⟨Greek *derma* skin⟩ **der·ma·ti·tis** [,dɜrmə'taɪtɪs] *n* inflammation of the skin. **der·ma·tol·o·gy** *n* the branch of medicine dealing with skin diseases. **der·ma·tol·o·gist** *n*. **der·ma·to·sis** *n* any skin disease.

der·nier cri [,dɛrnjei 'kri] *French* [dɛRnje'kRi] the latest fashion. ⟨= last cry⟩

der·o·gate ['dɛrə,geit] *v* **1** take away; detract: *She felt the committee's actions derogated from her authority.* **2** become worse; deviate (*from* a norm). **3** disparage; insult. **der·o·ga·tion** *n*. **de·rog·a·tive** *adj*. **de·rog·a·tive·ly** *adv*. ⟨Latin *de-* down from + *rogare* ask⟩ **de·rog·a·to·ry** [dɪ'rɒgə,tɔri] *adj* **1** disparaging; expressing a low opinion of a person or thing. **2** lessening the value. **de·rog·a·to·ri·ly** *adv*.

der·rick ['dɛrɪk] *n* **1** a large machine with a long arm for lifting or moving heavy objects. **2** a towerlike framework over an oil or gas well. ⟨*Derrick* 17c hangman in London, UK⟩

der·ri·ère *or* **der·ri·ere** [,dɛri'ɛr] *n* *Slang* buttocks. ⟨French = behind⟩

der·ring–do ['dɛrɪŋ 'du] *n* *Archaic* heroic daring; daring deeds. ⟨alteration of Middle English *dorryng don* daring to do⟩

der·vish ['dɜrvɪʃ] *n* a member of any of several Muslim religious orders. In some, the dervishes perform rites that include whirling, dancing, etc. ⟨Persian *darvīsh* beggar⟩

de·sal·i·nate [di'sælə,neit] *v* remove salt from, esp from seawater. **de·sal·i·na·tion** *n*.

des·cant ['dɛskænt] *n* *Music* **1** a separate melody or counterpoint sung above the basic melody. **2** the highest part or melody in harmonic music.
v [dɛ'skænt] talk at length; discourse freely: *to descant upon the wonders of nature.* ⟨Latin *discantare; dis-* away + *cantus* song⟩

de·scend [dɪ'sɛnd] *v* **1** go or come down (in space, value, pitch, etc.). **2** pass from an earlier to a later time: *superstitions descending from the Middle Ages.* **3** come from a source or ancestor (usually passive): *She is descended from a pioneer family.* **4** invade or attack suddenly (with *on* or *upon*): *Hordes of tourists descended on the town each summer.* **5** lower oneself: *She descended so far as to cheat on her exam.* **de·scent** [dɪ'sɛnt] *n*. ⟨Latin *descendere; de-* down + *scandere* climb⟩ **de·scend·ant** *n* **1** a person tracing his or her parentage to a certain individual, family, or group. **2** something derived from an earlier form: *Grand opera is the descendant of opéra bouffe.* *adj* going or coming down. **de·scend·er** *n* the part of a written or printed character, such as *p* or *g*, that goes below the line. Compare ASCENDER.

de·scram·ble [di'skræmbəl] *v* make (a scrambled television signal) intelligible again. **de·scram·bler** *n*.

de·scribe [dɪˈskraɪb] v **1** tell or write about; tell what something or someone is like: *He described the accident in detail.* **2** make the outline of: *The skater described a figure 8.* **de·scrib·a·ble** adj. **de·scrib·er** n. ⟨Latin *de-* from + *scribere* write⟩

de·scrip·tion [dɪˈskrɪpʃən] n **1** the act of describing or words that describe. **2** kind or sort: *cars of every description.* **de·scrip·tive** adj. **de·scrip·tive·ly** adv. **de·scrip·tive·ness** n.

de·scry [dɪˈskraɪ] v catch sight of: *The sailor descried a small island on the horizon.* ⟨French *descrier* proclaim; *des-* away + *crier* cry⟩

des·e·crate [ˈdɛsəˌkreɪt] v treat or use with gross disrespect; disregard the sacredness of: *They desecrated the church by using it as a stable.* **des·e·cra·tion** n. ⟨*de-* + *(con)secrate*⟩

de·seg·re·gate [diˈsɛgrəˌgeɪt] v abolish any law or practice in (a place) that requires the members of different races (or sexes, etc.) to be isolated from one another: *to desegregate the schools.* **de·seg·re·ga·tion** n.

de·sen·si·tize [diˈsɛnsəˌtaɪz] v make less sensitive or insensitive: *treatment desensitizing a person to an allergen. Daily exposure has desensitized us to violence.* **de·sen·si·ti·za·tion** n.

des·ert[1] [ˈdɛzərt] n **1** a dry, barren region. **2** a region that is not inhabited or cultivated. **3** any infertile or unstimulating environment: *a cultural desert.* ⟨Latin *desertum* abandoned; *deserere.* See DESERT[2].⟩

de·sert·i·fi·ca·tion n. deterioration of arid land into desert due to climate change or overuse.

> **CONFUSABLES**
> A **desert** is a region with little water and not much plant or animal life. A **dessert** is a sweet course served at the end of a meal.

de·sert[2] [dɪˈzɜrt] v **1** leave (someone who needs or relies on one): *to desert one's family.* **2** run away from (duty, military service, etc.). **3** fail: *His courage deserted him.* **de·sert·er** n. **de·ser·tion** n. ⟨Latin *desertare,* from *deserere* abandon; *de-* dis- + *serere* join⟩

> **SYNONYMS**
> **Desert** emphasizes breaking a promise, evading a duty, or disappointing someone, and therefore implies blame: *She deserted her friend in his hour of need.* **Forsake** emphasizes breaking off sentimental attachments and thus has emotional connotations, but does not necessarily suggest blame: *He forsook the farm for a career in banking.* **Abandon** emphasizes that the action is final and complete, whether necessary or justifiable or not: *They abandoned the wrecked plane.*

de·sert[3] [dɪˈzɜrt] n the fact of deserving, or (esp in the phrase **just deserts**) what is deserved: *The robber got his just deserts when he was sentenced to five years in prison.* ⟨Old French *deserte* pp of *deservir.* See DESERVE.⟩

de·serve [dɪˈzɜrv] v have a claim or right to; be worthy of or have due to one: *Good work deserves good pay. You deserve to be fired.* ⟨Latin *deservire* serve well; *de-* (intensive) + *servire*⟩ **de·serv·ed·ly** [dɪˈzɜrvɪdli] adv as deserved:

deservedly punished. **de·serv·ing** adj worthy (of something): *deserving of praise. Give the award to a deserving student.*

de·sex [diˈsɛks] v **1** remove the sex organs, sex drive, or sexual characteristics of. **2** dissociate from sex. Also, **de·sex·u·al·ize.**

des·ic·cate [ˈdɛsəˌkeɪt] v **1** dry thoroughly. **2** preserve by drying, as raisins or coconut. **des·ic·cant** adj, n. **des·ic·ca·tion** n. ⟨Latin *desiccare; de-* out + *siccus* dry⟩

de·sid·er·a·tum [dɪˌzɪdəˈrætəm] or [dɪˌsɪdə-] n, pl **-ta** [-tə] something desired or needed. ⟨Latin, pp of *desiderare* long for⟩

de·sign [dɪˈzaɪn] n **1** a drawing, sketch, etc. made to serve as a plan or pattern: *a design for a machine.* **2** an artistic arrangement of detail, form, and colour: *a wallpaper design in tan and brown.* **3** a plan in mind. **4** order that suggests a plan; organization of parts in relation to a whole and its purpose: *evidence of design in the universe.*
v **1** produce a first pattern, model, or sketch of something to be made: *to design a dress.* **2** plan in the mind; invent; contrive. **3** make to suit a specific purpose, user, etc.: *a house designed for blind people.* **de·sign·er** n. ⟨Latin *designare; de-* (intensive) + *signum* mark⟩
by design a on purpose: *Whether by accident or by design, he broke the lamp.* **b** by virtue of the original purpose and form. **have designs on** have a secret intention for, often evil or self-serving: *The thief had designs on the safe.* **de·sign·ed·ly** [dɪˈzaɪnɪdli] adv intentionally; on purpose. **de·sign·ing** adj scheming.

des·ig·nate [ˈdɛzɪgˌneɪt] v **1** mark out; point out: *Red lines designate main roads on this map.* **2** name; entitle: *She has been designated Chief Engineer.* **3** appoint: *to designate for a task.*
adj [ˈdɛzɪgnɪt] or [-ˌneɪt] selected; appointed. **des·ig·nat·ed** adj. **des·ig·na·tion** n. ⟨See DESIGN.⟩

de·sire [dɪˈzaɪr] v **1** wish strongly for; wish (to do). **2** want (someone) sexually. **3** ask for, esp formally: *The queen desires your presence.* **de·sire** n. ⟨Old French *desirer;* Latin *desiderare* long for⟩
de·sir·a·ble adj **1** good; worth wishing for or having. **2** arousing desire. **de·sir·a·bil·ity** n. **de·sir·a·bly** adv. **de·sir·ous** adj longing; having or showing desire (with *of*): *desirous of fame.*

de·sist [dɪˈsɪst] v stop; cease (often with *from*): *The judge ordered him to desist from fighting.* ⟨Latin *de-* from + *sistere* stop⟩

desk [dɛsk] n **1** a piece of furniture with drawers and a flat top on which to write or put a computer. **2** a counter in a department: *the information desk of a library, the customer service desk.* **3** in an orchestra, the place or status of a musician: *first desk.* ⟨Italian *desco;* Latin *discus* quoit, dish, Greek *diskos*⟩
desk·top n *Computers* a screen from which files or applications are opened.
adj **1** of a computer, fitting on a desk. **2** using such computers more or less exclusively. v **-topped, -top·ping** make or do by means of desktop computers. **desktop publishing** the

preparation of copy for printing, using only a computer.

des·o·late ['dɛsəlɪt] *or* ['dɛzəlɪt] *adj* 1 barren; inhospitable; empty and bleak: *desolate land.* 2 forlorn; lonely; wretched: *a ragged, hungry, desolate child.*
v ['dɛsə,leit] *or* ['dɛzə,leit] make desolate: *The Vikings desolated the land they attacked. He was desolated by the passing of his old friend.* **des·o·late·ly** *adv.* **des·o·la·tion** *n.* ⟨Latin *de-* (intensive) + *solus* alone⟩

de·spair [dɪ'spɛr] *n* 1 complete loss of hope: *Despair seized us as we felt the boat sinking.* 2 a cause of this: *She is the despair of her parents.*
v lose or give up hope: *The doctors despaired of saving the woman's life.* **de·spair·ing** *adj.* ⟨Latin *desperare; de-* not + *sperare* to hope⟩

des·per·ate ['dɛsprɪt] *adj* 1 having lost all hope: *He'd have to be desperate before he asked for help.* 2 made reckless by loss of hope: *a desperate criminal.* 3 giving little or no hope of improvement: *The situation is desperate.* 4 having an urgent need or desire: *desperate for something to do.* 5 extreme: *in desperate need.* **des·per·ate·ly** *adv.* **des·per·a·tion** *n.*

CONFUSABLES
Despair suggests hopelessness expressed in a resigned, depressed, or dejected attitude: *In his despair over losing his job he sold all his possessions and became a drifter.* **Desperation** suggests a recklessness caused by despair and expressed in rash or frantic action as a last resort: *He had no job and no money, and in desperation he robbed a bank.*

des·per·a·do [,dɛspə'rɑdou] *n, pl* -**does** or -**dos** a bold, reckless, dangerous outlaw. ⟨Old Spanish; Latin *desperatus.* See DESPAIR.⟩

de·spise [dɪ'spaɪz] *v* 1 look down on; feel contempt for: *People despise a traitor.* 2 dislike very much. ⟨Old French *despis-* stem of *despire,* Latin *despicere; de-* down + *specere* look at⟩ **des·pic·a·ble** [dɪ'spɪkəbəl] *or* ['dɛspɪkəbəl] *adj* to be despised; contemptible. **des·pic·a·bly** *adv.*

de·spite [dɪ'spaɪt] *prep* in spite of: *We went on foot despite the rain.* ⟨Old French *despit,* Latin *despectus* pp of *despicere.* See DESPISE.⟩

de·spoil [dɪ'spɔɪl] *v* rob; plunder. **de·spoil·er** *n.* **de·spo·li·a·tion** [dɪ,spoʊli'eiʃən] *n.* ⟨Latin *de-* completely + *spolium* armour, booty⟩

de·spond [dɪ'spɒnd] *v* lose heart or hope. **de·spond·ent** *adj.* **de·spond·en·cy** *n.* ⟨Latin *de-* away + *spondere* lose heart⟩

des·pot ['dɛspət] *or* ['dɛspɒt] *n* a tyrant or oppressive dictator. **des·pot·ic** [dɪ'spɒtɪk] *adj.* **des·pot·ism** *n.* ⟨Greek *despotēs* master⟩

des·sert [dɪ'zɜrt] *n* 1 a sweet course served at the end of a meal. 2 a food suitable for this course. ⟨French, from *desservir* clear the table; *des-* from + *servir* serve, Latin *servire*⟩

de·sta·bil·ize [di'steibə,laɪz] *v* deprive of stability; make unstable: *to destabilize a country's economy.* **de·sta·bi·li·za·tion** *n.*

des·tine ['dɛstən] *v* 1 assign or appoint in advance for a given purpose: *destined from birth to be a king.* 2 cause by fate: *My letter was destined never to reach her.* ⟨Latin *destinare* make fast, fix; *de-* (intensive) + *stare* stand⟩

destined for a headed toward; going to: *a ship destined for England.* **b** intended for; set apart for: *destined for the ministry.*

des·ti·na·tion *n* the place to which a person or thing is headed or sent. **des·ti·ny** *n* 1 what becomes of a person or thing in the end. 2 what is predetermined to happen.

des·ti·tute ['dɛstə,tjut] *or* ['dɛstə,tut] *adj* 1 very poor; lacking necessities such as food, clothing, and shelter. 2 lacking something good or needed (with *of*): *a region destitute of trees.* **des·ti·tu·tion** *n.* ⟨Latin *destitutus* pp of *destituere* forsake; *de-* away + *statuere* put⟩

de·stroy [dɪ'strɔɪ] *v* 1 ruin or wreck by tearing down, breaking, etc.: *Hail destroyed their crop.* 2 bring to nothing: *A heavy rain destroyed all hope of a picnic.* 3 kill: *The injured dog had to be destroyed.* **de·struc·tion** *n.* ⟨Latin *destruere; de-* un- + *struere* pile, build⟩

de·stroy·er *n* 1 one that destroys. 2 a small, fast warship. **de·struct·i·ble** [dɪ'strʌktəbəl] *adj* capable of being destroyed. **de·struc·tive** *adj* 1 habitually destroying things: *a destructive child.* 2 tending to destroy (often with *of*): *Such conduct is destructive of trust.* 3 having only a negative effect: *destructive criticism.* **de·struc·tive·ly** *adv.* **de·struc·tive·ness** *n.*

des·ul·to·ry ['dɛsəl,tɔri] *or* ['dɛzəl,tɔri] *adj* going randomly from one thing to another: *desultory thoughts. Systematic study of a few books is better than a desultory reading of many.* **des·ul·to·ri·ly** *adv.* **des·ul·to·ri·ness** *n.* ⟨Latin *desultorius* of a leaper; *de-* down + *salire* leap⟩

de·tach [dɪ'tætʃ] *v* 1 loosen and remove: *She detached a charm from her bracelet.* 2 separate (a group) from a main body for special duty: *A squad was detached to scout the area.* 3 make aloof or uninvolved: *to detach oneself from a situation.* **de·tach·a·ble** *adj.* ⟨French *détacher; dé-* away + Old French *tache* nail⟩

de·tached *adj* 1 of a house, standing alone, not joined to others: *a detached house.* 2 not emotionally involved and hence impartial. **de·tach·ed·ly** [dɪ'tætʃɪdli] *adv.* **de·tach·ment** *n* 1 the act of detaching or condition or quality of being detached. 2 *Military* a group of soldiers, tanks, etc. assigned to some special duty. 3 ✱ the smallest unit of organization of the Royal Canadian Mounted Police.

de·tail ['diteil] *or* [dɪ'teil] *n* 1 a minor fact in a story, report, etc.: *Skip the details.* 2 a small element of a design, complex object, etc.: *The two skirts are alike in every detail.* 3 details in general, or the work of dealing with them one by one: *He doesn't like the detail involved in accounting.* 4 a reproduction of part of a work of art, often enlarged. 5 *esp Military* **a** a group sent on some special duty: *a detail of six soldiers to guard the road.* **b** the duty.
v 1 give the particulars of: *He detailed all the things he had seen and done on his trip.* 2 send on special duty: *Police were detailed to hold back the crowd.* **de·tail·er** *n.* ⟨French *détaillir* cut in pieces; *de-* completely + *tailler* cut⟩

go into detail give all the details: *There's no*

time to go into detail. **in detail** with all the details.

de·tailed *adj* including or handling many details: *a detailed map, detailed work.*

de·tain [dɪ'tein] *v* **1** hold (someone) back; delay. **2** put or keep in custody: *Police have detained a suspect.* **de·tain·ment** *n.* ⟨Old French *detenir*, Latin *detinere; de-* away + *tenere* hold⟩ **de·tain·ee** [ˌditei'ni] *n* a person held in custody. **de·ten·tion** [dɪ'tɛnʃən] *n* **1** the act of detaining or condition of being detained. **2** a school punishment in which a student is kept in after school or during recess.

de·tect [dɪ'tɛkt] *v* **1** notice; find: *to detect an odour.* **2** discover or find out the truth about (a crime). **de·tect·a·ble** or **de·tect·i·ble** *adj.* **de·tec·tion** *n.* ⟨Latin *detectus* pp of *detegere; de-* un- + *tegere* cover⟩ **de·tec·tive** *n* **1** a police officer whose work is investigating crimes. **2** a private investigator. **de·tec·tive** *adj.* **de·tec·tor** *n* a device that detects and reports the presence of metal, radioactivity, smoke, etc.

dé·tente [dei'tɒnt] *French* [de'tãt] *n* the easing of tension, esp between nations or political groups: *a détente in the cold war.* ⟨French from *détendre; dé-* un + *tendre* stretch⟩

de·ten·tion See DETAIN.

de·ter [dɪ'tɜr] *v* discourage by the prospect of something unpleasant: *The extreme heat deterred us from going outdoors.* **de·ter·rence** *n.* ⟨Latin *de-* from + *terrere* frighten⟩ **de·ter·rent** *adj* deterring. *n* anything that deters, esp the prospect of punishment.

de·ter·gent [dɪ'tɜrdʒənt] *n* **1** a powder or liquid for cleansing: *laundry detergent.* **2** any chemical compound that keeps dirt particles suspended in water. **de·ter·gent** *adj.* ⟨Latin *detergere; de-* off + *tergere* wipe⟩

de·te·ri·o·rate [dɪ'tiriəˌreit] *v* become worse in condition, quality, or effectiveness: *A car deteriorates without proper care. The discussion quickly deteriorated into a shouting match.* **de·te·ri·o·ra·tion** *n.* ⟨Latin *deterior* worse⟩

de·ter·mine [dɪ'tɜrmən] *v* **1** make up one's mind firmly: *He determined to become the best Scout in his troop.* **2** find out definitely or exactly: *to determine a ship's position.* **3** be the deciding factor in: *Today's events will determine whether we are to go or stay.* **4** limit; define: *The meaning of a word is partly determined by context.* ⟨Latin *determinare* set limits to; *de-* completely + *terminus* end⟩ **de·ter·mi·na·ble** *adj* capable of being settled or decided. **de·ter·mi·nant** *n Mathematics* the sum of all the products formed from a square matrix. **de·ter·mi·nate** *adj* well-defined; with exact limits. **de·ter·mi·na·cy** *n.* **de·ter·mi·na·tion** *n* **1** the act of determining. **2** firmness of mind or strength of will; resolute character. **3** a firm decision. **de·ter·mined** *adj* with one's mind firmly made up; resolute. **de·ter·min·er** *n Grammar* a specifying word such as *the, a, her,* or *this,* before a noun. **de·ter·min·ism** *n* the doctrine that all events including human actions are

necessary results of antecedent causes. **de·ter·min·ist** *n.* **de·ter·mi·nis·tic** *adj.*

de·test [dɪ'tɛst] *v* dislike very much; hate. **de·test·a·ble** *adj.* **de·tes·ta·tion** *n.* ⟨Latin *detestari* curse with the gods as witness; *de-* (intensive) + *testari* witness⟩

de·throne [di'θroun] *v* **1** deprive of the power to rule; depose. **2** remove (someone) from any high position. **de·throne·ment** *n.*

det·o·nate ['dɛtəˌneit] *v* explode or cause to explode with noise and violence; fire; set off. **det·o·na·tion** *n.* ⟨Latin *de-* (intensive) + *tonare* thunder⟩ **det·o·na·tor** *n* a fuse, percussion cap, etc. used to set off an explosive.

de·tour ['ditur] *or* [dɪ'tur] *n* a route taken instead of the normal or more direct route. **de·tour** *v.* ⟨French *détour* from *détourner* turn aside; *de-* away from + *tourner* turn⟩

de·tox·i·fy [di'tɒksəˌfaɪ] *v* remove a toxic substance or its effect from; specifically, cure an addict by forced withdrawal: *to detoxify an alcoholic.* **de·tox·i·fi·ca·tion** *n.* Both informally shortened to **de·tox.**

de·tract [dɪ'trækt] *v* take away (quality, value, beauty, etc.): *That tacky frame detracts from the picture.* ⟨Latin *detractus* pp of *detrahere; de-* away + *trahere* draw⟩ **de·trac·tion** *n* **1** a taking away. **2** the act of speaking evil or disparaging. **de·trac·tive** *adj.* **de·trac·tive·ly** *adv.* **de·trac·tor** *n* a person who disparages or speaks evil of another.

de·train [di'trein] *v* get off or put off a railway train. **de·train·ment** *n.*

det·ri·ment ['dɛtrəmənt] *n* damage; harm: *He continued working, without detriment to his health.* **det·ri·men·tal** *adj.* ⟨Latin *detrimentum* from *deterere; de-* away + *terere* wear⟩

de·tri·tus [dɪ'traɪtəs] *n* **1** particles of rock or other material worn from a mass. **2** any debris; disintegrated matter: *The detritus left by the flood covered the highway.* **de·tri·tal** *adj.* ⟨Latin = a rubbing away⟩

deuce¹ [djus] *or* [dus] *n* **1** a playing card marked with a 2. **2** the side of a die having two spots. **3** *Tennis* a score of 40 each. ⟨Old French *deus* two; Latin *duos* accusative of *duo*⟩

deuce² [djus] *or* [dus] *Informal interj* a mild oath expressing annoyance: *What the deuce does he want now?* (probably Low German *duus* deuce¹, unlucky throw at dice) **deu·ced** [djust] *or* [dust], ['djusɪd] *or* ['dusɪd] *adj* damned. **deu·ced·ly** *or* **deu·ced·ly** *adv.*

de·us ex ma·chi·na [ˌdiəs ɛks 'mækənə] *or* [ˌdeiəs-] *Latin* in a story, a person, event, force, etc. that comes, in a contrived way, just in time to solve a difficulty. ⟨literally, god from the machinery (with reference to a stage device in the ancient theatre)⟩

deu·te·ri·um [dju'tiriəm] *or* [du'tiriəm] *n* an isotope of hydrogen having a mass double that of ordinary hydrogen; heavy hydrogen. *Symbol* **D** ⟨Greek *deutereion* having second place; *deuteros* second⟩

de·va ['deivə] *n* **1** *Hinduism, Buddhism* a god. **2** *Zoroastrianism* evil spirit. ⟨Sanskrit = god⟩

de·val·ue [di'vælju] *v* **1** Also, **de·val·u·ate** officially reduce the value of (currency) in relation to other currencies or gold. **2** lessen or attack the value of. **3** attach little importance or value to. **de·val·u·a·tion** *n*.

De·va·na·ga·ri [ˌdevə'nɑgəri] *n* the alphabet of Sanskrit and various other north Indic languages. ⟨Sanskrit = city of the gods⟩

dev·as·tate ['devəˌsteit] *v* **1** make desolate; destroy: *A long war devastated the border town.* **2** overwhelm with disappointment, grief, or hurt feelings; crush: *devastated by harsh criticism.* **dev·as·tat·ing** *adj.* **dev·as·ta·tion** *n*. ⟨Latin *devastare; de-* (intensive) + *vastus* waste⟩

de·vel·op [dɪ'veləp] *v* **1** acquire, make, or come into being gradually, by stages: *Plants develop from seeds. He developed a fondness for her.* **2** grow or mature, or cause to do so: *Exercise develops healthy bodies.* **3** work out in greater detail, depth, fullness, etc.: *to develop an argument or theme.* **4** change, esp by means of construction work: *to develop a park area, to develop the old downtown area.* **5** make or become more industrialized, modern, etc.: *developing nations.* **6** occur; transpire: *Let's see what develops before we decide.* **7** *Photography* treat (film or a plate) with chemicals to bring out the image recorded on it; of an image, be so brought out. ⟨French *développer* unwrap⟩

de·vel·op·er *n* **1** a person or company whose business is developing real estate on a large scale. **2** *Photography* a chemical used to bring out the picture on exposed film, plates, etc.

de·vel·op·ment *n* **1** the process of developing. **2** a happening: *the latest developments in science.* **3** a group of buildings built in an area by one company: *The new development will include schools.* **de·vel·op·men·tal** *adj* to do with development, esp the physical, cognitive, etc. development of children.

De·vi ['deivi] *n Hinduism* a goddess, the wife of Siva. ⟨Sanskrit = goddess⟩

de·vi·ate ['divi,eit] *v* turn, or cause to turn, aside: *to deviate from the truth.*
n, adj ['diviət] deviant. ⟨Latin *deviare; de-* aside + *via* way⟩
de·vi·ant *adj* deviating markedly from a norm, esp from social norms. *n* a deviant person, esp with reference to sexual behaviour. **de·vi·ance** *n.* **de·vi·a·tion** *n* **1** the act of deviating: *No deviation from the rules is allowed.* **2** *Statistics* the difference between the mean of a set of values and one value in the set, as a measure of variation from the norm.

de·vice [də'vəis] *n* **1** a mechanical invention used for a special purpose: *a device for lighting a gas stove.* **2** a plan; trick: *by some device or other.* **3** a design or symbol, esp a coat of arms or part of one. **4** *Literature, music* a feature introduced to achieve a particular effect. **5** a motto or inscription. ⟨Old French *devise*, Latin *divisus* pp of *dividere* divide⟩
leave to one's own devices leave to do as one chooses: *The teacher left us to our own devices while she met briefly with the principal.*

dev·il ['devəl] *n* **1 the Devil** in some faiths, the chief spirit of evil; Satan. **2** an evil spirit; demon. **3** an evil or cruel person. **4** *Informal* **a** a dashing, spirited, or mischievous person. **b** a person: *The poor devil didn't know what hit him.* **5** *Informal* something hard to handle, solve, etc.: *That last question was a real devil.*
v **-illed** or **-iled, -il·ling** or **-il·ing 1** prepare with hot spices: *devilled eggs.* **2** harass.
interj exclamation or intensifier expressing surprise, disbelief, annoyance, etc.: *Helped? The devil you did! What the devil do you mean?* ⟨Old English *deofol*; Greek *diabolos*⟩
between the devil and the deep (blue) sea between two equally bad alternatives. **devil of a** *Informal* very difficult, awkward, etc.: *We had the devil of a time getting the piano into the basement.* **give the devil his due** be fair even to a disliked person. **go to the devil a** go to ruin. **b** (imperative) damn you. **like the devil** *Informal* with great force, speed, etc.: *to work like the devil.* **speak of the devil** the person talked about has just appeared. **the devil take (someone** or **something)** someone or something be damned. **the devil take the hindmost** it doesn't matter what happens to the loser or last one. **the devil to pay** much trouble ahead as a result.
dev·il·ish *adj* **1** to do with devils; wicked, mischievous, etc.: *a devilish scheme.* **2** *Slang* extreme: *a devilish hurry.* **dev·il–may–care** *adj* careless or reckless: *a devil-may-care attitude toward authority.* **dev·il·ment** *n* See DEVILTRY.
devil's advocate 1 *Roman Catholic Church* an official appointed to argue against a proposed beatification or canonization. **2** a person who argues in order to provoke discussion or to test the strength of opposing arguments.
devil's food cake a rich dark chocolate cake.
devil's paintbrush a perennial weed of North America with orange flowers. **dev·il·try** or **dev·il·ry** *n* evil or mischievous plans or behaviour.

de·vi·ous ['diviəs] *adj* **1** winding; twisting; roundabout: *a devious route through little side streets.* **2** not straightforward; sneaky or tricky. **de·vi·ous·ly** *adv.* **de·vi·ous·ness** *n.* ⟨Latin *devius; de-* out of + *via* the way⟩

de·vise [dɪ'vaɪz] *v* **1** think up; invent: *to devise a scheme for earning money.* **2** *Law* leave (land or buildings) by a will.
n Law **1** the act of devising property. **2** a will, or part of a will, leaving property. **3** property so left. **de·vis·a·ble** *adj.* ⟨Old French *deviser* dispose in portions; Latin *dividere* divide⟩

de·vi·tal·ize [di'vəitəˌlaɪz] *v* take away the life, vitality, etc. of. **de·vi·tal·i·za·tion** *n.*

de·void [dɪ'vɔɪd] *adj* completely lacking (with *of*): *a speech devoid of humour.* ⟨Middle English *devoid* cast out; Old French *desvoidier*⟩

de·volve [di'vɒlv] or [dɪ'vɒlv] *v* of a duty, responsibility, etc. transfer or be transferred to someone else, esp at a lower level (with *on*). ⟨Latin *de-* down + *volvere* roll⟩

dev·o·lu·tion [ˌdevə'luʃən] or [ˌdivə'luʃən] *n* **1** a progression through time from stage to stage, often worsening. **2** a rightful passing

of property or rights from person to person.
3 a devolving of responsibility or authority.
4 *Biology* a development toward simpler
structure; degeneration. **de·vo·lu·tion·ary** *adj.*
de·vo·lu·tion·ism *n.* **de·vo·lu·tion·ist** *n.*

de·vote [dɪ'voʊt] *v* **1** give up wholly to some
person or purpose: *She devoted herself to her
children.* **2** set apart for a given purpose: *I
devote an hour a day to writing.* ⟨Latin *devotus*
pp of *devovere; de-* entirely + *vovere* vow⟩
dev·o·tee [ˌdɛvə'ti] *or* [ˌdivə'ti] *n* a person
devoted to something; a devoted follower.
de·vo·tion *n* **1** intense loyalty and love. **2** the
act of devoting. **3** earnestness, commitment,
etc. in religion. **de·vot·ed** *adj.* **de·vo·tion·al** *adj*
to do with or expressing religious devotion
or used for devotions. *n* a short Christian
homily or meditation. **devotions** *pl* prayer,
meditation, etc., either privately or informally
and intimately in a group.

de·vour [dɪ'vaʊr] *v* **1** eat hungrily or greedily.
2 consume; destroy: *Fire devoured the building.*
3 totally absorb the attention of: *devoured by
curiosity.* **de·vour·er** *n.* ⟨Latin *de-* + *vorare* gulp⟩

de·vout [dɪ'vaʊt] *adj* **1** sincerely religious.
2 earnest; sincere; hearty: *a devout follower.*
de·vout·ly *adv.* **de·vout·ness** *n.* ⟨Old French
devot, Latin *devotus.* See DEVOTE.⟩

dew [dju] *or* [du] *n* moisture from the air
that collects in small drops on cool surfaces
at night. **dew·y** *adj.* ⟨Old English *dēaw*⟩
dew·claw *n* a small, useless hoof or toe on
the feet of deer, pigs, dogs, etc. **dew·drop** *n* a
drop of dew. **dew·fall** *n* **1** the formation of
dew. **2** the time in the evening when this
begins. **dew·lap** *n* a loose fold of skin under
the throat of some animals and birds. **dew
point** the temperature at which water vapour
condenses as dew. **dew–worm** *n* ✸ any large
earthworm that comes to the surface at night
when there is dew. **dew·y–eyed** *adj* naive.

Dew·ey decimal system ['djui] *or* ['dui] a
system for classifying books, pamphlets, etc.
by subject, used in libraries. ⟨Melvil *Dewey*
(1851-1931), US librarian who devised it⟩

dex·ter·i·ty [dɛk'stɛrəti] *n* **1** manual skill;
quickness and precision in using the hands.
2 mental quickness and skill; cleverness.
dex·ter·ous ['dɛkstərəs] *or* ['dɛkstrəs] *adj.*

> **SYNONYMS**
> **Dexterous** suggests naturally easy, quick,
> smooth movements and lightness and
> sureness of touch: *a dexterous pianist.* **Deft**
> adds the idea of expert skill and efficiency
> coming from much practice: *a surgeon's deft
> fingers.* **Adroit** suggests quick-wittedness and
> cleverness or resourcefulness; it is often used
> in the context of mental activity: *The adroit
> lawyer got the truth out of the witness.*

dex·trose ['dɛkstrous] *n* a form of glucose.
⟨*dexter* + *(gluc)ose*⟩

dhar·ma ['dɑrmə] *n* **1** *Buddhism* law; true
teaching. **2** *Hinduism* **a** right behaviour;
virtue. **b** cosmic law or order. ⟨Sanskrit⟩

dho·ti ['douti] *n* a garment for the lower body

worn especially by Hindu men, consisting of
a piece of cloth passed between the legs,
secured at the waist and loosely wrapping
the legs to mid-calf or ankle. ⟨Hindi⟩

dhur·rie ['dɜri] *n* an Indian woven mat in
cotton or wool. ⟨Hindi⟩

di– *prefix* **1** twice; twofold, as in *dicotyledon.*
2 with two atoms, etc., of a given substance,
as in *dioxide.* Also, **dis–** before *s.* ⟨Greek⟩

dia– *prefix* through; across; thoroughly, as in
diameter. Also, **di–** before vowels. ⟨Greek⟩

di·a·be·tes [ˌdaɪə'bitɪs] *or* [ˌdaɪə'bitiz] *n* any
of several diseases characterized by excessive
urine and abnormal thirst; esp, DIABETES
MELLITUS. **di·a·bet·ic** [-'bɛtɪk] *adj, n.* ⟨Greek =
passing through; *dia-* through + *bainein* go⟩
diabetes mel·li·tus [mə'laɪtəs] *or* [mə'litəs] a
form of diabetes characterized by excessive
sugar in the urine and caused by failure to
produce insulin. ⟨Latin *mel* honey⟩

di·a·bol·i·cal [ˌdaɪə'bɒləkəl] *adj* devilish;
wicked; fiendish. ⟨Greek *diabolos.* See DEVIL.⟩

di·ac·o·nate [daɪ'ækənɪt] *or* [di'ækənɪt] *n*
1 the office of a deacon. **2** a group of
deacons. **di·ac·o·nal** *adj.* ⟨See DEACON.⟩

di·a·crit·i·cal [ˌdaɪə'krɪtəkəl] *adj* making or
seeing a distinction. **di·a·crit·i·cal·ly** *adv.*
⟨Greek *diakritikos; dia-* apart + *krinein* separate⟩
di·a·crit·ic *adj* diacritical. *n* DIACRITICAL MARK.
diacritical mark a mark such as ¨ ^ ¯ ˏ ´ or ˋ
added to a letter to show pronunciation, etc.

di·a·dem ['daɪəˌdɛm] *n* a crown. ⟨Greek
diadēma; dia- across + *deein* bind⟩

di·aer·e·sis See DIERESIS.

di·ag·no·sis [ˌdaɪəg'noʊsɪs] *n, pl* **-ses** [-siz]
1 the process of identifying the disease or
problem affecting a specific individual or
case. **2** any decision reached after a study of
facts. **3** a statement of either of these.
di·ag·nose [-'noʊs] *or* [-'noʊz] *v.* ⟨Greek *dia-*
apart + *gignōskein* learn to know⟩
di·ag·nos·tic [ˌdaɪəg'nɒstɪk] *adj* to do with
diagnosis: *a diagnostic survey. n* **1** **diagnostics**
pl (with sg verb) the art of making medical
diagnoses. **2** a symptom; characteristic sign:
*Frequent turnover is a diagnostic of employee
dissatisfaction.* **di·ag·nos·ti·cian** *n.*

di·ag·o·nal [daɪ'ægənəl] *adj* **1** *Geometry* that
joins two non-adjacent angles or vertices of a
polygon or polyhedron. **2** slanted, esp at a
45° angle to the horizontal or vertical.
n a diagonal line or plane. **di·ag·o·nal·ly** *adv.*
⟨Greek *dia-* across + *gōnia* angle⟩

di·a·gram ['daɪəˌgræm] *n* an informative or
technical drawing; a drawing illustrating an
idea, structure, relationship, system, etc.
⟨Greek *dia-* + *-gramma; graphein* to mark⟩
di·a·gram·mat·ic *adj* **1** in the form of a
diagram. **2** in outline only; sketchy.

di·al ['daɪəl] *n* **1** a marked surface, esp a
circular one, on which a moving pointer
indicates a measurement of some kind. **2** the
disk on a rotary telephone. **3** a knob that one
can turn to different settings to control
volume, choose radio frequency, etc.

v -**alled** or -**aled, -al·ling** or -**al·ing 1** enter (a number) on a rotary telephone or, loosely, on any telephone. **2** enter the number of (someone) in this way. ⟨probably Latin *rota dialis* daily (wheel); *dies* day⟩

dial direct make a telephone call without using an operator.

dial tone the humming sound heard when a telephone receiver is lifted, indicating that the line is in service and open for use.

di·a·lect [ˈdaɪəˌlɛkt] *n* **1** a form of a language characteristic of a region: *the dialect of English spoken in Newfoundland.* **2** one of a group of very closely related languages. **di·a·lec·tal** *adj.* ⟨Greek *dialektos; dia-* between + *legein* speak⟩ **di·a·lec·tol·o·gy** *n* the study of dialects. **di·a·lec·tol·o·gist** *n.*

> **USAGE**
> **Dialects** exist because of the separation of groups of speakers either regionally or socially. Where several regional dialects exist, one may attain higher status because it is spoken in the area containing the centre of government, education, or trade. A dialect is a valid form of a language, not to be confused with either informal or substandard usage or with argot.

di·a·lec·tic [ˌdaɪəˈlɛktɪk] *n* **1** logical debate or argument used to test or analyze a theory. **2** *Logic* **a** formal rhetorical reasoning. **b** a method based on resolution of contradictory opposites, thesis and antithesis, leading to synthesis. Also, **di·a·lec·tics. di·a·lec·tic** or **di·a·lec·ti·cal** *adj.* **di·a·lec·ti·cal·ly** *adv.*

dialectical materialism the socialist doctrine formulated by Karl Marx and Friedrich Engels using a dialectic method, that advocates a classless society emerging as the result of a long struggle between economic classes. **di·a·lec·ti·cian** *n* one skilled in dialectic.

di·a·logue [ˈdaɪəˌlɒg] *n* **1** conversation, or a particular conversation, between two or more people. **2** conversation as an element of a story, film, etc.: *Dialogue is difficult for some writers.* **3** communication or discussion between groups with different viewpoints: *interfaith dialogue.* **di·a·logue** *v.* ⟨Greek *dia-* between + *logos* speech⟩

di·al·y·sis [daɪˈæləsɪs] *n, pl* -**ses** [-ˌsiz] **1** the separation of crystalloids from colloids in solution. **2** *Medicine* the separation of waste matter from the blood in a machine using this process to replace the kidneys. **di·a·lyse** or **di·a·lyze** [ˈdaɪəˌlaɪz] *v.* **di·a·lyt·ic** [-ˈlɪtɪk] *adj.* ⟨Greek *dialysis; dia-* apart + *lyein* loose⟩

di·am·e·ter [daɪˈæmətər] *n* **1** a straight line passing from one side to the other through the centre of a circle, sphere, etc. **2** *Optics* a unit measuring the magnifying power of a lens. ⟨Greek *dia-* across + *metron* measure⟩ **di·a·met·ric** *adj* **1** of or along a diameter. **2** of opposites, direct; exact. **di·a·met·ri·cal·ly** *adv.*

di·a·mond [ˈdaɪmənd] *or* [ˈdaɪəmənd] *n* **1** a precious stone, pure carbon in crystal form. It is the hardest substance known and is also used for cutting. **2** a plane figure shaped like this ♦. **3** a playing card bearing this figure. **4** *Baseball* the space inside the lines that connect the bases. ⟨Old French *diamant;* Latin *diamantis,* alteration of *adamantis* adamant⟩

diamond in the rough a person with good character but poor manners.

dia·mond·back *n* **1** a large, very dangerous rattlesnake with diamond-shaped markings. **2** in full, **diamondback terrapin** an edible turtle having a shell marked with diamond shapes. **3** a moth with wings that fold into a diamond shape. **diamond willow ✻** willow wood with a diamond-patterned grain.

di·a·per [ˈdaɪpər] *or* [ˈdaɪəpər] *n* a thick pad of cloth or other absorbent material, used as underpants for a baby.

v put a diaper on (a baby). ⟨Old French *diapre,* Greek *diaspros; dia-* thorough + *aspros* white⟩

di·aph·a·nous [daɪˈæfənəs] *adj* **1** Usually of fabric, light and transparent; gauzy. **2** vague. ⟨Greek *dia-* through + *phainein* show⟩

di·a·phragm [ˈdaɪəˌfræm] *n* **1** a partition of muscle separating the chest and abdomen. **2** a thin partition in some animals and plants. **3** a thin disk or cone that vibrates rapidly, used in sound equipment. **4** a device that controls the light entering a camera or optical instrument. **5** a contraceptive device for women, consisting of a flexible, moulded cap fitting over the entrance to the uterus. ⟨Greek *dia-* across + *phragma* fence⟩

di·ar·rhe·a or **di·ar·rhoe·a** [ˌdaɪəˈriə] *n* the condition of having too many and too loose movements of the bowels. **di·ar·rhe·al** *adj.* ⟨Greek *diarrhoia; dia-* through + *rheein* flow⟩

di·a·ry [ˈdaɪəri] *or* [ˈdaɪri] *n* **1** an account of what one has done, thought, etc. during each day. **2** a book for keeping such an account. **di·a·rist** *n.* ⟨Latin *diarium; dies* day⟩

Di·as·po·ra [daɪˈæspərə] *n* **1** the scattering of the Jews after their captivity in Babylon. **2** diaspora any community whose members are scattered. ⟨Greek = a thorough sowing⟩

di·as·to·le [daɪˈæstəli] *n* the normal, rhythmic dilation of the heart. Compare SYSTOLE. **di·as·tol·ic** [ˌdaɪəˈstɒlɪk] *adj.* ⟨Greek = expansion; *dia-* apart + *stellein* send⟩.

diastolic pressure blood pressure measured when the heart is refilling after pumping blood, hence lower than SYSTOLIC PRESSURE.

di·a·tom [ˈdaɪəˌtɒm] *n* any of numerous unicellular, aquatic algae with hard shells. ⟨Greek *dia* through; in half + *tome* a cutting⟩ **di·a·to·ma·ceous** [ˌdaɪətəˈmeɪʃəs] *adj* **1** to do with diatoms. **2** consisting of their fossil remains: *diatomaceous earth.*

di·a·ton·ic [ˌdaɪəˈtɒnɪk] *adj Music* of or using only the eight tones of a standard major or minor scale. ⟨Greek *dia-* through + *tonos* tone⟩

di·a·tribe [ˈdaɪəˌtraɪb] *n* a bitter and violent denunciation. ⟨Greek *diatribē* pastime, study, discourse; *dia-* away + *tribein* wear⟩

di·a·ze·pam [daɪˈæzəˌpæm] *n* a drug used to relieve anxiety; a minor tranquillizer.

di·az·i·non [daɪˈæzəˌnɒn] *n* an insecticide often used on fruit trees.

dibs [dɪbz] *n pl Informal* **1** a prior claim to a desired object: *I have first dibs on the ice cream.* **2** one's share (of profits, etc.). ⟨origin uncertain⟩

dice [dəɪs] *n pl* of **die³ 1** small cubes used in games, with a different number of spots (one to six), or occasionally some other mark, on each side. **2** a game of chance played with such cubes (with sg verb).
v **1** play dice; throw or gamble with dice. **2** take serious risks: *dicing with death.* **3** cut into small cubes: *to dice carrots.* **dic·er** *n.*
load the dice *Informal* decide the outcome unfairly in advance. **no dice** *Slang* **a** no (in answer to a request). **b** total lack of success. **dic·ey** *adj Informal* risky; uncertain.

di·chot·o·my [dəɪ'kɒtəmi] *n* **1** a division into two opposed categories: *the dichotomy of living and non-living things.* **2** a sharp contrast or polarizing distinction. **3** *Biology* repeated branching into two parts. **di·chot·o·mize** *v.* **di·chot·o·mous** *adj.* ⟨Greek *dicha* in two + *tome* a cutting⟩

dick·ens [ˈdɪkənz] *n, interj Informal* devil.

Dick·en·si·an [dɪˈkɛnziən] *adj* of Charles Dickens, 19c English novelist, or his style.

dick·er [ˈdɪkər] *v* engage in petty bargaining. ⟨*dicker*, n, earlier, a lot of ten hides⟩

dick·ey¹ [ˈdɪki] *n* a false shirt or blouse front. Also, **dickie, dicky.** ⟨*Dick*, proper name⟩

dick·ey² [ˈdɪki] *n* ✱ a long, hooded outer pullover made of duffel or skins; parka; ATIGI. Also, **dick·ie, dick·y.** ⟨Inuktitut *atigi*⟩

di·cot·y·le·don [ˌdaɪkɒtəˈlidən] *n Botany* any flowering plant having two seed leaves (cotyledons) in the embryo. Compare MONOCOTYLEDON. **di·cot·y·le·don·ous** *adj.*

dic·ta [ˈdɪktə] *n* a pl of DICTUM.

dic·tate [ˈdɪkteit] *or* [dɪkˈteit] *v* **1** say aloud for another person to write: *to dictate a letter, to dictate spelling words.* **2** give orders: *No one is going to dictate to me.*
n a direction that is to be obeyed: *to follow the dictates of one's conscience.* **dic·ta·tion** *n.* ⟨Latin *dictare* say often; *dicere* tell, say⟩
dic·ta·tor *n* **1** a totalitarian ruler. **2** a person whose authority is accepted: *a dictator of men's fashions.* **3** one who dictates words for another to record. **dic·ta·to·ri·al** [ˌdɪktəˈtɔriəl] *adj* **1** totalitarian. **2** overbearing: *a dictatorial tone.* **dic·ta·tor·ship** [dɪkˈteitərˌʃɪp] *n.* **dic·tion** *n* **1** style of speaking or writing, esp in regard to choice of words. **2** enunciation in speaking or singing: *clear diction.* **dic·tion·ar·y** *n* **1** a book of words arranged alphabetically, with information about their meanings, forms, pronunciation, and history. **2** a similar reference work but limited to a special field or using some other arrangement, e.g., a thematic arrangement, labelled pictures, etc.: *a law dictionary, a plant dictionary.* **3** a book of any of these kinds, giving equivalent words in another language: *a French-English dictionary.* **dic·tum** *n, pl* **-tums** or **-ta** [-tə] **1** a formal, authoritative comment or judgment: *the dictums of literary critics.* **2** maxim; saying.

did [dɪd] *v* pt of DO¹.
did·n't [ˈdɪdənt] contraction of *did not.*

di·dac·tic [daɪˈdæktɪk] *or* [dɪˈdæktɪk] *adj* **1** intended to instruct: *The fables of Aesop are didactic stories.* **2** inclined to instruct others: *He was called "Professor" because of his didactic manner.* **di·dac·ti·cal·ly** *adv.* **di·dac·ti·cism** *n.* ⟨Greek *didaktikos; didaskein* teach⟩

did·dle [ˈdɪdəl] *v Informal* **1** swindle. **2** waste time. **3** fiddle or fool (*with*). ⟨origin uncertain⟩
did·dly *n* DIDDLY-SQUAT. *adj Informal* **1** fiddly. **2** trivial. **did·dly–squat** *Slang* nothing at all.

die¹ [daɪ] *v* **died, dy·ing 1** stop living; become dead. **2** lose force or strength; cease to exist or function. **3** *Informal* (in progressive) want very much: *I'm dying to meet her.* **4** suffer great agony: *to die of shame.* ⟨Old English *díegan*⟩
die away stop or end little by little: *The music died away.* **die down** grow less; subside. **die hard** resist to the very end. **die–hard** *adj, n.* **die off** die one by one until all are dead: *The whole herd of cattle died off in the epidemic.* **die out a** die away. **b** die off. **die to** cease to care about; become insensitive to: *to die to worldly pleasure.* **to die for** *Informal* superlatively good: *cheesecake to die for.*
die·back *n* any disease of trees or bushes that kills the twigs and tips of branches first and spreads back from there.

die² [daɪ] *n* **1** a tool or device for shaping or cutting things by stamping or punching. **2** a mould for shaping things . ⟨*die³*⟩
die–cast *v* shape out of metal by pouring it molten into a mould (die).

die³ [daɪ] *n* sg of DICE. ⟨Old French *de;* Latin *datum* given (i.e., by fortune), pp of *dare* give⟩
the die is cast the decision has been made and cannot be changed.

dief·fen·bach·ia [ˌdifənˈbækiə] *or* [-ˈbɑxiə] *n* a tropical plant of the arum family with large, glossy, poisonous leaves. ⟨E. Dieffenbach 19c German botanist⟩

di·e·lec·tric [ˌdaɪɪˈlektrɪk] *adj* not conducting electricity. **di·e·lec·tric** *n.*

di·er·e·sis or **di·aer·e·sis** [daɪˈɛrəsɪs] *or* [ˌdaɪəˈrɪsɪs] *n, pl* **-ses** [-siz] two dots (¨) placed over the second of two consecutive vowels to indicate that it is to be pronounced as a separate syllable. *Example: naïve.* ⟨Greek *diairesis* separation; *dia-* apart + *haireein* take⟩

die·sel [ˈdizəl] *or* [ˈdisəl] *n* a vehicle powered by a **diesel engine,** an internal-combustion engine that burns fuel oil ignited by the heat from compressed air. **die·sel** *adj.* **die·sel·ize** *v.* ⟨R. Diesel (1858-1913), its inventor⟩
diesel oil a light fuel oil.

di·et¹ [ˈdaɪət] *v* **1** the usual food and drink for a person or animal. **2** a special selection of food and drink eaten for health reasons or in an attempt to lose or gain weight.
v eat special food and drink, especially to lose weight. **di·e·tar·y** *adj.* **di·et·er** *n.* ⟨Greek *diaita* way of life⟩
di·e·tet·ic *adj* to do with diet or a particular diet. **di·e·tet·ics** *n* the science that deals with

the amount and kinds of food needed by the body (with sg verb). **di·e·ti·tian** or **di·e·ti·cian** *n* a person trained to plan meals with the proper proportion of various kinds of food.

di·et² ['daɪət] *n* a formal assembly. ⟨Latin *dieta* day's work, council session; same source as *diet¹* but influenced by *dies* day⟩

dif·fer ['dɪfər] *v* **1** be unlike (also with *from*). **2** disagree (also with *with*). ⟨Latin *differre* set apart; *dis-* apart + *ferre* carry⟩ **dif·fer·ence** ['dɪfrəns] *n* **1** the condition of being unlike. **2** a particular feature or point in which things are unlike: *I see several differences.* **3** what is left after subtracting one number from another. **4** disagreement. **make a difference a** matter; be important; have an effect or influence. **b** give or show different treatment; show partiality. **make all the difference** be the critical factor. **same difference** *Slang* it makes no difference. **split the difference a** divide what is left in half. **b** meet halfway; compromise. **what's the difference?** it doesn't matter. **dif·fer·ent** *adj* **1** not alike. **2** separate: *I went three different times.* **3** unusual. **4** miscellaneous; various: *talking about different things.* **dif·fer·ent·ly** *adv.* **differently–abled** *adj* alternative term for 'disabled', intended to connote appreciation for diversity and the competence of people with disabilities. **dif·fer·en·tial** [ˌdɪfəˈrenʃəl] *adj* **1** varying according to circumstances: *differential rates, charges, etc.* **2** contrastive; distinguishing. **3** *Physics, mechanics* to do with the difference of two or more forces. *n* **1** *Mathematics* **a** an infinitesimal difference between consecutive values of a variable quantity. **b** a function in which this difference varies with some other variable. **2** in a motor vehicle, an arrangement of gears that allows one of the rear wheels to turn faster than the other. **3** *Statistics* a derivative of a function times the increase in the independent variable. **dif·fer·en·tial·ly** *adv.* **differential calculus** the branch of calculus dealing with differentials and their relations. **dif·fer·en·ti·ate** *v* **1** make or constitute a difference: *What differentiates real kindness from mere politeness?* **2** discriminate: *It was almost impossible to differentiate between the twins.* **3** make or become different: *The words* metal *and* mettle *have the same origin but have differentiated over the centuries.* **4** *Mathematics* find the derivative of. **5** *Biology* become different or specialized: *The cells of an embryo differentiate into organs and parts as it grows.* **dif·fer·en·ti·a·tion** *n.* **dif·fer·en·ti·a·tor** *n* .

Different. In formal English, the standard expression is *different from*; informal usage is divided, sometimes using *different than.* The latter is especially common when the object is a clause: *The house was a good deal different than* (= *from how*) *he remembered it.*

dif·fi·cult ['dɪfəˌkʌlt] *adj* **1** hard to do, solve, or understand: *a difficult problem.* **2** hard to get along with: *Don't be difficult.* ⟨Latin *difficultas* from *difficilis; dis-* not + *facilis* easy⟩

dif·fi·cul·ty *n* **1** the fact or degree of being difficult: *the difficulty of a job.* **2** much effort. **3** trouble. **4** a difficult thing; problem. **in difficulties** in (usually financial) trouble. **make difficulties** cause trouble.

dif·fi·dent ['dɪfədənt] *adj* unassertive; timid or shy; tentative. **dif·fi·dence** *n.* ⟨Latin *diffidens* ppr of *diffidere; dis-* + *fidere* trust⟩

dif·frac·tion [dɪˈfrækʃən] *n Physics* **1** the breaking up of a ray of light into a series of bands. **2** a similar breaking up of sound waves, electricity, etc. **dif·fract** *v.* ⟨Latin *diffractus* pp of *diffringere; dis-* + *frangere* break⟩

dif·fuse [dɪˈfjuz] *v* **1** scatter widely; disperse. **2** *Physics* mix by spreading into one another, with the molecules moving but keeping their structure. *adj* [-ˈfjus] **1** spread out: *diffuse light.* **2** wordy: *a diffuse writer.* **dif·fu·sion** *n.* ⟨Latin *diffusus* pp of *diffundere; dis-* + *fundere* pour⟩

dig [dɪg] *v* **dug** or *(archaic)* **digged, dig·ging 1** use a spade, hands, claws, etc., to make a hole or passage, or to turn over soil, snow, or other material. **2** get by digging: *to dig clams.* **3** make a thorough search: *digging through one's pockets, digging for information.* **4** jab: *The rider dug her spurs into the horse's side.* **5** *Slang* **a** understand. **b** appreciate: *I dig the way she talks.* **c** observe; notice: *Dig that car!* *n* **1** an archaeological excavation. **2** a jab: *a dig in the ribs.* **3** a sarcastic remark: *She made several nasty little digs about their escapade.* ⟨Middle English *dygge(n)*⟩ **dig in a** begin a meal or job with gusto. **b** make a protective trench. **c** secure one's position: *He's really dug in at the factory.* **dig into** *Informal* work hard at or partake heartily of. **dig up a** unearth. **b** excavate: *They've dug up the whole field.* **c** find out by active inquiry. **dig·ger** *n* **1** any tool for digging. **2** Usually, **Digger** *Informal* an Australian or New Zealander. **3 Digger** a member of any of the Western American peoples who dug roots for food.

Dig·by chicken ['dɪgbi ♣ a small, smoke-cured herring. ⟨*Digby*, Nova Scotia⟩

di·gest [daɪˈdʒɛst] or [dɪˈdʒɛst] *v* **1** change (food) in the stomach, etc., so that it can be absorbed into the body as nourishment. **2** understand and absorb mentally: *to digest new ideas.* **3** summarize. *n* ['daɪdʒɛst] **1** a summary. **2** a periodical, etc., containing a collection of condensed versions: *a book-review digest.* **di·gest·i·ble** *adj.* **di·ges·tion** *n.* ⟨Latin *digestus* pp of *digerere* separate, dissolve; *dis-* apart + *gerere* carry⟩ **di·ges·tif** [diʒɛˈstif] *n* an after-dinner liqueur. **di·ges·tive** *adj* **1** to do with digestion: *digestive juices in the stomach.* **2** aiding digestion: *a digestive biscuit. n* an aid to digestion.

dig·it ['dɪdʒɪt] *n* **1** a finger or toe. **2** any of the figures 1, 2, 3, 4, 5, 6, 7, 8, 9, and 0, esp as occupying a place in a number. ⟨Latin *digitus* finger⟩ **dig·it·al** ['dɪdʒətəl] *adj* **1** to do with the recording and processing of information in the form of binary digits. **2** to do with fingers or toes. **3** to do with numerals; of a clock, meter, etc. having no dial or hands but giving information only by means of numerals, generally in a liquid-crystal display. *n* **1** a finger. **2** a key on a keyboard (of an organ, piano, etc.). **dig·it·al·ly** *adv.* **digital audio tape** a cassette tape containing digitally recorded sound. *Abbrev* **DAT**. **digital computer** a computer that processes data as binary digits. Compare ANALOGUE COMPUTER. **dig·i·tal·is** [ˌdɪdʒəˈtælɪs] *n* a drug used to stimulate the heart, obtained from the purple foxglove (*Digitalis purpurea*). **dig·i·tize** put (images, sounds, or other data) into digital form. **dig·i·ti·za·tion** *n.* **dig·i·tiz·er** *n.*

dig·ni·ty [ˈdɪgnəti] *n* **1** a manner, character, rank, etc. that commands respect or shows self-respect: *She had great dignity of bearing.* **2** true worth or nobility: *the dignity of labour.* ⟨Latin *dignitas; dignus* worthy⟩
beneath one's dignity too low or humble, or not noble enough, for one: *She says washing floors is beneath her dignity.*
dig·ni·fied *adj* full of dignity; commanding or showing respect; solemn. **dig·ni·fy** *v* **1** give dignity to: *The little house was dignified by the great elms around it.* **2** give undue dignity to: *Don't dignify that question with an answer. This is just liver dignified by a French name.* **dig·ni·tar·y** *n* a person in a position of honour.

dig·ox·in [dɪˈdʒɒksən] *n* a preparation of digitalis used to treat congestive heart failure.

di·graph [ˈdaɪɡræf] *n* two letters which together spell one sound, such as *sh* in *shop.* Compare LIGATURE def. 5. **di·graph·ic** *adj.* ⟨*di-* double + Greek *graphē* a writing⟩

di·gress [daɪˈgrɛs] *v* **1** get off the main topic in talking or writing. **2** swerve. **di·gres·sion** *n* **di·gres·sive** *adj.* ⟨Latin *digressus* pp of *digredi; dis-* aside + *gradi* to step⟩

Dijon mustard [diˈʒɒn] *French* [diˈʒɔ̃] a good quality mustard containing white wine, originally made in Dijon, France.

dike [daɪk] *n* **1** a dam or wall built as a defence against flooding. **2** a channel for water. **3** a low wall of earth or stone for defence. **4** causeway.
v **1** provide with a dike or dikes. **2** drain with a ditch or channel for water. Also, **dyke**. ⟨Old Norse *dik*⟩

di·lap·i·date [dɪˈlæpəˌdeɪt] *v* fall into ruin by neglect. **di·lap·i·dat·ed** *adj.* **di·lap·i·da·tion** *n.* ⟨Latin *dilapidare* take apart stone by stone; *di-* apart + *lapis* stone⟩

di·late [daɪˈleɪt] *or* [ˈdaɪleɪt] *v* **1** make or become larger or wider: *The pupils of the eyes dilate when the light is dim.* **2** speak or write in detail: *to dilate upon a subject.* **di·lat·ed** *adj.* **di·la·tion** *n.* ⟨Latin *dis-* apart + *latus* wide⟩
dil·a·ta·tion [ˌdaɪləˈteɪʃən] *or* [ˌdɪləˈteɪʃən] *n* an enlargement; stretched condition. **dilatation and curettage** a medical procedure in which the walls of the uterus scraped to remove tissue. *Abbrev* **D and C**. **di·la·tor** *n* **1** a muscle that dilates some part of the body. **2** a

surgical instrument for dilating wounds, canals of the body, etc.

dil·a·to·ry [ˈdɪləˌtɔri] *adj* **1** tending to delay; not prompt. **2** causing delay. **dil·a·to·ri·ly** *adv.* **dil·a·to·ri·ness** *n.* ⟨Latin *dilatus* pp of *differre* defer, delay. See DIFFER.⟩

dil·do [ˈdɪldou] *n* a device shaped like an erect penis, used for sexual stimulation. ⟨origin unknown⟩

di·lem·ma [dɪˈlɛmə] *n* **1** a difficult choice: *Give up the trip or miss the wedding: what a dilemma!* **2** any very problematic situation. ⟨Greek *dilemma < di-* two + *lemma* premise⟩

dil·et·tan·te [ˌdɪləˈtɑnt] *or* [ˈdɪləˌtɑnt] *n, pl* **-tes** [-tiz] *or* **-ti** [-ti] *n* one whose interest in an art or other subject is just for amusement; dabbler. **dil·et·tan·te** *adj.* **dil·et·tant·ism** *n.* ⟨Italian *dilettare*, Latin *delectare*. See DELIGHT.⟩

dil·i·gence [ˈdɪlədʒəns] *n* careful effort; the will to work hard and steadily: *Her diligence was rewarded with high marks.* **dil·i·gent** *adj.* ⟨Latin *diligens* ppr of *diligere* value highly, love; *dis-* apart + *legere* choose⟩

dill [dɪl] *n* a herb of the parsley family whose leaves and seeds are used to flavour soups, pickles, etc. ⟨Old English *dile*⟩
dill pickle a pickle flavoured with dill.

dil·ly [ˈdɪli] *n Slang* an extraordinary person or thing. ⟨apparently < *de*lightful + *-y²*⟩

dil·ly–dal·ly [ˈdɪli ˌdæli] *v* waste time; loiter; fool around. ⟨reduplication of *dally*⟩

di·lute [dɪˈlut] *or* [daɪˈlut] *v* **1** make weaker by adding water or other liquid. **2** lessen the force, effect, or high quality of.
adj **1** diluted. **2** present only in solution, esp a weak solution: *a dilute acid.* **di·lut·ed** *adj.* **di·lu·tion** *n.* ⟨Latin *dilutus* pp of *diluere; dis-* apart + *luere* wash⟩
dil·u·ent *adj* used to dilute. **dil·u·ent** *n.*

di·lu·vi·al [dɪˈluviəl] *or* [daɪˈluviəl] *adj* **1** to do with a flood. **2** made up of debris left by a flood or glacier. ⟨Latin *diluvium*. See DELUGE.⟩

dim [dɪm] *adj* **dim·mer**, **dim·mest 1** not bright: *a dim light.* **2** vague; not distinct or clear: *dim memories.* **3** not promising: *Her future looks dim.* **4** *Informal* stupid; slow. **dim, dimmed, dim·ming** *v.* **dim·ly** *adv.* **dim·ness** *n.* ⟨Old English *dimm*⟩
take a dim view of look on with disfavour: *He takes a dim view of practical jokes.*
dim·mer *n* a device for dimming an electric light. **dim·wit** *n Informal* a stupid person.

dime [daɪm] *n* a ten-cent coin of Canada or the US. ⟨Old French *disme*, Latin *decima* tenth; *decem* ten⟩
a dime a dozen *Informal* cheap and plentiful. **on a dime** precisely: *to stop on a dime.*
dime store a store selling a variety of articles in a low price range.

di·men·sion [dɪˈmɛnʃən] *or* [daɪˈmɛnʃən] *n* **1** a measure of length, width, or thickness. **2** size; extent: *a project of huge dimensions.* **3** element or factor: *to add a new dimension to one's character.* **4** *Mathematics* a property of length, area, and volume. A figure with length only (a line) has one dimension; a figure with area (e.g., a rectangle) has two dimensions ; a figure with volume (e.g., a cube) has three dimensions. **5** *Physics* any basic quantity, such as distance, time, mass, through which one can define all others. **di·men·sion·al** *adj.* **di·men·sion·al·ly** *adv.* **di·men·sion·al·i·ty** *n.* ⟨Latin *dimensio; dis-* out + *mensura* measure⟩

di·min·ish [dɪ'mɪnɪʃ] *v* **1** make or become less, esp gradually: *measures to diminish the safety risk, diminishing strength.* **2** *Music* reduce (a major or minor interval) by a half-tone. **3** *Architecture* taper. **di·min·ish·ing** *adj.* **di·min·ish·ment** *n.* ⟨blend of *diminue* (Latin *dis-* + *minuere* lessen) and *minish* (Old French *menuisier* make small; Latin *minutus* small)⟩
diminished chord *Music* a chord including a diminished interval. **law of diminishing returns** the principle that after a given point, the same or increased input or effort tends to produce smaller and smaller results.

di·min·u·en·do [dɪˌmɪnju'ɛndou] *n Music* a gradual decrease of volume. ⟨Italian = diminishing⟩

dim·i·nu·tion [ˌdɪmə'njuʃən] *or* [-'nuʃən] *n* reduction; decrease. ⟨Latin *diminutio*⟩
di·min·u·tive [dɪ'mɪnjətɪv] *adj* very small. *n Grammar* a word or affix, such as *-let* in English, meaning 'small'. **di·min·u·tive·ness** *n.* ⟨Latin *diminutus* pp of *diminuere* lessen⟩

dim·ple ['dɪmpəl] *n* **1** a small hollow in the surface of a plump part of the body, such as in the cheek. **2** any small depression or dent. *v* **1** make dimples in: *Rain dimpled the surface of the pond.* **2** form dimples: *Her cheek dimples when she smiles.* ⟨Middle English *dympull*⟩

dim sum ['dɪm 'sʊm] Chinese food consisting of a variety of dishes served in small portions, often small, steamed dumplings with a variety of fillings.

din [dɪn] *n* a loud, prolonged noise. *v* **1** make a din. **2** teach by saying over and over (with *into*): *The importance of honesty was dinned into us from infancy.* ⟨Old English *dynn*⟩

dine [daɪn] *v* eat dinner. ⟨Old French *disner;* Latin *disjejunare* to breakfast; *dis-* + *jejunium* fast[2]⟩
dine out eat dinner away from home.
din·er *n* **1** a person who is eating dinner. **2** a small eating place, usually near a highway. **di·nette (set)** *n* a set of chairs and a table for a small dining room or kitchen. **dining car** a railway car in which meals are served. **dining room** a room in which meals are served.

ding [dɪŋ] *v* **1** make a light ringing sound. **2** *Informal* damage by striking; dent. **ding** *n.* ⟨imitative⟩
ding–a–ling ['dɪŋ ə ˌlɪŋ] *n* **1** a tinkling or jangling sound. **2** *Slang* nitwit. **ding–dong** *n* **1** the sound of a swinging bell or a doorbell. **2** *Slang* nitwit.

ding·bat ['dɪŋˌbæt] *n* **1** *Slang* a stupid, silly, or crazy person. **2** any of the characters or symbols in a particular font (**Dingbats**) consisting entirely of such. ⟨origin uncertain⟩

din·ghy ['dɪŋi] *or* ['dɪŋgi] *n* a small boat. ⟨Hindi *dingi*⟩

din·go ['dɪŋgou] *n, pl* **-goes** a wild dog of Australia. ⟨native Australian name⟩

din·gy ['dɪndʒi] *adj* shabby, poorly lit, and dirty-looking; not bright, fresh, and clean. **din·gi·ly** *adv.* **din·gi·ness** *n.* ⟨origin uncertain⟩

dink·y ['dɪŋki] *adj Slang* small. ⟨Scottish or N English dial. *dink* trim + *-y*[2]⟩

din·ner ['dɪnər] *n* **1** the noon or evening meal, usually whichever is largest. **2** a formal social event including dinner: *They're going to a charity dinner.* **dinner jacket** TUXEDO (def. 1). **dinner theatre 1** a dinner with a dramatic performance presented during or after the meal. **2** an establishment that offers this. **din·ner·time** *n* the time at which dinner is eaten. **din·ner·ware** *n* plates, serving dishes, etc. used at dinner.

di·no·saur ['daɪnəˌsɔr] *n* **1** any of a group of extinct reptiles of the Mesozoic era. **2** a very old-fashioned person or thing. ⟨Greek *deinos* terrible + *sauros* lizard⟩

dint [dɪnt] *n* a dent, esp a small one. **dint** *v.* ⟨Old English *dynt*⟩
by dint of by means of (some action): *by dint of hard work.*

di·o·cese ['daɪəˌsis], ['daɪəsɪs], *or* ['daɪəˌsiz] *n* the district over which a Christian bishop has authority. **di·oc·e·san** *adj.* ⟨Greek *dioikēsis* province; *oikeein* inhabit⟩

di·ode ['daɪoud] *n* an electronic component consisting of a semiconductor and two attached electrodes, used mainly to convert alternating current to direct current. Also called **semiconductor diode.** ⟨*di-* + electro*de*⟩

di·o·ram·a [ˌdaɪə'ræmə] *n* a 3-D scene to be viewed through a peephole. **di·o·ram·ic** *adj.* ⟨Greek *dia-* through + *horama* sight⟩

di·ox·ide [daɪ'ɒksaɪd] *n Chemistry* an oxide with two atoms of oxygen per molecule.

di·ox·in [daɪ'ɒksən] *n* any of a family of aromatic hydrocarbons, some highly toxic, produced as industrial by-products in the manufacture of chlorinated phenols.

dip [dɪp] *v* **dipped, dip·ping 1** put or go into a liquid, esp just under the surface, and take or come quickly out again: *I dipped my hand into the pool.* **2** immerse (an animal) in disinfectant. **3** put (one's hand, a spoon, etc.) in and take something out: *to dip into a sugar bowl.* **4** take a small amount from (with *into*): *to dip into one's savings.* **5** lower and raise again quickly: *to dip a flag as a salute.* **6** go down slightly or briefly: *The road dips after the bridge. Production dipped last month.*
n **1** a short swim. **2** a sudden short drop. **3** a creamy mixture eaten by dipping into it with a raw vegetable, potato chip, etc. **4** an ice cream cone dipped in melted chocolate. **5** liquid disinfectant for dipping animals: *sheep dip.* **6** any act of dipping. **7** *Slang* an idiot or odd person. ⟨Old English *dyppan*⟩
dip·per *n* **1** a deep, long-handled utensil for dipping liquids. **2** any of a genus of diving

birds that feed on insects, etc. in fast-flowing streams. **dippy** *Slang adj* foolish; silly. **dip·stick** *n* **1** a rod for measuring the level of liquid in a container, esp oil in an engine. **2** *Slang* DIP (def. 7).

diph·the·ri·a [dɪf'θiriə] *or* [dɪp'θiriə] *n* an acute, infectious disease of the throat, usually accompanied by the formation of membranes that hinder breathing. ⟨Greek *diphthera* hide, leather; for the membranes⟩

diph·thong ['dɪfθɒŋ] *or* ['dɪpθɒŋ] *n* a vowel sound made up of two identifiable vowel sounds produced in one syllable, as the *i* [aɪ] in *die*. **diph·thon·gal** [-'θɒŋgəl] *or* [-'θɒŋəl] *adj*. **diph·thong·ize** *v.* ⟨Greek *di-* double + *phthongos* sound⟩

di·plod·o·cus [dɪ'plɒdəkəs] *n* a plant-eating dinosaur of North America. ⟨Greek *diploos* twofold + *dokos* supporting beam. Coined by O.C. Marsh, 19c US paleontologist.⟩

dip·loid ['dɪplɔɪd] *adj* double; twofold. *n* a diploid nucleus, cell, or organism. Compare HAPLOID. ⟨Greek *diploos* double⟩

di·plo·ma [də'ploumə] *n* a certificate given by a school, college, or university to its graduating students. ⟨Greek *diplōma* paper folded double; *diploos* double⟩ **diploma mill** a non-accredited establishment which grants diplomas of little value.

dip·lo·mat ['dɪplə,mæt] *n* **1** an official representative of one nation, stationed in another. **2** a person of great tact, skill in negotiating, etc. **di·plo·ma·cy** [də'plouməsi] *n*. **dip·lo·mat·ic** *adj*. **dip·lo·mat·i·cal·ly** *adv*. ⟨See DIPLOMA.⟩ **diplomatic corps** all of the diplomats of foreign nations stationed in a given capital. **diplomatic immunity** special privileges for diplomats, their families and staffs, such as freedom from arrest, search, and taxation, granted by international agreement.

di·pole ['daɪ,poul] *n* **1** two opposite, equal electric charges or magnetic poles separated by a small distance. **2** a molecule in which the centres of positive and negative charge are separated. **3** in full, **dipole antenna**, a radio or television antenna consisting of a straight metal rod divided so as to form a lozenge shape at the centre. **di·po·lar** *adj*.

dip·so·ma·ni·a [,dɪpsə'meiniə] *n* an abnormal craving for alcohol. **dip·so·ma·ni·ac** *n.* ⟨Greek *dipsa* thirst + *mania* mania⟩

dip·tych ['dɪptɪk] *n* **1** an ancient writing tablet with two halves hinged together along one side like a book, their inner surfaces waxed for writing on with a stylus. **2** a pair of paintings or carvings on two hinged panels. ⟨Greek *di-* twice + *ptychē* fold⟩

dire [daɪr] *adj* **1** dreadful; terrible: *dire threats.* **2** desperate; extreme: *in dire need.* **dire·ly** *adv*. **dire·ness** *n.* ⟨Latin *dirus*⟩

di·rect [dɪ'rɛkt] *or* [daɪ'rɛkt] *v* **1** manage; guide; give leadership to: *Who is directing this operation?* **2** plan, guide, conduct rehearsals for, and otherwise take artistic responsibility for (a play, opera, film, etc.). **3** tell (to do

something): *The captain directed the men to advance.* **4** tell or show the way: *Can you direct me to the mall?* **5** aim or send: *to direct a stream of water at something.* **6** address (words): *That remark was directed at me.* *adj* **1** straight: *a direct route.* **2** exact: *direct opposites.* **3** by an unbroken line of descent: *a direct descendant of the queen.* **4** immediate: *direct action.* **5** straightforward: *a direct answer.* **di·rec·tion** *n*. **di·rect·ly** *adv*. **di·rect·ness** *n*. **di·rec·tor** *n.* ⟨Latin *directus* pp of *dirigere*; *dis-* apart + *regere* guide⟩

direct access RANDOM ACCESS. **direct current** a steady electric current that flows in one direction. *Abbrev* **DC**. **direct discourse** discourse in which the exact words of a speaker are quoted. *Example: "I'll think it over,"* *he replied.* Compare INDIRECT DISCOURSE. **di·rec·tion** *n* **1** the place or part of space toward which a thing faces, points, or moves, or from which it comes. **2** a line of action, tendency, etc.: *if things should continue to develop in this direction.* **3 directions** *pl* instructions, usually for using a product or reaching a place. **4** the act or process of directing. **di·rec·tion·al** *adj Radio* fitted for determining the direction of origin of signals, or for sending signals in one direction only. **di·rec·tive** *n* an order. **direct mail** advertising sent directly to large numbers of people at their home or business addresses. **direct object** *Grammar* the word or words naming the thing directly undergoing the action. In *The car struck me*, *me* is the direct object. Compare INDIRECT OBJECT. **di·rec·tor·ate** *n* **1** the position of a director. **2** a group of directors. **di·rec·to·ri·al** *adj* having to do with a director or directorate. **director's chair** a folding chair with a canvas back and seat, of the kind used by a film director on the set. **di·rec·to·ry** *n* **1** a list of names and addresses, phone numbers, etc.: *a copy of the school directory.* **2** *Computers* an index, with multiple levels of organization, of stored files. **direct question** a question quoted directly and enclosed in quotation marks. *Example: She asked, "Who is it?"* Compare INDIRECT QUESTION. **direct tax** a tax which the government collects directly, such as income tax.

SYNONYMS

Direct = going straight from one to another in an unbroken line, though there may be many steps between: *Overwork and stress were the direct cause of her death.* **Immediate** = going from one thing to the next, without anything between: *A heart attack was the immediate cause of her death.*

dirge [dɜrdʒ] *n* **1** a song of lamentation for a person's death. **2** any slow, sad, solemn song, tune, or poem. ⟨contraction of Latin *dirige* direct, first word in mass for the dead⟩

dir·i·gi·ble [dɪ'rɪdʒəbəl] *or* ['dirədʒəbəl] *n* an aircraft kept aloft by a long, inflated hull with a steering and propelling mechanism underneath; airship. *adj* that can be steered. ⟨Latin *dirigere* direct⟩

dirn·dl ['dɜrndəl] *n* **1** an Alpine peasant

woman's costume consisting of a blouse, a tight, laced bodice, and a full skirt gathered at the waist. **2** a dress imitating this design. ⟨German dialect = girl; *Dirne* maid⟩

dirt [dɜrt] *n* **1** mud, dust, earth, loose soil, etc. **2** grime, stains, marks left by spills, etc.; whatever makes a thing not clean. **3** lewd or obscene words or thoughts. **4** nastiness or corruption. **5** *Informal* **a** news; information. **b** malicious gossip: *to dig up dirt on someone.* ⟨Old Norse *drit* excrement⟩
eat dirt submit to a humiliating experience. **treat like dirt** treat with contempt.
dirt bike a small motorcycle for off-road use. **dirt–cheap** *adj* very cheap. **dirt–poor** *adj* lacking basic necessities; extremely poor. **dirt·y** *adj* **1** soiled by dirt. **2** that makes dirty: *a dirty job.* **3** unpleasant: *dirty weather.* **4** low; mean: *a dirty trick.* **5** obscene: *a dirty joke.* **6** cheating; unsporting: *dirty tactics. adv* in a dirty way: *to talk dirty. v* make or become dirty. **dirt·i·ness** *n.* **dirty end of the stick** the hardest share of the work. **do the dirty on someone** or **do someone dirty** treat someone unfairly. **dirty linen** or **laundry** embarrassing private matters. **air** (or **hang** or **wash**) **one's dirty linen in public** make a public spectacle of family quarrels, etc. **dirty look** an angry or threatening look. **dirty pool** mean, dishonest, or unfair conduct. **dirty word 1** an obscene or other taboo word. **2** a word for something unacceptable: *Homework is a dirty word here.* **dirty work** tasks consisting of hard, unpleasant, or illicit activity: *The drug lord lets others do his dirty work.* **Dirty Thirties** the 1930s, years of drought and depression.

dis or **diss** [dɪs] *v* **dissed, dis·sing** *Slang* show disrespect or contempt for. ⟨*disrespect*⟩

dis– *prefix* **1** the opposite of; not: *discontent.* **2** undo an action: *disentangle.* Also, before certain consonants, **di-**; before *f*, **dif-**. ⟨Latin⟩

dis·a·bil·i·ty [ˌdɪsəˈbɪləti] *n* **1** a physical or mental condition consisting in the absence or impairment of a specific faculty or ability: *a hearing disability, a learning disability.* **2** *Law* something that disqualifies. **3** disadvantage: *Not knowing French is a disability in this job.*
dis·a·ble *v* **1** make nonfunctional: *Pulling this lever disables the whole system.* **2** cause to have a disability: *The accident disabled her.* **3** disqualify legally. **dis·a·bled** *adj.*

dis·a·buse [ˌdɪsəˈbjuz] *v* make free (*of a* deception or error): *Education should disabuse people of prejudice.*

dis·ad·van·tage [ˌdɪsədˈvæntɪdʒ] *n* **1** a fact, condition, or feature that makes success less likely: *The new student suffered the disadvantage of having missed the whole first term.* **2** an unfavourable position: *Her injury put her at a disadvantage for racing.*
to one's disadvantage unfavourable to one. **dis·ad·van·taged** *adj* suffering from social or economic disadvantage. **dis·ad·van·ta·geous** [ˌdɪsˌædvənˈteɪdʒəs] *adj* unfavourable.

dis·af·fect [ˌdɪsəˈfɛkt] *v* alienate the affections, loyalty, commitment, etc. of. **dis·af·fect·ed** *adj* **1** no longer loyal to a given

cause: *a disaffected Communist.* **2** disillusioned or discontented; alienated: *disaffected youth.* **dis·af·fec·tion** *n.*

dis·a·gree [ˌdɪsəˈgri] *v* **1** differ in opinion or viewpoint. **2** quarrel. **3** be in conflict; fail to correspond: *Your results disagree with mine.* **4** have a bad effect: *Cherries disagree with her.* **dis·a·gree·a·ble** *adj* **1** not to one's liking. **2** bad-tempered; cross. **dis·a·gree·ment** *n.*

dis·al·low [ˌdɪsəˈlaʊ] *v* **1** refuse to allow or grant. **2** ✱ of the Federal Government, nullify an Act of a provincial legislature. **dis·al·low·ance** *n.*

dis·am·big·u·ate [ˌdɪsæmˈbɪgjuˌeɪt] *v* make clear by getting rid of an ambiguity.

dis·ap·pear [ˌdɪsəˈpɪr] *v* **1** pass from sight. **2** pass out of existence or use; be lost. **3** be killed, esp secretly by political enemies, terrorists or a criminal organization. **dis·ap·pear·ance** *n.*

dis·ap·point [ˌdɪsəˈpɔɪnt] *v* **1** fail to please or to fulfil the expectations of. **2** fail to keep a promise to (someone). **dis·ap·point·ment** *n.*

dis·ap·prove [ˌdɪsəˈpruv] *v* **1** have or express an opinion against (often with *of*). **2** refuse consent to: *The judge disapproved the verdict.* **dis·ap·prov·al** *n.* **dis·ap·prov·ing·ly** *adv.*

dis·arm [dɪsˈɑrm] *v* **1** take weapons away from: *The police disarmed the bandits.* **2** stop having armed forces or military weapons. **3** remove fear and mistrust from: *I was suspicious, but her frankness disarmed me.* **4** deactivate (a bomb, etc.). **dis·arm·ing** *adj.*
dis·ar·ma·ment *n* the reduction of armed forces and military weaponry.

dis·ar·range [ˌdɪsəˈreɪndʒ] *v* mess up; disturb the orderly arrangement of: *hair disarranged by the wind.* **dis·ar·range·ment** *n.*

dis·ar·ray [ˌdɪsəˈreɪ] *n* disorder. **dis·ar·ray** *v.*

dis·as·sem·ble [ˌdɪsəˈsɛmbəl] *v* take apart.

dis·as·so·ci·ate [ˌdɪsəˈsoʊʃiˌeɪt] *or* [ˌdɪsəˈsoʊsiˌeɪt] *v* dissociate.

dis·as·ter [dɪˈzæstər] *n* **1** an event that causes much suffering or loss: *earthquakes and other disasters.* **2** a total failure: *The play is a disaster.* **dis·as·trous** *adj.* **dis·as·trous·ly** *adv.* ⟨Latin *dis-* without + *astrum* (lucky) star; Greek *astron*⟩
disaster area 1 an area that has suffered a natural disaster and may become entitled to special government assistance. **2** *Informal* a site of confusion; extremely messy place.

dis·band [dɪsˈbænd] *v* **1** dismiss from service: *The army was disbanded after the war.* **2** of a group, break up. **dis·band·ment** *n.*

dis·bar [dɪsˈbɑr] *v* **-barred, -bar·ring** punish (a lawyer) by depriving him or her of the right to practise law. **dis·bar·ment** *n.*

dis·be·lief [ˌdɪsbɪˈlif] *n* inability to believe. **dis·be·lieve** *v* refuse or be unable to believe.

dis·burse [dɪsˈbɜrs] *v* pay out (funds); expend. **dis·burse·ment** *n.* ⟨Old French *des-* away from + *bourse* purse; Greek *byrsa*⟩

disc [dɪsk] *n* **1** a phonograph record or a compact disc. **2** a blade of a DISC HARROW.

3 Also, **disk,** any of various round, thin, flat objects. ⟨See DISK.⟩
disc brake or **disk brake** a brake in a motor vehicle in which flat pads are pressed against both sides of a disc (def. 3) attached to a wheel. **disc harrow** a harrow that turns soil by means of rows of revolving, round, flat blades. **disc jockey** a person who chooses, plays, and introduces recorded music for a radio program, dance, etc. *Abbrev* **DJ** or **D.J.**
dis·co *n* **1** a night club where one may listen and dance to recorded music. **2** the style of music or dance characteristic of such clubs. **disc·o·thèque** ['dɪskə,tɛk] DISCO (def. 1).

dis·card [dɪ'skɑrd] *v* **1** throw away; give up as useless or worn out. **2** *Cards* get rid of (cards) by laying them aside or playing them. **dis·card** ['dɪskɑrd] *n.* ⟨< *dis-* + *card¹*⟩

dis·cern [dɪ'sɜrn] *or* [dɪ'zɜrn] *v* perceive or recognize; distinguish, esp something subtle or hard to see. **dis·cern·i·ble** *adj.* ⟨Latin *dis-* off + *cernere* separate⟩
dis·cern·ing *adj* perceptive or insightful; discriminating. **dis·cern·ment** *n.*

dis·charge [dɪs'tʃɑrdʒ] *v* **1** shoot: *to discharge a gun.* **2** release from prison, hospital, duty, etc.; dismiss. **3** empty: *The river discharged into a bay.* **4** give off; let out: *The clouds discharge electricity in the form of lightning.* **5** withdraw electricity from: *to discharge a battery.* **6** pay: *to discharge a debt.* **7** carry out: *to discharge one's duty.* **8** of a wound, sore, or bodily opening, ooze (pus, mucus, etc.). **dis·charge** ['dɪstʃɑrdʒ] *or* [dɪs'tʃɑrdʒ] *n.*

dis·ci·ple [də'saɪpəl] *n* **1** a follower. **2** one of the first twelve followers of Jesus.
v train (someone) as a disciple. **dis·ci·ple·ship** *n.*
⟨Latin *discipulus* pupil; *discere* learn⟩

dis·ci·pline ['dɪsəplɪn] *v* **1** train to obey, to work hard, or to lead a life of order and self-restraint. **2** punish: *The rebellious convicts were severely disciplined.*
n **1** the process of disciplining or the resulting condition of order and obedience: *a school with good discipline.* **2** self-restraint, industry, moderation, etc. **3** punishment. **4** a field of study. **dis·ci·pli·nar·y** *adj.* **dis·ci·plin·er** *n.*
⟨Latin *disciplina; discipulus.* See DISCIPLE.⟩
dis·ci·pli·nar·i·an *n* a person who believes in or exercises strict discipline.

dis·claim [dɪs'kleɪm] *v* **1** refuse to recognize as one's own: *The motorist disclaimed all responsibility for the accident.* **2** give up all claim to: *She disclaimed any share in the profits.*
dis·claim·er *n* a written statement denying responsibility or liability.

dis·close [dɪ'sklouz] *v* **1** lay open to view; uncover. **2** make known; tell. **dis·clo·sure** *n.*

dis·col·our or **dis·col·or** [dɪs'kʌlər] *v* **1** spoil or alter the colour of; stain: *Smoke had discoloured the new paint work.* **2** become changed in colour. **dis·col·or·a·tion** *n.*

dis·com·bob·u·late [,dɪskəm'bɒbjə,leɪt] *v Informal* disconcert; confuse.
dis·com·bob·u·la·tion *n.* ⟨fanciful alteration and extension, perhaps of *discomfit*⟩

dis·com·fort [dɪs'kʌmfərt] *n* **1** mild pain: *She felt some discomfort after the operation.* **2** a feeling of embarrassment, uneasiness, etc.
v make uncomfortable or uneasy.

dis·com·pose [,dɪskəm'pouz] *v* disturb the self-possession of; make uneasy or confused. **dis·com·po·sure** *n.*

dis·con·cert [,dɪskən'sɜrt] *v* **1** disturb the calmness or confidence of: *I was disconcerted by his unnaturally cheery tone.* **2** upset; put into disorder: *Our plans were disconcerted by our guest's late arrival.* **dis·con·cert·ing** *adj.*

dis·con·nect [,dɪskə'nɛkt] *v* undo or break the connection of: *She disconnected the electric fan by pulling out the plug.* **dis·con·nec·tion** *n.*
dis·con·nect·ed *adj* **1** not connected; not plugged in. **2** without meaningful order; random or incoherent: *disconnected remarks.*

dis·con·so·late [dɪs'kɒnsəlɪt] *adj* cheerless; very sorrowful and unable to be comforted. **dis·con·so·late·ly** *adv.* ⟨Latin *dis-* not + *consolatus* pp of *consolari* console⟩

dis·con·tent [,dɪskən'tɛnt] *n* restlessness or dissatisfaction; lack of contentment.
v cause such a feeling in. **dis·con·tent·ed** *adj.* **dis·con·tent·ment** *n.*

dis·con·tin·ue [,dɪskən'tɪnju] *v* stop doing, making, offering, etc.: *Bus service along this route has been discontinued.* **dis·con·tin·u·ance** or **dis·con·tin·u·a·tion** *n.*
dis·con·ti·nu·i·ty [,dɪskɒntə'njuəti] *or* [-'nuəti] *n* **1** lack of connectedness or unity: *The discontinuity of the plot made the novel hard to understand.* **2** lack of stability. **3** *Mathematics* the value of the independent variable at the point where a function is interrupted. **dis·con·tin·u·ous** *adj* broken, interrupted.

dis·cord ['dɪskɔrd] *n* **1** a conflict of opinion; disagreement; quarrelling. **2** harsh, clashing sounds. **3** *Music* **a** a lack of harmony. **b** an unharmonious chord leading to a resolution. ⟨Latin *discordare; dis-* apart + *cor, cordis* heart⟩
dis·cord·ant *adj* unharmonious; conflicting.

disc·o·thèque See DISC.

dis·count [dɪs'kaʊnt] *or* ['dɪskaʊnt] *v* **1** deduct (an amount) from a cost: *The store discounts five percent on seniors' purchases.* **2** reduce the price of: *discounted goods.* **3** disregard; reject as false: *Discount everything she says.*
n ['dɪskaʊnt] a deduction from a price.
adj ['dɪskaʊnt] **1** of prices, marked down. **2** sold or selling at a reduced price: *discount merchandise, a discount store.* ⟨Middle French *des-* away + *conter* count, Latin *computare*⟩
at a discount a at less than the regular price. **b** easy to get because not in demand.

dis·cour·age [dɪ'skɜrɪdʒ] *v* **1** lessen the hope or confidence of: *Repeated failures discouraged him.* **2** try to prevent by disapproving: *We discourage gum-chewing.* **dis·cour·ag·ing** *adj.* **dis·cour·age·ment** *n.* ⟨Old French *descoragier; des-* away + *curage.* See COURAGE.⟩

dis·course ['dɪskɔrs] *n* **1** a formal speech or writing: *Lectures and sermons are discourses.* **2 a** connected speech or text in general. **b** the characteristic way in which they are

formed in a particular language. **3** all the vocabulary, arguments, etc. characteristic of an ideology or philosophy: *Kantian discourse.* *v* [dɪ'skɔrs] talk or write at some length. ⟨Latin *discursus; dis-* + *currere* run⟩
dis·cur·sive [dɪ'skɜrsɪv] *adj* **1** shifting often from one subject to another. **2** founded on rational argument, not intuition.

dis·cour·te·ous [dɪs'kɜrtiəs] *adj* not polite. **dis·cour·te·ous·ly** *adv.* **dis·cour·te·sy** *n.*

dis·cov·er [dɪ'skʌvər] *v* **1** find or find out for the first time. **2** bring (a talented person) into public prominence. **dis·cov·er·a·ble** *adj.* **dis·cov·er·er** *n.* **dis·cov·er·y** *n.* ⟨Old French *descovrir; des-* away + *covrir*⟩

dis·cred·it [dɪs'krɛdɪt] *v* **1** show to be untrustworthy: *This information discredits the witness.* **2** refuse to believe: *to discredit a statement.* **3** damage the reputation of. **dis·cred·it** *n* **1** loss of good name or standing. **2** a source of this. **3** grounds for disbelief. **dis·cred·it·a·ble** *adj* bringing discredit.

dis·creet [dɪ'skrit] *adj* **1** showing restraint, judgment, tact, etc. esp by respecting people's confidences and privacy. **2** not lavish or ostentatious: *discreet elegance.* **dis·creet·ly** *adv.* **dis·creet·ness** *n.* ⟨Latin *discretus* pp of *discernere.* See DISCERN.⟩
dis·cre·tion *n* **1** the freedom to judge or choose: *left to your own discretion.* **2** the quality of being discreet. **at one's discretion** as one sees fit. **dis·cre·tion·ar·y** *adj* with, or to do with, the freedom to decide or choose.

dis·crep·an·cy [dɪ'skrɛpənsi] *n* lack of consistency or correspondence. **dis·crep·ant** *adj.* **dis·crep·ant·ly** *adv.*

dis·crete [dɪ'skrit] *adj* **1** separate; distinct. **2** consisting of distinct parts. **dis·crete·ly** *adv.* **dis·crete·ness** *n.* ⟨See DISCREET.⟩

dis·cre·tion See DISCREET.

dis·crim·i·nate [dɪ'skrɪmə,neit] *v* **1** make or see a distinction; distinguish: *to discriminate between lies and exaggeration.* **2** make an unfair difference in how people are treated: *The law must not discriminate against any race. adj* [dɪ'skrɪmənɪt] paying due attention to important distinctions. **dis·crim·i·nate·ly** *adv.* **dis·crim·i·na·tion** *n.* ⟨Latin *discrimen* separation; *discernere* discern⟩
dis·crim·i·nat·ing *adj* **1** having the ability to discriminate well: *a woman of discriminating taste.* **2** distinctive: *The discriminating mark of measles is a rash.* **3** *Business* differential: *a discriminating import tax.* **dis·crim·i·na·to·ry** *adj* discriminating unfairly: *discriminatory laws.*

dis·cur·sive See DISCOURSE.

dis·cus ['dɪskəs] *n* a heavy, circular plate used in athletic games as a test of skill and strength in throwing. ⟨Greek *diskos* quoit⟩

dis·cuss [dɪ'skʌs] *v* **1** talk about together. **2** deal with various aspects of in speech or writing: *Her new book discusses the future of the arts in Canada.* **dis·cus·sion** *n.* ⟨Latin *discussus* pp of *discutere; dis-* apart + *quatere* shake⟩

dis·dain [dɪs'dein] *v* look down on; scorn: *He*

took his bike, disdaining to walk. **dis·dain** *n.* **dis·dain·ful** *adj.* ⟨Old French *desdeignier; des-* away + *deignier* deign, Latin *dignari*⟩

dis·ease [dɪ'ziz] *n* **1** sickness. **2** a specific sickness: *Chicken pox is an infectious disease.* **3** a socially, psychologically, or morally unhealthy condition. **dis·eased** *adj.* ⟨Old French *desaise; des-* away + *aise* ease⟩

dis·em·bark [,dɪsəm'bark] *v* leave or cause to leave a ship or aircraft. **dis·em·bar·ka·tion** *n.*

dis·em·bod·y [,dɪsəm'bɒdi] *v* separate from the body or from its usual material form. **dis·em·bod·i·ment** *n.*

dis·em·bow·el [,dɪsəm'bauəl] *v* **-elled** or **-eled, -el·ling** or **-el·ing** rip out the bowels of. **dis·em·bow·el·ment** *n.*

dis·en·chant [,dɪsən'tʃænt] *v* **1** free from a magic spell or illusion. **2** disillusion; cause to be disappointed (*with*). **dis·en·chant·ed** *adj.* **dis·en·chant·ing** *adj.* **dis·en·chant·ment** *n.*

dis·en·fran·chise [,dɪsən'fræntʃaɪz] *v* disfranchise. **dis·en·fran·chise·ment** *n.*

dis·en·gage [,dɪsən'geidʒ] *v* **1** release: *She disengaged her hand from mine.* **2** *Military* go away from contact with (an enemy). **dis·en·gaged** *adj* **1** not busy; not in use. **2** released; detached. **dis·en·gage·ment** *n.*

dis·en·tan·gle [,dɪsən'tæŋgəl] *v* free from tangles or complications. **dis·en·tan·gle·ment** *n.*

dis·e·qui·lib·ri·um [dɪs,ikwə'lɪbriəm] or [,dɪsikwə'lɪbriəm] *n* loss or lack of balance.

dis·es·tab·lish [,dɪsɪ'stæblɪʃ] *v* withdraw official recognition or support from. **dis·es·tab·lish·ment** *n.*

dis·fa·vour or **dis·fa·vor** [dɪs'feivər] *n* **1** disapproval: *Employees looked with disfavour on any attempt to change the cafeteria.* **2** an injurious act: *to do someone a disfavour.* **dis·fa·vour** or **dis·fa·vor** *v.*

dis·fig·ure [dɪs'fɪgjər] or [dɪs'fɪgər] *v* spoil the appearance of; make ugly: *Huge billboards disfigured the landscape.* **dis·fig·ure·ment** *n.*

dis·fran·chise [dɪs'fræntʃaɪz] *v* **1** take the rights of citizenship away from. **2** take a right or privilege from; especially, deprive of social power or economic opportunity.

dis·gorge [dɪs'gɔrdʒ] *v* **1** throw up (what has been swallowed). **2** pour forth: *Swollen creeks disgorged their waters into the river.* ⟨Old French *desgorger; des-* + *gorge* throat⟩

dis·grace [dɪs'greis] *n* **1** loss of favour or respect. **2** a cause of this: *You're a disgrace!* *v* **1** cause to lose favour or respect: *Her conduct disgraced her family.* **2** humiliate: *Delinquent officers will be publicly disgraced.* **dis·grace·ful** *adj* scandalous; shameful.

SYNONYMS
Disgrace suggests losing the approval of others through social misconduct: *He was in disgrace after his ungentlemanly behaviour.* **Dishonour** is worse; it suggests losing one's honour or dignity through serious moral failure: *He brings dishonour on the whole regiment by his cowardice.*

dis·grun·tle [dɪs'grʌntəl] *v* put in a bad mood; dissatisfy: *the customer was disgruntled by the poor service.* **dis·grun·tle·ment** *n.* ⟨*dis-* + obsolete *gruntle* grunt, grumble⟩

dis·guise [dɪs'gaɪz] *v* 1 make (a person or thing) look, sound, etc. like someone or something else: *The spy disguised himself as an old man.* 2 hide; hide the true character of: *I cannot disguise my dislike for her.* ⟨Old French *desguisier; des-* down + *guise* guise⟩
dis·guise *n* 1 clothes, make-up, etc. used to suggest a false identity. 2 the act of disguising or the state of being disguised: *in disguise.* 3 a false appearance; act; pretence: *Her friendliness is just a disguise.*

dis·gust [dɪs'gʌst] *n* 1 an intense, sickening dislike: *The foul odour filled him with disgust.* 2 weary indignation: *Her excuses were so silly that I finally hung up in disgust.* **dis·gust** *v.* **dis·gust·ed** *adj.* **dis·gust·ing** *adj.* ⟨Middle French *desgoust; des-* apart + *goust* taste, Latin *gustus*⟩

dish [dɪʃ] *n* 1 any container for food, usually shallow. 2 **dishes** *pl* cups, saucers, glasses, plates, bowls, etc. 3 a particular prepared food: *My favourite dish is peaches and cream.* 4 anything shallow and hollow like a dish, such as a reflector for an antenna. 5 *Slang* an attractive person.
v shape like a dish. **dish·ful** *n.* ⟨Old English *disc;* Latin *discus* dish, Greek *diskos*⟩
dish it out *Slang* deliver insults, sarcasm, rough treatment, etc.: *She can dish it out, but she can't take it.* **dish out** a serve (food) to individuals. **b** give or dispense freely: *to dish out punishment or compliments.* **dish up** a put (food) in a dish ready for serving or eating. **b** present or offer attractively: *to dish up a good argument.*
dish antenna a radio or television antenna with a reflector shaped like a dish. **dish·cloth** or **dish·rag** *n* a cloth to wash dishes with. **dish·pan** *n* a large basin in which to wash dishes. **dishpan hands** hands that show the effects of exposure to hot water. **dish·tow·el** *n* a cloth for drying dishes. **dish·wash·er** *n* 1 a machine for washing and drying dishes. 2 a person employed to wash dishes. **dish·wa·ter** *n* 1 water in which dishes are washed. 2 weak or lukewarm coffee, soup, etc.

dis·har·mo·ny [dɪs'harməni] *n* lack of harmony; conflict or disunity.

dis·heart·en [dɪs'hartən] *v* discourage; demoralize; depress. **dis·heart·en·ing** *adj.* **dis·heart·en·ment** *n.*

di·shev·el [dɪ'ʃɛvəl] *v* **-elled** or **-eled, -el·ling** or **-el·ing** disarrange or rumple (hair, clothing, etc.). ⟨Old French *descheveler; des-* away + *chevel* hair, Latin *capillus*⟩

dis·hon·est [dɪs'ɒnɪst] *adj* not honest; using, involving, or obtained by fraud or pretence: *a dishonest merchant, dishonest praise, dishonest gain.* **dis·hon·est·ly** *adv.* **dis·hon·es·ty** *n.*

dis·hon·our or **dis·hon·or** [dɪs'ɒnər] *n* 1 loss of honour or reputation. 2 a cause of this.
v 1 cause to lose honour or reputation.

2 refuse to recognize. 3 refuse to pay (a bill). **dis·hon·our·a·ble** or **dis·hon·or·a·ble** *adj* not noble or decent; worthy of dishonour.

dis·il·lu·sion [ˌdɪsɪ'luʒən] *v* make bitter or cynical by disappointment. **dis·il·lu·sion** *n.* **dis·il·lu·sion·ed** *adj.* **dis·il·lu·sion·ment** *n.*

dis·in·cen·tive [ˌdɪsɪn'sɛntɪv] *n* deterrent.

dis·in·cline [ˌdɪsɪn'klaɪn] *v* make unwilling. **dis·in·cli·na·tion** *n.* **dis·in·clined** *adj.*

dis·in·fect [ˌdɪsɪn'fɛkt] *v* destroy potentially harmful micro-organisms in or on: *Surgical instruments are disinfected before use.* **dis·in·fect·ant** *n* an agent that disinfects, esp a chemical such as alcohol, chlorine, or carbolic acid.

dis·in·for·ma·tion [ˌdɪsɪnfər'meɪʃən] *n* 1 false information, intended to mislead. 2 the act of spreading such information.

dis·in·gen·u·ous [ˌdɪsɪn'dʒɛnjuəs] *adj* not frank; insincere; with an ulterior motive. **dis·in·gen·u·ous·ly** *adv.* **dis·in·gen·u·ous·ness** *n.*

dis·in·her·it [ˌdɪsɪn'hɛrɪt] *v* cut out of one's will; deprive of a rightful inheritance.

dis·in·te·grate [dɪs'ɪntə,greɪt] *v* 1 crumble or fall apart; undergo complete loss of structure and organization: *The old paper disintegrated into a pile of dust. After Mom died the family disintegrated.* 2 *Physics* change in nuclear structure through bombardment by charged particles. **dis·in·te·gra·tion** *n.* **dis·in·te·gra·tor** *n* a machine for disintegrating a substance.

dis·in·ter [ˌdɪsɪn'tɜr] *v* **-terred, -ter·ring** 1 take out of a grave or tomb; dig up. 2 bring to light; reveal. **dis·in·ter·ment** *n.*

dis·in·ter·est [dɪs'ɪntrɪst] *n* 1 impartiality. 2 loosely, indifference. **dis·in·ter·est·ed** *adj.*

CONFUSABLES

Many people avoid using **disinterested** to mean 'indifferent; not caring or paying any attention', a meaning which is more properly expressed by **uninterested**. A weaker contrast exists between the nouns, **disinterest** and **uninterest**, as the latter is infrequently used.

---

dis·joint [dɪs'dʒɔɪnt] *v* 1 put out of joint; dislocate. 2 put out of order; disarrange or disrupt. 3 take apart at the joints: *to disjoint a carcass prior to butchering.* **dis·joint·ed** *adj* lacking continuity and coherence. **disjoint set** *Mathematics* one of two or more sets that have no numbers in common. **dis·junc·tion** [dɪs'dʒʌŋkʃən] *n* a separation.

disk [dɪsk] *n* 1 a round, thin, flat object. 2 the round, central part of the flower head of most composite plants: *The daisy has a yellow disk.* 3 *Anatomy* any of the masses of fibrous cartilage between the vertebrae. 4 *Computers* a plate on which a computer stores data through the use of optical or magnetic technology. 5 See DISC for other senses. **disk·like** or **disc·like** *adj.* ⟨Greek *diskos*⟩ **disk drive** *Computers* a system component that reads data stored on disks. **disk·ette** *Computers n* a small flexible disk encased in rigid plastic, on which data can be stored. **disk flower** any of the tiny flowers that make up the central disk of the flower head of a composite plant. **disk operating system** *Computers* a program that runs a computer's internal functions. *Abbrev* **DOS**.

dis·like [dɪs'laɪk] *n* a feeling of not liking; a feeling against. **dis·like** *v.*

dis·lo·cate [ˌdɪslou'keɪt] *or* ['dɪslou,keɪt] *v* **1** cause one or more of the bones of (a joint) to be shifted out of place: *to dislocate one's shoulder.* **2** put out of order; upset: *This will dislocate all our careful plans.* **dis·lo·ca·tion** *n.*

dis·lodge [dɪs'lɒdʒ] *v* force (something) out of a place where it is stuck or entrenched: *to dislodge a heavy stone.*

dis·loy·al [dɪs'lɔɪəl] *adj* not loyal; unfaithful: **dis·loy·al·ly** *adv.* **dis·loy·al·ty** *n.*

dis·mal ['dɪzməl] *adj* **1** dark; gloomy: *Damp caves are dismal.* **2** dreary; miserable: *Sickness made me feel dismal.* **dis·mal·ly** *adv.* ⟨Anglo-French *dis mal* evil days; Latin *dies mali*⟩

dis·man·tle [dɪs'mæntəl] **1** take apart (any thing assembled or built): *I had to dismantle the bookcase to move it.* **2** get rid of or destroy (an institution, program, etc.) in planned stages: *dismantling the welfare system.* **3** strip of covering, equipment, furniture, guns, etc. ⟨Middle French *des-* away + *mantel* mantle⟩

dis·may [dɪ'smeɪ] *n* a loss of courage or hope because of a serious, sudden threat, setback, or difficulty. **dis·may** *v.* ⟨Latin *dismagare* deprive of strength⟩

dis·mem·ber [dɪs'mɛmbər] *v* **1** cut or tear the limbs from. **2** divide into parts: *The Austro-Hungarian Empire was dismembered after the First World War.* **dis·mem·ber·ment** *n.*

dis·miss [dɪ'smɪs] *v* **1** allow or tell to leave (usually at the end of a session of some kind): *At noon the teacher dismissed the class.* **2** remove from a position or office. **3** put out of mind: *She dismissed the magazine article with a laugh.* **4** refuse to consider: *to dismiss a charge in court.* **dis·miss·al** *n.* ⟨Latin *dismissus*; *dis-* away + *missus* pp of *mittere* send⟩ **dis·mis·sive** *adj* expressing dismissal: *a dismissive gesture.* **dis·mis·sive·ly** *adv.*

dis·mount [dɪs'maʊnt] *v* **1** get off a horse, bicycle, etc. **2** take (a thing) from its setting or support: *The cannon was dismounted for shipping to another fort.*

dis·o·bey [ˌdɪsə'beɪ] *v* fail or refuse to follow (rules or orders or the person issuing them). **dis·o·be·di·ence** [-'bidiəns] *n.* **dis·o·be·di·ent** *adj.*

dis·or·der [dɪs'ɔrdər] *n* **1** a lack of order or system; confusion; mess: *The room was in disorder.* **2** a public disturbance; riot. **3** a sickness or abnormal condition: *a disorder of the stomach.* **dis·or·der** *v.* **dis·or·dered** *adj.* **dis·or·der·ly** *adj* **1** not orderly; in confusion: *a disorderly pile.* **2** disturbing public peace and order: *a disorderly mob, disorderly conduct.* **dis·or·der·li·ness** *n.*

dis·or·gan·ize [dɪs'ɔrgə,naɪz] *v* disturb the

systematic or orderly arrangement of: *Heavy snowstorms disorganized the train schedule.* **dis·or·gan·i·za·tion** *n.* **dis·or·gan·ized** *adj* without system or orderly arrangement; lacking method and planning.

dis·o·ri·ent [dɪs'ɔri,ɛnt] *v* **1** cause to lose sense of direction. **2** cause to lose one's grasp of what is going on, what one's role is, etc.: *His sudden rise to fame disoriented him at first.* **dis·o·ri·en·ta·tion** *n.* ⟨French *désorienter,* from Latin *oriens* direction of sunrise; *oriri* rise⟩

dis·own [dɪs'oun] *v* refuse to recognize as one's own.

dis·par·age [dɪ'spɛrɪdʒ] *or* [dɪ'spærɪdʒ] *v* **1** speak slightingly of; belittle: *Cowards disparaged the hero's brave rescue attempt.* **2** harm the reputation of. **dis·par·ag·ing** *adj.* **dis·par·age·ment** *n.* ⟨Old French *desparagier* match unequally; *des-* apart + *parage* rank⟩

dis·pa·rate ['dɪspərɪt] *adj* different in kind. ⟨Latin *disparare; dis-* apart + *parare* get⟩ **dis·par·i·ty** [dɪ'spɛrəti] *or* [dɪ'spærəti] *n* **1** lack of equality. **2** the degree of difference.

dis·pas·sion [dɪs'pæʃən] *n* freedom from emotion or prejudice; calmness; impartiality. **dis·pas·sion·ate** *adj.* **dis·pas·sion·ate·ly** *adv.*

dis·patch or **des·patch** [dɪ'spætʃ] *v* **1** send off to some place or for some purpose: *to dispatch a messenger, to dispatch an ambulance.* **2** get (something) done promptly or speedily. **3** kill, eat up, or otherwise get rid of. *n* [dɪ'spætʃ] *or* ['dɪspætʃ] **1** the act of sending off or otherwise dispatching. **2** a written message or report sent by a government agency, news reporter, etc. **3** an agency that conveys or dispatches goods. **4** speed and promptness in getting a thing done. ⟨Italian *dispacciare* hasten⟩ **mention in dispatches** *Military* commend for bravery, distinguished service, etc., in the official report of an action. **dispatch case** a flat, stiff case for documents. **dis·patch·er** *n* a person or firm that ships or dispatches, esp one that dispatches taxis, ambulances, etc. when called for.

dis·pel [dɪ'spɛl] *v* **-pelled, -pel·ling** drive away (feelings or thoughts): *Laughter dispelled our fears.* ⟨Latin *dis-* away + *pellere* drive⟩

dis·pense [dɪ'spɛns] *v* **1** give out: *to dispense food, clothing, and medicine to refugees. This pump dispenses shampoo.* **2** apply; administer: *to dispense justice.* **3** exempt or excuse (from): *They were dispensed from their oath.* ⟨Latin *dis-* out + *pendere* weigh⟩ **dispense with a** get rid of: *The new system dispenses with oral exams.* **b** manage without: *She found she could dispense with rich food.* **dispensable** *adj* that may be done without; not essential. **dis·pen·sa·ry** *n* **1** a place where medicines and medical advice are given free or at low cost. **2** the part of a hospital or clinic where medicine is kept. **dis·pen·sa·tion** *n* **1** the act of dispensing. **2** a particular regime or system of management: *England under the dispensation of Elizabeth I.* **3** *Roman Catholic Church* official permission to disregard a law, etc., without penalty. **dis·pens·er** *n* a device made to release its contents one at a time or in measured amounts: *a coffee dispenser.*

dis·perse [dɪ'spɜrs] *v* **1** send or go in various directions; scatter: *The crowd dispersed when the game was over.* **2** distribute: *to disperse flyers.* **3** *Physics* divide (white light) into its coloured rays. **4** *Chemistry* scatter (particles of a colloid) throughout another substance. **dis·per·sal** *n.* **dis·per·si·ble** *adj.* ⟨Latin *dispersus* pp of *dispergere; dis- + spargere* scatter⟩ **dis·per·sion** *n* **1** the act of dispersing or state of being dispersed. **2** *Chemistry* a system consisting of dispersed colloidal particles and the medium in which they are dispersed. **3** *Statistics* the scatter of data around some central value. **4** DIASPORA.

dis·pir·it [dɪ'spɪrɪt] *v* depress; discourage. **dis·pir·it·ed** *adj.*

dis·place [dɪs'pleɪs] *v* **1** take over the place of; cause to be set aside: *The car has displaced the horse and buggy.* **2** remove from a position of authority. **3** move (a certain amount of a substance) by taking up its place, as a solid body does in a liquid. **displaced person** a person forced out of his or her home or country by war, famine, etc.; refugee. *Abbrev* **DP** or **D.P. dis·place·ment** *n* **1** the volume or mass of a fluid displaced by a solid in it. **2** specifically, the volume in a pump or engine cylinder that is displaced by a stroke of the piston. **3** *Psychiatry* an unconscious defensive process transferring the focus of an emotion to another object.

dis·play [dɪ'spleɪ] *v* **1** expose to view, esp attractively or for effect: *Many ancient weapons are displayed in the museum.* **2** show: *to display tact in a delicate situation.* **3** present (electronic signals) in visual form, as on a video screen. *n* **1** an act or way of displaying. **2** a thing or set of things being displayed. **3** showing off; showiness: *Her fondness for display led her to buy the most outrageous clothes.* **4** a pretended or affected show: *to put on a display of grief.* **5** *Zoology* behaviour serving to attract a mate. ⟨Old French *despleier,* Latin *displicare; dis-* apart + *plicare* fold⟩ **on display** being displayed.

dis·please [dɪs'pliz] *v* offend or annoy. **dis·pleas·ing** *adj.* **dis·pleas·ure** [dɪs'plɛʒər] *n.*

dis·pose [dɪ'spouz] *v* **1** put in a certain order or position: *to dispose troops.* **2** arrange (matters). **3** make willing: *More pay disposed her to take the new job.* **4** make liable: *Lack of proper rest disposes you to getting sick.* ⟨Old French *dis-* variously + *poser* place⟩ **dispose of a** sell, throw out, or give away: *to dispose of property.* **b** eat up: *We disposed of a whole pie.* **c** deal with conclusively: *to dispose of an item of business.* **dis·pos·a·ble** *adj* **1** to be thrown away after a single use. **2** that can be got rid of or lost without ill effect: *treating soldiers as if they were disposable.* **3** available for free use: *disposable income.* **disposables** *n pl* consumer goods designed to be thrown away after a

single use. **dis·pos·al** *n* **1** the act or manner of disposing. **2** the act or means of getting rid of or dealing with: *garbage disposal.* **at someone's disposal** ready for one's use at any time: *Does he have a car at his disposal?* **dis·posed** *adj* having a particular attitude; inclined: *How was he disposed toward the plan? She is disposed to get angry at the least thing.* **dis·po·si·tion** *n* **1** one's habitual attitude and way of behaving: *a cheerful disposition.* **2** a tendency: *He has a disposition to argue.* **3** the act or manner of disposing: *the disposition of troops in battle.*

dis·pos·sess [,dɪspə'zɛs] *v* **1** force to give up a house, land, etc.: *The farmer was dispossessed for not paying her rent.* **2** deprive: *Fear dispossessed him of his senses.* **dis·pos·ses·sion** *n.*

dis·pro·por·tion [,dɪsprə'pɔrʃən] *n* a lack of proper proportion. **dis·pro·por·tion** *v.* **dis·pro·por·tion·ate** or **dis·pro·por·tion·al** *adj* not in proportion; too much or too little: *a disproportionate amount of time spent on details.* **dis·pro·por·tion·ate·ly** *adv.*

dis·prove [dɪs'pruv] *v* prove incorrect or false; refute. **dis·prov·a·ble** *adj.*

dis·pute [dɪ'spjut] *v* **1** argue; debate. **2** quarrel. **3** disagree with (a statement); challenge: *The insurance company disputed her claim.* **4** fight over: *The sisters are disputing ownership of the car.* **dispute** *n.* **dis·put·a·ble** *adj.* **dis·pu·tant** [dɪ'spjutənt] *or* ['dɪspjətənt] *n.* ⟨Latin *disputare* examine, discuss; *dis-* item by item + *putare* calculate⟩ **beyond dispute a** absolutely certain. **b** final. **in dispute** being disputed. **dis·pu·ta·tion** *n* **1** the process, act, or manner of disputing. **2** formal debate. **dis·pu·ta·tious** *adj* fond of disputing; inclined to argue.

dis·qual·i·fy [dɪs'kwɒlə,faɪ] *v* make or declare unfit or ineligible to do something: *His injury disqualified him from playing.* **dis·qual·i·fi·ca·tion** *n.*

dis·qui·et [dɪs'kwaɪət] *v* make uneasy or anxious. **dis·qui·et** *n.* **dis·qui·et·ing** *adj.* **dis·qui·e·tude** *n.*

dis·qui·si·tion [,dɪskwɪ'zɪʃən] *n* a long, formal speech or writing on a given subject. ⟨Latin *disquisitio; dis-* (intensive) + *quaerere* seek⟩

dis·re·gard [,dɪsrɪ'gɑrd] *v* **1** pay no attention to. **2** treat without due respect. **dis·re·gard** *n.* **dis·re·gard·ful** *adj.*

dis·re·mem·ber [,dɪsrɪ'mɛmbər] *v* *Informal* fail to remember; forget.

dis·re·pair [,dɪsrɪ'pɛr] *n* bad condition; need of repairs: *The house was in disrepair.*

dis·re·pute [,dɪsrɪ'pjut] *n* the state of having lost respect or good reputation: *Many old remedies are now in disrepute.* **dis·rep·u·ta·ble** [dɪs'rɛpjətəbəl] *adj* **1** having a bad reputation. **2** lowering one's reputation: *disreputable conduct.* **3** shabby; much worn: *a disreputable old hat.* **dis·rep·u·ta·bly** *adv.*

dis·re·spect [,dɪsrɪ'spɛkt] *n* a lack of respect or courtesy; rudeness. **dis·re·spect·ful** *adj.*

dis·robe [dɪs'roub] *v* undress.

dis·rupt [dɪs'rʌpt] v 1 break up; split: *Their relationship was disrupted by a violent dispute.* 2 destroy the order, calm, or continuity of: *to disrupt telephone service, to disrupt family life.* **dis·rup·tion** n. **dis·rup·tive** adj. ⟨Latin *disruptus* pp of *disrumpere*; *dis-* apart + *rumpere* break⟩

dis·sat·is·fy [dɪs'sætɪs,faɪ] v fail to satisfy; make unhappy or restless. **dis·sat·is·fac·tion** n. **dis·sat·is·fied** adj.

dis·sect [dəɪ'sɛkt] or [dɪ'sɛkt] v 1 cut into parts to study the structure. 2 examine carefully part by part; analyze in detail: *to dissect a theory.* **dis·sec·tion** n. ⟨Latin *dissectus* pp of *dissecare*; *dis-* apart + *secare* cut⟩

dis·sem·ble [dɪ'sɛmbəl] v 1 disguise or hide (feelings, etc.): *anger dissembled by a smile.* 2 pretend: *The bored listener politely dissembled an interest she did not feel.* **dis·sem·bler** n. **dis·sem·bling** adj. ⟨obsolete *dissimule*, Latin *dissimulare*; altered by analogy with *resemble*⟩

dis·sem·i·nate [dɪ'sɛmə,neɪt] v spread (ideas, information, etc.) widely. **dis·sem·i·na·tion** n. ⟨Latin *dis-* in every direction + *semen* seed⟩

dis·sent [dɪ'sɛnt] v 1 express a difference of opinion: *Two of the judges dissented from the majority decision.* 2 refuse to conform to an established ideology or religion. **dis·sent** n. **dis·sent·er** n.   **dis·sent·ing**   adj. ⟨Latin *dissentire*; *dis-* differently + *sentire* feel, think⟩ **dis·sen·sion** [dɪ'sɛnʃən] n angry disputes.

dis·ser·ta·tion [,dɪsər'teɪʃən] n a formal discussion of a subject, esp a thesis for a doctoral or other graduate degree. ⟨Latin *disserere*; *dis-* (intensive) + *serere* join words⟩

dis·serv·ice [dɪs'sɜrvɪs] or [dɪ'sɜrvɪs] n an injustice, usually unwitting.

dis·si·dent ['dɪsədənt] adj disagreeing, esp with established ideology. **dis·si·dent** n. **dis·si·dence** n. ⟨Latin *dissidere*; *dis-* apart + *sedere* sit⟩

dis·sim·i·lar [dɪ'sɪmələr] adj quite unlike; not similar. **dis·sim·i·lar·ly** adv. **dis·sim·i·lar·i·ty** n. **dis·si·mil·i·tude** n unlikeness; difference.

dis·si·pate ['dɪsə,peɪt] v 1 spread in different directions; scatter: *The crowd soon dissipated.* 2 disappear or cause to disappear gradually: *The fog had dissipated by noon.* 3 spend foolishly: *to dissipate a fortune.* ⟨Latin *dis-* in different directions + *sipare* throw⟩ **dis·si·pat·ed** adj wild, irresponsible, dissolute, etc. **dis·si·pa·tion** n 1 the act of dissipating. 2 a dissipated lifestyle.

dis·so·ci·ate [dɪ'souʃi,eɪt] or [dɪ'sousi,eɪt] v 1 break the connection of: *to dissociate oneself from one's colleagues. Try to dissociate your past experience from the present situation.* 2 *Chemistry* separate the molecules of (a substance) into their constituent ions or atoms. 3 *Psychiatry* separate (an idea, feeling, etc.) from the main stream of consciousness, sometimes giving rise to multiple personality. **dis·so·ci·a·tion** n. **dis·so·ci·a·tive** adj. ⟨Latin *dis-* apart + *socius* ally⟩

dis·so·lute [,dɪsə'lut] adj living an immoral life. **dis·so·lute·ly** adv. **dis·so·lu·tion** n. ⟨Latin *dissolutus* pp of *dissolvere*. See DISSOLVE.⟩

dis·solve [dɪ'zɒlv] v 1 become part of a liquid: *Salt dissolves in water.* 2 break up; end: *to dissolve a partnership, to dissolve Parliament before an election.* 3 fade or cause to fade away: *The dream dissolved when she woke up.* 4 break down into parts. **dis·so·lu·tion** n. **dis·sol·u·ble** [dɪ'sɒljəbəl] or **dis·solv·a·ble** adj. ⟨Latin *dis-* (intensive) + *solvere* loose⟩ **dissolve in(to) tears** give way to weeping.

dis·so·nance ['dɪsənəns] n 1 *Music* lack of harmony, or a chord that is not harmonious. 2 disagreement; inconsistency. Compare CONSONANCE. **dis·so·nant** adj. ⟨Latin *dis-* apart + *sonare* sound⟩

dis·suade [dɪ'sweɪd] v persuade not to do something (with *from*): *to dissuade someone from quitting.* **dis·sua·sion** n. **dis·sua·sive** adj. ⟨Latin *dis-* against + *suadere* to urge⟩

dis·tance ['dɪstəns] n 1 the space between two points, or a measure of this space: *The distance from here to town is 5 km.* 2 a long way: *The farm is a distance from the road.* 3 the fact of being far away or removed in place or time: *At this distance I can't tell.* 4 emotional detachment, often giving a more balanced perspective: *I need to get some distance from the issue.* 5 lack of warmth or familiarity; aloofness. 6 perspective in a picture. v 1 leave far behind; outdo by far. 2 cause to be emotionally detached or distant (*from*). 3 dissociate. **dis·tant** adj. **dis·tant·ly** adv. ⟨Latin *distans* ppr of *distare*; *dis-* off + *stare* stand⟩ **go the distance** endure anything to the end. **in the distance** quite far away. **keep at a distance** treat with reserve or coolness: *We tried to be friendly but she kept us at a distance.* **keep one's distance a** remain some distance away: *The dog is nervous, so keep your distance.* **b** be not too friendly: *She keeps her distance with her employees.* **c** keep involvement to a minimum (often with *from*). **put (some) distance between oneself and** get away from. **distance learning** education for students working with no instructor present. Material is provided by mail, e-mail, TV, and the Internet.

dis·taste [dɪs'teɪst] n dislike; aversion: *His distaste showed on his face.* **dis·taste·ful** adj unpleasant; offensive.

dis·tem·per¹ [dɪs'tɛmpər] n 1 an infectious disease of dogs and other animals. 2 any sickness or disorder. ⟨Latin *dis-* not + *temperare* mix in proper proportion⟩

dis·tem·per² [dɪs'tɛmpər] n a method of painting in which powdered colours are mixed with glue. **dis·tem·per** v. ⟨Latin *dis-* thoroughly + *temperare* mix⟩

dis·tend [dɪ'stɛnd] v swell out: *His cheeks distended with each blast on his bugle.* **dis·ten·si·ble** adj. **dis·ten·sion** or **dis·ten·tion** n. ⟨Latin *dis-* apart + *tendere* stretch⟩

dis·til or **dis·till** [dɪ'stɪl] v **-tilled, -til·ling** 1 heat (a liquid) and condense the vapour given off. **2** obtain by this method: *Gasoline is distilled from crude oil.* **3** condense so only the essence is left. **4** extract (the essence of): *to distil the truth from a report.* **5** fall, let fall, or give off in drops: *Flowers distil nectar.* **dis·tilled** *adj.* ⟨Latin *de-* down + *stilla* drop⟩ **dis·til·late** ['dɪstəlɪt] *or* [-ˌleɪt] *n* a product of distilling. **dis·til·la·tion** *n* the process or result of distilling: *The book is a distillation of the author's thinking.* **dis·till·er** *n* one that distils, esp a maker of whisky, rum, brandy, etc. **dis·till·er·y** *n* a place where this is done.

dis·tinct [dɪ'stɪŋkt] *adj* **1** not to be confused, merged, or lumped together: *There are two distinct questions at issue.* **2** clear; easy to perceive, identify, etc.: *distinct images, a distinct lisp, a distinct advantage.* **dis·tinct·ly** *adv.* **dis·tinct·ness** *n.* ⟨Latin *distinctus* pp of *distinguere.* See DISTINGUISH.⟩ **dis·tinc·tion** *n* **1** the act of distinguishing or making a difference: *She treated all alike, without distinction.* **2** a difference; something that distinguishes one thing from another: *Is there any distinction between ducks and geese?* **3** honour, or excellence that brings honour: *a writer of distinction.* **distinction without a difference** a false distinction. **dis·tinc·tive** *adj* unique; uniquely identifying: *the distinctive style of a particular author.* **dis·tinc·tive·ly** *adv.* **dis·tinc·tive·ness** *n.* **distinct society ✴** in constitutional discussions, a status proposed for the province of Québec that assumes a unique cultural identity and certain powers of self-government not available to other provinces.

dis·tin·guish [dɪ'stɪŋgwɪʃ] *v* **1** see, make, or constitute a difference (often with *between*, *among*, or *from*): *It's hard to distinguish between her voice and her sister's. The ability to talk distinguishes humans from animals.* **2** make out; see or hear clearly: *I can't distinguish the path in the dark.* **3** be a unique feature of: *a style distinguished by dry humour.* **4** make famous: *She distinguished herself by winning six times.* **dis·tin·guish·a·ble** *adj.* ⟨Latin *dis-* between + *stinguere* to prick⟩ **dis·tin·guished** *adj* famous for excellence: *a distinguished artist.*

SYNONYMS
Distinguish emphasizes keenness or accuracy of perception: *to distinguish between an acoustic piano and an electric one by sound.* **Differentiate** emphasizes precision in defining categories and in recognizing or articulating which differences are important: *The teacher differentiated between Milton's sonnets and Shakespeare's.* **Discriminate** suggests insight, special knowledge, or expertise: *The detective was able to discriminate between genuine bills and counterfeit.*

dis·tort [dɪ'stɔrt] *v* **1** pull or twist out of the usual shape: *Rage distorted his face.* **2** present in a biassed way so as to give a false impression: *to distort facts or meaning.* **dis·tor·ted** *adj.* **dis·tor·tion** *n.* ⟨Latin *distortus* pp of *distorquere; dis-* (intensive) + *torquere* twist⟩

dis·tract [dɪ'strækt] *v* **1** draw away the mind, attention, etc., of: *Distract the baby while I give him the injection.* **2** confuse and make unable to concentrate: *So many people talking at once distracted me.* **3** make frantic or crazed (only in the passive): *nearly distracted by the thought of his missing sister.* **dis·tract·ed** *adj.* **dis·tract·ing** *adj.* ⟨Latin *distractus* pp of *distrahere; dis-* away + *trahere* pull⟩ **dis·trac·tion** *n* **1** the act of distracting or state of being distracted. **2** anything that distracts. **3** something that relieves the mind or spirit: *Movies are a popular distraction.* **4** madness. **dis·traught** [dɪ'strɔt] *adj* **1** in a state of mental conflict and confusion. **2** crazed.

dis·tress [dɪ'strɛs] *n* **1** great mental or physical pain. **2** a desperate situation: *a ship in distress.* **dis·tress** *v.* **dis·tress·ing** *adj.* ⟨Old French *distrece;* Latin *districtus* pp of *distringere; dis-* apart + *stringere* draw⟩ **dis·tressed** *adj* **1** troubled; in great mental pain. **2** in difficulty, often specifically financial or economic: *a distressed ship, a distressed area.* **3** treated so as to give an impression of age or wear: *distressed fabric.*

dis·trib·u·tar·y [dɪs'trɪbjʊˌteri] *n* a branch of a river that flows away from, rather than into, the main stream and never rejoins it.

dis·trib·ute [dɪ'strɪbjut] *v* **1** give some of to each: *to distribute candy.* **2** spread: *Distribute the paint evenly over the wall.* **3** divide by assigning to groups: *The schoolchildren were distributed into three groups for the tour.* **4** sell (goods) to a certain market. **dis·tri·bu·tion** *n.* ⟨Latin *distribuere; dis-* + *tribuere* assign (by tribe), from *tribus* tribe⟩ **dis·trib·u·tive** *adj* **1** *Mathematics* designating an operation that has the same result on a set as it has on members of the set. *Example: a(b + c)* is the same as *ab + ac.* **2** *Grammar* designating each individual of a group separately. *Each, every, either,* and *neither* are distributive words. **dis·trib·u·tor** *n* **1** a person or firm that sells goods made by a producer. **2** a part of a gasoline engine that distributes electricity to spark plugs. **dis·trib·u·tor·ship** *n.*

dis·trict ['dɪstrɪkt] *n* **1** a part of a larger area, showing certain characteristics: *a residential district of town. Northern Manitoba is a large nickel-producing district in Canada.* **2** an area marked off for administrative purposes: *a school district.* ⟨Latin *districtus.* See DISTRESS.⟩

dis·trust [dɪs'trʌst] *v* not trust; put no confidence in. **dis·trust** *n.* **dis·trust·ful** *adj.* **dis·trust·ful·ly** *adv.* **dis·trust·ful·ness** *n.* **distrustful of** lacking confidence in.

dis·turb [dɪ'stɜrb] *v* **1** destroy the peace of: *The noise disturbed us so much that we couldn't sleep.* **2** interrupt the work or activity of: *Don't disturb the class.* **3** put out of order: *Someone has disturbed my papers.* **4** trouble: *They were disturbed by the results of the survey.* **5** *Psychology* cause to be poorly adjusted or emotionally unbalanced (as past participle): *Disturbed children often do poorly in school.* **dis·turb·er** *n.* **dis·turb·ing** *adj.* **dis·turb·ance** *n.* ⟨Latin *dis-* (intensive) + *turba* commotion⟩.

dis·u·nite [ˌdɪsjə'nəit] *v* **1** separate. **2** destroy the unity of; cause dissension in. **dis·u·ni·ty** *n*. **dis·un·ion** *n* separation; separated condition.

dis·use [dɪs'jus]*n* lack of use: *The old tools were rusted from disuse.* *v* [dɪs'juz] stop using: *a long-disused method.*

di·syl·lab·ic [ˌdaɪsɪ'læbɪk] *or* [ˌdɪsɪ'læbɪk] *adj* made up of two syllables.

ditch [dɪtʃ] *n* **1** a trench dug in the earth, usually to carry away water. **2** specifically, the trench along the side of a road. *v* **1** drive (a vehicle) into a ditch. **2** land (an aircraft not equipped for it) on water. **3** *Informal* discard or abandon: *She ditched her husband.* ⟨Old English *dīc*⟩ **ditch·dig·ger** *n* a person or machine that digs ditches.

dith·er ['dɪðər] *n* *Informal* a state of quivering excitement or hesitation: *We were all in a dither, waiting for the results.* *v* hesitate because of indecision; waver. ⟨origin uncertain⟩ **dith·er·ing** *n* *Computers* a way of softening jagged edges in an image.

dit·to ['dɪtou] *Informal n* the same thing: *"I'll have a muffin." "Ditto for me."* *v* copy or repeat: *She simply dittos what I say.* *interj* I say the same; I agree. ⟨Italian = said⟩ **ditto mark** a small mark (") used in lists, tables, etc., directly under something written to show that it is repeated.

dit·ty ['dɪti] *n* a short, simple song. ⟨Old French *dite;* Latin *dictare* dictate⟩

di·u·ret·ic [ˌdaɪə'rɛtɪk] *adj* increasing the production of urine. **di·u·ret·ic** *n*. ⟨Greek *diourētikos; dia-* through + *oureein* urinate⟩

di·ur·nal [daɪ'ɜrnəl] *adj* **1** to do with the daytime. **2** *Zoology, botany* active or opening during the day and sleeping or closing at night. **3** lasting a day. **4** occurring every day. **di·ur·nal·ly** *adv*. ⟨Latin *diurnalis; dies* day⟩

di·va ['divə] *n* a prima donna; famous woman singer. ⟨Italian; Latin *diva* goddess⟩

Di·va·li [dɪ'vɑli] *n* See DIWALI.

di·van [dɪ'væn] *or* ['daɪvæn] *n* a low, usually backless and armless couch. ⟨Turkish *divān,* Persian *dēvān* book of accounts; couches of this type were originally in council chambers⟩

dive [daɪv] *v* **dived** or **dove, dived, div·ing** **1** plunge headfirst, usually into water. **2** go out of sight suddenly: *She dived into an alley.* **3** plunge the hand suddenly into anything: *He dived into his pocket and fished out a dollar.* **4** of an aircraft, missile, submarine, etc., descend at a steep angle. *n* **1** an act of diving. **2** *Informal* a shabby, cheap, disreputable place. ⟨Old English *dȳfan*⟩ **dive into** embark on with eager enthusiasm. **take a dive** *Informal* **a** *Boxing* fall down deliberately to feign a knockout. **b** in other sports, fall deliberately and strategically. **dive bomber** a bomber that releases its bomb load just before it pulls out of a dive toward the target. **dive–bomb** *v*. **div·er** *n* **1** a person or thing that dives. **2** a person who does

work under water. **diving board** a board with a spring, fixed over a pool and used to dive from. **diving suit** a waterproof suit with a helmet into which air is pumped through a tube, worn for work under water.

USAGE
Both **dived** and **dove** are standard forms for the past tense in Canadian English, but **dived** seems to be more widely preferred in writing and formal contexts.

di·verge [daɪ'vɜrdʒ] *v* **1** move in different directions from a point: *Our paths diverged at the fork in the road.* **2** differ: *Their opinions diverged on this matter.* **3** become gradually different: *Her tastes diverged from mine as we grew older.* **4** *Mathematics* (of a series) increase indefinitely as more terms are added. Compare CONVERGE. **di·ver·gence** *n*. **di·ver·gent** *adj*. ⟨Latin *dis-* in different directions + *vergere* slope⟩

di·verse [dɪ'vɜrs], [daɪ'vɜrs], *or* ['daɪvɜrs] *adj* **1** different: *The authors represent two very diverse outlooks.* **2** varied; various: *diverse articles of clothing, a person of diverse talents.* **di·verse·ly** *adv*. **di·verse·ness** *n*. **di·ver·si·ty** *n*. ⟨Latin *diversus*⟩ **di·ver·si·fy** [dɪ'vɜrsə,faɪ] *v* **1** vary; introduce variety to: *to diversify one's interests.* **2** extend (business activity) into different fields: *The company has begun to diversify.* **3** distribute (investments, etc.) among different securities to reduce risk. **di·ver·si·fi·ca·tion** *n*.

di·vert [dɪ'vɜrt] *or* [daɪ'vɜrt] *v* **1** turn aside: *to divert water from a stream.* **2** *Rare* entertain: *a book to divert her during the flight.* **3** distract: *Her jokes diverted me from my work.* ⟨Latin *dis-* aside + *vertere* turn⟩ **di·ver·sion** *n* **1** a manoeuvre to draw attention away from a planned activity: *You create a diversion while I slip into the vault.* **2** pastime; entertainment. **3** a turning aside: *a diversion of water to another area.* **di·ver·sion·ar·y** *adj*.

di·vest [dɪ'vɛst] *or* [daɪ'vɛst] *v* **1** strip; rid; free: *to divest oneself of all preconceived ideas.* **2** force to give up something: *divested of one's rights.* **3** take away or sell off (property). **di·vest·i·ture, di·vest·ure,** or **di·vest·ment** *n*. ⟨Latin *divestire* lit., unclothe; *vestire* clothe⟩

di·vide [dɪ'vaɪd] *v* **1** separate into parts. **2** *Mathematics* split into equal parts and find the size of each part: *Divide 8 by 2, and you get 4.* **Symbol** ÷ **3** share: *Divide the candy among you.* **4** mark off in units; graduate: *a ruler divided into centimetres.* **5** split or be split by a difference of feeling or opinion: *We were divided on that issue.* **6** form a boundary between: *A river divides the two countries.* *n* a ridge of land separating regions drained by two different river systems. **di·vid·ed** *adj*. ⟨Latin *dividere*⟩ **divided highway** a road with a median strip between lanes of traffic going in opposite directions. **div·i·dend** ['dɪvə,dɛnd] *or* [-dənd] *n* **1** *Mathematics* a number to be divided by another: *In 8 ÷ 2, 8 is the dividend.* **2** a sum of money to be shared by those to whom it belongs; especially, the profits of a company divided among its shareholders. **3** one share of such a sum. **4** benefit: *An active lifestyle brings important dividends.* **di·vid·er** *n* **1** a device separating an indoor area into sections; partition. **2** a piece of cardboard separating sections of a notebook, diskette storage box, card index, etc. **di·vis·i·ble** [dɪ'vɪzəbəl] *adj* capable of being divided without leaving a remainder: *Any even number is divisible by 2.* **di·vi·sion** [dɪ'vɪʒən] *n* **1** a dividing or being divided. **2** a thing that divides; boundary. **3** one of the parts into which a thing is divided: *He works in the company's sales division.* **4** disunity; dissension. **5** *Military* a major unit under single command. **6** *Biology* a major category in the classification of plants. **di·vi·sion·al** *adj*. **division of labour** or **labor** the assignment of different tasks to specialists, or to different genders or age groups, etc. **di·vi·sive** [dɪ'vəɪsɪv] *or* [dɪ'vɪzɪv] *adj* tending to divide, disunite, etc. **di·vi·sor** [dɪ'vaɪzər] *n* a number by which another is divided: *In 8 ÷ 2, 2 is the divisor.* **div·vy** ['dɪvi] *v Slang* divide or share (often with *up*).

di·vine [dɪ'vaɪn] *adj* **1** of, from, or for God or a god. **2** possessing the nature of God or a god. **3** *Informal* delightful; excellent: *"What a divine dress!" she cried.* **di·vine·ly** *adv.* *n* a theologian or member of the clergy. *v* **1** find out or foretell by supernatural means. **2** find out by guessing or intuition: *She divined their plan and immediately set out to stop them.* **3** locate (water, minerals, etc.) underground by means of a DIVINING ROD. **div·i·na·tion** [,dɪvə'neɪʃən] *n.* **di·vin·er** *n.* **di·vine·ness** *n.* ⟨Latin *divinus; divus* deity⟩ **divine right of kings** the right to rule, alleged to be given to kings by God rather than by people. **divining rod** a forked stick used to indicate the location of water or metal underground. **di·vin·i·ty** [dɪ'vɪnəti] *n* **1** a divine being; god. **2 the Divinity** God. **3** divine nature: *the divinity of Jesus.* **4** theology: *divinity school.*

di·vis·ible, di·vis·ion, di·vi·sor See DIVIDE.

di·vorce [dɪ'vɔrs] *n* **1** the legal ending of a marriage. **2** complete separation: *the divorce of church and state.* **di·vorce** *v.* ⟨Latin *divortium* separation; *divertere.* See DIVERT.⟩ **di·vor·cee** [dɪ,vɔr'si] *or* [dɪ'vɔrsi] *n* a divorced person.

div·ot ['dɪvət] *n* a piece of turf dug up by the stroke of a golf club. ⟨origin uncertain⟩

di·vulge [dɪ'vʌldʒ] *or* [daɪ'vʌldʒ] *v* reveal (secret information). **di·vulg·ence** *n.* ⟨Latin *divulgare* publish; *dis-* away + *vulgus* people⟩

Di·wa·li [dɪ'vali] *n* a Hindu festival celebrated in fall, dedicated to Lakshmi; often called **Festival of Lights.** Also, **Divali.** ⟨Hindi⟩

Dix·ie·land or **dix·ie·land** ['dɪksi,lænd] *n* a style of orchestral jazz with a strong rhythm in 4/4 time. ⟨*Dixie,* nickname for S US⟩

di·zy·got·ic twins [,daɪzaɪ'gɒtɪk] twins derived from two zygotes; fraternal twins.

diz·zy ['dɪzi] *adj* **1** feeling as if things are spinning around and one is losing one's balance; light-headed. **2** dazed or confused; bewildered. **3** likely to cause dizziness: *a dizzy height.* **4** *Informal* silly. **diz·zi·ly** *adj.* **diz·zi·ness** *n.* ⟨Old English *dysig* foolish⟩

DJ or **D.J.** DISC JOCKEY.

djinn [dʒɪn] See JINN.

dm decimetre(s).

DNA a long, helical molecule made up of acids that is an essential component of all living matter and contains the genetic codes determining heredity. ⟨abbreviation of *deoxyribonucleic acid*⟩ **DNA fingerprint** a unique pattern of DNA bands obtained from any piece of living or once-living matter and used for conclusive identification. **DNA testing** the process of obtaining a DNA fingerprint.

do¹ [du] *v pres sg* **does;** *pt* **did;** *pp* **done;** *ppr* **do·ing 1** carry out; perform: *easier said than done.* **2** complete: *to do an assignment.* **3** make: *to do a film.* **4** be the cause of; bring about: *to do justice. A holiday will do you good.* **5** have as a livelihood: *What does his mother do?* **6** deal with as the case may require: *to do one's hair, to do the dishes.* **7** get along: *How are they doing?* **8** be satisfactory: *Any kind of paper will do.* **9** act; behave: *You have done wisely.* **10** cover: *We did 100 km yesterday.* **11** *Informal* go at a speed of: *That car was doing at least 120 km/h.* **12** *Informal* cheat; trick: *to do someone out of their life savings.* **13** *Informal* spend (time) in jail as an inmate: *She did six months.* **14** *Slang* use (a drug): *to do heroin.* **15 Do** is also used with a purely structural, auxiliary function with *not,* in questions, and in other constructions, as well as to refer to a verb already used: *Do you dance? I did not know that. He doesn't work the same hours that I do.* *n* **1** *Informal* celebration: *They had a big do for us.* **2** *Informal* something required by rule or custom: *the do's and don'ts of etiquette.* **do·a·ble** ['duəbəl] *adj.* ⟨Old English *dōn*⟩ **do away with a** abolish: *do away with a rule.* **b** kill. **do by** act or behave toward. **do for** look after the needs of, as housekeeper, etc: *Who did for her while she was sick?* **do in** *Informal* **a** ruin or kill: *That's enough to do anybody in.* **b** tire out: *I'm all done in.* **do one's bit.** See BIT². **do or die** succeed no matter what the cost. **do-or-die** *adj.* **do over** *Informal* **a** redo. **b** renovate or redecorate. **do up a** close the fastenings of: *to do up a coat.* **b** wrap up: *to do up a package.* **c** clean and get ready for use: *to do up a room.* **d** style one's hair. **do with** enjoy or use (preceded by *can* or *could*): *I could do with a mug of tea now.* **do without** get along without. **have** (or **be**) **to do with** relate to: *Abstract art has little to do with everyday experience.* **how do you do?** (in formal introductions) Pleased to meet you. **do·er** ['duər] *n* **1** one that does. **2** an active, energetic person who accomplishes a lot. **do-good·er** *n Informal* a person who is too eager to set things right. **do·ings** ['duɪŋz] *n pl*

1 behaviour. 2 activities. **do–it–your·self** *adj* designed to be done or used by amateurs: *a do-it-yourself tiling kit.* **do–it–your·self·er** *n* *Informal* one who likes to try to do skilled work without the help of a professional. **done** [dʌn] 1 finished: *The job is done. Are you done with this newspaper?* 2 fully cooked. 3 proper according to social convention: *the done thing. That's simply not done.* **done for** *Informal* ruined; doomed. **done with** finished; dealt with: *Let's get this over and done with.*

do² [dou] *n Music* 1 the first or last tone of an eight-tone scale; the tonic note. 2 the tone C. ⟨Italian *do* used for the *ut* of *gamut*⟩

Do·ber·man pin·scher ['doubərmən 'pɪnʃər] a breed of large, short-haired dog, popular as a watchdog. ⟨L. *Doberman*, its German breeder + German *Pinscher* terrier⟩

do·cile ['dousaɪl] *or* ['dɒsaɪl] *adj* 1 meekly obedient. 2 easily trained. **do·cile·ly** *adv.* **do·cil·i·ty** [-'sɪləti] *n.* ⟨Latin *docilis; docere* teach⟩

dock¹ [dɒk] *n* 1 a platform over the water, for loading and unloading boats or ships. 2 the water between two piers, permitting the entrance of ships. 3 a large basin or compartment equipped with floodgates to receive ships for loading, unloading, and repair. 4 a bay or platform for loading and unloading trucks, aircraft, etc. *v* 1 come or bring into or alongside a dock. 2 join (spacecraft) together in space. ⟨Middle Dutch *docke*⟩
dock·age *n* a charge for using a dock. **dock·work·er** *n* a worker who loads and unloads cargo. **dock·yard** *n* a place where ships are built, equipped, and repaired.

dock² [dɒk] *n* the part of a tail left after cutting or clipping. *v* 1 cut short (an animal's tail or ears). 2 cut; deduct (an amount) from, esp as a penalty: *to dock someone's pay, to dock points for poor spelling.* ⟨Old English *-docca*, as in *finger-docca* finger muscle⟩

dock³ [dɒk] *n* the place where an accused person stands in court. ⟨Flemish *dok* pen⟩

dock⁴ [dɒk] *n* any of numerous herbs of the buckwheat family, some of which are troublesome weeds. ⟨Old English *docce*⟩

dock·et ['dɒkɪt] *n* 1 a list of cases to be tried by a court. 2 a list of decisions made in a court. 3 any list of items to be dealt with. 4 a label giving the contents of a package, document, etc. **dock·et** *v.* ⟨origin uncertain⟩

doc·tor ['dɒktər] *n* 1 a person licensed to treat diseases. 2 a holder of the highest degree in a university: *a Doctor of Philosophy. Abbrev* **Dr.** 3 any learned person. *v* 1 give medical treatment to. 2 alter or add finishing touches to: *to doctor an essay. You can doctor your own tea.* 3 tamper with in a dishonest way: *to doctor accounts.* ⟨Latin = teacher; *docere* teach⟩
doc·tor·al *adj* to do with a doctor (def. 2) or doctorate. **doc·tor·ate** *n* the degree of Doctor given by a university.

doc·trine ['dɒktrən] *n* 1 the body of beliefs held and taught by a religion, philosophy, political ideology, etc. 2 one of these beliefs. **doc·tri·nal** [,dɒk'traɪnəl] *or* ['dɒktrənəl] *adj.* ⟨Latin *doctrina; doctor.* See DOCTOR.⟩
doc·tri·naire [,dɒktrə'nɛr] *adj* 1 applying a theory rigidly without considering practical consequences in a given case. 2 dogmatic.

doc·u·ment ['dɒkjəmənt] *n* 1 something written that gives information or official proof of some fact. 2 *Computers* a text file. *v* ['dɒkjə,mɛnt] 1 prove or support by means of official papers or authoritative references: *a well-documented fact.* 2 record or show in a book, film, etc.: *The film documents the history of the North.* ⟨Latin *documentum* example, proof; *docere* show, teach⟩
doc·u·dra·ma *or* **doc·u–dra·ma** ['dɒkju,dræmə] *or* [-,drɑmə] *n* a factual film with fictional elements added for dramatic interest. **doc·u·men·ta·rist** *n* a maker of documentaries. **doc·u·men·ta·ry** [,dɒkjə'mɛntəri] *adj* 1 that consists of documents: *documentary evidence.* 2 presenting factual information in an artistic way: *a documentary film. n* a documentary film, television show, etc. **doc·u·men·ta·tion** *n* 1 documents collectively; official papers. 2 print material explaining the use of some equipment, piece of computer software, etc. 3 the act of documenting.

dod·der ['dɒdər] *v* move unsteadily or with trembling: *He dodders around as if he were ninety.* **dod·der·er** *n.* ⟨origin uncertain⟩

do·dec·a·gon [dou'dɛkə,gɒn] *n* a plane figure with 12 sides. ⟨Greek *dōdeka* twelve + *gōnia* angle⟩
do·dec·a·he·dron [,doudɛkə'hidrən] *n, pl* **-drons** *or* **-dra** [-drə] a solid with 12 faces.

dodge [dɒdʒ] *v* 1 move quickly in order to avoid being hit or caught by (a person or thing). 2 escape (an obligation, question, etc.) by trickery or evasion. **dodge** *n.* **dodg·er** *n.* ⟨origin uncertain⟩
dodge·ball *n* a game in which players forming a circle or two lines try to hit opponents with a large, inflated ball.

do·do ['doudou] *n, pl* **-dos** *or* **-does** 1 either of two extinct species of large, heavy bird with small flightless wings. 2 *Informal* a stupid person. 3 *Informal* an old-fashioned person. ⟨Portuguese *doudo* fool⟩
dead as a dodo defunct or obsolete, with no chance of revival: *That issue is dead as a dodo.* **go the way of the dodo bird** cease to exist.

doe [dou] *n* the female of a deer, antelope, and most other animals whose male is called a buck. See also HIND². ⟨Old English *dā*⟩
doe–eyed *adj* naive; innocent. **doe·skin** *n* soft leather made from the hide of a doe.

doff [dɒf] *v* 1 take off: *to doff one's clothes.* 2 tip or lift (one's hat) in greeting: *He doffed his hat.* 3 get rid of. ⟨contraction of *do off*⟩

dog [dɒg] *n* 1 a domesticated, meat-eating mammal, kept as a pet or used for herding, guarding, hunting, or leading the blind. 2 any of various animals closely or vaguely

resembling a dog, such as the prairie dog.
3 *Informal* a very inferior, unattractive, or
unpleasant person or thing. **4** *Informal*
fellow: *Lucky dog!* **5** a device for gripping
things. **6** *Informal* short for HOT DOG.
v **dogged, dog·ging 1** follow closely and
persistently like a dog. **2** worry as if by a dog:
dogged by financial crises for several years.
dog·gy *adj.* **dog·like** *adj.* ⟨Old English *docga*⟩
a dog's age a very long time: *I haven't spoken
to her in a dog's age.* **every dog has his day**
everyone gets some attention or good fortune
sometime. **go to the dogs** be ruined. **let
sleeping dogs lie** don't stir up unnecessary
trouble. **put on the dog** *Informal* behave or
dress in a showy, affected manner. **teach an
old dog new tricks** get an older person to
accept new ideas or methods.
dog·cart *n* **1** a small cart pulled by a dog or
dogs. **2** a small, open, usually two-wheeled
carriage with two seats that are back to back.
dog·catch·er *n* a person whose job is to take
stray dogs to the pound. **dog collar 1** a collar
for a dog. **2** *Informal* a clerical collar. **dog
days** in the northern hemisphere, a period of
very hot and humid weather during July and
August ⟨with reference to the rising of Sirius,
or the Dog Star⟩. **dog–ear** *n* a folded-down
corner of a page in a book. **dog–ear** *v.*
dog–eared *adj.* **dog–eat–dog** *adj* marked by
ruthless competition. **dog·fight** *n Informal* **1** a
fight between dogs. **2** any rough fight or
uproar. **3** combat between fighter planes.
dog·fish *n* **1** any of several species of small
shark, esp the **spiny dogfish. 2** bowfin.
dog·ged [ˈdɒgɪd] *adj* stubborn; persistent:
dogged efforts. **dog·ged·ly** *adv.* **dog·ged·ness**
n. **dog·gie** *n* a child's word or a pet name for
a dog. **doggie bag** a bag supplied by a
restaurant for taking home leftovers from
one's meal. **dog·house** *n* a small shelter for a
dog. **in the doghouse** *Informal* in disfavour.
dog in the manger a person who prevents
others from enjoying something of no value
to himself or herself. **dog·leg** *n* a sharp bend,
as in a road. **dog·leg, -legged, -leg·ging** *v.*
dog·nap, -napped, -nap·ping *v* steal (a dog or
dogs) for ransom or resale. **dog paddle** an
unsophisticated swimming stroke in which
the body remains more or less vertical, the
arms pump up and down, and the legs move
as in a running position. **dog·sled** *n* ✶ a sled
pulled by dogs. **dog's life** a miserable life.
dog tag 1 *Informal* an identification disk
worn on a neck chain by a member of the
armed forces. **2** a metal disk attached to a
dog's collar, showing that a licence has been
paid for, and often giving the dog's name
and address. **dog team** *n* a number of dogs
trained to pull a vehicle together, esp a sled.
dog–tired *adj* very tired. **dog·tooth** *n,
pl* **-teeth** a canine tooth. **dog·tooth violet** any
of a genus of plants of the lily family, with
long, pointed leaves. **dog·trot** *n* a gentle trot.
dog·wood *n* any of a genus of trees, shrubs,
and herbs having clusters of small flowers
and red, dark blue, or white fruit. The

western flowering dogwood is the floral
emblem of British Columbia.
doge [doudʒ] *Italian* [ˈdodʒe] *n* the chief
magistrate of Venice or Genoa when they
were republics. ⟨Italian = leader; Latin *dux*⟩
dog·ger·el [ˈdɒgərəl] *n* poetry that is trivial
and poorly written. ⟨Middle English⟩
dog·gone [ˈdɒgˈgɒn] *Slang adj, adv* damned:
a doggone fool. ⟨alteration of *God damn*⟩
do·gie [ˈdougi] *n* in W Canada and the US, a
motherless calf in a range herd. Also, **do·gy.**
⟨origin uncertain⟩
dog·ma [ˈdɒgmə] *n, pl* **-mas** or **-ma·ta** [-mətə]
1 a belief or body of beliefs authorized by a
church. **2** any doctrine or belief. **3** opinion
asserted arrogantly as if it were authoritative.
⟨Greek *dogma* opinion; *dokeein* think⟩
dog·mat·ic *adj* **1** insisting too strictly and
rigidly on orthodox belief about something.
2 speaking or acting as if one's opinions were
authoritative. **dog·ma·tism** *n.* **dog·ma·tist** *n.*
do–good·er See DO.
Dog·rib [ˈdɒgrɪb] *n, pl* **-rib** or **-ribs 1** a
member of a First Nations people of the
Northwest Territories. The Dogrib are one of
the Dene peoples and traditionally occupied
the region between Great Bear and Great
Slave Lakes. **2** their Athapascan language.
Dog·rib *adj.*
dog·wood See DOG.
doi·ly [ˈdɔɪli] *n* a small, decorative piece of
linen, lace, or paper used on serving plates,
under vases or centrepieces, etc. ⟨name of
17c London dry-goods dealer⟩
do·ings, do–it–yourself See DO.
do·jo [ˈdoudʒou] *n* a gymnasium or studio
where martial arts are taught. ⟨Japanese⟩
dol·drums [ˈdɒldrəmz] *or* [ˈdoul-] *n pl*
1 certain regions of the ocean near the
equator where the wind is very light or
changeable, formerly often immobilizing
sailing ships. **2** the calm or windless weather
there. **3** low spirits: *We were in the doldrums
because of the constant drizzle. This should get
rid of the doldrums.* ⟨probably related to *dull*⟩
dole [doul] *n* **1** a portion of money, food,
etc. given in charity. **2 the dole** government
assistance in the form of employment
insurance or welfare payments. **3** a portion
of anything given out.
v deal (*out*) in portions. ⟨Old English *dāl* part.
Related to DEAL.⟩
dole·ful [ˈdoulfəl] *adj* sad; gloomy.
doll [dɒl] *n* **1** a child's plaything made to
look like a person. **2** *Slang* a very attractive or
likable person.
v Slang dress in a stylish or showy way. (with
up): *They were all dolled up for the party.*
doll–like *adj.* ⟨pet name for *Dorothy*⟩
doll·house or **doll's house** a miniature house
for dolls, used as a toy. **doll·y** *n* **1** a child's
name for a doll. **2** a small, low frame on
wheels, used to move heavy objects or to lie
on while working under vehicles, machinery,
etc. **3** a small truck on which a movie or

television camera is moved around. *v* move a camera on a dolly: *The cameraman dollied in for the final scene.*

dol·lar ['dɒlər] *n* the basic unit of money in Canada and other countries, divided into 100 cents. *Symbol* $ ⟨German *(Joachims)thaler* coin of St. Joachim's valley (in Bohemia)⟩
dollar diplomacy a rich country's use of economic aid to needy nations to advance its own interests. **dollar sign** the symbol $, meaning dollar(s). **top dollar** a very high price or wage: *to pay top dollar.*

dol·lop ['dɒləp] *n* a portion, small or large, of something soft: *a dollop of ice cream. v* apply or serve in dollops. ⟨Scandinavian⟩

dol·man sleeve ['doulmən] *or* ['dɒl-] *n* a sleeve tapering from narrow at the wrist to very wide at the shoulder. ⟨Turkish *dōlāmān* a type of robe⟩

dol·men ['doulmən] *or* ['dɒl-] *n* a prehistoric monument, generally regarded as a tomb, consisting of a large, flat stone laid across upright ones. ⟨Breton *tol* table + *men* stone⟩

dol·o·mite ['dɒlə,məit] *or* ['doulə-] *n* a rock consisting mainly of magnesium carbonate and calcium. **dol·o·mit·ic** [-mɪtɪk] *adj.* ⟨D.G. de *Dolomieu* (1750-1801), French geologist⟩

do·lour or **do·lor** ['doulər] *n Poetic* sorrow; grief. **dol·or·ous** ['dɒlərəs] *or* ['doulərəs] *adj.* ⟨Latin *dolor*⟩

dol·phin ['dɒlfən] *n* 1 any of various small, highly intelligent toothed whales having a beaklike snout. 2 loosely, porpoise. ⟨Old French *daulphin;* Greek *delphis*⟩

dolt [doult] *n* a dull, stupid person. **dolt·ish** *adj.* ⟨obsolete *dold* pp of Middle English **dole(n)* to dull, Old English *dol* dull⟩

–dom *suffix* 1 the position, rank, or realm of: *kingdom.* 2 the condition of being: *martyrdom.* 3 all those who are: *fandom.* ⟨Old English⟩

do·main [də'mein] *n* 1 the territory under the control of a ruler or government. 2 the land owned by one person. 3 a field of thought, action, etc.: *the domain of politics.* 4 *Computers* one of a set of addresses on the Internet, identified by a common suffix representing a country, organization, network, etc. A **domain name** is the sequence of characters beginning with www. that identifies a network connection on the Internet. 5 *Mathematics* the set of values taken on by the independent variable of a function. ⟨Latin *dominium; dominus,* lord, *domus* house⟩

dome [doum] *n* 1 *Architecture* a rounded roof on a circular base. 2 something like a high rounded roof: *the dome of the sky.* 3 any building with such a roof, esp a sports stadium. 4 a clear, bubble-like projection in the roof of a railway car enhancing the view for passengers. 5 *Slang* the head.
v 1 furnish with a dome. 2 form into the shape of a dome. **domed** *adj.* **dome-like** *adj.* ⟨Greek *dôma* roof, house⟩
dome fastener ✱ a fastener consisting of two parts, one with a rounded projection in the

centre that snaps into a hole in the other.

do·mes·tic [də'mɛstɪk] *adj* 1 of the home or family affairs: *a domestic scene.* 2 fond of home and family life. 3 of animals, not wild. 4 of or from one's own country; not foreign: *domestic cars, domestic news.*
n a household servant. **do·mes·ti·cal·ly** *adv.* **do·mes·tic·i·ty** [,doumə'stɪsəti] *n.* ⟨Latin *domesticus; domus* house⟩
do·mes·ti·cate *v* 1 tame. 2 make fond of home and family life. **do·mes·ti·ca·tion** *n.*

dom·i·cile ['dɒmə,saɪl] *or* ['dɒməsəl] *n* 1 a dwelling place. 2 *Law* a place of permanent residence.
v settle in a domicile. ⟨Latin *domicilium; domus* house⟩

dom·i·nant ['dɒmənənt] *adj* 1 controlling; very influential: *a dominant influence.* 2 rising high above its surroundings: *the dominant hills to the west.* 3 *Music* to do with the fifth note in a standard major or minor scale. 4 *Genetics* to do with the one gene, out of a corresponding pair, that gets expressed as a trait in the organism. Compare RECESSIVE.
n 1 *Music* the fifth tone in an eight-tone scale. 2 *Genetics* dominant gene or character. 3 *Ecology* the most extensive species in a community, determining the kind and abundance of the others. **dom·i·nance** *n.* ⟨Latin *dominari* dominate; *dominus* lord⟩
dom·i·nate *v* 1 be or become dominant (in): *Our team dominates the league.* 2 control by superior power or force of character: *Her parents dominate her.* 3 rise or tower above. **dom·i·na·tion** *n.* **dom·i·neer** [,dɒmə'nir] *v* rule at one's own will; tyrannize (with *over*). **dom·i·neer·ing** *adj* aggressively trying to control others. **do·min·ion** [də'mɪnjən] *n* 1 supreme authority; control. 2 a territory under the rule of one person or government. 3 **Dominion** a name formerly used for Canada and certain other self-governing countries in the British Commonwealth. **Dominion Day** old name for **Canada Day.**

SYNONYMS
Dominant = more influential, powerful, or important, more frequent or noticeable than most others: *Freedom is a dominant theme in his novels.* **Predominant** = surpassing all others in these qualities: *Of all the things that motivated him, love was predominant.*

dom·i·no ['dɒmə,nou] *n, pl* **-noes** or **-nos** 1 **dominoes** (*pl* with *sg* verb) a game played with rectangular tiles that are either blank or marked with dots on one side. 2 one of the tiles in this game. 3 a masquerade costume consisting of a long, loose, hooded cloak and a mask. ⟨Latin, form of *dominus* master⟩
domino effect the effect of an act or event which triggers a series of similar events. ⟨with reference to the way dominoes standing in a row all fall when one is toppled⟩

don[1] [dɒn] *Spanish* [don] *n* 1 in some Canadian universities and colleges, an official in charge of a student residence. 2 in the UK, a university teacher. 3 **Don** a Spanish title meaning Mr. or Sir. **4** a Spanish gentleman. ⟨Spanish; Latin *dominus* lord⟩

Don Juan [ˌdɒn ˈwɒn] *or* [ˌdɒn ˈhwɒn] any man notorious for seducing women and living a dissolute life. ⟨after a legendary Spanish nobleman⟩ **don·nish** *adj* pedantic or formal like a university don. **Don Qui·xo·te** [kiˈhouti] *Spanish* [kiˈxote] a person of high but ridiculously impractical ideals. ⟨hero of a satirical novel by Spanish writer Cervantes⟩

don² [dɒn] *v* **donned, don·ning** put on (clothes). ⟨contraction of *do on*⟩

do·nate [douˈneit] *or* [ˈdouneit] *v* give freely, esp to a public institution or charitable cause: *My mother donates blood regularly. He donated a computer to the school.* **do·na·tion** *n.* ⟨Latin *donare; donum* gift⟩ **do·nor** [ˈdounər] *n* **1** a person who donates. **2** *Physics* in a covalent bond, the atom which supplies the shared pair of electrons.

done See DO.

Don Juan See DON¹.

don·key [ˈdɒŋki] *n* **1** a domestic animal resembling a horse but smaller, with longer ears, a shorter neck and mane, and smaller hooves. **2** a stubborn, silly, or stupid person. **3** DONKEY ENGINE. ⟨perhaps from *Duncan*⟩ **donkey engine** a small steam engine. **donkey engineer. donkey's years** *Informal* a very long time: *We haven't seen her in donkey's years.* **don·key–work** *n* difficult and dull work.

do·nor See DONATE.

Don Qui·xo·te See DON¹.

doo·dad [ˈdudæd] *n Informal* **1** a fancy, trifling ornament. **2** doohickey.

doo·dle [ˈdudəl] *v* make drawings or designs while thinking of something else: *He doodled while talking on the phone.* **doo·dle** *n.* ⟨German *dudeln* play the bagpipe⟩

doo·hick·ey [ˈdu,hɪki] *n Informal* any small device whose name has been temporarily forgotten. ⟨humorous coinage based on *do*⟩

doom [dum] *n* **1** fate. **2** an unhappy or terrible fate; ruin; death: *The soldiers marched to their doom in battle.* **3** judgment; sentence. *v* destine; assign to a given fate, esp an unhappy one. ⟨Old English *dōm*⟩ **doomed** *adj* bound for failure, death, or ruin. **doom·say·er** *n* one who habitually forecasts disaster. **dooms·day** *n* **1** the end of the world; day of God's final judgment of humankind. **2** any day of disaster or of settling accounts.

door [dɔr] *n* **1** a movable hinged or sliding structure designed to close up an entrance to a room, cupboard, etc. **2** doorway: *He came through the door.* **3** the house or room to which a door leads: *Her office is the third door on the right.* **4** any means of access. **5** an opportunity. ⟨Old English *duru*⟩ **close, shut,** or **slam the door on** preclude; exclude: *The car accident slammed the door on our hopes of a summer trip.* **darken the door of** visit. **lay at someone's door** blame someone for. **out of doors** outdoors. **show someone the door** ask or order a person to leave.

door·bell *n* a bell at a door, used by a visitor to signal his or her arrival. **door·jamb** [-ˌdʒæm] or **door·post** *n* the upright piece forming the side of a doorway. **door·keeper** *n* **1** a person who guards a door or entrance. **2** doorman. **door·knob** *n* a knob on a door that releases the latch of the door when turned. **door·man** *n, pl* **-men** a person whose work is opening the door of a hotel, apartment building, etc. for people going in or out. **door·mat** *n* **1** a mat at an outside door of a house for wiping dirt off shoes before entry. **2** *Informal* one who is easily imposed upon. **door·nail** *n* a nail with a large head. **dead as a doornail** entirely dead. **door·plate** *n* a metal plate on a door with a name, number, etc. on it. **door prize** a prize whose winner is drawn at random from those present at a public function. **door·sill** *n* threshold. **door·step** *n* a step leading from an outside door to the ground. **door·stop** *n* a device to hold a door open or to keep it from opening too far. **door–to–door** *adj* **1** making a call at each address in turn in a particular area: *a door-to-door salesperson.* **2** going all the way from the original starting point to the final destination: *door-to-door delivery.* **door–to–door** *adv.* **door·way** *n* an entrance.

do·pa·mine [ˈdoupəˌmin] *n* **1** a drug used to treat shock resulting from certain heart conditions. **2** a neurotransmitter in the brain. ⟨*d*(ihydr)*o*(xy)*p*(henyl) + *amine*⟩

dope [doup] *Slang n* **1** a harmful narcotic drug, such as heroin. **2** a substance taken or administered illegally to enhance athletic performance. **3** information: *the latest dope on the scandal.* **4** a prediction. **5** a stupid person. **6** lubricant for machinery. *v* **1** give or apply dope to (often with *up*). **2** adulterate with another substance. **dop·er** *n.* ⟨Dutch *doop* dipping sauce; *dopen* dip⟩ **dope out** *Slang* figure out; work out. **dope fiend** *Slang* drug addict. **dope–sheet** *n* a sheet giving spectators information about a horse race. **dope·y** or **dop·y** *adj Slang* **1** drowsy from drugs. **2** very stupid.

dop·pel·gäng·er [ˈdʌpəlˌgɛŋər] *n* a person's ghostly double. ⟨German = doublegoer⟩

Doppler effect [ˈdɒplər] *Physics* an apparent shift in the frequency of sound, light, and other waves caused by relative movement between the source and the observer. ⟨C. *Doppler*, 19c Austrian physicist⟩

do·ré [ˈdɔrei] *or* [ˈdɔri] *n* **1** ✹ WALLEYE (def. 7). **2** [dɔˈrei] gilded. ⟨Cdn. French = golden⟩

dorm [dɔrm] *n Informal* dormitory.

dor·mant [ˈdɔrmənt] *adj* in a long-term state of inactivity: *a dormant volcano. Many plants are dormant over winter.* **dor·man·cy** *n.* ⟨Latin *dormire* sleep⟩

dor·mer [ˈdɔrmər] *n* a small gablelike structure projecting from a sloping roof, with a window set in it. ⟨orig a sleeping room. See DORMANT.⟩

dor·mi·to·ry [ˈdɔrməˌtɔri] *n* a sleeping room containing a number of beds.

adj of a community, serving as a residential satellite to a nearby city. ⟨Latin *dormitorium; dormire* sleep⟩

dor·mouse ['dɔr,maʊs] *n, pl* -**mice** any of numerous mouselike rodents of the Old World. ⟨probably English dialect *dorm* sleep (Latin *dormire*) + mouse⟩

dor·sal ['dɔrsəl] *adj* **1** *Zoology* to do with the back: *a dorsal fin.* **2** *Botany* of the side of a leaf, branch, etc. away from the axis. **dor·sal·ly** *adv.* ⟨Latin *dorsum* back⟩

Dor·set ['dɔrsɪt] *n* an indigenous culture of NE Canada and N Greenland, lasting from about 900 B.C. to A.D. 1000 and characterized by skill in carving and by seal and caribou hunting. ⟨Cape *Dorset*, Baffin Island⟩

do·ry[1] ['dɔri] *n* a rowboat with a flat bottom and high sides, often used by ocean fishers. ⟨Central American Indian *dóri* dugout⟩

do·ry[2] ['dɔri] *n* ❋ **1** John Dory, an edible sea fish. **2** WALLEYE (def. 7); doré. ⟨*doré*⟩

DOS DISK OPERATING SYSTEM.

dose [doʊs] *n* **1** the amount of a medicine to be taken at one time. **2** the amount of anything thought to be necessary: *a dose of flattery, a dose of hard work.* **3** the amount of radiation to which a person is exposed over a given period.
v give medicine to in doses: *They dosed him with quinine.* ⟨Greek *dosis* giving; *didonai* give⟩ **dos·age** *n* the size and frequency of a dose. **do·sim·e·ter** [doʊ'sɪmətər] *n* an instrument for measuring a dose.

do–si–do or **do–se–do** ['doʊ si 'doʊ] *n* a figure in many folk dances in which two partners start out facing, revolve round each other back to back, and return to their initial positions. ⟨French *dos–à–dos* back to back⟩

dos·si·er ['dɒsi,eɪ] *n* a file; collection of documents on a person or thing. ⟨French⟩

dot [dɒt] *n* **1** a tiny round mark. **2** a short sound or flash of light used in Morse code.
v **dot·ted, dot·ting 1** mark with a dot: *to dot one's i's.* **2** be scattered here and there in: *Trees dotted the landscape.* ⟨Old English *dott* head of a boil⟩
dot one's i's and cross one's t's be very meticulous. **on the dot (of)** at exactly (the given time): *at 5:15, on the dot. She arrived on the dot of six.*
dot·com [dɒt'kɒm] *n Informal* any company doing business on the Internet ⟨from URLs ending in *.com*⟩. **dot·com** *adj.* **dot matrix printer** a computer printer which prints letters made up of dots. **dot·ted** *adj* **1** marked with a dot or dots. **2** made up of dots: *a dotted line.* **3** *Music* of a note or rest, followed by a dot adding half to its time value: *a dotted eighth.* **sign on the dotted line** commit oneself. **dot·ty** *adj* **1** *Informal* a bit crazy; eccentric. **2** *Informal* very enthusiastic. **3** full of dots. **dot·ti·ly** *adv.* **dot·ti·ness** *n.*

dote [doʊt] *v* be foolishly fond of (with *on* or *upon*): *He dotes on his daughter.* **dot·ing** *adj.* ⟨Middle English *doten*⟩
dot·age *n* an enfeebled mental condition sometimes accompanying old age. **do·tard** *n* a person in this condition.

dot·ty See DOT.

dou·ble ['dʌbəl] *adj* **1** twice as much, as many, as large, etc.: *double pay.* **2** for two: *a double bed.* **3** made up of two similar parts: *double doors.* **4** combining two in one: *The word 'bear' has a double meaning.* **5** *Botany* having multiple sets of petals. **6** insincere: *a double tongue.*
adv **1** twice. **2** as a pair or by pairs: *They rode double on the motorcycle.*
n **1** a number or amount that is twice as much: *I was paid double for that.* **2** a person or thing just like another: *I saw your double in the store yesterday.* **3** *Baseball* a hit that gets the batter to second base. **4 doubles** *pl* a game with two players per side. **5** in a film or play, a substitute: *She uses a stunt double.*
v **1** make or become twice as much, great, many, etc. **2** fold; bend: *to double one's fists. He doubled over in pain.* **3** go around: *The ship doubled the cape.* **4** move or cause to move at a run. **5** *Baseball* get a two-base hit. **6** *Music* play the same note or part as (another), an octave higher or lower. **dou·bly** *adv.* ⟨Old French; Latin *duplus*⟩
double back a fold over: *She doubled back the cloth to make a hem.* **b** go back the same way that one came. **double up a** fold up. **b** bend the upper part of the body toward the lower: *She doubled up in pain.* **c** share a room, a bed, etc. with another: *When guests came, the two brothers had to double up.* **on the double** quickly. **see double** see two of everything because of disturbed vision.
double agent a person supposedly working as a secret agent for one side but in fact working for the other, or deceiving both sides. **double bar** *Music* a double line on a staff, marking the end of a piece of music. **dou·ble–bar·relled** or **dou·ble–bar·reled** *adj* **1** with two barrels: *a double-barrelled shotgun.* **2** having a twofold purpose, effect, or meaning. **double bass** a stringed instrument with a deep bass tone, the largest member of the modern violin family. **double bassoon** a large bassoon, an octave lower in pitch than the ordinary bassoon. **double bill** two plays, movies, etc. presented on one program. **double bind** a situation in which two courses of action are required or expected, but it is impossible to do both. **double–blind** *adj* to do with an experiment in which neither the subject nor the researcher knows which treatment a given subject is receiving. **double–blind** *n.* **double boiler** a pair of pots, one of which fits onto the other. The food in the upper pot is cooked gently by the heat from the boiling water in the lower one. **double bond** *Chemistry* a bond in which two atoms in a molecule share two pairs of electrons. **dou·ble–breast·ed** *adj* of clothing, overlapping enough to make two thicknesses across the breast. **dou·ble–check** *v* check twice. **dou·ble–check** *n.* **double chin** a soft fold of flesh under the chin. **double–click** *v* *Computers* press twice on the mouse in rapid

succession. **double cross** *Informal* an act of treachery. **dou·ble–cross** *v.* **dou·ble–cros·ser** *n.* **double date** a DATE (def. 3) for two couples. **double–date** *v.* **dou·ble–deck·er** *n* a structure with two decks, floors, layers, levels, etc. **dou·ble–deck·er** *adj.* **dou·ble–dig·it** *adj* of a number or percentage, ranging from 10 to 99: *double-digit inflation.* **double Dutch** a skipping game in which two ropes are swung at a time. **dou·ble–edged** *adj* **1** two-edged. **2** having two contrary or complementary effects: *a double-edged compliment.* **dou·ble en·ten·dre** ['dʌbəl ɒn'tɒndrə] *or* ['dubəl-] *n* a word or expression with two meanings, one usually indelicate or improper. **double entry** a system of bookkeeping in which each transaction is recorded twice, once on the credit side of one account and once on the debit side of another. **double exposure** *Photography* two negatives superimposed onto the same print. **double feature** DOUBLE BILL. **double flat** *Music* a sign (♭♭) showing that a note must be lowered two half tones. **dou·ble–glazed** *adj* of a window, having two layers of glass with air between. **double glazing** *n.* **dou·ble–head·er** *n* **1** two baseball games between the same teams on the same day. **2** a railway train pulled by two engines. **double helix** the spiral character of each molecule of DNA, the base sequence on one strand being complementary to the sequence on the other. **double indemnity** in life insurance, a clause binding the insurance company to pay twice the face value of the policy in case of the accidental death of the insured. **dou·ble–joint·ed** *adj* having very flexible joints. **double negative** the use of two negatives in a sentence where only one is intended. *Example: There wasn't no butter in the store* to mean *There was no butter* or *There wasn't any butter.* **dou·ble–park** *v* park (a car, etc.) beside another which already fills the legitimate parking area. **double play** *Baseball* a play in which two base runners are put out. **double pneumonia** pneumonia affecting both lungs. **dou·ble–quick** *adj* very quick. *adv* in double-quick time. **double sharp** *Music* a sign (×) showing that a note must be raised two half tones. **dou·ble–space** *v* write or key in (text) leaving a space equal to one full line between lines. **dou·ble·speak** *n* deliberately ambiguous or misleading speech. **double standard** rules for behaviour (especially sexual) that are more liberal for men than for women. **dou·blet** *n* **1** a short, fitted jacket, worn by European men from about the 1400s to the 1600s. **2** a pair, or one of a pair, of two similar things. **dou·ble–take** *n* a delayed reaction to a situation, joke, etc., often used for comic effect. **dou·ble·think** *n* simultaneous acceptance of principles or concepts that are in fact contradictory. **double time 1** payment at twice the normal rate: *double time for working on Sundays.* **2** a rate of marching in which 180 paces, each about 90 cm, are taken in a minute. **3** *Music* **a** two beats to the bar. **b** of tempo, twice as fast as the previous tempo. **double–time** *v.*

double vision a disturbance of vision causing one to see two images of everything.

dou·bloon [dʌ'blun] *n* a former Spanish gold coin. ⟨Spanish *doblón*⟩

doubt [daʊt] *v* not believe; not be sure (of): *to doubt a claim, to doubt someone's sincerity. n* a lack of belief or certainty. **doubt·er** *n.* **doubt·ing** *adj.* ⟨Latin *dubitare*⟩
beyond doubt certain(ly). **in doubt** not sure. **no doubt** very likely: *Even if he had money, he'd no doubt expect me to pay the bill.* **without doubt** certainly.
doubt·ful *adj* **1** unclear; not at all certain: *a doubtful advantage.* **2** feeling uncertain: *You look doubtful.* **3** open to suspicion: *of doubtful reputation.* **doubt·ful·ly** *adv.* **doubt·ful·ness** *n.* **doubt·less** *adv* certainly or very likely: *He will doubtless understand at once.*

douche [duʃ] *n* a jet of water applied on or into any part of the body. **douche** *v.* ⟨French = shower⟩

dough [doʊ] *n* **1** a mixture of flour, liquid, and other ingredients for baking. **2** any soft, thick mass like this. **3** *Slang* money. ⟨Old English *dāg*⟩
dough·nut ['doʊˌnʌt] *n* a small deep-fried cake, often ring-shaped. **dough·y** *adj* **1** of crust, cake, etc., not fully cooked. **2** soft and flabby, pale, etc. like dough.

dough·ty ['daʊti] *adj Poetic* brave and strong. **dough·ti·ly** *adv.* **dough·ti·ness** *n.* ⟨Old English *dohtig; dugan* be good⟩

Doug·las fir ['dʌɡləs] any of a small genus of trees of the pine family native to W North America and E Asia. ⟨David *Douglas* (1798-1834), Scottish botanist and explorer⟩
Douglas maple a variety of maple growing on cliffs and rocky ledges along the northern Pacific coast, in sheltered valleys in the Rockies, and in the foothills of Alberta.

Douk·ho·bour or **Douk·ho·bor** ['dukəˌbɔr] *n* a member of a Christian sect, originally from Russia, traditionally holding that personal conscience supersedes any outside authority in all moral questions. Many Doukhobours settled in W Canada in the late 1890s. ⟨Russian *dukh* spirit + *borcy* wrestlers⟩

dour [dur] *or* [daʊr] *adj* gloomily stern. **dour·ly** *adv.* **dour·ness** *n.* ⟨Latin *durus* hard⟩

douse [daʊs] *v* **1** throw water on; drench. **2** plunge into liquid. **3** *Informal* put out (a light): *Douse the candles.* ⟨origin uncertain⟩

dove[1] [dʌv] *n* **1** any of various species of pigeon, esp any of the smaller, wild ones. **2** one who seeks a peaceful resolution of disputes. Compare HAWK[1] (def. 2). **dove·like** *adj*. **dov·ish** *adj*. ⟨Old English *dūfe*⟩

dove·cote ['dʌv,kout] *n* a shelter for doves or pigeons.   **dove·tail** *n* a wedge-shaped projection that fits into a corresponding gap to form a joint. *v* **1** join together in this way. **2** fit together perfectly: *Their strengths dovetailed to make them a great team.*

dove[2] [douv] *v* a pt of DIVE.

dow·a·ger ['dauədʒər] *n* **1** a woman who holds some title or property from her dead husband: *the queen dowager.* **2** *Informal* any dignified elderly woman. ⟨Old French *douage* dower; *douer* endow, Latin *dotare*⟩

dow·dy ['daudi] *adj* **1** dressed in dull, unstylish clothes. **2** of clothes, dull and unstylish. **dow·di·ly** *adv.* **dow·di·ness** *n.* ⟨origin uncertain⟩

dow·el ['dauəl] *n* a cylindrical peg fitted into corresponding holes on two parts to form a joint. **dow·el, -elled** or **-eled, -el·ling** or **-el·ing** *v.* ⟨related to German *Döbel* plug, tap⟩
dow·el·ling or **dow·el·ing** *n* wood in slender rods that can be cut up to make dowels.

dow·er ['dauər] *n Law* a widow's share of her dead husband's property. ⟨See DOWAGER.⟩

dow·itch·er ['dautʃər] *n* a shore bird of the same family as sandpipers and snipes, having a very long, straight bill. ⟨Iroquois⟩

down[1] [daun] *adv* **1** in or to a low or lower place or condition. **2** to a sitting or lying position: *She sat down.* **3** to or in a place or condition thought of as lower: *down south.* **4** at or to a smaller amount, degree, station, etc.: *The temperature has gone down.* **5** to a position or condition that prevents evasion, loss, etc.: *to track something down.* **6** from an earlier to a later time or person: *handed down from mother to daughter.* **7** to a less excited state: *Settle down, quiet down.* **8** in writing: *Take down what I say.* **9** actually; really: *Get down to the basics.* **10** in cash at the time of purchase: *I paid $30 down.*
adj **1** going or pointing down: *the down escalator.* **2** sad: *feeling down.* **3** having lost a given amount: *I'm down $5.* **4** *Computers* not working. **5** sick. **6** of one or more things in a series, dealt with: *One exam down, two to go!*
prep downward along or through: *to ride down a hill, to walk down a street.*
v **1** get down: *She downed the medicine at one swallow.* **2** defeat: *to down the favourite team.*
n **1** a downward movement. **2** a period of bad luck or unhappiness: *the ups and downs of life.* **3** *Football* a chance to move the ball forward. In Canadian football, a team has three downs in which to move the ball forward ten yards. ⟨Old English *adūne*, earlier *of dūne* from (the) hill⟩
be down on *Informal* **a** carry a grudge against. **b** oppose; disapprove of. **come down with** contract (an illness). **down and out** completely without money, friends, etc.

down–and–out·er *n.* **down to the ground** thoroughly: *a Conservative down to the ground.*
down with —— ! formula expressing strong opposition: *Down with TV!* **put down** belittle; humiliate; disparage.

down·beat *n Music* the first beat in a bar. *adj* gloomy. **down·cast** *adj* **1** directed downward: *downcast eyes.* **2** sad; dejected: *He was downcast after failing to make the team.* **down·draft** *n* a gust of air coming down (usually a chimney). **down East** See EAST. **down·er** *n Slang* **1** a depressant drug, such as a tranquillizer. **2** a depressing experience or situation: *That interview was a downer.* **down·fall** *n* **1** ruin, or a cause of ruin: *the downfall of an empire.* **2** a heavy fall of snow, etc. **down·grade** *n* a downward slope. *v* **1** lower the status or value of: *The position has been downgraded.* **2** speak slightingly of; belittle. **down·heart·ed** *adj* in low spirits; discouraged. **down·hill** *adv* down the slope of a hill. *adj* **1** going downward: *a downhill run.* **2** to do with skiing down high slopes. **go downhill** deteriorate; get worse and worse: *The business has been going downhill for some time.* **it's all downhill from here** the hardest part is over. **down·link** *n* the sending of signals from a satellite or spaceship to a receiver on earth. **down·load** *v Computers* transfer (files, programs, etc.) from one computer to another smaller or remote one. Compare UPLOAD. **down payment** a partial payment made at the time of purchase. **down·play** *v* treat as not very important. **down·pour** *n* a heavy rainfall. **down·right** *adj* **1** complete; absolute: *a downright lie.* **2** plain; straightforward and direct. **down·right** *adv.* **down·right·ness** *n.* **down·scale** ['daun,skeil] *adj* not catering to the wealthy, prestigious, etc. *v* **1** reduce the size or scope of. **2** make less opulent. **down·shift** *v* shift from a higher to a lower gear. **down·side** *n* disadvantage; negative aspect: *Good plan, but the downside is that she is away that day.* **down·size** *v* reduce the size or scope of (an operation, company, etc.), often by getting rid of staff. **down·spout** *n* a vertical pipe attached to an eavestrough to carry rainwater to the ground. **down·stage** *adj, adv* in a theatre, toward or at the front of the stage. **down·stairs** *adv* down the stairs. **2** on or to a lower floor: *I looked downstairs but couldn't find it. adj* on a lower floor: *downstairs rooms. n* a lower floor: *He rents out the downstairs.* **down·stream** *adv, adj* in the direction of the current of a river; farther along in the course of a river: *The sawmill was downstream from the town.* **down·swing** *n* a downward movement or trend: *a sharp downswing in sales.* **down time** or **down·time 1** time when equipment is not working. **2** a period of rest: *I need some down time from the stress of work.* **down–to–earth** *adj* practical and realistic. **down·town** *adv, adj* to or in the main or business section of a town: *to go downtown, in downtown Vancouver. n* the main or business section of a town. **down·trend** or **down·turn** *n* an economic decline. **down·trod·den** *adj* oppressed. **down under**

or **Down Under** the region of Australia, New Zealand, etc. **down·ward** *adv, adj* **1** toward a lower or worse place, degree, or condition. **2** from an earlier to a later time. Also (*adv*), **down·wards**. **down·wind** *adj, adv* **1** in the direction that the wind is blowing. **2** on the side opposite that from which the wind is blowing: *Keep downwind of the lion, so it can't smell you.*

down² [daʊn] *n* **1** the short, soft, fluffy feathers beneath the outer feathers of adult birds and forming the plumage of young birds. **2** soft hair or fluff: *The down on a boy's chin develops into a beard.* ⟨Old Norse *dúnn*⟩ **down–filled** *adj* filled with down from birds: *down-filled pillows.* **down·y** *adj* **1** covered with soft feathers or hair. **2** like down; soft; fluffy.

down³ [daʊn] *n* Usually **downs** *pl* a stretch of high, rolling, grassland. ⟨Old English *dūn*⟩

Down syndrome [daʊn] a congenital condition that typically results in a broad face, skin folds on the upper eyelids, and, often, development impairment. It is caused by a chromosomal defect. ⟨Langdon *Down*, 19c English physician⟩

dow·ry [ˈdaʊri] *n* the money, property, etc. that a bride brings to her husband. ⟨Anglo-French *dowarie*. See DOWER.⟩

dowse [daʊz] *v* use a DIVINING ROD to locate water, minerals, etc. **dows·er** *n*. ⟨dialect; perhaps Middle English *dushen* push down⟩

dox·ol·o·gy [dɒkˈsɒlədʒi] *n* a Christian hymn or poem praising God. ⟨Greek *doxa* glory, praise + *logos* speaking⟩

doy·en [ˈdɔɪən] *or* [dwɑˈjɛ̃] *n* a leader or senior member of a group. ⟨French = dean⟩ **doy·enne** [dɔɪˈjɛn] *or* [dwɑˈjɛn] *n* a woman who is a leader or senior member of a group.

doze [doʊz] *v* sleep lightly. **doze** *n*. ⟨related to Danish *döse* make dull⟩ **doze off** fall into a light sleep. **doz·y** *adj* **1** drowsy; sleepy. **2** mentally slow; stupid. **doz·i·ly** *adv*. **doz·i·ness** *n*.

doz·en [ˈdʌzən] *n, pl* **-ens** or (*after a number*) **-en** a group of 12. **doz·enth** *adj, n*. ⟨Old French *dozeine; douse* twelve, Latin *duodecim*⟩

DP or **D.P. 1** displaced person. **2** data processing.

dpi *Computers* a measure of the density of the image on a screen or produced by a printer. ⟨*dots per inch*⟩

Dr. or **Dr 1** Doctor. **2** Drive (in street names).

drab [dræb] *adj* **drab·ber**, **drab·best** dull; colourless or monotonous. *n* **1** a dull brownish grey. **2** a khaki drill uniform: *The soldiers wore drab on manoeuvres.* **drab·ly** *adv*. **drab·ness** *n*. ⟨variant of *drap* cloth; French. See DRAPE.⟩

drach·ma [ˈdrɑkmə] *or* [ˈdrækmə] *n, pl* **-mas** or **-mae** [-mi] the basic unit of currency in Greece, divided into 100 lepta. ⟨Greek *drachmē* handful⟩

dra·co·ni·an [dreiˈkouniən] *or* [drəˈkouniən] *adj* of rules or laws, harsh; unduly restrictive. ⟨*Draco*, Athenian legislator of the 7c B.C.⟩

draft [dræft] *n* **1** a current of air inside an enclosed space. **2** a device regulating air flow, as on a fireplace. **3** a rough, unpolished version of a drawing, plan, piece of writing, etc. **4 a** the process of selecting people for a special purpose, such as playing on a sports team. **b** the people so selected. **5** *esp US* the systematic selection of people for compulsory military service. **6** a written order requiring that the bearer be paid a stated amount of money. **7** the depth of water that a ship needs for floating. **8** an act of drinking or inhaling, or the amount drunk or inhaled at one time: *He emptied the glass in one draft. She took in a draft of fresh air.* **9** beer, ale, etc. drawn from a keg as ordered: *Do they sell draft?*
adj **1** used to pull loads: *draft horses.* **2** of ale or beer, on tap; drawn from a keg as ordered.
v **1** prepare a sketch or rough version of. *to draft new legislation.* **2** select from a group for some purpose or duty. ⟨variant of *draught*, Middle English *draht*; Old English *dragan* draw⟩ **on draft** of beer or ale, available to be drawn directly from a keg, etc. when ordered.
draft–dodg·er *n* one who evades compulsory military service, esp in the US. **draft·ee** [dræfˈti] *n* a person drafted for military service. **draft horse** a heavily built horse used for hauling heavy loads, pulling a plough, etc. **drafts·man** or **draughts·man** *n, pl* **-men 1** one who makes plans or sketches of things to be built. **2** one who drafts legal or official documents. **3** someone skilled at drawing. **draft·y** or **draught·y** *adj* letting in currents of air: *a drafty room.* **draft·i·ly** *adv*. **draft·i·ness** *n*.

drag [dræg] *v* **dragged, drag·ging 1** pull or move along heavily or slowly: *A team of horses dragged the log out of the forest.* **2** trail along the ground: *Your scarf is dragging.* **3** go too slowly: *Time drags when there's nothing to do.* **4** search (an area or body of water) by pulling a net, hook, etc. over the ground or bottom. **5** *Computers* move (an object displayed on a screen) using a mouse. **6** go or cause to go reluctantly or wearily: *to drag oneself out of bed.* **7** involve unnecessarily: *Don't drag her into this.* **8** *Slang* take part in or challenge to a DRAG RACE. **9** *Slang* inhale (*on* a cigarette).
n **1** a net, hook, etc., used in dragging. **2** the act of dragging. **3** the friction on a body as it moves through a fluid, acting in a direction opposite to the body's motion. **4** a device used to slow something down by means of friction. **5** any person or thing that holds back: *Such ideas are a drag on progress.* **6** *Slang* a puff on a cigarette. **7** *Slang* a person or thing that is boring or disappointing: *This party is a drag. What a drag that he's quitting!* **8** women's clothing worn by a man: *in drag.* ⟨Old Norse *draga* or variant of *draw*, Old English *dragan*⟩
drag and drop *Computers* the easy movement and release of items on a screen by means of the mouse. **drag one's feet** or **heels** act or work slowly on purpose. **drag out** (or **on**) make (or be) too slow or long: *to drag out a story. The reception dragged on till midnight.* **drag·gy** *adj* **1** dragging. **2** boring. **drag·net** *n*

1 a net used to drag (def. 4) an area of land or body of water. **2** a careful, extensive search for criminals, etc.: *a police dragnet.* **drag race** a contest with motor vehicles to see which can accelerate fastest.

drag·on ['drægən] *n* **1** a mythical monster, usually imagined as a huge, fierce, lizardlike or snakelike creature, often winged and breathing out fire and smoke. **2** a fierce or extremely stern person, esp a woman. **3** any of numerous small, brightly coloured S Asian tree lizards with winglike membranes. **drag·on·like** *adj.* ⟨Greek *drakōn*⟩
drag·on·fly *n* any of a suborder of insects having a long, slender body and four long, iridescent wings.

dra·goon [drə'gun] *n* **1** formerly, a soldier mounted on a horse and armed with a heavy musket. **2** a soldier in a cavalry regiment.
v force or bully (*into* something): *She was dragooned into signing a false statement.* ⟨French *dragon* dragon, pistol; later, soldier⟩

drain [drein] *v* **1** of liquid, flow or cause to flow off, esp gradually: *to drain water from a swamp, to drain cooked pasta. The water drains into a river.* **2** take away (from) slowly: *to drain money from an account. The long war had drained the country of its resources.* **3** use up the strength, vitality, etc. of (a person): *I was totally drained by the experience.* **4** empty by drinking: *He drained his glass.*
n **1** a means, such as a pipe, for carrying off liquid. **2** its opening in a floor, basin, etc. **3** the act or a cause of draining: *a drain of talent to other regions. That car is a drain on her budget.* **drain·age** *n.* ⟨Old English *drēahnian*⟩
down the drain (gone) to nothing or to waste: *That's $50 down the drain on that stupid play.*
drain·age *n* **1** the act or process of draining. **2** what is drained off. **drainage basin** the area drained by a river system. **drain·board** *n* a grooved board next to a sink, for draining water from washed dishes. **drain·er** *n* a pan, vat, etc. for draining off liquid. **drain·pipe** *n* a pipe for carrying off water or other liquid.

drake [dreik] *n* an adult male duck. ⟨Old English *draca;* Greek *drakōn* dragon⟩

dram [dræm] *n* **1** a small unit in various systems of weight **2** a small drink of spirits. ⟨Old French *drame;* See DRACHMA.⟩

dra·ma ['dræmə] *or* ['drɑmə] *n* **1** a story to be acted out on stage or film, etc.; a play, esp a serious one. **2** a series of events suggesting such a play: *The history of Canada is a great and thrilling drama.* **3** plays as a branch of literature. **4** pathos, excitement, heroism, etc.: *the drama of a rescue at sea.* ⟨Greek *drama* play, deed; *draein* do⟩
dra·ma·tic *adj* **1** to do with plays. **2** full of, or arousing, pathos or excitement: *After a dramatic pause, he turned on his heel and left.* **dra·mat·i·cal·ly** *adv.* **dra·mat·ics** *n pl* **1** the art of acting or producing plays (usually with sg verb). **2** exaggerated emotional behaviour: *Pay no attention to his dramatics.* **dram·a·tis per·so·nae** ['dræmətɪs pər'souni] *or* [-'sounaɪ] the characters or actors in a play. **dram·a·tist** *n*

a playwright. **dram·a·tize** *v* **1** adapt as a play: *to dramatize a novel.* **2** portray in a dramatic (def. 2) way. **dram·a·ti·za·tion** *n.*

Dramatic suggests genuine excitement of the imagination and emotions: *a dramatic reunion between the war veterans with their wives.*
Theatrical suggests a deliberate effort to impress or arouse the emotions by artificial behaviour including posture, gestures, tone of voice, etc.: *a theatrical show of gratitude.*
Melodramatic emphasizes sensationalism or exaggeration, especially in storytelling, writing, etc.: *a melodramatic soap opera.*

drank [dræŋk] *v* pt of DRINK.

drape [dreip] *v* **1** decorate or cover with cloth falling in graceful folds: *The buildings were draped with red and white bunting.* **2** arrange (clothes, etc.) in graceful folds: *The designer draped the robe around the model's shoulders.*
n **1 drapes** *pl* large, heavy curtains made to hang in folds. **2** the way a garment hangs on the body: *the drape of a skirt.* ⟨Old French *drap* cloth; Latin *drappus*⟩
drap·er·y *n* **1** cloth or garments hung in graceful folds, as on painted or carved figures. **2** fabric for drapes. **3 draperies** *pl* drapes.

dras·tic ['dræstɪk] *adj* extreme or radical; severe: *drastic measures.* **dras·ti·cal·ly** *adv.* ⟨Greek *drastikos* effective; *draein* do⟩

drat [dræt] *interj, v Informal* confound; darn; damn. **drat·ted** *adj.* ⟨(Go)d rot⟩

draught [dræft] an older spelling of DRAFT.

draw [drɒ] *v* **drew, drawn, draw·ing 1** make a picture of with pencil, pen, crayon, etc. **2** pull: *The horse drew the wagon.* **3** pull out, up, or back: *to draw the cork from a bottle, to draw one's bow and shoot, to draw money from an account.* **4** bring out; take out: *The bite drew blood.* **5** close (a curtain or blind). **6** attract: *The parade always draws a crowd.* **7** move: *We drew near the fire to get warm.* **8** get; receive: *He draws his pay each Friday.* **9** make a current of air to carry off smoke: *The chimney is not drawing well.* **10** of time, etc., pass gradually: *The day drew to a close.* **11** take (a breath). **12** arrive at (a logical conclusion). **13** of a boat or ship, need (a given depth) for floating. **14** of tea or other infusions, steep. **15** get or select by lottery: *to draw names, to draw first prize.*
draw a blank See BLANK. **draw and quarter a** formerly, execute by tying each limb to a different horse and sending the horses in various directions. **b** disembowel and cut up (a carcass). **c** punish or scold severely. **draw on a** come nearer. **b** use as a resource: *to draw on one's experience.* **draw oneself up** a stand erect. **b** become indignant. **draw out a** extend, often tediously. **b** persuade to talk: *We tried to draw him out because we knew he was shy.* **draw the line** set a limit or criterion to guide behaviour: *Pranks are OK, but I draw the line at actually hurting people.* **draw up a** make (a list, plan, chart, etc.). **b** write out in proper form: *The will was drawn up by a*

lawyer. **c** come or bring to a stop: *A taxi drew up at the door.*

draw·back *n* a disadvantage or hindrance.

draw·bridge *n* a bridge that can be wholly or partly lifted to prevent passage across it or to let boats pass under it. **draw·er** ['drɔər] *n* **1** a person or thing that draws. **2** [drɔr] a box built to slide in and out of a dresser, desk, etc. **3 drawers** [drɔrz] *pl humorous* pants or underpants. **draw·ing** *n* **1** a picture made by hand. **2** the art or act of making such pictures. **drawing board** a board, usually tilted, used as a support for drawing on paper. **go back to the drawing board** start all over with a new approach. **on the drawing board** in the planning stage. **drawing card** something intended to attract or interest people. **drawing room** a room for formally entertaining guests. **drawn** *adj* distorted with pain or worry; anxious: *His face was tired and drawn.* **drawn–out** *adj* tiresomely long. **draw·string** *n* a cord running through the hem around an opening so that it can be drawn tight: *a hood with a drawstring.*

drawl [drɔl] *v* talk slowly and with long, broad vowel sounds. **drawl** *n.* ⟨perhaps *draw*⟩

dread [drɛd] *v* **1** look forward to with fear or extreme reluctance: *I dread that interview with the boss tomorrow.* **2** regard with fear or awe: *Everyone dreaded the school bully.* *n* fear, esp of something to come. *adj* dreaded; inspiring dread: *a dread tyrant.* ⟨Old English *drǣdan*⟩ **dread·ful** *adj* **1** causing dread: *The dragon was a dreadful creature.* **2** *Informal* very bad: *a dreadful cold.* **dread·ful·ness** *n.* **dread·ful·ly** *adv.* **1** in a dreadful manner. **2** *Informal* very: *She's dreadfully upset.* **dread·locks** *n pl* thin braids all over the head, the ends often decorated with beads, coloured thread bindings, etc.

dream [drim] *n* **1** something imagined during sleep. **2** a lofty and often unrealistic hope: *The boy had dreams of being a hero.* **3** a beautiful or ideal person or thing. *adj* perfect; ideal: *a dream holiday.* *v* **dreamed** or **dreamt**, **dream·ing 1** have (a dream or dreams); imagine while sleeping. **2** have a daydream or fantasy: *She dreamed of being a queen.* **3** have a lofty hope, often an unrealistic one: *to dream of winning the Nobel Prize.* **4** imagine (usually negative): *I never dreamed he'd actually believe it.* **dream·less** *adj.* **dream·like** *adj.* ⟨Old English *drēam* joy, music; influenced by Old Norse *draumr* dream⟩ **a dream come true** something ideal. **a ——'s dream** something perfect for a ——: *This old house is a renovator's dream.* **dream on!** or **in your dreams!** *Informal* that is just wishful thinking! **dream up** think up; invent. **like a dream** very easily, smoothly, etc.: *This thing works like a dream.* **not dream of** not consider: *I wouldn't dream of hurting an animal.* **dream·boat** *n Slang* an attractive person. **dream·er** *n* **1** an impractical person; visionary. **2** one who often daydreams. **dream·land** *n* **1** a place where a person seems to be when dreaming. **2** DREAM WORLD. **in dreamland** asleep or dreaming. **dream world** an ideal imagined world. **dream·y** *adj* **1** like a dream; vague; dim: *a dreamy recollection.* **2** fond of daydreaming. **3** soothing: *dreamy music.* **4** *Informal* wonderful; perfect. **dream·i·ly** *adv.*

drear·y ['driri] *adj* **1** gloomy; cheerless. **2** tiresome: *a long, dreary speech.* **drear·i·ly** *adv.* **drear·i·ness** *n.* ⟨Old English *drēorig*⟩

dredge [drɛdʒ] *n* a machine with a scoop for removing mud or other things from the bottom of a river, harbour, etc. *v* **1** clear out (a channel, harbour, etc.) with a dredge. **2** collect and remove with a dredge. **dredg·er** *n.* ⟨Middle English *dreg*⟩ **dredge up** bring up (past events or little known facts, often embarrassing ones).

dregs [drɛgz] *n pl* **1** the solid bits of matter that settle to the bottom of tea, wine, etc. **2** the lowest or worst part: *the dregs of society.* ⟨Scandinavian; compare Icelandic *dreggjar*⟩

drei·del ['dreidəl] or ['draidəl] *n* a four-sided top with Hebrew letters on each side, used by Jewish children in a game, esp at Hanukkah. ⟨Yiddish *dreydl; drey(en)* to turn⟩

drench [drɛntʃ] *v* wet thoroughly; soak. ⟨Old English *drencan; drincan* drink⟩

dress [drɛs] *n* **1** a garment worn by women and girls that includes a skirtlike part not divided into legs. **2** clothing, esp with reference to style: *casual dress, modern dress. They care very little about dress.* **3** formal clothes: *in full dress.* *adj* to do with, or requiring, formal dress: *a dress occasion, a dress shirt.* *v* **1** put clothes on: *to dress a doll. He got up and dressed.* **2** clothe oneself attractively or strategically: *to dress for success. She knows how to dress.* **3** put formal clothes on: *They always dress for dinner.* **4** decorate or create a display in (a window). **5** put medicine or a bandage on (a wound or sore). **6** prepare (a bird, etc.) for cooking. **7** put garnishes, condiments, sauce, etc. on. **8** give a finish to (processed leather or fabric).⟨Old French *dresser* arrange; Latin *directus* straight⟩ **dress down a** scold severely. **b** dress casually. **dress up a** put on one's best clothes. **b** wear or cause to wear a costume. **c** represent more attractively: *stinginess dressed up as thrift.* **dress circle** an expensive section of seats in a theatre, usually upstairs. **dress·er** *n* **1** a piece of furniture with drawers for clothes. **2** a person who helps entertainers dress for their performances. **3** one who dresses in a given way: *He's a neat dresser.* **dress·ing** *n* **1** a sauce for salad. **2** stuffing for roast chicken, turkey, etc. **3** the bandage, medicine, etc. on a wound or sore. **4** fertilizer. **dress·ing–down** *n* a severe scolding. **dressing gown** a loose robe worn while resting, before dressing in the morning, after a bath, etc. **dressing room** a room in which to change clothes or dress, esp for actors. **dressing table** a table with a mirror at which one can sit to put on makeup, etc. **dress·mak·er** *n* a person who makes women's clothes. **dress·mak·ing** *n.* **dress rehearsal** a final rehearsal of a play with costumes and scenery. **dress uniform** military wear for formal occasions. **dress·y** *adj* of clothes, fairly formal.

dres·sage [drɛ'sɑʒ] *or* ['drɛsɪdʒ] *n* the art and skill of show riding, or of training a horse for it. ⟨French⟩

drew [dru] *v* pt of DRAW.

drib·ble ['drɪbəl] *v* **1** flow or let flow in drops: *Gasoline dribbled from the leak.* **2** let saliva run from the mouth. **3** move (a ball) along by bouncing it or giving it short kicks. *n* **1** a trickle. **2** a very light rain. **3** the act of dribbling. **drib·bler** *n.* ⟨*drib* variant of *drip*⟩ **in dribs and drabs** in small instalments.

drift [drɪft] *v* **1** carry or be carried along by a current. **2** move aimlessly: *People drifted in and out of the meeting.* **3** of snow, sand, etc., be heaped up by the wind. **4** lead a passive, ambitionless, often nomadic life. *n* **1** the act or direction of drifting: *the drift of an iceberg.* **2** a general tendency: *The drift of opinion was against war.* **3** the basic sense: *I got the drift of her speech, but not the details.* **4** a quantity of snow, sand, etc. heaped up by the wind or moved and deposited by a river or glacier. **drift·er** *n.* ⟨Old English *drīfan* drive⟩ **drift apart** gradually cease to be friends. **drift fence 1** a snow fence. **2** a deer fence. **drift–ice** *n* ✱ small masses of ice drifting in the sea. **drift net** a fishing net with anchors on the bottom and floats along the top to let it move with the current or tide. **drift·wood** *n* wood drifting in the water or washed ashore.

drill¹ [drɪl] *n* **1** a tool for making holes in wood, concrete, etc. **2** instruction or training in the form of repetitive exercises: *The teacher gave the class plenty of drill in arithmetic.* **3** *Informal* the approved procedure: *You know the drill.* **drill** *v.* **drill·er** *n.* ⟨Middle Dutch *dril*⟩ **drill·mas·ter** *n* an instructor who teaches by drilling, esp soldiers in marching, etc. **drill press** a machine for drilling holes, esp in metal. **drill sergeant 1** a sergeant who puts soldiers through training exercises. **2** a strict disciplinarian.

drill² [drɪl] *n* a machine for planting seeds in rows. **drill** *v.* ⟨origin uncertain⟩

drill³ [drɪl] *n* a strong, twilled cotton fabric used for work clothes, etc. ⟨German *Drillich*, Latin *trilix*; *tri-* three + *licium* thread⟩

drink [drɪŋk] *v* **drank, drunk, drink·ing 1** consume; swallow (liquid). **2** absorb; soak (*up*): *The dry ground drank up the rain.* **3** use liquor: *I don't drink.* **4** abuse liquor. **5** drink in honour of; toast: *They drank his health.* *n* **1** any liquid meant for drinking: *pop, juice, and other cold drinks.* **2** a quantity of this consumed: *He had a drink of milk.* **3** liquor. **4** abuse of liquor: *to take to drink. She drives me to drink.* **5** *Slang* **the drink** a body of water. **drink·a·ble** *adj.* ⟨Old English *drincan*⟩ **drink deep(ly) of** feel (an experience or emotion) intensely. **drink in** take in eagerly with the senses or mind. **drink to** drink in honour of; toast. **drink up** drink all of

(something). **I'll drink to that** I heartily agree. **drink·er** *n* a person who drinks liquor as a habit or to excess. **drinking fountain** a public water spout over a basin, delivering a jet of drinking water when a control is pressed.

drip [drɪp] *v* **dripped, drip·ping** fall or let fall in drops. *n* **1** the process of falling in drops. **2** a drop that falls. **3** *Slang* a stupid or socially inept person. **4** *Medicine* a constant intravenous dispensing of fluid. **drip·py** *adj.* ⟨Old English *dryppan; dropa* a drop⟩ **drip–dry** *adj* made to dry by being hung up after washing, usually with little or no ironing needed afterward: *drip-dry curtains.* **drip–dry** *v.* **drip·ping** *adj* very wet. **drip·pings** *n pl* melted fat and juice that drip from roasting meat.

drive [draɪv] *v* **drove, driv·en, driv·ing 1** operate (a car or other vehicle). **2** make go: *Drive those pesky geese away. Wind drives the windmill.* **3** make go by hitting: *to drive a nail into wood.* **4** force into or out of some state or condition: *You drive me crazy.* **5** negotiate (a bargain). **6** compel to make great efforts: *He drives himself too hard.* **7** *Golf* hit (the ball) from the tee. **8** driveway. **9** (in street names) a fairly quiet, wide road. *n* **1** a trip taken in a car or other vehicle. **2** ambition or self-motivation; will to work hard. **3** impelling force: *The need for approval is a strong drive in people.* **4** a campaign: *a charity drive.* **5** a hard, fast hit. **6** *Golf* the act of hitting the ball from the tee. **7** the process of moving a large number of things along, such as cattle on land, logs down a river, etc. **8** the group of things so moved, or the route followed. **9** *Computers* a device to hold and read stored data in a given format: *a tape drive, a floppy drive.* **10** a system of propulsion in a machine: *a car with front-wheel drive.* **driv·er** *n.* ⟨Old English *drīfan*⟩ **drive at** mean; intend: *I don't get what you're driving at.* **drive in** *Baseball* of a player at bat, cause (a run) to be scored or (another player) to score by means of a hit. **the driver's seat** the position of power.

drive–in *n* a place where customers may eat, watch a movie, etc. while seated in their cars. **drive–in** *adj.* **driv·en** *adj* **1** drifted: *driven snow.* **2** of a person, compelled by a strong ambition, competitiveness, etc. **drive shaft** a shaft that transmits power or motion, such as the one connecting a car's gear system to its wheels. **drive–through** *n* a facility of a bank, fast-food establishment, etc. that lets patrons transact business from their cars by driving up to a service window and then driving on when finished. **drive–through** *adj.* **drive·train** *n* the mechanism that sends the turning power to a car's wheels. **drive·way** *n* a lane from a house to a road. **driv·ing** *adj* forceful: *the driving rhythm, a driving rain.*

driv·el ['drɪvəl] *v* **-elled** or **-eled, -el·ling** or **-el·ing 1** drool. **2** talk nonsense. **driv·el** *n.* **driv·el·ler** or **driv·el·er** *n.* ⟨Old English *dreflian*⟩

driz·zle ['drɪzəl] *v* **1** rain steadily in very fine drops. **2** sprinkle: *Drizzle the shaved chocolate* *over the cake.* **driz·zle** *n.* ⟨Middle English *drese* to fall; Old English *drysnian*⟩

driz·zly ['drɪzli] *adj* with a steady, fine rain.

droll [droul] *adj* amusingly odd; quaintly funny. **droll·er·y** *n.* **drol·ly** *adv.* **droll·ness** *n.* ⟨French *drôle;* Dutch *drol* little fat fellow⟩

drom·e·dar·y ['drɒmə,dɛri] *n* a swift camel, esp the one-humped Arabian camel. ⟨Latin *dromedarius;* Greek *dromados* runner⟩

drone [droun] *n* **1** a male bee, esp a honeybee, whose sole function is to mate with the queen. **2** a lazy, inactive person. **3** continuous hum; dull monotone: *the drone of engines, the drone of a speaker's voice.* **4** one of the pipes on a bagpipe that make a continuous background tone. **5** a pilotless aircraft directed by remote control.
v **1** make a continuous humming sound. **2** talk in a monotone. ⟨Old English *drān*⟩

drool [drul] *v* **1** let saliva run from the mouth as a baby does. **2** *Informal* make an excessive show of enthusiasm (*over*): *drooling over a rock star.* **drool** *n.* ⟨contraction of *drivel*⟩

droop [drup] *v* **1** hang down limply. **2** grow weak or discouraged. **droop** *n.* **droop·ing** *adj.* **droop·y** *adj.* ⟨Old Norse *drúpa*⟩

drop [drɒp] *n* **1** a small, roundish mass of liquid: *a drop of blood.* **2** a small roundish candy: *a cough drop.* **3** a very small amount of anything: *a drop of kindness.* **4 drops** *pl* liquid medicine applied in tiny amounts. **5** a sudden fall: *a drop in prices.* **6** the distance down: *a drop of 10 m.* **7** a chute: *a letter drop.* **8** the act of dropping or a thing dropped, as supplies from an aircraft. **9** a secret place where illegal goods are left, the goods left there, or the act of leaving them.
v **dropped, drop·ping 1** fall or go down: *Gas prices have dropped. The land drops here.* **2** let fall: *Drop your gun. The river drops its soil at the mouth.* **3** lower: *Drop your voices.* **4** fall from exhaustion: *so tired I could drop.* **5** let go; leave off or out: *Members who do not pay will be dropped from the club. Drop the 'e' in 'drive' and add 'ing'.* **6** abandon: *Drop the subject.* **7** unload (passengers or cargo) (often with *off*): *Just drop me at the corner. I'll drop it off at your place when I'm done.* **8** spend (money), esp wastefully: *They dropped $400 for that chair!* ⟨Old English *dropa*⟩
at the drop of a hat at the least provocation or suggestion. **drop a brick** make a tactless comment. **drop a curtsy** curtsy. **drop in** (or **by** or **over**) make a brief stop or visit. **drop in the bucket** a comparatively insignificant amount. **drop names** try to impress others by casually mentioning important people in conversation. **drop off** a get less; decrease: *Sales have dropped off.* **b** fall asleep. **drop out** leave school, etc., without finishing. **get** (or **have**) **the drop on** get (or have) an advantage over. **wait for the other shoe to drop** wait for the next logical development.
drop·cloth *n* a large sheet of plastic, cloth, etc., used to protect a floor or furniture from paint drips. **drop cookie** a cookie for which dough is simply dropped by spoonfuls onto a sheet for baking. **drop curtain** a stage curtain that is raised or lowered rather than drawn across. **drop–down menu** *Computers* a menu that appears in list form under a heading when the heading is selected. **drop–in** (**centre**) an informal place where youth, parents with preschoolers, street people, or other groups can come for help, recreation, or companionship. **drop kick** a kick given to a football just as it touches the ground after being dropped from the hands. **drop–kick** *v.* **drop leaf** a hinged section of a tabletop, folded down when not in use. **drop–leaf** *adj.* **drop·let** *n* a tiny drop. **drop–off** *n* **1** a sharp slope down. **2** a sudden decline. **3** a place to unload passengers or cargo. **drop–out** *n* a person who leaves school, etc., without finishing. **drop·per** *n* a tube with a small opening at one end from which a liquid can be made to fall in drops. **drop·pings** *n pl* dung of animals or birds.

drop·sy ['drɒpsi] *n* an accumulation of fluid in some part of the body. **drop·si·cal** *adj.* ⟨Latin *hydropisis,* Greek *hydrōps; hydōr* water⟩

dross [drɒs] *n* **1** the waste or scum that comes to the surface of molten metals; slag. **2** worthless stuff; rubbish. ⟨Old English *drōs*⟩

drought [draut] *n* a long period of dry weather. **drought·y** *adj.* ⟨Old English *drūgath*⟩

drove[1] [drouv] *v pt* of DRIVE.

drove[2] [drouv] *n* **1** a group of cattle, sheep, etc., moving along together. **2** a crowd: *The tourists came in droves.* ⟨Old English *drāf*⟩

drown [draun] *v* **1** suffocate under water or other liquid. **2** cover with water; flood. **3** overcome with a much louder sound, stronger emotion, etc. (usually with *out*): *The boat's whistle drowned out her warning.* **4** get rid of by drinking: *to drown one's sorrows.* ⟨Old English *druncnian.* Related to DRINK.⟩
drowning in overwhelmed by an excess of.

drowse ['drauz] *v* be sleepy or half asleep. *n* the state of being sleepy or half asleep. **drow·sy** *adj.* **drow·si·ly** *adv.* **drow·si·ness** *n.* ⟨Old English *drūs(i)an* sink, become slow⟩

drub [drʌb] *v* **drubbed, drub·bing 1** beat with a stick. **2** defeat by a large margin. **drub·bing** *n.* ⟨Arabic *daraba* beat⟩

drudge [drʌdʒ] *n* a person who does hard, tiresome, or disagreeable work. **drudge** *v.* **drudg·er·y** *n.* ⟨Middle English *drugge(n);* related to Old English *drēogan* work, suffer⟩

drug [drʌg] *n* **1** a substance (other than food) used as a medicine. **2** any narcotic, sedative, or other mind-altering substance.
v **drugged, drug·ging 1** give drugs to, esp harmful ones or sedatives. **2** put such drugs in (food or drink). **3** affect as if by drugs. ⟨Middle Low German *droge-fate* dry barrels; *droge-* taken as name of contents⟩ **drug on the market** an article that is too abundant or no longer in demand.
drug abuse use of a drug to a harmful or addictive extent. **drug abuser. drug culture** people who use illegal drugs, regarded as a distinct segment of society. **drug·gist** *n* a

pharmacist. **drug·store** *n* a store that sells medicines and other sundries.

Dru·id or **dru·id** ['druɪd] *n* a member of an ancient Celtic religious order of poet-priests. **Dru·id·ic** or **dru·id·ic** *adj.* **Dru·id·ism** *n.* ⟨Gaulish; compare Old Irish *drui* sorcerer⟩

drum [drʌm] *n* **1** a hollow percussion instrument with a flat surface for striking. **2** the sound made when a drum is beaten, or any sound like this. **3** a large cylindrical container: *an oil drum.* **4** a spool-like part.
v **drummed, drum·ming 1** beat a drum. **2** beat again and again: *Stop drumming on the table with your fingers.* **3** force into the mind by repetition: *The work ethic was drummed into me from infancy.* **4** sound like a drum: *The noise drummed in his ears.* **drum·mer** *n.* ⟨Dutch or Low German *trommel*⟩
beat the drums for support vigorously. **drum out** send away in disgrace. **drum up** muster or summon; gather: *to drum up one's courage, to drum up volunteers or support.*
drum·beat *n* the sound made when a drum is beaten. **drum dance** ✲ any of various expressive or ritual dances of the Inuit or the First Nations, accompanied by drums. **drum dancer. drum·fish** *n, pl* **-fish** or **-fish·es** any of various carnivorous fishes found along the warm western shores of the Atlantic and making a drumming sound. **drum·head** *n* the membrane stretched tightly over the end of a drum. **drum major** the leader of a marching band. **drum ma·jo·rette** [ˌmeidʒəˈrɛt] a woman who accompanies a marching band, twirling a baton. **drum· stick** *n* **1** a stick for beating a drum. **2** the lower, meaty part of the leg of a cooked chicken, turkey, or other edible bird.

drum·lin ['drʌmlən] *n* a ridge or oval hill made by glacial deposit. ⟨*drumling* diminutive of *drum* ridge; Irish and Scots Gaelic *druim*⟩

drunk [drʌŋk] *adj* **1** intoxicated by liquor. **2** very much excited: *drunk with success.* **3** impaired by alcohol: *drunk driving.*
n Slang **1** a person who is drunk or often drunk. **2** a drinking spree: *a three-day drunk.* **drunk·ard** *n* a person who is often drunk. **drunk·en** *adj* **1** drunk. **2** caused or affected by too much alcohol: *drunken behaviour.* **drunk·en·ly** *adv.* **drunk·en·ness** *n.*

USAGE
As an adjective standing before the noun, the form **drunken** is preferred, except in the set phrases *drunk driver, drunk driving.*

drupe [drup] *n* any soft, fleshy fruit with a skin and a hard stone that contains the seed. Cherries and plums are drupes. ⟨Latin *drupa;* Greek *dryppa* very ripe olive⟩

druth·ers ['drʌðərz] *n pl Informal, dialect* a free choice or one's own way: *If I had my druthers, I'd quit tomorrow.* ⟨shortening of *I'd rather,* influenced by *other*⟩

dry [draɪ] *adj* **1** not wet; containing no liquid. **2** with little or no humidity or rain: *a dry climate.* **3** too lacking in moisture; parched: *dry skin.* **4** unaccompanied by tears,

mucus, etc.: *a dry sob, a dry cough.* **5** stale: *dry bread.* **6** dull: *a dry speech.* **7** understated or ironic: *dry humour.* **8** without butter, jam, etc.: *dry toast.* **9** of wine, not sweet: *dry wine.* **10** *Informal* thirsty or causing thirst: *dry work.* **11** having or favouring laws against liquor. **12** no longer productive.
v **1** make or become dry. **2** preserve by dehydrating. **dry·a·ble** *adj.* **dry·ly** or **dri·ly** *adv.* **dry·ness** *n.* ⟨Old English *drȳge*⟩
dry out a make or become completely dry. **b** *Informal* take treatment for alcoholism. **dry up a** disappear or become dry and hard, as a result of evaporation or lack of water supply. **b** *Slang* stop talking. **c** make or become unproductive. **suck dry** exhaust the vitality or productivity of.
dry battery a set of connected dry cells producing an electric current. **dry cell** an electrochemical cell in which the electrolyte is a paste that cannot spill. **dry–clean** *v* clean fabrics without water, using a solvent. **dry cleaner, dry cleaning. dry dock** an area set between two piers, built watertight so that water may be pumped out for repairing ships. **dry–dock** *v.* **dry·er** or **dri·er** *n* **1** a machine for drying things quickly, esp by heat or blown air: *a hair dryer, clothes dryer.* **2** a stand or rack for hanging clothes to dry. **dry–eyed** *adj* not crying. **dry goods** cloth, ribbon, lace, etc. **dry ice** a solid formed by compressing and cooling carbon dioxide. It changes from a solid directly back to gas, creating an illusion of fog. **dry law** a law prohibiting the making and selling of liquor. **dry measure** a system of units for measuring things like grain or fruit. The bushel and peck are units of dry measure. **dry rot** the decay of seasoned wood, causing it to crumble to a dry powder by the action of various fungi. **dry run** a trial or practice session. **dry·wall** *n* **1** plasterboard in sheets, for making interior walls without wet plaster. **2** this method of construction. **dry·wall** *adj, v.*

dry·ad ['draɪæd] *or* ['draɪəd] *n, pl* **-ads** or **-a·des** [-ə,diz] *Greek myth* a nymph that lives in a tree. **dry·ad·ic** *adj.* ⟨Greek *drys* tree⟩

D.S. or **d.s.** *Music* repeat from the point indicated. (for Italian *dal segno* from the sign)

du·al ['djuəl] *or* ['duəl] *adj* consisting of two; double. **du·al·i·ty** *n.* ⟨Latin *duo* two⟩
du·al·ism *n Philosophy* the doctrine that all phenomena are explained by two contrasting forces or principles, such as mind and matter or good and evil. **du·al·ist** *n.* **du·al·is·tic** *adj.* **du·al–pur·pose** *adj* having two functions.

dub¹ [dʌb] *v* **dubbed, dub·bing 1** make (a person) a member of an order of knighthood by striking his shoulder lightly with a sword. **2** name; nickname: *They dubbed him 'Whitey'.* ⟨Old English *dubbian*⟩

dub² [dʌb] *v* **dubbed, dub·bing 1** make or replace the soundtrack for (a film, a radio or television broadcast, a recording, etc.). **2** add (sounds) to a film, etc. (usually with *in*). **3** copy (a recording). ⟨short for *double*⟩

du·bi·ous ['djubiəs] *or* ['dubiəs] *adj* **1** that is

open to doubt: *dubious authorship.* **2** feeling doubt. **3** of questionable character: *a dubious scheme.* **du·bi·e·ty** [dju'baɪəti] *or* [du-] *n.* **du·bi·ous·ly** *adv.* **du·bi·ous·ness** *n.* ⟨Latin *dubius; du-* two (compare 'in two minds')⟩ **du·bi·ta·ble** *adj* liable to doubt or question.

du·cal See DUKE.

duch·ess ['dʌtʃɪs] *n* **1** the wife or widow of a duke. **2** a woman with a rank equal to that of a duke. ⟨Old French *duchesse; duc* duke⟩ **duch·y** ['dʌtʃi] *n* the territory under the rule of a duke or duchess.

duck¹ [dʌk] *n* **1** any of numerous aquatic birds with a thick body, short neck and legs, flat bill, and webbed feet. **2** the adult female of a duck. Compare DRAKE. **3** *Informal* darling; pet. **4** *Slang* person: *odd duck.* ⟨Old English *dūce.* Related to DUCK².⟩
like water off a duck's back without any effect.
duck·bill *n* platypus. **duck·ling** *n* a young duck. **duck soup** *Slang* something very easy. **duck·tail** *n* a haircut in which the sides are brushed back and cut to look like a duck's tail. **duck·weed** *n* any of a genus of tiny floating plants found in stagnant water. **duc·ky** *adj Informal* (often ironic) lovely.

duck² [dʌk] *v* **1** plunge suddenly under water. **2** lower (the head) or bend (the body) suddenly to avoid being hit. **3** move quickly in order to escape notice: *He ducked into a store.* **4** *Informal* avoid: *ducking responsibility.* **duck** *n.* ⟨Middle English *duke(n)*⟩

duck³ [dʌk] *n* **1** a strong cloth, lighter than canvas. **2 ducks** *pl Informal* pants made of this. ⟨Dutch *doek* cloth⟩

duct [dʌkt] *n* **1** a tube carrying liquid, air, wires, etc. **2** a tube in the body, carrying a fluid: *tear ducts.* **duct·less** *adj.* ⟨Latin *ductus* pp of *ducere* lead⟩

duc·tile ['dʌktaɪl] *or* ['dʌktəl] *adj* **1** of metal, capable of being hammered out thin or drawn out into a wire. **2** easily shaped, as wax. **3** docile. **duc·til·i·ty** [dʌk'tɪləti] *n.* ⟨Latin *ductilis; ducere* lead⟩

dud [dʌd] *n Informal* **1** a useless person or thing. **2 duds** *pl* **a** clothes. **b** belongings. ⟨Middle English *dudde;* of unknown origin⟩

dude [djud] *or* [dud] *n* **1** in W Canada and US, a city-bred person, esp one who spends a holiday on a ranch. **2** *Slang* any person. **3** a man who cares too much about his clothes; dandy. ⟨origin unknown⟩
dude ranch a ranch run as a tourist resort.

dudg·eon ['dʌdʒən] *n Archaic* resentment; anger. ⟨origin unknown⟩
in high dudgeon very angry; indignant.

due [dju] *or* [du] *adj* **1** owed as a debt. **2** rightful; deserved: *due reward.* **3** enough; appropriate: *Use due care when crossing streets.* **4** expected: *The train is due at noon.*
n **1** something owed as a debt or right: *Take it; it's your due.* **2 dues** *pl* fees paid to a club or union as a condition of membership.
adv straight: *due east.* ⟨Old French *deü* pp of *devoir* owe; Latin *debere*⟩

due to a caused by: *The accident was due to her careless use of the gun.* **b** *Informal* because of: *The rally was postponed due to the bad weather.* **fall due** be required to be paid (at a given time). **give a person his or her due** be fair to a person. **pay one's dues** suffer the hardships or carry out the obligations which earn (one) certain privileges or rights.
du·ly *adv* **1** properly; rightfully: *The documents were duly signed.* **2** when due; at the proper time: *The debt was duly paid.*

> **USAGE**
>
> In formal English many writers use **due to** only to introduce an adjective phrase, i.e., one modifying a noun: *Her success was due to hard work* (modifies *success*). Informally, however, **due to** is routinely used to introduce adverb phrases: *Due to her hard work, she succeeded.* This use can be avoided by the substitution of *because of* or *on account of: She succeeded because of* (or *on account of*) *her hard work.*

du·el ['djuəl] *or* ['duəl] *n* **1** a formal fight between two people armed with swords or firearms. **2** any fight or contest between two opponents: *a duel of wits.* **du·el, -elled** *or* **-eled, -el·ling** *or* **-el·ing** *v.* **du·el·list** *or* **du·el·ist** *n.* ⟨Latin *duellum*⟩

du·et [dju'ɛt] *or* [du'ɛt] *n* **1** a piece of music sung or played by two people. **2** two singers or players performing together. ⟨Italian *duetto* diminutive of *duo.* See DUO.⟩

duff [dʌf] *n Slang* buttocks. ⟨origin uncertain⟩

duf·fel or **duf·fle** ['dʌfəl] *n* **1** coarse woollen cloth. **2** things carried by a hunter, camper, soldier, etc. ⟨*Duffel* a town near Antwerp⟩
duffel bag a large bag of heavy cloth used by campers, hunters, sailors, etc. to carry their things. **duffel coat** a knee-length, usually hooded coat of duffel or similar material. **duffel sock** in the North: **1** one of a pair of wrap-around leggings made of long strips of duffel or blanketing. **2** an outer sock worn between a sock and a boot or mukluk.

duff·er ['dʌfər] *n Informal* **1** a small boy or old man; a term of endearment. **2** a useless, clumsy, or stupid person. ⟨origin uncertain⟩

dug [dʌg] *v* pt and pp of DIG.
dug·out *n* **1** a boat made by hollowing out a large log. **2 a** a small shelter at the side of a baseball field, used by those players not in the game. **b** a rough shelter made by digging into the side of a bank, trench, etc., as those made by soldiers on a battlefield. **3** ❋ on the Prairies, a large excavation used to hold water from the spring thaw and from rainfall.

du·gong ['dugɒŋ] *n* a large sea mammal of warm Pacific waters. ⟨Malay *dūyong*⟩

du jour [du 'ʒur] *French* [dy'ʒuʀ] of items on a menu, served on this day: *soupe du jour.* ⟨French = of the day⟩

duke [djuk] *or* [duk] *n* **1** a nobleman ranking next below a prince. **2** a prince who rules a small state called a duchy. **3 dukes** *pl Slang* fists. **du·cal** *adj.* **duke·dom** *n.* ⟨Old French *duc;* Latin *dux, ducis* leader⟩

dul·cet ['dʌlsɪt] *adj* soothing, esp to the ear; sweet; pleasing. ⟨Latin *dulcis*⟩

dul·ci·mer ['dʌlsəmər] *n* a musical instrument having metal strings which the player plucks, or strikes with two hammers. ⟨Latin *dulcis* sweet + *melos* song⟩

dull [dʌl] *adj* **1** not sharp: *a dull knife, a dull pain.* **2** not bright: *dull eyes.* **3** boring: *a dull book.* **4** slow or sluggish: *a dull mind. Business is dull these days.* **dull** *v.* **dull·ish** *adj.* **dul·ly** *adv.* **dull·ness** *n.* ⟨Middle English *dul*⟩
dull·ard *n* a slow-witted person.

dulse [dʌls] *n* an edible, reddish seaweed found along the coasts of the North Atlantic. ⟨Irish and Scots Gaelic *duileasg*⟩

du·ly See DUE.

dumb [dʌm] *adj* **1** not having, by nature, the power of speech: *dumb animals.* **2** saying nothing, because unwilling or too confused, surprised, etc.: *dumb with embarrassment. They kept questioning him, but he remained dumb.* **3** not expressed in or accompanied by words: *dumb grief.* **4** *Archaic* having a permanent disability which prevents speech; mute: *deaf and dumb.* **5** *Informal* stupid. **dumb·ly** *adv.* **dumb·ness** *n.* ⟨Old English *dumb* influenced by German *dumm* stupid⟩
dumb down *Informal* adapt for a less educated or less intelligent audience or user.
dumb·bell *n* **1** a short bar with a spherical weight on each end, used for weightlifting. **2** *Slang* a stupid person. **dumb·found** or **dum·found** [,dʌm'faʊnd] or ['dʌm,faʊnd] *v* amaze to the point of speechlessness. **dumb show** gestures without words. **dumb·struck** *adj* speechless with surprise. **dumb·wait·er** *n* especially formerly, a small box pulled up and down a shaft like an elevator, to carry dishes, food, etc. from floor to floor. **dum·my** *n* **1** a figure of a person, used to crash-test cars, display clothing, etc. **2** an imitation used for display, as a stage prop, etc.: *This gun is a dummy.* **3** *Informal* a stupid person. **4** a passive person or one controlled by another. *adj* of, for, or being a dummy: *dummy swords.*

dump [dʌmp] *v* **1** empty out; unload in a mass: *Dump the soil on the driveway.* **2** unload garbage: *No dumping.* **3** *Slang* get rid of; abandon: *to dump one's boyfriend.* **4** *Computers* copy, move, or print out (stored data). **5** put (goods) on the market in large quantities at low price, to get rid of them.
n **1** a place where garbage is unloaded. **2** a place to temporarily store military supplies: *an ammunition dump.* **3** *Informal* a shabby or otherwise depressing house, town, etc.: *Life in this dump is unbearable.* **4** any act of or like dumping, or a mass dumped or seemingly dumped: *a huge dump of snow.* **5** *Computers* the act, process, or result of dumping stored data. ⟨perhaps Scandinavian; compare Danish *dumpe* fall with a thud⟩
dump on *Slang* **a** vilify. **b** *Slang* vent one's ill feeling on: *So you lost! Don't dump on me!*
Dump·ster *n Trademark* a large metal boxlike container for garbage. **dump truck** a truck with a large boxlike structure that tips and

opens at the bottom to dump its contents.

dump·ling ['dʌmplɪŋ] *n* **1** a lump of dough boiled, baked, or steamed, with or without something inside it. **2** a short, plump person or animal. ⟨*dump* a badly shaped piece + *-ling*⟩ **dump·y** *adj* short and fat.

dumps [dʌmps] *n pl Informal*
(down) in the dumps feeling gloomy or sad. ⟨probably Dutch *domp* haze, dullness⟩

dun¹ [dʌn] *v* **dunned, dun·ning** repeatedly demand payment of a debt from (someone). *n* **1** a demand for payment, esp of a debt. **2** a creditor who persistently demands payment. ⟨variant of *din*⟩

dun² [dʌn] *adj* dull greyish brown. *n* a horse of this colour. ⟨Old English *dunn*⟩

dunce [dʌns] *n* a stupid person. ⟨*Dunsman*, name applied by his attackers to any follower of John *Duns Scotus*, a medieval theologian⟩

dun·der·head ['dʌndər,hɛd] *n* a stupid, foolish person. ⟨*dunder* of uncertain origin⟩

dune [djun] or [dun] *n* a mound or ridge of loose sand heaped up by the wind. ⟨Middle Dutch. Related to DOWN³.⟩
dune buggy a small vehicle for use on sand dunes or rough terrain.

dung [dʌŋ] *n* animal excrement; manure. ⟨Old English⟩
dung beetle any of various beetles that feed on dung as adults and larvae.

dun·ga·ree ['dʌŋɡə,ri] or [,dʌŋɡə'ri] *n* **1** a coarse cotton cloth used for work clothes. **2** dungarees *pl* overalls made of this cloth. ⟨Hindi *dungrī*⟩

dun·geon ['dʌndʒən] *n* **1** an underground prison in a castle. **2** any similarly dark, confining, grim place. ⟨Old French *donjon*⟩

dunk [dʌŋk] *v* **1** dip into a liquid: *to dunk a doughnut in coffee.* **2** *Informal* push (someone) under water. **3** *Basketball* jump up and drop (the ball) through the basket. **dunk·er** *n.* **dunk shot.** ⟨Low German *dunken*⟩

Dun·ne·za ['dʊnə'za] *n* **1** a First Nations people of the Peace River Valley in Alberta. **2** their language. **Dunne·za** *adj.* Also called **Beaver.**

du·o ['djuou] or ['duou] *n* a pair; team of two. ⟨Italian; Latin *duo* two⟩
du·o·tone *adj Printing* printed in two tones of the same colour.

du·o·de·num [,djuou'dinəm] or [,duou-] *n, pl* **-na** [-nə] the first part of the small intestine, just below the stomach. **du·o·de·nal** *adj.* ⟨Latin *duodeni* twelve each; with reference to its length, about twelve finger breadths⟩

dupe [djup] or [dup] *n* a person easily tricked. **dupe** *v.* ⟨Old French *d'uppe*; Latin *upupa* (name of a bird thought to be stupid)⟩

du·plex ['djuplɛks] or ['duplɛks] *n* ✱ **1** a building consisting of two dwellings under one roof, either side by side or one above the other. **2** one of the dwellings.
adj **1** double; twofold. **2** *Computers, telegraphy* to do with a system permitting simultaneous

two-way transmission of messages over one circuit. ⟨Latin, from *du-* two + *plicare* fold⟩

du·pli·cate ['djuplə,keit] *or* ['duplə,keit] *v* **1** make an exact copy of. **2** do or produce again: *to duplicate the results of an experiment.* **3** make redundant by doing the same thing: *You'll end up duplicating my work.*
n [-kɪt] an exact copy.
adj [-kɪt] **1** of two things, identical. **2** having two identical parts. **du·pli·ca·tion** *n.* ⟨Latin *du-* two + *plicare* fold⟩
in duplicate in two identical copies: *This application must be made out in duplicate.*

du·plic·i·tous [dju'plɪsətəs] *or* [du'plɪsətəs] *adj* pretending to be one thing while secretly being another. **du·plic·i·ty** *n.* ⟨Latin *duplicitas* doubleness; *duplex.* See DUPLEX.⟩

du·ra·ble ['djʊrəbəl] *or* ['dʊrəbəl] *adj* able to last a long time; tough; hard-wearing. **du·ra·bil·i·ty** *n.* ⟨Latin *durare* to last; *durus* hard⟩
du·ra·tion *n* the time a thing lasts: *a strike of short duration.* **for the duration** until the end.

du·ress [dju'rɛs] *or* [dʊ'rɛs], ['djʊrɛs] *or* ['dʊrɛs] *n* torture or imprisonment, or the threat of either, used to force or constrain. ⟨Old French *duresse,* Latin *duritia* hardness; *durus* hard⟩

Dur·ga Pu·ja ['dʊrgə ,pudʒə] a ten-day Hindu fall festival honouring Durga, the goddess of power. ⟨Hindi = worship of Durga⟩

dur·ing ['djʊrɪŋ] *or* ['dʊrɪŋ] *prep* **1** for the whole time of: *We're closed during weekends.* **2** at some point in: *Drop in anytime during the day.* ⟨ppr of obsolete *dure* endure; Latin *durare*⟩

du·rum ['djʊrəm], ['dʊrəm] *or,* esp on the Prairies, ['dɜrəm] *n* a species of wheat with a high gluten content, used especially for pastas. ⟨Latin = hard⟩

dusk [dʌsk] *n* **1** the time just before dark. **2** gloom. ⟨variant of Old English *dux* dark⟩
dusk·y *adj* **1** somewhat dark or dark-coloured. **2** dim. **3** gloomy.

dust [dʌst] *n* **1** fine, dry earth. **2** any fine powder. **3** what is left of a dead body after decay. **4** an act of dusting: *to do a quick dust of the furniture.*
v **1** remove dust from (also with *off*): *to dust a table, to dust off one's hat.* **2** sprinkle (plants) with insecticide powder. **3** bring back to use (with *off*): *to dust off an old tune and rerecord it.* **4** sprinkle with something powdery: *cupcakes dusted with icing sugar.* ⟨Old English *dūst*⟩
bite the dust a *Slang* fall dead or wounded *The outlaws bit the dust.* **b** be defeated. **eat someone's dust** be humiliatingly outdone by someone. **make the dust fly** be very quick or energetic. **shake the dust off one's feet** go away full of anger or scorn. **throw dust in someone's eyes** mislead a person
dust bowl esp in W Canada and US, a region subject to severe dust storms due to long periods of drought. **dust bunny** *Informal* a mass of dust, dirt, cobwebs, and so on that has formed under a bed, in a corner, etc. **dust devil** a small whirlwind that stirs up a column of dust, leaves, etc. as it moves along. **dust·er** *n* **1** a cloth, brush, etc., used to

remove dust. **2** a device for blowing dry insecticide onto plants. **3** a light house dress that fastens down the front. **4** *Informal* DUST STORM. **dusting powder** a fine, perfumed powder for dusting on the body after a bath, etc. **dust jacket** a removable paper cover for a book. **dust·pan** *n* a broad, flat, shovel-like receptacle for sweeping dust into from the floor. **dust·proof** *adj* impervious to dust. **dust ruffle** a decorative trim around the bottom of a mattress. **dust storm** a strong wind carrying clouds of dust. **dust·up** *n Slang* a violent quarrel; disturbance. **dust·y** *adj* **1** covered with or full of dust. **2** like dust; dry and powdery. **3** greyish: *a dusty pink.* **dust·i·ness** *n.*

Dutch [dʌtʃ] *n* **1** the official language of The Netherlands. **2 the Dutch** the people of The Netherlands.
adj of or from The Netherlands. ⟨Middle Dutch *dutsch*⟩
Dutch door a door divided into an upper and lower section, each opening separately. **Dutch elm disease** a killing fungal disease affecting elm trees. **Dutch oven** a large pot, roasting pan, or casserole dish with a high lid. **Dutch treat** *Informal* a meal or entertainment in which each person pays for himself or herself.

du·ty ['djuti] *or* ['duti] *n* **1** the thing that a person is obligated to do, either morally or as part of his or her job: *a list of the mail clerk's duties. It is your duty to obey the law.* **2** a sense of obligation: *She acted more out of duty than love.* **3** a tax, esp one on imports. ⟨Anglo-French *duete; du* owed. See DUE.⟩
do duty for serve in place of. **in duty bound** compelled by duty. **off duty** away from work: *She's off duty till six.* **on duty** at or to work.
du·ti·a·ble *adj* subject to a tax: *dutiable goods.* **du·ti·ful** *adj* acting or done out of duty. **duty–bound** *adj* obligated. **duty–free** *adj, adv* exempt from import tax.

du·vet [dju'vei] *or* [du'vei] *n* a down-filled quilt or comforter with a removable cover.

D.V. 1 God willing (Latin *deo volente*). **2** DV digital video; digital image reproduction.

DVD short for **digital videodisc,** a compact disc playable by a CD-ROM drive and holding a full-length, digitally recorded movie.

dwarf [dwɔrf] *n, pl* **dwarfs** or **dwarves** [dwɔrvz] **1** a person, animal, or plant much smaller than the usual size for its kind. **2** in fairy tales, a tiny person with magic power.
v **1** keep from growing; stunt. **2** cause to seem small by contrast or distance: *a tower dwarfed by the mountains.* **dwarf·ism** *n.* ⟨Old English *dweorg*⟩

dweeb [dwib] *n Slang* nerd. ⟨origin unknown⟩

dwell [dwɛl] *v* **dwelt** or **dwelled, dwell·ing** **1** *Formal, poetic* make one's home; live. **2** keep the attention fixed (*on* or *upon*): *to dwell on one's misfortunes.* **dwell·er** *n.* ⟨Old English *dwellan* delay⟩
dwell·ing *n* or (*Poetic*) **dwelling place** home.

dwin·dle ['dwɪndəl] *v* grow or cause to grow less and less. ⟨Old English *dwīnan* waste away⟩

dy·ad ['daɪæd] *n* **1** a whole composed of two parts; a pair. **2** *Biology* a pair of chromosomes formed during the division of a TETRAD. **3** *Chemistry* any atom, radical, etc. having a valence of two. **4** *Sociology* two people in an interdependent and ongoing relationship. **dy·ad·ic** *adj.* ⟨Latin *dyadis*; Greek *dyo* two⟩

dye [daɪ] *n* colouring matter, esp one used for organic substances.
v **dyed, dye·ing 1** colour (cloth, hair, etc.) by treating with a liquid containing colouring matter. **2** stain with colour: *The spilled grape juice dyed the rug purple.* ⟨Old English *dēag*⟩
dyed–in–the–wool *adj* thoroughgoing and loyal: *a dyed-in-the-wool Liberal.* **dye·stuff** *n* any substance yielding or used as a dye.

dy·ing ppr of DIE.

dyke [dəik] *n, v.* See DIKE.

USAGE

In Canada, **dyke** is a relatively infrequent variant of **dike** ('a wall to keep water out'). It may be confused with the slang word **dyke** of completely different origin, still considered by most people a term of offence (= lesbian).

dy·nam·ic [daɪ'næmɪk] *adj* **1** energetic or communicating energy; inspiring, forceful, etc.: *a dynamic personality.* **2** to do with dynamics.
n **1 dynamics** the branch of physics dealing with motion and the forces producing it. **2** (usually *pl*) a complex set of interacting forces that operate in a group or a sphere of activity: *dynamics of family life.* **3 dynamics** *pl Music* expressive effects of variation in tempo, loudness, etc. **dy·nam·i·cal·ly** *adv.* ⟨Greek *dynamis* power⟩
dy·na·mism *n* **1** dynamic quality. **2** any of various doctrines seeking to explain all natural phenomena by the action of some force. **dy·na·mo** ['daɪnə,mou] **1** GENERATOR. **2** *Informal* a very dynamic person. **dy·na·mom·e·ter** [,daɪnə'mɒmətər] *n* an instrument measuring force or power.

dy·na·mite ['daɪnə,məit] *n* **1** a powerful explosive made of nitroglycerin, usually in the form of a stick with a wick. **2** *Informal* anything likely to cause intense controversy. **3** *Informal* a very exciting thing or person.
v blow up, mine, or charge with dynamite.
adj spectacular; exciting: *What a dynamite idea!* **dy·na·mit·er** *n.* ⟨Greek *dynamis* power; named by Alfred Nobel, 19c inventor⟩

dy·nas·ty ['daɪnəsti] *or* ['dɪnəsti] *n* **1** a succession of rulers from the same family: *the Bourbon dynasty.* **2** their reign. ⟨Greek *dynastes; dynasthai* be powerful⟩
dy·nast [-næst] *n* a member of a dynasty; hereditary ruler. **dy·nas·tic** *adj.*

dyne [daɪn] *n* a unit of force equal to ten micronewtons. ⟨Greek *dynamis* power⟩

dys– *prefix* bad; abnormal: *dysfunction.* ⟨Greek⟩

dys·en·ter·y ['dɪsən,tɛri] *or* ['dɪsəntri] *n* a painful intestinal disorder producing severe diarrhea. ⟨Greek *dys-* bad + *entera* intestines⟩

dys·func·tion [dɪs'fʌŋkʃən] *n* a failure to function normally. **dys·func·tion·al** *adj.*

dys·lex·i·a [dɪs'lɛksiə] *n* an impairment of the ability to read. **dys·lex·ic** *adj, n.* ⟨Greek *dys-* faulty, bad + *lexis* speech⟩

dys·men·or·rhea [,dɪsmɛnə'riə] *n* painful menstruation. ⟨Greek *dys* -bad + *men* month + *rhein* to flow⟩

dys·pep·si·a [dɪs'pɛpsiə] *n* poor digestion; indigestion. ⟨Greek *dys-* bad + *pep-* digest⟩
dys·pep·tic *adj* **1** to do with or affected with dyspepsia. **2** gloomy; pessimistic. *n* a person who has dyspepsia. **dys·pep·ti·cal·ly** *adv.*

dys·pha·si·a [dɪs'feiʒə] *n* impairment of the ability to speak or understand speech. **dys·pha·sic** *adj.* ⟨Greek *dys-* bad + *-phasis* utterance⟩

dys·pho·ri·a [dɪs'fɔriə] *n Medicine* a chronic feeling of general discontent and illness. ⟨Greek *dys-* ill, bad + *phorein* to bear, suffer⟩

dys·pro·si·um [dɪs'prouziəm] *n* a rare and highly magnetic chemical element. *Symbol* **Dy** ⟨Greek *dysprositos* hard to get at⟩

dys·to·pi·a [dɪs'toupiə] *n* an imagined place or social condition where everything is bad and people lead a wretched life. Compare UTOPIA. **dys·to·pi·an** *adj.* ⟨*dys-* bad + *(u)topia.* Coined by 19c English philosopher J.S. Mill.⟩

dys·tro·phy ['dɪstrəfi] *n Medicine* **1** defective nutrition. **2** degeneration or defective development of tissue: *muscular dystrophy.* ⟨Greek *dys-* bad + *trophē* nourishment⟩
dys·troph·ic [dɪs'trɒfɪk] *or* [dɪs'troufɪk] *adj* **1** to do with dystrophy. **2** *Ecology* to do with a body of water derived from a bog as a result of a decline in nutrients required for aquatic plant life.

Ee

e or **E** [i] *n, pl* **e's** or **E's 1** the fifth letter of the English alphabet, or any speech sound represented by it. **2** the fifth person or thing in a series. **3** *Music* the third tone in the scale of C major. **4** *Mathematics* the base of the system of natural logarithms, equal to about 2.718 28. **5** a grade or mark indicating work well below average.

e 1 *Physics* erg. **2** *Baseball* error.

e–¹ *prefix* out of; from: *educe, emerge, erase, evoke.* It is the form of **ex-¹** used before consonants except *c, f, p, q, s, t.*

e–² *combining form* electronically carried out over the Internet: *e-mail, e-commerce.* Also, **E–**.

E or **E. 1** east; eastern. **2** English. **3** earth.

each [itʃ] *adj* every one of two or more people or things: *Each dog has a name.*
pron every single one: *She gave a pen to each.*
adv for each: *These pencils cost ten cents each.* ⟨Old English *ælc; ā* ever + *gelīc* alike⟩
each other one another: *The three boys struck each other.*

SYNONYMS

Each emphasizes that one and all of a number are thought of singly, as individuals: *Each dog has a name* means that, as individuals, all the dogs in the group have names of their own. **Every** means that all in the group are included, with no exceptions: *Every dog has a name* means none of the dogs was left without a name.

---

ea·ger [ˈigər] *adj* wanting very much: *The child is eager to please.* **ea·ger·ly** *adv.* **ea·ger·ness** *n.* ⟨Old French *aigre* keen; Latin *acer, acris*⟩
eager beaver *Informal* an especially or excessively enthusiastic person.

ea·gle [ˈigəl] *n* **1** any of a number of large, strong birds of prey, with very keen eyes. **2** *Golf* two strokes less than par for any hole on a course. ⟨Old French *aigle;* Latin *aquila*⟩
eagle eye 1 keen vision. **2** careful watch; lookout: *keeping an eagle eye out for bargains.*
ea·gle–eyed *adj* able to see far and clearly.
ea·glet [ˈiglɪt] *n* a young eagle.

ear¹ [ir] *n* **1** the organ of hearing and balance in the higher vertebrates. In mammals it consists typically of three parts: the **external ear middle ear** and **inner ear**. **2** the ability to distinguish small differences in sounds: *That musician has a very good ear.* **3** favourable attention: *to give ear to a request.* **eared** *adj.*
ear·less *adj.* ⟨Old English *ēare*⟩
all ears *Informal* listening attentively or eagerly. **believe one's ears** believe what one hears. **bend someone's ear** *Slang* talk to someone at great length. **by ear** without reading or reproducing written music: *to play by ear.* **go in one ear and out the other** be heard but make no impression. **have** or **keep an ear to the ground** *Informal* pay attention to what people are doing and saying so that one can act accordingly. **have the ear of** able to influence (someone). **in one ear and out the other** heard but disregarded. **lend an ear** listen. **play it by ear** *Informal* **a** proceed instinctively, without a plan. **b** eavesdrop. **set by the ears** stir up trouble between. **set something on its ear** *Informal* put into a state of excitement or upheaval: *a young designer setting the fashion world on its ear.* **up to the ears** *Informal* thoroughly involved; almost overcome. **wet behind the ears** *Informal* inexperienced.
ear·ache *n* pain in the ear. **ear·drum** *n* the thin membrane stretched across the middle ear. **ear·flap** *n* a part of a cap that can be turned down over the ear to keep it warm. **ear·ful** *n* **1** enough of what is being said. **2** a scolding. **3** gossip. **ear·lobe** *n* the soft tissue at the lowest part of the external ear.
ear·mark *n* **1** *Informal* a mark made on the ear of an animal to show who owns it. **2** a special mark or feature that sets a person or thing apart. *v* **1** make an earmark on. **2** identify: *Careful work earmarks a good student.* **3** set aside for some special purpose: *Five hundred dollars is earmarked to buy books.*
ear·muffs *n pl* a pair of coverings, attached to a headband, to put over the ears to keep them warm. **ear·phone** *n* a receiver for a radio, hearing aid, etc. that fits over or is inserted into the ear. **ear·piece** *n* a part of something that is connected to the ear: *the earpiece of a telephone.* **ear·plug** *n* something inserted into the ear to keep out water or noise. **ear·ring** *n* an ornament for the ear. **ear·shot** *n* the distance at which a sound can be heard: *out of earshot.* **ear·split·ting** *adj* of a noise, painfully loud. **ear·wig** *n* any of numerous insects with a pair of appendages at the tail end that are like forceps.

ear² [ir] *n* the mature spike of cereal plants, containing the seeds, or kernels.
v of such plants, develop ears; mature: *Soon the corn will ear.* ⟨Old English *ēar*⟩

earl [ɜrl] *n* in the UK, a nobleman ranking below a marquess. The wife or widow of an earl is a countess. **earl·dom** *n.* ⟨Old English *eorl*⟩

ear·ly [ˈɜrli] *adv* **1** near the beginning: *early in the day.* **2** before the usual or expected time: *I left 15 minutes early.* **3** long ago: *early in history.* **ear·ly** *adj.* **ear·li·ness** *n.* ⟨Old English *ǣr* ere + *-līce* -ly¹⟩
early on at an early stage: *They learned early on not to push her.*
early bird *Informal* a person who gets up or arrives early.

earn [ɜrn] *v* **1** be paid: *She earns ten dollars an hour.* **2** bring or get as deserved: *to earn respect.* **3** *Baseball* score (a run) not due to an opponent's error. ⟨Old English *earnian*⟩
earned run average *Baseball* the average number of runs scored not due to an error by a player in nine innings. *Abbrev* **ERA**. **earn·ings** *n pl* money earned from work or investment.

ear·nest [ˈɜrnɪst] *adj* **1** firm in purpose. **2** to be taken seriously. **ear·nest·ly** *adv.* **ear·nest·ness** *n.* ⟨Old English *eornost*⟩ **in earnest a** serious or seriously: *I speak in earnest.* **b** with or as if with determination and purpose: *It began to rain in earnest.*

earth [ɜrθ] *n* **1 Earth** the planet on which we live, third from the sun. **2** dry land. **3** soil; dirt: *The earth in the garden is soft.* **4** *Electricity* the connection of a conductor with the earth. **5** the hole of a burrowing animal. *v* connect (a conductor) with the earth. ⟨Old English *eorthe*⟩ **come back to earth** stop dreaming and get back to practical matters. **down to earth** realistic and practical. **earth·bound** *adj* **1** bound or limited to this earth. **2** headed for the earth: *earthbound meteors.* **earth–con·scious** *adj* environmentally aware. **Earth Day** a day (April 22) set aside to celebrate the environment. **earth·en** [ˈɜrθən] *adj* made of earth or baked clay. **earth·en·ware** *n* a porous type of pottery. **earth–friend·ly** *adj* not harmful to nature. **earth·ling** *n* an inhabitant of the earth; human being. **earth·ly** *adj* to do with the natural world, and not with heaven. **earth·mov·er** *n* bulldozer. **earth·quake** *n* a shaking of the earth's surface. **earth science** any of a group of sciences concerned with the origin and physical features of the earth. **earth–shak·ing** *adj* of extreme importance. **earth tone** any of the colours beige, tan, brown, etc., found in soil or vegetation. **earth·ward** *adv, adj* toward the earth. Also *(adv)*, **earthwards. earth·work** *n* a bank of earth piled up for a fortification. **earth·worm** *n* any of various worms that live in soil. **earth·y** *adj* natural; unsophisticated. **earth·i·ly** *adv.* **earth·i·ness** *n.*

ear·wig See EAR¹.

ease [iz] *n* **1** freedom from pain or trouble. **2** freedom from trying hard: *He enjoyed the ease of his part-time job.* **3** natural manner. *v* **1** make free from pain or trouble. **2** lessen: *This medicine eased my pain.* **3** loosen: *The belt is too tight; ease it a little.* **4** move slowly and carefully: *She eased the big box through the narrow door.* ⟨Old French *aise* comfort, elbow room; Latin *adjacens* adjacent⟩ **at ease a** comfortable. **b** with the hands behind the back and the feet apart: *The soldiers stood at ease.* **ease in** break in with light work. **ease off** or **up** a lessen. **b** loosen. **take one's ease** relax. **with ease** easily. **ease·ment** *n Law* a right held by one party in land owned by another. **eas·i·ly** *adv* **1** without difficulty or discomfort. **2** by far: *She is easily the best singer in the choir.* **3** very likely: *A war may easily begin.* **eas·y** *adj* **1** requiring little effort: *easy work.* **2** free from pain, discomfort, trouble, or worry: *an easy life.* **3** not severe: *easy terms.* **4** *Informal* ready to agree: *Choose whichever one you wish: I'm easy.* **5** not awkward: *easy manners.* **easy come, easy go** *Informal* ephemeral; easily lost. **easy does it!** *Informal* relax. **easy on the eyes** *Informal* good to look at. **go easy on** *Informal* **a** treat gently. **b** use sparingly. **on**

easy street well off. **take it easy** relax. **easy chair** a comfortable chair. **eas·y·go·ing** *adj* taking matters easily: *an easygoing person.* **easy mark** or **target** a person who is easily imposed on.

SYNONYMS

Easy = not too much work needed: *Lunch was easy to prepare.* **Simple** = not complicated: *He can work out simple puzzles.* **Effortless** = easy either by nature or by training: *the effortless movements of a cat.*

ea·sel [ˈizəl] *n* a support for holding an artist's canvas, a chalkboard, etc. upright. ⟨Dutch *ezel* literally, ass; Latin *asinus*⟩

east [ist] *n* **1** the direction of the sunrise. **2 the East a** the part of any country toward the east, esp the eastern part of Canada and the United States. **b** Asia. **east** or **East** *adj.* **east** *adv.* ⟨Old English *ēast*⟩ **back East** or **down East ✹** any point to the east of Winnipeg, esp that part of the country east of Québec: *He's from down East.* **east of** farther east than. **east·bound** *adj* going toward the east. **east·er·ly** *adj, adv* **1** toward the east. **2** from the east: *easterly winds.* **east·ern** *adj* **1** toward the east. **2** from the east. **3** of or in the east **4** of or in Asia. **East·ern·er** *n* a native of the eastern part of the country. **east·ern·ize** *v* cause to adopt eastern ideas, customs, etc. **east·ern·most** *adj* farthest east. **Eastern Orthodox Church** the Greek and Russian orthodox Christian churches. **Eastern rite** the liturgy and organization of the Eastern Orthodox Church. **Eastern Townships ✹** most of that part of Québec lying south of the St. Lawrence River Valley and west of Québec City. **East Indian** *n* a native or inhabitant of the Indian subcontinent, or a person of East Indian descent. **East Indies** formerly, the name that was given to the region of S Asia that includes India and SE Asia. **East·main** *n* **✹** the eastern shore of Hudson Bay. **east–north·east** *n* a direction midway between east and northeast. *adj, adv* in, from, or toward this direction. **east–south·east** *n* a direction midway between east and southeast. **east·ward** *adj, adv* toward the east: *an eastward slope, to ride eastward.* Also *(adv)*, **east·wards. east·ward·ly** *adj, adv.*

East·er [ˈistər] *n* the yearly Christian celebration commemorating Christ's rising from the dead, on the first Sunday after the first full moon after March 21. ⟨Old English *ēastre* name of a dawn goddess; *ēast* east⟩ **Easter egg** an egg, real or made of chocolate, glass, etc. used as a gift or ornament at Easter.

eat [it] *v* **ate, eat·en, eat·ing 1** take into the mouth and swallow. **2** have a meal: *Where shall we eat?* **3** waste as if by eating (usually with *up, through, into,* etc.): *The acid has eaten into the metal.* **4** *Informal* make annoyed or anxious: *What's eating her?* **eat·er** *n.* ⟨Old English *etan*⟩ **eat crow** be humbled. **eat one's heart out** *Informal* be consumed with envy. **eat one's words** take back what one has said. **eat out**

eat in a restaurant. **eat out of someone's hand** be completely submissive to someone. **eat up a** eat all of. **b** *Informal* receive eagerly: *They applaud and he just eats it up.* **eat·a·ble** *adj* fit to eat. *n* Usually, **eatables** *pl* food. **eat·er·y** *n Informal* restaurant. **eat·ing** *adj* for eating: *eating apples.* **good eating** good to eat. **eats** *n Informal* food; a meal.

eau de Co·logne [ou də kə'loun] cologne. ⟨French = water of Cologne, Germany⟩ **eau de toilette** [ou də twɑ'lɛt] a fragrant liquid, weaker than perfume.

eaves [ivz] *n pl* the lower edges of a roof projecting beyond the wall of a building. ⟨Old English *efes*⟩ **eaves·drop** *v* -dropped, -drop·ping listen to what one is not supposed to hear. **eaves·drop·per** *n.* **eaves·trough** *n* a trough placed along the eaves of a roof to carry rainwater away. **eaves·trough·ing** *n* material with which to make eavestroughs.

ebb [ɛb] *n* **1** Also, **ebb tide** a flowing of the tide away from the shore. **2** a decline. **3** a point of decline. **ebb** *v.* ⟨Old English *ebba*⟩ **ebb and flow 1** the falling and rising of the tide. **2** bad times and good times: *the ebb and flow of business.*

eb·on·y ['ɛbəni] *n* the hard, almost black wood of any of various tropical trees. ⟨Latin *ebeninus;* Egyptian⟩

e·bul·lient [ɪ'bʊljənt] *or* [ɪ'bʌljənt] *adj* **1** overflowing with excitement, liveliness, etc.; very enthusiastic. **2** boiling; bubbling. **e·bul·lience** *n.* **eb·ul·li·tion** [ˌɛbə'lɪʃən] *n.* ⟨Latin *ebullire; ex-* out + *bullire* boil⟩

e–business or **E–business** ['i ˌkɒmərs] *n* financial and other business transactions carried out over the Internet. Also, **e–commerce** or **E–commerce.**

ec·cen·tric [ɛk'sɛntrɪk] *adj* **1** odd; unconventional. **2** not having a perfectly circular path or shape: *the eccentric orbit of a planet.* **3** having its axis off centre: *an eccentric wheel. n* an eccentric person. **ec·cen·tri·cal·ly** *adv.* **ec·cen·tric·i·ty** *n.* ⟨Greek *ek-* out + *kentron* centre⟩

ec·cle·si·as·tic [ɪˌklizi'æstɪk] *n* a member of the clergy. ⟨Greek *ekklesia* church⟩ **ec·cle·si·as·ti·cal** *adj* to do with the church. **ec·cle·si·as·ti·cal·ly** *adv.* **ec·cle·si·as·ti·cism** *n.* excessive adherence to ecclesiastical form.

ECG electrocardiogram.

ech·e·lon ['ɛʃəˌlɒn] *n* **1** a level of command. **2** an arrangement of troops, ships, etc. in a steplike formation. **3** a group, esp a military unit, performing a special task: *a support echelon.* ⟨French *échelon; échelle* ladder⟩

e·chid·na [ɪ'kɪdnə] *n, pl* **-nas** or **-nae** [-ni] *or* [-naɪ] either of two species of egg-laying mammal of Australasia. ⟨Greek *echidna* viper⟩

e·chi·no·derm [ɪ'kaɪnəˌdɜrm] *or* ['ɛkənəˌdɜrm] *n* any of a phylum of invertebrate animals that live on the sea bottom, including starfish and sea urchins. ⟨Greek *echinos* sea urchin, orig, hedgehog + *derma* skin⟩

ech·o ['ɛkou] *n, pl* **ech·oes 1** a repeating of a sound as it is reflected by a surface. **2** a radio wave that has been reflected. **ech·o, ech·oed, ech·o·ing** *v.* **ech·o·like** *adj.* ⟨Greek *ēchē* sound⟩ **echo chamber** in recording and broadcasting, a room or microphone producing hollow sound effects. **e·cho·ic** *adj* in imitation of natural sounds. *Buzz* is an echoic word. **ech·o·ism** *n.* **ech·o·la·lia** [ˌɛkou'leiliə] *n* a disorder characterized by compulsive repetition of the speech of others. **ech·o·lo·ca·tion** *n* the determination of the position of an object by means of its reflection of sound waves. **echo sounder** a device that finds the depth of water by timing reflected sound waves. **echo sounding.**

é·clair [ei'klɛr] *or* [i'klɛr] *n* a piece of puff pastry filled with whipped cream or custard and covered with chocolate icing. ⟨French = lightning; *éclairer* lighten, Latin *exclarare*⟩

ec·lec·tic [ɪ'klɛktɪk] *adj* selecting what seems best from various sources. **ec·lec·ti·cal·ly** *adv.* **ec·lec·ti·cism** *n.* ⟨Greek *ek-* out of + *legein* pick⟩

e·clipse [ɪ'klɪps] *n* **1** a darkening of the sun, moon, etc. when some heavenly body cuts off its light as seen from the earth. A **solar eclipse** occurs when the moon passes between the sun and the earth. A **lunar eclipse** occurs when the moon enters the earth's shadow. **2** any blocking out of light. ⟨Greek *ek-* out + *leipein* leave⟩ **e·clipse** *v* **1** cut off the light from. **2** make less outstanding by comparison. **e·clip·tic** [ɪ'klɪptɪk] *n* the great circle on the celestial sphere that is the apparent annual path of the sun around the earth.

eco– *combining form* to do with the natural environment: *ecosystem.* ⟨Greek *oikos* house ⟩ **ec·o·cide** ['ikəˌsaɪd] *or* ['ɛkəˌsaɪd] *n* the destruction of the earth's natural environment. **e·col·o·gy** *n* the branch of biology that deals with the relation of living organisms to their environment. **e·co·log·i·cal** [ˌikə'lɒdʒəkəl] *or* [ˌɛkə-] *adj.* **ec·o·log·i·cal·ly** *adv.* **e·col·o·gist** *n.* **e·co·sys·tem** ['ikouˌsɪstəm] *or* ['ɛkou-] *n* the interaction of all the living things of an environment with each other and with their habitat. **e·co·zone** ['ikouˌzoun] *n* an area with characteristic climate patterns, ocean conditions, landscape, plants, and animals. A wetland is an ecozone.

E. coli [i 'koulaɪ] *Escherichia coli,* a species of bacteria found in human and animal intestines, and responsible for water pollution. ⟨T. *Escherich,* German physician + Latin *coli* of the colon⟩

e–commerce See E-BUSINESS.

e·con·o·my [ɪ'kɒnəmi] *n* **1** the managing of money or resources: *fuel economy.* **2** an instance of this: *She stretched her income by many little economies.* **3** a system of managing the production, distribution and consumption of goods: *feudal economy. adj* offered at a lower price: *an economy flight.* ⟨Greek *oikos* house + *nemein* manage⟩

e·co·nom·ic [ˌɛkə'nɒmɪk] *or* [ˌikə-] *adj* to do with economics or with economy. **e·co·nom·i·cal** *adj* avoiding waste: *An efficient engine is economical in its use of fuel.* **e·co·nom·i·cal·ly** *adv.* **e·co·nom·ics** *n* the science of the production, distribution, and consumption of wealth. **e·con·o·mist** *n.* **economies of scale** economic conditions favouring mass production by causing the price of an item to decrease as production increases. **e·con·o·mize** *v* **1** manage (a resource) thriftily. **2** cut down expenses.

> **CONFUSABLES**
> **Economic** means 'having to do with economics' while **economical** refers to saving: *an economic crisis, a more economical car.*

ec·ru or **é·cru** [ei'kru] *n, adj* pale beige. ⟨French = unbleached; Latin *crudus* raw⟩

ec·sta·sy ['ɛkstəsi] *n* **1** a state of great joy. **2** any strong feeling that completely absorbs the mind: *an ecstasy of rage.* **3** a stimulating, hallucinogenic drug. **ec·stat·ic** [ek'stætɪk] *adj.* **ec·stat·i·cal·ly** *adv.* ⟨Greek *ekstasis* trance; *ek-* out + *histanai* to place⟩

–ectomy *combining form* surgical removal of a part of the body: *tonsillectomy.* ⟨Greek *ek-* out + *-tomia* a cutting⟩

ectopic pregnancy [ek'tɒpɪk] the lodging of the embryo in a Fallopian tube, where it cannot develop and must be removed.

ec·u·men·i·cal [ˌɛkjə'mɛnəkəl] *adj* **1** general; universal. **2** representing the whole Christian Church. **3** promoting unity of all Christian denominations. **ec·u·men·i·cal·ly** *adv.* ⟨Greek *oikoumenē* inhabited; *oikos* dwelling⟩ **ec·u·men·i·cal·ism** [ˌɛkjə'mɛnəkə,lɪzəm] *n.*

ec·ze·ma ['ɛksəmə] *or* [ɛg'zimə] *n* an inflammation of the skin. **ec·ze·ma·tous** *adj.* ⟨Greek *ekzema; ek-* out + *zeein* to boil⟩

–ed[1] *suffix* forming the past tense of most English verbs. ⟨Old English⟩

–ed[2] *suffix* **1** forming the past participle of most English verbs. **2 a** having; supplied with: *long-legged, bearded.* **b** having the characteristics of: *honeyed.* ⟨Old English⟩

ed. editor; edition; edited.
eds. **1** editions. **2** editors.

ed·dy ['ɛdi] *n* **1** water, air, etc. moving against the current, often with a whirling motion. **2** any similar current, as of thought: *Eddies of controversy grew around the theory.* **ed·dy** *v.* ⟨Old English *ed-* turning + *ēa* stream⟩

e·del·weiss ['eidəl,vəis] *n* a small Alpine plant of the composite family. ⟨German *Edelweiss; edel* noble + *weiss* white⟩

e·de·ma [ɪ'dimə] *n, pl* **-ma·ta** [-mətə] **1** a swelling caused by an accumulation of watery fluid in the body. **2** excessive swelling in plants as a result of excess water. **e·dem·a·tous** [ɪ'dɛmətəs] *adj.* ⟨Greek *oidēma; oidos* tumour⟩

E·den ['idən] *n* **1** a delightful spot; paradise. **2** in the Bible, the garden Adam and Eve first lived in. ⟨Hebrew *'edēn*, pleasure, delight⟩

e·den·tate [ɪ'dɛnteit] *n* any of an order of New World mammals having only cheek teeth or no teeth at all, like sloths. ⟨Latin *ex-* without + *dens, dentis* tooth⟩

edge [ɛdʒ] *n* **1** a place where something ends. **2** a sharp side that cuts: *the edge of a blade.* **3** *Geometry* a line at which two surfaces of a solid meet. **4** sharpness; keenness. **5** *Informal* an advantage.
v **1** put an edge on. **2** move in a sideways manner: *She edged through the crowd.* **3** move little by little: *He edged his chair nearer to the fire.* **4** *Informal* win a narrow victory over: *Our team edged them 3-2.* **5** tilt (a ski) so that the edge cuts the snow. ⟨Old English *ecg*⟩ **edge in** manage to get in. **edge out** *Informal* defeat by a narrow margin. **edge·wise** *adv* with the edge forward. **get a word in edgewise** manage to say something to a talkative person or in a talkative group. **on edge** nervous; tense with eagerness. **set one's teeth on edge**, irritate one extremely. **take the edge off** deprive of force, bitterness, or enjoyment.
edg·ing *n* anything forming an edge. **edg·y** *adj* **1** sharp: *edgy outlines.* **2** irritable. **3** innovative. **edg·i·ly** *adv.* **edg·i·ness** *n.*

ed·i·ble ['ɛdəbəl] *adj* fit to eat; eatable: *Not all mushrooms are edible.*
n Usually, **edibles** *pl* things fit to eat; food. **ed·i·bil·i·ty** *n.* ⟨Latin *edibilis; edere* eat⟩

e·dict ['idɪkt] *n* **1** an order from an authority. **2** any order. ⟨Latin *ex-* out + *dicere* say⟩

ed·i·fice ['ɛdəfɪs] *n* **1** a building, esp a large or imposing building. **2** any elaborate construction or organization. ⟨Latin *aedificium; aedis* temple + *facere* make⟩

ed·i·fy ['ɛdə,fai] *v* improve morally; instruct. **ed·i·fi·ca·tion** *n.* ⟨Latin *aedificare* build (up). See EDIFICE.⟩

ed·it ['ɛdɪt] *v* **1** prepare, esp for publication, correcting errors, checking facts, etc. **2** have charge of (a newspaper, dictionary, etc.). **3** revise or give final form to (film, tape recordings, etc.) by cutting, splicing, etc. **4** *Computers* compile or modify (a computer file or program). ⟨Latin *editus* pp of *edere; ex-* out + *dare* give⟩
e·di·tion [ɪ'dɪʃən] *n* **1** all the copies of a book, newspaper, etc. issued at the same time: *the second edition of the book.* **2** an issue of the same newspaper, book, etc. published at different times with changes: *the afternoon edition, a foreign edition.* **ed·i·tor** *n* **1** a person who prepares material for publication or broadcasting. **2** a device used for editing movies, tape, etc., including a splicer, etc. **ed·i·to·ri·al** *n* an article or a broadcast, giving the speaker's opinion. **ed·i·to·ri·al** *adj.* **ed·i·to·ri·al·ist** *n.* **ed·i·to·ri·al·ize** *v.* **ed·i·to·ri·al·i·za·tion** *n.* **ed·i·to·ri·al·ly** *adv.* **ed·i·tor–in–chief** *n, pl* **ed·i·tors–in–chief** the person who is the head of the editorial staff of a publication or publishing house.

ed·u·cate ['ɛdʒə,keit] *v* develop in skill, knowledge, etc. by training, study, or experience. **ed·u·ca·tion** *n.* **ed·u·ca·tion·al** *adj.*

ed·u·ca·tion·al·ly *adv.* **ed·u·ca·tor** *n.* ⟨Latin *educare* bring up, raise⟩
ed·u·ca·ble *adj* capable of being educated.
educated guess an estimate based on experience.

–ee *suffix* **1** a person who is——: *absentee* = a person who is absent. **2** a person who is——ed: *appointee* = person who is appointed. **3** a person to whom something is——ed: *mortgagee* = person to whom something is mortgaged. ⟨French *-é*, masculine pp ending⟩

EEG *Medicine* electroencephalogram.

eel [il] *n* any of an order of snakelike fishes having a smooth skin and no pelvic fins. **eel–like** *adj.* ⟨Old English *ǣl*⟩

e'er [ɛr] *adv Poetic* ever.

–eer *suffix* **1** a person who is concerned with, or deals with: *auctioneer.* **2** a person who produces: *pamphleteer.* **3** deal with (sometimes pejorative): *electioneer.* ⟨French *-ier*⟩

EER energy efficiency ratio, a formula to show the efficiency of a machine; output of work as a ratio of the input of energy.

ee·rie ['iri] *adj* causing fear; weird: *an eerie scream.* **ee·ri·ly** *adv.* **ee·ri·ness** *n.* ⟨Middle English *eri, erg;* Old English *earg* cowardly⟩

ef·face [ɪ'feis] *v* **1** wipe out: *inscriptions effaced by time.* **2** keep (oneself) from being noticed: *The boy effaced himself by staying in the background.* **ef·face·a·ble** *adj.* **ef·face·ment** *n.* ⟨French *effacer; es-* away + *face* face⟩

ef·fect [ɪ'fɛkt] *n* **1** whatever is produced by a cause. **2** the power to produce results. **3** influence: *The medicine had an immediate effect.* **4 effects** *pl* personal property.
v produce as an effect; make happen. **for effect** to impress others. **in effect a** in fact. **b** in operation: *The rules are in effect.* **into effect** into operation. **of** or **to no effect** with no result. **take effect** begin to operate. **to the effect** with the meaning or purpose *(that).* ⟨Latin *effectus; ex-* out + *facere* make⟩
ef·fec·tive *adj* **1** producing the desired effect. **2** in operation: *effective as of today.* **3** striking. **ef·fec·tive·ly** *adv.* **ef·fec·tive·ness** *n.* **ef·fec·tu·al** *adj* producing the effect desired. **ef·fec·tu·al·ly** *adv.* **ef·fec·tu·ate** [ɪ'fɛktʃu,eit] *v* make happen; bring about; **ef·fec·tu·a·tion** *n.* ⟨French *effectuer;* Latin *effectus.* See EFFECT.⟩

Most commonly, **effect** is a noun, meaning 'result', and **affect** is a verb, meaning 'to influence': *We don't know what effect the new rule will have. The new rule will affect all of us.* However, in formal English, **effect** is also used as a verb meaning 'get done': *She effected an improvement in the plan.* Thus to **affect** a proposal means to make a change in it, while to **effect** a proposal means to get it done.

ef·fem·i·nate [ɪ'fɛmənɪt] *adj* of males, showing weakness or delicacy. **ef·fem·i·na·cy** *n.* **ef·fem·i·nate·ly** *adv.* ⟨Latin *effeminare* make a woman of; *ex-* out + *femina* woman⟩

ef·fer·vesce [,ɛfər'vɛs] *v* **1** give off bubbles of gas: *Ginger ale effervesces.* **2** be lively and happy; be excited. **ef·fer·ves·cence** *n.* **ef·fer·ves·cent** *adj.* **ef·fer·ves·cent·ly** *adv.* ⟨Latin *ex-* out + *fervescere* start to boil; *fervere* be hot⟩

ef·fete [ɪ'fit] *adj* **1** no longer vigorous or productive; worn out. **2** lacking in character. **ef·fete·ly** *adv.* **ef·fete·ness** *n.* ⟨Latin *effetus* worn out by bearing; *ex-* out + *fe-* breed, bear⟩

ef·fi·ca·cy ['ɛfəkəsi] *n* the power to produce a desired effect **ef·fi·ca·cious** [,ɛfə'keiʃəs] *adj.* **ef·fi·ca·cious·ly** *adv.* **ef·fi·ca·cious·ness** *n.* ⟨Latin *efficacia; efficere* accomplish. See EFFICIENT.⟩

ef·fi·cient [ɪ'fɪʃənt] *adj* able to produce the effect wanted without waste of time, energy, etc. **ef·fi·cient·ly** *adv.* ⟨Latin *efficere; ex-* out of + *facere* do, make⟩
ef·fi·cien·cy *n* **1** the ability to produce the effect wanted without waste of time, energy, etc. **2** the ratio of work done to the energy used, expressed as a percentage. **efficiency apartment** a one-room apartment with kitchenette and bathroom.

ef·fi·gy ['ɛfədʒi] *n, pl* **-gies** a statue, etc. of a person; image. ⟨Latin *effingere; ex-* out + *fingere* form⟩
burn or **hang someone in effigy** burn or hang an image of a person to show hatred.

ef·flo·resce [,ɛflə'rɛs] *v* **1** burst into bloom. **2** *Chemistry* **a** a change to a powder by loss of water of crystallization when exposed to air. **b** become covered with a crusty deposit when water evaporates. **ef·flo·res·cent** *adj.* ⟨Latin *efflorescere; ex-* out + *flos, floris* flower⟩
ef·flo·res·cence *n* **1** flowering. **2** anything resembling a mass of flowers. **3** *Chemistry* **a** a change that occurs when crystals lose their water of crystallization and become powder. **b** the formation of a crusty deposit when water evaporates from a solution.

ef·flu·ent ['ɛfluənt] *adj* flowing out or forth. *n* **1** a stream flowing out of another stream, lake, etc. **2** liquid industrial waste, sewage, etc. ⟨Latin *effluere; ex-* out + *fluere* flow⟩
ef·flu·vi·um [ɪ'fluviəm] *n, pl* **-vi·a** or **-vi·ums** an unpleasant odour. **ef·flu·vi·al** *adj.*

ef·fort ['ɛfərt] *n* **1** the use of energy to do something: *Climbing a steep hill takes effort.* **2** a strong attempt. **3** *Physics* the amount of energy required to perform a physical task: *To lift a mass of one kilogram requires effort equivalent to ten newtons.* **ef·fort·less** *adj.* **ef·fort·less·ly** *adv.* **ef·fort·less·ness** *n.* ⟨Latin *ex-* out + *fortis* strong⟩

ef·fron·ter·y [ɪ'frʌntəri] *n* shameless boldness; impudence. ⟨Latin *effrons; ex-* without + *frons* forehead, ability to blush⟩

ef·fu·sion [ɪ'fjuʒən] *n* **1** a pouring out: *the effusion of blood.* **2** an unrestrained expression of feeling, etc. in talking or writing. **3** the seeping of a fluid into a cavity. **ef·fu·sive** [ɪ'fjusɪv] *adj* showing too much feeling. **ef·fu·sive·ly** *adv.* **ef·fu·sive·ness** *n.*

e.g. for example (for Latin *exempli gratia*).

e·gal·i·tar·i·an [ɪ,gælə'tɛriən] *n* a person who believes in social equality. **e·gal·i·tar·i·an** *adj.* **e·gal·i·tar·i·an·ism** *n.* ⟨Old French *egalité* equality⟩

egg[1] [ɛg] *n* **1** a roundish body, covered with a shell, that is laid by the female of animals that do not bring forth live young. **2** *Biology* a female reproductive cell. **3** specifically, a hen's egg as used for food. **egg·less** *adj.* **egg·like** *adj.* **eg·gy** *adj.* ⟨Old Norse⟩ **have egg on one's face** *Informal* be completely embarrassed. **have** or **put all one's eggs in one basket** risk everything that one has on one chance. **lay an egg** commit a public blunder .
egg·beat·er *n* **1** a kitchen utensil for beating or whipping eggs, cream, etc. **2** *Slang* helicopter. **egg·head** *n* *Informal* an intellectual. **egg·nog** *n* a drink made of eggs, milk, sugar, and spices, often containing rum, brandy, etc. **egg·plant** *n* a plant with an egg-shaped fruit used as a vegetable. **egg roll** a small, deep-fried pastry containing vegetables and, often, pieces of chicken, shrimp, etc. **egg·shell** *n* the shell covering an egg. *adj* **1** like an eggshell; very thin and delicate. **2** a semi-mat finish on paint.

egg[2] [ɛg] *v* urge; encourage (*on*): *The other boys egged him on to fight.* ⟨Old Norse *eggja; egg* edge, point⟩

e·go [ˈigou] *n* **1** the self. **2** *Informal* conceit. **3** *Psychoanalysis* the part of the personality that is conscious of the environment and adapts itself to it. ⟨Latin = I⟩
e·go·cen·tric [ˌigouˈsɛntrɪk] *adj* seeing everything in relation to oneself. **e·go·ism** [ˈigou͵ɪzəm] *n* **1** selfishness. **2** talking too much about or thinking too well of oneself. **3** *Philosophy* the doctrine that self-interest motivates conduct. **e·go·ist** *n.* **e·go·is·tic** *adj.* **e·go·is·ti·cal·ly** *adv.* **e·go·ma·ni·a** [ˌigouˈmeiniə] *n* the state of being extremely self-centred. **e·go·ma·ni·ac** *n.* **e·go·ma·ni·a·cal** [ˌigouməˈnaiəkəl] *adj.* **e·go·ma·ni·a·cal·ly** *adv.* **e·go·tism** [ˈigə͵tɪzəm] *n* the habit of thinking, talking, or writing too much of oneself. **e·go·tist** *n.* **e·go·tis·tic** or **e·go·tis·ti·cal** *adj.* **e·go·tis·ti·cal·ly** *adv.* **ego trip** *Informal* an experience whose primary purpose is to enhance the feeling of power of the person involved. **e·go–trip·per** *n.*

e·gre·gious [ɪˈgridʒəs] *adj* **1** remarkably bad. **2** extraordinary. **e·gre·gious·ly** *adv.* ⟨Latin *ex*-out + *grex, gregis* herd, flock⟩

e·gress [ˈigrɛs] *n* **1** a going out: *No egress through this door.* **2** an exit. ⟨Latin *egressus* pp of *egredi; ex*- out + *gradi* step, go⟩

e·gret [ˈigrɪt] or [ˈɛgrɪt] *n* any of various herons that grow tufts of beautiful plumes. ⟨French *aigrette*⟩

eh [ei] *interj* **1** an exclamation of doubt, surprise, or failure to hear. **2** ✱ *Informal* an all-purpose tag question: *So that's what you think, eh?* **3** ✱ *Informal* a filler, like 'you know' or 'you see': *It's late, eh, so I'd better go.*

ei·der [ˈaidər] *n* any of several large sea ducks that breed in the Arctic. Also, **eider duck**. ⟨Icelandic *æthr*⟩
ei·der·down *n* **1** the soft feathers from the breasts of eiders, used to stuff pillows, etc. **2** a quilt stuffed with these feathers.

Eid ul–Adha [ˌid ul ˈədə] one of the two most important Islamic festivals, taking place in mid-December. The other is **Eid ul–Fitr** [ˌid ul ˈfɪtrə], at the end of Ramadan.

eight [eit] *n* **1** one more than seven; 8. **2** any set of eight persons or things. **3** a playing card having eight spots: *the eight of diamonds.* **4** *Rowing* a crew of eight rowers. **eight** *adj.* ⟨Old English *eahta*⟩
eight ball *Pool* a form of pool in which one side must pocket all other balls before the one numbered 8. **behind the eight ball** *Slang* in an unfavourable position. **eight·fold** *adj, adv* eight times as much. **eighth** *adj, n* **1** next after the seventh; 8th. **2** one, or being one, of eight equal parts. **eighth·ly** *adv.* **eighth note** *Music* one eighth of a note.

eight·een [ˈeitˈtin] *n* **1** eight more than ten; 18. **2** any set of 18 persons or things. **eight·een** *adj.* ⟨Old English *eahtatēne*⟩
eight·eenth *adj, n* **1** next after the 17th; 18th. **2** one, or being one, of 18 equal parts.

eight·y [ˈeiti] *n* **1** eight times ten; 80. **2 eighties** *pl* the years from 80 through 89, esp of a century or of a person's life: *My aunt is in her eighties.* **3** any set of 80 persons or things. **eight·y** *adj.* ⟨Old English *eahtatig*⟩
eight·i·eth *adj, n* **1** next after the 79th; 80th. **2** one, or being one, of 80 equal parts.

ein·stein·i·um [ainˈstainiəm] *n* an artificial, radioactive element. *Symbol* **Es** ⟨A. *Einstein*, 20c German physicist⟩

ei·ther [ˈiðər] or [ˈaiðər] *adj* **1** one or the other of two: *Either coat will do.* **2** each of two: *On either side of the river lie cornfields. pron* **1** one or the other of two: *Either of the coats will do.* **2** each of two: *Her hands were full, as she had a bag of groceries in either hand. adv* any more than another; also (with negatives): *If you don't go, I won't go either. conj* one or the other of two possibilities: *Either come in or go out.* ⟨Old English *ǣghwæther; ā* always + *gehwæther* each of two⟩

e·jac·u·late [ɪˈdʒækjə͵leit] *v* **1** of a man, eject semen. **2** say suddenly and briefly. **e·jac·u·la·tion** *n.* **e·jac·u·la·to·ry** *adj.* ⟨Latin *ex*-out + *jaculum* javelin; *jacere* throw⟩

e·ject [ɪˈdʒɛkt] *v* **1** throw out. **2** force out: *The landlord ejected the tenant.* **e·jec·tion** *n.* **e·jec·tor** *n.* ⟨Latin *ex*- out + *jacere* throw⟩
e·jec·ta *n* matter ejected, such as lava from a volcano.

eke [ik] *v Archaic, dialect* increase; enlarge. ⟨Old English *ēcan; ēaca* addition⟩
eke out a barely make (a living) by various schemes or makeshifts. **b** use (something) very thriftily to make it go as far as possible.

e·lab·o·rate [ɪˈlæbərɪt] *adj* worked out with great care; having many details; complicated. *v* [ɪˈlæbə͵reit] **1** add details to: *The architect spent months elaborating her plans.* **2** talk, write, etc. in detail: *The witness was asked to elaborate on his statements.* **e·lab·o·rate·ly** *adv.* **e·lab·o·rate·ness** *n.* **e·lab·o·ra·tion** *n.* ⟨Latin *elaborare; ex-* out + *labor* work⟩

e·lan or **é·lan** [ei'lɑn] *n* liveliness combined with flair. ⟨French, from *élancer* throw forth⟩

e·land ['ilənd] *n* either of two large, oxlike antelopes of Africa, with straight, spiral horns. ⟨Dutch = elk⟩

e·lapse [ı'læps] *v* slip away; glide by; pass: *Hours elapsed while she slept like a log.* ⟨Latin *elapsus* pp of *elabi; ex-* away + *labi* glide⟩

e·las·tic [ı'læstık] *adj* **1** able to spring back to its original size, shape, or position after being stretched, squeezed, etc. **2** springy: *an elastic step.* **3** being able to recover quickly from weariness, low spirits, etc.: *elastic spirits.* *n* **1** tape or fabric woven partly of rubber threads. **2** RUBBER BAND. **e·las·ti·cal·ly** *adv.* ⟨Greek *elastikos* driving; *elaunein* drive⟩ **e·las·tic·i·ty** [ılæ'stısəti] *n* **1** an elastic quality: *Rubber has elasticity.* **2** flexibility: *elasticity of meaning.* **e·las·ti·cize** *v* weave or make with elastic: *an elasticized belt.* **e·las·to·mer** [ı'læstəmər] *n* an elastic substance such as rubber. **e·las·to·mer·ic** [-'merık] *adj.*

e·late [ı'leit] *v* put in high spirits. **e·lat·ed** *adj.* **e·lat·ed·ly** *adv.* **e·la·tion** *n.* ⟨Latin *ex-* out, away + *latus* pp of *ferre* carry⟩

el·bow ['ɛlbou] *n* **1** the joint between the upper arm and forearm. **2** a joint in the forelimb of a four-legged animal that corresponds to this. **3** something resembling a bent elbow, such as a sharp bend in a road. *v* push with the elbow: *Somebody elbowed her off the sidewalk.* ⟨Old English *eln* length of lower arm + *boga* bow²⟩ **at someone's elbow** near at hand. **out at (the) elbows** ragged or very poor. **rub elbows with** mingle with (people). **up to the elbows in** deeply involved in.

elbow grease *Informal* hard work. **elbow room** *n* plenty of room.

eld·er¹ ['ɛldər] *adj* older; senior: *my elder sister, an elder statesman.* *n* **1** an older person: *The children showed respect for their elders.* **2** one of the older people of a group or community; a chief, ruler, member of council, etc. **3** any of various officers of certain churches. ⟨Old English *eldra; eald* old⟩ **eld·er·ly** *adj* **1** near old age. **2** to do with old people. *n* the elderly people who are old. **eld·er·li·ness** *n.* **eld·er·ship** *n* **1** the office or position of an elder in a church. **2** a group or court of elders. **elder statesman** any influential person whose political advice is deeply respected. **eld·est** *adj* oldest.

el·der² ['ɛldər] *n* any of a genus of shrubs or small trees of the honeysuckle family having edible berries. ⟨Old English *ellærn*⟩ **el·der·ber·ry** *n* **1** the edible fruit of an elder, used for jam, wine, etc. **2** ELDER².

El·do·ra·do [ˌɛldə'rɑdou] *n, pl* **-dos 1** a legendary city of great wealth sought by early explorers in South America. **2** any fabulously wealthy place. Also, **El Dorado.** ⟨Spanish *El Dorado* the gilded⟩

eld·ritch ['ɛldrıtʃ] *adj* weird. ⟨probably Middle English *elf, elve* elf + *-rice* kingdom⟩

e·lect [ı'lɛkt] *v* **1** choose for an office by voting. **2** choose: *We elected to play baseball.* **3 the elect** *pl* **a** a group of people who have special rights and privileges. **b** *Christianity* those who have been chosen by God for salvation and eternal life. *adj* **1** elected but not yet in office (after a noun): *the chair elect.* **2** specially chosen. **e·lec·tion** *n.* ⟨Latin *ex-* + *legere* choose⟩ **e·lec·tion·eer** [ı,lɛkʃə'nir] *v* work for the success of a candidate or party in an election. **e·lec·tive** *adj* **1** filled by an election: *an elective office.* **2** open to choice: *elective surgery.* **3** *Chemistry* tending to combine with certain substances rather than others. *n* a course of study that is not required. **e·lec·tive·ly** *adv.* **e·lec·tor** *n* a person who has the right to vote in an election. **e·lec·tor·al** [ı'lɛktərəl] *adj.* **e·lec·tor·al·ly** *adv.* **electoral college** *US* people chosen by the voters to elect the President and Vice-President of the US. **e·lec·tor·ate** *n* the persons having the right to vote in an election.

e·lec·tric [ı'lɛktrık] *adj* **1** to do with electricity: *an electric current.* **2** using electronic amplification: *an electric guitar.* **3** thrilling: *an electric atmosphere.* ⟨Greek *ēlektron* amber (which, under friction, has the property of attracting)⟩ **e·lec·tri·cal** *adj* to do with electricity. **e·lec·tri·cal·ly** *adv.* **electrical engineering** the branch of engineering which deals with electricity. **electric chair** a chair used in electrocuting criminals. **electric eel** a fish with an electric organ which can produce a shock strong enough to stun a person. **electric eye** a cell in which variations in electric current are produced by variations in the light falling on it. **e·lec·tri·cian** [ılɛk'trıʃən] *n* a person whose work is installing or repairing electric wires, lights, etc. **e·lec·tric·i·ty** [ılɛk'trısəti] *n* **1** a form of energy that can produce light, heat, magnetism, and chemical changes. **2** excitement. **electric storm** a storm accompanied by thunder and lightning. **e·lec·tri·fy** *v* **1** charge with electricity. **2** equip to use electricity. **3** thrill. **e·lec·tri·fi·ca·tion** *n.* **e·lec·tro·car·di·o·gram** *n* a tracing made by an electrocardiograph. *Abbrev* ECG, EKG. **e·lec·tro·car·di·o·graph** *n* an instrument that records the electric current produced by the action of the heart muscle. **e·lec·tro·car·di·og·ra·phy. e·lec·tro–con·vul·sive therapy** [-kən'vʌlsıv] the treatment of mental disorders through shock induced by electrical means. *Abbrev* ECT. **e·lec·tro·cute** [ı'lɛktrə,kjut] *v* kill by an electric current. **e·lec·tro·cu·tion** *n.* **e·lec·trode** [ı'lɛktroud] *n* a conductor through which an electric current enters or leaves a conducting medium. **e·lec·tro·dy·nam·ic** [-daı'næmık] *adj* to do with the force of electricity in motion. **e·lec·tro·dy·nam·ics** *n* the branch of physics that deals with the action of electricity.

e·lec·tro·en·ceph·a·lo·gram [-ɛn'sɛfələˌgræm] *n* a tracing made by an electroencephalograph. *Abbrev* **EEG**. **e·lec·tro·en·ceph·a·lo·graph** *n* an instrument for measuring the electrical activity of the brain. **e·lec·trol·y·sis** [ɪlɛk'trɒləsɪs] *n* **1** the chemical decomposition of an electrolyte by the passage of an electric current through it. **2** the destruction of unwanted body tissues such as hair roots, by means of an electric current. **e·lec·tro·lyte** [ɪ'lɛktrəˌlaɪt] *n* **1** a solution that conducts an electric current. **2** an active substance in the brain, such as potassium. **e·lec·tro·lyt·ic** [-lɪtɪk] *adj*. **e·lec·tro·mag·net** [-ˌmægnɪt] *n* a strong magnet made by coiling wire around an iron core and passing an electric current through the wire. **electromagnetic force** [-mæg'nɛtɪk] a force arising from an electric charge in motion. **electromagnetic wave** a wave of energy resulting from variations in the intensity of electric and magnetic fields vibrating at right angles to each other. **e·lec·tro·mag·net·ism** *n* magnetism produced by electricity. **e·lec·tro·mag·net·ic** *adj*. **e·lec·tro·mag·net·i·cal·ly** *adv*.
e·lec·trom·e·ter [ɪlɛk'trɒmətər] *n* an instrument for measuring differences in electrical charge. **e·lec·tro·mo·tive** [-'moutɪv] *adj* producing a flow of electricity. **electromotive force** the amount of energy derived from an electric source in one second when one unit of current is passing through the source, commonly measured in volts. *Abbrev* **EMF, e.m.f.**, or **emf**. **e·lec·tron** [ɪ'lɛktrɒn] *n* a particle present in all atoms, consisting of a negative electric charge. **electron beam** a stream of electrons moving in the same direction at the same speed. **e·lec·tron·ic** [ɪlɛk'trɒnɪk] *adj* **1** to do with electrons or electronics. **2** to do with computers. **e·lec·tron·i·cal·ly** *adv*. **electronic banking** banking activities performed at a machine. **electronic mail** messages sent from one terminal to another by users of a computer network system; e-mail. **electronic music** music created from sound made by electronic generators and filters. **e·lec·tron·ics** [ɪlɛk'trɒnɪks] *n* the branch of physics that deals with the production, activity, and effects of electrons in motion (with sing. verb). **electron microscope** a microscope that uses beams of electrons instead of beams of light. **electron tube** a device for producing a controlled flow of electrons, consisting of a sealed tube through which the electrons can move. **e·lec·tron·volt** [-ˌvoult] *n* a unit used with the SI for measuring the kinetic energy of electrons. One electronvolt is equal to the energy acquired by an electron when it is accelerated through a potential difference of one volt. *Symbol* **eV**. **e·lec·tro·plate** [-ˌpleit] *v* cover with a coating of metal by means of electrolysis. *n* silverware, etc., covered in this way. **e·lec·tro·stat·ic** [-'stætɪk] *adj* to do with stationary electric charges. **e·lec·tro·stat·i·cal·ly** *adv*. **e·lec·tro·stat·ics** *n* the branch of physics that deals with objects charged with electricity. **e·lec·tro·ther·a·py** [-'θɛrəpi] *n* the treatment of disease by electricity. **e·lec·tro·ther·a·pist** *n*.

el·e·gant ['ɛləgənt] *adj* **1** having or showing good taste: *The palace had elegant furnishings.* **2** *Informal* fine; excellent; superior. **el·e·gance** *n*. **el·e·gant·ly** *adv*. ⟨Latin *elegans*⟩

el·e·gy ['ɛlədʒi] *n*, *pl* **-gies** a poem that is a lament for the dead. **el·e·gize** *v*. ⟨Greek *elegeia*; *elegos* mournful poem⟩
el·e·gi·ac [ˌɛlə'dʒaɪək] *adj* **1** of or suitable for an elegy. **2** sad; mournful; melancholy.

el·e·ment ['ɛləmənt] *n* **1** a substance composed of atoms that are chemically alike. **2** one of the parts of which anything is made up: *Honesty and industry are elements of good living.* **3** one of the four substances—earth, water, air, and fire—once thought to make up all other things. **4** the place, condition, etc. preferred: *She's in her element tinkering with cars.* **5 the elements** *pl* the atmospheric forces. **6** *Mathematics* any member of a set. **7** in an electric oven, heater, etc., the metal coil which reddens with heat. **8** *Computers* any piece of data in an array. ⟨Latin *elementum* rudiment, first principle⟩
el·e·men·tal [ˌɛlə'mɛntəl] *adj* **1** of the forces of nature: *Many indigenous peoples worship elemental gods, such as the sun, thunder, etc.* **2** as found in nature: *Survival is an elemental instinct.* **3** being a necessary or essential part. **el·e·men·tal·ly** *adv*. **el·e·men·ta·ry** *adj* **1** introductory; basic. **2** *Chemistry* made up of only one chemical element. **elementary particle** *Physics* one of the basic components of matter, sharing the properties of an energy wave and a particle. **elementary school** a school of six, seven, or eight grades for children aged six and over, which is followed by high school or junior high school.

SYNONYMS
Elementary emphasizes the idea of basic things: *elementary arithmetic*. **Rudimentary** is a formal word used particularly to mean 'consisting of the first parts and principles': *a rudimentary knowledge of mathematics.* **Primary** emphasizes coming first: *Children attend primary school before high school.*

el·e·phant ['ɛləfənt] *n* either of two huge mammals of Africa and Asia having tough, grey skin and a flexible, muscular proboscis called a trunk. **el·e·phan·tine** [ˌɛlə'fæntaɪn] *or* ['ɛləfənˌtaɪn] *adj*. ⟨Greek *elephas*, *-antis* elephant, ivory⟩

el·e·vate ['ɛləˌveit] *v* **1** lift up; raise. **2** raise in rank: *The soldier was elevated to knighthood for bravery.* **el·e·vat·ed** *adj*. ⟨Latin *elevare*; *ex-* out + *levare* lighten, raise⟩
elevated railway a railway raised above the ground for traffic to pass underneath. **el·e·va·tion** *n* **1** a raised place: *A hill is an elevation.* **2** height above the earth's surface: *The airplane fell from an elevation of 1000 m.* **3** height above sea level: *The elevation of Calgary is 1045 m.* **4** the act of elevating: *the elevation of Caesar to be the ruler of Rome.* **5** a flat drawing of the front, rear, or side of a

building. **6** *Astronomy* the altitude of any heavenly body above the horizon. **7** *Surveying* the angular distance of an object above the horizontal plane through the observation point. **e·le·va·tor** *n* **1** a moving platform or cage to carry people and freight up and down in a building, mine, etc. **2** a building for storing grain. **3** a horizontal piece on an aircraft that is lowered or raised to make the aircraft climb or descend.

e·lev·en [ɪ'lɛvɪn] *n* **1** one more than ten; 11. **2** any set of eleven persons or things. **3** *Cricket, soccer, etc.* a team of eleven players. **e·lev·en** *adj*. ⟨Old English *endleofan* one left (over ten)⟩
e·lev·enth *adj, n* **1** next after the tenth; 11th. **2** one, or being one, of 11 equal parts. **eleventh hour** the latest possible moment.

elf [ɛlf] *n, pl* **elves 1** a tiny, mischievous fairy. **2** a small, mischievous person. **elf·ish** *adj*. **elf·like** *adj*. ⟨Old English *ælf*⟩
elf·in ['ɛlfən] *adj* **1** like an elf in delicacy, mischievousness, etc.: *elfin grace*. **2** to do with fairies. **3** tiny.

e·lic·it [ɪ'lɪsɪt] *v* draw forth: *to elicit a reply, to elicit applause*. **e·lic·it·or** *n*. **e·lic·i·ta·tion** *n*. ⟨Latin *elicere; ex-* out + *lacere* entice⟩

e·lide [ɪ'laɪd] *v* **1** omit or slur over (a syllable or vowel) in pronunciation. **2** omit (a written word, passage, etc.). **3** ignore or suppress. **e·lid·i·ble** *adj*. **e·li·sion** [ɪ'lɪʒən] *n*. ⟨Latin *ex-* out + *laedere* dash⟩

e·li·gi·ble ['ɛlədʒəbəl] *adj* fit to be chosen; qualified: *an eligible bachelor, to be eligible for the school team*. **e·li·gi·bil·i·ty** *n*. **e·li·gi·bly** *adv*. ⟨Latin *eligere* pick out, choose. See ELECT.⟩

e·lim·i·nate [ɪ'lɪmə,neɪt] *v* **1** get rid of. **2** omit: *The architect eliminated furniture in figuring the cost of the house*. **3** *Mathematics* get rid of (an unknown quantity) by combining algebraic equations. **4** put out of a competition by reason of defeat: *Our team was eliminated in the first round of the playoffs*. **e·lim·i·na·tor** *n*. **e·lim·i·na·to·ry** [ɪ'lɪmənə,tɔri] *adj*. **e·lim·i·na·tion** *n*. ⟨Latin *eliminare; ex-* out + *limen* threshold⟩

e·li·sion See ELIDE.

e·lite or **é·lite** [ɪ'lit] *or* [ei'lit] *n* the part of a group regarded as the most distinguished, intelligent, rich, etc. **e·lite** or **é·lite** *adj*. ⟨French; Old French *eslite* pp of *eslire*, Latin *eligere*. See ELECT.⟩
e·lit·ism or **é·lit·ism** *n* control or leadership by an elite. **e·lit·ist** or **é·lit·ist** *adj, n*.

e·lix·ir [ɪ'lɪksər] *n* **1** a universal remedy. **2** a medicine made of drugs or herbs mixed with alcohol and syrup. ⟨Arabic *al-iksīr*⟩

elk [ɛlk] *n, pl* **elks** or (esp collectively) **elk** a large mammal, the second largest member of the deer family. The adult male has large antlers. ⟨Old English *eolh*⟩

ell [ɛl] *n* **1** an extension of a building at one end, forming a letter L. **2** a pipe or tube with a right-angled bend. Also, **el**.

el·lipse [ɪ'lɪps] *n, pl* **el·lip·ses** [ɪ'lɪpsiz]

Geometry the oval path of a point that moves so that the sum of its distances from two fixed points remains the same. ⟨See ELLIPSIS.⟩
el·lip·soid [ɪ'lɪpsɔɪd] a solid of which all plane sections are ellipses or circles **el·lip·soid** or **ellipsoidal** *adj*. **el·lip·ti·cal** [ɪ'lɪptəkəl] *adj* **1** to do with an ellipse. **2** to do with ellipsis. **3** extremely concise or economical of words. **el·lip·ti·cal·ly** *adv*.

el·lip·sis [ɪ'lɪpsɪs] *n, pl* **-ses** [ɪ'lɪpsiz] **1** *Grammar* the omission of a word or words that could complete the construction of a sentence. *Example:* In *She is as tall as her brother*, there is a permissible ellipsis of *is tall* after *brother*. **2** in writing or printing, marks (. . . or * * *) used to show an omission. ⟨Greek *elleipsis; elleipein* come short, leave out⟩

elm [ɛlm] *n* any of a genus of tall trees native mainly to north temperate regions, valued as shade and timber trees. ⟨Old English⟩

El Niño [ɛl 'ninjou] a warm current sometimes occurring off the west coast of South America, having widespread influence on the weather. Compare LA NIÑA. ⟨Spanish = the (Christ) child⟩

el·o·cu·tion [,ɛlə'kjuʃən] *n* the art of speaking clearly in public. **el·o·cu·tion·ar·y** *adj*. **el·o·cu·tion·ist** *n*. ⟨Latin *ex-* out + *loqui* speak⟩

e·lon·gate [ɪ'lɒŋgeit] *v* stretch: *to elongate a rubber band to several times its normal length*. *adj* **1** lengthened. **2** long and thin. ⟨Latin *ex-* out + *longus* long⟩
e·lon·ga·tion *n* **1** a lengthening. **2** a lengthened part. **3** *Astronomy* the angular distance from the sun to any planet or the moon, measured from the earth.

e·lope [ɪ'loup] *v* run away with a lover. **e·lope·ment** *n*. ⟨Middle English *lope(n)* run⟩

el·o·quent ['ɛləkwənt] *adj* **1** speaking with grace and force. **2** highly expressive: *an eloquent look*. **el·o·quence** *n*. **el·o·quent·ly** *adv*. ⟨Latin *eloquens* ppr of *eloqui*. See ELOCUTION.⟩

else [ɛls] *adj* **1** other: *Who else was there?* **2** in addition: *I'm here; do you expect anyone else?* *adv* **1** differently: *How else can we do it?* **2** otherwise: *Hurry, else you'll be late*. ⟨Old English *elles*⟩
or else *Informal* or suffer for it: *Return my bike, or else*.
else·where *adv* in or to some other place.

USAGE
The possessive ending is transferred to **else** when this word follows a pronoun: *someone else's, who else's* (not *whose else*).

e·lu·ci·date [ɪ'lusə,deit] *v* make clear; explain: *She elucidated her theory by a simple experiment*. **e·lu·ci·da·tion** *n*. **e·lu·ci·da·tive** *adj*. ⟨Latin *ex-* out + *lucidus* bright⟩

e·lude [ɪ'lud] *v* **1** slip away from: *The sly fox eluded the dogs*. **2** escape discovery by: *The cause of cancer has eluded research*. **e·lu·sion** [ɪ'luʒən] *n*. ⟨Latin *ex-* out + *ludere* play⟩
e·lu·sive [ɪ'lusɪv] *adj* **1** hard to describe or understand. **2** tending to elude: *The elusive fox got away*. **e·lu·sive·ly** *adv*. **e·lu·sive·ness** *n*.

elves [ɛlvz] n pl of ELF.
elv·ish ['ɛlvɪʃ] adj elfish; elflike. **elv·ish·ly** adv.

'em or **em** [əm] pron pl Informal them.

e·ma·ci·ate [ɪ'meisi,eit] or [ɪ'meiʃi,eit] v cause to lose flesh: A long illness had emaciated the invalid. **e·ma·ci·at·ed** adj. **e·ma·ci·a·tion** n. ⟨Latin ex- (intensive) + macies leanness⟩

e—mail ELECTRONIC MAIL.

em·a·nate ['ɛmə,neit] v 1 spread out or come forth: Fragrance emanated from the flowers. 2 give out; emit; produce. **em·a·na·tion** n. **em·a·na·tive** adj. ⟨Latin ex- out + manare flow⟩

e·man·ci·pate [ɪ'mænsə,peit] v release from slavery or restraint; set free. **e·man·ci·pa·tion** n. **e·man·ci·pa·tor** n. ⟨Latin ex- away + manceps purchaser; manus hand + capere take⟩

e·mas·cu·late [ɪ'mæskjə,leit] v 1 remove the male glands of. 2 destroy the force of: The editor emasculated the speech by poor cutting. adj [ɪ'mæskjəlɪt] weakened. **e·mas·cu·la·tion** n. ⟨Latin ex- away + masculus male⟩

em·balm [ɛm'bɑm] or [ɛm'bɒlm] v 1 treat (a dead body) with chemicals to keep it from decaying. 2 preserve: fine sentiments embalmed in poetry. 3 fill with sweet scent: Roses embalmed the air. **em·balm·er** n.

em·bank·ment [ɛm'bæŋkmənt] n a raised bank of earth, stones, etc., used to hold back water, support a roadway, etc.

em·bar·go [ɛm'bɑrgou] n, pl **-goes** 1 a ban on engaging in commerce with a country: an embargo on oil exports. 2 any restriction put on commerce by law. 3 a restriction. **em·bar·go, -goed, -go·ing** v. ⟨Spanish, from embargar restrain; Latin in- in + barra bar⟩

em·bark [ɛm'bɑrk] v go on board a plane, bus, etc. as a passenger. **em·bar·ka·tion** n. ⟨French embarquer; en- in + barque boat⟩
embark on begin or enter upon: The young woman embarked on a business career.

em·bar·rass [ɛm'bɛrəs] or [ɛm'bærəs] v 1 make awkward and self-conscious: Meeting strangers embarrassed him. 2 burden with debt. **em·bar·rassed** adj. **em·bar·rass·ing** adj. ⟨French embarrasser, literally, to block; Latin barra bar⟩
em·bar·rass·ment n 1 an embarrassing or being embarrassed. 2 something that embarrasses: The naughty girl was an embarrassment to her parents.

em·bas·sy ['ɛmbəsi] n, pl **-sies** 1 the official residence, office, etc. of an ambassador in a foreign country. 2 an ambassador and his or her staff of assistants. An embassy ranks next above a legation. 3 a group officially sent to a foreign government with a special errand. ⟨Old French ambassee; related to Gothic andbahti service⟩

em·bat·tle [ɛm'bætəl] v 1 prepare for battle. 2 involve in or beset with conflict. **em·bat·tled** adj.

em·bed [ɛm'bɛd] or [ɪm'bɛd] v **-bed·ded, -bed·ding** 1 fix in a surrounding mass: Precious stones are found embedded in rock. 2 fix firmly (in the mind): Every detail of the accident is embedded in my memory. 3 place or code in a text or computer program.

em·bel·lish [ɛm'bɛlɪʃ] v 1 decorate; adorn. 2 make more interesting by adding details: She embellished the old stories so that they sounded new. **em·bel·lish·ment** n. ⟨Old French embellir; bel handsome, Latin bellus⟩

em·ber ['ɛmbər] n a piece of wood or coal still glowing in the ashes of a fire. ⟨Old English æmerge⟩

em·bez·zle [ɛm'bɛzəl] v steal by putting to one's own use (money held in trust): The treasurer embezzled $2000 from the club's funds. **em·bez·zle·ment** n. **em·bez·zler** n. ⟨Old French besillier maltreat; of uncertain origin⟩

em·bit·ter [ɛm'bɪtər] v make bitter: I was embittered by my loss. **em·bit·ter·ment** n.

em·bla·zon [ɛm'bleizən] v 1 display conspicuously. 2 decorate: The knight's shield was emblazoned with his coat of arms. 3 honour publicly: His deeds were emblazoned in song and story. **em·bla·zon·ment** n.

em·blem ['ɛmbləm] n an object that stands for a quality, idea, etc.: The dove is an emblem of peace. **em·blem·at·ic** adj. ⟨Greek embléma insertion; en- in + ballein throw⟩

em·bod·y [ɛm'bɒdi] v 1 put into visible form: The building embodied the idea of the architect. 2 bring together in, or make part of, a single book, system, etc.: The Constitution Act, 1967, embodies the conditions of Confederation. **em·bod·i·ment** n.

em·bold·en [ɛm'bouldən] v make bold.

em·bo·lism ['ɛmbə,lɪzəm] n the obstruction of an artery. ⟨Greek embolismos; emballein. See EMBLEM.⟩

em·bon·point [ãbɔ̃'pwɛ̃] n French plumpness.

em·boss [ɛm'bɒs] v decorate with a design that stands out from the surface: Coins are embossed with figures. **em·boss·ment** n. ⟨Old French embocer; en- in + boce swelling⟩

em·brace [ɛm'breis] v 1 hug. 2 take up or accept: to embrace an opportunity. 3 include: The book embraces all her writings. **em·brace** n. **em·brace·a·ble** adj. ⟨Old French embracer take into one's arms; Greek brachion arm⟩

em·bra·sure [ɛm'breiʒər] n 1 an opening in a wall for a gun. 2 Architecture a slanting of the wall on the inner sides of a window or door. ⟨French embraser widen an opening⟩

em·broi·der [ɛm'brɔidər] v 1 ornament (cloth, etc.) with a design made with a needle and thread. 2 add imaginary details to; exaggerate: He didn't exactly tell lies, but he did embroider his stories. **em·broi·der·er** n. **em·broi·der·y** n. ⟨obsolete broider; Old French broder⟩

em·broil [ɛm'brɔil] v 1 involve (a person, country, etc.) in a quarrel. 2 throw (affairs, etc.) into confusion. **em·broil·ment** n. ⟨French en- in + brouiller to disorder⟩

em·bry·o ['ɛmbriou] n 1 the unborn young of a vertebrate. 2 the undeveloped plant within a seed. 3 a beginning or undeveloped state of something. **em·bry·on·ic** [,embri'ɒnɪk] *adj.* **em·bry·on·i·cal·ly** *adv.* ⟨Greek *embryon; en-* in + *bryein* swell⟩ **in embryo** in an undeveloped state. **em·bry·ol·o·gy** *n* the branch of biology that deals with the development of embryos. **em·bry·o·log·i·cal** *adj.* **em·bry·o·log·i·cal·ly** *adv.* **em·bry·ol·o·gist** *n*.

em·cee ['em'si] *Informal n* master of ceremonies. **em·cee, -ceed, -cee·ing** *v.* Also, **M.C.** ⟨the initials *M.C.*⟩

e·mend [ɪ'mend] *v* correct. **e·mend·a·ble** *adj.* **e·men·da·tion** [,imɛn'deiʃən] *n.* ⟨Latin *ex-* out of + *mendum* fault⟩

em·er·ald ['emərəld] *n* a bright green precious stone; transparent green beryl. ⟨Old French *esmeralde;* Greek *smaragdos*⟩

e·merge [ɪ'mɜrdʒ] *v* **1** come into view: *The sun emerged from behind a cloud.* **2** become known: *Many facts emerged during the day.* **e·mer·gence** *n.* ⟨Latin *ex-* out + *mergere* dip⟩ **e·mer·gen·cy** *n* a sudden need for immediate action: *for use in an emergency. adj* for a time of sudden need: *an emergency brake.* **e·mer·gent** *adj* becoming politically and economically independent.

e·mer·i·tus [ɪ'mɛrətəs] *adj pl* **e·mer·i·ti** [-,ti] *or* [-,taɪ] retired, but retaining one's title as an honour: *a professor emeritus.* ⟨Latin, pp of *emerere; ex-* (intensive) + *merere* serve⟩

em·er·y ['emri] *n* a hard mineral used for grinding, smoothing, and polishing. ⟨French *émeri;* Greek *smyris* abrasive powder⟩ **emery board** a flat strip of cardboard coated with powdered emery, used as a nail file. **emery paper** a fine grade of sandpaper.

e·met·ic [ɪ'mɛtɪk] *adj* causing vomiting. *n* something that causes vomiting. ⟨Greek *emetikos; emeein* vomit⟩

–emia *suffix* blood; condition of the blood: *leukemia.* ⟨Greek *-aimia; haima* blood⟩

em·i·grate ['emə,greit] *v* leave one's own country or region to settle in another. Compare IMMIGRATE. **em·i·gra·tion** *n.* ⟨Latin *ex-* out + *migrare* move⟩ **em·i·grant** ['eməgrənt] *n* a person who leaves his or her own country to settle in another. **em·i·grant** *adj.* **é·migré** ['emə,grei] *n* a refugee; a political exile.

CONFUSABLES
Emigrate = leave a country to settle in another: *My family emigrated from India to Canada.* Immigrate = go to settle in a country from another country: *My family immigrated to Canada from India.*

em·i·nence ['emənəns] *n* **1** a position above all or most others; greatness. **2** a high place. **3** Eminence *Roman Catholic Church* the title of honour given to a cardinal: *his Eminence.* **4** *Anatomy* a projection, esp on a bone. **em·i·nent** *adj.* **em·i·nent·ly** *adv.* ⟨Latin *eminere; ex-* out + *minere* jut⟩ **é·mi·nence grise** [eminãs 'gʀiz] *n, pl* **é·mi·nences grises** [eminãs 'gʀiz] *French* a person who exercises power behind the

scenes; literally, grey eminence. ⟨nickname of Père Joseph, secretary of Cardinal Richelieu⟩

e·mir [ə'mir] *n* **1** a Muslim title given to rulers, governors, and commanders. **2** a title of dignity given to the descendants of Muhammad. ⟨Arabic *amir* commander⟩ **e·mir·ate** *n* **1** the rank or authority of an emir. **2** the territory governed by an emir.

em·is·sar·y ['emə,sɛri] *n* a person sent on a mission, esp one sent secretly. ⟨Latin *emissus* pp of *emittere.* See EMIT.⟩

e·mit [ɪ'mɪt] *v* **e·mit·ted, e·mit·ting 1** give off: *The sun emits light.* **2** utter: *The trapped lion emitted roars of rage.* **e·mis·sion** [ɪ'mɪʃən] *n.* ⟨Latin *ex-* out + *mittere* send⟩ **emission control** a device attached to a vehicle to reduce pollution from the exhaust. **emission spectrum** the unique spectrum of the electromagnetic radiation emitted by a substance. **e·mit·ter** *n* the electrode in a transistor that is the source of electrons.

Em·my ['emi] *n, pl* an annual award presented in the US by the Academy of Television Arts and Sciences for outstanding achievement in the field of television. ⟨*Immy*, slang shortening of *image orthicon*⟩

e·mol·lient [ɪ'mɒljənt] *adj* softening; soothing. **e·mol·lient** *n.* ⟨Latin *ex-* (intensive) + *mollis* soft⟩

e·mol·u·ment [ɪ'mɒljəmənt] *n* the salary or fee from a job, office, or position. ⟨Latin *emolumentum* profit; *ex-* out + *molere* grind⟩

e·mo·tion [ɪ'mouʃən] *n* **1** feeling as opposed to reason. **2** agitation: *a voice choked with emotion.* **e·mo·tion·less** *adj.* **e·mo·tion·less·ly** *adv.* ⟨French *émotion* from *émouvoir* stir up; Latin *ex-* out + *movere* move⟩ **e·mote** [ɪ'mout] *v* act a role in an exaggerated way. **e·mo·ti·con** [ɪ'moutə,kɒn] *n* Computers an icon used in e-mail, etc., made up of punctuation marks. *Examples:* :-) for a smile, :-(for a frown. **e·mo·tion·al** *adj* **1** to do with the emotions: *an emotional plea for money.* **2** easily affected by emotion: *Emotional people may cry if they hear sad music.* **e·mo·tion·al·ly** *adv.* **e·mo·tion·al·ism** *n* a tendency to display emotion too easily. **e·mo·tive** *adj* to do with the emotions.

em·pa·thy ['empəθi] *n* the ability to imagine another's feelings. **em·pa·thet·ic** [,empə'θɛtɪk] *or* **em·path·ic** [em'pæθɪk] *adj.* **em·pa·thet·i·cal·ly** *adv.* ⟨Greek *en-* in + *pathos* feeling⟩ **em·pa·thize** feel empathy (*with*): *to empathize with someone's aspirations.*

em·per·or See EMPIRE.

em·pha·sis ['emfəsɪs] *n, pl* **-ses** [-,siz] stress; importance: *emphasis on scientific studies.* **em·pha·size** *v.* **em·phat·ic** *adj.* **em·phat·i·cal·ly** *adv.* ⟨Greek, from *emphainein; en-* (intensive) + *phainein* show⟩

em·phy·se·ma [,emfə'zimə] *or* [-'simə] *n* a lung condition that causes impaired breathing. **em·phy·se·mat·ic** [-zə'mætɪk] *adj.* ⟨Greek = bodily inflation⟩

em·pire ['ɛmpaɪr] *n* **1** a group of countries under the same government, one country having some control over the rest: *the Roman Empire.* **2** a country ruled by an emperor or empress: *the Japanese Empire.* **3** a large business conglomerate controlled by one person or group. ⟨Latin *imperium*⟩
Em·pire ['ɛmpaɪr] *adj* to do with the first French Empire (1804-1815). **em·per·or** ['ɛmpərər] *n* a man who is the ruler of an empire. **em·press** ['ɛmprɪs] *n* **1** the wife of an emperor. **2** a woman who is the sovereign ruler of an empire.

em·pir·i·cal [ɛm'pɪrəkəl] *adj* **1** based on experiment and observation: *Chemistry is largely an empirical science.* **2** based on practical experience, without regard to theory: *The doctor's assistant had only an empirical knowledge of medicine.* Also, **em·pir·ic. em·pir·i·cal·ly** *adv.* ⟨Greek *en-* in + *peira* experience⟩
em·pir·i·cism *n* **1** the use of methods based on experiment and observation. **2** *Philosophy* the theory that all knowledge is based on sense experience. **em·pir·i·cist** *n.*

em·ploy [ɛm'plɔɪ] *v* **1** use the services of: *to employ many workers.* **2** use: *You employ a spoon in eating.* **3** keep busy; occupy: *Instead of wasting time, she employed herself in reading. n* employment: *There are many workers in the employ of the government.* **em·ploy·a·ble** *adj.* **em·ploy·ee** [ɛm'plɔɪi] *or* [ɛmplɔɪ'i] *n.* **em·ploy·er** *n.* **em·ploy·ment** *n.* ⟨French *employer*, Latin *implicare; in-* in + *plicare* fold⟩
employment insurance a government program providing payments of money to persons temporarily unemployed. *Abbrev* **EI**

em·po·ri·um [ɛm'pɔriəm] *n, pl* **-ri·ums** or **-ri·a** [-riə] a large store selling many different things. ⟨Greek *emporos* travelling merchant; *en-* on + *poros* voyage⟩

em·pow·er [ɛm'paʊər] *v* **1** give authority to: *The assistant was empowered to sign contracts.* **2** enable, esp in making one more in control of circumstances: *to empower single parents.* **em·pow·er·ment** *n.*

em·press See EMPIRE.

emp·ty ['ɛmpti] *adj* **1** with nothing in it. **2** unoccupied: *an empty room.* **3** not real; meaningless: *an empty threat.*
v **1** make or become empty: *Empty this box.* **2** flow out: *The St. Lawrence River empties into the Gulf of St. Lawrence.* **emp·ti·ly** *adv.* **emp·ti·ness** *n.* ⟨Old English ǣmtig; ǣmetta leisure⟩
empty of without; lacking. .
emp·ty–hand·ed *adj* bringing nothing: *We expected him to bring a present, but he arrived empty-handed.* **emp·ty–head·ed** *adj* silly. **empty nester** one whose children have become independent and left home. **empty nest syndrome** depression felt by a parent whose children have left home to be independent. **empty set** *Mathematics* a set that has no members.

e·mu ['imju] *n* a very large, flightless bird of Australia, resembling an ostrich but smaller. ⟨Portuguese *ema* ostrich, crane⟩

em·u·late ['ɛmjə,leɪt] *v* **1** try to equal or excel: *Try to emulate the industry of the ant.* **2** be an imitation or simulation of: *This program emulates software produced by another company.* **em·u·la·tion** *n.* **em·u·la·tor** *n.* ⟨Latin *aemulari; aemulus* striving to equal⟩

e·mul·sion [ɪ'mʌlʃən] *n* **1** a mixture of liquids that do not dissolve in each other. **2** *Pharmacy* a milky liquid containing very tiny drops of fat, oil, etc. **e·mul·si·fi·ca·tion** *n.* **e·mul·si·fi·er** *n.* **e·mul·si·fy** *v.* **e·mul·sive** *adj.* ⟨Latin *emulsio*, from *emulgere; ex-* out + *mulgere* milk⟩

en–[1] *prefix* **1** cause to be: *enfeeble.* **2** cause to have: *encourage.* Adding *en-* rarely changes the meaning of a verb except to make it more emphatic. **3** described as specified: *drunken, mistaken.* ⟨Old French; Latin *in-*⟩

en–[2] *prefix* in; on: *encephalon.* ⟨Greek⟩

–en[1] *suffix* **1** cause to be: *sharpen.* **2** cause to have: *strengthen.* ⟨Old English *-nian*⟩

–en[2] *suffix* made of: *silken, wooden, woollen.* ⟨Old English⟩

en·a·ble [ɛ'neɪbəl] *v* **1** make able: *Airplanes enable people to travel fast.* **2** make possible.

en·act [ɛ'nækt] *v* **1** pass (a bill) giving it validity as law. **2** put into practice: *to enact an idea.* **3** play the part of: *In her time, she had enacted many Shakespearean characters.* **en·act·ive** *adj* able to establish as a law. **en·act·ment** *n* **1** an enacting or being enacted. **2** law.

e·nam·el [ɪ'næməl] *n* **1** a glasslike substance melted and then cooled to make a smooth, hard surface. **2** a paint that gives a hard, glossy surface. **3** the outer layer of the teeth. *v* **-elled** or **-eled, -el·ling** or **-el·ing** decorate with, or as if with, enamel. **e·nam·el·ler** or **e·nam·el·er** *n.* **e·nam·el·list** or **e·nam·el·ist** *n.* ⟨Anglo-French *en-* on + *amayl* enamel⟩
e·nam·el·ware *n* pots, pans, etc. made of metal coated with enamel.

en·am·our or **en·am·or** [ɛ'næmər] *v* arouse to love: *Her beauty enamoured the prince.* ⟨Old French *en-* in + *amour* love; Latin *amor*⟩
en·am·oured or **en·am·ored** *adj* very much in love (usually with *of, with,* or *by*): *He was enamoured of his neighbour's daughter.*

en·camp [ɛn'kæmp] *v* **1** make a camp: *It took the soldiers only an hour to encamp.* **2** stay in a camp: *They encamped there for three weeks.* **en·camp·ment** *n.*

en·cap·su·late [ɛn'kæpsə,leɪt] *or* [ɛn'kæpsjə,leɪt] *v* **1** enclose in or as if in a capsule. **2** concisely express the essential features of something. **3** condense; abridge. **en·cap·su·la·tion** *n.*

en·case [ɛn'keɪs] *v* cover completely: *Armour encased the knight's body.* **en·case·ment** *n.*

–ence *suffix* **1** the act, fact, quality, or state of——ing: *abhorrence, dependence, indulgence.* **2** the quality or state of being——ent:

absence, confidence, competence, independence, prudence. See also -ENCY. ⟨Latin *-entia*⟩

en·ce·phal·ic [ˌɛnsəˈfælɪk] *adj* to do with the brain. ⟨Greek *enkephalos* brain⟩ **en·ceph·a·li·tis** [ɛnˌsɛfəˈlaitɪs] *n* inflammation of the brain. **en·ceph·a·lit·ic** [-ˈlɪtɪk] *adj.* **en·ceph·a·lo·gram** *n* an X-ray of the brain. **en·ceph·a·lon** [ɛnˈsɛfəˌlɒn] *n* the brain.

en·chant [ɛnˈtʃænt] *v* 1 use magic on: *The witch enchanted the princess.* 2 delight greatly; charm. **en·chant·er** *n.* **en·chant·ing** *adj.* **en·chant·ing·ly** *adv.* **en·chant·ment** *n.* **en·chan·tress** *n.* ⟨French *enchanter*, Latin *incantare; in-* against + *cantare* chant⟩

en·chi·la·da [ˌɛntʃɪˈlɑdə] *n* a tortilla rolled around a filling of meat, cheese, etc. **the whole enchilada** *Slang* the whole thing. ⟨Spanish *en-* in + Nahuatl *chili* chili⟩

en·ci·pher [ɛnˈsaifər] *v* convert a text into coded form.

en·cir·cle [ɛnˈsɜrkəl] *v* 1 form a circle around: *Trees encircled the pond.* 2 go in a circle around: *The moon encircles the earth.* **en·cir·cle·ment** *n.*

en·clave [ˈɛnkleiv] *or* [ˈɒnkleiv] *n* 1 a district surrounded by the territory of another country. 2 a small group distinguished by its culture from the dominant group which surrounds it: *an enclave of Russians in Paris.* ⟨French, from *enclaver* enclose⟩

en·close [ɛnˈklouz] *v* 1 surround. 2 put a wall or fence around. 3 include along with something else: *I enclosed a photo with the letter.* **en·clo·sure** *or* **in·clo·sure** *n* 1 something that encloses, such as a fence. 2 an enclosed area: *Cows are kept in this enclosure.* 3 something enclosed, esp in a letter.

en·code [ɛnˈkoud] *v* put into code: *to encode a message before sending it.* **en·cod·er** *n.*

en·co·mi·um [ɛnˈkoumiəm] *n, pl* **-mi·ums,** **-mi·a** [-miə] an elaborate expression of praise; eulogy. ⟨Greek *enkōmion* laudatory; *en-* in + *kōmos* revelry⟩ **en·co·mi·ast** [-ˌæst] *or* [-əst] *n* a eulogist.

en·com·pass [ɛnˈkʌmkpəs] *v* 1 surround completely: *The atmosphere encompasses the earth.* 2 contain. **en·com·pass·ment** *n.*

en·core [ˈɒŋkɔr] *or* [ˈɒnkɔr] *interj* once more. *n* an extra performance in response to audience demand. ⟨French = again⟩

en·coun·ter [ɛnˈkaʊntər] *v* 1 meet unexpectedly. 2 meet as an enemy. **en·coun·ter** *n.* ⟨Latin *in-* in + *contra* against⟩ **encounter group** a group of people engaged in training to enhance emotional sensitivity.

en·cour·age [ɛnˈkɜrɪdʒ] *v* 1 give courage to: *Success encourages you to do better.* 2 be favourable to: *High prices for farm products encourage farming.* 3 urge; recommend (*to*): *Students are encouraged to register as early as possible.* **en·cour·ag·er** *n.* **en·cour·ag·ing·ly** *adv.* **en·cour·age·ment** *n.* ⟨Old French *en-* in + *corage* courage; Latin *cor* heart⟩

en·croach [ɛnˈkroutʃ] *v* 1 go beyond proper limits: *The sea encroached upon the shore and* *submerged the beach.* 2 trespass upon the property or rights of another: *He will not encroach upon our time.* **en·croach·ment** *n.* ⟨Old French *encrochier; en-* in + *croc* hook⟩

en·crust [ɛnˈkrʌst] *v* 1 cover with a crust: *The inside of a kettle is encrusted with lime.* 2 form a crust (*on*): *The cold weather had encrusted the snow.* 3 decorate with a layer of costly material: *a crown encrusted with jewels.* **en·crus·ta·tion** *n.*

en·cum·ber [ɛnˈkʌmbər] *v* 1 hold back (from running, doing, etc.): *Heavy shoes encumber the wearer.* 2 make difficult to use: *Old boxes encumbered the fire escape.* 3 burden: *The doctor is encumbered with the care of too many patients.* 4 of property, put under a mortgage: *The farm was encumbered with a heavy mortgage.* **en·cum·brance** *or* **in·cum·brance** *n.* ⟨Old French *en-* in + *combre* barrier⟩

–ency suffix. 1 the act, fact, quality, or state of——ing: *dependency.* 2 the quality or state of being——ent: *frequency.* See also -ENCE. ⟨Latin *-entia*⟩

en·cyc·li·cal [ɛnˈsɪkləkəl] *n Roman Catholic Church* a letter from the Pope to his clergy. *adj* intended for wide circulation. ⟨Greek *enkyklios; en-* in + *kyklos* circle⟩

en·cy·clo·pe·di·a *or* **en·cy·clo·pae·di·a** [ɛnˌsaikləˈpidiə] *n* 1 a book or books giving information on all branches of knowledge. 2 a book treating one subject very thoroughly: *a medical encyclopedia.* ⟨Greek *enkyklios paideia* well-rounded education⟩ **en·cy·clo·pe·dic** *or* **en·cy·clo·pae·dic** *adj* possessing wide and varied information. **en·cy·clo·pe·di·cal·ly** *adv.* **en·cy·clo·pe·dist** *or* **en·cy·clo·pae·dist** *n* a person who makes or compiles an encyclopedia.

end [ɛnd] *n* 1 the last part: *the end of the book.* 2 the outside limit: *Those trees mark the end of their property.* 3 a purpose: *The end of work is to get something done.* 4 a result: *It is hard to tell what the end will be.* 5 death. 6 *Football* the player at either end of the line of scrimmage. 7 *Curling* one of the divisions of a game: *Our team was beaten in the last end.* *v* 1 have a boundary: *Their property ends here.* 2 stop: *when the summer ends.* 3 form the end of: *This chapter ends the book.* 4 kill. 5 arrive at a particular final stage, condition, etc. (often with *up*): *She ended up a judge.* ⟨Old English *ende*⟩ **at loose ends** not settled or busy doing something. **end to end** with the end of one object set next to the end of another. **in the end** finally: *Everything will turn out all right in the end.* **jump** *or* **go off the deep end** *Slang* act rashly. **keep** *or* **hold one's end up** sustain one's part in an undertaking. **make an end of** do no more. **make (both) ends meet** just manage to live on what one has. **no end (of)** *Informal* very much: *We had no end of trouble with that car.* **on end** a upright in position: *She stood the dominoes on end.* b one after another: *It snowed for days on end.* **put an end to** do away with; destroy. **the ends of the earth** the most distant areas.

end·game n 1 *Chess* the last stage of a chess game. 2 the last stage of anything. **end·ing** n 1 the last part. 2 death. **end·less** adj 1 having no end; lasting forever: *the endless motion of the stars.* 2 appearing to have no end: *an endless task.* 3 with the ends joined: *A bicycle chain is an endless chain.* **end·less·ly** adv. **end·less·ness** n. **end·most** adj nearest to the end. **end·note** n a footnote placed at the end of an essay, book, etc. rather than at the bottom of the page. **end of steel ✱ 1** the limit to which tracks have been laid for a railway. 2 a town at the end of a railway line; the terminus of a northern railway. **end·pa·per** n a folded sheet of paper half of which is pasted to the inside of either cover of a book. **end user** or **end–user** n the actual user of a product. **end–us·er** adj. **end·ways** or **end·wise** adv 1 on end; upright. 2 with the end forward. 3 end to end. **end zone 1** *Football* the part of the field between each goal line and the corresponding end of the field. 2 *Hockey* the ice between each blue line and the corresponding end of the rink.

SYNONYMS

End suggests a stop or natural close: *My holidays ended when school started.* **Conclude** suggests a formal ending of a speech, action, etc.: *Singing the national anthem concludes the meeting.* **Finish** suggests ending only after getting everything done that should be done: *I never finish my homework on time.*

---

en·dan·ger [ɛn'deɪndʒər] v expose to loss or injury: *Fire endangered the hotel's guests.*
endangered species any species that is threatened with extinction.
en·dear [ɛn'dir] v make dear: *Her kindness endeared her to all of us.* **en·dear·ing** adj. **en·dear·ing·ly** adv.
en·dear·ment n an act or word showing love.
en·deav·our or **en·deav·or** [ɛn'dɛvər] v attempt to achieve a goal: *endeavour to do better.* **en·deav·our** or **en·deav·or** n. ⟨Middle English -en-¹ + *dever* duty; Latin *debere* owe⟩
en·dem·ic [ɛn'dɛmɪk] adj regularly found in a particular people or locality: *Cholera is endemic in India.*
n 1 an endemic disease. 2 an animal or plant that is endemic to a particular region. **en·dem·i·cal·ly** adv. ⟨Greek *endēmos* native; *en-* in + *dēmos* people⟩
en·dive [ˈɛndaɪv] or [ˈɒndiv] n a kind of chicory. ⟨Latin *endivia*, earlier *intibus*; Greek *entybon*⟩
en·do·carp [ˈɛndou,kɑrp] n *Botany* the inner layer of a fruit or ripened ovary of a plant. A peach stone is an endocarp. See EPICARP. ⟨Greek *endo-* inside + *karpos* fruit⟩
en·do·crine [ˈɛndou,kraɪn], [ˈɛndoukrɪn], or [ˈɛndou,krin] adj 1 producing secretions that pass directly into the blood or lymph. 2 to do with the endocrine glands or the hormones they secrete. Compare EXOCRINE. ⟨Greek *endo-* inside + *krinein* separate⟩
endocrine gland any of various ductless glands that secrete hormones.

en·do·cri·nol·o·gy n the study of endocrine glands. **en·do·cri·nol·o·gist** n.
en·dog·a·my [ɛn'dɒgəmi] n 1 the custom of marrying within one's own group, etc. 2 pollination of a flower by pollen from another flower on the same plant. **en·dog·a·mous** or **en·dog·a·mic** adj. ⟨Greek *endo-* inside + *gamos* marriage⟩
en·dog·e·nous [ɛn'dɒdʒənəs] adj *Biology* originating or produced from within. ⟨Greek *endo-* inside + *-genes*; *gignesthai* be born⟩
en·do·me·tri·um [,ɛndou'mitriəm] n, pl **en·do·me·tri·a** [-triə] the membrane lining the uterus. **en·do·me·tri·al** adj. ⟨Greek *endo-* inside + *metra* uterus⟩
en·dor·phin [ɛn'dɔrfɪn] n in the central nervous system, any polypeptide produced internally to relieve pain. ⟨French *endorphine; endo(gène)* endogenous + *(m)orphine*⟩
en·dorse [ɛn'dɔrs] v 1 write one's name, etc. on the back of (a cheque or other document). 2 approve: *Parents endorsed the plan for a school playground.* 3 recommend: *to endorse a product.* **en·dors·a·ble** adj. **en·dors·er** n. **en·dor·see** [ɛn,dɔr'si] or [,ɛndɔr'si] n. ⟨Old French *endosser; en-* on + *dos* back, Latin *dorsum*⟩
en·dorse·ment n 1 a name, instructions, etc. written on the back of a cheque or other document. 2 approval. 3 a provision in an insurance contract by which the coverage may be increased or diminished. 4 a contract under which a celebrity, for a fee, publicly endorses a product or service.
en·do·scope [ˈɛndou,skoup] n a slender instrument for examining a hollow body organ. **en·do·scop·ic** [,ɛndou'skɒpɪk] adj. **en·dos·co·py** [ɛn'dɒskəpi] n. **en·dos·co·pist** n. ⟨Greek *endo-* inside + -SCOPE⟩
en·do·skel·e·ton [,ɛndou'skɛlətən] n the internal support structure of all vertebrates and other animals such as starfish. Compare EXOSKELETON. **en·do·skel·e·tal** adj. ⟨Greek *endo-* inside + SKELETON⟩
en·do·sperm [ˈɛndou,spɜrm] n *Botany* nourishment for the embryo enclosed with it in a plant seed. ⟨Greek *endo-* inside + SPERM⟩
en·do·therm·ic [,ɛndou'θɜrmɪk] adj causing the absorption of heat. ⟨Greek *endo-* inside + *thermē* heat⟩
en·dow [ɛn'daʊ] v 1 give money to provide an income for: *The rich man endowed the college he had attended.* 2 furnish at birth: *Nature endowed her with brains.* 3 attribute certain qualities to (something not actually having them): *endow storms with anger.* **en·dow·ment** n. ⟨Old French *en-* in + *douer* endow; Latin *dotare*⟩
en·due [ɛn'dju] or [ɛn'du] v 1 provide with a quality or power: *The wisest man is not endued with perfect wisdom.* 2 put on; don. 3 clothe. ⟨Old French *enduire*, Latin *inducere* lead into, confused with *induere* put on⟩
en·dure [ɛn'djur] or [ɛn'dur] v 1 keep on; last: *These statues have endured for a thousand*

years. **2** bear: *Those brave people endured much pain.* **en·dur·a·ble** *adj.* **en·dur·a·bly** *adv.* **en·dur·ance** *n.* **en·dur·er** *n.* **en·dur·ing** *adj.* **en·dur·ing·ly** *adv.* ⟨Latin *indurare* make hard; *in-* (causative) + *durus* hard⟩

ENE or **E.N.E.** east-northeast, a direction halfway between east and northeast.

en·e·ma [ˈɛnəmə] *n* an injection of liquid into the rectum to flush the bowels. ⟨Greek *enema; en-* in + *hienai* send⟩

en·e·my [ˈɛnəmi] *n* **1** a person or group that hates and tries to harm another. **2** anything harmful: *Frost is an enemy of plants.* **en·mi·ty** [ˈɛnməti] *n.* ⟨Latin *inimicus; in-* not + *amicus* friendly⟩
enemy alien a foreigner living in a country at war with the foreigner's own country.

en·er·gy [ˈɛnərdʒi] *n* **1** active strength or force: *Young people usually have more energy than old people.* **2** force; power. **3** *Physics* the capacity for doing work. Energy is measured in joules. **4** natural resources such as oil, needed to make things work: *We must conserve energy.* ⟨Greek *en-* in + *ergon* work⟩ **en·er·get·ic** *adj* **1** eager to work. **2** full of force. **en·er·get·i·cal·ly** *adv.* **en·er·gize** *v* **1** make active. **2** *Electricity* charge. **en·er·giz·er** *n.*

en·er·vate [ˈɛnərˌveit] *v* weaken: *A hot, damp climate enervates people who are not used to it.* *adj* [ɪˈnɜrvɪt] weakened. **en·er·va·tion** *n.* ⟨Latin *ex-* away + *nervus* sinew, nerve⟩

en·fant ter·ri·ble [ɑ̃ˈfɑ̃ˈtɛˈʀibl] *French* a person who shocks others by flouting convention.

en·fee·ble [ɛnˈfibəl] *v* make feeble; weaken. **en·fee·ble·ment** *n.*

en·fold [ɛnˈfould] *v* **1** fold in; wrap up: *enfolded in a shawl.* **2** embrace; clasp: *The mother enfolded her baby in her arms.*

en·force [ɛnˈfɔrs] *v* **1** force obedience to: *Police enforce the laws.* **2** force; compel: *The robbers enforced obedience by threats of violence.* **en·force·a·ble** *adj.* **en·force·ment** *n.* **en·forc·er** *n.*

en·fran·chise [ɛnˈfræntʃaɪz] *v* **1** give the right to vote: *For federal elections, Canadian citizens are enfranchised at the age of 18.* **2** release from slavery or restraint. **en·fran·chise·ment** *n.* **en·fran·chis·er** *n.*

en·gage [ɛnˈgeidʒ] *v* **1** keep busy; occupy: *Work engages much of her time.* **2** hire: *She engaged a cook for the summer.* **3** reserve: *We engaged a room in the hotel.* **4** bind (oneself or another) by a promise or contract: *I will engage to be there on time.* **5** promise to marry: *He is engaged to her.* **6** catch and hold: *Bright colours engaged the baby's attention.* **7** fit into: *The teeth of one gear engage with the teeth of another.* **8** come into contact with in battle: *to engage the enemy.* **9** secure the participation of (someone) in an activity: *to engage someone in conversation.* **10** activate. **en·gaged** *adj.* **en·gage·ment** *n.* ⟨French *engager; en gage* under pledge⟩
engage in a take part in; be active in: *She engages in many sports.* **b** occupy with: *They*

were engaged in repairing the car.
en·gag·ing *adj* very attractive; charming.

en·gen·der [ɛnˈdʒɛndər] *v* produce; cause: *Filth engenders disease.* ⟨Latin *in-* in + *generare* create⟩

en·gine [ˈɛndʒən] *n* **1** a machine that applies power to do some work, esp a machine that can start others moving. **2** a machine that pulls a railway train. ⟨Latin *ingenium* inborn qualities, talent; *in-* in + *gen-*, root of *gignere* produce, beget⟩
en·gi·neer *n* **1** a person who takes care of or runs engines. **2** a person trained in a branch of engineering. *v* manage; guide: *Although many opposed his plan, he engineered it through to final approval.* **en·gi·neer·ing** *n* the application of science to such practical uses as the design of structures and machines.

Eng·lish [ˈɪŋglɪʃ] *n* **1 the English** *pl* **a** the people of England. **b ✱** English Canadians. **2** the English language. **Eng·lish** *adj.* **Eng·lish·ness** *n.* ⟨Old English *Englisc; Engle* the English people⟩
English Canadian a Canadian of English ancestry or one whose principal language is English. **Eng·lish–Ca·na·di·an** *adj.* **Eng·lish·ism** *n* an English custom or expression. **English muffin** a muffin of yeast dough, cooked on a griddle. **English saddle** a saddle with a padded leather seat. It does not have the horn of the Western saddle.

en·gorge [ɛnˈgɔrdʒ] *v* **1** fill to bursting. **2** *Medicine* congest with blood or other fluid. **en·gorged** *adj.* **en·gorge·ment** *n.*

en·grave [ɛnˈgreiv] *v* **1** carve artistically: *initials engraved on a watch.* **2** impress deeply: *His mother's face was engraved on his memory.* **en·grav·er** *n.* ⟨*en-¹* + obsolete *grave* carve; Old English *grafan*⟩
en·grav·ing *n* a picture printed from an engraved plate, block, etc.

en·gross [ɛnˈgrous] *v* **1** take up all the attention of: *She was engrossed in a story.* **2** express in legal form. **3** *Business* buy all or much of (the supply of some commodity) so as to control prices. **en·gross·ment** *n.* ⟨(defs. 1, 3) French *en gros* in bulk; (def. 2) Anglo-French *en-* in + *grosse* document⟩
en·gros·sing *adj* **1** absorbing. **2** controlling.

en·gulf [ɛnˈgʌlf] *v* swallow up; submerge: *A wave engulfed the small boat.*

en·hance [ɛnˈhæns] *v* improve; add to: *The gardens enhanced the beauty of the house.* **en·hance·ment** *n.* **en·hanc·er** *n.* ⟨Anglo-French *enhauncer* raise; Latin *altus* high⟩

e·nig·ma [ɪˈnɪgmə] *n* a baffling or puzzling statement, problem, situation, person, etc.: *The queer behaviour of the child was an enigma to her parents.* **en·ig·mat·ic** [ˌɛnɪgˈmætɪk] *adj.* **en·ig·mat·i·cal·ly** *adv.* ⟨Greek *ainigma; ainissesthai* speak darkly; *ainos* fable⟩

en·join [ɛnˈdʒɔɪn] *v* **1** order; urge: *Parents enjoin good behaviour on their children.* **2** *Law* issue an authoritative command. **in·junc·tion** [ɪnˈdʒʌŋkʃən] *n.* ⟨Old French *enjoindre*, Latin *injungere* attack, charge; *in-* on + *jungere* join⟩

en·joy [ɛn'dʒɔɪ] *v* **1** have or use with joy. **2** have as an advantage: *She enjoyed good health.* **3** be happy; have a good time (with reflexive pronoun): *Did you enjoy yourself at the party?* **en·joy·a·ble** *adj.* **en·joy·a·bly** *adv.* **en·joy·a·ble·ness** *n.* **en·joy·ment** *n.* ⟨Old French *en-* in + *joir* rejoice, Latin *gaudere*⟩

en·large [ɛn'lɑrdʒ] *v* **1** make or become larger: *Enlarge the photograph.* **2** talk or write in greater detail (with *on* or *upon*): *to enlarge on an earlier statement.* **en·large·ment** *n.*

en·light·en [ɛn'laɪtən] *v* **1** instruct. **2** make free from prejudice, ignorance, etc. **en·light·en·er** *n.* **en·light·en·ment** *n.*

en·list [ɛn'lɪst] *v* **1** enrol in some branch of the armed forces. **2** secure the support of: *The mayor enlisted the churches of our city to work for more parks.* **en·list·er** *n.* **en·list·ment** *n.*

en·liv·en [ɛn'laɪvən] *v* make cheerful: *to enliven a talk with humour.* **en·liv·en·er** *n.* **en·liv·en·ing·ly** *adv.* **en·liv·en·ment** *n.*

en masse [ˌɒn 'mæs] *or* [ˌɛn 'mæs]; *French* [ɑ̃'mas] in a group; all together. ⟨French⟩

en·mesh [ɛn'mɛʃ] *v* catch in or as if in a net; entangle. **en·mesh·ment** *n.*

en·mi·ty See ENEMY.

en·no·ble [ɛn'noubəl] *v* **1** give a title of nobility to. **2** make more noble in nature: *Her character was ennobled through suffering.* **en·no·ble·ment** *n.* **en·no·bler** *n.*

en·nui [ɒn'wi]; *French* [ɑ̃'nyi] *n* a deep feeling of weariness and discontent. ⟨French = boredom⟩

e·nor·mous [ɪ'nɔrməs] *adj* **1** extremely large. **2** extremely wicked. **e·nor·mous·ly** *adv.* **e·nor·mous·ness** *n.* ⟨Latin *ex-* out of + *norma* pattern, norm⟩
e·nor·mi·ty *n* **1** extreme wickedness: *The murderer realized the enormity of his crime.* **2** great magnitude: *the enormity of the task.*

e·nough [ɪ'nʌf] *adj* as much or as many as needed: *Buy enough food for the picnic.* *n* an adequate quantity or number: *I have had enough to eat.* *adv* **1** sufficiently: *Have you played enough?* **2** quite: *She feels well enough to go.* *interj* stop! no more! ⟨Old English *genōg*⟩

en pas·sant [ɑ̃pa'sɑ̃] *French* in passing.

en·quire [ɛn'kwaɪr] *v* inquire. **en·quir·y** [ɛn'kwaɪri] *or* ['ɛnkwəri] *n* inquiry.

en·rage [ɛn'reɪdʒ] *v* put into a rage; make very angry; make furious. **en·rage·ment** *n.*

en·rap·ture [ɛn'ræptʃər] *v* fill with great delight: *We were enraptured by his rich voice.*

en·rich [ɛn'rɪtʃ] *v* **1** make rich or richer: *An education enriches your mind.* **2** raise the nutritive value of (a food) by adding vitamins and minerals. **3** *Education* expand the range of (a course of study): *an enriched program.* **en·rich·ment** *n.*

en·rol *or* **en·roll** [ɛn'roul] *v* **-rolled, -rol·ling** **1** write, or have one's name written, in a list. **2** make or become a member. ⟨Old French *enroller; en-* in + *rolle* roster; Latin *rota* wheel⟩

en·rol·ment *or* **en·roll·ment** *n* the number enrolled: *an enrolment of 200 students.*

en route [ɒn 'rut]; *French* [ɑ̃'ʀut] on the way: *We'll stop at Yellowknife en route from Whitehorse to Edmonton.* ⟨French⟩

en·sconce [ɛn'skɒns] *v* **1** shelter safely: *The soldiers were ensconced in fortified trenches.* **2** settle comfortably and firmly: *The cat ensconced itself in the armchair.* ⟨*en-* + earlier *sconce* fortification; probably Dutch *schans*⟩

en·sem·ble [ɒn'sɒmbəl]; *French* [ɑ̃'sɑ̃bl] *n* **1** all the parts of a thing considered together. **2** *Music* **a** a performance by the full number of singers, dancers, etc. **b** a group of musicians or the instruments used: *Two violins, a cello, and a harp made up the string ensemble.* **3** a group of dancers, actors, etc. **4** a harmonious set of clothes. ⟨French; Latin *in- + simul* at the same time⟩

en·shrine [ɛn'ʃraɪn] *v* **1** enclose in a shrine: *A fragment of the Cross is enshrined in the cathedral.* **2** cherish: *Memories of happier days were enshrined in her heart.* **en·shrine·ment** *n.*

en·sign ['ɛnsən] *n* **1** a flag: *the Red Ensign.* **2** the lowest commissioned officer in the US navy. ⟨French *enseigne*; Latin *insignia* insignia⟩

en·si·lage ['ɛnsəlɪdʒ] *n* **1** the preservation of green fodder by packing it in a silo. **2** green fodder preserved in this way. **en·sile** [ɛn'saɪl] *or* ['ɛnsaɪl] *v.* ⟨French. See SILO.⟩

en·slave [ɛn'sleɪv] *v* reduce to slavery: *an enslaved people, enslaved by alcohol.* **en·slave·ment** *n.*

en·snare [ɛn'snɛr] *v* catch in a snare; trap. **en·snare·ment** *n.*

en·sue [ɛn'su] *v* **1** come after: *the ensuing year.* **2** happen as a result: *He hit the man, and a fight ensued.* ⟨Old French *ensuivre; suivre* follow, Latin *sequi*⟩

en suite [ɒn 'swit] forming part of a whole: *a bedroom with en suite bathroom.* ⟨French⟩

en·sure [ɛn'ʃur] *v* **1** make sure or certain. **2** make safe: *Proper clothing ensured us against the cold.*

CONFUSABLES

Ensure is the usual spelling for 'make sure': *Check your work to ensure its accuracy.*
Insure means 'arrange for payment in case of loss, accident, or death': *They insured their house against fire.*

–ent *suffix* **1** ——ing: *absorbent, indulgent, coincident.* **2** one that——s: *correspondent, president, superintendent.* ⟨Latin *-ens, -entis*⟩

en·tail [ɛn'teil] *v* **1** impose; require: *Owning an automobile entailed great expense.* **2** *Law* limit inheritance to a specified line of heirs. *n* **1** an entailed inheritance. **2** the order of descent specified for an entailed estate. **en·tail·ment** *n.* ⟨Middle English *en-¹* + Old French *taille* tax, cutting; *taillier* cut⟩

en·tan·gle [ɛn'tæŋgəl] *v* **1** catch in a net. **2** become twisted together: *Loose string is easily entangled.* **3** cause to get into difficulty:

The villain tried to entangle the hero in an evil scheme. **en·tan·gle·ment** *n.* **en·tan·gling·ly** *adv.*

en·tente [ɑn'tɑnt]; *French* [ã'tãt] *n* an understanding; agreement between two or more governments. ⟨French, from *entendre* hear, understand⟩

en·ter ['ɛntər] *v* 1 go or come into. 2 become a part or member of: *He entered the armed forces.* 3 obtain admission for: *Parents enter their children in school.* 4 begin (often with *on* or *upon*): *to enter the practice of law.* 5 begin to take part (often with *into*): *to enter a contest.* 6 write or print in a book, list, etc.: *Enter the words in alphabetical order.* 7 form a part of (with *into*): *The possibility of failure didn't even enter into her calculations.* 8 *Computers* input (data or instructions). 9 submit an official statement to a court: *to enter a plea.* ⟨Old French *entrer*; Latin *intra* within⟩

en·trance ['ɛntrəns] *n* 1 the act of entering: *The actor's entrance was greeted with applause.* 2 a place by which to enter. 3 permission to enter. **en·trance·way** *n* a place by which to enter. **en·trant** *n* 1 a new member in a profession, club, etc. 2 a person who enters a contest. **en·try** ['ɛntri] *n* 1 the act of entering. 2 a place by which to enter. 3 the right to enter. 4 something written or printed in a book, list, etc. 5 a person or thing that takes part in a contest. 6 *Law* the act of taking possession of lands or buildings by entering or setting foot on them. **en·try·way** *n* an opening or passage that gives entrance. **entry word** *n* in a dictionary, one of the words listed and followed by information concerning its pronunciation, meanings, etc.

en·ter·ic [ɛn'tɛrɪk] *adj* intestinal. ⟨Greek *entera* intestines⟩

en·ter·i·tis [ˌɛntə'raɪtɪs] *n* an inflammation of the intestines.

en·ter·prise ['ɛntər,praɪz] *n* 1 an important, difficult, or dangerous undertaking. 2 a project: *a business enterprise.* 3 readiness to start projects. See PRIVATE ENTERPRISE. ⟨Old French *entre-* between + *prise* pp of *prendre* take, Latin *prehendere*⟩
en·ter·pris·ing *adj* ready to try important or difficult plans. **en·ter·pris·ing·ly** *adv.*

en·ter·tain [ˌɛntər'teɪn] *v* 1 amuse; interest. 2 have as a guest: *She entertained ten people at dinner.* 3 consider: *to entertain an idea.* **en·ter·tain·a·ble** *adj.* **en·ter·tain·ing** *adj.* **en·ter·tain·ing·ly** *adv.* ⟨French *entre-* among + *tenir* hold, Latin *tenere*⟩
en·ter·tain·er *n* a singer, musician, dancer, etc. who takes part in public entertainments. **en·ter·tain·ment** *n.*

en·thral or **en·thrall** [ɛn'θrɒl] *v* **-thralled**, **-thrall·ing** 1 captivate: *The explorer enthralled the audience with his adventures.* 2 enslave. **en·thral·ment** or **en·thrall·ment** *n.*

en·throne [ɛn'θroun] *v* set on a throne. **en·throne·ment** *n.*

en·thu·si·asm [ɛn'θuzi,æzəm] *n* 1 eager interest. 2 an activity that creates interest.

en·thu·si·as·tic *adj.* **en·thu·si·as·ti·cal·ly** *adv.* ⟨Greek *enthousiasmos; entheos* god-possessed; *en-* in + *theos* god⟩

en·thuse *v Informal* 1 show enthusiasm. 2 fill with enthusiasm. **en·thu·si·ast** [-,æst] *or* [-əst] *n* a person ardently interested in something: *a baseball enthusiast.*

en·tice [ɛn'taɪs] *v* attract by offering some reward: *The robber enticed us into a cave by promising to show us a gold mine.* **en·tic·er** *n.* **en·tic·ing** *adj.* **en·tice·ment** *n.* ⟨Old French *enticier* stir up; *en-* in + Latin *titio* firebrand⟩

en·tire [ɛn'taɪr] *adj* 1 having all the parts: *The entire platoon was wiped out.* 2 not broken; in one piece. 3 total: *entire trust.* ⟨Old French *entier*; Latin *integer.* See INTEGER.⟩
en·tire·ly *adv* 1 completely. 2 solely. **en·tire·ty** [ɛn'taɪrti] *or* [ɛn'taɪrəti] *n* 1 wholeness; completeness. 2 a complete thing. 3 *Law* possession by one person only. **in its entirety** wholly: *She enjoyed the concert in its entirety.*

en·ti·tle [ɛn'taɪtəl] *v* 1 give the title of: *She read a poem entitled "Trees."* 2 give a claim or right to: *Their age and experience entitle old people to the respect of young people.* 3 bestow a title of an honorary nature on.
en·ti·tle·ment *n* 1 the state of being entitled. 2 something to which one is entitled.

en·ti·ty ['ɛntəti] *n* 1 something that has a real and separate existence either actually or in the mind. Persons, mountains, languages, and beliefs are entities. 2 existence. ⟨Latin *entitas*, from *ens, entis* ppr of *esse* be⟩

en·tomb [ɛn'tum] *v* place in a tomb or as if in a tomb. **en·tomb·ment** *n.*

en·to·mol·o·gy [ˌɛntə'mɒlədʒi] *n* the branch of zoology that deals with insects. **en·to·mo·log·i·cal** [ˌɛntəmə'lɒdʒəkəl] *adj.* **en·to·mol·o·gist** *n.* ⟨Greek *entomon* insect; *entomos* notched; *en-* in + *temnein* cut (with reference to their segmented bodies)⟩
en·to·moph·a·gous [ˌɛntə'mɒfəgəs] *adj* having a diet consisting mainly of insects.

en·tou·rage ['ɒntʊ,rɑʒ] *or* [ˌɒntʊ'rɑʒ] *n* a group of people usually accompanying a person. ⟨French from *entourer* surround⟩

en·tr'acte [ɑn'trækt]; *French* [ã'trakt] *n* an interval between two acts of a play, ballet, opera, etc. ⟨French = between-act⟩

en·trails ['ɛntreilz] *or* ['ɛntrəlz] *n pl* 1 the intestines of a human or animal. 2 any inner parts. ⟨Latin *intralia; intra* inside⟩

en·trance¹ See ENTER.

en·trance² [ɛn'træns] *v* 1 put into a trance. 2 fill with joy; charm. **en·trance·ment** *n.* **en·tranc·ing·ly** *adv.* ⟨*en-¹* + *trance*⟩

en·trap [ɛn'træp] *v* **-trapped**, **-trap·ping** 1 catch in a trap. 2 bring into difficulty by trickery: *The lawyer entrapped the witness into contradicting himself.* **en·trap·ment** *n.*

en·treat [ɛn'trit] *v* ask earnestly: *The captives entreated the pirates not to kill them.* **en·treat·ing** *adj.* **en·treat·y** [ɛn'triti] *n.* ⟨Old French *en-* (intensive) + *traitier* treat, in sense of parley; Latin *tractare*⟩

en·tree or **en·trée** [ɒn'treɪ] *or* ['ɒntreɪ] *n* a main dish served at dinner or lunch. ⟨French, pp of *entrer* enter⟩

en·trench [ɛn'trɛntʃ] *v* **1** surround with a trench as fortification. **2** establish firmly: *Giving birthday gifts is a custom entrenched in people's minds.* **3** trespass: *Do not entrench upon the rights of others.* **en·trench·ment** *n*.

en·tre·pre·neur [ˌɒntrəprə'nɜr] *n* a person who organizes and manages a business, taking the risk of a loss. **en·tre·pre·neur·i·al** [ˌɒntrəprə'nʊriəl] *adj*. **en·tre·pre·neur·ship** *n*. ⟨French, from *entreprendre* undertake. See ENTERPRISE.⟩

en·tro·py ['ɛntrəpi] *n* **1** *Physics* **a** in a thermodynamic system, a measure of the energy that is not available for conversion to mechanical work. **b** a measure of the degree of molecular disorder in a system. **2** the tendency of the universe toward increasing disorder. **3** *Communications* a statistical measure of the predictable accuracy of a system in transmitting information. ⟨German *Entropie*, influenced by Greek *entropia* a turning in; *en-* + *tropē* a turning⟩

en·trust [ɛn'trʌst] *v* **1** charge with a trust: *The club entrusted the treasurer with its money.* **2** hand over for safekeeping: *They entrusted their son to his grandparents.* **en·trust·ment** *n*.

en·try See ENTER.

en·twine [ɛn'twaɪn] *v* **1** twine together. **2** twine around: *Roses entwined the little cottage.* **en·twine·ment** *n*.

e·nu·mer·ate [ɪ'njumə,reɪt] *or* [ɪ'numə,reɪt] *v* **1** name one by one: *She enumerated the provinces of Canada.* **2** count. **3** ✷ make up a list of (voters in an area) or enter (a person) in such a list. **e·nu·mer·a·tion** *n*. **e·nu·mer·a·tive** *adj*. ⟨Latin *enumerare; ex-* out + *numerus* number⟩
e·nu·mer·a·tor *n* ✷ a person appointed to list the eligible voters in a polling area.

e·nun·ci·ate [ɪ'nʌnsi,eɪt] *or* [ɪ'nʌnʃi,eɪt] *v* **1** pronounce (words) clearly and articulately. **2** state definitely: *After performing many experiments, the scientist enunciated a new theory.* **e·nun·ci·a·tion** *n*. ⟨Latin *enuntiare; ex-* out + *nuntius* messenger⟩

en·u·re·sis [ˌɛnjə'risɪs] *n* involuntary passing of urine. **en·u·ret·ic** [ˌɛnjə'rɛtɪk] *adj*. ⟨Greek *enourein* urinate in; *en-*in + *ourein* urinate⟩

en·vel·op [ɛn'vɛləp] *v* **1** wrap. **2** surround: *Our soldiers enveloped the enemy and captured them.* **3** hide: *Fog enveloped the village.* **en·vel·op·ment** *n*. ⟨Old French *enveloper; en-* in + *voloper* wrap⟩
en·ve·lope ['ɛnvə,loup] *or* ['ɒnvə,loup] *n* **1** a sealable paper cover in which a letter can be mailed. **2** something that covers and contains. **3** *Biology* any enclosing covering, such as a membrane or a shell. **4** *Geometry* a curve touching a continuous series of curves. **5** *Astronomy* a nebulous mass surrounding the nucleus of a comet on the side nearest the sun. **6** a bag that holds the gas in a balloon. **7** the set of constraints within which a system may operate safely. **push the envelope** extend the limits of what is possible.

en·vi·a·ble See ENVY.

en·vi·ron·ment [ɛn'vaɪərnmənt] *n* **1** all the conditions that affect the development of a living thing. **2** **the environment**, the air, water, and land around us. **3** the setting within which something is done: *learning environment.* **en·vi·ron·men·tal** *adj*. **en·vi·ron·men·tal·ly** *adv*.
en·vi·ron·men·tal·ism *n* **1** *Psychology* the theory that environment is more influential than heredity in an individual's development. **2** emphasis on protecting the natural environment. **en·vi·ron·men·tal·ist** *n, adj*.
en·vi·rons [ɛn'vaɪrənz] *n pl* surrounding districts; suburbs.

envisage [ɛn'vɪzɪdʒ] *v* foresee: *I envisage no difficulty.* ⟨French *en-* in + *visage* face⟩

en·vi·sion [ɛn'vɪʒən] *v* have a mental picture of: *to envision a state of permanent peace.*

en·voy ['ɛnvɔɪ] *or* ['ɒnvɔɪ] *n* **1** messenger. **2** a diplomat ranking next below an ambassador. ⟨French *envoyer* send; Latin *in via* on the way⟩

en·vy ['ɛnvi] *n* **1** discontent at another's good fortune because one wishes it were one's own. **2** the object of such feeling: *She was the envy of the younger girls in the school.* **en·vy** *v*. ⟨Old French *envie*, Latin *invidia; in-* against + *videre* see⟩
en·vi·a·ble *adj* to be envied; worth having: *She has an enviable record.* **en·vi·a·bly** *adv*. **en·vi·ous** *adj* full of envy. **en·vi·ous·ly** *adv*.

SYNONYMS

Envy = feel discontent and jealousy because of something a person has that one wants: *She envies famous people. She envies her fame.*
Covet = feel a great desire for something, especially something belonging to someone else: *He covets his neighbour's new car.*

en·zyme ['ɛnzaɪm] *n* a chemical substance, produced in cells, that can cause changes in other substances in the body. ⟨Greek *en-* in + *zymē* leaven, yeast⟩
en·zy·mol·o·gy [ˌɛnzə'mɒlədʒi] *n* the study of enzymes. **en·zy·mol·o·gist** *n*.

E·o·cene ['iə,sin] *Geology n* the second epoch of the Tertiary period, beginning about 60 million years ago. ⟨Greek *ēōs* dawn + *kainos* recent⟩

e·on ['iən] *or* ['iɒn] *n* **1** the longest period of geological time. **2** a very long period of time; many thousands of years: *Eons passed before life existed on the earth.* Also, **aeon**. ⟨Greek *aiōn* lifetime, age⟩

ep·au·lette or **ep·au·let** [ˌɛpə'lɛt] *or* ['ɛpə,lɛt] *n* an ornamental tab or piece on the shoulder of a uniform. ⟨French, from *épaule* shoulder⟩

é·pée [ei'pei] *n* a sword used in fencing, esp one with a sharp point and no cutting edge. **é·pée·ist** *n*. ⟨French, from Old French *espee;* Greek *spathē* blade, sword⟩

e·phem·er·a [ɪ'fɛmərə] *n, pl* **-ae** [-i] *or* [-aɪ] *or* **-as 1** any short-lived person or thing: *Of the* *many books published in a year, the majority are ephemerae.* **2** ephemeral things collectively. **3** printed matter intended for short-term use, such as a playbill, sought by collectors. ⟨Greek *ephēmeros* living a day; *epi-* upon + *hēmera* day⟩

e·phem·er·al *adj* lasting for only a day; lasting for only a very short time.

ep·ic ['ɛpɪk] *n* **1** a long poem that tells of the adventures of great heroes. **2** *Informal* a spectacular motion picture or other entertainment. *adj* like an epic; grand in style; heroic. **ep·i·cal·ly** *adv.* ⟨Greek *epikos; epos* word, story⟩

ep·i·can·thus [ˌɛpə'kænθəs] *n* a fold in the upper eyelid, associated with some Asian peoples; the **epicanthic fold**, covering the inner corner of the eye. ⟨Greek *epi-* on, in + *kanthos* corner of the eye⟩

ep·i·carp ['ɛpə,karp] *n* the outer layer or skin of a fruit. ⟨Greek *epi-* on + *karpos* fruit⟩

ep·i·cene ['ɛpə,sin] *adj* **1** of common gender. Nouns like *fish, mouse* are epicene. **2** not clearly of either sex. ⟨Greek *epi-* upon + *koinos* common⟩

ep·i·cen·tre ['ɛpə,sɛntər] *n* **1** the point from which earthquake waves seem to go out. It is situated directly above the true centre of the earthquake. **2** any focal point of great tension, disturbance, etc.: *the epicentre of a revolt.* Also, **ep·i·cen·ter. ep·i·cen·tral** *adj.* ⟨Greek *epi-* on, in + CENTRE⟩

ep·i·cure ['ɛpə,kjʊr] *n* a person who has a refined taste in eating and drinking. ⟨*Epicurus,* ancient Greek philosopher who taught that pleasure is the highest good and that virtue alone produces pleasure⟩

ep·i·cur·ism *n* the lifestyle of an epicure. **ep·i·cu·re·an** [ˌɛpəkjə'riən] *or* [ˌɛpə'kjʊriən] *adj* fond of pleasure and luxury. **ep·i·cu·re·an** *or* **Ep·i·cu·re·an** *n.* **ep·i·cu·re·an·ism** *or* **Ep·i·cu·re·an·ism** *n.*

ep·i·cy·cle ['ɛpə,səikəl] *n* **1** a small circle on the circumference of another circle. The movement of such a circle around the larger one explained the motion of the planets. **2** *Geometry* a circle which rolls around the outside or the inside of another circle. **ep·i·cy·clic** *adj.* **ep·i·cy·cloid** [ˌɛpə'səiklɔid] *n* a curve made by the motion of a point on the circumference of a circle which is rolling around the outside of a stationary circle.

ep·i·dem·ic [ˌɛpə'dɛmɪk] *n* **1** a rapid spreading of a disease: *an epidemic of measles.* **2** the rapid spread of an idea, fashion, etc. *adj* affecting many people at the same time: *The rumours had reached epidemic proportions.* **ep·i·dem·ic** *adj.* **ep·i·dem·i·cal·ly** *adv.* ⟨Greek *epidēmia; epi-* among + *dēmos* people⟩

ep·i·de·mi·ol·o·gy [ˌɛpə,dimi'ɒlədʒi] *n* the branch of medicine dealing with epidemic diseases. **ep·i·de·mi·o·log·ic·al** *adj.* **ep·i·de·mi·ol·o·gist** *n.*

ep·i·der·mis [ˌɛpɪ'dɜrmɪs] *n* **1** the outer layer of the skin of vertebrates. **2** the outer covering on the shells of many molluscs. **3** a

skinlike layer of cells in seed plants and ferns. **ep·i·der·mal** or **ep·i·der·mic** *adj.*

ep·i·du·ral [ˌɛpɪ'dʊrəl] or [-'dʒʊrəl] *n* an anesthetic inserted into a space in the spinal chord, used in childbirth. ⟨Greek *epi-* through + Latin *dura mater* hard mother⟩

ep·i·glot·tis [ˌɛpə'glɒtɪs] *n* a plate of cartilage that covers the entrance to the windpipe during swallowing, so that food, etc. does not get into the lungs. **ep·i·glot·tal** *adj.* ⟨Greek *epi-* on + *glotta* tongue⟩

ep·i·gram ['ɛpə,græm] *n* **1** a short, pointed, witty saying. *Example*: *"The only way to get rid of temptation is to yield to it."* **2** a short poem ending in a witty or clever turn of thought. **ep·i·gram·mat·ic** [ˌɛpəgrə'mætɪk] *adj.* **ep·i·gram·mat·i·cal·ly** *adv.* ⟨Greek *epigramma* a writing on; *epigraphein.* See EPIGRAPH.⟩

SYNONYMS
A special type of epigram is the **paradox**, which makes a statement that contradicts fact or itself, and yet suggests a truth: *All generalizations are false, including this one.* Closely related to the epigram is the **aphorism**—a pithy statement but not necessarily witty: *A living dog is better than a dead lion.*

ep·i·graph ['ɛpə,græf] *n* **1** a quotation at the beginning of a book or chapter. **2** an inscription on a building, monument, etc. **ep·i·graph·ic** *adj.* ⟨Greek *epi-* on + *graphein* write⟩

ep·i·lep·sy ['ɛpə,lɛpsi] *n* a chronic disorder of the central nervous system characterized by attacks involving loss of consciousness and, usually, convulsions. **ep·i·lep·tic** *adj.* ⟨Greek *epi-* on + *lepsia* seizing; *lambanein* take⟩

ep·i·logue ['ɛpə,lɒg] *n* **1** a concluding section added to a novel, poem, etc. **2** a speech after the end of a play, addressed to the audience and spoken by one of the actors. **3** any concluding act or event. ⟨Greek *epi-* in addition + *legein* speak⟩

E·piph·a·ny [ɪ'pɪfəni] *n* **1** the yearly Christian celebration commemorating the coming of the Wise Men to Christ at Bethlehem; in most Christian churches, January 6; in Orthodox Churches, January 19. **2 epiphany** a moment or experience of revelation. ⟨Greek *epi-* upon + *phainein* show⟩

ep·i·phe·nom·e·non [ˌɛpəfə'nɒmənən] *n, pl* **-na** [-nə] any secondary phenomenon, such as a complication in an illness. ⟨Greek *epi-* in addition + PHENOMENON⟩

ep·i·phyte ['ɛpə,fəit] *n* **1** any plant that is attached to another plant for support but does not derive its nourishment from its host; air plant. **2** a parasitic plant that lives on the outer surface of an animal. **ep·i·phyt·ic** [ˌɛpə'fɪtɪk] *adj.* **ep·i·phyt·i·cal·ly** *adv.* ⟨Greek *epi-* on + *phyton* plant⟩

e·pis·co·pal [ɪ'pɪskəpəl] *adj* **1** to do with bishops. **2 Episcopal** to do with the Church of England, the Anglican Church of Canada, etc. **E·pis·co·pa·lian** [ɪ,pɪskə'peiliən] *n, adj.*

E·pis·co·pa·lian·ism *n.* ⟨Greek *episkopos* overseer; *epi-* over + *skopeein* watch⟩

e·pis·co·pa·cy [ɪ'pɪskəpəsi] or **e·pis·co·pate** [ɪ'pɪskəpɪt] *n* **1** the government of a church by bishops. **2** bishops as a group. **3** the position, rank, or term of office of a bishop.

e·pi·si·ot·om·y [ɪˌpizi'ɒtəmi] *n* incision of the perineum to allow room for birth. ⟨Greek *epision* pubic area + *tome* cutting⟩

ep·i·sode ['ɛpəˌsoud] *n* **1** an incident that stands out from others: *an important episode in my life.* **2 a** a set of events within a novel, story, etc. but complete in itself. **b** *Music* a similar digression in a composition. **3** in classical Greek tragedy, the part between two choric songs. **4** a portion of a serial play, film, etc. **5** an incident or series of incidents complete in itself but belonging to a larger event: *an episode in the Reformation.* ⟨Greek *episodion* coming in addition; *epi-* on + *eis* into + *hodos* way⟩
ep·i·sod·ic [ˌɛpə'sɒdɪk] *adj* **1** like an episode; incidental; occasional. **2** consisting of a series of episodes: *Her new novel is loosely episodic.* **ep·i·sod·i·cal·ly** *adv.*

e·pis·te·mol·o·gy [ɪˌpɪstə'mɒlədʒi] *n* the part of philosophy that deals with the origin, nature, and limits of knowledge. **e·pis·te·mo·log·i·cal** *adj.* **e·pis·te·mo·log·i·cal·ly** *adv.* **e·pis·te·mol·o·gist** *n.* ⟨Greek *epistēmē* knowledge⟩

e·pis·tle [ɪ'pɪsəl] *n* **1** a letter, esp an instructive or a formal one. **2** a literary work written in the form of a letter. **3 Epistle a** a letter written by one of Christ's Apostles. **b** a selection from one of these, read as part of certain Christian church services. **e·pis·to·lar·y** *adj.* ⟨Greek *epistolē*; *epi-* to + *stellein* send⟩

ep·i·taph ['ɛpəˌtæf] *n* **1** a short statement in memory of a dead person, usually put on his or her tombstone. **2** any brief writing resembling this. **ep·i·taph·ic** *adj.* ⟨Greek *epi-* on + *taphos* tomb⟩

ep·i·the·li·um [ˌɛpə'θiliəm] *n, pl* **-li·a** [-liə] *Biology* a thin layer of cells forming a tissue that covers surfaces and lines hollow organs. **ep·i·the·li·al** *adj.* ⟨Greek *epi-* on + *thēlē* nipple⟩

ep·i·thet ['ɛpəθət] *n* **1** a descriptive expression. In *Richard the Lion-Hearted* the epithet is *the Lion-Hearted.* **2** a word or phrase (sometimes insulting) used in place of a person's name. **3** that part of the scientific name of an animal or plant which denotes a species, variety, or other division of a genus. **ep·i·thet·ic** or **ep·i·thet·i·cal** *adj.* ⟨Greek *epitheton* added; *epi-* on + *tithenai* place⟩

e·pit·o·me [ɪ'pɪtəmi] *n* **1** a condensed account. **2** an ideal or typical example: *Solomon is spoken of as the epitome of wisdom.* **e·pit·o·mize** *v.* ⟨Greek *epitomē* a cutting short; *epi-* into + *temnein* cut⟩

e·poch ['ipɒk] or ['ɛpək] *n* **1** a period of time; era. **2** a period of time in which striking things happened. **3** one of the divisions of time into which a geological period is divided: *the Holocene epoch of the Quaternary period.* **4** a date marking the start of an epoch. **5** *Astronomy* an arbitrary point in time used as a reference. **ep·och·al** ['ɛpəkəl] *adj.* ⟨Greek *epochē* fixed point in time; *epi-* up + *echein* hold⟩
e·poch–mak·ing *adj* beginning an epoch; causing important changes.

ep·o·nym ['ɛpəˌnɪm] *n* **1** a person from whom a nation, group, place, etc. gets or is reputed to get its name: *Romulus is the eponym of Rome.* **2** a person whose name is a synonym for something: *Ananias is the eponym of liar.* ⟨Greek *epi-* to + (dial.) *onyma* name⟩
e·pon·y·mous [ɪ'pɒnəməs] *adj* giving one's name to a nation, group, place, book, etc. **e·pon·y·my** *n.*

e·pox·y [ɪ'pɒksi] *adj* containing oxygen as a bond between two different atoms already united in another way: *Epoxy resins are extremely durable plastics.* ⟨Greek *epi-* + OXY(GEN)⟩

Epstein–Barr virus ['ɛpstaɪn 'bɑr] a kind of virus causing infectious mononucleosis, as well as certain cancers. ⟨M.A. *Epstein* and Y.M. *Barr,* UK physicians⟩

eq·ua·ble ['ɛkwəbəl] or ['ikwəbəl] *adj* **1** changing little; uniform. **2** even; tranquil: *an equable temperament.* **eq·ua·bil·i·ty** *n.* **eq·ua·bly** *adv.* ⟨Latin *aequare* make uniform; *aequus* even, just⟩

e·qual ['ikwəl] *adj* **1** the same in amount, size, number, value, degree, rank, nature, quality, etc. **2** evenly matched: *an equal contest.* **3** having the strength, capacity, ability, etc. necessary for a task (with *to*): *She certainly proved to be equal to the task.* *n* a person or thing that is equal to another: *In swimming he had no equal.*
v **e·qualled** or **e·qualed, e·qual·ling** or **e·qual·ing 1** be the same as: *Four times five equals twenty.* Symbol = **2** make or do something equivalent to: *He tried hard to equal the scoring record.* **e·qual·i·ty** [ɪ'kwɒlɪti] *n.* **e·qual·ly** *adv.* ⟨Latin *aequalis; aequus* even, just⟩
e·qual·i·za·tion *n* **1** the act of equalizing or the state of being equalized. **2** ✵ the practice of the federal government to pay money to the less wealthy provinces in order to bring their standard of living nearer to that of the resource-rich provinces. **e·qual·ize** *v* **1** make equal. **2** make even. **e·qual·iz·er** *n.* **equal opportunity 1** the principle of giving everyone the same chance or treatment regardless of sex, religion, colour, etc. **2** of a company, etc., operating on such a principle: *an equal opportunity employer.*

SYNONYMS
Equal = exactly the same in any quality that can be measured: *The pieces of pie are equal.* **Equivalent,** applying to things otherwise different, means equal in a quality that cannot be physically measured: *A CEGEP course may be regarded as equivalent to the first two years of university.*

e·qua·nim·i·ty [ˌikwə'nɪməti] *or* [ˌɛkwə-] *n* evenness of mind or temper; calmness: *A wise person bears misfortune with equanimity.* **e·quan·i·mous** [ɪ'kwænɪməs] *adj.* ⟨Latin *aequus* even + *animus* mind, temper⟩

e·quate [ɪ'kweɪt] *v* make, consider, treat, or represent as equal *(with).* ⟨Latin *aequare* make equal; *aequus* equal⟩ **e·qua·tion** [ɪ'kweɪʒən] *n* **1** a statement of equality between two quantities. **2** an expression using chemical formulas showing the substances in a chemical reaction.

e·qua·tor [ɪ'kweɪtər] *n* **1** an imaginary circle around the middle of the earth, halfway between the North Pole and the South Pole. **2** a similarly situated circle on any heavenly body. **3** CELESTIAL EQUATOR. **e·qua·to·ri·al** [ˌɛkwə'tɔriəl] *or* [ˌikwə-] *adj.* ⟨Latin *aequator* equalizer (of day and night); *aequare.* See EQUATE.⟩

e·ques·tri·an [ɪ'kwɛstriən] *adj* to do with horseback riding: *equestrian skill.* *n* a rider or performer on horseback. ⟨Latin *equestris* of a horseman; *equus* horse⟩

e·qui·an·gu·lar [ˌikwi'æŋgjələr] *or* [ˌɛkwi-] *adj* having all angles equal: *A square is equiangular.*

e·qui·dis·tant [ˌikwə'dɪstənt] *or* [ˌɛkwə-] *adj* equally distant: *All points of the circumference of a circle are equidistant from the centre.* **e·qui·dis·tant·ly** *adv.* **e·qui·dis·tance** *n.*

e·qui·lat·er·al [ˌikwə'lætərəl] *or* [ˌɛkwə-] *adj* having all sides equal in length. **e·qui·lat·er·al·ly** *adv.* ⟨Latin *aequus* equal + *latus, lateris* side⟩

e·qui·lib·ri·um [ˌikwə'lɪbriəm] *or* [ˌɛkwə-] *n* **1** a state of balance: *Scales are in equilibrium when the weights on each side are equal.* **2** the state of a chemical system when no further change occurs in it. **3** a condition of balance between things of any kind. **4** mental poise: *She is a sensible person and will not let petty annoyances upset her equilibrium.* **e·quil·i·brate** [ɪ'kwɪlə,breit] *or* [ˌikwə'laɪbreit] *v.* **e·quil·i·bra·tion** *n.* **e·quil·i·bra·tor** *n.* ⟨Latin *aequus* equal + *libra* balance⟩

e·quine ['ikwaɪn] *or* ['ɛkwaɪn] *adj* to do with horses. *n* a horse. ⟨Latin *equinus; equus* horse⟩

e·qui·nox ['ikwə,nɒks] *or* ['ɛkwə-] *n* either of the two times in the year when day and night are of equal length all over the earth. The **vernal** (spring) **equinox** occurs in the northern hemisphere about March 21, the **autumnal equinox** about September 22. **e·qui·noc·tial** *adj, n.* ⟨Latin *aequus* equal + *nox* night⟩

e·quip [ɪ'kwɪp] *v* **e·quipped, e·quip·ping** **1** furnish with all that is needed: *The fort was equipped with guns, ammunition, and food.* **2** prepare (oneself) mentally for a particular purpose. **e·quip·ment** *n.* ⟨Old French *esquiper;* Old Norse *skipa* to man a ship; *skip* ship⟩

eq·ui·ty ['ɛkwəti] *n* **1** fairness; justice. **2** *Law* a system of rules and principles based on fairness and justice. Equity covers cases in which fairness and justice require a settlement not covered by common law. **3** the amount that a property, business, etc. is worth beyond what is owed on it. ⟨Latin *aequitas; aequus* even, just⟩ **eq·ui·ta·ble** *adj* **1** fair: *Paying a person what she has earned is equitable.* **2** *Law* to do with equity. **eq·ui·ta·ble·ness** *n.* **eq·ui·ta·bly** *adv.*

e·quiv·a·lent [ɪ'kwɪvələnt] *adj* **1** equal in value, measure, force, effect, meaning, etc.: *Nodding one's head is equivalent to saying yes.* **2** *Chemistry* equal in value to a (stated) quantity of another substance. **3** *Geometry* having the same extent: *A triangle and a square that are equivalent have the same area.* *n* something equivalent: *He accepted the equivalent of his wages in groceries.* **e·quiv·a·lence** *n.* **e·quiv·a·lent·ly** *adv.* ⟨Latin *aequus* equal + *valere* be worth⟩

e·quiv·o·cal [ɪ'kwɪvəkəl] *adj* **1** having two or more meanings; intentionally vague: *an equivocal answer.* **2** uncertain: *The result was equivocal.* **3** rousing suspicion: *equivocal behaviour.* **e·quiv·o·cal·ly** *adv.* **e·quiv·o·cal·ness** *n.* ⟨Latin *aequus* equal + *vocare* call⟩ **e·quiv·o·cate** *v* **1** use expressions of double meaning in order to mislead. **2** avoid taking a stand. **e·quiv·o·ca·tion** *n.*

er [ɜr] *interj* an expression of hesitation in speech.

–er[1] *suffix* **1** a person or thing that——s: *admirer.* **2** a native or inhabitant of——: *villager.* **3** a person that works with——: *hatter.* **4** a person or thing that is or has : *two-wheeler.* ⟨Old English *-ere;* Latin *-arius*⟩

–er[2] *suffix* forming the comparative degree: **1** of certain adjectives: *softer, smoother.* **2** of certain adverbs: *faster.* ⟨Old English *-ra, -re,* for adj., *-or* for adv.⟩

e·ra ['ɛrə] *or* ['irə] *n* **1** a historical period distinguished by significant happenings. **2** a system of reckoning time from some important happening, given date, etc. The Christian era is the period of time reckoned from about four years after the birth of Christ. **3** an extensive expanse of time in geological history. ⟨Latin *aera* number, epoch, pl of *aes* brass (counter)⟩

ERA *Baseball* EARNED RUN AVERAGE.

e·rad·i·cate [ɪ'rædə,keit] *v* **1** get rid of entirely: *Yellow fever has been eradicated in many countries.* **2** pull out by the roots: *to eradicate weeds from a lawn.* **e·rad·i·ca·ble** *adj.* **e·rad·i·ca·tion** *n.* ⟨Latin *ex-* out + *radicis* root⟩

e·rase [ɪ'reis] *v* **1** rub out. **2** remove all trace of: *The blow on his head erased from his memory the details of the accident.* **3** remove marks or recorded information from: *Please erase the entire disk.* **e·ras·a·ble** *adj.* ⟨Latin *erasus* pp of *eradere; ex-* out + *radere* scrape⟩ **e·ras·er** *n* a piece of rubber or other substance for erasing marks made with pencil, ink, etc. **e·ra·sure** [ɪ'reiʃər] *n* an erased word, letter, mark, etc.

er·bi·um ['ɜrbiəm] *n* a rare metallic element. *Symbol* **Er** ⟨(*ytt*)*erbium*⟩

ere [ɛr] *Poetic, archaic prep, conj* before. ⟨Old English *ǣr*⟩

e·rect [ɪ'rɛkt] *adj* **1** upright: *That flagpole stands erect.* **2** raised; sticking out straight: *The cat faced the dog with fur erect.*
v **1** set upright: *to erect a mast on a firm base.* **2** build: *That house was erected last year.* **3** set up: *to erect a roadblock; to erect a machine from components.* **4** *Physiology* make rigid. **e·rect·ly** *adv.* **e·rect·ness** *n.* **e·rect·or** *n.* ⟨Latin *erectus* pp of *erigere; ex-* up + *regere* direct⟩
e·rec·tile [ɪ'rɛktaɪl] *adj* of body tissue or an organ, capable of becoming rigid or erect when filled with blood. **e·rec·tion** *n* **1** construction: *the erection of a building.* **2** a building or other structure. **3** the rigid state or condition of erectile tissue or an organ, esp of the penis or clitoris when filled with blood due to sexual excitement.

erg¹ [ɜrg] *n* a unit for measuring work or energy, equal to 0.1 microjoules. *Abbrev* **e** ⟨Greek *ergon* work⟩

erg² [ɜrg] *n* a large area of sand dunes in the desert. ⟨Arabic *'irq*⟩

er·go ['ɛrgou] *or* ['ɜrgou] *adv, conj* Latin therefore.

er·go·nom·ics [,ɜrgə'nɒmɪks] *n* (with a sg verb) *Biotechnology* the scientific study of the relationship between people and their working environment with a view to increasing efficiency. **er·go·nom·ic** *adj.* **er·gon·o·mist** [ɜr'gɒnəmɪst] *n.* ⟨Greek *ergon* work + (ECON)OMICS⟩

er·got ['ɜrgət] *n* **1** a disease of cereals in which the grains are replaced by fungous growths. **2** a medicine made from these growths, used to stop bleeding and contract muscles. ⟨Old French *argot* cock's spur⟩

er·mine ['ɜrmɪn] *n, pl* **-mines** or (esp collectively) **-mine** a small carnivorous mammal of northern and arctic regions, closely related to the weasels, having thick, soft fur which in winter changes to white except for the tip of the tail, which remains black. ⟨Latin *Armenius (mus)* Armenian (rat)⟩

e·rode [ɪ'roud] *v* **1** eat or wear away gradually: *Water erodes rocks.* **2** be eaten or worn away gradually. **3** make (something) decay, or undergo such decay: *to erode traditional values.* **e·ro·sion** *n.* **e·ro·sive** [ɪ'rousɪv] *adj.* ⟨Latin *ex-* away + *rodere* gnaw⟩

e·rog·e·nous [ɪ'rɒdʒənəs] *adj* to do with any area of the body that can produce sexual excitement when stimulated. ⟨Greek *eros* sexual love + -GENOUS⟩

e·rot·ic [ɪ'rɒtɪk] *adj* to do with sexual desire. **e·rot·i·cal·ly** *adv.* ⟨Greek *eros* sexual love⟩
e·rot·i·ca *n* erotic literature, art, etc.
e·rot·i·cism *n* **1** an erotic quality. **2** sexual arousal or desire. **3** preoccupation with sex.
e·rot·o·gen·ic [,ɛrətə'dʒɛnɪk] *adj* erogenous.
e·rot·o·ma·nia [ɪ,rɒtə'meiniə] *n Psychiatry* an abnormal and persistent desire for sex.

err [ɛr] *or* [ɜr] *v* **1** make mistakes. **2** do wrong: *To err is human; to forgive, divine.* ⟨Latin *errare* wander⟩

er·rat·ic [ɪ'rætɪk] *adj* **1** uncertain; irregular: *An erratic mind jumps from one idea to another.* **2** odd; unusual: *erratic behaviour.* **er·rat·i·cal·ly** *adv.* **er·ra·tum** [ɪ'rɑtəm] *or* [ɪ'reitəm] *n, pl* **-ta 1** an error in printing or writing. **2** Usually, **errata** *pl* a list of errors in a printed work.
er·ro·ne·ous [ɪ'rouniəs] *adj* of ideas, statements, etc., wrong: *Years ago many people held the erroneous belief that the earth was flat.* **er·ro·ne·ous·ly** *adv.* **er·ro·ne·ous·ness** *n.*
er·ror ['ɛrər] *n* **1** something wrong; a mistake. **2** wrongdoing; sin. **3** *Baseball* a faulty play that permits the batter to remain at bat or allows a runner to advance who should have been put out. **4** in measurements, the difference between the observed amount and the actual amount. **in error a** mistaken: *I was in error.* **b** by mistake: *I took your coat in error.*

er·rand ['ɛrənd] *n* a trip to do something, often for someone else: *The little boy runs errands for his parents.* ⟨Old English *ǣrende*⟩
errand boy 1 a boy who does errands. **2** *Informal* a man who acts entirely under others, without using his own initiative.

er·rant ['ɛrənt] *adj* **1** travelling in search of adventure: *a knight errant.* **2** of thoughts, conduct, etc., straying from the regular path. **3** of a wind, changing frequently. ⟨Old French *errer* travel (Latin *iterare*) and French *errer* wander (Latin *errare*)⟩

er·satz ['ɛrzɑts], ['ɛrzæts], *or* [ɛr'zɑts] *adj, n* substitute, often poor in quality. ⟨German⟩

erst·while ['ɜrst,waɪl] *adv Archaic* some time ago; in time past; formerly.
adj former; past. ⟨Old English *ǣrst* superlative of *ǣr* ere + *hwil* while⟩

er·u·dite ['ɛrə,daɪt] *or* ['ɛrjə,daɪt] *adj* scholarly; learned. **er·u·dite·ly** *adv.* **er·u·dite·ness** *n.* ⟨Latin *erudire* instruct; *ex-* away + *rudis* rude⟩
er·u·di·tion *n* acquired knowledge; scholarship; learning.

e·rupt [ɪ'rʌpt] *v* **1** burst forth: *Hot water erupted from the geyser.* **2** throw forth lava, etc.: *The volcano erupted.* **3** break out in a rash: *Her skin erupted when she had measles.* **4** break out suddenly and dramatically: *War erupted in the south.* **e·rup·tion** *n.* **e·rup·tive** *adj.* **e·rup·tive·ly** *adv.* ⟨Latin *eruptus* pp of *erumpere; ex-* out + *rumpere* burst⟩

-ery *suffix* **1** a place for——ing: *cannery.* **2** a place for——s: *nunnery.* **3** the occupation or business of a——: *cookery.* **4** the state or condition of a——: *slavery.* **5** the qualities, actions, etc. of a——: *knavery.* **6** ——s as a group: *machinery.* ⟨Old French *-erie*⟩

e·ryth·ro·cyte [ə'rɪθrou,saɪt] *n* one of the red blood cells that carry oxygen to cells, and carbon dioxide back to the lungs. **e·ryth·ro·cyt·ic** [-'sɪtɪk] *adj.* ⟨Greek *erythros* red + -CYTE⟩

es·ca·la·tor ['ɛskə,leitər] *n* a continuous moving stairway. ⟨*Escalator* former trademark; blend of *escalade* a climbing with ladders (Latin *scala* ladder) + *elevator*⟩

es·ca·late *v* increase by stages in amount, intensity, etc.: *escalating costs.* **es·ca·la·tion** *n.*

es·ca·pade ['ɛskə,peid] *n* a wild adventure or prank. ⟨French, from Italian *scappata; scappare* escape⟩

es·cape [ɛ'skeip] *v* **1** get free: *to escape from prison.* **2** keep free or safe from: *We all escaped the measles.* **3** avoid capture, trouble, etc.: *The thief has escaped.* **4** come out of (unintentionally): *A cry escaped her lips.* **5** fail to remember or notice: *Her name escapes me.* *n* **1** an act of escaping. **2** a way of escaping: *There was no escape from the trap.* **3** relief from boredom, trouble, etc.: *to find escape in mystery stories.* ⟨Latin *ex-* out of + *cappa* cloak⟩ **escape artist** a performer whose skill consists in getting free from confinement. Also, **es·cap·ol·o·gist. escape clause** a clause that frees a signer of a contract from certain responsibilities under specified circumstances. **es·cap·ee** [ɛ,skei'pi] *or* [ɛ'skeipi] *n* a person who has escaped, esp one who has escaped from prison. **escape (key)** *Computers* a key that interrupts a current operation. **escape mechanism 1** *Psychiatry* a thought or action that permits avoidance of an unpleasant reality. **2** any device or apparatus, such as an ejection seat in an aircraft, designed to permit escape. **escape velocity** *Physics* the minimum speed an object must attain to get free of a gravitational field. **es·cap·ism** [ɛ'skeipɪzəm] *n* avoidance of unpleasant realities by recourse to imagination or to entertainment. **es·cap·ist** *n, adj.*

es·cape·ment [ɛ'skeipmənt] *n* a device in a timepiece consisting of a notched wheel and a lever, by which the clockwork is controlled.

es·car·got [,ɛskɑr'gou] *or* [ɛ'skɑrgou]; *French* [ɛskaʀ'go] *n* an edible snail. ⟨French⟩

es·ca·role ['ɛskə,roul] *n* a kind of endive with broad leaves, used for salads. ⟨French⟩

es·carp·ment [ɛ'skɑrpmənt] *n* **1** a long, steep slope. **2** the ground made into a steep slope as part of a fortification. ⟨French *escarpe* a steep slope; Germanic⟩

es·cha·tol·o·gy [,ɛskə'tɒlədʒi] *n* the body of doctrines concerning the four last things: death, judgment, heaven, and hell. **es·cha·to·log·i·cal** *adj.* ⟨Greek *eschatos* last, final⟩

es·chew [ɛs'tʃu] *v* keep away from using, doing, etc.: *to eschew bad company, to eschew sweets.* **es·chew·er** *n.* ⟨Old French *eschiver*⟩

es·cort ['ɛskɔrt] *n* **1** a person or group going with another to give protection, show honour, etc.: *an escort of ten Mounties.* **2** a man or boy who accompanies a woman or girl on a walk, to a dance, etc., or vice versa. **3** one or more ships, aircraft, etc. serving as a guard: *During World War II, Canada's destroyers served as escorts to many convoys.* *v* [ɛ'skɔrt] accompany as an escort. ⟨French *escorte;* Italian *scorta; scorgere* guide⟩

es·crow ['ɛskrou] *or* [ɛ'skrou] *n Law* a written agreement put in the charge of a third person until certain conditions are fulfilled by two other parties.
in escrow held by a third party in accordance with an agreement. ⟨Old French *escroue* scrap, scroll⟩

es·cutch·eon [ɛ'skʌtʃən] *n* **1** a shield on which a coat of arms is put. **2** a protective metal plate around a keyhole, door handle, etc. **3** the panel on a ship's stern bearing its name.
blot on the escutcheon a disgrace to honour or reputation. ⟨Latin *scutum* shield⟩

–ese *suffix* **1** to do with: *Japanese* = to do with Japan. **2** a native or inhabitant of: *Portuguese* = a native, inhabitant of Portugal. **3** the language of: *Vietnamese* = a language of Vietnam. **4** a typical style or vocabulary: *journalese* = newspaper style. ⟨Old French *-eis;* Latin *-ensis*⟩

ESE or **E.S.E.** east-southeast, a direction halfway between east and southeast.

es·ker ['ɛskər] *n* a winding ridge of sand, gravel, etc. believed to have been deposited by meltwater streams flowing inside the retreating glaciers of the Ice Age. ⟨Irish *eiscir*⟩

Es·ki·mo ['ɛskə,mou] *adj, n, pl* **-mos** or **-mo 1** See INUIT and YUPIK (def. 1). **2** See INUKTITUT, INUPIAT, and YUPIK (def. 2). ⟨ultimate origin uncertain⟩

> **USAGE**
> **Eskimo** is a disparaging name derived from a word in a First Nations language and later applied to the Inuit and Yupik by Europeans. Although still used in the US, in Canada it is considered offensive.

ESL English as a second language.

e·soph·a·gus [ɪ'sɒfəgəs] *n, pl* **-gi** [-,dʒaɪ] *or* [-,gaɪ] the passage for food from the mouth to the stomach. ⟨Greek *oiso-* carry + *phagein* eat⟩

es·o·ter·ic [,ɛzə'tɛrɪk] *or* [,ɛsə-] *adj* **1** understood only by the select few. **2** private; secret. **es·o·ter·i·cal·ly** *adv.* ⟨Greek *esōterikos; esō* within⟩
es·o·ter·ica *n* esoteric items.

esp or **esp.** or **espec.** especially.

ESP or **E.S.P.** EXTRASENSORY PERCEPTION.

es·pa·drille ['ɛspə,drɪl] *or* [,ɛspə'drɪl] *n* a sandal with a canvas upper attached to a rope sole. ⟨French, from Spanish *esparto,* Greek *sparton* a kind of grass⟩

es·pe·cial [ɛ'spɛʃəl] *adj* special; exceptional: *of no especial value.* **es·pe·cial·ly** *adv.* ⟨Old French; Latin *specialis.* See SPECIAL.⟩

Es·pe·ran·to [,ɛspə'rɑntou] *or* [,ɛspə'ræntou] *n* an artificial language for international use. ⟨Dr. *Esperanto* (= 'hoping'), pseudonym of its inventor, Polish philologist Dr. Zamenhof⟩

es·pi·o·nage ['ɛspiə,nɑʒ] *or* ['ɛspiənɪdʒ] *n* spying or the use of spies. ⟨French *espion* spy⟩

es·pla·nade [,ɛsplə'neid] *or* [,ɛsplə'nɑd] *n* any open, level space used for public walks or drives. ⟨Spanish *esplanada;* Latin *ex-* out + *planus* level⟩

es·pouse [ɛ'spaʊz] v **1** marry. **2** take up or make one's own: *Late in life she espoused a new religion.* ⟨Old French *espouser;* Latin *sponsus* pp of *spondere* betroth⟩
es·pous·al [ɛ'spaʊzəl] n **1** adoption (of a cause, etc.). **2** the ceremony of becoming engaged or married. **3 espousals** pl a betrothal or a wedding.

es·pres·so [ɛ'spresou] n a very strong coffee brewed under steam pressure. ⟨Italian from Latin. See EXPRESS.⟩

esprit de corps [ɛ'spri də 'kɔr]; *French* [ɛspʀid'kɔʀ] a sense of union and of common responsibilities in some group: *The regiment has a strong esprit de corps.* ⟨French = group spirit⟩

es·py [ɛ'spaɪ] v catch sight of something, esp something far away, small, or partly hidden. ⟨Old French *espier;* Germanic⟩ **es·pi·al** [ɛ'spaɪəl] n **1** the act of spying. **2** the act of watching.

–esque *suffix* **1** in the——style; resembling the——style: *Romanesque* **2** like a——; like that of a——: *statuesque.* ⟨French from Germanic. Akin to -ISH.⟩

es·quire [ɛ'skwaɪr] *or* ['ɛskwaɪr] n in the Middle Ages, a young man of noble family who attended a knight until he himself was made a knight. ⟨Old French *esquier;* Latin *scutarius* shieldbearer, *scutum* shield⟩

–ess *suffix* female: *heiress, hostess, lioness.* ⟨French -*esse;* Greek -*issa*⟩

USAGE
This feminine suffix is to be avoided in names of occupations (actress, stewardess, etc.), where it has acquired a quasi-diminutive connotation that is offensively sexist.

es·say ['ɛsei] n **1** a literary composition on a certain subject. **2** a written theme assigned as an exercise in a high school, college, etc. **3** [ɛ'sei] a try; attempt.
v [ɛ'sei] try; attempt: *She essayed a very difficult jump.* ⟨Old French *essai;* Latin *exagium* a weighing⟩
es·say·ist ['ɛseiɪst] n a writer of essays.

es·sence ['ɛsəns] n **1** that which makes a thing what it is: *Kindness is the essence of politeness.* **2** any concentrated substance that has the characteristic flavour, fragrance, or effect of the plant, fruit, etc. from which it is obtained. **3** *Philosophy* the intrinsic nature of something, separate from its physical appearance. ⟨Latin *essentia; esse* be⟩
in essence, essentially. **of the essence**, most important: *Speed is of the essence.*
es·sen·tial [ɪ'sɛnʃəl] adj **1** needed to make a thing what it is: *Good food is essential to good health.* **2** being or containing the essence of a plant or other material: *essential odours.* **3** being such by its nature: *essential happiness, essential poetry.* n an absolutely necessary thing, element, or quality: *Learn the essentials first; then learn the details.* **es·sen·tial·ly** adv.
essential oil an oil having the characteristic fragrance or flavour of the plant or fruit from which it is extracted.

–est *suffix* forming the superlative degree of adjectives and adverbs: *warmest, soonest.* ⟨Old English -*est,* -*ost*⟩

es·tab·lish [ɪ'stæblɪʃ] v **1** set up firmly or permanently: *to establish a business.* **2** settle in a position: *She established herself in that chair.* **3** bring about permanently: *to establish a custom.* **4** prove: *to establish a fact.* ⟨Old French *establir,* Latin *stabilire; stabilis* stable, firm⟩
es·tab·lish·ment [ɪ'stæblɪʃmənt] n **1** the act of establishing or the state of being established: *the establishment of a scholarship fund.* **2** something established, such as a business, church, or code of laws. **3 the Establishment a** the Church of England or the Presbyterian Church of Scotland. **b** the people having the greatest influence in a society and being opposed to change. **es·tab·lish·men·tar·i·an** adj to do with the Establishment. n a person who supports the Establishment. **es·tab·lish·men·tar·i·an·ism** n.

es·tate [ɪ'steit] n **1** a large piece of land belonging to a person: *a beautiful estate with a cottage on it.* **2** property; possessions. **3** a condition or stage in life: *the estate of womanhood.* **4** a class or order of persons. The traditional estates (called **the three estates**) were the nobility, the clergy, and the commons (the third estate), each with different political rights. See also FOURTH ESTATE. ⟨Old French *estat;* L atin *status* state⟩

es·teem [ɪ'stim] v **1** regard highly: *We esteem people of good character.* **2** consider: *People have often esteemed happiness the greatest good.* n a very favourable opinion; high regard. ⟨Latin *aestimare* value⟩

es·ter ['ɛstər] n a compound resulting from the reaction of an acid with an alcohol. Animal and vegetable fats and oils are esters. ⟨German *esther; es(sig)* vinegar + *(ä)ther* ether⟩

es·thete, es·thet·ic·ian, es·thet·ics
See AESTHETE.

es·ti·ma·ble ['ɛstəməbəl] adj worthy of esteem. **es·ti·ma·bly** adv. ⟨See ESTEEM.⟩

es·ti·mate ['ɛstəmɪt] n **1** a judgment about how much, how many, how good, etc.: *My estimate of the length of the room was 7 m; it actually measured 6.56 m.* **2** a statement of what a certain job will cost: *The painter's estimate for painting the house was $1500.* **es·ti·mate** ['ɛstə,meɪt] v. **es·ti·ma·tor** n. ⟨See ESTEEM.⟩
es·ti·ma·tion n **1** judgment; opinion: *In my estimation, your plan will not work.* **2** esteem: *to hold in high estimation.*

es·ti·vate ['ɛstə,veɪt] v **1** spend the summer. **2** *Zoology* spend the summer in a dormant condition. Compare HIBERNATE. Also, **aes·ti·vate.** ⟨Latin *aestivas* of summer; *aestas* summer⟩
es·ti·va·tion n **1** *Zoology* the state of being in a dormant condition during the summer. **2** *Biology* the arrangement of the parts of a flower in the bud.

es·trange [ɪ'streindʒ] v **1** turn (a person)

from affection to indifference or hatred: *A quarrel had estranged him from his family.* **2** keep apart; keep away. **es·trange·ment** *n.* ⟨Old French *estranger*. See STRANGE.⟩.

es·trus ['ɛstrəs] *or* ['istrəs] *n* a period in the sexual cycle of all female placental mammals (except the higher primates) in which they are receptive to copulation with males and are capable of conceiving; heat. **es·trous** *adj.* ⟨Latin *oestrus* sting, frenzy; Greek *oistros*⟩ **es·tro·gen** ['ɛstrədʒən] *n* a hormone that induces physiological changes in females, esp in the sexual organs.

es·tu·ar·y ['ɛstʃu,ɛri] *n* a mouth of a river flowing into the sea. **es·tu·ar·i·al** *adj.* ⟨Latin *aestuarium; aestus* tide⟩

ETA estimated time of arrival.

ét·a·gère [,eitɔ'ʒɛr] *n* a piece of furniture with open shelves. ⟨French⟩

e–tail *n* retail selling carried out over the Internet.

et al. 1 and others (for Latin *et alii*). **2** and elsewhere (for Latin *et alibi*).

et cet·er·a [ɛt'sɛtərə] **1** and others; and so forth. **2** or something similar. *Abbrev* **etc.** ⟨Latin *et* and + *cetera* other things⟩ **et·cet·er·as** *n pl* usual additions.

etch [ɛtʃ] *v* **1** engrave (a drawing) by using acid to eat into a metal plate, glass, etc. **2** impress vividly: *The scene was etched on her mind.* **etch·ant** *n.* **etch·er** *n.* ⟨Dutch *etsen;* German *ätzen*⟩ **etch·ing** *n* an etched drawing or design.

ETD estimated time of departure.

e·ter·nal [ɪ'tɜrnəl] *adj* **1** existing before, throughout, and beyond all time. **2** always the same. **3** seeming to go on forever. **4** *Metaphysics* not subject to time or change. *n* **the Eternal** God. **e·ter·nal·ly** *adv.* ⟨Latin *aeternalis*⟩ **e·ter·ni·ty** *n* **1** time without beginning or ending. **2** the endless period after death. **3** a seemingly endless period of time.

eth·ane ['ɛθein] *n* a colourless, odourless, flammable hydrocarbon, present in natural gas and coal gas. ⟨*ether*⟩ **eth·a·nol** ['ɛθə,noul] *or* ['ɛθə,nɒl] *n* ETHYL ALCOHOL.

e·ther ['iθər] *n* **1** *Chemistry* any of a group of organic compounds formed by the action of acids on alcohols. **2** *Poetic* clear sky. **3** the invisible substance formerly supposed to exist through space. ⟨Greek *aithēr* upper air⟩ **e·the·re·al** *or* **ae·the·re·al** [ɪ'θiriəl] *adj* **1** light; airy; delicate: *ethereal beauty.* **2** heavenly or spiritual. **3** to do with the upper regions of space. **e·ther·ize** ['iθə,raɪz] *v* make unconscious with ether fumes. **e·ther·i·za·tion** *n.*

eth·ic ['ɛθɪk] *n* a set of moral principles or code of conduct: *the work ethic.* **eth·i·cal** *adj.* **eth·i·cal·ly** *adv.* ⟨Greek *ēthikos; ēthos* moral character⟩ **eth·i·cist** *n* one concerned with ethical matters. **eth·ics** *n* **1** the study of standards of right and wrong (with a sg verb). **2** formal or professional rules of right and wrong (with a plural verb): *Medical ethics do not permit doctors and surgeons to advertise.*

eth·nic ['ɛθnɪk]*adj* **1** to do with various groups of people by nationality, and their customs and languages. **2** ❋ *Informal* to do with immigrants who are not native speakers of English or French: *the ethnic vote.* *n* ❋ *Informal* an immigrant who is not a native speaker of English or French. **eth·ni·cal·ly** *adv.* ⟨Greek *ethnos* nation⟩ **ethnic cleansing** the forced removal or wholesale killing of people of a certain ethnic group from an area. **eth·nic·i·ty** [ɛθ'nɪsəti] *n* ethnic quality, character, or status. **eth·no·cen·tric** [,ɛθnou'sɛntrɪk] *adj* characterized by preoccupation with one's own cultural or national group. **eth·no·cen·tri·cal·ly** *adv.* **eth·no·cen·trism** or **eth·no·cen·tric·i·ty** *n.* **eth·no·cul·tur·al** *adj* to do with a particular ethnic group. **eth·no·ling·ui·stics** [,-lɪŋ'gwɪstɪks] *n* the study of a language in relation to its culture. **eth·nol·o·gy** *n* the branch of anthropology that deals with the comparison of various cultural groups of people. **eth·no·log·i·cal** *adj.* **eth·no·log·i·cal·ly** *adv.* **eth·nol·o·gist** *n.* **eth·no·mu·si·col·o·gy** [-,mjuzɪ'kɒlədʒi] *n* the study of the folk music of various cultures.

e·thos ['iθɒs] *n* the essential and distinctive character or spirit of a race or people, or of a system, culture, institution, etc. ⟨Greek *ēthos* character, nature⟩

eth·yl ['ɛθəl] *n* a univalent radical present in many organic compounds. ⟨*ether*⟩ **ethyl alcohol** ordinary alcohol, made by the fermentation of grain, sugar, etc. **eth·yl·ene** ['ɛθə,lin] *n* a colourless, flammable gas with an unpleasant odour, used as an anesthetic, in making organic compounds, and for colouring and ripening citrus fruits. **ethylene glycol** a colourless, viscous liquid used in cooling systems.

e·ti·o·late ['itiə,leit] *v* **1** *Botany* of a plant, make or become pale through lack of sunlight. **2** make weak, dull, colourless: *Her literary style was bland and etiolated.* **e·ti·o·la·tion** *n.* ⟨French *étioler*⟩

e·ti·ol·o·gy [,iti'ɒlədʒi] *n* **1** the branch of philosophy that deals with origins or causes. **2** the origin of a disease. **e·ti·o·log·i·cal** *adj.* **e·ti·o·log·i·cal·ly** *adv.* ⟨Greek *aitia* cause⟩

et·i·quette ['ɛtəkɪt] *n* **1** the rules for polite behaviour in society. **2** the conventions governing conduct in a profession, official ceremony, etc.: *medical etiquette.* ⟨French *étiquette* ticket (giving instructions)⟩

–ette *suffix* **1** small: *kitchenette.* **2** imitation: *leatherette* ⟨French, fem. diminutive suffix⟩

é·tude [ei'tjud] *or* [ei'tud] *n* a piece of music intended to develop skill in technique. ⟨French = study⟩

et·y·mol·o·gy [,ɛtə'mɒlədʒi] *n* **1** an explanation of the origin of a word and a

description of the changes it has gone through. **2** the branch of linguistics dealing with word origins. **et·y·mo·log·i·cal** *adj*. **et·y·mo·log·i·cal·ly** *adv*. **et·y·mol·o·gist** *n*. ⟨Greek *etymon* original, true sense or form of a word⟩
et·y·mon *n* the original form from which a word has developed historically.

eu– *prefix* good; well: *eulogy, euphony.* ⟨Greek⟩

eu·ca·lyp·tus [ˌjukəˈlɪptəs] *n* **-tus·es** *or* **-ti** [-taɪ] any of a genus of evergreen trees of the myrtle family. ⟨Greek *eu-* well + *kalyptos* covered; with reference to bud covering⟩
eucalyptus oil an oil extracted from eucalyptus leaves, used in antiseptics.

eu·ca·ry·ote [juˈkɛri,out] *or* [juˈkæri,out] *n* an organism with a membrane-bound nucleus. Also, **eu·ka·ry·ote.** Compare PROCARYOTE. ⟨Greek *eu-* good, well + *karyon* nut, kernel⟩

Eu·cha·rist [ˈjukərɪst] *n* **1** the Christian sacrament of the Lord's Supper; Holy Communion. **2** the consecrated bread and wine used. **Eu·cha·ris·tic** *adj*. ⟨Greek *eucharistia* thankfulness; *eu-* well + *charizesthai* show favour⟩

eu·chre [ˈjukər] *n* a simple card game for two, three, or four players, using the highest cards in the pack.
v **1** defeat at euchre. **2** *Informal* outwit; defeat. ⟨origin uncertain⟩

Eu·clid·e·an *or* **Eu·clid·i·an** [juˈklɪdiən] *adj* to do with Euclid, a Greek mathematician.

eu·gen·ic [juˈdʒɛnɪk] *adj* to do with improvement of the race: *eugenic breeding.* **eu·gen·i·cal·ly** *adv*. ⟨Greek *eu-* well + *genos* birth⟩
eu·gen·ics [juˈdʒɛnɪks] *n sg, pl* the science of improving the human race by a careful selection of parents. **eu·gen·i·cist** *n*

eu·lo·gy [ˈjulədʒi] *n* **1** a speech or writing in praise of a person, action, etc., esp someone who has just died. **2** high praise. **eu·lo·gist** *n*. **eu·lo·gis·tic** *adj*. **eu·lo·gis·ti·cal·ly** *adv*. **eu·lo·gize** *v*. ⟨Greek *eu-* well + *legein* speak⟩

eu·nuch [ˈjunək] *n* **1** a castrated man. **2** a castrated man in charge of a harem or the household of an Oriental ruler. **3** an ineffectual person. ⟨Greek *eunouchos; eunē* bed + *echein* keep⟩

eu·phe·mism [ˈjufə,mɪzəm] *n* a mild expression used instead of one that is unpleasantly direct. *Pass away* is a euphemism for *die.* **eu·phe·mis·tic** *adj*. **eu·phe·mis·ti·cal·ly** *adv*. **eu·phem·ize** *v*. ⟨Greek *eu-* good + *phēmē* speaking⟩

eu·pho·ny [ˈjufəni] *n* **1** agreeableness of sound. **2** the tendency in a language to change sounds so as to favour ease of utterance. **3** a combination of harmonious sounds. **eu·phon·ic** *adj*. **eu·phon·i·cal·ly** *adv*. **eu·pho·ni·ous** *adj*. **eu·pho·ni·ous·ly** *adv*. ⟨Greek *euphōnia; eu-* good + *phōnē* sound⟩

eu·pho·ri·a [juˈfɔriə] *n Psychology* a feeling of exaltation. **eu·phor·ic** *adj*. **eu·phor·ic·al·ly** *adv*. ⟨Greek *eu-* good + *pherein* bear⟩

eu·phor·iant *adj* producing euphoria. *n* a substance that produces euphoria.

Eur·a·sia [juˈreiʒə] *n* the continents of Europe and Asia.
Eur·a·sian *adj* **1** to do with Europe and Asia or its people. **2** of mixed European and Asian parentage. *n* a person of mixed European and Asian parentage.

eu·re·ka [juˈrikə] *interj* an exclamation of triumph about a discovery or a solution to a problem. ⟨Greek *heurēka* I have found (it); *heuriskein* find⟩

Europe [ˈjurəp] *n* a continent in the west part of Eurasia. ⟨Greek *Europa*⟩
eu·ro the unit of currency of the European Economic Community. **Eu·ro·pe·an** *adj* to do with Europe or its inhabitants. *n* **1** a native or inhabitant of Europe. **2** a person whose recent ancestors came from Europe. **European plan** a hotel system by which guests pay for only room and service, meals being extra. Compare AMERICAN PLAN. **European Union** a trading and political association of W European countries. *Abbrev* **EU.**

eu·ro·pi·um [jəˈroupiəm] *n* a rare metallic element. *Symbol* **Eu** ⟨See EUROPE.⟩

Eu·sta·chi·an tube [juˈsteiʃən] a slender canal between the pharynx and the middle ear. ⟨B. *Eustachio,* 16c Italian anatomist⟩

eu·tha·na·sia [ˌjuθəˈneiʒə] *n* a painless killing, esp to end an incurable disease; mercy killing. **eu·tha·nize** *v*. ⟨Greek *eu-* easy, good + *thanatos* death⟩

eu·troph·ic [juˈtrɒfɪk] *or* [juˈtroufɪk] *adj* of a lake or river, having excessive plant growth due to a high concentration of nutrients. Compare OLIGOTROPHIC. **eu·troph·i·ca·tion** [ju,trɒfɪˈkeiʃən] *n*. **eu·troph·y** [ˈjutrəfi] *n*. ⟨Greek *eu-* good, well + *trophē* nourishment⟩

eV electronvolt.

e·vac·u·ate [ɪˈvækju,eit] *v* **1** leave empty: *to evacuate a city.* **2** withdraw: *to evacuate all foreign residents from the war zone.* **3** make empty: *to evacuate the bowels.* **4** remove contents (air, water, etc.) from a container. **e·vac·u·a·tion** *n*. ⟨Latin *ex-* out + *vacuus* empty⟩
e·vac·u·ee [ɪ,vækjuˈi] *n* one who is removed to a place of greater safety.

e·vade [ɪˈveid] *v* **1** get away from by trickery. **2** avoid (the truth, a commitment, an issue, etc.) by indefinite or misleading statements. **3** baffle: *The solution evades me.* **e·va·sion** *n*. **e·va·sive** [ɪˈveisɪv] *adj*. **e·va·sive·ly** *adv*. **e·va·sive·ness** *n*. ⟨Latin *ex-* away + *vadere* go⟩

e·val·u·ate [ɪˈvælju,eit] *v* **1** judge the worth, quality, or importance of: *to evaluate a statement.* **2** find or decide the value of: *An expert evaluated the old clock at $900.* **3** *Mathematics* obtain the numerical value of (a function). **e·val·u·a·tion** *n*. **e·val·u·a·tive** *adj*. **e·val·u·a·tor** *n*. ⟨French *évaluer; valu* pp of *valoir* be worth⟩

ev·a·nesce [ˌɛvəˈnɛs] *v* disappear gradually;

fade away. **ev·a·nes·cence** *n.* **ev·a·nes·cent** *adj.* **ev·a·nes·cent·ly** *adv.* ⟨Latin *ex-* out + *vanescere* vanish; *vanus* insubstantial⟩

e·van·gel·i·cal [ˌivænˈdʒɛləkəl] *or* [ˌɛvən-] *adj* **1** to do with the four Gospels of the New Testament. **2** to do with the Protestant churches that emphasize Christ's atonement and salvation by faith as the most important parts of Christianity. **3** evangelistic. **4 Evangelical** designating those Protestant churches deriving from Lutheranism, rather than Calvinism. Compare REFORMED. **e·van·gel·i·cal·ly** *adv.* **e·van·gel·i·cal·ism** *n.* **e·van·gel·ism** [ɪˈvændʒə,lɪzəm] *n* **1** a preaching of the Gospel. **2** a missionary zeal for any cause. **e·van·gel·ist** *n* **1** a preacher of the Gospel. **2** a travelling preacher who urges people to make a religious commitment. **3 Evangelist** any one of the four apostles, Matthew, Mark, Luke, or John. **4** a zealous proponent of any doctrine. **e·van·gel·is·tic** *adj.* **e·van·gel·is·ti·cal·ly** *adv.* **e·van·gel·ize** *v.* **e·van·gel·i·za·tion** *n.* ⟨Greek *euangelion* good news; *eu-* good + *angellein* announce⟩

e·vap·o·rate [ɪˈvæpə,reit] *v* **1** change into a vapour: *The heat of the sun evaporated the puddles.* **2** remove moisture, esp water, from: *Heat is used to evaporate milk.* **3** vanish; fade away: *Her good resolutions soon evaporated.* **e·vap·o·ra·ble** *adj.* **e·vap·o·ra·tion** *n.* **e·vap·o·ra·tive** *adj.* ⟨Latin *ex-* out + *vapor* vapour⟩ **evaporated milk** whole milk that has been concentrated by evaporation of some of its water. **e·vap·o·ra·tor** *n* an apparatus for evaporating water or other liquid.

e·va·sion See EVADE.

eve [iv] *n* **1** the evening or day before some special day: *New Year's Eve.* **2** the time just before: *the eve of the battle.* **3** *Poetic* evening. ⟨variant of archaic *even;* OE *æfen*⟩

e·ven [ˈivən] *adj* **1** flat; smooth: *even country.* **2** at the same level: *The snow was even with the window.* **3** always the same: *an even motion.* **4** equal: *even shares.* **5** exact: *an even dozen.* **6** owing nothing and owed nothing: *When she had paid all of her debts, she was even.* **7** fair: *Justice is even treatment.* *v* **1** make equal: *to even the score.* **2** make level: *She evened the edges by trimming them.* *adv* **1** in an even manner. **2** exactly: *She left even as you came.* **3** indeed: *He is ready, even eager, to go.* **4** fully: *faithful even unto death.* **5** though one would not expect it: *Even the least noise disturbs her.* **6** still; yet: *You can do even better if you try.* **e·ven·ly** *adv.* **e·ven·ness** *n.* ⟨Old English *efen*⟩ **break even** *Informal* have equal gains and losses. **even out** become more even: *The path evened out and the going became easier.* **even though** although. **get** (*or* **be**) **even a** owe nothing. **b** get revenge. **e·ven–hand·ed** *adj* impartial: *He meted out even-handed justice.* **e·ven–hand·ed·ly** *adv.* **e·ven–hand·ed·ness** *n.* **even number** a number that has no remainder when divided

by 2: *The even numbers are 2, 4, 6, 8, etc.* **e·ven–tem·pered** *adj* calm.

eve·ning [ˈivnɪŋ] *n* **1** the last part of day and early part of night. **2** the last part: *Old age is the evening of life.* ⟨Old English *æfnung; æfnian* become evening; *æfen* evening⟩ **evening dress** formal clothes worn in the evening. **evening gown** a woman's evening dress, usually long. **eve·nings** *adv* in the evenings; every evening. **evening star** a bright planet seen in the western sky after sunset. Venus is often the evening star.

e·vent [ɪˈvɛnt] *n* **1** a happening; *current events.* **2** an important happening: *The discovery of oil in Alberta was certainly an event.* **3** an item in a program of sports or other planned happenings: *The broad jump was the last event.* ⟨Latin *eventus* pp of *evenire; ex-* out + *venire* come⟩ **at all events** or **in any event** whatever happens. **in the event of** in case of: *In the event of rain the party will be held indoors.* **in the event that** supposing: *In the event that the roads are icy, we will not come.* **e·vent·ful** *adj* **1** full of events: *Our day at the fall fair was highly eventful.* **2** having important results: *July 1, 1867 was an eventful day for Canada.* **e·vent·ful·ly** *adv.* **e·vent·ful·ness** *n.*

SYNONYMS

Event applies particularly to a happening of some importance: *Graduation from high school is an event that most students eagerly look forward to.* **Incident** applies to a less important happening: *The unexpected meeting with a girl I used to know was an amusing incident.* **Occurrence** is the general word for any happening, event, or incident: *Going to school is an everyday occurrence.*

e·ven·tu·al [ɪˈvɛntʃuəl] *adj* coming in the end: *eventual success after several failures.* **e·ven·tu·al·ly** *adv.* **e·ven·tu·al·i·ty** *n* a possibility: *We hope for rain but are ready for the eventuality of drought.* **e·ven·tu·ate** *v* come out in the end; result. **e·ven·tu·a·tion** *n.*

ev·er [ˈɛvər] *adv* **1** at any time: *Is she ever at home?* **2** at all times: *ever at your service.* **3** at all: *What did I ever do to you?* **4** *Informal* very: *Am I ever hungry!* ⟨Old English *æfre*⟩ **ever so** *Informal* very. **for ever and ever** always; eternally. **ev·er·green** *adj* **1** having leaves or needles all year: *evergreen tree.* **2** enduring: *an evergreen hope.* *n* **1** an evergreen tree, shrub, or herb. **2 evergreens** *pl* evergreen twigs or branches used for decoration, esp at Christmas. **ev·er·last·ing** *adj* **1** lasting forever. **2** lasting a long time. **3** lasting too long; tiresome: *his everlasting complaints.* *n* any of numerous plants of the composite family having papery flowers that keep their form when they are dry. **ev·er·last·ing·ly** *adv.* **ev·er·last·ing·ness** *n.* **ev·er·more** *adv, n* always; forever.

eve·ry [ˈɛvri] *adj* **1** all, regarded singly or separately: *Every written word is made of letters.* **2** all possible: *We gave her every consideration.*

3 at a regular interval of: *A bus leaves every two hours.* ⟨Old English *æfre* ever + *ælc* each⟩ **every now and then** from time to time. **every other** each alternating: *The courier makes deliveries every other day.* **every so often** from time to time. **every which way** *Informal* in all directions. *He had packed his suitcase every which way.*

eve·ry·bod·y ['ɛvrɪ,bʌdi] *or* [-,bɒdi] *pron* every person. **eve·ry·day** *adj* **1** daily: *Accidents are everyday occurrences.* **2** for every ordinary day: *everyday clothes.* **3** ordinary: *an everyday writer.* **Every·man** ['ɛvrɪ,mæn] *or* [-mən] *n* **1** an early morality play symbolizing the journey through life. **2** the chief character in this play, personifying humanity. **3** the average person. **eve·ry·one** *pron* every person. **eve·ry·thing** *pron* all things. *n* something extremely important: *This news means everything to us.* **eve·ry·where** *adv* in or to every place: *We looked everywhere for the dog.* *n* all places: *Everywhere was lit up.*

USAGE

Everyday is written as one word when it is an adjective, but as two words when **day** is a noun modified by **every**: *This was an everyday occurrence. Every day seemed a year.*

Everyone is written as one word when it is a pronoun, but as two words when **one** is a pronoun modified by **every**: *Everyone wants to attend the concert. Winning this game depends upon every one of you.*

Everything is written as one word when it is a noun or pronoun, but as two words when **thing** is a noun modified by **every**: *Everything has its proper place. There is a noun for every thing or idea you can think of.*

e·vict [ɪ'vɪkt] *v* **1** expel by a legal process from land, a building, etc.: *Because he had not paid his rent, the tenant was evicted.* **2** put out by force: *The soldiers evicted the enemy from the building.* **e·vic·tion** *n.* ⟨Latin *evictus* pp of *evincere.* See EVINCE.⟩

ev·i·dence ['ɛvədəns] *n* **1** whatever makes clear the truth or falsehood of something: . **2** *Law* facts established and accepted in a court of law. **3** an indication: *A smile gives evidence of pleasure.*
v make easy to see or understand: *Her smile evidenced her pleasure.* **ev·i·dent** *adj.* **ev·i·dent·ly** ['ɛvədəntli] *or* ['ɛvɪ,dɛntli] *adv.* ⟨Latin *ex-* out + *videre* see⟩ **in evidence** easily seen or noticed: *A crying baby is much in evidence.*

e·vil ['ivəl] *adj* **1** morally bad; wicked: *an evil character.* **2** causing harm: *an evil plan.* **3** unfortunate: *an evil fate.* **4** offensive; corrupt: *evil-smelling.* **e·vil** *n.* **e·vil·ly** *adv.* **e·vil·ness** *n.* ⟨Old English *yfel*⟩ **e·vil·do·er** ['ivəl,duər] *n* a person who does evil. **e·vil·do·ing** *n.* **evil eye** the power that some people are thought to have of causing harm to others by a look. **e·vil–eyed** *adj.* **e·vil–mind·ed** *adj* **1** wicked. **2** inclined to interpret anything in a lewd way. **Evil One** the Devil; Satan.

e·vince [ɪ'vɪns] *v* **1** show clearly: *The dog evinced its dislike of strangers by growling.* **2** show that one has (a certain quality, trait, etc.). ⟨Latin *evincere* claim for oneself; *ex-* out + *vincere* conquer⟩

e·vis·cer·ate [ɪ'vɪsə,reit] *v* **1** remove the bowels from. **2** weaken by depriving of some vital part: *The abridgment leaves the book somewhat eviscerated.* **3** *Surgery* remove the contents of (an organ). **e·vis·cer·a·tion** *n.* ⟨Latin *ex-* out + *viscera* entrails⟩

e·voke [ɪ'vouk] *v* call forth; bring out: *A good joke evokes a laugh.* ⟨Latin *ex-* out + *vocare* call⟩ **ev·o·ca·tion** [,ɛvə'keiʃən] *n* an evoking. **e·voc·a·tive** [ɪ'vɒkətɪv] *adj* tending to produce or arouse an emotional response, a vivid mental image, etc. **e·voc·a·tive·ly** *adv.* **e·voc·a·tive·ness** *n.*

ev·o·lu·tion [,ɛvə'luʃən] *or* [,ivə'luʃən] *n* **1** gradual development: *the evolution of the tanker from the first crude boat.* **2** *Biology* the theory that all living things developed from a few simple forms of life or from a single form. **3** a pattern of movements: *the graceful evolutions of a dancer.* **ev·o·lu·tion·ar·y** *adj.* ⟨Latin *evolutio* from *evolvere*; *ex-* out + *volvere* roll⟩ **ev·o·lu·tion·ist** *n* a student of, or believer in, a theory of evolution. **ev·o·lu·tion·ism** *n.* **e·volve** [ɪ'vɒlv] *v* develop or be developed gradually: *The girls evolved a plan for earning money.*

ewe [ju] *n* a female sheep. ⟨Old English *ēowu*⟩

ew·er ['juər] *n* a large water jug with a wide mouth. ⟨Old French *eviere, aiguiere,* Latin *aquarius* of or for water; *aqua* water⟩

ex¹ [ɛks] *prep* **1** out of. *Ex elevator* means free of charges until the time of removal from the grain elevator. **2** without. *Ex-dividend stocks* are stocks on which the purchaser will not receive the next dividend to be paid. ⟨Latin⟩

ex² [ɛks] *n Informal* a former spouse, boyfriend, girlfriend, etc.: *She saw her ex downtown yesterday.* ⟨*ex-* (def. 3)⟩

Ex [ɛks] *n Informal* an exhibition, esp the Canadian National Exhibition held annually in Toronto.

ex– *prefix* **1** out of, from, or out: *exit, export.* **2** thoroughly: *exterminate.* **3** former or formerly: *ex-president, ex-member.* **4** remove or release: *excommunicate.* ⟨Latin⟩

ex·ac·er·bate [ɛg'zæsər,beit] *or* [ɛk'sæsər,beit] *v* make worse. **ex·ac·er·ba·tion** *n.* ⟨Latin *ex-* completely + *acerbus* harsh, bitter⟩

ex·act [ɛg'zækt] *adj* **1** without any error or vagueness: *the exact amount.* **2** characterized by strict accuracy: *an exact thinker.*
v **1** demand and get: *to exact payment.* **2** require: *A hard piece of work exacts effort and patience.* **ex·act·a·ble** *adj.* **ex·ac·tion** *n.* **ex·act·ness** *n.* ⟨Latin *exactus* pp of *exigere* weigh precisely; *ex-* out + *agere* weigh⟩ **ex·act·ing** *adj* **1** making severe demands: *an exacting employer.* **2** requiring effort, care, or attention: *Flying an airplane is exacting work.*

ex·act·i·tude [ɛg'zæktə,tjud] or [ɛg'zæktə,tud] n exactness. ex·act·ly adv 1 in an exact manner. 2 just so; quite right. exact science a science in which facts can be accurately observed and results can be accurately predicted.

ex·ag·ger·ate [ɛg'zædʒə,reit] v 1 make (something) seem greater than it is: She exaggerated the dangers in order to frighten us. 2 go beyond the truth: He always exaggerates. 3 abnormally increase (features, gestures, etc.). ex·ag·ger·a·tion n. ex·ag·ger·a·tor n. ⟨Latin ex- out, up + agger heap⟩

ex·alt [ɛg'zɒlt] v 1 raise in rank, honour, power, etc.: Election to high office exalts a person. 2 fill with pride, joy, or noble feeling. 3 praise; honour; glorify. ex·al·ta·tion n. ⟨Latin ex- out, up + altus high⟩

ex·am·ine [ɛg'zæmən] v 1 look at closely and carefully. 2 test the knowledge or qualifications of. 3 question (a witness) formally. ex·am·in·a·ble adj. ex·am·i·na·tion n. ex·am·i·nee n. ex·am·in·er n. ⟨Latin examen a weighing; exigere. See EXACT.⟩
ex·am n Informal examination.

ex·am·ple [ɛg'zæmpəl] n 1 one thing taken to show what others are like: Vancouver is an example of a busy city. 2 a model: That father is a good example to his sons. 3 a sample to illustrate something: The problems in the mathematics textbook were accompanied by examples. ⟨Latin exemplum orig, taken out (i.e., as a sample); pp of eximere. See EXEMPT.⟩
for example for instance. make an example of treat severely as a warning or deterrent after someone has committed a crime or has misbehaved. set an example be a model or pattern of conduct.

SYNONYMS
Example applies to an individual thing, fact, etc. that shows what the type is like or how a general rule works: This chair is an example of period furniture. Sample applies to a part taken out of a thing to show the quality of the whole thing, which is considered exactly like it: The doctor examined a sample of her blood.

ex·as·per·ate [ɛg'zæspə,reit] v irritate very much; make angry. ex·as·per·at·ed adj. ex·as·per·at·ed·ly adv. ex·as·per·a·tion n. ⟨Latin ex- thoroughly + asper rough⟩

ex ca·the·dra [,ɛks kə'θidrə] or [-'kæθədrə] with authority. ⟨Latin ex cathedra from the chair⟩

ex·ca·vate ['ɛkskə,veit] v 1 make a hole by removing dirt, rock, etc. 2 get or uncover by digging: They excavated the ancient buried city. ex·ca·va·tion n. ⟨Latin ex- out + cavus hollow⟩
ex·ca·va·tor n a person who or thing that excavates. A steam shovel is an excavator.

ex·ceed [ɛk'sid] v go beyond: The sum of 5 and 7 exceeds 10. The success of the party exceeded our best expectations. ⟨Latin ex- out + cedere go⟩
ex·ceed·ing adj surpassing; very great; unusual; extreme. ex·ceed·ing·ly adv.

ex·cel [ɛk'sɛl] v be better than; do better than. ex·cel·lent ['ɛksələnt] adj. ex·cel·lent·ly adv. ⟨Latin excellere⟩
ex·cel·lence n superiority: the pursuit of excellence. ex·cel·len·cy n 1 excellence. 2 Excellency a title of honour used in speaking to or of the Governor General, an ambassador, a bishop, etc. Abbrev Exc.

ex·cept [ɛk'sɛpt] prep other or otherwise than: every day except Sunday.
conj with the exception (that): I'd go, except that my car won't start.
v 1 take out or leave out; exclude: All of us, the baby excepted, were helping to clean up. 2 object (to or against). ⟨Latin exceptus pp of excipere; ex- out + capere take⟩
except for other than: It's a good movie, except for a few boring scenes near the end.
ex·cept·ing prep except. ex·cep·tion n 1 a case that does not follow the rule: She usually arrives on time; today was an exception. 2 a person or item excluded: I loved the books, with one exception. 3 a disagreement; controversy: a paper liable to exception. 4 Law an objection raised in the course of a trial. take exception a object or protest (with to): She took exception to the editorial. b be offended. ex·cep·tion·a·ble adj objectionable. ex·cep·tion·a·bly adv. ex·cep·tion·al adj 1 unusual. 2 challenged or gifted physically or mentally: exceptional children. ex·cep·tion·al·ly adv.

ex·cerpt ['ɛgzɜrpt] or ['ɛksɜrpt]n a selected passage: excerpts from several medical books. ex·cerpt [ɪg'zɜrpt] or [ɛk'sɜrpt] v. ex·cerp·tion n. ⟨Latin excerpere; ex- out + carpere pluck⟩

ex·cess [ɛk'sɛs] n 1 an amount beyond what is usual or right: an excess of grief. 2 the amount by which one thing is more than another: to pay for an excess of 5 kg on luggage. 3 extreme or outrageous behaviour: excesses caused by drinking.
adj ['ɛksɛs] 1 more than the usual permitted: excess baggage. 2 more than is needed or desired: excess fat. ⟨Latin excessus pp of excedere. See EXCEED.⟩
in excess of more than: theft in excess of $500. to excess too much: He laughs to excess. ex·ces·sive [ɛk'sɛsɪv] adj too much: The price was excessive. ex·cess·ive·ly adv.

ex·change [ɛks'tʃeindʒ] v 1 give for something else: She would not exchange her house for a palace. 2 give and receive (things of the same kind): to exchange letters. 3 switch or reverse the positions of. 4 replace or have replaced (a purchase): We cannot exchange swimsuits.
n 1 an exchanging: Ten dimes for a dollar is a fair exchange. 2 a place where things are exchanged or traded: the stock exchange. 3 a conversation. 4 exchanges pl the cheques or drafts sent to a clearing house for settlement. ex·change·a·ble adj. ⟨Old French eschangier, Latin excambiare; ex- out + cambiare change; Celtic⟩
exchange rate the ratio at which the currency of one country can be exchanged

for that of another. **exchange student** a student who studies for a time in another institution or country.

ex·cheq·uer [ɛks'tʃɛkər] *n* **1** a treasury, esp the treasury of a nation. **2** *Informal* finances; funds. ⟨Old French *eschequier* chessboard; accounts were kept on a table marked in squares⟩

ex·cise[1] ['ɛksaɪz] *n* **1** a tax or duty on certain articles made, sold, or used within a country. **2** the fee paid to obtain a licence for fishing, hunting, etc. **ex·cis·a·ble** *adj*. **ex·cise** *v*. ⟨apparently Old French *acceis* tax; Latin *ad-* to + *census* tax⟩

ex·cise[2] [ɛk'saɪz] *v* remove by cutting out: *to excise a tumour, to excise a passage from a book.* **ex·cis·a·ble** *adj*. **ex·ci·sion** [ɛk'sɪʒən] *n*. ⟨Latin *excisus* pp of *excidere*; *ex-* out + *caedere* cut⟩

ex·cite [ɛk'saɪt] *v* **1** stir up the feelings of. **2** produce a response in (an organ, etc.): *to excite a nerve.* **ex·cit·a·ble** *adj*. **ex·cit·a·bil·i·ty** *n*. **ex·ci·ta·tion** *n*. **ex·cit·ed** *adj*. **ex·cit·ing** *adj*. ⟨Latin *excitare*; *ex-* out + *ciere* set in motion⟩ **ex·cite·ment** *n* **1** the state of being excited. **2** something that excites. **3** noisy activity; commotion: *What's all the excitement?*

ex·claim [ɛk'skleɪm] *v* cry out. **ex·cla·ma·tion** *n*. ⟨< F < L *exclamare* < *ex-* + *clamare* cry out⟩ **exclamation mark** a punctuation mark (!) used after a word or sentence to show that it is an exclamation. **ex·clam·a·to·ry** [ɛk'sklæmə,tɔri] *adj* using, containing, or expressing an exclamation: *an exclamatory sentence.*

ex·clude [ɛk'sklud] *v* **1** shut out; keep out: *Blinds exclude light.* **2** keep from including: *Professional players are excluded from the competition.* **3** EXPEL (def. 2). **ex·clu·sion** *n*. ⟨Latin *excludere*; *ex-* out + *claudere* shut⟩ **to the exclusion of** so as to exclude: *She worked away at her science project to the exclusion of everything else.* **ex·clud·ing** *prep* except for. **ex·clu·sion·ism** *n* the practice of denying rights or privileges to all but certain people. **ex·clu·sion·ar·y** *adj*. **ex·clu·sion·ist** *n*. **ex·clu·sive** [ɛk'sklusɪv] *adj* **1** each shutting out the other. *Baby* and *adult* are exclusive terms since a person cannot be both. **2** shutting out other things: *He demanded our exclusive attention.* **3** not shared with others: *exclusive rights.* **4** excluding certain people or groups for social, financial, or other reasons: *an exclusive club.* **5** not available elsewhere or to anyone else: *an exclusive interview. n* something exclusive, esp a story published by only one periodical. **ex·clu·sive·ness** *n*. **exclusive of** not counting: *There are 26 days in that month, exclusive of Sundays.* **ex·clu·sive·ly** *adv* with the exclusion of all others: *That selfish girl looks out for herself exclusively.* **ex·clu·siv·i·ty** *n*.

ex·com·mu·ni·cate [,ɛkskə'mjunə,keit] *v* cut off from membership in a church. *adj* [-kɪt] excommunicated. *n* [-kɪt] an excommunicated person. **ex·com·mu·ni·ca·tion** *n*. ⟨Latin *ex-* out of + *communitas* fellowship, community⟩

ex·co·ri·ate [ɛk'skɔri,eit] *v* **1** rub off the skin of. **2** denounce violently. **ex·co·ri·a·tion** *n*. ⟨Latin *ex-* off + *corium* hide, skin⟩

ex·cres·cent [ɛk'skrɛsənt] *adj* **1** forming an unnatural growth or a disfiguring addition. **2** *Phonetics* of a sound, present for no historical or grammatical reason, as *b* in *thimble*, derived from Old English *thymle*. ⟨Latin *ex-* out + *crescere* grow⟩ **ex·cres·cence** *n* **1** an unnatural growth, such as a wart. **2** an unnecessary addition: *excrescences of interpretation.*

ex·crete [ɛk'skrit] *v* **1** discharge (waste matter) from the body **2** *Botany* get rid of (waste) from the cells. **ex·cre·tion** *n*. **ex·cre·tive** *adj*. ⟨Latin *excretus* pp of *excernere*; *ex-* out + *cernere* sift⟩ **ex·cre·ment** ['ɛkskrəmənt] *n* waste matter discharged from the bowels; feces. **ex·cre·ment·al** *adj*. **ex·cre·ta** [ɛk'skritə] *n pl* waste matter discharged from the body, such as sweat or urine. **ex·cre·tal** *adj*. **ex·cre·to·ry** ['ɛkskrə,tɔri] *or* [ɛks'kritəri] *adj* to do with excretion: *The kidneys are excretory organs.*

ex·cru·ci·ate [ɛk'skruʃi,eit] *v* torture. **ex·cru·ci·a·tion** *n*. ⟨Latin *ex-* utterly + *cruciare* torture, crucify; *crux, crucis* cross⟩ **ex·cru·ci·at·ing** *adj* **1** very painful; causing great suffering. **2** intense; so extreme as to be unbearable: *in excruciating detail.* **ex·cru·ci·at·ing·ly** *adv*.

ex·cul·pate ['ɛkskəl,peit] *or* [ɛk'skʌlpeit] *v* free from blame; prove innocent. **ex·cul·pa·ble** *adj*. **ex·cul·pa·tion** *n*. ⟨Latin *ex-* out + *culpa* guilt⟩ **ex·cul·pa·to·ry** *adj* tending to exculpate or capable of exculpating.

ex·cur·sion [ɛk'skɜrʒən] *n* **1** a short pleasure trip. **2** a round trip at a reduced fare. **3** *Physics* a single movement of something from a centre by oscillation. **ex·cur·sive** *adj*. ⟨Latin *ex-* out + *currere* run⟩

ex·cuse [ɛk'skjuz] *v* **1** overlook (a fault, etc.). **2** give or be a reason for (something). **3** free from duty or obligation; let off: *Those who passed the first test are excused from the second. n* [ɛk'skjus] a real or pretended reason. **a poor excuse for** a substandard example of: *That was a poor excuse for a paper that you handed in.* **excuse me** I apologize. **b** please may I leave? **excuse oneself a** ask to be pardoned. **b** ask permission to leave. **make one's excuses** regretfully decline an invitation to attend some gathering. **ex·cus·a·ble** *adj*. **ex·cus·a·bly** *adv*. ⟨Latin *excusare*; *ex-* away + *causa* cause⟩ . **ex·cu·sa·to·ry** *adj* designed as an excuse.

ex·ec [ɛg'zɛk] *n* an executive.

ex·e·crate ['ɛksə,kreit] *or* ['ɛgzə-] *v* **1** express or feel extreme loathing for: *The former leader's cruelty was execrated by his followers.* **2** curse. **ex·e·cra·tion** *n*. **ex·e·cra·to·ry** *adj*. ⟨Latin *ex-* completely + *sacer* accursed⟩ **ex·e·cra·ble** ['ɛksəkrəbəl] *or* ['ɛgzə-] *adj* **1** abominable; detestable: *an execrable crime.*

2 *Informal* very bad: *execrable taste in art.*
ex·e·cra·bly *adv.*

ex·e·cute ['ɛksə,kjut] *v* **1** carry out: *The nurse executed the doctor's orders.* **2** put to death according to law: *The convicted murderer was executed.* **3** make according to a plan: *The tapestry was executed with great skill.* **4** perform or play (a piece of music). **5** *Law* make (a contract, will, etc.) complete by signing or doing whatever is necessary. **6** *Computers* follow (an instruction). **ex·e·cu·tion** *n.* ⟨Latin *ex(s)ecutus* pp of *exsequi; ex-* out + *sequi* follow⟩ **ex·e·cu·tion·er** *n* **1** a person who carries out the death penalty according to law. **2** any person who puts another to death. **ex·ec·u·tive** [ɛɡ'zɛkjətɪv] *adj* **1** to do with managing affairs: *an executive committee.* **2** suitable or designed for managers of an organization: *an executive suite.* **3** having the power of putting the laws into effect: *the executive branch of a government.* **ex·ec·u·tive** *n.* **ex·ec·u·tive·ly** *adv.* **Executive Council** in Canada, the Cabinet of a provincial or territorial government, consisting of the premier and his or her ministers. **executive officer** the manager of a company. **ex·ec·u·tor** [ɛɡ'zɛkjətər] *n* a person named in a will to carry out the provisions of the will. **ex·ec·u·to·ry** *adj Law* to be carried out. **ex·ec·u·tor·i·al** *adj.*

ex·e·ge·sis [,ɛksə'dʒisɪs] *n, pl* **-ses** [-siz] **1** a scholarly interpretation of written work, esp of a passage in the Bible. **2** an explanation or interpretation of a word, sentence, etc. ⟨Greek, from *ex-* out + *hēgeesthai* lead, guide⟩ **ex·e·gete** ['ɛksɪ,dʒit] *n* one skilled in exegesis. **ex·e·get·i·cal** or **ex·e·get·ic** *adj.* **ex·e·get·ics** *n* the science of exegesis.

ex·em·plar [ɛɡ'zɛmplər] *or* [-plɑr] *n* **1** an ideal model or pattern. **2** a typical case: *the exemplar of the insecure child.* ⟨Latin, from *exemplum.* See EXAMPLE.⟩ **ex·em·pla·ry** *adj* **1** worth imitating: *exemplary conduct.* **2** of a punishment, serving as a warning: *a sentence of exemplary severity.* **3** typical: *exemplary passages from a book.* **ex·em·pla·ri·ly** *adv.* **ex·em·pla·ri·ness** *n.* **exemplary damages** *Law* damages that exceed the value of actual loss, meant to serve as punishment. **ex·em·pli·fy** *v* **1** show by example: *The knights exemplified courage.* **2** show something as typical. **ex·em·pli·fi·ca·tion** *n.* **ex·em·pli gra·ti·a** [ɛɡ'zɛmpli 'ɡratiə] *Latin* for example; for instance. *Abbrev* **e.g. ex·empt** [ɛɡ'zɛmpt] *v* make free from a duty, rule, etc.: *to be exempted from the final exam.* **ex·empt** *adj.* **ex·emp·ti·ble** *adj.* **ex·emp·tion** *n.*

ex·er·cise ['ɛksər,saɪz] *n* **1** activity to train the body or keep it healthy. **2** active use or practice: *the exercise of one's right to vote.* **3** a task or activity used to practise a skill: *exercises at the end of the chapter.* **4 exercises** *pl* a formal activity; ceremony: *graduation exercises.* **ex·er·cise** *v.* ⟨Latin *exercere* not allow to rest; *ex-²* + *arcere* keep away⟩

ex·er·cis·er *n* **1** one who exercises. **2** a machine for exercising the body.

SYNONYMS

Exercise emphasizes repeated use of mental or physical powers to develop health and energy: *Exercise of the mind increases its power.* **Practice** applies to action repeated to develop skill: *Learning to play the piano well takes much practice.* **Drill** = constant repetition of an exercise to develop correct habits: *Some children benefit from drill in spelling.*

ex·ert [ɛɡ'zɜrt] *v* **1** exercise or bring to bear: *to exert an influence.* **2** try hard; strive (with a reflexive pronoun): *We'll have to exert ourselves to make the deadline.* **ex·er·tion** *n.* **ex·ert·ive** *adj.* ⟨Latin *ex(s)ertus* pp of *ex(s)erere* thrust out; *ex-* out + *serere* attach⟩

ex·e·unt ['ɛksiənt] *or* ['ɛksiʊnt] *v Latin* in stage directions, the signal for actors to leave the stage. It is the plural form of EXIT and means "They go out."

ex·fo·li·ate [ɛks'fouli,eit] *v* **1** cast or be cast off as flakes or scales. **2** *Geology* of some minerals, split. ⟨Latin *ex-* out + *folium* leaf⟩

ex gratia [ɛks 'ɡreiʃə] *or* [ɛks' ɡratiə] not required but as a favour. ⟨Latin⟩

ex·hale [ɛks'heil] *v* **1** breathe out. **2** give off (air, vapour, smoke, odour, etc.). **ex·ha·la·tion** [,ɛkshə'leiʃən] *n.* ⟨Latin *ex-* out + *halare* breathe⟩

ex·haust [ɛɡ'zɒst] *v* **1** empty completely: *to exhaust a well.* **2** use up: *to exhaust one's money.* **3** tire very much: *The climb up the hill exhausted us.* **4** deprive wholly of essential properties: *to exhaust the soil.* *n* the used steam, gas, etc. that escapes from a machine. **ex·haust·ed** *adj.* **ex·haust·i·ble** *adj.* **ex·haus·tion** *n.* **ex·haust·less** *adj.* ⟨Latin *exhaustus* pp of *exhaurire; ex-* out + *haurire* draw⟩ **ex·haus·tive** *adj* missing nothing important; thorough: *an exhaustive study of the play.* **ex·haust·ive·ly** *adv.* **ex·haust·ive·ness** *n.* **exhaust pipe** in an internal-combustion engine, the tube that leads gases out of the engine.

ex·hib·it [ɛɡ'zɪbɪt] *v* **1** show; display. **2** show in court as evidence. **ex·hib·it** *n.* **ex·hib·i·tor** or **exhibiter** *n.* ⟨Latin *exhibere; ex-* out + *habere* hold⟩ **ex·hi·bi·tion** *n* **1** display: *an exhibition of bad manners.* **2** a public show: *The art school holds an exhibition every year.* **3** a public showing of livestock, manufactured goods, etc., accompanied by amusements such as sideshows: *the Canadian National Exhibition.* **ex·hi·bi·tion·ism** *n* **1** an excessive tendency to show off one's abilities. **2** a compulsive tendency to expose the genitals in public. **ex·hi·bi·tion·ist** *n.* **ex·hi·bi·tion·is·tic** *adj.*

ex·hil·a·rate [ɛɡ'zɪlə,reit] *v* **1** invigorate: *The girls were exhilarated by their swim.* **2** put into high spirits: *She was exhilarated by the prospect of getting home a day early.* **ex·hil·a·ra·tion** *n.* ⟨Latin *ex-* thoroughly + *hilaris* merry⟩

ex·hort [ɛg'zɔrt] *v* urge strongly: *The preacher exhorted them to live out their faith.* **ex·hor·ta·tion** [ˌɛgzɔr'teiʃən] *or* [ˌɛksɔr'teiʃən] *n.* ⟨Latin *ex-* thoroughly + *hortari* urge strongly⟩

ex·hume [ɛks'hjum] *or* [ɛg'zjum] *v* take out of a grave or out of the ground; dig up. **ex·hu·ma·tion** *n.* ⟨Latin *ex-* out of + *humus* ground⟩

ex·i·gent ['ɛksədʒənt] *or* ['ɛgzə-] *adj* demanding immediate attention; urgent: *the exigent pangs of hunger.* **ex·i·gent·ly** *adv.* ⟨Latin *exigere*. See EXACT.⟩
ex·i·gen·cy [ɛg'zɪdʒənsi] *or* ['ɛksə-] *n* **1** the state or quality of being urgent. **2 exigencies** *pl* urgent needs: *The exigencies of business kept her from going home.* **3** an urgent case.

ex·ile ['ɛgzaɪl] *or* ['ɛksaɪl] *v* force (a person) to leave his or her country or home. *n* **1** banishment: *Napoleon's exile to Elba was brief.* **2** an exiled person. **3** any prolonged absence from one's own country. **4 the Exile** the captivity of the Jews in Babylon during the 6th century B.C. ⟨Latin *exiliare; ex(s)ilium*⟩

ex·ist [ɛg'zɪst] *v* **1** be real. **2** have life: *A person cannot exist without air.* **3** occur: *Such cases exist, but they are rare.* **ex·ist·ence** *n.* **ex·ist·ent** *adj.* ⟨Latin *ex-* forth + *sistere* stand⟩
ex·is·ten·tial [ˌɛgzɪ'stɛnʃəl] *or* [ˌɛksɪ-] *adj* **1** to do with actual experience. **2** to do with existentialism: *an existential play.* **ex·is·ten·tial·ly** *adv.* **ex·is·ten·tial·ism** *n* a system of philosophy that avoids abstract theories on life and emphasizes personal experience. **ex·is·ten·tial·ist** *adj, n.*

ex·it ['ɛgzɪt] *or* ['ɛksɪt] *n* **1** a way out. **2** a departure. **3** *Theatre* the departure of an actor from the stage: *a graceful exit.* **4** death. **ex·it** *v.* ⟨Latin = goes out⟩
exit poll a survey of voters leaving a polling booth.

ex li·bris [ˌɛks 'librɪs] *or* [ˌɛks 'laɪbrɪs] from the books (of); an inscription on a book, followed by the name of the book's owner. ⟨Latin⟩

ex ni·hi·lo [ˌɛks 'nihəˌlou] *or* [ˌɛks 'naɪəˌlou] from nothing: *Epics are not created ex nihilo.* ⟨Latin⟩

ex·o·carp ['ɛksouˌkarp] *n* EPICARP.

ex·o·crine ['ɛksəkrɪn] *adj* of a gland, secreting by means of a duct. Compare ENDOCRINE. ⟨Greek *exo-* outside + (*endo*)*crine*⟩

ex·o·dus ['ɛksədəs] *n* **1** a departure, esp of a large number of people: *Every summer there is an exodus from the city.* **2 Exodus** the departure of the Israelites from Egypt under Moses. ⟨Greek *exodos; ex-* out + *hodos* way⟩

ex of·fi·ci·o [ˌɛks ə'fɪʃiˌou] by virtue of one's office: *The secretary is, ex officio, a member of all committees.* ⟨Latin⟩

ex·og·a·my [ɛk'sɒgəmi] *n* marriage to a person outside one's own group, tribe, etc. **ex·og·a·mous** *adj.* ⟨Greek *exo-* outside + *gamos* marriage⟩

ex·og·e·nous [ɛk'sɒdʒənəs] *adj Biology* originating or produced from outside. ⟨Greek *exo-* outside + *-genes; gignesthai* be born⟩

ex·on·er·ate [ɛg'zɒnəˌreit] *v* **1** free from blame: *Witnesses to the accident completely exonerated the driver of the truck.* **2** relieve of a duty, task, obligation, etc. **ex·on·er·a·tion** *n.* ⟨Latin *ex-* off + *onus, oneris* burden⟩

ex·or·bi·tant [ɛg'zɔrbətənt] *adj* going far beyond what is right or reasonable: *exorbitant prices.* **ex·or·bi·tance** *n.* **ex·or·bi·tant·ly** *adv.* ⟨Latin *ex-* out of + *orbita* track⟩

ex·or·cise ['ɛksərˌsaɪz] *v* drive out (an evil spirit) by prayers, ceremonies, etc. **ex·or·cism** *n.* **ex·or·cist** *n.* ⟨Greek *exorkizein* bind by oath, conjure, exorcise; *ex-* + *horkos* oath⟩

ex·o·skel·e·ton [ˌɛksou'skɛlətən] *n* the hard, external structure that supports the bodies of many invertebrates, such as insects. Compare ENDOSKELETON. **ex·o·skel·e·tal** *adj.* ⟨Greek *exo-* outside + SKELETON⟩

ex·o·sphere ['ɛksouˌsfir] *n* the outermost rim of the earth's atmosphere. ⟨Greek *exo-* outside + SPHERE⟩

ex·o·therm·ic [ˌɛksou'θɜrmɪk] *adj Chemistry* to do with a chemical change that generates heat. ⟨Greek *exo-* outside + *thermē* heat⟩

ex·ot·ic [ɛg'zɒtɪk] *adj* **1** not native: *Many exotic plants are grown as house plants.* **2** strikingly unusual: *an exotic glamour.* **3** *Physics, chemistry* resulting from complicated technical procedures: *exotic compounds.* **ex·ot·ic** *n.* **ex·ot·i·cal·ly** *adv.* ⟨Greek *exōtikos; exō-* outside⟩
ex·ot·i·ca *n pl* things that are different, in an intriguing or exciting way: *He has interested himself in such exotica as geodesic houseboats.* **exotic dancer** a striptease dancer. **ex·ot·i·cism** [ɛg'zɒtəˌsɪzəm] *n* something unusual, such as a foreign word or phrase.

ex·pand [ɛk'spænd] *v* **1** increase in size. **2** spread out: *A bird expands its wings before flying.* **3** speak or write (*on*) in greater detail: *She expanded on the theme in the second chapter.* **4** *Mathematics* express (a quantity) as a sum of terms, product of terms, etc. **ex·pan·da·ble** *adj.* **ex·pand·er** *n.* **ex·pand·ing·ly** *adv.* ⟨Latin *ex-* out + *pandere* spread⟩
ex·panse *n* a large, unbroken space or stretch: *The Pacific Ocean is a vast expanse of water.* **ex·pan·si·ble** *adj.* **ex·pan·si·bil·ity** *n.*
ex·pan·sile [ɛk'spænsaɪl] *or* [ɛk'spænsəl] *adj* **1** capable of expanding. **2** to do with expansion. **ex·pan·sion** *n* **1** the act or process of expanding or the fact of being expanded. **2** a thing that is the result of expanding: *The thesis is an expansion of a paper she wrote last year.* **3** the development of a topic. **4** *Mathematics* the expression of a quantity as a sum of terms, product of terms, etc. **expansion card** *Computers* a circuit board inserted into an **expansion slot** in a computer to add to its capacity. **ex·pan·sion·ism** *n* a policy of territorial or commercial expansion. **ex·pan·sion·ist** *n, adj.* **ex·pan·sion·is·tic** *adj.* **ex·pan·sive** *adj* **1** tending

to expand. **2** wide. **3** taking in much or many things. **4** showing one's feelings freely and openly. **ex·pan·sive·ly** *adv.* **ex·pan·sive·ness** *n.*

ex·pa·ti·ate [ɛk'speiʃi,eit] *v* **1** write or talk much (*on*): *She expatiated on the thrills of her trip.* **2** roam freely. **ex·pa·ti·a·tion** *n.* **ex·pa·ti·a·tor** *n.* ⟨Latin *ex(s)patiari* walk around; *ex-* out + *spatium* space⟩

ex·pa·tri·ate [ɛks'peitri,eit] *v* **1** banish; exile. **2** withdraw (oneself) from one's country. **ex·pa·tri·ate** [ɛks'peitriɪt] *adj, n.* **ex·pa·tri·a·tion** *n.* ⟨Latin *ex-* out of + *patria* fatherland⟩

ex·pect [ɛk'spɛkt] *v* **1** think likely to happen. **2** count on as reasonable, necessary, or right: *A soldier is expected to be properly dressed.* **3** *Informal* think; suppose: *I expect they'll be coming by car.* **4** await the birth of: *My sister is expecting her first baby.* **ex·pect·ant** *adj.* **ex·pect·ant·ly** *adv.* ⟨Latin *ex(s)pectare; ex-* out + *specere* look⟩

ex·pect·an·cy *n* **1** a showing or feeling of expectation. **2** the expected amount based on statistical information: *a life expectancy of 77 years.* **ex·pec·ta·tion** *n* **1** anticipation. **2** something expected. **3** Usually, **expectations** *pl* a reason for expecting something: *They say she has great expectations.* **4** *Statistics* the expected value of any random variable. **in expectation (of)** expecting: *in expectation of a reward* **ex·pect·ing** *adj Informal* pregnant.

ex·pec·to·rate [ɛk'spɛktə,reit] *v* cough up and spit out (phlegm, etc.). **ex·pec·to·ra·tion** *n.* ⟨Latin *ex-* out of + *pectus, pectoris* chest⟩ **ex·pec·to·rant** *adj* causing or helping the discharge of phlegm, etc. *n* a medicine that promotes expectoration.

ex·pe·di·ent [ɛk'spidiənt] *adj* **1** suitable under the circumstances: *She decided it would be expedient to take an umbrella.* **2** prompted by a concern for personal advantage. *n* a means of bringing about a desired result: *The prisoner tied sheets together and escaped by this expedient.* **ex·pe·di·en·cy** or **ex·pe·di·ence** *n.* **ex·pe·di·ent·ly** *adv.* ⟨Latin *expedire* set free from a net; *ex-* out + *pes, pedis* foot⟩

ex·pe·dite ['ɛkspə,dəit] *v* make easy and quick: *If everyone will help, it will expedite matters.* **ex·pe·dit·er** *n.* ⟨Latin *expeditus* pp of *expedire.* See EXPEDIENT.⟩ **ex·pe·di·tious** [,ɛkspə'dɪʃəs] *adj* efficient and prompt. **ex·pe·di·tious·ly** *adv.* **ex·pe·di·tious·ness** *n.* **ex·pe·di·tion** *n* **1** a journey for some special purpose. **2** efficient and prompt action: *He completed his work with expedition.* **ex·pe·di·tion·ar·y** *adj.*

ex·pel [ɛk'spɛl] *v* **-pelled, -pel·ling 1** force out: *When the gunpowder exploded, the bullet was expelled from the gun.* **2** dismiss permanently: *A troublesome pupil may be expelled from school.* **ex·pul·sion** [ɛk'spʌlʃən] *n.* **ex·pul·sive** *adj*

ex·pend [ɛk'spɛnd] *v* spend; use up. **ex·pend·er** *n.* ⟨Latin *ex-* out + *pendere* weigh, pay⟩

ex·pend·a·ble *adj* **1** normally used up in service: *Pencils are expendable items.* **2** that may be sacrificed if necessary: *People don't think of themselves as being expendable in their jobs.* *n* Usually, **expendables** *pl* expendable persons or things. **ex·pend·i·ture** *n* the amount of money, time, etc. spent or used up: *Limit your expenditures to what is necessary.* **ex·pense** *n* **1** the cost: *the expense of the trip.* **2** a cause of spending: *Running a car is an expense.* **3 expenses** *pl* the charges incurred in doing one's job. **ex·pen·sive** *adj.* **ex·pen·sive·ly** *adv.* **ex·pen·sive·ness** *n.* **at the expense of a** paid by. **b** with the loss or sacrifice of: *He achieved prosperity at the expense of his health.* **c** with (someone) as the object: *They had many a laugh at his expense.* **expense account** a statement of expenses that will be repaid.

ex·pe·ri·ence [ɛk'spɪriəns] *n* **1** something that has happened to one: *an exciting experience.* **2** a living through something: *He has learned a lot by experience.* **3** everything gone through that makes up the life of a person, community, etc.: *in human experience.* **4** skill or wisdom gained by observing, doing, or living through things: *a person of wide experience.* **ex·pe·ri·ence** *v.* **ex·pe·ri·enced** *adj.* ⟨Latin *experientia; experiri* test, try out⟩ **ex·pe·ri·en·tial** *adj* to do with experience. **ex·pe·ri·en·tial·ly** *adv.*

ex·per·i·ment [ɛk'spɛrə,mɛnt] *v* try in order to find out: *He has been experimenting with dyes to get the colour he wants.* *n* [ɛk'spɛrəmənt] a test or trial to find out something new or to demonstrate something that is known. **ex·per·i·ment·er** *n.* ⟨Latin *experimentum; experiri.* See EXPERIENCE.⟩ **ex·per·i·men·tal** *adj* **1** based on experiments: *Chemistry is an experimental science.* **2** used for experimentation: *an experimental farm.* **3** based on experience, not on theory. **4** for testing: *They are growing an experimental variety of wheat at the university farm.* **ex·per·i·men·tal·ly** *adv.* **ex·per·i·men·ta·tion** *n* the act or process of experimenting: *More experimentation is needed to confirm the results.* **ex·per·i·men·tal·ism** *n.* **ex·per·i·men·tal·ist** *n.*

ex·pert ['ɛkspərt] *n* a person with a great deal of skill and knowledge. *adj* ['ɛkspərt] *or* [ɛk'spɜrt] knowing a great deal about some special field of knowledge. **ex·pert·ly** *adv.* **ex·pert·ness** *n.* ⟨Latin *expertus* pp of *experiri.* See EXPERIENCE.⟩ **ex·per·tise** *n* an overall grasp of a subject, process, etc., produced by ability, experience, and skill.

ex·pi·ate ['ɛkspi,eit] *v* make amends for (a wrong, sin, etc.): *The king tried to expiate the injustices of his uncle's rule.* **ex·pi·a·ble** *adj.* **ex·pi·a·tion** *n.* **ex·pi·a·tor** *n.* ⟨Latin *ex-* completely + *piare* appease; *pius* devout⟩ **ex·pi·a·to·ry** *adj* intended to expiate.

ex·pire [ɛk'spaɪr] *v* **1** come to an end *You must obtain a new automobile licence before your old one expires.* **2** die. **3** breathe out: *to expire used air from the lungs.* **ex·pi·ra·tion** *n.* ⟨Latin *ex-* out + *spirare* breathe⟩

ex·pi·ry [ɛk'spaɪri] *or* ['ɛkspəri] *n* 1 coming to an end. 2 death.

ex·plain [ɛk'spleɪn] *v* 1 make clear. 2 tell the significance of: *to explain his strange behaviour.* 3 give a reason for: *She couldn't explain her absence.* **ex·plain·a·ble** *adj.* ⟨Latin *ex-* out + *planus* flat⟩
explain away make insignificant by giving reasons: *to explain away someone's fears.* **explain oneself a** make one's meaning clear. **b** justify or give reasons for one's conduct: *Why did you leave your little brother alone? Explain yourself.*
ex·pla·na·tion [ˌɛksplə'neɪʃən] *n* 1 the act or process of explaining. 2 something that explains: *That book was a good explanation of the principle of atomic fission.* **ex·plan·a·to·ry** [ɛk'splænə,tɔri] *adj* helping to explain: *Read the explanatory part of the lesson first.*

ex·ple·tive [ɛk'splitɪv] *or* ['ɛksplətɪv] *n* 1 an oath: *The expressions* Damn! *and* My goodness! *are expletives.* 2 a syllable, word, or phrase added to fill out a line of verse, etc. without adding anything to the sense. 3 *Grammar* **a** in English, a word used to take the normal place of the subject or object, which is identified later. *There* in the following sentence is an expletive: *There is a book on the table.* **b** in some other languages, a word required by the grammar but having no independent meaning. *Ne* is often an expletive in French. ⟨Latin *expletus* pp of *explere; ex-* out + *plere* fill⟩

ex·pli·cate ['ɛksplə,keɪt] *v* 1 develop the meaning of (a principle, doctrine, etc.). 2 explain. **ex·plic·a·ble** ['ɛkspləkəbəl] *or* [ɛk'splɪkəbəl] *adj.* **ex·pli·ca·tion** *n.* **ex·pli·ca·tor** *n.* ⟨Latin *explicare.* See EXPLICIT.⟩
ex·pli·ca·to·ry ['ɛksplɛkə,tɔri] *or* [ɛk'splɪkə,tɔri] *adj* that explains.

ex·plic·it [ɛk'splɪsɪt] *adj* 1 clearly expressed: *explicit directions.* Compare IMPLICIT (def. 2). 2 outspoken: *The description of the victim's injuries was so explicit that it shocked us.* 3 obvious; evident. **ex·plic·it·ly** *adv.*
ex·plic·it·ness *n.* ⟨Latin *explicitus* pp of *explicare* unfold; *ex-* out + *plicare* fold⟩

ex·plode [ɛk'sploʊd] *v* 1 blow up: *The bomb exploded.* 2 react suddenly with noise or violence: *The audience exploded with laughter.* 3 destroy belief in: *Columbus helped to explode the theory that the earth was flat.* 4 increase rapidly: *an exploding population.* **ex·plo·sion** [ɛk'sploʊʒən] *n.* ⟨Latin *ex-* out + *plaudere* clap⟩
ex·plod·ed *adj* designating a diagram showing the parts of a machine, apparatus, etc. separated from each other, as if by an explosion. **ex·plo·sive** [ɛk'sploʊsɪv] *or* [ɛk'sploʊzɪv] *adj* 1 capable of exploding; likely to explode. 2 tending to burst forth noisily: *an explosive temper.* 3 to do with sudden outbursts: *an explosive situation. n* a substance capable of exploding: *Explosives are used in making fireworks.* **ex·plo·sive·ly** *adv.* **ex·plo·sive·ness** *n.*

ex·ploit ['ɛksplɔɪt] *n* a daring deed: *the exploits of famous heroes.*

v [ɛk'splɔɪt] 1 make use of: *A mine is exploited for its minerals.* 2 make unfair or selfish use of. 3 promote through public relations. **ex·ploit·a·ble** *adj.* **ex·ploi·ta·tion** *n.* **ex·ploit·er** *n.* ⟨Old French *esploit;* Latin *explicitum* achievement, pp of *explicare.* See EXPLICIT.⟩
ex·ploit·a·tive *or* **ex·ploit·ive** *adj* to do with exploitation, esp when selfish.

ex·plore [ɛk'splɔr] *v* 1 travel for the purpose of finding out about geographical features, etc. 2 search through (a place, etc.), in order to find out about it: *to explore one's surroundings.* 3 investigate: *to explore all the possibilities.* **ex·plo·ra·tion** *n.* **ex·plor·er** *n.* ⟨Latin *explorare* spy out; orig, cry out (at sight of game, etc.); *ex-* out + *plorare* weep⟩
ex·plor·a·to·ry [ɛk'splɔrə,tɔri] *adj* to do with exploration: *exploratory surgery.*

ex·plo·sion See EXPLODE.

ex·po ['ɛkspoʊ] *n Informal* exposition: *Expo 86.*

ex·po·nent [ɛk'spoʊnənt] *n* 1 a person or thing that explains, interprets, etc. 2 a person who favours (with *of*): *She is an exponent of the guaranteed annual wage.* 3 a person or thing that stands as an example or symbol of something: *This woman is a famous exponent of self-education.* 4 *Algebra* a small number written above a symbol or quantity to show how many times the symbol or quantity is to be used as a factor. *Example:* 2^3 = 2 × 2 × 2 ⟨Latin *exponere.* See EXPOUND.⟩
ex·po·nen·tial [ˌɛkspə'nɛnʃəl] *adj* 1 to do with algebraic exponents. 2 of any growth or increase, occurring more and more rapidly. **ex·po·nen·tial·ly** *adv.*

ex·port [ɛk'spɔrt] *or* ['ɛkspɔrt] *v* 1 send (goods) out of a country for sale in another. 2 *Computers* send from one application into another. **ex·port** ['ɛkspɔrt] *n, adj.* **ex·por·ta·tion** *n.* **ex·port·er** *n.* ⟨Latin *ex-* out + *portare* carry⟩

ex·pose [ɛk'spoʊz] *v* 1 lay open; make vulnerable: *His foolish actions exposed him to ridicule.* 2 lay open to view, esp something that was hidden. 3 reveal: *The investigators exposed the takeover plot.* 4 *Photography* allow light to act on (a sensitive film, paper, etc.). 5 put out without shelter: *The ancient Spartans used to expose unwanted babies.* ⟨Old French *ex-* forth (Latin *ex-*) + *poser* put. See POSE¹.⟩
ex·po·sé [ˌɛkspoʊ'zeɪ] *or* ['ɛkspoʊ,zeɪ] *n* 1 the showing up of a crime, of dishonesty, fraud, etc. 2 something, as an article, film, etc., that does this. **ex·po·sure** [ɛk'spoʊʒər] *n* 1 the act or instance of exposing: *public exposure.* 2 appearance in public: *Her campaign manager thought she needed more television exposure.* 3 a position in relation to the sun and wind: *a southern exposure.* 4 *Photography* **a** the time during which light reaches and acts on a film or plate. **b** the part of a film used for one picture. **c** the total amount of light on a film in making a picture. **die of exposure** die from hypothermia due to lack of shelter or adequate clothing.

ex·po·si·tion [ˌɛkspə'zɪʃən] *n* 1 a public show. 2 a detailed explanation: *the exposition of a* *scientific theory.* **3** a speech or a piece of writing explaining a process or idea. **4** *Music* the first section of a movement, in which the subjects are presented. **5** *Literature* the part which sets out the story, esp of a drama. **ex·pos·i·to·ry** or **ex·pos·i·tive** *adj.* ⟨Latin *expositus* pp of *exponere*. See EXPOUND.⟩

ex·pos·i·tor [ɛk'spɒzətər] *n* a person who explains; interpreter or commentator.

ex·pos·tu·late [ɛk'spɒstʃə,leit] *v* reason earnestly with a person: *They expostulated with their son about the foolishness of leaving school.* **ex·pos·tu·la·tion** *n.* **ex·pos·tu·la·to·ry** *adj.* ⟨Latin *ex-* (intensive) + *postulare* demand⟩

ex·po·sure See EXPOSE.

ex·pound [ɛk'spaʊnd] *v* **1** make clear; interpret. **2** state in detail. ⟨Old French *espondre;* Latin *ex-* forth + *ponere* put⟩

ex·press [ɛk'sprɛs] *v* **1** put into words: *Express your ideas clearly.* **2** show by look, voice, or action: *Your smile expresses joy.* **3** press out: *to express juice from grapes.*
adj **1** clear: *an express wish.* **2** particular: *She came for the express purpose of seeing you.*
n **1** a quick or direct means of sending things. **2** a train, bus, elevator, etc. travelling fast and making few stops. **ex·press** *adj.*
ex·press·i·ble *adj.* ⟨Latin *expressus* pp of *exprimere; ex-* out + *premere* press⟩
ex·pres·sion *n* **1** a putting into words: *Clarity of expression is important in style.* **2** a group of words used as a unit: *'Wise guy' is a slang expression.* **3** a showing by look, voice, or action: *Her sigh was an expression of sadness.* **4** a bringing out the meaning or beauty of something read, spoken, played, sung, etc.: *Try to read with more expression.* **5** a showing by a sign, figure, etc. **6** a symbol or group of symbols expressing a mathematical process or quantity. **7** a pressing out: *the expression of oil from plants.* **ex·pres·sion·ism** *n* a movement in art and literature marked by the attempt to express subjective feelings without regard for accepted forms. **ex·pres·sion·ist** *n, adj.* **ex·pres·sion·is·tic** *adj.* **ex·pres·sion·less** *adj* without expression: *an expressionless voice.* **ex·pres·sive** *adj* **1** representing (with *of*): *Alas is a word expressive of sadness.* **2** full of expression. **ex·pres·sive·ly** *adv.* **ex·pres·sive·ness** *n* **ex·pres·siv·i·ty** *n* expressive quality. **ex·press·ly** *adv* **1** clearly: *You were expressly forbidden to touch it.* **2** specially: *She came expressly to see you.* **ex·press·way** *n* a divided highway for fast driving.

SYNONYMS
Expressive emphasizes showing a meaning or feeling in a lively way: *An expressive shrug revealed her contempt.* **Significant** emphasizes being full of meaning: *She ended every remark with a significant smile.*

ex·pro·pri·ate [ɛk'sproupri,eit] *v* take (property) away from an owner, esp for public use. **ex·pro·pri·a·tion** *n.* **ex·pro·pri·a·tor** *n.* ⟨Latin *ex-* away from + *proprius* one's own⟩

ex·pul·sion See EXPEL.

ex·punge [ɛk'spʌndʒ] *v* remove completely;: *He was directed to expunge certain accusations from the record.* **ex·punc·tion** *n.* ⟨Latin *ex-* out + *pungere* prick⟩

ex·pur·gate ['ɛkspər,geit] *v* remove objectionable passages or words from (a book, letter, etc.). **ex·pur·ga·tion** *n.* ⟨Latin *ex-* out + *purgare* purge⟩

ex·quis·ite [ɛk'skwɪzɪt] or ['ɛkskwɪzɪt] *adj* **1** lovely in a delicate way: *exquisite lace.* **2** of highest excellence: *exquisite taste.* **3** sharp; intense: *exquisite joy.* **ex·quis·ite·ly** *adv.* **ex·quis·ite·ness** *n.* ⟨Latin *exquisitus* pp of *exquirere; ex-* out + *quaerere* seek⟩

ex·tant ['ɛkstənt] or [ɛk'stænt] *adj* still in existence: *Some of Captain Vancouver's charts are extant.* ⟨Latin *ex-* out, forth + *stare* stand⟩

ex·tem·po·re [ɛk'stɛmpərei] or [ɛk'stɛmpəri] *adj, adv* on the spur of the moment; without preparation; offhand or impromptu: *Each pupil will be called on to speak extempore.* **ex·tem·po·ra·ne·ous** [ɛk,stɛmpə'reiniəs] *adj.* **ex·tem·po·rize** *v.* **ex·tem·po·ri·za·tion** *n.* ⟨Latin *ex tempore* according to the moment⟩

ex·tend [ɛk'stɛnd] *v* **1** stretch out: *She extended her hand to the visitor.* **2** continue in time, space, or direction: *The beach extended for more than a kilometre in each direction.* **3** lengthen or enlarge: *to extend a ski trail another 3 km, to extend one's knowledge.* **4** give *to extend credit.* **ex·tend·i·ble** or **ex·tend·a·ble** *adj.* **ex·tend·a·bil·i·ty** *n.* ⟨Latin *ex-* out + *tendere* stretch⟩
ex·tend·ed *adj* **1** widespread; prolonged; widened. **2** spread out. **extended family** a family whose members are of several generations and branches. **ex·ten·si·ble** or **ex·ten·sile** [ɛk'stɛnsaɪl] or [ɛk'stɛnsəl] *adj* of a bodily or mechanical part, capable of being protruded, stretched, or opened out: *an extensible tongue.* **ex·ten·si·bil·i·ty** *n.* **ex·ten·sion** *n* **1** an extending or being extended. **2** a part that extends something: *the new extension to the school.* **3** an extra telephone connected to a line. **4** an increase in the time allowed for something: *I got an extension on my essay because I had been sick.* **5** an educational program for people who cannot take regular courses: *People who have full-time jobs can upgrade their education by taking evening classes through extension.* **6** *Physics* that property of a body by which it occupies a portion of space. **ex·ten·sion·less** *adj.* **extension cord** an electrical cord having a plug at one end and a socket at the other, used to lengthen the cord attached to an electrical appliance. **extension ladder** a ladder having movable parts enabling it to be extended to varying heights. **ex·ten·sive** *adj* **1** of great extent *an extensive park, extensive knowledge.* **2** affecting many things: *extensive change.* **ex·ten·sive·ly** *adv.* **ex·ten·sive·ness** *n.* **ex·tent** *n* **1** the size, space, length, amount, or degree to which a thing extends: *the whole extent of the country. The extent of a judge's power is limited by law.* **2** something extended; an extended space: *a*

vast extent of prairie. **3** *Physics* an object or body having length, area, or volume.

ex·ten·u·ate [ɛk'stɛnju,eit] *v* **1** make (guilt, a fault, an offence, etc.) seem less: *extenuating circumstances.* **2** make less or weaker. **ex·ten·u·a·tion** *n.* **ex·ten·u·at·ing** *adj.* ⟨Latin *ex-* out + *tenuis* thin⟩

ex·te·ri·or [ɛk'stiriər] *n* **1** an outer surface or part: *The exterior of the house was of brick.* **2** an outdoor scene on the stage.
adj **1** on the outside: *The skin of an apple is its exterior covering.* **2** happening outside: *exterior influences.* **3** suitable for use outside: *exterior paint.* **ex·te·ri·or·ly** *adv.* ⟨Latin = further outside; *exterus* outside⟩
exterior angle *Geometry* **1** any of the four angles formed on the outer sides of two lines by a straight line cutting through them. **2** the angle formed on the outside of a polygon between one of its sides and an extension of a side next to it.

ex·ter·mi·nate [ɛk'stɜrmə,neit] *v* destroy completely: *This poison will exterminate rats.* **ex·ter·mi·na·tion** *n.* **ex·ter·mi·na·tor** *n.* ⟨Latin *exterminare* drive out; *ex-* out of + *terminus* boundary⟩

ex·ter·nal [ɛk'stɜrnəl] *adj* **1** to do with the outer surface: *the external wall of a house.* **2** coming from without: *external influences.* **3** having existence outside one's mind: *external reality.* **4** for outward appearance: *Her politeness is only external.* **5** having to do with international affairs: *external affairs.* *n* **1** an outer surface or part. **2 externals** *pl* clothing, manners, etc: *He judges people by such externals as length of hair.* **ex·ter·nal·ly** *adv.* ⟨Latin *externus; exterus* outside⟩
external ear the fleshy part of the ear attached to the head. **ex·ter·nal·ism** *n* excessive attention to matters of form in religion. **ex·ter·nal·ize** *v* give objective shape or form to (things in the mind or emotions).

ex·tinct [ɛk'stɪŋkt] *adj* **1** no longer in existence: *The dinosaur is an extinct animal.* **2** no longer active: *an extinct volcano.* **ex·tinc·tion** *n.* ⟨Latin *ex(s)tinctus* pp of *ex(s)tinguere.* See EXTINGUISH.⟩

ex·tin·guish [ɛk'stɪŋgwɪʃ] *v* **1** put out: *Water extinguished the fire.* **2** put an end to: *One failure after another extinguished her hopes.* **ex·tin·guish·a·ble** *adj.* ⟨Latin *ex-* out + *stinguere* quench⟩
ex·tin·guish·er *n* a device for quenching fires.

ex·tir·pate ['ɛkstər,peit] *v* **1** destroy completely: *to extirpate a prejudice.* **2** tear up by the roots. **ex·tir·pa·tion** *n.* ⟨Latin *ex-* out + *stirps* root⟩

ex·tol or **ex·toll** [ɛk'stoul] *v* **-tolled, -tol·ling.** praise highly. ⟨Latin *ex-* up + *tollere* raise⟩

ex·tort [ɛk'stɔrt] *v* **1** obtain (money, a promise, etc.) from a person by threats. **2** obtain (something) by persistent demands: *The children extortied a promise of a picnic at the beach from their parents.* **ex·tor·tion** *n.* ⟨Latin *extortus* pp of *extorquere; ex-* out + *torquere* twist⟩

ex·tor·tion·ate [ɛk'stɔrʃənɪt] *adj*
1 characterized by extortion: *extortionate demands.* **2** much too great; exorbitant: *an extortionate price.* **ex·tor·tion·ate·ly** *adv.* **ex·tor·tion·er** or **ex·tor·tion·ist** *n* a person who is guilty of extortion.

ex·tra ['ɛkstrə] *adj* **1** more, greater, or better than what is usual: *extra pay.* **2** not included in the price: *Bread is extra in this restaurant.* *n* **1** something for which an additional charge is made: *The sunroof is an extra.* **2** something in addition to what is usual. **3** a special edition of a newspaper. **4** a person hired by the day to act in crowd scenes, etc. in a motion picture. **5** BYE[1].
adv **1** more than usually: *They like their coffee extra strong.* **2** in addition: *Dessert costs extra.* ⟨probably short for *extraordinary*⟩

extra– *prefix* outside, beyond, besides: *extraordinary.* ⟨Latin⟩

ex·tract [ɛk'strækt] *v* **1** pull out: *to extract a tooth.* **2** obtain by pressing, distilling, etc.: *to extract oil from olives.* **3** obtain against a person's will: *to extract a confession.* **4** deduce: *to extract a principle from a collection of facts.* **5** derive: *to extract pleasure from a situation.* **6** select (a passage) from a book, speech, etc. **ex·tract** ['ɛkstrækt] *n.* **ex·tract·a·ble** or **ex·tract·i·ble** *adj.* ⟨Latin *extractus* pp of *extrahere; ex-* out + *trahere* draw⟩
ex·trac·tion *n* **1** an extracting or being extracted: *the extraction of a tooth.* **2** descent; origin: *She is of Spanish extraction.* **ex·trac·tive** *adj* **1** tending to extract. **2** capable of being extracted. **3** of production in which materials are derived directly from nature, as in mining or farming. **ex·trac·tor** *n* something or someone that extracts.

ex·tra–cur·ric·u·lar [,ɛkstrə kə'rɪkjələr] *adj* outside the regular course of study: *Debating is an extra-curricular activity in high school.*

ex·tra·dite ['ɛkstrə,dəit] *v* give up or deliver (a fugitive) to another local authority for trial. **ex·tra·di·tion** *n.* ⟨Latin *ex-* out + *traditio* a delivering up; *tradere* hand over⟩
ex·tra·dit·a·ble *adj* for which a person can be extradited: *Murder is an extraditable offence.*

ex·tra·ju·dic·ial [,ɛkstrədʒu'dɪʃəl] *adj* beyond the authority of a court. **ex·tra·ju·dic·ial·ly** *adv.*

ex·tra·mar·i·tal [,ɛkstrə'mɛrətəl] or [-'mærətəl] *adj* outside the limits or bonds of marriage.

ex·tra·mu·ral [,ɛkstrə'mjurəl] *adj* **1** occurring outside the boundaries of a school or college: *extramural activities.* **2** between schools or colleges: *extramural hockey.* **3** to do with studies outside the normal program of a university, college, etc. **4** beyond the boundaries or walls of a city. ⟨Latin *extra muros* outside the walls⟩

ex·tra·ne·ous [ɛk'streiniəs] *adj* **1** coming from outside: *Sand, some other extraneous matter had got into the butter.* **2** irrelevant: *In her talk on conservation, she made extraneous remarks about wildlife photography.*

ex·tra·ne·ous·ly *adv.* **ex·tra·ne·ous·ness** *n.* ⟨Latin *extraneus; extra* outside⟩

ex·tra·or·di·naire [ɛk,strɔrdɪ'nɛr] *adj* (*placed after the noun*) extraordinary; striking; unusual: *a comedian extraordinaire.* ⟨French⟩

ex·tra·or·di·nar·y [ɛk'strɔrdə,nɛri] *or* [,ɛkstrə'ɔrdə,nɛri] *adj* **1** far beyond what is ordinary: *Two metres is an extraordinary height for a woman.* **2** outside of or additional to the regular class of officials (placed after the noun): *Ambassador Extraordinary.* **3** unplanned: *an extraordinary session of Parliament.* **ex·tra·or·di·nar·i·ly** *adv.*

ex·trap·o·late [ɛk'stræpə,leit] *v* **1** *Mathematics* project (new values of a series) from those already known. **2** infer (something) by projecting from known facts. **ex·trap·o·la·tion** *n.* ⟨*extra-* + (INTER)POLATE⟩

ex·tra·sen·so·ry [,ɛkstrə'sɛnsəri] *adj* beyond the normal scope or range of the senses: **extrasensory perception** mental telepathy.

ex·tra·ter·res·tri·al [,ɛkstrə tə'rɛstriəl] *adj* coming from or existing beyond the limits of the earth's atmosphere: *extraterrestrial life.* *n* a supposed creature from another planet.

ex·tra·ter·ri·to·ri·al [,ɛkstrə ,tɛrə'tɔriəl] *adj* **1** outside the laws of the country that a person is living in. Any ambassador to a foreign country has certain extraterritorial privileges. **2** beyond territorial limits or jurisdiction. **ex·tra·ter·ri·to·ri·al·ity** *n.* **ex·tra·ter·ri·to·ri·al·ly** *adv.*

ex·trav·a·gant [ɛk'strævəgənt] *adj* **1** spending carelessly and lavishly. **2** highly exaggerated: *extravagant praise, extravagant price.* **3** costing more than is proper: *an extravagant dinner.* **ex·trav·a·gance** *n.* **ex·trav·a·gant·ly** *adv.* ⟨Latin *extra-* outside + *vagari* wander⟩

ex·trav·a·gan·za *n* a lavish entertainment, piece of music, party, etc.

ex·treme [ɛk'strim] *adj* **1** much more than usual. **2** very severe: *extreme measures.* **3** farthest from the centre.
n **1** one of two things, places, parts, etc. as far or as different as possible from each other: *Love and hate are two extremes of feeling.* **2** an extreme degree or condition: *Joy is happiness in the extreme.* **3** *Mathematics* the first or last term in a proportion: *In the proportion, 2 is to 4 as 8 is to 16, 2 and 16 are the extremes; 4 and 8 are the means.* **4** involving physical risk and requiring great skill and endurance: *extreme sports.* **ex·treme·ly** *adv.*
ex·treme·ness *n.* ⟨Latin *extremus* furthest outside *exterus* outside⟩
go to extremes do or say too much; resort to extreme measures.
extremely high frequency the highest range of frequencies in the radio spectrum, between 30 and 300 gigahertz. *Abbrev* **EHF** or **ehf.** **extremely low frequency** the lowest range of frequencies in the radio spectrum, between 30 and 300 hertz. **extreme unction** *Roman Catholic Church* the sacrament given by a priest to a dying person. **ex·trem·ism** *n* a

tendency to go to political or ideological extremes. **ex·trem·ist** *n, adj.* **ex·trem·i·ty** [ɛk'strɛməti] *n* **1** the very end; the farthest possible place. **2** an extreme need, danger, suffering, etc.: *In their extremity the people on the sinking ship bore themselves bravely.* **3** the highest degree: *Joy is the extremity of happiness.* **4** an extreme action: *The soldiers were forced to the extremity of firing their rifles to scatter the angry mob.* **5** the **extremities** *pl* the hands and feet.

> **USAGE**
> Although **extremer** and **extremest** are used as the comparative and superlative, **more extreme** and **most extreme** are found more frequently in general usage.

ex·tri·cate ['ɛkstrə,keit] *v* set free (from entanglements, difficulties, etc.): *I extricated my young brother from the barbed-wire fence.* **ex·tri·ca·ble** *adj.* **ex·tri·ca·tion** *n.* ⟨Latin *ex-* out of + *tricae* perplexities⟩

ex·trin·sic [ɛk'strɪnzɪk] *or* [ɛk'strɪnsɪk] *adj* **1** not essential; caused by external circumstances. **2** being, coming, or acting from outside of a thing: *extrinsic aid.* Compare INTRINSIC. **ex·trin·si·cal·ly** *adv.* ⟨Latin *extrinsecus* coming from outside; earlier **extrim* from outside + *secus* following⟩

ex·tro·vert ['ɛkstrə,vɜrt] *n* a person more interested in what is going on than in his or her thoughts and feelings; a person who is active and talkative rather than thoughtful. Compare INTROVERT. **ex·tro·vert·ed** *or* **ex·tro·vert** *adj.* **ex·tro·ver·sion** [,ɛkstrə'vɜrʒən] *n.* ⟨Latin *extra* outside + *vertere* turn⟩

ex·trude [ɛk'strud] *v* **1** squeeze, force, or push out. **2** shape (metal, plastic, etc.) by forcing through a die. **ex·tru·sion** *n.* ⟨Latin *ex-* out + *trudere* thrust⟩

ex·u·ber·ant [ɛg'zubərənt] *adj* **1** having or showing high spirits: *an exuberant welcome.* **2** elaborate or lavish: *an exuberant use of bright colours.* **3** very abundant: *exuberant good health, exuberant vegetation.* **ex·u·ber·ance** *n.* **ex·u·ber·ant·ly** *adv.* ⟨Latin *exuberare* grow luxuriantly; *ex-* thoroughly + *uber* fertile⟩

ex·ude [ɛg'zud] *v* **1** come or send out in drops or as a smell: *Sweat exudes from the skin.* **2** show conspicuously: *She exudes confidence.* **ex·u·da·tion** *n.* ⟨Latin *ex-* out + *sudare* sweat⟩

ex·ult [ɛg'zʌlt] *v* rejoice greatly: *The winners exulted in their victory.* **ex·ult·ant** *adj.* **ex·ult·ant·ly** *adv.* **ex·ul·ta·tion** [,ɛgzʌl'teiʃən] *n.* **ex·ult·an·cy** [ɛg'zʌltənsi] *n.* ⟨Latin *ex(s)ultare* frequentative of *exsilire; ex-* forth + *salire* leap⟩

eye [aɪ] *n* **1** either of the two organs by which people and animals see. **2** any organ or machine that is sensitive to light. **3** the ability to see small differences in things: *A good artist must have an eye for colour.* **4** a look: *He cast an eye in her direction.* **5** Often, **eyes** *pl* a judgment: *She can do no wrong in his eyes.* **6** something like an eye: *the eye of a needle.* **7** the calm, clear area at the centre of a hurricane, cyclone, etc. **8** *Slang* PRIVATE EYE.

v **eyed**, **eye·ing** or **ey·ing 1** fix the gaze on: *He sat there, curiously eyeing everything in the room.* **2** look at watchfully: *The dog eyed the stranger.* **eye·like** *adj.* ⟨Old English *ēage*⟩ **an eye for an eye** punishment as severe as the offence. **be all eyes** watch attentively: *The children were all eyes as he opened the box.* **catch someone's eye** attract someone's attention. **cry one's eyes out** *Informal* sob tempestuously. **eyes right** or **eyes left** a military order to turn the head to the right or to the left as a salute while marching. **feast one's eyes on** admire (something attractive). **give someone the eye** *Slang* look at in a flirtatious manner. **have an eye for** be a sound and appreciative judge of: *She has an eye for a good painting.* **have an eye to** pay attention to. **have eyes for** *Informal* admire. **in a pig's eye** *Slang* not ever. **in the eye of the wind** *Nautical* against the direction of the wind. **in the eye(s) of** in the judgment of: *In the eyes of most doctors, smoking is dangerous to health.* **in the public eye** often seen in public or often mentioned in newspaper articles, etc. **keep an eye on** take care of. **keep an eye out for** be wary of: *You had better keep an eye out for pickpockets in the crowd.* **keep one's eyes open** (or **peeled** or **skinned**), watch (for). **look someone in the eye** look directly at someone's eyes. **make eyes at** look at in a flirtatious way. **my eye** *Informal* an exclamation used to express disagreement or contradiction: *Tired, my eye! She's just lazy.* **open someone's eyes** make a person see what is really happening. **run one's eye(s) over** give a cursory glance at. **see eye to eye** agree entirely: *They often don't see eye to eye, but they never actually fight.* **set** (or **lay** or **clap**) **eyes on** look at. **shut one's eyes to** refuse to consider. **under the eye of** supervised by. **up to one's** (or **the**) **eyes in** having more of than one can handle. **with an eye to** considering. **with one's eyes shut** *Informal* very easily; effortlessly.

eye·ball *n* the ball-shaped part of the eye apart from the lids and bony socket. *v Slang* look at closely or intently. **eyeball to eyeball** *Informal* face to face. **eye bolt** a bolt with a loop at one end to hold a rope or hook. **eye·brow** *n* the arch of hair above the eye. **raise an eyebrow** or **one's eyebrows** look surprised. **raise eyebrows** (or **an eyebrow**) arouse interest or excitement: *His outlandish get-up raised a few eyebrows.* **eye–catch·ing** *adj Informal* striking; appealing. **eye–catch·er** *n.* **eye contact** the act of looking someone in the eye. **eye·drop·per** *n* DROPPER (def. 2).

eye·ful [ˈaɪ.fʊl] *n* **1** as much as the eye can see at one time. **2** *Informal* a good look. **3** *Slang* a person who is unusually good-looking. **eye·glass** *n* **1** a lens for aiding or correcting vision, esp a monocle. **2** eyepiece. **3 eyeglasses** *pl* a pair of lenses held in a frame and worn to aid vision; spectacles. **eye·lash** *n* one of the hairs on the edge of the eyelid or below the eye. **eye·less** *adj* blind or without eyes. **eye·let** *n* **1** a small hole for a lace to go through. **2** a small hole edged with fine stitches, used as a decorative pattern in embroidery. **eye·lid** *n* the movable fold of skin over the eye. **eye·lin·er** *n* a coloured cosmetic applied as a fine line on the eyelids. **eye–o·pen·er** *n* **1** a happening that comes as a revelation: *Her behaviour was an eye-opener; I had no idea she could be so mean.* **2** a drink of liquor taken early in the day. **eye–o·pen·ing** *adj* enlightening or revealing. **eye·piece** *n* the lens nearest to the eye of the user in a telescope, microscope, etc. **eye rhyme** the final words of lines of verse that appear to rhyme because of their similar spelling. The words *cough*, *tough*, and *though* are eye rhymes. **eye·shade** *n* a visor to shield the eyes in bright light. **eye·shadow** a cosmetic in any of various colours applied to the eyelids. **eye·sight** *n* **1** the power of seeing. **2** the range of vision. **eye·sore** *n* something unpleasant to look at. **eye·stalk** *n Zoology* the stalk or peduncle upon which the eye is borne in lobsters, shrimp, etc. **eye·strain** *n* a tired or weak condition of the muscles of the eyes. **eye·tooth** *n*, *pl* **-teeth**. either of the two pointed, upper teeth between the incisors and the bicuspids. **give one's eyeteeth for** *Informal* go to great lengths to get or achieve. **eye·wash** *n* **1** a liquid preparation to clean or heal the eyes. **2** *Slang* deceiving flattery. **3** *Slang* nonsense. **eye·wit·ness** *n* a person who actually sees or has seen some act or happening.

ey·rie [ˈiri] or [ˈɛri] *n* **1** the nest of an eagle or other bird of prey high on a mountain or cliff. **2** a house, castle, etc. built in a high place. ⟨Old French *aire* area, Latin *ager* field; spelling influenced by Middle English *ey* egg⟩

e–zine *n* **1** a magazine devoted to matters of interest to Web users. **2** a magazine on the Web.

Ff

f or **F** [ɛf] *n, pl* **f's** or **F's 1** the sixth letter of the English alphabet, or any speech sound represented by it. **2** the sixth person or thing in a series. **3** *Music* the fourth tone in the scale of C major. **4 F** a failing grade in a rating system.

f 1 female. **2** *Music* forte. **3** *Mathematics* function. **4** folio. **5** the following page: *p. 83f means page 83 and the following page.*
ff. 1 and the following pages: *p. 26 ff. means page 26 and the following few pages.* **2** folios.

F or **F. 1** Fahrenheit. **2** French. **3** Friday. **4** February. **5** Father. **6** farad.

fa [fɑ] *n Music* **1** the fourth tone of an eight-tone major scale. **2** the tone F ⟨See GAMUT⟩

fa·ble ['feibəl] *n* **1** a story made up to teach a lesson. **2** an untrue story. **3** a myth. ⟨Latin *fabula; fari* speak⟩
fa·bled *adj* **1** told about in fables or legends: *the fabled Sasquatch.* **2** fictitious.

fab·ric ['fæbrɪk] *n* **1** cloth. **2** something constructed of combined parts: *the fabric of society.* ⟨Latin *fabrica* workshop⟩
fab·ri·cate *v* **1** build; construct; manufacture. **2** make up; invent (stories, lies, excuses, etc.). **3** forge (a document). **fab·ri·ca·tion** *n.*

fab·u·lous ['fæbjələs] *adj* **1** not believable: *fabulous prices.* **2** imaginary: *The phoenix is a fabulous bird.* **3** *Informal* wonderful: *We had a fabulous time at the party.* **fab·u·lous·ly** *adv.* ⟨Latin *fabulosus; fabula.* See FABLE.⟩

fa·çade [fə'sɑd] *n* **1** the front part of a building. **2** a front part of anything, esp when thought of as concealing something: *a façade of honesty.* Also, **fa·cade.** ⟨French, from *face.* See FACE.⟩

face [feis] *n* **1** the front part of the head. **2** an expression: *His face was sad.* **3** a distortion of the face, expressing annoyance, etc. or meant to amuse: *She made a face at me.* **4** outward appearance: *a different face on the matter.* **5** the outer surface of something: *the face of the earth.* **6** the main side of something: *the face of a clock.* **7** *Mathematics* one of the plane surfaces of a solid: *A cube has six faces.* **8** *Mining* the surface where work is in progress. **9** self-respect or prestige: *loss of face.* **10** impudence: *She had the face to return.* *v* **1** have the face turned toward: *Our house faces east.* **2** be opposite to: *Look at the picture facing page 60.* **3** meet bravely: *He faced the angry mob.* **4** present itself to: *A problem now faced us.* **5** cover the surface of with a layer of different material: *a wooden house faced with brick.* ⟨French *face;* Latin *facies* form⟩
face down disconcert. **face off** ✻ *Hockey* put (a puck) into play. **face–off** *n.* **face up to** meet bravely and boldly: *to face up to an enemy.* **face with** present with (a problem): *They faced her with an impossible request.* **fly in the face of** oppose. **in the face of a** in the

presence of: *in the face of danger.* **b** in spite of: *in the face of difficulties.* **lose face** lose dignity or prestige. **on the face of it** as it appears. **pull a long face** look unhappy or disapproving. **put a good** (or **brave**, etc.) **face on** make the best of. **put one's face on** *Informal* apply makeup. **show one's face** appear. **to someone's face** boldly, in the presence of: *She repeated the gossip to the teacher's face.*
face card a playing card that is a king, queen, or jack. **face·cloth** *n* a small cloth for washing the face or body. **face cord** a stack of firewood about 1.2 m × 2.4 m, cut in 60 cm lengths. **face·less** *adj* **1** without a face: *a faceless clock.* **2** without individual character. **face·lift** *n* **1** an operation designed to improve the appearance by tightening the skin, removing wrinkles, etc. **2** *Informal* a change designed to improve: *The whole company needs a facelift.* **face·lift** *v.* **face–sav·ing** *adj* that is intended to preserve one's dignity, self-respect, etc.: *a face-saving gesture.* **face value 1** the value stated on a bond, cheque, coin, etc. **2** the apparent meaning: *She took the compliment at face value and did not worry about any hidden meaning.* **fa·cial** ['feiʃəl] *adj* to do with the face: *facial expression, facial tissue. n Informal* a cosmetic treatment of the face. **fa·cial·ly** *adv.* **fac·ing** *n* **1** a layer of material covering a surface: *The front of the courthouse has a marble facing.* **2** a lining along the inside edges of the front opening, neckline, etc. of a garment.

SYNONYMS
Face is the common word, but especially emphasizes the physical features: *That child has a pretty face.* **Countenance** is formal and emphasizes the looks, especially as they show a person's thoughts or feelings: *He has a cheerful countenance.*

fac·et ['fæsɪt] *n* **1** any of the flat surfaces of a cut gem. **2** the surface of any of the segments of a compound eye of an insect, etc. **3** an aspect, as of a personality: *Selfishness was a facet of his character that we seldom saw.* ⟨French *facette; face.* See FACE.⟩
fac·et·ed *adj* (in combination) having facets: *multifaceted.*

fa·ce·tious [fə'siʃəs] *adj* **1** attempting to be humorous. **2** not to be taken seriously. **fa·ce·tious·ly** *adv.* **fa·ce·tious·ness** *n.* ⟨Latin *facetia* jest; *facetus* witty⟩

fac·ile ['fæsail] *or* ['fæsəl] *adj* **1** easily done, used, etc.: *facile methods.* **2** moving, working, etc. with ease: *a facile tongue.* **3** superficial or insincere: *facile answers to complex questions.* **fac·ile·ly** *adv.* **fac·ile·ness** *n.* ⟨Latin *facilis* easy; *facere* do⟩
fa·cil·i·tate [fə'sɪlə,teit] *v* **1** make easy; assist: *A vacuum cleaner facilitates housework.* **2** help (a meeting) to go well. **fa·cil·i·ta·tive** *adj.* **fa·cil·i·ta·tion** *n.* **fa·cil·i·ta·tor** *n.* **fa·cil·i·ty** *n* **1** ease: *the facility of communication.* **2** the ability to do anything easily. **3** Usually, **facilities,** *pl* something, such as equipment, that makes an activity easier: *sports facilities.*

fac·sim·i·le [fæk'sɪməli] *n* **1** an exact copy. **2** a process for transmitting printed matter and photographs by telephone and reproducing them on paper at the receiving set; fax. ⟨Latin *fac* (imperative) make + *simile* like⟩

fact [fækt] *n* **1** anything known to be true. **2** the quality of being real: *fact, not fantasy.* **3** a criminal act: *an accessory after the fact.* **fac·tu·al** *adj.* **fac·tu·al·ly** *adv.* ⟨Latin *factum* done, pp of *facere* do⟩
as a matter of fact, in fact, or **in point of fact** in truth; actually. **facts and figures** factual information.
fact–find·ing *n* the determination of the facts of a situation. **fact–find·ing** *adj.* **fact–find·er** *n.*
fact of life 1 a part of life that cannot be changed, esp an unpleasant part. **2 facts of life** *pl Informal* information about human sexual functions. **fact·oid** *n* an assumption accepted as a fact.

USAGE
The **fact that** is often a circumlocution for which **that** alone would be more acceptable: *He was quite aware [of the fact] that his visitor had arrived.*

fac·tion [ˈfækʃən] *n* **1** a group in a political party, church, etc., usually in opposition to another such group: *A faction often seeks to promote only its own interests at the expense of the group as a whole.* **2** quarrelling among the groups within a political party, church, etc. ⟨Latin *factio* party, orig, a doing; *facere* do⟩
fac·tion·al·ism *n* a condition characterized by faction: *a democracy threatened by regional factionalism.* **fac·tious** *adj* to do with causing strife. **fac·tious·ly** *adv.* **fac·tious·ness** *n.*

fac·ti·tious [fækˈtɪʃəs] *adj* not natural: *Advertising can cause a factitious demand for an article.* **fac·ti·tious·ly** *adv.* **fac·ti·tious·ness** *n.* ⟨Latin *facticius* artificial; *facere* do, make⟩

fac·tor [ˈfæktər] *n* **1** anything that helps to bring about a result: *Endurance is an important factor of success.* **2** *Mathematics* any of the numbers, algebraic expressions, etc. that produce a given number or quantity when multiplied together: *5, 3, and 4 are factors of 60.* **3** ✹ a person who acts as a representative of a company: *The Hudson's Bay Company formerly employed many factors.* *v Mathematics.* separate into factors. ⟨Latin *factor* doer, maker; *facere* do, make⟩
factor in (or **out**), include (or exclude) as a variable.
fac·tor·i·al [fækˈtɔriəl] *n Mathematics* the product of an integer and all the positive integers below it, down to 1. *Example:* 4 factorial = $4 \times 3 \times 2 \times 1 = 24$ *Symbol* **n!**

fac·to·ry [ˈfæktəri] *n* **1** a building or group of buildings where things are manufactured. **2** ✹ formerly, a trading post: *Moose Factory, Ontario.* ⟨Latin *factoria; factor.* See FACTOR.⟩

fac·ul·ta·tive [ˈfækəltətɪv] *or* [ˈfækəl,teitɪv] *adj* **1** giving permission. **2** optional. **3** of an animal or plant, able to survive in several modes or environments. **4** possible; not certain to happen. ⟨Latin *facultas* possibility of doing, from *facilis* doable; *facere* do⟩

fac·ul·ty [ˈfækəlti] *n* **1** a power of the mind or body: *the faculty of hearing.* **2** the power to do some special thing: *a faculty for arithmetic.* **3** the teaching staff of a university or college. **4** a department of learning in a university: *the faculty of theology, the faculty of law.* **5** the members of a profession: *The medical faculty is made up of physicians, surgeons, etc.* ⟨See FACULTATIVE.⟩

fad [fæd] *n* something people are very interested in for a short time. **fad·dy** *adj.* ⟨origin uncertain⟩
fad·dish *adj* inclined to follow fads. **fad·dish·ly** *adv.* **fad·dism** *n* the following of fads or temporary fashions. **fad·dist** *n.*

fade [feid] *v* **1** lose colour or brightness. **2** wither. **3** disappear: *The sound of the train faded in the distance.* **4** *Slang* make a bet against (the dicer or thrower). ⟨Old French *fade* pale, weak; Latin *fatuus* silly, tasteless⟩
fade in (or **out**) of a screen image or electronic signal, slowly become more (less) distinct or louder (quieter). **fade–in** *n.* **fade–out** *n.*

Fahr·en·heit [ˈfɛrən,həit] *or* [ˈfærən,həit] *adj* to do with a scale for measuring temperature, on which 32 degrees marks the freezing point of water and 212 degrees the boiling point. *Abbrev* **F.**, **F**, or **Fahr.** ⟨G. D. *Fahrenheit* (1686-1736), German physicist⟩

fail [feil] *v* **1** not succeed: *She tried hard, but failed.* **2** be unsuccessful in (an examination, etc.). **3** give a mark of failure to: *The teacher failed a third of the class.* **4** fall far short of what is expected: *The crops failed.* **5** not remember or choose (to do): *He failed to follow our advice.* **6** stop performing or operating: *The engine failed.* **fail·ure** *n.* ⟨Old French *faillir*; Latin *fallere* deceive⟩
without fail surely; certainly.
fail·ing *n* a fault; defect. *prep* in the absence of: *Failing good weather, the party will be held indoors.* **fail–safe** *adj* **1** of a mechanism, incorporating an element that enables it to return to a safe condition in the event of a malfunction. **2** proof against failure: *I have a fail-safe recipe for banana bread.*

faint [feint] *adj* **1** dim: *a faint idea.* **2** weak: *a faint voice.* **3** done feebly: *a faint attempt.* **4** about to faint: *I feel faint.* **5** lacking courage: *Faint heart ne'er won fair lady.* **6** remote: *a faint chance.*
n a condition in which a person is unconscious for a time. **faint** *v.* **faint·ly** *adv.* **faint·ness** *n.* ⟨Old French, pp of *faindre, feindre.* See FEIGN.⟩
faint·heart *n Archaic, poetic.* a faint-hearted person. **faint–heart·ed** *adj* lacking courage. **faint–heart·ed·ly** *adv.* **faint–heart·ed·ness** *n.*

fair¹ [fɛr] *adj* **1** honest: *a fair judge.* **2** according to the rules: *fair play.* **3** pretty good: *a fair understanding of the subject.* **4** not dark; blond: *fair hair.* **5** not cloudy: *fair weather.* **6** beautiful: *fair words.* **7** of good size: *a fair piece of property.* **8** easily read: *fair handwriting.* **9** favourable: *fair wind.*
adv **1** honestly: *to play fair.* **2** directly;

straight: *The stone hit him fair on the head.*
fair·ish *adj.* **fair·ness** *n.* ⟨Old English *fæger*⟩
fair and square *Informal* **a** accurately.
b honestly. **fair enough** an expression of
agreement. **fair to middling** moderately
good. **in a fair way** likely: *She's in a fair way to
be chosen as the valedictorian.* **no fair** *Informal*
unfair (used by children as an interjection).
fair ball *Baseball* a batted ball that is not a
foul. **fair game** a person or thing that is
considered a legitimate object of attack:
Politicians are fair game for cartoonists.
fair–haired *adj* having light-coloured hair.
fair·ly *adv* **1** in a fair manner. **2** to a fair
degree: *fairly good.* **3** actually: *He fairly
beamed when he saw us.* **fair–mind·ed** *adj*
impartial. **fair·mind·ed·ness** *n.* **fair play 1** fair
dealings in any contest. **2** just and equal
treatment of all. **fair sex** women, collectively.
fair shake *esp US Informal* fair treatment.
fair·way *n* **1** an unobstructed way. **2** the part
in a golf course where the grass is kept short,
between the tee and the putting green.
fair–weath·er *adj* failing in time of need: *He
is only a fair-weather friend.*

fair² [fer] *n* **1** a gathering for the purpose of
showing goods, products, etc., often with a
midway: *the Royal Winter Fair, the county fair.*
2 a gathering to buy and sell, often held at
regular times during the year: *a trade fair.*
3 an entertainment and sale of articles: *Our
club held a fair to raise money.* ⟨Old French
feire; Latin *feria* holiday⟩
fair·ground *n* an outdoor space where fairs
are held.

fair·ing ['ferɪŋ] *n* a structure fitted around a
part of an aircraft, motor vehicle, etc. to
reduce drag: *a motorcycle fairing.* ⟨fair¹⟩

fair·y ['feri] *n* a supernatural being of folklore
having magical powers. **fair·y·like** *adj.* ⟨Old
French *faerie; fae* fairy; Latin *fatum.* See FATE.⟩
fair·y·land *n* **1** the imaginary place where the
fairies live. **2** any pleasant place. **fairy tale 1** a
story about beings with magic powers. **2** an
untrue story, esp one intended to deceive;
lie. **fair·y–tale** *adj.*

fait ac·com·pli ['fɛt əkɒm'pli] something
done and so no longer worth opposing.
⟨French = accomplished fact⟩

faith [feiθ] *n* **1** a believing without proof.
2 belief in God, religion, or spiritual things.
⟨Old French *feid;* Latin *fides*⟩
bad faith dishonesty. **break faith** fail to keep
one's word. **good faith** honesty: *to act in good
faith.* **keep faith** keep one's promise; be loyal
or faithful. **keep the faith,** uphold a
particular organization.
faith·ful *adj* **1** worthy of trust: *a faithful
friend.* **2** accurate: *The witness gave a faithful
account of the events. n* **the faithful** a true
believers. **b** loyal followers. **faith·ful·ly** *adv.*
faith·ful·ness *n.* **faith healing** supernatural
healing by touch. **faith healer. faith·less** *adj*
1 unworthy of trust: *A traitor is faithless.*
2 not reliable. **3** without faith; unbelieving.
faith·less·ly *adv.* **faith·less·ness** *n.*

fake [feik] *v* **1** falsify: *The picture was faked.*

2 intentionally give a false appearance of: *to
fake an illness.* **3** improvise: *She got through the
exam by faking.*
n a fraud: *The beggar's limp was a fake.*
adj **1** false: *a fake testimonial.* **2** imitation;
simulated: *fake diamonds.* **fak·er** *n.* **fak·er·y** *n.*
⟨origin uncertain⟩
fake it bluff: *If you don't know the words to the
song, just fake it.* **fake someone out** *Informal*
get the better of someone by deception.

fa·la·fel [fə'lafəl] *n* a Middle Eastern dish of
chick peas and other vegetables, stuffed into
the pocket of a pita. ⟨Arabic *falafil*⟩

fal·con ['fælkən] *or* ['fɒlkən] *n* any of a
family of birds of prey that are active during
the day. ⟨Latin *falcis* sickle; for the hooked
talons⟩
fal·con·er *n* a person who hunts with (or
breeds, or trains) falcons. **fal·con·ry** *n* the
sport of hunting with falcons.

fall [fɒl] *v* **fell, fall·en, fall·ing 1** come down
from a higher level. **2** be depressed: *His spirits
fell when he heard they weren't going.* **3** lose
position, dignity, etc.: *The dictator fell from
the people's favour.* **4** be captured: *The fort fell
to the enemy.* **5** be killed in battle.
6 become: *She fell asleep.* **7** be placed: *The
primary stress of farmer falls on the first syllable.*
n **1** a drop from a higher level. **2** the amount
that falls: *a heavy fall of snow.* **3** the distance
that anything falls. **4** a coming down
suddenly from an erect position: *a bad fall.*
5 destruction. **6** autumn. **7** *Wrestling* a being
thrown on one's back. **b** a contest. **8 falls** *pl* a
waterfall. **9 the Fall** in the Bible, the sin of
Adam and Eve in eating the forbidden fruit.
⟨Old English *feallan*⟩
fall (all) over oneself, be too eager (to help,
please, etc.). **fall apart** disintegrate. **fall back**
retreat. **fall back on a** go back to for safety.
b turn to for help: *He knew he could fall back
on his father.* **fall behind a** fail to keep up.
b be in arrears in paying. **fall down a:** *Our
plans could fall down if we're not careful.* **fall
down on** *Informal* prove a failure at through
lack of effort. **fall flat** fail completely: *The
poor performance fell flat.* **fall for** *Slang* **a** be
deceived by. **b** fall in love with. **fall foul (of)**
a become entangled (with). **b** come into
conflict (with). **fall from grace a** *Informal* lose
favour. **b** turn aside into sin. **fall heir to**
inherit. **fall in a** collapse: *The roof fell in from
the weight of the snow.* **b** *Military* line up in
the correct formation. **fall in with a** meet by
chance: *We fell in with some interesting people.*
b agree with: *They fell in with our plans.* **fall
off** become less: *Attendance at baseball games
falls off late in the season.* **fall on** *or* **upon
a** attack: *Thieves fell on the man and stole his
money.* **b** come across. **c** be incumbent on: *It
falls on me to thank our speaker.* **fall out
a** *Military* leave one's place in line. **b** stop
being friends. **c** turn out; happen. **fall short
(of)** fail to reach some goal. **fall through** fail:
Her plans fell through. **fall to** begin to fight.
b begin to eat. **fall under a** be classified as.
b be subject to: *to fall under her influence.* **ride
for a fall** act so as to get into trouble.

fall·back *n* **1** anything kept in reserve as a backup. **2** a retreating. **fall·en** *adj* shrunken: *fallen cheeks*. *n* **the fallen** *pl* all those killed in battle. **fall fair** ✱ a fair held in the fall, for judging livestock, produce, and crafts, often with entertainment. **fall goose** ✱ a wild goose, esp the snow goose. **fall guy** *Slang* **1** the member of a comic act who is the butt of the jokes. **2** a scapegoat. **fall·off** *n* a decline. **falling–out** *n*, *pl* **fallings–out** *Informal* a quarrel. **falling star** meteor. **fall·out** *n* **1** the radioactive particles that fall to earth after a nuclear explosion. **2** a side effect.

USAGE

Falls is ordinarily used with a plural verb: *The falls are almost dry in August.* When **Falls** is part of a place name, the name is used with a singular verb: *Niagara Falls is receding.*

fal·la·cy ['fæləsi] *n* **1** a false idea: *It is a fallacy that riches always bring happiness*. **2** a mistake in reasoning. **fal·la·cious** *adj*. **fal·la·cious·ly** *adv*. **fal·la·cious·ness** *n*. ⟨Latin *fallax* deceptive; *fallere* deceive⟩

fal·li·ble ['fæləbəl] *adj* **1** liable to be deceived or mistaken. **2** liable to be false. **fal·li·bil·i·ty** *n*. **fal·li·bly** *adv*. ⟨Latin *fallibilis*; *fallere* deceive⟩

fal·low ['fælou] *or, esp in the Prairie Provinces*, ['fɒlou] *adj* of land, left unseeded. ⟨Old English *fealga* pl of *fealh* fallow land⟩
lie fallow be dormant: *Her plan lay fallow until she had money to implement it.*

false [fɒls] *adj* **1** not true; wrong: *false statements*. **2** not real or natural: *a false tooth*. **3** made or done so as to deceive: *to leave a false trail*. **4** *Music* not true in pitch: *a false note*. **false** *adv*. **false·ly** *adv*. **false·ness** *n*. ⟨Latin *falsus*; *fallere* deceive⟩
play false deceive; cheat; trick; betray.
false alarm 1 a warning signal given when no danger exists. **2** a situation that arouses a reaction which proves to be unjustified. **false face** a mask. **put on a false face** assume a certain behaviour in order to deceive. **false·heart·ed** *adj* deceitful; treacherous. **false·hood** *n* **1** lack of truth. **2** a lie. **false step 1** a stumble: *One false step and the climber would fall to her death*. **2** a mistake: *The police were waiting for the suspect to make a false step*. **false teeth** dentures. **fal·set·to** *n* an adult male voice pitched artificially high. **fal·si·fy** *v* **1** make a false version of. **2** lie. **fal·si·fi·ca·tion** *n*. **fal·si·fi·able** *adj*. **fal·si·ty** *n* **1** incorrectness: **2** something false; lie.

fal·ter ['fɒltər] *v* **1** hesitate; waver: *The soldiers faltered as their captain fell*. **2** move unsteadily. **3** come forth in hesitating, broken sounds: *Her voice faltered*. **fal·ter** *n*. **fal·ter·ing** *adj*. ⟨Middle English *faltren*⟩

fame [feim] *n* **1** the condition of being well known. **2** reputation. **famed** *adj*. **fa·mous** *adj*. **fa·mous·ly** *adv*. ⟨Latin *fama*; *fari* speak⟩

fa·mil·iar [fə'mɪljər] *adj* **1** often experienced: *a familiar tune*. **2** well acquainted: *familiar with French culture*. **3** intimate: *familiar friends*. **4** too friendly: *a familiar manner*. *n* **1** a close friend. **2** a demon supposed to serve a particular person. **fa·mil·iar·ly** *adv*. ⟨Latin *familiaris*; *familia*. See FAMILY.⟩
fa·mil·iar·i·ty [fə,mɪli'ɛrəti] *or* [-'ærəti] *n* **1** close acquaintance. **2** a freedom of behaviour suitable only to friends. **fa·mil·iar·ize** *v* make well acquainted: *Familiarize yourself with the rules*. **fa·mil·iar·i·za·tion** *n*.

fam·i·ly ['fæməli] *n* **1** a parent, his or her spouse or partner if any, and his or her child or children. **2** the children of a father and mother: *Do they have a family?* **3** a group of related people living in the same house. **4** all of a person's relatives. **5** *Biology* a major category, more specific than the order and more general than the genus. **6** *Linguistics* a group of related languages. **7** *Ecology* a community of organisms belonging to the same species. **8** *Mathematics* a group of curves, functions, etc., that have some property in common. **9** any group of related or similar things. **fa·mil·ial** [fə'mɪljəl] *or* [fə'mɪliəl] *adj*. ⟨Latin *familia* household; *famulus* servant⟩
in the family way *Informal* pregnant.
family allowance 1 an allowance paid to members of the armed forces, often to cover expenses overseas. **2 Family Allowance** ✱ formerly, an allowance paid by the federal government for children up to the age of 16 who are maintained by parents and guardians. It has been replaced by the Child Tax Benefit (or Credit). **family name 1** surname; last name. **2** the reputation of a family. **family planning** birth control. **family room** a room in a house used informally for conversation, games, etc. **family skeleton** a cause of shame that a family tries to keep secret: *Their family skeleton was the desertion of their grandfather to the enemy*. **family tree** a diagram showing the relationships of all the members of a family.

fam·ine ['fæmɪn] *n* **1** starvation. **2** a lack of food in a place: *famines in India*. **3** a very great shortage of anything: *a coal famine*. ⟨French, from *faim* hunger; Latin *fames*⟩

fam·ish ['fæmɪʃ] *v* be or make extremely hungry. **fam·ished** *adj*. ⟨Latin *fames* hunger; modelled on verbs in *-ish*⟩

fa·mous See FAME.

fan[1] [fæn] *n* **1** a device with which to stir the air: *A hand fan opens out to be wide at the top*. **2** anything spread out like an open hand fan. **3** any of various devices with blades revolving round a central hublike part. *v* **fanned, fan·ning 1** make a current of (air) with a fan, etc. **2** stir up: *Cruel treatment fanned their dislike into hate*. **3** *Baseball Slang* strike out: *The pitcher fanned five batters*. **fan·like** *adj*. ⟨Old English *fann*; Latin *vannus* winnowing fan⟩
fan out spread out like an open hand fan.
fan belt the belt that drives the fan to cool an automobile engine or other machine. **fan hitch** ✱ a method, first used by the Inuit, of harnessing sled dogs with a lead dog up in front and others on shorter traces fanning out behind it. **fan·jet** *n* turbojet. **fan·light** *n* a

semicircular window like an open fan. **fan·tail** *n* a part spread out like an open fan. **fan·wise** *adv* spread out like an open fan.

fan² [fæn] *n Informal* **1** a person extremely interested in a sport, one of the performing arts, etc., esp as a spectator: *a hockey fan.* **2** an enthusiastic supporter of anything: *a great fan of herbal remedies.* ⟨*fanatic*⟩ **fan club** an organized group of fans of a celebrity. **fan mail** the mail received by a celebrity from fans. **fan·zine** *n Informal* a fan magazine.

fa·nat·ic [fə'nætɪk] *n* a person who is carried away beyond reason by his or her beliefs. **fa·nat·ic** or **fa·nat·i·cal** *adj*. **fa·nat·i·cal·ly** *adv*. **fa·nat·i·cism** *n*. ⟨Latin *fanaticus* god-possessed; *fanum* temple⟩

fan·cy ['fænsi] *n* **1** imagination: *Poetic fancy has produced some great works of literature.* **2** something imagined: *Is it just fancy, or do I hear a sound?* **3** a notion: *a sudden fancy to go for a swim.* **4** a liking based mainly on whim: *They took a fancy to each other right away.* *v* **1** imagine: *Can you fancy yourself living in that house?* **2** suppose: *I fancy she is about sixty.* **3** like or be fond of: *He fancied the idea.* *adj* **1** having great technical skill and grace: *fancy dancing.* **2** not plain or simple: *a fancy costume.* **fan·ci·ly** *adv*. **fan·ci·ness** *n*. ⟨*fantasy*⟩ **fancy oneself** think too highly of oneself: **fan·ci·er** *n* a person who is knowledgeable about the breeding of particular kinds of plants or animals: *a dog fancier.* **fan·ci·ful** *adj* **1** quaint; whimsical: *fanciful decorations.* **2** influenced by fancy: *a fanciful mood.* **3** unreal: *a fanciful account of the events.* **fan·ci·ful·ness** *n*. **fancy dress** a costume for a masquerade. **fan·cy–free** *adj* not in love.

fan·dan·go [fæn'dæŋgou] *n* **1** a lively Spanish dance in three-four time. **2** a piece of foolery or nonsense. ⟨Spanish⟩

fan·fare ['fænfɛr] *n* **1** a short tune sounded by trumpets, hunting horns, etc. **2** a loud show of activity, talk, etc. ⟨French *fanfarer* blow a fanfare; Arabic *farfār* talkative⟩

fang [fæŋ] *n* **1** a long, sharp tooth by which certain animals, such as dogs, wolves, etc., seize and hold prey. **2** a hollow or grooved tooth by which a poisonous snake injects poison into its prey. **fanged** *adj*. ⟨Old English⟩

fan·ny ['fæni] *n Slang* buttocks. ⟨origin unknown⟩ **fanny pack** *Slang* a small pouch worn around the waist, to hold money, etc.

fan·ta·sy ['fæntəsi] *n* **1** imagination: *The idea of space travel was once pure fantasy.* **2** a fanciful idea. **3** wild imagining: *living in a world of fantasy.* **4** fiction featuring fantastic events in a coherent setting: The Lord of the Rings *is a fantasy.* ⟨Greek *phantastikos; phantazesthai* appear⟩ **fan·ta·si·a** [fæn'teiʒə] *n Music* **1** a composition in which form depends on the composer's fancy. **2** a medley of popular tunes. **3** a literary composition of a similar kind. **fan·tas·tic** [fæn'tæstɪk] *adj* **1** very

fanciful: *The idea of space travel seemed fantastic a hundred years ago.* **2** unreal: *There are fantastic creatures in* The Wizard of Oz. **3** very odd: *The firelight cast fantastic shadows on the walls.* **4** *Informal* unbelievably good, quick, etc.: *fantastic prices.* **fan·tas·ti·cal·ly** *adv.* **fan·ta·size** ['fæntə,saɪz] *v* indulge in extravagant daydreams.

FAQ frequently asked questions.

far [fɑr] *adj* **far·ther** or **fur·ther**, **far·thest** or **fur·thest 1** distant: *a far country.* **2** more distant: *the far side of the hill.* **3** a long way (*from*): *far from home. She is far from stupid.* *adv* **1** a long way off in time or space: *to travel far.* **2** very much: *It is far better to be cautious than to be careless in driving.* **3** to an advanced point, time, or degree: *She studied far into the night.* ⟨Old English *feorr*⟩ **a far cry a** a long way (*from*). **b** completely different (*from*). **as far as a** to a given point: *as far as I can.* **b** with regard to: *There's no problem as far as finances.* **by far** very much: *He was by far the better swimmer.* **far and away** unquestionably: *She's far and away the best player.* **far and wide** everywhere. **far be it from me** I do not dare or want. **far from it** not at all: *Agree with you? Far from it!* **far gone** in an advanced state of decay. **far out a** *Slang* excellent. **b** *Informal* very advanced: *His taste in art is far out.* **far–out** *adj.* **go far a** last long: *That new shampoo doesn't go very far.* **b** tend very much: *A sincere apology goes far toward mending a relationship.* **c** get ahead: *She should go far.* **in so far as** to the extent that. **so far** or **thus far a** to this or that point: *He accepts teasing just so far and then he gets angry.* **b** until now or then: *Our team has won every game so far.* **so far as** to the extent that. **so far so good** until now everything has been fine. **far·a·way** *adj* **1** distant: *faraway countries.* **2** dreamy: *a faraway look in her eyes.* **Far East** China, Japan, and other parts of E Asia. **far–fetched** *adj* hard to believe: *a far-fetched excuse.* **far–flung** *adj* widely spread. **Far North** in Canada, the Arctic and sub-Arctic regions. **far–off** *adj* distant: *far-off lands.* **far–rang·ing** *adj* **1** able to travel over a great distance: *far-ranging missiles.* **2** covering a wide area (of thought, subject matter, etc.): *a far-ranging debate.* **far–reach·ing** *adj* having a wide influence or effect. **far–see·ing** *adj* planning wisely for the future. **far–sight·ed** *adj* **1** having better vision for distant objects than for near objects. Compare NEAR-SIGHTED. **2** looking ahead; planning for the future. **far·sight·ed·ness** *n*.

CONFUSABLES
In formal English, **farther** is used for physical distance and **further** for abstract senses: *We have moved our campsite farther from the road. Her criticisms of the film went further than mine.* Informally, further is often used in all senses.

far·ad ['fɛrəd] *or* ['færəd] *n* an SI unit of electrical capacity. *Symbol* **F** ⟨M. *Faraday* (1791-1867), English physicist and chemist⟩ **far·a·day** *n* a unit of electricity equal to about 96 500 coulombs.

farce [fɑrs] *n* **1** a play intended merely to make people laugh, full of improbable situations. **2** absurd pretence: *The trial was a mere farce.* **far·ci·cal** *adj.* **far·ci·cal·ly** *adv.* ⟨French = stuffing; orig a comic interlude⟩

fare [fɛr] *n* **1** money paid to ride in an aircraft, bus, etc. **2** food: *hearty fare.*
v **1** get along: *If you fare well, you have success.* **2** *Poetic* go; travel. ⟨Old English *faran*⟩
fare·well *n* **1** an expression of good wishes at parting. **2** a departure; leave-taking.

farm [fɑrm] *n* **1** a tract of land where crops or livestock are raised. **2** a tract of land or water where a specific thing is raised for market. See FISH FARM.
v **1** raise crops or animals on a farm. **2** cultivate (land): *They farm 100 hectares.* **farm·er** *n.* **farm·ing** *n.* ⟨Old French *ferme* a lease; *fermer* make a deal; Latin *firmus* firm⟩
farm out a *Sports* send (a professional athlete) to a less advanced league so that he or she can gain experience. **b** turn over to a person, company, etc. for a special purpose: *He farms out the right to pick berries on his land.*
farm club or **team** *Sports* a minor-league team that trains players for the major leagues.
farm hand a person employed to work on a farm. **farm·house** *n* the dwelling on a farm. **farm·land** *n* land used for farming.

far·o [ˈfɛrou] *n* a gambling game played by betting on the order in which certain cards will appear. ⟨*Pharaoh,* from the image on the original cards⟩

far·row [ˈfɛrou] *or* [ˈfærou] *n* a litter of pigs.
v give birth to (a litter of pigs): *She farrowed a litter of six.* ⟨Old English *fearh*⟩

far·ther See FURTHER.

far·thing [ˈfɑrðɪŋ] *n* **1** a former British coin worth a fourth of a penny. **2** something having little value. ⟨Old English *fēorthung; fēortha* fourth⟩

fas·ci·a [ˈfeiʃə] **1** a long, flat band or surface. **2** *Biology* a broad band of contrasting colour. **3** [ˈfæʃə] *or* [ˈfæʃiə] *pl* **-ci·ae** [-i,i] *or* [-i,ɑɪ] a sheet of connective tissue beneath the skin, enclosing and separating layers of muscle. Also, **fa·ci·a. fas·ci·al** *adj.* ⟨Latin *fascis* bundle⟩

fas·ci·cle [ˈfæsəkəl] *n Botany* a small cluster of flowers, leaves, roots, etc. ⟨Latin *fasciculus* diminutive of *fascis* bundle⟩

fas·ci·nate [ˈfæsə,neit] *v* **1** attract very strongly: *The actor's charm fascinated everyone.* **2** hold motionless by strange power: *Snakes are said to fascinate birds.* **fas·ci·nat·ing** *adj.* **fas·ci·na·tion** *n.* **fas·ci·nat·ing·ly** *adv.* ⟨Latin *fascinare; fascinum* spell⟩

fas·cism [ˈfæʃɪzəm] *n* **1** Also, **Fascism,** a strongly nationalistic political party that seized control of the Italian government in 1922. **2** any system of government in which property is privately owned, but all labour is regulated by a national government, while all opposition is rigorously suppressed. **fas·cist** or **Fas·cist** *n, adj.* **fas·cis·tic** *adj.* ⟨Italian *fascio* bundle (as political emblem); Latin *fascis*⟩

fash·ion [ˈfæʃən] *n* **1** a manner; way: *Crabs walk in a peculiar fashion.* **2** current custom in dress, manners, speech, etc.
v **1** create: *She fashioned a whistle out of the stick.* **2** modify to suit a particular use. **fash·ion·a·ble** *adj.* **fash·ion·a·bly** *adv.* ⟨Anglo-French; Latin *factio* a doing or making⟩
after a fashion in some way; not very well. **fashion after** or **on** model after: *My dress is fashioned after yours.* **set the fashion** fix the fashion for others to follow.
fashion plate a person who wears stylish clothes.

fast¹ [fæst] *adj* **1** swift: *a fast runner.* **2** indicating a time ahead of the correct time: *My watch is fast.* **3** not restrained in pleasures: *a fast life of drinking and gambling.* **4** firm: *a fast hold on a rope.* **5** loyal: *fast friends.*
adv **1** swiftly. **2** firmly. **3** thoroughly: *fast asleep.* ⟨Old English *fæst*⟩
play fast and loose be tricky or unreliable: *to play fast and loose with the truth.* **pull a fast one** play a trick or hoax.
fast·ball *n* **1** a variety of softball having a number of features to add speed and action. **2** *Baseball* a basic pitch in which the ball travels at great speed in a direct trajectory. **fast buck** *Slang* money made quickly, often in a dubious manner. **fast food** restaurant food prepared quickly, often for taking out. **fast–food** *adj.* **fast–forward** a mode of operating a tape recorder, in which the tape is wound on at high speed. **fast lane 1** part of the highway reserved for traffic travelling quickly. **2** a hectic, busy life: *life in the fast lane.* **fast·ness** *n* a stronghold: *a mountain fastness.* **fast talk** persuasive patter. **fast–talk** *v.* **fast track** a career path promising rapid promotion. **fast–track** *v.*

fast² [fæst] *v* go without food. **fast** *n.* ⟨Old English *fæstan*⟩
break one's fast eat food for the first time after fasting.

fas·ten [ˈfæsən] *v* **1** fix firmly in place so as to close. **2** impose: *He tried to fasten the blame upon his companions.* **3** direct; fix (the gaze, etc.): *The dog fastened its eyes on the stranger.* ⟨Old English *fæstnian; fæst* fast¹⟩
fasten on or **upon a** take hold of. **b** choose. **c** single out or focus on.
fas·ten·er or **fas·ten·ing** *n* an attachment, device, etc. used to fasten a door, garment, etc.

fas·tid·i·ous [fəˈstɪdiəs] *adj* extremely refined or critical: *a fastidious eater.* **fas·tid·i·ous·ly** *adv.* **fas·tid·i·ous·ness** *n.* ⟨Latin *fastidium* loathing⟩

fat [fæt] *n* **1** any of various kinds of oily substance formed in the bodies of animals and also in some seeds. **2** the richest or best part of anything. **3** ✵ **a** seal blubber. **b** sealskins with attached blubber. **c** seals, esp whitecoats, as the object of the hunt. **4** excessive weight: *Fat increases the risk of heart attack.* **5** anything surplus or not needed: *Government departments have been asked to trim the fat from their budgets.*
adj **fat·ter, fat·test 1** containing fat: *fat meat.* **2** abounding in some desirable element: *fat*

land. **3** profitable: *a fat job.* **4** prosperous: *He grew fat from his vast holdings of land.* **5** fleshy. **6** too fat. **7** *Slang* not much: *a fat chance.* **fat·like** *adj.* **fat·ness** *n.* ⟨Old English *fætt*⟩

chew the fat *Slang* chat. **in** or **into the fat** ✳ among the seal herd: *The hunt began yesterday, with all 11 ships in the fat.* **live off the fat of the land** have the best of everything. **the fat is in the fire** it is too late to prevent unpleasant results.

fat cat *Slang* a person who is rich, privileged, and powerful. **fat farm** *Informal* a resort where people go to lose excess weight. **fat·head** *n Slang* a stupid or slow person. **fat·head·ed** *adj.* **fat·ten** *v* **1** make (a stock animal, etc.) fat or fleshy (often with *up*): *The hogs were being fattened for market.* **2** swell. **3** become fat or fatter. **fatten on** or **upon** take advantage of in order to live well: *He has been fattening on his sons for years.* **fat·ten·ing** *adj* tending to add fat to the body. **fat·tish** *adj* somewhat fat. **fat·ty** *adj* containing fat, or like fat. **fat·ti·ly** *adv.* **fat·ti·ness** *n.* **fatty acid** *Chemistry* any of a group of organic acids, some of which are found in animal and vegetable fats and oils.

fa·tal ['feitǝl] *adj* **1** causing death: *fatal accidents.* **2** causing destruction: *The loss of all our money was fatal to our plans.* **3** decisive; fateful: *the fatal day of the contest.* **fa·tal·ly** *adv.* ⟨Latin *fatalis; fatum.* See FATE.⟩ **fa·tal·i·ty** [fǝ'tælǝti] *n* **1** a fatal accident: *fatalities on the roads.* **2** a fatal influence or effect: *The fatality of many types of cancer has been reduced.* **3** the condition of being controlled by fate: *a struggle against fatality.*

SYNONYMS

Fatal is used of something that is sure to cause death: *a fatal disease.* **Deadly** refers to something likely to cause death: *a deadly weapon.* **Mortal** is used to refer to a state, but not to a weapon: *a mortal wound.* **Lethal** is used of something sure to kill: *a lethal dose.*

---

fate [feit] *n* **1** a power thought to control everything. **2** one's fortune. **3** death; ruin. *v* preordain by destiny. **fate·ful** *adj.* **fate·ful·ly** *adv.* ⟨Latin *fatum* spoken (i.e., by the gods), pp of *fari* speak⟩

fa·tal·ism *n* submission to everything that happens as inevitable. **fa·tal·ist** *n.* **fa·tal·is·tic** *adj.* **fat·ed** *adj* **1** controlled by fate. **2** doomed: *a fated social assistance program.*

fa·ther ['fɒðǝr] *n* **1** a male parent. **2** a person who is like a father. **3** a male ancestor. **4** a founder, inventor, oldest member, etc.: *Alexander Graham Bell was the father of the telephone.* **5** a title of respect used in addressing priests. **6 the Father** God. *v* **1** produce or bring forth, as a father: *to father children.* **2** take care of as a father does. **3** make. **4** foist: *They fathered the crime on him.* **fa·ther·like** *adj.* ⟨Old English *fæder*⟩ **father figure** a man regarded as having the qualities of an ideal father. **fa·ther·hood** *n* the condition of being a father. **fa·ther–in–law** *n,* *pl* **fa·thers–in–law** the father of one's spouse. **fa·ther·land** *n* one's native country.

fa·ther·less *adj.* **fa·ther·ly** *adj.* **fa·ther·li·ness** *n.* **Fathers' Day** a day honouring fathers, celebrated on the third Sunday in June. **Fathers of Confederation** ✳ the men, led by Sir John A. Macdonald, who in 1867 brought about the confederation of the original four provinces of Canada.

fath·om ['fæðǝm] *n* a unit equal to 1.83 m, used in measuring the depth of water. *v* get to the bottom of; understand fully. **fath·om·a·ble** *adj.* ⟨Old English *fæthm* width of outstretched arms⟩ **fath·om·less** *adj* **1** too deep to be measured. **2** impossible to be fully understood.

fa·tigue [fǝ'tig] *n* **1** weariness. **2** any exertion producing weariness. **3** a weakening (of metal) caused by continuous use or strain. **fa·tigue** *v.* ⟨French; Latin *fatigare* tire⟩

fat·u·ous ['fætʃuǝs] *adj* stupid but self-satisfied. **fat·u·ous·ly** *adv.* ⟨Latin *fatuus* foolish⟩ **fa·tu·i·ty** [fǝ'tjuti] *or* [fǝ'tuti] *n* **1** self-satisfied stupidity. **2** a foolish remark or act.

fat·wa ['fætwǝ] *n* a ruling of religious law made by an Islamic authority.

fau·cet ['fɒsɪt] *n esp US* a water tap. ⟨French *fausset; fausser* bore through⟩

fault [fɒlt] *n* **1** a flaw; error. **2** a responsibility: *Whose fault was it?* **3** *Geology* a break in a mass of rock, with one side pushed up. *v* find fault with: *Her work could not be faulted.* **fault·less** *adj.* **fault·less·ly** *adj.* ⟨Old French *faute;* Latin *fallere* deceive⟩ **at fault** deserving blame. **find fault (with)** object (to); criticize: *The teacher was always finding fault with badly done homework.* **to a fault** too much; very: *generous to a fault.* **fault·find·er** *n* a complainer. **fault·find·ing** *n, adj.* **fault·y** *adj* having faults. **fault·i·ly** *adv.* **fault·i·ness** *n.*

faun [fɒn] *n Roman myth* a minor rural god, having a goat's hind legs and a lustful character. ⟨Latin *Faunus* a rural deity⟩

fau·na ['fɒnǝ] *n* all the animals of a particular region or time: *the fauna of Australia.* **faun·al** *adj.* ⟨Latin *Fauna* a rural goddess, wife of Faunus⟩

faux [fou]; *French,* [fo] *adj* imitation; artificial: *faux pearls.* ⟨French⟩ **faux pas** [,fou 'pɑ] *pl* **faux pas** [,fou 'pɑz] a slip in speech, conduct, manners, etc.; blunder. ⟨French = false step⟩

fa·vour or **fa·vor** ['feivǝr] *n* **1** an act of kindness. **2** approval: *to look with favour on a plan.* **3** a gift or token: *The knight wore his lady's favour on his helmet.* *v* **1** show kindness to. **2** approve. **3** treat better than other people. **4** support: *to favour legal reform.* **5** be to the advantage of. **6** treat unusually gently: *The dog favours its sore foot when it walks.* **7** look like: *She favours her mother.* **fa·vour·a·ble** or **fa·vor·a·ble** *adj.* **fa·vour·a·bly** or **fa·vor·a·bly** *adv.* ⟨Latin *favor; favere* show kindness to⟩ **find favour with** win the approval of. **in favour of a** on the side of. **b** to the advantage of. **in one's favour** for one's benefit.

fa·voured or **fa·vored** *adj* **1** treated with favour. **2** having certain advantageous features. **3** having a given appearance (in compounds): *ill-favoured.* **fa·vour·ite** or **fa·vor·ite** *adj* liked better than others. *n* **1** a person or thing liked better than others. **2** a person treated with special favour. **3** *Sports* a person, horse, etc. expected to win a contest. **fa·vour·it·ism** or **fa·vor·it·ism** *n* a favouring of one or some more than others.

fawn¹ [fɒn] *n* a young deer less than a year old. **fawn·like** *adj.* ⟨Old French *faon;* Latin *fetus* fetus⟩

fawn² [fɒn] *v* **1** cringe to get favour: *Flattering relatives fawned on the rich woman.* **2** of dogs, etc., show fondness by crouching, wagging the tail, etc. **fawn·ing** *adj.* ⟨Old English *fagnian; fægen* fain (willing, eager)⟩ .

fax [fæks] *n, pl* **fax·es** a system for transmitting material by electronic means such as telephone or cable. It is received as an exact hard copy at the other end. **fax** *v.* ⟨shortening and respelling of *facsimile*⟩

faze [feiz] *v Informal* (usually negative) disturb; worry. ⟨Old English *fēsian* drive⟩

FBI *US* Federal Bureau of Investigation, a government agency that investigates violations of federal laws.

feal·ty [ˈfilti] *n* **1** in the Middle Ages, the loyalty owed by a vassal to his feudal lord: *to swear fealty to the king.* **2** loyalty; allegiance. ⟨Old French *feaulte;* Latin *fidelitas*⟩

fear [fir] *n* **1** the state of being afraid. **2** a cause for fear: *There is no fear of our losing.* **fear** *v.* **fear·less** *adj.* **fear·less·ly** *adv.* **fear·less·ness** *n.* ⟨Old English *fær* peril⟩
for fear of in order to prevent: *We went as quietly as we could, for fear of arousing the dog.*
without fear or favour impartially.
fear·ful *adj* **1** causing fear: *a fearful sight.* **2** afraid: *fearful of the dark.* **3** *Informal* very unpleasant: *a fearful cold.* **fear·ful·ly** *adv.* **fear·ful·ness** *n.* **fear·some** *adj* causing fear: *a fearsome monster.* **fear·some·ness** *n.*

fea·si·ble [ˈfizəbəl] *adj* **1** capable of being done easily: *a feasible plan.* **2** probable: *The explanation sounded feasible.* **3** suitable: *The road was too rough to be feasible for travel by automobile.* **fea·si·bil·i·ty** *n.* **fea·si·bly** *adv.* ⟨Old French *faisable,* from *faire* do; Latin *facere*⟩

feast [fist] *n* **1** an elaborate meal on some special occasion. **2** an unusually delicious or abundant meal. **3** a special treat: *a feast for the eyes.* **4** a religious festival or celebration: *Easter is an important Christian feast.* **feast** *v.* ⟨Latin *festa*⟩

feat [fit] *n* a great or unusual deed. ⟨Old French *fait,* Latin *factum* (thing) done⟩

feath·er [ˈfɛðər] *n* one of the light, thin growths that cover a bird's skin.
v **1** cover with feathers. **2** turn (an oar) so that the blade is parallel to the surface of the water. **3** turn (the blade of an airplane propeller) to decrease wind resistance. **4** apply pressure lightly and intermittently: *to feather brakes.* **5** provide with a very thin edge. **feath·ered** *adj.* **feath·er·less** *adj.* **feath·er·like** *adj.* ⟨Old English *fether*⟩
feather in one's cap something to be proud of. **feather one's nest** take advantage of chances to get rich. **in fine** (or **high** or **good**) **feather** in very good humour.
feather bed 1 a mattress filled with feathers. **2** *Informal* an easy way of living. **feath·er–bed, -bed·ded, bed·ding** *v* provide with luxuries. **feath·er·edge** *n* a very thin edge. **fea·ther·ing** *n* plumage, or anything suggesting it. **feath·er·weight** *n* **1** a boxer who weighs between 55 kg and 57 kg. **2** an unimportant person: *a featherweight on the political scene.* **feath·er·weight** *adj.* **feath·er·y** *adj.* **feath·er·i·ness** *n.*

fea·ture [ˈfitʃər] *n* **1** a part of the face. **2 features** *pl* the face. **3** any characteristic. **4** a main attraction, esp a full-length movie. **5** a special article, comic strip, etc. in a newspaper or magazine.
v give special prominence to: *The movie featured a young actor.* ⟨Old French *feture,* Latin *factura* formation; *facere* make⟩
feature film a full-length fictional film. **feature–length** *adj* of the usual length of a feature film. **fea·ture·less** *adj* not distinctive or impressive: *a featureless landscape.*

fe·brile [ˈfibraɪl] or [ˈfibrəl], [ˈfɛb-] *adj* **1** feverish. **2** caused by fever. ⟨Latin *febris* fever⟩

Feb·ru·ar·y [ˈfɛbruˌɛri] or [ˈfɛbjuˌɛri] *n* the second month of the year. It has 28 days except in leap years, when it has 29. ⟨Latin *februa* Roman feast of purification, Feb. 15⟩

fe·ces [ˈfisiz] *npl* **1** the waste matter discharged from the intestines. Also, **faeces.** **2** dregs; sediment. **fe·cal** or **fae·cal** *adj.* ⟨Latin *faeces* dregs⟩

feck·less [ˈfɛklɪs] *adj* **1** futile; ineffective. **2** careless: *feckless behaviour.* **3** worthless. **feck·less·ly** *adv.* **feck·less·ness** *n.* ⟨obsolete *feck* vigour, variant of *fect* from *effect*⟩

fe·cund [ˈfikənd] or [ˈfɛkənd] *adj* fruitful; productive; fertile: *Edison had a fecund mind.* **fe·cun·di·ty** *n.* ⟨Latin *fecundus*⟩

fed¹ [fɛd] *v* pt and pp of FEED.
fed up (**with**) annoyed; tired; wearied (by).

fed² [fɛd] *n Slang* **1** a member or official of the federal government. **2 the feds** *pl* the federal government. **3** *US* an agent or official of the FBI. Also, **Fed.**

fed·er·al [ˈfɛdərəl] *adj* **1** to do with an agreement among groups establishing a central organization to handle common affairs while the groups keep control of local affairs: *The Canadian Federation of Agriculture is a federal organization of farm representatives.* **2** Also, **Federal** to do with the central government of Canada. **3 Federal** in the United States: **a** to do with the Federalist Party. **b** supporting the central government during the Civil War. **fed·er·al·ly** *adv.* ⟨Latin *foederis* compact⟩
Federal Court of Canada a court that has exclusive jurisdiction over suits against the

Crown in federal affairs. **Federal Government** or **federal government** the government of Canada, located in Ottawa. **fed·er·al·ism** *n* the federal principle of government. **fed·er·al·ist** *n*. **fed·er·al·ize** *v*. **fed·er·al·i·za·tion** *n*. **fed·er·ate** *v* join in a league, federal union, etc. **fed·er·a·tion** *n* 1 the formation of a federal union. 2 a nation formed by such an act: *Canada is a federation*. 3 a union formed by agreement of organizations, states, or nations: *a federation of students*. **fed·er·a·tive** *adj*.

fe·do·ra [fə'dɔrə] *n* a soft felt hat with a curved brim and a crown creased lengthwise. ⟨probably the play *Fédora* by Sardou, French playwright⟩

fee [fi] *n* 1 a charge: *Doctors get fees for their services*. 2 **fees** *pl* the money paid for instruction at a school or university. 3 in a feudal society, land held by a vassal. ⟨Old French *fieu*, medieval Latin *feudum*; compare Old English *feoh* money, cattle⟩
hold in fee have absolute legal possession of.

fee·ble ['fibəl] *adj* 1 lacking strength. 2 lacking in force: *a feeble attempt*. **fee·ble·ness** *n*. **fee·bly** *adv*. ⟨Old French *feble*, Latin *flebilis* lamentable; *flere* weep⟩
fee·ble–mind·ed *adj* lacking normal intelligence. **fee·ble–mind·ed·ness** *n*.

feed [fid] *v* **fed, feed·ing** 1 give food to. 2 of animals, eat: *Don't disturb the cows while they're feeding*. 3 be sufficient food for: *One of their burgers feeds two people*. 4 supply (material): *to feed stories to a reporter, to feed paper into the printer*. 5 *Theatre* supply (another actor) with (cues). 6 *Sports* pass or give (the puck, ball, etc.) to (a teammate). **feed** *n*. ⟨Old English *fēdan; fōdu* food⟩
feed on a live at the expense of. **b** derive satisfaction, support, etc. from. **off one's feed** too sick to eat.
feed·back *n* information on the results of one's actions that will influence one's future actions. **feed·bag** *n* a bag that can be hung over a horse's head for holding oats, etc. **feed·er** *n* 1 a device that supplies food to a person or animal: *a bird feeder*. 2 anything that supplies something else with material.

feel [fil] *v* **felt, feel·ing** 1 touch, esp in order to know the texture, temperature, etc.: *Feel this cloth*. 2 try to find (one's way) by touch: *to feel your way in a dark room*. 3 have the feeling of being: *I feel lonely*. 4 have sympathy: *She feels for all who suffer*. 5 believe: *I feel that we will win*. 6 have feelings: *Do insects feel?* 7 seem, to the touch or to one's emotional nature: *This cloth feels like silk. Every criticism feels like a rejection*. *n* 1 the way in which something feels to the touch: *the feel of silk*. 2 atmospheric effect: *I don't like the feel of that alley*. 3 a natural talent (*for*): *That tailor has a feel for leather*. ⟨Old English *fēlan*⟩
feel for or **with** sympathize with. **feel like a** want: *I feel like an ice-cream cone*. **b** seem as if there will be: *It feels like rain*. **feel out** find out about in a cautious way: *Talk to them and*

see if you can feel out their reactions to the proposed changes. **feel up to** feel able to do something. **get the feel of** become used to: *Get the feel of that car before you drive to Montréal*. **make (something) felt** behave so that others notice (something): *The critic made his displeasure felt*.
feel·er *n* 1 a special part of an animal's body for touching with. 2 a suggestion, question, etc. made to find out what others are thinking. **feel·ing** *n* 1 the sense of touch. 2 emotion: *Joy and anger are feelings*. 3 sensitivity to the higher emotions: *His work shows feeling*. 4 pity; sympathy. 5 the quality felt to belong to anything: *There is a weird feeling about the place*. 6 **feelings** *pl* susceptibilities: *You hurt her feelings with that remark*. 7 a hunch: *I had a feeling this would happen*. *adj* sensitive. **feel·ing·ly** *adv*.

feet [fit] *n* pl of **foot**.
carry or **sweep off one's feet a** make very enthusiastic. **b** impress. **drag one's feet** act slowly on purpose. **feet of clay** ordinary qualities instead of superhuman. **get (or have) cold feet** See COLD FEET. **get one's feet wet** *Informal* try some new experience. **get to one's feet** stand up. **have one's feet on the ground** be sensible. **on one's feet** self-sufficient: *She helped her relatives until they were on their feet financially*. **stand on one's own feet** be independent.

feign [fein] *v* 1 pretend: *Some animals feign death when in danger*. 2 invent falsely: *to feign an excuse*. ⟨Old French *feign-*, stem of *feindre*; Latin *fingere* form⟩
feigned *adj* 1 not real. 2 invented to deceive: *a feigned headache*. **feign·ed·ly** *adv*. **feint** [feint] *n* 1 a sham attack. 2 a false appearance. **feint** *v*.

feist·y [fəisti] *adj* 1 aggressively energetic. 2 quarrelsome: *My cat is feisty*. **feist·i·ness** *n*. ⟨Middle English *fysten* literally, to fart⟩

USAGE
Feisty is used of people or animals that are small, so their aggressiveness is unexpected.

feld·spar ['feld,spɑr] *n* any of several crystalline minerals composed mostly of aluminum silicates. Also, **fel·spar**. ⟨German *Feld(spath)* literally, field spar + *spar³*⟩

fe·lic·i·ty [fə'lɪsəti] *n* 1 happiness. 2 good fortune. 3 appropriateness: *The writer phrased my ideas with felicity*. 4 a fortunate quality or feature. ⟨Latin *felicitas; felix* happy⟩
fe·lic·i·ta·tion *n* a congratulation. **fe·lic·i·tous** *adj* 1 well chosen for the occasion: *The poem was full of felicitous similes*. 2 fortunate. **fe·lic·i·tous·ly** *adv*.

fe·line ['filaɪn] *adj* 1 to do with the cat family. 2 stealthy; sly: *feline movements*. *n* any animal belonging to the cat family. ⟨Latin *felis* cat⟩

fell¹ [fel] *v* pt of FALL.

fell² [fel] *v* 1 knock down: *One blow felled him to the ground*. 2 cut down (a tree). *n* all the trees cut down in one season. ⟨Old English *fellan; feallan* fall⟩

fell³ [fɛl] *adj* **1** cruel; fierce; terrible: *a fell blow*. **2** deadly; destructive: *a fell disease*. **fel·ly** *adv*. **fell·ness** *n*. ⟨Old French *fel*. Probably related to FELON¹.⟩

fel·la·tio [fəˈleiʃou] *n* sexual activity in which the penis is taken into the partner's mouth. ⟨Latin *fellatus* pp of *fellare* suck⟩

fel·low [ˈfɛlou] *n* **1** *Informal* a man or boy (often as a familiar form of address). **2** a companion. **3** a graduate student who has a fellowship in a university or college. **4** an honoured member of a learned society. *adj* united by the same work, interests, aims, etc.: *fellow citizens, fellow sufferers*. ⟨Old English *fēolaga*, partner (literally, fee-layer)⟩ **fellow feeling** sympathy. **fel·low·ship** *n* **1** companionship. **2** a group of people having similar tastes, interests, etc. **3** a position or sum of money given to enable a person to go on with his or her studies.

fel·on [ˈfɛlən] *n* a person who has committed a felony. ⟨Old French *felon*; ultimate origin uncertain⟩ **fe·lo·ni·ous** *adj* **1** criminal. **2** wicked. **fe·lo·ni·ous·ly** *adv*. **fe·lo·ni·ous·ness** *n*. **fel·on·ry** *n* felons as a group. **fel·o·ny** *n* indictable offence; a major crime such as rape or murder.

felt¹ [fɛlt] *v* pt and pp of FEEL.

felt² [fɛlt] *n* cloth made by rolling and pressing together wool, hair, or fur. *v* of fibres, become pressed or matted together like felt. ⟨Old English⟩

fe·male [ˈfimeil] *adj* **1** to do with the sex that gives birth to young or produces eggs. **2** to do with women or girls: *a female voice*. *n* a person, animal, or plant that is female. **fe·male·ness** *n*. ⟨Latin *femella* diminutive of *femina* woman; form influenced by *male*⟩

fem·i·nine [ˈfɛmənɪn] *adj* **1** having qualities considered characteristic of women. **2** effeminate. **3** *Grammar* to do with the grammatical gender that includes words for female persons and animals. Compare MASCULINE, NEUTER. **4** *Music* of a phrase, ending in a chord or note that does not bear an accent. **fem·i·nine·ly** *adv*. **fem·i·nin·ity** *n*. **fem·in·ize** *v*. **fem·in·i·za·tion** *n*. ⟨Latin *femina* woman⟩ **fem·i·nism** *n* a philosophy advocating rights and opportunities for women which are equal to those that exist for men. **fem·i·nist** *n*, *adj*. **femme fa·tale** [ˌfam faˈtal] *pl*. **femmes fa·tales** [ˌfam faˈtal] *French* a disastrously seductive woman; siren.

fe·mur [ˈfimər] *n*, *pl* **fe·murs** or **fem·o·ra** [ˈfɛmərə] **1** thighbone. **2** *Zoology* a corresponding leg bone in animals and insects. **fem·o·ral** *adj*. ⟨Latin = thigh ⟩

fen [fɛn] *n* a marsh. ⟨Old English *fenn*⟩

fence [fɛns] *n* **1** a railing, wall or other means of enclosing a yard, field, etc. **2** a person who buys and sells stolen goods. *v* **1** put a fence around **2** fight with long, slender swords. **3** use evasive tactics, as in debate. **4** buy and sell (stolen goods). **fenc·er** *n*. ⟨variant of *defence*⟩

mend one's fences *Informal* **a** look after one's neglected political interests. **b** improve one's popularity. **on the fence** *Informal* not having made up one's mind which side to take. **fenc·ing** *n* **1** the act of one that fences. **2** the material for making fences.

fend [fɛnd] *v* ⟨variant of *defend*⟩ **fend for oneself**, *Informal* provide for oneself. **fend off** ward off; keep off. **fend·er** *n* **1** a protective covering over the wheels of an automobile, truck, etc. **2** a guard hung over the sides of a boat or a dock to protect the boat. **3** a device attached to the front of a locomotive, streetcar, etc. to reduce injury in case of a collision. **fender bender** *Informal* a minor car accident.

fen·nel [ˈfɛnəl] *n* a herb of the parsley family, cultivated for its aromatic seeds and leaves. ⟨Old English *fenol*; Latin *fenum* hay⟩

fe·ral [ˈfɛrəl] *or* [ˈfirəl] *adj* **1** untamed. **2** savage. **3** of a human being, living in the wild and not brought up by humans: *Feral children never learn language*. ⟨Latin *fera* beast⟩ **fer·i·ty** [ˈfɛrəti] *n* **1** a wild state. **2** ferocity.

fer·ment [fərˈmɛnt] *v* **1** cause or undergo a reaction in which sugar is converted to ethyl alcohol. **2** agitate or be agitated. *n* [ˈfɜrmɛnt] excitement; agitation; unrest. **fer·ment·a·ble** *adj*. **fer·men·ta·tion** *n*. **fer·ment·a·tive** *adj*. ⟨Latin *fermentum* leaven; *fervere* boil⟩

fermium [ˈfɜrmiəm] *n* an artificial, radioactive, metallic element. *Symbol* **Fm** ⟨Enrico *Fermi*, 20c US nuclear physicist⟩

fern [fɜrn] *n* any of a class of flowerless plants reproducing by means of spores. **fern·like** *adj*. **fern·y** *adj*. ⟨Old English *fearn*⟩

fe·ro·cious [fəˈrouʃəs] *adj* **1** fierce. **2** intense: *a ferocious appetite*. **fe·ro·cious·ness** *n*. **fe·ro·cious·ly** *adv*. **fe·roc·i·ty** [fəˈrɒsəti] *n*. ⟨Latin *ferox* fierce⟩

fer·ret [ˈfɛrət] *n* a domesticated form of the European polecat. *v* **1** drive out of hiding (usually with *out*): *to ferret out a criminal*. **2** find or find out by persistent searching (usually with *out*): *to ferret out the truth of the matter*. **3** search; rummage; dig: *ferreting around in his pockets for a quarter*. ⟨Old French *furet*; Latin *fur* thief⟩

fer·ric [ˈfɛrɪk] *adj* of or containing iron, esp trivalent iron. ⟨Latin *ferrum* iron⟩ **fer·ri·tin** [ˈfɛrətɪn] *n* an iron-storing protein found in the liver, spleen, and bone marrow. **fer·ro·mag·net·ic** [ˌfɛroumægˈnɛtɪk] *adj* easily susceptible to magnetization, as iron is. **fer·ro·mag·net·ism** *n*. **fer·rous** [ˈfɛrəs] *adj* of or containing iron, esp divalent iron. Compare FERRIC.

Fer·ris wheel [ˈfɛrɪs] a large, revolving framework of steel like an upright wheel, with swinging seats that hang from its rim: *Ferris wheels are found in the amusement areas of fairs, exhibitions, and carnivals*. ⟨19c US engineer G.W.G. *Ferris*, its inventor⟩

fer·rule [ˈfɛrul] *or* [ˈfɛrəl] *n* a metal cap around the end of a cane, umbrella, etc. to protect it. Also, **fer·ule**. ⟨Latin *viriola* diminutive of *viriae* bracelets; form influenced by *ferrum* iron⟩

fer·ry ['fɛri] *n* a boat that carries people and goods back and forth across a narrow stretch of water. Also, **fer·ry·boat**.
v carry people or goods back and forth. ⟨Old English *ferian; fær* fare⟩

fer·tile ['fɜrtaɪl] *or* ['fɜrtəl] *adj* **1** capable of reproduction. **2** of soil, capable of producing plants. **3** producing many young: *Rabbits are fertile creatures.* **4** productive of many ideas: *a fertile mind.* **5** *Biology* capable of developing into an individual: *fertile eggs.* **fer·tile·ly** *adv.* ⟨Latin *fertilis; ferre* bear⟩
fer·til·i·ty [fər'tɪləti] *n* the condition or degree of being fertile. **fer·ti·lize** *v* **1** make fertile: *A crop of alfalfa fertilized the soil by adding nitrates to it.* **2** put fertilizer on. **3** *Biology* of a male reproductive cell or sperm, unite with (a female reproductive cell). **fer·ti·li·za·tion** *n.* **fer·ti·liz·er** *n* a substance put on land to make it able to produce more.

fer·vent ['fɜrvənt] *adj* showing warmth of feeling; intense: *a fervent plea.* **fer·ven·cy** *n.* **fer·vent·ly** *adv.* ⟨Latin *fervere* boil⟩
fervid ['fɜrvɪd] *adj* **1** showing great warmth of feeling; intensely emotional. **2** intensely hot. **fer·vid·ly** *adv.* **fer·vour** *or* **fer·vor** ['fɜrvər] *n* great warmth of feeling; intense emotion: *The patriot's voice trembled with the fervour of his emotion.*

fes·cue ['fɛskju] *n* any of a genus of grasses native to temperate and cold regions of the northern hemisphere. ⟨Old French *festu;* Latin *festuca*⟩

–fest *Combining form* a festival: *songfest.* ⟨German *Fest* festival, celebration⟩

fes·ter ['fɛstər] *v* **1** form pus: *The neglected wound festered.* **2** cause pain or bitterness: *Resentment festered in her heart.* **3** decay; rot. ⟨Old French *festre;* Latin *fistula* pipe, ulcer⟩

fes·ti·val ['fɛstəvəl] *n* **1** a special time of celebration: *a Mozart festival.* **2** a competition among drama groups, orchestras, etc.: *a music festival.* **fes·tive** *adj.* **fes·tive·ness** *n.* ⟨Latin *festivalis,* from *festum* feast⟩
fes·tal ['fɛstəl] *adj* of a feast, festival, or holiday; joyous: *A birthday is a festal occasion.* **fes·tal·ly** *adv.* **Festival of Lights 1** Hanukkah. **2** Divali. **fes·tiv·i·ty** *n* **1** (often pl) a festive activity: *Are you attending the festivities?* **2** merriment.

fes·toon [fɛ'stun]*n* a hanging curve of flowers, ribbons, etc.: *The flags were hung on the wall in colourful festoons.*
v **1** decorate with festoons. **2** hang in curves: *Draperies were festooned over the window.* ⟨Italian *festone; festa* festival, feast⟩

fet·a ['fɛtə] *n* a cheese made from sheep's or goat's milk. ⟨Modern Greek *tyri pheta; tyri* cheese + *pheta* from Italian *fetta* slice⟩

fe·tal See FETUS.

fetch [fɛtʃ] *v* **1** go and get: *to fetch the newspaper.* **2** be sold for: *Eggs were fetching a good price that year.* **3** *Informal* attract: *Flattery*

will *fetch her.* **4** *Informal* hit; strike: *He fetched him one on the nose.* ⟨Old English *feccan*⟩
fetch and carry do small jobs. **fetch up** *Informal* arrive; stop.
fetch·ing *adj Informal* attractive; charming: *a fetching outfit.* **fetch·ing·ly** *adv.*

fete *or* **fête** [feit] *or* [fɛt]; *French* [fɛt] *n* a festival; a gala entertainment or celebration, usually held outdoors.
v honour with a fete: *The engaged couple were feted by their friends.* ⟨French = feast⟩
Fête nationale ['fɛt nasjə'nal] June 24, in the province of Québec a holiday celebrating French-Canadian culture, formerly (and still, unofficially) called **St. Jean Baptiste Day.**

fet·id ['fɛtɪd] *or* ['fitɪd] *adj* smelling very bad. Also, **foe·tid. fet·id·ly** *adv.* **fe·tor** *or* **foe·tor** *n.* ⟨Latin *foetidus; foetere* to smell⟩

fet·ish ['fɛtʃ] *n* **1** a material object believed to have magical powers. **2** anything regarded with unreasoning reverence: *Some people make a fetish of style.* **3** a condition in which sexual excitement is derived from an object or a non-sexual part of the body. ⟨French *fétiche;* Latin *facticius* artificial⟩
fet·ish·ism *n* **1** a belief in fetishes. **2** behaviour characterized by a FETISH (def. 3). **fet·ish·ist** *n.* **fet·ish·is·tic** *adj.*

fet·lock ['fɛt,lɒk] *n* **1** the tuft of hair above a horse's hoof on the back part of the leg. **2** the part of a horse's leg where this tuft grows. ⟨Middle English *fetlok*⟩

fet·ter ['fɛtər] *n* **1** a shackle for the feet to prevent escape. **2** Usually, **fetters** *pl* anything that shackles or binds. **fet·ter** *v.* ⟨Old English *feter.* Related to FOOT.⟩

fet·tle ['fɛtəl] *n* condition; trim: *The horse is in fine fettle.* ⟨possibly Middle English *fettel(en)* gird up; Old English *fetel* belt⟩

fet·tu·ci·ne [,fɛtu'tʃini] *n sg and pl* narrow, flat strips of pasta. Also, **fet·tu·cci·ne, fet·tu·ci·ni.** ⟨Italian⟩

fe·tus ['fitəs] *n* the unborn young of a vertebrate, esp a mammal, and esp during the later period of its development. Compare EMBRYO. Also, **foe·tus.** **fe·tal** *or* **foe·tal** *adj.* ⟨Latin⟩
fetal alcohol syndrome a syndrome of characteristic congenital malformations and mental retardation, resulting from prenatal exposure to alcohol.

feud [fjud] *n* **1** a deadly quarrel between families, tribes, etc., passed down from generation to generation. **2** a prolonged and bitter quarrel. **feud** *v.* ⟨Old French *fe(i)de;* Old High German *fehida* enmity⟩

feu·dal·ism ['fjudə,lɪzəm] *n* **1** the social, economic, and political system of Western Europe in the Middle Ages. **2** any system that resembles this. Also, **feudal system. feu·dal** *adj.* **feu·dal·ist** *n.* **feu·dal·is·tic** *adj.* ⟨Medieval Latin *feudum;* Germanic. Compare FEE.⟩

fe·ver ['fivər] *n* **1** an unhealthy condition of the body in which the temperature is higher than normal. **2** any of various diseases that cause fever. **3** an excited, restless condition.

fe·vered *adj.* **fe·ver·ish** *adj.* **fe·ver·ish·ly** *adv.* **fe·ver·ish·ness** *n.* ⟨Old English *fefer;* Latin *febris*⟩

fever blister COLD SORE. **fe·ver·few** *n* a plant believed to be useful in reducing a fever and preventing migraines. **fever pitch** a state of intense excitement or frenzied activity.

few [fju] *adj* not many.
n **1** a small number: *Only a few had bicycles.* **2 the few** a small, privileged group. **few·ness** *n.* ⟨Old English *fēawe*⟩
few and far between very few or infrequent. **quite a few** *Informal* a good many: *We caught ten fish, but quite a few got away.*

CONFUSABLES
Fewer refers only to number and to things that are counted: *Fewer cars were on the road.* Except in informal usage, **less** refers only to amount: *There was even less sunshine than the summer before.*

fey [fei] *adj* unusual in any of many different ways, including supernatural, psychic, or otherworldly. **fey·ly** *adv.* **fey·ness** *n.* ⟨Middle English *feie;* Old English *fǣge* fated⟩

fez [fɛz] *n, pl* **fez·zes** a brimless felt cap, usually red, ornamented with a tassel. ⟨Turkish; after *Fez*, in Morocco⟩

fi·an·cé [ˌfiɑnˈsei] *or* [fiˈɑnsei] *n* a man to whom a woman is engaged to be married. ⟨French, pp of *fiancer* betroth⟩
fi·an·cée [ˌfiɑnˈsei] *or* [fiˈɑnsei] *n* a woman to whom a man is engaged to be married.

fi·as·co [fiˈæskou] *n, pl* **-cos** *or* **-coes** a scandalous or embarrassing failure. ⟨Italian = flask; development of meaning uncertain⟩

fi·at [ˈfiɑt] *or* [ˈfiæt] *n* **1** any authoritative command; decree. **2** sanction: *He acted under the fiat of the queen.* ⟨Latin = let it be done⟩

fib [fɪb] a lie about some small matter. **fib, fibbed, fib·bing** *v.* ⟨possibly *fibble-fable,* from *fable*⟩

fi·bre [ˈfaɪbər] *n* **1** one of the threadlike structures that form certain plant or animal tissues. **2** a long, slender filament of wool, cotton, glass, etc. used especially for making cloth. **3** texture: *cloth of coarse fibre.* **4** essential character: *a strong moral fibre.* **5** ROUGHAGE. Also, **fi·ber. fi·brous** *adj.* **fi·brous·ly** *adv.* ⟨Latin *fibra*⟩
fi·bre·board or **fiberboard** *n* a building material made by compressing fibrous materials such as wood. **fi·bre·fill** or **fiberfill** *n* synthetic fibres used as a filling for winter coats, sleeping bags, etc. **fi·bre·glass** or **fiberglass** *n* **1** glass spun into fine fibres. **2** a thick material consisting of matted fibreglass, used for insulation. **3** a material consisting of plastic mixed with fibreglass, used for making boats, etc. **fibre optics** the technology of using glass or acrylic fibre for transmitting light. **fi·bre–op·tic** *adj.* **fi·bril·la·tion** [ˌfaɪbrəˈleiʃən] *or* [ˌfɪbrəˈleiʃən] *n* irregular, usually rapid, twitching of individual muscle fibres within a muscle. **fi·bril·late** *v.* **fi·bro·blast** *n* a type of cell that forms the fibres in connective tissue.

fi·bro·blas·tic *adj.* **fi·broid** *adj* made up of fibres. *n* a tumour made up of fibres.

fib·u·la [ˈfɪbjələ] *n, pl* **-lae** [-ˌli] *or* [-ˌlaɪ] *or* **-las 1** *Anatomy* the outer, thinner of the two bones in the human lower leg, extending from the knee to the ankle. **2** *Zoology* the corresponding bone in the hind leg of an animal. **fib·u·lar** *adj.* ⟨Latin = clasp, brooch⟩

fick·le [ˈfɪkəl] *adj* likely to change without reason: *fickle fortune, a fickle friend.* **fick·le·ness** *n.* ⟨Old English *ficol* deceitful⟩

fic·tion [ˈfɪkʃən] *n* **1** prose writings that tell about imaginary happenings. **2** what is imagined or made up: *He exaggerated so much that it was impossible to separate fact from fiction.* **fic·tion·al** *adj.* **fic·tion·al·ly** *adv.* ⟨Latin *fictio* something formed; *fingere* to form, fashion⟩
fic·tion·al·ize *v* make into fiction: *a highly fictionalized account of frontier life.* **fic·tion·al·i·za·tion** *n.* **fic·ti·tious** [fɪkˈtɪʃəs] *adj* **1** not real; made-up: *Characters in novels are usually fictitious.* **2** false: *The criminal used a fictitious name.* **fic·ti·tious·ly** *adv.* **fic·tive** *adj* **1** imaginary. **2** creative of fiction.

fi·cus [ˈfaɪkəs] *n, pl* **fi·cus** or **fi·cus·es** a tree of the mulberry family. ⟨Latin = fig⟩

fid·dle [ˈfɪdəl] *n* **1** *Informal* a violin. **2** *Slang* deception or fraud.
v **1** *Informal* play on a violin. **2** make aimless movements: *to fiddle with a button.* **3** tamper (with): *Don't fiddle with the controls.* **4** *Slang* swindle; cheat. **fid·dler** *n.* ⟨Old English *fithele;* Latin *vitula.*⟩
fit as a fiddle in excellent physical condition. **play second fiddle** take a secondary part. **fid·dle–de–dee** [ˌfɪdəl di ˈdi] *n, interj* nonsense. **fid·dle–fad·dle** *Informal n* trifling action. *interj* nonsense. *v* busy oneself about trivial things. **fid·dle·head** or **fid·dle·neck** *n* one of the young, curled fronds of certain ferns eaten as a delicacy. **fid·dle·sticks** *interj* nonsense! **fid·dly** *adj* requiring delicate handling. **fid·dli·ness** *n.*

fi·del·i·ty [fəˈdɛləti] *n* **1** steadfast faithfulness. **2** reliability in the performance of duty. **3** accuracy: *The reporter wrote her story with absolute fidelity.* ⟨Latin *fidelitas; fides* faith⟩

fidg·et [ˈfɪdʒɪt] *v* move about restlessly.
n **1** a person who moves about restlessly. **2 the fidgets** *pl* a fit of restlessness. **fidg·et·y** *adj.* **fidg·et·i·ness** *n.* ⟨obsolete *fidge* move restlessly⟩

fi·du·ci·ar·y [fəˈdjuʃiˌɛri] *or* [fəˈduʃiˌɛri] *adj* **1** held in trust: *fiduciary estates.* **2** to do with trust and confidence: *A guardian acts in a fiduciary capacity.*
n a trustee. ⟨Latin *fiducia* trust⟩

fief [fif] *n* in feudal times, land held from a lord in return for services. ⟨See FEE.⟩

field [fild] *n* **1** a piece of land used for crops or pasture. **2** a piece of land used for some special purpose: *a playing field.* **3** *Military* the place where a battle is or has been fought. **4** *Sports* **a** an area for athletics. **b** all those participating in a contest or outdoor sport: *A*

Canadian was leading the field. **c** a defensive football, baseball, etc. team. **5** a range of interest: *the field of science.* **6** a place where a scientist, linguist, etc., collects data, samples, etc. **7** *Physics* the space throughout which a force operates. **8** *Computers* **a** a location where a data item is entered. **b** the data so appearing.
v **1** *Baseball, etc.* catch and return (a ball). **2** bring in as player, candidate, etc.: *The party fielded only a handful of candidates.* **3** handle skilfully (esp questions). ⟨Old English *feld*⟩
play the field a *Informal* take a broad sphere of action. **b** *Slang* go out with many different persons of the opposite sex. **take the field** begin a battle, game, etc.
field corn corn grown for fodder. **field day 1** a day set aside for outdoor sports. **2** a day when soldiers perform drills, mock fights, etc. **3** a day of unusual activity, display, or success. **4** a day spent by a scientist, etc., in field work. **field·er** *n Baseball* a player who is stationed to stop the ball and throw it in. **field glasses** binoculars. **field goal 1** *Football* a goal scored by kicking the ball between the uprights and above the bar of the goal post. **2** *Basketball* a goal made while the ball is in play. **field hockey** a game played on a grass field with curved sticks. **field marshal** an officer of the highest rank in the armies of certain countries *Abbrev* **F.M. field·stone** *n* rough stones used for houses, walls, etc. **field test** a test made of a new product, system, etc. in the environment for which it is intended. **field–test** *v.* **field trip** a trip to give students special opportunities for observing facts relating to a particular field of study. **field work** the work done in the field by geologists, linguists, etc. gathering data. **field·work·er** or **field worker** *n.*

fiend [find] *n* **1** an evil spirit. **2** an extremely wicked person. **3** *Informal* a person who indulges excessively in some habit, game, etc.: *She is a fiend for work.* **fiend·like** *adj.* ⟨Old English *fēond* orig ppr of *fēogan* hate⟩
fiend·ish *adj* **1** extremely cruel or wicked: *fiendish tortures.* **2** *Informal* very difficult: *a fiendish exam.* **fiend·ish·ly** *adv.* **fiend·ish·ness** *n.*

fierce [firs] *adj* **1** savage; wild: *a fierce lion.* **2** violent: *a fierce wind.* **3** very eager: *a fierce determination to win.* **4** *Informal* intense: *The heat was fierce.* **fierce·ly** *adv.* **fierce·ness** *n.* ⟨Old French *fers, fiers;* Latin *ferus* wild⟩

fi·er·y See FIRE.

fi·es·ta [fi'estə] *n* **1** a religious festival. **2** a celebration; festivity. ⟨Spanish = feast⟩

fife [faif] *n* a small musical instrument like a flute. **fife** *v.* **fif·er** *n.* ⟨German *Pfeife* pipe⟩

fif·teen ['fɪf'tɪn] *n* **1** five more than ten; 15. **2** any set of 15 persons or things. **fif·teen** *adj.* ⟨Old English *fīftēne*⟩
fif·teenth *adj, n* **1** next after the 14th; 15th. **2** one, or being one, of 15 equal parts.

fifth [fɪfθ] *n* **1** next after the fourth; 5th. **2** one of five equal parts. **3** *Music* the fifth tone from the tonic or keynote of a scale; the dominant. **4** *Slang* a bottle of liquor containing one-fifth of a US gallon, about 800 mL. **fifth** *adj.* **fifth·ly** *adv.* ⟨alteration of Old English *fifta*⟩
fifth column any group of persons within a country who secretly aid its enemies. **fifth columnist. fifth wheel** *Informal* **1** a person or thing that is not needed and is in the way. **2** a trailer or camper.

fif·ty ['fɪfti] *n* **1** five times ten; 50. **2** a 50-dollar bill. **3 fifties** *pl* the years from 50 through 59, esp of a century or of a person's life: *Her grandfather is in his fifties.* **4** any set of 50 persons or things. **fif·ty** *adj.* ⟨Old English *fiftig*⟩
fif·ti·eth ['fɪftiiθ] *adj, n* **1** next after the 49th; 50th. **2** one, or being one, of 50 equal parts. **fif·ty–fif·ty** *adv, adj Informal* half-and-half.

fig [fɪg] *n* **1** any of a genus of trees and shrubs of the mulberry family, bearing seedlike fruits in a fleshy, pear-shaped receptacle. **2** something of little or no value (with negatives): *I don't care a fig for your opinion.* ⟨Old French *figue;* Latin *ficus*⟩

fight [fait] *n* **1** a struggle. **2** an angry dispute. **3** the will to fight: *There's plenty of fight left in him yet.* **4** a boxing match. **fight, fought, fight·ing** *v.* ⟨Old English *feoht,* n., *feohtan,* v.⟩
fight back offer resistance. **fight it out** fight until one side wins. **fight off a** turn back: *Fight off an enemy attack.* **b** overcome: *to fight off a cold.* **fight shy of** keep away from. **put up a fight** offer vigorous resistance.
fight·er *n* **1** one that fights. **2** a professional boxer. **3** FIGHTER PLANE. **fighter plane** a highly manoeuvrable and heavily armed airplane used mainly for attacking enemy aircraft. **fighting chance** *Informal* the possibility of success with a long, hard struggle. **fighting words** a statement that provokes hostility.

fig·ment ['fɪgmənt] *n* something imagined; a made-up story. ⟨Latin *figmentum; fingere* form, fashion⟩

fig·ure ['fɪgər] *or* ['fɪgjər] *n* **1** a symbol for a number. **2** a form enclosing a surface or space: *geometrical figures.* **3** a character: *Samuel de Champlain is a great figure in Canadian history.* **4** a human form: *The poor old woman was a figure of distress.* **5** an illustration: *Figures are used to help explain the process.* **6** a design: *Wallpaper often has figures on it.* **7 figures** calculations using figures: *She was never very good at figures.*
v **1** be conspicuous: *The names of great leaders figure in the story of human progress.* **2** *Informal* think; consider. **3** *Informal* make sense: *That figures.* ⟨Latin *figura; fingere* to form⟩
figure in include as a factor in calculations. **figure on** *Informal* expect: *I didn't figure on spending this much on renting an apartment.* **figure out** *Informal* **a** calculate: *to figure out how much a thing costs.* **b** think out: *to figure out what was meant.* **fig·ur·a·tive** *adj* **1** of words or their use, going beyond literal meaning. **2** having many figures of speech. **3** representing by a symbol: *A globe is a figurative model of the world.* **4** to do with representational art. **fig·ur·a·tive·ly** *adv.*

fig·ur·a·tive·ness *n.* **fig·ured** *adj* decorated with a design. **figure eight** the shape of a figure 8, as traced by a skater, plane, etc. **fig·ure·head** *n* **1** a person who is the head in name only. **2** a carving decorating the bow on a ship. **figure of speech** an expression in which words are used out of their literal meaning to add beauty or force. Metaphors are figures of speech. **figure skate** an ice skate for use in figure skating. **fig·ure–skate** *v.* **fig·ure–skat·er** *n.* **figure skating** *n.* **fig·ur·ine** *n* a small ornamental figure made of stone, metal, etc.

fil·a·ment ['fɪləmənt] *n* **1** a very fine thread. **2** *Botany* the stalklike part of a stamen. ⟨Latin *filamentum; filum* thread⟩
fil·a·men·tous *adj* threadlike.

filch [fɪltʃ] *v* steal (small things): *He filched pens from the teacher's desk.* ⟨origin uncertain⟩

file¹ [faɪl] *n* **1** a folder, cabinet, or drawer for keeping papers, etc. in order. **2** a set of papers kept in order. **3** a line of persons, animals, or things one behind another. **4** one of the vertical lines of squares on a chessboard, extending from player to player. Compare RANK. **5** *Computers* a collection of information stored in a computer under a single name.
v **1** put away (papers, etc.) in order. **2** make application: *to file for citizenship.* **3** move in a file: *The class filed out of the room.* ⟨French *fil* thread (Latin *filum*) and *file* row (Latin *filare* spin a thread)⟩
in single file one after another: *We walked in single file.* **on file** kept in order in a file: *All the reports are on file.*
filing cabinet a cabinet containing drawers for storing files.

file² [faɪl] *n* a steel tool with many small ridges on it, used to smooth, roughen, or shape a surface. **file** *v.* ⟨Old English *fíl*⟩
fil·ings *n pl* the small pieces of iron, wood, etc. that have been removed by a file.

fi·let [fɪ'leɪ] *or* ['fɪleɪ] *n* **1** a net with a square mesh. **2** FILLET (def. 3). ⟨French. See FILLET.⟩
filet mignon [mi'njɔ̃] a small, round, thick piece of choice beef, cut from the tenderloin. ⟨French *mignon* = dainty, pleasing⟩

fil·i·al ['fɪliəl] *adj* of a son or daughter: *The children treated their parents with filial respect.* **fil·i·al·ly** *adv.* ⟨Latin *filius* son, *filia* daughter⟩

fil·i·bus·ter ['fɪlə,bʌstər] *n* the deliberate hindering of the passage of a bill by long speeches. **fil·i·bus·ter** *v.* ⟨Spanish *filibustero*, French *fribustier*; Dutch *vrijbuiter.* See FREEBOOTER.⟩

fil·i·gree ['fɪlə,gri] *n* lacelike ornamental work of gold or silver wire. **fil·i·gree** *v, adj.* ⟨Italian *filigrana*; Latin *filum* thread + *granum* grain⟩

fill [fɪl] *v* **1** make or become full: *to fill a cup. The hall filled rapidly.* **2** satisfy the hunger of. **3** supply what is needed for: *A store fills orders, prescriptions, etc.* **4** stop up by putting something in: *A dentist fills decayed teeth.* **5** do the duties of (a position, office, etc.). **6** permeate, as a smell or sound: *The smell of*

garlic filled the kitchen. **7** fulfil or meet (a need, requirements, standards, etc.).
n **1** enough to fill something. **2** all that is wanted: *Eat and drink your fill.* **3** earth used to make uneven land level. ⟨Old English *fyllan; full* full⟩
fill in a fill with something put in: *Fill in the blanks.* **b** inform: *Fill me in as to what happened.* **c** substitute (*for*): *Can you fill in for me tonight?* **fill–in** *n* a person or thing used to fill a vacancy. **fill out 1** provide information: *to fill out a form.* **2** make or grow larger: *The baby has really filled out.* **fill the bill** come up to requirements. **fill up** fill completely.
filled gold a combination of gold plate with some base metal. **fill·er** ['fɪlər] *n* something used to fill an empty time or space or to increase bulk: *Those quotes in her essay are just filler.* **fill·ing** *n* anything put in to fill something. **filling station** a place where gasoline and oil for motor vehicles are sold.

fil·let ['fɪlɪt] *n* **1** a narrow band or strip of any material. **2** [fɪ'leɪ] a slice of fish, meat, etc. without bones or fat; filet.
v [fɪ'leɪ] cut (fish, meat, etc.) into fillets. ⟨French *filet* diminutive of *fil* thread; Latin *filum*⟩

fil·lip ['fɪləp] *n* a stimulus. **fil·lip** *v.* ⟨probably imitative⟩

fil·ly ['fɪli] *n* a young female horse, less than four or five years old. ⟨Old Norse *fylja*⟩

film [fɪlm] *n* **1** a very thin layer: *a film of oil.* **2** cellulose material used in making photographic negatives or transparencies. **3** a movie. **4** filmmaking as an art form.
v **1** cover or become covered with a film (sometimes with *over*): *His eyes filmed with tears.* **2** make a movie. **film·like** *adj.* ⟨Old English *filmen*; related to *fell* skin⟩
film·go·er *n* a person who goes to see movies regularly. **film·ic** *adj* to do with movies, esp with regard to visual features or qualities. **film·mak·er** *n* a person who makes movies. **film·mak·ing** *n.* **film noir** [nwar] a movie that is shot in sombre tones, and characterized by a mood of cynicism. **film·strip** *n* a series of still pictures put on film, to be projected in sequence. **film·y** *adj* like a film; very thin: *a filmy nightgown.* **film·i·ly** *adv.* **film·i·ness** *n.*

fil·ter ['fɪltər] *n* **1** a device for straining out substances from a liquid or gas. **2** the porous material used in such a device: *coffee filters.* **3** a device for controlling certain light rays, electric currents, etc. **4** any means of preventing or permitting the progress of certain elements: *This questionnaire acts as a filter for new applicants.* **fil·ter** *v, adj.* ⟨Latin *filtrum* felt; Germanic⟩
filter tip a cigarette with an attached filter. **fil·ter–tip** *or* **fil·ter–tipped** *adj.* **fil·trate** *n* liquid that has been passed through a filter. *v* pass through a filter. **fil·tra·tion** *n.*

filth [fɪlθ] *n* **1** foul, disgusting dirt: *garbage and other filth.* **2** obscene words, images, or thoughts. **filth·y** *adj.* **filth·i·ly** *adv.* **filth·i·ness** *n.* ⟨Old English *fylth; fúl* foul⟩

fin [fɪn] *n* **1** a movable, winglike part of a

fish's body. **2** something like a fin in shape or use. **fin·like** *adj.* **finned** *adj.* ⟨Old English *finn*⟩ **fin·back** *n* rorqual.

fi·na·gle [fə'neigəl] *v Informal* **1** manage to get craftily: *He finagled his way into the job.* **2** cheat; swindle. **fi·na·gler** *n.* ⟨UK dialect *fainaigue* renege at cards; origin uncertain⟩

fi·nal ['faɪnəl] *adj* **1** at the end: *a final consonant.* **2** settling the question: *The judge's decision is final.* *n* **1 finals** *pl* the last or deciding set in a series of contests, examinations, etc. **2** *Music* a tonic note. **fi·nal·ize** *v.* **fi·nal·ly** *adv.* ⟨Latin *finalis; finis* end⟩

fi·na·le [fə'næli] *or* [fə'nɑli] *n* the last part of an artistic performance. **fi·nal·ist** *n* a person who takes part in the deciding set in a series of contests, etc. **fi·nal·i·ty** [fə'næləti] *or* [faɪ'næləti] *n* the fact of being final or settled: *an air of finality.*

fi·nance ['faɪnæns] *or* [fə'næns]*n* **1** money matters. **2** the management of large sums of public or private money. **Public finance** is the management of government revenue and expenditure. **3 finances** *pl* money matters; money; funds; revenues. *v* provide or get money for: *Her friends helped her finance a business.* **fi·nan·cial** *adj.* **fi·nan·cial·ly** *adv.* ⟨Old French *finance* ending, settlement of a debt; *fin* end, Latin *finis*⟩ **fin·an·cier** [ˌfaɪnən'sir], [ˌfɪnən'sir], *or* [fə'nænsiər] *n* a person skilled in matters involving large sums of money.

finch [fɪntʃ] *n* any of a family of songbirds having a short, conical bill for crushing seeds. ⟨Old English *finc*⟩

find [faɪnd] *v* **found, find·ing 1** come upon: *I found him waiting for me.* **2** look for and get: *Please find my hat for me.* **3** discover: *See what I've found!* **4** get the use of: *Can you find time to do this?* **5** *Law* decide: *The jury found the accused man guilty.* *n* something found, esp something exciting or valuable: *This rare old book was quite a find.* **find·er** *n.* ⟨Old English *findan*⟩ **find oneself a** become aware of being: *He found himself in trouble.* **b** learn one's abilities and make good use of them. **find out a** learn about. **b** cause the true character of (something or someone) to become known: *Their carelessness will find them out.* **find·ing** *n* (often *pl*) a conclusion reached after an examination of facts, data, etc. by a commission, judge, etc.: *The Commission will publish its findings next spring.*

fin de siè·cle [fɛ̃dəˈsjɛkl] *French* the end of the century.

fine¹ [faɪn] *adj* **1** of very high quality: *a fine speech.* **2** very small or thin: *fine wire.* **3** sharp: *a tool with a fine edge.* **4** not coarse: *fine linen.* **5** subtle: *The law makes fine distinctions.* **6** pleasant; bright: *fine weather.* **7** in good health: *I feel fine.* *v* make fine or finer; become fine or finer. *adv Informal* excellently. **fine·ly** *adv.* **fine·ness** *n.* ⟨Old French *fin* fine; Latin *finire* finish⟩ **in fine a** finally. **b** in a few words; briefly.

fine art 1 works of art. **2** any of music, dance, drama, literature, or the visual arts. **3** any skill requiring dexterity, creativity, etc. (sometimes used facetiously): *the fine art of wine-tasting.* **fine–drawn** *adj* **1** drawn out until very thin. **2** very subtle: *fine-drawn distinctions.* **fine print** details printed in small print on a document. **fin·er·y** *n* showy clothes, ornaments, etc. **fi·nesse** [fə'nɛs] *n* **1** delicacy of execution: *That artist shows wonderful finesse.* **2** the skilful handling of a delicate situation. **fi·nesse** *v.* **fine–toothed** *adj* having very closely set teeth: *a fine-toothed saw.* **go over with a fine–toothed comb** examine carefully. **fine–tune** *v* **1** make small adjustments to the tuning of (a radio, TV set, etc.). **2** make small adjustments to (a plan of action, idea, etc.) to make it better.

SYNONYMS

Fine is the general word: *He does fine work.* **Choice** = of fine quality, usually carefully picked: *She selected a choice piece of jade.*

fine² [faɪn] *n* money paid as a punishment. *v* cause to pay a fine. ⟨Old French *fin*. See FINANCE.⟩

fin·ger ['fɪŋgər] *n* **1** one of the five end parts of the hand, esp the four besides the thumb. **2** anything shaped or used like a finger. *v* **1** touch with the fingers. **2** *Slang* point out; betray. ⟨Old English⟩ **burn one's fingers** get into trouble by meddling. **have a finger in the pie a** take part in doing something. **b** meddle; interfere. **have (or keep) one's fingers crossed** wish for good luck. **lay a finger on** touch to any degree (in the conditional or negative): *If you lay a finger on the child, you'll be sorry!* **lift a finger,** expend the least effort (in the negative): *He didn't lift a finger to help.* **put one's finger on** point out exactly. **put the finger on** *Slang* single out for slaying (by a gang). **twist around one's little finger** manage (a person) easily. **work one's fingers to the bone** work extremely hard.

fin·ger·board *n* a strip of wood on the neck of a violin, guitar, etc. against which the strings are pressed. **finger bowl** a small bowl to hold water for rinsing the fingers during or after a meal. **finger food** snack food to be eaten with the fingers, such as raw vegetables and dip. **fin·ger·ing** *n* **1** a touching with the fingers. **2** a way of using the fingers in playing certain musical instruments, or the signs on a piece of music to show this. **fin·ger·ling** *n* a young fish. **fin·ger·nail** *n* the hard layer of hornlike substance at the end of a finger. **fin·ger·paint** *v* paint with the fingers, palms, etc. instead of with brushes. **finger paint. finger painting. fin·ger·print** *n* **1** the markings on the inner surface of the last joint of a finger or thumb. **2** any identifying feature. *v* take an ink impression of the fingerprints of. **fin·ger·tip** *n* the very end or tip of the finger. **have at one's fingertips** be ready with. **(right down) to the (or one's) fingertips** to the depth of one's being: *a perfectionist to the fingertips.*

fin·i·al ['fɪnɪəl] *or* ['faɪnɪəl] *n Architecture* an ornament on the top of a roof, the end of a curtain rod, etc. ⟨Latin *finium,* from *finis* end⟩

fin·ick·y ['fɪnɪki] *adj* too precise or fussy: *He's terribly finicky about his food.* ⟨obsolete *finical,* from FINE[1]⟩

fin·ish ['fɪnɪʃ] *v* **1** bring (action, speech, etc.) to an end. **2** come to an end: *The race didn't finish until after dark.* **3** achieve a place in a contest: *to finish third.* **4** use up completely. *n* **1** the end. **2** a polished condition. **3** the mode of completion of something: *a slow finish.* **5** demise or downfall: *This expedition will be the finish of me.* **fin·ished** *adj.* **fin·ish·er** *n.* ⟨Old French *feniss-,* stem of *fenir;* Latin *finire*⟩
finish off a complete something. **b** destroy. **finish up a** complete. **b** use up completely. **finish with a** complete. **b** stop being friends with. **c** finish using: *Have you finished with my book yet?* **in at the finish** present at the end.
finishing touch a detail that completes by adding beauty or style.

fi·nite ['faɪnaɪt] *adj* **1** having limits: *our finite existence.* **2** *Mathematics* **a** of a number, capable of being reached by counting. **b** of a set, containing a definite number of elements. ⟨Latin *finitus* pp of *finire* finish⟩

fink [fɪŋk] *n Slang* **1** informer. **2** strikebreaker. **3** any unpleasant person. *v* be a tattletale; inform (*on*). ⟨German = finch; applied 18c by students at Jena to those not in any fraternity⟩

fiord [fjɔrd] *n* a narrow bay of the sea between high cliffs. Also, **fjord.** ⟨Norwegian⟩

fir [fɜr] *n* any of a genus of evergreen trees of the pine family, with leaves shaped like flattened needles and bearing upright cones. ⟨possibly Old English *fyrh* or Old Norse *fyri-*⟩

fire [faɪr] *n* **1** the flame, heat, and light caused by something burning. **2** a burning mass of fuel: *Put more wood on the fire.* **3** a destructive burning: *A fire destroyed the factory.* **4** passion; enthusiasm. **5** the shooting or discharge of guns, etc.: *enemy fire.* *v* **1** cause to burn. **2** begin to burn. **3** dry with heat: *Bricks are fired to make them hard.* **4** arouse: *to fire the imagination.* **5** shoot: *to fire a rocket.* **6** direct with force and speed: *to fire questions at someone.* **7** *Informal* dismiss from a job. **8** ignite fuel inside an engine: *The engine fired at once.* ⟨Old English *fȳr*⟩
catch fire begin to burn. **fight fire with fire,** respond in kind to an opponent's attack. **fire away** *Informal* begin to speak. **fire up a** start a fire in a furnace, etc. **b** make enthusiastic. **c** set a machine in operation. **go through fire and water** endure many troubles or dangers. **hang fire** be slow in acting. **on fire a** burning. **b** excited. **open fire** begin to shoot. **play with fire** meddle with something dangerous. **set fire to** cause to burn. **set on fire** cause to burn. **set the world on fire** become brilliant and famous. **take fire a** become enthusiastic. **b** become suddenly and intensely active, successful, or popular. **under fire a** exposed to enemy guns.

b attacked; blamed.

fi·er·y ['faɪri] *adj* **1** to do with fire: *a fiery red.* **2** full of spirit: *a fiery speech.* **3** easily aroused: *a fiery temper.* **fi·er·i·ly** *adv.* **fi·er·i·ness** *n.* **fire alarm** a device that signals that a fire has broken out. **fire·arm** *n* rifle, pistol, or other weapon to shoot with. **fire·ball** *n* **1** anything that looks like a ball of fire, such as a ball of lightning, or a large meteor. **2** *Informal* a person who possesses great enthusiasm. **fire·bomb** *n* an incendiary bomb. *v* attack with firebombs. **fire·bomb·er** *n.* **fire·bomb·ing** *n.* **fire·box** *n* **1** the place for the fire in a furnace, indoor fireplace, etc. **fire·brand** *n* a person who stirs up others, for good or ill. **fire·break** *n* a strip of land that has been cleared to prevent the spreading of a fire. **fire brigade** a body of people organized to fight fires. **fire·bug** *n Informal* a person who has a mania for setting things on fire. **fire chief** the head of a fire department. **fire·crack·er** *n* a paper roll containing gunpowder. **fire department** a municipal department in charge of fighting fires. **fire door** a door made of fireproof material. **fire drill** drill for pupils in a school, etc., to train them in case of fire. **fire–eat·er** *n* **1** an entertainer who pretends to eat fire. **2** a person who is too ready to fight. **fire engine** or **fire·truck** a truck with equipment to put out fires. **fire escape** a stairway, ladder, etc. to use in case of fire. **fire extinguisher** a container of chemicals that can be sprayed upon fire to put it out. **fire·fight·er** *n* **1** a member of a fire department. **2** a person who fights forest fires. **fire·fight·ing** *n.* **fire·fly** *n* any of a family of nocturnal beetles with an abdominal organ by means of which they produce flashes of light. **fire hall** or **fire station** ✱ **1** a building in which firefighting equipment is kept. **2** the headquarters of a fire department. **fire hydrant** a connection to the water main for firefighters, placed at intervals along a street. **fire irons** tools, such as a poker, needed for tending a fire. **fire·light** *n* the light from a fire. **fire opal** an orange-red opal. **fire·place** *n* a place built to hold a fire. **fire·pow·er** *n* the amount of fire deliverable by a military unit, by a particular weapon, etc. **fire·proof** *adj* almost impossible to burn: *A building made entirely of steel and concrete is fireproof. v* make fireproof. **fire rang·er** *n* ✱ a government employee hired to prevent and put out forest fires on Crown lands. **fire sale** a sale of goods damaged as a result of a fire. **fire·side** *n* **1** the space around a fireplace. **2** the home. **fire–spot·ter** *n* a person whose work is watching for and locating forest fires. **fire·storm** *n* **1** a large fire with strong winds, such as started by a nuclear explosion. **2** a violent outburst: *a firestorm of protest.* **Fire Temple** *Zoroastrianism* a shrine in which a sacred fire is always burning. **fire tower** a tower from which to keep watch for forest fires. **fire·trap** *n* **1** a building hard to get out of in case of fire. **2** a building that will burn very easily. **fire·wall** *n* **1** a fireproof wall. **2** a fireproof shield behind the engine of an automobile or airplane **3** *Computers* a system that prevents unauthorized access to a network. **fire·wa·ter** *n Informal* any strong alcoholic drink. **fire·weed** *n* any of several plants that flourish mainly in newly burned areas, with spikes of purplish flowers. It is the floral emblem of Yukon Territory. **fire·wood** *n* wood for burning as fuel. **fire·work** *n* a (often pl) firecracker, rocket, etc. that makes a loud noise or a fiery display. **firing line 1** any line where soldiers are stationed to shoot at the enemy, a target, etc. **2** the foremost position in a controversy. **firing range 1** an area used for shooting practice. **2** the distance within which specific weapons are effective: *The robber was within firing range.* **firing squad** a detachment of troops assigned to shoot to death a condemned person.

firm¹ [fɜrm] *adj* **1** not yielding easily to pressure; solid: *firm flesh.* **2** not easily moved: *a tree firm in the earth.* **3** steady in motion or action: *a firm grasp.* **4** not easily changed: *a firm purpose.* **5** not changing: *a firm price.* **6** settled: *a firm order.* **firm** *v, adv.* **firm·ly** *adv.* **firm·ness** *n.* ⟨Latin *firmus*⟩
firm up a make or become firm. **b** *Informal* arrange definitely: *Can we firm up the date for our meeting?* **stand** (or **hold**) **firm** remain set in one's convictions despite opposition.
firm·ware *n Computers* the programs stored permanently on a computer's ROM chip.

firm² [fɜrm] *n* a company of two or more persons in business or professional practice together: *an old and trusted firm.* ⟨Italian, Portuguese *firma* signature on a contract; Latin *firmus* firm¹⟩

fir·ma·ment [ˈfɜrməmənt] *n Poetic* the sky. ⟨Latin *firmamentum; firmus* firm¹⟩

first [fɜrst] *adj* **1** happening before all others; 1st: *a baby's first birthday.* **2 a** first in importance: *first vice-president.* **b** surpassing all others in performance: *first in the class.* **3** to do with the lowest gear of a vehicle. **4** *Music* **a** highest in pitch. **b** being the leading player in an orchestra section: *first violin.* **first** *adv.* **first·ly** *adv.*⟨Old English *fyrst*⟩
at first in the beginning. **first and foremost** chiefly. **first and last** taking all together. **first things first** what is most important must come first. **from the first** since the beginning. **in the first place** before anything else. **of the first water** the highest grade. **(the) first thing a** at the earliest possible moment. **b** even the most basic facts (with a negative): *He doesn't know the first thing about hockey.*
first aid the emergency treatment given before a doctor comes. **first–aid** *adj.* **first base 1** *Baseball* the base that must be touched first by a runner. **2** the one playing first base. **get to first base** *Informal* make the first step toward success: *The new worker will never get to first base if she is not punctual.* **first–born** *adj* oldest. *n* the first-born child. **first class 1** the best quality. **2** the class of mail that includes letters, postcards, etc. **first–class** *adj.* **first**

cousin the child of one's father's or mother's sister or brother. **first floor 1** in North America, the ground floor of a building. **2** in Britain and Europe, and sometimes in Québec, the floor above the ground floor. **first fruits** the first products or results. **first–generation** *adj* to do with immigrants who came as adults, or their customs. **first–hand** *adj, adv* from the original source: *first-hand information.* **First Lady** the wife of the president of the United States. **first light** dawn. **First Meridian ✳** the basic north-south line from which lands were surveyed in the Northwest Territories and are now surveyed in the Prairie Provinces. The First Meridian is located just west of Winnipeg at 97°W. **First Ministers ✳** the prime minister and all the provincial premiers. **First Nation ✳ 1** a group of Aboriginal people that make up a cultural community, usually one that is recognized as a band by the Federal Government. **2 First Nations** of or designating any of these peoples. **first night 1** the opening performance of a live show. **2 First Night** New Year's Eve. **first offender** someone convicted of having broken the law for the first time. **First Peoples** the Aboriginal peoples living in Canada. **first person** *Grammar* the form used to refer to the speaker. **first–per·son** *adj.* **first quarter** the period between the new moon and the first half moon. **first–rate** *adj* **1** of the highest class. **2** *Informal* excellent. **first–strike** *adj* of nuclear armaments, offensive as opposed to defensive. **first string** the starting lineup in a sport. **first–string** *adj.*

USAGE

First and last refer to items in a series, usually of more than two: *Her first act in office was to appoint a new chairperson. We left before the start of the last act.* Latest refers to a series that is still continuing: *Have you seen the latest episode?* Last refers either to the final item of a completed series or to the most recent item of a series: *I was pleased with the last election.*

fis·cal [ˈfɪskəl] *adj* **1** financial. **2** to do with government revenue: *fiscal policy.* **fis·cal·ly** *adv.* ⟨Latin *fiscalis; fiscus* purse⟩
fiscal year a year calculated for taxation or accounting purposes: *The company's fiscal year began in April.*

fish [fɪʃ] *n, pl* **fish** or (esp for different species) **fish·es 1** any of a group of cold-blooded aquatic vertebrates that breathe by means of gills. **2** any of various other aquatic creatures (usually in compounds): *crayfish, jellyfish.* **3** *Informal* a person lacking some desirable human trait: *a poor fish.*
v **1** try to catch fish. **2** try to pick up as if with a hook, etc. (with *for*): *He fished for the quarter with a bent wire.* **3** search by groping inside something: *She fished in her purse for a coin.* **4** try to get, usually by indirect means (with *for*): *fishing for compliments.* **fish·like** *adj.* **fish·ing** *n.* ⟨Old English *fisc*⟩
a fish out of water a person who is uncomfortable as a result of being out of his

or her usual environment. **drink like a fish** drink a lot of alcohol. **fish in troubled waters** take advantage of confusion to get what one wants. **fish or cut bait** attack a task head-on or abandon it altogether. **fish out** exhaust the supply of fish in (a lake, etc.) by fishing. **have other fish to fry** *Informal* have more important things to do.

fish and chips pieces of fish fried in a batter and served with French fries. **fish·bowl** *n* **1** a glass enclosure for keeping small fish. **2** any lifestyle in which one is unusually exposed to public view. **fish cake** or **ball** a ball of ground fish, often combined with mashed potato. **fish·er** *n* **1** a North American mammal of the weasel family, with dark fur. **2** a person who fishes. **fish·er·man** *n, pl* **-men** a man who fishes for a living or for pleasure. **fish·er·wom·an** *n, pl* **-wom·en.** **fish·er·y** *n* **1** a place for catching fish: *the Pacific fisheries.* **2** a place where fish are farmed or processed. **fish–eye lens** a wide-angle photographic lens that produces a circular image. **fish farm** a place where fish are bred for the market. **fish flake** a slatted platform for drying fish. **fish hawk** osprey. **fish–hook** *n* a barbed hook used for catching fish. **fishing ground** a place where fish are plentiful. **fishing hut** a small hut towed out onto the ice of a lake, to shelter ice fishers. **fishing lodge 1** a primitive cabin for fishers. **2** a resort for sport fishers. **fishing rod** or **pole** a slender rod for fishing, with a line attached. **fishing smack** a small ship used in fishing at sea. **fishing tackle** rods, lines, hooks, etc. used in catching fish. **fish ladder** fishway. **fish meal** ground-up dried fish used as feed for livestock or as fertilizer. **fish oil** oil obtained from fish. **fish·pond** *n* a pond in which there are fish, esp an ornamental pool. **fish stick** frozen fish fillets in the form of a short, oblong stick. **fish story** *Informal* an unbelievable story. **fish·tail** *adj* like a fish's tail in shape or action. *v* of a motor vehicle, etc., have the rear end swing from side to side out of control. **fish·way** *n* a series of pools built to enable fish to pass over a dam or falls on their way upstream. Also called **fish ladder** or **fish pass. fish·wife** *n, pl* **-wives** a woman who uses abusive language. **fish·y** *adj* **1** like a fish in smell, taste, or shape. **2** of fish. **3** *Informal* doubtful. **fish·i·ly** *adv.* **fish·i·ness** *n.*

fis·sion ['fɪʃən] *n* **1** division into parts. **2** *Biology* a method of reproduction in which the body of the parent divides to form two or more individuals. **3** *Physics* the splitting that occurs when the nucleus of an atom under bombardment absorbs a neutron. *v* undergo or cause to undergo fission. ⟨Latin *fissio* from *fissus* pp of *findere* cleave⟩ **fis·sile** ['fɪsaɪl] *or* ['fɪsəl] *adj* easily split. **fis·sil·i·ty** *n.* **fis·sion·a·ble** *adj* capable of nuclear fission.

fis·sure ['fɪʃər] *n* **1** a split: *a fissure in a rock.* **2** a division into parts. **3** *Anatomy* a cleft in the body. ⟨Latin from *findere* cleave⟩

fist [fɪst] *n* **1** the hand closed tightly. **2** *Informal* the hand. **3** *Informal* handwriting. **4** the grasp. **fist·like** *adj.* ⟨Old English *fўst*⟩ **fist·fight** *n* a fight with the fists. **fist·ful** *n.* **fist·i·cuffs** *n pl* blows with the fists. **fist·note** *n* in printed texts, a special note preceded by the symbol of a pointing fist.

fis·tu·la ['fɪstʃələ] *n, pl* **-las** or **-lae** [-ˌli] **1** a tube or pipe. **2** an abnormal or surgically made tubelike passage connecting the surface of the body with an internal organ or cavity. ⟨Latin = pipe, ulcer⟩

fit¹ [fɪt] *adj* **fit·ter, fit·test 1** appropriate: *fit for a queen.* **2** having the necessary qualifications: *fit for active service.* **3** ready: *fit to receive visitors.* **4** in good physical condition: *They exercise daily to keep fit.* *v* **fit** or **fit·ted, fit·ting 1** be or make suitable to: *Let the punishment fit the crime.* **2** have the right shape (for): *The last piece of the puzzle didn't fit.* **3** measure (someone) for something to be fitted: *They fitted her for her artificial leg.* **4** equip (often with *out* or *up*): *The car is fitted with radial tires.* **5** accommodate: *to fit an appointment into a schedule.* **6** agree with: *Her story doesn't fit the facts.* **7** belong: *She doesn't fit well in our group.* **8** install. *n* the manner in which one thing fits another: *a tight fit.* ⟨Middle English *fyt*⟩ **fit the bill** meet the requirements exactly. **fit to be tied** *Informal* overcome with frustration. **see** (or **think**) **fit** consider it suitable, right, etc. (*to*): *She may see fit to ignore the whole incident.* **fit·ly** *adv* **1** in a suitable manner. **2** at a proper time. **fit·ness** *n* **1** suitability. **2** physical health. **fitness club** facilities for exercise. **fit·ted** *adj* made to follow the contours of the body, furniture, etc.: *a fitted sheet.* **fit·ter** *n.* **fit·ting** *adj* proper; suitable. *n* **1** a trying on of unfinished clothes to see if they will fit. **2** a small part used to join other parts. **3** **fit·tings** *pl* furnishings. **fit·ting·ly** *adv.*

fit² [fɪt] *n* **1** a sudden attack of illness: *a fit of colic.* **2** any sudden attack or outburst: *a fit of laughter.* ⟨Old English *fitt* conflict⟩ **by fits and starts** irregularly; starting, stopping, beginning again, and so on. **have** (or **throw** or **take**) **a fit** have a violent negative reaction. **fit·ful** *adj* going on and then stopping: *a fitful sleep.* **fit·ful·ly** *adv.* **fit·ful·ness** *n.*

five [faɪv] *n* **1** one more than four; 5. **2** any set of five persons or things. **3** a playing card or side of a die having five spots. **4** a five-dollar bill. **five** *adj.* ⟨Old English *fīf*⟩ **five–and–ten** or **five–and–dime** *n* a store selling cheap items, that formerly cost five or ten cents. **five–and–dime** *adj.*

five·fold *adj* **1** five times as much or as many. **2** having five parts. *adv* five times as much or as many. **Five Nations** a former confederacy of Iroquois peoples of the First Nations, consisting of the Mohawks, Oneidas, Onondagas, Cayugas, and Senecas. Members of the Five Nations (now the Six Nations with the inclusion of the Tuscarora) lived in Ontario and Québec. **five·pin bowling** bowling using five pins. **five–star** *adj* **a** of a movie, resort, hotel, etc., of the very best class. **b** having the highest military rank: *a five-star general.*

fix [fɪks] *v* **1** make or become firm; fasten or be fastened tightly: *We fixed the post in the ground.* **2** set: *He fixed the price at one dollar.* **3** mend. **4** hold steady (eyes, attention, etc.). **5** *Informal* get revenge upon. **6** *Chemistry* bring about the combining of (atmospheric nitrogen) with other compounds to create nitrates, ammonia, etc. **7** *Informal* spay or castrate: *Has your cat been fixed?* **8** *Informal* influence the outcome of (a game, race, trial, etc.) by a bribe: *The jury had been fixed.* *n Informal* **1** a position hard to get out of. **2** the position of a ship, aircraft, etc. as determined by obtaining radio signals. **3** a dose of a narcotic. **fix·a·ble** *adj.* **fixed** *adj.* ⟨Latin *fixus* pp of *figere* fix⟩ **be fixed for** *Informal* supplied with: *How are you fixed for baby clothes?* **fix on** or **upon** select. **fix up** *Informal* **a** mend. **b** put in order; arrange. **c** provide with something needed: *We fixed her up with a date.*

fix·ate ['fɪkseɪt] *v* (usually passive) have, or cause (someone) to have, an obsessive attachment (with *on*). **fix·a·tion** *n* **1** a treatment to keep something from changing: *the fixation of a photographic film.* **2** *Chemistry* the process of changing into a more stable form. **3** *Psychoanalysis* a morbid attachment. **fix·a·tive** ['fɪksətɪv] *n* a substance used to keep something from changing. *adj* that prevents change. **fix·ed·ly** ['fɪksɪdli] *adv* in a fixed manner: *to stare fixedly.* **fix·ed·ness** *n.* **fix·ings** *n pl Informal* **1** furnishings; trimmings. **2** ingredients. **fix·i·ty** ['fɪksəti] *n* a fixed condition or quality. **fix·ture** *n* **1** something put in place to stay: *bathroom fixtures.* **2** a person or thing that stays in one place, job, etc.: *He is considered a fixture in the factory.*

fizz [fɪz] *v* effervesce; give off gas bubbles. *n Informal* bubbles; effervescence. Also, **fiz.** **fizz·y** *adj.* ⟨imitative⟩

fiz·zle ['fɪzəl] *v* **1** sputter weakly: *The firework fizzled.* **2** *Informal* fail. **fiz·zle** *n.* ⟨obsolete *fise* breaking of wind. See FEISTY.⟩ **fizzle out** end in failure.

fjord [fjɔrd] See FIORD.

flab·ber·gast ['flæbər,gæst] *v Informal* make speechless with surprise; amaze. ⟨possible blend of *flap* or *flabby* + *aghast*⟩

flab·by ['flæbi] *adj* lacking firmness or force; soft; weak: *flabby cheeks.* **flab·bi·ly** *adv.* **flab·bi·ness** *n.* ⟨variant of earlier *flappy; flap*⟩ **flab** *n* loose flesh on the body.

flac·cid ['flæksɪd] *or* ['flæsɪd] *adj* limp; weak:

flaccid muscles, a flaccid will. **flac·cid·ly** *adv.* **flac·cid·i·ty** *n.* ⟨Latin *flaccidus; flaccus* flabby⟩

flack¹ [flæk] *Slang n* **1** a publicity or press agent. **2** public relations material; publicity. *v* act as a publicity agent: *flacking for an author.* ⟨origin uncertain⟩

flack² [flæk] See FLAK.

flag¹ [flæg] *n* **1** a piece of cloth that shows the emblem of a country, or of some other organization: *the regimental flag.* **2** a piece of cloth that has a special meaning: *A red flag is a sign of danger.* **3** a mark or symbol drawing attention to. **4** *Music* a line added to the stem of a written note less than a quarter note. *v* **flagged, flag·ging** *v* **1** signal, esp by waving a flag: *to flag a train.* **2** draw attention to: *to flag an error.* ⟨possibly from *flag³*⟩ **flag·pole** or **flag·staff** *n* a pole from which a flag is flown. **flag·ship** ['flæg,ʃɪp] *n* **1** the ship that carries the officer in command of a fleet and displays his or her flag. **2** the most outstanding member of any group. *adj* main; leading: *The chain's flagship store is in Ottawa.* **flag·wav·ing** *n* **1** behaviour designed to provoke patriotic feelings. **2** any display of patriotism. **flag·wav·er** *n.* **flag·wav·ing** *adj.*

flag² [flæg] *n* any of various plants having swordlike leaves, such as the blue flag (a wild iris). ⟨Scandinavian; compare Danish *flæg*⟩

flag³ [flæg] *v* **flagged, flag·ging** get tired; grow weak: *My interest in this magazine is flagging.* ⟨related to Dutch *vlaggheren* flutter⟩

flag⁴ [flæg] *n* a flagstone. *v* **flagged, flag·ging** lay flagstones for a path, patio, etc. ⟨possible variant of *flake*⟩

flag·el·late ['flædʒə,leɪt] *v* whip; flog. *adj* ['flædʒəlɪt] *or* [tlə'dʒɛlɪt] **1** long, slender, and flexible, as a flagellum or whiplash. **2** *Zoology* having flagella. **3** *Botany* having runnerlike branches. *n* ['flædʒəlɪt] *or* [flə'dʒɛlɪt] a flagellate organism. ⟨Latin *flagellum* diminutive of *flagrum* whip⟩ **flag·el·la·tion** *n* a whipping. **fla·gel·lum** [flə'dʒɛləm] *n, pl* **-la** [-lə] *or* **-lums 1** *Biology* a long, whiplike tail or part. **2** a whip. **3** *Botany* a runner of a plant. **4** *Zoology* the end of the antennae in certain insects.

flag·on ['flægən] *n* **1** a container for liquids, usually having a handle and a spout, and often a cover. **2** a bottle holding about two litres. ⟨Old French *flascon.* Related to FLASK.⟩

fla·grant ['fleɪgrənt] *adj* notorious. **fla·gran·cy** *n.* **fla·grant·ly** *adv.* ⟨Latin *flagrare* burn⟩ **fla·gran·te de·lic·to** [flə'græntei dɪ'lɪktou] *Law* in the very act of committing the crime, literally, while the crime is blazing.

flag·stone ['flæg,stoun] *n* a large, flat stone, used for paving walks, patios, etc.

flail [fleɪl] *n* an instrument for threshing grain by hand. *v* beat; thrash: *to flail one's arms about.* ⟨Old English *fligel*⟩

flair [flɛr] *n* **1** a natural talent: *a flair for*

making clever rhymes. **2** discriminating taste: *She dresses with flair.* **3** bold creativity. ⟨French *flair* scent, *flairer* smell; Latin *fragrare*⟩

flak [flæk] *n* **1** gunfire from the ground, directed against aircraft. **2** *Informal* insistent criticism: *She got a lot of flak for what she said.* ⟨German, acronym for *Fl(ieger)a(bwehr)k(anone)* anti-aircraft gun⟩

flake[1] [fleik] *n* **1** a soft, loose bit: *a flake of snow.* **2** a thin, flat piece: *flakes of rust.* **3** *Informal* an eccentric or unpredictable person.
v come off or take off in flakes: *The paint had flaked off.* **flak·i·ly** *adv.* **flak·i·ness** *n.* **flak·y** *adj.* ⟨possibly Scandinavian⟩
flake out *Slang* drop with exhaustion.

flake[2] [fleik] *n* a slatted platform used for drying fish; fish flake. ⟨Old Norse *flake, fleke* hurdle, wicker shield⟩

flambé [flɑmˈbei]; *French* [flɑˈbe] *adj* (after a noun) of food, served with alcoholic liquor poured over it and set alight: *peach flambé.* **flambé, -béd** or **-béed, -bé·ing** *v.* ⟨French⟩

flam·boy·ant [flæmˈbɔiənt] *adj* **1** gorgeously brilliant: *flamboyant colours.* **2** excessively decorated: *flamboyant architecture.* **3** given to display: *a flamboyant person.* **flam·boy·ance** *n.* **flam·boy·ant·ly** *adv.* ⟨French, ppr of *flamboyer* to flame⟩

flame [fleim] *n* **1** one of the glowing tongues of light that shoot out from a fire. **2** burning gas or vapour. **3** *Informal* sweetheart. *v* **1** burn with flames. **2** grow hot, red, etc.: *Her cheeks flamed.* **3** give out a bright light. **4** subject to flame.
adj bright reddish yellow. **flame·less** *adj.* **flame·like** *adj.* ⟨Latin *flamma*⟩
flame out of jet engines, fail to function. **flame up** (or **out** or **forth**) burst out quickly and hotly; flare up.
flame·proof *adj* not liable to burn when in contact with flames. **flame–re·sist·ant** *adj* resistant to flame; not easily burned. **flame thrower** or **flame·throw·er** a weapon that directs a jet of burning gasoline mixture, napalm, etc. through the air. **flam·ing** *adj* **1** burning with flames. **2** like a flame, very bright. **3** showing or arousing strong feeling. **flam·ma·ble** *adj* easily set on fire; inflammable. **flam·ma·bil·i·ty** *n.*

> **USAGE**
> **Flammable** and **inflammable** both mean 'easily set on fire'. **Flammable** is used in industry, on warning labels, etc., to avoid all possibility of misinterpretation. The negative is **non–flammable**.

fla·men·co [fləˈmɛŋkou] *n* a style of Spanish Gypsy dance performed with castanets to fast, fiery rhythms. ⟨Spanish = Flemish (of Gypsies' dance celebrating 19c departure from Germany, later confused with Flanders)⟩

fla·min·go [fləˈmɪŋgou] *n, pl* **-gos** or **-goes** any of a family of large wading birds having a very long neck and legs, and plumage ranging from pale pink to scarlet. ⟨Portuguese; Latin *flamma* flame⟩

flan [flæn] *n* a tart or open pastry filled with fruit, custard, gelatin, etc. ⟨Middle French *flaon* tart⟩

flange [flændʒ] *n* a projecting edge on an object for attaching it to another object, strengthening it, etc. ⟨variant of obsolete *flanch*; Old French *flanchir* bend⟩

flank [flæŋk] *n* **1** the part of the side between the ribs and the hip, esp on an animal. **2** the side of a mountain, building, etc. **3** the far right or left side of an army, fleet, etc.
v **1** be at the side or both sides of: *High buildings flanked the alley.* **2** get around the far right or the far left side of. **flank·ing** *adj.* ⟨Old French *flanc*; Germanic⟩

flan·nel [ˈflænəl] *n* **1** a soft, woollen cloth. **2** flannels *pl* **a** clothes, esp pants, made of flannel. **b** woollen underwear. ⟨Middle English *flanen*, Welsh *gwlanen; gwlan* wool⟩
flan·nel·board *n* a board with flannel stretched across it, to which cut-outs will cling on contact, used primarily in nursery and elementary schools as a teaching aid. **flan·nel·ette** *n* a soft cotton cloth with a fuzzy surface.

flap [flæp] *v* **flapped, flap·ping 1** swing or cause to swing loosely: *The curtains flapped in the wind.* **2** move (wings, arms, etc.) up and down. **3** *Slang* become excited. *n* **1** a flapping motion. **2** a flat piece, usually hanging: *The coat had flaps on the pockets.* **3** *Slang* a state of excitement or anger. **flap·like** *adj.* **flap·py** *adj.* ⟨Middle English; probably imitative⟩
in a flap *Informal.* upset; confused.
flap·jack *n* a pancake.

flare [flɛr] *v* **1** flame up briefly: *Wind made the torches flare.* **2** blaze out suddenly (often with *up*). **3** spread or cause to spread outward from a narrower part: *a flared skirt.* *n* **1** a bright, unsteady light: *the flare of a match.* **2** a dazzling light used for signalling. **3** a sudden outburst: *a flare of bad temper.* **flar·ing** *adj.* ⟨Scandinavian; compare Norwegian *flara* blaze⟩
flare–up *n Informal* a sudden outburst of anger, violence, etc.

flash [flæʃ] *n* **1** a brief appearance: *a flash of yellow.* **2** a brief feeling or display: *a flash of wit.* **3** a very brief time. **4** a brief news report. *v* **1** give out a sudden, brief light. **2** pass quickly. **3** *Informal* briefly expose the genitals publicly. **4** *Informal* show off: *to flash a diamond ring.*
adj **1** flashy. **2** using a flash: *a flash camera.* **3** happening or done in a flash. **flash·y** *adj.* **flash·i·ly** *adv.* **flash·i·ness** *n.* ⟨Middle English *flasshe*(n), apparently imitative⟩
flash back of a film or book plot, return to an earlier time. **flash·back** *n.* **flash in the pan** a sudden, showy attempt or effort, often one that fails. **in a flash** in a very short time. **flash bulb** or **flash·bulb** a bulb used to give a bright light for taking photographs in dim light. **flash burn** a severe burn caused by instantaneous thermal radiation, such as that from an atomic bomb. **flash card** one of

a set of cards displaying letters, pictures, etc., used for drills in school subjects. **flash drive** *Computers* a removable device that plugs into a USB port, used to store data and transfer it from one computer to another. **flash·er** *n* **1** *Informal* ✻ a bright piece of metal used to attract fish to a lure. **2** *Informal* a person who exposes his or her genitals in public. **flash fire** a sudden fire that spreads rapidly. **flash flood** a very sudden, violent flooding of a river, stream, etc. **flash for·ward** *n* in a novel, play, etc., introduce some event supposed to take place at a later time. **flash–for·ward** *n*. **flash·ing** *n* the pieces of sheet metal used to cover the joints of a building to make them watertight. **flash·light** *n* a portable electric light. **flash paper** chemically treated paper that vanishes when ignited. **flash·point** *n* *Physical chemistry* the lowest temperature at which vapour from a combustible substance will ignite if exposed to flame.

flask [flæsk] *n* any bottle-shaped container. ⟨Old English *flasce*; Germanic⟩

flat¹ [flæt] *adj* **flat·ter**, **flat·test** **1** level. **2** touching all over: *He put his chest flat against the X-ray machine.* **3** of a shoe, having little or no heel. **4** with little air in it: *a flat tire.* **5** not to be changed: *a flat rate.* **6** without much interest, flavour, etc.: *a flat voice.* **7** not shiny: *a flat yellow.* **8** *Music* **a** below the true pitch. **b** one half step or half note below natural pitch.
n **1** a shallow box or basket. **2** a piece of theatrical scenery made of a wooden frame covered with canvas. **3** *Music* **a** a tone or note that is one half step or half note below natural pitch. **b** the sign ♭ that shows such a tone or note. *adv* **1** *Music* below the true pitch. **2** in a flat manner. **3** in or into a flat position: *flat on the floor.* **4** directly. **5** *Informal* completely: *flat broke.* **flat·ly** *adv.* **flat·ness** *n.* ⟨Middle English; Old Norse *flatr*⟩
fall flat fail completely. **flat out a** at maximum speed or effort. **b** bluntly: *She refused flat out.* **that's flat** that's final.
flat·bed *n* a truck or trailer without top or sides, used for carrying heavy machinery. **flat·bread** *n* a thin, dry cracker. **flat·car** *n* a railway freight car without a roof or sides. **flat·fish** *n, pl* **-fish** or **-fish·es** any of an order of marine fishes having a flattened body and both eyes on one side. **flat·foot** *n, pl* **-feet** a foot with a flattened arch. **flat·foot·ed** *adj* **1** having feet with flattened arches. **2** *Informal* **a** not to be changed or influenced. **b** plain. **3** clumsy. **4** unprepared: *to catch someone flat-footed.* **flat–foot·ed·ly** *adv.* **flat·i·ron** *n* an early form of IRON (def. 4), heated on a stove. **flat·land** *n* sometimes, **flatlands** *pl*, level ground with no hills. **flat–out** *adj Informal* absolute: *a flat-out insult.* *adv Informal* absolutely: *flat-out mistaken.* **flat·ten** *v* make or become flat. **flatten out** spread out flat. **flat·tish** *adj* somewhat flat. **flat·ware** *n* knives, forks, and spoons. **flat·worm** *n* any of a phylum of invertebrates having an unsegmented, usually flat body.

flat² [flæt] *n* an apartment all on one floor and generally not self-contained. ⟨Old English *flet* floor, home. Related to FLAT¹.⟩

flat·ter [ˈflætər] *v* **1** praise insincerely. **2** show to be better looking than is actually the case: *This picture flatters her.* **3** cause to feel honoured. **flat·ter·er** *n.* **flat·ter·ing** *adj.* **flat·ter·y** *n.* ⟨possibly extended use of Middle English *flateren* float⟩
flatter oneself a be gratified to know or think. **b** overestimate oneself.

flat·u·lent [ˈflætʃələnt] *adj* **1** having or causing gas in the stomach or intestines. **2** pompous. **flat·u·lence** *n.* **flat·u·lent·ly** *adv.* ⟨Latin *flatus* a blowing; *flare* blow⟩

flaunt [flɒnt] *v* **1** show off. **2** wave proudly: *banners flaunting in the breeze.* **flaunt** *n.* **flaunt·ing·ly** *adv.* ⟨possibly Scandinavian; compare Norwegian *flanta* gad about⟩

CONFUSABLES

Because of their form and the common ingredient of 'pride' in their meanings the words **flaunt** and **flout** are often confused. One **flaunts** something that one feels is superior, but **flouts** something for which one feels contempt.

flau·tist [ˈflʌutɪst] *or* [ˈflɒtɪst] *n* flutist.

fla·vour *or* **fla·vor** [ˈfleivər] *n* **1** a characteristic taste: *Chocolate and vanilla have different flavours.* **2** a characteristic quality: *stories with a flavour of the sea.* **3** *Physics* any kind of quarks or leptons.
v **1** season: *spices to flavour food.* **2** give an interesting quality to. **fla·vour·less** or **fla·vor·less** *adj.* **fla·vour·ful** or **fla·vor·ful** *adj.* ⟨Old French *flaur*; Latin *fragrare* emit odour⟩
fla·vour·ing or **fla·vor·ing** *n* something used to give a certain taste: *vanilla flavouring.*

flaw [flɒ] *n* **1** a defective place: *A flaw in the dish caused it to break.* **2** a fault; defect.
v make or become defective. **flaw·less** *adj.* **flaw·less·ly** *adv.* **flaw·less·ness** *n.* ⟨Scandinavian; compare Swedish *flaga*⟩

flax [flæks] *n* any of a genus of herbs cultivated for its seeds which yield linseed oil and the fibre of its stems which is woven into linen cloth. ⟨Old English *fleax*⟩
flax·en *adj* **1** made of flax. **2** pale yellow, as flax is: *flaxen hair.* **flax·seed** *n* linseed.

flay [flei] *v* **1** strip the skin from by whipping. **2** scold severely: *The angry man flayed his servant with his tongue.* **3** rob; cheat; extort. ⟨Old English *flēan*⟩

flea [fli] *n* any of an order of small, wingless, jumping insects with mouthparts adapted for sucking blood. ⟨Old English *flēah*⟩
flea in one's ear a severe scolding
flea·bane [ˈfli,bein] *n* any of a genus of plants traditionally believed to ward off fleas. **flea·bite** *n* **1** a bite from a flea **2** a small pain or annoyance. **flea–bit·ten** *adj Informal* shabby. **flea collar** a collar permeated with insecticides, used on cats and dogs. **flea market** a market selling a mixture of junk, antiques, etc. **flea·pit** *n* an apartment, cinema, etc. that is shabby and squalid.

fleck [flɛk] *n* **1** a spot of colour, light, etc.: *Freckles are brown flecks on the skin.* **2** a small particle; flake.
v sprinkle with spots or patches of colour, light, etc. ⟨Middle English; Old Norse *flekkr*⟩

fled [flɛd] *v* pt and pp of FLEE.

fledg·ling or **fledge·ling** [ˈflɛdʒlɪŋ] *n* **1** a young bird just able to fly. **2** a young and inexperienced person.
adj new and untried: *a fledgling organization.* ⟨compare Old English *unfligge* unfledged, unfit to fly⟩

flee [fli] *v* **fled, flee·ing. 1** run away; try to get away by running. **2** pass away; cease: *The shadows flee as day breaks.* ⟨Old English *flēon*⟩

fleece [flis] *n* **1** the wool that covers a sheep or similar animal. **2** a fabric with a soft pile.
v **1** cut the fleece from. **2** strip of money; cheat: *The gamblers fleeced him of a large sum.* **fleece·like** *adj.* ⟨Old English *flēos*⟩
fleec·y *adj* like a fleece; soft and fluffy: *fleecy clouds.* **fleec·i·ness** *n.*

fleet¹ [flit] *n* **1** a group of warships under one command; navy: *the Canadian fleet.* **2** a group of boats, aircraft, automobiles, etc. moving or working together: *a fleet of trucks.* ⟨Old English *flēot* ship, vessel; *flēotan* float⟩

fleet² [flit] *adj* swift; rapid. **fleet·ly** *adv.* **fleet·ness** *n.* ⟨Old English *flēotan*; Old Norse *fljótr.* Related to FLOAT.⟩
fleet·ing *adj* passing swiftly; soon gone. **fleet·ing·ly** *adv.*

flense [flɛns] *v* strip skin or blubber from (a seal or whale). **flens·er** *n.* ⟨Dutch *flensen* or Danish and Norwegian *flense*⟩

flesh [flɛʃ] *n* **1** the soft substance of a body that covers the bones and is covered by skin. **2** meat, esp of a sort not usually eaten by human beings. **3** the physical side of human nature, as distinguished from the spiritual or moral side. **4** the soft part of fruits or vegetables: *The McIntosh apple has crisp, juicy, white flesh.*
v **1** make or become fleshy (often with *out*): *He was skinny, but has fleshed out.* **2** give substance to (usually with *out*): *to flesh out a plot outline.* **flesh·less** *adj.* ⟨Old English *flǣsc*⟩
in the flesh in person. **press the flesh** *Informal* shake hands, esp as a politician. **flesh and blood 1** the body. **2** human nature: *The temptation was more than flesh and blood could resist.* **3** one's relatives by birth. **flesh–eating** *adj* meat-eating. **flesh–eating disease** an acute disease caused by bacteria that rapidly destroy bodily tissue. The technical name is **necrotizing fasciitis** [ˈnɛkrəˌtaɪzɪŋ ˌfæʃiˈaɪtəs]. **flesh·ly** *adj* **1** of the flesh; bodily. **2** sensual. **flesh·li·ness** *n.* **flesh·pot** *n* Usually, **fleshpots** *pl* establishments offering sensual entertainment: *the fleshpots of the city.* **flesh wound** a wound that injures the flesh only. **flesh·y** *adj* **1** having much flesh: *The calf is the fleshy part of the lower leg.* **2** plump. **3** of or like flesh. **flesh·i·ly** *adv.* **flesh·i·ness** *n.*

fleur–de–lis [ˌflɜr də ˈli] or [-ˈlis]; *French*
[flœrdˈli] *n, pl* **fleurs–de–lis** [-ˈliz] or [-ˈli] *French* [flœrdˈli] **1** *Heraldry* a design representing a lily. **2** the emblem of the province of Québec. ⟨French = flower of the lily⟩

flew [flu] *v* pt of FLY².

flex [flɛks] *v* **1** bend: *He flexed his arm.* **2** of muscles, tighten and relax alternately.
n **1** a bend or contraction of a muscle. **2** insulated wire used to connect electric appliances. ⟨Latin *flexus* pp of *flectere* bend⟩
flex·i·ble *adj* **1** easily bent. **2** easily adapted to fit various uses, purposes, etc.: *an actor's flexible voice.* **3** willing to accommodate the wants of others. **flex·i·bil·i·ty** *n.* **flex·i·bly** *adv.* **flex·ion** *n Physiology* a bending of some part of the body. **flex·time** *n* a flexible system of working hours, whereby employees can choose their starting and finishing times.

flib·ber·ti·gib·bet [ˈflɪbərtiˌdʒɪbɪt] *n* **1** a frivolous, flighty person. **2** chatterbox. ⟨Middle English *flypergebet*; origin uncertain⟩

flick [flɪk] *n* **1** a quick, light blow: *a flick of a whip.* **2** a sudden jerk: *a flick of her wrist.* **3** *Slang* movie. **flick** *v.* ⟨probably imitative⟩

flick·er¹ [ˈflɪkər] *v* **1** shine with a wavering light. **2** move quickly and lightly in and out: *The tongue of a snake flickers.*
n **1** a wavering light or flame. **2** a quick, light movement. **3** a dying spurt of energy, emotion, etc.: *a flicker of enthusiasm.* ⟨Old English *flicorian*⟩

flick·er² [ˈflɪkər] *n* any of several North American woodpeckers having a conspicuous white rump. ⟨perhaps imitative of its note⟩

flight¹ [flaɪt] *n* **1** the act of flying. **2** the distance flown by a bird, bullet, etc. **3** a group of things flying through the air: *a flight of six birds.* **4** a trip in an aircraft. **5** a set of stairs. **flight·less** *adj.* ⟨Old English *flyht.* Related to FLY².⟩
take flight fly away.
flight attendant a person employed to look after passengers during a flight. **flight bag** a bag designed to be carried as hand luggage on an airplane, etc. **flight deck 1** a separate compartment in some aircraft for the pilot and crew. **2** the uppermost deck on an aircraft carrier, which functions as a takeoff and landing area. **flight·path** or **flight path** *n* **1** the course taken by an aircraft, missile, etc. **2** a course indicated by an electronic beam as a navigation aid.

flight² [flaɪt] *n* **1** the act of running away: *The defeated army was in flight.* **2** escape: *The flight of the prisoners was soon discovered.* ⟨Middle English *fliht*; Old English *flēon* flee⟩
put to flight force to flee. **take to flight** flee.

flight·y [ˈflaɪti] *adj* **1** likely to have sudden fancies. **2** slightly crazy. **flight·i·ness** *n.*

flim·flam [ˈflɪmˌflæm] *Informal n* **1** nonsense; rubbish. **2** deception; a low trick.
v **-flammed, -flam·ming** cheat (a person) out of money; trick. **flim·flam·mer** *n.* ⟨possible reduplication of *flam* deceptive trick⟩

flim·sy [ˈflɪmzi] *adj* **1** light or poorly constructed. **2** inadequate: *a flimsy excuse.*

n a sheet of thin paper. **flim·si·ly** *adv.*
flim·si·ness *n.* ⟨possible alteration of *film* +
-sy, adj. suffix⟩

flinch [flɪntʃ] *v* 1 draw back from difficulty,
danger, or pain. 2 wince. **flinch** *n.* ⟨probably
Old French *flenchir;* Frankish **hlankjan* bend⟩

fling [flɪŋ] *v* **flung, fling·ing** *v* 1 throw
forcefully. 2 move rapidly: *She flung angrily
out of the room.* 3 move (a part of the body) in
an impulsive, unrestrained way: *The girl flung
her arms around her mother's neck.*
n 1 a violent throw. 2 a time of doing as one
pleases: *He had his fling when he was young,
and now he must work.* 3 *Informal* a shortlived
love affair. ⟨possibly Old Norse *flengja* flog⟩
have or **take a fling at** *Informal* **a** try;
attempt. **b** make scornful remarks about.

flint [flɪnt] *n* 1 a hard quartz that makes a
spark when struck against steel. 2 anything
very unyielding: *a heart of flint.* **flint·y** *adj.*
flint·i·ly *adv.* **flint·i·ness** *n.* ⟨Old English⟩

flip¹ [flɪp] *v* **flipped, flip·ping** *v* 1 move with a
snap of a finger and thumb: *to flip a coin.*
2 flip a coin to decide something by chance:
They flipped to see who would go. 3 turn
quickly: *to flip the pages of a book.* 4 invert: *to
flip a switch.* **flip** *n.* ⟨probably imitative⟩
flip one's lid *Informal* lose control of oneself.
flip out *Slang* lose one's composure in anger,
excitement, etc. **flip through** look at (a book,
magazine) quickly and randomly.
flip·chart *n* a large pad of paper on an easel.
Each sheet can be turned over the back of
the easel, leaving the next sheet available for
writing. **flip–flop** *Informal n* 1 a sudden
change of opinion. 2 **flip–flops** *pl* rubber
sandals with thongs. **flip–flop, -flopped,
-flop·ping** *v* abruptly change opinion: *She
flip-flopped on the issue of free trade.* **flip·per** *n*
1 a broad fin specially adapted for
swimming. 2 a flat piece of rubber or plastic
that fits onto the foot, used by swimmers for
extra power.

flip² [flɪp] *adj* **flip·per, flip·pest** *Informal*
flippant; cheeky.

flip·pant ['flɪpənt] *adj* pert in speech; not
respectful: *a flippant answer.* **flip·pan·cy** *n.*
flip·pant·ly *adv.* ⟨perhaps *flip¹* + *-ant*⟩

flirt [flɜrt] *v* 1 try to win the affection of
someone by amorous behaviour. 2 trifle; toy:
He flirted with the idea of going to Europe.
3 flutter: *She flirted her fan impatiently.*
n 1 a person who flirts. 2 a quick movement:
With a flirt of its tail, the bird flew away. 3 a
toss; jerk. ⟨ultimately imitative⟩
flir·ta·tion *n* 1 a love affair that is not serious.
2 a flirting or toying. **flir·ta·tious** *adj.*
flir·ta·tious·ly *adv.* **flir·ta·tious·ness** *n.*

flit [flɪt] *v* **flit·ted, flit·ting** 1 fly lightly and
quickly. 2 pass lightly and quickly: *Many idle
thoughts flitted through her mind.* **flit** *n.* ⟨Old
Norse *flytja.* Related to FLEET².⟩

float [flout] *v* 1 be held up by, or cause to be
held up by, air or liquid. 2 initiate (a
company, plan, idea, etc.). 3 of currency,
interest rates, etc., be allowed to find a level
on the market based on supply and demand.
n 1 a cork, bob, etc. on a fishing line. 2 an
air-filled part on an aircraft for landing on
water. 3 a hollow ball that regulates the level
of a liquid. 4 a flat car that carries something
to be shown in a parade. 5 a drink consisting
of ginger ale or a similar beverage with ice
cream in it. 6 a sum of money put in a cash
register so that change can be made.
float·a·ble *adj.* **flo·ta·tion** *n.* ⟨Old English
flotian; flēotan. Related to FLEET².⟩
float·er *n* 1 *Sports* a ball that travels slowly
and appears to hang in the air. 2 a person
who can fill in for anyone absent from work.
float·ing *adj* not fixed. **float plane** a
seaplane equipped with floats.

flock¹ [flɒk] *n* 1 animals of one kind that
move about in a group, esp sheep or birds.
2 a crowd. 3 people of a church regarded as
the charges of their pastor.
v come crowding: *The children flocked around
the teacher.* ⟨Old English *flocc*⟩

flock² [flɒk] *n* 1 a tuft of wool. 2 waste wool
or cotton used to stuff cushions. ⟨Old French
floc; Latin *floccus* tuft of wool⟩

floe [flou] *n* a floating piece of ice broken off
from an ice sheet. ⟨perhaps Norwegian *flo*⟩

flog [flɒg] *v* **flogged, flog·ging.** 1 whip hard.
2 *Slang* sell or try to sell. **flog·ger** *n.* ⟨perhaps
school slang for Latin *flagellare* whip⟩
flog a dead horse pursue a futile argument or
a lost cause. **flog to death** be too persistent,
causing a person to lose interest: *It wasn't a
bad idea, but she flogged it to death.*

flood [flʌd] *n* 1 a flow of water over its
normal confines, esp over what is usually dry
land. 2 *Poetic* ocean; sea; lake; river. 3 a great
outpouring of anything: *a flood of words.*
4 *Informal* floodlight. 5 **the Flood** in the
Bible, the water that deluged the earth in the
time of Noah.
v 1 flow over or into: *The river rose and flooded
our fields.* 2 become covered or filled with
water: *During the thunderstorm, our cellar
flooded.* 3 pour out like a flood: *Sunlight
flooded into the room.* 4 allow or receive too
much fuel into the carburetor of (an engine)
so that it fails to start. ⟨Old English *flōd*⟩
in flood filled with an unusual amount of
water: *The river was in flood.*
flood·gate *n* 1 a gate in a canal, river, stream,
etc. to control the flow of water. 2 something
that controls any flow. **flood·light** *n* a lamp
that gives a broad beam of light *v* **-light·ed** or
-lit, -light·ing illuminate with floodlights.
flood plain a plain bordering a river and
made of soil deposited by floods. **flood tide**
the flowing of the tide toward the shore.
flood·way *n* a giant ditch dug to divert spring
flood waters away from a city.

floor [flɔr] *n* 1 the inside bottom covering of
a room. 2 a storey of a building. 3 the part of
a room where an assembly sits: *the floor of the
House of Commons.* 4 the right to speak in an
assembly: *The chair decides who has the floor.*
5 the bottom of the sea, a cave, or area of
land: *the ocean floor.*

v **1** put a floor in or over. **2** knock down. **3** *Informal* defeat. **4** *Informal* confuse completely: *The last question on the exam floored us all.* ⟨Old English *flōr*⟩
floor it *Informal* bear down on the accelerator of a car so that the pedal is down to the floor. **floor·board** *n* one of the strips of wood in a wooden floor. **floor hockey** an indoor game derived from hockey, in which the players pass a plastic puck or a ring. **floor·ing** *n* material for making floors. **floor plan** a scale map of one floor of a building.

flop [flɒp] *v* **flopped, flop·ping 1** move loosely or heavily or fall: *The fish flopped helplessly on the deck.* **2** *Informal* fail. **3** *Slang* sleep; spend the night: *Can I flop here?*
n Informal a failure: *The new play was a flop.* ⟨imitative variant of *flap*⟩
flop·house *n* a cheap rooming house. **flop·py** *adj Informal* tending to flop: *a hat with a floppy brim.* **flop·pi·ly** *adv.* **flop·pi·ness** *n.* **floppy disk** *Computers* a thin, magnetized plate used for storing data; diskette.

flo·ra ['flɔrə] *n* the plants of a particular region or time: *the flora of the West Indies.* ⟨Latin *floris* flower⟩
flo·ral *adj* to do with flowers: *floral decorations.* **flo·res·cence** *n* **1** the act or period of blossoming. **2** a time of success. **flo·res·cent** *adj.* **flo·ret** *n Botany* one of the small flowers in the flower head of a composite plant, such as an aster. **flo·ri·cul·ture** *n* the cultivation of flowering plants. **flo·ri·cul·tur·ist** *n.* **flo·rist** ['flɔrɪst] *n* a person who raises or sells flowers.

flor·id ['flɔrɪd] *adj* **1** highly coloured: *a florid complexion.* **2** elaborately ornamented. **flor·id·ly** *adv.* **flor·id·ness** *n.* ⟨Latin *floridus*; from *floris* flower⟩

floss [flɒs] *n* **1** a soft, shiny, untwisted thread used for embroidery. **2** DENTAL FLOSS.
v use dental floss to clean (teeth). ⟨apparently related to FLEECE⟩

flo·ta·tion See FLOAT.

flo·til·la [flou'tɪlə] *or* [flə'tɪlə] *n* **1** a small fleet. **2** a fleet of small ships. ⟨Spanish, diminutive of *flota* fleet; Old Norse *floti* fleet⟩

flot·sam ['flɒtsəm] *n* the wreckage of a ship found floating on the sea. Compare JETSAM. ⟨Anglo-French *floteson*; *floter* float⟩
flotsam and jetsam a wreckage found floating on the sea or washed ashore. **b** odds and ends; useless things.

flounce¹ [flaʊns] *v* go with an angry or impatient movement of the body: *She flounced out of the room in a rage.* **flounce** *n.* **floun·cy** *adj.* ⟨possibly Scandinavian; compare Swedish *flunsa* plunge⟩

flounce² [flaʊns] *n* a wide ruffle. ⟨Old French *fronce* wrinkle; Germanic⟩

floun·der¹ ['flaʊndər] *v* **1** struggle awkwardly without making much progress; *Horses were floundering in the deep snowdrifts.* **2** be clumsy and make mistakes: *The frightened girl could only flounder through her song.* ⟨possible blend of *founder¹* and *blunder*⟩

floun·der² ['flaʊndər] *n, pl* **-der** or **-ders** any of numerous flatfishes including plaice, halibut, and turbot. ⟨Scandinavian⟩

flour [flaʊr] *or* ['flaʊər] *n* **1** a fine, powdery substance made by grinding wheat or other grain. **2** any fine, soft powder.
v cover with flour. **flour·y** *adj.* ⟨special use of *flower*; the flower (best, finest) of the meal⟩

flour·ish ['flɜrɪʃ] *v* **1** grow with vigour. **2** be in the best time of activity. **3** wave (a sword, arm, etc.) in the air. **4** make a showy display.
n **1** a waving in the air. **2** a showy decoration in handwriting. **3** *Music* a showy trill: *a flourish of trumpets.* **4** the state of being in the best time of life: *in full flourish.* **flour·ish·ing** *adj.* ⟨Old French *florir*, Latin *floris* flower⟩

flout [flaʊt] *v* treat with contempt; openly disregard: *to flout good advice.* ⟨variant of *flute*, v.⟩

flow [flou] *v* **1** run like water. **2** move easily. **3** of hair, etc., hang loosely. **4** be plentiful: *a land flowing with milk and honey.* **5** of the tide, flow in. **6** *Geology* alter in shape due to pressure, without breaking or splitting off.
n **1** any continuous movement like that of water in a river: *a rapid flow of speech.* **2** the rate of flowing. **3** *Physics* the directional movement in a current that is a characteristic of all fluids, as air or electricity. ⟨Old English *flōwan*⟩
flow from originate in. **go with the flow** *Informal* let things be.
flowchart or **flow chart** a diagram showing the relationship between different elements of a complex system. **flow·ing** *adj* **1** moving in a stream: *flowing water.* **2** moving smoothly: *flowing words.* **3** hanging loosely: *flowing robes.* **flow·ing·ly** *adv.*

SYNONYMS

Flow emphasizes the continuous forward movement of water: *Water flowed through the streets.* **Gush** = flow forth suddenly in quantity from an opening: *Oil gushed from the new well.* **Stream** = flow steadily in the same direction: *Rain streamed down the gullies.*

flow·er ['flaʊər] *n* **1** the part of a plant that includes the reproductive organs. **2** the finest part: *The flower of the country's youth was killed in the war.* **3** **flowers** *pl Chemistry* a fine powder produced by sublimation or condensation: *flowers of sulphur.*
v **1** produce flowers: *Our lilac didn't flower this year.* **2** reach one's best. **flow·er·er** *n.* **flow·er·less** *adj.* **flow·er·like** *adj.* ⟨Old French *flour*; Latin *floris*⟩
in full flower at the peak of attainment: *At 19 her creative ability was in full flower.*
flower bed or **flowerbed** an area of earth in a garden in which flowers are grown. **flower child** hippie. **flower girl** a girl who carries the flowers for a bride at her wedding. **flower head** a bloom composed of many tiny flowers grouped together. **flow·er·ing** *adj* having flowers. **flow·er·pot** *n* **1** a pot to hold earth for a plant. **2** *Geology* a pillar of rock left behind as the escarpment of which it

formed part has eroded. **flow·er·y** ['flaʊəri] *adj* **1** having many flowers. **2** containing many fanciful expressions.

flown [floun] *v* pp of FLY².

FLQ Front de Libération du Québec, a Québec Separatist terrorist organization.

flu [flu] *n Informal* influenza.

flub [flʌb] *v* **flubbed, flub·bing** *v* do (something) very clumsily; make a mess of. *n* a failure in performance; mistake; error.

fluc·tu·ate ['flʌktʃu,eit] *v* **1** rise and fall: *The temperature fluctuates from day to day.* **2** move in waves. **fluc·tu·a·tion** *n.* ⟨Latin *fluctus* wave⟩

flue [flu] *n* a tube for conveying smoke: *Our chimney has several flues.* ⟨origin uncertain⟩

flu·ent ['fluənt] *adj* **1** flowing smoothly or easily: *fluent French.* **2** speaking or writing easily and rapidly. **3** not fixed or stable. **flu·en·cy** *n.* **flu·ent·ly** *adv.* ⟨Latin *fluere* flow⟩

fluff [flʌf] *n* **1** soft, light particles: *a ball of fluff.* **2** *Informal* a mistake in reading, speaking, etc. on the stage, on television, etc. **3** light or inconsequential writing, etc. *v* **1** shake up into a soft, light mass: *I fluffed the pillows when I made the bed.* **2** become fluffy. **3** *Informal* make a mistake in reading (one's lines, etc.). ⟨apparently variant of *flue* downy matter (related to Old English *flēogan* to fly); influenced by *puff*⟩ **fluff·y** *adj* **1** soft and light like fluff: *Whipped cream is fluffy.* **2** covered with fluff: *fluffy baby chicks.* **fluff·i·ly** *adv.* **fluff·i·ness** *n.*

flu·id ['fluɪd] *n* **1** any substance that flows: *Water, mercury, air, and oxygen are fluids.* **2** liquid to drink: *Due to a severe digestive disorder, she is restricted to fluids.* *adj* **1** to do with fluids. **2** changing easily. **3** ready to be converted into cash: *fluid assets.* **flu·id·i·ty** *n.* **flu·id·ize** *v.* **flu·id·ly** *adv.* ⟨Latin *fluere* flow⟩ **flu·id·ics** [flu'ɪdɪks] *n* (with sg verb) the technology of systems that depend on the flow of a fluid in small jets. **flu·id·ic** *adj.* **fluid ounce** a non-metric unit for measuring liquids, equal to about 28 cm³.

fluke¹ [fluk] *n* **1** the pointed part of an anchor that catches in the ground. **2** the barbed head a harpoon, etc. **3** either half of a whale's tail. ⟨perhaps special use of *fluke³*⟩

fluke² [fluk] *Informal n* **1** *Billiards, pool* a lucky shot. **2** a lucky chance; fortunate accident. ⟨origin uncertain⟩ **fluk·y** or **fluk·ey** ['fluki] *adj Informal* **1** obtained by chance rather than by skill. **2** uncertain: *fluky weather.* **flu·ki·ness** *n.*

fluke³ [fluk] *n* **1** any of numerous parasitic flatworms. **2** a flatfish, esp any of various flounders. ⟨Old English *flōc*⟩

flume [flum] *n* **1** a deep, narrow valley with a stream running through it. **2** a large, inclined trough for carrying water. ⟨Latin *flumen* river; *fluere* flow⟩

flum·mox ['flʌməks] *v Informal* confuse; bewilder; confound. ⟨perhaps dialect *flummocks* maul, mangle⟩

flung [flʌŋ] *v* pt and pp of FLING.

flunk [flʌŋk] *Informal v* fail or cause to fail (school work). ⟨origin uncertain⟩ **flunk out** dismiss or be dismissed from school, college, etc. because of inferior work.

flunk·ey ['flʌŋki] *n, pl* **-eys 1** a manservant who wears livery. **2** a person who does tasks for another, esp in an obsequious way. Also, **flunk·y.** ⟨alteration of *flanker* one posted on the flank. See FLANK.⟩

fluo·res·cence [flə'rɛsəns] *or* [flɔ'rɛsəns] *n Physics, chemistry* a giving off of light from a substance exposed to X rays and ultraviolet rays. **fluo·resce** *v.* **fluo·res·cent** *adj.* ⟨*fluor(ite)* + *(phosphor)escence*⟩ **fluorescent lamp** a type of electric lamp that produces fluorescent light when acted on by an electric current.

fluor·ine ['flɔrin] *or* ['flʊrin] *n* a gaseous element similar to chlorine. *Symbol* **F** ⟨*fluor(ite)*; because found in it⟩ **fluor·i·date** *v* add small amounts of fluoride to (drinking water). **fluor·i·da·tion** *n.* **fluor·ide** *n* a compound of fluorine and another element or radical. **fluor·ite** *n* a mineral occurring in many colours and used for making glass, etc.; calcium fluoride.

flur·ry ['flɜri] *n* **1** a sudden gust of wind. **2** a light fall of snow. **3** a sudden excitement, or rush: *a flurry of activity.* *v* excite; confuse; disturb: *Noise in the audience flurried the actor so that he forgot his lines.* ⟨possible blend of *flutter* and *hurry*⟩

flush¹ [flʌʃ] *v* **1** blush or cause to blush: *Exercise flushed his face.* **2** wash with a rapid flow of water: *The streets were flushed every night.* **3** of a toilet, empty itself with a flow of water; cause (a toilet) to so empty itself. **flush** *n.* ⟨possible blend of *flash* and *blush*⟩

flush² [flʌʃ] *adj* **1** level: *The edge of the new shelf must be flush with the old one.* **2** well supplied: *flush with money.* **3** of printed text, having no indentations: *flush left.* **flush** *adv.* ⟨perhaps extended use of *flush¹*⟩

flush³ [flʌʃ] *v* start up suddenly or cause to start up suddenly: *The hunter's dog flushed a partridge in the woods.* ⟨origin uncertain⟩

flush⁴ [flʌʃ] *n Card games* a hand all of one suit. ⟨Old French *flus, flux;* Latin *fluxus* flow⟩

flus·ter ['flʌstər] *v* make or become nervous and excited. **flus·ter** *n.* ⟨Scandinavian; compare Icelandic *flaustr* bustle, *flaustra* be flustered⟩

flute [flut] *n* **1** a woodwind instrument consisting of a slender tube, with holes stopped for producing the different tones, and a mouth hole in the side near one end. **2** a long, rounded groove, as in the shaft of a column, etc. **3** a tall, narrow wine glass, used to serve champagne. *v* **1** sing, speak like a flute. **2** make rounded grooves in. **flut·ed** *adj.* **flute·like** *adj.* ⟨Old French *fleüte;* Latin *flatus* pp of *flare* blow⟩ **flut·ing** *n* a type of decoration consisting of long, rounded grooves. **flut·ist** or **flau·tist** *n* a person who plays a flute.

flut·ter ['flʌtər] v **1** wave back and forth quickly. **2** move about restlessly. **3** beat feebly and irregularly: *Her pulse fluttered.* **4** excite. *n* **1** the action of fluttering. **2** an excited condition: *Her appearance caused a flutter in the crowd.* **3** a heart condition with rapid beating. ⟨Old English *flotorian; flēotan* float⟩

flu·vi·al ['fluviəl] *adj* of, found in, or produced by a river: *A delta is a fluvial deposit.* ⟨Latin *fluvius* river⟩

flux [flʌks] *n* **1** a flow. **2** continuous change: *a state of flux.* **3** an unnatural discharge from the body. **4** a substance used to help metals fuse together: *Rosin is used as a flux in soldering.* **5** the rate of flow of a fluid, heat, etc. across a certain surface or area. *v* fuse together. ⟨Latin *fluxus; fluere* flow⟩

fly¹ [flaɪ] *n, pl* **flies 1** any of an order of two-winged insects, esp the housefly. **2** any of various other winged insects (usually in compounds): *dragonfly.* **3** a fish-hook with feathers, tinsel, etc. attached to make it resemble an insect. ⟨Old English *flēoge; flēogan* fly²⟩
fly in the ointment a small thing that spoils something else. **no flies on someone** *Informal* someone is clear-thinking and alert.
fly·blown *adj* spoiled by flies having laid eggs in it. **fly·catch·er** *n* a small songbird characterized by the habit of darting out to catch insects. **fly–fish·ing** *n* fishing with natural or artificial flies as bait. **fly-fish** *v.* **fly·pa·per** *n* a paper coated with a sticky substance to catch flies. **fly swatter** a device for killing flies, usually consisting of a long handle to which is attached a flexible piece of perforated plastic, etc. **fly·weight** *n* a boxer who weighs between 49 kg and 51 kg.

fly² [flaɪ] *v* **flew, flown, fly·ing 1** move or cause to move through the air: *to fly a kite.* **2** move swiftly. **3** run away. **4** *Informal* of a project, etc., be a success: *That new design won't fly!* **5** *Baseball* **flied, fly·ing** hit a ball high into the air with the bat.
n **1** a zipper in the front of pants. **2** an outer flap for a tent. **3** *Baseball* a ball hit high into the air with a bat. **4 flies** *pl* in a theatre, the space above the stage. **5 ✿** a sheet of canvas or hide erected for protection against the weather. **fly·a·ble** *adj.* ⟨Old English *flēogan*⟩
fly at attack violently. **fly in the face of.** See FACE. **fly off the handle.** See HANDLE. **let fly a** shoot; throw: *The hunter let fly an arrow.* **b** speak violently. **on the fly a** while still in the air. **b** without interrupting what one is doing: *We worked all day, eating on the fly.*
fly–beer ['flaɪ ˌbɪr] *n* ✿ *Maritimes* beer brewed from potatoes and hop yeast mixed with molasses. **fly·by** *n* a flight past a point by a spacecraft. **fly–by–night** *adj* not reliable. *n Informal* **1** a person who avoids paying debts by leaving secretly at night. **2** an unreliable person. **fly·er** or **fli·er** *n* **1** a person or thing that flies. **2** a very fast train, ship, etc. **3** *Slang* a reckless financial venture. **4** *Informal* a try. **5** a small handbill, used for advertising. **fly–in** *adj* ✿ of a fishing camp,

accessible only by airplane. **fly·ing** *adj* **1** moving through the air. **2** swift; like flight: *a flying leap.* **3** short and quick: *a flying visit.* **4** of cattle brands, wavy. **with flying colours** or **colors** successfully: *He passed the exam with flying colours.* **flying buttress** an arched support built between the wall of a building and a supporting column. **flying fish** any of a family of marine fishes that can glide some distance through the air after leaping from the water. **flying saucer** a disklike object that some people claim to have seen flying in the sky at great speed; UFO. **flying start** any advantage: *Knowing how to read will give you a flying start in school.* **flying wing ✿** *Football* a player whose position is variable behind the line of scrimmage. **fly·leaf** *n* a blank sheet of paper at the beginning or end of a book, etc. **fly·past** *n* a display in which aircraft in formation fly over a reviewing stand. **fly·wheel** *n* a heavy wheel attached to machinery to keep the speed even.

FM or **F.M.** FREQUENCY MODULATION.

foal [foul] *n* a young horse, donkey, etc. *v* give birth to (a foal). ⟨Old English *fola*⟩

foam [foum] *n* **1** a mass of very small bubbles. **2** a spongy, flexible material made from plastics, rubber, etc. **3** *Poetic* the sea. *v* **1** form foam or cause to foam. **2** break into foam: *The stream foams over the rocks.* **foam·i·ly** *adv.* **foam·i·ness** *n.* **foam·less** *adj.* **foam·like** *adj.* **foam·y** *adj.* ⟨Old English *fām*⟩
foam at the mouth be greatly enraged.
foam rubber a firm, spongy foam.

fob [fɒb] *v* **fobbed, fob·bing** trick; cheat. *n* a trick. ⟨origin uncertain⟩
fob off get rid of by a trick.

fo'c'sle ['fouksəl] *n Nautical* forecastle.

fo·cus ['foukəs] *n, pl* **-cus·es** or **-ci** [-saɪ] *or* [-si]; *n* **1** a point at which rays of light, heat, etc. meet or from which they seem to diverge after being reflected or refracted. **2** FOCAL LENGTH. **3** the correct adjustment of a lens, the eye, etc. to make a clear image: *to bring a telescope into focus.* **4** the central point of attention. **5** *Geometry* either of two fixed points used in **a** determining an ellipse. **b** a point used in determining some other curve. *v* **-cus·es** or **-cus·ses, -cused** or **-cussed, -cus·ing** or **-cus·sing 1** bring (rays of light, heat, etc.) to a point. **2** adjust (a lens, the eye, etc.) to make a clear image. **3** meet at a focus. **4** concentrate: *When studying, she focused her mind on her lessons.* **fo·cal** *adj.* **fo·cal·ly** *adv.* ⟨Latin *focus* hearth⟩
in focus clear; distinct. **out of focus** blurred.
focus group a representative group of people gathered to discuss a product, issue, etc.
focal length or **focal distance** *Optics* the distance of a focus from the optical centre of a lens or concave mirror.

fod·der ['fɒdər] *n* coarse food for horses, cattle, etc.: *Hay and cornstalks are fodder.* ⟨Old English *fōdor; fōda* food⟩

foe [fou] *n* enemy. ⟨Old English *fāh* hostile⟩

fog [fɒg] *n* **1 a** a cloud of fine drops of water

that forms just above the earth's surface. **b** a layer of such mist condensed on glass or plastic. **2** a confused condition: *His mind was in a fog during most of the examination.* **3** any vaporized liquid, such as insecticide.
v **fogged, fog·ging 1** cover or become covered with fog. **2** confuse. **3** spray with insecticide: *We'll have to fog the whole house.* **fog·gy** *adj.* **fog·gi·ly** *adv.* **fog·gi·ness** *n.* 〈Scandinavian; compare Danish *fog* spray〉
fog bank a dense mass of fog. **fog·bound** *adj* **1** kept from travelling, esp from sailing, by fog. **2** of an airport or port, unable to operate because of fog. **fog·horn** *n* a horn used in foggy weather to warn ships of danger from rocks, collision, etc.

fo·gey ['fougi] *n, pl* **-geys** one who is behind the times or lacks enterprise. Also, **fogy.** **fo·gey·ish** *adj.* **fo·gey·ism** *n.* 〈origin uncertain〉

foi·ble ['fɔɪbəl] *n* a weakness in character: *Talking too much is one of her foibles.* 〈French *foible*, older form of modern *faible* feeble〉

foie gras [fwɒ 'grɑ]; *French* [fwa'gʀa] See PÂTÉ DE FOIE GRAS.

foil¹ [fɔɪl] *v* **1** prevent (someone) from carrying out plans: *The hero foiled the villain.* **2** prevent (a scheme, plan, etc.) from succeeding. 〈Old French *fouler* trample, full (cloth); Latin *fullare* from *fullo* a fuller〉

foil² [fɔɪl] *n* **1** metal in a very thin sheet: *aluminum foil.* **2** a person who or thing that makes another seem better by contrast. 〈Old French; Latin *folium* leaf〉

foil³ [fɔɪl] *n* a narrow sword with a knob on the point to prevent injury, used in fencing. 〈origin uncertain〉

foist [fɔɪst] *v* **1** palm off as genuine: *to foist inferior goods on customers.* **2** put in secretly: *The translator has foisted several passages into that book.* **3** compel (someone) to accept (something): *My aunt is always foisting more food on me.* 〈probably dialect Dutch *vuisten* take in hand; *vuist* fist〉

fold¹ [fould] *v* **1** double over on itself. **2** put the arms around and hold tenderly. **3** enclose. **4** *Informal* close on account of failure: *They folded the business after only two months.* **5** *Informal* collapse: *The student folded under the pressure of exams.*
n **1** a layer of something folded. **2** a hollow made by folding: *Fold up the map along the original folds.* **3** *Geology* a bend in a layer of rock. 〈Old English *fealdan*〉
fold in in cooking, add to a mixture by gently turning with a spoon: *Fold in beaten egg whites.* **fold out**, unfold, open out. **fold up** make or become smaller by folding.
fold·a·way *adj* usually of a piece of furniture, made so as to fold up into a smaller space: *a foldaway cot.* **fold·er** *n* **1** a holder for papers, made by folding a piece of cardboard. **2** *Computers* a collection of files, shown onscreen as a small file folder. **folding door** a door that opens and closes by folding and unfolding. **folding money** *Informal* paper money, as opposed to coins. **fold·out** *n* an

extra wide page inserted into a magazine or book, which the reader unfolds to look at a map, picture, etc.

fold² [fould] *n* **1** a pen to keep sheep in. **2** a faith or community. 〈Old English *falod*〉
return to the fold return to active membership in one's faith or community.

–fold *suffix* **1** ——times as great: *tenfold.* **2** composed of——parts: *manifold.* 〈Old English *-feald.* Related to FOLD¹.〉

fol·i·age ['fouliɪdʒ] *n* the leaves of a plant. 〈French *feuillage; feuille* leaf, Latin *folia* leaves〉
fo·li·ate ['fouliɪt] *adj* **1** having leaves. **2** leaflike. *v* ['fouli,eɪt] **1** put forth leaves. **2** split into leafplates. **3** shape like a leaf. **fo·li·a·tion** *n.*

fo·lic acid ['foulɪk] *or* ['fʊlɪk] *Biochemistry* a compound of the vitamin B complex, found in green leaves and some animal tissue and used in the treatment of anemia. 〈Latin *folium* leaf〉

fo·li·o ['fouli,ou] *n* **1** a large sheet of paper folded once to make two leaves, or four pages, of a book, etc. **2** a book of the largest size, having pages made by folding large sheets of paper once. **3** a case for loose papers, etc. 〈Latin *folio*, form of *folium* leaf〉

folk [fouk] *n, pl* **folk** or **folks 1** people as a group: *city folk.* **2** a tribe; nation. **3** **folks** *pl* a people. **b** *Informal* one's own family.
adj **1** to do with people, their beliefs, customs, etc. **2** to do with folk songs or folk music: *a folk festival.* 〈Old English *folc*〉
folk dance a dance originating and handed down among the common people. **folk hero** a popular hero, often mythological: *Johnny Canuck is a folk hero.* **folk·lore** *n* the beliefs, legends, customs, etc. of a people, etc. **folk·lor·ic** *adj.* **folk·lor·ist** *n.* **folk medicine** popular remedies, often herbal, passed down the generations. **folk music** music originating among the common people. **folk–rock** *n* rock music with folk-song themes or lyrics. **folk song** a song originating, as a rule, among the common people: *"Alouette" is a well-known French-Canadian folk song.* **folk singer. folk·sy** *adj Informal* **1** friendly: *a nice, folksy evening.* **2** unpretentious. **3** artificially simple: *The movie was full of folksy stupidity.* **folk·si·ness** *n.* **folk·si·ly** *adv.* **folk tale** a story originating among the common people.

fol·li·cle ['fɒləkəl] *n* a small cavity, sac, or gland: *Hair grows from follicles.* 〈Latin *folliculus* diminutive of *follis* bellows〉

fol·low ['fɒlou] *v* **1** go or come after: *Night follows day.* **2** result from: *If you eat too much candy, a stomach ache will follow.* **3** go along: *Follow this road to the corner.* **4** go along behind: *My dog followed me to school.* **5** take as a guide: *Follow her advice.* **6** keep the mind on: *I found it hard to follow the conversation.* **fol·low·er** *n.* 〈Old English *folgian*〉
as follows the following: *The duties of the various officers are as follows.* **b** in the

following way: *Assemble frame as follows.* **follow out** carry out to the end. **follow through a** continue a motion through to the end: *Most golfers follow through after hitting the ball.* **b** carry out fully: *When one begins a job, one should try to follow it through.* **follow–through** *n.* **follow up** increase the effect of by further action: *He followed up his first request by asking again a week later.* **fol·low–up** *n, adj.*

fol·low·ing *n* **1** a group of followers. **2 the following** the persons, things, etc. now to be named, etc. *adj* **1** to be mentioned next: *The following people will stay behind.* **2** of the tide or wind, flowing in the same direction as a ship or aircraft. *prep* immediately after: *Following lunch, he took a nap.*

SYNONYMS

Follow is the general word meaning 'go after': *He has arrived, and she will follow later.* **Succeed** = come next in order of time, and usually suggests taking the place of someone or something: *He succeeded his father as president of the company.* **Ensue**, formal, means 'follow as a result': *A lasting friendship ensued from our working together.*

fol·ly ['fɒli] *n* **1** unwise conduct. **2** a foolish act or idea. **3** a costly, foolish undertaking. ⟨Old French *folie; fol* foolish. See FOOL.⟩

fo·ment [fou'mɛnt] *v* **1** promote (trouble, rebellion, etc.). **2** apply hot cloths, etc. to (a hurt). **fo·men·ta·tion** *n.* ⟨Latin *fomentum* a warm application; *fovere* warm⟩

fond [fɒnd] *adj* **1** expressing affection: *a fond look.* **2** foolishly naive or optimistic. **3** cherished: *fond hopes.* **fond·ly** *adv.* **fond·ness** *n.* ⟨Middle English *fonned* pp of *fonne(n)* be foolish⟩
be fond of a have a liking for: *fond of children.* **b** like to eat: *Cats are fond of fish.*

fon·dle ['fɒndəl] *v* caress lovingly: *The mother fondled her baby's hands.* **fon·dler** *n.* ⟨*fond*, v., special use of *fond*, adj.⟩

fon·due [fɒn'du] *or* ['fɒndu] *n* **1** a dish of melted Swiss cheese, white wine, and seasonings into which cubes of bread are dipped and then eaten. **2** any of various similar dishes consisting of small pieces of food cooked in a hot liquid at the table. ⟨French *fondue* pp of *fondre* melt. See FOUND³.⟩

font¹ [fɒnt] *n* **1** a basin holding holy water. **2** *Poetic, archaic* fountain or source: *the font of truth.* ⟨Latin *fontis* spring⟩

font² [fɒnt] *n Printing, Computers* a complete set of type of one size and style. ⟨French *fonte* from *fondre* melt. See FOUND³.⟩

fon·ta·nel [ˌfɒntə'nɛl] *n Anatomy* a gap between the bones of the growing skull of an infant or fetus. ⟨French *fontanelle* diminutive of *fontaine.* See FOUNTAIN.⟩

food [fud] *n* **1** what an animal or plant takes in to live and grow. **2** solid nourishment: *food and drink.* **3** what sustains in any way: *food for thought.* ⟨Old English *fōda*⟩
food bank an organization which collects

food, to be given free to the unemployed, the homeless, or those with low incomes. **food chain** a series of organisms in a community, each of which feeds on, and in turn is eaten by, other organisms in the chain. **food fish** a fish used as food. **foo·die** *n Informal* one with great interest in culinary delicacies. **food·land** *n* land used to grow edible crops: *the Ontario foodland.* **food poisoning** sickness from eating contaminated food. **food processor** a kitchen appliance for performing a variety of functions, such as slicing, blending, etc. **food·stuff** *n* any material for food: *Grain is a foodstuff.* **food value** the nutritional content of food. **food web** the inter-related feeding patterns of a community of living things.

fool [ful] *n* **1** a person without sense. **2** formerly, a jester. **3** a dupe.
v **1** act like a fool for fun: *Don't fool during class.* **2** make a fool of.
adj Informal of a resistant object: *That fool door!* **fool·ish** *adj.* **fool·ish·ly** *adv.* **fool·ish·ness** *n.* ⟨Old French *fol* madman; probably Latin *follis* empty-headed, orig bag, bellows⟩
be nobody's fool be clever. **fool around** *Informal* **a** waste time foolishly. **b** engage in illicit sex or in playful sexual activity. **c** meddle (with). **play the fool** clown around. **fool·er·y** *n* foolish action. **fool·har·dy** *adj* foolishly bold. **fool·har·di·ness** *n.* **fool·proof** *adj* so safe or simple that even a fool can use or do it: *a foolproof safety catch.* **fool's cap** a cap or hood worn by a fool or jester. **fools·cap** *n* writing paper in sheets usually about 21 cm wide by 35 cm long. **fool's errand** a useless undertaking. **fool's gold** a mineral that looks like gold; iron pyrites or copper pyrites. **fool's paradise** happiness based on false beliefs or hopes.

foot [fut] *n, pl* **feet** **1** the end part of a leg. **2** the lowest part. **3** the end opposite the head: *the foot of the table.* **4** soldiers that go on foot; infantry. **5** a non-metric unit for measuring length, equal to about 30 cm. *Symbol* ' **6** *Prosody* one of the metrical parts into which a line of verse is divided.
v **1** walk. **2** *Informal* pay (a bill, etc.). ⟨Old English *fōt*⟩
foot it *Informal* **a** travel on foot. **b** run. **get off on the wrong foot** make a bad beginning. **get** (or **have**) **one's foot in the door** *Informal* be in a good position for success. **my foot!** *Informal* an interjection denoting strong scepticism: *Sick, my foot! He was jogging this morning.* **on foot** walking. **put one's best foot forward** *Informal* **a** do one's best. **b** try to make a good impression. **put one's foot down** *Informal* act firmly. **put one's foot in one's mouth** say something unintentionally rude or embarrassing. **put one's foot in it** *Informal* get into trouble by saying or doing something tactless. **set foot on** or **in** enter: *I've never set foot in her apartment.* **under foot a** in the way. **b** on the ground: *damp under foot.* **with one foot in the grave** almost dead; dying.
foot·age *n* **1** a quantity of film: *We shot some*

good footage today. **2** an extent of something measured in feet: *square footage.* **foot–and–mouth disease** a contagious virus disease of cattle and some other animals. **foot·ball** *n* **1** a game played by two teams, in which each side tries to kick, pass, or carry a ball across the opposing team's goal line. **2** the oval ball used in playing this game. **3** *Informal* any subject of discussion that is passed around: *a political football.* **foot·board** *n* an upright piece across the foot of a bed. **foot·bridge** *n* a bridge for pedestrians only. **foot–dragging** *n* delay. **foot·er** *n* a line of text, esp one automatically inserted by software, at the foot of each page of a document. **foot·fall** *n* the sound of a step. **foot·hill** *n* a low hill at the base of a mountain: *the foothills of the Rockies.* **foot·hold** *n* **1** a place to put a foot: *footholds in cracks in the rock.* **2** a firm position: *It is hard to break a habit that has gained a foothold.* **foot·ing** *n* **1** a firm position: *to lose one's footing.* **2** a basis of understanding: *Canada and the US are on a friendly footing.* **3 footings** *pl* the concrete foundations of a building, wall, etc. **foot·lights** *n pl* a row of lights on the floor at the front of a stage, now rarely used. **foot·lock·er** *n* a small chest in which a soldier's personal belongings are kept, often at the foot of the bed. **foot·loose** *adj Informal* free to go anywhere. **foot·man** *n, pl* -**men** a male servant who answers the bell, waits on table, etc., now found mainly in royal palaces. **foot·mark** *n* footprint. **foot·note** *n* **1** a note at the bottom of a page about something in the text. **2** a subsidiary comment or event. **foot·note** *v.* **foot·path** *n* a path for pedestrians only. **foot–pound–second** *adj* of or designating the non-metric measurement system. **foot·print** *n* **1** the mark made by a foot. **2** a specification of something in terms of the area affected or occupied by it. **foot·rest** *n* a support on which to rest the feet. **foot·sie** ['fʊtsi] *n Informal* foot (esp a child's term). **play footsie** *Informal* **a** touch feet, knees, etc. in a flirtatious way, esp secretly. **b** flirt with, esp in a secretive way. **foot·slog, -slogged, -slog·ging** *v* march or plod, esp as through difficult terrain. **foot·slog·ger** *n.* **foot soldier** a soldier who fights on foot. **foot·sore** *adj* having sore feet, esp from walking. **foot·step** *n* **1** a person's step. **2** the sound of a step. **follow in someone's footsteps** do as another has done. **foot·stool** *n* a low stool on which to rest the feet. **foot·wear** *n* shoes, slippers, stockings, etc. **foot·work** *n* the way of using the feet: *Footwork is important in boxing and dancing.*

fop [fɒp] *n* a vain man who is fond of clothes and has affected manners. **fop·pish** *adj.* **fop·per·y** *n.* ⟨Middle English *foppe*⟩

for [fɔr] *prep* **1** as: *We used boxes for chairs.* **2** in support of: *I voted for her.* **3** representing: *A lawyer acts for her client.* **4** in return for: *We thanked him for his kindness.* **5** with the object of taking, achieving, etc.: *He went for a walk.* **6** suited to: *books for children.* **7** because of: *to*

shout for joy. **8** in honour of: *A party was given for her.* **9** with respect to: *bad for one's health.* **10** throughout; during: *to walk for 2 km, to sit for an hour.* **11** in the amount of: *a cheque for $20.* **12** scheduled at or on: *His appointment is for 2:30.*

conj because: *He felt happy, for he knew she had arrived safely.* ⟨Old English⟩

for·as·much as because; since.

for·age ['fɒrɪdʒ] *n* food for horses, cattle, etc. *v* **1** supply with food. **2** hunt for anything, esp food: *The girls foraged in the kitchen till they found some cookies.* **for·ag·er** *n.* ⟨Old French *fourrager; fuerre* fodder; Germanic⟩

for·ay ['fɒrei] *n* **1** a raid for plunder. **2** a brief attempt at something: *a foray into commerce.* **for·ay** *v.* ⟨Old French *fourrier; fuerre* fodder. See FORAGE.⟩

for·bear [fɔr'bɛr] *v* -**bore, -borne, -bear·ing** keep from (doing, etc.): *She forbore to hit back because the boy was smaller.* **for·bear·ance** *n.* **for·bear·ing** *adj.* ⟨Old English *forberan*⟩

for·bid [fɔr'bɪd] *v* -**bade** or -**bad, -bid·den** or -**bid, -bid·ding** order (someone) not to do something. ⟨Old English *forbēodan*⟩ **for·bid·den** *adj* not allowed. **forbidden fruit** any pleasure that is prohibited. **for·bid·ding** *adj* causing fear; looking dangerous: *a rocky and forbidding coast.* **for·bid·ding·ly** *adv.*

force [fɔrs] *n* **1** active power: *the force of running water.* **2** strength used against a person or thing: *to rule by force.* **3** mental or moral strength: *force of character.* **4** a group of people acting together: *our office force.* **5 forces** *pl* armed forces. **6** *Physics* any cause that produces, changes, or stops the motion of a body. **7** a source of power likened to a physical force: *social forces.*
v **1** use force on. **2** make by an unusual effort. **3** hurry the development of, by unnatural means: *to force rhubarb by growing it in a dark place.* **forced** *adj.* **for·ced·ly** ['fɔrsədli] *adv.* ⟨French; Latin *fortis* strong⟩
force in *Baseball* of a pitcher, cause (a run) to be scored by issuing a walk when the bases are loaded. **in force a** in effect or operation. **b** in great numbers.
force–feed, -fed, -feed·ing *v* **1** feed (an animal or person) by forcible means, as by passing a tube into the stomach. **2** force (someone) to accept or take in (ideas, etc.). **force·ful** *adj* powerful; vigorous: *a forceful manner.* **force·ful·ly** *adv.* **force·ful·ness** *n.* **force majeure** ['fɔrs ma'ʒɜr] *Law* any event that may allow a party to break a contract. **for·ci·ble** *adj* **1** made or done by force: *a forcible entry into a house.* **2** showing force: *a forcible speaker.* **for·ci·bly** *adv.*

CONFUSABLES
Both **forceful** and **forcible** mean 'showing force, powerful', but only **forcible** means 'done by force': *a forceful style, a forcible entry.*

for·ceps ['fɔrsɛps] *n, pl* -**ceps** a pair of small tongs used by surgeons, dentists, etc. for holding and pulling. ⟨Latin; from *formus* hot + *capere* take⟩

ford [fɔrd] *n* a place where a river is shallow enough to walk or drive through it. **ford** *v*. **ford·a·ble** *adj*. ⟨Old English⟩

fore¹ [fɔr] *adj, adv* at the front; forward. *n* the front, esp of a ship or boat. ⟨Old English⟩

fore² [fɔr] *interj Golf* a shout of warning to persons ahead on the fairway who are liable to be struck by the ball. ⟨perhaps for *before*⟩

fore– *prefix* **1** at or near the front: *foremast*. **2** before; beforehand: *foresee*. ⟨Old English *fore* before⟩

fore·arm¹ [ˈfɔr,arm] *n* the part of the arm between the elbow and wrist.

fore·arm² [fɔrˈarm] *v* prepare for trouble ahead of time; arm beforehand.

fore·bear [ˈfɔr,bɛr] *n* an ancestor; forefather. ⟨*fore-* + *be* + *-er* one who was before⟩

fore·bode [fɔrˈboud] *v* **1** give warning of: *Black clouds forebode a storm.* **2** have a feeling that something bad is going to happen. **fore·bod·ing** *n, adj.* **for·bod·ing·ly** *adv*.

fore·brain [ˈfɔr,brein] *n Anatomy* the front section of the brain.

fore·cast [ˈfɔr,kæst] *v* -cast or -cast·ed, -cast·ing predict: *Cooler weather is forecast for tomorrow.* **fore·cast** *n*. **fore·cast·er** *n*.

fore·cas·tle [ˈfouksəl] or [ˈfɔr,kæsəl] *n Nautical* **1** the upper deck in front of the foremast of a ship. **2** the sailors' quarters in a merchant ship, formerly in the forward part of the ship.

fore·check [ˈfɔr,tʃɛk] *v ✹ Hockey* check an opposing player in his or her own defensive zone, to prevent the opposing team from organizing an attack. **fore·check·er** *n*. **fore·check·ing** *n*.

fore·close [fɔrˈklouz] *v* **1** shut out; prevent. **2** *Law* take possession of a mortgaged property as a result of someone's failure to make the payments. **fore·clos·a·ble** *adj*. **fore·clo·sure** *n*. ⟨Old French *forclos* pp of *forclore* exclude; *for-* out (Latin *foris*) + *clore* shut (Latin *claudere*)⟩

fore·fa·ther [ˈfɔr,fɒðər] *n* ancestor.

fore·fin·ger [ˈfɔr,fɪŋgər] *n* the finger next to the thumb; first finger; index finger.

fore·foot [ˈfɔr,fʊt] *n, pl* -feet one of the front feet of an animal.

fore·front [ˈfɔr,frʌnt] *n* the place of greatest importance, activity, etc.

fore·go·ing [ˈfɔr,gouɪŋ] *adj* previous. *n* **the foregoing**, that which has already been referred to. **fore·gone** [fɔrˈgɒn] or [ˈfɔrgɒn] *adj* previous. **foregone conclusion** a fact that was expected: *She's so popular; her re-election was a foregone conclusion.*

fore·ground [ˈfɔr,graʊnd] *n* **1** the part of a scene nearest one. **2** focus of attention.

fore·hand [ˈfɔr,hænd] *adj* made with the palm of the hand turned forward. **fore·hand** *adv*.

fore·head [ˈfɔr,hɛd] *n* the part of the face above the eyes. ⟨Old English *forhēafod*⟩

for·eign [ˈfɔrɪn] *adj* **1** coming from outside one's own country: *a foreign language.* **2** not belonging: *Sitting still all day is foreign to my nature.* **3** not belonging naturally to the place where found: *a foreign object in the eye.* **for·eign·ness** *n*. ⟨Old French *forain*; Latin *foras* outside⟩

foreign correspondent a reporter who sends news from the foreign country where he or she is based. **for·eign·er** *n* **1** a person from another country. **2** *Informal* a person strange to one's own customs, ideas, etc. **foreign exchange** a place where one can change one's money into a foreign currency.

fore·leg [ˈfɔr,lɛg] *n* one of the front legs of an animal.

fore·man [ˈfɔrmən] *n, pl* -men **1** a person in charge of a group of workers. **2** a chairperson of a jury.

fore·most [ˈfɔr,moust] *adj* **1** first. **2** most notable. *adv* **1** first: *He stumbled and fell head foremost.* **2** in the first place: *first and foremost.* ⟨Old English *formest*; double superlative of *forma* first, superlative of *fore* before; infl. by *most*⟩

fore·name [ˈfɔr,neim] *n* a person's first name.

fore·noon [ˈfɔr,nun] *n* the time between early morning and noon. **fore·noon** *adj*.

fo·ren·sic [fəˈrɛnsɪk] *adj* **1** to do with a law court or public debate. **2** to do with the application of science to police work. ⟨Latin *forensis; forum* forum⟩

fore·paw [ˈfɔr,pɒ] *n* a front paw.

fore·play [ˈfɔr,plei] *n* the period of mutual sexual activity preceding intercourse.

fore·run·ner [ˈfɔr,rʌnər] *n* **1** a person going before to show that someone else is coming. **2** a sign or warning of something to come: *Black clouds are often the forerunners of a storm.*

fore·see [fɔrˈsi] *v* -saw, -seen, -see·ing know beforehand: *Mother foresaw how hungry we would be.* **fore·see·a·ble** *adj*. **fore·see·a·bly** *adv*. ⟨Old English *foresēon*⟩

fore·sight [ˈfɔr,sait] *n* **1** the power to realize beforehand what is likely to happen. **2** careful thought for the future. **3** a view into the future. **fore·sight·ed** *adj* having or showing foresight. **fore·sight·ed·ness** *n*.

fore·shad·ow [fɔrˈʃædou] *v* indicate beforehand: *Black clouds foreshadow a storm.* **fore·shad·ow·ing** *n*.

fore·shore [ˈfɔr,ʃɔr] *n* the part of the shore between the high-water mark and low-water mark.

fore·short·en [fɔrˈʃɔrtən] *v* **1** in a drawing or painting, represent (lines, etc.) as of less than true length in order to give the proper impression to the eye. **2** abridge; condense. **fore·short·en·ing** *n*.

fore·sight See FORESEE.

fore·skin [ˈfɔr,skɪn] *n* the fold of skin that covers the end of the penis; prepuce.

for·est ['fɒrɪst] *n* **1** a large area of land covered with trees. **2** the trees themselves. **for·est** *adj.* **for·est·ed** *adj.* **for·est·less** *adj.* ⟨Old French *forest*; Latin *foris* outdoors⟩ **for·est·a·tion** *n* the planting or taking care of forests. **for·est·er** *n* a person trained in forestry. **forest ranger** a government official in charge of guarding a forest and its wildlife. **for·est·ry** *n* the science of managing forests.

fore·stall [fɔr'stɒl] *v* prevent by acting first: *He forestalled a riot by having the police ready.*

fore·taste ['fɔr,teist] *n* a preliminary taste: *He got a foretaste of business life by working during his vacation.*

fore·tell [fɔr'tɛl] *v* -**told**, -**tell·ing** tell or show beforehand.

fore·thought ['fɔr,θɒt] *n* **1** previous thought or consideration. **2** careful thought for the future: *Forethought will often prevent mistakes.*

fore·to·ken [fɔr'toukən] *v* be an omen of. **fore·to·ken** ['fɔr,toukən] *n.*

for·ev·er [fə'rɛvər] *adv* **1** for always. **2** *Informal* all the time: *forever talking.* *n Informal* an excessively long time. **for·ev·er·more** [fə,rɛvər'mɔr] *adv* forever.

fore·warn [fɔr'wɔrn] *v* warn beforehand.

fore·wom·an ['fɔr,wʊmən] *n, pl* -**wom·en** **1** a woman in charge of a group of workers. **2** the chairwoman of a jury.

fore·word ['fɔr,wɜrd] *n* a short preface to a book or other writing, esp a note on the work of the author by a distinguished writer, scholar, public figure, etc.

for·feit ['fɔrfɪt] *v* lose as a penalty for a fault: *He forfeited his deposit when he lost the video.* *n* something lost as a penalty. **for·feit** *adj.* **for·feit·a·ble** *adj.* ⟨Old French *forfait* pp of *forfaire* transgress; *for-* (Latin *foris* outside) + *faire* do (Latin *facere*)⟩ **for·fei·ture** ['fɔrfətʃər] *n* **1** the loss of something as a penalty. **2** penalty; fine.

for·gave [fər'geiv] *v* pt of FORGIVE.

forge¹ [fɔrdʒ] *n* a furnace where metal is heated to a high temperature before being hammered into shape. *v* **1** heat (metal) and then hammer it into shape. **2** shape or form: *They forged a lasting friendship.* **3** make a fraudulent imitation of: *to forge a signature.* **forg·er** *n.* **for·ger·y** *n.* ⟨Old French *forge*; Latin *fabrica* workshop⟩

forge² [fɔrdʒ] *v* move forward slowly but steadily: *to forge ahead.* ⟨origin uncertain⟩

for·get [fər'gɛt] *v* -**got**, -**got·ten** or -**got**, -**get·ting** **1** be unable to remember. **2** omit without meaning to: *She forgot to send him a card.* **3** leave behind unintentionally: *I forgot my purse.* **4** put aside: *Let's forget our quarrel.* **forget it** *Informal* **a** don't concern yourself about this. **b** absolutely not. **forget oneself a** be unselfish. **b** do something inappropriate. **for·get·ta·ble** *adj.* ⟨Old English *forgietan*; *for-* away + Old Norse *geta* get⟩ **for·get·ful** *adj* **1** having a poor memory. **2** heedless: *forgetful of danger.* **for·get·ful·ly** *adv.*

for·get·ful·ness *n.* **for·get—me—not** *n* any of a genus of herbs of the borage family.

for·give [fər'gɪv] *v* -**gave**, -**giv·en**, -**giv·ing** **1** give up the wish to punish or get even with. **2** give up all claim to: *to forgive a debt.* **for·giv·a·ble** *adj.* **for·giv·a·bly** *adv.* **for·give·ness** *n.* ⟨Old English *forgiefan*; *for-* away + *giefan* give⟩ **for·giv·ing** *adj* willing to forgive. **for·giv·ing·ly** *adv.* **for·giv·ing·ness** *n.*

for·go [fɔr'gou] *v* -**went**, -**gone**, -**go·ing** do without; give up: *Forgo the movies and do your essay.* ⟨Old English *forgān*; *for-* away + *gān* go⟩

for·got [fər'gɒt] *v* a pt and a pp of FORGET.

fork [fɔrk] *n* **1** an instrument having a handle and pointed prongs, or tines. **2** anything shaped like a fork, such as a tuning fork. **3** the place where a tree, or stream divides into two branches. *v* **1** divide into two parts: *The road forks.* **2** lift or dig with a fork. **3** *Chess* threaten two pieces with one move. **fork·like** *adj.* ⟨Old English *forca;* Latin *furca*⟩ **fork out** *Slang* spend. **fork over** *Slang* hand over.

forked [fɔrkt] *adj* **1** divided into branches. **2** zigzag: *forked lightning.* **fork·lift** *n* a vehicle having a forklike device for lifting objects.

for·lorn [fɔr'lɔrn] *adj* **1** neglected: *The kitten, a forlorn little animal, was wet.* **2** unhappy; hopeless. **for·lorn·ly** *adv.* **for·lorn·ness** *n.* ⟨Old English *forloren* lost; pp of *forlēosan*⟩ **forlorn hope** a desperate hope, almost sure not to be fulfilled.

form [fɔrm] *n* **1** shape. **2** body of a person or animal. **3** an orderly arrangement of parts: *The effect of a story comes from its form as well as its content.* **4** a way of doing something: *He is fast, but his form in running is bad.* **5** a record of previous behaviour: *According to form, this horse should win.* **6** a document with printing on it and blank spaces to be filled in. **7** the way in which a thing exists: *Water exists in the forms of ice, snow, and steam.* **8** kind; sort: *Heat is a form of energy.* **9** a good condition of body or mind: *Athletes exercise to keep in form.* *v* **1** give shape to or take shape: *Clouds form in the sky.* **2** make up: *Parents and children form a family.* **3** organize: *We formed a club.* **4** put together (opinions, images, etc.), in one's mind. ⟨Latin *forma* form, mould⟩ **bad (good) form,** behaviour contrary to (in accord with) accepted customs. **form·less** *adj* shapeless. **form·less·ly** *adv.* **form·less·ness** *n.* **form letter** a letter copied from a pattern. **for·ma·tion** *n* **1** arrangement; order: *troops in battle formation.* **2** the thing formed: *Clouds are formations of tiny drops of water.* **3** *Geology* a series of layers of the same kind of rock. **4** *Ecology* the most populous plant community in a particular region, as tundra, prairie, etc. **form·a·tive** ['fɔrmətɪv] *adj* **1** to do with formation: *Mom was a formative influence in my life.* **2** *Biology* that can produce new cells or tissues: *formative yolk.* **for·ma·tive·ly** *adv.* **form·fit·ting** *adj* closely following the shape of the body.

for·mal ['fɔrməl] *adj* **1** with strict attention to ceremony: *The judge had a formal manner in court.* **2** done with the proper forms: *A written contract is a formal agreement to do something.* **3** to do with a formal occasion: *formal dress.* **4** of language, conforming to an official or conservative style in vocabulary, syntax, and pronunciation. **5** to do with institutions: *a formal education.*
n **1** a social gathering at which formal dress is worn. **2** a gown worn to formal social gatherings: *She was dressed in her first formal.* **for·mal·ly** *adv.* ⟨Latin *formalis; forma* form⟩
for·mal·ism *n* strict attention to outward forms and ceremonies. **for·mal·ist** *n.* **for·mal·is·tic** *adj.* **for·mal·i·ty** *n* **1** a procedure required by custom or rule. **2** attention to customs: *Visitors at the court of a king are received with formality.* **3** stiffness of manner. **for·mal·ize** *v* **1** make formal or official. **2** give a definite form to. **for·mal·i·za·tion** *n.*

form·al·de·hyde [fɔr'mældə,haɪd] *n Chemistry* a gas with a sharp odour, used in solution as a preservative. ⟨*form(ic acid) + aldehyde*⟩
For·ma·lin ['fɔrməlɪn] *n Trademark* a solution of formaldehyde in water.

for·mat ['fɔrmæt] *n* **1** the design or arrangement of anything: *the format of a television show.* **2** *Computers* a particular means by which data may be processed. **3** the medium in which sound may be reproduced: *cassette format.*
v prepare (a computer disk) for use by having the operating system write certain data on it: *to format the diskette.* Also called **initialize.** ⟨Latin *formatus* pp of *formare* to form⟩

for·ma·tion See FORM.

for·mer ['fɔrmər] *adj* **1** designating the first of two: *the former case.* **2** earlier or previous: *a former classmate.*
n **the former** the first of two: *When I am offered ice cream or pie, I always choose the former.* Compare LATTER. ⟨Middle English *formere,* comparative back-formation from *formest.* See FOREMOST.⟩
for·mer·ly *adv* in the past; some time ago.

for·mi·da·ble ['fɔrmədəbəl] *or* [fɔr'mɪdəbəl] *adj* **1** hard to overcome; hard to deal with. **2** *Informal* impressive. **for·mi·da·ble·ness** *n.* **for·mi·da·bly** *adv.* ⟨Latin *formidare* dread⟩

for·mu·la ['fɔrmjələ] *n, pl* **-las** *or* **-lae** [-,li] *or* [-,laɪ] **1** a set form of words: *"How do you do?"* is a formula of greeting. **2** a statement of religious belief or doctrine: *The Apostles' Creed is a formula of the Christian faith.* **3** a rule for doing something, esp one used by those who do not know the reason on which it is based. **4** a recipe: *a formula for making soup.* **5** a mixture, esp one for feeding a baby. **6** *Chemistry* an expression showing by symbols the composition of a compound: *The formula for water is H_2O.* **7** *Mathematics* an expression showing by algebraic symbols a rule, principle, etc. $(a + b)^2 = a^2 + 2ab + b^2$ is an algebraic formula. **8** a ranking of racing cars, usually by engine power: *Formula one.* ⟨Latin, diminutive of *forma* form⟩

for·mu·la·ic *adj* based on formulas.
for·mu·late *v* **1** express in systematic form: *Our ideas of fair treatment for all Canadians are formulated in a Bill of Rights.* **2** invent. **for·mu·la·tion** *n.*

for·ni·ca·tion [,fɔrnə'keɪʃən] *n* voluntary sexual intercourse other than between a married couple. **for·ni·cate** *v.* **for·ni·ca·tor** *n.* ⟨Latin *fornicari; fornix* brothel⟩

for·sake [fər'seɪk] *v* **-sook, -sak·en, -sak·ing.** give up; leave alone; abandon. **for·sak·en** *adj* . **for·sak·en·ly** *adv.* ⟨Old English *forsacan; for-* away + *sacan* dispute, deny⟩

for·swear [fɔr'swɛr] *v* **-swore, -sworn, -swear·ing** **1** swear to give up. **2** be untrue to one's sworn word. **for·sworn** *adj.* ⟨Old English *forswerian; for-* away + *swerian* swear⟩

for·syth·i·a [fər'sɪθjə] *n* any of a genus of shrubs of the olive family having yellow flowers that appear early in spring, before the leaves. ⟨W. *Forsyth,* 18c English horticulturist⟩

fort [fɔrt] *n* **1** a strong building that can be defended against an enemy. **2** formerly, a trading post. In the early days of the fur trade, these posts were usually fortified: *Winnipeg is built on the site of Fort Garry, an old Hudson's Bay Company post.* ⟨French; Latin *fortis* strong⟩
hold the fort, *Informal* keep things functioning.
for·ti·fy *v* **1** strengthen against attack. **2** strengthen. **3** add something to (food or drink) that strengthens: *Brandy is used to fortify port wine.* **for·ti·fi·ca·tion** *n.* **for·ti·fi·er** *n.*

forte[1] ['fɔrteɪ] *or* [fɔrt] *n* something a person does very well; strong point: *Cooking is her forte.* ⟨French, fem. of *fort* strong; Latin *fortis*⟩

for·te[2] ['fɔrteɪ] *Music adj, adv* loud. ⟨Italian *forte* strong, loud; Latin *fortis*⟩
for·tis·si·mo [fɔr'tɪsə,moʊ] *adj, adv* very loud.

forth [fɔrθ] *adv* **1** forward. **2** into view or consideration; out. **3** away. ⟨Old English⟩
and so forth and so on; and the like: *We ate cake, candy, nuts, and so forth.*
forth·com·ing ['fɔrθ,kʌmɪŋ] *or* [,fɔrθ'kʌmɪŋ] *adj* **1** about to appear: *the forthcoming week.* **2** ready when wanted: *She needed help, but none was forthcoming.* **3** friendly and communicative.
forth·right ['fɔrθ,raɪt] *adj* outspoken; direct. **forth·right·ly** *adv.* **forth·right·ness** *n.*
forth·with [,fɔrθ'wɪθ] *or* [-'wɪð] *adv* at once: *She said she would be there forthwith.*

for·ti·eth See FORTY.

for·ti·tude ['fɔrtə,tjud] *or* ['fɔrtə,tud] *n* courage in facing pain, danger, or trouble. ⟨Latin *fortitudo; fortis* strong⟩

fort·night ['fɔrt,naɪt] *n* two weeks. **fort·night·ly** *adv.* ⟨Middle English *fourtenight;* Old English *fēowertēne niht* fourteen nights⟩

for·tress See FORT.

for·tu·i·tous [fɔr'tjuətəs] *or* [fɔr'tuətəs] *adj* **1** accidental: *a fortuitous meeting.*

2 happening by lucky chance: *a fortuitous discovery such as penicillin.* **for·tu·i·tous·ly** *adv.* **for·tu·i·tous·ness** *n.* **for·tu·i·ty** *n* 1 chance; accident. 2 fortuitous quality. ⟨Latin *fortuitus; fors, fortis* chance⟩

for·tune ['fɔrtʃən] *n* 1 a great deal of money or property. 2 what is going to happen to a person: *to predict someone's fortune.* 3 good luck. 4 chance: *Fortune was against us; we lost.* ⟨Latin *fortuna; fors, fortis* chance⟩
a small fortune a large sum of money: *That can of caviar cost a small fortune.*
for·tu·nate *adj* 1 lucky. 2 bringing good luck. **for·tu·nate·ly** *adv.* **fortune cookie** a small cookie served with Chinese food, containing a slip of paper bearing advice, a motto, etc. **fortune hunter** a person who tries to get a fortune by marrying someone rich. **for·tune·tell·er** *n* a person who claims to be able to tell what is going to happen to others.

SYNONYMS
Fortunate suggests being favoured by circumstances that could not have been counted on: *He made a fortunate decision when he went into advertising.* **Lucky** is less formal and emphasizes the idea of accident or pure chance: *It was lucky that he missed his train the day it was wrecked.*

for·ty ['fɔrti] *n* 1 four times ten; 40. 2 **forties** *pl* the years from 40 through 49, esp of a century or of a person's life: *She achieved success as a playwright in her forties.* 3 any set of 40 persons or things. **for·ty** *adj.* ⟨Old English *fēowertig*⟩
for·ti·eth ['fɔrtiɪθ] *adj, n* 1 next after the 39th; 40th. 2 one, or being one, of 40 equal parts.
forty winks *Informal* a short nap.

fo·rum ['fɔrəm] *n* 1 the public square in ancient Rome, used for public assemblies and business. 2 an occasion or place for public discussion: *The* Opinions *page is a forum for readers' comments.* ⟨Latin⟩

for·ward ['fɔrwərd] *adv* 1 onward: *Go forward.* 2 toward the front. 3 into consideration: *He brought forward some ideas.* 4 later in time: *We put the clocks forward in April.* 5 earlier in time: *Move the meeting forward.*
adj 1 toward the front: *the forward part of a ship.* 2 advanced: *forward for one's age.* 3 pert; bold. 4 ready; eager: *He knew his lesson and was forward with his answers.*
v 1 send on further: *Please forward my mail to my new address.* 2 help along: *She did all she could to forward her friend's plan.*
n Sports a player whose position is in the front line. **for·ward·ly** *adv.* **for·ward·ness** *n.* ⟨Old English *forweard*⟩
forward–looking *adj* anticipating the future.

fos·sil ['fɒsəl] *n* 1 the remains of prehistoric animals or plants preserved in rocks where they have become petrified: *Bone fossils of dinosaurs have been discovered in Alberta.* 2 *Informal* a very old-fashioned person.
adj derived from the remains of living things: *fossil fuels.* **fos·sil–like** *adj.* ⟨Latin *fossilis* from *fossus* pp of *fodere* dig⟩

fossil fuels fuels obtained from the fossilized remains of living organisms within the earth, such as petroleum and natural gas. **fos·sil·ize** *v* 1 make into a fossil. 2 make or become out-of-date or rigid: *fossilized ideas.* **fos·sil·i·za·tion** *n.*

fos·ter ['fɒstər] *v* 1 help the development of: *Ignorance fosters superstition.* 2 bring up; rear. *adj* to do with an arrangement in which a child is given parental care in a home, without being legally adopted: *a foster child.* ⟨Old English *fōstrian* nourish; *fōster* nourishment⟩

fought [fɒt] *v* pt and pp of FIGHT.

foul [faʊl] *adj* 1 very dirty; impure; nasty: *foul air.* 2 very wicked: *Murder is a foul crime.* 3 obscene: *foul language.* 4 against the rules. 5 unfavourable: *a foul wind.*
n something done contrary to the rules.
adv in a foul way. **foul·ly** *adv.* **foul·ness** *n.* ⟨Old English *fūl*⟩
fall (or **run**) **foul of a** get tangled up with. **b** get into trouble or difficulties with: *to run foul of the law.* **foul out a** *Baseball* be put out by hitting a ball that is caught outside the foul lines. **b** *Basketball* be put out of a game for having committed too many fouls. **foul up** *Informal* make a mess of. **foul–up** *n.*
foul ball *Baseball* a ball hit so that it falls outside the foul lines. **foul line** 1 in various games, the boundary of normal play area. 2 *Basketball* a line from which foul shots are made. **foul–mouthed** [-,maʊθt] *or* [-,maʊðd] *adj* habitually using vile, offensive language. **foul play** 1 unfair play 2 treachery; violence. **foul shot** *Basketball* a free throw.

found¹ [faʊnd] *v* pt of FIND.
adj of a work of art, made from material found by chance: *found art.*
found·ling *n* a child found abandoned.

found² [faʊnd] *v* 1 establish: *Champlain founded Québec in 1608.* 2 rest for support; base: *He founded his claim on facts.* **found·er** *n.* ⟨Middle English; Old French *fonder;* Latin *fundare, fundus* bottom⟩
foun·da·tion *n* 1 the base: *the foundation of a house.* 2 the basis of a belief, idea, argument, etc.: *The report has no foundation in fact.* 3 an institution founded and endowed: *a charitable foundation.* 4 a cosmetic applied on the face as a base for rouge, powder, etc. **foun·da·tion·al** *adj.* **foun·da·tion·al·ly** *adv.*
Founder's Day *Buddhism* the festival celebrated in October, commemorating the introduction of Buddhism to Canada.

found³ [faʊnd] *v* melt and mould (metal). ⟨French *fondre* melt; Latin *fundere* pour⟩
found·ry *n* a place where metal is melted and moulded.

foun·der¹ See FOUND².

foun·der² ['faʊndər] *v* 1 fill or cause to fill with water and sink: *A ship foundered in the storm.* 2 bog down in soft ground. 3 go lame or stumble, or cause to do so: *Her horse foundered.* ⟨Old French *fondrer;* Latin *fundus* bottom⟩

fount [faʊnt] *n* an abundant source: *a fount of knowledge.* ⟨Latin *fontis* spring⟩

foun·tain ['faʊntən] *n* **1** a stream of water rising into the air. **2** a decorative structure through which water is forced into the air in a stream. **3** a device by which a jet of water is forced upward so that people may get a drink. **4** SODA FOUNTAIN. **5** an abundant source: *a fountain of wisdom.* **foun·tain·head** *n* **1** the source of a stream. **2** a chief or original source of anything. **fountain pen** a pen that supplies liquid ink from a tube inside.

four [fɔr] *n* **1** one more than three; 4. **2** any set of four persons or things. **3** a playing card or side of a die having four spots. **4** *Rowing* a crew of four rowers, or the boat they use. **four** *adj.* ⟨Old English *fēower*⟩
on all fours on hands and knees.
four–flush·er *n Informal* a person who pretends to be other than he or she really is. **four–flushing** *adj.* **four·fold** *adj* **1** four times as much or as many. **2** having four parts. *adv* four times as much or as many. **four–foot·ed** *adj* having four feet. **four–letter word** any of a group of one-syllable vulgar or taboo words. **four·plex** *n* ※ a building containing four dwelling units. **four–poster** *n* a bed having a column at each corner, supporting a canopy. **four·score** *adj, n* four times twenty; 80. **four·some** *n* a group of four people. **four·square** *adj* **1** square. **2** frank; outspoken. **3** not yielding. *adv* **1** in a square form. **2** without yielding. **four–stroke** *adj Machinery* to do with an engine requiring four piston strokes to complete a fuel cycle. **fourth** *adj, n* **1** next after the third; 4th. **2** one, or being one, of four equal parts. **fourth·ly** *adv.* **fourth estate** the press; newspapers and those who work for them. See ESTATE (def.4). **four–wheel drive** describing a vehicle in which power is transmitted to all four wheels at once. *Abbrev* **4WD**. Also known as **all-wheel drive.** *Abbrev* **AWD**.

four·teen ['fɔrt'tin] *n* **1** four more than ten; 14. **2** any set or series of 14 persons or things. **four·teen** *adj.* ⟨Old English *fēowertēne*⟩
four·teenth *adj, n* **1** next after the 13th; 14th. **2** one, or being one, of 14 equal parts.

fowl [faʊl] *n, pl* **fowls** or (esp collectively) **fowl** **1** a chicken or domestic turkey. **2** any of various other birds, esp those hunted as game. ⟨Old English *fugol*⟩

fox [fɒks] *n* **1** any of various mammals of the dog family that do not hunt in packs and that have a bushy tail. **2** a cunning person. *v* **1** *Informal* trick in a crafty way. **2** of beer, turn or be turned sour. **3** of the pages of a book, discolour or become discoloured. **4** confuse. **fox·like** *adj.* ⟨Old English⟩
fox·glove *n* any of a genus of herbs of the figwort family, esp one cultivated as a source of the drug digitalis. **fox·hole** *n* a hole in the ground for protection against enemy fire. **fox trot** a dance with short, quick steps. **fox–trot, -trot·ted, -trot·ting** *v.* **fox·y** *adj* **1** sly; crafty. **2** discoloured. **3** of certain wines,

tasting like wild grapes. **4** *Slang* sexy; seductive. **fox·i·ly** *adv.* **fox·i·ness** *n.*

foy·er ['fɔɪei] *n* an entrance hall in a theatre, etc.; lobby. ⟨French = hearth; Latin *focus*⟩

Fr. 1 France; French. **2** Father. **3** Friday.

fra·cas ['frækəs] *or* ['freikəs] *n* a noisy quarrel or fight; disturbance; uproar; brawl. ⟨French; Italian *fracasso* from *fracassare* smash⟩

frac·tal ['fræktəl] *adj* **1** to do with natural forms that show a pattern, but with small random variations. **2** *Computers* to do with software programmed to generate infinite random variations on a pattern, as a way of reproducing natural images. ⟨Latin *fractus* pp of *frangere* break⟩

frac·tion ['frækʃən] *n* **1** *Mathematics* one of the equal parts of a whole. **2** a very small amount. **frac·tion·al** *adj.* **frac·tion·al·ly** *adv.* ⟨Latin *fractio; fractus* pp of *frangere* break⟩

frac·tious ['frækʃəs] *adj* **1** cross; fretful. **2** hard to manage; unruly. **frac·tious·ly** *adv.* **frac·tious·ness** *n.* ⟨*fraction* (in earlier sense of discord, brawling), on model of *captious*, etc.⟩

frac·ture ['fræktʃər] *v* break; crack: *She fractured her arm.* **frac·ture** *n.* ⟨Latin *fractura; fractus* pp of *frangere* break⟩

frag·ile ['frædʒaɪl] *or* ['frædʒəl] *adj* **1** easily broken. **2** slight; ineffectual: *a fragile hope.* **3** *Informal* nervous; easily upset: *I feel fragile today.* **frag·ile·ly** *adv.* **fra·gil·i·ty** [frə'dʒɪləti] *n.* ⟨Latin *fragilis;* related to *frangere* break⟩

frag·ment ['frægmənt] *n* **1** a broken piece. **2** an incomplete or disconnected part: *She could hear only fragments of the conversation.* *v* [fræg'mɛnt] break or divide into fragments. **frag·men·tar·y** ['frægmən,tɛri] *or* [fræg'mɛntəri] *adj.* **frag·men·ta·tion** *n.* **frag·ment·ize** *v.* **frag·ment·i·za·tion** *n.* ⟨Latin *fragmentum;* related to *frangere* break⟩

fra·grance ['freigrəns] *n* **1** a pleasing odour. **2** a prepared perfume. **fra·grant** *adj.* **fra·grant·ly** *adv.* ⟨Latin *fragrare* emit odour⟩

frail [freil] *adj* **1** weak; physically delicate: *a frail child.* **2** easily broken: *a very frail support.* **3** morally weak. **frail·ly** *adv.* ⟨Old French *fraile;* Latin *fragilis* fragile. See FRAGILE.⟩
frail·ty *n* the fact or quality of being frail: *human frailty.*

frame [freim] *n* **1** a structure over which something is stretched or built: *the frame of a house.* **2** anything made of parts fitted together. **3** bodily structure: *a man of heavy frame.* **4** the border in which a thing is set: *a window frame.* **5** one of a series of pictures on a strip of film. **6** one turn at bowling. **7** *Informal Baseball* an inning. **8** *Pool, snooker* **a** the triangular form used to arrange the balls at the start of a game. **b** the period of play between two placings of the balls. **9** a glass box protecting plants outdoors. *v* **1** build frames of buildings. **2** shape: *to frame one's life according to a noble pattern.* **3** put together: *Laws are framed in Parliament.* **4** enclose with a frame. **5** *Informal* make seem guilty. **6** compose in speech: *She framed her*

excuses timidly. **fram·er** *n.* ⟨Old English *framian* to profit; *fram* forth⟩
frame house a house made of a wooden framework covered with boards. **frame of mind** mood. **frame of reference** the entire circumstances within which something exists. **frame–up** *n Informal* **1** a dishonest arrangement made beforehand. **2** a scheme made to have a person falsely accused. **frame·work** *n* **1** an open frame over which something is stretched or built or in which something is encased. **2** the way in which a thing is put together.

fran·chise ['fræntʃaɪz] *n* **1** a right granted by a government. **2** the right to vote: *A Canadian citizen receives the federal franchise at the age of 18.* **3** the authorization to sell the products of a manufacturer or providing a company's service in a given area, or the business so authorized. **4** authorization to own a member team, granted by a professional sports league, or the team so authorized. ⟨Old French *franchise* a freeing; *franc* free. See FRANK¹.⟩
fran·chi·see [,fræntʃaɪ'zi] *n* a person or business that holds a franchise.

fran·ci·um ['frænsiəm] *n* a rare radioactive element. *Symbol* **Fr** ⟨Latin; after *France*⟩

fran·cize or **fran·cise** ['frænsaɪz] *v* **-cized, -ciz·ing ✷** make or become French or French-speaking. **fran·ci·za·tion** *n.*

Fran·co– *combining form.* **1** French or French-speaking: *Francophile* **2** French and——: *the Franco-Prussian war.* **3** French-Canadian: *Franco-Albertan.*
Fran·co·phile ['fræŋkə,faɪl] *n* **1** a person who greatly admires France, its people, and its culture. **2 ✷** a non-French-Canadian who shows particular sympathy with the policies and culture of French-speaking Canada. **Fran·co·phobe** ['fræŋkə,foub] *n* **1** a person who hates or fears French people or French influences. **2 ✷** a person who is hostile to the policies, culture, etc. of French-speaking Canada. **Fran·co·phone** ['fræŋkə,foun] *n* a person in a bilingual or multilingual country whose native or principal language is French. **Fran·co·phone** *adj.*

fran·gi·ble ['frændʒəbəl] *adj* breakable. ⟨French; Latin *frangere* break⟩
fran·gi·pan·i [,frændʒə'pæni] *n, pl* **-pan·is** or **-pan·i** any of various tropical shrubs or trees of the dogbane family having fragrant flowers. ⟨M. *Frangipani* 16c Italian marquis, supposed perfume inventor⟩

Fran·glais [frɑŋ'glei]; *French* [fʀɑ̃'glɛ] *n ✷* *Informal* French spoken with many English words and expressions. Also, **Franglish.** ⟨French *français* French + *anglais* English⟩

frank¹ [fræŋk] *adj* **1** free in expressing one's thoughts: *When giving her opinion on any subject, she is always frank.* **2** plain; downright: *frank mutiny.*
v mark (a letter, etc.) for free mailing.
n a mark to show that a letter, package, etc. is to be sent without charge. **frank·ly** *adv.*

frank·ness *n.* ⟨Old French *franc* free, sincere (orig, a Frank, freedom in early France being confined to the dominant Franks)⟩

SYNONYMS
Frank = free in expressing one's thoughts: *Her eyes are frank and honest.*
Outspoken = speaking out, even when it involves giving offence: *He was outspoken in his criticism.* **Candid** = completely truthful: *Her candid account of her failure surprised us.*

frank² [fræŋk] *n Informal* frankfurter.
frank·furt·er ['fræŋk,fərtər] or **frankfurt** *n* wiener. ⟨German *Frankfurter* of Frankfurt⟩

Frank·en·stein ['fræŋkɪn,staɪn] *n* **1** any person brought down by his or her invention. **2** Also, **Frankenstein's monster** a thing that causes the ruin of its creator. ⟨in a 19c novel by Mary Shelley, a character who creates an uncontrollable monster⟩

frank·in·cense ['fræŋkɪn,sɛns] *n* a resin that gives off a spicy odour when burned. ⟨Old French *franc encens* pure incense⟩

fran·tic ['fræntɪk] *adj* **1** wild with fright, pain, rage, or frustration. **2** marked by wild, uncontrolled action: *She made a frantic effort to stop the car.* **fran·ti·cal·ly** *adv.* ⟨Old French *frénétique.* See FRENETIC.⟩

frap·pé [fræ'pei] *adj* iced; cooled.
n any frozen or iced food or drink. ⟨French, pp of *frapper* chill, beat⟩

fra·ter·nal [frə'tɜrnəl] *adj* **1** brotherly. **2** to do with a fraternity, society, etc. **3** of twins, developing from separately fertilized eggs. Compare IDENTICAL (def. 3). **fra·ter·nal·ly** *adv.*
fra·ter·nal·ism *n.* ⟨Latin *frater* brother⟩
fra·ter·ni·ty *n* **1** a male students' society in a university or college, usually having secret rites and a name made up of Greek letters. Compare SORORITY. **2** people having similar interests, work, etc.: *the publishing fraternity.* **3** brotherhood. **frat·er·nize** ['frætər,naɪz] *v* **1** be friendly. **2** associate with citizens of a hostile nation during occupation of their territory. **frat·er·ni·za·tion** *n.* **frat·er·niz·er** *n.*
frat·ri·cide *n* **1** the act of killing one's brother, sister, relative, or compatriot, as in a civil war. **2** a person who commits fratricide. **frat·ri·cid·al** *adj.*

fraud [frɒd] *n* **1** dishonesty. **2** a dishonest act. **3** *Informal* a person who is not what he or she pretends to be. **4** *Law* deception used to induce an individual to give up property or money. **fraud·u·lence** ['frɒdʒələns] *n.* **fraud·u·lent** *adj.* **fraud·u·lent·ly** *adv.* ⟨Latin *fraudis* cheating⟩

fraught [frɒt] *adj* loaded; filled: *A battlefield is fraught with horror.* ⟨pp of obsolete *fraught* to load; Middle Dutch *vracht* freight⟩

fray¹ [frei] *n* a noisy fight. ⟨Old French *affrei*; Latin *ex-* out of + Germanic *fridhu* peace⟩

fray² [frei] *v* **1** make or become ragged along the edge. **2** become weakened beyond its strength. **3** cause strain on (something); upset: *The constant tension frayed their nerves.* ⟨French *frayer*; Latin *fricare* rub⟩

frazil ['fræzəl] *or* [frə'zil] *n* ❋ *Geology* ice crystals or flakes formed in the turbulent waters of rivers, rapids, etc. and often accumulating as icebanks along the shore. Also, **frazil ice.** ⟨Cdn. French; French *fraisil* coal cinders; Latin *fax, facis,* torch⟩

fraz·zle ['fræzəl] *Informal v* **1** tear to shreds; wear out. **2** tire out; weary. **fraz·zle** *n.* ⟨blend of *fray²* and obsolete *fazle;* Middle English *faselyn* unravel, Old English *fæs* a fringe⟩

freak [frik] *n* **1** an event, object, etc. that is very strange: *a freak of nature.* **2** a person or animal having some extreme abnormality or deformity. **3** *Slang* enthusiast: *a hockey freak.* *adj* very strange or unusual: *a freak storm.* ⟨compare Old English *frīcian* dance⟩
 freak out *Slang.* **a** experience or cause to experience the disorientation brought on by psychedelic drugs. **b** make or become extremely excited, afraid, angry, etc.: *The new roller coaster ride really freaked her out.*
 freak·ish *adj* strange, unusual, or capricious. **freak·ish·ly** *adv.* **freak·ish·ness** *n.* **freak·y** *adj* *Slang* very odd or unconventional: *freaky clothes.* **freak·i·ness** *n.*

freck·le ['frɛkəl] *n* a brown spot on the skin. *v* make freckles on or become spotted with freckles: *The sun freckles the skin of some people.* **freck·ly** *adj.* ⟨probably from earlier *frecken;* Old Norse *freknur,* pl⟩
 freck·le–faced *adj* having many freckles.

free [fri] *adj* **fre·er, fre·est 1** not under another's control. **2** not held back or shut up. **3** clear *(of* or *from);* exempt from: *free of error.* **4** allowed: *You are free to speak.* **5** open to all: *a free port.* **6** without cost. **7** not following rules or words exactly: *free verse.* **8** *Chemistry* not combined with something else: *Oxygen exists free in the atmosphere.*
 adv **1** without cost. **2** in a free manner. *v* **freed, free·ing 1** make free: *to be freed early for good behaviour.* **2** let loose: *to free a boat from weeds.* **3** clear: *He must free himself of this charge.* **free·ly** *adv.* ⟨Old English *frēo, frīo*⟩
 for free *Informal* without costing anything. **free and easy** paying little attention to rules or customs. **free from** (or **of**) without. **free with** giving or using freely. **make free (with)** a use as if one owned. **b** take liberties. **set free** let loose. **with a free hand** generously.
 free agent a professional athlete who is free to sign with any team. **free association** *Psychology* a technique of letting the patient's mind wander at will, inadvertently focussing on subconsciously important matters. **free–as·so·ci·ate** *v.* **free·base** *n Informal* a form of cocaine specially prepared for smoking. **free·base** *v.* **free·bie** ['fribi] *n Slang* something free, esp a gift offered as a perquisite or a promotional gimmick. **free·boot·er** *n* a pirate. **free·born** *adj* born free, not in slavery. **freed·man** *n, pl* **-men** a man freed from slavery. **free·dom** *n* **1** the state or condition of being free. **2** free use: *We give all guests the freedom of our home.* **3** lack of restraint; frankness. **4** ease of movement or action. **freedom of the press** freedom to

publish anything without restriction. **Free·dom·ite** *n* ❋ a member of the Sons of Freedom, a Doukhobour sect. **freed·wom·an** *n, pl* **-wom·en** a woman freed from slavery. **free enterprise** an economic system with a minimum of government control. **free fall** the fall of a body when it is unrestrained by anything except gravity. **free flight** the flight of a spaceship after the power is shut down. **free–floating** *adj Informal* widespread but lacking a clear cause: *free-floating anxiety.* **free–for–all** *adj* open to all. *n* a fight, race, etc., open to all or in which everybody participates. **free–form** *adj* free from convention: *free-form sculpture.* **free·hand** *adj* done by hand without using instruments, measurements, etc.: *freehand drawing.* **free·hand** *adv.* **free hand** the authority to act as one sees fit: *The committee was given a free hand to spend the money.* **free·hand·ed** *adj* generous. **free·hold** *n Law* a piece of land held for life or with the right to transfer it to one's heirs. **free·hold·er** *n.* **free·lance** or **free·lanc·er** *n* a writer, artist, etc. who works independently and sells his or her work to anyone who will buy it. **free·lance** *adj, v.* **free–living** *adj* **1** eating and drinking freely, according to one's desires. **2** of an organism, existing independently of any other. **free·load** or **free–load** *v Slang* **1** attend a party, convention, etc. chiefly for the free food and drink. **2** take liberally, without contributing anything. **free·load·er** *n.* **free·man** *n, pl* **-men 1** a person who is not a slave or a serf. **2** a person who has civil or political freedom. **free market** an economic system in which prices are determined by supply and demand, and are not subject to government controls. **free·ma·son** *n* **1** formerly, a member of a guild of stoneworkers in the Middle Ages, who had passwords and secret signs by which they recognized each other. **2 Freemason** a member of the Ancient Free and Accepted Masons, a worldwide society pledged to brotherliness, mutual aid, and charity. **free·ma·son·ry** or **Free·ma·son·ry** *n.* **free port 1** a port open to traders of all countries. **2** a port where no taxes or duties have to be paid. **free radical** *Chemistry* an atom or molecule having one unpaired electron. **free–range** *adj* to do with fowl that are allowed to roam freely rather than being shut up in a small space. **free ride** or **lunch** *Informal* any service acquired without the usual payment. **free–standing** *adj* not attached to any other structure: *The CN Tower in Toronto is one of the tallest free-standing structures in the world.* **free·stone** *n* a fruit stone that can be easily separated from the pulp. **free·style** *adj* to do with a performance, as in a sports competition, in which the performer is not confined to a specific style. **free·think·er** *n* a person who forms opinions independently of authority or tradition. **free throw** *Basketball* an unchallenged throw of the ball at the net from a special point (the **free–throw line**) as a penalty. **free trade** international trade free from tariffs. **free verse** poetry not restricted by the usual conventions. **free·ware** *n* computer software available at no charge, often over the Internet. **free·way** *n esp US* a high-speed highway on which no tolls are charged. **free·wheel** *n* **1** in a car, etc., a device that lets the drive shaft run freely when it is turning faster than the engine shaft. **2** on a bicycle, a device that lets the wheels turn while the pedals are held still. **free·wheel** *v.* **free·wheel·ing** *adj* independent: *a freewheeling lifestyle.* **free·will** *adj* voluntary: *a freewill offering.* **free will** freedom of decision. **free world** the non-communist nations.

SYNONYMS

Freedom emphasizes the power to control one's own life. **Liberty** emphasizes the right to do as one pleases, without restraint: *Freedom of speech does not mean liberty to tell lies.*

–free *combining form* without; not containing: *sugar-free, fat-free.*

free·sia ['friʒə] *n* any of a genus of plants of the iris family having fragrant flowers. ⟨F.H.T. *Freese* 19c German botanist⟩

freeze ['friz] *v* **froze, fro·zen, freez·ing** **1** harden by cold: *to freeze ice cream.* **2** feel or be very cold: *You'll freeze outside today.* **3** be of the degree of cold at which water becomes ice: *It is freezing tonight.* **4** make or become stiff and unfriendly. **5** chill or be chilled with fear, etc. **6** become suddenly motionless: *The cat froze when it saw the bird.* **7** fix (prices, wages, etc.) at a definite amount, usually by governmental decree. **8** make numb by applying an anesthetic: *to freeze the gum before extracting a tooth.*
n a state of extreme coldness: *The freeze last night damaged the crop.* ⟨Old English *frēosan*⟩
freeze out *Informal* exclude socially: *The clique's unfriendliness froze out all newcomers.* **freeze over** form ice on the surface. **freeze–dry** *v* preserve (food, vaccine, etc.) by quick-freezing and then evaporating the frozen moisture content. **freeze–dried** *adj.* **freeze–dry·ing** *n.* **freeze–frame** *n* a picture held still in a movie or television program. **freez·er** *n* an insulated cabinet for freezing and storing perishable foods. **freeze–up** *n* ✸ the time of year when rivers and lakes freeze over. **freez·ing** *n* FREEZING POINT: *It's below freezing outside. adj Informal* very cold: *It's freezing in here.* **freezing point** the temperature at which a liquid freezes. *Abbrev* **F.P., f.p.,** or **fp.**

freight [freit] *n* **1** the load of goods carried on a train, ship, etc. **2** the carrying of goods on a train, ship, etc., or the charge for this. *v* send as freight. ⟨Middle Dutch *vrecht*⟩
freight car a railway car for carrying freight. **freight·er** *n* a ship or aircraft for carrying freight. **freight train** a railway train made up exclusively of freight cars.

French [frentʃ] *n* **1 the French,** *pl* **a** the people of France. **b** ✸ the people of French Canada. **2** the French language. **French** *adj.*

⟨Old English *Frencisc; Franca* Frank⟩
French braid a woman's hairstyle in which braiding is begun at the top of the head. **French bread** crusty yeast bread in a long, narrow loaf. **French Canada 1** all French Canadians. **2** the part of Canada inhabited mainly or entirely by French Canadians, esp the province of Québec. **French Canadian 1** a Canadian whose ancestors came from France or whose first language is French. **2** to do with French Canada or French Canadians. **3** the language of the French Canadians. **French doors** or **French windows** a pair of doors with panes of glass all the way down like a window. **French dressing** a salad dressing made of olive oil, vinegar, spices, etc. **French fact** ✸ the existence of French Canada as a distinct cultural entity. **French fry** or **french fry** a strip of potato that has been fried in oil or fat until brown and crisp **French–fry** or **french–fry** *v.* **French–fried** *adj.* **French Shore** ✸ **1** the west coast of Newfoundland, where the French held rights from 1713 till 1904. **2** an area originally settled by the Acadians, on the SW coast of Nova Scotia. **French toast** bread dipped in a mixture of egg and milk and then fried.

fre·net·ic [frə'nɛtɪk] *adj* frenzied; frantic. **fre·net·i·cal·ly** *adv.* ⟨Greek *phrenetikos; phrenitis* disease of the mind; *phren* mind⟩

fren·zy ['frɛnzi] *n* **1** a state of near madness: *a frenzy of grief.* **2** a state of very great excitement: *The spectators were in a frenzy after the home team scored the winning goal.* **fren·zied** *adj.* **fren·zied·ly** *adv.* ⟨Old French *frenesie,* Latin *phrenesis;* Greek. See FRENETIC.⟩

Fre·on ['friɒn] *n Chemistry Trademark* any of a class of fluorated hydrocarbons formerly used especially as refrigerants and as propellants for aerosol sprays. ⟨f(lourine) + re(frigerant) + -on modelled on *neon*⟩

fre·quent ['frikwənt] *adj* **1** occurring often, near together, or every little while. **2** regular: *She is a frequent caller at our house.*
v [frɪ'kwɛnt] or ['frikwənt] go often to: *Frogs frequent ponds.* **fre·quent·er** *n.* **fre·quent·ly** *adv.* ⟨Latin *frequens* crowded⟩
fre·quency ['frikwənsi] *n* **1** frequent occurrence. **2** the rate of occurrence. **3** *Physics* the number of times that any regularly repeated event occurs in a given unit of time. **4** the number of complete cycles per second of any type of wave motion: *Different radio stations broadcast at different frequencies.* **5** *Mathematics* the ratio of the number of times an event actually occurs to the number of times it might occur, in a given period. **6** *Statistics* for a collection of data, the number of items in a given category. The ratio of this number to the total number of items gives the relative frequency. **frequency band** *Television, radio, etc.* a certain range of wavelengths; channel. **frequency modulation** *Radio* a method of transmitting sound signals by changing the frequency of the carrier waves. Compare AMPLITUDE MODULATION. *Abbrev* **FM** or **F.M.**

fres·co ['freskou] *n, pl* **-coes** or **-co 1** the art of painting with water colours on damp, fresh plaster. **2** a picture so painted. **fres·co, -coed, -co·ing** *v*. ⟨Italian = cool, fresh⟩

fresh [freʃ] *adj* **1** newly made, arrived, or obtained: *fresh footprints*. **2** not known, seen, or used before. **3** another: *After her failure she made a fresh start.* **4** not salty: *There is fresh water in the Great Lakes.* **5** not spoiled; not stale; not artificially preserved. **6** not tired. **7** creative or original: *a fresh approach to the problem.* **8** not faded or worn. **9** clean: *a fresh shirt.* **10** pure; refreshing: *a fresh breeze.* **11** fairly strong: *a fresh wind.* **12** *Informal* too bold; impudent. **fresh·en** *v*. **fresh·ly** *adv*. **fresh·ness** *n*. ⟨Old English *fersc*; influenced by Old French *fresche*, fem. of *freis*⟩ **fresh out of** *Informal* having just used or sold the last of. **freshen up** do something to make, or feel, fresh: *He freshened up by taking a shower.* **fresh·man** *n, pl* **-men** *n* **1** a student in the first year of a university course. **2** beginner. **fresh·wa·ter** *adj* to do with water that is not salty: *a freshwater fish.*

fresh·et ['freʃɪt] *n* **1** a flood caused by heavy rains or melted snow. **2** a rush of fresh water flowing into the sea. ⟨*fresh* fresh water + diminutive *-et*⟩

fret¹ [fret] *v* **fret·ted, fret·ting 1** be or make peevish or worried. **2** eat away. **3** roughen. *n* **1** worry. **2** a hole worn through by fretting. ⟨Old English *fretan* eat⟩ **fret·ful** *adj* **1** inclined to fret. **2** agitated; seething: *the fretful sea.* **3** gusty: *the fretful wind.* **fret·ful·ly** *adv*. **fret·ful·ness** *n*.

fret² [fret] *n* an ornamental pattern made of straight lines bent or combined at angles. *v* **fret·ted, fret·ting** decorate with frets. **fret·ted** *adj*. ⟨Old French *frete* trellis work⟩ **fret saw** a saw with a very narrow, fine blade used for cutting open designs in thin wood. **fret·work** *n* ornamental openwork or carving.

fret³ [fret] *n* one of a series of ridges on a guitar, banjo, etc. to show where to put the fingers to produce tones. ⟨origin uncertain⟩

Freud·i·an ['frɔɪdiən] *adj* to do with Austrian physician Sigmund Freud (1856-1939), who developed a technique of psychoanalysis. **Freudian slip** a slip of the tongue that seems to reveal what one is really thinking.

fri·a·ble ['fraɪəbəl] *adj* easily crumbled: *Dry soil is friable.* **fri·a·bil·i·ty** *n*. ⟨Latin *friare* crumble⟩

fri·ar ['fraɪər] *n* a member of certain religious orders. ⟨Old French *frere*, Latin *frater* brother⟩ **fri·ar·y** *n* **1** a building where friars live; monastery. **2** a brotherhood of friars.

fric·tion ['frɪkʃən] *n* **1** a rubbing of one object against another. **2** *Physics* the resistance to motion of surfaces that touch. **3** conflict of differing ideas, opinions, etc.: *Political differences caused friction between the two countries.* **fric·tion·al** *adj*. **fric·tion·al·ly** *adv*. ⟨Latin *frictio*; *fricare* rub⟩

Fri·day ['fraɪdei] *n* the sixth day of the week, following Thursday. ⟨Old English *Frīgedæg* Frigg's day; *Frīg* + *dæg* day⟩.

man Friday or **girl Friday** a reliable and devoted assistant, so called after Robinson Crusoe's servant in the novel by Daniel Defoe.

fridge [frɪdʒ] *n* *Informal* refrigerator. ⟨shortening of *refrigerator* or *Frigidaire* (a trademark)⟩

friend [frend] *n* **1** a person who knows and likes another. **2** a person who belongs to the same side or group: *Are you friend or foe?* **3 Friend** a member of the Society of Friends; Quaker. **4** anything helpful: *A flashlight is a good friend in the wilderness.* **friend·less** *adj*. ⟨Old English *frēond*, ppr of *frēogan* love⟩ **a friend at court** a person who can help to influence others. **be friends with** be a friend of. **make friends with** become a friend of. **friend·ly** *adj* **1** having the attitude of a friend: *a friendly greeting.* **2** on good terms: *friendly relations between countries.* **3** favourable: *a friendly breeze.* **4** not harmful to or difficult for the person or thing specified (in combination): *user-friendly.* *adv* in a friendly manner. **friend·li·ness** *n*. **friend·ship** *n* **1** the state of being friends. **2** friendly behaviour.

fries [fraɪz] *n pl* FRENCH FRIES.

frieze [friz] *n* **1** a horizontal band of decoration around a room, building, etc. **2** *Architecture* a horizontal band forming part of the upper section of a wall, often ornamented with sculpture. ⟨French *frise*; Latin *Phrygium* of Phrygia⟩

fright [fraɪt] *n* **1** sudden fear. **2** *Informal* a person or thing that is ugly, shocking, or ridiculous. ⟨Old English *fryhto*⟩ **take fright**, become alarmed; panic. **fright·en** *v* **1** scare. **2** become afraid. **3** persuade by making afraid: *The gunshot frightened them into silence.* **fright·ened** *adj*. **fright·en·ing** *adj*. **fright·en·ing·ly** *adv*. **fright·ful** *adj* **1** causing fright: *a frightful thunderstorm.* **2** *Informal* very great. **3** *Informal* disagreeable: *a frightful cough.* **fright·ful·ly** *adv*. **fright·ful·ness** *n*.

Frighten is the general word: *The snake frightened me.* **Scare** particularly suggests suddenly giving sharp fear: *The firecrackers scared the puppy.* **Alarm** = fill with intense fear and anxiety: *Her failure to come home at midnight alarmed us.*

frig·id ['frɪdʒɪd] *adj* **1** very cold: *a frigid climate.* **2** cold in manner: *a frigid reception.* **3** of a woman, sexually unresponsive. **frig·id·i·ty** *n*. **frig·id·ly** *adv*. ⟨Latin *frigus* cold⟩

frill [frɪl] *n* **1** a RUFFLE (def. 2). **2** *Informal* anything added merely for show. **3** anything desirable but inessential: *Curriculum planners often treat music as a frill.* **4** a fringe of feathers, hair, etc. around the neck of a bird or animal. **fril·ly** *adj*. ⟨origin uncertain⟩

fringe [frɪndʒ] *n* **1** a trimming made of threads, cords, etc., either loose or in small bunches. **2** anything like this: *a fringe of hair.* **3** anything thought of as marginal rather than central: *the radical fringe of the labour movement.* **4** *Optics* the dark or light bands

due to diffraction of light or interference.
v **1** put a border on. **2** be a border for; border: *Bushes fringed the road.* **fringe** *adj.* ⟨Old French *frenge;* Latin *fimbria*⟩
fringe benefit 1 any employment benefit given over and above regular wages: *Pensions and medical insurance are fringe benefits.* **2** any desirable side effect or by-product.

Fris·bee ['frızbi] *n Trademark* a light disk shaped like an upside-down saucer. It is spun through the air in various ways. ⟨Mother Frisbie's Pie Co. in Bridgeport, CT, whose pie plates were formerly used in a similar way⟩

frisk [frısk] *v* **1** run and jump about playfully. **2** *Informal* search (a person) for concealed weapons, etc. by running a hand over the person's clothes. **frisk·y** *adj* playful. **frisk·i·ly** *adv.* **frisk·i·ness** *n.* ⟨orig adj; Old French *frisque* lively, brisk; Germanic⟩

fris·son [fri'sɔ̃] *n French* a shiver, as of pleasure or fear; thrill. ⟨French⟩

frit·ter¹ ['frıtər] *v* waste little by little (with *away*). ⟨Old French *freture, fraiture.* See FRACTURE.⟩

frit·ter² ['frıtər] *n* a small cake of batter, fried in fat: *corn fritters.* ⟨Old French *friture,* Latin *frictura* a frying; *frigere* fry⟩

fritz [frıts] *n*
on the fritz *Slang* out of order; not working or functioning: *The TV is on the fritz again.* ⟨origin unknown⟩

friv·o·lous ['frıvələs] *adj* **1** lacking seriousness: *Frivolous behaviour is out of place in church.* **2** of little worth: *She wasted her time on frivolous matters.* **fri·vol·i·ty** *n.* **friv·o·lous·ly** *adv.* **friv·o·lous·ness** *n.* ⟨Latin *frivolus*⟩

frizz or **friz** [frız] *v* **frizzed, friz·zing** form into small, crisp curls; curl. Also, **friz·zle.**
n, pl **friz·zes** hair curled in small, crisp curls or a very close crimp. **friz·zy** *adj.* **friz·zi·ness** *n.* ⟨apparently French *friser*⟩

fro [frou] *adv*
to and fro first one way and then back again; back and forth. ⟨Old Norse *frá.* Akin to FROM.⟩

frock [frɒk] *n* **1** a gown; dress. **2** a robe worn by a member of the clergy.
v invest with clerical authority. ⟨Old French *froc*⟩

frog [frɒg] *n* **1** any of a family of tailless amphibians with smooth skin and strong hind legs adapted for leaping. Compare TOAD. **2** a device on a rail where a railway track crosses or branches from another. **3** a pad of horny substance in the bottom of a foot of a horse, donkey, etc. **4** a perforated or spiked device for holding flowers upright in a vase, bowl, etc. **5** the part by which the bow of a stringed instrument is held. ⟨Old English *frogga*⟩
frog in one's throat *Informal* hoarseness.
frog kick *Swimming* a movement in which the swimmer draws his or her knees forward and then kicks out to the sides and brings both legs together again. **frog·man** ['frɒg,mæn] *or* ['frɒgmən] *n, pl* **-men** a skindiver, esp one working for the armed

forces. **frog run ✳** in sugaring-off operations, the second run of sap in the maple trees, inferior to the first. Compare with ROBIN RUN.

frol·ic ['frɒlık] *n* **1** a merry prank; fun. **2** a merry game or party.
v **-icked, -ick·ing** play; have fun; make merry. **frol·ic·some** *adj.* ⟨Dutch *vrolijk;* Middle Dutch *vrō* glad + *-lijk* -ly⟩

from [frʌm] *prep* **1** out of: *Bricks are made from clay.* **2** starting out at: *the train from Montréal.* **3** because of: *to act from a sense of duty.* **4** as being unlike: *Anyone can tell apples from oranges.* **5** off; out of: *He took a shirt from the drawer.* **6** out of the control or possession of: *He took the knife from the baby.* **7** out of proximity to: *Keep the baby away from the barbecue.* **8** less than; subtract: *Take three from six.* **9** so as not to be: *refrain from chattering.* **10** given by: *a gift from my sister.* ⟨Old English *fram, from*⟩

frond [frɒnd] *n* **1** a divided leaf of a fern, palm, etc. **2** a leaflike part of a seaweed, lichen, etc. ⟨Latin *frondis* leaf⟩

front [frʌnt] *n* **1** the foremost part: *the front of a car.* **2** *Military* the area where active fighting is going on. **3** a sphere of activity combining different groups in a political or economic battle: *the labour front.* **4** *Informal* an appearance of wealth, importance, etc. **5** *Informal* a person appointed to add respectability to an enterprise. **6** *Informal* a person or thing that serves as a cover for illegal activities. **7 ✳ a** the settled, civilized part of the country at the edge of the frontier. **b** in Newfoundland and Labrador and Nova Scotia, the area where the spring seal hunt took place, at the edge of the Arctic ice fields. **8** the dividing surface between two dissimilar air masses: *a cold front moving south.*
v **1** face (often with *on*). **2** oppose. **3** *Informal* serve as a cover for an illegal activity, etc. **front** *adj.* ⟨Latin *frontis* forehead⟩
in front of in a position before (a person or thing): *Stand in front of me.*
front·age ['frʌntıdʒ] *n* the front of a building or of a lot. **fron·tal** *adj* **1** to do with the front. **2** of the forehead. **front·al·ly** *adv.* **frontal lobe** *Anatomy* the front part of each hemisphere of the brain. **front bench 1** in a legislative chamber, the front seats on either side, reserved for the leading party members. **2** the leading party members. **front·bench·er** *n.* **front ice ✳** ice near the shore, esp the shore east of Labrador. **fron·tier** [frɒn'tir] *or* [frʌn'tir] *n* **1** the farthest part of a settled country, where the wilds begin: *Yukon is part of Canada's present-day frontier.* **2** an uncertain or undeveloped region: *the frontiers of science.* **fron·tier** *adj.* **fron·tis·piece** ['frʌntıs,pis] *or* ['frɒntıs-] *n* a picture facing the title page of a book. **front line** *Military* the part of the front nearest to enemy positions in battle. **front man 1** one who officially represents a group or organization. **2** one who fronts for another. **front–page** *adj* suitable for the front page of a newspaper: *front-page news.*

front–run·ner *n* the leader in any contest.
front–wheel drive describing a type of car in which power is transmitted to the front wheels instead of the rear wheels.

frosh [frɒʃ] *n Slang* a first-year student in high school or university. ⟨altered from *freshman*⟩

frost [frɒst] *n* 1 a freezing condition: *There was frost last night.* 2 the moisture frozen on or in a surface: *frost on windows.* 3 a coldness of manner or feeling. 4 *Slang* failure. *v* 1 cover or become covered with frost. 2 cover with icing: *to frost a cake.* 3 bleach (strands of hair). **frost·y** *adj.* **frost·i·ly** *adv.* **frost·i·ness** *n.* ⟨Old English⟩
frost·bite *n* an injury to a part of the body caused by severe cold. **frost·bit·ten** *adj.*
frost·ed 1 covered with frost: *a frosted window.* 2 finished with a surface suggesting frost: *frosted glass.* 3 covered with icing: *a frosted cake.* 4 frozen. **frost·ing** ['frɒstɪŋ] *n* 1 a mixture of sugar, butter, etc., spread over a cake. 2 a dull finish on glass, metal, etc.

froth [frɒθ] *n* 1 a mass of very small bubbles: *The bottle of pop was half froth.* 2 foaming saliva. 3 something light and trifling. *v* [frɒθ] *or* [frɒð] foam or cause to foam. **froth·y** ['frɒθi] *or* ['frɒði] *adj.* **froth·i·ly** *adv.* **froth·i·ness** *n.* ⟨Old Norse *frotha*⟩

frown [fraʊn] *n* 1 a drawing together of the brows. 2 any show of disapproval. **frown** *v.* **frown·ing·ly** *adv.* ⟨Old French *froignier;* Celtic⟩ **frown on** disapprove of.

frowz·y ['fraʊzi] *adj* slovenly; dirty; untidy. Also, **frows·y. frowz·i·ly** *adv.* **frowz·i·ness** *n.* ⟨obsolete *frowze* ruffle, rumple⟩

froze [froʊz] *v* pt of FREEZE.
fro·zen ['froʊzən] *adj* 1 hardened by cold: *a frozen dessert.* 2 very cold: *the frozen north.* 3 kept below freezing to prevent spoiling: *frozen foods.* 4 killed or injured by frost. 5 covered or clogged with ice: *a frozen water main.* 6 too frightened or stiff to move: *frozen to the spot in horror.* 7 temporarily forbidden to be sold or exchanged: *frozen assets.* 8 of prices, wages, etc., fixed at a particular amount or level.

fruc·tose ['frʊktous], ['fruk-], *or* ['frʌk-] *n* a sugar found in fruit juices, honey, etc. ⟨Latin *fructus*⟩

fru·gal ['frugəl] *adj* 1 avoiding waste: *A frugal housekeeper buys and uses food carefully.* 2 so sparing as to be barely sufficient: *She ate a frugal supper of bread and milk.* **fru·gal·i·ty** [fru'gæləti] *n.* **fru·gal·ly** *adv.* ⟨Latin *frugis* fruit, profit⟩

fru·giv·or·ous [fru'dʒɪvərəs] *adj* fruit-eating, as certain bats. ⟨Latin *frugis* fruit + *vorare* devour⟩

fruit [frut] *n* 1 the edible, seed-bearing product of a tree, shrub, or vine. 2 *Botany* the part of a plant that contains the seeds. 3 a product: *Her invention was the fruit of much effort.* *v* produce or cause to produce fruit. **fruit·like** *adj.* ⟨Old French; Latin *fructus*⟩

fruit bat any species of bat that lives on fruit.
fruit·cake *n* 1 a rich cake containing preserved fruits. 2 *Slang* a very eccentric person.
fruit cup mixed fruits served in a cup or glass.
fruit fly any of a family of small, two-winged flies whose larvae feed on plant tissues.
fruit·ful ['frutfəl] *adj* 1 productive or fertile: *fruitful soil.* 2 producing good results: *a fruitful discussion.* **fruit·ful·ly** *adv.* **fruit·ful·ness** *n.*
fruiting body *Botany* an organ that produces spores. **fru·i·tion** [fru'ɪʃən] *n* fulfilment: *Her plans have at last come to fruition.* **fruit·less** *adj* 1 unsuccessful. 2 barren. **fruit·less·ly** *adv.* **fruit·less·ness** *n.* **fruit stand** a small store or stand where fruit is sold. **fruit sugar** 1 fructose. 2 a powdered form of cane sugar. **fruit·y** *adj* 1 tasting or smelling like fruit. 2 *Informal* mellow and rich in quality: *a fruity voice.* **fruit·i·ness** *n.*

frump [frʌmp] *n* a dowdy, unattractive woman or girl. **frump·y** or **frump·ish** *adj.* **frump·i·ly** *adv.* **frump·i·ness** *n.* ⟨origin uncertain⟩

frus·trate ['frʌstreit] *v* 1 bring to nothing: *Rain frustrated our plan for a picnic.* 2 prevent from succeeding: *to frustrate an opponent.* 3 make discouraged by preventing the realization of a desire: *It's very frustrating to stand in line for an hour and then not get seats.* **frus·trat·ed** *adj.* **frus·tra·tion** *n.* ⟨Latin *frustrari; frustra* in vain⟩

SYNONYMS
Frustrate emphasizes making all efforts vain, thus keeping a person from achieving his or her aim: *The girl's waywardness frustrated her father's plans for her future.* **Thwart** = block someone's effort by some contrary action: *The sudden storm thwarted the men who were trying to reach the wrecked plane.*

frus·tum ['frʌstəm] *n* **-tums** or **-ta** [-tə] *Geometry* the part of a cone-shaped solid or pyramid left after the top has been cut off parallel to the base. ⟨Latin *frustum* piece⟩

fry¹ [fraɪ] *v* 1 cook in a pan over direct heat, usually in fat or oil. 2 *Slang* wreck: *You'll fry your brains studying day and night.*
n 1 fried food. 2 a social gathering at which food is fried and eaten: *a fish fry.* ⟨Old French *frire;* Latin *frigere*⟩
fry·er *n* 1 a chicken tender enough for frying. 2 a utensil for deep-frying food. **frying pan** a shallow pan with a long handle, used for frying food. **out of the frying pan into the fire** straight from one danger or difficulty into a worse one.

fry² [fraɪ] *n, pl* **fry** 1 a young fish, from the time that it is hatched. 2 small adult fish, such as sardines, that live together in large schools. 3 See SMALL FRY. ⟨Old Norse *frjó* seed⟩

fuch·sia ['fjuʃə] *n* any of a genus of shrubs of the evening-primrose family having showy, hanging flowers of pink, purple, or red. ⟨L. *Fuchs* 16c German botanist⟩

fud·dle ['fʌdəl] *v* 1 make stupid with alcohol. 2 confuse; muddle. *n Informal* a confused state. ⟨origin uncertain⟩

fud·dy–dud·dy [ˈfʌdi ˌdʌdi] *Informal n* a fussy or stuffy old-fashioned person. **fud·dy–dud·dy** *adj.* ⟨origin uncertain⟩

fudge¹ [fʌdʒ] *n* a soft candy made of sugar, milk, and butter. ⟨origin uncertain⟩

fudge² [fʌdʒ] *n* **1** an item of last-minute news added to a newspaper page. **2** nonsense; empty talk: *That's a lot of fudge.* *v* **1** avoid committing oneself on an issue: *Don't let her fudge on the issue.* **2** put together in a makeshift or dishonest way; fake. ⟨origin uncertain⟩

fu·el [ˈfjuəl] *n* **1** something burned to provide heat or power. **2** a material from which atomic energy can be obtained, as in a reactor. **3** material that supplies nutrients for a living organism: *Your body needs fuel to live and grow.* **4** anything that keeps up or increases a feeling, thought, or action: *His insults were fuel to her hatred.* *v* **-elled** or **-eled, -el·ling** or **-el·ing 1** supply with fuel. **2** be an impetus for: *The ongoing indignation of students fuelled a program of administrative reform.* ⟨Old French *fouaille*; Latin *focus* hearth⟩ **fuel cell** an electric cell that produces electrical energy from the oxidation of a fuel. **fu·el–ef·fi·cient** *adj* economical of fuel. **fuel efficiency. fuel injection** a system of distributing gasoline under pressure to the cylinders of a vehicle. **fuel oil** oil used for fuel, esp in diesel engines. **fuel rod** a group of long tubes containing nuclear fuel.

fu·gi·tive [ˈfjudʒətɪv] *n* **1** a person who is fleeing or who has fled: *a fugitive from justice.* **2** something short-lived or hard to grasp. *adj* **1** runaway. **2** lasting a very short time: *fugitive thoughts.* ⟨Latin *fugitivus; fugere* flee⟩

fugue [fjug] *n* **1** *Music* a composition in which different voices or instruments repeat the same melody with slight variations. **2** *Psychiatry* a mental condition in which the sufferer does not remember actions he or she has performed. ⟨French; Latin *fuga* flight⟩

–ful *suffix* **1** full of——: *cheerful.* **2** characterized by or having the qualities of——: *careful.* **3** having a tendency or the ability to——: *forgetful.* ⟨Old English; representing *full*, adj.⟩

ful·crum [ˈfʌlkrəm] or [ˈfʊlkrəm] *n, pl* **-crums, -cra** [-krə] **1** a support on which a lever turns in moving or lifting something. **2** anything on which something else depends. ⟨Latin *fulcrum* bedpost; *fulcire* support⟩

ful·fil or **ful·fill** [fʊlˈfɪl] *v* **-filled, -fill·ing 1** carry out (a promise, prophecy, etc.). **2** do or perform (a duty). **3** satisfy (a requirement, condition, etc.): *to fulfil a need.* **4** complete: *to fulfil a contract.* **ful·fill·er** *n.* **ful·fil·ment** or **ful·fill·ment** *n.* ⟨Old English *fullfyllan*⟩

full [fʊl] *adj* **1** able to hold no more: *a full cup.* **2** complete: *a full supply.* **3** of the greatest size, extent, etc.: *at full speed.* **4** plump: *a full face.* **5** having a large amount or number (*of*): *The lake is full of fish.* **6** completely taken up with (with *of*): *He's full of his latest project.*

7 thorough: *a full description.* *adv* **1** completely. **2** directly: *The blow hit him full in the face.* **3** very: *to know full well.* **full·ness** or **fulness** *n.* ⟨Old English⟩ **in full a** to or for the complete amount: *paid in full.* **b** with all the words; not shortened: *Write your name in full.* **in full swing** in full operation: *The party was in full swing.* **to the full** completely; entirely: *He satisfied his ambition to the full.* **full·back** *n* *Football, etc.* a player whose position is farthest behind the front line. **full blast** *Informal* at highest speed or largest capacity. **full–blood·ed** *adj* **1** of pure breed, or strain. **2** vigorous; hearty. **3** real; genuine. **full–blown** *adj* **1** in full bloom. **2** completely developed. **full–bod·ied** *adj* having considerable flavour, etc.: *a full-bodied wine.* **full dress** the formal clothes worn for important occasions. **full–dress** *adj* **1** to do with full dress: *a full-dress reception.* **2** utilizing all resources: *a full-dress report.* **full·fledged** *adj* **1** of a bird, having a complete set of feathers and therefore able to fly. **2** fully developed. **3** of full rank or standing. **full–grown** *adj* mature. **full house 1** *Theatre, etc.* the state of every seat being occupied. **2** *Poker* a hand made up of three cards of one kind and two of another, such as three sixes and two kings. **full–length** *adj* **1** for the full length of the human figure: *a full-length mirror.* **2** reaching almost to the floor: *full-length drapes.* **3** of standard size, length, duration, etc.: *a full-length novel.* **full moon** the moon seen with the whole disk illuminated. **full–scale** *adj* **1** made in the actual size: *a full-scale drawing.* **2** involving all available resources: *a full-scale investigation.* **full–throat·ed** *adj* **1** clamorous and loud. **2** rich and full in sound. **full tilt** at top speed or with full force. **full time** for the usual number of hours per week: *The plant employs workers full time.* **full–time** *adj.* **ful·ly** *adv* **1** completely: *fully awake.* **2** abundantly: *fully covered by insurance.* **3** at least: *fully three hours later.*

ful·mi·nate [ˈfʌlməˌneit] or [ˈfʊlməˌneit] *v* **1** thunder forth threats, protests, denunciations, etc.: *The newspapers fulminated against the crime wave.* **2** explode violently; cause to explode. **3** of a disease, develop suddenly. *n* *Chemistry* a salt of fulminic acid. Fulminates explode with great violence. **ful·mi·na·tion** *n.* ⟨Latin *fulminare; fulmen* lightning⟩

ful·some [ˈfʊlsəm] *adj* **1** offensive because of excessiveness, insincerity, etc.: *fulsome praise.* **2** abundant; profuse: *fulsome detail.* **ful·some·ly** *adv.* **ful·some·ness** *n.* ⟨*full* + *-some¹*; influenced in meaning by *foul*⟩

fum·ble [ˈfʌmbəl] *v* **1** search awkwardly: *He fumbled about in his pockets for the ticket.* **2** handle awkwardly: *She fumbled the introduction.* **3** *Sports* fail to catch and hold (a ball). **fum·ble** *n.* **fum·bling** *adj.* ⟨compare Low German *fummeln*⟩

fume [fjum] *n* **1** Usually, **fumes** *pl* a vapour, esp if odorous: *the fumes of the acid.* **2** an angry mood: *She was obviously in a fume.* *v* **1** give off fumes. **2** be in a state of anger or great irritation. ⟨Old French *fum;* Latin *fumus* smoke⟩

fu·mi·gate ['fjumə,geit] *v* expose to fumes in order to kill vermin or to disinfect. **fumi·ga·tion** *n.* **fu·mi·ga·tor** *n* **1** a person who fumigates. **2** an apparatus for fumigating.

fun [fʌn] *n* **1** lively playfulness: *a day full of fun.* **2** a source of amusement: *That game is fun.* **3** ridicule: *a figure of fun.* ⟨possibly orig *v,* variant of obsolete *fon* befool⟩
for fun for sheer enjoyment or amusement. **in fun** as a joke: *meant in fun.* **like fun** *Slang* an exclamation of scornful incredulity. **make fun of** or **poke fun at** laugh at.
fun house a carnival attraction, consisting of rooms with crooked floors, distorting mirrors, etc. **fun·ny** *adj* **1** amusing: *a funny story.* **2** intended to amuse: *She was just being funny.* **3** *Informal* strange; peculiar. **4** tricky: *Don't try anything funny, you might get hurt.* *n* **1** **funnies** *pl Informal* comic strips. **2** a joke; an amusing story: *I told a funny.* **get funny with** *Informal* be fresh with. **fun·ni·ly** *adv.* **fun·ni·ness** *n.* **funny bone** **1** the part of the elbow over which a nerve passes, being a pun on *humerus,* the bone of the upper arm. **2** sense of humour: *The comment struck her funny bone and she burst out laughing.* **funny money** *Informal* counterfeit bills. **funny paper** or **papers** the section of a newspaper containing the comic strips.

func·tion ['fʌŋkʃən] *n* **1** the proper work of something: *The function of the stomach is to digest food.* **2** a formal gathering for some purpose: *All the local dignitaries attended the great function.* **3** *Mathematics* an association between two sets where exactly one object from one set (the range) is paired with one object from the other set (the domain): *The volume of a sphere is a function of the radius.* **4** anything having two variables in consistent relation to each other: *Success is a function of attitude.*
v **1** work; be used: *My new pen does not function very well.* **2** have a function; serve (*as*): *That stone functions as a doorstop.* **func·tion·less** *adj.* ⟨Latin *functio; functus* pp of *fungi* perform⟩
func·tion·al ['fʌŋkʃənəl] *adj* **1** having a function. **2** stressing usefulness instead of beauty: *a functional approach to furniture design.* **3** *Medicine* affecting the function of a part of the body, but not its structure: *functional heart disease.* **func·tion·al·ly** *adv.* **functional illiterate** a person whose ability to read is too poor for practical purposes. **functional illiteracy. functionally illiterate.** **func·tion·al·ism** *n Architecture and design* the principle that the design of a structure should be determined primarily by its purpose or function. **func·tion·al·ist** *n.* **func·tion·al·ist·ic** *adj.* **func·tion·ar·y** *n, adj* official. **function key** *Computers* a keyboard key that causes some specialized operation to

take place (save, exit, etc.). **function word** *Grammar* a word having little or no meaning of its own, used to show relationships between other words. Words like *of* and *but* are function words.

fund [fʌnd] *n* **1** a sum of money set aside for a special purpose: *a fund of $1000 to buy books.* **2** a stock ready for use: *There is a fund of information in a dictionary.* **3** **funds** *pl* money available for use: *to run out of funds.* *v* provide funds for: *funded by the government.* ⟨Latin *fundus* bottom, a piece of land⟩
fund·ing *n* money for a special purpose: *funding for a new project.* **fund·rais·er** *n* **1** a person who raises donations. **2** a gathering, entertainment, etc. organized to raise funds. **fund·rais·ing** *n* the act of raising donations of money for a special purpose.

fun·da·men·tal [,fʌndə'mɛntəl] *adj* **1** basic: *fundamental principles.* **2** affecting a basic structure: *a fundamental change of attitude.* **3** main: *The fundamental aim of her campaign is to block the legislation.* **4** *Music* **a** to do with the lowest note of a chord. **b** to do with the primary tone of a harmonic series.
n **1** a principle, rule, law, etc. that forms a foundation: *the fundamentals of grammar.* **2** *Music* the lowest note of a chord. **3** *Physics* the component of a wave that has the greatest wavelength. **fun·da·men·tal·ly** *adv.* ⟨Latin *fundamentum* foundation; *fundus* bottom⟩
fun·da·men·tal·ism *n* **1** in Christianity, the belief that all the actual words of the Bible were directly inspired by God and should be followed more or less literally. **2** a parallel movement, often militant, in any faith. **3** a dogmatic or extreme version of any ideology. **fun·da·men·tal·ist** *n.*

fu·ner·al ['fjunərəl] *n* the ceremonies that accompany the burial or cremation of the dead. **fu·ner·al** *adj.* ⟨Latin *funeris* funeral⟩
be one's funeral *Informal* be one's own responsibility, esp in the case of disagreeable consequences.
funeral director a person who manages a FUNERAL HOME; undertaker. **funeral home** a business establishment that arranges funeral services and has facilities for preparing the bodies of the dead for burial or cremation. **funeral parlour** or **parlor** FUNERAL HOME. **fu·ner·ar·y** ['fjunə,rɛri] *adj* of a funeral or burial: *a funerary urn.* **fu·ne·re·al** [fju'niriəl] *adj* **1** of or suitable for a funeral. **2** sad; gloomy; dismal. **fu·ne·re·al·ly** *adv.*

fun·gus ['fʌŋgəs] *n, pl* **fun·gi** or **fun·gus·es** **1** any of a group of plantlike organisms that lack chlorophyl, are parasitic, and reproduce by means of spores. The group includes moulds, mushrooms, etc. **2** a diseased, spongy growth on the skin. **fun·gus·like** *adj.* ⟨Latin; probably akin to Greek *sphongos* sponge⟩
fun·gal ['fʌŋgəl] *adj* fungous. **fun·gi·cide** ['fʌndʒə,saɪd] or ['fʌŋgə,saɪd] *n* any substance that destroys fungi. **fun·gi·cid·al** *adj.* **fun·gous**

adj **1** spongy. **2** springing up suddenly, but not lasting. **3** caused by a fungus.

fu·nic·u·lar [fju'nɪkjələr] *adj* of, hanging from, or operated by a rope or cable. A **funicular railway** is a railway system in which the cars are moved by cables. ⟨Latin *funiculus* diminutive of *funis* rope⟩

funk¹ [fʌŋk] *Informal n* **1** a state of extreme fear; panic. **2** often, **blue funk**, a depressed mood. **3** coward.
v **1** be afraid to do (something). **2** frighten. ⟨origin uncertain⟩
funk·y *adj Informal* being in a state of panic or mental depression.

funk² [fʌŋk] *n* a type of popular music developed from rock, blues, and soul.
funk·y *adj Informal* **1** *Music* of or having an earthy, emotional blues style. **2** offbeat, esp in a campy or earthy way: *funky clothes.* ⟨black slang, literally smelly, hence musty, earthy; obsolete *funk* smell, smoke; Latin *fumigare*⟩

fun·nel ['fʌnəl] *n* **1** a tapering tube with a wide mouth, used for pouring something into a container with a small opening: *She used a funnel to pour the gas into the tank.* **2** anything shaped like a funnel: *the funnel of a tornado.* **3** a cylindrical metal chimney: *The steamship had two funnels.*
v **-nelled** or **-neled**, **-nel·ling** or **-nel·ing** pass or feed through or as if through a funnel. ⟨Old French *fonel;* Latin *(in)fundibulum; in-* in + *fundere* pour⟩

fur [fɜr] *n* **1** the thick covering of hair on the skin of certain animals. Usually, **furs** *pl* a garment made of fur. **3** a furlike coating, such as the whitish matter on the tongue during illness.
v **furred, fur·ring** coat or become coated with a furlike matter, such as on the tongue during illness. **fur** *adj.* **fur·less** *adj.* ⟨Old French *forrer* line, encase; *forre* sheath⟩
make the fur fly *Informal* **a** cause trouble; quarrel; fight. **b** achieve a great deal swiftly.
fur·ri·er ['fɜriər] *n* **1** a dealer in furs. **2** a person whose work is making and repairing fur garments. **fur·ry** *adj* **1** covered with or wearing fur: *a furry animal.* **2** looking or feeling like fur. **fur·ri·ness** *n.*

fu·ri·ous See FURY.

fur·long ['fɜrlɒŋ] *n* a non-metric unit for measuring distance, equal to 0.2 km. ⟨Old English *furlang; furh* furrow + *lang* long⟩

fur·lough ['fɜrlou] *n* a leave of absence, esp for a soldier or missionary. ⟨Dutch *verlof* permission⟩

fur·nace ['fɜrnɪs] *n* **1** an enclosed structure for providing heat for buildings by warming water or air. **2** an enclosed structure for providing intense heat for use in separating metal from ore, in treating metal, etc. ⟨Old French *fornais,* Latin *fornax; fornus* oven⟩

fur·nish [ˌfɜrnɪʃ] *v* **1** supply; provide: *The sun furnishes heat.* **2** supply (a room, house, etc.) with furniture, equipment, etc. ⟨Old French *furnir* accomplish; Germanic⟩

fur·nish·ings *n pl* **1** the furniture or equipment for a room, house, etc. **2** articles of clothing: *That store sells men's furnishings.*

SYNONYMS

Furnish = provide things or services necessary or wanted: *The garage furnished both cars and drivers.* **Equip** = fit out with what is needed to do work: *Our parents equipped us with the confidence to try anything new.*

fur·ni·ture ['fɜrnətʃər] *n* the movable articles needed in a room: *Beds, chairs, tables, and desks are furniture.* ⟨French *fourniture* from *fournir* furnish⟩

fu·ror ['fjʊrɔr] *or* ['fjʊrər] *n* **1** an outburst of wild enthusiasm: *There was a great furor in the crowd when we scored.* **2** an inspired or excited mood: *He wrote the poem in a furor.* **3** fury; rage. ⟨Latin *furor; furere* rage⟩

fur·row [ˈfɜrou] *n* **1** a long, narrow groove cut in the ground by a plough. **2** any long, narrow groove or track: *deep furrows in the muddy road.* **3** a deep wrinkle. **fur·row** *v.* ⟨Old English *furh*⟩

fur·ther ['fɜrðər] *(adj, adv, a comparative of far) adj* **1** more: *Have you any further need of me?* **2** more distant: *on the further side.*
adv **1** to a greater extent. **2** at or to a greater distance. **3** besides: *He said further that he would support us in any way he could.*
v help forward; promote. ⟨Old English *furthra,* adj, *furthor,* adv; *forth* forth⟩
fur·ther·ance *n* an act of furthering; promotion. **fur·ther·more** *adv* besides. **fur·ther·most** *adj* furthest. **fur·thest** *(adv, adj* a superlative of FAR) **1** to or at the greatest degree or extent. **2** to or at the greatest distance in space or time.

fur·tive ['fɜrtɪv] *adj* **1** done stealthily; secret: *a furtive attempt to read his sister's letter.* **2** sly; stealthy: *a furtive manner.* **fur·tive·ly** *adv.* **fur·tive·ness** *n.* ⟨Latin *furtivus; fur* thief⟩

fu·ry ['fjʊri] *n* **1** wild, fierce anger; a rage. **2** violence; fierceness. **3** a raging or violent person. **4** unrestrained energy, speed, etc.: *work with fury.* **fu·ri·ous** ['fjʊriəs] *adj.* **fu·ri·ous·ly** *adv.* ⟨Latin *furia* fury⟩
like fury *Informal* violently; very rapidly.

fuse¹ [fjuz] *n* **1** a wick filled with combustible powder used to ignite an explosive charge from a safe distance. **2** any of various devices for detonating a bomb, shell, etc. ⟨Italian *fuso;* Latin *fusus* spindle⟩
have a short fuse anger easily.

fuse² [fjuz] *n Electricity* in a circuit, a safety device that melts when the current exceeds a specific amperage, thus breaking the circuit.
v **fused, fus·ing** **1** melt, esp by the action of heat. **2** blend as if by melting together. **3** cease or cause to cease functioning because of the melting of a fuse: *The lights fused when we turned on the heater.* **fu·si·ble** *adj.* **fu·si·ble·ness** or **fu·si·bil·i·ty** *n.*
fu·si·bly *adv.* ⟨Latin *fusus* pp of *fundere* pour, melt⟩
blow a fuse a cause the safety device to trip. **b** burst out in anger.

fuse box a compartment in which electric fuses are stored. **fu·sion** *n* **1** a melting: *Bronze is made by the fusion of copper and tin.* **2** a blending: *A new party was formed by the fusion of two political groups.* **3** *Nuclear physics* the combining of two nuclei to create a nucleus of greater mass. **4** *Music* a type of popular music dating from the 1970s in which elements of jazz, funk, rock, etc. are blended. **5** a style of cuisine that blends dishes and techniques from different cultures.

fu·se·lage ['fjuzə,laʒ] *or* ['fjuzəlɪdʒ] *n* the body of an aircraft. ⟨French, from *fuselé* spindle-shaped. See FUSE¹.⟩

fu·sil·lade [,fjuzə'lad] *or* [,fjuzə'leid] *n* **1** a discharge of many firearms at the same time. **2** something that resembles a fusillade: *a fusillade of questions.* ⟨French, from *fusiller* shoot; *fusil* musket⟩

fuss [fʌs] *n* **1** too much bother about small matters. **2** a state of great nervousness. **3** a dispute or quarrel. **4** elaborate and noisy enjoyment: *a fuss over the new baby.* *v* **1** make a fuss. **2** make nervous or worried. **3** of a baby, make fretful noises. **fuss·er** *n*. ⟨origin uncertain⟩

fuss around, *Informal* engage in a pointless, irritating, or tiresome activity: *I can't be bothered fussing around with that broken tap.*

fuss·budg·et ['fʌs,bʌdʒɪt] *n Informal* a fussy person. **fuss·y** *adj* **1** inclined to fuss. **2** with much trimming or decoration: *fussy clothes.* **3** full of details; requiring much care: *a fussy job.* **fuss·i·ly** *adv.* **fuss·i·ness** *n.*

fust·y ['fʌsti] *adj* **1** having a stale smell. **2** old-fashioned; out-of-date. **fust·i·ly** *adv.* **fust·i·ness** *n.* ⟨Old French *fust* wine cask; Latin *fustis* staff⟩

fu·tile ['fjutaɪl] *or* ['fjutəl] *adj* **1** not successful; useless. **2** not important; trifling. **3** occupied with things of no value or importance: *a futile life.* **fu·tile·ly** *adv.* **fu·til·i·ty** [fju'tɪləti] *n.* ⟨Latin *futilis*⟩

fu·ton ['futɒn] *or* ['fjutɒn] **1** a Japanese quilted pad that can be placed on the floor to sleep on. **2** a piece of furniture consisting of a wooden frame covered by a quilted pad and typically used as a bed at night and a couch by day. ⟨Sino-Japanese, orig round cushions filled with cattails; Mandarin *fu* cattail + *ton* round⟩

fu·ture ['fjutʃər] *n* **1** the time to come: *She hopes to do well in the future.* **2** what is to come: *She claims she can foretell the future.* **3** an expectation of success and prosperity: *a young woman with a future.* **4** *Grammar* a tense of verbs indicating events yet to happen. **5** **futures** *pl* commodities or stocks to be received at a future date. **fu·ture** *adj.* **fu·ture·less** *adj.* ⟨Latin *futurus* future participle of *esse* be⟩

future perfect *Grammar* in English, a verb tense formed by adding *will have* to the past participle, expressing action to be completed before a future reference point: *By next week, he will have gone.* **future shock** inability of people to adjust to rapid change, esp technological change ⟨coined by Alvin Toffler, after *culture shock*⟩ **fu·tur·is·tic** *adj* to do with the future or what is thought of as characteristic of the future: *a futuristic movie, set in the year 2050.* **fu·tur·is·ti·cal·ly** *adv.* **fu·tu·ri·ty** [fju'tʃʊrəti] *n* **1** the time to come; future. **2** a future state or event.

fuzz [fʌz] *n* **1** fine, light fibres or hairs: *Peaches and some caterpillars are covered with fuzz.* **2** an audio distortion produced by deliberately overloading an amplification circuit. Also, **fuzz tone**. **3** *Slang* Usually, **the fuzz** the police or a police officer. *v* make or become fuzzy: *The blanket is fuzzing.* ⟨Dutch *voos* spray⟩ **fuzz·y** *adj* **1** of fuzz:, like fuzz, or covered with fuzz. **2** not clear or distinct: *Everything looks fuzzy when I don't have my glasses on.* **fuzz·i·ly** *adv.* **fuzz·i·ness** *n.*

–fy *suffix* **1** make or make into; cause to be: *simplify, intensify.* **2** become: *solidify.* **3** make like: *citify.* ⟨French *-fier*, Latin *-ficare; facere* do, make⟩

FYI for your information.

Gg

g or **G** [dʒi] *n, pl* **g's** or **G's 1** the seventh letter of the English alphabet, or any speech sound represented by it. **2** the seventh person or thing in a series. **3** *Music* the fifth tone of the scale of C major. **4 g** a unit of acceleration equal to the force of gravity upon a body at rest. **5 G** a force equal to the gravitational pull of the earth.

g 1 gram(s). **2** gravity.

G 1 German. **2** giga- (an SI prefix). **3** *Slang* a grand; one thousand dollars.

gab [gæb] *n Informal* chatter; gabble. *v* **gabbed, gab·bing** talk too much; chatter. **gab·by** *adj.* **gab·bi·ness** *n.* ⟨probably imitative⟩ **gift of the gab** fluency of speech; glibness. **gab·fest** *n Informal* **1** a long conversation. **2** an informal gathering for discussion.

gab·ble ['gæbəl] *v* **1** make unintelligible or animal sounds: *Geese gabble.* **2** talk rapidly, without making much sense: *She was gabbling on about a fire.* **gab·ble** *n.* ⟨gab, variant of *gob;* Gaelic *gob* mouth⟩

ga·ble ['geibəl] *n* the end of a ridged roof, with the triangular upper part of the wall that it covers. **ga·bled** *adj.* **ga·ble·like** *adj.* ⟨Old French *gable;* Old Norse *gafl*⟩

gad [gæd] *v* **gad·ded, gad·ding 1** go about looking for pleasure or excitement: *gadding about town.* **2** move about restlessly. *n* **1** the act of gadding. **2** gadabout. *He is a born gad.* ⟨possibly back-formed from obsolete *gadling* companion; Old English *gædling*⟩ **gad·a·bout** *n Informal* a person who goes about looking for pleasure or excitement.

gad·fly ['gæd,flaɪ] *n* **1** any of several flies that sting cattle, horses, etc. **2** a person who rouses others from a state of self-satisfaction by calling attention to their faults, etc. ⟨obsolete *gad* goad + *fly*[1]⟩

gadg·et ['gædʒɪt] *n Informal* a small device: *a gadget for the car.* ⟨origin uncertain⟩ **gadg·et·ry** *n* gadgets collectively.

gad·o·lin·i·um [,gædə'lɪniəm] *n* a rare, magnetic, metallic element. *Symbol* Gd ⟨J. *Gadolin* 19c Finnish chemist.⟩

Gael·ic ['geilik]; *also, esp Scottish* ['gɑlik] *adj* to do with the Gaels, original Celtic people of Scotland, or their language. *n* the language of the Gaels.

gaff [gæf] *n* **1** a hook for pulling large fish out of the water. **2** a pole extending along the upper edge of a fore-and-aft sail. **3** *Slang* a hoax, fraud, or trick. **4** a steel point on a climber's iron. *v* **1** hook or pull (a fish) out of the water with a gaff. **2** *Slang* **a** deceive or trick. **b** fix for the purpose of cheating: *to gaff the dice.* ⟨French *gaffe;* Celtic⟩ **blow the gaff** *Slang* give away a secret.

gaffe [gæf] *n* a tactless or indiscreet remark, action, etc.; faux pas. ⟨French⟩

gaf·fer ['gæfər] *n* **1** *Informal* an old man. **2** the chief electrician on the set of a television program or film. **3** a foreperson. ⟨alteration of *godfather*⟩

gag [gæg] *n* **1** something thrust into a person's mouth to keep him or her from crying out, etc. **2** anything used to silence a person. **3** *Informal* an amusing remark or trick. **4** a device used by dentists to keep the patient's mouth open. *v* **gagged, gag·ging** *v* **1** keep from talking, crying out, etc. by means of a gag. **2** force to keep silent. **3** say something to cause a laugh. **4** choke or strain or cause to choke or strain in an effort to vomit. ⟨probably imitative⟩ **gag rule** a prohibition on publication.

ga·ga ['gɑ,gɑ] *adj Slang* **1** mentally confused. **2** wildly enthusiastic: *They went gaga over the show.* ⟨French = old fool⟩

gage See GAUGE.

gag·gle ['gægəl] *n* **1** a flock of geese. **2** *Informal* a group of people or things: *a gaggle of autograph hunters.* **3** a gabbling sound, as that made by geese. *v* make gabbling or cackling sounds. ⟨Middle English *gagelen* to cackle⟩

gai·e·ty ['geiəti] *n* merriment; cheerful liveliness. See also GAY. ⟨French *gaieté*⟩

gai·ly ['geili] *adv* **1** happily; merrily. **2** brightly: *a gaily decorated room.* See also GAY.

gain [gein] *v* **1** get: *The king gained possession of more lands.* **2** get as a profit. **3** make progress: *The sick child is gaining and will soon be well.* **4** reach: *The swimmer gained the shore.* **5** of a timepiece, run too fast. **6** begin to catch up or catch up (*on*). **7** put on (weight): *I've gained two kilos in a month.* *n* **1** an increase in profit, advantage, etc. **2** the act of getting wealth: *Greed is love of gain.* **3** *Electronics* amplification of a radio signal, etc. **4 gains** *pl* profits. **gain·er** *n.* ⟨French *gagner*⟩ **gain·ful** *adj* bringing in money or advantage: *gainful employment.* **gain·ful·ly** *adv.*

gait [geit] *n* **1** the kind of step used in walking or running. **2** carriage of the body in moving: *He has a lame gait because of an injured foot.* ⟨Old Norse *gata* way⟩

ga·la ['gælə], ['geilə], *or* ['gɑlə] *n* a festive occasion; festival. **ga·la** *adj.* ⟨French from Italian⟩

gal·ax·y ['gæləksi] *n* **1** *Astronomy* any of the many systems of stars making up the universe. **2 Galaxy** the Milky Way, the band of countless stars that stretches across the sky. **3** a brilliant group: *a galaxy of brave knights.* **ga·lac·tic** [gə'læktik] *adj.* ⟨Greek *galaxias; galaktos* milk; for the Milky Way⟩

gale [geil] *n* **1** a strong wind. **2** *Meteorology* a wind with a speed of 50-88 km/h. Winds of gale force are represented by the numbers 7 to 9 on the Beaufort scale. **3** a noisy outburst: *gales of laughter.* ⟨origin uncertain⟩

ga·lette [gə'lɛt] *n* ✹ a flat, unleavened cake made by baking in a frying pan or covering with hot ashes in a fireplace. ⟨French⟩

gall¹ [gɒl] *n* **1** bile, esp animal bile used in medicine, etc. **2** anything very bitter. **3** bitterness: *Her heart was filled with gall.* **4** *Informal* excessive boldness: *He had a lot of gall to talk to his employer in such a nasty way.* ⟨Old English *gealla*⟩
gall bladder or **gall·blad·der** a sac attached to the liver, in which excess bile is stored until needed. **gall·stone** *n* a pebblelike mass that sometimes forms in the gall bladder.

gall² [gɒl] *v* **1** make or become sore by rubbing: *The rough strap galled the horse's skin.* **2** annoy. **gall** *n.* ⟨extended use of *gall¹*⟩
gall·ing *adj* bitterly disappointing; very annoying or irritating: *a galling defeat.*

gall³ [gɒl] *n* a growth, or tumour, on the leaves, stems, or roots of plants, caused by insects, fungi, bacteria, etc. ⟨Latin *galla*⟩

gal·lant ['gælənt] *adj* **1** noble: *a gallant knight.* **2** stately: *a gallant ship.* **3** [gə'lænt] *or* [gə'lɒnt] very attentive to women. *n* [gə'lænt] *or* [gə'lɒnt] a man who is very attentive to women. **gal·lant·ly** *adv.* ⟨Old French *galant* ppr of *galer* make merry⟩
gal·lant·ry *n* **1** dashing courage. **2** chivalrous attention to women.

gal·le·on ['gæliən] *or* ['gæljən] *n* formerly, a large, heavy sailing ship. ⟨Spanish *galeón;* Medieval Greek *galēa* galley⟩

gal·ler·y ['gæləri] *n* **1** a narrow passage projecting from the wall of a building. **2** a projecting upper floor in a church, theatre, etc.; balcony. **3** the highest floor of this kind in a theatre. **4** a covered walk. **5** a room or building where works of art are shown. **6** a room for use as a shooting range, etc. ⟨Italian *galleria*⟩
play to the gallery *Informal* try to get the praise of the common people.

gal·ley ['gæli] *n* **1** a ship propelled mainly by banks of oars, used in ancient and medieval times. **2** the kitchen of a ship or aircraft. **3** a long, narrow kitchen. **4** *Printing* **a** a tray for holding type that has been set. **b** a proof taken from the type in a galley, used to make corrections. ⟨Medieval Greek *galēa*⟩
galley slave 1 a person compelled to row a galley. **2** a drudge, esp in a kitchen.

Gal·lic ['gælɪk] *adj* **1** to do with Gaul or its people. **2** French. ⟨Latin *Gallus* a Gaul⟩
Gal·li·cism or **gal·li·cism** ['gælə,sɪzəm] *n* **1** a French idiom or expression. **2** a French trait.

gal·li·um ['gæliəm] *n* a metallic element similar to mercury. *Symbol* **Ga** ⟨Latin *gallus* cock, translation of discoverer's name *Lecoq de Boisbaudran*⟩

gal·li·vant ['gælə,vænt] *v* **1** travel for pleasure: *They're gallivanting around Europe.* **2** go around frivolously or indiscreetly with members of the opposite sex. ⟨perhaps altered from *gallant*⟩

gal·lon ['gælən] *n* a non-metric unit for measuring liquids. The traditional Canadian gallon is about 4.55 L; the US gallon is about 3.79 L. *Abbrev* **gal** ⟨Old Norman French *galon*⟩

gal·lop ['gæləp] *n* **1** the fastest gait of horses and other four-footed animals, where all four feet are off the ground together once in each stride. **2** a fast pace: *talking at a gallop.* *v* **1** go at a gallop or cause to gallop. **2** go very fast. ⟨French *galoper;* Germanic⟩

gal·lows ['gælouz] *n, pl* **-lows** or **-lows·es 1** a wooden structure used for hanging persons condemned to death. **2 the gallows** punishment by hanging. ⟨Old English *galga*⟩

Gal·lup poll ['gæləp] a poll of public opinion, taken from a representative sample. ⟨George *Gallup*, 20c US statistician⟩

ga·lore [gə'lɔr] *adj* in abundance (used after the noun): *Over Christmas we had parties galore.* ⟨Irish *go leōr* to sufficiency⟩

ga·losh [gə'lɒʃ] *n* an overshoe worn in wet or snowy weather: *I hate wearing galoshes.* Also, **go·losh.** ⟨French *galoche*⟩

ga·lumph [gə'lʌmf] *v* move heavily or clumsily: *galumphing up the stairs in his great boots.* ⟨blend of *gallop* and *triumph*; coined by Lewis Carroll⟩

gal·van·ic [gæl'vænɪk] *adj* **1** producing a direct current of electricity. **2** of or caused by an electric current. **3** stimulating: *a galvanic personality.* **4** produced as if by an electric shock: *a galvanic reaction.* **gal·van·i·cal·ly** *adv.* ⟨Luigi *Galvani*, 18c Italian physicist⟩
gal·va·nize ['gælvə,naɪz] *v* **1** apply an electric current to. **2** arouse suddenly. **3** cover (iron or steel) with a coating of zinc to prevent rust. **gal·va·ni·za·tion** *n.*

gam·bit ['gæmbɪt] *n* **1** *Chess* a way of opening a game by purposely risking a piece to gain advantage. **2** any risky stratagem intended to gain an advantage: *His opening gambit was to call for an investigation.* **3** a way of starting anything, such as a conversation. ⟨Provençal *cambi* an exchange; Latin *cambiare* to change; possibly Celtic⟩

gam·ble ['gæmbəl] *v* **1** play games of chance for some prize. **2** take a risk in order to gain some advantage: *to gamble by refusing a job offer and hoping for a better one.* **3** bet; wager. **4** lose by gambling (with *away*): *He gambled away his inheritance.* *n Informal* a risky venture. **gam·bler** *n.* **gam·bling** *n, adj.* ⟨probably related to GAME, *v*⟩

gam·bol ['gæmbəl] *v* **-bolled** or **-boled, -bol·ling** or **-bol·ing** run and jump in play: *Lambs gambolled in the meadow.* **gam·bol** *n.* ⟨French *gambade,* Italian *gambata; gamba* leg⟩

game¹ [geɪm] *n* **1** an activity done for entertainment: *Football and chess are games.* **2** any one of a number of contests making up a series: *I won four games out of six.* **3** any activity that tests one's skill: *the game of life.* **4** *Informal* any business venture, profession, etc.: *the acting game.* **5** a scheme: *We saw through her game.* **6** wild animals, birds, or fish hunted or caught for sport or for food. *adj* **1** to do with game: *game laws.* **2** brave: *a game fight.* **3** having enough spirit: *She was game for any adventure.* *v* gamble. **game·ly** *adv.* **game·ness** *n.* ⟨Old English *gamen* joy⟩

ahead of the game in an advantageous position. be off (or on) one's game play badly (or well). game over the end of all hope (for). play the game Informal follow the rules; be a good sport.

game·keep·er n a person employed to breed and look after game animals and birds on an estate. game plan a course of action for achieving an aim. game point a final point needed to win a game, esp of tennis. game preserve or reserve ✷ land set aside by the government for the protection of wildlife. game show a radio or esp a television program in which contestants can win prizes. games·man·ship n the art of defeating an opponent by manoeuvres to gain a psychological advantage: political gamesmanship. game warden ✷ an official whose duty it is to enforce the game laws in a certain district. gam·ing n the playing of games of chance for money. gam·y or gamey adj 1 having a taste or smell characteristic of the meat of wild animals or birds. 2 scandalous. gam·i·ness n.

game² [geim] adj Informal lame; injured: a game leg. ⟨origin uncertain⟩

gam·ete ['gæmit] or [gə'mit] n Biology a mature sexual reproductive cell. ga·met·ic [gə'mɛtɪk] adj. ⟨Greek gametē wife⟩

gam·in ['gæmən] n 1 a boy left to roam about the streets. 2 any small, lively person. adj like an urchin; impudent. ⟨French⟩
gam·ine [gæ'min]; French [ga'min] n 1 a young girl, abandoned and living on the streets. 2 an impish or tomboyish girl.

gam·ma ['gæmə] n the third letter of the Greek alphabet (Γ, γ = English G, g). gamma rays electromagnetic radiation similar to X rays but shorter in wavelength.

gam·ut ['gæmət] n 1 Music a the whole series of recognized notes. b the complete scale of any key, esp the major scale. 2 the entire range of anything: the gamut of feeling from hope to despair. ⟨contraction of Latin gamma ut, notes of the medieval scale⟩

gan·der ['gændər] n 1 an adult male goose. 2 a fool; simpleton. ⟨Old English gandra⟩
take a gander look: Take a gander at the outfit!

gang [gæŋ] n 1 a group of people acting together, esp for antisocial purposes. 2 a group of people associated for social purposes: We're having the gang over for coffee. ⟨Old English gang a going⟩
gang up on oppose as a group: Let's gang up on that bully.
gang·land n the world of organized criminal gangs. gang·ster n a member of an organized gang of criminals. gang·ster·ism n.

gan·gli·on ['gæŋgliən] n, pl -gli·a or -gli·ons. 1 a mass of nerve cells forming a nerve centre outside of the brain or spinal cord. 2 a centre of force or energy. gang·li·on·ic adj. ⟨Latin ganglion a type of swelling; Greek⟩

gan·gly ['gæŋgli] adj awkwardly tall and slender. Also, gan·gling. ⟨apparently ultimately from gang, v⟩

gang·plank ['gæŋ,plæŋk] n a movable bridge used in getting on and off a ship, etc.
gang·way ['gæŋ,wei] n 1 passageway. 2 gangplank. ⟨Old English gang a going⟩

gan·grene ['gæŋgrin] or [gæŋ'grin] n the decay of tissue when the blood supply is interfered with. gan·gre·nous ['gæŋgrənəs] adj. ⟨Greek gangraina⟩

gan·net ['gænɪt] n any of several fish-eating sea birds. ⟨Old English ganot⟩

gan·try ['gæntri] n a movable framework with platforms at different levels, used for servicing a rocket on its launching pad, for carrying a crane, etc. ⟨Latin canterius beast of burden; Greek kanthēlios pack ass⟩

gap [gæp] n 1 a hole, as in a fence, wall, etc. 2 an empty part: Why is there this gap in your employment history? 3 a difference of opinion, character, etc.. the generation gap. 4 a narrow way between things. ⟨Old Norse gapa. Related to GAPE.⟩
bridge (or close, or fill, or stop) a gap make up a deficiency.
gap-toothed ['gæp,tuθt] or ['gæp,tuðt] adj having a gap between two teeth.

gape [geip] v 1 open wide; be wide open: A deep crevasse gaped before us. 2 open the mouth wide. gape n. ⟨Old Norse gapa⟩

ga·rage [gə'rɑʒ] or [gə'rædʒ] n 1 a shelter for cars, trucks, etc. 2 an establishment for repairing and servicing cars, trucks, etc.
v put or keep in a garage. ⟨French, from garer park, put in shelter⟩
garage sale an informal sale of personal possessions, furniture, etc., usually held in a private garage or driveway. See also YARD SALE.

garb [gɑrb] n 1 the way one is dressed: a doctor's garb. 2 the outward covering.
v clothe: The doctor was garbed in white. ⟨Italian garbo grace⟩

gar·bage ['gɑrbɪdʒ] n 1 waste matter; trash. 2 Informal inferior or offensive speech, writings, etc.: That argument is a lot of garbage. ⟨Middle English, animal entrails; origin uncertain⟩
garbage fish ✷ fish of no commercial value.
garbage in, garbage out Computers the principle that inaccurate data produces inaccurate output. Abbrev GIGO

gar·ble ['gɑrbəl] 1 make misleading selections from (statements, writings, etc.): a garbled account of the premier's speech. 2 confuse (statements, etc.) unintentionally. ⟨Arabic gharbala sift; probably Latin cribellare; cribrum sieve⟩

gar·den ['gɑrdən] n a piece of ground used for growing vegetables, flowers, or fruits.
v make, take care of, or work in a garden. gar·den adj. gar·den·er n. gar·den·like adj. ⟨Norman French gardin; Germanic⟩
gar·den–var·i·e·ty adj common; ordinary: a garden-variety poet.

gar·de·nia [gɑr'dinjə] n any of a genus of trees and shrubs of the madder family, having fragrant flowers with waxy petals. ⟨Alexander Garden, 18c US botanist⟩

gar·gan·tu·an [gɑr'gæntʃuən] *adj* enormous; gigantic: *a gargantuan meal.* ⟨*Gargantua* a giant in a satire by Rabelais⟩

gar·gle ['gɑrgəl] *v* rinse the throat with liquid kept in motion in the throat. *n* **1** a liquid used for gargling. **2** a sound like that produced by gargling. ⟨probably imitative; influenced by Old French *gargoule* throat; Latin *gurgulio* windpipe⟩

gar·goyle ['gɑrgɔɪl] *n* a spout for carrying off rainwater from the gutter of a building and usually having the form of a grotesque creature. ⟨Old French *gargole* water spout⟩

gar·ish ['gɛrɪʃ] *or* ['gærɪʃ] *adj* **1** unpleasantly bright. **2** gaudy. **gar·ish·ly** *adv.* **gar·ish·ness** *n.* ⟨perhaps from obsolete *gaure* stare⟩

gar·land ['gɑrlənd] *n* a wreath of flowers, leaves, etc. worn on the head or hung as a decoration. *v* decorate with a garland. ⟨Old French *gerlande*⟩

gar·lic ['gɑrlɪk] *n* a plant of the lily family, widely grown for its strong-tasting bulb. **gar·lick·y** ['gɑrlɪki] *adj.* ⟨Old English *gārlēac; gār* spear + *lēac* leek⟩

gar·ment ['gɑrmənt] *n* any article of clothing. ⟨Old French *garnement; garnir.* See GARNISH.⟩

gar·ner ['gɑrnər] *v* **1** gather and store away: *Squirrels garner nuts in the fall.* **2** earn: *to garner respect.* ⟨Old French *gernier, grenier,* Latin *granarium.* See GRANARY.⟩

gar·net ['gɑrnɪt] *n* a mineral occurring mainly in red crystals. **gar·net·like** *adj.* ⟨Old French *grenat* grained (stone), Latin *granatum; granum* grain, seed⟩

gar·nish ['gɑrnɪʃ] *n* **1** something laid on or around food as a decoration: *a garnish of parsley.* **2** a decoration; trimming. **gar·nish** *v.* ⟨Old French *garniss-* a stem of *garnir* fit out; Germanic⟩ **garnish with** embellish with: *writing garnished with anecdotes.*
gar·nish·ee [,gɑrnə'ʃi] *v* **-nish·eed, -nish·ee·ing** *Law v* take (money or property) from a person, by authority of a court, to pay a debt. **gar·nish·ee** *n.*

gar·ret ['gɛrɪt] *or* ['gærɪt] *n* a space in a house just below a sloping roof. ⟨Old French *garite* watchtower; *garir* defend⟩

gar·ri·son ['gɛrəsən] *or* ['gærəsən] *n* **1** the soldiers stationed in a fort, town, etc. **2** a place where such troops are stationed. *v* station troops in (a fort, town, etc.) for defence. ⟨Old French *garison; garir.* See GARRET.⟩

gar·rote [gə'rɒt] *or* [gə'rout] *n* a cord used for strangling in a surprise attack, etc. *v* attack or kill with a garrote. Also, **ga·rotte, gar·rotte. gar·rot·er** *n.* ⟨Spanish *garrote* stick for twisting cord⟩

gar·ru·lous ['gɛrələs] *or* ['gærələs] *adj* talking too much about trivial matters. **gar·ru·li·ty** [gə'ruləti] *n.* **gar·ru·lous·ly** *adv.* ⟨Latin *garrulus; garrire* chatter⟩

gar·ter ['gɑrtər] *n* **1** a band, usually of elastic, used to hold up a stocking or sock.

2 an elastic band worn around the arm to keep the sleeve pushed up. ⟨Old French *gartier; garet* bend of the knee; Celtic⟩
garter belt an elastic belt with garters attached, worn for keeping up stockings. **garter snake** any of various harmless snakes having yellow or red stripes along the body.

gas¹ [gæs] *n* **1** not a solid or liquid. **2** any gas or mixture of gases except air. **3** gas in the stomach, usually as a result of a stomach disorder. **4** *Slang* empty or boasting talk. **5** *Slang* a person or thing that is very amusing, exciting, etc.: *The party was a gas.* *v* **gassed, gas·sing 1** supply with gas. **2** attack with gas. **3** *Slang* talk idly or boastfully. **gas·e·ous** ['gæsiəs], ['geisiəs], *or* ['gæfəs] *adj.* **gas·like** *adj.* **gas·sy** *adj.* ⟨alteration of Greek *chaos* chaos; coined by Jean B. van Helmont, 17c Flemish physicist⟩
gas·bag *n Slang* a person who talks too much. **gas chamber** a room for the execution of people by means of poisonous gas. **gas·i·fy** ['gæsɪ,faɪ] *v* change into a gas. **gas·i·fi·ca·tion** *n.* **gas jet** a small nozzle at the end of a gas fixture where the gas comes out. **gas·light** *n* **1** light made by burning gas. **2** to do with a period when gaslight was used: *a gaslight melodrama.* **gas main** a large underground pipe to carry gas. **gas·man** *n, pl* **-men** a person whose work is to read consumers' gas meters. **gas mask** a mask with a filter containing chemicals to neutralize poisons. **gas·works** *n* an industrial plant that manufactures gas.

gas² [gæs] *Informal n* gasoline. *adj* powered by gas: *a gas lawn mower.* *v* **gassed, gas·sing** fill the tank of a motor vehicle with gasoline (usually with *up*): *We gassed up before we left the city.*
step on the gas a push down the accelerator of a motor vehicle. **b** go faster: *We'd better step on the gas and get these dishes done.*
gas guzzler *Informal* a vehicle such as a car that uses a lot of fuel. **gas·o·hol** ['gæsə,hɒl] *n* a mixture of gasoline and alcohol used as a fuel for motor vehicles. **gas·o·line** [,gæsə'lin] *n* a liquid consisting of a mixture of hydrocarbons made by distilling petroleum. **gas pedal** the pedal controlling the flow of gasoline to a motor vehicle engine. **gas station** a place for supplying motor vehicles with gasoline, motor oil, water, etc.

gash [gæʃ] *n* a long, deep wound. **gash** *v.* ⟨earlier *garsh;* Norman French *garser* scarify⟩

gas·ket ['gæskɪt] *n* a strip of rubber, cork, etc. packed around the inside of a joint to make it leakproof. ⟨probably French *garcette;* Old French *garcete* small cord, orig little girl; *garce* feminine of *gars* boy⟩
blow a gasket *Slang* lose one's temper.

gasp [gæsp] *n* a sudden, short intake of breath through the mouth. *v* **1** catch the breath with difficulty. **2** breathe with gasps. **3** long (*for*): *I was gasping for a drink of water.* ⟨Old Norse *geispa* yawn⟩
at the last gasp a about to die. **b** at the final moment.

gas·pe·reau [ˌgæspə'rou] *n, pl* **gas·pe·reaux** **✹** the alewife, an Atlantic food fish. ⟨Cdn. French⟩

gas·tric ['gæstrɪk] *adj* to do with the stomach. ⟨Greek *gastros* stomach⟩
gastric juice the digestive fluid secreted by glands in the stomach. **gastric ulcer** an ulcer in the stomach lining. **gas·tri·tis** [gæ'straɪtɪs] *n Medicine* an inflammation of the stomach. **gas·tro·en·ter·i·tis** [ˌgæstrouˌɛntə'raɪtɪs] *n Medicine* inflammation of the the stomach and intestines. **gas·tro–in·tes·tin·al** *adj* to do with the stomach and intestines. **gas·tron·o·my** *n* the art or science of good eating. **gas·tro·nome** ['gæstrə,noum] a person who is expert in gastronomy; epicure. **gas·tro·no·m·ic** *adj.* **gas·tro·nom·i·cal·ly** *adv.* **gas·tro·pod** *n* any of a class of molluscs, most of which move by means of a single foot attached to the undersurface of their bodies.

gate [geit] *n* **1** a movable part for closing an opening in a wall or fence. **2** a way to go in or out. **3** a barrier intended to prevent entrance: *Level crossings are often equipped with gates.* **4** the number of people who pay to see a performance, or the amount of money received from these people: *a gate of $3250.* **5** *Skiing* an obstacle in a slalom course, consisting of two upright poles. **gate·like** *adj.* ⟨Old English *gæt;* compare Old Icelandic *gat* opening, passage⟩
get the gate *Slang* be dismissed. **give someone the gate** *Informal* **a** dismiss or turn away. **b** *Hockey* award a player a penalty, thus putting him or her off the ice. **gate–crash** *v Informal* attend a social function without being invited or without a ticket. **gate–crash·er** *n.* **gate·house** *n* **1** a house at or over a gate, used as the gatekeeper's quarters. **2** a structure at the gate of a reservoir, dam, etc., with machinery for regulating the flow of water. **gate·keep·er** *n* a person employed to guard a gate and control passage through it. **gate·leg** *n* a folding leg that supports a drop leaf of a table. **gateleg table** or **gatelegged table**. **gate·post** *n* one of the posts on either side of a gate. **gate·way** *n* **1** an opening in a wall, fence, etc., fitted with a gate or other barrier. **2** a way to get to or attain something: *a gateway to success.*

gath·er ['gæðər] *v* **1** bring into one place. **2** assemble: *A crowd gathered.* **3** collect: *Tears gathered in her eyes.* **4** pick and collect: *Farmers gather their crops.* **5** gain little by little: *The train gathered speed.* **6** collect (oneself) for an effort. **7** conclude: *I gathered from her voice that she was upset.* **8** pull together in folds: *a skirt gathered at the waist.* **gath·er·er** *n.* ⟨Old English *gaderian; geador* (to)gether⟩
gather oneself together prepare oneself mentally.
gath·er·ing *n* an assembly; party; crowd.

gauche [gouʃ] *adj* awkward or clumsy in social situations; tactless. **gauche·ly** *adv.* **gauche·ness** *n.* ⟨French = left-handed⟩

gau·che·rie ['gouʃəri] *or* [ˌgouʃə'ri] *n* **1** gaucheness. **2** a gauche act or remark.

gau·cho ['gʌutʃou] *n* a cowboy of the southern plains of South America. ⟨Spanish⟩

gaud·y [gɒdi] *adj* bright or ornate in a cheap and tasteless way: *gaudy jewellery.* **gaud·i·ly** *adv.* **gaud·i·ness** *n.* ⟨obsolete *gaud* trinket, Anglo-French *gaude; gaudir* rejoice⟩

gauge [geidʒ] *n* **1** a standard scale to which something must conform. **2** an instrument for measuring. **3** a means of estimating. **4** size, capacity, or extent. **5** the diameter of the bore of a firearm.
v **1** measure accurately with a device: *to gauge the width of the metal strip.* **2** estimate; judge: *to gauge the character of a stranger.* Also, **gage**. **gauge·a·ble** *adj.* **gaug·er** *n.* ⟨French⟩

gaunt [gɒnt] *adj* **1** very thin. **2** looking bare and gloomy: *a gaunt landscape.* **gaunt·ly** *adv.* **gaunt·ness** *n.* ⟨origin uncertain⟩

gaunt·let¹ ['gɒntlɪt] *n* **1** a heavy glove that was part of a knight's armour. **2** a heavy glove used for protection in industry, etc. ⟨Old French *gantelet* diminutive of *gant* glove⟩
take up (or **throw down**) **the gauntlet a** accept (issue) a challenge. **b** take up the defence of a person, opinion, etc.

gaunt·let² ['gɒntlɪt] *n* formerly, a military punishment in which the offender had to run between two rows of men who struck him with clubs as he passed. Also, **gant·let**. ⟨Swedish *gatlopp; gata* lane + *lopp* course⟩
run the gauntlet a expose oneself to a series of dangers: *In war, convoys run the gauntlet of enemy submarines.* **b** be exposed to unfriendly attacks, criticism, etc.

gauss [gʌus] *n* a unit of magnetic induction. ⟨K.F. *Gauss,* 19c German mathematician and astronomer⟩

gauze [gɒz] *n* a very thin, light cloth. **gauze·like** *adj.* **gauz·y** *adj.* ⟨French *gaze; Gaza,* capital of the Gaza Strip, SW of Israel⟩

gave [geiv] *v* pt of GIVE.

gav·el ['gævəl] *n* a mallet used by a presiding officer to signal for order. ⟨origin uncertain⟩

gawk [gɒk] *n* an awkward person.
v Informal stare rudely or stupidly. **gawk·er** *n.* ⟨origin uncertain⟩
gawk·y *adj* awkward; clumsy. **gawk·i·ly** *adv.* **gawk·i·ness** *n.*

gay [gei] *adj* to do with homosexuals. *n* homosexual. ⟨French *gai*⟩

USAGE
Former meanings of **gay** (full of fun, bright) are now avoided by most people because of the widespread use of the meaning 'homosexual'.

gaze [geiz] *v* look long and steadily. **gaze** *n.* ⟨Scandinavian; compare Norwegian, Swedish dialect *gasa*⟩

ga·ze·bo [gə'zibou] *n, pl* -bos or -boes a summerhouse, balcony, etc. that commands a wide view. ⟨supposedly from *gaze,* on the pattern of Latin future tenses in -*bo*⟩

ga·zelle [gə'zɛl] *n* any of a genus of antelope

having a slender, graceful body, and lustrous eyes. **ga·zelle·like** *adj.* ⟨French; Arabic *ghazāl*⟩

ga·zette [gə'zɛt] *n* an official government journal containing lists of appointments, promotions, etc. ⟨Italian *gazzetta* orig, coin; from the price of a paper⟩
gaz·et·teer [ˌgæzə'tir] *n* a dictionary or index of geographical names.

GB *Computers* gigabyte.

gear [gir] *n* **1** a wheel having teeth that fit between the teeth of another wheel. **2** machinery: *the steering gear of a car.* **3** the equipment for some purpose: *hiking gear.*
v **1** connect by gears. **2** make subordinate (*to*) in order to serve: *Industry was geared to the needs of war.* **gear·less** *adj.* ⟨Old Norse *gervi*⟩
gear up (or **down**), a shift to a higher (or lower) gear in a vehicle. **b** increase (or decrease) speed or activity. **in** (or **out of**) **gear a** connected to (disconnected from) the motor, etc. **b** in (or out of) working order. **in** (or **into**) **high gear** in (or into) a state of speed or efficiency: *The campaign moved into high gear.* **shift gears a** change from one gear to another. **b** change topic, mood, etc.
gear·ing *n* a set of gears, chains, etc. for transmitting motion or power. **gear·shift** *n* a device for connecting a motor, etc. to a set of gears. **gear·wheel** *n* a wheel with teeth that fit between the teeth of another wheel.

geck·o ['gɛkou] *n, pl* **geck·os** or **geck·oes** any of several insect-eating lizards found in the tropics, having suction pads on its toes for climbing. ⟨Malay *gekok*; imitative of its cry⟩

gee [dʒi] *interj* an exclamation or mild oath. ⟨a shortened form of *Jesus*⟩

geek [gik] *n Slang* **1** an odd person; misfit. **2** a very unfashionable, usually intelligent person, often devoted to a given pursuit: *computer geek.* ⟨dialect *geck* fool; Dutch *gek* madman, fool⟩

geese [gis] *n* pl of GOOSE.

gee·zer ['gizər] *n Slang* a fellow, usually odd, esp an elderly one. ⟨dialect pronunciation of *guiser* someone in disguise, mummer⟩

Gei·ger counter ['gaɪgər] a device used to measure radioactivity. ⟨Hans *Geiger*, 20c German physicist⟩

gei·sha ['geiʃə] *or* ['giʃə] *n, pl* **-sha** or **-shas** a Japanese girl trained in singing, dancing, the art of conversation, etc., in order to act as a hostess or companion for men. ⟨Japanese⟩

gel [dʒɛl] *n* a jellylike material.
v **gelled**, **gel·ling** form a gel. **gel·a·tion** [dʒɛ'leiʃən] *or* [dʒə'leiʃən] *n.* ⟨shortened form of *gelatin*⟩

gel·a·tin ['dʒɛlətən] *n* **1** a substance obtained by boiling animal tissues, bones, hoofs, etc. Gelatin dissolves easily in hot water and becomes jellylike when cool. **2** a transparent material, usually in the form of a sheet (**gelatin slide**) in any of several colours, put over stage lights to produce a certain effect. **ge·lat·i·nous** [dʒə'lætənəs] *adj.* ⟨Italian *gelatina; gelata* jelly; Latin *gelare* freeze⟩

geld [gɛld] *v* **geld·ed** or **gelt**, **geld·ing** remove the testicles of (an animal), esp a horse; castrate. ⟨Old Norse *gelda* castrate; *geldr* barren⟩
geld·ing *n* a gelded horse or other animal.

gel·id ['dʒɛlɪd] *adj* cold as ice; frosty. ⟨Latin *gelidus; gelum* cold⟩

gem [dʒɛm] *n* **1** a precious stone; **2** a person or thing that is very precious, beautiful, etc.: *The gem of her collection was a rare Thai stamp.* **gem·like** *adj.* ⟨Latin *gemma* gem, bud⟩
gem·mol·o·gy or **gem·ol·o·gy** *n* the study of gems, their origins, uses, etc. **gem·mol·o·gist** or **gem·ol·o·gist** *n.* **gem·stone** *n* a precious or semiprecious stone, capable of being cut and polished to make a gem.

Gem·i·ni ['dʒɛmə,naɪ] *or* [-,ni] *n pl* (with sg verb) **1** *Astronomy* a northern constellation containing the two bright stars, Castor and Pollux. **2** any of a series of two-person spacecraft launched by the US. ⟨Latin = twins⟩
gem·i·nate ['dʒɛmə,neit] *v* make or become double; combine in pairs. **gem·i·nate** ['dʒɛmənɪt] *adj.* **gem·i·na·tion** *n.*

–gen *suffix* producing or produced: *antigen, nitrogen.* ⟨Greek *-genēs; gignesthai* be born⟩

gen·der ['dʒɛndər] *n* **1** *Grammar* a system of grouping nouns, either arbitrarily or according to features such as sex, social rank, shape, etc. **2** sex (def. 2) viewed as a sociological category. ⟨Old French *gendre;* Latin *genus, generis* kind, sort⟩
gen·der–neu·tral *adj* taking care to apply equally to men and women: *gender-neutral language.*

USAGE

Many languages have special endings for masculine, feminine, and neuter nouns and for adjectives modifying them. English lost such formal distinctions several hundred years ago. Now, except in pronouns and a few nouns borrowed from other languages (for example, masseur/masseuse), gender is indicated only by the meaning of the word: man/woman, nephew/niece, rooster/hen.

gene [dʒin] *n Genetics* a part of a cell that determines the nature and development of an inherited characteristic. ⟨Greek *genea* breed, kind⟩
gene mapping the process of finding the location of specific genes on the chromosomes. **gene map** *n.* **gene pool** the full set of genes in a population. **ge·net·ic** [dʒə'nɛtɪk] *adj* **1** to do with origin and natural growth. **2** to do with or determined by genes. **ge·net·i·cal·ly** *adv.* **genetic code** the system by which genes transmit instructions that pass on hereditary characteristics. **genetic engineering** the ways in which genetic material can be altered to change hereditary characteristics. **genetic material** DNA in almost all organisms. **ge·net·ics** *n* **1** the branch of biology dealing with the principles of heredity. **2** the genetic make-up of an organism. **ge·net·i·cist** [dʒə'nɛtəsɪst] *n.* **ge·nome** ['dʒinoum] *n* the complete set of

genes in a cell or organism: *human genome.*
gen·o·type ['dʒinə,təip] *or* ['dʒenə,təip] *n*
1 the arrangement of genes in an organism.
2 the genetic make-up of the individual. **3** a
group of organisms each having the same
combinations of hereditary characteristics.

ge·ne·al·o·gy [,dʒini'ɒlədʒi] *n* **1** a record of
the descent of a person from ancestors. **2** the
study of lines of descent. **ge·ne·a·log·i·cal** *adj.*
ge·ne·al·o·gist *n.* ⟨Greek *genea* generation⟩

gen·er·al ['dʒenərəl] *adj* **1** of all; for all; from
all: *A government takes care of the general
welfare.* **2** common to many or most: *a
general interest in sports.* **3** not specialized: *a
general reader.* **4** sufficient for practical
purposes: *general instructions.* **5** indefinite;
vague: *She referred to her trip in a general way.*
6 of or for all those forming a group: *The
word* cat *can be used as a general term for cats,
lions, and tigers.* **7** of highest rank: *a general
manager, the Solicitor General.*
n Canadian Forces the highest-ranking officer
in Mobile Command and Air Command.
Abbrev **Gen. gen·er·al·ly** *adv.* ⟨Latin *genus,
generis* class, race⟩
in general a referring to all or most of those
in a given class. **b** usually: *In general, people
get along fairly well together.*
General Assembly the legislative body of the
United Nations. **general delivery** a
department of a post office that handles mail
which is not addressed to a street number or
box number. **general election 1** an election
involving all the voters of a country. **2 ✱** an
election in which a new federal Parliament is
elected. **gen·er·al·ist** *n* a person who does not
specialize in any one field of study but has a
wide general knowledge. **gen·er·al·ism** *n.*
gen·er·al·i·ty [,dʒenə'ræləti] *n* **1** a general
statement: *He spoke in generalities, giving no
details of the plan.* **2** a general principle or
rule: *"Nothing happens without a cause" is a
generality.* **3** general quality or condition: *A
rule of great generality has few exceptions.*
gen·er·al·ize *v* **1** refer to in one general
statement: *Men and women can be generalized
under the term 'human being'.* **2** talk vaguely;
use generalities. **3** infer (a general rule) from
particular facts: *If you have seen cats, lions,
leopards, and tigers eat meat, you can generalize
that the cat family eats meat.* **4** state in a more
general form: *The statement that 5 + 3 = 8 and
50 + 30 = 80 can be generalized to the form 5a +
3a = 8a.* **gen·er·al·iz·er** *n.* **gen·er·al·iz·a·ble** *adj.*
gen·er·al·i·za·tion *n.* **general practitioner** a
medical doctor who does not specialize in
one branch of medicine. **gen·er·al–pur·pose**
adj suitable for use for a number of different
purposes. **general store** a small store that
carries a wide variety of goods for sale but is
not divided into departments. **general strike**
a stopping of work in many or all industries.

gen·er·ate ['dʒenə,reit] *v* **1** produce: *Rubbing
generates heat.* **2** produce (offspring).
3 *Mathematics* form (a line, surface, figure, or
solid) by moving a point, line, or plane.
⟨Latin *generare; genus, -neris* race⟩
gen·er·a·ble *adj* capable of being produced.

gen·er·a·tion [,dʒenə'reiʃən] *n* **1** all the
people born about the same time. **2** the time
from the birth of one generation to the birth
of the next, about 30 years. **3** the production
of offspring. **4** production: *Water power is
used for the generation of electricity.* **5** *Biology*
the process of reproduction: *the asexual
generation of a fern.* **6** one stage in the
development of something: *an earlier
generation of computers.* **gen·er·a·tion·al** *adj.*
generation gap a wide difference in attitudes
between young and older people.
gen·er·a·tive *adj* to do with the production
of offspring. **gen·er·a·tive·ly** *adv.* **gen·er·a·tor** *n*
a machine that changes mechanical energy
into electrical energy.

ge·ner·ic [dʒə'nerɪk] *adj* **1** to do with a genus
of plants or animals: *Cats and lions show
generic differences.* **2** to do with a group of
similar things; not specific: *Liquid is a generic
term.* **3** to do with a group as distinct from a
brand name: *Most drugs have a generic name
as well as one or more brand names.*
ge·ner·i·cal·ly *adv.* ⟨Latin *genus, generis* kind⟩

gen·er·ous ['dʒenərəs] *adj* **1** unselfish.
2 willing to forgive. **3** large: *a generous serving.*
gen·er·os·i·ty [,dʒenə'rɒsəti] *n.* **gen·er·ous·ly** *adv.*
⟨Latin *generosus* of noble birth; *genus, generis*
race, stock⟩

gen·e·sis ['dʒenəsɪs] *n, pl* **-ses** [-,siz] origin;
creation. ⟨Greek⟩

ge·net·ic See GENE.

gen·ial ['dʒinjəl] *or* ['dʒiniəl] *adj* **1** cheerful
and friendly: *a genial welcome.* **2** helping
growth; comforting: *genial sunshine.*
ge·ni·al·i·ty [,dʒini'æləti] *n.* **gen·ial·ly** *adv.*
⟨Latin *genialis* literally, belonging to the
genius. See GENIUS.⟩

–genic *combining form.* **1** to do with
production: *carcinogenic = producing cancer.*
2 suitable for: *photogenic = suitable for
photography.* ⟨See -GEN⟩

ge·nie ['dʒini] *n* a spirit; jinni: *When Aladdin
rubbed his lamp, the genie came and did
whatever Aladdin asked.* ⟨French *génie*; Latin
genius. See GENIUS.⟩

gen·i·tal ['dʒenətəl] *adj* to do with sexual
reproduction or the sex organs. ⟨Latin
genitalis; gignere beget⟩
gen·i·ta·lia [,dʒenɪ'teiliə] *or* **gen·i·tals** *n* the
external sex organs.

gen·ius ['dʒinjəs] *n, pl* **gen·ius·es** *for 1-3*,
ge·ni·i ['dʒini,aɪ] *for 4, 5* **1** very great natural
power of mind. **2** a great natural ability of a
specified kind: *Mozart had a genius for
composing.* **3** the special character or spirit of
a person, nation, age, language, etc.: *the
genius of Elizabethan England.* **4** a guardian
spirit of a person, place, institution, etc.: *the
genius of the hill.* **5** either of two spirits, one
good and one evil, supposed to influence a
person's fate. ⟨Latin *genius* god presiding over
birth; *gignere* beget⟩

gen·o·cide ['dʒenə,saɪd] *n* systematic
extermination of a national, cultural,
religious, or racial group. **gen·o·cid·al** *adj.*

⟨Greek *genos* race + *-cide¹*; coined by R. Lemkin in 1944⟩

gen·ome See GENE.

gen·re ['ʒɒnrə] *or* ['ʒɒnər]; *French* [ʒɑ̃ʀ] *n* kind; sort; style, esp of works of literature, art, etc.: *The novel and the drama are two literary genres.* ⟨French; Latin *genus, generis* kind⟩

gen·teel [dʒɛn'til] *adj* **1** suited to polite society. **2** polite; well-bred; fashionable. **3** trying to be aristocratic, but not really being so. **gen·teel·ly** *adv.* **gen·teel·ness** *n.* ⟨French *gentil,* Latin *gentilis* of the same people, family, or race; *gens, gentis* race, clan⟩

gen·tian ['dʒɛnʃən] *n* any of a genus of plants with stemless leaves.
gentian violet a derivative of aniline that forms a violet solution in water, used as a dye, chemical indicator, and antiseptic.

gen·tile or **Gen·tile** ['dʒɛntaɪl] *n* a person who is not a Jew. **gen·tile** or **Gen·tile** *adj.* ⟨Latin *gentilis* foreign, orig, of a people, family or race. See GENTEEL.⟩

gen·tle ['dʒɛntəl] *adj* **-tler, -tlest** **1** not violent; mild: *a gentle tap.* **2** moderate: *a gentle slope.* **3** *Archaic* noble; gallant: *a gentle knight.* **4** refined; polite.
v treat in a soothing way: *The rider gentled her excited horse.* **gen·tle·ness** *n.* **gen·tly** *adv.* ⟨Old French *gentil.* See GENTEEL.⟩
gen·til·i·ty [dʒɛn'tɪləti] *n* **1** membership in the aristocracy or upper class. **2** good manners: *an air of gentility.* **3** pretended refinement. **gen·tle·folk** *n pl* people of the upper class. **gen·tle·man** *n, pl* **-men** **1** a man who is honourable and considerate of others. **2** a polite term for any man, also used (in the plural) as a form of address: *Ladies and gentlemen, welcome!* **3** a man of the upper class. **4** a personal servant of a gentleman, esp in the phrase *gentleman's gentleman.* **gen·tle·man·like** *adj.* **gen·tle·man·ly** *adj.* **gentleman's agreement** or **gentlemen's agreement** an unwritten agreement that is not legally binding but depends only on the honour of those who participate in it. **gen·tle·wom·an** *n, pl* **-wom·en** **1** a woman who is courteous and cultured. **2** a woman of the upper class. **gen·tle·wom·an·ly** *adj.* **gen·try** ['dʒɛntri] *n* formerly, in the UK, members of an upper class of wealthy landowners ranking just below the nobility. **gen·tri·fy** *v* to renovate old houses in urban areas. **gen·tri·fi·ca·tion** *n*

gen·u·flect ['dʒɛnjə,flɛkt] *v* bend the knee as an act of reverence. **gen·u·flec·tion** *n.* ⟨Latin *genu* knee + *flectere* bend⟩

gen·u·ine ['dʒɛnjuən] *or* ['dʒɛnju,aɪn] *adj* **1** real; true: *genuine leather.* **2** without pretence; sincere; frank: *genuine sorrow.* **gen·u·ine·ly** *adv.* **gen·u·ine·ness** *n.* ⟨Latin *genuinus* native, natural; *gignere* beget⟩

ge·nus ['dʒinəs] *n, pl* **gen·er·a** or **ge·nus·es** **1** *Biology* a major category in the classification of plants and animals, more specific than the family and more general than the species. **2** any kind or sort. ⟨Latin⟩

geo— *combining form* earth; land, as in *geocentric.* ⟨Greek *geō-; gē* earth⟩

ge·o·cen·tric [,dʒiou'sɛntrɪk] *adj* **1** as viewed or measured from the earth's centre. **2** having or representing the earth as a centre: *a geocentric view of the universe.* Compare HELIOCENTRIC. **ge·o·cen·tri·cal·ly** *adv.*

ge·ode ['dʒioud] *n* a rock having a cavity lined with crystals. ⟨Greek *geōdēs* earthy; *gē* earth + *eidos* form⟩

ge·o·des·ic [,dʒiə'dɛsɪk] *or* [,dʒiə'dizɪk] *n* the shortest distance between two points along a surface, esp a curved surface.
adj **1** to do with the geometry of curved lines. **2** *Architecture* built with short struts forming a spherical grid of polygons. ⟨Greek *gē* earth + *daisia* division; *daiein* divide⟩
geodesic dome a dome made of light materials forming polygons that interlock.

ge·og·ra·phy [dʒi'ɒgrəfi] *n* **1** the science that deals with the earth's surface, its division into continents and countries, the climate, animal and plant life, peoples, resources, industries, and products. **2** the surface features of a place. **ge·og·ra·pher** *n.* **ge·o·graph·i·cal** *adj.* **ge·o·graph·i·cal·ly** *adv.* ⟨Greek *geō-* earth + *graphein* describe⟩
geographical information system a computerized system used to gather, store, process, and display spatial data. *Abbrev:* GIS

ge·ol·o·gy [dʒi'ɒlədʒi] *n* **1** the science that deals with the earth's crust, the layers of which it is composed, and their history. **2** the features of the earth's crust in a place; rock formation of an area. **ge·o·log·i·cal** *adj.* **ge·o·log·i·cal·ly** *adv.* **ge·ol·o·gist** *n.* ⟨*geo-* + *-logy*⟩
geological time time measured by developments in the earth and its crust, divided into geological periods and often linked to the evolution of various forms of life.

ge·om·e·try [dʒi'ɒmətri] *n* the branch of mathematics that deals with lines, angles, surfaces, and solids. ⟨Greek *geō-* earth + *metron* measure⟩
ge·o·met·ric or **ge·o·met·ri·cal** *adj* **1** to do with the principles of geometry: *geometric proof.* **2** characterized by straight lines, circles, triangles, etc.; symmetrical: *a geometric design.* **ge·o·met·ri·cal·ly** *adv.*
geometric progression a sequence of numbers in which the ratio of each term to its predecessor is constant. Compare ARITHMETIC PROGRESSION.

ge·o·phys·ics [ˌdʒiou'fızıks] *n* the science that deals with the relations between the features of the earth and the forces that produce these features. Geophysics includes magnetism, meteorology, oceanography, seismology, etc. **ge·o·phys·i·cal** *adj.* **ge·o·phys·i·cist** *n.*

ge·o·sta·tion·ary [ˌdʒiou'steıʃə,nɛri] *adj* moving at the same speed as the earth, therefore apparently stationary.

ge·o·tech·nol·o·gy [ˌdʒioutɛk'nɒlədʒi] *n, pl* –gies any means used to determine location or any other spatial characteristic. Surveying, GLOBAL POSITIONING SYSTEMS, aerial photography, maps, and even Geiger counters are examples of geotechnology. **ge·o·tech·no·log·i·cal** *adj.*

ge·ot·ro·pism [dʒi'ɒtrə,pızəm] *n Biology* a response to gravity. **Positive geotropism** is a tendency to move down into the earth, as roots do. **Negative geotropism** is a tendency to move upward. **ge·o·trop·ic** [ˌdʒiə'trɒpık] *adj.* ⟨Greek *geo-* earth+ *tropē* turning⟩

ge·ra·ni·um [dʒə'reinjəm] *or* [dʒə'reiniəm] *n* any of various cultivated plants, having showy clusters of flowers. ⟨Greek *geranion; geranos* crane; pod resembles a crane's bill⟩

ger·bil ['dʒɜrbəl] *n* any of a subfamily of small burrowing rodents, having soft fur and a long, hairy tail. ⟨Latin *gerbillus* diminutive of *gerbo* jerboa, small jumping rodent of Asia⟩

ger·i·at·rics [ˌdʒɛri'ætrıks] *n* the branch of medicine that deals with the study of old age and its diseases. Compare GERONTOLOGY. **ger·i·at·ric** *adj.* **ger·i·a·tric·ian** *n.* ⟨Greek *gēras* old age + *iatreia* healing⟩

germ [dʒɜrm] *n* **1** a micro-organism, esp one that causes disease. **2** the earliest form of a living thing; seed; bud. **3** the beginning of anything. **germ·less** *adj.* **germ·like** *adj.* ⟨Latin *germen* sprout⟩
germ cell 1 in the embryo, a primordial cell of the type that eventually gives rise to reproductive cells. **2** one of the reproductive cells in a sexually reproducing animal or plant. Compare SOMATIC CELL. **ger·mi·cide** *n* any substance that kills germs, esp disease germs. **ger·mi·cid·al** *adj.* **ger·mi·nal** *adj* **1** to do with germs or germ cells. **2** in the earliest stage of development. **ger·mi·nate** *v* **1** grow or sprout, or cause to grow or sprout. **2** start growing or developing: *An idea was germinating in his head.* **ger·mi·na·tion** *n.* **germ warfare** the spreading of germs to produce disease among the enemy in wartime.

ger·mane [dʒər'mein] *adj* to the point; pertinent: *Your statement is not germane to the discussion.* ⟨*german,* of the same parents, Latin *germanus.* See GERM.⟩

ger·ma·ni·um [dʒər'meiniəm] *n* a rare, brittle, metallic element. *Symbol* **Ge** ⟨Latin *Germania* Germany⟩

German measles a contagious viral disease resembling measles, but milder.

ger·on·tol·o·gy [ˌdʒɛrən'tɒlədʒi] *n* the branch of science that studies the aging process and the problems of old people. Compare GERIATRICS. **ger·on·to·log·ic·al** *adj.* **ger·on·tol·o·gist** *n.* ⟨Greek *geron* old man⟩

ger·ry·man·der ['dʒɛri,mændər] *v* **1** arrange the boundaries of (the political constituencies of a region) so as to give the party in power an undue advantage in an election. **2** manipulate unfairly. ⟨*Gerry* + (*sala*)*mander*; Massachusetts Governor Gerry rearranged districts in 1812; one district became roughly salamander-shaped⟩

ger·und ['dʒɛrənd] *n Grammar* a verb form used as a noun; present participle. *Examples: eating, running.* ⟨Latin *gerundium; gerere* bear⟩

ges·so ['dʒɛsou] *n* a coating used to give surfaces the correct finish for painting. Gesso usually contains plaster of Paris. ⟨Italian gypsum, chalk⟩

Ges·talt [gə'ʃtalt] *or* [gə'stɒlt] *n, pl* **s** *or* **-en** [-ən] *Psychology* the total structure or pattern of various elements, so integrated as to constitute a whole greater than the sum of its parts. ⟨German = form, configuration⟩

ges·tate ['dʒɛsteit] *v* **1** carry (young) during pregnancy. **2** develop slowly. **ges·ta·tion** *n.* ⟨Latin *gestare* carry⟩

ges·ture ['dʒɛstʃər] *n* **1** a movement of the hands, or any part of the body, to help express an idea: *a gesture of dismissal.* **2** any action made to impress others: *Her refusal was merely a gesture; she really wanted to go.* **ges·ture** *v.* **ges·tur·al** *adj.* ⟨Latin *gestura; gestus* pp of *gerere* to bear, conduct⟩
ges·tic·u·late [dʒə'stıkjə,leit] *v* use excited or vehement gestures. **ges·tic·u·la·tion** *n.*

SYNONYMS

Gesture applies to any motion used to take the place of words or add to the meaning expressed by the words: *She did not speak, but with a gesture indicated that I should follow.* **Gesticulation** applies only to wild, excited, or clumsy gestures: *Her gesticulations suggested she was losing her temper rapidly.*

Ge·sund·heit [gə'zʊnthəit] *interj* a wish for good health to a person who has just sneezed. ⟨German = health⟩

get [gɛt] *v* **got, got** *or* **got·ten, get·ting 1** obtain: *I got a new coat.* **2** arrive (*at*): *I got home early last night.* **3** go and bring: *Get the ball!* **4** cause; cause to be: *I can't get this thing to work.* **5** become: *to get sick.* **6** *Informal* understand: *I don't get what you mean.* ⟨Middle English *gete(n)*; Old Norse *geta*⟩
get about a become widely known. **b** go to many social events. **get across (to)** *Informal* **a** make understand: *You can't get anything across to her when she's in that mood.* **b** become clear (*to*) or understood: *It finally got across to him that he wasn't welcome.* **get after a** scold. **b** urge. **get ahead** advance one's career. **get along a** go away. **b** be on good terms: *He doesn't get along with his neighbours.* **get around a** go from place to place. **b** become widely known. **c** win over: *Her winning smile helped her to get around her father.* **get around to** finally deal with. **get at**

a find out: *to get at the truth.* **b** *Informal* tamper with. **c** imply: *What are you getting at?* **get away a** leave. **b** escape. **get away with** *Informal* succeed in taking or doing (something) and escaping safely: *He thought he could get away with being late.* **get back a** return. **b** recover. **get back at** *Informal* get revenge on. **get behind a** support. **b** fail to keep up to schedule. **get by** *Informal* do well enough: *I got by on my small salary.* **get down to** begin: *to get down to work.* **get even** obtain revenge (used with *with*): *He promised to get even with his sister for twisting his arm.* **get in** arrive: *I just got in.* **get into a** end up in: *get into trouble.* **b** *Informal* become interested in: *She got into music at an early age.* **get it** *Informal* **a** be reprimanded or punished: *I'll get it if I'm late again.* **b** understand. **get off a** escape the full punishment deserved: *The naughty boy got off with a scolding.* **b** send: *I must get this letter off today.* **c** say or express (a joke or funny remark). **get on a** advance. **b** be on good terms. **c** grow old. **get one's own back** be revenged. **getting on for** approaching (a time). **get on to a** learn. **b** communicate with. **get out a** go out. **b** escape. **c** become known. **get over a** recover from: *He was a long time getting over his illness.* **b** *Informal* make clear or convincing. **get set** get ready. **get someone down** discourage; depress: *The hot weather was getting him down.* **get something over with** dispose of (an unpleasant task). **get there** succeed. **get through a** get to the end of: *She gets through her homework quickly.* **b** make or get a telephone connection. **c** make oneself understood: *No one can get through to her when she's angry.* **get to** *Informal* affect: *Her grief really gets to you, doesn't it?* **get together** *Informal* **a** meet. **b** come to an agreement. **get up a** get out of bed, etc. **b** stand up.

get·a·way *n Informal* **1** the act of getting away; escape. **2** the start of a race. **get–out** ['gɛt ˌʌut] *or* [gɛt 'ʌut] *n Informal* a way of avoiding a problem. **as all get–out** *Informal* to an extreme extent: *It's cold as all get-out.* **get·ter** *n* **1** a chemically active substance such as magnesium, used in vacuum tubes to clear gases. **2** ✱ poisoned bait used in exterminating wolves, gophers, etc. **3** (in combination) a person or thing that atains something desirable: *attention-getter.* **get–to·geth·er** *n Informal* an informal social gathering. **get–up** *n Informal* dress; costume. **get–up–and–go** *Informal n* energy; initiative.

Got and **gotten** are both acceptable as past participle of **get**: *I wish you had gotten here earlier. Hasn't he got rid of that thing yet?* But **got** is considered more correct by some, especially as a causative with another verb (in this case, *stamped*): Come back when you have got your book stamped. It is always used in the idiomatic construction *have got* to mean *have* (*I've only got 50 cents*).

gey·ser ['gaɪzər] *n* a spring that sends a column of hot water and steam into the air at intervals. ⟨Icelandic *geysir* a gusher⟩

ghast·ly ['gæstli] *adj* **1** horrible: *Murder is a ghastly crime.* **2** like a dead person or ghost; deathly pale: *The sick man's face was ghastly.* **3** *Informal* shocking: *a ghastly failure.* **ghast·li·ness** *n.* **ghast·ly** *adv.* ⟨Old English *gāstlic; gāst* ghost⟩

Ghastly suggests a connection with death, and emphasizes the horrifying appearance of what is described: *We saw a ghastly accident.* **Grisly** emphasizes being so horrible, and sometimes unearthly, as to cause a person to shudder with horror: *Robbing graves is a grisly occupation.*

gher·kin ['gɜrkən] *n* the small, prickly, cucumberlike fruit of a vine, used for pickles. ⟨earlier Dutch *agurkje* diminutive of *agurk;* ultimately Iranian *angorah* watermelon⟩

ghet·to ['gɛtou] *n, pl* **-tos. 1** a part of a city inhabited mainly by a minority group that is obliged to live there for reasons of poverty, prejudice, or government policy. **2** formerly, a part of a European city where Jews were obliged to live. **3** a part of a city given over to one purpose: *the industrial ghetto.* ⟨Italian; origin uncertain⟩
ghet·to·ize *v* separate as if in a ghetto.

ghost [goust] *n* **1** the spirit of a dead person, supposed to appear as a pale form. **2** anything pale, dim, or shadowy like a ghost: *a ghost of a chance.* **3** *Television* a secondary image resulting from the reflection of a transmitted signal. **ghost·like** *adj.* **ghost·li·ness** *n.* **ghost·ly** *adj.* ⟨Old English *gāst*⟩
give up the ghost die.
ghost town a town that has become empty of people. **ghost·write** or **ghost–write** *v* **-wrote, -writ·ten, -writ·ing** write (something) for another who is nominally the author. **ghostwriter, ghost-writer,** or **ghost writer.**

ghoul [gul] *n* **1** a horrible demon believed to feed on corpses. **2** a person who robs graves or corpses. **3** a person who enjoys what is revolting, brutal, and horrible. **ghoul·ish** *adj.* **ghoul·ish·ly** *adv.* **ghoul·ish·ness** *n.* ⟨Arabic *ghūl* ogre, monster⟩

GHz gigahertz.

gi·ant ['dʒaɪənt] *n* **1** a legendary being having superhuman size and strength. **2** a person or thing of unusual size, strength, importance, etc. **gi·ant** *adj.* ⟨Old French *geant;* Greek *gigantos*⟩
giant star any of a class of unusually large stars. **gi·gan·tic** [dʒaɪ'gæntɪk] *adj* **1** like a giant: *a gigantic wrestler.* **2** huge: *a gigantic building project.* **gi·gan·ti·cal·ly** *adv.* **gi·gan·tism** or **gi·ant·ism** *n* **1** abnormal growth or size. **2** *Medicine* pathological overdevelopment caused by malfunction of the pituitary gland.

gib·ber ['dʒɪbər] *v* chatter senselessly; talk rapidly and indistinctly. **gib·ber** *n.* ⟨imitative⟩

gib·ber·ish *n* meaningless or unintelligible language: *the gibberish of monkeys.*

gib·bon ['gɪbən] *n* any of a genus of small, long-armed, humanlike apes. ⟨French; probably native word⟩

gibe or **jibe** [dʒaɪb] *v, n* jeer; scoff; sneer. **gib·ing·ly** *adv.* ⟨Old French *giber* handle roughly; *gibe* staff⟩

gib·let ['dʒɪblɪt] *n* **giblets** *pl* the heart, liver, and gizzard of a fowl. ⟨Old French *gibelet* stew of game⟩

G.I.C. or **GIC** guaranteed investment certificate.

gid·dy ['gɪdi] *adj* **1** dizzy. or causing dizziness: *a giddy height.* **2** rarely serious: *Nobody can tell what that giddy fool will do next.* **gid·di·ly** *adv.* **gid·di·ness** *n.* ⟨Old English *gydig* mad, possessed (by a spirit); *god* a god⟩

gift [gɪft] *n* **1** a present. **2** the act of giving: *The house came to her by gift from an aunt.* **3** a natural ability: *a gift for painting.*
v give a gift to: *Heredity has gifted him with great intelligence.* ⟨Old Norse *gipt.* Akin to GIVE.⟩
look a gift horse in the mouth question the value of a gift.
gift·ed *adj* having natural ability or special talent: *a gifted musician.* **gift–wrap, –wrapped, –wrap·ping** *v* wrap using decorative paper, ribbon, etc. **gift–wrap** *n.*

gig [gɪg] *n Slang* an engagement for a band, singer, etc. to perform, esp for one night only. ⟨origin uncertain⟩

giga– *SI prefix* one billion. A gigametre is one billion metres. Compare KILO-, MEGA-. *Symbol* **G** ⟨Greek *gigas, gigantos* giant⟩
gi·ga·byte ['gɪgə,baɪt] or ['dʒɪgə-] *n Computers* a measure of the storage capacity of a computer system, roughly equal to one billion bytes. *Abbrev* **GB.** **gi·ga·hertz** ['gɪgə,hɜrts] or ['dʒɪgə-] *n* one billion hertz. *Abbrev* **GHz** **gi·ga·volt** ['gɪgə,voult] or ['dʒɪgə] *n* one billion volts. *Abbrev* **GV**

gi·gan·tic See GIANT.

gig·gle ['gɪgəl] *v* laugh in a silly or nervous way. **gig·gle** *n.* **gig·gly** *adj.* ⟨imitative⟩

GIGO *Computers* GARBAGE IN, GARBAGE OUT.

gig·o·lo ['dʒɪgəlou] or ['ʒɪgəlou] *n* **1** a man who is paid for being a dancing partner or escort for a woman. **2** a man supported by a woman. ⟨French, from *giguer* dance⟩

Gi·la monster ['hilə] a large, poisonous lizard found in the SW United States and N Mexico. ⟨*Gila* River, Arizona⟩

gild [gɪld] *v* **1** cover with a thin layer of gold or gold-coloured material. **2** make (something) shine as if with gold: *The light from the setting sun gilded the windows.* **3** make (something) seem better than it is. **gild·ed** or **gilt** *adj.* ⟨Old English *gyldan; gold* gold⟩
gild the lily **a** adorn unnecessarily. **b** praise something beautiful unnecessarily.
gild·ing or **gilt** *n* **1** a thin layer of gold or gold-coloured material. **2** an attractive outer appearance hiding an unattractive or unpleasant reality. **gilt on the gingerbread**

an additional adornment to something that is already attractive. **gilt–edged** *adj* of the very best quality: *gilt-edged stocks.*

gill [gɪl] *n* **1** an organ of aquatic animals such as fish, that enables them to obtain oxygen from the water. **2** any of the thin, structures on the underside of a mushroom cap. **3** gills *pl* **a** the hanging flesh under the throat of a fowl. **b** the flesh below a person's jaws. ⟨Old Norse; compare Swedish *gäl*⟩
green about the gills of a person, looking sick.
gill net a net for catching fish by entangling their gills in its meshes. **gill·net·ter** *n.*

gim·bals ['dʒɪmbəlz] or ['gɪmbəlz] *n pl* an arrangement for keeping an object horizontal, as a compass on a ship. ⟨Middle English *gemels* hinge; Old French *gemel* twin; Latin *gemellus*⟩

gim·let ['gɪmlɪt] *n* a hand tool for boring small holes in wood. ⟨Old French *guimbelet*⟩
gim·let–eyed ['gɪmlɪt ,aɪd] *adj* having sharp and piercing eyes.

gim·mick ['gɪmɪk] *n* **1** *Informal* any small device, esp one used in a tricky manner. **2** a trick. **3** something to attract attention. **gim·mick·y** *adj.* ⟨origin uncertain⟩
gim·mic·kry *n* the use of gimmicks.

gimp [gɪmp] *n* **1** braidlike trim for curtains, furniture, etc. **2** coloured plastic lacing, used for weaving bracelets and for other crafts. ⟨French *guimpe;* Germanic⟩

gin¹ [dʒɪn] *n* an alcoholic drink made from grain and usually flavoured with juniper berries. ⟨shortened from *geneva* liquor⟩

gin² [dʒɪn] *n* **1** a machine for separating cotton from its seeds. **2** a trap; snare. **3** a machine used to raise heavy things.
v **ginned, gin·ning 1** separate (cotton) from its seeds. **2** trap. ⟨Old French *(en)gin* engine⟩

gin·ger ['dʒɪndʒər] *n* **1** the aromatic, underground stem of an East Indian plant, used as a spice. **2** *Informal* liveliness; energy: *That horse has plenty of ginger.*
v Informal make spirited or enliven (with *up*): *The new manager soon gingered up the company.* **gin·ger·y** *adj.* ⟨Old French *gingiber,* Greek *zingiberis;* Malayalam *inchi-ver*⟩
ginger ale a non-alcoholic, carbonated drink flavoured with ginger. **ginger beer** a drink similar to ginger ale, but with a stronger taste. **gin·ger·bread** *n* **1** a cake flavoured with molasses and ginger. **2** a kind of cookie made of similar ingredients. **3** intricate wooden decoration, such as carving on the gables of houses, etc. *adj* **1** to do with intricate wooden decoration. **2** of ornamentation on furniture, etc., tasteless. **gin·ger·ly** *adv* very carefully, esp to avoid hurting or breaking.

ging·ham ['gɪŋəm] *n* a fabric usually of cotton and usually having a two-colour pattern of checks or stripes. ⟨French *guingan;* Malay *ginggang* orig, striped⟩

gin·gi·val ['dʒɪndʒəvəl] or [dʒɪn'dʒaɪvəl] *adj* to do with the gums. ⟨Latin *gingiva* gum⟩
gin·gi·vi·tis [,dʒɪndʒə'vaɪtɪs] *n* inflammation of the gums.

gink·go ['gɪŋkou] *or* ['dʒɪŋkou] *n, pl* **-goes** a large deciduous tree native to China and Japan, with fan-shaped leaves. ⟨Japanese⟩

gin·seng ['dʒɪnsɛŋ] *n* either of two herbs having a thick, forked, aromatic root used in medicine, esp in China. ⟨Mandarin *jên shên (jên* man, from shape of the root)⟩

gi·raffe [dʒə'ræf] *n* a large African mammal having a very long neck and legs. It is the tallest of living mammals, reaching a height of 5.5 m or more. ⟨French; Arabic *zarāfah*⟩

gird [gɜrd] *v* **girt** *or* **gird·ed, gird·ing** *Poetic* **1** put a belt or band around. **2** surround; enclose. **3** get ready for action: *They girded themselves for battle.* ⟨Old English *gyrdan*⟩
gir·dle ['gɜrdəl] *n* **1** a belt worn around the waist. **2** anything that surrounds or encloses: *a girdle of trees around the pond.* **3** a support like a corset worn about the hips or waist. **4** a ring made around a tree trunk, etc. by cutting the bark. **gir·dle** *v*.

gird·er ['gɜrdər] *n* a supporting beam. ⟨*gird*⟩

girl [gɜrl] *n* **1** a female child. **2** a daughter. **3** a female servant. **4** *Informal* a young, unmarried woman. **girl·hood** *n*. **girl·ish** *adj*. ⟨Middle English; origin uncertain⟩
girl·friend *n* **1** a female romantic partner. **2** a girl who is one's friend.

girth [gɜrθ] *n* **1** the measure around anything: *the girth of a tree.* **2** a strap that keeps a saddle, etc. in place on a horse's back. ⟨Old Norse *gjörth* girdle. Akin to GIRD.⟩

GIS GEOGRAPHICAL INFORMATION SYSTEM.

gist [dʒɪst] *n* **1** the essential part; the substance of an argument. **2** *Law* grounds for legal action. ⟨Old French *gist* (it) consists (in), depends (on); Latin *jacet* it lies⟩

Git·chi Man·i·tou ['gɪtʃi 'mænɪ,tu] the supreme deity of the Cree, Ojibwa, and related peoples. ⟨Algonquian = great spirit⟩

Git·xsan ['gɪtksæn] *n, pl* **-san** *or* **-sans 1** a member of a First Nations people living in British Columbia. **2** either of the dialects of Nass-Gitxsan, a Tsimshian language. **Git·xsan** *adj*. Also, **Git·ksan**.

give [gɪv] *v* **gave, giv·en, giv·ing 1** hand over as a present: *My sister gave me this watch.* **2** deliver: *to give one's word.* **3** cause to have: *Please give me a drink.* **4** offer: *She gave a lecture.* **5** do; utter: *He gave a cry of pain.* **6** yield to force: *The lock gave when she battered the door.* **7** provide a view or passage: *This window gives onto the courtyard.* **8** host (a party, social function, etc.): *They gave a party for their daughter's birthday.*
n a yielding to force or pressure; elasticity: *You need a fabric with give for this pattern.* **giv·er** *n*. ⟨Middle English *yive(n)*; initial *g* from Old Norse *gefa* give⟩
give and take exchange evenly or fairly. **give away a** give as a present. **b** ritually give (a bride) to her husband. **c** reveal; betray: *to give away secrets.* **give back** return. **give in** stop fighting and admit defeat. **give it to** *Informal* **a** punish. **b** scold. **give off** send out; put forth

(an odour, radiation, etc.). **give or take** add or subtract (a few): *The distance is two kilometres, give or take a few metres.* **give out a** distribute: *The girls gave out handbills.* **b** announce: *It was given out that the duke had died.* **c** become used up or worn out: *The food gave out during the famine.* **give over** stop. **give rise to** cause. **give up a** hand over. **b** stop having or doing. **c** stop trying. **d** have no more hope for: *They've given her up for dead.* **e** devote entirely: *He gave himself up to work.* **what gives?** *Informal* what's going on?
give–and–take *n* **1** an even or fair exchange. **2** good-natured exchange of talk. **give·a·way** *n Informal* **1** an obvious sign. **2** Sometimes, **giveaway show**, a radio or television show in which contestants receive prizes. **3** anything given away or sold cheaply to promote business, good relations, etc. **giv·en** *adj* **1** stated: *You must finish the test in a given time.* **2** assigned as a basis of calculating, reasoning, etc.: *Given that the radius is 19 cm, find the circumference. n* any fact assumed to be correct: *It is a given that the sun will rise every day.* **given name** a personal name: *Gordon and Charles are the given names of Gordon Charles Malan; Malan is his surname, or last name.* **given to** inclined toward: *The old soldier was given to boasting.*

SYNONYMS
Give is the general word: *He gave me these books.* **Present** = give in a formal way, often with ceremony: *The Board of Trade presented a trophy to the football team.* **Confer** = give in a courteous way, as to an inferior, or as an honour: *She conferred her smiles on the admiring crowd.*

giz·mo ['gɪzmou] *n* a word used for the name of an object that one cannot recall. ⟨origin uncertain⟩

giz·zard ['gɪzərd] *n* a bird's second stomach, where the food is ground up. ⟨Old French *gister*; Latin *gigeria* cooked entrails of a fowl⟩

gla·cial ['gleiʃəl] *adj* **1** relating to a glacial period. **2** made by the movement of ice or glaciers: *a glacial plain.* **3** icy: *a glacial stare.* **4** moving as slowly as a glacier: *at glacial speed.* **5** *Chemistry* resembling ice in its appearance. **gla·cial·ly** *adv*. ⟨Latin *glacies* ice⟩
gla·ci·ate ['gleiʃi,eit] *or* ['gleisi,eit] *v* **1** cover with ice or glaciers. **2** freeze. **gla·ci·a·tion** *n*.
gla·cier ['gleiʃər] *or* ['gleisjər] *n* a large mass of ice formed on high ground wherever winter snowfalls exceed summer melting.

glad [glæd] *adj* **glad·der, glad·dest. 1** feeling joy or bringing joy: *glad news.* **2** caused by or expressing happiness: *a glad shout.* **3** very willing: *glad to help.* **glad·ly** *adv*. **glad·ness** *n*. ⟨Old English *glæd* bright, shining⟩
glad·den *v* make or become glad. **glad hand** a very warm welcome. **glad–hand** *v*. **glad rags** *Slang* one's best clothes. **glad·some** *adj Poetic or archaic* glad or causing gladness.

glade [gleid] *n* an open space in a wood or forest. ⟨probably related to *glad*. See GLAD.⟩

glad·i·a·tor ['glædi,eitər] *n* in ancient Rome,

a slave, captive, or paid fighter who fought at the public shows. ⟨Latin, from *gladius* sword⟩

glad·i·o·lus [ˌglædi'ouləs] *n, pl* **-li** [-lai] *or* [-li] any of a genus of plants of the iris family, having large, showy flowers all growing on one side of the stem. ⟨Latin, diminutive of *gladius* sword⟩

glam·our ['glæmər] *n* **1** an exciting fascination: *the glamour of show business.* **2** a magic influence. Sometimes, **glam·or.**
glam·or·ize *v.* **glam·or·i·za·tion** *n.*
glam·or·ous *adj.* **glam·our·less** *adj.* ⟨alteration of *grammar* or its variant *gramarye* occult learning; orig a spell⟩

glance [glæns] *v* **1** look quickly. **2** hit and go off at a slant. **3** make a passing reference to (with *at*). **glance** *n.* **glanc·ing** *adj.* ⟨variant of Middle English *glace(n)*; Old French *glacier* to slip; Latin *glacies* ice⟩
glance off fail to affect: *Criticism just seems to glance off her.*

gland [glænd] *n* **1** an organ in the body by which substances are separated from the blood and changed into some secretion for use in the body. **2** *Botany* a secreting organ or structure, generally on or near a surface.
glan·du·lar ['glændʒələr] *or* ['glændjələr] *adj.*
glan·du·lar·ly *adv.* ⟨Latin *glans, glandis* acorn⟩

glare [glɛr] *n* **1** a strong, bright light: *the glare from the ice.* **2** a fierce, angry stare. **3** excessive brightness and showiness. **glare** *v.*
glar·ing *adj.* **glar·ing·ly** *adv.* **glar·ing·ness** *n.* ⟨Middle English *glaren* glassy⟩
glare ice ✹ ice that has a glassy surface.

glass [glæs] *n* **1** a hard, brittle substance that is usually transparent. **2** a drinking vessel made of glass, plastic, etc. **3 glasses** *pl* **a** a pair of lenses together with the frame that holds them in place, worn to correct defective vision or to protect the eyes. **b** binoculars. **4** mirror. **5** barometer.
v enclose or protect with glass (often used with *in*): *to glass in a porch.* **glass·like** *adj.* ⟨Old English *glæs*⟩
see through rose–coloured glasses be very often unduly optimistic about something.
glass blowing the art of shaping glass by blowing it while it is still hot and soft. **glass blower. glass ceiling** an unacknowledged barrier to advancement, based on gender, race, etc. **glass cutter 1** one who cuts sheets of glass into various shapes and sizes. **2** the tool used to cut these sheets. **glass·ful** *n* as much as a drinking glass holds. **glass·mak·er** *n* one who makes glass. **glass·ware** *n* articles made of glass. **glass wool** glass spun in very fine threads. **glass·y** *adj* **1** like glass: *a glassy lake.* **2** having a fixed, expressionless stare: *The dazed man's eyes were glassy.* **glass·i·ly** *adv.*
glass·i·ness *n.* **glaze** [gleiz] *v* **1** put glass in; cover with glass. **2** make a glassy surface on (china, food, etc.). **3** become glassy (often with *over*). **4** coat with a thin sheet of ice.
n **1** a smooth, glassy surface: *the glaze on a china cup.* **2** a substance used to make such a surface or coating on things. **gla·zier** ['gleiʒər] *n* a person whose work is putting

glass in windows, picture frames, etc.
glazed *adj.* **glaz·ing** *n.*

glau·co·ma [glɒ'koumə] *or* [glʌu'koumə] *n* a disease of the eye, characterized by increased pressure in the eyeball causing gradual loss of sight. **glau·com·a·tous** *adj.* ⟨Greek *glaukoma; glaukos* grey⟩

glaze See GLASS.

gleam [glim] *n* **1** a flash or beam of light. **2** a short or faint light. **3** a short appearance: *After one gleam of hope, they grew discouraged.*
gleam *v.* ⟨Old English *glǣm*⟩

SYNONYMS
Gleam applies to a steady light that comes out of the darkness and disappears: *We saw the gleam of headlights through the rain.*
Glimmer applies to a light shining feebly or unsteadily: *We saw the glimmer of a distant light through the trees.*

glean [glin] *v* **1** gather (grain) left on a field by reapers. **2** gather little by little or slowly: *We gleaned information from all the brochures.*
glean·er *n.* **glean·ings** *n pl.* ⟨Old French *glener,* Latin *glennare;* Celtic⟩

glee [gli] *n* **1** joy; delight; mirth. **2** a song for three or more, usually male, voices each singing a different part. **glee·ful** *adj.*
glee·ful·ly *adv.* **glee·ful·ness** *n.* ⟨Old English *glēo*⟩
glee club a group organized for singing glees or other part songs.

glen [glɛn] *n* a small, narrow valley. ⟨Scots Gaelic *gleann*⟩

glib [glɪb] *adj* **glib·ber, glib·best 1** speaking too smoothly to be sincere: *a glib sales talk.* **2** without depth; superficial: *a glib solution.*
glib·ly *adv.* **glib·ness** *n.* ⟨glibbery slippery; compare Dutch *glibberig*⟩

glide [glaɪd] *v* **1** move along smoothly, evenly, and easily. **2** of an aircraft, come down slowly without using a motor. **3** *Music* pass from one tone to another without a break. **glide** *n.* ⟨Old English *glīdan*⟩
glid·er *n* **1** an aircraft like an airplane but with no motor, kept in the air by rising air currents. **2** a chair with a sliding base.

glim·mer ['glɪmər] *n* **1** a faint or unsteady light. **2** a vague or faint appearance: *a glimmer of understanding.* **glim·mer** *v.*
glim·mer·ing *n.* ⟨Middle English. Related to GLEAM.⟩

glimpse [glɪmps] *n* **1** a short, quick view: *a glimpse of the falls as the train went by.* **2** a short, faint appearance. **glimpse** *v.* ⟨Middle English. Related to GLIMMER.⟩

glint [glɪnt] *v, n* gleam; flash. **glint·ing** *adj.* ⟨Scandinavian; compare Swedish *glinta*⟩

glis·ten ['glɪsən] *v, n* sparkle; shine.
glis·ten·ing *adj.* ⟨Old English *glisnian*⟩

glitch [glɪtʃ] *n* **1** *Slang* a malfunction. **2** a brief, sudden irregularity. ⟨Yiddish⟩

glit·ter ['glɪtər] *v* **1** shine with a bright, sparkling light: *New coins glitter.* **2** be bright and showy. **3 ✹** become covered with ice after a freezing rain. **glit·ter** *n*. **glit·ter·y** *adj*. **glit·ter ice ✹** ⟨Old Norse *glitra*⟩

glitz [glɪts] *n Informal* GLITTER (def. 2). **glit·zy** *adj*.

gloam·ing ['gloumɪŋ] *n Poetic* evening twilight; dusk. ⟨Old English *glōmung; glōm* twilight; influenced by *glow*⟩

gloat [glout] *v* **1** ponder with self-indulgent pleasure: *The miser gloated over his gold.* **2** show malicious pleasure: *They gloated over her failure.* ⟨Old Norse *glotta* smile scornfully⟩

glob [glɒb] *n* a large drop or mass of thick liquid: *globs of raspberry jam.* ⟨*globule*⟩

globe [gloub] *n* **1** anything round like a ball. **2** the earth; world. **3** a sphere with a map of the earth on it. **globe·like** *adj*. ⟨Latin *globus*⟩ **glob·al** *adj* **1** of the earth as a whole; worldwide: *global war.* **2** comprehensive: *global dysfunction.* **3** shaped like a globe. **4** *Computers* applying through an entire document, etc.: *to perform a global search.* **glob·al·ly** *adv*. **glob·al·ize** *v* especially of the economy, move to an international level of management, subject to worldwide trends. **global positioning system** a system for navigation, using radio signals from satellites. *Abbrev* **GPS**. **global village** the world regarded as a small community (coined by Marshall McLuhan, 20c Canadian writer). **global warming** a gradual, steady increase in the average temperature worldwide, beginning about 150 years ago and thought to be due to the GREENHOUSE EFFECT. **globe·trot·ter** *n* a person who travels widely over the world, esp for pleasure. **globe·trot·ting** *n, adj*. **glob·ule** ['glɒbjul] *n* a small sphere or ball; a drop: *globules of sweat.* **glob·u·lar** *adj*.

glob·u·lin ['glɒbjəlɪn] *n* any of a group of proteins, found in plant and animal tissues, that are soluble in weak salt solutions but insoluble in water.

glom [glɒm] *v* **glommed, glom·ming** *Slang* **glom onto** seize; grab; acquire. ⟨earlier *glaum*, Scottish dialect; probably Gaelic *glaim* snatch⟩

gloom [glum] *n* **1** deep shadow; darkness. **2** low spirits. **3** a dejected or sad look. **gloom** *v*. **gloom·y** *adj*. **gloom·i·ly** *adv*. **gloom·i·ness** *n*. ⟨Middle English *gloume(n)* look sullen, lower²; origin uncertain⟩

Gloos·cap ['gluskæp] *n* a legendary trickster hero of the Mi'kmaw, Maliseet and kindred First Nations. Also, **Glu·skap**. ⟨Algonquian⟩

glo·ry ['glɔri] *n* **1** great praise and honour. **2** that which brings praise and honour: *Her real glory was not her beauty but her success as a doctor.* **3** adoring praise. **4** magnificence. **5** the splendour and bliss of heaven. *v* rejoice or take pride (*in*): *Her father gloried in her success.* ⟨Old French *glorie;* Latin *gloria*⟩ **in one's glory** *Informal* in a state of greatest satisfaction: *He's in his glory with a dish of ice cream.* **glo·ri·fy** ['glɔrə,faɪ] *v* **1** make glorious. **2** praise; worship. **3** cause to seem more splendid, important, etc. than is actually the

case: *This literary essay is just a glorified plot summary.* **glo·ri·fi·ca·tion** *n*. **glo·ri·ous** *adj* **1** having or deserving glory. **2** magnificent: *a glorious pageant.* **3** *Informal* admirable; fine: *a glorious day.* **glo·ri·ous·ly** *adv*. **glo·ri·ous·ness** *n*.

gloss¹ [glɒs] *n* **1** a smooth, shiny surface: *Varnished furniture has a gloss.* **2** an outward appearance that covers faults underneath. *v* **1** put a shiny surface on. **2** become glossy. ⟨Old Norse *glossi* flame⟩ **gloss over** explain away (a fault, error, etc.): *He tried to gloss over his negligence.* **glos·sy** *adj* shiny. *n* **1** *Informal* a photograph printed on glossy paper. **2** a magazine printed on glossy paper. **gloss·i·ly** *adv*. **gloss·i·ness** *n*.

gloss² [glɒs] *n* **1** an explanation or definition. **2** an interlinear or other rough translation. **gloss** *v*. ⟨Greek *glōssa, glōtta* tongue⟩ **glos·sa·ry** *n* a list of technical or difficult words with explanations or comments: *a glossary of terms used in chemistry.*

glot·tis ['glɒtɪs] *n* the opening in the upper part of the windpipe, between the vocal cords. **glot·tal** *adj*. ⟨Greek *glōttis*. See GLOSS².⟩

glove [glʌv] *n* **1** a covering for the hand, having separate sections for each of the four fingers and the thumb. **2** a padded covering to protect the hand: *a boxing glove.* *v* **1** cover or provide with a glove or gloves. **2** *Baseball* catch (a ball) with a glove. **glove·less** *adj*. **glove·like** *adj*. ⟨Old English *glōf*⟩ **fit like a glove** fit perfectly. **hand in glove** or **hand and glove** in intimate relationship. **handle with (kid) gloves** treat carefully. **glove compartment** a compartment in the dashboard of a vehicle, for holding small articles.

glow [glou] *n* **1** the shine from something very hot. **2** any similar shine: *a firefly's glow.* **3** a warm feeling or colour of the body: *the glow of health.* **4** an eager look on the face: *a glow of excitement.* **glow** *v*. ⟨Old English *glōwan*⟩ **glow·ing** *adj* **1** radiant; shining. **2** rosy, warm, etc. from good health or exertion. **3** very positive; enthusiastic: *a glowing report.* **glow–worm** *n* any of various insects that emit a glow from the abdomen.

glow·er ['glauər] *v* stare angrily; scowl: *The fighters glowered at each other.* **glow·er** *n*. **glow·er·ing** *adj*. ⟨obsolete *glow*, v., stare⟩

glu·cose ['glukous] *n* a sugar occurring naturally in fruits. ⟨Greek *glykys* sweet⟩ **glu·ca·gon** ['glukə,gɒn] *n* a pancreatic hormone that raises the concentration of blood sugar and acts against insulin.

glue [glu] *n* a substance used to stick things together. *v* **glued, glu·ing** **1** stick together with glue. **2** attach firmly: *Her hands were glued to the steering wheel.* **3** look at fixedly: *glue your eyes to the road.* **glu·er** *n*. **glu·ey** *adj*. **glu·ey·ness** *n*. ⟨Old French *glu;* Latin *glus, glutis*⟩ .

glug [glʌg] *v* **glugged, glug·ging** *v* **1** drink in gulps. 2 make a gurgling noise like a liquid being poured into a bottle. **glug** *n.* ⟨imitative⟩

glum [glʌm] *adj* **glum·mer, glum·mest** gloomy; sullen: *a glum look.* **glum·ly** *adv.* **glum·ness** *n.* ⟨Germanic; compare Low German *glum* turbid, muddy. Akin to GLOOM.⟩

glu·on ['gluɒn] *n* a particle supposed to hold quarks together. ⟨*glue* + *-on*, suffix forming nouns⟩

glut [glʌt] *v* **glut·ted, glut·ting 1** feed or satisfy fully: *Years of war had glutted his appetite for adventure.* **2** fill too full: *The prices for wheat dropped when the market was glutted with it.* **3** eat too much.
n too great a supply. ⟨obsolete *glut*, n, glutton; Old French⟩

glu·ten ['glutən] *n* a tough, sticky substance that remains in flour when the starch is taken out. **glu·te·nous** *adj.* ⟨Latin = glue⟩

glu·ti·nous ['glutənəs] *adj* sticky. **glu·ti·nous·ly** *adv.* **glu·ti·nous·ness** *n.*

glut·ton ['glʌtən] *n* **1** a greedy eater. **2** a person who never seems to have enough of something: *a glutton for punishment.* **glut·ton·ous** *adj.* **glut·ton·y** *n.* ⟨Old French *glouton;* Latin *glutto*⟩

glyc·er·ol ['glɪsə,rɒl] *or* [-,roul] *n* a syrupy liquid obtained from fats and oils, used in ointments, lotions, antifreeze solutions, etc. Also, **glyc·er·in** ['glɪsərɪn] *or* **glycerine** [-rɪn] *or* [-,rin] ⟨French *glycérine;* Greek *glykeros* sweet⟩

gly·co·gen ['glaɪkədʒən] *n* a starchlike substance in the liver that is changed into glucose when needed. **gly·co·gen·ic** *adj.* **gly·col** ['glaɪkɒl] *n* Chemistry a liquid obtained from ethylene compounds and used as an antifreeze, solvent, etc. **gly·co·side** ['glaɪkə,saɪd] *n* any of various derivatives of sugar, widespread in plants.

glyph [glɪf] *n* a pictograph or other symbol, esp one etched in a surface. ⟨Greek *glyphe* a carving; *glyphein* carve, cut⟩

gm gram.

gnarl [narl] *n* a knot in wood.
v make knotted and rugged like an old tree; contort; twist. ⟨variant of *knurled*⟩ **gnarled** *adj* **1** knotty and twisted: *a gnarled old cypress.* **2** rugged and sinewy.

gnash [næʃ] *v* grind (the teeth) together. ⟨apparently Old Norse *gnastan*⟩

gnat [næt] *n* any of various two-winged flies that bite, such as black flies. **gnat·like** *adj.* ⟨Old English *gnætt*⟩

gnaw [nɒ] *v* **gnawed, gnawed** or **gnawn, gnaw·ing 1** wear away by biting: *to gnaw a bone.* **2** wear away. **3** torment: *A feeling of guilt gnawed my conscience.* **gnaw·ing** *adj.* ⟨Old English *gnagan*⟩

gneiss [naɪs] *n* a rock composed of quartz, feldspar, and mica. It is distinguished from granite by its layered structure. ⟨German; perhaps Middle High German *gneist* spark⟩

gnome [noum] *n* **1** Folklore a dwarf that lives underground and guards treasures of gold, jewels, etc. **2** an odd-looking person. **gnome·like** *adj.* ⟨Latin *gnomus;* invented by Paracelsus (16c)⟩

Gnos·ti·cism ['nɒstə,sɪzəm] *n* a religious and philosophical doctrine of pre-Christian and early Christian times. It regarded matter as evil and mystical knowledge as the key to salvation. **Gnos·tic** ['nɒstɪk] *n, adj.* ⟨Greek *gnōstikos* of knowledge; *gignōskein* know⟩

GNP or **G.N.P.** GROSS NATIONAL PRODUCT.

gnu [nju] or [nu] *n, pl* **gnu** or **gnus** either of two large antelopes having an oxlike head, curved horns, and a long, tufted tail; wildebeest. ⟨Hottentot⟩

go [gou] *v* **went, gone, go·ing 1** proceed: *Go straight home.* **2** leave: *It is time to go.* **3** work: *Does your watch go well?* **4** become: *to go mad.* **5** attend on a regular basis: *He goes to the local school.* **6** be known: *She went under a false name.* **7** pass: *The summer holidays go quickly.* **8** be given or sold: *First prize goes to the winner.* **9** have a certain result: *How did the game go?* **10** belong: *This book goes on the top shelf.* **11** have certain words, melody, rules, etc.: *How does that poem go?* **12** break down or be used up: *His eyesight is going.* **13** die: *His wife went first.* **14** Informal urinate or defecate. **15** be able to be divided (*into*): *6 goes into 18 three times.*
n pl **goes 1** Informal spirit; energy. **2** Informal a try: *Have another go at this problem.* **3** a success: *He is making a go of his new store.*
adj Slang in the launching of space capsules, etc., ready to proceed: *All systems are go.* ⟨Old English *gān*⟩

as people (or things) go considering how other people (or things) are. **from the word 'go'** from the very beginning. **go about a** be busy at. **b** approach (a task). **go ahead a** carry on: *He went ahead with his plan in spite of their objections.* **b** advance. **go all out** strive to the utmost. **go along** agree; co-operate. **go around** be enough to give some to all. **go at a** attack: *With a snarl, the dog went at the intruder.* **b** Informal make a start on: *The boys went at the dinner as if they were starving.* **go back on.** See BACK. **go by a** be guided by; follow: *to go by the rules.* **b** be known by: *She goes by the nickname 'Smiler'.* **go down a** sink. **b** be defeated. **c** be accepted: *Her motion did not go down with the assembly.* **d** be swallowed: *The jello went down easily.* **e** Slang happen. **go for** Informal. **a** try to get. **b** be attracted to. **c** attack. **go in for** Informal spend time and energy at: *She used to go in for basketball.* **go into a** investigate. **b** become involved with: *to go into music.* **go in with** share with. **go it** Informal go fast (imperative only). **go it alone** act without assistance. **go off a** leave. **b** explode: *The gun went off accidentally.* **c** stop functioning: *The hydro went off during the storm.* **d** of food, become tainted. **go on a** go ahead. **b** continue: *The noise went on for another two hours.* **c** start functioning: *The radio goes on when you turn this switch.* **d** behave: *If you go on that way,* *you'll get into trouble.* **e** happen: *What's going on here?* **f** talk a lot. **go out a** leave a room, one's home, etc. **b** stop burning or shining: *Don't let the candle go out.* **c** go to parties, movies, about town, etc. **d** date: *Are she and your brother still going out?* **e** of the heart, feelings, etc., feel sympathy (for a person or persons): *His heart went out to them.* **f** go on strike. **g** cease to be fashionable. **h** ✵ of ice, break up in spring and move with the current. **go over** *Informal* **a** look at carefully. **b** do again. **c** change sides, political parties, etc.: *go over to the opposition.* **go someone one better** outdo in some way. **go through a** go to the end of: *I went through two books over the weekend.* **b** experience: *He went through some hard times.* **c** search: *He went through his pockets to find a nickel.* **d** use up: *She went through all her money.* **go through with** complete: *He disliked the job so much that he refused to go through with it.* **go together a** match: *Pink and orange don't go together.* **b** keep steady company. **go under** be overwhelmed. **go up a** increase: *The price went up.* **b** be built: *New houses are going up quickly.* **go with a** keep company with: *He's been going with my sister for a long time.* **b** be in harmony with: *That tie goes with your suit.* **go without** do without the thing stated or implied. **let go a** allow to escape. **b** give up one's hold (*of*). **c** give up. **d** fire from a job. **let oneself go a** give way to one's feelings. **b** fail to keep oneself in good condition. **no go** *Informal* impossible. **on the go** *Informal* always moving: *on the go from morning till night.* **to go** of prepared food, for taking away from the place where it was bought, to be eaten elsewhere.

go–a·head *Informal n* **1** ambition; spirit. **2** authority to proceed. **go–be·tween** *n* a person who goes back and forth between others with proposals, suggestions, etc.: *She acted as a go-between during the strike.* **go–dev·il** *n* **1** ✵ *Mining and lumbering* a sleigh used to move ore, logs, etc. **2** a device flushed through a pipeline to clean it. **go·fer** ['goufər] *n Informal* a person who runs errands. **go–get·ter** *n Informal* an aggressive person who usually gets what he or she wants. **go–go** *adj* to do with a dance characterized by rapid, rhythmic body movements: *a go-go dancer.* **go·ing** *n* **1** a departure: *His going was sudden.* **2** the condition of the ground: *The going is bad on a muddy road.* *adj* **1** moving; working. **2** current: *the going price for gold.* **be going to** will: *It is going to rain soon.* **going on** almost: *It is going on four o'clock.* **going concern** a company, person, etc. that is busy and doing well. **go·ing–o·ver** *n* **1** *Informal* a thorough study. **2** *Slang* **a** a scolding. **b** a beating. **go·ings–on** *n pl* behaviour, esp when viewed with disapproval: *Her parents were unhappy about the goings-on at the party.* **gone** [gɒn] *adj* **1** moved away; left. **2** lost; hopeless: *a gone case.* **3** dead. **4** used up. **5** pregnant: *She's six months gone.* **6** *Slang* **a** very good: *the gone blues sung by Bessie Smith.* **b** transported: *a*

gone look on his face. **far gone a** deeply involved. **b** near death or ruin. **gone on** *Informal* in love with: *She's totally gone on him.* **gon·er** ['gɒnər] *n Informal* a person or thing that is dead, ruined, past help, etc.

goad [goud] *n* **1** a sharp-pointed stick for driving cattle, etc. **2** anything that drives or urges one on. **goad** *v.* ⟨Old English *gād*⟩

goal [goul] *n* **1** *Sports* **a** the space into which a player tries to shoot a puck, kick a ball, etc. in order to score: *Shoot for the goal!* **b** the act of scoring in such a manner: *She scored the winning goal.* **2** one's aim or object in doing something: *Her goal was to be a great doctor.* **goal·less** *adj.* ⟨Middle English *gol*; origin uncertain⟩
goal·ie, goal·keep·er *n Sports* the player who guards the goal to prevent scoring. **goal·keep·ing** *n.* **goal line** the line marking the goal in a game. **goal post** *Sports* one of a pair of posts with a bar across them, forming a goal. **goal·ten·der** *n* goalkeeper.

goat [gout] *n, pl* **goats** or **goat 1** any of a genus of bovid mammals with backward-curving horns. **2** *Informal* scapegoat. **goat·like** *adj.* ⟨Old English *gāt*⟩
get someone's goat *Informal* make someone annoyed or angry.
goat·ee [gou'ti] *n* a small, pointed beard on a man's chin. **goat·herd** *n* a person who tends goats. **goat·skin** *n* **1** leather made from the hide of goats. **2** something made of goatskin, such as a container for water.

gob [gɒb] *n* **1** *Informal* a lump; mass: *a gob of honey.* Also (*literary*), **gob·bet.** **2** *Slang* saliva. ⟨apparently Old French *gobe*⟩

gob·ble[1] ['gɒbəl] *v* **1** eat fast and greedily. **2** *Informal* seize or accept eagerly (with *up*): *He gobbled up every piece of information he could find on the rock group.* ⟨*gob*⟩

gob·ble[2] ['gɒbəl] *v* make the throaty sound that a male turkey does. **gob·ble** *n.* ⟨imitative⟩
gob·bler *n* a male turkey.

gob·ble·dy·gook or **gob·ble·de·gook** ['gɒbəldi,guk] *n Informal* speech or writing that is unnecessarily complicated: *official documents full of gobbledygook.* ⟨coined by US Congressman M. Maverick, 1944⟩

gob·let ['gɒblɪt] *n* a drinking glass with a base and stem. ⟨Old French *gobelet* diminutive of *gobel* cup⟩

gob·lin ['gɒblɪn] *n Folklore* an ugly, evil or mischievous sprite. ⟨Middle French *gobelin*; perhaps Middle High German *kobold* sprite⟩

go·by ['goubi] *n, pl* **-by** or **-bies** any of a family of fishes that have a suction cup which permits them to cling to rocks, etc. ⟨Latin *gobius* a kind of fish; Greek *kōbios*⟩

god [gɒd] *n, interj n* **1 God** in the Christian, Jewish, Muslim, and certain other religions, the creator and ruler of the universe. **2** a being considered worthy of worship. **3** a person or thing intensely admired and respected: *His father was a god to him.* *interj* Often, **God** *Slang* an exclamation or oath, often used in expressions such as **My God!** or **God in Heaven! god·like** *adj* ⟨Old English⟩

god·child *n, pl* -**chil·dren** a child that an adult sponsors at its baptism. **god·daugh·ter** *n.* **god·son** *n.* **god·damned** *adj* cursed by God (used as an expletive). **god·dess** *n* **1** a female god. **2** a very beautiful or charming woman. **3** a woman who is intensely admired and respected. **god·fa·ther** *n* **1** a man who sponsors a child when it is baptized. **2** a leading person in an organization. **god·moth·er** *n.* **god·par·ent** *n.* **god·for·sak·en** ['gɒdfər,seikən] *adj* **1** Often, **Godforsaken** apparently forsaken by God. **2** totally depraved. **3** desolate; wretched. **God·head** *n* God. **god·hood** *n* divine character. **god·less** *adj* **1** not believing in God; not religious. **2** wicked. **god·less·ly** *adv.* **god·less·ness** *n.* **god·ly** *adj* obeying God's laws; pious. **god·li·ness** *n.* **god·send** *n* something unexpected and very welcome, as if sent from God. **God·speed** *n* a wish of success to a person starting on a journey or undertaking.

gog·gle ['gɒgəl] *v* stare with wide-open eyes. *n* Usually, **goggles** *pl* large, close-fitting spectacles to protect the eyes from dust, etc. *adj* bulging: *the goggle eyes of a frog.* ⟨Middle English *gogel(en)*; origin uncertain⟩
gog·gle–eyed *adj* having rolling, bulging, or staring eyes.

goi·tre ['gɔitər] *n* chronic enlargement of the thyroid gland, producing a swelling in the throat. Also, **goi·ter. goi·trous** *adj.* ⟨French *goitre*; Latin *guttur* throat⟩

gold [gould] *n* **1** a shiny, yellow, metallic element that is a precious metal. *Symbol* **Au** (for Latin *aurum*). **2** money in large sums; wealth. **3** a gold medal: *She won gold in the Olympics.* **4** a bright, beautiful, or precious thing: *a heart of gold.* *adj* **1** made of gold or resembling gold: *a book with gold lettering.* **2** of a CD, tape, etc., selling a large number of copies. ⟨Old English⟩ **gold brick 1** gilded metal passed off as gold. **2** *Informal* anything that looks good at first, but turns out to be worthless. **gold·brick** *Slang v* **1** swindle, as by means of a gold brick. **2** pretend illness to avoid duties. **gold·brick** or **gold·brick·er** *n.* **gold digger** *Slang* a person whose primary motive for being involved romantically with another person is one of material gain. **gold dust** gold in a fine powder. **gold·en** *adj* **1** made of gold or resembling gold: *a golden buckle.* **2** shining like gold: *The windows were golden from the light of the sun.* **3** blond: *golden hair.* **4** most precious. **5** extremely favourable: *a golden opportunity.* **6** very happy and prosperous: *a golden age.* **Golden Age 1** *Greek and Roman myth* the first age of humankind, an era of perfect prosperity, happiness, and innocence. **2** a legendary age of perfect human happiness. **gold·en·eye** *n, pl* -**eye** or -**eyes** either of two northern diving ducks with yellow eyes. **golden handshake** *Informal* a pension or sum of money given at early retirement. **golden mean** the avoidance of extremes; moderation. **golden oldie** ['ouldi] *Informal* a piece of popular music, etc. that has withstood the test of time. **gold·en·rod** *n* any of a genus of plants of the composite family having tiny yellow flower heads. **golden rule** a rule of conduct that people should treat others as they themselves would want to be treated. **gold·eye** *n, pl* -**eye** or -**eyes ⚹** an edible freshwater fish. **gold–filled** *adj* made of cheap metal covered with a layer of gold. **gold·finch** *n* any of several small songbirds. **gold·fish** *n, pl* -**fish** or -**fish·es** a freshwater fish widely raised as an ornamental fish, selectively bred for a golden colour. Also called **golden carp. gold leaf** gold beaten into thin sheets. **gold medal** the highest award for an event in the Olympic games and other contests. **gold mine 1** a mine where ore yielding gold is obtained. **2** the source of something of great value: *Her real estate business is a gold mine.* **gold plate** cutlery or crockery plated with gold. **gold–plate** *v.* **gold reserve** the gold at the disposal of the government of a nation. **gold rush** a sudden movement of people to a place where gold has just been found. **gold·smith** *n* a person whose work is making articles of gold. **gold standard** the use of gold as the standard of value for money.

golf [gɒlf] *n* an outdoor game played with a small, hard ball and a set of long-handled clubs. **golf** *v.* **golf·er** *n.* ⟨origin uncertain⟩
golf club 1 a long-handled club used in playing golf. **2** a group of people joined together for the purpose of playing golf. **golf course** or **links** a place where golf is played, having tees, greens, and a fairway.

gol·ly ['gɒli] *interj* a word used to express surprise, etc. ⟨euphemism for *God*⟩

–gon *combining form* a figure having angles: *octagon.* ⟨Greek *gonon* having angles⟩

go·nad ['gounæd] *n* an organ in which reproductive cells develop. **go·nad·al** *adj.* ⟨Greek *gonē* seed; *gignesthai* be born⟩

gon·do·la ['gɒndələ] or [gɒn'doulə] *n* **1** a long boat with a high peak at each end, used on the canals of Venice. **2** a flat-bottomed river boat with pointed ends. **3** a freight car that has low sides and no top. **4** a car that hangs under a dirigible and holds the motors, passengers, etc. **5 ⚹** a broadcasting booth up near the roof of a hockey arena. **6** a car that hangs from and moves along a cable: *We went up the mountain in the gondola.* ⟨dialect Italian, from *gondolare* to rock⟩
gon·do·lier [,gɒndə'lir] *n* one who rows or poles a gondola (def. 1).

gone See GO.

gong [gɒŋ] *n* a platelike metal disk that is struck with a hammer. ⟨Malay⟩

gon·or·rhe·a or **gon·or·rhoe·a** [ˌgɒnəˈriə] *n* a contagious, sexually transmitted disease. ⟨Greek *gonos* seed + *rhoia* flow⟩

goo [gu] *n Slang* **1** any thick, sticky substance. **2** sentimentalism. **goo·ey** *adj.* ⟨origin uncertain⟩

good [gʊd] *adj* **bet·ter, best 1** moral. **2** admirable: *a good book.* **3** right; proper: *Do what seems good to you.* **4** well-behaved: *a good boy.* **5** honourable; worthy: *my good friend.* **6** genuine: *It is hard to tell counterfeit money from good money.* **7** agreeable; pleasant: *Have a good time.* **8** beneficial; useful: *drugs good for a fever.* **9** not spoiled; sound: *a good apple.* **10** thorough; complete: *to do a good job.* **11** skilful; clever: *to be good at arithmetic.* **12** more than a little: *a good while.* **13** best: *her good china.*
n **1** benefit; advantage: *work for the common good.* **2** that which is good: *He always looked for the good in people.* ⟨Old English *gōd*⟩
as good as almost; virtually: *The day is as good as over.* **come to no good** end badly. **feel good** *Informal* feel well or elated. **for good** permanently: *He has left Canada for good.* **good and** *Informal* very: *She was good and angry.* **good for a** able to last for. **b** able to pay. **c** worth: *a coupon good for a free ride.* **d** resulting in: *good for a laugh.* **e** an expression of praise: *Good for you!* **make good a** make up for: *She made good the damage done by her car.* **b** fulfil (a promise). **c** succeed: *His parents expected him to make good.* **to the good** on the side of profit or advantage. **up to no good** misbehaving.
good-bye, good–bye, or **good–by** *interj, n* farewell. **good–for–noth·ing** *adj* worthless; useless. **good–for–noth·ing** *n.* **Good Friday** the Friday before Easter. **good–heart·ed** *adj* kind and generous. **good–heart·ed·ness** *n.* **good–hu·moured** or **good–hu·mored** *adj* cheerful; pleasant. **good·ish** *adj Informal* considerable: *a goodish amount of work.* **good–look·ing** *adj* attractive: *a good-looking woman.* **good looks. good·ly** *adj* considerable: *a goodly quantity.* **good–na·tured** *adj* pleasant; kindly. **good·ness** *n* **1** the quality or state of being good. **2** the best part. *interj* often, **my goodness** an exclamation of surprise. **goods** *n pl* **1** personal property. **2** things for sale. **3** *Slang* what is needed or wanted. **catch with the goods a** catch with stolen goods. **b** catch in the act of committing a crime. **deliver the goods** *Slang* do what is expected or wanted. **get** (or **have**) **the goods on** *Slang* find out or know something bad about. **Good Samaritan** [səˈmɛrətən] any person who is unselfish in helping others. **good–sized** *adj* somewhat large. **good–tem·pered** *adj* easy to get along with; cheerful. **good turn** a kind or friendly act. **good will 1** a kindly feeling. **2** willingness. **3** the reputation that a business has with its customers. **good·y** *Informal n* **1** something very good to eat. **2** anything desirable: *a list of election goodies.* *interj* a child's exclamation of pleasure.

good·y–good·y or **goody two–shoes** *n* a person who makes a show of being good. **good·y–good·y** *adj.*

Careful speakers maintain the distinction between **good** and **well,** using **good** as an adjective only: *Her playing is good.* (adj) *She plays well.* (adv)

goof [guf] *Slang n* **1** a stupid or foolish person. **2** an obvious or careless error. *v* **1** make a mistake. **2** bungle (*up*): *I'm sure to goof it up.* ⟨French *goffe* awkward, stupid⟩
goof off or **around** waste time; shirk work. **goof·ball** *n Slang* **1** a barbiturate pill. **2** an odd, peculiar, or crazy person.

goo·gle [ˈgugəl] *v Trademark* to search for information on the Internet, particularly by using the Google search engine. ⟨Google™ is the trademark of Google Technologies Inc.⟩

goo·gol [ˈgugəl] *n* a number represented by one followed by a hundred zeros; 10^{100}. ⟨coined by Dr. Edward Kasner, 20c US mathematician, as hypothetical child's word for a very large number⟩
goo·gol·plex [ˈgugəlˌplɛks] *n* a number represented by one followed by a googol zeros; $10^{10^{100}}$.

goon [gun] *n Slang* **1** a ruffian hired to disrupt labour strikes. **2** a stupid person. ⟨dialect *gooney* idiot⟩

goose [gus] *n, pl* **geese** for 1 & 2, **goos·es** for 3 & 4 **1** any of various waterfowl belonging to the same family as ducks and swans. **2** a female goose as distinguished from the male (gander). **3** a silly person. **4** a prod in the buttocks.
v **1** feed gasoline suddenly to (an engine). **2** prod in the buttocks. ⟨Old English *gōs*⟩
cook someone's goose *Informal* ruin someone's chances, plans, etc. **kill the goose that lays the golden eggs** sacrifice future profit to satisfy present needs or greed.
goose bumps or **pimples** or **flesh** skin that has become rough like that of a plucked goose, from cold or fright. **gooseneck lamp** an electric light supported by a flexible tube like a goose's neck. **goose step** a marching step with the leg swung high with straight, stiff knee. **goose–step, -stepped, -step·ping** *v.* **gos·ling** [ˈgɒzlɪŋ] *n* a young goose.

goose·ber·ry [ˈgusˌbɛri] *n* any of various shrubs bearing berries, some of which have prickly skins. ⟨French *groseille* + *berry*⟩

go·pher [ˈgoufər] *n* a burrowing ground squirrel, one of the commonest mammals of the Canadian Prairies. ⟨Cdn. French *gaufre,* literally honeycomb, from burrow structure⟩

gore[1] [gɔr] *n* blood that is shed; clotted blood: *Her injured arm was covered with gore.* ⟨Old English *gor* dirt, dung⟩
gor·y [ˈgɔri] *adj* **1** bloody. **2** characterized by bloodshed, etc. **gor·i·ly** *adv.* **gor·i·ness** *n.*

gore[2] [gɔr] *v* wound with a horn or tusk: *The savage bull gored the farmer to death.* ⟨Middle English *gorre(n)*; origin uncertain⟩

gore[3] [gɔr] *n* **1** a tapering piece of cloth put in a skirt, sail, etc. to give greater width or change the shape. **2 ✻** an unassigned tract of land remaining after the marking out of a township into lots. ⟨Old English *gār* spear⟩

gorge [gɔrdʒ] *n* **1** a deep valley. **2** a feeling of disgust, resentment, etc. **3** a mass stopping up a narrow passage: *An ice gorge blocked the river.* **4** the contents of the stomach.
v stuff (oneself) with food. **gorg·er** *n.* ⟨Old French = throat; Latin *gurges*, orig, abyss⟩

gor·geous [ˈgɔrdʒəs] *adj* beautiful in a rich or spectacular way. **gor·geous·ly** *adv.* **gor·geous·ness** *n.* ⟨Old French *gorgias* fashionable, with reference to a ruff for the throat. See GORGE.⟩

go·ril·la [gəˈrɪlə] *n* the largest and most powerful anthropoid ape. ⟨W African word, according to a traveller in 5c B.C.⟩

gor·mand·ize See GOURMAND.

gosh [gɒʃ] *interj* a mild oath. ⟨euphemism for *God*⟩

gos·hawk [ˈgɒs,hɒk] *n* any of several short-winged hawks. ⟨Old English *gōshafoc; gōs* goose + *hafoc* hawk⟩

gos·ling See GOOSE.

gos·pel [ˈgɒspəl] *n* **1** the teachings of Jesus and the Apostles. **2** Usually, **Gospel** any one of the first four books of the New Testament. **3** *Informal* anything earnestly believed or taken as a guide for action. **4** the absolute truth. **5** music originating in black churches of the southern US, characterized by vocals with much embellishment. ⟨Old English *gōd* good + *spel* story⟩

gos·sa·mer [ˈgɒsəmər] *or* [ˈgɒzəmər] *n* **1** a thread of cobweb. **2** anything very light and thin. **gos·sa·mer** *adj.* ⟨Middle English, probably *gossomer* goose summer (Indian summer), when goose was eaten and cobwebs plentiful⟩

gos·sip [ˈgɒsɪp] *n* **1** idle talk about people. **2** a person who gossips a good deal. **gos·sip** *v.* **gos·sip·y** *adj.* ⟨Old English *godsibb* orig, godparent; *sibb* relative⟩
gos·sip·mon·ger [-ˌmɒŋgər] *or* [-ˌmʌŋgər] *n* a person who spreads gossip.

got [gɒt] *v* pt and a pp of GET.

Goth·ic [ˈgɒθɪk] *n* **1** *Architecture* a style characterized by pointed arches. **2** Often, **gothic,** *Printing* a family of heavy, angular typefaces based on medieval scripts.
adj **1** medieval. **2** to do with a style of literature that emphasizes the supernatural and the grotesque, usually having a medieval setting. ⟨the *Goths*, a Germanic people that overran the Roman Empire in S Europe⟩

got·ten [ˈgɒtən] *v* a pp of GET.

gouache [gwɑʃ] *n* a method of painting with opaque water colours. ⟨French; Italian *guazzo* water colour, mire; earlier, watering place, Latin *aquatio*⟩

gouge [gaʊdʒ] *n* **1** a chisel used for cutting grooves or holes. **2** a groove: *a long gouge in the desktop.* **3** *Informal* a trick; cheat; swindle.

v **1** cut with a gouge or something like it: *to gouge a piece of wood.* **2** make by gouging: *to gouge a channel.* **3** dig or tear (*out*): *to gouge dirt out of a crack.* **4** *Informal* overcharge or swindle. **goug·er** *n.* ⟨French; Latin *gulbia*⟩

gou·lash [ˈgulɑʃ] *or* [ˈgulæʃ] *n* a highly seasoned stew. ⟨Hungarian *gulyás (hús)* herdsman's (meat)⟩

gourd [gʊrd] *n* the hard-shelled fruit of any of various vines, often dried and used for making bowls, etc. **gourd·like** *adj.* ⟨Old French *cohorde,* Latin *cucurbita*⟩

gour·mand [gʊrˈmɑnd], [ˈgʊrmænd], *or* [ˈgʊrmənd] *n* **1** a person who is fond of good eating. **2** glutton. Also, **gour·mand.** ⟨French *gourmand* gluttonous; *gourmet* gourmet⟩
gour·mand·ize [ˈgɔrmən,daɪz] *v* eat good food greedily. **gour·mand·iz·er** *n.* **gour·mand·ise** [ˌgʊrmən'diz]; *French* [ɡuʀmɑ̃'diz] *n* a taste for good food.

> **CONFUSABLES**
> A **gourmand** eats a lot of good food.
> A **gourmet** appreciates good food, but does not overeat.

gour·met [gʊrˈmei]; *French* [guʀˈmɛ] *n* a person who is expert in judging fine foods, wines, etc.; epicure. ⟨Old French *gourmet, groumet* wine taster; *gromet* servant⟩

gout [gaʊt] *n* **1** a painful disease of the joints, often characterized by a swelling of the big toe. **2** a drop; splash; clot: *gouts of blood.* ⟨Old French *goute;* Latin *gutta* a drop, with reference to medieval theory of body humours⟩
gout·y *adj* affected with gout (def. 1).

gov·ern [ˈgʌvərn] *n* control; manage: *to govern a country, to govern one's temper.* **gov·ern·a·ble** *adj.* ⟨Old French *governer,* Latin *gubernare;* Greek *kybernaein* steer⟩
gov·ern·ance *n* control; control. **gov·ern·ess** *n* a woman who teaches children in their home. **gov·ern·ment** [ˈgʌvərmənt] *or* [ˈgʌvərnmənt] *n* **1** the rule or authority over a country, province, district, etc. **2** the person or persons ruling a country, state, district, etc. **3** a system of ruling: *a democratic government.* **4** rule; control. **gov·ern·men·tal** *adj.* **gov·ern·men·tal·ly** *adv.* **Government House ✻ 1** the official residence of the Governor General in Ottawa, also known as Rideau Hall. **2** in some provinces, the official residence of the Lieutenant-Governor. **gov·er·nor** *n* **1** an official appointed to govern a colony, province, city, fort, etc. **2** in the US, an official elected as the executive head of a state. **gov·er·nor·ship** *n.* **Governor General** *pl* **Governors General** in Canada, the representative of the Crown, appointed for five years.

Govt. or **govt.** government.

gown [gaʊn] *n* **1** a woman's formal dress. **2** a loose outer garment with very wide sleeves, such as those worn by judges, clergy, etc. **3** a loose garment worn in hospital by patients. **gown·less** *adj.* **gowned** *adj.* ⟨Old French *goune;* Latin *gunna*⟩

G.P. or **GP** *Medicine* GENERAL PRACTITIONER.

GPS global positioning system.

grab [græb] *v* **grabbed, grab·bing 1** seize suddenly. **2** take possession of in an unscrupulous manner: *to grab land*. **3** get or take in a hurry: *to grab a coffee*. **4** *Slang* strike the attention of: *How does that idea grab you?* *n* **1** the act of snatching: *She made a grab for the apple*. **2** a mechanical device for firmly holding something that is to be lifted. ⟨probably Middle Dutch *grabben*⟩
up for grabs *Informal* available.
grab bag *Informal* any varied assortment.
grab·by *adj* avaricious.

grace [greis] *n* **1** beauty of form, movement, or manner. **2** mercy; pardon. **3** *Christian theology* the influence of God operating in humans to strengthen them. **4** a short prayer of thanks said before or after a meal. **5** an allowance of time: *The bank gave her three days' grace*. **6** Usually, **Grace** a title used in speaking to or of a duke, duchess, or archbishop: *his Grace the Duke of Charford*. *v* give or add grace to. **grace·ful** *adj*. **grace·ful·ly** *adv*. **grace·ful·ness** *n*. ⟨French; Latin *gratia; gratus* pleasing⟩
have the grace have the goodness or courtesy: *He had the grace to say he was sorry*. **in someone's bad** (or **good**) **graces** out of (or in) favour with someone: *in the teacher's bad graces* **with** (**bad**) **good grace** (un)pleasantly; (un)willingly. **grace·less** *adj* **1** without grace. **2** not caring for what is right and proper: *a graceless rascal*. **grace·less·ness** *n*. **grace note** *Music* a note or group of notes added for ornament. **gra·cious** *adj* **1** courteous. **2** generous. **3** to do with sophisticated taste, coming from affluence: *gracious living*. *interj* an exclamation of surprise. **gra·cious·ly** *adv*. **gra·cious·ness** *n*.

grack·le ['grækəl] *n* any of several large American blackbirds having dark, iridescent plumage. ⟨Latin *graculus* jackdaw⟩

grade [greid] *n* **1** in schools, any one division, or class, arranged according to the pupil's progress. **2** a step in a course or process. **3** a degree in a scale of rank, quality, value, etc.: *grade A milk*. **4** a number or letter that shows how well one has done. **5** the slope of a road, railway track, etc. *v* **1** arrange according to size, value, etc.: *Apples are graded by size*. **2** give a grade to: *to grade papers*. **3** make more nearly level: *They graded the land around the house*. **4** go through a series of stages: *Red and yellow grade into orange*. ⟨French; Latin *gradus* step, degree⟩
make the grade perform up to standard.
gra·date [grei'deit] *or* ['greideit] *v* **1** pass from one degree of colour to another. **2** arrange according to grades. **gra·da·tion** *n*. **grad·er** *n* a machine for levelling earth. **grade school** ELEMENTARY SCHOOL. **gra·di·ent** ['greidiənt] *n* **1** the rate at which a road, railway track, etc. rises. **2** *Physics* the rate at which temperature or pressure changes. **grad·u·al** ['grædʒuəl] *adj* little by little: *a gradual increase in sound*. **grad·u·al·ly** *adv*.

grad·u·al·ness *n*. **grad·u·ate** ['grædʒu‚eit] *v* **1** finish a course of study, then receive a diploma, usually at a ceremony. **2** mark with degrees for measuring: *A thermometer is graduated*. **3** arrange in regular stages. *n* ['grædʒuit] a person who has graduated. *adj* ['grædʒuit] to do with graduates: *a graduate dinner*. **grad·u·a·tion** *n*. **grad·u·and** *n* ['grædʒu‚ænd] a student about to graduate.

graf·fi·ti [grə'fiti] *n*, *pl. of* **graffito** sayings or pictures drawn on a public surface such as a wall. ⟨Italian = scribblings; Greek *graphein* draw, write⟩

graft[1] [græft] *v* **1** insert (a shoot, bud, etc.) from one plant into a slit in another so that it will grow there permanently. **2** transfer (a piece of skin, bone, etc.) from one part of the body to another so that it will grow there. **graft** *n*. ⟨earlier *graff*, Old French *grafe;* Greek *grapheion* stylus (*graphein* write); for its shape⟩

graft[2] [græft] *v* *Informal* make (money) dishonestly through one's job, esp in political positions. **graft** *n*. **graft·er** *n*. ⟨origin uncertain⟩

gra·ham ['greiəm] *adj* to do with a finely ground, unsifted, whole-wheat flour: *graham crackers*. ⟨Sylvester *Graham*, 19c US reformer of dietetics⟩

Grail [greil] *n* **1** the cup supposed to have been used by Christ at the Last Supper; the object of medieval quests. **2** anything long sought for; the ultimate prize. ⟨Old French *graal*, Latin *gradale, cratale* from *crater* bowl; Greek *kratēr*⟩

grain [grein] *n* **1** a single seed of wheat or similar cereal grasses. **2** the seeds of such plants in the mass. **3** a tiny, hard particle of sand, salt, sugar, etc. **4** a unit for measuring mass, equal to about 0.065 g. *Abbrev* **gr 5** the smallest possible amount: *a grain of truth*. **6** the arrangement or direction of fibres in wood, layers in stone, etc. ⟨Old French; Latin *granum* grain, seed⟩
go against the grain be contrary to one's natural disposition.
grain elevator a building for storing grain. **grain·y** *adj* **1** of wood, etc., having a grain. **2** made of grains; granular. **gra·niv·o·rous** *adj* eating grain and other seeds: *Finches are granivorous birds*. **gran·a·ry** ['grænəri] *or* ['greinəri] *n* a building where grain is stored. **gran·u·lar** *adj* **1** to do with grains or granules. **2** having a coarsely textured surface. **gran·u·late** *v* **1** form into grains or granules. **2** roughen on the surface. **3** develop granulations. **gran·u·lat·ed** *adj*. **gran·u·la·tion** *n* a formation of, or into, granules or grainlike bodies, esp such a formation in healing tissue. **gran·ule** ['grænjul] *n* **1** a small grain, or a small bit or spot like a grain. **2** any of the small, brilliant marks in the sun's photosphere.

gram [græm] *n* an SI unit of mass, equal to one one-thousandth of a kilogram: *A nickel has a mass of about five grams. Symbol* **g** ⟨Greek *grámma* marked weight, something written; *graphein* mark, write⟩

–gram *combining form* something written; message:　　*monogram*. ⟨Greek　*grámma* something written; *graphein* write⟩

gram·mar ['græmər] *n* the system of the forms and uses of words in a particular language. **gram·mat·i·cal** [grə'mætəkəl] *adj.* **gram·mat·i·cal·ly** *adv.* ⟨Old French *grammaire*; Greek *grammatikē (technē)* (art) of writing. See -GRAM.⟩

gram·mar·i·an [grə'mɛriən] *n* a person knowledgable about grammar.

gran·a·ry See GRAIN.

grand [grænd] *adj* **1** large and of fine appearance: *grand mountains.* **2** dignified; splendid. **3** highest or very high in rank: *a grand master in chess.* **4** great; important. **5** *Informal* very pleasing: *a grand time.* **6** in terms of kinship, of the second generation before or after: *grandmother, grandson.* *n Slang* a thousand dollars. **grand·ly** *adv.* **grand·ness** *n.* ⟨Middle French *grant, grand*; Latin *grandis* big⟩
gran·dad or **grand·dad** *n Informal* GRANDFATHER (def. 1). **Grand Banks** or **Grand Bank** a shallow region of the ocean lying southeast of Newfoundland. **grand·child** *n, pl* -**chil·dren** a child of one's son or daughter. **grand·daugh·ter** *n.* **grand·son** *n.*
grand·dad·dy *n Informal* **1** grandfather. **2** the largest one of its kind: *the granddaddy of all the fish.* **gran·deur** ['grændjər] *n* greatness; majesty; nobility; dignity; splendour. **grand·fa·ther** *n* **1** the father of one's father or mother. **2** forefather. **grand·fa·ther·ly** *adj.* **grandfather clock** a pendulum clock in a tall case that stands on the floor. **gran·dil·o·quent** [græn'dɪləkwənt] *adj* using lofty or pompous words. **gran·dil·o·quence** *n.* **gran·di·ose** [,grændi'ous] *or* ['grændi,ous] *adj* **1** grand in an imposing way. **2** grand in an affected or pompous way. **gran·di·ose·ly** *adv.* **gran·di·os·i·ty** [-'ɒsəti] *n.* **grand jury** a special jury called to examine a charge against a person to determine if there is sufficient evidence. Grand juries have been abolished in most of the Canadian provinces that had them. **grand·ma** ['græmə] *or* ['græ,mɑ] *n Informal* GRANDMOTHER (def. 1). **grand mal** ['grænd 'mæl] a type of epilepsy characterized by seizures and loss of consciousness. Compare PETIT MAL. **grand·moth·er** *n* **1** the mother of one's father or mother. **2** a female ancestor. **grand·moth·er·ly** *adj.* **grand·neph·ew** *n* the son of one's nephew or niece. **grand·niece** *n* the daughter of one's nephew or niece. **grand·pa** ['græmpə] *or* ['græm,pɑ] *n Informal* GRANDFATHER (def. 1). **grand·par·ent** *n* a grandfather or grandmother. **grand piano** a large piano with horizontal frame and strings. Compare UPRIGHT PIANO. **Grand Prix** ['grɑn 'pri] any one of several road races for motor vehicles. **grand slam 1** *Bridge* the winning of all the tricks in a hand. **2** *Tennis, golf, etc.* the winning of several major tournaments in one season. **3** *Baseball* a home run with three runners on base. **4** a multiple victory in any series: *a grand slam in*

the final examinations. **grand·stand** *n.* the main seating place for people at an athletic field, racetrack, parade, etc., usually having a roof. *v* **-stand·ed, -stand·ing** act or speak ostentatiously to impress an audience. **grand·stand·er** *n.*

Grand emphasizes greatness that makes the person or thing described stand out: *Under the leadership of that grand old man, the nation flourished.* **Stately** emphasizes impressive dignity: *She was moved by the stately rhythm of processional music.* **Noble** emphasizes an imposing greatness in appearance: *The Rocky Mountains are a noble sight.*

gran·ite ['grænɪt] *n* a hard igneous rock consisting chiefly of quartz and feldspar. **gra·nit·ic** [grə'nɪtɪk] *adj.* ⟨Italian *granito* grained; *grano* grain, Latin *granum*⟩
gran·ite·ware *n* ironware covered with grey enamel to look like granite.

gra·niv·o·rous See GRAIN.

gran·nie or **gran·ny** ['græni] *n Informal* **1** grandmother. **2** an old woman. **3** a fussy person.
grannie knot or **granny knot** a knot differing from a square knot in having the ends crossed a different way. **Granny Smith** a tart, green apple, good for eating and cooking.

gra·no·la [grə'noulə] *n* a breakfast cereal consisting of oats, wheat germ, nuts, seeds, etc. ⟨coined late 19c; perhaps Latin *granum* grain + *-ola* Italian diminutive suffix⟩

grant [grænt] *v* **1** give what is asked: *to grant a request.* **2** admit to be true: *I grant that you are right.* **3** transfer or convey (the ownership of property), esp by deed or writing. *n* something granted, such as a privilege, right, sum of money, or tract of land. **grant·a·ble** *adj.* **grant·er** or **grant·or** *n.* ⟨Old French *graanter* variant of *creanter* promise; Latin *credens* ppr of *credere* trust⟩
take for granted a assume to be true. **b** assume the support or help of (someone). **grant·ee** [græn'ti] *n* a person to whom a grant is made.

gran·ule See GRAIN.

grape [greip] *n* a small, juicy, thin-skinned fruit that grows in bunches on vines. *adj* designating the family of mainly tropical, climbing shrubs that includes grapes and the Virginia creeper. **grape·like** *adj.* ⟨Old French *grape* hook, later, bunch of grapes; *graper* pick grapes⟩
grape·shot *n* a cluster of small iron balls formerly used to load a cannon. **grape·vine** *n* **1** any of numerous vines of the grape family. **2** *Informal* a means of circulating information, etc. unofficially or secretly from person to person.

grape·fruit ['greip,frut] *n, pl* -**fruit** or -**fruits** a large, edible citrus fruit with a thick, yellow rind and juicy pulp.

graph [græf] *n* **1** a line or diagram showing how one quantity changes with another.

2 *Mathematics* any line or lines representing an equation or function. **3** any of the most basic symbols in a writing system; letter. *v* draw (a line) representing some change. ⟨Greek *graphein* write, draw⟩ **–graph** *combining form* **1** make a picture, draw, or write: *photograph.* **2** a machine that makes a picture, draws, or writes: *seismograph.* **3** drawn or written: *autograph.* **4** something drawn or written: *lithograph.* **graph·ic** *adj* **1** lifelike; vivid: *a graphic account.* **2** to do with diagrams. **3** to do with drawing, painting, engraving, or etching: *the graphic arts.* **4** to do with handwriting: *graphic symbols.* **graph·i·cal·ly** *adv.* **graphical user interface** *Computers* a display of windows, icons, and menus that allows a user to execute commands by clicking on a mouse. *Abbrev* **GUI. graphic arts** drawing, painting, engraving, etching, etc. **graph·ics** *n* (with sg verb) **1** the art of drawing. **2** the art or science of making architectural plans. **3** the science of calculating by using diagrams. **graph paper** paper with small ruled squares for the drawing of diagrams, graphs, etc.

graph·ite ['græfaɪt] *n* a soft, black form of carbon used for pencil leads, as a lubricant for machinery, etc. **gra·phit·ic** [gra'fɪtɪk] *adj.* ⟨German *Graphit;* Greek *graphein* write⟩

grap·nel ['græpnəl] *n* **1** an instrument with hooks for seizing something. **2** an anchor with three or more hooks. ⟨Middle English *grapenel* diminutive of Old French *grape.* See GRAPE.⟩

grap·ple ['græpəl] *v* **1** seize and hold fast. **2** struggle: *The wrestlers grappled.* **3** use a grappling iron. **4** try to deal (*with*): *She grappled with the problem for an hour.* *n* grapnel. ⟨Old French *grapil, grape* hook⟩ **grappling iron** grapnel.

grasp [græsp] *v* **1** seize and hold fast by closing the fingers around. **2** seize eagerly: *to grasp an opportunity.* **3** understand. **grasp** *n.* ⟨Middle English *graspe(n)*⟩ **grasp at** accept eagerly: *I grasped at the opportunity.* **grasp at a straw** seize even the slightest opportunity. **grasp·ing** *adj* eager to get all that one can; greedy. **grasp·ing·ly** *adv.* **grasp·ing·ness** *n.*

grass [græs] *n* **1** non-woody green plants that grow in pastures and are suitable for food for grazing animals. **2** any of a family of plants having jointed, non-woody stems, and long, narrow leaves. Wheat, corn, sugar cane, etc. are grasses. **3** land covered with grass: *Keep off the grass.* **4** *Slang* marijuana. *v* **1** grow grass over or on. **2** feed on grass: *to grass livestock.* **grass·less** *adj.* **grass·like** *adj.* **grass·y** *adj.* **grass·i·ness** *n.* ⟨Old English *gærs, græs*⟩ **let the grass grow under one's feet** waste time. **grass·hop·per** ['græs,hɒpər] *n* any insect having biting mouthparts, two pairs of wings, and long, strong hind legs adapted for jumping. **grass·land** *n* **1** land with grass on it, used for pasture. **2** prairie. **grass roots** *Politics*

people and party organizations at the local level. **grass–roots** *adj.* **grass snake** any of various harmless snakes.

grate[1] [greit] *n* **1** a framework of iron bars to hold a fire. **2** a framework of bars over a window or opening. **3** *Mining* a screen used for separating or grading ore. **grate·like** *adj.* ⟨Latin *grata;* earlier *cratis* hurdle⟩ **grat·ing** *n* **1** a framework of bars over an opening. **2** *Physics* a band of parallel lines on glass or polished metal to diffract light into optimal spectra.

grate[2] [greit] *v* **1** irritate: *Her rude manners grate on other people.* **2** rub harshly together: *to grate the teeth.* **3** grind off in small pieces: *to grate cheese.* ⟨Old French *grater* scratch⟩ **grat·er** *n* a device with a rough surface for wearing vegetables, cheese, etc. into shreds. **grat·ing** *adj.* **1** irritating. **2** harsh or jarring in sound: *a grating voice.*

grate·ful ['greitfəl] *adj* feeling or causing gratitude: *a grateful breeze.* **grate·ful·ly** *adv.* **grate·ful·ness** *n.* ⟨obsolete *grate* agreeable, Latin *gratus*⟩ **grat·i·fy** ['græta,faɪ] *v* **1** please: *Flattery gratifies a vain person.* **2** satisfy: *to gratify a craving for chocolate.* **grat·i·fi·ca·tion** *n.* **grat·i·fy·ing** *adj.* **grat·i·tude** *n* a kindly feeling because of a favour received; thankfulness.

grat·is ['grætɪs] *adv, adj* for nothing; free. ⟨Latin, from *gratia* favour⟩

gra·tu·i·ty [grə'tjuəti] *or* [grə'tuəti] *n* a present, usually of money, given in return for a service; tip. ⟨Latin *gratuitas* gift; earlier adj. *gratuitus* free⟩ **gra·tu·i·tous** *adj* **1** freely given or obtained. **2** unnecessary: *a gratuitous remark.* **gra·tu·i·tous·ly** *adv.* **gra·tu·i·tous·ness** *n.*

grave[1] [greiv] *n* **1** a hole dug in the ground in which a dead body is to be buried. **2** a mound or monument over it. **3** any place that becomes the receptacle of what is dead: *a watery grave.* **4** death. **grave·like** *adj.* ⟨Old English *græf*⟩ **have one foot in the grave** be near death. **make someone turn over in his or her grave** say or do something that someone who is dead would have objected to strongly. **secret as the grave** kept as a close secret. **grave·dig·ger** *n* a person whose work is digging graves. **grave·stone** *n* a stone that marks a grave. **grave·yard** *n* **1** a place for burying the dead. **2** a lot, yard, etc. in which objects are discarded. **graveyard shift** *Slang* the working hours between midnight and the morning shift; night shift.

grave[2] [greiv] *adj* **1** important: *a grave decision.* **2** serious; threatening: *grave news.*

3 solemn: *a grave face.* **4** sombre: *grave colours.*
n a GRAVE ACCENT. **grave·ly** *adv.* **grav·i·ty** ['grævəti] *n.* ⟨French; Latin *gravis* serious⟩
grave accent [grɑv] *or* [græv] a mark (`) placed over a vowel to indicate stress, pitch, quality of sound (as in French *père*), or syllabic value (as in *belovèd*).

SYNONYMS
Grave emphasizes dignity, especially in looks, behaviour, and attitude, and suggests having a great problem on one's mind: *Her expression was grave.* Serious emphasizes being thoughtful, concerned with important things, and free from frivolity: *He became serious when he spoke of finding a job.* Sober suggests a settled or self-restrained seriousness, especially in looks, behaviour, and speech: *Her words were sober and wise.*

grav·el ['grævəl] *n* pieces of rock coarser than sand.
v **-elled** or **-eled, -el·ling** or **-el·ing** *v* cover with gravel: *to gravel a road.* ⟨Old French *gravele* diminutive of *grave* sand, seashore; Celtic⟩
grav·el·ly *adj* **1** to do with gravel. **2** rough; rasping; grating: *a gravelly voice.*

gra·ven ['greivən] *adj* **1** engraved; carved. **2** deeply impressed; firmly fixed.
graven image idol.

grav·id ['grævɪd] *adj* pregnant. ⟨Latin *gravidus; gravis* heavy⟩

grav·i·ty ['grævəti] *n* **1 a** the natural force that causes objects to move toward the centre of the earth, the moon, or a planet. **b** the natural force that makes objects move or tend to move toward each other. **2** heaviness; weight (used especially in **centre of gravity**): *a low centre of gravity.* **3** a solemn manner: *a look of gravity.* **4** a serious or critical character: *the gravity of the situation.* ⟨Latin *gravitas; gravis* heavy⟩
grav·i·tate *v* **1** move or cause to move by gravitation. **2** settle down; sink: *The sand in the water gravitated to the bottom of the bottle.* **3** be strongly attracted. **gra·vi·ta·tion** *n* **1** *Physics* the force that makes bodies in the universe tend to move toward one another. **2** a sinking. **3** a natural tendency toward some object of influence: *the gravitation of population to the cities.* **grav·i·ta·tive** *adj.* **grav·i·ta·tion·al** *adj.* **gra·vi·ta·tion·al·ly** *adv.*

gra·vy ['greivi] *n* **1** a sauce, often made from the juice that comes out of meat in cooking. **2** *Slang* easy profit over and above what would be expected: *We've covered all our expenses; the rest is gravy.* **3** *Slang* easy money illegally gained. ⟨Middle English *grave* misreading of Old French *grané* sauce, orig, properly seasoned; Latin *granum* seed⟩
gravy boat a jug used for serving gravy. **gravy train** *Slang* a situation in which sizable profits can be realized with little effort. **ride a gravy train a** realize easy profits. **b** enjoy an easy life.

gray·beard ['grei,bird] See GREYBEARD.

gray·ling ['greilɪŋ] *n* any of a genus of freshwater fishes famous as a food and game fish and for their beautiful colouring.

graze¹ [greiz] *v* **1** feed on growing grass, or put (cattle, sheep, etc.) to feed on growing grass. **2** *Informal* eat small amounts of a variety of foods at frequent intervals. **3** *Informal* sample a lot of different foods at one sitting. **graz·er** *n.* ⟨Old English *grasian; græs* grass⟩
gra·zing *n* the growing grass that cattle, sheep, etc. feed on; pasture.

graze² [greiz] *v* **1** touch lightly in passing. **2** scrape the skin from: *He grazed his knee.* **graze** *n.* ⟨origin uncertain⟩

grease [gris] *n* **1** animal fat that has been melted and then cooled to a soft solid. **2** any thick, oily substance.
v **1** put grease on or in: **2** *Slang* give money to as a bribe. **grease·less** *adj.* ⟨Old French *graisse;* Latin *crassus* fat⟩
grease gun a grease-filled cylinder for lubricating bearings, etc. **grease monkey** *Slang* a motor vehicle mechanic. **grease·paint** *n* make-up used in the theatre. **grease pencil** a writing device of compressed and coloured grease for writing on smooth surfaces. **greas·er** *n* a young man who affects the look of motorcycle gang members of the 1950s, with greased hair, leather jacket, etc. **greas·y** *adj* **1** smeared with grease. **2** containing much grease: *greasy food.* **3** slippery like grease: *The roads were greasy after the rain.* **4** too smooth in manner. **greas·i·ly** *adv.* **greas·i·ness** *n.* **greasy spoon** *Slang* a cheap restaurant.

great [greit] *adj* **1** big; much: *a great crowd, great ignorance.* **2** important; remarkable: *a great composer.* **3** most important; main: *the great seal.* **4** much in use: *That is a great habit of hers.* **5** *Informal* very good: *a great time at the party.* **6** *Informal* skilful: *He's great at skiing.* **7** in kinship terms, of the next generation before or after: *great-grandmother, great-grandson.*
adv Informal very well: *Things are going great.*
n Usually, **greats** *pl Informal.* a great or outstanding person: *the greats of show business.* **great·ness** *n.* ⟨Old English *grēat*⟩
go great guns *Slang.* move vigorously ahead; advance at full speed.
great ape any of various primates such as the gorilla, chimpanzee, and orangutan. **great–aunt** *n* an aunt of one's father or mother. **Great Britain** the principal island of the United Kingdom, including England, Scotland, and Wales. **great circle 1** any circle on the surface of a sphere having its plane passing through the centre of the sphere. The equator is one of the great circles of the earth. **2** the line of shortest distance between two points on the earth's surface. **great·coat** *n* a long, heavy overcoat like that of a soldier. **Great·er** *adj* denoting a large city with its adjacent suburbs and towns: *Greater Victoria.* **great–grand·child** *n pl* **-chil·dren** a grandchild of one's son or daughter.

great–grand·daugh·ter *n.* **great–grand·son** *n.*
great–grand·fa·ther *n* a grandfather of one's
father or mother. **great–grand·moth·er** *n* a
grandmother of one's father or mother.
great–grand·par·ent *n.* **great grey owl** a very
large owl having a round head with a very
large face, and grey plumage. **great–heart·ed**
adj **1** noble. **2** brave. **great–heart·ed·ness** *n.*
great horned owl a large owl with hornlike
tufts of feathers on the head. **Great Lakes**
Lakes Superior, Michigan, Huron, Erie, and
Ontario. **great·ly** *adv* to a great degree; very
much. **Great Spirit** an English name for the
supreme deity worshipped by certain First
Nations peoples; a translation of GITCHI
MANITOU. **great–un·cle** *n* an uncle of one's
father or mother. **Great War** the First World
War, from 1914 to 1918. **great white trillium**
a wildflower, the largest of the trilliums and
the floral emblem of Ontario.

SYNONYMS

Great chiefly means 'more than usual' (in
degree), but sometimes is used to describe
physical size that is impressive in some way:
We saw the great redwoods (size). *They are
trees of great age* (degree). **Large** = of great
size, amount, etc., but never degree: *We saw
many large trees.* **Big** particularly emphasizes
weight or significance: *big problems.*

---

grebe [grib] *n* any of a family of water birds
resembling loons. ⟨French *grèbe*⟩

greed [grid] *n* the wanting of more than
one's share; excessive desire: *a miser's greed
for money.* **greed·y** *adj.* **greed·i·ly** *adv.*
greed·i·ness *n.* ⟨Old English *grǣdig*⟩

Greek Orthodox Church the established
church of Greece, a member of the Eastern
Orthodox Church.

green [grin] *n* **1** the colour of most growing
plants. **2** grassy land. **3** putting green.
4 greens *pl* **a** green leaves and branches used
for decoration. **b** leaves and stems of plants
used as food: *salad greens.*
adj **1** having the colour green. **2** covered with
growing plants: *green fields.* **3** composed of
leafy, green vegetables: *green salad.*
4 characterized by visibly green vegetation: *a
green Christmas.* **5** vigorous: *a garden still
green.* **6** not dried, cured, or otherwise
prepared for use: *green tobacco.* **7** not ripe:
green peaches. **8** not trained or experienced;
not mature in age, judgment, etc.: *a green
employee.* **9** easily fooled. **10** recent; fresh;
new: *a green wound.* **11** having a pale colour
because of fear, jealousy, or sickness.
12 helping to maintain a healthy, natural
environment: *green products.*
v make or become green. **green·ish** *adj.*
green·ness *n.* ⟨Old English *grēne*⟩
green bean any of various cultivated
varieties of bean whose long green pods are
used as a vegetable. **green·belt** a circle of
parks and undeveloped land around a city.
Green Chamber ✱ a name given to the
Canadian House of Commons because of the
colour of the rugs, draperies, etc. in the room
in which the House meets. **green·er·y** *n*

1 green plants, grass, or leaves. **2** a place
where green plants are grown or kept.
green·horn *n Informal* **1** a person without
experience. **2** a person easy to trick or cheat.
green·house *n* a building with glass roof and
sides, used for growing plants in a controlled
atmosphere. **greenhouse effect** *Ecology* the
trapping of heat on the planet by a layer of
carbon dioxide and other gases such as
methane and ozone, known as **greenhouse
gases. green light** *Informal* permission to
proceed on a particular task. **green onion** a
young onion pulled before it is mature.
green paper a government document
intended to promote public discussion.
green pepper the unripe fruit of various
peppers, used as a vegetable. **green·stick
fracture** a breaking of part of a bone, leaving
the rest intact. It is particularly common in
children. **green tea** tea made from leaves
that have been steamed and then dried
without fermenting. **green thumb** a
remarkable ability to grow plants.
green·wood ['grin,wʊd] *n Poetic* the forest.

Green·wich (Mean) Time ['grɛnɪtʃ] the
basis for standard time, reckoned from the
prime meridian passing through Greenwich,
England. *Abbrev* **G.M.T.**

greet [grit] *v* **1** address in welcome.
2 receive: *Her speech was greeted with cheers.*
3 present itself to; meet: *A strange sight greeted
her eyes.* ⟨Old English *grētan*⟩
greet·ing *n* **1** the act or words of a person
who greets another. **2 greetings** *pl* friendly
wishes on a special occasion: *birthday
greetings.* **greeting card** a folded card,
illustrated and usually bearing a printed
message, for giving on a special occasion.

gre·gar·i·ous [grə'gɛriəs] *adj* **1** living in
flocks, herds, or other groups: *Sheep and cattle
are gregarious.* **2** fond of being with others.
gre·gar·i·ous·ly *adv.* **gre·gar·i·ous·ness** *n.*
⟨Latin *gregarius; gregis* flock⟩

Gregorian calendar the calendar now in use
in most countries, introduced by Pope
Gregory XIII in 1582.

grem·lin ['grɛmlɪn] *n* an imaginary
mischievous spirit, esp one supposed to
trouble airplane pilots. ⟨origin uncertain⟩

gre·nade [grə'neid] *n* **1** a small bomb,
usually thrown by hand. **2** a round, glass
bottle filled with chemicals that scatter as
the glass breaks. ⟨French; Old French *(pome)
grenate* pomegranate, seedy fruit. See GARNET.⟩
gren·a·dier [,grɛnə'dir] *n* **1** originally, a
soldier who threw grenades. **2** today, a
soldier in any one of several infantry
regiments.

gren·a·dine ['grɛnə,din] *or* [,grɛnə'din] *n* a
syrup made from pomegranate juice. ⟨French
grenadin; grenade. See GRENADE.⟩

grew [gru] *v* pt of GROW.

grey [grei] *n* the colour made by mixing
black and white.
adj **1** having a colour between black and

white. **2** having grey hair: *She's very grey.* **3** ancient. **4** dismal: *a grey day.* **5** being intermediate or indeterminate in character, condition, or situation: *There are too many grey areas in our club's constitution.*
v make or become grey. Also, **gray. grey·ish** or **grayish** *adj.* **grey·ly** *adv.* **grey·ness** *n.* ⟨Old English græg⟩
grey·beard or **gray·beard** *n* an old man. **Grey Cup ✻** a trophy awarded annually to the champion professional football team in Canada. **grey–head·ed** or **gray–head·ed** *adj* having grey hair. **grey·hound** *n* a breed of tall, slender, swift dog. **grey jay** CANADA JAY. **grey matter 1** the greyish tissue in the brain and spinal cord that contains nerve cells. **2** *Informal* intelligence; brains. **grey power** the power of elderly people, organized politically. **grey–scale** *adj Computers* to do with black-and-white images composed of pixels of different shades of grey, so as to minimize unwanted contrast. **grey wolf** TIMBER WOLF.

grid [grɪd] *n* **1** a framework of parallel iron bars. **2** the numbered squares drawn on maps and used for map references. **3** an arrangement of evenly-spaced horizontal and vertical lines for any purpose. **4** the lead plate in a storage battery. **5** an electrode in a vacuum tube that controls the flow of current. **6** a network of electric power lines and connections. **7** *Theatre* a framework above the stage, from which scenery, lights, etc. are hung. ⟨clipping of *gridiron*, Middle English *gredire, gredile* (see GRIDDLE); final element assimilated to *iron*⟩
grid·lock ['grɪd,lɒk] *n* **1** any impasse. **2** a total paralysis of traffic because key intersections are blocked by vehicles. **grid road ✻** a municipal road that follows a grid line established by survey.
grid·dle ['grɪdəl] *n* a heavy, flat plate of metal, used for cooking bacon, pancakes, etc. ⟨Middle English *gredile*, Old French *gredil*; Latin *craticula*. See GRILL.⟩
grid·dle·cake *n* a thin, flat cake of batter cooked on a griddle; pancake; flapjack.

grief [grif] *n* **1** deep sadness caused by trouble or loss. **2** a cause of sadness or sorrow: *Her son's illness was a great grief to her.* ⟨Old French *grief*; *grever* grieve; Latin *gravis* heavy⟩
come to grief have trouble; fail: *Although she worked hard, her plan came to grief.*
grief–stricken *adj* consumed with sorrow. **griev·ance** *n* **1** a real or imagined wrong. **2** *Labour* an objection to the breaking of a union agreement or policy. **grieve** [griv] *v* **1** feel grief: *She grieved over her kitten's death.* **2** cause to feel grief. **3** in labour relations, raise an objection. **griev·ing** *adj.* **griev·ous** *adj* **1** causing great pain or suffering: *grievous cruelty.* **2** atrocious: *a grievous wrong.* **3** causing or showing grief: *a grievous loss, a grievous cry.* **griev·ous·ly** *adv.* **griev·ous·ness** *n.*
grif·fin ['grɪfən] *n* a mythical creature with the head, wings, and forelegs of an eagle,

and the body, hind legs, and tail of a lion. Also, **grif·fon, gryph·on.** ⟨Old French *grifon;* Latin *gryphus, grypus* Greek *gryps*⟩

grift [grɪft] *v* obtain money by fraud. **grift·er** *n.* ⟨probably altered from *graft*⟩

grill [grɪl] *n* **1** a cooking utensil consisting of thin, metal bars on which meat, fish, etc. is cooked. **2** a restaurant specializing in broiled meat, fish, etc.
v **1** cook by direct heat, as on a grill; broil. **2** torment with heat: *grilled by the hot desert sun.* **3** question severely and persistently: *The detectives grilled the prisoner until he confessed.* **grilled** *adj.* ⟨French *gril,* Old French *greil, gredil,* Latin *craticula; cratis* latticework⟩
grille [grɪl] or **grillwork** *n* an ornamental metal grating used as a barrier or screen.

grim [grɪm] *adj* **grim·mer, grim·mest. 1** without mercy; stern. **2** not yielding; not relenting. **3** unappealing or unattractive. **4** depressing or worrying. **5** dark and without mirth: *grim humour.* **grim·ly** *adv.* **grim·ness** *n.* ⟨Old English *grimm* fierce⟩

gri·mace ['grɪmɪs] *n* a twisting of the face; an ugly or funny smile. **gri·mace** *v.* **gri·mac·ing** *adj.* ⟨Spanish *grimazo* panic⟩

grime [graɪm] *n* dirt rubbed deeply into a surface: *the grime on a miner's hands.* **grime** *v.* **grim·y** *adj.* **grim·i·ly** *adv.* **grim·i·ness** *n.* ⟨perhaps Old English *grīma* mask⟩

grin [grɪn] *v* **grinned, grin·ning** smile broadly. **grin** *n.* **grin·ning·ly** *adv.* ⟨Old English *grennian*⟩
grin and bear it put up with life's trials.

grind [graɪnd] *v* **ground, grind·ing 1** crush into bits: *Our back teeth grind food.* **2** crush by harshness: *The slaves were ground down by their masters.* **3** sharpen, smooth, or wear by rubbing on something rough: *An axe is ground on a grindstone.* **4** rub harshly (*on, into, against,* or *together*): *to grind one's heel into the earth.* **5** produce by turning a crank: *to grind out music on a hand organ.* **6** *Informal* work or study long and hard. **7** *Slang* rotate the hips in dancing.
n **1** the act of grinding. **2** *Informal* long, hard work or study. **3** a dull and laborious task. **4** *Informal* a person who works long and hard at his or her studies. **grind·ing** *adj.* ⟨Old English *grindan*⟩
grind·er *n* a person who or thing that grinds or sharpens: *a coffee grinder.* **grind·stone** *n* a flat, round stone used to sharpen or to smooth. **have** (or **keep** or **put**) **one's nose to the grindstone** work long and hard.

grip [grɪp] *n* **1** a firm hold. **2** a handle: *the grip of a suitcase.* **3** a small suitcase. **4** firm control or mastery: *in the grip of winter.* **5** a stagehand or a member of a film production crew who adjusts sets or scenery and props.
v **gripped, grip·ping 1** take a firm hold on. **2** get and keep the interest and attention of: *An exciting story grips the reader.* **grip·less** *adj.* ⟨Old English *gripe; grīpan* grasp⟩
come to grips with attempt to deal with (a problem, situation, etc.).

grip·ping *adj* that holds the attention or interest: *a gripping story.* **grip·ping·ly** *adv.*

gripe [graip] *v* **1** *Informal* complain in an ill-tempered manner. **2** cause to feel sudden, sharp pain in the abdomen.
n **1** *Informal* a grievance or complaint. **2** Usually, **gripes** *pl* colic. **grip·er** *n.* ⟨Old English *grīpan*⟩

gris·ly ['grɪzli] *adj* frightful; horrible; ghastly. **gris·li·ness** *n.* ⟨Old English *grislic*⟩

grist [grɪst] *n* **1** grain to be ground. **2** grain that has been ground; meal or flour. ⟨Old English *grīst; grindan* grind⟩
grist to (or **for**) **someone's mill** useful experience, knowledge, or material.

gris·tle ['grɪsəl] *n* cartilage; tough, elastic tissue. **gris·tly** ['grɪsli] *adj.* **grist·li·ness** *n.* ⟨Old English⟩

grit [grɪt] *n* **1** very fine bits of gravel or sand: *grit in the spinach.* **2** the abrasive quality of a sanding disk, cloth, paper, etc. **3** *Informal* courage: *The fighter showed plenty of grit.* **4 Grit** ✸ *Informal* a member of the Liberal party in Canada.
v **grit·ted, grit·ting** grind; clench: *He gritted his teeth and plunged into the water.* **grit·ty** *adj.* **grit·ti·ly** *adv.* **grit·ti·ness** *n.* ⟨Old English *grēot*⟩

grits [grɪts] *npl* **1** coarsely ground corn, oats, etc., with the husks removed. **2** *US* coarse hominy. ⟨Old English *grytte*⟩

griz·zle ['grɪzəl] *n* greying hair.
v make or become grey. ⟨Middle French *grisel* diminutive of *gris* grey; Germanic⟩
griz·zled *adj.* **1** grey; greyish. **2** grey-haired.
griz·zly *adj* grizzled. *n* GRIZZLY BEAR. **grizzly bear** a large bear found in W North America.

groan [groun] *n* a deep-throated sound expressing grief, pain, or disapproval.
v **1** give a groan. **2** be overburdened (*with*): *The table groaned with food.* ⟨Old English *grānian*⟩
groan·er *n* a bad pun or joke.

SYNONYMS

Groan suggests a heavier sound than **moan** and implies suffering too hard to bear and, often, rebelliousness: *the groans of people caught in the wreckage, the groans of slaves under a yoke.* **Moan** implies a more continuous and involuntary cry of pain or some similar sound: *the moan of the wind.*

groats [grouts] *n pl* hulled grain; hulled and crushed grain. ⟨Old English *grotan*, pl.⟩

gro·cer ['grousər] *n* a merchant who sells food and household supplies. ⟨Old French *grossier*, Latin *grossarius* orig, one who sells in bulk; *grossus* thick⟩
gro·cer·y *n* **1** a store that sells food and household supplies. **2 groceries** *pl* commodities sold by a grocer, esp food. **gro·ce·te·ri·a** [ˌgrousə'tiriə] *n* ✸ a small grocery store.

grog [grɒg] *n* **1** a drink made of rum or any other alcoholic liquor diluted with water. **2** any strong alcoholic liquor. ⟨*grogram* coarse wool fabric, nickname of UK Admiral

Vernon, for his cloak; he diluted sailors' rum⟩
grog·gy *adj Informal* **1** shaky. **2** drunk. **3** sluggish from tiredness or anesthetic, etc. **grog·gi·ly** *adv.* **grog·gi·ness** *n.*

groin [grɔin] *n* **1** the hollow on either side of the body where the thigh joins the abdomen. **2** *Architecture* a curved edge or line where two vaults of a roof intersect. ⟨Middle English *grynde*, influenced by *loin*⟩

grom·met ['grɒmɪt] *n* **1** a metal eyelet. **2** a ring of rope, used as an oarlock, to hold a sail on its stays, etc. ⟨obsolete French *gromette* curb of bridle; *gourmer* curb⟩

groom [grum] *n* **1** a man who has charge of horses. **2** a man just married or about to be married; bridegroom.
v **1** feed and take care of (horses); rub down and brush (a domestic animal). **2** take care of the appearance of. **3** prepare (a person) to fill some office or superior social niche. ⟨Middle English *grome* boy, origin uncertain; compare Old French *gromet* servant⟩
grooms·man *n, pl* **-men** a man who attends the bridegroom at a wedding.

groove [gruv] *n* **1** a long, narrow channel, esp one cut by a tool. **2** any similar channel; rut: *Wheels leave grooves in a dirt road.* **3** a fixed way of doing things: *It is hard to get out of a groove.*
v **1** make a groove or grooves in. **2** *Slang* feel mellow enjoyment (often *with on*): *He grooves on classical jazz.*
groove·less *adj.* **groove·like** *adj.* ⟨Middle Dutch *groeve* furrow, ditch⟩
in the groove *Slang* **a** performing well. **b** excellent; fashionable.
groov·y *adj Slang* **1** fashionable and exciting: *a groovy new singer.* **2** excellent.

grope [group] *v* **1** feel about with the hands: *to grope for the light switch.* **2** search uncertainly: *The detectives groped for some clue to the murder.* **3** *Slang* touch (someone) sexually, esp when unwanted. **grope** *n.* **grop·ing·ly** *adv.* ⟨Old English *grāpian*⟩

gros·beak ['grous,bik] *n* any of various common finches with a strong, cone-shaped bill. ⟨French *grosbec; gros* large + *bec* beak⟩

gross [grous] *adj* **1** with nothing taken out esp before accounting for taxes, expenses, etc.: *gross sales, gross income.* **2** obviously bad; glaring: *gross misconduct.* **3** coarse; vulgar: *gross manners.* **4** too big and fat. **5** heavy; dense: *the gross growth of a jungle.* **6** concerned with large masses or outlines; general. **7** *Informal.* disgusting.
n **1** *pl* **gross·es** the whole sum; total amount. **2** *pl* **gross** a unit consisting of 144.
v earn a total of, before taxes, expenses, etc.: *We plan to gross $60 000 next year.* **gross·ly** *adv.* **gross·ness** *n.* ⟨Old French *gros;* Latin *grossus* thick⟩
gross national product the total market value of a nation's goods and services, before deductions. *Abbrev* **GNP** or **G.N.P.**

gro·tesque [grou'tesk] *adj* **1** odd in shape, appearance, manner, etc.: *hideous dragons and*

other grotesque monsters. **2** ridiculous: *The monkey's grotesque antics made the children laugh.* **3** of painting, etc., combining designs in a fantastic or unnatural way.
n **1** a painting, etc. combining designs in a fantastic or unnatural way. **2** a fantastic character in a play or film. **3** a grotesque quality. **gro·tesque·ly** *adv.* **gro·tesque·ness** *n.* **gro·tes·que·ry** or **grotesquerie** *n.* ⟨Italian *grottesco*, from *grotta*. See GROTTO.⟩

grot·to ['grɒtou] *n, pl* **-toes** or **-tos 1** a cave. **2** an artificial cave made for coolness or pleasure. ⟨Italian *grotta*, Latin *crypta*; Greek *kryptē* vault⟩

grot·ty ['grɒti] *adj Slang* dirty or seedy. **grot·ti·ness** *n.* ⟨*grotesque*⟩

grouch [grʌutʃ] *Informal v* complain; sulk.
n **1** a sulky person. **2** a sulky, discontented feeling. **grouch·y** *adj.* **grouch·i·ly** *adv.* **grouch·i·ness** *n.* ⟨variant of obsolete *grutch*; Old French *groucher* murmur, grumble⟩

ground¹ [graʊnd] *n* **1** the solid part of the earth's surface. **2** earth; soil; dirt. **3** Often, **grounds**, the basis; justification: *grounds for complaint.* **4** background: *a blue pattern on a white ground.* **5 grounds** *pl* the land around a house, school, etc. **6** land for some special use. **7 grounds** *pl* the small bits that sink to the bottom of a drink such as coffee. **8** the connection of an electrical conductor with the earth.
v **1** cause to touch the ground. **2** run aground. **3** establish firmly. **4** instruct in the first principles: *The class is well grounded in grammar.* **5** connect (an electric wire or other conductor) with the earth. **6** prohibit (an aircraft) from flying. **7** restrict (a child) from participating in certain social activities, as a punishment. **8** *Baseball* hit a grounder. ⟨Old English *grund* bottom⟩
break ground a dig; plough. **b** begin building. **break new ground** do something for the first time, or in an original manner. **cover ground a** go over a certain distance or area. **b** do a certain amount of work, etc. **cut the ground from under someone's feet** spoil a person's argument by meeting it in advance. **down to the ground** *Informal* completely. **from the ground up** thoroughly: *She learned the family business from the ground up.* **gain ground a** progress. **b** become more widespread. **get off the ground** make a successful beginning. **give ground** retreat. **hold one's ground** not retreat. **lose ground a** retreat; yield. **b** give up what has been gained. **c** become less widespread **on one's own ground** in a context one finds familiar. **on the grounds of** because of. **run into the ground** *Informal* **a** overdo: *You've run that topic into the ground.* **b** use something, esp a motor vehicle, until it is beyond repair. **shift one's ground** use a different defence or argument. **stand one's ground** refuse to retreat.
adj to do with the ground.
ground bass *Music* repeated notes in the bass, giving harmony for the upper notes.

ground·break·ing *adj* new or original, and with important consequences. **ground–cherry** *n* any of various plants belonging to the nightshade family, bearing small red berries. **ground control** the personnel on the ground who control an aircraft or spacecraft before, during, and after its flight. **ground cover** any low-growing and spreading plant used to control weeds. **ground·er** *n Baseball* a ball hit or thrown so as to roll along the ground. **ground floor 1** the floor of a building at street level. **2** the beginning of a venture: *to get in on the ground floor.* **ground·hog** *n* a marmot with a flat head on a very short neck, and short, rounded ears. Also called **woodchuck. Groundhog Day** February 2, when the groundhog is supposed to come out of its burrow to see whether the sun is shining. If it sees its shadow, the groundhog returns to its burrow for six more weeks of winter; if the sky is overcast, it expects an early spring. **ground·less** ['graʊndlɪs] *adj* without foundation, basis, or reason. **ground·less·ly** *adv.* **ground·nut** *n* any of various plants having nutlike underground seeds, such as the peanut. **ground plan 1** the plan of a floor of a building. **2** the first or fundamental plan. **ground rule** one of a set of basic rules for action or procedure. **ground·sheet** *n* a waterproof sheet used under a tent, etc. to protect against damp from the ground. **ground·speed** *n* the speed of an airborne aircraft in relation to the ground it flies over. **ground squirrel** any of a genus of small, burrowing rodents belonging to the same family as squirrels. **groundswell** *n* **1** the broad, deep waves caused by a distant storm, earthquake, etc. **2** a great rise in the amount or force of anything, such as popular opinion. **ground water** water that seeps through the ground into springs and wells. **ground·work** *n* a foundation or first part. **ground zero** the exact point where a bomb strikes the ground or, in an atomic explosion, the area directly beneath the core of radiation.

ground² [graʊnd] *v* pt and pp of GRIND.

group [grup] *n* **1** a number of persons or things together. **2** a number of persons or things classed together: *Wheat belongs to the grain group.* **3** a number of musicians playing or singing together. **4** *Chemistry* **a** a radical. **b** a set of elements sharing similar properties.
v **1** form a group or put in a group. **2** arrange in groups. ⟨French *groupe*, Italian *gruppo*; ultimately Germanic⟩
group home a home where several people live who need a sheltered environment, such as ex-convicts. **group·ie** *n Slang* **1** a fan who follows members of touring musical groups, sports teams, etc., esp one who seeks sexual intimacy with them. **2** any avid fan or follower. **group·ing** *n* **1** a placing or manner of being placed in a group. **2** the resulting group. **Group of Seven ✹** a group of seven painters who organized themselves in 1920 to promote a movement in Canadian landscape painting.

group·er ['grupər] *n, pl* **-er** or **-ers** any of numerous large-mouthed food fishes found in warm seas. ⟨Portuguese *garupa*⟩

grouse[1] [graus] *n, pl* **grouse** any of numerous birds hunted as game, having a plump body. ⟨origin uncertain⟩

grouse[2] [graus] *Informal v* grumble. *n* **1** complaint. **2** a grumbler. ⟨Old French *groucer*, variant of *groucher* murmur, grumble⟩

grout [graut] *n* thin mortar used to fill cracks, etc. **grout** *v*. ⟨Old English *grūt*⟩

grove [grouv] *n* a group of trees standing together. ⟨Old English *grāf*⟩

grov·el ['grɒvəl] *v* **-elled** or **-eled, -el·ling** or **-el·ing** lie or crawl face downward at someone's feet: *The frightened slaves grovelled before their cruel master.* **grov·el·ler** or **grov·el·er** *n.* **grov·el·ling** or **grov·el·ing** *adj.* ⟨backformed from Middle English *groveling* on the face; *on grufe* prone, Old Norse *á grúfu*⟩

grow [grou] *v* **grew, grown, grow·ing** **1** become bigger by taking in food, as plants and animals do. **2** exist: *a tree growing only in the tropics.* **3** increase: *Her fame grew.* **4** become: *to grow cold, to grow rich.* **5** cause or allow to grow: *to grow corn.* ⟨Old English *grōwan*⟩
grow on or **upon** become increasingly attractive to: *The habit grew on me.* **grow out of** grow too big or too old for. **grow up a** develop. **b** begin to behave maturely.

grow·er *n* **1** a person who grows something: *a fruit grower.* **2** a plant that grows in a certain way: *a quick grower.* **growing pains 1** pains during childhood and youth, supposed to be caused by growing. **2** troubles that arise when something new is just developing. **grown** *adj* arrived at full growth. **grown–up** *adj* ['groun ˈʌp], *n* ['groun ˌʌp] adult. **growth** *n* **1** the process of growing. **2** the amount of growing: *one year's growth.* **3** what has grown or is growing: *a thick growth of bushes.* **4** an abnormal mass of tissue formed in or on the body. Cancer causes a growth. *adj* to do with stocks, or an industry, whose value or earnings multiply at a higher than average rate.

growl [graʊl] *v* **1** make a deep, angry sound. **2** complain angrily: *The soldiers growled about the poor food.* **growl** *n.* ⟨probably imitative⟩
growl·er *n* **1** a person who or animal that growls. **2** a floating piece of ice broken off from a glacier or larger iceberg.

grub [grʌb] *n* **1** a wormlike form of an insect. **2** a drudge. **3** *Informal* food. *v* **grubbed, grub·bing** **1** dig: *Pigs grub for roots.* **2** drudge; toil. **3** search or rummage. ⟨Middle English *grubbe(n)*; related to Old High German *grubilōn* dig⟩
grub·by *adj* **1** dirty: *grubby hands.* **2** mean or contemptible: *a grubby little con artist.* **3** infested with grubs. **grub·bi·ness** *n.* **grub·stake** *n* **1** the food, money, etc. supplied to a prospector or other entrepreneur on the condition of sharing in eventual profits. **2** ✹ the money or the means to buy provisions

for a certain period. **3** ✹ a store of provisions. **grub·stake** *v.* **grub·stak·er** *n.*

grudge [grʌdʒ] *n* ill will; a sullen feeling against; dislike of long standing. *v* **1** feel anger or dislike toward (a person) because of (something): *He grudged me my little prize even though he had won a bigger one.* **2** give or let have unwillingly: *The mean man grudged his horse the food that it ate.* ⟨earlier meaning, grumble; variant of *grutch*. See GROUCH.⟩
bear a grudge have and keep a grudge. **grudg·ing** *adj* unwilling.

gru·el ['gruəl] *n* a thin food made by boiling oatmeal, etc. in water or milk.

gru·el·ling ['gruəlɪŋ] *adj* very tiring. Also, **gruel·ing.** ⟨Old French *gruel*; Germanic⟩

grue·some ['grusəm] *adj* horrible; revolting. **grue·some·ly** *adv.* **grue·some·ness** *n.* ⟨obsolete *grue* shudder⟩

gruff [grʌf] *adj* **1** of a voice, deep and harsh. **2** rough; rude; unfriendly: *a gruff manner.* **gruff·ly** *adv.* **gruff·ness** *n.* ⟨Middle Dutch *grof*⟩

grum·ble ['grʌmbəl] *v* **1** mutter in discontent. **2** rumble: *Her stomach grumbled from hunger.* **grum·ble** *n.* **grum·bler** *n.* ⟨related to Old English *grymettan* roar, and *grim*⟩

grump [grʌmp] *n.* an ill-tempered person. *v* grumble. **grump·y** *adj.* **grump·i·ly** *adv.* **grump·i·ness** *n.* ⟨origin uncertain⟩

grunge [grʌndʒ] *n* **1** dirt. **2** a a fashion movement featuring loose, unkempt, layered clothing. **b** a style of rock music. ⟨a blend of *grimy, mangy,* and *grunt* childish euphemism for defecate⟩
grun·gy *adj Slang* unkempt, unattractive, dirty, etc.: *a grungy hotel.*

grunt [grʌnt] *n* the deep, hoarse sound that a pig makes, or a sound like this: *The old man got out of his chair with a grunt.* **grunt** *v.* ⟨Old English *grunnettan; grunian* grunt⟩

GST ✹ the **Goods and Services Tax,** a federal sales tax paid by the consumer on most goods and services.

G string 1 on a musical instrument, a string tuned to G. **2** a narrow loincloth held up by a cord around the waist.

G–suit ['dʒi ˌsut] *n* ANTI-G SUIT.

gua·ca·mo·le [ˌgwɑkɑ'mouli] *n* a dip or sauce made from seasoned avocado pulp. ⟨American Spanish; Nahuatl *a:waka* avocado + *mo:lli* a sauce⟩

gua·nine ['gwɒnin] *n* a constituent of RNA and DNA.

gua·no ['gwɑnou] *n* **1** the manure of sea birds or bats used as fertilizer. **2** an artificial fertilizer made from fish. ⟨Spanish; Quechua (Peru) *huanu*⟩

guar [gwɑr] *n* an annual plant of the legume family, cultivated for forage and for its seeds, which yield a gum used in industry. ⟨Hindi⟩

guar·an·tee [ˌgɛrən'ti], [ˌgærən'ti], *or* [ˌgɑrən'ti] *n* **1** a promise to pay or do something if another fails; a pledge to

replace goods if they are not as represented. **2** something given or taken as security. **3** an assurance; promise: *Wealth is not a guarantee of happiness.*
v **1** give a guarantee for. **2** secure (with *against* or *from*): *Her insurance guaranteed her against money loss in case of fire.* **3** promise (to do something): *I will guarantee to prove every statement I made.* **4** make sure or certain: *Wealth does not guarantee happiness.* ⟨Old French *guarantie; guarantir* to warrant⟩
guar·an·tor *n* someone who gives a guarantee.

guard [gɑrd] *v* **1** watch over carefully; defend: *The dog guards the house. The goalie guards the goal.* **2** keep in check; hold back; keep under control: *Guard your tongue.*
n **1** a person or group that guards. **2** anything that gives protection: *A guard was placed in front of the fire.* **3** a careful watch: *A soldier kept guard over the prisoners.* **4** defence. **5** *Sports* a position of defence.⟨French *garde(r)* (earlier *guarde(r)*); Germanic. Related to WARD.⟩
guard against prevent by being careful: *Guard against getting your feet wet.* **off one's guard** unprepared. **on guard** ready to defend or protect. **stand guard** do sentry duty.
guard·ed *adj* careful; cautious: *"Maybe" is a guarded answer to a question.* **guard·ed·ly** *adv.* **guard·ed·ness** *n.* **guard·house** *n* **1** a building used as a jail for soldiers. **2** a building used by soldiers on guard. **guard·i·an** ['gɑrdiən] *n* **1** a person who takes care of another or of some special thing. **2** a person appointed by law to take care of the affairs of someone who is young or cannot take care of them himself or herself. *adj* protecting: *a guardian angel.* **guard·i·an·ship** *n.* **guard·rail** *n* a rail or railing for protection.

gua·va ['gwɑvə] *n* any of several tropical trees and shrubs of the myrtle family, widely cultivated for its sweet, edible, pear-shaped fruit. ⟨Spanish *guayaba;* native name⟩

gu·ber·na·to·ri·al [ˌgubərnə'tɔriəl] *adj esp US* to do with a governor. ⟨Latin *gubernator* orig, pilot. See GOVERN.⟩

guck [gʌk] *n Informal* anything oozy, slimy, or similarly distasteful. ⟨perhaps blend of *goo* + *muck*⟩

guer·ril·la [gə'rɪlə] *n* a member of a band of fighters who harass the enemy by sudden raids, ambushes, etc. **guer·ril·la** *adj.* Also, **gue·ril·la.** ⟨Spanish, diminutive of *guerra* war⟩

guess [gɛs] *v* **1** form an opinion (of) without really knowing: *to guess the height of a tree.* **2** find out by guessing: *to guess a riddle.* **3** think; believe; suppose. **guess** *n.* **guess·er** *n.* ⟨Middle English; Scandinavian⟩

guess·ti·mate ['gɛstəmət] *n Informal* an estimate based mainly on guesswork. **guess·ti·mate** ['gɛstəˌmeit] *v.* **guess·work** *n* action or result based on guessing: *There is a lot of guesswork involved in buying a used car.*

guest [gɛst] *n* **1** a person who is received at another's home, club, restaurant, etc. **2** a visitor. **3** a person staying at a hotel, motel, boarding house, etc. **4** a person appearing on a show by invitation. *adj* **1** of or for guests: *a guest room.* **2** being a guest: *a guest lecturer.* ⟨Old English *giest* stranger; Old Norse *gestr.* Related to HOST².⟩ **be my guest** *Informal* help yourself: *"May I use your phone?" "Certainly; be my guest."* **guest of honour** the most important guest at a social function; the guest in honour of whom the function is held.

guff [gʌf] *n Informal* foolish talk, esp when used in an attempt to hide the real facts. ⟨probably imitative⟩

guf·faw [gʌ'fɔ] *n* a loud, coarse burst of laughter. **guf·faw** *v.* ⟨imitative⟩

GUI ['gui] GRAPHICAL USER INTERFACE

guide [gaɪd] *v* **1** show (someone) the way. **2** manage; control; regulate.
n **1** a person who or thing that shows the way: *Tourists sometimes hire guides.* **2** a part of a machine for directing or regulating motion or action. **3** guidebook. **4** a handbook giving instructions or assistance on some subject: *an income tax guide.* ⟨Old French *guider*⟩
guid·ance *n* **1** leadership; direction: *Under her mother's guidance she learned to cook.* **2** *Education* studies and counselling intended to help students make the most of their opportunities and plan for the future. **3** *Aeronautics* the regulation of the path of rockets, missiles, etc. in flight. **guide·book** *n* a book of directions and information, esp one for tourists. **guide dog** a dog specially trained to guide a blind person. **guided missile** a missile whose course may be controlled during flight. **guide·line** *n* a principle or instruction set forth as a guide. **guide·post** *n* a post with signs and directions on it for travellers. **guide word** in dictionaries and similar reference works, either of two words appearing at the top of a page, one indicating the first entry word and the other showing the last entry word on the page.

guild [gɪld] *n* **1** a society for mutual aid or for some common purpose: *the Canadian Guild of Potters.* **2** in the Middle Ages, a union of those in one trade, formed to keep standards high and to protect their interests: *the guild of silversmiths.* ⟨Old Norse *gildi*⟩
guild·hall *n* **1** the hall in which a guild meets. **2** a town hall; city hall.

guile [gaɪl] *n* crafty deceit; craftiness; sly tricks: *A swindler uses guile; a robber uses force.* ⟨Old French; Germanic. Akin to WILE.⟩
guile·less *adj* honest. **guile·less·ness** *n.*

guil·le·mot [ˈgɪlə,mɒt] *n* any of a genus of black-and-white northern sea birds of the auk family. ⟨French *guillemot* probably pet form of *Guillaume* William⟩

guil·lo·tine *n* [ˈgɪlə,tin] **1** a machine for beheading persons by means of a heavy blade that slides down between two posts. **2** a machine for cutting paper. **guil·lo·tine** [ˌgɪləˈtin] *v.* ⟨Joseph I. *Guillotin*, 18c French physician and advocate of its use⟩

guilt [gɪlt] *n* the fact or state of having done wrong. **guilt·i·ly** *adv.* **guilt·i·ness** *n.* **guilt·less** *adj.* **guilt·y** *adj.* ⟨Old English *gylt* offence⟩

guin·ea [ˈgɪni] *n* a former British gold coin. ⟨*Guinea* in W Africa; coin was originally made of gold from there⟩
guinea pig 1 a plump-bodied rodent extensively used as a pet and in scientific research. **2** any person or thing serving as a subject for experiment.

guise [gaɪz] *n* **1** a style of dress, esp when used as a disguise. *The soldier went into the village in the guise of a monk.* **2** external appearance: *an old idea in a new guise.* **3** an assumed appearance: *Under the guise of friendship she plotted treachery.* ⟨Old French⟩

gui·tar [gəˈtɑr] *n* a musical instrument having usually six strings that are plucked with the fingers or a pick. **gui·tar·ist** *n.* ⟨Spanish *guitarra*, Greek *kithara* type of lyre⟩

gu·lag [ˈgulæg] *n* in the former Soviet Union, a forced labour camp notorious for bad conditions. ⟨Russian acronym for *G(lavnoe) u(pravlenie ispravitel' no trudovykh) lag(erei)*, Chief Administration of Corrective Labour Camps⟩

gulch [gʌltʃ] *n* a deep, narrow ravine with steep sides, esp one marking the course of a stream. ⟨origin unknown⟩

gulf [gʌlf] *n* **1** a large bay; an arm of a sea extending into the land. **2** a very deep break or cut in the earth. **3** a wide separation: *The quarrel left a gulf between us.* **gulf·like** *adj.* ⟨Old French *golfe*, Italian *golfo*; Greek *kolpos*, orig, bosom⟩

gull¹ [gʌl] *n* any of numerous aquatic birds having webbed feet and mainly white plumage. ⟨Middle English; perhaps from Welsh *gwylan*⟩
gull·er·y *n* a breeding place of gulls.

gull² [gʌl] *v* deceive; cheat.
n a person who is easily deceived or cheated. ⟨origin uncertain⟩

gul·li·ble *adj* easily deceived. **gul·li·bil·i·ty** *n.* **gul·li·bly** *adv.*

gul·let [ˈgʌlɪt] *n* **1** a passage for food from the mouth to the stomach; esophagus. **2** the throat. ⟨Old French *goulet*; Latin *gula* throat⟩

gul·ly [ˈgʌli] *n* **1** a small ravine. **2** a channel made by heavy rains or running water: *After the storm, the newly-seeded lawn was full of gullies.* ⟨possibly variant of *gullet*⟩

gulp [gʌlp] *v* **1** swallow eagerly or greedily. **2** keep in; choke back: *The disappointed girl gulped down a sob.* **3** gasp; choke.
n **1** the act of swallowing. **2** the amount swallowed at one time. ⟨imitative⟩

gum¹ [gʌm] *n* **1** a sticky juice, obtained from certain plants, that hardens in the air and dissolves in water. **2** any similar secretion, such as resin, gum resin, etc. **3** CHEWING GUM. **4** mucilage; glue.
v **gummed, gum·ming 1** smear, stick together, or stiffen with gum. **2** make or become sticky. **gum·my** *adj.* **gum·mi·ness** *n.* ⟨Old French *gomme*; Greek *kommi*⟩
gum up *Slang* mess up; put out of order.
gum arabic the gum obtained from acacia trees, used in candy, medicine, mucilage, etc. **gum·boot** *n* a high rubber boot. **gum·drop** *n* a jellylike piece of candy made of gum arabic, gelatin, etc. **gum·shoe** *n Slang* detective. **gum tree** any of various trees that yield gum.

gum² [gʌm] *n* Often, **gums** *pl* the flesh around the teeth. ⟨Old English *gōma* palate⟩

gum·bo [ˈgʌmbou] *n* **1** the pods of the okra plant. **2** soup thickened with okra pods: *chicken gumbo soup.* **3** soil that contains much silt and becomes very sticky when wet, esp that found on the western prairies. ⟨native African language⟩

gump·tion [ˈgʌmpʃən] *n Informal* **1** energy; resourcefulness. **2** common sense; good judgment. ⟨Scots dialect; origin uncertain⟩

gun [gʌn] *n* **1** a weapon with a metal tube for shooting shells, bullets, shot, etc. **2** a device for ejecting or discharging something: *a grease gun.* **3** See BIG GUN.
v **gunned, gun·ning 1** hunt or hunt (*for*) with a gun. **2** shoot (someone) with a gun (usually used with *down*): *He was gunned down as he left his car.* **3** go after, with intent to hurt, destroy, etc. (with *for*): *They'll be gunning for you when they read the report.* **4** cause to accelerate suddenly: *She gunned the engine.* ⟨Old Norse *Gunna* shortened from *Gunnhilda* woman's name applied to engines of war⟩
gun it *Informal* speed up greatly. **jump** (or **beat**) **the gun a** of a competitor in a race, etc., start before the signal is given. **b** act prematurely. **spike someone's guns.** See SPIKE. **stick to one's guns** keep one's position under opposition or attack. **under the gun** *Informal* in a difficult position.
gun barrel the metal tube of a gun. **gun·boat** *n* a small warship. **gun·fight** *n* a fight in which guns are used. **gun·fight·er** *n.* **gun·fire** *n* the shooting of a gun, or the

sound of shooting. **gun·man** *n*, *pl* **-men** a man who uses a gun to rob or kill. **gun·met·al** *n* any of various dark grey alloys used for chains, buckles, handles, etc. **gun·ner** *n* 1 a person trained to fire artillery pieces. 2 a naval officer in charge of a ship's guns. 3 a person, esp a private, serving in the artillery. **gun·point** *n* the tip or point of a gun barrel. **at gunpoint** being threatened by a gun. **gun·pow·der** *n* a powder that explodes when brought into contact with fire. **gun·run·ning** *n* the bringing of guns into a country illegally. **gun·run·ner** *n*. **gun·shot** *n* 1 a shot fired from a gun. 2 the distance that a gun will shoot. **gun·sling·er** *n* *Slang* gunman. **gun·smith** *n* a person whose work is making or repairing small guns. **gun·stock** *n* the wooden support to which the barrel of a gun is fastened. **gun·wale** or **gunnel** ['gʌnɔl] *n* the reinforced top edge of the side of a boat, formerly used to support guns.

gung–ho ['gʌŋ 'hou] *adj Slang* full of unrestrained energy and enthusiasm. *He's just starting out in business and is very gung-ho.* ⟨Mandarin *kung-ho* work together⟩

gunk [gʌŋk] *n Informal* any unpleasant, heavy, oily or sticky matter; guck.

gunny sack a sack or bag made of gunny, a strong, coarse fabric.

gup·py ['gʌpi] *n* a small, brightly coloured, freshwater fish that bears live young instead of laying eggs as most fish do. ⟨Robert J.L. *Guppy*, 19c, Trinidad, who supplied first specimens⟩

gur·dwa·ra [gər'dwarə] *n* a Sikh temple in which services of worship are held on Sundays. It also serves as a Sikh community centre. ⟨Sanskrit *guru* teacher; *dwara* door⟩

gur·gle ['gɜrgəl] *v* 1 flow with a bubbling sound: *Water gurgles when it is poured out of a bottle.* 2 make a bubbling sound: *The baby gurgled happily.* **gur·gle** *n*. ⟨imitative⟩

gur·ney ['gɜrni] *n* a stretcher on wheels, used in a hospital to move sick people. ⟨origin unknown⟩

gu·ru ['guru] or ['guru] *n* 1 *Hinduism* a personal religious adviser or teacher. 2 a person who guides others, esp in a spiritual way. 3 any expert, esp one hailed as a popular leader: *a guru of pop culture.* ⟨Hindi *gurū*⟩ **Gu·ru** *Sikhism* 1 any of the ten founding teachers of Sikhism. 2 the honorific title given to the Granth, the Sikh holy book. **Gu·ru Granth Sa·hib** the sacred scriptures containing the teachings of the Gurus.

gush [gʌʃ] *v* 1 rush out suddenly. 2 *Informal* talk in a silly way about one's affections or enthusiasms. 3 have an abundant flow of blood, tears, etc. **gush** *n*. **gush·ing** *adj*. ⟨probably imitative⟩ **gush·er** *n* 1 an oil well that flows copiously without being pumped. 2 *Informal* a gushy person. **gush·y** *adj* effusive; sentimental. **gush·i·ly** *adv*. **gush·i·ness** *n*.

gus·set ['gʌsɪt] *n* 1 a triangular piece of

material inserted in a dress, etc. to give greater strength or more room. 2 a bracket used to reinforce the joints of a structure. ⟨Old French *gousset; gousse* husk⟩

gus·sy ['gʌsi] *v Slang* make seemly or attractive; spruce (*up*): *The girls gussied themselves up for the party.* ⟨origin uncertain⟩

gust [gʌst] *n* 1 a sudden, violent rush of wind. 2 a sudden burst of rain, sound, etc. 3 an outburst of anger, laughter, etc. *v* to blow or rush in gusts. **gust·y** *adj*. **gust·i·ly** *adv*. **gust·i·ness** *n*. ⟨Old Norse *gustr*⟩

gus·ta·to·ry ['gʌstə,tɔri] *adj* of the sense of taste; to do with tasting: *Eating fine foods gives gustatory pleasure.* ⟨Latin *gustare* to taste⟩

gus·to ['gʌstou] *n* 1 hearty enjoyment: *The hungry boy ate his dinner with gusto.* 2 a liking or taste. 3 spirited activity. ⟨Italian *gusto* orig, taste; Latin *gustus*⟩

gut [gʌt] *n* 1 intestine. 2 **guts** *pl* entrails; bowels. 3 **guts** *pl Informal* **a** courage. **b** the inner or essential part: *the guts of a car, the guts of the problem.* *v* **gut·ted, gut·ting** 1 remove the entrails of. 2 plunder or destroy the inside of: *Fire gutted the building and left only the walls standing.* *adj* 1 *Slang* vital; basic: *The gut issue is the demand for higher wages.* 2 *Informal* arising from deep, basic feelings: *a gut reaction.* ⟨Old English *guttas*, pl.⟩ **gut·buck·et** *adj* of jazz, played in a noisy, vigorous style as in the bars of New Orleans. **gut·less** *adj* cowardly; lacking force or persistence. **gut·sy** *Slang* courageous or forceful; having guts: *a gutsy political leader.*

gut·ter ['gʌtər] *n* 1 a channel along the side of a road to carry off water. 2 eavestrough. 3 any channel or groove, such as the channel along each side of a bowling lane. **4 the gutter** a wretched, poverty-stricken, or deprived environment: *a child of the gutter.* 5 *Printing* the white space formed by the inner margins of two facing pages of a book. *adj* to do with a depraved environment: *gutter language, gutter journalism.* *v* 1 form gutters in. 2 flow or melt in streams: *A candle gutters when the melted wax runs down its sides.* ⟨Anglo-French *gotere*; Latin *gutta* drop⟩

gut·tur·al ['gʌtərəl] *adj* 1 of the throat. 2 formed in the throat; harsh: *a guttural voice.* **gut·tur·al·ly** *adv*. **gut·tur·al·ness** *n*. ⟨Latin *guttur* throat⟩

guy[1] [gaɪ] *n* a rope, chain, etc. attached to something to steady or secure it. ⟨Old French *guier* to guide; Germanic⟩

guy[2] [gaɪ] *n* 1 *Informal* fellow. 2 *Informal* any person of either sex and any age. ⟨*Guy Fawkes*, member of a conspiracy (1605) to blow up the British King and Parliament⟩

guz·zle ['gʌzəl] *v* drink greedily; drink too much. **guz·zler** *n*. ⟨probably Old French *gosiller* vomit; French *gosier* throat⟩

Gwich'in ['gwɪtʃɪn] *n*, *pl* **-in** 1 a member of a First Nations people of the Northwest Territories. The Gwich'in are one of the Dene peoples. **2** the Athapascan language of these people. **Gwich'in** *adj.* Also, **Kut·chin.**

gybe [dʒaɪb] See JIBE¹.

gym·na·si·um [dʒɪmˈneɪʒiəm] *or* [-ˈneɪziəm] *n, pl* **-si·ums** or **si·a** [-ʒiə] or [-ziə] a room, building, etc. fitted up for physical exercise or training and for indoor athletic sports. Also, **gym.** ⟨Latin; Greek *gymnasion* from *gymnazein* exercise (naked); *gymnos* naked⟩ **gym·nast** [ˈdʒɪmnəst] *or* [ˈdʒɪmnæst] *n* an expert in gymnastics. **gym·nas·tic** *adj* to do with bodily exercise. **gym·nas·ti·cal·ly** *adv.* **gym·nas·tics** *n pl* **1** physical exercises for developing the muscles, such as are performed in a gymnasium. **2** the sport of doing exercises in agility and balance.

gym·no·sperm [ˈdʒɪmnəˌspɜrm] *n* any of a division of plants producing seeds not enclosed in an ovary. Many gymnosperms, such as pines, bear their seeds on cones. **gym·no·sper·mous** *adj.* ⟨Greek *gymnospermos; gymnos* naked + *sperma* seed⟩

gy·ne·col·o·gy [ˌgaɪnəˈkɒlədʒi] *or* [ˌdʒaɪnə-] *n* the branch of medicine dealing with the diseases and reproductive functions specific to women. Also, **gy·nae·col·o·gy.** **gy·ne·co·log·i·cal** *adj.* **gy·ne·col·o·gist** *n.* ⟨Greek *gynē, gynaikos* woman⟩

gyp [dʒɪp] *v* **gypped, gyp·ping** *Slang* cheat; swindle: *She gypped me out of three dollars. n* **1** a swindle; fraud: *That show was a big gyp; it wasn't anything like the ad.* **2** a swindler. ⟨shortened from *gypsy*⟩

gyp·sum [ˈdʒɪpsəm] *n* a mineral used for making plaster of Paris, fertilizer, etc.; hydrated calcium sulphate. ⟨Latin; Greek *gypsos* chalk, plaster⟩

Gyp·sy [ˈdʒɪpsi] *n* **1** Sometimes, **gypsy** a member of a wandering people who originally migrated to Europe from N India and now live throughout the world. **2** Romany, the language of the Gypsies. **3 gypsy** a drifter. **gypsy** *adj.* ⟨*Egyptian*; Gypsies were thought to have originated in Egypt⟩

gy·rate [ˈdʒaɪreɪt] *v* move in a circle or spiral; whirl; rotate: *A top gyrates.* **gy·ra·tor** *n.* **gy·ra·tion** *n.* ⟨Greek *gyros* circle, turning⟩

gyr·fal·con [ˈdʒɜrˌfɒlkən] *or* [ˈdʒɜrˌfælkən] *n* the largest falcon, found mainly in arctic and subarctic regions. ⟨Old French *girfaucon;* Old High German *gir* hawk⟩

gy·ro·com·pass [ˈdʒaɪrouˌkʌmpəs] *n* a compass using a motor-driven gyroscope instead of a magnetic needle. It points to the geographic North Pole instead of to the magnetic pole. ⟨Greek *gyros* circle, turning⟩ **gy·ro·scope** [ˈdʒaɪrəˌskoup] *n* a heavy disk mounted so that its axis can turn freely in one or more directions. **gy·ro·scop·ic** *adj.* **gy·ro·scop·i·cal·ly** *adv.*

gy·ros [ˈjirous] *or* [ˈjirɒs] *n* a Greek dish comprising various seasoned meats mixed and cooked on a rotating vertical spit, then shaved off and served in a pita. ⟨Greek *gyros* circle, turning, because a spit rotates⟩

Hh

h or H [eitʃ] *n, pl* **h's** or **H's 1** the eighth letter of the English alphabet, or any speech sound represented by it. **2** the eighth person or thing in a series. **3 H** a symbol used on pencils to indicate the degree of hardness of the lead.

h 1 hour. **2** hecto- (an SI prefix).

H 1 hydrogen. **2** *Physics* **a** intensity of magnetic field. **b** the horizontal component of Earth's magnetic field. **3** *Electricity* henry. **4** *Slang* heroin.

ha [hɑ], [hɒ], *or* [hæ] *interj* **1** an exclamation of surprise, joy, triumph, etc.: *"Ha! I've caught you!" she cried.* **2** in writing, a way of indicating laughter: *"Ha! ha! ha!" they laughed.*

ha hectare.

ha·be·as cor·pus ['heibiəs 'kɔrpəs] *Law* an order requiring that a prisoner be brought before a judge to decide whether he or she is being held lawfully. ⟨Latin = you may have the person⟩

hab·it ['hæbɪt] *n* **1** a tendency to act in a certain way: *His habit is to do the hardest job first.* **2** disposition: *a man of morose habit.* **3** a pattern of behaviour acquired by repetition: *the habit of brushing one's teeth.* **4** addiction. **5** the distinctive costume worn in some religious orders: *The Grey Nuns traditionally wore a grey habit.* **6** the characteristic form, mode of growth, etc., of an animal or plant: *The honeysuckle is of a twining habit.* ⟨Latin *habitus; habere* hold, live in, stay⟩
take the habit become a nun.
ha·bit·u·al [həˈbɪtʃuəl] *adj* **1** done by habit; caused by habit: *a habitual smile.* **2** usual: *Snow is a habitual sight in arctic regions.*
ha·bit·u·al·ly *adv.* **ha·bit·u·al·ness** *n.* **ha·bit·u·ate** [həˈbɪtʃu,eit] *v* **1** make used *(to)*; accustom: *Loggers are habituated to hard work.* **2** go to (a place) frequently. **ha·bit·u·a·tion** *n.* **ha·bit·u·é** [həˌbɪtʃuˈei] *or* [həˈbɪtʃu,ei] *n* a person who has the habit of going to a place frequently: *a habitué of the theatre.*

SYNONYMS
Habit refers more to a personal practice, something one does without thinking about it: *Biting one's fingernails is a bad habit.*
Custom refers especially to practice consciously adopted and continued over a long period of time: *It was a custom in her family to play euchre every Friday evening.*

hab·it·ant ['hæbə,tɒnt] *or* [,hæbəˈtã] *French* [abiˈta] ✹ *n* formerly, a rural French-Canadian; farmer.
adj to do with rural French Canadians or rural French Canada, esp historically. ⟨Cdn. French; Latin *habitare* live in⟩

hab·i·tat ['hæbə,tæt] *n* **1** the place where an animal or plant naturally lives or grows: *The jungle is the habitat of tigers.* **2** a dwelling place. ⟨Latin = it inhabits⟩
hab·it·a·ble *adj* fit to live in. **hab·it·a·ble·ness** *n.*

hab·it·a·bly *adv.* **hab·i·ta·tion** *n* a place to live in; home; dwelling.

hack¹ [hæk] *v* **1** cut with repeated rough blows: *She hacked the crate apart with an old axe.* **2** make (one's way) by cutting away vegetation: *hacking our way through the underbrush.* **3** *Slang* handle (something) successfully (often with *it*): *She couldn't hack the long hours.* **4** cough in short bursts. **5** *Basketball* commit the foul of hitting the arm of (an opponent who has the ball).
n **1** a rough cut. **2** *Curling* a notch cut in the ice at one end of a rink, used as a foothold when a player throws a rock. **3** a short, dry cough. **4** *Basketball* a personal foul committed by striking the arm of a player who has the ball. ⟨Old English *haccian*⟩
hack·er *n* a person skilled in the use of computers, esp one who uses this skill to gain access illegally to data. **hack·saw** *n* a fine-toothed saw for cutting metal.

hack² [hæk] *n* **1** a carriage for hire. **2** *Informal* taxi. **3** a worn-out horse. **4** a horse for ordinary riding. **5** a person hired to do routine literary work. **6** a faithful but undistinguished worker in an organization, as a political party: *an old party hack.*
v **1** ride on horseback over roads. **2** *Informal* drive a taxi. **3** write or act as a hack. *adj* done merely for money. ⟨short for *hackney; Hackney,* borough of London, UK⟩
hack·ney *n* **1** a horse for ordinary riding. **2** a carriage for hire. *adj* hired. *v* use too often. **hack·neyed** *adj* commonplace: *"White as snow" is a hackneyed comparison.*

hack·le ['hækəl] *n* **1** the neck plumage of certain birds. **2** *Fishing* the part of an artificial fly corresponding to the legs of an insect. **3 hackles** *pl* the erectile hairs on the back of a dog's neck. ⟨Middle English *hakell*⟩
raise the hackles of *Informal* arouse the suspicion or anger of.

hack·ma·tack ['hækmə,tæk] *n* ✹ any of various evergreens, esp the tamarack. ⟨Algonquian⟩

hack·ney See HACK².

had [hæd] *v* pt and pp of HAVE.

had·dock ['hædək] *n, pl* **-dock** or **-docks** an important food fish resembling the cod, but smaller. ⟨Middle English *haddok;* origin uncertain⟩

Ha·des ['heidiz] *n* **1** *Greek myth* **a** the home of the dead, below the earth. **b** the god of the lower world, also called Pluto. **2** Often, **hades** *Informal* hell. ⟨Greek *Haidēs*⟩

had·ron ['hædrɒn] *n Physics* any of a class of particles, including protons and neutrons, whose constituent particles are quarks. **ha·dron·ic** *adj.* ⟨Greek *hadros* strong, thick⟩

ha·fiz ['hɑfɪz] *n Islam* a title of respect for a Muslim who can recite the entire Koran from memory. ⟨Arabic⟩

haf·ni·um ['hæfniəm] *n* a rare, metallic, element somewhat like zirconium. *Symbol* **Hf** ⟨*Hafnia* Latin name of Copenhagen⟩

haft [hæft] *n* the handle of a knife, sword, dagger, etc. ⟨Old English *hæft*⟩

hag [hæg] *n* **1** a very ugly old woman, esp one who is vicious or malicious. **2** witch. **hag·like** *adj.* **hag·gish** *adj.* **hag·gish·ness** *n.* ⟨Middle English *hagge*⟩

hag·fish *n, pl* **-fish** or **-fish·es** any of several species of eel-like, marine vertebrates with horny teeth that they use to bore into the bodies of fish, eating them from inside.

Hag·ga·dah or **Hag·ga·da** [hə'gɑdə] *n, pl* **-doth** [-douθ] or **-dot** [-dout] *Judaism* **1** in the Talmud, a story that explains the Jewish law. **2** the text of the Seder service on the first, or the first two, evenings of Passover. **hag·ga·dic** *adj.* ⟨Hebrew = story; *higgid* relate⟩ **hag·ga·dist** *n* a writer of the Haggadah.

hag·gard ['hægərd] *adj* wild-looking from pain, fatigue, worry, etc. **hag·gard·ly** *adv.* **hag·gard·ness** *n.* ⟨Middle French *hagard* of the hedges, untamed; Middle High German *hag* hedge⟩

hag·gis ['hægɪs] *n Scottish* the heart, lungs, and liver of a sheep mixed with suet and oatmeal and boiled in the stomach of the animal. ⟨probably Scottish *hag* chop⟩

hag·gle ['hægəl] *v* dispute about a price or the terms of a bargain. **hag·gle** *n.* **hag·gler** *n.* ⟨Scottish *hag* chop, hack; Old Norse *höggva*⟩

hag·i·og·ra·phy [,hægi'ɒgrəfi] *n* the writing of the lives of the saints. **hag·i·o·graph·ic** *adj.* ⟨Greek *hagios* holy + *graphos* thing written⟩ **hag·i·og·ra·pher** *n* **1** a writer of the lives of the saints. **2** any writer on sacred subjects.

Hai·da ['haɪdə] *n, pl* **Hai·da** **1** a member of a First Nations people of western British Columbia and Alaska. **2** their language. **Hai·da** *adj.*

hai·den [haɪ'dɛn] *n* the small outer shrine of a Shinto temple which worshippers may enter for their devotions. ⟨Japanese⟩

hai·ku ['haɪku] *n, pl* **hai·ku** a Japanese verse form consisting of three lines of five, seven, and five syllables respectively. ⟨Japanese⟩

hail¹ [heil] *v* **1** shout in welcome to; cheer: *The crowd hailed the winner.* **2** call loudly to; shout to: *The captain hailed the passing ship.* *interj Poetic* welcome! congratulations! **hail** *n.* ⟨earlier *be hail!*; Old Norse *heill* healthy⟩ **hail from** come from. **within hail** near enough to hear a call or shout.

hail² [heil] *n* **1** rounded lumps of ice that fall instead of rain under certain conditions (with a sg verb): *The hail was coming down hard.* **2** a forceful rush of something: *a hail of abuse, a hail of bullets.* *v* **1** be the case that hail is falling (with the subject *it*): *It hailed yesterday.* **2** pour down like hail: *The critics hailed scorn on his performance.* ⟨Old English *hægel*⟩ **hail·stone** *n* a piece of hail. **hail·storm** *n* a storm with hail.

hair [hɛr] *n* **1** a threadlike outgrowth from the skin of human beings and animals. **2** a threadlike growth from the outer layer of plants. **3** something very small: *She won the race by a hair.* **hair** *adj.* **hair·less** *adj.* ⟨Old English *ǽr*⟩

get in someone's hair annoy. **have by the short hairs** *Informal* be in a position to coerce (someone) to do something. **let one's hair down** be informal or unconventional; relax. **not turn a hair** not show any sign of being disturbed. **split hairs** make excessively fine distinctions. **to a hair** exactly; just right.

hair·brush *n* a brush for the hair. **hair·cut** *n* **1** the act of cutting the hair of the head. **2** the result of cutting the hair; hairstyle. **hair·do** *n* the way in which the hair, esp of a woman, is arranged. **hair·dress·er** *n* a person whose work is cutting and taking care of people's hair. **hair·dress·ing** *n.* **hair·line** *n* **1** the natural margin where hair growth ends on the head. **2** a very thin line. *adj* very thin or narrow: *a hairline crack in a wall.* **hair·piece** *n* **1** a wig worn to cover baldness. **2** an extra length of hair worn to add bulk or length. **hair·pin** *n* **1** a pin used to keep the hair in place. **2** a sharp bend in a road, river, etc., like a hairpin in shape. **hair·rais·ing** *adj Informal* making the hair seem to stand on end; terrifying. **hair's–breadth** or **hairs·breadth** ['hɛrz ,brɛdθ] or [-,brɛtθ] *adj* very narrow; extremely close: *a hairbreadth escape.* *n* a very narrow space. **hair·split·ting** *n* the making of excessively fine distinctions. *adj* excessively subtle. **hair·spring** *n* a very fine spring that regulates the motion in a watch or clock. **hair·style** *n* a way of arranging the hair. **hair·styl·ing** *n.* **hair·styl·ist** *n.* **hair trig·ger** a trigger that operates by very slight pressure. **hair–trig·ger** *adj* set off by the slightest pressure: *a hair-trigger temper.* **hair·y** *adj* **1** having much hair. **2** *Slang* difficult; disturbing; dismaying; frightening: *a hairy situation.* **hair·i·ly** *adv.* **hair·i·ness** *n.*

Hai·sla ['haɪslə] *n, pl* **Hai·sla** or **Hai·slas** a member of the northern branch of the Kwakiutl people of British Columbia. Also called **Kitimat.**

hajj or **haj** [hɑdʒ] *n Islam* a pilgrimage to the sacred shrine at Mecca, to be undertaken at least once in the lifetime of all devout Muslims. ⟨Arabic⟩ **haj·ji** ['hɑdʒi] *n* one who has done the HAJJ.

hake [heik] *n, pl* **hake** or **hakes** any of several marine food fishes of the cod family. ⟨dialect variant of *hook*, for hooklike growth under lower jaw⟩

ha·kim¹ [hə'kɪm] *n* in Muslim countries, a physician. ⟨Arabic *hakīm* wise man⟩

ha·kim² ['hakɪm] *n* in Muslim countries, a ruler; judge or governor. ⟨Arabic *hākim* ruler⟩

hal·al [halɑl] *adj* permitted under Islamic religious law: *halal meats.* The opposite is **haram.**

hal·cy·on ['hælsiən] *adj* calm; peaceful: *halcyon days.* *n Archaic or poetic* a bird that was supposed to calm the waves; kingfisher. ⟨Greek *halkyon* variant of *alkyon* kingfisher⟩

hale [heil] *adj* strong and well; healthy. **hale·ness** *n*. ⟨Old English *hāl*⟩

half [hæf] *n, pl* **halves** *n* **1** one of two equal parts. **2** in certain games, one of two equal periods. **3** one of two nearly equal parts: *Which is the bigger half?* *adj* **1** being or making half of. **2** being only part of: *A half-truth is often no better than a lie.* *adv* **1** to half of the full amount or degree: *half full of milk.* **2** partly: *half understood.* ⟨Old English *healf*⟩ **by half** by far. **half past** thirty minutes after a specified hour: *It's half past four.* **not half a** to a very slight extent. **b** *Informal.* not at all; the reverse of: *not half bad.*

half–and–half *adj* **1** half one thing and half another. **2** not clearly one thing or the other. *adv* in two equal parts. *n* a mixture of milk and cream. **half·back** *n Sports* in football or soccer, a player whose position is behind the forward line. **half–baked** *adj* **1** *Informal* not fully worked out; incomplete. **2** *Informal* not experienced; showing poor judgment. **half brother** a brother related through one parent only. **half sister. half cock** the position of the hammer of a gun when it is pulled back halfway. At half cock the trigger is locked and the gun cannot be fired. **go off at half cock** act without sufficient thought. **half–cocked** *adj*. **half–heart·ed** *adj* lacking interest or enthusiasm: *a half-hearted attempt.* **half–heart·ed·ly** *adv*. **half–heart·ed·ness** *n*. **half hitch** a knot formed by passing the end of a rope under and over its standing part and then inside the loop. **half–hour** *n* thirty minutes. **half–hour** *adj*. **half–hour·ly** *adv, adj*. **half–life** *n* **1** *Nuclear physics* the time in which half of the original radiant energy of a radioactive substance is given off. **2** of any substance, usually harmful, the time it takes for the amount of the substance in the environment to be reduced by half by decay. **half–light** *n* a dim light, as of early evening. **half–mast** *n* a position part way down from the top of a mast, staff, etc. **half moon** the moon when only half of its surface appears bright. **half nelson** *Wrestling* a hold applied by hooking one arm under an opponent's armpit and putting a hand on the back of the opponent's neck. **half note** *Music* a note held half as long as a whole note. **half rest** *Music* a rest lasting as long as a half note. **half–section** *n* ✹ an area of land covering 130 ha. **half slip** a woman's undergarment like a skirt. **half–time** *n* **1** *Sports* the interval between two halves of a game. **2** *Music* a tempo half as fast as the previous tempo. **half–time** *adj*. **half tone** *Music* the smallest interval in a scale, equivalent to that between two adjacent keys on a piano. **half–tone** *n* a process used in making pictures for books and magazines, by breaking the image into tiny dots. **half–track** or **half·track** *n* an army motor vehicle that has wheels in front and short tracks in the rear. **half–truth** *n* a statement that is only partly true. **half·way** *adv* half the required distance: *The rope reached only halfway to the boat.*

adj **1** midway: *a halfway point.* **2** not going far enough; inadequate: *halfway measures.* **go** (or **meet**) **halfway** do one's share toward reaching an agreement. **halfway house 1** a resting place at a midway point on a route. **2** a place offering a structured environment to help recently released convicts, mental patients, etc. become adjusted to society. **half·wit** *n* **1** a feeble-minded person. **2** a foolish, stupid person. **half·wit·ted** *adj*. **half·wit·ted·ly** *adv*. **half·wit·ted·ness** *n*. **halve** [hæv] *v* **1** divide into two equal parts. **2** reduce to half: *The new machine halves the time of doing the work.* **by halves** in a half-hearted way. **go halves** share equally.

hal·i·but [ˈhæləbət] *n, pl* **-but** or **-buts** a flatfish highly valued as a commercial food fish. ⟨Middle English *haly* holy + *butte* flatfish; eaten on holy days⟩

Hal·i·go·ni·an [ˌhælɪˈgouniən] *n* a native or inhabitant of Halifax, Nova Scotia.

hal·i·to·sis [ˌhæləˈtousɪs] *n* a disorder characterized by persistent bad breath. ⟨Latin *halitus* breath⟩

hall [hɒl] *n* **1** a passageway; corridor. **2** a room at the entrance of a building. **3** a large room for holding meetings, banquets, etc. **4** a building for public business: *The mayor's office is in the town hall.* **5** a building of a school, college, or university. **6** a mansion, esp the manor of an estate. ⟨Old English *heall*⟩ **Hall of Fame** a society into which outstanding professional sports players are inducted. **hall·way** *n* a passageway.

hal·le·lu·jah or **hal·le·lu·iah** [ˌhæləˈlujə] *interj* praise the Lord! Also, **al·le·lu·ia.** ⟨Hebrew *halleluyah* praise Yah (Jehovah)⟩

hall·mark [ˈhɒlˌmɑrk] *n* **1** an official mark indicating standard of purity, put on gold and silver articles. **2** a mark or sign of good quality: *Courtesy is the hallmark of a gentleman.* ⟨Goldsmiths' *Hall* in London, UK, seat of the Goldsmiths' Co., who legally regulated stamping⟩

hal·loo [həˈlu] *interj* a shout to attract attention. ⟨Old French *halloer* chase with shouts; *hale, hare* (the shout)⟩

hal·low [ˈhælou] *v* **1** make holy; make sacred. **2** honour as sacred. **hal·lowed** *adj*. ⟨Old English *hālgian; hālig* holy⟩ **Hal·low·een** or **Hal·low·e'en** [ˌhæləˈwin] *n* the evening of October 31. The next day is Allhallows or All Saints' Day.

hal·lu·ci·na·tion [həˌlusəˈneɪʃən] *n* **1** the perception of an object that is not in fact present. **2** any false notion. **hal·lu·ci·nate** *v*. **hal·lu·ci·na·tive** *adj*. **hal·lu·ci·na·to·ry** *adj*. ⟨Latin *hallucinari* wander; Greek *haluein* be delirious; form influenced by Latin *vaticinari* rave⟩ **hal·lu·cin·o·gen** [həˈlusənədʒən] *n* a drug or substance that produces hallucinations. **hal·lu·cin·o·gen·ic** *adj*.

ha·lo [ˈheɪlou] *n, pl* **-los** or **-loes** *n* **1** a series of coloured rings appearing around the sun or moon when it is seen through a cloud or ice crystals. **2** a circle of light shown around the head of a saint or divine being in a painting, etc. **3** a kind of glamour that surrounds an idealized person or thing: *A halo of romance surrounds King Arthur.* ⟨Latin; Greek *halōs* disk, threshing floor (for circular path of ox)⟩

hal·o·gen [ˈhælədʒən] *or* [ˈheilədʒən] *n* any one of the elements iodine, bromine, chlorine, fluorine, and astatine, that combine directly with metals to form salts. ⟨Greek *hals, halos* salt + -GEN⟩

halt¹ [hɒlt] *v* stop or cause to stop for a time. **halt** *n.* ⟨German *halten* stop, hold⟩ **call a halt** (*to*), cause something to stop.

halt² [hɒlt] *v* hesitate; waver: *Shyness made her halt as she talked.* **halt·ing** *adj.* ⟨Old English *haltian*⟩

hal·ter [ˈhɒltər] *n* **1** a headstall with an attached strap for leading a horse, cow, etc. **2** a woman's sleeveless top, fastened behind at the neck and just above the midriff so as to leave the shoulders and back bare. Also, **halter top.**
v put a halter on (an animal). ⟨Old English *hælftre*⟩

hal·vah or **hal·va** [ˈhɑlvə] *n* a confection of ground sesame seeds and honey, etc. ⟨Arabic *halwa*⟩

halve See HALF.

hal·yard [ˈhæljərd] *n* on a ship, a rope or tackle used to raise or lower a sail, flag, etc. ⟨Middle English *hallyer* from *hale* haul⟩

ham [hæm] *n* **1** salted and smoked meat from the upper part of a pig's hind leg. **2** Often, **hams** *pl* the back of the thigh **3** the part of the leg behind the knee. **4** *Informal* **a** an actor who exaggerates speeches, gestures, etc. **b** any person who behaves in an exaggerated way before an audience, photographer, etc. **5** *Informal* an amateur radio operator.
v **hammed, ham·ming** *Informal* overact or behave in an exaggerated way ⟨Old English *hamm* bend of the knee⟩

ham·burg·er [ˈhæmˌbɜrgər] *n* **1** ground beef. **2** this meat shaped into flat cakes and fried or broiled. Also, **ham·burg.** ⟨*Hamburg* city in Germany⟩

ham·let [ˈhæmlɪt] *n* a small group of houses, smaller than a village and with no local government of its own. ⟨Old French *hamelet* diminutive of *hamel* village; Germanic⟩

ham·mer [ˈhæmər] *n* **1** a tool used to drive nails and beat metal into shape. **2** a small mallet used by auctioneers to indicate by a rap the sale of an article. **3** one of the padded mallets for striking the string of a piano. **4** a lever with a hard head for striking a bell, as in a clock. **5** the part of the firing mechanism of a gun that explodes the charge. **6** *Track and field* a metal ball attached to a steel wire with a handle on the other end by which it is twirled around and thrown for distance.
v **1** drive, hit, or work with a hammer. **2** beat again and again: *He hammered on the door*

with his fist. **3** work (something) out with much effort. **ham·mer·like** *adj.* ⟨Old English *hamor*⟩

hammer and tongs with all one's force and strength: *The two girls fought hammer and tongs.* **hammer away a** keep working: *She hammered away at her homework.* **b** keep nagging: *He hammered away at his mother till he got what he wanted.* **hammer out** work (something) out with much effort. **under the hammer** for sale at an auction.

ham·mer·head *n* any of a genus of sharks having a head resembling a double-headed hammer. **hammer lock** *Wrestling* a hold in which an opponent's arm is twisted and held behind the opponent's back.

ham·mock [ˈhæmək] *n* a swinging bed made of canvas, cord, etc. that is suspended at both ends. ⟨Spanish *hamaca;* Carib⟩

ham·per¹ [ˈhæmpər] *v* hold back; hinder: *The unwieldy bundle severely hampered his progress.* ⟨Middle English *hampre(n)*; origin uncertain⟩

ham·per² [ˈhæmpər] *n* a large container, often a wicker basket, usually having a cover: *a picnic hamper.* ⟨obsolete *hanaper*, Old French *hanapier* basket for documents; *hanap* cup⟩

ham·ster [ˈhæmstər] *n* any of various rodents having a short tail and large cheek pouches. ⟨German⟩

ham·string [ˈhæmˌstrɪŋ] *n* **1** in a human being, one of the tendons at the back of the knee. **2** in a four-footed animal, the great tendon at the back of the hock.
v **-strung** or (*rare*) **-stringed, -string·ing** **1** cripple by cutting the hamstring. **2** destroy the activity, efficiency, etc. of.

Han [han] *n, pl* **Han 1** a member of a First Nations people living along the Yukon River. **2** their Athapascan language. **Han** *adj.*

hand [hænd] *n* **1** the end of a limb that grasps, holds, or clings. **2** something resembling a hand in shape, appearance, or use: *the hands of a watch.* **3** a hired worker who uses his or her hands: *a farm hand.* **4** a member of a ship's crew. **5** Usually, **hands** *pl* **a** possession; control: *The property is no longer in my hands.* **b** care or charge: *The sick child was taken off his hands.* **6** a share in doing something: *no hand in the matter.* **7** one's style of handwriting: *He writes in a clear hand.* **8** skill; ability: *The artist's work showed a master's hand.* **9** a round of applause or clapping: *The crowd gave the winner a big hand.* **10** a measure used in giving the height of horses, etc., about 10 cm. **11** *Card games* **a** the cards held by a player in one round of a card game. **b** one round of a card game.
v **1** give with the hand: *Please hand me the butter.* **2** help with the hand: *The doorman handed the lady into her car.* ⟨Old English⟩

all hands a all sailors of a ship's crew. **b** *Informal* all members of a group. **at first hand** from direct experience. **at hand** within reach; ready. **at second hand** from a source other than the original source. **at the hand** (or **hands**) **of** from (a person, as giver, doer, etc.): *We have received many favours at her hands.* **by hand** by using the hands, not machinery. **change hands** pass from one person to another: *A lot of money changed hands.* **clean hands** freedom from crime or dishonesty. **eat out of someone's hand** submit to someone's authority. **force someone's hand** make a person do something, or show what he or she is going to do. **from hand to mouth** without being able to put something aside for the future: *to live from hand to mouth.* **hand–to–mouth** *adj.* **give a hand** help. **hand down a** pass along. **b** *Law* announce (a decision, opinion, etc.). **hand in** give or pass to a person in authority. **hand in (or and) glove (with)** in close relations. **hand in hand a** holding hands. **b** together. **hand it to** *Informal* acknowledge as commendable: *You've got to hand it to him; he's quite a salesman.* **hand out** give out. **hand over** give to another. **hand over fist** rapidly, or in great quantity, esp of making money. **hands down** easily: *She won the contest hands down.* **hand to hand** close together: *to fight hand to hand.* **hand–to–hand** *adj, adv.* **have one's hands full** have as much to do as one can manage. **in hand a** under control. **b** in progress; being done. **join hands** become partners. **keep one's hand in** keep in practice. **lay hands on a** seize. **b** arrest. **c** attack. **d** bless by touching with the hands. **lend a hand** help. **on hand** within reach; ready: *The supermarket has lots of oranges on hand.* **on the one hand** from this point of view. **on the other hand** from the opposite point of view: *On the one hand, I want a bicycle; on the other hand, I can't afford to buy it.* **out of hand a** out of control. **b** at once: *The boy was expelled out of hand.* **show one's hand** reveal one's real intentions. **sit on one's hands** *Informal* **a** fail to applaud. **b** do nothing. **take in hand a** bring under control: *That child should be taken in hand by someone.* **b** start to deal with: *The supervisor promised to take the matter in hand.* **tie someone's hands** make someone unable to do something. **to hand** within reach; near. **try one's hand at** try to do: *trying his hand at politics.* **turn one's hand to** work at. **wait on someone hand and foot** serve diligently. **wash one's hands of** have no more to do with; refuse to be responsible for.

hand·bag *n* **1** a small bag for money, keys, etc. **2** a small travelling bag to hold clothes, etc. **hand·ball** *n* a game in which players use their hands to hit a rubber ball against the walls of a court. **hand·basket** a basket with a handle. **going to hell in a handbasket** deteriorating very quickly. **hand·bell** *n* a bell with a handle. **hand·bill** *n* a printed notice to be handed out to people. **hand·book** *n* a small book of directions or reference: *a handbook of engineering.* **hand brake** a brake operated by a manual lever. **hand·car** *n* a small car used on railway tracks, driven by a hand lever. **hand·cart** *n* a small cart pulled or pushed by hand. **hand·craft** *n* work done with the hands: *a display of handcrafts including pottery. v* make by hand: *She*

handcrafted the furniture. **hand·cuff** *n* Usually, **handcuffs** *pl* a device to secure a prisoner, usually consisting of a pair of metal rings that are fastened about the wrists. **hand·cuff** *v.* **hand·ful** *n* **1** as much or as many as the hand can hold. **2** a small number or quantity. **3** *Informal* a person or thing that is hard to control: *That girl is quite a handful.* **hand·gun** *n* a firearm that is held and fired with one hand. **hand–held** *adj* of an appliance, designed to be operated while being held in the hand: *a hand-held electric mixer.* **hand·hold** *n* a place to put the hands for holding on, such as in a climb. **hand·i·craft** ['hændi,kræft] handcraft. **hand·i·work** *n* **1** work done with the hands. **2** the result of a person's action. **hand·ker·chief** ['hæŋkərtʃɪf] *n* **1** a piece of fine cotton, silk, etc., used especially for wiping the nose. **2** kerchief. **hand·made** *adj* made by hand, not machinery. **hand–me–down** *Informal n* a second-hand article. **hand·out** *n* **1** food or money handed out. **2** a story issued to the press by a business organization, government agency, etc. **3** a set of notes issued to students in connection with their courses, to people attending a public lecture, etc. **hand–picked** *adj* carefully selected: *a hand-picked successor.* **hand·rail** *n* a railing used as a guard on a stairway, platform, etc. **hand·saw** *n* a saw used with one hand and not motorized. **hand·set** *n* a telephone that has the receiver, keypad, and mouthpiece in the same unit. **hand·shake** *n* a clasping and shaking of hands by two people as a sign of friendship. **hands–on** *adj* making use of personal, esp physical, involvement: *a hands-on learning process.* **hand·spring** *n* a somersault made from a standing position, in which the person comes down first on the hands. **hand·stand** *n* an act of supporting the body on the hands alone, while the trunk and legs are stretched in the air. **hand·work** *n* work done by hand, not by machinery. **hand·writ·ing** *n* a manner or style of writing: *He recognized his mother's handwriting on the envelope.* **hand·writ·ten** *adj.* **(hand)writing on the wall a** in the Bible, handwriting seen by Belshazzar, King of Babylon, on the wall of his palace, which Daniel interpreted as a prophecy of the fall of Babylon. **b** a portent of doom. **see** or **read the (hand)writing on the wall a** perceive that an institution, way of life, etc. is coming to an end. **b** see things as they really are. **hand·y** *adj* **1** easy to reach or use: *handy shelves, a handy tool.* **2** skilful with the hands: *She's handy with tools.* **hand·i·ly** *adv.* **hand·i·ness** *n.* **come in handy** be useful. **hand·y·man** *n, pl* **-men 1** someone who does odd jobs. **2** someone good at fixing things.

hand– *combining form* made or done by hand, not by machinery: *hand-woven.*

hand·i·cap ['hændi,kæp] *n* **1** something that puts a person at a disadvantage. **2** a contest where nobody has an unfair advantage or is at an unfair disadvantage. **3** a disadvantage

assigned to a superior competitor to make a contest more equal: *a golf handicap of four.*
v -**capped**, -**cap·ping 1** put at a disadvantage: *The pitcher was handicapped by a sore arm.* **2** give a handicap to: *The Sports Committee handicapped me 5 m.* **hand·i·capped** *adj.* **hand·i·cap·per** *n.* ⟨*hand in cap*; apparently with reference to an old game⟩

hand·i·craft See HAND.

han·dle [ˈhændəl] *n* **1** the part of a thing made to be held by the hand. **2** *Slang* a name or title.
v **1** touch, hold, or move with the hand. **2** manage: *The captain handles the soldiers well.* **3** perform in a certain way when driven, managed, directed, etc.: *This car handles easily.* ⟨Old English *handle; hand* hand⟩
fly off the handle *Slang* get angry or excited. **handle to one's name** *Slang* a title of nobility, etc.
han·dle·bars *n pl* the bars by which a bicycle, etc. is guided. **han·dler** *n* **1** a person who helps to train a boxer. **2** a person who guides a politician, etc. **3** a person who shows dogs or cats, etc. in a contest.

hand·maid [ˈhændˌmeid] *n* a female servant or attendant. Also, **hand·maid·en.**

hand·some [ˈhænsəm] *adj* **1** good-looking. **2** fairly large: *a handsome amount of money.* **3** generous: *a handsome gift.* **hand·some·ly** *adv.* **hand·some·ness** *n.* ⟨Middle English *handsom* easy to handle, ready at hand; *hand* + *-some¹*⟩

hang [hæŋ] *v* **hung, hang·ing** *v* **1** fasten or be fastened to something above. **2** fasten or be fastened so as to turn freely: *to hang a door on its hinges.* **3 hung** or **hanged, hang·ing** put or be put to death by hanging with a rope around the neck. **4** decorate with things that hang: *The walls were hung with pictures.* **5** bend down; let droop: *He hung his head in shame.* **6** *Computers* of a computer system, program, etc., stop working suddenly and inexplicably. **7** attach (wallpaper, pictures, etc.) to walls. **8** depend. **9** be wearisome: *Time hangs on her hands.*
n the way that something hangs: *I don't like the hang of the skirt.* ⟨Old English *hōn* (past *hēng*) suspend, and *hangian* be suspended⟩
get the hang of *Informal* **a** discover how to operate, do, etc.: *to get the hang of driving a car.* **b** understand the meaning of: *I didn't quite get the hang of what he said.* **give** (or **care**) **a hang** *Informal* care about (usually negative): *He doesn't give a hang about anybody.* **hang around a** loiter with no definite purpose in mind. **b** wait near: *a crowd hanging around the door.* **hang back** be unwilling to go forward. **hang in** *Informal* not give up. **hang in the balance** be undecided. **hang it (all)!** an expression of annoyance. **hang on a** hold tight. **b** be unwilling to let go, stop, or leave. **c** depend on. **d** listen to very carefully: *She hung on the teacher's every word.* **e** wait, esp on the telephone. **hang one's head** be ashamed. **hang onto a** try to keep control or possession of. **b** depend for support on: *Hang onto this*

thought, *it may help you.* **hang out a** lean out. **b** *Slang* live; stay. **c** *Slang* loiter habitually (*at* or *in* a place). **hang over a** be about to happen to: *The possibility of being punished hung over her for days.* **b** *Informal* remain from an earlier time or condition. **hang together** be coherent or consistent: *The story does not hang together.* **hang up a** put on a hook. **b** put (a telephone receiver) back in place. **c** detain. **d** ❋ *Lumbering* of the movement of logs, slow down or stop en route from forest to mill.

hang·er [ˈhæŋər] *n* anything on which something else is hung: *a coat hanger.* **hang·er–on** *n, pl* **hang·ers–on** an undesirable follower. **hang–glid·er** *n* a motorless aircraft with an attached harness, designed to carry people through the air for a short while. **hang–glide** *v.* **hang–glid·ing** *n* the sport of gliding through the air while suspended from a hang-glider. **hang·ing** *n* **1** death by hanging with a rope around the neck. **2** something that hangs from a wall, bed, etc. *adj* **1** deserving to be punished by hanging: *a hanging crime.* **2** fastened to something above. **3** leaning over or down. **4** located on a height or steep slope: *a hanging lake.* **hang·man** [ˈhæŋmən] *or* [ˈhæŋˌmæn] *n, pl* -**men** a man who hangs criminals sentenced to death by hanging. **hang·out** *n Slang* **1** a place one lives in or goes to often. **2** a rendezvous, esp for criminals. **hang·o·ver** [ˈhæŋˌouvər] *n* **1** *Informal* something that remains from an earlier time. **2** *Slang* a condition characterized by headache and nausea resulting from consumption of alcohol the previous night. **hang–up** *n* **1** *Slang* a personal or emotional difficulty. **2** ❋ *Lumbering* a log caught on a snag or obstruction when being transported.

USAGE
In formal English, the preferred form of the past tense and past participle for def. 3 only is **hanged:** *The murderer was hanged.* In informal English, however, **hung** is often used: *He was hung for his crimes.*

hang·ar [ˈhæŋər] *n* **1** a shed for aircraft. **2** a shed. ⟨Latin *angarium* shed for shoeing horses⟩

hang·dog [ˈhæŋˌdɒg] *adj* ashamed; sneaking; degraded: *a hangdog look.*

hang·nail [ˈhæŋˌneil] *n* a bit of skin that hangs partly loose near a fingernail. ⟨Old English *angnœgl, ang-* compressed, painful + *nœgl* nail; influenced by *hang*⟩

hank [hæŋk] *n* a coil; loop. ⟨Old Norse *hönk*⟩

han·ker [ˈhæŋkər] *v* wish; crave (with *for* or *after*). ⟨origin uncertain⟩ **han·ker·ing** [ˈhæŋkərɪŋ] *n* a longing; craving: *I have a hankering for a large, juicy steak.*

hank·y [ˈhæŋki] *n, pl* **hank·ies** *Informal* handkerchief. Also, **hank·ie.**

hank·y–pank·y [ˈhæŋki ˈpæŋki] *n Slang* questionable behaviour: *Was there any hanky-panky involved in his getting the contract?*

Han·sard [ˈhænsərd] *n* the printed record of

the proceedings of the Canadian or British Parliaments. ⟨Luke *Hansard* (1752-1828), first compiler⟩

Hansen's disease ['hænsənz] an infectious disease which causes sores, and which may result in paralysis and deformity; leprosy. ⟨A. *Hansen* (1841-1912), Norwegian physician⟩

Ha·nuk·kah or **Ha·nuk·ka** ['hʌnəkə] *or* ['hɑnəkə] *Hebrew* ['xɑnʊˌkɑ] *n* the Feast of Dedication or the Feast of Lights, a Jewish festival falling in December. Also, **Cha·nu·kah** or **Cha·nuk·kah.** ⟨Hebrew = dedication⟩

hap·haz·ard [ˌhæp'hæzərd] *adj* random; not planned: *Haphazard answers are usually wrong.* **hap·haz·ard·ly** *adv.* **hap·haz·ard·ness** *n.* ⟨obsolete *hap* chance, luck + HAZARD⟩

hap·less ['hæplɪs] *adj* unlucky; u nfortunate. **hap·less·ly** *adv.* **hap·less·ness** *n.*

hap·loid ['hæplɔɪd] *Biology adj* designating a nucleus, cell, or organism possessing a single set of unpaired chromosomes. Compare DIPLOID. ⟨Greek *haploeidēs; haplous* single + *eidos* form⟩

hap·pen ['hæpən] *v* **1** occur. **2** take place by chance: *Accidents will happen.* **3** chance (*to*): *She happened to sit next to me.* ⟨Middle English *happene(n); hap* chance; luck⟩
  as it happens by chance: *As it happens, I have no money with me.* **happen on** (or **upon**) meet or find by chance: *She happened on a dime while looking for her ball.* **happen to** be the fate of; become of: *Nobody knew what happened to the last explorer.*
  hap·pen·ing *n* anything that happens. **hap·pen·stance** ['hæpənˌstæns] *n Informal* a situation resulting from chance: *His success came more by happenstance than good planning.*

hap·py ['hæpi] *adj* **1** feeling pleasure and joy. **2** lucky: *a happy chance.* **3** clever and fitting: *a happy choice of words.* **4** (in compounds) much given to using a given thing: *trigger-happy.* **hap·pi·ly** *adv.* **hap·pi·ness** *n.* ⟨Middle English, from *hap.* See HAPPEN.⟩
  hap·py–go–luck·y *adj* taking things easily; trusting to luck. **happy hour** the time of day when some bars sell drinks at cheaper prices.

har·a–ki·ri ['hɛrə 'kiri], ['hærə-], *or* ['hɑrə-] *n* the national form of honourable suicide in Japan. Also, **hara–kari, hari–kari.** ⟨Japanese *hara* belly + *kiri* cutting⟩

ha·rangue [hə'ræŋ] *n* **1** a noisy speech. **2** a long, pompous speech. **ha·rangue** *v.* ⟨Middle English; Old French *arenge*⟩

har·ass [hə'ræs], ['hɛrəs], *or* ['hærəs] *v* **1** trouble by repeated attacks: *Pirates harassed the coastal villages.* **2** disturb; worry; torment. **har·ass·ment** *n.* ⟨French *harasser;* Old French *harer* call dogs on. See HALLOO.⟩

har·bin·ger ['hɑrbɪndʒər] *n* one that goes ahead to announce another's coming: *The robin is a harbinger of spring.* **har·bin·ger** *v.* ⟨Old French *herbergere* provider of shelter (thus, one who goes ahead), *herberge* lodging. Compare HARBOUR.⟩

har·bour or **har·bor** ['hɑrbər] *n* **1** a

sheltered area of deep water where ships may dock or anchor. **2** any place of shelter. *v* **1** give shelter to: *to harbour a criminal.* **2** keep in the mind: *Don't harbour unkind thoughts.* **3** be the habitat of: *This forest harbours deer.* **har·bour·less** or **har·bor·less** *adj.* ⟨Old English *hereberg* lodgings; *here* army + *beorg* shelter⟩
  har·bour·age or **har·bor·age** *n* **1** a shelter for ships. **2** any shelter. **harbour master** an officer who has charge of a harbour or port.

hard [hɑrd] *adj* **1** solid to the touch: *Rocks are hard.* **2** firmly formed: *Her muscles were hard.* **3** difficult: *a hard problem.* **4** causing much pain, trouble, etc.: *a hard illness.* **5** unfeeling: *a hard master.* **6** not gentle: *a hard face.* **7** acting with energy, persistence, etc.: *a hard worker.* **8** violent: *a hard storm.* **9** containing much alcohol: *hard liquor.* **10** *Informal* real and significant: *hard news.* **11** *Phonetics* of the consonants *c* and *g,* pronounced as [k] (*corn*) and [g] (*get*), not as in *city* and *gem.* Compare SOFT (def. 8). **12** of a drug, seriously addictive and harmful: *hard drugs such as heroin and cocaine.* Compare SOFT (def. 11). **13** of currency, fully backed by gold or silver. Compare SOFT (def. 12).
  adv **1** so as to be solid: *frozen hard.* **2** firmly: *Don't hold so hard.* **3** with difficulty: *to breathe hard.* **4** with steady effort or much energy: *Try hard.* **5** with vigour or violence: *She hit hard.* **6** intently: *look hard at a person.* **hard·ness** *n.* ⟨Old English *heard*⟩
  go hard with cause severe trouble or pain to: *It will go hard with the murderer when she is caught.* **hard by** near; close to. **hard put (to it)** in much difficulty. **hard up** *Informal* needing money or anything very badly.
  hard and fast that cannot be changed or broken; strict. **hard–and–fast** *adj.* **hard–bit·ten** *adj* stubborn. **hard–boiled** *adj* **1** boiled until hard: *hard-boiled eggs.* **2** *Informal* not very emotional; tough. **hard·bound** or **hard·back** *adj* of a book, having relatively rigid covers. **hard cash** actual money. **hard cider** fermented cider, containing alcohol. **hard–code** *v Computers* write fixed values into a program. **hard copy** information that can be read without equipment, such as a computer printout. **hard–cop·y** *adj.* **hard core** the most lasting part of any thing. **hard–core** *adj* **1** showing explicit sex: *hard-core movies.* **2** solidly committed: *hard-core disco fans.* **hard·cov·er** *adj, n* hardbound. **hard disk** *Computers* an internal storage device used to retain programs and data. **hard drive** *Computers* the component of a computer system that holds and reads the HARD DISK. **hard·en** *v* **1** make or become hard. **2** make or become capable of endurance. **3** make or become unfeeling. **hard feelings** resentment. **hard hat** *n* a rigid helmet worn for protection against falling objects. **hard–hat** *adj.* **hard–head·ed** *adj* **1** shrewd. **2** stubborn. **hard–head·ed·ness** *n.* **hard–heart·ed** *adj* without pity; cruel. **hard–heart·ed·ness** *n.* **hard labour** or **labor** hard work in addition to imprisonment.

hard line a stern attitude: *taking a hard line against drunk driving.* **hard–line** *adj.* **hard–lin·er** *n.* **hard–nosed** *adj Informal* unsentimental, often to the point of ruthlessness. **hard of hearing** somewhat deaf. **hard palate** the front, bony part of the roof of the mouth. **hard·pan** *n* hard, underlying earth. **hard pressed** confronted with the necessity to act quickly: *She was hard pressed to get the essay ready.* **hard put** barely able: *He was hard put to think of an excuse.* **hard return** *Computers* a RETURN (def. 7) inserted by the user, that starts a new paragraph. Compare SOFT RETURN. **hard·rock** ✱ *n* **1** *Mining* rock that can be removed only by drilling or blasting. **2** *Slang* a strong, rough person. **hard rock** *Music* very loud, fast rock. **hard–scrab·ble** *adj* giving a small return for hard work: *a hard-scrabble farm.* **hard sell** *Informal* an aggressive approach to selling. Compare SOFT SELL. **hard–sell** *adj.* **hard·ship** *n* something hard to bear: *Hunger, cold, and sickness are hardships.* **hard sledding** difficult going. **hard·tack** *n* a very hard biscuit which keeps well and is used on ships. **hard·top** *Informal n* an automobile having a body design like a convertible, but with a rigid top. **hard·ware** *n* **1** articles made from metal. Nails are hardware. **2** *Military* equipment such as guns, tanks, etc. **3** *Computers* the structural parts of a computer. Compare SOFTWARE. **hard water** water with minerals that hinder the action of soap. **hard·wear·ing** or **hard–wear·ing** able to withstand rough treatment: *hardwearing material.* **hard·wood** *n Forestry* any tree that has broad leaves or does not have needles. Maple is a hardwood; pine is a softwood. **hard·wood** *adj.* **hard·work·ing** *adj* industrious.

har·di·hood See HARDY.

hard·ly [ˈhɑrdli] *adv* **1** only just: *We hardly had time for breakfast.* **2** not quite: *hardly strong enough.* **3** most probably not: *She will hardly come now.* **4** with trouble or effort: *money hardly earned.* **5** in a hard manner; harshly: *to deal hardly with a person.*

When used at the beginning of a sentence, **hardly** and **scarcely** are followed by inverted word order: *Hardly had she left when it began to rain. Scarcely had he asked when the reply arrived.*

har·dy [ˈhɑrdi] *adj* **1** able to bear hard treatment; strong. **2** able to withstand the cold of winter in the open air: *hardy plants.* **3** bold. **4** too bold. **har·di·ly** *adv.* ⟨Old French *hardi* pp of *hardir* harden; Germanic⟩ **har·di·hood** *n* boldness; daring. **har·di·ness** *n* **1** endurance; strength. **2** hardihood.

hare [hɛr] *n, pl* **hare** or **hares** any of several mammals related to rabbits, but larger and having longer ears and legs. *v* hurry; run: *They hared off after the thief.* **hare·like** *adj.* ⟨Old English *hara*⟩ **hare·brained** *adj* reckless. **hare·lip** *n* a deformity caused when parts of the lip fail to grow together before birth. **hare·lipped** *adj.*

Hare [hɛr] *n* **1** a member of a First Nations people living in the Mackenzie Valley. **2** the Athapascan language of these people. **Hare** *adj.*

Hare Krishna [ˈhɑri ˈkrɪʃnə] *or* [ˈhɛri] *n* a Hindu religion based on Vedic writings.

har·em [ˈhɛrəm] *n* **1** the part of a Muslim house where the women live. **2** the wives, female relatives, female servants, etc. of a Muslim household. **3** of fur seals and certain other animals, a number of females controlled by one male. ⟨Arabic *haram, harim* forbidden; because off limits to males⟩

hark [hɑrk] *v* listen. **hark back** return to a previous point or subject; revert: *Whenever we chat together, he is always harking back to his time in the army.* ⟨Middle English *herkien*⟩

harlequin duck a small diving duck.

har·lot [ˈhɑrlət] *n* prostitute. ⟨Old French = vagabond⟩ **har·lot·ry** *n* prostitution.

harm [hɑrm] *n* **1** hurt; damage: *The accident did a lot of harm to the car.* **2** evil; wrong: *What harm is there in "borrowing" a bicycle?* *v* injure. **harm·ful** *adj.* **harm·ful·ly** *adv.* **harm·ful·ness** *n.* **harm·less** *adj.* **harm·less·ly** *adv.* **harm·less·ness** *n.* ⟨Old English *hearm*⟩

Harm = injure, but is a more informal word, and especially suggests injuring a person so as to cause suffering of some kind: *Unfounded and malicious rumours harmed his reputation.* **Damage** = hurt or harm so as to lessen the value or appearance of a person or thing: *The furniture was damaged in the fire.*

har·mon·ic [hɑrˈmɒnɪk] *adj* **1** *Music* **a** to do with harmony as distinguished from melody and rhythm. **b** to do with overtones heard along with the main tone. **c** musical. **2** to do with harmony or agreement. **3** *Physics* to do with wave frequencies that are integral multiples of the fundamental frequency. *n* **1** *Music* **a** a tone produced on a stringed instrument by a light pressure at a point on a string. **b** an overtone whose rate of vibration is an integral multiple of the main tone. **2** a fainter and higher tone heard along with the main tone; overtone. **har·mon·i·cal·ly** *adv.* ⟨Greek *harmonia* concord, a joining; *harmos* joint⟩ **har·mon·i·ca** *n* a reed instrument played by using the tongue and lips; mouth organ. **har·mon·ics** *n* the science of musical sounds. **har·mo·ny** [ˈhɑrməni] *n* **1** an agreement of feeling, ideas, or actions: *to live in perfect harmony.* **2** a pleasing arrangement of parts: *a harmony of design and colour.* **3** *Music* a sounding together of tones in a chord. **4** the act of harmonizing, esp of singing voices. **har·mo·ni·ous** *adj.* **har·mo·nize** *v.*

har·ness [ˈhɑrnɪs] *n* **1** the leather straps used to hitch an animal to a carriage, plough, etc. **2** an arrangement of straps to fasten or hold: *a parachute harness.* *v* **1** put harness on. **2** control so as to use the power of. Water in a stream is harnessed by allowing it to accumulate behind a dam. ⟨Old French *harneis*; possibly Scandinavian⟩ **in harness** at one's regular work: *back in harness after a holiday.*

harp [hɑrp] *n* a musical instrument played by plucking strings with the fingers. **harp·ist** *n.* ⟨Old English *hearpe*⟩ **harp on** keep on tiresomely talking or writing about; refer continually to.

harp seal a hair seal found in the Atlantic, with a horseshoe-shaped marking on its back.

har·poon [hɑr'pun] *n* a barbed spear used for catching whales and other sea animals. **har·poon** *v.* **har·poon·er** *or* **har·poon·eer** *n.* ⟨French *harpon;* Middle French *harper* grip⟩

harp·si·chord ['hɑrpsə,kɔrd] *n* a stringed musical instrument resembling a piano. **harp·si·chord·ist** *n.* ⟨French *harpe* harp + *chorde* string of a musical instrument; Greek⟩

har·py ['hɑrpi] *n* a very greedy person who preys upon others. ⟨Greek *Harpyia;* probably related to *harpazein* snatch⟩

har·ri·dan ['hɛrədən] *or* ['hærədən] *n* a bad-tempered, disreputable, old woman. ⟨probably French *haridelle* worn-out horse⟩

har·row ['hɛrou] *or* ['hærou] *n Agriculture* a heavy frame with iron teeth or upright disks. *v* **1** *Agriculture* draw a harrow over (land, etc.). **2** hurt; wound. **3** distress; torment. **har·row·er** *n.* ⟨Middle English *harwe*⟩ **har·row·ing** *adj.* painful; moving to pity: *a harrowing account of the ordeal.*

har·ry ['hɛri] *or* ['hæri] *v* **1** raid and rob with violence: *The pirates harried the towns along the coast.* **2** worry; torment: *harried by fear of losing his job.* ⟨Old English *hergian;* here army⟩

harsh [hɑrʃ] *adj* **1** rough to the senses: *a harsh voice.* **2** cruel; severe: *a harsh man.* **3** grim: *a harsh expression.* **4** rugged; bleak: *a harsh landscape.* **harsh·ly** *adv.* **harsh·ness** *n.* ⟨variant of Middle English *harsk*⟩

har·um–scar·um ['hɛrəm 'skɛrəm] *adj* rash; thoughtless: *a harum-scarum child.* **har·um–scar·um** *adv.* ⟨apparently *hare* frighten + *scare*⟩

har·vest ['hɑrvɪst] *n* **1** a gathering in of natural products: *The oyster harvest was small this year.* **2** the consequences: *reaping the harvest of one's mistakes.* **har·vest** *v.* **har·vest·a·ble** *adj.* ⟨Old English *hœrfest*⟩ **har·vest·er** *n* **1** a person who works in a harvest field; reaper. **2** a machine for harvesting crops, esp grain. **harvest moon** the full moon at harvest time, or about September 23.

has–been ['hæz ,bɪn] *or* [-,bɪn] *n Informal* a person or thing whose best days are past.

hash¹ [hæʃ] *n* **1** a mixture of cooked meat, potatoes, etc. chopped into small pieces and fried or baked. **2** a mixture. **3** a muddle. *v* **1** chop into small pieces. **2** make a mess or muddle of. **3** *Informal* talk about in detail; (often with *over, through,* etc.): *The two leaders spent hours hashing over their problems.* ⟨French *hacher; hache* hatchet⟩

make a hash of make a mess of: *She made a hash of mounting stamps in her album.* **settle someone's hash** *Informal* subdue someone completely; get even with someone.

hash browns a dish consisting of potatoes boiled and then cut up and sautéed.

hash² [hæʃ] *n Slang* hashish.

hash·ish ['hæʃiʃ], ['hæʃiʃ], *or* [hə'ʃiʃ] *n* an extract from the hemp plant, that is smoked, chewed, or drunk for its intoxicating effect. Compare CANNABIS, MARIJUANA. ⟨Arabic⟩

Ha·sid ['hɑsɪd] *or* [hə'sɪd] *n, pl* **Hasidim** ['hɑsədɪm] *or* [hə'sidɪm] a member of a Jewish sect emphasizing mysticism, prayer, and religious zeal. Also, **Cha·sid. Ha·sid·ic** [hə'sɪdɪk] *adj.*

hasp [hæsp] *n* a hinged metal clasp that is fastened by a padlock. ⟨variant of Old English *hœpse*⟩

has·sle ['hæsəl] *Informal n* **1** an argument: *There was a hassle about who was going to ride in the front seat of the car.* **2** trouble: *Driving is too much hassle.* **has·sle** *v.* ⟨origin uncertain⟩

has·sock ['hæsək] *n* **1** a padded footstool or thick cushion to rest the feet on, sit on, or kneel on. **2** a tuft of coarse grass. ⟨Old English *hassuc* coarse grass⟩

haste [heist] *n* **1** a trying to be quick; hurrying: *The king's business required haste.* **2** quickness without care: *Haste makes waste.* ⟨Old French from Germanic⟩ **in haste a** in a hurry. **b** without careful thought. **make haste** hurry; be quick. **has·ten** ['heisən] *v* **1** cause to be quick; hurry: *She hastened the children off to bed.* **2** be quick: *Let me hasten to explain.* **hast·y** *adj* **1** quick: *a hasty visit.* **2** rash: *hasty decisions.* **3** easily angered. **hast·i·ly** *adv.* **hast·i·ness** *n.*

hat [hæt] *n* **1** a covering for the head. **2** any of a person's roles, positions, etc.: *I'm wearing my director's hat today.* **hat·less** *adj.* ⟨Old English *hætt*⟩ **pass the hat** take up a collection. **take off one's hat to** honour as if by removing one's hat: *I take my hat off to anybody who can make that jump.* **throw one's hat into the ring** *Informal* enter a contest, esp for election to a public office. **under one's hat** *Informal* as a secret: *Keep it under your hat.* **hat·band** *n* a band around the crown of a hat, just above the brim. **hat·rack** *n* a rack, or set of hooks, to put hats on. **hat·ter** *n* a person who makes or sells hats. **hat trick 1** *Hockey, soccer, etc.* three goals scored in a single game by the same player. **2** *Informal* any feat consisting of three or more victories in a row.

hatch¹ [hætʃ] *v* **1** bring forth (young) from an egg: *A hen hatches chickens.* **2** plan, esp in secret: *to hatch an evil scheme.* **hatch** *n.* ⟨Middle English *hœche(n)*⟩ **hatch·er·y** *n* a place for hatching eggs of fish, hens, etc.

hatch² [hætʃ] *n* **1** an opening in a ship's deck through which the cargo is loaded, or the trap door covering this. **2** an opening in the floor or roof of a building, etc.: *an escape hatch.* ⟨Old English *hæcc*⟩

hatch·back *n* a sloping back on an automobile, which swings up like a hatch for loading cargo. **hatch·way** *n* 1 an opening in the deck of a ship to the lower part. 2 a similar opening in a floor, roof, etc.

hatch³ [hætʃ] *v* draw, cut, or engrave fine parallel lines on: *The artist hatched parts of the picture to darken them.* **hatch·ing** *n.* ⟨French *hacher* chop, hatch. See HASH¹.⟩

hatch·et ['hætʃɪt] *n* a small axe. ⟨Old French *hachette* diminutive of *hache* axe⟩

hatchet job *Informal* a vicious attack in speech or writing. **hatchet man** *Informal* 1 a person hired to make vicious attacks. 2 a hired murderer. 3 a person hired to get rid of employees.

hate [heit] *v* 1 dislike very strongly: *I hate that shade of blue.* 2 be unwilling: *I hate to disturb you late at night.* **hate** *n.* **hat·er** *n.* **ha·tred** *n.* ⟨Old English *hatian*⟩

hate·ful *adj* 1 causing hate. 2 feeling hate. **hate·ful·ness** *n.* **hate·mong·er** ['heit,mɒŋgər] or [-,mʌŋgər] *n* one who tries to stir up hatred against a certain group.

SYNONYMS

Hate, the general word, suggests very strong dislike and a feeling of hostility: *The prisoners hated the guards.* Detest suggests strong dislike mixed with scorn for something or someone disgusting: *I detest a coward.* Abhor suggests a dislike that makes one shrink away from something extremely disagreeable: *I abhor filth of any kind.*

haugh·ty ['hɒti] *adj* too scornful of others: *a haughty smile.* **haugh·ti·ly** *adv.* **haugh·ti·ness** *n.* ⟨Old French *haut* high, Latin *altus*⟩

haul [hɒl] *v* 1 drag with force. 2 transport by truck or railway: *Those trains haul coal.* *n* 1 the act of hauling. 2 the amount won, taken, etc. at one time: *a good haul of fish.* ⟨Middle English *hale,* French *haler;* Germanic⟩ **haul·age** *n* a charge made for hauling.

haunch [hɒntʃ] *n* 1 the part of the body around the hip. 2 the hind quarter of an animal. ⟨Old French *hanche*⟩

haunt [hɒnt] *v* 1 of a ghost, appear frequently. 2 visit frequently: *They haunt the new bowling alley.* 3 come into: *Memories of his youth haunted the old man.* *n* 1 a place often visited: *returning to their old haunts.* 2 a place where wild animals habitually come to drink or feed. **haunt·ing** *adj.* ⟨Old French *hanter*⟩ **haunt·ed** *adj.* 1 visited by ghosts. 2 harried or harassed, as if by ghosts.

haute cou·ture [otku'tyʀ] *French* the clothes made by leading designers and dressmakers. **haute cui·sine** [otkwi'zin] *French* cooking as a fine art, esp as practised by acknowledged master chefs.

hau·teur [hou'tɜr] *or* [ou'tɜr] *n* haughtiness; a haughty manner or spirit. ⟨French, from *haut* high⟩

have [hæv] *v pres 1* **have** *2* **have** *3* **has** *pl* **have;** *pt and pp* **had;** *ppr* **hav·ing** 1 hold: *I have a book in my hand.* 2 own: *She has a big house.* 3 have as a part, quality, etc.: *The house has many windows.* 4 cause to, or cause to be: *Have them send an extra copy.* 5 be compelled: *We all have to eat.* 6 take: *Have a seat.* 7 experience: *to have a pain.* 8 be afflicted with: *I have a bad cold.* 9 hold in the mind: *to have an idea.* 10 *Slang* fool or cheat: *I think I've been had.* 11 become the parent of: *She had her baby yesterday.* ⟨Old English *habban*⟩ **have had it** *Slang* a become disgusted. b reach an end. **have it in for** *Informal* have a grudge against. **have it out** fight or argue until a question is settled. **have nothing on** have no advantage of. **have on** a be wearing b have scheduled. **have to be** be undeniably: *That has to be the stupidest excuse I've ever heard.* **have to do with** a be connected with. b associate with. **let someone have it** scold or punish someone severely.

have-not *n* a person, province, or country that has little or no wealth. **have-not** *adj.*

ha·ven ['heivən] *n* 1 a harbour, esp one providing shelter from a storm. 2 a place of shelter and safety. ⟨Old English *hæfen*⟩

hav·oc ['hævək] *n* very great destruction or injury: *Tornadoes create widespread havoc.* ⟨Anglo-French; Old French *havot* plundering, devastation⟩ **play havoc with** damage severely; ruin.

hawk¹ [hɒk] *n* 1 any of a genus of birds of prey that are active during the day. 2 a person who takes an aggressive stand in controversial issues, esp one who favours a policy of military strength. Compare DOVE¹ (def. 2). *v* 1 hunt with trained hawks. 2 hunt or pursue like a hawk. **hawk·like** *adj.* ⟨Old English *hafoc*⟩ **hawk·ing** *n* the act of hunting with hawks; falconry. **hawk·ish** *adj* aggressive.

hawk² [hɒk] *v* 1 carry (goods) about for sale as a street peddler does. 2 advertise by shouting that goods are for sale. 3 spread (a report) around. ⟨back-formed from *hawker;* probably Middle Low German *hoker*⟩ **hawk·er** *n* a person who carries wares around and offers them for sale by shouting; peddler.

haw·thorn ['hɒ,θɔrn] *n* any of a genus of thorny shrubs and small trees of the rose family, having red fruits called haws. ⟨Old English *hagathorn; haga* hedge + *thorn* thorn⟩

hay [hei] *n* 1 grass, alfalfa, clover, etc. that has been cut and dried for use as food for cattle, horses, etc. 2 grass ready for mowing. *v* cut and dry grass, alfalfa, clover, etc. for hay: *The workers are haying in the east field.* ⟨Old English *hēg.* Related to HEW.⟩ **hit the hay** *Slang* go to bed. **make hay (while the sun shines)** *Informal* take advantage of some opportunity.

hay·cock *n* a small, cone-shaped pile of hay in a field. **hay fever** an allergy caused by the pollen of ragweed and other plants. **hay·field** *n* a field where crops such as grass are grown.

hay·loft *n* the upper storey of a stable or barn, where hay is stored. Also, **hay·mow**. **hay·rack** *n* **1** a frame used for holding hay to be eaten by cattle, horses, etc. **2** a framework on a wagon used in hauling hay, straw, etc. **hay·ride** *n* a ride for fun on a wagon filled with hay. **hay·seed** *n* **1** grass seed, esp that shaken out of hay. **2** the chaff that falls from hay. **3** *Slang* an unsophisticated person from the country. **hay·stack** *n* a large pile of hay outdoors. **hay·wire** *n* wire used to tie up bales of hay. *adj* **1** tangled up. **2** *Slang* stop-gap; flimsy: *a haywire repair job.* **3** ✹ *Lumbering slang* poorly organized and equipped. **go haywire** act in an excited or confused manner.

haz·ard ['hæzərd] *n* **1** risk; danger: *Life is full of hazards.* **2** chance. **3** *Golf* any obstruction on a course that can trap a ball.
v risk: *I would hazard my life on her honesty.* **haz·ard·ous** *adj.* **haz·ard·ous·ness** *n.* ⟨Old French *hasard;* Arabic *al-zahr* the die⟩

haze¹ [heiz] *n* **1** a small amount of mist, smoke, etc. in the air. **2** vagueness of the mind during which one sees things indistinctly: *After he was hit on the head, everything was in a haze for him.*
v make or become hazy (with *over*). ⟨origin uncertain⟩
ha·zy *adj* **1** misty; smoky: *hazy air.* **2** confused; vague: *hazy ideas.* **ha·zi·ly** *adv.* **ha·zi·ness** *n.*

haze² [heiz] *v* **1** force to do tasks as part of an initiation process: *The new student resented being hazed by the older students.* **2** in western Canada and the US, drive (cattle, etc.) from horseback. **haz·ing** *n.* ⟨perhaps Old French *haser* irritate, harass⟩

ha·zel ['heizəl] *n* any of a genus of shrubs and small trees of the birch family bearing edible nuts. ⟨Old English *hæsel*⟩
ha·zel·nut *n* the edible nut of a hazel; filbert.

H–bomb ['eitʃ ,bɒm] *n* HYDROGEN BOMB.

HDL high-density lipoprotein, that helps rid the bloodstream of cholesterol.

HDTV high-definition television, a TV system with a sharp image and a wide-screen format.

he [hi] *pron, subj* **he** *obj* **him** *poss* **his** *pl subj* **they** *pl obj* **them** *pl poss* **theirs** a boy, man, or male animal that has just been referred to: *My son has to work hard, but he likes his job.*
n, pl **he's** a male human being or animal: *Is the cat a he or a she?* ⟨Old English *hē*⟩
he–man *Informal n* a virile, rugged man.

head [hɛd] *n* **1** the top part of a body holding the eyes, mouth, etc. **2** the top part of anything: *the head of a pin.* **3** the foremost part of anything: *the head of a procession.* **4** the chief person; leader; commander. **5** *pl* **head** a unit, used in counting animals: *fifty head of cattle.* **6** anything rounded like a head: *a head of lettuce.* **7** mind: *a wise head.* **8** a topic: *He arranged his speech under four main heads.* **9** headline. **10** *Slang* one who uses drugs: *an acid head.* **11** a decisive point: *Her sudden refusal brought matters to a head.* **12** pressure of water, steam, etc. **13** froth, as on beer. **14** the device in a recorder that records or deletes information on a magnetic tape or disk. **15** *Computers* the component of a disk drive that contacts the recording surface for purposes of reading or writing data. Also called **read/write head**.
adj **1** at the top or front of: *the head division of a parade.* **2** coming from in front: *a head wind.* **3** chief; leading; commanding.
v **1** be or go at the top or front of: *to head a parade.* **2** move or go, or cause to move or go, in a certain direction: *to head a boat toward shore.* **3** be the head of. **4** *Soccer* direct the movement of (the ball) with one's head: *He headed the ball.*
adv **heads** of a coin, with the head side uppermost. **head·like** *adj.* ⟨Old English *hēafod*⟩
come to a head a of boils, pimples, etc., reach the stage where they are about to break through the skin. **b** reach a decisive stage: *The international crisis came to a head and war was declared.* **give someone his** or **her head** let someone go as he or she pleases. **go to one's head a** make one dizzy or intoxicated. **b** make one conceited. **hang** (or **hide**) **one's head** show that one is ashamed. **head off a** get in front of and turn back: *to head off a stampeding herd.* **b** prevent: *to head off possible trouble.* **c** leave. **head over heels a** in a somersault. **b** completely. **heads up** watch out. **heads–up** *adj.* **keep one's head** stay calm. **keep one's head above water** keep out of financial difficulty. **lay** (or **put**) **heads together a** confer. **b** conspire. **lose one's head** lose one's self-control. **make head or tail of** understand. **on** (or **upon**) **one's head** on one's responsibility. **one's head off** (do something) very much: *to laugh one's head off.* **out of** (or **off**) **one's head** *Informal* insane. **over someone's head a** beyond one's power to understand. **b** bypassing someone of lesser authority. **take it into one's head** intend. **talk someone's head off** talk endlessly. **turn someone's head** make someone conceited.
head·ache *n* **1** pain in the head. **2** *Informal* anything that causes worry or trouble. **head·ach·y** *adj.* **head·band** *n* **1** a band of cloth, etc. worn around the head to hold the hair in place or for ornament, for warmth, etc. **2** a flexible band that holds earphones or earmuffs over the ear. **head·board** *n* a board that forms the head of a bed. **head cold** the common cold when it affects mostly the sinus passages. **head·dress** *n* a covering or decoration for the head. **head·er** *n* **1** *Informal* a plunge headfirst: *a header into the water.* **2** a running title appearing at the top of each page of a chapter, section, etc. **3** *Masonry* a brick or stone laid with its length across the thickness of a wall. Compare STRETCHER def. 3. **4** *Carpentry* a beam set across and supporting the ends of joists, etc. to form one side of an opening. **5** *Soccer* the act of hitting the ball with the head. **head·first** or **head·fore·most** *adv* with the head first. **head·gear** *n* a covering for the head; hat, cap, etc.

head–hunt·ing *n* **1** the traditional practice, among certain peoples, of trying to get the heads of enemies as a sign of victory, adulthood, etc. **2** the search to find highly skilled people to work for a particular company. **head–hunt·er** *n*. **head·ing** *n* **1** the title of a page, chapter, etc.; topic. **2** the direction of a ship or aircraft as indicated by a compass. **head·lamp** *n* **1** a small lamp worn on the cap or the forehead. **2** a headlight on a train, automobile, etc. **head·land** *n* a point of land jutting out into water. **head·less** *adj* **1** having no head. **2** without a leader. **3** without brains; stupid. **head lettuce** a variety of lettuce whose leaves form a solid head. **head·light** *n* **1** of vehicles such as automobiles, one of two large lights at the front. **2** a large single light at the front of a locomotive, streetcar, etc. **head·line** *n* **1** the words printed at the top of an article in a newspaper or magazine to indicate the topic. **2** a summary of radio or television news, read before giving details. **3** **headlines** publicity: *He's the kind of person who gets plenty of headlines.* **make headlines** receive publicity. **head·lin·er** *n* one who makes headlines; a star. **head·lock** *n Wrestling* a hold in which a person's head is held between the body and arm of the opponent. **head·long** *adv, adj* **1** headfirst. **2** moving with great speed. **3** without stopping to think: *rushing headlong into trouble.* **head·man** ['hɛd,mæn] *n, pl* **-men** a chief; leader. **head·mas·ter** *n Brit* a school principal. **head·mis·tress** *n*. **head–on** *adj* with the head or front first: *a head-on collision.* *adv* in a direct way: *to tackle the issue head-on.* **head·phone** *n* a telephone or radio receiver held on the head, against the ears. **head·quar·ters** *n pl or sg* **1** the place from which the commanding officer of an army, police force, etc. sends out orders. **2** the centre from which any organization is controlled. **head·rest** *n* a support for the head: *The dentist's chair has a headrest.* **head·room** *n* clearance; headway: *Some bridges do not have enough headroom to allow trucks to pass underneath.* **head·set** *n* earphones, often with a microphone attached. **head·shrink·er** *n Slang* psychiatrist. **head·stand** *n* a position in which the head is on the floor while the rest of the body, supported by the hands, is upright. **head start** **1** an advantage allowed someone at the beginning of a race: *The smaller boy was given a head start.* **2** any advantage. **head·stone** *n* a tombstone. **head·strong** *adj* rashly or foolishly determined to have one's own way. **head–to–head** *adj* directly opposed. **head·wa·ters** *n pl* the sources of a river. **head·way** *n* **1** forward motion: *The ship could make no headway against the strong wind.* **2** progress with work, etc. **head·wind** a wind blowing straight against the front of a ship, plane, etc. **head·word** *n* **1** a word that is modified by other words; the main word of a phrase. **2** ENTRY WORD. **head·y** *adj* apt to make one dizzy; intoxicating. **head·i·ly** *adv*. **head·i·ness** *n*.

heal [hil] *v* **1** make or become whole, sound, or well; **2** make free from anything bad, such as a quarrel. **heal·er** *n*. ⟨Old English *hǣlan; hāl* well, whole⟩

health [hɛlθ] *n* **1** freedom from sickness. **2** a condition of body or mind: *in poor health.* **healthy** *adj*. **health·i·ly** *adv*. **health·i·ness** *n*. ⟨Old English *hǣlth; hāl* well, whole⟩
drink someone's health drink a toast to a person with a wish that she or he may be healthy and happy: *To the bride's health.*
✳ **health card** a card that identifies a person as eligible for provincially funded treatment. **health care** services provided by the medical profession. **health club** FITNESS CLUB. **health food** natural foodstuffs chosen for their healthy effect. **health–food** *adj*. **health·ful** *adj* good for the health: *healthful exercise.* **health·ful·ly** *adv*. **health·ful·ness** *n*.

> **USAGE**
> Formal usage tends to distinguish between the words **healthful** and **healthy**, using **healthful** to mean 'giving health', and **healthy** to mean 'having good health'. Places and food are healthful; persons and animals are healthy.

heap [hip] *n* **1** a pile of things together: *a heap of stones.* **2** *Informal* a large amount.
v **1** form into a heap. **2** give generously: *His mother heaped potatoes on his plate.* **3** fill to the point of overflowing: *a plate heaped with potatoes.* ⟨Old English *hēap*⟩

hear [hir] *v* **heard, hear·ing 1** perceive by the ear: *to hear sounds.* **2** listen to: *to hear a person's explanation.* **3** give a formal hearing to, as a judge does.
interj **hear! hear!** shouts of approval. **hear·er** *n*. **hear·ing** *n*. ⟨Old English *hēran*⟩
hear from a receive news from: *Have you heard from your friend?* **b** receive a reprimand from. **hear of** have some knowledge of: *I've never heard of her.* **hear out** listen to till the end. **will not hear of it** will not listen to, think of, agree to, or allow it.
hearing aid a device used to improve hearing. **hear·ing–im·paired** *adj* deaf or somewhat deaf. **hear·say** ['hir,sei] *n* common talk; gossip. **hearsay evidence** *Law* evidence based on the testimony of another person, rather than on the knowledge of the witness. Such evidence is usually not admissible.

hark·en ['hɑrkən] *v Archaic* listen; listen attentively. Also, **hark·en.** ⟨Old English *hercnian, heorcnian*⟩

hearse [hɜrs] *n* an automobile, carriage, etc. used in funerals to carry a dead person to his or her grave. ⟨Old French *herce*, Latin *hirpicis* harrow; orig a frame like a harrow⟩

heart [hɑrt] *n* **1** the organ that pumps the blood throughout the body. **2** the region of the heart; breast. **3** the feelings; mind; soul: *She has a kind heart.* **4** the source of love: *to give one's heart.* **5** kindness: *to have no heart.* **6** spirit; courage: *The losing team showed plenty of heart.* **7** the innermost part: *in the heart of the forest.* **8** the main part: *the heart of*

the matter. **9** a conventional figure shaped somewhat like a heart. ⟨Old English *heorte*⟩ **after one's own heart** just as one likes it. **at heart** in one's deepest thoughts or feelings. **break the heart of** crush with envy or grief. **by heart** from memory. **change of heart** a complete reversal of opinion. **eat one's heart out** feel great envy, grief, or worry. **from one's heart** with deepest feeling. **get to the heart of** find out the significance of. **have a heart** *Informal* be kind. **have one's heart in one's boots** (or **mouth**) be very frightened. **have one's heart in the right place** have good intentions. **have the heart** be hard-hearted enough: *I hadn't the heart to refuse his request.* **heart and soul** with all one's affections and energies. **heart of gold** an extremely kind nature. **in one's heart of hearts** in one's deepest thoughts or feelings. **lose one's heart to** fall in love with. **near to one's heart** of great value or interest to one. **set one's heart at rest** reassure one. **set one's heart on** be determined to have or do. **steal one's heart** cause one to love. **take heart** be encouraged. **take to heart** think seriously about. **to one's heart's content** as much as one wants. **with all one's heart** a sincerely. **b** gladly.
heart·ache *n* sorrow; grief. **heart attack** a sudden instance of heart disease. **heart·beat** *n* one complete contraction and dilation of the heart. **heart·break** *n* a crushing sorrow. **heart·break·ing** *adj*. **heart·break·ing·ly** *adv*. **heart·brok·en** *adj*. **heart·brok·en·ly** *adv*. **heart·burn** *n* a burning sensation in the chest, generally caused by digestive juices. **heart·en** *v* encourage. **heart failure** a sudden stopping of the heartbeat. **heart·felt** *adj* sincere; genuine. **heart·land** *n* any area that is the centre of an institution, country, etc. **heart·less** *adj* unfeeling; cruel. **heart·less·ness** *n*. **heart–rend·ing** *adj* very distressing. **heart–rend·ing·ly** *adv*. **heart·sick** *adj* very unhappy. **heart·sore** *adj* feeling or showing grief. **heart·strings** *n pl* deepest feelings: *The new baby tugs at my heartstrings.* **heart–throb** *n Informal* a person with whom one is infatuated. **heart–to–heart** *adj* without reserve; frank: *a heart-to-heart talk.* **heart–to–heart** *n Informal* a frank, intimate talk. **heart·warm·ing** *adj* able to stir up warm feelings. **heart·wood** *n* the hard, central wood of a tree. **heart·worm** *n* a nematode worm parasitic on dogs and cats. **heart–wrenching** *adj* very distressing. **heart·y** *adj* **1** warm and friendly: *a hearty welcome.* **2** strong and well: *hale and hearty.* **3** full of energy: *a hearty laugh.* **4** with plenty to eat or requiring much food: *a hearty meal, a hearty eater.* **heart·i·ly** *adv*. **heart·i·ness** *n*.

hearth [harθ] *n* **1** the floor of a fireplace. **2** the home; fireside: *The soldier longed for his own hearth.* ⟨Old English *heorth*⟩ **hearth·stone** *n* a stone forming a hearth.

heat [hit] *n* **1** the quality or state of being hot. **2** the temperature. **3** *Physics* a form of energy that consists in the motion of the molecules of a substance. **4** hot weather. **5** the artificial warming of a house or apartment: *Does the rent include heat?* **6** intensity of feeling. **7** most violent or active state: *In the heat of the fight he lost his temper.* **8** *Slang* pressure; torture. **9** one trial in a race: *She won the first heat.* **10** a periodically recurring condition of sexual excitement in female mammals; estrus.
v **1** make hot or warm; become hot or warm (often with *up*). **2** excite; become excited. ⟨Old English *hætu*. Related to HOT.⟩
in heat of female mammals, in a condition of sexual excitement, and so able to mate.
heat·er *n* a device that gives heat or warmth: *an electric heater.* **heat exchanger** a device by means of which heat is transferred from one medium to another as a source of power, as in an atomic power plant. **heat exhaustion** a condition due to prolonged exposure to heat, characterized by sweating and dizziness. Compare HEATSTROKE. **heat pump** a device using mechanical energy to transfer heat from one place to another that is at a higher temperature. **heat shield** a coating of special material on the nose cone of a spacecraft to protect it from the heat produced when it re-enters the earth's atmosphere. **heat sink** a device for storing heat absorbed by a cooling system. **heat·stroke** *n* a serious illness produced by long exposure to extreme heat, in which the body temperature rises dangerously high. Compare HEAT EXHAUSTION. **heat wave** a long period of very hot weather.

hea·then ['hiðən] *n, pl* **-thens** or (esp collectively) **-then** a person thought to have no religion or culture. **hea·then** *adj*. **hea·then·ish** *adj*. ⟨Old English *hæthen* orig heath dweller; *hæth* heath, open wasteland⟩

heath·er ['hɛðər] *n* any of several species of heath, esp a plant having clusters of usually purplish flowers. **heath·er·y** *adj*. ⟨probably from *heath*. See HEATHEN.⟩

heave [hiv] *v* **heaved** or **hove, heav·ing** *v* **1** lift with effort: *He heaved the big box into the wagon.* **2** utter with effort: *to heave a sigh of relief.* **3** rise and fall rhythmically: *the heaving sea.* **4** bulge: *The ground heaved during the earthquake.* **5** pant. **6** try to vomit. **heave** *n*.
interj **heave ho!** a sailor's cry when pulling on any rope or cable, or when throwing something overboard. ⟨Old English *hebban*⟩
give something the (old) **heave–ho** *Informal* discard; get rid of. **heave to** stop (a ship) as by trimming the sails, etc.

heav·en ['hɛvən] *n* **1** in various belief systems, the place where God or the gods live and where the blessed go after death, thought of as beyond the sky. Compare HELL (def. 1). **2** a place or condition of greatest happiness: *It was heaven to relax at home.* **3** Usually, **heavens** *pl* sky: *stars shining in the heavens.* **heav·en·ly** *adj*. **heav·en·li·ness** *n*. ⟨Old English *heofon*⟩
for heaven's sake or **good heavens!** an exclamation of surprise or protest. **move heaven and earth** do everything possible.

heav·en·ward *adj, adv* toward heaven. Also *(adv)*, **heavenwards**.

heav·y ['hevi] *adj* 1 of great mass: *a heavy load*. 2 of great density: *heavy metal*. 3 of more than usual mass for its kind: *heavy silk*. 4 of great amount or intensity: *heavy rain*. 5 sorrowful: *heavy news*. 6 coarse: *heavy features*. 7 dull: *heavy reading*. 8 *Informal* emotionally involving.
n 1 *Theatre* the villain in a play. 2 *Informal* any person who tries to accomplish matters by force. **heav·y** *adv*. **heav·i·ly** *adv*. **heav·i·ness** *n*. ⟨Old English *hefig; hebban* heave⟩
hang heavy of time, pass slowly and boringly: *Time hung heavy on his hands*. **heavy-duty** *adj* 1 built to withstand hard use: *a heavy-duty vacuum cleaner*. 2 *Informal* serious, thorough, big, etc.: *a heavy-duty talk, heavy-duty changes*. **heav·y–hand·ed** *adj* 1 awkward: *heavy-handed attempts at humour*. 2 harsh; cruel. **heav·y–hand·ed·ness** *n*. **heav·y–heart·ed** *adj* sad; gloomy. **heav·y–heart·ed·ness** *n*. **heavy industry** the manufacture of large objects for use by other industries. **heav·y·set** *adj* of a sturdy and often stout build: *a heavyset man*. **heavy water** *Chemistry* water used to control nuclear reactions, composed of oxygen and deuterium, an isotope of hydrogen present in very small quantities in ordinary water. **heav·y·weight** *n* 1 a boxer weighing more than 81 kg. 2 *Informal* a person of great influence: *a heavyweight in the political field*.

heck [hɛk] *interj, n Informal* a mild form of the word **hell**, used to express anger, etc.

heck·le ['hɛkəl] *v* harass (a speaker, etc.) by asking bothersome questions, etc. **heck·ler** *n*. ⟨*heckle* comb for flax or hemp, Middle English *hekele*⟩

hec·tic ['hɛktɪk] *adj* 1 to do with great excitement or confusion: *a hectic life*. 2 showing signs of a fever: *a hectic flush*. **hec·ti·cal·ly** *adv*. ⟨Greek *hektikos* habitual, consumptive; *hexis* habit⟩

hecto– *SI prefix* hundred. *Symbol* h ⟨Greek *hekaton*⟩
hect– *SI prefix* a form of **hecto–** used before a vowel. **hec·tare** ['hɛktɛr] *or* ['hɛktɑr] *n* a unit used with the SI for measuring land area, equal to 10 000 m². *Symbol* **ha**

hedge [hɛdʒ] *n* 1 a thick fence of bushes or trees. 2 any barrier. 3 a means of defence.
v 1 enclose or separate with a hedge: *to hedge a garden*. 2 avoid giving a direct answer: *Stop hedging and tell us what you want to do*. 3 protect oneself from losing money on (a bet, investment, etc.) by making other bets. ⟨Old English *hecg*⟩
hedge in surround on all sides: *The town was hedged in by mountains and a forest*.
hedge·hog *n* any of a subfamily of small mammals, having short spines on the back.
hedge·row *n* a thick row of bushes or small trees forming a hedge.

he·don·ism ['hidə,nɪzəm] *n* 1 *Philosophy* the doctrine that pleasure is the highest good.

2 *Psychology* the theory that human behaviour always aims to achieve pleasure and avoid pain. 3 the pursuit of sensual pleasure as a lifestyle. **he·don·ist** *n*. ⟨Greek *hēdonē* pleasure⟩

–hedron *combining form* face; a geometric figure with a given number of faces: *tetrahedron*. ⟨Greek *hedra* seat, side⟩

heed [hid] *v* give careful attention (to): *Now heed what I say*.
n careful attention; notice: *She paid no heed to the warning signal*. **heed·er** *n*. **heed·ful** *adj*. **heed·ful·ness** *n*. **heed·less** *adj*. **heed·less·ness** *n*. ⟨Old English *hēdan*⟩

hee·haw ['hi,hɒ] *n* 1 the braying sound made by a donkey. 2 a loud, coarse laugh. **hee·haw** *v*. ⟨imitative⟩

heel¹ [hil] *n* 1 the back part of a person's foot, below the ankle. 2 the part of an animal's hind leg that corresponds to a person's heel. 3 anything shaped, used, or placed at an end like a heel. The end crust of a loaf of bread is sometimes called a heel. 4 *Informal* a contemptible person.
v 1 follow closely behind (someone): *I'm teaching my dog to heel*. 2 put a heel on. 3 touch or drive forward with the heel or as if with the heel: *She heeled the horse*. ⟨Old English *hēla*⟩
cool one's heels *Informal* be kept waiting a long time. **down at (the) heel** or **heels a** of a shoe or shoes, with the heels worn down. **b** in a shabby condition: *The whole place looked very down at the heel*. **drag one's heels a** slow up on purpose. **b** work without enthusiasm. **kick up one's heels** have fun. **out at the heels a** with the heel of the stocking or shoe worn through. **b** shabby and run-down. **take to one's heels** run away. **to heel a** close behind: *The dog walked to heel*. **b** under control: *He brought the crew to heel*.

heel² [hil] *v* lean over to one side: *The ship heeled as it turned*. ⟨alteration of earlier *heeld*, Old English *h(i)eldan; heald* inclined⟩

heft [heft] *Informal n* mass or heaviness.
v 1 judge the mass of by lifting: *She hefted the baseball bat to get the feel of it*. 2 lift; heave. ⟨*heave*, by analogy with *thieve, theft,* etc.⟩
heft·y ['hɛfti] *adj Informal* 1 weighty; heavy: *a hefty load*. 2 large: *a hefty bill for repairs*. 3 big and strong. **hef·ti·ly** *adv*. **hef·ti·ness** *n*.

he·gem·o·ny [hə'dʒɛməni] *or* ['hɛdʒə,mouni] *n* political domination, esp, leadership by one state over others in a group. **heg·e·mon·ic** [,hɛdʒə'mɒnɪk] *adj*. ⟨Greek *hēgemōn* leader; *hēgeesthai* lead⟩

heif·er ['hɛfər] *n* a young cow that has not yet had a calf. ⟨Old English *hēahfore*⟩

height [həit] *n* 1 the measurement from top to bottom: *My father's height is 187 cm*. 2 the distance above sea level. 3 a fairly great distance up: *rising at a height above the valley*. 4 a high point or place: *on the mountain heights*. 5 the highest part: *She had reached the height of her career by the age of forty*. ⟨Old English *hīehthu; hēah* high⟩

height·en v 1 make or become higher. 2 make or become stronger, more intense, etc.: *The background music heightened the feeling of suspense.* **height of land 1** a region higher than its surroundings. **2** ✷ a watershed: *A height of land marks the boundary between Labrador and Québec.*

Heil·tsuk ['haɪltsʊk] n 1 a member of a First Nations people living on the coast of British Columbia. 2 their Wakashan language. **Heiltsuk** *adj.* Also called **Bella Bella.**

Heimlich manoeuvre ['haɪmlɪk] an emergency procedure used to dislodge food from a person's airway by pressing one's fist into the victim's abdomen and giving upward thrusts. ⟨H.J. *Heimlich*, US physician⟩

hei·nous ['heinəs] or ['hinəs] adj very wicked; abominable: *a heinous crime.* **hei·nous·ly** adv. **hei·nous·ness** n. ⟨Old French *haïnos; haïr* to hate⟩

heir [ɛr] n 1 a person who has the right to receive property after the death of its owner. 2 a person to whom some trait, ideal, task, etc. passes from someone who lived before him or her. ⟨Latin *heres* heir⟩ **heir apparent** pl **heirs apparent** a person who will be the first to succeed to a property or title. **heir·ess** ['ɛrɪs] n 1 a female heir. 2 a female heir to great wealth. **heir·loom** n a possession handed down from generation to generation. **heir presumptive** pl **heirs presumptive** a person who will be heir unless someone with a stronger claim is born.

heist [haɪst] *Slang* v rob or steal. **heist** n. ⟨alteration of *hoist*⟩

held [hɛld] v pt and pp of HOLD[1].

hel·i·cal See HELIX.

hel·i·cop·ter ['hɛlə,kɒptər] n an aircraft having horizontal propellers by means of which it can take off and land vertically, and move forward, backward, or sideways. ⟨Greek *helikos* (form of *helix*) spiral + *pteron* wing⟩ **hel·i·pad** n a small piece of level surface for helicopters to land or take off. **hel·i·port** n a place for helicopters to land or take off.

he·li·o·cen·tric [,hiliou'sɛntrɪk] adj to do with having the sun as a centre: *The Copernican system of astronomy is heliocentric.* Compare GEOCENTRIC. ⟨Greek *helios* sun + CENTRE⟩

he·li·o·trope ['hiliə,troup] or ['hiljə,troup] n any of a genus of herbs of the borage family, having flowers that always turn to face the sun. ⟨Greek *hēlios* sun + *tropos* a turning⟩ **he·li·ot·ro·pism** [,hili'ɒtrə,pɪzəm] n of certain plants and other organisms, a tendency to respond to sunlight by turning toward it or away from it. **he·li·o·trop·ic** [,hiliə'trɒpɪk] adj. **he·li·o·trop·i·cal·ly** adv.

hel·i·pad, hel·i·port See HELICOPTER.

he·li·um ['hiliəm] n an inert gas that will not burn. *Symbol* **He** ⟨Greek *hēlios* sun⟩

he·lix ['hiliks] n, pl **hel·i·ces** ['hɛlə,siz] or **he·lix·es 1** a spiral shape or form. 2 *Anatomy* the inward-curving rim of the outer ear.

hel·i·cal ['hɛləkəl] adj. **hel·i·cal·ly** adv. ⟨Greek *helix, helikos* a spiral⟩

hell [hɛl] n 1 in various belief systems, the home of the Devil, where wicked persons suffer punishment after death, thought of as below or within the earth. Compare HEAVEN (def. 1). 2 a place or state of wickedness or misery: *War is hell.* 3 *Informal* a severe scolding: *Her mother gave her hell for being rude.* 4 *Informal* wild, mischievous spirits: *The kids were full of hell that day.*
interj Slang an exclamation of annoyance: *Hell! There goes another fuse.* **hell·ish** adj. **hell·ish·ness** n. ⟨Old English⟩
come hell or high water *Informal* whatever difficulties arise: *I'm going, come hell or high water.* **like hell a** *Informal* very hard, fast, etc.: *I worked like hell.* **b** *Slang* an exclamation expressing strong disagreement: *Like hell is she going to use my car!* **raise hell** *Informal* cause trouble; make a disturbance: *The disgruntled prisoners started raising hell.*
hell·bent *Slang adj* recklessly determined (usually with *for* or *on*): *He was hellbent on spending all his money. adv* recklessly or wildly: *She came tearing hellbent around the corner.* **hellbent for leather** at extremely high speed. **hell·cat** n 1 a spiteful woman. 2 witch. **hell·fire** n the fire of hell; punishment in hell. **hell·hole** n *Informal* a place of great discomfort, filth, squalor, etc.

hel·le·bore ['hɛlə,bɔr] n any of a genus of poisonous plants of the buttercup family. ⟨Greek *helleboros*⟩

Hel·len·ic [hə'lɛnɪk] or [hə'linɪk] adj Greek. ⟨Greek *Hellēn* mythical father of the Greeks⟩ **Hel·len·ist** n a scholar skilled in the ancient Greek language, literature, and culture. **Hel·len·ize** ['hɛlə,naɪz] v use or imitate the Greek language, ideals, or customs. **Hel·len·i·za·tion** n.

hel·lion ['hɛljən] n *Informal* a mischievous or troublesome person. ⟨origin uncertain⟩

hel·lo [hɛ'lou] or [hə'lou] *interj* an exclamation used in greeting or to express surprise or attract attention. Also, **hal·lo, hul·lo.**

helm [hɛlm] n 1 the handle or wheel by which a ship is steered. 2 a position of control *The situation improved after the new director took over the helm.* ⟨Old English *helma*⟩ **helms·man** n, pl **-men** the person at the helm of a ship.

hel·met ['hɛlmɪt] n a covering to protect the head. ⟨Old French *helmet* diminutive of *helme* protective head covering; Germanic⟩

help [hɛlp] v 1 provide with what is needed. 2 assist: *to help someone with her work.* 3 make better: *medicine to help a cough.* 4 avoid; keep from: *He can't help yawning.* 5 serve with food (usually with a reflexive pronoun): *They helped themselves to some sandwiches.*
n 1 anything done or given in aid: *Your advice is a great help.* 2 assistance: *I need some help with my work.* 3 a person or thing that helps.

4 a means of making better: *The medicine was a help.* **help·er** *n.* **help·ful** *adj.* **help·ful·ly** *adv.* **help·ful·ness** *n.* ⟨Old English *helpan*⟩
cannot help but *Informal* cannot fail to: *I cannot help but admire her endurance.* **help oneself a** take what one wishes, etc.: *Help yourself to a drink.* **b** control oneself: *She couldn't help herself.* **help out** give temporary help. **so help me (God)** a mild oath meaning: I speak the truth.
help·ing *n* a portion of food. **help·less** *adj* **1** not able to help oneself; weak. **2** without help, protection, etc. **help·less·ness** *n.*

SYNONYMS
Help emphasizes actively providing whatever support another needs for any purpose: *He helps his mother at home.* Assist suggests standing by to help in any way needed: *A nurse assists a doctor.*

hel·ter–skel·ter [ˈhɛltər ˈskɛltər] *adv* with disorderly haste: *The children ran helter-skelter when the dog rushed at them.* ⟨imitative⟩

hem¹ [hɛm] *n* **1** a finished edge on an article of cloth. **2** any rim or margin. **hem, hemmed, hem·ming** *v.* ⟨Old English *hemm*⟩
hem in around (or **about**) **a** surround on all sides. **b** keep from getting away.
hem·line *n* the relative length of a skirt.

hem² [hɛm] *interj* a word to represent the sound of clearing the throat. **hem, hemmed, hem·ming** *v.* ⟨imitative⟩
hem and haw hesitate in order to avoid committing oneself: *She hemmed and hawed for weeks and then handed the problem to me.*

he–man See HE.

hem·a·tite [ˈhɛməˌtait] *or* [ˈhiməˌtait] *n* a naturally occurring mineral, a valuable ore of iron. Also, **haem·a·tite.** ⟨Greek *haimatitēs* bloodlike; *haima, haimatos* blood⟩

he·ma·tol·o·gy [ˌhiməˈtɒlədʒi] *or* [ˌhɛmə-] *n* the branch of physiology that deals with the structure, function, and diseases of the blood. **he·ma·tol·o·gist** or **hae·ma·tol·o·gist** *n.* ⟨Greek *haima* blood ⟩
he·ma·to·ma [ˌhiməˈtoumə] *or* [ˌhɛmə-] *n, pl* **-mas** or **-ma·ta** [-mətə] a swelling filled with blood. **he·mo·glo·bin** [ˈhiməˌgloubən] *n Biochemistry* the protein matter in the red corpuscles of the blood, which carries oxygen from the lungs and carbon dioxide to the lungs. **he·mo·phil·i·a** [ˌhiməˈfiliə] *or* [ˌhɛmə-] *n Pathology* an inherited condition in which the blood does not clot normally. **he·mo·phil·i·ac** *n* a person suffering from hemophilia. **hem·or·rhage** [ˈhɛmərɪdʒ] *n* **1** a discharge of blood from the blood vessels. **2** a steady loss of something vital, such as money. **hem·or·rhage** *v.* **hem·or·rhag·ic** [ˌhɛməˈrædʒɪk] *adj.* **hem·or·rhoids** [ˈhɛməˌrɔidz] *n pl* swollen veins near the anus caused by the dilation of blood vessels.

hem·i·ple·gia [ˌhɛməˈplidʒiə] *n* paralysis of one side of the body.
hem·i·ple·gic [ˌhɛməˈplidʒɪk] *adj.* ⟨Greek *hēmi-* half + *plēgē* stroke⟩
hem·i·sphere [ˈhɛmɪˌsfir] *n* **1** a half of a

sphere or globe. **2** a half of the earth's surface. **3** *Anatomy* CEREBRAL HEMISPHERE. **hem·i·spher·ic** [ˌhɛmɪˈsfɛrɪk] *adj.* ⟨Greek *hēmi-* half + *sphaira* sphere⟩

hem·lock [ˈhɛmlɒk] *n* **1** any of a genus of evergreen trees of the pine family having bark that is rich in tannin. **2** a poisonous plant of the parsley family. ⟨Old English *hymlice*⟩

hemo– See HEMATOLOGY.

hemp [hɛmp] *n* **1** a plant of the mulberry family whose tough fibres are made into rope, coarse cloth, etc. **2** hashish, marijuana, or some other drug obtained from the female hemp plant. ⟨Old English *henep*⟩

hen [hɛn] *n* **1** the adult female of the domestic fowl. **2** the adult female of certain other birds and a few animals: *a hen sparrow, a hen lobster.* **hen·like** *adj.* ⟨Old English *henn*⟩
scarce as hen's teeth *Informal* very scarce.
hen·house *n* a shelter for poultry. **hen·pecked** *adj Informal* domineered over by one's wife: *He's a tyrant at work, but henpecked at home.*

hence [hɛns] *adv* **1** therefore: *The attempts to raise money have failed; hence the project will have to be abandoned.* **2** from now: *A year hence, the incident will have been forgotten.* **3** *Archaic* from here: *Get thee hence.* **4** from this origin: *Hence came several problems.* ⟨Middle English *hennes;* Old English *heonan + -s,* adv ending⟩
hence·forth *adv* from now on.

USAGE
Hence is a formal word for the less formal consequently or therefore and the general so: *She has not answered our last letter; hence it would seem she is not interested.*

hench·man [ˈhɛntʃmən] *n, pl* **-men 1** a follower who obeys orders without scruple: *One of his henchmen collected the blackmail money.* **2** a trusted attendant or follower. ⟨Middle English *henxtman;* Old English *hengest* horse + *man;* orig groom or squire⟩

hen·na [ˈhɛnə] *n* a shrub of the loosestrife family which yields a dark orange-red dye.
adj reddish brown.
v colour with henna: *to henna one's hair.* ⟨Arabic *henna'*⟩

hen·ry [ˈhɛnri] *n, pl* **-ries** or **-rys** *Electricity* an SI unit for measuring inductance. When a current varying at the rate of one ampere per second induces an electromotive force of one volt, the circuit has inductance of one henry. *Symbol* **H** ⟨J. Henry, 19c US physicist⟩

he·pat·ic [həˈpætɪk] *adj* to do with the liver. ⟨Greek *hēpatos* liver⟩
hep·a·ti·tis [ˌhɛpəˈtaitɪs] *n* inflammation of the liver.

hepta– *combining form* seven: *heptagon.* ⟨Greek = seven⟩
hep·ta·gon [ˈhɛptəˌgɒn] *n* a figure having seven sides. **hep·tag·o·nal** [hɛpˈtægənəl] *adj.* **hep·ta·he·dron** [ˌhɛptəˈhidrən] *n, pl* **-drons** or **-dra** a solid with seven faces. **hep·ta·he·dral** *adj.* **hep·tam·e·ter** [hɛpˈtæmətər] *n* a line of

verse having seven metrical feet. *Example*:
And thríce I he róut I ed áll I his foés, I
and thríce I he sléw I the sláin.
hept·a·met·ric *adj*.

her [hɜr] *pron* the objective form of SHE.
adj **1** a possessive form of SHE. **2 Her** a word
used as part of any of certain formal titles:
Her Majesty the Queen. ⟨Old English *hire*⟩
hers *pron* a possessive form of SHE. **of hers**
associated with her: *He's a friend of hers*.
her·self *pron* **1** a reflexive pronoun, the form
of **she** used as an object: *She asked herself if it
was really worth the trouble*. **2** a form of **she** or
her added for emphasis: *She did it herself*.
3 her usual self: *She is not herself today*.

> **USAGE**
> Her and hers are possessive forms of she.
> Her is a determiner and is always followed by
> a noun: *This is her bicycle*. Hers is a pronoun
> and stands alone: *This bicycle is hers*.

her·ald ['herəld] *n* **1** a person who carries
official messages, or makes announcements.
2 a forerunner: *Dawn is the herald of day*.
v **1** give news of: *The robins heralded the
arrival of spring*. **2** greet enthusiastically; hail:
Her election was heralded by the newspapers.
⟨West Germanic *heriwald* army chief⟩
he·ral·dic [hə'rældɪk] *adj* to do with heraldry
or heralds. **her·ald·ry** *n* the art dealing with
coats of arms.

herb [hɜrb] *or* [ɜrb] *n* **1** any flowering plant
whose stalk lives only one season. **2** any of
many plants having aromatic leaves, roots,
etc. that are used for flavouring food, in
medicines., etc. **herb·like** *adj*. ⟨Latin *herba*⟩
her·ba·ceous [hər'beiʃəs] *adj* **1** of or like a
herb. **2** *Botany* having the colour, texture,
etc. of leaves: *a flower with herbaceous sepals*.
herb·al ['hɜrbəl] *or* ['ɜrbəl] *adj* to do with
herbs: *herbal tea*. *n* a book about herbs, esp
one that describes their uses as medicine.
herb·al·ist *n* a person who deals in herbs.
her·bi·cide ['hɜrbə,saɪd] *n* any chemical
substance used to destroy plants or stop their
growth. **her·bi·vore** ['hɜrbə,vɔr] *n* any animal
that eats plants, esp a hoofed animal such as
a cow. **her·biv·o·rous** *adj*.

her·cu·le·an [,hɜrkjə'liən] *or* [hər'kjuliən] *adj*
having or requiring great strength or
courage. ⟨*Hercules*, in Greek myth a hero of
great strength and courage⟩

herd [hɜrd] *n* **1** a number of animals of one
kind together. **2** people as a mass: *the
common herd*. **3** the keeper of a herd (usually
in compounds): *cowherd, goatherd*.
v **1** bring or come together as if in a herd: *The
cattle were herded into the corral*. **2** drive or
take care of cattle, sheep, etc.: *Her job is
herding sheep*. ⟨Old English *heord*⟩
herds·man *pl* **-men** or **herd·er** *n* a manager or
keeper of a herd of animals.

here [hir] *adv* **1** in, at, or to this place. **2** at
this point in an argument, conversation,
etc.: *Here the speaker paused*. **3** a word used to
call attention: *Here, take your scarf*.
n this place: *Fill the bottle up to here*.

interj an exclamation of indignation, rebuke,
etc.: *Here, give me that!* ⟨Old English *hēr*⟩
here! present! (in answer to a roll call). **here
and there** in various places. **here goes!**
Informal announcement of something bold
about to be done. **here's to** a wish for health
or success to. **here, there, and everywhere** in
many different places. **here you are** here is
what you want. **neither here nor there** off
the subject; unimportant. **the here and now**
the present time and place.
here·a·bouts [,hirə'bʌuts] *or* ['hirə,bʌuts] *adv*
around here. **here·af·ter** *adv* **1** in the future.
2 in life after death. *n* **the hereafter** life after
death. **here·by** [,hir'baɪ] *or* ['hir,baɪ] *adv
Formal* by this means: *I hereby certify that I am
over 21*. **here·in** [,hir'ɪn] *adv Formal* in this
place, book, etc. **here·to·fore** [,hirtə'fɔr] *or*
['hirtə,fɔr] *adv Formal* before this time.
here·un·der [,hir'ʌndər] *adv Formal* **1** in a
book, document, etc., below: *according to the
terms specified hereunder*. **2** in accordance with
this. **here·up·on** [,hirə'pɒn] *or* ['hirə,pɒn] *adv
Formal* **1** upon this. **2** right after this, usually
as a result. **here·with** [,hir'wɪθ] *or* [,hir'wɪð]
adv Formal with this.

he·red·i·ty [hə'rɛdəti] *n* **1** *Biology* the
transmission of characteristics from parent
to offspring through genes. **2** the
transmission from one generation to another
of property, titles, customs, etc. by
inheritance or tradition. ⟨Latin *hereditas*
inheritance; *heredis* heir⟩
he·red·i·tar·y *adj* **1** coming by inheritance: *a
hereditary title*. **2** *Biology* transmitted or
caused by heredity: *Colour blindness is
hereditary*. Compare CONGENITAL. **3** derived
from one's ancestors: *a hereditary enemy*.
her·it·a·bil·i·ty [,herətə'bɪləti] *n* a statistical
measure of the variation in a trait in a
population, that is caused by genetics rather
than environment or chance. **her·it·a·ble** *adj*
capable of being inherited, or capable of
inheriting. **her·it·age** *n* **1** what is or may be
handed on to a person from his or her
ancestors. **2** something that a person has as a
result of having been born in a certain time,
condition, etc.: *a heritage of violence*.

her·e·sy ['herəsi] *n* a belief different from the
accepted belief of a church, school,
profession, etc. ⟨Greek *hairesis* a taking,
choosing; *haireein* take⟩
her·e·tic ['herətɪk] *n, adj* holding such a belief.
he·ret·i·cal [hə'rɛtəkəl] *adj*.

her·maph·ro·dite [hər'mæfrə,daɪt] *n*
1 *Biology* an animal or plant having the
reproductive organs of both sexes. **2** a person
or thing that combines opposite qualities.
her·maph·ro·dite *adj*. **her·maph·ro·dit·ic**
[hər,mæfrə'dɪtɪk] *adj*. ⟨*Hermaphroditos*, in
Greek myth a son of Hermes and Aphrodite,
who became united in body with a nymph⟩

her·me·neu·tics [,hɜrmə'njutɪks] *or* [-'nutɪks]
n (with sg verb) the study of the principles of
literary and scriptural interpretation.
her·me·neu·tic *adj*. **her·me·neu·ti·cal·ly** *adv*.
⟨Greek *hermēneus* interpreter, translator⟩

her·met·ic [hər'mɛtɪk] *adj* **1** airtight. **2** of a poem, very difficult to interpret. **3** magical. **her·met·i·cal·ly** *adv.* ⟨Latin *hermeticus; Hermes* Trismegistus, supposed author of a work on magic and alchemy⟩

her·mit ['hɜrmɪt] *n* a person who lives alone in some lonely place, often for religious reasons. **her·mit·like** *adj.* ⟨Greek *erēmitēs; erēmia* desert, *erēmos* uninhabited⟩ **her·mit·age** *n* a place to live away from other people. **hermit crab** any of various crustaceans resembling crabs, that live in and carry around the empty shells of molluscs.

her·ni·a ['hɜrniə] *n, pl* **-ni·as** *or* **-ni·ae** [-ni,i] *or* [-ni,aɪ] *Pathology* the protrusion of a part of the intestine or some other organ through a break in its surrounding walls; a rupture. **her·ni·al** *adj.* ⟨Latin⟩

he·ro ['hirou] *n, pl* **-roes 1** a person admired for doing brave deeds. **2** a person admired for contributing to a particular field: *a football hero.* **3** the most important male person in a story, play, motion picture, etc. **4** *Myth and legend* a man of more than human qualities, such as Hercules. ⟨Greek *heros*⟩ **he·ro·ic** [hɪ'rouɪk] *adj* **1** brave; noble: *heroic deeds.* **2** to do with heroes and their deeds: *The* Iliad *and the* Odyssey *are heroic poems.* **3** unusually daring or bold: *Only heroic measures could save the town from the flood.* **4** unusually large. *n* **heroics** *pl* words or actions that seem noble but are only for effect. **he·ro·i·cal·ly** *adv.* **heroic couplet** two successive and rhyming lines of verse in iambic pentameter. **heroic verse** a poetic form used in heroic and other long poems. **her·o·ine** ['hɛrouɪn] *n* **1** a female hero: *Roberta Bondar is a space heroine.* **2** the most important female person in a story, play, motion picture, etc. **3** *Myth and legend* a woman or girl having more than human qualities, such as Medea. **her·o·ism** ['hɛrou,ɪzəm] *n* great bravery. **he·ro–wor·ship** ['hirou-] *v* **-shipped** *or* **-shiped, -ship·ping** *or* **-ship·ing** *v* idolize; worship as a hero. **he·ro–wor·ship** *or* **hero worship** *n.* **he·ro–wor·ship·per** *or* **he·ro–wor·ship·er** *n.*

her·o·in ['hɛrouɪn] *n* a habit-forming sedative drug made from morphine. ⟨German, former trademark; possibly *hero*⟩

her·on ['hɛrən] *n* any of various wading birds having a long neck that is doubled back in flight. ⟨Old French *hairon*⟩

her·pes ['hɜrpiz] *n* any of several virus diseases of the skin or mucous membranes, characterized by blisters. **Herpes simplex** is a type of herpes marked by watery blisters, esp on the mouth, lips, or genitals. ⟨Greek *herpēs* shingles; *herpein* creep⟩

her·ring ['hɛrɪŋ] *n, pl* **-ring** *or* **-rings** a small, silvery fish, one of the most important food fishes in the world. ⟨Old English *hæring*⟩ **her·ring·bone** *n* **1** a zigzag pattern, resembling the spine of a herring. **2** cloth with a small zigzag pattern. **3** *Skiing* a method of going up a slope by pointing the front of the skis outward and putting the

weight on the inner side. **herring choker** ✴ *Slang* a person from the Maritime Provinces, esp one from New Brunswick.

hers See HER.

hertz [hɜrts] *n, pl* **hertz** an SI unit for measuring the frequency of waves and vibrations, equal to one cycle per second. *Symbol* **Hz** ⟨H. R. *Hertz* 19c German physicist⟩

hes·i·tate ['hɛzə,teit] *v* **1** hold back because one feels doubtful. **2** be reluctant because of scruples: *I hesitated to ask you because you were so busy.* **3** pause: *He hesitated before asking the question.* **hes·i·tat·ing·ly** *adv.* **hes·i·ta·tion** *n.* ⟨Latin *haesitare; haerere* stick fast⟩ **hes·i·tan·cy** ['hɛzətənsi] *n* hesitation; doubt; indecision. **hes·i·tant** *adj.* **hes·i·tant·ly** *adv.*

SYNONYMS

Hesitate emphasizes holding back, unable to act promptly: *I hesitated about taking the job.* **Falter** suggests giving way after starting to act: *I went to apologize, but faltered at the door.* **Waver** suggests being unable to stick firmly to a decision: *My confidence in him wavers.*

het·er·o·dox ['hɛtərə,dɒks] *adj* differing from an acknowledged standard; not orthodox: *a heterodox belief.* **het·er·o·dox·y** *n.* ⟨Greek *heteros* other + *doxa* opinion⟩

het·er·o·ge·ne·ous [,hɛtərə'dʒiniəs] *adj* **1** different in kind. **2** made up of unlike elements. Compare HOMOGENEOUS. **3** *Mathematics* of different kinds and having no common integral division except 1. **het·er·o·ge·ne·i·ty** [,hɛtərədʒə'niəti] *n.* **het·er·o·ge·ne·ous·ly** *adv.* ⟨Greek *heteros* other + *genos* kind⟩

het·er·o·sex·u·al [,hɛtərə'sɛkʃuəl] *adj* **1** *Biology* to do with the different sexes. **2** to do with sexual feeling for a person of the opposite sex. Compare HOMOSEXUAL. ⟨Greek *heteros* other + SEX⟩ **het·er·o·sex·u·al** *n.* **het·er·o·sex·u·al·ly** *adv.* **het·er·o·sex·u·al·i·ty** *n.*

heu·ris·tic [hjʊ'rɪstɪk] *adj* **1** guiding or helping one to discover: *heuristic reasoning.* **2** *Education* to do with encouraging students to use personal investigation to find things out for themselves. *n* *Computers* a procedure used to solve a problem in a way that imitates human intelligence. **heu·ris·ti·cal·ly** *adv.* ⟨Greek *heuristein* to find⟩

hew [hju] *v* **hewed, hewed** *or* **hewn, hew·ing** **1** cut with an axe, sword, etc. **2** conform (*to*): *The newspaper hews strictly to the party line.* **hewn** *adj.* ⟨Old English *hēawan*⟩

hex [hɛks] *Informal v* practise witchcraft on. *n* a magic spell. ⟨German *Hexe* witch⟩

hexa– ['hɛksə] *combining form* six: *hexagon.* ⟨Greek *hex* six⟩

hex·a·gon ['hɛksə,gɒn] *n* a figure with six sides. **hex·ag·o·nal** [hɛk'sægənəl] *adj.*

hex·a·gram *n* a six-pointed star formed of two equilateral triangles. **hex·a·he·dron** [,hɛksə'hidrən] *n, pl* **-drons** *or* **-dra** a solid with six faces. **hex·a·he·dral** *adj.*

hex·am·e·ter [hɛk'sæmətər] *n* a line of poetry having six metrical feet. **hex·a·met·ric** *adj*.

hey [hei] *interj* a sound made to attract attention, to express surprise or other feeling, or to ask a question.

hey·day ['hei,dei] *n* the period of greatest strength, vigour, spirits, prosperity, etc. ⟨origin uncertain⟩

hi [hai] *interj Informal* a call of greeting; hello.

hi·a·tus [hai'eitəs] *n, pl* -**tus·es** or -**tus** an empty space; gap. ⟨Latin, from *hiare* to gape⟩

hi·ba·chi [hɪ'bɑtʃi] *n* a container in which charcoal is burned for cooking, heating, etc. ⟨Japanese *hi* fire + *bachi* bowl⟩

hi·ber·nate ['haibər,neit] *v* spend the winter in an inactive condition, as bears do. Compare ESTIVATE. **hi·ber·na·tion** *n*. ⟨Latin *hibernare; hibernus* wintry⟩
hi·ber·nal [hai'bɜrnəl] *adj* to do with winter.

hi·bis·cus [hə'bɪskəs] *or* [hai'bɪskəs] *n* any of a genus of shrubs and trees of the mallow family, cultivated for their large flowers. ⟨Latin⟩

hic·cup ['hɪkʌp] *or* ['hɪkəp] *n* **1** a sudden, involuntary contraction of the diaphragm, producing a characteristic, short, clicking sound. **2 the hiccups** *pl* the state of having one hiccup after another. **hic·cup, hic·cupped, hic·cup·ping** *v*. Also, **hic·cough** ['hɪkʌp]. ⟨probably imitative⟩

hick [hɪk] *Slang n* **1** a farmer or farm worker. **2** an unsophisticated person. **hick** *adj*. ⟨*Hick*, form of *Richard*, a man's name⟩

hick·ey ['hɪki] *n Informal* a lovebite.

hick·o·ry ['hɪkəri] *n* any of a genus of trees of the walnut family. The nuts of some species are edible. ⟨Algonquian⟩

hide¹ [haid] *v* **hid, hid·den** or **hid, hid·ing 1** conceal. **2** keep secret: *She hid her anxiety.*
n a shelter for hiding from birds or animals; blind. **hid·den** *adj*. ⟨Old English *hȳdan*⟩
hide out remain concealed: *The bandits hid out for several weeks.*
hide–and–(go–)seek *n* a children's game in which one player has to find the others, who are hidden in different places. **hide·a·way** *n* **1** a place of concealment. **2** a quiet, restful place. **hide·out** *n* a place for hiding or being alone. **hid·ey–hole** or **hid·y–hole** *n Informal* hideaway. **hid·ing** *n*. the condition of being hidden; concealment.

SYNONYMS
Hide is the general word: *I hid the present in my closet.* **Conceal** is more formal and usually suggests hiding with intent to deceive: *She concealed the note in her dress.*

hide² [haid] *n* **1** the skin of an animal, either raw or tanned. **2** a person's skin. ⟨Old English *hȳd*⟩
neither hide nor hair nothing at all.
hide·bound *adj* **1** of cattle, etc., with the skin sticking close to the bones. **2** stubborn and narrow-minded. **hid·ing** *n Informal* beating.

hid·e·ous ['hɪdiəs] *adj* **1** very ugly; frightful: *a hideous monster.* **2** terrible; revolting; abominable: *a hideous crime.* **hid·e·ous·ly** *adv*. **hid·e·ous·ness** *n*. ⟨Old French *hide* fear, horror⟩

hi·er·ar·chy ['hai,rɑrki] *n* **1** the order of higher and lower ranks in an organization. **2** church government by a body of clergy according to rank. **hi·er·ar·chi·cal** or **hi·er·arch·ic** *adj*. **hi·er·ar·chi·cal·ly** *adv*. ⟨Greek *hieros* sacred + *archos* ruler⟩

hi·er·at·ic [,haiə'rætɪk] *or* [hai'rætɪk] *adj* **1** to do with the priestly caste. **2** to do with a form of Egyptian writing used by the early priests in their records. **3** to do with certain styles in art in which earlier methods, fixed by religious tradition, are conventionally followed. Also, **hi·er·at·i·cal. hi·er·at·i·cal·ly** *adv*. ⟨Greek *hieros* sacred (one)⟩

hi·er·o·glyph·ic [,haiə'glɪfɪk] *n* **1** a character or picture of an object standing for a word, idea, or sound. **2** a secret symbol. **3** a letter or word that is hard to read. **4 hieroglyphics** *pl* **a** any system of writing that uses hieroglyphics. **b** *Informal* writing that is hard to read. Also (defs 1-3) **hi·er·o·glyph. hi·er·o·glyph·ic** *adj*. **hi·er·o·glyph·i·cal·ly** *adv*. ⟨Greek *hieros* sacred + *glyphē* carving⟩

hi–fi ['hai 'fai] *Informal adj* high-fidelity.
n high-fidelity reproduction of music, etc. or the equipment for such reproduction.

hig·gle·dy–pig·gle·dy ['hɪgəldi 'pɪgəldi] *adv* in jumbled confusion. ⟨imitative⟩

high [hai] *adj* **1** of more than usual height: *a high building.* **2** being a specified distance from top to bottom (following a noun): *The mountain is 6100 m high.* **3** far above the ground: *an airplane high in the air.* **4** senior to others in rank or position: *a high official.* **5** superior: *a person of high character.* **6** great; intense: *high temperature.* **7** most important: *the high altar.* **8** costly: *Berries are high in winter.* **9** above the normal pitch: *a high voice.* **10** smelling bad as a result of decay: *I prefer to eat game after it has become high.* **11** *Slang* excited by or as if by alcohol or drugs.
adv at or to a high point, rank, amount, degree, price, pitch, etc.: *The eagle flies high.*
n **1** a high point, level, position, etc.: *Food prices reached a new high last month.* **2** *Meteorology* an area of high barometric pressure: *a high is approaching from the west.* **3** *Slang* a state of euphoria produced by or as if by drugs. ⟨Old English *hēah*⟩
from on high from heaven. **high and dry a** out of the water: *The fish was high and dry on the beach.* **b** without help: *She has left me high and dry with all this work to do.* **high and low** everywhere: *We looked high and low but couldn't find the letter.* **on high** in or to heaven. **run high** reach a high pitch: *Tempers ran high at election time.*
High Arctic * the arctic islands and the northeastern part of the arctic mainland of Canada. **high·ball** *n* **1** whisky, brandy, etc. mixed with soda water or ginger ale. **2** a railway signal to proceed. *v* **1** *Slang* **a** move or drive at high speed. **b** run on an accelerated

schedule. **2** signal to (the engineer of a train) to proceed. **high·born** *adj* of noble birth. **high·brow** *Informal n* a person who has strong intellectual interests, esp one thought to have a feeling of superiority because of this. **high·brow** *adj.* **high·chair** *n* a baby's tall chair for feeding. **High Church** a branch of the Anglican Communion laying great emphasis on ceremonial observances, etc. Compare LOW CHURCH. **high–class** *adj* of or for a high social class. **High Commission** the embassy of one Commonwealth country in another. **High Commissioner. higher education** education beyond the level of secondary school. **high·er–up** *n Informal* a person occupying a superior position. **high·fa·lu·tin** [ˈhaɪfəˈlutən] *adj Informal* pompous; pretentious. **high–fi·del·i·ty** [ˈhaɪ fəˈdɛləti] *adj Electronics* indicating reproduction of the full audio range with a minimum of distortion. **high flier** or **high flyer** *n* a person who is extravagant or has pretentious ideas, ambitions, etc. **high–flown** *adj* **1** aspiring; extravagant. **2** attempting to be eloquent: *high-flown compliments.* **high frequency** the range of radio frequencies between 3 MHz and 30 MHz. *Abbrev* **HF, H.F.,** or **h.f. high–fre·quen·cy** *adj.* **high–grade** *adj* **1** of fine quality: *a high-grade performance.* **2** *Mining* to do with gold-bearing ore of a high assay value. *v* ✹ **1** steal small quantities of the best ore from (a mine). **2** *Logging* take only the best timber from (a stand). **high–hand·ed** *adj* disregarding the feelings of others: *a high-handed way of running things.* **high–hand·ed·ly** *adv.* **high–hand·ed·ness** *n.* **high hat** a top hat. **high jinks** or **hi·jinks** [ˈhaɪ ˌdʒɪŋks] boisterous merrymaking. **high jump** an athletic event in which the contestants try to jump as high as possible over a bar. **high·land** *n* a region that is higher and hillier than the neighbouring areas. **Highland fling** a lively dance originating in the Highlands of Scotland. **high life** a fashionable lifestyle. **high·light** *n* **1** the representation of light falling on a part of something: *dramatic highlights in a painting.* **2** the most interesting part, event, etc.: *The highlight of our trip was the drive along the Cabot Trail. v* **1** emphasize (a part of a painting, etc.) with light or bright colour. **2** make prominent: *The new product was highlighted in the company's brochures.* **high·lin·er** ✹ *n* in a Maritime fishing fleet: **1** the boat making the largest catch within a specified time. **2** the captain of such a boat. **high·ly** *adv* **1** in a high degree. **2** with much approval. **3** at a high price. **High Mass** a complete ritual of the Mass sung by the priest. Compare LOW MASS. **high–mind·ed** *adj* having high principles: *a high-minded person.* **high·mind·ed·ness** *n.* **Highness** a title of honour given to members of royal families. **high noon** exactly midday. **high–pitched** *adj* **1** of high tone or sound: *a high-pitched whistle.* **2** of a roof, having a steep slope. **3** marked by intense feeling: *the high-pitched excitement of the chase.* **high point** the climax.

high–pow·ered *adj* having much energy: *a high-powered sales talk.* **high priest 1** a chief priest. **2** the head of the ancient Jewish priesthood. **high relief** a relief sculpture in which the modelled forms project well out from the background. **high·rise** *n* a building with many storeys: *an apartment highrise.* **high·rise** *adj.* **high·road** *n* **1** a main road; highway. **2** a direct and easy way: *There is no highroad to success.* **high school** a school attended after elementary school. **high–school** *adj.* **high seas** the open ocean. The high seas are outside the jurisdiction of any country. **high sign** *Informal* any gesture used as a signal. **high–spir·it·ed** *adj* **1** having a bold, proud, or energetic spirit: *a high-spirited horse.* **2** happy. **high–spir·it·ed·ness** *n.* **high spirits** *n.* **high·stick** *v* **high·sticked, high·sticking** *Hockey and lacrosse* illegally strike or hinder (an opposing player) with one's stick raised above shoulder level. **high·stick·ing** *n.* **high–strung** *adj* very sensitive; nervous. **high·tail** *v Slang* run away at full speed. **hightail it** hurry. **high tech** [tɛk] *Informal* **1** a style of interior design that exploits the materials and features of industrial design. **2** HIGH TECHNOLOGY. **high–tech** *adj.* **high technology** advanced modern technology. **high tide 1** the highest level of the tide. **2** the time when the tide is highest. **3** a culminating point. **high time 1** the time just before it is too late: *It is high time that we left.* **2** *Informal* a lively time at a party, etc. **high–toned** *adj* **1** having a high character or principles. **2** *Informal* stylish. **high treason** treason against one's government. **high water 1** the highest level of water. **2** HIGH TIDE. **high–water mark 1** the highest level of water in a river or lake. **2** any highest point. **high·way** *n* **1** a main road connecting cities or towns. **2** ✹ a high-speed, controlled-access expressway. **3** a direct way to some end. **high·way·man** *n, pl* **-men** formerly, a man who robbed travellers on a public road.

SYNONYMS
High, the general word, describes things, not people, that rise to more than usual height: *High hills surround the valley.* **Tall** = higher than the average of its kind, and is used to describe people or something that is both high and narrow: *He is a tall man. The corn grows tall here.* **Lofty,** more literary, means 'very high, rising to an impressive height': *We saw the lofty Mount Robson.*

high muck·a·muck [ˈmʌkəˌmʌk] ✹ *Slang* a leader; big-shot. ⟨Chinook jargon *hyiu muckamuck* a good big meal⟩

hi·jack [ˈhaɪˌdʒæk] *v* **1** stop (a vehicle) in transit by force in order to steal it or its cargo. **2** seize control of (an aircraft) in flight by force in order to obtain money or some other concession. **hi·jack·er** *n.* **hi·jack·ing** *n.* ⟨origin uncertain⟩

hi–jinks *n* HIGH JINKS.

hike [haɪk] *Informal v* **1** take a long walk. **2** raise with a jerk: *He hiked himself up onto*

the platform. **3** raise; increase: *to hike wages.*
hike *n.* **hik·er** *n.* ⟨possibly related to HITCH⟩

hi·lar·i·ous [hə'lɛriəs] *adj* **1** noisily cheerful: *a hilarious party.* **2** very funny: *The joke was hilarious.* **hi·lar·i·ous·ly** *adv.* **hi·lar·i·ous·ness** *n.* **hi·lar·i·ty** [hə'lɛrəti] *or* [hə'lærəti] *n.* ⟨Greek *hilaros* merry⟩

hill [hɪl] *n* **1** a raised part on the earth's surface, smaller than a mountain. **2** a heap, of earth, sand, etc. **3 the Hill ✱** *Informal* **a** Parliament Hill. **b** Parliament.
v **1** put a little heap of soil over and around. **2** form into a heap. **hill·y** *adj.* **hill·i·ness** *n.* ⟨Old English *hyll*⟩
over the hill *Informal* past one's prime.
hill·bil·ly ['hɪl,bɪli] *Informal n* a person who lives in the backwoods or a mountain region, esp in the S United States. **hill·side** *n* the side of a hill. **hill·top** *n* the top of a hill.

hilt [hɪlt] *n.* the handle of a sword, dagger, etc. ⟨Old English⟩
to the hilt thoroughly; completely.

him [hɪm] *pron* the objective form of HE. ⟨Old English *him*, dative of *hē* he⟩
him·self *pron* **1** a reflexive pronoun, the form of **he** used as an object: *He cut himself.* **2** a form of **he** or **him** added for emphasis: *Did you see my brother himself?* **3** his usual self: *He feels himself again.*

Him·a·la·yan [,hɪmə'leiən] *or* [hə'maliən] *adj* **1** to do with the Himalayas, a mountain range along the border between India and Tibet. **2** a breed of domestic cat, a cross between Persian and Siamese.

Hi·na·ya·na [,hinə'janə] *n* a branch of Buddhism that follows the Pali scriptures and stresses meditation. ⟨Sanskrit *hina* lesser + *yanum* way⟩

hind¹ [haɪnd] *adj* **hind·er**, **hind·most** or **hind·er·most** back; rear: *The mule kicked up its hind legs.* ⟨Old English *hindrian*⟩
hind·most *adj* farthest back. **hind·quar·ter** *n* **1** the hind leg and loin of a carcass of beef, etc. **2 hindquarters**, the hind part of any four-legged animal. **hind·sight** *n Informal* the ability to see, after the event is over, what should have been done.

hind² [haɪnd] *n, pl* **hind** or **hinds** a female deer. ⟨Old English⟩

hin·der ['hɪndər] *v* keep or hold back; make difficult: *problems that hinder completion of a project.* ⟨Old English *hindrian*⟩
hin·drance ['hɪndrəns] *n* an obstacle.

Hin·du ['hɪndu] *n* a person who believes in Hinduism. **Hin·du** *adj.* ⟨Persian *Hindū; Hind* India⟩
Hin·du·ism *n* a religion and way of life that is practised mainly in India, characterized by the doctrine of transmigration of souls.

hinge [hɪndʒ] *n* **1** a movable joint by which a door, lid, etc. moves on its post, base, etc. **2** that on which something depends.
v depend (with *on* or *upon*): *The success of the enterprise will hinge on the dedication of the people involved.* **hinged** *adj.* ⟨Middle English *heng.* Related to HANG.⟩

hint [hɪnt] *n* **1** a slight indication: *A black cloud gave a hint of the coming storm.* **2** an indirect suggestion. **3** a piece of practical information: *helpful hints.* *v* give a hint (often with *at*): *The unsettled weather hinted at a storm.* **hint·ing** *adj.* ⟨obsolete *hent* seize; Old English *hentan*⟩

SYNONYMS

Hint = say something in a roundabout way: *She hinted that it was time to go to bed by saying, "Do you often stay up this late?"* **Insinuate** = suggest something unkind or nasty in a sly or underhand way: *Are you insinuating that I am a liar?*

hin·ter·land ['hɪntər,lænd] *n* **1** the region behind a coast; the inland region. **2** a region remote from major urban centres. ⟨German *hinter* behind + *Land* land⟩

hip¹ [hɪp] *n* **1** hipbone. **2** Usually, **hips** *pl* the part of the body between the waist and the thighs. ⟨Old English *hype*⟩
straight from the hip very candidly.
hip·bone *n* either of the large bones that form the main part of the pelvis in mammals. **hip roof** a roof with sloping ends and sides. **hip wader** a long rubber boot reaching to the hip, used when fishing, etc.

hip² [hɪp] *n* a pod containing the ripe seed of a rosebush. ⟨Old English *hēope*⟩

hip³ [hɪp] *adj Slang* showing knowledge about the latest trends in music, fashion, etc.: *She's hip to the music.* ⟨origin uncertain⟩
hip·pie *Slang n* **1** any of the young people of the 1960s who rejected the customs of conventional society and expressed their ideas through communal living, mysticism, the use of drugs, etc. **2** any person of a later time who adopts similar habits and attitudes.

hip·po·pot·a·mus [,hɪpə'pɒtəməs] *n, pl* **-mus·es** or **-mi** [-,mai] *or* [-,mi] a very large, plant-eating mammal having a large head with an enormous mouth. Also, **hip·po** *Informal.* ⟨Greek; *hippos* horse + *potamos* river⟩

hire [haɪr] *v* **1** take on as an employee. **2** agree to pay for the temporary use of (a thing) or the services of (a person): *He hired a car and a woman to drive it.* **3** give the use of (a thing) or the services of (a person), in return for payment (usually with *out*): *She hired out as a carpenter.*
n payment for the use of a thing or the services of a person. ⟨Old English *hȳrian*⟩
for hire available for use or work in exchange for payment: *boats for hire.*
hire·ling *n* a person available for hire. *adj* mercenary.

hir·sute [hər'sut] *or* ['hɜrsut] *adj* hairy.
hir·sute·ness *n.* ⟨Latin *hirsutus*⟩

his [hɪz] *adj* **1** the possessive form of HE. **2 His** a word used as part of certain formal titles: *His Majesty the King.*
pron the possessive form of HE. ⟨Old English *his*, genitive of *hē* he⟩
of his associated with him: *She's just a friend of his.*

hiss [hɪs] *v* **1** make a sound like that of the *s* in *see: The snake hissed.* **2** make this sound as a sign of disapproval. **hiss** *n.* ⟨imitative⟩

his·ta·mine ['hɪstə,min] *or* ['hɪstəmɪn] *n* Biochemistry an amine released by the body in allergic reactions. ⟨*hist(idine)*, an amino acid (Greek *histos* web, tissue) + *amine*⟩

his·tol·o·gy [hɪ'stɒlədʒi] *n* **1** the branch of biology dealing with the structures of animal and plant tissues as seen through a microscope. **2** the tissue structure of an animal or plant. **his·to·log·i·cal** or **his·to·log·ic** *adj.* **his·to·log·i·cal·ly** *adv.* **his·tol·o·gist** *n.* ⟨Greek *histos* web, tissue⟩

his·to·ry ['hɪstri] *or* ['hɪstəri] *n* **1** a statement of what has happened. **2** a written account of a person, nation, movement, etc.: *a history of the fur trade.* **3** all past events considered together: *one of the greatest achievements in history.* **4** *Informal.* something that is over and done with: *That whole affair is history now.* **5** CASE HISTORY. ⟨Greek *historia* inquiry, record, story⟩

make history a influence the course of history. **b** do something worthy of remembrance.

his·to·ri·an [hɪ'stɔriən] *n* **1** a person who has much knowledge of history. **2** a person who records events. **his·tor·ic** *adj* famous or important in history: *Kingston is a historic city.* **his·tor·i·cal** *adj* **1** to do with history: *a historical term.* **2** based on history: *historical fact.* **his·tor·i·cal·ly** *adv.* **historical present** the present tense used in describing past events to make them seem more vivid. **his·to·ric·i·ty** [,hɪstə'rɪsəti] *n* authenticity proved by history.

CONFUSABLES
Historic refers to being famous in history: *Halifax is a historic city.* Historical means 'to do with history': *a historical museum.*

his·tri·on·ic [,hɪstri'ɒnɪk] *adj* **1** theatrical and insincere; deliberately affected. **2** having to do with actors or acting; dramatic. *n* **histrionics** *pl* a deliberately dramatic show of emotions, for effect. **his·tri·on·i·cal·ly** *adv.* ⟨Latin *histrio* actor⟩

hit [hɪt] *v* **hit, hit·ting 1** strike: *He hit the ball with the bat.* **2** get to (what is aimed at): *Her arrow hit the bull's-eye.* **3** have a painful effect on: *The death of his sister hit him hard.* **4** occur suddenly: *when the tornado hit.* **5** reach (a certain point): *Prices hit a new high.* **6** *Baseball* make (a base hit): *She hit a double.* *n* **1** a blow; stroke. **2** the act of reaching a target. **3** a sharp attack. **4** a very successful person or thing: *My brother was a big hit at my party.* **5** *Baseball* a base hit. **hit·less** *adj.* **hit·ta·ble** *adj.* ⟨Old English *hittan;* Old Norse *hitta* meet with⟩

hard hit affected deeply: *She was hard hit by the news of her mother's death.* **hit back** retaliate. **hit below the belt** be unfair to (an opponent). **hit it off** *Informal* get along well with someone: *He hit it off with his new neighbour right away.* **hit off** mimic or represent cleverly or accurately. **hit on** (or **upon**) **a** discover by chance: *They've hit on a new idea for the contest.* **b** *Slang* make sexual advances to. **hit or miss** showing a lack of care or planning. **hit–or–miss** *adj.* **hit the books** *Informal* begin to study. **hit the nail on the head.** See NAIL. **hit the roof** (or **ceiling**) *Informal* react with a burst of anger or shock. **hit–and–run** *adj* to do with a driver who runs into another person or vehicle and drives away without stopping. *n* **1** such an accident. **2** *Baseball* a play in which the batter tries to hit the ball to protect a runner who has already left base. **hit list** *Slang* a list of people designated to be eliminated by a particular person. **hit man** *Slang* a hired murderer. **hit·ter** *n* esp in sports, a person who hits: *She's a good hitter, but not much of a fielder.*

hitch [hɪtʃ] *v* **1** fasten with a hook, rope, etc.: *She hitched her horse to a post.* **2** harness to a wagon, etc. (with *up*): *She hitched up the team and drove to town.* **3** become fastened or caught; fasten; catch. **4** *Informal* obtain by hitchhiking: *She hitched a ride home.* *n* **1** a fastening. **2** a short, sudden pull: *He gave his pants a hitch.* **3** an obstacle: *A hitch in their plans made them miss the train.* **4** a kind of knot used for temporary fastening: *She put a hitch in the rope.* **5** *Informal* a free ride from a passing automobile. **6** *Slang* a period of time, esp a period of service in the armed forces. ⟨Middle English *hyche(n)*; origin uncertain⟩

get hitched *Slang* get married. **without a hitch** smoothly; successfully.

hitching post a post for hitching horses, etc.

hitch·hike ['hɪtʃ,haik] *Informal v* travel by asking for free rides from motorists: *They hitchhiked across the country.* *n* a journey made in this way. **hitch·hik·er** *n.*

hith·er ['hɪðər] *adv* to or toward this place. *adj* on this side; nearer. ⟨Old English *hider.* Related to HERE.⟩

hither and thither or **hither and yon** in all directions: *The frightened hens ran hither and thither.* **hith·er·to** ['hɪðər,tu] *or* [,hɪðər'tu] *adv* until now.

HIV acronym for **human immunovirus**, a virus that destroys the body's capacity for immunity, and so causes AIDS.

hive [haiv] *n* **1** a box for bees to live in. **2** a large number of bees living together. **3** a busy place full of people: *On Saturdays the department store is a hive.* *v* **1** put (bees) in a hive. **2** of bees, enter a hive. **3** store up (honey) in a hive. **4** lay up for future use. **5** live close together like bees. ⟨Old English *hȳf*⟩

hives [haivz] *n* a condition characterized by small, very itchy, fluid-filled swellings on the skin, usually caused by an allergic reaction. ⟨Scottish; origin unknown⟩

ho [hou] *interj* **1** an exclamation of surprise, joy, or scorn. **2** an exclamation used to attract attention: *Land ho!*

hoar [hɔr] *n* **1** hoariness. **2** hoarfrost. ⟨Old English *hār*⟩
hoar·frost *n* a film of tiny ice crystals that sometimes forms on a cold surface. **hoar·y** *adj* **1** of hair, grey or white. **2** white or grey with age: *a hoary old man.* **3** very old. **hoar·i·ness** *n.* **hoar·y–head·ed** *adj* having white or grey hair. **hoary marmot ✺** a large grey marmot found in the mountains of western Canada. Also, **whis·tler.**

hoard [hɔrd] *n* a supply stored away. *v* save and store away: *A squirrel hoards nuts for the winter.* **hoard·er** *n.* ⟨Old English *hord*⟩

hoard·ing [ˈhɔrdɪŋ] *n* a temporary board fence put up around a construction site. ⟨*hoard* fence; apparently Anglo-French *hurdis*⟩

hoarse [hɔrs] *adj* rough and deep in sound: *a hoarse voice.* **hoarse·ly** *adv.* **hoarse·ness** *n.* ⟨Old English *hās; r* inserted from Old Norse⟩
hoars·en [ˈhɔrsən] *v* make or become hoarse.

hoax [houks] *n* a mischievous trick: *The report of an attack from Mars was a hoax.* **hoax** *v.* ⟨probably altered from *hocus*⟩

hob [hɒb] *n* a shelf at the back or side of a fireplace, used for keeping things warm. ⟨variant of HUB⟩
hob·nail *n* a nail with a large head, used to protect the soles of boots. **hob·nailed** *adj.*

hob·ble [ˈhɒbəl] *v* **1** move awkwardly: *She managed to hobble to the phone without using the crutches.* **2** put a strap, rope, etc. around the legs of (an animal, esp a horse) so that it cannot run away. **3** hinder. *n* **1** an awkward walk; limp. **2** a strap used to hobble a horse, etc. ⟨Middle English *hobelen*⟩

hob·by [ˈhɒbi] *n* something a person likes to work at apart from his or her main business or occupation. **hob·by·ist** *n.* ⟨Middle English *hoby*, from *Robin.* See HOBGOBLIN.⟩
ride a hobby give too much time or attention to one's hobby.
hob·by·horse *n* **1** a stick with a horse's head, used as a toy by children. **2** a favourite topic: *He is on his hobbyhorse of cutting costs.*

hob·gob·lin [ˈhɒbˌgɒblən] *n* **1** a mischievous elf; goblin. **2** something imaginary that gives rise to fear. ⟨*Hob* Middle English nickname for *Robert, Robin* + *goblin*⟩

hob·nob [ˈhɒbˌnɒb] *v* **-nobbed, -nob·bing** *Informal* **1** talk together on familiar terms. **2** drink together. ⟨from drinking phrase *hob or nob* give or take; Old English *hæbbe* have + *næbbe* not have⟩

ho·bo [ˈhoubou] *n, pl* **-bos** or **-boes** an itinerant worker. ⟨origin uncertain⟩

hock¹ [hɒk] *n* the joint in the hind leg of a horse, cow, etc. above the fetlock joint. ⟨Old English *hōh*⟩

hock² [hɒk] *v Informal* PAWN¹. ⟨orig noun; compare Dutch *hok* pen, jail⟩
hock·shop *n Informal* a store where goods may be pawned.
in (or **out of**) **hock a** in (or no longer in) another's possession as security; in pawn.

b in (or no longer in) debt: *She is in hock to her mother for the down payment on the house.*

hock³ [hɒk] *v Slang* steal: *Who hocked my pen?* ⟨origin uncertain⟩

hock·ey [ˈhɒki] *n* **1** a game played on ice by two teams of six players wearing skates, in which the members of each team use hooked sticks to try to shoot a small, thick, black rubber disk (the puck) into the opposing team's goal; ice hockey. **2** FIELD HOCKEY. ⟨*hock* hooked stick, variant of *hook*⟩
hockey stick a hooked or curved stick used in playing hockey.

ho·cus–po·cus [ˈhoukəs ˈpoukəs] *n* **1** sleight of hand; magic. **2** any meaningless talk or action designed to cover up a deception: *All his talk about our beautiful house and garden was just hocus-pocus.* ⟨sham Latin used by jugglers, etc.; probably alteration of *hoc est corpus* (this is the Body) from the Eucharist⟩

hod [hɒd] *n* a trough or tray on a long handle, used for carrying bricks, mortar, etc. ⟨Middle Dutch *hodde*⟩

hodge·podge [ˈhɒdʒˌpɒdʒ] *n* a confused mess; jumble. ⟨variant of *hotchpotch* from *hotchpot*; Old French *hochepot* stew; *hocher* shake + *pot* pot⟩

Hodg·kin's disease [ˈhɒdʒkənz] a cancer characterized by chronic enlargement of the lymph nodes, spleen, and, often, the liver. ⟨T. *Hodgkin*, 19c English physician⟩

hoe [hou] *n, v* **hoed, hoe·ing** *n* a tool used to loosen soil and cut weeds. **hoe** *v.* ⟨Old French *houe*⟩
hoe·down [ˈhouˌdaʊn] *n* **1** a lively dance, esp a square dance. **2** a party featuring hoedowns: *There's a hoedown Saturday night.*

hog [hɒg] *n* **1** a domestic pig, esp a full-grown, castrated male raised for meat. **2** *Informal* a selfish, greedy person. *v* **hogged, hog·ging** *Informal* take more than one's share of: *Don't hog the blanket.* **hog·like** *adj.* **hog·gish** *adj.* **hog·gish·ness** *n.* ⟨Old English *hogg*⟩
go whole hog do something thoroughly. **live** (or **eat**) **high off the hog** *Informal* live well. **hog·back** *n Geology* a low, sharp ridge with steep sides. **hog line** *Curling* a line marked across the ice 6.4 m in front of each tee, the minimum distance for a rock to remain in play. **hogs·head** *n* a large barrel or cask, esp one having a capacity of from 455 L to 635 L. **Hog·town** *n* ✺ an old name for Toronto. **hog·wash** *n* **1** refuse given to hogs; swill. **2** *Slang* worthless stuff; nonsense. **hog–wild** *adj Slang* frenzied; wildly going to extremes.

ho–hum or **ho·hum** [ˈhouhʌm] *adj* dull; routine. ⟨imitative of yawning⟩

hoi pol·loi [ˌhɔɪ pəˈlɔɪ] ordinary people; the general populace. ⟨Greek = the many⟩

hoist [hɔɪst] *v* **1** lift up, often with ropes and pulleys: *hoist sails.* **2** *Slang* drink (liquor). *n* an apparatus for lifting heavy loads. ⟨earlier *hoise;* Dutch *hijschen*⟩
hoist with one's own petard See PETARD.

hoi·ty–toi·ty [ˈhɔɪti ˈtɔɪti] *adj* **1** haughty or pompous. **2** flighty or silly.
interj an exclamation of indignant surprise. ⟨reduplication of earlier *hoighty;* origin uncertain⟩

hok·ey [ˈhouki] *adj Slang* exaggerated or contrived. ⟨*hokum*⟩

ho·key–po·key [ˈhouki ˈpouki] *n* **1** trickery; hocus-pocus. **2** a singing and dancing game performed usually by children. ⟨*hocus-pocus*⟩

ho·kum [ˈhoukəm] *n Informal* **1** pretentious nonsense. **2** elements such as crude comedy, corny sentimentality, etc., introduced into a play, show, etc. merely for their effect on the audience. ⟨perhaps from *hocus(-pocus)*⟩

hold[1] [hould] *v* **held, held, hold·ing 1** take in the hands or arms and be or stay: *Please hold my watch.* **2** keep in some condition: *Hold the paper steady while you draw.* **3** not give way: *The dike held during the flood.* **4** oblige (a person) to adhere (*to* a promise), etc.: *They held him to his promise.* **5** defend: *Hold the fort.* **6** contain: *This theatre holds 500 people.* **7** reserve: *Please hold the room for me till eight o'clock.* **8** have and keep as one's own: *to hold a valid driver's licence.* **9** have and take part in: *to hold a meeting.* **10** keep or have in mind: *to hold a belief.* **11** think: *People once held that the earth was flat.* **12** stay on a telephone: *Please hold.* **13** be in force or effect: *The rule holds in all cases.* **14** *Music* keep on singing or playing (a note). **15** *Informal* leave out; omit (from a food order): *Hold the anchovies.*
n **1** the act of holding (on): *to release one's hold.* **2** something to hold by: *She looked for a hold on the rock.* **3** a holding back; delay: *a hold in the launching of a missile.* **4** an order to temporarily halt something. **5** a controlling influence: *A habit has a hold on you.* **6** *Wrestling* a way of holding one's opponent. ⟨Old English *healdan*⟩
get hold of get in touch with (someone). **hold against** a blame for: *Don't hold it against me; it's not my fault.* **b** continue to resent (someone). **hold back** a avoid disclosing: *to hold back the truth.* **b** withhold (money, wages, etc.). **hold down** a keep under control. **b** *Informal* have and keep: *to hold down a job.* **hold forth** a talk (often disparagingly).
b offer. **hold in** restrain: *He was so angry he couldn't hold in his temper.* **hold it!** stop! **hold off** a keep at a distance. **b** keep from acting or attacking. **c** delay acting. **hold on** *Informal* **a** keep on; continue. **b** wait a minute! **hold one's own** maintain one's position in the face of opposition. **hold out** a continue; last: *The water would not hold out much longer.* **b** stretch forth: *Hold out your hand.* **c** keep resisting: *The soldiers held out for six days.* **d** *Slang* keep back something expected or due (*on* someone): *Don't hold out on me, just tell the truth.* **hold out for** continue action to get: *The strikers held out for more pay.* **hold over** a keep longer than scheduled: *The movie was held over for a week.* **b** postpone: *The game has been held over until next week.* **hold the fort** be

in charge to see that nothing goes wrong. **hold up** a continue; endure. **b** stop: *The police officer held up the traffic.* **c** *Informal* rob. **d** delay: *We were held up by an accident on the highway.* **hold with** approve of. **lay** (or **take**) **hold of** seize. **no holds barred** any method is acceptable. **on hold** waiting on the telephone **hold·back** *n* **1** something that holds back. **2** the act of holding back. **3** something held back. **hold·er** *n* **1** a person who holds a bill, cheque, etc. and is entitled to receive payment on it. **2** a person who owns or occupies property. **3** a device for holding something (usually in compounds): *a potholder.* **hold·ing** *n* **1** land, esp a piece of land rented from someone else. **2** Usually, **holdings** *pl* property, esp in the form of stocks or bonds. **3** *Sports* the illegal hindering of an opponent's movements. **holding company** a company that owns stocks of other companies and thus often controls them. **holding pattern** the usually circular pattern of movement of a plane waiting in the air for landing instructions. **hold·out** *n Informal* a person or group that refuses to accept an agreement. **hold·o·ver** *n* a person or thing held over from another time or place: *She was a holdover from last year's team.* **hold·up** *n* **1** the act of forcibly stopping and robbing. **2** delay: *She got out of her car to see what the holdup was.*

hold[2] [hould] *n* **1** the interior of a ship below the deck. **2** a similar cargo compartment in an aircraft. ⟨variant of *hole*⟩

hole [houl] *n* **1** an opening in something, often a break: *a hole in a sock.* **2** a place lower than the parts around it: *a hole in the road.* **3** burrow: *Rabbits live in holes.* **4** a dark or dirty place: *I don't want to live in that hole.* **5** *Informal* a flaw: *That argument has several holes in it.* **6** *Informal* an embarrassing or difficult position.
v **1** make a hole in: *The side of the ship was holed by an iceberg.* **2** hit or drive into a hole. **hol·ey** *adj.* ⟨Old English *hol*⟩
burn a hole in one's pocket of money, make one want badly to spend: *His birthday gift is burning a hole in his pocket.* **hole in one** *Golf* a hit made from the tee so that the ball goes into the hole. **hole out** hit a golf ball into a hole. **hole up** a of animals, go into a hole. **b** *Slang* go into hiding. **in the hole** in financial difficulties. **make a hole in** use up a large amount of: *The computer made a hole in my savings.* **pick holes in** find fault with. **the hole** solitary confinement in a prison.
hole–and–corner *adj Informal* furtive; underhand. **hole–in–the–wall** *adj Informal* insignificant; shabby.

Hole is the common word applying to an opening: *Fire burned a hole in the roof.* **Cavity** is chiefly scientific or technical, and applies only to a hollow space inside a solid mass: *The dentist filled several cavities in my teeth.*

Ho·li [ˈhouli] *n Hinduism* a popular spring festival generally dedicated to Krishna.

hol·i·day ['hɒlə,dei] n 1 a day free of work. 2 a day on which general business is suspended: *Labour Day is a holiday as specified by law.* 3 Often, **holidays** pl vacation. 4 a holy day; religious festival.
v take a holiday: *They are holidaying in the tropics.* ⟨Old English *hāligdæg* holy day⟩
on holiday taking a vacation.
holiday–maker n someone taking a vacation.

ho·li·ness See HOLY.

ho·lism ['houlɪzəm] n *Philosophy* the theory that living nature consists of wholes that are more than just the sum of their parts. Also, **who·lism. ho·list** n. ⟨Greek *hólos* whole⟩
ho·lis·tic or **who·lis·tic** adj emphasizing the relationship between parts and wholes: *holistic medicine.* **ho·lis·ti·cal·ly** adv.

hol·ler ['hɒlər] *Informal* v shout. **hol·ler** n.

hol·low ['hɒlou] adj 1 having a cavity inside: *A tube is hollow.* 2 having an inward curve: *hollow cheeks.* 3 sounding as if coming from something hollow: *a hollow groan.* 4 worthless or false: *hollow promises.* 5 empty: *a hollow stomach.*
n 1 a hollow place: *a hollow in the road.* 2 a small valley: *They built their house in a hollow.*
v make or form by hollowing (usually with out): *She hollowed out a canoe from a log.*
hol·low·ly adv. **hol·low·ness** n. ⟨Old English *holh*⟩
beat (all) hollow *Informal* defeat soundly in a competition.
hol·low·ware n bowls and pitchers of silver.

hol·ly ['hɒli] n any of a genus of trees and shrubs having thick, shiny leaves with spiny points along the edges, and clusters of bright red berries. ⟨Old English *holegn*⟩

hol·ly·hock ['hɒli,hɒk] n a tall plant of the mallow family, widely grown for its spikes of large, showy flowers. ⟨Middle English *holihoc*; Old English *hālig* holy + *hocc* mallow⟩

Hol·ly·wood ['hɒli,wʊd] n the American film industry. ⟨*Hollywood*, section of Los Angeles, California, where major studios are⟩

hol·mi·um ['houlmiəm] n a rare metallic element belonging to the yttrium group. *Symbol* Ho ⟨Stock*holm*⟩

hol·o·caust ['hɒlə,kɒst] or ['houlə,kɒst] n 1 a sacrificial offering, all of which is burned. 2 great destruction of life, esp by fire. 3 **the Holocaust** the systematic killing of Jews by the Nazi regime in Germany before and during World War II. ⟨Greek *holos* whole + *kaustos* burned⟩

Hol·o·cene ['hɒlə,sin] or ['houlə,sin] n *Geology* the second epoch of the Quaternary period, beginning about 11 000 years ago. **Hol·o·cene** adj. Also called **Re·cent**. ⟨Greek *holos* whole + *kainos* recent⟩

hol·o·gram ['hɒlə,græm] or ['houlə,græm] n *Optics* a photograph obtained by holography. ⟨Greek *holos* whole + *gramma* something written⟩

ho·log·ra·phy [hə'lɒgrəfi] n a photographic process for making three-dimensional pictures, in which a beam of laser light causes a diffraction pattern that is reconstructed in visible light. **hol·o·graph** ['hɒlə,græf] or ['houlə,græf] adj in the handwriting of the person in whose name it appears: *a holograph will.* n a holograph manuscript, letter, document, etc. **hol·o·graph·ic** adj.

hol·ster ['houlstər] n a leather case for a pistol. ⟨Dutch *holster;* compare Old Norse *hulstr* sheath⟩

ho·ly ['houli] adj 1 belonging to or coming from God or a god: *the Holy Bible.* 2 morally and spiritually blameless: *a holy life.* 3 devoted to the service of God or a god: *a holy man.* 4 declared sacred by religious authority: *a holy day.* 5 worthy of deep respect. **hol·i·ly** adv. ⟨Old English *hālig*⟩
ho·li·er–than–thou ['houliər ðən 'ðaʊ] adj *Informal* self-righteous. **ho·li·ness** n 1 a being holy. 2 **Holiness** a title used in speaking to or of the Pope, orthodox patriarchs, and the Dalai Lama. **Holy Communion** *Christianity* the commemoration of Christ's Last Supper, in which bread and wine are consecrated and consumed. **Holy Father** *Roman Catholic Church* a title of the Pope. **Holy Ghost** See HOLY SPIRIT. **Holy Land** Israel and Palestine. **holy of holies** 1 the inner shrine of the Jewish tabernacle and temple. 2 any place that is most sacred. **holy orders** *Christianity* the rite by which someone becomes a member of the clergy. **take holy orders** become a member of the Christian clergy. **Holy Spirit** or **Holy Ghost** *Christianity* the third person in the Trinity, considered to be God as spiritually active in the world. **holy water** water blessed by a priest. **Holy Week** *Christianity* the week before Easter. **Holy Writ** the Bible; the Scriptures.

hom·age ['hɒmɪdʒ] or ['ɒmɪdʒ] n 1 respect; honour: *Everyone paid homage to the great leader.* 2 in feudal times, a formal acknowledgment by a vassal that he owed loyalty and service to his lord. ⟨Old French *homage; hom* man, vassal, Latin *homo*⟩

home [houm] n 1 one's own house. 2 one's own town or country. 3 the social unit formed by a family, etc. living together in one house or apartment: *He comes from a broken home.* 4 a house built for occupation by one family: *luxury homes for sale.* 5 the natural habitat of an animal or plant: *The beaver makes its home in the water.* 6 any place where a person can rest and be safe. 7 the place of origin or development of something. 8 *Games* the objective or goal.
adv 1 to the thing aimed at: *to drive a nail home.* 2 to the core: *Her accusing words struck home and they were ashamed.* 3 at, to, or toward one's own home: *She's not home.*
v of birds, return home. **home** adj. ⟨Old English *hām*⟩
at home a in one's own home or country. **b** at ease; comfortable. **c** ready to receive visitors. **bring home to** make clear to. **close to (or near home)** affecting one deeply. **come home to** be understood or realized by. **drive home a** make secure with a hammer. **b** make

someone understand: *He thumped the table to drive home his argument.* **home free** *Informal* sure of success: *One more game and then we're home free.* **home (in) on** be guided toward (a goal). **see someone home** escort a person to that person's home. **to write home about** remarkable: *He's nothing to write home about.* **home·bo·dy** *n* one chiefly interested in home life. **home·bound** *adj* **1** headed for home. **2** restricted to the house or apartment. **home·boy** *n esp US slang* a member of one's gang. **home·brew** *n* **1** an alcoholic liquor made at home, esp beer. **2** ✴ *Slang* **a** in Canadian professional football, a native-born player. **b** a local player in any sport. **c** any person or thing of native origin. **home·com·ing** *n* an annual celebration held at many universities and colleges for alumni. **home fries** slices of boiled potato cut and fried. **home front** in war, civilians and their activities. **home–grown** *adj* of produce, grown locally. **home·land** ['houm,lænd] *n* one's own or native land. **home·less** *adj* having no home. *n* **the homeless** *n pl* **home·less·ness** *n.* **home·like** *adj* friendly; familiar; comfortable. **home·ly** *adj* **1** not good-looking: *a homely face.* **2** suited to home life; everyday: *homely pleasures.* **home·li·ness** *n.* **home·made** *adj* **1** made at home. **2** amateurish. **home·mak·er** *n* a person who manages a home, esp one who is a spouse and parent. **home·mak·ing** *n.* **home–own·er** *n* a person who owns his or her own home. **home page** *Computers* the first document reached at an address on the WORLD WIDE WEB. **home plate** *Baseball* the block beside which a player stands to hit the ball. **hom·er** *n* **1** *Baseball Informal* HOME RUN. **2** *Slang* a referee, umpire, etc. who is said to favour the home team. **3** *Slang* a supporter of the hometown team. **4** *Slang* a player or team that plays well in home games. **5** HOMING PIGEON. **home·room** or **home room** *n* **1** the classroom where a given class meets first every day to show attendance, hear announcements, etc. **2** the classroom in an elementary school, where a given class is taught most subjects, usually by the same teacher. **3** the period during which a class meets in the homeroom. **home rule** the management of the affairs of a country, district, or city by its own people. **home run** *Baseball* a run made by a player on a hit that enables him or her to make the entire circuit of the bases without a stop. **home·sick** *adj* ill or depressed because one is away from home. **home–sick·ness** *n.* **home·spun** *adj* **1** spun or made at home. **2** not polished; simple: *homespun manners. n* cloth made of yarn spun at home. **home·stead** *n* **1** a house or farm with its land and other buildings. **2** ✴ formerly, in the West, a parcel of public land, usually 65 ha, granted under certain conditions by the federal government. *v* **1** settle on such land: *His grandfather homesteaded in Saskatchewan.* **2** settle and work (land, etc.). **home·stead·er** *n.* **home stretch 1** the part of a track over which the

last part of a race is run. **2** the last part of any undertaking. **home town 1** the town or city where one grew up or spent most of one's early life. **2** the town or city of one's principal residence. **home·town** *adj.* **home·ward** *adv, adj* toward home. Also (*adv*), **homewards. home·work** *n* **1** lessons to be studied or prepared outside the classroom. **2** any work done at home. **3** work done in preparation for something: *The interviewer's searching questions showed that she had done her homework.* **home·y** *adj* **hom·i·er, hom·i·est** *Informal* like home; cosy and comfortable. **hom·ing** *adj* **1** able to find its way back to its place of origin. **2** assisting in guiding home. **homing pigeon** a pigeon trained to fly home from great distances.

ho·me·op·a·thy [,houmi'ɒpəθi] *n* a system of treating disease by giving very small doses of a drug that in large quantities would produce symptoms of the disease in healthy persons. Compare ALLOPATHY. 〈Greek *homoios* similar + *patheia* disease〉 **ho·me·o·path** ['houmiə,pæθ] *n* a person who practises homeopathy. **ho·me·o·path·ic** *adj* to do with homeopathy or homeopaths. **ho·me·o·path·i·cal·ly** *adv.*

ho·me·o·sta·sis [,houmiə'steisɪs] *or* [-'stæsɪs] *n* **1** the state of equilibrium between the different body activities of an organism. **2** the maintenance of equilibrium between interdependent elements of a group, society, etc. **ho·me·o·stat·ic** [-'stætɪk] *adj.*

hom·i·cide ['hɒmə,saɪd] *n* the killing of one human being by another. Intentional homicide is murder. **hom·i·cid·al** *adj.* **hom·i·cid·al·ly** *adv.* 〈Latin *homo* man + *caedere* kill〉

hom·i·ly ['hɒməli] *n* **1** a sermon, usually based on some part of the Bible. **2** a serious moral talk or writing. **hom·i·list** *n.* 〈Greek *homilia; homilos* throng; because addressed to congregation〉 **hom·i·let·ics** [,hɒmə'lɛtɪks] *n* the art of writing and preaching sermons. **hom·i·let·ic** *adj.*

hom·i·nid ['hɒmənɪd] *n* any of a family of primate mammals, including modern humans (*Homo sapiens*), the only surviving member of the group. **hom·i·nid** *adj.* 〈Latin *homo, hominis* man〉

hom·i·noid ['hɒmə,nɔɪd] *n* a member of the superfamily that includes humans and the great apes; a hominoid animal. *adj* like a human; of the form of a human. 〈Latin *hominis* man + -OID〉

hom·i·ny ['hɒməni] *n* dried, hulled corn. **Hominy grits** is coarsely ground hominy that is boiled in water or milk for food. 〈short for *rockahominy*; Algonquian〉

ho·mo¹ ['houmou] *n, pl* **hom·i·nes** ['hɒmə,niz] any member of the genus *Homo*, which includes present and extinct peoples. 〈Latin = man〉 **Ho·mo sa·pi·ens** ['seipiənz] *or* ['sæpiənz] the specific name given to modern humans. 〈Latin = knowing man〉

ho·mo² ['houmou] *n* ✹ *Informal* homogenized whole milk.

ho·mo·ge·ne·ous [,houmə'dʒiniəs] *or* [,hɒmə-] *adj* **1** of the same kind; similar: *homogeneous interests.* **2** composed of similar elements or parts: *a homogeneous rock.* Compare HETEROGENEOUS (defs. 1, 2) **3** *Mathematics* of the same kind or of the same degree or dimensions. Also (def 2), **ho·mo·ge·nous** [hə'mɒdʒənəs]. **ho·mo·ge·ne·i·ty** [,houmədʒə'niəti] *or* [,hɒmə-] *n.* **ho·mo·ge·ne·ous·ly** *adv.* ⟨Greek *homos* same + *genos* kind⟩

ho·mog·e·nize [hə'mɒdʒə,naɪz] *v* **1** make homogeneous. **2** break up the fat globules of (whole milk) into extremely small particles. **ho·mog·e·ni·za·tion** *n.*

hom·o·graph ['hɒmə,græf] *n* one of two or more words having the same spelling but different meanings, origins, and, often, pronunciations. *Mail,* meaning 'letters', and *mail,* meaning 'armour', are homographs. **ho·mo·graph·ic** [,houmə'græfɪk] *or* [,hɒmə-] *adj.* Compare HOMOPHONE, HOMONYM. ⟨Greek *homos* same + *graphē* writing⟩

ho·mol·o·gous [hə'mɒləgəs] *adj* **1** corresponding in position, proportion, value, structure, etc. **2** *Biology* corresponding in structure and in origin but not necessarily in function. The wing of a bird and the foreleg of a horse are homologous. **3** *Genetics* referring to a pair of matching chromosomes. One member of the pair is received from each parent at conception. ⟨Greek *homologos* agreeing; *homos* same + *logos* reasoning, relation⟩

hom·o·nym ['hɒmə,nɪm] *n* one of two or more words having the same pronunciation and spelling but different meanings and origins. *Rose,* past tense of the verb *rise,* and *rose,* meaning the flower, are homonyms. Compare HOMOGRAPH, HOMOPHONE. ⟨Greek *homos* same + dialect *onyma* name⟩

ho·mo·pho·bia [,houmə'foubiə] *n* hatred or fear of homosexuals.

hom·o·phone ['hɒmə,foun] *n* **1** one of two or more words having the same pronunciation but different meanings, origins, and, usually, spellings. *Pear, pair,* and *pare* are homophones. **2** one of two or more letters or symbols having the same sound. The letters *c* and *k* are homophones in the word *cork.* **ho·moph·o·nous** [hə'mɒfənəs] *adj.* Compare HOMOGRAPH, HOMONYM. ⟨Greek *homos* same + *phōnē* sound⟩ **ho·moph·o·ny** [hə'mɒfəni] *n* **1** sameness of sound. **2** homophonous music.

ho·mo·sex·u·al [,houmə'sekʃuəl] *adj* to do with having sexual desire for one of the same sex. Compare HETEROSEXUAL. **ho·mo·sex·u·al** *n.* **ho·mo·sex·u·al·i·ty** *n.* **ho·mo·sex·u·al·ly** *adv.*

ho·mun·cu·lus [hə'mʌŋkjələs] *n, pl* **-li** [-,laɪ] *or* [-,li] a small or miniature person; dwarf. ⟨Latin, diminutive of *homo* man⟩

Hon. 1 Honourable. **2** Honorary. **3** Honours.

hon·don [hɒn'dɒn] *n Shintoism* the inner shrine of a temple which worshippers may not enter, and in which the chief treasure of the shrine is housed. ⟨Japanese⟩

hone [houn] *n* a fine-grained whetstone on which to sharpen cutting tools. *v* **1** sharpen on a hone. **2** make more precise, effective, etc. ⟨Old English *hān* a stone⟩

hon·est ['ɒnɪst] *adj* **1** not lying, cheating, or stealing: *an honest person.* **2** obtained by fair means: *honest profits.* **3** not hiding one's real nature: *my honest opinion.* **4** genuine: *honest goods.* **hon·est·ly** *adv.* **hon·es·ty** *n.* ⟨Latin *honestus; honos, honor* honour⟩

hon·est–to–good·ness *adj Informal* genuine.

SYNONYMS

Honesty emphasizes fairness in relations with others, and refusal to steal, lie, cheat, or misrepresent: *He shows honesty in all his business affairs.* **Integrity** applies more directly to character than to actions, having very high standards of right and wrong: *A woman of integrity can be trusted.*

hon·ey ['hʌni] *n* **1** a thick, sweet, liquid that bees make. **2** sweetness. **3** darling; sweetheart. **4** *Informal* a person or thing that is very attractive: *a honey of a boat.* **hon·ey·like** *adj.* ⟨Old English *hunig*⟩

hon·ey·bee *n* any of various social bees that produce honey. **hon·ey·comb** *n* **1** a structure of wax containing rows of six-sided cells made by bees, in which they store honey, pollen, and their eggs. **2** anything like this. *v* **1** make in a pattern like a honeycomb. **2** pierce with many holes: *The rock was honeycombed with passages.* **3** weaken by spreading through: *That city is honeycombed with crime.* **hon·ey·dew** *n* **1** a sweet substance that oozes from the leaves of certain plants in hot weather. **2** a sweet, sticky substance excreted by aphids or scale insects, found as a deposit on plants. **3** a variety of muskmelon. **hon·eyed** *or* **hon·ied** ['hʌnid] *adj* **1** sweetened with honey. **2** smooth; flattering: *honeyed words.* **hon·ey·moon** *n* **1** the holiday spent together by a newly married couple. **2** the initial period of marriage. **3** the initial period of any new arrangement, when things are harmonious. *v* have a honeymoon. **hon·ey·moon·er** *n.* **hon·ey·suck·le** ['hʌni,sʌkəl] *n* any of a genus of shrubs or vines cultivated for their showy, often fragrant, flowers.

honk [hɒŋk] *n* **1** the cry of the wild goose. **2** any similar sound: *the honk of a car horn.* **honk** *v.* ⟨imitative⟩ **honk·er** *n* **1** ✹ *Informal* CANADA GOOSE. **2** *Slang* a large nose.

hon·ky–tonk ['hɒŋki ,tɒŋk] *Slang n* **1** a cheap drinking place, esp one playing lowbrow music. **2** a low-class dance hall, night club, etc. **3** the kind of music played there. **hon·ky–tonk** *adj.* ⟨perhaps imitative of the music typically found there⟩

hon·our *or* **hon·or** ['ɒnər] *n* **1** glory; fame. **2** credit for acting well: *It was greatly to his honour that he refused the reward.* **3** honours *or*

honors *pl* **a** special favours or courtesies. **b** a special credit given to a student for unusually excellent work. **4** great respect: *We pay honour to heroes.* **5 Honour** or **Honor** a title used for a judge, mayor, etc.
v **1** respect greatly. **2** confer dignity upon; favour **3** accept and pay (a bill, draft, note, etc.) when due. ⟨Latin *honor, honos*⟩
do honour to a treat with great respect. **b** bring honour to. **do the honours** act as host or hostess. **on** or **upon one's honour** pledged to do what is expected: *He was on his honour not to speak.*
hon·o·rar·i·um *n, pl* **-rar·i·ums** or **-rar·i·a** an honorary fee for professional services on which no fixed price is set: *The guest speaker received an honorarium.* **hon·or·ar·y** *adj* **1** given or done as an honour: *an honorary degree.* **2** without pay or regular duties: *an honorary secretary.* **3** of an obligation, depending on one's honour for fulfillment, but not enforceable otherwise. **hon·or·ee** *n* the recipient of an honour. **hon·or·if·ic** *adj* doing or giving honour. *n* a title of respect. *Sir* is an honorific. **hon·our·a·ble** or **hon·or·a·ble** *adj* **1** having a sense of what is right and proper. **2** accompanied by honour or honours: *an honourable burial.* **3** worthy of honour. **4** showing respect. **5** having a title, rank, or position of honour. **hon·our·a·ble·ness** or **hon·or·a·ble·ness** *n.* **hon·our·a·bly** or **hon·or·a·bly** *adv.* **Hon·our·a·ble** or **Hon·or·a·ble** *adj* in Canada, a title given to members of the Privy Council (which includes the Federal Cabinet), to the Speakers of both the House of Commons and the provincial legislative assemblies, and to certain senior judges. **honourable mention** a citation given to a competitor who has done well, but not well enough for a prize. **honours course 1** a university program of study offered to superior scholars for specialization in certain major subjects. **2** a school course of advanced studies for certain students. **honours degree. honours list** a list of persons receiving special honours or recognition. **honour system** a system of trusting people to obey the rules, pay their fare, etc. without being watched or forced.

SYNONYMS

Honour = respect shown in appreciation of a person's high character, ability, or position: *We pay honour to heroes.* **Deference** = respect shown to a person by putting his or her wishes before one's own: *In deference to his mother's wishes, he stopped smoking at home.* **Homage** = honour paid with reverence: *He bowed in homage to the Unknown Soldier.*

---

hooch [hutʃ] See HOOTCH.
hood¹ [hʊd] *n* **1** a covering for the head and neck. **2** a metal covering over the engine of an automobile. **3** anything like a hood. *v* cover with a hood. **hood·ed** *adj.* **hood·less** *adj.* **hood·like** *adj.* ⟨Old English *hōd*⟩ **hood·wink** *v* mislead by a trick. **hood·wink·er** *n.*
hood² [hʊd] *n Slang* HOODLUM.
–hood *noun-forming suffix* **1** the state of being:

boyhood. **2** the character of: *sainthood.* **3** a group of: *priesthood.* ⟨Old English *hād* state⟩
hood·lum [ˈhʊdləm] *n Informal* **1** a street ruffian. **2** a criminal, esp one who uses force. **hood·lum·ism** *n.* ⟨probably German dialect *Hodalum, Huddellump*⟩
hoo·ey [ˈhʊi] *n Slang* nonsense.
hoof [hʊf] *or* [hʊf] *n, pl* **hoofs** or **hooves 1** a hardcovering on the feet of horses, cattle, and other animals. **2** the whole foot of such animals. **3** *Slang* the human foot. **hoofed** [hʊft] *or* [hʊft] *adj.* **hoof·less** *adj.* **hoof·like** *adj.* ⟨Old English *hōf*⟩ **hoof it** *Slang* **a** go on foot. **b** dance. **on the hoof** of beef cattle, etc. alive, not yet killed. **hoof·beat** *n* the sound made by an animal's hoofs.
hoo·ha [ˈhʊha] *n Informal* fuss.
hook [hʊk] *n* **1** a piece of stiff material, curved for holding something: *a clothes hook.* **2** a curved piece of wire for catching fish: *a fish-hook.* **3** anything curved like a hook. *v* **1** attach with a hook. **2** catch with a hook. **3** be curved like a hook. **4** catch by a trick. **5** *Informal* steal. **6** *Hockey* impede the progress of (a puck-carrier) illegally by catching at his or her body from the side or rear with one's hockey stick. **hook·like** *adj.* ⟨Old English *hōc*⟩
by hook or by crook by fair means or foul. **get one's hooks into** *Informal* influence (a person). **hook, line, and sinker** *Informal* **a** the whole lot. **b** completely. **hook up a** attach with a hook. **b** connect (an electric appliance). **off the hook a** *Informal* free of responsibility. **b** of a telephone receiver, not on its rest, thus preventing incoming calls. **on the hook** *Informal* obligated.
hook and eye a fastener for a garment, etc., consisting of a loop and a hook. **hooked** *adj* **1** curved like a hook. **2** *Informal* addicted, esp to drugs. **3** *Informal* engaged or married. **hook·er** *n* **1** *Slang* prostitute. **2** *Informal* thief. **3** a drink of straight liquor: *a hooker of whisky.* **hook shot** *Basketball* a shot at the basket made from behind the head. **hook·up** *n* **1** the arrangement of the parts of a radio or television set, telephone, broadcasting facilities, etc. **2** facilities for connecting a trailer to water, electricity, etc. **hook·worm** *n* any of various parasitic roundworms having hooked mouthparts that attach to the intestinal lining.
hook·ah [ˈhʊkə] *or* [ˈhukɑ] *n* a tobacco pipe with a tube by which the smoke is drawn through water for cooling. ⟨Arabic *huqqah*⟩
hook·y [ˈhʊki] *n* **play hooky** *Informal* stay away from school without permission. ⟨possibly Dutch *hoekje* hide-and-seek; *hoek* corner + *-je* (diminutive)⟩
hoo·li·gan [ˈhuləgən] *n Informal* one of a gang of street ruffians; hoodlum. **hoo·li·gan·ism** *n.* ⟨perhaps an Irish surname⟩
hoop [hup] *n* **1** a band in the form of a circle: *A hoop holds together the staves of a barrel.* **2** a circular frame formerly worn to

spread out a woman's skirt. **3** *Croquet* one of the arches through which players try to hit the balls. **hoop·like** *adj.* ⟨Old English *hōp*⟩

hoop·la ['huplɑ] *n Slang* **1** uproar. **2** sensational advertising; ballyhoo. ⟨orig a coach driver's exclamation⟩

hoo·ray [hə'rei] *interj, n, or v* hurrah.

hoot [hut] *n* **1** the sound that an owl makes, or a sound like that: *the hoot of a car horn.* **2** a sound to show disapproval or scorn. **3** *Informal* a bit (only in the negative): *I don't give a hoot what happens.* **4** *Informal* something causing laughter: *Her costume was a hoot.* **hoot** *v.* ⟨Middle English *hute(n)*; probably imitative⟩

hootch or **hooch** [hutʃ] *n* **1** hootchinoo. **2** *Slang* any alcoholic liquor, esp cheap whisky. ⟨shortening of HOOTCHINOO⟩

hoo·tchi·noo ['hutʃə,nu] *n* in the Yukon and Alaska, a potent alcoholic liquor distilled illegally. ⟨name of Aboriginal settlement in S Alaska; Tlingit *khutsnuwu* grizzly bear fort⟩

hoo·te·nan·ny ['hutə,næni] *n* an informal party featuring folk singing. ⟨developed from *hoot*⟩

hooves [huvz] *or* [hʊvz] *n* a pl of HOOF.

hop¹ [hɒp] *v* **hopped, hop·ping 1** spring on one foot. **2** spring with both or all feet at once: *Many birds hop.* **3** *Informal* get on or in (a train, plane, etc.): *I'll hop a bus and be there in 20 minutes.* **4** jump quickly (onto, out of, etc.): *She hopped off the bus.*
n **1** a spring. **2** *Informal* a dancing party. **3** a short trip. ⟨Old English *hoppian*⟩
hopping mad very angry. **hop to it** *Informal* be quick; hurry up.
hop·per *n* **1** a grasshopper. **2** a container into which grain, etc. is poured in order to be fed evenly into another container. **hop·scotch** *n* a children's game in which the players hop over lines drawn on the ground.

hop² [hɒp] *n* **1** a vine of the mulberry family. **2 hops** *pl* the dried flowers of the hop vine, used to flavour beer. ⟨Middle Dutch *hoppe*⟩

hope [houp] *n* **1** an expectation that what one desires will happen. **2** optimism about the future. **3** a person or thing in which one places hope: *She is the hope of the family.* **4** something hoped for. **hope** *v.* ⟨Old English *hopa*⟩
hope against hope keep on hoping even though there is no good reason to hope.
hope chest a chest in which a woman collects articles that will be useful after she marries. **hope·ful** *adj* showing or giving hope: *a hopeful smile, a hopeful sign. n* a person who expects to achieve something: *many young hopefuls waiting for auditions.* **hope·ful·ly** *adv.* **hope·ful·ness** *n.* **hope·less** *adj* feeling or giving no hope: *a hopeless illness.* **hope·less·ly** *adv.* **hope·less·ness** *n.*

horde [hɔrd] *n* **1** a crowd; swarm. **2** a wandering group: *Hordes of Mongols and Turks invaded Europe during the Middle Ages.* ⟨Turkish *ordu* camp⟩

ho·ri·zon [hə'raizən] *n* **1** the line where the earth and sky seem to meet. **2** Usually, **horizons** *pl* the limit of one's thinking. **3** *Geology* a distinct layer or group of layers of rock or soil. **ho·ri·zon·less** *adj.* ⟨Greek *horizōn (kyklos)* bounding (circle); *horos* limit⟩

hor·i·zon·tal [,hɔrə'zɒntəl] *adj* **1** parallel to the horizon; at right angles to a vertical line. **2** flat; level: *a horizontal surface. n* something horizontal, such as a line. **hor·i·zon·tal·ly** *adv.*

hork [hɔrk] *v ✽ Slang* spit.

hor·mone ['hɔrmoun] *n* **1** *Physiology* a substance in the bloodstream that influences the activity of some organ. **2** *Botany* a substance in the sap of plants that acts similarly. **hor·mo·nal** [hɔr'mounəl] *adj.* ⟨Greek *hormōn* setting in motion⟩

horn [hɔrn] *n* **1** a hard growth, usually pointed, on the heads of some animals. **2** anything that sticks up on the head of an animal: *a snail's horns.* **3** a musical instrument shaped like a horn. **4** anything that projects like a horn or is shaped like a horn: *a saddle horn.*
v hit or wound with horns; gore. **horned** *adj.* **horn·less** *adj.* **horn·like** *adj.* ⟨Old English⟩
blow one's own horn speak in praise of oneself. **draw** (or **pull in**) **one's horns** restrain oneself. **horn in** *Slang* intrude: *She kept trying to horn in on our conversation.* **lock horns** engage in conflict (*with*). **on the horns of a dilemma** having two unpleasant choices, one of which must be taken.
horn·bill *n* any of a tropical family of birds having a large bill with a bony lump, or casque, on the top of it. **horned toad** any of several lizards having spines on the back and tail. **horn of plenty** CORNUCOPIA (def. 2). **horn·pipe** *n* a lively dance, formerly popular among sailors. **horn·y** *adj* **1** made of horn or a substance like it. **2** hard like horn: *The farmer's hands were horny from work.* **3** *Slang* sexually eager or excited. **horn·i·ness** *n.*

hor·net ['hɔrnɪt] *n* any of several large wasps that live in colonies. ⟨Old English *hyrnet(u)*; form influenced by *horn*⟩
hornet's nest a situation likely to be troublesome.

horn·swog·gle ['hɔrn,swɒgəl] *v* swindle; cheat. ⟨invented⟩

hor·o·scope ['hɔrə,skoup] *n Astrology* **1** the position of the planets and stars at a person's birth, regarded as influencing his or her life. **2** a diagram of the heavens, used in telling fortunes. **3** a fortune told by this means.
cast a horoscope discover the influence that the stars and planets are supposed to have on a person's life. **ho·ro·scop·ic** [-'skɒpɪk] *adj.* ⟨Greek *hōra* time + *skopos* watcher⟩

hor·ror ['hɔrər] *n* **1** terror caused by something frightful. **2** a very strong dislike. **3** a cause of horror. **4** *Informal* something very bad. **5 the horrors** *Informal* **a** a fit of horror, as in delirium tremens. **b** extreme depression. ⟨Latin *horror; horrere* to bristle⟩
hor·ren·dous [hə'rɛndəs] *adj* frightful. **hor·ren·dous·ly** *adv.* **hor·ri·ble** *adj* **1** causing horror. **2** *Informal* extremely unpleasant: *a*

horrible noise. **hor·ri·bly** *adv.* **hor·rid** *adj Informal* very unpleasant; *a horrid child.* **hor·rid·ly** *adv.* **hor·rif·ic** [hɔr'ɪfɪk] *adj* producing horror. **hor·ri·fy** ['hɔrə,faɪ] *v* **1** cause to feel horror. **2** *Informal* shock. **hor·ror–struck** or **horror–stricken** *adj* horrified.

hors d'oeu·vre [ˌɔr 'dɜrv] *French* [ɔR'dœvʀ] *pl* **hors d'oeu·vres** [ˌdɜrvz] *French* ['dœvʀ] light food served before the regular courses of a meal. ⟨French *hors d'œuvre,* literally, apart from (the main) work⟩

horse [hɔrs] *n, pl* **hors·es** or (esp collectively) **horse** **1** a large, four-legged animal with solid hoofs, used for riding, and pulling loads. **2** *Gymnastics* an apparatus to vault over. **3** a frame with legs to support something. ⟨Old English *hors*⟩
a horse of a different colour something different. **back the wrong horse** forecast inaccurately. **hold one's horses** *Informal* restrain oneself. **horse around** *Slang.* **a** fool around. **b** engage in horseplay. **look a gift horse in the mouth** be ungrateful. **on one's high horse** *Informal* behaving in an arrogant way. **the horse's mouth** the original source: *news straight from the horse's mouth.*
horse–and–bug·gy *adj* old-fashioned: *horse-and-buggy ideas.* **horse·back** *n* the back of a horse. *adv* on the back of a horse. **horse chestnut** a large tree whose seeds resemble chestnuts, but are poisonous. **horse–drawn** *adj* pulled by horses. **horse·flesh** *n* **1** horses for riding, driving, and racing. **2** meat from horses. **horse·fly** *n* any of a family of large flies that suck the blood of horses, cattle, etc. **horse·hair** *n* stiff fabric made from the hair from the mane or tail of a horse. **horse·hide** *n* leather made from the hide of a horse. **horse latitudes** two regions where there is often very calm weather and that extend around the world at about 30° N and 30° S of the equator. **horse laugh** *Informal* a loud, boisterous laugh. **horse·man** *n, pl* **-men 1** a man skilled in managing horses. **2** ✷ *Slang* a member of the Royal Canadian Mounted Police. **3** a rancher who raises horses. **horse·man·ship** *n* skill in managing horses. **horse·meat** *n* the flesh of a horse, esp when used for food. **horse·play** *n* rough, boisterous play. **horse·pow·er** *n* a non-metric unit used for measuring the power of engines, motors, etc. One horsepower is about three-quarters of a kilowatt. *Symbol* **hp.** **horse·rad·ish** *n* a herb of the mustard family, cultivated for its pungent root. **horse sense** *Informal* common sense. **horse·shoe** ['hɔrʃ,ʃu] *n* **1** a U-shaped metal plate nailed to a horse's hoof to protect it. **2** anything shaped like a horseshoe: *a horseshoe of flowers.* **3 horseshoes** a game in which the players try to throw horseshoes over or near a stake 12 m away (with sg verb). **horse trader 1** a buyer or seller of horses. **2** a shrewd negotiator. **horse·whip** *n* a whip for driving or controlling horses. **horse·whip, -whipped, -whip·ping** *v.* **horse·wom·an** *n, pl* **-wom·en** a woman skilled in managing horses. **hors·y** or **horsey** *adj* **1** dressing or talking like people

who spend much time with horses. **2** *Slang* large and awkward in appearance. **hors·i·ly** *adv.* **hors·i·ness** *n.*

hor·ti·cul·ture ['hɔrtə,kʌltʃər] *n* the cultivation of flowers, fruits, vegetables, etc. **hor·ti·cul·tur·al** *adj* **hor·ti·cul·tur·ist** *n.* ⟨Latin *hortus* garden⟩

ho·san·na [hou'zænə] *interj, n* a shout of praise to the Lord. ⟨Hebrew *hoshi'ahnna* save now, we pray⟩

hose [houz] *n* **1** *pl* **hose** stockings or socks. Also, **ho·sier·y.** **2** *sg, pl* **hos·es** a tube made of material that will bend, used to carry liquids for short distances.
v **1** put water on with a hose (often with *down*): *She hosed down the lawn furniture.* **2** *Slang* get the better of, esp by unfair means: *He said the team was tired of being hosed by the officials.* ⟨Old English *hosa*⟩

ho·ser ['houzər] ✷ *Slang* an endearingly dense, loud, and opinionated lowbrow.

hos·pice ['hɒspɪs] *n* an institution providing homelike care for the terminally ill. ⟨Latin *hospitium; hospitis* guest, host⟩

hos·pi·ta·ble [hə'spɪtəbəl] *or* ['hɒspətəbəl] *adj* **1** giving friendly treatment to guests: *a hospitable family.* **2** willing to consider: *hospitable to new ideas.* **hos·pi·ta·bly** *adv.* **hos·pi·tal·i·ty** *n.* ⟨Latin *hospitis* guest, host⟩
hospitality suite at a convention, etc., a room where free refreshments are offered, esp alcoholic drinks.

hos·pi·tal ['hɒspətəl] *n* **1** a place where sick or injured people are cared for. **2** a similar place for sick or injured animals. ⟨Latin *hospitalia* guest rooms; *hospitis* guest, host⟩
hos·pi·tal·ize *v* put in a hospital to be treated or cared for. **hos·pi·tal·i·za·tion** *n.*

host¹ [houst] *n* **1** a person who entertains another as a guest. **2** the keeper of a hotel. **3** a country or city staging an event such as the Olympic Games. **4** one who conducts a talk show on radio or television. **5** *Biology* a plant or animal on which a parasite lives: *The oak tree is the host of the mistletoe that grows on it.* **6** *Computers* a computer that makes files, esp Internet documents, available to other computers on the same network. **host** *v.* ⟨Latin *hospitis* guest, host⟩

host² [houst] *n* a large number; multitude: *A host of stars glittered in the sky.* ⟨Latin *hostis* army, enemy (orig stranger)⟩

Host [houst] *n Christianity* the bread or wafer used in Holy Communion. ⟨Latin *hostia* animal sacrificed; form influenced by *host¹*⟩

hos·tage ['hɒstɪdʒ] *n* a person held as a pledge that certain agreements will be carried out. ⟨Old French *hostage, ostage* status of guest; Latin *hospitis* guest⟩

hos·tel ['hɒstəl] *n* **1** a supervised lodging place. **2** an inn; hotel. **3** ✷ *North* In full, **hostel school** a residential boarding school for Inuit or First Nations children. ⟨Old French *hostel, ostel.* See HOSPITAL.⟩
hos·tel·ry *n* an inn; hotel.

hos·tile [ˈhɒstaɪl] or [ˈhɒstəl] adj **1** to do with an enemy: *the hostile army.* **2** unfriendly: *a hostile look.* **3** unfavourable: *a hostile climate.* **hos·tile·ly** adv. ⟨Latin *hostis* enemy, stranger⟩ **hos·til·i·ty** [hɒˈstɪləti] n **1** unfriendliness. **2** opposition. **3** a hostile act. **4 hostilities** pl acts of war; warfare; fighting.

SYNONYMS

Hostile emphasizes being opposed: *Their hostile looks showed that he was unwelcome.* **Unfriendly** places less emphasis on ill will, and suggests being unwilling to be agreeable: *We sat around in an unfriendly silence.*

hot [hɒt] adj **hot·ter, hot·test 1** warmer than the body: *a hot fire.* **2** feeling uncomfortable due to heat: *I'm too hot to sit in the sun.* **3** spicy: *This chili is not too hot.* **4** full of any strong feeling: *hot with rage.* **5** full of great enthusiasm. **6** *Slang* stolen: *hot diamonds.* **7** *Informal* likely to succeed: *a hot team.* **8** *Slang* fashionable. **9** ✳ *Mining* potentially rich in minerals: *a hot mineral area.* adv in a hot manner: *The sun beat hot on the sand.* **hot·ly** adv. ⟨Old English *hāt*⟩ **blow hot and cold** waver in mind or opinion. **hot under the collar** very angry. **hot up** make or become intense: *as the situation hots up.* **make it hot for** *Informal* make trouble for. **hot air** *Slang* empty, pompous talk. **hot·bed** n any place favourable to rapid growth: *These slums are a hotbed of crime.* **hot·blood·ed** adj **1** easily angered. **2** rash. **3** passionate. **hot·cake** a flapjack or pancake. **go** (or **sell**) **like hotcakes** be in great demand. **hot cross bun** a bun marked with a cross, eaten esp on Good Friday. **hot dog 1** a sandwich made of a hot wiener enclosed in a long roll **2** wiener. **hot–dog** v **-dogged, -dog·ging** do stunts while skiing or surfing. **hot–dog·ger** n. **hot·foot** v *Informal* go in great haste (usually with *it*): *We hotfooted it to the airport.* **hot·head** n a quick-tempered person. **hot–head·ed** adj **hot·house** n a greenhouse that is heated for growing plants. adj needing careful handling, as if in a hothouse: *She's no hothouse creature.* **hot·line** n **1** a phone line which people can call to get counsel or to listen to recorded information: *a weather hotline.* **2** a phone line enabling listeners to call into a talk show to express their views. **3** a direct means of communication for use in emergencies. **hot·link** n, v *Computers* link using hypertext. **hot·list** n *Computers* a list of frequently accessed websites, coded so the user can click on any name in the list to go to that site. v Add a website to such a list. **hot pants** very brief, tight shorts for women. **hot plate** an electrically heated metal plate for cooking food or keeping it hot. **hot potato** *Slang* something too controversial to handle. **hot rod** *Slang* a car with a supercharged engine. **hot rod·der** a person who drives a hot rod. **hot seat 1** *Slang* ELECTRIC CHAIR. **2** an embarrassing predicament. **3** the chair occupied by the victim of an aggressive interview. **hot·shot** n *Slang* a person who is skilful in a flashy way.

hot spot 1 a fashionable nightclub, resort, etc. **2** a place of unrest or violence. **3** a point in the earth's crust where a volcano is likely to form. **hot spring** Usually, **hot springs** pl a natural spring whose water has a high temperature. **hot–tem·pered** adj easily angered. **hot tub** a large tub filled with hot water, in which several people can soak at the same time. **hot water** *Informal* trouble. **hot–wire** *Informal* start (a vehicle) without a key by connecting a wire carrying current.

ho·tel [houˈtɛl] n **1** a building where rooms may be rented on a day-to-day basis. **2** ✳ *Informal* a place where beer and wine are sold for drinking on the premises. ⟨French *hôtel*, Old French *hostel*. See HOSPITAL.⟩ **ho·tel·ier** [houˈtɛljər] or [ˌhoutəˈlir] *French* [otɛlˈje] n the owner or manager of a hotel.

hound [haʊnd] n **1** any of various breeds of hunting dog, most of which hunt by scent. **2** any dog. v **1** keep on chasing: *The police hounded the thief until they caught her.* **2** keep urging or pestering: *His parents hounded him to do his homework.* ⟨Old English *hund*⟩ **hound's–tooth** a pattern of broken checks. **hound's–tooth** adj.

hour [aʊr] n **1** a unit used with the SI for measuring time, equal to 3600 seconds or 60 minutes. *Symbol* **h 2** a short space of time: *After his hour of glory, he was soon forgotten.* **3** the present time: *the man of the hour.* **4** fifteen degrees of longitude. **5 hours** pl the time for work, study, etc.: *Our store hours are 9 to 6.* ⟨Old French *hure*; Latin, Greek *hōra* season, time, hour⟩ **hour·glass** n two glass bulbs joined by a very narrow neck and containing fine sand. It takes one hour for the sand to run from the upper bulb to the lower one. **hour hand** the short hand on a clock or watch. **hour·ly** adj done, happening, coming, etc. every hour: *hourly news reports.* adv every hour.

house [haʊs] n, pl **hous·es** [ˈhaʊzɪz] **1** a building designed for people to live in. **2** the people living in a house: *The whole house was awake by 7 o'clock.* **3 House** a lawmaking body: *the House of Commons.* **4** an audience: *A large house heard the singer.* **5** a noble or royal family: *the house of Hanover.* **6** *Curling* the goal or target. adj prepared by a particular restaurant: *the house dressing.* v [haʊz] **1** provide with a house: *Where can we house all these children?* **2** place in a secure or protected position, as mechanical parts in a case. **house·ful** n. ⟨Old English *hūs*⟩ **bring down the house** *Informal* be vigorously applauded. **clean house a** set a house in order. **b** get rid of bad conditions. **keep house** manage a home and its affairs. **like a house on fire a** very well. **b** very rapidly. **on the house** free: *After visiting the candy factory, I was given a box of chocolates on the house.* **put** (or **set**) **one's house in order** arrange one's affairs. **house arrest** confinement to one's house by order of a court. **house·boat** *n* a boat that can be used as a place to live in. **house·bound** *adj* confined to the house: *He is housebound because of his arthritis.* **house·break·er** *n* a person who breaks into a house to steal. **house·break·ing** *n.* **house·bro·ken** *adj* of a pet such as a dog or cat, trained to urinate and defecate only outdoors or in a special place indoors. **house call** a visit to a home to give medical care: *Do you know a doctor who makes house calls?* **house·clean** *v* clean the house or apartment. **house·clean·ing** *n.* **house·coat** *n* a woman's informal garment for wearing at home. **house·fly** *n* a two-winged fly that lives around houses, feeding on food and garbage. **house·hold** *n* all the people living in a house. *adj* **1** to do with a household: *household expenses.* **2** common or familiar: *a household word.* **house·hold·er** *n* a person who owns or lives in a house. **house·hus·band** *n* a man who stays at home to look after the house and, usually, children, while the woman goes out to work. **house·keep·er** *n* a person hired to manage a home and its affairs. **house·keep·ing** *n* **1** the managing of a home and its affairs. **2** the everyday operations of an organization. **house lights** *n* the lighting in the audience part of a theatre or cinema. **house·mate** *n* one who shares a house, apartment, etc. with another person. **house·moth·er** *n* a woman who supervises and takes care of a group of people living together as a family. **House of Assembly ✱** in Nova Scotia, and in Newfoundland and Labrador, the provincial legislature. **house of cards** anything that can be easily knocked down. **House of Commons** in Canada, the elected representatives who meet in Ottawa to make laws and debate questions of government. **house of correction** any of various institutions for the confinement of juvenile offenders or persons who have committed minor offences. **House of Lords** in the UK, the upper, non-elective branch of the lawmaking body, composed of nobles and clergy. **Houses of Parliament ✱** the federal legislative body consisting of an elected lower house and an appointed upper house. **House of Representatives 1** in the United States: the lower branch of the federal lawmaking body or of the lawmaking body of certain states. **2** the lower branch of the Parliament of Australia, or of the General Assembly of New Zealand. **house organ** a newsletter printed for internal distribution in a company. **house·par·ent** *n* one of a married couple in charge of a residence at a school, college, or other institution. **house physician** a resident physician of a hotel, hospital, etc. **house plant** a plant grown indoors in a pot. **house–proud** *adj* proud of the appearance of one's house. **house–rais·ing** *n* the building of a house by a group of neighbours. **house–sit, house–sat, house–sit·ting** *v* live in a house to look after it while the owners are away. **house–to–house** *adj* from one house to the next, stopping at each: *a house-to-house campaign.* **house–train** *v* train (a pet) to

urinate and defecate only outdoors or only in a special place indoors. **house·wares** *n pl* equipment for a household, esp dishes, kitchen utensils, small appliances, etc. **house·warm·ing** *n* a party given when a person or family moves into a new residence. **house·wife** *n,* *pl* **-wives** a woman who manages a home for her family. **house·wife·ly** *adj.* **house·work** *n* the work to be done in housekeeping, such as cleaning, and cooking. **hous·ing** *n* **1** the provision of houses as homes. **2** houses. **3** a shelter; covering. **4** a frame for holding together and protecting the parts of a machine. **housing start** the building of houses, as an economic indicator: *Housing starts are up this quarter.*

hove [houv] *v* a pt and a pp of HEAVE.

hov·el [ˈhʌvəl] *or* [ˈhɒvəl] *n* a house that is small, crude, and unpleasant to live in; shack. ⟨Middle English; origin uncertain⟩

hov·er [ˈhʌvər] *or* [ˈhɒvər] *v* **1** stay in or near one place in the air: *The hummingbird hovered in front of the flower.* **2** stay in or near one place: *The dogs hovered around the kitchen door.* **3** be in an uncertain condition: *The sick woman hovered between life and death.* ⟨Middle English hover(en), hoven; origin uncertain⟩
hover over threaten: *The fear of failure hovered over the young executive.*
Hov·er·craft [ˈhʌvər.kræft] *or* [ˈhɒvər-] *n* a motorized vehicle capable of travelling just above the surface of water or land on a cushion of air created by powerful fans blowing downward.

how [haʊ] *adv* **1** in what way; by what means: *Tell her how to do it.* **2** to what degree, extent, etc.: *How long will it take?* **3** in what state or condition: *Tell me how she is.* **4** for what reason: *How is it you are late?* **5** to what effect; with what meaning: *How do you mean?* *n* a way of doing: *She considered all the hows and wherefores.* ⟨Old English hū⟩
how come? *Informal* what is the reason?: *How come you didn't call last night?* **how so?** why is it so? **how's that?** what did you say?
how·ev·er *conj* nevertheless *It is his; however, you may use it. adv* **1** to whatever extent, degree, etc: *However you do it, the effect will be the same.* **2** by whatever means: *However did you manage to get here?* **how–to** *adj* giving instructions for making or doing something.

howl [haʊl] *v* **1** give a mournful cry: *Wolves howl.* **2** make a sound like this: *Listen to the wind howling in the trees.* **3** give a cry of pain, rage, distress, etc. **4** yell: *We howled with laughter.* **5** force by howling: *The angry mob howled him off the platform.* **howl** *n.* ⟨Middle English houle(n)⟩
howl·er *n Informal* a ridiculous mistake.

hp horsepower.

HP, H.P., or **h.p.** **1** high pressure. **2** horsepower. **3** *Electricity* high power.

HQ or **hq** headquarters.

HTML *Computers* acronym for **Hypertext Markup Language** a computer programming language used to create and display hypertext files on the Internet.

hu·a·ra·che [wɑ'rɑtʃi] *n* a Mexican sandal with leather straps to cover the upper foot. ⟨Mexican Spanish⟩

hub [hʌb] *n* **1** the central part of a wheel. **2** any centre of interest, importance, activity, etc.: *London is the hub of the Commonwealth.* ⟨origin uncertain⟩
hub·cap *n* the cap that fits over the hub of an automobile wheel.

hub·bub ['hʌbʌb] *n* a noisy tumult; uproar. ⟨imitative⟩

hu·bris ['hjubrɪs] *or* ['hubrɪs] *n* insolence; arrogance; wanton or contemptuous pride. **hu·bris·tic** *adj.* ⟨Greek *hybris*⟩

huck·le·ber·ry ['hʌkəl,bɛri] *n* any of a genus of shrubs of the heath family, bearing berries resembling blueberries. ⟨probably alteration of *hurtleberry;* dialect *hurt*, Old English *horte* whortleberry⟩

huck·ster ['hʌkstər] *n* **1** peddler. **2** *esp US Informal* a person in the advertising business. **3** an unfair trader. **huck·ster** *v.* ⟨perhaps Middle Dutch *hokester*, orig fem. Related to HAWK².⟩

hud·dle ['hʌdəl] *v* **1** crowd close: *The sheep huddled in a corner of the field.* **2** curl oneself up: *The swimmer sat huddled in a blanket.* **3** of football players, group together to receive signals. **4** *Informal* hold a secret, casual conference. **hud·dle** *n.* ⟨Compare Middle English *hudrc(n)*⟩

Hudson Bay ['hʌdsən] an inland sea in N Canada. ⟨Henry *Hudson*, English explorer, died 1611⟩
Hudson's Bay Company ⚓ a trading company chartered in 1670, as the Company of Adventurers of England trading into Hudson's Bay, to carry on the fur trade with the aboriginal peoples of North America.

hue¹ [hju] *n* **1** that property of colour by which it can be distinguished from grey: *all the hues of the rainbow.* **2** a variety of a colour. **3** aspect or type: *politicians of every hue.* ⟨Old English *hīw*⟩

hue² [hju] *n Archaic* (except in **hue and cry**). shouting.
hue and cry a shouts of alarm or protest. **b** an alarm formerly raised to call people to pursue a criminal, in which they were obliged by law to join. ⟨French *huer* shout⟩

huff [hʌf] *n* a fit of anger or peevishness. ⟨imitative⟩
huff·y *adj* tending to be easily offended; touchy. **huff·i·ly** *adv.* **huff·i·ness** *n.*

hug [hʌg] *v* **hugged, hug·ging 1** put the arms around and hold close. **2** cling firmly to: *They still hug their belief in her.* **3** keep close to: *The boat hugged the shore.* **hug** *n.* **hug·ga·ble** *adj.* ⟨apparently Old Norse *hugga* to comfort⟩

huge [hjudʒ] *adj* **1** extremely large in size, quantity, etc. **2** unusually great in extent, scope, degree, or capacity: *a huge undertaking.* **huge·ly** *adv.* **huge·ness** *n.* ⟨Old French *ahuge*⟩

hu·la ['hulə] *n* a native Hawaiian dance characterized by movement of the hips and hand gestures that tell a story. ⟨Hawaiian⟩
Hula Hoop *Trademark* a plastic hoop designed to be rotated around the body by swinging the hips.

hulk [hʌlk] *n* **1** the body of a worn-out ship. **2** a big, clumsy person or thing.
v **1** be unwieldy. **2** slouch. **3** rise in an impressive way. ⟨Old English *hulc* a fast ship⟩
hulk·ing or **hulk·y** *adj* big and clumsy.

hull¹ [hʌl] *n* **1** the outer covering of a seed. **2** the calyx of some fruits. The green leaves at the stem of a strawberry are called its hull. **3** any outer covering.
v remove the hulls from: *to hull strawberries, to hull grain.* **hull·er** *n.* ⟨Old English *hulu*⟩

hull² [hʌl] *n* **1** the body or frame of a ship. **2** the frame of a seaplane, airship, etc. ⟨extended use of *hull¹*⟩

hul·la·ba·loo [,hʌləbə'lu] *n* a loud noise or disturbance; uproar. ⟨imitative; probably reduplication of *hullo*⟩

hul·lo [hə'lou] *interj, n* hello.

hum [hʌm] *v* **hummed, hum·ming 1** make a murmuring sound like that of a bee: *The sewing machine hums busily.* **2** sing with closed lips, not sounding words. **3** bustle. **4** *Informal* be busy and active: *The new president made things hum.* **hum** *n.* **hum·ma·ble** *adj.* ⟨imitative⟩
hum·ming·bird *n* any of a family of tiny birds noted for their ability to hover in the air as they feed and also for the humming sound made by their rapidly beating wings.

hu·man ['hjumən] *adj* **1** to do with people: *human nature.* **2** having qualities natural to people, as opposed to machines, animals, or divine beings: *human error.* **3** warm, open, etc.: *She's more human now that she knows us.* *n* a human being; person. ⟨Latin *humanus*⟩
human being a man, woman, or child; person. **hu·mane** [hju'mein] *adj* **1** kind. **2** tending to humanize and refine: *humane studies.* **hu·mane·ly** *adv.* **hu·mane·ness** *n.* **hu·man·ism** *n* a philosophy of life based on the principle that human beings alone are responsible for giving meaning and purpose to their lives. **hu·man·ist** *n.* **hu·man·is·tic** *adj.* **hu·man·is·ti·cal·ly** *adv.* **hu·man·i·tar·i·an** [hju,mænə'tɛriən] *adj* **1** helpful to humanity. **2** to do with humanitarianism. *n* a person who is devoted to the welfare of all human beings. **hu·man·i·tar·i·an·ism** *n* **1** humanitarian principles. **2** the doctrine that people's obligations are concerned wholly with the welfare of the human race. **hu·man·i·ty** *n* **1** human beings taken as a group. **2** good human character. **3** kindness: *Treat animals with humanity.* **4** the humanities arts, philosophy, and the social sciences. **hu·man·ize** *v* **1** give a human character or quality to. **2** cause to be kind. **hu·man·i·za·tion** *n.* **hu·man·kind** *n* the human

race; people. **hu·man·ly** *adj* **1** in a human manner. **2** by human means: *humanly impossible.* **hu·man·oid** ['hjumə,nɔɪd] *adj* having human characteristics: *humanoid robots. n* any creature closely resembling a human being: *Science fiction often deals with humanoids from other planets.* **human resources 1** the personnel department in a company. **2** resources in the form of human energy, employable people, etc. **human rights** the rights of an individual that are considered basic in any human society.

> **CONFUSABLES**
> **Human** suggests any quality belonging specially to people as distinct from animals or God, but particularly suggests their feelings or faults. **Humane** chiefly suggests a person's compassionate feelings toward animals or people who are helpless or suffering.

hum·ble ['hʌmbəl] *adj* **1** low in position or condition: *a humble place to live.* **2 a** having a feeling that one is unimportant, weak, poor, etc. **b** modest in spirit. **3** deeply respectful. *v* **1** make humble; bring down. **2** make lower in position, condition, or pride. **hum·bly** *adv.* ⟨Old French; Latin *humilis* low, *humus* ground⟩ **hu·mil·i·ate** [hju'mɪli,eit] *v* lower the pride of. **hu·mil·i·at·ed** *adj.* **hu·mil·i·at·ing** *adj.* **hu·mil·i·a·tion** *n.* **hu·mil·i·ty** *n* lack of pride.

humble pie an inferior pie made of the inward parts of an animal, formerly served to the servants after a hunt. ⟨variant of *umble pie; umbles, numbles* entrails; Latin *lumbulus* diminutive of *lumbus* loin⟩ **eat humble pie a** be forced to do something humiliating. **b** apologize.

hum·bug ['hʌm,bʌg] *n* **1** a person who pretends to be what he or she is not. **2** a cheat. **3** pretence. **4** nonsense: *Dad says our argument is humbug. v* **-bugged, -bug·ging** deceive with a sham. ⟨origin unknown⟩

hum·ding·er ['hʌm,dɪŋər] *n Slang* a person or thing that is first-rate: *a humdinger of a car.*

hum·drum ['hʌm,drʌm] *adj* without variety; commonplace; dull. *n* a humdrum routine. ⟨varied reduplicaton of *hum*, v.⟩

hu·mer·us ['hjumərəs] *n, pl* **-mer·i** [-mə,raɪ] *or* [-mə,ri] the long bone in the upper part of the forelimb or arm, reaching from the shoulder to the elbow. ⟨Latin *umerus*⟩

hu·mid ['hjumɪd] *adj* moist; damp: *The air is very humid here.* **hu·mid·ly** *adv.* ⟨Latin *umidus; umere* be moist⟩ **hu·mi·dex** ['hjumɪ,dɛks] *n* 🐾 an index of discomfort resulting from a combination of humidity and heat. ⟨blend of *humid*(ity) + (*ind*)*ex;* coined by Toronto Weather Office in 1965⟩ **hu·mid·i·fi·er** *n* a device for keeping air moist. **hu·mid·i·fy** *v* make more humid. **hu·mid·i·fi·ca·tion** *n.* **hu·mid·i·ty** *n* **1** the state of the atmosphere with respect to the amount of water vapour present in it. **2** moistness, esp of the atmosphere: *The*

humidity today is worse than the heat. **hu·mi·dor** ['hjumə,dɔr] *n* **1** a box, jar, etc. for keeping tobacco moist. **2** any similar device.

hu·mil·i·ate, hu·mil·i·ty See HUMBLE.

hum·mock ['hʌmək] *n* **1** a very small, rounded hill. **2** a bump or ridge in a field of ice. ⟨origin unknown⟩

hum·mus ['hʌməs] *or* ['hʊməs] *n* a Middle Eastern dish consisting of finely ground chick peas and spices. ⟨Turkish *humus*⟩

hu·mong·ous [hju'mʌngəs] *or* [hju'mɒngəs] *adj Informal* very large.

hu·mour *or* **hu·mor** ['hjumər] *n* **1** a funny or amusing quality: *I see no humour in your tricks.* **2** a state of mind: *Success puts you in good humour.* **3** a whim. **4** any of various body fluids formerly supposed to determine a person's health and disposition. They were blood, phlegm, choler, and melancholy. **5** any clear body fluid. *v* **1** give in to the whims of (a person). **2** act so as to agree with. **hu·mour·less** *or* **hu·mor·less** *adj.* ⟨Anglo-French; Latin *umor* fluid⟩ **sense of humour** the ability to see the amusing side of things. **hu·mor·ist** *n* a person who tells or writes jokes and funny stories. **hu·mor·ous** *adj* amusing. **hu·mor·ous·ly** *adv.*

hump [hʌmp] *n* **1** a rounded lump: *Some camels have two humps.* **2** a mound; a hill. *v* **1** rise or cause to rise up into a hump: *The cat humped its back when it saw the dog.* **2** *Slang* make an effort. ⟨related to Dutch *homp* lump⟩ **over the hump** past a difficult period. **hump·back** *n* **1** hunchback. **2** a large baleen whale with a rounded back that shows as a hump above the water just before the whale sounds. Also called **humpback whale. hump·backed** *adj* hunchbacked.

humph [hʌmpf] *interj, n* an exclamation of doubt, disgust, contempt, etc.

hu·mus ['hjuməs] *n* the dark brown part of soil formed from decayed leaves and other vegetable matter. ⟨Latin *humus* earth⟩

hunch [hʌntʃ] *v* **1** hump. **2** form into a hump: *He sat hunched up with his chin on his knees.* **3** move, push, or shove by jerks. *n* **1** a hump. **2** *Informal* an intuition: *I had a hunch we would win.* ⟨origin unknown⟩ **hunch·back** *n* a crooked back that has a hump at the shoulders, or a person with such a back. **hunch·backed** *adj.*

hun·dred ['hʌndrəd] *n, pl* **-dreds** *or* (after a number, etc.) **-dred 1** ten times ten; 100. **2** a 100-dollar bill. **3 hundreds** *pl* the numbers between 100 and 999. **hun·dred** *adj.* ⟨Old English *hund* 100 + *red* reckoning⟩ **hun·dred·fold** *adj* **1** a hundred times as much or as many. **2** having 100 parts. *adv* a hundred times as much or as many. **hun·dredth** *adj, n* **1** next after the 99th; 100th. **2** one, or being one, of 100 equal parts. **hun·dred·weight** *n, pl* **-weights** *or* (after a number, etc.) **-weight** a non-metric unit for measuring mass equal to 100 pounds (about 45 kg) in Canada.

hung [hʌŋ] *v* a pt and a pp of HANG.
hung over having a hangover. **hung up** *Informal* delayed: *to be hung up in traffic.* **hung up on** *Informal* disturbed by; absorbed in: *to be hung up on one's anxieties.*
hung jury a jury that cannot agree on a verdict.

hun·ger ['hʌŋgər] *n* **1** an uncomfortable or painful feeling caused by lack of food. **2** a desire or need for food. **3** a strong desire: *a hunger for kindness.* **hun·ger** *v.* **hun·gry** *adj.* **hun·gri·ly** *adv.* ⟨Old English *hungor*⟩
hunger strike a refusal to eat until certain demands are met.

hunk [hʌŋk] *n* **1** *Informal* a big lump, piece, or roughly cut slice. **2** *Slang.* a good-looking man. ⟨related to Flemish *hunke* hunk⟩

hun·ker ['hʌŋkər] *v* squat on one's haunches (with *down*). ⟨origin uncertain⟩

hunk·y–do·ry ['hʌŋki 'dɔri] *adj Slang* fine; just right; satisfactory. ⟨dialect slang *hunkey* all right, safe; Dutch *honk* home, goal⟩

hunt [hʌnt] *v* **1** go after (wild creatures) to kill them for food or sport. **2** persecute. **3** look thoroughly: *to hunt through drawers.*
n **1** the act of hunting: *a duck hunt.* **2** a group of persons hunting together. **3** a careful search. ⟨Old English *huntian*⟩
hunt down a hunt for until caught or killed. **b** look for until found. **hunt out** seek and find. **hunt up** find by search.
hunt·er *n* **1** a person who hunts. **2** a horse or dog trained for hunting. **hunter's moon** the full moon after the harvest moon. **hunting ground** a place for hunting.

hur·dle ['hɜrdəl] *n* **1** in a race, a barrier for people or horses to jump over. **2** **hurdles** *pl* a race in which the runners jump over hurdles. **3** an obstacle, difficulty, etc.
v jump over. **hur·dler** *n.* ⟨Old English *hyrdel*⟩

hurl [hɜrl] *v* **1** throw with force. **2** speak with strong feeling: *to hurl insults.* **3** vomit.
n a violent throw. **hurl·er** *n.* ⟨related to Low German *hurreln*⟩

Hu·ron ['hjʊrɒn] *or* ['hjʊrən] *n* **1** a member of a First Nations people formerly living in the region between Lakes Huron and Ontario. **2** their Iroquoian language. **Hu·ron** *adj.* ⟨French = unkempt person, ruffian; *hure* dishevelled head of hair⟩

hur·rah [hə'rɑ] *interj*, *n* a shout of joy, approval, etc. Also, **hoo·ray**, **hur·ray.**

hur·ri·cane ['hɜrə,kein] *n* **1** a tropical cyclone that forms over the Atlantic Ocean, with winds of more than 120 km/h and, usually, very heavy rain. **2** any wind with a speed of more than 117 km/h. ⟨Spanish *huracán*; Carib⟩
hurricane lamp an oil lamp with a chimney to protect the flame from wind.

hur·ry ['hɜri] *v* **1** drive, move, etc. quickly. **2** move with more than a natural speed. **3** urge to great speed: *Don't hurry the driver.*
n **1** hurried movement or action. **2** an eagerness to have or do quickly. **3** need of haste: *There is no hurry.* ⟨origin uncertain⟩
hur·ried *adj* **1** done in a hurry: *a hurried reply.* **2** forced to hurry. **hur·ried·ly** *adv.*

hurt [hɜrt] *v* **hurt**, **hurt·ing 1** cause pain. **2** feel pain; suffer: *My ankle hurts.*
n **1** a wound or injury. **2** a bad effect, or a cause of this: *Failure was a hurt to her pride.* **hurt·ful** *adj.* **hurt·ful·ly** *adv.* **hurt·ful·ness** *n.* ⟨probably Old French *hurter* strike⟩
be hurting for *Informal* need very much: *We're hurting for time, folks.*

hur·tle ['hɜrtəl] *v* rush noisily or violently: *The express train hurtled past.* **hur·tle** *n.* ⟨Middle English, frequentative of *hurten* strike. See HURT.⟩

hus·band ['hʌzbənd] *n* the man one is married to.
v manage carefully: *Sick people must husband their strength.* **hus·band·ly** *adj.* ⟨Old English *hūs* house + *bonda* head of family⟩
hus·band·ry *n* **1** careful management. **2** farming, esp as a science or art.

hush [hʌʃ] *v* **1** stop making a noise. **2** calm.
n a stopping of noise; silence; quiet.
interj stop the noise! keep quiet! ⟨Middle English *hussht* orig interj, silence!⟩
hush up a stop discussion of. **b** *Informal* be silent.
hush–hush *adj Informal* secret: *hush-hush plans.* **hush money** *Informal* money to keep a person from telling something.

husk [hʌsk] *n* **1** the dry outer covering of certain seeds or fruits. **2** the dry or worthless outer covering of anything.
v remove the husk from. **husk·like** *adj.* ⟨Middle English *huske*; related to *house*⟩
husking bee formerly, a community gathering where neighbours husked corn and had a party.

husk·y¹ ['hʌski] *adj* **1** hoarse: *a husky cough.* **2** big and strong: *a husky young man.* **husk·i·ly** *adv.* **husk·i·ness** *n.* ⟨husk, n⟩

husk·y² ['hʌski] *n* ✱ any northern working dog. ⟨abbreviation of an early variant of *Eskimo*⟩

hus·sar [hə'zɑr] *n* **1** a light-armed cavalry soldier. **2** a member of certain armoured regiments. ⟨Old Serbian *husar, kursar;* Italian *corsaro* runner. Related to CORSAIR.⟩

hus·sy ['hʌsi] *n* a bad-mannered, bold, or immoral woman. ⟨*huswif* housewife⟩

hus·tings ['hʌstɪŋz] *n pl or sg* **1** a platform from which speeches are made in a political campaign. **2** the campaign route taken by a political candidate. ⟨Old Norse *hústhing* council; *hús* house + *thing* assembly⟩

hus·tle ['hʌsəl] *v* **1** hurry. **2** force hurriedly: *The police hustled the tramps out of town.* **3** push roughly. **4** *Informal* go or work quickly or with tireless energy: *He had to hustle to earn enough money to support his family.* **5** *Slang* sell or solicit, esp in an aggressive or deceitful way. *n* **1** a hurry. **2** a rough pushing or shoving; rude jostling. **3** *Informal* tireless energy. **hus·tler** *n.* ⟨Middle Dutch *hutselen* shake⟩

hut [hʌt] *n* a small, roughly built house. **hut·like** *adj.* ⟨Middle High German *hütte*⟩

hutch [hʌtʃ] *n* **1** a pen for rabbits, etc. **2** a cupboard with shelves, set on top of a buffet. ⟨Old French *huche*; Latin *hutica* chest⟩

Hut·ter·ite ['hʌtə,rəit] ✻ *n* a member of a religious and ethnic group of communal farmers living mainly in Alberta and Manitoba. **Hut·ter·ite** *adj.* ⟨Jacob *Hutter*, 16c founder⟩

hy·a·cinth ['haɪə,sɪnθ] *n* any of a genus of plants of the lily family, cultivated for their fragrant flowers. ⟨Greek *hyakinthos*⟩

hy·brid ['haɪbrɪd] *n* **1** the offspring of two animals or plants of different species, varieties, etc. **2** anything of mixed origin. **hy·brid** *adj.* ⟨Latin *hybrida* variant of *ibrida* mongrel, hybrid⟩ **hybrid card** a car with a hybrid propulsion system, such as an internal combustion engine and an electric motor. **hy·brid·ism** *n* **1** the production of hybrids. **2** a hybrid condition. **hy·brid·ize** *v* produce or cause to produce hybrids. **hy·brid·i·za·tion** *n.*

hy·dra ['haɪdrə] *n, pl* **-dras** or **-drae** [-dri] *or* [-draɪ] **1 Hydra** *Greek myth* a monstrous serpent having nine heads, each of which, after being cut off, was replaced by two heads unless the wound was cauterized. **2** any persistent evil. **3** a kind of freshwater polyp, so called because when the tubelike body is cut into pieces, each piece forms a new individual. ⟨Greek *hydra* water serpent⟩

hy·dran·gea [haɪ'dreɪndʒə] *or* [-dʒiə] *n* any of a genus of shrubs or vines of the saxifrage family, cultivated for their large, showy flower clusters. ⟨Greek *hydōr* water + *angeion* vessel; for its cup-shaped seed capsule⟩

hy·drant ['haɪdrənt] *n* a large pipe with a valve for drawing water directly from a water main. ⟨Greek *hydōr* water⟩

hy·drate ['haɪdreɪt] *Chemistry n* a compound produced when any of certain other substances unite with water. *v* combine with water to form a hydrate. ⟨Greek *hydōr* water⟩ **hy·dra·tion** *n* the process of combining with water, esp to form a hydrate.

hy·drau·lic [haɪ'drɒlɪk] *adj* **1** to do with water or other liquid in motion. **2** to do with hydraulics: *a hydraulic engineer.* **hy·drau·li·cal·ly** *adv.* ⟨Greek *hydōr* water + *aulos* pipe⟩. **hy·drau·lics** *n* the branch of science dealing with water and other liquids in motion (with sg verb).

hy·dro ['haɪdrou] *n* ✻ **1** hydro-electric power. **2** electricity as a utility distributed by a power company: *The hydro was off for two hours during the storm.* ⟨Greek *hydōr* water⟩ **hydro–** *combining form* **1** to do with water: *hydrostatics.* **2** combined with hydrogen: *hydrochloric.* Also, **hydr-**, before vowels. **hy·dro–e·lec·tric** *adj* to do with the generation of elecricity by water power. **hy·dro–e·lec·tric·i·ty** *n.*

hy·dro·car·bon [,haɪdrou'kɑrbən] *n Chemistry* any of a class of compounds containing only hydrogen and carbon.

hy·dro·ceph·a·lus [,haɪdrə'sɛfələs] *n Pathology* an accumulation of fluid within the cranium, esp in infancy, often causing great enlargement of the head. **hy·dro·ce·phal·ic** [,haɪdrousə'fælɪk] *or* **hy·dro·ceph·a·lous** [,haɪdrə'sɛfələs] *adj.* ⟨*hydro-* + Greek *kephalē* head⟩ .

hydrochloric acid [,haɪdrə'klɒrɪk] *Chemistry* a corrosive solution of hydrogen chloride.

hy·dro·dy·nam·ics [,haɪdroudaɪ'næmɪks] *n* the branch of physics dealing with the forces exerted by liquids. **hy·dro·dy·nam·ic** *adj.* **hy·dro·dy·nam·i·cal·ly** *adv.*

hy·dro·foil ['haɪdrə,fɔɪl] *n* one of a set of blades attached to the hull of a boat so that the boat is lifted just clear of the water.

hy·dro·gen ['haɪdrədʒən] *n* a gaseous element that burns easily and weighs less than any other known element. Hydrogen combines chemically with oxygen to form water. *Symbol* **H** ⟨Greek *hydōr* water + *-genēs* born⟩ **hy·dro·ge·nate** [haɪ'drɒdʒə,neɪt] *or* ['haɪdrədʒə,neɪt] *v Chemistry* combine an unsaturated organic compound with hydrogen. **hydrogen bomb** a bomb that uses the fusion of atoms to cause an explosion of tremendous force. **hydrogen peroxide** a liquid often in dilute solution as an antiseptic, a bleaching agent, etc. **hydrogen sulphide** or **sulfide** *Chemistry* a flammable, poisonous gas having an offensive odour, found especially in mineral waters and decaying matter.

hy·drog·ra·phy [haɪ'drɒgrəfi] *n* the study of oceans, lakes, rivers, etc., esp with reference to their use for navigation and commerce.

hy·drol·o·gy [haɪ'drɒlədʒi] *n* the branch of physical geography that deals with the laws, properties, distribution, etc. of water. **hydrologic cycle** [,haɪdrə'lɒdʒɪk] the circular process in which water evaporates from the ocean, falls to earth as rain or snow, and runs to the ocean from rivers fed by rain or snow.

hy·drol·y·sis [haɪ'drɒləsɪs] *n, pl* **-ses** [-,siz] *Chemistry* a chemical decomposition that changes a compound into other compounds by taking up the elements of water. **hy·dro·lyt·ic** [,haɪdrə'lɪtɪk] *adj.* **hy·dro·lyze** *v.* ⟨*hydro-* + Greek *lysis* a loosening⟩

hy·drom·e·ter [haɪ'drɒmətər] *n* a graduated instrument for finding the specific gravity of a liquid.

hy·dro·pho·bi·a [,haɪdrə'foubiə] *n* **1** a

morbid dread of water. **2** rabies, esp in human beings, so called because one of the symptoms is a fear of water.
hy·dro·pho·bic *adj* **1** to do with hydrophobia. **2** *Chemistry* not easily mixed with or made wet by water.

hy·dro·plane ['haɪdrə,pleɪn] *n* **1** a light speedboat with hydrofoils so that the hull will rise out of the water at high speeds. **2** a horizontal rudder on a submarine for making it go up and down.
v of a vehicle, ride on a film of water that is built up under the tires on a wet road, thus losing control over brakes and steering.

hy·dro·pon·ics [,haɪdrə'pɒnɪks] *n* the growing of plants in water containing the necessary nutrients instead of in soil. **hy·dro·pon·ic** *adj.* **hy·dro·pon·i·cal·ly** *adv.* ⟨hydro- + Latin *ponere* to place⟩

hy·dro·sphere ['haɪdrə,sfɪr] *n* **1** the water on the surface of the globe. **2** the water vapour in the atmosphere.

hy·dro·stat·ics [,haɪdrə'stætɪks] *n* the branch of physics that deals with the equilibrium and pressure of liquids. **hy·dro·stat·ic** *adj.* **hy·dro·stat·i·cal·ly** *adv.*

hy·dro·ther·a·py [,haɪdrə'θɛrəpi] *n* the treatment of diseases by means of water, esp bathing or exercising in water.

hy·drot·ro·pism [haɪ'drɒtrə,pɪzəm] *n* *Biology* a tendency to turn or move toward or away from water. **hy·dro·trop·ic** *adj.* ⟨hydro- + Greek *tropos* a turning⟩

hy·drous ['haɪdrəs] *adj* containing water, usually in combination.

hy·e·na [haɪ'inə] *n* any of a family of wolflike carnivores that live mainly as scavengers. ⟨Greek *hyaina*; *hys* pig⟩

hy·giene ['haɪdʒin] *n* **1** the principles of preventing disease. **2** practices such as cleanliness that help to preserve health: *personal hygiene.* **hy·gien·ic** [haɪ'dʒinɪk] *or* [-'dʒɛnɪk] *adj.* **hy·gien·i·cal·ly** *adv.* ⟨Greek *hygieinē*; *hygiēs* healthy⟩
hy·gien·ist [haɪ'dʒɛnɪst], ['haɪdʒinɪst], *or* [haɪ'dʒinɪst] *n* a person trained in hygiene, such as a dental hygienist.

hy·grom·e·ter [haɪ'grɒmətər] *n* any instrument for determining the amount of moisture in the air. ⟨Greek *hygros* wet⟩

hy·men ['haɪmən] *n* *Anatomy* a fold of mucous membrane extending partly across the opening of the vagina, usually ruptured the first time sexual intercourse takes place. **hy·men·al** *adj.* ⟨Greek = membrane⟩

hymn [hɪm] *n* **1** a song of praise to God. **2** any song of praise. **hymn** *v.* **hymn·like** *adj.* ⟨Greek *hymnos*⟩
hym·nal *n* a book of hymns.

hype [haɪp] *Informal n* sensational or exaggerated advertising. **hype** *v.* ⟨hyperbole⟩

hyp·er ['haɪpər] *adj Informal* overwrought or overexcited. ⟨Greek = exceedingly, beyond⟩
hyper– *prefix* exceedingly; to excess: *hyperacidity, hypersensitive.*

hy·per·ac·tiv·i·ty [,haɪpəræk'tɪvəti] *n* excessive activity or restlessness, associated with physical or psychological disorders, esp in children. **hy·per·ac·tive** *adj.*

hy·per·bo·la [haɪ'pɜrbələ] *n, pl* **-las** *Geometry* a curve formed when a cone is cut by a plane. ⟨Greek *hyperbolē*; *hyper-* beyond + *ballein* throw⟩
hy·per·bo·le [haɪ'pɜrbəli] *n* exaggeration for effect. *Example: Waves high as mountains broke over the reef.* Compare LITOTES. **hy·per·bol·ize** *v.* **hy·per·bol·ism** *n* the use of hyperbole. **hy·per·bol·ic** [,haɪpər'bɒlɪk] *adj* **1** to do with hyperbole; exaggerated; exaggerating. **2** to do with hyperbolas. **hy·per·bol·i·cal·ly** *adv.*

hy·per·crit·i·cal [,haɪpər'krɪtəkəl] *adj* excessively critical. **hy·per·crit·i·cal·ly** *adv.* **hy·per·crit·i·cism** *n*

hy·per·gly·ce·mi·a [,haɪpərglaɪ'simiə] *n* an abnormally high concentration of sugar in the blood. **hy·per·gly·ce·mic** *adj.* ⟨hyper- + Greek *glyko-* sweet + -EMIA⟩

hy·per·me·di·a [,haɪpər'midiə] *n* *Computers* the hypertext system that allows downloading graphics, sound files, video files, and text.

hy·per·o·pi·a [,haɪpər'oupiə] *n* far-sightedness. **hy·per·op·ic** [-'ɒpɪk] *adj.* ⟨Greek *hyper-* beyond + *ōps* eye⟩

hy·per·sen·si·tiv·i·ty [,haɪpər,sɛnsə'tɪvəti] *n* excessive sensitiveness. **hy·per·sen·si·tive** *adj.* **hy·per·sen·si·tive·ness** *n.*

hy·per·son·ic [,haɪpər'sɒnɪk] *adj* **1** of speed five or more times faster than that of sound. **2** able to travel at this speed.

hy·per·ten·sion [,haɪpər'tɛnʃən] *n* abnormally high blood pressure.

hy·per·text ['haɪpər,tɛkst] *n* *Computers* **1** in a document, Web page, etc., a feature whereby text, graphics, and sound can be accessed by selecting a specially marked word on the screen (**hyperlink text**) or, sometimes, an icon. **2** loosely, **a** a document or documents using this feature. **b** the word embodying the link. ⟨Greek *hyper-* beyond, over + TEXT⟩

hy·per·thy·roid·ism [,haɪpər'θaɪrɔɪ,dɪzəm] *n* excessive activity of the thyroid gland. Compare HYPOTHYROIDISM.

hy·per·ven·ti·late [,haɪpər'vɛntə,leɪt] *v* breathe abnormally fast and deeply. **hy·per·ven·ti·la·tion** *n.*

hy·phen ['haɪfən] *n* a mark (-) used to connect words to form certain compounds (*double-dealer, light-hearted, door-to-door*); to separate certain affixes to indicate special meaning (*re-creation* vs. *recreation*) or facilitate recognition of word elements (*re-enter*); to indicate a break in a word at the end of a line of printing or writing. ⟨Greek *hyphen*; *hypo-* under + *hen* one⟩
hy·phen·ate write or print with a hyphen. **hy·phen·at·ed** *adj* **1** joined with a hyphen. **2** of foreign or mixed birth: *a hyphenated Canadian.* **hy·phen·a·tion** *n.*

hyp·no·sis [hɪp'noʊsɪs] *n*, *pl* **-ses** [-siz] a state resembling deep sleep, in which a person acts according to the suggestions of the person who induced the hypnosis. ⟨Greek *hypnos* sleep, n.⟩
hyp·no·ther·a·py [ˌhɪpnoʊ'θɛrəpi] *n* the use of hypnotism to treat behavioural disorders. **hyp·no·ther·a·pist** *n*. **hyp·not·ic** [hɪp'nɒtɪk] *adj* **1** to do with hypnosis. **2** easily hypnotized. **3** causing or tending to cause sleep: *the hypnotic monotone of his voice. n* a drug or other means of causing sleep. **hyp·not·i·cal·ly** *adv*. **hyp·no·tism** *n* the inducing of hypnosis. **hyp·no·tize** *v* **1** put into a hypnotic state. **2** *Informal* control by suggestion. **hyp·no·tist** *n*. **hyp·no·tiz·a·ble** *adj*.
hypo– *prefix* **1** under; beneath; below: *hypodermic*. **2** less than; less than normal: *hypothyroid*. ⟨Greek⟩
hy·po·al·ler·gen·ic [ˌhəipo͟ˌælər'dʒɛnik] *adj* having little or no tendency to cause an allergic reaction.
hy·po·chon·dri·a [ˌhəipə'kɒndriə] *n* unnatural anxiety about one's health. **hy·po·chon·dri·ac** *n*, *adj*. ⟨Greek *hypo-* under + *chondros* cartilage (of breastbone); supposed seat of melancholy⟩
hy·poc·ri·sy [hɪ'pɒkrəsi] *n* the act of putting on a false appearance, esp of goodness or religion. **hyp·o·crite** ['hɪpəˌkrɪt] *n*. **hyp·o·crit·i·cal** [ˌhɪpə'krɪtəkəl] *adj*. **hyp·o·crit·i·cal·ly** *adv*. ⟨Greek *hypokrisis* acting, pretence; *hypo-* under + *krinein* judge⟩
hy·po·der·mic [ˌhəipə'dɜrmɪk] *adj* for injecting under the skin: *a hypodermic needle. n* a syringe used to inject medicine under the skin. **hy·po·der·mi·cal·ly** *adv*. ⟨*hypo-* + Greek *derma* skin⟩
hy·po·gly·ce·mi·a [ˌhəipəɡləi'simiə] *n* an abnormally low concentration of sugar in the blood. **hy·po·gly·ce·mic** *adj*. ⟨*hypo-* + Greek *glyko-* sweet + -EMIA⟩
hy·pot·e·nuse [həi'pɒtəˌnjus] *or* [-ˌnus], [-ˌnjuz] *or* [-ˌnuz] *n* *Geometry* the side of a right triangle opposite the right angle. ⟨Greek *hypoteinousa*, ppr of *hypoteinein; hypo-* under + *teinein* stretch⟩

hy·po·thal·a·mus [ˌhəipə'θæləməs] *or* [ˌhɪpə-] *n* *Anatomy* the part of the brain beneath the thalamus. It controls hunger, thirst, temperature, and growth. **hy·po·tha·lam·ic** [ˌhəipəθə'læmɪk] *or* [ˌhɪpə-] *adj*.
hy·po·ther·mi·a [ˌhəipə'θɜrmiə] *n* abnormally low body temperature. ⟨*hypo-* + Greek *thermē* heat⟩
hy·poth·e·sis [həi'pɒθəsɪs] *n*, *pl* **-ses** [-ˌsiz] **1** something assumed because it seems likely to be a true explanation; theory. **2** a proposition assumed as a basis for reasoning. **hy·poth·e·size** *v*. ⟨Greek *hypo-* under + *thesis* a placing⟩
hy·po·thet·i·cal [ˌhəipə'θɛtəkəl] *adj* of or based on a hypothesis; proposed for the sake of argument, but not real. Also, **hy·po·thet·ic**. **hy·po·thet·i·cal·ly** *adv*.
hy·po·thy·roid·ism [ˌhəipə'θaɪrɔɪˌdɪzəm] *n* *Pathology* insufficient activity of the thyroid gland. Compare HYPERTHYROIDISM.
hys·sop ['hɪsəp] *n* a herb of the mint family, used as flavouring and, formerly, as a medicine. ⟨Greek *hyssōpos;* Semitic⟩
hys·ter·ec·to·my [ˌhɪstə'rɛktəmi] *n* surgical removal of the uterus. ⟨Greek *hystera* uterus + -ECTOMY⟩
hys·te·ri·a [hɪ'stiriə] *or* [hɪ'stɛriə] *n* **1** a nervous disorder that causes violent fits of laughing and crying, imaginary or real illnesses, lack of self-control, etc. **2** a state of uncontrolled excitement, esp involving laughing or crying. **hys·ter·ic** [hɪ'stɛrɪk] *n*. **hys·ter·i·cal** or **hys·ter·ic** *adj*. **hys·ter·i·cal·ly** *adv*. ⟨Greek *hystera* uterus; it was formerly thought that women are more often affected than men⟩
hys·ter·ics *n pl* HYSTERIA (def. 2)
Hz HERTZ.

Ii

i or **I** [aɪ] *n, pl* **i's** or **I's** **1** the ninth letter of the English alphabet, or any speech sound represented by it. **2** the ninth person or thing in a series. **3** the Roman numeral for 1.

I [aɪ] *pron subj* **I** *obj* **me** *poss* **mine** *pl subj* **we** *pl obj* **us** *pl poss* **ours.**
n, pl **I's** **1** the person who is speaking or writing. **2** the ego or individual self. ⟨Old English *ic*⟩

> **USAGE**
> The pronoun **I** is written with a capital because in old handwritten manuscripts a small **i** was likely to be lost or get attached to a neighbouring word.

i·am·bic [aɪˈæmbɪk] *Prosody adj* to do with a metrical foot consisting of two syllables, the first one having a weak stress and the second a strong stress. *Example:*
  The sún I that bríef I Decém I ber dáy
  Rose chéer I less ó I ver hílls I of gréy.
n Usually, **iambics** *pl* iambic verse. ⟨Greek *iambos*⟩
iambic pentameter a poetic metre based on five iambic feet in a line of verse.

i·at·ro·gen·ic [aɪˌætrəˈdʒɛnɪk] *adj* of a disease or symptoms, caused or induced by medical treatment. ⟨Greek *iatros* doctor + -GENIC⟩

i·bex [ˈaɪbɛks] *n, pl* **i·bex·es, ib·i·ces** [ˈɪbəˌsiz] *or* [ˈaɪbəˌsiz], *or* (esp collectively) **i·bex** any of several wild goats having large horns that curve back in a semicircle. ⟨Latin⟩

ibid. in the same place (for Latin *ibidem*).

> **USAGE**
> The term **ibid.** is used in a footnote to refer to the book, article, etc. mentioned in the immediately preceding footnote.

i·bis [ˈaɪbɪs] *n, pl* **i·bis·es** or (esp collectively) **i·bis** any of various wading birds having a slender, downward-curved bill. ⟨Egyptian⟩

–ible *adjective-forming suffix* that can be――ed: *perfectible, reducible.* ⟨Old French; Latin *-ibilis*⟩

i·bu·pro·fen [ˌaɪbjuˈproufən] *or* [ˌɪbju-] *n* an analgesic and anti-inflammatory drug.

–ic *suffix* **1** to do with: *atmospheric, artistic.* **2** *Chemistry* implying a smaller proportion of the element that *-ous* implies, as in *sulphuric.* ⟨French *-ique*, Latin *-icus*, or Greek *-ikos*⟩

ICBM intercontinental ballistic missile.

ice [aɪs] *n* **1** frozen water. **2** a frozen surface for skating, curling, hockey, etc. **3 the ice** ✹ esp in Newfoundland and Labrador, the edge of the Arctic icefields where seal hunting takes place. **4** a frozen dessert, usually made of sweetened fruit juice. **ice** *adj.*
v **1** cool with ice. **2** freeze (*over*): *The lake ices over in January.* **3** cover with icing. **4** *Hockey* **a** shoot (a puck) from the defensive zone past the red line at the opposite end of the rink. **b** put (a team) into play: *Our town iced a*

good hockey team. **5** *Slang* kill. **ice·less** *adj.* **i·cy, i·ci·er, i·ci·est** *adj.* **i·ci·ly** *adv.* **i·ci·ness** *n.* ⟨Old English *īs*⟩
break the ice *Informal* overcome first difficulties in getting acquainted. **cut no ice** *Informal* have little or no effect. **on ice** ready and waiting. **on thin ice** in a dangerous or difficult position.

ice age 1 any of the times in geological history when much of the earth was covered with glaciers. **2** Often, **Ice Age** the most recent such time, the Pleistocene epoch. **ice·berg** *n* a large mass of ice floating in the sea. **tip of the iceberg** a small part of something much larger. **ice–blind** *adj* ✹ temporarily blind from exposure to the glare from ice. Compare SNOW-BLIND. **ice·blink** *n* a glare in the sky over an ice field, caused by reflection. **ice·bound** *adj* **1** held fast by ice: *The ship was icebound.* **2** shut in by ice: *The port at Churchill is icebound for about 10 months of the year.* **ice–box** or **ice·box** *n* an insulated box in which food is kept cool by ice. **ice·break·er** *n* **1** a ship designed for breaking a passage through ice. **2** something, such as a joke, which helps to put people at their ease at gatherings. **ice bridge 1** a winter road over a frozen river, lake, etc. **2** ✹ a bridge of ice formed by the jamming of ice in a river. **ice·cap** *n* a permanent covering of ice over an area. **ice carnival** ✹ an organized social activity featuring winter sports, ice sculpture, etc. **ice–chisel** *n* ✹ an ice-cutting tool. **ice–cold** *adj* as cold as ice. **ice cream** a frozen dessert made of cream. **ice–cream parlour** or **parlor** a small cafe that sells ice cream. **ice cube** a small chunk of ice used for chilling drinks or food. **iced** *adj* **1** cooled with ice. **2** covered with icing. **ice field** a large sheet of ice floating in the sea, or covering land. **ice fishing** fishing through a hole cut through ice. **ice fisher. ice hockey** HOCKEY (def. 1). **ice·house** *n* **1** a building where ice is stored. **2** a structure with insulated walls, used for cold storage. **3** ✹ a snow house. **4** an ice-making plant. **ice hut** a small building towed onto the ice and used by ice fishers as a shelter while angling. **ice milk** a sweet food made with frozen skim milk. **ice pack 1** a large expanse of floating ice, consisting of many small floes packed together. **2** a bag containing ice for application to the body to relieve pain, swelling, itch, etc. **ice pan** or **pan ice** ✹ a fairly substantial slab of ice broken off from a large expanse of ice. **ice pick** a sharp-pointed tool for breaking up ice. **ice sheet** a thick sheet of ice covering a large area for a long time. **ice skate** SKATE¹ (def. 1). **ice–skate** *v.* **ice–skat·er** *n.* **ice storm** a freezing rain that covers exposed surfaces with a layer of glistening ice; SILVER THAW (def. 1). **ice time 1** *Hockey* the time actually spent on the ice by a player or players during a game. **2** the time during which the ice at a rink is available to a group, or individuals. **i·ci·cle** [ˈaɪsəkəl] *n* **1** a pointed, hanging stick of ice formed by the freezing of dripping water.

2 anything resembling this. **i·ci·cled** *adj.*

ic·ing *n* **1** a sweet mixture used to cover cakes, etc., made of sugar and some liquid, flavouring, etc. **2** in hockey, the shooting of the puck from within one's own defensive zone across the opponent's goal line. **icing sugar** powdered sugar used in making icing, candy, etc.

I Ching ['i 'tʃɪŋ] an ancient Chinese book of divination; the Book of Changes.

ich·thy·ol·o·gy [ˌɪkθiˈɒlədʒi] *n* the branch of zoology dealing with fish. **ich·thy·o·log·i·cal** *adj.* **ich·thy·ol·o·gist** *n.* ⟨Greek *ichthys* fish⟩

i·ci·cle See ICE.

ick·y ['ɪki] *Slang* **1** repulsive. **2** sticky. ⟨imitative⟩

i·con ['aikɒn] *n* **1** a sacred picture of Christ, an angel, a saint, etc. **2** any picture or image. **3** *Computers* a symbol that represents an object (file, application, etc.) or an operation (delete, print, etc.). ⟨Greek *eikōn*⟩ **i·con·ic** [əiˈkɒnɪk] *adj* **1** to do with icons. **2** of memorial sculptures, etc., conventional in style. **i·con·o·clasm** [əiˈkɒnəˌklæzəm] *n* the belief of iconoclasts. **i·con·o·clast** *n* **1** a person who attacks cherished institutions. **2** a person opposed to the use of images in religious worship. **i·con·o·clas·tic** *adj.* **i·con·o·clas·ti·cal·ly** *adv.* **i·co·nog·ra·phy** [ˌəikəˈnɒgrəfi] *n* **1** the study of illustrating by means of symbols, etc. **2** the representation of an individual in portraits, statues, etc. **i·co·nol·o·gy** *n* the historical study of icons.

i·co·sa·he·dron [ˌəikousəˈhidrən] *n* a solid with 20 faces. ⟨Greek *eikosi* twenty⟩

ICT information and communication technologies.

ICU intensive care unit.

i·cy See ICE.

id [ɪd] *n Psychoanalysis* that part of the self which is subconscious and instinctive. ⟨Latin = it; translation of German *Es* primal urge⟩

ID card ['ai 'di] identification card, an official card or other document such as a driver's licence, that helps to establish one's identity.

i·de·a [aiˈdiə] *n* **1** an abstraction: *the idea of immortality.* **2** an opinion: *to force one's ideas on others.* **3** a plan, suggestion, or invention: *She told them her idea for the campaign.* **4 ideas** *pl* creative thinking: *full of ideas.* **5** the purpose: *The idea of a vacation is to relax.* **6** the slightest knowledge: *I have no idea what time it is.* ⟨Greek = form, kind; base *id-* see⟩ **get ideas (into one's head)** expect too much.

i·de·al *n* a model to be imitated: *Her mother is her ideal. adj* **1** just as one would wish: *an ideal day for a picnic.* **2** existing only in thought: *A point without length, breadth, or thickness is an ideal object.* **i·de·al·ism** *n* **1** the practice of acting according to one's ideals, regardless of circumstances. **2** a cherishing of fine ideals. **3** the idealized treatment of things in art or literature as opposed to a faithful rendering of nature. **4** *Philosophy* the belief that all knowledge derives from ideas, not from objects. **i·de·al·ist** *n.* **i·de·al·is·tic** [ˌaidiəˈlɪstɪk] *adj.* **i·de·al·is·ti·cal·ly** *adv.*

i·de·al·ize [aiˈdiəˌlaiz] *v* think of as perfect rather than as is actually the case: *He idealized his older sister.* **i·de·al·i·za·tion** *n.* **i·de·al·ly** *adv* **1** perfectly. **2** in theory.

id·e·o·gram or **id·e·o·graph** ['ɪdiə,-] *or* ['aidiə,-] *n* a symbol that represents a thing without representing the sounds of the word for the thing. **id·e·og·ra·phy** [ˌɪdiˈɒgrəfi] *n* the representation of ideas by symbols. **id·e·o·graph·ic** *adj.* **i·de·ol·o·gy** [ˌaidi'-] *or* [ˌɪdi'-] *n* **1** a body of concepts about social, political, or economic systems. **2** the combined doctrines of a social or political movement. **i·de·o·log·i·cal** *adj.* **i·de·o·log·i·cal·ly** *adv.* **i·de·ol·o·gist** *n.* **i·de·o·logue** *n* a person who supports a particular ideology.

i·dée fixe [ideiˈfiks] *French* an obsession.

i·den·ti·cal [aiˈdɛntəkəl] *adj* **1** the same: *The composer of this song is identical with the lyricist.* **2** exactly alike: *The copy is identical to the original.* **3** of twins, developing from a single egg cell that split in two. Compare FRATERNAL (def. 3). **i·den·ti·cal·ly** *adv.* ⟨Latin *identicus*, from *idem* same⟩ **i·den·ti·fi·ca·tion** *n* something used to identify a person or thing. **i·den·ti·fy** *v* **1** recognize as being a certain person or thing: *He identified the bag as his by what it contained.* **2** make the same: *The king identified his people's welfare with his own.* **3** connect closely: *He identified himself with the revolutionary movement.* **i·den·ti·fi·able** *adj.* **i·den·ti·ty** *n* **1** being oneself and not another: *The writer concealed her identity under an assumed name.* **2** exact likeness: *an identity of interests.* **3** the state of being the same one as described: *the identity of these pearls with the ones reported missing.* **identity theft** the stealing of someone's personal information in order to defraud that person, or for other criminal activities like terrorism.

id·i·o·cy See IDIOT.

id·i·om ['ɪdiəm] *n* **1** an expression whose meaning is not predictable from its constituent elements. *Example: chew the fat* means *chat.* **2** dialect: *the idiom of the Ottawa Valley.* **3** a people's way of expressing themselves: *In the Hopi idiom, time is not an important category.* **id·i·o·mat·ic** *adj.* **id·i·o·mat·i·cal·ly** *adv.* ⟨Greek *idioma; idios* one's own⟩

id·i·o·syn·cra·sy [ˌɪdiəˈsɪŋkrəsi] *n* a personal peculiarity of behaviour, taste, etc. **id·i·o·syn·crat·ic** [ˌɪdiəsɪŋˈkrætɪk] *adj.* **id·i·o·syn·crat·i·cal·ly** *adv.* ⟨Greek *idios* one's own + *synkrasis* temperament (*syn* together + *kerannynai* mix)⟩

id·i·ot ['ɪdiət] *n* **1** a person who does not develop mentally beyond the age of three or four years. **2** a very stupid or foolish person: *I was an idiot to refuse that offer.* **id·i·ot·ic** [ˌɪdiˈɒtɪk] *adj.* **id·i·ot·i·cal·ly** *adv.* ⟨Greek *idiōtēs; idios* one's own⟩

id·i·o·cy *n* **1** the state of being an idiot. **2** very great stupidity. **3** a stupid act or remark. **idiot box** *Slang* television. **idiot savant** ['ɪdiət sə'vant] person with a serious mental handicap but with one extraordinary gift, such as mathematics. **idiot stick ✷** *Slang* a low-priced souvenir totem pole.

i·dle ['aɪdəl] *adj* **1** not busy; not working: *idle hands.* **2** lazy. **3** worthless: *idle pleasures.* **4** without any good reason: *idle fears.*
v **1** waste time; do nothing: *Are you going to spend your whole vacation just idling?* **2** run slowly without transmitting power: *The motor of a car idles when it is out of gear.* **i·dle·ness** *n.* **i·dly** *adv.* ⟨Old English *idel*⟩
idle away spend wastefully: *She idled away many hours lying in the hammock.*
i·dler *n* a lazy person.

i·dol ['aɪdəl] *n* **1** an object worshipped as a god. **2** in the Bible, a false god. **3** a person or thing worshipped too much. **i·dol·ize** *v.* **i·dol·i·za·tion** *n.* ⟨Greek *eidōlon* image; *eidos* form⟩
i·dol·a·ter [aɪ'dɒlətər] *n* **1** a person who worships idols. **2** an admirer. **i·dol·a·trous** *adj.* **i·dol·a·trous·ly** *adv.* **i·dol·a·try** *n.*

i·dyll or **i·dyl** ['aɪdəl] *or* ['ɪdəl] *n* **1** in poetry or prose, a short description of a scene of country life. **2** a simple and charming event or experience. **3** a long narrative poem on a major theme: *Idylls of the King.* **i·dyl·lic** *adj.* **i·dyl·li·cal·ly** *adv.* ⟨Greek *eidyllion* diminutive of *eidos* form⟩

–ie *suffix* little; darling: *dearie.* ⟨variant of *-y*⟩

i.e. that is. ⟨Latin *id est*⟩

if [ɪf] *conj* **1** on condition that: *I'll go if you will.* **2** whether: *I wonder if he will go.*
n a condition or supposition. ⟨Old English *gif*⟩
as if as it would be if. **if not a** otherwise: *I assume you'll be there; if not, let me know.* **b** even though not: *a wholesome meal, if not a very tasty one.* **c** indeed: *She should be reprimanded, if not fired.*
if·fy ['ɪfi] *adj Informal* uncertain, undecided, or risky: *an iffy proposition.*

i·gloo ['ɪglu] *n* **1** an Inuit dwelling, esp a domed structure built of blocks of snow. **2** any structure resembling this in shape. Also, **iglu.** ⟨Inuktitut *iglu, igdlu* abode, dwelling⟩

Ig·lu·lik [ɪ'glulɪk] *n, pl* **-lik 1** a member of an Inuit people of the eastern Arctic. **2** their dialect of Inuktitut.

ig·ne·ous ['ɪgniəs] *adj* **1** to do with fire. **2** *Geology* to do with rock formed by the solidification of molten matter: *Granite is igneous rock.* ⟨Latin *igneus; ignis* fire⟩

ig·nite [ɪg'naɪt] *v* **1** set on fire or begin to burn. **2** *Chemistry* heat to the point of combustion or chemical change. **ig·nit·a·ble** or **ig·nit·i·ble** *adj.* ⟨Latin *ignire; ignis* fire⟩
ig·ni·tion [ɪg'nɪʃən] *n* **1** a setting on fire or a catching fire. **2** the apparatus for igniting the vapour in an internal-combustion engine. **3** the heating of a substance to produce a complete chemical change.

ig·no·ble [ɪg'noubəl] *adj* **1** mean; without honour: *To betray a friend is ignoble.* **2** not of noble birth or position. **ig·no·bil·i·ty** *n* **ig·no·bly** *adv.* ⟨Latin *ignobilis; in-* not + early form *gnobilis* noble⟩

ig·no·min·i·ous [ˌɪgnə'mɪniəs] *adj* **1** shameful; dishonourable. **2** contemptible. **ig·no·min·i·ous·ly** *adv.* ⟨Latin *ignominia; in-* not + *nomen* name; form influenced by *gnoscere* come to know⟩
ig·no·min·y *n* **1** public shame and disgrace. **2** shameful action or conduct.

ig·nore [ɪg'nɔr] *v* pay no attention to ⟨Latin *ignorare* not know; *in-* not + *gnarus* aware⟩
ig·no·ra·mus [ˌɪgnə'reɪməs] *or* [ˌɪgnə'ræməs] *n* an ignorant person. **ig·no·rant** *adj* **1** knowing little or nothing: *A person who has not had opportunity to learn may be ignorant without being stupid.* **2** showing lack of knowledge: *an ignorant remark.* **3** uninformed; unaware: *He was ignorant of the fact that his house had been burned.* **ig·no·rance** *n.* **ig·no·rant·ly** *adv.*

i·gua·na [ɪ'gwɑnə] *n* any of the larger lizards of the tropical American family *Iguanidae.* ⟨Spanish; Carib⟩

ik·tas ['ɪktɑs] *n pl* **✷** *Informal* on the West Coast, goods or belongings: *We've got food and all the iktas we need.* Also, **ic·tas.** ⟨Chinook Jargon⟩

il–¹ *prefix* a form of IN-¹ occurring before *l*: *illegal.*

il–² *prefix* a form of IN-² occurring before *l*: *illuminate.*

ilk [ɪlk] *n* kind. ⟨Old English *ilca* same⟩
of that ilk a of the same place or name. **b** of that kind or sort.

ill [ɪl] *adj* **worse, worst 1** sick. **2** evil: *an ill deed.* **3** unfavourable: *an ill wind.* **4** cruel.
adv **worse, worst 1** harmfully. **2** unfavourably: *to fare ill.* **3** in an unkind manner: *He speaks ill of his former friends.* **4** with difficulty: *You can ill afford to waste your money.*
n **1** a sickness; disease. **2** an evil; a harm; a trouble: *Poverty is an ill.* ⟨Old Norse *illr*⟩
go ill with affect badly. **ill at ease** uncomfortable. **take ill** become ill. **take something ill** take offence at (something). **ill–ad·vised** *adj* unwise. **ill–ad·vis·ed·ly** [ˌɪləd'vaɪzɪdli] *adv.* **ill–bred** *adj* rude. **ill breeding. ill–con·sid·ered** or **ill–con·ceived** *adj* unwise; unsuitable. **ill–de·fined** *adj* not clearly explained. **ill–dis·posed** *adj* unfriendly; unfavourable. **ill–equipped** *adj* poorly prepared. **ill fame** a bad reputation. **ill–fat·ed** *adj* **1** sure to have a bad end. **2** unlucky. **ill–fa·voured** or **ill–fa·vored** *adj* **1** ugly to look at. **2** unpleasant; offensive. **ill feeling** dislike: *There has been ill feeling between them since the quarrel.* **ill–found·ed** *adj* without a good reason. **ill–got·ten** *adj* acquired by unfair, dishonest, or evil means. **ill health** poor health. **ill humour** or **humor** a cross, unpleasant mood. **ill–hu·moured** or **ill–hu·mored** *adj.* **ill–man·nered** *adj* rude. **ill nature** disagreeableness. **ill–na·tured** *adj.* **ill·ness** *n* a sickness. **ill–suit·ed** *adj* unsuitable.

ill temper bad temper. **ill–tem·pered** *adj*.
ill–timed *adj* done or happening at a bad
time. **ill–treat** *v* treat badly or cruelly; abuse.
ill–treat·ment *n*. **ill will** unkind or unfriendly
feeling; hostility.

il·le·gal [ɪ'ligəl] *adj* **1** prohibited by law:
illegal parking. **2** prohibited by an accepted
set of rules, esp in sports: *an illegal punch in
boxing.* **il·le·gal·ly** *adv*. **il·le·gal·i·ty** *n*.

il·leg·i·ble [ɪ'lɛdʒəbəl] *adj* hard or impossible
to read. **il·leg·i·bil·i·ty** *n*. **il·leg·i·bly** *adv*.

il·le·git·i·mate [ˌɪlə'dʒɪtəmɪt] *adj* **1** born of
parents who are not married to each other.
2 not according to the law. **il·le·git·i·ma·cy** *n*.
il·le·git·i·mate·ly *adv*.

il·lib·er·al [ɪ'lɪbərəl] *adj* **1** prejudiced.
2 stingy. **il·lib·er·al·i·ty** *n*. **il·lib·er·al·ly** *adv*.

il·lic·it [ɪ'lɪsɪt] *adj* **1** not permitted by
common custom: *an illicit love affair.*
2 ILLEGAL (def. 1): *illicit gambling.* **il·lic·it·ly** *adv*.
il·lic·it·ness *n*.

il·lit·er·ate [ɪ'lɪtərɪt] *adj* **1** unable to read or
write. **2** unable to read or write as well as
expected: *illiterate university students.*
n a person who is illiterate, often in a
particular field: *a computer illiterate.*
il·lit·er·a·cy *n*. **il·lit·er·ate·ly** *adv*.

il·log·ic [ɪl'lɒdʒɪk] *n* a lack of logic.
il·log·i·cal [ɪ'lɒdʒəkəl] *adj* **1** not according to
the rules of logic. **2** not reasonable: *an
illogical fear of the dark.* **il·log·i·cal·ly** *adv*.
il·log·i·cal·i·ty *n*.

il·lu·mi·nate [ɪ'lumə,neit] *v* **1** light up: *The
room was illuminated by four lamps.* **2** make
clear: *Our teacher could illuminate almost any
subject.* **3** decorate with lights: *The streets were
illuminated for the celebration.* **4** decorate with
gold and designs. **il·lu·mi·na·ble** *adj*.
il·lu·mi·na·tion *n*. **il·lu·mi·na·tive** [ɪ'lumənətɪv]
or [ɪ'lumə,neitɪv] *adj*. ⟨Latin *illuminare; in-* in
+ *lumen* light⟩
il·lu·mi·na·ti [ɪ,lumə'nɑti] *n pl* people
claiming special knowledge. **il·lu·mine**
[ɪ'lumən] *v* make or become bright; light up:
A smile can often illumine a homely face.

il·lu·sion [ɪ'luʒən] *n* **1** something that
deceives by giving a false idea: *an illusion of
reality.* **2** a false impression: *She's under the
illusion that she's popular.* **il·lu·sion·al** or
il·lu·sion·ary *adj*. ⟨Latin *illusio* from *illudere*
mock; *in-* at + *ludere* play⟩
il·lu·sion·ist *n* one who produces illusions;
conjurer. **il·lu·so·ry** [ɪ'lusəri] or [ɪ'luzəri] *adj*
unreal or misleading. **il·lu·so·ri·ly** *adv*.
il·lu·so·ri·ness *n*.

> **CONFUSABLES**
> An **illusion** is a misleading appearance: *an
> illusion of wealth.* An **allusion** is an indirect
> reference or slight mention: *He made several
> allusions to recent novels.*

il·lus·trate [ɪ'lə,streit] *v* **1** make clear by
pictures, examples, etc.: *A pump was used to
illustrate the action of the heart in circulating
blood.* **2** provide with pictures, diagrams, etc.
that explain or decorate: *This book is well

illustrated.* **il·lus·tra·tion** *n*. **il·lus·tra·tion·al** *adj*.
⟨Latin *in-* in + *lustrum*, orig lighting⟩
il·lus·tra·tive [ɪ'lʌstrətɪv] or [ɪ'lə,streitɪv] *adj*
helping to explain: *illustrative examples.*
il·lus·tra·tive·ly *adv*. **il·lus·tra·tor** [ɪ'lə,streitər] *n*
an artist who makes illustrations for books, etc.

il·lus·tri·ous [ɪ'lʌstriəs] *adj* outstanding: *an
illustrious statesman, an illustrious deed.*
il·lus·tri·ous·ly *adv*. **il·lus·tri·ous·ness** *n*. ⟨Latin
illustris lighted up, bright; *lustrum* lighting⟩

im–¹ *prefix* a form of IN-¹ occurring before *b, m,
p: imbalance, immoral, impatient.*

im–² *prefix* a form of IN-² occurring before *b, m,
p: imbibe, immure, impart.*

im·age ['ɪmɪdʒ] *n* **1** an artificial likeness of a
person or thing: *an image of a god.* **2** a person
or thing resembling another: *She is the very
image of her mother.* **3** a picture in the mind.
4 the way a person, nation, etc. is regarded
by the world at large: *Canada's foreign image.*
5 the impression of something produced
optically, as by a lens or mirror. A **real image**
is projected by a lens (by refraction) and a
virtual image is reflected in a mirror. **6** the
optical impression produced by an electronic
device: *an image on a television screen.* ⟨Old
French; Latin *imago*⟩
im·age·ry ['ɪmɪdʒri] *n* descriptions and
figures of speech that help the mind to form
pictures. **i·mag·i·nar·y** *adj* not real: *The
equator is an imaginary line circling the earth.*
imaginary number *Mathematics* a COMPLEX
NUMBER in which the coefficient of the
imaginary part is not zero. **i·mag·i·na·tion** *n*
1 the power of forming pictures in the mind.
2 the ability to create new ideas.
i·mag·i·na·tive [ɪ'mædʒənətɪv] *adj* showing
imagination: *an imaginative solution, an
imaginative child.* **i·mag·i·na·tive·ly** *adv*.
i·mag·ine [ɪ'mædʒɪn] *v* **1** picture in one's
mind. **2** suppose; guess: *I cannot imagine what
you mean.* **3** have the delusion that: *She
imagined someone was watching her.*
i·mag·i·na·ble *adj*. **i·mag·i·na·bly** *adv*.
im·ag·ism *n* a movement in poetry that
advocates the use of precise imagery and
opposes symbolism. **im·ag·ist** *n*. **im·ag·is·tic** *adj*.
im·ag·is·ti·cal·ly *adv*.

i·mam [ɪ'mɑm] *n Islam* **1** in the Sunni
tradition, a leader of worship in a mosque.
2 in the Shiite tradition, a spiritual leader
whose authority derives directly from
Muhammad. ⟨Arabic *imam; amma* go before⟩

im·bal·ance [ɪm'bæləns] *n* **1** the state of
being out of balance. **2** *Medicine* a lack of
co-ordination in glands, muscles, etc.

im·be·cile ['ɪmbə,saɪl] or ['ɪmbəsəl] *n* a very
stupid or foolish person **im·be·cile** *adj*.
im·be·cil·ic [-'sɪlɪk] *adj*. **im·be·cil·i·ty** *n*.
⟨Latin *imbecillus* weak⟩

im·bibe [ɪm'baɪb] *v* **1** drink. **2** absorb: *The
roots of a plant imbibe moisture from the earth.*
im·bib·er *n*. **im·bi·bi·tion** [ˌɪmbɪ'bɪʃən] *n*.
⟨Latin *in-* in + *bibere* drink⟩

im·bro·glio [ɪm'broʊljoʊ] *n* a complicated
or difficult situation. ⟨Italian⟩

im·bue [ɪmˈbju] v **1** fill; inspire: *She imbued her son's mind with the ambition to succeed.* **2** fill with moisture or colour. **im·bue·ment** n. ⟨Latin *imbuere* soak⟩

IMF INTERNATIONAL MONETARY FUND.

im·i·tate [ˈɪməˌteɪt] v **1** try to act like: *The boy imitated his father.* **2** copy: *A parrot imitates the sounds it hears.* **3** look like: *Plastic is often made to imitate wood.* **im·i·ta·ble** adj. **im·i·ta·bil·i·ty** n. ⟨Latin *imitari*⟩ **im·i·ta·tion** n **1** the act of imitating. **2** a copy: *an imitation of an antique chair.* adj made to look like something else: *imitation pearls.* **in imitation of** in order to be like. **im·i·ta·tion·al** adj. **im·i·ta·tive** adj **1** inclined to imitate others. **2** of a word, imitating a sound. *Bang* is an imitative word. **im·i·ta·tive·ly** adv. **im·i·ta·tive·ness** n. **im·i·ta·tor** n.

im·mac·u·late [ɪˈmækjəlɪt] adj **1** without stain: *The laundered shirts were immaculate.* **2** without fault: *Her appearance was immaculate.* **3** without sin. **im·mac·u·late·ly** adv. **im·mac·u·la·cy** n. ⟨Latin *in-* not + *macula* spot⟩

im·ma·nent [ˈɪmənənt] adj **1** remaining within; inherent. **2** of God, pervading the universe. **im·ma·nence** or **im·ma·nent·ly** adv. ⟨Latin *in-* in + *manere* stay⟩

im·ma·ter·i·al [ˌɪməˈtɪriəl] adj **1** not important. **2** spiritual rather than physical. **im·ma·te·ri·al·ly** adv. **im·ma·te·ri·al·ness** n.

im·ma·ture [ˌɪməˈtʃʊr] adj **1** not fully developed. **2** of an adult, behaving irresponsibly. **im·ma·ture·ly** adv. **im·ma·tu·ri·ty** n.

im·meas·ur·a·ble [ɪˈmɛʒərəbəl] adj too vast to be measured. **im·meas·ur·a·bly** adv. **im·meas·ur·a·bil·i·ty** n.

im·me·di·ate [ɪˈmidɪt] adj **1** without delay: *an immediate reply.* **2** with nothing between: *in immediate contact.* **3** direct: *the immediate result.* **4** closest: *my immediate neighbour.* **5** to do with the very near future: *our immediate plans.* **6** closely related: *my immediate family.* **im·me·di·a·cy** n. **im·me·di·ate·ly** adv. ⟨Latin *immediatus; in-* not + *medius* middle⟩

im·me·mo·ri·al [ˌɪməˈmɔriəl] adj extending back beyond the bounds of memory: *time immemorial.* **im·me·mo·ri·al·ly** adv.

im·mense [ɪˈmɛns] adj very big; huge; vast: *The Pacific Ocean is an immense body of water.* **im·mense·ly** adv. **im·men·si·ty** n. ⟨Latin *in-* not + *mensus* pp of *metiri* measure⟩

im·merse [ɪˈmɜrs] v **1** lower into a liquid until covered by it. **2** baptize by dipping under water. **3** involve deeply; absorb: *immersed in business affairs.* ⟨Latin *immersus* pp of *immergere; in-* in + *mergere* plunge⟩ **im·mersed** adj **1** Biology embedded in the surrounding parts, as an organ may be. **2** Botany growing under water. **im·mers·i·ble** adj that can be immersed without damage: *an immersible frying pan.* **Im·mer·sion** [ɪˈmɜrʒən] n **1** a baptism by dipping a person under water. **2** ✹ a method of teaching an additional language to a person by means of intensive exposure to the language.

im·mi·grate [ˈɪməˌgreɪt] v come into a country or region to live. Compare EMIGRATE. **im·mi·gra·tion** n. ⟨Latin *in-* into + *migrare* move⟩ **im·mi·grant** [ˈɪməgrənt] n **1** a person who comes into a country or region to live. Compare EMIGRANT. **2** a new plant or animal in an area. **im·mi·grant** adj.

im·mi·nent [ˈɪmənənt] adj likely to happen soon: *A storm is imminent.* **im·mi·nence** n. **im·mi·nent·ly** adv. ⟨Latin *in-* in + *minere* hang⟩

SYNONYMS
Imminent means 'likely to happen at any moment': *Swept along by the swift current, he was in imminent danger of going over the falls.* **Impending** suggests hanging over one, often indefinitely, and means 'near and about to take place': *impending disaster.*

im·mis·ci·ble [ɪˈmɪsəbəl] adj incapable of being mixed: *Water and oil are immiscible.* **im·mis·ci·bly** adv.

im·mo·bile [ɪˈmoubaɪl] or [ɪˈmoubəl] adj **1** not movable. **2** motionless. **im·mo·bil·i·ty** n. **im·mo·bi·lize** v. **im·mo·bi·li·za·tion** n.

im·mod·er·ate [ɪˈmɒdərɪt] adj not moderate; more than is right. **im·mod·er·ate·ly** adv. **im·mod·er·a·cy** n. **im·mod·er·a·tion** n.

im·mod·est [ɪˈmɒdɪst] adj **1** bold or rude. **2** indecent or improper. **im·mod·est·ly** adv. **im·mod·es·ty** n.

im·mo·late [ˈɪməˌleɪt] **1** kill as a sacrifice. **2** sacrifice. **3** destroy. **im·mo·la·tion** n. ⟨Latin *immolare* sacrifice, sprinkle with sacrificial meal; *in-* on + *mola* sacrificial meal⟩

im·mor·al [ɪˈmɔrəl] adj **1** morally wrong; wicked. **2** lewd; unchaste. **im·mo·ral·i·ty** n. **im·mor·al·ly** adv.

im·mor·tal [ɪˈmɔrtəl] adj **1** living forever. **2** likely to be remembered forever. n **1 immortals** pl the gods of ancient Greek and Roman mythology. **2** a person likely to be remembered forever: *Shakespeare is one of the immortals.* **im·mor·tal·ity** n. **im·mor·tal·ize** v. **im·mor·tal·i·za·tion** n. **im·mor·tal·ly** adv.

im·mov·a·ble [ɪˈmuvəbəl] adj **1** that cannot be moved. **2** not moving. **3** firm; steadfast; unyielding. **4** unfeeling; impassive. n **immovables** pl Law land, buildings, and other property that cannot be carried about. **im·mov·a·bly** adv. **im·mov·a·bil·i·ty** n.

im·mune [ɪˈmjun] adj **1** protected from or resistant to infections and toxins. (with *to*): *Some people are immune to poison ivy; they can touch it without getting a rash.* **2** free from some duty or obligation (with *from*): *immune from taxes.* **im·mu·ni·ty** n. ⟨Latin *immunis,* orig free from obligation⟩ **immune deficiency** a failure of the body's immune system to guard against infection. **immune response** the mechanisms by which the body responds to foreign antigens. **im·mu·nize** [ˈɪmjəˌnaɪz] v make immune: *Vaccination immunizes people against smallpox.* **im·mu·ni·za·tion** n. **im·mu·nol·o·gy** n the branch of medicine dealing with the immune system. **im·mu·no·log·i·cal** adj.

im·mu·nol·o·gist *n.* **im·mu·no·sup·pres·sion** [,ımjənousə'prɛʃən] *n* the suppression of immunity, esp to prevent rejection of a transplant. **im·mu·no·sup·pres·sant** or **im·mu·no·sup·pres·sive** *adj.*

im·mure [ı'mjʊr] *v* **1** imprison. **2** confine. **im·mure·ment** *n.* ⟨Latin *in-* in + *murus* wall⟩

im·mu·ta·ble [ı'mjutəbəl] *adj* never changing; unchangeable. **im·mu·ta·bil·i·ty** *n.* **im·mu·ta·bly** *adv.* ⟨Latin *in-* not + *mutabilis* changeable; *mutare* change⟩

imp [ımp] *n* **1** a young or small demon. **2** a mischievous child. **imp·ish** *adj.* **imp·ish·ly** *adv.* **imp·ish·ness** *n.* ⟨Old English *impe* a shoot, graft; Latin *imputus,* Greek *emphytos* engrafted⟩

im·pact ['ımpækt] *n* **1** a striking (of one thing against another): *The impact of the two swords broke both of them.* **2** a forceful effect: *the impact of automation on society.*
v **1** *Informal* affect strongly. **2** make contact forcefully (usually with *on, upon, against,* etc.): *The bat impacted against the ball with a crack.* **3** [ım'pækt] drive or press closely or firmly into something. ⟨Latin *impactus* pp of *impingere* strike against. See IMPINGE.⟩
im·pact·ed [ım'pæktıd] *adj* **1** firmly wedged in place. **2** of a tooth, pressed between the jawbone and another tooth.

im·pair [ım'pɛr] *v* make worse; damage: *Poor food impaired his health.* **im·pair·a·ble** *adj.* **im·pair·ment** *n.* ⟨Old French *empeirer*; Latin *in-* + *pejor* worse⟩
im·paired *adj* ✷ *Law* of a driver of a motor vehicle, under the influence of alcohol or narcotics: *She was charged with driving while impaired.* **impaired driving.**

im·pa·la [ım'pælə] *or* [ım'pɑlə] *n, pl* **-las** or (esp collectively) **-la** an antelope, the adult males having horns that curve in an S. ⟨Zulu⟩

im·pale [ım'peil] *v* **1** pierce through with something pointed: *The butterflies were impaled on small pins.* **2** torture by thrusting upon a pointed stake. **im·pale·ment** *n.* ⟨Latin *in-* on + *palus* stake⟩

im·pal·pa·ble [ım'pælpəbəl] *adj* that cannot be perceived by touch: *Sunlight is impalpable.* **im·pal·pa·bly** *adv.* **im·pal·pa·bil·i·ty** *n.*

im·part [ım'pɑrt] *v* **1** give: *The furnishings imparted an air of elegance to the room.* **2** communicate: *The interviewer asked her to impart the secret of her success.* **im·par·ta·tion** *n.* ⟨Latin *in-* + *pars, partis* part⟩

im·par·tial [ım'pɑrʃəl] *adj* showing no favour to either side of any contest or conflict. **im·par·tial·ly** *adv.* **im·par·ti·al·i·ty** *n.*

im·pass·a·ble [ım'pæsəbəl] *adj* so that one cannot go through or across: *Deep mud made the road impassable.* **im·pass·a·bil·i·ty** *n.* **im·pass·a·bly** *adv.*

im·passe ['ımpæs] *or* [ım'pæs] *n* **1** a position from which there is no escape; deadlock. **2** a road closed at one end; blind alley. ⟨French⟩

im·pas·sioned [ım'pæʃənd] *adj* full of strong feeling; ardent; rousing: *an impassioned speech.* **im·pas·sion·ed·ly** *adv.*

im·pas·sive [ım'pæsıv] *adj* **1** expressionless: *an impassive face.* **2** not feeling any emotion, pain, or injury. **im·pas·sive·ly** *adv.* **im·pas·sive·ness** *n.* **im·pas·siv·i·ty** *n.* ⟨Latin *in-* not + *passivus,* from *pati* suffer⟩

im·pa·tiens [ım'peiʃəns] *n* any of a genus of plants cultivated for its bright flowers. ⟨Latin = not enduring, not bearing⟩

im·pa·tient [ım'peiʃənt] *adj* **1** not willing to bear delay, opposition, etc.: *too impatient to attend to details.* **2** restless: *They were impatient to see the puppy.* **3** showing lack of patience: *an impatient answer.* **im·pa·tience** *n.* **im·pa·tient·ly** *adv.*
impatient of unwilling to endure; not liking.

im·peach [ım'pitʃ] *v* **1** cast doubt on: *to impeach the testimony of a witness.* **2** charge with wrongdoing. **3** bring a (public official) to trial for wrong conduct during office: *The judge was impeached for taking a bribe.* **im·peach·a·ble** *adj.* **im·peach·ment** *n.* ⟨Old French *empêechier* hinder, Latin *in-* on + *pedica* shackle; *ped-* foot⟩

im·pec·ca·ble [ım'pɛkəbəl] *adj* **1** faultless. **2** sinless. **im·pec·ca·bly** *adv.* **im·pec·ca·bil·i·ty** *n.* ⟨Latin *in-* not + *peccare* sin⟩

im·pe·cu·ni·ous [,ımpə'kjuniəs] *adj* having little or no money. **im·pe·cu·ni·ous·ly** *adv.* **im·pe·cu·ni·ous·ness** *n.* ⟨*in-¹* + Latin *pecunia* money; *pecu* head of cattle⟩

im·pede [ım'pid] *v* hinder. ⟨Latin *impedire; in-* on + *pes, pedis* foot⟩
im·ped·ance *n* **1** *Electricity* the apparent resistance in an alternating-current circuit, made up of reactance and ohmic resistance. **2** *Physics* the ratio of pressure in a sound wave to the product of the particle velocity and the area of a cross section of the wave. **im·ped·i·ment** [ım'pɛdəmənt] *n* **1** hindrance. **2** a defect in speech: *Stuttering is an impediment.* **3** *Law* a bar to the making of a valid marriage contract. **im·ped·i·men·ta** [ım,pɛdə'mɛntə] *n pl* equipment, baggage, etc. that hinders progress.

im·pel [ım'pɛl] *v* **-pelled, -pel·ling 1** drive; force: *Hunger impelled the lazy man to work.* **2** cause to move: *The wind impelled the boat to shore.* ⟨Latin *in-* on + *pellere* push⟩

im·pend [ım'pɛnd] *v* **1** be likely to happen soon: *When war impends, people try to prevent it.* **2** hang threateningly. **im·pend·ing** *adj.* ⟨Latin *in-* over + *pendere* hang⟩

im·pen·e·tra·ble [ım'pɛnətrəbəl] *adj* **1** that cannot be entered, pierced, or passed: *Thick steel is impenetrable by an ordinary bullet.* **2** not open to ideas, influences, etc. **3** impossible to explain or understand: *an impenetrable mystery.* **4** *Physics* of a body, excluding all other bodies from the space it occupies. **im·pen·e·tra·bil·i·ty** *n.* **im·pen·e·tra·bly** *adv.*

im·pen·i·tent [ım'pɛnətənt] *adj* feeling no regret for having done wrong. **im·pen·i·tence** *n.* **im·pen·i·tent·ly** *adv.*

im·per·a·tive [ım'pɛrətıv] *adj* **1** urgent; necessary: *It is imperative that a very sick child stay in bed.* **2** expressing a command.

3 *Grammar* denoting the mood of a verb that expresses a command, request, or advice. "Go!" is in the **imperative mood**. Compare INDICATIVE, SUBJUNCTIVE.
n **1** a command: *The great imperative is "Love your neighbour."* **2** a necessary thing. **im·per·a·tive·ly** *adv.* **im·per·a·tive·ness** *n.* ⟨Latin *imperare* command⟩

im·per·cep·ti·ble [ˌɪmpərˈsɛptəbəl] *adj* **1** very slight. **2** that cannot be perceived. **im·per·cep·ti·bil·i·ty** *n.* **im·per·cep·ti·bly** *adv.*

im·per·fect [ɪmˈpɜrfɪkt] *adj* **1** having some defect. **2** not complete. **3** *Grammar* expressing continued or customary action or state in the past. **4** *Music* denoting any interval other than a fourth, fifth, or octave. **im·per·fec·tion** *n.* **im·per·fect·ly** *adv.*

im·pe·ri·al [ɪmˈpiriəl] *adj* **1** to do with an empire or its ruler. **2** to do with the rule of one country over other countries and colonies. **3** designating a system of weights and measures traditionally used in the UK.
n **1** a pointed beard growing beneath the lower lip. **2** a size of paper, 58.4 × 78.7 cm. **im·pe·ri·al·ly** *adv.* ⟨Latin *imperium* empire⟩
imperial gallon the traditional British gallon, equal to 160 fluid ounces (about 4.55 dm³). It is almost identical with the traditional Canadian gallon, and is about 20 percent bigger than the US gallon. **im·pe·ri·al·ism** *n* extending the rule of one country over other countries and territories. **im·pe·ri·al·ist** *n, adj.* **im·pe·ri·al·is·tic** *adj.* **im·pe·ri·al·is·ti·cal·ly** *adv.*

im·per·il [ɪmˈpɛrəl] *v* **-illed** or **-iled**, **-il·ling** or **-il·ing** put in danger. **im·per·il·ment** *n.*

im·pe·ri·ous [ɪmˈpiriəs] *adj* haughty; arrogant. **im·pe·ri·ous·ly** *adv.* **im·pe·ri·ous·ness** *n.* ⟨Latin *imperiosus* commanding⟩

im·per·ish·a·ble [ɪmˈpɛrɪʃəbəl] *adj* everlasting; indestructible. **im·per·ish·a·bil·i·ty** *n.* **im·per·ish·a·bly** *adv.*

im·per·ma·nent [ɪmˈpɜrmənənt] *adj* not lasting; temporary. **im·per·ma·nence** *n.* **im·per·ma·nent·ly** *adv.*

im·per·me·a·ble [ɪmˈpɜrmiəbəl] *adj* **1** that cannot be passed through. **2** not permitting the passage of fluid through the pores, etc. **im·per·me·a·bil·i·ty** *n.* **im·per·me·a·bly** *adv.*

im·per·son·al [ɪmˈpɜrsənəl] *adj* **1** referring to all or any persons, not to any special one. **2** not affected by personal feelings: *an impersonal approach to the case.* **3** *Grammar* of a verb, having nothing but an indefinite *it* for a subject. *Example:* rained in *It rained today.* **im·per·son·al·i·ty** *n.* **im·per·son·al·ly** *adv.*
impersonal pronoun a pronoun that is used to refer to a person or thing not named. In English, *it, one, they,* and *you* can function as impersonal pronouns: *You should be careful when crossing the street.*

im·per·son·ate [ɪmˈpɜrsəˌneɪt] *v* **1** pretend to be: *The thief impersonated a police officer.* **2** act the part of: *to impersonate Hamlet.* **im·per·son·a·tion** *n.* **im·per·son·a·tor** *n.*

im·per·ti·nent [ɪmˈpɜrtənənt] *adj* impudent; disrespectful. **im·per·ti·nence** *n.* **im·per·ti·nent·ly** *adv.* ⟨Latin *in-* not + *pertinere* relate, belong⟩

SYNONYMS
Impertinent = disrespectful: *Talking back to older people is impertinent.* **Impudent** adds the idea of defiance: *The impudent girl made faces at the teacher.*

im·per·turb·a·ble [ˌɪmpərˈtɜrbəbəl] *adj* characterized by great calmness. **im·per·turb·a·bil·i·ty** *n.* **im·per·turb·a·bly** *adv.*

im·per·vi·ous [ɪmˈpɜrviəs] *adj* **1** not letting anything pass through: *Rubber cloth is impervious to moisture.* **2** not open to or affected by argument, suggestions, etc.: *She is impervious to all the gossip about her.* **im·per·vi·ous·ly** *adv.* **im·per·vi·ous·ness** *n.* ⟨*in-* + Latin *pervius; per-* through + *via* way⟩

im·pet·u·ous [ɪmˈpɛtʃuəs] *adj* **1** acting hastily or with sudden feeling: *Children are usually more impetuous than adults.* **2** moving with great force or speed: *the impetuous rush of water over Niagara Falls.* **im·pet·u·os·i·ty** *n.* **im·pet·u·ous·ly** *adv.* **im·pet·u·ous·ness** *n.* ⟨Latin *impetuosus; impetus* attack⟩

im·pe·tus [ˈɪmpətəs] *n* **1** the force with which a moving body tends to maintain its velocity and overcome resistance: *the impetus of a moving automobile.* **2** a driving force: *Ambition is an impetus.* ⟨Latin = attack, n; *impetere* attack⟩

im·pi·e·ty [ɪmˈpaɪəti] *n* **1** lack of reverence for God. **2** lack of respect. **3** an impious act. **im·pi·ous** [ˈɪmpiəs] or [ɪmˈpaɪəs] *adj.* **im·pi·ous·ly** *adv.*

im·pinge [ɪmˈpɪndʒ] *v* **1** hit; strike (with on): *Rays of light impinge on the eye.* **2** encroach; infringe. **im·pinge·ment** *n.* ⟨Latin *impingere; in-* on + *pangere* strike⟩

im·pi·ous See IMPIETY.

im·plac·a·ble [ɪmˈplækəbəl] or [ɪmˈpleikəbəl] *adj* that cannot be placated or appeased; relentless. **im·plac·a·bly** *adv.* **im·plac·a·bil·i·ty** *n.* ⟨See PLACATE.⟩

im·plant [ɪmˈplænt] *v* **1** instil; fix deeply: *A good parent implants high ideals in children.* **2** insert: *A steel tube is implanted in the socket.* **3** set (a piece of skin, bone, etc.) into the body. *n* [ˈɪmplænt] tissue or other substance set or grafted into the body. **im·plan·ta·tion** *n.*

im·plau·si·ble [ɪmˈplɔzəbəl] *adj* lacking the appearance of truth or trustworthiness. **im·plau·si·bil·i·ty** *n.* **im·plau·si·bly** *adv.*

im·ple·ment [ˈɪmpləmənt] *n* **1** a useful piece of equipment. **2** an agent or means.
v [ˈɪmpləmənt] put (something) into effect: *to implement an order.* **im·ple·men·ta·tion** *n.* **im·ple·men·tal** *adj.* ⟨Latin *implementum,* that which fills a need; *in-* in + *-plere* fill⟩

im·pli·cate [ˈɪmpləˌkeɪt] *v* show to be connected with a crime, fault, etc.: *The thief's confession implicated two other people.* ⟨Latin *in-* in + *plicare* fold⟩
im·pli·ca·tion *n* **1** the act or fact of implicating or of being implicated. **2** See IMPLY.

im·plic·it [ɪmˈplɪsɪt] *adj* **1** without doubting, hesitating, or asking questions: *implicit trust.* **2** meant, but not distinctly stated: *His silence gave implicit consent.* Compare EXPLICIT. **3** involved as a necessary part or condition. **im·plic·it·ly** *adv.* **im·plic·it·ness** *n.* ⟨Latin *implicitus* pp of *implicare.* See IMPLICATE.⟩

im·plode [ɪmˈploud] *v* burst or cause to burst inward: *External pressure can cause a vacuum tube to implode.* **im·plo·sion** *n.* ⟨*im-¹ + (ex)plode*⟩

im·plore [ɪmˈplɔr] *v* beg earnestly for. **im·plor·ing** *adj.* ⟨Latin *implorare,* invoke with tears; *in-* to + *plorare* weep⟩

im·ply [ɪmˈplaɪ] *v* **1** indicate without saying outright: *Silence often implies consent.* **2** involve as a necessary part or condition: *Speech implies the existence of a speaker.* **im·plied** *adj.* ⟨Old French *emplier,* Latin *implicare.* See IMPLICATE.⟩

im·pli·ca·tion *n* **1** something implied; an indirect suggestion: *There was no implication of dishonesty in her failure in business.* **2** *Logic* the relationship between two propositions that makes one an outcome of the other.

CONFUSABLES
Imply = indicate without saying: *By putting on a sad face, the speaker implied that the news was bad.* Infer = suppose: *I inferred from the speaker's sad face that the news was bad.*

im·po·lite [ˌɪmpəˈlaɪt] *adj* rude. **im·po·lite·ly** *adv.* **im·po·lite·ness** *n.*

im·pol·i·tic [ɪmˈpɒləˌtɪk] *adj* in human relationships, unwise: *It is impolitic to offend people who could be of help.* **im·pol·i·tic·ly** *adv.*

im·pon·der·a·ble [ɪmˈpɒndərəbəl] *adj* that cannot be explained, or measured exactly: *Faith and love are imponderable forces.* **im·pon·der·a·ble** *n.* **im·pon·der·a·bly** *adv.* **im·pon·der·a·bil·i·ty** *n.*

im·port [ɪmˈpɔrt] *or* [ˈɪmpɔrt] *v* **1** bring in from a foreign country for sale or use: *Canada imports coffee from Brazil.* **2** *Computers* bring from one application into another. **3** signify: *Tell me what your remark imports.* *n* [ˈɪmpɔrt] **1** anything imported. **2** significance. **3** importance: *a matter of great import.* **4** ❉ **a** in professional football, a non-Canadian player who has played less than five years in Canada. **b** in other sports, a player who is not a native of the country or area in which he or she is playing. **im·port·a·bil·i·ty** *n.* **im·port·a·ble** *adj.* **im·por·ta·tion** *n.* **im·port·er** [ɪmˈpɔrtər] *or* [ˈɪmpɔrtər] *n.* ⟨Latin *in-* on + *portare* carry⟩

im·por·tant [ɪmˈpɔrtənt] *adj* **1** having value or significance. **2** having social position or influence. **3** acting as if important: *He rushed around in an important manner, giving orders.* **im·por·tance** *n.* **im·por·tant·ly** *adv.* ⟨Latin *importans* ppr of *importare.* See IMPORT.⟩

im·por·tune [ˌɪmpɔrˈtjun], [-ˈtʃun], *or* [-ˈtun] *v* ask urgently or repeatedly. **im·por·tu·nate** [ɪmˈpɔrtʃənɪt] *adj.* **im·por·tu·nate·ly** *adv.* **im·por·tu·ni·ty** *n.* ⟨Latin *importunus* ; *in-* not + *opportunus* convenient. See OPPORTUNE.⟩

im·pose [ɪmˈpouz] *v* **1** put (a burden, tax, punishment, etc.) (*on*): *The judge imposed a fine of $500 on the convicted man.* **2** force one's authority or one's company (*on* another). **im·pos·a·ble** *adj.* **im·po·si·tion** *n.* ⟨French *in-* on + *poser* put, place. See POSE.⟩

im·pos·ing *adj* impressive because of size or dignity; commanding attention: *The Peace Tower of the Parliament Buildings is an imposing landmark.* **im·pos·ing·ly** *adv.*

im·pos·si·ble [ɪmˈpɒsəbəl] *adj* **1** that cannot be done: *an impossible task.* **2** that cannot happen: *It is impossible for two and two to be six.* **3** that cannot be true: *an impossible story.* **4** not able to be tolerated: *an impossible person.* *n* something that is or seems impossible: *The sergeant always demanded the impossible of his men.* **im·pos·si·bil·i·ty** *n.* **im·pos·si·bly** *adv.*

im·pos·tor [ɪmˈpɒstər] *n* a person who assumes a false name or character. ⟨Latin, from *imponere* impose; *in* on + *ponere* put⟩

im·po·tent [ˈɪmpətənt] *adj* **1** not having power; helpless: *an impotent rage.* **2** in a male, incapable of having an orgasm or an erection. **im·po·tence** *n.* **im·po·tent·ly** *adv.*

im·pound [ɪmˈpaʊnd] *v* **1** shut up in or as if in a pound: *to impound stray animals.* **2** take and hold in the custody of the law: *to impound documents for use as evidence in court.* **im·pound·ment** *n.* ⟨*im-² + POUND³*⟩

im·pov·er·ish [ɪmˈpɒvərɪʃ] *v* **1** make poor. **2** exhaust the resources of: *to impoverish the soil.* **im·pov·er·ished** *adj.* **im·pov·er·ish·ment** *n.* ⟨Latin *in-* + *pauper* poor⟩

im·prac·ti·ca·ble [ɪmˈpræktəkəbəl] *adj* impossible to be done or put into practice: *impracticable suggestions.* **im·prac·ti·ca·bil·i·ty** *n.* **im·prac·ti·ca·bly** *adv.*

im·prac·ti·cal [ɪmˈpræktəkəl] *adj* **1** not practical; unrealistic: *To build a bridge across the Atlantic Ocean is an impractical scheme.* **2** idealistic. **im·prac·ti·cal·ly** *adv.*

CONFUSABLES
Impractical describes things that are useless or people who have a very unrealistic view of life: *Buying useless things because they are on sale is impractical.* Impracticable describes things that have been proved unusable or that are impossible to put into practice: *Most schemes to abolish poverty are impracticable.*

im·pre·cate [ˈɪmprəˌkeɪt] *v* call down (curses, evil, etc.): *He imprecated ruin on his enemies.* **im·pre·ca·tion** *n.* **im·pre·ca·to·ry** *adj.* ⟨Latin *imprecare; in -* on + *prex, precis* prayer⟩

im·pre·cise [ˌɪmprɪˈsaɪs] *adj* inexact. **im·pre·cise·ly** *adv.* **im·pre·ci·sion** *n.*

im·preg·na·ble [ɪmˈpregnəbəl] *adj* able to resist attack: *an impregnable fortress, an impregnable argument.* **im·preg·na·bil·i·ty** *n.* **im·preg·na·bly** *adv.* ⟨Old French *imprenable* not takable; *prendre* take. Infl by *impregnate.*⟩

im·preg·nate [ɪmˈpregneɪt] *v* **1** make pregnant or fertilize: *to impregnate an egg cell.* **2** fill (with): *Sea water is impregnated with salt.*

im·preg·na·tion *n.* **im·preg·na·tor** *n.* ⟨Latin *impraegnare; in-* + *praegnans* pregnant⟩

im·pre·sa·ri·o [,ımprə'seri,ou] *or* [-'sɑri,ou] *n* a person who manages a concert tour, an opera or ballet company, or other live entertainment. ⟨Italian, from *impresa* undertaking; Latin *in-* on + *prehendere* take⟩

im·press [ım'prɛs] *v* **1** have a strong effect on: *He impressed us with his courage.* **2** fix in the mind: *to impress words in one's memory.* **3** make marks on by pressing: *to impress wax with a seal.*
n ['ımprɛs] a special mark or quality: *The author left the impress of her personality on her work.* **im·press·er** *n.* ⟨Latin *impressus* pp of *imprimere; in-* in + *premere* press⟩

im·pres·sion *n* **1** an effect produced on a person: *Punishment made no impression on her.* **2** an idea: *I have an impression that I left the door open.* **3** something produced by pressure: *The thief left an impression of his feet in the garden.* **4** a result produced by work: *Washing the floor made some impression on the dirt.* **5** any mould, such as dentists make of the teeth. **6** an impersonation of someone. **im·pres·sion·a·ble** *adj* easily influenced. **im·pres·sion·a·bil·i·ty** *n.* **im·pres·sion·is** *n* Often, **Impressionism** a school of painting characterized by the use small dabs of colour to suggest reflected light. **im·pres·sion·ist** *n* **1** Usually, **Impressionist** a painter of the school of Impressionism. **2** an entertainer who does impressions. **im·pres·sion·is·tic** *adj.* **Im·pres·sion·ist·i·cal·ly** *adv.* **im·pres·sive** *adj* making an impression on the mind, feelings, conscience, etc.: *an impressive ceremony.* **im·pres·sive·ly** *adv.* **im·pres·sive·ness** *n.*

im·pri·ma·tur [,ımprı'mɑtər] *n* **1** an official licence to print a book, etc., now generally used of works sanctioned by the Roman Catholic Church. **2** sanction; approval. ⟨Latin = let it be printed⟩

im·print ['ımprınt] *n* **1** a mark made by pressure: *the imprint of a foot in the sand.* **2** a mark: *Suffering left its imprint on her face.* **3** a publisher's name, with the place and date of publication, in a book; a printer's name and address as printed on his or her work.
v [ım'prınt] **1** mark by pressing or stamping; print: *to imprint a postmark on an envelope.* **2** impress: *a scene imprinted on the memory.* **im·print·ing** *n* **1** the process by which certain characteristics are transferred from one person or animal to another. **2** the process by which a young animal treats the first creature it sees as its mother. **3** *Genetics* the phenomenon by which an allele of a gene pair is altered depending on whether it has been inherited from the mother or from the father.

im·pris·on [ım'prızən] *v* **1** put in prison. **2** confine closely; restrain. **im·pris·on·ment** *n.*

im·prob·a·ble [ım'prɒbəbəl] *adj* **1** not likely to happen. **2** not likely to be true: *an improbable story.* **im·prob·a·bil·i·ty** *n.* **im·prob·a·bly** *adv.*

im·promp·tu [ım'prɒmptu] *adj, adv* without previous thought or preparation: *an* *impromptu speech, a speech made impromptu.* ⟨Latin *in promptu* in readiness⟩

im·prop·er [ım'prɒpər] *adj* **1** not according to rules of conduct; not polite: *improper language.* **2** inappropriate: *improper clothing for a hike.* **3** incorrect: *an improper conclusion.* **4** not properly so called: *an improper fraction.* **im·prop·er·ly** *adv.* **im·pro·pri·e·ty** *n.*
improper fraction a fraction greater than 1. *Example: 7/4.*

im·prov ['ımprɒv] *Informal n* improvisation.

im·prove [ım'pruv] *v* **1** make better or become better: *Her health is improving.* **2** increase the value of (land or property). **3** ✱ formerly, clear (land) in preparation for seeding. **im·prov·a·ble** *adj.* **im·prove·ment** *n.* ⟨Anglo-French *emprouer;* Old French *en-* in + *prou* profit⟩
improve on a make better; b do better than.

im·prov·i·dent [ım'prɒvədənt] *adj* not careful in providing for the future. **im·prov·i·dence** *n.* **im·prov·i·dent·ly** *adv.*

im·pro·vise ['ımprə,vaız] *v* **1** compose, perform, etc. without preparation. **2** engage in role-playing without a script: *Come and watch the children improvising.* **3** make, using whatever resources are available: *The girls improvised a tent out of two blankets.* **im·pro·vi·sa·tion** *n.* **im·pro·vi·sa·tion·al** *adj.* **im·pro·vis·er** *n.* ⟨Italian *improvvisare;* Latin *in-* not + *pro-* beforehand + *videre* see⟩

im·pru·dent [ım'prudənt] *adj* rash; unwise: *an imprudent decision.* **im·pru·dence** *n.* **im·pru·dent·ly** *adv.*

im·pu·dent ['ımpjədənt] *adj* rudely bold; insolent. **im·pu·dence** *n.* **im·pu·dent·ly** *adv.* ⟨Latin *in-* not + *pudere* be modest⟩

im·pugn [ım'pjun] *v* attack by words; challenge as false. **im·pugn·a·ble** *adj.* **im·pug·na·tion** [,ımpʌg'neıʃən] *n.* ⟨Latin *in-* against + *pugnare* fight⟩

im·pulse ['ımpʌls] *n* **1** a sudden, driving force: *the impulse of a wave.* **2** a sudden inclination to act: *A mob is influenced more by impulse than by reasoning.* **3** the stimulating force of emotion: *The murderer acted on impulse.* **4** *Mechanics* the product obtained by multiplying the value of a force by the time during which it acts. ⟨Latin *impulsus* pp of *impellere.* See IMPEL.⟩
im·pul·sive *adj* **1** acting upon impulse. **2** able to impel: *an impulsive force.* **3** of a force, acting at brief intervals. **im·pul·sive·ly** *adv.* **im·pul·sive·ness** *n.*

im·pu·ni·ty [ım'pjunəti] *n* freedom from punishment or other consequences: *If laws are not enforced, crimes are committed with impunity.* ⟨Latin *impunitas; in-* without + *poena* punishment⟩

im·pure [ım'pjur] *adj* **1** dirty; unclean. **2** mixed with a substance of lower value. **3** immoral: *impure thoughts.* **im·pure·ly** *adv.*
im·pu·ri·ty *n* **1** the state of being impure. **2** Often, **impurities** *pl* anything that makes something else impure: *Unfiltered water has impurities.*

im·pute [ɪm'pjut] *v* charge (a fault, etc.) to a person: *I impute her failure to laziness.* **im·put·a·bil·i·ty** *n.* **im·put·a·ble** *adj.* **im·put·a·bly** *adv.* **im·pu·ta·tion** *n.* **im·put·a·tive** *adj.* ⟨Latin *in-* in, to + *putare* reckon⟩

in [ɪn] *prep* **1** inside: *in the box.* **2** into: *Put it in the fire.* **3** with: *to wrap in paper.* **4** from among: *one in a hundred.* **5** because of: *to act in self-defence.* **6** concerning: *a course in Canadian history.*
adv **1** in or into some place, condition, etc.: *to come in.* **2** present: *She's is not in today.* **3** *Informal* in fashion: *Cocktail parties are in.*
adj Informal fashionable: *Red is the in colour.*
n **1** *Informal* **a** a way of approach: *an in to a career in business.* **b** a position of familiarity: *an in with the company president.* **2 ins** *pl* the group in office or in power. ⟨Old English⟩
in for unable to avoid: *We are in for a storm.*
in on taking part in: *A lot of people were in on the planning.* **ins and outs** the details: *The manager knows the ins and outs of the business.* **in that** because. **in with a** friendly with. **b** partners with. **in–group** *n* a group of people sharing a sense of being exclusive, esp such a group having power or prestige. **in–house** *adj, adv* using an organization's own resources: *an in-house magazine. We can check that in-house.* **in–pa·tient** *n* a patient who lives in a hospital while being treated. Compare OUT-PATIENT. **in–serv·ice** *adj* to do with a program for the training of employees: *in-service courses for civil servants.*

CONFUSABLES
In generally shows location (literal or figurative); **into** generally shows direction:
He was in the house. She came into the house.
He was in a stupor. She fell into a deep sleep.

in–¹ *prefix* not; the opposite or absence of: *inexpensive, inattention, inconvenient.* Also: **i-** (before *gn*), **il-** (before *l*), **im-** (before *b*, *m*, *p*), **ir-** (before *r*). ⟨Latin⟩

in–² *prefix* in, into, on, or upon: *inscribe.* ⟨Latin⟩

in·a·bil·i·ty [ˌɪnə'bɪləti] *n* a lack of ability, power, or means; condition of being unable.

in ab·sen·tia [ɪn æb'sɛnʃə] *Latin* while absent.

in·ac·ces·si·ble [ˌɪnək'sɛsəbəl] *adj* **1** that cannot be reached. **2** hard to reach or enter: *The fort on top of the steep hill is inaccessible.* **in·ac·ces·si·bil·i·ty** *n.* **in·ac·ces·si·bly** *adv.*

in·ac·cu·rate [ɪn'ækjərɪt] *adj* not accurate; faulty: *an inaccurate report.* **in·ac·cu·ra·cy** *n.* **in·ac·cu·rate·ly** *adv.*

in·ac·tive [ɪn'æktɪv] *adj* **1** not active. **2** idle. **in·ac·tion** *n.* **in·ac·tive·ly** *adv.* **in·ac·tiv·i·ty** *n.*

in·ad·e·quate [ɪn'ædəkwɪt] *adj* not as much as is needed: *inadequate preparation for a test.* **in·ad·e·qua·cy** *n.* **in·ad·e·quate·ly** *adv.*

in·ad·mis·si·ble [ˌɪnəd'mɪsəbəl] *adj* **1** not allowable. **2** not to be admitted. **in·ad·mis·si·bil·i·ty** *n.* **in·ad·mis·si·bly** *adv.*

in·ad·vert·ent [ˌɪnəd'vɜrtənt] *adj* **1** not attentive. **2** not done on purpose. **in·ad·vert·ence** *n.* **in·ad·vert·ent·ly** *adv.* ⟨*in-¹* + Latin *advertere.* See ADVERT.⟩

in·ad·vis·a·ble [ˌɪnəd'vaɪzəbəl] *adj* unwise. **in·ad·vis·a·bil·i·ty** *n.* **in·ad·vis·a·bly** *adv.*

in·al·ien·a·ble [ɪn'eiliənəbəl] *adj* that cannot be given away or taken away: *Every person has the inalienable right of equality before the law.* **in·al·ien·a·bil·i·ty** *n.* **in·al·ien·a·bly** *adv.*

in·ane [ɪ'nein] *adj* silly or foolish: *inane remarks.* **in·ane·ly** *adv.* **in·an·i·ty** [ɪ'nænəti] *n.* ⟨Latin *inanis* empty⟩

in·an·i·mate [ɪn'ænəmɪt] *adj* **1** not having life: *the inanimate desert. Stones are inanimate.* **2** not animated: *an inanimate face.* **in·an·i·mate·ly** *adv.* **in·an·i·ma·tion** *n.*

in·ap·pli·ca·ble [ˌɪnə'plɪkəbəl] *or* [ɪn'æpləkəbəl] *adj* not applying to the case in question. **in·ap·pli·ca·bil·i·ty** *n.* **in·ap·pli·ca·bly** *adv.*

in·ap·pro·pri·ate [ˌɪnə'proupriɪt] *adj* not suitable; not fitting. **in·ap·pro·pri·ate·ly** *adv.* **in·ap·pro·pri·ate·ness** *n.*

in·apt [ɪn'æpt] *adj* **1** not suitable: *Jokes are inapt at funerals.* **2** unskilful: *an inept performance.* **in·apt·ly** *adv.* **in·ap·ti·tude** *n.* ⟨Latin *in-* not + *aptus* apt⟩

in·ar·tic·u·late [ˌɪnɑr'tɪkjəlɪt] *adj* **1** not like regular speech: *an inarticulate groan.* **2** unable to speak in words: *Cats and dogs are inarticulate.* **3** unable to talk comprehensibly. **4** not expressed: *inarticulate grief.* **5** *Zoology* not jointed: *A jellyfish's body is inarticulate.* **in·ar·tic·u·late·ly** *adv.* **in·ar·tic·u·late·ness** *n.*

in·at·ten·tive [ˌɪnə'tɛntɪv] *adj* not attentive; careless; heedless; negligent. **in·at·ten·tion** *n.* **in·at·ten·tive·ly** *adv.* **in·at·ten·tive·ness** *n.*

in·au·di·ble [ɪn'ɒdəbəl] *adj* that cannot be heard. **in·au·di·bil·i·ty** *n.* **in·au·di·bly** *adv.*

in·au·gu·rate [ɪn'ɒgjə,reit] *v* **1** install in office with a ceremony: *The new mayor will be inaugurated at noon.* **2** make a formal beginning of: *The development of the airplane inaugurated a new era in transportation.* **3** open for use with a ceremony. **in·au·gu·ral** *adj.* **in·au·gu·ra·tion** *n.* ⟨Latin *inaugurare; in-* for + *augur* taker of omens⟩

in·aus·pi·cious [ˌɪnɒ'spɪʃəs] *adj* showing signs of probable failure; unlucky. **in·aus·pi·cious·ly** *adv.* **in·aus·pi·cious·ness** *n.*

in–be·tween ['ɪn bɪ'twin] *adj* **1** belonging in the middle: *He is at that in-between age, neither boy nor man.* **2** neutral; indifferent. *n* a person or thing that is in-between.

in·board ['ɪn,bɔrd] *adv, adj* **1** inside the hull of a ship. **2** close to the fuselage of an aircraft. Compare OUTBOARD.

in·born ['ɪn,bɔrn] *adj* **1** instinctive: *an inborn sense of rhythm.* **2** inherited.

in·breed ['ɪn,brid] *or* [ɪn'brid] *v* **-bred, -breed·ing** breed from closely related persons, animals, or plants. **in·breed·ing** *n.* Compare INTERBREED.
in·bred ['ɪn,brɛd] *adj.* **1** inborn; natural: *an inbred courtesy.* **2** bred for generations from ancestors closely related.

inc. 1 Usually, **Inc.** incorporated. **2** inclusive.

In·ca ['ɪŋkə] *n* a member of an Indian people

of South America that held power in Peru. **In·can** n, adj. ⟨Spanish, from Quechua *ynca* prince of the ruling family⟩

in·cal·cu·la·ble [ɪn'kælkjələbəl] adj **1** too great in number to be counted: *The sands of the beach are incalculable.* **2** not able to be reckoned beforehand: *A flood in the valley would cause incalculable losses.* **3** uncertain. **in·cal·cu·la·bly** adv. **in·cal·cu·la·bil·i·ty** n.

in cam·e·ra [ɪn 'kæmərə] **1** *Law* in the privacy of a judge's chambers, rather than in open court. **2** in a closed session, as of a committee. ⟨Latin = in a room or chamber⟩

in·can·des·cent [ˌɪnkæn'dɛsənt] adj **1** glowing with heat. **2** intensely bright. **3** to do with a material that gives light by incandescence. An **incandescent lamp** (light bulb) is an electric lamp with a fine wire that becomes white-hot when current flows through it. **in·can·des·cence** n. **in·can·des·cent·ly** adv. ⟨Latin *incandescere* begin to glow; *in-* in + *candere* gleam white⟩

in·can·ta·tion [ˌɪnkæn'teɪʃən] n a set of words spoken to cast a magic spell. ⟨Latin *in-* against + *cantare* chant⟩

in·ca·pa·ble [ɪn'keɪpəbəl] adj not competent: *An employer cannot afford to hire incapable workers.* **in·ca·pa·bil·i·ty** n. **in·ca·pa·bly** adv. **incapable of a** without the ability: *incapable of lying.* **b** not legally qualified for: *Certain beliefs make a person incapable of jury duty.* **c** not susceptible to: *incapable of exact measurement.*

in·ca·pac·i·tate [ˌɪnkə'pæsə,teɪt] v **1** deprive of ability or power: *His injury incapacitated him for working.* **2** legally disqualify. **in·ca·pac·i·ty** n.

in·car·cer·ate [ɪn'kɑrsə,reɪt] v **1** imprison. **2** confine; shut in. **in·car·cer·a·tion** n. ⟨Latin *in-* in + *carcer* jail⟩

in·car·nate [ɪn'kɑrnɪt] adj **1** embodied in human form: *The villain was an incarnate fiend.* **2** personified (follows the noun): *evil incarnate.* **3** *Botany* flesh-coloured or crimson. v [ɪn'kɑrneɪt] **1** embody: *She incarnates all womanly virtues.* **2** put into an actual form: *The sculptor incarnated his vision in a beautiful statue.* ⟨Latin *incarnare*; *in-* in + *carnis* flesh⟩ **in·car·na·tion** n **1** the taking on of human form by a spiritual being. **2** embodiment. **3** a person or thing that represents some quality: *A miser is an incarnation of greed.* **4 the Incarnation** the Christian doctrine of the union of divine nature and human nature in the person of Jesus Christ.

in·cen·di·ar·y [ɪn'sɛndi,ɛri] adj **1** to do with the malicious setting on fire of property. **2** used to start a fire: *incendiary bombs.* **3** stirring up strife: *incendiary speeches.* n **1** a person who maliciously sets fire to property. **2** a person who deliberately stirs up strife. **3** a bomb containing chemical agents that cause fire. ⟨Latin *incendium* fire⟩

in·cense¹ ['ɪnsɛns] n a substance giving off a sweet smell when burned. ⟨Latin *incensus* pp of *incendere* burn, kindle⟩

in·cense² [ɪn'sɛns] v make very angry; fill with rage: *Cruelty incenses most people.* ⟨Latin *incensare* frequentative of *incendere* kindle⟩

in·cen·tive [ɪn'sɛntɪv] n something that urges a person on; a motive; stimulus. adj motivating. ⟨Latin *in-* in + *canere* sing⟩

in·cep·tion [ɪn'sɛpʃən] n a beginning. ⟨Latin *inceptio* from *incipere* begin⟩

in·ces·sant [ɪn'sɛsənt] adj never stopping: *The roar of Niagara Falls is incessant.* **in·ces·sant·ly** adv. ⟨Latin *in-* not + *cessare* cease⟩

in·cest ['ɪnsɛst] n the crime of sexual intercourse between persons so closely related that their marriage is prohibited by law. **in·ces·tu·ous** adj. **in·ces·tu·ous·ly** adv. **in·ces·tu·ous·ness** n. ⟨Latin *incestus*; *in-* not + *castus* chaste⟩

inch [ɪntʃ] n a non-metric unit for measuring length, equal to about 2.54 cm. *Symbol* " v move little by little: *The worm inched along.* ⟨Old English *ynce;* Latin *uncia,* orig a twelfth. Related to OUNCE.⟩ **every inch** completely. **within an inch of** very close to: *The man was within an inch of death.*

in·cho·ate [ɪn'koʊt] adj incomplete; undeveloped. **in·cho·ate·ly** adv. **in·cho·ate·ness** n ⟨Latin *incohare* begin, orig harness; *in-* on + *cohum* yoke fastener⟩

in·ci·dent ['ɪnsədənt] n **1** a happening. **2** a minor event that causes a public crisis. adj **1** liable to happen: *Hardships are incident to the life of an explorer.* **2** falling (*upon*): *rays of light incident on a mirror.* ⟨Latin *incidere* happen; *in-* on + *cadere* to fall⟩ **in·ci·dence** n **1** the fact or rate of occurrence: *a high incidence of traffic accidents during the weekend.* **2** *Physics* the direction a line, ray, etc. takes in falling on a surface. **in·ci·den·tal** [ˌɪnsə'dɛntəl] adj **1** happening along with something more important: *Certain discomforts incidental to camping.* **2** occurring by chance. n Often, **incidentals** pl something incidental: *We spent $350 for bus fares, and $28 for incidentals such as magazines.* **in·ci·den·tal·ly** adv. **incidental music** music played as accompaniment to a film, play, etc.

in·cin·er·ate [ɪn'sɪnə,reɪt] v burn or be burned to ashes. **in·cin·er·a·tion** n. ⟨Latin *in-* into + *cineris* ashes⟩ **in·cin·er·a·tor** n a furnace for burning garbage.

in·cip·i·ent [ɪn'sɪpiənt] adj just beginning; in an early stage. **in·cip·i·ent·ly** adv. ⟨Latin *incipere.* See INCEPTION.⟩

in·cise [ɪn'saɪz] v cut into with a sharp tool. **in·ci·sion** [ɪn'sɪʒən] n. ⟨Latin *incisus* pp of *incidere; in-* into + *caedere* cut⟩ **in·cised** adj **1** engraved. **2** having notches around the edge: *an incised leaf.* **in·ci·sive** adj sharp; penetrating: *an incisive criticism.* **in·ci·sive·ly** adv. **in·ci·sive·ness** n. **in·ci·sor** n a tooth having a sharp edge for cutting.

in·cite [ɪn'saɪt] v urge on; stir up; rouse. **in·cite·ment** n. **in·cit·er** n. ⟨Latin *incitare; in-* on + *ciere* cause to move⟩

in·clem·ent [ɪn'klɛmənt] adj **1** rainy:

inclement weather. **2** severe: *an inclement ruler.*
in·clem·en·cy [ɪn'klɛmənsi] *n.* **in·clem·ent·ly** *adv.*
in·cline [ɪn'klaɪn] *v* **1** be in favour of: *Dogs incline to meat as a food.* **2** slope; slant: *That roof inclines steeply.* **3** bend; bow.
n ['ɪnklaɪn] a slope; slant. **in·clined** *adj.* ⟨Latin *in-* in + *clinare* bend⟩
in·cli·na·tion [ˌɪnklə'neɪʃən] *n* **1** a liking: *a strong inclination for sports.* **2** tendency: *an inclination to become fat.* **3** a bending. **4** a slope. **in·cli·na·tion·al** *adj.* **inclined plane** a plane surface set at an angle to the horizontal.
in·clude [ɪn'klud] *v* **1** contain: *The farm includes about 65 ha.* **2** put in a total: *The number of people lost included the captain of the ship.* **3** allow to participate: *He tried to include her in all his activities.* **in·clud·a·ble** *adj.* ⟨Latin *includere; in-* in + *claudere* shut⟩
in·clud·ed *adj* **1** counted in a total. **2** formed between two intersecting lines: *an included angle.* **in·clud·ing** *prep* counting as a part: *He took my purse, including all my money.* **in·clu·sion** *n* **1** something included. **2** the including of all members of society. **in·clu·sive** *adj* **1** including the extremes mentioned: *pages 10 to 20 inclusive* means *pages 10 and 20 and all those in between.* **2** including everything concerned: *an inclusive list of expenses.* **3** welcoming diversity of viewpoints, backgrounds, etc. **inclusive of** including. **in·clu·sive·ly** *adv.* **in·clu·sive·ness** *n.*
in·cog·ni·to [ˌɪnkɒg'nitou] *adj, adv* with one's name, character, rank, etc. concealed: *The prince travelled incognito.* ⟨Latin *in-* not + *cognitus* pp of *cognoscere* come to know⟩
in·co·her·ent [ˌɪnkou'hirənt] *adj* confused in thought or speech. **in·co·her·ence** *n.* **in·co·her·ent·ly** *adv.*
in·come ['ɪnkʌm] *n* what comes in from property, business, work, etc.
income tax a tax on a person's income.
in·com·ing *adj* coming in: *The incoming tenant will pay a higher rent. interj Informal* a warning of an approaching missile, often used jocularly. *n* **incomings** *pl* revenue.
in·com·men·su·ra·ble [ˌɪnkə'mɛnʃərəbəl] *or* [ˌɪnkə'mɛnsərəbəl] *adj* **1** that cannot be compared because not measurable in the same units: *Money and human life are incommensurable.* **2** *Mathematics* having no common integral divisor except 1. *Example:* 8, 17, and 11. **in·com·men·su·ra·bly** *adv.* **in·com·men·su·rate** [ˌɪnkə'mɛnʃərɪt] *or* [ˌɪnkə'mɛnsərɪt] *adj* **1** not in proportion; not adequate: *strength incommensurate to a task.* **2** having no common measure; incommensurable. **in·com·men·su·rate·ly** *adv.*
in·com·mu·ni·ca·ble [ˌɪnkə'mjunəkəbəl] *adj* not capable of being communicated or told. **in·com·mu·ni·ca·bly** *adv.* **in·com·mu·ni·ca·bil·i·ty** *n.*
in·com·mu·ni·ca·do [ˌɪnkəˌmjunə'kɑdou] *adj* deprived of or refusing communication with others: *The prisoner was being held incommunicado.* ⟨Spanish *incomunicado*⟩

in·com·pa·ra·ble [ɪn'kɒmpərəbəl] *or* [ˌɪnkəm'pɛrəbəl] *adj* **1** without equal; matchless: *incomparable beauty.* **2** unsuitable for comparison. **in·com·pa·ra·bly** *adv.* **in·com·pa·ra·bil·i·ty** *or* **in·com·par·a·ble·ness** *n.*
in·com·pat·i·ble [ˌɪnkəm'pætəbəl] *adj* **1** not able to live together peaceably: *My cat and my dog are incompatible.* **2** inconsistent: *Late hours are incompatible with health.* **3** to do with drugs, blood types, etc. that cannot be used together because of undesirable reactions. **4** of two propositions, unable to be true simultaneously. **in·com·pat·i·bil·i·ty** *n.* **in·com·pat·i·bly** *adv.*
in·com·pe·tent [ɪn'kɒmpətənt] *adj* **1** lacking ability or fitness. **2** not legally qualified. **in·com·pe·tence** *n.* **in·com·pe·tent·ly** *adv.*
in·com·plete [ˌɪnkəm'plit] *adj* lacking some part; unfinished. **in·com·plete·ly** *adv.* **in·com·plete·ness** *n.*
in·com·pre·hen·si·ble [ˌɪnkɒmprɪ'hɛnsəbəl] *adj* impossible to understand. **in·com·pre·hen·sion** *n.* **in·com·pre·hen·si·bly** *adv.*
in·con·ceiv·a·ble [ˌɪnkən'sivəbəl] *adj* **1** impossible to imagine: *A circle without a centre is inconceivable.* **2** hard to believe: *The new jet can travel at an inconceivable speed.* **in·con·ceiv·a·bil·i·ty** *n.* **in·con·ceiv·a·bly** *adv.*
in·con·clu·sive [ˌɪnkən'klusɪv] *adj* not settling or deciding something doubtful: *The evidence against the prisoner was inconclusive.* **in·con·clu·sive·ly** *adv.* **in·con·clu·sive·ness** *n.*
in·con·gru·ent [ɪn'kɒŋgruənt] *adj* not congruent. **in·con·gru·ent·ly** *adv.* **in·con·gru·ence** *n.*
in·con·gru·ous [ɪn'kɒŋgruəs] *adj* **1** not appropriate: *Heavy walking shoes would be incongruous with evening dress.* **2** not consistent. **3** made up of disparate parts. **in·con·gru·i·ty** *n.* **in·con·gru·ous·ly** *adv.*
in·con·nu ['ɪnkəˌnu] *n, pl* **-nu** or **-nus** ✱ a whitefish, valued as a food fish. ⟨French = unknown, because little known to anglers⟩
in·con·se·quent [ɪn'kɒnsəˌkwɛnt] *or* [ɪn'kɒnsəkwənt] *adj* **1** not logically connected: *an inconsequent argument.* **2** off the subject: *an inconsequent remark.* **in·con·se·quent·ly** *adv.* **in·con·se·quen·tial** [ˌɪnkɒnsə'kwɛnʃəl] *adj* unimportant; trivial. **in·con·se·quen·tial·ly** *adv.* **in·con·se·quen·ti·al·i·ty** *n.*
in·con·sid·er·ate [ˌɪnkən'sɪdərɪt] *adj* not thoughtful of the feelings of others. **in·con·sid·er·ate·ly** *adv.* **in·con·sid·er·ate·ness** *n.*
in·con·sist·ent [ˌɪnkən'sɪstənt] *adj* **1** lacking in agreement: *The police officer's accepting the bribe was inconsistent with her reputation for honesty.* **2** failing to keep to the same principles, course of action, etc.: *An inconsistent person's opinions change without reason.* **in·con·sist·en·cy** *n.* **in·con·sist·ent·ly** *adv.*
in·con·sol·a·ble [ˌɪnkən'souləbəl] *adj* not to be comforted. **in·con·sol·a·bly** *adv.* **in·con·sol·a·bil·i·ty** *n.*
in·con·spic·u·ous [ˌɪnkən'spɪkjuəs] *adj*

attracting little or no attention. **in·con·spic·u·ous·ly** *adv.* **in·con·spic·u·ous·ness** *n.*

in·con·stant [ɪnˈkɒnstənt] *adj* changeable; variable. **in·con·stan·cy** *n.* **in·con·stant·ly** *adv.*

in·con·test·a·ble [ɪnkənˈtɛstəbəl] *adj* unquestionable. **in·con·test·a·bly** *adv.* **in·con·test·a·bil·i·ty** *n.*

in·con·ti·nent [ɪnˈkɒntənənt] *adj* **1** *Medicine* unable to control natural discharges or evacuations. **2** without self-restraint. **3** not chaste. **4** incapable of holding back (used with *of*): *incontinent of tears.* **in·con·ti·nence** *n.* **in·con·ti·nent·ly** *adv.*

in·con·tro·vert·i·ble [ˌɪnkɒntrəˈvɜrtəbəl] *adj* unquestionable. **in·con·tro·vert·i·bil·i·ty** *n.* **in·con·tro·vert·i·bly** *adv.*

in·con·ven·ient [ˌɪnkənˈvinjənt] *adj* causing trouble or bother. **in·con·ven·ient·ly** *adv.* **in·con·ven·ience** *n* **1** trouble; bother. **2** a cause of trouble. *v* cause trouble: *Would it inconvenience you to carry this package for me?*

in·cor·po·rate [ɪnˈkɔrpəˌreit] *v* **1** make (a thing) part of something else: *We shall incorporate your idea into our plan.* **2** form into a corporation: *When the business became large, the owners incorporated it.* **3** give material form to: *to incorporate one's thoughts in an article.* *adj* [ɪnˈkɔrpərɪt] united; incorporated. **in·cor·po·ra·ble** *adj.* **in·cor·po·rat·ed** *adj.* **in·cor·po·ra·tion** *n.* ⟨Latin *incorporare; in-* into ι *corporis* body⟩

in·cor·po·re·al [ˌɪnkɔrˈpɔriəl] *adj* not of any material substance. **in·cor·po·re·al·ly** *adv.* **in·cor·po·re·i·ty** [ɪnˌkɔrpəˈriiti] or **in·cor·po·re·al·i·ty** *n.*

in·cor·rect [ˌɪnkəˈrɛkt] *adj* **1** containing errors or mistakes; wrong; faulty. **2** not proper. **in·cor·rect·ly** *adv.* **in·cor·rect·ness** *n.*

in·cor·ri·gi·ble [ɪnˈkɔrədʒəbəl] *adj* so firmly fixed (in a bad habit) that nothing else can be expected: *an incorrigible liar.* **in·cor·ri·gi·bil·i·ty** *n.* **in·cor·ri·gi·bly** *adv.* ⟨Latin *incorrigibilis; in-* not + *corrigere* to correct⟩

in·cor·rupt·i·ble [ˌɪnkəˈrʌptəbəl] *adj* **1** honest: *an incorruptible judge.* **2** not capable of decay: *Diamonds are incorruptible.* **in·cor·rupt·i·bly** *adv.* **in·cor·rup·ti·bil·i·ty** *n.*

in·crease [ɪnˈkris] *v* make or become greater in size, number, degree, etc.. **in·crease** [ˈɪnkris] *n.* ⟨Latin *increscere; in-* in + *crescere* grow⟩ **on the increase** increasing: *The movement of people to the cities is on the increase.* **in·creas·ing·ly** *adv* more and more.

in·cred·i·ble [ɪnˈkrɛdəbəl] *adj* **1** unbelievable. **2** *Informal* extraordinary: *Her last race was incredible; I've never seen anything like it.* **in·cred·i·bil·i·ty** *n.* **in·cred·i·bly** *adv.*

CONFUSABLES
Incredible = unbelievable, and **incredulous** = showing a lack or belief: *Her story of having seen a ghost seemed incredible to her family. If they are incredulous, show them the evidence.*

in·cred·u·lous [ɪnˈkrɛdʒələs] or [ɪnˈkrɛdjələs] *adj* **1** not willing or likely to believe: *Most people are incredulous about ghosts.* **2** showing a lack of belief: *an incredulous smile.* **in·cre·du·li·ty** [ˌɪnkrəˈdjuləti] or [-ˈduləti] *n.* **in·cred·u·lous·ly** *adv.*

in·cre·ment [ˈɪnkrəmənt] or [ˈɪŋkrəmənt] *n* **1** an increase or the amount by which something increases. **2** one of a series of usually small increases: *an annual increment in pay.* **3** *Mathematics* the amount by which the value of a variable changes. *v* [ˈɪnkrəˌment] or [ˈɪŋkrəˌment] increase by small stages. **in·cre·ment·al** *adj.* ⟨Latin *incrementum; increscere.* See INCREASE.⟩

in·crim·i·nate [ɪnˈkrɪmə,neit] *v* **1** show to be guilty. **2** implicate: *In her confession the thief incriminated two of her accomplices.* **in·crim·i·na·tion** *n* **in·crim·i·na·to·ry** *adj.* ⟨Latin *in-* against + *crimen* charge⟩

in·cu·bate [ˈɪnkjə,beit] or [ˈɪŋkjə,beit] *v* **1** keep (an egg, embryo, etc.) under conditions that will enable it to hatch, develop, etc. **2** of a disease, go through INCUBATION (def. 2). **in·cu·ba·tive** *adj.* ⟨Latin *in-* on + *cubare* lie⟩ **in·cu·ba·tion** *n* **1** an incubating or being incubated. **2** the stage of a disease from the time of infection until the appearance of the symptoms. **in·cu·ba·tion·al** *adj.* **in·cu·ba·tor** *n* **1** an apparatus for keeping eggs warm so that they will hatch. **2** a similar apparatus for protecting babies born very small or prematurely. **3** an apparatus in which bacterial cultures are developed.

in·cu·bus [ˈɪnkjəbəs] or [ˈɪŋkjəbəs] *n, pl* **-bi** [-,baɪ] or [-,bi] or **-bus·es** an evil spirit supposed, in medieval times, to descend upon sleeping persons, esp women. Compare SUCCUBUS. ⟨Latin, from *incubare.* See INCUBATE.⟩

in·cul·cate [ɪnˈkʌlkeit] or [ˈɪnkʌl,keit] *v* teach persistently. **in·cul·ca·tion** *n.* ⟨Latin *inculcare* orig trample in; *in-* in + *calx* heel⟩

in·cul·pate [ɪnˈkʌlpeit] or [ˈɪnkʌl,peit] *v* **1** accuse. **2** incriminate. **in·cul·pa·tion** *n.* **in·cul·pa·to·ry** *adj.* ⟨Latin *in-* in + *culpa* blame⟩

in·cum·bent [ɪnˈkʌmbənt] *adj* **1** lying, leaning *(on).* **2** resting (on a person) as a duty: *She felt it incumbent upon her to speak.* **3** currently in office: *the incumbent minister.* *n* a person holding a position, church living, etc. ⟨Latin *incumbere* lie down on⟩ **in·cum·ben·cy** *n* **1** the holding of an office: *During my incumbency as mayor, the city prospered.* **2** an obligation.

in·cur [ɪnˈkɜr] *v* **-curred, -cur·ring 1** experience (something unpleasant): *to incur expenses.* **2** bring on oneself: *to incur someone's anger.* **in·cur·rence** *n.* ⟨Latin *in-* upon + *currere* run⟩ **in·cur·sion** [ɪnˈkɜrʒən] *n* **1** an invasion; raid: *The pirates made incursions along the coast.* **2** a flowing in: *Dikes protected the lowland from incursions of the sea.*

in·cur·a·ble [ɪnˈkjʊrəbəl] *adj* not capable of being cured or remedied: *an incurable invalid.* **in·cur·a·bil·i·ty** *n.* **in·cur·a·bly** *adv.*

in·cu·ri·ous [ɪnˈkjʊriəs] *adj* unobservant; indifferent. **in·cu·ri·ous·ly** *adv.* **in·cu·ri·os·i·ty** *n.*

in·debt·ed [ɪnˈdɛtɪd] *adj* owing money or gratitude: *We are indebted to scientists for many of our comforts.* **in·debt·ed·ness** *n.*

in·de·cent [ɪnˈdisənt] *adj* improper: *an indecent haste to sell off his father's belongings.* **in·de·cen·cy** *n.* **in·de·cent·ly** *adv.*

in·de·ci·pher·a·ble [ˌɪndɪˈsəifərəbəl] *adj* incapable of being deciphered; illegible. **in·de·ci·pher·a·bil·i·ty** *n.* **in·de·ci·pher·a·bly** *adv.*

in·de·ci·sive [ˌɪndɪˈsəisɪv] *adj* 1 having the habit of hesitating and putting off decisions. 2 not settling the matter: *an indecisive battle.* **in·de·ci·sion** *n.* **in·de·ci·sive·ly** *adv.* **in·de·ci·sive·ness** *n.*

in·dec·o·rous [ɪnˈdɛkərəs] *adj* not suitable; improper; unseemly. **in·dec·o·rous·ly** *adv.* **in·de·co·rum** [ˌɪndɪˈkɔrəm] *n* improper behaviour, speech, dress, etc.

in·deed [ɪnˈdid] *adv* in fact; really; truly; surely: *War is indeed terrible.* *interj* an expression of surprise, doubt, contempt, sarcasm, etc.

in·de·fat·i·ga·ble [ˌɪndɪˈfætəgəbəl] *adj* never getting tired or giving up; tireless. **in·de·fat·i·ga·bil·i·ty** *n.* **in·de·fat·i·ga·bly** *adv.* ⟨Latin *in-* not + *de-* (intensive) + *fatigare* tire⟩

in·de·fen·si·ble [ˌɪndɪˈfɛnsəbəl] *adj* 1 that cannot be defended: *an indefensible island.* 2 not justifiable: *an indefensible lie.* **in·de·fen·si·bil·i·ty** *n.* **in·de·fen·si·bly** *adv.*

in·de·fin·a·ble [ˌɪndɪˈfaɪnəbəl] *adj* that cannot be defined. **in·de·fin·a·bil·i·ty** *n.* **in·de·fin·a·bly** *adv.*

in·def·i·nite [ɪnˈdɛfənɪt] *adj* 1 not precise; vague: *"Maybe" is a very indefinite answer.* 2 not limited: *We have an indefinite time to finish this work.* 3 *Grammar* not specifying precisely. *Some, any, many,* and *few* are indefinite pronouns. **in·def·i·nite·ly** *adv.* **in·def·i·nite·ness** *n.* **indefinite article** *Grammar* in English, either of the articles A or AN.

in·del·i·ble [ɪnˈdɛləbəl] *adj* 1 that cannot be erased: *He left an indelible impression on us.* 2 capable of making a permanent mark: *indelible ink.* **in·del·i·bil·i·ty** *n.* **in·del·i·bly** *adv.* ⟨Latin *in-* not + *delebilis* able to be destroyed; *delere* destroy⟩

in·del·i·cate [ɪnˈdɛləkɪt] *adj* 1 coarse; crude. 2 improper; immodest. **in·del·i·cate·ly** *adv.* **in·del·i·cate·ness** *n.* **in·del·i·ca·cy** [ɪnˈdɛləkəsi] *n* 1 lack of delicacy. 2 an instance of vulgar language.

in·dem·ni·fy [ɪnˈdɛmnəˌfaɪ] *v* 1 compensate for damage or expense incurred: *She promised to indemnify me for my losses.* 2 insure. **in·dem·ni·fi·ca·tion** *n.* **in·dem·ni·fi·er** *n.* ⟨Latin *indemnis* without loss⟩ **in·dem·ni·ty** [ɪnˈdɛmnəti] *n* 1 the payment for damage or expense incurred. 2 insurance. 3 ✹ the remuneration paid to an MP or MLA.

in·dent [ɪnˈdɛnt] *v* 1 make notches in (an edge, line, border, etc.): *an indented coastline.* 2 begin (a line) farther from the edge of a page than the other lines. 3 order (goods, etc.) by an indent. **in·dent** [ˈɪndɛnt] *or* [ɪnˈdɛnt] *n.* ⟨Latin *in-* in + *dentis* tooth⟩ **in·den·ta·tion** *n* a dent; notch; cut. **in·den·ture** *n* 1 a written agreement. 2 Usually, **indentures** *pl* a contract by which a person is bound to serve someone else, esp as an apprentice. **indentured** *adj.*

in·de·pend·ent [ˌɪndɪˈpɛndənt] *adj* 1 done without help from others: *independent work.* 2 not influenced by others: *An independent person votes as she pleases.* 3 not under another's rule: *Canada is an independent country.* 4 *Mathematics* of a variable, that can be assigned any value. *n* 1 a person who votes without regard to party. 2 **Independent** a person who stands for election without being a representative of any political party. **in·de·pend·ent·ly** *adv.* **independent of** without regard to: *independent of the feelings of others.* **independently of** apart from. **in·de·pend·ence** *n* freedom from dependence on or control by another. **independent clause** *Grammar* a subject and predicate that can function alone as a sentence. **independent variable** *Mathematics* a variable whose value determines the value of the dependent variable.

in–depth [ˈɪn ˈdɛpθ] *adj* going below the surface; deep; detailed: *an in-depth study.*

in·de·scrib·a·ble [ˌɪndɪˈskraɪbəbəl] *adj* that cannot be described. **in·de·scrib·a·bly** *adv.* **in·de·scrib·a·ble·ness** *n.*

in·de·struct·i·ble [ˌɪndɪˈstrʌktəbəl] *adj* that cannot be destroyed. **in·de·struct·i·bil·i·ty** *n.* **in·de·struct·i·bly** *adv.*

in·de·ter·mi·na·ble [ˌɪndɪˈtɜrmənəbəl] *adj* 1 not capable of being settled or decided. 2 not capable of being found out exactly. **in·de·ter·mi·na·bly** *adv.*

in·de·ter·mi·nate [ˌɪndɪˈtɜrmənɪt] *adj* not determined; not fixed; indefinite; vague. **in·de·ter·mi·na·cy** *n.* **in·de·ter·mi·nate·ly** *adv.*

in·dex [ˈɪndɛks] *n, pl* **in·dex·es** or **in·di·ces** [ˈɪndəˌsiz] 1 a list of the contents of a book, giving page references for each subject. 2 an alphabetical list of the items in any collection. 3 an annual listing of all the works that have appeared in a particular field. 4 a sign: *A person's face is often an index of his or her mood.* 5 a number that indicates the relative amount, intensity, value, etc. of something: *the cost-of-living index, a pollution index.* 6 *Mathematics* a an exponent. b the number indicating the root. *v* 1 provide with an index. 2 arrange for (income, tax, etc.) to be adjusted according to the cost of living: *to index a pension.* **in·dex·er** *n.* **in·dex·less** *adj.* ⟨Latin *index* orig that which points out; *indicare.* See INDICATE.⟩ **in·dex·a·tion** *n* the policy of indexing income, taxes, etc. **index finger** the finger next to the thumb; forefinger.

In·di·an ['ɪndiən] *n* **1** a native or inhabitant of the Republic of India. **2** a member of the indigenous peoples of the Americas, excepting the Inuit and the Métis. **In·di·an** *adj.*

Indian agent formerly, a federal government official in charge of affairs relating to Aboriginal peoples. **Indian corn** dried cobs of corn whose kernels are orange, purple, brown, and gold. **Indian Days ✸** a festival during which First Nations people exhibit their customs, often in conjunction with a stampede, rodeo, or powwow. **Indian paintbrush** any of various plants of the figwort family having scarlet or orange leaves just below the flowers. **Indian reserve ✸** a tract of land set aside by the Federal Government for the exclusive use of a First Nations band, usually by treaty. **Indian summer** a time of mild weather that sometimes occurs after the first frosts of autumn. **Indian wrestling** a form of wrestling in which contestants try to overcome their opponents by the pressure of their hands against the opponent's hands.

> **USAGE**
> The name **Indian** arose from Columbus's mistaken idea that he had reached India when he landed in the Americas in 1492. It is still widely used in the US and Central and South America to designate aboriginal peoples. In Canada, the term is potentially offensive, but is used without offence by many, including aboriginal peoples. Acceptable substitutes for **Indian** are Aboriginal; Native; Indigenous; and First Peoples, all of which include Indians, Métis, and Inuit. The First Nations comprise many distinct groups, whose specific names (e.g., Cree, Ojibwa, Tsimshian) should be used whenever applicable.

in·di·cate ['ɪndə,keɪt] *v* **1** point to: *The arrow indicates the way to go.* **2** show: *A thermometer indicates temperature.* **3** require: *an old book for which leather binding is indicated.* **4** state in general terms: *The government has indicated its intention to lower taxes.* **in·di·cat·a·ble** *adj.* **in·di·ca·tion** *n.* ⟨Latin *indicare; in-* towards + *dicare* proclaim⟩

in·dic·a·tive [ɪn'dɪkətɪv] *adj* **1** being a sign (*of*): *A headache can be indicative of eye strain.* **2** *Grammar* expressing a state as actual. In *I am going, Did you go?* and *She isn't here* the verbs are in the **indicative mood**. **in·dic·a·tive·ly** *adv.* **in·di·ca·tor** *n* **1** the pointer, etc. on an instrument that measures something. **2** *Chemistry* a substance used to indicate chemical conditions. **3** *Ecology* a plant whose existence shows that its environment is of a certain kind.

in·di·ces ['ɪndə,siz] *n* a pl. of INDEX.

in·dict [ɪn'daɪt] *v* **1** charge with an offence. **2** of a grand jury, find enough evidence against (a person) to justify a trial. **in·dict·a·ble** *adj.* **in·dict·ment** *n.* ⟨Latin *in-* in + *dictare* dictate, express in writing⟩

indictable offence *Law* a crime, such as armed robbery, that is more serious than a summary offence. A person charged with an indictable offence in Canada may be arrested without a warrant. Compare SUMMARY OFFENCE.

in·dif·fer·ent [ɪn'dɪfrənt] *or* [ɪn'dɪfərənt] *adj* **1** having no interest: *an indifferent attitude toward the environment.* **2** unimportant: *an indifferent success.* **3** not bad, but less than good: *an indifferent player.* **in·dif·fer·ence** *n.* **in·dif·fer·ent·ly** *adv.*

in·di·gen ['ɪndədʒən] *n* a person, animal, or plant native to an area. Also, **indi·gene** ['ɪndə,dʒin]. ⟨Latin *indigena* a native⟩ **in·dig·e·nous** *adj* **1** native to a particular country, region, etc.: *indigenous peoples.* **2** originating within a given culture: *indigenous customs.* **in·dig·e·nize** *v.* **in·dig·e·niz·a·tion** *n.* **in·dig·e·nous·ly** *adv.* **in·dig·e·nous·ness** *n.*

in·di·gent ['ɪndɪdʒənt] *adj* poor and needy. *n* an indigent person. **in·di·gence** *n.* **in·di·gent·ly** *adv.* ⟨Latin *indigere* to need⟩

in·di·gest·i·ble [,ɪndə'dʒɛstəbəl] *or* [,ɪndaɪ'dʒɛstəbəl] *adj* hard to digest. **in·di·gest·i·bil·i·ty** *n.* **in·di·gest·i·bly** *adv.* **in·di·ges·tion** [,ɪndə'dʒɛstʃən] *n* the pain from an inability to digest food properly.

in·dig·nant [ɪn'dɪgnənt] *adj* angry at something unworthy, unjust, or mean. **in·dig·nant·ly** *adv.* **in·dig·na·tion** *n.* ⟨Latin *in-* not + *dignus* worthy⟩

in·dig·ni·ty [ɪn'dɪgnəti] *n* **1** an injury to dignity. **2** a state of humiliation.

in·di·go ['ɪndə,gou] *n, pl* **-gos** or **-goes** a blue dye. ⟨Spanish; Greek *indikon* Indian (dye)⟩

in·di·rect [,ɪndə'rɛkt] *or* [,ɪndaɪ'rɛkt] *adj* **1** not straight: *an indirect route.* **2** not directly connected: *Happiness is an indirect consequence of doing one's work well.* **3** not straightforward: *an indirect answer.* **in·di·rect·ly** *adv.* **in·di·rect·ness** *n.*

indirect discourse discourse in which a speaker's words are reported indirectly. Compare DIRECT DISCOURSE. **indirect object** *Grammar* the person or thing to which something is said, given, or shown. *Example:* In *I gave him a book, him* is the indirect object, and *book* is the direct object. Compare DIRECT OBJECT. **indirect question** a reported question. *Example: She asked if they were hungry.* Compare DIRECT QUESTION. **indirect tax** a tax paid indirectly by the consumer because it is included in the price of an article or service.

in·dis·creet [,ɪndɪ'skrit] *adj* not wise and judicious; imprudent: *an indiscreet remark.* **in·dis·creet·ly** *adv.* **in·dis·creet·ness** *n.* **in·dis·cre·tion** [,ɪndɪ'skrɛʃən] *n.*

in·dis·crim·i·nate [,ɪndɪ'skrɪmənɪt] *adj* **1** confused: *She tipped everything out of her suitcase in an indiscriminate mass.* **2** done, made, etc. with no attention to important differences: *indiscriminate reading.* **in·dis·crim·i·nate·ly** *adv.*

in·dis·pen·sa·ble [,ɪndɪ'spɛnsəbəl] *adj* absolutely necessary. **in·dis·pen·sa·bil·i·ty** *n.*

in·dis·posed [ˌɪndɪˈspouzd] *adj* **1** slightly ill. **2** unwilling: *They were indisposed to work nights.* **in·dis·pose** *v* **1** make unwilling: *Hot weather indisposes me to work hard.* **2** make slightly ill. **3** make unfit or unable. **in·dis·po·si·tion** *n.*

in·dis·put·a·ble [ˌɪndɪˈspjutəbəl] *adj* unquestionable. **in·dis·put·a·bil·i·ty** *n.* **in·dis·put·a·bly** *adv.*

in·dis·sol·u·ble [ˌɪndɪˈsɒljəbəl] *adj* not capable of being dissolved, undone, or destroyed. **in·dis·sol·u·bil·i·ty** *n.* **in·dis·sol·u·bly** *adv.* ⟨Latin *in-* not + *dissolubilis; dissolvere* dissolve⟩

in·dis·tinct [ˌɪndɪˈstɪŋkt] *adj* not clear to the eye, ear, or mind; confused. **in·dis·tinct·ly** *adv.* **in·dis·tinct·ness** *n.*

in·dis·tin·guish·a·ble [ˌɪndɪˈstɪŋgwɪʃəbəl] *adj* **1** virtually identical. **2** not easily perceptible. **in·dis·tin·guish·a·bly** *adv.*

in·di·um [ˈɪndiəm] *n* a rare, metallic element that is soft and easily fusible. *Symbol* **In** ⟨Latin *indicum* See INDIGO.⟩

in·di·vid·u·al [ˌɪndəˈvɪdʒuəl] *n* **1** person: *a clever individual.* **2** a distinctive person, animal, or thing: *She tries to remain an individual.*
adj **1** single; separate: *an individual question.* **2** for one only: *an individual serving.* **3** distinctive: *an individual style of arranging her hair.* ⟨Latin *in-* not + *dividuus* divisible⟩ **in·di·vid·u·al·ism** *n* any theory that emphasizes the importance of individuals as opposed to that of a group. **in·di·vid·u·al·ist** *n.* **in·di·vid·u·al·is·tic** *adj.* **in·di·vid·u·al·is·ti·cal·ly** *adv.* **in·di·vid·u·al·i·ty** *n* the sum of the qualities that make one person or thing different from any other. **in·di·vid·u·al·ize** **1** give a distinctive character to. **2** specify. **in·di·vid·u·al·i·za·tion** *n.* **in·di·vid·u·al·ly** *adv* each one separately; one at a time: *The teacher helps us individually.*

in·di·vis·i·ble [ˌɪndəˈvɪzəbəl] *adj* **1** not capable of being divided. **2** not capable of being divided without leaving a remainder. **in·di·vis·i·bil·i·ty** *n.* **in·di·vis·i·bly** *adv.*

in·doc·tri·nate [ɪnˈdɒktrəˌneit] *v* **1** teach a principle to. **2** instruct. **in·doc·tri·na·tion** *n.* **in·doc·tri·na·tor** *n.* ⟨Latin *in-* in + *doctrinare* teach; *doctrina* doctrine⟩

in·do·lent [ˈɪndələnt] *adj* lazy; disliking work. **in·do·lence** *n.* **in·do·lent·ly** *adv.* ⟨Latin *in-* not + *dolere* suffer pain⟩

in·dom·i·ta·ble [ɪnˈdɒmətəbəl] *adj* unconquerable: *indomitable courage.* **in·dom·i·ta·bil·i·ty** *n.* **in·dom·i·ta·bly** *adv.* ⟨Latin *in-* not + *domare* tame⟩

in·door [ˈɪnˌdɔr] *adj* done, played, used, etc. in a house or building: *indoor tennis.* **in·doors** *adv* in or into a building: *go indoors.*

in·du·bi·ta·ble [ɪnˈdjubətəbəl] *or* [ɪnˈdubətəbəl] *adj* not to be doubted; certain. **in·du·bi·ta·bly** *adv.* **in·du·bi·ta·bil·i·ty** *n.* ⟨Latin *in-* not + *dubitare* doubt⟩

in·duce [ɪnˈdjus] *or* [ɪnˈdus] *v* **1** persuade: *Advertising induces people to buy.* **2** cause: *Her labour was induced.* **3** *Electricity* produce (an electric current, electric charge, etc.) without direct contact. **4** *Logic* infer by reasoning from particular facts to a general rule. **in·duc·i·ble** *adj.* ⟨Latin *in-* in + *ducere* lead or bring in, introduce⟩

in·duce·ment *n* **1** an incentive: *Prizes are inducements to try hard to win.* **2** *Law* an introductory statement to explain a plea.

in·duct [ɪnˈdʌkt] *v* **1** bring in; introduce (into a place, seat, position, office, etc.). **2** *US* take into or enrol in military service. ⟨Latin *inductus* pp of *inducere*. See INDUCE.⟩

in·duct·ance *n Electricity* **1** the property of an electrical conductor or circuit that makes INDUCTION possible. **2** the lag in an electric circuit when the current goes on or off. **in·duc·tee** [ɪndʌkˈti] *n* a person who is soon to be inducted. **in·duc·tion** *n* **1** *Electricity* the process by which electrical or magnetic properties are transferred without direct contact. **2** *Logic* the act of reasoning from particular facts to a general rule. Compare DEDUCTION def. 2. **3** the ceremony of installing a person in office. **4** the act of producing or inducing: *induction of a hypnotic state.* **5** the drawing of the fuel mixture into an internal-combustion engine. **induction coil** *Electricity* a device for producing a high voltage from a current of low voltage. **in·duc·tive** *adj* **1** *Logic* reasoning by induction. **2** producing a response in an organism. **3** introductory. **in·duc·tive·ly** *adv.*

in·dulge [ɪnˈdʌldʒ] *v* **1** yield to the wishes of: *We often indulge a sick person.* **2** give in to one's pleasures (often with *in*): *He indulges in tobacco.* **3** let (oneself) have, use, or do (usually with *in*): *to indulge oneself in dreaming.* **in·dulg·ing·ly** *adv.* ⟨Latin *indulgere*⟩ **in·dul·gence** *n* **1** the act of yielding to the wishes of another or allowing oneself one's own desires. **2** something indulged in. **3** a favour. **4** *Roman Catholic Church* remission of the punishment still due for a sin, after the guilt has been forgiven. **in·dul·gent** *adj* lenient, often excessively so: *an indulgent parent.* **in·dul·gent·ly** *adv.*

in·dus·try [ˈɪndəstri] *n* **1** any branch of business, trade, or manufacture: *the steel industry.* **2** manufacturing in general: *She would rather teach than work in industry.* **3** steady effort: *Industry favours success.* **in·dus·tri·al** [ɪnˈdʌstriəl] *adj.* **in·dus·tri·al·ly** *adv.* ⟨Latin *industria* diligence⟩ **in·dus·tri·al·ism** *n* a system of social and economic organization in which industrial activities prevail. **in·dus·tri·al·ist** *n* a person who conducts or owns an industrial enterprise. **in·dus·tri·al·ize** *v* develop large industries as an important feature in an economic system. **in·dus·tri·al·i·za·tion** *n.* **industrial park** a small area of low-rise buildings housing offices and light industry. **in·dus·tri·ous** *adj* working hard and steadily: *an industrious student.* **in·dus·tri·ous·ly** *adv.* **in·dus·tri·ous·ness** *n.*

–ine[1] *suffix* characteristic of; having the nature of; being: *crystalline, elephantine.* ⟨Latin *-inus*⟩

in·e·bri·ate [ɪ'nibri,eit] *v* make drunk. *n* [ɪ'nibriɪt] a habitual drunkard. *adj* [ɪ'nibriɪt] drunk. **in·e·bri·a·tion** *n*. ⟨Latin *in-* + *ebrius* drunk⟩

in·ed·i·ble [ɪn'ɛdəbəl] *adj* not fit to eat: *Some toadstools are inedible.* **in·ed·i·bil·i·ty** *n*.

in·ed·u·ca·ble [ɪn'ɛdʒəkəbəl] *adj* incapable of being educated.

in·ef·fa·ble [ɪn'ɛfəbəl] *adj* **1** not to be expressed in words, or too great to be described. **2** too sacred to be spoken. **in·ef·fa·bil·i·ty** *n*. **in·ef·fa·bly** *adv*. ⟨Latin *ineffabilis*; *in-* not + *ex-* out + *fari* speak⟩

in·ef·fec·tive [,ɪnɪ'fɛktɪv] *adj* **1** of little or no use. **2** incapable. **in·ef·fec·tive·ly** *adv*. **in·ef·fec·tive·ness** *n*.

in·ef·fec·tu·al [,ɪnɪ'fɛktʃuəl] *adj* failing or unable to have the effect wanted; useless. **in·ef·fec·tu·al·ly** *adv*. **in·ef·fec·tu·al·i·ty** *n*.

in·ef·fi·ca·cious [,ɪnɛfə'keiʃəs] *adj* not able to produce the effect wanted. **in·ef·fi·ca·cious·ly** *adv*. **in·ef·fi·ca·cy** [ɪn'ɛfəkəsi] *n*.

in·ef·fi·cient [,ɪnɪ'fɪʃənt] *adj* **1** not able to produce an effect without waste of time, energy, etc.: *A machine that uses too much power is inefficient.* **2** incapable: *an inefficient worker.* **in·ef·fi·cien·cy** *n*. **in·ef·fi·cient·ly** *adv*.

in·e·las·tic [,ɪnɪ'læstɪk] *adj* stiff; inflexible. **in·e·las·tic·i·ty** [,ɪnɪlæ'stɪsəti] *n*.

in·el·e·gant [ɪn'ɛləgənt] *adj* not graceful or fine. **in·el·e·gance** *n*. **in·el·e·gant·ly** *adv*.

in·el·i·gi·ble [ɪn'ɛlədʒəbəl] *adj* not suitable; not qualified: *Her youth makes her ineligible for the post.* **in·el·i·gi·bil·i·ty** *n*. **in·el·i·gi·bly** *adv*.

in·e·luc·ta·ble [,ɪnɪ'lʌktəbəl] *adj* inescapable; inevitable. **in·e·luc·ta·bil·i·ty** *n*. **in·e·luc·ta·bly** *adv*. ⟨Latin *in-* not + *ex-* out + *luctari* struggle⟩

in·ept [ɪn'ɛpt] *adj* **1** not suitable: *He would be an inept choice as captain.* **2** awkward; incompetent: *an inept performance.* **3** foolish: *inept ideas.* **in·ept·ly** *adv*. **in·ept·ness** *n*. ⟨Latin *ineptus*; *in-* not + *aptus* apt⟩

in·ept·i·tude *n* **1** unfitness. **2** a foolish or inappropriate act or remark. **3** incompetence.

SYNONYMS
Inapt and inept have similar meanings, but only inept can mean 'foolish, absurd'.

in·e·qual·i·ty [,ɪnɪ'kwɒləti] *n* **1** the state of being unequal in amount, rank, etc. **2** *Mathematics* an expression showing that two quantities are not equal, such as $a < b$ (*a* is less than *b*). Also called an **in·e·qua·tion**.

in·eq·ui·ta·ble [ɪn'ɛkwətəbəl] *adj* unfair; unjust. **in·eq·ui·ta·bly** *adv*. **in·eq·ui·ty** *n*.

in·e·rad·i·ca·ble [,ɪnɪ'rædəkəbəl] *adj* that cannot be got rid of. **in·e·rad·i·ca·bil·i·ty** *n*. **in·e·rad·i·ca·bly** *adv*.

in·ert [ɪn'ɜrt] *adj* **1** having no power to move or act; lifeless: *A stone is an inert mass of matter.* **2** inactive. **3** *Chemistry* with few or no active properties: *Helium is an inert gas.* **in·ert·ly** *adv*. **in·ert·ness** *n*. ⟨Latin *inertis* idle, unskilled; *in-* without + *ars, artis* art, skill⟩

in·er·tia [ɪn'ɜrʃə] *n* **1** a tendency to remain in the state one is in and not start changes. **2** *Physics* the tendency of matter to stay still, or go on moving in the same direction, unless acted on by some outside force.

in·es·cap·a·ble [,ɪnɪ'skeipəbəl] *adj* that cannot be avoided. **in·es·cap·a·bly** *adv*.

in·es·sen·tial [,ɪnɪ'sɛnʃəl] *adj* **1** not essential. **2** without essence or being.

in·es·ti·ma·ble [ɪn'ɛstəməbəl] *adj* too good, great, precious, etc. to set a value on: *Freedom is an inestimable privilege.* **in·es·ti·ma·bil·i·ty** *n*. **in·es·ti·ma·bly** *adv*.

in·ev·i·ta·ble [ɪn'ɛvətəbəl] *adj* not avoidable. *n* **the inevitable** that which is bound to happen. **in·ev·i·ta·bil·i·ty** *n*. **in·ev·i·ta·bly** *adv*. ⟨Latin *in-* not + *evitare* avoid⟩

in·ex·act [,ɪnɪg'zækt] *adj* with errors or mistakes; not just right. **in·ex·act·i·tude** *n*. **in·ex·act·ly** *adv*. **in·ex·act·ness** *n*.

in·ex·cus·a·ble [,ɪnɪk'skjuzəbəl] *adj* that cannot be justified. **in·ex·cus·a·bly** *adv*. **in·ex·cus·a·ble·ness** *n*.

in·ex·haust·i·ble [,ɪnɪg'zɒstəbəl] *adj* **1** very abundant. **2** tireless. **in·ex·haust·i·bil·i·ty** *n*. **in·ex·haust·i·bly** *adv*.

in·ex·o·ra·ble [ɪn'ɛgzərəbəl] *or* [ɪn'ɛksərəbəl] *adj* **1** relentless; not influenced by entreaties: *an inexorable force.* **2** unalterable. **in·ex·o·ra·bil·i·ty** *n*. **in·ex·o·ra·bly** *adv*. ⟨Latin *in-* not + *ex-* (intensive) + *orare* entreat⟩

in·ex·pe·di·ent [,ɪnɪk'spidiənt] *adj* not wise, practicable, or suitable. **in·ex·pe·di·en·cy** *or* **in·ex·pe·di·ence** *n*. **in·ex·pe·di·ent·ly** *adv*.

in·ex·pen·sive [,ɪnɪk'spɛnsɪv] *adj* low-priced. **in·ex·pen·sive·ly** *adv*. **in·ex·pen·sive·ness** *n*.

in·ex·pe·ri·ence [,ɪnɪk'spiriəns] *n* lack of skill gained from experience. **in·ex·pe·ri·enced** *adj*.

in·ex·pert [ɪn'ɛkspərt] *adj* unskilled. **in·ex·pert·ly** *adv*. **in·ex·pert·ness** *n*.

in·ex·pi·a·ble [ɪn'ɛkspiəbəl] *adj* that cannot be atoned for: *Murder is an inexpiable crime.* **in·ex·pi·a·bly** *adv*.

in·ex·plic·a·ble [,ɪnɪk'splɪkəbəl] *or* [ɪn'ɛkspləkəbəl] *adj* impossible to explain or understand. **in·ex·plic·a·bil·i·ty** *n*. **in·ex·plic·a·bly** *adv*.

in·ex·press·i·ble [,ɪnɪk'sprɛsəbəl] *adj* that cannot be expressed; beyond expression. **in·ex·press·i·bil·i·ty** *n*. **in·ex·press·i·bly** *adv*.

in ex·tre·mis [ɪn ɛkstrɛmɪs] *Latin* at the point of death. ⟨Latin = amid the final things⟩

in·ex·tri·ca·ble [ɪn'ɛkstrəkəbəl] *or* [,ɪnɪk'strɪkəbəl] *adj* **1** that one cannot get out of. **2** that cannot be disentangled or solved. **in·ex·tri·ca·bil·i·ty** *n*. **in·ex·tri·ca·bly** *adv*.

in·fal·li·ble [ɪn'fæləbəl] *adj* **1** that cannot be mistaken: *an infallible rule.* **2** absolutely reliable: *infallible obedience.* **3** *Roman Catholic Church* incapable of error in the exposition of doctrine (said of the Pope as head of the Church). **in·fal·li·bil·i·ty** *n*. **in·fal·li·bly** *adv*.

in·fa·mous ['ɪnfəməs] *adj* **1** deserving a very bad reputation. **2** in public disgrace: *an infamous traitor.* **in·fa·mous·ly** *adv*. **in·fa·my** ['ɪnfəmi] *n*.

in·fant ['ɪnfənt] *n* **1** a baby; very young child. **2** a minor.
adj **1** of or for an infant. **2** in an early stage. **in·fan·cy** *n*. **in·fant·hood** *n*. **in·fant·like** *adj*. ⟨Latin *infans* orig not speaking⟩
in·fan·ti·cide [ɪn'fæntə,saɪd] *n* the act of killing a baby under a year old. **in·fan·tile** ['ɪnfən,taɪl] *or* ['ɪnfəntəl] *adj* **1** to do with infants: *infantile diseases*. **2** childish: *infantile behaviour*. **3** in an early stage.

in·fan·try ['ɪnfəntri] *n* soldiers trained to fight on foot. ⟨Italian *infanteria; infante* foot soldier; orig a youth.⟩

in·farct [ɪn'fɑrkt] *n Pathology* an area of dead tissue resulting from obstruction of the blood supply to that area. **in·farct·ed** *adj*. ⟨Latin *infarctus* pp of *infarcire; in-* in + *farcire* stuff⟩
in·farc·tion [ɪn'fɑrkʃən] *n Pathology* a sudden insufficiency of blood due to a blood clot, etc. in a vein or artery that results in the death of a portion of tissue or an organ.

in·fat·u·ate [ɪn'fætʃu,eit] *v* inspire with an unreasoning passion. **in·fat·u·at·ed** *adj*. **in·fat·u·at·ed·ly** *adv*. **in·fat·u·a·tion** *n*. ⟨Latin *in-* in + *fatuus* foolish⟩

in·fect [ɪn'fɛkt] *v* **1** cause illness by means of disease-producing organisms: *A person who has influenza may infect other people*. **2** affect with a particular character, mood, belief, etc.: *The soldiers were infected with their captain's courage*. **3** *Computers* introduce a computer virus into. ⟨Latin *infectus* pp of *inficere* dye, orig put in; *in-* in + *facere* make, do⟩
in·fec·tion *n* **1** the multiplication of harmful micro-organisms within the body: *The wound was cleaned to avoid infection*. **2** an infectious disease. **in·fec·tious** *adj* **1** of a disease, communicable by infection. Compare CONTAGIOUS. **2** capable of producing an infection: *infectious agents such as viruses*. **3** catching: *an infectious laugh*. **in·fec·tious·ly** *adv*. **in·fec·tious·ness** *n*.

in·fe·lic·i·tous [,ɪnfə'lɪsətəs] *adj* **1** unsuitable; not appropriate. **2** unfortunate; unhappy. **in·fe·lic·i·tous·ly** *adv*. **in·fe·lic·i·ty** *n*.

in·fer [ɪn'fɜr] *v* **-ferred, -fer·ring** conclude: *Seeing my frown, she inferred that I was displeased*. See also IMPLY. **in·fer·a·ble** *adj*. **in·fer·a·bly** *adv*. **in·fer·ence** ['ɪnfərəns] *n*. **in·fer·en·tial** *adj*. **in·fer·en·tial·ly** *adv*. ⟨Latin *in-* in + *ferre* bring⟩

in·fe·ri·or [ɪn'firiər] *adj* **1** below average: *an inferior grade of coffee*. **2** lower in importance, quality, etc. **3** lower in position or rank. **4** *Biology* below others of the same kind, or below the normal position.
n **1** a person who is lower in rank or station. **2** an inferior thing. **in·fe·ri·or·i·ty** *n*. ⟨Latin, comparative of *inferus* low, situated below⟩
inferiority complex 1 *Psychology* an abnormal feeling of being inferior to other people. **2** any lack of self-confidence.

in·fer·no [ɪn'fɜrnou] *n* hell, or something like hell: *Within half an hour of the start of the fire, the whole building was a raging inferno*. ⟨Italian = hell; Latin *inferus* below⟩

in·fer·nal *adj* **1** hellish: *infernal heat*. **2** *Informal* abominable. **in·fer·nal·ly** *adv*.

in·fer·tile [ɪn'fɜrtaɪl] *or* [ɪn'fɜrtəl] *adj* not fruitful; sterile. **in·fer·tile·ly** *adv*. **in·fer·til·i·ty** [,ɪnfər'tɪləti] *n*

in·fest [ɪn'fɛst] *v* disturb frequently or in large numbers (with *by* or *with*): *Swamps are often infested with mosquitoes*. **in·fes·ta·tion** [,ɪnfɛ'steɪʃən] *or* [,ɪnfə'steɪʃən] *n*. ⟨Latin *infestare* attack; *infestus* hostile⟩

in·fi·del ['ɪnfədəl] *n* **1** a person who does not believe in religion. **2** a person who opposes a faith, esp Christianity or Islam. **in·fi·del** *adj*. ⟨Latin *in-* not + *fidelis* faithful⟩
in·fi·del·i·ty [,ɪnfə'dɛləti] *n* **1** lack of religious faith. **2** unfaithfulness, esp of husband or wife; disloyalty.

in·field ['ɪn,fild] *n* **1** *Baseball* **a** the part of the field within the base lines; DIAMOND (def. 4). **b** the first, second, and third base players and shortstop of a team: *That team has a good infield*. **2** *Agriculture* **a** the part of farm lands nearest the buildings. **b** land regularly tilled. Compare OUTFIELD.
in·field·er *n Baseball* a player of the infield.

in·fight·ing ['ɪn,faitɪŋ] *n* **1** *Informal* internal conflict: *Infighting among staff lost their company the contract*. **2** *Boxing* fighting at close quarters. **in·fight·er** *n*.

in·fil·trate ['ɪnfɪl,treit] *or* [ɪn'fɪltreit] *v* **1** *Military* pass into as if by filtering: *Enemy troops infiltrated the front lines*. **2** filter into or through. **3** enter secretly or by deception. **in·fil·tra·tion** *n*. **in·fil·tra·tive** *adj*. **in·fil·tra·tor** *n*.

in·fi·nite ['ɪnfənɪt] *adj* **1** without limits. **2** extremely great: *infinite patience*. ⟨Latin *in-* not + *finis* boundary⟩
in·fi·nite·ly *adv* **1** to an infinite degree. **2** *Informal* very much: *I'm infinitely obliged to you*. **in·fi·ni·tes·i·mal** [,ɪnfənə'tɛsəməl] *adj* **1** so small as to be almost nothing: *A millionth of a centimetre is an infinitesimal length*. **2** *Mathematics* less than any assignable quantity or magnitude. **in·fi·ni·tes·i·mal·ly** *adv*. **in·fin·i·tude** [ɪn'fɪnə,tjud] *or* [-,tud] *n* **1** the state of being infinite. **2** an infinite extent, amount, or number. **in·fin·i·ty** *n* **1** the state of being infinite: *the infinity of space*. **2** an infinite distance, space, or time. **3** an infinite or very large amount or extent. **3** *Mathematics* **a** an infinite quantity or magnitude. **b** the limit that a function is said to approach in certain conditions. **to infinity** without limits.

in·fin·i·tive [ɪn'fɪnətɪv] *n Grammar* a form of a verb not limited by person, number, tense, voice, or mood. In *We want to go now, to go* is the infinitive. **in·fin·i·tiv·al** [,ɪnfɪnə'taɪvəl] *adj*. ⟨Latin *infinitivus* from *infinitus* unrestricted. See INFINITE.⟩

in·firm [ɪn'fɜrm] *adj* **1** weak; feeble. **2** weak in character. **in·fir·mi·ty** *n*. **in·firm·ly** *adv*. ⟨Latin *infirmus*⟩
in·fir·ma·ry *n* a place for the care of the sick or injured, esp a small hospital in a school or other institution.

in·flame [ɪn'fleim] *v* **1** become or cause to

become on fire. **2** arouse or become aroused to violent emotion: *Her speech inflamed the crowd.* **3** become inflamed, or produce inflammation in: *The smoke inflamed my eyes.* **in·flam·ma·ble** [ɪnˈflæməbəl] *adj.* **in·flam·ma·bly** *adv.* **in·flam·ma·bil·i·ty** *n.* See also FLAMMABLE. ⟨Latin *in-* in + *flamma* flame⟩ **in·flam·ma·tion** [ˌɪnfləˈmeɪʃən] *n* a diseased condition marked by heat, swelling, and pain. **in·flam·ma·to·ry** *adj* **1** tending to arouse: *an inflammatory speech.* **2** to do with inflammation.

in·flate [ɪnˈfleɪt] *v* **1** swell with air or gas: *to inflate a balloon.* **2** increase (prices, etc.) beyond a reasonable amount. **in·flat·ed** *adj.* ⟨Latin *in-* into + *flare* blow⟩
in·flat·a·ble *n* an inflatable boat, raft, etc.
in·fla·tion *n* **1** a swelling (with air, gas, etc.) **2** an increase of the currency of a country by issuing much paper money. **3** a sharp and sudden rise of prices. Compare DEFLATION. **in·fla·tion·ar·y** *adj.* **inflationary spiral** rapidly rising prices resulting from increasing costs of labour and services. **in·fla·tion·ism** *n* the practice of inflation through expansion of currency. **in·fla·tion·ist** *n, adj.*

in·flect [ɪnˈflɛkt] *v* **1** change the tone or pitch of (the voice). **2** *Grammar* vary the form of (a word) to show case, number, etc. By inflecting *who,* we have *whose* and *whom.* **3** bend; curve. **in·flect·ed** *adj.* **in·flec·tion** *n.* **in·flec·tion·al** *adj.* **in·flec·tion·less** *adj.* **in·flec·tive** *adj.* ⟨Latin *in-* in + *flectere* bend⟩

In·flex·i·ble [ɪnˈflɛksəbəl] *adj* **1** unyielding: *inflexible determination.* **2** that cannot be changed. **3** not easily bent: *an inflexible steel rod.* **in·flex·i·bil·i·ty** *n.* **in·flex·i·bly** *adv.*

SYNONYMS

Inflexible = unyielding, holding to what one has made up one's mind to do: *It is a waste of time to argue with someone whose attitude is inflexible.* **Inexorable** = not to be affected by pleading: *The principal was inexorable in her decision.* **Unrelenting** = not softening in force: *He was unrelenting in his hatred.*

---

in·flict [ɪnˈflɪkt] *v* cause someone to have or suffer. *to inflict a penalty.* **in·flic·tion** *n.* ⟨Latin *inflictus* pp of *infligere; in-* on + *fligere* dash⟩

in–flight [ˈɪn ˈflaɪt] *adj* served or shown during a flight: *an in-flight movie.*

in·flo·res·cence [ˌɪnfləˈrɛsəns] *n Botany* **1** the arrangement of flowers on the stem. **2** a flower cluster. **3** the state of being in flower. **in·flo·res·cent** *adj.* ⟨Latin *in-* in + *floris* flower⟩

in·flow [ˈɪnˌfloʊ] *n* **1** a flowing in or into. **2** that which flows in; influx.

in·flu·ence [ˈɪnfluəns] *n* **1** the power to act on others, seen only in the effect: *the influence of the moon on the tides.* **2** the power to affect without using force: *A person may have influence by his or her wealth.* **3** a person who or thing that has such power. **4** *Electricity* electrostatic induction.
v have power over: *The moon influences the tides.* **in·flu·ence·a·ble** *adj.* ⟨Latin *influentia* orig a flowing in; *in-* in + *fluere* flow⟩

in·flu·en·tial *adj* having much influence: *influential friends.* **in·flu·en·tial·ly** *adv.*

in·flu·en·za [ˌɪnfluˈɛnzə] *n* an acute, contagious viral disease; flu. **in·flu·en·zal** *adj.* ⟨Italian; Latin *influentia.* See INFLUENCE.⟩

in·flux [ˈɪnflʌks] *n* **1** a flowing in: *the influx of immigrants into a country.* **2** the point where a river flows into another river, a lake, or the sea. ⟨Latin *in-* in + *fluxus* pp of *fluere* flow⟩

in·fo [ˈɪnfoʊ] *n Slang* information.
infobot [ˈɪnfoʊˌbɒt] *n* an electronic message sent automatically: *I e-mailed a letter to the editor of the newspaper and got an infobot back.* **in·fo·ma·ni·ac** [ˌɪnfoʊˈmeɪniæk] *n Informal* a person who collects facts for their own sake. **in·fo·mer·cial** [ˈɪnfoʊˌmɜrʃəl] *n* a television program which is one long advertisement.

in·form [ɪnˈfɔrm] *v* **1** give knowledge to. **2** give the police incriminating information (*against* or *on*). ⟨Latin *in-* in + *forma* form⟩
in·form·ant *n* a person who gives information to another. **in·for·ma·tion** *n* **1** facts: *A dictionary gives information about words.* **2** the act of informing: *A guidebook is for the information of travellers.* **in·for·ma·tion·al** *adj.* **information highway** *Computers* all electronic media and communication systems. **information management** the work of planning and overseeing the use of information technology. **information technology** all the technology involved in generating, storing, retrieving, etc. information electronically by computers, the Internet, etc. *Abbrev* **IT.** **information theory** the study of the efficiency of any communication system. **in·form·a·tive** *adj* giving information; instructive. **in·form·a·tive·ly** *adv.* **in·form·er** *n* a person who gives information about a criminal activity to the police.

in·for·mal [ɪnˈfɔrməl] *adj* **1** without ceremony: *an informal party.* **2** used in everyday English, but not in formal speech or writing. *Kids* is an informal term for *children.* Compare COLLOQUIAL. **in·for·mal·ly** *adv* **in·for·mal·i·ty** *n*

in·frac·tion [ɪnˈfrækʃən] *n* a breaking of a law or obligation: *Reckless driving is an infraction of the law.* ⟨Latin *infractio* from *infractus* pp of *infringere.* See INFRINGE.⟩

in·fra·red [ˈɪnfrəˈrɛd] *adj* to do with the long, invisible light waves beyond the red end of the colour spectrum. ⟨Latin *infra-* below + RED⟩

in·fra·struc·ture [ˈɪnfrəˌstrʌkʃər] *n* the essential elements of a structure: *Roads and sewer are part of the infrastructure of a city.* ⟨Latin *infra-* below + STRUCTURE⟩

in·fre·quent [ɪnˈfrikwənt] *adj* scarce; rare. **in·fre·quen·cy** *n.* **in·fre·quent·ly** *adv.*

in·fringe [ɪnˈfrɪndʒ] *v* **1** violate (a law, obligation, right, etc.): *A false label infringes the laws relating to food.* **2** trespass (*on*): *to infringe on the rights of another.* **in·fringe·ment** *n.* ⟨Latin *in-* in + *frangere* break⟩

in·fu·ri·ate [ɪnˈfjʊriˌeɪt] *v* fill with extreme anger; make furious. **in·fu·ri·at·ing·ly** *adv.* ⟨Latin *in-* into + *furia* fury⟩

in·fuse [ɪnˈfjuz] *v* **1** fill someone with (a principle, idea, etc.) (with *into*): *The captain infused courage into his soldiers.* **2** inspire (with *with*): *He infused the soldiers with courage.* **3** soak in a liquid to draw out flavour, etc.: *We infuse tea leaves in hot water.* ⟨Latin *infusus* pp of *infundere; in-* in + *fundere* pour⟩
in·fu·sion [ɪnˈfjuʒən] *n* **1** the act of infusing. **2** a liquid extract obtained by soaking, as tea.

–ing¹ *suffix forming nouns* the performance, result, material, etc. of some activity or thing: *hard thinking, the art of painting, a beautiful drawing.* ⟨Old English *-ing, -ung*⟩

–ing² *suffix* **1** an element forming the present participle of verbs: *raining, staying, talking.* **2** that——s: *lasting.* ⟨Middle English *-ing, -ind, -end*; Old English *-ende*⟩

in·gen·ious [ɪnˈdʒinjəs] *adj* **1** clever; skilful in planning or making: *an ingenious girl.* **2** cleverly made: *an ingenious device.* **in·ge·ni·ous·ly** *adv.* **in·ge·nu·ity** [ˌɪndʒəˈnjuəti] *or* [-ˈnuəti] *n.* ⟨Latin *ingeniosus; ingenium* natural talent⟩

> **CONFUSABLES**
> **Ingenious** = clever; skilful: *She is so ingenious that she is sure to think of a way of doing this work more easily.* **Ingenuous** = frank; simple: *The ingenuous child had never thought of being suspicious of what others told her.*

in·gé·nue [ˌænʒəˈnu]; *French, sg and pl* [ɛ̃ʒeˈny] *n* a simple, innocent girl or young woman, esp as represented on the stage, in film, etc. ⟨French = ingenuous (fem)⟩

in·gen·u·ous [ɪnˈdʒɛnjuəs] *adj* **1** frank; open; sincere. **2** simple; natural; innocent. **in·gen·u·ous·ly** *adv.* **in·gen·u·ous·ness** *n.* ⟨Latin *ingenuus* orig native, free born⟩

in·gest [ɪnˈdʒɛst] *v* **1** take (food, etc.) into the body for digestion. **2** take in: *He ingested the new idea slowly.* **in·gest·i·ble** *adj.* **in·gest·ion** *n.* **in·gest·ive** *adj.* ⟨Latin *ingestus* pp of *ingerere; in-* in + *gerere* carry⟩

in·glo·ri·ous [ɪnˈɡlɔriəs] *adj* bringing no glory; shameful. **in·glo·ri·ous·ness** *n.* **in·glo·ri·ous·ly** *adv.*

in·go·ing [ˈɪnˌɡouɪŋ] *adj* going in; entering.

in·got [ˈɪŋɡət] *n* a block or bar of metal. ⟨Old English *in-* in + *goten* pp of *gēotan* pour⟩

in·grain [ɪnˈɡrein] *v* fix deeply and firmly: *Certain habits are ingrained in one's nature.* **in·grained** *adj.* ⟨⟨dyed⟩ in grain⟩

in·grate [ˈɪnɡreit] *n* an ungrateful person. **in·grat·i·tude** [ɪnˈɡrætəˌtjud] *or* [-ˌtud] *n.* ⟨Latin *in-* not + *gratus* thankful⟩

in·gra·ti·ate [ɪnˈɡreiʃiˌeit] *v* bring (oneself or someone) into favour (usually with *with*): *He tried to ingratiate himself with the teacher by giving her presents.* **in·gra·ti·a·tion** *n.* **in·gra·ti·at·ing** *adj.* **in·gra·ti·at·ing·ly** *adv.* ⟨Latin *in gratiam* into favour⟩

in·gre·di·ent [ɪnˈɡridiənt] *n* one of the parts of a mixture: *the ingredients of a cake.* ⟨Latin *ingrediens* ppr of *ingredi; in-* in + *gradi* go⟩

in·gress [ˈɪnɡrɛs] *n* **1** a going in: *A high fence prevented ingress to the field.* **2** a way in; entrance. **3** a right to go in. **in·gres·sion** *n.* ⟨Latin *ingressus* pp of *ingredi.* See INGREDIENT.⟩

in·grown [ˈɪnˌɡroun] *adj* **1** grown within; grown inward. **2** grown into the flesh.

in·hab·it [ɪnˈhæbɪt] *v* **1** live in (a place, region, house, cave, tree, etc.): *Fish inhabit the sea.* **2** exist within: *Thoughts inhabit the mind.* **in·hab·it·a·ble** *adj.* **in·hab·it·a·bil·i·ty** *n.* **in·hab·it·ant** *n.* **in·hab·i·ta·tion** *n.* ⟨Latin *in-* in + *habitare* dwell; *habere* have, dwell⟩

in·hale [ɪnˈheil] *v* draw into the lungs. ⟨Latin *in-* in + *halare* breathe⟩
in·hal·ant [ɪnˈheilənt] *n* a medicine to be inhaled. **in·ha·la·tion** [ˌɪnhəˈleiʃən] *n* **1** the act of inhaling. **2** a medicine to be inhaled. **in·hal·er** *n* an apparatus used in inhaling medicine, a gas, etc. Also called **in·ha·la·tor** [ˈɪnhəˌleitər].

in·har·mo·ni·ous [ˌɪnhɑrˈmouniəs] *adj* **1** discordant. **2** not congenial; disagreeable. **in·har·mo·ni·ous·ly** *adv.* **in·har·mo·ni·ous·ness** *n.*

in·here [ɪnˈhir] *v* belong to as an essential quality or attribute: *Greed inheres in human nature.* ⟨Latin *in-* in + *haerere* stick⟩
in·her·ent [ɪnˈhɛrənt] *or* [ɪnˈhirənt] *adj* existing as a basic quality: *the inherent sweetness of sugar.* **in·her·ence** *n.* **in·her·ent·ly** *adv.*

in·her·it [ɪnˈhɛrɪt] *v* **1** get after a person dies: *Her niece inherited the farm.* **2** get from one's ancestors: *I have inherited my father's brown hair.* **3** receive from predecessors: *The new government inherited a financial crisis.* **in·her·it·a·bil·i·ty** *n.* **in·her·it·a·ble** *adj.* **in·her·i·tor** *n.* ⟨Old French *enheriter*, Latin *inhereditare; in-* in + *heredis* heir⟩
in·her·it·ance *n* anything inherited.

in·hib·it [ɪnˈhɪbɪt] *v* **1** restrain: *The soldier's sense of duty inhibited his impulse to desert.* **2** forbid. **3** *Chemistry* decrease the rate of action of (a reaction). **in·hib·it·a·ble** *adj.* ⟨Latin *inhibitus; in-* in + *habere* hold⟩
in·hi·bi·tion [ˌɪnəˈbɪʃən] *or* [ˌɪnhə-] *n* **1** the act of inhibiting. **2** the state of being inhibited. **3** an inner force that restrains impulses. **in·hib·i·tor** *or* **inhibiter** *n Chemistry* anything that interferes with a reaction: *Antifreeze is an inhibitor.* **in·hib·i·to·ry** *adj* tending to inhibit.

in·hos·pi·ta·ble [ˌɪnhɒˈspɪtəbəl] *or* [ɪnˈhɒspɪtəbəl] *adj* providing no shelter: *They encountered a rocky, inhospitable shore.* **in·hos·pi·ta·bly** *adv.* **in·hos·pi·tal·i·ty** *n* a lack of hospitality; inhospitable behaviour.

in·hu·man [ɪnˈhjumən] *adj* **1** without kindness; cruel. **2** showing qualities not considered natural to a human being: *almost inhuman powers of endurance.* **3** not up to normal standards for humans: *inhuman living conditions.* **in·hu·man·i·ty** *n.* **in·hu·man·ly** *adv.*

in·hu·mane [ˌɪnhjuˈmein] *adj* lacking in compassion, humanity, or kindness. **in·hu·mane·ly** *adv.* ⟨variant of INHUMAN⟩

in·im·i·cal [ɪˈnɪməkəl] *adj* **1** hostile. **2** unfavourable: *Lack of ambition is inimical to success.* **in·im·i·cal·i·ty** *n.* **i·nim·i·cal·ly** *adv.* ⟨Latin *inimicus; in-* not + *amicus* friendly⟩

in·im·i·ta·ble [i'nɪmətəbəl] *adj* that cannot be imitated or copied; matchless. **i·nim·i·ta·bly** *adv.* **i·nim·i·ta·bil·i·ty** *n.*

in·iq·ui·tous [ɪ'nɪkwətəs] *adj* very unjust; wicked. **i·niq·ui·tous·ly** *adv.* **in·iq·ui·ty** *n.* ⟨Latin *iniquitas* from *iniquus; in-* not + *aequus* just⟩

in·i·tial [ɪ'nɪʃəl] **-tialled** or **-tialed, -tial·ling** or **-tial·ing** *adj* occurring at the beginning; first. *n* **1** the first letter of a word or name. **2 initials** the first letters of one's surname and given name(s) used instead of one's signature. *v* mark or sign with initials: *Chris Allen Lee initialled the note C.A.L.* ⟨Latin *initium* beginning, from *inire* begin; *in* -in + *ire* go⟩ **in·i·tial·ize** *v Computers* **1** FORMAT. **2** set to an initial value or state: *The total was initialized to zero on January 1st.* **in·i·tial·ly** *adv* at the beginning. **in·i·ti·ate** [ɪ'nɪʃi,eit] *v* **1** begin. **2** admit (a person) by special ceremonies (into secret knowledge, or a society). *n* [ɪ'nɪʃiɪt] a person who is initiated. **in·i·ti·a·tion** *n.* **in·i·ti·a·tor** *n.* **in·i·ti·a·tive** *n* the active part in taking the first steps in any undertaking: *She takes the initiative in making acquaintances.* **in·i·ti·a·to·ry** *adj* introductory.

in·ject [ɪn'dʒɛkt] *v* force (liquid) into a passage, cavity, or tissue: *to inject cortisone into a muscle.* **in·ject·a·ble** *adj.* **in·jec·tion** *n.* ⟨Latin *injectus; in-* in + *jacere* throw⟩

in·ju·di·cious [,ɪndʒə'dɪʃəs] *adj* showing lack of judgment; unwise; not prudent. **in·ju·di·cious·ly** *adv.* **in·ju·di·cious·ness** *n.*

in·junc·tion [ɪn'dʒʌŋkʃən] *n* **1** a command: *Injunctions of secrecy did not prevent the news from leaking out.* **2** *Law* an order issued by a court or judge ordering a person to refrain from doing something. **in·junc·tive** *adj.* ⟨Latin *injunctio* from *injungere.* See ENJOIN.⟩

in·jure ['ɪndʒər] *v* cause damage to: *She injured her arm when she fell. Her pride has been injured.* ⟨Latin *injuria; in-* not + *juris* right⟩ **in·ju·ri·ous** [ɪn'dʒʊriəs] *adj* **1** harmful: *Hail is injurious to crops.* **2** unfair. **3** slanderous. **in·ju·ri·ous·ly** *adv.* **in·ju·ri·ous·ness** *n.*

in·ju·ry ['ɪndʒəri] *n* **1** damage; harm: *She escaped from the train wreck without injury.* **2** unfairness; injustice; wrong: *You did me an injury when you said I lied.*

in·jus·tice [ɪn'dʒʌstɪs] *n* **1** a lack of justice. **2** an unjust act.

ink [ɪŋk] *n* **1** a coloured substance used for writing, printing, or drawing. **2** a dark liquid squirted out for protection by squids, etc. *v* **1** colour or stain with ink. **2** put (a contract, etc.) in writing. **ink·like** *adj.* ⟨Old French *enque,* Greek *enkauston; en* in + *kaiein* burn⟩ **ink in** fill in (an outline) with ink. **ink·y** *adj* **1** dark or black, like ink: *inky shadows.* **2** marked or stained with ink. **ink·i·ly** *adv.* **ink·i·ness** *n.*

ink·ling ['ɪŋklɪŋ] *n* a vague notion; hint. ⟨Middle English *inclen* whisper, hint⟩

in·laid See INLAY.

in·land ['ɪn,lænd] or ['ɪnlənd] *adj* **1** away from the coast or the border: *an inland sea.*

2 domestic; not foreign: *inland trade.* *adv* in or toward the interior.

in–law ['ɪn ,lɒ] *n Informal* a relative by marriage. ⟨Middle English *inlawen;* Old English *inlagian*⟩

in·lay [ɪn'lei] or ['ɪn,lei] *v* **-laid, -lay·ing** set as a decoration onto a surface: *to inlay strips of gold.* *n* ['ɪn,lei] *n* **1** an inlaid decoration. **2** a shaped piece of porcelain, etc. cemented in a tooth as a filling. **in·laid** [ɪn'leid] or ['ɪn,leid] *adj.*

in·let ['ɪn,let] or ['ɪnlət] *n* a narrow strip of water extending into the land or between islands. ⟨Middle English⟩

in-line skates ['ɪn,laɪn] roller skates having four wheels in a single row, one behind the other. **inline skating.**

in lo·co pa·ren·tis [ɪn 'loukou pɑ'rɛntɪs] *Latin* in the place of a parent.

in·mate ['ɪn,meit] *n* a person who lives with others in the same building, esp one confined in a prison, hospital, etc.

in me·di·as res [ɪn 'midiəs 'reis] or ['riz] *Latin* in the midst of things.

in me·mo·ri·am ['ɪn mə'mɔriəm] *Latin* in memory (of); to the memory (of).

inn [ɪn] *n* a public house for lodging and caring for travellers. ⟨Old English⟩ **inn·keep·er** *n* a person who owns, manages, or keeps an inn.

in·nards ['ɪnərdz] *n pl Informal* **1** the internal organs of the body. **2** the internal workings of any mechanism. ⟨variant of *inward*⟩

in·nate [ɪ'neit] *adj* **1** natural; inborn: *an innate talent for drawing.* **2** existing as a natural characteristic: *the innate complexity of the problem.* **in·nate·ly** *adv.* **in·nate·ness** *n.* ⟨Latin *in-* in + *natus* pp of *nasci* be born⟩

in·ner ['ɪnər] *adj* **1** farther in: *an inner room.* **2** close to the central part: *the inner circle of government, inner thoughts.* ⟨Old English *innera* comparative of *inne* within⟩ **inner city** the older, central part of a large city. **in·ner–cit·y** *adj.* **in·ner·most** *adj* **1** farthest in: *the innermost parts.* **2** most secret.

in·ning ['ɪnɪŋ] *n* **1** *Baseball* the period of play in which each team has a turn at bat. **2** Usually, **innings**, the time when a person or group has a chance for action (usually with sg verb). ⟨Old English *innung* a getting in⟩

in·no·cent ['ɪnəsənt] *adj* **1** free from wrongdoing: *an innocent bystander.* **2** not guilty **3** without knowledge of evil: *as innocent as a baby.* **4** lacking (usually with *of*): *a bare room innocent of all decoration.* *n* a person who is naive. **in·no·cence** *n.* **in·no·cent·ly** *adv.* ⟨Latin *in-* not + *nocere* harm⟩

SYNONYMS

Innocent emphasizes having consciously done no wrong: *The truck driver was proved innocent of manslaughter.* **Blameless** = not to be held responsible, whether or not wrong has been done: *He was held blameless, although the child was killed.* **Guiltless** = without guilt in thought, intention, or act: *The other driver was not guiltless.*

in·noc·u·ous [ɪ'nɒkjuəs] *adj* **1** not capable of damage: *an innocuous medicine.* **2** not likely to arouse strong feelings: *innocuous remarks.* **in·noc·u·ous·ly** *adv.* **in·noc·u·ous·ness** *n.* ⟨Latin *in-* not + *nocuus* hurtful; *nocere* to harm⟩

in·no·vate ['ɪnə,veit] *v* bring in something new. **in·no·va·tion** *n.* **in·no·va·tion·al** *adj.* **in·no·va·tive** *adj.* **in·no·va·tor** *n.* ⟨Latin *innovare; in-* in + *novus* new⟩

In·nu ['ɪnu] *n* **1** a member of a First Nations people living in northern Québec. **2** their Cree dialect; Montagnais or Naskapi. **In·nu** *adj.*

in·nu·en·do [,ɪnju'ɛndou] *n, pl* **-does** an indirect hint or reference, esp against someone's reputation. ⟨Latin *innuendo* by giving a nod to; *in-* in + *-nuere* nod⟩

in·nu·mer·a·ble [ɪ'njumərəbəl] *or* [ɪ'nu-] *adj* too many to count: *innumerable stars.* **in·nu·mer·a·bil·i·ty** *n.* **in·nu·mer·a·bly** *adv.* ⟨Latin *in-* not + *numerabilis* countable⟩

in·nu·mer·ate [ɪ'njumərɪt] *or* [ɪ'numərɪt] *adj* unable to do simple calculations; the mathematical equivalent of **illiterate.** **in·nu·mer·acy** *n.* ⟨Latin *numerus* number, by analogy with *illiterate*⟩

in·oc·u·late [ɪ'nɒkjə,leit] *v* infect (a person or animal) with a mild form of a disease, thus reducing the individual's chances of contracting the disease thereafter. **in·oc·u·la·tion** *n.* ⟨Latin *inoculare* implant; *in-* in + *oculus* bud, eye⟩

in·of·fen·sive [,ɪnə'fɛnsɪv] *adj* harmless; not arousing objections. **in·of·fen·sive·ly** *adv.* **in·of·fen·sive·ness** *n.*

in·op·er·a·ble [ɪn'ɒpərəbəl] *adj* **1** unworkable: *an inoperable plan.* **2** unable to be cured by surgery: *an inoperable cancer.* **in·op·er·a·bil·i·ty** *n.*

in·op·er·a·tive [ɪn'ɒpərətɪv] *or* [ɪn'ɒpə,reitɪv] *adj* not working; without effect. **in·op·er·a·tive·ness** *n.*

in·op·por·tune [ɪn,ɒpər'tjun] *or* [-'tun] *adj* coming at a bad time: *an inopportune call.* **in·op·por·tune·ly** *adv.* **in·op·por·tune·ness** *n.* **in·op·por·tu·ni·ty** *n.*

in·or·di·nate [ɪn'ɔrdənɪt] *adj* much too great; *He spends an inordinate amount of time tinkering with his car.* **in·or·di·nate·ly** *adv.* ⟨Latin *in-* not + *ordinis* order⟩

in·or·gan·ic [,ɪnɔr'gænɪk] *adj* **1** to do with matter that is not animal or vegetable: *Minerals are inorganic.* **2** *Chemistry* to do with the branch of chemistry that deals with inorganic compounds and elements. **in·or·gan·i·cal·ly** *adv.*

in·put ['ɪn,pʊt] *n* **1** the amount of material, energy, etc. put in: *an increased input of funds.* **2** data fed into a computer system. *v* **in·put, in·put·ting** feed (data) into a computer or data-processing system.

in·quest ['ɪnkwɛst] *n* **1** a legal inquiry to determine the cause of a sudden death. **2** any investigation into the cause of an event, situation, etc. ⟨Latin *inquisita* pp of *inquirere.* See INQUIRE.⟩

in·qui·e·tude [ɪn'kwaɪə,tjud] *or* [-,tud] *n* restlessness; uneasiness.

in·quire [ɪn'kwaɪr] *v* **1** ask. **2** make an investigation. Also, **en·quire.** **in·quir·er** *n.* **in·quir·ing** *adj.* **in·quir·y** [ɪn'kwaɪri] *or* ['ɪnkwəri] *or* **en·quiry** *n.* ⟨Latin *inquirere; in-* into + *quaerere* ask⟩

in·qui·si·tion [,ɪnkwə'zɪʃən] *n* **1** an official investigation. **2 the Inquisition** a court established by the Roman Catholic Church in 1229 to discover heresy. **3** any severe questioning. **in·qui·si·tion·al** *adj.* **in·quis·i·tive** *adj* **1** curious. **2** prying into other people's affairs. **in·quis·i·tive·ly** *adv.* **in·quis·i·tive·ness** *n.* **in·quis·i·tor** *n* **1** an official investigator. **2** a person who conducts an inquiry in a very harsh or hostile manner. **in·quis·i·to·ri·al** *adj.* **in·quis·i·to·ri·al·ly** *adv.*

in re [ɪn 'ri] *or* [ɪn 'rei] *Latin* concerning; in the matter of. ⟨literally, in the thing⟩

in·road ['ɪn,roud] *n* **1** a raid. **2** Usually, **inroads** *pl* a penetration that destroys, injures, or lessens something: *The unusual expenses made serious inroads on her savings.*

in·rush ['ɪn,rʌʃ] *n* a rushing in; inflow. **in·rush·ing** *n, adj.*

in·sa·lu·bri·ous [,ɪnsə'lubriəs] *adj* unfavourable to health. **in·sa·lu·bri·ous·ly** *adv.* **in·sa·lu·bri·ty** *n.*

in·sane [ɪn'sein] *adj* **1** mentally deranged. **2** extremely foolish: *an insane plot to overthrow the government.* **in·sane·ly** *adv.* **in·san·i·ty** [ɪn'sænəti] *n.*

in·san·i·tar·y [ɪn'sænə,teri] *adj* not clean; unhealthy. **in·san·i·tar·i·ness** *n.*

in·sa·tia·ble [ɪn'seiʃəbəl] *adj* that cannot be satisfied: *an insatiable appetite for sweets.* **in·sa·tia·bly** *adv.* **in·sa·tia·bil·i·ty** *n.*

in·scribe [ɪn'skraɪb] *v* **1** write on a surface: *Her initials were inscribed on the bracelet.* **2** *Geometry* draw (a figure) inside another figure so that their boundaries touch in as many places as possible. **in·scrib·a·ble** *adj.* **in·scrib·er** *n.* **in·scrip·tion** [ɪn'skrɪpʃən] *n.* ⟨Latin *in-* on + *scribere* write⟩

in·scru·ta·ble [ɪn'skrutəbəl] *adj* so obscure that one cannot make out its meaning: *an inscrutable look.* **in·scru·ta·bil·i·ty** *n.* **in·scru·ta·bly** *adv.* ⟨Latin *in-* not + *scrutari* examine, ransack; *scruta* trash⟩

in·sect ['ɪnsɛkt] *n* any of a large class of invertebrates having three pairs of legs and, usually, one or two pairs of wings. **in·sect·ile** [ɪn'sɛktaɪl] *adj.* **in·sect·like** *adj.* ⟨Latin *insectum* pp of *insecare; in-* into + *secare* cut; for their segmented bodies⟩ **in·sec·ti·cide** [ɪn'sɛktə,saɪd] *n* a substance for killing insects. **in·sec·ti·ci·dal** *adj.* **in·sec·ti·vore** [ɪn'sɛktə,vɔr] *n* any insect-eating animal or plant. **in·sec·tiv·o·rous** [,ɪnsɛk'tɪvərəs] *adj.*

in·se·cure [,ɪnsɪ'kjur] *adj* **1** not safe from danger, failure, etc.: *insecure investments.* **2** liable to give way: *an insecure lock.* **3** lacking confidence: *an insecure child.* **in·se·cure·ly** *adv.* **in·se·cu·ri·ty** *n.*

in·sem·i·nate [ɪn'sɛmə,neit] v impregnate; fertilize. **in·sem·i·na·tion** n. **in·sem·i·na·tor** n. ⟨Latin in- not + seminare to sow; semen seed⟩

in·sen·sate [ɪn'sɛnsɪt] or [ɪn'sɛnseit] adj 1 without sensation; inanimate: the insensate stones. 2 unfeeling: insensate cruelty. 3 senseless; stupid: insensate folly. **in·sen·sate·ly** adv. **in·sen·sate·ness** n.

in·sen·si·ble [ɪn'sɛnsəbəl] adj 1 not having the power to perceive: A blind person is insensible to colours. 2 unconscious: The man hit by the truck was insensible for hours. 3 not aware: The girls in the boat were insensible of the danger. **in·sen·si·bil·i·ty** n. **in·sen·si·bly** adv.

in·sen·si·tive [ɪn'sɛnsətɪv] adj 1 not responsive to beauty, the feelings of others, etc.: an insensitive nature. 2 not able to be affected by touch, light, etc: The injection made my tooth insensitive. **in·sen·si·tive·ly** adv. **in·sen·si·tive·ness** n. **in·sen·si·tiv·i·ty** n.

in·sen·ti·ent [ɪn'sɛnʃiənt] or [ɪn'sɛnʃənt] adj unable to feel; lifeless. **in·sen·ti·ence** n.

in·sep·a·ra·ble [ɪn'sɛprəbəl] adj that cannot be separated or parted: inseparable pals. **in·sep·a·ra·bly** adv. **in·sep·a·ra·bil·i·ty** n.

in·sert [ɪn'sɜrt] v 1 thrust or set into: to insert a key in a lock, to insert a letter into a word. n ['ɪnsərt] something set in: The dress has lace inserts. **in·sert·a·ble** adj. **in·ser·tion** n. ⟨Latin insertus pp of inserere; in- in + serere entwine⟩

in·set ['ɪn,sɛt] n a small map, photograph, etc. set within a larger one, to show detail.

in·shore ['ɪn'ʃɔr] adj near the shore. adv in toward the shore.

in·side ['ɪn'saɪd] n 1 inner part: the inside of a house. 2 Often, insides pl Informal the parts inside the body. adj 1 to do with the inside: an inside seat. 2 Informal done or known by those within an organization: inside information. 3 that is nearer the centre of a curve: the inside skate. 4 Baseball of a pitch, close to the batter and missing the strike zone. adv on, at, or to the inside of a place or thing: Please go inside. prep on, at, or to the inside of: We left the blankets inside the trunk. **inside of** Informal within the limits of: inside of a week. **inside out a** with the inside showing: She turned her pockets inside out. **b** completely: He learned his lessons inside out. **inside job** a crime committed by a person or persons closely associated with the victim. **in·sid·er** [,ɪn'saɪdər] or ['ɪn,saɪdər] n someone in an organization who has power, or access to important information. **insider trading** the crime of using private information to trade on the stock market. **inside track 1** on a race track, the lane nearest the inside of the curve. 2 Informal an advantageous position or situation.

in·sid·i·ous [ɪn'sɪdiəs] adj 1 sly; treacherous: an insidious plot. 2 developing without attracting attention: an insidious disease. **in·sid·i·ous·ly** adv. **in·sid·i·ous·ness** n. ⟨Latin insidiae ambush; in- in + sedere sit⟩

in·sight ['ɪn,saɪt] n 1 an understanding based on a seeing of the inner nature of something. 2 wisdom in dealing with people or with facts. 3 Psychology a the relatively sudden awareness of a solution to a problem. b understanding of oneself. **in·sight·ful** [ɪn'saɪtfəl] or ['ɪn,saɪtfəl] adj. ⟨Middle English⟩

in·sig·ni·a [ɪn'sɪgniə] n pl (often used as sg) 1 the emblems of a high position, military order, etc.: The crown, orb, and sceptre are the insignia of monarchs. 2 a distinguishing badge, logo, etc. of an organization. ⟨Latin, pl of insigne badge; in- on + signum mark⟩

in·sig·nif·i·cant [,ɪnsɪg'nɪfəkənt] adj 1 having little importance or influence: an insignificant position in the company. 2 having little or no meaning: insignificant chatter. **in·sig·nif·i·cance** n. **in·sig·nif·i·cant·ly** adv.

in·sin·cere [,ɪnsɪn'sir] adj not candid. **in·sin·cere·ly** adv. **in·sin·cer·i·ty** [,ɪnsɪn'sɛrəti] n.

in·sin·u·ate [ɪn'sɪnju,eit] v 1 suggest (something) indirectly, in scheming way: She insinuated that the mayor had accepted bribes. 2 introduce by gradual and stealthy means: to insinuate doubt into a person's mind. **in·sin·u·a·tion** n. **in·sin·u·a·tive** adj. ⟨Latin insinuare; in- in + sinus a curve, winding⟩ **in·sin·u·a·ting** adj 1 tending to cause doubt. 2 winning favour artfully. **in·sin·u·a·ting·ly** adv.

in·sip·id [ɪn'sɪpɪd] adj 1 without much taste: A mixture of milk and water is an insipid drink. 2 uninteresting: insipid writing. **in·sip·id·ly** adv. **in·sip·id·ness** n. ⟨Latin in- not + sapidus tasty⟩

in·sist [ɪn'sɪst] v keep firmly to some position: to insist on something. **in·sist·ence** n. ⟨Latin in- on + sistere take a stand⟩ **in·sist·ent** adj 1 insisting: She was insistent about going for a walk. 2 pressing; urgent: an insistent knocking at the door. **in·sist·ent·ly** adv.

in si·tu ['sɪtu] or ['situ] Latin in its original place; in position.

in·so·far [,ɪnsou'far] or [,ɪnsə'far] adv to such a degree (usually with as): He should be told the facts insofar as they concern him.

in·sole ['ɪn,soul] n a shaped piece of material laid on the sole inside a shoe or boot.

in·so·lent ['ɪnsələnt] adj boldly rude; insulting. **in·so·lence** n. **in·so·lent·ly** adv. ⟨Latin insolens spurning custom; in- not + solere be accustomed⟩

in·sol·u·ble [ɪn'sɒljəbəl] adj 1 that cannot be dissolved: Diamonds are insoluble. 2 that cannot be explained: an insoluble mystery. **in·sol·u·bil·i·ty** n. **in·sol·u·bly** adv.

in·sol·vent [ɪn'sɒlvənt] adj 1 not able to pay one's debts. 2 to do with bankruptcy. **in·sol·ven·cy** [ɪn'sɒlvənsi] n.

in·som·ni·a [ɪn'sɒmniə] n sleeplessness. ⟨Latin; in- not + somnus sleep⟩ **in·som·ni·ac** n a person who has trouble getting enough sleep. **in·som·ni·ac** adj.

in·sou·ci·ant [ɪn'susiənt] adj carefree; unconcerned: an insouciant disposition. **in·sou·ci·ance** n. **in·sou·ci·ant·ly** adv. ⟨French in- not + souciant ppr of soucier care⟩

in·spect [ɪn'spɛkt] *v* **1** look over carefully: *A dentist inspects my teeth twice a year.* **2** examine officially: *The restaurant was inspected annually.* **in·spect·a·ble** *adj.* **in·spec·tion** *n.* ⟨Latin *inspicere; in-* on + *specere* look⟩

in·spec·tor *n* **1** an official appointed to inspect. **2** a police officer, usually ranking next below a superintendent. **in·spec·to·ral** or **in·spec·tor·i·al** *adj.* **in·spec·tor·ship** *n.*

in·spire [ɪn'spaɪr] *v* **1** put thought, feeling, force, etc. into: *The speaker inspired the crowd.* **2** breathe in. **in·spir·a·ble** *adj.* **in·spi·ra·tion** [ˌɪnspə'reɪʃən] *n.* **in·spi·ra·tion·al** *adj.* **in·spir·ing** *adj.* ⟨Latin *in-* in + *spirare* breathe⟩

in·sta·bil·i·ty [ˌɪnstə'bɪləti] *n* the state of being unstable: *the instability of the dollar.*

in·stall or **in·stal** [ɪn'stɒl] *v* **1** place formally in a position: *to install a new judge.* **2** put in a place; settle: *The cat installed itself in a chair.* **3** put in position for use: *to install a program on a computer.* **in·stal·la·tion** [ˌɪnstə'leɪʃən] *n.* **in·stall·er** *n.* ⟨Latin *in-* in + *stallum* stall'; Germanic⟩

in·stal·ment or **in·stall·ment** [ɪn'stɒlmənt] *n* **1** a sum of money to be paid at regular times: *to pay in instalments.* **2** any of the parts of a series: *The magazine has a serial story in six instalments.* ⟨*stall* agree to payment of (a debt) by instalments; Germanic⟩

in·stance ['ɪnstəns] *n* **1** a person or thing serving as an example: *an instance of bad manners.* **2** a stage in an action: *He said he preferred, in this instance, to remain at home.* *v* refer to as an example. ⟨Latin *instantia; instans*. See INSTANT.⟩

for instance as an example.

in·stant ['ɪnstənt] *n* **1** a particular point in time: *Stop talking this instant!* **2** a very short time: *She paused for an instant.* *adj* **1** without delay: *instant relief from pain.* **2** urgent: *an instant need for action.* **3** prepared beforehand and requiring little cooking, etc: *instant coffee.* **in·stant·ly** *adv.* ⟨Latin *instans* ppr of *instare* stand near; *in-* in + *stare* stand⟩

the instant just as soon as: *The instant she came in the door, everyone stopped talking.*

in·stan·ta·ne·ous [ˌɪnstən'teiniəs] *adj* done in an instant: *an instantaneous reaction.* **in·stan·ta·ne·ous·ly** *adv.* **in·stan·ta·ne·ous·ness** *n.*

instant messaging *Computers* a form of real-time conversation on a network.

instant replay an immediate retelecast of a situation, esp of professional sports.

in·stead [ɪn'stɛd] *adv* in place of someone or something: *If you cannot go, let her go instead.* ⟨earlier *in stead* in place⟩

instead of rather than: *Instead of studying, she read a story.*

in·step ['ɪn,stɛp] *n* the inner arch of the human foot between the toes and the heel.

in·sti·gate ['ɪnstə,geit] *v* set in motion, esp something undesirable: *to instigate a rebellion.* **in·sti·gat·ing·ly** *adv.* **in·sti·ga·tion** *n.* **in·sti·ga·tor** *n.* ⟨Latin *instigare* goad on⟩

at the instigation of instigated by.

in·stil or **in·still** [ɪn'stɪl] *v* **-stilled, -still·ing** put in little by little: *Reading good books instils a love for fine literature.* **in·stil·la·tion** *n.* **in·stil·ment** or **in·still·ment** *n.* ⟨Latin *instillare* let drip in; *in-* in + *stilla* a drop⟩

in·stinct ['ɪnstɪŋkt] *n* an inborn tendency: *Birds do not learn to fly; they fly by instinct.* **in·stinc·tive** or **in·stinc·tu·al** *adj.* **in·stinc·tive·ly** or **in·stinc·tu·al·ly** *adv.* ⟨Latin *instinctus* pp of *instinguere* impel; *stinguere* to prick⟩

in·sti·tute ['ɪnstɪ,tjut] *or* ['ɪnstɪ,tut] *n* **1** an organization for the support of a particular cause: *the Canadian National Institute for the Blind.* **2** an educational institution: *a collegiate institute.* *v* originate or set going: *The police instituted an inquiry into the causes of the accident.* ⟨Latin *in-* in + *statuere* establish, *status* position⟩

in·sti·tu·tion *n* **1** an organization established for some public purpose: *A church is an institution.* **2** an established custom: *Giving presents on birthdays is an institution.* **3** a setting up: *Many people favour the institution of more clubs for young people.* **4** *Informal* a very familiar person or thing: *He's an institution around here.* **in·sti·tu·tion·al** *adj.* **in·sti·tu·tion·al·ly** *adv.* **in·sti·tu·tion·al·ize** *v* **1** make into an acceptable custom: *to institutionalize gambling in the form of lotteries.* **2** commit to a public institution for care. **3** make accustomed to an institution: *After three years in the hospital, she had become institutionalized.* **in·sti·tu·tion·al·i·za·tion** *n.*

in·struct [ɪn'strʌkt] *v* **1** teach formally. **2** give orders to: *The owner instructed her agent to sell the property.* **3** inform: *My lawyer instructs me that payment is due.* **4** *Law* of a judge, give (the jury) an explanation of the points of law in a case. **in·struc·tion** *n.* **in·struc·tion·al** *adj.* **in·struc·tive·ly** *adv.* **in·struc·tive** *adj.* **in·struc·tive·ly** *adv.* **in·struc·tive·ness** *n.* **in·struc·tor** *n.* ⟨Latin *instructus* pp of *instruere; in-* on + *struere* pile, arrange, furnish⟩

in·stru·ment ['ɪnstrəmənt] *n* **1** a precision tool: *surgical instruments.* **2** a device for producing musical sounds: *wind instruments.* **3** a device for measuring, recording, or controlling. **4** a person or thing by means of which something is done. **5** a formal legal document, such as a contract, deed, or grant. **in·stru·men·ta·tion** *n.* ⟨Latin *instrumentum; instruere*. See INSTRUCT.⟩

in·stru·men·tal *adj* **1** serving as a means: *His aunt was instrumental in getting him a job.* **2** written for a musical instrument: *instrumental music.* *n* a piece of music for musical instruments, without vocal accompaniment. **in·stru·men·tal·ly** *adv.*

in·stru·men·tal·ist *n.* **in·stru·men·tal·i·ty** *n* usefulness or helpfulness. **instrument flying** the directing of an aircraft by instruments only. **instrument panel** on an aircraft or other machine, a panel displaying gauges, indicator lights, etc., permitting the operator to check on and control specific functions of the machine.

in·sub·or·di·nate [ˌɪnsəˈbɔrdənɪt] *adj* resisting authority; disobedient; unruly. **in·sub·or·di·nate·ly** *adv.* **in·sub·or·di·na·tion** *n.*

in·sub·stan·tial [ˌɪnsəbˈstænʃəl] *adj* 1 frail; flimsy: *A cobweb is insubstantial.* 2 unreal; imaginary: *Dreams are insubstantial.* **in·sub·stan·ti·al·i·ty** *n.* **in·sub·stan·tial·ly** *adv.*

in·suf·fer·a·ble [ɪnˈsʌfərəbəl] *adj* intolerable; unbearable: *insufferable insolence.* **in·suf·fer·a·ble·ness** *n.* **in·suf·fer·a·bly** *adv.*

in·suf·fi·cient [ˌɪnsəˈfɪʃənt] *adj* not enough. **in·suf·fi·cien·cy** *n.* **in·suf·fi·cient·ly** *adv.*

in·su·lar [ˈɪnsələr] *or* [ˈɪnsjələr] *adj* 1 to do with islands or islanders: *a moderate, insular climate.* 2 like people who live in isolation, thought of as narrow-minded: *an insular point of view.* **in·su·lar·ism** *n.* **in·su·lar·i·ty** *n.* **in·su·lar·ly** *adv.* ⟨Latin *insula* island⟩

in·su·late [ˈɪnsəˌleɪt] *or* [ˈɪnsjəˌleɪt] *v* 1 keep from transferring heat, etc. by surrounding with a non-conducting material. 2 set apart; isolate. **in·su·la·tion** *n.* **in·su·la·tor** *n* something that insulates, esp a material that prevents the transfer of electricity or heat.

in·su·lin [ˈɪnsəlɪn] *n* 1 a hormone that enables the body to use sugar and other carbohydrates. 2 a preparation containing this, used in the treatment of diabetes. ⟨Latin *insula* island (i.e., of the pancreas)⟩

in·sult [ɪnˈsʌlt] *v* treat with scorn or abuse: *The rebels insulted the flag by burning it.* *n* [ˈɪnsʌlt] a remark or an act that insults. **in·sult·ing·ly** *adv.* ⟨Latin *insultare* frequentative of *insilire* leap on; *salire* leap⟩

in·su·per·a·ble [ɪnˈsupərəbəl] *adj* that cannot be passed over or overcome: *an insuperable barrier.* **in·su·per·a·bly** *adv.* **in·su·per·a·bil·i·ty** *n.* ⟨Latin *in-* not + *superare* surmount; *super* over⟩

in·sup·port·a·ble [ˌɪnsəˈpɔrtəbəl] *adj* 1 unbearable. 2 that cannot be justified: *insupportable rudeness.* **in·sup·port·a·bly** *adv.*

in·sure [ɪnˈʃʊr] *v* 1 arrange for money payment in case of loss, accident, sickness, or death: *to insure a house.* 2 make safe or certain; ensure. **in·sur·a·ble** *adj.* **in·sur·a·bil·i·ty** *n.* **in·sur·ance** *n* 1 an insuring of property, person, or life. 2 the money for which a person or thing is insured: *He has $100 000 insurance.* ⟨variant of *ensure*⟩ **in·sured** *n* a person who is insured. **in·sur·er** *n* a person or company, etc. that insures.

in·sur·gent [ɪnˈsɜrdʒənt] *n* a member of a political group who rebels. *adj* 1 rising in revolt; rebellious. 2 rushing in. **in·sur·gence** *or* **in·sur·gen·cy** *n.* ⟨Latin *in-* against + *surgere* rise (pp *surrectum*)⟩

in·sur·rec·tion [ˌɪnsəˈrɛkʃən] *n* a rising against established authority. **in·sur·rec·tion·al** *adj.* **in·sur·rec·tion·ist** *n.*

in·sur·mount·a·ble [ˌɪnsərˈmaʊntəbəl] *adj* that cannot be overcome. **in·sur·mount·a·bly** *adv.* **in·sur·mount·a·bil·i·ty** *n.*

in·sur·rec·tion See INSURGENT.

in·tact [ɪnˈtækt] *adj* with no part missing or damaged: *The dishes were intact.* **in·tact·ly** *adv.*

in·tact·ness *n.* ⟨Latin *in-* not + *tactus* pp of *tangere* touch⟩

in·take [ˈɪnˌteɪk] *n* 1 a place where water, air, gas, etc. enters a channel or other narrow opening. 2 a taking in. 3 the thing taken in.

in·tan·gi·ble [ɪnˈtændʒəbəl] *adj* 1 not capable of being touched or felt: *Sound is intangible.* 2 not easily grasped by the mind: *She had that intangible quality called charm.* *n* something intangible. **in·tan·gi·bil·i·ty** *n.* **in·tan·gi·ble·ness** *n.* **in·tan·gi·bly** *adv.*

in·te·ger [ˈɪntədʒər] *n* any positive or negative whole number or zero: *The numbers 4, –37, 106, etc. are integers.* ⟨Latin = whole⟩ **in·te·gral** [ˈɪntəgrəl] *or* [ɪnˈtɛgrəl] *adj* 1 essential: *an integral part.* 2 complete. 3 *Mathematics* having to do with whole numbers. *n* a whole number. **integral calculus** the branch of mathematics dealing with integrals and the solution of differential equations. Compare DIFFERENTIAL CALCULUS.

in·te·grate [ˈɪntəˌgreɪt] *v* 1 make more unified: *The government should integrate its approach to unemployment.* 2 bring in (individuals or groups) as part of a larger group: *to integrate immigrants into Canadian society.* 3 desegregate. 4 *Mathematics* calculate the integral of. **in·teg·ra·ble** *adj.* **in·te·gra·tion** *n.* **in·te·gra·tion·ist** *n.* ⟨Latin *integer* whole⟩ **integrated circuit** *Electronics* a miniature electronic system incorporated into a chip of semiconducting material. **in·te·gra·tive** *adj* fostering integration: *an integrative approach.*

in·teg·ri·ty [ɪnˈtɛgrəti] *n* 1 uprightness; honesty: *Her poetry is too commercial to have integrity.* 2 wholeness. 3 the condition of being uncorrupted: *Scholars have questioned the integrity of the text.* ⟨Latin *integer* whole⟩

in·teg·u·ment [ɪnˈtɛgjəmənt] *n* a natural outer covering of an animal or plant. **in·teg·u·men·ta·ry** *adj.* ⟨Latin *integumentum* from *integere* cover; *in-* on + *tegere* cover⟩

in·tel·lect [ˈɪntəˌlɛkt] *n* 1 the power of understanding as distinguished from feeling. 2 great intelligence. 3 a person having high mental ability: *Einstein was one of the greatest intellects of all time.* ⟨Latin *intellectus* pp of *intelligere.* See INTELLIGENT.⟩ **in·tel·lec·tu·al** *adj* to do with the intellect: *an intellectual process.* *n* a person interested in intellectual things. **in·tel·lec·tu·al·ly** *adv.* **in·tel·lec·tu·al·ism** *n* 1 devotion to intellectual pursuits. 2 *Philosophy* the doctrine that knowledge is derived from pure reason. **in·tel·lec·tu·a·list** *n.* **in·tel·lec·tu·a·lis·tic** *adj.* **in·tel·lec·tu·al·is·ti·cal·ly** *adv.* **in·tel·lec·tu·al·ize** *v* express (feelings, attitudes, etc.) in intellectual terms. **in·tel·lec·tu·al·i·za·tion** *n.*

in·tel·li·gent [ɪnˈtɛlədʒənt] *adj* 1 having intelligence; rational: *Is there intelligent life on other planets?* 2 having a high degree of intelligence: *an intelligent remark.* 3 of a computer-operated device, having ARTIFICIAL INTELLIGENCE. **in·tel·li·gent·ly** *adv.* ⟨Latin *intelligere* understand⟩ **in·tel·li·gence** *n* 1 the ability to learn and know. **2** information, esp secret information. **3** a group engaged in obtaining secret information: *military intelligence.*

intelligence quotient a number used to describe intelligence. *Abbrev* **IQ** or **I.Q.**

in·tel·li·gent·si·a [ɪn͵tɛləˈdʒɛntsɪə] *or* [-ˈɡɛntsɪə] *n sg or pl* people who represent the superior intelligence of a society. **in·tel·li·gi·ble** [ɪnˈtɛlədʒəbəl] *adj* capable of being understood. **in·tel·li·gi·bil·i·ty** *n.* **in·tel·li·gi·bly** *adv.*

in·tem·per·ate [ɪnˈtɛmpərɪt] *adj* **1** not moderate; lacking in self-control: *an intemperate appetite.* **2** drinking too much intoxicating liquor. **3** extreme in temperature: *an intemperate climate.* **in·tem·per·ance** *n.* **in·tem·per·ate·ly** *adv.*

in·tend [ɪnˈtɛnd] *v* **1** plan: *We intend to go home soon.* **2** mean for a particular purpose or use: *That gift was intended for you.* ⟨Latin *in-* toward + *tendere* stretch⟩

in·tense [ɪnˈtɛns] *adj* **1** very strong; extreme: *intense pain.* **2** of activity, etc., strenuous: *intense thought.* **3** having strong feeling: *an intense person.* **in·tense·ly** *adv.* **in·tense·ness** *n.* ⟨Latin *intensus* a pp of *intendere.* See INTEND.⟩ **in·ten·si·fi·er** *n Grammar* an intensive. **in·ten·si·fy** *v* strengthen; increase: *Blowing on a fire intensifies the heat.* **in·ten·si·fi·ca·tion** *n.* **in·ten·si·ty** *n* **1** very great strength, force, etc. **2** the strength of a colour. **3** *Physics* the amount of heat, light, sound, etc. per unit of area, volume, etc. **in·ten·sive** *adj* **1** deep and thorough: *An intensive study of a few books is more valuable than a superficial reading of many.* **2** to do with a system of farming in which work is spent on a small area to produce larger crops. *n Grammar* a word element, phrase, etc. that adds force but has little meaning of its own. The prefix *super* in *superstar* is an intensive. **in·ten·sive·ly** *adv.*

in·tent¹ [ɪnˈtɛnt] *n* **1** that which is intended; purpose: *with intent to kill.* **2** meaning: *What is the intent of that sentence?* ⟨Old French *entent(e);* Latin *intentus.* See INTENT².⟩

to all intents and purposes in almost every way; practically.

in·ten·tion *n* **1** determination to act in a certain way. **2** a purpose: *It was my intention to go home.* **3** intentions *pl Informal.* purpose with respect to marrying. **in·ten·tion·less** *adj.* **in·ten·tion·al** *adj* done on purpose. **in·ten·tion·al·ly** *adv.* **in·ten·tioned** *adj* having a specific intention.

in·tent² [ɪnˈtɛnt] *adj* **1** very attentive: *an intent look.* **2** much interested; determined (used with *on*): *He is intent on making money.* **in·tent·ly** *adv.* **in·tent·ness** *n.* ⟨Latin *intentus* a pp of *intendere.* See INTEND.⟩

in·ter [ɪnˈtɜr] *v* **-terred, -ter·ring** bury. **in·ter·ment** *n.* ⟨Latin *in-* in + *terra* earth⟩

CONFUSABLES
Inter = bury, and **intern** = confine. One **inters** a dead body; one **interns** a live person who might cause trouble.

inter– *prefix* **1** one with the other: *intercommunicate* = communicate with each other. **2** between: *interpose* = put between. **3** between or among members of a group: *interscholastic* = between or among schools. ⟨Latin, between, among, during⟩

in·ter·act [͵ɪntərˈækt] *v* act on another. **in·ter·ac·tion** *n.* **in·ter·ac·tive** *adj Computers* involving direct communication between a computer system and a user.

in·ter a·li·a [͵ɪntər ˈɑliə] *or* [ˈeiliə] *Latin* among other things.

in·ter·breed [͵ɪntərˈbrid] *v* **-bred, -breed·ing.** breed by using different varieties or species of animals or plants. Compare INBREED.

in·ter·cede [͵ɪntərˈsid] *v* plead in another's behalf: *Friends of the condemned man interceded with the authorities for a pardon.* ⟨Latin *inter-* between + *cedere* go⟩ **in·ter·ces·sion** [͵ɪntərˈsɛʃən] *n* **1** the act or fact of interceding. **2** a prayer in behalf of another person. **in·ter·ces·sion·al** *adj.* **in·ter·ces·sor** [͵ɪntərˈsɛsər] *n* a person who intercedes. **in·ter·ces·so·ry** *adj.*

in·ter·cept [͵ɪntərˈsɛpt] *v* **1** take or stop (a person, vehicle, etc.) on the way from one place to another: *to intercept a pass in football.* **2** intersect. **3** *Mathematics* cut off (part of a line or plane). *n* [ˈɪntərˌsɛpt] *Mathematics* the distance from the origin to the point where a line crosses an axis on a graph. ⟨Latin *intercipere; inter-* between + *capere* catch⟩ **in·ter·cep·tion** *n.* **in·ter·cep·tive** *adj.* **in·ter·cep·tor** or **intercepter** *n* an aircraft or missile designed to stop enemy aircraft or missiles.

in·ter·ces·sion See INTERCEDE.

in·ter·change [͵ɪntərˈtʃeindʒ] *v* **1** put each of (two or more persons or things) in the other's place. **2** cause to follow one another alternately: *to interchange laughter with tears.* **in·ter·change** [ˈɪntərˌtʃeindʒ] *n.* **in·ter·change·a·ble** *adj.* **in·ter·change·a·bil·i·ty** *n.* **in·ter·change·a·bly** *adv.* ⟨Old French *entrechangier, entre-* between; see CHANGE.⟩

in·ter·com [ˈɪntərˌkɒm] *n Informal* a system of communication between rooms of a building, parts of a ship or aircraft, etc. ⟨shortened from *intercommunication system*⟩

in·ter·con·nect [͵ɪntərkəˈnɛkt] *v* connect with each other. **in·ter·con·nec·tion** *n.*

in·ter·con·ti·nen·tal [͵ɪntərˌkɒntəˈnɛntəl] *adj* extending or carried on between or among continents: *intercontinental travel.*

in·ter·cos·tal [͵ɪntərˈkɒstəl] *adj* between the ribs. **in·ter·cos·tal·ly** *adv.* ⟨Latin *inter-* between + *costa* rib⟩

in·ter·course [ˈɪntərˌkɔrs] *n* **1** exchange of thoughts, services, feelings, etc.: *Airplanes make intercourse between different parts of the country far easier.* **2** SEXUAL INTERCOURSE. ⟨Old French *entrecours,* Latin *intercursus* a running between; see COURSE. Later influenced by *inter-*.⟩

in·ter·de·nom·i·na·tion·al [͵ɪntərdɪˌnɒməˈneiʃənəl] *adj* between or involving different religious denominations.

in·ter·de·part·men·tal [ˌɪntərˌdipɑrt'mɛntəl] *adj* between departments.
in·ter·de·part·men·tal·ly *adv.*

in·ter·de·pend·ent [ˌɪntərdɪ'pɛndənt] *adj* dependent each upon the other.
in·ter·de·pend·ence or **in·ter·de·pend·en·cy** *n.*
in·ter·de·pend·ent·ly *adv.*

in·ter·dict ['ɪntər,dɪkt] *n* **1** an official prohibition. **2** *Roman Catholic Church* a censure excluding a place or person from certain privileges.
v [ˌɪntər'dɪkt] **1** place under an interdict: *to interdict a parish.* **2** prohibit by authority: *to interdict trade with other countries.*
in·ter·dic·tion *n.* ⟨Latin *interdicere* prohibit⟩

in·ter·dis·ci·plin·a·ry [ˌɪntər'dɪsɪplə,nɛri] *adj* involving two or more academic disciplines.

in·ter·est ['ɪntrɪst] *or* ['ɪntrest] *n* **1** a feeling of wanting to know or take part in: *He has no interest in sports.* **2** the power of arousing such a feeling: *A dull book lacks interest.* **3** something that stirs up such feelings. **4** a share in property and actions: *She bought a half interest in the farm.* **5** advantage: *Each person should look after his or her own interest.* **6** money paid for the use of money.
v **1** hold the attention of. **2** cause (a person) to take a share in something: *He tried to interest us in buying a car.* ⟨Latin = it makes a difference; *inter-* between + *esse* be⟩
in the interest of a in behalf of. **b** with the objective of. **with interest** with something extra given in return: *She returned our favour with interest.*
in·ter·est·ed ['ɪntrɪstɪd] *or* ['ɪntə,rɛstɪd] *adj* **1** feeling or showing interest. **2** concerned: *A meeting will be held for all interested parties.* **3** influenced by personal considerations: *interested motives.* **in·ter·est·ed·ly** *adv.*
in·ter·est·ing ['ɪntrɪstɪŋ] *or* ['ɪntə,rɛstɪŋ] *adj* arousing interest; holding one's attention.
in·ter·est·ing·ly *adv.*

in·ter·face ['ɪntər,feis] *n* **1** a surface that forms a common boundary between two regions, bodies, etc.: *the interface of air and water.* **2** an area where systems influence each other: *Taxation is the most critical interface between government and business.* **3** *Computers* a program or device that enables a user to communicate with a computer, or two pieces of hardware or software to operate jointly. **in·ter·face** *v.*
in·ter·fa·cing *n* a stiff material placed between two layers of fabric in a collar, cuff, etc. to give shape or body to it.

in·ter·fere [ˌɪntər'fir] *v* **1** come between in a way that hinders: *I will come on Saturday if nothing interferes.* **2** meddle: *Don't interfere.* **3** *Sports* hinder the action of an opposing player in an illegal way. **4** *Physics* of waves, act upon one another so as to increase, lessen, neutralize, etc. each other. ⟨Latin *inter-* between + *ferire* strike⟩
interfere with a obstruct: *The rain interfered with our plans.* **b** distort by interfering.
in·ter·fer·ence [ˌɪntər'firəns] *n* **1** the act of interfering. **2** *Physics* the effect that waves have on each other, to intensify or neutralize each other, produce beats, etc. **3** *Radio and television* confusion of radio signals, producing static, distortion of sound, etc. **4** *Football* the legal blocking of an opposing player to clear the way for the ball carrier. **5** *Sports* the illegal hindering of an opposing player. **run interference (for) a** *Football* clear the way for the ball carrier. **b** act as a screen: *She never has to deal directly with the public because her assistant runs interference for her.*
in·ter·fer·on [ˌɪntər'firɒn] *n* *Biochemistry* a protein produced in virus-infected cells to counteract infection.

in·ter·file [ˌɪntər'fail] *v* combine two or more sets of items into one set.

in·ter·ga·lac·tic [ˌɪntərgə'læktɪk] *adj* occurring or situated between galaxies: *intergalactic travel.*

in·ter·gen·er·a·tion·al [ˌɪntər,dʒɛnə'reiʃənəl] *adj* taking place between two different generations: *intergenerational conflict.*

in·ter·gla·cial [ˌɪntər'gleiʃəl] *adj* *Geology* to do with the period between two glacial epochs.

in·ter·im ['ɪntərɪm] *n* meantime.
adj temporary: *an interim report.* ⟨Latin = in the meantime; *inter* between⟩

in·te·ri·or [ɪn'tiriər] *n* **1** the inside: *The interior of the house was beautifully decorated.* **2** the part of a region away from the coast or border. **3 ✱ Interior,** the inland area of British Columbia. **in·te·ri·or** *adj.* ⟨Latin = inner⟩
interior decoration the colours, materials, furnishings, etc. used in a room. **interior decorator 1** a person whose work is painting or wallpapering the interiors of buildings. **2** a person whose work is planning decor, etc. for the interior of a building. **interior design** the art of planning furnishings for the interiors of buildings. **interior designer. interior monologue** *Literature* a form of writing that gives the innermost thoughts of a character. **Interior Salish 1** a member of a First Nations people, including the **Okanagan** and **Lillooet** bands, living in southern British Columbia and neighbouring states of the US. **2** their dialect of Salish.

in·ter·ject [ˌɪntər'dʒɛkt] *v* insert abruptly: *Every now and then the speaker interjected some witty remark.* ⟨Latin *interjectus* pp of *interjicere*; *inter-* between + *jacere* throw⟩
in·ter·jec·tion *n* **1** something interjected, such as a word or remark. **2** *Grammar* an exclamation of surprise, sorrow, delight, etc. *Oh! Ah! Ouch!* and *Um* are interjections.
in·ter·jec·tion·al *adj.*

in·ter·lace [ˌɪntər'leis] *v* **1** arrange (threads, strips, branches, etc.) so that they go over and under each other. **2** intersperse: *a speech interlaced with jokes.* **in·ter·lace·ment** *n.*

in·ter·lard [ˌɪntərˈlɑrd] *v* mix so as to give variety to: *The speaker interlarded his speech with amusing stories.* ⟨French *entrelarder;* Latin *inter-* between + *lardum* fat⟩

in·ter·leaf [ˈɪntərˌlif] *n, pl* **-leaves** a leaf of paper put between others, as in a book, for notes, etc. **in·ter·leave** *v.*

in·ter·lin·e·ar [ˌɪntərˈlɪniər] *adj* **1** inserted between the lines: *an interlinear translation.* **2** containing two different languages or versions in alternate lines. **in·ter·lin·e·ar·ly** *adv.*

in·ter·lin·ing [ˈɪntərˌlaɪnɪŋ] *n* an extra lining between the outer fabric of a garment and the lining: *a woollen interlining.*

in·ter·link [ˌɪntərˈlɪŋk] *v* link together.

in·ter·lock [ˌɪntərˈlɒk] *v* **1** join tightly together: *The antlers of the two stags were interlocked.* **2** be connected so that all action is synchronized.

in·ter·loc·u·tor [ˌɪntərˈlɒkjətər] *n* a person who takes part in a conversation or dialogue. ⟨Latin *inter-* between + *loqui* speak⟩

in·ter·lop·er [ˈɪntərˌloupər] *v* one who intrudes or interferes in the affairs of others. **in·ter·lope** *v.* ⟨Dutch *enterloper;* *enter-* between (Latin *inter-*) + *lopen* run, walk⟩

in·ter·lude [ˈɪntərˌlud] *n* **1** anything thought of as filling the time between two things: *a few interludes of fair weather during the rainy season.* **2** *Music* a composition played between the parts of a song, play, etc. **3** an entertainment between the acts of a play. ⟨Latin *inter-* between + *ludus* play⟩

in·ter·lu·nar [ˌɪntərˈlunər] *adj* to do with the period between the old moon and the new moon, when the moon is not visible.

in·ter·mar·ry [ˌɪntərˈmɛri] *or* [ˌɪntərˈmæri] *v* **1** of families, peoples, etc., connect by marriage. **2** marry with close relations. **in·ter·mar·riage** *n.*

in·ter·me·di·ate [ˌɪntərˈmidiɪt] *adj* in a middle stage: *beginning and intermediate French.* ⟨Latin *inter-* between + *medius* in the middle⟩ **in·ter·me·di·ar·y** *n* a person who deals with each side in negotiations: *She acted as intermediary between the city and the developer.* *adj* **1** acting as an intermediary: *an intermediary agent.* **2** intermediate.

in·ter·ment See INTER.

in·ter·mez·zo [ˌɪntərˈmɛtsou] *or* [-ˈmɛdzou] *n, pl* **-mez·zos, -mez·zi** [-ˈmɛtsi] *or* [-ˈmɛdzi] *Music* a short composition between the main divisions of an extended musical work. ⟨Italian⟩

in·ter·mi·na·ble [ɪnˈtɜrmənəbəl] *adj* endless or seemingly endless: *an interminable speech.* **in·ter·mi·na·ble·ness** *n.* **in·ter·mi·na·bly** *adv.*

in·ter·min·gle [ˌɪntərˈmɪŋgəl] *v* mix together.

in·ter·mis·sion [ˌɪntərˈmɪʃən] *n* **1** a pause, esp between acts of a play, parts of a musical performance, etc.: *two fifteen-minute intermissions.* **2** a stopping for a time: *It rained without intermission.* ⟨Latin *intermissio* from *intermittere; inter-* between + *mittere* put⟩

in·ter·mit·tent *adj* stopping and beginning again. **in·ter·mit·tent·ly** *adv.* **in·ter·mit·tence** or **·in·ter·mit·ten·cy** *n.*

in·tern¹ [ɪnˈtɜrn] *v* force to stay in a certain place, esp during a war: *Aliens are sometimes interned in wartime.* *n* [ˈɪntɜrn] one who is interned; internee. **in·tern·ment** *n.* ⟨French *interner; interne* inner⟩

in·tern² [ˈɪntɜrn] *n* **1** a medical doctor working as an assistant in a hospital. **2** a recent graduate, etc. in any of various other fields undergoing supervised training. *v* act as an intern. **in·tern·ship** *n.* ⟨French *interne.* See INTERN¹.⟩

in·ter·nal [ɪnˈtɜrnəl] *adj* **1** on the inside: *internal injuries.* **2** to be taken inside the body: *internal remedies.* **3** to do with affairs within a country: *internal disturbances.* **4** of the mind; subjective: *Thoughts are internal.* **in·ter·nal·ly** *adv.* ⟨Latin *internus* within⟩ **internal–combustion engine** an engine in which the power comes from explosions within each cylinder. **in·ter·na·lize** *v* **1** give a subjective character to. **2** adopt (the values of another). **in·ter·na·li·za·tion** *n.* **internal medicine** the branch of medicine dealing with the non-surgical treatment of diseases. **in·ter·nist** [ɪnˈtɜrnɪst] *n* a specialist in internal medicine, as distinguished from a surgeon. **internal revenue** government income from taxes. **internal rhyme** a rhyme in which a rhyming syllable is in the middle of the line rather than at the end.

in·ter·na·tion·al [ˌɪntərˈnæʃənəl] *adj* **1** to do with being among nations: *international trade.* **2** accepted by many or all nations: *an international driver's licence.* **in·ter·na·tion·al·i·ty** *n.* **in·ter·na·tion·al·ly** *adv.* **International Court of Justice** WORLD COURT. **International Date Line** DATE LINE (def. 1). **in·ter·na·tion·al·ism** *n* international co-operation. **in·ter·na·tion·al·ist** *n.* **in·ter·na·tion·al·ize** *v* bring (territory) under the control of several nations. **in·ter·na·tion·al·i·za·tion** *n.* **international law** the body of rules that most nations recognize as binding in international relations. **International Monetary Fund** an agency affiliated with the United Nations and intended to stabilize world currencies. *Abbrev* **IMF**

in·ter·ne·cine [ˌɪntərˈnisən], [ˌɪntərˈnisaɪn], *or* [ˌɪntərˈnɛsɪn] *adj* **1** destructive to both sides. **2** to do with a dispute within a group: *internecine conflict.* ⟨Latin *inter-* between + *necare* kill; *necis* slaughter, n⟩

In·ter·net [ˈɪntərˌnɛt] *n* *Computers* an international computer network giving access to a broad range of information and providing electronic communication services such as e-mail. Also called **the Net.**

in·tern·ment See INTERN¹.

in·ter·of·fice [ˌɪntərˈɒfɪs] *adj* between offices of an organization: *an interoffice memo.*

in·ter·per·son·al [ˌɪntər'pɜrsənəl] *adj* describing relations between two persons. **in·ter·per·son·al·ly** *adv.*

in·ter·plan·e·tar·y [ˌɪntər'plænə,tɛri] *adj* 1 within the solar system, but outside the atmosphere of any of the planets or the sun: *interplanetary space.* 2 carried on between planets: *interplanetary travel.*

in·ter·play ['ɪntər,pleɪ] *n* the action of things on each other: *the interplay of light and shadow.* **in·ter·play** [ˌɪntər'pleɪ] *v.*

in·ter·po·late [ɪn'tɜrpə,leɪt] *v* 1 alter (a book, passage, etc.) by putting in new words. 2 *Mathematics* insert (intermediate terms) in a series. 3 insert or introduce (something additional) between other things. **in·ter·po·la·tion** *n.* ⟨Latin *interpolare* alter, falsify; i.e., by inserting new material⟩

in·ter·pose [ˌɪntər'pouz] *v* 1 put between; insert. 2 introduce as an interruption: *She interposed an objection.* 3 intervene in a dispute: *He interposed between the angry children.* **in·ter·pos·al** *n.* **in·ter·pos·a·ble** *adj.* **in·ter·pos·ing·ly** *adv.* **in·ter·po·si·tion** *n.* ⟨French *inter-* between + *poser* place. See POSE.⟩

in·ter·pret [ɪn'tɜrprɪt] *v* 1 explain the meaning of: *to interpret a difficult passage in a book.* 2 bring out the meaning of (a character, music, etc.) in performing it. 3 understand according to one's own judgment: *We interpreted your silence as consent.* 4 translate orally for speakers of different languages: *I interpret for my parents in school interviews.* **in·ter·pret·a·bil·i·ty** *n.* **in·ter·pret·a·ble** *adj.* **in·ter·pre·ta·tion** *n.* **in·ter·pre·ta·tion·al** *adj.* ⟨Latin *interpretis* negotiator; perhaps from *pretium* price⟩ **in·ter·pret·er** *n* a person who interprets, esp one whose work is translating a language orally. **in·ter·pre·tive** or **in·ter·pre·ta·tive** *adj* used for interpreting. **in·ter·pre·tive·ly** *adv.*

in·ter·pro·vin·cial [ˌɪntərprə'vɪnʃəl] *adj* between or among provinces. **in·ter·pro·vin·cial·ly** *adv.*

in·ter·ra·cial [ˌɪntər'reɪʃəl] *adj* between or involving different races. **in·ter·ra·cial·ly** *adv.*

in·ter·reg·num [ˌɪntər'rɛgnəm] *n, pl* **-nums** or **-na** [-nə] 1 the time between the end of one ruler's reign and the beginning of the next one. 2 any time during which a nation is without its usual government. 3 a period of inactivity; pause. **in·ter·reg·nal** *adj.* ⟨Latin *inter-* between + *regnum* reign⟩

in·ter·re·late [ˌɪntərrɪ'leɪt] *v* relate to one another: *The two proposals are interrelated.* **in·ter·re·la·tion** or **in·ter·re·la·tion·ship** *n.*

in·ter·ro·gate [ɪn'tɛrə,geɪt] *v* ask questions of, esp formally: *to interrogate a witness.* **in·ter·ro·ga·tion** *n.* **in·ter·ro·ga·tor** *n.* ⟨Latin *inter-* between + *rogare* ask⟩ **in·ter·rog·a·tive** [ˌɪntə'rɒgətɪv] *adj* 1 of or having the form of a question: *an interrogative tone of voice.* 2 *Grammar* used in asking questions: *an interrogative pronoun.* *n Grammar* an interrogative word: *Who* is an interrogative. **in·ter·rog·a·tive·ly** *adv.*

in·ter·rupt [ˌɪntə'rʌpt] *v* 1 break in upon (talk, work, rest, a person speaking, etc.). 2 break the continuity of: *A wall interrupts the view from our window.* **in·ter·rup·tion** *n.* **in·ter·rup·tive** *adj.* ⟨Latin *interruptus* pp of *interrumpere; inter-* between + *rumpere* break⟩ **in·ter·rupt·ed** *adj Botany* of leaves on a stem, not evenly arranged. **in·ter·rupt·er** *n* 1 one that interrupts. 2 *Electricity* a device for opening and closing an electric circuit.

in·ter·scho·las·tic [ˌɪntərskə'læstɪk] *adj* between schools: *interscholastic competition.*

in·ter·sect [ˌɪntər'sɛkt] *v* 1 cut or divide by crossing: *Draw a line to intersect two parallel lines.* 2 cross each other: *Streets often intersect at right angles.* ⟨Latin *intersectus* pp of *intersecare; inter-* between + *secare* cut⟩ **in·ter·sec·tion** [ˌɪntər'sɛkʃən] or ['ɪntər,sɛkʃən] *n* 1 a place where two or more things cross each other: *The light changed just before we got to the intersection.* 2 *Mathematics* the set of elements common to two or more given sets. **in·ter·sec·tion·al** *adj.*

in·ter·sperse [ˌɪntər'spɜrs] *v* 1 vary with other things put here and there: *The lawn was interspersed with beds of flowers.* 2 scatter: *He interspersed jokes throughout his talk.* **in·ter·sper·sion** [-'spɜrʒən] *n.* ⟨Latin *interspersus* pp of *interspergere; inter-* between + *spargere* scatter⟩

in·ter·state ['ɪntər,steɪt] *adj* between states: *an interstate highway.*

in·ter·stel·lar [ˌɪntər'stɛlər] *adj* 1 existing between or among the stars: *interstellar space.* 2 carried on between stars or star systems: *dreams of interstellar travel.*

in·ter·stice [ɪn'tɜrstɪs] *n* a small or narrow space between things or parts; CHINK[1]. **in·ter·sticed** *adj.* ⟨Latin *interstitium; inter-* between + *stare* to stand⟩ **in·ter·sti·tial** [ˌɪntər'stɪʃəl] *adj* 1 to do with interstices. 2 *Anatomy* situated between the cellular elements. **in·ter·sti·tial·ly** *adv.*

in·ter·twine [ˌɪntər'twaɪn] *v* twine around each other: *Two vines intertwined on the wall.*

in·ter·ur·ban [ˌɪntər'ɜrbən] *adj* between cities or towns: *an interurban highway.*

in·ter·val ['ɪntərvəl] *n* 1 an intervening period of time: *an interval of several weeks.* 2 the time or space between: *intervals of freedom from pain.* 3 *Music* the difference in pitch between two tones. 4 *Mathematics* a set of all the numbers between two given numbers. An **open interval** contains neither of its end parts; a **closed interval** contains both of its end parts. ⟨Latin *intervallum* orig space between palisades⟩ **at intervals a** now and then: *Stir the pudding at intervals.* **b** here and there: *We saw many lakes at intervals along the way.*

in·ter·vene [ˌɪntər'vin] *v* 1 come or be (between): *A week intervenes between Christmas and New Year's Day.* 2 come in to help settle a dispute: *She was asked to intervene in the strike.* **in·ter·ven·i·ent** *adj.* ⟨Latin *inter-* between + *venire* come⟩

in·ter·ven·tion [ˌɪntərˈvɛnʃən] *n* **1** the act of intervening. **2** interference, esp by one nation in the affairs of another. **3** *Medicine* taking medical action rather than letting a disease take its course. **in·ter·ven·tion·ist** *n,* *adj.* **in·ter·ven·tion·ism** *n.*

in·ter·view [ˈɪntərˌvju] *n* **1** a meeting of people face to face: *a job interview.* **2** a meeting between a reporter, commentator, etc. and a person from whom information is sought. **in·ter·view** *v.* **in·ter·view·er** *n.* **in·ter·view·ee** [ˌɪntərvjuˈi] *n.* ⟨French *entrevue* from *entrevoir* glimpse; *entre-* between + *voir.*⟩

in·ter·weave [ˌɪntərˈwiv] *v* **-wove, -wo·ven, -weav·ing** **1** weave together. **2** intermingle; connect closely: *In his book he has interwoven the stories of two families.*

in·tes·tate [ɪnˈtɛsteit] *or* [ɪnˈtɛstɪt] *adj* having made no will. **in·tes·ta·cy** *n.* ⟨Latin *intestatus; in-* not + *testare* make a will⟩

in·tes·tine [ɪnˈtɛstən] *n Anatomy* **1** either of the two parts of the alimentary canal extending from the stomach to the anus. The **small intestine** is about 640 cm long; the **large intestine** is about 165 cm long. **2 intestines** *pl* the intestine; the bowels. *adj* within the country. Intestine strife is civil war. **in·tes·ti·nal** *adj.* **in·tes·ti·nal·ly** *adv.* ⟨Latin *intestina* internal (things); *intus* within⟩ **intestinal fortitude** *Informal* courage; guts.

in·ti·mate[1] [ˈɪntəmɪt] *adj* **1** very familiar: *an intimate friend.* **2** resulting from close familiarity: *intimate knowledge.* **3** personal: *A diary is a very intimate book.* **4** engaged in or characterized by sexual relations. *n* a close friend. **in·ti·mate·ly** *adv.* ⟨Latin *intimus* superlative of *in* in. See INTIMATE[2].⟩ **in·ti·ma·cy** [ˈɪntəməsi] *n* **1** close association. **2** an intimate act. **3** sexual intercourse.

in·ti·mate[2] [ˈɪntəˌmeit] *v* suggest indirectly; *She intimated that an arrest would be made soon.* **in·ti·ma·tion** *n.* ⟨Latin *intimatus* pp of *intimare* orig press in; *intimus.* See INTIMATE[1].⟩

in·tim·i·date [ɪnˈtɪməˌdeit] *v* **1** frighten, esp in order to influence. **2** overcome with awe: *Her expertise intimidates me.* **in·tim·i·da·tion** *n.* ⟨Latin *in-* + *timidus* fearful⟩

in·to [ˈɪntu] *prep* **1** to the inside of: *to go into the house.* **2** to the condition of: *to get into mischief.* **3** to a further time or place in: *He worked on into the night.* **4** against: *He wasn't watching and ran into the wall.* **5** *Informal* involved or concerned with: *He's really into philosophy.* ⟨Old English. See IN, TO.⟩

in·tol·er·a·ble [ɪnˈtɒlərəbəl] *adj* unbearable. **in·tol·er·a·bil·i·ty** *n.* **in·tol·er·a·bly** *adv.* **in·tol·er·ant** *adj* **1** unwilling to let others do as they choose. **2** unwilling to accept persons of different races, backgrounds, etc. as equals. **3** unable or unwilling to endure (used with *of*): *intolerant of criticism.* **4** sensitive or allergic to a food, drug, etc.: *intolerant to penicillin.* **in·tol·er·ance** *n.* **in·tol·er·ant·ly** *adv.*

in·tone [ɪnˈtoun] read or recite in a singing voice. ⟨Latin *intonare; in-* in + *tonus* tone⟩ **in·to·nate** [ˈɪntəˌneit] *v* speak with a

particular tone. **in·to·na·tion** *n* **1** *Linguistics* the sound pattern of speech produced by differences in stress and pitch: *Rising intonation generally indicates a question.* **2** singing or playing in tune: *Intonation is a major problem for cellists.* **3** the act of intoning: *the intonation of a psalm.*

in to·to [ɪn ˈtoutou] *Latin* as a whole.

in·tox·i·cate [ɪnˈtɒksəˌkeit] *v* **1** make drunk: *Too much wine intoxicates people.* **2** of a drug, make (a person) lose control. **3** excite greatly: *The early election returns intoxicated her with thoughts of victory.* **in·tox·i·cat·ed** *adj.* **in·tox·i·cat·ed·ly** *adv.* **in·tox·i·ca·tion** *n.* **in·tox·i·cat·ing** *adj.* **in·tox·i·cat·ing·ly** *adv.* ⟨Latin *in-* in + *toxicum* poison. See TOXIC.⟩ **in·tox·i·cant** *n* something that intoxicates.

intra– *prefix* within; inside: *intravenous.* ⟨Latin⟩

in·tra·cel·lu·lar [ˌɪntrəˈsɛljələr] *adj* within a cell or cells.

in·trac·ta·ble [ɪnˈtræktəbəl] *adj* **1** hard to manage; stubborn. **2** difficult to remedy. **in·trac·ta·bil·i·ty** *n.* **in·trac·ta·bly** *adv.*

in·tra·mu·ral [ˌɪntrəˈmjʊrəl] *adj* within the walls of some institution. In intramural games, all the players belong to the same school. Compare EXTRAMURAL.

in·tran·si·gent [ɪnˈtrænzədʒənt] *adj* unwilling to agree or compromise. **in·tran·si·gence** *n.* **in·tran·si·gent·ly** *adv.* ⟨Latin *in-* not + *transigere* reach agreement; *trans-* through + *agere* drive⟩

in·tran·si·tive [ɪnˈtrænzətɪv] *adj Grammar* not taking a direct object. The verbs *belong,* and *seem* are intransitive. **in·tran·si·tive·ly** *adv.* **in·tran·si·tive·ness** *n.*

in·tra·u·ter·ine [ˌɪntrəˈjutərɪn] *or* [-ˌraɪn] *adj* within the uterus. **intrauterine device** a contraceptive device usually in the form of a coil that is inserted and left in the uterus. *Abbrev* **IUD**

in·tra·ve·nous [ˌɪntrəˈvinəs] *adj* **1** within a vein. **2** into a vein: *an intravenous injection.* **in·tra·ve·nous·ly** *adv.* ⟨intra- + Latin *vena* vein⟩

in·trep·id [ɪnˈtrɛpɪd] *adj* fearless; courageous; very brave. **in·tre·pid·i·ty** *n.* **in·trep·id·ly** *adv.* ⟨Latin *in-* not + *trepidus* alarmed⟩

in·tri·cate [ˈɪntrəkɪt] *adj* **1** entangled or complicated: *an intricate knot, an intricate plot.* **2** complex; obscure or puzzling: *an intricate problem.* **3** detailed. **in·tri·ca·cy** *n.* **in·tri·cate·ly** *adv.* **in·tri·cate·ness** *n.* ⟨Latin *intricare* entangle; *in-* in + *tricae* hindrances⟩

in·trigue [ɪnˈtrig] *or* [ˈɪntrig] *n* **1** underhand planning: *The palace was filled with intrigue.* **2** a crafty plot. **3** a secret love affair. *v* [ɪnˈtrig] **1** plot. **2** excite the curiosity and interest of: *The book's unusual title intrigued me.* **3** have a secret love affair. **in·tri·guer** *n.* **in·tri·guing·ly** *adv.* ⟨French; Italian *intrigare,* Latin *intricare* entangle. See INTRICATE.⟩

in·trin·sic [ɪnˈtrɪnzɪk] *adj* **1** belonging to a thing by its very nature: *The intrinsic value of a five-dollar bill is only that of the paper it is* *printed on.* **2** *Anatomy* originating inside the part on which it acts: *the intrinsic muscles of the larynx.* Compare EXTRINSIC. **in·trin·si·cal·ly** *adv.* ⟨Latin *intrinsecus* internal, inwardly⟩

in·tro·duce [ˌɪntrəˈdjus] *or* [ˌɪntrəˈdus] *v* **1** bring in: *to introduce a new subject into the conversation.* **2** put in: *The doctor introduced a tube into my throat.* **3** bring into use, notice, etc.: *to introduce a reform.* **4** make known: *The hostess introduced the speaker to the audience.* **5** bring (a person) to acquaintance with something: *I introduced my cousin to the city by showing her the sights.* **6** start: *He introduced his speech with a joke.* **in·tro·duc·i·ble** *adj.* ⟨Latin *intro-* in + *ducere* lead⟩

in·tro·duc·tion [ˌɪntrəˈdʌkʃən] *n* **1** an introducing or being introduced. **2** a preliminary part of a book, speech, etc. that leads into the main part. **3** a first course, etc. in a field of study. *an introduction to biology.* **4** a thing brought into use: *Radios are a later introduction than telephones.* **in·tro·duc·to·ry** [ˌɪntrəˈdʌktəri] *adj* used to introduce; preliminary. **in·tro·duc·to·ri·ly** *adv.*

Introduction applies to a part of the book, play, etc. that leads into the main part. **Preface** applies to a separate section coming before the actual book, explaining something such as the purpose, method, etc. **Foreword** applies especially to an introductory note on the book or the author by a distinguished writer, scholar, or public figure: *A foreword by the president came before the author's preface.*

in·tro·spect [ˌɪntrəˈspɛkt] *v* examine one's inner feelings. **in·tro·spec·tion** *n.* **in·tro·spec·tive** *adj.* **in·tro·spec·tive·ly** *adv.* **in·tro·spec·tive·ness** *n.* ⟨Latin *introspectus* pp of *introspicere; intro-* into + *specere* look⟩

in·tro·vert [ˈɪntrəˌvɜrt] *n* a person more interested in his or her own thoughts than in what is going on around him or her. Compare EXTROVERT.
v [ˌɪntrəˈvɜrt] **1** introspect. **2** *Zoology* pull (a tubular part or organ) inward by invagination. **3** fold (something) inward. **in·tro·ver·sion** [ˌɪntrəˈvɜrʒən] *n* **1** a tendency toward reflection rather than social interaction. **2** the act or fact of turning inward. **in·tro·ver·sive** *adj.* **in·tro·ver·tive** *adj.* ⟨*intro-* + Latin *vertere* turn⟩

in·trude [ɪnˈtrud] *v* **1** come unasked: *If you are busy, I will not intrude.* **2** force in: *Do not intrude your opinions upon others.* **in·trud·er** *n.* **in·tru·sion** *n.* **in·tru·sive** *adj.* **in·tru·sive·ly** *adv.* **in·tru·sive·ness** *n.* ⟨Latin *in-* in + *trudere* thrust⟩

in·tu·i·tion [ˌɪntjuˈɪʃən] *or* [ˌɪntuˈɪʃən] *n* immediate perception of truths, facts, etc. without reasoning. **in·tu·i·tion·al** *adj.* ⟨Latin *intuitio* a gazing at; *in-* at + *tueri* look, *v*⟩
in·tu·it [ɪnˈtjuɪt] *or* [ɪnˈtuɪt] *v* know or learn by intuition. **in·tu·it·a·ble** *adj.* **in·tu·i·tive** *adj* **1** perceiving by intuition: *an intuitive person.* **2** acquired by intuition: *intuitive knowledge.* **in·tu·i·tive·ly** *adv.*

I·nu·it [ˈɪnuɪt] *or* [ˈɪnjuɪt] *n pl, sg* **I·nuk** [ˈɪnʊk] an Aboriginal people living mainly in the Canadian Arctic and along the NW coasts of Alaska. They are one of the two main groups formerly called Eskimos, the other group being the Yupik. **I·nu·it** *adj.* ⟨Inuktitut, pl of *inuk* man, person⟩

The English names applied by Europeans to Inuit communities, usually with reference to some aspect of culture or environment (Caribou Inuit, Copper Inuit, etc.), are still used by many people, including some Inuit. However, some find these names offensive because they are completely non-indigenous. The Inuit have their own Inuktitut names for their different communities.

i·nuk·shuk [ˈɪnʊkˌʃʊk] *or* [ɪˈnʊkʃʊk] *n, pl* **-shuks** *or* **-shu·it** [-ʃuɪt] ✱ a stone cairn having the rough outline of a human figure. Inukshuks were traditionally built by the Inuit to serve as landmarks or, in long rows, to drive caribou toward waiting hunters. Also, **i·nuk·suk**, **i·nuk·shook**. ⟨Inuktitut = thing in the shape of a man⟩

I·nuk·ti·tut [ɪˈnʊktəˌtut] *n* ✱ a language of the Inuit, also called **Inuinnaqtun** [ɪˈnuɪnɑkˌtun] in the W Arctic and **Inuvialuktun** [ɪˈnuviəlʊkˌtun] in the Delta region. There are six major dialects of Inuktitut, with varying degrees of mutual intelligibility. Also, **I·nuk·ti·tuk** [ɪˈnʊktəˌtʊk] *n.* ⟨Inuktitut *inuk* man, person + *titut* speech⟩

in·un·date [ˈɪnənˌdeɪt] *v* **1** overflow; flood. **2** overwhelm: *The radio station was inundated with requests.* **in·un·da·tion** *n.* ⟨Latin *in-* onto + *undare* flow; *unda* wave⟩

I·nu·pi·at [ɪˈnupiˌæt] *n* a language of the Inuit, mutually intelligible with Inuktitut. Also, **I·nu·pi·aq.**

in·ure [ɪˈnjʊr] *v* **1** harden; accustom: *Many years in the wilderness had inured them to hardship.* **2** esp of a law or agreement, take or have effect: *The agreement inures to the benefit of the employees.* **in·ure·ment** *n.* ⟨*in* + Anglo-French *ure* use *n.*; Latin *opera* work⟩

in·vade [ɪnˈveɪd] *v* **1** enter as an enemy. **2** interfere with; violate: *to invade the rights of others.* **in·vad·er** *n.* **in·va·sion** *n.* **in·va·sive** *adj.* ⟨Latin *in-* in + *vadere* go, walk⟩

in·va·lid¹ [ˈɪnvəlɪd] *n* a person who is weak because of sickness or injury.
v **1** make weak or sick. **2** release from active service because of sickness or injury: *He was invalided out of the army.* **in·va·lid** *adj.* ⟨Latin *in-* not + *validus* strong; *valere* be strong⟩

in·val·id² [ɪnˈvælɪd] *adj* not valid; without force: *If a will is not signed, it is invalid.* **in·va·lid·i·ty** [ˌɪnvəˈlɪdəti] *n.* **in·val·id·ly** *adv.* ⟨Latin *invalidus.* See INVALID¹.⟩

in·val·i·date [ɪnˈvælɪˌdeɪt] *v* make valueless. **in·val·i·da·tion** *n.*

in·val·u·a·ble [ɪnˈvæljəbəl] *adj* priceless. **in·val·u·a·bly** *adv.* **in·val·u·a·ble·ness** *n.*

in·var·i·a·ble [ɪnˈvɛriəbəl] *adj* unchanging.

n anything that never changes. **in·var·i·a·bly** *adv.* **in·var·i·a·ble·ness** or **in·var·i·a·bil·i·ty** *n.*

in·var·i·ant *adj* unchanging. **in·var·i·ant·ly** *adv.*

in·va·sion See INVADE.

in·vec·tive [ɪn'vɛktɪv] *n* a violent attack in words; abusive language. **in·vec·tive·ness** *n.* **in·vec·tive·ly** *adv.* ⟨Latin *invectus* pp of *invehi* launch an attack; *in-* against + *vehere* carry⟩ **in·veigh** [ɪn'veɪ] *v* make a violent attack in words; complain bitterly (*against*): *He inveighed against the poor working conditions.*

in·vei·gle [ɪn'veɪgəl] *v* win over by trickery; entice; lure: *The saleswoman inveigled the poor girl into buying four dresses.* **in·vei·gle·ment** *n.* ⟨probably French *aveugle(r)* blind; Latin *aboculus, ab-* without + *oculus* eye⟩

in·vent [ɪn'vɛnt] *v* **1** think out (something new): *Alexander Graham Bell invented the telephone.* **2** think up: *to invent an excuse.* **in·ven·tion** *n.* **in·ven·tive** *adj.* **in·ven·tive·ly** *adv.* **in·ven·tive·ness** *n.* **in·ven·tor** *n.* ⟨Latin *inventus* pp of *invenire; in-* in + *venire* come⟩

in·ven·to·ry ['ɪnvən,tɔri] *n* **1** a detailed list of articles. **2** a collection of articles that are or may be so listed: *a sale to reduce inventory.* *v* make a detailed list of: *Some stores inventory their stock once a month.* **in·ven·to·ri·al** *adj.* ⟨Latin *inventorium* from *inventus.* See INVENT.⟩ **take inventory** make a detailed list.

in·verse [ɪn'vɜrs] *or* ['ɪnvɜrs] *adj* reversed in position, direction, or tendency: *DCBA is the inverse order of ABCD.* *n* **1** direct opposite: *Evil is the inverse of good.* **2** *Mathematics* **a** the reciprocal of a quantity, also called **multiplicative inverse**: *4/3 is the multiplicative inverse of 3/4.* **b** the negation of a quantity, also called **additive inverse**: *3 is the additive inverse of –3.* **in·verse·ly** *adv.* ⟨Latin *inversus* pp of *invertere.*⟩

in·ver·sion [ɪn'vɜrʒən] *n* **1** the fact of inverting or being inverted. **2** something inverted. **3** *Grammar* any reversal of the usual word order. **4** *Music* the transposition from bass to tenor or treble. **in·vert** [ɪn'vɜrt] *v* **1** turn upside down: *to invert a glass.* **2** reverse in position, direction, order, etc. **3** *Music* change by making the lowest note an octave higher or the highest note an octave lower. **in·vert·i·bil·i·ty** *n.* **in·vert·i·ble** *adj.* **invert sugar** ['ɪnvɜrt] a mixture of glucose and fructose.

in·ver·te·brate [ɪn'vɜrtəbrɪt] *or* [ɪn'vɜrtə,breɪt] *n* *Zoology* any animal lacking a backbone. *adj* **1** to do with the invertebrates. **2** *Informal* lacking character, conviction, or purpose.

in·vest [ɪn'vɛst] *v* **1** use (money) to buy something expected to produce a profit: *She invested her money in land.* **2** put in (time, energy, etc.) for later benefit: *The group invested its energies in developing new playgrounds.* **3** give power to: *He invested his lawyer with complete power to act for him.* **4** install in office with a ceremony: *A monarch is invested by being crowned.* **in·vest·a·ble** or **in·vest·i·ble** *adj.* ⟨Latin *investire; in-* in + *vestis* clothing⟩ **in·ves·ti·ture** *n* a formal investing of a person with an office, dignity, honour, right, etc. **in·vest·ment** *n* **1** a laying out of energy, time, or money. **2** something that is expected to yield a profitable return. **in·ves·tor** *n* a person who invests money.

in·ves·ti·gate [ɪn'vɛstə,geɪt] *v* search into: *to investigate a complaint.* **in·ves·ti·ga·tion** *n.* **in·ves·ti·ga·tive** *adj.* **in·ves·ti·ga·tor** *n.* ⟨Latin *in-* in + *vestigare* track, trace⟩

in·vet·er·ate [ɪn'vɛtərɪt] *adj* **1** confirmed in a habit, feeling, etc.: *an inveterate liar.* **2** long and firmly established: *Cats have an inveterate dislike of dogs.* **in·vet·er·a·cy** *n* a settled, fixed condition; the nature of a fixed habit. **in·vet·er·ate·ly** *adv.* ⟨Latin *inveteratus* pp of *inveterascere* make old; *in-* in + *veteris* old⟩

in·vid·i·ous [ɪn'vɪdiəs] *adj* likely to arouse ill will or resentment: *invidious comparisons.* **in·vid·i·ous·ly** *adv.* **in·vid·i·ous·ness** *n.* ⟨Latin *invidia* envy. See ENVY.⟩

in·vig·i·late [ɪn'vɪdʒə,leɪt] *v* supervise students, etc. writing an examination. **in·vig·i·la·tion** *n.* **in·vig·i·la·tor** *n.* ⟨Latin *in-* on + *vigilare* keep watch⟩

in·vig·or·ate [ɪn'vɪgə,reɪt] *v* fill with energy. **in·vig·or·at·ing** *adj.* **in·vig·or·a·tive** *adj.* **in·vig·or·a·tion** *n.*⟨Latin *in-* in + *vigor*⟩

in·vin·ci·ble [ɪn'vɪnsəbəl] *adj* unconquerable: *an invincible opponent.* **in·vin·ci·bil·i·ty** *n.* **in·vin·ci·bly** *adv.* ⟨Latin *in-* not + *vincere* conquer⟩

in·vi·o·la·ble [ɪn'vaɪələbəl] *adj* **1** that must not be violated: *an inviolable sanctuary.* **2** that cannot be violated: *The gods are inviolable.* **in·vi·o·la·bil·i·ty** *n.* **in·vi·o·la·bly** *adv.* **in·vi·o·late** [ɪn'vaɪəlɪt] *adj* not violated; unbroken; not profaned. **in·vi·o·late·ly** *adv.* **in·vi·o·late·ness** or **in·vi·o·la·cy** [ɪn'vaɪələsi] *n.*

in·vis·i·ble [ɪn'vɪzəbəl] *adj* **1** not capable of being seen: *Thought is invisible.* **2** not easily seen: *invisible mending.* **3** *Business* not listed in financial statements: *an invisible asset.* **in·vis·i·bil·i·ty** *n.* **in·vis·i·bly** *adv.* **invisible ink** ink that is colourless and thus invisible until treated by a heat, light, etc.

in·vite [ɪn'vaɪt] *v* **1** ask (someone) politely to do something: *We invited her to join our club.* **2** make a polite request for: *The author invited our opinion of her story.* **3** give grounds for: *The letter invites some questions.* **4** give a desire to do: *The calm water invited us to swim.* *n* ['ɪnvaɪt] *Slang* invitation. **in·vi·ta·tion** [,ɪnvə'teɪʃən] *n.* ⟨Latin *invitare*⟩ **in·vi·ta·tion·al** *adj* restricted to invited persons. *n Sports* a tournament by invitation. **in·vit·ing** *adj* tempting. **in·vit·ing·ly** *adv.*

in vit·ro [ɪn 'vitrou] *Biology* in a test tube or other artificial environment made of glass: *in vitro fertilization.* ⟨Latin = in glass⟩ **in vitro fertilization** the process of fertilizing ova with sperm in a laboratory.

in·vo·ca·tion See INVOKE.

in·voice ['ɪnvɔɪs] *n* a form listing goods or services sent to a purchaser showing prices, amounts, shipping charges, etc.

v submit an invoice to. ⟨earlier *invoyes* pl of *invoy* variant of *envoy*. See ENVOY.⟩

in·voke [ɪn'vouk] *v* **1** call on in prayer: *The tribe invoked their rain gods.* **2** appeal to for judgment: *to invoke an authority.* **3** call forth by magic: *Aladdin invoked the genie of the magic lamp.* **4** use: *The governor general invoked her power of veto.* **in·vo·ca·ble** *adj.* **in·vo·ca·tion** *n.* **in·vo·ca·tion·al** or **in·vo·ca·to·ry** [ɪn'vɒkə,tɔri] *adj.* ⟨Latin *in-* on + *vocare* call⟩

in·vol·un·tar·y [ɪn'vɒlən,tɛri] *adj* **1** not done of one's own free will or with one's consent. **2** not controlled by the will: *Breathing is mainly involuntary.* **in·vol·un·tar·i·ly** *adv.* **in·vol·un·tar·i·ness** *n.*

in·vo·lute ['ɪnvə,lut] *adj* **1** intricate. **2** rolled up on itself. **3** *Botany* of a leaf or petal, having the margins rolled in to the centre. **4** *Zoology* of a shell, having coiled whorls. *v* [,ɪnvə'lut] or ['ɪnvə,lut] become involute. ⟨Latin *involutus* pp of *involvere*. See INVOLVE.⟩ **in·vo·lu·tion** *n* **1** entanglement; complexity. **2** *Mathematics* the raising of a quantity to any power. **3** *Biology* degeneration. **4** *Botany* a rolling inward from the edge. **5** *Medicine* **a** regressive changes in the body due to old age. **b** the shrinking of an organ, as the uterus after childbirth.

in·volve [ɪn'vɒlv] *v* **1** include: *Housekeeping involves cooking.* **2** affect: *This involves the interests of all of us.* **3** bring (into difficulty, danger, etc.): *One mistake can involve you in trouble.* **4** complicate: *A sentence that is involved is generally hard to understand.* **5** take up the attention of: *I was involved in a book.* **in·volve·ment** *n.* ⟨Latin *in-* in + *volvere* roll⟩ **in·volved** *adj* **1** intricate. **2** affected. **3** *Informal* in a romantic relationship (*with*).

in·vul·ner·a·ble [ɪn'vʌlnərəbəl] *adj* **1** that cannot be injured: *Achilles was invulnerable except for his heel.* **2** not easily assailable: *an invulnerable argument.* **in·vul·ner·a·bil·i·ty** *n.* **in·vul·ner·a·bly** *adv.*

in·ward ['ɪnwərd] *adv* **1** toward the inside: *a passage leading inward.* **2** into the mind or soul: *Turn your thoughts inward.* *adj* **1** internal: *the inward parts of the body.* **2** directed toward the inside: *an inward slant of the eyes.* **3** in mind or soul: *inward peace.* **in·ward·ly** *adv.* ⟨Old English *inweard*⟩ **in·ward·ness** *n* **1** inner nature or meaning. **2** spirituality. **in·wards** *adv* inward.

i·o·dine ['aɪə,daɪn]; *in Chemistry* ['aɪə,din] *n* **1** an element of the halogen group with an irritating odour. *Symbol* **I.** **2** a brown liquid, **tincture of iodine** used as an antiseptic. ⟨French *iode*; Greek *ion* violet⟩ **i·o·dize** *v* combine or treat with iodine or an iodide: *iodized salt.* **i·o·diz·er** *n.* **i·o·di·za·tion** *n.*

i·on ['aɪɒn] or ['aɪən] *n Physics, chemistry* an atom or group of atoms having a negative or positive electric charge as a result of having lost or gained one or more electrons. **Positive ions** (cations) are formed by the loss of electrons. **Negative ions** (anions) are formed by the gain of electrons. **i·on·ize** *v.* separate into ions. **i·on·i·za·tion** *n.* **i·on·iz·er** *n.* ⟨Greek *ion* ppr of *ienai* go⟩

i·on·o·sphere [aɪ'ɒnə,sfir] *n* a region of ionized layers of air above the stratosphere. **i·on·o·spher·ic** [aɪ,ɒnə'sfɛrɪk] *adj.*

–ion *suffix* **1** the act of——ing: *attraction.* **2** the condition or state of being——ed: *fascination.* **3** the result of——: *collection.* ⟨French; Latin *-io, -ionis* noun ending⟩

i·o·ta [aɪ'outə] *n* **1** the ninth letter of the Greek alphabet (I, ι). **2** a small quantity: *There is not an iota of truth in that story.* ⟨Greek⟩

IOU or **I.O.U.** a note acknowledging a debt: *Write me an IOU for ten dollars.* ⟨for *I owe you*⟩

IPA or **I.P.A.** International Phonetic Alphabet.

IP address *Computers* a numeric address, usually four sets of numbers separated by periods, that is given to servers and users connected to the Internet.

ip·e·cac ['ɪpə,kæk] *n* a plant of the madder family whose roots are used as an emetic or purgative. ⟨Portuguese; Tupi-Guarani *ipe-kaa-guéne* creeping plant causing nausea⟩

ip·so fac·to ['ɪpsou 'fæktou] *Latin* by that very fact; by the fact itself.

IQ or **I.Q.** *Psychology* INTELLIGENCE QUOTIENT.

ir–¹ *prefix* the form of IN-¹ occurring before *r*: *irrational, irresolute.*

ir–² *prefix* the form of IN-² occurring before *r*: *irrigate, irradiate.*

i·ras·ci·ble [ɪ'ræsəbəl] *adj* easily made angry; irritable. **i·ras·ci·bil·i·ty** *n.* **i·ras·ci·bly** *adv.* ⟨Latin *irasci* grow angry; *ira* anger⟩

ire [aɪr] *n* anger; wrath. ⟨Latin *ira* anger⟩ **i·rate** [aɪ'reit] or ['aɪreit] *adj* angry. **i·rate·ly** *adv.*

ir·i·des·cent [,ɪrɪ'dɛsənt] *adj* displaying the colours of the rainbow. **ir·i·des·cence** *n.* **ir·i·des·cent·ly** *adv.* ⟨Latin *iridis* rainbow⟩

i·rid·i·um [ɪ'rɪdiəm] or [aɪ'rɪdiəm] *n* a rare, metallic element that resembles platinum. *Symbol* **Ir** ⟨See IRIDESCENT; with reference to its iridescence in solution.⟩

i·ris ['aɪrɪs] *n, pl* **i·ris·es** **1** *Botany* any of a genus of plants, having sword-shaped leaves and showy flowers. **2** *Anatomy* the coloured part of the eye. ⟨Greek *iris* rainbow⟩

irk [ɜrk] *v* weary; annoy; bore: *It irks us to wait for people who are always late.* ⟨Middle English *irke(n)* tire; Scandinavian⟩ **irk·some** *adj* tiresome. **irk·some·ly** *adv.* **irk·some·ness** *n.*

i·ron ['aɪərn] *n* **1** a hard, metallic element. *Symbol* **Fe** **2** a tool made from this metal. **3** great hardness and strength: *women of iron.* **4** an appliance with a flat surface for smoothing cloth. **5** a golf club with an iron or steel head. **6 irons** *pl* handcuffs; shackles. *adj* **1** to do with iron. **2** like iron; hard or strong: *an iron will.* **3** harsh or cruel: *the iron hand of fate.* *v* smooth or press (cloth, etc.) with a heated iron. **i·ron·like** *adj.* ⟨Old English *īren*⟩ **iron out** straighten out: *to iron out problems.*

Iron Age a period characterized by the use of tools, weapons, etc. made of iron. In Europe, the Iron Age began about 1000 B.C. **i·ron·clad** *adj* **1** protected with iron plates. **2** very hard to change or get out of: *an ironclad agreement.* *n* formerly, a warship protected with iron plates. **i·ron·fist·ed** *adj* cruel; despotic. **iron hand** strict control. **i·ron—hand·ed** *adj.* **i·ron·hand·ed·ness** *n.* **i·ron·ware** *n* articles made of iron. **i·ron—willed** *adj* having an exceptionally firm will. **i·ron·wood** *n* any of various trees having very hard, heavy wood. **i·ron·work** *n* **1** works made of iron. **2 ironworks** a place where iron or steel is smelted or fashioned into heavy products. **i·ron·work·er** *n* **1** a person who makes things of iron. **2** a person whose work is building the framework of bridges, skyscrapers, etc.

i·ro·ny ['aɪrəni] *or* ['aɪərni] *n* **1** a method of expression in which the intended meaning is the opposite of that expressed. **2** an outcome contrary to what would naturally be expected: *It was an amusing irony when a fake diamond was stolen instead of the real one.* **3 dramatic irony**, a situation in which the audience knows something which a character does not. **4** feigned ignorance in an argument, sometimes called **Socratic irony**. **i·ron·ic** [aɪ'rɒnɪk] *adj.* **i·ron·i·cal·ly** *adv.* ⟨Greek *eirōneia* pretence; *eirōn* pretender⟩

CONFUSABLES

Irony emphasizes deliberately saying the opposite of what one means, depending on tone to show the real meaning. **Sarcasm** applies only to contemptuous remarks that may be stated ironically but are always intended to hurt. **Satire** is the formal use of irony, sarcasm, and other kinds of humour to expose, criticize, or attack follies or vices.

Ir·o·quois ['irə,kwɒ] *n sg or pl* a member of any of a group of First Nations peoples and Native Americans called the FIVE NATIONS (later, the SIX NATIONS) living mostly in Québec, Ontario, and New York State. **Ir·o·quois** *adj.* **Ir·o·quoi·an** [,irə'kwɔɪən] *n* **1** a family of First Nations and Native American languages, including Huron, Oneida, Kanien'keha, Onondaga, Cayuga, Seneca, Tuscarora, and Cherokee. **2** a First Nations person or Native American from any of these people groups; an Iroquois. **Ir·o·quoi·an** *adj.*

ir·ra·di·ate [ɪ'reidi,eit] *v* **1** shine upon; illuminate. **2** radiate; give out. **3** expose to radiation. **ir·ra·di·a·tive** *adj.* **ir·ra·di·ant** *adj* radiant; shining. **ir·ra·di·ance** or **irradiancy** *n.* **ir·ra·di·a·tion** *n* **1** the process of irradiating. **2** a stream of light. **3** enlightenment of the mind or spirit. **4** *Optics* the apparent enlargement of an object seen against a dark background.

ir·ra·tion·al [ɪ'ræʃənəl] *adj* **1** unreasonable: *It is irrational to be afraid of the number 13.* **2** unable to think clearly. **3** *Mathematics* **a** a number whose decimal expansion neither terminates nor repeats. √3 is an irrational number. **b** of functions, that cannot be

expressed as the ratio of two polynomials. **ir·ra·tion·al·i·ty** *n.* **ir·ra·tion·al·ly** *adv.* **ir·ra·tion·al·ism** [ɪ'ræʃənə,lɪzəm] *n* thought or behaviour that is not rational.

ir·rec·on·cil·a·ble [ɪ'rɛkən,saɪləbəl] *or* [,ɪrɛkən'saɪləbəl] *adj* that cannot agree. **ir·rec·on·cil·a·bil·i·ty** *n.* **ir·rec·on·cil·a·bly** *adv.*

ir·re·cov·er·a·ble [,ɪrɪ'kʌvərəbəl] *adj* **1** that cannot be regained or got back: *Wasted time is irrecoverable.* **2** that cannot be remedied: *irrecoverable sorrow.* **ir·re·cov·er·a·bly** *adv.*

ir·re·duc·i·ble [,ɪrɪ'djusəbəl] *or* [,ɪrɪ'dusəbəl] *adj* that cannot be reduced. **ir·re·duc·i·bil·i·ty** *n.* **ir·re·duc·i·bly** *adv*

ir·ref·u·ta·ble [ɪ'rɛfjətəbəl] *or* [,ɪrɪ'fjutəbəl] *adj* that cannot be refuted or disproved. **ir·ref·u·ta·bil·i·ty** *n.* **ir·ref·u·ta·bly** *adv.*

ir·reg·u·lar [ɪ'rɛgjələr] *adj* **1** erratic: *irregular breathing.* **2** without symmetry: *irregular features.* **3** not according to law or morals: *irregular behaviour.* **4** *Military* not in the regular army. **5** *Grammar* not inflected in the usual way. *Be* is an irregular verb. **ir·reg·u·lar·ly** *adv.* **ir·reg·u·lar·i·ty** [ɪ,rɛgjə'lɛrəti] *or* [ɪ,rɛgjə'lærəti] *n* **1** a lack of regularity. **2** something irregular. **3** lack of regularity of bowel movements.

ir·rel·e·vant [ɪ'rɛləvənt] *adj* not to the point; off the subject: *A question about economics is irrelevant in a music lesson.* **ir·rel·e·vance** or **ir·rel·e·van·cy** *n.* **ir·rel·e·vant·ly** *adv.*

ir·re·mov·a·ble [,ɪrɪ'muvəbəl] *adj* that cannot be removed. **ir·re·mov·a·bil·i·ty** or **ir·re·mov·a·ble·ness** *n.* **ir·re·mov·a·bly** *adv.*

ir·rep·a·ra·ble [ɪ'rɛpərəbəl] *adj* that cannot be repaired. **ir·rep·a·ra·bil·i·ty** *n.* **ir·rep·a·ra·bly** *adv.* ⟨Latin *in-* not + *reparare* repair⟩

ir·re·place·a·ble [,ɪrɪ'pleisəbəl] *adj* impossible to replace with another. **ir·re·place·a·bil·i·ty** *n.* **ir·re·place·a·bly** *adv.*

ir·re·press·i·ble [,ɪrɪ'prɛsəbəl] *adj* that cannot be repressed or restrained. **ir·re·press·i·bil·i·ty** *n.* **ir·re·press·i·bly** *adv.*

ir·re·proach·a·ble [,ɪrɪ'proutʃəbəl] *adj* free from blame; faultless: *an irreproachable life.* **ir·re·proach·a·bil·i·ty** *n.* **ir·re·proach·a·bly** *adv.*

ir·re·sist·i·ble [,ɪrɪ'zɪstəbəl] *adj* too great to be withstood; overwhelming: *an irresistible desire to laugh.* **ir·re·sist·i·bil·i·ty** *n.* **ir·re·sist·i·bly** *adv.*

ir·res·o·lute [ɪ'rɛzə,lut] *adj* **1** unable to make up one's mind. **2** lacking in resoluteness: *An irresolute person makes a poor leader.* **ir·res·o·lute·ly** *adv.* **ir·res·o·lu·tion** *n.*

ir·re·spec·tive [,ɪrɪ'spɛktɪv] *adj* regardless: *Any person, irrespective of age, may join the club.* **ir·re·spec·tive·ly** *adv.*

ir·re·spon·si·ble [,ɪrɪ'spɒnsəbəl] *adj* without a sense of responsibility: *It was irresponsible to leave the broken glass on the sidewalk.* **ir·re·spon·si·bil·i·ty** *n.* **ir·re·spon·si·bly** *adv.*

ir·re·triev·a·ble [,ɪrɪ'trivəbəl] *adj* that cannot be restored to its former condition. **ir·re·triev·a·bil·i·ty** *n.* **ir·re·triev·a·bly** *adv.*

ir·rev·er·ent [ɪ'rɛvərənt] *adj* disrespectful. **ir·rev·er·ence** *n*. **ir·rev·er·ent·ly** *adv*.

ir·re·vers·i·ble [ˌɪrɪ'vɜrsəbəl] *adj* not capable of being reversed. **ir·re·vers·i·bil·i·ty** *n*. **ir·re·vers·i·bly** *adv*.

ir·rev·o·ca·ble [ɪ'rɛvəkəbəl], [ˌɪrə'vɒkəbəl], or [ˌɪrə'voukəbəl] *adj* not to be recalled, withdrawn, or revoked: *an irrevocable decision*. **ir·rev·o·ca·bil·i·ty** *n*. **ir·rev·o·ca·bly** *adv*. ⟨Latin *in-* not + *re-* back + *vocare* call⟩

ir·ri·gate ['ɪrəˌgeit] *v* 1 supply (land) with water by means of ditches, sprinklers, etc. 2 *Medicine* wash out (a wound, cavity) with a flow of some liquid: *to irrigate the nose and throat with warm water*. **ir·ri·ga·ble** *adj*. **ir·ri·ga·bly** *adv*. **ir·ri·ga·tion** *n*. **ir·ri·ga·tion·al** *adj*. ⟨Latin *in-* in + *rigare* to lead water⟩

ir·ri·tate ['ɪrɪˌteit] *v* 1 make impatient or angry: *The boy's foolish questions irritated his father*. 2 make unnaturally sensitive: *Too much sun irritates the skin*. 3 *Biology* stimulate (an organ, muscle, tissue, etc.) to perform some characteristic action: *A muscle contracts when it is irritated by an electric shock*. **ir·ri·ta·ble** *adj*. **ir·ri·ta·bil·i·ty** *n*. **ir·ri·ta·bly** *adv*. **ir·ri·tat·ed·ly** *adv*. **ir·ri·tat·ing·ly** *adv*. **ir·ri·ta·tion** *n*. ⟨Latin *irritare* enrage, provoke⟩

ir·ri·tant *n* a thing that causes irritation: *A mustard plaster is an irritant*. **ir·ri·tant** *adj*. **ir·ri·tan·cy** *n*.

ir·rupt [ɪ'rʌpt] *v* 1 rush in suddenly. 2 of an animal population, increase suddenly in numbers. **ir·rup·tion** *n*. **ir·rup·tive** *adj*. **ir·rup·tive·ly** *adv*. ⟨Latin *irruptus* pp of *irrumpere* invade⟩

is [ɪz] *v* 3rd person singular, present indicative of BE. ⟨Old English⟩
as is as it is now; in its present condition.

ISBN International Standard Book Number.

–ish *suffix* 1 somewhat: *sweetish*. 2 resembling: *childish*. 3 to do with; belonging to: *Turkish*. 4 inclined to: *bookish*. 5 near, but usually somewhat past: *fortyish*. ⟨Old English *-isc*⟩

Is·lam [ɪs'lɑm] or [ɪz'lɑm] *n* 1 the religion of Muslims, following the teachings of Muhammad as the prophet of Allah. 2 Muslims as a group. 3 the civilization of Muslim peoples. 4 all the countries in which Islam is the main religion. **Is·lam·ic** *adj*. **Is·lam·ic·al·ly** *adv*. ⟨Arabic *islām* submission (to God); *aslama* he surrendered himself⟩

is·land ['ailənd] *n* 1 a body of land completely surrounded by water. 2 something resembling this. **is·land·like** *adj*. ⟨Old English *igland; īg* island + *land* land; ⟩
is·land·er *n* a native or inhabitant of an island. **isle** [ail] *n* island. **is·let** *n* a small island.

–ism *suffix* 1 an action; practice: *criticism*. 2 a doctrine: *socialism*. 3 a quality; state: *heroism*. 4 an instance: *witticism*. 5 an unhealthy condition caused by——: *alcoholism*. ⟨Greek *-ismos, -isma*⟩

ISO the international name of an organization which sets quality standards for various industries. Its English name is International

Organization for Standardization; ISO is not an acronym but a full name. ⟨Greek *iso-* equal⟩

iso– *combining form* 1 equal: *isosceles, isometric*. 2 *Chemistry* isomeric. ⟨Greek *iso-; isos* equal⟩

i·so·bar ['aɪsəˌbɑr] *n* 1 *Meteorology* a line on a weather map connecting places with the same atmospheric pressure. 2 an atom with the same atomic weight as, but usually a different atomic number from, another atom. ⟨*iso-* + Greek *baros* weight⟩

i·so·late ['aɪsəˌleit] *v* 1 separate from others: *to isolate people with contagious diseases*. 2 *Chemistry* obtain (a substance) in an uncombined form: *to isolate the oxygen from water*. **i·so·late** ['aɪsəlɪt] *n, adj*. **i·so·la·tion** *n*. ⟨French *isoler*, Latin *insulare; insula* island⟩
in isolation without reference to related matter: *Considered in isolation, the whole thing assumes a less significant aspect*.
i·so·la·tion·ist [ˌaɪsə'leiʃənɪst] *n* one who objects to his or her country's participation in international affairs. **i·so·la·tion·ism** *n*.

i·so·mer ['aɪsəmər] *n* 1 *Chemistry* a compound composed of the same elements, but with a difference in the arrangement of atoms. 2 *Physics* one of a set of atomic nuclei differing in behaviour but having the same atomic number. **i·so·mer·ic** [ˌaɪsə'mɛrɪk] *adj*. **i·so·mer·i·cal·ly** *adv*. ⟨*iso-* + Greek *meros* part⟩

i·so·met·ric [ˌaɪsə'mɛtrɪk] *adj* to do with equality of measure. Also, **i·so·met·ri·cal**. **i·so·met·ri·cal·ly** *adv*. ⟨*iso-* + Greek *metron* measure⟩
isometric exercise exercise which involves alternate tensing and relaxing muscles.

i·so·mor·phic [ˌaɪsə'mɔrfɪk] *adj* 1 *Biology* having similar appearance, but different ancestry. 2 isomorphous. **i·so·morph** *n*. **i·so·morph·ism** *n*. ⟨*iso-* + Greek *morphē* form⟩
i·so·mor·phous *adj* 1 *Chemistry* crystallizing in the same form or related forms. 2 *Biology* showing similarity of form.

i·sos·ce·les [ai'sɒsəˌliz] *adj* of a triangle, with two sides equal. ⟨*iso-* + Greek *skelos* leg⟩

i·so·therm ['aɪsəˌθɜrm] *n* *Meteorology* a line on a weather map connecting places with the same temperature. ⟨*iso-* + Greek *thermē* heat⟩

i·so·ton·ic [ˌaɪsə'tɒnɪk] *adj* 1 *Physical chemistry* having the same osmotic pressure. 2 *Physiology* having to do with muscle contractions caused by tension. 3 *Music* characterized by equal tones. **i·so·ton·i·cal·ly** *adv*. **i·so·to·nic·i·ty** [ˌaɪsətə'nɪsəti] *n*. ⟨*iso-* + Greek *tonos* a stretching⟩

i·so·tope ['aɪsəˌtoup] *n* *Chemistry* any of the atoms of an element with the same number of protons but a different number of neutrons and different physical properties. **i·so·top·ic** [ˌaɪsə'tɒpɪk] *adj*. **i·sot·o·py** [ai'sɒtəpi] *n*. ⟨*iso-* + Greek *topos* place⟩

i·so·trop·ic [ˌaɪsə'trɒpɪk] *adj* *Physics* having the same properties, such as elasticity or conduction, in all directions. **i·sot·ro·py** *n*. ⟨Greek *isos-* + *tropos* turn, way⟩

ISP Internet service provider.

is·sue [ˈɪʃju] *or* [ˈɪʃu] *v* **1** send out: *The government issues stamps.* **2** come out; go out: *Smoke issues from the chimney.* **3** publish, or be published. **4** distribute: *Books were issued to all.* *n* **1** a quantity (of copies of a magazine, etc.) sent out at one time. **2** a coming forth: *an issue of blood from the nose.* **3** a point to be debated: *political issues.* **4** a child or children: *She died without issue.* **is·su·a·ble** *adj.* **is·su·er** *n.* ⟨Old French *eissue* pp of *eissir* , Latin *exire; ex-* out + *ire* go⟩ **at issue** to be considered. **burning issue** a matter of great importance. **face the issue** do what must be done. **join issue** take opposite sides in an argument. **make an issue** cause to become a point of debate. **take issue** disagree: *I take issue with you on that point.*

is·su·ance *n* an issuing; issue.

–ist *suffix* **1** a person who does or makes: *theorist.* **2** one who knows about: *biologist.* **3** one engaged in: *machinist.* **4** one who believes in: *abolitionist.* ⟨Greek *-istēs*⟩

isth·mus [ˈɪsməs] *n, pl* **-mus·es** or **-mi** [-maɪ] *or* [-mi] a narrow strip of land connecting two large bodies of land. ⟨Latin; Greek *isthmos* neck of land⟩

it [ɪt] *pron. subj or obj* **it** *poss* **its** *pl subj* **they** *pl obj* **them** *pl poss* **theirs** **1** a thing, animal, or person already mentioned: *The plan is sound, but it is too complicated.* **2** the subject of an impersonal verb: *It is snowing.* **3** a subject of a clause that anticipates the real subject : *It is hard to believe that he is dead.* **4** a direct object without specific meaning: *I've had it, I'm going!* **5** *Informal* the final thing: *That's it, I quit.* *n* **1** in certain children's games, the player who must catch, find, guess, etc. **2** something neither male nor female:. ⟨Old English *hit*⟩

its [ɪts] *adj* of, or done by it or itself: *The dog hurt its paw. pron* that which belongs to it: *A dog's kennel is its and its alone.* **it·self** [ɪtˈsɛlf] *pron* **1** a reflexive pronoun: *The horse tripped and hurt itself.* **2** a form of **it** added for emphasis: *The land itself is worth more than the house.* **3** its usual self. **it's 1** it is: *It's my turn.* **2** it has: *It's been a good day.*

CONFUSABLES
The **'s** in **it's** means that something has been left out: *it is* or *it has.* Nothing is left out of **its.**

IT information technology.

i·tal·ic [aɪˈtælɪk] *or* [ɪˈtælɪk] *adj* **1** of or designating a style of type in which the letters and numerals slant to the right. *This sentence is in italic.* Compare ROMAN. **2 Italic** a style of handwriting or calligraphy. *n* Usually, **italics** *pl* italic type or print. **i·tal·i·cize** [aɪˈtælə,saɪz] *or* [ɪˈtælə,saɪz] *v.* **i·tal·i·ci·za·tion** *n.* ⟨Latin *Italicus; Italia* Italy⟩

itch [ɪtʃ] *n* **1** a tickly feeling in the skin that makes one want to scratch. **2** a restless, feeling : *an itch to get away.* **itch** *v.* **itch·y** *adj.* ⟨Middle English *yicchen;* Old English *gyccan*⟩

–ite[1] *suffix* **1** a native or inhabitant of: *Israelite.* **2** a person associated with: *labourite.* **3** a mineral, a fossil, or a rock substance: *hematite.* **4** esp in the names of manufactured products, having the property of: *dynamite.* ⟨Greek *-itēs*⟩

–ite[2] *suffix* a salt of——: *phosphite, sulphite.* ⟨French *-ite* ,variant of *-ate* suffix for salts⟩

i·tem [ˈaɪtəm] *n* **1** a separate thing: *This list contains twelve items.* **2** a piece of news: *an items in today's paper.* ⟨Latin = likewise⟩ **i·tem·ize** *v* list by items. **i·tem·i·za·tion** *n.*

it·er·ate [ˈɪtə,reit] *v* repeat, often with slight modifications. **it·er·a·tion** *n.* ⟨Latin *iterare* < *iterum* again⟩

i·tin·er·ant [aɪˈtɪnərənt] *or* [ɪˈtɪnərənt] *adj* travelling from place to place. *n* a person who travels from place to place. **i·tin·er·an·cy** or **i·tin·er·a·cy** *n.* **i·tin·er·ant·ly** *adv.* ⟨Latin *itinerari* travel; *iter, itineris* journey⟩ **i·tin·er·ar·y** *n* the route or plan of a journey. *adj* of travelling or routes of travel.

–itis *suffix* **1** inflammation of: *appendicitis.* **2** *Informal* an abnormal use: *telephonitis.* ⟨Greek *-itis,* fem. of *-itēs.* Related to *-ite*[1].⟩

its See IT.

IUD INTRAUTERINE DEVICE.

IV intravenous.

–ive *suffix* **1** of or having to do with: *interrogative, inductive.* **2** tending to; likely to: *active, appreciative, imitative.* ⟨Latin *-ivus*⟩

i·vo·ry [ˈaɪvəri] *n* **1** form of dentine, composing the tusks of elephants, walruses, etc. **i·vo·ry** *adj.* ⟨Anglo-French *ivorie;* Latin *eboreus* of ivory, *ebur* ivory; Egyptian⟩ **ivory tower** a withdrawal from the world of practical affairs into a world of ideas.

i·vy [ˈaɪvi] *n* any of a genus of climbing or trailing plants. **i·vied** *adj.* Old English *īfig*⟩ **Ivy League** a group of eight universities of the eastern US, including Harvard, Yale, and Princeton, so named because many of the buildings were ivy-covered. **i·vy–league** *adj.*

–ize *suffix* **1** make or become: *legalize, centralize, crystallize, materialize.* **2** engage in; be busy with; use: *apologize, theorize.* **3** treat or combine with: *macadamize, oxidize.* ⟨Latin *-izare,* Greek *-izein*⟩

Jj

j or J [dʒei] *n*, *pl* **j's** or **J's** **1** the tenth letter of the English alphabet, or any speech sound represented by it. **2** the tenth person or thing in a series.

J **1** January. **2** joule.

jab [dʒæb] *v* **jabbed**, **jab·bing** **1** thrust (something pointed): *to jab a fork into a potato.* **2** punch with a short blow. **jab** *n*. ⟨Middle English *jobbe*(*n*); probably imitative⟩

jab·ber ['dʒæbər] *v* talk fast in a senseless way. **jab·ber** *n*. **jab·ber·er** *n*. **jab·ber·ing·ly** *adv*. ⟨probably imitative⟩

jack [dʒæk] *n* **1** any of various devices for raising a heavy object a short distance. **2** Also, **Jack**, a sailor. **3** a playing card with a knave on it. **4 jacks**, a game in which pieces are tossed up and caught between bounces of a ball (with a sg verb). **5** an electrical device to receive a plug, as a telephone jack.
v **1** raise with a jack (often with *up*): *to jack up a car*. **2** *Informal* raise (usually with *up*): *to jack up prices*. ⟨Middle English *Jakke*, a popular peasant name⟩
every man jack everyone.

jack·a·napes ['dʒækə,neips] *n* **1** an insolent fellow. **2** a saucy or mischievous child. **jack·ass** *n* **1** a male donkey. **2** a fool. **jack·boot** *n* a heavy, military boot reaching up to the knee. **jack·boot·ed** *adj*. **jack·daw** *n* a common bird closely related to the crow. **Jack·flsh** *n*, *pl* -**fish** or -**fish·es** ✹ a common game fish of the pike family. **Jack Frost** freezing cold weather personified. **jack·fruit** *n* a tree native to tropical America, with edible fruit. **jack·ham·mer** *n* a tool for drilling rock, concrete, etc., driven by compressed air. **jack herring** ✹ BC a small male herring used as bait in angling. **jack–in–the–box** or **jack–in–a–box** *n* a toy consisting of a box containing a figure that springs up when the lid is unfastened. **jack–in–the–pul·pit** *n* any of several woodland plants of the arum family. **jack–knife** or **jack·knife** *n*, *pl* -**knives** **1** a large pocketknife. **2** a headfirst dive in which the diver touches the feet with the hands and then straightens out again. *v* **1** double up like a jack-knife. **2** of a tractor-trailer, etc., double up at the connecting hitch when the vehicle is thrown off course. **jack·light** ✹ *n* a light used for hunting or fishing at night. *v* hunt or fish (*for*) using a jacklight, esp when it is illegal. **jack·light·er** *n*. **jack·light·ing** *n*. **jack of all trades** a person who can do many different kinds of work fairly well. **jack–o'–lan·tern** [,dʒæk ə 'læntərn] *n* **1** a pumpkin hollowed out and cut to look like a face, used as a lantern at Halloween. **Jack pine** ✹ a pine with cones that are often curved. **jack·pot** *n* **1** a pool of money that is competed for regularly and that increases as contestants fail to win it. **2** any large gain. **hit the jackpot a** win a jackpot. **b** have a stroke

of good luck. **jack–rab·bit** *n* any of several large hares. **Jack Tar** or **jack tar** a sailor.

jack·al ['dʒækəl] *n* any of several wild animals closely related to the dog. ⟨Turkish *chakal*; Persian *shagal*⟩

jack·et ['dʒækɪt] *n* **1** an outer garment for the upper part of the body. **2** any outer covering such as the skin of a potato. **3** DUST JACKET. **4** LIFE JACKET. **jack·et·ed** *adj*. **jack·et·less** *adj*. **jack·et·like** *adj*. ⟨Middle French *jaquet* diminutive of *jaque* peasant's tunic.⟩

jac·quard [dʒə'kɑrd] or ['dʒækɑrd] *adj* to do with an elaborate figured design woven on a loom. ⟨Joseph *Jacquard* 18c French weaver who invented the loom⟩

jade[1] [dʒeid] *n* a hard mineral found in a variety of colours, esp green. **jade** *adj*. ⟨French; Spanish *(piedra de) ijada* (stone of) colic, which it was thought to cure⟩

jade[2] [dʒeid] *n* an inferior or worn-out horse. *v* **1** wear out; tire; weary. **2** dull by long use. **jad·ed** *adj*. **jad·ed·ly** *adv*. **jad·ed·ness** *n*. ⟨origin uncertain; compare Old Norse *jalda* mare⟩

jag[1] [dʒæg] *n* a sharp point sticking out. *v* **jagged**, **jag·ging** **1** make notches in. **2** tear unevenly. ⟨late Middle English *jagge* a cut⟩ **jag·ged** ['dʒægɪd] *adj* with sharp points sticking out. **jag·ged·ly** *adv*. **jag·ged·ness** *n*.

jag[2] [dʒæg] *n* **1** *Informal* a state of intoxication. **2** *Informal* a period of uncontrolled indulgence or behaviour: *a crying jag*. ⟨origin uncertain⟩

jag·uar ['dʒægwɑr] *n* a large animal of the cat family having a tawny coat with black spots. ⟨Portuguese; Tupi *jaguara*⟩

jail [dʒeil] *n* **1** a prison. **2** imprisonment. *v* put or keep in jail. **jail·less** *adj*. **jail–like** *adj*. ⟨Old French *jaiole*; Latin *cavea* cage⟩ **break jail** escape from jail. **jail·break** *n*. **jail·bird** *n* *Slang* **1** a prisoner in jail. **2** a person who has been in jail many times. **jail·er** or **jail·or** ['dʒeilər] *n* a person who keeps someone or something confined.

Jain [dʒain] or [dʒein] *n* an adherent of **Jain·ism**, a religion of India having Hindu and Buddhist elements. **Jain** *adj*. ⟨Hindi *Jaina*; *jina* victorious⟩

ja·la·pe·ño [,hɑlə'peinjou] *n* a Mexican hot pepper. ⟨Mexican Spanish⟩

ja·lop·y [dʒə'lɒpi] *n* *Informal* an old car in a poor state of repair. ⟨origin uncertain⟩

jal·ou·sie ['ʒælʊ,zi] or ['dʒælə,si] *n* a window shutter made of adjustable slats. ⟨French = jealousy; for possibility of looking through without being seen⟩

jam[1] [dʒæm] *v* **jammed**, **jam·ming** **1** press; squeeze: *The ship was jammed between two rocks*. **2** crush: *Her fingers were jammed in the door*. **3** shove: *to jam one more book into the bookcase*. **4** block up: *The river was jammed with logs*. **5** stick or cause to stick so as not to work properly: *The window has jammed*. **6** make (radio signals, etc.) unintelligible by sending out others of approximately the same frequency. **7** have a JAM SESSION.

n **1** a mass of people or things crowded together: *a traffic jam*. **2** *Informal* a difficult or tight spot. ⟨perhaps imitative⟩

jam on *Informal* apply hastily: *jam on the brakes*.

jam·bo·ree [ˌdʒæmbəˈri] *n* **1** *Informal* a noisy party. **2** a large rally or gathering of Scouts.

jam–packed *adj Informal* filled to capacity.

jam session an informal gathering of musicians at which they improvise.

jam² [dʒæm] *n* a preserve made by boiling fruit with sugar until thick. **jam·like** *adj*. **jam·my** *adj*. ⟨perhaps special use of *jam¹*⟩

jamb [dʒæm] *n* the upright piece forming the side of a doorway, window, fireplace etc. ⟨Old French *jambe* literally, leg⟩

jam·ba·la·ya [ˌdʒʌmbeˈlaɪə] *n* a Creole dish consisting of tomatoes, shrimps, herbs, and rice. ⟨American French; Provençal *jambalaia*⟩

jan·gle [ˈdʒæŋɡəl] *v* **1** make or cause to make a loud, clashing noise. **2** quarrel. **3** make tense or strained: *Their complaints jangled her nerves*. **jan·gle** *n*. **jan·gler** *n*. **jan·gly** *adj*. ⟨Old French *jangler;* probably imitative⟩

jan·i·tor [ˈdʒænətər] *n* a person hired to take care of and clean a building, offices, etc.; caretaker. **jan·i·tor·ial** *adj*. **jan·i·tor·ship** *n*. ⟨Latin = doorkeeper; *janus* arched passageway⟩

Jan·u·ar·y [ˈdʒænjuˌɛri] *n* the first month of the year. It has 31 days. ⟨Latin *Janus* Roman god of exits and entrances. See JANITOR.⟩

January thaw ✳ a spell of mild weather in January, causing the snow to melt.

jape [dʒeip] *n, v* joke or jest. **jap·er** *n*. **jap·er·y** *n*. **jap·ing·ly** *adv*. ⟨Middle English; origin uncertain⟩

jar¹ [dʒɑr] *n* a container with a wide mouth and a lid. ⟨French *jarre;* Arabic *jarrah*⟩

jar² [dʒɑr] *v* **jarred, jar·ring 1** cause to shake: *The aftershock jarred my desk*. **2** have a harsh effect on: *The children's playful yells jarred her nerves*. **3** clash; be in conflict: *Our opinions jar*. **jar** *n*. **jar·ring·ly** *adv*. ⟨probably imitative⟩

jar·gon [ˈdʒɑrɡən] *n* **1** language that fails to communicate because it is full of long, fancy words. **2** the language of a particular group profession etc.: *the jargon of sailors*. ⟨Old French; probably ultimately imitative⟩

USAGE
Definition 2 carries no criticism but is a technical sense of **jargon** as used by linguists. This should not be confused with definition 1, which does suggest poor expression.

jas·mine [ˈdʒæzmɪn] *n* any of a large genus of shrubs and vines of the olive family cultivated for their highly fragrant flowers. ⟨French *jasmin;* Arabic; Persian *yasmin*⟩

jas·per [ˈdʒæspər] *n* a variety of quartz. ⟨Old French *jaspre;* Greek *iaspis;* Semitic⟩

jaun·dice [ˈdʒɒndɪs] *n* **1** *Pathology* a liver disease, characterized by yellow skin. **2** a cynical outlook due to envy, jealousy, etc. *v* prejudice the mind or judgment of by envy, discontent, etc. ⟨Old French *jaunisse; jaune* yellow Latin *galbinus*⟩

jaunt [dʒɒnt] *n* a short pleasure trip. **jaunt** *v*. ⟨origin uncertain⟩

jaun·ty *adj* **1** sprightly: *to walk with jaunty steps*. **2** stylish: *a jaunty cap*. **jaun·ti·ly** *adv*. **jaun·ti·ness** *n*. ⟨French *gentil* noble. See GENTEEL.⟩

jave·lin [ˈdʒævlɪn] *n* **1** a light spear thrown by hand. **2** a spear thrown for distance in track and field contests. ⟨French *javeline*⟩

jaw [dʒɒ] *n* **1** either of the two sets of bones that form the framework of the mouth in most vertebrates. **2** jaws *pl* **a** the mouth with its jawbones and teeth. **b** the parts in a tool that grip: *the jaws of a vise*. **3** *Slang* gossip. *v Slang* **1** talk; gossip. **2** find fault with; scold. **jaw·less** *adj*. ⟨perhaps related to CHEW; influenced by French *joue* cheek⟩

jaw·bone *n* the bone of the lower jaw. *v* talk vehemently to. **jaw·break·er** *n* **1** *Informal* a big, hard candy. **2** *Informal* a word hard to pronounce. **3** a machine for crushing ore. **jaw·break·ing** *adj*. **jaw·break·ing·ly** *adv*. **Jaws of Life** *Trademark* a large tool used to pry open wrecked vehicles, to free people trapped inside.

jay [dʒei] *n* any of various birds of the same family as crows, noted for being noisy and aggressive. The bluejay and Canada jay are common Canadian birds. ⟨Latin *gaius* special use of *Gaius* masculine name⟩

jay·walk *v* walk across a street at a place other than a regular crossing or without paying attention to traffic. **jay·walk·er** *n*.

jazz [dʒæz] *n* **1** a style of music characterized by complex rhythms and improvisation of a basic melody. **2** any popular dance music having a pronounced rhythm. **3** *Slang* anything considered tiresome, affected, etc.: *I'm tired of all that jazz about how rich she is*. *v Slang* make more exciting or decorative (usually with *up*): *to jazz up a dull colour scheme*. **jazz·er** *n*. ⟨origin uncertain⟩

jaz·zy *adj Informal* loud or flashy: *jazzy clothes*. **jazz·i·ly** *adv*. **jazz·i·ness** *n*.

jeal·ous [ˈdʒɛləs] *adj* **1** fearful that a person one loves may prefer another. **2** envious (often with *of*): *I am jealous of her marks*. **3** watchful in guarding something: *A democracy is jealous of its freedom*. **jeal·ous·ly** *adv*. **jeal·ous·y** *n*. ⟨Old French *gelos,* Latin *zelosus; zelus* zeal, Greek *zēlos*⟩

jean [dʒin] *n* **jeans** *pl* pants made of denim. ⟨probably French *Gênes* Genoa, Italy⟩

Jeep [dʒip] *n Trademark* an all-wheel drive vehicle able to travel over rugged terrain. ⟨origin uncertain⟩

jeer [dʒir] *v* make fun rudely or unkindly. *n* a jeering remark; rude sarcastic comment. **jeer·er** *n*. **jeer·ing·ly** *adv*. ⟨origin uncertain⟩

Jehovah See YAHWEH.

Jehovah's Witnesses [dʒəˈhouvəz] a Christian sect founded in Pennsylvania in the 1870s. One of their beliefs is that religious conviction is above civil authority.

je·june [dʒɪ'dʒun] *adj* **1** lacking nourishing qualities. **2** flat and uninteresting. **3** naive. **je·june·ly** *adv.* **je·june·ness** *n.* **je·ju·ni·ty** *n.* ⟨Latin *jejunus* meagre; orig hungry⟩

jel·ly ['dʒɛli] *n* **1** a food that is liquid when hot but firm when cold. **2** a jellylike substance: *petroleum jelly.*
v **-lied, -ly·ing 1** turn into jelly. **2** prepare in or cover with jelly. **jel·ly·like** *adj.* ⟨Old French *gelée*; Latin *gelata* pp of *gelare* congeal⟩
jell *v* **1** make or become jelly. **2** *Informal* take definite form: *Our plans have jelled.* **jel·lied** *adj* **1** turned into jelly. **2** prepared in or covered with jelly: *jellied eels.* **jel·ly bean** *n* a small bean-shaped candy. **jel·ly·fish** *n, pl* **-fish** or **-fishes 1** any of a class of invertebrate marine animals having a jellylike body. **2** *Informal* a person of weak will or character.

je ne sais quoi [ˌʒənsɛ'kwa] *French* an indefinable thing (literally, *I don't know what*).

jen·ny ['dʒɛni] *n* the female of certain animals and birds. ⟨orig diminutive of *Jane*⟩

jeop·ard·y ['dʒɛpərdi] *n* risk; danger: *The firefighters put their lives in jeopardy when they entered the burning building.* **jeop·ard·ize** *v.* ⟨Old French *jeu parti* even or divided game⟩

Jer·e·mi·ah [ˌdʒɛrə'maɪə] *n* a pessimistic person who sees mainly evil and predicts a terrible future. ⟨*Jeremiah,* a Hebrew prophet who denounced the evils of his time⟩
jer·e·mi·ad [-'maɪəd] *n* a long, sad complaint.

jerk¹ [dʒɜrk] *n* **1** a sudden, sharp pull. **2** *Slang* an unpleasant or stupid person. *v* **1** pull suddenly. **2** move with jerks: *The old wagon jerked along.* **3** twitch. **jerk·y** *adj.* **jerk·i·ly** *adv.* **jerk·i·ness** *n.* ⟨probably imitative⟩

jerk² [dʒɜrk] *v* **1** preserve (meat) by cutting it into slices and drying it in the sun. **2** prepare meat by spicing and barbecuing it. **jerk** *n, adj.* ⟨Spanish *charquear; charquí* jerked meat; Quechua⟩
jerk·y *n* ✻ strips of dried beef.

jer·kin ['dʒɜrkɪn] *n* a short outer vest. ⟨origin uncertain⟩

jer·o·bo·am [ˌdʒɛrə'bouəm] *n* a wine bottle holding 3.64 L. ⟨*Jeroboam* a king of ancient Israel⟩

jer·ry–build ['dʒɛri ˌbɪld] *v* **-built, -building** build cheaply. **jer·ry·build·er** *n.*

jer·sey ['dʒɜrzi] *n pl* **-seys 1** a soft fabric made with a plain stitch. **2** a knitted garment for the upper body. **3** *Jersey* a breed of dairy cattle that give very rich milk. **jer·seyed** *adj.* ⟨*Jersey* one of the Channel Islands⟩

jess [dʒɛs] *n* a short strap fastened around a falcon's leg and attached to the leash. **jess** *v.* ⟨Old French *ges*; Latin *jacere* to throw⟩

jest [dʒɛst] *v* **1** act or speak playfully. **2** make fun of; laugh at.
n a joke. **jest·ful** *adj.* **jest·ing·ly** *adv.* ⟨Old French *geste* orig story, exploit⟩
in jest in fun.
jest·er *n* a person who jests. In the Middle Ages, kings often had jesters to amuse them.

Jes·u·it ['dʒɛzjuɪt] *or* ['dʒɛʒuɪt] *n* Roman Catholic Church a member of a religious order called the Society of Jesus. ⟨Latin *Jesuita; Jesus*⟩

Je·sus ['dʒizəs] *n* Jesus of Nazareth, regarded by Christians as divine prophet or the Son of God. ⟨Hebrew *Yeshua* Jehovah saves⟩
Jesus Christ Jesus.

jet¹ [dʒɛt] *n* **1** a stream of gas or liquid, sent with force: *A fountain sends up a jet of water.* **2** a jet-propelled aircraft.
v **jet·ted, jet·ting 1** gush out. **2** travel or carry by jet aircraft. ⟨French, from *jeter* throw⟩
jet engine an engine that produces motion by jet propulsion. **jet lag** *n* a delayed effect of fatigue after a long flight in an aircraft. **jet·lin·er** *n* a large jet aircraft used for carrying passengers. **jet plane** an aircraft that is driven by jet engine. **jet–pro·pelled** *adj* **1** driven by jet propulsion. **2** moving fast. **jet propulsion** propulsion in a given direction by a jet of air, gas, etc. forced in the opposite direction. **jet set** wealthy people who frequent fashionable places, travelling by jet. **jet·set·ter** *n.* **jet–ski** *n* a motorized craft with a seat and a ski, for skimming over water. **jet stream 1** a current of air travelling at very high speed from west to east at high altitudes. **2** the stream of exhaust from a rocket engine.

jet² [dʒɛt] *n* a black variety of lignite. ⟨Old French *jaiet,* Greek *Gagas,* town in Asia Minor⟩
jet–black *adj* deep black.

jet·sam ['dʒɛtsəm] *n* **1** goods thrown overboard to lighten a ship in distress. **2** such goods washed ashore. **3** anything tossed aside as useless. Compare FLOTSAM. ⟨variant of *jettison*; Latin *jactatio; jacere* throw⟩
jet·ti·son ['dʒɛtəsən] *or* ['dʒɛtəzən] *v* **1** throw (goods) overboard to lighten a ship, aircraft, etc. in distress. **2** throw away; discard.

jet·ty ['dʒɛti] *n* **1** a breakwater. **2** landing place; pier, or dock. ⟨Old French *jetée* thrown out; pp of *jeter* throw, Latin *jacere*⟩

Jew [dʒu] *n* **1** a person descended from the ancient Israelites; Hebrew. **2** a person whose religion is Judaism. **Jew·ish** *adj.* **Jew·ish·ness** *n.* ⟨Old French *giu jueu* Greek *Ioudaios;* Hebrew *y'hudi* of the tribe of Judah⟩
Jew·ry *n* Jews as a group; the Jewish people.

jew·el ['dʒuəl] *n* **1** a precious stone; gem. **2** a person or thing that is very precious. **jew·el–like** *adj.* ⟨Anglo-French *juel* trinket, plaything, Latin *jocalis; jocus* joke, game⟩
jew·el·ler or **jew·el·er** *n* a person who makes, sells, or repairs jewellery, watches, etc. **jew·el·ler·y** or **jew·el·ry** ['dʒuəlri] *or* ['dʒuləri] *n* ornaments set with gems.

jews'–harp or **jew's–harp** ['dʒuz ˌhɑrp] *n* a simple musical instrument held between the teeth and played by striking with a finger. ⟨*jaws'-harp*⟩

Jez·e·bel ['dʒɛzəˌbɛl] *or* ['dʒɛzəbəl] *n* any shameless, immoral woman. Also, **jez·e·bel.** ⟨the depraved wife of Ahab, King of Israel⟩

jib¹ [dʒɪb] *n* Nautical on a ship or boat, a triangular sail in front of the foremast. ⟨origin uncertain⟩
cut of one's jib one's outward appearance.

jib² [dʒɪb] *v* **jibbed, jib·bing** move sideways or backward instead of forward. ⟨origin uncertain⟩
jib at *Informal* refuse to face or deal with: *The horse jibbed at the high fence.*

jib³ [dʒɪb] *n* the projecting arm of a crane or derrick. ⟨probably *gibbet*⟩

jibe¹ [dʒaɪb] *v Nautical* of a sail, shift from one side of a ship to the other when sailing before the wind. Also, **jib.** ⟨Dutch *gijben*⟩

jibe² See GIBE.

jibe³ [dʒaɪb] *v Informal* be in harmony; agree. Also, **jive.** ⟨origin uncertain⟩

jif·fy [ˈdʒɪfi] *n Informal* a very short time: *I'll be there in a jiffy.* ⟨origin uncertain⟩

jig¹ [dʒɪg] *n* a lively dance.
in jig time quickly; rapidly: *I'll do it in jig time.* **the jig is up** *Slang* it's all over: *She knew the jig was up when she heard the police sirens.*
v **jigged, jig·ging 1** dance a jig. **2** move jerkily. **jig·like** *adj.* ⟨Old French *giguer* dance; *gigue* fiddle; Germanic⟩
jig·gle [ˈdʒɪgəl] *v* jerk slightly. **jig·gle** *n.*
jig·gly *adj.* **jig·saw** *n* a saw worked with an up-and-down motion, used to cut curves.
jigsaw puzzle a picture cut into irregular pieces that can be fitted together again.

jig² [dʒɪg] *n* **1** a fishing lure weighted with a bright metal. **2** a guide for a drill, file, etc.
v **jigged, jig·ging** fish with a jig. ⟨origin uncertain⟩

jig·ger·y–pok·er·y [ˈdʒɪgəri ˈpoukəri] *n Slang* humbug; fraud; bunk.

ji·had [dʒɪˈhɑd] *n Islam* a holy war; any crusade against rival beliefs. ⟨Arabic *jihād* struggle, strife⟩

jil·lion [ˈdʒɪljən] *n Informal* an extremely large quantity. ⟨by analogy with *million, billion,* etc.⟩

jilt [dʒɪlt] *v* cast off (a lover or sweetheart) after giving encouragement.
n someone who jilts a lover. ⟨origin uncertain⟩

jim–dan·dy [ˈdʒɪm ˈdændi] *Informal adj* excellent; great: *Everything is jim-dandy.*
n an excellent person or thing.

jim·jams [ˈdʒɪm,dʒæmz] *n pl Slang*
1 DELIRIUM TREMENS. **2** jitters; a creepy uneasy feeling. ⟨coined word⟩

jim·my [ˈdʒɪmi] *n* a crowbar used to force windows, doors, etc. **jim·my** *v.* ⟨apparently a special use of *Jimmy* diminutive of *James*⟩

jin·gle [ˈdʒɪŋgəl] *n* **1** a sound like that of little bells. **2** a song that has a catchy rhythm: *advertising jingles.*
v make a jingling sound: *The sleigh bells jingle as we ride.* **jing·ler** *n.* **jin·gly** *adj.* ⟨imitative⟩

jin·go·ism [ˈdʒɪŋgou,ɪzəm] *n* the favouring of aggressive foreign policy likely to lead to war. **jin·go·ist** *n, adj.* **jin·go·is·tic** *adj.* **jin·go·is·ti·cal·ly** *adv.* ⟨by *jingo* phrase in refrain of song adopted by supporters of Disraeli 19c UK statesman; *jingo,* magician's term⟩

jin·ni or **jin·nee** [dʒɪˈni] or [ˈdʒɪni] *n, pl* **jinn** (jinn often used as sg) *Muslim myth* a spirit that can appear in human or animal form

and do good or harm to people. Also, **djin·ni djinn.** ⟨Arabic *jinn* pl of *jinni* demon⟩

jinx [dʒɪŋks] *Slang n* a person or thing that is believed to bring bad luck. **jinx** *v.* ⟨Latin *iynx* bird used in magic; Greek⟩

jit·ter [ˈdʒɪtər] *v Informal* act nervously.
n pl **the jitters** *Slang* extreme nervousness. **jit·ter·y** *adj.* ⟨possible variant of dialect *chitter* shiver, tremble; variant of *chatter*⟩
jit·ter·bug *Informal n* a lively dance. **jit·ter·bug, -bugged, -bug·ging** *v.*

ji·va [ˈdʒivə] *n Jainism* **1** the individual soul of every living thing. **2** the vital energy of life, opposite of AJIVA. ⟨Sanskrit *jiva* living⟩

jive¹ [dʒaɪv] *n Slang n* **1** lively jazz; swing music. **2** dancing to jive music. **3** the talk of swing enthusiasts. **4** the latest slang.
v **jived, jiv·ing 1** dance to jive music. **2** play jive music. ⟨origin uncertain⟩

jive² [dʒaɪv] See JIBE³.

job [dʒɒb] *n* **1** a piece of work. **2** employment: *My sister is hunting for a job.* **3** anything a person has to do: *I'm not washing the dishes; that's her job.* **4** *Informal* an affair; matter.
v **jobbed, job·bing 1** buy (goods) from manufacturers and sell to retailers in smaller lots. **2** let out (work) to different contractors, workers, etc. ⟨origin uncertain⟩
a good job good work: *You did a good job on that garden.* **on the job a** at the workplace. **b** attending to one's work or duty.
job·ber *n* **1** a person who buys goods from manufacturers and sells to retailers in smaller lots. **2** a person who works by the job. **3 ✻** *Logging* an operator who undertakes to log a certain area for a specified price. **job·hold·er** *n* a person regularly employed. **job·less** *adj* not having regular work. *n* **the jobless** *pl* people who are unemployed. **job·less·ness** *n.*

Job [dʒoub] *n* any patient, enduring person. ⟨in the Bible, a man who kept his faith in God despite many troubles⟩
Job's comforter a person who increases the misery of the person he or she pretends to comfort. **patience of Job** great self-control despite trouble or irritation.

jock¹ [dʒɒk] *n Informal* jockey.

jock² [dʒɒk] *n* **1** *Slang* a male athlete or sports enthusiast. **2** *Informal* jockstrap. ⟨*jock* formerly, the male genitals; origin uncertain⟩

jock·ey [ˈdʒɒki] *n, pl* **-eys** a person whose occupation is riding horses in races.
v **1** ride (a horse) in a race. **2** trick; cheat: *Swindlers jockeyed her into buying some worthless land.* **3** manoeuvre to get advantage: *The crews were jockeying their boats to get into the best position for the race.* ⟨orig a proper name, diminutive of Scottish *Jock* Jack⟩
jockey for try to win by taking advantage: *jockeying for first place in the competition.*
jockey shorts underpants for boys or men which fit tightly at the crotch. **jock·strap** *n Informal* an elastic supporter for the genitals, used by men when participating in sports.

jo·cose [dʒəˈkous] *adj* jesting; humorous; playful: *jocose remarks.* **jo·cose·ly** *adv.*

jo·cose·ness n. **jo·cos·i·ty** [dʒə'kɒsɪti] n. ⟨Latin *jocosus; jocus* jest⟩
joc·u·lar ['dʒɒkjələr] adj **1** fond of joking. **2** jesting: *a jocular remark*. **joc·u·lar·ly** adv. **joc·u·lar·i·ty** n. **joc·und** ['dʒɒkənd] or ['dʒoʊ-] adj cheerful. **joc·und·ly** adv. **jo·cun·di·ty** n.

jodh·purs ['dʒɒdpərz] n pl breeches for horseback riding, loose above the knees and fitting closely below. ⟨*Jodhpur*, India⟩

jog¹ [dʒɒg] v **jogged, jog·ging 1** shake with a push: *I jogged her elbow to get her attention.* **2** stir up with a reminder: *to jog one's memory.* **3** move up and down with a jerking motion: *The old horse jogged me up and down on its back.* **4** go (on) in a steady fashion: *He is not very enterprising but just jogs along.* **5** run at a slow, steady rate: *I go jogging every day.* **jog** n. **jog·ger** n. ⟨Middle English; origin uncertain⟩ **jog·gle** v shake or jolt slightly: *The milk spilled because you joggled my elbow.* **jog·gle** n.

jog² [dʒɒg] n **1** a part that sticks out or in: *a jog in a wall.* **2** a temporary change in direction: *a jog in the road.* **jog** v. ⟨variant of *jag*⟩

john [dʒɒn] n *Informal* **1** toilet. **2** any man, esp one who is vulnerable to a con game. **3** the male client of a prostitute. ⟨*John* common masculine name⟩
John Doe 1 a fictitious name used in legal forms, proceedings, etc. to represent an unspecified person. **2** an anonymous average man. **John Henry** ['hɛnri] pl **John Henries** *Informal* a person's signature: *Put your John Henry at the bottom of this form.* **Johnny Canuck ✱** a Canadian, esp a member of the armed forces of the First or Second World War. **John·ny–come–late·ly** n, pl **John·ny–come–late·lies, John·nies–come–late·ly** *Informal* a newcomer.

joie de vi·vre [ʒwad'vivʀ] *French* joy of living; enjoyment of life.

join [dʒɔɪn] v **1** bring together: *to join hands.* **2** come together: *The two roads join here.* **3** *Geometry* draw a connecting line between (two points). **4** unite: *to join in marriage.* **5** become a member (of): *to join a club.* n a place or line of joining; seam. ⟨Old French *joindre;* Latin *jungere*⟩
join battle begin to fight. **join forces** give mutual support. **join hands** a shake or clasp hands. **b** agree; co-operate. **join in** take part. **join up** enlist in the armed forces.
join·er n **1** a skilled woodworker. **2** *Informal* a person who joins many clubs, societies, etc.
joint n **1** the place at which two things are joined together. **2** *Anatomy* the junction between two bones that allows movement. **3** a piece of meat for roasting. **4** *Slang* a a low-class place for cheap eating, drinking, or entertainment. **b** any place, building, etc. **5** *Slang* a marijuana cigarette. v **1** connect by a joint. **2** divide at the joints: *Please joint this chicken.* adj shared by two or more persons: *joint efforts.* **out of joint** a out of place at the joint. **b** in bad condition. **joint committee 1 ✱** a committee with members from the Commons and the Senate. **2** any committee with members from different groups. **joint·ed**

adj having joints. **joint·ed·ly** adv. **joint·ly** adv together: *We owned the boat jointly.*

> **SYNONYMS**
> **Join** does not suggest how lasting the association may be: *The two clubs joined forces during the campaign.* **Combine** emphasizes blending one to one, for a common purpose: *He combines business with pleasure.* **Unite** emphasizes the loss of separate interests, etc.: *The members of her family united to help her.*

joist [dʒɔɪst] n one of the horizontal pieces of timber extending across a building. ⟨Old French *giste* pp of *gesir;* Latin *jacēre* to lie²⟩

joke [dʒoʊk] n **1** something said or done to make somebody laugh. **2** a person or thing laughed at. **3** something that is not in earnest. **joke** v. **jok·ing·ly** adv. ⟨Latin *jocus*⟩
crack a joke tell a joke. **no joke** a serious matter: *Poverty is no joke.*
jok·er n **1** a person who tells funny stories or plays tricks on others. **2** *Slang* any person: *Who does that joker think he is?* **3** *Card games* an extra card added in some games as a wild card. **4** *Informal* a phrase in a law, contract, etc. inserted to defeat the original purpose.

jol·ly ['dʒɒli] adj full of fun. adv *Informal* very: *You can jolly well wait.* v *Informal* **1** flatter. **2** tease playfully. n Usually, **jollies** pl *Slang* good times, fun. **jol·li·ly** adv. **jol·li·ness** n. ⟨Old French *joli*⟩ **get one's jollies** *Slang* obtain pleasure: *She gets her jollies by putting people down.* **jol·li·fi·ca·tion** n festivity; merrymaking. **jol·li·fy** v cheer up. **jol·li·ty** n fun; festivity. **Jolly Rog·er** a traditional pirates' flag, with a skull and crossbones on a black background.

jolt [dʒoʊlt] v **1** shake up: *The wagon jolted us when it went over a rock.* **2** move with jerks: *The car jolted across the rough ground.* **3** shock: *She was jolted out of her complacency by news of the firm's bankruptcy.* **jolt** n. **jolt·i·ness** n. **jolt·ing·ly** adv. **jolt·y** adj. ⟨origin uncertain⟩

jon·quil ['dʒɒŋkwɪl] n a plant of the amaryllis family, widely cultivated for its fragrant flowers. ⟨French; Spanish *junquillo* diminutive of *junco* reed; Latin *juncus*⟩

josh [dʒɒʃ] *Slang* v tease playfully. **josh** n. **josh·er** n. ⟨origin uncertain⟩

joss stick a slender stick of fragrant paste, burned as incense. ⟨pidgin English form of Portuguese *deos* god; Latin *deus*⟩

jos·tle ['dʒɒsəl] v **1** push against: *She was jostled by the crowd.* **2** compete (for): *to jostle for position.* **jos·tle** n. **jos·tler** n. ⟨*joust*⟩

jot [dʒɒt] v **jot·ted, jot·ting** write briefly or in haste: *The clerk jotted down the order.* n the tiniest bit or amount: *I do not care a jot.* **jot·ter** n. ⟨Latin, Greek *iōta* iota, smallest letter in the Greek alphabet⟩ **jot·ting** n a short, informal note.

joual [ʒwɑl], [ʒu'ɑl], or [ʒu'æl] n ✱ uneducated or dialectal Canadian French. ⟨Cdn. French pronunciation of *cheval* horse⟩

joule [dʒul] n *Physics* an SI unit for measuring energy. One joule is the amount of work done in applying one newton of force to move a body one metre. *Symbol* **J** ⟨James Prescott *Joule* 19c English physicist⟩

jour·nal [ˈdʒɜrnəl] *n* **1** a daily record such as a diary, or written records of the meetings of a society. **2** a newspaper or magazine. **3** *Bookkeeping* **a** a book in which every item of business is written down to be entered later under the proper account. **b** a daybook. ⟨Old French; Latin *diurnalis* daily; *dies* day⟩ **jour·nal·ese** *n* a loose style of writing such as is sometimes used in newspapers, magazines etc. **jour·nal·ism** *n* the work of writing for editing, or publishing a newspaper or magazine. **jour·nal·ist** *n*. **jour·nal·is·tic** *adj*. **jour·nal·is·ti·cal·ly** *adv*.

jour·ney [ˈdʒɜrni] *n pl* **-neys** **1** a trip, esp a fairly long one: *a journey around the world.* **2** a passage from one stage to another: *one's journey through life.* **jour·ney** *v*. ⟨Old French *journée* a day's travel; Latin *diurnus* of one day; *dies* day⟩

jour·ney·man [ˈdʒɜrnimən] *n pl* **-men** **1** a worker who has completed an apprenticeship, but who is not a master or employer. **2** a person who is a competent worker or performer, but is not outstanding. ⟨orig paid by the day. See JOURNEY.⟩

joust [dʒaust] *n* **1** formerly, a combat between two knights on horseback, in which each tried to unseat the other with his lance. **2** Usually, **jousts** *pl* a tournament consisting of a series of such combats. **joust** *v*. **joust·er** *n*. Compare TILT. ⟨Old French *jouster*; Latin *juxtare* be next to *juxta* beside⟩

Jove [dʒouv] *n Roman myth* Jupiter. **jo·vi·al** *adj* good-hearted and full of fun. ⟨Latin *Jovialis* of Jupiter; for supposed traits of those born under the planet's sign⟩ **jo·vi·al·ly** *adv*. **jo·vi·al·ness** *n*. **jo·vi·al·i·ty** *n* merriment.

jowl [dʒaul] *n* **1** the lower jaw. **2** cheek. **3** a fold of flesh hanging from the neck. **jowled** *adj*. **jowl·y** *adj*. ⟨Old English *ceafl* influenced by French *joue* cheek⟩

joy [dʒɔɪ] *n* **1** a strong feeling of pleasure. **2** something that causes gladness: *It was a joy to see her.* **3** outward rejoicing. **joy·ful** *adj*. **joy·ful·ly** *adj*. **joy·ful·ness** *n*. **joy·less** *adj*. **joy·less·ly** *adv*. **joy·less·ness** *n*. ⟨Old French *joie* Latin *gaudia* pl of *gaudium* joy⟩ **joy·ous** *adj* joyful; glad: *a joyous song.* **joy·ous·ly** *adv*. **joy·ous·ness** *n*. **joy ride** *Informal* a ride in a car for pleasure, esp when the car is driven recklessly or is used without permission. **joy–ride** *v*. **joy–rid·er** *n*. **joy·stick** *n Computers* a computer input device in which the movement of a small lever causes a corresponding movement on the screen.

J.P. JUSTICE OF THE PEACE.

Jr. or **jr.** junior.

ju·bi·lant [ˈdʒubələnt] *adj* rejoicing; exulting: *The people were jubilant when the war was over.* **ju·bi·lant·ly** *adv*. **ju·bi·la·tion** *n*. ⟨Latin *jubilare* shout with joy; *jubilum* wild shout⟩

ju·bi·lee [ˌdʒubəˈli] or [ˈdʒubə,li] *n* **1** an anniversary thought of as a time of rejoicing: *a fiftieth wedding jubilee.* **2** a time of rejoicing: *to have a jubilee in celebration of a victory.* **3** *Roman Catholic Church* a year in which punishment for sin is remitted, after repentance and the performance of certain acts. **4** in the Old Testament, a year of rest, and redistribution of wealth, which was to happen every 50 years. ⟨Latin *jubilaeus*; Hebrew *yobel* trumpet; orig ram's horn, ram⟩

Ju·da·ism [ˈdʒudi,ɪzəm] or [ˈdʒudei,ɪzəm] *n* the religion of the Jews, based on the teachings of Moses and the prophets as found in the Bible and in the Talmud. ⟨Latin *Judaeus* Jew. See JEW.⟩ **Ju·dae·o–Chris·tian** or **Judeo–Christian** [dʒuˈdeiou-] *adj* common to both Christianity and Judaism: *the Judaeo-Christian heritage.* **Ju·da·ic** [dʒuˈdeiɪk] *adj* of the Jews; Jewish. **Ju·da·i·cal** *adj*. **Ju·da·i·cal·ly** *adv*. **Ju·da·i·ca** *n pl* books about Jewish life and Judaism.

judge [dʒʌdʒ] *n* **1** a government official appointed or elected to hear cases in court. In Canada all judges are appointed. **2** a person chosen to settle a dispute. **3** a person who can decide how good a thing is. *v* **1** hear in a court of law. **2** settle (a dispute). **3** form an opinion of: *to judge the merits of a book.* **4** condemn: *to judge a person harshly.* **5** think; conclude: *I judged that you had forgotten to come.* **judg·er** *n*. **judge·a·ble** *adj*. **judge·like** *adj*. **judge·ship** *n*. ⟨Old French *juge* Latin *judex; jus* law + root of *dicere* say⟩ **judg·ment** or **judge·ment** [ˈdʒʌdʒmənt] *n* **1** the act of judging. **2** *Law* **a** a decision given by a judge or court of law. **b** a debt arising from a judge's decision. **3** an opinion: *It was a bad plan, in my judgment.* **4** good sense. **5** a decision made by anybody who judges. **6** condemnation. **7** a misfortune considered as a punishment from God: *The neighbours considered his broken leg a judgment for his deeds.* **judg·men·tal** or **judge·men·tal** *adj* too ready to criticize. **Judgment Day** the day of God's final judgment of humankind at the end of the world. **ju·di·ca·to·ry** [ˈdʒudəkə,tɔri] *adj* to do with the administration of justice. *n* **1** the administration of justice. **2** a court of law. **ju·di·cial** [dʒuˈdɪʃəl] *adj* **1** to do with the administration of justice. **2** ordered by a court of law. **3** impartial: *a judicial decision.* **ju·di·cial·ly** *adv*. **ju·di·ci·ar·y** [dʒuˈdɪʃəri] or [dʒuˈdɪʃi,eri] *n* **1** the branch of government that administers justice. **2** judges as a group. *adj* to do with the administration of justice. **ju·di·cious** [dʒuˈdɪʃəs] *adj* showing good judgment: *a judicious use of money.* **ju·di·cious·ly** *adv*. **ju·di·cious·ness** *n*.

ju·do [ˈdʒudou] *n* a form of jujitsu, a martial art. **ju·do·ist** *n*. ⟨Japanese *ju* gentle + *do* art⟩

jug [dʒʌg] *n* **1** a container for liquids, usually with a handle **2** *Slang* jail. *v* **jugged, jug·ging 1** *Slang* jail. **2** stew in an earthenware container: *to jug hare.* ⟨probably orig proper name, alteration of *Joan*⟩

Jug·ger·naut [ˈdʒʌgər,nɒt] *n* **1** *Hinduism* **a** Krishna. **b** an idol of Krishna that is pulled through the streets on a huge chariot at an annual festival. **2 juggernaut** a huge, overpowering force that destroys everything in its path. ⟨Hindi *Jagannath*, Sanskrit *Jagannatha; jagat* world + *natha* lord⟩

jug·gle [ˈdʒʌgəl] *v* **1** keep (several objects) in the air by rapidly tossing them and catching them as they fall. **2** manage to keep (several activities, etc.) going at the same time: *juggling two jobs.* **3** manipulate so as to cheat: *juggling accounts to hide a theft.* **jug·gle** *n.* **jug·gling·ly** *adv.* **jug·gler** *n.* **jug·gler·y** *n.* ⟨Old French *jogler;* Latin *joculari* to joke; *jocus* jest⟩

jug·u·lar [ˈdʒʌgjələr] *adj* **1** of the neck or throat. **2** of the jugular vein. ⟨Latin *jugulum* collarbone, diminutive of *jugum* yoke⟩
go for the jugular *Slang* attack the weakest part (of an argument, speech, etc.).
jugular vein one of the two large veins on either side of the neck that return blood from the head to the heart.

juice [dʒus] *n* **1** the liquid in fruits, meats, and vegetables. **2** *Slang* electricity. **3** *Slang* gasoline. **juice·less** *adj.* ⟨Latin *jus* broth⟩
juic·er *n* an apparatus for squeezing juice out of fruits or vegetables. **juic·y** *adj* **1** full of juice. **2** full of interest. **juic·i·ly** *adv.* **juic·i·ness** *n.*

ju·jit·su [dʒuˈdʒɪtsu] *n* a traditional Japanese method of fighting without weapons. Also, **ju·jut·su, jiu·jit·su, jiu·jut·su.** ⟨Japanese *jū* soft + *jutsu* art⟩

ju·jube [ˈdʒudʒub] *n* a candy made of gelatin. ⟨French *jujube* or Latin *jujuba;* Greek *zizyphon*⟩

juke box [dʒuk] *Informal* a machine that plays music when money is deposited in a slot. ⟨Gullah *juke* disorderly, wicked; for machine's origin in cheap inns⟩

Julian calendar [ˈdʒuliən] a calendar in which the average length of a year was 365 days, introduced by Julius Caesar in 46 B.C.

ju·li·enne [ˌdʒuliˈɛn] *adj* (after the noun) of vegetables, cut into strips: *potatoes julienne.*
n a clear soup containing vegetables cut into strips or small pieces. ⟨French⟩

Ju·ly [dʒəˈlaɪ] *n* the seventh month of the year. It has 31 days. ⟨Latin *Julius (Caesar)*⟩

jum·ble [ˈdʒʌmbəl] *v* mix: *She jumbled up everything in the drawer.*
n a confused mixture. **jum·ble·ment** *n.* **jum·bler** *n.* **jum·bly** *adj.* ⟨perhaps imitative⟩

jum·bo [ˈdʒʌmbou] *Informal n* something unusually large of its kind.
adj very big: *a jumbo burger.* ⟨*Jumbo,* elephant exhibited by P.T. Barnum, 19c US showman⟩
jumbo jet a very large passenger airplane.

jump [dʒʌmp] *v* **1** leap: *to jump high.* **2** cause to jump: *to jump a horse over a fence.* **3** give a sudden start: *You made me jump.* **4** rise suddenly: *Prices jumped.* **5** *Checkers* pass over and capture (an opponent's piece). **6** pounce upon: *The robbers jumped the shopkeeper.*
n **1** the act of jumping. **2** something to be jumped over. **3** the distance jumped. **4** a contest in jumping. **5** a sudden nervous start.

6 a sudden rise. **7** a sudden and abrupt transition from one thing to another. **8 the jumps** *Informal* a nervous condition characterized by sudden starts or jerks. **jump·a·ble** *adj.* ⟨probably imitative⟩
get or **have the jump on** *Slang* get or have an advantage over. **jump a claim** seize a piece of land claimed by another. **jump at** accept eagerly. **jump** (or **skip**) **bail** fail to appear for trial after having been released on bail. **jump on** *Slang* blame; scold. **jump ship a** desert a vessel. **b** leave a commitment before the proper time. **jump the track** of a train, leave the rails suddenly. **jump to conclusions** make an unfair assessment based on little evidence. **jump to it!** *Informal* be quick! **on the jump** *Informal* rushing around; busy.
jump ball *Basketball* the putting of the ball into play by the referee, who tosses it between two opposing players. **jump·er** *n* **1** a person who or thing that jumps. **2** a sleigh on low wooden runners. **3** a short length of wire used to bypass part of an electric circuit. **jumper cables** BOOSTER CABLES. **jumping bean** a seed of any of various shrubs of the spurge family that contains a moth caterpillar whose movements cause the seed to jump. **jumping jack 1** a toy that can be made to jump by pulling a string. **2** an exercise imitating the movement of such a toy. **jump·ing–off place** or **point 1 ⚓** *esp North* a place, usually a town, where one leaves the railway or other link with civilization to proceed into the wilderness. **2** any starting place. **3** any place considered the ultimate in wilderness. **jump–off** *adj* beginning; starting: *a jump-off place for exploration parties.* **jump shot** or **pass** *Basketball* a play in which a player throws the ball while at the height of his or her jump. **jump–start** *v* **1** start a vehicle by the use of booster cables. **2** vitalize with an infusion of money, energy, etc.: *The politician jump-started her campaign by funding a huge picnic.* **jump·suit** *n* a one-piece garment consisting of a top and pants, orig applied to a suit worn by parachutists. **jump·y** *adj* **1** moving by jumps. **2** easily excited or frightened. **jump·i·ly** *adv.* **jump·i·ness** *n.*

SYNONYMS
Leap emphasizes springing high, and suggests more grace than **jump**: *She leaped lightly to the opposite bank of the stream.*

jump·er[1] See JUMP.
jump·er[2] [ˈdʒʌmpər] *n* **1** a sleeveless dress usually worn over a blouse. **2** a loose short jacket, esp as part of a sailor's uniform. ⟨*jump* short coat; perhaps from French *juppe;* Arabic *jubbah* long open coat⟩

junc·tion [ˈdʒʌŋkʃən] *n* **1** a joining or being joined: *the junction of two rivers.* **2** a place where things meet. **3** a connection between parts of a transmission line. ⟨Latin *junctio; jungere* join⟩

junc·ture [ˈdʒʌŋktʃər] *n* **1** a point of time. **2** a state of affairs. **3** crisis. **4** joint. **5** a joining or being joined. ⟨Latin *junctura; jungere* join⟩

June [dʒun] *n* the sixth month of the year. It has 30 days. ⟨Latin *Junius* orig a Roman name⟩

jun·gle ['dʒʌŋgəl] *n* **1** wild tropical region thickly overgrown with bushes, vines, etc. **2** a tangled mass. **3** a place of vicious competition: *The city is a jungle.* **jun·gled** *adj.* **jun·gly** *adj.* ⟨Sanskrit *jāngala* desert, forest⟩

jun·ior ['dʒunjər] *adj* **1** of lower position, rank, or standing: *a junior officer.* **2** to do with students in grades 4 to 6. **3** of or for young people: *a junior tennis match.* **junior** *n.* ⟨Latin comparative of *juvenis* young⟩
be someone's junior be younger than someone.
junior college a college giving only the first year or two of a university degree program.
junior high school any school intermediate between elementary school and high school.

ju·ni·per ['dʒunəpər] *n* any of a genus of evergreens of the cypress family, having fragrant wood. ⟨Latin *juniperus*⟩

junk¹ [dʒʌŋk] *n* **1** old metal, paper, rags, etc. **2** *Informal* trash. **3** *Slang* a narcotic drug such as heroin or morphine; dope.
v Informal throw away: *We junked the old chairs last fall.* **junk·y** *adj.* ⟨origin uncertain⟩
junk bond any bond that promises a yield that it cannot make. **junk food** prepackaged food having a little nutritive value. **junk·ie** *n Slang* **1** a drug addict. **2** a person who is addicted to anything: *an Internet junkie.* **junk mail** unsolicited mail consisting of advertisements. **junk·yard** *n* a yard for the collection and resale of junk.

junk² [dʒʌŋk] *n* a sailing ship traditionally used esp by the Chinese, with sails stiffened by horizontal battens. ⟨Portuguese *junco*; probably Javanese *jong*⟩

jun·ket ['dʒʌŋkɪt] *n* **1** a feast, picnic. **2** *Informal* an unnecessary trip taken by an official at the expense of the government or the firm he or she works for. **jun·ket** *v.* **jun·ket·er** or **jun·ke·teer** *n.* ⟨dialect Old French *jonquette* basket; *jonc* reed Latin *juncus*⟩

jun·ta ['hʊntə], ['dʒʊntə], *or* ['dʒʌntə]; *Spanish* ['xʊnta] *n* a group of people forming a government, esp as the result of a revolution: *a military junta.* ⟨Spanish, from Latin *jungere* join⟩

Jupiter ['dʒupətər] *n* **1** *Roman myth* the chief god, corresponding to the Greek god Zeus. **2** the largest planet, fifth from the sun.

Ju·ras·sic [dʒɔ'ræsɪk] *n Geology* the middle period of the Mesozoic era, starting about 208 million years ago. **Ju·ras·sic** *adj.* ⟨French *jurassique*; Jura Mountains⟩

ju·ris·dic·tion [,dʒʊrɪs'dɪkʃən] *n* **1** the right of administering law. **2** the extent of authority: *The case was not within this jurisdiction.* **ju·ris·dic·tion·al** *adj.* ⟨Latin *jurisdictio; juris* law + *dicere* say⟩

ju·ris·pru·dence [,dʒʊrɪs'prudəns] *n* **1** the science of law. **2** a branch of law: *medical jurisprudence.* **ju·ris·pru·den·tial** *adj.*
ju·ris·pru·den·tial·ly *adv.* ⟨Latin *jurisprudentia; juris* law + *prudentia* prudence⟩

ju·rist *n* **1** an expert in law. **2** a civil lawyer. **3** a judge.

ju·ry ['dʒʊri] *n pl* **ju·ries 1** a group of persons selected to give a verdict based on the evidence. **2** a group of persons chosen to decide the winner in a contest. **ju·ror** *n.* ⟨Anglo-French *jurie; jurer* swear, Latin *jurare*⟩

ju·ry–rigged ['dʒʊri ˌrɪgd] *adj* rigged for temporary usually emergency use. ⟨*jury* makeshift; probably Old French *ajurie, adjutorie* help. See ADJUTANT.⟩

just [dʒʌst] *adj* **1** fair. **2** righteous: *a just life.* **3** deserved: *just rewards.* **4** lawful: *a just claim. adv* **1** exactly: *just a metre.* **2** very close: *a picture just above the fireplace.* **3** a short while ago: *She has just gone.* **4** barely: *I just managed to catch the train.* **5** only: *just an ordinary man.* **6** *Informal* truly: *just perfect.* **just·ness** *n.* **just·ly** *adv.* ⟨Latin *justus* upright; *jus* right law⟩
just now a exactly at this moment. **b** a very short time ago: *I saw her just now.*

jus·tice ['dʒʌstɪs] *n* **1** fair dealing: *a sense of justice.* **2** well-founded reason: *He complained with justice of the bad treatment he had received.* **3** deserved reward or punishment. **4** the administration of law. **5** Justice in Canada and the UK, the title of a judge. **bring someone to justice** do what is necessary so that a person shall be legally punished. **do justice to a** treat fairly. **b** show appreciation for: *She did justice to the dinner.* **do oneself justice** do as well as one can do. **justice of the peace** a provincial judicial officer who tries cases involving infractions of by-laws, administers oaths, etc. *Abbrev* **J.P. jus·ti·fy** *v* **1** show to be just: *The fine quality justifies the high price.* **2** show a good reason for (something done). **3** *Printing* adjust the spaces between the words of (a line) so that the line gives an even right-hand margin.
jus·ti·fi·a·ble *adj.* **jus·ti·fi·a·bil·i·ty** *n.*
jus·ti·fi·a·bly *adv.* **jus·ti·fi·ca·tion** *n.* **jus·ti·fi·er** *n.*

jut [dʒʌt] *v* **jut·ted, jut·ting** stick out: *The pier juts out into the water.* **jut** *n.* ⟨variant of *jet*¹⟩

jute [dʒut] *n* a fibre used for making sacks, rope, etc. ⟨Sanskrit *jata* mat of hair⟩

ju·ve·nile ['dʒuvə,naɪl] *or* ['dʒuvənəl] *adj* **1** youthful. **2** of or for young people: *juvenile books.* **3** behaving younger than one's years. *n* **1** a young person. **2** an actor who plays youthful parts. **3** a young bird. ⟨Latin *juvenis* young⟩
juvenile court a law court where cases involving children and adolescents are heard. **juvenile delinquency** criminal behaviour by adolescents and children. **juvenile delinquent.**

jux·ta·pose [,dʒʌkstə'pouz] *v* put side by side. **jux·ta·po·si·tion** *n.* ⟨French *juxtaposer;* Latin *juxta* beside + French *poser* place. See POSE¹.⟩

Kk

k or **K** [kei] *n, pl* **k's** or **K's** **1** the eleventh letter of the English alphabet, or any speech sound represented by it. **2** the eleventh person or thing in a series. **3** *Slang* kilometre: *It's 24 k's to the nearest town.*

k **1** kilo- (an SI prefix). **2** karat.

K¹ **1** potassium (for Latin *Kalium*). **2** kelvin(s). **3** karat.

K² **1** one thousand. **2** a unit of computer memory. One K of computer memory is 1024 bytes. ⟨*kilo-*⟩

Kaa·ba ['kɑbə] *n* the most sacred Muslim shrine, a small structure within the Great Mosque at Mecca, toward which Muslims face when praying. Also, **Caa·ba**. ⟨Arabic *ka'bah*, literally, a square building⟩

Kab·loo·na or **kab·loo·na** [kæb'lunə] *n* ✱ a white person; person of European descent. Also, **Kad·loo·na**. ⟨Inuktitut *kabluna(k)* one with big eyebrows⟩

kad·dish ['kɑdɪʃ] or [kɑ'dɪʃ] *n, pl* **kad·dish·im** [-im] *Judaism* a prayer used as a public or official prayer of mourning for a dead relative. ⟨Aramaic *qaddish* holy⟩

ka·fuf·fle [kə'fʌfəl] *n* disorder; fuss. Also, **ker·fuf·fle**.

Kah·na·wa·ke [ˌgɑnɑ'wɑgi] *n* a member of First Nations people living near Montréal. **Kahnawake** *adj.* Also called **Caughnawaugha**.

Kai·la ['kaɪlə] *n* the supreme god of the Inuit. ⟨Inuktitut⟩

Kai·nai ['kaɪnaɪ] *n* **1** a member of a First Nations people living in Alberta. **2** their language. **Kainai** *adj.* Also called **Blood**.

kai·ser¹ ['kaɪzər] *n* the former title of the emperors of Germany and of Austria. ⟨Latin *Caesar*⟩

kai·ser² ['kaɪzər] *n* a large bun used especially for sliced meat sandwiches. Also called **kaiser bun, kaiser roll.** ⟨short for German *kaisersemmel* kaiser bun, emperor's bun; invented for Emperor Frederick V, 1487.⟩

kale [keil] *n* any of various kinds of cabbage that have loose leaves instead of a compact head. ⟨variant of *cole*, Old English *cāl*; Latin *caulis* cabbage⟩

ka·lei·do·scope [kə'laɪdə,skoup] *n* **1** a tube containing bits of coloured glass and mirrors. As it is turned, it reflects changing patterns. **2** anything that changes continually. **ka·lei·do·scop·ic** [kə,laɪdə'skɒpɪk] *adj.* **ka·lei·do·scop·i·cal·ly** *adv.* ⟨Greek *kalos* pretty + *eidos* shape + -SCOPE⟩

Ka·li ['kɑli] *n Hinduism* goddess of life and death, the wife of Shiva.

ka·lo·tik ['kælətɪk] *n* a special hook for towing home a seal. ⟨Inuktitut⟩

Ka·ma·su·tra [ˌkɑmə'sutrə] *n* the Hindu manual of erotic love, written in Sanskrit. Also, **Kama sutra.** ⟨Sanskrit *kama* love + *sutra* guideline, manual⟩

ka·mi ['kɑmi] *n, pl* **ka·mi** *Shintoism* any divine spirit. ⟨Japanese⟩

ka·mik ['kɑmɪk] *n* ✱ a soft, knee-length boot of sealskin or caribou hide, worn in eastern arctic regions; mukluk. ⟨Inuktitut⟩

ka·mi·ka·ze [ˌkɑmɪ'kɑzi] *n* **1** a member of a Japanese air corps in World War II that carried out suicide missions in which an aircraft was deliberately crashed on a target. **2** *Informal* a person who behaves in a self-destructive manner. **ka·mi·ka·ze** *adj.* ⟨Japanese = divine wind⟩

ka·na ['kɑnə] *n* Japanese syllabic writing. ⟨Japanese⟩

kan·ga·roo [ˌkæŋgə'ru] *n, pl* **-roos** or (esp collectively) **-roo** any of a family of marsupials, typically having hind legs adapted for leaping. See also WALLABY. **kan·ga·roo·like** *adj.* ⟨origin uncertain⟩

kangaroo court *Informal* an unauthorized court held by a group in order to try someone suspected of a crime, esp without good evidence.

Kan·i·en'·ke·ha [kæn,jən'kei,hæ] *n, pl* **Kan·i·en'·ke·ha·ka** [-kæ] **1** a member of a First Nations people living in Ontario and Québec. **2** their language. **Kanien'keha** *adj.* Also called **Mohawk**.

kan·ji ['kɑndʒi] *n, pl* **-ji** or **-jis** ideographic Japanese script using Chinese symbols. ⟨Japanese *kan* Chinese + *ji* ideograph⟩

ka·o·lin or **ka·o·line** ['keiəlɪn] *n* a fine, white clay, used in making porcelain. ⟨*Kaoling* mountain in China which yielded the first kaolin sent to Europe; *kao* high + *ling* hill⟩

ka·on ['kei,ɒn] *n Physics* a K-meson, any of four mesons whose mass is almost a thousand times that of an electron. ⟨*K- meson; K* symbol for one thousand + *meson*⟩

ka·pok ['keipɒk] *n* the silky fibres around the seeds of a certain tropical tree, used for stuffing pillows, life preservers, etc. ⟨Malay⟩

Ka·po·si's sar·co·ma [kə'pouziz sɑr'koumə] a skin cancer due to a deficiency in the immune system. ⟨M.K. *Kaposi* 19c Hungarian dermatologist⟩

ka·put [kə'pʊt] *adj Informal* ruined, broken, useless, etc. (never before a noun): *All our plans are kaput.* ⟨German, from French *être capot* be without a score in piquet⟩

ka·ra·o·ke [ˌkɛri'ouki] or [ˌkæri'ouki] *n* a system allowing a person to sing to recorded music. ⟨Japanese⟩

kar·at ['kɛrət] or ['kærət] *n* a unit used to specify the proportion of gold in an alloy; one of 24 equal parts. An 18-karat gold ring is 18 parts pure gold and 6 parts alloy. *Symbol* **K** or **k.** Compare CARAT.

ka·ra·te [kə'rɑti] *n* a Japanese system of self-defence without weapons, using hand and foot strokes capable of crippling or killing. ⟨Japanese, literally, empty-handed⟩

kar·ma ['kɑrmə] *n* 1 *Buddhism, Hinduism* the totality of a person's thoughts, actions, etc. that are supposed to affect his or her fate in his or her next incarnation. 2 destiny; fate. **kar·mic** *adj.* ⟨Sanskrit *karma* deed, fate⟩

kart [kɑrt] *n* go-kart.
v take part in a go-kart race. **kart·er** *n.*

kar·y·o·type ['kɛriə,taɪp] *or* ['kæriə,taɪp] *n Genetics* the chromosome constitution of an individual. **kar·y·o·typ·ic** [-'tɪpək] *or* **kar·y·o·typ·i·cal** *adj.*

kash·ruth [kɑʃ'rut] *or* ['kɑʃrut] *n* dietary laws prescribed for Jews. ⟨Hebrew, literally, fitness⟩

Kas·ka ['kaskə] *n, pl* **-ka** *or* **-kas** 1 a member of a First Nations people living in northern British Columbia and the Yukon. 2 their Athapascan language. **Kas·ka** *adj.*

ka·ty·did ['keiti,dɪd] *n* any large grasshopper. ⟨imitative of the insect's sound⟩

kay·ak ['kaɪæk] *n* a light, narrow boat with pointed ends, made of skins, etc. over a frame, leaving an opening for the user. It is propelled by a double-bladed paddle. **kay·ak·er** *n.* **kay·ak·ing** *n.* ⟨Inuktitut⟩

Ka·yon·kwe'·ha·ka See CAYUGA.

ka·za·chok [,kɑzɑ'tʃouk] *n* a Russian folk dance in which the dancer kicks vigorously with alternate legs while in a squatting position. ⟨Russian *Kazakh* Cossack⟩

ka·zoo [kə'zu] *n* a toy musical instrument made of a tube sealed off at one end. ⟨imitative⟩

KB *Computers* kilobyte.

ke·bab [kə'bɒb] *n* a dish comprising pieces of meat and vegetables cooked on a skewer. Also, **ka·bob.** ⟨Arabic *kabab*⟩

keek·wil·lie (house) ['kikwɪli] *n* ✹ a large subterranean winter dwelling formerly used by certain First Nations peoples. ⟨Chinook Jargon = below; Chinook *gigwalix*⟩

keel [kil] *n* 1 *Nautical* the main timber or steel piece that extends the whole length of the bottom of a boat. 2 *Botany, zoology* a longitudinal ridge on a leaf or bone. ⟨Middle English *kele*; Old Norse *kjölr*⟩
keel over a turn upside down: *The sailboat keeled over in the storm.* **b** *Informal* fall over. **on an even keel a** horizontal. **b** steady: *His business affairs are on an even keel again.*
keel·haul ['kil,hɒl] *v* formerly, haul (a person) from side to side under the keel of a ship as a punishment.

keen[1] [kin] *adj* 1 sharp enough to cut well: *a keen blade.* 2 sharp; piercing: *a keen wind.* 3 vigorous: *keen competition.* 4 able to do its work quickly and accurately: *a keen sense of smell.* 5 *Informal* full of enthusiasm (often with *about, for,* etc.): *a keen player.* **keen·ly** *adv.* **keen·ness** *n.* ⟨Middle English *kene*; Old English *cēne*⟩

be keen on a like: *She's very keen on desserts.* **b** approve of: *I'm not keen on your staying out so late.*
keen·er *n Slang* an enthusiastic participant.

keen[2] [kin] *n* a wailing lament for the dead. *v* wail; lament. **keen·er** *n.* ⟨Irish *caoine*⟩

keep [kip] *v* **kept, keep·ing** 1 have permanently: *You may keep this book.* 2 not let go: *They were kept in prison.* 3 take care of: *My uncle keeps chickens.* 4 have; hold: *keep this in mind.* 5 hold back: *What is keeping her from accepting?* 6 restrain oneself (*from*): *The little boy couldn't keep from crying.* 7 maintain or stay in good condition: *to keep a house.* 8 be postponable without ill effect: *This matter will keep.* 9 continue or cause to continue in some stated place, condition, etc.: *to keep awake.* 10 make regular entries in: *to keep books.* 11 celebrate: *to keep Thanksgiving.* 12 be faithful (to): *to keep a promise.* 13 provide for: *He is not able to keep himself, much less a family.*
n 1 food and a place to sleep; maintenance: *She earns her keep.* 2 the strongest part of a castle or fort. ⟨Old English *cēpan* observe⟩
for keeps a for the winner to keep his or her winnings. **b** *Informal* forever. **keep in with** *Informal* keep acquaintance with. **keep on** continue: *The boys kept on swimming.* **keep time a** of watches, clocks, etc., go correctly. **b** maintain a tempo: *The choir kept time well.* **keep to oneself a** not mix with others. **b** not reveal to others. **keep up a** continue. **b** maintain in good condition. **c** not fall behind. **keep up with a** not fall behind. **b** live or do as well as: *She tried hard to keep up with her wealthy neighbours.* **c** stay up to date with: *She keeps up with the news.*
keep·er *n* 1 a person who keeps or looks after something or someone. 2 a person who owns or runs some establishment: *the keeper of an inn.* 3 *Informal* anything that one wishes to keep. **keep·er·less** *adj.* **keep·ing** *n* 1 care: *She left the jewels in my keeping.* 2 agreement: *His actions are not in keeping with his promises.* **keep·sake** *n* something kept in memory of the giver.

SYNONYMS
Keep is the general word meaning 'not let go from one's possession or care': *They were kept in prison.* **Retain,** more formal, emphasizes continuing to hold on to in spite of difficulties: *The patient retained her sense of humour.*

keg [kɛg] *n* a small barrel. ⟨Old Norse *kaggi*⟩

kelp [kɛlp] *n* any of the large, brown seaweeds. ⟨Middle English *culp(e)*⟩

kel·vin ['kɛlvɪn] *adj Physics* **Kelvin** to do with a scale of temperature on which 0 represents absolute zero, theoretically the coldest possible state. Zero on the Kelvin scale is equal to –273.16°C.
n an SI unit of temperature. One kelvin is equal to one degree Celsius. *Symbol* **K** ⟨Lord *Kelvin* 19c English physicist⟩

ken [kɛn] *n* 1 the range of sight. 2 the range of knowledge: *What happens on Mars is* *beyond our ken.* ⟨Old English *cennan* make declaration; *cann* know, can[1]⟩

ken·nel ['kɛnəl] *n* 1 a house for a dog. 2 Often, **kennels** *pl* **a** a place where dogs are bred. **b** a place where dogs and cats may be lodged and cared for. ⟨Latin *canis* dog⟩

ke·no ['kinou] *n* a gambling game resembling bingo in which the players cover numbers on their cards. ⟨French *quine* five winning numbers; Latin *quini* five each⟩

kep·i ['keipi] *or* ['kɛpi] *n, pl* **kep·is** a cap with a round, flat top, worn by French soldiers. ⟨French *képi*; German *Kappe* cap⟩

kept [kɛpt] *v* pt and pp of KEEP.

ker·a·tin ['kerətɪn] *n* Zoology a complex protein, the chief constituent of horn, nails, hair, feathers, etc. **ke·rat·i·nous** or **ke·rat·i·noid** [kə'ræt-] *adj*. ⟨Greek *keras, -atos* horn⟩

ker·chief ['kɜrtʃɪf] *n* a piece of cloth worn over the head or around the neck. **ker·chiefed** *adj*. ⟨Old French *couvrechief; couvrir* cover + *chief* head⟩

ker·nel ['kɜrnəl] *n* 1 the softer part inside the shell of a nut or inside the stone of a fruit. 2 a seed of a grain like wheat. 3 the central part: *the kernel of an argument.* ⟨Old English *cyrnel* diminutive of *corn* seed, grain⟩

ker·o·sene ['kerə,sin] *or* [,kerə'sin] *n* ✸ a thin oil, a mixture of hydrocarbons, used as a fuel in lamps, stoves, etc. ⟨Greek *kēros* wax⟩ **kerosene lamp** ✸ a lamp that burns kerosene.

kes·trel ['kɛstrəl] *n* any of several small falcons noted for their habit of hovering against the wind just before diving. ⟨probably Old French *cresserelle*; Latin *crista* crest⟩

ket·a ['kɛtə] *or* ['kitə] *n, pl* **ket·a** ✸ a species of Pacific salmon, the chum. ⟨origin uncertain⟩

ketch [kɛtʃ] *n* Nautical a sailing ship with a mainmast toward the bow and a smaller mast toward the stern. ⟨perhaps from *catch*⟩

ketch·up ['kɛtʃəp] *or* ['kætʃəp] *n* a sauce made of tomatoes, onions, salt, sugar, and spices. Also, **cat·sup**. ⟨Malay *kechap* sauce⟩

ke·tone ['kitoun] *n* Chemistry one of a group of organic compounds such as acetone. **ke·ton·ic** [ki'tɒnɪk] *adj*. ⟨German *keton*; French *acétone*⟩

ket·tle ['kɛtəl] *n* 1 a metal container for boiling liquids, cooking fruit, etc. 2 Geology a depression in glacial drift remaining after the melting of an isolated mass of buried ice. ⟨Old English *cetel;* Latin *catillus* diminutive of *catinus* vessel⟩ **kettle of fish** an awkward state of affairs. **ket·tle·drum** *n* a drum consisting of a hollow metal hemisphere and a parchment top.

key¹ [ki] *n, pl* **keys** *n* 1 an instrument that locks and unlocks. 2 anything like this in shape or use: *a key to open a can of sardines.* 3 something that explains or answers: *the key to a puzzle.* 4 an important or essential person, thing, etc. 5 a device to turn a bolt or nut, etc. 6 one of a set of parts pressed down by the fingers in playing a piano, a woodwind instrument, etc. and in keyboarding. 7 *Music* a scale of related tones based on a particular tone: *a song written in the key of B flat.* 8 an explanation of symbols used in a map, etc. 9 a means to achieve something: *the key to success.* 10 *Basketball* the space, including the foul line, in front of each basket. 11 *Botany* a seed with winglike appendages.
adj very important: *key industries.*
v 1 *Music* regulate the pitch of: *to key a piano for a concert.* 2 give a particular style, etc. to: *Her performance is keyed to a young audience.* **key·less** *adj*. ⟨Old English *cǣg*⟩ **key in** enter data, etc. by means of a keyboard. **keyed up a** excited. **b** make or be overexcited: *too keyed up to concentrate.* **key up** raise the courage or nerve of: *The coach keyed up the team for the big game.*
key block a large, conical block of snow, dropped into place at the centre of an igloo dome, serving to lock the structure firmly together. **key·board** ['ki,bɔrd] *n* 1 the set of keys on a piano, calculator, computer, etc. 2 any musical instrument having a keyboard, such as a synthesizer. *v* operate the keyboard of a computer. **key·board·ing** *n*. **key·chain** *n* a small chain to which keys may be attached. **keyed** *adj* having keys: *a keyed flute.* **key·hole** *n* an opening in a lock through which a key is inserted. **key·note** *n* 1 *Music* the note on which a scale is based. 2 the main idea: *World peace was the keynote of her speech.* **keynote speech** or **keynote address** a speech, that addresses the principal issues in which those present are interested. **key·pad** *n* 1 that part of a computer keyboard that contains numbers and special keys. 2 the panel of keys or buttons on a calculator, phone, etc. **key·stone** *n* 1 *Architecture* the middle stone at the top of an arch, holding the other stones in place. 2 the part on which other associated parts depend: *Freedom is the keystone of our policy.* **key·stroke** *n* a stroke of a key on a keyboard. **key·word** *n* Computers a word used as a reference point for finding information by retrieving a document on the Internet.

key² [ki] *n, pl* **keys** a low island; reef. ⟨Spanish *cayo;* Taino (aboriginal language of West Indies) *cayo, caya* small island⟩

kg kilogram(s).

KGB the secret police of the former Soviet Union. ⟨Russian *K(omitet) G(osudarstvennoi) B(ezopasnosti)* State Security Committee⟩

khak·i ['kæki], ['kɑki], *or* ['kɑrki] *n* 1 a dull, yellowish brown. 2 a stout cloth of this colour, used for soldiers' uniforms. **khak·i** *adj*. ⟨Hindi = dust-coloured; Persian *khak* dust⟩

Khal·sa ['kɑlsə] *n* Sikhism the worldwide community of baptized members.

khan [kɑn] *or* [kæn] *n* a title of dignity in Iran, Afghanistan, India, etc. ⟨Turkish⟩

kha·tib [kə'tib] *n* Islam the preacher, usually a mullah, who delivers the teaching (**khutba**) in a mosque. ⟨Arabic *khataba* to preach⟩

kHz or **khz** kilohertz.

kib·ble ['kɪbəl] *n* a substance consisting of coarse particles, esp dog food or cat food. *v* grind into coarse particles. ⟨origin uncertain⟩

kib·butz [kɪ'bʊts] *n, pl* **kib·butz·im** [-'ɪm] *Hebrew* a communal settlement or farm co-operative in Israel. ⟨literally, a gathering⟩ **kib·butz·nik** *n* a member of a kibbutz.

kib·itz ['kɪbɪts] *v Informal* **1** look on as an outsider and offer unwanted advice, as in a card game. **2** joke or make wisecracks. **kib·itz·er** *n*. ⟨Yiddish⟩

kib·lah ['kɪb‚lɑ] *n Islam* **1** the direction Muslims face when they pray. **2** in a mosque, a mark indicating this direction. ⟨Arabic *qibla* something put opposite; *qabala* be opposite⟩

ki·bosh ['kaɪbɒʃ] *n Informal* nonsense. *v* put an end to.
put the kibosh on finish off: *The boss put the kibosh on long coffee breaks.* ⟨origin uncertain; probably Yiddish⟩

kick [kɪk] *v* **1** strike with the foot: *The horse kicked the boy.* **2** move by kicking: *to kick a ball.* **3** spring back when fired: *This gun kicks.* **4** *Informal* complain. **5** *Slang* make oneself free of (a habit).
n **1** the act of kicking. **2** the recoil of a gun when it is fired. **3** *Slang* a complaint; cause for complaint. **4** Often, **kicks** *pl Slang* thrill: *We just did it for kicks.* **5** *Slang* the power of a drink, drug, etc. to intoxicate. **6** *Slang* a period of intense interest (in something): *She is on a classical music kick.* **kick·a·ble** *adj*. **kick·less** *adj*. ⟨origin uncertain⟩
kick around or **about** *Informal* **a** lie around. **b** go around aimlessly. **c** consider. **d** toy with: *You won't have me to kick around any more.* **kick back** *Informal* **a** spring back suddenly and unexpectedly. **b** *Informal* return (money received by some illegal or secret agreement or by coercion). **kick·back** *n*. **kick in** *Slang* **a** die. **b** contribute: *If everyone kicks in $3, we can order a large pizza.* **c** begin taking effect. **kick off a** *Football* put a ball in play with a kick. **b** *Informal*. begin. **c** *Slang*. die. **kick·off** *n*. **kick out** *Informal* expel: *She should be kicked out of our club.* **kick the bucket** See BUCKET. **kick up** *Slang* cause: *to kick up a lot of trouble.* **kickboxing** boxing using blows with the hands and feet. **kickboxer.** **kick·er** ['kɪkər] *n* **1** a person who or animal or thing that kicks. **2** *Informal* an outboard motor. **3** *Slang* a surprising twist: *The contract seemed generous; the kicker was that we would get no money until all the work was finished.* **kick·stand** *n* a lever attached to the rear wheel of a cycle, used to support the vehicle when it is not in use. **kick–start** *v* **1** start (a motorcycle engine) by vigorously kicking downward against a pedal at the side. **2** start something by a sudden powerful injection of resources, etc. **kick–start** *n*.

kid¹ [kɪd] *n* **1** a young goat or antelope. **2** *Informal* a child or young person. *adj Informal* younger: *my kid sister.* **kid·like** *adj*. **kid·dish** *adj*. ⟨Old Norse *kith*⟩

kid·die or **kid·dy** *n Informal* a child. **kid·do** ['kɪdou] *n Informal* child (a term of address or endearment). **kid–glove** or **kid–gloved** *adj Informal* careful; considerate: *a kid-glove approach.* **handle with kid gloves** treat with special care. **kid gloves** smooth gloves made of soft kidskin. **kid·nap** *v* **-napped** or **-naped**, **-nap·ping** or **-nap·ing** carry off and hold (a person) against his or her will by force or by fraud. **kid·nap·per** or **kid·nap·er** *n*. **kids' lit** or **kid·lit** *Informal* children's literature.

kid² [kɪd] *v* **kid·ded, kid·ding** *Slang* **1** tease playfully; talk jokingly; banter. **2** deceive. **kid·der** *n*. **kid·ding·ly** *adv*. ⟨perhaps from *kid¹* in sense of 'treat as a child'⟩
kid around joke. **no kidding! a** an expression of incredulity. **b** I mean this; I am not joking.

kid·dush [kɪ'duʃ] or ['kɪdəʃ] *n Judaism* the prayer or blessing recited over wine or bread on the Sabbath eve. ⟨Hebrew *qiddūsh* sanctification⟩

kid·ney ['kɪdni] *n, pl* **-neys** **1** *Anatomy* in vertebrates, one of the pair of organs that separate waste matter from the blood and pass them off through the bladder. **2** nature; kind: *We must guard our leaders against terrorists, assassins, and people of that kidney.* **kid·ney·like** *adj*. ⟨Middle English *kiden-* of uncertain meaning and origin + *ey* egg⟩
kidney bean the kidney-shaped seed of any of several cultivated varieties of bean. **kidneystone** *Pathology* an abnormal stone found in the kidney.

kill [kɪl] *v* **1** put to death. **2** put an end to: *to kill odours.* **3** cancel (a word, paragraph, item, etc.). **4** defeat or veto (a legislative bill). **5** *Informal* use up (time): *We killed an hour at the zoo.* **6** *Hockey* overcome the disadvantage of (a penalty) by thwarting the opposing team's attempts to score: *Our team killed the penalty and were then able to score a goal.* **7** stop: *She killed the engine.* **8** *Informal* overcome completely: *My foot is killing me.*
n **1** the act or an instance of killing. **2** an animal or animals killed, as in a hunt. **3** an enemy aircraft, ship, etc. destroyed in battle. **kill·a·ble** *adj*. ⟨Middle English *kyllen, cullen*⟩
kill off exterminate; wipe out.
kill·er *n* **1** a person, animal, or thing that kills. **2** *Slang* a criminal who recklessly or wantonly kills others. **3** *Slang* anything that is very difficult: *That climb is a killer.* **4** *Slang* something excellent or impressive. **killer bee** a honeybee which attacks when provoked. **killer whale** a black-and-white whale which preys on fish, seals, sea otters, narwhals, etc. and even larger baleen whales. Also called **orca. kill·ing** *adj* **1** deadly; destructive: *a killing frost.* **2** overpowering; : *a killing pace.* **3** *Informal* extremely funny.
n **1** murder; slaughter. **2** *Informal* a sudden great financial success: *She made a killing in one day on the stock market.* **kill·ing·ly** *adv*.

kill–joy or **killjoy** *n* a person who spoils other people's fun.

Kill is the general word, meaning 'put to death or cause the death of a person, animal, or plant': *Overwork killed her. Lack of water kills flowers.* **Murder** emphasizes wicked and cold-blooded killing, and means 'kill a person unlawfully, usually deliberately': *He murdered his rich uncle.* **Slay**, chiefly literary or journalistic, means 'kill with violence, in battle, or by murdering': *All the captives were slain.*

kill·deer [ˈkɪlˌdir] *n, pl* **-deers** or (esp collectively) **-deer** a plover noted for its loud, penetrating call. ⟨imitative of its call⟩

kil·lick [ˈkɪlɪk] *n* an anchor made of wooden poles or sticks bound around a rock or rocks, used esp in the Maritimes and New England. Also, **kil·lock**. ⟨origin uncertain⟩

kiln [kɪln] or [kɪl] *n* a furnace or oven for burning, baking, or drying something. ⟨Old English *cylen*; Latin *culina* kitchen⟩ .
kiln–dry [ˈkɪln ˌdraɪ] or [ˈkɪl ˌdraɪ] *v* **-dried, -dry·ing** dry (a material such as wood) in a kiln instead of letting it weather naturally.

ki·lo [ˈkiloʊ] *n* kilogram.

kilo– *SI prefix* *one* thousand. A kilowatt is one thousand watts. Compare MEGA-, GIGA-. *Symbol* **k** ⟨French; Greek *chilioi*⟩

kil·o·byte [ˈkɪləˌbaɪt] *n Computers* The storage capacity of a computer system, roughly equal to one thousand bytes. *Symbol* **kB**

kil·o·gram [ˈkɪləˌɡræm] *n* an SI unit for measuring mass. The kilogram is one of the seven base units in the SI. *Symbol* **kg**. Also, **kil·o·gramme**.

kil·o·hertz [ˈkɪləˌhɜrts] *n, pl* **kil·o·hertz** *Physics* an SI unit for measuring frequency of waves, equal to 1000 hertz. *Symbol* **kHz**

ki·lo·me·tre [kəˈlɒmətər] or [ˈkɪləˌmitər] *n* an SI unit for measuring length or distance, equal to 1000 m. *Symbol* **km**. Also, **ki·lo·me·ter**. **kil·o·met·ric** *adj*.

kil·o·pas·cal [ˈkɪləˌpæskəl] *n* an SI unit for measuring pressure, equal to 1000 pascals. *Symbol* **kPa**

kil·o·volt [ˈkɪləˌvoʊlt] *n Electricity* a unit equal to 1000 volts. *Symbol* **kV**

kil·o·watt [ˈkɪləˌwɒt] *n* an SI unit for measuring power, equal to 1000 watts. *Symbol* **kW**

kilowatt hour *Electricity* a unit for measuring electrical energy, defined as the number of kilowatts of electrical power used per hour. One kilowatt hour is equivalent to 3.6 megajoules. *Symbol* **kWh**

kilt [kɪlt] *n* a pleated, knee-length tartan skirt, often worn by Scottish men. **kilt·like** *adj*. ⟨probably Scandinavian; compare Danish *kilte* tuck⟩

kil·ter [ˈkɪltər] *n Informal* good condition: *Our radio is out of kilter.* ⟨origin uncertain⟩

ki·mo·no [kəˈmoʊnə] or [kəˈmoʊnoʊ] *n, pl* **-nos 1** a loose outer garment held in place by a sash, often worn by Japanese people. **2** a loose dressing gown. ⟨Japanese⟩

kin [kɪn] *n* **1** a person's family or relatives: *All our kin came to the family reunion.* **2** family relationship: *What kin is she to you?*
next of kin nearest living relative: *His next of kin is his mother.* **kin·less** *adj.* ⟨Old English *cynn*⟩
kin·dred [ˈkɪndrɪd] *n* **1** family relationship. **2** one's family or relatives. *adj* **1** related: *kindred peoples.* **3** similar: *We are studying about dew, frost, and kindred facts of nature.* **kins·folk** [ˈkɪnzˌfoʊk] or **kin·folk** *n pl* relatives. **kin·ship** *n* a family relationship. **kins·man** *n, pl* **-men** a male relative. **kins·wom·an** *n, pl* **-wom·en** a female relative.

–kin *suffix* little: *lambkin.* ⟨Middle English⟩

kind¹ [kaɪnd] *adj* helpful, considerate, generous, etc. **kind·less** *adj.* **kind·less·ly** *adv.* **kind·less·ness** *n.* **kind·ness** *n.* ⟨Old English *(ge)cynde* natural. Compare KIND².⟩
kind–heart·ed *adj* kindly; sympathetic. **kind–heart·ed·ly** *adv.* **kind–heart·ed·ness** *n.* **kind·ly** *adj* **1** friendly: *kindly faces.* **2** pleasant: *a kindly rain shower.* *adv* **1** in a kind or friendly way. **2** please (in formal requests or to express impatience, etc.): *Kindly return this portion of the bill with your payment. Will you kindly get your feet off the chair!* **kind·li·ness** *n.* **take kindly to** like or accept: *She does not take kindly to criticism.*

kind² [kaɪnd] *n* **1** class; sort; variety: *many kinds of candy.* **2** a natural group. ⟨Old English *(ge)cynd* nature, origin⟩
after one's (or **its**) **kind** *Archaic* according to one's or its own nature. **in kind a** in goods or produce, not in money. **b** in something of the same sort: *If you do me this favour, I'll pay you back in kind.* **c** in characteristic quality: *The difference is in kind, not merely in degree, between a hound and a terrier.* **kind of** *Informal* nearly; somewhat: *The room was kind of dark.* **of a kind a** alike: *She and her mother were two of a kind—tight-fisted.* **b** of a poor quality: *Two boxes and a plank make a table of a kind.*

Kind and **sort** can be singular or plural:
This kind of apple is likely to be wormy.
These sorts of behaviour are out of place here.
Avoid using a plural determiner with a singular noun, as in *these kind of shoes* (which should be *this kind of shoes*) or *those sort of ideas* (which should be *that sort of ideas*).

kin·der·gar·ten [ˈkɪndərˌɡɑrtən] or [-ˌɡɑrdən], [ˈkɪndə-] *n* **1** the year (or two years) of school before grade 1. **2** a school for younger children. **kin·der·gart·ner** *n.* ⟨German; *Kinder* children + *Garten* garden⟩

kin·dle [ˈkɪndəl] *v* **1** set on fire or catch fire: *This damp wood will never kindle.* **2** stir up or become stirred up: *Her cruelty kindled our anger.* **3** light up: *The boy's face kindled as he told about the circus.* **kin·dler** *n.* ⟨Old Norse *kynda* kindle⟩
kin·dling *n* small pieces of wood for starting a fire.

ki·net·ic [kɪ'nɛtɪk] *adj* **1** of motion. **2** caused by motion. ⟨Greek *kinētikos; kineein* move⟩
kin·e·mat·ics [ˌkɪnə'mætɪks] *n* the branch of mechanics dealing with the different kinds of motion that are possible for a body. **kinetic energy** *Physics* the energy of a given body that depends on its motion. **ki·net·ics** [kɪ'nɛtɪks] *n* the branch of mechanics dealing with the effects of forces in causing or changing the motion of bodies (with sg verb). **kinetic theory** the theory that the constituent particles of matter are in constant motion, and that the temperature of a substance is proportional to the velocity of the particles.

king [kɪŋ] *n* **1** the male ruler of a nation. **2** a person or animal or thing that is best or most important in a certain sphere or class: *The lion is called the king of the beasts.* **3** *Chess* the chief piece. **4** *Checkers* a piece that has moved entirely across the board. **5** a playing card bearing a picture of a king. **king·less** *adj*. **king·like** *adj*. **king·ship** *n*. ⟨Old English *cyning*⟩
king·bird *n* any of several flycatchers. **king cobra** a very large, poisonous snake that feeds mainly on other snakes. The king cobra is the largest poisonous snake in the world. **king·craft** *n* the art of ruling. **king·dom** *n* **1** a country that is governed by a king or a queen. **2** realm; domain: *The mind is the kingdom of thought.* **3** one of the five major divisions of living things. Animals, plants, fungi, protists, and monerans are kingdoms. **king·fish·er** *n* any of a family of birds having a large head, and a large, sharp bill, with most species having brightly coloured plumage and a crest. **king·let** *n* either of two small birds having a small patch on the crown of the head. **king·ly** *adj* **1** of royal rank. **2** fit for a king: *a kingly crown.* **3** regal or noble: *a kingly bearing.*
adv regally. **king·li·ness** *n*. **king·mak·er** *n* **1** a person who establishes a king. **2** a person of consequence who can influence the choice of candidates for political office. **king·mak·ing** *n, adj*. **king·pin** *n* **1** *Bowling* the pin in front or in the centre. **2** *Informal* the most important person or thing. **king–size** or **king–sized** *adj* **1** unusually large: *a king-size sandwich.* **2** largest in a standard range of sizes: *a king-size bed.* **king snake** any snake of the genus *Lampropeltis,* having red or yellow markings. **king's ransom** *Informal* a very large amount of money: *They paid a king's ransom for that furniture.*

kink [kɪŋk] *n* **1** a small, tight twist in thread, hair, etc. **2** a pain or stiffness in the muscles of the neck, back, etc. **3** a mental twist. **4** a hindrance or complication: *There are a few kinks in your plan.*
v make or form a kink: *The rope kinked when he stretched it out.* ⟨probably Dutch *kink* twist⟩
kink·y *adj* **1** twisted; curly. **2** *Informal* very unconventional, esp in sexual practices. **kink·i·ly** *adv*. **kink·i·ness** *n*.

kin·ka·jou ['kɪŋkə,dʒu] *n* a nocturnal mammal of the raccoon family. ⟨French *quincajou;* Tupi-Guarani⟩

kin·ni·kin·nick or **kin·ni·kin·ik** [ˌkɪnəkə'nɪk] *n* ✱ **1** a mixture of various ingredients, such as bearberry, sumac, or dogwood leaves, used by Canadian First Nations people for smoking. **2** a plant, esp the bearberry, from which this mixture is made. Also, **kin·ni·kin·nic.** ⟨Algonquian *kinikinic* that which is mixed⟩

ki·osk ['kiɒsk] *or* [ki'ɒsk] *n* **1** a small building, usually with one or more sides open, used as a newsstand, bus shelter, telephone booth, etc. **2** *Computers* an information booth where data may be accessed from a CD-ROM or from the Internet. ⟨Turkish *kiushk* pavilion⟩

kip·per ['kɪpər] *n* a herring, salmon, etc. that has been salted and dried or smoked. **kip·per** *v*. ⟨Old English *cypera* male salmon⟩

kirsch [kirʃ] *n* a brandy made from fermented wild black cherries. ⟨German *Kirschwasser* cherry water⟩

kis·met ['kɪzmɪt] *n* fate; destiny. ⟨Arabic *qisma(t); qasama* divide⟩

kiss [kɪs] *v* **1** touch with the lips as a sign of love, greeting, or respect. **2** touch gently: *A soft wind kissed the treetops.*
n **1** a touch with the lips. **2** a gentle touch. **3** a piece of candy containing nuts, etc, and wrapped in a twist of paper. **kiss·a·ble** *adj*. **kiss·a·bil·i·ty** *n*. ⟨Old English *cyssan*⟩
kiss away put, bring, take, etc. by kissing: *He kissed away her tears.* **kiss goodbye** lose one's chances at: *You can kiss that job goodbye.* **kiss off** *Slang* reject. **kiss–off** *n*.
kiss·er *n* **1** a person who kisses. **2** *Slang* the face or mouth. **kiss of death** a destructive relationship or action: *The yellow tabloid's story on the candidate was the kiss of death for her campaign.* **kiss of life** mouth-to-mouth resuscitation.

kit[1] [kɪt] *n* **1** a set of materials or tools required for a particular purpose: *a first-aid kit.* **2** a set of parts intended to be put together to make a particular thing: *a model airplane kit.* **3** a set of printed materials issued for instruction and information: *a visitor's kit.* **4** the clothing and equipment required for a certain activity: *a soldier's kit.* **5** a bag or other holder containing a set of materials or equipment. ⟨probably Middle Dutch *kitte* jug, tankard⟩
the whole kit and caboodle *Informal* the complete group: *They met the children and their friends at the theatre and took the whole kit and caboodle out to supper.*
kit–bag *n* a bag, usually closed at the top by a drawstring, for carrying belongings.

kit[2] [kɪt] *n* **1** the young of certain fur-bearing wild animals such as the beaver. **2** kitten. **kit fox** SWIFT (def. *n* 2).

Ki·tab–i–Aq·das [kɪ'tɑb i æk'dɑs] *n Bahaism* the laws and teachings of Baha-ullah, the most sacred portion of the Bahai scriptures.

kitch·en ['kɪtʃən] *n* a room with facilities for preparing and cooking food. ⟨Old English *cycene,* Latin *coquina; coquus* a cook⟩

kitch·en·ette *n* a very small, compactly arranged kitchen. **kitchen garden** a garden where vegetables and fruit are grown. **kitch·en·ware** *n* kitchen utensils.

kite [kəit] *n* **1** a light frame covered with paper, cloth, or plastic, designed to be flown in the air on the end of a long string. **2** a hawk having long, pointed wings. **3** an aircraft pulled by a towline and supported by air currents. **kite·like** *adj.* ⟨Old English *cӯta*⟩ **fly a kite** propose something simply to get a reaction. **go fly a kite** *Slang* go away.

kith [kɪθ] *n* friends. **kith and kin** friends and relatives. ⟨Old English *cӯththe* acquaintance; *cunnan* know⟩

Kit·i·mat See HAISLA.

kitsch [kɪtʃ] *n* **1** mass-produced decorative articles, esp when gaudy or pretentious. **2** trite, uninspired art or literature. **kitsch·y** *adj.* ⟨German *kitschen* to throw together a work of art; from dialect⟩

kit·ten ['kɪtən] *n* **1** a young cat. **2** the young of certain other animals, such as rabbits. ⟨Old French *cheton; chat* cat, Latin *cattus*⟩ **have kittens** *Slang* be extremely shocked and upset about something. **kit·ten·ish** *adj* **1** like a kitten. **2** coquettish. **kit·ten·ish·ly** *adv.* **kit·ten·ish·ness** *n.* **kit·ty** *n, pl* **-ties** *Informal* kitten.

kit·ti·wake ['kɪti,weik] *n* a medium-sized oceanic gull with black-tipped grey wings. ⟨imitative of its call⟩

kit·ty¹ See KITTEN.

kit·ty² ['kɪti] *n, pl* **-ties 1** *Poker* **a** the stakes. **b** a fund made up of contributions from each person's winnings, used to buy refreshments, etc. for the players. **2** a fund of money pooled by a group of people for a particular use: *a monthly contribution for the grocery kitty.* **3** *Card games* a number of cards set aside that may be used by the player making the highest bid, etc. ⟨origin uncertain⟩

kit·ty–cor·ner ['kɪti ,kɔrnər] *adj* diagonally opposite: *There is a small drugstore kitty-corner from the garage.* *adv* diagonally. Also, **kitty–cornered.** ⟨*catty-corner*, variant of *cater-corner;* French *quatre* four + CORNER⟩

ki·wi ['kiwi] *n, pl* **-wis 1** any of a small genus of flightless birds of New Zealand having shaggy plumage and a long, slender bill. **2 Kiwi** *Informal* a New Zealander. **3** KIWI FRUIT. ⟨Maori⟩ **kiwi fruit** or **ki·wi·fruit** *n* the edible fruit of a subtropical Asian vine, having a hairy, brownish skin and sweet, bright green pulp.

KKK See KU KLUX KLAN.

Klee·nex ['klinɛks] *n Trademark* a very soft, absorbent tissue, used as a handkerchief, for removing cosmetics, etc.

klep·to·ma·ni·a [,klɛptə'meiniə] *n* an uncontrollable impulse to steal. **klep·to·ma·ni·ac** *n.* ⟨Greek *kleptēs* thief + MANIA⟩

klick [klɪk] *Slang* kilometre: *It's 24 klicks to the next town.*

Klon·dike ['klɒndəik] *n* ✽ a region of the Yukon where gold was discovered in 1897. **Klondike fever** ✽ formerly, the excitement and lust for gold generated by the Klondike gold rush. **Klon·dik·er** *n* ✽ a person who took part in the Klondike gold rush to the Yukon, 1897-1899. **Klondike Trail** ✽ formerly, a route through the western prairies and British Columbia leading to the Klondike.

klutz [klʌts] *n Slang* a physically clumsy or socially inept person. **klutz·y** *adj.* ⟨Yiddish; German *klotz* wooden block, lout⟩

km kilometre(s). **km/h** kilometres per hour: *The top speed of this car is 120 km/h.*

kn knot (unit of speed).

knack [næk] *n* **1** a special skill. **2** the power to do something easily. ⟨origin uncertain⟩

knack·wurst ['nɑk,wɜrst] *n* a smooth, bland sausage. ⟨German; *knacken* to crack, break + *wurst* sausage⟩

knap·sack ['næp,sæk] *n* a bag for provisions, having straps for carrying on the back. ⟨Low German; *knappen* eat + *Sack* sack¹⟩

knave [neiv] *n* **1** a dishonest person; rogue. **2** the jack, a playing card with a picture of a servant or soldier on it. **3** *Archaic* a male servant; a man of humble birth or position. ⟨Old English *cnafa* boy⟩ **knav·er·y** *n* **1** behaviour characteristic of a knave. **2** a tricky, dishonest act. **knav·ish** *adj* tricky; dishonest. **knav·ish·ly** *adv.* **knav·ish·ness** *n.*

knead [nid] *v* **1** work (dough, clay, etc.) by pressing with the hands until it has the proper consistency. **2** massage: *Stiffness in the muscles may be taken away by kneading.* **knead·er** *n.* **knead·a·bil·i·ty** *n.* **knead·a·ble** *adj.* **knead·ing·ly** *adv.* ⟨Old English *cnedan*⟩

knee [ni] *n* **1** the joint between the thigh and the lower leg. **2** anything like a bent knee in shape or position. *v* **kneed, knee·ing** strike with the knee. ⟨Old English *cnēo*⟩ **bring to one's knees** force to yield. **on one's knees a** pleading humbly: *I'm on my knees to you.* **b** in a state of near collapse or defeat. **knee breeches** breeches reaching to or just below the knees. **knee·cap** *n* the flat, movable bone at the front of the knee; patella. *v* **-capped, -cap·ping** shoot (a person) in the kneecaps, esp as an act of terrorism. **knee–deep** *adj* so deep as to reach the knees. **knee–high** ['ni 'hai] *adj* so high as to reach the knees. *n* ['ni ,hai] a knee-high sock made of stocking material. **knee jerk** a reflex extension of the leg as a result of a tap on the patellar tendon. **knee–jerk** *adj Informal* responding in an unthinking way: *a knee-jerk reaction.* **kneel** *v* **knelt** or **kneeled, kneel·ing** go down on one's knee or knees. **kneel·ing** *adj.* **kneel·er** *n* a stool, cushion, etc. to kneel on. **knee·pad** *n* a pad worn around the knee for protection.

knell [nɛl] *n* **1** the sound of a bell rung slowly after a death. **2** a sign of death, failure, etc.: *Their refusal rang the knell of our hopes.* ⟨Old English *cnyll(an)*⟩

knelt [nɛlt] *v* a pt and a pp of KNEEL.

knew [nju] *or* [nu] *v* pt of KNOW.

knick·ers ['nɪkərz] *n pl* **1** short, loose-fitting pants gathered at the knee. **2 a** a woman's undergarment for the lower part of the body. **b** *Informal* underpants. ⟨short for *knickerbockers;* from the costume shown in illustrations in Washington Irving's *Knickerbocker's History of New York*)⟩

knick·er·bock·ers ['nɪkər,bɒkərz] *n pl* KNICKERS (def. 1).

knick–knack ['nɪk ,næk] *n* a pleasing trifle; ornament; trinket. Also, **nick–nack.** ⟨varied reduplication of *knack*⟩

knife [nəif] *n, pl* **knives** *n* a thin, flat blade, usually of metal, fastened in a handle.
v **knifed, knif·ing. 1** cut or stab with a knife. **2** pierce as with a knife: *The wind knifed through her thin jacket.* **knife·like** *adj.* **knife·less** *adj.* ⟨Old English *cnīf*⟩
knife in the back an act of betrayal: *I thought she was my friend, but her gossiping about me was a knife in the back.* **under the knife** *Informal* undergoing a surgical operation: *She went under the knife this morning, and is now in stable condition in the recovery room.*

knight [nəit] *n* **1** in the Middle Ages, a man raised to an honourable military rank and pledged to do good deeds. **2** in modern times, a man raised to an honourable rank because of personal achievement. A knight has the title *Sir* before his name. **3** *Chess* a piece usually shaped like a horse's head.
v raise to the rank of knight. **knight·ly** *adj.* **knight·li·ness** *n.* ⟨Old English *cniht* boy⟩
knight errant ['nəit 'ɛrənt] *n, pl* **knights errant 1** formerly, a knight travelling in search of adventure. **2** a person of great chivalry. **3** an adventurous person, usually impractical. **knight errantry. knight·hood** *n* **1** the rank or dignity of a knight. **2** knights as a group or class: *All the knighthood of France came to the aid of the king.*

knish [knɪʃ] *or* [kə'nɪʃ] *n* in Jewish cookery, dough stuffed with some filling and baked or fried. ⟨Yiddish; Polish⟩

knit [nɪt] *v* **knit·ted** or **knit, knit·ting 1** make (an article) by looping yarn together. **2** join closely together, or be joined closely: *A broken bone knits.* **3** wrinkle (one's brow): *She knitted her brow in concentration as she studied the crossword puzzle.*
n knitted fabric: *a cotton-polyester knit.*
knit·ta·ble *adj.* **knit·ter** *n.* ⟨Old English *cnyttan; cnotta* knot[1]⟩
knit·ting *n* knitted work. **knitting needle** one of a pair of long needles used in knitting. **knit·wear** *n* knitted clothing, including clothing made of machine-knitted fabric .

knives [nəivz] *n* pl of KNIFE.

knob [nɒb] *n* **1** a rounded lump. **2** the handle of a door, drawer, etc. **knob·like** *adj.*

⟨Middle Low German *knobbe*⟩
knobbed *adj* having a knob or knobs. **knob·by** *adj* **1** covered with knobs. **2** rounded like a knob. **knob·bi·ness** *n.*

knock [nɒk] *v* **1** hit: *She knocked him on the head.* **2** hit and cause to fall: *He knocked all the books onto the floor.* **3** make a noise by hitting: *to knock on a door.* **4** make a noise: *The engine is knocking.* **5** *Slang* criticize: *Don't knock the food; it's all we've got.* **knock** *n.* ⟨Old English *cnocian*⟩
knock around or **about** *Informal* **a** wander from place to place. **b** hit repeatedly. **knock down a** signify the sale of (an article) to the highest bidder at an auction by a blow of the mallet. **b** take apart: *We knocked down the bookcase and packed it in the car.* **c** strike down. **knock it off** *Slang* stop it. **knock off** *Informal* **a** deduct: *to knock off 10 dollars from the price.* **b** stop work: *We knock off at noon for lunch.* **c** do quickly: *She knocked off a new poem in just a few minutes.* **d** *Slang* defeat or kill.
knock out a hit so hard as to make helpless or unconscious. **b** defeat. **knock together** put together hastily: *We knocked together a bookcase out of some planks and bricks.* **knock up a** exhaust. **b** *Slang* make pregnant.
knock·a·bout *n* *Nautical* a small sailboat equipped with one mast but no bowsprit. *adj* noisy; boisterous: *a knockabout farce.* **knock–down** *adj* made to be taken apart or put together easily. **knock·er** *n* a knob, ring, etc. fastened on a door for use in knocking. **knock–knee** *n* **1** an inward curving of the legs, so that the knees knock together in walking. **2 knock–knees** *pl* knees that curve in this way. **knock–kneed** *adj.* **knock·out** *n* **1** the act of rendering unconscious or helpless by a punch: *The boxer won the fight by a knockout.* **2** *Slang* a person or thing considered outstanding: *The party was a knockout.* **knockout drops** *Informal* any drug put in a drink to make a person unconscious.

knoll [noul] *n* a small, rounded hill; mound. ⟨Old English *cnoll*⟩

knot [nɒt] *n* **1** a fastening made by tying together pieces of rope, string, etc. **2** an accidental twisting of rope, string, etc., usually drawn tight. **3** a group; cluster: *a knot of people.* **4** a hard mass of wood formed where a branch grows from a tree. **5** a hard lump: *I feel a knot in this back muscle.* **6** a unit for measuring the speed of a ship or aircraft; one nautical mile per hour.
v **knot, knot·ted, knot·ting. knot·less** *adj.* **knot·like** *adj.* ⟨Old English *cnotta*⟩
tie the knot *Informal* marry: *They tied the knot last spring.*
knot·hole *n* a hole in a board where a knot has fallen out. **knot·ted** *adj* having a knot or knots; knotty. **knot·ty** *adj* **1** full of knots: *knotty wood.* **2** difficult; puzzling: *a knotty problem.* **knot·ti·ly** *adv.* **knot·ti·ness** *n.*

know [nou] *v* **knew, known, know·ing 1** be sure of: *He knows the facts of the case.* **2** have firmly in the mind: *to know a lesson.* **3** be aware (of): *to know a person's name.* **4** be acquainted with: *I know her.* **5** have an understanding of: *She knows Canadian literature.* **6** recognize: *You would hardly know her since her illness.* **know·a·ble** *adj.* ⟨Old English *cnāwan*⟩

in the know *Informal* having inside information. **know what's what** *Informal* be well-informed.

know–all *n Informal* know-it-all. **know–how** *n Informal* the ability to do something. **know·ing** *adj* **1** well-informed. **2** clever. **3** suggesting secret understanding of matters: *His only answer was a knowing look.* **4** deliberate: *I will not tolerate knowing disobedience.* **know·ing·ly** *adv* **1** in a knowing way. **2** with knowledge; on purpose: *She would not knowingly hurt anyone.* **know–it–all** *n Slang* a person having pretensions to knowing everything, and who thinks other people are wrong or ill-informed. Also, **know–all. knowl·edge** *n* **1** what one knows: *His knowledge of the subject is limited.* **2** all that is known or can be learned. **knowl·edge·a·ble** *adj* well-informed. **knowl·edge·a·bly** *adv.* **known** *adj* in the knowledge of everyone; widely recognized: *a known fact, a known artist.* **know–noth·ing** *n* an ignorant person.

> **SYNONYMS**
> **Know** emphasizes being well acquainted with a subject: *She knows more about Mexico than anyone else in Canada.* **Understand** emphasizes having a thorough grasp of both facts and meaning: *She understands the workings of the stock market.*

knuck·le [ˈnʌkəl] *n* **1** a finger joint; esp the joint between a finger and the rest of the hand. **2** the knee or hock joint of an animal used as food: *boiled pigs' knuckles.* *v* press or rub with the knuckles. ⟨Middle Low German *knokel* diminutive of *knoke* bone⟩

knuckle down *Informal* **a** work hard: *Let's knuckle down and get the job done.* **b** knuckle under. **knuckle under** *Informal* submit.

knuckle ball *Baseball* a pitch made by holding the ball with the thumb and the knuckles of the first two or three fingers. **knuck·le·bone** *n* **1** a bone forming part of a knuckle. **2** in quadrupeds, a bone corresponding to a wrist, ankle, or finger bone in humans. **knuck·le·dust·er** *n Informal* a piece of metal worn over the knuckles as a weapon. **knuck·le·head** *n Slang* a thoughtless or inept person.

knurl [nɜrl] *n* **1** a knot; knob. **2** a small ridge, such as on the edge of a coin or on the cap of a tube of toothpaste. **knurl·y** *adj.* ⟨apparently diminutive of *knur* knot, Middle English *knor(re)*⟩

KO or **K.O.** [ˈkeiˈou] *v* **KO'd** or **K.O.'d, KO'ing** or **K.O.'ing** *Slang v* knock out: *He was KO'd in the fourth round.* *n, pl* **KO's** *n* knockout.

ko·a·la [kouˈɑlə] *n* a furry, grey, arboreal marsupial of Australia that feeds on the leaves and shoots of eucalyptus trees. ⟨aboriginal name⟩

ko·an [ˈkouan] *n, pl* **-ans** or **-an** *Zen Buddhism* a seemingly meaningless puzzle designed to heighten awareness of truth. ⟨Japanese *kō* public + *an* proposal, design⟩

Ko·di·ak bear [ˈkoudiˌæk] a subspecies of the brown bear, found on Kodiak Island off the southern coast of Alaska and adjacent coastal areas. It is the largest living carnivorous animal, averaging 2.7 m in length. ⟨Russian⟩

Kog·mol·ik [kɒgˈmoulɪk] *n, pl* **-ik** or **-iks** **1** a member of the Inuit peoples living to the east of Mackenzie Delta in the Coronation Gulf area. **2** the language of these people. **Kog·mol·ik** *adj.*

kohl·ra·bi [koulˈrɑbi] *or* [ˈkoulˌrɑbi] *n, pl* **-bies** a cultivated variety of cabbage with a thickened, turnip-shaped stem that is eaten as a vegetable. ⟨German; Italian *cavoli rape*⟩

ko·ji·ki [kouˈdʒiki] *n Shintoism* one of the most highly revered of ancient texts, covering the history of Japan from the creation of the world to the middle of the 7th century. ⟨Japanese⟩

ko·ka·nee [ˈkoukəˌni] *n* ✱ a freshwater form of the sockeye salmon, common in British Columbia. Compare OUANANICHE. ⟨perhaps from *Kokanee* Creek, B.C.⟩

ko·la [ˈkoulə] *n* either of two trees of the same family as the cacao, cultivated extensively in tropical regions for their seeds, called kola nuts. Also called **kola tree.** ⟨native African⟩
kola nut the caffeine-containing seed of the kola tree, used as a flavouring in soft drinks and medicines.

kol·khoz [ˈkɒl, kɒz] *n* in the former Soviet Union, a collective farm. ⟨Russian *kol(lektivnoe) khoz(yaistvo)* collective farm⟩

kom·a·tik [ˈkɑməˌtɪk] *n* ✱ *North* a large, wooden dogsled made of closely spaced crossbars lashed to two broad runners. Also, **kam·u·tik.** ⟨eastern Inuktitut *qamutik* dual form of *qamut* sled runner⟩

Ko·mo·do dragon [kəˈmoudou] the largest living lizard, found in southeast Asia. ⟨*Komodo* Island, Indonesia⟩

kook [kuk] *n Slang* a peculiar or eccentric person; screwball. **kook·y** *adj.* **kook·i·ness** *n.* ⟨perhaps from *cuckoo*⟩

kook·a·bur·ra [ˈkʊkəˌbɜrə] *n* a large Australian kingfisher noted for its cry that resembles loud, harsh laughter; laughing jackass. ⟨Wiradjuri *gugubarra*; imitative⟩

Koo·ten·ay See KTUNAXA.

Ko·ran See QUR'AN.

ko·sher [ˈkouʃər] *adj* **1** right or clean according to Jewish ritual law: *kosher meat.* **2** *Slang* all right; legitimate: *It's not kosher to change the rules once the game has started.* ⟨Hebrew *kasher* proper⟩

kow·tow ['kaʊ,taʊ] v **1** kneel and touch the ground with the forehead to show deep respect, submission, or worship. **2** show slavish respect or obedience (*to*). *n* the act of kowtowing. **kow·tow·er** *n*. ⟨Mandarin *k'o-t'ou*, literally, knock (the) head⟩

kPa kilopascal.

kraft [kræft] *n* a tough, brown wrapping paper made from chemically treated wood pulp. ⟨German *Kraft* strength⟩

kra·ken ['krɑkən] *n* a mythical monster supposed to live in Norwegian waters. ⟨Norwegian⟩

Krem·lin ['krɛmlɪn] *n* **1** the citadel of Moscow. The chief offices of the Russian government are in the Kremlin. **2** the government of Russia. ⟨Russian *kreml* citadel; Tatar⟩

krill [krɪl] *n*, *pl* **krill** any of the tiny, shrimplike crustaceans that occur in swarms, esp in polar seas. ⟨Norwegian *kril* young fry (of fish)⟩

Krish·na ['krɪʃnə] *n* an incarnation of the Hindu god Vishnu, occurring in many forms, but esp as the divine flute player, calling the human soul to God. **Krish·na·ism** *n*. ⟨Sanskrit⟩

Kriss Krin·gle ['krɪs 'krɪŋgəl] Santa Claus. ⟨German dialect *Christkindl* Christ child, Christmas gift⟩

kryp·ton ['krɪptɒn] *n* a rare, inert, gaseous element. *Symbol* **Kr** ⟨Greek = hidden⟩

Ktu·na·xa [ktʊ'næksə] *n* **1** a member of a First Nations people living near Kootenay Lake in British Columbia. **2** their language. **Ktunaxa** *adj.* Also called **Kootenay**, **Kutenai**.

kud·lik ['kudlɪk] *n* ✽ a dishlike soapstone lamp that burns caribou or seal oil, traditionally used by Inuit. ⟨Inuktitut *gudlik*⟩

ku·dos ['kudouz] *or* ['kudous] *n Informal* prestige; glory; fame; praise or credit. ⟨Greek *kydos*⟩

ku·du ['kudu] *n* either of two large antelopes, both having spirally curved horns. ⟨Hottentot⟩

Ku·fic ['kufɪk] *adj* to do with an early form of the Arabic alphabet used to make copies of the Koran.

Ku Klux Klan ['ku 'klʌks 'klæn] *n US* a secret society formed in the S United States after the Civil War to regain and maintain control by local white people, later opposing Blacks, Jews, Catholics, and foreigners. *Abbrev* **KKK**. **Ku Klux Klan·ner** *n*. ⟨probably Greek *kyklos* circle + CLAN⟩
the Klan *n* KU KLUX KLAN. **Klans·man** *n*, *pl* **-men** a member of the Ku Klux Klan.

kuk·ri ['kʊkri] *n* a knife with a curved, very sharp blade, used as a weapon by Gurkhas. ⟨Nepali⟩

ku·lak ['kulɑk] *n* **1** in Russia, formerly, a well-to-do peasant, farmer, or trader who opposed collectivization. **2** a Russian peasant who owns and tills his or her land for his or her own profit. ⟨Russian = fist; hence, tight-fisted⟩

ku·le·tuk ['kulə,tʌk] *n* ✽ a hooded jacket made of skin, often trimmed with fur; parka. ⟨Inuktitut⟩

kum·quat ['kʌmkwɒt] *n* a fruit resembling a small orange, used especially for preserves and candy. ⟨Cantonese⟩

kung fu ['kʊŋ 'fu] a Chinese art of fighting similar to karate, that dates back to ancient times. ⟨Mandarin *ch'uan-fa* = boxing principles⟩

Kut·chin See GWICH'IN.

Ku·te·nai See KTUNAXA.

kvetch [kvɛtʃ] *Informal v* gripe; complain petulantly.
n a person who habitually does this. ⟨Yiddish⟩

kW kilowatt(s).

Kwa·kwa·ka'·wakw [kwa'kwɑkɪ,wɑk] *n*, *pl* **Kwakwakawakw 1** a member of a First Nations people living on the shores of Queen Charlotte Sound and on N Vancouver Island. **2** the Wakashan language of this people. Also called **Kwakiutl**. **Kwakwakawakw** *adj.*

Kwan·zaa ['kwɑn zə] *n* a festival held by some Blacks in North America to celebrate their culture. It runs from December 26 to January 1.

kWh kilowatt hour(s).

kwu·nu·se·la ['kwunusələ] *n* ✽ *Pacific coast* thunderbird. ⟨Kwakiutl⟩

Ll

l or L [ɛl] *n, pl* **l's** or **L's 1** the twelfth letter of the English alphabet, or any speech sound represented by it. **2** the twelfth person or thing in a series. **3 L** the Roman numeral for 50.

la [lɑ] *n Music* **1** the sixth tone of an eight-tone major scale. **2** the tone A. Also, **lah.** ⟨See GAMUT.⟩

lab [læb] *n Informal* laboratory.

la·bel [ˈleibəl] *n* **1** a slip of material attached to anything and marked to show what or whose it is, or where it is to go. **2** a short phrase used to describe some person, thing, or idea: *'Land of Opportunity' is a label often given to Canada.*
v **-belled** or **-beled, -bel·ling** or **-bel·ing 1** put a label on. **2** describe as: *He labelled the boastful man a liar.* **la·bel·ler** or **la·bel·er** *n.* ⟨Old French *label* ribbon, strip; Germanic⟩

la·bi·al [ˈleibiəl] *adj* to do with lips. **la·bi·al·ly** *adv.* ⟨Latin *labium* lip⟩

lab·o·ra·to·ry [ˈlæbrə,tɔri] or [ləˈbɔrə,tɔri] *n* **1** a place where scientific work is done. **2** a place fitted up for manufacturing chemicals, etc. ⟨Latin *laboratorium; labor* work⟩

la·bour or **la·bor** [ˈleibər] *n* **1** work: *He was well paid for his labour.* **2** *Economics* the work of human beings that produces goods or services. **3** workers as a group: *Labour favours safe working conditions.* **4** the process of childbirth: *in labour.*
v **1** work hard: *He laboured all day in the mill.* **2** elaborate with effort or in detail: *The speaker laboured the point so much that we lost interest.* **3** move slowly and heavily: *The ship laboured in the high waves.* **4** be burdened, troubled, or distressed. **5** act or function at a disadvantage (usually with *under*): *to labour under a delusion.* ⟨Old French; Latin *labor*⟩ **la·bo·ri·ous** [ləˈbɔriəs] *adj* requiring much work: *Climbing a mountain is laborious.* **la·bo·ri·ous·ly** *adv.* **la·bo·ri·ous·ness** *n.* **Labour Day** the first Monday in September, a legal holiday in Canada and the US in honour of workers. **la·boured** or **la·bored** *adj* done with effort; not easy or natural. **la·bour·er** or **la·bor·er** *n* **1** a worker. **2** a person whose job requires strength rather than skill or training. **la·bour–in·ten·sive** requiring a huge labour force in relation to the amount of capital required. **labour party** any political party organized to protect and promote the interests of workers. **la·bour–sav·ing** *adj* that takes the place of or lessens labour. **labour union** an association of workers organized to protect and promote their common interests and to deal collectively with employers.

Lab·ra·dor [ˈlæbrə,dɔr] or [,læbrəˈdɔr] *n* a region on the NE coast of Canada, the mainland part of the province of Newfoundland and Labrador.
Labrador retriever [ˈlæbrə,dɔr] ✹ a breed of retriever originating in Newfoundland,

having a thick coat. **Labrador tea** ✹ a common bog plant having leathery leaves.

la·bret [ˈleibrɛt] *n* an ornament of bone, shell, etc. stuck into or through the lower lip to stretch it, worn by various peoples, e.g., formerly, the Tlingit. ⟨Latin *labrum* lip + *-et*⟩

lab·y·rinth [ˈlæbə,rɪnθ] *n* **1** a place through which it is hard to find one's way; maze. **2** a confusing, complicated state. **lab·y·rin·thine** [,læbəˈrɪnθin] or [-θɪn] *adj.* ⟨Greek *labyrinthos*⟩

lace [leis] *n* **1** a delicate, netlike fabric. **2** a cord, string, etc. for pulling together.
v **1** put laces through. **2** mark with streaks; streaked: *a white petunia laced with purple.* **3** add a dash of brandy, etc. to (a beverage). **lace·less** *adj.* **lace·like** *adj.* ⟨Old French *laz;* Latin *laqueus* loop, noose⟩
lace into *Informal* **a** attack. **b** criticize severely: *to lace into someone for incompetence.* **lace·work** *n* openwork like lace. **lac·ing** *n* **1** a cord, string, etc. for pulling or holding something together. **2** gold or silver braid used for trimming. **lac·y** *adj* **1** of lace. **2** like lace; having an open pattern: *the lacy leaves of a fern.* **lac·i·ly** *adv.* **lac·i·ness** *n.*

lac·er·ate [ˈlæsə,reit] *v* **1** tear roughly: *The bear's claws lacerated the man's flesh.* **2** distress: *Your sharp words lacerated my feelings.*
adj [ˈlæsərɪt] or [-,reit] *Botany, zoology* deeply or irregularly indented as if torn: *lacerate leaves.* Also, **lac·er·a·ted. lac·er·a·tion** *n.* **lac·er·a·tive** *adj.* ⟨Latin *lacer* mangled⟩

lach·ry·mal [ˈlækrəməl] *adj* to do with tears. ⟨Latin *lacrima* tear⟩ **lach·ry·mose** [ˈlækrə,mous] *adj* tearful; sad. **lach·ry·mos·i·ty** [,lækrəˈmɒsəti] *n.*

lack [læk] *v* **1** have less than enough: *A desert lacks water.* **2** be without: *A homeless person lacks a home.* **3** be absent or missing. **lack** *n.* ⟨perhaps Middle Dutch *lac*⟩
supply the lack supply what is needed.
lack·ing *adj* **1** not having enough: *A weak person is lacking in strength.* **2** absent: *Water is lacking in a desert.* *prep* without: *Lacking anything better, use what you have.* **lack·lus·tre** or **lack·lus·ter** [ˈlæk,lʌstər] *adj* **1** not shining. **2** lacking vitality: *a lacklustre production.*

lack·a·dai·si·cal [,lækəˈdeizəkəl] *adj* languid; listless; dreamy; lazy. **lack·a·dai·si·cal·ly** *adv.* **lack·a·dai·si·cal·ness** *n.* ⟨*lackaday* variant of *alack a day!*⟩

lack·ey [ˈlæki] *n, pl* **-eys 1** a male servant; footman. **2** a slavish follower. ⟨French *laquais;* Spanish *lacayo* foot soldier⟩

la·con·ic [ləˈkɒnɪk] *adj* using few words. **la·con·i·cal·ly** *adv.* **lac·o·nism** [ˈlækə,nɪzəm] *n.* ⟨Greek *lakōnikos* Spartan; Spartans were noted for brevity or terseness of speech⟩

lac·quer [ˈlækər] *n* **1** a varnish consisting of shellac dissolved in a solvent. **2** a dressing for the hair, made from gum or resin.
v coat with lacquer. **lac·quer·er** *n.* ⟨French; Portuguese *laca* resin secreted by insect⟩

la·crosse [ləˈkrɒs] *n* ✹ a game played, either indoors (**box lacrosse**) or outdoors (**field lacrosse**) by two teams, in which a rubber ball is carried and passed from player to player in an attempt to score a goal. ⟨Cdn. French *la crosse* the stick used in the game⟩ **lacrosse stick** ✹ an L-shaped stick strung with leather thongs that form a kind of pouch for carrying the ball in the game of lacrosse.

lac·tate [ˈlækteit] *v* secrete milk. ⟨Latin *lactare* suckle; *lac, lactis* milk⟩
lac·ta·tion *n* **1** the secretion of milk. **2** the time during which a mother gives milk. **lac·ta·tion·al** *adj.* **lac·ta·tion·al·ly** *adv.* **lac·tic** *adj* to do with milk. **lactic acid** *Biochemistry* an organic acid produced by the action of bacteria on the lactose of milk in the process of souring. **lac·tose** [ˈlæktous] *n Biochemistry* a crystalline sugar present in milk.

la·cu·na [ləˈkjunə] *n, pl* **-nas** or **-nae** [-ni] *or* [-nai] **1** a gap: *There were several lacunas in her letter where words had been erased.* **2** *Biology* a tiny cavity in bones or tissues. **la·cu·nal** *adj.* ⟨Latin = hole; *lacus* cistern, lake⟩

lad [læd] *n* **1** a boy; young man. **2** *Informal* man. **lad·dish** *adj.* **lad·hood** *n.* ⟨Middle English *ladde,* Old English *Ladda* (a nickname)⟩
lad·die [ˈlædi] *n Scottish* a boy.

lad·der [ˈlædər] *n* **1** a set of rungs or steps fastened to two sidepieces, for use in climbing. **2** an ascending series of little pools for fish to swim upstream past a dam or falls. **3** anything resembling or suggesting a ladder: *This company has an elaborate promotion ladder.* **4** a run in a knitted garment such as a stocking.
v of knitted garments, esp stockings, develop ladders as the result of the breaking of a thread. **lad·der·less** *adj.* **lad·der·like** *adj.* ⟨Old English *hlǣder*⟩

lade [leid] *v* **lad·ed, lad·en** or **lad·ed, lad·ing** **1** put a burden on; load. **2** dip; scoop; ladle. **3** take on cargo. ⟨Old English *hladan*⟩
lad·en *adj* loaded; burdened. **lad·ing** *n* **1** the act of loading. **2** load; cargo.

la–di–da [ˈlɑ di ˈdɑ] *adj Informal* affected in behaviour or pronunciation.

la·dle [ˈleidəl] *n* a large, cup-shaped spoon with a long handle, for dipping out liquids. *v* dip out. **la·dler** *n.* ⟨Old English *hlǣdel; hladan* load⟩
ladle out *Informal* give freely, usually something bad: *That teacher is too fond of ladling out punishments.*

la·dy [ˈleidi] *n* **1** a woman of refinement or of high social position. **2** any woman: *She's a courageous lady.* **3 Lady** in the UK, a title given to women of certain ranks of nobility. **4 Our Lady** *Roman Catholic Church* the Virgin Mary. ⟨Old English *hlǣfdīge,* literally, loaf-kneader; *hlāf* loaf + *-dīg-* knead⟩
la·dy·bug *n* any of numerous small beetles having a rounded back, usually red or orange with black spots. **la·dy–in–wait·ing** *n, pl* **la·dies–in–wait·ing** a lady who is an attendant of a queen or princess. **la·dy–kill·er** *n Slang* a man supposed to be dangerously fascinating to women. **la·dy·like** *adj* **1** well-bred or refined: *a ladylike cough.* **2** suitable for a lady:

a ladylike costume. **la·dy·love** *n Informal* a sweetheart. **La·dy·ship** *n* in the UK, a title used in speaking to or of a woman having the rank of LADY (def. 3): *your Ladyship.* **la·dy's–slip·per** or **lady–slipper** *n* any of several wild orchids found in temperate regions, having flowers whose shape suggests a slipper. The **pink lady's–slipper** is the provincial flower of Prince Edward Island.

lag [læg] *v* **lagged, lag·ging** fall behind in movement, development, etc. (often with *behind*): *She lagged because she was tired.* *n* **1** the act of lagging. **2** the amount by which a person or thing lags. **3** an interval of time, esp between related events, such as an action and its effect. **lag·ger** *n.* **lag·ging** *adj.* ⟨Scandinavian; compare Norwegian *lagga* go slowly⟩
lag·gard [ˈlægərd] *n* a person who moves too slowly or falls behind. *adj* slow; backward. **lag·gard·ly** *adj,* *adv.* **lag·gard·li·ness** *or* **lag·gard·ness** *n.* **lag·ging** *adj* dragging.

la·ger [ˈlɑgər] *or* [ˈlɒgər] *n* a light beer. ⟨German *Lagerbier; Lager* storehouse + *Bier* beer⟩

la·goon [ləˈgun] *n* **1** a pond connected with a larger body of water. **2** shallow water separated from the sea by sandbanks. **3** the water within a ring-shaped coral island. ⟨Italian *laguna,* Latin *lacuna* hole, pond⟩

la·hal [ləˈhɑl] *n* ✹ *esp Pacific coast* a First Nations gambling game taking various forms, the winner being the player to whom falls a marked object (as a disk) mixed with several similar but unmarked objects.

la·ic See LAY³.

laid [leid] *v* pt and pp of LAY¹.
laid up a put away for future use. **b** *Informal* forced by illness to stay indoors. **c** of ships, dismantled and put in dock. **laid–back** *adj* **1** placed in a backward position: *The horse had laid-back ears.* **2** *Slang* unexcited or unexcitable: *The whole evening was laid-back and low-key.*

lain [lein] *v* pp of LIE².

lair [ler] *n* **1** the den of a wild animal. **2** *Informal* any refuge. ⟨Old English *leger; licgan* lie²⟩

lais·sez faire or **lais·ser faire** [ˈlɛsei ˈfɛr] **1** the principle of letting people do as they please. **2** *Economics* the absence of governmental interference in trade, industry, etc. **lais·sez–faire** *adj.* ⟨French = allow to do⟩

la·i·ty See LAY³.

lake [leik] *n* a large body of fresh water usually surrounded by land. ⟨Latin *lacus*⟩
lake boat ✹ a vessel designed for service on the Great Lakes. **lake carrier** ✹ a freighter designed for service on the Great Lakes. **lake char** ✹ LAKE TROUT. **lake chub** ✹ a freshwater fish found across Canada and north to

Hudson Bay. **lake·front** *n* land at the edge of a lake. **Lake·head** or **lakehead** *n* the city of Thunder Bay, Ontario, and the surrounding region, on the northwest shore of Lake Superior. **lak·er** *n* **1** a lake boat, esp one operating on the Great Lakes. **2 ✱** a lake fish, esp a lake trout. **Lakes** *n* GREAT LAKES. **lake·side** *n* the land next to a lake. *adj* beside a lake: *a lakeside cottage*. **lake trout** a char native to the lakes of N North America.

Lak·shmi ['lʌkʃmi] *n Hinduism* the goddess of good fortune, to whom the Festival of Lights is dedicated.

lam [læm] *n Slang* a quick escape; flight.
on the lam a escaping. **b** in hiding. ⟨origin unknown⟩

la·ma ['lɑmə] or ['læmə] *n* in Tibet and Mongolia, a Buddhist priest or monk. ⟨Tibetan *blama*⟩
la·ma·ser·y ['lɑmə,sɛri] or ['læmə,sɛri] *n, pl* in Tibet and Mongolia, a place where lamas live, work, and worship.

lamb [læm] *n* **1** a young sheep. **2 the Lamb** or **Lamb of God** *Christianity* Jesus Christ. **3** a young, dear, or innocent person.
v give birth to a lamb or lambs. **lamb·like** *adj*. ⟨Old English⟩
like a lamb a meekly; timidly. **b** easily fooled.
lamb·kin ['læmkɪn] *n* **1** a little lamb. **2** a young or dear person. **lamb·skin** *n* **1** the skin of a lamb, esp with the wool on it. **2** leather made from the skin of a lamb. **3** parchment.

lam·baste [læm'beist] *v* **-bast·ed, -bast·ing** *Slang* **1** beat; thrash. **2** scold roughly. ⟨perhaps Scandinavian *lam* beat, thrash + obsolete *baste* beat or scold, Old Norse *beysta*⟩

lam·bent ['læmbənt] *adj* **1** moving lightly over a surface: *a lambent flame*. **2** softly bright: *Moonlight is lambent*. **lam·ben·cy** *n*. ⟨Latin *lambere* lick⟩

lame [leim] *adj* **1** not able to walk properly. **2** stiff and sore: *Her arm is lame from playing ball*. **3** *Informal* poor; unsatisfactory: *Sleeping too long is a lame excuse for being late*.
v make lame or become lame: *The accident lamed her for life*. **lame·ly** *adv*. **lame·ness** *n*. ⟨Old English *lama*⟩
lame duck 1 *Informal* a helpless person or thing. **2** *Esp US* an elected representative or any administrator, who is serving the last part of the current term.

la·mé [læ'mei] or [lɑ'mei] *n* a rich fabric made wholly or partly of metal threads. ⟨French *lamé* lit., laminated; *lame* metal leaf⟩

la·ment [lə'mɛnt] *v* **1** mourn for: *to lament the dead*. **2** regret: *We lamented his absence*.
n **1** an expression of grief. **2** a poem or tune that expresses grief. **lam·en·ta·tion** *n*. **la·ment·er** *n*. **la·ment·ing** *adj*. ⟨Latin *lamentum* a wailing⟩
lam·en·ta·ble ['læməntəbəl] or [lə'mɛntəbəl] *adj* **1** giving cause for sorrow: *a lamentable accident*. **2** inferior: *The singer gave a lamentable performance*. **lam·en·ta·bly** *adv*.

lam·i·nate ['læmə,neit] *v* **1** cover with a thin layer, esp of plastic. **2** make by putting layer on layer. **3** beat (metal) into a thin plate.
n ['læmənɪt] or [-,neit] **1** a laminated plastic. **2** any laminated product. **lam·i·nat·ed** *adj*. **lam·i·na·tion** *n*. ⟨*lāmina* thin piece or plate⟩
lam·i·nar *adj* to do with thin layers.

lamp [læmp] *n* **1** a device that provides artificial light: *a floor lamp*. **2** a similar device that gives heat: *a spirit lamp*. **3** a device producing radiation: *a sun lamp*. **4** an electric light bulb. ⟨Greek *lampas; lampein* shine⟩
lamp·black *n* a fine, black soot deposited when oil, gas, etc. burn incompletely. **lamp·fish** *n* ✱ oolichan. **lamp·light** *n* the light from a lamp. **lamp·post** *n* a post used to support a street lamp. **lamp·shade** *n* a cover put over a lamp, to reflect and diffuse the light.

lam·poon [læm'pun] *n* a piece of writing that ridicules a person in a highly satirical way. **lam·poon** *v*. ⟨French *lampon* drinking song; *lampons* let us drink⟩
lam·poon·ist *n* a writer of lampoons.

lam·prey ['læmpri] or ['læmprei] *n, pl* **-preys** any of a family of fishes, having an eel-like body and a round, sucking mouth ⟨Old French *lampreie*, Latin *lampreda* earlier *naupreda*, influenced by *lambere* lick⟩

LAN [læn] *Computers* LOCAL AREA NETWORK.

lance [læns] *n* a long, wooden spear with a sharp metal head.
v **1** pierce with a lance. **2** cut open with a lancet: *The dentist lanced the infected gum*. ⟨French; Latin *lancea*⟩
lanc·er *n* formerly, a mounted soldier armed with a lance. **lan·cet** *n* **1** a surgical knife **2** a narrow, sharply pointed arch or window.

land [lænd] *n* **1** the solid part of the earth's surface: *dry land*. **2** soil: *This is good land for a garden*. **3** ground used as property: *The farmer invested in land and machinery*. **4** *Economics* anything furnished by nature without the help of humans, such as soil, mineral deposits, water, etc. *Land, labour, and capital* are the three principal factors of production.
v **1** come to land; bring to land: *The ship landed at the pier*. **2** go ashore: *The passengers landed*. **3 ✱** enter or be permitted to enter Canada as an immigrant. **4** arrive: *We landed in the ditch*. **5** *Informal* catch; get: *to land a fish*. **6** *Slang* get (a blow) home: *I landed one on his chin*. **land·like** *adj*. ⟨Old English⟩
how the land lies what the state of affairs is.
land·ed *adj* **1** owning land: *landed gentry*. **2** consisting of land. Landed property is real estate. **landed immigrant ✱** a person admitted to Canada as a settler and potential Canadian citizen. **land·fall** *n* **1** a sighting of land. **2** the land sighted or reached after a voyage or flight: *The explorer's landfall was near the mouth of the St. Lawrence*. **land·fill** *n* the disposal of waste by burying it under a shallow layer of ground. **land·form** *n Geology* a natural physical feature of the land. **land grant** a grant of land. **land·hold·er** *n* a person who owns or occupies land. **land·hold·ing** *adj, n*. **land·ing** *n* **1** a coming or bringing to land: *The army made a landing in*

France. **2 ✹** formal admission into Canada as an immigrant. **3** a place where persons or goods are landed from a ship, helicopter, etc. **4** a platform at the top of a flight of stairs. **5** *Logging* a place where logs are gathered before being transported to a sawmill. **landing field** a field for aircraft to land on and take off from safely. **landing gear** the wheels, pontoons, etc. of an aircraft. **landing pad** helipad. **landing strip** airstrip. **land·la·dy** *n* **1** a woman who owns buildings or land that she rents to others. **2** a woman who keeps a boarding house, lodging house, or inn. The legal term, regardless of gender, is **landlord. land·less** *adj* without land; owning no land. **land·less·ness** *n.* **land·locked** *adj* shut in, or nearly shut in, by land: *a landlocked harbour.* **land·lord** *n* **1** a person who owns buildings or land that he or she rents to others. **2** the keeper of a boarding house, lodging house, or inn. **land·lord·ship** *n.* **land·lubber** *n* a person not used to being on ships. **land·lub·ber·ish** *adj.* **land·mark** *n* **1** something familiar or easily seen, used as a guide. **2** an important fact or event. **3** a stone or other object that marks the boundary of a piece of land. **land mass** *Geology* a vast, unbroken area of land. **land mine** a container filled with explosives, on the ground or lightly covered, usually set off by the weight of something passing over it. **Land of the Little Sticks ✹** a region of stunted trees at the southern limits of the Barren Ground in northern Canada. **Land of the Midnight Sun ✹** the Far North. **land·own·er** *n* a person who owns lands. **land·own·er·ship** *n.* **land·own·ing** *n, adj.* **land·scape** *n* a view of scenery on land. *v* make (land) more pleasant to look at by arranging trees, shrubs, flowers, etc. **land·scap·er** *n.* **land·slide** *n* **1** a sliding down of a mass of soil on a steep slope. **2** an overwhelming majority of votes for one political party or candidate. **3** any overwhelming victory: *She won by a landslide.* **lands·man** *n, pl* **-men 1** a person who lives or works on land. **2** an inexperienced sailor. **land·ward** *adv, adj* toward the land. Also *(adv),* **land·wards.**

lan·dau ['lændɒ], ['lændaʊ], *or* ['lændoʊ] *n* **1** a four-wheeled carriage with a top that can be folded back. **2** an automobile with a similar top. ⟨*Landau,* town in Germany, where first made⟩

lane [leɪn] *n* **1** a narrow road or path. **2** any narrow way: *a highway with four lanes, the inside lane on a track.* ⟨Old English *lanu*⟩

lan·guage ['læŋgwɪdʒ] *n* **1** human speech. **2** the distinct form of speech common to a people, nation, or group of peoples: *the French language.* **3** a form or style of verbal expression: *bad language.* **4** communication of meaning in any way: *the language of dance.* **5** a set of attitudes, often held by a group: *He just doesn't speak my language.* **6** *Computers* a set of specifications that defines the form in which instructions for a computer are to be written. ⟨Old French *langage; langue* tongue, Latin *lingua*⟩

language arts the part of the school curriculum directly concerned with reading, speaking, listening, and writing. **language laboratory** a room equipped with headphones, etc. that enable students to practise a language they are studying.

lan·guid ['læŋgwɪd] *adj* **1** without energy: *A hot, sticky day makes a person feel languid.* **2** without interest. **lan·guid·ly** *adv.* **lan·guid·ness** *n.* ⟨Latin *languere* be faint⟩

lan·guish ['læŋgwɪʃ] *v* **1** become weak or weary. **2** suffer under unfavourable conditions: *Wild animals often languish in captivity.* **3** grow less intense: *His vigilance never languished.* **4** pine *(for)*: *She languished for home.* **5** assume a tender look for effect. **lan·guish·ing** *adj.* **lan·guish·ing·ly** *adv.* **lan·guor** ['læŋgər] *n.* **lan·guor·ous** *adj.*

La Ni·ña [læ'ninjə] a cooling of the ocean surface off the west coast of South America. Compare EL NIÑO. ⟨Spanish = the girl⟩

lank [læŋk] *adj* **1** long and thin: *a lank boy.* **2** straight and flat: *lank hair.* **lank·ly** *adv.* **lank·ness** *n.* ⟨Old English *hlanc*⟩

lank·y ['læŋki] *adj* awkwardly long and thin. **lank·i·ly** *adv.* **lank·i·ness** *n.*

lan·o·lin ['lænəlɪn] *n* fat or grease obtained from wool, used in ointments, etc. Also, **lan·o·line.** ⟨Latin *lana* wool + *oleum* oil⟩

lan·tern ['læntərn] *n* **1** a case to protect a light from wind, rain, etc. **2** the room at the top of a lighthouse where the light is. **3** an upright structure on a roof or dome, for letting in light and air or for decoration. ⟨Latin *lanterna*⟩ **lan·tern–jawed** *adj* having hollow cheeks and long, thin jaws.

lan·than·um ['lænθənəm] *n* a rare-earth element that tarnishes easily. *Symbol* **La** ⟨Greek *lanthanein* lurk unseen⟩

lan·yard ['lænjərd] *n* **1** a cord used on ships to fasten rigging. **2** a cord with a hook at one end, used in firing cannon. Also, **lan·iard.** ⟨*lanyer* (French *lanière* thong) + *yard²*⟩

lap¹ [læp] *n* **1** the front part from the hips to the knees of a person sitting down, with the clothing that covers it. **2** a loosely hanging edge of clothing; flap. ⟨Old English *læppa*⟩ **in the lap of luxury** in luxurious circumstances. **lap dog** a small pet dog. **lap·ful** *n* as much as a lap can hold. **lap·top (computer)** a computer small enough to fit on a person's lap.

lap² [læp] *v* **lapped, lap·ping 1** overlap: *We lapped shingles on the roof.* **2** extend beyond a limit: *The reign of Queen Elizabeth I lapped into the 1600s.* **3** wrap or be wrapped *(around)*: *He lapped the blanket around him.* **4** in a race, get a lap or more ahead of (other racers). *n* **1** a lapping over. **2** one time around a racetrack. **3** a part of any course travelled: *The last lap of the hike was the toughest.* ⟨Middle English *lappen* fold, wrap; akin to LAP¹⟩

lap³ [læp] *v* **lapped, lap·ping 1** drink by lifting with the tongue: *Cats lap water.* **2** move gently with a slight slapping sound: *Little waves lapped against the boat.* **lap** *n.* ⟨Old English *lapian*⟩
lap up *Informal* consume eagerly: *The advanced students lapped up the math course.*

la·pel *n* the part of the front of a coat or jacket that is folded back just below the collar. ⟨*lap¹* + diminutive suffix *-el*⟩

lap·i·dar·y [ˈlæpəˌdɛri] *n* a person who cuts, polishes, or engraves precious stones.
adj **1** to do with cutting precious stones. **2** characteristic of inscriptions; grandiose: *lapidary language.* ⟨Latin *lapidis* stone⟩

lapse [læps] *n* **1** a slight mistake. **2** a slipping away from what is right: *a moral lapse.* **3** a slipping by: *A minute is a short lapse of time.* **4** the ending of a right or privilege because it was not renewed: *the lapse of a lease.* **lapse** *v.* **lap·sed** *adj.* ⟨Latin *lapsus* fall; *labi* to slip⟩

lar·board [ˈlɑrbərd] *or* [ˈlɑrˌbɔrd] *Nautical n* the side of a ship to the left when one looks from the stern toward the bow; port. ⟨Middle English *ladeborde* loading side⟩

lar·ce·ny [ˈlɑrsəni] *n, pl* **-nies** *Legal* theft. **lar·ce·nous** *adj.* **lar·ce·nous·ly** *adv.* ⟨Anglo-French *larcin*, Latin *latrocinium; latro* bandit⟩

larch [lɑrtʃ] *n* any of a genus of trees of the pine family, having needlelike leaves that are shed in the fall. ⟨German *Lärche*; Latin *laricis*⟩

lard [lɑrd] *n* the fat of pigs, melted then hardened to a white solid used in cooking. *v* **1** insert strips of bacon or salt pork in (meat poultry, etc.) before cooking. **2** grease. **3** give variety to; enrich: *to lard a long speech with stories.* **lard·like** *adj.* ⟨Latin *lardum*⟩
lar·der *n* **1** a pantry; place where food is kept. **2** a supply of food.

large [lɑrdʒ] *adj* **1** of more than the usual size, amount, or number: *Canada is a large country.* **2** of great scope: *a person of large experience.* **large·ness** *n.* ⟨Latin *largus* copious⟩
at large a at liberty; free: *Is the escaped prisoner still at large?* **b** altogether: *the people at large.* **in large** or **in the large** on a big scale. **large·ly** *adv* **1** to a great extent: *This region consists largely of desert.* **2** much. **large–scale** *adj* extensive: *a large-scale disaster.* **larg·ish** *adj Informal* rather large.

lar·gesse [lɑrˈdʒɛs] *or* [lɑrˈʒɛs] *n* **1** generous giving. **2** a generous gift or gifts. ⟨Old French *largesse; large* large. See LARGE.⟩

lar·go [ˈlɑrgou] *Music adj* slow and dignified. ⟨Italian *largo* broad, slow; Latin *largus* large⟩

lar·i·at [ˈlɛriət] *or* [ˈlæriət] *n* a long rope with a running noose at one end; lasso. ⟨Spanish *la reata* the rope⟩

lark¹ [lɑrk] *n* any of a family of songbirds that live mainly on the ground. ⟨Old English *lāwerce*⟩

lark² [lɑrk] *Informal n* a merry time; frolic or prank. **lark** *v.* ⟨origin uncertain⟩

lar·ri·gan [ˈlɛrəgən] *or* [ˈlærəgən] *n* ✳ an oiled leather moccasin, usually with a flexible sole. ⟨origin uncertain⟩

lar·va [ˈlɑrvə] *n, pl* **-vae** [-vi] *or* [-vaɪ] the wingless form of many insects from the time they leave the egg until they become a pupa. ⟨Latin *larva* ghost, skeleton⟩
lar·val *adj* **1** to do with larvae. **2** of a disease, latent; undeveloped.

lar·ynx [ˈlɛrɪŋks] *or* [ˈlærɪŋks] *n, pl* **la·ryn·ges** [ləˈrɪndʒiz] or **lar·ynx·es** *Anatomy* the cavity at the upper end of the human windpipe, containing the vocal cords. **la·ryn·ge·al** [ləˈrɪndʒəl] *or* [-dʒiəl] *adj.* ⟨Greek⟩
lar·yn·gi·tis [ˌlɛrənˈdʒaɪtɪs] *or* [ˌlærən-] *n* inflammation of the larynx, often accompanied by a temporary loss of voice.

la·sa·gna [ləˈzɑnjə] *n* a dish consisting of flat noodles baked in layers with tomato, cheese, and meat or vegetables. ⟨Italian⟩

las·civ·i·ous [ləˈsɪviəs] *adj* lustful. **las·civ·i·ous·ly** *adv.* **las·civ·i·ous·ness** *n.* ⟨Latin *lascivia* wantonness; *lascivus* wanton⟩

la·ser [ˈleizər] *n* a device for amplifying and concentrating light waves into a single beam of light. ⟨*l*ight *a*mplification by *s*timulated *e*mission of *r*adiation⟩
laser beam a beam of intense radiation from a laser, used in surgery and industry. **laser disk** a disk to be read by a machine using a laser beam. **laser printer** *Computers* a printer that uses laser technology. **laser surgery** surgery using laser beams, as in eye surgery.

lash¹ [læʃ] *n* **1** a whip. **2** a stroke with a whip. **3** a sudden, swift movement. **4** eyelash.
v **1** beat with a whip. **2** beat back and forth: *The lion lashed its tail.* **3** strike violently: *The rain lashed against the windows.* **4** attack severely with words: *The editorial lashed the government for its indifference.* **lash·ing** *adj.* ⟨Middle English *lasche*, perhaps imitative⟩
lash out strike at, with or as if with a whip: *In his book he lashes out at those who wronged him.* **lash·ing** *n* **1** a whipping. **2** a severe attack in words. **3 lashings** *pl* an abundance (*of*).

lash² [læʃ] *v* tie or fasten with a rope, cord, etc. ⟨Middle English *lasschyn*⟩

lass [læs] *n* a girl; young woman. ⟨Middle English *lasse*; origin uncertain⟩

las·si·tude [ˈlæsɪˌtjud] *or* [ˈlæsɪˌtud] *n* lack of energy. ⟨Latin *lassitudo; lassus* tired⟩

las·so [ˈlæˈsu], [ləˈsu], *or, esp US,* [ˈlæsou] *n, pl* **-sos** *or* **-soes** a long rope with a running noose at one end; lariat.
v **-soed, -so·ing** catch with a lasso. **las·so·er** *n.* ⟨Spanish *lazo*; Latin *laqueus* loop, noose⟩

last¹ [læst] *adj* **1** coming after all others: *the last page of the book.* **2** previous: *last week.* **3** being the only one remaining *my last dollar.*
n **1** a person or thing that comes after all others: *She was the last in the line.* **2** the end: *You have not heard the last of this.*
adv **1** after all others: *I arrived last.* **2** on the most recent occasion: *When did you last see her?* ⟨Old English *lætest; læt* late⟩
at last or **at long last** after a long time: *So you have come home at last!* **breathe one's last** die.

see the last of not see again.
last–ditch *adj* **1** serving as a last line of defence: *a last-ditch move.* **2** resisting to the last extremity: *last-ditch survivors of the attack.* **Last Judgment** or **Judgement** *Christianity* God's final judgment of all humankind at the end of the world. **last·ly** *adv* finally. **last name** surname; family name. **last offices** prayers for a dead person. **last post** in the armed forces, the bugle call that gives the hour of retiring. It is blown also at military funerals, Remembrance Day ceremonies, etc. **last quarter** the period between the second half moon and the new moon. **last rites** religious rites performed for a dying person. **last straw** the last of a series of troublesome things resulting in a collapse, outburst, etc. **Last Supper** the supper of Jesus and His disciples on the evening before He was crucified. **last word 1** the most conclusive thing said on a subject. **2** *Informal* the most up-to-date style: *the last word in casual wear.* **3** *Informal* something that cannot be improved on.

SYNONYMS

Last = coming after all others in a series: *the last day of school.* **Final** emphasizes the idea of completing a series of events: *final exams.* **Ultimate** = the last that can ever be reached by going forward or by tracing backward: *The ultimate cause of this disease is unknown.*

last² [læst] *v* **1** go on; endure: *The storm lasted three days.* **2** continue in good condition, force, etc.: *I hope these shoes last a year.* **3** be enough: *while our money lasts.* ⟨Old English *lǣstan* <*lǣst* track. Related to LAST³.⟩
last·ing *adj* that will last. **last·ing·ly** *adv.*

last³ [læst] *n* a block shaped like a person's foot, on which shoes and boots are formed or repaired. ⟨Old English *lǣste; lǣst* track⟩

latch [lætʃ] *n* a catch for fastening a door, window, etc. **latch** *v.* ⟨Old English *læccan* grasp⟩ **on the latch** fastened only with a latch. **latch on** *Informal* understand. **latch onto** *Informal* **a** seize. **b** get. **c** understand. **d** stick closely to (a person or group of people).
latch·key *n* a key used to open a door.

late [leit] *adj* **lat·er** or **lat·ter**, **lat·est** or **last 1** happening after the usual time: *a late lunch.* **2** happening at an advanced time: *success late in life.* **3** recent: *The late storm did much damage.* **4** recently dead: *My late brother was a fine man.* **5** gone out of office: *The late prime minister is still working actively.*
adv **lat·er, lat·est** or **last 1** after the usual time: *He worked late.* **2** at an advanced time: *It rained late in the day.* **3** recently. **late·ness** *n.* ⟨Old English *læt*⟩
of late lately: *I haven't seen him of late.*
late·com·er *n* a person who or thing that arrives later than expected. **late·ly** *adv* recently. **lat·ish** *adj, adv Informal* rather late.

la·tent [ˈleitənt] *adj* present, but not visible or active: *a latent infection.* **la·ten·cy** *n.* **la·tent·ly** *adv.* ⟨Latin *latere* lie hidden⟩
latent heat *Physics* the amount of heat

absorbed or released when a substance changes its state.

lat·er·al [ˈlætərəl] *adj* **1** to do with a side. **2** of thinking, exploiting indirect relationships. Compare LINEAR.
n **1** a lateral outgrowth. **2** *Mining* **a** a drift other than the main drift. **b** a connecting tunnel. **lat·er·al·ly** *adv.* ⟨Latin *lateris* side⟩

la·tex [ˈleiteks] *n, pl* **lat·i·ces** [ˈlæti,siz] or **la·tex·es 1** a milky liquid present in certain plants, that is the basis of rubber and chicle. **2** *Chemistry* an emulsion of synthetic rubber or plastic in water, used in paints, adhesives, etc. ⟨Latin *latex* something liquid⟩

lath [læθ] *n, pl* **laths** [læðz] or [læθs] *n* a narrow strip of wood used to support the plaster of a wall, or to make a lattice. **lath·like** *adj.* ⟨Middle English *laththe*⟩
lath·ing or **lath·work** *n* laths collectively.

lathe [leið] *n* a machine for holding pieces of wood, metal, etc. and turning them against a cutting tool that shapes them. ⟨Middle English *lath* stand; Scandinavian⟩

lath·er [ˈlæðər] *n* **1** the foam made from soap or detergent mixed in water. **2** foam formed in sweating: *the lather on a horse.*
v **1** put lather on, or form a lather. **2** *Informal* beat; flog. ⟨Old English *lēathor*⟩
in (or **into**) **a lather** *Informal* in (or into) a greatly excited state: *to work oneself into a lather about nothing.*

Lat·in [ˈlætin] *n* **1** the language of the ancient Romans. **2** a member of any of the peoples whose languages come from Latin: *The French are Latins.*
adj to do with Latin, the Romance languages, or Latin America. ⟨Latin *Latinus* of Latium⟩
Latin America South America, Central America, Mexico, and much of the West Indies. **Lat·in–A·mer·i·can** *n, adj.* **La·tin·ate** *adj* using many Latin constructions.

lat·i·tude [ˈlæti,tjud] or [ˈlæti,tud] *n* **1** *Geography* the distance north or south of the equator, measured in degrees. Compare LONGITUDE. **2** room to act or think: *An artist is allowed more latitude than a bricklayer.* **lat·i·tu·di·nal** *adj.* ⟨Latin *latitudo; latus* wide⟩

lat·ke [ˈlɑtkə] *n* a Jewish potato pancake. ⟨Yiddish; Russian *latka* patch⟩

la·trine [ləˈtrin] *n* a toilet in a camp, factory, etc. ⟨Latin *latrina* washroom; *lavare* wash⟩

lat·ter [ˈlætər] *adj* later; nearer the end: *Friday comes in the latter part of the week.*
n **the latter** the second of two: *Canada and the US are in North America; the former lies north of the latter.* Compare FORMER. **lat·ter·ly** *adv.* ⟨Old English *lætra* later⟩
lat·ter–day *adj* of recent times: *latter-day religions.*

lat·tice [ˈlætis] *n* **1** a structure of crossed strips with open spaces between them. **2** any pattern or decoration resembling a lattice. **3** *Physics* the geometric structure of materials in a nuclear reactor. **lat·tice·like** *adj.* ⟨Old French *lattis; latte* lath; Germanic⟩
lat·tice·work *n* a lattice or lattices.

laud [lɒd] *v* praise.
n a song of praise. ⟨Latin *laudare* praise, v; *laus, laudis* praise, n⟩
laud·a·ble *adj* praiseworthy. **laud·a·bil·i·ty** *n.*
laud·a·bly *adv.* **laud·a·to·ry** *adj* expressing praise.

laugh [læf] *v* make sounds and movements that show amusement at humour: *We all laughed at the joke.* **laugh** *n.* **laugh·a·ble** *adj.*
laugh·a·ble·ness *n.* **laugh·a·bly** *adv.* **laugh·ter** *n.*
⟨Old English *hliehhan*⟩
last laugh a victory that defies the expectations of others: *When his old car won, he had the last laugh.* **laugh at a** make fun of. **b** disregard or make light of: *to laugh at danger.* **laugh in** (or **up**) **one's sleeve** laugh to oneself. **laugh off** pass off with a laugh. **laugh on the other** (or **wrong**) **side of one's face** (or **mouth**) be made to change from amusement to sorrow.
laugh·ing *adj* **1** that laughs or seems to laugh: *the laughing brook.* **2** accompanied by laughter. **laugh·ing·ly** *adv.* **no laughing matter** a matter that is serious. **laughing gas** nitrous oxide, which makes some people laugh. **laugh·ing·stock** *n* an object of ridicule.

launch¹ [lɒntʃ] *v* **1** set afloat. **2** set going: *to launch someone in business.* **3** send out: *to launch a rocket.* **launch** *n.* **launch·a·ble** *adj.*
⟨Anglo-French *launcher* use a lance. See LANCE.⟩
launch out begin; start.
launching pad a platform from which a rocket is launched into the air.

launch² [lɒntʃ] *n* a motorboat used for pleasure trips. ⟨Spanish, Portuguese *lancha;* Malay *lanchāran* speedboat; *lanchar* speed⟩

laun·der ['lɒndər] *v* **1** wash and iron (clothes, linens, etc.). **2** *Informal* disguise the source of (money obtained illegally).
laun·der·a·bil·i·ty *n.* **laun·der·a·ble** *adj.*
laun·der·er *n.* ⟨Middle English *lander* washer of linen; Latin *lavare* wash⟩
laun·dress ['lɒndrɪs] *n* a woman whose work is washing and ironing clothes, linens, etc.
Laun·dro·mat ['lɒndrə,mæt] *n Trademark* a self-service laundry with coin-operated washing machines and dryers. **laun·dry** *n*
1 an establishment or room where clothes, linens, etc. are washed and ironed. **2** clothes, etc. washed or to be washed.

lau·rel ['lɔrəl] *n* **1** any of a genus of evergreen trees or shrubs; especially **bay**, believed to be the leaves used by the ancient Greeks for wreaths to crown victors and heroes.
2 laurels *pl* honour or victory: *The laurels went to a young athlete who had not competed before.* **lau·relled** or **lau·reled** *adj.* ⟨Old French *lorier, laurier;* Latin *laurus*⟩
look to one's laurels guard one's reputation from rival competitors. **rest on one's laurels** be satisfied with honours already won.
lau·re·ate ['lɔriit] *adj* **1** crowned with a laurel wreath as a mark of honour. **2** honoured.

Lau·ren·tia [lə'rɛnʃiə] *n ❋ Often poetic* the region north of the St. Lawrence River, formerly New France and its hinterland. ⟨feminine of Latin *Laurentius* Lawrence⟩

Lau·ren·tian *adj* **1** to do with the St. Lawrence River and adjoining lands. **2** *Geology* to do with granites found in the rocks of the Canadian Shield. **Laurentian Shield ❋** CANADIAN SHIELD.

la·va ['lævə] or ['lɑvə] *n* the molten rock flowing from a volcano, or the rock formed when it cools. ⟨dialect Italian *lava* stream; Latin *lavare* wash⟩

lav·a·to·ry ['lævə,tɔri] *n* **1** washroom; toilet. **2** washbasin. ⟨Latin *lavatorium; lavare* wash⟩

lav·en·der ['lævəndər] *n* a small evergreen shrub which yields an essential oil used in perfumes. ⟨Latin *lavendula*⟩

lav·ish ['lævɪʃ] *adj* **1** very free in giving: *A rich person can afford to be lavish with money.* **2** very abundant: *many lavish gifts.* **lav·ish** *v.*
lav·ish·ly *adv.* **lav·ish·ness** *n.* ⟨Old French *lavasse* flood, *laver* wash, Latin *lavare*⟩

law [lɒ] *n* **1** a body of rules recognized as binding. **2** one of these rules: *a law against slavery.* **3** the controlling influence of these rules: *maintain law and order.* **4** a body of such rules concerned with a particular subject: *criminal law.* **5** the legal profession: *enter the law.* **6 a** legal authorities. **b** *Informal* a police officer or detective. **7** *Philosophy, sciences* a statement of a relation invariable under the same conditions: *the law of gravitation.* **law·like** *adj.* ⟨Old English *lagu*⟩
go to law take legal action. **lay down the law** give orders that must be obeyed. **read law** study to be a lawyer. **take the law into one's own hands** take steps to gain one's rights without going to court.
law·a·bid·ing *adj* obedient to the law.
law·break·er *n* a person who breaks the law.
law·break·ing *n, adj.* **law·ful** *adj* **1** according to law: *lawful arrest.* **2** allowed by law: *lawful demands.* **law·ful·ly** *adv.* **law·ful·ness** *n.*
law·giv·er *n* a person who prepares a system of laws. **law·less** *adj* **1** paying no attention to the law: *a lawless life.* **2** hard to control: *a lawless mob.* **3** having no laws: *a lawless frontier town.* **law·less·ness** *n.* **law·mak·er** *n* a person who helps to make laws; legislator.
law·mak·ing *n, adj.* **law of averages 1** *Statistics* the principle that the number of occurrences of an event is predictable from its number of random trials. **2** *Informal* the principle that the greatest influence on any occurrence is probability. **law·suit** *n* a civil case in a court of law. **law·yer** ['lɔiər] *n* a person whose profession is giving advice about the laws or acting for others in a court of law. **law·yer·like** *adj.* **law·yer·ly** *adj.*

lawn [lɒn] *n* land covered with grass kept cut. ⟨Middle French *lande* glade; Celtic⟩
lawn bowling a game played on a bowling green with a wooden ball that is rolled toward a target ball (the jack). **lawn mower** a machine with revolving blades for cutting the grass on a lawn. **lawn tennis** tennis played outdoors.

law·ren·ci·um ['lɔrɛnsiəm] *n* an artificial, radioactive element. *Symbol* **Lr** ⟨E.O. *Lawrence,* 20c American physicist.⟩

lax [læks] *adj* **1** loose or slack. **2** not strict: *lax behaviour.* **lax·ly** *adv.* **lax·ness** *n.* **lax·i·ty** *n.* ⟨Latin *laxus*⟩
lax·a·tive *n* a medicine that makes the bowels move. **lax·a·tive** *adj.*

lay¹ [lei] *v* **laid, lay·ing 1** put down: *Lay your book on the table.* **2** place; set: *He lays great emphasis on good manners.* **3** wager: *I lay five dollars that she will not come.* **4** produce (an egg) from the body: *Birds lay eggs.*
n **1** the way in which a thing is laid or lies: *the lay of the ground.* **2 ✱** formerly, a lease to work a gold claim for a share of the proceeds. ⟨Old English *lecgan* causative of *licgan* lie²⟩
lay about strike out on all sides. **lay a course** *Nautical* sail in a certain direction. **lay aside** (or **away**) save: *I laid away ten dollars a week.* **lay·a·way** *n.* **lay by a** put away for future use. **b** *Nautical* of a ship, come to a standstill. **lay in** get and save: *to lay in supplies for the winter.* **lay into** *Informal* beat; *v Slang* scold. **lay it on thick** See THICK. **lay low** bring down. **lay off a** *Slang* stop teasing: *Lay off the new kid.* **b** put out of work. **lay·off** *n.* **lay oneself out** make an effort. **lay open** expose (*to*): *I laid myself open to ridicule.* **lay out a** spread out: *Supper was laid out on the table.* **b** prepare (a dead body) for burial. **c** arrange or plan: *to lay out a program.* **d** mark off: *They laid out a tennis court.* **e** *Slang* spend: *They laid out two hundred dollars in repairs.* **f** *Slang.* knock unconscious. **lay·out** *n.* **lay over** *Informal* break a journey: *We'll lay over in Vancouver for a few days.* **lay·o·ver** *n.* **lay to** *Nautical* of ships, head into the wind and stand still. **lay up a** put away for future use. **b** cause to stay indoors because of illness: *He was laid up with the flu.* **c** *Nautical* put (a ship) in dock.
lay·a·bout *n* a lazy, shiftless person. **lay·er** *n* **1** one that lays: *This hen is a good layer.* **2** one thickness. *v* arrange in layers. **lay** (or **lie**) **of the land 1** the position of hills, water, trees, etc. **2** the existing situation.

> ┌─────────────┐
> │ **CONFUSABLES** │
> └─────────────┘
> **Lay** always takes an object: *We laid a new floor in the kitchen. Lay the book on the table.*
> **Lie** does not take an object: *I'm going to lie down for a rest. She lay down for a rest.*

lay² [lei] *v* pt of LIE².
lay³ [lei] *adj* **1** not of the clergy. **2** not of lawyers, doctors, etc.: *The lay mind understands little of the cause of the disease.* ⟨Old French *lai;* Latin *laicus*⟩
la·i·ty ['leiəti] *n* the people as distinguished from the clergy or from professionals: *Lawyers use words that the laity do not understand.*
lay·man ['leimən] *n, pl* **-men 1** a male member of the church who is not a member of the clergy: *The priest and several laymen planned the church budget.* **2** a man who is not a member of a particular profession: *It is hard for most laymen to understand doctors' prescriptions.* ⟨*lay³* + *man*⟩
lay⁴ [lei] *n* a poem or song. ⟨Old French *lai,* Germanic; compare Old High German *leih*⟩

lay·ette [lei'ɛt] *n* clothes, bedding, etc. for a newborn baby. ⟨French, from *laie* chest⟩
lay·up or **lay-up** ['leiʌp] *n Basketball* a shot on the basket at close range, often bounced off the backboard.
la·zy ['leizi] *adj* **1** not willing to work or be active: *too lazy to get up and turn off the TV.* **2** to do with idleness: *a lazy summer day.* **3** not very active: *a lazy stream.* **la·zi·ly** *adv.* **la·zi·ness** *n.* ⟨perhaps Middle Low German *lasich* weak, feeble⟩
laze *v* be lazy or idle. **la·zy·bones** *n pl or sg Informal* a lazy person. **lazy eye** an eye with poor vision caused by underuse. **lazy Su·san** a revolving tray for holding different kinds of food, condiments, etc.
lb. [paʊnd] pound (sg or collective pl); *pl* **lbs.** [paʊndz]. ⟨Latin *libra,* pl *librae*⟩
l.c. 1 LOWER CASE. **2** LOC. CIT.
LCD 1 *Computers* LIQUID-CRYSTAL DISPLAY. **2** LEAST COMMON DENOMINATOR.
LCM LEAST COMMON MULTIPLE.
lea [li] *n* a grassy field. ⟨Old English *lēah*⟩
leach [litʃ] *v* **1** run (water, etc.) through slowly. **2** dissolve out by running water through slowly: *Potash is leached from wood ashes.* **leach·a·bil·i·ty** *n.* **leach·a·ble** *adj.* ⟨Old English *leccan* wet⟩
lead¹ [lid] *v* **led, lead·ing 1** guide: *She led us through the forest.* **2** be a means of effecting a certain result: *Hard work leads to success.* **3** spend (life, time, etc.): *He leads a quiet life.* **4** afford passage: *This road leads to the city.* **5** guide in action, opinion, etc.: *Such actions led us to distrust her.* **6** be at the head of: *The clowns led the parade.* **7** *Card games* make first play at cards. **8** *Curling* throw first on a team.
n **1** example: *to follow someone's lead.* **2** the foremost place. **3** the distance, number of points, etc. that one is ahead: *a lead of 3 m at the halfway mark.* **4** *Card games* the right to play first. **5** something that leads. **6** *Theatre, film* the principal role in a play, etc. **7** leash. **8** a clue: *The librarian gave me some good leads.* **9** *Electricity* a conductor conveying electric current. **10** *Curling* the person on a team who throws first in each end. **lead·ing** *adj.* ⟨Old English *lǣdan*⟩
lead astray a give false information to. **b** encourage to do wrong. **lead nowhere** lead to a dead end. **lead off** begin. **lead on a** influence. **b** deceive. **c** take the lead. **lead up to** prepare the way for.
lead dog in a dog team, the dog that leads the team, setting the pace. **lead·er** *n* **1** a person or thing that leads: *a band leader.* **2** LEADING ARTICLE. **3** a length of nylon, etc. used to attach the lure to a fishing line. **4** an article offered at a low price to attract customers. **lead·er·less** *adj.* **lead·er·ship** *n.* **lead–in** *n* **1** a wire that runs from an antenna to a receiver or transmitter. **2** introduction: *a short lead-in.* **lead·ing** *adj* most important; principal: *the leading scientist in her field.* **leading article, lead article,** or **leader** an important editorial in a newspaper, etc.

leading lady an actor who plays the chief female part in a play or film. **leading man. leading question** a question worded to make the desired answer unavoidable. **lead-off** *n* 1 the beginning of something. 2 *Baseball* the opening hitter. **lead time** the period needed to develop and manufacture a product.

lead² [lɛd] *n* 1 a soft metallic element. *Symbol* **Pb** 2 a weight on a line used to find the depth of water. 3 bullets. 4 a thin piece of graphite or other substance in or for a pencil. 5 **leads** *pl* a strips of lead used to cover roofs. b the frames of lead in which glass is set. **lead** *adj.* **lead·less** *adj.* **lead–free** *adj.* ⟨Old English *lēad*⟩
lead·en *adj* 1 made of lead: *a leaden coffin.* 2 heavy: *The runner's legs felt leaden.* 3 grey and gloomy: *leaden clouds.* **lead·en·ly** *adv.* **lead·en·ness** *n.* **lead·ing** *n* 1 a frame of lead. 2 the space between lines of type. **lead pencil** an ordinary pencil with a graphite core. **lead–pipe cinch** *Slang* 1 something absolutely certain. 2 a very easy thing to do.

leaf [lif] *n, pl* **leaves** 1 one of the green parts that grow on the stem of a plant. 2 a sheet of paper. 3 a thin piece of metal, etc.: *gold leaf.* 4 a piece serving as an extension to a table.
v 1 put forth leaves: *These trees leaf in spring.* 2 (with *through*) turn pages. **leaf·less** *adj.* **leaf·less·ness** *n.* **leaf·like** *adj.* ⟨Old English *lēaf*⟩
in leaf having completely developed foliage. **take a leaf from someone's book** *Informal* follow someone's example. **turn over a new leaf** start all over again.
leaf·hop·per *n* any of a family of insects which are agricultural pests because they suck the juices of plants. **leaf·let** *n* a small sheet of printed matter: *advertising leaflets.* **leaf mould** compost made mainly of leaves. **leaf·y** *adj* 1 having many leaves. 2 resembling a leaf: *fabric with a leafy design.* **leaf·i·ness** *n.*

league [lig] *n* 1 an association of persons, countries, etc., formed to help one another. 2 a group of teams that play against each other: *a bowling league.* 3 *Informal* a class or level: *The two are just not in the same league.* **leagu·er** *n.* ⟨French *ligue,* Italian *liga, lega; legare* bind; Latin⟩
in league united: *in league with the enemy.*

leak [lik] *n* 1 a hole that lets something in or out: *a leak in a tire.* 2 an escape or loss: *a news leak.* **leak** *v.* **leak·i·ness** *n.* **leak·y** *adj.* ⟨Middle English *leken*; Scandinavian⟩
leak·age *n* 1 the act of leaking: *a leakage in a pipeline.* 2 the rate of leaking: *The leakage was about 40 L an hour.* **leak·proof** *adj* that will not allow anything to leak in or out.

lean¹ [lin] *v* **leaned** or **leant** [lɛnt], **lean·ing** 1 bend: *A small tree leans over in the wind.* 2 rest in a sloping position: *Lean against me.* 3 set in a leaning position: *Lean the picture against the wall.* 4 rely: *to lean on a friend's advice.* 5 tend: *Her favourite sport was tennis, but now she leans toward golf.*
n inclination: *The old barn has more of a lean this year.* ⟨Old English *hlinian*⟩
lean on apply force to persuade. **lean over**

backward See BEND.
lean–to *n* 1 a building partly supported by another. 2 a crude shelter built against posts, trees, rock, etc.: *We keep wood in this lean-to.*

lean² [lin] *adj* 1 with little or no fat: *a lean horse.* 2 producing little: *a lean harvest.* **lean·ly** *adv.* **lean·ness** *n.* ⟨Old English *hlǣne*⟩

leap [lip] *n* a jump.
v **leaped** or **leapt** [lɛpt], **leap·ing** 1 jump: *A frog leaps.* 2 come as if with a leap: *An idea leaped to her mind.* 3 jump over: *to leap a fence.* ⟨Old English *hlȳp,* n, *hlēapan,* v⟩
by leaps and bounds fast and very much. **leap at** *Informal* accept with eagerness: *to leap at the chance.* **leap in the dark** an action taken without knowing what its results will be.
leap·frog *n* a game in which one player jumps over the bent back of another.
v **-frogged, -frog·ging** 1 leap as in the game of leapfrog. 2 skip over. **leap year** a year having 366 days, the extra day being February 29. A year is a leap year if its number divides exactly by four, except years at the end of a century, which must be exactly divisible by 400; 2004 and 2000 are leap years, whereas 2005 and 2100 are not.

learn [lɜrn] *v* **learned** or **learnt, learn·ing.** 1 gain knowledge, skill, or habit by study, instruction, or experience: *to learn French.* 2 memorize: *He learned the poem in five minutes.* 3 find out: *She tried to learn the details of the train wreck.* 4 acquire (a habit). 5 become able by discipline or practice: *to learn to control one's temper.* **learn·a·ble** *adj* **learned** *adj.* ⟨Old English *leornian*⟩
learn·ed ['lɜrnɪd] *adj* having much knowledge; scholarly: *a learned woman, a learned book.* **learn·ed·ly** *adv.* **learn·ed·ness** *n.* **learn·er** *n* beginner. **learn·ing** *n* 1 the gaining of knowledge or skill. 2 the possession of knowledge gained by study. 3 knowledge.

CONFUSABLES

The verbs **learn** and **teach** are not synonyms: *I learned how to play chess. She taught me how to play chess.* The usage *She learned me how to play chess* is unacceptable.

lease [lis] *n* 1 a contract giving the right to use property for a length of time, usually by paying rent. 2 the length of time for which such an agreement is made: *They have a year's lease on the property.*
v give or take a lease on. **leas·a·ble** *adj.* **lease·less** *adj.* ⟨Middle English *les;* Anglo-French *lesser* to lease, Latin *laxāre*⟩
new lease on life the chance to live a longer, better, or happier life: *The successful surgery gave her a new lease on life.*
lease·hold *n* real estate held by a lease. **lease·hold·er** *n.* **les·see** [lɛ'si] *n* a person to whom a lease is granted. **les·sor** ['lɛsɔr] or [lɛ'sɔr] *n* a person who grants a lease.

leash [liʃ] *n* a strap for restraining a dog or other animal.
v hold with a leash. ⟨Old French *laisse* loose⟩
strain at the leash try to go ahead despite restraint.

least [list] *adj* less than any other; smallest: *The least bit of dirt in a watch may make it stop.* *n* the least amount: *It's the least you can do.* *adv* to the least extent: *She liked that book least of all.* ⟨Old English *lǣst*⟩
at least or **at the least a** at the lowest estimate: *The temperature was at least 35°C.* **b** at any rate: *He was late but at least he came.* **c** as a minimum requirement, offer, etc.: *You must be at least six years old to join.* **not in the least** not at all.
least (or **lowest**) **common denominator** *Mathematics* the lowest common multiple of all the denominators of a group of fractions. *Abbrev* **LCD**. **least common multiple** the least quantity that contains two or more given quantities exactly. *Abbrev* **LCM**. **least·wise** or **leastways** *adv Informal* at least; at any rate.

leath·er [ˈlɛðər] *n* animal skin that has been prepared for use by tanning it. ⟨Old English *lether*⟩
leath·er·ette *n* imitation leather. **leath·er·y** *adj* like leather in appearance or toughness. **leath·er·i·ness** *n*.

leave[1] [liv] *v* **left**, **leav·ing 1** go away: *We leave tonight.* **2** let remain: *I left a book on the table.* **3** let remain when one dies: *She left a large fortune.* **4** let (a person, etc.) alone to do something: *Leave me to settle the matter.* **5** let remain uneaten, unused, etc.: *to leave one's dessert.* **6** not attend to: *I will leave my homework till tomorrow.* ⟨Old English *lǣfan*⟩
leave off stop: *Continue the story from where I left off.* **leave out** omit: *She left out two words when she read the sentence.*
leav·ings *n pl* leftovers; remnants.

leave[2] [liv] *n* **1** permission; consent: *They gave him leave to go.* **2** permission to be absent from duty, or the length of time that such permission lasts. ⟨Old English *lēaf*⟩
by your leave with your consent. **on leave** absent from duty with permission. **take leave** (*of*), say goodbye (to): *We took leave of our hostess.* **take one's leave** say goodbye and depart. **leave–tak·ing** *n*.
leave of absence the length of time that absence from duty is permitted.

leav·en [ˈlɛvən] *n* **1** any substance, such as yeast, that will make dough rise. **2** a tempering or modifying element: *The solemn speech had a leaven of humour.* **leav·en** *v.* ⟨Old French *levain;* Latin *levamen* lifting, *levare* lift⟩
leav·en·ing *n* something that leavens.

leaves [livz] *n* **1** pl of LEAF. **2** pl of LEAVE[2].

lech·er·y [ˈlɛtʃəri] *n* lewdness; gross indulgence of lust. **lech·er** *n.* **lech·er·ous** *adj.* **lech·er·ous·ly** *adv.* ⟨Old French *lecheor* glutton, libertine⟩

le·ci·thin [ˈlɛsəθɪn] *n Biochemistry* any fatty substance as found in animal tissues. ⟨Greek *lekithos* yolk of an egg⟩

lec·tern [ˈlɛktərn] *n* a reading desk or stand with a sloping top. ⟨Old French *lettrun,* Latin *lectrum; legere* read⟩

lec·ture [ˈlɛktʃər] *n* **1** a speech on a chosen subject, usually for instruction. **2** a scolding. **lec·ture** *v.* **lec·tur·er** *n.* ⟨Latin *lectura*⟩

led [lɛd] *v* pt and pp of LEAD[1].

LED or **L.E.D.** LIGHT-EMITTING DIODE.

ledge [lɛdʒ] *n* **1** a narrow shelf: *a window ledge.* **2** a shelf of rock. **ledge·less** *adj.* ⟨Middle English, from *legge(n)*; akin to LAY[1]⟩

ledg·er [ˈlɛdʒər] *n* a book in which a business keeps a record of all money transactions. ⟨Middle English *legger* a book. See LEDGE.⟩

lee [li] *n* **1** the side sheltered from the wind: *the lee of the house.* **2** the direction toward which the wind is blowing. **lee** *adj.* ⟨Old English *hlēow* shelter⟩
lee·ward [ˈliwərd] *or, in nautical use,* [ˈluərd] *adj, adv* **1** on the side away from the wind. **2** in the direction toward which the wind is blowing. *n* the side away from the wind. **lee·ward·ly** *adv.* **lee·way** *n* **1** *Nautical* the side movement of a ship to leeward. **2** more space, time, money, etc. than is needed: *She made it to work with five minutes' leeway.* **3** sufficient room or scope for action.

leech [litʃ] *n* **1** any of a class of mostly freshwater worms having a segmented body with a sucker at either end. Many leeches live by sucking the blood of other animals. **2** *Informal* a person who persistently tries to get what he or she can out of others. *v Informal* live off others without contributing anything. **leech·like** *adj.* ⟨Old English *lǣce*⟩

leek [lik] *n* an edible plant of the lily family, closely related to the onion. ⟨Old English *lēac*⟩

leer [lir] *n* a sly, evil, or lewd glance. **leer** *v.* **leer·ing** *adj.* ⟨perhaps Old English *hlēor* cheek, for idea of looking askance, over one's cheek⟩
leer·y *adj Informal* **1** suspicious. **2** afraid. **3** sly. **leer·i·ly** *adv.* **leer·i·ness** *n.*

lees [liz] *n pl* dregs. ⟨French *lie;* Celtic⟩

left[1] [lɛft] *adj* **1** of the side that is toward the west when the main side faces north: *a person's left hand.* **2** Often, **Left** *Politics* to do with the Left.
adv on or to the left side: *turn left.*
n **1** the left side or hand. **2 the Left** or **the left a** a liberal, radical, or revolutionary group. **b** esp in some legislatures, the members sitting on the left of the presiding officer by virtue of their more liberal views. ⟨dialect Old English *left* (for *lyft*) weak⟩
left face a turn to the left. **left–hand** *adj* **1** on or to the left. **2** to do with the left hand. **left–hand·ed** *adj* **1** using the left hand more easily and readily than the right. **2** turning from right to left: *a left-handed screw.* **left–hand·ed·ly** *adv.* **left–hand·ed·ness** *n.* **left–hand·er** *n.* **left·ist** *Politics n* a person who favours the LEFT[1] (def. 2). *adj* to do with the Left: *leftist ideas.* **left·ism** *n.* **left wing 1** *Politics* the more liberal faction of a group. **2** *Hockey, lacrosse, etc.* the position to the left of centre of a forward line. **left–wing** *adj.* **left–wing·er** *n.* **left·y** *n Informal* a left-handed person.

left[2] [lɛft] *v* pt and pp of LEAVE[1].

left·o·ver *n* anything that is left. Scraps of food from a meal are leftovers. **left·o·ver** *adj*.

leg [lɛg] *n* **1** one of the limbs on which humans and animals support themselves and walk. **2** anything shaped or used like a leg: *a table leg*. **3** one of the distinct stages of any course: *the last leg of a trip*.
v **legged, leg·ging** *Informal* walk; run: *We could not get a ride, so we legged it*. **leg·less** *adj*. **leg·like** *adj*. ⟨Old Norse *leggr*⟩
give someone a leg up *Informal* help (up). **have not a leg to stand on** *Informal* have no defence. **on one's last legs** about to fall, die, etc. **pull someone's leg** fool someone. **shake a leg** *Slang* hurry up: *Shake a leg or we'll be late*.
-leg·ged ['lɛgɪd] *or* [lɛgd] *adj* having a leg or legs of a specified number or kind: *a three-legged stool, a long-legged bird*. **leg·gings** *n pl* **1** outer coverings for the legs, for use outdoors. **2** tight, stretchy pants for women. **leg·gy** *adj* having long legs. **leg·gi·ness** *n*. **leg warmers** coverings for the legs, used especially by dancers.

leg·a·cy ['lɛgəsi] *n* **1** the property left to a person by a will. **2** anything passed on from a predecessor. ⟨Latin *legatia*, earlier *legatum* bequest; *legare*. See LEGATE.⟩

le·gal ['ligəl] *adj* **1** of law: *legal knowledge*. **2** of lawyers. **3** according to law; lawful. **le·gal·ly** ['ligəli] *adv*. ⟨Latin *lex, legis* law⟩
legal aid *Law* the provision of legal assistance to needy people. **le·gal·ese** [,ligə'liz] *n* the jargon of the legal profession. **le·gal·ist·ic** *adj*. to do with overly strict adherence to law. **le·gal·is·ti·cal·ly** *adv*. **le·gal·i·ty** [lɪ'gæləti] *n* **1** accordance with law; lawfulness. **2** a legal requirement. **le·gal·ize** *v* make legal. **le·gal·i·za·tion** *n*. **le·gal-size** *adj* of paper, 22 cm by 36 cm. Compare LETTER-SIZE. **legal tender** money that must, by law, be accepted in payment of debts.

leg·ate ['lɛgɪt] *n* **1** a representative of the Pope. **2** any representative. **leg·ate·ship** *n*. ⟨Latin *legatus* pp of *legare* provide with a contract; *lex, legis* contract, law⟩
le·ga·tion [lɪ'geɪʃən] *n* **1** the diplomatic representative of a country and his or her staff of assistants. **2** the official residence, offices, etc. of such a representative in a foreign country.
le·ga·to [lɪ'gɑtou] *Music adj* smooth and connected. *Legato* is the opposite of *staccato*. ⟨Italian *legato* pp of *legare* bind, Latin *ligāre*⟩

leg·end ['lɛdʒənd] *n* **1** a story coming down from the past: *The stories about King Arthur are legends, not history*. **2** the explanation of the symbols on a map or diagram. ⟨Latin *legenda* (things) to be read; *legere* read⟩
leg·end·ar·y ['lɛdʒən,dɛri] *adj* **1** to do with a legend. **2** famous. **leg·end·ar·i·ly** *adv*. **leg·end·ry** *n* legends as a group.

┌─ USAGE ─────────────────────────────
│ A **legend** relates to a people's past and usually
│ glorifies a person or event. A **myth** relates to a
│ people's religion, and is usually about gods or
│ other supernatural beings; its aim is to explain
│ a belief or some aspect of life or nature.
└────────────────────────────────────

leg·er·de·main [,lɛdʒɜrdə'mein] *n* **1** SLEIGHT OF HAND. **2** trickery. **leg·er·de·main·ist** *n*. ⟨French *léger de main* quick of hand⟩

leg·i·ble ['lɛdʒəbəl] *adj* easy to read: *legible handwriting*. ⟨Latin *legere* read⟩
leg·i·bil·i·ty *n*. **leg·i·ble·ness** *n*. **leg·i·bly** *adv*.

le·gion ['lidʒən] *n* **1** in the ancient Roman army, a body of soldiers consisting of 3000 to 6000 foot soldiers and 300 to 700 cavalry. **2** a great many; a very large number. **3 Legion** ROYAL CANADIAN LEGION.
adj very numerous: *His problems are legion*. ⟨Latin *legio; legere* choose⟩
le·gion·ar·y *adj* to do with a legion. *n* a soldier of a legion. **Le·gion·naire** [,lidʒə'nɛr] *n* a member of the Royal Canadian Legion.

leg·is·late ['lɛdʒə,sleit] *v* **1** make laws: *Parliament legislates for Canada*. **2** force by legislation: *The council legislated her out of office*. **leg·is·la·tion** *n*. **leg·is·la·tor** *n*. ⟨Latin *legis lator* proposer (lit., bearer) of a law⟩
leg·is·la·tive *adj* **1** to do with making laws: *legislative reforms*. **2** having the duty and power of making laws: *Parliament is a legislative body*. **leg·is·la·tive·ly** *adv*. **Legislative Assembly** ✳ the group of representatives elected to the legislature of any of certain provinces or the Yukon Territory. **leg·is·la·ture** *n* **1** persons having the power to make laws for a country, province, or state. **2** the place where they meet.

le·git·i·mate [lə'dʒɪtəmɪt] *adj* **1** lawful: *the legitimate heir to the throne*. **2** acceptable: *a legitimate reason for absence from work*. **3** born of parents who are married. **4** logical: *a legitimate conclusion*. **5** to do with drama acted on stage, as opposed to film and other stage entertainment: *the legitimate theatre*.
v [lə'dʒɪtə,meit] make or declare lawful. **le·git·i·ma·cy** [lə'dʒɪtəməsi] *n*. **le·git·i·mate·ly** *adv*. **le·git·i·ma·tion** *n*. ⟨Latin *legitimus* lawful; *lex, legis* law⟩
le·git [lə'dʒɪt] *adj Slang* shortened form of legitimate. **le·git·i·mize** *v* make or declare to be legitimate. **le·git·i·mi·za·tion** *n*.

leg·ume ['lɛgjum] *n* the fruit or seed of plants of the pea family, esp beans or peas. **le·gu·mi·nous** [lə'gjumənəs] *adj*. ⟨French *légume* vegetable; Latin *legumen*⟩

lei [lei] *n* a wreath of flowers, leaves, etc. ⟨Hawaiian⟩

lei·sure ['lɛʒər] *or* ['liʒər] *n* time free from required work. **lei·sure·less** *adj*. ⟨Old French *leisir*; Latin *licere* be allowed⟩
at leisure a free; not busy. **b** taking plenty of time. **at one's leisure** at one's convenience. **lei·sure·ly** *adj, adv* without hurry. **lei·sure·li·ness** *n*. **leisure wear** casual, comfortable clothing.

leit·mo·tif *or* **leit·mo·tiv** ['laitmou,tif] *n* **1** *Music* a theme repeated throughout a work and associated with a person, situation, or idea. **2** any repeating theme. ⟨German⟩

lem·ming ['lɛmɪŋ] *n* any of various small, mouselike arctic rodents having greyish or brownish fur, and furry feet. ⟨Norwegian⟩

lem·on ['lɛmən] *n* **1** an acid-tasting, light yellow citrus fruit. **2** *Slang* a thing (usually a car) that is constantly troublesome. ⟨Old French *limon;* Arabic *laimun,* Persian *limun*⟩ **lem·on·ade** [ˌlɛmə'neɪd] *or* ['lɛməˌneɪd] *n* a drink made of lemon juice, sugar, and water.

le·mur ['limər] *n* any of a family of primates found mainly in Madagascar. ⟨Latin *lemures* pl, ghosts; for their nocturnal habits⟩

lend [lɛnd] *v* **lent, lend·ing 1** let another have or use for a time. **2** give the use of (money) for payment: *Banks lend money.* **3** give; add: *Flowers lend charm to a room.* **lend·er** *n.* ⟨Old English *lǣnan; lǣn* loan⟩ **lend a hand** help. **lend itself to** be suitable for: *The old engine lent itself to our purposes.* **lend oneself to** make oneself available for: *Don't lend yourself to foolish schemes.* **lend–lease** *n* a system of making a loan of equipment in return for some service.

length [lɛŋkθ] *n* **1** how long a thing is: *the length of your arm.* **2** the extent in time: *the length of a visit.* **3** a piece of given length: *a length of rope.* **4** the distance from end to end of a boat, horse, etc., as a measurement in racing: *The grey horse finished two lengths ahead of mine.* ⟨Old English; from *lang* long[1]⟩ **at arm's length** See ARM[1]. **at full length** with the body stretched out flat. **at length a** with all the details: *She told her story at length.* **b** at last; finally: *At length, after a delay, the meeting started.* **c** continuously and for a long time. **go to any length** do everything possible. **length·en** *v* make longer or become longer. **length·wise** or **length·ways** *adv, adj* in the direction of the length. **length·y** *adj* long or too long: *Her directions were so lengthy that I got confused.* **length·i·ly** *adv.* **length·i·ness** *n.*

le·nient ['linjənt] *adj* mild; merciful: *a lenient punishment.* **le·ni·ent·ly** *adv.* **le·nien·cy, le·nience,** or **len·i·ty** ['lɛnəti] *n.* ⟨Latin *lenientis* pp of *lenire* soften; *lenis* mild⟩

lens [lɛnz] *n* **1** a piece of transparent substance having a curved surface, used to focus rays of light passing through it. **2** a lens-shaped structure in the eye that focusses light rays on the retina. **lens·less** *adj.* **lens·like** *adj.* ⟨Latin *lens, lentis* lentil; for its shape⟩ **len·tic·u·lar** [lɛn'tɪkjələr] *adj* shaped like a lens.

lent [lɛnt] *v* pt and pp of LEND.

Lent [lɛnt] *n* the forty weekdays before Easter, observed in many Christian churches as a time for fasting and repenting of sins. **Lent·en** or **lent·en** *adj.* ⟨Old English *lencten* spring, akin to *lang* long; for the longer days⟩

len·til ['lɛntəl] *n* a plant of the pea family with seeds shaped like lenses. ⟨French *lentille,* Latin *lenticula* diminutive of *lens, lentis* lentil⟩

le·o·nine ['liəˌnaɪn] *adj* of or like a lion. ⟨Latin *leoninus; leo* lion, Greek *leōn*⟩

leop·ard ['lɛpərd] *n* a large animal of the cat family, having fur with small, black spots. ⟨Greek *leopardos; leōn* lion + *pardos* leopard⟩

le·o·tard ['liəˌtɑrd] *n* **1** a one-piece garment extending just to the thighs. **2 leotards** *pl* tights. ⟨J. *Léotard,* 19c French gymnast⟩

lep·er See LEPROSY.

lep·i·dop·ter·an [ˌlɛpə'dɒptərən] *n* any of an order of insects comprising butterflies, moths, and skippers, all having four broad wings covered with scales. Also, **lep·i·dop·ter·on. lep·i·dop·ter·ist** *n.* **lep·i·dop·ter·ous** *adj.* ⟨Greek *lepidos* scale + *pteron* wing⟩

lep·re·chaun ['lɛprəˌkɒn] *n Irish folklore* a sprite or goblin resembling a little old man. ⟨Irish *leipreachán, lupracán,* Old Irish *lúchorpán; lú* small + *corp* body, Latin *corpus*⟩

lep·ro·sy ['lɛprəsi] *n* an infectious disease that causes sores on the skin and injury to the nerves, and that may result in paralysis and deformity; HANSEN'S DISEASE. **lep·er** *n.* **lep·rous** *adj.* **lep·rous·ly** *adv.* **lep·rous·ness** *n.* ⟨Greek *lepra* leprosy; *lepein* to peel⟩

lep·ton ['lɛptɒn] *n Physics* any of a class of elementary particles that include electrons, muons, neutrinos, and their antiparticles. ⟨Greek *leptos* small, thin; *lepein* to peel⟩

les·bi·an ['lɛzbiən] *n* a homosexual woman. **les·bi·an** *adj.* **les·bi·an·ism** *n.* ⟨*Lesbos,* home of Greek poetess Sappho, supposed homosexual⟩

le·sion ['liʒən] *n* **1** an injury. **2** *Medicine* a diseased condition often causing a change in the structure of an organ or tissue. ⟨Latin *laesio* injury; *laedere* to strike⟩

less [lɛs] *adj* **1** not so much: *of less width.* **2** fewer: *Five is less than seven.* **3** lower in age or importance: *no less a person than the king.* *n* a smaller amount: *less than five dollars.* *adv* to a smaller extent: *less important.* *prep* without; minus: *a year less two days.* ⟨Old English *lǣs(sa)*⟩ **more or less a** somewhat: *I was more or less impatient.* **b** about: *fifty dollars, more or less.* **less·en** *v* make or become less. **less·er** *adj* **1** smaller. **2** less important or of lower quality.

CONFUSABLES
Both **less** and **lesser** are used as comparatives of **little**. **Less** usually refers to size or quantity: *less time, less food;* **Lesser** refers to value or importance: *a lesser poet, the lesser of two evils.*

–less *suffix* **1** without——: homeless. **2** that does not——: ceaseless. **3** that one cannot——: countless. ⟨Old English *-lēas; lēas* free from⟩

les·see See LEASE.

les·son ['lɛsən] *n* **1** something learned. **2** a unit of learning or teaching. **3** a meeting with a teacher to study a given subject: *a piano lesson.* **4** a selection from the Bible or other sacred writings, read as part of a religious service. ⟨Old French *leçon;* Latin *lectionis* reading, *legere* read⟩

les·sor See LEASE.

lest [lɛst] *conj* **1** for fear that: *Be careful lest you fall.* **2** that: *They feared lest he should come too late.* ⟨Middle English *leste*⟩

let [lɛt] *v* **let, let·ting 1** permit: *Let the dog have a bone.* **2** allow to run out: *Doctors used to let blood from people to lessen a fever.* **3** rent or be rented. **4** *Let* is used in suggestions: *Let's go home.* ⟨Old English *lǣtan*⟩

let down a lower. **b** disappoint: *Don't let us down today.* **let·down** *n.* **let go a** release: *to let go a rope.* **b** give up: *He let go all thought of winning.* **c** dismiss from a job. **let in** permit to enter. **let in for** expose to: *He let his friends in for a lot of questioning when he left town so suddenly.* **let in on** reveal (privileged information) to. **let loose** allow to go free. **let off a** release: *let off poisonous gases, to let off with a small fine.* **b** free from: *The teacher would not let us off homework.* **let off steam** *Informal* give way to one's feelings: *She let off steam by shouting.* **let on** *Informal* **a** allow to be known: *He didn't let on his surprise at the news.* **b** pretend: *She let on that she didn't see me.* **let oneself go a** cease to restrain oneself. **b** cease to take care of one's appearance. **let out a** permit to go out. **b** make (a garment) larger. **c** rent: *Has the room been let out yet?* **d** dismiss or be dismissed: *School lets out at 3:30.* **e** make known. **let up** *Informal* **a** stop. **b** lessen. **let·up** *n.*

–let *suffix* **1** little——: *booklet.* **2** a thing worn on——: *anklet.* ⟨Old French *-el* (Latin *-ittus* diminutive⟩

le·thal ['liθəl] *adj* causing death; deadly: *lethal weapons, a lethal dose.* **le·thal·ly** *adv.* ⟨Latin *let(h)alis; letum* death⟩

leth·ar·gy ['lɛθərdʒi] *n, pl* **-gies 1** drowsy dullness; lack of energy. **2** a condition of unnatural drowsiness or prolonged sleep. **le·thar·gic** *adj.* **le·thar·gi·cal·ly** *adv.* ⟨Greek *lēthargos; lēthē* forgetfulness + *argos* lazy⟩

let·ter ['lɛtər] *n* **1** a symbol that represents speech. **2** a message, usually delivered by mail. **3** the exact wording: *the letter of the law but not the spirit.* **4 letters** *pl* literature.
v inscribe (something) in letters. **let·ter·er** *n.* **let·ter·less** *adj.* ⟨Old French; Latin *littera*⟩
to the letter exactly: *I carried out your order to the letter.*
letter bomb an explosive device contained in an envelope. **letter carrier** a person who collects or delivers mail. **let·tered** *adj* **1** able to read and write. **2** knowing literature. **let·ter·head** *n* **1** the name and address of a person or company, printed at the top of a sheet of writing paper. **2** paper so printed. **let·ter·ing** *n* **1** letters drawn, painted, stamped, etc. **2** calligraphy. **letter of credit** a document issued by a bank, allowing the person named in it to draw money. **letter opener** a long knife for opening sealed envelopes. **let·ter–per·fect** *adj* correct in every detail. **let·ter–qual·i·ty** *adj* of computer printing, sufficiently clear to be used in a formal letter. **letter–size** *adj* of paper, 22 cm by 28 cm. Compare LEGAL-SIZE. **letters patent** *Law* an official document giving a person or a corporation authority from a government to have some right, such as a patent.

let·tuce ['lɛtəs] *n* a vegetable grown in several varieties, all having large leaves on a short stalk. ⟨Old French *laitues*, pl, Latin *lactuca; lac, lactis* milk; for its milky juice⟩

leu·co·cyte or **leu·ko·cyte** ['lukə,saɪt] *n Anatomy* any of the white or colourless cells in the blood. ⟨Greek *leukos* white + -CYTE⟩

leu·ke·mi·a [lu'kimjə] *n Pathology* a type of cancer characterized by the abnormal growth of white blood cells.

lev·ee[1] ['lɛvi] *n* a bank built to keep a river from overflowing ⟨French *levée* pp of *lever* raise; Latin *levare*⟩

lev·ee[2] or **lev·ée** ['lɛvi], [lə'vi], *or* [lə'veɪ] *n* **1** a usually formal reception, esp one held during the day: *the Governor General's levee.* **2** formerly, a reception held by a person of high rank on rising from bed. ⟨French *levé, lever* a rising; *lever.* See LEVEE[1].⟩

lev·el ['lɛvəl] *adj* **1** completely flat: *level ground.* **2** of equal height: *The table is level with the window sill.* **3** *Informal* steady: *She's got a level head.* **4** equal in degree, quality, etc.: *They were level in rank, but not in salary.*
n **1** an instrument for showing whether a surface is horizontal. **2** height: *eye level.* **3** degree, rate, or style: *the noise level.* **4** in a structure, a horizontal section: *the basement level of a parking garage.*
v **-elled** or **-eled, -el·ling** or **-el·ing 1** make level: *to level rough ground.* **2** come to a level position (usually with *off* or *out*): *The path climbs and then levels off.* **3** demolish: *The tornado levelled every house in the village.* **4** raise and hold level for shooting: *The soldier levelled her rifle.* **5** aim (words, intentions, etc.): *She levelled a stinging rebuke at the speaker.* **6** *Slang* be honest and frank (used with *with*): *You can level with me.* **7** bring to a common level: *Death levels all human ranks.* **lev·el·ler** or **lev·el·er** *n.* **lev·el·ly** *adv.* **lev·el·ness** *n.* ⟨Old French *livel;* Latin *libella* diminutive of *libra* balance, scale⟩
find one's level arrive at the most natural position, rank, etc.: *After failing as a painter, he found his level as a political cartoonist.* **one's level best** *Informal* one's very best. **on the level** *Informal* honest and straightforward: *Is that offer on the level?*
level crossing a place where a railway track crosses a street. **lev·el–head·ed** *adj* sensible. **lev·el–head·ed·ly** *adv.* **lev·el–head·ed·ness** *n.*

le·ver ['livər] *or, esp for v,* ['lɛvər] *n* **1** a bar used to move something. **2** anything used as a tool to influence: *He used my name as a social lever.* **3** a simple machine consisting of a bar turning on a fixed point called the fulcrum, using effort to move a mass: *A wheelbarrow is one kind of lever.* **le·ver** *v.* ⟨Old French *leveor; lever* raise, Latin *levare*⟩

lev·er·age ['lɛvərɪdʒ] *n* **1** the advantage gained by using a lever. **2** increased power of action. **leveraged buy–out** *Business* the purchase of a company using as collateral the assets of the company to be bought.

le·vi·a·than [lə'vaɪəθən] *n* **1** in the Bible, a huge sea animal. **2** a huge ship. **3** any great and powerful person or thing. ⟨Hebrew *livyathan* dragon⟩

lev·i·tate ['lɛvə,teɪt] *v* rise or cause to rise in the air. **lev·i·ta·tion** *n.* **lev·i·ta·tion·al** *adj.* **lev·i·ta·tive** *adj.* **lev·i·ta·tor** *n.* ⟨Latin *levitas* lightness (see LEVITY); modelled on *gravitate*⟩

lev·i·ty ['lɛvəti] *n* lightness of spirit or mind; frivolity: *The issue is serious and should not be treated with levity.* ⟨Latin *levitas; levis* light⟩

lev·y ['lɛvi] *v* **1** order to be paid: *The government levies taxes.* **2** draft for an army: *to levy troops in time of war.*
n **1** money collected by authority or force. **2** the troops drafted for an army. ⟨French *levée.* See LEVEE[1].⟩

lewd [lud] *adj* designed to arouse sexual desire, esp in a coarse or offensive way: *lewd pictures.* **lewd·ly** *adv.* **lewd·ness** *n.* ⟨Old English *lǽwede* lay, unlearned⟩

lex·i·con ['lɛksə,kɒn] *or* ['lɛksəkən] *n* **1** a dictionary, esp of Greek, Latin, or Hebrew. **2** the total vocabulary of a particular speaker or writer or of a particular subject. **3** *Linguistics* the total stock of morphemes in a language. ⟨Greek *lexikon* wordbook; *lexis* word, *legein* say⟩
lex·i·cal *adj* **1** to do with words as separate units of meaning, rather than as elements of phrases, sentences, etc. **2** to do with lexicography or a lexicon. **lex·i·cal·i·ty** *n.* **lex·i·cal·ly** *adv.* **lex·i·cog·ra·phy** [,lɛksə'kɒgrəfi] *n* the science of compiling dictionaries. **lex·i·cog·ra·pher** *n.* **lex·i·co·graph·i·cal** *or* **lex·i·co·graph·ic** *adj.* **lex·i·co·graph·i·cal·ly** *adv.* **lex·i·col·o·gy** [,lɛksə'kɒlədʒi] *n* the study of the history, form, and meaning of words. **lex·i·co·log·i·cal** *adj.* **lex·i·col·o·gist** *n.*

l.h. or **L.H.** left hand.

li·a·ble ['laɪəbəl] *adj* **1** likely: *Glass is liable to break.* **2** in danger of having, doing, etc.: *We are all liable to diseases.* **3** legally responsible: *The company is not liable for damage.* **4** under obligation: *Citizens are liable to jury duty.* ⟨French *lier* bind; Latin *ligare*⟩
li·a·bil·i·ty *n* **1** the state of being susceptible: *liability to disease.* **2** the state of being under obligation: *liability for a debt.* **3** Usually, **liabilities** *pl* debts. **4** a person or thing that acts as a disadvantage: *Her short temper is a liability in dealing with people.*

li·ai·son [li'eizɒn] *or* ['liə,zɒn] *French* [ljɛ'zɔ̃] *n* **1** communication in order to co-ordinate activities. **2** any close bond. **3** an illicit love affair. ⟨French; Latin *ligatio; ligare* bind⟩
li·aise [li'eiz] *v Informal* set up liaison *(with)*: *An envoy liaises with a foreign government.*

li·a·na [li'ɑnə] *or* [li'ænə] *n* any of various woody vines found in tropical rainforests, that are rooted in the ground and twine around the trunks of trees, etc. for support. Also, **liane.** ⟨French *liane,* earlier *liorne*⟩

li·ar See LIE[1].

li·ard ['liərd], [li'ɑr], *or* [li'ɑrd] *n* ✸ especially in the North, the balsam poplar; tacamahac. ⟨Cdn. French; Old French *liard* grey⟩

lib [lɪb] *n Informal* liberation: *women's lib.*

li·ba·tion [laɪ'beiʃən] *n* a pouring out of wine, water, etc. as an offering to a god. ⟨Latin *libare* pour out⟩

li·bel ['laɪbəl] *n Law* a written statement, picture, etc. tending to damage a person's reputation. Compare SLANDER. **li·bel, -belled** or **-beled, -bel·ling** or **-bel·ing** *v.* **li·bel·ler** or **li·bel·er** *n.* **li·bel·lous** or **li·bel·ous** *adj.* ⟨Latin *libellus* diminutive of *liber* book⟩

lib·er·al ['lɪbrəl] *adj* **1** generous. **2** plentiful: *a liberal supply of wood.* **3** broad-minded. **4** favouring or following the principles of liberalism. **5 Liberal a** to do with a political party advocating moderate progress and reform. **b** in Canada, to do with the Liberal Party. **6** giving the general thought: *a liberal interpretation of the speaker's ideas.*
n **1** a person who favours principles of liberalism. **2 Liberal** a member of a Liberal Party. **lib·er·al·ly** *adv.* **lib·er·al·ize** *v.* **lib·er·al·i·za·tion** *n.* ⟨Latin *liberalis; liber* free⟩
liberal arts subjects such as literature and philosophy as distinct from technical or professional subjects. **liberal education** an education in the liberal arts. **lib·er·al·ism** *n* **1** a political philosophy that emphasizes belief in progress, individual freedom, and democratic government. **2 Liberalism** the principles of a Liberal political party. **lib·er·al·ist** *n.* **lib·er·al·is·tic** *adj.* **lib·er·al·i·ty** [,lɪbə'ræləti] *n* **1** generosity. **2** a tolerant and progressive nature. **3** broad-mindedness. **Liberal Party** one of the principal political parties of Canada.

lib·er·ate ['lɪbə,reit] *v* **1** set free. **2** *Chemistry* set free from combination: *liberate a gas.* **3** *Slang* steal. **lib·er·a·tor** *n.* ⟨Latin *liber* free⟩
lib·er·a·tion *n* **1** the act of liberating, or the state of being liberated. **2** a movement striving for equal status and rights: *women's liberation, gay liberation.*

lib·er·tine ['lɪbər,tin] *n* a person who lives without regard to accepted moral standards, esp one who leads a dissolute life; **lib·er·tine** *adj.* **lib·er·tin·ism** *n.* ⟨Latin *libertinus* freedman; *liber* free⟩

lib·er·ty ['lɪbərti] *n* **1** freedom. **2** the right to do as one pleases: *liberty of speech.* **3** the right of being in, using, etc.: *We give our dog the liberty of the yard.* **4** too great freedom in action or speech: *Her use of his first name and other liberties annoyed him greatly.* ⟨Latin *libertas; liber* free⟩
at liberty a free: *The escaped lion is still at liberty.* **b** allowed: *You are at liberty to make a choice.* **c** not busy: *She will see you as soon as she is at liberty.* **take liberties with** be too familiar with: *The soldiers soon gave up trying to take liberties with their new sergeant.*
lib·er·tar·i·an [,lɪbər'tɛriən] *n* **1** an advocate of full civil liberty with minimal government intervention. **2** one who believes in freedom of the will. **lib·er·tar·i·an·ism** *n.*

li·bi·do [lə'bidou] *n* **1** sexual desire. **2** energy in general. ⟨Latin = desire; *libere* be pleasing⟩
li·bid·i·nous [lə'bɪdənəs] *adj* lustful; lewd. **li·bid·i·nous·ly** *adv.* **li·bid·i·nous·ness** *n.*

li·brar·y ['laɪbrɛri] *or* ['laɪbrəri] *n* **1** a room or building where a collection of books, periodicals, tapes, etc. is kept to be used or borrowed. **2** a collection of books, periodicals, etc., esp a large collection: *They*

have an extensive library of rare books. **3** a set of books having something in common: *a publisher's Library of Classics.* ⟨Latin *librarium* bookcase; *liber* book⟩
li·brar·i·an [laɪˈbrɛriən] *n* a person trained to organize, administer, or assist in a library.
li·bret·to [ləˈbrɛtou] *n* the words of an opera, oratorio, etc. **li·bret·tist** [ləˈbrɛtɪst] *n*. ⟨Italian, diminutive of *libro* book⟩
lice [laɪs] *n* pl of LOUSE.
li·cence [ˈlaɪsəns] *n* **1** permission given by law to do something, or the paper, card, etc. showing such permission: *The barber hung his licence on the wall.* **2** freedom of action, speech, etc. that is permitted. **3** abuse of liberty. **li·cence·less** *adj.* Also, **li·cense**. ⟨Old French *licence*, Latin *licentia; licere* be allowed⟩
licence plate metal plates bearing the registration number of a vehicle. **li·cense** [ˈlaɪsəns] *v* **1** give a licence to: *to license a new driver.* **2** permit, esp by law: *A doctor is licensed to practise medicine.* **3** abuse of moral. **li·cens·er** *n.* **li·censed** *adj* **1** holding a government licence to sell alcoholic liquors for drinking on the premises: *a licensed restaurant.* **2** holding any other kind of licence: *a licensed driver.* **li·cen·see** [ˌlaɪsənˈsi] *n* a person to whom a licence is given. **li·cen·tious** [laɪˈsɛnʃəs] *adj* disregarding accepted moral principles. **li·cen·tious·ly** *adv.* **li·cen·tious·ness** *n.*

li·chee [ˈlitʃi] See LITCHI.
li·chen [ˈlaɪkən] *n* any of a large group of complex plants made up of an alga and a fungus in a permanent relationship. **li·chen·like** *adj.* **li·chen·ous** *adj.* ⟨Greek *leichēn* what eats around itself; *leichein* lick⟩
li·chen·ol·o·gy *n* the study of lichens. **li·chen·o·log·i·cal** *adj.* **li·chen·ol·o·gist** *n.*
lic·it [ˈlɪsɪt] *adj* lawful; permitted. **lic·it·ly** *adv.* **lic·it·ness** *n.* ⟨Latin *licitus; licere* be allowed⟩
lick [lɪk] *v* **1** pass the tongue over. **2** lap up with the tongue. **3** play (over) as a tongue would: *The flames were licking the roof.* **4** *Informal* beat: *I could lick him easily.*
n **1** a stroke of the tongue. **2** a place where salt is found or provided, and where animals go to lick it up. **3** *Informal* a blow: *I got in a few good licks.* **4** a small quantity: *She didn't do a lick of work.* **5** *Informal* **licks** pl chance: *You'll get your licks in later.* **6** *Informal* speed: *moving at a great lick.* **7** *Informal* a bold, improvised musical embellishment, esp on the guitar. ⟨Old English *liccian*⟩
lick into shape *Informal* make presentable.
lick·e·ty–split [ˌlɪkəti ˈsplɪt] *adv Informal* at a great speed: *She was off lickety-split before I could stop her.* **lick·ing** *n Informal* **1** a thrashing. **2** a defeat or setback. **lick·spit·tle** [ˈlɪkˌspɪtəl] *n* a contemptible flatterer.
lic·o·rice [ˈlɪkərɪʃ] *n* a sweet, black, gummy

substance obtained from the roots of a plant of the pea family, used as a flavouring and as a laxative. ⟨Anglo-French *lycorys;* Greek *glykyrrhiza; glykys* sweet + *rhiza* root⟩
lid [lɪd] *n* **1** a movable cover. **2** *Slang* a hat. **3** *Informal* a restraint: *put the lid on gambling.* **lid·ded** *adj.* **lid·less** *adj.* ⟨Old English *hlid*⟩
blow the lid off *Slang* reveal: *to blow the lid off a government's waste of public funds.* **flip one's lid** *Slang* get very excited. **keep a lid on it!** *Slang* keep it quiet!
lie¹ [laɪ] *n* a false statement. **li·ar** [ˈlaɪər] *n.* **lie, lied, ly·ing** *v.* **ly·ing** *adj, n.* ⟨Old English *lyge*, n, *lēogan*, v⟩
give the lie to a accuse of lying. **b** show to be false: *Her dissertation gives the lie to rumours of her incompetence.*
lie² [laɪ] *v* **lay, lain, ly·ing** **1** have one's body in a flat position on a horizontal surface: *to lie on the grass.* **2** assume such a position (with *down*): *to lie down on the grass.* **3** be in a horizontal position: *The book was lying on the table.* **4** be kept or stay in a given position, state, etc.: *to lie idle.* **5** be found: *The lake lies to the south of us. The cure lies in education.* **6** be in the grave: *Her body lies in Fredericton.* **7** *Archaic* spend the night; lodge.
n the manner, position, or direction in which something lies. ⟨Old English *licgan*⟩
lie around a be lazy. **b** be scattered around: *Don't leave your clothes lying around.* **lie behind** be the reason for. **lie down on the job** not give full attention to one's obligations. **lie in a** be confined in childbirth. **b** stay in bed later than usual. **lie off** *Nautical* of a ship, etc., stay not far from: *The ship lay off the coast of Norway.* **lie over** be left waiting until a later time. **lie to** *Nautical* of a ship, etc., come almost to a stop, facing the wind. **take a thing lying down** yield to something: *He won't take that insult lying down.*
lie (or **lay**) **of the land** **1** the natural features of a landscape. **2** the condition in which things are. **ly·ing–in** *n* confinement in childbirth.

liege [lidʒ] or [liʒ] *n* formerly, in the Middle Ages: **1** a lord having a right to the homage of his vassals. **2** a vassal obliged to give homage to his lord. **liege** *adj.* ⟨Old French; Latin *leticus* from *letus* freedman; Germanic⟩
liege lord a feudal lord.
lien [lin] or [ˈliən] *n Law* a claim placed on the property of another as a safeguard for payment of a debt. **lien·a·ble** *adj.* ⟨French = bond, Latin *ligamen; ligare* bind⟩
lieu [lu] *n Archaic* (except in **in lieu of**) place; stead. ⟨French; Latin *locus*⟩
in lieu of in place of: *They gave the landlord produce in lieu of money for rent.*
lieu·ten·ant [lɛfˈtɛnənt] or, esp US, [luˈtɛnənt]

n **1** a person who acts for someone senior to him or her: *She was one of the gang leader's lieutenants.* **2** *Canadian Forces* **a** an officer ranking below a captain. *Abbrev* **Lt.** or **Lt** **b** in Maritime Command, the equivalent of a captain. *Abbrev* **Lt.(N)** or **Lt(N)** **lieu·ten·an·cy** *n.* ⟨French, from *lieu* a place (see LIEU) + *tenant* ppr of *tenir* hold; Latin *tenere*⟩

lieutenant–governor *n* ✹ in Canada, the official representative of the Crown in a province. *Abbrev* **Lt.Gov.**

life [ləif] *n, pl* **lives 1** the condition of being alive. **2** the time of being alive: *a short life.* **3** the time of existence: *the life of a battery.* **4** a living being, esp a person: *Five lives were lost in the fire.* **5** living things considered together: *The island had almost no animal life.* **6** a way of living: *a dull life.* **7** a biography: *He's writing a life of Mackenzie King.* **8** vigour: *Put more life into your work.* **9** the living form as represented in art: *The portrait was painted from life.* **10** a sentence of imprisonment for life: *He got life.* **11** a particular part of a person's life: *her love life.* ⟨Old English *līf*⟩

as large (or **as big**) **as life** in person. **for dear life** as if to save one's life: *He ran for dear life.* **for life** during the rest of one's life. **for the life of me** (or **him, her,** etc.) *Informal* even if my (or his, her, etc.) life depended on it (used only in negative expressions): *I can't for the life of me remember where I put my keys.* **see life** *Informal* get experience: *Most young people want to see life before they settle down.* **take (one's own) life** kill (oneself). **to the life** exactly. **true to life** true to reality. **life and limb** physical safety: *The old bridge is a danger to life and limb.* **life·blood** *n* a source of strength: *The young people became the lifeblood of the organization.* **life·boat** *n* **1** a boat specially built for saving lives at sea. **2** a boat carried on a ship for use in an emergency. **life buoy** LIFE PRESERVER. **life cycle** the various stages through which an organism goes in the course of its life. **life expectancy** the number of years one can reasonably expect to live. Compare LIFE SPAN. **life·guard** *n* a person who is responsible for the safety of swimmers. **life insurance** insurance that provides for the payment of a money on the death of the insured. **life jacket** (or **vest**) a life preserver in the form of a vest which is buoyant or inflatable. **life·less** *adj* **1** inanimate: *a lifeless statue.* **2** dead: *lifeless bodies on the battlefield.* **3** having no living things: *a lifeless planet.* **4** dull: *a lifeless performance.* **life·less·ly** *adv.* **life·less·ness** *n.* **life·like** *adj* like the real thing. **life·line** *n* **1** a rope for saving life, such as one thrown to a ship from the shore. **2** a line across a deck or passageway of a ship to prevent falling overboard. **3** anything that helps to maintain something that cannot exist by itself: *The bus service was a lifeline to the remote community.* **life·long** *adj* lasting all one's life. **life of Ri·ley** an easy, luxurious life. **life preserver** a device made of buoyant or inflatable material, to keep a person from drowning. **lif·er** ['ləifər] *n Slang* a convict in prison for life. **life raft** a raft for saving lives in a shipwreck or from the wreck of an aircraft at sea. **life·sav·er** *n Informal* a person who or thing that saves one from trouble, discomfort, etc.: *The interruption was a lifesaver, because I didn't know what to say to her any more.* **life·sav·ing** *n* the practice of saving lives, esp by preventing drowning. **life·sav·ing** *adj.* **life sciences** the sciences dealing with living organisms, for example, biology and botany. **life–size** or **life-sized** *adj* of an image, having the same size as the living person, animal, etc.: *a life-size statue.* **life·span** *n* the length of time that a person, animal, machine, etc. may be expected to live or function. Compare LIFE EXPECTANCY. **life·style** *n* a way of life: *a casual lifestyle.* **life·time** *n* the length of time that someone is alive or that something functions: *In his whole lifetime he had never been in an airplane.* *adj* lasting for such a length of time: *a lifetime commitment.* **life vest** LIFE JACKET. **life·work** *n* work that takes or lasts a whole lifetime.

lift [lɪft] *v* **1** raise or rise. **2** pull upward. **3** *Slang* steal: *lift things from a store.* **4** plagiarize.

n **1** an elevating influence. **2** the act of lifting. **3** a free ride: *She often gave me a lift to school.* **4** elevated carriage (of the head, neck, eyes, etc.): *a haughty lift of the chin.* **5** *Informal* an improvement in spirits: *The promotion gave her a lift.* **6** *Aeronautics* the force exerted on an airfoil by a flow of air over and around it. **lift·a·ble** *adj.* **lift·er** *n.* ⟨Old Norse *lypta* to raise; akin to *lopt* air. See LOFT.⟩

lift off rise from the ground: *The spaceship will lift off in two hours.* **lift·off** *n.*

lig·a·ment ['lɪgəmənt] *n* a band of strong tissue that connects bones or holds organs in place. ⟨Latin *ligamentum; ligare* bind⟩

lig·a·ture ['lɪgətʃər] *or* ['lɪgə,tʃʊr] *n* **1** a thread used in surgery to tie up a blood vessel, etc. **2** something that unites or connects. **3** a binding or tying up. **4** *Music* **a** a slur. **b** a group of notes connected by a slur. **5** *Printing* letters joined. Æ and Œ are ligatures. Compare DIGRAPH.

v bind or tie up with a ligature. ⟨Latin *ligatura; ligare* bind⟩

light¹ [ləit] *n* **1** the form of radiant energy that acts on the eye. **2** anything that gives light. **3** a bright part: *light and shade.* **4** daytime. **5** something with which to start something else burning: *Give me a light so I can start the fire.* **6** knowledge: *We need more light on this subject.*

adj **1** having much light: *a light room.* **2** bright; clear: *It is as light as day.* **3** pale in colour; whitish: *light hair, light blue.*

v **light·ed** or **lit, light·ing 1** cause to give light: *She lit the lamp.* **2** provide with light: *The room is lighted by six windows.* **3** make or become bright: *Her face was lighted by a smile.* **4** become light: *The sky lights up at sunrise.* **5** show the way by giving light: *His flashlight lighted us through the tunnel.* **6** set fire to. **7** take fire. **light·ness** *n.* ⟨Old English *lēoht*⟩

according to one's lights following one's own ideas. **bring to light** reveal. **come to light** be revealed. **in light of** considering. **in the light of** as informed by. **see the light** (or **see the light of day**) **a** come into being. **b** be made public. **c** come to understand something: *After struggling with the issue, he finally saw the light.* **shed** (or **cast**, or **throw**) **light on** explain. **strike a light** make a flame.

light bulb or **lightbulb** a glass bulb containing a fine wire or a gas that glows when an electric current flows through it. **light-e·mit·ting diode** a semiconductor diode that emits light when voltage is applied. *Abbrev* **LED** or **L.E.D.** **light·en** *v* **1** make or become brighter. **2** make or become paler in colour: *The sun lightened her hair.* **light·en·er** *n.* **light·er** *n* a device used to light a cigarette, pipe, barbecue, etc. **light·house** *n* a tower with a bright light that shines far over the water. **light·ing** *n* the way in which lights are arranged, esp on the stage. **light·ning** *n* a flash of light in the sky caused by a discharge of electricity between clouds. *adj* very fast or sudden: *a lightning decision.* **lightning bug** firefly. **lightning rod** a metal rod used to conduct lightning into the earth or water to prevent fire. **light pen** *Computers* an electronic device allowing the user to manipulate data on a screen by pointing to it. **light·proof** *adj* that will not let light in. **light–year** *n Astronomy* a unit of distance equal to that travelled by light in one year, about 9 460 500 000 000 km. **light–years** *adv Informal* a long way: *Her work is light-years ahead of those of her competitors.*

light² [lait] *adj* **1** not heavy. **2** less than usual in mass, amount, density, force, etc.: *light clothing, a light sleep.* **3** not hard or severe: *light punishment.* **4** moving easily: *light on one's feet.* **5** cheerfully careless: *a light laugh.* **6** not serious: *light reading.* **7** containing little alcohol: *a light wine.* **8** built small and without much weight: *a light truck.* **9** not involving heavy machinery: *light industry.* *adv* **1** lightly. **2** with as little luggage as possible: *to travel light.* ⟨Old English *līht*⟩ **light in the head a** dizzy. **b** silly. **c** crazy. **make light of** treat as of little importance. **light·en** *v* **1** make or become lighter in weight. **2** make or become less of a burden: *to lighten taxes.* **3** make or become more cheerful: *The good news lightened their hearts.* **light–fin·gered** *adj* skilful at stealing. **light–foot·ed** *adj* stepping lightly. **light–head·ed** *adj* **1** dizzy. **2** not sensible. **light–head·ed·ness** *n.* **light–heart·ed** *adj* carefree. **light–heart·ed·ness** *n.* **light heavyweight** a boxer weighing between 76 kg and 81 kg. **light·ly** *adv* **1** with little

pressure, force, etc. **2** to a small degree: *lightly clad.* **3** easily: *She jumped lightly aside.* **4** cheerfully: *to take bad news lightly.* **5** indifferently: *This is too important to be treated lightly.* **light–mind·ed** *adj* not serious. **light–mind·ed·ness** *n.* **light·ness** *n.* **lights** *n pl* the lungs of sheep, pigs, etc., so called because of their light weight. **light·weight** ['lait,weit] *n* **1** a person or thing of less than average mass. **2** a boxer weighing between 58 kg and 60 kg. **3** a person of little influence: *a lightweight in the music world.* **light·weight** *adj.*

light³ [lait] *v* **light·ed** or (*esp in idioms*) **lit**, **light·ing 1** come down to the ground; alight: *He lighted from his horse.* **2** come down from flight: *A bird lighted on the branch.* **3** come by chance: *Her eye lighted upon a familiar face in the crowd.* ⟨Old English *līhtan* to lighten, relieve of a weight; see LIGHT²⟩ **light into** *Slang* **a** attack. **b** scold. **light out** *Slang* leave suddenly; go away quickly.

lig·nin ['lignin] *n Botany* an organic substance which, together with cellulose, makes up the woody tissues of plants. **lig·ne·ous** *adj.* ⟨Latin *lignum* wood⟩ **lig·nite** *n* a soft coal. **lig·nit·ic** [lig'nitik] *adj.*

like¹ [laik] *prep* **1** similar to: *I am like my sister.* **2** similarly to: *She can run like a deer.* **3** typical of: *Isn't that just like him?* **4** in the right state of mind for doing: *He felt like working.* **5** such as: *They offer technical courses like mechanics, drafting, and plumbing.*

adj similar: *Her uncle promised her $200 if she could earn a like sum.*

conj Informal **1** the same as; as: *He reacted just like I did.* **2** as if: *It looks like we'll have to do it.*

n a person or thing like another: *We will not see her like again.*

adv Informal probably (usually with *enough*): *Like enough it will rain.* ⟨Old English *(ge)līc*⟩

and the like and so forth: *He studied music, painting, and the like.* **like anything** (or **crazy** or **mad**, etc.) *Informal* very much. **nothing like** *Informal* **a** not at all: *She is nothing like her brother.* **b** not nearly: *It's nothing like as cold today.* **something like** *Informal* something similar to: *The tune goes something like this.* **the likes** (or **like**) **of** *Informal* anyone or anything like.

like–mind·ed *adj* sharing the same tastes. **like–mind·ed·ness** *n.* **lik·en** *v* compare: *The poet likens life to a dream.* **like·ness** *n* **1** a resemblance: *There is a strong likeness between the boy and his father.* **2** a representation, esp a painting, drawing, or photograph: *The portrait is a good likeness of her.* **3** the appearance: *The wizard assumed the likeness of a very old man.* **like·wise** *adv* in the same way: *See what I do. Now do likewise.*

like² [ləik] *v* **liked, lik·ing 1** enjoy: *Do you like milk?* **2** have a friendly feeling toward: *They like their new math teacher.* **3** want (with would): *I would like a glass of milk.* **4** be inclined: *Come whenever you like.*
n **likes** *pl* preferences: *My mother knows my likes and dislikes.* ⟨Old English *līcian* to please⟩ **lik·a·ble** or **like·a·ble** *adj* popular. **lik·a·bil·i·ty** *n*. **lik·a·bly** *adv*. **lik·ing** *n* **1** a preference: *She had a liking for apples.* **2** a fondness or kindly feeling: *She had a liking for children.*

–like *suffix* **1** like——: *wolflike*. **2** like that of ——: *childlike*. **3** suited to——: *businesslike*. ⟨*like¹*, adj.⟩

USAGE
-like is a productive suffix that can be freely added to nouns to form adjectives.

like·ly [ˈləikli] *adj* **1** probable: *One likely result of the heavy rains is a flood.* **2** suitable: *Is there a likely place to fish?* **3** promising: *a likely boy.* **4** plausible: *a likely story.*
adv probably: *I'll very likely be home all day.* **like·li·hood** *n*. ⟨Old Norse *líkligr*⟩

li·lac [ˈlaɪlɑk], [ˈlaɪlæk] *or* [ˈlaɪlək] *n* any of various shrubs or small trees of the olive family, widely cultivated for its fragrant flowers. ⟨Persian *lilak*⟩

lilt [lɪlt] *v* sing or play (a tune), speak, or move in a light, swinging manner. **lilt** *n*. ⟨Middle English *lulte*⟩

lil·y [ˈlɪli] *n* any of a genus of plants that grow from bulbs, having showy flowers. The **prairie lily** is the provincial flower of Saskatchewan; the **Madonna lily** is the provincial flower of Québec.
adj like a lily in being white, beautiful, fragile, pure, etc. **lil·y·like** *adj*. ⟨Old English *lilie*; Latin *lilium*⟩
gild the lily. See GILD¹.
lil·y–liv·ered [ˈlɪli ˌlɪvərd] *adj* cowardly. **lily pad** one of the floating leaves of a water lily. **lil·y–white** *adj* **1** white as a lily. **2** uncorrupted: *a lily-white politician.*

limb [lɪm] *n* **1** a leg, arm, or wing. **2** a large branch of a tree. **3** a person or thing thought of as a part, member, etc. **limb·less** *adj*. ⟨Old English *lim*⟩
out on a limb *Informal* in or into a dangerous position: *The producer was left out on a limb when her backers withdrew their support.* **tear limb from limb 1** tear (a body) violently apart. **2** *Informal* attack; criticize harshly.

lim·ber [ˈlɪmbər] *adj* bending easily; flexible: *A pianist has to have limber fingers.*
v make or become supple (with *up*): *We did some exercises to limber up before the game.* **lim·ber·ness** *n*. ⟨perhaps from *limp²* or *limb*⟩

lim·bo¹ [ˈlɪmbou] *n* **1** Often, **Limbo** *Roman Catholic theology* a place for those dead who have not received the grace of Christ while living, but have not deserved the punishment of impenitent sinners. **2** a condition of neglect or disregard: *The belief that the earth is flat belongs to the limbo of outworn ideas.* **3** an indefinite condition or place: *He was left in limbo for some time before*

he was told he definitely had the job. ⟨Latin *(in) limbo* on the edge⟩

lim·bo² [ˈlɪmbou] *n* a dance in which dancers bend over backward and pass under a low bar. ⟨perhaps from *limber*⟩

lime¹ [laɪm] *n* **1** calcium oxide; quicklime. **2** a deposit from hard water found on the inside of kettles, pipes, etc.
v put lime on. ⟨Old English *līm*⟩
lime·light *n* **1** an intense white light produced by heating lime, formerly used as a stage spotlight in theatres. **2** the centre of public attention: *Some politicians try to avoid the limelight.* **lime·stone** *n* rock formed consisting mostly of calcium carbonate.

lime² [laɪm] *n* a citrus tree bearing fruit with a green rind. ⟨French; Arabic *līma*⟩

lim·er·ick [ˈlɪmərɪk] *n* a kind of humorous poem consisting of five lines, with the first two lines rhyming with the last, and the third and fourth shorter lines rhyming with each other. *Example:*
There was a young lady named Lynn
Who was so exceedingly thin
That when she essayed
To drink lemonade
She slid down the straw and fell in. ⟨apparently from a song about *Limerick*, Irish Republic⟩

lim·it [ˈlɪmɪt] *n* **1** the farthest point or edge: *the limit of one's vision.* **2** *Mathematics* a value toward which terms of a sequence, values of a function, etc. approach indefinitely near. **3** in betting games, the agreed maximum amount of any bet or raise. **4** *Logging* ✱ a concession; timber limit. **5** **limits** *pl* **a** boundary: *Keep within the limits of the school grounds.* **b** constraints; limitations. **6** the maximum quantity of fish or game that the law allows one to take in a specified period. **7 the limit** *Informal* something very trying: *Isn't that just the limit? I couldn't believe it.*
v set a limit to: *Limit your expenditure to $60.* **lim·it·a·ble** *adj*. ⟨Latin *limes, limitis* boundary⟩ **lim·i·ta·tion** *n* **1** the act of being limited. **2** something that limits. **3** *Law* a period of time after which a claim, suit, etc. cannot be brought in court. A **statute of limitations** is a statute that fixes such a period of time. **lim·it·ed** *adj* restricted. **limited company** a corporation in which the liability of stockholders is limited to a specified amount. **limited edition 1** an edition of a book, etc. limited to a certain number of copies. **2** any other collector's item, such as a doll, of which few copies are made. **lim·it·less** *adj* without limits; infinite. **lim·it·less·ness** *n*.

lim·o [ˈlɪmou] *n Informal* limousine.

lim·ou·sine [ˈlɪməˌzin] *or* [ˌlɪməˈzin] *n* **1** a large, luxurious automobile, esp one driven by a chauffeur. **2** a large automobile or small bus used to carry passengers to and from an airport, etc. ⟨probably early French dialect *limousine* a coach⟩

limp¹ [lɪmp] *n* a lame step or walk.
v **1** walk with a limp. **2** proceed in a halting or laboured manner: *The new project limped*

along, as no one seemed very interested in it.
limp·ing·ly *adj.* ⟨perhaps Old English *lemphealt* lame⟩

limp² [lɪmp] *adj* not stiff or firm: *The lettuce was weeks old and quite limp.* **limp·ly** *adv.* **limp·ness** *n.* ⟨origin uncertain; compare Old Norse *limpa* weakness⟩

lim·pet [ˈlɪmpɪt] any of various marine gastropod molluscs having a single shell and a fleshy foot by which they cling to rocks, etc. ⟨Old English *lempedu;* Latin. See LAMPREY.⟩

lim·pid [ˈlɪmpɪd] *adj* clear; transparent: *limpid water, limpid eyes.* **lim·pid·ly** *adv.* **lim·pid·i·ty** *n.* ⟨Latin *limpidus* clear⟩

linch·pin [ˈlɪntʃ͵pɪn] *n* **1** a locking pin inserted through a hole in the end of an axle to keep the wheel on. **2** something or someone that is key to any endeavour. ⟨Old English *lynis* linchpin + *pin*⟩

line¹ [laɪn] *n* **1** a piece of rope, cord, or wire. **2** a long, narrow mark: *Draw two lines along the margin.* **3** a wrinkle or crease: *the lines in his face.* **4** a straight line: *The lower edges of the two pictures are about on a line.* **5** *Geometry* the path that a point may be imagined to make as it moves. **6 lines** *pl* **a** outline: *a ship of fine lines.* **b** plan of construction: *The two books were written on the same lines.* **c** the words that an actor speaks in a play: *I forgot my lines.* **7** a limit: *That hedge marks our property line.* **8** a row of persons or things: *a line of cars.* **9** a row of words in a column: *a page of 40 lines.* **10** a connected series of persons or things following one another in time: *The Stuarts were a line of English kings.* **11 the line a** the equator. **b** the border between two countries, esp that between Canada and the United States: *south of the line.* **c** the soldiers, ships, or aircraft that do all the fighting. **12** in a telephone, telegraph, etc. system: **a** a wire or wires connecting points or stations. **b** the system itself. **13** any rope, pipe, etc. running from one point to another. **14 a** one branch of a system of transportation: *the main line of a railway.* **b** a whole system of transportation or conveyance: *the Northern Line.* **15** a branch of business: *the dry-goods line.* **16** a kind or brand of goods: *a good line of hardware.* **17** *Slang* an exaggerated story: *She gave me a line about why she was late.* **18** ✱ in Ontario, CONCESSION ROAD.

v **1** mark (paper, etc.) with lines. **2** cover with lines: *Age had lined his face.* **3** form a line along: *Cars lined the road for a kilometre.* **4** *Baseball* hit a liner. **5** ✱ float a canoe downstream by guiding it from the shore with ropes attached to the bow and stern (often with *down*): *We often lined down rapids instead of portaging.* **lin·a·ble** or **line·a·ble** *adj.* **lin·ed** *adj.* **line·less** *adj.* **line·like** *adj.* ⟨Latin *linea* line, linen thread; *linum* flax⟩

all along (or **down**) **the line** everywhere. **bring into line** cause to conform: *She will bring the other members into line.* **come into line** conform. **draw the line** See DRAW. **get** (or **have**) **a line on** *Informal* get or have

information about. **hold the line a** wait on the phone. **b** withstand an attack. **in line a** in alignment. **b** in agreement. **c** in order: *next in line.* **in line with** agreeing or conforming to. **in the line of duty a** in the course of doing military duty. **b** while pursuing one's career. **lay it on the line** state things firmly. **line up a** form or wait in a line of people. **b** organize. **c** put in a line. **on a line** even; level. **on the line a** in between; neither one thing nor the other. **b** at risk: *A politician's job is on the line at election time.* **out of line** not suitable or proper. **read between the lines.** See READ. **string** (or **feed**) **someone a line** tell someone an untrue and exaggerated story. **toe the line** See TOE.

lin·age or **line·age** [ˈlaɪnɪdʒ] *n* **1** the number of lines of printed or written matter on a page, making up an article or advertisement, etc. **2** payment according to the number of lines. **lin·e·age** [ˈlɪniɪdʒ] *n* one's descent in a direct line from an ancestor. **lin·e·al** [ˈlɪniəl] *adj* **1** in the direct line of descent: *a lineal descendant.* **2** hereditary: *by lineal right.* **lin·e·al·ly** *adv.* **lin·e·a·ment** [ˈlɪniəmənt] *n* **1** a part. **2** a part of a face with attention to its outline. **lin·e·ar** [ˈlɪniər] *adj* **1** to do with lines: *linear symmetry.* **2** *Mathematics* involving measurement in one dimension only: *linear measure.* **3** of thinking, using direct relationships. Compare LATERAL. **lin·e·ar·ly** *adv.* **linear equation** *Mathematics* an equation whose graph is a straight line. **linear measure** any system of units for measuring length. **line·back·er** *n* *Football* a defensive player whose playing position is just behind the line of scrimmage. **line dancing** dancing in which dancers perform steps in rows, all facing the same way. **line drive** *Baseball* a ball hit in a straight line. **line·man** *n, pl* **-men 1** a person who repairs telegraph, telephone, or electric wires. **2** *Football* a centre, guard, tackle, or end. **3** a person who inspects railway tracks. **line of credit** credit advanced by a bank to a borrower up to a stated limit. **line of fire 1** the path of a bullet, shell, etc. **2** any very dangerous position. **lin·er** *n* **1** a ship or airplane belonging to a transportation line or system. **2** *Baseball* a ball hit so that it travels not far above the ground. **lines·man** *n, pl* **-men 1** lineman. **2** *Sports* a person who watches the lines that mark out the field, rink, court, etc. to assist the umpire or referee. **line·up** or **line–up** *n* **1** a number of people arranged in a line; especially, a group including a suspected offender, lined up for identification. **2** *Sports* the list of players on a team arranged according to position of play, etc. **3** a queue of people waiting for something: *There was a long lineup for tickets.*

line² [laɪn] *v* **1** put a lining inside (something). **2** fill: *to line one's pockets with money.* **lin·ed** *adj.* ⟨Old English *līn* flax⟩
lin·er [ˈlaɪnər] *n* something that serves as a lining: *a diaper liner.* **lin·ing** *n* a layer of material covering the inner surface of something.

lin·en ['lɪnən] *n* **1** thread spun from flax. **2** cloth made from flax. **3** Often **linens** *pl*, articles traditionally made of linen or cotton. Tablecloths and serviettes are called **table linen**; sheets, pillow cases, etc. are called **bed linen**. ⟨Old English *līnen*, adj; *līn* flax⟩
wash one's dirty linen in public See DIRTY LINEN.

ling [lɪŋ] *n, pl* **ling** or **lings** any of several edible fishes of the cod family. ⟨Middle English *lenge;* Old English *lang* long¹⟩

–ling *suffix* **1** little, young, or unimportant ——: duckling, princeling. **2** one that is——: underling. **3** one belonging to or concerned with——: earthling, hireling. ⟨Old English⟩

lin·ger ['lɪŋgər] *v* **1** put off departure: *Several fans lingered at the stage door.* **2** continue to stay, although gradually dying or becoming less: *Daylight lingers long in the summertime.* **3** go slowly; dally. **4** persist, esp in the mind: *The tune lingers in my mind.* **lin·ger·er** *n.* **lin·ger·ing** *adj.* ⟨frequentative of earlier *leng* delay, Old English *lengan; lang* long¹⟩

lin·ge·rie [ˌlɑʒəˈrei] *or* [ˈlɑʒəˌrei] *French* [lɛ̃ʒˈʀi] *n* women's underwear, nightgowns, etc. ⟨French *lingerie; linge* linen⟩

lin·go ['lɪŋgou] *n, pl* **-goes** *Informal* language, esp a dialect, jargon, etc.: *the lingo of sports writers.* ⟨Provençal *lengo* and Italian *lingua;* Latin *lingua* tongue⟩

lin·gua fran·ca ['lɪŋgwə 'fræŋkə] *pl* **lingua francas** or **linguae francae** ['lɪŋgwi 'frænsi] **1** a language or dialect used as a means of communication between peoples having different native languages: *Swahili is the lingua franca of central Africa.* **2** a hybrid language developed for this purpose: *Chinook Jargon was the lingua franca of Canada's Pacific coast.* **3** any system used as communication between people having different languages, backgrounds, etc.: *Pop music is the new lingua franca.* ⟨Italian *lingua franca* Frankish language⟩

lin·gual ['lɪŋgwəl] *adj* **1** to do with the tongue: *a lingual defect.* **2** to do with speech or languages. ⟨Latin *lingua* tongue⟩
lin·guist *n* **1** a person trained in linguistics. **2** a person skilled in a number of languages. **3** philologist. **lin·guis·tics** *n* the study of the structures, sounds, forms, etc. of language and languages (with sg verb). Compare PHILOLOGY. **lin·guis·tic** *adj.* **lin·guis·ti·cal·ly** *adv.*

lin·gui·ne [lɪŋˈgwini] *n* narrow strips of pasta. Also, **lin·gu·ini**. ⟨Italian pl of *linguino* diminutive of *lingua* tongue⟩

lin·i·ment ['lɪnəmənt] *n* a liquid for rubbing on the skin to relieve soreness, sprains, bruises, etc. ⟨Latin *linimentum; linere* anoint⟩

link [lɪŋk] *n* **1** one loop of a chain. **2** a fact or thought that connects others: *a link in a chain of evidence.* **3** *Chemistry* a bond. **4** *Computers* connection; a path along which signals are sent, or a component of such a path: *video link.* **link** *v.* **link·ed** *adj.* ⟨Scandinavian⟩
link·age *n* **1** a linking or being linked. **2** an arrangement or system of links. **linking verb**

a verb (such as **be, become,** or **seem**) that does not express action and is not followed by an object. *Examples*: I *am* sleepy. He *turned* pale. She *is* a doctor. They *became* friends.

USAGE
Many verbs with full meanings of their own (such as **taste, feel, act, look**) can also be used as linking verbs: *The butter tastes rancid. She felt sad. He acts old. This looks excellent.*

li·no·le·um [ləˈnouliəm] **1** *n* formerly, a floor covering made of ground cork mixed with linseed oil on a canvas back. **2** a similar floor covering made of vinyl. ⟨coined from Latin *linum* flax + *oleum* oil⟩

lin·seed ['lɪn,sid] *n* the seed of flax. ⟨Old English *līn* flax + SEED⟩
linseed oil an oil pressed from linseed, used especially in making paints and ink.

lint [lɪnt] *n* tiny bits of fibre from cloth, often accumulating in clothes dryers. **lint·less** *adj.* ⟨Latin *linum* or Old English *līn* flax⟩

lin·tel ['lɪntəl] *n* a horizontal beam or stone over a door, window, etc., that carries the weight of the wall above it. ⟨Old French; Latin *limes, limitis* boundary⟩

li·on ['laɪən] *n* **1** a large animal of the cat family, having, in the adult male, a mane around the neck and shoulders. **2** a very brave or strong person. **3** a famous or important person: *a literary lion.* **li·on·like** *adj.* ⟨Anglo-French; Latin *leo,* Greek *leōn*⟩
beard the lion in his den defy a powerful person in his or her own home, office, etc. **put one's head in the lion's mouth** put oneself in a dangerous position. **twist the lion's tail** intentionally provoke a government or other authority.
li·on·ess *n* a female lion. **li·on·heart** *n* someone very brave. **li·on–heart·ed** *adj.* **li·on·ize** *v* treat as very important: *The visiting artist was lionized by the press.* **li·on·i·za·tion** *n.* **lion's share** the biggest or best part: *the lion's share of the dessert.*

lip [lɪp] *n* **1** either of the two fleshy, movable edges of the mouth. **2** a folding edge of any opening: *the lip of a pitcher.* **3** *Music* the mouthpiece of a musical instrument. **4** *Slang* impudent talk: *Don't give me any lip.*
v **lipped, lip·ping** use the lips in playing a musical wind instrument. **lip·less** *adj.* **lip·like** *adj.* ⟨Old English *lippa*⟩
bite one's lip keep strong feeling under control. **button one's lip** *Slang* keep quiet. **hang on the lips of** listen to with great admiration. **keep a stiff upper lip** be brave or firm. **read my lips** I mean exactly what I said. **smack one's lips** enjoy, especially food, in anticipation.
lip gloss a cosmetic applied to the lips to make them shiny. **lipped** [lɪpt] *adj* **1** having a lip or lips. **2** having lips of a specified kind (in compounds): *tight-lipped.* **lip·py** *adj Slang* insolent. **lip–read, -read** [-ˌrɛd], **-read·ing** *v* understand (speech) by watching the lip movements of the speaker. **lip reader** *n.* **lip reading** *n.* **lip–serv·ice** *n* service expressed in

words only; insincerity. **lip·stick** *n* **1** a cosmetic paste for the lips, usually coloured. **lip–sync** or **–synch** ['lɪp ˌsɪŋk] *v* mouth the words of (a song) while it is played, to make it seem that one is singing.

lip·id ['lɪpɪd] *or* ['ləipɪd] *n Biochemistry* any of a group of natural organic compounds, including fats, oils, and steroids, that are insoluble in water but soluble in organic solvents such as alcohol. ⟨Greek *lipos* fat⟩
lip·o·suc·tion ['lɪpou,sʌkʃən] *or* ['ləipou,sʌkʃən] *n* surgical removal of fatty tissue by suction.

li·queur [lɪˈkjʊr] *n* a syrupy, highly flavoured alcoholic drink. ⟨French; Latin *liquor*⟩

liq·uid ['lɪkwɪd] *n* a substance that is neither a solid nor a gas.
adj **1** in the form of a liquid: *liquid soap.* **2** clear and smooth-flowing in sound: *the liquid notes of a bird.* **3** easily turned into cash: *Savings bonds are a liquid investment.* **liq·uid·i·ty** *n*. ⟨Latin *liquidus; liquere* be fluid⟩
liq·ue·fy ['lɪkwə,faɪ] *v* make or become liquid. **liq·ue·fac·tion** *n*. **liq·ue·fi·a·ble** *adj*. **liq·ue·fier** *n*. **liquid assets** things easily converted into cash. **liq·ui·date** ['lɪkwɪ,deɪt] *v* **1** settle the accounts of (a business, etc.); clear up the affairs of (a bankruptcy). **2** convert into cash. **3** get rid of, esp by killing. **liq·ui·da·tion** *n*. **liq·ui·da·tor** *n*. **liquid crystal display** *Computers* a means of displaying characters on a calculator, digital clock, etc., using a liquid with crystalline properties. *Abbrev* **LCD**
liquid measure any system of units for measuring liquids.

liq·uor ['lɪkər] *n* **1** an alcoholic drink, such as whisky. **2** any liquid, esp a liquid in which food is canned or cooked. ⟨Latin⟩
liquor control board ✹ a government board regulating the distribution and sale of alcoholic beverages within a province.

lisp [lɪsp] *v* **1** produce a *th* sound instead of the sound of *s* or *z* in speaking, as 'thing' for 'sing'. **2** speak like a baby or child. **lisp** *n*. **lisp·ing** *adj*. ⟨Old English *wlisp* adj, lisping⟩

lis·some or **lis·som** ['lɪsəm] *adj* **1** lithe; supple. **2** nimble; active. **lis·some·ly** or **lis·som·ly** *adv*. **lis·some·ness** or **lis·som·ness** *n*. ⟨variant of lithesome⟩

list¹ [lɪst] *n* a series of names, numbers, words, or other items: *a shopping list.*
v make a list of; enter in a list. ⟨French *liste*⟩
list·ing *n* **1** a piece of real estate for sale: *three new listings today.* **2** *Computers* a document produced by a computer, consisting of printed lines of information. **list price** the price given in a catalogue or list.

list² [lɪst] *n* a tipping to one side; tilt: *the list of a ship.* **list** *v*. ⟨extended use of *list* desire, be inclined, Old English *lystan; lust* pleasure⟩

lis·ten ['lɪsən] *v* **1** pay attention so as to hear. **2** give heed (to advice, etc.): *Politicians should listen to their constituents.* **lis·ten·er** *n*. ⟨Old English *hlysna; hlyst* hearing⟩
listen in listen to others talking: *I listened in on the extension.*

list·less ['lɪstlɪs] *adj* seeming too tired to care about anything: *a dull and listless mood.* **list·less·ly** *adv*. **list·less·ness** *n*. ⟨obsolete *list* desire; see LIST².⟩

lists [lɪsts] *n pl* in the Middle Ages, a field where knights fought in tournaments. ⟨blend of obsolete *list* woven border and Old French *lice* place of combat; Germanic⟩
enter the lists join in a contest.

lit¹ [lɪt] *v* a pt and a pp of LIGHT¹ and LIGHT³.

lit² [lɪt] *n Informal* literature.

lit·a·ny ['lɪtəni] *n* **1** a form of prayer for use in church services, with fixed responses from the congregation. **2** any account involving much repetition: *a litany of complaints.* ⟨Greek *litaneia; litesthai* entreat⟩

li·tchi ['litʃi] *n* the fruit of a Chinese tree of the soapberry family, having juicy pulp. Also, **li·chee** or **ly·chee**. ⟨Mandarin *li chih*⟩
litchi nut the fruit of the litchi.

lit·er·al ['lɪtərəl] *adj* **1** following the exact words of the original: *a literal translation.* **2** taking words in their basic meaning: *When we say* He flew down the stairs, *we do not mean* fly *in the literal sense of the word.* **3** concerned mainly with facts: *a literal type of mind.* **4** true to fact: *a literal account.* **lit·er·al·ness** *n*. ⟨Latin *lit(t)era* letter⟩
lit–crit *n Informal* literary criticism.
lit·er·al·ism *n* **1** keeping to the literal meaning. **2** in visual art, utter realism. **lit·er·al·ist** *n*. **lit·er·al·is·tic** *adj*. **lit·er·al·is·ti·cal·ly** *adv*. **lit·er·al·ly** ['lɪtərəli] *adv* **1** word for word: *to translate literally.* **2** without exaggeration: *I was literally penniless.* **3** *Informal* virtually. **lit·er·ar·y** *adj* **1** to do with literature: *a literary treatise.* **2** to do with books: *a literary agent.* **3** to do with writers, scholars, etc., or writing as a profession: *a literary journal.* **4** knowing much about literature: *They are a very literary family.*
lit·er·ate *adj* **1** able to read and write. **2** acquainted with literature. **3** minimally competent in a given field. *n* a literate person. **lit·er·a·cy** *n*. **lit·er·ate·ly** *adv*. **lit·e·ra·ti** [,lɪtəˈrɑti] *n pl* scholarly or literary people. **lit·er·a·ture** ['lɪtərətʃər] *n* **1** the writings of a period or of a country: *Canadian literature.* **2** all the books and articles on a subject: *the literature of stamp collecting.* **3** printed matter of any kind: *Election campaign literature informs people about the candidates.*

–lith *combining form* rock; stone: *megalith.* ⟨Greek *lithos*⟩

lithe [laɪð] *adj* bending easily; flexible: *lithe of body, a lithe willow.* **lithe·ly** *adv.* **lithe·ness** *n.* ⟨Old English *līthe* mild⟩ **lithe·some** *adj* lithe.

lith·i·um [ˈlɪθiəm] *n* a metallic element similar to sodium. Lithium is the lightest of all the metals. *Symbol* **Li** ⟨Greek *lithos* stone⟩

li·thog·ra·phy [ləˈθɒɡrəfi] *n* the art of transferring an image onto paper from a metal plate, by preparing the surface so that certain parts receive ink while other parts repel it. ⟨Greek *lithos* stone + -GRAPH⟩ **lith·o·graph** [ˈlɪθəˌɡræf] *n* a picture, print, etc. made by lithography. **li·thog·ra·pher** *n.* **lith·o·graph·ic** *adj.* **lith·o·graph·i·cal·ly** *adv.*

li·thol·o·gy [ləˈθɒlədʒi] *n* the study of rocks. ⟨Greek *lithos* stone⟩

lith·o·sphere [ˈlɪθəˌsfir] *n* the solid outer shell of the earth, including the continental and oceanic crusts. ⟨Greek *lithos* stone + SPHERE⟩

lit·i·gate [ˈlɪtəˌɡeit] *v* **1** engage in a lawsuit. **2** contest in a lawsuit. **lit·i·ga·ble** *adj.* **lit·i·ga·tion** *n.* **lit·i·ga·tor** *n.* ⟨Latin *litigare; lis, litis* lawsuit + *agere* drive⟩ **lit·i·gant** [ˈlɪtəɡənt] *n* a person engaged in a lawsuit. **li·ti·gious** [ləˈtɪdʒəs] *adj* having the habit of going to law. **li·ti·gious·ness** *n.*

lit·mus [ˈlɪtməs] *n* a blue colouring matter that turns red in an acid solution and back to blue in an alkaline solution. ⟨Old Norse *litmose* dyer's herb; *litr* colour + *mosi* moss⟩ **litmus paper** a strip of paper treated with litmus. **litmus test 1** *Chemistry* a test using litmus paper to see whether a solution is acidic or alkaline. **2** any test dependent on one crucial factor.

li·to·tes [ˈlaɪtəˌtiz], [ˈlɪtəˌtiz], *or* [ləˈtoutiz] *n, pl* **-tes** *Rhetoric* a form of understatement in which something is said by denying its opposite. *Example: He had not a little to drink.* *Compare* HYPERBOLE. ⟨Greek *litotēs; litos* plain⟩

li·tre [ˈlitər] *n* a unit used with the SI for measuring volume or capacity, equal to one cubic decimetre. *Symbol* **L** ⟨French; Latin, Greek *litra* a unit of weight⟩

lit·ter [ˈlɪtər] *n* **1** scattered rubbish. **2** the animals born at the same time from one mother: *a litter of puppies.* **3** gravel or other material put in a cat's litter box. **4** a stretcher for carrying a sick person. **5** a framework to be carried on peoples' shoulders or by beasts of burden, consisting of a couch usually enclosed by curtains. *v* **1** leave things lying around. **2** give birth to (animals). ⟨Anglo-French *litere,* Latin *lectus* bed⟩ **litter box** a box containing gravel or other material, for use as a toilet by a cat. **lit·ter·bug** *n Informal* one who leaves litter lying about in public places.

lit·tle [ˈlɪtəl] *adj* **less** or **less·er, least;** or **lit·tler, lit·tlest 1** small: *A grain of sand is little.* **2** not much: *little hope.* **3** short: *a little walk.* **4** mean and narrow in thought or feeling: *Only a little man would manipulate a child.* *adv* **less, least 1** to a small extent: *He travels*

little. **2** not at all: *He little knows the outcome.* *n* **1** a small amount, quantity, or degree: *to add a little.* **2** a short time or distance: *Go a little to the left.* **lit·tle·ness** *n.* ⟨Old English *lȳtel*⟩ **in little** on a small scale. **little by little** gradually: *She recovered little by little.* **make little of** treat as of little importance: *She made little of her troubles.* **not a little** much; very: *He was not a little upset by the accident.* **think little of** consider as worthless.

Little Dipper the seven principal stars in the constellation Ursa Minor. Compare BIG DIPPER. **little people 1** in folklore, small imaginary beings, such as fairies, elves, leprechauns, etc. **2** the common people, esp the working class. **3** children. **little theatre** a small, usually amateur theatre group.

lit·to·ral [ˈlɪtərəl] *adj* to do with a shore, esp of the sea. *n* the region along a shore, esp the zone between the marks of high and low tide. ⟨Latin *litoris* shore⟩

lit·ur·gy [ˈlɪtərdʒi] *n* **1** a ritual for public worship. **2** Often, **Liturgy** the Eucharistic service, esp in the Eastern Orthodox Church. **li·tur·gi·cal** *adj.* **li·tur·gi·cal·ly** *adv.* ⟨Greek *leitourgia* public worship; *leitos* public + *ergon* work⟩

live [lɪv] *v* **1** have life; exist: *All creatures have an equal right to live.* **2** remain alive: *He managed to live through the war.* **3** support oneself: *live on one's income.* **4** subsist; feed: *Rabbits live mainly on grass.* **5** dwell: *My aunt lives in Victoria.* **6** have a full life: *Those people know how to live!* ⟨Old English *lifian, libban*⟩ **live for** have a passion for: *She lives for dancing.* **live in** live at the place where one works. **live–in** *adj* **1** living at one's place of employment: *a live-in nanny.* **2** cohabiting. *n* **1** a live-in employee. **2** a cohabiting lover. **live it up** *Slang* enjoy life to the full. **live off** (or **on**) **a** support oneself by. **b** have as one's main diet. **c** use (someone) as a source of income. **live out a** live away from where one works. **b** last through. **live something down** live so worthily that some fault of the past is overlooked. **live together** have a common-law marriage. **live up to** act according to: *The car has not lived up to the salesperson's description.* **live with a** accept. **b** be in a common-law marriage with.

liv·a·ble or, *esp US* **liveable** *adj* **1** fit to live in: *livable surroundings.* **2** easy to live with. **3** worth living: *A good friend often helps make life livable.* **liv·a·ble·ness** *n.* **liv·a·bil·i·ty** *n.* **live** [laɪv] *adj* **1** alive: *a live dog.* **2** full of energy: *She is a very live girl, always on the go.* **3** *Electricity* carrying an electric current: *a live wire.* **4** of telephones, microphones, etc., not shut off. **5** *Radio, television* broadcast as performed and not from tape or film made beforehand. *adv* of recordings or broadcasts, made as performed before an audience. **live-bear·er** [ˈlaɪvˌberər] *n* any fish that bears live young instead of laying eggs, such as the guppy. **live·li·hood** [ˈlaɪvliˌhʊd] *n* a means of obtaining the money necessary to buy food, clothing, and shelter. **live load** a variable weight that a structure carries in addition to its own weight, such as traffic on a bridge. Compare DEAD LOAD. **live·long** ['lɪv,lɒŋ] *adj* the whole length of: *the livelong day.* **live·ly** *adj* 1 full of life. 2 vivid. *adv* in a lively manner. **live·li·ness** *n.* **liv·en** ['laɪvən] *v* make or become more lively or interesting (often with *up*): *The show isn't bad, but they could liven it up a little.* **live·stock** *n* farm animals. **live wire** 1 *Electricity* a wire through which an electric current is flowing. 2 *Informal* an energetic person. **liv·ing** ['lɪvɪŋ] *adj* 1 having life: *a living plant.* 2 full of life: *a living faith.* 3 in actual existence: *a living language.* 4 true to life: *a living picture.* 5 for living in: *living conditions.* 6 enough to live on: *a living wage.* *n* 1 the condition of being alive: *the joy of living.* 2 **the living** *pl* all the people who are alive. 3 livelihood. 4 a manner of life: *healthful living.* 5 a position in certain Christian churches, including the income attached to it. **in living memory** within the lifetime of people still living. **living quarters** a place to live. **living room** a room used for the general activities of the occupants, for entertaining guests, etc. **living wage** a wage sufficient to enable a person or family to live in reasonable comfort and security. **living will** a document stating a person's wishes for a future time when he or she may be dependent on life-support machines.

liv·er ['lɪvər] *n Anatomy* in vertebrates, a large organ that secretes bile and helps in the absorption of food. ⟨Old English *lifer*⟩ **liv·er·ish** *adj* having a sour or peevish disposition. **liv·er·wurst** ['lɪvər,wɜrst] *or* [-,wurst] *n* sausage consisting largely of ground liver. Also called **liver sausage.**

liv·er·y ['lɪvəri] *n* 1 any special uniform provided for the servants of a household, or adopted by any group or profession. 2 the business of stabling or hiring out horses, formerly often with carriages. 3 the keeping of cars, bicycles, or other vehicles for hire. ⟨Anglo-French *livere; livrer* dispense, Latin *liberare;* orig, provisions given to servants⟩ **liv·er·ied** *adj* clothed in a livery (def. 1). **livery stable** a place where horses and vehicles are kept for hire or where horses are fed and stabled.

lives *n* pl of LIFE.

live·yere, liv·ere, *or* **liv·ier** ['lɪvjər] *n* ✱ *Newfoundland and Labrador* a permanent resident, as opposed to those who come for the fishing or sealing season only. ⟨*livier* manorial worker with certain property rights. See LIVERY.⟩

liv·id ['lɪvɪd] *adj* 1 having a dull bluish colour, as from a bruise: *livid marks on an arm.* 2 very pale: *livid with shock.* 3 flushed: *livid with anger.* 4 *Informal* very angry: *The insults made her livid.* **liv·id·ly** *adv.* **liv·id·ness** or **li·vid·i·ty** *n.* ⟨Latin *lividus; livere* be bluish⟩

liz·ard ['lɪzərd] *n* any of a suborder of reptiles belonging to the same order as snakes, having external ears, eyes with movable lids,

and, in most species, four short legs. **liz·ard·like** *adj.* ⟨Old French *lesard*⟩

lla·ma ['læmə] *or* ['lɑmə] *n, pl* **-mas** *or* (esp collectively) **-ma** a domesticated South American hoofed mammal having thick, shaggy wool. ⟨Spanish; Quechua⟩

lo [lou] *interj Archaic, poetic* look! behold! ⟨Old English *lā*⟩

load [loud] *n* 1 whatever is being carried: *a load of hay.* 2 the amount usually carried at one time (often in compounds): *a planeload of tourists.* 3 **loads** *pl Informal* a great quantity or number: *loads of food.* 4 something that weighs down: *That's a load off my mind!* 5 *Mechanics* the weight supported by a structure or part. 6 *Slang* enough liquor to make one drunk.
v 1 place on or in a carrier of some kind: *The dockhands are loading grain.* 2 burden (often with *down*): *loaded down with debt.* 3 supply amply: *They loaded her with compliments.* 4 put a charge in (a gun). 5 place (something) into (a device): *to load a cassette into a tape recorder.* 6 *Computers* transfer (programs, data, etc.) from auxiliary storage into a computer's main memory. **load·er** *n.* **load·less** *adj.* ⟨Old English *lād* course, carrying; compare *lode*⟩ **load·ed** *adj* 1 carrying a load. 2 with a charge in it: *a loaded gun.* 3 *Slang* drunk. 4 *Slang* rich. 5 *Informal* full of half-hidden assumptions: *loaded questions.* 6 *Informal.* well equipped: *This new car is loaded with options.*

loaf¹ [louf] *n, pl* **loaves** [louvz] 1 a quantity of bread baked as one piece. 2 any mass of food shaped like a loaf and baked: *a meat loaf.* ⟨Old English *hlāf*⟩

loaf² [louf] *v* spend time idly; do nothing: *We loafed all day Saturday.* ⟨origin uncertain⟩ **loaf·er** *n* 1 a person who loafs. 2 **Loafer** *Trademark* a comfortable, casual shoe resembling a moccasin.

loam [loum] *n* rich, fertile earth. **loam·i·ness** *n.* **loam·y** *adj.* ⟨Old English *lām*⟩

loan [loun] *n* 1 the act of lending: *She asked for the loan of his pen.* 2 anything that is lent, esp money: *He asked his brother for a loan.* **loan** *v.* **loan·a·ble** *adj.* ⟨Old Norse *lān*⟩ **on loan** lent or granted for temporary use: *The book was out on loan so I had to wait.* **loan·er** *n* a loaned item, esp a replacement for something being repaired. **loan shark** *Informal* a person who lends money at an extremely high or unlawful rate of interest. **loan–shark·ing** *n.* **loan·word** or **loan word** *n* a word taken from another language, often being slightly changed in the process.

USAGE
Although some people object to the use of **loan** as a verb, its use as both a verb and a noun is standard current English: *I said I would loan (or lend) him my tuxedo. She asked me for a loan of five dollars.*

loath [louθ] *or* [louð] *adj* unwilling: *The little girl was loath to leave her mother.* Also, **loth.** ⟨Old English *lāth* hostile⟩ **nothing loath** willing; willingly.

loathe ['louð] *v* feel strong disgust for. **loath·ing** *n.* **loath·some** ['louðsəm] *or* ['louθsəm] *adj.* **loath·some·ness** *n.*

loaves [louvz] *n* pl of LOAF[1].

lob [lɒb] *n* **1** *Tennis* a ball hit high to the back of the opponent's court. **2** a slow, underarm throw. **lob, lobbed, lob·bing** *v.* **lob·ber** *n.* ⟨Middle English *lobbe(n)* move clumsily⟩
lob shot *n Hockey* a deceptive, slow-moving shot on goal.

lob·by ['lɒbi] *n* **1** a large entrance hall in a theatre, hotel, etc. **2** a group of people that tries to influence legislators.
v try to influence legislators: *The textile manufacturers are lobbying for a tax on imported fabrics.* **lob·by·ist** *n.* ⟨Latin *lobia* covered walk⟩

lobe [loub] *n* a rounded, projecting part. The lobe of the ear is the rounded, lower end. **lobed** *adj.* ⟨Greek *lobos*⟩
lo·bate ['loubeit] *adj* having a lobe or lobes; having the form of a lobe. The liver is lobate.

lo·bot·o·my [lə'bɒtəmi] *n* a surgical operation involving incision into the frontal lobe of the brain. **lo·bot·o·mize** *v.* ⟨Greek *lobos* lobe + *tome* a cutting⟩

lob·ster ['lɒbstər] *n* any of a family of edible sea crustaceans with a pair of large pincers at the front. ⟨Old English *loppestre;* Latin *locusta* locust, influenced by Old English *loppe* spider⟩ **lobster pot** a trap for lobsters.

lob·stick ['lɒb,stɪk] *n* ✹ in the North, a tall, prominently situated spruce or pine trimmed of all but its topmost branches, originally used by the First Nations people as a talisman and landmark. Also, **lop·stick.** ⟨*lopped stick*⟩

lo·cal ['loukəl] *adj* **1** to do with a certain place or places: *local news.* **2** restricted to one part of the body: *a local pain.*
n **1** a train, bus, etc. that stops at all of the stations on its route. **2** a local inhabitant. **3** a branch of a union, fraternity, etc. **4** a person, team, etc. from a given locality. **5** a local anesthetic. **lo·cal·ly** *adv.* ⟨Latin *locus* place⟩
local area network *Computers* a set of computers connected to communicate or share resources. *Abbrev* **LAN local colour** *or* **color** the customs, peculiarities, etc. of a certain place or period, used in writing by people who have visited the place, to make the story seem more real. **lo·cale** [lou'kæl] *n* location, site, or place, esp with reference to events connected with it. **local government** the system of administration of local affairs in a township, city, etc. by its own people through their elected representatives. **lo·cal·ism** *n* **1** a local custom, practice, etc. **2** a word or expression, etc. peculiar to a certain area: *Outport,* meaning *an outlying fishing village,* is a Newfoundland localism. **3** attachment to a certain place. **lo·cal·ist** *n.* **lo·cal·is·tic** *adj.* **lo·cal·i·ty** [lou'kæləti] *n* a particular place: *Are there any stores in this locality?* **lo·cal·ize** ['loukə,laɪz] *v* limit to a

particular place: *The infection was localized in the foot.* **lo·cal·i·za·tion** *n.* **lo·cate** [lou'keit] *or* ['loukeit] *v* **1** establish in a place: *He located his new store in Yellowknife.* **2** establish oneself in a place: *Early settlers located where there was water.* **3** find out the exact position of: *The general tried to locate the enemy's camp.* **4** ✹ formerly, establish (someone) legally as a settler under terms set by the government. **lo·cat·a·ble** *adj.* **lo·ca·tion** *n.* **be located** be situated. **on location** at a place outside the studio for the purpose of filming a movie.

loc. cit. in the place cited (for Latin *loco citato*).

lo·ci ['lousaɪ] *or* [-si], ['loukaɪ] *or* [-ki] *n* pl of LOCUS.

lock[1] [lɒk] *n* **1** a means of fastening doors, boxes, etc. **2** an enclosed section in a canal, dock, etc. which permits vessels to be raised or lowered to different water levels. **3** an airtight chamber providing entrance to a compartment in which there is compressed air. **4** the complete turning circle of a vehicle: *This car has a wide lock.*
v **1** fasten with a lock: *to lock a door.* **2** hold fast: *The ship was locked in ice.* **3** join or link together: *The girls locked arms.* **4** fasten (a wheel) to keep from turning. **5** make certain to accomplish or get (with *up*): *We've got the championship locked up.* **lock·a·ble** *adj.* **lock·ed** *adj.*
lock·less *adj.* ⟨Old English *loc* fastening, bar⟩ **lock in** invest (money) so that it cannot be taken out before a specified time. **lock out** refuse to give work to (workers) until they accept the employer's terms. **lock, stock, and barrel** *Informal* completely. **lock up a** lock a building for the night: *Be sure to lock up as you leave.* **b** keep (money) in an account that cannot be used until a certain date: *Our savings are locked up in G.I.C.s.* **under lock and key** locked up.
lock·age ['lɒkɪdʒ] *n* **1** the use or operation of locks in canals or streams. **2** the toll paid for passage through a lock. **lock·er** *n* **1** a chest, drawer, closet, or cupboard that can be locked. **2** a large, refrigerated compartment for storing frozen food for a long time. **3** any person or thing that locks or locks something. **locker room** a room in a sports facility where players can shower, keep their clothes in a locker, etc. **locker–room** *adj* of language, typical of locker rooms; vulgar or bawdy. **lock·et** ['lɒkɪt] *n* a small ornamental case of gold, silver, etc. for holding a picture of someone. **lock·jaw** *n* tetanus. A characteristic symptom of the disease is a stiffness of the jaw muscles. **lock·out** *n* the closure of a factory, office, etc. or the refusal of work by an employer in order to make the employees agree to terms. **lock·smith** *n* a person who makes or repairs locks and keys. **lock step** marching in step close together. **lock·up** *n* **1** the act or time of locking up. **2** *Informal* jail.

lock[2] [lɒk] *n* **1** a curl of hair. **2 locks** *pl* the hair of the head: *curly locks.* ⟨Old English *locc* lock of hair⟩

lo·co ['loukou] *n, pl* **-cos** *n* **1** locoweed. **2** the disease caused by eating this weed.
adj Slang crazy. ⟨Spanish *loco* insane⟩
lo·co·weed *n* any of various plants of the pea family, that are poisonous to livestock.

lo·co·mo·tion [,loukə'mouʃən] *n* the act or power of moving from place to place. ⟨Latin *loco* from a place + MOTION⟩
lo·co·mo·tive [,loukə'moutɪv] *n* an engine that runs on rails on its own power.
adj moving from place to place: *locomotive bacteria.* **lo·co·mo·tor** *adj* to do with locomotion.

lo·cus ['loukəs] *n, pl* **lo·ci 1** place or locality. **2** *Mathematics* the set of all points whose location satisfies given conditions. **3** *Genetics* **a** the position of a particular gene on a chromosome. **b** the gene itself. ⟨Latin⟩

lo·cust ['loukəst] *n* **1** any of a family of grasshoppers that migrate in swarms, often destroying all vegetation in the areas they pass through. **2** any of various hardwood trees of the pea family. ⟨Latin *locusta*⟩

lo·cu·tion [lou'kjuʃən] *n* **1** a particular form of expression characteristic of a particular region, group of people, etc. **2** style of speech: *He has no sense of formal locution.* ⟨Latin *locutio; loqui* speak⟩

lode [loud] *n* **1** a vein of metal ore: *The miners struck a rich lode of copper.* **2** a plentiful source of anything. ⟨Old English *lād* carrying⟩
lode·star or **load·star** *n* **1** a star that shows the way, esp the North Star. **2** a guiding principle. **lode·stone** or **load·stone** *n* **1** iron oxide (magnetite) that is naturally magnetic. **2** a person or thing that attracts strongly: *Gold was the lodestone that drew us to the Yukon.*

lodge [lɒdʒ] *v* **1** live in a place for a time, or provide with a place: *Can you lodge us tonight?* **2** get caught in a place: *My kite lodged in that tree.* **3** put before some authority: *We lodged a complaint with the police.*
n **1** an inn or resort hotel, etc. **2** a small or temporary house: *My uncle rents a lodge in the mountains every summer.* **3** a branch of a fraternal organization. **4** the den of an animal such as a beaver or otter. **5** a First Nations dwelling or household. **lodge·a·ble** *adj.* ⟨Old French *loge* arbour, covered walk⟩
lodge·pole pine ✷ a pine found throughout British Columbia and western Alberta, occurring in two forms: a short, often crooked tree along the coast and a tall, straight, slender tree inland. **lodg·er** *n* a person who lives in rented rooms. **lodg·ing** *n* **1** a place to live in for a time. **2 lodgings** *pl* a rented room or rooms in a house. **lodging house** a house in which rooms are rented. **lodg·ment** or **lodge·ment** *n* **1** a lodging or being lodged: *the lodgment of a complaint.* **2** something lodged or deposited: *a lodgment of earth on a ledge or rock.*

loft [lɒft] *n* **1** attic. **2** a room under the roof of a barn or stable. **3** the partly open floor of an apartment building or warehouse: *a studio loft.* **4** *Golf* **a** the backward slope of the face of a club to give elevation to a struck ball. **b** a

stroke that drives a ball upward. **5** the natural resiliency of wool, down, etc., enabling it to act as insulation.
v **1** *Golf* hit (a ball) high up into the air. **2** propel or lift high in the air. ⟨Old Norse *lopt* air, sky, loft⟩
loft·y ['lɒfti] *adj* **1** very high: *lofty mountains.* **2** high in character or spirit: *lofty ideals.* **3** proud; haughty: *a lofty contempt for others.* **loft·i·ly** *adv.* **loft·i·ness** *n.*

log¹ [lɒg] *n* **1** a length of wood just as it comes from the tree. **2** any piece of cut firewood. **3** *Nautical* the daily record of a ship's voyage. **4** the record of an airplane trip, performance of an engine, etc. **5** a personal diary of a journey. **6** *Nautical* a float for measuring the speed of a ship.
v **logged, log·ging 1** cut down trees. **2** enter in a logbook or log. **3** travel (a particular distance) or reach (a particular speed): *We logged 800 km the first day.* **log·like** *adj.* ⟨Middle English *logge*; origin uncertain⟩
log in mark one's arrival in a book. **log off** (or **out**) end a session of work on a computer. **log on** (or **in**) begin a session of work on a computer by entering a password or other identification. **log out** mark one's departure in a book.
log·book *n* **1** a book containing a permanent record of all the details of the voyage of a ship or aircraft. **2** any book containing a record of performance over a period of time. **log cabin** a small house built entirely of logs, squared off and caulked with clay. **log drive ✷** the transportation of logs by means of water. **log driver** *n* ✷ a person whose work is felling trees and getting the logs to the mill. **log·ger·head** *n* **1** *Archaic, dialect* a stupid person. **2** any of various large-headed marine turtles. **at loggerheads** in disagreement. **log·in** *n* **1** the act of logging on to a computer. Also, **log·on**. **2** the password or other identification keyed in by a person logging on. **log·ging** *n* ✷ the work of cutting down trees and removing them from the forest. **log·jam** *n* **1** an accumulation of floating logs jammed together in the water. **2** any deadlock or blockage, often figurative, as a backlog of paperwork. **log·roll** *v* **1** roll logs by walking on them. **2** *Informal esp US* get (a bill) passed by giving political aid in return for a favour. **log·roll·er** *n.* **log·rolling** *n.*

log² [lɒg] *n* logarithm.
log·a·rithm ['lɒgə,rɪðəm] *n Mathematics* an exponent of the power to which a fixed number (usually 10) must be raised in order to produce a given number. **log·a·rith·mic** *adj.* ⟨Greek *logos* proportion + *arithmos* number⟩

lo·gan ['lougən] *n* ✷ pokelogan.

log·ic ['lɒdʒɪk] *n* **1** the science of getting new information by reasoning from facts that one already knows. **2** reasoning; the use of argument: *The lawyer won her case because her logic was sound.* **3** sound sense: *There is much logic in what you say.* **log·i·cal** *adj.* **log·i·cal·ly** *adv.* **log·i·cal·i·ty** *n.* ⟨Greek *logikē (technē)* reasoning (art); *logos* word, reason⟩

logic bomb *Computers* a set of instructions in a computer program that can cause a program to fail in certain circumstances, especially when these instructions have been created intentionally. **lo·gi·cian** [lə'dʒɪʃən] *n* a person trained in logic.

lo·gis·tics [lə'dʒɪstɪks] *n* 1 the art of planning and carrying out military movement, evacuation, and supply. 2 the handling of any complex operation. **lo·gis·tic** *adj*. **lo·gis·ti·cal·ly** *adv*. ⟨French *logistique; loger* lodge⟩

lo·go ['lougou] *n* an identifying symbol used as a trademark, in advertising, etc.

log·o·gram ['lɒgə,græm] *or* ['lougə,græm] *n* a character or symbol used to represent a whole word, such as ¢ for *cent*.

lo·gom·a·chy [lə'gɒməki] *n* 1 an argument about words. 2 a meaningless battle of words. ⟨Greek *logos* word + *machia* battle⟩

log·o·phile ['lɒgə,faɪl] *or* ['lougə,faɪl] *n* a lover of words. ⟨<Greek *logos* word⟩

log·or·rhea [,lɒgə'riə] *n* excessive, esp compulsive, wordiness or talkativeness. **log·or·rhe·ic** *adj*. ⟨Greek *logos* word + *rhoia; rheein* to flow⟩

lo·gy ['lougi] *or* ['lɒgi] *adj Informal* heavy; sluggish; dull. ⟨perhaps Dutch *log* heavy, dull⟩

–logy *combining form* 1 an account, doctrine, or science of: *biology*. 2 writing; discussion: *eulogy, trilogy*. ⟨Greek *-logia; logos* word, reason or (more often) *legein* speak (of), mention⟩

loin [lɔɪn] *n* 1 Usually, **loins** *pl* the part of the body between the ribs and the hips. 2 a piece of meat from this part of an animal: *a loin of pork*. ⟨Old French *loigne*; Latin *lumbus*⟩
gird up one's loins get ready for action.

loin·cloth *n* a piece of cloth fastened around the waist and covering the thighs.

loi·ter ['lɔɪtər] *v* 1 stand around idly. 2 dawdle. 3 spend (time) idly (with *away*). **loi·ter·er** *n*. ⟨Middle Dutch *loteren* be loose⟩

loll [lɒl] *v* 1 recline in a lazy manner: *to loll on a chesterfield*. 2 hang out loosely or droop: *A dog's tongue lolls out in hot weather*. **loll** *n*. ⟨Middle English *lolle(n)*⟩
loll about rest comfortably and lazily.

lol·li·pop or **lol·ly·pop** ['lɒli,pɒp] *n* a piece of hard candy on the end of a small stick; sucker. ⟨dialect *lolly* tongue + *pop*⟩

lone [loun] *adj* 1 alone; solitary: *We met a lone traveller on our way*. 2 lonely: *a lone life*. ⟨variant of *alone*⟩
lone·ly ['lounli] *adj* 1 longing for company. 2 without many people: *a lonely road*. 3 alone: *a lonely tree*. **lone·li·ness** *n*. **lon·er** *n Informal* a person who prefers to be alone. **lone·some** *adj* 1 feeling lonely or making one feel lonely. 2 desolate: *a lonesome road*. 3 solitary: *a lonesome pine*. **lone·some·ness** *n*. **lone wolf** *Informal* a person who prefers to work or live alone

long[1] [lɒŋ] *adj* 1 measuring much from end to end in space or time: *a long distance, a long speech*. 2 continuing for too much time: *a long wait*. 3 having a specified length in space or time: *five metres long, two hours long*. *adv* 1 throughout the whole length of: *all night long*. 2 for a long time: *a reform long overdue*. 3 at a point of time far distant from the time indicated: *long before*.
n 1 a long time: *I haven't worked here for long*. 2 a long sound, syllable, or signal: *Morse code consists of longs and shorts*. ⟨Old English *lang*⟩
a long face a sad expression. **as long as** or **so long as** provided that. **before long** soon. **in the long** (or **short**) **run** See RUN. **so long** *Informal* goodbye. **the long and the short of it** the upshot: *The long and the short of it is that she needs a job*.
long·bow ['lɒŋ,bou] *n* a bow drawn by hand and shooting a long feathered arrow. **long–dis·tance** *adj* 1 to do with telephone service to another town, city, etc. 2 for or over great distances: *a long-distance moving van*. **long–drawn** *adj* prolonged to great length: *the long-drawn howl of a coyote*. **long·hair** *adj Informal* a person who prefers classical music to popular music. **long·hair** or **long–haired** *adj*. **long·hand** *n* ordinary writing, not keyed. **long·horn** *n* a breed of cattle having very long horns. **long·house** *n* a large dwelling of certain First Nations or Native American peoples in which several families of a community lived together. **long·ish** *adj*. rather long. **long·johns** or **long–johns** ['lɒŋ,dʒɒnz] *n* *pl Informal* 1 underpants with long legs. 2 LONG UNDERWEAR. **long jump** 1 an athletic event in which contestants try to jump over as much ground as possible. **long·line** *n* a fishing line, sometimes several kilometres long, that has many baited hooks, used for deep-sea fishing. **long·lin·er** *n* a fishing vessel that uses longlines. **long–lived** ['lɒŋ 'lɪvd] *adj* lasting a long time. **long–range** *adj* 1 future: *long-range plans*. 2 capable of covering a great distance: *long-range missiles*. **long shot** 1 *Informal* a bet against great odds. 2 *Informal* any venture involving great risk, but offering great rewards. 3 a movie or television scene photographed from a distance. **by a long shot** by any means; to any degree: *The campaign isn't over by a long shot*. **long slide** *Curling* a style of play in which the curler takes a long slide along the ice when delivering his or her stone from the hack. **long–stand·ing** *adj* having lasted for a long time: *a long-standing feud*. **long–suf·fer·ing** *adj* enduring trouble or pain long and patiently. **long–suf·fer·ing·ly** *adv*. **long suit** 1 *Card games* the suit in which one has most cards. 2 something in which a person excels: *Patience is not her long suit*. **long–term** *adj* lasting or intended to last for a long time: *a long-term lease*. **long–term memory** memory of far distant events, such as over a lifetime. Compare SHORT-TERM MEMORY. **long underwear** ankle-length underpants and a top with sleeves, often made in one piece. **long wave** a radio wave of frequency less than 300 kilohertz. **long–wave** *adj*. **long·ways** *adv* lengthwise. **long–wind·ed** *adj* 1 capable of long effort without getting out of breath:

A long-distance runner must be long-winded.
2 long and tiresome: *a long-winded speech.*
long–wind·ed·ness *n.*

long² [lɒŋ] *v* wish very much; have a strong desire: *to long for peace.* **long·ing** *n, adj.* **long·ing·ly** *adv.* ⟨Old English *lang* long¹⟩

lon·gev·i·ty [lɒn'dʒɛvəti] *n* long life. ⟨Latin *longaevus* long-lived; *longus* long + *aevum* age⟩

lon·gi·tude ['lɒŋgɪ,tjud] *or* ['lɒŋgɪ,tud], ['lɒndʒɪ-] *n Geography* a distance east or west on the earth's surface, measured in degrees from a certain meridian. On maps, lines through the Poles represent longitudes. Compare LATITUDE. ⟨Latin *longitudo* length⟩
lon·gi·tu·di·nal [-'tjudənəl] *or* [-'tudənəl] *adj* **1** to do with length: *longitudinal measurement.* **2** to do with changes over a period of time: *a longitudinal study.* **3** of longitude. **lon·gi·tu·di·nal·ly** *adv*

long·shore·man ['lɒŋ,ʃɔrmən] *n, pl* **-men** a man whose work is loading and unloading ships. ⟨for *alongshoreman*⟩

look [lʊk] *v* **1** try to see (often with *at*). **2** examine (with *at*): *Look at all the facts.* **3** search: *I looked everywhere for my socks.* **4** seem; appear: *She looks pale.*
n **1** a glance. **2** a search. **3** appearance. **4** looks *pl* personal appearance: *to have good looks.* ⟨Old English *lōcian*⟩
look after take care of. **look alive** *Informal* hurry. **look around** (or **round**) consider many possibilities. **look askance** at regard with disfavour. **look at** examine. **look back** think about the past. **look bad** seem improper. **look black** seem hopeless: *After he lost his job, his future looked black.* **look daggers** look angrily: *He looked daggers at me.* **look down on** despise. **look for a** search for. **b** expect: *We'll look for you tonight.* **c** act so as to cause: *looking for trouble.* **look forward to** expect, esp with pleasure: *We look forward to seeing you.* **look in** make a short visit: *She said she'd look in today.* **look into** investigate. **look on a** watch without taking part: *The teacher conducted the experiment while we looked on.* **b** consider: *I look on her as a very able person.* **look oneself** look well: *He has been quite ill and still doesn't look himself.* **look out** be careful; watch out: *Look out for cars as you cross the street.* **look out for** take care of: *He always looked out for his little sister.* **look over** inspect. **look sharp** *Informal* be quick. **look through** examine: *She looked through the merchandise carefully.* **look to a** do something about. **b** turn to for help. **look up a** find: *She looked up the word in the dictionary.* **b** *Informal* call on; visit: *Look me up when you come to town.* **c** *Informal* improve: *Hopefully, things will look up soon.* **look up to** respect.
look–a·like *n* a person who or thing that closely resembles one that is famous or popular. **look–a·like** *adj.* **look·er** *n Slang* a person who is good-looking. **looking glass** *Archaic* mirror. **look·out** *n* **1** a careful watch, or the person or group that keeps such a watch. **2** a place from which to watch. **3** *Informal* something to be cared for or

worried about: *That is his lookout.* **be on the lookout** (for), watch (for): *on the lookout for bargains.* **lookout tower** a high tower from which to watch for forest fires. **look–see** *n Informal* a quick look: *She went to the book sale to have a look-see.*

loom¹ [lum] *n* a machine for weaving cloth. ⟨Old English *(ge)lōma* implement⟩

loom² [lum] *v* appear dimly as a large, often threatening shape: *An iceberg loomed through the thick, grey fog.* ⟨origin uncertain⟩
loom large seem important.

loon¹ [lun] *n* any of a genus of diving birds of northern regions having legs set far back on its body. ⟨earlier *loom;* Old Norse *lómr*⟩.
⋆loon·ie *n Informal.* a Canadian one-dollar coin. A loon is pictured on it.

loon² [lun] *n Informal* a crazy person. ⟨Compare Middle Dutch *loen* stupid fellow⟩
loon·y ['luni] *Slang adj* crazy. **loon·y** *n.* **loon·i·ness** *n.* ⟨obsolete *luny; lunatic*⟩

loop [lup] *n* **1** the shape of a curve that crosses itself. **2** *Computers* a program, or instruction that repeats continuously.
v **1** make or form a loop or loops. **2** fasten with a loop: *She looped the sail to the mast with rope.* ⟨Middle English *loupe,* perhaps from Celtic; compare Gaelic *lub* loop, bend⟩
throw or **knock for a loop** *Informal* surprise very much: *Her proposal threw him for a loop.* **loop the loop** of an aircraft, roller coaster, etc., make a vertical circle in the air. **out of the loop** not one of the influential people, or not up-to-date, in business, politics, etc.

loop·hole ['lup,houl] *n* **1** a small opening in a wall to shoot through, look through, or let in light and air. **2** a means of escape or evasion. ⟨perhaps Middle Dutch *lupen* peer⟩

loose [lus] *adj* **1** not firmly fastened: *a loose tooth.* **2** not tight: *loose clothing.* **3** not shut in: *We leave the dog loose at night.* **4** not exact: *a loose translation.* **5** having too little restraint: *a loose tongue.* **6** lewd or unchaste. **7** *Informal* relaxed. **8** *Chemistry* of a chemical element, free; uncombined.
v **1** set free. **2** make loose; unfasten.
adv in a loose manner. **loose·ly** *adv.*
loose·ness *n.* ⟨Old Norse *lauss*⟩
break loose a break a connection. **b** free oneself. **c** *Slang.* go on a spree. **cast loose** unfasten. **cut loose a** break loose; **b** abandon restraint: *She cuts loose on weekends.* **let, set,** or **turn loose** set free. **on the loose** *Informal* **a** free. **b** on a spree.
loose end usually, **loose ends** *pl* unfinished detail: *We've finished the main job, but there are still a few loose ends to tie up.* **at loose ends** in an unsettled or disorganized condition: *She has finished university, but is still at loose ends about what she wants to do.* **loose·leaf** *adj* of a notebook, etc., having pages that can be taken out: *a looseleaf binder. n* sheets of lined paper with holes for use in a ring binder. **loos·en** *v* make or become loose or looser. **loosen up a** warm up one's muscles with exercise. **b** be or become more relaxed.

loose·strife ['lus,strəif] *n* any of a genus of herbs, esp a weed having spikes of purple flowers. ⟨literal translation of Greek *Lysimachos*, the supposed discoverer⟩

loot [lut] *n* **1** spoils; plunder: *loot taken by soldiers from a captured town.* **2** *Slang* **a** money or other capital: *That's a lot of loot to spend for a CD player!* **b** gifts received. *v* plunder; rob. **loot·er** *n.* ⟨Hindi *lūt*⟩

lop [lɒp] *v* **lopped, lop·ping. 1** cut (usually with *off*): *We lopped off a big chunk of cheese.* **2** trim by cutting off branches, twigs, etc.: *to lop a tree.* ⟨origin uncertain⟩

lope [loup] *v* run with a long, easy stride. **lope** *n.*⟨Old Norse *hlaupa* leap⟩

lop–eared ['lɒp ,ird] *adj* having ears that hang loosely or droop.

lop·sid·ed ['lɒp,saɪdɪd] *adj* larger or heavier on one side than the other; leaning to one side. **lop·sid·ed·ly** *adv.* **lop·sid·ed·ness** *n.*

lop·stick ['lɒp,stɪk] *n* ✹ See LOBSTICK.

lo·qua·cious [ləˈkweiʃəs] *adj* talking much. **lo·qua·cious·ly** *adv.* **lo·quac·i·ty** [ləˈkwæsəti] *n.* ⟨Latin *loquax* talkative; *loqui* talk⟩

lo·quat ['loukwɒt] *or* ['loukwæt] *n* an evergreen tree of the rose family, having edible fruit. ⟨Cantonese *lo kwat* rush orange⟩

lo·ran ['lɔræn] *n* a device by which a navigator can determine position from signals sent out by two or more radio stations. ⟨long range navigation⟩

lord [lɔrd] *n* **1** a ruler, master, or chief. **2** a feudal superior. **3 the Lord a** God. **b** Christ. **4 Lord a** in the UK, a titled nobleman. **b** a title given to men holding certain positions: *Lord Chief Justice.* **lord·like** *adj.* **lord·ship** *n.* ⟨Old English *hlāford*; *hlāf* loaf + *weard* keeper⟩ **lord it over** domineer over. **lord·ly** *adj* **1** like or suitable for a lord; grand. **2** haughty; insolent. **lord·ly** *adv.* **lord·li·ness** *n.* **Lord's Day** *Christianity* Sunday. **Lord's Prayer** in the Bible, a prayer given by Jesus to His disciples.

lore [lɔr] *n* **1** the facts and stories about a certain subject. **2** learning; knowledge. ⟨Old English *lār*⟩

lose [luz] *v* **lost, los·ing 1** not have any longer. **2** be unable to find: *to lose a book.* **3** fail to get, catch, see, hear, or understand: *to lose a train, to lose a sale.* **4** be defeated: *Our team lost.* **5** bring to destruction: *The ship and its crew were lost.* **6** of a clock or watch, run less than the exact time: *My watch is losing again.* **7** evade; shake off (a pursuer). ⟨Old English *losian* be lost; *los* destruction⟩ **lose oneself a** let oneself go astray. **b** become absorbed: *to lose oneself in a good book.* **lose out** fail; be unsuccessful. **los·er** ['luzər] *n* **1** one who loses. **2** a person who is habitually unsuccessful. **3** one who takes defeat in a particular way: *a poor loser.* **los·ing** *adj* **1** that cannot be won: *a losing game.* **2** who or that loses: *the losing team.* **loss** [lɒs] *n* **1** a losing or being lost. **2** a person or thing lost: *The house was a complete*

loss. **3** the harm caused by losing something. **4** a defeat. **at a loss a** in difficulty: *He was at a loss for words.* **b** unable: *She was at a loss to explain her anxiety.* **c** for less than its original cost: *They sold their house at a loss.* **loss leader** an article sold at a loss in order to attract customers. **lost** [lɒst] *adj* **1** no longer kept: *lost friends.* **2** missing: *lost articles.* **3** no longer visible, audible, or recognizable: *He was lost in the crowd.* **4** wasted: *lost time.* **5** having gone astray: *We were soon lost in the forest.* **6** bewildered: *She looked completely lost.* **7** absorbed (with *in*): *lost in thought.* **get lost** *Slang* go away. **lost on** wasted on: *Sarcasm is lost on her.* **lost to a** no longer possible for: *The chance of promotion was lost to him.* **b** no longer belonging to: *After that incident, her son was lost to her.* **c** insensible to: *lost to all sense of duty.* **lost cause** an undertaking certain to be defeated.

lot [lɒt] *n* **1** a large number or amount: *a lot of books. This one is a lot thicker.* **2** lots *Informal* a large number or amount: *lots of money.* **3** a number of persons or things considered as a group: *This lot of tickets still has to be sold.* **4** a plot of ground, esp one having fixed boundaries: *a corner lot.* **5** a film studio together with the surrounding property. **6** an object used to decide something by chance: *We drew lots to decide who should be captain.* **7** one's fate; fortune: *a happy lot.* **8** an item for sale at an auction: *When are these lots being sold?* *adv* **lots** *Informal* much: *This table is lots nicer than that one.* ⟨Old English *hlot*⟩ **cast** (or **draw**) **lots** use objects to decide something by chance. **cast** or **throw in one's lot with** share the fate of. **lot·ter·y** ['lɒtəri] *n* a method of raising money by selling numbered lots (tickets) and picking at random the winning one.

loth See LOATH.

lo·tion ['louʃən] *n* a liquid medicine or cosmetic applied to the skin. ⟨Latin *lotio* a washing; *lavere* wash⟩

lot·us ['loutəs] *n* **1** any of various tropical water lilies. **2** the fruit eaten by the ancient Greek lotus-eaters that was supposed to cause a dreamy and contented forgetfulness. Also, **lot·os.** ⟨Greek *lōtos* the lotus plant⟩ **lo·tus–eat·er** *n* a person who leads a life of indolent ease. **lotus land** ✹ *Informal* British Columbia, esp Vancouver, so called because of its laid-back way of life.

loud [laʊd] *adj* **1** noisy. **2** clamorous; insistent: *loud demands for higher pay.* **3** *Informal* flashy or vulgar: *loud clothes.* *adv* in a loud manner. **loud·ly** *adv.* **loud·ness** *n.* ⟨Old English *hlūd*⟩ **out loud** loud enough to be heard. **loud·ish** *adj* rather loud. **loud-mouthed** ['laʊd,mʌʊθt] *or* [-,maʊðd] *adj* offensively noisy. **loud·mouth** *n.* **loud·speak·er** *n* a device for amplifying the sound of a speaker's voice, music, etc.

lounge [laʊndʒ] *v* **1** stand, stroll, sit, or lie at ease. **2** idle at one's ease.

n **1** a comfortable and informal room, in which one can lounge and be at ease. **2** a sofa having a headrest at one end but no back. **3** a bar featuring comfortable chairs, etc. and, often, live music. **loung·er** *n.* ⟨Scottish dialect; perhaps from *lungis* laggard⟩

louse [laʊs] *n* **1** *pl* **lice** any of a group of insects that are parasites of mammals and birds. **2** *pl* **lous·es** *Slang* a mean, contemptible person. ⟨Old English *lūs*⟩
louse up *Slang* make a mess; botch: *We loused up the job so badly, we had to do it over again.*
lous·y ['laʊzi] *adj* **1** *Slang* inferior; bad: *The pay is lousy.* **2** *Slang* nasty; mean: *a lousy swindler.* **3** *Slang* well-supplied (with): *lousy with money.* **4** infested with lice. **lous·i·ly** *adv.* **lous·i·ness** *n.*

lout [laʊt] *n* an awkward, stupid person. **lout·ish** *adj.* **lout·ish·ly** *adv.* **lout·ish·ness** *n.* ⟨perhaps Old Norse *lútr* bent down, stooped⟩

lou·vre or **lou·ver** ['luvər] *n* **1** an opening covered with horizontal strips of wood, glass, etc., set slanting to keep out rain or light but provide ventilation. **2** a ventilating slit. **lou·vred** *adj.* ⟨Middle French *lover* skylight⟩

love [lʌv] *n* **1** a deep feeling of fondness: *love of one's family.* **2** a loved one. **3** selfless kindness. **4** a strong liking: *a love of books.* **5** sexual passion. **6** *Tennis, etc.* no score. **love** *v.* **lov·a·ble** or **love·a·ble** *adj.* **lov·a·ble·ness** *n.* **lov·a·bly** *adv.* **love·less** *adj.* **love·less·ness** *adj.* ⟨Old English *lufu*, n, *lufian*, v⟩
fall in love (with) begin to love. **for love** for pleasure; not for money. **for the love of** for the sake of. **in love** feeling love, usually romantic. **make love** engage in sexual play or intercourse. **no love lost** dislike: *There is no love lost between the two brothers.* **not for love or money** not on any terms.
love affair 1 a romantic relationship between two people who are not married to each other. **2** an intense enthusiasm about something: *a love affair with the opera.*
love·bird *n* **1** any of various small parrots, that appear to show great affection for their mates. **2 lovebirds** *pl* two people very obviously in love with each other. **love child** a child born out of wedlock. **love game** *Tennis* a game in which one's opponent does not win a point. **love handles** *Informal* a roll of flesh around a person's middle, just below the waist. **love·lorn** ['lʌv,lɔrn] *adj* forsaken by the person whom one loves. **love·ly** ['lʌvli] *adj* **1** having beauty, harmony, or grace: *a lovely person.* **2** *Informal* very pleasing: *a lovely holiday.* **love·li·ness** *n.* **love·making** *n* sexual intimacy. **love match** a marriage for love, not for money or social position. **lov·er** *n* **1** a person who is in love with another. **2 lovers** *pl* two people who are in love with each other. **3** a person who has a sexual relationship with another, esp outside marriage. **4** a person in terms of his or her physical skill at lovemaking: *a good lover.* **5** a person having a strong liking for something: *a lover of books.* **lov·er·like** *adj.* **love seat** a small couch seating two persons. **love·sick**

adj languishing because of love. **love triangle** the relationships involving a person and his or her two rival lovers. **lov·ing** *adj* affectionate. **lov·ing·ly** *adv.* **lov·ing–kind·ness** *n* **1** deep affection. **2** kind behaviour arising from love.

low¹ [loʊ] *adj* **1** not high or tall. **2** of less than ordinary height, amount, or degree: *The river is low this year.* **3** near the ground: *a low shelf.* **4** almost used up: *Supplies were low.* **5** not loud: *a low sound.* **6** small in amount, value, etc.: *a low price.* **7** not advanced in development, organization, etc.: *Bacteria are low organisms.* **8** humble: *She rose from a low position to president of the company.* **9** lacking health or vitality: *Her mother is very low.* **10** unfavourable: *a low opinion.* **11** mean: *a low trick.* **12** of a neckline, cut so as to leave part of the breast exposed. **low–cut** *adj.* **13** *Music* deep in pitch: *a low note.*
adv **1** at or to a low position, amount, rank, degree, pitch, etc.: *The lamp hangs too low.* **2** in a low manner.
n **1** a low position or state. **2** *Meteorology* an area of low barometric pressure. **low·ness** *n.* ⟨Old Norse *lágr*⟩
lay low bring down: *The first blow laid him low.* **lie low** *Informal* stay hidden; keep still: *The robbers will lie low for a time.*
low blow 1 *Boxing* an illegal hit below the belt. **2** any unfair action. **low·born** *adj* of humble birth. **low·brow** *Informal n* a person lacking in appreciation of intellectual things. **low·brow** *adj.* **low–cal·o·rie** ['loʊ 'kæləri] *adj* containing few calories. **Low Church** a tradition in the Anglican Church, laying little stress on church authority and ceremonies. Compare HIGH CHURCH. **low comedy** broadly humorous comedy. **low·down** *n Slang* the actual facts or truth: *Give me the lowdown on what happened.* **low–down** *adj Informal* mean: *a low-down trick.* **low·er** *v* See LOWER¹. **lower oneself a** behave improperly. **b** condescend: *She could hardly lower herself to speak to us.* **Lower Canada** ['loʊər] **1** a traditional name for the province of Québec. **2** until 1841, the official name of the region between the Ottawa River and New Brunswick. Lower Canada was lower down the St. Lawrence River than Upper Canada. **lower case** *Printing* small letters, not capital. **low·er–case** *adj Abbrev* **l.c. Lower Chamber** or **lower chamber** LOWER HOUSE. **lower class** Often, **lower classes** *pl* the people having the lowest social status. **low·er–class** *adj.* **Lower House** or **lower house** the more representative branch of a bicameral legislature. The members of the Lower House of a legislature are usually elected. **Lower Lakes** the most southerly of the Great Lakes, Lakes Erie and Ontario. **Lower Mainland** the lowland area around Vancouver. **low·er·most** *adj* lowest. **Lower Town** the part of a town lying closest to the waterfront. **lowest common denominator 1** *Mathematics* LEAST COMMON DENOMINATOR. **2** the level of the feelings, opinions, etc. supposedly common to the majority of

people. **low frequency** the range of radio frequencies between 30 kHz and 300 kHz. **low–fre·quen·cy** *adj.* **low–grade** *adj* of poor quality; inferior. **low–key** *adj* subdued or restrained: *a low-key attack on government policy.* **low·land** ['loulənd] *or* ['lou,lænd] *n* land that is lower and flatter than the neighbouring country. **low·land** *adj.* **low·life** *n, pl* **-lifes** *Slang* **1** a debased or vile person; a criminal. **2** immoral people or surroundings. **low·life** *adj.* **low·ly** *adj* low in rank: *a lowly servant.* **low·li·ness** *n.* **Low Mass** a Mass that is simpler in form than a High Mass. **low–mind·ed** *adj* having a vulgar mind. **low–mind·ed·ness** *n.* **low–necked** *adj* of a dress, etc., cut low so as to show part of the bosom. **low profile** an attitude concerned with keeping quiet about one's activities: *to keep a low profile.* **low–rise** *adj* having only a few storeys: *low-rise apartments.* **low–rise** *n.* **low spirits** depression. **low–spir·it·ed** *adj.* **low tide** the lowest level of the tide, or the time when the tide is lowest. **low water 1** the lowest level of water in a lake or river. **2** LOW TIDE. **low–water mark 1** a mark showing low water. **2** the lowest point of anything.

low² [lou] *v* make the sound of a cow mooing; moo. **low** *n.* ⟨Old English *hlōwan*⟩

low·er¹ ['louər] *v* **1** let down or haul down. **2** reduce in amount, force, etc.: *to lower the volume of the music.* **3** become lower: *The sun lowered slowly.* **4** *Music* depress in pitch. ⟨*low¹*⟩

low·er² ['lauər] *v* **1** become or appear dark and threatening. **2** frown or scowl.
n a frowning or threatening appearance. **low·er·ing** *adj.* ⟨Middle English *loure(n)* frown⟩

lox [lɒks] *n* thinly sliced smoked salmon. ⟨Yiddish *laks,* Middle High German *lacs*⟩

loy·al ['lɔɪəl] *adj* **1** faithful to love or duty. **2** faithful to one's government, or country: *a loyal citizen.* **loy·al·ly** *adv.* **loy·al·ty** *n.* ⟨French; Latin *legalis* legal, *lex, legis* law⟩ **loy·al·ist** *n* **1** a person who supports the existing government, esp in time of revolt. **2 Loyalist a** UNITED EMPIRE LOYALIST. **b** any of the colonists who remained loyal to Britain during the American Revolution. **3 Loyalist** in Spain, a person loyal to the Republic during the Civil War (1936-1939). **loy·al·ist** *adj.* **Loyalist Province** ✹ New Brunswick, because it was originally settled by United Empire Loyalists.

loz·enge ['lɒzɪndʒ] *n* **1** a small tablet of medicine or a piece of candy: *Cough drops are sometimes called lozenges.* **2** a design or figure shaped like a diamond. ⟨Old French *losenge;* Latin *lausa* slab; Celtic⟩

LRT light rapid transit.

LSD lysergic acid diethylamide.

Ltd. limited.

Lt.Gov. LIEUTENANT-GOVERNOR.

lu·au ['luaʊ] *n* a Hawaiian feast, usually including entertainment. ⟨Hawaiian *lu'au*⟩

lub·ber ['lʌbər] *n* **1** a clumsy, stupid fellow.

2 *Nautical* a clumsy sailor. **lub·ber·ly** *adj.* **lub·ber·li·ness** *n.* ⟨Middle English *lober*⟩

lube [lub] *n Informal* a lubricant. ⟨short form⟩

lu·bri·cant ['lubrəkənt] *n* a substance such as oil for putting on surfaces to reduce friction. **lu·bri·cant** *adj.* ⟨Latin *lubricus* slippery⟩ **lu·bri·cate** *v* **1** put a lubricant on. **2** make slippery or smooth. **3** make easy: *to lubricate the peace talks.* **lu·bri·ca·tion** *n* **1** a lubricating or being lubricated. **2** oil, grease, etc. used for lubricating. **lu·bri·cious** ['lubrɪʃəs] *adj* **1** lewd. **2** oily. **lu·bri·ci·ty** *n.* ⟨Latin *lubricare; lubricus* slippery⟩

lu·ces ['lusiz] *n* a pl of LUX.

lu·cid ['lusɪd] *adj* **1** easy to understand: *a lucid explanation.* **2** shining; bright. **3** having a clear mind: *Insane people sometimes have lucid intervals.* **4** clear: *a lucid stream.* **lu·cid·ly** *adv.* **lu·cid·i·ty** *n.* ⟨Latin *lucidus; lux, lucis* light⟩

Lu·ci·fer ['lusəfər] *n* in the Bible, the chief rebel angel who was cast out of heaven; Satan, esp before his fall. ⟨Latin = lightbearer; *lux, lucis* light + *ferre* bear⟩

luck [lʌk] *n* **1** chance. **2** good fortune: *Lots of luck and joy to you.* **luck·less** *adj.* **luck·y** *adj.* **luck·i·ly** *adv.* ⟨Middle Low German *(ge)lucke*⟩ **down on one's luck** *Informal* having bad luck. **in luck** having good luck: *I'm in luck today; I found a five-dollar bill.* **luck in** *Informal* have the good luck to be included. **luck out** *Informal* be very lucky. **out of luck** having bad luck. **push** (or **crowd**) **one's luck** take unnecessary chances when things are going favourably: *You've won every game so far, but don't push your luck.* **try one's luck** see what one can do: *Try your luck with this puzzle.* **worse luck** unfortunately.

lu·cra·tive ['lukrətɪv] *adj* bringing in money; profitable. **lu·cra·tive·ly** *adv.* **lu·cra·tive·ness** *n.* ⟨Latin *lucrari* to gain; *lucrum* gain⟩

lu·cre ['lukər] *n Archaic, facetious* money.

lu·di·crous ['ludəkrəs] *adj* amusingly absurd; ridiculous. **lu·di·crous·ly** *adv.* **lu·di·crous·ness** *n.* ⟨Latin *ludicrus; ludus* sport⟩

lug¹ [lʌg] *v* **lugged, lug·ging** pull along or carry with effort. ⟨Middle English *luggen*⟩ **lug·gage** ['lʌgɪdʒ] *n* suitcases, bags, etc. for carrying belongings on a trip.

lug² [lʌg] *n* **1** a projecting part used to hold something. **2** a stud projecting from a wheel to increase traction. **3** *Slang* a clumsy or stupid person. ⟨Scandinavian; compare Swedish *lugg* forelock⟩

luge [luʒ] *n* a small sled that a person rides lying on his or her back. ⟨French⟩

lu·gu·bri·ous [lə'gubriəs] *adj* sad; mournful, esp in an exaggerated or affected way. **lu·gu·bri·ous·ly** *adv.* **lu·gu·bri·ous·ness** *n.* ⟨Latin *lugubris; lugere* mourn⟩

luke·warm ['luk'wɔrm] *adj* **1** of a liquid, fairly warm. **2** showing little enthusiasm: *a lukewarm greeting.* **luke·warm·ly** *adv.* **luke·warm·ness** *n.* ⟨dialect *luke* lukewarm⟩

lull [lʌl] *v* **1** hush to sleep: *The mother lulled the crying baby.* **2** make or become more

nearly calm: *The wind lulled.* **3** set at rest: *to lull people into a false sense of security.*
n a temporary period of less noise or activity: *a lull in a storm.* **lull·ing** *adj.* ⟨Middle English *lulle(n)*, sing a lullaby; probably imitative⟩
lul·la·by ['lʌlə,baɪ] *n* **1** a song to lull a baby to sleep. **2** any soothing piece of music.

lum·bar ['lʌmbər] *or* ['lʌmbɑr] *adj* to do with the loins. ⟨Latin *lumbaris;* Latin *lumbus* loin⟩
lum·ba·go [lʌm'beigou] *n* an injury of the muscles in the lower back producing pain.

lum·ber[1] ['lʌmbər] *n* timber, logs, beams, boards, etc. roughly cut and prepared for use. ⟨*lombard* pawnshop⟩
lum·ber·jack *n* **1** logger. **2** CANADA JAY.
lum·ber·man *n, pl* **-men** a man dealing in timber or lumber. **lum·ber·yard** *n* a place where lumber is sold.

lum·ber[2] ['lʌmbər] *v* move along heavily and noisily. **lum·ber·ing** *adj.* ⟨Middle English *lomeren;* Scandinavian⟩

lu·men ['lumən] *n, pl* **-mi·na** [-mənə] *Optics* an SI unit for measuring the rate of emission of light rays from a given light source. *Symbol* **lm** ⟨Latin *lūmen* light, window⟩
lu·mi·nar·y ['lumə,nɛri] *n* **1** the sun, moon, or other light-giving body. **2** a distinguished person, esp one who enlightens. **lu·mi·nesce** [,lumə'nɛs] *v* exhibit luminescence. **lu·mi·nes·cence** *n* an emission of light by a process other than incandescence, including phosphorescence, fluorescence, and the light produced by fireflies. **lu·mi·nes·cent** *adj.* **lu·mi·nous** ['lumənəs] *adj* **1** shining by its own light: *The sun is luminous.* **2** full of light. **3** treated with some substance that glows in the dark. **lu·mi·nos·i·ty** [,lumə'nɒsəti] *n.* **lu·mi·nous·ly** *adv.*

lum·mox ['lʌməks] *n Informal* an awkward, stupid person. ⟨origin uncertain⟩

lump[1] [lʌmp] *n* **1** a solid mass of no particular shape. **2** a swelling: *a lump on the head.* **3** a lot; mass. **4** *Informal* an awkward, dull, or stupid person. **5 lumps** *pl Informal* a beating or defeat: *to take your lumps.*
v **1** become lumpy. **2** put together: *We will lump all our expenses.* ⟨Middle English; Scandinavian⟩
lump·ec·to·my [lʌm'pɛktəmi] *n* the surgical removal of a tumour in an organ, without removing the whole organ. **lump·ish** *adj* **1** like a lump; heavy and clumsy. **2** stolid; stupid. **lump·ish·ly** *adv.* **lump·ish·ness** *n.* **lump sugar** small blocks of sugar. **lump sum** a sum of money given in payment at one time: *He paid off the last $500 of his loan in a lump sum.* **lump–sum** *adj.* **lump·y** *adj* **1** full of lumps: *lumpy gravy.* **2** covered with lumps: *lumpy ground.* **3** of water in a lake, etc., rough. **lump·i·ly** *adv.* **lump·i·ness** *n.*

lump[2] [lʌmp] *v Informal* put up with; endure: *If you don't like it, you can lump it.* ⟨origin uncertain⟩

lu·na·cy See LUNATIC.

lu·nar ['lunər] *adj* to do with the moon. ⟨Latin *luna* moon⟩

lunar eclipse an eclipse of the moon when it lies within the earth's shadow. **lunar module** an independent unit designed for use on the moon. **lunar month** the period of one complete revolution of the moon around the earth; the interval between one new moon and the next, about 29 days. **lunar year** a period of twelve lunar months.

lu·na·tic ['lunə,tɪk] *n* **1** an insane person. **2** an extremely foolish person. **lu·na·tic** *adj.* **lu·na·cy** ['lunəsi] *n.* ⟨Latin *lunaticus; luna* moon; for its alleged crazy-making influence⟩
lunatic fringe *Informal* members of the periphery of any group, whose zeal goes beyond the views held by most members.

lunch [lʌntʃ] *n* a light meal between breakfast and dinner. Also, **lunch·eon** ['lʌntʃən] *n.* **lunch** *v.* **lunch·er** *n.* ⟨dialect *luncheon* hunk of food⟩
no free lunch you never get something for nothing. **out to lunch** *Slang* crazy.
lunch·room or **lunch–room** *n* a room in a plant, school, etc. where workers, teachers, or students may eat the lunches they have brought. **lunch·time** *n* the time when lunch is served and eaten, usually around midday.

lung [lʌŋ] *n* in vertebrates, one of the pair of breathing organs by means of which the blood receives oxygen and is relieved of carbon dioxide. ⟨Old English *lungen*⟩
at the top of one's lungs as loudly as possible.
lung·fish *n, pl* **-fish** or **-fish·es** any of several species of freshwater fishes having an air-breathing lung as well as gills.

lunge [lʌndʒ] *n* any sudden forward movement: *The catcher made a lunge toward the bull.* **lunge** *v.* ⟨French *allonger,* Latin *ad-* toward + *longus* long⟩

lu·pine ['lupaɪn] *adj* of or like a wolf. ⟨Middle English; Latin *lupinus; lupus* wolf⟩

lu·pus ['lupəs] *n* **1** a skin disease, also called **lupus vulgaris**, caused by the tubercle bacillus. **2** a chronic immunological disorder, also called **lupus erythematosus** affecting the skin and sometimes also the nervous system, joints, kidneys, and lungs. ⟨Latin = wolf⟩

lurch[1] [lɜrtʃ] *v* **1** lean suddenly to one side. **2** stagger. **lurch** *n.* ⟨origin uncertain⟩

lurch[2] [lɜrtʃ] *n*
leave in the lurch leave in a helpless condition or a difficult situation. ⟨French *lourche*, name of a game⟩

lure [lur] *n* **1** attraction: *the lure of the sea.* **2** a decoy; bait. **lure** *v.* **lur·ing** *adj.* ⟨Old French *loire;* Germanic⟩

lu·rid ['lurɪd] *adj* **1** lighted up with a fiery glare: *The sky was lurid with the flames of the burning city.* **2** causing horror; gruesome: *a lurid crime.* **3** sensational: *a lurid account of the kidnapping.* **4** glaring in brightness or colour: *a lurid yellow.* ⟨Latin *luridus*⟩

lurk [lɜrk] *v* **1** stay around without arousing attention; wait out of sight. **2** be hidden. **lurk·er** *n.* **lurk·ing·ly** *adv.* ⟨apparently from *lour* variant of *lower*[2]⟩

lus·cious ['lʌʃəs] *adj* **1** delicious; richly sweet: *a luscious peach*. **2** very pleasing to the senses. **lus·cious·ly** *adv*. **lus·cious·ness** *n*. ⟨Middle English; perhaps variant of *delicious*⟩

lush¹ [lʌʃ] *adj* **1** growing thick and green: *lush grass*. **2** characterized by abundant growth: *lush fields*. **3** rich in ornament: *lush description*. **lush·ly** *adv*. **lush·ness** *n*. ⟨Middle English *lusch* slack⟩

lush² [lʌʃ] *Slang n* a person who habitually drinks excessive amounts of alcoholic liquor. ⟨perhaps from *lush¹*⟩

lust [lʌst] *n* **1** sexual desire, esp when intense. **2** any strong desire: *a lust for power*. *v* feel a strong desire (with *after* or *for*): *A miser lusts after gold*. **lust·ful** *adj*. **lust·ful·ly** *adv*. **lust·ful·ness** *n*. ⟨Old English *lust* pleasure⟩ **lust·y** *adj* strong and healthy; full of vigour and enthusiasm. **lust·i·ly** *adv*. **lust·i·ness** *n*.

lus·tre ['lʌstər] *n* **1** a bright shine on the surface: *the lustre of pearls*. **2** brightness: *Her eyes had no lustre*. Also, **lus·ter**. **lus·tre·less** *adj*. **lus·trous** *adj*. **lus·trous·ly** *adv*. **lus·trous·ness** *n*. ⟨French; Italian *lustro*; *lustrare* light up; Latin⟩

lute [lut] *n* a stringed musical instrument like a large mandolin. **lu·ten·ist** ['lutənɪst] *n*. ⟨Old French; Provençal *laut*, Arabic *al'ud*⟩

lu·te·ti·um [lu'tiʃəm] *n* a rare, metallic element. *Symbol* **Lu** ⟨Latin *Lutetia* Paris⟩

Lu·ther·an ['luθrən] *n* a member of any of the churches together constituting a large Protestant denomination, originating in the 1520s as a result of the teachings of Martin Luther (1483-1546). **Lu·ther·an** *adj*.

lux [lʌks] *n*, *pl* **lux·es** or **lu·ces** ['lusiz] *Optics* an SI unit for measuring illumination by a source of light per unit area on a surface. *Symbol* **lx** ⟨Latin *lūx* light¹⟩

lux·u·ry ['lʌkʃəri] or ['lʌgʒəri] *n* **1** an abundance of the comforts of life. **2** anything that one particularly enjoys, usually something costly. **3** something pleasant but not necessary. **lux·u·ri·ous** [lʌg'ʒʊriəs] or [lʌk'ʃʊriəs] *adj*. **lux·u·ri·ous·ly** *adv*. **lux·u·ri·ous·ness** *n*. ⟨Latin *luxus* excess⟩ **in the lap of luxury** See LAP. **lux·u·ri·ant** [lʌg'ʒʊriənt] or [lʌk'ʃʊriənt] *adj* **1** thick and lush: *a luxuriant head of hair*. **2** producing abundantly. **3** rich in ornament. **lux·u·ri·ance** *n*. **lux·u·ri·ant·ly** *adv*. **lux·u·ri·ate** *v* **1** indulge oneself: *luxuriating in a hot bath*. **2** grow very abundantly.

–ly¹ *adverb-forming suffix* indicating: **1** manner: *cheerfully*. **2** aspect: *financially*. **3** degree or extent: *greatly*. **4** direction: *northwardly*. **5** place in a series: *thirdly*. **6** time: *recently*. **7** frequency: *yearly*. ⟨Old English *-līce; -līc* -ly²⟩

–ly² *adjective-forming suffix* **1** like: *ghostly*. **2** suited to or typical of: *brotherly*. **3** occurring once per given interval: *daily*. **4** located in, made of, etc.: *heavenly*. ⟨Old English *-līc*, suffixal use of LIKE¹⟩

ly·cée [li'sei] *n*, *pl* in France, a public secondary school. ⟨French, from Latin. See LYCEUM.⟩

ly·ce·um [ləi'siəm] or ['ləisiəm] *n* **1** a lecture hall. **2** **Lyceum** an outdoor gymnasium near Athens, where Aristotle taught. ⟨Greek *Lykeion*; for nearby temple of Apollo, *Lykeios*⟩

ly·chee ['litʃi] *n* See LITCHI.

lye [lai] *n* *Chemistry* any strong, alkaline substance obtained by leaching wood ashes, esp sodium hydroxide or potassium hydroxide. ⟨Old English *lēag*⟩

ly·ing¹ See LIE¹.

ly·ing² ['laiɪŋ] *v* ppr of LIE².

lymph [lɪmf] *n* *Anatomy, physiology* a nearly colourless liquid in the tissues of the body, containing white blood cells but no red blood cells. **lym·phat·ic** [lɪm'fætɪk] *adj*. ⟨Latin *lympha* clear water⟩ **lymph node** or **gland** one of the masses of tissue lying along the course of the lymphatic vessels. **lym·pho·cyte** ['lɪmfə,sait] *n* *Physiology* one of the colourless cells of lymph produced in the lymph nodes. **lym·pho·cyt·ic** [,lɪmfə'sɪtɪk] *adj*.

lynch [lɪntʃ] *v* kill, usually by hanging, through mob action and without a trial. **lynch·er** *n*. **lynch·ing** *n*. ⟨W. *Lynch*, an 18c US magistrate⟩

lynx [lɪŋks] *n*, *pl* **lynx·es** or (esp collectively) **lynx** a medium-sized wildcat having long legs with large paws, tufted ears, and a short tail. **lynx·like** *adj*. ⟨Greek⟩

lyre [lair] *n* an ancient, stringed musical instrument like a small harp. **lyr·ist** ['lairɪst] *n*. ⟨Greek *lyra*⟩

lyr·ic ['lirɪk] *n* **1** a short poem expressing emotion. **2** **lyrics** *pl* the words for a song. *adj* **1** to do with a lyric or lyrics (def. 1): *a lyric poet*. **2** having a melodic singing voice: *a lyric soprano*. ⟨Greek *lyrikos* of or for a lyre⟩ **lyr·i·cal** ['lirɪkəl] *adj* **1** expressing great enthusiasm and emotion: *She was lyrical in her praise of the new auditorium*. **2** lyric. **lyr·i·cal·ly** *adv*. **lyr·i·cism** ['liri,sizəm] *n* **1** a lyric style, quality, or form of expression: *Keats's lyricism*. **2** high-flown sentiments; exuberance. **lyr·i·cist** ['lirisist] *n* **1** a writer of song lyrics. **2** a lyric poet.

Mm

m or **M** [ɛm] *n, pl* **m's** or **M's 1** the thirteenth letter of the English alphabet, or any speech sound represented by it. **2** the thirteenth person or thing in a series. **3 M**, the Roman numeral for 1000.

m 1 metre(s). **2** milli- (an SI prefix).

M mega- (an SI prefix).

ma [mɑ] *or* [mɒ] *n Informal* mother.

ma'am [mæm] *or* [mɑm] *n* madam.

ma·ca·bre [mə'kɑbər],   [mə'kɑb],   *or* [mə'kɑbrə] *adj* gruesome; horrible. ⟨French⟩

mac·ad·am [mə'kædəm] *n* material for making roads, consisting of stones mixed with tar or asphalt ⟨John L. McAdam (1756-1836), Scottish engineer⟩ **mac·ad·am·ize** *v* construct or surface (a road) with macadam. **mac·ad·am·i·za·tion** *n*.

ma·ca·da·mia [,mækə'deimiə] *n* Usually, **macadamia nut**, the edible seed of an Australian tree. ⟨J. *Macadam*, 19c Australian chemist⟩

ma·caque [mə'kɑk] *or* [mə'kæk] *n* any of a genus of short-tailed or tailless Old World monkeys. ⟨French; Portuguese *macaco* monkey⟩

mac·a·ro·ni [,mækə'rouni] *n, pl* **-nis** or **-nies** flour paste that has been dried, to be cooked for food. ⟨earlier Italian *maccaroni*, pl; Greek *makaria* barley broth⟩ **mac·a·ron·ic** [,mækə'rɒnɪk] *adj* **1** composed of a mixture of languages, esp of Latin and English. **2** jumbled. **mac·a·ron·i·cal·ly** *adv*.

mac·a·roon [,mækə'run] *n* a very sweet, chewy cookie. ⟨French *macaron*; Italian *maccarone*, sg. See MACARONI.⟩

ma·caw [mə'kɒ] *n* any parrot belonging to either of two genera of brilliantly coloured, tropical parrots. ⟨Portuguese *macao* parrot; origin uncertain⟩

mace[1] [meis] *n* **1** a staff used as a symbol of authority. **2** in the Middle Ages, a war club having a heavy metal head. ⟨Old French; Latin *mattea*, earlier *matteola* hammer⟩

mace[2] [meis] *n* a spice made from the dried outer covering of nutmegs. ⟨Old French *macis*; Latin *macir*, Greek *makir* rind of Indian root⟩

Mace [meis] *n Trademark* a liquid chemical similar in effect to tear gas, producing tears and temporary blindness.

mac·er·ate ['mæsə,reit] *v* **1** soften by soaking for some time. **2** soften (food) by the digestive process. **mac·er·a·tion** *n*. **mac·er·a·tor** *n*. **mac·er·a·tive** *adj*. ⟨Latin *macerare* soften⟩

ma·chet·e [mə'ʃɛti] *or* [mə'tʃɛti] *n* a large, heavy knife used as a tool and weapon. ⟨Spanish; Latin *mactare* kill⟩

Mach·i·a·vel·li·an or **Mach·i·a·vel·i·an** [,mækiə'vɛliən] *adj* **1** to do with Niccolo Machiavelli (1469-1527), Italian statesman who wrote *The Prince*, a detailed study of unscrupulous methods used to gain power. **2** characterized by subtle or unscrupulous cunning. **Mach·i·a·vel·li·an·ism** *n*.

ma·chic·o·la·tion [mə,tʃɪkə'leiʃən] *n Architecture* **1** in medieval fortresses, an opening in the floor through which missiles might be cast on attackers. **2** a projecting gallery or parapet with such openings. **ma·chic·o·lat·ed** *adj*. ⟨Provençal *machacol* projection, balcony; *macar* crush + *col* neck, Latin *collum*⟩

mach·i·nate ['mækə,neit] *or* ['mæʃə,neit] *v* plot. **mach·i·na·tor** *n*. ⟨Latin *machinari*; *machina*. See MACHINE.⟩ **mach·i·na·tion** *n* Usually, **machinations**, *pl* a scheme with an evil purpose.

ma·chine [mə'ʃin] *n* **1** a device with interrelated parts, designed for a particular kind of work: *a calculating machine*. **2** *Mechanics* a device for transmitting power, energy, or motion. **3** a motor vehicle, aircraft, bicycle, etc. **4** a highly organized group of people: *the party machine*. *v* make or finish by machine. **ma·chine·like** *adj*. ⟨French; Latin *machina*, Greek *machana*, *mēchanē* device, means⟩ **machine gun** a gun that uses ammunition automatically. **ma·chine–gun**, **-gunned**, **-gun·ning** *v*. **machine language** *Computers* a language for instructions that can be used directly by the central processing unit of a computer. **ma·chin·er·y** *n* **1** machines: *There is a lot of machinery in a shoe factory.* **2** the works of a machine: *the machinery of a watch*. **3** any combination of persons or things by which something is kept going: *Police officers are part of the machinery of the law*. **machine shed ✱** a farm building in which implements are kept. **machine shop** a workshop where machines are made or repaired. **machine tool** a tool, such as a lathe, used in manufacturing machinery. **ma·chin·ist** *n*.

Mach number [mɑk] *or* [mæk] a number representing the ratio of the speed of an object to the speed of sound. Mach 1 equals the speed of sound, and Mach 2 is twice the speed of sound. ⟨Ernst *Mach*, 19c Austrian physicist⟩

ma·cho ['mɑtʃou] *adj* robust and virile in an exaggerated way: *a macho swagger*. ⟨Spanish *macho* male⟩ **ma·chis·mo** [mə'tʃɪzmou] *n* exaggerated or aggressive masculinity.

mack·er·el ['mækərəl] *n, pl* **-el** or **-els** an important marine food fish. ⟨Anglo-French *makerel*⟩

mack·i·naw ['mækə,nɒ] *n* **1** MACKINAW COAT. **2** MACKINAW BLANKET. **3** MACKINAW BOAT. ⟨Cdn. French *Mackinac*; *Michilimackinac* Mackinac Island, Algonquian (Ojibwa) *mitchimakinak* large turtle⟩ **mackinaw blanket** a blanket that often has bars of colour, used in the North and West by First Nations people, trappers, etc. **mackinaw boat** a flat-bottomed boat, formerly used in the Upper Great Lakes region. **mackinaw coat** or **jacket** a short coat made of heavy cloth, often plaid.

mac·ro ['mækrou] *n Computers* a set of detailed computer instructions generated by a single command.

macro– *combining form* large; long: *macrocosm.* Compare MICRO-. ⟨Greek *makrós*⟩

mac·ro·bi·ot·ics [ˌmækroubaɪ'ɒtɪks] *n* (with a sg verb) a diet consisting mainly of whole grains and vegetables. **mac·ro·cosm** ['mækrəˌkɒzəm] *n* **1** universe. **2** any system composed of smaller units. **mac·ro·cos·mic** *adj.*
mac·ro·cos·mi·cal·ly *adv.* **mac·ro·e·co·nom·ics** *n* (with a sg verb) the study of the economy of a country as a whole. Compare MICRO-ECONOMICS. **mac·ro·e·co·nom·ic** *adj.* **mac·ro·scop·ic** [ˌmækrə'skɒpɪk] *adj* **1** that can be seen with the naked eye. **2** having to do with large groups. **mac·ro·scop·i·cal·ly** *adv.*

mad [mæd] *adj* **mad·der, mad·dest 1** out of one's mind; crazy; insane. **2** angry. **3** much excited: *The dog made mad efforts to catch up with the car.* **4** foolish: *a mad scheme.* **5** very lively: *a mad party.* **6** very enthusiastic: *mad about boats.* **mad·ness** *n.* ⟨Old English *(ge)mæded; gemæden* drive mad⟩
like mad, *Slang* furiously: *He ran like mad to catch the train.* **mad as a hatter** or **mad as a March hare** completely crazy.
mad·cap *adj* impulsive or foolish: *a madcap escapade.* *n* a person who habitually does impulsive things. **mad·den** ['mædən] *v* **1** make crazy. **2** make very angry or excited. **mad·den·ing** *adj.* **mad·house** *n* **1** formerly, an asylum for the insane. **2** a place of uproar: *The arena was a madhouse after the home team won.* **mad·ly** *adv* **1** insanely; wildly. **2** with desperate haste: *The girl pedalled madly to get to school on time.* **3** *Informal* very much: *They were madly in love.* **mad·man** ['mæd,mæn] or [-mən] *n, pl* **-men** *Informal* **1** an insane man. **2** a man whose behaviour is so unconventional as to appear irrational. **mad·wom·an** *n, pl* **-wom·en.**

USAGE

Mad is most often used to mean very reckless or foolish: *Crossing the Pacific on a raft seems a mad thing to do.* **Crazy** usually suggests a more wild or disturbed state: *crazy with fear.*

---

mad·am ['mædəm] *n* **1** a formal title used in speaking to a woman. **2** a woman who runs a brothel. ⟨Old French *ma dame* my lady⟩
ma·dame [mə'dæm] *French* [ma'dam] *n, pl* **mes·dames** [mei'dam] *French* [me'dam] a title of respect for a married woman; Mrs. *Abbrev* **Mme. mad·e·moi·selle** [ˌmædəmə'zɛl] *n French* [madmwa'zɛl] *pl* **mad·e·moi·selles** [ˌmædəmə'zɛlz] *or* **mes·de·moi·selles** [medmwa'zɛl] a title of respect for an unmarried woman; Miss. *Abbrev* **Mlle.**

made [meid] *v* pt and pp of MAKE.
adj **1** formed. **2** artificially produced: *made land.* **3** successful: *a made man.*
made–to–meas·ure *adj* of clothing, made to the buyer's measurements. **made–to–or·der** *adj* made according to the buyer's wishes. **made–up** *adj* **1** invented: *a made-up story.* **2** painted, etc. with cosmetics: *made-up lips.*

mad·e·moi·selle See MADAM.

Ma·don·na [mə'dɒnə] *n Christianity* Usually, **the Madonna**, Mary, the mother of Jesus. ⟨Italian *madonna* my lady⟩
Madonna lily a garden lily having pure white flowers. It is the floral emblem of Québec.

ma·dra·sa or **ma·dra·sah** [mə'dræsə] *n* a school in which Islamic subjects are taught, esp the Koran, the Arabic language, the Hadith, and jurisprudence. ⟨Arabic⟩

mad·ri·gal ['mædrəgəl] *n* a medieval or Elizabethan song for several voices, without instrumental accompaniment. **mad·ri·gal·ist** *n.* ⟨Latin *matricale* original, chief; *matrix* womb⟩

mael·strom ['meilstrəm] *n* **1** a turbulent whirlpool. **2** a violent confusion. ⟨Dutch *maelstroom; malen* grind + *stroom* stream⟩

ma·es·tro ['maistrou] *Italian* [ma'estro] *n, pl* **-tros** *or (Italian)* **ma·es·tri** [ma'estri] **1** a great composer, teacher, or conductor of music. **2** a master of any art. ⟨Latin *magister* master⟩

Ma·fi·a ['mafiə] *or* ['mæfiə] *n* **1** a worldwide organization of criminal elements engaged in illicit activities such as racketeering. **2 mafia,** any group thought to dominate in an underhanded way some aspect of society: *an intellectual mafia.* ⟨Italian *mafia* boldness⟩
ma·fi·o·so [ˌmafi'ousou] *n, pl* **-si** [-si] a member of the Mafia.

mag·a·zine [ˌmægə'zin] *or* ['mægə,zin] *n* **1** a publication issued at regular intervals, which contains stories, photographs, etc. by various contributors. **2** a room in a fort or warship for keeping explosives. **3** a holder on a gun for the cartridges to be fed into the chamber. ⟨French *magasin,* Italian *magazzino,* Arabic *makhzan* storehouse⟩

ma·gen·ta [mə'dʒɛntə] *n* a purplish red dye. ⟨Battle of *Magenta,* Italy, 1859; discovered in that year⟩

mag·got ['mægət] *n* a fly in the larval stage, just after leaving the egg. **mag·go·ty** *adj.* ⟨Middle English *magot;* Scandinavian⟩

Mag·i ['mædʒaɪ] *or* ['meidʒaɪ] *n pl, sg* **Mag·us** in the Bible, three wise men who brought gifts to the infant Jesus. ⟨Latin *magus.* See MAGIC.⟩

mag·ic ['mædʒɪk] *n* **1** the use of charms, spells, etc. to try to call up occult powers. **2** something that produces results as if by magic: *the magic of music.* **3** the art of illusion: *She made the rabbit disappear by magic.* **mag·ic** *adj.* **ma·gi·cian** [mə'dʒɪʃən] *n.*
mag·i·cal *adj* **1** to do with magic **2** mysterious. **mag·i·cal·ly** *adv.* ⟨Old French *magique,* Greek *magikos; magos* astrologer; Old Persian⟩

mag·is·trate ['mædʒə,streit] *or* ['mædʒəstrɪt] *n* a government official appointed to hear cases in a magistrate's court. **mag·is·tra·cy** *n.* ⟨Latin *magistratus; magister* master⟩
mag·is·te·ri·al [ˌmædʒə'stiriəl] *adj* **1** of or suited to a magistrate. **2** showing authority: *a magisterial voice.* **3** overbearing.
mag·is·te·ri·al·ly *adv.* **magistrate's court** a court dealing with minor cases.

mag·ma ['mægmə] *n Geology* the very hot, fluid substance from which lava is formed. **mag·mat·ic** *adj.* **mag·ma·tism** *n.* ⟨Greek = an unguent; *massein* knead, mould⟩

mag·na cum lau·de ['mægnə kʊm 'laʊdei] *or* [kʌm 'lɒdei] with high honours. ⟨Latin = with great praise⟩

mag·nan·i·mous [mæg'nænəməs] *adj* 1 noble in soul or mind. 2 showing a generous spirit: *a magnanimous offer.* **mag·na·nim·i·ty** [ˌmægnə'nɪməti] *n.* **mag·nan·i·mous·ly** *adv.* ⟨Latin *magnus* great + *animus* spirit⟩

mag·nate ['mægneit] *or* ['mægnɪt] *n* a powerful person, esp in business or industry: *an oil magnate.* ⟨Latin *magnatis; magnus* great⟩

mag·ne·si·um [mæg'niʒəm] *n* a metallic element that burns with a dazzling white light. *Symbol* **Mg** ⟨*Magnesia,* in Thessaly⟩ **mag·ne·sia** *n* magnesium oxide, a tasteless powder used in medicine, fertilizers, etc..

mag·net ['mægnɪt] *n* 1 a piece of iron, steel, etc. that attracts metals to it. 2 anything that attracts: *Our pet rabbits were a magnet for the children.* **mag·net·ic** [mæg'nɛtɪk] *adj.* **mag·net·i·cal·ly** *adv.* **mag·net·ism** *n.* **mag·net·ize** *v.* **mag·net·iz·a·ble** *adj.* **mag·net·i·za·tion** *n.* **mag·net·iz·er** *n.* ⟨Greek *Magnētis lithos* Magnesian stone. See MAGNESIUM.⟩ **magnetic disk** *Computers* a device able to store information in a computer. **magnetic equator** an imaginary line around the earth, where the lines of force of the earth's magnetic field are parallel to the earth's surface. **magnetic field** the region of magnetic force around a magnet. **magnetic flux** *Physics* the strength of a magnetic field in an area. **magnetic north** the direction in which the magnetic needle of a compass points. **magnetic pole** 1 one of the two poles of a magnet. 2 **Magnetic Pole,** one of the two points on the earth toward which a magnetic needle points. The **North Magnetic Pole** is at about 77.8°N 95°W; the **South Magnetic Pole** is at about 64.7°S 154°E. **magnetic storm** a temporary fluctuation in the earth's magnetic field. **magnetic tape** a ribbon coated on one side with a substance that magnetizes easily, used for recording. **mag·ne·to** [mæg'nitou] *n* a small machine which uses a magnetic field to produce an electric current. **mag·ne·to·sphere** *n* the region around the earth in which ionized particles are controlled by the earth's magnetic field.

mag·nif·i·cent [mæg'nɪfəsənt] *adj* 1 richly decorated; splendid: *a magnificent palace.* 2 impressive: *magnificent words.* 3 superb: *a magnificent view.* **mag·nif·i·cence** *n.* **mag·nif·i·cent·ly** *adv.* ⟨Latin *magnificentia; magnificus* noble. See MAGNIFY.⟩

mag·ni·fy ['mægnə,fai] *v* 1 increase the apparent size of (an object). 2 go beyond the truth. **mag·ni·fi·ca·tion** *n.* **mag·ni·fi·er** *n.* **mag·ni·fi·a·ble** *adj.* ⟨Latin *magnificare* esteem greatly; *magnus* great + *facere* make⟩

magnifying glass a lens that makes objects appear larger than they really are.

mag·ni·tude ['mægnə,tjud] *or* ['mægnə,tud] *n* 1 greatness of size, extent, importance, etc.: *The magnitude of the crime called for a long sentence.* 2 relative size, extent, etc.: *the magnitude of an angle.* 3 *Astronomy* a measure of the brightness of a heavenly body. ⟨Latin *magnitudo; magnus* large⟩ **of the first magnitude,** of great importance.

mag·no·lia [mæg'nouliə] *n* any of a genus of shrubs and trees whose flowers bloom in early spring, in some cases before the leaves. ⟨Pierre *Magnol,* 17c French botanist⟩

mag·num ['mægnəm] *n* a bottle that holds 2.3 L, used for spirits. ⟨Latin = great⟩ **mag·num o·pus** ['oupəs] *Latin* a great work of literature, music, or art, esp the greatest work of a particular artist, writer, etc.

mag·pie ['mæg,pai] *n* any of several mainly black-and-white birds of the crow family, having a chattering call. ⟨*Mag,* for *Margaret* + *pie,* orig name for it; Old French *pie,* Latin *pica*⟩

ma·ha·ra·jah [ˌmɑhə'rɑdʒə] *n* any of certain ruling princes in India. Also, **ma·ha·ra·ja.** ⟨Sanskrit *maha-* great + *raja* rajah, king⟩ **ma·ha·ra·ni** [ˌmɑhə'rɑni] *n* 1 the wife of a maharajah. 2 a woman holding in her own right a rank equal to that of a maharajah. Also, **ma·ha·ra·nee.** ⟨Sanskrit *rani* queen⟩

ma·ha·ri·shi [ˌmɑhə'rɪʃi] *n* Hindu sage who teaches others; guru. ⟨Hindi *mahā* great + *rishi* sage⟩

ma·hat·ma [mə'hɑtmə] *or* [mə'hætmə] *n* in India and Tibet, a wise and holy person. ⟨Sanskrit *maha-* great + *atman* soul⟩

Ma·ha·vi·ra [mə,hɑ'virə] *n* the chief founder of the Jain religion.

mah–jong *or* **mah–jongg** ['mɑ 'dʒɒŋ] *or* ['mɑ 'ʒɒŋ] *n* a western version of a Chinese game played with 136 or 144 dominolike tiles. ⟨former TM *Mah–Jongg,* from Mandarin for 'sparrow'; for image on one tile⟩

ma·hog·a·ny [mə'hɒgəni] *n* any of various tropical American trees whose hard wood is highly valued for timber. ⟨obsolete Spanish *mahogani,* probably of West Indian origin⟩

maid [meid] *n* 1 a woman servant: *a kitchen maid.* 2 a young, unmarried woman; girl. 3 a virgin. ⟨shortened from *maiden,* Old English *mægden*⟩ **maid of honour** or **honor** an unmarried woman who is the chief attendant of the bride at a wedding. **maid·en** ['meidən] *n* 1 a young, unmarried woman; girl. 2 a virgin. 3 a racehorse that has never won a race. *adj* 1 to do with a maiden: *maiden blushes.* 2 unmarried: *a maiden aunt.* 3 first: *a ship's maiden voyage.* 4 untried: *maiden ground.* **maid·en·hair** ['meidən,hɛr] *n* any of a genus of ferns with delicate fronds. **maid·en·hood** *n.* **maid·en·ly** *adj.* **maid·en·li·ness** *n.* **maiden name** the surname a woman used before her marriage. **maid·serv·ant** *n* a female servant.

mail¹ [meil] *n* a public system of collection and delivery of letters, parcels, etc., usually run by a government. **2** messages left by E-MAIL or VOICE MAIL.
v send by mail. ⟨Middle English *male*, Old French *malle* satchel, bag⟩
mail·box *n* **1** a public box for depositing outgoing mail. **2** a private box outside a dwelling, cubbyhole in an office, etc. where mail is delivered. **mail·er** *n* **1** a machine for stamping or addressing letters, etc. **2** a container in which to mail things. **mail·man** *n, pl* **-men** a man whose work is delivering mail; letter carrier. **mail order** an order for goods sent by mail. **mail–or·der** *adj.*

mail² [meil] *n* flexible armour made of metal rings or plates linked together. ⟨Old French *maille;* Latin *macula* a mesh in a net⟩

mail·lot [mɑ'jou] *n, pl* **mail·lots** [mɑ'jouz]; *French sg, pl* [mɑ'jo] **1** a bathing suit, esp a one-piece suit. **2** a one-piece, garment worn by dancers, gymnasts, etc.

maim [meim] *v* cause permanent damage to a part of the body: *He was not seriously maimed, but did lose two toes from frostbite.* ⟨Middle English *mayme* variant of *mayhem*⟩

main [mein] *adj* most important.
n **1** *Archaic* physical strength. **2** a large pipe for water, gas, etc.: *a water main.* **3** *Poetic* the open sea; ocean. ⟨Old English *mægen* power⟩
by main force or **strength** by using full strength. **in the main** for the most part: *His grades were excellent in the main.* **with might and main** with all one's force.
main clause *Grammar* a clause that can stand by itself as a sentence; independent clause. **main drag** *Slang* the chief road of a town or city. **main·frame** *Computers adj* to do with a central computer serving several terminals. Compare MICROCOMPUTER. **main·land** ['mein,lænd] *or* ['meinlənd] *n* the principal part of a land mass, apart from outlying islands. **main·land·er** *n.* **main·line** *n* the principal line of a railway, etc. *v Slang* inject (a drug, such as heroin) directly into a principal vein. **main·lin·er** *n.* **main·ly** *adv* mostly; chiefly. **main·mast** ['mein,mæst] *or* ['meinməst] *n Nautical* the principal mast of a sailing ship. **main·sail** ['mein,seil] *or* ['meinsəl] *n Nautical* the largest sail on the mainmast of a ship. **main·spring** *n* **1** the principal spring in a clock, watch, etc. **2** the main cause, motive, or influence. **main·stay** *n* **1** *Nautical* a supporting rope from the maintop to the foot of the foremast. **2** the main support: *His friends were his mainstay through his time of trouble.* **main·stream** *n* the main trend of a fashion, body of opinion, etc.: *the mainstream of modern art. v* integrate (a child with a disability) into a regular class. **main·stream** *adj.* **main·street·ing** *n* ✱ the practice, by a politician, etc., of walking about main streets in order to greet potential supporters. **main·street** *v.*

main·tain [mein'tein] *v* **1** carry on: *to maintain one's composure.* **2** keep in good condition: *to maintain a fleet of trucks.* **3** pay the expenses of: *She maintains a family of four.* **4** uphold; argue for: *to maintain an opinion.* **5** declare to be true: *He maintained that he was innocent.* **main·tain·a·ble** *adj.*
main·tain·er *n.* ⟨Old French *maintenir;* Latin *manu tenere* hold by the hand⟩
main·te·nance ['meintənəns] *n* **1** support: *A government collects taxes to pay for its maintenance.* **2** upkeep: *The army devotes much time to the maintenance of its equipment.* **3** *Law* the payment of money by a person to a former spouse for the support of the former spouse and any children. Compare ALIMONY.

mai·tre d' [,meitər 'di] *or* [,meitrə 'di] *n, pl* **mai·tre d's** *Informal* MAÎTRE D'HÔTEL. ⟨French⟩
maî·tre d'hô·tel ['meitər dou'tɛl] *n, pl* **maîtres d'hôtel** ['meitər dou'tɛl]; *French sg, pl* [mɛtʀdo'tɛl] a headwaiter, literally, master of the hotel.

maj·es·ty ['mædʒəsti] *n* **1** grandeur; nobility; stateliness: *the majesty of the ceremony.* **2** supreme authority: *the majesty of the law.* **3 Majesty,** a title used to or of a king, queen, emperor, empress, etc.: *Your Majesty, His Majesty, Her Majesty.* ⟨Latin *majestas*⟩
ma·jes·tic [mə'dʒɛstɪk] *adj* grand; noble; dignified. **ma·jes·ti·cal·ly** *adv.*

ma·jor ['meidʒər] *adj* **1** greater: *the major share of the profits.* **2** of the first rank: *a major poet.* **3** very serious: *a major disaster.* **4** of legal age. **5** to do with a student's principal course of study. **6** *Music* **a** of an interval, greater by a half step than the minor: *a major second.* **b** of a scale, key, or mode, in which the interval between the tonic and the third step is a major third (two whole steps): *C major scale or key.* **c** of a chord, containing a major third.
n **1** an officer in the armed forces ranking next above a captain. *Abbrev* **Maj.** or **Maj 2** *Sports* **the majors,** *pl* the MAJOR LEAGUES.
v of a student, give most of one's attention to (a subject) (used with *in*): *to major in botany.* ⟨Latin, comparative of *magnus* great⟩
ma·jor–do·mo ['meidʒər 'doumou] *n* a man in charge of a royal or noble household. **ma·jor·ette** *n* DRUM MAJORETTE. **ma·jor·i·ty** [mə'dʒɔrəti] *n* **1** the greater part. **2** the number of votes by which one candidate's return exceeds the total number of votes for all other candidates. **3** the legal age of responsibility. **major league 1** *Baseball* either of the two chief leagues of American professional baseball teams. **2** *Hockey* the National Hockey League. **major–league** *adj.* **major penalty** *Hockey* a five-minute penalty awarded for certain serious infractions. **major premise** See SYLLOGISM.

make [meik] *v* **made, mak·ing 1** build; form. **2** have the qualities needed for: *Dry wood makes a good fire.* **3** force to: *He made me go.* **4** cause to be or become: *to make a room warm.* **5** get; obtain: *to make one's living.* **6** do: *to make an attempt.* **7** cause the success of: *That one deal made the young businesswoman.* **8** *Informal* get a place on: *He made the football team.* **9** attend: *I can't make tonight's meeting.*
n **1** the way in which a thing is made: *Do you*

like the make of that coat? **2** a kind; brand: *What make of car is this?* ⟨Old English *macian*⟩ **make after** pursue. **make as if** pretend that. **make away with a** get rid of. **b** kill. **c** steal: *The treasurer made away with the club's funds.* **make believe** pretend. **make–be·lieve** *n, adj.* **make for a** go toward: *Make for the hills!* **b** help bring about: *Careful driving makes for fewer accidents.* **make fun.** See FUN. **make good.** See GOOD. **make good time ✻** travel at a swift pace. **make it** *Informal* **a** succeed. **b** *Slang* have sexual intercourse (with). **c** reach a destination: *Can you make it to the meeting?* **make like** *Slang* **a** imitate. **b** perform the services of: *to make like a cook.* **make off** run away. **make off with** steal: *He made off with some apples.* **make or break** cause to succeed or fail. **make out a** write out: *He made out his application for camp.* **b** show (to be): *That makes me out a liar.* **c** understand: *to make out a problem.* **d** see with difficulty: *I can barely make out the horizon.* **e** *Slang* engage in extensive kissing and caressing, and, often, sexual intercourse. **make over a** alter: *to make over a dress.* **b** transfer ownership of: *Grandfather made over his farm to my mother.* **make something of** make an issue of. **make time** go with speed. **make tracks (for) ✻** start out (for a place), usually in haste. **make up a** invent: *to make up a story.* **b** become friends again after a quarrel. **c** put cosmetics on (the face). **d** complete: *We need two more eggs to make up a dozen.* **e** constitute: *The committee is made up of women.* **make up for a** give or do something in place of: *to make up for lost time.* **b** compensate for: *Her kindness more than makes up for her shyness.* **make up one's mind** decide. **make up to** flatter. **on the make** *Informal* trying for success, profit, etc. **mak·er** *n* **1** a person who or thing that makes. **2 Maker** God. **meet one's Maker** die. **make·shift** *n* a temporary substitute: *When the power went off, we used candles as a makeshift.* **make·shift** *adj.* **make–up** or **make·up** *n* **1** the way of being put together. **2** one's nature: *a nervous make-up.* **3** cosmetics. *adj* referring to a course or examination taken to make up for one missed or failed: *a make-up test.* **make–work** *n* **1** the finding of unnecessary jobs. **2** the providing of work for unemployed people. **make–work** *adj.* **mak·ing** *n* **1** the cause of a person's success: *Early hardships were the making of him.* **2 makings** *pl* ingredients; contributory factors. **in the making** in the process of being made.

mal– *combining form* bad or badly; poor or poorly: *malnutrition, maltreat.* ⟨French *mal*, Latin *male* badly; *malus* bad⟩

mal·ad·just·ed [ˌmælə'dʒʌstɪd] *adj* not in harmony with one's environment and conditions of life. **mal·ad·just·ment** *n.*

mal·a·droit [ˌmælə'drɔɪt] *adj* unskilful; awkward. **mal·a·droit·ly** *adv.* **mal·a·droit·ness** *n.*

mal·a·dy ['mælədi] *n* **1** a sickness or disease. **2** any unwholesome or disordered condition: *Poverty is a social malady.* ⟨Old French *maladie; malade* ill, Latin *male habitus* doing poorly⟩

ma·laise [mæ'leiz] *n* **1** a general feeling of bodily discomfort and weakness. **2** weakness tending toward disruption or decline: *Apathy is the malaise of democracy.* ⟨French *malaise; mal-* ill + *aise* ease⟩

mal·a·mute ['mælə,mjut] *n* a breed of dog having a heavy coat and a tail that curls over the back. Malamutes have long been used as sled dogs in the North. Also, **mal·e·mute.** ⟨*Malemiut* a Yupik people of W Alaska⟩

mal·a·prop·ism ['mæləprɒ,pɪzəm] *n* a ridiculous misuse of words that sound alike, as *immortality/immorality* in *They believe in the immorality of souls.* ⟨Mrs. *Malaprop*, character in Sheridan's play *The Rivals*⟩

mal·ap·ro·pos [ˌmælæprə'pou] *adj* at the wrong time or place; inappropriate. *adv* inappropriately. ⟨French *mal à propos*⟩

ma·lar·i·a [mə'lɛriə] *n Pathology* a disease characterized by chills and fever, transmitted by the anopheles mosquitoes. **ma·lar·i·al** *adj.* ⟨Italian, from *mala aria* bad air⟩

mal·con·tent [ˌmælkən'tent] *or* ['mælkən,tent] *adj* discontented or rebellious. *n* a discontented person.

male [meil] *adj* **1** to do with the sex that produces sperm cells that fertilize the eggs of a female to produce young: *the male organs.* **2** to do with men or boys: *a male voice.* *n* a person, animal, or plant that is male. **male·ness** *n.* ⟨Latin *masculus,* diminutive of *mas* male⟩

Mal·e·cite See MALISEET.

mal·e·dic·tion [ˌmælə'dɪkʃən] *n* the uttering of a curse. **mal·e·dic·tive** *adj.* **mal·e·dic·to·ry** *adj.* ⟨Latin *male* ill + *dictio; dicere* speak⟩

mal·e·fac·tor ['mælə,fæktər] *n* a criminal or evildoer. ⟨Latin *male* ill + *factor; facere* do⟩

ma·lev·o·lent [mə'lɛvələnt] *adj* malicious; spiteful: *a malevolent smile.* **ma·lev·o·lence** *n.* **ma·lev·o·lent·ly** *adv.* ⟨Latin *male* ill + *volens; velle* wish⟩

mal·fea·sance [mæl'fizəns] *n Law* misconduct by a public official: *A judge is guilty of malfeasance if he or she accepts a bribe.* **mal·fea·sant** *adj, n.* ⟨French *malfaisance; mal-* badly + *faire* do⟩

mal·for·ma·tion [ˌmælfər'meiʃən] *n* an irregular or abnormal structure: *A hunchback is a malformation of the spine.* **mal·formed** *adj.*

mal·func·tion [mæl'fʌŋkʃən] *n* failure to work or perform: *a mechanical malfunction in a machine.* **mal·func·tion** *v.*

mal·ice ['mælɪs] *n* **1** active ill will; spite. **2** *Law* intent to commit an act which will harm another person without justification.

ma·li·cious [mə'lɪʃəs] *adj.* **ma·li·cious·ly** *adv.* **ma·li·cious·ness** *n.* ⟨Old French; Latin *malitia; malus* evil⟩

malice aforethought *Law* committed with intent.

ma·lign [mə'laɪn] *v* speak evil of, often falsely; slander: *You malign him when you call him stingy, for he gives all he can afford to give. adj* 1 evil; injurious: *a malign influence.* 2 hateful; malicious. 3 potentially fatal. **ma·lign·er** *n.* **ma·lign·ly** *adv.* ⟨Latin *malignare; malignus,* from *malus* evil + *gen-* birth⟩

ma·lig·nant [mə'lɪgnənt] *adj* 1 extremely evil or malicious. 2 extremely harmful. 3 *Pathology* of a disease, very infectious: *malignant cholera.* 4 *Pathology* of a tumour, cancerous. Compare BENIGN (def. 2). **ma·lig·nan·cy** or **ma·lig·nance** *n.* **ma·lig·nant·ly** *adv.*

ma·lin·ger [mə'lɪŋgər] *v* pretend to be sick in order to escape work or duty; shirk. **ma·lin·ger·er** *n.* ⟨French *malingre* sickly; Old French *mal* badly (Latin *male*) + *heingre* sick⟩

Mal·i·seet ['mælə,sit] *or* [,mælə'sit] *n, pl* **-seet** or **-seets** *n* 1 a member of a First Nations people living in New Brunswick, eastern Québec, and northern Maine. 2 the Algonquian language of this people. **Mal·i·seet** *adj.* Also, **Mal·e·cite.**

mall [mɒl] *n* 1 SHOPPING MALL. 2 a walk lined with stores. ⟨Old French *ma(i)l* mallet; orig mallet used in pall-mall, old game played in a lane or alley. See MALLET.⟩

mal·lard ['mælərd] *n, pl* **-lards** or (esp collectively) **-lard** a wild duck having a blue wing patch. ⟨Old French *mallart*⟩

mal·le·a·ble ['mæliəbəl] *adj* 1 capable of being hammered into shapes without being broken. 2 adaptable; yielding: *A malleable person is easily persuaded to change his plans.* **mal·le·a·bil·i·ty** *n.* **mal·le·a·bly** *adv.* ⟨Latin *malleare* hammer, v; *malleus,* n⟩

mal·let ['mælɪt] *n* a hammer having a head of wood, rubber, or other relatively soft material. ⟨Old French *maillet* diminutive of *mail;* Latin *malleus* hammer⟩

mal·low ['mælou] *n* any of a genus of herbs having lobed leaves and usually large, showy flowers. ⟨Old English *mealwe,* Latin *malva*⟩

mal·nour·ished [mæl'nɜrɪʃt] *adj* suffering from lack of food or nutritious food.

mal·nu·tri·tion [,mælnjə'trɪʃən] *or* [,mælnə-] *n* poor nourishment; lack of nourishment.

mal·oc·clu·sion [,mælə'kluʒən] *n* failure of the upper and lower teeth to close properly.

mal·o·dor·ous [mæl'oudərəs] *adj* smelling bad. **mal·o·dor·ous·ly** *adv.* **mal·o·dor·ous·ness** *n.*

mal·peque [mæl'pik] *or* ['mælpɛk] *n* ✳ a variety of oyster, found in Malpeque Bay, Prince Edward Island.

mal·prac·tice [mæl'præktɪs] *n* criminal neglect or unprofessional treatment in any professional position. **mal·prac·ti·tion·er** [,mælpræk'tɪʃənər] *n.*

malt [mɒlt] *n* grain soaked in water until it sprouts, then dried and aged.

v change or be changed into malt. **malt·y** *adj.* ⟨Old English *mealt*⟩

malted milk a drink made from milk and malt, mixed with ice cream and flavouring.

mal·treat [mæl'trit] *v* treat roughly or cruelly; abuse: *Only vicious persons maltreat animals.* **mal·treat·ment** *n.*

ma·ma or **mam·ma** ['mʌmə], ['mɑmə], *or* ['mɒmə] *n Informal* mother. ⟨reduplication of an infantile sound⟩

mam·ba ['mɑmbə] *or* ['mæmbə] *n* any of a genus of very poisonous snakes belonging to the same family as the cobras and coral snakes. ⟨South African *m'namba*⟩

mam·bo ['mɑmbou], ['mɒm-], *or* ['mæm-] *n* a fast ballroom dance of Caribbean origin. ⟨Haitian Creole⟩

mam·mal ['mæməl] *n* any of a class (Mammalia) of warm-blooded, vertebrate animals, the females of which have glands (mammae) that produce milk for feeding their young. **mam·ma·li·an** [mə'meiliən] *adj, n.* **mam·ma·like** *adj.* ⟨Latin *mamma* breast⟩

mammary gland *Anatomy, zoology* an organ in female mammals that produces milk. **mam·mo·gram** *n* a printout from a mammography. **mam·mog·ra·phy** [mə'mɒgrəfi] *n* examination of the breasts by X ray. **mam·mo·graph·ic** *adj.*

Mam·mon or **mam·mon** ['mæmən] *n* 1 material wealth thought of as an object of worship. 2 greed for wealth. **Mam·mon·ism** *n.* ⟨Aramaic *mamon* riches⟩

mam·moth ['mæməθ] *n* any of an extinct genus of elephants of the Pleistocene epoch having a hairy skin and long, curved tusks. *adj* huge; gigantic. ⟨earlier Russian *mammot*⟩

man [mæn] *n, pl* **men** 1 an adult male person. 2 the human race: *Man has existed for thousands of years.* See Usage box below. 3 a male servant. 4 *Informal* a husband or lover. 5 one of the pieces used in chess, etc.

v **manned, man·ning** *v* supply with a crew: *We can man ten ships.*

interj Informal an exclamation of surprise, excitement, etc., or for effect: *Man, what a player!* **man·hood** *n.* ⟨Old English *mann*⟩

as one man unanimously. **be one's own man (or woman) a** be free to do as one pleases. **b** have complete control of oneself. **to a man** all: *We accepted his idea to a man.*

man about town a man who spends much of his time in fashionable clubs, theatres, etc. **man·ful** *adj* having or showing courage, etc. **man·ful·ly** *adv.* **man·ful·ness** *n.* **man·han·dle** *v* 1 treat roughly. 2 move by human strength without mechanical appliances. **man·hole** *n* a hole for a worker to enter a sewer, steam boiler, etc. **man–hour** *n* an hour of work done by one person, used as a time unit in industry. **man·hunt** *n* a hunt for a criminal. **man·kind** *n* 1 [,mæn'kaɪnd] the human race. 2 ['mæn,kaɪnd] men collectively, as opposed to women. **man·like** *adj* 1 of an animal, having characteristics of a human being: *The chimpanzee is the most manlike of the apes.*

2 like or characteristic of men. **3** suitable for a man; masculine. **man·ly** adj **1** as a man should be. **2** suitable for a man; masculine. **man·li·ness** n. **man–made** adj synthetic: Nylon is a man-made fibre. **man·nish** adj **1** peculiar to a man: a mannish way of holding a baby. **2** of clothes or manners, generally associated with a man rather than a woman: She has a mannish style of dress. **man·nish·ly** adv. **man·nish·ness** n. **man–of–war** n, pl **men–of–war** **1** warship. **2** Portuguese **man–of–war**, a stinging jellyfish. **man·pow·er** n the power supplied by human physical work. **man·serv·ant** n, pl **men·serv·ants** a male servant. **man·slaugh·ter** n Law the unlawful killing of another human being accidentally. **man–to–man** adj straightforward: a man-to-man talk. adv honestly; sincerely. **men·folk** n pl Informal **1** men collectively. **2** a group of men, such as the male members of a family.

USAGE

Many people consider the use of **man** and words like **mankind** and **man-made** to be offensive when referring to human beings in general. Non-sexist words such as **person**, **people**, **humankind**, **synthetic**, etc. can be used instead. Similarly, words like **chairman**, **fireman**, **spokesman** can be replaced by **chair**, **firefighter**, **spokesperson**. A good thesaurus will provide non-sexist synonyms.

M.A.N. Member of the National Assembly (for Membre de l'Assemblée Nationale).

man·a·cle ['mænəkəl] n **1** Usually, **manacles** pl a handcuff. **2** any restraint. **man·a·cle** v. ⟨Old French; Latin manicula diminutive of manica sleeve; manus hand⟩

man·age ['mænɪdʒ] v **1** control; direct: manage a business, manage a horse. **2** succeed in accomplishing: I finally managed to get the job done. **3** get along: manage on one's income. **4** get one's way with (a person) by craft; handle. **man·age·a·ble** adj. **man·age·a·bil·i·ty** n. **man·age·a·bly** adv. ⟨Italian maneggiare; mano hand, Latin manus⟩
man·age·ment ['mænɪdʒmənt] n **1** control; direction. **2** the people that manage a business or an institution. **man·ag·er** n **1** a person who manages: a bank manager. **2** a person skilled in managing (affairs, time, money, etc.): She is not much of a manager, but the family gets along somehow. **3** a person who directs the activities of a team, performer, etc. **man·a·ge·ri·al** [,mænə'dʒɪriəl] adj. **man·a·ge·ri·al·ly** adv. **man·a·ge·ri·al·ism** n.

ma·ña·na [mʌn'jɑnə] n, adv tomorrow; some time in the future. ⟨Spanish⟩

man·a·tee ['mænə,ti] or [,mænə'ti] n any of a genus of sea mammals, having a whalelike body. ⟨Spanish manati; Carib⟩

man·da·rin ['mændərɪn] n **1** an orange with a thin, very loose, peel. **2** Mandarin the main language of modern China, the standard form being the one used in Beijing. **3** formerly, in the Chinese empire, an official of high rank. **4** a person whose government work has considerable political or social influence: the mandarins of Ottawa. ⟨Chinese Pidgin English; Portuguese mandar⟩
mandarin collar a narrow collar that stands up straight and does not meet at the front.

man·date ['mændeit] or ['mændɪt] n **1** a command. **2** a direction given to a government by the votes of the people in an election: a mandate to increase taxes.
v ['mændeit]v order (something) to be done; make mandatory. ⟨Latin mandare order⟩
man·da·to·ry ['mændə,tɔri] adj **1** giving a command. **2** required by a command. **man·da·to·ri·ly** adv.

man·di·ble ['mændəbəl] n **1** a mouth part of an insect, lobster, etc. **2** either part of the beak of a bird, octopus, etc. **3** the jaw of a vertebrate; lower jaw. See MAXILLA. **man·dib·u·lar** adj. ⟨Latin mandibula; mandere chew⟩

man·do·lin ['mændəlɪn] or [,mændə'lɪn] n a musical instrument having a pear-shaped body. **man·do·lin·ist** [,mændə'lɪnɪst] n. ⟨French; Italian mandolino; Greek pandoura three-stringed instrument⟩

man·drake ['mændreik] n a plant of the nightshade family, with a forked root thought of as resembling the human form and so having magical powers. ⟨by folk etymology from Greek mandragoras⟩

man·drill ['mændrəl] n a terrestrial monkey. The adult male has bare patches of red, blue, and pink skin on the face and buttocks. ⟨man + drill baboon; probably W African⟩

mane [mein] n the long, heavy hair growing on the back or around the neck of a horse, lion, etc. **mane·less** adj. ⟨Old English manu⟩

ma·nège [mɑ'neʒ] or [mɑ'neiʒ] n **1** the art of training or riding horses. **2** a riding school. ⟨French; Italian maneggio; maneggiare manage⟩

man·ga·nese ['mæŋgə,niz] n a brittle, metallic element. Symbol Mn ⟨Italian manganese alteration of Latin magnesia. See MAGNESIUM.⟩

mange [meindʒ] n an itchy skin disease of dogs, horses, cattle, etc., in which the hair falls off in patches. ⟨Old French manjue or mangeue itch⟩
man·gy ['meindʒi] adj **1** affected with or caused by the mange: a mangy dog. **2** shabby, dirty, scruffy, etc.: a mangy old rug. **3** contemptible. **man·gi·ness** n. **man·gi·ly** adv.

man·ger ['meindʒər] n a trough in which to put hay for horses or cows to eat. ⟨Old French mangeoire; manger eat, Latin manducare⟩

man·gle¹ ['mæŋgəl] v **1** cut or tear roughly: His arm was badly mangled in the accident. **2** do or play badly: to mangle a song. ⟨perhaps Old French mahaignier injure⟩

man·gle² ['mæŋgəl] n a machine for pressing and smoothing cloth by passing it between rollers. **man·gle** v. ⟨Dutch mangel, earlier mange; Latin manganum contrivance⟩

man·go ['mæŋgou] n, pl **-goes** or **-gos** a juicy fruit having yellow or orange flesh. ⟨Portuguese; Tamil mankay⟩

man·grove ['mæŋgrouv] *n* any of a genus of tropical evergreen trees or shrubs that grow in swampy land, having roots that grow down from the branches. ⟨Spanish *mangle*, Malay *manggi-manggi*; influenced by *grove*⟩

ma·ni·a ['meiniə] *n* **1** a form of mental disorder characterized by extremes of joy or rage, often followed by depression. **2** an excessive fondness: *a mania for ice cream.* **man·ic** ['mænɪk] *adj, n.* ⟨Greek = madness⟩ **ma·ni·ac** *n* **1** a person who behaves in a wild or irresponsible way: *That driver is a maniac.* **2** a person who has an excessive fondness for something. **ma·ni·a·cal** [mə'naɪəkəl] *adj.* **ma·ni·a·cal·ly** *adv.* **man·ic–de·pres·sive** *adj* designating a psychosis characterized by periods of extreme confidence alternating with deep depression. **man·ic–de·pres·sive** *n.*

man·i·cure ['mænə,kjʊr] *v* **1** trim, clean, and polish (the fingernails). **2** trim closely. *n* a treatment for the fingernails. **man·i·cur·ist** *n.* ⟨Latin *manus* hand + *cura* care⟩

man·i·fest ['mænə,fest] *adj* obvious: *The thief left so many clues that her guilt was manifest.* *v* show plainly. *n* **1** a list of a ship's cargo. **2** a list of passengers, freight, etc. on an airplane flight. **man·i·fest·ly** *adv.* **man·i·fest·ness** *n.* ⟨Latin *manifestus* near at hand; *manus* hand⟩ **man·i·fes·ta·tion** *n* **1** something that manifests: *A brave deed is a manifestation of courage.* **2** the occurrence of a spiritualistic materialization: *No manifestation occurred at the first séance.* **man·i·fes·to** [,mænə'festou] *n, pl* **-os** or **-oes** a public declaration of intentions, purposes, or motives.

man·i·fold ['mænə,fould] *adj* **1** of many kinds: *manifold duties.* **2** having many parts. *n* a pipe having openings for connection with other pipes. *v* make manifold; multiply. ⟨Old English *manigfeald; manig* many + *feald* fold⟩

man·i·kin ['mænə,kɪn] *n* **1** a little man. **2** mannequin. Also, **man·ni·kin.** ⟨Dutch *manneken* diminutive of *man* man⟩

ma·nil·a or **ma·nil·la** [mə'nɪlə] *adj* made from manila paper or hemp: *a manila envelope.* ⟨*Manila*, Philippines⟩ **Manila hemp** a strong fibre made from the leafstalks of the abaca, a plant related to the banana. **Manila paper** a strong wrapping paper, made originally from Manila hemp.

man·i·oc ['mæni,ɒk] *n* CASSAVA. ⟨Tupi-Guarani *manioca*⟩

ma·nip·u·late [mə'nɪpjə,leit] *v* **1** handle skilfully. **2** manage by use of unfair influence: *She so manipulated the team that she was elected captain.* **3** change for one's own advantage: *to manipulate a company's accounts to cover up his theft.* **ma·nip·u·la·tor** *n.* **ma·nip·u·lat·a·ble** or **ma·nip·u·la·ble** *adj.* **ma·nip·u·la·tion** *n.* ⟨Latin *manipulus* handful; *manus* hand⟩ **ma·nip·u·la·tive** *adj* **1** tending to manipulate others. **2** to do with manipulation. *n, pl* **manipulatives** *Education* small items such as

blocks and counters, which children can manipulate to develop their reasoning skills.

Man·i·to·ba [,mænə'toubə] *n* a central province of Canada. *Abbrev* **MB. Man·i·to·ban** *n, adj.* **Manitoba maple** ✻ a maple common on the Prairies, the only Canadian maple normally having compound leaves.

man·i·tou or **man·i·tu** ['mænə,tu] *n* in the traditional religion of the Algonquian peoples: **1** any of the spirits representing the power that dwells within all things in nature. **2** Often, **Manitou**, the impersonal supreme being or supernatural force, author of life and all things; the chief of the manitous, called **gitche** (or **kitshe**) **manitou**, often translated as 'Great Spirit'. ⟨Algonquian⟩

man·na ['mænə] *n* in the Bible, the food that miraculously fell from heaven. ⟨Hebrew *man* what?⟩

man·ne·quin ['mænəkɪn] *n* **1** a model of a human figure, used by artists, tailors, stores, etc. **2** a woman whose work is modelling clothes for designers, retail stores, etc. ⟨French; Dutch *manneken*. See MANIKIN.⟩

man·ner ['mænər] *n* **1** the way something happens or is done: *The trouble arose in a curious manner.* **2** a way of behaving: *a kind manner.* **3** a style: *He dresses in a strange manner.* **4** kind or kinds: *We saw all manner of birds in the forest.* **5** **manners** *pl* ways or customs. ⟨Anglo-French *manere*, Latin *manuaria* of the hand; *manus* hand⟩ **in a manner of speaking** in a way. **to the manner born a** accustomed to wealthy conditions. **b** naturally suited to (an activity). **man·nered** *adj* **1** having manners of a certain kind: *well-mannered.* **2** affected. **man·ner·ism** *n* an idiosyncratic habit. **man·ner·less** *adj* having bad manners. **man·ner·less·ness** *n.* **man·ner·ly** *adj* having good manners. *adv* politely. **man·ner·li·ness** *n.*

ma·noeu·vre [mə'nuvər] *n* **1** a planned movement of troops: *The army practises warfare by holding manoeuvres.* **2** a skilful plan. **ma·noeu·vre** *v.* Also, **ma·neu·ver.** **ma·noeu·vra·ble** *adj.* **ma·noeu·vra·bil·i·ty** *n.* ⟨French; Latin *manu operare* work by hand⟩

ma·nom·e·ter [mə'nɒmətər] *n* an instrument for measuring the pressure of fluids. **man·o·met·ric** [,mænə'mɛtrɪk] *adj.* **man·o·met·ri·cal·ly** *adv.* **ma·nom·e·try** *n.* ⟨Greek *manos* thin + *metron* measure⟩

man·or ['mænər] *n* **1** in the Middle Ages, a feudal estate. **2** a large holding of land. **3** a large house on an estate, esp a manor house. **ma·no·ri·al** [mə'nɔriəl] *adj.* ⟨Anglo-French *maner*; Latin *manere* stay⟩

man·qué [mɑŋ'kei] *French* [mã'ke] *adj* (only after the noun) frustrated or unfulfilled: *a novelist manqué teaching creative writing courses.* ⟨French, pp of *manquer* to miss⟩

man·sard ['mænsɑrd] *or* ['mænsərd] *n* a four-sided roof having two slopes on each side. **man·sard·ed** *adj.* ⟨François *Mansard*, 17c French architect⟩

manse [mæns] *n* a minister's house. ⟨Latin *mansa* dwelling, n; fem. pp of *manere* stay⟩

man·sion ['mænʃən] *n* a large, stately house. ⟨Latin *mansio; manere* stay⟩

man·sue·tude ['mænswə,tjud] *or* ['mænswə,tud] *n* gentleness in behaviour. ⟨Latin *mansuētūdō* tameness; *manus* hand + *suetus* pp of *suescēre* grow accustomed⟩

man·ta ['mæntə] *n* devilfish. Also, **manta ray**.

man·tel ['mæntəl] *n* a shelf above a fireplace. Also, **man·tel·piece**. ⟨variant of *mantle*⟩

man·tis ['mæntɪs] *n, pl* **-tis·es** or **-tes** [-'tiz] any of a large family of carnivorous insects, having the habit of raising their foremost pair of legs raised, suggesting praying. ⟨Greek *mantis* prophet; for its praying posture⟩

man·tle ['mæntəl] *n* **1** a cloak. **2** anything that covers like a cloak: *a mantle of snow*. **3** *Geology* the solid rock part of the earth's interior, between the crust and the core.
v become covered with a coating or scum: *The pond was mantled*. ⟨Latin *mantellum* diminutive of *mantum* cloak⟩

man·tra ['mæntrə] *or* ['mɑntrə] *n* *Hinduism or Buddhism* **1** any of the metrical hymns of praise in the Veda. **2** a sacred word or formula used for incantation or meditation. ⟨Sanskrit = instrument of thought; *man* think⟩

man·u·al ['mænjuəl] *adj* **1** to do with using the hands: *manual labour*. **2** done by hand, not automatically: *a manual choke*. *n* a book that helps its readers to understand or use something. **man·u·al·ly** *adv*. ⟨Latin *manus* hand⟩

man·u·fac·ture [,mænjə'fæktʃər] *v* **1** make: *This factory manufactures outboard motors.* **2** invent: *The dishonest lawyer manufactured evidence.* ⟨Latin *manu facere* make by hand⟩
man·u·fac·tur·er *n* a person or company whose business is manufacturing.

ma·nure [mə'njʊr] *or* [mə'nʊr] *n* a substance, esp animal waste, put in soil as fertilizer. ⟨Anglo-French *maynoverer* work with the hands⟩

man·u·script ['mænjə,skrɪpt] *n* an unpublished book, paper, etc. written by hand or with a typewriter or computer. **man·u·script** *adj. Abbrev* **MS.**, **MS**, **ms.**, or **ms** ⟨Latin *manu scriptus* written by hand⟩

man·y ['mɛni] *adj* **more**, **most** in great number; numerous: *many years ago*.
n a large number of people or things: *There were many at the fair*. ⟨Old English *manig*⟩
a good many a fairly large number. **a great many** a very large number. **one too many for** more than a match for. **the many a** most people. **b** the common people.

Ma·o·ri ['maʊri] *or* ['maʊri] *n* **1** a member of a Polynesian people of New Zealand. **2** their Polynesian language. **Ma·o·ri** *adj*.

map [mæp] *n* **1** a drawing representing the earth's surface or part of it. **2** a maplike drawing of anything: *a road map*.
v **mapped, map·ping 1** make a map of. **2** plan; arrange in detail: *to map out the week's work*. **3** transfer by or as if by a mathematical

transformation. ⟨Latin *mappa mundi* map of the world; special use of *mappa* napkin⟩
off the map *Informal* of no importance. **put on the map** *Informal* make well-known.

ma·ple ['meipəl] *n* any of a large genus of trees and shrubs, having fruits with two winglike extensions, each containing a seed. *adj* made with maple sugar or syrup: *maple candy*. **ma·ple·like** *adj*. ⟨Old English *mapel*⟩
maple bush ✳ a grove of sugar maple trees. **maple candy ✳** candy made from maple sap. **maple leaf 1** a leaf of the maple tree. **2** this leaf as a Canadian emblem. **maple sugar** sugar made from the sap of the sugar maple. **maple syrup** syrup made from the sap of the sugar maple.

mar [mɑr] *v* **marred, mar·ring** spoil the beauty of; damage. ⟨Old English *merran* waste⟩

ma·ra·ca [mə'rɑkə] *n* a percussion instrument resembling a rattle. ⟨Portuguese⟩

maraschino cherries [,mɛrə'ʃinou] *or* [,mær'ʃinou] cherries preserved in syrup flavoured with a sweet cherry liqueur.

mar·a·thon ['mɛrə,θɒn] *or* ['mærə,θɒn] *n* **1** a long-distance foot race, officially measured at 42.195 km. **2** any long-distance endurance contest: *a dance marathon*. ⟨*Marathon*, site of Greek victory over Persians; a messenger ran 37 km to Athens to announce it.⟩

ma·raud [mə'rɒd] *v* go about in search of plunder; make raids for booty. **ma·raud·er** *n*. ⟨French = rascal⟩

mar·ble ['mɑrbəl] *n* **1** limestone that is capable of taking a high polish. **2** a sculpture made of marble. **3** a small ball of glass, stone, etc. used in games. **4 marbles** a game played with such little balls (with a sg verb). **5 marbles** *pl Slang* wits, common sense, or brains: *I don't think he's got all his marbles*.
adj **1** made of marble. **2** resembling marble; hard, cold, streaked, mottled, or unfeeling: *a marble heart, a marble cake*. **mar·ble·like** *adj*. ⟨Old French *marbre*; Greek *marmaros* gleaming stone⟩

march¹ [mɑrtʃ] *v* **1** walk in time and with equal steps. **2** proceed steadily. **3** cause to go: *The police officer marched the thief off to jail.* **4** advance or progress inexorably.
n **1** the movement of troops: *The army is prepared for the march*. **2** *Music* a composition to march to, usually in 4/4 time. **3** a long, hard walk. **4** a demonstration made by walking. **5** inexorable advance or progress: *History records the march of events*. **march·er** *n*. ⟨Old French *marchier* to tread⟩
on the march advancing inexorably.
marching orders a command to move on. **march·past** *n* a parade, in which troops, etc. march past a reviewing stand.

march² [mɑrtʃ] *n* land along the border of a

country. ⟨Old English *gemearc* boundary + Old French *marche* boundary; both Germanic⟩

March [mɑrtʃ] *n* the third month of the year. It has 31 days. ⟨Latin *Martius* of Mars⟩

Mar·di Gras ['mɑrdi 'grɑ] **1** the last day before Lent; Shrove Tuesday. **2** a traditional public carnival celebrating this day. ⟨French = fat (i.e., meat-eating) Tuesday⟩

mare¹ [mɛr] *n* a fully mature female horse, donkey, etc. ⟨Old English *mere*⟩

mare's–nest *n* **1** something supposed to be a great discovery that turns out to be a mistake or joke. **2** *Informal* a confused situation.

mare² ['mɑrei] *or* ['mɛrei] *n, pl* **ma·ri·a** ['mɑriə] *or* ['mɛriə] *Astronomy* one of the dark areas on the moon and Mars, thought by Galileo to be seas. ⟨Latin = sea⟩

mar·ga·rine ['mɑrdʒərɪn] *or* [,mɑrdʒə'rin] *n* a compound of vegetable oils, used as a substitute for butter. ⟨French⟩

mar·gin ['mɑrdʒən] *n* **1** an edge. **2** the blank space around the writing on a page. **3** an extra amount: *Allow a margin of 15 minutes to catch a train.* **4** the difference between the cost and selling price. **5** a condition beyond which something ceases to be possible: *the margin of subsistence.* ⟨Latin *margo, marginis* edge⟩
mar·gin·al *adj.* **1** to do with a margin. **2** barely acceptable or profitable. **3** slight. **mar·gin·al·i·ty** *n.* **mar·gin·al·ly** *adv.* **mar·gi·na·li·a** [,mɑrdʒə'neiliə] *n pl* notes written in the margin of a book, etc. **mar·gin·al·ize** *v* deprive of power or the opportunity to be involved; keep on the fringes of society or of any group. **mar·gin·al·i·za·tion** *n.*

mar·gue·rite [,mɑrgə'rit] *n* a garden plant of the composite family with daisylike flowers. ⟨French = daisy, pearl; Latin *margarita* pearl⟩

mar·i·gold ['mɛrɪ,gould] *or* ['mærɪ,gould] *n* any of various plants of the composite family, widely cultivated for their showy yellow, orange, or red flowers. ⟨Middle English *Mary* (the Virgin) + *gold*⟩

mar·i·jua·na or **mar·i·hua·na** [,mɛrə'wɒnə] *or* [,mærə'wɒnə] *n* **1** hemp. **2** the dried leaves and flowers of the female hemp plant, esp when smoked for its intoxicating effect. Compare CANNABIS, HASHISH. ⟨Mexican Spanish *mariguana, marihuana*⟩

ma·rim·ba [mə'rɪmbə] *n* a percussion instrument resembling a xylophone. ⟨Bantu⟩

ma·ri·na See MARINE.

mar·i·nate ['mɛrə,neit] *or* ['mærə,neit] *v* soak in brine, marinade, or oil and vinegar. ⟨French *mariner*; *marin* marine. See MARINE.⟩
mar·i·nade [,mɛrə'neid] *or* [,mærə'neid] *n* a spiced vinegar, wine, etc. in which meat, fish, etc. are soaked before being cooked. **mar·i·nade** ['mærə,neid] *or* ['mɛrə,neid] *v.*

ma·rine [mə'rin] *adj* to do with the sea, with shipping, or with a navy: *marine animals, marine law, marine power.*
n **1** shipping: *our merchant marine.* **2** a soldier

formerly serving only at sea, now also participating in land and air action: *Canada has no marines.* ⟨Latin *marina; mare* sea⟩
ma·ri·na [mə'rinə] *n* a place on a waterfront where pleasure boats may be moored and where fuel may be bought. **mar·i·ner** ['mɛrənər] *or* ['mærənər] *n* a sailor; seaman. **mar·i·time** ['mɛrə,taɪm] *or* ['mærə,taɪm] *adj* **1** on or near the sea: *St. John's is a maritime city.* **2** to do with the sea or with shipping and sailing: *maritime law.* **3** **Maritime** to do with the MARITIME PROVINCES. **Maritime Command** ✹ a major element of the Canadian Forces, whose role is to provide seagoing forces. **Maritime Provinces** the provinces along the east coast of Canada, including New Brunswick, Nova Scotia, and Prince Edward Island. **Mar·i·tim·er** *n* ✹ a native or long-term resident of these provinces. **Mar·i·times** *n* MARITIME PROVINCES.

USAGE
The Atlantic Provinces include the **Maritime Provinces** and Newfoundland and Labrador.

mar·i·o·nette [,mɛriə'nɛt] *or* [,mæriə'nɛt] *n* a puppet moved by strings. ⟨French; *Marie Mary*⟩

mar·i·tal See MARRY.

mar·jo·ram ['mɑrdʒərəm] *n* any of various plants of the mint family. ⟨Old French *majorane*, Latin *majorana, majoraca*⟩

mark [mɑrk] *n* **1** a trace made by some object on the surface of another. **2** an object, put as a sign. **3** something that indicates a quality: *Courtesy is a mark of good breeding.* **4** a grade or rating: *My mark in arithmetic was B.* **5** a target. **6** impression: *Great people leave their mark on whatever they do.* **7** *Informal* a person who is an easy prey for tricksters, etc. *v* **1** make a mark on: *Be careful not to mark the table.* **2** show by means of a sign. **3** give grades to. **4** *Archaic* notice: *Mark how carefully he moves.* **5** select as if by mark: *She was marked for promotion.* ⟨Old English *mearc*⟩ **beside the mark a** not relevant. **b** not precise. **hit the mark a** succeed in doing what one tried to do. **b** be exactly right. **make one's mark** become famous. **mark down** mark for sale at a lower price. **mark·down** *n, adj.* **mark off** or **out** make lines, etc. to show the position of. **mark (out) for** select for. **mark time a** move the feet as in marching, but stay in the same spot. **b** go through the motions without accomplishing anything. **mark up** mark for sale at a higher price. **mark·up** *n, adj.* **miss the mark a** fail to do what one tried to do. **b** be not exactly right. **of mark** important: *a woman of mark.* **wide of the mark a** inaccurate. **b** irrelevant.
marked *adj* **1** having a mark on it. **2** very noticeable: *a marked difference between a grape and an orange.* **3** distinguished as if by a mark: *marked for success.* **mark·ed·ly** ['mɑrkɪdli] *adv.* **mark·ed·ness** *n.* **marked man** a person who is picked out as someone to watch: *After he was spotted near the scene of the murder, he was a marked man.* **mark·er** *n* **1** a pen similar to a ballpoint, but with a tip made of felt. **2** a

person or thing that keeps the score in games. **3** *Slang* a pledge of future payment: *You hold my marker for $350.* **mark·ing** *n* arrangement of marks: *I like the marking on your cat's coat.* **marks·man** ['mɑrksmən] *n, pl -men* a person who shoots well. **marks·man·ship** *n*.

mar·ket ['mɑrkɪt] *n* **1** a meeting of people for the purpose of buying and selling: *a fruit market.* **2** a store for the sale of provisions: *a fish market.* **3** the demand (for goods): *enough milk to supply the market.* *v* sell: *He markets the goods he makes.* **mar·ket** *adj.* **mar·ket·er** *n.* **mar·ket·a·ble** *adj.* **mar·ket·a·bil·i·ty** *n.* ⟨Norman French; Latin *mercatus* trade; *merx, mercis* merchandise⟩ **be in the market for** be a possible buyer of: *He's in the market for a new car.* **play the market** speculate on the stock exchange. **price out of the market** lose business by setting a price above what buyers will pay: *We must not price our grain out of the market.* **mar·ket·ing** *n* **1** planning for the promotion, sale, and distribution of goods or services. **2** grocery shopping. **mar·ket·place** *n* **1** a place where a market is held. **2** the world of business and commerce. **market research** research that asks consumers what they like, as a guide to production. **market researcher.** **market value** or **price** the current price.

mar·lin ['mɑrlən] *n* any of several large marine fishes related to the sailfishes. ⟨short for *marlinespike* spike used to separate rope strands; Dutch *marren* tie + *lijn* line + SPIKE⟩

mar·ma·lade ['mɑrmə,leid] *n* a preserve made of oranges or other citrus fruit. ⟨Portuguese *marmelo* quince⟩

mar·mo·set ['mɑrmə,sɛt] or ['mɑrmə,zɛt] *n* any of numerous small monkeys having claws instead of nails, and a long, furry tail. ⟨Old French *marmouset* grotesque figurine⟩

mar·mot ['mɑrmət] *n* any of a genus of burrowing rodents belonging to the same family as squirrels, having a thickset body. ⟨French *marmottaine;* Latin *mus* (*muris*) *montanus* mouse of the mountains⟩

ma·roon[1] [mə'run] *n, adj* dark brownish red. ⟨Italian *marrone* chestnut⟩

ma·roon[2] [mə'run] *v* **1** put (a person) ashore in a lonely place and leave him or her there. **2** leave in a lonely, helpless position. *n* a descendant of escaped black slaves. ⟨American Spanish *cimarron* wild⟩

mar·quee [mɑr'ki] *n* **1** a large tent, often used for an outdoor party. **2** a rooflike shelter over an entrance, esp to a theatre. ⟨Old French *(tente) marquise* officers' tent⟩

mar·que·try ['mɑrkətri] *n* decoration made with thin pieces of wood, ivory, etc. fitted together to form a design on furniture. ⟨French *marqueter* inlay; *marque* mark⟩

mar·riage See MARRY[1].

mar·row ['mɛrou] or ['mærou] *n* **1** the soft tissue that fills the cavities of most bones. **2** the inmost part: *I was chilled to the marrow.* **3** VEGETABLE MARROW. ⟨Old English *mearg*⟩

mar·ry ['mɛri] or ['mæri] *v* **1** join as husband and wife. **2** unite closely. **mar·ried** *adj.* ⟨Old French *marier,* Latin *maritare; maritus* husband⟩ **mar·i·tal** ['mɛrətəl] or ['mærətəl] *adj* to do with marriage. **mar·i·tal·ly** *adv.* **mar·riage** ['mɛrɪdʒ] or ['mærɪdʒ] *n* **1** married life. **2** a wedding. **3** a close union: *the marriage of words and melody.* **mar·riage·a·ble** *adj* fit for or old enough to marry. **mar·riage·a·bil·i·ty** *n.*

Mars [mɑrz] *n* **1** *Roman myth* the god of war. **2** the planet next beyond the earth and fourth in order from the sun. **Mar·tian** ['mɑrʃən] *n* a supposed inhabitant of the planet Mars.

Mar·seil·laise [,mɑrsə'leiz] *French* [maʀsɛ'jɛz] *n* the national anthem of France. ⟨*Marseilles*⟩

marsh [mɑrʃ] *n* an area of wet, muddy land sometimes partly covered with water. ⟨Old English *mersc; mere* lake⟩ **marsh gas** methane. **marsh·land** *n* marshy land. **marsh·mal·low** ['mɑrʃ,mɛlou] or [-,mælou] *n* a confection orig made from the root of the MARSH MALLOW. **marsh mallow** a perennial herb of the mallow family, with a root that secretes a gummy substance. **marsh rabbit** or **hare** ✱ muskrat, esp when eaten as food. **marsh·y** *adj* **1** soft and wet like a marsh. **2** of marshes. **marsh·i·ness** *n.*

mar·shal ['mɑrʃəl] *n* **1** an officer; person in charge: *a fire marshal.* **2** in the armed forces, an officer of high rank: *a field marshal.* *v* **-shalled** or **-shaled, -shal·ling** or **-shal·ing** **1** arrange properly: *to marshal arguments for a debate.* **2** arrange in military order: *to marshal troops.* **mar·shal·ler** or **mar·shal·er** *n.* ⟨Old French *mareschal;* Latin *mariscalcus* groom⟩

mar·su·pi·al [mɑr'supiəl] *n* any of an order of mammals whose young are born at a very early stage of development, continuing their growth while inside a pouch, or marsupium. **mar·su·pi·al** *adj.*

mart [mɑrt] *n* a market; a centre of trade. ⟨Middle Dutch, variant of *markt* market⟩

mar·ten ['mɑrtən] *n, pl* **-tens** or (esp collectively) **-ten** any of several small carnivorous mammals related to the weasels. ⟨Dutch *martren,* Old French *martrine*⟩

mar·tial ['mɑrʃəl] *adj* **1** to do with war: *martial music.* **2** fond of fighting: *martial spirit.* **mar·tial·ly** *adv.* ⟨Latin *Mars, Martis* Mars, god of war⟩ **martial art** any form of exercise used for self-defence, such as karate, judo, etc. **martial law** temporary rule by the army instead of by the usual civil authorities.

Mar·tian See MARS.

mar·tin ['mɑrtən] *n* any of various swallows. ⟨for its migration around feast of St. Martin⟩

mar·ti·net [,mɑrtə'nɛt] or ['mɑrtə,nɛt] *n* a person who enforces very strict discipline. ⟨Jean *Martinet* 17c French general⟩

mar·ti·ni [mɑr'tini] *n* a cocktail made of gin and dry vermouth. ⟨*Martini* and Rossi, vermouth and wine makers⟩

mar·tyr ['mɑrtər] *n* **1** a person who chooses

to die or suffer rather than renounce his or her faith. **2** a person who suffers great pain or anguish. **3** a person who puts on a false appearance of suffering to attract attention. *v* **1** torture or kill (a person) because of his or her beliefs. **2** torture. **mar·tyr·dom** *n.* **mar·tyr·like** *adj.* ⟨Greek = witness⟩

mar·vel ['mɑrvəl] *n* an astonishing thing: *Television is one of the marvels of invention.* *v* **-velled** or **-veled, -vel·ling** or **-vel·ing** be astonished: *She marvelled at the beautiful sunset.* ⟨Old French *merveil;* Latin *mirabilia* wonders, *mirus* strange⟩ **mar·vel·lous** or **mar·vel·ous** *adj* **1** causing wonder. **2** *Informal* excellent: *a marvellous time.* **mar·vel·lous·ly** or **·mar·vel·ous·ly** *adv.* **mar·vel·lous·ness** or **mar·vel·ous·ness** *n.*

Marx·ism ['mɑrksɪzəm] *n* the political and economic theories of Karl Marx (1818-1883) and Friedrich Engels (1820-1895), German writers who believed in communal ownership of all resources. **Marx·ist** *n, adj.*

mar·zi·pan ['mɑrzə,pæn] or ['mɑrdzə,pæn] *n* a paste of ground almonds and sugar. ⟨German; Italian *marzapane* medieval coin⟩

mas·car·a [mæ'skɛrə] or [mæ'skærə] *n* a cosmetic for darkening the eyelashes. ⟨Spanish *máscara* mask⟩

mas·cot ['mæskɒt] or ['mæskət] *n* **1** an animal, person, or thing supposed to bring good luck. **2** anything adopted as a symbol. ⟨Provençal *mascotto,* little witch⟩

mas·cu·line ['mæskjəlɪn] *adj* **1** having qualities considered characteristic of men. **2** mannish. **3** *Grammar* to do with the grammatical gender that includes words for male persons and animals. Compare FEMININE, NEUTER. **mas·cu·line·ly** *adv.* **mas·cu·lin·i·ty** *n.* ⟨Latin *masculinus; mas* male⟩

ma·ser ['meizər] *n* a device for amplifying microwaves to produce a narrow, intense beam of radiation. ⟨*m*icrowave *a*mplification by *s*timulated *e*mission of *r*adiation⟩

mash [mæʃ] *n* **1** a soft mixture. **2** any mixture of ground grain used as feed for poultry, livestock, etc. **3** crushed malt or meal soaked in water for making beer or whisky. *v* **1** beat into a soft mass. **2** mix (crushed malt or meal) with water in brewing. **mash·er** *n.* ⟨Old English *māsc-*⟩

mas·jid ['mʌsdʒɪd] *n* mosque. Also, **mus·jid.** ⟨Arabic⟩

mask [mæsk] *n* **1** a covering for the face, worn for disguise or in fun: *a Halloween mask.* **2** anything that disguises: *He hid his evil plans under a mask of friendship.* **3** a covering for the face, worn for protection: *a surgical mask.* **4** a device covering the nose and mouth, designed to aid breathing: *an oxygen mask.* **5** a cosmetic preparation spread over the face to recondition the skin. *v* **1** hide; disguise: *A smile masked her disappointment.* **2** cover with masking tape: *We masked the edges of the window panes before painting the frame.* **mask·er** *n.* **mask·like** *adj.* ⟨Latin *masca* mask, ghost⟩

masked *adj* **1** wearing a mask: *a masked gunman.* **2** hidden or disguised: *masked jealousy.* **masking tape** adhesive tape used to cover areas that are not to be painted.

mas·kin·onge ['mæskə,nɒndʒ] *n, pl* **mas·kin·onge** ✷ muskellunge. ⟨Cdn. French *masquinongé;* Algonkian⟩

mas·och·ism ['mæsə,kɪzəm] *n* a condition in which sexual pleasure results from being beaten, dominated, etc. Compare SADISM. **mas·och·ist** *n.* **mas·o·chis·tic** *adj.* **mas·o·chis·ti·cal·ly** *adv.* ⟨L. Von Sacher-*Masoch* 19c Austrian novelist who described it.⟩ .

ma·son ['meisən] *n* **1** a person whose work is building with stone, brick, or similar materials. **2** Usually, **Mason** Freemason. ⟨Old French *masson* Latin *machionis,* Germanic.⟩ **Ma·son·ite** ['meisə,nɑit] *n Trademark* a wood fibre pressed into sheets and used in building. **ma·son·ry** *n* **1** stonework, brickwork, etc. **2** something constructed of stone, brick, etc., such as a chimney or wall.

mas·quer·ade [,mæskə'reid] *n* **1** a party at which masks and fancy costumes are worn. **2** a false pretence; disguise. *v* go about under false pretences: *The prince masqueraded as a beggar.* **mas·quer·ad·er** *n.* ⟨Spanish *mascarada, mascara* mask⟩

mass¹ [mæs] *n* **1** a lump. **2** a large quantity together: *a mass of flowers.* **3** the majority. **4** bulk; size. **5** *Physics* a measure of the amount of matter a body contains. **6 the masses** the general population: *Most television programs are made for the masses.* *adj* **1** done on a large scale: *a mass protest.* **2** to do with the general population: *a book designed for a mass market.* *v* assemble. ⟨Latin *massa* lump of kneaded dough Greek *maza; massein* knead⟩ **in the mass** as a whole. **mass–energy equation** *Physics* the equivalence expressed by the Einstein equation $E = mc^2$. **mass·less** *adj Physics* having no mass. **mass·less·ness** *n.* **mass market** the general population considered as a homogeneous market for goods or services. **mass-mar·ket** *adj.* **mass media** the various modern means of communication that reach a vast audience. **mass noun** *Grammar* a noun that stands for something which cannot be counted, such as *milk.* **mass production** the making of goods in quantity by machinery. **mass–pro·duce** *v.* **mass–pro·duc·er** *n.*

USAGE

A **mass noun** cannot be used with an indefinite article or in the plural.

Mass or **mass²** [mæs] *n* the central service of worship in the Roman Catholic Church and some other Christian churches. ⟨Old English *mæsse;* Latin *missa* pp of *mittere* send away⟩

mas·sa·cre ['mæsəkər] *n* a wholesale slaughter of people or animals. **mas·sa·cre** *v.* ⟨French; Old French *macecle* slaughterhouse⟩

mas·sage [mə'sɑʒ] or [mə'sɑdʒ] *v* **1** knead the body to make muscles and joints more supple. **2** manipulate (statistics, data, etc.).

mas·sage *n.* ⟨French; *masser* knead. See MASS¹.⟩
massage parlour 1 an establishment offering
body rubs. **2** a euphemism for a brothel.
mas·seur [mæ'sɜr] *or* [mə'sɜr] *French* [ma'sœʀ]
n a man whose work is massaging. **mas·seuse**
[mæ'sʊz], [mə'suz], *or* [mə'sus] *French* [ma'søz] *n*
a woman whose work is massaging.

mas·sa·sau·ga [ˌmæsə'sɒgə] *n* ✳ a small
rattlesnake found in southern Ontario.
⟨*Mississauga* River, Ontario; Ojibwa *misi* great
+ *sauk* river mouth⟩

mas·sif ['mæsɪf] *French* [ma'sif] *n Geology* **1** a
main part or mass of a mountain range. **2** a
large block of the earth's crust that has
shifted as a unit and is bounded by faults.
⟨French = massive⟩

mas·sive ['mæsɪv] *adj* **1** big and heavy: *a
massive building*. **2** imposing; impressive.
3 extensive: *a massive assault*. **4** *Geology*
without definite structural divisions.
mas·sive·ly *adv.* **mas·sive·ness** *n.*

mast¹ [mæst] *n* **1** a long pole set upright to
support the sails and rigging of a ship. **2** any
upright pole: *a flag mast, a TV mast*. **mast·less**
adj. **mast·like** *adj.* ⟨Old English *mæst*⟩
before the mast *Archaic* serving as an
ordinary sailor. Sailors (not officers) used to
sleep in the forward part of the ship.
mast·head *n* **1** *Nautical* the top of a ship's
mast. **2** the part of a newspaper or magazine
that gives the title, the names of the owners
and editors, and the publication address.

mast² [mæst] *n* acorns, chestnuts, etc. that
have accumulated on the ground. ⟨Old
English *mæst*⟩

mas·tec·to·my [mæ'stɛktəmi] *n* the surgical
removal of a breast. ⟨Greek *mastos* breast +
-ECTOMY⟩

mas·ter ['mæstər] *n* **1** a person who has
power or authority. **2** the captain of a
merchant ship. **3** a great artist, or a picture
by a great artist: *an old master*. **4** an expert.
5 the Master Jesus. **6** an initial recording,
stencil, etc. used for making duplications.
adj **1** of or by a master. **2** main; controlling: *a
master switch, a master plan*.
v **1** conquer; control. **2** become expert in.
mas·ter·dom *n.* **mas·ter·less** *adj.* ⟨Old French
maistre, Latin *magister; magis* more⟩
mas·ter–at–arms *n, pl* **mas·ters–at–arms** a
naval police officer who keeps order on a
ship. **mas·ter·ful** *adj* **1** fond of power or
authority. **2** expert: *a masterful performance*.
mas·ter·ful·ly *adv.* **mas·ter·ful·ness** *n.* **master
key** a key that opens all the different locks in
a building. **mas·ter·ly** *adj* expert: *a masterly
painter*. **mas·ter·ly** *adv.* **mas·ter·li·ness** *n.*
mas·ter·mind *n* a person who plans and
directs a complex project. **mas·ter·mind** *v.*
master of ceremonies a person in charge of a
ceremony who announces the successive
events and makes sure that they take place in
the proper order. *Abbrev* **M.C. mas·ter·piece** *n*
1 anything done or made with wonderful
skill. **2** a person's greatest work. **master
stroke** a very skilful act or achievement.
mas·ter·y *n* **1** control. **2** victory: *Two teams*

competed for mastery. **3** great skill: *Our teacher
has a mastery of many subjects*.

mas·tic ['mæstɪk] *n* **1** a resin used in making
varnish, chewing gum, incense, and as an
astringent. **2** any of various cements. ⟨Greek
mastichē chewing gum⟩
mas·ti·cate *v* **1** chew. **2** crush to a pulp.
mas·ti·ca·ble ['mæstəkəbəl] *adj.*
mas·ti·ca·tion *n.*

mas·to·don ['mæstəˌdɒn] *n* any of several
extinct elephantlike mammals that
flourished from the Miocene to the
Pleistocene epochs. ⟨Greek *mastos* breast +
odōn tooth; for projections on its molars⟩

mas·toid ['mæstɔɪd] *n* the projection of bone
behind the ear. ⟨Greek *mastos* breast; for its
form⟩

mas·tur·bate [ˌmæstər'beit] *n* manipulate
the genitals to induce sexual gratification.
mas·tur·ba·tion *n.* **mas·tur·ba·tor** *n.* ⟨Latin
masturbari; manus hand + *stuprare* defile⟩

mat¹ [mæt] *n* **1** a piece of coarse fabric like a
rug, made of straw, rope, etc. **2** a piece of
material to put under a dish, vase, lamp, etc.
3 a large, thick pad on the floor of a ring, etc.
to protect wrestlers or gymnasts. **4** anything
packed thickly together: *a mat of hair*.
v **mat·ted, mat·ting** pack or tangle together
like a mat: *The swimmer's wet hair was matted*.
⟨Old English *matt;* Latin *matta*⟩

mat² [mæt] *n* a border for a picture, usually
between the picture and the frame. ⟨See
MATTE.⟩
v **mat·ted, mat·ting** put a mat around.

mat·a·dor ['mætəˌdɔr] *n* the chief performer
in a bullfight. ⟨Spanish; Latin *mactātor;
mactāre* kill⟩

match¹ [mætʃ] *n* a short piece of wood or
paper tipped with a mixture that takes fire
when rubbed on a rough or prepared surface.
⟨Old French *mesche*; Greek *myxa* wick⟩
match·book *n* a paper folder to hold safety
matches. **match·box** *n* a cardboard box for
matches. **match·stick** *n* a thin stick of wood
from which a match is made. **match·wood** *n*
1 wood for making matches. **2** splinters.

match² [mætʃ] *n* **1** a person or thing equal to
another. **2** two persons or things that go well
together. **3** a contest: *a tennis match*.
4 marriage: *She made a good match*.
v **1** be equal to. **2** go well together. **3** find one
like. **4** fit together. **5** oppose. **match·a·ble** *adj.*
match·less *adj.* **match·less·ly** *adv.*
match·less·ness *n.* ⟨Old English *(ge)mæcca*
companion⟩
match·mak·er *n* a person who arranges
marriages for others. **match·mak·ing** *n, adj.*
match point *Tennis, golf, etc.* the final point
needed to win a match.

mate¹ [meit] *n* **1** one of a pair. **2** a husband
or wife. **3** *Nautical* a ship's officer next below
the captain. **4** a companion or fellow worker:
Those two were mates in the army.
v **1** put or come together as a pair: *Birds mate
in the spring*. **2** marry. **mate·less** *adj.* ⟨Middle
Low German *mate* messmate. Related to MEAT.⟩

mate² [meit] *Chess* *n* a checkmate. *v* checkmate; defeat. ⟨Old French. See MATTE.⟩

ma·te·ri·al [mə'tiriəl] *n* **1** what a thing is made from: *building materials.* **2** cloth. **3** anything serving as raw matter for working upon: *enough material for a book.* *adj* **1** of matter; physical. **2** of the body: *Food and shelter are material comforts.* **3** to do with the things of this world rather than with spiritual things. **4** important: *Hard work is a material factor in success.* **5** *Law* likely to influence a case: *material evidence.* ⟨Latin *materia* timber, matter *mater* trunk (of tree)⟩ **ma·te·ri·al·ism** *n* a tendency to care more for material possessions than for spiritual needs. **ma·te·ri·al·ist** *n.* **ma·te·ri·al·is·tic** *adj.* **ma·te·ri·al·is·ti·cal·ly** *adv.* **ma·te·ri·al·ize** *v* **1** become an actual fact: *Our plans did not materialize.* **2** appear or cause to appear in bodily form: *A spirit materialized from the smoke of the wizard's fire.* **ma·te·ri·al·i·za·tion** *n.* **ma·te·ri·al·ly** *adv* **1** physically. **2** considerably. **3** *Philosophy* in substance; not in form. **ma·té·ri·el** [mə,tiri'el] *n* equipment.

ma·ter·nal [mə'tɜrnəl] *adj* **1** motherly. **2** related on the mother's side of the family: *maternal grandparents.* **3** inherited from a mother. **ma·ter·nal·ly** *adv.* ⟨Latin *mater* mother⟩ **ma·ter·ni·ty** *n* **1** motherhood. **2** motherliness. *adj* **1** for an expectant mother: *a maternity dress.* **2** for women in and after childbirth: *a maternity ward.* **maternity leave** paid leave of absence from work for a mother before and after the baby is born.

math·e·mat·ics [,mæθə'mætɪks] *n* (with a sg verb) the science dealing with the properties and relationships of quantities. **math·e·ma·ti·cian** [,mæθəmə'tɪʃən] *n.* ⟨Greek *mathēmatos* learning, knowledge⟩ **math·e·mat·i·cal** *adj* **1** to do with mathematics. **2** exact; accurate. **math·e·mat·i·cal·ly** *adv.*

mat·i·née or **mat·i·nee** [,mætə'nei] *or* ['mætə,nei] *n* a performance held in the afternoon. ⟨French; *matin* morning⟩

ma·tins ['mætənz] *n pl* **1** *Roman Catholic Church* the first of the canonical hours in the breviary. **2** *Anglican Church* morning service. ⟨Latin *matutinus* of or in the morning⟩

ma·tri·arch ['meitri,ark] *n* **1** a mother who is the ruler of a family or tribe. **2** a venerable old woman. **ma·tri·ar·chal** *adj.* ⟨Latin *mater* mother) + Greek *-arkhes* ruler⟩ **ma·tri·ar·chate** ['meitri,arkɪt] *n* a society governed by women. **ma·tri·ar·chy** *n* a form of social organization in which descent is traced through the mother, as the ruler of the - the act of killing one's mother. **ma·tri·cid·al** *adj.* **ma·tri·lin·e·al** [,mætrə'lɪniəl] *adj* to do with kinship through the maternal line: *a matrilineal tradition.* Compare PATRILINEAL. **ma·tri·lin·e·al·ly** *adv.* **mat·ri·mo·ny** ['mætrə,mouni] *n* **1** married life. **2** the act of marrying. **mat·ri·mo·ni·al** *adj.* **mat·ri·mo·ni·al·ly** *adv.*

ma·tri·ces ['meitrə,siz] *n pl* of MATRIX.

ma·tric·u·late [mə'trɪkjə,leit] *v* enrol as a student in a college or university. **ma·tric·u·la·tor** *n.* ⟨Latin *matricula*, diminutive of Latin *matrix* register⟩

ma·trix ['meitrɪks] *n, pl* **ma·tri·ces** ['meitrə,siz] or **ma·trix·es** **1** that which gives form to something enclosed within it. The rock in which gems are embedded is called a matrix. **2** a series of related things, as mathematical terms, arranged in a rectangular array of rows and columns. ⟨Latin = womb⟩

ma·tron ['meitrən] *n* **1** a married woman or widow, esp a dignified older woman. **2** a woman who supervises the inmates of a school, hospital, or other institution. **ma·tron·ly** *adj.* **ma·tron·li·ness** *n.* ⟨Latin *matrona; mater* mother⟩ **matron of honour** or **honor** a married woman who is the chief attendant of the bride at a wedding.

matte [mæt] *adj* dull; not glossy. *n* a dull surface. ⟨French *mat, matte* dull, dead⟩

mat·ter ['mætər] *n* **1** the substance of the material world. **2** an instance: *a matter of fact.* **3** things written or printed: *reading matter.* **4** importance. **5** a substance secreted by a living body, esp pus. *v* be important: *Nothing seems to matter when you are very sick.* ⟨Anglo-French *matere;* Latin *materia.* See MATERIAL.⟩ **as a matter of fact.** See FACT. **for that matter** so far as that is concerned. **matter of life and death** something of crucial importance. **matter of opinion** a debatable assertion. **no matter a** it is not important. **b** regardless of: *He wants a car, no matter what it costs.* **what is the matter?** what is wrong? **matter of course** something that follows inevitably. **matter–of–course** *adj.* **mat·ter–of–fact** *adj* not imaginative: *a matter-of-fact report.* **mat·ter–of–fact·ly** *adv.* **mat·ter–of–fact·ness** *n.*

mat·tock ['mætək] *n* a tool like a pickaxe, used for loosening soil and cutting roots. ⟨Old English *mattuc*⟩

mat·tress ['mætrɪs] *n* a thick, soft, or resilient pad used to form a bed. ⟨Italian *materasso;* Arabic *matrah* cushion⟩

ma·ture [mə'tʃʊr] *adj* **1** ripe, full-grown or in full excellence: *mature forest.* **2** having full development of the body, mind, etc.: *mature thinking.* **3** due; payable: *a mature loan.* **ma·ture** *v.* **ma·ture·ly** *adv.* **ma·tu·ri·ty** *n.* ⟨Latin *maturus* ripe⟩ **mat·u·ra·tion** [,mætʃə'reiʃən] *n* **1** a discharge of pus. **2** a maturing. **mat·u·ra·tion·al** *adj.*

matz·o ['matsou] *n, pl* **matz·oth** ['matsout] or **matz·os** ['matsouz] a thin piece of unleavened bread, eaten esp during Passover. ⟨Hebrew *matstsōth,* pl of *matstsāh,* a cake of unleavened bread⟩

maud·lin ['mɒdlɪn] *adj* **1** sentimental in a silly way: *maudlin sympathy.* **2** sentimental and tearful as a result of drinking too much alcoholic liquor. ⟨alteration of Mary *Magdalene,* often painted as weeping⟩

maul [mɒl] *v* beat and pull about: *The lion mauled its keeper badly.* *n* a very heavy hammer or mallet. ⟨Middle English *malle;* Old French *mail* mallet⟩

maun·der ['mɒndər] *v* talk in a rambling, foolish way. **maun·der·er** *n.* ⟨origin uncertain⟩

mau·so·le·um [,mɒzə'liəm] *or* [,mɒsə'liəm] *n,* *pl* **-le·ums** *or* **-le·a** [-'liə] **1** Mausoleum the tomb of King Mausolos, one of the seven wonders of the ancient world. **2** a large, magnificent tomb. ⟨Greek *Mausōleion*⟩

mauve [mouv] *n, adj* delicate, pale purple. ⟨French Latin *malva* mallow⟩

ma·ven *or* **ma·vin** ['meivən] *n* a person who knows all about a certain subject: *a railway maven.* ⟨Yiddish Hebrew, connoisseur⟩

mav·er·ick ['mævrɪk] *n* **1** a calf or other animal not marked with an owner's brand. **2** *Informal* one who refuses to affiliate with a regular political party. **3** *Informal* any person or organization that is unwilling to conform. ⟨probably S. *Maverick* 19c Texan rancher⟩

maw [mɒ] *n* **1** the mouth and throat of an animal, esp a carnivorous animal. **2** the stomach of an animal or bird. **3** anything thought of as resembling this in appetite: *Nations continue to pour wealth into the maw of war.* ⟨Old English *maga*⟩

mawk·ish ['mɒkɪʃ] *adj* **1** sickening. **2** sickly sentimental. **mawk·ish·ly** *adv.* **mawk·ish·ness** *n.* ⟨dialect *mawk* maggot, Old Norse *mathkr*⟩

max. maximum.

max·i ['mæksi] *n Informal* anything that is the biggest of a series or of its kind.

max·il·la [mæk'sɪlə] *n, pl* **max·il·lae** [-'sɪli] *or* [-'sɪlaɪ] **1** in vertebrates, the jaw; upper jawbone. **2** either of a pair of appendages just behind the mandibles of insects, crabs, etc. **max·il·lar·y** ['mæksə,lɛri] *or* [mæk'sɪləri] *adj, n.* ⟨Latin *maxilla* jaw⟩

max·im ['mæksəm] *n* a short rule of conduct; proverb: *"Look before you leap"* is a maxim. ⟨Latin *maxima propositio* greatest proposition⟩

max·i·mum ['mæksəməm] *n, pl* **-mums** *or* **-ma 1** the upper limit: *a maximum of $1000.* **2** *Mathematics* the greatest value of a function within a given interval of the domain. *adj* greatest possible: *The maximum score on the test is 100.* ⟨Latin = greatest⟩ **max·i·mal** *adj* being the greatest possible. **max·i·mal·ly** *adv.* **max·i·mize** *v* **1** increase as much as possible. **2** treat as important. **max·i·mi·za·tion** *n.* **max·i·miz·er** *n.*

may [mei] *auxiliary v* **might** May is used to express: **1** opportunity or permission: *You may enter.* **2** a wish or prayer: *May you be very happy.* **3** contingency, esp in clauses expressing condition, etc.: *I write so that you may know my plans.* ⟨Old English *mæg*⟩

May [mei] *n* the fifth month of the year. It has 31 days. ⟨Latin *Maius*⟩ **may·ap·ple** *or* **May apple** *n* a herb of the barberry family, having an edible fruit. **May Day** May 1, traditionally celebrated as a festival of spring. **may·flow·er** *n* **1** TRAILING ARBUTUS. **2** Mayflower the ship on which the Pilgrim Fathers came to America in 1620. **may·fly** *n* any of an order of insects the larva of which is aquatic. **May·pole** *or* **may·pole** *n* **1** a high pole decorated with flowers and ribbons, around which merrymakers dance on May Day. **2** ✽ lobstick. **May queen** a girl honoured as queen on May Day.

Ma·ya ['maɪə] *n, pl* **Ma·ya** *or* **Ma·yas** a member of a group of peoples mainly of Yucatán, Belize, and Guatemala, who speak Mayan languages. **Ma·yan** ['maɪən] *n* a language family of Mexico and Central America. **Ma·yan** *adj.*

may·be ['meibi] *or* ['mɛbi] *adv* perhaps.

CONFUSABLES
Maybe is an adverb meaning 'perhaps': *Maybe you'll have better luck next time.* **May be** is a verb form: *I may be there.*

May·day ['mei,dei] *n* an international signal of distress, used in emergencies by ships and aircraft. ⟨French *m'aider* help me⟩

may·hem ['meihɛm] *n* confusion and willful violence. ⟨Anglo-French *mahaym* maim; origin uncertain⟩

ma·yo ['meiou] *n Informal* mayonnaise.

may·on·naise ['meiə,neiz] *or* [,meiə'neiz] *n* a dressing for salads, made of egg yolks, oil, vinegar or lemon juice, and seasoning. ⟨French; *Mahón*, seaport in Minorca⟩

may·or ['meiər] *n* the person at the head of the government of a city, town, or village. ⟨Old French *maire, maor;* Latin *major.*⟩ **may·or·al·ty** *n* **1** the position of mayor. **2** a mayor's term of office.

maze [meiz] *n* **1** a complicated network of paths. **2** any complicated arrangement. **3** a state of confusion. ⟨variant of *amaze*⟩ **maz·y** ['meizi] *adj* like a maze, intricate: *mazy paths.* **maz·i·ly** *adv.* **maz·i·ness** *n.*

MB 1 *Computers* megabyte. **2** Manitoba.

M.C. 1 Military Cross. **2** MASTER OF CEREMONIES.

McCar·thy·ism [mə'karθi,ɪzəm] *n* the act of making sensational public accusations of political disloyalty or corruption. ⟨J.R. McCarthy (1909-1957), chair of US Senate Permanent Investigations Committee⟩

Mc·Coy [mə'kɔɪ] *n Informal* **the real McCoy** a genuine person or thing. ⟨origin uncertain⟩

Mc·In·tosh ['mækɪn,tɒʃ] *n* ✽ a bright red winter apple having crisp, white flesh. Also called **McIntosh Red.** ⟨John *McIntosh*, 18c Ontario farmer⟩

me [mi] *pron* the objective form of I: *The dog bit me. This is for you and me.* ⟨Old English *mē*⟩

USAGE
It is good English to say **It is me** (or **It's me**) in speech, though some people consider **It is I** to be correct in writing. On the other hand, **me** is always the correct form to use as the object (of a verb or of a preposition): *between you and me.* In this situation, some speakers mistakenly use *between you and I.*

mead [mid] *n* an alcoholic drink made from fermented honey. ⟨Old English *medu*⟩

mead·ow ['mɛdou] *n* a piece of grassy land. **mead·ow·less** *adj.* **mead·ow·y** *adj.* ⟨Old English *mǣdwe*⟩

mead·ow·lark either of two songbirds of the blackbird family.

mea·gre ['migər] *adj* **1** scanty: *a meagre meal.* **2** thin: *a meagre face.* Also, **mea·ger.** **mea·gre·ly** *adv.* **mea·gre·ness** *n.* ⟨Old French *maigre*; Latin *macer* thin⟩

meal¹ [mil] *n* breakfast, lunch, dinner, supper, or tea. ⟨Old English *mǣl*⟩ **meal ticket** *Slang* someone or something that provides a living for another. **meal·time** *n* the usual time for eating a meal.

meal² [mil] *n* **1** ground grain. **2** anything ground to a powder. ⟨Old English *melu*⟩ **meal·y** *adj* **1** like meal; powdery. **2** of or covered with meal. **3** pale. **meal·i·ness** *n.* **meal·y–mouthed** [,mauðd] *or* [,mʌuθt] *adj* using insincere words.

mean¹ [min] *v* **meant, mean·ing 1** signify: *What does this word mean?* **2** indicate: *Keep out; that means you.* **3** communicate: *What is that look supposed to mean?* **4** intend: *I do not mean to go.* **5** design for a definite purpose: *a toy meant for young children.* **6** destine: *Fate meant us for each other.* ⟨Old English *mǣnan*⟩ **mean well by** have kindly feelings toward. **mean·ing** *n* significance. *adj* expressive: *a meaning look.* **mean·ing·ly** *adv.* **mean·ing·ful** *adj.* **mean·ing·ful·ly** *adv.* **mean·ing·ful·ness** *n.* **mean·ing·less** *adj* **1** without meaning. **2** not significant. **mean·ing·less·ly** *adv.* **mean·ing·less·ness** *n.*

mean² [min] *adj* **1** stingy. **2** ill-tempered and selfish; vicious; unkind. **3** *Slang* expert: *She plays a mean guitar.* **4** small-minded: *mean thoughts.* **5** *Informal* hard to manage: *a mean horse.* **6** low in quality or grade; of poor appearance: *a mean house.* **7** low in social position: *of mean birth.* **8** of little importance: *the meanest flower.* **mean·ly** *adv.* **mean·ness** *adj.* ⟨Old English *(ge)mǣne* common⟩ **no mean** very good: *no mean artist.* **mean·ie** *n Informal* a mean person.

mean³ [min] *adj* **1** average: *The mean temperature for July in Yarmouth is 16.4°C.* **2** intermediate in kind, quality, or degree. *n* **1** the average: *the mean for the course.* **2** a condition halfway between two extremes: *the golden mean.* **3** **means** the method by which something is brought about (with a sg or plural verb): *a means of transportation.* **4** **means** *pl* **a** money resources: *to live within one's means.* **b** wealth: *a woman of means.* ⟨Old French *meien*; Latin *medianus* middle⟩ **by all means** certainly. **by any means** in any possible way. **by means of** by the use of: *by means of a notice in the paper.* **by no means** certainly not: *by no means easy.* **means to an end** a way of getting or doing something. **means test** an inquiry into the income of a person applying for public funds. **mean·time** *n* the time between: *The carnival opens Friday; in the meantime we will make our costumes.*

adv meanwhile. **mean·while** *adv* **1** in the time between: *Classes finish at 12 and start again at 2; meanwhile we can have lunch.* **2** at the same time, esp in a different place.

USAGE
Means meaning 'what a thing is done by' is plural in form, and singular or plural in use: *A means of communication is lacking. The means of helping others are never lacking.* **Means** meaning 'wealth' is plural in form and in use: *His means permit him to live well.*

me·an·der [mi'ændər] *v* **1** follow a winding course: *A brook meanders through the meadow.* **2** wander aimlessly: *We meandered along.* **me·an·der** *n.* **me·an·der·er** *n.* **me·an·der·ing** *adj.* ⟨Greek *Maiandros*, winding river in Asia Minor⟩

mea·sles ['mizəlz] *n* (with a sg verb) an infectious disease characterized by red spots on the skin. ⟨Middle English *mesel* spot⟩ **mea·sly** ['mizli] *adj* **1** to do with measles. **2** *Slang* meagre: *He earns a measly $5 per hour.* **3** *Slang* poor: *a measly performance.*

meas·ure ['mɛʒər] *v* **1** find out the size, quantity, etc. of (something). **2** be of specified dimensions: *This brick measures 5 cm by 10 cm by 20 cm.* **3** assess: *to measure a person's character by his or her actions.* *n* **1** the process of finding the size, quantity, etc. of something. **2** the size, dimensions, etc. thus found: *His waist measure is 70 cm.* **3** a system of measuring: *dry measure.* **4** a unit of measuring. *Centimetre, kilogram, litre,* and *hour* are measures. **5** quantity; extent: *The measure of her courage was remarkable.* **6** rhythm, as in poetry or music: *the stately measure of blank verse.* **7** *Music* **a** a unit of rhythm, consisting of one strong beat and one or more weak beats. **b** a bar. **8** a dance or dance movement. **9** a course of action: *take measures to relieve suffering.* **meas·ur·a·ble** *adj.* **meas·ur·a·bil·i·ty** *n,* **meas·ur·a·bly** *adv.* **meas·ur·er** *n.* ⟨Old French *mesure,* Latin *mensura; mensus,* pp of *metiri* measure, v⟩ **beyond measure** beyond a reasonable limit. **for good measure** as something extra. **full measure** all it should be. **in some measure** partly. **made to measure** of a garment, custom-made. **measure out a** distribute by measuring. **b** distribute carefully. **measure up** meet a required standard: *The party did not measure up to her expectations.* **take measures** do something: *The police are taking measures to counteract street fighting.* **take someone's measure** judge someone's character or abilities. **meas·ured** *adj* **1** regular. **2** rhythmical. **3** deliberate and restrained. **meas·ured·ly** *adv.* **meas·ured·ness** *adj.* **meas·ure·less** *adj* too great to be measured. **meas·ure·less·ly** *adv.* **meas·ure·less·ness** *n.* **meas·ure·ment** *n* **1** the act of measuring. **2** the size found by measuring: *The measurements of the room are 6 m by 4.5 m.* **measuring cup** a pitcher with a scale for making measurements.

meat [mit] *n* **1** animal flesh used as food. **2** *Poetic* food of any kind: *meat and drink.* **3** the part that can be eaten: *the meat of a nut.*

4 the essential part: *the meat of an argument.*
meat·less *adj.* ⟨Old English *mete*⟩
meat·ball *n* ground meat shaped into a ball.
meat·loaf or **meat loaf** *n* ground meat mixed with breadcrumbs and spices and baked.
meat·y *adj* **1** giving food for thought: *The speech was very meaty; it contained many ideas.* **2** heavily fleshed. **meat·i·ly** *adv.*

Mec·ca [ˈmɛkə] *n* **1** the birthplace of Muhammad and holy city of the Muslims. **2** mecca, a place that many people visit: *a tourist mecca.* **3** mecca, a place that many people long for as a goal.

me·chan·ic [məˈkænɪk] *n* a worker who repairs machinery. ⟨Greek *mēchanē* machine⟩
me·chan·i·cal *adj* **1** to do with machinery. **2** automatic; without expression: *Her reading is very mechanical.* **me·chan·i·cal·ly** *adv.*
mechanical advantage the ratio of the output of a machine to the input. **mechanical engineering** the branch of engineering that deals with machines. **me·chan·ics** *n* (with a sg verb) **1** the branch of physics dealing with motion, including kinematics, kinetics, and statics. **2** the mechanical or technical part of something: *the mechanics of playing the piano.*
mech·a·nism [ˈmɛkəˌnɪzəm] *n* **1** a machine or its parts: *the mechanism of a refrigerator.* **2** a system working as the parts of a machine do: *The bones and muscles are parts of the mechanism of the body.* **3** the means by which something is done: *Committees are a useful mechanism for getting things done.* **4** *Psychology* a response unconsciously selected to protect oneself: *a defence mechanism.* **mech·a·nize** *v* **1** make mechanical. **2** do by machinery, rather than by hand. **3** replace people or animals by machinery in (a business, etc.) **mech·a·ni·za·tion** *n.*

med·al [ˈmɛdəl] *n* a small, flat piece of metal with an inscription: *a medal for bravery.* ⟨Italian *medaglia*; Latin *metallum* metal⟩
me·dal·lion [məˈdæljən] *n* **1** a large medal. **2** a round or oval design. **3** a round or oval piece of cooked meat. **med·al·list** [ˈmɛdəlɪst] or **medalist** *n* a person who has won a medal.

med·dle [ˈmɛdəl] *v* busy oneself with other people's affairs without being asked. **med·dler** *n.* **med·dling** *adj.* ⟨Old French *medler* mix⟩
med·dle·some *adj* fond of meddling in other people's affairs. **med·dle·some·ly** *adv.* **med·dle·some·ness** *n.*

me·di·a [ˈmidiə] **1** *n pl* all the forms of communication that reach a mass audience, such as TV, newspapers, film, or the Internet. **media literacy** the ability to interpret and evaluate these communications. **media literate** *adj.* **2** a pl of MEDIUM.

me·di·al [ˈmidiəl] *adj* **1** in the middle. **2** to do with a mathematical mean. **me·di·al·ly** *adv.* ⟨Latin *medius* middle⟩

me·di·an [ˈmidiən] *adj* **1** to do with the middle. **2** *Statistics* having as many above as below a certain number: *The median age of the population was 21; the average age was 25.* *n* **1** the middle number of a series: *The median of* 1, 3, 4, 8, 9 *is* 4. **2** a line or point in the middle. **3** on a highway, a central strip of grass or pavement. ⟨Latin *medius* middle⟩

me·di·ate [ˈmidiˌeit] *v* **1** act to bring about an agreement: *to mediate between labour and management.* **2** be a connecting link between: *Canada is said to mediate between the United States and the United Kingdom.* *adj* [ˈmidiɪt] connected through some other person or thing. **me·di·a·tion** *n.* **me·di·a·tive** *adj.* **me·di·a·tor** *n.* **me·di·a·to·ry** *adj.* ⟨Latin *mediari* be in the middle; *medius* middle⟩

med·ic [ˈmɛdɪk] *n Informal* **1** physician. **2** a member of the medical branch of any of the armed forces. ⟨shortened form of *medical*⟩

med·i·cal [ˈmɛdɪkəl] *adj* to do with healing or with the science of medicine: *medical advice, medical schools, medical treatment.* *n Informal* medical examination. **med·i·cal·ly** *adv.* ⟨Latin *medicus* doctor⟩
med·i·ca·ble *adj* capable of being cured or relieved by medical treatment. **medical examiner** a physician appointed to perform autopsies. **med·i·care** [ˈmɛdəˌkɛr] *n* a government-sponsored program of health insurance. **med·i·cate** *v* treat with medicine. **med·i·ca·tive** *adj.* **med·i·cat·ed** *adj* containing medicine: *medicated gauze.* **med·i·ca·tion** *n* MEDICINE (def. 1).

med·i·cine [ˈmɛdəsɪn] *n* **1** any substance used to improve health. **2** the science of treating sickness and maintaining health. **3** the branch of this discipline that deals with the non-surgical treatment of disease. **4** among First Nations and Native American peoples: **a** an object or ceremony believed to have power over natural or supernatural forces. **b** supernatural power. ⟨Latin *medicina*; *medicus* doctor⟩
give someone a taste of their own medicine treat someone as they have treated others. **take one's medicine** accept a disagreeable result of one's own actions.
me·dic·i·nal [məˈdɪsənəl] *adj* having value as medicine. **me·dic·i·nal·ly** *adv.* **medicine bag** a bag used by First Nations people to carry objects traditionally believed to have magical powers in protecting the bearer. **medicine man** a man traditionally believed by aboriginal peoples to have supernatural power over diseases, evil spirits, and other things. **medicine woman. medicine wheel** a circle of stones found at old First Nations and American Indian encampments on the prairies, believed to be associated with the religious life of those who constructed them.

me·di·e·val [mɛdˈivəl], [ˌmɛdiˈivəl], or [ˌmidiˈivəl] *adj* to do with the Middle Ages, the period from about A.D. 500 to about A.D. 1500. Also, **me·di·ae·val. me·di·e·val·ly** *adv.* ⟨Latin *medium* middle + *aevum* age⟩
me·di·e·val·ism or **me·di·ae·val·ism** *n* **1** medieval thought, religion, and art. **2** a medieval belief or custom. **me·di·e·val·ist** or **me·di·ae·val·ist** *n.*

me·di·o·cre [ˌmidiˈoukər] *adj* neither good nor bad; average: *a mediocre cake.* ⟨Latin *mediocris* middling; *medius* middle⟩

me·di·oc·ri·ty [ˌmidiˈɒkrəti] *n* **1** mediocre quality or ability **2** a mediocre person.

med·i·tate [ˈmɛdəˌteit] *v* **1** think quietly and deeply; reflect: *Monks meditate on holy things.* **2** think about; consider. **med·i·ta·tion** *n.* **med·i·ta·tive** *adj.* **med·i·ta·tive·ly** *adv.* **med·i·ta·tive·ness** *n.* ⟨Latin *meditari*⟩

Med·i·ter·ra·ne·an [ˌmɛdətəˈreiniən] *adj* to do with the Mediterranean Sea, the lands around it or their inhabitants. ⟨Latin *medius* middle + *terra* land⟩

me·di·um [ˈmidiəm] *n, pl* **-di·a 1** an agency through which anything acts: *TV is a medium of communication.* **2** a means of artistic expression: *The sculptor's medium was wood.* **3** an environment: *Water is the medium in which fish live.* **4** a nutritive substance in which micro-organisms are grown for study. **5** a liquid with which paints are mixed. **6** *pl* **-di·ums** a person through whom spirits of the dead can supposedly communicate with the living. *adj* having a middle position; moderate. *adv* moderately: *medium loud.* ⟨Latin = middle⟩ **medium frequency** the range of radio frequencies between 300 and 3000 kilohertz. **medium of exchange** money or its equivalent. **me·di·um–sized** *adj* neither large nor small of its kind: *a medium-sized car.*

USAGE
Careful writers and speakers avoid using **media** as a singular: *She gave up the medium of painting and took to other media instead.*

med·ley [ˈmɛdli] *n, pl* **-leys 1** a mixture of things that ordinarily do not belong together. **2** *Music* a composition made up of tunes or excerpts from other pieces. ⟨Middle English *medlee.* See MEDDLE.⟩

me·dul·la [məˈdʌlə] *n, pl* **-dul·las** or **-dul·lae** [-ˈdʌli] *or* [-ˈdʌlaɪ] **1** *Anatomy* a bone marrow. **b** the innermost part of an organ. **2** *Botany* the pith of plants. ⟨Latin = marrow⟩ **medulla ob·lon·ga·ta** [ˌɒblɒŋˈgɑtə] *or* [-geitə] *Anatomy* the lowest part of the brain, at the top end of the spinal cord.

me·du·sa [məˈdjusə] *or* [məˈdusə] *n, pl* **-sas** or **-sae** [-si] *or* [-saɪ] *Zoology* a jellyfish. **me·du·san** *adj.* **me·du·soid** *adj.* ⟨*Medusa* monster of Greek myth, with snakes for hair⟩

meek [mik] *adj* **1** patient; mild. **2** submitting when ordered about or injured: *He was meek as a lamb when he was reproved.* **meek·ly** *adv.* **meek·ness** *n.* ⟨Middle English *meoc*⟩

meet¹ [mit] *v* **met meet·ing 1** come to face to face. **2** be united: *a nature in which courage and caution meet.* **3** come into company with by arrangement: *Meet me at one o'clock.* **4** be introduced to: *Have you met my sister?* **5** respond to: *to meet obligations, etc.* **6** assemble: *Parliament will meet next month.* *n* a gathering; a competition: *an athletic meet.* **meet·ing** *n.* ⟨Old English *mētan*⟩ **meet halfway** compromise (with). **meet the eye** or **the ear** be seen or heard. **meet up with** meet. **meet with** talk with face to face.

meet² [mit] *adj Archaic* suitable; fitting: *It is*

meet that we should help our friends. **meet·ly** *adv.* **meet·ness** *n.* ⟨Old English *(ge)mǣte*⟩

me·ga [ˈmɛgə] *Slang adv* very much: *mega talented.* *adj* very big: *a mega science test.* ⟨Greek *megas* great⟩ **mega–** *combining form* **1** great; large: *megalith.* **2** *SI prefix* one million. A megavolt is one million volts. Compare GIGA-, KILO-. *Symbol* **M.**

meg·a·bucks [ˈmɛgəˌbʌk] *n Slang* a vast amount of money.

meg·a·byte [ˈmɛgəˌbait] *n Computers* a measure of the storage capacity of a computer system, roughly equal to one million bytes. *Abbrev* **MB**

meg·a·cit·y [ˈmɛgəˌsiti] *n* a large metropolitan area administered by one government.

meg·a·cy·cle [ˈmɛgəˌsaikəl] *n* megahertz.

meg·a·dose [ˈmɛgəˌdous] *n* a dose of a vitamin or drug many times the normal size.

meg·a·hertz [ˈmɛgəˌhɜrts] *n, pl* **meg·a·hertz** an SI unit for measuring frequency, equal to one million hertz. *Symbol* **MHz**

meg·a·lith [ˈmɛgəˌliθ] *n* a stone of great size, esp in ancient construction work. **meg·a·lith·ic** *adj.* ⟨*mega-* + Greek *lithos* stone⟩

meg·a·lo·ma·ni·a [ˌmɛgəlouˈmeiniə] *n Psychiatry* a mental illness characterized by delusions of greatness, wealth, etc. **meg·a·lo·ma·ni·a·cal** [ˌmɛgəlouməˈnaiəkəl] *or* **meg·a·lo·man·ic** [ˌmɛgələˈmænɪk] *adj.* **meg·a·lo·ma·ni·ac** [ˌmɛgələˈmeiniˌæk] *n.* ⟨Greek *megalou, megas* great + MANIA ⟩

meg·a·lop·o·lis [ˌmɛgəˈlɒpəlɪs] *n* **1** a city of great size, esp one thought of as a centre of the power of a country. **2** a heavily populated area made up of several cities. ⟨Greek *mega, megalou* great + *polis* city⟩ **meg·a·lo·pol·i·tan** [ˌmɛgələˈpɒlətən] *n, adj.*

meg·a·phone [ˈmɛgəˌfoun] *n* a funnel-shaped horn used to increase the loudness of the voice. **meg·a·phon·ic** [-ˈfɒnɪk] *adj.* **meg·a·phon·i·cal·ly** *adv.*

meg·a·ton [ˈmɛgəˌtʌn] *n* a measure of atomic power equivalent to one million tons of high explosive. **meg·a·ton·ic** [-ˈtɒnɪk] *adj.*

meg·a·vi·ta·min [ˈmɛgəˌvaitəmɪn] *n* an abnormally large amount of any vitamin.

me·gil·lah [məˈgɪlə] *n* **1** *Slang* a long-winded story. **2** [megiˈla] *pl* **-gil·loth** [-giˈlout] a scroll containing Hebrew scriptures, read on certain days. Also, **me·gil·la.** ⟨Yiddish *megile* scroll⟩ **the whole megillah** *Slang* the entirety of anything.

mei·o·sis [maiˈousɪs] *n, pl* **-ses** [-siz] **1** *Biology* the division of a living germ cell to produce gametes. Compare MITOSIS. **2** *Rhetoric* litotes; understatement. **mei·ot·ic** [maiˈɒtɪk] *adj.* **mei·o·ti·cal·ly** *adv.* ⟨Greek *meiōn* less⟩

mel·a·mine [ˈmɛləˌmin] *n* a strong plastic, used for making moulded articles, adhesives, and surface coatings. ⟨mel(am), a chemical compound + amine⟩

mel·an·chol·y ['mɛlən,kɒli] n 1 low spirits; a tendency to be sad. 2 Archaic black bile, one of the four humours of ancient physiology, believed to cause low spirits. adj 1 sad. 2 deplorable: a melancholy fact. ⟨Greek melas black + cholē bile⟩

mé·lange [me'lɑ̃ʒ] n, pl -langes [-'lɑ̃ʒ] French a mixture; medley. ⟨French, from mêler mix⟩

mel·a·nin ['mɛlənɪn] n Biochemistry the dark brown or black pigment present in the skin, hair, and eyes of humans and animals. ⟨Greek melano, melas black⟩
mel·a·no·ma [,mɛlə'noumə] n, pl -mas or -mata [-mətə] Pathology a malignant tumour developed from cells that form melanin.

meld [mɛld] v merge or become merged. **meld** n. ⟨blend of melt + weld⟩

me·lee or **mê·lée** [mɛ'lei] or [mei'lei] French [mɛ'le] n 1 a confused fight. 2 any similar state of hectic confusion. ⟨French mêlée pp of mêler mix⟩

mel·io·rism ['miljə,rɪzəm] or ['miliə,rɪzəm] n the doctrine that human effort can improve the state of the world, socially, economically, and spiritually. **mel·io·rist** n. **mel·io·ris·tic** adj.

mel·lif·lu·ous [mə'lɪfluəs] adj sweetly or smoothly flowing: a mellifluous speech. **mel·lif·lu·ous·ly** adv. **mel·lif·lu·ous·ness** n. ⟨Latin mel, mellis honey + fluere to flow⟩

mel·low ['mɛlou] adj 1 full-flavoured from ripeness: a mellow apple. 2 soft, warm, and rich: a violin with a mellow tone. 3 softened and made wise by age and experience. 4 slightly tipsy. 5 Informal relaxed. v make or become mellow. **mel·low·ly** adv. **mel·low·ness** n. ⟨Old English mearu soft⟩

me·lo·de·on [mə'loudiən] n a small organ in which air is sucked inward by a bellows. ⟨pseudo-Greek form of melodium; melody⟩

mel·o·dra·ma ['mɛlə,dræmə] or ['mɛlə,drɑmə] n any sensational drama, writing, speech, etc., with exaggerated appeal to the emotions. **mel·o·dra·mat·ic** [-drə'mætɪk] adj. **mel·o·dra·mat·i·cal·ly** adv. **mel·o·dram·a·tize** v. ⟨Greek melos song + drama drama⟩
mel·o·dra·mat·ics n pl 1 melodramatic writing. 2 melodramatic behaviour.

mel·o·dy ['mɛlədi] n 1 any agreeable succession of sounds. 2 Music the main tune in a harmonized composition. ⟨Greek melos song + ōidē song⟩
me·lod·ic [mə'lɒdɪk] adj to do with melody. **me·lod·i·cal·ly** adv. **me·lo·di·ous** [mə'loudiəs] adj 1 pleasing to the ear: a melodious voice. 2 having a melody: a melodious song. **me·lo·di·ous·ly** adv. **me·lo·di·ous·ness** n.

mel·on ['mɛlən] n the juicy fruit of various plants of the gourd family. **mel·on·like** adj. ⟨Latin melo short for melopepo; Greek mēlon apple + pepōn gourd⟩

melt [mɛlt] v **melt·ed, melt·ed** or **mol·ten, melt·ing 1** change or be changed from solid to liquid. **2** dissolve: Sugar melts in water. **3** disappear or cause to disappear gradually: The clouds melted away. **4** blend gradually: In the rainbow, colours melt into one another. **melt·a·bil·i·ty** n. **melt·a·ble** adj. **melt·ing·ly** adv. ⟨Old English meltan⟩
melt·down n a situation in a nuclear reactor where the holder for the fuel melts, ending in a violent explosion. **melting point** Physical chemistry the temperature at which a solid substance melts. **melting pot** a country or city thought of as a place in which various peoples are assimilated. **melt·wa·ter** n water from melting glaciers or snows. **mol·ten** ['moultən] adj of metal, rock, etc., made liquid by heat: molten lava.

mem·ber ['mɛmbər] n 1 a person belonging to a group. 2 Usually, **Member**, a person elected to a legislative body. 3 Mathematics one of the objects that belongs to a set. 4 a part of a body or of a plant, esp a leg, arm, wing, or branch. 5 the penis. **mem·ber·less** adj. ⟨Latin membrum limb, part⟩ **Member of Parliament** in Canada, a title given to each of the representatives elected to the Federal Parliament. Abbrev **MP** or **M.P. Member of the Provincial Parliament ✳** in Ontario, a member of the Legislative Assembly. Abbrev **MPP** or **M.P.P.**
Member of the House of Assembly ✳ in Newfoundland and Labrador, a member of the Legislative Assembly. Abbrev **MHA** or **M.H.A.**
Member of the Legislative Assembly ✳ a title given to each of the representatives elected to the legislatures of most Canadian provinces. Abbrev **MLA** or **M.L.A.**
Member of the National Assembly ✳ in Québec, a member of the provincial legislature. Abbrev **MNA** or **M.N.A.**
mem·ber·ship n 1 the fact of being a member. 2 the members. 3 the number of members.

mem·brane ['mɛmbrein] n 1 a thin layer of plant or animal tissue. 2 a thin, pliable sheet used to line or cover something. **mem·brane·less** adj. ⟨Latin membrana skin covering body part; membrum member⟩

me·men·to [mə'mɛntou] n, pl -tos or -toes something serving as a reminder, warning, or remembrance. ⟨Latin = remember!⟩
memento mori [mə'mɔri] something serving as a reminder of death. ⟨Latin mori die⟩

mem·o ['mɛmou] n Informal memorandum.

mem·oir ['mɛmwɑr] n 1 biography, esp one written from special sources. 2 a report of a scientific or scholarly study. 3 **memoirs** pl a record of events written from personal knowledge. **mem·oir·ist** n. ⟨French mémoire; Latin memoria memory⟩

mem·o·ran·dum [,mɛmə'rændəm] n, pl -dums or -da [-də] 1 a note to aid the memory. 2 an informal letter, note, or report.

mem·o·ry ['mɛməri] n, pl 1 the ability to remember. 2 what a person remembers. 3 reputation after death. 4 Computers the part of a drive from which data can be retrieved. **mem·o·rize** v. **mem·o·riz·a·ble** adj.

mem·o·ri·za·tion *n.* **mem·o·riz·er** *n.* ⟨Latin *memoria.* See MEMOIR.⟩

in memory of as a remembrance of: *On November 11 we observe a two-minute silence in memory of those who died for their country.*

mem·o·ra·bil·i·a [ˌmɛmərəˈbɪliə] *or* [-ˈbɪliə] *n pl* objects of personal or historical significance.

mem·o·ra·ble *adj* worth remembering.

mem·o·ra·bly *adv.* **mem·o·ra·bil·i·ty** *n.*

me·mo·ri·al [məˈmɔriəl] *n* something that is a reminder of some important event or person. *adj* helping people to remember some person or event: *memorial services.* **me·mo·ri·al·ly** *adv.* **me·mo·ri·al·ize** *v.* **me·mo·ri·al·iz·er** *n.*

me·mo·ri·al·i·za·tion *n.* **memory bank** **1** everything that a person remembers. **2** the archives of an organization or nation.

memory board *Computers* a detachable storage device that provides additional memory. **memory card** *Computers* a plug-in chip for extra storage and retrieval of data.

Memory emphasizes the ability to keep in the mind or call back something once learned: *That vacation lives in her memory.* **Recollection** emphasizes calling back to mind, often with effort, something not thought of for a long time: *I have little recollection of my childhood.*

mem·sa·hib [ˈmɛmˌsab] *or* [ˌmɛmˈsab] *n* formerly, a title of respect used in the Indian subcontinent for a married European lady. ⟨Hindi *mem* (English *ma'am*) + *sahib* sir⟩

men [mɛn] *n* pl of MAN.

men·ace [ˈmɛnɪs] *n* a threat: *Forest fires are a menace in dry weather.* **men·ace** *v.* **men·ac·ing** *adj.* ⟨Latin *minācia; minax* threatening⟩

mé·nage *or* **me·nage** [meiˈnaʒ] *French* [meˈnaʒ] *n, pl* **-nages** [-ˈnaʒɪz]; *French* [-ˈnaʒ] **1** a household; domestic establishment. **2** housekeeping. ⟨French⟩

ménage a trois [menaʒaˈtʀwa] *n French* any continuous relationship, usually sexual, involving three people who live together.

me·nag·er·ie [məˈnæʒəri] *or* [məˈnaʒəri] *n* a collection of wild animals kept in cages for exhibition. ⟨French *ménagerie,* housing for domestic animals⟩

mend [mɛnd] *v* **1** repair. **2** improve: *He should mend his manners.* **3** get back one's health. **mend** *n.* **mend·a·ble** *adj.* **mend·er** *n.* ⟨variant of *amend*⟩

on the mend a improving. **b** getting well. **mend·ing** *n* items to be mended.

men·da·cious [mɛnˈdeiʃəs] *adj* **1** untruthful. **2** false; untrue. **men·da·cious·ly** *adv.* **men·da·cious·ness** *n.* **men·dac·i·ty** [-ˈdæsəti] *n.* ⟨Latin *mendax* lying⟩

men·di·cant [ˈmɛndəkənt] *adj* begging: *mendicant friars.* *n* a beggar. **men·di·can·cy** *n.* ⟨Latin *mendicare* beg; *mendicus* beggar⟩

men·folk See MAN.

me·ni·al [ˈminiəl] *adj* to do with a servant; low; mean. *n* **1** a servant who does the humblest and most unpleasant tasks. **2** a low, mean, or servile person. **me·ni·al·ly** *adv.* ⟨Middle English *meynie* household⟩

me·nin·ges [məˈnɪndʒiz] *n pl, sg* **me·ninx** [ˈmɪnɪŋks] *Anatomy* the three membranes that surround the brain and spinal cord. **me·nin·ge·al** *adj.* ⟨Greek *mēninx* membrane ⟩ **men·in·gi·tis** [ˌmɛnɪnˈdʒaitɪs] *n Pathology* a serious disease in which the meninges are inflamed. **men·in·git·ic** [-ˈdʒɪtɪk] *adj.*

me·nis·cus [məˈnɪskəs] *n, pl* **-nis·cus·es, -nis·ci** [-ˈnɪsai] *or* [-ˈnɪskai], [ˈnɪsi] *or* [-ˈnɪski] **1** the curved upper surface of a column of liquid, produced by surface tension. **2** *Optics* a lens that is concave on one side and convex on the other. ⟨Greek *mēniskos,* diminutive of *mēnē* moon⟩

Men·non·ite [ˈmɛnəˌnait] *n* a member of any of several Christian churches whose tenets include pacificism and the baptism of adult believers. **Men·non·ite** *adj.* ⟨after *Menno Simons* 16c Dutch founder⟩

me·nom·i·nee [məˈnɒməni] *n* ✱ wild rice. ⟨Cree⟩

men·o·pause [ˈmɛnəˌpɒz] *n* the period in a woman's life during which menstruation ceases permanently. **men·o·pausal** *adj.* ⟨Greek *mēn* month + *pausis* pause⟩

men·o·rah *or* **Men·o·rah** [məˈnɔrə] *n* a candelabrum used in Jewish worship. ⟨Hebrew *manorah*⟩

men·serv·ants *n pl* of MANSERVANT.

men·stru·a·tion [ˌmɛnstruˈeiʃən] *or* [mɛnˈstreiʃən] *n* the regular discharge of blood and tissue from the uterus, normally occurring about every four weeks in non-pregnant women from puberty to menopause. **men·stru·al** *adj.* **men·stru·ate** *v.* ⟨Latin *menstruare; mensis* month⟩ **men·ses** [ˈmɛnsiz] *n pl* menstruation.

men·su·ra·tion [ˌmɛnʃəˈreiʃən] *n* **1** the act of measuring. **2** the branch of mathematics that deals with finding lengths, areas, and volumes. **men·su·ra·tive** *adj.* **men·su·ra·tion·al** *adj.* ⟨Latin *mensura.* See MEASURE.⟩

–ment *noun-forming suffix* **1** the act or state of——ing: *enjoyment.* **2** the state or condition of being——ed: *amazement.* **3** the result of ——ing: *pavement.* **4** a means or instrument for——ing: *inducement.* ⟨Latin *-mentum*⟩

men·tal [ˈmɛntəl] *adj* **1** to do with the mind: *mental processes.* **2** without being spoken or written down: *a mental calculation.* **3** to do with a disorder of the mind: *mental illness.* **men·tal·ly** *adv.* ⟨Latin *mens, mentis* mind⟩

mental age *Psychology* an estimate of the level of mental development as measured against age. **men·tal·ism** *n Philosophy* the doctrine that the material world exists only as a perception of the mind. **men·tal·is·tic** *adj.* **men·tal·is·ti·cal·ly** *adv.* **men·tal·ist** *n* **1** a person who believes in mentalism. **2** mind reader. **men·tal·i·ty** *n* **1** mental capacity: *of average mentality.* **2** attitude: *the Western mentality.* **mental telepathy** telepathy.

men·thol ['mɛnθɒl] *n Chemistry, pharmacy* a substance obtained from oil of peppermint, used in medicine. **men·tho·lat·ed** *adj.* ⟨German; Latin *mentha* mint + *oleum* oil⟩

men·tion ['mɛnʃən] *v* speak about; refer to. *n* a short statement; reference. **men·tion·a·ble** *adj.* ⟨Latin *mentio*⟩ **make mention of** speak of. **not to mention** in addition to.

men·tor ['mɛntər] *or* ['mɛntɔr] *n* a wise and trusted adviser. *v* be a mentor to. ⟨in Greek myth, *Mentor*, Odysseus' trusted friend⟩

men·u ['mɛnju] *n* **1** a list of the food served at a meal. **2** *Computers* a list of topics, operations, etc. that allows the user to make a selection. ⟨French = small, detailed; Latin *minutus*⟩ **menu–driven** *adj* of software, relying on menus to guide users to choose programs.

me·ow [mi'aʊ] *n* the sound made by a cat. **me·ow** *v*. Also, **mi·aow** or **mi·aou**. ⟨imitative⟩

Meph·is·to·phe·li·an [ˌmɛfɪstə'filiən] *or* [məˌfɪstə'filiən] *adj* wicked and crafty; sardonic; scoffing. Also, **Meph·is·to·phe·le·an**. ⟨*Mephistopheles*, the devil in legend of Faust⟩

mer·can·tile See MERCHANT.

Mer·ca·tor projection [mər'keitər] a method of drawing maps with straight lines for latitude and longitude. ⟨Gerhardus *Mercator* 16c Flemish mapmaker⟩

mer·ce·nar·y ['mɜrsəˌnɛri] *adj* acting with money as the sole motive. *n* a soldier serving for pay in a foreign army. **mer·ce·nar·i·ly** *adv*. **mer·ce·nar·i·ness** *n*. ⟨Latin *mercenarius*; *merces* wages⟩

mer·chant ['mɜrtʃənt] *n* a person who buys and sells commodities for profit. *adj* to do with trade: *merchant ships.* **mer·chant·like** *adj.* ⟨Old French *marchëant*; Latin *mercari* trade⟩ **mer·can·tile** ['mɜrkənˌtaɪl] *adj* to do with merchants or trade: *a mercantile venture.* **mer·can·til·ism** ['mɜrkəntəˌlɪzəm] *n* an economic system that stressed the holding of precious metals, a greater volume of exports than imports, and the exploitation of colonies. **mer·can·til·ist** *n, adj.* **mer·chan·dise** ['mɜrtʃənˌdaɪs] *or* [-ˌdaɪz] *n* goods for sale. *v* ['mɜrtʃənˌdaɪz] **1** buy and sell. **2** strive for increased sales by advertising, etc. **mer·chan·dis·er** *n*. **mer·chant·man** *n, pl* -men a ship used in commerce. **merchant marine** ships used in commerce.

mer·cu·ry ['mɜrkjəri] *n* **1** a metallic element that is liquid at ordinary temperatures. *Symbol* **Hg**. **2 Mercury a** *Roman myth* the messenger of the gods, the god of commerce. **b** the planet that is the smallest and nearest to the sun. ⟨Latin *Mercurius*⟩ **mer·cu·ri·al** [mər'kjʊriəl] *adj* **1** sprightly. **2** changeable; fickle. **3** to do with mercury: *mercurial poisoning.* **mer·cu·ri·al·ly** *adv*.

mer·cy ['mɜrsi] *n* **1** more kindness than justice requires: *The judge showed mercy.* **2** kindly treatment; pity. **3** something to be thankful for: *It's a mercy that they arrived safely.* **mer·ci·ful** *adj.* **mer·ci·ful·ly** *adv*. **mer·ci·less** *adj.* **mer·ci·less·ly** *adv*. **mer·ci·less·ness** *n*. ⟨Old French *merci*; Latin *merces* reward⟩ **at the mercy of** in the power of: *Without shelter we were at the mercy of the storm.* **mercy flight** ✳ esp in the North, an aircraft flight to fetch a person to hospital for treatment. **mercy killing** euthanasia.

mere[1] [mir] *adj* nothing more than; only: *The cut was a mere scratch.* ⟨Latin *merus* pure⟩ **mere·ly** *adv* simply; only; and nothing more.

mere[2] [mir] *n Poetic or dialect* lake. ⟨Old English⟩

mer·e·tri·cious [ˌmɛrə'trɪʃəs] *adj* **1** attractive in a showy way: *Wood painted to look like marble is meretricious.* **2** plausible but not genuine. **mer·e·tri·cious·ly** *adv*. **mer·e·tri·cious·ness** *n*. ⟨Latin *meretrix* prostitute; *mereri* earn⟩

merge [mɜrdʒ] *v* **1** combine or cause to combine into one: *to merge two businesses.* **2** blend: *merging traffic.* **3** *Computers* combine (two or more files, etc.). ⟨Latin *mergere* dip⟩ **merg·er** *n* any combination of companies.

me·rid·i·an [mə'rɪdiən] *n* **1** *Geography* **a** an imaginary circle passing through the North and South Poles. **b** the half of such a circle from pole to pole. **2** the highest point that the sun or a star reaches in the sky. **3** the highest point: *the meridian of life.* *adj* **1** highest. **2** around midday. ⟨Latin *meridies* noon; *medius* middle + *dies* day⟩

me·ringue [mə'ræŋ] *n* a mixture of egg white and sugar, beaten until stiff. ⟨French⟩

mer·it ['mɛrɪt] *n* **1** worth. **2** anything that deserves praise or reward. **3** Usually, **merits** *pl* actual qualities, whether good or bad: *The judge will consider the case on its merits.* *v* deserve. **mer·it·less** *adj.* ⟨Latin *meritum* pp of *mereri* earn⟩ **mer·i·toc·ra·cy** *n* a system in which individuals achieve status on the basis of intellect, rather than birth or wealth. **mer·i·to·ri·ous** *adj* deserving reward or praise. **mer·i·to·ri·ous·ly** *adv*. **mer·i·to·ri·ous·ness** *n*.

mer·lin ['mɜrlən] *n* the usual European name for the pigeon hawk. ⟨Anglo-French *merilun* Old French *esmeril*⟩

mer·maid ['mɜrˌmeid] *n* an imaginary sea maiden having the form of a fish from the waist down. **mer·man** ['mɜrˌmæn] *or* ['mɜrmən] *n, pl* -men. ⟨See MERE[2], MAID.⟩

mer·ry ['mɛri] *adj* **1** full of fun. **2** happy; joyful. **mer·ri·ly** *adv*. **mer·ri·ment** *n*. **mer·ri·ness** *n*. ⟨Old English *myrge*⟩ **make merry** laugh and be happy; have fun. **mer·ry–go–round** *n* **1** a set of figures with seats on a circular platform, that people ride for fun. **2** any rapid round: *The holidays were a merry-go-round of parties.* **mer·ry·mak·ing** *n* **1** laughter and gaiety; fun. **2** a joyous festival. **mer·ry·mak·er** *n*. **mer·ry·mak·ing** *adj.*

me·sa ['meisə] *n US* a flat-topped hill with steep sides. ⟨Spanish = table; Latin *mensa*⟩

mes·cal [mɛ'skæl] *n* **1** an alcoholic drink made from the leaves of any of various agaves. **2** a spineless cactus that yields mescaline. ⟨Spanish; Nahuatl *mexcalli*⟩
mes·cal·ine or **mescalin** ['mɛskə,lin] *or* ['mɛskəlɪn] *n* a narcotic drug that produces hallucinations and is related to LSD.

mesh [mɛʃ] *n* **1** a fabric of thread, cord, wire, etc. woven with holes: *a fly swatter made of wire mesh.* **2 meshes** web; network: *Seaweed was caught in the meshes of the net.*
v **1** engage or become engaged: *The teeth of the small gear mesh with the teeth of a larger one.* **2** be in harmony: *Their ideas do not mesh.* ⟨Old English *mæscre* net⟩

mes·mer·ism ['mɛzmə,rɪzəm] *n* hypnotism. **mes·mer·ist** *n.* **mes·mer·ize** *v.* **mes·mer·iz·er** *n.* ⟨F.A. Mesmer 18c Austrian hypnotist⟩

me·son ['mɛzɒn] *or* ['mizɒn] *n Physics* a highly unstable particle in the nucleus of an atom, having a positive, neutral, or negative charge and a short lifetime. ⟨Greek *mesos* middle⟩

Mes·o·zo·ic [,mɛzə'zouɪk] *Geology n* the era before the present era, beginning about 245 million years ago. **Mes·o·zo·ic** *adj.* ⟨Greek *mesos-* middle + *zōē* life⟩

mes·quite [mɛ'skit] *or* ['mɛskit] *n* a spiny tree or shrub of the pea family. ⟨Spanish *mezquite*; Nahuatl *mizquitl*⟩

mess [mɛs] *n* **1** a dirty or untidy condition. **2** *Informal* a person in a dirty or untidy state. **3** confusion or difficulty: *His affairs are in a mess.* **4** an unpleasant or unsuccessful state of affairs: *She made a mess of her finals.* **5** in the armed forces: **a** an organization for social purposes: *He was secretary of the sergeants' mess.* **b** the dining room used by members of such an organization.
v take one's meals *(with).* **messy** *adj.* **mess·i·ness** *n.* **mes·si·ly** *adv.* ⟨Old French *mes*; Latin *missus* pp of *mittere* put (i.e., on the table)⟩
mess around (or **about**) *Informal* **a** busy oneself without seeming to accomplish anything. **b** *Slang* waste time. **mess up a** spoil (something): *to mess up your chances.* **b** make dirty or untidy: *to mess up a room.* **c** *Informal* commit a misdeed: *I really messed up.*
mess hall in the armed forces, a place where a group of people eat together regularly.

mes·sage ['mɛsɪdʒ] *n* **1** information sent from one person to another. **2** a lesson implied in a work of fiction, movie, etc. **3** a radio or television commercial. **mes·sen·ger** ['mɛsəndʒər] *n.*
mes·sag·ing *n* the sending of a message, usually by cellphone. ⟨Old French; Latin *missus* pp of *mittere* send⟩
get the message take the hint.

Mes·si·ah [mə'saɪə] *n* **1** *Judaism* according to some interpretations, the deliverer promised to the Hebrews. **2** *Christianity* Jesus Christ, the fulfillment of these prophecies. **3 messiah** a person thought of as a great saviour. **Mes·si·an·ic** [,mesi'ænɪk] *adj.* **Mes·si·an·i·cal·ly** *adv.* ⟨Hebrew *mashiah* anointed⟩

Messrs. ['mɛsərz] *n* pl of MR.: *Messrs Rankin and Majid.*

met [mɛt] *v* pt and pp of MEET¹.

me·ta– *prefix* **1** beyond: *metalanguage.* **2** change of state: *metamorphosis.* **3** between: *metatarsal.* **4** transposed: *metathesis.* Also, before a vowel, **met-**. ⟨Greek = beyond, over⟩

me·tab·o·lism [mə'tæbə,lɪzəm] *n Physiology* the processes of building up food into living matter and using living matter so that it is broken down into waste. **met·a·bol·ic** [,mɛ'tə'bolɪk] *adj.* **met·a·bol·i·cal·ly** *adv.* **me·tab·o·lize** *v.* **me·tab·o·liz·a·ble** *adj.* ⟨meta- + Greek *bolē* a throwing; *ballein* throw⟩
me·tab·o·lite [mə'tæbə,laɪt] *n Biology, physiology.* any organic compound produced by metabolism.

met·a·car·pus [,mɛtə'kɑrpəs] *n, pl* **-pi** [-paɪ] *or* [-pi] **1** *Anatomy* the part of the hand between the wrist and the fingers. **2** *Zoology* the corresponding part in an animal's foreleg. **met·a·car·pal** *adj.* ⟨meta- + Greek *karpos* wrist⟩

met·al ['mɛtəl] *n* **1** a substance that is a good conductor of heat and electricity. **2** *Chemistry* any element that can form a salt by replacing the hydrogen of an acid. **3** material: *Cowards are not made of the same metal as heroes.* **me·tal·lic** [mə'tælɪk] *adj.* **me·tal·li·cal·ly** *adv.* **met·al·like** *adj.* ⟨Greek *metallon* mine⟩
metal fatigue the deterioration and breakdown of metal as a result of stress. **met·al·lif·er·ous** [mɛtə'lɪfərəs] *adj* containing or yielding metal: *metalliferous rocks.* **met·al·lur·gy** ['mɛtə,lɜrdʒi] *n* the science of working with metals. **met·al·lur·gic** or **met·al·lur·gi·cal** *adj.* **met·al·lur·gi·cal·ly** *adv.* **met·al·lur·gist** *n.* **met·al·work** *n* things made out of metal. **met·al·work·er** *n.* **met·al·work·ing** *n.*

met·a·lang·uage ['mɛtə,læŋgwɪdʒ] *n* a symbolic system used in talking about language or in discussing another language.

met·a·mor·pho·sis [,mɛtə'mɔrfəsɪs] *n, pl* **-ses** [-,siz] **1** a dramatic change. **2** the changed form. **3** *Zoology* a marked change in the form of an animal after the embryonic stage. **4** *Botany* the modification of a plant during its development. **met·a·mor·phose** [,mɛtə'mɔrfouz] *or* [,-'mɔrfous] *v.* ⟨meta- + Greek *morphē* form⟩
met·a·mor·phic [,mɛtə'mɔrfɪk] *adj* **1** to do with change of form. **2** *Geology* designating rock that has undergone changes through the action of pressure, heat, moisture, etc.

met·a·phor ['mɛtə,fɔr] *or* ['mɛtəfər] *n* a figure of speech in which a word or phrase that ordinarily means one thing is used of another thing, in order to suggest a likeness between the two things. *Examples: She had a heart of stone. we basked in his melting smile.* Compare SIMILE. **met·a·phor·ic** or **met·a·phor·i·cal** *adj.* **met·a·phor·i·cal·ly** *adv.* ⟨meta- + Greek *pherein* carry⟩
mix metaphors use incompatible metaphors

in the same expression: *Put your shoulder to the wheel and become a tower of strength.*

USAGE

A **metaphor** compares implicitly by speaking of one thing as if it were another: *This play is a mirror of reality.* A **simile** says explicitly that one thing is like another, using **like** or **as**: *This play reflects reality as a mirror does.*

met·a·phys·ics [ˌmɛtəˈfɪzɪks] *n* (with a sg verb) the branch of philosophy that tries to explain the first principles of reality and knowledge. **met·a·phy·si·cian** [ˌmɛtəfəˈsɪʃən] *n.* **met·a·phys·i·cal** *adj* 1 about the real nature of things. 2 highly abstract. **met·a·phys·i·cal·ly** *adv.*

me·tas·ta·sis [məˈtæstəsɪs] *n, pl* -**ses** [-ˌsiz] *Pathology* the spread of disease from one part of the body to another. **met·a·stat·ic** [ˌmɛtəˈstætɪk], *adj.* **met·a·stat·i·cal·ly** *adv.* **me·tas·ta·size** [mɛˈtæstəˌsaɪz] *v.* ⟨*meta-* + STASIS⟩

met·a·tar·sus [ˌmɛtəˈtɑrsəs] *n, pl* -**si** [-saɪ] *or* [-si] 1 *Anatomy* the part of the foot between the heel and ankle and the toes. 2 *Zoology* the corresponding part in a bird's foot and an animal's hind leg. **met·a·tar·sal** *adj.* **met·a·tar·sal·ly** *adv.*

me·tath·e·sis [məˈtæθəsɪs] *n, pl* -**ses** [-ˌsiz] 1 *Phonology* the transposition of sounds, syllables, or letters in a word. *Example:* aks for ask. 2 *Chemistry* the interchange of atoms between molecules. **met·a·thet·ic** [ˌmɛtəˈθɛtɪk] or **met·a·thet·i·cal** *adj.* ⟨*meta-* + THESIS⟩

mete [mit] *v* (usually with *out*) give to each a share of; distribute; allot. ⟨Old English *metan*⟩

me·te·or [ˈmitiər] *n* a mass of stone or metal that comes toward the earth from outer space at great speed. **me·te·or·like** *adj.* ⟨Greek *meteōron* (thing) in the air; *aeirein* lift⟩ **me·te·or·ic** [ˌmitiˈɔrɪk] *adj* 1 of meteors. 2 brilliant and soon ended. **me·te·or·i·cal·ly** *adv.* **me·te·or·ite** *n* a fallen meteor. **me·te·or·it·ic** [-ˈɪtɪk] *adj.* **me·te·or·ol·o·gy** *n* the science of the atmosphere, especially as it relates to weather. **me·te·or·o·log·i·cal** *adj.* **me·te·or·o·log·i·cal·ly** *adv.* **me·te·or·ol·o·gist** *n.* **meteor shower** *Astronomy* the meteors seen when the earth passes through a group of them.

me·ter [ˈmitər] *n* a device that measures: *a parking meter.* ⟨Greek *metron* measure⟩ **–me·ter** *combining form* 1 a device for measuring: *speedometer.* 2 verse having a specified number of metrical feet per line: *pentameter.*

meth·a·done [ˈmɛθəˌdoun] *n* a narcotic drug similar to morphine. ⟨*dimethyl* + *amino* + *diphenyl* + *-one.* 20c.⟩

meth·am·phet·a·mine [ˌmɛθæmˈfɛtəˌmin] *or* [-ˈfɛtəmɪn] *n* a mood-elevating drug. ⟨*methyl* + *amphetamine.* 20c.⟩

meth·ane [ˈmɛθein] *n Chemistry* a highly flammable gas. ⟨*methyl*⟩ **meth·a·nol** [ˈmɛθəˌnɒl] *n Chemistry* a poisonous, flammable liquid. Also called **methyl alcohol.** [ˈmɛθəl]

meth·od [ˈmɛθəd] *n* 1 a set way of doing

something involving various ordered steps. 2 order in getting things done: *If you used more method, you wouldn't waste so much time.* 3 **Method,** an acting technique in which the actor attempts to think like the character. **meth·od·less** *adj.* ⟨Greek *methodos* pursuit; *meta-* + *hodos* a travelling⟩ **method in one's madness** system and sense underlying apparent folly. **me·thod·i·cal** *adj* 1 done with a method: *a methodical procedure.* 2 tending to act according to a method: *a methodical thinker.* **me·thod·i·cal·ly** *adv.* **me·thod·i·cal·ness** *n.* **Meth·od·ist** *n* a member of any of the Protestant churches that grew out of an 18c reform movement. **meth·od·ol·o·gy** *n* 1 a system of procedures used in a particular field. 2 the branch of logic that deals with the analysis of such procedures. **meth·od·o·log·i·cal** *adj.* **meth·od·o·log·i·cal·ly** *adv.* **meth·od·ol·o·gist** *n.*

methyl alcohol See METHANE.

me·tic·u·lous [məˈtɪkjələs] *adj* extremely or excessively careful about small details. **me·tic·u·lous·ly** *adv.* **me·tic·u·lous·ness** *n.* ⟨Latin *meticulosus; metus* fear⟩

mé·tier [meiˈtjei] *n* the kind of work for which one has special ability. ⟨French; Latin *ministerium.* See MINISTER.⟩

Mé·tis or **Mé·tis** [ˈmeiti], or [meiˈti], *n, pl* -**tis** ✱ *n* a person descended from Europeans and First Nations peoples, esp those who established themselves in the Red, Assiniboine, and Saskatchewan river valleys during the 19th century. The Métis form a distinct cultural group. **Mé·tis** or **Mé·tis** *adj.* ⟨Cdn. French; Latin *misticius* of mixed heritage⟩ **Mé·tisse** [meiˈtis] *n, pl* -**tisses** [-ˈtis] or [-ˈtisɪz] ✱ a female Métis.

me·ton·y·my [məˈtɒnəmi] *n Rhetoric* the use of the name of one thing for another which it suggests. *Example:* In *the pen is mightier than the sword*, the word *pen* is used to mean *power of literature* and *sword* is used to mean *military force.* **met·o·nym·ic** [ˌmɛtəˈnimɪk] *adj.* ⟨*meta-* + Greek *onyma* name⟩ **met·o·nym** [ˈmɛtəˌnim] *n* any word used in metonymy.

me·tre[1] [ˈmitər] *n* 1 *Prosody* the rhythmical pattern resulting from the arrangement of stressed and unstressed syllables in regularly recurring groups (feet). 2 *Music* the combining of beats or notes into rhythmic groups, or the pattern formed in this way. Also, **me·ter.** ⟨Greek *metron* measure⟩

me·tre[2] [ˈmitər] *n* an SI unit for measuring length. Also, **me·ter.** *Symbol* m ⟨French *mètre;* Greek *metron* measure⟩ **metre–stick** *n* a graduated measuring stick that is one metre long. **met·ric** [ˈmɛtrɪk] *adj* to do with the METRIC SYSTEM. **met·ri·cal** *adj* 1 written in verse, not in prose: *a metrical translation of Homer.* 2 to do with measurement. **met·ri·cal·ly** *adv.* **met·ri·cate** *v* express in a metric system of measurement.

met·ri·ca·tion *n.* **metric system** a decimal system of measurement.

met·ro ['mɛtrou] *n Informal* **1** the territory of a METROPOLITAN (*adj*, def. 2) government. **2** the subway train system in Montréal. **3** Metro ✹ metropolitan Toronto.

me·trol·o·gy [mə'trɒlədʒi] *n, pl* **-gies 1** the science of weights and measures. **2** a system of weights and measures. **me·tro·log·i·cal** *adj.* **me·tro·log·i·cal·ly** *adv.* ⟨Greek *metron* measure⟩

met·ro·nome ['mɛtrə,noum] *n* a device used by persons practising musical instruments to help keep time. **met·ro·nom·ic** [,mɛtrə'nɒmɪk] *adj.* **met·ro·nom·i·cal·ly** *adv.* ⟨Greek *metron* measure + *-nomos* rule⟩

me·trop·o·lis [mə'trɒpəlɪs] *n* a large city. ⟨Greek *mētēr* mother + *polis* city⟩ **met·ro·pol·i·tan** [,mɛtrə'pɒlətən] *adj* **1** to do with a large city. **2** designating a form of government based on a federation of municipalities that form a large urban area. **3** to do with the chief diocese of a church or province. **4** to do with the mother city or the mainland territory of the parent state: *metropolitan France. n* **1** a person who lives in a large city and knows its ways. **2** *Eastern Orthodox Church* the head of an ecclesiastical province. **3** *Roman Catholic and Anglican Churches* an archbishop having authority over an ecclesiastical province. **met·ro·pol·i·tan·ism** *n.* **metropolitan area** the area including a large city and its suburbs.

met·tle ['mɛtəl] *n* **1** temperament. **2** spirit; courage. ⟨variant of *metal*⟩ **on one's mettle** ready to do one's best.

mew [mju] *n* the sound made by a cat or kitten. **mew** *v.* ⟨imitative⟩

mewl [mjul] *v* whimper. ⟨imitative⟩

mez·za·nine ['mɛzə,nin] *n* **1** a partial storey between two main floors of a building. **2** in a theatre, the lowest balcony. ⟨Italian *mezzanino; mezzano* middle Latin *medianus*⟩

mez·zo-so·pran·o ['mɛtsou sə'prænou] *n* an adult female singing voice having a range between soprano and alto. ⟨Italian *mezzo* half⟩

mez·zo·tint ['mɛtsou,tɪnt] *or* ['mɛzou,tɪnt] *n* an engraving on copper or steel, made by scraping away parts of a roughened surface, or a print made from such an engraving. **mez·zo·tint** *v.* ⟨Italian *mezzotinto* half-tint⟩

MFD multifunction device, a machine that acts as a printer, photocopier, scanner and fax machine.

mg milligram(s).

MHA or **M.H.A.** MEMBER OF THE HOUSE OF ASSEMBLY.

MHz megahertz.

mi [mi] *n Music* **1** the third tone of an eight-tone major scale. **2** the tone E. ⟨See GAMUT.⟩

mi·as·ma [maɪ'æzmə] *n, pl* **-mas** or **-ma·ta** [-mətə] **1** a poisonous vapour rising from the earth and infecting the air. **2** an influence that corrupts: *a miasma of evil thoughts.*

mi·as·mal or **mi·as·mat·ic** *adj.* **mi·as·mic** *adj.* ⟨Greek = pollution; *miainein* pollute⟩

mi·ca ['maɪkə] *n* a mineral that divides into thin layers. ⟨Latin = grain, crumb⟩ **mi·ca·ceous** [maɪ'keɪʃəs] *adj* like mica in structure or composition.

mice [maɪs] *n* pl of MOUSE.

mick·ey ['mɪki] *n Slang* **1** ✹ a half bottle of liquor or wine. **2** an alcoholic drink to which a drug like chloral hydrate has been added. ⟨slang term for an Irishman; nickname for *Michael*⟩ **take the mickey out of** tease.

Mickey Mouse *Informal* not worthwhile or serious; trivial: *a Mickey Mouse rehab program.* ⟨name of Walt Disney's cartoon character⟩

Mic·mac See MI'KMAW.

micro ['maɪkrou] *adj* small; small-scale: *micro decision-making.* ⟨Greek *mikros* small⟩ **micro–** *combining form* **1** very small: *microfilm.* Compare MACRO–. **2** abnormally small: *microcephalic.* **3** involving the use of a microscope: *microbiology.* **4** *SI prefix* millionth: *microsecond.*

mi·crobe ['maɪkroub] *n* a micro-organism, esp a disease-producing bacterium. **mi·crobe·less** *adj.* **mi·cro·bi·al** or **mi·cro·bic** *adj.* ⟨Greek *mikros* small + *bios* life⟩

mi·cro·bi·ol·o·gy [,maɪkroubaɪ'ɒlədʒi] *n* the biology of micro-organisms. **mi·cro·bi·o·log·i·cal** *adj.* **mi·cro·bi·ol·o·gist** *n.*

mi·cro·chip ['maɪkrə,tʃɪp] *n Computers* a very small piece of material containing the information for a computer circuit.

mi·cro·com·put·er ['maɪkroukəm,pjutər] *n Computers* a miniature, portable computer. Compare MAINFRAME.

mi·cro·cosm ['maɪkrou,kɒzəm] *n* **1** a universe in miniature. **2** a person or community thought of as a miniature representation of the universe. **mi·cro·cos·mic** *adj.* **mi·cro·cos·mi·cal·ly** *adv.* ⟨Greek *mikros* small + *kosmos* world⟩

mi·cro–e·co·nom·ics [,maɪkrou ,ɛkə'nɒmɪks] *or* [,ɪkə-] *n* the economy of one product or a single consumer (with a sg verb). Compare MACRO-ECONOMICS. **mi·cro·e·co·nom·ic** *adj.*

mi·cro–e·lec·tron·ics or **mi·cro·e·lec·tron·ics** [,maɪkrou ɪlɛk'trɒnɪks] *or* [,ɪlɛk'trɒnɪks] *n* (with a sg verb) the branch of electronics that deals with electronic components of miniature size. **mi·cro–e·lec·tron·ic** or **mi·cro·e·lec·tron·ic** *adj.*

mi·cro·fiche ['maɪkrou,fiʃ] *n, pl* **-fich·es** [-,fiʃ] *or* [-,fiʃɪz] a single sheet of microfilm, carrying microcopies of numerous pages of printed matter. ⟨*micro-* + French *fiche* card⟩

mi·cro·film ['maɪkrou,fɪlm] *n* a film for making very small photographs of pages of a book, documents, etc. to preserve them in a very small space. **mi·cro·film** *v.*

mi·crom·e·ter [maɪ'krɒmətər] *n* an instrument for measuring very small distances, angles, objects, etc.

mi·cro·me·tre ['məikrou,mitər] *n* one-millionth of a metre. Also, **mi·cro·me·ter.** *Symbol* μm

mi·cron ['məikrɒn] *n, pl* **mi·crons** or **mi·cra** ['məikrə] micrometre. ⟨Greek *micron* form of *mikros* small⟩

mi·cro–or·gan·ism or **mi·cro·or·gan·ism** [,məikrou 'ɔrgə,nizəm] *n* any organism too small to be seen with the naked eye.

mi·cro·phone ['məikrə,foun] *n* an instrument for increasing the loudness of sounds or for transmitting sounds. **mi·cro·phon·ic** [,məikrə'fɒnɪk] *adj.*

mi·cro·pro·ces·sor [,məikrou'prousesər] or [-'prɒsɛsər] *n Computers* an integrated circuit that controls all the functions of a central processing unit in a computer or other electronic device.

mi·cro·scope ['məikrə,skoup] *n* an instrument with a lens or combination of lenses for making small things look larger. **mi·cro·scop·ic** [,məikrə'skɒpɪk] or **1** that cannot be seen without a microscope. **2** like a microscope: *a microscopic eye for mistakes.* **3** to do with a microscope. **mi·cro·scop·i·cal·ly** *adv.* **mi·cros·co·py** [məi'krɒskəpi] *n* microscopic investigation.

mi·cro·sec·ond ['məikrə,sekənd] *n* one-millionth of a second. *Symbol* μs

mi·cro·wave ['məikrou,weiv] *n* a very short electromagnetic wave.
microwave oven an oven in which food is cooked by means of the heat produced by microwaves penetrating the food.

mid [mɪd] *adj* in the middle; middle. ⟨Old English *midd*⟩

mid– *combining form.* middle; mid; the middle point or part of: *midair.* ⟨Old English. See MID.⟩

mid·air or **mid–air** ['mɪd 'ɛr] *n* **1** the sky; air: *The parachute floated in midair.* **2** uncertainty: *With the contract still in midair, the board recessed.* **mid·air** or **mid–air** *adj.*

Mi·das ['maidəs] *n* **1** *Greek legend* a king of Phrygia whose touch turned everything to gold. **2** *Informal* a man of great moneymaking ability. **Mi·das·like** *adj.*
the Midas touch the ability to make money easily.

mid·day ['mɪd,dei] *n* the middle of the day; noon. **mid·day** *adj.* ⟨Old English *middæg*⟩

mid·den ['mɪdən] *n Dialect* a dunghill; refuse heap. ⟨Scandinavian; compare Danish *mög dynge* muck heap⟩

mid·dle ['mɪdəl] *adj* **1** that is halfway between. **2** medium: *a man of middle size.* *n* the part that is the same distance from each end. ⟨Old English *middel*⟩
middle age the time of life between youth and old age. **mid·dle–aged** *adj.* **Middle Ages** the period of European history between ancient and modern times, from about A.D. 500 (or from A.D. 476, the date of the fall of Rome) to about A.D. 1450. **middle–age spread** weight gain in the middle years of

life, esp on the waist and hips. **mid·dle·brow** *n* one who has an average interest in intellectual or arts topics. **mid·dle·brow** *adj.* **middle C** *Music* the note on the first added line below the treble staff and the first above the bass staff. **middle class** people between the wealthy and the working class. **mid·dle–class** *adj.* **middle distance 1** the part of a scene between the foreground and the background. **2** *Sports* a category of footrace between the sprints and the distance races **middle–distance** *adj.* **Middle East** the region between the E Mediterranean and India. **middle finger** the finger between the forefinger and the ring finger. **mid·dle·man** *n, pl* **-men** a trader who buys goods from the producer and sells them to a retailer or to the consumer. **middle management** the mid-level of supervisory management in a company, between managers and workers. **mid·dle–of–the–road** *adj* moderate. **mid·dle–of–the–road·er** *n.* **Middle Path** *Buddhism* a way of life midway between materialism and self-denial. **middle school** a school midway between elementary and high school, usually comprising grades six through eight. **mid·dle·weight** *n* a boxer weighing between 71 kg and 75 kg. **mid·dling** *adj* medium in size, quality, grade, etc. *adv Informal or dialect* moderately.

midge [mɪdʒ] *n* **1** any of a family of small flies usually found in swarms around ponds and streams. **2** a very small person or animal. ⟨Old English *mycg*⟩

midg·et ['mɪdʒɪt] *n* **1** a person very much smaller than normal. **2** anything much smaller than the usual size for its type. *adj* **1** much smaller than usual for its type: *a midget submarine.* **2** *Sports* of or for very young or very small players. ⟨*midge*⟩

mid·life crisis ['mɪd,ləif] a turning point during the middle years of life, brought about by stressful events such as menopause or children leaving home.

mid·night ['mɪd,nəit] *n* the middle of the night; esp 12 o'clock at night. *adj* of, at, or like midnight; very dark: *midnight blue.*
burn the midnight oil work or study far into the night.
midnight sun the sun seen at midnight in the arctic and antarctic regions during the summer. **land of the midnight sun** the Arctic or Antarctic.

mid·point ['mɪd,pɔint] *n* a point at or near the centre or middle: *the midpoint of a line.*

mid·riff ['mɪdrɪf] *n* the muscular wall separating the chest cavity from the abdomen. ⟨Old English *midd* mid + *hrif* belly⟩

midst [mɪdst] *n* the middle. *prep* amidst; amid. Also, **'midst.** **in our** (or **your** or **their**) **midst** among us (or you or them): *a traitor in our midst.* **in the midst of a** in the middle of. **b** during: *The announcement was made in the midst of the program.* ⟨Old English *tō middes* in the middle; and *mid* + *-est*⟩

mid·stream ['mɪd'strim] *n* **1** the middle of a stream. **2** the middle of any process. *adv* in midstream.

mid·sum·mer ['mɪd'sʌmər] *or* ['mɪd,sʌmər] *n* around June 21, the summer solstice. **mid·sum·mer** *adj*.

mid·term ['mɪd,tɜrm] *n* **1** the middle of a term. **2** an examination held in the middle of a term or semester. **mid·term** *adj*.

mid·way ['mɪd'wəi] *adv, adj* halfway; in the middle: *midway between the two towns* (adv), *a midway point on the chart* (adj). *n* ['mɪd,wei] at a fair or exhibition, the place for games, rides, and other amusements. ⟨Old English *midweg*⟩

mid·week ['mɪd,wik] *n* the middle of the week. **mid·week** *adj*. **mid·week·ly** *adv*.

mid·wife ['mɪd,wəif] *n, pl* -wives a person who helps women in childbirth. ⟨Old English *mid* with + *wīf* woman⟩
mid·wife·ry [mɪd'wɪfəri] *n* the science of helping women in childbirth.

mid·win·ter ['mɪd'wɪntər] *n* around December 21, the winter solstice. **mid·win·ter** *adj*.

mid·year ['mɪd,jir] *n* the middle of the year. **mid·year** *adj*.

mien [min] *n* a way of acting and looking: *The manager had the mien of a soldier.* ⟨probably related to DEMEANOUR; influenced by French *mine* facial expression; Celtic⟩

miff [mɪf] *Informal n* a petty quarrel. *v* be or make offended. ⟨origin uncertain⟩

might¹ [məit] *v* pt of MAY.

might² [məit] *n* great power; strength. **with might and main** with all one's strength. ⟨Old English *miht*⟩
might·y *adj* **1** powerful: *a mighty blow.* **2** very great: *a mighty famine.* *adv Informal* very; extremely: *a mighty cold day.* *n* the mighty, *pl* all those who are mighty. **might·i·ly** *adv*.

mi·graine ['maigrein] *n* a severe headache, often accompanied by nausea and sensitivity to light. **mi·grain·ous** ['maigrənəs] *adj*. ⟨Greek *hemikrania; hemi-* half + *kranion* skull⟩

mi·grate ['maigreit] *v* **1** move from one place to settle in another. **2** go from one region to another with the change in the seasons. **mi·gra·to·ry** ['maigrə,tɔri] *adj*. ⟨Latin *migrare*⟩
mi·grant *n* a person, animal, bird, or plant that migrates. **mi·grant** *adj*. **mi·gra·tion** *n* **1** a number of people or animals migrating together. **2** *Chemistry* **a** a movement of atoms from one place to another within the molecule. **b** the movement of ions between the two electrodes during electrolysis. **mi·gra·tion·al** *adj*.

mi·ka·do [mə'kɑdou] *n* the ancient title of the emperor of Japan. ⟨Japanese *mi* honourable + *kado* door, gate⟩

mike [məik] *n Informal* microphone. *v* provide with a microphone.

Mi'kmaw ['mɪkmɒw] *n, pl* -maq **1** a member of a First Nations people living in the Maritimes. **2** their Algonquian language. **Mi'kmaw** *adj*. Also, **Mic·mac**. ⟨Algonquian, literally, allies⟩

mild [maild] *adj* **1** gentle; kind: *a mild old gentleman.* **2** warm; not harsh or severe: *a mild climate.* **3** not sharp or strong in taste: *mild cheese.* **mild·ly** *adv*. **mild·ness** *n*. ⟨Old English *milde*⟩

mil·dew ['mɪldju] *or* ['mɪldu] *n* **1** any of various fungi that attack plants or grow on food, cloth, etc., esp in damp conditions. **2** a furry coating caused by the growth of such fungi. **mil·dew** *v*. **mil·dew·y** *adj*. ⟨Old English *mildēaw* honeydew⟩

mile [mail] *n* **1** a non-metric unit of distance, equal to about 1.609 km. **2** NAUTICAL MILE. **3** miles *pl* a relatively great distance: *We were miles from home.* Abbrev **mi** ⟨Old English *mīl*; Latin *milia passuum* a thousand paces; *mille* thousand⟩
mile·age *n* **1** the total number of miles travelled: *What's the mileage on your car?* **2** the distance a motor vehicle can go on a given amount of fuel: *We get good mileage on our new car.* **3** an allowance for travelling expenses at a fixed rate per unit of distance: *She gets mileage on trips she makes for the company.* **4** the use a person gets out of something: *He's getting a lot of mileage out of that one joke.* **mile·stone** *n* an important event: *The invention of printing was a milestone in the progress of education.*

mi·lieu [mɪl'jʊ] *French* [mi'ljø] *n* surroundings; environment.

mil·i·tar·y ['mɪlə,tɛri] *adj* to do with soldiers or war.
n the military the armed forces; soldiers: *The military did rescue work during the flood.* ⟨Latin *militaris; miles* soldier⟩
mil·i·tant *adj* **1** aggressive; warlike. **2** aggressively active in serving a cause: *a militant environmentalist.* **mil·i·tant** *n*. **mil·i·tan·cy** *n*. **mil·i·tant·ly** *adv*. **mil·i·ta·rism** *n* the policy of making military power very strong. **mil·i·ta·rist** *n*. **mil·i·ta·ris·tic** *adj*. **mil·i·ta·ris·ti·cal·ly** *adv*. **mil·i·ta·rize** *v* make the military organization of (a country) very powerful. **mil·i·ta·ri·za·tion** *n*. **military law** a system of regulations governing the armed forces. **mil·i·tate** *v* operate *(against)*: *Bad weather militated against the success of the picnic.* **mi·li·tia** [mə'lɪʃə] *n* a part of an army made up of citizens who are not regular soldiers but who undergo training for emergency duty.

milk [mɪlk] *n* **1** the white liquid secreted by the mammary glands of female mammals for the nourishment of their young. **2** any liquid resembling this: *coconut milk*.
v **1** draw milk from: *to milk cows*. **2** drain strength, wealth, etc. from: *The dishonest treasurer milked the club funds.* **milk·less** *adj*. ⟨Old English *milc, mioluc*⟩
cry over spilt milk waste regret on what has happened and cannot be remedied.
milk·er 1 *n* a cow, goat, etc. that gives a specified quantity or quality of milk: *a good milker.* **2** a person who or machine that milks. **milk·ing** *n* one of the regularly scheduled times when cows are milked. **milk of human kindness** natural sympathy and affection. **milk of magnesia** a milky-white medicine, used as a laxative and antacid. **milk shake** a drink consisting of milk, flavouring, and often ice cream, shaken until frothy. **milk snake** a harmless snake that eats small rodents. **milk·sop** [ˈmɪlk,sɒp] *n* a weak person; a coward. **milk sugar** lactose. **milk tooth** one of the first set of teeth. **milk·weed** *n* any of various weeds whose stem contains a white juice that looks like milk. **milk–white** or **milky–white** *adj* white as milk. **milk·y** *adj* **1** white as milk. **2** containing milk. **3** mild; weak; timid. **milk·i·ness** *n*. **Milky Way 1** a broad band of faint light across the sky at night. It is made up of countless stars. **2** the galaxy in which these countless stars are found. The earth, sun, and all the planets around the sun are part of the Milky Way.

mill¹ [mɪl] *n* **1** a machine for grinding: *a coffee mill.* **2** a building containing a machine for grinding grain. **3** a building where manufacturing is done: *A paper mill makes paper from wood pulp.*
v **1** grind: *Some wheat will be milled before it is exported.* **2** manufacture. **3** cut a series of fine ridges on the edge of (a coin): *A dime is milled.* **4** of people or animals in a group, move around in an aimless way (often with *around* or *about*): *There were many people milling around after the parade.* ⟨Old English *mylen*; Latin *molinum; mola* millstone⟩
go (or **put**) **through the mill** *Informal* learn (or teach) by hard or painful experience.
mill·er *n* a person who owns or runs a mill, esp a flour mill. **mill·pond** *n* a pond supplying water to drive a mill wheel. **mill·race** *n* a current of water that drives a mill wheel. **mill·stone** *n* **1** either of a pair of stones used for grinding corn, wheat, etc. **2** a heavy burden: *The old house was a millstone around her neck.* **3** anything that grinds or crushes. **mill·stream** *n* the stream in a millrace. **mill wheel** a wheel that is turned by water and supplies power for a mill. **mill·wright** *n* **1** a person who sets up mills or machinery for mills. **2** a mechanic who takes care of the machinery in a factory, etc.

mill² [mɪl] *n* $.001, or one-tenth of a cent. Mills are used in accounting, but not as coins. ⟨Latin *millesimum* one thousandth; *mille* thousand⟩
mill rate a rate used for calculating municipal taxes. A mill rate of 45.6 means that a property owner pays a tax of 45.6 mills ($0.0456) for every dollar of the assessed value of the property.

mil·len·ni·um [məˈlɛniəm] *n, pl* **mil·len·ni·ums** or **mil·len·ni·a** [məˈlɛniə] **1** a period of a thousand years: *The world is many millenniums old.* **2 the millennium** the period of a thousand years during which, according to the Bible, Christ is prophesied to reign on earth. **mil·len·ni·al** *adv*. ⟨Latin *mille* thousand + *annus* year⟩

mil·let [ˈmɪlɪt] *n* any of various grasses grown for grain or fodder. ⟨Middle French, diminutive of *mil* millet, Latin *milium*⟩

milli– *SI prefix* thousandth: *millilitre. Symbol* **m** ⟨Latin *mille*⟩

mil·li·bar [ˈmɪlə,bɑr] *n* an SI unit for measuring pressure, equal to 0.1 kilopascals. *Symbol* **mbar**

mil·li·gram [ˈmɪlə,græm] *n* one thousandth of a gram. Also, **mil·li·gramme.** *Symbol* **mg**

mil·li·li·tre [ˈmɪlə,litər] *n* one thousandth of a litre. Also, **mil·li·li·ter** *Symbol* **mL**

mil·li·me·tre [ˈmɪlə,mitər] *n* one thousandth of a metre. Also, **mil·li·me·ter** *Symbol* **mm**

mil·li·ner [ˈmɪlənər] *n* a person who makes, trims, or sells women's hats. ⟨*Milaner* dealer from Milan, Italy, famous for straw⟩
mil·li·ner·y [ˈmɪlənəri] *or* [ˈmɪlə,nɛri] *n* women's hats.

mil·lion [ˈmɪljən] *n* **1** one thousand thousand; 1 000 000. **2 mil·lions** a very large but unstated number. **mil·lion** *adj*. ⟨Italian *milione*; Latin *mille* thousand⟩
mil·lion·aire [ˈmɪljə,nɛr] *or* [ˌmɪljəˈnɛr] *n* **1** a person whose wealth is equal to more than a million dollars, pounds, etc. **2** any very wealthy person. **mil·lionth** *adj*, *n* one, or being one, of a million equal parts.

mil·li·pede [ˈmɪlə,pid] *n* any of a class of arthropod having a segmented body with most segments bearing two pairs of legs each. Also, **mil·le·pede.** ⟨Latin *mille* thousand + *pedis* foot⟩

mil·li·sec·ond [ˈmɪlə,sɛkənd] *n* one thousandth of a second. *Symbol* **ms**

milque·toast [ˈmɪlk,toust] *n* an extremely timid person. ⟨Mr. *Milquetoast*, a comic-strip character⟩

milt [mɪlt] *n* the sperm cells of male fishes together with the milky fluid containing them. ⟨earlier *milk*; *milt* spleen; Dutch⟩

mime [maɪm] *n* **1** a form of drama in which the actors use movement and gestures but no words. **2** communication through gestures but without words: *She told her story in mime.* **3** an actor communicating through gestures only. **mime** *v*. ⟨Greek *mimos*⟩

mim·ic [ˈmɪmɪk] *v* -**icked**, -**ick·ing 1** make fun of by imitating. **2** imitate: *A parrot can mimic a person's voice.* **3** of things, be an imitation of. *n* **1** a person or thing that imitates. **2** a performer whose act is mimicking.

adj not real, but imitated for some purpose: *a mimic battle*. **mim·ick·er** *n.* **mim·ic·ry** *n.* ⟨Greek *mimikos; mimos* mime⟩

mi·me·sis [maɪˈmisɪs] *or* [mɪˈmisɪs] *n* **1** mimicry. **2** *Biology* protective markings in a plant, animal, etc. **3** the representation of reality in art or literature. **4** *Pathology* the assuming of the symptoms of one disease by another disease. **mi·met·ic** [-ˈmɛtɪk] *adj.*

min minute(s).

min·a·ret [ˌmɪnəˈrɛt] *or* [ˈmɪnəˌrɛt] *n* a high tower of a Muslim mosque, from which a muezzin or crier calls the people to prayer. ⟨Spanish; Arabic *manāret* lighthouse⟩

mince [mɪns] *v* **1** grind into very small pieces. **2** speak or move in a prim, affected way. **3** soften (words, etc.), as when stating unpleasant facts: *The judge addressed the jury bluntly, without mincing words.* ⟨Old French *mincier*; Latin *minutus* small⟩
not to mince matters to speak plainly.
mince·meat *n* a mixture of chopped apples, raisins, etc., used as a filling for pies. **make mincemeat of** *Informal* reduce as if into little pieces: *Our team made mincemeat of the rest of the league.* **mince pie** a pie filled with MINCEMEAT. **minc·ing** *adj* affectedly elegant or dainty. **minc·ing·ly** *adv.*

mind [maɪnd] *n* **1** that part of a person which knows, thinks, feels, etc. **2** intellect. **3** a person who has intelligence: *a great mind.* **4** sanity: *be out of one's mind.* **5** a way of thinking and feeling: *change one's mind.*
v **1** take notice. **2** be careful concerning: *Mind the step.* **3** take care of: *Mind the baby.* **4** feel concern about: *We mind parting from a friend.* **mind·er** *n.* ⟨Old English *(ge)mynd*⟩
bear in mind remember. **be in** (or **of**) **two minds** vacillate between two intentions or opinions. **be of one mind** agree. **call to mind a** recall. **b** remember. **give someone a piece of one's mind** speak to angrily. **have a mind of one's own** have definite opinions. **have a mind** (*to*) intend to: *I have a mind to watch hockey tonight.* **have half a mind** (*to*) be somewhat inclined. **have in mind a** think of; consider. **b** intend. **keep in mind** remember. **know one's own mind** know what one really thinks. **make up one's mind** decide. **mind the store.** See STORE. **mind you** on the other hand: *He's very amusing; mind you, that can be tiresome at times.* **on one's mind** in one's thoughts; troubling one. **put someone in mind** (*of*) remind. **set one's mind on a** want very much. **b** concentrate. **speak one's mind** give one's frank opinion. **take one's mind off** distract one's attention from. **to one's mind** in one's opinion.
mind–blow·ing *adj* so amazing as to defy understanding: *a sum of money of mind-blowing proportions.* **mind–bog·gling** *adj* mind-blowing. **mind·ful** *adj* having in mind: *Mindful of your advice, I drove slowly.* **mind·ful·ly** *adv.* **mind·ful·ness** *n.* **mind·less** *adj* **1** stupid. **2** careless. **3** not requiring intelligence: *a mindless job.* **mind·less·ly** *adv.* **mind·less·ness** *n.* **mind reader** a person who

professes to be able to perceive another's thoughts directly. **mind·set** *n* a habitual mental attitude. **mind's eye** imagination.

mine¹ [maɪn] *pron* a possessive form of **I**: *The dog is mine.*
of mine associated with me: *She's a friend of mine.* ⟨Old English *mīn*⟩

mine² [maɪn] *n* **1** a large hole dug in the earth to get out valuable minerals: *a gold mine.* **2** a rich source: *a mine of information.* **3** a container holding an explosive charge that is exploded by propeller vibrations (**acoustic** or **sonic mine**) or by magnetic attraction (**magnetic mine**) or by contact with a person, vehicle, etc. (**land mine**). **mine** *v.* **min·er** *n.* ⟨French; Celtic⟩
mine·field *n* **1** an area where explosive mines have been laid. **2** a controversial issue or situation. **min·er·al** [ˈmɪnərəl] *n* **1** any inorganic, naturally occurring, solid element or compound having a crystalline structure. **2** any natural substance that is neither plant nor animal. *adj* to do with minerals: *mineral water.* **min·er·al·ize** *v* convert into mineral; petrify. **min·er·al·i·za·tion** *n.* **min·er·al·o·gy** [ˌmɪnəˈrɒlədʒi] *or* [ˌ-ˈrælədʒi] *n* the science that deals with the properties of minerals. **min·er·al·og·i·cal** *adj.* **min·er·al·og·i·cal·ly** *adv.* **min·er·al·o·gist** *n.* **mineral oil** an oil obtained from petroleum, used as a laxative and as a base for cold creams, etc. **mineral right** a right to the mineral deposits in a given piece of land. **mineral water** water containing mineral salts or gases. **mine·sweep·er** *n* a warship equipped for dragging the sea to remove or disarm enemy mines.

min·e·stro·ne [ˌmɪnəˈstrouni] *n* a soup containing vegetables, vermicelli, etc. ⟨Italian⟩

Ming [mɪŋ] *n* a type of fine porcelain. **Ming** *adj.* ⟨name of ruling Chinese dynasty (14-17c) when made⟩

min·gle [ˈmɪŋɡəl] *v* **1** mix or blend: *The Fraser and Thompson Rivers mingle their waters near Lytton, BC.* **2** associate: *to mingle with important people.* **min·gler** *n.* ⟨Middle English *mengele(n)*, Old English *mengan* mix⟩

min·i [ˈmɪni] *n* *Informal* something small, short, etc. for its kind, such as a miniskirt, minicar, or minibus. ⟨*miniature*⟩
mini– *combining form* small for its kind; very small, very short, etc.: *minicomputer.* **min·i·bike** *n* a small motorcycle. **min·i·bus** *n* a small bus used for short runs, as between an airport and a hotel, etc. **min·i·skirt** *n* a very short skirt ending well above the knees.

min·i·skirt·ed *adj.* **min·i·van** *n* a motor vehicle able to seat several passengers, whose rear seats can be removed to accommodate cargo.

min·ia·ture ['mɪnətʃər] *or* ['mɪniətʃər] *n* **1** a small model: *In the museum there is a miniature of the ship* Victory. **2** a very small painting, usually a portrait. *adj* tiny: *miniature furniture for a doll house.* **min·ia·tur·ize** *v.* **min·i·a·tur·i·za·tion** *n.* ⟨Italian *miniatura* Latin *miniare* illuminate (a manuscript), paint red *minium* red lead; confused with Latin *minutus* small⟩ **in miniature** reduced in size.

min·i·mum ['mɪnəməm] *n, pl* **-mums** or **-ma** [-mə] **1** the least amount or smallest quantity possible: *a minimum of eight hours sleep.* **2** *Mathematics* the least value of a function within an interval of the domain. *adj* least possible: *a minimum rate.* ⟨Latin = smallest⟩ **min·i·mal** ['mɪnəməl] *adj* to do with a minimum: *The side effects of the drug were minimal.* **min·i·mal·ly** *adv.* **min·i·mize** *v* **1** reduce to the least possible amount or degree: *Take every precaution to minimize the dangers of your trip.* **2** make the least of: *The ungrateful girl minimized the help we had given.* **min·i·mi·za·tion** *n.* **min·i·miz·er** *n.* **minimum wage** the lowest wage allowed by law.

min·ion ['mɪnjən] *n* a servile follower. ⟨French *mignon* darling, dainty⟩

min·is·ter ['mɪnɪstər] *n* **1** a member of the clergy serving a church. **2** a member of the cabinet who is in charge of a government department: *the Minister of Labour.* **3** a diplomat ranking below an ambassador: *the British Minister to Canada.* *v* **1** act as a servant or nurse (*to*): *She ministers to the sick.* **2** be helpful. **min·is·te·ri·al** [,mɪnɪ'stiriəl] *adj.* **min·is·te·ri·al·ly** *adv.* ⟨Latin = servant; *minus* less; on analogy of *magister* master⟩ **min·is·tra·tion** *n* the act of ministering: *ministration to the sick.* **min·is·tra·tive** *adj.* **min·is·try** *n* **1** the office or term of a minister. **2** the ministers of a church. **3** the ministers of a government. **4** in Canada, Europe, etc.: **a** a government department under a minister. **b** the offices of such a department.

mink [mɪŋk] *n, pl* **mink** or **minks** any of several mammals closely related to the weasels, having soft, lustrous fur. **mink·like** *adj.* ⟨Scandinavian; compare Swedish *mänk*⟩

min·now ['mɪnou] *n* any of various small, freshwater fishes. ⟨Middle English *minwe;* Old English *myne*⟩

mi·nor ['maɪnər] *adj* **1** smaller; less important: *a minor poet.* **2** under legal age. **3** *Music* of an interval, less by a half step than the corresponding major interval. *n* **1** a person who is legally considered not an adult. **2** *Music* a minor interval, key, scale, chord, etc. **3** a subject or course of study to which a student gives less time than to a major subject. **4** *Hockey* MINOR PENALTY. **5 the minors** *pl Sports* the minor leagues. *v* have or take as a minor subject of study (with *in*): *to minor in Chemistry.* ⟨Latin = lesser⟩

mi·nor·i·ty [mə'nɔrəti] *or* [maɪ'nɔrəti] *n* **1** the smaller part: *The minority must often accept what the majority decides to do.* **2** a group that differs in race, religion, or national origin from the larger part of the population. **3** the condition being under the legal age of responsibility. **mi·nor·i·ty** *adj.* **minor penalty** *Hockey* a two-minute penalty awarded for certain infractions of the rules. **minor premise** See SYLLOGISM.

min·ster ['mɪnstər] *n* a large or important church; cathedral. ⟨Old English *mynster;* Latin *monasterium*⟩

min·strel ['mɪnstrəl] *n* any of a class of medieval entertainers, esp a singer or musician. ⟨Latin *ministerialis.* See MINISTER.⟩ **min·strel·sy** *n* **1** a collection of songs and ballads. **2** a company of minstrels.

mint¹ [mɪnt] *n* any of a genus of strongly scented herbs, esp any of several species used for flavouring food. ⟨Latin *mentha;* Greek *minthē*⟩

mint² [mɪnt] *n* **1** a place where money is made by government authority. **2** *Informal* a large amount, esp of money: *She made a mint when she sold her house.* *adj* of a stamp or coin, in perfect condition, as issued. *v* **1** make (coins, medals, etc.): *This quarter was minted in 1938.* **2** make or originate. ⟨Old English *mynet* coin; Latin *moneta*⟩ **in mint condition** as good as new: *an old car in mint condition.*

min·u·et [,mɪnju'ɛt] *n* a slow, stately dance, popular in the 1700s. ⟨French *menuet,* diminutive of *menu* small⟩

mi·nus ['maɪnəs] *prep* **1** decreased by: *Five minus two is three.* **2** *Informal* without or lacking: *a book minus its cover.* *n* the sign (–) meaning that the quantity following it is to be subtracted. *adj* **1** less than (never before a noun): *A mark of B minus is not as high as B.* **2** less than zero: *a minus quantity.* ⟨Latin = less⟩ **min·u·end** ['mɪnju,ɛnd] *n* *Mathematics* a number or quantity from which another is to be subtracted.

mi·nus·cule ['mɪnə,skjul] *adj* **1** very small. **2** *Paleography* written in small letters, or in lower case letters. *n* a lower case letter. ⟨Latin *minuscula* slightly smaller; *minus* less⟩

min·ute¹ ['mɪnɪt] *n* **1** an SI unit for measuring time, equal to sixty seconds or one-sixtieth of an hour. *Symbol* **min 2** any short period of time: *He paused for a minute to listen.* **3** *Geometry* an SI unit for measuring angles, equal to sixty seconds or one-sixtieth of a degree. *Symbol* ′ **4** a written record. **5 minutes** *pl* the record of the proceedings at a meeting of a society, board, committee, etc. *v* **min·ut·ed, min·ut·ing** put in the minutes: *Have you minuted that?* ⟨Old French; Latin *minuta* small part, *minutus* small; *minus* less⟩ **up to the minute** up to date. **minute hand** on a watch or clock, the longer of the two hands, indicating the minutes. It moves around the dial once every hour.

SYNONYMS

Minute usually suggests a measurable, although very short, amount of time: *May I rest a minute?* Moment is more vague, suggesting a very brief period that is noticeable but not measurable: *I'll be with you in a moment.* Instant is more definite and suggests a point of time or a period too brief to be noticed: *Come here this instant!*

mi·nute² [maɪ'njut] *or* [maɪ'nut] *adj* **1** tiny: *a minute speck of dust.* **2** to do with very small details: *minute instructions.* **mi·nute·ly** *adv.* **mi·nute·ness** *n.* ⟨Latin *minutus* small; *minus* less⟩

mi·nu·ti·ae [mɪ'njuʃi,i] *or* [mɪ'nuʃi,i]; [-,aɪ] *or* [mɪ'nuʃi,aɪ] *n pl* very small matters; trifling details.

minx [mɪŋks] *n* a bold or impudent girl. **minx·ish** *adj.* ⟨perhaps Low German *minsk*, impudent woman⟩

min·yan ['mɪnjɑn] *or* [min'jɑn] *n, pl* **min·yan·im** [mɪn'jɒnɪm] *or* [,minja'nim] *Judaism* a quorum of ten adults needed to hold a service, a funeral, etc. ⟨Hebrew, orig = number, quantity⟩

Mi·o·cene ['maɪə,sin] *Geology n* the fourth epoch of the Tertiary period, beginning about 24 million years ago. **Mi·o·cene** *adj.* ⟨Greek *meiōn* less + *kainos* new⟩

mip·ku ['mɪpku] *n* ✹ dried caribou meat. ⟨Inuktitut⟩

mir·a·cle ['mirəkəl] *n* **1** a happening that is contrary to the known laws of nature: *It would be a miracle if the earth stood still in the sky for an hour.* **2** a remarkable example: *a miracle of patience.* **mi·rac·u·lous** [mə'rækjələs] *adj.* **mi·rac·u·lous·ly** *adv.* **mi·rac·u·lous·ness** *n.* ⟨Latin *miraculum; mirari* wonder at, *mirus* wonderful⟩

miracle drug a new drug that treats conditions previously thought untreatable. **miracle play** any of a class of medieval religious dramas.

mi·rage [mə'rɑʒ] *n* **1** a misleading appearance in which some distant scene is viewed as being close and, often, inverted. **2** an illusion; a thing that does not exist. ⟨French, from *mirer* gaze at⟩

Mi·ran·da [mə'rɑndə] *US adj* to do with the right to remain silent, etc., of which police are obliged to inform a person being arrested. **Mi·ran·dize** *v.* ⟨*Miranda*, defendant's surname in the case (1966) giving rise to this⟩

mire [maɪr] *n* **1** soft, deep mud. **2** a bog. *v* **1** stick or cause to stick in mire: *He mired his car and needed help.* **2** soil with mire. **3** hold back, as if in a mire: *She got mired in a traffic jam.* **mir·y** *adj.* **mir·i·ness** *n.* ⟨Old Norse *myrr*⟩

mir·ror ['mirər] *n* **1** a surface that reflects light. **2** whatever reflects or gives a true description: *This book is a mirror of the author's life.* **mir·ror** *v.* **mir·ror·like** *adj.* ⟨Old French *mirour*. See MIRAGE.⟩

mirth [mɜrθ] *n* merriment accompanied by laughter: *She shook with mirth.* **mirth·ful** *adj.* **mirth·ful·ly** *adv.* **mirth·ful·ness** *n.* **mirth·less** *adj.* **mirth·less·ly** *adv.* **mirth·less·ness** *n.* ⟨Old English *myrgth; myrge* merry⟩

mis– *prefix* **1** bad: *misinformation.* **2** badly: *misbehave.* **3** wrong: *mispronunciation.* **4** wrongly: *misunderstand.* ⟨Old English⟩

mis·ad·ven·ture [,mɪsəd'vɛntʃər] *n* an unfortunate accident.

mis·al·ly [,mɪsə'laɪ] *v* **-lied, -ly·ing** associate unsuitably. **mis·al·li·ance** *n* an unsuitable association, esp in marriage.

mis·an·dry ['mɪsəndri] *or* ['mɪsændri] *n* hatred of men or of males. **mis·an·drist** *n.* ⟨Greek *misos* hatred + *andros* man⟩

mis·an·thro·py [mɪ'sænθrəpi] *n* a hatred or distrust of human beings. **mis·an·thrope** ['mɪsən,θroup] *n.* **mis·an·throp·ic** [-'θrɒpɪk] *adj.* **mis·an·throp·i·cal·ly** *adv.* ⟨Greek *misos* hatred + *anthrōpos* person⟩

mis·ap·ply [,mɪsə'plaɪ] *v* make a wrong use of. **mis·ap·pli·ca·tion** *n.* **mis·ap·pli·er** *n.*

mis·ap·pre·hend [,mɪsæprɪ'hɛnd] *v* misunderstand. **mis·ap·pre·hen·sion** *n.*

mis·ap·pro·pri·ate [,mɪsə'proupri,eit] *v* make use of without authority or right: *The treasurer had misappropriated the club funds.* **mis·ap·pro·pri·a·tion** *n.*

mis·be·got·ten [,mɪsbɪ'gɒtən] *adj* **1** illegitimate: *a misbegotten child.* **2** poorly done; pitiable: *She was ready to throw out the whole misbegotten plan.*

mis·be·have [,mɪsbɪ'heiv] *v* behave oneself badly. **mis·be·hav·iour** *or* **mis·be·hav·ior** *n.*

mis·be·lief [,mɪsbɪ'lif] *n* a false or mistaken belief.

mis·cal·cu·late [mɪs'kælkjə,leit] *v* calculate wrongly; judge wrongly: *Her arrow fell short because she had miscalculated the distance.* **mis·cal·cu·la·tion** *n.* **mis·cal·cu·la·tor** *n.*

mis·car·riage [mɪs'kɛrɪdʒ] *or* [mɪs'kærɪdʒ] *n* **1** a failure: *a miscarriage of justice.* **2** ['mɪskɛrɪdʒ] the involuntary expulsion of a fetus from the womb before it has developed enough to survive. **mis·car·ry** [mɪs'kɛri] *or* [mɪs'kæri] *v.*

mis·cast [mɪs'kæst] *v, -cast, -cast·ing* cast in an unsuitable role: *The young actor was badly miscast as a grandfather.*

mis·ce·ge·na·tion [,mɪsədʒə'neiʃən] *or* [mɪ,sɛdʒə'neiʃən] *n* marriage or sexual relations between people of different races. ⟨Latin *miscere* mix + *genus* race⟩

mis·cel·la·ne·ous [,mɪsə'leiniəs] *adj* consisting of different things, not arranged in a particular system: *a miscellaneous collection of stamps.* **mis·cel·la·ne·ous·ly** *adv.* **mis·cel·la·ne·ous·ness** *n.* ⟨Latin *miscellus* mixed; *miscere* mix⟩

mis·cel·la·ny [mə'sɛləni] *or* ['mɪse,leini] *n* a mixture of various things.

mis·chance [mɪs'tʃæns] *n* bad luck.

mis·chief ['mɪstʃɪf] *n* **1** conduct that causes harm, often unintentionally: *Mischief with matches may cause a serious fire.* **2** merry teasing: *Her eyes were full of mischief.* **3** harm or injury, esp when done by a person: *He'll do you a mischief if he can.* **mis·chie·vous** ['mɪstʃəvəs] *adj.* **mis·chie·vous·ly** *adv.* **mis·chie·vous·ness** *n.* ⟨Old French *meschief, mes-* bad + *chever* come to an end⟩

mis·ci·ble ['mɪsəbəl] *adj* especially of liquids, capable of being mixed to form a substance having the same composition throughout. Water and alcohol are miscible; water and oil are not. **mis·ci·bil·i·ty** *n.* ⟨Latin *miscere* mix⟩

mis·con·ceive [ˌmɪskən'siv] *v* have a wrong idea about. **mis·con·cep·tion** *n.*

mis·con·duct [mɪs'kɒndʌkt] *n* **1** bad or dishonest management: *The ambassador was censured by the government for misconduct of diplomatic affairs.* **2** bad behaviour. **3** *Hockey* a ten-minute penalty awarded for improper behaviour.
v [ˌmɪskən'dʌkt] **1** manage badly or dishonestly. **2** behave (oneself) badly.

mis·con·strue [ˌmɪskən'stru] *v* misinterpret: *Shyness is sometimes misconstrued as rudeness.* **mis·con·struc·tion** *n.*

mis·count [mɪs'kaʊnt] *v* count incorrectly. *n* ['mɪs,kaʊnt] an incorrect count.

mis·cre·ant ['mɪskriənt] *adj* depraved. *n* villain. ⟨Old French *mes-* wrong + *creant,* pp of *creire* believe, Latin *credere*⟩

mis·cue ['mɪskju] *or* [mɪs'kju] *n* **1** *Billiards* a bad stroke in which the cue slips and does not hit the ball squarely. **2** *Informal* a slip-up. *v* [mɪs'kju] **1** make a miscue. **2** *Theatre* miss one's cue; respond to a wrong cue.

mis·deal [mɪs'dil] *v* -dealt, -deal·ing *Card games v* deal incorrectly. **mis·deal** ['mɪsdil] *n.*

mis·deed [mɪs'did] *or* ['mɪsdid] *n* a bad or wicked act; offence.

mis·de·mean·our *or* **mis·de·mean·or** [ˌmɪsdɪ'minər] *n* **1** an offence, esp a minor one. **2** *Law esp US* a minor criminal offence, less serious than a felony. A misdemeanour is similar to a summary conviction offence in Canada.

mis·di·ag·nose [ˌmɪsdaɪəg'nous] *or* [-'nouz] *v* diagnose incorrectly.

mis·di·rect [ˌmɪsdə'rɛkt] *or* [ˌmɪsdaɪ'rɛkt] *v* direct incorrectly. **mis·di·rec·tion** *n.*

mise en scène [mizɑ̃'sɛn] *French* the general direction of a play or film, including staging, lighting, etc.

mi·ser ['maɪzər] *n* a person who loves money for its own sake, esp one who lives poorly in order to keep money. **mi·ser·ly** *adj.* **mi·ser·li·ness** *n.* ⟨Latin *miser* wretched⟩

mis·er·a·ble ['mɪzərəbəl] *adj* **1** unhappy; wretched. **2** causing trouble or unhappiness: *a miserable cold.* **3** poor; pitiful: *They live in a miserable, cold house.* **4** pitiable; deplorable: *a miserable failure.* **mis·er·a·ble·ness** *n.* **mis·er·a·bly** *adv.* ⟨Latin *miserare* to pity; *miser* wretched⟩

mis·er·y ['mɪzəri] *n* **1** an extremely unhappy state of mind. **2** poor or mean conditions: *Some very poor people live in misery.* **3** *Informal* a wretched person: *She's an old misery.*

mis·file [mɪs'faɪl] *v* file (papers, books, etc.) incorrectly.

mis·fire [mɪs'faɪr] *v* **1** of a firearm, etc., fail to discharge. **2** of an internal-combustion engine, fail to ignite properly. **3** fail to have an intended effect: *The robber's scheme misfired.* **mis·fire** ['mɪs,faɪr] *n.*

mis·fit ['mɪsfɪt] *n* **1** a bad fit, such as of a garment. **2** a person who is not suited to his or her environment. **mis·fit** [mɪs'fɪt] -fit·ted, -fit·ting *v.*

mis·for·tune [mɪs'fɔrtʃən] *n* **1** bad luck. **2** a piece of bad luck; unlucky accident.

mis·give [mɪs'gɪv] *v* -gave, -giv·en, -giv·ing cause to feel doubt, suspicion, or anxiety: *My heart misgave me.* **mis·giv·ing** *n.*

mis·gov·ern [mɪs'gʌvərn] *v* manage badly. **mis·gov·ern·ment** *n.*

mis·guide [mɪs'gaɪd] *v* lead into mistakes or wrongdoing; mislead. **mis·guid·ed** *adj.*

mis·han·dle [mɪs'hændəl] *v* **1** handle roughly or harshly: *to mishandle a horse.* **2** manage badly or ignorantly; mismanage: *to mishandle a business deal.*

mis·hap ['mɪshæp] *n* an unlucky accident. ⟨*mis-* + obsolete *hap* chance, luck; Old Norse *happ*⟩

mis·hear [mɪs'hir] *v* -heard, -hear·ing hear (especially words) inaccurately: *You must have misheard me, I said 'same' not 'shame'.*

mish·mash ['mɪʃ,mæʃ] *n* a jumble: *a mishmash of styles.* ⟨probable reduplication of *mush*⟩

Mish·nah *or* **Mish·na** ['mɪʃnə] *n,* pl **Mish·na·yoth** [ˌmɪʃnə'jout] *or* -yos [ˌ-'jous] *Judaism* the collection of the interpretations of the law of Moses. **Mish·na·ic** [mɪʃ'neiɪk] *or* **Mish·nic** *adj.* ⟨Hebrew = instruction; *shanah* teach, learn⟩

mis·in·form [ˌmɪsɪn'fɔrm] *v* give incorrect or misleading information to. **mis·in·form·er** *n.* **mis·in·for·ma·tion** *n.*

mis·in·ter·pret [ˌmɪsɪn'tɜrprɪt] *v* give a wrong meaning to: *to misinterpret a signal.* **mis·in·ter·pret·a·ble** *adj.* **mis·in·ter·pre·ta·tion** *n.* **mis·in·ter·pret·er** *n.*

mis·judge [mɪs'dʒʌdʒ] *v* **1** judge or estimate wrongly: *The archer misjudged the distance to the target and his arrow fell short.* **2** judge unfairly: *The teacher soon discovered that she had misjudged the boy's capabilities.* **mis·judg·er** *n.* **mis·judg·ing·ly** *adv.* **mis·judg·ment** *or* **mis·judge·ment** *n.*

mis·la·bel [mɪs'leibəl] *v* -la·belled, -label·ling label (something) incorrectly: *The $500 dress had been mislabelled $200.*

mis·lay [mɪs'lei] *v* -laid, -lay·ing put (a thing) in a place and forget where it is: *Mother is always mislaying her glasses.* **mis·lay·er** *n.*

mis·lead [mɪs'lid] *v* -led, -lead·ing cause to go in a wrong direction or to believe in something that is wrong: *His cheerfulness misled us into believing that everything was all right.* **mis·lead·ing** *adj.* **mis·lead·ing·ly** *adv.*

mis·man·age [mɪsˈmænɪdʒ] *v* manage badly. **mis·man·ag·er** *n.* **mis·man·age·ment** *n.*

mis·match [mɪsˈmætʃ]*v* match unsuitably, or fail to match: *a mismatched pair of socks.* **mis·match** [ˈmɪsmætʃ] *n.*

mis·name [mɪsˈneim] *v* call by a wrong or unsuitable name: *The slow horse was misnamed 'Lightning'.*

mis·no·mer [mɪsˈnoumər] *n* a wrong or unsuitable name or term: *'Lightning' is a misnomer for that slow old horse.*

mi·sog·a·my [mɪˈsɒgəmi] *n* a hatred of marriage. **mis·o·gam·ous** *adj.* **mi·sog·a·mist** *n.* ⟨Greek *misos* hatred + *gamos* marriage⟩

mi·sog·y·ny [mɪˈsɒdʒəni] *n* a hatred of women. **mi·sog·y·nist** *n.* **mi·sog·y·nous** *adj.* ⟨Greek *misos* hatred + *gynē* woman⟩

mis·place [mɪsˈpleis] *v* **1** put in the wrong place: *a misplaced adjective.* **2** put (something) in a place and then forget where it is. **3** place (one's affections, trust, etc.) on an unworthy object. **mis·place·ment** *n.*

mis·print [ˈmɪsˌprɪnt] a mistake in printing. **mis·print** [mɪsˈprɪnt] *v.*

mis·pro·nounce [ˌmɪsprəˈnaʊns] *v* say in a way considered incorrect. **mis·pro·nounc·er** *n.* **mis·pro·nun·ci·a·tion** [ˌmɪsprəˌnʌnsiˈeiʃən] *n.*

mis·quote [mɪsˈkwout] *v* quote incorrectly. **mis·quo·ta·tion** *n.* **mis·quote** *n.* **mis·quot·er** *n.*

mis·read [mɪsˈrid] *v* **-read** [-ˈrɛd], **-read·ing** **1** read wrongly: *I misread tapering as papering.* **2** misinterpret: *She misread his silence as agreement.* **mis·read·er** *n.*

mis·rep·re·sent [ˌmɪsrɛprɪˈzɛnt] *v* **1** give a wrong idea of, esp in order to deceive: *She misrepresented the car when she said it was in good running order.* **2** be a bad representative of: *His new novel misrepresents his status as a writer.* **mis·rep·re·sen·ta·tion** *n.* **mis·rep·re·sen·ta·tive** *adj.* **mis·rep·re·sent·er** *n.*

miss¹ [mɪs] *v* **1** fail to hit (a target). **2** fail to find, get, do, etc.: *miss a train.* **3** avoid: *I just missed being hit.* **4** notice the absence of: *I did not miss my purse till later.* **5** feel keenly the absence of. **6** leave out: *to miss a word in reading.* **7** be without (only in progressive tenses): *The bicycle is missing one pedal.* *n* a failure to hit, attain, etc.: *a near miss.* ⟨Old English *missan*⟩ **a miss is as good as a mile** a narrow miss is no better or worse than a wide miss. **give something a miss** *Slang* not go to (an event) on purpose. **miss one's guess** guess wrongly. **miss·ing** *adj.* **1** out of the usual place: *a missing shoe.* **2** absent: *Two students were missing from class.* **3** lacking or wanting: *It was a good dinner, but there was something missing.* **missing link** an animal of indeterminate form needed to prove the evolution of one known animal to another.

miss² [mɪs] *n* **1** a girl or young woman. **2 Miss** a title put before a girl's or unmarried

woman's name. **3 Miss,** a form of address used in place of the name of a girl or an unmarried woman: *I beg your pardon, Miss.* ⟨short for *mistress*⟩

mis·sal [ˈmɪsəl] *n* **1** *Roman Catholic Church* a book containing the prayers, etc. for celebrating the Mass throughout the year. **2** any book of prayers, etc. ⟨Latin *missa* Mass⟩

mis·shape [mɪsˈʃeip] *v* **-shaped, -shaped** or **-shap·en, -shap·ing** shape badly; deform; make in the wrong shape. **mis·shap·en** *adj* badly shaped; deformed. **mis·shap·en·ly** *adv.* **mis·shap·en·ness** *n.*

mis·sile [ˈmɪsail] *or* [ˈmɪsəl] *n* **1** an object that is thrown or shot at a target. **2** a rocket containing explosives. ⟨Latin *missilis* throwable; *missus* pp of *mittere* send⟩

mis·sion [ˈmɪʃən] *n* **1** special business on which a person or group is sent. **2** a group of persons sent on some special business: *She was one of a trade mission.* **3** an organization for the spread of a religious faith or for humanitarian work, or the headquarters of such a mission. **4** a program of religious services for converting unbelievers or stimulating faith. **5** a place where persons may go for aid, such as food, shelter, or counsel. **6** a purpose in life: *He felt that his mission was to care for his brother's children.* ⟨Latin *missio* a sending; *missus.* See MISSILE⟩ **mis·sion·ar·y** [ˈmɪʃəˌnɛri] *n* **1** a person sent by a church, etc. on a religious mission. **2** a person who works to advance some cause or idea: *a missionary for science. adj* to do with missions or missionaries: *He spoke with missionary zeal of a new social order.* **mission furniture** heavy, plain furniture. **mission statement** a paper issued by an organization, setting forth its objectives and future plans.

mis·sive [ˈmɪsɪv] *n Literary* a written message; letter. ⟨Latin *missus.* See MISSILE.⟩

mis·spell [mɪsˈspɛl] *v* **-spelled** or **-spelt, -spell·ing** spell incorrectly. **mis·spell·ing** *n.*

mis·spend [mɪsˈspɛnd] *v* **-spent, -spend·ing** spend wrongly; waste: *The woman regretted having misspent her youth.* **mis·spend·er** *n.*

mis·state [mɪsˈsteit] *v* make misleading or wrong statements about. **mis·state·ment** *n.*

mis·step [mɪsˈstɛp] *or* [ˈmɪsstɛp] *n* **1** a wrong step: *A single misstep would have plunged him into the abyss.* **2** an error in judgment; blunder: *A misstep now could ruin her career.*

mis·sus [ˈmɪsəz] *n* Often, **the missus** *Informal* wife: *You'll have to ask the missus about that.* Also, **miss·is.** ⟨*mistress*⟩

miss·y [ˈmɪsi] *n Informal* little miss; miss.

mist [mɪst] *n* **1** a cloud of fine drops of water in the air. **2** anything that obscures: *The ideas were lost in a mist of long words.* *v* **1** rain in fine drops. **2** cover or become covered with or as if with mist (often with *over* or *up*): *Tears misted her eyes.* ⟨Old English⟩ **mist·y** *adj* **1** full of or covered with mist: *misty air.* **2** not clearly seen: *a misty shape.* **3** vague; indistinct. **mist·i·ly** *adv.* **mist·i·ness** *n.*

mis·take [mɪ'steik] *n* a misunderstanding; error; blunder: *I used your towel by mistake.* *v* -**took,** -**tak·en,** -**tak·ing** 1 misunderstand what is seen or heard: *She gave me the address but I mistook the street name and got lost.* 2 take to be some other person or thing: *I mistook that stick for a snake.* **mis·tak·a·ble** *adj.* **mis·tak·a·bly** *adv.*
and no mistake without a doubt; surely.
mis·tak·en *adj* 1 wrong in opinion; having made a mistake: *A mistaken person should admit his or her error.* 2 wrongly judged: *It was a mistaken kindness to give that girl more candy.* **mis·tak·en·ly** *adv.*

mis·ter ['mɪstər] *n* 1 **Mister** the spoken form of MR., a title for a man, used before his last name or the name of his rank or office: *He always called his teacher 'Mister'.* 2 *Informal* a title used in speaking to a man (used alone, not with a name): *Hey, mister! You dropped your wallet.* ⟨variant of *master*⟩

USAGE
When used as a title before a name or office, **Mister** is generally written in its abbreviated form: **Mr.** See also MISTRESS, def. 5.

mis·time [mɪs'taɪm] *v* 1 say or do at the wrong time. 2 misstate the time of.

mis·tle·toe ['mɪsəl,tou] *n* a shrub traditionally used as a Christmas decoration. ⟨Old English *mistel* mistletoe + *tān* twig⟩

mis·took [mɪs'tʊk] *v* pt of MISTAKE.

mis·tral ['mɪstrəl] *or* [mɪs'trɑl] *n* a cold, dry, northerly wind common in S France. ⟨Provençal = orig dominant, Latin *magistralis; magister* master⟩

mis·trans·late [,mɪstrænz'leit] *or* [mɪs'trænzlcit] *v* translate incorrectly. **mis·trans·la·tion** *n.*

mis·treat [mɪs'trit] *v* treat badly; abuse. **mis·treat·ment** *n.*

mis·tress ['mɪstrɪs] *n* 1 a woman who has power or authority, such as the female head of a household. 2 a woman or girl as owner: *The dog was waiting for its mistress.* 3 a woman having a thorough mastery (of something): *mistress of the art of fencing.* 4 a woman who has a continuing sexual relationship with a man who supports her, without being married to him. 5 **Mistress** *Archaic, dialect* a title for a woman, used before the name. It is replaced in modern use by **Mrs.** (pronounced ['mɪsəz]), **Miss,** or **Ms.** ⟨Old French *maistress; maistre.* See MASTER.⟩

mis·tri·al ['mɪs,traɪəl or [mɪs'traɪəl] *n* 1 a trial declared void because of some error in the proceedings. 2 a trial that is inconclusive because the jury has failed to reach a verdict.

mis·trust [mɪs'trʌst] *v* have no confidence in: *She mistrusted her ability to learn to swim.* **mis·trust** *n.* **mis·trust·ing** *adj.*
mis·trust·ful *adj* doubting; suspicious. **mis·trust·ful·ly** *adv.*

mis·un·der·stand [,mɪsʌndər'stænd] *v* -**stood,** -**stand·ing** take in a wrong sense; give the wrong meaning to.
mis·un·der·stand·ing *n* 1 a failure to understand. 2 a disagreement: *After their misunderstanding, they scarcely spoke to each other for months.* **mis·un·der·stand·ing·ly** *adv.* **mis·un·der·stood** *adj* not understood or properly appreciated: *As a child, he had always felt misunderstood.*

mis·use [mɪs'juz] *v* 1 use for the wrong purpose: *He misuses his knife at the table by lifting food with it.* 2 abuse; ill-treat: *She misuses her sled dogs by driving them too hard.* *n* [mɪs'jus] wrong, improper, or harsh usage: *the misuse of public funds.*

mite [maɪt] *n* 1 any of a large number of tiny arachnids that are often parasites on plants or animals. 2 any very small object or creature: *I'll have just a mite of toast.* 3 a small sum of money: *Though poor herself, she gave her mite to charity.* 4 *Informal* bit; tad: *She's a mite greedy.* ⟨Old English⟩

mit·i·gate ['mɪtə,geit] *v* make or become less severe: *to mitigate a person's anger.* **mit·i·ga·ble** *adj.* **mit·i·ga·ting** *adj.* **mit·i·ga·tion** *n.* ⟨Latin *mitigare; mitis* gentle⟩

mi·to·sis [məi'tousɪs] *or* [mɪ'tousɪs] *n Biology* the division of the nucleus of a living animal or plant cell to produce two daughter nuclei that are identical to the parent. Compare MEIOSIS. **mi·tot·ic** [məi'tɒtɪk] *or* [mɪ'tɒtɪk] *adj.* **mi·tot·i·cal·ly** *adv.* ⟨Greek *mitos* thread⟩

mi·tral valve ['maɪtrəl] *Anatomy* the heart valve between the left atrium and the left ventricle.

mi·tre ['məitər] *n* 1 a tall cap worn by bishops and abbots during certain ceremonies. 2 the headdress of the ancient Jewish high priests. 3 a finished or hemmed corner on a garment, tablecloth, etc. *v* 1 join or prepare (ends of wood) for joining in a mitre joint. 2 finish (a corner of a hem) in a mitre joint. Also, **mi·ter. mi·tred** or **mi·tered** *adj.* ⟨Greek *mitra* headband⟩
mitre box *Carpentry* a box designed to guide a saw in cutting a mitre joint. **mitre joint** a right-angled joint made by cutting the ends of two pieces of wood, etc. on equal slants and fitting them together.

mitt [mɪt] *n* 1 mitten. 2 a padded glove used for catching the ball in baseball, etc. 3 a mittenlike covering or pad worn over the hand, designed for a particular use: *oven mitts.* 4 *Slang* a hand. ⟨short for *mitten*; French *mitaine,* Old French *mite*⟩
mit·ten ['mɪtən] *n* a glove covering the fingers together and the thumb separately.

mix [mɪks] *v* 1 stir well together: *mix ingredients for a cake.* 2 join: *mix business and pleasure.* 3 be mixable: *Milk and water mix.* 4 make friends easily: *She found it difficult to mix with strangers.* 5 confuse (usually with up): *Don't mix me up; I'm trying to count.* *n* 1 mixture. 2 a mixed preparation: *a cake mix.* 3 ginger ale, soda water, etc. to mix with alcoholic drinks. **mix·a·bil·i·ty** *n.* **mix·a·ble** *adj.* ⟨Latin *mixtus* pp of *miscere* mix⟩
mixed [mɪkst] *adj* 1 of different kinds combined: *mixed emotions.* 2 of different

kinds; assorted: *mixed candy.* **3** of or for persons of both sexes: *mixed company.* **mixed up** involved esp in something dishonest (with *in* or *with*): *She was mixed up in a plot to overthrow the king.* **mixed bag** *Informal* a collection of different people or things: *The guests at the party were really a mixed bag.* **mixed blessing** an advantage that has some disadvantageous aspects. **mixed doubles** *Tennis, etc* a match for two couples, each a man and a woman. **mixed farm** a farm on which both crops and livestock are raised. **mixed farming. mixed marriage** a marriage between persons of different races or religions. **mixed metaphor** See METAPHOR. **mixed number** a number consisting of a whole number and a fraction, such as 1 $3/4$. **mixed–up** *adj* bewildered; emotionally unbalanced: *a mixed-up youth.* **mix·er** *n* **1** an appliance for mixing foods, etc. **2** a person who gets along well with others: *a good mixer.* **3** MIX (def. 3). **4** an informal party where people can mingle. **mix·ture** *n* **1** something made by mixing: *Green is a mixture of blue and yellow.* **2** *Chemistry* a substance made of ingredients that keep their individual properties and can be separated by non-chemical means: *A mixture of sugar and water can be separated by boiling off the water.* Compare COMPOUND[1] (def. 2). **mix–up** *n Informal* confusion; mess.

SYNONYMS
Mix emphasizes forming a compound in which the parts are well spread into one another: *Mix the dry ingredients before adding a liquid.* Blend = mix smoothly together, so that each part loses its distinct existence: *Blend the flour into the butter.*

mL millilitre(s).

MLA or **M.L.A.** MEMBER OF THE LEGISLATIVE ASSEMBLY.

Mlle or **Mlle.** *pl* **Mlles** or **Mlles.** Mademoiselle.

mm millimetre(s).

Mme or **Mme.** *pl* **Mmes** or **Mmes.** Madame.

MNA or **M.N.A.** MEMBER OF THE NATIONAL ASSEMBLY.

mne·mon·ic [nɪˈmɒnɪk] *adj* **1** intended to aid memory: *mnemonic symbols.* **2** to do with memory: *great mnemonic power.* *n* a device to aid the memory. ⟨Greek *mnēmonikos; mnammasthai* remember⟩ **mne·mon·i·cal·ly** *adv.*

M.O. See MODUS OPERANDI.

moan [moun] *n* **1** a low sound of suffering. **2** any similar sound: *the moan of the wind.* **moan** *v.* **moan·ing** *adj.* ⟨Middle English *man*⟩

moat [mout] *n* a ditch dug around a castle or town as a protection against enemies. Moats were usually kept filled with water. ⟨Old French *mote* mound⟩

mob [mɒb] *n* **1** a crowd. **2** an uncontrollable crowd. **3** *Slang* **a** a gang of criminals. **b the mob** the Mafia. **4 the mob a** the common mass of people, thought of as lacking taste, culture, judgment, etc.

v **mobbed, mob·bing 1** attack with violence, as a mob does. **2** crowd around too closely: *Autograph hunters mobbed the singer outside her hotel.* ⟨Latin *mobile vulgus* fickle populace⟩ **mob·ster** *n Slang* a member of a gang of criminals.

mo·bile [ˈmoubaɪl] *or* [ˈmoubəl] *adj* **1** capable of moving or of being moved: *A car is a mobile machine.* **2** easily changed: *mobile features.* **3** allowing or undergoing movement from one social class to another: *a mobile society.* **mo·bil·i·ty** [mouˈbɪləti] *n.* ⟨Latin *mobilis* movable; *movere* move⟩ **mo·bile** [ˈmoubaɪl] *or* [ˈmoubil] *n* a construction of shapes suspended from wires, so that the shapes will move in a current of air. **mobile home** a large trailer used as a more or less permanent home. Compare MOTOR HOME. **mobile phone** a telephone linked to a cellular radio system. **mo·bi·lize** [ˈmoubəˌlaɪz] *v* **1** call (troops, warships, etc.) into active military service. **2** prepare for war: *The troops mobilized quickly.* **3** put into active use: *mobilize the wealth of a country.* **mo·bi·liz·a·ble** *adj.* **mo·bi·li·za·tion** *n.* **mo·bi·liz·er** *n.*

Mö·bi·us strip [ˈmoubiəs] *German* [ˈmœbiʊs] a one-sided, continuous surface, made by twisting one end of a rectangular strip through 180° and joining it to the other end. Also, **Moe·bi·us strip.** ⟨A.F. *Möbius* 19c German mathematician⟩

moc·ca·sin [ˈmɒkəsən] *n* **1** a leather shoe or boot having the bottom and sides made of a single piece of leather which is joined to the rounded piece forming the top. Moccasins were the traditional footwear of many Native American and First Nations peoples. **2** a shoe or slipper similar in construction or appearance. ⟨Algonquian⟩ **moccasin flower** ✱ any of several lady's-slippers.

mo·cha [ˈmoukə] *n* **1** a variety of coffee originally coming from the Arabian peninsula. **2** a flavouring made from coffee or a mixture of coffee and chocolate. ⟨*Mocha,* a port in SW Yemen⟩

mock [mɒk] *v* **1** make fun of. **2** imitate; copy. **3** scoff. *adj* imitation: *a mock battle.* **mock·er** *n.* **mock·er·y** *n.* **mock·ing** *adj.* **mock·ing·ly** *adv.* ⟨Old French *mocquer*⟩ **make mock of** or **make mockery of** ridicule. **mock·ing·bird** *n* a songbird famous for being able to imitate the songs of other birds. **mock–up** *n* a full-sized model of an aircraft, landscape, etc., built accurately to scale.

mode [moud] *n* **1** the way in which a thing is done. **2** *Grammar* MOOD[2]. **3** *Music* **a** any of various arrangements of the tones of an octave. **b** either of the two main scale systems in modern music: *major and minor modes.* **4** the mineral composition of a sample of igneous rock, stated quantitatively in percentages by mass. **5** *Computers* the state of a device or program indicating the operations it is ready to perform. **6** the style that prevails; the way most people are behaving, dressing, etc. **7** *Mathematics* the member of a set of measurements that occurs most often. ⟨Latin *modus* measure⟩

mo·dal *adj* **1** *Grammar* to do with a verb form that expresses in terms of possibility rather than fact. The auxiliary verbs *may, can, must, would,* and *should* are modal verbs. **2** to do with mode, manner, or form. **mo·dal·i·ty** *n* **1** the fact, state, or quality of being modal. **2** form. **3** mode; method. **mod·ish** *adj* fashionable. **mod·ish·ly** *adv.* **mod·ish·ness** *n.*

mod·el ['mɒdəl] *n* **1** a small copy: *a model of a ship.* **2** a particular style of a thing: *Some car makers produce a new model every year.* **3** a descriptive hypothesis: *the Copernican model of the universe.* **4** a thing or person to be imitated. **5** a person who poses for artists, photographers, etc. **6** a person employed to wear clothing for customers to see.
v **-elled** or **-eled, -el·ling** or **-el·ing 1** make; design: *model a bird's nest in clay.* **2** follow as a model: *He modelled himself on his father.* **3** work as a model.
adj **1** used or serving as a model. **2** just right, esp in conduct: *a model child.* **mod·el·ler** or **mod·el·er** *n.* ⟨Italian *modo* mode⟩
on the model of in imitation of.
mod·el·ling or **mod·el·ing** *n* **1** the occupation of a model. **2** the making of solid forms in clay, wax, etc., esp by shaping with the hands. **3** in drawing or painting, the showing of the effects of light and shade to give a three-dimensional appearance.

mo·dem ['moudəm] *n* *Computers* a device that enables a computer to receive and send data over telephone lines. ⟨*mo(dulator)* + *dem(odulator)*⟩

mod·er·ate ['mɒdərɪt] *adj* **1** not extreme: *moderate expenses.* **2** not violent: *moderate winds.* **3** medium: *a moderate profit.*
n a person who holds moderate opinions.
v ['mɒdə,reit] **1** make or become less extreme: *The wind is moderating.* **2** act as moderator. **mod·er·ate·ly** *adv.* **mod·er·a·tion** *n.* ⟨Latin *moderare* regulate; *modus* measure⟩
in moderation not going to extremes: *He eats sweets in moderation.*
mod·er·a·tor *n* **1** a presiding officer. **2** an arbitrator. **3** the chief elected officer of certain churches. **4** material used in a reactor to slow down nuclear fission. **5** *Computers* a person who volunteers to screen messages sent to a NEWSGROUP or CHAT ROOM.

mod·ern ['mɒdərn] *adj* **1** of the present time or recent past: *Television is a modern invention.* **2** up-to-date; not old-fashioned.
n a person of the present time or of times not long past: *He is studying English dramatists, specializing in the moderns.* **mod·ern·ly** *adv.*
mod·ern·ness *n.* ⟨Latin *modernus,* from *modo* just now; *modus* measure⟩
mod·ern·ism *n* **1** modern attitudes, methods, etc. or sympathy with what is modern. **2** Usually, **Modernism** the tendency to interpret the teachings of the Bible or the Christian church in accordance with modern scientific theories. **mod·ern·ist** *n.* **mod·ern·is·tic** *adj.* **mod·ern·is·ti·cal·ly** *adv.*
mo·der·ni·ty [mə'dɜrnəti] *n* **1** something modern. **2** modern times. **mod·ern·ize** *v* **1** bring up to present ways or standards. **2** adopt modern ideas. **mod·ern·i·za·tion** *n.* **mod·ern·iz·er** *n.*

mod·est ['mɒdɪst] *adj* **1** having a moderate estimate of one's own merits. **2** unassertive or diffident: *modest behaviour.* **3** not extreme: *a modest request.* **4** not pretentious: *a modest living room.* **mod·est·ly** *adv.* **mod·es·ty** *n.* ⟨Latin *modestus* in due measure; *modus* measure⟩

mod·i·cum ['mɒdəkəm] *n* a moderate quantity: *a modicum of good sense.* ⟨Latin = moderate; *modus* measure⟩

mod·i·fy ['mɒdə,faɪ] *v* **1** change somewhat: *to modify the terms of a lease.* **2** make less: *to modify one's demands.* **3** *Grammar* limit the meaning of; qualify. Adverbs modify verbs, adjectives, and other adverbs. **4** *Biology* make structural changes. A tusk is a modified tooth. **mod·i·fi·a·ble** *adj.* **mod·i·fi·ca·tion** *n.* ⟨Latin *modus* measure + *facere* make⟩
mod·i·fi·er *n* *Grammar* a word that limits the meaning of another word. In *a very tight coat,* the adjective *tight* is a modifier of *coat,* and the adverb *very* is a modifier of *tight.*

mod·u·late ['mɒdʒə,leit] or ['mɒdjə,leit] *v* **1** adjust; tone down. **2** *Music* change from one key to another. **3** *Radio* vary the frequency of (electrical waves). **mod·u·la·tion** *n.* ⟨Latin *modulari; modus* measure⟩
mod·u·la·tor *n* a device for varying the frequency of a signal in radio, television, etc.

mod·ule ['mɒdʒul] or ['mɒdjul] *n* **1** a standard or unit for measuring. **2** an independent unit that forms part of a larger structure, program, etc. **mod·u·lar** *adj.* ⟨Latin *modulus,* diminutive of *modus* measure⟩

mod·u·lus ['mɒdʒələs] or ['mɒdjələs] *n, pl* **-li** [-,laɪ] *or* [-,li] *Mathematics* **1** of a complex number, the numerical length of the vector representing the complex number. **2** an integer which can be divided exactly into the difference between two other integers. *Example: a modulus of 4 and 14 is 5.* **mod·u·lar** *adj.* ⟨See MODULE.⟩

mo·dus o·pe·ran·di ['moudəs ,ɒpə'rændaɪ] *or* [-di] *Latin* a habitual way of working; the characteristic way a person does something. *Abbrev* **M.O.**

mo·gul¹ ['mougəl] *n* **1** **Mogul** one of the Mongol conquerors of India in the 16th century or one of their descendants. **2** an important or influential person. ⟨Arabic; Persian *Mugul* Mongol⟩

mo·gul² ['mougəl] *n* a mound or bump of hard snow on a ski run. ⟨Norwegian⟩

mo·hair ['mouher] *n* yarn made from the long, silky hair of the Angora goat. ⟨Arabic *mukhayyar;* influenced by *hair*⟩

Mo·ham·med [mou'hɑmɪd] *or* [mou'hæmɪd] *n* See MUHAMMAD.

Mo·hawk ['mouhɒk] *n* See Kanien'keha. *adj* to do with a haircut leaving only a central raised portion: *a Mohawk cut.*

Mohs scale [mouz] a scale according to which minerals are categorized by their relative hardness, with diamond being the hardest at 10 and talc the softest at 1. ⟨F. *Mohs,* 19c German mineralogist⟩

moi·e·ty ['mɔɪəti] *n* **1** half. **2** an indefinite part: *Only a moiety of high-school graduates go to college.* ⟨Middle French *moitié;* Latin *medietas* half; *medius* middle⟩

moil [mɔɪl] *v* work hard; drudge. *n* **1** hard work. **2** trouble; confusion. ⟨Old French *moillier* moisten; Latin *mollis* soft⟩

moiré or **moire** [mwɑ'rei], [mwɑr], or [mɔ'rei] *n* **1** cloth having an irregular, wavy finish. **2** the watery pattern itself. *adj* having such a finish: *moiré taffeta.* ⟨French *moire,* from English *mohair*⟩

moist [mɔɪst] *adj* **1** slightly wet. **2** humid. **3** full of tears: *His eyes were moist, but he did not cry.* **moist·en** *v.* **moist·ly** *adv.* **moist·ness** *n.* ⟨Old French *moiste,* Latin *muccidus; mucus* mucus⟩
mois·ture *n* a slight wetness. **mois·tur·ize** *v* restore moisture to: *a cream to moisturize the skin.* **mois·tur·iz·er** *n.*

mo·ksha ['moukʃə] *n Buddhism, Hinduism, Jainism* spiritual release and freedom from the ongoing cycle of death and rebirth; the final state of mystical bliss. ⟨Sanskrit⟩

mol MOLE[3].

mo·lar[1] ['moulər] *n* a tooth with a broad surface for grinding. *adj* **1** capable of grinding. **2** to do with the molar teeth. ⟨Latin *mola* mill⟩

mo·lar[2] See MOLE[3].

mo·las·ses [mə'læsɪz] *n* a sweet syrup obtained in making sugar from sugar cane. ⟨Latin *mellaceum; mel* honey⟩

mole[1] [moul] *n* a small, permanent spot on the skin, usually brown and slightly raised. ⟨Old English *māl*⟩

mole[2] [moul] *n* **1** any of a family of burrowing mammals having soft fur, weak eyes, and a pointed snout. **2** a spy who gains a position of trust in an organization over a long period of time. **mole·like** *adj.* ⟨Middle English *molle*⟩
mole·hill *n* a mound of earth raised up by moles burrowing under the ground. **make a mountain (out) of a molehill** give great importance to something which is really insignificant, esp a hindrance. **mole·skin** *n* **1** a strong cotton fabric used for sports and work clothing. **2 moleskins** *pl* pants made of this fabric.

mole[3] [moul] *n* an SI base unit for measuring substances that take part in chemical reactions. One mole of an element, compound, etc. corresponds to its molecular weight. *Symbol* **mol** ⟨German *Mol* for *Molekül* molecule⟩

mo·lar ['moulər] *adj* **1** *Physics* of mass, pertaining to a body of matter as a whole. **2** *Chemistry* **a** to do with, or measured by the mole. **b** of a solution, containing one mole of solute per litre. **mo·lar·i·ty** *n.*

mol·e·cule ['mɒlə,kjul] *n* **1** the smallest part into which a substance can be divided without chemical change. **2** any very small particle. **mo·lec·u·lar** *adj.* ⟨Latin *molecula* diminutive of *moles* mass⟩

mo·lest [mə'lɛst] *v* **1** persecute, esp so as to injure: *It is cruel to molest animals.* **2** abuse or harass sexually. **mo·lest·er** *n.* **mo·les·ta·tion** [,moulə'steiʃən] or [,mɒlə'-] *n.* ⟨Latin *molestare; moles* burden⟩

mol·li·fy ['mɒlə,faɪ] *v* **1** soothe; appease: *The angry child refused all our attempts to mollify him.* **2** soften: *His anger was finally mollified.* **mol·li·fi·ca·tion** *n.* **mol·li·fi·er** *n.* **mol·li·fi·a·ble** *adj.* ⟨Latin *mollis* soft + *facere* make⟩

mol·lusc or **mol·lusk** ['mɒləsk] *n* any of a phylum of invertebrate animals having soft bodies covered with a hard shell. ⟨Latin *molluscus* soft (of nutshells)⟩

mol·ly·cod·dle ['mɒli,kɒdəl] *n* a person accustomed to being fussed over and pampered. **mol·ly·cod·dle** *v.* **mol·ly·cod·dler** *n.* ⟨See CODDLE.⟩

Mol·o·tov cocktail ['mɒlə,tɒf] or [-,tɒv] a simple incendiary hand grenade consisting of a gasoline-filled bottle with a short fuse that is ignited just before being thrown. ⟨V.M. *Molotov,* 20c Russian statesman⟩

mol·ten See MELT.

mo·lyb·de·num [mə'lɪbdənəm] or [,mɒlɪb'dinəm] *n* a metallic element of the chromium group. *Symbol* **Mo** ⟨Greek *molybdaina; molybdos* lead⟩

mom [mʌm] or [mɒm] *n Informal* mother. ⟨*mama* imitative of infantile sound⟩
mom·my *n Informal* mother; mom.

mo·ment ['moumənt] *n* **1** a very short, space of time. **2** a particular point of time: *at the same moment.* **3 the moment** right now: *He's busy at the moment.* **4** importance: *a matter of moment.* **5** *Physics* the product of a force and its distance from an axis, measured in newton metres. ⟨See MOMENTUM.⟩
mo·men·tar·i·ly [,moumən'tɛrəli] *adv* **1** for a moment: *hesitate momentarily.* **2** from moment to moment: *The danger was momentarily increasing.* **3** at any moment: *We expect him to arrive momentarily.* **mo·men·tar·y** ['moumən,tɛri] *adj* lasting only a moment. **moment of truth** the moment when a critical decision must be made. **mo·men·tous** [mou'mɛntəs] *adj* very important. **mo·men·tous·ly** *adv.* **mo·men·tous·ness** *n.*

mo·men·tum [mou'mɛntəm] *n, pl* **-tums** or **-ta** [-tə] **1** the force with which a body moves, the product of its mass and its velocity. **2** the impetus resulting from movement: *The runner's momentum carried her beyond the finish line.* **3** the power (of a campaign, social movement, etc.) to continue its advance. ⟨Latin = movement; *movere* move⟩

mon·ad ['mɒnæd] *or* ['mounæd] *n* **1** *Philosophy* a fundamental metaphysical unit or entity. **2** *Biology* a one-celled organism. **3** *Chemistry* an atom, element, or radical having a valence of one. **4** unit; one. ⟨Greek *monados* unit; *monos* alone⟩

mon·arch ['mɒnɑrk] *or* ['mɒnərk] *n* **1** a ruler or sovereign head of state with the title of king or queen, or emperor or empress. **2** a person or thing having supreme power or pre-eminence. **mo·nar·chi·c** [mə'nɑrkık] *or* **mo·nar·chi·cal** *adj.* **mo·nar·chi·cal·ly** *adv.* ⟨Greek *monos* alone + *archein* rule⟩ **monarch butterfly** a butterfly having orange and black wings with white spots. **mo·nar·chism** ['mɒnər,kızəm] *n* **1** the principles of monarchy. **2** attachment to monarchy. **mon·ar·chist** *n.* **mon·ar·chy** *n* government by a monarch.

mon·as·ter·y ['mɒnə,stɛri] *n* a building where monks or nuns live and work. **mon·as·te·ri·al** [,mɒnə'stiriəl] *adj.* ⟨Greek *monastērion; monos* alone⟩ **mo·nas·tic** [mə'næstık] *adj* **1** to do with monks or nuns: *monastic vows.* **2** to do with monasteries. **3** like that of monks or nuns: *He lives an almost monastic life. n* a monk or nun. **mo·nas·ti·cal·ly** *adv.* **mo·nas·ti·cism** *n* the system of living under religious vows, usually in a monastery or convent.

mon·au·ral [mɒn'ɔrəl] *adj* MONOPHONIC.

Mon·day ['mʌndei] *n* the second day of the week, following Sunday. ⟨Old English *mōn(an)dæg* moon's day⟩

mon·er·an [mə'nirən] *n* a member of the KINGDOM (def. 3) **Monera** of living things, comprising the bacteria, blue-green algae, and other cells without a visible nucleus. ⟨Greek *moneres* single; *monos* alone⟩

mon·ey ['mʌni] *n, pl* **-eys** *or* **-ies 1** officially issued coins and notes used as a medium of exchange. **2** wealth: *She has a lot of money.* **3 money** or **moneys a** sums of money: *He was responsible for the moneys entrusted to him.* **b** more than one type of money: *a collection of the moneys issued by different countries.* **mon·ey·less** *adj.* ⟨Old French *moneie,* Latin *moneta; Moneta,* title of Juno whose temple served as a mint⟩ **for my money** *Informal* in my opinion. **in the money** doing well financially. **make money** earn or receive money. **mon·e·tar·ism** *n* the theory that economic growth depends primarily on the regulation of the money supply, esp through the control of interest rates. **mon·e·tar·ist** *n.* **mon·e·tar·y** ['mɒnə,tɛri] *or* ['mʌnə,tɛri] *adj* to do with money: *a monetary reward.* **mon·e·tar·i·ly** *adv.* **mon·ey·bags** *n Slang* a wealthy person. **mon·eyed** *or* **mon·ied** *adj* **1** wealthy. **2** representing money or people having money: *moneyed resources.* **mon·ey·grub·ber** *n*

Informal a person whose main concern is making or saving money. **mon·ey·grub·bing** *adj, n.* **mon·ey·lend·er** *n* a person whose business is lending money at interest. **mon·ey·mak·er** *n* **1** a person who is clever at making money. **2** a product, investment, etc. that yields large profits. **mon·ey–mak·ing** *n, adj.* **money order** an order issued by a post office or bank for the payment of a particular amount of money.

Exact sums of money are usually written in figures: *72 cents; $4.98; $5; $42 810.* Approximate amounts are more likely to be written in words: *half a million dollars.*

–monger *combining form* **1** a person who sells——: *fishmonger.* **2** a person who exploits——: *scandalmonger.* ⟨Old English *mangere,* Latin *mango* trader⟩

mon·goose ['mɒŋgus] *n, pl* **-goos·es** a ferretlike animal noted for its ability to kill poisonous snakes without being harmed. ⟨Marathi (language of India) *mangus*⟩

mon·grel ['mɒŋgrəl] *n* an animal or plant of mixed breed, esp a dog. *adj* of mixed breed, race, origin, nature, etc.: *a mongrel speech that was half English and half French.* ⟨Old English *gemong* mixture⟩

mon·ies ['mʌniz] *n* a pl of MONEY.

mon·i·ker *or* **mon·ick·er** ['mɒnəkər] *n Informal* a person's name, nickname, signature, or other identifying mark or sign. ⟨origin uncertain⟩

mon·ism ['mɒnızəm] *n Philosophy* **1** the doctrine that the universe can be explained by one principle. **2** the doctrine that reality is an indivisible, organic entity. **mon·ist** *n.* **mo·nis·tic** *adj.* **mo·nis·ti·cal·ly** *adv.* ⟨Greek *monos* alone⟩

mon·i·tor ['mɒnətər] *n* **1** a person, piece of equipment, etc. that checks, or gives warning. **2** a device used for checking radio and television transmissions, telephone messages, etc. as they are being recorded or broadcast. **3** any of a genus of large, tropical lizards. **4** *Computers* a device that provides a video display of a computer's output. *v* **1** check quality, intensity, etc. **mon·i·to·ri·al** *adj.* **mon·i·to·ri·al·ly** *adv.* ⟨Latin = *one who warns; monere* warn⟩

monk [mʌŋk] *n* a man who has taken vows to live in a way prescribed by a religious brotherhood, usually in a monastery. **monk·ish** *adj.* **monk·ish·ness** *n.* **monk·like** *adj.* ⟨Greek *monachos* individual; *monos* alone⟩

mon·key ['mʌŋki] *n* **1** any of the smaller, tree-living primates, as distinguished from humans, apes, etc. The **Old World monkeys** include langurs, baboons, and some tailless species. The **New World monkeys** include many arboreal species with prehensile tails. **2** any primate other than lemurs and humans. *v Informal* play: *Don't monkey with the TV set.* **mon·key·like** *adj.* ⟨probably *Moneke,* son of Martin the Ape in medieval tale⟩

monkey bars an open structure of bars, designed for children to climb and play on.

monkey business *Informal* **1** silly or mischievous acts: *Those kids are always full of monkey business, but they do not mean to hurt you.* **2** deceitful or treacherous acts: *There must have been some monkey business, because a few of the files were missing.* **mon·key·shines** *n pl Informal* mischievous tricks and jokes.

monkey wrench an adjustable wrench. **throw a monkey wrench into** *Informal* upset (plans, operations, etc.).

mon·o¹ ['mɒnou] *n Informal* mononucleosis.

mon·o² ['mɒnou] *adj Informal* MONOPHONIC.

mono– *combining form* one; single: *monotone. monosyllable.* Also, before vowels, **mon-** ⟨Greek *monos* single⟩

mon·o·chrome ['mɒnə,kroum] *n* a painting, drawing, etc. in a single colour. **mon·o·chro·mat·ic** *adj.* ⟨*mono-* + Greek *chrōma* colour⟩ **mon·o·chro·ma·tism** *n* colour blindness in which everything is seen in shades of grey.

mon·o·cle ['mɒnəkəl] *n* an eyeglass for one eye. **mon·o·cled** *adj.* ⟨Greek *monos* single + Latin *oculus* eye⟩ **mo·noc·u·lar** [mə'nɒkjələr] *adj* involving only one eye: *monocular vision.*

mon·o·cot·y·le·don [,mɒnə,kɒtə'lidən] *n* any flowering plant having a single seed leaf (cotyledon) in the embryo. Compare DICOTYLEDON. **mo·no·co·ty·le·don·ous** *adj.*

mo·nog·a·my [mə'nɒɡəmi] *n* **1** the practice of being married to only one person at a time. **2** *Zoology* the habit of having only one mate. **mo·nog·a·mist** *n.* **mo·nog·a·mis·tic** *adj.* **mo·nog·a·mous** *adj.* **mo·nog·a·mous·ly** *adv.* ⟨*mono-* + Greek *gamos* marriage⟩

mon·o·gram ['mɒnə,ɡræm] *n* a design made by combining letters, usually the initials of a person's name. **mon·o·gram·mic** *adj.*

mon·o·graph ['mɒnə,ɡræf] *n* a scholarly book or article on one aspect of a subject. **mon·o·graph·ic** *adj.* **mon·o·graph·i·cal·ly** *adv.*

mon·o·lin·gual [,mɒnə'lɪŋɡwəl] *or* [-'lɪŋɡjuəl] *adj* knowing or using only one language: *a monolingual person.*
n a person who knows or uses only one language. **mon·o·lin·gual·ism** *n.*

mon·o·lith ['mɒnə,lɪθ] *n* **1** a single large block of stone. **2** an organization that is massive, uniform, and rigid in its attitudes. **mon·o·lith·ic** *adj.* ⟨*mono-* + Greek *lithos* stone⟩

mon·o·logue ['mɒnə,lɒɡ] *n* **1** a long speech by one person. **2** a scene or short play for one actor. **mon·o·logu·ist** *n.* ⟨*mono-* + Greek *logos* discourse⟩

mon·o·ma·ni·a [,mɒnə'meiniə] *n* an excessive concern with one thing. **mon·o·ma·ni·ac** *n.* **mon·o·ma·ni·a·cal** [,mɒnəmə'naiəkəl] *adj.*

mon·o·mer ['mɒnəmər] *n* *Chemistry* a chemical compound consisting of single molecules that can join together to form a polymer or copolymer. **mon·o·mer·ic** [,mɒnə'mɛrɪk] *adj.* ⟨*mono-* + (POLY)MER)⟩

mo·no·mi·al [mə'noumiəl] *adj* consisting of a single word or term.
n Algebra an expression consisting of a single term. Compare BINOMIAL, POLYNOMIAL. ⟨*mono-* + (BI)NOMIAL⟩

mon·o·morph·ic [,mɒnə'mɔrfɪk] *adj* **1** *Biology* having only one form. **2** having uniform structure. Also, **mon·o·mor·phous.**

mon·o·nu·cle·o·sis [,mɒnə,njukli'ousɪs] *or* [,mɒnə,nukli'ousɪs] *n* an infectious disease characterized by an abnormal increase of leucocytes. Also called **infectious mononucleosis.**

mon·o·pho·bia [,mɒnə'foubiə] *n* abnormal fear of being alone. **mon·o·phobe** *n.* **mon·o·pho·bic** *adj.*

mon·o·phon·ic [,mɒnə'fɒnɪk] *adj* in sound reproduction, having only one channel for transmission: *a monophonic tape.*

mon·oph·thong ['mɒnəf,θɒŋ] *or* ['mɒnəp-] *n* a single vowel sound; a vowel without a glide. ⟨*mono-* + Greek *phthangos* sound⟩

mon·o·plane ['mɒnə,plein] *n* an airplane having one set of wings.

mon·o·ple·gia [,mɒnə'plidʒiə] *n* paralysis of one part of the body. **mon·o·ple·gic** *adj.* ⟨*mono-* + Greek *plēge* blow, stroke⟩

mo·nop·o·ly [mə'nɒpəli] *n* **1** control of a commodity or service for a particular market, with little or no competition. Compare OLIGOPOLY. **2** the exclusive possession or control of something: *No one has a monopoly on virtue.* ⟨*mono-* + Greek *pōleein* sell⟩ **mo·nop·o·lize** *v* **1** have or get exclusive control of. **2** keep entirely to oneself. **mo·nop·o·liz·a·tion** *n.* **mo·nop·o·liz·er** *n.*

mon·o·rail ['mɒnə,reil] *n* a railway in which cars run on a single rail.

mon·o·so·di·um glu·ta·mate [,mɒnə'soudiəm 'ɡlutə,meit] a powder made from various vegetable proteins and used for seasoning foods. *Abbrev* **MSG**

mon·o·syl·la·ble ['mɒnə,sɪləbəl] *n* a word of one syllable. *Yes* and *no* are monosyllables. **mon·o·syl·lab·ic** *adj.*

mon·o·the·ism ['mɒnəθi,ɪzəm] *n* the doctrine or belief that there is only one God. **mon·o·the·ist** *n.* **mon·o·the·is·tic** *adj.* **mon·o·the·is·ti·cal·ly** *adv.*

mo·no·tint ['mɒnou,tɪnt] *n* monochrome.

mon·o·tone ['mɒnə,toun] *n* sameness of tone, of style of writing, of colour, etc. **mon·o·tone** *adj.* **mo·not·o·nous** [mə'nɒtənəs] *adj* **1** continuing in the same tone: *a monotonous voice.* **2** tedious because of lack of variety: *monotonous food.* **mo·not·o·nous·ly** *adv.* **mo·not·o·ny** [mə'nɒtəni] *n.*

mon·o·va·lent [,mɒnə'veilənt] *adj Chemistry* having a valence of one.

mon·ox·ide [mə'nɒksaid] *or* ['mɒnək,said] *n* *Chemistry* an oxide with one oxygen atom in each molecule.

mon·o·zy·got·ic [,mɒnəzai'ɡɒtɪk] *adj* arising from a single zygote.

monozygotic twins a pair of twins derived from a single fertilized ovum. See TWIN. Monozygotic twins are identical.

mon·sieur [mə'sjø] *n, pl* **mes·sieurs** [me'sjø] French Mr.; sir. ⟨French = my lord⟩

Mon·si·gnor or **mon·si·gnor** [mɒn'sinjər] *Italian* [‚monsi'njɔr] *n, pl* **Mon·si·gnors** or **mon·si·gnors**; *Italian* **Mon·si·gno·ri** or **mon·si·gno·ri** [‚monsi'njɔri] *Roman Catholic Church* a title given to certain dignitaries. ⟨Italian, half-translation of French *monseigneur*⟩

mon·soon [mɒn'sun] *n* **1** a wind system that reverses its direction with the seasons. **2** in India and adjacent regions, the season when the monsoon blows from the southwest, characterized by heavy rains. **mon·soon·al** *adj.* ⟨Arabic *mausim* season⟩

mon·ster ['mɒnstər] *n* **1** an imaginary creature of strange appearance. **2** a huge creature or thing. **3** a person who is evil or cruel. *adj.* huge. **mon·ster·like** *adj.* ⟨Latin *monstrum* divine warning; *monstrare* show⟩
monster house an overlarge house occupying most of its lot. **mon·stros·i·ty** [mɒn'strɒsəti] *n* something monstrous. **mon·strous** ['mɒnstrəs] *adj* **1** enormous. **2** unnaturally formed. **3** shocking; dreadful. *adv Informal* very. **mon·strous·ly** *adv.*

mon·tage [mɒn'taʒ] *French* [mɔ̃'taʒ] *n* **1** the combination of several pictures to make a composite picture. **2** in movies or television, the use of a sequence of rapidly changing pictures. **3** any combining of different elements: *His latest novel is a montage of biography, history, and fiction.* ⟨French, from *monter* mount⟩

Mon·ta·gnais [‚mɒntə'njei] *n, pl* **-gnais** [-'njei] *or* [-'njeiz] *or* **-gnaises** [-'njeiz] Innu. ⟨French *montagne* mountain⟩

month [mʌnθ] *n* **1** one of the twelve parts into which the year is divided. **2** the period of time from any day of one month to the corresponding day of the next: *It will take us about a month to finish the project.* **3** *Astronomy* **a** the time it takes the moon to make one complete revolution around the earth; lunar month. **b** the time from one new moon to the next, about 29.53 days; synodical month. **c** one twelfth of a solar year, about 30.41 days; solar month. **d** a sidereal month (29.531 days). ⟨Old English *mōnath*⟩
month·ly *adj* done, happening, etc. every month. *n* **1** a magazine published every month. **2** menstrual period. *adv* every month; month by month.

In reference matter and informal writing, the names of months with more than four letters are abbreviated in dates: *Jan. 21, 2005, June 30, 2050.* When only the month or month and year are given, abbreviations are rare: *January 2005. She visits us every January.* In formal writing, the names of the months are not abbreviated. In the digital system, the months are shown as numbers: *2005 01 21.*

mon·u·ment ['mɒnjəmənt] *n* **1** something set up to preserve the memory of a person or an event. **2** anything that keeps alive the memory of a person or an event. **3** an enduring example: *The professor's publications were monuments of learning.* ⟨Latin *monumentum; monere* remind⟩
mon·u·men·tal *adj* **1** to do with a monument. **2** like a monument; weighty, lasting, and important: *The British North America Act is a monumental document.* **3** very great: *monumental ignorance.* **mon·u·men·tal·ly** *adv.*

moo [mu] *v* **mooed, moo·ing** make the sound of a a cow. **moo** *n.* ⟨imitative⟩

mooch [mutʃ] *v Slang* **1** sneak; skulk. **2** steal, usually food. **3** beg. **4** fish by drifting with light tackle. **mooch·er** *n.* ⟨origin uncertain⟩

mood¹ [mud] *n* **1** a state of mind or feeling. **2** **moods** *pl* fits of depression or bad temper. ⟨Old English *mōd* spirit⟩
mood·y *adj* **1** likely to have changes of mood. **2** often having gloomy moods. **3** sullen or gloomy. **mood·i·ly** *adv.* **mood·i·ness** *n.*

mood² [mud] *n Grammar* the form of a verb that shows whether the act or state is a fact (indicative mood), a command (imperative mood), or a possibility (subjunctive mood). ⟨*mode*; influenced by *mood¹*⟩

moo·lah or **moo·la** ['mulə] *n Slang* money. ⟨origin unknown⟩

moon [mun] *n* **1** a heavenly body that revolves around the earth from west to east once in about 28 days. **2** the moon at a certain period of time: **new moon** (a slender crescent), **half moon** (a half circle), **full moon** (a circle), **old moon** (waning). **3** about a month. **4** a satellite: *the moons of Jupiter.* *v* wander about or gaze idly or listlessly. **moon·like** *adj.* ⟨Old English *mōna*⟩
once in a blue moon. See BLUE.
moon·beam *n* a ray of moonlight. **moon·calf** *n* a foolish or absent-minded person. **moon·less** *adj* **1** lacking the light of the moon: *a moonless night.* **2** having no satellite: *a moonless planet.* **moon·light** *n* the light of the moon, actually reflected sunlight. *v Informal* work at a second job, usually at night. **moon·light·er** *n.* **moon·light·ing** *n.* **moon·lit** *adj* lighted by the moon. **moon·rise** *n* the rising of the moon above the horizon. **moon·scape** *n* a view of the details of the surface of the moon. **moon·shine** *n* **1** *Informal* intoxicating liquor made unlawfully, or smuggled. **2** empty talk. **3** moonlight. **moon·struck** *adj* dazed; crazed.

moor¹ [mur] *v* keep (a ship, etc.) in place by means of ropes or chains fastened to the shore or to anchors. ⟨Middle English *more(n)*⟩
moor·ing *n* **1** a place where a ship or aircraft is made fast. **2** **moorings** *pl* the ropes, etc. by which a ship, etc. is made fast.

moor² [mur] *n Brit* open wasteland, usually hilly or high up. ⟨Old English *mōr*⟩

moose [mus] *n, pl* **moose** the largest living member of the deer family. ⟨Algonquian⟩

moose·bird *n* ❋ CANADA JAY. **moose call** a device made to imitate the call of a moose, to entice a moose to come within the hunter's range. **moose·fly** *n* any one of several species of horsefly. **moose·hide** *n* the hide of the moose, valued as leather. **moose lily** ❋ the yellow, or pond, lily. **moose·meat** *n* the flesh of the moose, used as food. **moose·milk** *n* ❋ *Slang* 1 a drink made of rum or other liquor and milk. 2 in the North, home-distilled liquor. **moose pasture** ❋ *Slang* mining claims that are considered worthless. **moose·wood** *n* the striped maple tree. **moose yard** ❋ a space in the woods where moose in winter tread down the snow, remaining there for protection and warmth, feeding on tender shoots and saplings.

moot [mut] *adj* debatable: *a moot point.* *v* bring forward (a subject, etc.) for discussion. ⟨Old English *(ge)mōt* meeting⟩
moot court a mock court held in a law school to give students practice.

mop [mɒp] *n* 1 a bundle of yarn, rags, sponge, etc. fastened at the end of a stick, for cleaning floors, dishes, etc. 2 something like a mop: *a mop of hair.*
v **mopped, mop·ping** 1 clean with a mop. 2 wipe. ⟨Old French *mappe*; Latin *mappa* napkin⟩
mop up a finish. **b** *Military* clear out or rid (an area, town, etc.) of scattered or remaining enemy troops. **mop–up** *n, adj.*

mope [moup] *v* **moped, mop·ing** be listless, silent, and sad.
n a person who mopes. ⟨perhaps related to Dutch *moppen* pout⟩

mo·ped ['mou‚pɛd] *n* a motorized bicycle. ⟨*mo(tor)-* + *ped(al)*⟩

mop·pet ['mɒpɪt] *n* *Informal* child. ⟨obsolete *mop* doll⟩

mo·raine [mə'rein] *n* a mass or ridge of rocks, dirt, etc. deposited at the sides or end of a glacier after being carried down or pushed aside by the pressure of the ice. **mo·rain·al** or **mo·rain·ic** *adj.* ⟨French⟩

mor·al ['mɔrəl] *adj* 1 good in character or conduct: *a moral act.* 2 to do with the difference between right and wrong: *a moral question.* 3 teaching a good lesson: *a moral book.* 4 being so by virtue of its psychological effect: *moral support.*
n 1 **morals** *pl* character or behaviour in matters of right and wrong. 2 the lesson of a fable, a story, or an event: *The moral of the story was "Look before you leap."* **mor·al·ly** *adv.* ⟨Latin *mores* manners⟩
mo·ral·i·ty [mə'ræləti] *n* the rightness or wrongness of an action. **mor·al·ism** *n.* **mor·al·ist** *n.* **mor·al·is·tic** *adj.* **mor·al·is·ti·cal·ly** *adv.* **morality play** a form of drama popular during the 15th and 16th centuries, in which vices and virtues were personified. **morality squad** a police division that deals with the enforcement of laws concerning gaming and prostitution. **mor·al·ize** *v* 1 think, talk, or write about questions of right and wrong. 2 point out the moral lesson in something.

3 improve the morals of. **mor·al·i·za·tion** *n.* **mor·al·iz·er** *n.*

Moral = a lesson: *What's the moral of the story?* **Morale** = mental condition as regards courage, confidence, etc.: *The general was pleased with the morale of his soldiers.*

mo·rale [mə'ræl] *n* the mental attitude as regards confidence, enthusiasm, etc.: *The morale of the team was low after its defeat.* ⟨French *moral*⟩

mo·rass [mə'ræs] *n* 1 a piece of marshy ground. 2 a difficult situation; a puzzling mess. ⟨Dutch *moeras*; Old French *marais*⟩

mor·a·to·ri·um [‚mɔrə'tɔriəm] *n, pl* **-ri·ums** or **-ri·a** [-riə] 1 a legal authorization to delay payments of money due. 2 a temporary pause in any action. ⟨Latin *mora* delay, n⟩

mo·ray ['mɔrei] *n* any of numerous eels found in warm seas, having a large mouth with strong, sharp teeth. ⟨Portuguese *moreia*; Greek *muraina*⟩

mor·bid ['mɔrbɪd] *adj* 1 unhealthy: *His mother thinks his liking for horror movies is morbid.* 2 diseased: *Cancer is a morbid growth.* 3 horrible: *the morbid details of a murder.* **mor·bid·ly** *adv.* **mor·bid·ness** *n.* ⟨Latin *morbus* disease⟩
mor·bid·i·ty *n* 1 a morbid state or quality. 2 the proportion of sickness in a certain group or locality: *Morbidity statistics show that tuberculosis is on the decline in Canada.*

mor·dant ['mɔrdənt] *adj* biting; sarcastic: *mordant criticism.*
n an acid that eats into metal. **mor·dan·cy** ['mɔrdənsi] *n.* ⟨Old French *mordre* bite⟩

more [mɔr] (comparative of **much** and **many**; superlative **most**) *adj* 1 greater in number, degree, importance, etc: 2 additional: *Take more time.*
n a greater number, etc: *I want more.*
adv 1 in or to a greater extent or degree: *It hurts more to beg than to borrow.* 2 in addition; longer; again: *Sing once more.*
be no more be dead. **more or less a** somewhat: *Most people are more or less selfish.* **b** approximately: *The distance is 5 km, more or less.* ⟨Old English *māra*⟩
more·o·ver *adv* in addition to that: *His power is absolute and, moreover, hereditary.*

To form comparatives and superlatives, **more** and **most** are put before all adjectives and adverbs of three syllables or more, and before some adjectives and most adverbs of two syllables. Other adjectives and adverbs, apart from a few irregular ones, use **-er** and **-est** to form the comparative and superlative.

mo·rel [mə'rɛl] *n* any of a genus of edible fungus having a pitted head. ⟨French *morille*⟩

mo·rel·lo [mə'rɛlou] *n* a variety of very dark red, sour cherry. ⟨amarelle; influenced by Italian *morello* blackish⟩

mo·res ['mɔreiz] *or* ['mɔriz] *n pl Sociology*

customs prevailing among a social group that are accepted as right. ⟨Latin = manners⟩

morgue [mɔrg] *n* **1** a place in which unclaimed bodies of dead persons are kept until they can be identified. **2** that part of a hospital where autopsies are performed. **3** *Informal* in a newspaper office, the reference library. ⟨*Morgue* name of building in Paris⟩

mor·i·bund [ˈmɔrəˌbʌnd] *adj* dying. **mor·i·bun·di·ty** *n.* **mor·i·bund·ly** *adv.* ⟨Latin *moribundus; mori* die⟩

Mor·mon [ˈmɔrmən] *n* a member of The Church of Jesus Christ of Latter-day Saints, founded in the United States in 1830 by Joseph Smith. **Mor·mon** *adj.* **Mor·mon·ism** *n.* ⟨narrator of scripture *The Book of Mormon*⟩

morn [mɔrn] *n Poetic* dawn or morning. ⟨Old English *morgen*⟩

morn·ing [ˈmɔrnɪŋ] *n* **1** the early part of the day, ending at noon. **2** the first or early part of anything: *the morning of life.* **morn·ing** *adj.* ⟨Middle English *morwen* morn (Old English *morgen*) + -*ing* as in *evening*⟩

morning coat a man's coat used for formal daytime wear, cut away diagonally from the waist in front. **morning sickness** a feeling of nausea, often accompanied by vomiting, that occurs in the morning during pregnancy, esp in the first few months. **morning star** a planet, esp Venus, seen in the eastern sky before sunrise.

mo·roc·co [məˈrɒkou] *n* a fine leather made from goatskins, used in binding books. ⟨*Morocco,* where first made⟩

mo·ron [ˈmɔrɒn] *n Informal* a stupid or annoyingly ignorant person. **mo·ron·ic** [məˈrɒnɪk] *adj.* **mo·ron·i·cal·ly** *adv.* ⟨Greek = foolish, dull⟩

mo·rose [məˈrous] *adj* gloomy, sullen: *a morose look.* **mo·rose·ly** *adv.* **mo·rose·ness** *n.* ⟨Latin *morosus* fastidious; *moris* habit⟩

morph [mɔrf] *n* **1** *Linguistics* ALLOMORPH. **2** *Biology* any of the distinct forms of a species, as, for example, the worker bee versus the queen bee of a species of bee. *v* undergo or cause to undergo a radical change in form. ⟨Greek *morphē* form⟩

mor·pheme [ˈmɔrfim] *n Linguistics* the smallest meaningful element of a language, such as *un-, -ing, do, make,* or *snow* in English. **mor·phem·ic** *adj.* **mor·phem·i·cal·ly** *adv.* ⟨Greek *morphē* form; on analogy of *phoneme*⟩

mor·phine [ˈmɔrfin] *n* an addictive drug made from opium. ⟨*Morpheus* Greek god of dreams⟩

mor·phol·o·gy [mɔrˈfɒlədʒi] *n* **1** the study of forms and structure in any science, as of plants and animals in biology, or words in linguistics. **2** the form and structure of an organism or of one of its parts. **mor·pho·log·i·cal** *adj.* **mor·pho·log·i·cal·ly** *adv.* **mor·phol·o·gist** *n.* ⟨Greek *morphē* form⟩

mor·row [ˈmɔrou] *n Archaic, poetic* the

following day or time: *See you on the morrow.* ⟨Middle English *morwe(n)* morn. See MORNING.⟩

Morse code [mɔrs] a signalling system by which letters, numbers, etc. are represented by dots, dashes, and spaces or by long and short flashes of light. ⟨S.F.B. *Morse,* 19c US inventor⟩

mor·sel [ˈmɔrsəl] *n* **1** a small bite; mouthful. **2** a piece. **3** a dish of food: *a dainty morsel.* ⟨Old French diminutive of *mors* bite; Latin *morsum* pp of *mordere* bite⟩

mor·tal [ˈmɔrtəl] *adj* **1** sure to die sometime. **2** of humans. **3** causing death: *a mortal wound.* **4** causing spiritual death: *mortal sin.* *n* **1** a being that is sure to die sometime. **2** a human being. **mor·tal·ly** *adv.* ⟨Latin *mortis* death⟩

mor·tal·i·ty *n* **1** the state of being sure to die sometime. **2** a loss of life on a large scale: *The mortality from automobile accidents is very serious.* **3** the death rate. **mortality table** an actuarial table used by insurance companies to predict how many people will die at a given age, based on statistics. **mortal sin** *Christian theology* a sin so serious that it can cause spiritual death. Compare VENIAL SIN.

mor·tar [ˈmɔrtər] *n* **1** a mixture of lime, cement, sand, and water, used for holding bricks or stones together. **2** a bowl of very hard material, in which substances may be pounded to a powder. **3** a very short artillery piece for shooting shells at high angles. **mor·tar** *v.* ⟨Old French *mortier;* Latin *mortarium*⟩

mor·tar·board *n* **1** a flat, square board used by masons to hold mortar. **2** an academic cap topped by a flat, square piece, worn on ceremonial occasions.

mort·gage [ˈmɔrgɪdʒ] *n* a claim on property, given in case the money is not repaid. **mort·gage** *v.* ⟨Old French *mort* dead (Latin *mortuus*) + *gage* pledge⟩

mort·ga·gee [-ˈdʒi] *n* the creditor in a mortgage. **mort·gag·er** or **mort·ga·gor** [-ˈdʒɔr] *n* the debtor in a mortgage.

mor·ti·cian [mɔrˈtɪʃən] *n esp US* UNDERTAKER (def. 1).

mor·ti·fy [ˈmɔrtəˌfaɪ] *v* **1** make ashamed or embarrassed: *They were mortified by their cousin's rudeness to their friend.* **2** control (one's physical desires) through self-denial or pain. **3** *Pathology* become affected with or cause gangrene. **mor·ti·fi·ca·tion** *n.* **mor·ti·fi·er** *n.* ⟨Latin *mortis* death + *facere* make⟩

mor·ti·fied *adj* ashamed; humiliated.

mor·tise [ˈmɔrtɪs] *n* a hole in one piece of wood cut to receive a projection on another piece, called the **tenon,** so as to form a joint (**mortise and tenon joint**). *v* fasten by a mortise: *Some furniture is mortised together, not nailed.* Also, **mor·tice.** ⟨Old French *morteise;* Arabic *murtazz* fastened⟩

mor·tu·a·ry [ˈmɔrtʃuˌɛri] *n* **1** that part of a funeral parlour where bodies of dead people await burial. **2** a morgue. ⟨Latin *mortuarium; mortis* death⟩

mortuary pole ✹ a totem pole erected to the memory of certain First Nations chiefs, whose remains were kept in a box at the top of the pole.

mo·sa·ic [mou'zeɪɪk] *n* **1** a design made of small pieces of stone, glass, etc. **2** something made up of varied parts, like a mosaic: *Canada is often called a cultural mosaic.* **3** any of several plant diseases that cause the leaves to become spotted. **mo·sa·ic** *adj.* ⟨Latin *mosaicus, musaicus* of the Muses, artistic⟩

mo·sey ['mouzi] *v Slang* move in an aimless or leisurely manner. ⟨probably Spanish *vamos* let's go⟩

mosh [mɒʃ] *v* dance wildly, bumping into other dancers deliberately in the process, often at a concert in a **mosh pit** in front of the stage. **mosh·er** *n.* ⟨origin unknown⟩

Moslem See MUSLIM.

mosque [mɒsk] *n* a Muslim place of worship. ⟨French; Arabic *masjid*⟩

mos·qui·to [mə'skitou] *n, pl* **-toes** or **-tos** any of a large family of insects, the females of which pierce the skin of humans and animals and suck their blood. ⟨Spanish, dim. of *mosca,* Latin *musca* fly⟩
mosquito hawk the common nighthawk which feeds on flying insects.

moss [mɒs] *n* any of a class of flowerless and rootless plants usually growing as carpetlike masses on tree trunks, rocks, moist ground, etc. **moss·like** *adj.* ⟨Old English *mos* bog⟩
moss·y *adj* **1** covered with moss: *a mossy bank.* **2** like moss; *mossy green.* **moss·i·ness** *n.*

most [moust] *adj* (superlative of **many** and **much**) **1** greatest in number, degree, importance, etc.: *The winner gets the most money.* **2** the majority of; almost all: *Most children like candy.*
n the greatest quantity, amount, degree, or number: *He did most of the work.*
adv (superlative of **much**) **1** in or to the greatest extent or degree: *Which movie did you like most?* **2** to a very great degree: *a most persuasive argument.* **3** *Informal* almost: *We go there most every week.* ⟨Old English *māst*⟩
at (**the**) **most** not more than. **for the most part** mainly or usually. **make the most of** make the best use of.
most·ly *adv* almost all; mainly.

USAGE
Most is a common informal shortening of almost: *A drop in prices will appeal to most everybody.* It is ordinarily out of place in written English.

mote [mout] *n* a speck of dust. ⟨Old English *mot*⟩

mo·tel [mou'tel] *n* a hotel consisting of a building having rooms that can be reached directly from an outdoor parking area. ⟨*mo(tor)* + (*ho*)*tel*⟩

mo·tet [mou'tet] *n Music* a composition having a sacred theme, usually sung unaccompanied. ⟨Old French, diminutive of *mot* word⟩

moth [mɒθ] *n, pl* **moths** [mɒðz] *or* [mɒθs] any of a number of mostly nocturnal insects having broad wings. Compare BUTTERFLY. ⟨Old English *moththe*⟩
moth·ball *n* a ball made of naphthalene, or some other strong-smelling substance, used in clothes closets to keep moths away. *v* **1** put in protective storage: *to mothball a ship.* **2** set aside or postpone for an indefinite period: *to mothball a project.* **in mothballs** *Informal* **a** in protective storage. **b** in an inactive state or condition: *The plans have been put in mothballs.* **moth–eat·en** *adj* **1** having holes made by moths. **2** worn-out; out-of-date. **moth·proof** *adj* treated chemically so as to keep moths away. **moth·proof** *v.* **moth·y** *adj* **1** containing moths. **2** having holes made by moths.

moth·er ['mʌðər] *n* **1** a female parent. **2** the source: *Necessity is the mother of invention.* **3** the biggest or best: *the mother of all breadmaking machines.*
v **1** give birth to or produce. **2** act as mother to: *mothering a tearful child.*
adj **1** of, like, or being a mother: *mother love.* **2** native or innate: *English is my mother tongue.* **moth·er·less** *adj.* **moth·er·less·ness** *n.* ⟨Old English *mōdor*⟩
mother·board, mother board, or **main board** *n Computers* a circuit board in a computer, containing the major electronic components and usually expansion slots. **mother country** the country where a person was born. **Mother Goose 1** the imaginary author of a book of fairy tales by Charles Perrault (1628-1703). **2** the imaginary author of English nursery rhymes, actually of folk origin. **moth·er·hood** *n* **1** the state of being a mother. **2** mothers (with a sg verb): *The motherhood of our city wants more day-care centres.* **moth·er–in–law** *n, pl* **moth·ers–in–law** the mother of one's husband or wife. **moth·er·land** *n* **1** one's native country. **2** the land of one's ancestors. **mother lode** the main vein of ore in an area or mine. **moth·er·ly** *adj* **1** characteristic of a mother: *motherly advice.* **2** like a mother; kindly: *She's a warm, motherly person.* **moth·er·li·ness** *n.* **moth·er–of–pearl** *n* the pearly lining of certain marine shells. **Mother's Day** the second Sunday of May, set apart in honour of mothers. **mother ship** a fishing vessel, spacecraft, etc. that acts as a base for one or more smaller craft. **mother superior** a woman who is in charge of a convent of nuns. **mother tongue** one's native language.

mo·tif [mou'tif] *n* **1** *Art, literature* a dominant, usually recurring feature: *the Cinderella motif.* **2** a distinctive, often repeated figure in a design. **3** *Music* **a** a recurring melodic or rhythmic fragment of a theme or subject. **b** LEITMOTIF. ⟨French; Latin *motivus* moving⟩

mo·tion ['mouʃən] *n* **1** the state of moving: *Everything is either in motion or at rest.* **2** a movement: *the motion of the moving train.* **3** a formal proposal for action made in a meeting, etc. **4** *Law* an application made to a court or judge for an order, ruling, etc.

v **1** make a movement, as of the hand or head, to show one's meaning: *She motioned her disagreement.* **2** show (a person) what to do by such a motion: *He motioned me out.* **mo·tion·less** *adj.* **mo·tion·less·ness** *n.* ⟨Latin *motio; movere* move⟩
go through the motions act mechanically without commitment. **in motion** moving.
mo·tile ['moutaɪl] *or* ['moutəl] *adj Biology* able to move about. **mo·til·i·ty** [mou'tɪləti] *n.*
motion picture a movie. **motion sickness** nausea caused by motion, such as the pitching and rolling of a ship.

mo·tive ['moutɪv] *n* the thought that makes one act: *His motive in going was a wish to travel.* *adj* that makes something move. ⟨Latin *motivus* moving; *motus*, pp of *movere* move⟩
mo·ti·vate *v* make (someone) want to act: *His offer to help was motivated by a desire to please.* **mo·ti·va·tion** *n* **1** the act of furnishing with an incentive to action. **2** the incentive itself: *She doesn't have the motivation to do her homework.* **mo·ti·va·tion·al** *adj.*

mot juste [mo'ʒyst] *French* a word or phrase that exactly fits the situation.

mot·ley ['mɒtli] *adj* made up of different colours, different things, or different people: *a motley collection of old toys.*
n, pl **-leys** a suit of more than one colour worn by clowns: *At the party she wore motley.* ⟨Old English *mot* speck⟩

mo·tor ['moutər] *n* **1** *Electricity* a machine that converts energy into mechanical energy, used to operate another machine: *the motor of a pump.* **2** an internal-combustion engine. **3** a car or truck. **4** something that causes or imparts motion or activity.
adj **1** powered by a motor: *a motor car.* **2** of, by, or by means of automobiles: *a motor tour.* **3** to do with motion or action: *Motor nerves arouse muscles to action.*
v **1** travel or transport by automobile. **2** *Slang* move or go quickly. **mo·tor·less** *adj.* ⟨Latin = mover; *motus.* See MOTIVE.⟩
mo·tor·bike *n Informal* a motorcycle. **mo·tor·boat** *n* a boat propelled by a motor. **mo·tor·cade** *n* a parade of automobiles. **mo·tor·cy·cle** *n* a two-wheeled motor vehicle. **mo·tor·cy·cle** *v.* **mo·tor·cy·clist** *n.* **motor home** a large motor vehicle, having a completely enclosed body that is equipped for use as a travelling home. Compare MOBILE HOME. **mo·tor·ist** *n* a person who travels by automobile. **mo·tor·ize** *v* supply with motor-driven vehicles. **mo·tor·i·za·tion** *n.* **motor lodge** motel. **motor scooter** a light, two-wheeled motor vehicle. **motor vehicle** a vehicle that travels under its own power, designed for use on roads and highways.

mot·tle ['mɒtəl] *v* mark with spots of different colours. **mot·tle** *n.* **mot·tled** *adj.* ⟨Old English *mot* speck. Related to MOTLEY.⟩

mot·to ['mɒtou] *n, pl* **-toes** or **-tos** a brief sentence adopted as a rule of conduct: *"Think before you speak" is a good motto.* ⟨Italian; Latin *muttum* grunt, word⟩

moue [mu] *n* a grimace; pout. ⟨French⟩

mou·fle ['mufəl] *n* ❋ the thick, edible upper part of the snout of the moose. ⟨Cdn. French; French *mufle* flabby face⟩

mouf·lon or **mouf·flon** ['muflɒn] *n* a wild sheep, having a dark, reddish brown coat. ⟨French; Latin *mufro*⟩

mould¹ or **mold** [mould] *n* **1** a hollow shape in which anything is formed: *Molten metal is poured into a mould.* **2** the model according to which anything is shaped.
v shape. ⟨Old French *modle*; Latin *modulus*⟩
mould·ing or **mold·ing** *n* a shaped strip of wood or plaster.

mould² or **mold** [mould] *n* **1** a furry growth of fungus that appears on food and other things when they are left in a moist place. **2** any fungus that produces mould.
v make or become covered with mould. ⟨Middle English *muwle*, influenced by *mould³*⟩
mould·y or **mold·y** *adj* **1** covered with mould. **2** musty; stale: *a mouldy smell.* **3** outdated. **mould·i·ness** or **mold·i·ness** *n.*

mould³ or **mold** [mould] *n* earth mixed with decaying leaves, manure, etc. ⟨Old English *molde*⟩
mould·er or **mold·er** ['mouldər] *v* turn into dust by natural decay.

moult or **molt** [moult] *v* shed feathers, skin, shells, or horns periodically. **moult** or **molt** *n.* ⟨Middle English *mout*; Latin *mutare* change⟩

mound [maund] *n* **1** a heap of earth or stones. **2** *Baseball* the elevated ground from which a pitcher pitches. **3** a heap of anything.
v heap up. ⟨Old English *mund* protection; meaning influenced by *mount²*⟩
Mound Builders aboriginal peoples who lived in North America in prehistoric and early historic times. They built mounds of earth to bury their dead or for defence.

mount¹ [maunt] *v* **1** go up: *to mount stairs.* **2** increase: *The cost of living mounts steadily.* **3** get up on: *mount a platform.* **4** fix in a proper setting, backing, etc.: *to mount a picture on cardboard.* **5** set upon an elevation: *a small house mounted on poles.* **6** plan and begin: *to mount a campaign to get elected.*
n **1** a horse provided for riding. **2** that on which anything is placed: *the mount for a picture.* **mount·a·ble** *adj.* **mount·less** *adj.* ⟨Old French *monter*; Latin *montis* mount⟩
mount·ed *adj* **1** on horseback. **2** in a position for use: *a mounted gun.* **3** having a proper setting: *a mounted photograph.* **Mount·ie** or **mount·ie** *n* ❋ *Informal* a member of the ROYAL CANADIAN MOUNTED POLICE. **mount·ing** *n* a support, setting, or the like.

mount² [maunt] *n Poetic* (except before a proper name) a mountain: *Mount Everest.* ⟨Old English *munt*; Latin. See MOUNT¹.⟩

moun·tain ['mauntən] *n* **1** a very high hill. **2 mountains** *pl* a series of such hills. **3** a large heap of anything: *a mountain of rubbish.* **4** a huge amount: *a mountain of difficulties.* **moun·tain** *adj.* ⟨Old French *montaigne*; Latin *montanus* mountainous. See MOUNT¹.⟩

make a mountain (out) of a molehill. See MOLEHILL.

mountain avens any of a small genus of plants of the rose family. The white mountain avens is the official flower of the Northwest Territories. **moun·tain bike** a bicycle with wide, deeply treaded tires, designed for rough terrain. **moun·tain·eer** *n* **1** a person skilled in mountain climbing. **2 Mountaineer** a Montagnais or Naskapi. *v* climb mountains. **moun·tain·eer·ing** *n.* **mountain goat 1** a white mountain antelope. **2 ✱** a goatlike mammal found in the western mountains. **mountain lion** cougar. **moun·tain·ous** *adj* **1** covered with mountain ranges: *mountainous country.* **2** huge: *a mountainous wave.* **mountain range** a row of mountains. **mountain sickness** sickness (difficult breathing, headache, and nausea) caused by the rarefied air at high altitudes. **moun·tain·side** *n* the side of a mountain. **moun·tain·top** *n* the top of a mountain.

moun·te·bank ['mauntə,bæŋk] *n* **1** a person who sells quack medicines in public. **2** anybody who tries to deceive people by stories and jokes. ⟨Italian *monta in banco* mount on bench⟩

mourn [mɔrn] *v* **1** grieve. **2** feel sorrow over: *The girl mourned her dead grandfather.* **mourn·er** *n.* **mourn·ful** *adj* **1** sad. **2** gloomy. **mourn·ful·ly** *adv.* **mourn·ful·ness** *n.* ⟨Old English *murnan*⟩

mourn·ing *n* **1** the act of sorrowing. **2** the wearing of black or some other colour, or the flying of flags at half-mast, etc. as signs of sorrow for a person's death. **3** clothes worn to show sorrow: *The widow was dressed in mourning.* **mourn·ing** *adj.* **mourn·ing·ly** *adv.*

mouse [maus] *n, pl* **mice** [məis] **1** a small rodent having a long, scaly tail. Also called **house mouse. 2** any of numerous rodents resembling the house mouse but usually having a hairy tail, such as the **deer mouse. 3** *Informal* a timid person. **4** *Computers* a hand-held device that controls the location of an object or a cursor on a screen and allows commands to be entered. *v* [maus] *or* [mauz] of a cat, owl, etc., hunt for or catch mice. **mouse·like** *adj.* ⟨Old English *mūs*⟩ **mouse ear** the soft, feltlike bud of the pussy willow. **mous·er** ['mausər] *or* ['mauzər] *n* an animal that catches mice: *Our cat is a good mouser.* **mouse·trap** *n* a trap for catching mice. **build a better mousetrap** make something for which there is a demand. **mous·y** or **mousey** *adj* resembling a mouse in being timid, drab in colour, quiet, etc.: *mousy hair.* **mous·i·ly** *adv.* **mous·i·ness** *n.*

mous·sa·ka [mu'sɑkə] *n* a Greek dish consisting of layers of ground beef and eggplant, covered with a sauce. ⟨Greek⟩

mousse [mus] *n* **1** a dessert made with sweetened whipped cream or gelatin: *chocolate mousse.* **2** any other substance with a foamy texture, such as hair setting lotion. ⟨French = foam⟩

mous·tache See MUSTACHE.

mouth [mauθ] *n, pl* **mouths** [mauðz] **1** *Anatomy* the opening through which a person or an animal takes in food. **2** an opening suggesting a mouth: *the mouth of a cave.* **3** a part of a river, creek, etc. where its waters are emptied into some other body of water: *the mouth of the St. Lawrence River.* *v* [mauð] **1** utter (words) in an affected, insincere, or pompous way. **2** form (words) with the lips without speaking. **mouth·like** *adj.* **mouth·less** *adj.* ⟨Old English *mūth*⟩ **down in the mouth** *Informal* in low spirits. **have a big mouth** *Informal* have a tendency to talk indiscreetly. **laugh on the other side** (or **wrong side**) **of one's mouth.** See LAUGH. **mouth off** *Slang* talk boastfully or disrespectfully. **open one's big mouth** *Informal* talk indiscreetly. **put one's money where one's mouth is** support one's words with concrete actions. **shoot off one's mouth** *Slang* talk indiscreetly, boastfully, or disrespectfully. **the horse's mouth.** See HORSE. **mouth·ful** *n, pl* **-fuls 1** the amount that the mouth can easily hold. **2** a small amount. **3** *Slang* a significant statement: *You said a mouthful.* **4** a long word which is difficult to pronounce. **mouth organ** harmonica. **mouth·part** *n* usually, **mouthparts,** *pl* a structure near the mouth of arthropods, adapted for piercing, sucking, grasping, etc. **mouth·piece** *n* **1** the part of a musical instrument that is placed against or in the mouth of the player. **2** a piece forming the mouth of something: *the mouthpiece of a telephone.* **3** a person, newspaper, etc. used by other persons to express their views: *That newspaper is a mouthpiece for the government.* **mouth–to–mouth** *adj* to do with a method of artificial resuscitation in which the rescuer breathes air into the mouth of a person who has stopped breathing. **mouth·wash** *n* an antiseptic liquid for rinsing the inside of the mouth. **mouth–wa·ter·ing** *adj* appetizing: *a mouth-watering menu.* **mouth·y** ['mauθi] *or* ['mauði] *adj* given to disrespectful talk. **mouth·i·ly** *adv.* **mouth·i·ness** *n.*

move [muv] *v* **1** change the position of. **2** change place or position: *We moved out to the veranda for coffee.* **3** change one's place of living or working: *We move to the country next week.* **4** put or keep in motion: *The wind moves the leaves.* **5** of the bowels, empty or cause to be emptied. **6** act: *God moves in a mysterious way.* **7** affect with emotion: *to be moved to tears.* **8** make a formal request: *Mr. President, I move that we adjourn.* **9** carry oneself: *move with dignity and grace.* *n* **1** *Games* the moving of a piece: *a good move.* **2** movement. **3** an action, regarded strategically. ⟨Latin *movere*⟩ **get a move on** *Slang* hurry up. **make one's move** take strategic action. **move heaven and earth.** See HEAVEN. **move in** (or **out**) move oneself into (or out of) a place to live. **on the move** moving about: *to be always on the move.* **mov·a·ble** or **move·a·ble** *adj* **1** that can be moved. **2** changing from one date to another

in different years: *Easter is a movable holy day.*
n Usually, **movables** *pl Law* personal property. **mov·a·bil·i·ty** *n.* **mov·a·bly** *adv.*
move·ment *n* **1** the act of moving. **2** the moving parts of a machine. **3** *Music* **a** the type of rhythm: *a waltz movement.* **b** one section of a long composition: *the second movement of a symphony.* **4** a program by a group of people to bring about some one thing: *the movement for peace.* **5** an emptying of the bowels. **mov·er** *n* a person whose work is moving furniture, etc. from one residence to another. **mover and shaker** a person with influence in a given field. **mov·ie** *n* a motion picture; film. **mov·ie·go·er** *n* a person who goes to movies. **mov·ing** *adj.* **1** to do with movement. **2** causing an emotional response: *a moving story.* **mov·ing·ly** *adv.*

mow¹ [mou] *v* **mowed, mowed** or **mown, mow·ing 1** cut down with a machine or scythe. **2** destroy at a sweep, as if by mowing: *The machine guns mowed down our soldiers.* **mow·er** *n.* ⟨Old English *māwan*⟩ **mow·ing** ['mouɪŋ] *n* **1** the process of cutting grass, etc. **2** the hay mowed at one time.

mow² [mau] *or* [mou] *n* **1** the place in a barn where hay, grain, etc. is stored. **2** a pile of hay, grain, etc. in a barn. ⟨Old English *mūga*⟩

mox·ie ['mɒksi] *n Slang* courage; nerve. ⟨*Moxie*, former soft drink⟩

moz·za·rel·la [,mɒtsə'rɛlə] *or* [,mɒzə'rɛlə] *n* a mild, soft Italian cheese, used especially in pizza. ⟨Italian⟩

MP or **M.P. 1** MEMBER OF PARLIAMENT. **2** MILITARY POLICE.

MPP or **M.P.P.** MEMBER OF THE PROVINCIAL PARLIAMENT.

MP3 *Computers* a file format for compressing a computerized sound recording for downloading. ⟨short for MPEG 1 layer 3; *motion picture expert group*⟩

Mr. or **Mr** ['mɪstər] *pl* **Messrs** a title for a man, used before his last name or the name of his rank or office: *Mr. Einola, Mr. Speaker.* ⟨abbrev of MISTER⟩
Mrs. or **Mrs** ['mɪsɪz] *pl* **Mrs.** or **Mesdames** [mei'dæm] a title for a married woman, used before her husband's surname: *Mrs. Perlman.* ⟨abbrev of MISTRESS⟩ **Ms.** or **Ms** [mɪz] a title used in front of the surname of a woman or girl: *Ms. Joubert.*

USAGE

Mr. and Mrs. are written out only when not used as part of a name: *That's five dollars, mister. You'll have to ask the missus.* Such use is informal. Before the name of a rank or office, the word **madam** is normally used for a woman: *Madam President.*
Ms. is a form made up in the 1950s to parallel Mr. and Mrs. Unlike them, it is not an abbreviation but a title, but it imitates them in being followed by a period. Like Mr., Ms. does not identify a person's marital status.

MRI magnetic resonance imaging, a technique that produces an image, similar to an X ray, of a body part in cross section.

ms millisecond(s).

MS MULTIPLE SCLEROSIS.

MS., MS, ms., or **ms** manuscript.

MSG MONOSODIUM GLUTAMATE.

Msgr. 1 Monsignor. **2** Monseigneur.

Mt. *pl* **Mts.** Mount; Mountain.

much [mʌtʃ] *adj* in great quantity or degree: *much money, much time.*
adv **more, most 1** to a great extent or degree: *much pleased.* **2** about: *This is much the same as the others.* **3** a lot: *Do you go out much?*
n **1** a great deal: *Much of this is true.* **2** an important thing: *The rain did not amount to much.* ⟨Middle English *muche(l)*⟩
a bit (or **too**) **much** far-fetched. **as much as a** to the same extent as: *I like you as much as your sister.* **b** in effect: *She as much as told him to get lost.* **make much of** treat as of great importance. **much as a** although: *Much as I like opera, I had to decline her invitation.* **b** in almost the same way as. **much of a size, height, etc.** nearly the same size, height, etc. **not much of a** not a very good: *not much of a game.* **too much for** more than one can cope with: *The work is too much for him.*
much·ness *n* greatness; magnitude. **much of a muchness** much alike; nearly equivalent.

mu·ci·lage ['mjusəlɪdʒ] *n* **1** a gummy substance used to make things stick together. **2** a substance in plants that resembles glue. **mu·ci·lag·i·nous** [,mjusə'lædʒənəs] *adj.* ⟨Latin *mucilago* musty juice; *mucus* mucus⟩

muck [mʌk] *n* **1** dirt; filth. **2** anything filthy, or disgusting. **3** moist farmyard manure. **4** *Placer mining* unwanted earth, rock, etc. that is removed. **5** *Informal* mess. **muck·y** *adj.* ⟨Old Norse *myki* cow dung⟩
muck around (or **about**) waste time. **muck out** clean out (a stable, mine, etc.). **muck up** *Informal* ruin or spoil.
muck·rake *v* expose real or imagined misdeeds of prominent people. **muck·rak·er** *n.*

mu·cus ['mjukəs] *n* a slimy substance secreted by the mucous membranes. **mu·cos·i·ty** [mju'kɒsəti] *n.* **mu·cous** ['mjukəs] *adj.* ⟨Latin⟩
mucous membrane the tissue that lines cavities of the body that are open to the air.

mud [mʌd] *n* **1** soft, sticky, wet earth. **2** any place, situation, etc. that is mean or degrading. **3** muskeg, bog mud, etc. applied to the runners of a dogsled so that it freezes into a smooth-sliding surface. ⟨Middle English *mudde*⟩
clear as mud *Informal* incomprehensible. **drag in the mud** defame. **here's mud in your eye** *Informal* a toast. **one's name is mud** one is in disgrace.
mud·dy *adj* **1** of mud: *muddy footprints.* **2** resembling mud; dull, impure, etc.: *a muddy colour.* **3** confused: *muddy thinking.* *v* make or become muddy: *Erosion muddied the river.* **muddy the water** confuse matters. **mud·di·ly** *adv.* **mud·di·ness** *n.* **mud flat** the level land bordering a stream. **mud·guard** *n* a

guard to protect riders from the mud thrown up by the wheels of a vehicle. **mud·pie** n a shape made of mud by the use of a pail. **mud puppy** any of a genus of aquatic salamanders. **mud room** in a building, a room in which boots, etc. are deposited. **mud·sling·ing** n the use of offensive charges, misleading accusations, etc. against an opponent in a political campaign, or the like.

mud·dle ['mʌdəl] v **1** mix or mess up (often with *up*): *I muddled it up.* **2** make confused. n a mess; disorder; confusion. ⟨*mud*⟩ **make a muddle of** bungle. **muddle through** manage somehow. **mud·dling** adj.

mues·li ['mjuzli] n a breakfast cereal made of rolled oats, dried fruit, etc. ⟨Swiss German⟩

mu·ez·zin [mju'ɛzən] n a crier who, at certain hours, calls Muslims to prayer. ⟨Arabic *mu'adhdhin; adhana* proclaim⟩

muff [mʌf]n **1** a cylindrical covering into which the hands are thrust to keep them warm. **2** awkward handling; bungling. v **1** fail to catch a ball. **2** bungle. ⟨Dutch *mof*; Old French *moufle* thick glove⟩

muf·fin ['mʌfən] n a small quick bread made of wheat flour, cornmeal, etc. ⟨Low German *muffen* small cakes⟩

muf·fle ['mʌfəl] v **1** wrap in order to keep warm. **2** wrap in order to soften the sound: *A bell can be muffled with cloth.* ⟨Old French *mofler* stuff; *moufle*. See MUFF.⟩ **muf·fler** n **1** a scarf worn for warmth. **2** a device attached to an engine to reduce the noise of the exhaust. **muf·flered** adj.

muf·ti ['mʌfti] n **1** ordinary clothes, not a uniform: *The retired general appeared in mufti.* **2** a Muslim official who assists a judge. ⟨Arabic = JUDGE def. 1, for stage costume⟩

mug [mʌg] n **1** a drinking cup used without a saucer. **2** *Slang* the face. v **mugged**, **mug·ging 1** attack and rob a person. **2** *Slang* make faces, esp before an audience or camera: *to mug for the camera.* **mug·ful** n. ⟨Scandinavian; compare Norwegian *mugge.* Mugs were formerly shaped like faces.⟩ **mug·ger** n one who attacks and robs people. **mug·ging** n. **mug shot** a police photograph of a suspect.

mug·gy ['mʌgi] adj hot and humid. **mug·gi·ly** adv. **mug·gi·ness** n. ⟨Scandinavian; compare Old Norse *mugga* fine rain⟩

mug·wump ['mʌg,wʌmp] n **1** *Informal* any indecisive person. **2** *US* an independent in politics. ⟨Algonquian *mukquomp* great man⟩

Mu·ham·mad or **Mo·ham·med** [mu'hɑməd] or [mu'hæməd] n a prophet (570?-632) revered by followers of the Islamic faith, who believe that he received the final revelation from God which is recorded in the Qur'an.

muk·luk ['mʌklʌk] n ❋ a high, waterproof boot, often made of sealskin, worn by Inuit and others in the North. ⟨Inuktituk *muklok* bearded seal⟩

muk·tuk ['mʌktʌk] n ❋ the thin, outer skin of the beluga, used as food (often eaten raw) in the Arctic. ⟨Inuktitut⟩

mu·lat·to [mjə'lɑtou] or [mjə'lætou]; [mə-] n, pl **-toes** a person having both white and black ancestors. ⟨Spanish *mulato; mulo* mule; Latin⟩

mul·ber·ry ['mʌl,bɛri] n any of a genus of trees and shrubs having edible, usually purple, berrylike fruit. ⟨Old English *mōrberie*; Latin *morum* mulberry⟩

mulch [mʌltʃ] n straw, leaves, etc. spread on the ground around trees or plants. **mulch** v. ⟨Old English *mylsc* mellow⟩

mule[1] [mjul] n **1** the sterile offspring of a male donkey and a mare. **2** any hybrid animal or plant, esp one that is sterile. **3** *Informal* a stupid or stubborn person. ⟨Latin *mulus*⟩ **mule deer** a species of deer that has very long ears. **mule–skin·ner** n *Informal* muleteer, so called because the driver figuratively skins his mules with his whip. **mu·le·teer** [,mjulə'tir] n a driver of mules. **mul·ish** adj like a mule; stubborn. **mul·ish·ly** adv. **mul·ish·ness** n.

mule[2] [mjul] n a slipper or light shoe covering only the toes and part of the instep. ⟨Latin *mulleus* red leather shoe⟩

mull[1] [mʌl] v *Informal* think (about) (with *over*): *to mull over a problem.* ⟨origin uncertain⟩

mull[2] [mʌl] v make (wine, beer, etc.) into a hot drink, with sugar, spices, etc. ⟨origin uncertain⟩

mul·lah ['mʌlə] or ['mulə] n a title of respect for a Muslim who is learned in Islamic theology. ⟨Arabic *maula*⟩

mul·let ['mʌlɪt] n, pl **-let** or **-lets** any of a family of important food fishes, found in fresh water and salt water. ⟨Old French *mulet*; Latin *mullus*; Greek *myllos*⟩

mul·lion ['mʌljən] n a vertical bar between the panes of a window, or the like. **mul·lioned** adj. ⟨metathesis of Middle English *muniall*; Old French *meien*. See MEAN³.⟩

multi– *combining form* to do with several or many: *multicoloured, multinational, multimillionaire.* ⟨Latin, from *multus* much⟩

mul·ti·col·oured or **mul·ti·col·ored** ['mʌlti,kʌlərd] adj having many colours.

mul·ti·cul·tur·al [,mʌlti'kʌltʃərəl] adj to do with a number of distinct cultures existing side by side in the same country, province, etc.: *Canada is a multicultural country.* **mul·ti·cul·tur·al·ism** n a policy promoting the existence of distinct cultural groups within a country, province, etc.: *Canada has a federal minister responsible for multiculturalism.*

mul·ti·eth·nic [,mʌlti'ɛθnɪk] adj comprising people from many nations.

mul·ti·far·i·ous [,mʌltə'fɛriəs] adj having many different kinds; extremely varied: *multifarious talents.* **mul·ti·far·i·ous·ly** adv. **mul·ti·far·i·ous·ness** n. ⟨*multi-* many + Latin *fariam* parts⟩

mul·ti·lat·er·al [,mʌlti'lætərəl] adj **1** having

many sides. **2** involving two or more nations, parties, etc.: *a multilateral trade agreement.* **mul·ti·lat·er·al·ly** *adv.*

mul·ti·lin·gual [ˌmʌlti'lɪŋgwəl] *or* [-'lɪŋgjuəl] *adj* **1** able to speak several languages well. **2** expressed in or containing several languages: *a multilingual conversation.* **mul·ti·lin·gual·ly** *adv.* **mul·ti·lin·gual·ism** *n.*

mul·ti·me·di·a [ˌmʌlti'midiə] *adj* **1** involving several media together: *a multimedia sales presentation.* **2** *Computers* making use of sound, graphics, text, etc. within a single piece of software.

mul·ti·mil·lion·aire [ˌmʌlti'mɪljə,nɛr] *or* [ˌmʌlti,mɪljə'nɛr] *n* a person whose wealth amounts to many millions of dollars, pounds, etc.

mul·ti·na·tion·al [ˌmʌlti'næʃənəl] *adj* **1** to do with several nations: *a multinational agreement.* **2** of a business, having divisions in several nations: *a multinational food corporation.* *n* a multinational company.

mul·ti·part·ite [ˌmʌlti'pɑrtəit] *adj* having many parts.

mul·ti·ple ['mʌltəpəl] *adj* involving many parts, relations, etc.: *multiple interests.* *n Mathematics* a number that contains another number a certain number of times without a remainder: *Twelve is a multiple of three.* ⟨Latin *multiplus* manifold⟩ **multiple choice** a style of test requiring one to choose an appropriate response from a list. **multiple–choice** *adj.* **multiple sclerosis** a disease of the brain and spinal cord that usually eventually results in permanent paralysis. *Abbrev* **MS.** **mul·ti·plex** *adj Radio, television, etc.* capable of carrying distinct signals simultaneously. **mul·ti·pli·cand** [ˌmʌltəplə'kænd] *n* the number to be multiplied by another. In 5 times 497, the multiplicand is 497. **mul·ti·plic·i·ty** [ˌmʌltə'plɪsəti] *n* **1** a variety. **2** a great many: *a multiplicity of interests.* **mul·ti·pli·er** *n* the number that multiplies another. In 5 times 497, the multiplier is 5. **mul·ti·ply** ['mʌltə'plaɪ] *v* **1** increase or cause to increase: *The dangers multiplied.* **2** *Mathematics* take (a number or quantity) a given number of times. **3** increase by procreation. **mul·ti·pli·a·ble** *adj.* **mul·ti·pli·ca·tion** *n.*

mul·ti·ra·cial [ˌmʌlti'reiʃəl] *adj* involving many different races: *a multiracial society.*

mul·ti·stage ['mʌlti,steidʒ] *adj* **1** of a rocket or missile, having several sections. **2** having a number of stages for the completion of a process: *a multistage investigation.*

mul·ti·sto·rey [ˌmʌlti'stɔri] *adj* having more than two storeys.

mul·ti·task·ing ['mʌlti,tæskɪŋ] *n Computers* a feature of an operating system allowing it to run applications simultaneously.

mul·ti·tude ['mʌltə,tjud] *or* ['mʌltə,tud] *n* **1** a great many. **2 the multitude** the common people. ⟨Latin *multitudo; multus* much⟩ **mul·ti·tu·di·nous** *adj* **1** very numerous.

2 including many parts or features. **mul·ti·tu·di·nous·ly** *adv.* **mul·ti·tu·di·nous·ness** *n.*

mul·ti·va·ri·ate [ˌmʌltə'vɛriɪt] *adj Statistics* involving more than one variable.

mum¹ [mʌm] *adj* silent; saying nothing. *interj* say nothing! ⟨Middle English⟩ **mum's the word** keep silent.

mum² See MUMMER.

mum·ble ['mʌmbəl] *v* **1** speak indistinctly. **2** chew as a person does who has no teeth. *n* a mumbling sound. **mum·bler** *n.* **mum·bling** *adj.* ⟨Middle English *momelen*⟩

mum·bo jum·bo ['mʌmbou 'dʒʌmbou] **1** a meaningless ritual. **2** unintelligible language. ⟨possibly a West African language⟩

mum·mer ['mʌmər] *n* **1** a person who wears a mask or disguise for fun. **2** an actor. ⟨Old French *momer* mask oneself; *momon* mask⟩ **mum** *v* **mummed, mum·ming 1** act in a disguise. **2** masquerade. **mum·mer·y 1** a performance of mummers. **2** any useless or silly show or ceremony.

mum·mi·chog ['mʌmi,tʃɒg] *n* a fish of Atlantic coastal waters which often enters fresh water. ⟨Algonquian⟩

mum·my ['mʌmi] *n* **1** a dead body preserved from decay by the ancient Egyptian method. **2** a dead body dried and preserved by nature. **mum·mi·fi·ca·tion** *n.* **mum·mi·fy** *v.* ⟨Arabic *mumiya; mum* wax⟩

mumps [mʌmps] *n pl* (with a sg verb) a contagious disease with swelling below the ears. ⟨pl of obsolete *mump* grimace⟩

munch [mʌntʃ] *v* chew vigorously and steadily; chew noisily. ⟨apparently imitative⟩

mun·dane [mʌn'dein] *or* ['mʌndein] *adj* **1** ordinary; everyday; humdrum: *mundane matters of business.* **2** of this world, not of heaven. ⟨Latin *mundus* world⟩

mu·nic·i·pal [mju'nɪsəpəl] *adj* to do with the affairs of a city, town, or other municipality. **mu·nic·i·pal·ly** *adv.* ⟨Latin *munia* official duties + *capere* take on⟩ **municipal district ✳** a large rural municipality. **mu·nic·i·pal·i·ty** [mju,nɪsə'pæləti] *or* [ˌmjunəsə'pæləti] *n* a city, district, etc. having local self-government.

mu·nif·i·cent [mju'nɪfəsənt] *adj* extremely generous: *a munificent reward.* **mu·nif·i·cence** *adj.* **mu·nif·i·cent·ly** *adv.* ⟨Latin *munus* gift + *facere* make⟩

mu·ni·tion [mju'nɪʃən] *n* Usually, **munitions** *pl* material used in war: *Munitions are military supplies, such as guns, powder, or bombs.* *v* provide with military supplies. ⟨Latin *munitio; munire* fortify; *moenia* walls⟩

mu·on ['mjuɒn] *n Physics* a highly unstable, elementary particle having a positive or negative charge. ⟨*mu (mes)on; mu* twelfth letter of Greek alphabet + MESON, its former classification⟩

mu·ral ['mjurəl] *adj* to do with walls. *n* a painting done directly on a wall. **mu·ral·ist** *n.* ⟨Latin *murus* wall⟩

mur·der ['mɜrdər] *n* **1** *Law* the unlawful killing of a person by another. In Canada, **first-degree murder** is intentional killing, or accidental killing by someone committing any of certain crimes. **2** *Informal* something very hard, disagreeable, or dangerous: *The traffic was murder last night.*
v **1** *Law* commit the crime of murder against. **2** do (something) very badly: *He murdered that song.* **mur·der·er** *n.* **mur·der·ous** *adj.* **mur·der·ous·ly** *adv.* **mur·der·ous·ness** *n.* ⟨earlier *murther;* Old English *morthor*⟩
murder will out any great wrong will be found out. **scream** (or **yell**) **bloody** (or **blue**) **murder** scream or yell very loudly.

mu·rine ['mjʊrɪn] *or* ['mjʊraɪn] *adj* having to do with rodents. ⟨Latin *mūrīnus* of mice⟩

murk [mɜrk] *n* darkness; gloom. Also, **mirk**. ⟨Middle English *mirke;* Scandinavian⟩
murk·y *adj* **1** dark or gloomy. **2** misty; hazy: *murky smoke.* **3** obscure in meaning: *murky prose.* **murk·i·ly** *adv.* **murk·i·ness** *n.*

mur·mur ['mɜrmər] *n* **1** a low, indistinct sound: *the murmur of a stream.* **2** *Medicine* a sound due to a leaky valve in the heart. **3** quiet speech. **mur·mur** *v.* **mur·mur·er** *n.* **mur·mur·ing** *adj.* ⟨Latin = a hum; imitative⟩

> **SYNONYMS**
> **Murmur** = quiet speech: *He murmured his thanks.* **Mumble** = speak so that the sounds are not properly formed: *I'm not hard of hearing; you just mumble.* **Mutter** = mumble as if not wanting to be heard: *She muttered some rude remarks.*

mus·cle ['mʌsəl] *n* **1** animal tissue consisting of cells that contract and relax to produce movement. **2** strength: *It takes muscle to move a piano.* **3** *Informal* power or influence: *The organization has enough muscle to get its way.*
v Informal gain by force: *He muscled his way past me.* **mus·cle·less** *adj.* **mus·cly** ['mʌsəli] *adj.* ⟨Latin *musculus* diminutive of *mus* mouse⟩
muscle in *Slang* force oneself into a situation when one is not wanted. **not move a muscle** keep perfectly still.
mus·cle–bound *adj* having some muscles stiff or tight, as a result of exercise. **muscle car** a high-performance car. **muscle shirt** a tank top. **mus·cu·lar** ['mʌskjələr] *adj* **1** to do with muscle: *muscular strain.* **2** with well-developed muscles. **mus·cu·lar·i·ty** *n.* **mus·cu·lar·ly** *adv.* **muscular dystrophy** *Pathology* a disease characterized by wasting away of muscle fibres. **mus·cu·la·ture** ['mʌskjələtʃər] *n* an arrangement of muscles.

muse [mjuz] *v* **mused, mus·ing 1** think in a dreamy way. **2** look thoughtfully. **3** say thoughtfully. ⟨Old French *muser* loiter⟩

Muse [mjuz] *n* **1** *Greek myth* one of the nine goddesses of the fine arts and sciences. Their names are Calliope, Clio, Erato, Euterpe, Melpomene, Polyhymnia, Terpsichore, Thalia, and Urania. **2** **muse** a spirit that inspires a poet or composer. ⟨Greek *Mousa*⟩

mu·se·um [mju'ziəm] *n* a building where a collection of objects illustrating science, history, art, or other subjects is kept and displayed. ⟨Greek *mouseion* seat of the Muses⟩

mush[1] [mʌʃ] *n* **1** *esp US* cornmeal boiled in water. **2** any soft, thick mass. **3** *Informal* sentimentality; maudlin talk. **mush·y** *adj.* **mush·i·ly** *adv.* **mush·i·ness** *n.* ⟨variant of *mash*⟩

mush[2] [mʌʃ] **✻** *n* **1** a command to advance given to sled dogs. **2** a journey by dogsled.
v **1** urge (sled dogs) onward by shouting commands: *He mushed his dog team.* **2** follow a dogsled on foot: *He mushed across the barren lands.* **mush·er** *n.* ⟨French *marche!* go⟩

mush·room ['mʌʃrum] *n* any of various fast-growing fungi, many of which are edible. Compare TOADSTOOL.
v grow very fast: *His business mushroomed when he opened the new store.* ⟨Old French *mousseron* Latin *mussirio* (specific kind)⟩
mushroom cloud a mushroom-shaped cloud of radioactive matter that follows a nuclear explosion.

mu·sic ['mjuzɪk] *n* **1** the art of organizing sounds into melodic patterns. **2** written music: *a songbook with words and music.* **3** a pleasant sound: *the music of the wind.* **mu·sic·less** *adj.* ⟨Greek *mousikē technē* art of the Muse. See MUSE.⟩
face the music *Informal* accept difficulties or punishment resulting from one's actions. **set to music** compose a melody to accompany (a poem, etc.).
mu·si·cal *adj* **1** to do with music: *musical instruments.* **2** fond of music. *n* an entertainment in which a story is told through music as well as dialogue. **mu·si·cal·ly** *adv.* **mu·si·cal·i·ty** *n.* **musical chairs** **1** an elimination game in which players march to music around chairs numbering always one fewer than the players. When the music stops, everyone rushes to sit down and the person left standing is eliminated. **2** a situation in which a number of people exchange positions. **musical instrument** any instrument used in producing music. **music box** a box containing apparatus for producing music mechanically. **mu·si·cian** [mju'zɪʃən] *n* a person trained in music, esp one who earns a living by it. **mu·si·col·o·gy** *n* the study of music. **mu·si·co·log·i·cal** *adj.* **mu·si·co·log·i·cal·ly** *adv.* **mu·si·col·o·gist** *n.* **music video** a short videotape featuring a piece of music.

musk [mʌsk] *n* a substance with a lasting odour, used as a perfume base. It is obtained from a gland of the male **musk deer. musk·y** *adj.* ⟨Latin *muscus;* Sanskrit *mushka* testicle⟩
musk–ox or **musk·ox** *n, pl* **-ox** or **-ox·en** a large, bovid mammal having a musky odour.

mus·keg ['mʌskeg] *n* **1** a swamp. **2** an area of bog composed of decaying plant life, esp moss. ⟨Algonquian; compare Cree *muskak* swamp⟩

mus·kel·lunge ['mʌskə,lʌndʒ] *n, pl* **-lunge ✻** a freshwater fish of the pike family Also, *Informal* **mus·kie**. ⟨Algonquian (Objibwa) *mashkinonge* great pike⟩

mus·ket ['mʌskɪt] *n* an old gun used by soldiers before rifles were invented. ⟨Italian *moschetto*, orig a hawk; Latin *musca* fly⟩ **mus·ket·eer** *n* a soldier armed with a musket.

musk·rat ['mʌsk,ræt] *n, pl* **-rats** or (esp collectively) **-rat** a water rodent having webbed hind feet. ⟨*musquash* by folk etymology⟩

Mus·lim ['mʊslɪm] *or* ['mʌzləm] *n* a believer in Islam. **Mus·lim** *adj*. Also, **Mos·lem**. ⟨Arabic *muslim* one who submits⟩

mus·lin ['mʌzlən] *n* a cotton cloth made in a wide variety of weights. **mus·lin** *adj*. ⟨Italian *mussolina; Mussolo* Mosul, Iraq⟩

Mus·queam ['mʌskwəm] *n* a First Nations band living in Vancouver. **Mus·queam** *adj*.

muss [mʌs] *Informal v* put into disorder (often with *up*): *Don't muss up my hair.* **muss** *n*. **muss·y** *adj*. **muss·i·ly** *adv*. **muss·si·ness** *n*. ⟨variant of *mess*⟩

mus·sel ['mʌsəl] *n* any of a family of marine molluscs having a dark, elongated shell. ⟨Old English *mus(c)le*. See MUSCLE.⟩

must¹ [mʌst] *aux v* **1** need to: *We must eat to live.* **2** ought to: *I must go home soon.* **3** be certain to: *He must seem very rude.* **4** be supposed to: *You must have that book.* *n* something necessary: *This rule is a must. adj Informal* necessary: *a must item.* ⟨Old English *mōste*, pt of *mōt* have to⟩

must² [mʌst] *n* the unfermented juice of the grape. ⟨Latin *mustum* fresh (wine)⟩

mus·tache ['mʌstæʃ] *or* [mə'stæʃ] *n* the hair that grows on a person's upper lip. Also, **mous·tache**. **mus·tached** *adj*. ⟨Latin *mustacia;* Greek *mystax*⟩ **mus·ta·chio** [mə'staʃiou] *n* a large or fancy mustache.

mus·tang ['mʌstæŋ] *n* the small, wild or half-wild horse. ⟨Spanish *mestengo* untamed⟩

mus·tard ['mʌstərd] *n* a yellow powder or paste used as seasoning. ⟨Latin *mustum* MUST²⟩ **cut the mustard** *Slang* meet minimum standards.

mus·ter ['mʌstər] *v* **1** assemble: *to muster soldiers.* **2** summon: *muster up courage.* *n* **1** a bringing together of people or troops for review or service. **2** the list of those mustered. Also called **muster roll**. ⟨Old French *mostrer*, Latin *monstrare* show⟩ **pass muster** come up to required standards.

mus·ty ['mʌsti] *adj* **1** having a smell or taste suggesting mould or damp: *musty crackers.* **2** out-of-date: *musty laws.* **mus·ti·ly** *adv*. **mus·ti·ness** *n*. ⟨perhaps *moist* + *-y*⟩

mu·ta·tion [mju'teiʃən] *n* **1** a change. **2** *Biology* **a** a change in genetic structure that produces a new characteristic. **b** a new variety of animal or plant resulting from such a change. **mu·tate** ['mjuteit] *v*. **mu·ta·tive** *adj*. **mu·ta·tion·al** *adj*. **mu·ta·tion·al·ly** *adv*. ⟨Latin *mutare* change⟩ **mu·ta·ble** *adj* **1** liable to change: *mutable customs.* **2** fickle: *a mutable person.* **mu·ta·bil·i·ty** *n*. **mu·ta·bly** *adv*. **mu·ta·gen** ['mjutədʒən] *n* anything that causes

mutation by causing changes in DNA. **mu·ta·gen·ic** *adj*. **mu·ta·gen·i·cal·ly** *adv*. **mu·tant** *adj* to do with mutation. *n* a new variety resulting from mutation. **mu·ta·tis mu·tan·dis** [mju'teitɪs mju'tændɪs] *or* [mu'tatɪs mu'tandɪs] *Latin* the necessary changes having been made.

mute [mjut] *adj* **1** silent. **2** unable to speak. *n* **1** a person who cannot speak. **2** a device put on a musical instrument to soften the sound. *v* **1** soften or deaden the sound of: *He muted the strings of his violin.* **2** lessen the intensity of. **mute·ly** *adv*. **mute·ness** *n*. ⟨Latin *mutus*⟩

mu·ti·late ['mjutə,leit] *v* **1** cut or destroy a part of (a body). **2** deface (something) so as to damage it. **mu·ti·la·tion** *n*. **mu·ti·la·tor** *n*. ⟨Latin *mutilare; mutilus* maimed⟩

mu·ti·ny ['mjutəni] *n* an open rebellion against lawful authority, esp by sailors or soldiers against their officers. **mu·ti·ny** *v*. **mu·ti·neer** *n*. **mu·ti·nous** *adj*. **mu·ti·nous·ly** *adv*. ⟨Old French *mutiner; mutin* rebellious⟩

mutt [mʌt] *n Slang* a dog, esp a mongrel. ⟨origin uncertain⟩

mut·ter ['mʌtər] *v* **1** speak softly and indistinctly. **2** grumble; complain. *n* muttered words. **mut·ter·er** *n*. **mut·ter·ing** *adj*. ⟨Latin *muttire;* imitative⟩

mut·ton ['mʌtən] *n* the meat from a sheep. ⟨Old French *moton;* Latin *multonis,* ram⟩

mu·tu·al ['mjutʃuəl] *adj* **1** given and received: *mutual dislike.* **2** having the same relation each to the other: *mutual enemies.* **3** *Informal* belonging to each of several: *our mutual friend.* **mu·tu·al·i·ty** *n*. **mu·tu·al·ly** *adv*. ⟨Latin *mutuus* reciprocal⟩ **mutual fund** a financial fund that invests the pooled capital of those who buy units in it. **mutual insurance** or **plan** a system of insurance by which the policyholders share the gains and losses of a common fund. **mu·tu·al·ism** *n Biology* a relationship between two species of organisms in which both species benefit from the association. Compare PARASITISM.

muu·muu ['mu,mu] *n* a woman's long, loose, flowing gown that is gathered at the neckline. ⟨Hawaiian⟩

Mu·zak ['mjuzæk] *n Trademark* music that is transmitted by telephone or FM radio, used in public areas. ⟨alteration of *music*⟩

muz·zle ['mʌzəl] *n* **1** the nose and jaws of a four-footed animal. **2** a cover for putting over an animal's head to keep it from biting. **3** the open front end of a firearm. **4** *Informal* anything preventing free expression. *v* **1** put a muzzle on. **2** prevent from expressing views: *The government muzzled the newspapers during the rebellion.* **muz·zler** *n*. ⟨Old French *musel; muse*⟩

MVP *Sports* most valuable player.

my [mai] *adj* **1** a possessive form of I: *I hurt my arm.* **2** a word used as part of certain formal titles: *my lord.* **3** *Informal* a word used in addressing a person: *Hello, my boy.*

interj a word used as an exclamation of surprise: *My, what a big cat!* ⟨Old English *mīn*⟩

my·col·o·gy [maɪˈkɒlədʒi] *n* the branch of botany dealing with fungi. **my·co·log·i·cal** *adj.* **my·co·log·i·cal·ly** *adv.* **my·col·o·gist** *n.* ⟨Greek *mykēs* fungus⟩

my·na or **my·nah** [ˈmaɪnə] *n* any of various tropical Asian starlings. ⟨Hindi *maina*⟩

my·o·car·di·um [ˌmaɪouˈkɑrdiəm] *n, pl* -**di·a** [-diə] *Anatomy* the muscular layer of the wall of the heart. ⟨Greek *myo-* (*mys* muscle) + *kardia* heart⟩

myocardial infarction the destruction of part of the heart muscle as a result of a stop in blood supply. Compare CORONARY THROMBOSIS.

my·o·pi·a [maɪˈoupiə] *n* near-sightedness. **my·op·ic** [maɪˈɒpɪk] *adj.* ⟨Greek *myein* shut + *ōps* eye⟩

myr·i·ad [ˈmiriəd] *n* a very large number. *adj* 1 countless. 2 highly varied. ⟨Greek *myriados* ten thousand⟩

myrrh [mɜr] *n* a fragrant substance obtained from a shrub, used in medicines, perfumes, and incense. ⟨Latin *myrrha* Greek *myrra*⟩

myr·tle [ˈmɜrtəl] *n* any of a genus of evergreen shrubs. ⟨Greek *myrtos*⟩

my·self [maɪˈsɛlf] *pron, pl* **our·selves** 1 a reflexive pronoun, the form of I used as an object: *I hurt myself.* 2 a form of I or **me** added for emphasis: *I will go myself.* 3 my usual self: *I'm not myself today.*

mys·ter·y [ˈmɪstəri] *n* 1 something that is unknown. 2 a story, play, etc. telling of the solution of a crime: *a writer of mysteries.* 3 something that is not understood: *the mystery of the migration of birds.* 4 a religious idea that human reason cannot understand. 5 a secret religious rite for initiated persons only. **mys·te·ri·ous** [mɪˈstiriəs] *adj.* **mys·te·ri·ous·ly** *adv.* **mys·te·ri·ous·ness** *n.* ⟨Greek *mystērion; mystēs* an initiate; *myein* close (lips, eyes)⟩

mystery play a medieval, religious play based on the Bible. **mys·tic** [ˈmɪstɪk] *adj* 1 to do with the ancient religious mysteries: *mystic arts.* 2 to do with mystics. 3 mysterious. *n* a person who believes that truth or God can be known through spiritual insight. **mys·ti·cism** [ˈmɪstəˌsɪzəm] *n.* **mys·ti·cal** *adj* 1 to do with mystics: *a mystical experience.* 2 spiritually symbolic: *mystical symbols.* **mys·ti·cal·ly** *adv.* **mys·ti·fy** *v* 1 bewilder: *The conjuror's tricks mystified the audience.* 2 make mysterious. **mys·ti·fi·er** *n.* **mys·ti·fi·ca·tion** *n.* **mys·ti·fied** *adj.* **mys·ti·fy·ing** *adj.* **mys·tique** [mɪˈstik] *n* an aura of mystery and awe associated with a person, profession, etc.

myth [mɪθ] *n* 1 a traditional story about superhuman beings, such as gods, goddesses, and monsters. 2 an invented story. 3 an imaginary person or thing: *Her wealthy aunt was a myth invented to impress her friends.* 4 an opinion, belief, or ideal that has little or no basis in fact or truth. **myth·i·cal** or **mythic** *adj.* **myth·i·cal·ly** *adv.* ⟨Greek *mythos* word, story⟩ **my·thol·o·gy** *n* a body of myths relating to a particular culture: *Greek mythology.* **myth·o·log·i·cal** *adj.* **myth·o·log·i·cal·ly** *adv.*

Nn

n or **N** [ɛn] *n, pl* **n's** or **N's** **1** the fourteenth letter of the English alphabet, or any speech sound represented by it. **2** the fourteenth person or thing in a series.

n nano- (an SI prefix).

N **1** nitrogen. **2** north; northern. **3** newton(s).

nab [næb] *v* **nabbed, nab·bing** *Informal* **1** grab. **2** arrest: *The police soon nabbed the thief.* ⟨earlier *nap*; probably Scandinavian⟩

na·bob ['neibɒb] *n* **1** a wealthy man. **2** any important or powerful person. **na·bob·ism** *n*. ⟨Hindi *nabab*; Arabic *nuwwab*⟩

na·cho ['natʃou] *n* a highly spiced, baked tortilla chip. ⟨Spanish⟩

na·cre ['neikər] *n* mother-of-pearl. **na·cre·ous** *adj.* ⟨French; Latin *naggārah* shell⟩

Na–Dene [na 'deini] *or* [ˌna dei'nei] *n* a Native American and First Nations language grouping including Tlingit, Haidan, and Athapascan.

na·dir ['neidər] *or* ['neidir] *n* **1** *Astronomy* the point in the heavens directly beneath the place where one stands. **2** the lowest point: *the nadir of his career.* Compare ZENITH. ⟨Arabic = opposite (i.e., to zenith)⟩

nae·vus ['nivəs] *n* birthmark. Also, **ne·vus**. ⟨Latin⟩

NAFTA ['næftə] North American Free Trade Agreement, an agreement involving Canada, the US, and Mexico, to get rid of trade barriers among themselves.

nag[1] [næg] *v* **nagged, nag·ging 1** annoy by peevish complaints. **2** continue to cause annoyance: *a nagging headache.* **nag·ger** *n*. **nag·ging·ly** *adv.* ⟨Scandinavian; compare Icelandic *nagga* grumble⟩

nag[2] [næg] *n* **1** *Informal* a horse, esp one that is old. **2** *Slang* a racehorse regarded as useless. ⟨Middle English⟩

nai·ad ['naiæd] *n, pl* **-ads** or **-a·des** [-əˌdiz] **1** *Greek and Roman myth* a nymph guarding a stream or spring. **2** a larval form of the dragonfly. ⟨Greek *Naiados; naein* flow⟩

na·if or **na·ïf** See NAIVE.

nail [neil] *n* **1** a slender piece of metal with a head on one end and a point on the other, to be hammered into pieces of material to hold them together. **2** the hard substance covering the end of a finger or toe.
v **1** fasten with a nail **2** *Informal* keep fixed. **3** *Informal* seize. **4** *Informal* detect and expose (a lie, etc.). **nail·er** *n*. ⟨Old English *nægel*⟩
hard as nails a tough. **b** without pity. **hit the nail on the head** *Informal* say or do something just right. **nail down** *Informal* get with certainty: *He nailed down first place in the singing competition.* **on the nail** esp of making a payment, at once; immediately.
nail·file *n* a small file for smoothing fingernails. **nail polish** a liquid applied to

decorate fingernails, that hardens into a high gloss when dry.

na·ive or **na·ïve** [naɪ'iv] *or* [nɑ'iv] *adj* simple in nature, not sophisticated: *She was naive to believe their promises.* **na·ive·ly** or **na·ïve·ly** *adv.* ⟨French; Latin *nativus* native, rustic⟩
na·if or **na·ïf** [nɑ'if] *adj* naive. *n* a naive person. **na·ive·té** or **na·ïve·té** [naɪ'ivtei], [naɪ'ivəˌtei], *or* [ˌnaɪiv'tei] *n* **1** unspoiled freshness. **2** a naive action, remark, etc. **na·ive·ty** or **na·ïve·ty** [naɪ'ivti] *n* naiveté.

na·ked ['neikɪd] *adj* **1** with no clothes on. **2** stripped of usual cover: *The trees stood naked in the snow.* **3** plain: *the naked truth.* **na·ked·ly** *adv.* **na·ked·ness** *n*. ⟨Old English *nacod*⟩
naked eye the eye alone, not helped by any telescope or microscope: *too small to be seen with the naked eye.*

Na·ko·da [nə'kouda] *n, pl* **–da** or **–das 1** a member of a First Nations people living in Alberta and Saskatchewan. **2** their Siouan language. **Nakoda** *adj.* Also called **Stoney**.

Na·ko·ta [nə'kouta] *n, pl* **–ta** or **–tas 1** a member of a First Nations or Native American people living on the northern Great Plains. **2** their Siouan language. **Nakota** *adj.* Also called **Assiniboine**.

nam·by–pam·by ['næmbi 'pæmbi] *Informal adj* weakly simple or sentimental; insipid: *That valentine is too namby-pamby.*
n **1** namby-pamby talk or writing. **2** a namby-pamby person. ⟨*Nam*, short for Ambrose Philips 18c English poet ridiculed by Alexander Pope⟩

name [neim] *n* **1** the word by which someone or something is known: *Our dog's name is Sparky.* **2** reputation: *He made a name for himself as a writer.* **3** a famous person or thing: *She's a name in the industry.*
v **1** give a name to: *They named the baby Maya.* **2** mention by name: *Three persons were named in the report.* **3** give the right name for: *Can you name these flowers?* **4** specify or fix: *to name a price.* **nam·a·ble** or **nameable** *adj.* ⟨Old English *nama*⟩
call names insult by using bad names. **name–call·ing** *n*. **name–caller** *n*. **drop names** mention famous people one has met. **name–drop·ping** *n*. **name–drop·per** *n*. **in name only** supposed to be but not really so. **in the name of a** on the authority of; acting for: *He bought the car in the name of his father.* **b** for the sake of: *We did it in the name of charity.* **know (only) by name** know only by hearing about: *I know her by name but I've never met her.* **name after** (or for) give someone or something the same name as: *He was named for his father.* **to one's name** belonging to one: *I've got $10 to my name.*
name brand a product backed by the reputation of the manufacturer. **name–brand** *adj.* **name day** the feast day of the saint

whose name one bears. **name·less** *adj*
1 having no name: *a nameless baby.* **2** not
marked with a name: *a nameless grave.*
3 unknown: *a book by a nameless writer.*
4 that cannot be described: *a nameless
longing.* **5** not fit to be mentioned: *nameless
crimes.* **6** unknown to fame. **name·less·ly** *adv.*
name·less·ness *n.* **name·ly** *adv* that is to say:
*Only two students got a perfect mark, namely,
Jamil and Jeanne.* **name of the game** the main
objective. **name·plate** *n* a strip of metal,
plastic, etc. imprinted with a person's name.
name·sake *n* a person named after another,
or thing that has the same name as another.

Na·na·bo·zho [ˌnænəˈbouʒou] *n* a trickster
hero of Algonquian mythology. Also,
Na·na·bush ['nænəˌbuʃ].

nan·ny ['næni] *n* a woman with special
training hired to look after the children of a
family. ⟨*Nan* diminutive of *Anna*⟩
nan·ny goat a female goat.

nano– ['nænou] *SI prefix* billionth: *nanosecond.*
Symbol **n** ⟨Greek *nanos* dwarf⟩
na·no·me·tre *n* one billionth of a metre.
na·no·sec·ond *n* one billionth of a second.

na·nook ['nænuk] *n* ✸ polar bear. ⟨Inuktitut
nanuq⟩

nap¹ [næp] *v* **napped, nap·ping** take a short
sleep. **nap** *n.* ⟨Old English *hnappian* sleep
lightly⟩
catch napping take unprepared: *That test
caught me napping.*

nap² [næp] *n* **1** a fuzzy surface on cloth or
leather, consisting of fibres that have been
raised. **2** the direction in which these fibres
lie when smoothed down. **nap·less** *adj.*
nap·less·ness *n.* ⟨Middle Dutch *noppe*⟩

na·palm ['nei,pɒm] *Military n* a chemical
substance for use in incendiary bombs.
na·palm *v.* ⟨*na*phthenic and *palm*itic acids⟩

nape [neip] *n* the back of the neck. ⟨Middle
English; origin uncertain⟩

naph·tha ['næpθə] *or* ['næfθə] *n* any of
various flammable liquids distilled from
petroleum, coal tar, etc. used as a solvent,
paint thinner, etc. **naph·thous** *adj.* ⟨Greek⟩
naph·tha·lene or **naph·tha·line** [-,lin] *n*
Chemistry a crystalline hydrocarbon used in
mothballs.

nap·kin ['næpkɪn] *n* a piece of cloth or paper
used at meals for protecting the clothing or
for wiping the lips or fingers. ⟨Old French
nape cloth + diminutive suffix⟩

nap·pie or **nap·py** ['næpi] *n* a small dish for
serving fruit. ⟨Middle English *nap* bowl⟩

nar·cis·sus [nɑr'sɪsəs] *n, pl* **-cis·sus·es** or **-cis·si**
[-'sɪsaɪ] *or* [-'sɪsi] **1** any of a genus of plants of
the amaryllis family having spring-blooming
flowers. **2** **Narcissus** *Greek myth* a beautiful
youth who fell in love with his own
reflection. ⟨Greek *narkissos*; *narkē* numbness⟩
nar·cis·sism *n* excessive absorption in one's
own personal comfort, importance, etc.
nar·cis·sist *n.* **nar·cis·sis·tic** *adj.*

nar·co·lep·sy ['nɑrkə,lɛpsi] *n* a pathological
condition marked by periods of sudden, deep
sleep. **nar·co·lep·tic** *adj.* ⟨Greek *narkē*
numbness + *lepsis* seizure⟩

nar·cot·ic [nɑr'kɒtɪk] *n* **1** any of a group of
drugs that have a strong pain-killing effect
and produce drowsiness, dullness, or sleep.
2 any drug subject to legal restrictions
because of its effects or its potential for
dependence. **3** something that numbs or
dulls. **nar·cot·ic** *adj.* ⟨Greek *narkē* numbness⟩
nar·co·sis [nɑr'kousɪs] *n* a stupor or state of
insensibility, brought about by narcotics.

nar·rate [nə'reit], ['nɛreit], *or* ['næreit] *v*
1 tell (a story). **2** provide the narration for (a
film, etc.): *The travelogue was narrated by a
local journalist.* **nar·ra·tion** *n.* **nar·ra·tor** *n.*
⟨Latin *narrare* relate⟩
nar·ra·tive ['nɛrətɪv] *or* ['nærətɪv] *n* **1** a report,
account, story, etc. **2** the part of a literary
work that describes events, as distinguished
from dialogue, etc. **nar·ra·tive** *adj.*

nar·row ['nɛrou] *or* ['nærou] *adj* **1** having
little width. **2** limited in extent, amount,
opportunity, etc.: *a narrow circle of friends.*
3 prejudiced: *a narrow mind about art.* **4** close;
careful: *a narrow scrutiny.*
n **narrows**, *pl* the narrow part of a river,
strait, sound, valley, pass, etc.
v **1** decrease in width: *The road narrows here.*
2 fix the limits of (often with *down*): *to narrow
a search to three places.* **nar·row·ly** *adv.*
nar·row·ness *n.* ⟨Old English *nearu*⟩
nar·row–mind·ed *adj* prejudiced.
nar·row–mind·ed·ly *adv.*
nar·row–mind·ed·ness *n.*

nar·whal ['nɑrwəl] *n* a whale of the arctic
seas. The male has a long tusk extending
forward from a tooth in the upper jaw. Also,
nar·wal. ⟨Old Norse *nár* corpse + *hval* whale⟩

NASA ['næsɑ] National Aeronautics and Space
Administration, the US body administering
space travel and research.

na·sal ['neizəl] *adj* **1** to do with the nose:
nasal passages. **2** *Phonetics* spoken through
the nose. **na·sal·i·ty** [nei'zæləti] *n.* **na·sal·ly**
adv. ⟨Latin *nasus* nose⟩
na·sal·ize *v* pronounce with a nasal sound.
na·sal·i·za·tion *n.*

nas·cent ['næsənt] *or* ['neisənt] *adj* **1** in the
process of coming into existence. **2** *Chemistry*
of an element, being in a free or uncombined
state: *nascent chlorine.* ⟨Latin *nasci* be born⟩

NASDAQ ['næzdæk] National Association of
Securities Dealers Automated Quotations.

Nas·ka·pi ['næskəpi] *n, pl* **Nas·ka·pi** or
Nas·ka·pis 1 a member of an Algonquian
people of northern Québec and the interior
of Labrador. **2** the Cree dialect spoken by the
Naskapi. **Nas·ka·pi** *adj.*

> **USAGE**
> These people, together with the Montagnais,
> prefer to call themselves Innu.

Nass–Git·ksan ['næs 'gɪtksæn] *n* the
language of the Gitksan and Nisga'a.

na·stur·tium [nə'stɜrʃəm] *n* any of a genus
of plants having showy yellow, orange, or
red flowers, and sharp-tasting leaves. ⟨Latin

nas·ty ['næsti] *adj* **1** disgustingly dirty, etc.: *a nasty smell.* **2** sordid or obscene: *a nasty mind.* **3** very unpleasant: *a nasty temper.* **4** rather dangerous: *a nasty wound.* **5** difficult: *a nasty problem.* **6** selfish; disagreeable: *My brother is a nasty man.* **nas·ti·ly** *adv.* **nas·ti·ness** *n.* ⟨Middle English *nasti*⟩

na·tal ['neɪtəl] *adj* to do with birth: *Your natal day is your birthday.* ⟨Latin *nattus* pp of *nasci* be born.⟩

na·ta·to·ri·al [ˌneɪtə'tɔriəl] *or* [ˌnætə'tɔriəl] *adj* to do with swimming: *Ducks are natatorial birds.* Also, **na·ta·to·ry.** ⟨Latin *natare* swim⟩

na·ta·tion [nə'teɪʃən] *n* **1** the art of swimming. **2** the act of swimming. **na·ta·tion·al** *adj.*

na·tion ['neɪʃən] *n* **1** a community of people occupying a defined territory and united under one government. **2 the nation a** the people of such a community. **b** the territory of such a community. **3** a people having the same descent and history and, usually, language: *the French-Canadian nation.* **4** a confederacy of First Nations peoples. **5** one of the peoples making up such a confederacy. **na·tion·al** ['næʃənəl] *adj, n.* **na·tion·al·ly** *adv.* ⟨Latin *natio* stock; *natus.* See NATAL.⟩

National Aboriginal Day June 21, proclaimed in 1996 as an annual day to recognize the contributions of the First Nations, Inuit, and Métis peoples to Canada. **National Assembly** ✺ in Québec, the group of representatives elected to the provincial legislature. **na·tion·al·ism** *n* **1** patriotic feelings. **2** the desire and plans for national independence. **3** the desire of a people to preserve its own language, religion, traditions, etc. **na·tion·al·ist** *n* **1** an upholder of nationalism. **2 Nationalist** a member of a political party supporting national independence or a strong national government. **na·tion·al·ist** or **Nationalist** *adj.* **na·tion·al·is·tic** *adj.* **na·tion·al·is·ti·cal·ly** *adv.* **na·tion·al·i·ty** *n* **1** the fact of belonging to a nation: *His passport showed that his nationality was Canadian.* **2** an ethnic group: *Many nationalities benefit from the Heritage Language program.* **na·tion·al·ize** *v* bring (land, industries, etc.) under the ownership of a nation. **na·tion·al·i·za·tion** *n.* **national park** land kept by the government for people to enjoy for its scenery, historical interest, etc. **na·tion·hood** *n* the condition or state of being a nation. **na·tion·wide** *adj, adv* throughout the nation.

The primary meaning of **nation** refers to people under an independent government. But using **nation** as referring to people with common ties of birth, language, and culture has in recent years become more widely established. In Canada this use of the word has been reinforced by similar uses of the word **nation** in Canadian French.

na·tive ['neɪtɪv] *n* **1** a person born in a certain place or country: *a native of Whitehorse.* **2** Often, **Native** one of the original inhabitants of a region, as contrasted with settlers, visitors, etc.; aboriginal; in Canada, a First Nations, Métis, or Inuit person. **3** an indigenous animal or plant.
adj **1** born in a certain place: *a native son of Charlottetown.* **2** associated with one by birth: *one's native land.* **3** belonging to one because of his or her country or the nation to which he or she belongs: *one's native language.* **4** born in a person: *native ability.* **5** Often, **Native** aboriginal: *Native rights.* **6** originating, grown, or produced in a certain place: *The Manitoba maple is native to Canada.* **7** *Computers* of programming, designed and built into a system, esp its programs and programming language: *native anti-virus software.* **na·tive·ness** *n.* ⟨Latin *nativus* innate; *natus.* See NATAL.⟩

go native of a conqueror, settler, visitor, etc., give up one's own culture and live as the natives do.

Na·tive American *n* an Aboriginal person living in the United States. **Na·tive American** *adj.* **na·tive–born** *adj* born in a particular town, country, etc.: *My father is a native-born Canadian, but my mother was born in Iceland.*

Native emphasizes the idea of being born in a person, rather than being acquired: *He has native artistic talent.* **Natural** emphasizes being part of the nature of a person, animal, or thing, because of essential character: *Sugar has natural sweetness.*

Na·tiv·i·ty [nə'tɪvəti] *n* **1** the birth of Christ. **2** Christmas. ⟨Latin *nativitas.* See NATAL.⟩

NATO ['neɪtou] *n* North Atlantic Treaty Organization, a league of countries of North America and Europe, formed in 1949 for mutual defence.

nat·ter ['nætər] *v* talk on at length; chatter. ⟨earlier *gnatter*; origin uncertain⟩

nat·ty ['næti] *adj Informal* neatly smart in appearance: *a natty uniform.* **nat·ti·ly** *adv.* **nat·ti·ness** *n.* ⟨origin uncertain⟩

na·ture ['neɪtʃər] *n* **1** the sum total of the forces at work throughout the universe: *the laws of nature.* **2 Nature** the personification of all natural facts and forces. **3** the natural world, with all its plants and animals: *to love nature in all its colour and beauty.* **4** instinct: *It is against nature for a mother to kill her child.* **5** reality: *true to nature.* **6** the abilities with which a person or animal is born: *It is the nature of birds to fly.* **7** sort; kind. ⟨Latin *natura*; *natus.* See NATAL.⟩

by nature because of the essential character of the person or thing. **of** (or **in**) **the nature of** having the nature of: *The president was something in the nature of an autocrat.* **nat·u·ral** ['nætʃərəl] *adj* **1** produced by nature. **2** instinctive: *natural ability.* **3** normal: *a natural death.* **4** true to nature: *The picture looked natural.* **5** free from affectation: *a natural manner.* **6** to do with nature: *the natural sciences.* **7** *Music* neither sharp nor flat. **8** of food, having little interference such as processing or additives. *n* **1** *Music* **a** a natural tone or note. **b** a sign (♮) used to cancel the effect of a preceding sharp or flat. **c** a white key on a keyboard instrument. **2** *Informal* a person who seems especially suited for something: *He's a natural for the football team.* **nat·u·ral·ness** *n.*

natural childbirth childbirth with a minimum or no use of anesthetic. **natural gas** a combination of methane and other hydrocarbons that occurs in natural deposits in the earth. **natural history** the study of animals, plants, minerals, and other things in nature. **nat·u·ral·ism** *n* **1** a style in art and literature characterized by a realistic portrayal of nature, life, etc. **2** *Philosophy* a view of the world which posits the existence only of natural elements and forces, excluding the supernatural or spiritual. **nat·u·ral·ist** *n* a person who studies animals and plants. **nat·u·ral·is·tic** *adj* **1** to do with naturalism: *a naturalistic painting.* **2** of natural history or naturalists. **3** imitating nature. **nat·u·ral·ize** *v* **1** grant the rights of citizenship to (persons native to other countries). **2** adopt (a foreign word or custom): *The French word* chauffeur *has been naturalized in English.* **3** introduce and make at home in another country: *The English sparrow has become naturalized in parts of Canada.* **nat·u·ral·i·za·tion** *n.* **natural law** a rule of conduct supposedly based on reason inherent in nature. **nat·u·ral·ly** *adv* **1** in a natural way: *to speak naturally.* **2** by nature: *a naturally obedient child.* **3** as might be expected; of course. **natural number** any whole number other than zero. **natural parent** the biological parent of a child or children. **natural resource** any material supplied by nature that is useful or necessary to people: *Minerals are natural resources.* **natural science** any of the sciences that deal with nature and the physical world. **natural selection** the process by which animals and plants best adapted to their environment tend to survive and produce similar offspring. **na·tur·ism** ['neitʃə,rɪzəm] *n* nudism. **na·tur·ist** *n.* **na·tur·op·a·thy** [,nætʃə'rɒpəθi] *n* a method of treating diseases without surgery or synthetic drugs, relying instead on natural forces such as good nutrition, and the use of natural herbal medicines. **na·tur·o·path** ['nætʃərə,pəθ] *n.* **na·tur·o·path·ic** *adj.*

naught [nɒt] *n* nothing: *All his work went for naught.* ⟨Old English *nā* no + *wiht* wight⟩

naugh·ty ['nɒti] *adj* **1** not obedient. **2** improper. **naugh·ti·ly** *adv.* **naugh·ti·ness** *n.* ⟨Middle English *naught* wickedness⟩

nau·se·a ['nɒziə], ['nɒʒə], *or* ['nɒʃə] *n* **1** the feeling that one has when about to vomit. **2** extreme disgust. ⟨Greek *nausia; naus* ship⟩ **nau·se·ate** ['nɒzi,eit] *v* **1** cause nausea in. **2** feel nausea. **3** cause to feel loathing. **nau·se·at·ing·ly** *adv.* **nau·se·ous** ['nɒziəs], ['nɒʃəs], *or* ['nɒʒəs] *adj* **1** causing nausea. **2** affected with nausea or disgust. **3** disgusting; loathsome. **nau·seous·ly** *adv.*

nau·ti·cal ['nɒtɪkəl] *adj* to do with ships, sailors, or navigation. **nau·ti·cal·ly** *adv.* ⟨Latin Greek *nautikos,* ult. *naus* ship⟩ **nautical mile** a unit for measuring distance in air and sea navigation, equal to 1853.25 m. **nau·ti·lus** ['nɒtələs] *n, pl* **-lus·es** or **-li** [-,laɪ] *or* [-,li] any of a genus of molluscs having a chambered shell coiled in a flat spiral. Also called **pearly nautilus.** ⟨Greek *nautilos* sailor⟩

na·val See NAVY.

nave [neiv] *n* the main part of a cross-shaped church between the side aisles. ⟨Latin *navis* ship⟩

na·vel ['neivəl] *n* **1** the small scar, usually a hollow, in the middle of the abdomen, marking the place where the umbilical cord was attached before and at birth. **2** a central point; middle. ⟨Old English *nafela; nafu* hub⟩

nav·i·gate ['nævə,geit] *v* **1** steer (a ship, aircraft, etc.). **2** sail on or over (a sea, river, etc.): *Many ships navigate the St. Lawrence each year.* **3** plot the position and course of (a ship, aircraft, vehicle, etc.). **4** move along: *The snowplough could hardly navigate along the icy streets.* ⟨Latin *navis* ship + *agere* drive⟩ **nav·i·ga·ble** *adj* that ships can travel on: *The St. Lawrence River is deep enough to be navigable.* **nav·i·ga·bil·i·ty** *n.* **nav·i·ga·bly** *adv.* **nav·i·ga·tion** *n* the science of determining the position, course, and distance travelled of a ship, aircraft, or spacecraft. **nav·i·ga·tion·al** *adj.* **nav·i·ga·tor** *n* a person who is qualified to navigate.

na·vy ['neivi] *n* **1** all the ships of war of a country, together with their personnel. **2** Often, **Navy** the branch of the armed forces comprising warships and personnel. In Canada, the function of a navy is served by the Maritime Command of the Canadian Forces. ⟨Latin *navis* ship⟩ **na·val** *adj* **1** to do with warships or the navy: *a naval officer.* **2** having a navy: *Canada is among the naval powers.* **na·val·ly** *adv.* **navy blue** a dark blue, named for the colour of the navy uniform.

Naw Ruz [nɑ ruz] *n* in Bahaism and Zoroastrianism, the New Year festival celebrated at the vernal equinox.

nay [nei] *adv* **1** *Archaic* no. **2** *Formal* not only that, but also: *We are willing, nay, eager to go.* *n* **1** a denial or refusal. **2** a negative vote or voter. ⟨Old Norse *nei; ne* not + *ei* ever⟩ **nay·say·er** ['nei,seiər] *n* one who usually expresses a negative view.

Na·zi ['nætsi] *or* ['nɑtsi] *n, pl* **Na·zis** a supporter of the National Socialist German Workers' Party that controlled Germany from 1933 to 1945, under the leadership of Adolf Hitler. Compare FASCIST. **Na·zi** *adj.* **Na·zism** or **Nazi·ism** *n.* ⟨German *Nationalsozialist* National Socialist⟩

N.B. or **n.b.** NOTA BENE.

NDP or **N.D.P.** NEW DEMOCRATIC PARTY.

NE, N.E., or **n.e.** northeast; northeastern.

Ne·an·der·thal [ni'ændər,θɒl] *or* [-,tɒl] *n* an

extinct people widespread in Europe, N Africa, and parts of Asia in the early Stone Age. **Ne·an·der·thal** *adj.* 〈name of valley in Germany where evidence found〉

neap tide [nip] the tide that occurs when the difference in height between high and low tide is least, at the first and last quarters of the moon. 〈Old English *nep(flod)* neap tide〉

near [nir] *adv* **1** close by: *The train drew near.* **2** *Informal* almost: *near crazy with fright.* *adj* **1** close by: *The near house is yellow; the far one red.* **2** closely related: *a near relative.* **3** resembling closely: *near beer.* **4** on the left-hand side (of a horse, vehicle, etc.): *the near foreleg.* Compare OFF. **5** stingy. *prep* close to: *Our house is near the river.* *v* approach: *The ship neared the land.* **near·ness** *n.* 〈Old English; comparative of *nēah* nigh〉 **come near** (doing) almost do: *I came near forgetting my glasses again.* **near at hand a** within easy reach: *My pen is always near at hand.* **b** not far in the future: *The time for decision is near at hand.* **near·by** *adv, adj* close at hand: *They live nearby.* **Near East 1** the countries of SW Asia and Egypt. **2** MIDDLE EAST. **near·ly** *adv* **1** almost: *I nearly missed the train.* **2** closely: *a matter that concerns you very nearly.* **near miss** *n* **1** a narrow escape from danger. **2** anything approaching excellence. **near–sight·ed** *adj* having an eye condition in which a person has better vision for nearby objects than for distant objects. Compare FAR-SIGHTED. **near–sight·ed·ly** *adv.* **near–sight·ed·ness** *n.*

neat [nit] *adj* **1** clean and in order: *a neat desk.* **2** able to keep things in order: *a very neat person.* **3** skilful; clever: *a neat trick.* **4** esp of alcoholic liquor, undiluted. **5** *Informal* very pleasing: *a neat party.* **neat·ly** *adv.* **neat·ness** *n.* 〈French *net* Latin *nitere* shine〉 **neat·en** *v* make neat; tidy up.

neb·u·la ['nɛbjələ] *n, pl* **-lae** [-,li] *or* [-,laɪ] *or* **-las** *Astronomy* **a** a cloudlike cluster of stars or a mass of dust particles visible in the sky at night. **b** an exterior galaxy. **neb·u·lar** *adj.* 〈Latin = mist〉 **neb·u·lous** ['nɛbjələs] *adj* hazy; vague: *Our holiday plans are still somewhat nebulous.* **neb·u·lous·ly** *adv.* **neb·u·lous·ness** *n.*

nec·es·sar·y ['nɛsə,sɛri] *adj* indispensable: *Death is a necessary end.* *n* **1** something essential: *a necessary of life.* **2 necessaries** *pl Law* the things, as food, shelter, clothing, etc., required to support a person in a way suitable to his or her station. **nec·es·sar·i·ly** [,nɛsə'sɛrəli] *or* ['nɛsə,sɛrəli] *adv.* 〈Latin *ne-* not + *cess-* stem of *cedere* withdraw〉 **ne·ces·si·tate** *v* make necessary: *His broken leg necessitated an operation.* **ne·ces·si·ta·tion** *n.* **ne·ces·si·ty** *n* **1** the fact of being necessary: *the necessity of eating.* **2** anything that cannot be done without: *Water is a necessity.* **3** that which forces one to act in a certain way: *Necessity can drive people to do disagreeable things.* **4** that which is inevitable: *Night follows day as a necessity.* **5** poverty: *in great necessity.* **of necessity** because it must be: *We left early of necessity; there are no buses at night.*

Necessary applies to whatever is needed because of circumstances: *Work is a necessary part of life.* **Essential** implies that the existence of something depends on the thing referred to: *Good health is essential to happiness.*

neck [nɛk] *n* **1** the part of the body that connects the head with the shoulders. **2** the part of a garment that goes around the neck. **3** any narrow part. **4** a narrow strip of land. *v Informal* exchange passionate embraces, kisses, and caresses. 〈Old English *hnecca*〉 **get it in the neck** *Slang* receive a severe scolding, defeat, etc. **lose (win) by a neck a** lose (win) a horse race by the length of a head and neck. **b** lose (win) by a small margin. **neck and neck** being equal or even in a contest. **neck of the woods** *Informal* locality or region: *There are few good roads in this neck of the woods.* **neck or nothing** venturing all. **risk one's neck** risk one's life. **stick one's neck out** *Informal* put oneself in a dangerous position by foolish action. **neck·band** *n* the part of a shirt, blouse, etc. to which the collar is attached. **neck·er·chief** ['nɛkərtʃif] *n* a cloth worn round the neck. **neck·lace** ['nɛklɪs] *n* a string of jewels, gold, beads, etc. worn around the neck as an ornament. **neck·line** *n* the line formed by the neck opening of a garment: *a low neckline.* **neck·tie** *n* TIE (*n* def. 2).

nec·ro– *combining form* dead; corpse; death: *necrophobia.* 〈Greek *nekros* dead body〉 **nec·ro·man·cy** ['nɛkrə,mænsi] *n* **1** a supposed foretelling of the future by communicating with the dead. **2** magic; sorcery. **nec·ro·man·cer** *n.* **nec·ro·man·tic** *adj.* **nec·ro·man·ti·cal·ly** *adv.* **nec·ro·phil·i·a** [,nɛkrə'filiə] *n Psychiatry* a morbid fascination with death. **nec·ro·phile** ['nɛkrə,faɪl] *n.* **nec·ro·phil·i·ac** *adj, n.* **nec·ro·pho·bi·a** *n Psychiatry* an abnormal fear of death. **nec·ro·pho·bic** *adj.* **ne·crop·o·lis** [nə'krɒpəlɪs] *n* **1** cemetery. **2** an ancient burial ground. **ne·cro·sis** [nə'krousɪs] *n, pl* **-ses** [-siz] **1** the death of body cells resulting from damage caused by an outside agent. **2** any of various plant diseases characterized by spots of decayed tissue. **ne·crot·ic** [nə'krɒtɪk] *adj.*

nec·tar ['nɛktər] *n* **1** *Greek myth* the drink of the gods. **2** any delicious drink. **3** *Botany* a sweet liquid found in many flowers. **nec·tar·like** *adj.* **nec·tar·ous** *adj.* 〈Greek *nektar*〉 **nec·tar·ine** [,nɛktə'rin] *or* ['nɛktə,rin] *n* a fruit like a peach but having a smooth skin.

née *or* **nee** [nei] *adj* born. 〈French; fem pp of *naître* be born〉

Née is placed after the name of a married woman who has changed her surname, to show her birth name: *Mrs. Singan, née Adams.*

need [nid] *n* **1** lack of a necessary thing: *The loss by our team showed the need of practice.*

2 a useful or desired thing that is lacking. **3** requirement: *There is no need to hurry.* **4** a situation of difficulty: *a friend in need.* **5** extreme poverty.

v **1** have need of. **2** must; ought to: *He need not go.* **3** be in want: *Give to those that need.* **need·ful** *adj.* **need·ful·ly** *adv.* **need·ful·ness** *n.* ⟨Old English *nēd*⟩

have need to *Dialect* be required to. **if need be** if the necessity arises: *I'll do it if need be.* **need·less** *adj* not needed; unnecessary.

need·less·ly *adv.* **need·less·ness** *n.* **needs** *adv* necessarily: *A soldier must needs obey.* **need·y** *adj* very poor. **need·i·ness** *n.*

nee·dle ['nidəl] *n* **1** a slender tool, pointed at one end and having a hole, or eye, at the other to pass a thread through, used in sewing. **2** a slender rod used in knitting. **3** a thin pointer on a compass, on on a gauge, etc. **4** hypodermic syringe. **5** injection: *As part of his treatrment, the doctor gave him a needle.* **6** *Botany* the needle-shaped leaf of the fir, pine, etc.

v Informal tease: *I needled him into losing his temper.* **nee·dle·like** *adj.* ⟨Old English *nēdl*⟩

a needle in a haystack something hard to find. **nee·dle·point** *n* embroidery done on canvas. **nee·dle·work** *n* work done with a needle, esp embroidery or fine hand sewing.

ne'er–do–well ['ner du ,wel] *n* a worthless person. **ne'er–do–well** *adj.*

ne·far·i·ous [nɪ'feriəs] *adj* very wicked; villainous. **ne·far·i·ous·ly** *adv.* **ne·far·i·ous·ness** *n.* ⟨Latin *ne-* not + *fas* right, divine decree⟩

ne·gate [nɪ'geit] *v* deny; nullify. **ne·gat·or** *n.* ⟨Latin *negare* say no⟩

ne·ga·tion *n* **1** denial. **2** the absence or opposite of some positive thing: *Darkness is the negation of light.* **ne·ga·tion·al** *adj.* **neg·a·tive** ['nɛgətɪv] *adj* **1** saying no: *His answer was negative.* **2** consisting only in the absence of something: *Not being unkind is only negative kindness.* **3** not optimistic or helpful: *a negative attitude.* **4** *Mathematics, physics* minus: *Three below zero is a negative quantity.* **5** *Chemistry, physics* having more electrons than protons: *a negative particle.* **6** *Photography* showing the lights and shadows reversed: *the negative image on a photographic plate.* *n* **1** an affix, word, or statement that says no. **2** *Mathematics* a minus quantity, sign, etc. **3** *Photography* an image in which the lights and shadows are reversed. **neg·a·tive·ly** *adv.* **neg·a·tiv·i·ty** *n.* **in the negative** expressing disagreement by saying no: *Most of the replies were in the negative.* **neg·a·tiv·ism** *n* **1** a tendency to say or do the opposite of what is suggested. **2** *Psychology* behaviour marked by resistance to suggestion. **3** an attitude of pessimism. **neg·a·tiv·ist** *n, adj.* **neg·a·tiv·ist·ic** *adj.*

USAGE
Two **negatives** should not be used in a sentence where only one is required. *She won't tell us nothing* should be corrected to *She won't tell us anything.*

ne·glect [nɪ'glɛkt] *v* give too little care to: *to neglect one's health.* **ne·glect** *n.* **ne·glect·er** or **ne·glect·or** *n.* **ne·glect·ful** *adj.* **ne·glect·ful·ly** *adv.* ⟨Latin *neglectus,* pp of *negligere; nec* not (*ne-* not + *que* and) + *legere* pick up⟩

neg·li·gence ['nɛglədʒəns] *n* **1** a lack of proper care: *Because of negligence the house was in need of repair.* **2** *Law* failure to take due care, resulting in damage. **neg·li·gent** *adj.* **neg·li·gent·ly** *adv.* **neg·li·gi·ble** *adj* that can be disregarded; of little importance: *a negligible difference in price.* **neg·li·gi·bly** *adv.* **neg·li·gi·bil·i·ty** *n.*

neg·li·gee ['nɛglə,ʒei] *n* a woman's loose dressing gown. ⟨French *négligée* pp of *négliger* neglect⟩

ne·go·ti·ate [nɪ'gouʃi,eit] *v* **1** talk over and arrange terms: *The rebels negotiated for peace with the government.* **2** get past or over: *The car negotiated the sharp curve by slowing down.* **ne·go·tia·bil·i·ty** *n.* **ne·go·ti·a·ble** [nɪ'gouʃəbəl] or [nɪ'gouʃiəbəl] *adj.* **ne·go·ti·a·tion** *n.* **ne·go·ti·a·tor** *n.* **ne·go·ti·a·to·ry** *adj.* ⟨Latin *negotium* business; *neg-* not + *otium* ease⟩

Ne·gro ['nigrou] *n, pl* **-groes** a member of one of the major races of the world, which includes especially the people of Africa; a black. **Ne·gro** *adj.* ⟨Spanish *negro;* Latin *niger* black⟩

Ne·groid ['nigrɔid] *adj* to do with or like the Negro race.

neigh [nei] *n* the sound that a horse makes; whinny. **neigh** *v.* ⟨Old English *hnǣgan*⟩

neigh·bour or **neigh·bor** ['neibər] *n* **1** a person who lives near another: *next-door neighbours.* **2** a person or thing that is near another: *The big tree brought down several of its smaller neighbours as it fell.*

v be near or next to. **neigh·bour·less** or **neigh·bor·less** *adj.* ⟨Old English *nēahgebūr; nēah* nigh + *gebūr* countryman⟩

neigh·bour·hood or **neigh·bor·hood** *n* **1** the region near some place or thing. **2** a district: *an attractive neighbourhood.* **3** the people of a place or district: *The whole neighbourhood came to the big party. adj* to do with a neighbourhood: *a neighbourhood newspaper.* **in the neighbourhood of** *Informal* about: *The car cost in the neighbourhood of $29 000.*

neigh·bour·ing or **neigh·bor·ing** *adj* near. **neigh·bour·ly** or **neigh·bor·ly** *adj* to do with neighbours who get along with each other: *a neighbourly chat.* **neigh·bour·li·ness** or **neigh·bor·li·ness** *n.*

nei·ther ['niðər] or ['naɪðər] *conj* **1** not either: *Neither you nor I will go.* **2** nor yet: *"They toil not, neither do they spin."*
adj not either: *Neither statement is true.*
pron not either: *Neither of the statements is true.* ⟨Middle English *ne* not + *either*⟩

nel·son ['nɛlsən] *n* either of two holds in wrestling. See HALF NELSON and FULL NELSON. ⟨origin uncertain⟩

nem·a·tode ['nɛmə,toud] *n* any of a class of worms having a long, unsegmented body. ⟨Greek *nēmatos* thread; *neein* spin⟩

nem·e·sis ['nɛməsɪs] *n,* *pl* **-ses** [-ˌsiz]
1 Nemesis *Greek myth* the goddess of
retribution. **2** punishment for evil deeds. **3** a
person who punishes another for evil deeds.
⟨Greek; *nemein* give what is due⟩

neo– *combining form* new; recent: *neoclassicism.*
⟨Greek *neos*⟩

Ne·o·cene ['niəˌsin] *Geology* the later division
of the Tertiary period, comprising the
Miocene and Pliocene epochs. **Ne·o·cene** *adj.*
⟨*neo-* + Greek *kainos* recent⟩

ne·o·clas·si·cism [ˌniou'klæsəˌsɪzəm] *n Music,*
literature, arts the revival of classical ideals of
form, proportion, and restraint.
ne·o·clas·sic·al *adj.* **ne·o·clas·si·cist** *n.*

ne·o·co·lo·ni·al·ism [ˌniouka'louniəˌlɪzəm] *n*
1 the control of former colonies by economic
means. **2** the use of economic power to
influence a nation. **ne·o·co·lo·ni·al** *adj.*
ne·o·co·lo·ni·al·ist *n.*

ne·o·dym·i·um [ˌniou'dɪmiəm] *n* a metallic
element found in certain rare minerals.
Symbol **Nd** ⟨*neo-* + (*di*)*dymium*⟩

ne·o·fas·cism [ˌniou'fæʃɪzəm] *n* any
movement to restore the former beliefs or
principles of fascism. **ne·o·fas·cist** *n, adj.*

Ne·o·lith·ic [ˌniə'lɪθɪk] *adj* of the later Stone
Age. ⟨*neo-* + Greek *lithos* stone⟩

ne·ol·o·gism [nɪ'ɒləˌdʒɪzəm] *n* **1** a new word;
new meaning for an old word. **2** the use of
new words or new meanings for old words.
ne·ol·o·gist *n.* **ne·ol·o·gis·tic** *adj.* ⟨Greek *neos*
new + *logos* word⟩
ne·ol·o·gize *v* create new words or meanings.

ne·on ['niɒn] *n* an inert element that is a
colourless, odourless gas found in small
quantities in the atmosphere. *Symbol* **Ne**
⟨Greek, form of *neos* new⟩

ne·o·nate ['niouˌneit] *n* a newborn child,
esp one less than a month old. **ne·o·na·tal**
adj. **ne·o·na·tal·ly** *adv.* ⟨*neo-* + Latin *natus*
born⟩
ne·o·na·tol·o·gy *n* the care of newborns, esp
children born prematurely.
ne·o·na·tol·o·gist *n.*

ne·o–Na·zism [ˌniou 'nætsɪzəm] *or* [-'nɑtsɪzəm]
n any movement to restore the principles
and beliefs of Nazism. Also, **neo–Na·zi·ism**
[-sɪˌɪzəm]. **ne·o–Na·zi** *n, adj.*

ne·o·phyte ['niəˌfəit] *n* **1** a new convert. **2** a
beginner. **ne·o·phyt·ic** [ˌniə'fɪtɪk] *adj.* ⟨Greek
neos new + *phyton* plant⟩

neph·ew ['nɛfju] *n* **1** the son of one's
brother or sister. **2** the son of one's brother-
in-law or sister-in-law. ⟨Old French *neveu;*
Latin *nepos*⟩

ne·phri·tis [nɪ'frəitɪs] *n Pathology* inflammation
of the kidney. ⟨Greek *nephros* kidney⟩
ne·phrit·ic [nɪ'frɪtɪk] *adj* to do with the
kidneys; renal.

ne plus ul·tra [ni plʌs 'ʌltrə] *or* [nei plʊs
'ʊltrə] the height of excellence or
achievement. ⟨Latin = no more beyond⟩

nep·o·tism ['nɛpəˌtɪzəm] *n* the showing of
too much favour by one in power to his or
her relatives. **nep·o·tist** *n.* **nep·o·tis·tic** *adj.*
⟨Latin *nepos* nephew⟩

Nep·tune ['nɛptjun] *or* ['nɛptun] *n* **1** *Roman
myth* the god of the sea, corresponding to the
Greek god Poseidon. **2** *Astronomy* the fourth
largest planet in the solar system and the
eighth in distance from the sun.
nep·tu·ni·um *n* a radioactive element similar
to uranium. *Symbol* **Np**

nerd [nɜrd] *n Slang* **1** an ineffectual and
foolish person. **2** an intelligent person
concerned exclusively with one non-social
activity: *a computer nerd.* ⟨earlier slang *nert; nut*⟩

nerve [nɜrv] *n* **1** *Physiology* a fibre
connecting the brain or spinal cord with the
eyes, muscles, etc., or with other nerves.
2 courage: *The diver lost his nerve and wouldn't
go off the high board.* **3** *Informal* impudence.
4 *Biology* a vein of a leaf or an insect's wing.
5 nerves *pl* nervousness.
v put courage in (oneself): *The soldiers nerved
themselves for the battle.* ⟨Latin *nervus* sinew⟩
get on someone's nerves annoy someone.
have (got) one's nerve, show bravado: *She's
got her nerve pushing in front of us like that.*
strain every nerve exert oneself fully.
nerve centre 1 a group of nerve cells having
a common function. **2** a control centre: *the
economic nerve centre of the nation.* **nerve gas**
Chemical warfare a gas that attacks the
central nervous system, causing extreme
weakness or death. **nerve·less** *adj* **1** without
strength or vigour. **2** without courage.
3 without nerves. **4** self-controlled.
nerve·less·ly *adv.* **nerve–wrack·ing** or
nerve–rack·ing *adj* trying to the limit of
endurance. **nerv·ous** ['nɜrvəs] *adj* **1** of the
nerves. **2** having easily excited nerves.
3 deriving from a tense condition of the
nerves: *nervous energy.* **4** restless; uneasy;
timid. **nerv·ous·ly** *adv.* **nerv·ous·ness** *n.*
nervous breakdown (not in technical use) a
psychiatric disorder characterized by extreme
physical and mental fatigue. **nervous system**
Anatomy, zoology the system in the body that
interprets stimuli and conducts impulses to
the glands, muscles, etc. concerned. **nerv·y**
adj **1** *Slang* rude and bold. **2** showing
courage. **3** excitable. **ner·vi·ly** *adv.* **ner·vi·ness** *n.*
See also NEURAL.

–ness *noun-forming suffix* **1** the quality, state,
or condition of being ——: *preparedness.*
2 ——action; ——behaviour: *carefulness.* ⟨Old
English *-nes(s)*⟩

USAGE
-ness is a productive suffix and can be freely
used to form new words.

nest [nɛst] *n* **1** a structure used by birds,
insects, fish, etc. for depositing eggs or
young. **2** a snug retreat. **3** a set from large to
small such that each fits within another: *a
nest of tables.*
v **1** build or have a nest. **2** fit together in a
nest: *The tables were nested and put away.*
3 hunt for birds' nests. **nest·a·ble** *adj.*
nest·like *adj.* **nest·er** *n.* ⟨Old English⟩

feather one's nest make things comfortable for oneself.

nest egg 1 an egg left in a nest to induce a hen to continue laying. **2** something, usually money, as a reserve.

nes·tle ['nɛsəl] *v* **1** settle oneself or be settled cosily: *to nestle down in a big chair.* **2** press close (together) in love or for comfort: *The mother nestled her baby in her arms.* ⟨Old English *nestlian; nest* nest⟩

nest·ling ['nɛstlɪŋ] *or* ['nɛslɪŋ] *n* a bird too young to leave the nest.

net¹ [nɛt] **1** an open fabric made of string, wire, etc., knotted so as to leave regular holes: *Veils are made of very fine net.* **2** anything like a net; network. **3 the Net** *Computers* the Internet. **4** a trap or snare.
v **net·ted, net·ting 1** catch in or as if in a net: *net a fish.* **2** *Tennis, badminton, etc.* hit (a ball) into the net. **net·like** *adj.* ⟨Old English *nett*⟩
net·ting *n* a netted or meshed material: *mosquito netting.* **net·work** *n* **1** any netlike combination of lines or channels: *a network of highways.* **2** a group of radio or television stations so connected that the same program may be broadcast by all: *the French network of CBC radio.* **3** *Computers* a system of links interconnecting a set of computers. *v* meet with friends or colleagues to exchange ideas or further one's interests. **net·work·ing** *n.*

net² [nɛt] *adj* **1** free from deductions or additions. **2** final: *the net result.*
v **net·ted, net·ting** *v* gain (after deductions, etc.): *The sale netted me a good profit.* **net·ta·ble** *adj.* ⟨French. See NEAT¹.⟩

neth·er ['nɛðər] *adj* lower: *nether garments, nether regions.* ⟨Old English *neothera*⟩
neth·er·most *adj* lowest.

Net·sil·ik [nɛt'sɪlɪk] *n, pl* **-lik** a member of an Inuit people living in the central Arctic, mostly on the northern coast. **Net·sil·ik** *adj.*

net·tle ['nɛtəl] *n* any of a genus of plants having sharp hairs that sting the skin.
v irritate: *She was nettled by the interruptions.* **net·tle·like** *adj.* ⟨Old English *netele*⟩
net·tle·some *adj* **1** annoying. **2** easily annoyed.

neu·ral ['njʊrəl] *or* ['nʊrəl] *adj* to do with a nerve or the nervous system. **neu·ral·ly** *adv.* ⟨Greek *neuron* nerve⟩
neu·ral·gia *n* pain along the course of a nerve. **neu·ral·gic** *adj.* **neu·ri·tis** [-'rəitɪs] *n Pathology* inflammation of a nerve, causing muscular atrophy. **neu·rit·ic** [-'rɪtɪk] *adj.*

neuro– [,njʊ'rou] *combining form* nerve; sinew; tendon: *neurology.* Also (esp before a vowel), **neur-** ⟨See NEURAL.⟩
neu·ro·sur·ge·ry *n* surgery of the nervous system, esp of the brain.
neu·ro·sur·gi·cal *adj.* **neu·ro·sur·geon** *n.*
neu·ro·trans·mit·ter *n* a chemical substance such as serotonin, which passes messages between nerve cells in the brain.

neu·rol·o·gy [njʊ'rɒlədʒi] *or* [nʊ'rɒlədʒi] *n* the study of the nervous system and its diseases. ⟨See NEURAL.⟩

neu·ro·log·i·cal *adj.* **neu·ro·log·i·cal·ly** *adv.* **neu·rol·o·gist** *n.*

neu·ron ['njʊrɒn] *or* ['nʊrɒn] *n Anatomy* one of the conducting cells of which the brain, spinal cord, and nerves are composed. Also, **neurone. neu·ron·ic** *adj.* ⟨See NEURAL.⟩

neu·ro·sis [njʊ'rousɪs] *or* [nʊ'rousɪs] *n, pl* **-ses** [-siz] any of various mental disorders characterized by anxiety and obsessive behaviour. ⟨See NEURAL.⟩
neu·rot·ic [-'rɒtɪk] *adj* **1** to do with a neurosis. **2** *Informal* having a tendency toward erratic behaviour or obsession with unrealistic ideas. **neu·rot·ic** *n.* **neu·rot·i·cal·ly** *adv.* **neu·rot·i·cism** *n.*

neu·ter ['njutər] *or* ['nutər] *adj* **1** *Grammar* to do with the grammatical gender that includes words for many inanimate things and also words for persons or animals of which the sex is not specified. Compare FEMININE, MASCULINE. **2** *Zoology* of insects, etc., having no, or non-functional, sex organs: *Worker bees are neuter.* **3** *Botany* sterile. **4** taking no sides; neutral.
v castrate (an animal). **neu·ter** *n.* ⟨Latin *ne-* not + *uter* either⟩

neu·tral ['njutrəl] *or* ['nutrəl] *adj* **1** not taking part in a quarrel, contest, or war. **2** being neither one thing nor the other. **3** having little or no colour. **4** *Chemistry* neither acid nor alkaline. **5** *Electricity* neither positive nor negative. **6** *Biology* not developed in sex.
n **1** one not taking part in a quarrel or war. **2** *Machinery* the position of gears when they do not transmit motion to the working parts. **neu·tral·ly** *adv.* ⟨See NEUTER.⟩
neu·tral·ism *n* a policy of remaining neutral, esp in international conflicts. **neu·tral·ist** *n, adj.* **neu·tral·i·ty** *n.* **neu·tral·ize** *v* take away the effect of (something) by using an opposite power. **neu·tral·i·za·tion** *n.* **neu·tral·iz·er** *n.*

neu·tri·no [nju'trinou] *or* [nu-] *n Physics* an elementary particle that has no electric charge, produced in the process of radioactive decay. ⟨Italian, diminutive of *neutone* neutron⟩

neu·tron ['njutrɒn] *or* ['nutrɒn] *n* a nuclear particle having almost the same mass as a proton but having no electric charge. ⟨*neutral* + *-on* as in *electron, proton*⟩
neu·tron bomb a nuclear bomb designed to produce intense radiation over a wide area, thus causing great loss of life but relatively little destruction of property.

nev·er ['nɛvər] *adv* **1** not ever. **2** not at all. ⟨Old English *næfre; ne* not + *æfre* ever⟩
never mind a pay no attention to: *Never mind the noise.* **b** forget it: *Never mind; I'll do it.*
nev·er·more *adv* never again. **nev·er·the·less** [,nɛvərðə'lɛs] *adv* however; in spite of it: *She was very tired; nevertheless, she kept on working.*

ne·vus ['nivəs] *n* See NAEVUS.

new [nju] *or* [nu] *adj* **1** not existing before: *a new idea.* **2** not worn or used up: *a new path.* **3** as if new; fresh: *go on with new courage.*

4 not familiar: *a new country to me.* **5** being the later of two things of the same kind: *New France.* **6** recently bought: *a new car.*
adv newly; recently; freshly: *new-mown hay.* **new·ness** *n.* ⟨Old English *nīwe*⟩
New Age 1 a cultural movement of the late 20th century, characterized by spiritual sensitivity, holistic beliefs, and environmentalism. **2** a style of popular music designed to produce a relaxed mood. **new·born** *adj* **1** recently born: *a newborn baby.* **2** ready to start a new life; born again. *n* a newborn baby: *clothes for the newborns.* **New Bruns·wick** ['brʌnzwɪk] a Maritime province of Canada. *Abbrev* **NB. New Bruns·wick·er** *n.* **New Canadian** a person originally from another country who plans to become, or has recently become, a Canadian citizen. **new·com·er** *n* a person who has just arrived or who arrived not long ago. **New Democratic Party** a Canadian political party with socialist ties; one of the principal political parties of Canada. **New England** the NE part of the United States. **New Englander.** **new·fan·gled** [-ˌfæŋgəld] *adj* lately come into fashion; novel: *newfangled ideas.* **New·fie** [nju'fi] *or* ['nufi] *n* ✹ *Informal* a Newfoundlander. **New·found·land** [ˌnjufənd'lænd] *or* [ˌnu-]; ['njufəndlənd], ['nu-], *or* [nju-] *n* a large island off the east coast of Canada. Newfoundland and Labrador constitute a province. *Abbrev* **NF. New·found·land·er** *n.* **New France** the name of the territory in North America belonging to France from 1609 to 1763. It included Québec, Acadia, and the Louisiana Territory. **new·ly** *adv* **1** recently: *newly discovered.* **2** once again: *newly painted walls.* **3** in a new way: *newly arranged furniture.* **new·ly·wed** *n* a newly married person. **new moon 1** the phase of the moon when it is between the earth and the sun, so that its dark side is toward the earth and its face is invisible. **2** the thin crescent that appears at sunset two or three days after this phase, with the hollow side on the left. **news** *n* (with a sg verb) **1** information about something that has just happened or will soon happen: *The news that he had been fired was a tremendous shock.* **2** a report of current happenings in a newspaper, on television, radio, etc. **break the news** make something known. **news·cast** *n* a radio or television program devoted to current events, news bulletins, etc. **news·cast·er** *n.* **news·group** *n* on the Internet, a group of users who can read information on a subject and post responses. **news·let·ter** *n* an account of the activities of a society or company. **news·pa·per** ['njus,peipər] *or* ['nus-] *n* a publication usually printed daily or weekly, containing news stories and pictures, advertisements, etc. **news·print** ['njus,prɪnt] *or* ['nus-] *n* a cheap, coarse paper, the kind on which newspapers are usually printed. **news release** PRESS RELEASE. **news·room** *n* a room or section of a newspaper office or radio or television station where news is collected

and edited for publication or broadcasting. **news·stand** *n* a place where newspapers and magazines are sold. **news·wor·thy** *adj* interesting or important enough to be included in a newspaper or newscast: *The reporter tried to think of an angle that would make the story newsworthy.* **news·y** *adj Informal* full of news. **New Testament** the second part of the Christian Bible. **New World** the western hemisphere. **New World** *or* **new–world** *adj.* **new year 1** the year approaching or newly begun. **2 New Year** or **New Year's** the first day or days of the year. **New Year's Day** January 1, observed as a legal holiday in many countries, including Canada.

SYNONYMS
New describes something now existing, made, seen, or known for the first time: *They own a new house.* **Novel** adds and emphasizes the idea of being strikingly different: *Their house has a novel dining room.* **Modern** describes people and things characteristic of the present time, or recent times, and may suggest being up-to-date, not old-fashioned: *The architecture is modern.*

newt [njut] *or* [nut] *n* any of various small salamanders, usually aquatic only during the breeding season. ⟨Middle English *an ewt* (taken as *a newt)*⟩
new·ton ['njutən] *or* ['nutən] *n Physics* an SI unit for measuring force. One newton is the force required to give an acceleration of one metre per second squared to a mass of one kilogram. *Symbol* **N** ⟨Sir Isaac *Newton.* See NEWTONIAN.⟩
New·to·ni·an ['njutounian] *or* ['nu-] *adj* to do with Sir Isaac Newton (1642-1727), the English scientist and mathematician, or his discoveries: *Newtonian physics.* **newton metre** *Physics* an SI unit for measuring torque or moment of force. *Symbol:* **N•m**
next [nɛkst] *adj* nearest: *the next train.*
prep nearest to: *We own the house next the lake.*
adv in the place, time, or position that is nearest: *I am going to do math problems next.* ⟨Old English *nēhst,* superlative of *nēah* nigh⟩
next to a immediately adjacent to: *Who was the girl next to you?* **b** nearly: *It cost next to nothing.* **c** following in order of preference: *Next to eating I like sleeping.*
next door in or at the next house: *The woman next door owns two dogs.* **next door to** almost: *His silence was next door to an admission of guilt.* **next–door** *adj.* **next of kin** the nearest relative, or nearest relative by marriage.
nex·us ['nɛksəs] *n, pl* **nex·us 1** a connection. **2** a connected series. ⟨Latin, from *nectere* bind⟩
NGO non-government organization.
NHL or **N.H.L.** National Hockey League.
ni·a·cin ['naɪəsɪn] *n* NICOTINIC ACID. ⟨*ni(cotinic) ac(id)*⟩
nib [nɪb] *n* the point of a pen. ⟨Old English *nebb* beak, tip⟩

nib·ble ['nɪbəl] v 1 eat away with quick, small bites. 2 bite gently: *A fish nibbles at the bait.* 3 eat little or lightly. **nib·bler** n. ⟨Middle English *nebbylen* peck at⟩
nibble at *Informal* **a** be interested in: *The management are nibbling at my suggestion.* **b** take apart or attack, as if by taking small bites: *critics nibbling at a new play.* n 1 an act of nibbling: *We've been fishing all day and haven't had a nibble.* 2 a small piece, esp of food: *just a nibble of the cake.*

nibs [nɪbz] n *Slang* **his** (or **her**) **nibs** *Facetious* a title of pretended respect for someone: *How is his nibs today?* ⟨origin uncertain⟩

nice [nəis] adj 1 pleasing; satisfactory: *a nice day.* 2 kind: *He was nice to us.* 3 subtle; precise: *a nice distinction.* 4 requiring or using care, skill, or tact: *a nice problem.* 5 fastidious: *nice in his eating.* 6 proper; suitable. 7 refined; cultured: *nice manners.* **nice·ly** adv. **nice·ness** n. ⟨Old French = silly, Latin *nescius; ne-* not + *scire* know⟩
ni·ce·ty ['nəisəti] n 1 exactness; delicacy: *Television sets require nicety of adjustment.* 2 a fine point; small distinction. 3 something dainty or refined. **to a nicety** just right: *cakes browned to a nicety.*

niche [nɪʃ] or [nɪtʃ] n 1 a recess in a wall for a statue, etc. 2 a suitable place or position: *He will find his niche in the world.* 3 **a** the space occupied by an organism in its habitat. **b** the role of an organism including its position in the food chain, etc. ⟨French; origin uncertain⟩

nick [nɪk] n a place where a small bit has been cut or broken out: *She cut nicks in a stick to keep count of her score.*
v 1 make a nick in: *I nicked the edge of the plate.* 2 cut into or wounded slightly: *The bullet just nicked his arm.* 3 hit, guess, etc. exactly. ⟨origin uncertain⟩
in the nick of time just in time.

nick·el ['nɪkəl] n 1 a metallic element that is resistant to rust, used mainly in alloys. *Symbol* **Ni** 2 a five-cent piece. ⟨German *Kupfernickel* copper devil; for its deceptive resemblance to copper⟩
nick·el–and–dime v *Informal* 1 spend very little or too little (on). 2 haggle (with) over trifling amounts. **nick·el·o·de·on** [,nɪkə'loudiən] n 1 formerly, motion picture exhibitions to which the price of admission was five cents. 2 formerly, a juke box, esp one that started on the insertion of a nickel. **nickel plate** a thin coating of nickel deposited on a metal object to prevent rust. **nick·el·plate** v.

nick–nack ['nɪk ,næk] n See KNICK-KNACK.

nick·name ['nɪk,neim] n 1 a short form of a proper name: *Elizabeth's nickname is 'Betty'.* 2 a name used instead of a proper name: *Majid's nickname was 'Buzz'.* **nick·name** v. ⟨Middle English *an ekename* (taken as *a nekename*); *eke* additional (see EKE) + *name.*⟩

nic·o·tine ['nɪkə,tin] or [,nɪkə'tin] n *Chemistry* a poisonous alkaloid contained in the leaves of tobacco. **nic·o·tine·less** adj. ⟨Jacques *Nicot* 16c French ambassador; brought tobacco to France⟩
nic·o·tin·ic acid [,nɪkə'tɪnɪk] *Biochemistry* an acid of the vitamin B complex found in meat, eggs, wheat germ, etc.; niacin. **ni·co·tin·ism** ['nɪkəti,nɪzəm] or [,nɪkə'tinɪzəm] n nicotine poisoning.

nic·ti·tate ['nɪktə,teit] v wink. Also, **nic·tate.** ⟨Latin *nictitare* blink repeatedly⟩
nictitating membrane in reptiles, birds, and some other animals, a thin membrane that can be extended across the eye. Also called **third eyelid.**

niece [nis] n 1 the daughter of one's brother or sister. 2 a daughter of a brother or sister of one's spouse. ⟨Old French; Latin *neptis*⟩

nif·ty ['nɪfti] *Informal* adj excellent, esp by being ingenious, handy, or stylish: *a nifty way to solve the problem.*

nig·gard ['nɪgərd] n a stingy person. **nig·gard** adj. **nig·gard·li·ness** n. **nig·gard·ly** adj, adv. ⟨Middle English *nig* stingy + pejorative suffix *-ard*⟩

nig·gle ['nɪgəl] v 1 be concerned with petty things. 2 irritate or worry. **nig·gler** n. **nig·gling** adj. ⟨possibly Scandinavian⟩

nigh [nai] *Archaic, poetic, or dialect* adv 1 near: *Dawn was nigh.* 2 nearly: *He was nigh dead with fright.*
adj **nigh·er**, **nigh·est** or **next** near. ⟨Old English *nēah*⟩

night [nait] n 1 the period of darkness between evening and morning. 2 the dark: *She went out into the night.* **night** adj. **night·less** adj. **night·like** adj. ⟨Old English *niht*⟩
make a night of it celebrate until very late.
night·cap n 1 a cap for wearing in bed. 2 a drink taken just before going to bed. **night·club** n a place for dancing, eating, and entertainment, open only at night. **night·crawl·er** n *esp US* dew-worm. **night·dress** n nightgown. **night·fall** n the coming of night. **night·gown** n a loose garment for women and girls, for wearing in bed. **night·hawk** n 1 any of a genus of goatsuckers having dark plumage. 2 *Informal* NIGHT OWL. **night·ie** or **night·y** n *Informal* nightgown. **night·in·gale** ['naitən,geil] or ['naitɪŋ,geil] n any of several thrushes noted for the sweet song of the male, which it sings by night or day. **night light** a small lamp that provides a dim light, used especially beside the bed of a child or of a sick person at night. **night·long** adj lasting all night. **night·long** adv. **night·ly** adj 1 done every night. 2 done at night. **night·ly** adv. **night·mare** n 1 a frightening dream. 2 a frightening experience: *The dust storm was a nightmare.* **night·mar·ish** adj. **night·mar·ish·ly** adv. **night·mar·ish·ness** n. **night owl** *Informal* a person who often stays up late. **nights** adv regularly in the nighttime: *He works nights.* **night school** a school held in the evening for persons who work during the day. **night·shade** n any of various plants of the

nightshade family having berries that are often poisonous. **night shift 1** a working period during the night. **2** the workers who work at night. **night·shirt** *n* a loose garment for wearing in bed. **night·spot** *n Informal* nightclub. **night stand** a small table at the side of a bed. **night·stick** *n* a police officer's stick or club. **night terrors** a feeling of extreme fear and disorientation experienced on partial waking. **night·time** *n* the time between evening and morning. **night watch 1** a watch or guard kept during the night. **2** the person or persons keeping such a watch. **3** a period or division of the night. **night watchman.**

ni·hil·ism ['naɪə,lɪzəm] *or* ['niə,lɪzəm] *n* **1** the entire rejection of the usual beliefs in religion, morals, government, laws, etc. **2** *Philosophy* the denial that anything exists. **3** Nihilism, the beliefs of a 19th-century Russian revolutionary party, that advocated the removal of the old society by violence. **ni·hil·ist** *n.* **ni·hil·is·tic** *adj.* ⟨Latin *nihil* nothing⟩

nil [nɪl] *n* nothing. ⟨Latin = nothing, shortened from *nihil*⟩

nim·ble ['nɪmbəl] *adj* **1** able to move lightly and quickly: *nimble fingers.* **2** quick to understand: *a nimble mind.* **nim·ble·ness** *n.* **nim·bly** *adv.* ⟨Middle English *nymel;* Old English *niman* take⟩

nim·bus ['nɪmbəs] *n, pl* **-bus·es** or **-bi** [-baɪ] *or* [-bi] **1** a light disk about the head of a sacred person in a picture. **2** a bright cloud surrounding a god, person, or thing. **3** a rain cloud. ⟨Latin = cloud⟩ **nim·bo·stra·tus** [,nɪmbou'streɪtəs] *or* [-'strætəs] *n, pl* **-ti** [-taɪ] *or* [-ti] a low, grey cloud layer that brings rain or snow.

NIMBY ['nɪmbɪ] someone who opposes introducing some institution thought of as undesirable in the neighbourhood. ⟨for *not in my backyard*⟩

nin·com·poop ['nɪŋkəm,pup] *n* a fool; simpleton. ⟨origin uncertain⟩

nine [naɪn] *n* **1** one more than eight; 9. **2** any set of nine persons or things. **3** a playing card having nine spots. **4** *Golf* the first or last nine holes of an eighteen-hole course. **5 the Nine** the Muses. **nine** *adj.* ⟨Old English *nigon*⟩ **dressed (up) to the nines** *Informal* very formally dressed: *I showed up in my jeans and found that she was dressed to the nines.* **nine times out of ten** as a general rule. **the whole nine yards** everything: *He does daily workouts, natural foods, the whole nine yards.* **nine days' wonder** anything that causes a short period of excitement. **nine·fold** *adj* **1** nine times as much. **2** having nine parts. *adv* nine times as much or as many. **nine·pins** *n* a game in which nine wooden pins are set up to be bowled down with a ball (with a sg verb). **ninth** [naɪnθ] *adj, n* **1** next after the eighth; 9th. **2** one, or being one, of nine equal parts. **ninth·ly** *adv.*

nine·teen ['naɪn'tin] *n* **1** nine more than ten; 19. **2** any set of 19 persons or things. **nine·teen** *adj.* ⟨Old English *nigontēne*⟩ **nine·teenth** *adj, n* **1** next after the 18th; 19th. **2** one, or being one, of 19 equal parts.

nine·ty ['naɪnti] *n* **1** nine times ten; 90. **2 nineties** *pl* the years from 90 through 99, esp of a century or of a person's life: *She was in her nineties when she died.* **4** any set of 90 persons or things. **nine·ty** *adj.* ⟨Old English *nigontig*⟩ **nine·ti·eth** ['naɪntiɪθ] *adj, n* **1** next after the 89th; 90th. **2** one, or being one, of 90 equal parts.

nin·ja ['nɪndʒə] *n* **1** a Japanese mercenary of medieval times, highly skilled in the martial arts. **2** any modern-day fighter imitating the style of these mercenaries. ⟨Japanese⟩

nin·ny ['nɪni] *n* fool. ⟨perhaps *an innocent* naive person⟩

ni·o·bi·um [naɪ'oubiəm] *n* a rare metallic element, formerly called columbium. *Symbol* **Nb** ⟨*Niobe,* in Greek myth, a mother turned into a fountain⟩

nip¹ [nɪp] *v* **nipped, nip·ping 1** squeeze tight and suddenly. **2** take off by biting, pinching, or snipping. **3** stop or spoil the growth of: *a policy designed to nip inflation.* **4** injure with cold: *The flowers were all nipped by frost.* *n* **1** a sudden sharp pinch or bite. **2** stinging cold. **3** a sharp flavour: *cheese with a nip.* ⟨Middle English *nyppen*⟩ **nip and tuck** *Informal* in a contest, so evenly matched that the issue remains in doubt till the end. **nip in the bud** stop at the very beginning: *All her plans were nipped in the bud by the sudden death of her benefactor.* **nip·per** *n* **1** a big claw of a lobster or crab. **2 nippers** *pl* any tool that nips. **nip·py** *adj* **1** chilly; biting: *nippy weather.* **2** sharp; pungent: *nippy cheese.*

nip² [nɪp] *n* a small drink: *a nip of brandy.* *v* **nipped, nip·ping** drink nips. ⟨*nipperkin* small vessel; origin uncertain⟩

nip·ple ['nɪpəl] *n* **1** the round projection in the centre of the mammary gland which, in females, contains the outlet of the milk ducts. **2** the mouthpiece of a baby's bottle. **3** something shaped or used like a nipple. **nip·ple·less** *adj.* ⟨earlier *neble* diminutive of *neb.* See NIB.⟩

nir·va·na or **Nir·va·na** [nər'vænə] *or* [-'vɑnə] *n* **1** *Buddhism* the enlightened level of being of a person who has overcome the desires and the pain of worldly existence. **2** *Hinduism* freedom of the soul. **3** freedom from care and pain. ⟨Sanskrit = extinction; *nis-* out + *vā-* blow⟩

Ni·sei ['ni'seɪ] *n, pl* **-sei** a native-born Canadian or US citizen whose parents were Japanese immigrants. ⟨Japanese *ni* two + *sei* generation⟩

Nis·ga'a ['nɪʃgɑ] *n, pl* **-ga'a 1** a member of a people living in the Skeena River area of British Columbia. **2** their dialect of

Nass-Gitksan, a Tsimshian language. **Nis·ga'a** *adj.* Also, **Nish·ga.**

ni·si ['nəɪsaɪ] *or* ['nisi] *conj Law* not yet final: *a decree nisi.* ⟨Latin = unless⟩

Nis·sen hut ['nɪsən] a prefabricated shelter for soldiers, semicylindrical in shape, made of corrugated iron, with a concrete floor. Compare QUONSET HUT. ⟨Lt.Col. P.N. *Nissen,* 20c designer⟩

nit [nɪt] *n* the egg or the young of a louse or similar insect. **nit·ty** *adj.* ⟨Middle English *nite;* Old English *hnitu*⟩

nit·pick *v* find fault with unimportant details: *I welcome your criticism but try not to nitpick.* **nit·pick·er** *n.* **nit·pick·ing** *n.*

ni·tro·gen ['naɪtrədʒən] *n* a gaseous element that forms about four-fifths of the earth's atmosphere by volume. *Symbol* **N** **ni·trog·e·nous** [naɪ'trɒdʒənəs] *adj.* ⟨Greek *nitron* sodium carbonate + -GEN⟩

ni·trate *n* **1** a salt or ester of nitric acid. **2** POTASSIUM NITRATE or SODIUM NITRATE, used as a fertilizer. **ni·tre** ['naɪtər] *n* **1** potassium nitrate. **2** sodium nitrate, used as a fertilizer. Also, **ni·ter. nitric acid** a highly corrosive liquid. **ni·tri·fy** *v* **1** oxidize (ammonia compounds, etc.) to nitrates, esp by bacterial action. **2** impregnate (soil, etc.) with nitrates. **3** combine or treat with nitrogen or one of its compounds. **ni·tri·fi·ca·tion** *n.* **ni·tri·fi·er** *n.* **ni·tri·fi·a·ble** *adj.* **nitrogen cycle** the cycle of chemical changes that returns nitrogen to its original form after its use by plants and bacteria. **nitrogen dioxide** a gas found in automobile exhaust fumes. **nitrogen fixation** the conversion of atmospheric nitrogen into nitrogen compounds, thus providing nitrogen for plants. **ni·tro·glyc·er·in** or **ni·tro·glyc·er·ine** [,naɪtrou'glɪsərɪn] *n* an explosive liquid made by treating glycerin with nitric and sulphuric acids. **nitrous oxide** a gas having a sweet taste and smell, used as an anesthetic, esp in dentistry. Also called **laughing gas.**

nit·ty–grit·ty ['nɪti 'grɪti] *n Informal* basic reality: *Let's get down to the nitty-gritty of who is going to pay for the broken window.* ⟨nit + grit⟩

nit·wit ['nɪt,wɪt] *n Slang* a stupid or scatterbrained person. ⟨slang *nit* nothing (Yiddish) + *wit*⟩

nix [nɪks] *Slang n, interj* **1** no. **2** nothing. *v* reject or veto: *The city council nixed the proposal.* ⟨German, dialect variant of *nichts* nothing⟩

Nla·ka'·pa·mux [,ənhlɒ'kʊpəmə] *n* **1** a member of a First Nations people living in British Columbia. **2** their Salishan language. **Nlaka'pamux** *adj.* Also called **Thompson.**

NNE or **N.N.E.** north-northeast.

NNW or **N.N.W.** north-northwest.

no [nou] *n, pl* **noes 1** a word used to deny, refuse, or disagree. **2** a denial; refusal. **3** a negative vote or voter: *The noes have it. adj* not any; not a: *He has no friends.*

adv not at all: *He is no better.* ⟨variant of *none*⟩ **no–ac·count** *Informal adj* no good: *a no-account swindler. n* a person of no importance at all. **no–brain·er** *n Informal* something very easy to figure out or decide: *The first question was a no-brainer.* **no–fault** *adj* to do with a type of car insurance under which a person is compensated by his or her own insurance company, regardless of who is to blame. **no–hit·ter** *n Baseball* a game in which the pitcher prevents the opposing team from gaining any base hits. **no–holds–barred** *adj Informal* without restrictions: *a no-holds-barred effort.* **no·how** *adv Informal* in no way; not at all. **no–man's–land** or **no man's land** *n* **1** in war, the area between opposing armies. **2** a tract of land to which no one has an established claim. **3** any area of involvement that is not clearly defined: *a legal no-man's-land.* **no–name** *adj* to do with products marketed in generic packaging and without a brand name. **no–no** *n Informal* an action that is ill-advised or forbidden. **no one** or **no–one** ['nou ,wʌn] no person; nobody. **no–see–em** or **no–see–um** *n ✱* any of various tiny insects that have a nasty bite. **no–show** *n Informal* anyone who fails to show up for a reservation, appointment, etc. **no way** *Slang* definitely not or definitely no: *No way could he pass an exam like that!* **no–win** *adj* unsuccessful for all parties concerned: *The constitutional debate is a no-win situation.*

No. number (for Latin *numero; numerus* number).

nob [nɒb] *n Slang* **1** head. **2** a person of wealth or social importance. ⟨possible variant of *knob*⟩

no·bel·i·um [nou'biliəm] *n* an artificial radioactive element. *Symbol* **No** ⟨A.B. *Nobel,* who established the Nobel prizes⟩

No·bel prize [nou'bɛl] any of a group of prizes established by A.B. Nobel, 19c Swedish philanthropist, to be given annually to the person or persons who have contributed most in his or her field.

no·ble ['noubəl] *adj* **1** great by birth, rank, or title. **2** great in character or quality. **3** magnificent: *Niagara Falls is a noble sight.* **4** of metals, resisting oxidation or corrosion, as gold. **5** *Chemistry* of certain gaseous elements, chemically inert, as helium. *n* a person great by birth, rank, or title: *A duke is a noble.* ⟨Latin *nobilis* renowned⟩ **no·bil·i·ty** *n* **1** people of noble rank. **2** noble birth; noble rank. **3** noble character or quality. **no·ble·man** *n, pl* -**men** a man who belongs to the nobility. **no·blesse o·blige** [nou'blɛs ou'bliʒ] *French* the unwritten expectation that persons of noble rank should behave nobly. **no·ble·wom·an** *n, pl* -**wom·en** a woman who belongs to the nobility. **no·bly** *adv* **1** in a noble manner. **2** splendidly; magnificently. **3** of noble ancestry: *nobly born.*

no·bod·y ['nou,bʌdi], [-,bɒdi], *or* [-,bədi] *pron* no one; no person. *n pl* -**bod·ies** a person of no importance.

nock [nɒk] *n* a notch on a bow or arrow for the bowstring.
v fit (an arrow) to the bowstring for shooting. ⟨Middle English *nocke*⟩

noc·tur·nal [nɒk'tɜrnəl] *adj* 1 to do with night: *The stars are a nocturnal sight.* 2 of animals, active during the night instead of the day: *Raccoons are nocturnal.* 3 of plants, having flowers that open only at night: *One species of cactus is nocturnal.* **noc·tur·nal·ly** *adv.* ⟨Latin *nocturnalis; noctis* night⟩
noc·tam·bu·lism [nɒk'tæmbjə,lɪzəm] *n* sleepwalking. **noc·turne** ['nɒktɜrn] *n Music* a dreamy composition.

nod [nɒd] *v* **nod·ded, nod·ding** 1 bow (the head) slightly and raise it again quickly. 2 show agreement by nodding. 3 let the head fall forward and bob around when sleepy. **nod** *n.* ⟨Middle English *nodden*⟩
nodding acquaintance a casual acquaintance. **get** (or **give**) **the nod** *Informal* **a** receive or give approval. **b** receive or give a victory or decision to. **nod off** fall asleep.

node [noud] *n* 1 a knob; swelling. 2 *Botany* a joint in a stem. 3 *Physics* a point in a vibrating body at which there is comparatively no vibration. 4 a knotlike mass of specialized tissue in the body: *a lymph node.* 5 *Geometry* a point at which a curve intersects itself so that each of the branches has a distinct tangent. 6 a central point in a system. 7 *Astronomy* either of the two points at which the orbit of a heavenly body intersects the path of another heavenly body. **nod·al** *adj.* ⟨Latin *nodus* knot⟩
nod·ule ['nɒdʒul] *n* 1 a small knot, knob, or swelling. 2 a lump: *nodules of pure gold.* 3 *Botany* a tubercle. **nod·u·lar** *adj.*

no·ël [nou'ɛl] *n* 1 a Christmas song; carol. 2 **Noël** Christmas. ⟨French; Latin *natalis* natal. See NATAL.⟩

nog·gin ['nɒgən] *n* 1 a small mug. 2 a small measure of liquor. 3 *Informal* a person's head. ⟨origin uncertain⟩

noise [nɔɪz] *n* 1 a sound that is not musical or pleasant: *the noise of traffic.* 2 any sound: *the noise of rain on the roof.* 3 *Physics* a group of sound waves produced by irregular vibrations. 4 any undesired disturbance in a radio or television signal.
v Archaic spread the news of: *It was noised abroad that the king was dying.* **noise·less** *adj.* **noise·less·ly** *adv.* **noise·less·ness** *n.* **nois·y** *adj.* **nois·i·ly** *adv.* **nois·i·ness** *n.* ⟨Old French; Latin *nausea.* See NAUSEA.⟩
noise·mak·er *n* a horn, rattle, etc. used to make noise at a party, sports event, etc.

SYNONYMS

Noise applies to any loud sound made by people or things: *The noise kept me awake.* **Uproar** applies especially to the shouting of a crowd: *You should have heard the uproar when officials called back the touchdown.*

---

noi·some ['nɔɪsəm] *adj* 1 offensive; smelling bad: *a noisome slum.* 2 harmful: *a noisome*

pestilence. **noi·some·ly** *adv.* **noi·some·ness** *n.* ⟨*noy* (variant of *annoy*) + *-some¹*⟩

no·mad ['noumæd] *n* 1 a member of a people that moves from place to place so as to have pasture for its cattle or to be near its own food or water supply. The Inuit have traditionally been nomads. 2 wanderer. *adj* nomadic: *nomad peoples.* **no·mad·ic** *adj.* **no·mad·i·cal·ly** *adv.* **no·mad·ism** *n.* ⟨Greek *nomados; nemein* pasture⟩

nom de guerre [,nɒm də 'gɛr] *French* [nɔ̃də'gɛʀ] *French* an assumed name under which to pursue a profession, undertaking, or the like. ⟨literally, war name⟩

nom de plume [,nɒm də 'plum] a name used by a writer instead of his or her real name. ⟨literally, pen name⟩

no·men·cla·ture ['noumən,kleɪtʃər] *or* [nou'mɛnklətʃər] *n* a system of names used in a particular field of science, art, etc.: *the nomenclature of music.* ⟨Latin *nomen* name + *calare* call⟩

nom·i·nal ['nɒmənəl] *adj* 1 being so in name only; not real: *The president is the nominal head of the club, but the secretary really runs its affairs.* 2 so small that it is not worth considering: *a nominal rent.* 3 to do with a name. 4 *Grammar* to do with a noun. *Day* is the nominal root of *daily.* ⟨Latin *nomen* name⟩
nom·i·nal·ism *n Philosophy* the doctrine that abstractions exist only as names. **nom·i·nal·ist** *n.* **nom·i·nal·is·tic** *adj.* **nom·i·nal·is·ti·cal·ly** *adv.* **nom·i·nal·ly** *adv* 1 in a nominal way only. 2 by name. **nom·i·nate** *v* 1 suggest as candidate for an office. 2 appoint to an office or duty: *The prime minister nominated her Secretary of State.* **nom·i·na·tor** *n.* **nom·i·na·tion** *n.* **nom·i·na·tive** ['nɒmənətɪv] *adj* 1 to do with the grammatical case that shows that a noun, pronoun, or adjective is part of the subject of a sentence. 2 bearing a person's name, as on shares. **nom·i·nee** [,nɒmə'ni] *n* a person who is nominated.

non– *prefix* not; opposite of; lack of: *nonconformity, nonflammable, non-smoking.* ⟨Latin = not⟩

non·a·ge·nar·i·an [,nɒnədʒə'nɛriən] *or* [,noun-] *n* a person who is 90 years old or between 90 and 100 years old. **non·a·ge·nar·i·an** *adj.* ⟨Latin *nonagenarius* of ninety⟩

non·a·gon ['nɒnə,gɒn] *n* a polygon having nine sides. ⟨Latin *nonus* ninth + Greek *gōnia* angle⟩

nonce [nɒns] *n* the one occasion or purpose. *adj* serving a single occasion: *nonce use.* ⟨Middle English *for then ones* for the once, taken as *for the nones*⟩
for the nonce for the present time.
nonce word a word formed and used for a single occasion.

non·cha·lant [,nɒnʃə'lɒnt] *or* ['nɒnʃə,lɒnt] *adj* coolly unconcerned or indifferent. **non·cha·lance** *n.* **non·cha·lant·ly** *adv.* ⟨French *non-* not + *chaloir* be warm⟩

non·com·mit·tal [ˌnɒnkə'mɪtəl] *adj* not committing oneself. *I will think it over* is a noncommittal answer. **non·com·mit·tal·ly** *adv.*

non·con·form·i·ty [ˌnɒnkən'fɔrməti] *n* 1 failure or refusal to conform. 2 a failure or refusal to conform to an established church. **non·con·form·ist** *n.*

non·de·script ['nɒndəˌskrɪpt] *or* [ˌnɒndə'skrɪpt] *adj* 1 having no distinctive features; drab. 2 not easily classified: *eyes of nondescript shade, neither blue nor grey.* ⟨non- + Latin *descriptus* described⟩

none [nʌn] *pron* 1 not any: *We have none of that paper left.* 2 no one; not one: *None of these is a typical case.* 3 no persons or things. *adv* not at all: *Our supply is none too great.* ⟨Old English *nān; ne* not + *ān* one⟩ **none·such** or **non·such** ['nʌnˌsʌtʃ] *n* a person or thing without equal; paragon. **none·the·less** [ˌnʌnðə'lɛs] *adv* nevertheless.

> **USAGE**
> **None** may be either singular or plural: *As only ten jurors have been chosen so far, none of the witnesses were called. I have heard the whole story, and none of it is true.*

non·en·ti·ty [nɒn'ɛntəti] *n,* 1 a person or thing of little importance. 2 something that does not exist. 3 non-existence.

non–es·sen·tial [ˌnɒn ə'sɛnʃəl] *adj* not essential; not necessary. **non–es·sen·tial** *n.*

non·e·vent [ˌnɒnɪ'vɛnt] *n* a happening that is unimportant.

nonfic·tion [nɒn 'fɪkʃən] *n* prose literature that is not a form of writing based on imaginary people and events.

non·flam·ma·ble [n̂ɒn'flæməbəl] *adj* not easily set on fire and not fast-burning if set on fire; not flammable.

non·func·tion·al [nɒn'fʌŋkʃənəl] *adj* having no proper use. **non·func·tion·al·ly** *adv.*

non–in·ter·ven·tion [ˌnɒn ɪntər'vɛnʃən] *n* the avoidance of any interference by a nation in the affairs of other nations or of its own states, etc. **non·in·ter·ven·tion·ist** *adj, n.*

non·pa·reil [ˌnɒnpə'rɛl] *adj* having no equal. *n* a person or thing having no equal. ⟨French *non-* not (Latin) + *pareil* equal; Latin *par*⟩

non–par·ti·san [nɒn 'pɑrtəzən] *or* [-ˌzæn] *adj* not supporting any faction or political party.

non·per·son ['nɒn'pɜrsən] *n* someone who is ignored, esp by a government or organization, or treated as if non-existent.

non·plus [nɒn'plʌs] *v* -plussed or -plused, -plus·sing or -plus·ing puzzle completely: *We were nonplussed to see two roads leading off to the left where we had expected only one.* ⟨Latin = no further⟩

non–prof·it [nɒn 'prɒfɪt] *adj* not conducted to make a profit: *a non-profit organization.*

nonsec·tar·i·an [ˌnɒn sɛk'tɛriən] *adj* not connected with any religious denomination.

non·sense ['nɒnsɛns] *or* ['nɒnsəns] *n* 1 words, ideas, or acts without meaning. 2 foolish talk or doings: *It is nonsense to say that we can walk that far.* 3 impudent or silly behaviour: *She doesn't take any nonsense from her employees.* **non·sen·si·cal** *adj.* **non·sen·si·cal·ly** *adv.* ⟨non- + *sense*⟩

non se·qui·tur [nɒn 'sɛkwətər] or [-tʊr] 1 a statement that has no direct relationship with what has just been said. 2 *Logic* a conclusion that does not follow from the premises. ⟨Latin = it does not follow⟩

non–skid ['nɒn 'skɪd] *adj* made so as to prevent skidding: *non-skid tires.* Also called **non–slip.**

non–stand·ard ['nɒn 'stændard] *adj* 1 not conforming to accepted specifications, etc. 2 different from what is held to be normal.

non–start·er [nɒn 'stɑrtər] *n Informal* 1 something expected that does not happen. 2 a useless idea.

non–sta·tus ['nɒn 'stætəs] *adj* ✳ of a First Nations person, not registered with the Federal Government as a STATUS INDIAN under the Indian Act.

non–stop ['nɒn 'stɒp] *adj, adv* without stopping: *a non-stop flight.*

non–trea·ty ['nɒn 'triti] *adj* ✳ of First Nations people, not under the terms of a treaty with the Canadian government.

noo·dle¹ ['nudəl] *n* 1 *Informal* a very stupid person. 2 *Slang* the head. ⟨origin uncertain⟩

noo·dle² ['nudəlz] *n* a flat strip of pasta. ⟨German *Nudel*⟩

nook [nʊk] *n* 1 a cosy little corner. 2 a hidden spot; sheltered place. ⟨Middle English *noke*⟩

noon [nun] *n* twelve o'clock in the daytime. *adj* of noon. ⟨Old English *nōn*; Latin *nona (hora)* ninth (hour)⟩ **noon·day** *n* noon. *adj* of noon: *the noonday meal.* **noon hour** 1 noon; the time around noon. 2 lunch hour: *I'll see you at noon hour.* **noon–hour** *adj.* **noon·time** *n* noon.

noose [nus] *n* 1 a loop with a slip-knot that tightens as the rope is pulled. 2 anything that restricts or snares like a noose. 3 the noose death by hanging. *v* catch in a noose or as if in a noose. ⟨Old French *nos*; Latin *nodus* knot⟩

Noot·ka ['nʊtkə] *or* ['nutkə] See NUU-CHAH-NULTH.

nope [noup] *adv Informal* no.

nor [nɔr] *conj* and not; or not; neither; and not either. *Nor* is used with a preceding *neither* or negative: *She is neither friend nor foe. Not a boy nor a girl stirred.* ⟨Old English *nāther ne* not + *āther* either⟩

NORAD ['nɔræd] North American Air Defence (Command), a joint military organization of Canada and the US, monitoring air space for both countries.

Nor·dic ['nɔrdɪk] *adj* 1 to do with the Germanic peoples of northern Europe, esp of Scandinavia. 2 to do with a type of people characterized by tall stature, blond hair, and blue eyes. **3** of or designating cross-country skiing. 〈French *nord* north〉

norm [nɔrm] *n* the standard for a certain group; type; model; pattern: *In mathematics this class is above the norm for the senior year.* 〈Latin *norma* a rule, pattern〉

nor·mal ['nɔrməl] *adj* **1** regular; usual: *The normal temperature of the human body is 37°C.* **2** *Geometry* perpendicular. **3** *Medicine, psychology* of average intelligence, mental or physical health, etc. *n* **1** the usual state or level: *two kilograms above normal.* **2** *Geometry* a line or plane that is at right angles to another. **nor·mal·i·ty** *n.* **nor·mal·i·za·tion** *n.* **nor·mal·iz·er** *n.* **nor·mal·ly** *adv.* **nor·mal·cy** ['nɔrməlsi] *n* a normal condition. **nor·ma·tive** *adj* to do with, constituting, or conforming to a norm or standard: *normative grammar.* **nor·ma·tive·ly** *adv.*

Nor·man ['nɔrmən] *n* **1** a native or inhabitant of Normandy in France. **2** a member of the Scandinavian people who conquered Normandy in the 10th century A.D. **3** a member of the Norman-French people who conquered England in 1066. **Nor·man** *adj.*

Norse [nɔrs] *n* **1 the Norse** *pl* **a** the people of ancient Scandinavia; Norsemen. **b** the people of Norway. **2** the language of the ancient Scandinavians, often called Old Norse. *adj* **1** to do with ancient Scandinavia, its people, or their language. **2** to do with Norway or its people. 〈Dutch *Noorsch* Norwegian〉

north [nɔrθ] *n* **1** the direction to the right as one faces the setting sun. **2 the North a** the part of any country. **b** in Canada, the northern parts of the provinces from Québec westward and the territory north of these provinces. **north** or **North** *adj.* **north** *adv.* 〈Old English〉

north of farther north than.

North American a native or inhabitant of North America. **North American** *adj.* **north·bound** *adj* going toward the north. **north·east** *n* halfway between north and east. **north·east** *adj, adv.* **north·east·er** *n* a wind or storm from the northeast. **north·east·er·ly** *adj, adv.* **north·east·ern** *adj* to do with the northeast. **north·east·ward** *adv, adj* toward the northeast. Also (*adv*), **north·east·wards. north·east·ward·ly** *adj, adv.* **north·er·ly** *adj, adv* to do with the north. **north·ern 1** toward the north. **2** from the north. **3** of or in the north. **north·ern·er** *n* **1** a native or inhabitant of the north. **2 Northerner** a native or inhabitant of the Far North. **northern lights** the bands of light that appear in the northern sky at night; AURORA BOREALIS. **north·ern·most** *adj* farthest north. **north·ing** ['nɔrθɪŋ] *or* ['nɔrðɪŋ] *n* the distance measured in a northerly direction. **north·land** ['nɔrθ,lænd] *or* ['nɔrθlənd] *n* Usually, **Northland** the northern regions of Canada; the Far North. **north·land·er** *n.*

north–north·east *n* a direction halfway between north and northeast. **north–north·west** *n* a direction halfway between north and northwest. **North Pole** the northern end of the earth's axis. **North Star** the bright star almost directly above the North Pole. **north·ward** *adj, adv* toward the north. Also (*adv*), **north·wards. north·ward·ly** *adj, adv.* **north·west** *n* **1** halfway between north and west. **2 North·west** ✱ the region of Canada north and west of the Great Lakes. **north·west** *adj, adv.* **north·west·er** *n* a wind or storm from the northwest. **north·west·er·ly** *adj, adv.* **north·west·ern** *adj* to do with the northwest. **North West Mounted Police** ✱ a former name of the Royal Canadian Mounted Police. *Abbrev* **NWMP** or **N.W.M.P.** **Northwest Passage** ✱ a route for ships from the Atlantic to the Pacific along the northern coast of North America. **Northwest Rebellion** ✱ an armed uprising of Métis and First Nations peoples in Saskatchewan in 1885. **Northwest Territories** a large area of land in the northwest of Canada, having a territorial government. *Abbrev* **NT. north·west·ward** *adv, adj* toward the northwest. Also (*adv.*), **north·west·wards. north·west·ward·ly** *adj, adv.* **nor'west·er** *n* a waterproof coat worn by sailors.

Nos. numbers.

nose [nouz] *n* **1** the part of the face above the mouth, for breathing and as the organ of smell. **2** the sense of smell: *a dog with a good nose.* **3** a faculty for detecting: *a nose for news.* *v* **1** discover by smelling. **2** smell; sniff. **3** rub with the nose. **4** push with the nose or forward end. **5** search (*for*). **nose·less** *adj.* **nose·like** *adj.* 〈Old English *nosu*〉

count noses find out how many people are present. **follow one's nose a** go straight ahead. **b** be guided by one's instinct. **c** be guided by one's sense of smell. **lead by the nose** *Informal* have complete control over. **look down one's nose at** *Informal* feel contempt for. **nose out** find out by looking around. **on the nose a** exactly. **b** of a bet on a horse, that it will win. **pay through the nose** *Informal* pay a great deal too much. **poke one's nose into** pry into. **put someone's nose out of joint** *Informal* **a** take someone's place in another's favour. **b** destroy someone's hopes, plans, etc. **thumb one's nose (at)**. See THUMB. **turn up one's nose at** *Informal* treat with contempt. **under one's nose** in plain sight; very easy to notice.

nose bag a bag containing food, to be hung over a horse's head. **nose·bleed** *n* a bleeding from the nose. **nose cone** a cone-shaped cap at the forward end of a spacecraft, designed to streamline and to provide protection. **nose–dive** *n* **1** a plunge straight downward by an aircraft. **2** a sudden, sharp drop. **nose–dive** *v.* **nose·gay** *n* a bunch of flowers. **nose job** cosmetic surgery, usually to reduce the size of the nose; rhinoplasty. **nose ring** a ring in the nose of an animal such as a bull, for leading it. **nos·ey** or **nosy** *adj Informal* too curious about other people's business;

prying; inquisitive. **no·si·ly** adv. **no·si·ness** n. **Nosey Park·er** Informal a person showing a persistent and offensive curiosity about things which do not concern him or her.

nosh [nɒʃ] Slang n a snack or tidbit. v eat or chew. ⟨Yiddish nash snack⟩

nos·tal·gia [nɒ'stældʒə] or [nə-] n **1** homesickness. **2** a yearning for something in the past. **nos·tal·gic** adj. **nos·tal·gi·cal·ly** adv. ⟨Greek nostos homecoming + algos pain⟩

nos·tril ['nɒstrəl] n either of the two external openings in the nose. ⟨Old English nosthyrl; nosu nose + thyrel hole⟩

nos·trum ['nɒstrəm] n **1** a medicine prepared and recommended by the same person, usually without scientific evidence of its effectiveness. **2** a pet scheme for producing wonderful results; cure-all. ⟨Latin = ours⟩

not [nɒt] adv a word used to make a negative statement or to express denial, refusal, etc.: That is not true. ⟨unstressed variant of nought⟩

no·ta be·ne ['noutə 'beni] or ['bene] Latin note well; take notice. Abbrev **N.B.** or **n.b.**

no·ta·ry ['noutəri] n **1** NOTARY PUBLIC. **2** ✸ in Québec, a lawyer who has the same training as a barrister but who is not permitted to plead in court. ⟨Latin notarius clerk; nota note⟩
no·ta·rize v certify (a contract, deed, will, etc.) as a notary public or other legal official. **notary public** pl **notaries public** a person authorized to certify deeds and contracts, take oaths, and attend to certain other legal matters. Abbrev **N.P.**

no·ta·tion See NOTE.

notch [nɒtʃ] n **1** a V-shaped cut made in an edge or on a surface. **2** ✸ Newfoundland and Labrador an entrance to a harbour. **3** a grade; step.
v **1** make a notch in. **2** record by notches; tally. ⟨earlier an och (taken as a notch); Middle French oche⟩

note [nout] n **1** words written down to remind one of something. **2** a brief letter: Write your grandmother a note to thank her for the birthday gift. **3** a formal letter from one government to another. **4** a single sound of definite pitch made by a musical instrument or voice. **5** Music **a** a written sign to show the pitch and length of a sound. **b** any key of a keyboard instrument: to strike the wrong note. **6** a bird's song or call. **7** a tone of voice or way of expression: a note of anxiety.
v **1** write down as a thing to be remembered. **2** observe carefully: Now note what I do next. **3** mention specially. **note·less** adj. **not·er** n. ⟨Latin nota note, mark⟩
compare notes exchange ideas. **make a note of** write down as something to be remembered. **of note** that is important: a writer of note. **strike the right** (or **wrong**) **note** say or do something suitable (unsuitable). **take note of** give attention to or notice. **take notes** write down things to be remembered.
no·ta·ble adj **1** worthy of notice; important:

a notable event. **2** that can be noted; perceptible: a notable quantity. n an important or famous person. **no·ta·bil·i·ty** n. **no·ta·bly** adv. **no·ta·bi·lia** [,noutə'bɪliə] n pl matters worthy of notice. **no·ta·tion** n **1** a set of signs or symbols used to represent numbers, quantities, or other values. In arithmetic we use the Arabic notation (1, 2, 3, 4, etc.). **2** a note to assist memory.
no·ta·tion·al adj. **note·book** n **1** a book in which to write notes. **2** Computers a laptop computer. **not·ed** adj famous: Shakespeare is a noted English author. **note·pad** n a pad of paper for taking notes. **note·paper** n paper used for writing letters. **note·wor·thy** adj remarkable: noteworthy achievement. **note·wor·thi·ness** n.

noth·ing ['nʌθɪŋ] n **1** not anything; no thing. **2** something that does not exist: create a world out of nothing. **3** a thing of no importance or value; person of no importance: People regard him as a nothing. **4** zero; nought.
adv not at all: She is nothing like her sister in looks. **noth·ing·ness** n. ⟨no + thing⟩
bring to nothing ruin or frustrate completely. **make nothing of a** be unable to understand. **b** treat as unimportant. **nothing less than** just the same as. **think nothing of a** consider as easy to do. **b** treat as unimportant. **c** do without scruple: He thinks nothing of taking pencils home from the office.

USAGE
Nothing, and **nobody**, are singular: Nothing is further from the truth. Nobody thinks that his or her dog is a nuisance. Informally, **nobody** is sometimes followed by a plural pronoun: Nobody thinks their dog is a nuisance.

no·tice ['noutɪs] n **1** observation; attention: escape one's notice. **2** advance information: The whistle blew to give notice that the boat was about to leave. **3** a written or printed sign.
v **1** take notice of; perceive: I noticed a big difference at once. **2** mention; refer to. **no·tice·a·ble** adj. **no·tice·a·bly** adv. ⟨Latin notitia; notus pp of noscere come to know⟩
serve notice give warning. **take notice** give attention; observe; see.

no·ti·fy ['noutə,faɪ] v give notice to; inform: Our teacher notified us that there would be a test on Monday. **no·ti·fi·ca·tion** n. **no·ti·fi·er** n. **no·ti·fi·a·ble** adj. ⟨Latin notus known (see NOTICE) + facere make⟩

no·tion ['nouʃən] n **1** an idea: He has no notion of what I mean. **2** an opinion: It is a common notion that red hair means a quick temper. **3** an inclination: She had a notion to visit her grandmother. **4** notions pl small, useful articles, such as pins, needles, thread, tape, etc. **no·tion·less** adj. ⟨Latin notio; notus. See NOTICE.⟩

no·to·ri·ous [nə'tɔriəs] adj widely known because of some unfavourable quality, action, etc.: a notorious gossip. **no·to·ri·e·ty** [,noutə'raɪəti] n. **no·to·ri·ous·ly** adv. ⟨Latin notorius; notus known⟩

not·with·stand·ing [ˌnɒtwɪθ'stændɪŋ] *prep* in spite of: *He bought it notwithstanding the high price.*
conj in spite of the fact that.
adv nevertheless: *It is raining; but I shall go, notwithstanding.*
notwithstanding clause ✶ in the Canadian Charter of Rights and Freedoms, a clause (Section 33) that may be invoked by the federal and provincial parliaments to override other basic charter provisions.

nou·gat ['nugət] *n* a soft candy containing nuts and sometimes fruit. ⟨French; Provençal *noga*; Latin *nucis* nut⟩

nought [nɒt] *n* **1** zero; 0. **2** naught; nothing. ⟨See NAUGHT.⟩

noun [naun] *Grammar n* a word used as the name of a person, place, thing, quality, event, etc. ⟨Anglo-French *nom*; Latin *nomen* name⟩
noun clause *Grammar* a subordinate clause that acts as a noun. *Example*: I know *that you will come with us.* **noun phrase** *Grammar* a phrase consisting of a noun plus any modifiers. *Example*: *the small white duck.*

nour·ish ['nɜrɪʃ] *v* **1** keep alive and well, with food: *Milk nourishes a baby.* **2** foster: *to nourish a hope.* **nour·ish·er** *n.* **nour·ish·ing·ly** *adv.* **nour·ish·ment** *n.* ⟨Old French *norir;* Latin *nutrire* feed⟩

nou·veau riche ['nuvou 'riʃ] *French* [nuvo'Riʃ] *pl,* **nou·veaux riches** ['nuvou'riʃ] *French* one who has recently become rich.

no·va ['nouvə] *n, pl* **no·vae** ['nouvi] *or* ['nouvaɪ] *or* **no·vas** *Astronomy* a star that suddenly becomes brighter and then gradually fades away. ⟨Latin *nova* new⟩

No·va Sco·tia ['nouvə 'skouʃə] a Maritime province of Canada. *Abbrev* **NS. No·va Sco·tian** ['nouvə 'skouʃən] *n, adj.*

nov·el¹ ['nɒvəl] *adj* of a new kind: *a novel experience.* ⟨Old French; Latin *novellus,* diminutive of *novus* new⟩
nov·el·ty 1 newness; novel character: *After the novelty of the game wore off, we lost interest.* **2** a new or unusual thing: *Staying up late was a novelty to the children.* **3 novelties** *pl* small, unusual articles; toys, cheap jewellery, etc.

nov·el² ['nɒvəl] *n* a fictional story long enough to fill one or more volumes. **nov·el·like** *adj.* **nov·el·ist** *n.* ⟨Italian *novella;* Latin = new things. See NOVEL¹.⟩
no·vel·la [nou'vɛlə] a short novel or an extended short story.

No·vem·ber [nou'vɛmbər] *n* the eleventh month of the year. It has 30 days. ⟨Latin; *novem* nine; for original calendar order⟩

no·ve·na [nou'vinə] *n, pl* **-nas, -nae** [-ni] *or* [-naɪ] *Roman Catholic Church* a religious exercise consisting of prayers or services on nine days, usually as a petition for some special purpose: *a novena of nine first Fridays.* ⟨Latin *novem* nine⟩

nov·ice ['nɒvɪs] *n* **1** a beginner. **2** a person who has been received into a religious order

but has not yet taken final vows. ⟨Latin *novicius; novus* new⟩
no·vi·ti·ate or **no·vi·ci·ate** [nou'vɪʃiɪt] *n* **1** a period of probation before taking final vows in a religious order. **2** the state or period of being a beginner in anything.

no·vo·caine or **no·vo·cain** ['nouvəˌkein] *n* **1** an alkaloid compound, used as a local anesthetic. **2 Novocain** *Trademark.* ⟨Latin *novus* new + (CO)CAINE⟩

now [nau] *adv* **1** at the present time: *He is here now.* **2** at once: *Do it now!* **3** then; next: *We have signed the petition and it now goes to the mayor.*
n the present; this time.
conj since: *Now I am older, I have changed my mind.* ⟨Old English *nū*⟩
just now. See JUST¹. **now and again** from time to time; once in a while. **now and then** from time to time; once in a while.
now·a·days *adv* at the present day. *n* the present day; these times.

no·where ['nou,wɛr] *adv* in, at, or to no place. *n* a non-existent place. ⟨Old English *nahwær*⟩

nox·ious ['nɒkʃəs] *adj* extremely harmful; poisonous: *Fumes from the exhaust of an automobile are noxious.* **nox·ious·ly** *adv.* **nox·ious·ness** *n.* ⟨Latin *noxa* hurt⟩

noz·zle ['nɒzəl] *n* **1** a tip on a hose, pipe, can, etc. to allow one to control the outward flow of liquid or gas. **2** *Slang* nose. ⟨diminutive of *nose*⟩

ns nanosecond.

NSF or **nsf** not sufficient funds.

N.T. New Testament.

nth [ɛnθ] *adj Mathematics* being of the indefinitely large or small value or amount denoted by *n*: *the nth power.*
to the nth degree or **power a** to any degree or power. **b** *Informal.* to the utmost: *She was dressed to the nth degree for the occasion.*

nu·ance ['njuɑns] *or* ['nuɑns], ['njuəns] *or* [nuəns] *n* a shade of expression, meaning, etc. ⟨French; *nuer* shade; *nue* cloud⟩

nub [nʌb] *n* **1** a knob. **2** a lump or piece. **3** the point or gist of anything. ⟨apparently variant of *knob*⟩
nub·bin *n* **1** a small lump. **2** a small or imperfect ear of corn. **3** an undeveloped fruit.

nu·bile ['njubaɪl] *or* ['nubaɪl] *adj* of a girl or young woman: **1** old or mature enough to be married. **2** sexually developed. **nu·bil·i·ty** [-'bɪləti] *n.* ⟨Latin *nubere* take a husband⟩

nu·cle·us ['njukliəs] *or* ['nukliəs] *n, pl* **-cle·i** [-kli,aɪ] **or -cle·us·es 1** a central part around which other parts are collected: *The family is the nucleus of our society.* **2** *Physics* the group of particles forming the central part of an atom. **3** *Chemistry* a stable group of atoms in a compound: *the benzene nucleus.* **4** *Biology* a mass of protoplasm found in most cells, without which a cell cannot grow. ⟨Latin *nuc(u)leus* diminutive of *nucis* nut⟩
nu·cle·ar ['njukliər] *or* ['nukliər] *adj* **1** to do

with the nucleus of a cell: *nuclear membranes*. **2** to do with the nuclei of atoms: *nuclear physics*. **3** to do with using nuclear energy: *the nuclear age*. **4** to do with any kind of nucleus: *the nuclear family*. **nuclear energy** the energy released by any nuclear reaction. **nuclear family** *Anthropology* a parent or parents and their child or children living together, without people from other generations or other branches of the family. **nuclear fission** FISSION (def. 3). **nuclear fuel** a fissile substance that will sustain a chain reaction. **nuclear fusion** FUSION (def. 4). **nuclear medicine** the use of radioactive isotopes in the treatment of disease. **nuclear physics** the branch of physics that is concerned with the structure and reactions of atomic nuclei. **nuclear physicist. nuclear power** electrical or motive power from nuclear energy produced in a reactor. **nuclear reactor** an apparatus for producing controlled nuclear energy. **nuclear winter** a great cooling of the earth's temperature after a nuclear war. **nu·cle·ate** *v* ['njuklɪˌeɪt] form into a nucleus or around a nucleus. *adj* ['njuklɪt] having a nucleus. **nu·cle·a·tion** *n*. **nu·cle·ic acid** [nju'kliːɪk] *or* [nju'kleɪɪk]; [nju'-] *Biochemistry* any of a group of complex acids, including DNA and RNA, found especially in the nuclei of cells. **nu·cle·o·lus** [nju'kliːələs] *or* [nu'-] *n, pl* **-li** [-ˌlaɪ] *or* [-ˌli] *Biology* a small structure found within the nucleus in most cells. Also, **nu·cle·ole** ['njukli,oul] *or* ['nu-]. **nu·cle·o·lar** *adj*. **nu·cle·on** ['njuklɪˌɒn] *or* ['nu-] *n Physics* one of the atomic particles that make up the nucleus of an atom, such as a neutron or proton. **nu·cle·on·ic** *adj*. **nu·cle·o·tide** ['njuklɪəˌtaɪd] *or* ['nu-] *n Biochemistry* a molecule that is the unit of structure of nucleic acid. **nuke** [njuk] *or* [nuk] *Slang n* a nuclear weapon. *v* **1** destroy with or as if with atomic bombs. **2** cook or heat in a microwave oven.

nude [njud] *or* [nud] *adj* naked.
n **1** a representation of a naked person in painting, sculpture, etc. **2** a naked person. **nu·di·ty** *n*. ⟨Latin *nudus*⟩
in the nude without clothes on: *to go swimming in the nude*.
nud·ism *n* the practice of going naked, esp for one's health. **nud·ist** *n, adj*.

nudge [nʌdʒ] *v* **1** push slightly or jog with the elbow to attract attention. **2** stimulate: *to nudge one's memory*. **3** approach closely: *She is nudging forty*. **nudge** *n*. **nudg·er** *n*. ⟨origin uncertain⟩

nu·ga·to·ry ['njugəˌtɔri] *or* ['nugəˌtɔri] *adj* **1** trifling. **2** invalid. **3** ineffective; useless. ⟨Latin *nuga* trifle⟩

nug·get ['nʌgɪt] *n* **1** a small lump of gold in its natural state. **2** anything small but valuable: *a few nuggets of truth*. ⟨perhaps diminutive of dialect *nug* lump⟩

nui·sance ['njusəns] *or* ['nusəns] *n* a thing that or person who annoys or offends: *Flies are a nuisance*. ⟨Old French; *nuire* harm, Latin *nocere*⟩

nuke See NUCLEUS.

null [nʌl] *adj* **1** as if not existing: *A promise obtained by force is legally null*. **2** unimportant; useless. **3** not any; zero. ⟨Latin *nullus; ne-* not + *ullus* any⟩
null and void without legal force or effect.
null hypothesis *Statistics* a hypothesis that assumes that two variables are unrelated. **nul·li·fy** *v* **1** make not binding: *nullify a law*. **2** make unimportant; cancel: *The difficulties of the plan nullify its advantages*. **nul·li·fi·ca·tion** *n*. **nul·li·fi·er** *n*. **nul·li·ty** *n* **1** futility; nothingness. **2** a mere nothing. **3** something that is null, such as a nullified law. **null set** *Mathematics* an empty set.

numb [nʌm] *adj* having lost the power of feeling: *My fingers are numb with cold*.
v **1** make numb: *Shovelling snow has numbed my fingers and toes*. **2** dull the feelings of: *numbed with grief*. **numb·ly** *adv*. **numb·ness** *n*. ⟨Old English *nome(n)* pp of *niman* take, seize⟩

num·ber ['nʌmbər] *n* **1** a word or symbol used in counting. **2** the sum: *The number of your fingers is ten*. **3** a quantity: *a number of reasons*. **4** a particular number that identifies: *a licence number*. A common symbol for this is #. **5** a single item on a program, etc.: *The program consisted of four musical numbers*. **6** a song or other piece of music: *She sings many old numbers*. **7** a single issue of a periodical. **8** *Grammar* a system for varying the form of words to indicate reference to singular and plural number. **9 numbers** *pl* numerical preponderance: *win by force of numbers*.
v **1** distinguish with a number: *The pages of this book are numbered*. **2** be able to show: *This city numbers a million inhabitants*. **3** include as one of a collection: *I number you among my best friends*. **4** limit: *His days in office are numbered*. **num·ber·er** *n*. ⟨Old French *nombre*; Latin *numerus*⟩
a number of several. **beyond number** too many to count. **have someone's number** know someone's weak point, and so be able to take advantage of it. **someone's number is up** *Informal* someone is doomed. **without number** too many to be counted.
number cruncher *Informal* **1** a very powerful computer. **2** a researcher who relies on statistics. **number crunching**. **num·ber·less** *adj* **1** very numerous: *numberless fish in the sea*. **2** without a number. **number one** **1** *Informal* oneself: *He worries too much about number one*. **2** the first or best in a series.

Number is a collective noun, requiring a singular or plural verb according to whether the total or the individual units are meant: *A number of tickets have already been sold. The number of tickets sold is astonishing.*

nu·men ['njumɪn] *or* ['numɪn] *n, pl* **-mi·na** [-mənə] **1** *Roman myth* the presiding spirit of a place. **2** creative energy. **nu·mi·nous** *adj*. ⟨Latin: a nod, command⟩

nu·mer·al ['njumərəl] *or* ['numərəl] *n* a figure or figures standing for a number. 2, 15, and 100 are Arabic numerals. II, XV, and C are Roman numerals for 2, 15, and 100. ⟨Latin *numerus* number⟩

nu·mer·a·ble *adj* that can be counted. **nu·mer·a·cy** *n* the ability to read and use numbers. **nu·mer·ate** *v* ['njumə,reit] *or* ['nu-] 1 enumerate. 2 read (a numerical expression). *adj* ['njumərɪt] *or* ['nu-] able to read and use numbers. **nu·mer·a·tion** *n* 1 the process of numbering, counting, or calculating. 2 the expression in words of a written numeral. **nu·mer·a·tor** *n* 1 *Arithmetic* in a common fraction, the number above the line. 2 a person or thing that makes a count, takes a census, etc. **nu·mer·i·cal** [nju'mɛrəkəl] *or* **nu·mer·ic** *adj* 1 to do with a number or numbers. 2 *Mathematics* of a mathematical quantity, designating the value in figures without considering the sign. **nu·mer·i·cal·ly** *adv.* **nu·mer·ol·o·gy** *n* a system of foretelling the future, based on the supposed influence that numbers have on people's lives. **nu·mer·o·log·i·cal** *adj.* **nu·mer·ol·o·gist** *n.* **nu·mer·ous** *adj* 1 very many: *numerous acquaintances.* 2 consisting of great numbers. **nu·mer·ous·ly** *adv.* **nu·mer·ous·ness** *n.*

USAGE

Usage varies in writing **numerals** as parts of consecutive sentences. In general, newspapers and informal writing have numerals for numbers over ten, words for smaller numbers: *four days, 14 days*. A more formal style is to spell out all numbers that can be written in one or two words: four, fifteen, ninety-two, 114, one thousand. Practice within a piece of writing should be consistent.

nu·mis·mat·ics [,njumɪz'mætɪks] *or* [,nu-] *n* the study or collection of coins and medals (with a sg verb). **nu·mis·mat·ic** *adj.* **nu·mis·mat·i·cal·ly** *adv.* **nu·mis·ma·tist** *n.* ⟨Greek *nomisma* coin; *nomizein* have in use⟩

num·skull ['nʌm,skʌl] *n Informal* a stupid person; blockhead. ⟨for *numb skull*⟩

nun [nʌn] *n* a woman who is a member of a religious order and lives a life of prayer, worship, and service. ⟨Latin *nonna*⟩ **nun·ner·y** *n* a building where nuns live; convent.

Nu·na·vut ['nʊnəvʊt] *n* an area in central and eastern Northwest Territories, governed by First Nations and Inuit people as a separate territory since April 1, 1999. *Abbrev* **NU**. ⟨Inuktitut = our land⟩

nun·ny bag ['nʌni] ✹ in Newfoundland and Labrador, a haversack, often made of sealskin.

nup·tial ['nʌpʃəl] *or* ['nʌptʃəl] *adj* of marriage or weddings. *n* **nuptials** *pl* a wedding. **nup·tial·ly** *adv.* ⟨Latin *nuptialis; nubere* See NUBILE.⟩

nurse [nɜrs] *n* 1 a person who is trained to take care of the sick, the injured, or the old. 2 a woman who takes care of the young children of another person. *v* 1 be a nurse. 2 nourish and protect: *to nurse a hatred in the heart*. 3 treat with special care:

He nursed his sore arm by using it very little. 4 feed milk to (a baby) at the breast. 5 suck milk from the breast. ⟨Old French *nurrice*, Latin *nutricia; nutrire* feed, suckle⟩

nurse·maid *n* a maid employed to care for children. **nurs·er** *n* a baby's bottle. **nurs·er·y** *n* 1 a room set apart for the use of babies and children. 2 a day-care centre. 3 a place where young plants are grown for sale. 4 a place or condition that helps something to grow: *Slums are often nurseries of disease*. **nursery rhyme** a short, traditional poem for young children. **nursery school** a school for young children, usually for those under five. **nurs·ing** *n* the occupation of a nurse. **nursing home** a residence providing care for old, chronically ill, or disabled persons. **nursing station** 1 in a hospital, a location serving as a base for the nurses on duty. 2 ✹ in the North, a small hospital for emergency cases. **nurs·ling** *or* **nurse·ling** *n* 1 a baby that is being nursed. 2 any person or thing that is under tender care.

nur·ture ['nɜrtʃər] *v* 1 care for; rear. 2 nourish: *Minerals in the soil nurture plants*. *n* 1 a bringing up; training; education. 2 food; nourishment. 3 the sum of environmental factors acting on a person, as opposed to genetic makeup: *nature vs nurture*. **nur·tur·er** *n*. ⟨Old French *nourture*, Latin *nutritura; nutrire* See NURSE.⟩

nut [nʌt] *n* 1 a dry fruit or seed with a shell that has a kernel inside. 2 a small block having a threaded hole in the centre, by means of which it is screwed on to a bolt. 3 *Slang* the head. 4 *Slang* an eccentric person. 5 *Slang* an enthusiast: *a car nut*. *v* **nut·ted, nut·ting** gather nuts. *adj* **nuts** *Slang* eccentric or crazy. **nut·like** *adj.* ⟨Old English *hnutu*⟩ **hard nut to crack** *Informal* a difficult question, person, problem, or undertaking. **off one's nut** *Slang* crazy. **nut·crack·er** *n* an instrument for cracking the shells of nuts. **nut·meat** *n* the kernel of a nut. **nut·pick** *n* a pointed tool for getting the meat of a nut. **nuts and bolts** *Informal* practical details: *She knows the nuts and bolts of producing a book*. **nut·shell** *n* 1 the shell of a nut. 2 something extremely small in size or scanty in amount. **in a nutshell** in very brief form: *Let me tell you the whole story in a nutshell*. **nut·ty** *adj* 1 containing many nuts: *nutty cake*. 2 like nuts 3 *Slang* eccentric. 4 *Slang* very interested or enthusiastic (with *about*): *nutty about dancing*. **nut·ti·ly** *adv.* **nut·ti·ness** *n.*

nut·meg ['nʌtmɛg] *n* a hard, spicy seed, grated and used for flavouring food. ⟨Middle English half-translation of Old French *nois mugue* musky nut⟩

nu·tri·a ['njutriə] *or* ['nutriə] *n* the fur of the coypu. ⟨Spanish; Latin *lutra*⟩

nu·tri·tious [nju'trɪʃəs] *or* [nu'trɪʃəs] *adj* valuable as food; nourishing. ⟨Latin *nutritius; nutrire* feed⟩ **nu·tri·tious·ly** *adv.* **nu·tri·tious·ness** *n.*

nu·tri·ent *n* a nutritive substance.
adj nourishing. **nu·tri·tion** *n* nourishment: *A balanced diet gives good nutrition.*
nu·tri·tion·al or **nu·tri·tion·ar·y** *adj.*
nu·tri·tion·al·ly *adv.* **nu·tri·tion·ist** *n.*
nu·tri·tive *adj* **1** to do with foods and the use of foods. **2** nutritious. **nu·tri·tive·ness** *n.* **nu·tri·tive·ly** *adv.*

Nuu–chah–nulth [nu'tʃɒnul] *n* **1** a member of a First Nations people living mainly on Vancouver Island. **2** their Wakashan language. **Nuu-chah-nulth** *adj.* Also called **Nootka.**

Nux·alk ['nuksəlk] *n* **1** a member of a First Nations people living on the coast of British Columbia. **2** their Salishan language. **Nuxalk** *adj.* Also called **Bella Coola.**

nux vom·i·ca ['nʌks 'vɒməkə] a poisonous seed containing strychnine and other poisonous alkaloids. ⟨Latin = vomiting nut; *nux* nut + *vomere* vomit⟩

nuz·zle ['nʌzəl] *v* **1** poke or rub with the nose: *The calf nuzzles its mother.* **2** snuggle; cuddle. ⟨*nose*; influenced by *nestle*⟩

NW or **N.W.** northwest; northwestern.

NWMP or **N.W.M.P.** NORTH WEST MOUNTED POLICE.

N.W.T. NORTHWEST TERRITORIES.

ny·lon ['nailɒn] *n* an extremely strong, plastic substance, used to make textiles, utensils, bristles, etc. **ny·lon** *adj.* ⟨former trademark⟩

nymph [nɪmf] *n* **1** *Greek and Roman myth* one of a group of minor goddesses of nature. **2** *Poetic* a beautiful or graceful young woman. **3** any of certain insects in the stage of development between larva and adult. It resembles the adult but has no wings. **nymph·like, nym·phal,** or **nym·phe·an** ['nɪmfiən] *adj.* ⟨Greek *nymphē*⟩
nymph·et ['nɪmfət] *n* an attractive young girl who is at or close to the age of puberty and shows herself to be aware of her sexuality. **nym·pho·ma·ni·a** *n* uncontrollable sexual desire in a woman. **nym·pho·ma·ni·ac** *adj, n.*

Oo

o or **O**[1] [ou] *n, pl* **o's** or **O's 1** the fifteenth letter of the English alphabet, or any speech sound represented by it. **2** the fifteenth person or thing in a series. **3** zero. **4 O**, the type of human blood not containing either of the antigens A or B.

O[2] [ou] See OH.

USAGE

O is usually used only before a name or something treated as a name: *O Canada.* In other cases, the spelling is usually **Oh.**

o' [ə] *or* [ou] *prep* of: *man-o'-war.*

oaf [ouf] *n* a clumsy and usually stupid or boorish person. **oaf·ish** *adj.* **oaf·ish·ly** *adv.* **oaf·ish·ness** *n.* ⟨orig = elf's child, changeling; Old Norse *álfr* elf⟩

oak [ouk] *n* any of a genus of trees or shrubs of the beech family, bearing nuts called acorns. **oak·like** *adj.* ⟨Old English *āc*⟩
oak·en *adj Archaic, poetic* made of oak wood.

oar [ɔr] *n* a long pole with a broad blade at one end, used for rowing or steering a boat.
v row. ⟨Old English *ār*⟩
put one's oar in meddle. **rest on one's oars** stop working or trying and take a rest.
oar·lock *n* a support for an oar; rowlock.

o·a·sis [ou'eisɪs]*n, pl* **-ses** [-siz] **1** a fertile spot in the desert. **2** any pleasant place in a desolate region. ⟨Greek⟩

oat [out] *n* Usually, **oats** *pl* a tall cereal grass. **oat·like** *adj.* ⟨Old English *āte*⟩
feel one's oats *Slang* **a** be lively. **b** feel pleased and show it. **sow one's wild oats** See WILD OATS.
oat·cake *n* a thin cake made of oatmeal.
oat·en *adj* made of oats or oatmeal. **oat·meal** *n* **1** oats made into meal; ground or rolled oats. **2** porridge made from oats.

oath [ouθ] *n, pl* **oaths** [ouðz] *or* [ouθs] **1** a promise that something is true, esp when made to a judge. **2** the name of some holy person or thing used as an exclamation. **3** a swear word. ⟨Old English *āth*⟩
take oath or **take an oath** promise solemnly. **take oaths** or **take someone's oath** certify an oath: *A notary public is authorized to take oaths.* **under oath** bound by an oath: *to give evidence under oath.*

ob·bli·ga·to [ˌɒblə'gɑtou] *Music adj* accompanying a solo, but with independent importance. Also, **o·bli·ga·to.** ⟨Italian; literally, obliged⟩

ob·du·rate ['ɒbdjərɪt] *adj* **1** stubborn: *an obdurate refusal.* **2** not repentant: *an obdurate criminal.* **ob·du·ra·cy** *n.* **ob·du·rate·ly** *adv.* ⟨Latin *ob-* against + *durare* harden⟩

o·be·di·ence See OBEY.

o·bei·sance [ou'bisəns] *or* [ou'beisəns] *n* **1** a deep bow: *The men made obeisance to the king.* **2** deference. **o·bei·sant** *adj.* ⟨Old French = obedience, *obeir* obey; Latin. See OBEY.⟩

ob·e·lisk ['ɒbə,lɪsk] *or* ['oubə,lɪsk] *n* a tapering, four-sided shaft of stone with a top shaped like a pyramid. ⟨Greek *obeliskos* diminutive of *obelos* spit[2]⟩

o·bese [ou'bis] *adj* extremely fat. **o·bese·ly** *adv.* **o·be·si·ty** *n.* ⟨Latin *obesus; ob-* in addition + pp of *edere* eat⟩

o·bey [ou'bei] *v* **1** do what one is told. **2** act in accordance with: *to obey the laws.* **o·be·di·ence** [ou'bidiəns] *n.* **o·be·di·ent** *adj.* **o·be·di·ent·ly** *adv.* ⟨Old French *obéir* Latin *oboedire; ob-* to + *audire* listen⟩

ob·fus·cate ['ɒbfə,skeit] *or* ['ɒb'fʌskeit] *v* **1** confuse; stupefy: *A person's mind may be obfuscated by liquor.* **2** darken; obscure. **ob·fus·ca·tion** *n.* ⟨Latin *ob-* over + *fuscus* dark⟩

o·bi ['oubi] *n, pl* **o·bis** or **o·bi** a broad sash worn around the waist of a kimono. ⟨Japanese⟩

o·bit·u·a·ry [ou'bɪtʃu,ɛri] *n* a notice recording a death. **o·bit·u·ar·y** *adj.* **o·bit·u·ar·ist** *n.* ⟨Latin *obitus mortem* having met death⟩

ob·ject ['ɒbdʒɪkt] *or* ['ɒbdʒɛkt] *n* **1** anything that can be seen or touched. **2** a person or thing toward which feeling, thought, or action is directed: *an object of charity.* **3** something aimed at; purpose: *Is it your object to upset me?* **4** *Grammar* a word or words toward which the action of the verb is directed or to which a preposition expresses some relation.
v [əb'dʒɛkt] **1** be opposed: *Many people object to loud music.* **2** give a reason against something: *She objected that it was too wet to be outdoors.* **ob·ject·ing·ly** *adv.* ⟨Latin *ob-* against + *jectus* pp of *jacere* throw⟩
ob·jec·ti·fy [əb'dʒɛktə,fai] *v* make objective; externalize: *Kind acts objectify kindness.* **ob·jec·ti·fi·ca·tion** *n.* **ob·jec·tion** *n* **1** a reason or argument against something. **2** a feeling of disapproval or dislike. **ob·jec·tion·a·ble** *adj* unpleasant; disagreeable. **ob·jec·tion·a·bly** *adv.* **ob·jec·tive** *n* **1** something aimed at: *My objective is to play better tennis.* **2** *Optics* the lenses in a microscope or telescope that form the image of the object. *adj* **1** existing as an actual object; real. **2** dealing with objects, not with feelings: *The report was not objective, but was biassed in favour of one company.* Compare SUBJECTIVE (def. 2). **ob·jec·tive·ly** *adv.* **ob·jec·tiv·i·ty** [ˌɒbdʒɛk'tɪvɪti] *n.* **object lesson** **1** instruction conveyed by means of material objects. **2** a practical illustration of a principle: *Most road accidents are object lessons in the dangers of carelessness.* **ob·jet d'art** [ˌɒbʒei 'dɑr] *pl* **ob·jets d'art** [ˌɒbʒei 'dɑr] *French* a small picture, vase, etc. of artistic value.

ob·late[1] ['ɒbleit] *or* [ou'bleit] *adj* flattened at the poles, as the earth is. Compare PROLATE. **ob·late·ly** *adv.* **ob·late·ness** *n.* ⟨Latin *ob-* inversely + *(pro)latus* extended⟩

ob·late[2] ['ɒbleit] *n Roman Catholic Church* a member of any of various lay institutes devoted to religious work. ⟨Latin *oblatus* pp of *offerre* offer⟩
ob·la·tion [ə'bleiʃən] *n* an offering to God or a god. **ob·la·tion·al** or **ob·la·to·ry** ['ɒblɔ,tɔri] *adj.*

ob·li·gate ['ɒblə,geit] *v* bind morally or legally: *A witness in court is obligated to tell the truth.* **ob·li·ga·ble** ['ɒbləgəbəl] *adj.* ⟨Latin *ob*- to + *ligare* bind⟩

ob·li·ga·tion [,ɒblə'geiʃən] *n* **1** a duty: *a person's obligation to family.* **2** a contract: *The firm was not able to meet its obligations.* **3** being in debt for a favour, service, etc. **4** a service; favour: *An independent person likes to repay all obligations.* **ob·li·ga·tion·al** *adj.* **ob·lig·a·to·ry** [ə'blɪgə,tɔri] *adj* binding morally or legally. **ob·lig·a·to·ri·ly** *adv.* **o·blige** [ə'blaɪdʒ] *v* **1** bind by a promise, duty, etc.: *The law obliges parents to send their children to school.* **2** put under a debt of thanks for a favour: *She obliged us with a song.* **3** do a favour (to): *She asked for tea and he obliged immediately.* **be obliged** be grateful to someone for a service: *I am obliged to you for letting me stay at your house.* **o·blig·ing** *adj* willing to do favours; helpful. **o·blig·ing·ly** *adv.* **o·blig·ing·ness** *n.*

ob·lique [ə'blik] *adj* **1** slanting. **2** *Geometry* **a** containing no right angle: *an oblique triangle.* **b** having the axis not perpendicular to the base: *an oblique cone.* **3** indirect or not explicit: *an oblique glance.* *n* something oblique, esp a stroke or line. **ob·lique·ness** *n.* ⟨Latin *obliquus*⟩ **ob·liq·ui·ty** [ə'blɪkwəti] *n* conduct that is not upright and moral. **ob·liq·ui·tous** *adj.*

ob·lit·er·ate [ə'blɪtə,reit] *v* remove all traces of; destroy: *Rain obliterated the footprints.* **ob·lit·er·a·tion** *n.* **ob·lit·er·a·tive** *adj.* ⟨Latin *ob literas* (*scribere*) (draw) across the letters⟩

ob·liv·i·on [ə'blɪviən] *n* **1** the condition of being entirely forgotten: *Many ancient cities have passed into oblivion.* **2** the condition of being unaware of what is going on. ⟨Latin *oblivisci* forget; + *ob*- over + *levis* smooth⟩ **ob·liv·i·ous** *adj* forgetful; unaware (with *to* or *of*): *The book was so interesting that I was oblivious of my surroundings.* **ob·liv·i·ous·ly** *adv.* **ob·liv·i·ous·ness** *n.*

ob·long ['ɒblɒŋ] *adj* longer than broad: *an oblong tablecloth.* *n* a rectangle that is not square. ⟨Latin *ob*- (intensive) + *longus* long⟩

ob·lo·quy ['ɒbləkwi] *n* **1** public reproach; abuse. **2** disgrace. **ob·lo·qui·al** [ɒb'loukwiəl] *adj.* ⟨Latin *ob*- against + *loqui* speak⟩

ob·nox·ious [əb'nɒkʃəs] *adj* very disagreeable; offensive: *Her disgusting table manners made her obnoxious to us.* **ob·nox·ious·ly** *adv.* **ob·nox·ious·ness** *n.*

o·boe ['oubou] *n* a woodwind with a thin, poignant tone. **o·bo·ist** *n.* ⟨Italian French *hautbois, haut* high + *bois* wood⟩

ob·scene [əb'sin] *adj* **1** grossly indecent according to the standards of a community: *an obscene dance.* **2** offending a moral principle: *an obscene display of wealth.* **ob·scene·ly** *adv.* **ob·scen·i·ty** [əb'sɛnəti] *n.* ⟨Latin *obscenus*⟩

ob·scure [əb'skjʊr] *adj* **1** not clearly expressed: *an obscure sentence.* **2** not well-known: *an obscure poet.* **3** not distinct: *obscure sounds.*

v **1** hide from view; overshadow: *Clouds obscure the sun. Her talents were obscured by the brilliance of her rival.* **2** make unclear: *All their talk just obscures the issue.* **ob·scure·ly** *adv.* **ob·scure·ness** *n.* ⟨Latin *ob*- over + *scurus* covered⟩

ob·scu·rant·ism [,ɒbskjə'ræntɪzəm] *or* [əb'skjʊrən,tɪzəm] *n* **1** opposition to progress and the spread of knowledge. **2** an artistic or literary style characterized by deliberate complexity and obscurity. **ob·scu·rant·ist** *n, adj.* **ob·scu·ri·ty** *n* **1** a lack of clearness: *The obscurity of the inscription puzzled us.* **2** something obscure: *The movie had so many obscurities that we didn't enjoy it.* **3** the state of being unknown: *to rise from obscurity to fame.*

ob·se·quies ['ɒbsə,kwiz] *n pl* funeral rites or ceremonies. ⟨Latin *obsequiae,* pl, for Latin *exsequiae ex*- out + *sequi* follow⟩

ob·se·qui·ous [əb'sikwiəs] *adj* polite from hope of gain or from fear. **ob·se·qui·ous·ly** *adv.* **ob·se·qui·ous·ness** *n.* ⟨Latin *obsequiae* earlier *exsequiae; ex*- out + *sequi* follow⟩

ob·serve [əb'zɜrv] *v* **1** notice. **2** study: *An astronomer observes the stars.* **3** remark: *"Foul weather," he observed.* **4** follow in practice: *to observe a rule.* **5** celebrate: *to observe the Sabbath.* **ob·serv·a·ble** *adj.* **ob·serv·a·bly** *adv* **ob·serv·a·bil·i·ty** *n.* **ob·serv·ance** *n.* **ob·serv·a·tion** *n.* **ob·serv·ed·ly** *adv.* **ob·serv·ant** *adj* quick to notice; watchful. **ob·serv·ant·ly** *adv.* **ob·ser·va·tion·al** *adj* to do with observation, rather than with experiment. **ob·ser·va·tion·al·ly** *adv.* **ob·serv·a·to·ry** *n* a building with a telescope, etc. for observing heavenly bodies. **ob·serv·er** *n* **1** one who watches. **2** one who celebrates a rule, custom, etc.: *an observer of the Sabbath.* **3** one who attends a meeting but can take no official part in it. **4** someone sent to report on a situation by a body such as the United Nations. **ob·serv·ing** *adj* observant.

CONFUSABLES

Observation and **observance** are sometimes confused because both are related to the verb **observe**. **Observation** applies especially to noticing things, or to being noticed: *the observation of the stars.* **Observance** applies celebrating: *the observance of religious duties.*

---

ob·sess [əb'sɛs] *v* **1** keep the full attention of: *The fear that someone might steal her money obsesses her.* **2** think excessively: *Stop obsessing about your interview.* ⟨Latin *obsessus* pp of *obsidere* besiege⟩ **ob·ses·sion** *n* **1** the influence of an idea that a person cannot escape. **2** *Psychiatry* a compelling idea, usually irrational, over which a person has little conscious control. **ob·ses·sion·al** *adj.* **ob·ses·sion·al·ly** *adv.* **ob·ses·sive** *adj* to do with, or causing obsession. **ob·ses·sive·ly** *adv.*

ob·so·lete [,ɒbsə'lit] *adj* **1** no longer in use. **2** out-of-date: *an obsolete software program.* **ob·so·lete·ly** *adv.* ⟨Latin *obsoletus,* pp of *obsolescere; ob*- off + *solere* be customary⟩ **ob·so·les·cent** [,ɒbsə'lɛsənt] *adj* passing out

of use; becoming out-of-date. **ob·so·les·cence** *n*.
ob·so·les·cent·ly *adv*.

ob·sta·cle [ˈɒbstəkəl] *n* something that
stands in the way or stops progress. ⟨Latin
obstaculum ob- against + *stare* stand⟩
obstacle course a course that includes several
obstacles, such as walls or ditches.

ob·stet·rics [əbˈstɛtrɪks] *n* the branch of
medicine concerned with caring for women
before, during, and after childbirth (with a sg
verb). **ob·stet·ric** *adj*. **ob·ste·tri·cian** *n*. ⟨Latin
obstetrix midwife; *ob-* by + *stare* stand⟩

ob·sti·nate [ˈɒbstənɪt] *adj* **1** stubborn. **2** hard
to control or treat: *an obstinate cough*.
ob·sti·na·cy [ˈɒbstənəsi] *n*. **ob·sti·nate·ly** *adv*.
⟨Latin *obstinare; ob-* against + *stare* stand⟩

ob·strep·er·ous [əbˈstrɛpərəs] *adj* **1** noisy;
boisterous. **2** unruly; disorderly.
ob·strep·er·ous·ly *adv*. **ob·strep·er·ous·ness** *n*.
⟨Latin *ob-* against + *strepere* make noise⟩

ob·struct [əbˈstrʌkt] *v* be in the way of;
hinder: *Trees obstruct our view of the ocean*.
ob·struc·tion *n*. ⟨Latin *obstructus*, pp of
obstruere; ob- against + *struere* pile⟩
ob·struc·tion·ism *n* the deliberate hindering
of business in a meeting, legislature, etc.
ob·struc·tion·ist *n*. **ob·struc·tive** *adj* tending or
serving to obstruct; blocking; hindering.
ob·struc·tive·ly *adv*. **ob·struc·tive·ness** *n*.

ob·tain [əbˈtein] *v* **1** get through diligence or
effort: *We study to obtain knowledge*. **2** be
customary: *Different rules obtain in different
schools*. **ob·tain·a·ble** *adj*. **ob·tain·ment** *n*.
⟨Latin *obtinere ob-* to + *tenere* hold⟩

ob·trude [əbˈtrud] *v* **1** force: *Don't obtrude
your opinions on others*. **2** force oneself;
intrude. **3** thrust forward. *A turtle obtrudes its
head from its shell*. **ob·trud·er** *n*. **ob·tru·sion** *n*.
⟨Latin *ob-* toward + *trudere* thrust⟩
ob·tru·sive [əbˈtrusiv] *adj* **1** not blending or
fitting in: *obtrusive colours*. **2** protruding.
3 pushy. **ob·tru·sive·ly** *adv*. **ob·tru·sive·ness** *n*.

ob·tuse [əbˈtjus] *or* [əbˈtus] *adj* **1** not sharp
or acute. **2** slow in understanding: *He was too
obtuse to take the hint*. **ob·tuse·ly** *adv*.
ob·tuse·ness *n*. ⟨Latin *ob-* on + *tundere* beat⟩
obtuse angle an angle between 90° and 180°.

ob·verse [ˈɒbvərs] *n* **1** the side of a coin,
medal, etc. that has the principal design.
Opposed to REVERSE. **2** the face of anything
that is meant to be turned toward the
observer; front. **3** a counterpart.
adj [ɒbˈvərs] *or* [ˈɒbvərs] **1** turned toward the
observer. **2** being a counterpart to something
else. **3** having the base narrower than the top
or tip: *an obverse leaf*. **ob·verse·ly** *adv*. ⟨Latin
ob- to + *vertere* to turn⟩

ob·vi·ate [ˈɒbviˌeit] *v* **1** clear out of the way:
to obviate a difficulty. **2** foresee something and
thus make it unnecessary. **ob·vi·a·tion** *n*.
⟨Latin *obviare; obvius* in the way. See OBVIOUS.⟩

ob·vi·ous [ˈɒbviəs] *adj* easily seen or
understood. **ob·vi·ous·ly** *adv*. **ob·vi·ous·ness** *n*.
⟨Latin *obvius* in the way; *ob* across + *via* way⟩

oc·ca·sion [əˈkeiʒən] *n* **1** a particular time:

We have met on several occasions. **2** a special
event: *The jewels were worn for great occasions*.
3 a good chance. **4** a cause: *The dog that was
the occasion of the quarrel had run away*.
v cause; bring about: *Her odd behaviour
occasioned talk*. ⟨Latin *occasio; ob-* across +
casus pp of *cadere* fall⟩
on occasion now and then; once in a while.
oc·ca·sion·al *adj* **1** happening once in a while:
*We had fine weather except for an occasional
thunderstorm*. **2** caused by or used for some
special event: *a piece of occasional music to be
played at the opening concert*. **3** for use as
called for, not part of a set: *occasional chairs*.
oc·ca·sion·al·ly *adv* once in a while.

Oc·ci·dent [ˈɒksədənt] *n* **1** the countries in
Europe and America; the West. Compare
ORIENT. **2 occident** the west. **Oc·ci·den·tal** or
oc·ci·den·tal *n, adj*. ⟨Latin *occidere* go down;
ob- toward + *cadere* fall; for setting sun⟩

oc·cip·i·tal [ɒkˈsipətəl] *Anatomy adj* to do
with the back part of the skull. **oc·cip·i·tal·ly**
adv. ⟨Latin *occiput; ob-* behind + *caput* head⟩

oc·clude [əˈklud] *v* **1** stop up (a passage,
pores, etc.). **2** shut in, out, or off. **3** *Chemistry*
absorb and retain (gases). **4** *Dentistry* meet
closely. Upper teeth and lower teeth should
occlude. **5** *Meteorology* force (air) to rise, such
as when a cold front pushes under a warm
front. **oc·clu·dent** *adj*. **oc·clu·sion** *n*. ⟨Latin *ob-*
up + *claudere* close⟩

oc·cult [əˈkʌlt] *or* [ˈɒkʌlt] *adj* **1** mysterious.
2 outside the laws of the natural world:
Astrology and alchemy are occult sciences.
n **the occult** occult studies or beliefs.
oc·cult·ism *n*. **oc·cult·ist** *n*. ⟨Latin *occultus* pp
of *occulere; ob-* up + *celare* cover⟩
oc·cul·ta·tion *n* a hiding of one heavenly
body by another passing between it and the
observer: *the occultation of a star by the moon*.

oc·cu·pant See OCCUPY.

oc·cu·py [ˈɒkjəˌpai] *v* **1** take up; fill: *The
building occupies an entire block*. **2** keep busy:
Sports occupy her attention. **3** take possession
of: *The enemy occupied our fort*. **4** have; hold:
The judge occupies an important position. **5** live
in: *The owner and her family occupy the house*.
oc·cu·pant *n*. **oc·cu·pi·er** *n*. **oc·cu·pan·cy** *n*.
⟨Latin *occupare* seize *ob-* up + *capere* grasp⟩
oc·cu·pa·tion *n* **1** one's business or
employment. **2** an occupying or being
occupied: *the occupation of a town by the
enemy*. **oc·cu·pa·tion·al** *adj* to do with trades,
callings, etc.: *occupational hazards*.
oc·cu·pa·tion·al·ly *adv*. **occupational disease** a
disease that results from a particular
occupation: *Silicosis is an occupational disease
of coal miners*. **occupational therapy** *Medicine*
the treatment of persons having disabilities
through specific types of activities, work, etc.
to promote rehabilitation.

oc·cur [əˈkɜr] *v* **1** take place; happen: *Storms
often occur in winter*. **2** exist: E *occurs in English
more than any other letter*. **3** come to mind:
Did it occur to you to close the window?
oc·cur·rence *n*. ⟨Latin *ob-* across + *currere* run⟩

o·cean ['ouʃən] *n* **1** the great body of salt water that covers almost three-fourths of the earth's surface. **2** any of its four main divisions—the Atlantic, Pacific, Indian, and Arctic Oceans. **3** a vast expanse or quantity: *oceans of trouble*. ⟨Greek *ōkeanos*⟩
o·cean-go·ing *adj* to do with travel on the ocean: *an ocean-going ship*. **O·ce·an·i·a** [ˌouʃi'æniə] *n* Australia, New Zealand, and other islands of the Pacific Ocean. **o·ce·an·ic** [ˌouʃi'ænɪk] *adj* **1** of the ocean. **2** like the ocean; vast. **o·cean·og·ra·phy** *n* the branch of geography dealing with oceans and ocean life. **o·cean·og·ra·pher** *n*. **o·cean·o·graph·ic** *adj*. **o·cean·o·graph·i·cal·ly** *adv*.

o·ce·lot ['ɒsəˌlɒt] *n* a mammal of the cat family, having a buff coat spotted with black. ⟨Mexican *ocelotl*⟩

o·chre ['oukər] *n* any of various clays ranging in colour from yellow to brown, and red, used as pigments. Also, **o·cher**. **o·chre·ous** ['oukriəs] *adj*. ⟨Greek *ōchros* yellow⟩

o'clock [ə'klɒk] the time expressed in units of one hour: *It is one o'clock*. ⟨*of the clock*⟩

oc·ta– ['ɒktæ] *combining form* eight. Variant of **oc·to–**. ⟨Greek *oktō* eight⟩
oc·tad *n* **1** a group of eight. **2** anything with a valence of eight. **oc·ta·gon** [-ˌgɒn] *n* a polygon having eight sides. **oc·tag·o·nal** [ɒk'tægənəl] *adj*. **oc·ta·he·dron** [ˌɒktə'hidrən] *n, pl* **-drons** or **-dra** [-drə] a polyhedron having eight faces. **oc·ta·he·dral** *adj*. **oc·tant** ['ɒktənt] *n* an eighth of a circle. **oc·tave** ['ɒktɪv] *n* **1** *Music* the interval between one tone and the next of the same name. **2** *Prosody* an eight-line stanza. **oc·ta·val** [ɒk'teival] *adj*. **oc·ta·vo** [ɒk'teivou] *or* [ɒk'tævou] *n* the page size of a book in which each leaf is an eighth of a sheet of paper.

oc·tane ['ɒktein] *n Chemistry* any of a group of liquid hydrocarbons obtained from petroleum. ⟨Greek *oktō* eight + English *-ane*, chemical suffix⟩
octane number the number indicating the quality of a motor fuel.

oc·ten·ni·al [ɒk'tɛniəl] *adj* **1** lasting eight years. **2** happening every eighth year. **oc·ten·ni·al·ly** *adv*. ⟨Latin *octo* eight + *annus* year⟩

oc·tet [ɒk'tɛt] *n* **1** a musical composition for eight voices or instruments. **2** eight singers or players. **3** *Prosody* **a** the first eight lines of a sonnet. **b** an eight-line stanza; octave. **4** any group of eight. Also, **oc·tette**. ⟨Latin *oct-* eight + *-et* as in *duet*⟩

Oc·to·ber [ɒk'toubər] *n* the tenth month of the year. October has 31 days. ⟨Latin; *octo* eight, for original calendar⟩

oc·to·ge·nar·i·an [ˌɒktədʒə'nɛriən] a person who is 80 years old or between 80 and 90 years old. **oc·to·ge·nar·i·an** *adj*. ⟨Latin *octogenarius* containing eighty⟩

oc·to·pus ['ɒktəpəs] *n, pl* **-pus·es** or **-pi** [-ˌpaɪ] any of a genus of marine cephalopods having a soft body and eight arms, or tentacles. ⟨Greek *oktō* eight + *pous* foot⟩

oc·tu·ple [ɒk'tʌpəl], [-'tjupəl], *or* [-tupəl] *adj* **1** having eight parts. **2** eightfold. ⟨Latin *octuplus; octo* eight⟩

oc·u·lar ['ɒkjələr] *adj* to do with the eye. *n* the eyepiece of a telescope, microscope, etc. **oc·u·lar·ly** *adv*. ⟨Latin *oculus* eye⟩

OD ['ou'di] *n, pl* **OD's** *Slang n* an overdose of a narcotic. **OD, OD'd, OD'ing** (with *on*) *v*.

Od·a·wa [o'dɒwə] *n* **1** a member of a First Nations people formerly living along the Ottawa River, now mainly on Manitoulin Island, ON. **2** their Ojibwa language. **Od·a·wa** *adj*. Also, **Ot·ta·wa**.

odd [ɒd] *adj* **1** not divisible by two. **2** being one of a set when the other or others are missing: *an odd glove*. **3** occasional, extra, or random: *He earns a living doing odd jobs around town*. **4** somewhat more than a quantity specified (in compounds): *The whole job will cost 300-odd dollars*. **5** peculiar; strange: *It's odd that she's not back yet*. **odd·ly** *adv*. **odd·ness** *n*. ⟨Scandinavian⟩
odd·ball *Slang n* a person whose behaviour is eccentric or unconventional. **odd·ball** *adj*. **odd·i·ty** *n* **1** strangeness; peculiarity. **2** a strange or peculiar person or thing. **odd lot** *Stock exchange* in transactions, an amount less than the usual. **odd one** (or **man**, etc.) **out** *n* **1** one who does not fit into a group. **2** one who is left out of a group. **odd·ment** *n* a thing left over. **odd number** a number that has a remainder of 1 when divided by 2. **odds** *n pl or sg* **1** an advantage. In betting, odds of 3 to 1 mean that 3 will be paid if the bet is lost for every 1 that is received if the bet is won. **2** *Games* an extra allowance given to the weaker side.
at odds quarrelling or disagreeing: *They've been at odds for months*. **no odds** no difference: *It makes no odds to me*. **odds and ends** things left over; extra bits. **the odds are** the probability is: *The odds are we'll win*. **odds–on** *adj* having the odds in one's favour.

ode [oud] *n* a lyric poem, often addressed to some person or thing: *Ode to a Nightingale*. ⟨Greek *ōidē; aeidein* sing⟩

o·di·ous ['oudiəs] *adj* hateful. **o·di·ous·ly** *adv*. **o·di·ous·ness** *n*. ⟨Latin *odium* hatred⟩
o·di·um ['oudiəm] *n* **1** hatred. **2** blame.

o·dom·e·ter [ou'dɒmətər] *n* an instrument for measuring the distance a vehicle travels. ⟨Greek *hodos* way + *metron* measure⟩

o·dour *or* **o·dor** ['oudər] *n* **1** a smell or scent: *the odour of roses, the odour of garbage*. **2** repute: *They were in bad odour because of a suspected theft*. **3** a taste or quality characteristic of something: *an odour of impropriety*. **o·dour·ful** *or* **o·dor·ful** *adj*. **o·dour·less** *or* **o·dor·less** *adj*. ⟨Latin *odor*⟩ **o·dor·if·er·ous** *adj* giving forth an odour, esp an unpleasant one: *We heaped up all the dirty laundry into one odoriferous pile*. **o·dor·if·er·ous·ly** *adv*. **o·dor·if·er·ous·ness** *n*. **o·dor·ous** *adj* giving forth an odour: *Freshly ground spices are odorous*. **o·dor·ous·ly** *adv*. **o·dor·ous·ness** *n*.

oeu·vre ['œvʀ] *French n* all the works in the lifetime of a composer, writer, artist, etc. ⟨French = work⟩

of [ʌv] *prep* **1** belonging to: *the children of a family.* **2** made from: *a house of bricks.* **3** with: *a house of six rooms.* **4** that has as a quality: *a look of pity.* **5** named: *the city of Yellowknife.* **6** away from; from: *north of Brandon.* **7** about: *to think well of someone.* **8** that has as a purpose: *the hour of prayer.* **9** by: *the writings of Shakespeare.* **10** as a result of: *to die of grief.* **11** like: *smelling of onions.* **12** that connects nouns having the meaning of a verb with what would be the object of the verb: *The eating of fruit.* ⟨Old English⟩

> **USAGE**
> In formal English, using **of** after **off** is not normally acceptable: *She stepped off the sidewalk* (not *off of*).

off [ɒf] *prep* **1** into a position not on: *I fell off the curb.* **2** from; away from: *off the road.* **3** supported by: *She lived off her relatives.*
adv **1** from the correct position, condition, etc.: *He took off his hat.* **2** away; at a distance; to a distance: *to go off on a journey.* **3** distant in time: *My birthday is only five weeks off.* **4** so as to stop or lessen: *Turn the water off.* **5** without work: *an afternoon off.* **6** in full: *Pay off the debt.* **7** on one's way: *The train started and we were off on our trip.*
adj **1** no longer due to take place: *Our trip is off.* **2** stopped: *The electricity is off.* **3** not spent working: *He pursues his hobby during off hours.* **4** not up to average: *Last summer was an off season for fruit.* **5** deteriorated in quality, etc.: *The milk is off.* **6** possible but not likely: *I came on the off chance that I would find you.* **7** wrong: *Your figures are way off.* **8** more distant: *the off side of a wall.* **9** on the right-hand side (of a vehicle, etc.): *the off wheel.* Compare NEAR (def. 5).
be off go away. **off and on** at some times and not at others. ⟨Old English *of* (stressed)⟩
off·bal·ance *adj* unsteady; unprepared.
off·beat ['ɒf,bit] *n Music* a beat that has relatively little stress. *adj* **1** *Music* to do with offbeats. **2** ['ɒf'bit] *Informal* unconventional.
off·col·our or **off–col·or** *adj* **1** somewhat improper: *an off-colour joke.* **2** not well: *She was feeling off-colour yesterday.* **off–key** *adj* **1** *Music* not in the correct key. **2** improper; ill-timed: *an off-key remark.* **offline** *adv Computers* by means not controlled by a computer: *The labels will be produced offline.* *adj* to do with processing not controlled by a computer. **off·load** *v* unload. **off·print** *n* a separate reprint of a story, article, etc. from a journal, book, etc. **off–put·ting** *adj Informal* likely to deter one. **off·road vehicle** a vehicle designed for rough terrain. **off·screen** *adj* not seen on a movie or television screen: *an off-screen commentary.* **off·screen** *adv.* **off–sea·son** *n* the slow season of a business, sport, etc. **off·sea·son** *adj.* **off·shoot** *n* **1** *Botany* a branch growing from the main stem of a plant, tree, etc. **2** anything coming from a main part, stock, race, etc. **off·shore**

['ɒf'ʃɔr] *adj* **1** off or away from the shore: *an offshore wind.* **2** done or working away from the shore: *offshore fisheries. adv* toward the water: *The wind was blowing offshore.* **off·side** or **off–side** *adj Football, hockey, etc.,* of a player on the offensive, being ahead of the ball or puck and being penalized. **off·site** *adj, adv* away from the main site: *offsite storage.* **offstage** *adj* away from the part of the stage that the audience can see. *adv* when not performing: *Offstage, she is shy.* **off–street** *adj* away from the street: *off-street parking.* **off–track** *adj* not conducted at a race track: *off-track betting.* **off–white** *adj* almost white.

of·fal ['ɒfəl] *n* **1** the entrails and internal organs of a butchered animal. **2** garbage; refuse. ⟨*off + fall*⟩

of·fence [ə'fɛns]; *for defs. 5-6,* ['ɒfɛns] *n* **1** a breaking of the law. **2** something that causes displeasure: *Rudeness is an offence.* **3** hurt feelings, or the act of hurting someone's feelings: *No offence was intended.* **4** the act of attacking: *The army proved weak in offence.* **5** *Football, hockey, etc.* the attacking part of a team. Also, **of·fense.** ⟨Latin *offensa* pp of *offendere; ob-* against + *fendere* strike⟩
give (or **take**) **offence** offend (or be offended). **of·fend** [ə'fɛnd] *v* **1** displease or cause displeasure. **2** do wrong. **of·fend·ed** *adj.* **of·fend·er** *n.* **of·fen·sive** *adj* **1** annoying: *"Shut up" is an offensive retort.* **2** unpleasant; disgusting: *an offensive odour.* **3** to do with attack: *offensive weapons. n* **1** the attitude of attack: *The army took the offensive.* **2** an attack: *an offensive against polio.* **of·fen·sive·ly** *adv.* **of·fen·sive·ness** *n.*

of·fer ['ɒfər] *v* **1** hold out; present: *to offer help.* **2** volunteer: *He offered to help us.* **3** have as an advantageous feature: *Self-employment offers independence and adventure.* **4** bid as a price: *He offered twenty dollars for our old stove. n* **1** the act of offering: *an offer of money.* **2** a thing that is offered. **3** *Law* a proposal that, if accepted, will become a contract. **of·fer·a·ble** *adj.* ⟨Latin *ob-* to + *ferre* bring⟩
of·fer·ing ['ɒfrɪŋ] *n* **1** something offered. **2** a sacrifice of an animal, etc. made to a deity. **of·fer·to·ry** ['ɒfər,tɔri] *n* **1** a collection, usually of money, at a religious service. **2** the verses said or the music played while the offering is received. **3 a** *Christianity* the part of the service at which bread and wine are offered to God. **b** the prayers said at this time.

> **SYNONYMS**
> **Offer** is the common word meaning 'hold out' something to be taken or refused: *She offered him coffee.* **Proffer** is the literary word, suggesting offering with courtesy: *We accepted the proffered hospitality.* **Tender** is a formal word meaning 'offer formally' something like actions or services, not objects: *to tender a resignation, to tender a bid.*

off·hand *adj* ['ɒf'hænd] **1** done without previous planning: *offhand remarks.* **2** casual; informal. **3** impolite. Also, **off·handed.**

adv without previous preparation: *She could not tell offhand how much it would cost.* **off·hand·ed·ly** *adv.* **off·hand·ed·ness** *n.*

of·fice ['ɒfɪs] *n* **1** the place in which the work of a business or profession is done. **2** a position, esp in the public service: *The MP was appointed to the office of Minister of Defence.* **3** the staff working in an office: *Half the office is on vacation.* ⟨Latin *officium* service; *opus* work + *facere* do⟩

of·fice·hold·er *n* a government official. **of·fi·cer** *n* **1** a person who commands others in the armed forces. **2** a person who holds an office in the government, the church, etc.: *a health officer.* **3** a person appointed to an administrative position in a company, club, society, etc. **of·fi·cial** [ə'fɪʃəl] *n* **1** a person who holds a public position: *Postmasters are government officials.* **2** a person holding office; officer: *bank officials. adj* **1** to do with an office or officers: *an official uniform.* **2** having authority: *an official record.* **3** formal or ceremonial: *an official welcome to the city.* **of·fi·cial·ly** *adv.* **of·fi·cial·dom** *n* officials collectively. **of·fi·cial·ese** [ə,fɪʃə'liz] *n* pompous, involved, or obscure language thought of as characteristic of official reports, etc. **of·fi·cial·ism** *n* an excessive attention to official routine. **of·fi·cial·ize** *v* make official. **of·fi·cial·i·za·tion** *n.* **of·fi·ci·ate** [ə'fɪʃi,eɪt] *v* **1** perform the duties of any office: *The president officiates as chair at all meetings.* **2** serve as a referee or umpire in a sport. **of·fi·cious** *adj* too ready to offer services or advice. **of·fi·cious·ly** *adv.* **of·fi·cious·ness** *n.*

off·ing ['ɒfɪŋ] *n* the more distant part of the sea as seen from the shore.
in the offing a within sight. **b** due to come, happen, etc. soon: *An election is in the offing.*

off·set [,ɒf'sɛt] *v* **-set, -set·ing** make up for; counterbalance: *The better roads offset the greater distance.*
n ['ɒf,sɛt] **1** a counterbalance to something. **2** *Botany* a side shoot that starts a new plant. **3** an amount or distance that something is out of line. **4** *Printing* the process in which an inked impression is first made on a rubber roller and then on the paper. **5** *Surveying* a distance measured perpendicularly from a main line. **6** an abrupt bend in a pipe or bar to carry it past some obstruction.

off·spring ['ɒf,sprɪŋ] *n sg* or *pl* **1** the young of a person, animal, or plant: *Every one of her offspring had red hair.* **2** a result; effect.

of·ten ['ɒfən] or ['ɒftən] *adv* frequently. ⟨Middle English *ofte(n)*; Old English *oft*⟩
oft, of·ten·times, or **oft·times** *adv Poetic* often.

o·gee [ou'dʒi] or ['oudʒi] *n* an S-shaped curve or line. ⟨French *ogive*⟩

og·ham or **og·am** ['ɒgəm] or ['ouəm] *n* an alphabetical writing system used on monuments by the ancient Celts. ⟨Old Irish *ogam*; *Ogma*, legendary inventor⟩

o·give ['oudʒaɪv] or [ou'dʒaɪv] *n* **1** *Architecture* a pointed arch. **2** *Statistics* a

distribution curve showing cumulative frequencies. ⟨MF; origin uncertain⟩

o·gle ['ougəl] *v* look (at) with desire. **o·gle** *n.* **o·gler** *n.* ⟨Dutch *oogelen*; *oog* eye⟩

O·go·po·go [,ougou'pougou] *n* ✱ a legendary monster reported as being seen from time to time in Okanagan Lake, BC. ⟨name in a British music hall song⟩

o·gre ['ougər] *n* **1** *Folklore* a monster that supposedly eats people. **2** a terrifying person. **o·gre·ish** ['ougərɪʃ] *adj.* ⟨French; Latin *Orcus* god of hell⟩
o·gress ['ougrɪs] *n* a female ogre.

oh [ou] *interj* **1** a word used before names in addressing persons: *Oh Mary, look!* **2** an expression of surprise, joy, grief, pain, etc. Also, **O.**

O–Ha·rai ['ou ha'raɪ] *n* in Shinto, the purification ceremony observed in June and December. ⟨Japanese⟩

ohm [oum] *n Electricity* an SI unit for measuring resistance. A conductor has a resistance of one ohm if it takes a potential difference of one volt to send a current of one ampere through it. *Symbol* Ω ⟨G.S. *Ohm* 19c German physicist⟩
ohm·met·er *n* a device for measuring the resistance of a conductor. **Ohm's law** the electric current (I) in a circuit is directly proportional to the voltage (V) and inversely proportional to the resistance (R), that is, $V = IR$.

–oid *suffix* resembling; like: *alkaloid, planetoid.* ⟨Greek *-oeidēs*; *eidos* form⟩

oil [ɔɪl] *n* **1** any of several fatty liquids that do not dissolve in water. **2** petroleum. **3** Often, **oils** *pl* OIL PAINT.
v put oil on or in. ⟨Latin *oleum*; Greek *elaion*⟩
pour oil on troubled waters make things calm. **strike oil a** find oil by boring a hole in the earth. **b** find something very profitable; have good luck.
oil·can *n* a can with a spout, for oiling machinery, etc. **oil·cloth** *n* a cloth coated on one side with a mixture of oil, clay, and colouring. **oil colour** or **color 1** OIL PAINT. **2** a painting done in oil colours. **oil·er** *n* **1** a person or thing that oils. **2** OIL TANKER. **3 oilers** *pl* oilskins or other waterproof clothing. **oil field** an area where petroleum has been found. **oil paint** paint made by mixing pigment with an oil, such as linseed oil. **oil painting** a picture painted with oil paints. **oil pan** the bottom of the crankcase serving as an oil reservoir. **oil sand** any area of sand or rock that contains large deposits of oil. **oil·skin** *n* **1** cloth treated with oil to make it waterproof. **2 oilskins** *pl* a coat and trousers made of this cloth. **oil slick 1** a film of oil on water. **2** a similar film on the surface of a road. **oil tanker** a ship having special tanks to transport oil. **oil well** a well drilled in the earth to get oil. **oil·y** *adj* **1** to do with oil: *an oily smell.* **2** like oil; slippery. **3** disagreeably smooth: *an oily smile.* **oil·i·ness** *n.* **oil·i·ly** *adv.*

oint·ment ['ɔɪntmənt] *n* a substance made

from oil or fat, used on the skin to heal or to make it soft. ⟨Old French *oignement*; Latin *unguere*; influenced by *anoint*⟩

O·jib·wa See ANISHINABE.

OK or **O.K.** ['ou'kei] *v Informal adj, adv* all right; approved: *The new schedule is OK.* *v* **OK'd** or **O.K.'d, OK'ing** or **O.K.'ing** approve. *n, pl* **OK's** or **O.K.'s** *n* approval: *She has given us her OK.* Also, **o·kay.** ⟨*oll korrect*, deliberate misspelling of *all correct*⟩

O·ka ['oukə] *n* ✺ a cheese, cured with brine, made by Trappist monks in Oka, Québec.

O·kan·a·gan [ˌoukənægən] *n* **1** a member of a First Nations people living in British Columbia. **2** their Salishan language. **Okanagan** *adj.*

o·kra ['oukrə] *n* a herb of the mallow family, used as a vegetable. ⟨West African language⟩

o·lal·lie [ou'lɑli] *n* ✺ **1** any of several berries, esp the salmonberry. **2** the bush such berries grow on. ⟨Chinook Jargon = berry⟩

old [ould] *adj* **1** having existed long: *old friends.* **2** of (a specified) age: *She is one year old today.* **3** **old·er** or **eld·er, old·est** or **eld·est** advanced in age: *an old woman. He doesn't look old.* **4** Often, **Old** designating the earlier or earliest of two or more periods, types, etc.: *Old English, the old edition.* **5** showing the effects of age or use: *an old coat.* **6** former: *an old student of hers.* **7** experienced: *an old hand.* **8** *Informal* a word used as an intensifier: *a high old time at the party.* *n* **1 the old a** people who are old (with a pl verb): *The old have interesting stories to tell.* **b** things that are old (with a sg verb): *The old gives way to the new.* **2** a time long ago: *the heroes of old.* **old·ness** *n.* ⟨Old English *ald*⟩ **old–boy network** an exclusive group of people of a similar background, expected to give help to one another. **Old Country** the native land of persons living elsewhere: *To many Canadians, Italy is the Old Country.* **old·en** *adj Poetic* of old. **old–fash·ioned** *adj* **1** out-of-date. **2** keeping to old ways, ideas, etc. **old guard** the conservative members of a community, organization, etc. **old hand** an experienced person. **old hat 1** *Informal* familiar. **2** old-fashioned. **old·ie** *n Informal* an old thing: *The band played oldies.* **old·ish** *adj* somewhat old. **old master 1** any great painter who lived before 1800. **2** a painting by such a painter. **old moon** the moon when seen as a C-shaped waning crescent. **old school** people who have old-fashioned or conservative ideas. **old–school** *adj.* **old·ster** *n Informal* an older person. **Old Testament** the sacred Scriptures of the Hebrews, as constituting the first part of the Christian Bible. **old–time** *adj* of or like former times. **old–tim·er** *n Informal* a person who has long been a resident, worker, etc. in a place. **old–world** *adj* **1** to do with the ancient world: *an old-world mammoth.* **2** characteristic of a former period: *old-world courtesy.* **Old World** Europe, Asia, and Africa. **Old World** *adj.*

o·le·ag·i·nous [ˌouli'ædʒənəs] *adj* oily. **o·le·ag·i·nous·ly** *adv.* **o·le·ag·i·nous·ness** *n.* ⟨Latin *oleaginus; olea , oliva* olive⟩

o·le·fin ['ouləfɪn] *n* any unsaturated hydrocarbon. **o·le·fin·ic** *adj.* ⟨Latin *oleum* oil + *facere* make⟩

ol·fac·tion [ɒl'fækʃən] *or* [oul'-] *n* **1** the act of smelling. **2** the sense of smell. ⟨Latin *olere* emit odour + *facere* make⟩ **ol·fac·to·ry** [ɒl'fæktəri] *or* [oul-] *adj* to do with smelling; of smell.

ol·i·gar·chy ['ɒləˌgɑrki] *n* a form of government in which a few people have all the power. **ol·i·garch** *n* one of a small number of persons holding ruling power. **ol·i·gar·chic** or **ol·i·gar·chi·cal** *adj.* **ol·i·gar·chi·cal·ly** *adv.*

Ol·i·go·cene ['ɒləˌgouˌsin] *Geology n* the third epoch of the Tertiary period, beginning about 37 million years ago. **Ol·i·go·cene** *adj.* ⟨Greek *oligos* small + *kainos* new⟩

ol·i·gop·o·ly [ˌɒlə'gɒpəli] *n* a situation in which a few producers control an industry so that there is limited competition. Compare MONOPOLY. **ol·i·gop·o·list** *n.* **ol·i·gop·o·lis·tic** *adj.* ⟨Greek *oligos* few + (MONO)POLY⟩

ol·ive ['ɒlɪv] *n* an evergreen tree with edible fruits that are the source of olive oil. Latin *oliva* Greek *elaia*⟩ **olive branch 1** a branch of the olive tree as an emblem of peace. **2** anything offered as a sign of peace.

Olympic games or **Olympics** [ə'lɪmpɪk] *or* [ou'lɪmpɪk] **1** in ancient Greece, contests in athletics, poetry, and music, held every four years. **2** a modern event including only the athletic contests of these games. ⟨Mt. *Olympus*, mythical home of the gods⟩ **O·lym·pi·ad** or **o·lym·pi·ad** [ə'lɪmpiˌæd] *n* **1** in ancient Greece, a period of four years from one Olympic games to the next. **2** the celebration of the modern Olympic games. **O·lym·pi·an** *adj* **1** like a god; heavenly. **2** aloof and superior: *Olympian calm. n* **1** any of the major Greek gods. **2** a contender in the Olympics. **O·lym·pic** *adj.*

om·buds·man ['ɒmbədzmən] *n, pl* **-men** a government official appointed to investigate citizens' grievances against the government. ⟨Swedish; *ombud* commission⟩

o·meg·a [ou'mɛgə], ['oumɪgə], *or* [ou'migə] *n* **1** the last of any series; end. **2** the last letter of the Greek alphabet (Ω or ω). ⟨Greek *o mega* big *o*⟩

om·e·lette or **om·e·let** ['ɒmlɪt] *n* a food dish of beaten eggs. ⟨French, earlier *alemelle* blade, Latin *lamella*; for its flatness⟩

o·men ['oumən] *n* **1** a sign of what is to happen: *Spilling salt is said to be an omen of misfortune.* **2** prophetic meaning: *He believes black cats are creatures of ill omen.* ⟨Latin⟩ **om·i·nous** ['ɒmənəs] *adj* of bad omen; unfavourable: *The watchdog gave an ominous growl.* **om·i·nous·ly** *adv.* **om·i·nous·ness** *n.*

o·mis·sion See OMIT.

o·mit [ou'mɪt] *v* **o·mit·ted, o·mit·ting 1** leave out: *You have omitted a letter in this word.* **2** fail to do: *She omitted to make her bed.* **o·mis·si·ble** *adj.* **o·mis·sion** *n.* ⟨Latin *ob-* by + *mittere* let go⟩

omni– *combining form* all: *omnidirectional; omnipotence.* ⟨Latin *omnis*⟩

om·ni·bus ['ɒmnəbəs] *n* **1** a volume of works by a single author, or of similar works by several authors: *a Hemingway omnibus, a science fiction omnibus.* **2** [-,bʌs] a large passenger vehicle having seats inside. *adj* covering many things at once: *an omnibus law.* ⟨Latin *omnibus* for all⟩

om·ni·far·i·ous [,ɒmnə'fɛriəs] *adj* of all kinds. ⟨Latin *omni-* all + *fas*. See NEFARIOUS.⟩

om·nip·o·tent [ɒm'nɪpətənt] *adj* having all power; almighty: *an omnipotent ruler.* **om·nip·o·tence** *n.* **om·nip·o·tent·ly** *adv.*

om·ni·pres·ent [,ɒmnə'prɛzənt] *adj* present everywhere at the same time. **om·ni·pres·ence** *n.*

om·nis·cience [ɒm'nɪʃəns] *or* [ɒm'nɪsiəns] *n* knowledge of everything. **om·nis·cient** *adj.* ⟨*omni-* + Latin *scientia* knowledge⟩

om·niv·o·rous [ɒm'nɪvərəs] *adj* **1** eating every kind of food. **2** fond of all kinds: *An omnivorous reader reads all kinds of books.* **om·niv·o·rous·ly** *adv.* **om·niv·o·rous·ness** *n.* ⟨*omni-* + Latin *vorare* eat⟩

om·ni·vore ['ɒmnə,vɔr] *n* a creature that can eat every kind of food: *Humans are omnivores.*

on [ɒn] *prep* **1** supported by: *on the table.* **2** touching so as to cover, be around, etc.: *There's new paint on the ceiling.* **3** close to; along the edge of: *on the shore, on the next street.* **4** against: *the picture on the wall.* **5** in the condition of; in the process of; in the way of: *on purpose.* **6** at the time of: *They greeted us on our arrival.* **7** concerning: *a book on animals.* **8** for the purpose of: *He went on an errand.* **9** among: *I am on the committee.* **10** carried by: *He had a gun on him.* *adv* **1** on something: *The walls are up, and the roof is on.* **2** to something: *Hold on.* **3** toward something: *The others looked on.* **4** farther; more: *March on.* **5** in or into a condition, process, etc.: *Turn the gas on.* **6** from a time; forward: *later on, from that day on.* *adj* taking place or going to take place: *The race is on.* ⟨Old English⟩ **and so on** and more of the same. **be on about** talk a lot about. **on and off** at some times and not others. **on and on** without stopping. **on to** *Informal* aware of and able to see through (a deception, etc.): *We're on to her tricks.*

on·com·ing *adj* approaching: *oncoming cars.* *n* approach: *the oncoming of the storm.* **on·go·ing** *adj* actually going on; in process; continuing: *an ongoing social problem.* **online** *adj, adv* Computers involving interactive processing done while directly connected to a computer: *Her flight will now be booked through the on-line reservation system.*

on·look·er *n* a spectator. **on·rush** *n* a violent forward movement. **on·rush·ing** *adj.* **on·screen** *adj, adv* on a computer, television, or movie screen. **on·set** *n* **1** an attack: *The onset of the enemy took us by surprise.* **2** the beginning: *the onset of winter.* **on·shore** *adv, adj* **1** toward the land: *an onshore wind.* **2** on the land: *an onshore patrol.* **on·side** *adj, adv* **1** in a position allowed by the rules of a game. **2** prepared to co-operate. **on·site** *adj* at the actual location: *an onsite inspection.* **on·slaught** *n* a vigorous attack. **on·stage** *adj, onstage characters adv* on or onto the stage: *She carried the sword onstage.* **on·to** *prep* to a position on: *throw a ball onto the roof.* **on·ward** or **on·wards** *adv, adj* forward: *The army marched onward.*

> **USAGE**
> When **on** is an adverb and **to** is a preposition, they should be written as two words: *We got back in the car and drove on to the city.* When **on** and **to** are combined to make a compound preposition, they are usually written solid: *They looked out onto the park.*

once [wʌns] *adv* **1** one time: *I eat once a day.* **2** formerly: *a once powerful nation.* *conj* after: *Once you cross the river, you are safe.* *n* a single occasion: *Once is enough.* ⟨Old English *ānes; ān* one⟩ **all at once** suddenly. **at once a** immediately: *Come at once.* **b** at the same time: *Everyone shouted at once.* **for once** for one time at least. **just this once** for this time only. **once and for all** finally. **once in a while** now and then. **once or twice** a few times. **once upon a time** long ago (to begin a fairy tale). **once–o·ver** *n Informal* **1** a short, quick look. **2** a quick, superficial job: *He gave the furniture a once-over with a dust cloth.*

on·co·gene ['ɒŋkə,dʒin] *n Genetics* a gene that can convert a normal cell into a malignant cell. ⟨<Greek *onkos* swelling + GENE⟩ **on·col·o·gy** [ɒŋ'kɒlədʒi] *n* the branch of medicine dealing with the treatment of tumours. **on·co·log·i·cal** *adj.* **on·col·o·gist** *n.*

one [wʌn] *n* **1** the first natural number; 1. **2** a single person or thing: *a table for one.* **3** a playing card or side of a die with one spot; ace. *adj* **1** being a single unit: *one apple.* **2** some: *One day he will be sorry.* **3** the same: *They held one opinion.* **4** united: *We must be one.* *pron* **1** some person or thing: *One of her poems was selected.* **2** any person or thing: *One must work hard to achieve success.* **3** the same person or thing: *Dr. Jekyll and Mr. Hyde were one.* **4** the person or thing previously mentioned: *She has a black purse and a white one.* ⟨Old English (stressed) *ān*⟩ **all one** making no difference: *It is all one to me whether you stay or go.* **at one** in agreement: *The two judges were at one about the winner.* **one and all** everyone. **one and the same** the very same. **one by one** one after another. **one or two** a few. **one up on** *Informal* in a position of advantage over. **one another** each of several in an action or relation that is reciprocal: *They struck at one*

another. They were in one another's way.
one–horse *adj* worked by a single horse: *a one-horse sleigh.* **one–horse town** *Informal.* a town of little importance. **one–legged** ['wʌn 'lɛgɪd] *or* [-'lɛgd] *adj* **1** having only one leg. **2** of an argument or viewpoint, limited. **3** lacking some important element, so as to be ineffective: *a one-legged law.* **one–liner** *n* a one-line joke. **one·ness** ['wʌnnɪs] *n* **1** the quality of being one in number or the only one of its kind. **2** the quality of being the same in kind. **3** the fact of forming one whole. **4** harmony. **one–night stand 1** a single performance in one place. **2** *Informal* a single sexual encounter. **one–on–one** *adj* consisting of individual confrontation or interaction: *a one-on-one meeting.* *adv* individually: *I'd like to meet him one-on-one.* **one–piece** *adj* of a garment, consisting of a single piece: *a one-piece swimsuit.* **one·self** *pron* **1** a reflexive pronoun: *One might ask oneself if it is worth the trouble.* **2** a form of **one** added for emphasis: *One has to do the real work oneself.* **3** one's usual self: *It's nice to be oneself again after an illness.* **one–shot** *adj Informal* being the only one, not part of a series: *a one-shot effort.* **one–sid·ed** *adj* **1** seeing only one side of a question; prejudiced. **2** uneven; unequal: *a one-sided game.* **one–time** *adj* former: *my one-time best friend.* **one–to–one** *adj* **1** *Mathematics* allowing for one member of a class to pair with only one of another class. **2** one–on–one. **one–track** *adj Informal* preoccupied with only one thing at a time: *a one-track mind.* **one–two** *n* **1** *Boxing* a knockout punch. **2** a concluding argument. **one up 1** winning. **2** beating an opponent by one score: *At half-time we were one up on our rivals.* **3** one each: *The score was one up at half-time.* **one–up·man·ship** *n Informal* the art of getting the better of someone else in business, social life, etc. **one–way** *adj* moving or allowing movement in only one direction: *one-way traffic, a one-way flight.*

The use of the impersonal pronoun **one** is formal, especially if it must be repeated. *Informal: You can't be too careful, can you? Formal: One can't be too careful, can one?*

O·nei·da [ou'naɪdə] *n, pl* **-da** *or* **-das 1** a member of a Native American people belonging to the Five Nations confederacy, originally of New York State and later living in Ontario and Wisconsin. **2** the Iroquoian language of the Oneida. **O·nei·da** *adj.*

on·er·ous See ONUS.

on·ion ['ʌnjən] *n* a herb of the lily family, having an edible bulb. **on·ion·like** *adj.* ⟨French *oignon* Latin *unio*⟩
know one's onions *Informal* be well-informed. **onion rings** slices of onion battered and deep-fried. **on·ion·skin** *n* **1** the outer skin of an onion. **2** a thin, glossy, translucent paper.

on·ly ['ounli] *adj* **1** by itself or themselves; one and no more; these and no more; sole, single, or few of the kind or class: *an only son.*

Those were the only clothes he owned. This is the only road along the shore. **2** best; finest: *As far as she is concerned, he is the only writer.*
adv **1** merely; just: *He sold only two.* **2** and no one or nothing more; and that is all: *Only he remained. I did it only through friendship.*
conj **1** but: *I would have gone only I didn't have the money.* **2** it must be added that; however: *We camped right beside a stream, only the water was not fit to drink.* ⟨Old English *ānlīc*⟩
if only I wish: *If only wars would cease!*
only too very: *She was only too glad to help us.*

To avoid uncertainty, **only** as an adverb should be placed immediately before the word or words it modifies. The following sentences all have different meanings:
*He **only** e-mailed his parents last week.*
(That is, he didn't telephone.)
*He e-mailed **only** his parents last week.*
(That is, he didn't e-mail anyone else.)
*He e-mailed his parents **only** last week.*
(That is, he e-mailed them just last week).

on·o·mat·o·poe·ia [ˌɒnəˌmætə'piə] *n* **1** the naming of a thing or action by imitating the sound associated with it, as in *buzz, splash.* **2** the adaptation of the sound to the sense for effect, as in 'the murmuring of innumerable bees'. **on·o·mat·o·poe·ic** *or* **on·o·mat·o·po·et·ic** [ˌɒnəˌmætəpou'ɛtɪk] *adj.* **on·o·mat·o·po·et·i·cal·ly** *adv.* ⟨Latin; Greek *onomatos* name + *-poios* making⟩

On·on·da·ga [ˌɒnən'dɑgə] *or* [ˌɒnən'deigə] *n, pl* **-ga** or **-gas** *n* **1** a member of a First Nations people belonging to the Five Nations confederacy, living mainly near Brantford, ON. **2** the Iroquoian language of the Onondaga. **On·on·da·ga** *adj.* ⟨Iroquois *Ononta' gé* on top of the hill⟩

On·ta·ri·o [ɒn'tɛriou] *n* an eastern province of Canada. *Abbrev* **ON. On·tar·i·an** *n, adj.* ⟨Iroquois = good lake⟩

on·tog·e·ny [ɒn'tɒdʒəni] *n Biology* the development of an individual organism. ⟨Greek *ontos* being + *-geneia* origin. See -GEN.⟩

on·tol·o·gy [ɒn'tɒlədʒi] *n* the part of philosophy that deals with the nature of being. **on·to·log·i·cal** *adj.* **on·to·log·i·cal·ly** *adv.* **on·tol·o·gist** *n.* ⟨Greek *ontos* being⟩

o·nus ['ounəs] *n* a burden; responsibility: *Since he made the accusation, the onus is on him to prove it.* ⟨Latin *onus, oneris*⟩
on·er·ous ['ounərəs] *or* ['ɒnərəs] *adj* **1** burdensome: *an onerous task.* **2** *Law* in a contract, entailing a legal obligation greater than the benefits. **on·er·ous·ly** *adv.* **on·er·ous·ness** *n.*

on·yx ['ɒnɪks] *n* a translucent variety of quartz. ⟨Greek = nail, claw⟩

oo·dles ['udəlz] *n pl Informal* large or unlimited quantities; heaps; loads: *oodles of money.* ⟨*huddle* a mass of things⟩

oo·li·chan ['ulə,kɑn] *or* ['uləkən] *n, pl* **-chan** or **-chans ✱** a highly valued food fish of the smelt family found along the Pacific coast of

North America. Also, **eu·la·chon, oo·la·chan.** ⟨Chinook Jargon⟩

oolichan oil or grease ✻ an oil rendered from the oolichan and formerly a food and trade item among the Coast and Inland First Nations people of BC.

oomph [umf] *n Slang* **1** extreme vigour. **2** sex appeal. ⟨imitative⟩

ooze¹ [uz] *v* **1** leak slowly and quietly: *Blood oozed from her scraped knee. The news of their failure oozed to the public.* **2** drain away: *His courage oozed away as he waited.* *n* **1** a slow flow. **2** something that oozes. **ooz·y** *adj.* **ooz·i·ly** *adv.* **ooz·i·ness** *n.* ⟨Old English *wōs* juice⟩

ooze² [uz] *n* **1** a soft mud or slime, esp that at the bottom of a pond, lake, river, or ocean. **2** muddy ground. **ooz·y** *adj.* **ooz·i·ly** *adv.* **ooz·i·ness** *n.* ⟨Old English *wāse* mud⟩

op [ɒp] *n* opportunity: *photo op.*

o·pac·i·ty See OPAQUE.

o·pal ['oupəl] *n* a form of silica that is softer than quartz. ⟨Greek *opallios* Sanskrit *upala*⟩ **o·pal·es·cent** [,oupə'lɛsənt] *adj* showing a play of colours like that of the opal. **o·pal·es·cence** *n.* **o·pal·ine** ['oupə,laɪn], [-lɪn], *or* [-lɪn] *adj* of or like opal.

o·paque [ou'peɪk] *adj* **1** not letting light through; not transparent: *Muddy water is opaque.* **2** not shining; dull. **3** obscure; hard to understand. **4** stupid. *n* something opaque. **o·pac·i·ty** [ou'pæsəti] *n.* **o·paque·ly** *adv.* ⟨Latin *opacus* dark, shady⟩

op art [ɒp] a style of drawing that creates optical illusions by means of complex geometrical designs. ⟨shortened from *optical art,* on analogy with *pop art*⟩

op.cit. in the book, passage, etc. previously referred to. ⟨Latin *opere citato* in the work cited⟩

OPEC ['oupɛk] Organization of Petroleum Exporting Countries.

o·pen ['oupən] *adj* **1** not shut: *an open drawer.* **2** not closed in: *an open field.* **3** unfilled: *to have an hour open.* **4** that may be entered, used, shared, competed for, etc. by all: *an open meeting.* **5** ready for business: *The exhibition is now open.* **6** without restriction: *open season for hunting.* **7** undecided: *an open question.* **8** not obstructed: *an open view.* **9** unprejudiced: *an open mind.* **10** not secret: *open disregard of rules.* **11** having spaces or holes: *cloth of open texture.* **12** *Music* **a** of an organ pipe, not closed at the upper end. **b** of a string on a violin, cello, etc., not stopped by the finger. **c** of a note, produced by such a pipe or string, or without aid of slide, key, etc. **13** that is spread out; expanded: *an open flower.* **14** free from hindrance, esp from ice: *open water on the lake.* **15** *Electricity* of an electric circuit, not complete or closed. *n* **the open a** the open country, air, sea, etc.: *I spent the afternoon out in the open and got badly sunburned.* **b** public view or knowledge: *Bring the problem out into the open.* *v* **1** cause to become open: *Open the door.* **2** set going: *She*

has opened a new store. **3** begin the proceedings of: *to open negotiations.* **4** become or make accessible: *Open a path through the woods.* **5** make or become accessible to knowledge, sympathy, etc.: *Open your heart to them.* **6** expose to view; disclose. **7** expand, extend, or spread out. **8** *Computers* in software, prepare for use: *open a file.*

open to a willing to consider. **b** liable to: *open to criticism.* **c** to be used by: *open to the public.* **open up a** make or become open. **b** unfold. **c** open a way to and develop: *The early settlers opened up the West.* **o·pen·ly** *adv.* **o·pen·ness** *n.* ⟨Old English.⟩

open air the out-of-doors. **o·pen–air** *adj.* **o·pen–and–shut** *adj Informal* direct; obvious; straightforward: *an open-and-shut case.* **open book** someone or something that is easy to discover or interpret: *Her opinions are an open book.* **o·pen–end·ed** *adj* having no set boundary or limit; having no single right answer: *an open-ended agreement, open-ended questions.* **o·pen–end·ed·ness** *n.* **o·pen·er** *n* **1** a device for opening bottles, cans, letters, etc. **2** *Informal* the first game of a scheduled series. **3 openers** *Card games* cards of high enough value to allow the player to open the bidding. **for openers** *Informal* as a beginning. **o·pen–face** *adj* of a sandwich, made without the top slice of bread. **o·pen–hand·ed** *adj* generous. **o·pen–hand·ed·ness** *n.* **open–heart** *adj* designating surgery on the heart while its functions are performed by mechanical means. **o·pen–heart·ed** *adj* **1** candid. **2** kindly; generous. **o·pen–heart·ed·ness** *n.* **open house 1** an informal social event open to all: *They dropped in at their neighbour's open house.* **2** an occasion when a school, factory, etc. is opened for inspection by the public. **3** a time when a house for sale is open to inspection by buyers. **keep open house** offer food, or food and lodging, to all visitors. **o·pen·ing** *n* **1** a gap. **2** the first part: *the opening of a lecture.* **3** an official ceremony to mark the beginning of a new business, institution, etc. **4** a job, place, or position that is open or vacant. **5** a favourable opportunity: *She waited for an opening to ask to borrow the car.* **open letter** a letter addressed to a particular person but intended for publication in a newspaper, magazine, etc. **o·pen–line** *adj* hot-line: *an open-line radio show.* **open marriage** a marriage in which the partners agree that each is permitted sexual relationships with other people. **open mind** a mind ready to consider new ideas. **o·pen–mind·ed** *adj.* **o·pen–mind·ed·ness** *n.* **o·pen–mouthed** [-,maʊðd] *or* [,-,mʌʊθt] *adj* **1** gaping with surprise. **2** greedy. **o·pen–pit** *adj* worked on from the exposed surface, not underground: *open-pit mining.* **open question** a matter that has not been decided on and on which differences of opinion are accepted. **open season 1** a period during which it is legal to hunt fish or game that is protected by law at other times. **2** a situation in which anyone can criticize a given person, group, etc. with seeming impunity (with *on*): *open* *season on tourists.* **open secret** a matter that is supposed to be secret but that everyone knows about. **open sesame 1** in the *Arabian Nights*, the magic words that opened the door of the robbers' den. **2** anything that obtains easy access: *Her education was an open sesame to the job.* **open shop** a factory, shop, or other establishment that will employ both union and non-union workers. Compare CLOSED SHOP. **open water 1** water free of obstructions. **2 ✹** esp in the North: **a** the time when rivers and lakes become free of ice; break-up. **b** the time between break-up and freeze-up. **o·pen·work** *n* ornamental work in cloth, metal, etc. that has openings in the material.

op·er·a¹ ['ɒpərə] *n* drama set to music, in which the words are sung by the performers rather than spoken. **op·er·at·ic** *adj.* **op·er·at·i·cal·ly** *adv.* ⟨Italian *opera in musica* a work to music; Latin *opera*, pl of *opus* work⟩ **opera glasses** small, low-powered binoculars for use at the opera, in theatres, etc. **opera house 1** a theatre where operas are performed. **2** any theatre. **op·er·et·ta** *n* a short, amusing opera with some words spoken rather than sung.

op·er·a² ['ɒpərə] *n* a pl of OPUS.

op·er·a·ble See OPERATE.

op·er·ate ['ɒpə,reit] *v* **1** be working or keep at work: *The machinery operates night and day.* **2** *Medicine* perform a surgical operation. ⟨Latin *operare*; *opera*. See OPERA¹.⟩ **op·er·a·ble** *adj* fit for a surgical operation. **op·er·and** ['ɒpə,rænd] *n* *Mathematics* any symbol or quantity that is subject to an operation. **operating system** *Computers* a collection of computer programs that provide the overall control of a computer system. **op·er·a·tion** *n* **1** working: *The operation of a railway requires many people.* **2** the way a thing works: *the operation of a machine.* **3** *Medicine* a treatment in which instruments are used to cut into the body in order to remove, replace, or repair a part. **4** *Mathematics* something done to a number or quantity. Addition, subtraction, multiplication, and division are the four commonest operations in arithmetic. **in operation a** working. **b** in use or effect. **op·er·a·tion·al** *adj.* **op·er·a·tion·al·ly** *adv.* **op·er·a·tive** ['ɒpərətɪv] *adj* **1** operating: *the laws operative in a community.* **2** to do with productiveness: *operative departments of a manufacturing establishment.* **3** to do with a surgical operation. **4** relevant; of note: *the operative word in a sentence.* *n* **1** a person who operates a machine. **2** a private detective or secret agent. **op·er·a·tive·ly** *adv.* **op·er·a·tor** *n* **1** a person who operates something, esp a skilled worker who runs a machine. **2** *Informal* a person who is skilled in manipulating people for his or her own needs.

oph·thal·mol·o·gy [,ɒfθæl'mɒlədʒi] *or* [,ɒpθæl-]; [,ɒfθə-] *n* the branch of medicine that deals with the structure, functions, and diseases of the eye.

oph·thal·mic [ɒf'θælmɪk] *or* [ɒp'-] *adj.* **oph·thal·mol·o·gist** *n.* ⟨Greek *ophthalmos* eye⟩

USAGE

An **ophthalmologist** is a doctor who is trained to treat eye diseases as well as recommending corrective lenses. An **optometrist** is not a doctor but is trained to examine eyes and recommend corrective lenses. An **optician** prepares, fits, and sells glasses and contact lenses.

o·pi·ate See OPIUM.

o·pin·ion [ə'pɪnjən] *n* **1** a judgment formed in the mind: *I prefer to form my own opinion.* **2** a view or impression: *She has a poor opinion of such shoddy construction.* **3** a formal judgment made by an expert. **4** *Law* a statement by a judge or jury of the reasons for the decision of the court. ⟨Latin *opinio*⟩ **o·pine** [ou'paɪn] *v Informal* express or have an opinion; suppose: *He opined that the weather would improve by evening.* **o·pin·ion·at·ed** *adj* obstinate with regard to one's opinions. **o·pin·ion·at·ed·ly** *adv.* **o·pin·ion·at·ed·ness** *n.*

o·pi·um ['oupiəm] *n* **1** a powerful, addictive drug that causes sleep and eases pain, made from the unripe seeds of the opium poppy. **2** anything that has a dulling or tranquillizing effect. ⟨Greek *opion*; *opos* vegetable juice⟩ **o·pi·ate** ['oupiɪt] *n* **1** any powerful drug containing opium or a derivative of opium and used especially to dull pain or to bring sleep. **2** anything that quiets. **o·pi·ate** *adj.*

o·pos·sum [ə'pɒsəm] *n* any of a family of New World marsupials. Also called **pos·sum.** ⟨Algonquian⟩

op·po·nent [ə'pounənt] *n* a person who is on the other side in a fight, game, or argument. **op·po·nent** *adj.* **op·po·nen·cy** *n.* ⟨Latin *ob-* against + *ponere* put⟩

op·por·tune [,ɒpər'tjun] *or* [,ɒpər'tun] *adj* **1** suitable: *You have arrived at a most opportune moment.* **2** occurring at the right time: *an opportune meeting.* **op·por·tune·ly** *adv.* **op·por·tune·ness** *n.* **op·por·tu·ni·ty** *n.* ⟨Latin *ob portum* toward port (of wind)⟩ **op·por·tun·ism** [,ɒpər'tjunɪzəm] *or* [-tunɪzəm] *n* taking advantage of circumstances, esp with little regard for principles. **op·por·tun·ist** *n.* **op·por·tun·is·tic** *adj.* **op·por·tun·is·ti·cal·ly** *adv.*

op·pose [ə'pouz] *v* **1** act, fight, speak, or struggle against. **2** put in contrast: *to oppose European and North American culture.* **3** cause to face: *to oppose one's finger to one's thumb.* **op·pos·er** *n.* ⟨Old French *opposer;* Latin *ob-*⟩ against + *pos-* stem of *ponere* put⟩ **op·pos·a·ble** *adj* **1** capable of being opposed or resisted. **2** capable of being placed opposite something else. The human thumb is opposable to the fingers. **op·pos·a·bil·i·ty** *n.* **op·posed** *adj* placed in opposition; contrasted: *The two boys had strongly opposed characters, but they were friends.* **as opposed to** in contrast to: *I prefer fish as opposed to meat.*

op·po·site ['ɒpəzɪt] *or* ['ɒpəsɪt] *adj* **1** placed face to face, back to back, or at the other end or side: *the opposite side of the street.* **2** as different as can be: *Sour is opposite to sweet. n* a thing that or person who is opposite: *Black is the opposite of white. prep* **1** opposite to: *opposite the church.* **2** in a motion picture or play, acting as the leading lady or man of (an actor of the opposite sex): *She played opposite a famous actor in her first starring role.* **op·po·site·ly** *adv.* **opposite number** a person in an organization who holds a position equal to that of a person in another organization. **op·po·si·tion** [,ɒpə'zɪʃən] *n* **1** action against: *The mob offered opposition to the police.* **2** contrast: *His views were in opposition to mine.* **3** the political party or parties not in power: *the official opposition.* **4** any opponent: *We defeated the opposition.* **op·po·si·tion·al** *or* **op·po·si·tion·ar·y** *adj.* **op·po·si·tion·less** *adj.*

op·press [ə'prɛs] *v* **1** govern harshly. **2** weigh down; burden: *A fear of trouble ahead oppressed my spirits.* **op·pres·sion** *n.* **op·pres·sive** *adj.* **op·pres·sive·ly** *adv.* **op·pres·sive·ness** *n.* **op·pres·sor** *n.* ⟨Latin *ob-* against + *pressare*; *pressus* pp of *premere* press⟩

op·pro·bri·um [ə'proubriəm] *n* disgrace or reproach caused by shameful or vicious conduct. **op·pro·bri·ous** *adj.* **op·pro·bri·ous·ly** *adv.* ⟨Latin *ob-* at + *probrum* infamy⟩

opt [ɒpt] *v* make a choice, esp in favour of something: *She opted to stay.* **opt in** choose to join. **opt out** (**of**), decide to leave: *Several nations wanted to opt out of the alliance.* ⟨Latin *optare*⟩
op·tion *n* **1** the power to choose: *We have the option of rejecting this offer and waiting for a better one.* **2** something that may be chosen: *One of the options offered with this car model is air conditioning.* **3** a right to buy something at a certain price within a certain time: *to hold an option on land. v* obtain or grant an option in reference to (something). **op·tion·al** *adj* not required or standard: *optional equipment.* **op·tion·al·i·ty** *n.* **op·tion·al·ly** *adv.*

op·tic ['ɒptɪk] *adj* of the eye or the sense of sight. ⟨Greek *optikos; optos* seen, *ops* eye⟩
op·ti·cal *adj* to do with the eye or the sense of sight: *an optical illusion.* **op·ti·cal·ly** *adv.* **optical character recognition** the ability of a photo-electric machine to read letters and numbers. *Abbrev* **OCR. optical illusion** a drawing that deceives the eye. **op·ti·cian** [ɒp'tɪʃən] *n* a person who prepares, fits, and sells glasses and contact lenses. **optic nerve** the nerve that conducts visual stimuli from the eye to the brain. **op·tics** *n* (with a sg verb) the science that deals with light and vision.

op·ti·mism ['ɒptə,mɪzəm] *n* a tendency to be hopeful and confident about things. **op·ti·mist** *n.* **op·ti·mis·tic** *adj.* **op·ti·mis·ti·cal·ly** *adv.* ⟨Latin *optimus* best⟩
op·ti·mal *adj* most favourable or desirable. **op·ti·mal·ly** *adv.* **op·ti·mize** *v* make as satisfactory as possible: *She checked every detail to optimize the effect of the advertisement.*

op·ti·mi·za·tion *n.* **op·ti·mum** *n, pl* **-ma** [-mə] *or* **-mums** the best point, amount, etc. for a particular purpose. *adj* most favourable: *an optimum temperature for growth.*

op·tom·e·try [ɒp'tɒmətri] *n* the profession of examining the eyes for defects in vision and prescribing lenses or exercises to correct such defects. **op·tom·e·trist** *n.* ⟨Greek *optos* seen + *metron* measure⟩

op·u·lent ['ɒpjələnt] *adj* **1** wealthy; affluent. **2** abundant and luxuriant; lavish. **op·u·lence** ['ɒpjələns] *n.* **op·u·lent·ly** *adv.* ⟨Latin *opulens; ops* power, wealth⟩

o·pus ['oupəs] *n, pl* **o·pus·es** *or* **op·er·a** ['ɒpərə] a literary work or musical composition: *He played his own opus, No. 16.* ⟨Latin = work⟩

or [ɔr] *conj* **1** a word used to indicate: **a** a choice or difference: *Do you prefer coffee or tea?* **b** equivalence of two words: *This is the termination or end.* **c** approximate quantity, etc.: *They'll be gone for three or four days.* **2** otherwise: *Hurry, or you'll be late.* ⟨Old English *āther; ā* ever + *hwæther* either⟩

–or *suffix* **1** a person or thing that ――s: *actor, accelerator.* **2** an act, state, condition, quality, characteristic, etc., esp in words from Latin: *error, horror.* ⟨Latin⟩

or·a·cle ['ɔrəkəl] *n* **1** in ancient times: **a** an answer given by a god through a priest or priestess to some question. **b** the place where the god gave answers. **2** a person who gives wise advice. **3** something regarded as a reliable guide. ⟨Latin *oraculum; orare* pray⟩
o·rac·u·lar [ɔ'rækjələr] *adj* **1** of or like an oracle. **2** with a hidden meaning that is difficult to make out. **3** very wise. **o·rac·u·lar·ly** *adv.*

o·ral ['ɔrəl] *adj* **1** spoken; using speech. **2** of the mouth. **3** taken by mouth: *oral medicine. n* a spoken examination: *a PhD oral.* **o·ral·ly** *adv.* ⟨Latin *os, oris* mouth⟩

or·ange ['ɔrɪndʒ] *n* **1** a reddish yellow citrus fruit with a juicy pulp. **2** a colour made by mixing red and yellow. **or·ange** *adj.* **or·ange·like** *adj.* **or·ang·y** *or* **or·ange·y** *adj.* ⟨Old French *orenge*; Spanish *naranja*⟩
or·ange·ade [,ɔrɪn'dʒeid] *n* a drink made of orange juice, sugar, and water.

o·rang·u·tan, o·rang–u·tan, *or* **o·rang·u·tang** [ɔ'ræŋə,tæn] *or* [-æŋ] *n* a large anthropoid ape of the forests of Borneo and Sumatra, having long, reddish brown hair. Also, **orang·ou·tang** *or* **orang–ou·tang.** ⟨Malay *orang* man + *utan* wild⟩

o·ra·tion [ɔ'reiʃən] *n* **1** a formal speech delivered on a special occasion. **2** a speech given in an affected style. **o·rate** [ɔ'reit] *v.*

or·a·tor ['ɔrətər] *n.* **or·a·tor·i·cal** [,ɔrə'tɔrəkəl] *adj.*
or·a·tor·i·cal·ly *adv.* ⟨Latin *orare* pray, plead⟩
or·a·to·ry ['ɔrə,tɔri] *n* **1** the art of public speaking. **2** skill in public speaking. **3** language used in public speaking. **4** a small chapel; a room set apart for prayer.

or·a·to·ri·o [,ɔrə'tɔri,ou] *n, pl* **-ri·os** a musical drama performed without action, costumes, or scenery, and usually based on Biblical or historical themes. ⟨Italian; Latin *oratorium* place of prayer. See ORATION.⟩

orb [ɔrb] *n* **1** a sphere, esp a heavenly body such as the sun, moon, etc. **2** a jewelled sphere, esp a symbol of royal power. **orb·like** *adj.* ⟨Latin *orbis* circle⟩

or·bit [,ɔrbɪt] *n* **1** the path of a heavenly body, satellite, etc. around another body in space: *the earth's orbit around the sun.* **2** the regular course of life or experience.
v travel in an orbit around: *Artificial satellites are orbiting the earth.* **or·bit·al** or **or·bit·a·ry** *adj.* ⟨Latin *orbita* wheel track. See ORB.⟩

or·ca ['ɔrkə] *n* KILLER WHALE. ⟨Latin⟩

or·chard ['ɔrtʃərd] *n* an area in which fruit trees are grown. ⟨Old English *ort-* (Latin *hortus* garden) + *geard* yard[1]⟩

or·ches·tra ['ɔrkɪstrə] *n* **1** a large group of musicians organized to perform music together. **2** all the instruments played together by the musicians in such a group. **3** the part in a theatre just in front of the stage, where the musicians sit to play. Also, **orchestra plt.** **4** the main floor of a theatre, esp the part near the front. ⟨Greek space for dancing chorus at a drama; *orcheesthai* dance⟩
or·ches·tral [ɔr'kɛstrəl] *adj* of, composed for, or performed by an orchestra. **or·ches·tral·ly** *adv.* **or·ches·trate** ['ɔrkɪs,treit] *v* **1** compose or arrange (music) for performance by an orchestra. **2** arrange or control all the various stages or elements of (something) to achieve a particular effect. **or·ches·tra·tion** *n.* **or·ches·trat·or** *n.*

or·chid ['ɔrkɪd] any of a large family of plants obtaining their food and moisture from the air. Most orchids have showy flowers. ⟨Greek *orchis* testicle; for root shape⟩

or·dain [ɔr'dein] *v* **1** order by law: *The law ordains that convicted murderers shall be imprisoned.* **2** officially appoint as a member of the Christian clergy. **or·dain·a·ble** *adj.* ⟨Latin *ordinare; ordo, ordinis* order⟩
or·di·na·tion [,ɔrdə'neiʃən] *n* the ceremony or state of being admitted as a minister in a Christian church.

or·deal [ɔr'dil] *n* a severe test or experience. ⟨Old English *ordæl* verdict for judgment⟩

or·der ['ɔrdər] *n* **1** the way one thing follows another: *in order of size.* **2** a condition in which every part is in its right place: *to put a room in order.* **3** the way the world works: *the order of nature.* **4** the state of things in which the law is obeyed and there is no trouble: *The police officer tried hard to keep order.* **5** the rules by which a meeting is run. **6** a command. **7** a request for goods, or the goods so requested: *Mother asked when they would deliver our grocery order.* **8** a paper saying that money is to be given or paid: *a money order.* **9** a kind or sort: *to have ability of a high order.* **10** *Biology* a major category in the classification of plants and animals, more specific than a class and more general than a family. **11** Usually, **orders** HOLY ORDERS. **12** a society to which one is admitted as an honour: *the Order of Canada.* **13** a modern fraternal organization: *the Order of Freemasons, the Imperial Order Daughters of the Empire.* **14** a portion of food served in a restaurant, etc.: *an order of toast.*
v **1** put in order: *to order one's affairs.* **2** tell what to do. **3** give a request or directions (for): *Are you ready to order?* ⟨Old French *ordre;* Latin *ordo*⟩
by order according to an order given by the proper person: *by order of the premier.* **call to order** ask to be quiet and start work: *She called the meeting to order.* **in** (or **out of**) **order a** in the right (or wrong) arrangement: *Are all the pages in order?* **b** working (or not working) properly. **c** allowed by (or against) the rules of a meeting, etc. **in order that** so that: *The teacher spoke clearly in order that everyone could hear her.* **in order to** for the purpose of: *She worked hard in order to qualify for the scholarship.* **in short order** quickly. **made to order** made to fit or suit a certain person or place. **on order** having been ordered but not yet received. **on the order of** similar to: *a house on the order of ours.* **order around** or **about** tell to do this and that: *Stop ordering me around.* **take holy orders** become a member of the Christian clergy. **tall order** *Informal* something difficult to do.
or·dered *adj* **1** characterized by regular arrangement: *a quiet, ordered existence.* **2** *Mathematics, etc.* having elements arranged in a specific order: *an an ordered pair of numbers.* **or·der–in–coun·cil** *n, pl* **or·ders–in–coun·cil** a regulation made by the federal cabinet or by a provincial cabinet. **or·der·ly** *adj* **1** in order: *an orderly mind.* **2** well-behaved: *an orderly class.*
n **1** *Military* a person who attends a superior officer to carry messages, etc. **2** a hospital attendant who keeps things in order. **or·der·li·ness** *n.* **Order of Canada ✳** an order that honours Canadians for outstanding achievement and service to their country or to humanity at large. Memberships are in three categories: companion (**CC**), officer (**OC**), and member (**CM**). **ordinal number** ['ɔrdənəl] a number, such as first, twentieth, thousandth, etc., that shows the place an item has in an ordered sequence. Compare CARDINAL NUMBER.

or·di·nance ['ɔrdənəns] *n* **1** a rule made by authority: *an ordinance against burning leaves.* **2** a religious ceremony. ⟨See ORDAIN.⟩

or·di·nar·y ['ɔrdə,nɛri] *adj* **1** customary. **2** not special; average: *an ordinary person.* **or·di·nar·i·ly** [,ɔrdə'nɛrəli] or ['ɔrdə,nɛrəli] *adv.* **or·di·nar·i·ness** *n.* ⟨See ORDAIN.⟩
out of the ordinary unusual.

or·di·nate ['ɔrdənɪt] *n Mathematics* the second number in an ordered pair. Compare ABSCISSA. ⟨See ORDAIN.⟩

or·di·na·tion See ORDAIN.

ord·nance ['ɔrdnəns] *n* **1** artillery. **2** military weapons and equipment of all kinds. ⟨variant of *ordinance*⟩

or·dure ['ɔrdʒər] *n* **1** filth; dung. **2** something vile or objectionable. **or·dur·ous** *adj.* ⟨Old French; *ord* filthy, Latin *horridus* horrid⟩

ore [ɔr] *n* a naturally occurring mineral containing a valuable substance such as metal: *iron ore.* ⟨Old English *ār* brass⟩

o·reg·a·no [ə'rɛgə,nou] *or* [,ɔrə'gænou] *n* the dried leaves of any of several herbs of the mint family, used as a seasoning. ⟨Spanish; Greek *origanon* marjoram⟩

or·gan ['ɔrgən] *n* **1** a large musical wind instrument consisting of sets of pipes which are sounded by forcing air through them. **2** an instrument in which a similar sound is produced by electronic means. **3** any structure in an animal or plant, such as an eye, lung, stamen, or pistil, that is composed of cells and tissues organized to perform some particular function. **4** a group that performs a particular function within a larger group: *A court is an organ of government.* **5** a newspaper or magazine that gives the views of a political party or some other group. ⟨Greek *organon* instrument; *ergon* work⟩ **organ donor** a person who donates or bequeaths a bodily organ, for transplant or research. **or·gan·elle** [,ɔrgə'nɛl] *n Biology* a separate structure within the cytoplasm of a cell, such as a cilium or centriole, that functions as an organ. **organ grinder** a person who plays a hand organ by turning a crank. **or·gan·ic** *adj* **1** to do with a bodily organ: *an organic disease.* **2** to do with beings having organs or an organized physical structure: *organic substances.* **3** made up of related parts; organized: *Every part of an organic whole depends on every other part.* **4** forming part of the basic structure of something: *The music is an organic part of the film.* **5** to do with compounds of carbon: *Organic compounds exist naturally as constituents of animals and plants.* **6** designating a method of raising plants or animals without using chemical fertilizers, pesticides, or drugs: *organic gardening.* **or·gan·i·cal·ly** *adv.* **organic chemistry** the branch of chemistry that deals with compounds of carbon. **or·gan·ism** *n* **1** a living body having organs or an organized structure. **2** a very tiny animal or plant. **3** a complex structure of parts that work together, esp one that can change. A community may be spoken of as a social organism. **or·gan·is·mic** *or* **or·gan·is·mal** *adj.* **or·gan·is·mi·cal·ly** *adv.* **or·gan·ist** *n* a person who plays the organ. **or·gan·i·za·tion** [,ɔrgənə'zeiʃən] *or* [,ɔrgənaɪ'zeiʃən] *n* **1** a group of persons united for some purpose. **2** the act of organizing. **3** something made

up of related parts, each having a function: *A tree is an organization of roots, trunk, branches, leaves, and fruit.* **or·gan·i·za·tion·al** *adj.* **or·gan·i·za·tion·al·ly** *adv.* **or·gan·ize** *v* **1** arrange to work together as a whole: *The general organized his soldiers into a powerful fighting force.* **2** arrange in a system: *She organized her thoughts.* **3** *Informal* make oneself ready to do what is required: *Please wait—I'm not organized yet.* **4** bring or form into a labour union: *to organize the workers in a factory.* **or·gan·iz·a·ble** *adj.* **or·gan·iz·er** *n.* **organized labour** or **labor** workers who belong to labour unions.

or·gasm ['ɔrgæzəm] *n* **1** the climax or culmination of sexual excitement. **2** an instance of frenzied excitement or behaviour. **or·gas·mic** *adj.* ⟨Greek *orgasmos; orgaein* swell⟩

or·gy ['ɔrdʒi] *n* **1** a wild, drunken, or licentious revelry. **2** something resembling an orgy in lack of control: *an orgy of killing.* **3** Usually, **orgies** *pl* secret ceremonies in the worship of certain Greek and Roman gods. **or·gi·as·tic** *adj.* **or·gi·as·ti·cal·ly** *adv.* ⟨Greek *orgia* secret rites⟩

o·ri·ent ['ɔriənt] *n* **1** the Orient the Far East. Compare OCCIDENT. **2** a pearl of great value. *v* ['ɔri,ɛnt] **1** put or build facing east. **2** place in a certain position: *The building is oriented north and south. She is oriented toward a career in business.* **3** find the direction or position of. **O·ri·en·tal** or **o·ri·en·tal** *adj, n.* ⟨Latin *oriri* rise; for rising sun⟩ **orient oneself** find the right relationship with one's surroundings: *It takes a while to orient yourself in a strange city.* **o·ri·en·ta·tion** *n* **1** the process of orienting or the state of being oriented. **2** a general tendency of interest: *Her orientation toward the dramatic shows clearly in her dress designs.* **or·i·en·teer** *v* find one's way through unfamiliar territory by means of a map or compass or both. **or·i·en·teer·ing** *n.*

or·i·fice ['ɔrəfɪs] *n* an opening, such as a mouth, or vent through which something may pass. ⟨Latin *oris* mouth + *facere* make⟩

or·i·ga·mi [,ɔrɪ'gæmi] *or* [,ɔrɪ'gami] *n* a paper sculpture developed by the Japanese. ⟨Japanese *ori* a folding + *gami* paper⟩

or·i·gin ['ɔrədʒɪn] *n* **1** the thing from which anything comes; source: *the origin of a quarrel.* **2** ancestry: *a person of humble origin. The word beef is of French origin.* **3** *Mathematics* the intersection of co-ordinate axes or planes. ⟨Latin *originis; oriri* rise⟩ **o·rig·i·nal** [ə'rɪdʒənəl] *adj* **1** first; earliest: *the original settlers.* **2** fresh and unusual: *a very original story.* **3** inventive. **4** not copied or translated from something else: *the original manuscript. n* **1** the first version from which something is copied or translated. **2** the language in which a book was first written: *She has read* War and Peace *in the original.* **3** an unusual or eccentric person. **o·rig·i·nal·i·ty** *n.* **o·rig·i·nal·ly** *adv.* **original sin** *Christian theology* the state of sin in which all human beings exist from conception because

of Adam's disobedience to the word of God.
o·rig·i·nate [ə'rɪdʒə,neɪt] v 1 cause to be;
invent. 2 come into being. **o·rig·i·na·tor** n.

Or·mazd ['ɔrmæzd] n the chief deity of
Zoroastrianism. ⟨ɔld Persian *auramazdah*. See
AHURA MAZDA.⟩

or·na·ment ['ɔrnəmənt] n 1 something used
to add beauty, esp a part that has no
particular function: *Vases are ornaments.* 2 a
person or an act, quality, etc. that adds
beauty, grace, or honour: *He was an ornament
to his time.* **or·na·ment** ['ɔrnə,mɛnt] v.
or·na·men·tal adj. **or·na·men·tal·i·ty** n.
or·na·men·tal·ly adv. **or·na·men·ta·tion** n.
⟨Latin *ornamentum; ornare* adorn⟩

or·nate [ɔr'neɪt] adj 1 much ornamented: *She
liked ornate furniture.* 2 characterized by the
use of elaborate figures of speech, flowery
language, etc.: *an ornate style of writing*
or·nate·ly adv. **or·nate·ness** n.

or·ner·y ['ɔrnəri] adj *Informal* having an
irritable or mean disposition: *an ornery horse.*
or·ner·i·ness n. ⟨contraction of *ordinary*⟩

or·ni·thol·o·gy [,ɔrnə'θɒlədʒi] n a branch of
zoology dealing with birds. ⟨Greek *ornithos*
bird⟩
or·ni·tho·log·i·cal adj. **or·ni·tho·log·i·cal·ly** adv.
or·ni·thol·o·gist n.

or·phan ['ɔrfən] n a child whose parents are
dead.
v make an orphan of. **or·phan** adj. ⟨Greek
orphanos bereaved⟩
or·phan·age n a home for orphans.

or·tho·cen·tre ['ɔrθə,sɛntər] n *Geometry* the
point at which the three altitudes of a
triangle intercept. ⟨Greek *orthos* straight +
CENTRE⟩

or·tho·don·tics [,ɔrθə'dɒntɪks] n (with a sg
verb) the branch of dentistry that deals with
adjusting irregular or crooked teeth.
or·tho·don·tic adj. **or·tho·don·tist** n. ⟨Greek
orthos straight + *odontos* tooth⟩

or·tho·dox ['ɔrθə,dɒks] adj 1 conforming to
established doctrine, esp in religion: *an
orthodox Muslim.* 2 conforming to custom:
The orthodox Thanksgiving dinner is turkey.
3 **Orthodox a** to do with the Eastern
Orthodox Church or any of its member
churches. **b** to do with the branch of Judaism
following most closely the ancient laws.
⟨Greek *orthos* straightt + *doxa* opinion⟩
or·tho·dox·y n the holding of generally
accepted beliefs; orthodox religious practice.

or·thog·o·nal [ɔr'θɒgənəl] adj *Mathematics*
to do with right angles. **or·thog·o·nal·ly** adv.
⟨Greek *orthos* right + *gōnia* angle⟩

or·thog·ra·phy [ɔr'θɒgrəfi] n 1 the
representation of the sounds of a language
by written symbols. 2 the art of using
standard spelling. 3 the study of letters and
spelling. ⟨Greek *orthos* right + *graphien* write⟩
or·tho·graph·ic [,ɔrθə'græfɪk] adj 1 to do with
orthography. 2 *Mathematics* having
perpendicular lines. **or·tho·graph·i·cal·ly** adv.
orthographic projection the two-dimensional
representation of a three-dimensional object.

or·tho·pe·dics [,ɔrθə'pidɪks] n (with a sg
verb) the branch of surgery that deals with
bones and joints. Also, **or·tho·pae·dics.**
or·tho·pe·dic adj. **or·tho·pe·dic surgeon** n.
⟨Greek *orthos* right + *paideia* childrearing⟩

or·thot·ics [ɔr'θɒtɪks] n the branch of
medicine dealing with the manufacture and
fitting of devices for the correction of
orthopedic problems (with a sg verb).
or·thot·ic n a device used to aid a foot or
other part which has some orthopedic
problem. **or·thot·ic** adj. ⟨Greek *orthos* straight⟩

–ory suffix 1 ——ing: *contradictory.* 2 to do
with——; to do with——ion: *advisory,
auditory.* 3 characterized by——ion: *adulatory.*
4 serving to——: *expiatory.* 5 tending to——;
inclined to——: *conciliatory.* 6 establishment
for——ing: *depository.* ⟨Latin *-orius, -orium*⟩

o·ryx ['ɔrɪks] n, pl **o·ryx·es** ['ɔrɪksəz] or (esp
collectively) **o·ryx** any of a genus of large
antelope having long, nearly straight horns.
⟨Greek = antelope, pickaxe; for its horns⟩

OS *Computers* OPERATING SYSTEM.

Os·car ['ɒskər] n a small statuette awarded
annually by the American Academy of
Motion Picture Arts and Sciences for the best
performances, photography, etc. during the
year. ⟨name of person it allegedly resembles⟩

os·cil·late ['ɒsə,leɪt] v 1 move to and fro
between two points. 2 vary between
opposing opinions, theories, etc. 3 *Physics*
vary regularly above and below a mean
value. **os·cil·la·tion** n. ⟨Latin *oscillum* swing, n⟩
os·cil·la·tor n a person or thing that
oscillates, esp a device for producing the
oscillations that give rise to an alternating
electric current. **os·cil·lo·scope** [ə'sɪlə,skoup]
n an instrument for representing wave
oscillations on the screen of a cathode-ray
tube.

os·cu·la·tion [,ɒskjə'leɪʃən] n 1 the act of
kissing. 2 a kiss. ⟨Latin *osculum* a kiss⟩

–ose¹ suffix forming adjectives: *verbose,
comatose.* ⟨Latin *-osus*⟩

–ose² suffix used to form chemical terms, esp
names of carbohydrates: *fructose.* ⟨French
-ose in *glucose*⟩

–osis combining form 1 denoting an act,
process, or condition: *osmosis.* 2 *Medicine*
denoting an abnormal or diseased condition:
neurosis. ⟨Greek⟩

os·mi·um ['ɒzmiəm] n a metallic element,
the heaviest metal known. *Symbol* Os ⟨Greek
osmē odour, for its pungent oxide⟩

os·mo·sis [ɒz'mousɪs] or [ɒs'mousɪs] n
1 *Physical chemistry* the tendency of a less
concentrated solution to pass through a
porous partition into a more concentrated
solution, until the concentration on each
side is the same. 2 *Informal* a process of
gradual absorption that suggests osmosis: *He
thought he could learn German by osmosis,
without taking a course.* **os·mot·ic** [ɒz'mɒtɪk]
or [ɒs'mɒtɪk] adj. **os·mot·i·cal·ly** adv. ⟨Greek
ōsmos a thrust⟩

os·prey ['ɒspri] *or* ['ɒsprei] *n* a large hawk that feeds on fish. 〈Latin *ossifraga; os* bone + *frangere* break〉

os·si·fy ['ɒsə,faɪ] *v* **1** become bone: *The soft parts of a baby's skull ossify as the baby grows older.* **2** make or become rigid, or very conservative: *The once free exchange of ideas among the group members had ossified into mere ritual.* **os·si·fi·ca·tion** *n.* 〈Latin *os* bone〉

os·su·ary ['ɒsju,ɛri] *or* ['ɒfju,ɛri] *n* an urn or other place to hold the bones of the dead.

os·ten·si·ble [ɒ'stɛnsəbəl] *adj* apparent; pretended: *The ostensible reason for her leaving was not the true one.* **os·ten·si·bly** *adv.* 〈Latin *ostendere,* show; *ob-* toward + *tendere* stretch〉

os·ten·ta·tion [,ɒstən'teɪʃən] *n* a showing off. **os·ten·ta·tious** *adj.* **os·ten·ta·tious·ly** *adv.* 〈Latin ostentare frequentative of *ostendere.* See OSTENSIBLE.〉

os·te·o·ar·thri·tis [,ɒstiouɑr'θraɪtɪs] *n Pathology* arthritis caused by joint and cartilage degeneration. 〈Greek *osteon* bone + ARTHRITIS〉

os·te·o·my·e·li·tis [,ɒstiou,maɪə'laɪtɪs] *n Pathology* inflammation of the bone or bone marrow. 〈Greek *osteon* bone + MYELITIS〉

os·te·op·a·thy [,ɒsti'ɒpəθi] *n* a system of medical practice based on the theory that many diseases can be treated by manipulating the bones and muscles. **os·te·o·path·ic** [,ɒstiə'pæθɪk], *adj.* **os·te·o·path·i·cal·ly** *adv.* 〈Greek *osteon* bone + *pathein* SUFFER〉 **os·te·o·path** ['ɒstiə,pæθ] *n* a person who practises osteopathy.

os·te·o·po·ro·sis [,ɒstioupə'rousɪs] *n* a bone condition common in older women, characterized by loss of bone mass and easily broken bones, owing to loss of calcium. 〈Greek *osteon* bone + PORE²+ -OSIS〉

os·tra·cize ['ɒstrə,saɪz] *v* **1** shut out from society, from favour, from privileges, etc. **2** in Ancient Greece, banish by popular vote, without a trial or formal accusation. **os·tra·cism** ['ɒstrə,sɪzəm] *n.* **os·tra·ciz·a·ble** *adj.* 〈Greek *ostrakon* tile used as a ballot〉

os·trich ['ɒstrɪtʃ] *n* **1** a flightless bird, the largest living bird, with showy tail plumes valued for ornamentation. **2** *Informal* a person who avoids facing an approaching danger (from the ostrich's supposed habit of burying its head in the sand to avoid oncoming danger). 〈Old French *ostrusce,* Latin *avis struthio;* Greek〉

oth·er ['ʌðər] *adj* **1** remaining: *The youngest boy is here, but the other boys are at school.* **2** additional or further: *I have no other books with me.* **3** not the same as one already mentioned: *Come some other day.* **4** different: *I would not have him other than he is.* *pron* **1** the other one: *Each praises the other.* **2** another person or thing: *There are others to be considered.* *adv* differently: *I can't do other than to go.* 〈Old English *ōther*〉 **every other** alternate: *every other day.* **no** or **none other than** no one less than: *The* presentation was made by none other than the prime minister. **other than** apart from; except for: *Other than you, no one knew.* **the other day** (**night,** etc.) recently.

other half a different stratum of society: *seeing how the other half lives.* **oth·er·ness** *n* the quality of being distinct, or special in nature, character, etc. **oth·er·wise** *adv* **1** differently: *I could not do otherwise.* **2** in other ways: *He is noisy, but otherwise a very nice boy.* **3** under other circumstances: *He reminded me of what I should otherwise have forgotten. adj* different: *It might have been otherwise. conj* or else; if not: *Come at once; otherwise you will be too late.* **other world** life after death. **oth·er·world·ly** *adj* **1** of or devoted to another world, such as the world of the mind, or the world to come. **2** supernatural; weird. **oth·er·world·li·ness** *n.*

o·ti·ose ['oufɪ,ous] *adj* **1** having no real function: *The essay was wordy and full of otiose comments.* **2** *Archaic* lazy. **o·ti·ose·ly** *adv.* **o·ti·os·i·ty** *n.* 〈Latin *otium* leisure〉

Ot·ta·wa ['ɒtə,wɒ] *or* ['ɒtəwə] *n, pl* -**was** or -**wa 1** the capital city of Canada. **2** See ODAWA.

ot·ter ['ɒtər] *n, pl* -**ters** or (esp collectively) -**ter** any of several water mammals of the weasel family. 〈Old English *oter*〉

ot·to·man ['ɒtəmən] *n* **1** a low seat without back or arms. **2** a cushioned footstool. 〈*Ottoman* Turk; Arabic *Othmani,* for ancestor *Othman*〉

oua·na·niche [,wɑnə'nɪʃ] *or* [,wɑnə'niʃ] *n, pl* -**niche ✳** a landlocked Atlantic salmon native to Lac St-Jean and some other freshwater lakes in Québec and Ontario. Compare KOKANEE. 〈Cdn. French; Montagnais *wananish* little salmon)〉

ou·bli·ette [,ubli'ɛt] *n* a secret dungeon having a trapdoor in the ceiling as its only entrance. 〈French; *oublier* forget〉

ouch [ʌutʃ] *interj* an exclamation expressing sudden pain. 〈imitative〉

ought [ɒt] *auxiliary verb Ought* is used with an infinitive to express: **1** duty or obligation: *You ought to obey your parents.* **2** rightness or appropriateness: *The theatre ought to allow children in free.* **3** a sensible course: *I ought to go before it rains.* **4** an expectation by others: *You ought to know better.* **5** likelihood: *The fastest one ought to win.* 〈Middle English *oughten; oughte* pt of *oughen* owe〉

ounce [auns] *n* **1** a non-metric unit for measuring mass, about 28 g. **2** a non-metric unit for measuring liquids, about 28 cm³. **3** a little bit: *an ounce of prevention.* 〈Latin *uncia* twelfth part〉

our [aur] *or* [ɑr] *adj* a possessive form of **we:** *our garden, our coats.* 〈Old English *ūre*〉 **ours** [aurz] *or* [ɑrz] *pron* a possessive form of **we:** *That car is ours.* **of ours** associated with us: *They're friends of ours.* **our·self** [aur'sɛlf] *or* [ɑr-] *pron* myself (when **we** is used as the subject instead of **I** as by a sovereign, writer, or judge): *"We shall ourself reward the victor,"* said the queen. **our·selves** [aur'sɛlvz] *or* [ɑr-]

pron pl **1** a reflexive pronoun, the form of **we** used as an object: *We cannot see ourselves as others see us.* **2** a form of **we** or **us** added for emphasis: *We ourselves are responsible for what happened.* **3** our usual selves: *We weren't ourselves when we let them get away with that.*

CONFUSABLES

Our is a determiner and is always followed by a noun: *This is our car.* **Ours** is a pronoun and stands alone: *This car is ours.*

–ous *adjective-forming suffix* **1** having; characterized by; like: *joyous, thunderous.* **2** *Chemistry* implying a larger proportion of the element indicated than *-ic* implies: *ferrous.* ⟨Latin *-osus*⟩

oust [ʌust] *v* force out. ⟨Anglo-French; Latin *obstare* block. See OBSTACLE.⟩
oust·er *n* the act of ousting.

out [ʌut] *adv* **1** away: *to rush out.* **2** not in or at a place, state, etc.: *out of fashion.* **3** into the open air: *He went out at noon.* **4** to or at an end: *to fight it out.* **5** from the usual place, condition, etc.: *Put the light out.* **6** into or in existence, activity, or outward manifestation: *Fever broke out.* **7** aloud; loudly: *Speak out.* **8** to others: *Give out the books.* **9** from among others: *Pick out an apple.* **10** in the wrong: *to be out in one's calculations.* **11** at a money loss of: *to be out ten dollars.* **12** *Baseball, etc.* not in play; no longer at bat or on base.
adj **1** not in possession or control: *The Liberals are out, the Conservatives are in.* **2** not in use, action, fashion, etc. **3** without money, supplies, etc.: *Have you any bread left? No, I'm right out.* **4** *Baseball, etc.* of a player or side, not allowed to continue in play. **5** of a homosexual, no longer secretive about his or her sexuality.
n **1** a defence or excuse: *to have an out for stealing.* **2** *Baseball* an instance of putting out or being put out.
prep out through: *He went out the door.*
v **1** *Archaic* go or come out: *Murder will out.* **2** disclose the homosexual orientation of. ⟨Old English *ūt*⟩
at outs or **on the outs** disagreeing: *to be on the outs with a friend.* **out and away** by far: *She is out and away the best player.* **out and out** thoroughly: *out and out discouraged.* **out back** outside and behind the house or other building: *The kids are playing out back.* **out for** looking for: *We have a holiday and are out for a good time.* **out of a** from inside: *He came out of the house.* **b** away from: *60 km out of Calgary.* **c** so as to take away: *She was cheated out of her money.* **d** from: *a dress made out of silk.* **e** from among: *We picked our puppy out of that litter.* **f** because of: *I went only out of curiosity.* **g** of animals, borne by (a female). **out of hand.** See HAND. **out to** eagerly or earnestly trying to: *Their team is out to make the finals.* **out West** ✱ in or to the Prairie Provinces of Canada, or British Columbia.
out·age *n* **1** a time of interrupted service, esp in the case of gas, electric, or water power. **2** an interruption or failure in service, function, or use. **out–and–out** *adj* thorough:

an out-and-out lie. **out·back** *n* **1** in Australia, the unsettled part of the interior; back country. Also, **Outback.** **2** any similarly unsettled area. **out·er** *adj* **1** of or on the outside: *The outer door is locked.* **2** farther from the centre: *the outer suburbs of the city.*
out·er·most *adj* farthest out. **outer space** space beyond the earth's atmosphere, where the moon, stars, and other planets are. **out·er–space** *adj.* **out·er·ware** *n* clothing intended to be seen. Compare UNDERWEAR. **out·ing** *n* a short pleasure trip. **out–of–the–way** *adj* remote; secluded: *an out-of-the-way cottage.* **out·ward** *adj* **1** going toward the outside: *an outward glance.* **2** outer: *to all outward appearances.* **3** on the surface: *an outward transformation.* *adv* **1** toward the outside. **2** on the outside: *He folded the coat with the lining outward.* Also ⟨*adv*⟩, **out·wards. out·ward·ly** *adv.*

out– *prefix* **1** outward; away; forth: *outflow, outburst.* **2** outside: *outbuilding.* **3** better, more, longer, etc. than: *outdo, outlast, outrun.*
Note: See OUT for words derived from idioms with **out** (e.g., **out–and–out**) or formed by adding a suffix to **out** (e.g., **outing**).
out·bal·ance *v* outweigh. **out·board** *adj, adv* **1** outside the hull of a boat. **2** away from the middle of a boat. **outboard motor** a portable engine with a propeller, mounted on the outside of the stern of a small boat. **out·bound** *adj* outward bound. **out·break** *n* **1** a sudden occurrence or increase: *an outbreak of flu.* **2** a riot. **out·build·ing** *n* a building built near a main building: *Barns are outbuildings on a farm.* **out·burst** *n* a bursting forth: *an outburst of laughter, anger, etc.* **out·cast** *n* a person or animal cast out from home and friends: *Criminals are outcasts of society.* **out·cast** *adj.* **out·class** *v* be much better than: *He is a good runner, but his younger brother definitely outclasses him.* **out·come** *n* a result or consequence: *the outcome of the election.* **out·crop** *n* part of a rock formation that comes to the surface of the earth: *This outcrop proved to be very rich in gold.* **out·cry** *n* a strong protest: *a public outcry against the four-lane highway.* **out·dat·ed** *adj* old-fashioned: *The coal-oil lamp is outdated.* **out·dis·tance** *v* leave behind: *She outdistanced all the other runners and won the race.* **out·do** *v* **-did, -done, -do·ing** do more or better than; surpass. **out·doors·y** *adj Informal* suited to or enjoying the outdoors. **the outdoors** *n* the open air (with sg verb): *We spend all summer in the outdoors.* **out·door** *adj.* **out·doors** *adv.* **out·face** *v* **1** face boldly; defy. **2** stare at (a person) until he or she stops staring back. **out·field** *n Baseball* **1** the part of the field beyond the infield. **2** the three players in the outfield. **out·field·er** *n.* **out·fit** *n* **1** a set of clothes to be worn together: *a summer outfit.* **2** a group or organization thought of as a single unit: *He worked for the same outfit for five years.* **3** all the equipment necessary for an undertaking: *a sailor's outfit, the outfit for a camping trip.* **4** ✱ a vehicle and its team, such as a sled and dogs. *v* **-fit·ted, -fit·ting 1** equip:

He outfitted himself for camp. **2** supply: *The whole family was outfitted with new coats last winter.* **out·fit·ter** *n* **1** a person or company that sells gear and supplies for wilderness expeditions. **2** ❋ the manager of such an expedition. **out·flank** *v* **1** go beyond the flank of (an opposing army, etc.). **2** get the better of: *They outflanked us and won the debate.* **out·flow** *n* a flowing out: *the outflow from a water pipe, an outflow of sympathy.* **out·fox** *v* outwit; outsmart. **out·go·ing** ['ʌut,gouɪŋ] *adj* **1** departing: *the outgoing mail.* **2** retiring from office: *the outgoing president.* **3** [,ʌut'gouɪŋ] friendly; sociable: *She is very outgoing and likes parties.* **out·grow** [,ʌut'grou] *v* **-grew, -grown, -grow·ing 1** grow too large for: *He's outgrown all his clothes.* **2** grow away from: *to outgrow early friendships.* **3** grow faster than: *She outgrew her twin sister. The population is outgrowing the food supply.* **out·growth** ['ʌut,grouθ] *n* **1** a natural development: *This business is an outgrowth of the little store started ten years ago.* **2** a thing that has grown out of something else: *A corn is an outgrowth on a toe.* **out·house** *n* a small building in a park, at a cottage, etc., housing a non-flush toilet. **out·land·er** ['ʌut,lændər] *n* **1** a foreigner; alien. **2** *Informal* any outsider or stranger. **out·land·ish** [,ʌut'lændɪʃ] *adj* strange or ridiculous. **out·law** *n* **1** a person outside the protection of the law. **2** a criminal. *v* **1** declare (a person) an outlaw. **2** make or declare (something) illegal: *We should outlaw war.* **out·lay** *n* money, energy, etc. spent: *a large outlay for clothing.* **out·let** ['ʌutlɪt] *n* **1** a way out: *the outlet of a lake, an outlet for one's energies.* **2** a market for a product. **3** a store selling the products of a certain manufacturer: *The shoe manufacturer had several retail outlets.* **4** a place in a wall, etc. for inserting an electric plug. **out·line** *n* **1** the line that shows the shape of an object: *the outlines of mountains against the evening sky.* **2** a drawing that gives only outer lines. **3** a general plan: *Make an outline before beginning to write an essay.* **in outline a** with only the outline shown. **b** with only the main points or features. **out·line** *v.* **out·live** *v* live or last longer than; survive: *That idea has outlived its usefulness.* **out·look** *n* **1** what seems likely to happen: *Look at those black clouds; the outlook for our picnic is not good.* **2** an attitude of mind: *a gloomy outlook on life.* **3** a high place to watch from. **4** what one sees on looking out: *The window has a pleasant outlook.* **out·ly·ing** *adj* lying outside the boundary; remote: *the outlying houses in the settlement.* **out·ma·noeu·vre** [-mə'nuvər] *v* **1** outwit. **2** surpass in being manoeuvrable: *This car can outmanoeuvre any other car of its size on the market.* **out·mod·ed** *adj* out-of-date. **out·num·ber** *v* be more than: *They outnumbered us three to one.* **out·pace** *v* **1** run faster than. **2** outdo. **out·pa·tient** *n* a patient being treated at a hospital or clinic but not staying there. **out·per·form** *v* perform better or longer than. **out·port** *n* ❋ *Newfoundland and Labrador esp formerly,* any harbour town

other than St. John's, the capital. **out·port·er** *n.* **out·post** *n* **1** a guard placed at some distance from an army or camp to prevent surprise attack. **2** a settlement in an outlying place: *an outpost in the North.* **out·pour·ing** *n* an uncontrolled expression of thoughts or feelings. **out·put** *n* **1** the amount produced: *the daily output of automobiles.* **2** a putting forth: *a sudden output of effort.* **3** *Computers* information produced from the storage unit. **out·rank** *v* rank higher than. **out·reach** ['ʌut,ritʃ] *n* the act or extent of reaching out, esp in terms of communicating with, serving, and exerting an influence in a community: *The social aid program has little outreach into the community.* *v* [,ʌut'ritʃ] exceed: *Her accomplishments far outreached those of her predecessors.* **out·rid·er** *n* a servant or attendant riding on a horse before or beside a carriage, wagon, etc. **out·rig·ger** *n* **1** a float, extending outward from the side of a light boat to prevent upsetting. **2** a boat or canoe with an outrigger. **out·right** *adv* **1** entirely; not gradually: *sell a thing outright.* **2** openly: *I laughed outright.* **3** on the spot: *She fainted outright.* *adj* **1** complete: *an outright loss.* **2** downright; direct: *an outright refusal.* **out·run** *v* **-ran, -run, -run·ning 1** run faster than. **2** go beyond: *Your story outruns the facts.* **out·sell** *v* **-sold, -sell·ing 1** outdo in selling. **2** exceed in the number of items sold: *His second novel outsold his first.* **out·set** *n* a beginning: *At the outset, it looked like a nice day.* **out·shine** *v* **-shone, -shin·ing 1** shine longer or more brightly than. **2** surpass. **out·side** ['ʌut'saɪd] *or* ['ʌut,saɪd] *n* **1** the side or surface away from the centre or inside: *The coat is blue on the outside and grey on the inside.* **2** the external appearance: *You can't tell a person's character by looking at the outside.* **3** ❋ *North* the more southerly, settled parts of Canada. *adj* **1** forming the outer part: *the outside leaves of a cabbage.* **2** not belonging to a certain group, set, district, etc.: *Outside people tried to get control of the business.* **3** being or coming from beyond a wall, boundary, etc.: *Outside noises disturbed the class.* **4** maximum: *an outside estimate.* **5** of a possibility, slight: *an outside chance of winning.* *adv* **1** on or to the outside. **2** outdoors. *prep* beyond the limits of: *Stay outside the yard.* **at the outside** at the most: *It will take me a week at the outside.* **outside in** so that what should be outside is inside. **outside of** *Informal* with the exception of: *Outside of my aunt, none of us liked the play.* **out·sid·er** *n* **1** a person who does not belong to a particular group, company, party, etc. **2** ❋ a person who does not live in the North: *The people of Whitehorse call the people of Edmonton outsiders.* **3** a person, horse, etc. believed to have no chance of winning a competition. **out·size** *adj* larger than the usual size. **out·skirts** *n pl* the outer parts or edges of a town, district, etc. **out·smart** *v Informal* outdo in cleverness. **out·sourc·ing** *n* the practice of contracting the equipment and expertise of another organization to get work done. **out·spo·ken** *adj* frank: *outspoken criticism.* **out·spo·ken·ness** *n.* **out·spread** ['ʌut,sprɛd] *adj* extended: *outspread wings.* *v* [ˌʌut'sprɛd] **-spread, -spread·ing** to spread out. **out·stand·ing** *adj* **1** excellent: *an outstanding performance.* **2** important; striking: *one of the most outstanding events of this century.* **3** yet to be dealt with: *outstanding debts, outstanding orders.* **out·stand·ing·ly** *adv.* **out·stretch** [ˌʌut'strɛtʃ] *v* extend; reach out. **out·stretched** ['ʌut,strɛtʃt] *adj.* **out·strip** *v* **-stripped, -strip·ping 1** go faster than. **2** do better than. **out·take** *n* part of a film that is discarded and does not appear in the finished film. **out·vote** *v* defeat in a vote. **out·wear** *v* **-wore, -worn, -wear·ing 1** wear longer than. **2** wear out. **out·weigh** *v* exceed in weight, importance, influence, etc.: *The disadvantages outweigh the advantages.* **out·wit** *v* **-wit·ted, -wit·ting** be too clever for: *The prisoner outwitted the guards and escaped.* **out·worn** *adj* **1** worn out. **2** out-of-date.

SYNONYMS
Outline applies to the line marking the edge of a shape: *We could see the outline of a man.* **Contour** emphasizes the shape shown by the outline: *The contours of her face are delicate.* **Profile** applies to the side view of something: *You would stand up straight if you could see your profile when you slouch.*

out·rage ['ʌutreidʒ] *n* **1** an overturning of the rights of others by force; a grave insult or offence. **2** the shocked, angry feeling aroused by this.
v ['ʌutreidʒ] *or* [ˌʌut'reidʒ] offend very greatly by insult or injustice. ⟨Old French *outrage*; Latin *ultra* beyond⟩
out·ra·geous [ʌut'reidʒəs] *adj* shocking; very offensive. **out·ra·geous·ness** *n.*

ou·tré [u'trei] *adj* passing the bounds of what is usual; eccentric; bizarre. ⟨French *outrer* exaggerate; Latin *ultra* beyond⟩

ou·zo ['uzou] *n* a strong, colourless, Greek alcoholic liquor flavoured with aniseed. ⟨Greek *ouzon*⟩

o·va ['ouvə] *n* pl of OVUM.

o·va·ry *n* **1** *Anatomy, zoology* in female animals, the reproductive organ that produces the egg cells. **2** *Botany* in a seed-bearing plant, the part that contains the young seeds, called ovules. **o·var·i·an** *adj* .

o·val ['ouvəl] *adj* egg-shaped.
n something having an oval shape.
o·val·ly *adv.* ⟨Latin *ovum* egg⟩

o·va·tion [ou'veiʃən] *n* an enthusiastic public welcome; burst of applause. ⟨Latin *ovare* rejoice⟩

ov·en ['ʌvən] *n* **1** a space in a stove for baking food. **2** a small furnace for heating or drying. ⟨Old English *ofen*⟩
ov·en·proof *adj* able to stand the heat of an oven without cracking. **ov·en·ware** *n* dishes made to be ovenproof.

o·ver ['ouvər] *prep* **1** above in place or position: *the roof over one's head.* **2** above in authority, power, etc.: *We have a captain over*

us. **3** above and to the other side of: *to leap over a wall.* **4** on the other side of: *lands over the sea.* **5** more than: *It costs over ten dollars.* **6** in the course of: *over many years.* **7** about; because of: *He is very upset over the whole thing. They are fighting over chores again.*
adv **1** above: *The cliff hung over.* **2** so as to cover or affect a whole area: *Cover the tar over with sand until it has hardened. She travels all over.* **3** to or at some distance away: *He's over at the school. Let's go over to the community centre.* **4** to another; out of one's possession: *Hand the money over.* **5** down: *The ball went too near the edge and rolled over.* **6** again; afresh: *to start over. You'll have to do that assignment over.* **7** in excess: *He bought a coffee and still had fifty cents over. Shorten your essay, it's two pages over.* **8** from beginning to end: *Read this over and tell me what you think.* **9** so that what was at the top is at the bottom: *Turn the box over. It flipped over.*
adj **1** top: *the over crust of a pie.* **2** ended: *The play is over.*
n excess; extra. ⟨Old English *ofer*⟩
over again once more: *Let's do that over again.* **over against a** opposite to; in front of. **b** so as to bring out a contrast with. **over and above** besides. **over and over** again and again. **over (and done) with** *Informal* finished: *Let's get this over with today.* **think something over** think about something at length with a view to making a decision.
o·ver·age ['ouvərɪdʒ] *n* a surplus or extra amount, as of goods. **o·ver–the–count·er** *adj* of medicines, sold without a prescription.

o·ver– *prefix* **1** too much; too long, etc.: *overcrowded.* **2** extra: *oversize.* **3** above, across, or beyond: *overflow, overseas, overlord.* **4** so as to bring down or invert: *overthrow, overturn.*
o·ver·a·chieve *v* perform better than required. **o·ver·a·chieve·ment** *n.* **o·ver·a·chiev·er** *n.*
o·ver·act *v* act (a part) in an exaggerated way.
o·ver·age [ˌouvər'eidʒ] *adj* above a specified age limit. **o·ver·all** ['ouvər'ɒl] *adj* including all parts; total: *an overall estimate. adv* **1** as a whole; generally: *Overall, it was a successful meeting.* **2** in total: *It'll cost you $240 overall.*
o·ver·alls ['ouvər,ɒls] *n pl* a long-sleeved, one-piece garment that incorporates top and pants, worn over other clothes to keep them clean. Also called **cov·er·alls. o·ver·arm** *adj, adv* with the arm raised above the shoulder: *to throw overarm.* **o·ver·awe** *v* overcome with awe: *She was overawed by the grandeur of the estate.* **o·ver·bal·ance** *v* **1** lose, or cause to lose, balance: *He overbalanced and fell.* **2** outweigh: *The gains overbalanced the losses.*
o·ver·bear *v* **-bore, -borne, -bear·ing** overcome by weight or force: *His father overbore his objections.* **o·ver·bear·ing** *adj* **1** forcing others to one's own will. **2** of supreme importance. **o·ver·bear·ing·ly** *adv.* **o·ver·bite** *n Dentistry* a condition in which the upper front teeth project over the lower ones. **o·ver·blown** *adj* **1** pretentious: *Her speech was filled with flowery, overblown sentiments.* **2** of a flower, too fully open: *Petals dropped from the overblown rose.*

o·ver·board *adv* from a boat into the water: *He fell overboard.* **go overboard** go too far in an effort because of extreme enthusiasm: *She went overboard and bought more than she needed.* **throw overboard** get rid of: *We had to throw all our plans overboard and start again.* **o·ver·book** *v* issue reservations for (a flight, performance, etc.) to more people than there is room for. **o·ver·bur·den** *v* overload. **o·ver·cast** *adj* **1** cloudy; gloomy: *The sky was overcast before the storm.* **2** sad: *Her face was overcast.* *v* **-cast, -cast·ing** cover or be covered with clouds or darkness. *n* mist or cloud cover. **o·ver·charge** [ˌouvər'tʃɑrdʒ] *v* **1** charge too high a price. **2** load too heavily: *The battery was overcharged.* **o·ver·charge** *n*. **o·ver·coat** *n* a coat worn for warmth over regular clothing. **o·ver·come** *v* **-came, -come, -com·ing 1** get the better of; defeat: *to overcome an enemy, all difficulties.* **2** make weak: *to overcome by weariness.* **3** confuse: *The girl was so overcome by the noise that she couldn't speak.* **o·ver·com·pen·sate** *v* go too far in trying to make up for a feeling of inferiority: *She overcompensated for her shyness at the party by insulting half the guests.* **o·ver·com·pen·sa·tion** *n*. **o·ver·cor·rect** *v* **1** go too far in correcting so as to result in the opposite error, as in steering a car. **2** form an incorrect usage from trying too hard to avoid an error. *Example*: for you and I *instead of* for you and me. **o·ver·cor·rec·tion** *n*. **o·ver·do** *v* **-did, -done, -do·ing 1** attempt too much: *She overdoes exercise.* **2** exaggerate: *The funny scenes in the play were overdone.* **3** overcook: *Don't overdo the roast.* **4** exhaust; tire. **o·ver·done** *adj* cooked too much. **o·ver·dose** ['ouvər,dous] *n* too big a dose. *v* [ˌouvər'dous] *or* ['ouvər,dous] **1** give too large a dose to. **2** take too large a dose. **o·ver·draft** an overdrawing of a bank account. **o·ver·draw** *v* **-drew, -drawn, -draw·ing 1** draw from (a bank account) more money than is in it. **2** exaggerate: *The characters in the book were greatly overdrawn.* **o·ver·dress** *v* dress too elaborately or too warmly. **o·ver·drive** *n* an arrangement of gears that reduces the power required to maintain a desired speed. **o·ver·due** *adj* **1** late arriving: *The plane is overdue.* **2** due but not paid: *an overdue bill.* **o·ver·es·ti·mate** [-meit] *v* estimate at too high a value, amount, etc. *n* [-mɪt] an estimate that is too high. **o·ver·es·ti·ma·tion** *n*. **o·ver·ex·cite** *v* excite too much. **o·ver·ex·cit·a·ble** *adj*. **o·ver·ex·cite·ment** *n*. **o·ver·ex·ert** *v* put forth too much effort (usually with reflexive pronoun): *He hurt his back when he overexerted himself in gymnastics.* **o·ver·ex·er·tion** *n*. **o·ver·ex·pose** *v* **1** expose to too much light or radiation: *to overexpose a film.* **2** show to the public too often: *She is overexposed in this movie.* **o·ver·ex·po·sure** *n*. **o·ver·ex·tend** *v* commit (oneself) beyond what one can pay, do, etc. **o·ver·fill** [ˌouvər'fɪl] *v* fill too full. **o·ver·fish** *v* take too many fish from: *If you overfish these waters, the fisheries will close.* **o·ver·flow** [ˌouvər'flou] *v* **1** flow over the bounds (of): *The water*

overflowed the tub. **2** have the contents flowing over: *The bucket overflowed.* **3** be very abundant. **o·ver·flow** ['ouvər,flou]   *n*. **o·ver·grown** [ˌouvər'groun] *adj* **1** grown too big: *an overgrown tree.* **2** covered by growing vegetation: *The wall is overgrown with ivy.* **o·ver·growth** ['ouvər,grouθ] *n*. **o·ver·hand** *adj* done or made with the hand brought forward and down from above the shoulder. **o·ver·hand** *adv*. **o·ver·hang** [ˌouvər'hæŋ] *v* **-hung, -hang·ing 1** project over: *Trees overhang the street to form an arch of branches.* **2** threaten: *The threat of an invasion overhung the city.* *n* ['ouvər,hæŋ] something that projects: *the overhang of the roof.* **o·ver·haul** *v* [ˌouvər'hɒl] examine thoroughly so as to make any needed repairs. **o·ver·haul** ['ouvər,hɒl]   *n*.   **o·ver·head** *adv, adj* ['ouvər'hɛd] above one's head: *the stars shining overhead. Watch out for the overhead wires.* *n* ['ouvər,hed] general expenses of running a business, such as rent, lighting, etc. **o·ver·hear** *v* **-heard, -hear·ing** hear when one is not supposed to. **o·ver·in·dulge** *v* indulge to excess. **o·ver·in·dul·gent** *adj*. **o·ver·joyed** *adj* filled with great joy. **o·ver·kill** *n* **1** a capacity for destruction in excess of that required to destroy a target or enemy. **2** *Informal* the act of overdoing something. **o·ver·land** *adv, adj* on land; by land: *You cannot travel overland from Halifax to St. John's.* **o·ver·lap** *v* **-lapped, -lap·ping** place or be placed so that one piece covers part of the next. **o·ver·lap** ['ouvər,læp] *n*. **o·ver·lay** [ˌouvər'lei] *v* **-laid, -lay·ing 1** lay or place (one thing) over or upon (another). **2** cover with an ornamental layer of something: *overlaid with gold.* **o·ver·lay** ['ouvər,lei] *n*. **o·ver·leaf** *adj, adv* on the other side of the page. **o·ver·load** [ˌouvər'loud] *v* load too heavily. **o·ver·load** ['ouvər,loud] *n*. **o·ver·look** *v* **1** fail to see: *Here are the letters you overlooked.* **2** pay no attention to: *Her boss said he would overlook the mistake.* **3** have a view of from above: *This high window overlooks half the city.* **o·ver·lord** *n* a person who is lord over other lords: *The duke was the overlord of knights who held land from him.* **o·ver·ly** *adv* excessively; too: *overly sensitive to criticism.* **o·ver·much** *adj, adv* too much. *n* too great an amount. **o·ver·nice** *adj* too particular. **o·ver·nice·ness** *n*. **o·ver·night** ['ouvər'nəit] *adv* **1** for one night: *to stay overnight.* **2** immediately: *Change will not come overnight. adj* **1** done, occurring, etc. from one day to the next: *an overnight stop.* **2** for use for one night: *an overnight bag.* **3** immediate; sudden. *v* stay overnight: *Since it was late, we decided to overnight in Calgary before moving on to Victoria in the morning.* **o·ver·pass** *n* a bridge over a road, railway, canal, etc. **o·ver·play** *v* **1** play (a part, etc.) in an exaggerated way. **2** overestimate the strength of (one's position, etc.). **overplay one's hand a** *Cards* be too confident in the hand one has been dealt. **b** try too hard. **o·ver·pop·u·late** *v* permit or cause (a city, region, etc.) to become too densely populated. **o·ver·pop·u·la·tion** *n*.

o·ver·pow·er *v* **1** overcome: *to overpower one's enemies.* **2** be so much greater than, that nothing else is felt, heard, etc.: *Sudden anger overpowered every other feeling.* **o·ver·pow·er·ing·ly** *adv.* **o·ver·price** *v* set too high a price on. **o·ver·pro·tect** *v* exercise more control than is necessary in trying to protect from hurt: *an overprotected child.* **o·ver·pro·tec·tive** *adj.* **o·ver·qual·i·fied** *adj* having more education, training, or experience than a job calls for. **o·ver·rate** *v* estimate too highly: *The movie was overrated; it was not very good.* **o·ver·reach** *v* **1** reach over or beyond. **2** reach too far. **overreach oneself a** fail by attempting too much: *In trying to make peace between the two friends, she overreached herself.* **b** fail by being too tricky. **o·ver·re·act** *v* react too strongly and unreasonably. **o·ver·re·ac·tion** *n.* **o·ver·ride** [,ouvər'raɪd] *v* **-rode,** **-rid·den,** **-rid·ing 1** act in spite of: *to override advice.* **2** prevail over or negate (something done earlier): *The new regulation overrides all previous ones. n* ['ouvər,raɪd] an instance of overriding: *a price override on the cash register.* **o·ver·rule** *v* **1** decide authoritatively against (an argument, etc.): *The president overruled my plan.* **2** prevail over: *The majority overruled me.* **o·ver·run** [,ouvər'rʌn] *v* **-ran, -run, -run·ning** *v* **1** spread over rapidly or in great numbers: *Weeds had overrun the old garden.* **2** invade and conquer: *Enemy troops overran most of the country.* **3** exceed: *The speaker overran the time set for him. n* ['ouvər,rʌn] **1** a balance or surplus; an excess. **2** the amount of money by which a cost exceeds estimates. **o·ver·saw** *v* pt of OVERSEE. **o·ver·seas** ['ouvər'siz] *adv* to, in, or relating to countries across the sea: *to travel overseas, to increase overseas trade.* **o·ver·see** [,ouvər'si] *v* **-saw, -seen, -see·ing** look after and direct (work or workers). **o·ver·se·er** ['ouvər,siər] *n* **1** a person who oversees the work of others. **2 ✲** in certain provinces, the head of a township council. **o·ver·sexed** *adj* having excessive sexual desire or capacity. **o·ver·shad·ow** *v* **1** be or appear more important than: *The boy overshadowed his brother as a skater.* **2** cast a shadow over. **o·ver·shoe** *n* a waterproof shoe or boot worn over another shoe to keep the foot dry. **o·ver·shoot** [,ouvər'ʃut] *v* **-shot, -shoot·ing 1** of an aircraft, pass beyond the limit of (the runway or landing field) when trying to land. **2** shoot or go beyond (the target, limit, etc.). **overshoot the mark** do too much. **o·ver·shot** ['ouvər,ʃɒt] *adj* of the upper jaw, projecting beyond the lower. **o·ver·sight** *n* a failure to notice something: *Through an oversight, the bill was not paid.* **o·ver·sim·pli·fy** *v* simplify to the point of distortion: *She has oversimplified the problem; there are factors she did not even consider.* **o·ver·sim·pli·fi·ca·tion** *n.* **o·ver·size** *adj* **1** larger than the usual size. **2** too big: *an oversize sweater.* **o·ver·sleep** *v* **-slept, -sleep·ing** sleep beyond the time set for waking. **o·ver·spend** *v* **-spent, -spend·ing** spend extravagantly. **o·ver·state** *v* exaggerate. **o·ver·state·ment** *n.*

o·ver·stay *v* stay beyond the limits of: *to overstay one's welcome.* **o·ver·step** *v* **-stepped, -step·ping** exceed: *She overstepped the limits of politeness by asking personal questions.* **o·ver·stock** *v* stock or supply with more than is needed: *Stores often have sales when they're overstocked.* **o·ver·stuff** *v* stuff more than is necessary. **o·ver·stuffed** *adj* of furniture, having very thick stuffing: *a large, comfortable, overstuffed armchair.* **o·ver·take** *v* **-took, -tak·en, -tak·ing 1** catch up to: *If you hurry, you might be able to overtake her before she reaches her car.* **2** catch up with and pass: *They overtook us and arrived before we did.* **3** come upon suddenly: *A storm overtook the children.* **o·ver·tax** *v* **1** tax too heavily. **2** put too heavy a burden on. **o·ver·tax·a·tion** *n.* **o·ver·throw** [,ouvər'θrou] *v* **-threw, -thrown, -throw·ing 1** defeat: *to overthrow a government.* **2** put an end to: *to overthrow slavery. n* ['ouvər,θrou] a defeat; upset: *the overthrow of one's plans.* **o·ver·time** *n* **1** extra time; time beyond the regular hours. **2** wages for this period: *They don't pay overtime.* **3** *Sports* a period or periods beyond the normal game time. *adv* **1** beyond the regular hours: *She worked overtime.* **2** beyond the allotted or permitted time. *adj* **1** of or for overtime: *overtime work.* **2** being beyond the allotted time: *overtime parking.* **o·ver·tone** *n* **1** *Music* a harmonic. **2** a hint of something felt, believed, etc.: *an overtone of anger.* **o·ver·turn** *v* **1** turn over; upset: *The boat overturned.* **2** overthrow; destroy the power of: *The rebel forces overturned the government.* **o·ver·view** *n* a brief, general survey; a look at the main points. **o·ver·ween·ing** *adj* thinking too much of oneself; arrogant; presumptuous. **o·ver·ween·ing·ly** *adv.* **o·ver·weight** *adj* **1** of a person or animal, having a mass that is too great in proportion to build. **2** having a greater mass than allowed: *overweight baggage.* **o·ver·whelm** [-'wɛlm] *v* **1** overcome completely; crush: *to overwhelm with grief.* **2** cover completely as a flood would: *A wave overwhelmed the boat.* **o·ver·whelm·ing** *adj.* **o·ver·wind** [-'waɪnd] *v* **-wound, -wind·ing** wind (a clock or watch) too tightly. **o·ver·win·ter** *v* spend the winter (in a place). **o·ver·work** *v* **1** work or cause to work too hard or too long: *Don't overwork or you'll have a heart attack. She overworks her employees.* **2** *Informal* use too much or too often: *to overwork a pose of childlike innocence.* **3** develop at too great length; belabour: *to overwork an argument.* **o·ver·work** *n.* **o·ver·wrought** [-'rɒt] *adj* exhausted by too much excitement, grief, anxiety, etc.: *overwrought nerves.*

o·vert [ou'vɜrt] *or* ['ouvərt] *adj* open; not hidden: *Hitting someone is an overt act.* **o·vert·ly** [ou'vɜrtli] *adv.* ⟨Old French, pp of *ovrir* open; Latin *aperire*⟩

o·ver·ture ['ouvərtʃər] *n* **1** an introductory proposal (usually in the plural): *overtures for peace.* **2** *Music* a composition played as an introduction to an opera, oratorio, etc. ⟨Old French; Latin *apertura* opening.⟩

o·vi·duct, o·vi·form, etc. See OVUM.

o·vine ['ouvaɪn] *or* ['ouvɪn] *adj* to do with sheep. ⟨Latin *ovis* sheep⟩

o·vum ['ouvəm] *n, pl* **o·va** ['ouvə] the mature female reproductive cell produced by the ovary of a plant or animal. ⟨Latin = egg⟩ **o·vi·duct** *n* the tube through which the ovum, or egg, passes from the ovary. **o·vi·form** *adj* egg-shaped. **o·vip·a·rous** [ou'vɪpərəs] *adj* producing eggs that hatch outside the body, as birds do. Compare OVOVIVIPAROUS. **o·vi·pos·i·tor** [ˌouvə'pɒzɪtər] *n* an organ of certain insects, by which eggs are deposited. **o·void** *n* an egg-shaped object. **o·void** *adj.* **o·vo·vi·vi·par·ous** [ˌouvəvə'vɪpərəs] *adj* producing eggs that hatch in the body, as some fish, reptiles, and amphibians do. **ov·u·late** ['ɒvjə,leit] *or* ['ouvjə,leit] *v* produce an ovum. **ov·u·la·tion** *n.* **ov·ule** ['ɒʌjul] *or* ['ouvjul] *n* **1** *Biology* a small ovum, esp one in an early stage of growth. **2** *Botany* the part of a plant that develops into a seed.

owe [ou] *v* **1** have to pay: *I owe you $10.* **2** be obliged or indebted to or for. **3** be obliged to offer: *We owe friends our trust.* ⟨Old English *āgan*⟩ **ow·ing** *adj* due; owed: *to pay what is owing.* **owing to** because of: *The ball game was called off owing to rain.*

owl [aʊl] *n* any of an order of birds of prey having big eyes set in the front of the head. Most owls are active at night. **owl–like** *adj.* ⟨Old English *ūle*⟩ **owl·et** *n* **1** a young owl. **2** a small owl. **owl·ish** *adj* like an owl, esp in having large eyes or a seemingly wise expression: *an owlish look.* **owl·ish·ness** *n.*

own [oun] *adj* belonging to oneself or itself: *We have our own troubles.* *v* **1** possess: *She owns much land.* **2** admit, confess; acknowledge: *He owned his guilt.* *n* the one or ones belonging to oneself or itself. **own·er** *n.* **own·er·less** *adj.* **own·er·ship** *n.* ⟨Old English *āgen* orig pp of *āgan* owe⟩ **come into one's own** get the success or credit that one deserves. **get one's own back** get revenge. **hold one's own** not be forced back. **of one's own** belonging to oneself. **on one's own a** on one's own account, resources, etc. **b** alone: *The baby should never be left on her own.* **c** single: *Now she's divorced and on her own.* **own up (to)**, confess; admit: *The prisoner owned up to the crime.*

ox [ɒks] *n, pl* **ox·en** [ɒksən] a full-grown, castrated male of cattle. Compare STEER². **ox·like** *adj.* ⟨Old English *oxa*⟩ **ox·bow** ['ɒks,bou] *n* **1** a U-shaped frame that forms part of a yoke for an ox. **2** a U-shaped bend in a river. **oxbow lake** a lake which was part of an oxbow but which became a separated body of water when the river straightened its course. **ox·tail** *n* the tail of a cow, ox, or steer, cut up to make food.

ox·y·gen ['ɒksɪdʒən] *n* a gas that is the most abundant of all elements. *Symbol* **O** **ox·y·gen·ic** [-'dʒɛnɪk] *or* **ox·yg·e·nous** [ɒk'sɪdʒənəs] *adj.* ⟨French *oxygène*, intended as 'acidifying (principle)' Greek *oxys* sharp (acidic) + *-genēs* See -GEN.⟩ **ox·i·dant** *n* any reagent that oxidizes. **ox·i·da·tion** [ˌɒksə'deiʃən] *n.* **ox·ide** ['ɒksaɪd] *n* a compound of oxygen with another element. **ox·i·dize 1** combine with oxygen. **2** rust. **ox·y·a·cet·y·lene** [ˌɒksi'sɛtə,lin] *adj* to do with a mixture of oxygen and acetylene. **ox·y·gen·ate** *v* treat, combine, or supply with oxygen: *to oxygenate the blood.* **ox·y·gen·a·tion** *n.* **ox·y·gen·a·tor** *n.* **oxygen mask** a device worn over the nose and mouth through which oxygen is supplied. **oxygen tent** a plastic tent that can be placed over the head of a patient to provide a flow of oxygen.

ox·y·mo·ron [ˌɒksə'mɔrɒn] *n, pl* **-mo·ra** [-'mɔrə] a figure of speech in which contradictory words are placed together. *Example: Avoid accidents by making haste slowly.* **ox·y·mo·ron·ic** *adj.* ⟨Greek pointedly stupid; *oxys* sharp + *mōros* stupid⟩

oys·ter ['ɔɪstər] *n* **1** any of a family of bivalve molluscs having a rough shell; especially, any edible species. **2** something from which to take or derive advantage: *The world is her oyster.* ⟨Old French *oistre*; Greek *ostreon*⟩ **oyster bed** a place where oysters breed or are cultivated.

o·zone ['ouzoun] *n* a form of oxygen consisting of molecules composed of three atoms instead of the usual two, produced by electricity and present in the air, especially after a thunderstorm. *Symbol* O_3 ⟨Greek *ozein* smell + French *-one*, chemical suffix⟩ **o·zo·no·sphere** [ou'zounə,sfir] *n* a region of the upper stratosphere containing a high concentration of ozone that protects earth from excessive ultraviolet radiation from the sun. Also called **ozone layer**.

Pp

p or **P** [pi] *n, pl* **p's** or **P's 1** the sixteenth letter of the English alphabet, or any speech sound represented by it. **2** the sixteenth person or thing in a series.
mind one's p's and q's be careful about what one says or does.

p 1 *Music* piano (softly). **2** pico- (an SI prefix).

P.A. 1 PUBLIC ADDRESS (SYSTEM). **2** PRESS AGENT. **3** personal assistant.

Pab·lum ['pæbləm] *n Trademark* ✱ a type of soft, bland, cooked cereal food for infants. ⟨Latin *pabulum* fodder⟩

pace [peis] *n* **1** rate of movement: *a fast pace in walking.* **2** a step. **3** the length of a step in walking, used as a unit for measuring, about 76 cm. **4** a particular gait of some horses in which both legs on one side are raised at the same time.
v **1** set the pace for. **2** walk with regular steps. **3** measure by paces: *We paced off the distance.* **4** control the rate of progress of: *Pace yourself.* ⟨Latin *passus* step⟩
change of pace variation in tempo, mood, etc. **go through one's paces** show off one's abilities. **keep pace with** keep up with. **put someone through his or her paces** find out what someone can do. **set the pace a** set a speed for others to keep up with. **b** be an example or model for others to follow.
pace·mak·er *n Medicine* an electrical device for stimulating the heartbeat. **pace·set·ter** *n* a person leading the way in fashion, ideas, etc.

pach·y·derm ['pækə,dɜrm] *n* any of several thick-skinned, hoofed mammals, such as the elephant or rhinoceros. **pach·y·der·mal** *adj.* ⟨Greek *pachys* thick + *derma* skin⟩

pa·cif·ic [pə'sɪfɪk] *adj* **1** tending to make peace. **2** not warlike: *a pacific nation.* **3** peaceful; quiet: *a pacific nature.* **4 Pacific** to do with the Pacific Ocean: *a Pacific storm.* **pa·cif·i·cal·ly** *adv.* ⟨Latin *pacificus; pacis* peace + *facere* make⟩
Pacific Coast that part of Canada that borders the Pacific Ocean, esp British Columbia. **Pacific dogwood** a tree bearing green flowers surrounded by white petal-like bracts. It is the provincial flower of British Columbia. **Pacific Rim** the coastal areas and countries bordering the Pacific Ocean. **pac·i·fi·er** *n* a rubber nipple or ring given to a baby to suck. **pac·i·fism** *n* opposition to war or violence as a way of settling disputes. **pac·i·fist** *adj, n.* **pac·i·fis·tic** *adj.* **pac·i·fis·ti·cal·ly** *adv.* **pac·i·fy** *v* **1** quiet down: *Can't you pacify that screaming baby?* **2** reduce the anger of; make peace with. **pac·i·fi·ca·tion** *n.*

pack [pæk] *n* **1** a bundle of things wrapped together for carrying. **2** a set: *a pack of thieves, a pack of lies.* **3** a number of animals hunting together: *a pack of wolves.* **4** a package containing a standard number: *a six-pack of beer.* **5** backpack.
v **1** put together in a bundle, etc.: *Pack your clothes in this bag.* **2** crowd closely together: *We were packed into one small room.* **3** press together: *The heavy trucks packed the snow on the highway.* **4** put into a container to be sold: *Vegetables are often packed in cans.* **5** load (an animal) with a pack. **6** carry in a pack, on a pack animal, etc.: *He packed his supplies into the bush.* **7** protect with closely applied materials: *The fish was packed in ice.* **8** arrange unfairly. To pack a jury is to fill it unfairly with those who will favour one side.
adj trained to carry goods: *a pack dog.* **pack·a·ble** *adj.* ⟨Middle English *packe*⟩
pack it in give up an activity: *They packed it in for the day.* **pack off** send away: *The child was packed off to bed.* **pack up** *Informal* **a** stop working; cease operating; fail: *One of the aircraft's engines packed up.* **b** assemble one's things in preparation for leaving. **send packing** send away abruptly.
pack·age *n* **1** a bundle of things wrapped together; a parcel. **2** a receptacle for packing goods, printed with matter intended both to identify it and to attract buyers. **3** a finished product contained in a unit ready for immediate use: *a computer package.* **4** a group of goods, services, laws, etc., as an indivisible unit: *Our holiday package includes hotel and meals.* **5** *Computers* software and related materials sold as a unit: *a word-processing package.* *v* put in a package. **pack·ag·ing** *n.*
package deal a bargain in which a number of items are presented as a single offer. **package tour** an arrangement for a holiday including airfare, hotel, activities, etc. **pack animal** an animal used for carrying loads. **pack·er** *n* **1** a person or company whose business is packing meat, fruit, etc.: *a meat packer.* **2** someone who carries goods on a pack animal or on his or her own back. **3** someone who packs goods in a store or warehouse, after purchase. **4** a person who transports goods to remote places by vehicle. **pack·et** *n* **1** a small package. **2** *Informal* a lot of money. **packet boat** a boat that carries mail, passengers, and goods regularly on a fixed route. **pack ice** ice pushed by wind or current into a solid mass. **pack·ing** *n* **1** material used to pack or to make watertight, etc.: *the packing around the valves of a radiator.* **2** sterilized material used to fill a wound to allow drainage and prevent closure. *adj* of snow, of such consistency that it packs and binds together easily. **packing house** (or **plant**) a place where meat, fruit, vegetables, etc. are prepared and packed to be sold. **pack rat 1** a wood rat, well-known for hoarding objects of various kinds. **2** *Informal* a person who has a tendency to hoard objects, esp useless ones. **pack·sack** *n* a bag for carrying gear, clothing, etc., usually worn strapped to the back; knapsack.

pact [pækt] *n* an agreement; compact: *The two nations signed a peace pact.* ⟨Latin *pactum*, pp of *pacisci* covenant⟩

pad¹ [pæd] *n* **1** something soft used for comfort, protection, or stuffing. **2** one of the cushionlike parts on the the feet of dogs, and some other animals. **3** a large floating leaf of a water plant. **4** a number of sheets of paper fastened along an edge: *a writing pad.* **5** the launching platform for a rocket. **6** *Slang* a place where a person sleeps, such as a room, an apartment, etc.

v **pad·ded, pad·ding** *v* **1** fill with something soft. **2** make (a paper or speech) longer by using unnecessary words just to fill space or time: *Don't pad your essay.* **3** increase the amount of (a bill, expense account, etc.) by false entries. **pad·ding** *n.* ⟨origin uncertain⟩

pad² [pæd] *v* **pad·ded, pad·ding** walk softly: *a wolf padding through the bush.* **pad** *n.* ⟨perhaps Middle Dutch *pad* path⟩

pad·dle¹ ['pædəl] *v* **1** wade barefoot in water: *to paddle at the beach.* **2** move the hands or feet about in water. **pad·dler** *n.* **paddle wheel** a wheel having an arrangement of paddles around its rim, used for propelling a boat. ⟨apparently PAD²⟩

pad·dle² ['pædəl] *n* **1** a short oar with a broad blade at one or both ends. **2** a similar object with a rounded blade, used for table tennis, etc. **3** the act of paddling. **4** one of the boards fixed around a water wheel or a paddle wheel. **5** a handle with a wheel, by which the user can control the action in electronic games. **6** a canoe journey: *a short paddle away.* **pad·dle** *v.* **pad·dler** *n.* ⟨Latin *padela*; perhaps from *patella* pan⟩
paddle one's own canoe look after one's own affairs.

pad·dock ['pædək] *n* **1** a small field used for exercising animals or as a pasture. **2** an enclosure at a racetrack for displaying horses before they race. ⟨Old English *pearroc*; Latin *parricus* enclosure⟩

pad·dy ['pædi] *n* a field of rice. ⟨Malay *padi*⟩

paddy wagon *Slang* PATROL WAGON.

pad·lock ['pæd,lɒk] *n* a removable lock having a hinged bar that is snapped shut. **pad·lock** *v* fasten with such a lock.

pa·dre ['pɑdrei] *n* father. It is used as a name for a priest. ⟨Italian; Latin *pater* father⟩

paed·er·ast, paed·er·as·ty See PEDERAST.

pa·gan ['peigən] *n* a heathen. The ancient Greeks and Romans were pagans. *adj* **1** to do with the pagans: *pagan customs.* **2** not religious. **pa·gan·ism** *n.* ⟨Latin *paganus* rustic; *pagus* village⟩

> **USAGE**
> Both **pagan** and **heathen** have a basic connotation of 'unenlightened'. People belonging to established religions object to being called **pagan**. **Heathen** in particular, is used as a term of insult. The words, therefore, are best used in historical contexts: *Julius Caesar was a pagan. The Goths were heathen.*

page¹ [peidʒ] *n* **1** one side of sheet of paper: *The book has 350 pages.* **2** a sheet of paper. **3** *Computers* a unit of storage, esp the graphics and text that can be displayed one screen at a time.
v number the pages of: *Make sure you page*

your essay. ⟨Latin *pagina* something fixed; *pangere* fasten⟩
pag·i·nate ['pædʒə,neit] *v* number the pages of (books, etc.). **pag·i·na·tion** *n* **1** the figures with which pages are numbered. **2** the number and arrangement of pages in a book, etc., as described in a catalogue.

page² [peidʒ] *n* **1** a servant who runs errands for guests at hotels, etc. **2** a young person employed to carry messages for members of the House of Commons, the Senate, or a legislative assembly. **3** formerly, a young man preparing to be a knight.
v try to get a message to a person by means of an announcement, an electronic pager, or on a public address system. ⟨Italian *paggio*; Greek *paidion* lad⟩
page·boy *n* **1** a boy serving as a page. **2** a hairstyle with the hair curled under at the ends. **pag·er** *n* a portable electronic device used to page someone; beeper.

pag·eant ['pædʒənt] *n* **1** an elaborate spectacle: *The wedding was a splendid pageant.* **2** an entertainment that represents scenes from history or legend. ⟨Middle English *pagent* movable stage; Latin. See PAGE¹.⟩
pag·eant·ry *n* **1** a splendid show. **2** mere show; empty display.

pa·go·da [pə'goudə] *n* a temple with many storeys, and with a roof curving upward from each storey. ⟨Portuguese *pagode*; Tamil *pagavadi*; Sanskrit *bhagavati* goddess⟩

paid [peid] *v* pt of PAY.

pail [peil] *n* a container with a wide top and a handle that arches over the top. **pail·ful** *n.* ⟨Old French *paielle*; Latin *pagella* a measure⟩

pain [pein] *n* **1** an unpleasant sensation in the body: *a sharp pain in my back.* **2** mental suffering: *The memory gave her pain.* **3** pains *pl* effort: *He got nothing but trouble for his pains.* **4** *Informal* a bothersome person or thing.
v cause to suffer; give rise to pain; ache: *His tooth was paining him a great deal.* ⟨Old French *peine*; Greek *poinē* penalty⟩
be at pains make an effort: *She was at great pains to make them understand.* **on** (or **under**) **pain of** subject to the penalty of: *on pain of death.* **pain in the neck** *Informal* a bothersome person or thing. **take pains** be careful: *She took pains to do a good job.*
pained *adj* distressed, mentally hurt, etc. **pain·ful** *adj* **1** causing pain. **2** feeling pain. **3** difficult: *Balancing accounts can be a painful job.* **4** produced with difficulty: *a long, painful speech.* **pain·ful·ness** *n.* **pain·kill·er** *n* a drug that relieves pain. **pain·kil·ling** *adj.* **pain·less** *adj* causing no pain. **pain·less·ness** *n.* **pains·tak·ing** *adj* using great care or effort on the part of the doer. **pains·tak·ing·ly** *adv.*

paint [peint] *n* a liquid that dries as a coloured coating.
v **1** decorate with paint: *to paint a house.* **2** make pictures with paint. **3** picture vividly in words. ⟨Old French *peindre* paint; Latin *pingere*⟩
paint black represent as evil or wicked: *not so black as she is painted.* **paint oneself into a**

corner act in such a way as to leave oneself no choice. **paint the town red** See TOWN.

paint·brush n a brush for applying paint. **paint·er** n 1 a person who paints pictures. 2 a person who paints houses, etc. **paint·ing** n 1 a work produced by the art of painting. 2 the process of applying paint to a surface.

paint·er¹ See PAINT.

paint·er² ['peintər] n a rope, usually fastened to the bow of a boat, for tying it to a ship, pier, etc. ⟨Old French *pentoir* hanging cord⟩

pair [per] n, pl **pairs** or (sometimes after a numeral) **pair 1** a set of two. 2 a single thing made of two parts that cannot be used separately: *a pair of scissors*. 3 *Card games* two cards of the same value in different suits: *a pair of jacks, etc.*
v arrange or be arranged in pairs. ⟨Latin *paria* equals⟩
pair off or **up** arrange or form into pairs: *The guests paired off for the first dance.*

> **USAGE**
> When a **pair** is thought of as a unit, it takes a singular verb: *This pair of shoes is getting old.* When a **pair** is thought of as referring to two individual items, it takes a plural verb: *The pair of vases were both chipped.*

pa·ja·mas See PYJAMAS.

pal [pæl] *Informal* n a comrade; chum.
v **palled, pal·ling** v associate as pals. ⟨Romany brother⟩

pal·ace ['pælɪs] n 1 the official home of a king, queen, or some other important person. 2 a very fine house or official building: *the palace of justice*. **pa·la·tial** [pə'leifəl] *adj* fit for a palace; magnificent: *a palatial apartment*. **pa·la·tial·ly** *adv*. ⟨Old French *palais*; Latin *Palatium* Palatine Hill⟩

pal·ate ['pælɪt] n 1 the roof of the mouth. The bony part in front is the **hard palate;** the fleshy part at the back is the **soft palate.** 2 the sense of taste: *The new ice cream flavour pleased the children's palates*. **pal·at·a·ble** *adj*. **pal·at·a·bly** *adv*. ⟨Latin *palatum*⟩

pa·lav·er [pə'lævər] or [pə'lɑvər] n 1 formerly, a conference between European travellers and African natives. 2 empty talk. 3 flattery. 4 fuss and bother. ⟨Portuguese *palavra*; Latin *parabola* story⟩

pale¹ [peil] *adj* 1 without much colour: *Her face is pale after her illness.* 2 not intense or bright: *pale blue.* 3 feeble: *a pale foreign policy.*
v 1 turn or cause to turn pale: *Her face paled at the bad news.* 2 appear less significant by comparison: *Our troubles pale beside those of others*. **pale·ly** *adv*. **pale·ness** n. **pal·ish** *adj*. ⟨Latin *pallidus; pallere* be pale.⟩
pal·lid ['pælɪd] *adj* having less colour than usual; pale: *a pallid face*. **pal·lor** n a lack of colour from fear, illness, death, etc.; paleness.

pale² [peil] n 1 a board pointed at the top, used for fences. 2 enclosure. 3 the limits within which one has a right to protection: *Murder is an act outside the pale of society.* ⟨Latin *palus* stake⟩

beyond the pale outside the norm of usual behaviour: *Their bad behaviour was completely beyond the pale.*
pal·ing n 1 a fence of pales. 2 pales collectively, as fencing material.

paleo– *combining form* 1 old; ancient: *paleography* = ancient writing. 2 of a relatively early time division: *Paleocene* = the earliest epoch of the Tertiary period. 3 to do with a remote time period: *paleogeography*. Also, **palaeo-**. ⟨Greek *palaios* ancient⟩
Pa·le·o·cene ['peiliə,sin] *Geology* n the first epoch of the Tertiary period, beginning about 66 million years ago. **Pa·le·o·cene** *adj*. **pa·le·og·ra·phy** n 1 ancient writing. 2 the study of ancient writings. **pa·le·og·ra·pher** n. **pa·le·o·graph·ic** *adj*. **Pa·le·o·lith·ic** n the earlier part of the Stone Age. **pa·le·on·tol·o·gy** n the science that studies life existing long ago, as known from fossils. **pa·le·on·tol·o·gist** n. **Pa·le·o·zo·ic** n the era before the Mesozoic era, beginning about 600 million years ago. **Pa·le·o·zo·ic** *adj*.

pal·ette ['pælɪt] n 1 a thin board with a thumb hole at one end, used by painters to mix colours on. 2 the range or quality of colour used by an artist: *Gauguin used a bright palette*. ⟨French; Latin *pala* spade⟩

Pa·li ['pɑli] n the Indic language in which Buddhist sacred texts were written.

pa·li·mo·ny ['pælə,mouni] n *Informal* money paid to a lover on the breakup of their relationship. ⟨*pal* + *alimony*⟩

pal·imp·sest ['pælɪmp,sest] n a piece of writing material from which one writing has been erased to make room for another; a manuscript with one text written over another. ⟨Greek *palin* again + *psaein* rub smooth⟩

pal·in·drome ['pælɪn,droum] n a word, phrase, sentence, or number which reads the same backward as forward. *Madam, I'm Adam* is a palindrome, as is the number 2002. ⟨Greek *palin* again, back + *dromos* a running⟩

pal·i·sade [,pælɪ'seid] or ['pælə,seid] n 1 a high fence of pointed wooden stakes, built especially for defence. 2 Usually, **palisades** pl a line of high, steep cliffs. ⟨Latin *palus* stake⟩

pall¹ [pɒl] n 1 a heavy cloth spread over a coffin, a hearse, or a tomb. 2 a dark, gloomy covering: *A pall of smoke shut out the sun*. ⟨Old English *pæll*; Latin *pallium* cloak⟩
pall·bear·er n a person who helps to carry the coffin at a funeral.

pall² [pɒl] v 1 become distasteful or tiresome. 2 cloy (with *on*): *The thought of sitting through another long lecture palled on her*. ⟨variant of *appall*⟩

pal·la·di·um [pə'leidiəm] n a rare, metallic element, harder than platinum. *Symbol* **Pd** ⟨*Pallas*, asteroid named after Greek goddess *Pallas, Pallados*⟩

pal·let ['pælɪt] n 1 a straw bed. 2 a small, hard bed. ⟨Old French *paille* straw⟩

pal·li·ate ['pæli,eit] v **-at·ed, -at·ing** 1 lessen without curing; mitigate: *to palliate a disease*.

2 make appear less serious; excuse: *to palliate a fault*. **pal·li·a·tion** *n*. ⟨Latin *pallium* cloak⟩ **pal·li·a·tive** *adj* **1** useful to lessen or soften. **2** serving to control pain: *Palliative care is given to people not likely to live*. *n* something that lessens, softens, mitigates, or excuses.

pal·lid, pal·lor See PALE[1].

palm[1] [pɒm] *or* [pɒlm] *n* the inside of the hand between the wrist and the fingers. *v* conceal in the hand: *The magician palmed a nickel*. ⟨Latin *palma*⟩ **grease the palm** of bribe. **have an itching palm** be greedy for money. **palm off** get accepted by fraud: *The book she palmed off on me turned out to have some pages missing*. **pal·mate** ['pælmeit] *or* ['pɒlmeit] *adj* shaped like a hand with the fingers spread: *palmate antlers*. **palm·is·try** *n* the art of telling a person's future from the lines in the palm. **palm·ist** *n*.

palm[2] [pɒm] *or* [pɒlm] *n* **1** any of a family of trees, shrubs, etc., most species having a trunk crowned by large fan-shaped or feather-shaped leaves. **2** a leaf of a palm tree used as a symbol of victory or triumph. ⟨Latin *palma* PALM[1], for shape of leaves⟩ **pal·met·to** [pæl'mɛtou] *or* [pɒl'mɛtou] *n, pl* **-tos** or **-toes** any of a genus of palms with fan-shaped leaves. **palm oil** an edible fat obtained from the fruit of palms.

pal·o·mi·no [ˌpælə'minou] *n, pl* **-nos** a horse with a cream coat. ⟨Spanish; for colour⟩

pa·loo·ka [pə'lukə] *n Slang* **1** a poor or inferior boxer. **2** a stupid lout, esp a muscular one. ⟨coined word⟩

pal·pate ['pælpeit] *v* examine with the hands, esp for medical diagnosis. **pal·pa·tion** *n*. ⟨Latin *palpare* feel, pat⟩ **pal·pa·ble** *adj* **1** that can be touched or felt: *a palpable hit*. **2** readily seen or heard and recognized; obvious: *a palpable error*. **pal·pa·bil·i·ty** *n*. **pal·pa·bly** *adv*.

pal·pi·tate ['pælpəˌteit] *v* **1** beat very rapidly: *Your heart palpitates when you are excited*. **2** quiver; tremble: *His body palpitated with terror*. **pal·pi·ta·tion** *n*. ⟨Latin *palpitare* throb⟩

pal·sy ['pɒlzi] *n* paralysis, esp when accompanied by tremors. **pal·sied** *adj*. ⟨Middle English *palesie*⟩

pal·try ['pɒltri] *adj* **1** almost worthless. **2** petty; mean. **pal·tri·ly** *adv*. **pal·tri·ness** *n*. ⟨perhaps dialect *palt* trash⟩

pam·pas ['pɑmpəs] *or* ['pæmpəs] *Spanish* ['pampas] *n pl* the vast plains of South America. ⟨Spanish; Quechua *pampa* plain⟩

pam·per ['pæmpər] *v* **1** indulge too much: *to pamper a child*. **2** treat kindly: *Let our hotel staff pamper you*. ⟨Middle English *pamperen*⟩

pam·phlet ['pæmflɪt] *n* a short printed work: *an advertising pamphlet*. ⟨*Pamphilet*, popular name for 12c poem 'Pamphilus, or About Love'⟩ **pam·phlet·eer** *n* a writer of pamphlets.

pan[1] [pæn] *n* **1** a shallow dish for cooking and other household uses. **2** any area shaped like a pan, such as a small hollow in the ground. **3** hard subsoil. **4** *Slang* the human

face. **5** *Informal* a critical review of a play, film, etc. *v* **panned, pan·ning** **1** wash (gravel, sand, etc.) in a pan to get gold. **2** *Informal* criticize severely. ⟨Old English *panne*⟩ **pan out 1** *Informal* turn out well. **2 ✱** *Gold mining* to yield gold.

pan·cake *n* a thin cake of batter, fried in a pan or on a griddle. **pan·ful** *n* the contents of a pan: *a panful of potatoes*. **pan·han·dle** *n* a strip of land projecting like the handle of a pan: *the Alaska Panhandle*. *v Informal* beg from passers-by on the street, named from the pan used for collecting money. **pan·han·dler** *n*. **pan ice ✱** See ICE PAN. **pan·ner** *n* a prospector who seeks gold by panning.

pan[2] [pæn] *v* **panned, pan·ning** move (a film, video, or television camera) so as to take in a whole scene. ⟨*pan(orama)*⟩

pan·a·ce·a [ˌpænə'siə] *n* a remedy for all diseases or ills. **pan·a·ce·an** *adj*. ⟨Greek *panakeia; pan-* all + *akos* cure⟩

pa·nache [pə'næʃ] *n* behaviour marked by flair. ⟨French; *penna* feather; Latin⟩

pan·cre·as ['pæŋkriəs] *n Anatomy, zoology* a large gland that secretes digestive enzymes and insulin. **pan·cre·at·ic** [ˌpæŋkri'ætɪk] *adj*. ⟨Greek *pan-* all + *kreas* flesh⟩

pan·da ['pændə] *n* a black-and-white, bearlike mammal. Also called **giant panda.** ⟨Nepali⟩

pan·dem·ic [pæn'dɛmɪk] *adj* of a disease, affecting a large proportion of the population over an extensive geographical area: *a pandemic outbreak of influenza*. ⟨Greek *pan-* all + *demos* people⟩

pan·de·mo·ni·um [ˌpændə'mouniəm] *n* chaotic disorder. ⟨Greek *pan-* all + *daimōn* demon⟩

pan·der ['pændər] *n* **1** a person who helps people indulge evil designs or passions. **2** one who acts as a pimp in a sexual relationship. Also, **pan·der·er. pan·der** *v*. ⟨*Pandarus* character in a story by Chaucer⟩

pane [pein] *n* a sheet of glass enclosed in a frame as part of a window or door. ⟨Latin *pannus* piece of cloth⟩

pan·e·gyr·ic [ˌpænə'dʒairɪk] *or* [ˌpænə'dʒirɪk] *n* **1** something written or spoken in praise of a person or thing; eulogy. **2** enthusiastic praise. **pan·e·gyr·ic** *adj*. **pan·e·gyr·i·cal·ly** *adv*. **pan·e·gyr·ist** *n*. ⟨Greek *pan-* all + *agyris* assembly⟩

pan·el ['pænəl] *n* **1** a separate surface usually set off from what is around it. **2** a list of persons called as jurors. **3** a small group of persons selected for a special purpose, such as holding a discussion: *The panel gave its opinion on the recent election*. **4** a board containing the instruments used in operating an automobile, computer, etc. *v* **-elled** or **-eled, -el·ling** or **-el·ing** decorate with panels. ⟨Latin *pannellus; pannus* piece of cloth⟩ **pan·el·ling** or **pan·el·ing** *n* wooden panels forming a decorative wall surface. **pan·el·list** or **pan·el·ist** *n* one of a group of persons making up a panel. **panel truck** a small, light truck with a completely enclosed body.

pang [pæŋ] *n* **1** a sudden, short, sharp pain. **2** a sudden feeling of distress or anguish: *a pang of remorse.* ⟨origin uncertain⟩

pan·ic ['pænɪk]*n* a sudden fear that causes people to lose self-control. **pan·ic** *adj*. **pan·ic, -icked, -ick·ing** *v*. **pan·ick·y** *adj*. ⟨Greek *panikos* of god Pan (who caused fear)⟩
push (or **press** or **hit**) **the panic button** *Informal* react with panic in the face of a supposed emergency.
panic attack an attack of fear, accompanied by palpitations. **pan·ic–strick·en** [-ˌstrɪkən] *adj* frightened out of one's wits.

pan·ni·er ['pænjər] *n* one of a pair of containers slung across a beast of burden, or fitted on the back of a bicycle or motorcycle. ⟨Latin *panarium* bread basket⟩

pan·o·ply ['pænəpli] *n* **1** complete equipment or covering: *the panoply of war.* **2** any splendid display involving ceremonial dress: *the panoply of a coronation.* **pan·o·plied** *adj*. ⟨Greek *pan-* all + *hopla* arms⟩

pan·o·ram·a [ˌpænə'ræmə] *n* **1** a wide view. **2** a complete survey of some subject: *a panorama of the development of the car.* **pan·o·ram·ic** *adj*. **pan·o·ram·i·cal·ly** *adv*. ⟨Greek *pan-* + *horama* view⟩

pan·pipe ['pænˌpaip] *n* Usually, **panpipes** *pl* a musical instrument made of tubes. The player blows across their tops. ⟨*Pan* Greek god of flocks⟩

pan·sy ['pænzi] *n, pl* **-sies** a plant of the violet family. ⟨French *pensée* thought⟩

pant [pænt] *v* **1** breathe hard and quickly. **2** speak with short, quick breaths: *"We need help!" she panted.* **pant** *n*. ⟨Latin *phantasiare* suffer from a nightmare; Greek *phantasia* image⟩

pan·the·on ['pænθiˌɒn] *n* **1** **Pantheon** in Rome, a temple for all the gods. **2** all the gods of a people. **3** a group of illustrious people. ⟨Greek *pan-* all + *theos* god⟩
pan·the·ism *n* **1** the belief that God and the universe are identical. **2** the worship of the gods of all cultures together. **pan·the·ist** *n*. **pan·the·ist·ic** *adj*. **pan·the·ist·i·cal·ly** *adv*.

pan·ther ['pænθər] *n, pl* **-thers** or (esp collectively) **-ther 1** a leopard, esp of the black colour phase. **2** cougar. **3** jaguar. ⟨Greek⟩

pan·ties See PANTS.

pan·to·mime ['pæntəˌmaim] *n* **1** a play without words, in which the actors express themselves by gestures. **2** gestures without words. **3** a lavish stage entertainment, based on a traditional tale, featuring singing, dancing, and clowning.
v express by gestures. **pan·to·mim·ic** [ˌpæntə'mɪmɪk] *adj*. **pan·to·mim·ist** *n*. ⟨Latin; Greek *pantos* all + *mimos* mimic⟩

pan·try ['pæntri] *n* a small room used for storing food. ⟨Latin *panis* bread⟩

pants [pænts] *n pl* an outer garment for the lower body, reaching from the waist to the ankles, and covering each leg separately. ⟨*pantaloons, Pantalone* Italian comic character⟩
pan·ties *n pl* an undergarment worn by women and young children, covering the lower part of the torso and having separate leg holes. **pant·suit** *n* for women, pants and a matching jacket. **pan·ty·hose** or **pan·ty–hose** or **pan·ti·hose** *n pl* for women, stockings knitted in one piece with a pantie-like top.

pap [pæp] *n* **1** soft food for infants or invalids. **2** ideas or facts watered down to a characterless consistency. ⟨Latin *pappa* food⟩

pa·pa ['pɑpə] or ['pɒpə] *n* father; daddy. ⟨French⟩

pa·pal, pa·pa·cy See POPE.

pa·pa·raz·zi [ˌpɑpə'rɑtsi]*n pl, sg* **pa·pa·raz·zo** photographers who pursue celebrities. ⟨Italian⟩

pa·pa·ya [pə'paijə] *n* a treelike plant widely cultivated in warm regions, having a large, juicy, edible fruit. ⟨Spanish; Carib⟩

pa·per ['peipər] *n* **1** thin sheets made from wood pulp, rags, etc., used for writing, wrapping packages, etc. **2 papers** *pl* a collection of documents, such as journals, of an individual: *The Pearson papers are in the National Archives.* **3** newspaper. **4** an essay: *I read a paper on English grammar.* **5 papers** *pl* documents telling who a person is.
adj **1** made of paper: *paper dolls.* **2** to do with paper: *a paper clip.* **3** existing only on paper: *paper profits.*
v cover with wallpaper. ⟨Greek *papyros*⟩
on paper in theory: *The plan looks all right on paper but it may not work.*
pa·per·back *n* a book with a flexible paper cover. **pa·per·back** *adj*. **paper birch** the white birch, the bark of which was used to make canoes or as a surface for writing. **pa·per·board** *n* a thick type of cardboard. **pa·per·boy** *n* a boy who delivers newspapers. **pa·per·girl** *n*. **paper clip** a flat clip of bent wire used to hold sheets of paper together. **pa·per·hang·er** *n* **1** a person whose work is applying wallpaper. **2** *Slang* a person who makes a business of passing counterfeit bills or forged cheques. **paper money** money made of paper, not metal. **paper profits** profits existing on paper but not yet realized. **paper route** a contract to deliver newspapers to customers on a given route. **paper tiger** a person, country, etc. apparently posing a threat but actually powerless. **paper trail** all the documents by which an act, decision, etc. may be traced to its source. **pa·per·weight** *n* a small, heavy object put on loose papers to keep them from being scattered. **pa·per·work** *n* work done on or with paper, such as writing, filing, etc. **pa·per·y** *adj* thin, like paper.

pa·pier–mâ·ché [ˌpeipər mæ'ʃei] *French* [papjema'ʃe] *n* a paper pulp mixed with some stiffener and used for modelling. ⟨French = chewed paper⟩

pa·pil·la [pə'pɪlə] *n, pl* **-pil·lae** [-'pɪlai] or [-'pɪli]. **1** a small, nipplelike projection. **2** a protuberance concerned with touch, taste, or smell: *the papillae on the tongue.* **pap·il·lar·y** ['pæpəˌlɛri] *adj*. ⟨Latin = nipple⟩

papoose [pə'pus] *n* a small child or baby of First Nations parents. ⟨Algonquian⟩

USAGE
The use of **papoose** by non-Aboriginal people may be regarded as offensive because of its association with an attitude that patronized Aboriginal people.

pap·ri·ka [pə'prikə] *or* ['pæprəkə] *n* a mild, red-coloured pepper made of the dried pods of sweet pepper plants. ⟨Hungarian; Serbian *pàpar* pepper; Greek *peperi*⟩

Pap smear or **test** [pæp] a test for early stages of cancer of the uterus or cervix. ⟨G. *Papanicolaou* 20c US scientist⟩

pa·py·rus [pə'pairəs] *n, pl* **-ri** [-rai] *or* [-ri] 1 a water plant of the Nile valley from which the ancient Egyptians made paper. 2 a writing material made from the papyrus plant. ⟨Greek *papyros*⟩

par [par] *n* 1 an equal level: *The gains and losses are about on a par.* 2 an average amount, condition, etc.: *I'm feeling below par.* 3 the value of a bond, a share of stock, etc., that is printed on it; face value: *That stock is selling above par.* 4 *Golf* the number of strokes set as an expert score for any one hole.
adj 1 average. 2 of or at par. ⟨Latin = equal⟩
par for the course *Informal* what is normal or to be expected.
par·i·ty ['pɛriti] *or* ['pæriti] *n* equality. **par value** the value of a stock, bond, etc. printed on it.

para– ['pærə] *prefix* beside, near, or beyond. ⟨Greek⟩

par·a·ble ['pɛrəbəl] *or* ['pærəbəl] *n* a short, simple story used to teach a moral lesson. **par·a·bol·ic** *adj.* **par·a·bol·i·cal·ly** *adv.* ⟨Greek *para-* alongside + *bolē* a throwing⟩

pa·rab·o·la [pə'ræbələ] *n Geometry* a curve formed by the intersection of a cone with a plane parallel to a side of the cone. ⟨See PARABLE.⟩ **par·a·bol·ic** [ˌpɛrə'bɒlɪk] *or* [ˌpærə-] *adj* 1 to do with a parabola. 2 dish-shaped, as a TV satellite dish.

par·a·chute ['pɛrəˌʃut] *or* ['pærə-] *n* an apparatus shaped like an umbrella, made to give a gradual descent to a person or thing that jumps or is dropped from an aircraft.
v 1 airdrop. 2 ✴ **a** *Politics* introduce (a candidate) into a riding in an attempt to win the seat. **b** bring in (an outsider) to do a specific job. **par·a·chut·ist** *n.* ⟨French *para-* guard against + *chute* fall⟩
par·a·troop·er [-ˌtrupər] *n* a soldier trained to use a parachute for descent into a battle area.

pa·rade [pə'reid] *n* 1 a march for display: *The circus had a parade.* 2 a place to walk for display or pleasure. 3 a great display: *to make a parade of one's wealth.* 4 a military display or review of troops. **pa·rade** *v.* ⟨Spanish *parar* stop; Latin *parare* prepare⟩

par·a·digm ['pɛrəˌdaim] *or* ['pærə-] *n* 1 a system of related assumptions determining one's approach to things. 2 a pattern; example. **par·a·dig·mat·ic** [ˌpɛrəˌdɪgmætɪk] *adj.* ⟨Greek *para-* alongside + *deiknunai* show⟩

par·a·dise ['pɛrəˌdəis] *or* ['pærə-] *n* 1 heaven. 2 a place or condition of great happiness. 3 a place of great beauty. 4 Also, **Paradise** the Garden of Eden. ⟨Old Persian *pairidaeza* park⟩

par·a·dox ['pɛrəˌdɒks] *or* ['pærə-] *n* 1 a statement that seems to say two opposite things. *Example: More haste, less speed.* 2 a statement that is false because it says two opposite things. 3 a person or thing that seems full of contradictions. **par·a·dox·i·cal** *adj.* **par·a·dox·i·cal·ly** *adv.* ⟨Greek *para-* contrary to + *doxa* opinion⟩

par·af·fin ['pɛrəfɪn] *or* ['pærəfɪn] *n* 1 a flammable mixture of hydrocarbons obtained especially from petroleum. 2 *Chemistry* any hydrocarbon of the methane series. **par·af·fin·ic** *adj.* ⟨Latin *parum* not very; + *affinis* related (i.e., to other substances)⟩

par·a·gon ['pɛrəˌgɒn] *or* ['pærə-] *n* a model of excellence. ⟨Greek *parakonē* whetstone⟩

par·a·graph ['pærəˌgræf] *or* ['pɛrə-] *n* a group of sentences relating to the same topic. A paragraph begins on a new line. ⟨Greek *para-* beside + *graphein* write; for line in margin marking a break in sense⟩

par·a·keet ['pɛrəˌkit] *or* ['pærə-] *n* any of various small parrots. Also, **parr·a·keet**. ⟨Old French *paroquet, perrot* parrot. See PARROT.⟩

par·a·lan·guage ['pɛrəˌlæŋgwɪdʒ] *or* ['pærə-] *n* aspects of vocal utterances not strictly part of language, as volume, tempo, facial expressions, and gestures.
pa·ra·lin·guis·tic *adj.* ⟨*para-* + LANGUAGE⟩

par·a·lip·sis [ˌpɛrə'lɪpsɪs] *or* [ˌpærə-] *n, pl* **par·a·lip·ses** [-siz] a rhetorical device for emphasizing a point by making a passing reference to it. *Example: not to mention the danger involved.* ⟨*para-* + Greek *leipein* to leave⟩

par·al·lax ['pɛrəˌlæks] *or* ['pærə-] *n* the apparent change in the direction or position of an object as seen from two different points. **par·al·lac·tic** *adj.* ⟨Greek *parallaxis; para-* + *allasein* to change⟩

par·al·lel ['pɛrəˌlɛl] *or* ['pærə-] *adj* 1 being the same distance apart everywhere: *the parallel rails of a railway track.* 2 similar: *parallel points in the characters of two people.*
n 1 a parallel line or surface. 2 *Geography* any line of latitude: *the 49th parallel.* 3 something like another: *Their experience was a parallel to ours.* 4 a comparison to show likeness: *Draw a parallel between this winter and last winter.*
v **-lelled** or **-leled**, **-lel·ling** or **-lel·ing** 1 be at the same distance from throughout the length: *The street parallels the railway.* 2 be similar to: *Your story closely parallels what they told me.* **par·al·lel·ism** *n.* ⟨Greek *para allēlōn* beside one another⟩
parallel bars *Gymnastics* two bars mounted horizontally on posts. **par·al·lel·e·pi·ped** [ˌpærəˌlɛlə'pəipɪd] *n* a six-sided prism. **par·al·lel·o·gram** [ˌ-ˌgræm] *n* a four-sided plane figure having opposite sides parallel.

par·a·lyze or **par·a·lyse** ['pɛrəˌlaiz] *or* ['pærə-] *v* **-lyzed** or **-lysed**, **-lyz·ing** or **-lys·ing** 1 affect with a loss of the power of moving in the

body: *Her arm was paralyzed after the accident.*
2 make powerless or ineffective: *The project
was paralyzed when the funds were cut.* **3** stun:
paralyzed with fear. **pa·ral·y·sis** [pə'ræləsɪs] *n.*
par·a·lyt·ic ['perə,lɪtɪk] *or* ['pærə-] *adj.* ⟨*para-* +
Greek *lyein* to loosen⟩

par·a·me·ci·um [,perə'miʃiəm] *or* [,pærə-],
[,perə'misiəm] *or* [,pærə-] *n, pl* **-ci·a** [-ʃiə] *or* [-siə]
any of a genus of free-swimming protozoans
having a groove along one side leading into
the mouth. ⟨*para-* + Greek *mēkos* length⟩

par·a·med·i·cal *adj* [,perə'mɛdəkəl] *or* [,pærə-]
to do with auxiliary medical personnel such
as X-ray technicians, etc. **par·a·med·ic** *n.*

pa·ram·e·ter [pə'ræmətər] *n* **1** *Mathematics* a
quantity that is constant in a particular case
but varies in other cases. **2** any of a set of
measurable properties that determine the
characteristics or behaviour of something:
parameters of space and time. **3** any defining
feature: *They found the parameters of their life
too restricting.* ⟨*para-* + Greek *métron* meter⟩

par·a·mil·i·tar·y [,perə'mɪləteri] *or* [,pærə-]
adj to do with a group organized along
military lines: *a paramilitary police force.*

par·a·mount ['perə,maunt] *or* ['pærə-] *adj*
chief in importance: *Truth is of paramount
importance.* ⟨Anglo-French *par* by + *amont* up⟩

par·a·noi·a [,perə'nɔɪə] *or* [,pærə-] *n* **1** a
mental illness characterized by the belief
that one is being persecuted or by delusions
of self-importance. **2** an irrational feeling of
persecution. **par·a·noid** *or* **par·a·noi·ac** *adj, n.*
⟨*para-* + Greek *nous* mind⟩

par·a·nor·mal [,perə'nɔɪməl] *or* [,pærə-] *adj*
that cannot be explained in normal scientific
terms: *a paranormal experience.*
par·a·nor·mal·ly *adv.*

par·a·pet ['perəpət] *or* ['pærə-] *n* **1** a low
mound of stone, earth, etc., to protect soldiers.
2 a low wall at the edge of a roof, bridge, etc.
⟨Italian; *para* defend + *petto* breast⟩

par·a·pher·nal·ia [,perəfə'neiljə] *or* [,pærə-] *n
pl* **1** personal belongings. **2** equipment. ⟨*para*
+ Greek *phernē* dowry⟩

USAGE
Paraphernalia can be used with either a
singular or a plural verb.

par·a·phrase ['perə,freiz] *or* ['pærə-] *v* state
the meaning of (a passage) in other words.
par·a·phrase *n.* **par·a·phras·tic** *adj.*

par·a·ple·gi·a [,perə'plidʒiə] *or* [,pærə-] *n*
paralysis of the legs and the lower part of the
trunk. **par·a·ple·gic** *n, adj.* ⟨*para-* + Greek
plēgia stroke⟩

par·a·psy·chol·o·gy [,perəsəi'kɒlədʒi] *or*
[,pærə-] *n* the study of mental phenomena
not explainable in terms of physical laws,
such as telepathy. **par·a·psy·cho·log·i·cal** *adj.*

par·a·site ['perə,sait] *or* ['pærə-] *n* **1** a plant or
animal living in or on another from which it
receives food or other benefit; the host
receives no benefit and may be harmed. Lice
are parasites. **2** a person who lives on others.

par·a·sit·ic [-'sɪtɪk] *or* **par·a·sit·i·cal** *adj.*
par·a·sit·i·cal·ly *adv.* ⟨*para-* + Greek *sitos* food⟩
par·a·sit·ism *n* *Biology* a form of symbiosis in
which one organism lives in or on another.
Compare MUTUALISM. **par·a·si·tol·o·gy** *n* the
branch of biology that deals with the study
of parasites.

par·a·sol ['perə,sɒl] *or* ['pærə-] *n* a light
umbrella used as a protection from the sun.
⟨Italian *para* ward off + *sole* sun⟩

par·a·tax·is [,perə'tæksɪs] *or* [,pærə-] *n*
Grammar the placing together of related
clauses, phrases, etc. with no connecting word.
Example: Let's go, it's getting late. **par·a·tac·tic**
adj. ⟨*para-* + Greek *taxis; tassein* put⟩

par·a·troop·er See PARACHUTE.

par·boil ['par,bɔɪl] *v* **1** boil till partly cooked.
2 overheat. ⟨Latin *per-* thoroughly + *bullire*
boil; *par-* confused with *part*⟩

par·cel ['parsəl] *n* **1** a package. **2** a piece: *a
parcel of land.*
v **-celled** *or* **-celed**, **-cel·ling** *or* **-cel·ing** make a
parcel of. ⟨Old French *parcelle*; Latin *particula*,
diminutive of *partis* part⟩
parcel out distribute in portions.

parch [partʃ] *v* **1** make hot, dry, and thirsty:
The fever parched her. **2** dry by heating: *Corn is
sometimes parched.* ⟨Middle English *parchen*⟩

parch·ment ['partʃmənt] *n* **1** the skin of
sheep, goats, etc. prepared for use as a
writing material. **2** a kind of paper that looks
like parchment. ⟨Latin blending of *parthica*
Parthian (leather) + *pergamina* of Pergamum⟩

par·don ['pardən] *n* **1** forgiveness: *He asked
his mother's pardon for having insulted her.* **2** a
setting free from punishment. **par·don** *v.*
par·don·a·ble *adj.* **par·don·a·bly** *adv.* ⟨Latin
per- thoroughly + *donare* give⟩
pardon (me) *or* **I beg your pardon** a polite
expression of apology, disagreement, or
incredulity, or a request to someone to repeat
what he or she has just said.

pare [per] *v* **1** peel: *to pare an apple.* **2** lessen
little by little: *to pare expenses.* ⟨Latin *parare*
make ready⟩
par·ing *n* a part pared off; skin; rind.

par·e·gor·ic [,perə'gɔrɪk] *or* [,pærə-] *n* a
soothing medicine containing opium.
adj soothing. ⟨Greek *parēgorikos* soothing;
para- + *-agoros* speaking⟩

par·ent ['perənt] *n* **1** a mother, father; any
ancestor or progenitor. **2** any animal or plant
that produces offspring or seed. **3** a business
enterprise having subsidiary companies in
which it has a controlling interest.
v take care of a child: *Mothers learn to parent
by experience.* **pa·ren·tal** *adj.* **pa·ren·tal·ly** *adv.*
par·ent·hood *n.* ⟨Latin *parere* bring forth⟩
par·ent·age *n* family line; ancestry. **parental
leave** a leave of absence from a job for a
parent to look after a baby. **par·ent·ing** *n* the
skills necessary for raising children.
par·ent·ing *adj.* **Parent–Teacher Association**
an organization of teachers, parents and
guardians, set up to further the effectiveness

of the educational program in the school. *Abbrev* **PTA** or **P.T.A.**

pa·ren·the·sis [pə'rɛnθəsɪs] *n, pl* **-ses** [-siz] **1** *Grammar* words inserted to qualify something, usually set off by brackets, commas, or dashes. **2** either of two curved lines ( ) used to set off such an expression or to indicate that a group of symbols in mathematics, chemistry, etc., is regarded as a single term. **3** an often irrelevant episode. **pa·ren·the·size** *v.* **par·en·thet·ic** [ˌpɛrən'θɛtɪk] *or* [ˌpærən-], *or* **par·en·thet·i·cal** *adj.* **par·en·thet·i·cal·ly** *adv.* ⟨*para-* + Greek *en-* in + *thesis* a placing⟩

pa·re·sis [pə'risɪs], ['pɛrəsɪs], *or* ['pærəsɪs] *n* **1** an incomplete paralysis, affecting the ability to move but not the ability to feel. **2** a psychosis due to destruction of brain tissue, characterized by seizures, speech defects, progressive paralysis, etc. **pa·ret·ic** [pə'rɛtɪk] *adj.* ⟨Greek = a letting go⟩

par ex·cel·lence [par ˌɛksə'lɑns]; *French* [paʀɛksɛ'lɑ̃s] beyond comparison; above all others of the same sort.

par·fait [par'fei] *French* [paʀ'fɛ] *n* ice cream with syrup, whipped cream, etc., served in a tall glass. ⟨French = perfect⟩

pa·ri·ah [pə'raɪə] *n* **1** an outcast. **2** a member of a low caste in S India. ⟨Tamil *paraiyar* drummers; this caste provided drummers at festivals⟩

par·ing See PARE.

par·ish ['pɛrɪʃ] *or* ['pærɪʃ] *n* **1** a district that has its own church and clergy. **2** ✹ in New Brunswick, a political unit similar to a township. **3** ✹ in Québec, a civil district similar to a township. **pa·rish·ion·er** [pə'rɪʃənər] *n.* ⟨*para-* + Greek *oikos* dwelling⟩

pa·ro·chi·al [pə'roukiəl] *adj* **1** to do with a parish: *a parochial school.* **2** narrow; limited: *a parochial viewpoint.* **pa·ro·chi·al·ly** *adv.* **pa·ro·chi·al·ism** *n.* **parochial school** a local school maintained by a church.

par·i·ty See PAR.

park [park] *n* a piece of land set apart for public recreation. *v* **1** leave (an automobile, etc.) for a time in a certain place. **2** *Informal* place, put, or leave: *Just park your books on the table.* ⟨Old French *parc*; Latin *parricus* enclosure⟩ **par·kade** *n* ✹ a multistoreyed structure for parking automobiles. **park·ette** *n* ✹ a small park in a city. **parking lot** an area used for parking motor vehicles. **parking meter** a device for indicating the amount of parking time that has been bought for a vehicle. **park·land** *n* **1** land kept free from houses, factories, etc. and maintained as a public park. **2** ✹ the region between the foothills of the Rockies and the prairie. **3** ✹ the wooded region between the northern forests and the three Prairie Provinces. **park ranger** a government official who patrols and helps maintain a national or provincial park. **park·way** *n* a broad road or highway made attractive by grass, trees, flowers, etc.

par·ka ['parkə] *n* **1** a knee-length fur pullover with a hood, worn in the North. **2** a long winter coat with a hood. ⟨Yupik *purka* skin, coat⟩

Par·kin·son's disease ['parkənsənz] *Pathology* a progressive disorder of the central nervous system characterized by tremors. ⟨J. Parkinson 19c English surgeon⟩

par·lance ['parləns] *n* a way of speaking: *legal parlance.* ⟨Old French; *parler* speak⟩

par·lay ['parlei] *or* [par'lei] *v* **1** risk (an original bet and its winnings) on another bet. **2** build up (something) by taking risks with it: *She parlayed a few hundred dollars into a fortune.* ⟨Italian *paroli* grand cast at dice⟩

par·ley ['parli] *n* a conference, esp one with an enemy to discuss terms. **par·ley** *v.* ⟨French *parlée* pp of *parler* speak⟩

par·lia·ment ['parləmənt] *n* **1** **Parliament** the national lawmaking body of Canada, consisting of the Senate and the House of Commons. **2** the sitting members of a Parliament from one election to the next. **par·lia·men·ta·ry** *adj.* ⟨Old French *parlement*; *parler* speak⟩ **par·lia·men·tar·i·an** *n* a person skilled in parliamentary procedure or debate. **parliamentary secretary** ✹ a member of the House of Commons appointed to assist a Cabinet Minister. **Parliament Hill** the Parliament buildings in Ottawa.

par·lour *or* **par·lor** ['parlər] *n* **1** a sitting room or living room. **2** a room specially equipped for a certain kind of business: *a beauty parlour, a beer parlour.* ⟨Anglo-French; *parler* speak. See PARLEY.⟩

pa·ro·chi·al See PARISH.

par·o·dy ['pɛrədi] *or* ['pærədi] *n* **1** a humorous imitation of a serious piece of writing. **2** any work of art that makes fun of another. **3** a poor imitation. **par·o·dy** *v.* ⟨*para-* + Greek *ōidē* song⟩ **pa·rod·ic** [pə'rɒdɪk] *or* **pa·rod·i·cal** *adj.* **par·o·dist** *n.*

pa·role [pə'roul] *n* **1** a conditional release from prison before the full term is served. **2** conditional freedom allowed in place of imprisonment. **3** word of honour: *The prisoner gave his parole not to try to escape.* *v* give a parole: *He was paroled on condition that he report to the judge every three months.* **pa·rol·a·ble** *adj.* ⟨French = word; Latin *parabola* parable⟩ **out on parole** released from prison under certain conditions. **pa·rol·ee** [pərou'li] *n* one who is released from prison on parole.

par·ox·ysm ['pɛrək,sɪzəm] *or* ['pærək-] *n* **1** a convulsion: *a paroxysm of coughing.* **2** a sudden violent emotion, etc.: *a paroxysm of rage.* ⟨*para-* + Greek *oxynein* goad⟩

par·quet [par'kei] *n* a flooring made of inlaid pieces of wood. **par·quet** *adj.* ⟨French diminutive of *parc* park⟩

par·ri·cide ['pɛrə,saɪd] *or* ['pærə-] *n* the crime

of killing one's parent or a close relative. Compare PATRICIDE. **par·ri·cid·al** *adj.* ⟨Latin *parricidium* murder of kinsman⟩

par·rot ['pɛrət] *or* ['pærət] *n* **1** any of a family of birds of the tropics, having a stout, hooked bill. Parrots are excellent mimics. **2** a person who repeats words or acts without understanding them.
v repeat without understanding: *He parrots his elder brother.* **par·rot·like** *adj.* ⟨French *Perrot* diminutive of *Pierre* Peter⟩

par·ry ['pɛri] *or* ['pæri] *v* ward off (a thrust, question, etc.): *He parried the sword with his dagger. She parried our question by smiling.* **par·ry** *n.* ⟨French *parer* ward off⟩

parse [pɑrs] *v* **1** *Grammar* **a** analyze (a sentence) grammatically. **b** describe (a word) grammatically. **2** *Computers* analyze (a string) for the purpose of associating groups of characters with syntactic structures in the underlying grammar: *This program will parse English but not Swahili.* **pars·a·ble** *adj.* ⟨Latin *pars orationis* part of speech⟩

par·sec ['pɑr,sɛk] *n Astronomy* a unit used with the SI for measuring distance in interstellar space, about 3.26 light years. *Symbol* **pc** ⟨*par(allax)* + *sec(ond)*²⟩

par·si·mo·ni·ous [,pɑrsə'mouniəs] *adj* stingy. **par·si·mo·ny** ['pɑrsə,mouni] *n.* ⟨Latin *parsimonia; parcere* spare⟩

pars·ley ['pɑrsli] *n* a plant cultivated for its aromatic leaves, used as garnish. ⟨Old French *peresil*; Greek *petros* rock + *selinon* parsley⟩

par·son ['pɑrsən] *n* **1** an Anglican priest in charge of a parish. **2** *Informal* any member of the Protestant clergy. ⟨Latin *persona* person⟩
par·son·age *n* the house provided for a minister by his or her church.

part [pɑrt] *n* **1** something less than the whole. **2** each of several equal quantities into which a whole may be divided: *A dime is a tenth part of a dollar.* **3** a share: *Each girl must do her part.* **4** a character in a play, motion picture, etc.: *the part of Juliet.* **5** the words spoken by a character: *Actors have to learn their parts quickly.* **6** *Music* one of the voices or instruments. The four parts in singing are soprano, alto, tenor, and bass. **7 parts** *pl* a region: *I was born in these parts.*
adj less than the whole: *part-time.*
adv in some measure or degree; partly.
v **1** divide into pieces. **2** separate: *The friends parted in anger.* ⟨Latin *pars, partis* part⟩
for one's part as far as one is concerned: *For my part, I'd rather stay.* **for the most part** mostly. **in good part** in a friendly or gracious way: *She took the teasing in good part.* **in part** partly. **on someone's part** or **on the part of someone** done by someone: *There were improprieties on her part.* **part and parcel** an essential part: *Practising is part and parcel of learning to play the piano.* **part from** go away from; leave. **part with** give up; let go. **play a part** behave out of character, with the intention of deceiving: *After murdering her husband, she played the part of the grieving*

widow. **b** be an influential factor: *The lack of available jobs played a part in her decision.* **take part** take or have a share; participate.

par·tial ['pɑrʃəl] *adj* **1** not complete; not total: *a partial loss.* **2** biassed: *A father should not be partial to any one of his children.* **3** having a liking (with *to*): *I am partial to sports.* **par·tial·ly** *adv.* **par·ti·al·i·ty** [,pɑrʃi'æləti] *n* **1** bias. **2** a special fondness: *a partiality for candy.* **part·ing** *n* **1** a departure. **2** a separation. **3** a place or thing that separates: *Her hairstyle has a side parting.* **part·ing** *adj.* **parting shot** a violent criticism, threat, etc. made on departing. **par·ti·tion** *n* **1** a division into parts: *the partition of wealth.* **2** a thin inside dividing wall. **par·ti·tion** *v.* **par·ti·tive** *n Grammar* a word or phrase referring to a part of a collective or mass. *Some, few,* and *any* are partitives. **part·ly** *adv* in part. **part of speech** *Grammar* one of the nine classes into which words are grouped: noun, pronoun, adjective, verb, adverb, preposition, conjunction, interjection, and article. **part time** part of the time. **part–time** *adj.*

par·take [pɑr'teik] *v* **-took, -tak·en, -tak·ing** **1** to share in common with others: *We look forward to partaking in the ceremony.* **2** take or have a share (with *of*): *Would you care to partake of dessert?* ⟨part-taker⟩

par·the·no·gen·e·sis [,pɑrθənou'dʒɛnəsɪs] *n Biology* reproduction by development of an unfertilized ovum, occurring especially among the lower plants and invertebrate animals. **par·the·no·ge·net·ic** [-dʒə'nɛtɪk] *adj.* ⟨Greek *parthenos* virgin. See GENESIS.⟩

par·tic·i·pate [pɑr'tɪsə,peit] *v* take part: *The teacher participated in the children's games.* **par·tic·i·pa·tion** *n.* **par·tic·i·pant** *n.* ⟨Latin *partis* part + *capere* take⟩
par·tic·i·pa·to·ry [pɑr'tɪsəpə,tɔri] *adj* allowing participation.

par·ti·ci·ple ['pɑrtə,sɪpəl] *n Grammar* a verb form used principally as an adjective. *Examples:* the *dripping* tap, the *broken* vase. **par·ti·cip·i·al** [,pɑrtə'sɪpiəl] *adj.* ⟨Old French *participle*; Latin *participium* a sharing⟩

par·ti·cle ['pɑrtəkəl] *n* **1** a very small bit. **2** *Physics* **a** a minute mass of matter that is treated as a point without length, breadth, or thickness. **b** one of the fundamental units of matter, as the electron, neutron, photon, or proton. ⟨Latin *particula.* See PARCEL.⟩
par·ti·cle·board *n* a board made of sawdust or small pieces of wood pressed together with a binding agent.

par·tic·u·lar [pər'tɪkjələr] *adj* **1** considered separately: *That particular chair is already sold.* **2** belonging to some one person, thing, occasion, etc.: *A particular characteristic of a skunk is its smell.* **3** special: *a particular friend.*

4 hard to please: *She is very particular.*
n **1** an individual part: *complete in every particular.* **2** Often, **particulars** *pl* a specific item of information: *The police should be informed of the particulars of the break-in.* **par·tic·u·lar·i·ty** [pər,tɪkjə'lɛrəti] *or* [-lærəti] *n.* **par·tic·u·lar·ly** [pər'tɪkjələrli] *or* [-lɛrli] *adv.* ⟨Latin *particula.* See PARCEL.⟩
in particular especially.
par·tic·u·lar·ize *v* treat in detail; specify. **par·tic·u·lar·i·za·tion** *n.*

Parti Québécois [pɑr'ti ,keibɛk'wɑ] ✽ a major political party in Québec, formed as a separatist party in 1968.

par·ti·san ['pɑrtə,zæn] *or* ['pɑrtəzən] *n* **1** a strong supporter, esp one whose support is based on feeling. **2** a guerrilla. **par·ti·san** *adj.* ⟨French; Italian *partigiano; parte* part⟩
par·ti·san·ship *n* **1** strong loyalty to a party or cause. **2** the act of taking sides.

par·ti·tion, par·ti·tive See PART.

part·ner ['pɑrtnər] *n* **1** a member of a business partnership. **2** associate: *The thief climbed through the window while his partner watched the street.* **3** spouse. **4** either person of a couple dancing together. **5** *Sports and games* either of two players playing against another pair. **6** one who shares: *She was the partner of my walks.* **part·ner** *v.* **part·ner·ship** *n.* ⟨Anglo-French *parçon* partition; Latin *partitio*⟩

par·took [pɑr'tʊk] *v* pt of PARTAKE.

par·tridge ['pɑrtrɪdʒ] *n* **-tridg·es** or (esp collectively) **-tridge 1** any of numerous game birds. **2** the ptarmigan. ⟨Old French *perdriz;* Greek *perdix*⟩

par·tu·ri·tion [,pɑrtʃə'rɪʃən] *n* the act or process of giving birth to young. ⟨Latin *parturire* be in labour; *parere* bear⟩

par·ty ['pɑrti] *n, pl* **-ties** *n* **1** a gathering for pleasure. **2** a group of people doing something together: *a scouting party.* **3** a group of people having similar political aims: *the Liberal Party.* **4** one who takes part in, or knows about: *She was a party to our plot.* **5** each of the sides in a contract, lawsuit, etc. *v* **-tied, -ty·ing** attend a party: *partying till dawn.* ⟨Old French *partie;* pp of *partir* divide⟩
party away use up in partying: *We partied the night away. She partied all her money away.*
party line 1 a telephone line by which two or more subscribers share one circuit. **2** the official policy of a political party: *Members are expected to vote along party lines.* **par·ty–lin·er** *n* a person who follows closely the policies of his or her political party. **party politics** politics based on political parties, regardless of public interest. **party pooper** someone who spoils a party by refusing to take part in the activities. **party whip** a political official whose job it is to organize party members to vote on a certain issue.

pas·cal [pæ'skæl] *n* an SI unit for measuring pressure or stress, equal to the pressure produced by the force of one newton applied to an area of one square metre. *Symbol* **Pa** ⟨B. *Pascal* 17c French mathematician⟩

pass [pæs] *v* **1** move past. **2** go, or cause to go, to another: *Money passes from person to person.* **3** put (a rope, string, etc.): *He passed a rope around his waist for support.* **4** go away: *The pain will soon pass.* **5** overtake and leave behind. **6** discharge from the body. **7** be successful in (an examination, a course, etc.). **8** ratify: *to pass a law.* **9** be approved by (a law-making body, etc.): *The new law passed the city council.* **10** use; spend: *We passed the days pleasantly.* **11** *Football, hockey, etc.* transfer (the ball, etc.).
n **1** the act of passing. **2** success in an examination, etc. **3** a note, licence, etc. allowing one to do something: *He needed a pass to enter the fort.* **4** free ticket: *a pass to the circus.* **5** a motion of the hands. **6** a narrow passage through mountains. **7** *Football, hockey, etc.* a transference of a ball, puck, etc. **8** *Informal* a sexual approach. ⟨Old French *passer;* Latin *passus* step⟩
bring to pass accomplish. **come to pass** happen. **pass as** (or **for**) be accepted as: *Use a material that will pass as silk.* **pass away a** come to an end. **b** die. **pass off a** go away. **b** take place. **c** cause to be accepted under false pretenses. **pass on a** pass to another person. **b** die. **pass one's lips a** be uttered. **b** be eaten or drunk. **pass out a** hand out. **b** *Informal* faint. **pass over a** fail to notice; overlook: *The teacher passed over my mistake.* **b** ignore the claims of (a person) to promotion, honour, etc. **c** die **pass something by** disregard. **pass the time of day** greet and chat with someone. **pass up a** give up: *to pass up a chance at revenge.* **b** fail to take advantage of.
pass·a·ble *adj* **1** mediocre: *a passable performance.* **2** that can be travelled on: *the roads are barely passable.* **pass·a·ble·ness** *n.* **pass·a·bly** *adv* fairly; moderately. **pas·sage** *n* **1** a way through a building. **2** a way through: *to ask for passage through a crowd.* **3** right to pass: *The guard refused us passage.* **4** a passing: *the passage of time.* **5** a piece from a speech or musical composition. **6** a journey, esp by sea: *a stormy passage across the Atlantic.* **7** progression from one state to another: *rites of passage.* **8** an opening into, through, or out of something: *nasal passages.* **pas·sage·way** *n* a way along which one can pass. **pass·book** *n* bankbook. **pas·sen·ger** ['pæsəndʒər] *n* a traveller in a train, motor vehicle, etc. who has nothing to do with its operation. **pass·er–by** *n, pl* **pass·ers–by** a person who passes by: *The robbery was seen by a passer-by.* **pass·ing** *adj* **1** going past: *a passing motorist.* **2** not lasting: *a passing fashion.* **3** incidental: *a passing remark.* **4** designating satisfactory completion of a course of study: *a passing grade.* **5** to do with a track, lane, etc. for passing another vehicle. *n* the act of one who or that which passes: *the passing of summer. They mourned her passing.* **in passing** incidentally: *She mentioned in passing that she was planning a trip.* **pass·key** *n* **1** a master key. **2** a private key. **Pass·o·ver** ['pæs,ouvər] *n* an annual Jewish holiday, so called because,

according to the Bible, a destroying angel 'passed over' the houses of the Hebrew slaves when it killed the first-born child in every Egyptian home. **pass·port** *n* **1** an official document identifying the citizenship of the holder, and giving the holder permission to travel abroad under the protection of its government. **2** anything that gives one acceptance: *An interest in gardening was a passport to my aunt's favour.* **pass·word** *n* **1** a secret word that identifies a person speaking it and allows him or her to pass. **2** *Computers* a personal code that uniquely enables its possessor to use a computer by keying in the code. **pas·time** *n* something that causes the time to pass pleasantly; a form of recreation.

pas·sé [pæ'seɪ] *French* [pa'se] *adj* no longer useful or fashionable: *That expression is passé.* ⟨French = passed⟩

pas·sim ['pæsɪm] *adv Latin* in various places. (Used in footnotes in referring to material found throughout a book, article, etc.)

pas·sion ['pæʃən] *n* **1** very strong feeling: *Love and hate are passions.* **2** a rage: *He flew into a passion.* **3** intense love or sexual desire. **4** a very strong liking: *a passion for music.* **5** Usually, **the Passion** the sufferings of Jesus on the cross. **pas·sion·ate** *adj.* **pas·sion·ate·ly** *adv.* **pas·sion·less** *n.* ⟨Latin *passio; pati* suffer⟩

pas·sive ['pæsɪv] *adj* **1** not acting in return: *a passive victim.* **2** characterized by lack of initiative: *a passive disposition.* **3** *Grammar* to do with a form (called the passive voice) of a verb that shows the subject of a clause as the recipient of the action. In *The cup was broken by me,* the subject *the cup* receives the action represented by the passive *was broken.* Compare ACTIVE (def. 5). **pas·sive·ly** *adv.* **pas·sive·ness** or **pas·siv·i·ty** *n.* ⟨Latin *passivus; pati* suffer, undergo⟩
passive resistance resistance to authority by non-violent refusal to co-operate.

past [pæst] *adj* **1** gone by: *Our troubles are past.* **2** just gone by: *the past year.* **3** having served a term in office: *a past president.* **4** of former times. **5** *Grammar* to do with a verb form expressing actions that have ended at the time of the statement: *the past tense.*
n **1** time gone by. **2** a past history: *a glorious past.* **3** a person's past life, esp one of questionable morality: *a man with a past.*
prep **1** beyond: *The arrow went past the mark.* **2** after: *ten past two.*
adv so as to pass by or beyond: *The cars go past once an hour.* ⟨earlier pt of *pass*⟩
not put it past someone believe someone capable of something.
past participle *Grammar* in English, a participle used: **a** with the auxiliary verb *have* to form perfect tenses. *Example:* It *has rained* every day. **b** with the auxiliary verb *be* to form the passive voice. *Example:* The cheese *was eaten* by me. **c** as an adjective indicating a completed state. *Example: broken* glass.

CONFUSABLES
Past is not a verb. The past tense of the verb pass is passed.

pas·ta ['pɑstə] *or* ['pæstə] *n* a type of flour paste used to make foods such as spaghetti, noodles, etc. ⟨Italian; Latin; Greek. See PASTE.⟩

paste [peist] *n* **1** a mixture, such as flour and water, that will stick paper together. **2** a soft, doughlike mixture. **3** a glassy material used in making imitations of precious stones.
v **1** stick with paste: *to paste a label on a box.* **2** *Slang* hit with a hard blow. ⟨Greek *pasta* porridge; *passein* sprinkle⟩
paste·board ['peist,bɔrd] *n* a stiff material made of sheets of paper pasted together. *adj* **1** made of pasteboard. **2** flimsy; sham. **past·y** *adj* like paste in appearance or texture; especially, pale and flabby. **past·i·ness** *n.*

pas·tel [pæ'stɛl] *n* **1** a kind of crayon. **2** a drawing made with such crayons. **3** a soft, pale shade of some colour. ⟨Italian *pastello*; ; Greek *pasta.* See PASTE.⟩

pas·teur·ize ['pæstʃə,raɪz] *v* heat (milk, beer, etc.) to a high temperature and chill it, to destroy bacteria. **pas·teur·i·za·tion** *n.* ⟨L. *Pasteur* 19c French chemist⟩

pas·tiche [pæ'stiʃ] *n* **1** a piece of writing, music, etc., consisting mainly of bits borrowed from various sources. **2** an unlikely mixture of materials, styles, etc. ⟨French; Italian *pasticcio* pie⟩

pas·tille [pæ'stil] *n* **1** a flavoured or medicated lozenge. **2** a cone of aromatic paste, burnt as a disinfectant, incense, etc. ⟨French; Latin *pastillus* diminutive of *panis* bread⟩

pas·time See PASS.

pas·tor ['pæstər] *n* a priest or minister in charge of a Christian community. ⟨Latin = shepherd; *pascere* feed⟩
pas·tor·al *adj* **1** to do with shepherds or country life. **2** to do with the duties of a pastor. *n* a play, poem, etc., dealing in an idealized manner with rural life. **pas·tor·al·ly** *adv.* **pas·tor·ale** [,pæstə'ræl] *n Music* any piece in a simple style intended to suggest rural life.

pas·tra·mi [pə'strami] *n* smoked and highly seasoned beef. ⟨Yiddish⟩

pas·try ['peistri] *n, pl* -tries **1** a dough of flour and lard, butter, etc., used to make pie crusts, etc. **2** all fancy baked goods. ⟨*paste*⟩

pas·ture ['pæstʃər] *n* grasslands on which cattle, horses, etc., can feed.
v **1** put (cattle, etc.) out to pasture. **2** of land, provide (animals) with pasture: *This field will pasture 20 cattle.* ⟨Latin *pastura; pascere* feed⟩
put out to pasture *Slang* allow or force (older people) to retire or be less active: *It's time that group was put out to pasture.*

past·y See PASTE.

pat¹ [pæt] *v* **pat·ted, pat·ting 1** strike lightly with the hand or a flat object, to shape: *She patted the dough into a flat cake.* **2** tap lightly with the hand in affection: *to pat a dog.*
n **1** a light stroke with the hand or with something flat. **2** a small mass of butter. ⟨Middle English *patte*⟩
pat on the back a compliment, often condescending.

pat² [pæt] *adj* **1** suitable: *a pat reply.* **2** so perfect as to seem glib or memorized.
adv **1** exactly. **2** glibly; tritely. ⟨probably special use of *pat¹*⟩
have (down) pat or **know pat** *Informal* know thoroughly: *She has the history lesson pat.*
stand pat *Informal* refuse to change: *People were angry, but the prime minister stood pat.*

patch [pætʃ] *n* **1** a piece of material put on to mend a hole or to strengthen a weak place: *to sew a patch on a torn sleeve.* **2** a protective dressing applied to a sore or wound: *a patch over the right eye.* **3** a small area different from that around it: *a patch of brown on the skin.* **4** a piece of ground: *a garden patch.* **5** *Military* a small piece of fabric worn on the sleeve, indicating affiliation with a particular military unit. **6** a small membrane which releases a substance gradually through the skin: *a nicotine patch.*
v **1** put on a patch. **2** make with patches: *to patch a quilt.* **3** put an end to (usually with *up*): *to patch up a quarrel.* **4** connect circuits (usually with *through*): *I'll patch you through to the main office.* ⟨Middle English *pacche*, perhaps variant of *pece* piece. See PIECE.⟩
patch together improvise a temporary solution for: *We could patch together a plan that will do for the time being.* **patch up** put together or mend hastily or poorly: *I can patch it up for now, but it won't hold for long.*
patch logging ✳ a system of logging by which only patches of trees in a stand are cut down, the rest being left to ensure natural reseeding of the cutover patch. **patch·work** *n* **1** pieces of cloth of various colours or shapes sewed together. **2** anything like this: *a patchwork of fields and woods.* **patch·y** *adj* **1** characterized by patches: *a patchy lawn.* **2** not consistent: *a patchy performance.* **patch·i·ly** *adv.* **patch·i·ness** *n.*

pate [peit] *n* the top of the head; head: *a bald pate.* ⟨Middle English; origin uncertain⟩

pâ·té [pæ'tei] or [pɑ'tei] *French* [pɑ'te] *n* a meat paste, usually highly seasoned. ⟨French; Old French *pastee*⟩
pâté de foie gras [pæ'tei də ˌfwɑ 'grɑ] *French* [pɑtedfwɑ'grʀɑ] a rich paste made from the livers of specially fattened geese.

pa·tel·la [pə'tɛlə] *n, pl* **-tel·las** or **-tel·lae** [-'tɛli] or [-'tɛlaɪ] **1** kneecap. **2** *Biology* a cuplike formation. **pa·tel·lar** *adj.* ⟨Latin diminutive of *patina* pan.⟩

pat·ent ['pætənt] *n* **1** a right by which a person is the only one allowed to make, use, or sell a new invention for a number of years. **2** an official document from a government giving a right.
adj **1** protected by a patent: *a patent lock.* **2** ['peitənt] evident; plain: *She smiled at the patent ineptness of their scheme.*
v get a patent for: *If your invention is a good one, you must patent it.* **pat·ent·a·ble** *adj.* ⟨Latin *patere* lie open⟩
pa·ten·cy ['peitənsi] *n* obviousness. **patent** ['peitənt] **leather** leather with a very glossy, surface, made by a process formerly

patented. **pa·tent·ly** ['peitəntli] *adv* **1** plainly; obviously. **2** openly. **patent** ['peitənt] **medicine** a product sold without prescription as a remedy for certain ailments or illnesses.

pa·ter·nal [pə'tɜrnəl] *adj* **1** fatherly. **2** related on the father's side of the family: *a paternal aunt.* **3** inherited from a father. **pa·ter·nal·ly** *adv.* ⟨Latin *pater* father⟩
pa·ter·fa·mil·i·as [ˌpætərfə'miliəs] or [ˌpeitər-] *n, pl* **patres familias** ['pætreis fə'miliəs] a father or head of a family. **pa·ter·nal·ism** *n* the principle of managing the affairs of a group of people as a father manages the affairs of his children. **pa·ter·nal·ist** *n.* **pa·ter·nal·is·tic** *adj.* **pa·ter·nal·is·ti·cal·ly** *adv.* **pa·ter·ni·ty** *n* **1** fatherhood. **2** paternal origin.

path [pæθ] *n, pl* **paths** [pæðz] **1** a track made by people or animals walking. **2** a way made to walk, ride bicycles, etc. upon. **3** a route; track: *The moon has a regular path through the sky.* **4** a way of acting or behaving: *"Some choose paths of glory, some choose paths of ease."* **path·less** *n.* ⟨Old English *pæth*⟩
path·way *n* path.

pa·thet·ic See PATHOS.

path·o·gen ['pæθədʒən] *n* a disease-causing agent. **path·o·gen·ic** *adj.* ⟨Greek *pathos* disease + *gen-* produce⟩

pa·thol·o·gy [pə'θɒlədʒi] *n, pl* **-gies 1** the study of the nature and causes of disease. **2** any deviation from a normal or sound condition. **pa·thol·o·gist** *n.*
path·o·log·i·cal *adj* **1** due to disease: *a pathological condition of the blood cells.* **2** compulsive: *a pathological hatred of cats, a pathological liar.* **path·o·log·i·cal·ly** *adv.*

pa·thos ['peiθɒs] *n* the quality that arouses a feeling of pity. ⟨Greek *pathos* suffering⟩
pa·thet·ic [pə'θɛtɪk] *adj* **1** arousing pity: *A lost child is a pathetic sight.* **2** pitifully inadequate: *a pathetic attempt to amuse.* **pa·thet·i·cal·ly** *adv.* **pathetic fallacy** the attribution of human characteristics to nature or inanimate things. *Example: a stubborn cold.*

pa·tient ['peiʃənt] *adj* **1** having the ability to accept calmly things that trouble, or that require long waiting. **2** with steady effort: *patient research.*
n a person or animal who is being treated by a doctor, veterinarian, etc. **pa·tience** *n.* **pa·tient·ly** *adv.* ⟨Latin *pati* suffer⟩

pat·i·na ['pætənə] or [pə'tinə] *n* **1** a film formed naturally over time on the surface of copper. **2** a smooth surface produced by age and exposure on substances such as wood. **3** an aura assumed by something as a result of association, etc.: *the patina of success.* ⟨Italian = coating; Latin = pan⟩

pat·i·o ['pætiou] *n* a terrace or open courtyard for meals, lounging, etc. ⟨Spanish⟩

pat·ois [pæ'twɑ] or ['pætwɑ] *French* [pa'twɑ] *n, pl* **pat·ois** *French* [pa'twɑ] **1** a dialect different from the standard language of a country or district. **2** the special language of a particular group; jargon. ⟨French; Old French *patoier* handle clumsily; *pate* paw⟩

pa·tri·arch ['peitri,ɑrk] *n* **1** a father who is the ruler of a family or tribe. **2** a venerable old man. **3** a person thought of as the founder of something. **4** a high-ranking religious official, esp in the Roman Catholic Church and the Eastern Orthodox Church. **pa·tri·ar·chal** *adj.* ⟨Greek *patria* family + *archos* leader⟩

pa·tri·ar·chy *n* **1** a form of social organization in which descent is traced through the father, as the ruler of the family. **2** any type of social institution dominated by men. **3** systemic male domination. **pat·ri·cide** ['pætrə,saɪd] *or* ['peitrə-] *n* the act of killing one's father. Compare PARRICIDE. **pat·ri·cid·al** *adj.* **pat·ri·lin·e·al** [,pætrə'lɪniəl] *or* [,peitrə-] *adj* to do with kinship through the male line. Compare MATRILINEAL. **pat·ri·lin·e·al·ly** *adv.* **pat·ri·mo·ny** ['pætrə,mouni] *n* **1** property inherited from one's father or ancestors. **2** property belonging to a church, monastery, or convent. **3** any heritage. **pat·ri·mo·ni·al** *adj.*

pa·tri·ate ['peitri,eit] *or* ['pætri,eit] *v* ❋ bring (government, decision-making powers, etc.) under the direct control of the people of a given region, nation, etc.: *The British parliament voted in 1982 to patriate the Canadian constitution.* **pa·tri·a·tion** *n.* ⟨back formation from *repatriate*⟩

pa·tri·cian [pə'trɪʃən] *n* **1** in ancient Rome, **a** a member of the senatorial aristocracy. **b** later, a member of the nobility. Compare PLEBEIAN (def. 1). **2** a person of noble birth or high social rank. **3** any person of good background or refined taste. **pa·tri·cian** *adj.* ⟨Latin *patricius; patres* senators, fathers⟩

pat·ri·cide, pat·ri·lin·e·al, pat·ri·mo·ny
See PATRIARCH.

pa·tri·ot ['peitriət] *or* ['pætriət] *n* a person who loves and loyally supports the interests of his or her country. **pa·tri·ot·ic** *adj.* **pa·tri·ot·i·cal·ly** *adv.* **pa·tri·ot·ism** *n.* ⟨Greek *patriōtēs; patris* fatherland⟩

pa·trol [pə'troul] *v* **-trolled, -trol·ling** go around (a town, camp, etc.) to watch or guard. *n* **1** a person or group who patrol. **2** a making of the rounds to watch or guard: *on patrol.* **3** a group of soldiers, ships, or aircraft, sent to find out all they can about the enemy. ⟨French *patrouiller* paddle in mud⟩ **patrol car** a police car used for patrolling roads or districts. **patrol wagon** a closed van used by the police for carrying prisoners.

pa·tron ['peitrən] *n* **1** one who buys regularly at a given store, restaurant, hotel, etc. **2** a person who sponsors a person, cause, institution, etc.: *a patron of the arts.* *adj* guarding; protecting: *a patron saint.* ⟨Latin *patronus; pater* father⟩ **pa·tron·age** ['peitrənɪdʒ] *or* ['pætrənɪdʒ] *n* **1** the regular business given to a store, hotel, etc. by customers. **2** the support given by a patron. **3** favour given in a condescending way: *an air of patronage.* **4** the power to give jobs or favours: *the patronage of a premier.* **pa·tron·ize** *v.* **pa·tron·iz·ing** *adj.* **patron saint**

a saint regarded as the special guardian of a person, church, city, etc.

pat·ro·nym·ic [,pætrə'nɪmɪk] *n* a name derived from the name of a father or ancestor, esp through the use of an affix. *Johnson,* meaning *son of John,* is a patronymic. ⟨Greek *patēr* father + *onyma* name⟩

pat·sy ['pætsi] *n Informal* **1** one who is easily victimized or deceived. **2** a scapegoat. ⟨origin uncertain⟩

pat·ter¹ ['pætər] *v* **1** make rapid taps: *rain pattering against the window.* **2** move with light, rapid steps: *She pattered down the stairs.* **pat·ter** *n.* ⟨*pat¹*⟩

pat·ter² ['pætər] *n* **1** rapid and easy talk, such as that of a comedian. **2** the specialized vocabulary of a certain group, esp thieves, etc. ⟨*pater* in *paternoster* the Lord's prayer in Latin, for its first words⟩

pat·tern ['pætərn] *n* **1** an arrangement of shapes, colours, etc.: *a floral pattern.* **2** a model for making something: *a paper dressmaking pattern.* **3** a fine example. **4** a configuration suggesting a design: *traffic patterns.* **5** a standard group of qualities, acts, etc. that characterize a type or individual: *a behaviour pattern.* *v* make or do according to a pattern (often with *after* or *on*): *She patterned herself after her mother.* ⟨Old French *patron* (see PATRON); for a client's copying his or her patron⟩

pat·ty ['pæti] *n* **1** a small pie or filled pastry. **2** a flat cake of chopped food: *hamburger patties.* ⟨French *pâté*⟩

pau·ci·ty ['pɒsəti] *n* **1** a small number. **2** a scarcity; lack. ⟨Latin *paucus* few⟩

paunch [pɒntʃ] *n* **1** the belly; abdomen. **2** a protruding belly; POT BELLY. **paunch·y** *adj.* **paunch·i·ness** *n.*⟨Old Norman French *panche;* Latin *pantex*⟩

pau·per ['pɒpər] *n* **1** a very poor person. **2** a person supported by charity. **pau·per·ism** *n.* **pau·per·ize** *v.* **pau·per·i·za·tion** *n.* ⟨Latin = poor⟩

pause [pɒz] *v* stop for a time. *n* **1** a stop; rest. **2** a momentary hesitation or slight delay. **3** *Music* the holding of a note, chord, or rest beyond its written time value. ⟨Latin *pausa;* Greek *pausis; pauein* to stop⟩ **give one pause** cause one to reconsider.

pave [peiv] *v* cover (a street, sidewalk, etc.) with pavement. ⟨Latin *pavire* tread down⟩ **pave the way** prepare a smooth or easy way: *The maps made by the earliest explorers paved the way for those who followed.* **pave·ment** *n* **1** a covering for streets, sidewalks, etc., made of gravel, concrete, asphalt, etc. **2** a paved road, etc. **pav·ing** *n* the material for pavement.

pa·vil·ion [pə'vɪljən] *n* **1** a building, usually open-sided, used for shelter, pleasure, etc.: *a bathing pavilion.* **2** a large tent for entertainment or shelter: *We rented a pavilion for our wedding.* **3** any building that houses an exhibition at a fair. ⟨Latin *papilio* tent, butterfly⟩

paw [pɒ] *n* **1** the foot of an animal having claws. **2** *Informal* a large or clumsy hand.
v **1** touch with a paw: *The kitten pawed the ball of yarn.* **2** strike with or as if with a hoof: *The horse was pawing the ground, eager to go.* **3** touch awkwardly, rudely, or too intimately. ⟨Old French *powe*⟩

pawn¹ [pɒn] *v* give (something) as security that borrowed money will be repaid: *She pawned her watch to buy food.*
n something left as security. ⟨Old French *pan*⟩
pawn·bro·ker *n* a person who lends money at interest on articles that are left as security.
pawn·shop *n* a pawnbroker's shop.

pawn² [pɒn] *n* **1** *Chess* one of the 16 pieces, 8 black and 8 white, of lowest value. **2** a person or thing used by someone to further his or her own purposes: *She used her friends as pawns in her race for political power.* ⟨Old French *peon*; Latin. See PEON.⟩

pay [peɪ] *v* **paid, pay·ing** **1** give (a person) what is due for goods, services, work, etc. **2** hand over the amount of: *pay a debt.* **3** give; make: *to pay attention, to pay a visit.* **4** be worthwhile (*for*): *Crime does not pay.* **5** reward or punish: *She paid them for their insults by causing them trouble.* **6** suffer: *One who does wrong must pay the penalty.* **7 payed, pay·ing** let out (a rope, etc.) (with *out*).
adj **1** containing enough metal, oil, etc. to be worth mining, drilling, etc.: *a pay lode.* **2** made operable by the use of coins or credit cards: *a pay phone.* **3** concerning a service for which a fee is paid: *pay TV.* **pay** *n.* ⟨Old French *paier*; Latin *pacare* pacify; *pacis* peace⟩
in the pay of working for. **pay back a** return (borrowed money). **b** give the same treatment as received: *I'll pay her back for her hospitality by inviting her for dinner. I'll pay you back yet!* **pay down a** pay (part of the price) at the time of purchase, used in instalment buying. **b** pay in full. **pay off a** give all the money that is owed. **b** get even with. **c** *Informal* bribe. **pay up** pay in full.
paid *adj* **1** receiving money. **2** no longer owed. **pay·a·ble** *adj* **1** required to be paid: *accounts payable.* **2** that can be paid: *payable at any bank.* **pay·cheque** *n* a cheque issued to an employee in payment of wages or salary. **pay·day** *n* a day on which wages are paid. **pay dirt 1** ore containing enough metal to be worth mining. **2** *Informal* something that yields a beneficial result. **hit** (or **strike**) **pay dirt** find a source of wealth or success. **pay·ee** [peɪˈiː] *n* a person to whom money is to be paid. **pay·load** *n* **1** the part of a vehicle's load that produces revenue. **2** the warhead, instruments, etc. carried by a missile. **pay·ment** *n* **1** the act of paying. **2** the amount paid: *a monthly payment.* **3** reward or punishment: *He said his child's good health was payment enough.* **pay·off** *n* **1** returns for an enterprise. **2** a bribe. **3** *Slang* the climax of a story, situation, etc. **pay phone** a telephone operated by money or credit card. **pay·roll** *n* **1** an employer's list of persons to be paid, together with the amount that each is to receive. **2** the total amount to be distributed among these persons. **pay TV** a cable television service for which extra payment is made.

PC **1** PROGRESSIVE CONSERVATIVE. **2** PERSONAL COMPUTER. **3** POLITICALLY CORRECT.

PCB *pl* **PCB's** POLYCHLORINATED BIPHENYL.

PCP phenylcyclohexylpiperidine, a psychedelic drug, sometimes fatal; angel dust.

PDF *Computers* portable document format, a standardized format that allows any document to be displayed regardless of how it was created.

pea [piː] *n* **1** an annual vine grown in many varieties for its protein-rich seeds borne in pods. **2** any of various plants that are related to or resemble the garden pea (usually used in compounds): *chick pea, sweet pea.* ⟨Middle English *pees* sg taken as pl; Greek *pison* pea⟩
(as) like as two peas (**in a pod**) exactly alike.
pea·shoot·er *n* a toy blowgun for shooting dried peas or other small objects. **pea soup** a thick soup made from ham, dried peas, and other vegetables. **pea·soup·er** or **pea·soup** *n* *Informal* a thick, heavy fog.

peace [piːs] *n* **1** freedom from strife of any kind. **2** public quiet, order, and security. **3** quiet; calm; stillness: *peace of mind.* ⟨Old French *pais*; Latin *pacis*⟩
at peace a not in a state of war. **b** not quarrelling. **c** peaceful. **hold** or **keep one's peace** be silent. **keep the peace** maintain public order. **make one's peace with** come to accept (something or someone). **make peace** effect a reconciliation.
peace·a·ble *adj* liking peace. **peace·a·ble·ness** *n.* **peace·a·bly** *adv.* **peace·ful** *adj* **1** calm: *a peaceful scene.* **2** keeping peace: *peaceful neighbours.* **3** to do with peace: *peaceful uses for nuclear energy.* **peace·ful·ly** *adv.* **peace·ful·ness** *n.* **peace·keep·ing** *n* the enforcement of peace between hostile nations by means of an international body of soldiers. **peace·keep·er** *n.* **peace·mak·er** *n* a person who reconciles conflicts. **peace·mak·ing** *n, adj.* **peace offering** an offering made to obtain peace. **peace pipe** calumet. **peace·time** *n* a time of peace. **peace·time** *adj.*

peach [piːtʃ] *n* **1** a small tree of the rose family that bears a juicy fruit with a fuzzy skin. See also NECTARINE. **2** *Informal* a person or thing especially admired: *She's a peach of a girl and we all love her.* ⟨Old French *pesche*; Latin *Persicum malum* Persian apple⟩
peaches–and–cream 1 of a person's complexion, smooth and delicately coloured. **2** of corn, having white and yellow kernels. **peach·y** *adj Slang* fine; wonderful.

pea·cock ['pi,kɒk] *n, pl* **-cocks** or (esp collectively) **-cock** *n* **1** the male of a peafowl. **2** a person who is vain and fond of showing off. ⟨Old English *pēa* (Latin *pavo*) + *cock¹*⟩
pea·fowl *n* any of several brightly coloured birds of the same family as pheasants. The males usually have iridescent plumage. **pea·hen** *n* an adult female peafowl.

peak [pik] *n* **1** the top of a mountain or hill. **2** a mountain that stands alone. **3** the maximum or high point: *the peak of a career.* **4** a projecting brim at the front of a cap: *She wears her cap with the peak pushed to one side.* *v* come or cause to come to a high point: *The unemployment rate normally peaks in February.* **peaked** *adj.* ⟨variant of *pick²*⟩
peak·ed ['pikɪd] *adj* sickly in appearance; wan; thin: *He always looks a little peaked at the end of winter.* ⟨obsolete *peak* get pale and sickly⟩

peal [pil] *n* **1** the prolonged ringing of bells. **2** any loud, long, usually reverberating sound: *a peal of thunder.* *v* ring or cause (bells) to ring in peals. ⟨Middle English *pele*⟩

pea·meal bacon ['pi,mil] ✱ back bacon coated with ground cornmeal.

pea·nut ['pi,nʌt] *or* ['pinət] *n* **1** a plant of the pea family whose seeds are eaten as nuts and also yield an oil used in cooking, etc. **2** peanuts *Slang* something of little value, esp a small amount of money: *It costs peanuts to run this car.*
peanut butter a spread made from peanuts, used as a filling for sandwiches, etc.

pear [pɛr] *n* a tree of the rose family that bears a juicy fruit that is smaller toward the stem end. ⟨Old English *pere*; Latin *pirum*⟩

pearl [pɜrl] *n* **1** a rounded bead formed inside oysters and other bivalve molluscs from deposits of calcite around a nucleus such as a grain of sand. **2** a similar gem made artificially. **3** a very fine one of its kind. *v* *v* hunt or dive for pearls. **pearl·y** *adj.* **pearl·i·ness** *n.* ⟨Latin *perla*⟩
cast pearls before swine display something fine to a person who cannot appreciate it.

pea·sant ['pɛzənt] *n* a person who works on the land, esp a farm labourer. **pea·sant** *adj* of peasants: *peasant labour.* ⟨Old French *paysant*; *pays* country; Latin *pagus* district⟩
peas·ant·ry *n* peasants collectively.

peat [pit] *n* vegetable matter consisting of plants that have become partly carbonized, used as fertilizer and as a fuel when dried. **peat·y** *adj.* ⟨Middle English *pete*⟩
peat bog a bog composed of peat. **peat moss** any of a genus of mosses that grow only in wet, acid areas; sphagnum.

pea·vey ['pivi] *n, pl* **-veys** a strong lever, fitted with a sharp point of iron or steel and a hinged semicircular hook, used by loggers. Also, **pea·vy.** ⟨possibly from a J. *Peavey*, purported inventor⟩

peb·ble ['pɛbəl] *n* **1** a small stone, usually worn smooth by water. **2** a rough, uneven surface on leather, paper, etc. **peb·ble·like** *adj.* ⟨Old English *pæbbel* (in place names)⟩
peb·bly ['pɛbli] *adj* **1** covered with pebbles. **2** having a rough, uneven surface.

pe·can [pɪ'kæn], ['pikæn], *or* [pɪ'kɑn] *n* a large hickory tree bearing edible nuts. ⟨Algonquian *pakan* hard-shelled nut⟩

pec·ca·dil·lo [,pɛkə'dɪlou] *n, pl* **-loes** or **-los** a slight sin or fault. ⟨Spanish, diminutive of *pecado* sin; Latin *peccatum*⟩

peck¹ [pɛk] *n* **1** a unit for measuring volume of grain, fruit, etc., equal to about 9.09 dm³. **2** a great deal: *a peck of trouble.* ⟨Middle English *pec*⟩

peck² [pɛk] *v* **1** strike and pick with the beak or with something like a beak. **2** *Informal* kiss lightly and hurriedly. **peck** *n.* ⟨akin to *pick¹*⟩
peck at a *Informal* eat only a little, bit by bit: *She just pecked at her food.* **b** keep criticizing.
pecking order 1 an order of superiority established in flocks of chickens, etc., each bird enjoying the right of dominating those weaker than itself. **2** any similar order of precedence in human society. **peck·ish** *adj Informal* somewhat hungry.

pecs See PECTORAL.

pec·tin ['pɛktən] *n Biochemistry* a carbohydrate that occurs in ripe fruits and is used to stiffen jams and jellies. **pec·tic** *adj.* ⟨Greek *pēktos* congealed; *pēgnynai* stiffen⟩

pec·to·ral ['pɛktərəl] *adj* to do with the breast or chest: *the pectoral muscles.* ⟨Latin *pectoris* chest⟩
pecs [pɛks] *n pl Slang* pectoral muscles, esp those well developed by exercise. **pectoral fin** one of the two fins behind the head of a fish.

pe·cul·iar [pɪ'kjuljər] *adj* **1** strange; unusual: *The dog's peculiar behaviour frightened the children.* **2** belonging to only one person or thing: *Some minerals are peculiar to the Canadian Shield.* **pe·cu·li·ar·i·ty** [pɪ,kjuli'ɛrəti] *or* [-ærəti] *n.* **pe·cul·iar·ly** *adv.* ⟨Latin *peculium* property; *pecu* money, cattle⟩

pe·cu·ni·ar·y [pɪ'kjuni,ɛri] *adj* to do with money. ⟨Latin *pecunia* money. See PECULIAR.⟩

ped·a·go·gy ['pɛdə,gɒdʒi] *or* ['pɛdə,goudʒi] *n* **1** the profession of teaching. **2** the science or art of teaching. **3 a** a method of teaching a particular subject: *second language pedagogy.* **b** the method used by a particular teacher or school: *This is usual Montessori pedagogy.* **ped·a·gog·i·cal** *adj.* **ped·a·gog·i·cal·ly** *adv.* ⟨Greek *paidos* boy + *agōgos* leader⟩
ped·a·gogue ['pɛdə,gɒg] *n* a pedantic teacher.

ped·al ['pɛdəl] *n* a lever worked by the foot. **ped·al, -alled** or **-aled, -al·ling** or **-al·ing** *v.* **ped·al** *adj.* ⟨Latin *pedis* foot⟩
pedal pushers calf-length pants for women and girls, orig for bicycle riding.

ped·ant ['pɛdənt] *n* **1** a person who displays his or her knowledge in a tiresome way. **2** a narrow-minded scholar who places emphasis on detail. **pe·dan·tic** [pə'dæntɪk] *adj.* **pe·dan·ti·cal·ly** *adv.* **ped·ant·ry** *n.* ⟨Greek *paideuein* educate; *paidos* boy⟩

ped·dle ['pɛdəl] *v* **1** carry from place to place and sell. **2** sell or deal out in small quantities: *to peddle candy, to peddle gossip.* ⟨Middle English *pedlere; ped* basket⟩
ped·dler or **pedlar** *n* a person who travels about selling things that he or she carries in a pack, in a cart, etc.

ped·er·as·ty ['pɛdə,ræsti] *n* the practice of homosexual relations by a man with a boy. **ped·er·ast** *n.* **ped·er·as·tic** *adj.*
ped·er·as·ti·cal·ly *adv.* ⟨Greek *paidos* boy + *erastēs* lover⟩

ped·es·tal ['pɛdɪstəl] *n* **1** the base of a statue, large vase, lamp, etc. **2** any foundation, esp when used to display something.
put (or **set**) **on a pedestal** idolize or romanticize: *The newly engaged couple put each other on a pedestal.* ⟨Italian *piedestallo; pie* foot (Latin *pedis*) + *di* of + *stallo* stall[1] ⟩

pe·des·tri·an [pə'dɛstriən] *n* a person who goes on foot.
adj **1** to do with pedestrians: *a pedestrian crossing.* **2** without imagination; dull: *a pedestrian style in writing.* ⟨Latin *pedestris* on foot; *pedis* foot⟩
pe·des·tri·an·ism *n* the quality of being dull or commonplace.

pe·di·at·rics [,pidi'ætrɪks] *n* (with a sg verb) the branch of medicine dealing with children's diseases and the care and development of babies and children. **pe·di·at·ric** *adj.* **pe·di·a·tri·cian** [,pidiə'trɪʃən] *n.* ⟨Greek *paidos* child + *iatreia* treatment⟩

ped·i·cel ['pɛdəsəl] *n* **1** *Biology* a plant stalk that supports a single flower. **2** *Zoology* a short structure joining organs or parts. ⟨Latin *pedis* foot⟩

ped·i·cure ['pɛdə,kjur] *n* a cosmetic treatment for the feet, toes, and toenails. **ped·i·cur·ist** *n.* ⟨Latin *pedis* foot + *cura* care⟩

ped·i·gree ['pɛdə,gri] *n* **1** the ancestors of a person or animal; family tree. **2** derivation, as from a source: *the pedigree of a word.* **3** the recorded ancestry of a purebred animal.
adj of an animal, purebred: *a pedigree cat.* ⟨probably French *pied de grue* foot of a crane; for 3-branched mark used in genealogies⟩
ped·i·greed *adj* having a known pedigree.

ped·lar See PEDDLE.

pe·dol·o·gy [pɪ'dɒlədʒi] *n* the study of soils. **pe·do·log·i·cal** *adj.* **pe·dol·o·gist** *n.* ⟨Greek *pedan* ground⟩

ped·o·phil·ia [,pɛdə'fɪliə] *n* the abnormal sexual attraction of an adult for young children. ⟨Greek *paidos* boy + *phileein* love⟩
ped·o·phile ['pɛdə,faɪl] *n* an adult who has pedophilia.

pe·dun·cle [pɪ'dʌŋkəl] *n* **1** *Biology* a plant stalk that supports a solitary flower or flower cluster. **2** *Zoology* PEDICEL (def. 2). **3** *Anatomy* a stalklike bundle of nerve fibres connecting various areas of the brain. **pe·dun·cu·lar** *adj.* ⟨Latin *pedunculus* diminutive of *pedis* foot⟩

pee [pi] *Slang v* peed, pee·ing urinate. **pee** *n.* ⟨euphemism for *piss*, from the initial letter *p*⟩

peek [pik] *v* look quickly or secretly. **peek** *n.* ⟨Middle English *piken*⟩

peel [pil] *n* the outer covering of certain fruits or vegetables.
v **1** remove skin, bark, etc. from: *to peel an orange.* **2** come off, esp in flakes: *Her skin is peeling from the sunburn.* **3** remove (with *off*): *to peel off a bandage.* **4** leave a group or lineup (with *off*): *Each motorcycle in the line peeled off as it reached the barrier.* **peel·er** *n.* ⟨Old French *peler*; Latin *pilare* strip away hair⟩
keep one's eyes peeled *Informal* be on the alert: *Keep your eyes peeled for a gas station.*
peel·ing *n* a piece peeled off: *potato peelings.*

peep[1] [pip] *v* **1** look through a small hole. **2** look quickly or secretly. **3** show slightly, as if peeping: *a toe peeping through a hole in a sock.* **peep** *n.* ⟨Middle English *pepen*; Old French *piper*; Latin *pipare*⟩
peep·er *n* *Slang* **1** a person that peeps; voyeur. **2** *Informal* an eye: *Close your peepers and go to sleep.* **peep·hole** *n* a hole through which one may peep. **Peeping Tom** a man who derives pleasure from secretly watching women undressing, etc. **peep show** a film or an exhibition of objects or pictures viewed through a small opening.

peep[2] [pip] *n* **1** a short, high sound such as that made by a baby bird. **2** a feeble protest: *I don't want to hear another peep out of you.* **peep** *v.* ⟨imitative⟩
peep·er *n* any of several frogs that make peeping noises.

peer[1] [pir] *n* **1** a person of the same age, social situation, etc. as another: *a jury of one's peers.* **2** a member of the peerage; a noble. ⟨Old French *per*; Latin *par* equal⟩
peer·age *n* all the titled persons of a country. **peer·ess** *n* **1** a noblewoman. **2** the wife or widow of a peer. **peer group** the people of approximately the same age, social status, etc. within a culture. **peer·less** *adj* without an equal; matchless: *a peerless leader.* **peer·less·ly** *adv.* **peer·less·ness** *n.* **peer pressure** pressure one feels to conform to the styles, attitudes, etc. of a PEER GROUP. **peer-to-peer** *Computers* to do with a network in which each computer has access to the files, software, and peripheral devices of all the others.

peer[2] [pir] *v* look closely: *to peer at the small print.* ⟨probably variant of *appear*⟩

peeve [piv] *Informal v* annoy. **peeve** *n.* ⟨Middle English *pevysh*⟩
pee·vish *adj* cross; fretful; complaining. **pee·vish·ly** *adv.* **pee·vish·ness** *n.*

pee·wee ['piwi] *n* **1** a very small person or thing. **2** *Sports* ✱ a player aged between 8 and 12. **3** *Logging* an undersized log. ⟨*pewee* small bird; for its cry⟩

peg [pɛg] *n* **1** a piece of wood, metal, etc. used to fasten parts together, to hang things on, etc. **2** a step; degree: *to go up several pegs in someone's estimation.*
v **pegged, peg·ging 1** fasten or hold with pegs. **2** work hard and steadily (usually with

away): *pegging away at one's studies.* **3** *Informal* categorize: *She has been pegged as a militant feminist.* **4** keep (a price, commodity, etc.) at a set level: *The price of the shares was pegged at $25.00.* **peg·like** *adj.* ⟨Middle Dutch *pegge*⟩
a square peg in a round hole a person in a position for which he or she is totally unsuited. **take someone down a peg** lower the pride of someone.

Pei·gan See Piikani.

pe·jo·ra·tive [pɪ'dʒɔrətɪv] *adj* tending to make worse; disparaging. **pe·jo·ra·tive·ly** *adv.* ⟨Latin *pejor* worse⟩

Pe·king·ese [ˌpikə'niz] *or* [ˌpikɪŋ'iz] *n, pl* **-ese** a breed of small dog with a flat nose, orig developed in China. Also, **Pe·kin·ese**. ⟨*Peking* former name for Beijing, China⟩

pe·lag·ic [pə'lædʒɪk] *adj* to do with the ocean or the open sea. ⟨Greek *pelagos* sea⟩

pel·i·can ['pɛləkən] *n* any of a genus of fish-eating birds having a bill with a distensible pouch on the underside for scooping up and holding food. ⟨Greek *pelekan*⟩

pel·let ['pɛlɪt] *n* a little ball of paper, mud, metal, medicine, compressed food for animals, etc. **pel·let·like** *adj.* ⟨Old French *pelote;* Latin *pila* ball⟩

pel·li·cle ['pɛləkəl] *n* **1** a very thin skin; scum. **2** *Zoology* a non-living membrane secreted by animal cells such as protozoans. **pel·lic·u·lar** [pɛ'lɪkjələr] *adj.* ⟨Latin *pellicula,* diminutive of *pellis* skin⟩

pell–mell *or* **pell·mell** ['pɛl 'mɛl] *adv* **1** in a rushing, tumbling mass. **2** in headlong haste. *adj* headlong; tumultuous.
n violent disorder or confusion. ⟨French reduplication *pêle-mêle; mêler* mix⟩

pel·lu·cid [pə'lusɪd] *adj* **1** clear: *a pellucid stream.* **2** clearly expressed: *pellucid language.* **pel·lu·cid·ly** *adv.* **pel·lu·cid·i·ty** *n.* ⟨Latin *per-* through + *lucere* to shine⟩

pelt¹ [pɛlt] *v* **1** throw things at: *pelted with flowers.* **2** beat heavily: *The rain came pelting down.* **3** run quickly: *The thief pelted down the street.* ⟨Middle English *pelten*⟩
at full pelt fast.

pelt² [pɛlt] *n* the skin of a fur-bearing animal before it has been dressed or tanned. ⟨Old French *peleterie; pel* skin, Latin *pellis*⟩

pel·vis ['pɛlvɪs] *n, pl* **-vis·es** *or* **-ves** [-viz] *Anatomy* the basin-shaped structure in many vertebrates formed by the hipbones and the backbone. **pel·vic** *adj.* ⟨Latin = basin⟩

pem·mi·can ['pɛməkən] *n* dried, lean meat pounded into a paste with fat and sometimes berries. Pemmican keeps for a long time. ⟨Cree *pimii* fat, grease + *kan* prepared⟩

pen¹ [pɛn] *n* an instrument for writing with ink. *v* **penned, pen·ning** write. **pen·like** *adj.* ⟨Latin *penna* feather⟩
pen·knife *n, pl* **-knives** a small pocketknife, orig used for sharpening quills for pens. **pen·man·ship** *n* skill in writing with pen, pencil, etc. **pen name** a name used by a

writer instead of his or her real name: *Mark Twain* was the pen name of *Samuel Clemens.*

pen² [pɛn] *n* **1** a small, closed area for cows, pigs, etc. **2** any small place of confinement.
v **penned** *or* **pent, pen·ning 1** shut in a pen. **2** confine closely: *I kept the dog penned in a corner while they hunted for the leash.* **pen·like** *adj.* ⟨Old English *penn*⟩
pent *adj* closely confined (with *in* or *up*): *He was pent up in the house most of the winter because of illness.* **pent–up** *adj* confined; restrained; checked: *pent-up emotions.*

pen³ [pɛn] *n Slang* penitentiary.

pen⁴ [pɛn] *n* a female swan. ⟨origin unknown⟩

pe·nal ['pinəl] *adj* to do with punishment: *penal laws.* ⟨Greek *poinē* penalty⟩
penal code the laws and the punishments for breaking them. **pe·nal·ize** ['pinə,laɪz] *or* ['pɛnə,laɪz] *v* **1** declare punishable by law or by rule: *The City Council has penalized loud noises late at night.* **2** inflict a penalty on: *The player was penalized by having to forfeit a point.* **pen·al·ty** ['pɛnəlti] *n* **1** a punishment for breaking a law or rule: *The penalty for speeding is a fine.* **2** a disadvantage imposed on a side for breaking the rules of a sport or game: *There are six penalties in last night's game.* **3** a disadvantage attached to some act or condition: *the penalties of old age.* **4** a handicap imposed for breach of contract: *The penalty for cashing this bond before the due date is $100.* **penalty box** *Hockey, lacrosse* a special bench where penalized players serve their penalties. **pen·al·ty–kill·er** *or* **penalty killer** *n Hockey* a player put on the ice when his or her team is shorthanded as the result of a penalty, to prevent scoring by the other side. **pen·al·ty–kill·ing** *or* **penalty killing**.

pen·ance ['pɛnəns] *n* **1** any act done as a punishment borne to show sorrow for sin, and to obtain pardon for sin. **2** *Roman Catholic Church* the sacrament that includes contrition, confession, and absolution. ⟨Latin *paenitentia.* See PENITENCE.⟩
do penance perform some act, or undergo some penalty, in repentance for sin.

pen·chant ['pɛntʃənt] *n* a strong liking (with *for*): *a penchant for taking long walks.* ⟨French; *pencher* incline; Latin *pendere* hang⟩

pen·cil ['pɛnsəl] *n* a pointed tool to write or draw with, consisting of a tube of wood, metal, plastic, etc., having a thin piece of graphite or coloured material in the centre.
v **-cilled** *or* **-ciled, -cil·ling** *or* **-cil·ing** mark, write, or draw with a pencil. **pen·cil–like** *adj.* ⟨Latin *penicillus* paintbrush; diminutive of *penis* tail, penis⟩
pencil in book, as by writing on a calendar: *When can I pencil you in for an interview?* **pencil pusher** *Informal* a person whose work entails much writing or manual recording.

pend·ant ['pɛndənt] *n* a hanging ornament attached to an earring, necklace, or bracelet. Also, **pen·dent**.
adj hanging. **pend·ant·like** *adj.* ⟨Old French *pendre* hang; Latin *pendere*⟩

pend·ing ['pɛndɪŋ] *adj* waiting to be decided or settled: *The agreement was pending.*
prep **1** while waiting for: *Pending my return, get things ready.* **2** during: *pending the investigation.* ⟨Latin *pendere* hang⟩

pen·du·lous ['pɛndjələs] *adj* **1** hanging downward: *pendulous jowls.* **2** suspended so as to swing freely. **pen·du·lous·ness** *n.* ⟨Latin *pendulus*; *pendere* hang⟩
pen·du·lum *n* a body hung from a point so as to move to and fro under the forces of gravity and momentum.

pen·e·trate ['pɛnə,treɪt] *v* **1** pass through or into: *The bullet penetrated the wall.* **2** pierce through: *Our eyes could not penetrate the darkness.* **3** make a way through something: *The sunshine penetrated the clouds.* **4** spread through: *The smell penetrated the whole house.* **pen·e·tra·ble** *adj.* **pen·e·tra·bil·i·ty** *n.*
pen·e·tra·bly *adv.* **pen·e·tra·tion** *n.* ⟨Latin *penetrare*; *penitus* inmost⟩
pen·e·trat·ing *adj* **1** piercing: *a penetrating scream.* **2** keen: *a penetrating insight.*
pen·e·trat·ing·ly *adv.*

> **SYNONYMS**
> **Penetrate** suggests the driving force or keenness of what goes in: *The bullet penetrated the wall.* **Pierce** means stab through the surface with a sharp-pointed object: *The dagger pierced his side.*

pen·guin ['pɛŋgwɪn] *n* any of a family of flightless sea birds native to the cold regions of the southern hemisphere, having legs set far back on the body so that they walk erect, and wings modified into flippers for swimming. ⟨Welsh *pen* head + *gwyn* white⟩

pen·i·cil·lin [,pɛnə'sɪlən] *n* any of a group of very powerful antibiotic drugs, made from a penicillium mould or produced synthetically. ⟨Latin. See PENCIL.⟩
pen·i·cil·li·um *n, pl* **-cil·li·ums** or **-cil·li·a** [-'sɪlɪə] any of a genus of fungi occurring as green or blue mould on stale food.

pen·in·su·la [pə'nɪnsələ] *or* [pə'nɪnsjələ] *n* a piece of land almost surrounded by water.
pen·in·su·lar *adj.* ⟨Latin *paene* almost + *insula* island⟩

pe·nis ['pinɪs] *n, pl* **-nis·es** or **-nes** [-niz] the male sexual organ, which, in mammals, is also the organ through which urine is excreted. **pen·ile** *adj.* ⟨Latin = tail, penis⟩

pen·i·tence ['pɛnətəns] *n* repentance. ⟨Latin *paenitentia*; *paenitere* repent⟩
pen·i·tent *adj* sorry for doing wrong. *n* **1** a person who is sorry for wrongdoing. **2** *Roman Catholic Church* a person who confesses and does penance under the direction of a priest. **pen·i·tent·ly** *adv.*
pen·i·ten·tial *adj* to do with penitence or with penance. **pen·i·ten·tia·ry** [,pɛnə'tɛnʃəri] *n, pl* **-ries** a prison, esp a federal prison for serious crimes. *adj* **1** making one liable to punishment in a prison: *a penitentiary offence.* **2** used for punishment and reformation: *penitentiary measures.*

pen·knife, pen·man·ship, pen name See PEN.

pen·nant ['pɛnənt] *n* a flag, often tapering to a point, used on ships for signalling, as a banner, trophy, etc. ⟨blend of *pennon* (Old French *penon*; Latin *penna* feather) + *pendant*⟩

pen·ny ['pɛni] *n, pl* **pen·nies 1** one cent. **2** even the smallest sum of money: *I wouldn't give them a penny.* ⟨Old English *peni(n)g*⟩
a penny for your thoughts a remark made to someone obviously deep in thought. **a pretty penny** *Informal* a large sum of money: *That must have cost a pretty penny!*
pen·ni·less *adj* having no money; very poor.
pen·ny–pinch·ing *adj* too thrifty; miserly.
pen·ny–pinch·ing *n.* **pen·ny–pinch·er** *n.*
pen·ny–wise *adj* thrifty in regard to small sums. **penny–wise and pound–foolish** thrifty in small expenses and wasteful in big ones.
pen·ny·worth *n* a small amount.

pe·nol·o·gy [pi'nɒlədʒi] *n* the study of the treatment of prison inmates and the management of prisons. ⟨Greek *poinē* punishment⟩

pen·sion[1] ['pɛnʃən] *n* **1** money paid to people who have retired from regular work. **2** an allowance given by a patron to an artist.
pen·sion·a·ble *adj.* **pen·sion·less** *adj.* ⟨Latin *pensio*; *pendere* weigh out, pay⟩
pension off cause to retire from service with a pension.
pen·sion·er *n* one who receives a pension.

pen·sion[2] [pã'sjɔ̃] *n French* boarding house. ⟨Old French = rent. See PENSION[1].⟩

pen·sive ['pɛnsɪv] *adj* thoughtful in a sad way. **pen·sive·ly** *adv.* **pen·sive·ness** *n.* ⟨Old French *penser* think; Latin *pendere* weigh⟩

pent See PEN[2].

pen·ta– ['pɛntə] *prefix* five. ⟨Greek⟩
pent·a·gon [-,gɒn] *n* **1** a figure with five sides. **2 the Pentagon** in the US, a pentagon-shaped building that is the headquarters of the Department of Defense. **pen·tag·o·nal** [pɛn'tægənəl] *adj.* **pent·a·gram** *n* a five-pointed star. **pent·a·he·dron** [,pɛntə'hidrən] *n, pl* **-drons, -dra** a solid with five faces.
pent·a·he·dral *adj.* **pent·am·e·ter** [pɛn'tæmətər] *n* **1** a line of poetry having five metrical feet. **2** unrhymed verse, each line having five iambic feet; HEROIC VERSE; BLANK VERSE.
pent·a·met·ric *adj.* **Pen·ta·teuch** ['pɛntə,tjuk] *or* ['pɛntə,tuk] *n* the first five books of the Christian or Jewish scriptures: Genesis, Exodus, Leviticus, Numbers, and Deuteronomy.
pen·tath·lete *n* an athlete who competes in a pentathlon. **pen·tath·lon** [pɛn'tæθlɒn] *n* **1** an athletic contest consisting of five events: discus throw, javelin throw, long jump, 200 m dash, and 1500 m run. **2** the **modern pentathlon**, comprising a cross-country equestrian steeplechase, a cross-country run, a swim, foil fencing, and pistol shooting.
pen·ta·ton·ic *adj Music* having five tones in the scale.

Pen·te·cost ['pɛntə,kɒst] *n* **1** the seventh Sunday after Easter, a Christian festival commemorating the descent of the Holy Spirit upon the Apostles. **2** a Jewish religious holiday, celebrating the giving of the law to Moses. ⟨Greek *pentēkostē* fiftieth (day)⟩

Pen·te·cos·tal or **pen·te·cos·tal** *adj* to do with fundamentalist Protestant denominations that emphasize the activity of the Holy Spirit.

pent·house ['pɛnt,haʊs] *n* **1** an apartment or house built on the top of a building. **2** a luxury apartment on the top floor of a highrise. ⟨Middle English *pentis;* Latin *appendere* append; influenced by *house*⟩

pent–up See PEN[2].

pe·nul·ti·mate [pɪ'nʌltəmɪt] *adj* next to last. ⟨Latin *paene* almost + *ultima* last⟩

pe·num·bra [pɪ'nʌmbrə] *n, pl* **-brae** [-bri] or [-braɪ] or **-bras** the partial shadow outside the complete shadow formed by the sun, moon, etc. during an eclipse. ⟨Latin *paene* almost + *umbra* shadow⟩

pen·u·ry ['pɛnjəri] *n* great poverty. ⟨Latin *penuria*⟩
pe·nu·ri·ous [pə'njʊriəs] or [pə'nʊriəs] *adj* **1** poor: *penurious surroundings.* **2** stingy. **pe·nu·ri·ous·ly** *adv.* **pe·nu·ri·ous·ness** *n.*

pe·on ['pion] *n* in Latin America, a person doing work that requires little skill. ⟨Spanish; Latin *pedonis* foot soldier⟩

pe·o·ny ['piəni] *n* any of a genus of shrubby plants, cultivated for their showy flowers. ⟨Greek *paiōnia; Paiōn* physician of the gods⟩

peo·ple ['pipəl] *pl n* **1** men, women, and children; persons. **2** (functioning as sg) an ethnic group; nation. **3** the public. **4** the persons of a place, class, or group: *city people, Prairie people.* **5** the common people. **6** human beings considered indefinitely: *She's afraid of what people will think.*
v fill with inhabitants: *Canada was largely peopled by Europeans.* ⟨Latin *populus*⟩

SYNONYMS

People emphasizes cultural and social unity, arising from common responsibilities and interests: *The Pennsylvania Dutch are a people, not a nation.* **Race** refers to biological unity, having common descent, and is no longer in technical use: *Europeans are often said to belong to the Caucasian race.*
Nation can emphasize political unity, applying to a group united under one government: *Spaniards are a people and a nation, not a race.* However, **nation** is also used of a group united by history, language, and culture: *the First Nations.*

pep [pɛp] *Informal n* energy; enthusiasm. *v* **pepped, pep·ping** put new life into (with *up*): *to pep up a party.* ⟨*pepper*⟩
pep pill any of various stimulant drugs, such as amphetamine, in pill form. **pep·py** *adj* energetic; lively. **pep·pi·ness** *n.* **pep rally** a meeting organized to stimulate support and enthusiasm for a team, cause, campaign, etc. **pep talk** a short, emotional talk intended to encourage some activity.

pep·per ['pɛpər] *n* **1** a seasoning with a hot taste, made from the ground-up berries of a tropical shrub. **2** any of various capsicums.

v **1** season with pepper (def. 1). **2** sprinkle thickly: *Her face is peppered with freckles.* **3** hit with small objects sent thick and fast: *We peppered the enemy with shot.* ⟨Greek *peperi*⟩
pep·per·corn ['pɛpər,kɔrn] *n* a dried berry of the pepper shrub. **pepper mill** a hand mill used to grind peppercorns. **pep·per·mint** *n* **1** a species of mint yielding a sweet-smelling oil. **2** a candy flavoured with this oil. **pep·per·o·ni** [,pɛpə'rouni] *n* a spicy Italian sausage. **pepper shaker** a container with holes in the top for sprinkling pepper on food. **pep·pery** *adj* **1** to do with pepper: *a peppery stew.* **2** sharp; pungent. **3** having a hot temper. **pep·per·i·ness** *n.*

pep·sin ['pɛpsən] *n* an enzyme in the stomach that helps to digest proteins. ⟨Greek *pepsis* digestion⟩
pep·tic ['pɛptɪk] *adj* **1** promoting digestion. **2** to do with pepsin. **3** to do with the action of digestive juices: *a peptic ulcer.*

Pé·quiste [pei'kist] *n* ✱ a supporter of the Parti Québécois. Also, **pé·quiste**. ⟨French *P* [pe] *Q* (Parti Québécois) + *iste*⟩

per [pər] *prep* **1** for each: *We need two sandwiches per person.* **2** according to: *The order was sent out as per instructions.* ⟨Latin⟩
per an·num ['ænəm] *Latin* for each year: *Her salary was $89 000 per annum.* **per cap·i·ta** ['kæpətə] for each person: *$40 for eight people amounts to $5 per capita.* **per·cent** or **per cent** [pər'sɛnt] *n* **1** parts in each hundred. Five percent (5%) is 5 out of each 100, or of the whole. *Symbol %* **2** for each hundred: *Seven percent of the students failed.* **3** percentage: *A large percent of the apple crop was ruined.* **per·cent·age** *n* **1** the part of each hundred: *What percentage of children were absent?* **2** a part: *A large percentage of students finish high school now.* **3** *Slang* advantage or profit: *What's the percentage in that?* **per·cen·tile** [-taɪl] or [-təl] *n* any value in a series of points on a scale arrived at by dividing a group into a hundred equal parts in order of magnitude: *A student at the fiftieth percentile is at a point halfway between the top and the bottom of the group.* **per di·em** ['diəm] or ['daɪəm] *Latin* **1** for each day: *The room rate is $75.00 per diem.* **2** a daily allowance: *We were given a per diem of $85.00.* **per se** ['sei] *Latin* by, of, or in itself; intrinsically.

per·ceive [pər'siv] *v* **1** be aware of through the senses; see, hear, taste, smell, or feel. **2** take in with the mind: *I perceived that I could not make them change their minds.* ⟨Old French *perceivre;* Latin *per-* fully + *capere* grasp⟩
per·cept ['pɜrsɛpt] *n* that which is perceived. **per·cep·ti·ble** *adj* great enough to be perceived: *There was no perceptible change in her breathing.* **per·cep·ti·bil·i·ty** *n.* **per·cep·ti·bly** *adv.* **per·cep·tion** *n* **1** the act of perceiving. **2** the power of perceiving: *a keen perception.* **3** PERCEPT. **per·cep·tive** *adj* having the power of perceiving; insightful: *Her comments were always perceptive.* **per·cep·tive·ly** *adv.*
per·cep·tive·ness *n.* **per·cep·tu·al** *adj* to do with perception. **per·cep·tu·al·ly** *adv.*

perch¹ [pɜrtʃ] *n* **1** a bar, branch, or anything on which a bird can come to rest. **2** a rather high place or position.
v **1** alight and rest: *A robin perched on our porch railing.* **2** sit, esp on something rather high: *The child perched on a stool.* **3** place high up: *The village was perched on a hill.* ⟨Old French *perche*; Latin *pertica* pole⟩

perch² [pɜrtʃ] *n*, *pl* **perch** or **perch·es** any of a genus of small food fishes. ⟨Greek *perkē*⟩

per·co·late ['pɜrkə,leit] *v* **1** drip or drain through small holes. **2** filter through: *Water percolates sand.* **per·co·la·tion** *n*. ⟨Latin *per*- through + *colum* strainer⟩
per·co·la·tor ['pɜrkə,leitər] *n* a coffee pot in which boiling water continually bubbles up and drips down through ground coffee.

per·cus·sion [pər'kʌʃən] *n* **1** the striking of one body against another with force. **2** *Medicine* the technique of tapping a part of the body to find out the condition of the parts underneath by the resulting sound. **3** *Music* the section of an orchestra or band composed of PERCUSSION INSTRUMENTS. **per·cus·sive** *adj*. ⟨Latin *percussio*; *per*- (intensive) + *quatere* strike, beat⟩
percussion instrument a musical instrument played by striking it, such as a cymbal, or by shaking it, as a tambourine. **per·cus·sion·ist** *n*.

per·di·tion [pər'dɪʃən] *n* **1** the loss of one's soul and the joys of heaven; eternal death. **2** hell. ⟨Latin *perdere* destroy⟩

per·e·gri·nate ['pɛrəgrə,neit] *v* **1** journey, esp on foot. **2** travel across or through (a place). **per·e·gri·na·tion** *n*. ⟨Latin *peregrinus* from foreign parts; *per*- outside + *ager* territory⟩

per·emp·to·ry [pə'rɛmptəri] *adj* **1** imperious; dogmatic: *a peremptory boss.* **2** leaving no choice; absolute: *a peremptory decree.* **3** *Law* **a** not admitting of debate. **b** not requiring that cause be shown. **per·emp·to·ri·ly** *adv*. **per·emp·to·ri·ness** *n*. ⟨Latin *peremptorius* deadly, final; *per*- (intensive) + *emere* take⟩

per·en·ni·al [pə'rɛniəl] *adj* **1** lasting through the whole year: *a perennial stream.* **2** lasting for a long time: *the perennial beauty of the hills.* **3** producing flowers from the same root year after year: *perennial garden plants.*
n a perennial plant. Compare ANNUAL and BIENNIAL. **per·en·ni·al·ly** *adv*. ⟨Latin *per*- through + *annus* year⟩

per·es·troi·ka [,pɛrɛ'strɔika] *n* in the former Soviet Union, reforms of the late 1980s.

per·fect ['pɜrfɪkt] *adj* **1** without defect. **2** having all its parts: *The set was perfect.* **3** entire; utter: *a perfect stranger.* **4** *Grammar* of a verb form, showing an action, state, etc. thought of as being completed. See PERFECT TENSE. **5** correct in every detail: *a perfect copy.* **6** *Botany* having both stamens and pistils.
v [pər'fɛkt] remove all faults from: *The formula was perfected at last.* **per·fect·i·ble** [pər'fɛktəbəl] *adj*. **per·fect·i·bil·i·ty** *n*. ⟨Latin *perfectus* pp of *perficere*; *per*- fully + *facere* do⟩
per·fec·tion *n* **1** a perfect condition. **2** a perfect person or thing. **3** a making perfect: *The perfection of our plans will take another week.* **to perfection** perfectly: *He played the solo to perfection.* **per·fec·tion·ism** *n* a striving for absolute perfection. **per·fec·tion·ist** *n*. **per·fec·tion·is·tic** *adj*. **per·fect·ly** *adv* **1** completely and faultlessly: *a perfectly drawn circle.* **2** to an adequate extent: *This coat is perfectly good.* **perfect participle** *Grammar* the past participle preceded by *having*. In *Having written the letter, she mailed it, having written* is a perfect participle. **perfect tense** the form of a verb which shows that the action is completed now (**present perfect**); was completed in the past (**past perfect**); is to be completed in the future (**future perfect**).

per·fi·dy ['pɜrfədi] *n* base treachery. **per·fid·i·ous** [pər'fɪdiəs] *adj*. **per·fid·i·ous·ly** *adv*. ⟨Latin *per*- away + *fides* faith⟩

per·fo·rate ['pɜrfə,reit] *v* make a hole or holes through: *Sheets of postage stamps are perforated.* **per·fo·ra·tion** *n*. ⟨Latin *per*- through + *forare* bore⟩

per·force [pər'fɔrs] *adv Formal, archaic* by necessity. ⟨French *par* by + *force*⟩

per·form [pər'fɔrm] *v* **1** carry out (an action). **2** act, play an instrument, sing, dance, etc. in public. **per·form·ance** *n*. **per·form·er** *n*. ⟨Old French *par*- fully + *fournir* furnish⟩
per·form·a·tive *n* a gesture having a conventional linguistic meaning, as (in English) shaking the head for 'no' and nodding for 'yes'. **performing arts** any of the arts such as dance, drama, etc., that are performed before an audience.

per·fume ['pɜrfjum] *or* [pər'fjum] *n* **1** a pleasant scent: *the perfume of flowers.* **2** a substance that produces a pleasant scent.
v [pər'fjum] **1** fill with a sweet odour. **2** put a sweet-smelling substance on. ⟨Latin *per*- through + *fumare* smoke⟩

per·func·to·ry [pər'fʌŋktəri] *adj* done with little thought or effort: *The girl gave her face a perfunctory washing. The nurse was perfunctory in the performance of his duties.* **per·func·to·ri·ly** *adv*. **per·func·to·ri·ness** *n*. ⟨Latin *per*- to the end + *fungi* execute⟩

per·haps [pər'hæps] *adv* maybe. ⟨Middle English *per happes* by chances⟩

per·i·gee ['pɛrɪ,dʒi] *n* **1** the point in the orbit of a satellite where it comes closest to the earth. Compare APOGEE. **2** the lowest or closest point. ⟨Greek *peri*- near + *gē* earth⟩

per·i·he·li·on [,pɛrɪ'hiliən] *or* [,pɛrɪ'hiljən] *n*, *pl* **-he·li·a** [-'hiliə] *or* [-'hiljə] the point in the orbit of a planet or other heavenly body where it is closest to the sun. Compare APHELION. ⟨Greek *peri*- near + *hēlios* sun⟩

per·il ['pɛrəl] *n* a chance of harm. ⟨Latin *periculum*⟩
per·il·ous *adj* dangerous; full of peril: *a perilous journey.* **per·il·ous·ly** *adv*.

pe·rim·e·ter [pə'rɪmətər] *n* the boundary of a plane figure or an area: *There is a fence around the perimeter of the field.* **per·i·met·ric** [,pɛrɪ'mɛtrɪk] *adj*. ⟨Greek *peri*- around + *metron* measure⟩

pe·ri·od ['pirjəd] *n* **1** a span of time: *a short period.* **2** a portion of time marked off by events that recur. A month, from new moon to new moon, is a period. **3** *Geology* a subdivision of an era. **4** the portion of a game during which there is actual play: *There are three periods in a hockey game.* **5** one of the portions of time into which a school day is divided. **6** an occurrence of menstruation. **7** the punctuation mark (.) that indicates the end of a declarative sentence.
adj characteristic of a certain period of history: *period furniture.*
interj Informal **1** that's final! *The discussion is over, period!* **2** categorically: *"She dislikes big dogs?" "No, she dislikes dogs, period."* ⟨Greek *periodos* cycle; *peri-* around + *hodos* a going⟩
pe·ri·od·ic [,piri'ndɪk] *adj* **1** recurring at regular intervals: *periodic attacks of malaria.* **2** happening every now and then: *a periodic fit of tidying one's desk.* **pe·ri·od·i·cal·ly** *adv.* **pe·ri·od·i·cal** *n* a magazine that appears at regular intervals. **pe·ri·o·dic·i·ty** [,piriə'dɪsəti] *n* the tendency to happen at regular intervals. **periodic sentence** a complex sentence with the MAIN CLAUSE at the end. In *When he was ready, he left the room, he left the room* is the main clause. **periodic table** *Chemistry* a table in which the elements are shown in related groups. **period piece** a work of art, as a painting, literature, etc. that calls to mind a particular period of history.

per·i·o·don·tal [,pɛriə'dɒntəl] *adj Dentistry* to do with the tissues around the teeth: *periodontal disease.* ⟨Greek *peri-* + *odontos* tooth⟩
per·i·o·don·tics *n* (with a sg verb) the branch of dentistry dealing with diseases of the tissues and structures around the teeth. **per·i·o·don·tic** *adj.* **per·i·o·don·tist** *n.*

per·i·pa·tet·ic [,pɛripə'tɛtɪk] *adj* **1** walking about; itinerant. **2** jumping from one subject to another; discursive.
n a person who wanders or travels about from place to place. **per·i·pa·tet·i·cal·ly** *adv.* ⟨Greek *peri-* around + *pateein* walk⟩

pe·riph·er·y [pə'rɪfəri] *n,* **1** a boundary; perimeter. **2** an area outside the main area: *the periphery of a city.* **3** *Anatomy* the area surrounding a nerve ending, such as a muscle. ⟨Greek *peri-* around + *pherein* carry⟩
pe·riph·er·al *adj* **1** to do with a periphery. **2** incidental or minor: *peripheral issues.* **3** *Anatomy* to do with the surface of the body: *peripheral nerves.* **4** *Computers* to do with supplementary hardware connected to a computer to make up a computer system. Printers, monitors, and disk drives are peripheral devices. **pe·riph·er·al·ly** *adv.* **peripheral nervous system** all the nerves outside the brain and spinal cord. Compare

CENTRAL NERVOUS SYSTEM. **peripheral vision** the area of vision outside the line of direct sight.
pe·riph·ra·sis [pə'rɪfrəsɪs] *n, pl* -ses [-,siz] **1** a roundabout way of speaking or writing. *The wife of your father's brother* is a periphrasis for *your aunt.* **2** an expression using auxiliaries that has the same function as a word. *Examples: has gone = went, of the dog = dog's.* Also, **pe·riph·rase** ['pɛrəfreiz]. **per·i·phras·tic** [,pɛrə'fræstɪk] *adj.* **per·i·phras·ti·cal·ly** *adv.* ⟨Greek *peri* around + *phrazein* speak⟩

per·i·scope ['pɛrɪ,skoup] *n* an instrument with an arrangement of mirrors or prisms that permits a person to see things that are otherwise above and out of sight. ⟨Greek *peri* around + *skopein* look⟩
per·i·scop·ic [,pɛrɪ'skɒpɪk] *adj* giving vision obliquely as well as in a direct line.

per·ish ['pɛrɪʃ] *v* **1** die or be destroyed. **2** decay: *Fruit perishes quickly in hot weather.* ⟨Latin *perire; per-* (intensive) + *ire* go⟩
per·ish·a·ble *adj* likely to decay. *n* Usually, **perishables** *pl* things that are likely to decay, esp fresh food. **per·ish·a·bil·i·ty** *n.*

per·i·to·ne·um [,pɛritə'niəm] *n, pl* -ne·a [-'niə] *Anatomy* the membrane that lines the walls of the abdomen of a mammal. **per·i·to·ne·al** *adj.* ⟨Greek *peri-* around + *teinein* stretch⟩
per·i·to·ni·tis [,pɛritə'naitis] *n* inflammation of the peritoneum.

per·i·win·kle[1] ['pɛri,wɪŋkəl] *n* any of several evergreen plants of the dogbane family having blueish flowers. ⟨Latin *pervinca*⟩
per·i·win·kle[2] ['pɛri,wɪŋkəl] *n* any of various edible marine snails. ⟨Old English *pine-* (perhaps Greek *pinē* mussel) + *wincle* corner⟩

per·jure ['pɜrdʒər] *v* lie when under oath (with a reflexive pronoun): *The witness perjured herself.* **per·jured** *adj.* **per·jur·er** *n.* **per·ju·ry** *n.* ⟨Latin *per-* through + *jurare* swear⟩

perk[1] [pɜrk] *v* **1** move briskly or saucily. **2** raise briskly (often with *up*): *The sparrow perked up its tail.* **3** make smart (often with *out*): *They are all perked out in their best clothes.* **perk·y** *adj.* **perk·i·ly** *adv.* **perk·i·ness** *n.* ⟨Middle English *perken*⟩
perk up brighten up: *The whole garden perked up after the rain.*
perk[2] [pɜrk] *v Informal* percolate: *to hear the coffee perking.*
perk[3] [pɜrk] *n Informal* perquisite: *enjoying perks such as free theatre tickets.*

perm [pɜrm] *n Informal* PERMANENT WAVE.
v give (hair) a permanent wave.

per·ma·frost ['pɜrmə,frɒst] *n* ground or subsoil that is permanently frozen. ⟨blend of *permanent* + *frost*⟩
permafrost pit a storage pit for food, using the refrigerative properties of permafrost.

per·ma·nent ['pɜrmənənt] *adj* intended to last: *a permanent filling in a tooth.*
n Informal PERMANENT WAVE. **per·ma·nence** *n.* **per·ma·nent·ly** *adv.* ⟨Latin *per-* through + *manere* stay⟩
permanent press a chemical treatment given

to fabric to make it resistant to creases. **permanent–press** *adj.* **permanent tooth** one of the second set of teeth in a mammal that follow the baby teeth. **permanent wave** a wave produced in the hair by chemicals, that lasts even after washing the hair many times.

per·me·ate ['pɜrmi,eit] *v* spread through the whole of: *Smoke permeated the house. Water will not permeate this fabric.* **per·me·a·ble** *adj.* **per·me·a·tion** *n.* ⟨Latin *per-* through + *meare* pass⟩ **per·me·a·bil·i·ty** *n* 1 a measure of the ease with which liquid or gas can filter through a porous material. 2 *Physics* a measure of the ease with which magnetic induction can be established by a magnetic field.

per·mis·si·ble, per·mis·sion, per·mis·sive See PERMIT.

per·mit [pər'mɪt] *v* -mit·ted, -mit·ting *v* 1 allow (a person, etc.) to do something. 2 let (something) be done or occur: *The law does not permit smoking in this store.*
n ['pɜrmɪt] an official printed order giving the recipient permission to do something: *a parking permit, a liquor permit.* ⟨Latin *per-* through + *mittere* let go⟩
per·mis·si·ble [pər'mɪsəbəl] *adj* that may be permitted; allowable. **per·mis·si·bly** *adv.*
per·mis·si·bil·i·ty *n.* **per·mis·sion** *n* consent: *They asked her permission to leave early.* **per·mis·sive** *adj* not strict; indulgent: *permissive parents.* **per·mis·sive·ness** *n.*

SYNONYMS
Permit emphasizes the idea of giving consent: *His parents permitted him to borrow their car when he was eighteen.* **Allow** often means not forbid, without necessarily giving permission or approval: *That teacher allows too much noise in the room.*

per·mu·ta·tion [,pɜrmjə'teiʃən] *n* 1 complete rearrangement. 2 *Mathematics* a rearrangement of the order of a set of things. The permutations of *a*, *b*, and *c* are *abc, acb, bac, bca, cab, cba.* **per·mute** [pər'mjut] *v.* ⟨Latin *per-* across + *mutare* change⟩

per·ni·cious [pər'nɪʃəs] *adj* 1 causing harm: *pernicious habits.* 2 fatal: *a pernicious disease.* **per·ni·cious·ly** *adv.* **per·ni·cious·ness** *n.* ⟨Latin *per-* thoroughly + *necis* death⟩

per·nick·e·ty [pər'nɪkɪti] *adj Informal* 1 overly fastidious; fussy. 2 requiring precise and careful handling. ⟨origin uncertain⟩

pe·ro·gy [pə'rougi] *n* a dumplinglike pastry with a meat, cheese, or other filling. Also, **pie·ro·gi, pi·rog·i, py·roh·y.** ⟨Ukrainian⟩

per·o·ra·tion [,pɛrə'reiʃən] *n* 1 the last part of an oration, summing up what has been said. 2 a long speech, usually employing high-flown and pompous language. **per·o·rate** *v.* ⟨Latin *per-* to an end + *orare* orate⟩

per·ox·ide [pə'rɒksaɪd] *n* 1 *Chemistry* an oxide that contains the greatest amount of oxygen. 2 HYDROGEN PEROXIDE.
v bleach (hair) by applying hydrogen peroxide. ⟨Latin *per-* fully + OXIDE⟩

per·pen·dic·u·lar [,pɜrpən'dɪkjələr] *adj* 1 at right angles to the horizon; vertical; upright. 2 *Geometry* at right angles to a given line, plane, or surface. **per·pen·dic·u·lar** *n.* **per·pen·dic·u·lar·ly** *adv.* **per·pen·dic·u·lar·i·ty** *n.* ⟨Latin *perpendiculum* plumb line⟩

per·pe·trate ['pɜrpə,treit] *v* do or commit (a crime, fraud, or anything bad or foolish). **per·pe·tra·tor** *n.* ⟨Latin *per-* (intensive) + *patrare* perform⟩

per·pet·u·al [pər'pɛtʃuəl] *adj* 1 lasting for all time: *the perpetual orbit of the moon.* 2 lasting throughout life: *a perpetual income.* 3 continuous: *perpetual motion.* **per·pet·u·al·ly** *adv.* ⟨Latin *per-* to the end + *petere* seek⟩
per·pet·u·ate *v* cause to last indefinitely: *a monument to perpetuate the memory of someone.* **per·pet·u·a·tor** *n.* **per·pe·tu·i·ty** [,pɜrpə'tʃuəti] *or* [,pɜrpə'tuəti] *n* endless time. **in perpetuity** forever.

per·plex [pər'plɛks] *v* 1 trouble with doubt; puzzle: *This problem is hard enough to perplex even the instructor.* 2 complicate (something). **per·plex·ing** *adj.* **per·plex·ing·ly** *adv.* ⟨Latin *per-* completely + *plectere* intertwine⟩
per·plexed *adj* 1 puzzled and confused. 2 confusing; complicated: *a highly perplexed problem.* **per·plex·ed·ly** [pər'plɛksədli] *adv.* **per·plex·i·ty** *n.*

per·qui·site ['pɜrkwɪzɪt] *n* 1 anything received in addition to regular pay, esp something promised or expected: *The maid's perquisites were dresses no longer wanted by her employer.* 2 a tip. ⟨Latin *perquisitum* (thing) gained; *per-* thoroughly + *quaerere* seek⟩

per·se·cute ['pɜrsə,kjut] *v* 1 oppress, esp for religious, racial, or political reasons. 2 annoy: *persecute with many questions.* **per·se·cu·tor** *n.* **per·se·cu·to·ry** *adj.* **per·se·cu·tion** *n.* ⟨Latin *per-* (intensive) + *sequi* follow⟩

per·se·vere [,pɜrsə'vir] *v* continue steadily in doing something difficult: *The early explorers persevered in their efforts to find a westerly route to India.* **per·se·ver·ance** *n.* **per·se·ver·ing** *adj.* ⟨Latin *per-* very + *severus* strict⟩

per·si·flage ['pɜrsɪ,flɑʒ] *n* a frivolous or flippant style of treating a subject in speech or writing. ⟨French *persifler* banter; *per-* (Latin = through) + *siffler* whistle⟩

per·sim·mon [pər'sɪmən] *n* a tree of the ebony family, with orange-red fruit. ⟨Algonquian⟩

per·sist [pər'sɪst] *v* 1 refuse to stop or be changed: *She persisted till she had solved the problem.* 2 stay, esp past a usual time: *The cold weather will persist for days.* **per·sist·ence** *n.* **per·sist·ent** *adj.* **per·sist·ent·ly** *adv.* ⟨Latin *per-* to the end + *sistere* stand⟩

per·son ['pɜrsən] *n* 1 a man, woman, or child; human being. 2 bodily appearance: *He kept his person neat and trim.* 3 *Grammar* any of the three groups of pronoun or verb forms indicating distinction of person: **first person** (speaker), **second person** (person spoken to), or **third person** (person or thing spoken about). 4 *Law* a human being, or an entity such as a corporation, recognized by the law

as capable of having legal rights and duties.
in person by or with one's own action or presence: *The artist was there in person.* ⟨Latin *persona* character, actor's mask⟩

per·so·na [pər'sounə] *n, pl* **-nas** or **-nae** [-ni] *or* [-nai] **1** a personality that a person presents to the public: *In private life the premier drops his public persona.* **2** Usually, **personae** *pl* the characters in a novel, play, etc. **per·so·na non gra·ta** [nɒn 'grɑtə], ['grætə], *or* ['greitə] *Latin* a person who is not acceptable, usually said of diplomats no longer acceptable to the countries to which they have been assigned: *to be declared a persona non grata.* **per·son·a·ble** *adj* having a pleasing appearance and personality. **per·son·age** *n* a person of importance. **per·son·al** *adj* **1** to do with an individual: *personal opinion.* **2** private; intimate: *Don't ask personal questions.* **3** done in person: *a personal visit.* **4** *Grammar* showing person. *I, we, you, he, she, it,* and *they* are **personal pronouns.** *n* Usually, **personals** *pl* short paragraphs, in the classified section in a newspaper, directed toward a particular person advertising for a companion. **per·son·al·ly** *adv.* **personal computer** a computer designed for use by individuals, chiefly for word processing, data management, video games, etc. *Abbrev* **PC.** **per·son·al·i·ty** *n* **1** the qualities of character that make one person be different from another: *The two boys are quite unlike in personality.* **2** the attractive qualities of a person: *She has a lot of personality.* **3** a person of importance or renown: *a TV personality.* **per·son·al·ize** *v* make personal; especially, mark with one's name, etc.: *Personalized stationery has the owner's monogram, name, or name and address printed on it.* **per·son·al·i·za·tion** *n.* **per·son·i·fy** [pər'sɒnə,fai] *v* **1** represent a thing as a person or as having human qualities: *The sea is often personified in poetry.* **2** be the incarnation of: *She personifies kindness.* **per·son·i·fi·ca·tion** *n.* **per·son·nel** [,pɜrsə'nɛl] *n* persons employed in any business, service, etc.

per·spec·tive [pər'spɛktɪv] *n* **1** the art of picturing objects on a flat surface so as to give the appearance of distance. **2** the effect of distance on the appearance of objects: *Railway tracks seem to meet at the horizon because of perspective.* **3** the effect, as of calmness, objectivity, etc., that the distance of events has on the mind: *If you distanced yourself from the whole situation for a while, you could get some perspective on it.* **4** a view of facts in which they are in the right relation to one another: *This editorial puts the crisis in perspective.* **5** a view in front; distant view. **6** a mental viewpoint: *My perspective on this matter is quite different from yours.* **per·spec·tive·ly** *adv.* ⟨Latin *per-* through + *specere* look⟩

per·spi·ca·cious [,pɜrspɪ'keiʃəs] *adj* keen in observing and understanding; discerning: *a perspicacious judgment.* **per·spi·ca·cious·ly** *adv.* **per·spi·cac·i·ty** [-kæsəti] *n.* ⟨Latin *perspicacis.* See PERSPECTIVE.⟩

per·spic·u·ous [pər'spɪkjuəs] *adj* clear; easily understood: *a perspicuous style.* **per·spi·cu·i·ty** [,pɜrspɪ'kjuəti] *n.* **per·spic·u·ous·ly** *adv.* ⟨Latin *perspicuus.* See PERSPECTIVE.⟩

per·spire [pər'spair] *v* SWEAT (*v.* def. 1). **per·spi·ra·tion** [,pɜrspə'reiʃən] *n.* ⟨Latin *per-* through + *spirare* breathe⟩

per·suade [pər'sweid] *v* cause (a person) to do something or believe something by urging, arguing, etc. **per·suad·a·ble** or **per·sua·si·ble** [pər'sweisəbəl] *or* [-'sweizəbəl] *adj.* **per·sua·si·bil·i·ty** *n.* ⟨Latin *per-* thoroughly + *suadere* urge⟩
per·sua·sion *n* **1** a persuading: *All our persuasion was of no use; she would not come.* **2** a firm belief: *The two sisters were of different political persuasions.* **3** a religious belief: *All Christians are not of the same persuasion.* **4** *Facetious* kind; sort: *lawyers, and others of that persuasion.* **per·sua·sive** [pər'sweisɪv] *or* [-'sweizɪv] *adj* effective in persuading: *a very persuasive way of talking.*
per·sua·sive·ly *adv.* **per·sua·sive·ness** *n.*

SYNONYMS
Persuade emphasizes winning someone over to a desired belief by appealing to his or her feelings as well as to his or her mind.
Convince emphasizes overcoming a person's objections by proof or arguments, appealing to his or her reason and understanding:
I have convinced her that she needs a vacation, but I cannot persuade her to take one.

pert [pɜrt] *adj* **1** too forward in speech or action. **2** *Informal* lively. **3** chic and sprightly. **pert·ly** *adv.* **pert·ness** *n.* ⟨Old French *apert* open; Latin *apertus*⟩

per·tain [pər'tein] *v* **1** be connected as a part, possession, etc.: *the house and the land pertaining to it.* **2** refer (to): *an editorial pertaining to the election.* ⟨Latin *per-* across + *tenere* reach⟩
per·ti·nent ['pɜrtənənt] *adj* relating to the matter in hand. **per·ti·nence** or **per·ti·nen·cy** *n.* **per·ti·nent·ly** *adv.*

per·ti·na·cious [,pɜrtə'neiʃəs] *adj* **1** very persistent: *a pertinacious fighter.* **2** stubborn. **per·ti·na·cious·ly** *adv.* **per·ti·nac·i·ty** [-'næsəti] *n.* ⟨Latin *per-* very + *tenacis* tenacious⟩

per·ti·nence, per·ti·nent See PERTAIN.

per·turb [pər'tɜrb] *v* disturb greatly: *The management was perturbed at the possibility of a strike.* **per·tur·ba·tion** *n.* **per·turb·ing** *adj.* ⟨Latin *per-* thoroughly + *turbare* confuse⟩

pe·ruse [pə'ruz] *v* **1** read carefully. **2** read. **pe·rus·al** *n.* ⟨Latin *per-* to the end + *USE*⟩

per·vade [pər'veid] *v* spread throughout: *The smell of pines pervades the air.* **per·vad·ing** *adj.* **per·va·sion** *n.* **per·va·sive** *adj.* **per·va·sive·ly** *adv.* **per·va·sive·ness** *n.* ⟨Latin *per-* through + *vadere* go⟩

per·verse [pər'vɜrs] *adj* **1** contrary; stubborn: *The perverse child did just what we told her not to.* **2** wicked. **3** not correct: *perverse reasoning.* **4** of a distorted character, esp as regards sexual morality. **per·verse·ly** *adv.*

per·verse·ness or **per·vers·i·ty** *n.* ⟨Latin *perversus* pp of *pervertere; per-* away + *vertere* turn⟩

per·ver·sion *n* **1** a change to what is unnatural, abnormal, or wrong: *A tendency to eat sand is a perversion of appetite.* **2** a twisted or distorted shape or character: *perversion of facts.* **3** any of various sexual preferences and practices that are considered abnormal. **per·vert** *v* [pər'vɜrt] **1** lead or turn from the right way or from the truth: *Reading unwholesome books may pervert our taste for good books.* **2** give a wrong meaning to: *His enemies perverted his friendly remark into an insult.* **3** use for improper purposes: *A clever criminal perverts his talents. n* ['pɜrvərt] a person who practises sexual perversion. **per·vert·er** *n.* **per·vert·ed** *adj.* **per·vert·ed·ness** *n.*

Pe·sach ['peisɑx] *or* ['pesɑx] Passover. ⟨Hebrew *pesah*⟩

pes·ky ['peski] *adj Informal* annoying: *How can we get rid of these pesky wasps?* ⟨perhaps alteration of *pesty; pest*⟩

pes·si·mism ['pɛsə,mızəm] *n* a tendency to see the worst aspects of things, or regard them without hope. **pes·si·mist** *n.* **pes·si·mis·tic** *adj.* **pes·si·mis·ti·cal·ly** *adv.* ⟨Latin *pessimus* worst⟩

pest [pɛst] *n* any thing or person that causes trouble, annoyance, or destruction: *Mosquitoes are pests.* ⟨Latin *pestis* plague⟩

pes·ti·cide *n* any substance used to destroy plant or animal pests. **pes·ti·lent** *adj* **1** bringing contagious disease: *Rat bites may be pestilent.* **2** morally harmful: *the pestilent effects of war.* **3** troublesome: *Those pestilent rabbits have eaten all the lettuce plants.* **pes·ti·lence** *n.* **pes·ti·len·tial** *adj.* **pes·ti·len·tial·ly** *adv.* **pes·ti·lent·ly** *adv.*

pes·ter ['pɛstər] *v* **1** annoy; trouble: *pestered by flies.* **2** bother with repeated demands: *He kept pestering her till she gave in.* **pes·ter·er** *n.* **pest·er·ing** *adj.* ⟨Old French *empestrer* hobble (an animal); influenced by *pest*⟩

pes·tle ['pɛsəl] *n* a club-shaped tool used for crushing substances in a mortar. ⟨Old French *pestel*; Latin *pistillum*⟩

pet [pɛt] *n* **1** an animal kept as a favourite and treated with affection. **2** a favourite person or thing.
adj **1** showing affection: *a pet name.* **2** favourite. **3** *Informal* special: *a pet theory.*
v **pet·ted, pet·ting 1** treat as a pet. **2** stroke. **3** *Informal* fondle passionately. ⟨Scots Gaelic *peata,* perhaps Middle English *pety* small⟩

pet·al ['pɛtəl] *n* one of the parts of a flower that are often coloured. **pet·al–like** or · **pet·al·oid** *adj.* ⟨Greek *petalon* leaf⟩

pe·tard [pɪ'tɑrd] *n* an explosive device formerly used to break down a door or to breach a wall. ⟨French *pétard* explosive device; *péter* break wind⟩
hoist with one's own petard injured by one's own scheme for the ruin of others.

pe·ter ['pitər] *v Informal* gradually come to

an end (with *out*): *We rationed our food as supplies began to peter out.* ⟨origin unknown⟩

pet·i·ole ['pɛti,oul] *n* **1** *Botany* the stalk by which a leaf is attached to a stem. **2** *Zoology* a stalklike part. A petiole connects the thorax and abdomen of a wasp. **pet·i·ol·ar** *adj.* ⟨Latin *petiolus* diminutive of *pedis* foot⟩

pe·tite [pə'tit] *adj* little, esp with reference to a woman or girl. ⟨French = little⟩
pet·it four ['pɛti 'fɔr] *French* [pəti'fur] *pl* **pet·its fours** ['pɛti 'fɔrz] *French* [pəti'fur] a small fancy cake. **pe·tit mal** [pə'ti 'mæl] *Pathology* a mild type of epilepsy. Compare GRAND MAL. **petit point** ['pɛti] a diagonal needlepoint stitch.

pe·ti·tion [pə'tɪʃən] *n* **1** a formal request to one in authority for some privilege, benefit, etc.: *a petition asking the city council for a new sidewalk.* **2** *Law* a written application for an order of court for some action by a judge. *v* **1** make a petition (*to*). **2** pray. **pe·ti·tion·er** *n.* **pe·ti·tion·ar·y** *adj.* ⟨Latin *petitio; petere* seek⟩

pet·rel ['pɛtrəl] *n* any of various sea birds that roam far out at sea. ⟨apparently diminutive of St. *Peter,* who walked on a lake⟩

pe·tri dish ['pitri] a round, shallow glass container with a loose cover, used in laboratories to hold bacterial cultures. ⟨J. *Petri* 20c German bacteriologist⟩

pet·ri·fy ['pɛtrə,faɪ] *v* **1** turn into stony substance (usually in the passive): *Wood may become petrified over time.* **2** make or become stiff, dull, etc. **3** paralyze with fear. **pet·ri·fac·tion** *n.* **pet·ri·fied** *adj.* ⟨Greek *petra* rock⟩

pet·ro·glyph ['pɛtrə,glɪf] *n* a carving or inscription on rock, esp a prehistoric one. **pet·ro·glyph·ic** *adj.* ⟨Greek *petra* rock + *glyphē* carving⟩

pe·tro·le·um [pə'trouliəm] *n* a combustible oil that occurs in deposits within rock strata. It consists of a complex mixture of hydrocarbons. ⟨Greek *petra* rock + *oleum* oil⟩
pet·ro·chem·i·cal *n* any of various chemicals made from petroleum or natural gas, used in the manufacture of plastics, paints, etc. **pet·ro·chem·i·cal** *adj.* **pet·ro·dol·lar** *n* Usually, **petrodollars** *pl* money earned from the sale of petroleum, thought of as a source of economic or political power. **petroleum jelly** a greasy substance obtained from petroleum, used as an ointment and as a lubricant.

pet·ti·coat ['pɛti,kout] *n* a skirt worn beneath an outer skirt by women or girls. *adj* female; feminine: *petticoat government.* · ⟨orig, *petty coat* little coat⟩

pet·ti·fog·ger ['pɛti,fɒgər] *n* **1** a person who uses petty or underhanded methods. **2** a person who quibbles over small details. **pet·ti·fog, -fogged, -fog·ging** *v.* **pet·ti·fog·ge·ry** *n.* ⟨*petty* + obsolete *fogger*⟩

pet·ty ['pɛti] *adj* **1** having little importance: *a petty offence.* **2** making a fuss over small matters. **pet·ti·ly** *adv.* **pet·ti·ness** *n.* ⟨Old French *petit* little⟩
petty cash a sum of money kept on hand to

pay small expenses. **petty officer** in Maritime Command, one of the top ranks of non-commissioned officer. *Abbrev* **P.O.**

pet·u·lant ['pɛtʃələnt] *adj* subject to little fits of bad temper. **pet·u·lance** *or* **pet·u·lan·cy** **pet·u·lant·ly** *adv*. ⟨Latin *petulans, petere* seek⟩

Pe·tun [pə'tun] *n, pl* **Pe·tun** **1** a member of an extinct First Nations people who lived between Lakes Huron and Ontario, noted for their tobacco cultivation and trade. **2** the Iroquoian dialect of this people. ⟨Cdn. French; Middle French = tobacco; Tupi⟩

pew [pju] *n* in a church, a bench for people to sit on. ⟨Old French *puie;* Latin *podia* pl of *podium.* See PODIUM.⟩

pew·ter ['pjutər] *n* any of various alloys composed mainly of tin. ⟨Old French *peutre*⟩

pey·o·te [pei'outi] *Spanish* [pe'jote] *n* **1** any of several cactuses, esp mescal. Also, **pey·o·tl.** **2** mescaline. ⟨Spanish *peyote;* Nahuatl *peyotl* caterpillar; for its soft, fuzzy centre⟩

PG Parental Guidance, a movie rating informing parents that children may attend but that there may be some scenes or language unsuitable for young children.

pH *Chemistry* a symbol used to express acid or alkaline content. A pH of 14 denotes high alkaline content, and a pH of 0 indicates high acidity; pH 7 is taken as neutral. ⟨potential of Hydrogen⟩

phag·o·cyte ['fægə,sɔit] *n Physiology* a white blood corpuscle, or leucocyte. ⟨Greek *phagein* eat + -CYTE⟩

phal·anx ['fælæŋks] *n* **1** *pl* **phal·anx·es** or **phal·an·ges** [fə'lændʒiz] in ancient Greece, a special battle formation of infantry fighting with their shields joined and long spears overlapping each other. **2** *pl* **pha·lanx·es** a compact or closely massed body of persons, animals, or things: *a phalanx of trees.* **3** *Anatomy, zoology pl* **pha·lan·ges** any one of the bones of the fingers or toes. **pha·lan·ge·al** *adj*. ⟨Greek⟩

phal·lus ['fæləs] *n, pl* **phal·li** ['fælaɪ] or **phal·lus·es** **1** an image or model of the penis. **2** *Anatomy* the penis or the clitoris. **phal·lic** *adj*. ⟨Greek *phallós*⟩

phan·tasm ['fæn,tæzəm] *n* **1** a thing seen only in one's imagination. **2** a supposed appearance of an absent person, living or dead. **phan·tas·mal** or **phan·tas·mic** *adj*. ⟨Greek *phantasma* image; *phainein* show⟩ **phan·tas·ma·go·ria** [fæn,tæzmə'gɔriə] *n* **1** a shifting scene of real things, illusions, deceptions, and the like: *the phantasmagoria of a dream.* **2** any swiftly changing scene. **phan·tas·ma·go·ri·cal** or **phan·tas·ma·go·ric** *adj*.

phan·tom ['fæntəm] *n* **1** an illusory image of the mind. **2** a vague or shadowy appearance; ghost. **3** a mere show; appearance without material substance: *a phantom of a government.* **phan·tom** *adj*. ⟨Old French *fantosme;* Greek *phantasma* image⟩

Phar·aoh ['fɛrou] *or* ['færou] *n* a title given to the kings of ancient Egypt.

Phar·i·see ['fɛrə,si] *or* ['færə,si] *n* **1** in ancient times, a member of a strict Jewish sect. **2 pharisee a** a person who makes a show of religion rather than following its spirit. **b** a person who considers himself or herself much better than others. **phar·i·sa·ic** or **phar·i·sa·i·cal** *adj*. **phar·i·sa·i·cal·ly** *adv*. ⟨Greek *pharisaios;* Aramaic *perishaiya* separated⟩

phar·ma·cy ['fɑrməsi] *n* **1** the art of preparing medicines. **2** a drugstore. **phar·ma·cist** *n*. ⟨Greek *pharmakon* drug⟩ **phar·ma·ceu·ti·cal** [-'sutəkəl] *adj* **1** to do with pharmacy or pharmacists. **2** to do with drugs: *pharmaceutical treatment. n* a medicinal drug. **phar·ma·col·o·gy** [-'kɒlədʒi] *n* the science of drugs, including their properties, preparation, uses, and effects. **phar·ma·co·log·i·cal** *adj*. **phar·ma·col·o·gist** *n*.

phar·ynx ['fɛrɪŋks] *or* ['færɪŋks] *n, pl* **phar·ynx·es** or **pha·ryn·ges** [fə'rɪndʒiz] *Anatomy* in vertebrates, the muscular tube connecting the mouth cavity with the esophagus. **pha·ryn·ge·al** [fə'rɪndʒiəl] or **pharyngal** [fə'rɪŋgəl] *adj*. ⟨Greek = throat⟩

phase [feiz] *n* **1** one of stages of development of a person or thing. **2** *Astronomy* the shape of the moon or of a planet as it is seen at a given time. **3** *Zoology* a variation in colour in an animal that distinguishes it from typical members of its group: *A leopard of the black colour phase is usually called a panther.* ⟨Greek *phasis* appearance; *phainein* show⟩ **phase in** bring about (an innovation or reform) in orderly stages. **phase out** eliminate (an old system, order, etc.) gradually, in planned stages. **phase-out** *n*.

pheas·ant ['fɛzənt] *n, pl* **-ants** or (esp collectively) **-ant** any of various game birds, the male of which has brightly coloured plumage. ⟨Provençal *faisan;* Greek *phasianos* Phasian, of the river Phasis⟩

phe·nom·e·non [fə'nɒmə,nɒn] *or* [-nən] *n* **1** *pl* **phe·nom·e·na** an event that can be observed: *Fever and inflammation are phenomena of disease.* **2** *pl* **phe·nom·e·nons** something or someone extraordinary. **phe·nom·e·nal** *adj*. **phe·nom·e·nal·ly** *adv*. ⟨Greek *phainomenon* ppr of *phainesthai* appear⟩ **phe·nom·e·nol·o·gy** *n* a descriptive account of the phenomena of a particular field of study. **phe·nom·e·no·log·i·cal** *adj*.

phe·no·type ['finə,təip] *n Genetics* **1** the visible characteristics of an organism as determined by the interaction of its genetic inheritance (genotype) and its environment. **2** a group of organisms sharing such characteristics. **phe·no·typ·ic** [-'tɪpɪk] *adj*. ⟨Greek *phainein* show + TYPE⟩

pher·o·mone ['fɛrə,moun] *n Biochemistry* a substance exuded by certain organisms, such as insects, that serves as a communication with others of the same species, affecting their behaviour, etc. **pher·o·mon·al** *adj*. ⟨Greek *pherein* carry + (HOR)MONE⟩

phi·al ['faɪəl] *n* a small bottle; vial. ⟨Greek *phialē* a broad, flat vessel⟩

phi·lan·der [fə'lændər] *v* flirt. **phi·lan·der·er** *n*.
⟨Greek *philos* loving + *andros* man⟩

phi·lan·thro·py [fə'lænθrəpi] *n* love of people, esp as shown by practical kindness or gifts of money: *Charities appeal to one's philanthropy.* **phil·an·throp·ic** [ˌfɪlən'θrɒpɪk] *adj*. **phil·an·throp·i·cal·ly** *adv*. **phi·lan·thro·pist** *n*.
⟨Greek *philos* loving + *anthrōpos* human being⟩

phi·lat·e·ly [fə'lætəli] *n* the collecting of postage stamps. **phil·a·tel·ic** [ˌfɪlə'tɛlɪk] *adj*. **phi·lat·e·list** *n*. ⟨Greek *philos* loving + *ateleia* tax exemption (indicated by stamp)⟩

–phile *combining form* a lover of——: *discophile* = a person who is fond of discs. Also, **-phil**.
⟨Greek *philos* loving⟩
–philia *combining form* **1** tendency to——: *hemophilia*. **2** strong or unnatural attraction toward——: *Anglophilia, necrophilia*.

phil·har·mon·ic [ˌfɪlhɑr'mɒnɪk] *or* [ˌfɪlər-] *adj* loving music. A musical club is often called a philharmonic society.
n **Philharmonic** a symphony orchestra.
⟨Greek *philos* loving + *harmonia* music⟩

phi·lis·tine ['fɪlə,staɪn], [fə'lɪstin] *or* ['fɪlə,stən] *n* a person who is indifferent to artistic or intellectual values.
adj smugly uncultured. ⟨Greek *Philistinoi*; Hebrew *p'lishtim*⟩

phil·o·den·dron [ˌfɪlə'dɛndrən] *n*, *pl* **-drons** *or* **-dra** [-drə] any of a genus of plants of the arum family. ⟨Greek *philos* loving + *dendron* tree; it clings to trees⟩

phi·lol·o·gy [fə'lɒlədʒi] *n* the historical and comparative study of languages, esp through documents. Compare LINGUISTICS. **phil·o·log·i·cal** *adj*. **phil·o·log·i·cal·ly** *adv*. **phi·lol·o·gist** *n*.
⟨Greek *philos* loving + *logos* word⟩

phi·los·o·phy [fə'lɒsəfi] *n* **1** the study of the truth or principles underlying all knowledge. **2** an explanation or theory of the universe: *Hegelian philosophy*. **3** a system for guiding life, such as a body of principles of conduct. **4** a set of broad, general principles of a particular subject: *the philosophy of science*. **phi·los·o·pher** *n*. ⟨Greek *philos* loving + *sophos* wise⟩
phil·o·soph·ic·al *or* **phil·o·soph·ic**. *adj* **1** to do with philosophers or philosophy: *a philosophical journal*. **2** taking a calm attitude in the face of trouble: *He lost, but he was philosophical about it.* **phil·o·soph·i·cal·ly** *adv*.
phi·los·o·phize *v* **1** try to understand and explain things: *philosophizing about life and death*. **2** engage in superficial philosophical talk. **phi·los·o·phiz·er** *n*.

phish·ing ['fɪʃɪŋ] *n Computers* trying to discover sensitive information, such as passwords, by sending e-mails or instant messages that seem to be sent by a trustworthy person or business. ⟨fishing with lures⟩

phle·bi·tis [flə'baɪtɪs] *n Pathology* inflammation of the wall of a vein. **phle·bit·ic** [-'bɪtɪk] *adj*. ⟨Greek *phlebos* vein⟩

phlegm [flɛm] *n* **1** the discharge of mucus during a cold or other respiratory disease. **2** of the four humours of ancient physiology, believed to cause sluggishness. **3** calmness. **phleg·my** *adj*. ⟨Greek *phlegma* clammy humour⟩
phleg·mat·ic [flɛg'mætɪk] *adj* **1** sluggish or indifferent. **2** calm. **phleg·mat·i·cal·ly** *adv*.

phlo·em *or* **phlo·ëm** ['flouəm] *n* the soft tissue in the vascular system of plants or trees, that serves to transport and store food. Compare XYLEM. ⟨Greek *phloos* bark⟩

phlox [flɒks] *n* any of a genus of plants cultivated for their clusters of flowers. ⟨Greek; literally, flame⟩

–phobe *combining form* a person who has irrational hatred or fear of——: *Anglophobe* = a person who hates or fears the English or England. ⟨Greek *phobos* panic, fear⟩
–phobia *combining form* extreme or irrational hatred or fear of——: *Anglophobia*. **pho·bi·a** *n* an irrational fear of or aversion to a particular thing or situation. **pho·bic** *adj*.

phoe·nix ['finɪks] *n* a mythical bird, the only one of its kind, said to burn itself to ashes on a funeral pyre, and rise again. ⟨Greek *phoinix*, probably Egyptian *bonū* heron⟩

phone [foun] *n*, *v* **phoned**, **phon·ing** telephone. ⟨shortened form⟩
phone book TELEPHONE DIRECTORY. **phone card** a prepaid card for use in pay phones. **phone sex** an activity in which people pay to call a certain number and engage in sexually explicit conversation.

pho·neme ['founim] *n Linguistics* any of the speech sounds that distinguish one word from another. The words *cat* and *bat* are contrasted by their initial phonemes. **pho·ne·mic** *adj*. ⟨Greek *phōnēma*; *phōnē* sound⟩
pho·ne·mics *n* (with a sg verb) the description of the phonemes of a language. Compare PHONETICS.

pho·net·ic [fə'nɛtɪk] *adj* to do with speech sounds: *phonetic laws*. **pho·net·i·cal·ly** *adv*. ⟨Greek *phōnētikos*; *phōnē* sound⟩
pho·net·ics *n* (with a sg verb) *Linguistics* **1** the study of speech sounds. **2** a system of symbols for transcribing these sounds. Compare PHONEMICS. **pho·ne·ti·cian** *n*.

phon·ic ['fɒnɪk] *or* ['founɪk] *adj* **1** to do with sound. **2** to do with phonics. **phon·i·cal·ly** *adv*. ⟨Greek *phōnē* sound⟩
phon·ics *n* (with a sg verb) a method of learning to read by learning the relationship between the sounds and the letters.

pho·nol·o·gy [fə'nɒlədʒi] *n* **1** the study of human speech sounds. **2** the sound system of a given language at a particular time. **pho·no·log·i·cal** [ˌfounə-] *or* [ˌfɒnə-] *adj* **pho·no·log·i·cal·ly** *adv*. **pho·nol·o·gist** *n*.

pho·ny ['founi] *Informal adj* counterfeit.
n a fake; pretender. Also, **pho·ney** (*pl* **-neys**). **pho·ni·ness** *n*. ⟨*fawney*, a gilt brass ring used by swindlers; Irish Gaelic *fáinne* ring⟩

phos·phor ['fɒsfər] *n* **1** phosphorus. **2** any phosphorescent or fluorescent substance. ⟨Greek *phōs* light + *pherein* bring⟩

phos·phate *n* **1** a salt or ester of an acid containing phosphorus. **2** a fertilizer containing such salts. **phos·phat·ic** [fɒsˈfætɪk] *adj.* **phos·pho·res·cence** [ˌfɒsfəˈresəns] *n* **1** a giving out of light without burning. **2** *Physics* light given off by a substance as a result of absorbing rays, as X rays. **phos·pho·res·cent** *adj.* **phos·pho·resce** *v* be luminous without noticeable heat. **phos·pho·rus** [ˈfɒsfərəs] *n* a non-metallic element. *Symbol* **P**.

pho·tic [ˈfoutɪk] *adj* **1** to do with light. **2** *Biology* pertaining to the effect of light on organisms, or their generation of light. ⟨Greek *phōs, phōtos* light⟩

pho·to [ˈfoutou] *n, pl* **-tos** *Informal* photograph. **photo finish 1** *Sports* a finish so close that a photograph is required to decide the winner. **2** any contest decided by a narrow margin. **photo radar** radar that detects speeding vehicles and photographs the offender's licence plate.

photo– *combining form* **1** light: *photometry*. **2** photographic: *photo-engraving*. ⟨Greek *phōs, phōtos* light⟩ **pho·to·cop·i·er** *n* a machine for making photocopies. **pho·to·cop·y** *n* a photographic reproduction of printed matter. **pho·to·cop·y** *v*. **pho·to·fin·ish·ing** *n* the development of exposed film. **pho·to·gen·ic** [-ˈdʒɛnɪk] *adj* **1** looking attractive in photographs or motion pictures: *a photogenic face*. **2** *Biology* phosphorescent; luminescent. **3** due to or caused by light. **pho·to·gen·i·cal·ly** *adv.* **pho·to·graph** *n* a picture made with a camera. *v* **1** take photographs. **2** look good in a photograph: *She does not photograph well*. **pho·tog·ra·pher** [fəˈtɒɡrəfər] *n*. **pho·to·graph·ic** *adj* like a photograph as regards precise detail: *photographic accuracy*. **pho·to·graph·i·cal·ly** *adv.* **pho·tog·ra·phy** *n*. **pho·to·jour·nal·ism** *n* journalism in which photographs, rather than written material, are used to present the majority of news items. **pho·tom·e·ter** [fouˈtɒmətər] *n Optics* an instrument for measuring the intensity of light. **pho·to·sen·si·tive** *adj* sensitive to light. **pho·to·sen·si·tiv·i·ty** *n*. **pho·to·syn·the·sis** *n Biology, biochemistry* the process by which plant cells make sugar from carbon dioxide and water in the presence of chlorophyl and light. **pho·to·syn·thet·i·c** *adj*.

pho·ton [ˈfoutɒn] *n Physics* a quantum or unit particle of light, having a momentum equal to its energy and moving with the velocity of light. ⟨*phot(o electr)on*⟩

phrase [freiz] *n* **1** a combination of words that has meaning. **2** a short, striking expression. *Example: A war to end wars.* **3** *Grammar* a group of words with no subject or finite verb, used as a unit. In *He went to the house*, the words *to the house* form a phrase. **4** *Music* a short part of a composition. *v* express in a particular way: *She phrased her excuse politely*. **phras·al** *adj.* **phras·al·ly** *adv.* ⟨Greek *phrazein* say⟩ **phrase·book** *n* a collection of idioms and everyday phrases used in a foreign language,

with their translations. **phra·se·ol·o·gy** [ˌfreiziˈɒlədʒi] *n* the particular way in which a person expresses himself or herself. **phra·se·o·log·i·cal** *adj.* **phra·se·o·log·i·cal·ly** *adv.* **phras·ing** *n* **1** a phraseology. **b** the grouping of spoken words by pauses. **2** *Music* a grouping or dividing into phrases.

phy·lac·ter·y [fəˈlæktəri] *n* **1** either of two small cases containing texts from the Jewish law. **2** reminder. **3** a charm worn as a protection. ⟨Greek *phylaktērion* safeguard; *phylakos* watchman⟩

phyl·lo [ˈfɪlou] *n* a flaky pastry made in layers with butter, used for Greek pastries, etc. ⟨Greek *phyllon* leaf⟩

phy·log·e·ny [faɪˈlɒdʒəni] *n* **1** the origin and development of anything, esp of an animal or plant. **2** the historical development of a group of non-living things such as a family of languages. **phy·lo·gen·ic** [ˌfaɪləˈdʒɛnɪk] or **phy·lo·ge·net·ic** [-dʒəˈnɛtɪk] *adj.* **phy·lo·ge·net·i·cal·ly** *adv.* ⟨Greek *phylon* race + *-geneia* origin⟩

phy·lum [ˈfaɪləm] *n, pl* **-la** [-lə] *Biology* a major category in the classification of animals, more general than a class. It corresponds to a division in the classification of plants. ⟨Greek *phylon* race⟩

phys·i·cal [ˈfɪzɪkəl] *adj* **1** of the body: *physical exercise*. **2** sexual or carnal: *a physical attraction*. **3** to do with aggressive bodily activity: *Hockey is a very physical sport.* **4** of matter: *The tide is a physical force.* **5** according to the laws of nature: *It is a physical impossibility to stop the earth's movement around the sun.* **6** of the science of physics. *n Informal* a complete medical examination. **phys·i·cal·ly** *adv.* **phys·i·cal·i·ty** *n.* ⟨Greek *physis* nature; *phyein* produce⟩ **physical education** instruction in how to exercise and take care of the body. **physical geography** the branch of geography that deals with the study of landforms, climate, winds, etc. **physical sciences** physics, chemistry, geology, and other sciences dealing with inanimate matter. **phy·si·cian** [fəˈzɪʃən] *n* **1** any legally qualified doctor of medicine. **2** a medical doctor as distinct from a surgeon. **phys·ics** *n* (with a sg verb) **1** the science that deals with matter, energy, motion, and force. **2** the physical properties and processes of a specific thing: *the physics of a machine.* **phys·i·cist** [ˈfɪzəsɪst] *n*.

phys·i·og·no·my [ˌfɪziˈɒnəmi] *n* **1** the kind of features one has; one's face. **2** the art of estimating character from the features or the body. **3** the general aspect or looks of a countryside, a situation, etc. **phys·i·og·no·mist** *n.* **phys·i·og·nom·i·cal** *adj.* ⟨Greek *physis* nature + *gnōmōn* judge, one who knows⟩

phys·i·ol·o·gy [ˌfɪziˈɒlədʒi] *n* **1** the science dealing with the normal functions of living things: *plant physiology.* **2** all the functions and activities of a living thing. **phys·i·o·log·i·cal** *adj.* **phys·i·o·log·i·cal·ly** *adv.* **phys·i·ol·o·gist** *n.* ⟨Greek *physis* nature + *-logos* treating of⟩

phys·i·o·ther·a·py [ˌfɪziə'θɛrəpi] *n* the treatment of diseases and weaknesses by physical remedies, such as massage and exercise. Often informally shortened to **phy·si·o. phy·si·o·ther·a·pist** *n*.

phy·sique [fɪ'zik] *n* bodily structure: *a strong physique*. ⟨French = physical⟩

pi [paɪ] *n Mathematics* the ratio of the circumference of any circle to its diameter, equal to about 3.141 592. *Symbol* π ⟨Greek letter, initial of *periphereia* periphery⟩

pi·an·o¹ [pi'ænou] *n* a musical instrument having metal strings struck by felt-covered hammers operated by the keys on a keyboard. **pi·an·ist** ['piənɪst] *or* [pi'ænɪst] *n*. ⟨*pianoforte*; Italian *piano* soft + *forte* loud⟩
pi·an·o·for·te [pi,ænou'fɔrti] *or* [pi'ænou,fɔrt] *n* PIANO.

pi·a·no² [pi'ɑnou] *Music adj* soft. *adv* softly. *Abbrev* **p** ⟨Italian = *soft*⟩
pi·a·nis·si·mo [ˌpiə'nɪsə,mou] *adv* very softly. *Abbrev* **pp**

pic·a·resque [ˌpɪkə'rɛsk] *adj* **1** referring to a type of fiction originating in Spain and recounting the exploits of a roguish hero: *a picaresque novel*. **2** relating to rogues and vagabonds. ⟨Spanish *picaresco*; *picaro* rogue⟩

pic·a·yune [ˌpɪkə'jun] *adj* **1** of little value: *a lot of effort for picayune results*. **2** mean; petty. *n* anything trivial. ⟨Provençal *picaioun* coin⟩

pic·co·lo ['pɪkə,lou] *n* a small wind instrument of the flute family. ⟨Italian = small⟩

pick¹ [pɪk] *v* **1** choose. **2** gather: *We pick fruit.* **3** use something pointed to manipulate or remove things: *to pick one's teeth, to pick a lock*. **4** look for and hope to find: *to pick a quarrel*. **5** use the fingers on with a plucking motion: *to pick the strings of a banjo*.
n **1** a selection. **2** the best part. **3** something used to pluck the strings of a musical instrument. **4** a turn to choose: *It's your pick*. ⟨Middle English *picken*⟩
pick and choose be very particular about choosing. **pick apart** find flaws in. **pick at a** pull on with the fingers: *The invalid picked at the blankets*. **b** eat only a little of at a time. **pick off a** shoot one at a time. **b** *Baseball* catch (a runner) off base and throw him or her out. **pick on a** *Informal* find fault with. **b** *Informal* annoy; tease; bully. **pick one's way** or **pick one's steps** move with great care over treacherous ground, in a difficult situation, etc. **pick out a** choose. **b** distinguish something from the surroundings: *Can you pick me out in this group picture?* **pick over a** look over carefully and make selections. **b** sort and clean: *The berries need to be picked over before we can eat them.* **pick someone's brains** find out and use the ideas, skills, etc. of another, as one's own. **pick up a** take up: *She picked up the chance to make some money by baby-sitting.* **b** get by chance: *to pick up a bargain.* **c** give fresh energy, courage, etc.: *A good dinner will pick you up.* **d** acquire (a particular skill): *He picked up the trumpet after one lesson.* **e** take up into a vehicle: *to pick up passengers.* **f** go

faster. **g** take (a check) with intent to pay it: *Who'll pick up the tab?* **h** *Informal* meet (someone) casually, with intention of a sexual encounter. **pick up on** notice and understand. **pick up the pieces** salvage a situation after a failure, disappointment, etc **picked** *adj* specially chosen or selected for merit: *a crew of picked riders*. **pick·ings** *n pl* **1** things left over; scraps. **2** profits: *That investment brought in pretty slim pickings.* **pick–me–up** *n Informal* a stimulant or tonic. **pick·pock·et** *n* a person who steals from people's pockets, bags, etc. **pick·up** *n* **1** a picking up: *the daily pickup of mail.* **2** *Informal* improvement or power of acceleration: *a pickup in business. This car hasn't much pickup.* **3** *Sports* a catching or hitting of a ball very soon after it has bounced on the ground. **4** a small truck. Also, **pickup truck**. **5** *Informal* a person met casually, often in the hope that a sexual encounter will result. *adj* made up of available material, personnel, etc.: *a pickup meal, a pickup team*. **pick·y** *adj Informal* too fussy or particular.

pick² [pɪk] *n* **1** pickaxe. **2** a sharp-pointed tool for breaking ice, cleaning teeth, etc. ⟨variant of *pike* pike¹⟩
pick·axe or **pickax** *n* a heavy metal tool that is pointed at one or both ends, used for breaking up dirt, rocks, etc.

pick·er·el ['pɪkərəl] *n, pl* **-el** or **-els** any of three small fishes of the pike family ⟨diminutive of *pike²*⟩

pick·et ['pɪkɪt] *n* **1** a pointed stake placed upright to make a fence, to tie a horse to, etc. **2** troops, or a single person, posted to guard against surprise attack. **3** a person stationed by a labour union near a place of work where there is a strike, to prevent employees from working or customers from buying.
v act as a picket: *to picket a factory during a strike*. **pick·et·er** *n*. ⟨French *piquet* diminutive of *pic* PIKE¹.⟩
picket fence a fence made of pickets. **picket line** people picketing a business, factory, etc.

pick·le ['pɪkəl] *n* **1** a vegetable preserved in brine, vinegar, etc. **2** *Informal* a problematic situation; difficulty.
v preserve in pickle: *to pickle beets*. ⟨Middle Dutch *pekel*⟩

pic·nic ['pɪknɪk] *n* **1** a meal in the open air. **2** *Informal* a very easy job (usually negative): *The trip down here was no picnic.*
v **-nicked**, **-nick·ing** eat in picnic style. **pic·nick·er** *n*. ⟨French *piquenique*⟩

pic·to·graph, pic·to·ri·al See PICTURE.

pic·ture ['pɪktʃər] *n* **1** a drawing, painting, portrait, or photograph. **2** a mental image: *a clear picture of the problem.* **3** something beautiful: *She was a picture in her new dress.* **4** likeness: *That boy is the picture of his father.* **5** an example: *She was the picture of despair.*
v **1** draw, paint, etc. **2** imagine: *to picture life a hundred years ago.* **3** describe vividly: *The speaker pictured the suffering of the poor.* ⟨Latin *pictura*; *pictus* pp of *pingere* paint⟩
in (or **out**) **of the picture** part (or not part) of

any given situation. **picture perfect** so attractive that one would want its likeness to be preserved. **the big picture** a comprehensive view of a topic, situation, etc. **pic·to·graph** *n* 1 a picture used as a symbol. 2 a chart on which symbols represent quantities like population. **pic·to·graph·ic** *adj*. **pic·to·graph·i·cal·ly** *adv*. **pic·tog·ra·phy** *n* written communication using a system of pictures. **pic·to·ri·al** *adj* to do with pictures. *n* a magazine in which pictures are the main feature. **pic·to·ri·al·ly** *adv*. **pic·tur·esque** [ˌpɪktʃəˈrɛsk] *adj* 1 pretty enough to be used in a picture: *a picturesque old mill.* **pic·tur·esque·ly** *adv*. **pic·tur·esque·ness** *n*. **picture window** a large window that frames the view seen through it.

pid·dle [ˈpɪdəl] *v* 1 do anything in a trifling or ineffective way. 2 *Informal* urinate. *n Informal* urine. **pid·dler** *n*. ⟨origin uncertain⟩ **pid·dling** *adj* trifling; petty.

pid·gin [ˈpɪdʒən] *n* a simplified language developed between speakers of two or more different languages who need to communicate. Compare CREOLE. ⟨Chinese Pidgin English pronunciation of *business*⟩ **pidgin English** any of several types of very simple English used for communication.

pie [paɪ] *n* 1 food consisting of an upper pastry crust, an under crust, or both, usually baked, having a filling of meat, fruit, etc. 2 something desirable that may be divided into portions. ⟨Middle English *pye*⟩ **as easy as pie** extremely easy to do. **pie crust** pastry used for the bottom or top of a pie. **pie–in–the–sky** *n Slang* 1 unrealistic promises of benefits in the future: *Most of that party's platform is pie-in-the-sky.* 2 utopian plans unlikely to come to fruition. *adj* unrealistic: *pie-in-the-sky suggestions.* **pie social ✵** a social event to which those attending bring pies to raise money for charity.

pie·bald [ˈpaɪ,bɒld] *adj* spotted in two colours, esp black and white. ⟨*(mag)pie* (for dark colour) + *bald* (i.e., light-coloured)⟩ **pied** [paɪd] *adj* having patches of two or more colours; many-coloured.

piece [pis] *n* 1 one of the parts into which a thing is divided: *a piece of wood.* 2 a portion: *a piece of bread.* 3 a single work of art: *a piece of music.* 4 a share; financial interest: *a piece of the action.* 5 *Checkers, chess, etc.* a figure, disk, block, etc. used in playing. 6 ✵ formerly, a package of goods or furs weighing about 40 kg, the standard load. ⟨Old French *piece, pece*; Latin *petia*; Celtic⟩ **go to pieces** collapse: *When she left, he went to pieces.* **of a piece** of the same kind: *That plan is of a piece with the rest of their silly suggestions.* **piece of one's mind** *Informal* a candid opinion. **b** a scolding. **speak** (or **say**) **one's piece** voice one's opinions. **piece·meal** *adv* a little at a time: *work done piecemeal.* **piece·meal** *adj*. **piece·work** *n* work paid for the amount done, not by the time it takes. **piece·work·er** *n*.

pièce de ré·sis·tance [ˌpjɛs də reɪzɪˈstɑs] *French* [pjɛsdəʀɛziˈstɑs] 1 the chief dish of a meal. 2 the most important item in any collection or series.

pied See PIEBALD.

pied–à–terre [pjetaˈtɛʀ] *n, pl* **pieds–à–terre** *French* a house or apartment kept for occasional use: *They live in an isolated cabin but have a pied-à-terre in Whitehorse.* ⟨literally, foot on (the) ground⟩

pied·mont [ˈpid,mɒnt] *n* an area of land at the base of a mountain: *the piedmont of Alberta.* **pied·mont** *adj* near the base of a mountain or mountains: *the piedmont area of Alberta.* ⟨Latin *pedis* foot + *montis* mountain⟩

Pie·gan See PIIKANI.

pier [pir] *n* 1 a structure supported on columns extending into the water. 2 one of the solid supports on which the arches of a bridge rest. ⟨Middle English *per*; Latin *pera*⟩

pierce [pirs] *v* 1 make a hole in. 2 go into; go through: *A tunnel pierces the mountain.* 3 sound so loudly and keenly as to be almost painful to the hearer: *A sharp cry pierced the air.* 4 penetrate with the eye or mind: *to pierce a disguise.* ⟨Old French *percer*; Latin *pertusus* pp of *pertundere* pierce⟩ **pierc·ing** *adj* penetrating; keen: *a piercing look; piercing cold.* **pierc·ing·ly** *adv*. **pierc·ing·ness** *n*.

pie·ro·gi [pəˈrougi] See PEROGY.

pi·e·ty See PIOUS.

pi·e·zo·e·lec·tric [paɪˌizouˈlɛktrɪk] *adj* of certain crystals, alternately enlarging and growing smaller as a result of stress when subjected to an electric current. ⟨*piezo-* pressure (Greek *piezein* press) + ELECTRIC⟩

pif·fle [ˈpɪfəl] *Informal n, interj* silly talk; nonsense. **pif·fle** *v*. ⟨perhaps Old English *pyffan* puff⟩

pig [pɪg] *n* 1 a domestic mammal having a long snout and a heavy body. 2 *Informal* a dirty, disagreeable person. 3 *Informal* a person who eats a lot, often with bad table manners. 4 *Slang* a rude or arrogant person. *v* **pigged, pig·ging** 1 of a sow, give birth. 2 *Informal* Usually, **pig it** live in poor or dirty conditions. **pig·gish** *adj*. **pig·gish·ly** *adv*. **pig·gish·ness** *n*. ⟨Middle English *pigge*⟩ **buy a pig in a poke** buy something without seeing its real value. **make a pig of oneself** *Informal* overeat. **pig out** *Informal* eat to the point of discomfort. **pig·gy** *n pl Informal* a little pig. **pig·gy·back** *n* a carrying or being carried on the back or shoulders: *He gave the child a piggyback.* **pig·gy·back** *adv, adj, v.* **piggy bank** 1 a small container in the shape of a pig, with a slot in the top for coins. 2 any coin bank. **pig–head·ed** *adj* stupidly stubborn. **pig–head·ed·ness** *n*. **pig iron** crude iron. **pig·let** *n* a baby pig. **pig·pen** *n* 1 a pen where pigs are kept. 2 a filthy place. **pig·skin** *n* 1 leather made from the skin of a pig. 2 *Informal* the ball used in football. **pig·sty** [ˈpɪg,staɪ] *n* pigpen. **pig·tails** *n pl* braids.

pi·geon ['pɪdʒən] *n* **1** any of a family of birds having a stout body and small head. **2** *Slang* a person who is easily tricked. ⟨Old French *pijon*; Latin *pipionis* squab⟩

pi·geon·hole *n* one of a set of boxlike compartments for holding papers in a desk, a cabinet, etc. *v* **1** put in a pigeonhole; put away. **2** classify, often in a stereotypical way. **3** put aside with the idea of dismissing or neglecting: *The city council pigeonholed the request for a new park.* **pi·geon–toed** *adj* having the toes or feet turned inward.

pig·ment ['pɪgmənt] *n* **1** a colouring matter. **2** *Biology* the natural colouring matter of a cell. **pig·men·tar·y** *adj.* **pig·ment·ize** *v.* ⟨Latin *pigmentum*; *pingere* paint⟩

pig·men·ta·tion *n Biology* the colouring of an animal or plant resulting from pigment in the tissues.

Pii·kan·i ['pikænɪ] *n* **1** a member of a First Nations or Native American people, living in Alberta and Montana. **2** their Algonquian language. **Piikani** *adj.* Also called **Peigan, Piegan.**

pi·ka [pəikə] *n* any of a family of small, tailless mammals resembling guinea pigs. ⟨Tungus (Siberian language) *piika*⟩

pike[1] [pəik] *n* **1** a weapon having a long wooden handle and a pointed metal head, once carried by foot soldiers; spear. **2** a sharp point; spike. ⟨French *pique* spear; *pic* pick[2]⟩

pike·staff *n, pl* **-staves** [-,steivz] **1** the shaft of a pike or spear. **2** a staff with a metal spike, used by travellers on foot.

pike[2] [pəik] *n* a large, long fish having a long, narrow, pointed head with many sharp teeth. ⟨*pike*[1], for the shape of its snout⟩

pi·las·ter [pə'læstər] *n* a rectangular pillar. ⟨Italian *pilastro*; Latin *pila* pillar⟩

pi·lau or **pi·law** [pɪ'laʊ] *n* a dish consisting of rice flavoured with spices, and often including chopped meat, poultry, or fish. ⟨Persian⟩

pile[1] [pail] *n* **1** many things lying one upon another: *a pile of wood.* **2** a heap: *a pile of dirt.* **3** Often, **piles** *pl Informal* a large amount or number: *piles of dishes to wash, a pile of work to do.* **4** *Informal* a large amount of money: *He made a pile on that deal.* **5** NUCLEAR REACTOR. *v* **1** make or become heaped into a pile (often with *up*): *Snow had piled up against the door.* **2** move in a group, esp in a confused way (with *in, into, out, off,* etc.): *to pile out into the street.* ⟨Latin *pila* pillar⟩

pile something on *Informal* employ (flattery, humour, etc.) in great amounts or to excess: *Some authors like to pile on the sex and violence.* **pile–up** *n Informal* **1** a collision involving several or many vehicles. **2** a great jumble of people or things: *a pile-up on the football field.*

pile[2] [pail] *n* a heavy beam driven upright into the earth, to help support a bridge, wharf, building, etc. ⟨Latin *pilum* javelin⟩ **pile driver** a machine for driving down piles or stakes. **pil·ing** *n* piles.

pile[3] [pail] *n* the loops that form the surface of certain fabrics. ⟨Latin *pilus* hair⟩

piles [pailz] *n pl* a swelling of blood vessels at the anus; hemorrhoids. ⟨Latin *pila* ball⟩

pil·fer ['pɪlfər] *v* steal in small quantities. **pil·fer·er** *n.* **pil·fer·age** *n.* ⟨Middle French *pelfrer* rob⟩

pil·grim ['pɪlgrəm] *n* a person who goes on a journey to a holy place as an act of religious devotion. ⟨Latin *peregrinus* foreigner⟩ **pil·grim·age** *n* a pilgrim's journey.

pil·ing See PILE[2].

pill [pɪl] *n* **1** medicine in a small, solid mass. **2 the pill** or **the Pill** an oral contraceptive. *v* of fabric, become matted into small balls: *This sweater is pilling badly.* ⟨Latin *pilula* diminutive of *pila* ball⟩ **pill·box** *n* **1** a box for holding pills. **2** a small, low fortress with machine guns.

pil·lage ['pɪlɪdʒ] *v* rob with violence: *Pirates pillaged the towns along the coast.* *n* plunder; robbery. **pil·lag·er** *n.* ⟨Old French *piller* plunder; Latin *pileare* flay⟩

pil·lar ['pɪlər] *n* **1** a slender, upright structure. **2** an important support or supporter: *a pillar of the community.* **pil·lared** *adj.* ⟨Old French *piler*; Latin *pila* pillar⟩ **from pillar to post** from one thing or place to another without any definite purpose. **Pillars of Islam** the five bases of the Islamic faith: confession, prayer, almsgiving, fasting, and the pilgrimage to Mecca.

pil·lion ['pɪljən] *n* a pad behind a saddle on a horse or motorcycle for a passenger to sit on. *adv* on a pillion: *to ride pillion.* ⟨Scots Gaelic *pillean, pell* cushion; Latin *pellis* skin⟩

pil·lo·ry ['pɪləri] *n* **1** formerly, a device used for public punishment, consisting of a wooden frame with holes for a person's head and hands. **2** exposure to public ridicule. *v* expose to public ridicule, scorn, or abuse. ⟨Old French *pellori*⟩

pil·low ['pɪlou] *n* **1** a fabric bag filled with soft material, to support the head when sleeping. **2** anything used for a similar purpose. *v* rest as if on a pillow: *He pillowed his head on a pile of leaves.* **pil·low·like** or **pil·lo·wy** *adj.* ⟨Old English *pylu*; Latin *pulvinus*⟩ **pil·low·case** or **pil·low·slip** *n* a removable cover for a pillow. **pillow sham** an ornamental cover for a pillow.

pi·lot ['pailət] *n* **1** a person trained to operate the controls of an aircraft or spacecraft. **2** a person whose job is steering ships in or out of a harbour or through dangerous waters. **3** a television show produced as a sample of a projected series. *v* **1** act as the pilot of. **2** guide: *The manager piloted us through the factory.* **3** use as an advance or experimental version: *to pilot a book in a school.* **pi·lot** *adj.* ⟨Italian *pilota,* earlier *pedota*; Greek *pēdon*⟩ **pilot fish** a marine fish that often accompanies a shark. **pilot light** a small flame kept burning all the time and used to light a main burner. **pilot whale** any of a genus of small, toothed whales.

pi·men·to [pɪ'mɛntou] *n* any of various sweet red peppers, used especially as a relish. ⟨Spanish *pimiento*; Latin *pigmentum* spice⟩

pimp [pɪmp] *n* 1 a man, who solicits for or manages one or more prostitutes and takes part of their earnings. 2 a man who procures sexual entertainment for others. **pimp** *v.* ⟨perhaps Middle French *pimper* dress up⟩

pim·per·nel ['pɪmpər,nɛl] *or* ['pɪmpərnəl] *n* any of a genus of plants of the primrose family. ⟨Latin *piperinus; piper* pepper⟩

pim·ple ['pɪmpəl] *n* a small, inflamed swelling in the skin. **pim·pled** *adj.* **pim·ply** *adj.* ⟨Middle English *pymple*⟩

pin [pɪn] *n* 1 a short piece of wire with a point at one end and a head at the other, used for fastening things together. 2 a kind of badge with a pin to fasten it to clothing. 3 a brooch. 4 any of various fastenings: *a safety pin, a clothes pin.* 5 in a stringed musical instrument, a peg to which a string is fastened. 6 *Bowling* any of the pieces of wood used as targets. 7 **pins** *Informal* legs: *She's a little shaky on her pins.* 8 *Computers* a short piece of wire that forms part of an electronic connection.
v **pinned, pin·ning** 1 fasten with a pin or as if with a pin. 2 hold fast in one position: *When the tree fell, it pinned her shoulder to the ground.* **pin·like** *adj.* ⟨Old English *pinn* peg⟩
on pins and needles very anxious or uneasy. **pin down a** hold to a pledge. **b** fix firmly; establish. **pin someone's ears back** scold. **pin on** *Informal* fix blame for (something) on: *The police could not pin the crime on him.*

pin·ball *n* a game in which a ball rolls down a board studded with pins, into numbered compartments. **pinball machine** a gambling device used for playing pinball. **pin·cush·ion** *n* a small cushion to stick pins in for use. **pin·feath·er** *n* an undeveloped feather just emerging through the skin. **pin·head** *n* 1 the head of a pin. 2 something very small or unimportant. 3 *Informal* a very stupid person. **pin·head·ed** *adj Informal* very stupid or silly: *That was a pinheaded thing to do.* **pin·hole** *n* a tiny hole made as if by a pin. **pin money** 1 money set aside for buying extra or minor things. 2 formerly, an allowance of money given to a wife for her own use. **pin·point** *n* something very small or sharp: *a pinpoint of light. adj* extremely precise: *pinpoint accuracy. v* locate precisely: *to pinpoint the heart of the problem.* **pin·prick** *n* 1 a tiny puncture from something like a pin. 2 a minor irritation. **pin·stripe** *n* cloth having fine stripes. **pin–up** *n* 1 a picture of a sexually attractive person put up on a wall. 2 a person who has posed for such pictures. **pin–up** *adj.* **pin·wheel** *n* 1 a toy made of a wheel fastened to a stick by a pin so that it revolves in the wind. 2 a kind of firework that revolves when lighted. **pin·worm** *n* any of various small, threadlike worms that are intestinal parasites in vertebrates.

PIN [pɪn] personal identification number, a number identifying a person, esp for purposes of electronic banking. Often, **PIN number** or **PIN code.**

pin·a·fore ['pɪnə,fɔr] *n* a full apron worn by children or women to protect other clothes. ⟨*pin,* v + *afore* before⟩

pi·ña·ta [pɪn'jɑtə] *n* a Mexican papier-mâché or clay figure, usually of an animal, filled with candies. ⟨Spanish = pot⟩

pin·cer ['pɪnsər] *n* 1 a claw of a crab, lobster, etc., resembling a pair of pincers. 2 **pincers** *pl* a tool for gripping, made like scissors. **pin·cer·like** *adj.* ⟨Old French *pincier* to pinch⟩

pinch [pɪntʃ] *v* 1 squeeze between two hard edges, or with thumb and forefinger. 2 cause to become thin: *a face pinched by hunger.* 3 limit closely: *to be pinched for space.* 4 *Slang* arrest. 5 *Slang* steal. **pinch** *n.* (See PINCER.) **pinch–hit** *v* **-hit, -hit·ting** 1 *Baseball* bat for another player when a hit is badly needed. 2 take another's place in an emergency. **pinch·hit·ter** *n.* **pinch·pen·ny** *Informal adj* mean with money. *n* a miserly person.

pine¹ [paɪn] *n* any of a genus of evergreen trees, having needlelike leaves growing in tufts. **pine·like** *adj.* ⟨Latin *pinus*⟩
pine nut the edible seed of any of several pine trees. **pin·er·y** ['paɪnəri] *n* 1 a forest of pine trees. 2 a place where pineapples are grown. **pine tar** a tar obtained by distilling pine wood and used for roofing, paints, antiseptics, etc. **pin·y** or **pin·ey** *adj* to do with pine trees: *a piny fragrance, piny mountains.*

pine² [paɪn] *v* 1 yearn. 2 waste away with pain, hunger, grief, or desire. ⟨Old English *pīn* torture; Greek *poinē*⟩

pine·ap·ple ['paɪn,æpəl] *n* 1 a plant cultivated for its fruit, which resembles a large pine cone and has juicy, yellow flesh. 2 *Slang* a hand grenade or bomb.

pin·go ['pɪŋgou] *n, pl* **ping·os** or **ping·oes** a dome-shaped mound of soil, usually with a core of ice, found in tundra regions and produced by the pressure of water or ice accumulating underground and pushing upward. ⟨Inuktitut *pinguk*⟩

Ping–Pong ['pɪŋ ,pɒŋ] *n Trademark* TABLE TENNIS.

pin·ion¹ ['pɪnjən] *n* any of the stiff flying feathers of a bird's wing.
v 1 cut off or tie the pinions of (a bird) to prevent its flying. 2 bind: *His arms were pinioned behind his back.* ⟨Old French *pignon;* Latin *pinna* feather⟩

pin·ion² [pɪn,jən] *n Machinery* 1 a small gear with teeth that fit into those of a larger gear or rack. 2 a spindle with teeth that engage with a gear. ⟨Old French *pignon* battlement; Latin *pinna* pinnacle⟩

pink¹ [pɪŋk] *n* 1 a colour made by mixing red and white. 2 any of a genus of flowering plants having stems with swollen joints. 3 the highest degree: *the pink of health. adj* to do with the colour pink. **pink·ish** *adj.* ⟨*pink²,* for flower's serrated edges; colour is named for the flower.⟩

pink–col·lar *adj* referring to types of jobs traditionally performed by women, such as nursing, salesclerking, etc. Compare BLUE-COLLAR, WHITE-COLLER. **pink·eye** *n Pathology* an acute, contagious conjunctivitis of humans and some domestic animals. **pink slip** *Informal* notice of termination of employment, named for the colour of the paper on which the notice is often printed.

pink² [pɪŋk] *v* **1** prick with a sword, spear, etc. **2** cut the edge of (cloth) with special shears, leaving a serrated edge that prevents unravelling. ⟨Middle English *pynken;* Old English *pynca* point⟩
pink·ie or **pinky** *n Informal* the smallest finger. **pinking shears** shears for pinking cloth.

pin·na·cle [ˈpɪnɪkəl] *n* **1** *Architecture* a slender turret. **2** a high peak of rock. **3** the highest point of achievement: *at the pinnacle of her fame.* ⟨Latin *pinnaculum,* diminutive of *pinna* feather, wing, point⟩

pin·nate [ˈpɪnɪt] *or* [ˈpɪneit] *adj* **1** like a feather, esp in having parts arranged on opposite sides of an axis. **2** *Botany* of a leaf, consisting of leaflets arranged on opposite sides of the stalk. **pin·nate·ly** *adv.* ⟨Latin *pinna* feather⟩

pi·noch·le or **pi·noc·le** [ˈpinʌkəl] *or* [ˈpinɒkəl] *n* a game played with 48 cards, in which points are scored according to the value of certain combinations of cards. ⟨origin uncertain⟩

pint [paint] *n* a non-metric unit for measuring liquids, equal to about 0.57 dm³. ⟨Middle Dutch *pinte* plug⟩
pint–sized *adj Informal* small.

Pin·yin [ˈpɪnˈjɪn] *n* a system for romanizing Chinese words. Also, **pin·yin.** ⟨Mandarin⟩

pi·o·neer [ˌpaɪəˈnɪr] *n* **1** a person who settles in a region that has not been settled before. **2** a person who goes first and so prepares a way for others. **pi·o·neer** *v.* ⟨French *pionnier;* Old French *peon* foot soldier; Latin. See PEON.⟩

pi·ous [ˈpaɪəs] *adj* **1** having reverence for God; religious. **2** showing religious scruples in a smug way: *pious platitudes.* **pi·ous·ly** *adv.* **pi·e·ty** [ˈpaɪəti] *n.* ⟨Latin *pius*⟩
pi·e·tism *n* **1** an emphasis on personal piety at the expense of neglecting social righteousness. **2** pretended piety. **pi·e·tist** *n.* **pi·e·tis·tic** *adj.* **pi·e·tis·ti·cal·ly** *adv.*

SYNONYMS
Pious emphasizes showing religion or reverence for God by carefully observing religious duties and practices, and sometimes suggests that more religion is shown than felt: *They are pious enough to go to church in the morning but they gossip all afternoon.* **Devout** emphasizes feeling true reverence that usually is expressed in prayer or devotion to religious observances, but may not be outwardly shown at all.

pip¹ [pɪp] *n* the seed of an apple, orange, etc. ⟨short for *pippin,* type of apple⟩

pip² [pɪp] *n* one of the spots on playing cards, dominoes, or dice. ⟨origin uncertain⟩

pipe [pəip] *n* **1** a tube through which a liquid or gas flows. **2** a tube with a bowl at one end, for smoking. **3 pipes** *pl* **a** a set of musical tubes: *the pipes of Pan.* **b** bagpipe. **c** the singing voice. **4 ✸** formerly, in the fur trade: **a** a rest period on a journey, orig one in which to smoke a pipe. **b** a spell of travelling between rest periods.
v **1** carry by means of a pipe. **2** transmit (music, speech, etc.) by electronic means, esp from one room to another (with *in*): *The background music will be piped in.* **3** play on a pipe. **4** sing or speak in a shrill voice. **pipe·ful** *n.* **pipe·like** *adj.* ⟨Latin *pipare* chirp⟩
pipe down *Slang* be quiet. **pipe up** *Slang* speak, esp in a piping voice. **put that in your pipe and smoke it** see if you can accept that. **pipe cleaner** a short length of fine twisted wire covered with small tufts of yarn. **pipe dream** *Informal* an impractical idea. **pipe fitter** a worker who installs, repairs, and maintains pipe systems. **pipe·line** *n* **1** a line of pipes for carrying gas, oil, or other liquids. **2** a direct channel for supplying information, etc.: *She's got a pipeline into the manager's office.* **3** a flow of materials through a series of productive processes. **pip·er** *n* a person who plays on a pipe or bagpipe. **pay the piper** pay for one's pleasure; bear the consequences. **pi·pette** [pɪˈpɛt] *or* [pəiˈpɛt] *n* a slender pipe for transferring liquids. **pi·pette** *v.* **pip·ing** *n* **1** a system of pipes. **2** material that can be used for pipes. **3** a shrill sound: *the piping of frogs in the spring.* **4** a narrow band of material used for trimming edges of clothing, cushions, etc. **5** ornamental lines of icing, meringue, etc. *adj* shrill. **piping hot** very hot.

pip·squeak [ˈpɪpˌskwik] *n Slang* a small or insignificant person or thing. ⟨after small German shell of World War I, named for its sound in flight⟩

pi·quant *adj* **1** [piˈkɑnt] sharp or pungent in an agreeable way: *a piquant sauce.* **2** [ˈpikənt] intriguing: *a piquant bit of news.* **pi·quan·cy** *n.* **pi·quant·ly** *adv.* ⟨French = stinging⟩

pique [pik] *n* a feeling of anger at being slighted: *She left the party in a fit of pique.* *v* **1** cause a feeling of anger or resentment in. **2** stir up: *to pique one's curiosity.* ⟨French = sting⟩

pi·ra·cy See PIRATE.

pi·ra·nha [pəˈrɑnə] *or* [pəˈrænə] *n, pl* **-nhas** or (esp collectively) **-nha** any of various small freshwater fishes, a few species of which are carnivorous and noted for their voracity. ⟨Portuguese; Tupi *pira nya* toothed fish⟩

pi·rate [ˈpaɪrɪt] *n* **1** one who attacks and robs ships. **2** a person who publishes, reproduces, or uses a book, play, musical composition, etc. without permission. **pi·ra·cy** [ˈpaɪrəsi] *n.* **pi·rate** *v.* **pi·rate·like** *adj.* **pi·rat·i·cal** [pəˈrætɪkəl] *adj.* **pi·rat·i·cal·ly** *adv.* ⟨Greek *peiratēs; peiraein* attack⟩

pi·rosh·ki or **pi·rozh·ki** [pə'rʌʃki] *or* [pə'rɒʃki] *n pl* small pastry turnovers filled usually with a ground beef mixture. ⟨Russian⟩

pir·ou·ette [,piru'ɛt] *n* a whirling about on one foot or on the toes, as in dancing. **pir·ou·ette** *v*. ⟨French = spinning top⟩

pis·cine ['pəisin] *or* ['pɪsin] *adj* to do with fish or fishes. ⟨Latin *piscis* fish⟩ **pis·ca·to·ri·al** [,pɪskə'tɔriəl] *adj* to do with fishing. **pis·ca·to·ri·al·ly** *adv*. **pis·ci·cul·ture** ['pɪsɪ,kʌltʃər] *n* the breeding and rearing of fish by artificial means.

pis·ta·chi·o [pɪ'stæʃi,ou] *n* a small tree of the cashew family, with a greenish, edible nut. ⟨Italian; Greek *pistakion*; *pistakē* the tree⟩

pis·til ['pɪstəl] *n Botany* the part of a flower that produces seeds. ⟨Latin *pistillum* pestle⟩

pis·tol ['pɪstəl] *n* a small, short gun. ⟨French *pistole*; Czech *pišt'ala*⟩

pis·ton ['pɪstən] *n* **1** in an engine, pump, etc., a cylinder fitting inside a tube in which it is moved by the force of exploding vapour. **2** in a wind instrument, a sliding valve that, when pressed by the fingers, lowers the pitch. ⟨Italian *pistone*; Latin *pistus* pp of *pinsere* pound⟩

pit¹ [pɪt] *n* **1** a hole in the ground. **2** a little hole in the skin, such as is left by smallpox. **3** a usually sunken area in front of the stage of a theatre where the orchestra sits. **4** an enclosed place where animals or birds are made to fight each other: *a bear pit*. **5** an area alongside an automobile race track where cars are serviced during a race. *v* **pit·ted**, **pit·ting** **1** mark with small pits or scars. **2** set to fight or compete: *The man pitted his brains against the strength of the bear.* ⟨Old English *pytt*; Latin *puteus* well²⟩ **the pits** *Slang* the worst possible thing: *That exam was the pits.* **pit·fall** *n* **1** a hidden pit to catch animals in. **2** any trap, such as a likely error or difficulty. **pit lamp** ✹ *esp BC* a kind of jacklight, so called because of its resemblance to the light on a miner's helmet. **pit·lamp·ing** *n*. **pit stop** **1** *Auto racing* a stop in the PIT (def. 5) for repairs, etc. during a race. **2** *Informal* a pause made during a journey to eat, visit the rest room, etc. **3** any place for such a stop. **pit·ted** *adj* **1** having the pits removed: *pitted olives*. **2** marked with pits: *This silver dish is pitted.*

pit² [pɪt] *n* the seed of a cherry, peach, etc. *v* **pit·ted**, **pit·ting** remove pits from (fruit). ⟨Dutch = kernel⟩

pi·ta ['pitə] *n* a round, flat bread forming a pocket which can be stuffed with meat, vegetables, etc. ⟨Hebrew⟩

pitch¹ [pɪtʃ] *v* **1** throw; toss. **2** *Slang* try to sell (a product, service, etc.). **3** set up: *to pitch a tent.* **4** fall forward: *She lost her balance and pitched over the cliff.* **5** of a boat, plunge with the bow rising and then falling. **6** set at a certain point, degree, or level. **7** slope: *That roof is steeply pitched.* **8** ✹ travel from one camping place to another. *n* **1** a throw. **2** a point: *the lowest pitch of bad fortune.* **3** in music, speech, etc., the highness or lowness of a sound. **4** *Music* **a** the exact number of vibrations producing a particular tone. **b** a particular standard of pitch: *concert pitch.* **5** a spot in a street where a peddler, street performer, etc. is regularly stationed. **6** the amount of slope. **7** the piece of ground on which certain games are played: *a horseshoe pitch.* **8** a plunge forward or headlong; lurch. ⟨Middle English *picche(n)*⟩ **make a pitch for** *Informal* make a persuasive request for. **pitch in** *Informal* **a** contribute. **b** begin to work vigorously. **pitch into** *Informal* **a** attack. **b** start on vigorously: *The children pitched into their dinners.* **pitch on** (or **upon**) choose. **pitched battle** a planned battle with lines of troops, etc., arranged beforehand. **pitch·er** *n Baseball* the player who throws the ball to the batter. **pitch·fork** *n* a large fork used for throwing hay or straw. **pitch·fork** *v*.

pitch² [pɪtʃ] *n* **1** a black, sticky substance obtained from the distillation of tar, etc. **2** bitumen. **3** resin obtained from various evergreens. **pitch·y** *adj*. ⟨Latin *pix, picis*⟩ **pitch black** *adj* very dark or black: *Her hair is pitch black.* **pitch dark** *adj* very dark; with no light at all. **pitch pine** any of various pines from which pitch or turpentine is obtained.

pitch·blende ['pɪtʃ,blɛnd] *n* a mineral consisting largely of uranium oxide, occurring in black, pitchlike masses. It is a source of radium, uranium, and actinium. ⟨half-translation of German *Pechblende*⟩

pitch·er¹ ['pɪtʃər] *n* a container for holding and pouring liquids, with a lip on one side and a handle on the other. **pitch·er·ful** *n*. ⟨Old French *pichier*; Latin *bicarium*⟩ **pitcher plant** any of a genus of herbs having leaves modified into pitchers in which insects are trapped, to be digested by the plant. It is the provincial flower of Newfoundland and Labrador.

pitch·er² See PITCH¹.

pit·e·ous See PITY.

pith [pɪθ] *n* **1** *Botany* the central, spongy tissue in the stems of certain plants. **2** *Zoology* the soft inner substance of a bone, feather, etc. **3** an essential part: *the pith of a speech.* **4** strength. **pith·y** *adj*. **pith·i·ly** *adv*. **pith·i·ness** *n*. ⟨Old English *pitha*⟩

pit·i·a·ble, **pit·i·ful**, **pit·i·less** See PITY.

pi·ton ['piton] *or* [pɪ'tɒn] *French* [pi'tɔ̃] *n* **1** an iron spike with a ring at one end, used in mountain climbing. It can be driven into a crack in rock or ice and used to secure a rope. **2** a sharply pointed mountain peak. ⟨French = point, peak⟩

pit·tance ['pɪtəns] *n* a small amount or share. ⟨Old French *pitance* alms; Latin *pietas* piety⟩

pit·ter-pat·ter ['pɪtər ,pætər] *n* a rapid succession of light beats or taps, as of rain. **pit·ter-pat·ter** *adv, v*. ⟨reduplication of *patter*¹⟩

pi·tu·i·tar·y gland [pə'tuə,tɛri] *Anatomy* an endocrine gland situated at the base of the brain. It secretes hormones that promote growth. ⟨Latin *pituita* phlegm, mucus⟩

pit·y ['pɪti] *n* **1** sorrow for another's distress. **2** a cause for regret: *It is a pity to be inside in good weather.*
v feel pity for. **pit·y·ing** *adj.* ⟨Latin *pietas*⟩
have or **take pity on** show pity for. **pit·e·ous** ['pɪtiəs] *adj* deserving pity. **pit·e·ous·ness** *n.* **pit·i·a·ble** *adj* **1** deserving pity. **2** deserving contempt. **pit·i·a·ble·ness** *n.* **pit·i·a·bly** *adv.* **pit·i·ful** *adj* **1** deserving pity: *a pitiful sight.* **2** deserving contempt: *a pitiful performance.* **pit·i·ful·ly** *adv.* **pit·i·ful·ness** *n.* **pit·i·less** *adj* showing no pity or mercy: *a pitiless tyrant, a pitiless act.* **pit·i·less·ly** *adv.* **pit·i·less·ness** *n.*

CONFUSABLES

Pitiful emphasizes the effect on others, that of arousing pity, made by something felt to be touching or pathetic: *The crying children were pitiful.* Piteous emphasizes the quality in the thing itself that makes it appeal for pity and move the heart: *Their sad faces were piteous.*

---

piv·ot ['pɪvət] *n* **1** a point on which something turns. **2** a person, thing, etc. having a central role. **3** *Hockey* the player who plays centre in a forward line. *v* turn on a pivot: *to pivot on one's heel.* **piv·ot·al** *adj.* **piv·ot·al·ly** *adv.* ⟨Old French⟩

pix·el ['pɪksəl] *n* any of the many tiny dots which make up an image on a computer or television screen. ⟨*pict(ure)* + *el(ement)*⟩

pix·ie or **pix·y** ['pɪksi] *n* a fairy or elf. **pix·ie·ish** or **·pix·y·ish** *adj.* ⟨British dialect⟩ **pix·i·lat·ed** ['pɪksə,leitɪd] *adj* whimsical; eccentric. **pix·i·la·tion** *n.*

pizza ['pitsə] *n* a layer of dough covered with a mixture of tomatoes, cheese, olives, etc. and baked. Sometimes called **pizza pie.** ⟨Italian; possibly Greek *pitta* bread, cake⟩ **piz·ze·ri·a** [,pitsə'riə] or **pizza parlour** *n* a place where pizzas are made and sold, for taking out or eating on the premises.

piz·zazz [pə'zæz] *n Slang* glamorous vitality: *accessories to add pizzazz to a basic suit.* Also, **pi·zazz. piz·zaz·zy** *adj.* ⟨imitative⟩

pj's or **p.j.'s** ['pi,dʒeiz] *Informal* pyjamas.

pl or **pl.** plural.

plac·ard ['plækɑrd] *or* ['plækərd] *n* a notice to be posted in a public place. **plac·ard** *v.* ⟨French; *plaque* plaque⟩

pla·cate [plə'keit] *or* ['pleikeit] soothe; make peaceful: *to placate a person one has offended.* **pla·cat·ing** *adj.* **pla·ca·tion** *n.* ⟨Latin *placare*⟩ **plac·a·ble** ['plækəbəl] *adj* easily quieted. **plac·a·bil·i·ty** *n.* **plac·a·bly** *adv.*

place [pleis] *n* **1** a particular part of space: *a good place for a picnic.* **2** a city, town, village, district, etc. **3** a dwelling: *We all went to my place.* **4** the usual location: *The book is back in its place on the shelf.* **5** a suitable rank or position: *He has found his place in teaching.* **6** a position in time: *The performance was slow in several places.* **7** a step in order of proceeding: *In the first place, the room is too*

small; *in the second place, it is too dirty.* **8** *Mathematics* the position of a figure in a number: *in the third decimal place.* **9** a position in a competition: *I won first place.* *v* **1** put (in a spot, position, condition, or relation). **2** give the place, etc. associated with: *I remember her name, but I cannot place her.* **3** assign to a date, rank, category, value, age, etc. **4** entrust to an appropriate person, firm, etc. for action, treatment, disposal, etc.: *to place an ad.* **5** *Sports* **a** be among the leaders in a competition: *Our horse failed to place in the first race.* **b** finish second in a horse race. Compare WIN (def. 1) and SHOW (def. 10). ⟨Latin *plattia;* Greek *plateia (hodos)* broad (way); *platys* broad⟩

all over the place, *Informal* **a** everywhere. **b** very disordered. **give place** yield: *His anger gave place to remorse.* **go places** *Informal* advance rapidly toward success. **in place a** in the usual place. **b** ready for use: *All systems are in place for the first democratic election in this small country.* **in place of** instead of: *You can use water in place of milk in this recipe.* **know one's place** act according to one's (inferior) position in life. **out of place a** not in the usual place. **b** inappropriate. **put someone in his or her place** tell or show someone that he or she is conceited. **take place** happen; occur.
place card a small card with a person's name on it, to indicate where the guest is to sit at the table. **place·hold·er** *n Mathematics* the symbol zero when used to indicate the place value of another digit. In the number 40, the 0 is a placeholder (for the ones) indicating that the 4 is in the tens place. **place in the sun** as favourable a position as any occupied by others. **place kick** *Football* a kick given to a ball after it has been placed on the ground. **place–kick** *v.* **place·mat** *n* a mat that serves as an individual tablecloth at a meal. **place·ment** *n* **1** a location; arrangement. **2** the finding of a job for a person. **3** *Football* a placing of the ball on the ground for a place kick. **place setting** the dishes, etc. required to set one person's place at a table. **place value** *Mathematics* the value of a digit according to its position in a number. In *582,* the place values are $5 \times 100, 8 \times 10, 2 \times 1$.

pla·ce·bo [plə'sibou] *n, pl* **-bos** or **-boes 1** a pill, etc., containing no active substance, given to satisfy a patient or to serve as a control in an experiment to test a new drug. **2** something said only to flatter or mollify. ⟨Latin = I shall please⟩

pla·cen·ta [plə'sɛntə] *n, pl* **-tae** [-ti] *or* [-tai] or **-tas 1** *Anatomy* the organ by which the fetus is attached to the womb and nourished. **2** *Botany* the part of the ovary of flowering plants that bears the ovules. **pla·cen·tal** *adj.* ⟨Latin = flat cake, Greek *plakos* flat surface⟩

plac·er ['plæsər] *n Mining* a deposit of sand or gravel containing gold or other valuable minerals in particles that can be washed out. ⟨Spanish = sandbank⟩ **placer mining** the process of washing loose sand or gravel for gold or other minerals.

plac·id ['plæsɪd] *adj* calm; peaceful; quiet: *a placid lake*. **plac·id·ly** *adv*. **pla·cid·i·ty** or **plac·id·ness** *n*. ⟨Latin *placere* please⟩

pla·gia·rize ['pleɪdʒə,raɪz] *v* take and use as one's own (the thoughts, writings, etc. of another). **pla·gia·rism** *n*. **pla·gia·rist** *n*. ⟨Latin *plagiarius* kidnapper; *plaga* net⟩

plague [pleɪg] *n* **1** a dangerous disease that spreads rapidly and often causes death. **2** any epidemic disease. **3** anything or anyone that annoys: *Her hay fever is a plague this year*.
v annoy: *Stop plaguing me for money*. **pla·guy** or **pla·guey** *adj Informal*. ⟨Latin, dialect Greek *plaga* blow⟩

plaice [pleɪs] *n*, *pl* **plaice** or **plaic·es** a flounder that is an important food fish. ⟨Latin *platessa* flatfish; Greek *platys* flat⟩

plaid [plæd] *n* **1** a pattern of stripes crossing each other at right angles. **2** tartan. ⟨Scots Gaelic *plaide*⟩

plain [pleɪn] *adj* **1** easy to see, hear, or understand. **2** absolute: *plain foolishness*. **3** uncomplicated: *plain sewing*. **4** frank and honest: *plain speech*. **5** without ornament: *a plain dress*. **6** not rich or highly seasoned: *plain food*. **7** simple in manner: *They're plain people*. **8** not good-looking: *a plain face*. **9** not mixed with anything: *plain coffee*.
adv simply; clearly: *She's plain stubborn*.
n Often, **plains** *pl* a large, more or less flat and treeless stretch of land: *Buffalo used to roam the North American plains*. **plain·ly** *adv*. **plain·ness** *n*. ⟨Latin *planus* flat⟩
plain·clothes ['pleɪn ,klouz] *or* [,klouðz] *adj* wearing ordinary clothes, not a uniform. **plain·clothes** *n*. **plain sailing** unobstructed progress: *We had some problems but now it's plain sailing*. **Plains Cree 1** a member of one of the two main branches of the Cree people. The Plains Cree migrated to the Prairies from the eastern woodlands. **2** their Cree dialect. **Plains Cree** *adj*. **Plains peoples** any of the First Nations peoples including the Assiniboine, Blackfoot, and Plains Cree, who formerly inhabited the Great Plains area. **plain·song** *n* vocal music used in the Christian church from very early times, sung in unison and unaccompanied. Also called **Gregorian chant**. **plain–spo·ken** *adj* frank in speech.

plaint [pleɪnt] *n* **1** *Archaic, poetic* lamentation. **2** *Law* accusation or complaint. ⟨Old French *plainte*; Latin *planctus* pp of *plangere* lament⟩
plain·tiff *n* a person who begins a lawsuit. **plain·tive** *adj* mournful; sad. **plain·tive·ly** *adv*. **plain·tive·ness** *n*.

plait [pleɪt] *or* [plæt] *n*, *v* braid. ⟨Old French *pleit*; Latin *plicatus* a pp of *plicare* fold⟩

plan [plæn] *n* **1** a method for achieving an end: *a plan for attracting more tourists to the city*. **2** goal: *Her plan was to have the business established by the end of the year*. **3** a drawing showing how a floor of a building is arranged. **4** a detailed map of a small area such as a town, a property, etc.

v **planned, plan·ning 1** think out beforehand how (something) is to be done (sometimes with *out*): *to plan a program*. **2** make plans. **3** intend: *We are planning to take a trip this year*. **plan·ner** *n*. ⟨French, literally, plane; Latin *planus* flat; for sketch on a flat surface⟩
plan on a reckon on: *We are planning on 200 guests*. **b** intend: *I plan on going*.

plane¹ [pleɪn] *n* **1** any flat surface. **2** a level of thought, conduct, etc.: *He keeps his writing on a high plane*. **3** airplane. **4** *Geometry* a surface such that if any two points on it are joined by a straight line, the line will be contained wholly in the surface.
v of a speedboat, etc., rise slightly out of the water while moving. **plane** *adj*. ⟨Latin *planum* level place⟩
plane figure *Mathematics* in geometry, a figure which lies in a single PLANE¹. **plane geometry** *Mathematics* a branch of geometry dealing with plane figures. **plane·load** *n* the load of people or cargo carried by an airplane: *a planeload of supplies*.

plane² [pleɪn] *n* carpenter's tool with a blade for smoothing wood. **plane** *v*. ⟨French *plane*, Latin *plana; planare* to smooth⟩

plan·et ['plænɪt] *n Astronomy* one of the heavenly bodies (except comets and meteors) that move around a star in regular paths. Mercury, Venus, the Earth, Mars, Jupiter, Saturn, Uranus, Neptune, and Pluto are planets in our solar system. **plan·e·tar·y** *adj*. ⟨Greek *planētēs; planaesthai* wander⟩
plan·e·tar·i·um *n*, *pl* **-i·a** [-iə] or **-i·ums** a building with an apparatus that shows the movements of the sun, moon, planets, and stars by projecting lights on the inside of a dome. **plan·et·oid** *n* a minor planet; asteroid.

plan·gent ['plændʒənt] *adj* resounding loudly and mournfully, as a deep bell. ⟨Latin *plangere* bewail⟩

plank [plæŋk] *n* **1** a long piece of sawed timber. **2** an item in the platform of a political party, etc.
v cook and serve on a wooden board. **plank·like** *adj*. ⟨Latin *planca* board⟩
walk the plank be forced to walk off a plank extending from a ship's side. Pirates reputedly used to execute prisoners in this way. **plank house** among coastal First Nations peoples, a long, communal building built of cedar and capable of housing several families, now used chiefly for ceremonial affairs. Compare LONGHOUSE. **plank·ing** *n* a quantity of planks.

plank·ton ['plæŋktən] *n* the mass of very

small animal or plant life that drifts in salt and fresh water. **plank·ton·ic** [-tɒnɪk] *adj.* ⟨Greek *planktos* wandering⟩

plant [plænt] *n* **1** any living thing that is not an animal, fungus, moneran, or protist. **2** a living thing that has leaves, roots, and a soft stem. **3** the buildings, machinery, etc. used in manufacturing: *a steel plant.* **4** *Informal* a person or thing placed so as to trap: *The money found in her room was a plant.*
v **1** put in the ground to grow. **2** set firmly: *Plant your feet firmly and pull.* **3** *Informal* place (a person or thing) so as to trap or deceive: *The evidence was planted.* **plant·like** *adj.* ⟨Latin *planta* sprout⟩

plan·ta·tion *n* **1** a large farm, esp in a tropical country, on which cotton, sugar, etc. are grown. **2** a large group of trees or other plants that have been planted. **3** a colony; settlement: *Plantations were established in Newfoundland in the early 1600s.* **4** *Logging* a reforested tract of land that has previously been cut over. **plant·er** *n* **1** a person who runs a plantation: *a cotton planter.* **2** a box, pot, etc., used for growing plants indoors, on a patio or balcony, etc. **3** ✹ *Newfoundland and Labrador* a small trader; a person who hires others to fish for him or her, taking a share of the catch. **plant kingdom 1** one of the broad divisions of the natural world, ranging from small plants to large trees. Compare ANIMAL KINGDOM. **2** in present-day biology, one of the five divisions of living things. See also ANIMAL, FUNGUS, MONERAN, and PROTIST.

plan·tain¹ ['plæntən] *n* a tropical plant related to the banana. ⟨Spanish *plántano*⟩

plan·tain² ['plæntən] *n* any of a genus of plants having leaves that spread out from the base of the stem. ⟨Latin *plantaginis*; *planta* sole of the foot; for its flat leaves⟩

plan·tar ['plæntər] *adj* to do with the sole of the foot: *plantar warts.* ⟨Latin *planta* sole of the foot⟩

plan·ti·grade *adj* walking on the whole sole of the foot, as a human, bear, etc. does.

plaque [plæk] *n* **1** an inscribed tablet fastened to a wall, etc., and intended to inform. **2** *Dentistry* a thin film of saliva, mucus, etc., together with bacteria, that forms on the teeth and hardens into tartar. **3** *Medicine* an abnormal patch on the body, such as a spot of psoriasis. **4** a clear space in a bacterial culture, resulting from the localized destruction of cells by a virus. ⟨French; Dutch *plak* flat board⟩

plash [plæʃ] *v, n* splash. **plash·y** *adj.*

plas·ma ['plæzmə] *n* **1** *Physiology* the liquid part of blood or lymph. **2** the watery part of milk; whey. **3** *Physics* a highly ionized gas, consisting of almost equal numbers of free electrons and positive ions. **4** *Biology* protoplasm; cytoplasm. Also, (defs. 1, 2, & 4), **plasm.** ⟨Greek = something moulded; *plassein* mould⟩

plas·ter ['plæstər] **1** a soft mixture of lime, sand, and water that hardens in drying. **2** a

protective dressing that will stick to the body and protect cuts, relieve pain, etc.
v **1** cover (walls, ceilings, etc.) with plaster. **2** spread with anything thickly: *My shoes were plastered with mud.* **plas·ter·like** *adj.* ⟨Greek *emplastron*; *en-* on + *plassein* mould⟩

plas·ter·board *n* a thin board consisting of a layer of plaster between layers of pressed felt covered with paper. **plas·tered** *adj Slang* drunk. **plas·ter·er** *n* a person who plasters walls, etc. **plas·ter·ing** *n.* **plaster of Paris** a mixture of powdered gypsum and water, which hardens quickly.

plas·tic ['plæstɪk] *n* **1** any of various synthetic materials (polyethylene, vinyl, styrene, polyester, etc.) that can be moulded when subjected to heat, pressure, etc. **2** *Informal* credit card or cards.
adj **1** made of synthetic plastic: *plastic cups.* **2** to do with moulding or modelling: *Sculpture is a plastic art.* **3** easily moulded or shaped. **4** easily influenced: *Children's minds are plastic.* **5** artificial or phoney: *plastic food.* ⟨Greek *plastikos*; *plassein* to mould⟩

plastic art 1 three-dimensional artworks. **2** visual art as distinct from music or writing. **Plas·ti·cine** ['plæstɪˌsin] *or* [ˌplæstɪ'sin] *n Trademark* a modelling paste that remains malleable. **plas·tic·i·ty** *n* the capacity for being moulded. **plas·ti·cize** *v* **1** make or become plastic. **2** treat with a plastic: *a plasticized fabric for raincoats.* **plas·ti·ci·za·tion** *n.* **plastic surgery** a branch of surgery concerned with reconstructing parts of the body, or with improving appearance. **plastic surgeon.**

plat du jour ['plɑ du 'ʒʊr] *French* [plady'ʒuʀ] in a restaurant, the special dish of the day.

plate [pleit] *n* **1** a dish, usually round, and almost flat. **2** the food served to one person at a meal: *The dinner will cost $50 a plate.* **3** dishes covered with a layer of silver or gold: *silver plate.* **4** a thin, flat piece of metal, bone, horn, etc: *steel plates.* **5** any full-page inserted illustration forming part of a book. **6** *Baseball* **a** the place where the batter stands to hit a pitched ball; home base. **b** the place where the pitcher stands. **7** *Dentistry* **a** the part of a set of false teeth that fits to the gums: *an upper plate.* **b** an orthodontic device of similar shape.
v **1** cover with a thin layer of silver, gold, or other metal. **2** put food on a plate, in an attractive arrangement. ⟨Greek *platys* flat⟩
on a plate See PLATTER. **on one's plate** taking up one's time, effort, and attention.

plate·ful *n* the contents of a plate: *a plateful of cookies.* **plate glass** thick sheet glass. **plate·let** *n* one of the very tiny disks found in the blood of vertebrates, that assist in blood clotting. **plate tectonics** *Geology* the theory that the crust is made up of huge segments, called plates, that float on the mantle below. **plat·ing** *n* a thin layer of silver, gold, or other metal. **plat·ter** ['plætər] *n* a large plate, used especially for holding or serving a main dish. **on a platter** or **plate** *Informal* with no effort required: *The promotion was handed to her on a platter.*

pla·teau [plə'tou] *n, pl* **-teaus** or **-teaux** [-'touz] **1** a large level area of land in the mountains or rising sharply from a lower area. **2** a period or state of levelling off: *Our team improved rapidly at first, but then we reached a plateau.* ⟨French; *plat* flat. See PLATE.⟩

plat·form ['plætfɔrm] *n* **1** a raised, level surface. **2** a plan of action of a group. **3** an extra layer in a sole of a shoe, to give additional thickness. **4** *Computers* the environment in which applications are run, consisting of the operating system, type of CPU or other hardware, the way a system is configured, or any combination of these factors. ⟨French *plateforme* flat form⟩

plat·i·num ['plætənəm] *n* a precious, silver-coloured metallic element that does not tarnish easily. *Symbol* **Pt** *adj* designating an album or video of music that has sold over two million copies. ⟨Spanish *plata* silver⟩ **platinum blonde** a person having whitish silver hair.

plat·i·tude ['plætə,tjud] *or* ['plætə,tud] *n* **1** a commonplace remark: *Better late than never* is a platitude. **2** flatness; triteness; dullness. **plat·i·tu·din·ize** *v*. **plat·i·tu·di·nous** *adj*. ⟨French *plat* flat. See PLATE.⟩

Pla·ton·ic [plə'tɒnɪk] *adj* **1** to do with Plato (d. 347? B.C.), a Greek philosopher, or his philosophy. **2** Usually, **platonic** to do with affection between two people that is free from sexual overtones. **pla·ton·i·cal·ly** *adv*.

pla·toon [plə'tun] *n* **1** one of the formations of soldiers making up a company. **2** *Football, etc.* a group of players trained for a particular kind of play: *the punt-return platoon.* ⟨French *peloton* diminutive of *pelote* ball⟩

plat·ter See PLATE.

plat·y·pus ['plætəpəs] *n, pl* **-pus·es** or **-pi** [-,paɪ] an egg-laying water mammal of Australia. ⟨Greek *platys* flat + *pous* foot⟩

plau·dit ['plɒdɪt] *n* **1** a round of applause. **2** Usually, **plaudits** *pl* enthusiastic approval. ⟨Latin *plaudite* applaud!⟩

plau·si·ble ['plɒzəbəl] *adj* appearing true or reasonable: *a plausible liar.* **plau·si·bil·i·ty** *n*. **plau·si·bly** *adv*. ⟨Latin *plausus* pp of *plaudere* applaud⟩

play [pleɪ] *n* **1** something done to amuse oneself. **2** a turn, move, or act in a game: *The centre made a brilliant play.* **3** the act of carrying on a game: *Play was slow in the first half.* **4** a story written for or presented as a dramatic performance; drama. **5** freedom for action, movement, etc.
v **1** have fun: *a kitten playing with its tail.* **2** do for amusement or to deceive: *to play a joke on someone.* **3** take part in (a game): *to play tag.* **4** cause to play in a game: *Each coach played the best goalie.* **5** act a part: *to play in a tragedy.* **6** pretend to be, in fun: *to play cowboys.* **7** produce (music) on an instrument: *to play a tune.* **8** do something pointlessly: *Do not play with your food.* **9** bet on: *She plays the horses.* ⟨Old English *plegan* exercise⟩

in play a *Sports* of a ball, in a position to be legally played. **b** as a joke. **out of play** *Sports* of a ball, not in a position to be legally played. **play at** do (something) half-heartedly. **play down** make seem less important: *to play down the unfavourable results of the opinion poll.* **played out a** exhausted. **b** finished. **play fair** act in an honourable way. **play for time** delay so as to benefit oneself in the long run. **play into someone's hands** act so as to give a person an advantage over oneself. **play off a** pit (one person against another) by clever manipulation. **b** play an extra game to settle (a tie). **play on** (or **upon**) take advantage of: *She played on her mother's good nature.* **play out** play (drama, game, etc.) to the end. **play possum.** See POSSUM. **play second fiddle** take an inferior role. **play up** make the most of: *Her agent played up the singer's extensive background in classical music.* **play up to** *Slang* flatter: *to play up to a famous person.*

play·a·ble *adj* **1** that can be played. **2** fit to be played on. **play–act** *v* pretend. **play·back** *n* a replaying of a tape recording or videotape, esp when it has just been made. **play·bill** *n* **1** a handbill announcing a play. **2** the program of a play. **play·boy** *n* a man, usually rich, who devotes his time to the pursuit of pleasure. **play–by–play** *adj* giving each event as it happens or happened: *a play-by-play broadcast of a hockey game.* **play·er** *n* **1** a person who plays a game: *a baseball player.* **2** an actor in a theatre. **3** a person who plays a musical instrument. **4** *Informal* an influential person in a particular field. **5** a device that plays: *a CD player.* **play·ful** *adj* **1** full of fun. **2** not serious. **play·ful·ly** *adv*. **play·ful·ness** *n*. **play·go·er** *n* a person who goes to the theatre often. **play·ground** *n* **1** a place for outdoor play, esp an area equipped with swings, etc. for children. **2** a popular place for leisure activity, such as a resort area: *The French Riviera is a playground of the wealthy.* **play·house** *n* **1** a small house for children to play in. **2** a theatre for live dramatic performances. **playing box** *Lacrosse* an area in which box lacrosse is played. **playing card** one of a set of, usually, 52 cards used in games, having one side marked with numbers and symbols. **playing field** a piece of level ground where athletic events are held. **level playing field** equal opportunity. **play·mate** *n* a playing companion. **play·off** *n* **1** an extra game played to settle a tie. **2** one of a series of games played by the top teams in a league to determine the winner of the championship, of a special trophy, etc. **play on words** pun; punning. **play·pen** *n* a small, portable enclosure for babies to play in. **play·room** *n* a room for children to play in. **play therapy** a method of therapy in which children express their emotions and hidden problems through play. **play·thing** *n* toy. **play·time** *n* time for playing. **play·wright** ['pleɪ,raɪt] *n* a writer of plays; dramatist.

pla·za ['plæzə] *n* **1** a shopping centre. Also, **shopping plaza. 2** a public square in a city or town. ⟨Spanish; Greek⟩

plea [pli] *n* **1** an earnest appeal **2** an excuse: *The man's plea was that he had not seen the signal.* **3** *Law* **a** the answer made by a defendant to a charge in a court. **b** an argument made in support of one side in a lawsuit. ⟨Old French *plai, plaid;* Latin *placitum* that which pleases; *placere* please⟩

plea bargain an arrangement between a prosecutor and a defendant, whereby the defendant pleads guilty to lesser charges in return for having graver charges dropped. **plea–bar·gain** *v.* **plead** [plid] *v* **plead·ed** or **pled** [plɛd], **plead·ing** **1** make an earnest appeal. **2** offer as an excuse: *The woman pleaded poverty in her defence.* **3** *Law* **a** act as counsel for: *She had a good lawyer to plead her case.* **b** answer to a charge in court: *Do you plead guilty or not guilty?* **plead·ing** *adj.*

pleas·ant See PLEASE.

please [pliz] *v* **pleased, pleas·ing** **1** give pleasure (to): *Toys please children.* **2** wish: *Do what you please.* **3** if you would be so kind (used as a polite addition to requests): *Come here, please.* ⟨Old French *plaisir;* Latin *placere*⟩ **if you please a** if you like. **b** with your permission (may be an ironic exclamation of indignation). **please yourself** do what you like. **pleas·ant** [ˈplɛzənt] *adj* **1** giving pleasure. **2** friendly. **pleas·ant·ly** *adv.* **pleas·ant·ness** *n.* **pleas·ant·ry** *n* **1** a good-natured joke. **2** lively, good-humoured talk. **pleas·ing** [ˈplizɪŋ] *adj* giving pleasure; pleasant: *a pleasing manner.* **pleas·ing·ly** *adv.* **pleas·ur·a·ble** *adj* pleasant; agreeable. **pleas·ur·a·bly** *adv.* **pleas·ure** [ˈplɛʒər] *n* **1** a feeling of being pleased. **2** something that pleases. **3** sensual enjoyment. **4** one's desire or choice: *What is your pleasure in this matter?* *v* gratify oneself, often in a sexual way. **pleas·ure·ful** *adj.* **at one's pleasure** as or when one pleases. **take one's pleasure** *(in)* enjoy: *He takes his pleasure in hunting and fishing.*

CONFUSABLES

Pleasant emphasizes that the person or thing described has certain qualities that give pleasure: *We spent a pleasant evening.*
Pleasing emphasizes the effect on the one experiencing what is described: *The evening was pleasing to me because I wanted to see her.*

---

pleat [plit] *n* a flat fold made by doubling material on itself. **pleat** *v.* ⟨variant of *plait*⟩

ple·be·ian See PLEBISCITE.

pleb·i·scite [ˈplɛbəˌsɑɪt] *or* [ˈplɛbəsɪt] *n* a direct vote by the qualified voters of a country, province, municipality, etc. on some question. Compare REFERENDUM. ⟨Latin *plebs* common people + *scitum* decree⟩ **ple·be·ian** [pləˈbiən] *n* **1** a member of the **plebs**, or common people, of ancient Rome. Compare PATRICIAN (def. 1). **2** a member of the common people of any country. **3** a vulgar person. *adj* **1** to do with the common people. **2** vulgar in manner or style. **3** pedestrian in style. **ple·be·ian·ism** *n.*

plec·trum [ˈplɛktrəm] *n, pl* **-trums** or **-tra** [-trə] a small piece of ivory, metal, etc., used for plucking the strings of a guitar, etc. ⟨Latin; Greek *plēktron; plēssein* strike⟩

pled *v* a pt and a pp of PLEAD.

pledge [plɛdʒ] *n* **1** a solemn promise. **2** something that secures: *The knight left a jewel as pledge for the borrowed horse.* **3** a promised donation.
v **1** promise solemnly. **2** give as security. **3** promise to donate (a sum). **4** drink to the health of: *The guests pledged the couple in champagne.* ⟨Old French *plege*⟩
take the pledge promise not to drink alcoholic liquor.

Pleis·to·cene [ˈplɑɪstəˌsin] *Geology n* the first epoch of the Quaternary period, beginning about two million years ago; ICE AGE (def. 2). **Pleis·to·cene** *adj.* ⟨Greek *pleistos* most + *kainos* recent⟩

ple·na·ry [ˈplɛnəri] *or* [ˈplinəri] *adj* **1** complete; absolute: *plenary powers.* **2** attended or to be attended by all qualified members: *a plenary session.* **ple·na·ri·ly** *adv.* ⟨Latin *plenus* full⟩

plen·i·po·ten·ti·ar·y [ˌplɛnəpəˈtɛnʃəri] *or* [-pəˈtɛnʃiˌɛri] *n* a diplomatic agent having full power or authority. **plen·i·po·ten·ti·ar·y** *adj.* ⟨Latin *plenus* full + *potens* powerful⟩

plen·ty [ˈplɛnti] *n* **1** a full supply: *plenty of time.* **2** the quality of being plentiful: *years of peace and plenty.*
adj enough; plentiful: *Six loaves will be plenty.* *adv Informal* fully: *plenty good enough.* ⟨Latin *plenitas* fullness; *plenus* full⟩
plen·i·tude [ˈplɛnɪˌtjud] *or* [-ˌtud] *n* **1** fullness: *in the plenitude of health and vigour.* **2** abundance: *a plenitude of food.* **plen·te·ous** [ˈplɛntiəs] *adj* plentiful. **plen·te·ous·ly** *adv.* **plen·ti·ful** *adj* more than enough: *a plentiful supply of gas for the trip.* **plen·ti·ful·ly** *adv.*

ple·o·nasm [ˈpliəˌnæzəm] *n* the use of more words than are necessary to express an idea; redundancy; tautology. *Example:* The *two twins* arrived together. **ple·o·nas·tic** *adj.* **ple·o·nas·ti·cal·ly** *adv.* ⟨Greek *pleon* more⟩

pleth·o·ra [ˈplɛθərə] *n* excessive abundance. **ple·thor·ic** [pləˈθɔrɪk] *adj.* ⟨Greek *plēthorē; plēthein* be full⟩

pleu·ra [ˈplʊrə] *n, pl* **pleu·rae** [ˈplʊri] *or* [ˈplʊrɑɪ] *Anatomy* in mammals, either of the membranes folded back over the surface of the lung. **pleu·ral** *adj.* ⟨Greek *pleura* rib⟩ **pleu·ri·sy** [ˈplʊrɪsi] *n Pathology* inflammation of the pleura. **pleu·rit·ic** *adj.*

plex·us [ˈplɛksəs] *n, pl* **-us·es** or **-us** **1** a network of nerves, blood vessels, etc. The **solar plexus** is a collection of nerves behind the stomach. **2** an interwoven combination of parts in a system; network. **plex·al** *adj.* ⟨Latin *plexus; plectere* twine, braid⟩

pli·a·ble [ˈplɑɪəbəl] *adj* **1** easily bent; flexible; supple: *Willow twigs are pliable.* **2** easily influenced; yielding: *He is too pliable to be a good leader.* **pli·a·bil·i·ty** *n.* Also, **pli·ant** [ˈplɑɪənt] *adj.* **pli·an·cy** *adj.* **pli·ant·ly** *adv.* ⟨French *plier* bend, fold⟩

pli·ers ['plaɪərz] n (usually with a pl verb) small pincers with long jaws. ⟨ply¹⟩

plight¹ [plaɪt] n a difficult or dangerous state. ⟨Old French pleit orig, way of folding. See PLAIT. Influenced by plight²⟩

plight² [plaɪt] Archaic v pledge; promise.
plight one's troth a pledge one's word. **b** promise to marry. ⟨Old English pliht risk (i.e., undertaken in promising)⟩

plinth [plɪnθ] n **1** Architecture the square part of the base of a column. **2** any square base, as of a pedestal, etc. ⟨Greek plinthos⟩

Pli·o·cene ['plaɪə,sin] Geology n the fifth epoch of the Tertiary period, beginning about 11 million years ago. **Pli·o·cene** adj. Also, **Plei·o·cene.** ⟨Greek pleiōn more + kainos recent⟩

plod [plɒd] v **plod·ded, plod·ding 1** walk slowly or heavily. **2** proceed in a slow or dull way: He plods away at his lessons.
n heavy footsteps: The plod of the horses' hooves could be heard outside. **plod·der** n. **plod·ding** adj. ⟨perhaps imitative⟩

plonk [plɒŋk] n Informal cheap or inferior wine. ⟨perhaps French blanc white (wine)⟩

plop [plɒp] n a sound like that of a flat object striking water without a splash.
v **plopped, plop·ping 1** fall with a plopping sound: The stone plopped into the water. **2** fall or drop heavily: She plopped into the first soft chair she came to. ⟨imitative⟩

plot [plɒt] n **1** a secret plan, esp to do something wrong. **2** the main story of a play, novel, poem, etc. **3** a small piece of ground: a cemetery plot, a garden plot.
v **plot·ted, plot·ting 1** plan secretly with others. **2** mark (something) on a map or diagram: The nurse plotted the patient's temperature over several days. **3** Mathematics **a** determine the location of (a point) by means of its coordinates. **b** make (a curve) by connecting points marked out on a graph. ⟨Old English = patch of ground; sense influenced by French complot joint plot⟩
plot·ter ['plɒtər] n **1** one who plots. **2** Computers a computer-controlled device to produce diagrams and pictures on paper.

plough or **plow** [plaʊ] n **1** a farm implement for cutting the soil and turning it over. **2** Usually, **plow** a machine for removing snow. **plough** or **plow** v. ⟨Old English plōg⟩
plough back reinvest (profits) in the same business. **plough into** Informal **a** hit hard or at speed and travel into: The car went out of control and ploughed into the building. **b** start (an activity) vigorously or with energy and determination: to plough into one's homework. **plough through** work one's way through: I must plough through a lot of material for this course. **plough under a** plough into the ground to enrich the soil. **b** defeat; destroy.
ploughing or **plowing match ⚹** a competition among farmers to determine the best at ploughing. **plough·man** or **plow·man** n, pl -men **1** a man who guides a plough. **2** a

farm worker. **plough·share** or **plow·share** n the part of a plough that cuts the soil.

plov·er ['plʌvər] n any of numerous shore birds with long wings, and, usually, no hind toes. ⟨Anglo-French; Latin pluvia rain; bird was said to call before rain⟩

ploy [plɔɪ] n Informal an action or words by which advantage over another may be gained: a clever ploy. ⟨possibly from employ n⟩

pluck [plʌk] v **1** pull off; pick: to pluck flowers. **2** pick or pull (at): to pluck the strings of a violin. **3** pull off the feathers or hair from: to pluck one's eyebrows.
n **1** the act of picking or pulling. **2** courage. ⟨Old English pluccian⟩
pluck up one's spirits (or **courage**, etc.), take courage.
pluck·y adj having courage. **pluck·i·ly** adv.

plug [plʌg] n **1** a piece of wood, rubber, metal, etc., used to stop up a hole. **2** a device used to make an electrical connection by sticking it into an outlet. **3** Informal an advertisement: The interview was mainly a plug for her latest book.
v **plugged, plug·ging 1** stop up with a plug (often with up): to plug up a hole. **2** insert the plug of (an electrical appliance) into an outlet (with in or into). **3** Informal advertise, esp on a radio or television program: to plug a product. **plug·less** adj. **plug·like** adj. ⟨Middle Dutch plugge⟩
plug away (or **along**) **at** Informal work steadily at (something). **pull the plug** Informal put an end to something: The administration pulled the plug on our new project. **plug up** clog.

plum [plʌm] n **1** any of various trees and shrubs of the rose family producing edible fruit with a smooth skin. **2** something very desirable, esp a job. **plum·like** adj. ⟨Old English plūme; Latin prunum; Greek prounmon⟩
plum·my adj **1** Informal desirable: a plummy part in the new play. **2** of a voice, full in tone.
plum pudding a rich pudding with raisins, spices, etc., traditionally served at Christmas.

plum·age See PLUME.

plumb [plʌm] n a small weight used on the end of a line to keep the line vertical.
adj vertical.
adv **1** vertically. **2** Informal completely: plumb out of luck.
v **1** test by a plumb line: Our line was not long enough to plumb the depths of the lake. **2** get to the bottom of: No one could plumb the mystery. ⟨Latin plumbum lead (the metal)⟩
out of plumb or **off plumb** not truly vertical.
plumb line 1 a line with a plumb, used to find the depth of water or to test the vertical straightness of a wall. **2** any vertical line.

plumb·er ['plʌmər] n a person whose work is installing and maintaining water pipes and fixtures in buildings. ⟨See PLUMB.⟩
plumb·ing n **1** the work of a plumber. **2** the water pipes and fixtures in a building or part of a building: the bathroom plumbing.

plume [plum] n **1** a long feather. **2** feathers

worn as an ornament on a helmet, etc. **3** a moving column of something such as smoke: *Snow rose in a plume from the snowblower.* **plume·like** *adj.* ⟨Latin *pluma*⟩
plum·age *n* the feathers on a bird.

plum·met ['plʌmɪt] *v* plunge; drop. ⟨Old French *plommet*. See PLUMB.⟩

plump[1] [plʌmp] *adj* rounded out.
v make or become plump (often with *up*): *He plumped the pillows on the bed.* **plump·ness** *n.* ⟨Middle English *plompe* dull, rude⟩

plump[2] [plʌmp] *v* **1** fall or drop heavily: *She plumped down on a chair.* **2 a** drop: *to plump down one's bags at the station.* **b** pay at once and in one lot: *to plump down $100.*
n **1** *Informal* a heavy fall. **2** *Informal* the sound made by a plunge or fall.
adv heavily or suddenly: *He ran plump into me.* ⟨Middle English *plumpen,* probably imitative⟩
plump for a give one's complete support to: *to plump for lower taxes.* **b** vote for.

plun·der ['plʌndər] *v* rob by force.
n things taken in plundering; loot: *They carried off their plunder in ships.* **plun·der·er** *n.* ⟨German = household goods⟩

SYNONYMS
Plunder applies particularly to things carried off by invading soldiers during a war: *The soldiers returned home with their plunder.* **Loot** applies particularly to things carried off from a city destroyed in war, or at the scene of a fire, wreck, etc., but is used also of anything taken by robbery: *Much loot was taken during the rioting.*

plunge [plʌndʒ] *v* **1** thrust with force into something, esp a liquid. **2** throw violently into a certain condition: *to plunge the room into darkness.* **3** throw oneself (into water, danger, a fight, etc.). **4** slope abruptly, as a cliff or road. **5** *Slang* gamble heavily.
n **1** the act of plunging. **2** a swim. ⟨Old French *plungier;* Latin *plumbum* lead sounder⟩ **take the plunge** *Informal* dare to do something which requires courage
plung·er *n* a rubber suction cup on a long stick, used for unplugging drains, toilets, etc.

plunk [plʌŋk] *v* **1** pluck so as to produce a hollow sound: *to plunk a banjo string.* **2** put down heavily: *I plunked my books on the table.*
adv with a thud or twang: *She sat down plunk on the ground.* **plunk** *n.* ⟨imitative⟩
plunk down hand over (payment): *He plunked down ten thousand dollars for the car.* **plunk for** *Informal* plump for.

plu·ral ['plʊrəl] *adj* **1** *Grammar* signifying more than one. **2** to do with more than one: *plural citizenship.* **plu·ral·ize** *v.*
plu·ral·i·za·tion *n.* **plu·ral·ly** *adv.* ⟨Latin *pluralis; plus* more⟩
plu·ral·ism *n* a condition of society in which a number of diverse cultural, religious, or racial groups maintain their diversity within a single nation or civilization. **plu·ral·is·tic** *adj.* **plu·ral·is·ti·cal·ly** *adv.* **plu·ral·i·ty** [plʊ'rælɪti] *n* in a contest, the number of votes cast for the leading candidate when that number is not more than half the total number of votes: *He won by only a plurality, not a majority.*

plus [plʌs] *prep* added to.
adj **1** better than: *Her mark was B plus.* **2** greater than zero; positive: *a plus quantity.* **3** *Informal* additional: *a plus value.*
n **1** the plus sign (+). **2** something extra; a gain. **3** a positive quantity. **4** an advantage: *The members' hard work was a big plus.*
conj Informal and in addition: *The work of an engineer requires intelligence plus experience.* ⟨Latin = more⟩

plush [plʌʃ] *n* cloth having a very soft pile.
adj **1** to do with plush: *plush upholstery.* **2** luxurious and showy: *plush surroundings.* ⟨Middle French *peluche;* Latin *pilus* hair⟩

Plu·to ['plutou] *n* **1** *Greek myth* the god of the lower world, or Hades. **2** in our solar system, the furthest planet from the sun.
plu·to·ni·um [plu'touniəm] *n* a radioactive metallic element found naturally in uranium ores and produced from uranium in nuclear reactors. *Symbol* Pu

plu·to·crat ['plutə,kræt] *n* **1** a person who has power because of wealth. **2** any wealthy person. **plu·to·crat·ic** *adj.* **plu·to·crat·i·cal·ly** *adv.* ⟨Greek *ploutos* wealth + *kratos* power⟩
plu·to·cra·cy [plu'tɒkrəsi] *n* **1** a system of government in which the rich rule. **2** a ruling class of wealthy people.

plu·to·ni·um See PLUTO.

plu·vi·al ['pluviəl] *adj* **1** to do with rain. **2** *Geology* caused by the action of rain. ⟨Latin *pluvia* rain⟩

ply[1] [plaɪ] **1** work with: *The dressmaker plies her needle.* **2** work steadily at (something): *carpenters plying their trade.* **3** supply with in a pressing manner: *to ply a person with food.* **4** travel regularly along (a course or route): *Boats ply the river.* ⟨variant of *apply*⟩

ply[2] [plaɪ] *n* **1** a layer, as of laminated wood: *three-ply plywood.* **2** a strand, as of yarn: *six-ply embroidery thread.* ⟨French *pli; plier* fold⟩
ply·wood *n* a board made of several thin layers of wood glued together.

p.m. 1 after noon (for Latin *post meridiem*). **2** post-mortem.

P.M. 1 PRIME MINISTER. **2** after noon (for Latin *post meridiem*).

PMS PRE-MENSTRUAL SYNDROME.

pneu·mat·ic [nju'mætɪk] *or* [nu'mætɪk] *adj* to do with air, or gas: *a pneumatic drill.* **pneu·mat·i·cal·ly** *adv.* ⟨Greek *pneuma* breath⟩
pneu·mat·ics *n* (with a sg verb) the branch of physics that deals with the pressure, elasticity, mass, etc. of gases.

pneu·mo·nia [nju'mounjə] *or* [nu'mounjə] *n Pathology* a disease in which the lungs are inflamed. ⟨Greek *pneumōn* lung⟩

P.O. 1 POST OFFICE. **2** PETTY OFFICER.

poach[1] [poutʃ] *v* **1** take (game or fish) illegally. **2** steal (someone else's) ideas. **poach·er** *n.* ⟨Middle French *pocher* poke, thrust⟩

poach² [poutʃ] *v* cook by simmering in milk, water, etc. ⟨Old French *poche* cooking spoon⟩

pock [pɒk] *n* a pustule.
v mark with or as if with pocks. ⟨Old English *pocc*⟩
pock·mark *n* **1** a pit in the skin, such as those left by acne. **2** any small hollow suggesting such a scar: *The floor was covered with pockmarks made by spike-heeled shoes.* **pock·mark** *v*. **pock·marked** *adj.*

pock·et ['pɒkɪt] *n* **1** a pouch sewn into or onto clothing. **2** *Billiards, etc.* one of the pouches on a billiard table. **3** *Geology* a cavity in the earth containing ore, oil, etc. **4** any condition in the air that causes an aircraft to drop suddenly. **5** a small area different from the surrounding area: *a few Liberal pockets in a Conservative riding.*
adj small enough to go in a pocket: *a pocket calculator.*
v **1** put in one's pocket: *He pocketed his change.* **2** hold back: *He pocketed his pride and said nothing.* **3** take secretly: *The accountant pocketed the profits.* **4** *Billiards, etc.* drive into a pocket. ⟨Anglo-French *pokete* diminutive of Middle French *poque, poche*⟩
be out of pocket spend or lose (money). **in pocket** having or gaining money: *They were $100 in pocket at the end of the day.*
pock·et·book *n* **1** Often, **pocket book** a small paperback. **2** a small case for carrying money, papers, etc. in a pocket. **3** financial resources: *too expensive for my pocketbook.* **4** *esp US* a woman's purse. **pocket borough** an electoral riding where support for one party is so strong as to virtually guarantee its candidate's election. **pock·et·ful** *n* as much as a pocket will hold. **pock·et·knife** *n, pl* **-knives** a small knife with blades that fold into the handle. **pocket money** money for minor expenses. **pock·et–size** or **pocket–sized** *adj* **1** small enough to go in a pocket: *a pocket-size radio.* **2** *Informal* small for its kind: *a pocket-size country.*

pod¹ [pɒd] *n* **1** the fruit of a plant such as a bean, consisting of a case that contains several seeds in a row. **2** the case itself. **3** a part of a spacecraft that can be detached from the main part.
v **pod·ded, pod·ding** produce pods. **pod·like** *adj.* ⟨origin uncertain⟩

pod² [pɒd] *n* a small herd of whales, seals, etc. ⟨origin unknown⟩

po·di·a·try [pə'daɪətri] *n* the branch of medicine dealing with foot ailments. **po·di·a·trist** *n.* ⟨Greek *podos* foot + *iatreia* treatment⟩

po·di·um ['poudiəm] *n, pl* **-di·a** [-diə] **1** a small raised platform, esp one used by an orchestra conductor. **2** lectern. ⟨Latin; Greek *podion* diminutive of *podos* foot⟩

po·em ['pouəm] *n* **1** a piece of writing that uses language that is more evocative and concentrated than prose. **2** something very beautiful: *The runner was a poem in motion.* ⟨Greek *poēma; poieein* make, compose⟩

po·et ['pouɪt] *n* a person who writes poetry.

po·et·as·ter ['pouɪˌtæstər] *n* a writer of inferior poetry. **po·et·ic** *adj* **1** to do with poets or poetry: *poetic imagery.* **2** written in verse. **3** showing beautiful language or thought: *a poetic description of a scene.* **po·et·i·cal·ly** *adv.* **poetic justice** ironic justice, in that the punishment is matched to the individual's behaviour. **poetic licence** a freedom traditionally granted to writers to violate certain grammatical rules or to alter fact for effect. **po·et·ics** *n* (with a sg verb) the theory or study of poetry. **poet laureate** *pl* **poets laureate** the official poet of any country, state, etc. **po·et·ry** *n* **1** poems: *a book of poetry.* **2** the art or theory of writing poems. **3** lyrical feeling: *Her skating is pure poetry.*

po·gey or **po·gy** ['pougi] *n* ❋ *Slang* money given by the government to unemployed persons.
on (the) pogey drawing such relief. ⟨orig, hobo slang for 'workhouse'⟩

po·grom [pou'grɒm] or ['pɒgrəm] *n* an organized, often officially sanctioned, massacre, esp of Jews. ⟨Yiddish; Russian = devastation⟩

poign·ant ['pɔɪnjənt] *adj* **1** deeply affecting: *a poignant story.* **2** stimulating: *a subject of poignant interest.* **3** sharp in taste or smell. **poign·an·cy** ['pɔɪnjənsi] *n.* **poign·ant·ly** *adv.* ⟨Old French, ppr of *poindre* prick⟩

poin·ci·a·na [ˌpɔɪnsi'ænə] *n* any of a genus of tropical trees or shrubs of the pea family having showy red or orange flowers. ⟨de Poinci, 17c natural historian⟩

poin·set·ti·a [pɔɪn'sɛtə] or [pɔɪn'sɛtiə] *n* a shrub having small flowers surrounded by large, petal-like, scarlet, pink, or whitish bracts. ⟨J. R. *Poinsett*, its 19c discoverer⟩

point [pɔɪnt] *n* **1** a sharp end. **2** a dot. **3** *Mathematics* something that has position but no magnitude. **4** a particular place: *This is the point where we turned around.* **5** a particular time: *At this point they lost interest in the game.* **6** a particular state, condition, etc.: *boiling point.* **7** a detail: *She answered my questions point by point.* **8** the main idea: *I missed the point of the talk.* **9** each of the 32 positions indicating direction, marked on a compass. **10** a wedge of land sticking out into the water. **11** a unit of credit, scoring, or measuring: *We're three points ahead.* **12** *Hockey* a position at the opponents' blueline, taken by an offensive player when the puck is within their defensive zone. **13** *Lacrosse* one of the defencemen playing out in front of the goalie.
v **1** direct attention with, or as if with, the finger (with *at* or *out*): *She pointed out the suspect.* **2** have or face a specified direction: *The signboard points north.* **3** fill joints of (brickwork) with mortar (often with *up*). ⟨Old French; Latin *punctum* pp of *pungere* prick⟩
at the point of very near to. **beside the point** irrelevant. **in point** relevant: *the case in point.* **in point of** as regards. **in point of fact** as a matter of fact: *In point of fact, they never left*

the house at all. **make a point** convince a person that an argument is correct. **make a point of** be particular about: *Make a point of being on time.* **on the point of** on the verge of: *I'm on the point of going out.* **point out** show: *Please point out my mistakes.* **point up** put emphasis on. **strain** or **stretch a point a** exceed the limit. **b** make an exception: *Ordinarily, this is not allowed, but we can stretch a point for you.* **to the point** appropriate: *The speech was brief and to the point.*

point–blank *adj* **1** close enough to aim straight at the target: *point-blank range.* **2** plain and blunt: *a point-blank question.* **point–blank** *adv.* **point blanket ✹** a Hudson's Bay Company blanket having black marks or 'points' woven in. **point·ed** *adj* **1** having a sharp point. **2** aimed: *a pointed remark.* **3** conspicuous: *a pointed refusal.* **point·ed·ly** *adv.* **point·ed·ness** *n.* **point·er** *n* **1** a long stick used in pointing things out on a map, etc. **2** a hand of a clock, meter, etc. **3** any of several breeds of hunting dog. **4** *Informal* a useful hint. **5 ✹** a river boat that is pointed at both bow and stern and is of shallow draft, for use in logging drives. **poin·til·lism** ['pwæntə,lɪzəm] *n* a painting technique that uses tiny dots of colour placed close together so that they blend when seen from a distance. **poin·til·list** *n, adj.* **point·less** *adj* without purpose. **point·less·ly** *adv.* **point·less·ness** *n.* **point man 1** *Hockey* a player assigned to play the POINT (def. 12). Also, **point player. 2** a front rider in a cattle drive. **point of honour** a matter that seriously affects a person's principles: *It was a point of honour with her to pay bills promptly.* **point of no return** the stage in an action after which there is no turning back, so that one is obliged to continue. **point of order** a question raised as to whether proceedings are according to the rules. **point–of–sale** or **point–of–purchase** *adj* designed for, placed at, operating at, etc., the checkout area in a store. **point of view 1** a position from which objects are considered. **2** an attitude of mind.

poise [pɔɪz] *n* **1** composure. **2** the way in which the body, head, etc. are held; carriage: *He admired the actor's poise.*
v **1** balance: *Poise yourself on your toes.* **2** hold or carry steadily: *The athlete poised the weight in the air before throwing it.* ⟨Old French *pois, peis; peser* weigh, Latin *pensare*⟩

poi·son ['pɔɪzən] *n* **1** a substance that can cause death. **2** anything dangerous or deadly: *Hate is a poison in the mind.*
v **1** kill or harm by poison. **2** put poison in or on: *Her hot milk was poisoned.* **3** have a harmful effect on: *Lies poison the mind.* **poi·son·er** *n.* **poi·son·ous** *adj.* **poi·son·ous·ly** *adv.* **poi·son·ous·ness** *n.* ⟨Latin *potionis* potion; *potare* to drink⟩
poison ivy a vine or shrub of the cashew family, having leaves composed of three leaflets. It produces a toxic oil. **poison oak** a plant of the cashew family, having leaflets shaped like oak leaves. **poison pill** anything used by a company threatened with a hostile

takeover to make the takeover less attractive. **poison sumac** a shrub of the cashew family, having leaves with seven to thirteen leaflets.

Pois·son dis·tri·bu·tion [pwa'soun] *French* [pwa'sɔ̃] *Statistics* a frequency distribution which is a limiting form of the binomial probability distribution when the number of events is large and the probability of success becomes small. ⟨S.D. *Poisson,* 19c French mathematician⟩

poke[1] [pouk] *v* **1** push with something pointed. **2** push: *He poked his head in the window.* **3** *Informal* punch: *to poke someone in the nose.* **4** pry: *She's always poking into other people's business.* **5** go lazily: *poking along at 40 km/h.* **6** search or putter (usually with *around* or *about*): *poking around in the attic.* **poke** *n.* ⟨Middle Dutch *poken* thrust⟩
pok·er *n* a metal rod for stirring a fire. **pok·ey** or **pok·y** *adj* **1** annoyingly slow: *a pokey old horse.* **2** small and shabby: *a pokey room.* **3** shabby in dress. **pok·i·ly** *adv.* **pok·i·ness** *n.*

poke[2] [pouk] *n* **1** a small bag or sack. **2** a sleeping bag. **3** a wallet or purse. ⟨Middle French *poque* bag, pouch⟩
buy a pig in a poke buy something without seeing it first.

poke·lo·gan ['poukə,lougən] *n* ✹ *esp Maritimes* a small stagnant backwater or marshy place in a stream. Also, **lo·gan.** ⟨Algonquian⟩

pok·er[1] See POKE[1].

pok·er[2] ['poukər] *n* any of several card games in which players bet that the value of their cards is greater than that of the cards held by the other players. ⟨origin uncertain⟩
poker face *Informal* a facial expression that does not show one's thoughts, as of a poker player trying not to reveal the quality of his or her hand of cards. **po·ker–faced** *adj.*

pok·ey[1] or **pok·y**[1] ['pouki] *n, pl* **-eys** or **-ies** *Slang* jail. ⟨perhaps *pogey*⟩

pok·ey[2] or **pok·y**[2] See POKE[1].

po·lar, po·lar·i·ty, po·lar·i·za·tion See POLE[2].

pol·der ['pouldər] *n* an area of land reclaimed from the sea and protected by dikes. ⟨Dutch⟩

pole[1] [poul] *n* a long, slender piece of wood, metal, etc.: *a telephone pole.*
adj to do with a position on a racetrack nearest the infield: *the pole position in the Vancouver Indy.*
v move by pushing with a pole: *to pole a raft.* ⟨Old English *pāl;* Latin *palus* stake⟩
pole vault an athletic event in which contestants vault over a high bar, using a long, flexible pole. **pole–vault** *v.* **pole–vault·er** *n.*

pole[2] [poul] *n* **1** either end of the earth's rotational axis. The North Pole and the South Pole are opposite each other. **2** either of two points where opposite forces are strongest. **3** either of two opinions, forces, etc., considered as being opposite extremes. ⟨Latin *polus;* Greek *polos*⟩
poles apart very much different: *The two parties are poles apart with no sign of a settlement.* **po·lar** ['poulər] *adj* **1** to do with the North or

South Pole: *the polar wastes.* **2** to do with the poles of a magnet, battery, etc. **3** directly opposite in character: *Good and evil are polar elements.* **4** *Chemistry* ionizing when dissolved or fused. **polar bear** a large, white, semi-aquatic bear found in arctic regions. **po·lar·i·ty** *n* **1** *Physics* **a** the possession of two opposed poles. **b** a positive or negative polar condition, as in electricity. **2** the possession of two opposite tendencies. **po·lar·i·za·tion** *n* **1** the production or acquisition of polarity. **2** *Electricity* a process by which gases produced during electrolysis are deposited on electrodes of a cell, giving rise to a reverse electromotive force. **3** *Optics* a state in which waves of light move transversely in only one direction or plane or in two perpendicular planes. **4** the reduction of a spectrum of opinions, etc., to a pair of opposite extremes: *the polarization of the electorate on the issue of free trade.* **po·lar·ize** *v.* **polar lights** the AURORA BOREALIS in the northern hemisphere or the AURORA AUSTRALIS in the southern hemisphere. **pole·star** *n* **1** Polaris, the North Star. **2** a guiding principle. **3** a centre of interest.

pole·axe ['poul,æks] *n* an axe with a long handle and a spike opposite the blade. *v* fell with or as if with a poleaxe. ⟨Middle English *pol(le)* poll, head + *ax* axe⟩

pole·cat ['poul,kæt] *n* **1** a small carnivorous mammal of the weasel family. **2** the North American skunk. ⟨Old French *poule* hen + Middle English *cat*; it preys on poultry⟩

po·lem·ic [pə'lɛmɪk] *n* **1** a strong argument against or attack on an idea, opinion, etc.: *The book is a long polemic against conservatism.* **2** a line of argument: *the Marxist polemic.* **3** Usually, **polemics** the art or practice of argument (with a sg or pl verb): *This is not the time to indulge in polemics.* *adj* to do with disagreement: *a polemic writer.* Also, **po·lem·i·cal. po·lem·i·cal·ly** *adv.* **po·lem·i·cist** *n.* ⟨Greek *polemos* war⟩

po·len·ta [pou'lɛntə] *n* an Italian dish consisting of a thick cornmeal mush, usually baked or fried. ⟨Latin = pearl barley⟩

po·lice [pə'lis] *n* **1** the organized civil force whose duty is to guard lives and property, to preserve order, and to arrest those who commit crimes. **2** any organized body of people employed for a similar purpose. *v* keep order in: *to police the streets.* ⟨French; Latin *politia* state administration; Greek *politeia*⟩ **police dog** a dog trained for use in police work. **police force** the law-enforcing body of a country, province, state, etc. **police officer** a member of a police force. **po·lice·man** *n, pl* **-men. po·lice·wom·an** *n, pl* **-wom·en. police state** a country strictly controlled, esp with the aid of a secret police organization. **police station** the headquarters of the police of a particular area.

pol·i·cy¹ ['pɒləsi] *n* **1** a plan of action that guides or influences future decisions: *company policy. The candidate explained his party's policy.* **2** practical wisdom; prudence: *It is poor policy to promise more than you can give.* ⟨Old French *policie.* See POLICE.⟩

pol·i·cy² ['pɒləsi] *n* a written contract concerning insurance. **pol·i·cy·hold·er** *n.* ⟨Italian *polizza;* Latin *apodixa,* Greek *apodeixis* declaration⟩

po·li·o See POLIOMYELITIS.

po·li·o·my·e·li·tis [,pouliou,maɪə'laɪtɪs] *n* *Pathology* an acute infectious disease characterized by permanent paralysis of muscles. ⟨Greek *polios* grey + *myelos* marrow⟩

pol·ish ['pɒlɪʃ] *v* **1** make shiny by rubbing. **2** become smooth and shiny: *This leather polishes well.* **3** remove by smoothing (with *off* or *away*). **4** improve (often with *up*): *to polish an essay.* *n* **1** a substance used to give shine, remove dirt, etc.: *silver polish.* **2** shininess: *a high polish.* **3** culture; refinement: *a woman of breeding and polish.* **4** the act of polishing: *I gave the table a quick polish.* ⟨Old French *polir;* Latin *polire*⟩ **polish off** *Informal.* **a** get done with; finish. **b** consume eagerly.

po·lite [pə'laɪt] *adj* **1** having good manners. **2** refined; elegant. **po·lite·ly** *adv.* **po·lite·ness** *n.* ⟨Latin *politus* pp of *polire* polish⟩

SYNONYMS
Polite suggests having and showing good manners at all times: *That polite boy gave me his seat in the subway train.* **Courteous** adds to the idea of showing thoughtful attention to the feelings and wishes of others: *I go to that store because the clerks there are courteous.* **Civil** is being just polite enough not to be rude: *All I expect is a civil answer.*

pol·i·tic ['pɒlə,tɪk] *adj* **1** sensible and expedient: *It was not politic to arouse his irritation.* **2** scheming; crafty. **pol·i·tic·ly** *adv.* ⟨Greek *politikos; polis* city-state⟩

po·lit·i·cal [pə'lɪtɪkəl] *adj* to do with politics. or government: **po·lit·i·cal·ly** *adv.* ⟨See POLITIC.⟩ **political economy** a social science dealing with the ways in which political and economic processes are related to each other. **political economist. politically correct** anything that avoids what might be construed as racism, sexism, etc. *Abbrev* **PC political science** a social science dealing with the principles and conduct of government. **political scientist. pol·i·ti·cian** [,pɒlə'tɪʃən] *n* **1** a person holding or seeking a political office. **2** anyone, holding public office or not, regarded as being opportunistic and dishonest. **po·lit·i·cize** *v* **1** make politically aware: *a politicized electorate.* **2** give a political tone to: *to politicize a social issue.* **po·lit·i·ci·za·tion** *n.* **pol·i·tick** ['pɒlə,tɪk] *v* take part in political activity, esp in order to solicit votes: *He's politicking in the Maritimes this week.* **pol·i·tick·er** *n.* **pol·i·tics** *n* **1** the science and art of government (with a sg verb). **2** government as a business or profession (with a sg verb): *Politics was her first and only career.* **3** the activities, entailed by this (with a sg or pl verb): *party politics.*

4 methods for gaining or keeping power, often suggesting scheming (with a sg or pl verb): *The builder played politics to win the contract.* **5** views on the proper role of government (with a pl verb): *Their politics are very conservative.* **6** the relationships between people, esp as they involve authority or power (with a sg verb): *the politics of volunteer organizations.* **pol·i·ty** ['pɒləti] *n* **1** political organization. **2** a particular form or system of government. **3** a community with a government; state.

pol·ka ['poulkə] *or* ['poukə] *n, v* **-kaed, -ka·ing** *n* **1** a lively dance in four-four time. **2** the music for this dance. **pol·ka** *v.* 〈Czech *pulka* half-step; *pul* half〉
pol·ka dot a dot repeated to form a pattern on cloth. **pol·ka–dot** or **pol·ka–dot·ted** *adj.*

poll [poul] *n* **1** a collection of votes: *The class took a poll to decide where the picnic would be held.* **2** the number of votes cast: *If it rains on election day, there may be a light poll.* **3** the results of these votes. **4** a list of voters. **5** the place where votes are cast and counted: *The polls are open now.* **6** a survey of opinion concerning a particular subject. **7** the head, esp the part of it on which the hair grows.
v **1** receive (as votes): *The mayor polled a record vote.* **2** question or canvass in a public opinion poll. 〈Middle English *pol* head〉
polling booth an enclosed space in a polling station where a voter marks his or her ballot in privacy. **polling station** a room or building set up as a place to vote. **poll·ster** *n* a person who takes public opinion polls. **poll tax** a tax levied on each adult, regardless of his or her income or property.

pol·len ['pɒlən] *n* a fine, yellowish powder formed in the anthers of flowers, consisting of tiny grains that are the male sex cells. 〈Latin = mill dust〉
pollen count a count of pollen particles in the air. **pol·li·nate** *v Botany* carry pollen from stamens to pistils of. **pol·li·na·tion** *n.*

pol·lock ['pɒlək] *n, pl* **-locks** or (esp collectively) **-lock** a food fish of the cod family.

pol·lute [pə'lut] *v* make impure; especially, contaminate (the air, water, etc.) with waste materials: *the polluted air of cities.* **pol·lut·er** *n.* **pol·lu·tion** *n.* 〈Latin *polluere*〉
pol·lu·tant [pə'lutənt] *n* anything that pollutes: *Car exhaust is a major air pollutant.*

Pol·ly·an·na [ˌpɒli'ænə] *n* one who is always cheerful, or overly cheerful. 〈heroine of 20c stories by E. H. Porter〉

po·lo ['poulou] *n* **1** a game played by two teams on horseback, who use mallets to drive a wooden ball through the opposing team's goal. **2** WATER POLO. 〈perhaps Tibetan *pulu* ball〉

po·lo·ni·um [pə'louniəm] *n* a radioactive element that occurs naturally in uranium ores and is also produced artificially in nuclear reactors. *Symbol* **Po** 〈Latin *Polonia* Poland, homeland of the Curies, 20c scientists〉

pol·ter·geist ['poultər,gaist] *n* a ghost or spirit that is mischievous, supposedly responsible for noises such as door slamming. 〈German *poltern* noisy + *geist* ghost〉

poly– *combining form* **1** more than one; many; extensive: *polyangular.* **2** polymerized: *polyethylene.* 〈Greek; *polys* much, many〉

pol·y·an·dry ['pɒli,ændri] *or* [ˌpɒli'ændri] *n* the practice of having more than one male mate at one time. Compare POLYGAMY and POLYGYNY. **pol·y·an·drist** *n.* **pol·y·an·drous** *adj.* 〈*poly-* + Greek *andros* man, husband〉

pol·y·chlo·rin·at·ed biphenyl [ˌpɒli'klɔrə,neitɪd bai'fɛnəl] **PCB**, one of a group of highly toxic isomers of biphenyl in chlorinated form, now banned in use.

pol·y·chro·mat·ic [ˌpɒlikrə'mætɪk] *adj* having a variety of colours.

pol·y·es·ter [ˌpɒli'ɛstər] *n Chemistry* any of a group of synthetic organic polymers, prepared in the form of plastics, fibres, etc. 〈*poly-* + *ester*〉

pol·y·eth·y·lene [ˌpɒli'ɛθə,lin] *n Chemistry* any of various synthetic polymers of ethylene that are resistant to chemicals and moisture. Also, **pol·y·thene.**

po·lyg·a·my [pə'lɪgəmi] *n* the practice of having more than one spouse at one time. Compare POLYGYNY and POLYANDRY. **po·lyg·a·mist** *n.* **po·lyg·a·mous** *adj.* 〈*poly-* + Greek *gamos* marriage〉

pol·y·glot ['pɒli,glɒt] *adj* multilingual. *n* **1** a person who knows several languages. **2** a mixture or confusion of several languages. 〈*poly-* + Greek *glōtta* tongue〉

pol·y·gon ['pɒli,gɒn] *n Geometry* a closed plane figure having straight sides, esp one with more than four sides. **po·lyg·o·nal** [pə'lɪgənəl] *adj.* 〈*poly-* + Greek *gōnia* angle〉

pol·y·graph ['pɒli,græf] *n* an instrument for recording various physiological responses (such as changes in respiration, etc.) to verbal stimuli. Polygraphs are often used as lie detectors. **pol·y·graph·ic** *adj.*

po·lyg·y·ny [pə'lɪdʒəni] *n* the practice of having more than one wife or female mate at one time. Compare POLYGAMY and POLYANDRY. **po·lyg·y·nist** *n.* **po·lyg·y·nous** *adj.* 〈*poly-* + Greek *gynē* woman, wife〉

pol·y·he·dron [ˌpɒli'hidrən] *n, pl* **-drons** or **-dra** [-drə] a solid figure having four or more plane faces, all of which are polygons. **pol·y·he·dral** *adj.* 〈*poly-* + Greek *hedra* base〉

pol·y·math ['pɒli,mæθ] *n* a person of great and encyclopedic learning. **pol·y·math·ic** *adj.* 〈*poly-* + Greek *manthanein* learn〉

pol·y·mer ['pɒləmər] *n Chemistry* any of a number of compounds composed of very large molecules that are made up of many simple molecules chemically linked together. **pol·y·mer·ic** [-'mɛrɪk] *adj.* **po·lym·er·ize** [pə'lɪmə,raɪz] *or* ['pɒləmə,raɪz] *v,* **po·lym·er·i·za·tion** *n.* ⟨*poly-* + Greek *meros* part⟩

pol·y·morph ['pɒli,mɔrf] *n* 1 *Zoology, botany* a polymorphic organism. 2 *Chemistry* a substance able to crystallize in different forms. ⟨*poly-* + Greek *morphē* form⟩
pol·y·mor·phic *adj* having, assuming, or passing through various forms, stages, etc.
pol·y·mor·phism *n* 1 *Biology* the occurrence of different forms or different colour types in one species. 2 *Chemistry* the property of a compound of crystallizing in at least two distinct forms. 3 *Genetics* the presence together in a population of two or more relatively common alleles of a specific gene.
pol·y·mor·phous *adj* polymorphic.
pol·y·mor·phous·ly *adv.*

pol·y·no·mi·al [,pɒli'noumiəl] *n* 1 *Algebra* an expression consisting of two or more terms. $ab + x^2y$ is a polynomial. Compare MONOMIAL. 2 *Biology* a taxonomic name consisting of more than two terms, as for designating a subspecies. **pol·y·no·mi·al** *adj.* ⟨*poly-* + *(bi)nomial*⟩

pol·yp ['pɒlɪp] *n* 1 *Zoology* any of various simple water animals having a mouthlike opening surrounded by tentacles for gathering in food. 2 *Pathology* a growth arising from the surface of a mucous membrane. ⟨Greek *polypous, polys* many + *pous* foot⟩

pol·y·pro·pyl·ene [,pɒli'proupə,lin] *n Chemistry* a lightweight thermoplastic, harder than polychylene, used for insulating materials, etc.

pol·y·sac·cha·ride [,pɒli'sækə,raɪd] *or* [-'sækərɪd] *n Chemistry* any of a large group of natural carbohydrates, including starch, cellulose, and glycogen.

po·lys·e·my [pə'lɪsəmi] *n* the fact of one word having various meanings. The word *point* is an example of polysemy. **po·lys·e·mous** *adj.* ⟨*poly-* + Greek *sēma* sign⟩

pol·y·sty·rene [,pɒli'staɪrɪn] *n Chemistry* a synthetic organic polymer formed from styrene, used as an insulator and for many moulded products such as dishes, toys, etc.

pol·y·syl·lab·ic [,pɒlɪsɪ'læbɪk] *adj* 1 having three or more syllables. 2 of a style of writing or speaking, characterized by polysyllabic words. **pol·y·syl·lab·i·cal·ly** *adv.* **pol·y·syl·la·ble** *n.*

pol·y·tech·nic [,pɒli'tɛknɪk] *adj* to do with instruction in technical arts or applied sciences. *n* a polytechnic school.

pol·y·the·ism ['pɒliθi,ɪzəm] *n* belief in more than one god. **pol·y·the·ist** *n.* **pol·y·the·is·tic** *adj.* **pol·y·the·is·ti·cal·ly** *adv.*

pol·y·un·sat·u·rat·ed [,pɒliʌn'sætʃə,reitɪd] *adj* to do with a class of vegetable and animal fats whose molecules consist of long carbon chains with many double bonds. **pol·y·un·sat·u·rate** [-rɪt] *or* [-,reit] *n* any of a variety of polyunsaturated animal fats or vegetable oils.

pol·y·ur·e·thane [,pɒli'jʊrə,θein] *n Chemistry* any of a group of synthetic organic polymers that may be rubbery, resinous, or fibrous. Polyurethanes are most often made in the form of flexible foam.

pol·y·vi·nyl chlo·ride [,pɒlivaɪnəl] *Chemistry* a synthetic thermoplastic material produced by the polymerization of vinyl chloride. *Abbrev* **PVC**

pom·ace See POME.

po·made [pɒ'meid] *n* a perfumed ointment for the scalp and hair. ⟨Italian *pomata*; Latin *pomum* fruit, apple⟩

po·man·der ['poumændər] *or* [pə'mændər] *n* 1 a ball of mixed aromatic substances formerly carried for perfume or as a guard against infection. 2 an orange or lemon studded with cloves. ⟨Middle French *pome* (see POME) *ambre* amber fruit⟩

pome [poum] *n* an apple or any fruit consisting of firm flesh surrounding a core that contains several seeds. **po·ma·ceous** [pə'meiʃəs] *adj.* ⟨Latin *pomum* apple⟩
pom·ace ['pʌmɪs] *n* 1 apple pulp or similar fruit pulp before or after the juice has been pressed out. 2 the crushed matter left after oil has been pressed out of fish, seeds, etc.

pome·gran·ate ['pɒmə,grænɪt] *n* a tree or bush whose fruit has a thick, leathery skin and many seeds. ⟨Old French *pome* (see POME) + *grenate* seedy, Latin *granata; granum* grain⟩

pom·e·lo ['pɒməlou] *n* a tree bearing a large citrus fruit, like a grapefruit but sweeter. ⟨altered from Dutch *pompelmoes* grapefruit⟩

pom·mel ['pɒməl] *or* ['pʌməl] *n* 1 the part of a saddle that sticks up at the front. 2 a rounded knob on the hilt of a sword, dagger, etc. ⟨Old French *pomel* diminutive of *pome* (see POME); for the knobby shape⟩

pomp [pɒmp] *n* 1 a stately display: *The king was crowned with great pomp.* 2 an excessively showy display. ⟨Greek *pompē* parade⟩
pom·pous *adj* 1 tending to display oneself in an overly grand, self-important way. 2 of language, ostentatiously flowery. **pom·pos·i·ty** [pɒm'pɒsəti] *n.* **pom·pous·ly** *adv.*

pom·pa·dour ['pɒmpə,dɔr] *or* [-dʊr] *n* a hairstyle in which the hair is brushed straight up and back from the forehead. ⟨the Marquise de *Pompadour* 18c mistress of Louis XV of France⟩

pom·pa·no ['pɒmpə,nou] *n, pl* **-nos** *or* (esp collectively) **-no** a saltwater food fish having no teeth and a forked tail. ⟨Spanish⟩

pom·pom ['pɒm,pɒm] *n* an ornamental ball used on clothing, hats, shoes, etc. ⟨French *pompon; pompe* pomp⟩

pom·pous See POMP.

pon·cho ['pɒntʃou] *n, pl* **-chos** a cloak consisting of a large piece of cloth with a hole in the middle to put the head through. ⟨Spanish; Araucanian (Chile) *pontho*⟩

pond [pɒnd] *n* **1** a body of still water, smaller than a lake. **2** ✳ *esp Newfoundland and Labrador* a lake. **3** ✳ *Logging* an expanse of quiet water where logs, are penned till needed. ⟨orig, variant of *pound³*⟩
pond hockey ✳ **1** unorganized hockey played on frozen ponds, streams, etc. **2** *Slang* hockey of a low standard. **pond lily** WATER LILY. **pond scum** free-floating algae that form a green scum on water. **pond·weed** *n* any of a genus of aquatic plants having jointed stems.

pon·der [ˈpɒndər] *v* consider carefully. **pon·der·a·ble** *adj*. **pon·der·ing** *adj*. ⟨Latin *ponderare* weigh; *ponderis* weight⟩

pon·der·ous [ˈpɒndərəs] *adj* **1** very heavy. **2** heavy and clumsy: *Slowly he lifted his ponderous bulk from the chair.* **3** overly serious: *a ponderous way of speaking.* **pon·der·ous·ly** *adv*. **pon·der·ous·ness** or **pon·der·os·i·ty** *n*. ⟨Latin *ponderis* weight⟩

pons a·sin·o·rum [ˌpɒnz ˌæsɪˈnɔrəm] **1** *Geometry* a proposition from the first book of Euclid. **2** any problem difficult for beginners to master. ⟨Latin = bridge of asses⟩

pon·tiff [ˈpɒntɪf] *n* **1** the Pope. **2** a bishop. **3** a high priest. **4 Supreme Pontiff** the Pope. ⟨French *pontife*; Latin *pontifex* high priest⟩
pon·tif·i·cal [pɒnˈtɪfɪkəl] *adj* **1** to do with the Pope; papal. **2** to do with a bishop. **3** pompous or dogmatic. **pon·tif·i·cal·ly** *adv*. **pon·tif·i·cate** *v* speak dogmatically and pompously: *My parents loved to pontificate on the virtues of thrift.*

pon·toon [pɒnˈtun] *n* **1** a low, flatbottomed boat. **2** such a boat, or some other floating structure, used as one of the supports of a temporary bridge. **3** a boat-shaped float on an aircraft, used for landing on or taking off from water. ⟨Latin *pontonis*; *pontis* bridge⟩

pon·y [ˈpouni] *n* **1** a small horse. **2** *Informal* something that is small for its kind. ⟨obsolete French *poulenet*; Latin *pullus* foal⟩
pony up *Slang* settle an account.
po·ny·tail *n* a hairstyle in which the main length is pulled back and held tightly against the head with a ribbon, elastic band, etc.

pooch [putʃ] *n Slang* dog. ⟨origin uncertain⟩

poo·dle [ˈpudəl] *n* a breed of dog having thick, curly, wool-like hair that is not shed. **poo·dle·like** *adj*. ⟨German *Pudelhund*; dialect *pudeln* splash water + *Hund* dog⟩

pooh [pu] *interj, n* exclamation of contempt. **pooh–pooh** *v* express contempt for.

pool¹ [pul] *n* **1** a small pond. **2** a still, deep place in a stream. **3** a large puddle of liquid: *There was a pool of grease under the car.* **4** a large tank for swimming in. ⟨Old English *pōl*⟩

pool² [pul] *n* **1** a game played on a billiard table, using a cue ball and fifteen other numbered balls. Compare SNOOKER. **2** the things or money put together by different persons for common advantage. **3** ✳ in the West, a co-operative grain marketing organization among farmers. **4** the stake played for in some games. **5** money bet by members of a group on the outcome of a sports event.

v put (things or money) together for common advantage: *We pooled our savings for a year to buy a boat.* ⟨French *poule* booty, literally, hen; Latin *pulla* chick⟩
pool hall an establishment whose main attraction is a poolroom. **pool·room** *n* a room or place in which the game of pool is played. **pool table** a billiard table, having the usual six pockets but smaller than the standard table used for billiards or snooker.

poop¹ [pup] *n* a deck at the stern of a ship. Also, **poop deck.** ⟨Latin *puppis* stern⟩

poop² [pup] *v Slang* make exhausted (often with *out*): *All of us were pooped after the climb.* ⟨origin uncertain⟩

poop³ [pup] *Slang n* **1** waste matter; feces; manure. **2** the most recent or current inside information. **poop** *v*. ⟨origin uncertain⟩
poop sheet *Slang* a press release, etc., containing a concise list of information about a particular subject.

poor [pur] *adj* **1** not having enough income to maintain a standard of living regarded as normal in the community in which one lives: *They were poor, but never destitute.* **2** not good in quality: *poor soil.* **3** needing pity: *This poor child has been hurt.* **4** not favourable: *a poor chance for recovery.*
n **the poor** (with a pl verb) poor persons collectively. **pov·er·ty** [ˈpɒvərti] *n*. ⟨Old French *povre*; Latin *pauper*⟩
poor box a box in a church, into which donations for the poor can be put. **poor·house** *n* formerly, a place in which destitute people lived at public expense. **poor·ly** *adv* badly or inadequately. *adj Informal* in bad health: *I feel poorly today.* **poor–mouth** *n* a person who continually pleads poverty, often as an excuse for not paying bills, returning hospitality, etc. **poor–mouth** *v*.

SYNONYMS
Poverty emphasizes being in need, or having not enough for all the necessities of life: *Their cheap clothes and broken furniture indicated their poverty.* **Want** emphasizes extreme need: *Welfare agencies give help to those in want.* **Destitution** emphasizes complete lack of food and shelter: *Charitable organizations relieved the destitution following the floods.*

pop¹ [pɒp] *v* **popped, pop·ping 1** make a short, explosive sound. **2** thrust suddenly: *He popped a candy into his mouth.* **3** put (a question) suddenly. **4** burst open with a pop. **5** of the eyes, open very wide: *The surprise made her eyes pop.* **6** *Baseball* hit a short, high ball over the infield. **7** *Slang* take (a drug or drugs) habitually, esp in pill form: *He used to pop a lot of pills.*
n **1** a short, explosive sound. **2** *esp* ✳ a carbonated non-alcoholic drink. **3** *Baseball* a fly ball that can be easily caught. **4** *Slang* attempt: *She got it on the first pop.*
adv with a pop; suddenly. ⟨imitative⟩
a pop per person, or per turn, use, etc.: *Admission is $5 a pop.* **pop off** *Slang* **a** fall

asleep. **b** die. **c** complain loudly and angrily. **d** leave quickly: *I must pop off now.* **pop the question** *Informal* propose marriage.

pop·corn *n* a variety of corn whose kernels burst open and puff out in a white mass when heated. Also called **popping corn.**

pop·gun *n* a toy gun that shoots harmless pellets with a popping sound. **pop·o·ver** *n* a very light and hollow muffin. **pop·per** *n* a pan, pot, etc., or electrical appliance used for popping popcorn. **pop–up** *n* **1** a folding picture having parts that stand up. **2** *Computers* a window that suddenly appears on the screen. *adj* characterized by a mechanical feature that automatically raises something: *a pop-up toaster.*

pop² See POPULAR.

Pope or **pope** [poup] *n* **1** the supreme head of the Roman Catholic Church. **2 a** the Orthodox patriarch of Alexandria. **b** the Coptic patriarch of Alexandria. **c** in some Christian churches, a parish priest. **pa·pa·cy** ['peipəsi] *n*. **pa·pal** ['peipəl] *adj*. ⟨Latin *papa;* earlier, tutor, bishop; Greek *papas* father⟩

pop·in·jay ['pɒpɪn,dʒei] *n* conceited, silly person. ⟨Old French *papingay* parrot; Spanish⟩

pop·lar ['pɒplər] *n* any of a genus of trees having flowers in drooping catkins. ⟨Old French *poplier;* Latin *populus*⟩
poplar bluff ✳ BLUFF¹ (def. 2).

pop·lin ['pɒplən] *n* a strong fabric used for sportswear, raincoats, etc. ⟨Italian *papalina* papal, perhaps for former papal seat Avignon, source of the fabric⟩

pop·pet ['pɒpɪt] *n* a small or dainty person, esp a pretty child; pet. ⟨variant of *puppet*⟩

pop·py ['pɒpi] *n* any of a genus of plants having a milky sap, and seeds in a capsule. ⟨Latin *papaver*⟩
pop·py·seed *n* the very small, black seed of the poppy plant.

pop·py·cock ['pɒpi,kɒk] *n, interj Informal* nonsense; bosh. ⟨Dutch *pappekak* soft dung⟩

Pop·si·cle ['pɒpsɪkəl] *n Trademark* fruit-flavoured ice on a stick. ⟨*pop¹* + *icicle*⟩

pop·u·lar ['pɒpjələr] *adj* **1** liked by most acquaintances: *a popular girl.* **2** liked by many people: *a popular movie.* **3** intended to appeal to public taste: *popular science.* **4** to do with the people: *Canada has a popular government.* **5** widespread among many people: *the popular belief that black cats bring bad luck.* ⟨Latin *populus* people⟩
pop *Slang adj* aimed at or supposedly reflecting the tastes of the general population: *pop psychology. n* popular music. **pop art** an art style based on advertising art, comic strips, etc. **pops** *adj* to do with an orchestra that plays mainly light classics. **pop·u·lace** ['pɒpjəlɪs] *n* the people in general. **pop·u·lar·i·ty** *n* the state of being liked by most people. **pop·u·lar·ize** *v* **1** simplify so as to appeal to a great number of people: *to popularize the sciences.* **2** cause to be generally known: *to popularize a tune.* **pop·u·lar·i·za·tion** *n*. **pop·u·lar·ly** *adv* by the people in general: *The*

defendant was popularly believed to have been guilty, though she was acquitted. **popular vote** the number of votes cast as opposed to seats won. **pop·u·late** *v* **1** inhabit: *This city is densely populated.* **2** furnish with inhabitants: *Europeans populated much of the Canadian West.* **pop·u·la·tion** *n* **1** the people of a city or a country. **2** the total number of organisms of a specific kind in a given area: *the caribou population of the North.* **3** the total number from which samples are taken for statistical measurement. **pop·u·lism** *n* a political movement appealing to the interests of ordinary people. **pop·u·list** *n, adj.* **pop·u·lous** *adj* heavily populated. **pop·u·lous·ly** *adv.* **pop·u·lous·ness** *n.*

por·ce·lain ['pɔrsəlɪn] *n* a hard, white, translucent pottery. ⟨Italian *porcellana,* a kind of shell; Latin *porcus* hog; for the shell's shape⟩

porch [pɔrtʃ] *n* **1** a covered entrance to a building. **2** veranda. ⟨Old French *porche;* Latin *porticus*⟩

por·cine See PORK.

por·cu·pine ['pɔrkjə,paɪn] *n* any of a number of rodents having barbed spines mixed in with the hair of the back and tail. ⟨Latin *porcus* pig + *spina* thorn⟩

pore¹ [pɔr] *v* **1** study long and steadily (with *over*): *The historian pored over the old book for hours.* **2** ponder intently (with *over*): *to pore over a problem.* ⟨origin uncertain⟩

pore² [pɔr] *n* one of the openings in skin or leaves through which fluids are absorbed or excreted. ⟨Greek *poros* passage⟩
po·rous *adj* full of tiny holes; permeable by water, air, etc. **po·rous·ness** or **po·ros·i·ty** [pɔ'rɒsɪti] *n.*

pork [pɔrk] *n* the flesh of a pig, used for food. ⟨Latin *porcus* pig⟩
por·cine ['pɔrsaɪn] or ['pɔrsɪn] *adj* to do with pigs. **pork barrel** *Slang* government appropriations for projects that may not be needed but appeal to certain constituents. **pork–bar·rel** *adj.* **pork·er** *n* a pig, esp one fattened to eat. **pork·y** *adj* fat.

porn [pɔrn] *n* pornography.
adj pornographic: *a porn movie.* Also, **por·no.**

por·nog·ra·phy [pɔr'nɒgrəfi] *n* writings, pictures, films, etc. gratuitously depicting nudity and sexual activity, esp when connected with violence and abuse. **por·no·graph·ic** *adj.* **por·no·graph·i·cal·ly** *adv.* ⟨Greek *pornē* harlot + *graphein* write⟩

po·rous See PORE².

por·poise ['pɔrpəs] *n, pl* **-pois·es** or (esp collectively) **-poise** any of several small toothed whales allied to dolphins but smaller. *v* move forward with an up-and-down motion, as a porpoise does. ⟨Old French *porpeis;* Latin *porcus* hog + *piscis* fish⟩

por·ridge ['pɔrɪdʒ] *n* a breakfast food made of oatmeal or other cereal boiled in water or milk until it thickens. ⟨variant of *pottage*⟩

port¹ [pɔrt] *n* **1** a harbour. **2** a city or town

with a harbour. **3** any place where one can find shelter. ⟨Latin *portus*⟩

port of entry any harbour, airport, etc. that has customs facilities.

port² [pɔrt] *n* **1** an opening in a ship for letting in light and air. **2** an opening in a wall, ship's side, etc. through which guns may be fired. **3** an opening in machinery for steam, air, water, etc. to pass through. **4** *Curling, lawn bowling* an opening between stones or woods, large enough for another stone or wood to pass through. **5** *Electronics* a point at which signals, energy, etc. enter or leave an electronic device. **6** *Computers* a socket into which a device can be connected, esp one for communications. ⟨Latin *porta* gate⟩

port·hole *n* an opening in a wall, ship's side, furnace door, etc.

port³ [pɔrt] *Nautical n* the left side of a ship or aircraft when facing forward. **port** *adj*. Compare STARBOARD. ⟨for docking in port on a ship's left side (the steering oar stuck out on the right side)⟩

port⁴ [pɔrt] *n* a strong, sweet fortified wine. ⟨*Oporto*, city in Portugal⟩

port·a·ble ['pɔrtəbəl] *adj* **1** capable of being easily moved about. **2** usable anywhere because it is run by batteries: *a portable TV*. *n* a temporary building on school grounds, used as an extra classroom. **port·a·bil·i·ty** *n*. ⟨Latin *portare* carry⟩

por·tage [pɔr'taʒ] *n* **1** the act of carrying boats, provisions, etc. overland from one stretch of water to another. **2** a place where such a carrying takes place. **3** ['pɔrtɪdʒ] the act or cost of transporting or carrying. **por·tage** *v*. ⟨Old French; see PORTABLE.⟩

por·tal ['pɔrtəl] *n* a door, gate, or entrance, esp an imposing one. ⟨See PORT².⟩

por·tend [pɔr'tend] *v* be a portent of (usually something bad): *Black clouds portend a storm*. ⟨Latin *por-* before + *tendere* extend⟩

por·tent ['pɔrtent] *n* a sign of something (usually bad); omen. **por·ten·tous** *adj*. **por·ten·tous·ly** *adv*. **por·ten·tous·ness** *n*.

por·ter¹ ['pɔrtər] *n* **1** a person employed to carry luggage for patrons at a hotel, airport, etc. **2** an attendant on a railway train. **3** a hospital employee who moves patients, supplies, etc. ⟨Latin *portare* carry⟩

por·ter² ['pɔrtər] *n* **1** a person who guards a door or entrance. **2** janitor. ⟨Latin *porta* gate⟩

por·ter³ ['pɔrtər] *n* a heavy, dark brown beer. ⟨*porter's ale* (i.e., ale for a *porter¹*)⟩

port·fo·li·o [pɔrt'fouliou] *n* **1** a briefcase. **2** the position and duties of office of a cabinet minister or a minister of state: *The Minister of Defence resigned her portfolio*. **3** holdings in the form of stocks, bonds, etc. **4** a selection of works, such as drawings, academic papers, etc. ⟨Latin *portare* carry + *folium* sheet, leaf⟩

port·hole See PORT².

por·ti·co ['pɔrtɪkou] *n, pl* **-coes** or **-cos** a

porch having the roof supported by columns. ⟨Italian. See PORCH.⟩

por·tion ['pɔrʃən] *n* **1** a share. **2** the quantity of food served to one person. **3** one's fate. *v* divide into parts or shares. **por·tion·less** *adj*. ⟨Latin *portio*⟩

port·ly ['pɔrtli] *adj* stout; corpulent. **port·li·ness** *n*. ⟨*port* bearing, demeanour; Latin *portare* carry⟩

por·trait ['pɔrtrɪt] *n* **1** a painting or photograph of a person, esp when of the face or bust. **2** a picture in words; description. **por·trait·ist** *n*. ⟨French, orig pp of *portraire* portray. See PORTRAY.⟩

por·tray [pɔr'trei] *v* **1** describe or picture in words: *The book portrays life long ago*. **2** make a picture of. **3** represent on the stage. **por·tray·al** *n*. ⟨Old French *portraire*; Latin *protrahere*; *pro-* forth + *trahere* draw⟩

pose [pouz] *n* **1** a way of holding the body. **2** an affectation: *She takes the pose of being an invalid when really she is well*. **3** ✱ formerly, in the fur trade, one of several stopping places established on a long portage. *v* **1** hold a bodily position: *to pose for a portrait*. **2** put in a certain position: *The artist posed her before painting her picture*. **3** pretend: *He posed as a rich man though he owed more than he owned*. **4** state: *to pose a question*. ⟨French *poser*; Latin *pausare* pause; influenced by stem *pos-* of Latin *ponere* put, place⟩

pos·er¹ ['pouzər] *n* a person who poses. ⟨*pose*⟩

pos·er² ['pouzər] *n* a very puzzling problem. ⟨obsolete *pose* puzzle completely; *oppose*⟩

po·seur [pou'zɜr] *French* [po'zœʀ] *n* an affected person, one who puts on airs to impress others. ⟨French; *poser* pose⟩

posh [pɒʃ] *adj Informal* well-appointed; stylish. **posh·ly** *adv*. **posh·ness** *n*. ⟨origin uncertain; folk etymology suggests acronym *port out, starboard home* (best accommodation on ships to and from the East)⟩

pos·it ['pɒzɪt] *v* lay down or assume as a fact. ⟨Latin *positus* pp of *ponere* set, place⟩

po·si·tion [pə'zɪʃən] *n* **1** a place where a thing or person is. **2** a way of being placed: *a more comfortable position*. **3** the proper place. **4** a job. **5** a rank: *The manager was raised to the position of vice-president*. **6** a way of thinking: *What's your position on this question?* **7** the place held by a player on a team. *v* put in position. ⟨Latin *positio*. See POSIT.⟩ **po·si·tion·al** *adj* to do with position.

pos·i·tive ['pɒzətɪv] *adj* **1** without doubt. **2** affirmative: *a positive answer*. **3** definite: *a positive refusal*. **4** favourable: *a more positive attitude*. **5** practical: *positive help*. **6** greater than zero. **7** *Electricity* lacking electrons. *n* **1** a positive degree or quantity. **2** *Electricity* the positive terminal in a battery, etc. **3** *Photography* a print made from a negative. **4** *Grammar* the simple form of an adjective or adverb. *Fast* is the positive; *faster* is the comparative; *fastest* is the superlative.

pos·i·tive·ly *adv.* **pos·i·tive·ness** *n.* ⟨Latin *positivus*. See POSIT.⟩

pos·i·tiv·ism *n* a philosophical system that deals only with positive facts and phenomena, rejecting abstract speculation.

pos·i·tron ['pɒzə‚trɒn] *n Physics* the antiparticle of the electron, having the same mass, etc. as the electron and an equal but opposite electric charge. ⟨*positive* + *(elec)tron*⟩

pos·se ['pɒsi] *n* **1** a group of persons who could be summoned to help a law officer, esp in an emergency. **2 ✱** in western Canada, a troop of horses and riders trained for special exercises, often giving exhibitions at stampedes and rodeos. ⟨Latin = power; earlier, be able⟩

pos·sess [pə'zɛs] *v* **1** own: *He possessed great wisdom.* **2** of a spirit, control: *The devil must have possessed those kids today.* ⟨Latin *possessus* pp of *possidere* possess⟩
pos·sessed *adj* **1** dominated by passion, or as by an evil spirit. **2** owning: *The peacekeepers are possessed of great courage.* **3** maintaining calm: *She remained possessed throughout the interview.* **pos·ses·sion** *n* **1** ownership. **2** something possessed. **3** a territory under the rule of a country: *Ascension Island is a possession of the UK.* **pos·ses·sive** *adj* **1** to do with possession: *the possessive instinct.* **2** *Grammar* to do with the form of a noun or pronoun that shows that it refers to the possessor. *My* is the possessive form of *I* in *my books; bird's* is the possessive of *bird* in *a bird's wing.* **pos·ses·sive·ly** *adv.* **pos·ses·sive·ness** *n.* **pos·ses·sor** *n* one who or that which occupies, owns, or controls: *the proud possessor of a grand piano.*

pos·si·ble ['pɒsəbəl] *adj* **1** that can happen. **2** that may be true: *It is possible that he left by the rear exit.* **3** that can be done, chosen, etc. properly: *the only possible candidate.*
n a possible candidate, winner, etc.
pos·si·bil·i·ty *n.* **pos·si·bly** *adv.* ⟨Latin *posse* be able⟩

SYNONYMS
Possible means that with suitable conditions and methods something may exist, happen, or be done: *A cure for cancer is possible.* **Practicable** suggests that by available means something can be carried out, done, or used: *Using X rays is a practicable way of discovering unsuspected diseases.* **Feasible** suggests something that is not yet tried but seems likely to be practicable: *Would compulsory X rays be a feasible proposition?*

pos·sum ['pɒsəm] *n* opossum.
play possum pretend to be dead or asleep.

post¹ [poust] *n* **1** a length of timber, metal, etc. set upright: *a hitching post.* **2** the post, line, etc. where a race starts or ends: *The horses are ready at the post.*
v **1** fasten (a notice) up where it can be seen. **2** enter (a message) on a website, electronic mailing list, etc. for others to read. **3** offer publicly: *to post a reward.* **4** cover (a wall, etc.) with notices. **5** put up notices warning

people to keep out of (land or buildings): *When land is posted, no one may hunt there.* ⟨Latin *postis*⟩
keep someone posted keep someone informed of developments.
pos·ter *n* a large printed advertisement, picture, or notice. **post·ing** *n* a message entered on a computer bulletin board, etc.

post² [poust] *n* **1** a place where one is supposed to be when on duty. **2** a place where soldiers are stationed. **3** a job or position: *a post as district manager.* **4** a trading station, esp in unsettled country: *a Hudson's Bay Company post.*
v **1** send to a station or post: *We posted guards at the door.* **2** appoint to a post, unit, etc. ⟨Latin *positus* pp of *ponere* put, place⟩
post·ing *n* a position to which a person has been posted, esp in the military and the diplomatic corps.

post³ [poust] *n* the mail: *to send by post.*
v **1** travel with haste; hurry. **2** supply with up-to-date information: *Keep me posted.* **3** *Bookkeeping* make all requisite entries in (a ledger, etc.). **post·ed** *adj.* ⟨Italian *posta*; Latin *posita* fem pp of *ponere* put, place⟩
post·age *n* the amount paid on anything sent by mail. **post·al** *adj* to do with the mail or the post office. **postal code ✱** the part of an address that uses a system of six alternating letters and numerals to identify a particular postal delivery point. **post·card** *n* a card without an envelope for sending a short message by mail. **post·mark** *n* an official mark to cancel the postage stamp and record the place and date of mailing. **post·mark** *v.* **post·mas·ter** *n* the person in charge of a post office. **post·mas·ter·ship** *n.* **Postmaster General** *pl* **Postmasters General ✱** formerly, the federal cabinet minister responsible for the Post Office. **post office 1** Usually, **Post Office** an agency responsible for handling mail. **2** an office where stamps and money orders are sold and mail can be registered or insured, etc. *Abbrev* **P.O.** **post·paid** ['poust‚peid] *or* ['poust'peid] *adj* with the postage paid for in advance.

post– *prefix* **1** after: *postgraduate, post-mortem.* **2** behind: *postjugular.* ⟨Latin = after, behind⟩
post·date *v* **1** give (a letter, cheque, etc.) a later date than the actual date of writing. **2** follow in time. **post·di·lu·vi·an** [-də'luviən] *adj* after the biblical Flood. Compare ANTEDILUVIAN. **post·grad·u·ate** [-'grædʒuɪt] *n* a student who continues university studies at a level beyond that of a bachelor's degree. **post·grad·u·ate** *adj.* **post–im·pres·sion·ism** *n* a syle of painting which stresses either formal structure or the possibilities of colour. **post–im·pres·sion·ist** *n, adj.* **post·mod·ern** *adj* coming after and usually in reaction to modernism in the 20th century, esp in architecture, literature, and the arts. **post·mod·ern·ism** *n.* **post·mod·ern·ist** *n.* **post·na·tal** [-'neitəl] *adj* **1** to do with the mother of a newborn baby: *postnatal depression.* **2** having to do with the period just after birth: *postnatal diseases of children.*

post–op·er·a·tive [-'ɒpərətɪv] *adj* to do with the period immediately following a surgical operation: *a post-operative infection.* **post–op·er·a·tive·ly** *adv.* **post–sec·on·da·ry** *adj* to do with education beyond the secondary or high-school level. **post–test** *n* a test taken after instruction to test what has been learned. Compare PRE-TEST. **post–trau·mat·ic stress disorder** (or **syndrome**) a state of shock, with other symptoms, resulting from any form of severe stress, like battle fatigue. **post·war** *adj* to do with the period immediately following a war: *a postwar construction boom.*

pos·te·ri·or [pɒ'stiriər] *adj* **1** situated behind; back; rear; hind. **2** later; coming after. Compare ANTERIOR.
n Informal the buttocks. ⟨Latin, comparative of *posterus* subsequent; *post* after, behind⟩

pos·ter·i·ty [pɒ'stɛrəti] *n* the generations of the future: *documents preserved for posterity.* ⟨Latin *posteritas*; *posterus*. See POSTERIOR.⟩

pos·tern ['poustərn] *or* ['pɒstərn] *n* a back door or gate. ⟨Old French *posterne*; Latin *posterus*. See POSTERIOR.⟩

post·haste ['poust'heist] *adv* very speedily; in great haste. ⟨*post³* + *haste*⟩

post·hu·mous ['pɒstʃəməs] *adj* **1** born after the death of the father: *a posthumous son.* **2** happening after death: *posthumous fame.* **post·hu·mous·ly** *adv.* ⟨Latin *postumus* last, orig superlative of *post* after; influenced by *humus* earth, i.e., burial⟩

post·ing¹ See POST¹.

post·ing² See POST².

post·lude ['poustlud] *n* **1** a closing piece of music. **2** a final or concluding phase: *the postlude of an era.* ⟨*post-* + (*pre*)*lude*⟩

post–mor·tem [poust 'mɔrtəm] an autopsy; examination of a dead body. ⟨Latin = after death⟩

post·par·tum [poust'partəm] *adj* to do with the period following childbirth: *postpartum depression.* ⟨*post-* + Latin *partum* a bringing forth; *parere* bear⟩

post·pone [pous'poun] *v* put off till later. ⟨*post-* + Latin *ponere* put⟩
post·pone·ment *n.*

post·pran·di·al [poust'prændiəl] *adj* after dinner: *postprandial speeches.*
post·pran·di·al·ly *adv.* ⟨*post-* + Latin *prandium* lunch⟩

post·script ['pous,skrɪpt] *n* **1** an addition to a letter, written after the writer's name has been signed. **2** a supplementary part appended to any composition.

pos·tu·late ['pɒstʃəlɪt] *n* something assumed as a fundamental principle: *One postulate of geometry is that a straight line may be drawn between any two points.*
v ['pɒstʃə,leit] **1** assume without proof as a basis for reasoning. **2** require; demand. **pos·tu·la·tion** *n.* ⟨Latin *postulare* demand⟩
pos·tu·lant ['pɒstʃələnt] *n* **1** a candidate for

admission to a religious order. **2** a person who asks or applies for something.

pos·ture ['pɒstʃər] *n* **1** a position of the body: *good posture.* **2** a condition: *In the present posture of public affairs it is difficult to invest money safely.* **3** a mental attitude.
v **1** take a certain posture: *The dancer postured before the mirror.* **2** adopt an attitude for effect. **pos·tur·al** *adj.* ⟨Latin *positura*; *positum* pp of *ponere* place⟩

po·sy ['pouzi] *n* a bunch of flowers. ⟨variant of obsolete *poesy* poetry, Greek *poēsis*; *poiein*. See POEM.⟩

pot¹ [pɒt] *n* **1** a container made of metal, earthenware, glass, etc.: *a flower pot, a coffee pot.* **2** a basket used to catch fish, lobsters, etc. **3** *Informal* a large sum of money. **4** *Informal* all the money bet at one time.
v **pot·ted, pot·ting 1** put into a plant pot: *to pot tomato plants.* **2** *Billiards and snooker* successfully shoot (a ball) into one of the pockets. **pot·like** *adj.* ⟨Old English *pott*⟩
go to pot go to ruin: *After losing his job he took to drinking and went to pot.* **keep the pot boiling** *Informal* **a** make a living. **b** keep things going in a lively way. **shoot** or **trap for the pot** kill animals for food. **sweeten the pot.** See SWEETEN.
pot·bel·ly *n* a large, protruding belly; paunch. **pot·bel·lied** *adj.* **potbelly stove** or **potbellied stove** a bulging stove on feet, that burns wood or coal. **pot·boiler** *n* a mediocre work of literature, art, or music produced merely to make a living. **pot·bound** *adj* of plants, having roots that have outgrown the size of the pot, so that the plant cannot continue growing without being replanted. **pot·ful** *n* **1** as much as a pot will hold: *a potful of potatoes.* **2** a large amount: *a potful of money.* **pot·head** *n* ✹ *esp Newfoundland and Labrador* PILOT WHALE. **pot·herb** *n* **1** any plant whose leaves and stems are boiled as a vegetable, such as spinach. **2** any plant used as seasoning in cooking. **pot·hold·er** *n* a pad used for protecting the hands when handling hot pots, etc. **pot·hole** *n* **1** a deep, round hole. **2** a hole in the surface of a road. **3** ✹ SLOUGH¹ (def. 1). **4** ✹ DUGOUT (def. 3). **5** ✹ a circular depression on any rock surface. **6** a deep cave extending vertically from the ground surface. **pot·hook** *n* **1** an S-shaped hook for hanging a pot over a fire. **2** an S-shaped stroke made by children in learning to write. **pot·hunt·er** *n* **1** a person who shoots anything, regardless of rules of sport. **2** a person who takes part in contests merely to win prizes. **3** a person who hunts for food or for profit. **pot·luck** *n* **1** whatever food happens to be ready for a meal. **2** a meal to which all present have contributed: *a potluck lunch.* **3** whatever is available: *Students are having to take potluck with their courses this year.* **pot·pie** *n* a baked savoury pie. **pot·pour·ri** [,poupʊ'ri] *n* a fragrant mixture of dried flower petals and spices. **pot·sherd** ['pɒt,ʃɜrd] *n* a broken piece of earthenware, esp an ancient one. **pot shot 1** a shot at something without careful aim. **2** a passing

or random criticism. **pot·ted** *adj* **1** put into a pot. **2** cooked and preserved in pots or cans. **3** *Slang* drunk. **pot·ter** *n* a person who makes pottery. **pot·ter·y** *n* pots or other earthenware. **pot·ty** *n* a child's chamber pot.

pot² [pɒt] *n Informal* marijuana. ⟨Spanish *potiguaya*⟩

pot·head *n Slang* a person who habitually smokes marijuana.

po·ta·ble ['poutəbəl] *adj* fit for drinking. *n* Usually, **potables** *pl* anything drinkable. ⟨Latin *potare* to drink⟩

pot·ash ['pɒt,æʃ] *n* **1** any of several potassium salts, such as potassium chloride, processed for use in agriculture and industry. **2** potassium, or a potassium oxide. ⟨Dutch *potasch* literally, pot ash⟩

po·tas·si·um [pə'tæsiəm] *n* a soft, metallic element, occurring in nature only in compounds. *Symbol* **K** ⟨Latinization of *potash*⟩ **potassium nitrate** *Chemistry* a crystalline compound used as an oxidizing agent; nitre; saltpetre. *Formula*: KNO_3

po·ta·to [pə'teitou] *n*, *pl* **-oes** a starchy tuber, widely eaten as a cooked vegetable. ⟨Spanish *patata*; *Haitian*⟩ **potato chip 1** a thin slice of potato that has been fried in deep fat and is eaten as a snack. **2** FRENCH FRY.

po·tent ['poutənt] *adj* **1** having power or effectiveness in action: *a potent remedy for a disease.* **2** of a drink, etc., strong: *potent tea.* **3** powerful or mighty: *a potent leader.* **4** of males, capable of having an erection or reach orgasm. **po·ten·cy** *n.* **po·tent·ly** *adv.* ⟨Latin *potens*; *potere* be able⟩ **po·ten·tate** [-'teit] *n* any person possessing great power, esp a ruler.

po·ten·tial [pə'tɛnʃəl] *adj* possible as opposed to actual: *a potential danger.* *n* **1** a possibility. **2** *Electricity* the amount of electrification of a point with reference to some standard. **po·ten·tial·ly** *adv.* ⟨See POTENT.⟩ **potential energy** *Physics* the energy that something has that is due to its structure, not to motion. **po·ten·ti·al·i·ty** *n* possibility as opposed to actuality: *She has the potentiality of becoming a great dancer.*

poth·er ['pɒðər] *n* **1** confusion; disturbance. **2** mental excitement: *She was all in a pother about chairing the meeting.* ⟨origin uncertain⟩

po·tion ['pouʃən] *n* a drink, esp one used as a medicine or poison, or in magic. ⟨Latin *potio*; *potare* to drink⟩

pot·latch ['pɒtlætʃ] *n*, *v* ✹ *esp West Coast n* **1** among First Nations people of the west coast, esp the Kwa Kwa Ka'wakw (Kwakiutl), a gathering held to celebrate some special event such as an initiation, or to mourn the death of a person of high rank. The host would present valuable gifts to guests as an indication of their status and of his own. Present-day ceremonies emphasize the celebration aspects, although gifts are still given. **2** *Informal* any celebration. *v* **1** hold or take part in a potlatch. **2** give

(something) with the expectation of a gift in return. **3** give things to others freely. ⟨Chinook Jargon; Nootka *patshatl* gift⟩

pot·ter¹ See POT.

pot·ter² ['pɒtər] *v* PUTTER¹. **pot·ter·er** *n.* ⟨earlier *pote* poke, Old English *potian* push⟩

pot·ter·y ['pɒtəri] *n*, *pl* **-ter·ies.** **1** pots, dishes, vases, or other earthenware, esp as distinct from porcelain or stoneware. Pottery is not as strong as stoneware and not as fine as porcelain. **2** the art or craft of making pottery. **3** a place where pottery is made. ⟨*pot¹*⟩

pot·ty¹ See POT¹.

pot·ty² ['pɒti], *adj Informal* eccentric; mentally offbalance.

pouch [pautʃ] *n* **1** a bag or sack. **2** *Zoology* a baglike receptacle such as on the abdomen of a marsupial, in which the young are carried. **3** a loose fold of skin: *pouches under the eyes.* *v* form a pouch or form into a pouch. **pouch·like** *adj.* ⟨Old French *poche*, *pouche*⟩

pouf [puf] *n* **1** a loose roll of hair. **2** a soft ottoman. Also, **pouff** or **pouffe.** ⟨French = puff⟩

poul·tice ['poultɪs] *n* a soft, moist mass of mustard, herbs, etc., applied to the body as a medicine. **poul·tice** *v.* ⟨Latin *pultes* pl of *puls* mush⟩

poul·try ['poultri] *n* domesticated birds, such as chickens, raised for meat or eggs. ⟨Old French *pouleterie*; *poulet* diminutive of *poule* hen; Latin *pullus* young fowl⟩

pounce [pauns] *v* come down with a rush and seize (with *on*). **pounce** *n.* ⟨Old French *poinçon* awl; Latin *punctus* point (see POINT); for the talon of a bird of prey⟩

pound¹ [paund] **1** a non-metric unit for measuring mass, about 454 g. **2** the basic unit of money of the UK and elsewhere. ⟨Latin *(libra) pondo* a pound by weight; *pendere* weigh⟩ **pound cake** a rich cake, orig made from one pound each of sugar, flour, and butter.

pound² [paund] *v* **1** hit hard again and again: *to pound on a door.* **2** throb: *After running fast, you can feel your heart pound.* **3** crush to powder or pulp by beating: *Pound these spices for me and I will make curried vegetables.* **pound** *n.* ⟨Old English *pūnian*⟩

pound³ [paund] *n* **1** an enclosed place for keeping stray pets, until claimed by the owners. **2** any place of confinement. ⟨Old English *pund-* (found only in compounds)⟩

pound⁴ [paund] *n* the button on a telephone marked with the symbol #. Also called **pound key.**

pour [pɔr] *v* **1** cause to flow in a steady stream: *to pour milk.* **2** flow in a steady stream. ⟨Middle English *pouren*⟩ **it never rains but it pours** misfortunes come all together or not at all. **pour it on** *Informal* **a** to do something with great enthusiasm. **b** offer profuse flattery.

pout [pʌut] *v* **1** push out the lips, as a displeased child does. **2** show displeasure. **3** swell out; protrude. *n* **1** a pushing out of the lips when displeased. **2** a fit of sullenness. **pout·y** *adj.* ⟨Middle English *pouten*⟩

pou·tine [pu'tin] *n* ✹ a Québécois dish consisting of French fries topped with gravy or sauce and cheese curds. ⟨Cdn. French⟩

pov·er·ty See POOR.

P.O.W. or **POW** prisoner of war.

pow·der ['paudər] *n* **1** a solid reduced to dust by crushing: *talcum powder.* **2** fine snow. *v* **1** make into powder. **2** become powder. **3** sprinkle with powder. **4** apply powder to (the face, etc.). **pow·der·y** *adj.* ⟨Old French *poudre*; Latin *pulveris* dust⟩
powder burn a burn on the skin resulting from the explosion of gunpowder at close range. **powder keg 1** a small cask for holding gunpowder. **2** something that is liable to erupt in violence: *The whole country was a powder keg after the death of the dictator.* **powder room** a small rest room for women.

pow·er ['pauər] *n* **1** strength; might. **2** the ability to do or act: *I will give you all the help in my power.* **3** a particular ability: *powers of concentration.* **4** authority: *Parliament has the power to declare war.* **5** any person, thing, body, or nation having authority: *Five powers held a peace conference.* **6** *Mechanics* energy that can do work: *Running water produces power to run mills.* **7** electricity as a public utility: *The power is off.* **8** *Physics* the capacity for exerting mechanical force. In the SI, all power is expressed in watts. **9** *Mathematics* the product of a number multiplied by itself: *16 is the 4th power of 2.*
v provide with power: *a boat powered by an outboard motor.*
adj **1** operated by a motor: *power tools.* **2** conveying electricity: *power lines.* **pow·er·less** *adj.* **pow·er·less·ness** *n.* ⟨Old French *poeir*; Latin *potere* be able⟩
in power having control or authority: *the government in power.* **the powers that be** those who have control or authority.
pow·er dress·ing *n* cultivation of a powerful image by dressing in a style associated with high-level business professionals. **pow·er·ful** *adj* mighty; strong. **pow·er·ful·ly** *adv.* **pow·er·house** *n* **1** a building containing boilers, engines, etc. for generating electric power. **2** *Informal* a person or group having great power, energy, drive, etc. *adj* of a person or group, powerful; effective. **power lunch** *Informal* a lunch over which high-level business negotiations are made. **power of attorney** a written statement giving one person legal power to act for another. *Abbrev* **P.A.** **power plant** a building with machinery for generating power. **power play** *Hockey* a situation arising when one team has a temporary numerical advantage because of a penalty against the opposing team. **power station** POWERHOUSE (def. 1). **power steering** in a motor vehicle, a steering mechanism that uses power from the engine to help turn the steering wheel. **power tool** a tool, such as a drill, worked by a motor.

Power is the general word applying to any physical, mental, or moral ability or capacity, whether used or not: *Every normal, healthy person has power to think.* **Strength** suggests a power within the person or thing, to do, bear, or resist much: *She has strength of character.* **Force** emphasizes the use of power or strength to get something done: *We had to use force to get into the house.*

pow·wow ['pau,wau] *n* **1** among First Nations or Native American peoples, a celebration or ceremony, usually featuring feasting and dancing and certain rites, held before an expedition, hunt, council, or conference. **2** a council or conference of or with a First Nations or Native American people. **3** among some First Nations or Native American peoples, a medicine man, or a ritual ceremony conducted by one. **pow·wow** *v.* ⟨Algonquian⟩

pox [pɒks] *n* **1** any of several diseases that are characterized by pustules, or pocks (esp in compounds): *chicken pox, smallpox.* **2** Usually, **the pox,** syphilis. ⟨variant of *pocks.* See POCK.⟩

P.R. or **PR** PUBLIC RELATIONS.

prac·ti·cal ['præktɪkəl] *adj* **1** to do with practice rather than theory: *Earning a living is a practical matter.* **2** able to be put into practice with reasonable efficiency: *a practical plan.* **3** having good sense. **prac·ti·cal·i·ty** *n.* ⟨Greek *praktikos*; *prassein* do⟩ **prac·ti·ca·ble** ['præktɪkəbəl] *adj* capable of being put into practice: *a practicable idea.* **prac·ti·ca·bil·i·ty** *n.* **prac·ti·ca·bly** *adv.* **practical joke** a kind of trick that depends on someone being embarrassed or abused in some way. **practical joker. prac·ti·cal·ly** *adv* **1** almost: *We're practically home.* **2** virtually: *They practically ran the show.* **3** in a practical way: *reacting very practically to the crisis.*

Practicable emphasizes that it is possible (or not possible) for something to be done: *Building an apartment tower on soft marshland is not practicable.* **Practical** suggests that what can be done is (or is not) also reasonable: *Building on this drained swamp would cost too much for the project to be practical.*

prac·tice ['præktɪs] *n* **1** the doing of an action many times over in order to gain skill: *Piano practice is dull, but necessary.* **2** the process of doing something: *Her plan is good in theory, but not in practice.* **3** the custom: *It is the practice at the factory to blow a whistle at noon.* **4** the working at an occupation: *the practice of medicine.* **prac·tise** *v.* ⟨Old French *practiser, practiquer*; Latin *practicare* do, practise; *practicus.* See PRACTICAL.⟩
prac·tised *adj* experienced: *a practised liar.* **prac·tis·ing** *adj* actively engaged in some career or actively following a religion: *a practising lawyer, a practising Catholic.*

prac·ti·tion·er [præk'tɪʃənər] *n* a person engaged in the practice of a profession: *a medical practitioner.*

SPELLING

Practice is one of two pairs of words that in Canadian English are usually spelled differently as nouns and verbs. The preferred spelling for the noun is **practice** and for the verb **practise**. (The other pair of words is **licence** and **license**.)

prag·mat·ic [præg'mætɪk] *adj* 1 to do with practical values, not with ideals: *a pragmatic person.* 2 treating the facts of history systematically, with special reference to their causes and effects. **prag·mat·i·cal·ly** *adv.* **prag·ma·tism** *n.* **prag·ma·tist** *n.* ⟨Greek *pragmatikos; prassein* do⟩

prai·rie ['prɛri] *n* 1 a large area of fairly level land with grass but very few trees. 2 the **Prairies** *pl* a the great plain that covers much of central North America. b ✹ the part of this plain that covers much of central and southern Manitoba, Saskatchewan, and Alberta.
adj Often, **Prairie** to do with the PRAIRIE PROVINCES. ⟨French; Latin *prataria,* earlier *pratum* meadow⟩
prairie chicken 1 either of two grouse of the central North American plains. 2 *Slang, esp BC* a newcomer, esp one from the Prairies. **prairie crocus** See CROCUS. **prairie dog** any of several burrowing rodents found especially on the central North American plains. **prairie itch** ✹ a form of dermatitis caused by a freshwater hydra encountered in certain sloughs on the prairie. **prairie lily** a wild, orange-red lily found on the prairies. It is the provincial flower of Saskatchewan. **prairie oyster** 1 a raw egg seasoned with Worcestershire sauce, swallowed whole. 2 a testicle of a bull calf, prepared for eating. **Prairie Provinces** Manitoba, Saskatchewan, and Alberta. **prairie schooner** a covered wagon used by pioneers in crossing the plains. **prairie wolf** coyote.

praise [preiz] *v* 1 express approval or admiration of. 2 worship in words or song: *to praise God.* **praise** *n.* ⟨Old French *preisier;* Latin *pretiare* prize, v; *pretium* reward⟩
sing the praise or **praises of** praise with enthusiasm.
praise·wor·thy *adj* deserving approval.
praise·wor·thi·ly *adv.* **praise·wor·thi·ness** *n.*

SYNONYMS

Praise means to express in an enthusiastic way one's high opinion or admiration of someone or something: *The coach praised the team for its fine playing.* **Approve** means to think or express a favourable opinion: *Everyone in the room approved her idea.* **Commend** suggests a more formal expression of favourable opinion: *The mayor commended the teenagers for their quick thinking.*

pra·line ['preilin] *or* ['prɒlin] *n* a candy made of sugar and nuts. ⟨Marshal Duplessis-*Praslin,* 17c, whose cook invented it⟩

prance [præns] *v* 1 jump around on the hind legs. 2 swagger. 3 dance. **prance** *n.* **pranc·er** *n.* **pranc·ing** *adj.* ⟨Middle English *prancen*⟩

prank [præŋk] *n* a piece of mischief: *On April Fool's Day people play pranks on each other.* **prank·ish** *adj* full of pranks. **prank·ish·ly** *adv.* **prank·ish·ness** *n.* **prank·ster** *n* a person who plays pranks. ⟨origin uncertain⟩

pra·se·o·dym·i·um [ˌpreiziou'dɪmiəm] *or* [ˌpreisiou-] *n* a rare metallic element. *Symbol* **Pr** ⟨Greek *prasios* bluish green + *(di)dymium*⟩

prate [preit] *v* talk a great deal in a foolish way. **prate** *n.* **prat·er** *n.* **prat·ing** *adj.* ⟨Middle Dutch *praeten*⟩

prat·fall ['præt,fɒl] *n Slang* a fall on the backside, as part of a slapstick performance. ⟨Slang *prat* buttocks; origin unknown⟩

prat·tle ['prætəl] *v* talk as a child does; tell freely. **prat·tle** *n.* **prat·tler** *n.* ⟨*prate*⟩

prawn [prɒn] *n* any of various marine decapod crustaceans. Compare SHRIMP. ⟨Middle English *prane*⟩

prax·is ['præksɪs] *n, pl* **prax·is·es** or **prax·es** [-siz] 1 the practice of an art, science, etc., as opposed to the theory of it. 2 custom. ⟨Greek = action, doing; *prassein* do⟩

pray [prei] *v* 1 speak to God in worship. 2 make a request to God or to any other object of worship: *to pray for help.* 3 ask earnestly. ⟨Latin *precari; precis* prayer⟩
prayer [prɛr] *n* 1 an earnest request. 2 a form of words to be used in praying. 3 *Informal* a chance of success: *He doesn't have a prayer when it comes to getting that job.* **prayer wheel** a wheel or cylinder inscribed with prayers, each turn of the wheel counting as an uttered prayer, used by the Buddhists of Tibet. **praying mantis** mantis.

pre– *prefix* before in place, time, order, or rank: *prepay, pre-eminent.* ⟨Latin *prae-* before⟩

preach [pritʃ] *v* 1 speak publicly on a religious subject. 2 advise strongly: *The coach was always preaching exercise and fresh air.* 3 give advice, usually in a tiresome way: *He is forever preaching about good table manners.* **preach·er** *n.* ⟨Old French *prechier;* Latin *praedicare; prae-* forth + *dicare* proclaim⟩
preach·i·fy *v Informal* moralize too much. **preach·y** *adj.*

pre·am·ble [pri'æmbəl] *n* 1 a preliminary statement. 2 a preliminary fact, act, or circumstance. ⟨*pre-* + Latin *ambulum* walk, n⟩

pre·ar·range [ˌpriə'reindʒ] *v* arrange beforehand: *a prearranged signal.* **pre·ar·range·ment** *n.*

Pre·cam·bri·an or **Pre–Cam·bri·an** [ˌpri'kæmbriən] *or* [-'keimbriən] *Geology adj* to do with the earliest era of geological time.

pre·car·i·ous [prɪ'kɛriəs] *adj* 1 not safe or secure: *a precarious hold on a branch.* 2 poorly founded; doubtful: *a precarious conclusion.* **pre·car·i·ous·ly** *adv.* **pre·car·i·ous·ness** *n.* ⟨Latin *precarius* orig, obtainable only by entreaty; *precis* prayer⟩

pre·cau·tion [prɪˈkɒʃən] *n* something done beforehand to prevent harm: *Lock the door as a precaution against theft.* **pre·cau·tion·ar·y** *adj.*

pre·cede [prɪˈsid] *v* **1** go or come before: *The rain was preceded by a violent windstorm.* **2** be higher than in rank or importance: *A major precedes a captain.* ⟨pre- + Latin *cedere* go⟩
prec·e·dence [ˈprɛsɪdəns] *n* a higher position; greater importance: *to take precedence over all others.* **prec·e·dent** [ˈprɛsɪdənt] *n* **1** a case that may serve as an example for a later case. **2** *Law* a judicial decision that serves as a guide in future similar situations. **pre·ced·ing** *adj* previous: *the preceding page.*

CONFUSABLES

Precede means 'go or come before': *January precedes February.* Proceed means 'move forward': *The year proceeds slowly.*

---

pre·cept [ˈprisɛpt] *n* a general rule of behaviour: *"If at first you don't succeed, try, try, try again" is a familiar precept.* **pre·cep·tive** *adj.* ⟨Latin *praeceptum* pp of *praecipere*; *prae-* before + *capere* take⟩

pre·cinct [ˈprisɪŋkt] *n* **1** Usually, **precincts** *pl* a space enclosed by walls, a fence, etc.: *the school precincts.* **2** Often, **precincts** *pl* bounds; limit. **3** a district within certain boundaries: *a police precinct.* ⟨Latin *praecinctum* pp of *praecingere* enclose; *prae-* before + *cingere* gird⟩

pre·cious [ˈprɛʃəs] *adj* **1** valuable **2** much loved. **3** too fastidious; affected.
adv Informal very: *precious little money.* **pre·cious** or **pre·cious·ly** *adv.* ⟨Latin *pretiosus*; *pretium* price⟩
pre·ci·os·i·ty [ˌprɛʃiˈɒsɪti] *n* affectation of language, style, or taste. **precious metal** a valuable metal such as gold, or platinum. **precious stone** a jewel. Diamonds, rubies, emeralds, and sapphires are precious stones.

prec·i·pice [ˈprɛsəpɪs] *n* a very steep cliff. ⟨Latin *praecipitium*; *praecipitis* steep, headlong; *prae-* first + *caput* head⟩

pre·cip·i·tate [prɪˈsɪpɪˌteit] *v* **1** bring about suddenly: *to precipitate a war.* **2** *Chemistry* separate (a substance), or be separated out from a solution as a solid. **3** condense or be condensed from vapour, in the form of rain, dew, etc.
adj [prɪˈsɪpɪtɪt] **1** sudden: *a precipitate drop in the temperature.* **2** rash: *precipitate actions.*
n [prɪˈsɪpɪtɪt] or [-ˌteit] a substance, usually crystalline, separated out from a solution as a solid. **pre·cip·i·tate·ly** *adv.* **pre·cip·i·ta·tor** *n.* **pre·cip·i·ta·tive** *adj.* ⟨Latin *praecipitare.* See PRECIPICE.⟩
pre·cip·i·tant *n Chemistry* a substance that causes another substance in solution to be deposited in solid form. **pre·cip·i·tant·ly** *adv.* **pre·cip·i·ta·tion** [prɪˌsɪpɪˈteiʃən] *n* **1 a** the depositing of moisture in the form of rain, snow, etc. **b** something that is precipitated, such as rain, dew, or snow. **2 a** sudden bringing on: *the precipitation of a war without warning.* **3** unwise or rash speed. **4** *Chemistry* **a** the separating out of a substance from a solution as a solid. **b** the substance separated

out in this way. **pre·cip·i·tous** [prɪˈsɪpɪtəs] *adj* **1** like a precipice; very steep: *precipitous cliffs.* **2** hasty; rash: *Do not make any precipitous claims at the conference.* **3** sudden. **pre·cip·i·tous·ly** *adv.* **pre·cip·i·tous·ness** *n.*

pré·cis [preiˈsi] or [ˈpreisi] *n, pl* **-cis** [-siz] a summary of an essay, speech, book, etc. *v* make a précis of: *to précis a long magazine article.* ⟨French; Latin. See PRECISE.⟩

pre·cise [prɪˈsəis] *adj* **1** exact; definite: *The precise sum was $31.28.* **2** careful: *precise handwriting.* **pre·cise·ly** *adv.* **pre·cise·ness** *n.* ⟨Latin *praecisus* pp of *praecidere*; *prae-* in front + *caedere* cut⟩
pre·ci·sion [prɪˈsɪʒən] *n* exactness: *the precision of a machine.* *adj* marked by precision: *precision instruments.*

pre·clude [prɪˈklud] *v* make impossible: *Buying a car now would preclude any possibility of a holiday trip.* ⟨pre- + Latin *claudere* shut⟩

pre·co·cious [prɪˈkoʊʃəs] *adj* developed much earlier than normal in knowledge, skill, etc.: *a precocious child.* **pre·co·cious·ly** *adv.* **pre·co·cious·ness** or **pre·coc·i·ty** [prɪˈkɒsɪti] *n.* ⟨Latin *praecocis*; *prae-* before + *coquere* ripen⟩

pre·cog·ni·tion [ˌprikɒgˈnɪʃən] *n* prior knowledge. **pre·cog·ni·tive** [priˈkɒgnətɪv] *adj.*

pre·con·ceive [ˌprikənˈsiv] *v* form (an idea) before having any actual experience or knowledge: *a preconceived notion.* **pre·con·ceived** *adj.* **pre·con·cep·tion** *n.*

pre·con·di·tion [ˌprikənˈdɪʃən] *n* something that must be fulfilled before something else can take place, etc.; prerequisite.
v prepare in advance: *You have been preconditioned to react that way from childhood.*

pre–Con·fed·er·a·tion [ˌpri kənˌfɛdəˈreiʃən] *adj* ✱ to do with the period in Canada prior to 1867, when CONFEDERATION (def. 3) was established.

pre·con·scious [priˈkɒnʃəs] *adj* **1** not present in, but capable of easy recall to the conscious mind. **2** happening before the development of consciousness.
n the preconscious part of the mind.

pre·cook [priˈkʊk] *v* cook (food), partially or completely, ahead of time in order to shorten or simplify its final preparation.

pre·cur·sor [prɪˈkɜrsər] *n* a forerunner: *A severe cough may be the precursor of pneumonia.* **pre·cur·so·ry** *adj.*

pre·date [priˈdeit] *v* **1** to come before in time: *His teaching career predated his entry into politics.* **2** assign something to a date before its actual date: *She predated her letter to make it look as if she had written it a week earlier.*

pred·a·tor [ˈprɛdətər] *n* **1** an animal that lives by killing and eating other animals. **2** a person who lives by exploiting or preying on others. **pred·a·to·ry** *adj.* ⟨Latin *praeda* prey⟩
pre·da·tion [prɪˈdeiʃən] *n* the act of preying on other animals.

pre·de·cease [ˌpridɪˈsis] *v* die before (someone else): *Husbands frequently predecease their wives.* **pre·de·cease** *n.*

pred·e·ces·sor ['prɛdɪ,sɛsər] or ['pridɪ,sɛsər] n 1 a person holding a position before another: *Louis St. Laurent was the predecessor of John Diefenbaker.* 2 something that came before another which has replaced it. 3 ancestor. ⟨Latin *prae-* before + *decedere* retire; *de-* away + *cedere* go⟩

pre·des·ti·na·tion [pri,dɛstɪ'neiʃən] n 1 fate; destiny. 2 an action of God in deciding beforehand what will happen. 3 a doctrine that by God's decree certain souls will be saved and others lost. **pre·des·tine** v.

pre·de·ter·mine [,pridɪ'tɜrmɪn] v 1 decide beforehand: *The time for the meeting was predetermined.* 2 direct beforehand (to something): *Her love of children predetermined her to seek a career as a kindergarten specialist.* **pre·de·ter·mi·na·tion** n.

pre·dic·a·ment [prɪ'dɪkəmənt] n a difficult unpleasant, or dangerous situation. ⟨Latin *praedicamentum* category; *praedicare*. See PREDICATE.⟩

pred·i·cate ['prɛdɪkɪt] n 1 *Grammar* that part of a sentence or clause that contains a finite verb. *Example:* The committee *has organized a trip to Ottawa.* 2 *Logic* that which is said of the subject in a proposition. v ['prɛdɪ,keit] 1 base (a statement, action, etc.) on something. 2 declare to be true: *Most religions predicate life after death.* 3 imply. 4 *Logic* assert (something) about the subject of a proposition. **pred·i·ca·ble** ['prɛdɪkəbəl] adj. **pred·i·ca·bly** adv. **pred·i·ca·tion** n. **pred·i·ca·tive** ['prɛdɪkətɪv] or [prɪ'dɪkətɪv] adj. **pred·i·ca·tive·ly** adv. ⟨Latin *prae-* before + *dicare* make known⟩

GRAMMAR
The **predicate** of a sentence or clause is the verb with its modifiers, object, complement, etc. It may be a simple verb (*The bell* **tolled**), a verb and adverbial modifier (*The sun* **went behind the cloud**), a transitive verb and its modifiers and object (*He* **finally landed the fish**), or a linking verb and its complement (*My sister* **is an excellent skier**).

pre·dict [prɪ'dɪkt] v tell beforehand; forecast; prophesy: *The weather service predicts rain.* **pre·dict·a·bil·i·ty** n. **pre·dict·a·ble** adj. **pre·dict·a·bly** adv. **pre·dic·tion** [prɪ'dɪkʃən] n. **pre·dic·tive** adj. **pre·dic·tive·ly** adv. **pre·dic·tor** n. ⟨Latin *prae-* before + *dicere* say⟩

pre·di·gest [,pridaɪ'dʒɛst] v 1 cause (food) to be partly digested beforehand by some process: *Predigested food is used for persons whose digestion is impaired.* 2 simplify to make easier to use: *a predigested edition of Gulliver's Travels for children.* **pre·di·ges·tion** n.

pre·di·lec·tion [,prɛdə'lɛkʃən] or [,pri-] n a liking; preference. ⟨Latin *prae-* before + *dilectus* pp of *diligere* choose⟩

pre·dis·pose [,pridɪ'spouz] v 1 give a tendency to (with *to*): *A cold predisposes a person to other viruses.* 2 put into a suitable frame of mind: *He is predisposed to be generous.* **pre·dis·po·si·tion** [,pridɪspə'zɪʃən] n.

pre·dom·i·nate [prɪ'dɒmə,neit] v be greater in power, strength, numbers, etc. adj [-nɪt] predominant. **pre·dom·i·nant** adj 1 having more power, authority, or influence than others. 2 most noticeable or frequent. **pre·dom·i·nance** n. **pre·dom·i·nant·ly** adv. **pre·dom·i·nat·ing** adj.

pre–Dor·set [,pri 'dɔrsɪt] n an indigenous culture of northeastern Canada and N Greenland, earlier than the Dorset and dating from about 2000 B.C.

pree·mie ['primi] n *Informal* a baby born prematurely. ⟨*prem(ature)* + *ie*⟩

pre–em·i·nent [pri 'ɛmənənt] adj standing out above all others: *a pre-eminent scientist.* **pre–em·i·nence** n. **pre–em·i·nent·ly** adv.

pre–empt [pri 'ɛmpt] v 1 secure before someone else can: *The cat pre-empted the comfortable chair.* 2 take the place of: *The regular programs were pre-empted by the Grey Cup telecast.* **pre–emp·tor** n. ⟨*pre-emption*⟩ ⟨*pre-* + Latin *emptio* a buying; *emere* to buy⟩ **pre–emp·tion** n 1 a pre-empting or being pre-empted. 2 the purchase or appropriation of something before others have a chance to do so. **pre–emp·tive** adj initiated to prevent someone from acting first: *a pre-emptive strike against the enemy.* **pre–emp·tive·ly** adv.

preen [prin] v 1 of birds, smooth (the feathers) with the beak. 2 arrange (one's hair, clothing, etc.) in a fussy, self-satisfied way. ⟨perhaps obsolete *prune* preen, and Middle English *preonen* prick; Old French *prēon* pin⟩ **preen oneself on** show self-satisfaction in (an achievement or skill): *He preens himself on his dancing skill.*

pre–ex·ist [,pri ɛg'zɪst] v exist beforehand; exist before (something else). **pre–ex·ist·ence** n. **pre–ex·ist·ent** adj.

pre·fab ['pri,fæb] n *Informal* a prefabricated structure, esp a building.

pre·fab·ri·cate [pri'fæbrə,keit] v 1 make all standardized parts of at a factory, so that construction consists mainly of assembling the sections: *a prefabricated house.* 2 put together or prepare in advance, esp in an artificial way: *a prefabricated excuse.* **pre·fab·ri·ca·tion** n.

pref·ace ['prɛfɪs] n 1 an introduction to a written work describing its subject, purpose, etc. or giving background information. 2 the preliminary part of a speech. **pref·ace** v. **pref·a·to·ry** adj. **pref·a·to·ri·ly** adv. ⟨Latin *praefatio*; *prae-* before + *fari* speak⟩

pre·fect ['prifɛkt] n 1 in ancient Rome, etc., a title of various officers. Also, **prae·fect.** 2 in France, the chief administrative official of a department. 3 in Paris, France, the chief of police. 4 in some schools, a senior student who has some authority over other students. ⟨Latin *praefectus* pp of *praeficere*; *prae-* in front + *facere* make⟩ **pre·fec·ture** ['prifɛktʃər] n the office, jurisdiction, or official residence of a prefect.

pre·fer [prɪ'fɜr] v -**ferred**, -**fer·ring** 1 like

better: *I will come later, if you prefer.* **2** put forward: *to prefer charges of speeding against a driver.* **3** promote; advance. **4** give priority to (a client, etc.). ⟨Latin *prae-* before + *ferre* carry⟩ **pref·er·a·ble** ['prɛfrəbəl] *adj* more desirable: *I decided that going along was preferable to staying behind.* **pref·er·a·bly** *adv.* **pref·er·ence** ['prɛfrəns] *n* **1** the favouring of one thing or person above another. **2** in international trade, a granting of certain concessions. **pref·er·en·tial** [,prɛfə'rɛnʃəl] *adj* to do with receiving, or showing preference: *preferential treatment.* **pref·er·en·tial·ly** *adv.* **pref·er·en·tial·ism** *n.* **preferential shop** a business giving preference to union members in hiring, promotion, etc. Compare CLOSED SHOP. **pre·fer·ment** *n* **1** promotion: *to seek preferment in the army.* **2** a position, office, or honour to which a person is advanced: *a sought-after preferment.* **3** the act of putting forward a charge. **preferred stock** stock with guaranteed priority over common stock in the payment of dividends.

pre·fig·ure [pri'fɪgjər] *or* [pri'fɪgər] *v* show or suggest beforehand by a figure or type: *The shadow of the gallows across his path prefigured his ultimate fate.* **pre·fig·ur·a·tion** *n.* **pre·fig·ure·ment** *n.* **pre·fig·ur·a·tive** *adj.*

pre·fix ['prifɪks] *n* **1** *Grammar* a syllable or word put at the beginning of a word to change its meaning: *pre*paid, *under*line, *dis*appear. **2** a title put before a name. *Example: Dame Joan Sutherland.*
v [pri'fɪks] *or* ['prifɪks] put before: *We prefix 'Mr.' to a man's name.* Compare SUFFIX. **pre·fix·al** *adj.* **pre·fix·ion** *n.*

preg·nant ['prɛgnənt] *adj* **1** being with child or young. **2** filled: *a mind pregnant with ideas.* **3** filled with meaning: *a pregnant pause.* **preg·nan·cy** ['prɛgnənsi] *n.* **preg·nant·ly** *adv.* ⟨Latin *praegnans*; *prae-* before + *gen-* bear⟩

pre·heat [pri'hit] *v* of an oven, heat to a particular temperature before placing something in it to cook.

pre·hen·sile [pri'hɛnsaɪl] *or* [pri'hɛnsəl] *adj* adapted for seizing, grasping, or holding on: *New World monkeys have prehensile tails; Old World monkeys do not.* ⟨Latin *prehensus* pp of *prehendere* grasp⟩

pre·his·to·ry [pri'hɪstəri] *n* **1** all that occurred in time before the period of written history. **2** a history or account of the background of a situation or event. **pre·his·tor·ic** *adj* to do with periods before recorded history: *prehistoric animals.*

pre·judge [pri'dʒʌdʒ] *v* judge without knowing all the facts. **pre·judg·ment** *or* **pre·judge·ment** *n.*

prej·u·dice ['prɛdʒədɪs] *n* **1** an opinion based on irrelevant considerations: *a prejudice against doctors based on one unfortunate experience.* **2** unreasonable hostility toward a particular person, group, race, nation, etc.: *the battle against prejudice.* **3** disadvantage: *They feel that the new bylaw works to the prejudice of apartment dwellers.*

v **1** cause prejudice in: *The fact that I was her supervisor may prejudice me in her favour.* **2** damage: *He tried to say nothing that might prejudice their interests.* **prej·u·diced** *adj.* ⟨Latin *prae-* before + *judicium* judgment⟩ **prej·u·di·cial** *adj* causing prejudice; hurtful. **prej·u·di·cial·ly** *adv.*

prel·ate ['prɛlət] *n* a high-ranking member of the clergy, such as a bishop. **pre·lat·ic** [pri'lætɪk], *adj.* ⟨Latin *praelatus* pp to Latin *praeferre* prefer. See PREFER.⟩

pre·lim·i·nar·y [pri'lɪmɪ,nɛri] *adj* coming before the main business: *After preliminary remarks by the principal, the school play began.* *n* **1** something preparatory: *Intensive research is a necessary preliminary to any serious writing.* **2** a preliminary examination. **3** a game or match as a run-up to the main one: *to make it through the preliminaries.* **pre·lim·i·nar·i·ly** *adv.* ⟨Latin *prae-* before + *limen* threshold⟩

pre·lit·er·ate [pri'lɪtərɪt] *adj* to do with a society or culture that has not developed a written language.

prel·ude ['prɛljud], ['prilud], *or* ['preilud] *n* anything serving as an introduction. **prel·ude** *v* . ⟨Latin *prae-* before + *ludere* play⟩

pre·mar·i·tal [pri'mɛrɪtəl] *or* [pri'mærɪtəl] *adj* existing or happening before marriage: *premarital counselling.*

pre·ma·ture [,primə'tʃʊr] *or* [,prɛmə'tʃʊr] *adj* **1** born at less than 40 weeks of pregnancy. **2** happening before the proper time. **pre·ma·ture·ly** *adv.* **pre·ma·tu·ri·ty** *or* **pre·ma·ture·ness** *n.*

pre·med·i·cal [pri'mɛdɪkəl] *adj* preparing for the study of medicine: *a premedical student.* Usually shortened to **premed.**

pre·med·i·tate [pri'mɛdɪ,teit] *v* plan or consider (something) ahead of time: *to premeditate a murder.* **pre·med·i·tat·ed** *adj.* **pre·med·i·tat·ed·ly** *adv.*

pre–men·stru·al syndrome [pri'mɛnstruəl] *or* ['mɛnstrəl] a set of symptoms experienced by many women just before their menstrual periods, characterized by bloating and irritability. *Abbrev* **PMS**

pre·mier ['primjər] *or* [pri'mir] *n* **1 ✷** in Canada, the head of a provincial cabinet. **2** the chief officer of any government.
adj **1** first in rank or quality: *a novel of premier importance.* **2** earliest. **pre·mier·ship** *n.* ⟨French = first; Latin *primarius*. See PRIMARY.⟩

pre·mière or **pre·miere** [prəm'jɛr] *or* [pri'mir]; French [prə'mjɛr] *n* the first public performance: *the première of a play.*
v -**mièred** or -**miered**, -**mièr·ing** or -**mier·ing** **1** give or have a first public performance. **2** appear for the first time: **a** as a star: *He premièred last year in a musical comedy.* **b** in publication: *The magazine premiered in September 1993.*

prem·ise ['prɛmɪs] *n* **1** *Logic* a statement assumed to be true and used to draw a conclusion. See also SYLLOGISM. **2 premises** *pl* a house or building with its grounds.
v ['prɛməs] *or* [pri'maɪz] *v* set forth as an

introduction, assumption, or explanation. ⟨Latin *praemissa* pp of *praemittere*; *prae-* before + *mittere* put⟩

pre·mi·um ['primiəm] *n* **1** an extra payment or charge: *They had to pay a considerable premium to get first-quality goods.* **2** money paid regularly for an insurance policy. **3** something given away or offered at a reduced price to purchasers of a product, service, etc. **4** the excess value of one form of money over another of the same nominal value. **5** an unusually high value: *The company puts a premium on accuracy of work.* *adj* of a higher grade or quality. ⟨Latin *praemium*; *prae-* before + *emere* buy⟩ **at a premium** much valued and in demand: *Good housing is at a premium these days.*

pre·mo·lar [pri'moulər] *n* one of the permanent teeth in front of the molars.

prem·o·ni·tion [ˌpremə'nɪʃən] *or* [ˌprim-] *n* a feeling that something bad is about to happen; foreboding. **pre·mon·i·to·ry** *adj.* ⟨Latin *prae-* before + *monere* warn⟩

pre·na·tal [pri'neitəl] *adj* **1** to do with a woman who is expecting a child: *prenatal classes.* **2** before birth: *a prenatal diagnosis of defects.* **pre·na·tal·ly** *adv.*

pre·nup·tial [pri'nʌpʃəl] *or* [pri'nʌptʃəl] *adj* **1 a** before marriage: *a prenuptial contract.* **b** before a wedding: *a prenuptial party.* **2** *Zoology* before mating.

pre·oc·cu·py [pri'ɒkjə,paɪ] *v* take up all the attention of: *The problem preoccupied her mind.* **pre·oc·cu·pa·tion** *n.* **pre·oc·cu·pied** *adj.*

pre·op·er·a·tive [pri'ɒprə,tɪv] *adj* to do with the preparatory period preceding a surgical operation.

pre·or·dain [ˌpriɔr'dein] *v* decide or settle beforehand; foreordain. **pre·or·di·na·tion** *n.*

prep [prep] *adj Informal* preparatory. *v* **prepped, prep·ping 1** get training: *She prepped for her exams by extensive extra reading.* **2** prepare (a patient) for surgery. ⟨*preparatory* or *preparation*⟩

pre·pack·age [pri'pækɪdʒ] *v* package before sale according to certain grades, prices, etc.

pre·paid [pri'peid] *v* pt and pp of PREPAY.

pre·pare [pri'per] **1** make from ingredients or parts: *They prepared a delicious meal.* **2** get ready for some purpose: *to prepare for school.* **3** plan: *to prepare an adequate defence.* **pre·pared·ness** [pri'perdnɪs] *or* [-perɪdnɪs] *n.* ⟨Latin *prae-* before + *parare* make ready⟩ **prep·a·ra·tion** [ˌprepə'reiʃən] *n* **1** anything done to prepare for something: *He made no preparations for his holidays.* **2** a substance made by a special process: *The preparation included camphor.* **pre·par·a·tive** [pri'perətɪv] *or* [pri'pærətɪv] *adj* preparatory. *n* something that prepares. **prep·a·ra·to·ry** ['prepərə,tɔri], [pri'perə,tɔri], *or* [pri'pærə,tɔri] *adj* **1** of or for preparation. **2** as an introduction. **preparatory school** a private school educating students for college or university. **prep·py** *Informal n* a student or graduate of a preparatory school. *adj* **1** to do with a style of dress, hair, etc. that is neat, fashionable, and expensive, typical of private school students. **2** tending to be smart and self-opinionated.

pre·pay [pri'pei] *v* **-paid, -pay·ing** pay for in advance. **pre·pay·ment** *n.*

pre·pon·der·ate [pri'pɒndə,reit] *v* be the chief or most numerous element: *Maples preponderate in our eastern woods.* **pre·pon·der·ance** *n.* **pre·pon·der·ant** *adj.* **pre·pon·der·ant·ly** *adv.* ⟨Latin *praeponderare* outweigh; *prae-* before + *ponderare* weigh⟩

prep·o·si·tion [ˌprepə'zɪʃən] *n Grammar* a word that shows relationships of time, direction, position, etc. among other words or parts of a sentence. *With, for, by,* and *in* are prepositions in the following sentence: *A man with rugs for sale walked by our house in the morning.* **prep·o·si·tion·al** *adj.* **prep·o·si·tion·al·ly** *adv.* ⟨Latin *prae-* before + *positio*; *positum* pp of *ponere* put⟩

pre·pos·sess·ing [ˌpripə'zesɪŋ] *adj* making a favourable first impression; attractive: *The performer's appearance was not prepossessing.* **pre·pos·ses·sion** *n* bias; a favourable feeling or opinion formed beforehand.

pre·pos·ter·ous [pri'pɒstərəs] *adj* contrary to common sense: *It would be preposterous to shovel snow with a spoon.* **pre·pos·ter·ous·ly** *adv.* **pre·pos·ter·ous·ness** *n.* ⟨Latin *praeposterus* in reverse order; *prae-* before + *post* after⟩

prep·py See PREPARE.

pre·quel ['prikwəl] *n* a film or book using the characters from another work by the same author, but at an earlier age. ⟨*pre-* + (SE)QUEL; coined by J.R.R. Tolkien⟩

pre·re·cord [ˌpriri'kɔrd] *v* **1** *Radio and television* record for later broadcast. **2** *Film* record (music, sound effects, etc.) ahead of time for later inclusion. **pre·re·cord·ed** *adj* of commercial recording tapes, designating those which have images, sound, etc. recorded on them before sale.

pre·req·ui·site [pri'rekwəzɪt] *n* something required as a condition before something else can be considered: *A high-school diploma is the usual prerequisite to university studies.* **pre·req·ui·site** *adj.*

pre·rog·a·tive [pri'rɒgətɪv] *n* a privilege that nobody else has: *The government has the prerogative of coining money.* **pre·rog·a·tive** *adj.* ⟨Latin *prae-* before + *rogare* ask⟩

pres·age ['presɪdʒ] *n* **1** something that foreshadows a future event. **2** a feeling that something is about to happen. *v* ['presɪdʒ] *or* [pri'seidʒ] **1** give warning of: *Some think that a ring around the moon presages a storm.* **2** have a presentiment of: *The teacher presaged a disaster from the experiment.* ⟨Latin *prae-* before + *sagus* prophetic⟩

pres·by·o·pia [ˌprezbi'oupiə] *or* [ˌpres-] *n Ophthalmology* a form of farsightedness, usually occurring after middle age. **pres·by·op·ic** [-'ɒpɪk] *adj.* ⟨Greek *presbys* old + *ops* eye⟩

Pres·by·te·ri·an [ˌprɛzbɪ'tiriən] *or* [ˌprɛs-] *n* a member of any of several Christian churches that constitute the main branch of the Reformed churches, whose government is by presbyters (elders) and was first established by John Calvin. **Pres·by·te·ri·an** *adj*. **Pres·by·te·ri·an·ism** *n*. ⟨Greek *presbyteros* elder; *presbys* old⟩

pre·school ['pri,skul] *adj* to do with the period in a child's life after infancy and before the child begins elementary school: *preschool activities*. **pre·school·er** *n*.

pre·sci·ence ['priʃəns] *or* ['prɛʃəns] *n* a knowledge of things before they exist or occur. **pre·sci·ent** *adj*. **pre·sci·ent·ly** *adv*. ⟨Latin *prae-* before + *scientia* knowledge; *scire* know⟩

pre·scribe [prɪ'skraɪb] *v* **1** lay down as a rule: *to do what the law prescribes*. **2** order as treatment: *to prescribe an antibiotic*. ⟨Latin *prae-* before + *scribere* write⟩
pre·scrip·tion [prɪ'skrɪpʃən] *n* **1** an order. **2** a written order for a medicinal remedy or for eyeglasses. *Symbol* ℞ **pre·scrip·tive** *adj* that prescribes. **pre·scrip·tive·ly** *adv*.

pres·ence ['prɛzəns] *n* **1** the fact or condition of being present in a place: *I knew of his presence in the other room*. **2** the place within immediate proximity of a person or thing: *in the presence of two witnesses*. **3** personal appearance and bearing: *a woman of noble presence*. **4** a supernatural being felt to be near. ⟨Latin *praesentia; praesens* present; *prae-* before + *esse* be⟩
presence of mind the ability to think and act calmly and quickly when taken by surprise.
pres·ent *adj* **1** not absent. **2** at this time: *present prices*. **3** *Grammar* to do with a verb form expressing actions going on at the present time, or habitual action: *the present tense*. *n* the present time. **at present** now. **for the present** for the time being. **pres·ent–day** *adj* of the present time. **pres·ent·ly** *adv* **1** soon. **2** at present; now: *The prime minister is presently in Ottawa*. **3** *Archaic* at once.
present participle *Grammar* in English, a participle used **a** to express the same time as that expressed by the finite verb of the clause. In the sentence *Saying good night, they started for home, saying* is a present participle expressing the same time as the verb *started*. **b** with the auxilary verb *be* to form the progressive aspect of the present and past tenses of verbs: *We are leaving now. They were arguing*. **c** as an adjective in an active sense: *running water = the water is running*. In modern English the present participle always ends in **-ing**.

pres·ent¹ See PRESENCE.

pre·sent² [prɪ'zɛnt] *v* **1** make a formal gift to (with *with*): *The company presented him with a silver tray*. **2** offer for consideration: *She presented reasons for her action*. **3** bring before the public: *The school presented a play*. **4** introduce socially: *May I present my son?* **5** bring before a person of high rank: *She was presented to the Governor General*. **6** *Law* bring before a court, etc. for consideration: *to*

present a case. **7** turn in a particular direction: *The actor presented his profile to the camera*. *n* ['prɛzənt] a gift. **pres·en·ta·tion** *n*. **pre·sent·er** *n*. ⟨Latin *praesentare; praesens*. See PRESENCE.⟩

present arms salute by bringing a rifle, etc. to a vertical position in front of one's body.
pre·sent·a·ble [prɪ'zɛntəbəl] *adj* **1** fit to go into company: *to make oneself presentable again after cleaning the basement*. **2** suitable to be offered: *a very presentable gift*. **pre·sent·a·bly** *adv*.

pre·sen·ti·ment [prɪ'zɛntəmənt] *or* [-sɛntə-] *n* a feeling or impression that something is about to happen; premonition.

pre·serve [prɪ'zɜrv] *v* **1** keep from harm or change. **2** conserve and protect (wildlife) in a regulated area. **3** keep up; maintain. **4** keep from spoiling: *Ice helps to preserve food*. **5** prepare (food) to keep it from spoiling. *n* **1** an area where wild animals, fish, or plants are protected. **2** Usually, **preserves** *pl* fruit cooked and sealed from the air: *plum preserves*. **3** something regarded as the special domain of one person or group: *All original documents are the preserve of one retired history professor*. **pre·serv·a·ble** *adj*. **pres·er·va·tion** *n*. ⟨Latin *prae-* before + *servare* keep⟩
pres·er·va·tion·ist *n* a person who advocates preserving aspects of the environment such as historic sites and buildings, natural areas, endangered species, etc. **pre·serv·a·tive** *n* any substance that will prevent decay or injury. **pre·serv·er** *n* a person or thing that preserves or protects from danger: *a life preserver*.

pre·set [pri'sɛt] *v* -set, -set·ting set beforehand.

pre·shrink [pri'ʃrɪŋk] *v* -shrank, -shrunk, -shrink·ing expose (fabric or a garment) to conditions that cause shrinking, so that it will not shrink when washed or drycleaned after sale. **pre·shrunk** *adj*.

pre·side [prɪ'zaɪd] *v* **1** hold the place of authority. **2** have authority: *The manager presides over the business of the store*. **pre·sid·ing** *adj*. ⟨Latin *prae-* before + *sedere* sit⟩
pres·i·dent ['prɛzɪdənt] *n* **1** Often, **President**, the highest executive officer of a republic. **2** the head officer of a ·company, university, society, club, etc. **pres·i·den·cy** *n*. **pres·i·dent e·lect** *n* a president who has been elected but has not yet taken office. **pres·i·den·tial** *adj*. **pres·i·den·tial·ly** *adv*.

press¹ [prɛs] *v* **1** use force steadily (against): *Press the button*. **2** make smooth; flatten: *Press clothes with an iron*. **3** push forward: *We pressed on in spite of the wind*. **4** urge (a person): *Because it was so stormy, we pressed our guest to stay all night*. **5** insist on: *I hate to press the point, but I need the report now*. **6** harass: *enemies pressing on every side*. *n* **1** a pressure: *the press of ambition*. **2** any of various instruments for exerting pressure: *a garlic press*. **3** a machine for printing. **4** newspapers, magazines, and the people who work for them: *The concert was reported by the press*. **5** notice given in newspapers or magazines: *The actor got good press for her performance.* **6** a crowd. **7** *Basketball* a defensive measure in which offensive players are closely guarded over the whole court. **8** *Weightlifting* a technique in which the weight is pressed away from the body using the arms or legs. **press·er** *n.* ⟨Latin *pressare* frequentative of *premere* press⟩

be hard pressed (to) See HARD PRESSED.

be pressed for be constrained by the scarceness of: *pressed for time.* **go to press** begin to be printed: *The newspaper goes to press at midnight.* **press the flesh** *Informal* shake hands.

press agent an agent in charge of publicity for a person, organization, etc. **press baron** the chief executive or owner of a large newspaper or publishing company. **press box** at a sports stadium, arena, etc., an enclosed space set aside for reporters. **press conference** a meeting for the giving of information to reporters by a person or group. **press gallery** an area reserved for the news media, esp in a legislative assembly. **press·ing** *adj* **1** urgent. **2** persistent in making a request. **press·ing·ly** *adv.* **press release** a story or statement officially prepared and released to the press by a government agency, public relations firm, etc. Also called **news release**. **press secretary** a person responsible for media relations on behalf of a prominent figure or organization.

press² [prɛs] *v* **1** force into service, usually naval or military: *When the dishwasher broke, I was pressed into washing the supper dishes.* **2** make use of in other than the intended way: *When the roof leaked, every container in the house was pressed into service as a rain-catcher.* ⟨Old French *prester* furnish; Latin *praestro* ready⟩

press gang in former times, a group of men whose job it was to obtain men, often by force, for service in the navy or army.

pres·sure [ˈprɛʃər] *n* **1** the continued action of a force: *The pressure of the wind filled the sails of the boat.* **2** *Physics* the force per unit of area: *The tires of a bicycle need a pressure of about 300 kilopascals.* **3** a state of trouble or strain: *the pressure of poverty.* **4** a compelling force: *He changed his mind under pressure from others.* **5** the need for decisive action; urgency: *the pressure of business.*
v force or urge by exerting pressure: *The opposition pressured the government into debating the matter.* ⟨Latin *pressura*; *pressus* pp of *premere* press⟩

pressure cooker 1 an airtight metal pot for cooking with steam under pressure. **2** *Informal* something involving a great deal of pressure: *This job is a real pressure cooker.* **pressure group** any group that attempts to further its interests in the federal or provincial legislatures, or elsewhere, through the use of lobbying, propaganda, etc. **pressure ice** ridges of ice formed by vast areas of sea ice pressing against each other. **pressure point 1** any of a number of points on the surface of the body where an artery

passes close under the skin and in front of a bony structure so that pressure applied at that point will check bleeding. **2** an area, issue, etc. that is sensitive to political or other pressure. **pressure ridge** a ridge of PRESSURE ICE. **pres·sur·ize** *v* **1** keep the atmospheric pressure inside (the cabin of an aircraft, spacesuit, etc.) at a normal level in spite of the altitude. **2** place under high pressure: *At busy times, we are pressurized to work late.* **pres·sur·i·za·tion** *n.*

pres·ti·dig·i·ta·tor [ˌprɛstəˈdɪdʒə͵teitər] *n* a person skilled in sleight of hand. **pres·ti·dig·i·ta·tion** *n.* ⟨Latin *praestigiator* juggler; influenced by French *preste* quick and Latin *digitus* finger⟩

pres·tige [prɛˈstiʒ] *or* [prɛˈstidʒ] *n* good reputation, influence, or status derived from achievements, associations, wealth, etc. ⟨French = magic spell; Latin *praestigiae* tricks⟩ **pres·ti·gious** [prəˈstɪdʒəs] *adj* having or conferring prestige. **pres·ti·gious·ly** *adv.*

pres·to [ˈprɛstou] *interj* used when something is produced rapidly, almost as if by magic. ⟨Italian; Latin *praesto* ready⟩

pre·sume [prɪˈzum] *or* [prɪˈzjum] *v* **1** take for granted without proving: *The law presumes innocence until guilt is proved.* **2** dare: *May I presume to speak now?* **3** take unfair advantage of (with *on* or *upon*): *Don't presume on his good nature by borrowing money from him.* **4** assume something is the case: *Dr. Livingstone, I presume.* **pre·sum·a·ble** *adj.* **pre·sum·a·bly** *adv.* **pre·sump·tion** [prɪˈzʌmpʃən] *n.* ⟨Latin *prae-* before + *sumere* take⟩

presumption of innocence *Law* a presumption that an accused person is innocent until proven guilty. **pre·sump·tive** *adj* **1** presumed: *her presumptive.* **2** giving ground for presumption: *The man's running away was seen as presumptive evidence of guilt.* **pre·sump·tive·ly** *adv.* **pre·sump·tu·ous** *adj* acting without permission or right; too bold: *It is presumptuous of you to use my computer when I am out.* **pre·sump·tu·ous·ness** *n.*

pre·sup·pose [ˌprisəˈpouz] *v* **1** take for granted in advance: *Let us presuppose that most people are motivated by good intentions.* **2** imply: *A fight presupposes fighters.* **pre·sup·po·si·tion** [ˌprisʌpəˈzɪʃən] *n.*

pre·teen or **pre–teen** [ˌpriˈtin] *n* a young person before adolescence, usually aged 11 or 12 years.

pre·tend [prɪˈtɛnd] *v* **1** make believe. **2** claim falsely. **3** claim: *I don't pretend to be an artist.* *adj* make-believe; simulated: *pretend pearls.* **pre·tend·ed** *adj.* **pre·tend·ed·ly** *adv.* ⟨Latin *prae-* before + *tendere* stretch⟩

pre·tence *or (esp US)* **pre·tense** [ˈpritɛns] *or* [prɪˈtɛns] *n* **1** a false appearance: *Under pretence of picking up the book, she took the money.* **2** a false claim: *a pretence of knowing the answer.* **3** a claim. **4** make-believe: *His anger was all pretence.* **5** a showing off: *Her manner is free from pretence.* **pre·tend·er** *n* a person who makes claims to something (with *to*): *a pretender to the throne.* **pre·ten·sion** *n* a pretentious display. **pre·ten·tious** *adj* doing things for show: *a pretentious style of entertaining guests.* **pre·ten·tious·ness** *n.*

Pretend means speak or act as if one has or feels something: *They pretended ignorance of the whole affair.* **Affect** emphasizes putting on some characteristic or feeling, for some intended effect: *When she applied for a job, she affected simplicity.* **Assume** suggests putting on the appearance of feeling something, to cover up one's real feelings: *He assumed a look of sorrow.*

pre·ter·nat·u·ral [ˌpritər'nætʃərəl] *adj* **1** out of the ordinary; abnormal. **2** supernatural. **pre·ter·nat·u·ral·ly** *adv.* **pre·ter·nat·u·ral·ism** *n.* ⟨Latin *praeter-* beyond + NATURAL⟩

pre–test ['pri,test] *n* a test given at the beginning of a course to determine level of knowledge or understanding. Compare POST-TEST. **pre–test** ['pri'test] *v.*

pre·text ['pritɛkst] *n* a false reason concealing the real reason: *He used his sore finger as a pretext for not going to school.* ⟨Latin *prae-* in front + *texere* weave⟩

pret·ty ['prɪti] *adj* **1** attractive. **2** not at all pleasing: *a pretty mess.* **3** too dainty. **4** *Informal* considerable in amount or extent: *a pretty price.*
adv fairly; rather: *It is pretty late.* **pret·ti·ly** *adv.* **pret·ti·ness** *n.* ⟨Old English *prættig* cunning; *prætt* trick⟩
a pretty penny. See PENNY. **pretty up** make pretty. **sitting pretty** *Slang* in a good position. **pret·ti·fy** ['prɪtə,faɪ] *v* decorate, esp in an overly cute way. **pret·ti·fi·ca·tion** *n.*

pret·zel ['prɛtsəl] *n* a hard biscuit, usually made in the shape of a loose knot and salted on the outside. ⟨German *Brezel*⟩

pre·vail [prɪ'veɪl] *v* **1** be in general use: *That custom still prevails.* **2** be the most usual or strongest: *Sadness prevailed in our minds.* **3** win the victory: *The knights prevailed against their foe.* **pre·vail·ing** *adj.* ⟨Latin *prae-* before + *valere* have power⟩
prevail on (or **upon**, or **with**) persuade.
prev·a·lent ['prɛvələnt] *adj* widespread; common: *Colds are prevalent in the winter.* **prev·a·lence** *n.*

pre·var·i·cate [prɪ'vɛrə,keɪt] *or* [prɪ'værə,keɪt] *v* **1** tell a lie. **2** be evasive. **pre·var·i·ca·tion** *n.* **pre·var·i·ca·tor** *n.* ⟨Latin *praevaricari* speak evasively, walk crookedly; *prae-* before + *varicus* straddling; *varus* crooked⟩

pre·vent [prɪ'vɛnt] *v* **1** keep *(from)*: *Illness prevented him from doing his work.* **2** keep from happening: *Rain prevented the game.* **pre·vent·a·ble** or **pre·vent·i·ble** *adj.* **pre·ven·tion** *n.* ⟨Latin *prae-* before + *venire* come⟩
pre·ven·tive *adj* that prevents: *preventive measures against disease. n* something that prevents: *Vaccination is a preventive against flu.* **pre·ven·tive·ly** *adv.*

pre·view ['pri,vju] *n* **1** a previous view,

inspection, etc. **2** an advance showing of a motion picture, play, etc. to a select audience. **pre·view** *v.*

pre·vi·ous ['priviəs] *adj* **1** coming or going before. **2** *Informal* hasty; premature: *Don't be too previous about refusing.* **pre·vi·ous·ly** *adv.* ⟨Latin *prae-* before + *via* way⟩

Previous suggests earlier in time, or being the last one before the present: *I cannot go, as I have a previous engagement* (made before). **Prior** adds the idea of coming first in order of importance: *I have a prior engagement* (one that has first call). **Preceding** means coming immediately before in a series of similar things: *Check the preceding bank statement.*

prey [preɪ] *n* **1** an animal hunted for food, esp by another animal. **2** a person or thing injured: *to be a prey to disease.* ⟨Latin *praeda*⟩
prey on or **upon a** hunt or kill for food. **b** be a strain upon: *The memory of the accident preyed upon their minds.*

pri·ap·ic [praɪ'æpɪk] *adj* **1** phallic. **2** overly taken up with virility. ⟨*Priapos* Greek god symbolizing male generative power⟩
pri·a·pism ['praɪə,pɪzəm] **1** *Pathology* continuous and painful erection of the penis. **2** prurient or lascivious behaviour.

price [praɪs] *n* **1** cost to the buyer. **2** what must be given, done, etc. to obtain a thing: *a heavy price for victory.*
v **1** put a price on; set the price of. **2** *Informal* ask the price of; find out the price of: *to price a rug.* ⟨Old French *pris*; Latin *pretium*⟩
at any price at any cost: *to win at any price.*
beyond or **without price** so valuable that it cannot be bought.
price fixing the establishment of ceiling prices by a government, or illegally by producers of a commodity. **price index** a comparative index of the prices of goods and services, taking 100 as a base representing the prices of the same goods and services at a previous period. **price·less** *adj* **1** extremely valuable: *a priceless painting.* **2** *Informal* delightfully amusing: *a priceless story.* **price·less·ness** *n.* **price tag 1** a tag on merchandise showing its price. **2** *Informal* an estimated cost. **price war** a system in which sellers try to capture the market by undercutting the prices of competitors. **pric·ey** or **pric·y** *adj Informal* expensive.

Price means the amount of money for which something is sold: *The price of meat is high now.* **Charge** is the amount asked, especially for services: *There is no charge for delivery.* **Cost** means the amount paid for goods or services, and also whatever is given or spent, such as effort, to get anything: *The cost of renovating our old house was high.*

prick [prɪk] *n* **1** a little hole or mark made by a sharp point. **2** a sharp pain.
v **1** make a little hole in with a sharp point. **2** cause or feel a sharp pain. ⟨Old English *prica* point⟩

prick out (or **off**) transplant (seedlings) into larger containers. **prick up** point upward: *The dog's ears pricked up.*

prick·le ['prɪkəl] *n* **1** a small, sharp point; thorn. **2** a prickly, tingling sensation. *v* **1** feel a tingling, prickly sensation. **2** cause such a sensation in. **prick·ly** *adj* **1** having many sharp points: *a prickly rosebush.* **2** sharp and stinging: *a prickly rash.* **3** hard to deal with: *a prickly question.* **4** quick to take offence: *a prickly individual.* **prick·li·ness** *n.* **prickly heat** a rash caused by inflammation of the sweat glands. **prickly pear** any of a genus of cactuses having edible fruit. **prickly rose** a common North American wild rose, it is the provincial flower of Alberta.

pride [praɪd] *n* **1** a high opinion of one's own worth or abilities. **2** satisfaction in something concerned with oneself: *to take pride in a job well done.* **3** too high an opinion of oneself. **4** a group of lions. ⟨Old English *prýde; prúd* proud⟩

pride oneself on be proud about: *She prides herself on her mathematical ability.*

pride of place the most important position: *In his affections, his wife holds pride of place.*

SYNONYMS

Pride applies to a feeling of pleased satisfaction with what one is, has, or has done: *Pride in oneself is necessary for a healthy outlook on life; excessive pride is unattractive.* **Conceit** suggests much too high an opinion of one's own abilities and accomplishments: *Conceit makes criminals think they are too clever to be caught.*

prie–dieu ['pri 'djʊ] *French* [pʀi'djœ] *n* French a small desk for a prayer book, etc. with a lower piece on which to kneel. ⟨French = pray God⟩

pries [praɪz] *n* pl of PRY.
v 3rd person singular, present tense of PRY.

priest [prist] *n* **1** a member of the clergy or minister of certain Christian churches. **2** a minister of any religion: *a Buddhist priest.* **priest·ly** *adj.* **priest·li·ness** *n.* ⟨Old English *prēost;* Greek *presbyteros.* See PRESBYTERIAN.⟩

priest·ess ['pristɪs] *n* formerly, a woman who served at an altar or in sacred rites: *a priestess of the goddess Diana.* **priest·hood** *n* **1** the position of priest. **2** priests as a group.

prig [prɪg] *n* someone who is smug and thinks he or she is a better person than others. **prig·gish** *adj.* **prig·gish·ness** *n.* ⟨origin uncertain⟩

prim [prɪm] *adj* **prim·mer, prim·mest** stiffly precise, neat, proper, or formal. **prim·ly** *adv.* **prim·ness** *n.* ⟨Middle French *prim* fine, delicate; Latin *primus* first⟩

pri·ma·cy ['praɪməsi] *n,* *pl* **-cies** **1** the condition of being first in order, rank, etc. **2** *Roman Catholic Church* the supreme power of the Pope. ⟨Latin *primatia; primatis.* See PRIMATE.⟩

pri·ma don·na ['prima 'dɒnə] *pl* **pri·ma don·nas** **1** the principal woman singer in an opera. **2** *Informal* a temperamental person. ⟨Italian = first lady⟩

pri·ma fa·ci·e ['primə] *or* ['praɪmə 'feiʃi,i], ['feiʃi,ei], *or* ['feiʃi] *Latin* at first view; before investigation.

pri·mal ['praɪməl] *adj* **1** of early times; first; primeval. **2** chief; fundamental. **pri·mal·ly** *adv.* ⟨Latin *primus* first⟩

pri·ma·ry ['praɪmɛri] *or* ['praɪməri] *adj* **1** first in time. **2** original; fundamental. **3** first in importance. **4** *Ornithology* to do with one of the large flight feathers growing on the distal section of a bird's wing. **5** utilizing the crude products of nature as raw materials: *a primary industry.* **6** *Education* to do with grades 1, 2, and 3: *primary teachers.* **7** *Chemistry* involving or obtained from the replacement of one atom or group. **8** *Geology* of rocks, formed directly by sedimentation, precipitation, or solidification, and not altered subsequently. *n* **1** anything that is first in order, rank, or importance. **2** *Ornithology* a primary feather. ⟨Latin *primarius; primus* first⟩

pri·ma·ri·ly *adv* **1** chiefly: *Napoleon was primarily a general.* **2** originally. **primary colour** one of three colours that can be mixed together to make any other colour. Red, yellow, and blue are the primary colours in pigments; in light, they are red, green, and blue. **primary election** *US* an election to choose candidates for office from a certain political party.

pri·mate ['praɪmeit] *n* **1** any of an order of mammals that includes humans, apes, monkeys, etc. **2** ['praɪmeit] *or* [-mɪt] an archbishop or bishop ranking above all other bishops: *The Archbishop of Canterbury is the Primate of the Anglican Church.* ⟨Latin *primatis* of first rank; *primus* first⟩

pri·ma·tol·o·gy ['praɪmə-] *n* the branch of zoology dealing with the study of primates. **pri·ma·tol·o·gist** *n.*

prime¹ [praɪm] *adj* **1** first in rank; chief: *The prime object was to lower the tax rate.* **2** first in time or order. **3** first in quality: *prime beef.* *n* **1** the best time: *the prime of life.* **2** the best part. **3** the first part. **4** a PRIME NUMBER. **5** the mark (′) representing one of the sixty minutes of a degree. **6** *Music* the tonic, or keynote. **7** PRIME RATE. ⟨Latin *primus* first⟩

prime meridian the meridian from which the longitude east and west is measured. It passes through Greenwich, England, and its longitude is 0°. **prime minister** Often, **Prime Minister,** the chief minister in certain governments. *Abbrev* **P.M. prime number** *Mathematics* an integer not exactly divisible by any whole number other than itself and 1. Compare COMPOSITE NUMBER. **prim·er** ['prɪmər] *or* ['praɪmər] *n* **1** a first book in reading. **2** a beginner's book in any subject. **prime rate** the lowest rate of interest charged by a bank on commercial loans to its most preferred customers. **prime time** *Radio and television* the time when the largest audience can be expected, usually between 7 and 10 in the evening. **prime–time** *adj.*

prime² [praɪm] *v* **1** prepare by putting something in or on. **2** cover (a surface) with a coat of paint so that the finishing coat will not soak in. **3** equip (a person) with information, words, etc. **4** pour water into (a pump) to start action. ⟨probably from *prime¹*⟩ **prim·er** *n* a paint used for a first coat.

pri·me·val [praɪ'miːvəl] *adj* **1** to do with the earliest time: *In its primeval state the earth was without any form of life.* **2** ancient: *primeval forests.* **pri·me·val·ly** *adv.* ⟨Latin *primus* first + *aevum* age⟩

prim·i·tive ['prɪmɪtɪv] *adj* **1** of early times: *primitive people.* **2** first of the kind: *primitive Christians.* **3** very simple; crude: *A primitive way of making fire is by rubbing two sticks together.* **4** *Biology* **a** primordial. **b** to do with an ancient group or species.
n **1** an artist belonging to a period before the Renaissance. **2** an artist who imitates early painters, or who paints with simplicity. **3** *Mathematics* an expression from which another is derived. **4** a word from which another is derived. **prim·i·tive·ly** *adv.* **prim·i·tive·ness** *n.* ⟨Latin *primitivus; primus* first⟩

pri·mo·gen·i·ture [ˌpraɪmə'dʒenɪtʃər] *n Law* the right or principle of inheritance by the first-born, esp the inheritance by the eldest son. ⟨Latin *primus* first + *genitus* pp of *gignere* beget⟩

pri·mor·di·al [praɪ'mɔrdiəl] *adj* **1** existing at the very beginning. **2** *Biology* formed first in the course of development: *primordial leaves.* **3** original; elementary: *primordial laws.* **pri·mor·di·al·ly** *adv.* ⟨Latin *primordium* beginning; *primus* first + *ordiri* begin⟩

primp [prɪmp] *v* arrange (one's hair or clothing) in a fussy or careful way: *to primp in front of a mirror.* ⟨probable variant of *prim,* formerly a *v*⟩

prim·rose ['prɪm,roʊz] *n* any of a genus of plants having large leaves and showy flowers of many different colours. ⟨Latin *prima rosa* first rose⟩

Pri·mus stove ['praɪməs] *Trademark* a portable stove that burns vaporized oil, used by campers, etc.

prince [prɪns] *n* a human male who is: **1** a member of a royal family. **2** a sovereign. **3** in certain countries, a high-ranking member of the nobility. **4** the greatest or best of a group: *a merchant prince.* **5** a generous person: *He's a real prince of a fellow.* ⟨Latin *princeps* chief; *primus* first + *capere* take⟩
Prince Edward Island Canada's smallest province, an island in the Gulf of St. Lawrence. *Abbrev* **PE** or **P.E.I. Prince Edward Islander. prince·ly** *adj* **1** royal; noble. **2** fit for a prince; magnificent: *a princely salary.* **Prince of Darkness** the Devil. **Prince of Peace** a name for Jesus Christ. **Prince of Wales** in the UK, a title conferred on the heir apparent of the sovereign. **prin·cess** ['prɪnsɛs] *or* ['prɪnsɪs] *n* **1** a daughter of a reigning monarch, or of the son of a reigning monarch. **2** the wife or

widow of a prince. **3** a woman having the same rank as a prince. **4** any woman considered to have the characteristics of a princess, in being accomplished, charming, etc. or arrogant, spoiled, etc. **princess royal** the eldest daughter of a reigning monarch. **prin·ci·pal·i·ty** *n* a state ruled by a prince.

prin·ci·pal ['prɪnsəpəl] *adj* most important. *n* **1** the head of a school, college, etc. **2** a sum of money that has been borrowed. **3** a person who hires another person to act for him or her. **4** a person directly responsible for a crime. **5** a person taking a leading part, as in a play, opera, film, etc. ⟨Latin *principalis; princeps.* See PRINCE.⟩
prin·ci·pal·ly *adv* for the most part; chiefly.

> **CONFUSABLES**
> **Principal** as a noun means 'chief person' or 'main sum of money'. **Principle** is used only as a noun, meaning 'a basic idea', or 'a rule of conduct': *the principles of democracy, Good character depends upon high principles.*

prin·ci·ple ['prɪnsəpəl] *n* **1** a belief on which other ideas are based: *Science is based on the principle that things can be explained.* **2** a rule of conduct: *I make it a principle to save some money each week.* **3** uprightness; honour: *a woman of principle.* **4** a rule of science explaining how things act: *the principle of the lever.* **5** *Chemistry* a part of a substance that gives some special quality: *the bitter principle in a drug.* ⟨Latin *principium; princeps.* See PRINCE.⟩ **in principle** as regards the general rule: *to approve something in principle.* **on principle** for reasons of right conduct.
prin·ci·pled *adj* characterized by sound moral principles: *a principled act of protest.*

prink [prɪŋk] *v* primp. **prink·er** *n.* ⟨origin uncertain⟩

print [prɪnt] *v* **1** use type, plates, etc. and ink or dye to reproduce (words, pictures, or designs) on some surface. **2** publish. **3** make (words or letters) the way they look in print instead of in writing. **4** stamp with designs, patterns, etc.: *Machines print cloth, etc.* **5** fix: *The scene is printed on my memory.* **6** *Photography* produce a photograph. **7** *Computers* cause (a computer file) to be reproduced in printed form (often with *out*): *I want this file printed out today.*
n **1** printed words, letters, etc.: *clear print.* **2** printed publications. **3** a picture printed from an engraved block, plate, etc. **4** cloth with a pattern printed on it. **5** a mark made by pressing: *the print of a foot.* **6** *Photography* a photograph produced from a negative. ⟨Old French *priente* pp of *preindre, prembre;* Latin *premere* press⟩
in (or **out of**) **print** available (or not) available for purchase from the publisher.
print·a·ble *adj* fit to be printed. **print·a·bil·i·ty** *n.* **printed circuit** *Electronics* an electrical circuit in which some of the components have been printed in with electrically conductive ink. **print·er** *n* **1** a person whose business or work is printing or setting type. **2** a machine used for printing. **print·ing** *n* **1** the process of

producing printed matter. **2** printed words, letters, etc. **3** all the copies printed at one time. **4** letters made like those in print. **printing press** a machine for printing from type, plates, etc. **print·out** *n Computers* a printed record of the output of a computer.

pri·or ['praɪər] *adj* **1** coming before; earlier: *a prior engagement*. **2** of greater importance: *She regretted not being able to work the extra hours, but considered her family a prior responsibility*. *n* the head of a priory or monastery for men. **pri·or·ess** [-ɪs] *n*. ⟨Latin⟩ **prior to** coming before in time, order, or importance; earlier than; before. **pri·or·i·tize** [praɪˈɔrəˌtaɪz] *v* rank in order of priority. **pri·or·i·ty** *n* **1** a coming before in order or importance: *Fire engines have priority over other traffic*. **2** something of first importance: *Neatness is not a priority for her*. **pri·o·ry** *n* a monastery, convent, etc. governed by a prior or prioress.

prism ['prɪzəm] *n* **1** *Geometry* a solid whose ends are parallel and of the same size and shape, and whose other faces are parallelograms. **2** *Optics* a transparent prism having triangular bases and rectangular sides, used for separating white light into the colours of the spectrum. **3** any similar object. ⟨Greek *prisma* sawed-off piece; *priein* to saw⟩ **pris·mat·ic** *adj* **1** of or like a prism. **2** varied in colour. **pris·mat·i·cal·ly** *adv* by a prism. **prismatic colours** or **colors** red, orange, yellow, green, blue, indigo, and violet; the colours of the rainbow.

pris·on ['prɪzən]*n* **1** a public building in which criminals or those who have been arrested are detained. **2** any place that confines or restricts. *The small apartment was a prison to the big farm dog*. **pris·on·like** *adj*. ⟨Latin *prehensionis* arrest; *prehendere* seize⟩ **pris·on·er** *n* **1** a person who is under arrest or held in a prison. **2** a person who is confined against his or her will. **prisoner of war** a person taken by the enemy in war.

pris·sy ['prɪsi] *adj* **1** too precise and fussy. **2** too easily shocked. **pris·si·ly** *adv*. **pris·si·ness** *n*. ⟨blend of *prim* and *sissy*⟩ **priss** *n Informal n* someone who is too precise and fussy. *v* behave in such a manner.

pris·tine [prɪˈstin] or ['prɪstin] *adj* **1** as it was in its earliest state: *The colours inside the pyramid had kept their pristine freshness*. **2** pure; undefiled: *We drank from the pristine waters of the mountain stream*. **pris·tine·ly** *adv*. ⟨Latin *pristinus* former⟩

pri·va·cy See PRIVATE.

pri·vate ['praɪvɪt] *adj* **1** not for the public: *the private life of a movie star*. **2** secluded: *some private corner*. **3** having no public office: *a private citizen*. **4** secretive about one's personal life: *a very private couple*. **5** not owned or controlled by the government. *n* **1** a person holding the lowest rank in the armed forces. *Abbrev* **Pte.** or **Pte 2 privates** *pl* private parts; genitals. **pri·vate·ly** *adv*. ⟨Latin *privatus* pp of *privare* set apart; *privus* one's own⟩

in private a not publicly: *They met in private to discuss the salary increases*. **pri·va·cy** ['praɪvəsi] *n* **1** the state of being away from others: *in the privacy of one's home*. **2** secrecy: *He spoke in strict privacy*. **3** anyone's private affairs: *invasion of privacy*. **private enterprise** the production and sale of goods, etc. by industries under private control. **pri·va·teer** [ˌpraɪvəˈtir] *n* **1** an armed ship owned by private persons and holding a government commission to attack and capture enemy ships. **2** its commander or one of its crew. **private eye** *Informal* a person who engages in detective work on behalf of individuals or corporations. Also, **P.I. private member** backbencher. **private parts** genitals. **private school** a school that is not part of the public school system. Also called **independent school. private sector** privately owned business and industry. **pri·va·tize** *v* transfer (public property, services, etc.) from public or government control to private control. **pri·va·ti·za·tion** *n*.

pri·va·tion [praɪˈveɪʃən] *n* **1** the lack of the usual comforts or necessities of life: *the privations of a life as an explorer*. **2** the state of being deprived: *She felt the loss of her husband as a real privation*. ⟨Latin *privare* deprive, set apart. See PRIVATE.⟩

priv·et ['prɪvɪt] *n* any of a genus of shrubs and small trees of the olive family having small, dark green leaves. ⟨origin uncertain⟩

priv·i·lege ['prɪvəlɪdʒ] *n* a special favour. *v* give a privilege to. ⟨Latin *privus* individual + *legis* law⟩ **priv·i·leged** *adj* **1** having privileges: *the privileged classes of society*. **2** *Law* **a** not having to be revealed in a court of law: *privileged communication between lawyer and client*. **b** of a communication, not actionable as slander or libel.

SYNONYMS

Privilege suggests a special right given to people as a favour or due them because of their position, age, sex, citizenship, etc.: *Alumni have the privilege of buying football tickets at special rates*. **Prerogative** suggests a privilege or legal right belonging to a person by virtue of birth, office, position, etc.: *Calling an extraordinary meeting is the prerogative of the chair*.

priv·y ['prɪvi] *adj* private. *n* **1** an outhouse; outdoor toilet. **2** *Law* a person having an interest in a legal transaction. ⟨Old French *prive*; Latin *privatus*. See PRIVATE.⟩ **privy to** having secret knowledge of. **priv·i·ly** *adv* secretly. **privy council 1** a group of personal advisers to a ruler. **privy councillor** or **councilor. 2 Privy Council** in Canada, the honorary advisers to the Governor General, made up of current and former cabinet members, parliamentary speakers, the Supreme Court Chief Justice, and provincial premiers.

prize¹ [praɪz] *n* **1** a reward offered in a

contest. **2** that which is won in a lottery, sweepstake, etc. **3** something well worth working for.
adj **1** given as a prize. **2** that has won a prize. **3** worthy of a prize.
v value highly: *She prizes her books.* ⟨See PRICE.⟩
prize·fight *n* a boxing match fought for money. **prize·fight·er** *n*. **prize·fight·ing** *n*.

prize² [praɪz] *v* a person or thing taken or captured in war, esp a ship and its cargo. ⟨Old French *prise* seizure; pris pp of *prendre*, Latin *prehendere* seize⟩

pro¹ [prou] *adv* in favour; affirmatively.
adj in favour: *the number of pro responses.*
prep in favour of: *pro anything exotic.*
n **1** a reason in favour. The pros and cons of a question are the arguments for and against it. **2** a person who votes for or favours something. **3** a vote in favour of something. ⟨Latin = for; in favour of⟩

pro² [prou] *n, pl* pros; *adj Informal* professional.

pro–¹ *prefix* **1** forward: *proceed, project.* **2** forth; out: *prolong, proclaim.* ⟨Latin; Greek *pro*⟩

pro–² *prefix* **1** on the side of; in favour of: *pro-union.* **2** in place of; acting as: *pronoun, proconsul.* ⟨Latin *pro*⟩

pro·act·ive [prou'æktɪv] *adj* tending to take initiative or definitive action.

prob·a·ble ['prɒbəbəl] *adj* **1** likely to happen. **2** likely to be as described: *the probable culprit.* **prob·a·bly** *adv.* ⟨Latin *probabilis; probare* prove⟩
prob·a·bil·i·ty *n* **1** a good chance: *a probability that the trip will be cancelled.* **2** something likely to happen: *A storm is one of the probabilities for tomorrow.* **3** *Statistics* the ratio of the number of successful outcomes to the total number of possible outcomes. **in all probability** very likely, probably.

pro·bate ['proubeɪt] *Law n* the official proving of a will as genuine. **pro·bate** *v, adj.* ⟨Latin *probatum* pp of *probare* prove, make good; *probus* good⟩

pro·ba·tion [prou'beɪʃən] *n* **1** a testing of conduct, qualifications, etc.: *After a period of probation, the novice became a nun.* **2** *Law* the system of letting convicted persons go free under the supervision of a probation officer. ⟨Latin *probare* prove⟩
pro·ba·tion·al or **pro·ba·tion·ar·y** *adj* **1** to do with probation. **2** on probation. **pro·ba·tion·er** *n* a person who is on probation. **probation officer** an officer appointed to supervise offenders who have been placed on probation.

probe [proub] *v* **1** search into; examine thoroughly. **2** examine with a probe: *The doctor probed the wound to find the splinter.*
n **1** a thorough examination; investigation. **2** a slender instrument for exploring a wound, cavity in the body, etc. **3** an instrument, often electronic, used to test or explore. **4** an artificial satellite, etc. equipped to obtain information about other planets, conditions in outer space, etc. and transmit this information back to earth. **prob·ing** *adj.* ⟨Latin *proba* test, n; *probare* prove⟩

pro·bi·ty ['proubɪti] *n* uprightness; honesty; high principle. ⟨Latin *probitas; probus* good⟩

prob·lem ['prɒbləm] *n* **1** a difficult question. **2** a matter of difficulty.
adj that causes difficulty: *a problem child.*
prob·le·mat·ic *adj.* ⟨Greek *problēma; proballein* propose; *pro-* forward + *ballein* throw⟩

pro bono [ˌprou 'bounou] of services, provided free of charge by professional organizations or businesses to charitable groups, the poor, etc. ⟨Latin *pro bono publico* for the good of the people⟩

pro·bos·cis [prə'bɒsɪs] *or* [-'bɒskɪs] *n, pl* **-bos·ci·des** [-'bɒsɪdiz] **1** any long, flexible snout, as an elephant's trunk. **2** a tubular organ of some insects, such as mosquitoes, adapted for piercing or sucking. **3** *Facetious* a person's nose, esp when prominent. ⟨Greek *proboskis; pro-* for + *boskein* feed⟩

pro·ceed [prə'sid] *v* **1** go on after having stopped: *Please proceed with your story.* **2** carry on any activity: *She proceeded to eat the apple.*
n Usually, **proceeds** ['prousidz] *pl* money obtained from a sale, etc.: *the proceeds from the yard sale.* ⟨Latin *pro-* forward + *cedere* move⟩
pro·ce·dure [prə'sidʒər] *n* a method of doing things: *parliamentary procedure.* **pro·ce·dur·al** *adj.* **pro·ce·dur·al·ly** *adv.* **pro·ceed·ing** *n* **1** an action; course of action. **2** **proceedings** *pl* **a** the action in a case in a law court: *The bank initiated proceedings against the embezzler.* **b** a record of what was done at the meetings of a society, club, etc.; minutes. **c** the published version of the papers presented at a conference, etc.

pro·cess¹ ['prouses] *or* ['prɒses] *n* **1** a set of actions in a special order: *By what process is cloth made from wool?* **2** *Law* **a** a written summons to appear in a court of law. **b** the proceedings in a legal action.
v **1** treat or prepare by some special method. **2** deal with (someone) according to a formal procedure.
adj treated or prepared by some special method: *process cheese.* ⟨Latin *processus* progress; *procedere.* See PROCEED.⟩
in the process in the course (*of*): *In the process of looking for her keys she found many other mislaid items.*
process cheese or **processed cheese** a blend of cheeses and flavourings, etc. **pro·ces·sor** *n* **1** *Computers* the part of a computer that processes data. **2** FOOD PROCESSOR. **3** any person or thing that processes.

pro·cess² [prə'ses] *v* move in procession: *The graduands will process across the campus.* ⟨back formation from *procession*⟩

pro·ces·sion [prə'sɛʃən] *n* **1** an orderly series of people or things moving forward: *A funeral procession filled the street.* **2** the act of moving forward in such a way. ⟨Latin *processio; procedere.* See PROCEED.⟩
pro·ces·sion·al *adj* to do with a procession.
n **1** processional music: *The choir marched in,*

singing the processional. **2** a book containing hymns, etc., for use in religious processions.

pro–choice ['prou 'tʃɔɪs] *adj* supporting the right to choose whether or not to have a legal abortion: *pro-choice pamphlets.* **pro–choic·er** *n.*

pro·claim [prə'kleim] *v* **1** declare publicly: *War was proclaimed.* **2** praise enthusiastically in public: *The crowds proclaimed the Queen as she rode to her coronation.* ⟨Latin *pro-* forth + *clamare* shout⟩ **proc·la·ma·tion** [,prɒklə'meiʃən] *n* a public declaration: *A proclamation was issued to announce the forthcoming election.*

SYNONYMS

Proclamation = an official announcement by an executive or administrative officer: *The Prime Minister issued a proclamation declaring martial law in the disaster area.* **Edict** = an order or law proclaimed by the highest authority, usually a decree of a ruler with supreme authority: *The dictator issued an edict seizing the gold mines.*

---

pro·cliv·i·ty [prə'klɪvəti] *n* a tendency; inclination. ⟨Latin *pro-* forward + *clivus* slope⟩

pro·cras·ti·nate [prə'kræstə,neit] *v* delay; put things off until later. **pro·cras·ti·na·tion** *n.* **pro·cras·ti·na·tor** *n.* ⟨Latin *pro-* forward + *cras* tomorrow⟩

pro·cre·ate ['proukri,eit] *v* **1** become father to; beget. **2** produce offspring. **3** bring into being. **pro·cre·a·tion** *n.* **pro·cre·a·tive** *adj.* **pro·cre·a·tor** *n.* ⟨Latin *pro-* forth + *creare* create⟩

proc·tol·o·gy [prɒk'tɒlədʒi] *n* the branch of medicine dealing with diseases of the rectum and anus. **proc·to·log·i·cal** *adj.* **proc·tol·o·gist** *n.* ⟨Greek *proktos* anus, rectum⟩

proc·tor ['prɒktər] *n* in a university or school: **a** an official who keeps order. **b** a person who supervises students during an examination. **proc·to·ri·al** *adj.* **proc·tor·ship** *n.* ⟨short for *procurator*⟩

pro·cure [prə'kjʊr] *v* **1** obtain by care or effort: *A friend procured a position in the bank for my cousin.* **2** bring about: *to procure a person's death.* **3** obtain (persons) for prostitution. **pro·cur·a·ble** *adj.* **pro·cure·ment** *n.* ⟨Latin *procurare* manage; *pro-* for + *cura* care⟩ **pro·cur·er** *n* a person who obtains persons for prostitution. **pro·cur·ess** [prə'kjʊrɪs] *n* a female keeper of a brothel.

prod [prɒd] *v* **prod·ded, prod·ding** **1** a poke with something pointed: *to prod an animal with a stick.* **2** stir up: *to prod someone to action by threats and entreaties.* *n* **1** a poke or thrust. **2** a sharp-pointed stick. **3** a reminder. ⟨Old English *prod-*, as in *prodbor* borer⟩

prod·i·gal ['prɒdɪgəl] *adj* **1** wasteful: *to be prodigal of water.* **2** lavish: *prodigal expenditures.* *n* **1** a spendthrift. **2** a returning wanderer, wastrel, etc. **prod·i·gal·i·ty** *n.* **prod·i·gal·ly** *adv.* ⟨Latin *prodigus* wasteful; *prodigere* squander⟩ **prodigal son** a person who is welcomed back into a family after having been away, from

the story in the Bible of the wastrel son whose father welcomes him back.

prod·i·gy ['prɒdədʒi] *n, pl* **-gies** **1** a marvel. A child prodigy is remarkably brilliant in some respect. **2** a marvellous example: *The warriors performed prodigies of valour.* ⟨Latin *prodigium* omen⟩ **pro·di·gious** [prə'dɪdʒəs] *adj* **1** very great; vast: *The ocean contains a prodigious amount of water.* **2** marvellous: *a prodigious achievement.* **pro·di·gious·ly** *adv.* **pro·di·gious·ness** *n.*

pro·duce [prə'djus] *or* [prə'dus] *v* **1** make: *The factory produces stoves.* **2** cause: *Hard work produces success.* **3** bring forth (offspring, crops, products, dividends, interest, etc.): *Hens produce eggs.* **4** show: *Produce your proof.* **5** bring (a play, film, etc.) before the public. **6** *Mathematics* extend (a line or plane). *n* ['prɒdjus], ['proudjus], *or* ['proudus] **1** what is produced. **2** vegetables and fruit. **pro·duc·i·ble** *adj.* **pro·duc·tion** *n.* ⟨Latin *pro-* forth + *ducere* bring⟩ **make a production (out) of** *Informal* fuss needlessly: *to make a big production out of a misprint in the paper.* **pro·duc·er** *n* **1** a person who grows or makes things that are to be used by others. **2** a person in charge of presenting a play, film, television program, etc. **producer goods** machinery, raw materials, etc. that are used in the production of other goods. **prod·uct** ['prɒdəkt] *or* ['prɒdʌkt] *n* **1** the result of work or of growth: *farm products.* **2** *Mathematics* a quantity resulting from multiplying: *The product of 5 and 8 is 40.* **3** *Chemistry* a substance obtained from another substance through chemical change. **4** a generic word used commercially to refer to any specific manufactured substance or article: *Squeeze a small amount of product into your hand.* **production line** **1** a row of machines in a factory, along which workers oversee the various stages of production. **2** *Hockey Informal* a forward line that scores a large number of goals. **pro·duc·tive** *adj* **1** capable of producing. **2** producing food or articles of commerce: *productive labour.* **3** producing abundantly: *a productive farm.* **pro·duc·tive·ly** *adv.* **pro·duc·tiv·i·ty** *n.*

pro·fane [prə'fein] *adj* **1** with disregard for God or holy things: *profane language.* **2** not sacred; worldly: *Mozart wrote both religious and profane music.* *v* **1** treat (holy things) with contempt or disregard: *Soldiers profaned the temple by stabling horses there.* **2** put to wrong or unworthy use. **prof·a·na·tion** [,prɒfə'neiʃən] *n.* **pro·fane·ly** *adv.* ⟨Latin *pro-* in front of (i.e., outside) + *fanum* shrine⟩ **pro·fan·i·ty** [prə'fænɪti] *n* profane language.

pro·fess [prə'fes] *v* **1** claim: *I don't profess to be an expert.* **2** declare openly: *The soldiers professed their loyalty to their country.* **3** declare one's belief in: *Christians profess Christ and the Christian religion.* ⟨Latin *professus* pp of *profiteri; pro-* forth + *fateri* confess⟩ **pro·fessed** *adj* **1** alleged; pretended. **2** openly declared. **pro·fes·sion** *n* **1** an occupation requiring special postgraduate education and training, esp law, medicine, teaching, engineering, or the ministry. **2** open declaration: *I welcomed her profession of friendship.* **3** a declaration of belief in a religion. **the oldest profession** prostitution. **pro·fes·sion·al** *adj* **1** to do with a profession: *a professional manner.* **2** engaged in a profession: *A lawyer is a professional person.* **3** making a business of something that others do for pleasure: *a professional ballplayer.* **4** engaged in by professionals rather than amateurs: *a professional ballgame.* **5** making a business of something not properly a business: *a professional politician.* *n* **1** a person who makes a business or trade of something that others do for pleasure. **2** someone who follows a profession: *Most of these students are the children of professionals.* **3** a person affiliated with a sports club, such as golf, as an instructor, contestant, etc. **pro·fes·sion·al·ism** *n* the standing or methods of a professional, as distinguished from those of an amateur. **pro·fes·sion·al·ize** *v* make or become professional. **pro·fes·sion·al·ly** *adv.* **pro·fes·sor** *n* **1** any teacher at a university or college. **2** a teacher of the highest rank in a university or college. **prof·es·so·ri·al** [ˌprɒfəˈsɔriəl] *adj.* **prof·es·so·ri·al·ly** *adv.* **pro·fes·sor·ship** *n.*

prof·fer [ˈprɒfər] offer; present: *We proffered regrets at having to leave so early.* *n* an offer made: *The counsellor's proffer of advice was accepted.* ⟨Latin *pro-* forth + *offerre* offer. See OFFER.⟩

pro·fi·cient [prəˈfɪʃənt] *adj* advanced in any subject; skilled: *She was proficient in music.* **pro·fi·cien·cy** *n.* **pro·fi·cient·ly** *adv.* ⟨Latin *proficere* advance; *pro-* forward + *facere* make⟩

pro·file [ˈproufaɪl] *n* **1** a side view, esp of the human face. **2** an outline. **3** a concise description of a person's abilities, character, or career. **pro·file** *v.* ⟨Italian *profilare* draw in outline; Latin *pro-* forth + *filum* thread⟩

prof·it [ˈprɒfɪt] *n* **1** Often, **profits** *pl* the gain from a business. **2** benefit: *What profit is there in worrying?* **prof·it** *v.* **prof·it·a·ble** *adj.* **prof·it·a·bly** *adv.* **prof·it·a·bil·i·ty** *n.* **prof·it·less** *adj.* ⟨Latin *profectus* advance, n; *proficere*. See PROFICIENT.⟩

prof·i·teer *n* a person who makes an unfair profit by taking advantage of public necessity. **prof·i·teer** *v.*

prof·li·gate [ˈprɒfləgɪt] *adj* **1** very wicked; shamelessly bad. **2** recklessly extravagant. *n* a person who is very wicked or extravagant. **prof·li·ga·cy** *n.* **prof·li·gate·ly** *adv.* ⟨Latin *profligare* intensive of *profligere* ruin; *pro-* down + *fligere* strike⟩

pro for·ma [prou ˈfɔrmə] *adj* **1** done in a perfunctory manner or for the sake of form. **2** providing a set form or method: *a pro forma invoice, a pro forma balance sheet.* *n* a document setting out the rules, method, or format by which something is to be done: ⟨Latin = as a matter of form⟩

pro·found [prəˈfaʊnd] *adj* **1** very deep: *a profound sigh.* **2** deeply felt: *profound despair.* **3** having great depth of knowledge or understanding: *a profound thinker.* **4** radical; complete: *a profound reorganization.* **pro·found·ly** *adv.* **pro·found·ness** *n.* ⟨Latin *profundus; pro-* toward + *fundus* bottom⟩ **pro·fun·di·ty** *n* **1** the state of being profound. **2** a very deep thing or place.

pro·fuse [prəˈfjus] *adj* **1** very abundant: *profuse thanks.* **2** lavish; extravagant: *He was so profuse with his money that he is now poor.* **pro·fuse·ly** *adv.* **pro·fu·sion** *n.* ⟨Latin *profusus* pp of *profundere; pro-* forth + *fundere* pour⟩

SYNONYMS
Profuse suggests a quantity that is more than enough: *They were profuse in their praise.*
Lavish suggests showing no attempt to limit the amount, but implies excessive generosity or liberality: *It was a lavish display of gifts.*

pro·gen·i·tor [prəˈdʒɛnɪtər] *n* **1** an ancestor. **2** a source or predecessor of anything. ⟨Latin; *pro-* forth + *gen-* stem of *gignere* beget⟩

prog·e·ny [ˈprɒdʒəni] *n* children; offspring; descendants.

pro·ges·ter·one [prəˈdʒɛstəˌroun] *n* **1** *Biochemistry* a natural steroid hormone that prepares the uterus for reception of the fertilized ovum and maintains pregnancy. **2** *Pharmacy* a commercial preparation of this compound, used in the treatment of various uterine dysfunctions and as normal replacement therapy after menopause or complete hysterectomy. ⟨*pro-* + *ge(station)* + *ster(ol)* + *-one*⟩

prog·no·sis [prɒgˈnousɪs] *n, pl* **-ses** [-siz] **1** *Medicine* a forecast of the probable course of a disease. **2** an estimate of what will probably happen. ⟨Greek *pro-* before + *gnōsis* a knowing; *gignōskein* recognize⟩ **prog·nos·tic** *adj* indicating something in the future. *n* **1** an indication. **2** a prediction. **prog·nos·ti·cate** *v* forecast. **prog·nos·ti·ca·tion** *n.* **prog·nos·ti·ca·tor** *n.*

pro·gram or **pro·gramme** [ˈprougræm] or [ˈprougrəm] *n* **1** a list or schedule of items or events; list of performers, players, etc. **2** a plan of what is to be done: *a business program.* **3** *Computers* (**program** only) a set of instructions outlining the steps to be performed by the computer in a specific operation. **4** in education, a set of courses. **5** a presentation, esp a radio or television show. *v* **-grammed, -gram·ming** **1** draw up a program or plan (*for*). **2** *Computers* prepare a set of instructions for. **pro·gram·ming** *n.* ⟨Greek *pro-* forth + *gramma* something written⟩ **pro·gram·mer** *n* a person who prepares programs for a computer. **pro·gram·ming language** *Computers* a system of words and codes, like a language, which allows a person to put instructions into a computer in a form that the computer can recognize and process.

pro·gress [ˈprougrɛs] or [ˈprɒgrɛs] *n* **1** an

advance; improvement: *the progress of science:* **2** a moving forward: *to make rapid progress on a trip.* **pro·gress** [prə'grɛs] *v.* ⟨Latin *progressus* pp of *progredi; pro-* forward + *gradi* step⟩
pro·gres·sion [prə'grɛʃən] *n* **1** a moving forward: *a slow method of progression.* **2** *Mathematics* a succession in which there is always the same relation between each quantity and the one after it. 2, 4, 6, 8, 10 are in **arithmetical progression.** 2, 4, 8, 16 are in **geometrical progression. 3** *Music* a moving from one tone or chord to another.
pro·gres·sive [prə'grɛsɪv] *adj* **1** interested in new ideas in order to advance to something better: *a progressive nation.* **2** Often, **Progressive**, favouring moderate reform through government action. **3** moving forward; developing: *a progressive disease.* **4** *Education* to do with an educational system which places emphasis on the individual interests and capabilities of the child. **5** increasing in proportion to the increase of something else: *a progressive income tax.* *n* a person who favours or follows a progressive policy, as in politics or education. **pro·gres·sive·ly** *adv.* **pro·gres·sive·ness** *n.* **Progressive Conservative ✱** a person who supports the policies of a provincial Progressive Conservative party. *Abbrev* **PC**
pro·hib·it [prə'hɪbɪt] *v* **1** forbid by authority: *Picking flowers is prohibited.* **2** prevent: *The high price prohibits my buying the car.* ⟨Latin *prohibere; pro-* away + *habere* keep⟩
pro·hi·bi·tion [,proʊə'bɪʃən] *n* **1** the act of prohibiting. **2 Prohibition** a *US* the period (1920–1933) when the sale, manufacture, and consumption of alcoholic beverages was forbidden by law. **b** in some Canadian provinces, the enactment of laws against the sale and public consumption of alcohol. **pro·hi·bi·tion·ist** *n* one who favours laws against the manufacture and sale of alcohol. **pro·hib·i·tive** [prə'hɪbətɪv] *adj* preventing or discouraging purchase: *The cost of the car was prohibitive.* **pro·hib·i·tive·ly** *adv.*

> **USAGE**
> **Prohibited** is followed by **from**: *We are prohibited from parking in front of the building.* The noun **prohibition** is followed by **against**: *The prohibition against parking in front of the building is strictly enforced.*

proj·ect ['proudʒɛkt] *or* ['prɒdʒɛkt] *n* **1** a plan or undertaking. **2** a major school assignment. **3** a government subsidized housing development.
v [prə'dʒɛkt] **1** stick out: *The rocky point projects far into the water.* **2** cause to stick out. **3** throw: *A catapult projects stones.* **4** cause to fall on a surface: *Films are projected on a screen.* **5** cause (the voice) to be heard clearly at a distance: *Actors learn to project.* **6** forecast; extrapolate. **pro·jec·tion** *n.* ⟨Latin *projectus* pp of *projicere; pro-* forward + *jacere* throw⟩
pro·jec·tile [prə'dʒɛktaɪl] *or* [-'dʒɛktəl] *n* any object that is thrown, shot, etc., as a rocket, stone, etc. *adj* **1** capable of being thrown,

shot, etc. **2** forcing forward: *a projectile force.* **3** that can be thrust forward: *the projectile jaws of a fish.* **pro·jec·tor** *n* an apparatus for projecting a picture on a screen. **pro·jec·tion·ist** *n.*
pro·kar·y·ote [prou'kɛriət] *or* [prou'kæriət] *n Biology* a cell without a visible nucleus. Also, **pro·car·y·ote. pro·kar·y·ot·ic** *adj.* ⟨Greek *pro-* before + *karyon* kernel⟩
pro·lapse ['proulæps] *n Pathology* the falling down of an internal organ from its normal position. **pro·lapse** [prou'læps] *v.*
pro·le·tar·i·at [,proulə'tɛriət] *n* the lowest class in economic status, who possess no capital or property and so must work for wages, esp in industry, in order to survive. **pro·le·tar·i·an** *adj, n.* ⟨Latin *proles* offspring, their chief contribution to the state⟩
pro–life ['prou 'ləɪf] *adj* defending the right to life of all human beings at every stage of development, esp by opposing abortion. **pro–lif·er** *n.*
pro·lif·er·ate [prə'lɪfə,reɪt] *v* **1** grow by reproducing (new parts) by multiplication, as cell division, or by procreation. **2** produce (something) or be produced rapidly: *The administration is proliferating e-mail endlessly.* **pro·lif·er·a·tion** *n.* ⟨Latin *proles* offspring + *ferre* bear⟩
pro·lif·ic [prə'lɪfɪk] *adj* **1** producing offspring abundantly: *prolific animals.* **2** producing much: *a prolific imagination.* **pro·lif·i·cal·ly** *adv.*
pro·lix ['prouliks] *or* [prou'lɪks] *adj* using too many words; too long; tedious. **pro·lix·i·ty** or **pro·lix·ness** *n.* ⟨Latin *pro-* forth + *lixus* pp of *liquere* flow⟩
pro·logue ['proulɒg] *n* **1** a speech addressed to the audience at the beginning of a play, opera, etc. **2** an introduction to a literary work. **3** any introductory act or event. ⟨Greek *pro-* before + *logos* speech⟩
pro·long [prə'lɒŋ] *v* make longer; draw out. **pro·lon·ga·tion** *n.* ⟨Latin *prolongare; pro-* forth + *longus* long⟩
prom [prɒm] *n Informal* a dance or ball given by a college or high-school class. ⟨short for *promenade*⟩
PROM [prɒm] *n Computers* a programmable read-only memory chip, with contents that can be programmed to suit specific needs. ⟨from *programmable read-only memory*⟩
prom·e·nade [,prɒmə'neɪd] *or* [,prɒmə'nɑd] *n* **1** walk for pleasure or display: *the Easter promenade.* **2** a public place for such a walk. **3** a ball. **4** a square-dancing figure in which couples march once around the square, etc. *v* walk about for pleasure or for display: *He promenaded back and forth on the ship's deck.* **prom·e·nad·er** *n.* ⟨French *promener* take for a walk⟩
pro·me·thi·um [prə'miθiəm] *n* an artificial, radioactive element. *Symbol* **Pm** ⟨Greek myth, *Prometheus,* who stole fire from heaven⟩
prom·i·nent ['prɒmənənt] *adj* **1** important; well-known: *a prominent citizen.* **2** easy to see:

A single tree in a field is prominent.
3 projecting: *Some insects have prominent eyes.*
prom·i·nence *n.* **prom·i·nent·ly** *adv.* ⟨Latin *pro-* forward + *minere* jut⟩

pro·mis·cu·ous [prə'mɪskjuəs] *adj* lacking discrimination, esp in sexual relations: *promiscuous behaviour.* **prom·is·cu·i·ty** *n.* **pro·mis·cu·ous·ly** *adv.* ⟨Latin *pro-* (intensive) + *miscere* mix⟩

prom·ise ['prɒməs] *n* **1** the words by which one binds oneself to do something. **2** an indication of what may be expected: *The clouds give promise of rain.* **3** an indication of future excellence: *a young scholar who shows promise.* **prom·ise** *v.* ⟨Latin *promissum* pp of *promittere* promise; *pro-* before + *mittere* put⟩ **Prom·ised Land 1** in the Bible and the Koran, the country promised by God to Abraham and his descendants. **2** heaven. **3** promised land a place or condition of expected happiness: *Canada is a promised land for many immigrants.* **prom·is·ing** *adj* likely to turn out well: *a promising student.* **prom·is·ing·ly** *adv.* **prom·is·sory** note a written promise to pay a sum of money to a certain person at a certain time. *Abbrev* **P/N** or **p/n.**

pro·mo ['proumou] *Informal n* an advertisement on radio or television, etc. forming part of a campaign promoting a forthcoming product or program. ⟨*promotion*⟩

prom·on·to·ry ['prɒmən,tɔri] *n* a high point of land jutting into a body of water. ⟨Latin *pro-* forward + *montis* mountain⟩

pro·mote [prə'mout] *v* **1** raise or advance in rank, condition, or importance. **2** help to grow or develop: *to promote peace.* **3** further the sale of (an article) by advertising. **4** sponsor or secure capital for (an event, new business, etc.). **pro·mot·er** *n.* **pro·mo·tion** *n.* **pro·mo·tion·al** *adj.* ⟨Latin *promotus* pp of *promovere; pro-* forward + *movere* move⟩

SYNONYMS
Promote emphasizes causing an undertaking to move forward by giving active support and helping it develop: *Travel scholarships promote better understanding of the problems other countries face .* **Further** emphasizes helping a cause, project, etc. to keep going ahead: *Getting a travel scholarship will allow you to further your understanding of the problems other countries face.*

prompt [prɒmpt] *adj* **1** on time: *Be prompt to obey.* **2** done at once: *a prompt answer.* **3** used in prompting: *a prompt box on a stage.*
v **1** cause (someone) to do something: *Her curiosity prompted her to ask questions.* **2** suggest: *A kind thought prompted the gift.* **3** remind (a speaker, actor, etc.) of the words or actions needed. **4** *Computers* request input through a message on the screen.
n **1** something that prompts. **2** *Computers* a message on the screen requesting input. **3** *Business* a limit of time allowed for payment of goods purchased. **prompt·ly** *adv.* **prompt·ness** or **promp·ti·tude** *n.* ⟨Latin *promptus* pp of *promere; pro-* forth + *emere* take⟩

prompt·er *n* a person who supplies actors, speakers, etc. with their lines from off-stage, when they forget them.

prom·ul·gate ['prɒməl,geit] *or* [prə'mʌlgeit] *v* **1** proclaim formally. **2** spread far and wide: *Schools try to promulgate knowledge.* **prom·ul·ga·tor** *n.* **prom·ul·ga·tion** *n.* ⟨Latin *pro-* forward + *mulgere* press⟩

prone [proun] *adj* **1** liable (*to*): *prone to evil.* **2** very likely to have (in compounds): *She is accident-prone.* **3** lying face downward. Compare SUPINE. **prone·ness** *n.* ⟨Latin *pronus*⟩

prong [prɒŋ] *n* one of the pointed ends of a fork, antler, etc.
v pierce or stab with a prong. **pronged** *adj.* ⟨Middle English *prange*⟩

pro·noun ['prou,naun] *n Grammar* a word used to indicate without naming *I, we, you, he, it, they, who, whose, which, this, mine,* and *whatever* are pronouns in English. **pro·nom·i·nal** *adj.* **pro·nom·i·nal·ly** *adv.* ⟨Latin *pro-* for + *nomen* noun⟩

pro·nounce [prə'nauns] *v* **1** speak: *Pronounce your words clearly.* **2** articulate (a word) in the generally accepted way: *How do you pronounce rhinoceros?* **3** give an opinion: *Only an expert should pronounce on this case.* **4** declare (a person or thing) to be: *The doctor pronounced her cured.* **pro·nounce·a·ble** *adj.* ⟨Latin *pronuntiare; pro-* forth + *nuntius* messenger⟩ **pro·nounced** *adj* strongly marked; decided: *pronounced opinions.* **pro·nounce·ment** *n* **1** a declaration. **2** an opinion. **pro·nun·ci·a·tion** *n* the way of pronouncing.

pron·to ['prɒntou] *adv Informal* promptly; quickly; right away. ⟨Spanish; Latin *promptus.* See PROMPT.⟩

proof [pruf] *n* **1** a way of showing the truth of something. **2** *Law* convincing evidence. **3** the act of testing. **4** *Printing* a trial impression from type. **5** the standard strength of alcoholic liquors. See PROOF SPIRIT. *adj* **1** of tested strength: *We are proof against being taken by surprise.* **2** of an alcoholic liquor, of standard strength: *proof spirit.*
v **1** treat (something) to make it resistant to water, etc. **2** proofread. ⟨Old French *prueve,* Latin *proba; probare* prove⟩
proof·read *v* **-read** [-,rɛd], **-read·ing** read (printers' proofs, etc.) and mark errors to be corrected. **proof spirit** a mixture of alcohol with water, containing by volume a standard amount of ethyl alcohol at 15.6°C. In Canada and the UK, proof is 57.1 percent, and in the US, 50 percent. **prove** [pruv] *v* **proved, proved** or **prov·en, prov·ing 1** establish as true. **2** be found (to be): *This book proved interesting.* **prove oneself** show oneself to be: *He proved himself honest.* **prove out** show or be shown as true, satisfactory, etc.: *My plan proved out finally.* **prov·a·ble** *adj.* **prov·en** *adj* known to be authentic: *a proven treatment for bee stings.*

–proof *suffix* protected against; safe from: *fireproof, waterproof, bombproof.* ⟨See PROOF.⟩

prop[1] [prɒp] *v* **propped, prop·ping 1** hold

up with a support (often with *up*): *to prop up the clothesline with a stick.* **2** support (often with *up*): *to prop a failing cause.* **prop** *n.* ⟨Middle Dutch *proppe*⟩

prop² [prɒp] *n Informal* any article, such as a table or a weapon, used in staging a play. ⟨short for *(stage) property*⟩

prop·a·gan·da [ˌprɒpə'gændə] *n* efforts to spread opinions by distortion and deception. **prop·a·gan·dist** *n, adj.* **prop·a·gan·dize** *v.* ⟨Latin *propaganda fide* propagation of the faith. See PROPAGATE.⟩

prop·a·gate ['prɒpəˌgeit] *v* **1** produce offspring: *Trees propagate themselves by scattering seeds.* **2** increase in number: *During this hard winter, deep potholes have propagated on all the city streets.* **3** spread (news, knowledge, etc.): *Don't propagate unkind reports.* **prop·a·ga·ble** *adj.* **prop·a·ga·tor** *n.* **prop·a·ga·tion** *n.* ⟨Latin *propagare* to plant slips; *pangere* make fast⟩

pro·pane [prou'pein] *or* ['proupein] *n* a hydrocarbon gas of the methane series, found in petroleum. ⟨*prop(yl)* + *(meth)ane*⟩

pro·pel [prə'pɛl] *v* **-pelled, -pel·ling** drive forward: *to propel a boat by oars, a person propelled by ambition.* **pro·pel·la·ble** *adj.* ⟨Latin *pro-* forward + *pellere* push⟩
pro·pel·lant *n* something that propels, such as the fuel of a missile or the gas under that dispenses the contents of an aerosol container. **pro·pel·ler** *n* a device with blades, for driving forward boats and aircraft. **pro·pul·sion** [prə'pʌlʃən] *n* the process of driving forward. **pro·pul·sive** *adj.*

pro·pen·si·ty [prə'pɛnsɪti] *n* a natural inclination: *Many academics have a propensity for wordiness.* ⟨Latin *propensus* pp of *propendere*; *pro-* forward + *pendere* hang⟩

prop·er ['prɒpər] *adj* **1** correct; fitting: *Night is the proper time to sleep.* **2** strictly so called (usually after the noun): *The population of Vancouver proper does not include that of the suburbs.* **3** decent; respectable: *proper conduct.* **4** *Informal* **a** complete; thorough: *You must make a proper effort to sort out that pile of papers.* **b** excellent: *That was a proper meal, that was!* **5** overly concerned with correctness: *He is a very proper man and is easily scandalized.*
n Christianity the parts of a liturgy, such as the mass, that vary according to the day and time of day. **prop·er·ly** ['prɒpərli] *adv.* ⟨Latin *proprius* one's own⟩
proper adjective *Grammar* an adjective formed from a PROPER NOUN and always capitalized. *Example:* the French language. **proper fraction** *Mathematics* a fraction less than 1. **proper noun** or **name** *Grammar* a noun that identifies one particular person, place, organization, etc. *Sarah, Calgary,* and *Renaissance* are proper nouns. Compare COMMON NOUN.

prop·er·ty ['prɒpərti] *n* **1** possessions. **2** a piece of land: *She owns some property out West.* **3** a quality belonging to something: *Soap has* the property of removing dirt. **4 properties** *pl* the furniture, weapons, etc., used in staging a play, film, or television scene. ⟨Latin *proprietas.* See PROPER.⟩
prop·er·tied *adj* owning property.

SYNONYMS
Property suggests whatever someone legally owns, including land, buildings, animals, money, stocks, documents, objects, and rights: *Landed property is taxable.* **Goods** suggests movable personal property, as distinguished from land, buildings, etc., and applies chiefly to things such as furniture, furnishings, and implements, but never to money or papers, etc.: *Professional movers packed our goods.* **Effects** applies to personal possessions, including money, clothing, jewellery, personal belongings, and papers: *My sister and I packed all our effects.*

pro·phase ['prou,feiz] *n Biology* the first stage of mitosis, in which changes take place in the nucleus of a cell.

proph·e·cy ['prɒfəsi] *n* **1** the foretelling of future events. **2** a divinely inspired utterance, writing, etc. **proph·e·sy** ['prɒfə,saɪ] *v.* ⟨Greek *prophēteia*; *prophētēs* prophet; *pro-* for + *phanai* speak⟩
proph·et ['prɒfɪt] *n* **1** a person who tells what will happen. **2** someone who is believed to be inspired by God or a god: *Every religion has its prophets.* **3 the Prophet a** Muhammad. **b** Joseph Smith, the founder of the Mormon religion. **4 the Prophets** *pl* **a** the twenty-one books that constitute the second main division of the Hebrew Bible. **b** in Christian use, the sixteen books of the Old Testament that are named after prophets. **pro·phet·ic** *adj* **1** containing prophecy: *a prophetic saying.* **2** giving warning of what is to happen: *prophetic words.* **pro·phet·i·cal·ly** *adv.*

pro·phy·lac·tic [ˌprɒfə'læktɪk] *or* [ˌprou-] *adj* **1** protecting from disease. **2** protective; preservative; precautionary.
n **1** *Medicine* a treatment that protects against disease. **2** precaution. **3** a contraceptive device. **pro·phy·lac·ti·cal·ly** *adv.* ⟨Greek *pro-* before + *phylakos* a guard⟩
pro·phy·lax·is [ˌprɒfə'læksɪs] *or* [ˌprou-] *n* **1** protection from disease. **2** contraception.

pro·pin·qui·ty [prə'pɪŋkwəti] *n* **1** nearness in time or place, esp personal nearness. **2** nearness of blood; kinship. ⟨Latin *propinquitas*; *prope* near⟩

pro·pi·ti·ate [prə'pɪʃiˌeit] *v* prevent or reduce the anger of. **pro·pi·ti·a·tor** *n.* **pro·pi·ti·a·ble** *adj.* **pro·pi·ti·a·tive** *adj.* ⟨Latin *propitiare*; *propitius.* See PROPITIOUS.⟩
pro·pi·ti·a·tion *n* **1** the act of reducing anger, etc. **2** something that propitiates: *The flowers were a propitiation for my unkind words.* **pro·pi·ti·a·to·ry** *adj* intended to reduce anger, etc.; conciliatory: *a propitiatory offering.*

pro·pi·tious [prə'pɪʃəs] *adj* **1** favourable: *propitious weather for our trip.* **2** favourably inclined; gracious: *a propitious attitude.*

pro·pi·tious·ly *adv.* **pro·pi·tious·ness** *n.* ⟨Latin *propitius; pro-* forward + *petere* go toward⟩

pro·po·nent See PROPOUND.

pro·por·tion [prə'pɔrʃən] *n* **1** the relation in size, number, etc., of one thing to another: *the proportion of flour to milk in a recipe* **2** a proper relation between parts: *Her short legs were out of proportion with her long body.* **3 proportions** *pl* dimensions. **4** a part: *A large proportion of BC is rocky.* **5** *Mathematics* an equality of ratios: *Example: 4:2 = 10:5.* *v* fit (one thing to another) so that they complement each other in size or scale: *The designs in that rug are well proportioned.* ⟨Latin *proportio; pro portione* in relation to the part⟩ **pro·por·tion·al** *adj* in the proper relation: *Price is proportional to demand.* **pro·por·tion·al·ly** *adv.* **proportional representation** an electoral system in which the number of seats that each party or group is given is proportional to its share of the total number of votes cast. **pro·por·tion·ate** [-nɪt] *adj* in the proper proportion: *The profit from the bazaar was not proportionate to the effort we put into it.* **pro·por·tion·ate·ly** *adv.*

pro·pose [prə'pouz] *v* **1** put forward for consideration. **2** present (someone) for office, membership, etc. **3** present as the object of (a toast to be drunk): *May I propose a toast to the chair?* **4** intend: *She proposes to save half of all she earns.* **5** make an offer of marriage. **pro·pos·al** *n.* **pro·pos·er** *n.* ⟨French *pro-* forth + *poser* put. See POSE.⟩ **prop·o·si·tion** *n* **1** something presented for consideration. **2** *Logic* a statement affirming or denying something, that is to be proved true or false. **3** *Informal* a suggestion to engage in illicit sexual intercourse. *v Informal* make a suggestion to (someone), especially to engage in illicit sexual intercourse.

SYNONYMS
Proposal indicates a suggestion, offer, plan, or terms put forward for consideration and acceptance or action, but emphasizes the idea of offering for acceptance or refusal, or suggesting for consideration: *The young people made a proposal to the City Council.* **Proposition** emphasizes the specific arrangement put forward as a proposal, the statement of the terms, and the details of the plan, especially from a contractual point of view: *The Council approved the idea, but not the proposition set forth.*

pro·pound [prə'paʊnd] *v* put forward; propose: *to propound a theory.* **pro·pound·er** *n.* ⟨earlier *propoune*; Latin *pro-* before + *ponere* set⟩ **pro·po·nent** [prə'pounənt] *n* **1** one who makes a proposition. **2** a supporter.

pro·pri·e·tar·y [prə'praɪə,tɛri] *adj* controlled by a private person as property. A **proprietary medicine** can be made only by a certain person or persons. ⟨Latin *proprietas* ownership; *proprius* one's own⟩ **pro·pri·e·tor** *n* an owner, esp of a business. **pro·pri·e·tor·ship** *n.*

pro·pri·e·ty [prə'praɪəti] *n* **1** proper behaviour: *She acted with propriety.* **2 proprieties** *pl* the conventional standards of proper behaviour. ⟨Latin *proprietas* appropriateness. See PROPER.⟩

pro·pul·sion See PROPEL.

pro ra·ta ['prou 'rɑtə] *or* ['reitə] according to the share, interest, etc. of each. ⟨Latin *pro rata parte* according to the portion figured (for each). See RATE.⟩ **pro·rate** [,prou'reit] *v* distribute proportionally: *We prorated the money according to the number of hours each had worked.* **pro·ra·tion** *n.*

pro·rogue [prou'roug] *v* discontinue the meetings of (a lawmaking body) for a time: *Parliament will be prorogued for the summer recess.* ⟨Latin *pro-* forward + *rogare* ask for⟩

pro·sa·ic See PROSE.

pro·sce·ni·um [prou'siniəm] *n, pl* **-ni·a** [-niə] **1** the part of the stage in front of the curtain. **2** the curtain and the framework that holds it (**proscenium arch**). ⟨Greek *pro-* in front of + *skēnē* stage⟩

pro·sciut·to [prə'ʃutou] *Italian* [pro'ʃutto] *n* a dried Italian ham. ⟨Italian *prosciugare* dry out⟩

pro·scribe [prou'skraɪb] *v* **1** prohibit as wrong: *to proscribe cardplaying.* **2** outlaw. **3** banish. **4** formerly, publish (someone's name) as condemned to death, exile, etc. **pro·scrib·er** *n.* **pro·scrip·tion** [prou'skrɪpʃən] *n.* **pro·scrip·tive** *adj.* **pro·scrip·tive·ly** *adv.* ⟨Latin *pro-* publicly + *scribere* write⟩

prose [prouz] *n* language not arranged in poetic metre: *This writer's prose is better than most people's poetry.* ⟨Latin *prosa* straight; *pro(ve)rsus; pro-* forward + *vertere* turn⟩ **pro·sa·ic** [prou'zeiik] *adj* like prose; not imaginative; matter-of-fact. **pro·sa·i·cal·ly** *adv.* **pro·saic·ness** *n.* **pros·y** *adj* **1** like prose. **2** wordy. **3** commonplace; dull; tiresome. **pros·i·ly** *adv.* **pros·i·ness** *n.*

pros·e·cute ['prɒsə,kjut] *v Law* **1** bring before a court. **2** carry out: *The government prosecuted an inquiry into the company's failure.* ⟨Latin *prosecutus* pp of *prosequi; pro-* forth + *sequi* follow⟩ **pros·e·cu·tion** *n* **1** *Civil Law* the carrying on of a lawsuit: *She abandoned her prosecution of the case for damages.* **2** *Criminal Law* the side that institutes criminal proceedings against another. The prosecution makes charges that must be answered by the defence. **pros·e·cu·tor** *n.*

pros·e·lyte ['prɒsə,laɪt] *n* a convert from one opinion, religious belief, etc. to another. ⟨Greek *pros-* over + *elytos* one who has come⟩ **pros·e·lyt·ize** ['prɒsələ,taɪz] *v* make converts.

pros·o·dy ['prɒsədi] *n* **1** the science of poetic metres and versification. **2** *Linguistics* the stress and intonation of an utterance. ⟨Greek *pros* in addition to + *ōidē* song, poem⟩

pros·pect ['prɒspɛkt] *n* **1** anything expected or looked forward to. **2** expectation: *The prospect of a vacation is pleasant.* **3** the outlook for the future. **4** a person who may be a customer, candidate, etc.: *The sales rep had several prospects in mind.* **5** a view: *a fine prospect.* **6** *Mining* a mining area appearing to have attractive mineral deposits. *v* search (for minerals): *to prospect for gold.* ⟨Latin *pro-* forward + *specere* look⟩ **pro·spec·tive** *adj* probable; expected: *a prospective client.* **pro·spec·tive·ly** *adv.* **pros·pec·tor** ['prɒspɛktər] *n* a person who explores for gold, silver, oil, etc. **pro·spec·tus** *n* a booklet advertising something, like programs offered by a college, or stocks, etc. of interest to investors.

pros·per ['prɒspər] *v* **1** be successful. **2** make successful. **pros·per·i·ty** *n.* **pros·per·ous** *adj.* **pros·per·ous·ly** *adv.* ⟨Latin *prosperare*⟩

pros·tate ['prɒsteit] *Anatomy n* a gland surrounding the male urethra. It controls the release of urine. **pros·tate** *adj.* ⟨Greek *pro-* in front + *states* standing; *stenai* stand⟩

pros·the·sis [prɒs'θisɪs] *or* ['prɒsθəsɪs] *n, pl* -ses [-siz] a false tooth, artificial leg, etc. added to the body. **pros·thet·ic** *adj.* ⟨Greek *pros-* in addition to + *thesis; tithenai* put⟩ **pros·thet·ics** *n* (with sg verb) the branch of dentistry or surgery pertaining to prosthesis. **pros·the·tist** *n.*

pros·ti·tute ['prɒstə,tjut] *or* ['prɒstə,tut] *n* a person who accepts payment for sexual acts. *v* **1** offer (oneself or another person) for hire to engage in sexual acts. **2** give up (oneself or one's talents) to an unworthy cause: *He has prostituted his art by selling paintings that he knows are not well done.* **pros·ti·tu·tion** *n.* ⟨Latin *pro-* publicly + *statuere* cause to stand⟩

pros·trate ['prɒstreit] *v* **1** lay (oneself) down flat, face downward: *The captives prostrated themselves before the conqueror.* **2** make weak or helpless: *Sickness can prostrate people.* **pros·trate** *adj.* **pros·tra·tion** *n.* ⟨Latin *prostratus* pp of *prosternere; pro-* forth + *sternere* strew⟩

pros·y See PROSE.

pro·tac·tin·i·um [,proutæk'tɪniəm] *n* a radioactive metallic element found in uranium ores. *Symbol* **Pa** ⟨*proto-* + *actinium*⟩

pro·tag·o·nist [prə'tægənɪst] *n* **1** the main character in a play, story, or novel. **2** a person who takes a leading part; active supporter. ⟨Greek *prōtos* first + *agōnistēs* actor; *agōn* contest⟩

pro·te·an ['proutiən] *or* [prou'tiən] *adj* readily assuming different forms or characters; exceedingly variable. ⟨*Proteus* Greek sea god of variable form⟩

pro·tect [prə'tɛkt] *v* shield from harm; guard. **pro·tec·tive** *adj.* **pro·tec·tive·ly** *adv.* **pro·tec·tive·ness** *n.* **pro·tec·tor** *n.* ⟨Latin *pro-* in front + *tegere* to cover⟩ **pro·tec·tion** [prə'tɛkʃən] *n* **1** defence. **2** a thing or person that prevents damage: *This old shirt is my protection against paint splatters.* **3** *Economics* the system of taxing imported foreign goods so that people are more likely to buy goods made in their own country. **4** *Informal* the payment of money to gangsters in order not to be harmed. **pro·tec·tion·ism** *n Economics* the system of PROTECTION (def. 3). **pro·tec·tion·ist** *n, adj.* **pro·tec·tor·ate** *n* an underdeveloped country under the control of a strong country.

pro·té·gé ['proutə,ʒei] *n* a person under the patronage or protection of another. **pro·té·gée** *n fem.* ⟨French, pp of *protéger* protect. See PROTECT.⟩

pro·tein ['proutin] *n Biochemistry* a complex compound containing nitrogen that is a necessary part of the cells of animals and plants. ⟨Greek *prōteios* of the first quality⟩

pro tem·po·re [,prou 'tɛmpəri] *or* ['tɛmpərei] *Latin* for the time being; temporarily. Often shortened to **pro tem.**

pro·test ['proutɛst] a statement that denies or objects strongly. **pro·test** [prə'tɛst] *or* ['proutɛst] *v.* **pro·test·er** *n.* **pro·test·ing** *adj.* ⟨Latin *pro-* forth + *testari* testify⟩ **under protest** unwillingly.

Prot·es·tant ['prɒtəstənt] *n* generally, any Christian who is not a member of the Roman Catholic or Eastern Orthodox Churches. Baptists, Presbyterians, United Church members, and many others are Protestants. **Prot·es·tant** *adj.* **Prot·es·tant·ism** *n.* **prot·es·ta·tion** [,prɒtɪ'steɪʃən] *or* [,prou-] *n* a solemn declaration: *a protestation of innocence.*

Pro·tis·ta [prou'tɪstə] *n Biology* in some systems of classification, a kingdom of one-celled organisms having characteristics common to plants and animals alike, such as algae, bacteria, yeast, etc. ⟨Greek = very first ones; *protos* first⟩ **pro·tist** ['proutɪst] *n* any organism of the group Protista.

proto– *combining form* **1** first in time, rank, etc.: *prototype.* **2** **Proto–** designating the earliest reconstructed stage of a language: *Proto-Germanic.* ⟨Greek *protos* first⟩

pro·to·col ['proutə,kɒl] *or* ['proutə,koul] *n* **1** a first draft from which a treaty is prepared. **2** the rules of etiquette of the diplomatic corps. **3** the rules for any procedure. ⟨Greek *prōtos* first + *kolla* glue; for first leaf glued to a papyrus roll, giving date and contents⟩

pro·ton ['proutɒn] *n Physics, Chemistry* a nuclear particle carrying one unit of positive electric charge, found in the nucleus of every kind of atom. ⟨Greek = first⟩

pro·to·plasm ['proutə,plæzəm] *n Biology* a soft jelly that is the living substance of all plant and animal cells, consisting mainly of water, lipids, proteins, carbohydrates, and inorganic salts. **pro·to·plas·mic** *adj.* ⟨*proto-* + Greek *plasma* moulded thing; *plassein* mould⟩

pro·to·type ['proutə,taɪp] *n* the first type of anything: *A modern ship has its prototype in the hollowed log.* **pro·to·typ·i·cal** [-,tɪpɪkəl] *adj.*

pro·to·zo·an [,proutə'zouən] *n, pl* -**zo·ans** *or* -**zo·a** [-'zouə] any of a phylum of minute, single-celled organisms found throughout the world in fresh water, in the oceans at all depths, and in the soil. **pro·to·zo·an** *adj.* ⟨*proto-* + Greek *zōion* animal⟩

pro·tract [prə'trækt] *v* **1** lengthen in time: *to protract a visit.* **2** thrust out; extend. **pro·tract·ed** *adj.* **pro·tract·ed·ly** *adv.* **pro·tract·ed·ness** *n.* **pro·tract·i·ble** *adj.* **pro·trac·tion** *n.* ⟨Latin *protractus* pp of *protrahere*; *pro-* forward + *trahere* drag⟩ **pro·trac·tile** [prə'træktaɪl] *or* [-təl] *adj* capable of being lengthened out, or of being thrust forth. The turtle has a protractile head. **pro·trac·tor** [prə'træktər] *or* ['proutræktər] *n* an instrument for measuring angles.

pro·trude [prə'trud] *v* **1** stick out: *The saucy child protruded her tongue.* **2** be thrust forth: *Her teeth protrude too far.* **pro·trud·ent** *adj.* **pro·tru·sion** *n.* ⟨Latin *pro-* forward + *trudere* thrust⟩ **pro·tru·sile** [prə'trusaɪl] *or* [-səl] *adj* capable of being thrust out, as an elephant's trunk or the tongue of a hummingbird.

pro·tu·ber·ant [prə'tjubərənt] *or* [prə'tubərənt] *adj* bulging out; sticking out. **pro·tu·ber·ance** *n.* **pro·tu·ber·ant·ly** *adv.* ⟨Latin *pro-* forward + *tuber* lump⟩ **pro·tu·ber·ate** *v* swell out or bulge, so as to form a rounded projection.

proud [praʊd] *adj* **1** feeling gratified. **2** thinking too well of oneself. **3** highly gratifying: *a proud moment.* **pride** *n.* **proud·ly** *adv.* ⟨Old French *prod, prud* valiant; Latin *prode* useful; *prodesse* be useful⟩ **do someone** (or **oneself**) **proud** honour or distinguish: *Her generosity did her proud.* **proud of** thinking well of.

> **SYNONYMS**
> **Proud** may mean either holding oneself above anything low, mean, or contemptible or thinking oneself better than others, but usually also suggests a haughty or conceited manner or appearance: *She has a strong, proud face.* **Overbearing** suggests being rudely dictatorial or haughtily insulting in behaviour and speech: *Promoted too quickly, the conceited youth became overbearing.* **Supercilious** suggests conceit, but emphasizes a coolly scornful attitude: *With a supercilious smile she refused our invitation.*

prove See PROOF.

prov·e·nance ['prɒvənəns] *n* origin or source: *the provenance of a painting.* ⟨Latin *pro-* forth + *venire* come⟩

prov·erb ['prɒvərb] *n* **1** a saying expressing a general truth. *Examples: A stitch in time saves nine. Look before you leap.* **2** a well-known example: *He is a proverb for carelessness.* ⟨Latin *pro-* forth + *verbum* word, speech⟩ **pro·ver·bi·al** *adj* **1** to do with proverbs: *proverbial wisdom.* **2** that has become a proverb: *the proverbial stitch in time.* **3** well-known: *the proverbial loyalty of dogs.* **pro·ver·bi·al·ly** *adv.*

pro·vide [prə'vaɪd] *v* **1** supply: *Who will provide the costumes?* **2** supply means of support: *Parents provide for their children.* **3** take care for the future: *to provide against accident.* **pro·vid·er** *n.* ⟨Latin *pro-* ahead + *videre* see⟩

pro·vid·ed or **pro·vid·ing** *conj* provided that; if: *She will go provided I go too.* **prov·i·dence** *n* **1** God's care and help. **2** care or preparation for the future. **prov·i·dent** *adj* **1** careful in providing for the future. **2** economical; frugal. **prov·i·dent·ly** *adv.* **prov·i·den·tial** *adj* **1** fortunate: *The delay was providential, for the bus we had planned to take broke down.* **2** to do with divine influence. **prov·i·den·tial·ly** *adv.*

pro·vi·sion [prə'vɪʒən] *n* **1** a statement making a condition: *A provision of the lease is that the rent must be paid promptly.* **2** a taking care for the future. **3 provisions** *pl* a supply of food and drinks. **make provision** take care for the future. **pro·vi·sion·al** *adj* for the time being: *a provisional government.* **pro·vi·sion·al·ly** *adv.* **pro·vi·so** [prə'vaɪzou] *n, pl* **-sos** or **-soes** part of an agreement that states a condition: *He was admitted to the class with the proviso that he was to be put back if he failed.* **pro·vi·so·ry** *adj.* **pro·vi·so·ri·ly** *adv.*

prov·ince ['prɒvəns] *n* **1** one of the ten main political divisions, which, together with the territories, make up Canada. **2** a similar division in other countries. **3** proper extent of function: *It was within the province of the committee to make such decisions.* ⟨Latin *provincia* territory gained by conquest⟩ **pro·vin·cial** [prə'vɪnʃəl] *adj* **1** to do with the provinces, as opposed to the federal government of Canada: *Education is a provincial power in Canada, while justice is federal.* **2** narrow in outlook: *a provincial point of view.* **pro·vin·cial·ly** *adv.* **provincial park** ✳ land established by a provincial government as a wildlife preserve and as a holiday area.

pro·vi·sion See PROVIDE.

pro·vo·ca·teur [prə,vɒkə'tɜr] *French* [pʀɔvɔka'tœʀ] *n* one who stirs up trouble or provokes violence. **pro·vo·ca·teur** *adj* (after the noun). ⟨French⟩

pro·voke [prə'vouk] *v* **1** make angry; vex. **2** stir up: *An insult provokes a person to anger.* **3** call forth; bring about. **prov·o·ca·tion** *n.* ⟨Latin *pro-* forth + *vocare* call⟩ **pro·voc·a·tive** *adj* **1** irritating. **2** stimulating: *a remark provocative of mirth.* **3** arousing sexual interest. **pro·voc·a·tive·ly** *adv.* **pro·voc·a·tive·ness** *n.*

prow [praʊ] *n* **1** the pointed front part of a ship or boat; bow. **2** the projecting front part of anything: *the prow of an aircraft.* ⟨French *proue*; Greek *prōira*; *pro-* forward⟩

prow·ess ['praʊɪs] *n* **1** bravery; daring. **2** unusual skill or ability. ⟨Old French *proece*; *prod* valiant. See PROUD.⟩

prowl [praʊl] *v* **1** secretly hunt for something to eat or steal: *Many wild animals prowl at night.* **2** wander about (a place): *prowling the streets.* **prowl** *n.* **prowl·er** *n.* ⟨Middle English *prollen*⟩ **on the prowl** prowling about.

prox·im·i·ty [prɒk'sɪməti] *n* nearness. ⟨Latin *proximus* nearest⟩

prox·y ['prɒksi] *n* **1** a person authorized to act for another: *He acted as a proxy for the* *child's godfather.* 2 a statement authorizing a proxy to act or vote for a person. ⟨Middle English alteration of *procuracy* office of proctor⟩

prude [prud] *n* a person who shows excessive propriety or modesty, esp with regard to sexual matters. **prud·er·y** *n*. **prud·ish** *adj*. ⟨French *prudefemme* excellent woman; Old French *prod* (see PROUD) + *femme* woman⟩

pru·dent ['prudənt] *adj* 1 planning carefully ahead of time: *A prudent worker saves part of his or her wages.* 2 characterized by good judgment: *a prudent policy.* **pru·dence** *n*. **pru·dent·ly** *adv*. ⟨Latin *prudens* variant of *providens*. See PROVIDE.⟩

SYNONYMS

Prudence emphasizes common sense in directing one's affairs, giving thought to one's actions and their consequences, and usually suggests caution, watchfulness, and saving: *Prudence is wisdom in everyday life.* **Foresight** emphasizes ability to see what is likely to happen, and giving thought to being prepared: *They had the foresight to arrange for travel insurance before going on their trip.*

prune¹ [prun] *n* a dried plum. ⟨Latin *prunum*, Greek *proumnon*⟩

prune² [prun] *v* 1 cut out undesirable parts from: *to prune a wordy manuscript.* 2 cut undesirable branches from (a bush, tree, etc.), in order to improve productivity. ⟨Old French *prooignier; pro-* + *rooignier* clip, round off; Latin *rotundus* round⟩

pru·ri·ent ['prʊriənt] *adj* having or exciting lustful thoughts. **pru·ri·ence** *n*. **pru·ri·ent·ly** *adv*. ⟨Latin *prurire* itch, be wanton⟩

pry¹ [praɪ] *v* inquire into (other people's affairs) with curiosity. **pry·ing** *adj*. ⟨Middle English *prien*⟩

pry² [praɪ] *v* 1 move by force, esp by using a lever. 2 get with much effort: *We finally pried the secret out of her.*
n a lever for prying. ⟨obsolete *prize* lever, taken as pl; Old French *prise* a grasp⟩

P.S. postscript (for Latin *post scriptum*).

psalm [sɒm] *n* a sacred song or poem. ⟨Greek *psalmos* playing of a stringed instrument; *psallein* pluck⟩
psalm·o·dy ['sɒmədi] *or* ['sælmədi] *n* 1 the art of singing psalms or composing music for them. 2 psalms or hymns. **psalm·o·dist** *n*. **psal·mod·ic** [sæl'mɒdɪk] *adj*.

PSAT ['pisæt] Preliminary Scholastic Aptitude Test.

pse·phol·o·gy [sɛ'fɒlədʒi] *n* the study of election trends, based on statistical evidence. **pse·pho·log·i·cal** *adj*. **pse·phol·o·gist** *n*. ⟨Greek *psephos* pebble (used as ballot)⟩

pseudo– *combining form* false; spurious: *pseudo-intellectual, pseudonym.* Also, sometimes before a vowel, **pseud-**. ⟨Greek⟩

pseu·do·nym ['sudə,nɪm] *n* a name used by an author instead of his or her real name.

pseu·do·nym·i·ty *n*. **pseu·do·nym·ous** *adj*. ⟨*pseudo-* + Greek *onyma* name⟩

psi or **p.s.i.** pounds per square inch.

psi·lo·cybe ['saɪlə,saɪb] *or* ['sɪlə,saɪb] *n* the mushroom commonly called 'magic mushroom'. ⟨Greek *psilos* bare + *kybe* head⟩

psit·ta·co·sis [,sɪtə'koʊsɪs] *n* a contagious disease of parrots and other birds, communicable to people. ⟨Greek *psittakos* parrot⟩

pso·ri·a·sis [sə'raɪəsɪs] *n Pathology* a skin disease characterized by scaly red patches, and highly resistant to treatment. ⟨Greek *psorian* to itch⟩

psy·che ['saɪki] *n* 1 the human spirit. 2 the mind. ⟨Greek = breath, life⟩
psych out [saɪk] *Informal* a lose one's nerve. b upset (someone): *Her remark psyched out her opponent.* c figure out: *Psych it out for yourself.*
psych up *Informal* prepare mentally for a task, performance, etc.
psy·che·del·ic [,saɪkə'dɛlɪk] *adj* 1 to do with drugs that can produce abnormal changes in the mind. 2 suggesting the bizarre colours, sounds, etc. associated with the effects of psychedelic drugs: *psychedelic music.* **psy·chic** *adj* 1 mental: *illness due to psychic causes.* 2 outside the known laws of physics; supernatural. 3 very susceptible to psychic influences; clairvoyant, able to contact spirits, etc. *n* a psychic person; a medium. **psy·chi·cal·ly** *adv*.

psy·chi·a·try [sə'kaɪətri] *n* the branch of medicine dealing with mental disorders. **psy·chi·at·ric** [,saɪki'ætrɪk] *adj*.
psy·chi·at·ri·cal·ly *adv*. **psy·chi·a·trist** *n*. ⟨*psycho* + Greek *iatreia* treatment⟩

psy·chic See PSYCHE.

psy·cho ['saɪkoʊ] *Slang n* a psychopath or psychotic. **psy·cho** *adj*. ⟨shortened form⟩

psycho– *combining form* mind: *psychoanalysis.* Also, **psych–** before some vowels. ⟨Greek *psychē* soul, mind⟩
psy·cho·a·nal·y·sis *n* [-ə'næləsɪs] a method of treating mental disorders, by bringing to light any subconscious forces that have affected the person's mind. **psy·cho·an·a·lyt·ic** [-,ænə'lɪtɪk] *or* **psy·cho·an·a·lyt·i·cal** *adj*.
psy·cho·an·a·lyze *or* **psy·cho·an·a·lyse** *v*.
psy·cho·an·a·lyst *n*. **psy·cho·bab·ble** *n* talk that uses jargon from psychology or psychiatry in a trite or superficial way. **psy·cho·ki·ne·sis** [-kɪ'nisɪs] *n* control of objects by the force of the mind, without the use of any known physical energy. **psy·cho·mo·tor** *adj* to do with muscular activity resulting from mental processes. **psy·cho·path** ['saɪkə,pæθ] *n* one whose behaviour is characterized by extremely amoral and antisocial tendencies. **psy·cho·path·ic** *adj*. **psy·cho·path·i·cal·ly** *adv*. **psy·cho·so·mat·ic** [-sə'mætɪk] *adj* 1 to do with both mind and body. 2 to do with physical disorders caused by mental disturbances. **psy·cho·so·mat·i·cal·ly** *adv*. **psy·cho·ther·a·py** *n* the science of treating mental or physical disorders by psychological techniques.

psy·cho·ther·a·pist *n*. **psy·cho·trop·ic** [-'trɒpɪk] *or* [-'troupɪk] *adj* of a drug, capable of acting on the mind, as tranquillizers do.

psy·chol·o·gy [səi'kɒlədʒi] *n* the study of the mind and the ways of thought. **psy·chol·o·gist** *n*. ⟨Greek *psychē* soul, mind⟩ **psy·cho·log·i·cal** *adj* **1** of the mind. **2** to do with psychology or psychologists.
psy·cho·log·i·cal·ly *adv*. **psychological warfare** systematic efforts to affect morale, loyalty, etc., esp of large national groups.

psy·cho·mo·tor, psy·cho·path See PSYCHO-.

psy·cho·sis [səi'kousɪs] *n, pl* **-ses** [-siz] any severe form of mental disturbance or disease, which may or may not have an organic basis. **psy·chot·ic** *adj*. ⟨Greek *psychē* soul, mind⟩

psy·cho·so·mat·ic, psy·cho·ther·a·py See PSYCHO-.

psy·chot·ic See PSYCHOSIS.

psy·cho·trop·ic See PSYCHO-.

PTA or **P.T.A.** PARENT-TEACHER ASSOCIATION.

ptar·mi·gan ['tɑrməgən] *n, pl* **-gans** or (esp collectively) **-gan** any of several species of arctic and alpine grouse having plumage that is mainly white in winter and mainly brown in summer. ⟨Scots Gaelic *tarmachan, p* added by confusion with Greek *pteron* feather⟩

pter·o·dac·tyl [ˌtɛrə'dæktəl] *n* any of an order of extinct flying reptiles that lived during the Jurassic and Cretaceous periods. ⟨Greek *pteron* wing + *daktylos* finger⟩

pto·maine or **pto·main** ['toumein] *or* [tou'mein] *n* any of several chemical compounds produced by the decomposition of protein. ⟨Greek *ptōma* corpse⟩
ptomaine poisoning food poisoning, formerly attributed to ptomaines, caused by bacteria found in decaying food.

pub [pʌb] *Informal n* a beer parlour or tavern. ⟨short for *public house*⟩

pu·ber·ty ['pjubərti] *n* the stage when the body becomes capable of sexual reproduction. ⟨Latin *pubertas; pubes* adult⟩
pu·bes·cent *adj* **1** arriving or arrived at puberty. **2** *Botany, zoology* covered with down or fine hair: *a pubescent leaf.* **pu·bes·cence** *n*.
pu·bic *adj* to do with the the pubis, the lower front portion of the hipbone.

pub·lic ['pʌblɪk] *adj* **1** to do with the people as a whole: *public affairs.* **2** open to all the people: *a public park.* **3** known to many or all; not private: *The fact became public.*
n **the public** the people in general: *The public will not accept more restraints.* **pub·lic·ly** *adv*. ⟨Latin *publicus; poplicus* (influenced by *pubes* adult); *populus* people⟩
go public a issue shares for sale to the public, thus becoming a PUBLIC COMPANY. **b** reveal previously concealed information to the public. **in public** not in private; openly. **public address system** loudspeakers used to carry messages, music, etc. to an audience in a large room, in different rooms of one building, or in the open air. *Abbrev* **P.A.** **pub·li·ca·tion** *n* **1** anything that is published.

2 the act of making known. **public company** a company owned by shareholders whose shares can be freely traded on the Stock Exchange. **public domain** *Law* of works, material, etc., never copyrighted or having an expired copyright. **in the public domain** available for unrestricted use because unprotected by copyright or patent: *Gilbert and Sullivan's operas are now in the public domain.* **public enemy** a person who is a danger to the public. **pub·li·cist** *n* a public relations expert or press agent. **pub·lic·i·ty** [pə'blɪsəti] *n* **1** the act of bringing to public notice through newspapers, signs, radio, TV, etc.: *the recent publicity about environmental concerns.* **2** public notice: *the publicity that actors desire.* **pub·li·cize** *v*. **public relations 1** the relations of an organization, with the public. **2** the activities an organization undertakes to create a favourable public image of itself. *Abbrev* **P.R.** or **PR 3** the business of promoting such an image. **public school 1** in Canada and the US, a tax-supported school, esp an elementary school. **2** in the UK, a private boarding school. **public service 1** CIVIL SERVICE. **public servant. 2** a service given for the benefit of the community: *a drop-in centre run as a public service.* **public–service** *adj*. **pub·lic–spir·it·ed** *adj* having an unselfish desire for the public good. **public utility** a company formed to render services to the public, such as a company furnishing electricity. **public works** things built by the government at public expense and for public use, such as roads.

pub·lish ['pʌblɪʃ] *v* **1** prepare (a book, paper, map, piece of music, etc.) for sale. **2** publish the work of: *Some Canadian writers are published abroad before being published in Canada.* **3** make publicly known: *Don't publish your faults.* **pub·lish·a·ble** *adj*. ⟨Old French *publier;* Latin *publicus* public⟩
pub·lish·er *n* a person or company whose business is to publish books, newspapers, etc.

puce [pjus] *adj* dark purple. ⟨French = flea; Old French *pulce;* Latin *pulicis*⟩

puck [pʌk] *n* a hard, black rubber disk used in hockey. ⟨English dialect variant of *poke¹*⟩
puck–car·ri·er *n* the player in possession of the puck during play. **puck·chas·er, puck·push·er,** or **puck·ster** *n Slang* a hockey player. **puck shy** of a goalie, afraid of being hit by the puck.

puck·er ['pʌkər] *v* draw into wrinkles: *to pucker one's brow.* ⟨apparently; *poke²*⟩

puck·ish ['pʌkɪʃ] *adj* mischievous; impish. **puck·ish·ly** *adv*. **puck·ish·ness** *n*. ⟨Puck fairy prankster in Shakespeare's *A Midsummer Night's Dream*⟩

pud·ding ['pʊdɪŋ] *n* **1** a soft dessert: *rice pudding.* **2** a cakelike dessert: *plum pudding.* **3** a sausage, esp **blood pudding.** ⟨perhaps Old French *boudin* sausage or Old English *puduc* blister⟩

pud·dle ['pʌdəl] *n* a small pool of liquid. *v* make wet or muddy. **pud·dly** *adj*. ⟨Middle English *puddel* diminutive of *pudd* ditch⟩

pu·den·dum [pjuˈdɛndəm] *n, pl* **-da** [-də] *Anatomy* the external genitalia of either sex, but especially those of the female. ⟨Latin *pudere* be ashamed⟩

pudg·y [ˈpʌdʒi] *adj* short and fat or thick. **pudg·i·ly** *adv.* **pudg·i·ness** *n.* ⟨Scots dialect⟩

pueb·lo [ˈpweblou] *or* [ˈpweiblou] *n, pl* **-los** **1** a communal dwelling of certain Native American peoples of the SW United States, consisting of flat-roofed houses of adobe or stone. **2** a Native American village in the SW United States. **3 Pueblo** *pl* **-lo** *or* **-los** a member of any of several Native American peoples of the SW United States, who live or lived in pueblos. ⟨Spanish = people; Latin *populus*⟩

pu·er·ile [ˈpjʊrail] *or* [ˈpjʊrɪl] *adj* foolish for a grown person to say or do; childish. **pu·er·ile·ly** *adv.* **pu·er·il·i·ty** *n.* ⟨Latin *puer* child⟩

pu·er·per·al [pjuˈɜrpərəl] *adj* to do with childbirth. ⟨Latin *puer* child + *parere* bear⟩

puff [pʌf] *v* **1** blow with short, quick blasts. **2** breathe quickly and with difficulty. **3** smoke: *to puff a cigar.* **4 a** swell with fluid or air (sometimes with *up*): *My ankles are puffed up in this heat.* **b** swell with emotion: *She puffed out her cheeks with anger.* **5** praise in exaggerated language.
n **1** a short, quick blast: *a puff of wind.* **2** a quick, hard breath. **3** a small pad for putting powder on the skin, etc. **4** a light pastry filled with whipped cream, jam, etc. **5** extravagant praise. ⟨Old English *pyffan*; imitative⟩
puff·ball *n* any of various fungi having a ball-shaped body. **puffed–up** *adj* **1** swollen. **2** conceited. **puff·y** *adj* swollen. **puff·i·ness** *n.*

puff·er [ˈpʌfər] *n* **1** any of various marine fishes having a spiny body which can be inflated with air or water into a globelike shape when the fish is disturbed. **2** *Informal* a hand-held ventilator for asthmatics.

puf·fin [ˈpʌfən] *n* any of several diving birds of the auk family, having a bill with yellow, red, and blue stripes. ⟨Middle English *poffin*; perhaps related to *puff*, for its appearance⟩

pug [pʌg] *n* a breed of small dog having a turned-up nose. ⟨origin uncertain⟩
pug nose a short, often thick turned-up nose. **pug–nosed** *adj.*

pu·gi·lism [ˈpjudʒə,lɪzəm] *n* boxing. **pu·gi·list** *n.* **pu·gi·lis·tic** *adj.* **pu·gi·lis·ti·cal·ly** *adv.* ⟨Latin *pugil* boxer⟩

pug·na·cious [pʌgˈneiʃəs] *adj* fond of fighting. **pug·nac·i·ty** [-ˈnæsɪti] *n.* **pug·na·cious·ly** *adv.* ⟨Latin *pugnacis*; *pugnus* fist⟩

puis·ne [ˈpjuni] *adj* designating a superior court judge of subordinate rank. The Supreme Court of Canada is composed of a chief justice and eight puisne judges. ⟨Old French *puisné* born later. See PUNY.⟩

puke [pjuk] *n, v Slang* vomit. ⟨imitative⟩

puk·ka [ˈpʌkə] *adj Anglo-Indian* **1** reliable; good: *We got a really pukka blender.* **2** solid; substantial. Also, **puc·ka.** ⟨Hindi *pakka* cooked, ripe⟩

pul·chri·tude [ˈpʌlkrɪ,tjud] *or* [ˈpʌlkrɪ,tud] *n* beauty. **pul·chri·tu·di·nous** *adj.* ⟨Latin *pulcher* beautiful⟩

pull [pʊl] *v* **1** move (something) by drawing toward oneself: *Pull the door open; don't push it.* **2** take hold of and tug. **3** move, usually with effort: *I pulled ahead of the others in the race.* **4** tear; rip: *to pull a book to pieces.* **5** stretch too far: *to pull a ligament.* **6** row: *Pull for the shore.* **7** *Informal* do; commit: *Don't pull any tricks.*
n **1** the act of pulling. **2** a difficult effort: *It was a hard pull to get up the hill.* **3** something to pull by: *a curtain pull.* **4** *Informal* influence; advantage. ⟨Old English *pullian*⟩
pull apart a separate into pieces by pulling. **b** be severely critical of: *to pull apart a term paper.* **pull down** *Informal* receive as a salary: *She pulls down at least $80 000 in that job.* **pull for** *Informal* give encouragement to: *to pull for the underdog.* **pull in** a restrain. **b** *Informal* arrest: *pulled in for speeding.* **c** stop: *Let's pull in at the next doughnut shop we see.* **pull off** *Informal* do successfully: *They pulled off the merger in record time.* **pull one's punches** hold back, especially to keep from winning. **pull oneself together** gather one's energy, etc.: *I have to pull myself together if I want to get this job done on time.* **pull out (of)** withdraw from (a venture, etc.) **pull over** steer or cause to steer a vehicle toward the curb and stop: *The police pulled me over because one tail-light was out.* **pull through** get through a difficult situation. **pull together** work in harmony. **pull up** a stop. **b** rebuke: *The professor pulled the disrespectful student up sharply.*
pull·o·ver [ˈpʊl,ouvər] *n* a sweater put on by pulling it over the head.

SYNONYMS
Pull = draw (or try to draw) toward or after oneself or in a particular direction: *Pull the curtains across.* **Tug** = pull hard, but not necessarily successfully: *The dog tugged at the tablecloth.* **Jerk** = pull, push, or twist quickly and suddenly: *She jerked her hand away.*

pul·let [ˈpʊlɪt] *n* a young hen. ⟨Old French *poulette* diminutive of *poule* hen, Latin *pulla*⟩

pul·ley [ˈpʊli] *n, pl* **-leys** **1** a wheel with a grooved rim in which a rope, belt, or wire can run. **2** a set of such wheels used to increase the power applied. ⟨Old French *poulie*; Greek *polos* axle, pivot⟩

pull·o·ver See PULL.

pul·mo·nar·y [ˈpʌlmə,nɛri] *or* [ˈpʊl-] *adj* to do with the lungs. ⟨Latin *pulmo* lung⟩

pulp [pʌlp] *n* **1** the soft part of any fruit or vegetable, esp after the juice or oil has been pressed out of it. **2** a moist mixture of ground-up wood, rags, etc., from which paper is made. **3** any soft, wet mass.
adj to do with poorly-written published material, printed on cheap paper: *pulp fiction.*
v **1** reduce or be reduced to pulp. **2** remove pulp from. **pulp·less** *adj.* **pulp·like** *adj.* **pulp·y** *adj.* **pulp·i·ness** *n.* ⟨Latin *pulpa*⟩

pul·pit [ˈpʊlpɪt] *or* [ˈpʌlpɪt] *n* a platform in a

church from which the minister preaches. ⟨Latin *pulpitum* scaffold, platform⟩

pulse¹ [pʌls] *n* **1** the beating of the arteries caused by the rush of blood into them after each contraction of the heart. **2** any series of regular beats or vibrations: *the pulse of an engine.* **3** *Electricity* a sudden increase in the magnitude of a voltage or current. **4** feeling; sentiment: *the pulse of the nation.*
v throb: *a heart pulsing with excitement.* ⟨Latin *pulsus* pp of *pellere* beat⟩
pul·sar [-sɑr] *n* a body or mass of energy in space that emits regular, pulsating radio waves. **pul·sate** *v* **1** throb: *The patient's heart was pulsating rapidly.* **2** quiver. **pul·sa·tion** *n*.

pulse² [pʌls] *n* the edible seeds of certain leguminous plants, such as peas, beans, lentils, etc. ⟨Latin *puls* porridge⟩

pul·ver·ize [ˈpʌlvəˌraɪz] *v* **1** grind to dust. **2** become dust. **3** demolish. **pul·ver·i·za·tion** *n*. ⟨Latin *pulvis, pulveris* dust⟩

pu·ma [ˈpjumə] *n* cougar. ⟨Spanish; Quechua⟩

pum·ice [ˈpʌmɪs] *n* Often, **pumice stone**, a light stone thrown up from volcanoes, used for cleaning, smoothing, and polishing. **pum·ice** *v*. ⟨Latin *pumex, -micis*⟩

pum·mel [ˈpʌməl] *v* **-melled** or **-meled**, **-mell·ing** or **-mel·ing** beat; beat with the fists. Also, **pom·mel**. ⟨variant of *pommel* beat with the pommel of a sword⟩

pump¹ [pʌmp] *n* an apparatus for forcing liquids or gases into or out of things. *v* **1** move (liquids, air, etc.) by a pump. **2** force air into by blowing or suctioning. **3** move up and down like a pump handle. **4** *Informal* try to get information out of: *Don't let her pump you for directions to the picnic.* ⟨Middle Dutch *pompe*⟩
pump iron *Informal* do weightlifting exercises. **pump up a** inflate. **b** increase or strengthen: *to pump up a political campaign.* **c** rouse to enthusiasm: *to pump up a team.* **pumped** *adj Informal* excited; enthusiastic. **pump·er** *n* a firetruck equipped with hoses and a water tank to pump water at a fire.

pump² [pʌmp] *n* a low-cut shoe with no fastenings. ⟨origin uncertain⟩

pum·per·nick·el [ˈpʌmpərˌnɪkəl] *n* a heavy, dark, slightly sour bread made from unsifted rye flour. ⟨German *pumpern* break wind + *Nickel* goblin⟩

pump·kin [ˈpʌmpkɪn] *n* the edible fruit of two plants of the gourd family, usually with an orange rind and golden flesh that is used as a vegetable, for pies, etc. ⟨earlier *pump(ion)* + -*kin* diminutive; Greek *pepōn* melon⟩
pump·kin·seed *n* the seed of a pumpkin.

pun [pʌn] *n* a humorous use of a word having two or more different meanings. *Example: One berry to another: "If you hadn't been so fresh, we wouldn't be in this jam."*
pun, pun·ned, pun·ning *v*. ⟨perhaps first syllable of Italian *puntiglio* verbal quibble⟩
pun·ster *n* a person fond of making puns.

punch¹ [pʌntʃ] *v* **1** hit with the fist.

2 *Informal* deliver with effectiveness. **3** *esp Western Canada and US* herd (cattle); work as a cowhand.
n **1** a quick blow. **2** *Informal* vigorous force or effectiveness: *This story lacks punch.* ⟨perhaps variant of *pounce*⟩
beat to the punch be quicker than (someone). **punch in** (or **out**) **a** record one's time of arrival (or departure) by means of a time clock. **b** enter (or extract) data into a computer. **punch up a** use a keyboard to bring up (information) on a computer. **b** add liveliness to (a piece of writing).
punch–drunk *adj* **1** suffering from slight brain damage as a result of repeated blows to the head received in boxing. **2** *Informal* appearing bewildered or dazed. **punch·line** *n* a telling phrase, sentence, etc. that makes the point of a joke or narrative. **punch–up** *n Informal* a fight, esp with the fists **punch·y** *adj Informal* **1** forceful *punchy talk.* **2** PUNCH-DRUNK.

punch² [pʌntʃ] *n* a tool for piercing materials, forcing nails beneath a surface, driving bolts out of holes, etc. **punch** *v*. ⟨earlier *puncheon*, Old French *poinchon*; Latin *punctus* point⟩

punch³ [pʌntʃ] *n* a drink made of two or more liquids mixed together. ⟨probably Hindi *panch* five; for number of ingredients⟩

punc·til·i·o [pʌŋkˈtɪliˌou] *n, pl* -**i·os** **1** a detail of honour, conduct, ceremony, etc. **2** care in attending to such details. ⟨Italian; Latin *punctus* point⟩
punc·til·i·ous [pʌŋkˈtɪliəs] *adj* **1** very careful and exact: *A patient should be punctilious in following the doctor's orders.* **2** paying strict attention to details of conduct.
punc·til·i·ous·ly *adv*. **punc·til·i·ous·ness** *n*.

punc·tu·al [ˈpʌŋktʃuəl] *adj* on time. **punc·tu·al·i·ty** *n*. **punc·tu·al·ly** *adv*. ⟨Latin *punctualis; punctus* point⟩

punc·tu·ate [ˈpʌŋktʃuˌeit] *v* **1** use periods, commas, etc., in writing, to help make the meaning clear. **2** interrupt now and then: *The crowd punctuated the politician's speech with boos.* **3** give point or emphasis to. ⟨Latin *punctuare; punctus* point⟩
punc·tu·a·tion *n* the use of periods, commas, etc. in writing. **punctuation marks** Periods, commas, question marks, semicolons, colons, apostrophes, quotation marks, and exclamation marks are punctuation marks.

punc·ture [ˈpʌŋktʃər] *n* a hole made by something pointed. **punc·ture** *v*. ⟨Latin *punctura; punctus* pp of *pungere* prick⟩

pun·dit [ˈpʌndɪt] *n* an authority, esp self-proclaimed; often used ironically. **pun·dit·ry** *n*. ⟨Sanskrit *pandita* learned⟩

pun·gent [ˈpʌndʒənt] *adj* **1** sharply affecting the organs of taste and smell: *a pungent pickle.* **2** sharp; biting: *pungent criticism.* **3** *Biology* sharp-pointed; piercing. **pun·gen·cy** *n*. **pun·gent·ly** *adv*. ⟨Latin *pungere* prick⟩

pun·ish [ˈpʌnɪʃ] *v* **1** cause pain, loss, or discomfort to (a person) because of some fault or offence. **2** *Informal* deal with severely or roughly. **pun·ish·ment** *n*. ⟨Latin *punire; poena* penalty⟩

pun·ish·a·ble *adj* deserving punishment; liable to punishment: *a crime punishable by imprisonment, a punishable offence.* **pun·ish·a·bil·i·ty** *n*. **pu·ni·tive** ['pjunətɪv] *adj* **1** concerned with punishment. **2** quick to punish. **pu·ni·tive·ly** *adv*. **pu·ni·tive·ness** *n*.

punk[1] [pʌŋk] *n* **1** decayed wood used as tinder. **2** a preparation that burns slowly, used to light fireworks. ⟨origin uncertain⟩

punk[2] [pʌŋk] *n* **1** *Slang* a young person, esp one regarded as ill-mannered, etc. **2** *Slang* a petty gangster.
adj **1** *Slang* inferior in quality, condition, etc. **2** *Slang* somewhat unwell: *I was feeling punk yesterday.* **3** to do with a style associated with PUNK ROCK music, characterized by grotesque clothing, hairstyles, etc. ⟨perhaps *punk*[1], in sense of 'something rotten'⟩
punk rock a form of hard-driving, often deliberately offensive music originating in the late 1970s, that expresses anger and discontent. **punk rocker** or **punker.**

pun·kah or **pun·ka** ['pʌŋkə] *n* in India and the East Indies, a large swinging fan hung from the ceiling and kept in motion by a servant or by machinery. ⟨Hindi *pankha*⟩

punt[1] [pʌnt] *v Football* kick (a ball) before it hits the ground after being dropped from the hands. **punt** *n*. **punt·er** *n*. ⟨origin uncertain⟩

punt[2] [pʌnt] *n* a flat-bottomed boat, usually moved by pushing with a pole against the bottom of a river, etc. **punt** *v*. **punt·er** *n*. ⟨Latin *ponto* a kind of ship, pontoon⟩

pu·ny ['pjuni] *adj* **1** of less than usual size and strength; weak. **2** petty; not important. **pu·ni·ly** *adv*. **pu·ni·ness** *n*. ⟨Old French *puisne* later-born; *puis* afterward (Latin *postea*) + *ne* born; Latin *natus*⟩

pup [pʌp] *n* **1** a young dog. **2** a young seal. *v* **pupped, pup·ping** give birth to pups. ⟨*puppy*; probably French *poupée* doll; Latin *pupa*⟩
pup·py **1** a young dog. **2** a young fox, wolf, etc. **pup·py·like** or **pup·py·ish** *adj*. **pup·py·hood** *n*. **puppy love** sentimental love that often exists briefly between adolescent girls and boys. **pup tent** a small, easily portable two-person tent.

pu·pa ['pjupə] *n, pl* **-pae** [-pi], [-paɪ], *or* **-pei** [-pei] *or* **-pas** a stage between the larva and the adult in the development of many insects. **pu·pal** *adj*. ⟨Latin = girl, doll⟩
pu·pate *v* pass through the pupal stage. **pu·pa·tion** *n*.

pu·pil[1] ['pjupəl] *n* a person who is being taught by someone. ⟨Latin *pupillus* ward; *pupus* boy⟩

pu·pil[2] ['pjupəl] *n Anatomy* the opening in the centre of the iris of the eye which looks like a black spot. ⟨Latin *pupilla* diminutive of *pupa* girl, doll; for the reflection one sees of oneself in another's pupil⟩

pup·pet ['pʌpɪt] *n* **1** a figure moved by wires,

strings, rods, or the hands. **2** any person who is not independent. **pup·pet·like** *adj*. ⟨Old French *poupette;* Latin *pupa* doll⟩
pup·pe·teer [,pʌpɪ'tir] *n* a person who makes puppets or who manipulates puppets in puppet shows. **pup·pet·ry** *n* the act of making and manipulating puppets.

pup·py See PUP.

pur·blind ['pɜr,blaɪnd] *adj* **1** nearly blind. **2** slow to understand. **pur·blind·ness** *n*. ⟨earlier *pur blind* pure blind⟩

pur·chase ['pɜrtʃəs] *v* **1** buy. **2** get in return: *to purchase safety at the cost of happiness.*
n **1** the act of buying. **2** the thing bought. **3** a firm hold: *Wind the rope twice around the tree to get a better purchase.* **pur·chas·er** *n*. ⟨Anglo-French *pur-* forth (Latin *pro-*) + *chacer* chase. See CHASE.⟩

pur·dah ['pɜrdə] *n* among some Hindus and Muslims: **1** a curtain to screen women from the sight of men or strangers. **2** a veil worn by women to hide the face. **3** the condition of being kept hidden from men or strangers. ⟨Hindi; Persian *pardah* veil, curtain⟩

pure [pjʊr] *adj* **1** not mixed with anything else: *pure gold.* **2** perfectly clean: *pure air.* **3** correct; without defects: *Does anyone speak pure French?* **4** mere; sheer: *pure accident.* **5** without sin: *a pure mind.* **6** theoretical (opposed to APPLIED): *pure science.* **pure·ness** *n*. **pu·ri·fi·ca·tion** *n*. **pu·ri·fy** *v*. **pu·ri·fi·er** *n*. **pu·ri·fi·ca·to·ry** *adj*. **pu·ri·ty** *n*. ⟨Latin *purus*⟩
pure as the driven snow extremely virtuous.
pure·bred *adj* designating an animal or plant whose ancestors are known to have belonged to one breed: *purebred Holsteins.*
pure laine ['pyr 'lɛn] ❋ *French* to do with a francophone Québécois all of whose ancestors can be traced back to the original settlement of New France. **pure·ly** *adv* **1** in a pure manner. **2** entirely. **3** merely: *purely by chance.* **4** innocently. **pur·ist** *n* a person who is very careful about purity and correctness, esp in language. **pur·ism** *n*. **pu·ris·tic** *adj*. **pu·ris·ti·cal·ly** *adv*. **Pu·ri·tan** *n* **1** during the 1500s and 1600s, a member of a group in the Church of England who wanted simple forms of worship and stricter morals. **2 puritan** a person who is very strict in morals and religion. **Pu·ri·tan·ism** *n*. **pu·ri·tan·i·cal** *adj* like a puritan; very strict or too strict in morals or religion. **pu·ri·tan·i·cal·ly** *adv*.

pu·rée [pjʊ'rei] *n* **1** food boiled soft and put through a sieve or blender. **2** a thick soup. **pu·rée, -réed, -ré·ing** *v*. ⟨French; *purer* strain; Latin *purare* purify⟩

purge [pɜrdʒ] *v* **1** make clean. **2** become clean. **3** clear of any undesired thing or person, such as air in a water pipe or opponents in a nation. **4** empty (the bowels). **5** *Medicine* cause (someone) to have a bowel movement. **6** clear of guilt.
n **1** the act of purging. **2** a medicine that purges. **3** the elimination of unwanted people from a nation or party. ⟨Latin *purgare; purus* pure + *agere* drive, make⟩

pur·ga·tive ['pɜrgətɪv] *n* a medicine that empties the bowels. **pur·ga·to·ry** ['pɜrgə,tɔri] *n* **1** *Roman Catholic Church* a temporary condition in which the souls of those who have died penitent are purified from sin by punishment. **2** any place of temporary suffering or punishment. **pur·ga·to·ri·al** *adj*.

pu·ri·fy See PURE.

Pu·rim ['pjʊrɪm] *or* ['pʊrɪm] *Hebrew* [pu'rɪm] *n* a Jewish religious festival, celebrated each year in February or March, commemorating Esther's deliverance of the Jews from being massacred. ⟨Hebrew *purim* pl of *pur* lot⟩

pur·ism pur·ist, **pu·ri·ty**, etc. See PURE.

purl [pɜrl] *v* knit with inverted stitches. ⟨variant of obsolete *pirl* twist into a cord⟩

pur·lieu ['pɜrlu] *n* **1** a piece of land on the border of a forest. **2** one's haunt. **3** any outlying region. ⟨Anglo-French *puralee*; *por*- forth + *aler* go; influenced by *lieu* place⟩

pur·loin [pər'lɔɪn] *or* ['pɜrlɔɪn] *v* steal. **pur·loin·er** *n*. ⟨Anglo-French *purloigner* remove; *pur*- forth + *loin* afar; Latin *longe*⟩

pur·ple ['pɜrpəl] *n* **1** a colour made by mixing red and blue. **2** Usually, **the purple** noble or royal rank.
adj **1** of the colour purple. **2** noble or royal. **3** of rhetorical style, excessively elaborate: *purple prose*. **pur·plish** *adj*. ⟨Latin *purpura*, Greek *porphyra* shellfish yielding purple dye⟩ **turn purple** become very angry or furious. **purple loosestrife** a wildflower with purple flower spikes. It is considered a pest. **purple violet** See VIOLET.

pur·port [pər'pɔrt] *v* **1** claim: *The map purported to be genuine.* **2** have as its main idea.
n ['pɜrpɔrt] the meaning; main idea. **pur·port·ed** *adj*. **pur·port·ed·ly** *adv*. ⟨Anglo-French *pur*- forth + *porter* carry; Latin *portare*⟩

pur·pose ['pɜrpəs] *n* **1** aim; intention:. **2** an end for which a thing is made, done, used, etc.: *What is the purpose of this machine?* **3** purposeful quality: *a life of purpose.*
v plan; aim; intend. **pur·pose·less** *adj*. **pur·pose·less·ness** *n*. ⟨Old French *pourposer* propose; *pour*- (Latin *pro*-) + *poser*. See POSE.⟩ **on purpose** intentionally. **to good purpose** with good results. **to little** (or **no**) **purpose** with few (or no) results: *We shopped all day, to little purpose.* **pur·pose·ful** *adj* having determination: *a purposeful stride*. **pur·pose·ful·ly** *adv*. **pur·pose·ly** *adv* on purpose; intentionally.

purr [pɜr] *n* a low, murmuring sound such as a cat makes when pleased. **purr** *v*. ⟨imitative⟩

purse [pɜrs] *n* **1** handbag. **2** a case for carrying money. **3** money; resources: *The family purse cannot afford a vacation.*
v press into folds or wrinkles: *She pursed her lips in disapproval.* ⟨Greek *byrsa* skin; for leather pouch⟩
purs·er *n* an officer who keeps the accounts of a ship or airplane, and attends to other matters of business. **purse seine** a fishing net with ends can be pulled like a drawstring purse to enclose the fish. **purse–seine** *v*.

purse strings strings pulled to close a purse. **control** or **hold the purse strings** control the spending of money. **tighten** (or **loosen**) **the purse strings** be more sparing (or generous) in spending money.

purs·lane ['pɜrslən] *or* ['pɜrslein] *n* any of various low-growing plants with fleshy leaves. ⟨Old French *porcelaine*; Latin *porcilaca*, *portulaca*⟩

pur·sue [pər'su] *v* **1** follow to catch or kill; chase. **2** proceed along; follow: *He pursued a wise course, taking no chances.* **3** seek: *to pursue pleasure*. **pur·su·a·ble** *adj*. **pur·su·er** *n*. ⟨Anglo-French *pursuer*; Latin *prosequi*. See PROSECUTE.⟩ **pur·su·ant** *adj* following (usually with *to*): *pursuant to your instructions*. **pur·suit** *n* **1** the act of pursuing. **2** an occupation or pastime.

pu·ru·lent ['pjʊrələnt] *or* ['pjʊrjələnt] *adj* **1** to do with pus: *a purulent sore*. **2** corrupt; rotten. **pu·ru·lence** or **pu·ru·len·cy** *n*. **pu·ru·lent·ly** *adv*. ⟨Latin *pus*, *puris* pus⟩

pur·vey [pər'vei] *v* supply (food or provisions): *to purvey for a royal household*. **pur·vey·or** *n*. ⟨Anglo-French *porveier*; Latin *providere*. See PROVIDE.⟩

pur·view ['pɜrvju] *n* a range of operation, activity, concern, etc. ⟨Anglo-French *purveu* pp of *proveier* purvey. See PURVEY.⟩

pus [pʌs] *n* a liquid formed by inflammation of infected tissue in the body, consisting of white blood cells, bacteria, serum, etc. ⟨Latin⟩

push [pʊʃ] *v* **1** move (something) away by pressing against it: *Push the door; don't pull it.* **2** move by pressing: *Push the cat outdoors.* **3** go forward by force: *to push on at a rapid pace.* **4** force (one's way): *We had to push our way through the crowd.* **5** urge the use, sale, etc. of: *pushing her new book.*
n **1** Informal force; energy: *She has made a lot of successful deals, and that seems to give her even more push.* **2** the act of pushing. **3** a hard effort; determined advance. ⟨Old French *pousser*; Latin *pulsare* beat⟩
push around *Informal* bully. **push for** support strongly. **pushed for** constrained by the lack or scarceness of. **push it** overdo it. **push off** *Informal* leave: *Why don't you just push off?* **when push comes to shove** *Informal* when the time comes to face a problem.
push button a small knob that is pushed to close or open an electric circuit. **push–but·ton** *adj* **1** operated by a button: *a push-button phone*. **2** using automated systems that can be operated from a distance or with little effort: *push-button warfare*. **push·cart** *n* a light cart pushed by hand. **push·er** *n Slang* a person who sells drugs illegally. **push–o·ver** *n Slang* **1** something very easy to do. **2** a person very easy to beat in a contest. **3** a person easily influenced. **push·pin** *n* a thumbtack with a large head, used for marking maps, charts, etc. **push–up** or **push·up** *n* **1** an exercise in which the person, face down, raises and lowers the body by pushing up with the arms. **2** ✱ vegetation pushed by a muskrat into a

breathing-hole in the ice to keep it from freezing up. **push·y** *adj Informal* offensively forceful and aggressive.

pu·sil·lan·i·mous [ˌpjusəˈlænəməs] *adj* cowardly; timid. **pu·sil·la·nim·i·ty** *n*. **pu·sil·lan·i·mous·ly** *adv*. ⟨Latin *pusillus* little + *animus* spirit⟩

puss[1] [pʊs] *n Informal* a cat. ⟨Germanic **puss·y 1** a cat. **2** catkin. **puss·y·cat** *n* **1** a cat. **2** a gentle person: *Many very large men are real pussycats, especially around small children.* **puss·y·foot** *Informal v* **1** move cautiously to avoid being noticed. **2** be cautious about revealing one's opinions (often with *around*).

puss[2] [pʊs] *n Slang* the face; mouth. ⟨Irish Gaelic *pus* mouth, lips⟩

pus·tule [ˈpʌstʃul] *n* **1** a pimple containing pus. **2** any swelling like a pimple. ⟨Latin *pustula; pus* pus⟩ **pus·tu·late** *v* form or cover with pustules. **pus·tu·la·tion** [ˌpʌstʃəˈleiʃən] *n*.

put [pʊt] *v* **put, put·ting 1** place; lay: *I put sugar in my tea.* **2** cause to be in some state, condition, etc.: *Put your room in order.* **3** express: *to put things clearly.* **4** propose for consideration: *The executive put several questions to the membership.* **5** apply: *A doctor puts her skill to good use.* **6** impose: *to put a tax on gasoline.* ⟨late Old English *putian* to push⟩ **put about** change direction. **put across** *Informal* **a** carry out successfully. **b** carry out by trickery. **put ahead** (or **back**) move the hands of (a clock or watch) forward (or back). **put aside** or **by a** save for future use. **b** exclude from use. **put away a** *Slang* consume (food, drink, etc.). **b** *Slang* commit to a prison, etc.: *The judge put her away for ten years.* **put down a** put an end to. **b** write down. **c** belittle. **d** put (an animal) to death humanely. **put forward** suggest (an idea). **put in a** *Informal* spend (time). **b** do: *to put in a good day's work.* **c** make (a claim, plea, or offer): *She put in for a loan.* **put it on** *Slang* pretend; exaggerate. **put it** (or **her**) **there** *Slang* shake hands with me. **put off a** postpone: *Don't put off going to the dentist.* **b** get rid of. **put on a** clothe oneself with. **b** assume, esp as a pretence: *to put on an air of innocence.* **c** increase: *The driver put on speed.* **d** present (an entertainment): *The class put on a play.* **e** *Slang* fool (someone): *Are you putting me on?* **put out a** extinguish. **b** embarrass. **c** dislocate: *I put my knee out when I fell.* **d** spend; pay. **put over** *Informal* **a** carry out successfully. **b** impose (something false) on a person. **put someone on to** inform (someone) about (something). **put through** carry out successfully. **put to flight** cause to flee. **put up a** offer; make available: *to put up a house for sale, to put up the money for a car.* **b** build. **c** preserve (fruit, etc.). **d** give lodging to. **e** *Informal* incite: *Who put you up to this?* **put up a fuss** express extreme displeasure. **put upon** impose upon. **put up with** tolerate. **stay put** stay in the same position.

put–down *n Informal* **1** a belittling of a person or thing. **2** a comment, reply, etc.

intended to belittle. **put–on** *n* **1** a pretension or affectation. **2** *Slang* a mischievous joke or trick played for fun. **put–up** *adj Informal* planned beforehand, in a secret or crafty manner: *a put-up job.*

SYNONYMS

Put emphasizes the action of moving something into or out of a place, or bringing it into some condition, state, or relation: *Put the groceries away.* **Place** emphasizes the idea of a definite spot, condition, etc. more than the action: *Place your hands behind your head.* **Set** suggests a careful, purposeful, and directed 'putting': *Set the box down over there.*

pu·ta·tive [ˈpjutətɪv] *adj* supposed; reputed: *the putative author of a book.* **pu·ta·tive·ly** *adv*. ⟨Latin *putare* think⟩

pu·trid [ˈpjutrɪd] *adj* **1** rotten; foul. **2** thoroughly corrupt; extremely bad. **3** gangrenous: *putrid flesh.* **4** extremely unpleasant. ⟨Latin *puter, putris* rotten⟩ **pu·tre·fy** *v* rot; decay. **pu·tre·fac·tion** *n*. **pu·tres·cent** [pjuˈtresənt] *adj* becoming putrid; rotting. **pu·tres·cence** *n*.

putt [pʌt] *Golf v* strike (a ball) gently to roll it into the hole. **putt** *n*. ⟨variant of *put*⟩ **putt·er** a golf club with an upright face, used in putting. **putt·ing green** the smooth turf around a golf hole.

put·ter[1] [ˈpʌtər] *v* keep busy in a rather useless way. Also, **pot·ter. put·ter·er** *n*. ⟨variant of *potter*[2]⟩

putt·er[2] See PUTT.

put·ty [ˈpʌti] *n* a soft mixture of whiting and linseed oil, used for holding glass in window frames. ⟨French *potée* orig, potful; *pot* pot⟩

puz·zle [ˈpʌzəl] *n* **1** a difficult problem. **2** a problem to be done for fun. **3** a game such as a crossword puzzle, jigsaw puzzle, etc. *v* **1** make unable to solve something. **2** put forth intense mental effort on something (often with *over*): *to puzzle over arithmetic.* **puz·zled** *adj*. **puz·zle·ment** *n*. **puz·zling** *adj*. ⟨origin uncertain⟩ **puzzle out** find out by thinking hard: *to puzzle out the meaning of a sentence.*

PVC POLYVINYL CHLORIDE.

pyg·my [ˈpɪgmi] *n* **1 Pygmy** a member of a small people of equatorial Africa. **2** anything that is unusually small for its kind; dwarf. *adj* unusually small or insignificant. Also, **pig·my**. ⟨Greek *pygmaioi* dwarfish; *pygmē* cubit⟩

py·ja·mas [pəˈdʒæməz] or [pəˈdʒɑməz] *n pl* loose garments for sleeping or lounging in, consisting of a top and pants. Also (esp US), **pa·ja·mas**. ⟨Persian *pae* leg + *jamah* garment⟩

py·lon [ˈpaɪlɒn] *n* **1** a tower for guiding aircraft pilots. **2** a tall framework used to carry high-tension wires across country. **3** a small marker used to guide traffic, etc. **4** a gateway, particularly of an ancient Egyptian temple. ⟨Greek = gateway; *pylē* gate⟩

py·or·rhe·a or **py·or·rhoe·a** [ˌpaɪəˈriə] *n* *Pathology* a disease of the gums in which pockets of pus form about the teeth. ⟨Greek *pyon* pus + *rheein* flow⟩

pyr·a·mid ['pırə,mıd] *n* **1** *Geometry* a solid having a polygon for its base and having triangular sides meeting in a point. **2** any of the huge royal tombs, having four triangular sides, built by the ancient Egyptians. **py·ram·i·dal** [pı'ræmədəl] *adj.* ⟨Egyptian⟩
pyramid scheme, a tiered network for direct marketing of goods, in which each tier of agents is recruited in larger numbers by, and charges a higher price than, the one above, passing a portion of the profits upward.

pyre [paır] *n* a pile of wood on which a dead body is burned as a funeral rite. ⟨Greek *pyr* fire⟩

py·rene ['paırin] *n* *Chemistry* a hydrocarbon obtained from coal tar and thought to be carcinogenic. ⟨Greek *pyr* fire⟩

py·re·thrum [paı'riθrəm] *n* **1** any of several chrysanthemums cultivated for their showy flowers. **2** an insecticide prepared from the dried flower heads of some of these plants. ⟨Greek *pyrethron*; *pyr* fire⟩

py·rex·ia [paı'rɛksiə] *n* *Pathology* a fever. **py·ret·ic** [paı'rɛtık] *adj.* ⟨Greek; *pyr* fire⟩

py·rite ['paırait] *n* a common mineral consisting of iron sulphide, having a yellow colour and a metallic glitter that suggests gold; FOOL'S GOLD. ⟨Greek *pyritēs* flint; *pyr* fire⟩ **py·ri·tes** [paı'raitiz] *or* ['paıraits] *n, pl* **-tes** any of various compounds of sulphur and a metal: *Pyrite is the commonest pyrites.* **py·rit·ic** [-'rıtık] *adj.*

py·ro·man·cy ['paırə,mænsi] *n* the practice of claiming to foretell the future by flames or the forms appearing in fire. ⟨Greek *pyros* fire + *manteia* divination⟩

py·ro·ma·ni·a [,paırə'meiniə] *n* an obsessive desire to set things on fire. **py·ro·ma·ni·ac** *n, adj.* ⟨Greek *pyros* fire + -MANIA⟩
py·ro·ma·ni·a·cal [,paıroumə'naıəkəl] *adj* **1** caused by a pyromaniac. **2** of or having a tendency toward pyromania.

py·ro·pho·bia [,paırə'foubiə] *n* an abnormal fear of fire. **py·ro·phobe** *n.* ⟨Greek *pyros* fire + -PHOBIA⟩

py·ro·tech·nic [,paırə'tɛknık] *adj* **1** do with fireworks. **2** brilliant; sensational: *pyrotechnic eloquence.* **3** to do with activating systems in spacecraft, by igniting various materials and devices on command. Also, **py·ro·tech·ni·cal**. **py·ro·tech·ni·cal·ly** *adv.* ⟨Greek *pyros* fire + -TECHNICAL⟩
py·ro·tech·nics *n* **1** the making of fireworks. **2** a display of fireworks. **3** a brilliant or sensational display. **py·ro·tech·ni·cian** *n.*

Pyr·rhic victory ['pırık] a victory won at too great cost. ⟨*Pyrrhus* Greek King (3c B.C.) who won a battle with great loss of life⟩

Py·tha·gor·e·an theorem [pə,θægə'riən] *Geometry* the theorem that the square of the hypotenuse of a right-angled triangle is equal to the sum of the squares of the two adjacent sides. ⟨*Pythagoras* Greek philosopher and mathematician (6c B.C.)⟩

py·thon ['paıθɒn] *or* ['paıθən] *n* **1** any of a subfamily of large, nonvenomous snakes that kill their prey by constriction. **2** any large constricting snake. ⟨Greek⟩

pyx [pıks] *n Ecclesiastical* the box in which the bread of the Eucharist is kept or carried. ⟨Greek *pyxis*; *pyxos* boxwood⟩

Qq

q or **Q** [kju] *n, pl* **q's** or **Q's 1** the seventeenth letter of the English alphabet, or any speech sound represented by it. **2** the seventeenth person or thing in a series.

Q. 1 question. **2** quarto. **3** quarterly.

qag·gig ['kɑgɪg] *n* an Inuit festival marking the first sunrise of the new year and the beginning of the hunting season. ⟨Inuktitut⟩

qa·mu·tik ['kɑmʊtɪk] *n* komatik. ⟨Inuktitut⟩

Q and A or **Q & A** questions and answers.

QC or **Q.C.** QUEEN'S COUNSEL.

qiv·i·ut ['kɪvi,ʊt] *n* the soft, silky underfur of the arctic muskox, used as a textile fibre. ⟨Inuktitut⟩

q.t. or **Q.T.** *Slang* quiet.
on the q.t. very secretly; quietly.

quack¹ [kwæk] *n* the sound a duck makes. **quack** *v.* ⟨imitative⟩

quack² [kwæk] *n* **1** a person who practises as a doctor but lacks professional training. **2** an ignorant pretender to knowledge of any sort. *adj* **1** used by quacks. **2** not genuine: *quack medicine.* ⟨quacksalver; Dutch *quacken* boast + *salf* salve⟩
quack·er·y *n* the methods of a quack.

quad¹ [kwɒd] *n Informal* a quadrangle on a campus.

quad² [kwɒd] *n Informal* quadruplet.

quad·ran·gle ['kwɒ,dræŋgəl] *n* a four-sided space surrounded by buildings. ⟨quadri- four + *angulus* angle⟩

quad·rant ['kwɒdrənt] *n* **1** a quarter of a circle. **2** formerly, an instrument used in astronomy and navigation for measuring altitudes. **3** *Geometry* one of the four sections into which a plane surface is divided by two perpendicular lines. ⟨Latin *quadrans* a fourth⟩

quad·ra·phon·ics [,kwɒdrə'fɒnɪks] *n* (with a sg verb) a system for the reproduction of sound using four transmission channels that feed four separate loudspeakers.
quad·ra·phon·ic *adj.* ⟨quadri- four + Greek *phōnē* sound⟩

quad·rate ['kwɒdrɪt] *or* ['kwɒdreit] *n* something square or rectangular. **quad·rate** *adj.* *v* ['kwɒdreit] agree or conform (often with *with*). ⟨Latin *quadrus* square; *quattuor* four⟩
quadratic equation [kwɒ'drætɪk] *Algebra* an equation involving squares but no higher powers of the unknown quantity. **quad·ra·ture** *n* **1** *Mathematics* the finding of a square equal in area to a given surface bounded by a curve. **2** *Astronomy* the position of any planet or star that is 90° away from another.

quad·ren·ni·al [kwɒ'drɛniəl] *adj* **1** occurring every four years: *a quadrennial election.* **2** of or lasting for four years. **quad·ren·ni·al·ly** *adv.* ⟨quadri- four + *annus* year⟩

quad·ri·cen·ten·ni·al [,kwɒdrəsen'tɛniəl] *adj* to do with a four hundred year period: *The year* A.D. *2267 will be the quadricentennial anniversary of Confederation. n* a four hundredth anniversary.

quadri– ['kwɒ,drɪ] *prefix* four. Also, before a vowel, **quadr–**. ⟨Latin⟩

quad·ri·ceps ['kwɒdrə,sɛps] *n pl* **-ceps** or **-cep·ses** [-,sɛpsiz] *Anatomy* the large four-part extensor muscle of the front of the thigh. ⟨quadri- four + *caput* head⟩

quad·ri·lat·er·al [,kwɒdrə'lætərəl] *n* a plane figure having four sides and four interior angles.

qua·drille [kwɒ'drɪl] *n* a square dance for four couples. ⟨French; Latin *quadrus* square⟩

quad·ril·lion [kwɒ'drɪljən] *n* a cardinal number represented by 1 followed by 15 zeros. **quad·ril·lionth** *adj, n.* ⟨quadri- four + (M)ILLION⟩

quad·ri·ple·gia [,kwɒdrə'plidʒə] *n Pathology* complete paralysis of all four limbs or of the body from the neck down. **quad·ri·ple·gic** *adj, n.* ⟨quadri- four + Greek *plēge* stroke⟩

quad·ru·ped ['kwɒdrə,pɛd] *n* an animal, esp a mammal, that has four feet. **quad·ru·ped** *adj.* ⟨Latin *quadru-* four + *pedis* foot⟩

quad·ru·ple [kwɒ'drupəl] *or* [-'drʌpəl] *adj* **1** consisting of four parts. **2** four times as much or as many. **3** *Music* having four beats to each measure.
n a number, amount, etc. four times as great as another: *80 is the quadruple of 20.*
v make or become four times as great. **quad·ru·ply** *adv.* ⟨Latin *quadruplus; quadru-* four⟩

quad·ru·plet [kwɒ'druplɪt] *or* [-'drʌplɪt] *n* one of four children born at the same time from the same mother. **quad·ru·pli·cate** [kwɒ'druplɪkɪt] *adj* fourfold. **in quadruplicate** in four identical copies: *Please submit your résumé in quadruplicate.*

quaff [kwɒf] *v* drink in large drafts. ⟨origin uncertain⟩

quag·mire ['kwæg,maɪr] *n* soft muddy ground. ⟨obsolete *quag* to shake + *mire*⟩
quag·gy *adj* **1** swampy. **2** flabby; soft and wobbly: *quaggy flesh.*

qua·hog ['kwɒhɒg] *or* [kwə'hɒg] *n* an edible clam with a rounded shell. Also **qua·haug.** ⟨Algonquian⟩

quail¹ [kweil] *n pl* **quails** or (esp collectively) **quail** any of various game birds belonging to the same family as partridges and pheasants. ⟨Old French *quaille;* Germanic⟩

quail² [kweil] *v* be afraid; shrink back in fear. ⟨Middle English⟩

quaint [kweint] *adj* strange in an amusing way: *Old photographs seem quaint to us today.* **quaint·ly** *adv.* **quaint·ness** *n.* ⟨Old French *cointe* pretty, clever; Latin *cognitus* known⟩

quake [kweik] *v* tremble: *I quaked with fear.* *n* **1** a shaking; trembling. **2** earthquake. ⟨Old English *cwacian*⟩

Quak·er ['kweikər] *n* a member of a

Christian group called the Religious Society of Friends who favour simple religious services and refuse to fight in wars or take oaths. **Quak·er·ish** or **Quak·er·like** *adj.* **Quak·er·ism** *n.* ⟨*quake* v⟩

qual·i·fy [ˈkwɒlə͵faɪ] *v* **1** make competent: *to qualify oneself for a job.* **2** satisfy criteria: *Can you qualify for the Scouts?* **3** *Sports* gain the right to compete in a contest. **4** limit or modify. **qual·i·fi·a·ble** *adj.* **qual·i·fied** *adj.* **qual·i·fy·ing** *adj.* ⟨Latin *qualis* of what sort + *facere* make⟩

qual·i·fi·ca·tion *n* **1** that which makes a person fit for a job, task, etc. **2** a limitation; restriction: *The statement was made without any qualification.* **qual·i·fi·er** *n* **1** a person who or thing that qualifies. **2** *Grammar* a word that modifies the meaning of another word; adjectives and adverbs.

qual·i·ty [ˈkwɒləti] *n* **1** basic character or nature: *One quality of iron is hardness.* **2** a characteristic: *She has many fine qualities.* **3** grade of excellence: *a poor quality of cloth.* **4** nature: *Hardship tests a person's quality. adj* of high standard: *quality repair work.* **qual·i·ta·tive** *adj.* **qual·i·ta·tive·ly** *adv.* ⟨Latin *qualitas; qualis* of what sort⟩

qualitative analysis *Chemistry* the process of determining the chemical components of a substance. Compare QUANTITATIVE ANALYSIS.

qualm [kwɒm] *n* uneasiness; doubt: *I tried the test with some qualms.* ⟨Old English *cwealm* pain⟩

quan·da·ry [ˈkwɒndəri] *n* a state of uncertainty; dilemma. ⟨origin uncertain⟩

quan·ti·fy [ˈkwɒntə͵faɪ] *v* **1** count or measure. **2** *Logic* express explicitly the extent of by using such words as *all, some,* or *most.* **quan·ti·fi·a·ble** *adj.* **quan·ti·fied** *adj.* **quan·ti·fi·ca·tion** *n.* ⟨Latin *quantus* how much + *facere* make⟩

quan·ti·fi·er *n Grammar* a modifier that denotes the quantity of something. In the sentence *Few people really enjoy studying grammar, few* is a quantifier.

quan·ti·ty [ˈkwɒntəti] *n* **1** any amount of anything measurable: *equal quantities of nuts and raisins.* **2** a large amount: *The baker buys flour in quantity.* **3** something that is measurable. **quan·ti·ta·tive** *adj.* **quan·ti·ta·tive·ly** *adv.* ⟨Latin *quantitas; quantus* how much⟩

quantitative analysis *Chemistry* the process of determining the amount of each chemical component of a substance. Compare QUALITATIVE ANALYSIS.

quan·tum [ˈkwɒntəm] *n pl* **-ta** [-tə] **1** a portion. **2** *Physics* the smallest amount of energy capable of existing independently. ⟨Latin = how much⟩

quantum leap or **jump 1** *Physics* a sudden change of an atom, electron, etc. from one energy state to another. **2** any sudden major advance: *a quantum leap in technology.* **quantum mechanics** the branch of physics dealing with the behaviour of elementary particles on the basis of the QUANTUM THEORY.

quantum number *Physics* any number distinguishing among members of a family of elementary particles. **quantum theory** *Physics* the theory that, whenever radiant energy is transferred, the transfer occurs in stages, and the amount of energy transferred during each stage is of a definite quantity.

quar·an·tine [ˈkwɔrən͵tin] *or* [͵kwɔrənˈtin] *v* **1** isolate (people carrying a communicable or infectious disease), usually for a specific length of time. **2** isolate or exclude an undesirable person or group. **quar·an·tine** *n.* ⟨Italian *quaranta* forty, Latin *quadraginta*; original period was 40 days⟩

quark [kwɔrk] *or sometimes* [kwɑrk] *n Physics* any of the fundamental particles from which protons and neutrons are formed. ⟨nonsense word in a novel by James Joyce; applied by US physicist M. Gell-Mann to the particles⟩

quar·rel [ˈkwɔrəl] *n* an angry disagreement. *v* **-relled** or **-reled, -rel·ling** or **-rel·ing 1** disagree angrily. **2** find fault: *It is useless to quarrel with facts.* **quar·rel·ler** or **quar·rel·er** *n.* ⟨Latin *querella* complaint; *queri* complain⟩ **quar·rel·some** *adj* fond of fighting and disputing. **quar·rel·some·ness** *n.*

SYNONYMS
Quarrel particularly applies to a fight in words, or a dispute soon over or ending in severed relations: *The children had a quarrel over the division of the candy.* **Feud** suggests a long-lasting quarrel marked by violent attacks and revenge (when between two groups) or by unfriendly acts and verbal attacks (when between individuals): *The senator and the columnist had carried on a feud for years.*

quar·ry¹ [ˈkwɔri] *n* a place where stone is dug cut for use in building or sculpture. **quar·ry** *v.* ⟨Latin *quareia; quadrus* square; for squaring building stone⟩

quar·ry² [ˈkwɔri] *n* **1** an animal chased in a hunt. **2** anything hunted or eagerly pursued. ⟨Old French *cuir* hide, skin; Latin *corium*⟩

quart [kwɔrt] *n* a non-metric unit for measuring volume or capacity, equal to about 1.14 Latin. ⟨Latin *quartus* fourth⟩

quar·ter [ˈkwɔrtər] *n* **1** one-fourth. **2** in Canada, the US, etc., a coin worth 25 cents. **3** fifteen minutes: *a quarter to three.* **4** one-fourth of a year; three months: *Sales increased in the first quarter.* **5** one of the four phases of the moon. The quarters of the moon are four periods of about seven days each. **6** a region or district: *the Latin Quarter of the city.* **7** a section of a community, group, etc.: *The bankers' theory was not accepted in other quarters.* **8** any of the four divisions marked off by the four main compass points: *What quarter is the wind blowing from?* **9** mercy as shown to a defeated enemy: *He asked no quarter and was given none.* **10** *Football, basketball, etc* one of the four equal periods of play into which a game is divided. **11** **quarters** *pl* a place to live: *officers' quarters.* *v* **1** divide into quarters. **2** give a place to live in: *Soldiers were quartered in the town.* **3** cover (an area) by going over it from left to right and from right to left; search intensively. **4** cut the body of (a person or animal) into quarters. ⟨Latin *quartarius* a fourth.⟩ **at close quarters** fighting or living close together.

quar·ter·back *n* **1** *Football* the player whose position is immediately behind the centre of the line of scrimmage. **2** a person who directs any group or activity. *v* manage or direct any undertaking. **quar·ter·deck** *n Nautical* on a ship, the part of the upper deck between the mainmast and the stern, used especially by the officers. **quar·ter·fi·nal** *n* a stage in a sports tournament at which eight players or teams compete. **quarter horse** a horse orginally bred for racing on quarter-mile tracks. **quar·ter·ly** *adj* happening, done, etc. at four regular intervals a year. *adv* once each quarter of a year. *n* a magazine published four times a year. **quar·ter·mas·ter** *n Military* **a** an officer who has charge of providing quarters, clothing, etc. for troops. **b** *Navy* an officer who has charge of the steering, signals, etc. *Abbrev* **QM** or **Q.M. quarter note** *Music* a note equal to one-fourth of a whole note. **quarter rest** *Music* a rest lasting as long as a QUARTER NOTE. **quarter round** a convex moulding whose cross section is a quarter of a circle. **quarter section** a piece of land, usually square, containing 160 acres (about 65 hectares).

quar·tet or **quar·tette** [kwɔr'tɛt] *n* **1** a group of four musicians. **2** a piece of music for four voices or instruments. **3** any group of four. ⟨Italian *quartetto*. See QUART.⟩

quar·tic ['kwɔrtɪk] *n Algebra* an equation of the fourth degree. ⟨Latin *quartus* fourth⟩

quar·tile ['kwɔrtaɪl] *n Statistics* any of the three values of a variable that divide a population into four equal groups. ⟨Latin *quartus* fourth⟩

quartz [kwɔrts] *n* a crystalline mineral consisting of silica that is present in many rocks and solids. ⟨German *Quarz*⟩

qua·sar ['kweizɑr] or ['kweisɑr] *n Astronomy* any of various starlike bodies that are very distant from the earth and give off light and radio waves. ⟨*quasi* + (*stell*)*ar*⟩

quash [kwɒʃ] *v* **1** put down completely; crush: *to quash a revolt.* **2** make void; annul: *The judge quashed the charges against the prisoner.* ⟨Old French *quasser,* Latin *quassare* shatter⟩

qua·si ['kwɒzi] ['kweizaɪ] or ['kweisaɪ] *adj* not real; halfway: *quasi humour.* ⟨Latin *quam* as + *si* if⟩

quasi– *combining form* in some sense or to a certain extent: *quasi-historical, quasi-official.*

Qua·ter·na·ry [kwə'tɜrnəri] or ['kwɒtər,nɛri] *Geology n* the fourth chief period in time, which includes the Pleistocene and Holocene (Recent) epochs. **Qua·ter·na·ry** *adj.* ⟨Latin *quater* four times⟩

quat·rain ['kwɒtreɪn] *n* a stanza or poem of four lines, usually having an alternating

rhyme scheme *abab* or *abcb,* less frequently *abba.* ⟨French; *qquatre* four, Latin *quattuor*⟩

quat·re·foil ['kætrə,fɔɪl] or ['kætər,fɔɪl] *n* a leaf or flower composed of four leaflets or petals. ⟨Old French *quatre* four + *feuil* leaf; Latin *quattuor, folium*⟩

qua·ver ['kweɪvər] *v* sing or say in shaky tones. **qua·ver** *n.* **qua·ver·ing·ly** *adv.* **qua·ver·y** *adj.* ⟨Middle English *quave* shake⟩

quay [ki] *n* a landing place where ships load and unload. ⟨Old French; Celtic⟩

quea·sy ['kwizi] *adj* **1** easily upset. **2** feeling nauseated. **quea·si·ly** *adv.* **quea·si·ness** *n.* ⟨origin uncertain⟩

Qué·bec [kwɪ'bɛk] or [kə'bɛk] *French* [ke'bɛk] *n* an eastern province of Canada. *Abbrev* **QC Qué·beck·er** or **Qué·bec·er** *n.* **Qué·bé·cois** [keibɛ'kwɑ] *French* [kebe'kwɑ] *n pl* **Qué·bé·cois** a Québecker, esp a Francophone. **Qué·bé·coise** [keibɛ'kwɑz] *French* [kebe'kwaz] *n pl* **Qué·bé·coises** a female Québecker, esp a Francophone.

queen [kwin] *n* **1** a female ruler. **2** a woman judged to be first in importance, or best in beauty or some other quality: *the fashion queen.* **3** *Entomology* an egg-laying female in a colony of bees, ants, etc. **4** *Chess* a piece that can move any number of squares in any direction. **5** the chief, best, etc.: *The rose is the queen of flowers.* **6** *Slang* a male homosexual esp one who appears very effeminate. **queen·like** *adj.* ⟨Old English *cwēn*⟩ **queen it** *Informal* behave pretentiously or domineeringly. **queen consort** the wife of a reigning king. **queen crab ✿** a species of crab found on the east coast. **queen·dom** *n* the realm of a queen. **queen·hood** *n* the state of being a queen. **queen·ly** *adj* fit for a queen. *adv* in a queenly manner. **queen·li·ness** *n.* **queen mother** the widow of a former king and mother of a reigning king or queen. **Queen's Counsel** a lawyer who has been appointed counsel to the Crown. *Abbrev* **QC** or **Q.C.** Also, during the reign of a king, **King's Counsel. queen–size** *adj* of a bed or mattress, larger than double, usually 152 × 203 cm. Also, **queen–sized. Queen's Printer ✿** the printer of all government documents, federal and provincial.

queer [kwir] *adj* **1** different from normal; strange: *a queer noise.* **2** *Slang* homosexual. *n Slang* a homosexual. Although it has some currency in the gay community, the slang use of **queer** to mean 'homosexual' is offensive to many people. *v Slang* spoil: *to queer a deal.* **queer·ly** *adv.* **queer·ness** *n.* ⟨German *quer* oblique⟩

quell [kwɛl] *v* **1** put down (rebellion, etc.): *to quell a riot.* **2** put an end to; suppress: *to quell one's fears.* ⟨Old English *cwellan* kill⟩

quench [kwɛntʃ] *v* **1** put an end to: *to quench a thirst.* **2** drown out: *The rain quenched the fire.* **3** suppress: *Don't quench your feelings.* **quench·less** ['kwɛntʃlɪs] *adj.* ⟨Old English *cwencean*⟩

quer·u·lous [ˈkwɛrələs] *adj* complaining; fretful; peevish. **quer·u·lous·ness** *n*. ⟨See QUARREL.⟩

que·ry [ˈkwiri] *n* **1** a question. **2** doubt. **3** *Computers* a request for a file, website, etc. in a search engine or database. **que·ry** *v*. ⟨Latin *quaere* ask!⟩

que·sa·dil·la [ˌkeɪsəˈdijə] *n* a Mexican dish consisting of a crust covered with cheese and various items, like a pizza. ⟨Spanish *queso* cheese⟩

quest [kwɛst] *n* **1** the act of searching: *a quest for treasure*. **2** an expedition in search of something ideal or holy: *the quest for the Holy Grail*. **quest** *v*. ⟨Latin *quaesita; quaerere* seek⟩

ques·tion [ˈkwɛstʃən] *n* **1** an inquiry. **2** a matter of doubt: *A question arose about the ownership of the car.* **3** a matter to be investigated: *the question of automation.* *v* **1** ask; inquire. **2** doubt; dispute: *I question the truth of his story.* **ques·tion·er** *n*. **ques·tion·ing** *adj*. ⟨Latin *quaestio; quaerere* ask⟩ **beg the question** See BEG. **beside the question** off the subject. **beyond question** without doubt: *The statements in that book are true beyond question.* **call into** or **in question** dispute. **in question a** under consideration or discussion. **b** in dispute. **out of the question** not to be considered. **without question a** without a doubt: *She is, without question, the brightest student in the school.* **b** without challenging someone's authority: *to obey without question.*

ques·tion·a·ble *adj* **1** uncertain. **2** of doubtful honesty or morality. **ques·tion·a·bly** *adv*. **question mark** a punctuation mark (?) put after a question. **ques·tion·naire** [ˌkwɛstʃəˈnɛr] *n* questions designed to obtain statistical information: *to fill out a questionnaire.* **question period 1** in the House of Commons a short period in which ministers answer questions submitted in advance by Members of Parliament. **2** a similar period in any assembly.

SYNONYMS
Ask is the general word and suggests nothing more: *I asked him why he did it.* **Question** often means ask a series of questions: *We questioned the boy until he told all he knew.* **Interrogate** is a formal word meaning 'to question formally and methodically': *The intelligence officer interrogated the prisoners.*

quet·zal [kɛtˈsɑl] *n pl* **quet·zales** [kɛtˈsɑleis] a bird having brilliant plumage. The male has long flowing tail feathers. ⟨Spanish; Nahuatl⟩

queue [kju] *n* **1** a line of people, cars, etc.; line-up. **2** *Computers* a stored sequence of items such as messages, print jobs etc., waiting to be processed. *v* wait in a line (usually with *up*): *We had to queue up to get tickets.* ⟨French = tail; Latin *coda, cauda*⟩

quib·ble [ˈkwɪbəl] *n* **1** a petty evasion of the main point: *a legal quibble.* **2** a minor criticism: *a quibble about procedure.* **quib·ble** *v*. **quib·bler** *n*. ⟨obsolete *quib;* Latin

quibus form of *quo* who (representing legal jargon⟩

quiche [kiʃ] *n* an open pie filled with an egg and cream custard and various other ingredients such as ham, cheese, or seafood. ⟨French; German *Küche* cake⟩

quick [kwɪk] *adj* **1** fast and sudden: *a quick turn.* **2** begun and ended in a short time: *a quick visit.* **3** prompt: *a quick reply.* **4** not patient: *a quick temper.* **5** ready; lively: *a quick wit.* **6** eager or ready: *quick to help others.* *n* **1** sensitive flesh under a nail : *The child bit his nails down to the quick.* **2** the sensitive part of one's feelings: *Their insults cut him to the quick.* **3** *Archaic* **the quick** *pl* living persons: *the quick and the dead.* *adv* quickly: *Come quick!* **quick·ly** *adv*. **quick·ness** *n*. ⟨Old English *cwic* alive⟩
quick bread bread, biscuits, etc., made with baking powder, that does not require the dough to be left to rise before baking. **quick·en** *v* **1** accelerate: *His pulse quickened.* **2** make or become stimulated: *Her interest quickened when the discussion turned to travel.* **3** of a child in the womb, show life by movements. **quick·ie** [ˈkwɪki] *n Informal* **1** something done very quickly: *Her last film was just a quickie.* **2** an alcoholic drink consumed in a hurry. **quick·lime** *n* calcium oxide. **Quick march!** an order to begin marching in QUICK TIME. **quick·sand** *n* soft wet sand that will not support a heavy weight. **quick·sil·ver** *n* mercury. *adj* unpredictable: *a quicksilver temperament.* **quick·step** *n* a lively dance step. **quick–tem·pered** *adj* easily angered. **quick time** a marching rate of 120 paces per minute or about 5.5 km/h. **quick·wa·ter** *n* ✳ a stretch of a stream with sufficient fall to create a strong current but where there are no rapids. **quick–wit·ted** *adj* mentally alert. **quick–wit·ted·ness** *n*.

quid [kwɪd] *n* a bite of chewing tobacco. ⟨Old English *cwidu* cud⟩

quid·nunc [ˈkwɪdˌnʌŋk] *n* an inquisitive person; gossip. ⟨Latin = what now⟩

quid pro quo [ˌkwɪd prou ˈkwou] *Latin* one thing in return for another; compensation. ⟨Latin = something for something⟩

qui·es·cent [kwiˈɛsənt] *or* [kwaɪˈɛsənt] *adj* inactive; quiet; still. **qui·es·cence** *n*. **qui·es·cent·ly** *adv*. ⟨Latin *quiescere* rest⟩

qui·et [ˈkwaɪət] *adj* **1** moving very little: *a quiet river.* **2** with no or little noise: *quiet footsteps.* **3** saying little: *a quiet person.* **4** calm; gentle: *a quiet manner.* **5** not active: *a quiet life.* **6** peaceful: *a quiet mind.* **7** out of the way; secluded: *a quiet spot in the country.* *v* **1** make quiet: *to quiet a frightened child.* **2** become quiet: *The wind quieted down.* **3** calm; allay: *The guide quieted our fears.* *n* a state of rest or stillness: *the quiet of early morning.* **qui·et·ly** *adv*. **qui·et·ness** *n*. ⟨Latin *quietus* pp of *quiescere* rest⟩
qui·et·en [ˈkwaɪətən] *v* **1** cause to become quiet. **2** become quiet (usually with *down*): *The wind finally quietened down.* **Quiet Revolution** ✳ the period of social reform that

occurred in Québec in the 1960s, accompanied by the rise of Separatism.
qui·e·tude ['kwaɪə,tjud] *or* ['kwaɪə,tud] *n* quietness; stillness. **qui·e·tus** [kwaɪ'itəs] *n* **1** final extinction: *Lack of funds has given the quietus to the project.* **2** release from life; death.

quill [kwɪl] *n* **1** a large, stiff feather from a bird. **2** ✹ formerly, in the fur trade, a feather used as a token by traders bartering with First Nations people. **3** one of the spines of a porcupine or hedgehog. ⟨Middle English *quil*⟩

quilt [kwɪlt] *n* a bed covering made of two layers of cloth with a filling between them.
v stitch with lines through layers of cloth: *to quilt a traditional design.* ⟨Old French *cuilte*; Latin *culcita* cushion⟩
quilt·ing *n* **1** material used for making quilts. **2** the activity of making quilts. **quilting bee** a social gathering to work on a quilt.

quince [kwɪns] *n* a hard fruit used for making preserves and jelly. ⟨Middle English *coyns*; Latin *cotoneum*⟩

quin·cen·te·na·ry [,kwɪnsɛn'tɛnərɪ] *or* [-'tinərɪ] *n* a 500th anniversary. ⟨Latin *quinque* five + CENTENARY⟩

quin·cunx ['kwɪnkʌŋks] *n* **1** a group of five objects with four forming the corners of a rectangle and the fifth in the centre, such as the five on a playing card. **2** a set of five stories. **3** *Botany* a group of five petals or leaves. **quin·cun·cial** [kwɪn'kʌnʃəl] *adj.* ⟨Latin = five-twelfths; *quinque* five + *uncia* twelfth⟩

qui·nine ['kwaɪnaɪn] *n Chemistry, pharmacy* a bitter drug made from cinchona bark. ⟨Spanish *quina*; Quechua *kina* bark⟩

quin·quen·ni·al [kwɪn'kwɛniəl] *adj* **1** occurring every five years. **2** of or lasting for five years. **quin·quen·ni·al·ly** *adv.* ⟨Latin *quinque* five + *annus* year⟩
quin·quen·ni·um *n* a period of five years.

quint [kwɪnt] *n Informal* quintuplet.

quin·tain ['kwɪntən] *n* an object mounted on a post, used by knights as a target for tilting. ⟨obscure origin⟩

quin·tal ['kwɪntəl] *or* ['kæntəl]. *n* ✹ *Newfoundland and Labrador* a unit used for weighing fish equal to about 50.8 kg. ⟨Latin *quintale*; Arabic *qintar* hundred pounds⟩

quin·tes·sen·tial [,kwɪntə'sɛnʃəl] *adj* of the purest or most perfect kind: *the quintessential detective of modern fiction.* **quin·tes·sence** *n.* **quin·tes·sen·tial·ly** *adv.* ⟨Latin *quinta essentia* fifth essence⟩

quin·tet or **quin·tette** [kwɪn'tɛt] *n* **1** a group of five musicians. **2** a piece of music for five voices or instruments. **3** any group of five. ⟨Italian *quintetto*; Latin *quintus* fifth⟩

quin·til·lion [kwɪn'tɪljən] *n* a cardinal number represented by 1 followed by 18 zeros. **quin·til·lionth** *adj, n* ⟨Latin *quintus* fifth + (M)ILLION⟩

quin·tu·ple [kwɪn'tʌpəl], [-'tjupəl] *or* [-'tupəl] *adj* **1** consisting of five parts. **2** five times as much or as many.

n a number, amount, etc., five times as great. *v* make or become five times as great. ⟨Latin *quintus* fifth + (QUADR)UPLE⟩
quin·tu·plet [kwɪn'tʌplɪt], [-'tjuplɪt] *or* [-'tuplɪt] *n* one of five born at the same time from the same mother. **quin·tu·pli·cate** [kwɪn'tjupləkɪt], [-'tupləkɪt] *or* [-'tʌpləkɪt] *adj* fivefold. **in quintuplicate** in five identical copies.

quip [kwɪp] *n* a witty saying. **quip, quipped, quip·ping** *v.* ⟨earlier *quippy*, Latin *quippe* oh indeed⟩

quire [kwaɪr] *n* 24 or, sometimes, 25 sheets of paper of the same size and quality. ⟨Old French *quaier*; Latin *quaterni* four each⟩

quirk [kwɜrk] *n* **1** an odd mannerism. **2** an unexpected happening: *a quirk of fate.* **quirk·y** *adj.* **quirk·i·ly** *adv.* **quirk·i·ness** *n.* ⟨origin uncertain⟩

quis·ling ['kwɪzlɪŋ] *n* **1** a person who collaborates with an enemy. **2** a traitor. ⟨V. *Quisling*, Norwegian army officer who collaborated with the Nazis⟩

quit [kwɪt] *v* **quit** or **quit·ted, quit·ting** *v* **1** stop: *to quit work.* **2** give up; let go: *She quit her job.* ⟨Old French *quiter*; Latin *quietare* discharge.⟩
quits *adj* on even terms by repayment or retaliation (never before a noun): *After the book was returned undamaged the boys were quits.* **call it quits** stop doing something: *The mosquitoes got so bad that we finally had to call it quits and go home.* **quit·ter** *n Informal* a person who gives up too easily.

quite [kwaɪt] *adv* **1** completely: *That's not quite true.* **2** really: *It's quite the thing these days.* **3** to a considerable extent or degree: *She plays the piano quite well.*
quite a a a considerable (number, size etc.): *It cost quite a lot.* **b** *Informal* impressive: *He's quite a guy.* **quite so!** true!

quiv·er[1] ['kwɪvər] *v* tremble: *to quiver in fear.* **quiv·er** *n.* ⟨origin uncertain⟩

quiv·er[2] ['kwɪvər] *n* a case for holding arrows. ⟨Old French *quivre*⟩

qui vive [,ki 'viv] a sentry's challenge to someone demanding passage. ⟨French = long live who?⟩
on the qui vive watchful; alert.

quix·ot·ic [kwɪk'sɒtɪk] *adj* characterized by very high but impractical ideals or extravagant chivalry. **quix·ot·i·cal·ly** *adv.* ⟨DON QUIXOTE⟩

quiz [kwɪz] *n, pl* **quiz·zes** a short or informal test: *a quiz in geography.*
v **quizzed, quiz·zing** *v* **1** give such a test to: *to quiz a class in history.* **2** question; interrogate: *The lawyer quizzed the witness.* ⟨origin uncertain⟩
quiz show a radio or television program in which contestants are given prizes for answering questions correctly.

quiz·zi·cal *adj* **1** odd; comical. **2** teasing: *a quizzical smile.* **3** perplexed or puzzled: *a* *quizzical look on one's face.* **quiz·zi·cal·ly** *adv.* ⟨obsolete *quiz* odd person⟩

quoit [kwɔɪt]*n* **1** a flattish ring used in a game similar to horeshoes, in which it is thrown at a peg stuck in the ground. **2 quoits** the game in which quoits are thrown at a peg (with a sg verb). ⟨Old French *coite* cushion⟩

quon·dam ['kwɒndæm] *adj* that once was; former: *the quondam king of Romania.* ⟨Latin = at one time⟩

quo·rum ['kwɔrəm] *n* the number of members of any assembly that must be present if the business done is to be legal. ⟨Latin = of whom⟩

quo·ta ['kwoutə] *n* **1** a share that is required of or due to a person or group: *a quota of tickets to sell.* **2** a limited quantity that is allowed: *a government quota on imports.* ⟨Latin *quota pars* how large a part⟩

quo·ta·tion See QUOTE.

quote [kwout] *v* **quot·ed, quot·ing 1** repeat the exact words of: *to quote Shakespeare.* **2** give as an example: *The judge quoted various cases in support of her opinion.* **3** give (a price): *to quote a price on a home.*
n **1** *Informal* quotation. **2** *Informal* QUOTATION MARK. ⟨Latin *quotare* to number chapters; *quotus* what number (in a sequence)⟩
quot·a·ble *adj* worth quoting: *a quotable comment.* **quot·a·bil·i·ty** *n.* **quot·a·bly** *adv.* **quo·ta·tion** *n* **1** somebody's words repeated exactly by another person: *From what author does this quotation come?* **2** the stating of the current price of a stock, commodity, etc. **quotation mark** one of a pair of marks used to indicate the beginning and end of a quotation. The usual marks are (" ") for a quotation and (' ') for a quotation within a quotation.

A punctuation mark at the end of a **quotation** is normally placed before the closing quotation mark, if it is part of the quotation or precedes a phrase identifying the source.
A punctuation mark is placed outside the quotation marks if its function is to punctuate the main sentence and not the quotation:
Her abrupt reply was "What do you think?"
Have you heard "If you could read my mind"?

quoth [kwouθ] *v Archaic* said (always precedes the subject): *"I would never do anything so stupid" quoth he.* ⟨Old English *cwethan* say⟩

quo·tid·i·an [kwou'tɪdiən] *adj* **1** daily. **2** ordinary; commonplace; usual. ⟨Latin *quotidie* daily; *quotus* (see QUOTE) + *dies* day⟩

quo·tient ['kwouʃənt] *n Mathematics* the number obtained by dividing one number by another. In $26 \div 2 = 13$, the quotient is 13. ⟨Latin *quotiens* how many times⟩

Qur·'an or **Ko·ran** [ku'rɑn] [kə'rɑn] *or* [kə'ræn] *n* the sacred book of Islam consisting of the revelations believed to have been made to the prophet Muhammad by Allah through the angel Gabriel. ⟨Arabic *qurān* recitation; *qara'a* read⟩

q.v. see this word ⟨Latin *quod vide* which see⟩
The abbreviation **q.v.** is also used as an instruction to refer to another book, article, etc., just mentioned. It is now often replaced in reference works by the English word **see**.

QWERTY keyboard ['kwɜrti] a keyboard for a computer terminal having the alphabetical and numerical keys in the traditional order. ⟨for the first six alphabetical keys⟩

Rr

r or **R** ['ɑr] *n, pl* **r's** or **R's** **1** the eighteenth letter of the English alphabet, or any speech sound represented by it. **2** the eighteenth person or thing in a series.
the three R's the basic elements of an education; reading, writing, and arithmetic.

R or **R.** **1** River. **2** Restricted, a film rating indicating that only those above a specified age will be admitted. **3** *US* Republican. **4** King (for Latin *rex*). **5** Queen (for Latin *regina*). **6 r** radius. **7 R** or **r** roentgen(s).

rab·bi ['ræbaɪ] *n* **1** a title for a teacher of the Jewish law. **2** a Jewish religious leader, esp the head of a congregation. **rab·bin·i·cal** [rə'bɪnɪkəl] or **rab·bin·ic** *adj.* **rab·bin·i·cal·ly** *adv.* ⟨Hebrew = master⟩

rab·bit ['ræbɪt] *n* any of various vegetarian burrowing mammals related to hares. **rab·bit·like** *adj.* ⟨Middle English *rabet*⟩
rabbit ears *Informal* a small indoor television antenna consisting of two rods in a V shape.
rabbit punch a quick, hard blow to the base of the skull.

rab·ble ['ræbəl] *n* a disorderly crowd. ⟨Middle English *rabel* crowd; *rablen* jabber⟩
rab·ble–rous·er *n* a person who tries to stir up people to violence, as a form of protest. **rab·ble–rous·ing** *adj, n.*

rab·id ['ræbɪd] *adj* **1** affected with rabies: *a rabid dog.* **2** furious. **3** fanatical; violent: *a rabid idealist.* **rab·id·ly** *adv.* **ra·bid·i·ty** or **rab·id·ness** *n.* ⟨Latin *rabere* be mad⟩

ra·bies ['reibiz] *n* an infectious viral disease that can be transmitted by the bite of an animal that has the disease.

rac·coon [rə'kun] or [ræ'kun] *n* any of a genus of small, omnivorous mammals having a bushy, ringed tail, and a dark patch around the eyes. Also, **ra·coon.** ⟨Algonquian⟩

race¹ [reis] *n* **1** a contest of speed. **2** Often, **races** *pl* a series of horse races. **3** any contest that suggests a race: *a political race.* **4** a strong current of water: *a mill race.*
v **1** engage in a contest of speed. **2** move swiftly. **3** of an engine, run too fast when idling. ⟨Old Norse *rás*⟩
race·track or **race·course** *n* a prepared track for racing. **race·horse** *n* a horse bred for racing. **rac·er** *n* a person who races, or an animal, vehicle, etc. that is used for racing.

race² [reis] *n* **1** a traditional grouping of human beings, distinguished mainly by such traits as dominant blood types, skin colour, body proportions, etc. **2** one of the major divisions of living things: *the human race, the race of birds.* **3** a group of people having some feature in common: *the Scottish race, the Nordic race, the brave race of sailors.* ⟨French; Italian *razza*⟩
ra·cial ['reiʃəl] *adj* to do with a human race: *racial traits.* **ra·cial·ly** *adv.* **rac·ism** ['reisɪzəm] *n* **1** prejudice against a person or group because

of a difference of race or of cultural or ethnic background. **2** belief in the superiority of a particular race. **rac·ist** *n, adj.*

ra·ceme [rei'sim] or [rə'sim] *n Botany* a type of flower cluster having the flowers on short stalks along a stem. ⟨Latin *racemus* cluster⟩

rack¹ [ræk] *n* **1** a fixture with bars, shelves, etc., to keep things on: *a towel rack.* **2** a frame made of bars to hold hay and other food for cattle, etc. **3** a former instrument of torture that stretched the body of the victim. **4** *Billiards* a triangular frame used for arranging the balls. ⟨probably Middle Dutch *rec* framework⟩
v **1** hurt very much: *racked with grief.* **2** stretch; strain.
off the rack (of clothes) ready-made. **on the rack** in great pain. **rack one's brains** think as hard as one can. **rack up a** score (points, a victory, etc.). **b** *Billiards* set up (the balls) in the rack.

rack² [ræk] *n* wreck; destruction (now only in the phrase **rack and ruin**).
go to rack and ruin decay; become destroyed. ⟨variant of *wrack¹*⟩

rack³ [ræk] *n* broken clouds driven by the wind. *v* (of clouds) be driven by the wind. ⟨Scandinavian⟩

rack⁴ [ræk] *n* a rib section of lamb, mutton, or veal. ⟨origin uncertain⟩

rack·et¹ ['rækɪt] *n* **1** loud noise; uproar: *Who's making all the racket?* **2** *Informal* any dishonest scheme. **3** *Slang* any business or occupation: *What's your racket?*
v **1** move about in a noisy way. **2 a** take part in an exciting social life. **b** travel casually in search of adventure (used with *around*). ⟨perhaps imitative⟩
rack·et·eer *n* one who extorts money by threatening violence. *v* obtain money by such means. **rack·et·eer·ing** *n.*

rack·et² ['rækɪt] *n* See RACQUET.

rac·on·teur [ˌrækɒn'tɜr] *French* [ʀakɔ̃'tœʀ] *n* a person who is skilful at telling stories, anecdotes, etc. **rac·on·teuse** [-'tɜz] *French* ['ʀakɔ̃'tøz] *n.* ⟨French; *raconter* tell⟩

rac·quet ['rækɪt] *n* **1** a bat used in games like tennis, consisting of a network of nylon, gut, etc. stretched in a frame. **2** *Informal* the paddle used in table tennis. ⟨French *raquette; Arabic *rāḥat* palm of the hand⟩

rac·y ['reisi] *adj* **1** lively. **2** slightly indecent: *a racy novel.* **rac·i·ly** *adv.* **rac·i·ness** *n.* ⟨*race²*, in the sense of particular class⟩

rad¹ [ræd] *n* a unit of nuclear radiation equal to 100 ergs of energy per gram, for absorbed doses of radiation. ⟨*rad(iation)*⟩

rad² [ræd] *n Informal* radiator.

rad³ *Mathematics* **1** radical. **2** radian.

ra·dar ['reidɑr] *n* a system for determining the distance, direction, etc. of objects by the reflection of high-frequency radio waves. ⟨short for *radio detecting and ranging*⟩
radar trap a police apparatus that uses radar

to detect road vehicles travelling faster than the speed limit.

ra·di·al, ra·di·an See RADIUS.

ra·di·ance, ra·di·ant See RADIATE.

ra·di·ate ['reidi,eit] *v* **1** give out rays of: *The sun radiates light.* **2** issue in rays: *Heat radiates from those steam pipes.* **3** spread out as if from a centre: *Roads radiate from the city in every direction.* ⟨Latin *radiare; radius* ray⟩ **ra·di·ant** ['reidiənt] *adj* **1** expressing joy or good health: *a radiant smile.* **2** sending out rays of light or heat: *The sun is a radiant body.* **3** bright with light. **ra·di·ance** or **ra·di·an·cy** *n*. **ra·di·ant·ly** *adv*. **radiant energy** *Physics* a form of energy perceived as heat, light, X rays, etc. **radiant heating** a method of heating a room, etc., by means of pipes or wires concealed in walls, baseboards, etc. **ra·di·a·tion** *n* **1** the process of giving out radiant energy. **2** the energy radiated. **3** radioactive rays. **4** the process of using a radioactive material to kill diseased tissue. **radiation sickness** *Pathology* a disease resulting from an overdose of radiation from radioactive materials. **ra·di·a·tor** ['rædi,eitər] *n* **1** a heating device consisting of a set of pipes through which steam or hot water passes. **2** a device for circulating coolant in an engine.

rad·i·cal ['rædəkəl] *adj* **1** fundamental: *a radical change.* **2** *Grammar* of or pertaining to a root. **3** *Botany* arising from the root. **4** *Mathematics* having to do with or forming the root of a number or quantity.
n **1** a person who favours fundamental changes. **2** *Chemistry* an atom or group of atoms acting as a unit in reactions. **3** *Mathematics* the sign (√) to show that some root is to be extracted. **rad·i·cal·ly** *adv*. **rad·i·cal·ness** *n*. ⟨Latin *radicis* root⟩ **rad·i·cal·ism** *n* extreme views. **rad·i·cle** *n Botany* **1** the lower end of the stem of a plant embryo. **2** a small root.

ra·di·i ['reidi,aɪ] *n* a pl of RADIUS.

ra·di·o ['reidiou] *n* **1** an apparatus for receiving sounds sent as electromagnetic waves, without wires. **2** the business of radio broadcasting: *She got a job in radio.* **ra·di·o** *adj, v*. ⟨independent use of *radio-* (def. 1)⟩ **radio control** control by means of radio signals: *Our garage door is operated by radio control.* **ra·di·o–con·trolled** *adj*. **radio frequency** any frequency of electromagnetic waves between about 10 kHz and 300 000 MHz, used in transmitting radio and television signals. *Abbrev* **RF**. **radio source** *Astronomy* a supernova, quasar, or other celestial source of radio waves. **radio telescope** a radio receiver and antenna, for the study of radio waves from bodies in outer space. **radio wave** an electromagnetic wave of RADIO FREQUENCY.

radio– *combining form* **1** to do with radio: *radiotelegraphy.* **2** to do with rays or radiation: *radiograph.* **3** to do with radioactivity: *radioisotope.* **4** to do with a radius: *radiosymmetrical.*
ra·di·o·ac·tive *adj Chemistry Physics* giving off radiant energy in the form of alpha, beta, or

gamma rays as a result of the breaking up of atoms. **ra·di·o·ac·tiv·i·ty** *n*. **radioactive dating** a method of determining the age of anything of organic origin by measuring the rate of decay of radioactive isotopes. **ra·di·o·graph** *n* a picture produced by X rays, usually called an X ray. **ra·di·og·ra·phy** *n*. **ra·di·o·graph·ic** *adj*. **ra·di·og·ra·pher** *n*. **ra·di·o·i·so·tope** [,-'əisə,toup] *n* a radioactive isotope, esp one produced artificially. **ra·di·ol·o·gy** *n* the branch of medicine dealing with the use of radioactive substances in the treatment of disease. **ra·di·o·log·i·cal** *adj*. **ra·di·o·log·i·cal·ly** *adv*. **ra·di·ol·o·gist** *n*. **ra·di·os·co·py** *n* an examination by X ray. **ra·di·o·scop·ic** *adj*. **ra·di·o·sen·si·tive** *adj* sensitive to various forms of radiant energy such as X rays. **ra·di·o·sen·si·tiv·i·ty** *n*. **ra·di·o·sym·met·ri·cal** *adj* symmetrical about a central point. **ra·di·o·ther·a·py** [-'θɛrəpi] *n* the treatment of disease by means of radiation. **ra·di·o·ther·a·pist** *n*.

rad·ish ['rædɪʃ] *n* a herb of the mustard family, widely cultivated for its red-skinned, crisp root. ⟨Latin *radix* root⟩

ra·di·um ['reidiəm] *n* a radioactive metallic element found in uranium ores. *Symbol* **Ra** ⟨Latin *radius* ray⟩

ra·di·us ['reidiəs] *n, pl* **-di·i** [-di,aɪ] or **-di·us·es** **1** any straight line going from the centre to the outside of a circle or a sphere. **2** a circular area measured by the length of its radius: *The explosion could be heard within a radius of 10 km.* **3** range of influence, experience, etc.: *beyond the radius of her influence.* **4** *Anatomy* the shorter of the two bones of the forearm. ⟨Latin = ray⟩
ra·di·al ['reidiəl] *adj* arranged like rays from a centre: *radial symmetry.* **ra·di·al·ly** *adv*. **radial tire** a tire in which the cords extending to the edges of the tire are at right angles to the centre line of the tread. **ra·di·an** ['reidiən] *n* an SI unit equal to the angle formed between two radii of a circle that cut off an arc on the circumference equal in length to the radius. There are 2π radians in a circle. *Symbol* **rad**

ra·don ['reidɒn] *n* a radioactive gaseous element, the densest gas known. *Symbol* **Rn** ⟨*radium*⟩

raf·fi·a ['ræfiə] *n* a fibre from the leafstalks of a palm, used in making baskets, mats, etc. ⟨Malagasy *rafia*⟩

raf·fish ['ræfɪʃ] *adj* **1** crude; rowdy; vulgar. **2** rakishly unconventional. **raf·fish·ly** *adv*. **raf·fish·ness** *n*. ⟨*riffraff*⟩

raf·fle ['ræfəl] *n* a lottery.
v sell (an article) by a raffle (usually used with *off*): *to raffle off a quilt.* ⟨Old French *rafle* dice game⟩

raft¹ [ræft] *n* **1** a platform made of logs, boards, etc. used for transportation on water. **2** *Logging* pieces of timber lashed together for floating downstream. **3** an inflatable boat. **4** a floating ice formation resulting from the piling up of cakes of ice in layers.
v **1** travel by raft. **2** of ice, be piled high, layer

upon layer, as a result of pressure. **3 ⚒** *Logging* drive (logs, timber, etc.) by means of a raft. ⟨Old Norse *raptr* log⟩

raft² [ræft] *n Informal* a large number; abundance: *a raft of experience.* ⟨variant of *raff* heap; *riffraff*⟩

raf·ter ['ræftər] *n* a supporting beam, often slanting, of a roof. ⟨Old English *ræfter*⟩

rag¹ [ræg] *n* **1** a torn or waste piece of cloth. **2** any cloth used for cleaning, washing, etc. **3 rags a** *pl* tattered clothes. **b** *Informal* any clothes. **4** *Informal* a newspaper, esp one considered as inferior. **rag·like** *adj.* ⟨Old Norse *rögg* shaggy tuft⟩

rag·a·muf·fin ['rægə,mʌfən] *n* a ragged, dirty child. **rag doll 1** a doll made of cloth, esp scraps. **2** a person who is limp, passive, unenergetic, etc. **rag·ged** ['rægɪd] *adj* **1** worn into rags. **2** not straight and tidy; uneven. **rag·ged·ly** *adv.* **rag·ged·ness** *n.* **run ragged** exhaust completely by stress, overwork, etc. **rag·ged·y** *adj Informal* rather ragged or tattered. **rag·tag** *adj* **1** ragged or slovenly. **2** being an odd mixture of elements. *n* rabble, esp in **ragtag and bobtail. rag·weed** *n* any of a genus of plants whose flowers produce large amounts of pollen.

rag² [ræg] *v* **ragged, rag·ging** *Slang* **1** scold. **2** tease; torment. ⟨origin uncertain⟩

rag the puck *Hockey* keep control of the puck by skilful stick-handling and elusive skating, usually as a means of killing time when one's own team is shorthanded.

rag³ [ræg] *n* a piece of music in RAGTIME. ⟨*ragtime*⟩

rage [reidʒ] *n* **1** violent anger. **2** a fashion that is popular for a short time, esp in (**all**) **the rage**: *the rage for hotpants in the 60s.* *v* **1** speak or move with furious anger. **2** act violently: *A storm is raging.* ⟨Old French; Latin *rabia*, from *rabies*⟩

rag·time ['ræg,taɪm] *n* an early style of jazz performed esp on the piano, characterized by a strong rhythm base and a syncopated melody. ⟨possibly *ragged*, for the syncopation⟩

raid [reid] *n* **1** a sudden attack. **2** a deliberate attempt by speculators to force down prices on stock exchanges. **3** an aggressive attempt by a business to lure staff from a competitor. *v* **1** attack suddenly. **2** force a way into; enter and seize what is in: *The police raided the gambling house.* **raid·er** *n.* ⟨variant of Old English *rād*. See ROAD.⟩

rail¹ [reil] *n* **1** a bar extending between posts, brackets, etc., and used as a barrier: *the top rail of the fence.* **2** a series of bars forming a track for a train, etc. **3** railway: *They shipped their car by rail.* ⟨Old French *reille*; Latin *regula* straight rod⟩

off the rails a not functioning properly. **b** *Slang* mentally deranged. **rail in** enclose within a fence.

rail fence any of several kinds of fence made of rails split from logs. **rail·head** *n* **1** the end of a railway. **2** the farthest point to which the tracks of a railway under construction have been laid; END OF STEEL. **3** a point on a railway that serves as a depot for military supplies, etc. **rail·ing** *n* **1** a barrier made of rails, esp along the side of a staircase, etc. **2** material for making rails. **rail·road** *n esp US* railway. *v Informal* rush (a person or thing) through something, esp to prevent careful consideration: *to railroad a bill through a committee.* **rail·way** *n* **1** a track for trains, consisting of parallel steel rails on heavy wooden crosswise beams called **ties. 2** tracks, stations, etc., of a transportation system that uses rails: *He worked for the railway for years.* **rail·way·man** *n.*

rail² [reil] *v* complain bitterly; use violent language: *He railed at his hard luck.* **rail·ing** *n.* ⟨French *railler*; Latin *ragere* scream⟩

rail·ler·y *n* **1** good-humoured ridicule; teasing. **2** a bantering remark.

rail³ [reil] *n, pl* **rails** or (esp collectively) **rail** any of numerous wading birds having very long toes that allow them to run over the mud of marshes. ⟨French *râle*; Latin *rascla*⟩

rai·ment ['reimənt] *n Poetic* clothing; garments. ⟨short for *arraiment*; *array*⟩

rain [rein] *n* **1** water falling in the form of drops from clouds. **2** a thick, fast fall of anything: *a rain of bullets.* *v* **1** be the case that rain is falling (with the subject *it*): *It was raining when we left.* **2** pour down like rain: *Tears rained down his cheeks.* **rain·less** *adj.* ⟨Old English *regn*⟩

rain cats and dogs *Informal* rain very hard.

rained out of an outdoor sports event, etc., cancelled because of rain.

rain·bow *n* an arch of coloured light seen in the sky when the sun's rays shine through rain, mist, or spray. The colours of the rainbow are violet, indigo, blue, green, yellow, orange, and red. **rainbow trout** a trout having a greenish back and a pinkish band along each side. **rain check 1** a ticket for future use, given to the spectators at an outdoor performance stopped by rain. **2** any similar ticket. **3** *Informal* an understanding that an invitation will be renewed: *May I take a rain check on your invitation to dinner?* **rain·coat** *n* a waterproof coat. **rain·drop** *n* a drop of rain. **rain·fall** *n* **1** a shower of rain: *a heavy rainfall during the night.* **2** the amount of water in the form of rain that falls in a particular area over a certain period of time. **rain·for·est** a region of tropical evergreen forest, where rainfall is heavy throughout the year. **rain·mak·ing** *n* a making rain artificially. **rain·proof** *adj* not letting rain through: *The roof of our shed isn't rainproof any more.* **rain·storm** *n* a storm with much heavy rain. **rain·wa·ter** *n* water that has been collected from rain. **rain·wear** *n* clothing made to be worn in the rain, such as raincoats, etc. **rain·y** *adj* having much rain: *rainy weather.* **rain·i·ly** *adv.* **rain·i·ness** *n.* **rainy day** a time of need, or of boredom or leisure, in the future: *to save for a rainy day.*

raise [reiz] *v* **1** lift up: *to raise one's hand.*

2 increase in degree, amount, etc.: *to raise the rent.* **3** set upright: *to raise a totem pole.* **4** put into a higher position: *to raise a sales representative to manager.* **5** breed; grow: *The farmer raises cattle.* **6** cause: *to raise a laugh.* **7 a** bring forward: *The speaker raised an interesting point.* **b** utter, esp vigorously: *raise a cheer.* **8** build; set up: *to raise a fund.* **9** bring up; rear: *Parents raise their children.* **10** *Curling* hit (a rock of one's own team) into a position nearer to the button or house.
n an increase in amount, price, pay, etc. ⟨Old Norse *reisa;* Gmc. causative of *rīsan* rise⟩
raise Cain (**the devil, mischief, the roof,** etc.) *Slang* make a disturbance; create an uproar.
raised *adj* **1** embossed. **2** of cloth, having a fuzzy surface. **3** leavened with yeast as opposed to baking powder: *raised bread.*

SYNONYMS
Raise means to bring something to a higher level: *Raise your right hand.* Lift means to take something, usually heavy, up from the ground or some other low level: *Please lift the table.* Elevate chiefly means 'to raise to a higher rank': *Good reading elevates the mind.*

rai·sin ['reizən] *n* a sweet, dried grape. ⟨Old French; Latin *racemus* grape cluster⟩

rai·son d'être [Rɛzɔ̃'dɛtR] *French* reason for being; justification.

rake¹ [reik] *n* a long-handled garden tool having at one end a bar with prongs, for smoothing soil, gathering leaves, etc.
v **1** use a rake. **2** scratch: *He raked his arm on a loose nail.* **3** search carefully: *They raked the newspapers for descriptions of the accident.* **4** fire guns along the length of (a ship, line of soldiers, etc.). ⟨Old English *raca*⟩
rake in gather (something, esp money) in great amounts and very quickly. **rake over the coals** reprimand very severely. **rake up a** gather together as if by raking: *She raked up enough money to rent a canoe.* **b** bring to light unpleasant facts about (someone's past, a public scandal, etc.).

rake² [reik] *n* a dissolute man, esp one who belongs to fashionable society. ⟨short for *rakehell*, libertine; *rake¹* + *hell*⟩
rak·ish *adj* jaunty: *a hat set at a rakish angle.*

rake³ [reik] *n* a slant; slope: *The auditorium has a steep rake.* **rake** *v.* ⟨origin uncertain⟩

ral·ly ['ræli] *v* **1** bring or come together again: *to rally the fleeing troops.* **2** come to help a person, party, or cause: *She rallied to the side of her injured friend.* **3** recover health or confidence: *The first question threw her off, but she rallied and answered the rest with assurance.* **4** *Tennis, etc.* hit the ball back and forth several times. **ral·ly** *n.* ⟨French *rallier*; re- again + *allier* ally⟩

ram [ræm] *n* **1** a male sheep. **2** a part of a machine that strikes heavy blows. **3** BATTERING RAM.
v **rammed, ram·ming 1** strike head on: *One ship rammed the other ship.* **2** drive down or in by heavy force: *He rammed the bolt into the wall.* **3** force acceptance of: *to ram an*

unpopular bill through Parliament. ⟨Old English *ramm*⟩

RAM [ræm] *Computers* the main memory of a computer. ⟨random-access memory⟩

Ra·ma ['ramə] *n Hinduism* an incarnation of the god Vishnu, representing grace and justice toward people.

Ram·a·dan or **Ram·a·zan** [ˌramə'dan] *or* [ˌramə'zan] *n* the ninth month of the Muslim year, during which fasting is rigidly practised daily from dawn until sunset. ⟨Arabic *Ramadān*, orig. the hot month⟩

ram·ble ['ræmbəl] *v* **1** wander about for pleasure. **2** talk or write about one thing and then another with no clear connections. **3** grow irregularly in various directions: *Vines rambled over the wall.*
n a walk for pleasure. **ram·bler** *n.* **ram·bling** *adj.* ⟨Middle English *romblen; romen* roam⟩

ram·bunc·tious [ræm'bʌŋkʃəs] *adj* uncontrollably exuberant: *The kids were very rambunctious after travelling all day.* ⟨possibly *ram* knock around + variant of *bumptious*⟩

ram·ie ['reimi] *or* ['ræmi] *n* the fibre from a plant of the nettle family, used for fabrics. ⟨Malay *rami* plant⟩

ram·i·fi·ca·tion [ˌræməfə'keiʃən] *n* **1** a branching out of anything. **2** a branch; part. **3** a result, consequence, extension, etc.: *the ramifications of an idea.* **ram·i·fy** *v.* ⟨Latin *ramificare; ramus* branch + *facere* make⟩

ramp [ræmp] *n* **1** a sloping walk or roadway connecting two levels of a building, road, etc. **2** a sloping stretch from the shore into the water, for launching boats from a trailer. ⟨French *rampe; ramper* rear up⟩

ram·page ['ræmpeidʒ] *n* a spell of violent behaviour: *The mad elephant went on a rampage and killed its keeper.*
v [ræm'peidʒ] *or* ['ræmpeidʒ] rush wildly about; behave violently; rage. **ram·pa·geous** [ræm'peidʒəs] *adj.* **ram·pa·geous·ness** *n.* ⟨possibly French *ramper*⟩
on the rampage acting aggressively.

ramp·ant ['ræmpənt] *adj* **1** growing without any check: *Rampant vines covered the fence.* **2** passing beyond restraint or usual limits: *Anarchy was rampant after the dictator died.* **3** *Heraldry* (placed after the noun) of a beast, represented as standing up on the left hind leg, with the forelegs raised, in profile: *lions rampant.* **ramp·an·cy** *n.* **ramp·ant·ly** *adv.* ⟨Old French *ramper* rear up⟩
run rampant spread unchecked: *nasty rumours running rampant.*

ram·part ['ræmpart] *or* ['ræmpərt] *n* **1** a wide bank of earth built around a fort to help defend it. **2** ✱ in the Northwest: **a** a high bank on either side of a river flowing through a canyon. **b** the canyon itself. ⟨French *remparer* fortify; Latin *re-* back + *ante* before + *parare* prepare⟩

ram·pike ['ræmpəik] *n* ✱ a tall, dead tree, esp one that has been blackened and stripped of its branches by fire. ⟨origin uncertain⟩

ram·shack·le ['ræm,ʃækəl] *adj* loose and shaky; likely to come apart: *ramshackle old buildings.* ⟨possibly *ransack*⟩

ran [ræn] *v* pt of RUN.

ranch [ræntʃ] *n* a large farm with grazing land, for raising cattle, sheep, horses, etc. in large numbers.
v work on or operate a ranch. ⟨Spanish *rancho* camp⟩
ranch·er *n* a person who owns or operates a ranch. **ranch hand** a person employed on a ranch, esp a cattle ranch. **ranch house 1** the main building on a ranch. **2** ✸ on the West coast, a large communal dwelling of various coastal First Nations peoples. **3** a long, low, one-storey house. **ranch·land** *n* land used or suitable for ranching.

ranch·er·ie ['ræntʃəri] *n* ✸ *British Columbia* a village or settlement of First Nations people, esp the settled part of a First Nations reserve. ⟨Spanish *ranchería*⟩

ran·cid ['rænsɪd] *adj* **1** esp of fats or oils, stale; spoiled: *rancid butter.* **2** tasting or smelling like stale fat: *a rancid odour.* **ran·cid·ly** *adv.* **ran·cid·i·ty** or **ran·cid·ness** *n.* ⟨Latin *rancere* be rank⟩

ran·cour or **rancor** ['ræŋkər] *n* extreme hatred or spite. **ran·cor·ous** *adj.* **ran·cor·ous·ly** *adv.* ⟨Latin *ranco* ; *rancere* be rank⟩

R & B RHYTHM AND BLUES.

R and D or **R & D** *Informal* research and development: *They're spending millions on R and D in the energy field.*

ran·dom ['rændəm] *adj* **1** happening by chance or with no plan or pattern. **2** not regular or uniform: *wallpaper with a random pattern.* **3** *Statistics* to do with a method of statistical sampling in which each member of a set has an equal chance of being selected: *random sample.* **ran·dom·ly** *adv.* **ran·dom·ness** *n.* ⟨Old French *randon* rapid rush⟩ **at random** with no plan or criterion: *She took a book at random from the shelf.*
random access *Computers* a method of accessing data without searching through the data surrounding it. Also called **direct access.**
ran·dom–ac·cess *adj.* **ran·dom·ize** *v* make random, esp selection in a sample. **random walk** *Mathematics* the path of a point or quantity, each successive move of which is randomly determined.

SYNONYMS

Random emphasizes being undetermined by any criterion: *Random sampling is a basic statistical method.* **Haphazard** emphasizes giving no thought to fitness for a purpose: *Because of her haphazard way of choosing clothes, she never looks well dressed.*

R & R *Informal* **1** rest and recuperation or rest and relaxation (from *rest and recuperation* leave in the US military): *After working very hard on several presentations, she repaired to her cottage for some R & R.* **2** rock-and-roll.

ran·dy ['rændi] *adj* **1** coarse and boisterous in behaviour. **2** lustful. ⟨origin uncertain⟩

rang¹ [ræŋ] *v* pt of RING².

rang² [ræŋ] *n* ✸ *Québec* a series of long narrow lots, usually fronting on a road. ⟨French = row⟩

range [reɪndʒ] *n* **1** the distance between certain limits: *a range of prices between $50 and $100.* **2** the distance a gun, etc. can shoot. **3** the maximum distance that can be travelled by a vehicle without refuelling. **4** *Statistics* in a sample, the difference between the largest and smallest values. **5** *Music* the extent, from lowest tone to highest, of the pitch of a voice, musical instrument, or piece of music: *He has an extraordinary range and can sing tenor just as well as bass.* **6** a place to practise shooting: *a rifle range.* **7** extensive areas of grassland suitable for grazing. **8** a row of mountains. **9** the area in which certain plants or animals live. **10** an appliance that includes a stove and an oven: *a gas range.* **11** ✸ a row of lots, concessions, or townships.
v **1** vary within certain limits: *prices ranging from $5 to $10.* **2** wander; rove; roam: *His eyes ranged over the crowd.* **3** put in groups: *The swimming classes are ranged by age and ability.* **4** put or group on a given side of a conflict: *Loyal citizens ranged themselves with the king.* **5** find the distance of (a target). **6** be found; occur (in a habitat): *a plant ranging from Canada to Mexico.* ⟨Old French *ranger* array⟩
rangefinder an instrument for determining the distance between an object and an observer. **range·lil·y** *n* ✸ the wild orange-red lily. **rang·er** *n* **1** a person employed to guard a tract of forest. **2** ✸ In the North, a member of a First Nations or Inuit people who acts as a volunteer military scout or observer.

rang·y¹ ['reɪndʒi] *adj* slender and long-limbed: *a rangy horse.* **rang·i·ness** *n.* ⟨range⟩

rang·y² ['ræŋi] *adj Slang* of children, rambunctious because of restlessness. ⟨origin uncertain⟩

rank¹ [ræŋk] *n* **1** a line, esp of soldiers, placed side by side. **2 ranks** *pl* **a** soldiers and junior non-commissioned officers. **b** RANK AND FILE. **3** a grade; class: *the military rank of colonel.* **4** a high position: *A duke is a man of rank.* **5** any of the horizontal rows of squares on a chessboard. Compare FILE¹ (def. 4).
v **1** arrange in a row. **2** have a certain position in relation to others: *Bill ranked low in the test.* **3** assign a rank or position to: *Rank the continents in order of size.* **4** be more important than; outrank: *A major ranks a captain.* ⟨Old French *renc*⟩
break rank(s) a a step out of line. **b** depart from the practice, opinions, etc. of one's group. **pull rank** *Informal* use one's superior position to get one's own way.
rank and file 1 an armed force excluding its officers. **2** the members of an organization, society, etc., excluding the leaders: *The union leaders were in favour of the offer but it was rejected by a vote of the rank and file.*

rank·ing adj 1 having the highest rank: *the ranking officer present.* 2 recognized as being of high calibre: *Most of the association members are ranking artists.* n 1 a list of people or things in order of their position relative to some standard. 2 a position in such a list.

rank² [ræŋk] adj 1 large and coarse: *rank grass.* 2 having a strong, unpleasant smell or taste: *rank meat.* 3 strongly marked; extreme: *rank nonsense.* **rank·ly** adv. **rank·ness** n. ⟨Old English *ranc* proud⟩

ran·kle ['ræŋkəl] v cause anger, bitterness, or irritation (*in*): *Even after all those years, the memory of the insult still rankled.* ⟨Old French *rancler*; Latin *dracunculus* sore, *draco* serpent⟩

ran·sack ['rænsæk] v 1 search through thoroughly: *I ransacked the whole closet, but couldn't find the belt.* 2 go through with the intent of plundering or robbing: *Burglars had ransacked the house.* **ran·sack·er** n. ⟨Old Norse *rann* house + *-saka* search⟩

ran·som ['rænsəm] n the price paid or demanded before a captive is set free.
v obtain the release of (a captive) by paying a price. ⟨Old French *ranson*; Latin *redemptionis*⟩

rant [rænt] v speak wildly or violently.
n an extravagant or violent speech. **rant·er** n. **rant·ing·ly** adv. ⟨Middle Dutch *ranten*⟩
rant and rave scold violently; speak wildly and extravagantly at great length.

rap¹ [ræp] n 1 a quick, light blow. 2 *Slang* a blame. b conviction; prison sentence.
v **rapped, rap·ping** 1 knock sharply. 2 say sharply: *rap out an answer.* 3 *Slang* rebuke; criticize; condemn. ⟨imitative⟩
beat the rap *Slang* escape conviction or prison sentence. **bum rap** *Slang* an unfair judgment or penalty. **rap on the knuckles** *Informal* an unduly light punishment. **take the rap** *Slang* take the blame, often for someone else.
rap sheet *Slang* a record kept by law enforcement agencies of a person's arrests and convictions: *The RCMP had a long rap sheet on every member of the gang.*

rap² [ræp] n *Informal* the least bit: *I don't care a rap.* ⟨18c Irish counterfeit half-penny⟩

rap³ [ræp] **rapped, rap·ping** *Slang* v 1 talk informally; chat. 2 perform rap (*n* def. 2).
n 1 a free, informal talk. 2 a type of popular music consisting of rhyming verse, often improvised, chanted to a strong, repetitive beat. **rap·per** n. ⟨possibly special use of *rap¹*⟩

ra·pa·cious [rə'peɪʃəs] adj 1 seizing by force; plundering. 2 greedy. 3 of animals, living by the capture of prey. **ra·pa·cious·ly** adv. **ra·pac·i·ty** [rə'pæsɪti] or **ra·pa·cious·ness** n. ⟨Latin *rapacis* grasping; *rapere* seize⟩

rape¹ [reɪp] n 1 the crime of an individual having sexual intercourse with a person forcibly and without his or her consent. 2 any forcible or outrageous violation: *the rape of a country's natural resources.* **rape** v. ⟨Latin *rapere* seize⟩
rap·ist n a person who commits rape.

rape² [reɪp] n a plant of the mustard family, widely cultivated for its seeds (rapeseed) that yield rapeseed oil, and as a forage crop for sheep and hogs. See also CANOLA. ⟨Latin *rapa* turnip⟩

rap·id ['ræpɪd] adj 1 quick: *a rapid worker.* 2 going at a fast rate: *rapid growth.*
n Usually, **rapids** pl a part of a river's course where the water rushes quickly, often over rocks. **ra·pid·i·ty** [rə'pɪdəti] n. **rap·id·ly** adv. ⟨Latin *rapidus*; *rapere* hurry away⟩
rapid eye movement a rapid movement of the eyes under closed lids, characteristic of the stage of sleep during which a person dreams. *Abbrev* **REM**. **rap·id–fire** adj 1 firing or adapted for firing shots in quick succession. 2 done quickly or sharply: *a rapid-fire style of speaking.* **rapid transit** a system of fast public transportation by railway, often raised above the ground.

ra·pi·er ['reɪpiər] n a light, two-edged sword. **ra·pi·er·like** adj. ⟨Middle French *rapière*; *râpe* grater, for its perforated guard⟩

rap·pel [rə'pɛl] n a technique for descending a cliff, etc. by means of a double rope passed around the climber's body in such a way that he or she can control the rate of descent.
v -**pelled** or -**peled**, -**pel·ling** or -**pel·ing**. ⟨French; *rappeler* to recall⟩

rap·pé pie ['ræpeɪ] ✺ *Maritimes* a pie with grated onions, potatoes, and pork. ⟨Acadian French *tarte râpée*, literally grated pie⟩

rap·port [rə'pɔr] *French* [ʀa'pɔʀ] n a connection or relationship, esp a harmonious one: *He has no rapport with his students.* ⟨French; *rapporter* bring back⟩

rap·proche·ment [ˌræprʌʃ'mɑ̃] *French* [ʀapʀɔʃ'mɑ̃] n the establishment or renewal of friendly relations. ⟨French; *rapprocher* bring near⟩

rapt [ræpt] adj 1 completely engrossed. 2 caused by or showing delight: *a rapt smile.* **rapt·ly** adv. **rapt·ness** n. ⟨Latin *raptus*, pp of *rapere* seize⟩
rap·ture ['ræptʃər] n 1 a strong feeling that absorbs the mind; very great joy. 2 Often, **raptures** pl an expression of great joy. **rap·tur·ous** adj. **rap·tur·ous·ly** adv.

rap·tor ['ræptər] n BIRD OF PREY. ⟨Latin = robber; *rapere* seize⟩
rap·to·ri·al adj 1 to do with birds of prey. 2 adapted for seizing prey: *raptorial claws.*

ra·quette [ræ'kɛt] n ✺ snowshoe. Also **ra·quet**, **rack·et**, or **rac·quette**. ⟨Cdn. French⟩

rare¹ [rɛr] adj 1 seldom seen or occurring; uncommon: *A solar eclipse is a rare event.* 2 unusually good: *Shakespeare had rare powers as a dramatist.* 3 not dense: *The higher you go, the rarer is the air.* **rare·ness** n. ⟨Latin *rarus*⟩
rare–earth metal or **element** *Chemistry* any of the rare metallic elements that have atomic numbers from 57 to 71 inclusive. **rar·e·fy** ['rɛrə,faɪ] v make or become less dense: *The air in the mountains is rarefied.* **rar·e·fac·tion** [ˌrɛrə'fækʃən] n. **rare·ly** adv 1 not often: *Horse-drawn delivery carts are rarely seen these days.* 2 unusually well:

a rarely carved panel. **rar·i·ty** ['rɛrɪti] *n* **1** something rare: *A thirty-year-old car is a rarity*. **2** a lack of density: *The rarity of mountain air is bad for people with weak hearts*. **3** unusual excellence: *The rarity of her thesis won her the Governor-General's medal*.

SYNONYMS
Rare describes something uncommon or unusual at any time: *The Gutenberg Bible is a rare book*. Scarce describes something usually or formerly common or plentiful, but not existing in large enough quantity at the present time: *Water is becoming scarce in some parts of the country*.

rare² [rer] *adj* of meat, cooked so that the inside is still red. **rare·ness** *n*. ⟨Old English *hrēr*⟩

rar·ing ['rɛrɪŋ] *adj Informal* very eager: *raring to go*. ⟨*rare*, dialect var. of *rear²*⟩

ras·cal ['ræskəl] *n* **1** a dishonest person; rogue. **2** a mischievous person or animal. **ras·cal·ly** *adj, adv*. ⟨Old French *rasque* filth⟩

rash¹ [ræʃ] *adj* too hasty or too bold; reckless; impetuous. **rash·ly** *adv*. **rash·ness** *n*. ⟨Middle English *rasch* quick⟩

rash² [ræʃ] *n* **1** an eruption of spots on the skin, usually temporary, as a symptom of a disease, allergic reaction, etc.: *Perfumed soaps give me a rash*. **2** a sudden appearance of a large number of instances of something unpleasant or unhappy: *There was a rash of angry letters following the publication of the article*. ⟨Old French *rasche* scurf⟩

rasp [ræsp] *v* **1** make a grating sound: *The file rasped on the metal blade*. **2** utter with a harsh sound: *to rasp out a command*. **3** scrape with a rasp or other rough instrument.
n **1** a harsh, grating sound or effect: *a rasp in a person's voice*. **2** a coarse file with pointlike teeth. **rasp·ing** *adj*. **rasp·ish** *adj*. ⟨Old French *rasper*; Germanic⟩
rasp·y *adj* **1** harsh; rasping: *a raspy voice*. **2** irritable. **rasp·i·ly** *adv*. **rasp·i·ness** *n*.

rasp·ber·ry ['ræz,bɛri] *n* **1** any of several prickly shrubs of the rose family having edible, aggregate fruit. **2** *Slang* a sound of derision made with the tongue and lips. **rasp·ber·ry·like** *adj*. ⟨*raspis* raspberry (origin uncertain) + *berry*⟩

Ras·ta·far·i·an [,ræstə'fɛriən] *or* [,-'færiən] *adj* to do with a Jamaican religion based on the divinity of Haile Selassie (1892-1975), emperor of Ethiopia, that stresses Africa as the home to which black people must return. *n* one who follows this religion or identifies with Rastafarianism as a social and political movement. Also, **Ras·ta**. **Ras·ta·far·i·an·ism** *n*. ⟨*Ras Tafari* Prince Tafari, original name and title of Haile Selassie⟩

rat [ræt] *n* **1** any of numerous long-tailed rodents resembling the mouse, but larger. **2** *Slang* a contemptible, disloyal person. **3** ✱ *Northwest* a muskrat.
v **rat·ted**, **rat·ting** **1** hunt for rats. **2** ✱ *Northwest* trap muskrats. **3** *Slang* betray, inform on, or desert one's friends or

associates (usually with *on*): *She wouldn't rat on her friends*. **rat·tish** *adj*. ⟨Old English *rætt*⟩
rats *Slang* an exclamation of frustration, disgust, etc. **smell a rat** *Informal* suspect a trick. **rat's nest** a complicated situation. **rat race** *Informal* a fierce struggle, esp with reference to competing in the business world. **rat–tail** *adj* shaped like a rat's tail; long, thin, and tapered. *n Informal* a short haircut with a lock of hair left long at the back of the head. **rat·ter** *n* an animal that catches rats: *Our dog is a good ratter*. **rat–trap** *n* **1** a trap to catch rats. **2** a dirty, run-down building. **rat·ty** *adj* **1** of or like rats. **2** full of rats. **3** *Slang* poor; shabby: *a ratty old jacket*. **4** *Slang* angry or irritable: *The boss seems a little ratty today*.

ratch·et ['rætʃɪt] *n* a wheel or bar with teeth that strike against a catch fixed so that motion is permitted in one direction but not in the other. ⟨Italian *rocchetto*⟩

rate [reit] *n* **1** a quantity, degree, etc. measured in proportion to something else: *The car was travelling at a rate of 85 km/h*. **2** a price: *We pay the regular rate*. **3** speed or pace: *a rapid rate*. **4** a grade; rating.
v **1** put a value on: *We rated the house as worth $75 000*. **2** regard as: *He was rated one of the richest men in town*. **3** put in a certain class or grade. **4** *Informal* be worthy or be worthy of: *He doesn't rate*. ⟨Latin *rata* fixed (amount), pp of Latin *reri* reckon⟩
at any rate a under any circumstances. **b** at least. **at that (or this) rate** in that or this case; under such conditions.
rate·pay·er *n* a person who pays municipal taxes. **rat·ing** *n* **1** a rank; grade. **2** in some navies, a sailor of the lowest rank. **3** an amount fixed as a grade: *a rating of 80% in English*. **4** a specification of an engine, furnace etc., expressing its heat capacity, performance limit, etc. **5** a film classification. **6** a level of merit or popularity established by a survey.

rath·er ['ræðər] *adv* **1** more willingly; preferably: *I would rather go sooner than later*. **2** more properly: *This is rather for your parents to decide than for you*. **3** more precisely: *It was late Monday night or, rather, early Tuesday morning*. **4** in some degree: *rather good*. **5** on the contrary: *The sick man is no better today; rather, he is worse*. ⟨Old English *hrathor*, comparative of *hrathe* quickly⟩

rat·i·fy ['rætə,fai] *v* approve formally: *The countries will ratify the agreement made by their representatives*. **rat·i·fi·er** *n*. **rat·i·fi·ca·tion** *n*. ⟨Latin *ratus* fixed + *facere* make⟩

rat·ing See RATE.

ra·ti·o ['reiʃou] *n* **1** the relative magnitude. *Sheep and cows in the ratio of 10 to 1 means* there are ten sheep for every cow. **2** a quotient of two numbers or quantities. The ratio of 3 to 10 is 3/10. The ratio of 10 to 3 is 10/3. ⟨Latin = reckoning; *reri* reckon⟩

ra·tion ['ræʃən] *n* **1** Often, **rations** a fixed allowance of food. **2** a portion of anything dealt out: *a ration of sugar*.

v distribute in limited amounts: *to ration food in wartime.* ⟨French; Latin *ratio*. See RATIO.⟩

ra·tion·al [ˈræʃənəl] *adj* **1** sensible; reasonable: *Angry people seldom act in a rational way.* **2** able to think logically: *As children grow older, they become more rational.* **3** based on reasoning: *a rational explanation.* **ra·tion·al·i·ty** *n.* **ra·tion·al·ly** *adv.* ⟨Latin *ratio*. See RATIO.⟩

ra·tion·ale [ˌræʃəˈnæl] *n* the fundamental reason or logical basis. **ra·tion·al·ism** *n* the principle of accepting reason as the supreme authority in matters of opinion, belief, or conduct. **ra·tion·al·ist** *n.* **ra·tion·al·is·tic** *adj.* **ra·tion·al·is·ti·cal·ly** *adv.* **ra·tion·al·ize** *v* **1** find (often unconsciously) an excuse for (one's desires or actions): *I rationalize my overeating by thinking, "I must eat enough to keep up my strength."* **2** *Mathematics* eliminate radical signs from (an expression) without changing the value. **ra·tion·al·i·za·tion** *n.* **ra·tion·al·iz·er** *n.*

rational number *Mathematics* any number that can be expressed as a ratio between two integers, excluding zero as a denominator. The numbers 2, –0.5, and 3/4 are rational numbers.

rat·tan [rəˈtæn] *n* **1** any of several climbing palms having very long, jointed, pliable stems. **2** the stem of any of these palms, used for wickerwork, canes, etc. ⟨Malay *rotan*⟩

rat·tle [ˈrætəl] *v* **1** make a number of short, sharp sounds. **2** talk quickly, on and on (usually with *on*): *to rattle on about something.* **3** say quickly (often with *off*): *to rattle off a speech.* **4** *Informal* confuse; upset: *She was so rattled that she forgot her speech.* *n* **1** a number of short, sharp sounds: *the rattle of empty bottles.* **2** a toy, instrument, etc. filled with pellets so that it makes a noise when it is shaken. **3** a series of horny pieces at the end of a rattlesnake's tail. **rat·tly** *adj.* ⟨Middle English *ratelen*; probably imitative⟩

rattle around in *Informal* live or work in (a place) that is much larger than one needs.

rat·tler *Informal* rattlesnake. **rat·tle·snake** *n* any of the snakes that produce a warning rattle by vibrating the loosely connected horny segments at the end of its tail. **rat·tle·trap** *n* something shaky, rickety, or rattling, esp an old, worn-out car.

rau·cous [ˈrɒkəs] *adj* **1** harsh-sounding: *the raucous caw of a crow.* **2** loud and disorderly. **rau·cous·ly** *adv.* **rau·cous·ness** *n.* ⟨Latin *raucus*⟩

raun·chy [ˈrɒntʃi] *adj Slang* **1** lewd; indecent: *raunchy songs bordering on the obscene.* **2** smelly or dirty, esp from body odour: *raunchy sneakers.* **3** vulgarly exuberant: *Some of the fans got pretty raunchy.* **raun·chi·ly** *adv.* **raun·chi·ness** *n.* ⟨origin uncertain⟩

rav·age¹ [ˈrævɪdʒ] *v* damage greatly; destroy: *The forest fire ravaged huge areas of country.* *n* the resulting destruction; great damage: *War causes ravage.* **rav·age·ment** *n.* **rav·ag·er** *n.* ⟨French *ravager; ravir* ravish⟩

rav·age² [ˈrævɪdʒ] *n* ✸ a place where a group of moose, deer, or other animals stay for a time feeding on the surrounding vegetation before moving on. ⟨Cdn. French⟩

rave [reiv] *v* **1** talk wildly and incoherently, as when extremely excited, delirious, etc. **2** talk with much, or too much, enthusiasm: *She raved about the food.* *n* **1** *Informal* unrestrained praise, esp in a review of a play, film, etc.: *The play got raves in the press.* **2** a large, informally organized gathering of young people to dance and listen to fast electronic popular music. *adj* unrestrainedly enthusiastic: *rave reviews.* ⟨Old French *raver*, variant of *rêver* dream⟩

rav·ing *adj* **1** delirious; frenzied; raging. **2** *Informal* remarkable: *a raving beauty.* *n* Often, **ravings** delirious talk. **rav·ing·ly** *adv.*

rav·el [ˈrævəl] *v* **-elled** or **-eled**, **-el·ling** or **-el·ing** **1** separate the threads of; fray: *The sweater was ravelled at the wrist.* **2** tangle; confuse. ⟨Middle Dutch *ravelen; rafel* thread⟩

ra·ven [ˈreivən] *n* **1** a very large bird closely related to the crows, having glossy black plumage. **2 Raven** the trickster and divine culture-hero of Pacific Northwest First Nations folklore. ⟨Old English *hræfn*⟩

rav·en·ous [ˈrævənəs] *adj* **1** very hungry. **2** very eager or greedy: *The child was ravenous for praise.* **rav·en·ous·ly** *adv.* **rav·en·ous·ness** *n.* ⟨*raven* devour, Old French *ravine*⟩

rav·en·ing [ˈrævənɪŋ] *adj* **1** seeking eagerly for prey: *ravening wolves.* **2** voracious.

ra·vine [rəˈvin] *n* a long, deep, narrow gorge worn by running water or by the action of glaciers. ⟨French; Old French = violent rush⟩

rav·ing See RAVE.

rav·i·o·li [ˌræviˈouli] *n* small cases of pasta filled with meat, cheese, etc. ⟨Italian⟩

rav·ish [ˈrævɪʃ] *v* **1** fill with delight: *to be ravished by the sunset.* **2** rape. **rav·ish·er** *n.* ⟨Old French *ravir*; Latin *rapere* seize⟩

rav·ish·ing *adj* totally delightful; enchanting: *jewels of ravishing beauty.* **rav·ish·ing·ly** *adv.*

raw [rɒ] *adj* **1** not cooked: *raw oysters.* **2** in the natural state; not treated: *raw materials.* **3** unprocessed; unevaluated: *raw statistics.* **4** not trained: *a raw recruit.* **5** unpleasantly damp or cold: *raw weather.* **6** with the skin off: *a raw spot.* **7 a** having a crude quality; not refined in taste: *a raw story.* **b** so blunt as to be harsh or coarse. **8** *Slang* unjustly harsh; unfair: *a raw deal.* **raw·ly** *adv.* **raw·ness** *n.* ⟨Old English *hrēaw*⟩

in the raw a in an unrefined or crude state: *experiencing life in the raw.* **b** *Slang* naked: *to sleep in the raw.*

raw·hide *n* the untanned skin of cattle. **raw material 1** material intended to be manufactured into something else: *Petroleum is one of the basic raw materials of industry.* **2** a person or thing thought of as having potential for development: *some good raw material for the football team.*

SYNONYMS
Raw applies to a product that has not yet been processed: *Raw milk must be pasteurized to make it ready to drink.* **Crude** applies to a product in its natural state: *Crude rubber is treated with heat to make it more elastic.*

ray[1] [rei] *n* **1** a line or beam of light. **2** a stream of radiant energy in the form of heat, electricity, light, etc.: *X rays*. **3** anything like a ray, coming out from a centre. **4** *Geometry* a straight line extending from a point. **ray·less** *adj*. **ray·like** *adj* ⟨Old French *rai*; Latin *radius*⟩

ray[2] [rei] *n* any of an order of fishes having a flattened body with the eyes on the top of the head and having winglike pectoral fins. See also STINGRAY. ⟨Latin *raia*⟩

ray·on ['reiɒn] *n* a textile fibre made from cellulose. ⟨*ray*[1] (for its sheen) + (*cott*)*on*⟩

raze [reiz] *v* tear down; destroy completely: *The old school was razed and a new one was built in the same place.* ⟨French *raser* scrape; Latin *radere*⟩

ra·zor ['reizər] *n* a cutting instrument used for shaving or cutting hair: *an electric razor.* ⟨Old French *rasor; raser.* See RAZE.⟩ **ra·zor·back** *n* **1** a finback whale; rorqual. **2** a sharp ridge on a hill, mountain, etc.

razz [ræz] *Slang v* tease, ridicule, or heckle: *We razz her about the old car she drives.* ⟨*raspberry*⟩

RBI or **rbi** *n, pl* **RBIs, RBI's,** or **RBI**. *Baseball* run batted in.

R.C. ROMAN CATHOLIC.

RCMP or **R.C.M.P.** ROYAL CANADIAN MOUNTED POLICE.

Rd. Road.

RDA recommended daily allowance (used in reference to vitamins and other nutrients).

re[1] [rei] *n Music* **1** the second tone of an eight-tone major scale. **2** the tone D. ⟨Latin *resonare*, word sung on this note in a medieval song set to the scale⟩

re[2] [ri] *prep* with reference to; in the matter or case of; about; concerning. ⟨for Latin *in re* in the matter of⟩

re– *prefix* **1** again; once more: *reappear, rebuild, re-enter.* **2** again, but in a different way: *redesign, rearrange.* **3** back: *recall, repay, replace.* ⟨Latin⟩

USAGE
Most words beginning with **re-** are not hyphenated: *rearm, refine, remit.* However, a hyphen is often used if the letter following the **re-** is e: *re-entry, re-establish.* A hyphen is used to distinguish a word in which **re-** means 'again' from another word that would otherwise have the same spelling: *recover* 'get back, get better', *re-cover* 'cover again'.

reach [ritʃ] *v* **1** get to; arrive at: *to reach the top of a hill, an agreement, etc.* **2** stretch; stretch out: *to reach out one's hand.* **3** extend in space, time, effect, etc. (*to*): *The power of Rome reached to the ends of the known world.* **4** get at; influence: *Most people can be reached by flattery.* **5** establish communication with: *You can reach me at the following address.* **6** *Informal* make a claim, joke, etc., with too little foundation: *I may be reaching here, but I think it's the only clinic of its kind in Canada.* *n* **1** the extent of reaching: *out of one's reach.* **2** a continuous stretch: *a reach of woodland.*

3 a part of a river between bends, or of a canal between locks. ⟨Old English *ræcan*⟩

re·act [ri'ækt] *v* **1** act in response (with *to*): *Dogs react to kindness by showing affection.* **2** act in opposition to something or somebody (with *against*): *Some people react against fads.* **3 a** act chemically: *Acids react on metals.* **b** be affected by such a reaction: *Many people react badly to penicillin.* **re·ac·tion** *n*. **re·ac·tion·al** *adj*.

re·ac·tance *n Electricity* that part of the impedance of an alternating-current circuit that is due to inductance or capacitance or both. **re·ac·tant** *n Chemistry* any substance participating in a chemical reaction. **re·ac·tion·ary** *adj* to do with a tendency toward a previous system, esp in politics, economics, etc. *n* a person who favours such a previous system. **reaction time** *Psychology* the time between a stimulus and the response it elicits. **re·ac·tive** *adj* **1** to do with reaction. **2** tending to react. **re·ac·tive·ly** *adv*. **re·ac·tiv·i·ty** or **re·ac·tive·ness** *n*. **re·ac·tor** *n* **1** *Electricity* a device used to introduce reactance into an alternating-current circuit. **2** NUCLEAR REACTOR. **re·a·gent** [ri'eidʒənt] *n* **1** a person, force, etc. that reacts. **2** *Chemistry* **a** a substance that takes part in a reaction. **b** something that, when added to a substance, causes a reaction that helps determine the composition of the substance.

re·ac·ti·vate [ri 'ækti,veit] *v* make or become active or effective again.

read [rid] *v* **read** [rɛd], **read·ing** *v* **1** understand the meaning of (symbols in writing): *The blind read Braille with their fingers.* **2** speak (written words): *Read this story to me.* **3** show by letters, figures, signs, etc.: *The thermometer reads 20°.* **4** interpret: *to read a person's mind. Farmers read the sky.* **5** *Informal* understand (a person) clearly: *I don't want this to happen again, do you read me?* **6** produce a certain impression when read: *This does not read like work of a child.* **7** bring or put by reading: *He reads himself to sleep.* **8** *Computers* copy or transfer data by electronic means: *She used a bar-code scanner to read the product code.* *n* **1** a spell of reading. **2** a piece of reading matter considered in terms of the pleasure it gives: *That novel is a good read.* ⟨Old English *rædan* guess, read, counsel⟩

read between the lines discover a meaning or implication not stated outright in something. **read my lips** I mean what I just said. **read out a** read aloud: *She read out her answer to the class.* **b** *Computers* produce a readout of. **read the water a** ✱ scan the water from a boat for signs of danger such as shoals. **b** when fishing, scan the water seeking a good place to cast a fly or a lure. **read up (on)** acquire information (about) by reading.

read·a·ble *adj* **1** interesting or enjoyable to read: *Her novels are very readable.* **2** legible: *readable handwriting.* **3** able to be understood or processed by a person or machine. **read·a·bil·i·ty** *n*. **read·a·bly** *adv*. **read·er** *n* **1** a person who reads something or reads in a certain way: *a poor reader.* **2** a book for practising reading. **3** a person employed to read manuscripts and estimate their fitness for publication. **4** an employee who reads and records the totals on a meter, as for hydro, water, etc consumption. **5** *Computers* an electronic device that copies or transfers data from a source (bar code, etc.). **read·er·ship** *n* the reading audience of a particular publication or author. **read·ing** *n* **1** the act or process of getting the meaning of written words. **2** a public recital. **3** written matter: *There's good reading in this magazine.* **4** the information shown on the scale of an instrument: *The reading on the thermometer was 38°.* **5** an interpretation: *Each actor gave the lines a different reading.* **6** one of the three stages in the passage of a bill by a legislative assembly. *adj* used in reading: *reading glasses.* **read–on·ly memory** *Computers* computer memory whose contents can be retrieved but not modified. *Abbrev* **ROM. read·out** *Computers* information displayed by an electronic device (computer, calculator, etc.) on a screen or on paper.

re–ad·dress [ˌri əˈdrɛs] *v* **1** put a new address on: *to re-address a letter.* **2** deal with again.

read·y [ˈrɛdi] *adj* **1** prepared for immediate action or use: *Dinner is ready.* **2** willing: *The knights were ready to die for their lords.* **3** prompt: *a ready answer.* **4** likely; liable: *She is too ready to find fault.* **5** immediately available: *ready money.* *v* make ready. **read·i·ness** *n* ⟨Old English *ræde* ready⟩ **at the ready** ready for action: *The soldiers walked down the road with their guns at the ready.* **make ready** prepare. **the ready** *Informal* cash; money at hand. **read·i·ly** [ˈrɛdəli] *adv* **1** willingly or promptly: *She answered our questions readily.* **2** easily: *The parts fitted together readily.* **ready–made** *adj* **1** of clothes, made beforehand in standard sizes. **2** not original: *a magazine article filled with ready-made ideas.* **3** already established: *The server being down provided him with a ready-made excuse for not working.* **read·y–mix** [ˈrɛdi ˌmɪks] *or* [ˈmɪks] *adj* ready to cook or use after adding liquid and, sometimes, other ingredients: *ready-mix muffins, ready-mix concrete.* **read·y–to–wear** *n* clothing made in a range of standard sizes.

re·a·gent See REACT.

real [ril] *adj* **1** not imagined or made up: *a real experience, the real reason.* **2** genuine: *a real diamond.* **3** *Law* to do with immovable property, as land and houses. **4** *Optics* to do with an optical image formed by the actual convergence of light rays, as by a lens or mirror. **5** *Economics* measured by reference to actual purchasing power: *In a period of rising prices, real incomes fall if money incomes remain steady.* ⟨Latin *realis; res* thing⟩ **for real** *Slang* in fact; true or truly. **get real** *Slang* be serious. **in real life** in reality; actually: *He plays a gangster in the TV series, but in real life he's a very gentle man.*

real estate a piece of land, together with the buildings, trees, water, and minerals that belong with it. **real estate agent** a person dealing in REAL ESTATE. **re·al·ism** [ˈriəˌlɪzəm] *n* **1** practical tendency. **2** a style in literature and art characterized by trying to picture nature, people, etc. objectively and factually. **re·al·ist** *n.* **re·al·is·tic** [ˌriəˈlɪstɪk] *adj* **1** lifelike. **2** to do with realists or realism. **re·al·is·ti·cal·ly** *adv.* **re·al·i·ty** [riˈæləti] *n* **1** the quality or state of being real: *He was convinced of the reality of what he had seen.* **2** the quality, esp in art, of being true to life: *The dialogue lacks reality.* **3** a real thing, fact, or event: *Her dream became a reality.* **4** actual existence: *His writing may be an attempt to escape from reality.* **in reality** in fact: *I thought she was joking, but in reality she was serious.* **reality TV** programs that show how ordinary people behave when put into situations that make unusual demands on them. **re·al·ize** [ˈriəˌlaɪz] *v* **1** be fully aware of: *They realize how hard you worked.* **2** make real: *Her uncle's gift made it possible for her to realize her dream of going to college.* **3** change (property) into money: *Before going to France to live, he realized all his property in Canada.* **4** obtain as a return or profit: *They realized $10 000 from their investment.* **re·al·i·za·tion** [ˌriəlɪˈzeiʃən] *or* [ˌriəlaɪˈzeiʃən] *n.* **real·ly** [ˈrili] *adv* **1** actually: *things as they really are.* **2** truly: *a really magnificent house.* **3** *Informal* very; very much: *to run really fast. interj* an expression of surprise, disbelief, or disapproval: *Really! I don't believe it!* **real number** *Mathematics* a member of the set of numbers that includes all the RATIONAL NUMBERS and all the IRRATIONAL numbers. **Re·al·po·li·tik** [reiˈɑlˌpɒləˌtik] *n* policy based on power and expediency rather than ideals. **real time** *Computers* a mode of computer operation or any other system characterized by the nearly simultaneous occurring and recording of events. **real–time** *adj.* **real·tor** [ˈriltər] *n* a member of an organization engaged in the business of buying and selling real estate. **real·ty** [ˈrilti] *n* REAL ESTATE.

SYNONYMS

Real means that what is described is not imaginary, or made up: *Give your real name.* **Actual** means that what is described has happened, and is not merely capable of happening: *Name an actual case of bravery.*

realm [rɛlm] *n* **1** kingdom. **2** range; domain: *the realm of possibility.* ⟨Old French *reialme; reial* regal; Latin *regalis*⟩

ream[1] [rim] *n* **1** a quantity of sheets of paper of the same size and quality, usually 500. **2** Usually, **reams** *pl Informal* a very large quantity: *She took reams of notes. Abbrev* **rm.** ⟨Old French *rayme;* Arabic *rizmah* bundle⟩

ream[2] [rim] *v* enlarge clean out, or shape (a hole). ⟨Old English *ryman* widen; *rum* room⟩ **ream out** *Slang.* reprimand severely: *The teacher reamed me out for inattention.* **ream·er** [ˈrimər] *n* **1** a tool for shaping a hole, or for cleaning a pipe. **2** a similar utensil for squeezing the juice out of lemons, etc.

reap [rip] *v* **1** cut (grain). **2** gather (a crop) from. **3** get as a return or reward: *Kind acts often reap happy smiles.* ⟨Old English *repan*⟩ **reap·er** *n* a person who or machine that cuts grain or gathers a crop. **the (Grim) Reaper** the personification of death, often depicted as a hooded figure carrying a scythe.

rear¹ [rir] *n* **1** the back part: *the rear of the house.* **2** Often, **rear end**, *Slang* buttocks. *adj* located at the back. ⟨variant of *arrear*⟩ **at** (or **in**) **the rear of** behind. **bring up the rear** come or be last: *We filed through the woods, with me bringing up the rear.* **rear–end** *v* hit (another vehicle) from behind. **rear guard** that part of an army that protects the rear. **rear·most** ['rir,moust] *adj* farthest in the rear; last. **rear·view mirror** a mirror on a car, etc., attached so as to give a view of the area to the rear. **rear·ward** *adv, adj* toward the rear.

rear² [rir] *v* **1** make grow; bring up: *He was reared in the city.* **2** raise: *to rear one's head.* **3** esp of a horse, rise on the hind legs (sometimes with *up*): *The horse reared as the train roared past.* ⟨Old English *rǣran* raise⟩

re·arm [ri'ɑrm] *v* esp of a nation or a military force, arm again with new or better weapons. **re·ar·ma·ment** [ri'ɑrməmənt] *n*.

re·ar·range [,riə'reindʒ] *v* **1** arrange in a new or different way: *to rearrange furniture.* **2** arrange again. **re·ar·range·ment** *n*.

rea·son ['rizən] *n* **1** a cause for an action, feeling, etc.: *I have a reason for doing this.* **2** a justification: *What is the reason for such poor work?* **3** the ability to draw conclusions: *Reason separates humans from the lower primates.* **4** sanity: *Have you lost your reason?* *v* **1** think (about) logically: *Human beings can reason.* **2** conclude (that something is the case) from the relevant facts. **3** argue in a rational way: *You just can't reason with him.* **rea·son·er** *n.* **rea·son·less** *adj.* **rea·son·less·ly** *adv.* ⟨Old French *raison*; Latin *ratio* reckoning⟩ **beyond all reason** completely unreasonable or unreasonably. **bring to reason** cause to be reasonable. **by reason of** because of. **in** (or **within**) **reason** within reasonable limits. **reason away** get rid of by reasoning. **reason out** think through and come to a conclusion. **stand to reason** be reasonable: *It stands to reason that she would resent your insults.* **with reason** with justification. **rea·son·a·ble** *adj* **1** not absurd: *a reasonable explanation.* **2** not extreme: *a reasonable request.* **3** inexpensive: *I expected the dress to be expensive, but it was really very reasonable.* **4** ready to listen to reason: *Be reasonable.* **rea·son·a·bly** *adv.* **rea·son·ing** *n* the process of drawing conclusions from facts.

USAGE

The **reason is**, or **the reason was**, etc. should be followed by **that**, and not by **because**. Instead of *My reason for being late is because my car would not start,* say: *My reason for being late is that my car would not start.* Or avoid the word **reason** and say: *I was late because my car would not start.*

reas·sem·ble [,ri ə'sɛmbəl] *v* **1** come or bring together again. **2** assemble something that has been taken apart: *We reassembled the old clock piece by piece.*

re·as·sure [,riə'ʃur] *v* restore to confidence: *The captain's confidence during the storm reassured the passengers.* **re·as·sur·ance** *n.* **re·as·sur·ing·ly** *adv.*

re·bate ['ribeit] *n* the return of part of the money paid; discount. **re·bate** ['ribeit] *or* [ri'beit] *v.* ⟨Old French *rabattre* beat down; re- back + *abattre*. See ABATE.⟩

reb·el [rɪ'bɛl] *v* **re·belled**, **re·bel·ling 1** use force to oppose authority: *The troops rebelled against their commander.* **2** resist authority or control: *He rebelled against his parents.* **3** feel a great dislike: *We rebelled at the thought of having to stay home all weekend.* **re·bel** [rɛ'bəl] *n, adj.* ⟨Latin *rebellare*; re- back + *bellum* war⟩ **re·bel·lion** [rɪ'bɛljən] *n* **1** organized resistance against authority. **2** an attitude in opposition to some generally accepted code of behaviour. **re·bel·lious** *adj.* **re·bel·lious·ly** *adv.* **re·bel·lious·ness** *n.*

re·birth [ri'bɜrθ] *n* **1** a being born again; reincarnation. **2** spiritual renewal. **3** revival; reawakening: *the rebirth of nationalism, the rebirth of hope.* **re·born** [ri'bɔrn] *adj* renewed, or revived.

re·bound [rɪ'baund] *v* **1** bounce back. **2** echo. **3** make a vigorous recovery, as from illness: *Her courage rebounded.* *n* ['ri,baund] **1** a springing back or resounding. **2** *Basketball* a ball that bounds off the backboard when a scoring attempt has been missed. ⟨re- + bound²⟩ **on the rebound a** after a bounce off the wall, floor, etc. **b** (while) recovering from the failure of a relationship or from some other unhappy experience.

re·buff [rɪ'bʌf] *n* **1** a blunt rejection, as of a person who makes advances, offers help, makes a request, etc.; snub. **2** any setback. *v* give a rebuff to. ⟨Italian *ributto*⟩

re·build [ri'bɪld] *v* **-built**, **-build·ing 1** build again. **2** repair or renovate extensively: *rebuild a kitchen.*

re·buke [rɪ'bjuk] *v* speak disapprovingly to. *n* an expression of disapproval; scolding. ⟨Old French re- back + *buchier* strike⟩ **re·buk·er** *n.* **re·buk·ing** *adj.*

re·bus ['ribəs] *n* a puzzle in which a word or phrase is represented by pictures, letters, or signs suggesting the original sounds. A picture of a cat and a log is a rebus for *catalogue.* ⟨Latin *rebus* by means of objects⟩

re·but [rɪ'bʌt] *v* **-but·ted**, **-but·ting** oppose by formal argument (the evidence presented by the other side): *Each team in the debate was given two minutes to rebut the other's arguments.* **re·but·tal** *n.* ⟨Old French re- back + *boter* butt³⟩

re·cal·ci·trant [rɪ'kælsətrənt] *adj* **1** resisting authority or control. **2** hard to manage. **re·cal·ci·trant** *n.* **re·cal·ci·trance** *n.* ⟨Latin *recalcitrare* kick back; re- back + *calcis* heel⟩

re·call [rɪ'kɒl] v **1** remember. **2** call back, esp a defective product for repair or refund: *The manufacturer recalled all cars of that model in order to correct the exhaust system.* **3** bring back: *recalled to life.* **4** take back: *The order has been given and cannot be recalled.* **re·call** ['ri,kɒl] *or* [rɪ'kɒl] *n.*

re·cant [rɪ'kænt] v renounce (a statement, opinion, purpose, etc.): *Though he was tortured to make him change his story, the prisoner would not recant.* **re·can·ta·tion** *n.* ⟨Latin *recantare*; re- back + *cantare* chant⟩

re·cap¹ [ri'kæp] v **-capped, -cap·ping** put a cap or lid on again: *to recap a bottle of soda.*

re·cap² [ri'kæp] v **-capped, -cap·ping** *Informal* v recapitulate. **re·cap** ['ri,kæp] *n.*

re·ca·pit·u·late [,rikə'pɪtʃə,leit] v repeat or recite the main points of; sum up. **re·ca·pit·u·la·tion** *n.* **re·ca·pit·u·la·tive** *adj* **re·ca·pit·u·la·to·ry** [,rikə'pɪtʃələ,tɔri] *adj.* ⟨Latin re- again + *capitulum* chapter. See CHAPTER.⟩

re·cap·ture [ri'kæptʃər] v **1** capture or take again. **2** bring back; recall: *The picture album recaptured the days of the horse and buggy.* **re·cap·ture** *n.*

re·cast [ri'kæst] v **-cast, -cast·ing 1** cast again or cast differently: *recast a bell. She was recast as the heroine in the film version.* **2** remodel: *recast a sentence, recast the entire format.* **re·cast** ['ri,kæst] *n.*

re·cede [rɪ'sid] v **1** move back, down, or away. **2** slope backward: *He has a chin that recedes.* ⟨Latin re- back + *cedere* go⟩

re·ces·sion [rɪ'sɛʃən] *n* **1** a moving backward in time or space. **2** a backward slope. **3** a period of temporary business decline, shorter and less extreme than a depression.

re·ces·sion·ar·y *adj.* **re·ces·sive** *adj* **1** tending to go back; receding. **2** *Genetics* to do with a trait that appears in offspring only in the absence of a dominant corresponding gene. Compare DOMINANT. **re·ces·sive·ly** *adj.* **re·ces·sive·ness** *n.*

re·ceipt See RECEIVE.

re·ceive [rɪ'siv] v **1** take or get (something offered or sent): *to receive gifts, to receive new ideas.* **2** accept as true: *a theory widely received.* **3** react to in a given way: *Her idea was badly received by the rest of us.* **4** experience: *to receive a blow.* **5** let into one's house, society, etc.; welcome: *to receive strangers.* **6** admit to a state or condition: *to receive a person into the Christian faith.* **7** *Sports* catch or return (a serve, pass, ball, puck, etc.). **8** *Radio and television* change electromagnetic waves into sound or picture signals. ⟨Old French *receivre*; Latin *recipere*; re- back + *capere* take⟩

be on the receiving end *Informal* be subject to some action, frequently unpleasant: *He was on the receiving end of my bad temper.* **re·ceipt** [rɪ'sit] *n* **1** a written statement that money, a package, a letter, etc. has been received. **2** receiving or being received: *The goods will be sent on receipt of payment.* **3** Usually, **receipts** *pl* money, etc. received: *The expenses were greater than the receipts.*

v write on or stamp (a bill, etc.) to indicate that something has been received or paid for: *She asked the store to receipt the bill.*

re·ceiv·a·ble *adj* (after the noun) on which payment is to be received. *Accounts receivable* is the opposite of *accounts payable.* *n pl* **receivables** bills or accounts receivable.

re·ceived *adj* accepted as standard: *Received wisdom has it that oysters are an aphrodisiac.*

re·ceiv·er *n* **1** anyone or anything that receives. **2** a device in a telephone, radio, or television set that converts electrical impulses or electromagnetic waves into sound or picture signals. **3** *Law* one appointed to take charge of the property of bankrupts, or to care for property under litigation. **re·ceiv·er·ship** *n.* **4** *Sports* **a** the player or side whose turn it is to RECEIVE (def. 7). **b** *Football* the player intended to receive a forward pass. **5** a person who knowingly receives stolen goods. **receiving blanket** a small, lightweight blanket for wrapping a newborn baby. **receiving line** a group of people, usually the hosts, who stand in a row at wedding receptions or other formal occasions in order to welcome each guest individually. **re·cip·i·ent** [rɪ'sɪpiənt] *n* a person who or thing that receives something: *The recipients of the prizes had their names printed in the paper.* adj receiving or willing to receive.

SYNONYMS

Receive carries no suggestion of positive action and means nothing more than to take in what is given: *She received a prize.* **Accept** always suggests being willing to take what is offered: *She received a gift from him, but refused to accept it.*

re·cent ['risənt] *adj* **1** that has happened or been done not long ago: *a recent quarrel.* **2** to do with a time comparatively near to the present: *recent history, the most recent ice age.* **3** **Recent** to do with the most recent geological epoch, forming the last part of the Quaternary period, beginning about 11 thousand years ago. Also called **Holocene.** **re·cen·cy** *n.* **re·cent·ly** *adv.* **re·cent·ly** *adv.* ⟨Latin *recens*⟩

re·cep·ta·cle [rɪ'sɛptəkəl] *n* **1** any container used to put things in. **2** a wall socket for an electrical plug. **3** *Botany* **a** the base of the flower to which all the parts of the flower are attached. **b** the structure bearing the reproductive organs or spores. ⟨Latin *receptaculum*. See RECEIVE.⟩

re·cep·tion [rɪ'sɛpʃən] *n* **1** the act of receiving: *calm reception of bad news.* **2** the fact of being received: *a warm reception.* **3** a social gathering to receive and welcome people. **4** the quality of the sound in a radio or of the sound and picture signals in a television set. ⟨Latin *receptio*. See RECEIVE.⟩

re·cep·tion·ist *n* a person employed in an office to welcome visitors, direct them, give out information, etc. **re·cep·tive** *adj* **1** quick, to receive ideas, impressions, etc.: *a receptive mind.* **2** to do with reception or receptors.

re·cep·tive·ly *adv.* **re·cep·tive·ness** *n.*
re·cep·tiv·i·ty *n.* **re·cep·tor** *n Physiology* a cell or group of cells sensitive to stimuli.

re·cess [rɪ'sɛs] *or esp def. 1* ['rises] *n* **1** a time during which work, classes, or any other proceeding temporarily stops: *There will be a short recess before the next meeting.* **2** an alcove; niche. **3** an inner place or part: *the recesses of a cave,*
v [rɪ'sɛs] stop or cause to stop for a break: *The judge recessed the court until the following day.* ⟨Latin *recessus* pp of *recedere*. See RECEDE.⟩

re·ces·sion, re·ces·sive See RECEDE.

re·ces·sion·al [rɪ'sɛʃənəl] *n* a hymn or other piece of music sung or played while the clergy and the choir leave at the end of a church service.

re·charge [ri'tʃɑrdʒ] *v* to charge again. **re·charge** ['ri,tʃɑrdʒ] *n.*

re·cher·ché [rəˌʃɛr'ʃei] *or* [rə'ʃɛrʃei] *French* [ʀəʃɛʀ'ʃe] *adj* **1** devised with care. **2 a** too studied; far-fetched: *That metaphor is a bit recherché.* **b** affected: *His poetry is apt to be too recherché for the general taste.* ⟨French = sought after; *re-* again + *chercher* search⟩

re·cid·i·vism [rɪ'sɪdɪ,vɪzəm] *n* a tendency to chronic relapse into crime or antisocial behaviour. ⟨Latin *re-* back + *cadere* fall⟩ **re·cid·i·vist** *n* a habitual criminal. **re·cid·i·vist** *or* **re·cid·i·vis·tic** *adj.*

rec·i·pe ['rɛsəpi] *n* **1** a set of directions for preparing something to eat or drink. **2** a set of directions for preparing anything by combining ingredients: *a recipe for making soap.* **3** a means of reaching some state or condition: *a recipe for happiness.* ⟨Latin = take!, first word in a recipe, *recipere* take, receive. See RECEIVE.⟩

re·cip·i·ent See RECEIVE.

re·cip·ro·cate [rɪ'sɪprɪ,keit] *v* **1** give, do, feel, etc. in return: *She loves me, and I reciprocate her love.* **2** give or do something in return: *They invited us to lunch, so we must reciprocate.* **3** move with a backward and forward motion: *a reciprocating valve.* **re·cip·ro·ca·tion** *n.* **re·cip·ro·ca·tor** *n.* **re·cip·ro·ca·to·ry** *adj.* ⟨Latin *reciprocus* alternating⟩
re·cip·ro·cal *adj* **1** done or given in exchange: *a reciprocal gift.* **2** mutual: *reciprocal friendship.* **3** *Mathematics* inverse. *n Mathematics* a number so related to another that when multiplied together they give 1: *The reciprocal of 3 is 1/3, and the reciprocal of 1/3 is 3.* **re·cip·ro·cal·i·ty** *n.* **re·cip·ro·cal·ly** *adv.* **rec·i·proc·i·ty** [ˌrɛsə'prɒsɪti] *n* **1** mutual action, influence, or dependence. **2 a** mutual exchange, esp an exchange of privileges in regard to trade between two countries.

re·cite [rɪ'sait] *v* **1** tell in detail: *He recited the day's adventures.* **2** mention in order: *They recited a long list of grievances.* **3** repeat (a poem, etc.) before an audience. **re·cit·er** *n.* ⟨Latin *re-* again + *citare* summon⟩
re·cit·al *n* **1** a telling of facts in detail: *Her recital of the day's events fascinated her hearers.* **2** a story; account. **3** a program of music or dance given by one or more performers, or by a small ensemble. **re·cit·al·ist** *n.* **rec·i·ta·tion** [ˌrɛsə'teiʃən] *n* a repetition of something from memory, esp before an audience. **rec·i·ta·tive** [ˌrɛsitə'tiv] *n Music* a style halfway between speaking and singing.

reck·less ['rɛklɪs] *adj* rash; heedless; careless: *Reckless of consequences, the boy played truant. Reckless driving causes many automobile accidents.* **reck·less·ly** *adv.* **reck·less·ness** *n.* ⟨Old English *recceléas*⟩

reck·on ['rɛkən] *v* **1** count: *Reckon the cost before you decide.* **2** consider: *She is reckoned the best player in the league.* **3** *Informal* think; suppose: *I reckon that's the truth.* **4** calculate; compute; do arithmetic. **reck·on·er** *n.* ⟨Old English *gerecenian*⟩
reckon on take into account: *He didn't reckon on breaking his leg when he decided to try skiing.* **reckon up** count up: *Before you buy a car, reckon up all the hidden costs.* **reckon with** take into account: *We must reckon with higher prices for food.* **to be reckoned with** worthy of serious thought: *a writer to be reckoned with.* **reck·on·ing** *n* **1 a** a calculation. **b** an estimation: *We should be there in around ten minutes, by my reckoning.* **2** the settlement of an account, or the giving of rewards or penalties for any action. **3** Usually, **dead reckoning** *Nautical* the calculation of the position of a ship. **day of reckoning** a time when one must account for or be punished for one's actions: *There will be a day of reckoning for your foolish behaviour.*

re·claim [rɪ'kleim] *v* **1** make available for cultivation, etc.: *to reclaim a swamp.* **2** recover from discarded products: *to reclaim tin from cans.* **3** obtain the return of: *The library sent a notice reclaiming the book.* **re·claim·a·ble** *adj.* **rec·la·ma·tion** [ˌrɛklə'meiʃən] *n.* ⟨Latin *re-* back + *clamare* cry out⟩
re·claimed lake ✳ a lake that has been restocked with trout following a drop in the number of species in it.

re·cline [rɪ'klain] *v* **1** lean back or lie down: *to recline on a couch.* **2** lay (something) back or down: *He reclined his head on the pillow.* ⟨Latin *re-* back + *-clinare* lean⟩
re·clin·er *n* a type of armchair with an adjustable back and seat.

re·cluse ['rɛklus] *or* [rɪ'klus] *n* a person who lives shut up or withdrawn from the world. **re·clu·sion** [rɪ'kluʒən] *n.* **re·clu·sive** *adj.* ⟨Latin *reclusus* pp of *recludere*; *re-* back + *claudere* shut⟩

SYNONYMS
A **recluse** withdraws for any of a variety of reasons, including a desire for complete privacy. The term **hermit** usually refers to someone who has withdrawn in order to concentrate on spiritual things or to lead a lifestyle based on values so radical as to be incompatible with general society.

rec·og·nize ['rɛkəg,naiz] *v* **1** know as a person or thing familiar to one: *I could scarcely recognize my old friend.* **2** identify: *to* *recognize a person from a description.* **3** know the significance of: *She recognized his qualities at once.* **4** acknowledge: *He recognized his duty to his family.* **5** take notice of: *Stand up and don't speak till the chairperson recognizes you.* **6** show appreciation of. **7** acknowledge and deal with: *For years, certain nations did not recognize the new government.* **rec·og·ni·tion** *n.* **rec·og·niz·a·ble** *adj.* **rec·og·niz·a·bly** *adj.* **rec·og·niz·a·bil·i·ty** *n.* ⟨Latin *re-* again + *cognoscere* know. See COGNITION.⟩

re·coil [rɪ'kɔɪl] *v* **1** draw back: *Most people would recoil at seeing a snake in their path.* **2** spring back: *The gun recoiled after I fired.* **3** backfire: *Revenge often recoils on the avenger.* **re·coil** ['rikɔɪl] *or* [rɪ'kɔɪl] *n.* ⟨Old French *reculer* back up; Latin *re-* back + *culus* rump⟩

rec·ol·lect [ˌrɛkə'lɛkt] *v* remember: *He didn't recollect the details.* ⟨*re-* + *collect* with narrowed meaning⟩
rec·ol·lec·tion *n* **1** memory. **2** something remembered.

rec·om·mend [ˌrɛkə'mɛnd] *v* **1** speak in favour of. **2** advise. **3** make pleasing or attractive: *The position of the cottage recommends it as a summer home.* **rec·om·men·da·tion** *n.* ⟨Latin *re-* again + *commendare* commend⟩

rec·om·pense ['rɛkəmˌpɛns] *v* **1** pay (a person); pay back; reward: *They were well recompensed for their efforts.* **2** make a fair return for (an action, anything lost, damage done, etc.): *The loss of property must be recompensed.* **rec·om·pense** *n.* ⟨Latin *re-* back + *com-* with + *pendere* weigh out in payment⟩

rec·on·cile ['rɛkənˌsaɪl] *v* **1** make or become friends again. **2** make agree: *It is impossible to reconcile his story with the facts.* **3** make satisfied or content with something: *It is hard to reconcile oneself to being sick for a long time.* ⟨Latin *re-* back + *concilium* bond of union⟩
rec·on·cil·a·ble *adj.* **rec·on·cil·er** *n.* **rec·on·cil·i·a·tion** *n.*

rec·on·dite ['rɛkənˌdaɪt] *or* [rɪ'kɒndaɪt] *adj* **1** hard to understand. **2** little known; obscure; esoteric. **rec·on·dite·ly** *adv.* **rec·on·dite·ness** *n.* ⟨Latin *reconditus* pp of *recondere* store away⟩

re·con·di·tion [ˌrikən'dɪʃən] *v* restore to a good condition by repairing, replacing parts, etc.: *a completely reconditioned motor.*

re·con·nais·sance [rɪ'kɒnəsəns] *n* an examination or survey, esp for military purposes. ⟨French *reconnaissance*⟩

rec·on·noi·tre [ˌrɛkə'nɔɪtər] *or* [ˌrikə'nɔɪtər] *v* **-tred, -tring** **1** make a survey of (the enemy's strength or position, a region, etc.) in order to gain information for military purposes. **2** approach a place and make a survey of it: *It seemed wise to reconnoitre before entering the town.* Also, **rec·on·noi·ter.** **rec·on·noi·trer** *n.* ⟨Old French *reconoistre*; Latin. See RECOGNIZE.⟩

re·con·sid·er [ˌrikən'sɪdər] *v* consider with a view to changing a position or decision: *The assembly voted to reconsider the bill.* **re·con·sid·er·a·tion** *n.*

re·con·sti·tute [ri'kɒnstəˌtjut] *or* [-ˌtut] *v* constitute anew; esp, restore (a condensed or dehydrated substance) to its original liquid state by adding water: *to reconstitute orange juice.* **re·con·sti·tu·tion** *n.*

re·con·struct [ˌrikən'strʌkt] *v* **1** rebuild. **2** try to discover (a sequence of events) by organizing in the mind all available information: *When the police reconstructed the crime, they realized who the murderer must be.* **3** build or rebuild, from available evidence, a model or duplicate of (something that existed previously): *Upper Canada Village is a reconstructed pioneer community.* **re·con·struc·tion** *n.* **re·con·struc·tive** *adj.*

re·cord [rɪ'kɔrd] *v* **1** preserve for remembrance: *History is recorded in books.* **2** reproduce accurately in written or graphic form: *The machine records the patient's heart rhythms.* **3** put on disc or magnetic tape. **4** measure and indicate: *The thermometer records temperatures.* *n* ['rɛkərd] **1** the permanent form of any event, speech, etc. **2** *Law* **a** an official written account. **b** an authoritative copy of an official document: *a record of a deed.* **3** the known facts about what a person, team, etc. has done: *a fine school record.* **4** a criminal record: *They say he has a record.* **5** a great performance, esp the best achievement in a sport: *to hold the record for the high jump.* **6** *Computers* a set of information fields treated as a unit in a database. *adj* unequalled: *a record crop.* ⟨Latin *recordari* remember; *re-* back + *cordis* heart, mind⟩
a matter of record a recorded event. **break a record** improve on an unequalled standard previously set in some athletic event, etc. **go on record** state one's views publicly. **off the record** not intended to be quoted: *The Prime Minister was speaking off the record.* **on record** written down or otherwise made available: *The facts of the murder are now on record.* **set the record straight** correct an erroneous view of what was said or done.

re·cord·er [rɪ'kɔrdər] *n* **1** a person who records, esp one whose work is making written accounts. **2** an apparatus or machine that records. **3** TAPE RECORDER. **4** a musical wind instrument resembling a flute. **re·cord·ing** [rɪ'kɔrdɪŋ] *n* **1** a sound record made on disc or tape. **2** the act of transcribing any sound or combination of sounds. *adj* that records: *a recording studio.*

re·count [rɪ'kaʊnt] *v* tell in detail; give an account of: *He recounted all the happenings of the day.* ⟨Old French *re-* again + *conter* tell (the story of)⟩

re–count [ri 'kaʊnt] *v* count again. *n* ['ri ˌkaʊnt] *n* a second count, as of votes.

re·coup [rɪ'kup] *v* **1** make up for; regain: *He recouped his losses.* **2** repay. ⟨French *recouper; re-* back + *couper* cut⟩

re·course ['rikɔrs] *or* [rɪ'kɔrs] *n* **1** the act of turning to a person, organization, course of action, etc. when in need of help (usually in **have recourse to**): *to have recourse to the Internet.* **2** a person, organization, course of action, etc. turned to for help or protection: *The child's recourse was always her mother.* **3** *Commerce* the right to collect payment from the maker or endorser of a cheque or similar negotiable instrument. ⟨Latin *recursus* retreat; *re-* back + *currere* run⟩

re·cov·er [rɪ'kʌvər] *v* **1** get back (something lost, taken away, or stolen). **2** make up for (something lost or damaged): *recover lost time.* **3** come back to life, health, one's senses, etc.: *He recovered quickly from surgery.* **4** check (oneself): *He started to fall but recovered himself. She was about to make a rude comment but recovered herself just in time.* **5** *Law* obtain by judgment in a court. **6** *Sports* take back control or possession of (a ball, puck, etc.). **7** reclaim, as in useful substances recovered from materials that used to be thrown away. **re·cov·er·er** *n.* **re·cov·er·y** *n.* ⟨Old French *recovrer*; Latin *recuperare*⟩

recovery room in a hospital, a room in which patients are placed after surgery, to recover from the effects of the anesthetic.

SYNONYMS

Recover = get something back again in one's possession after losing it: *We recovered the stolen TV.* **Reclaim** = bring back into usable condition from a lost state: *Part of her farm is reclaimed swamp.* **Retrieve** = recover by effort or search: *I threw the stick so that the dog could retrieve it.*

re—cov·er [ri 'kʌvər] *v* cover again or anew; esp, provide (a piece of upholstered furniture) with a new covering.

rec·re·a·tion [,rɛkri'eiʃən] *n* **1** a refreshing of the body and spirit through play or amusement. **2** a form of play or amusement that serves this purpose: *Her favourite recreation is tennis.* **re·cre·ate** ['rɛkri,eit] *v.* **rec·re·a·tion·al** *adj.* ⟨Latin *recreare* restore; *re-* again + *creare* create⟩

rec·re·a·tion·al vehicle any type of vehicle (such as a camper, trailer, etc.) fitted out as living quarters and used for camping, travelling, etc. *Abbrev* **RV. recreation room** **1** in a hotel, apartment building, etc., a room for playing games, lounging, dancing, and other informal activities. **2** in a private home, a family room. Also, **rec room.**

re—cre·ate [,ri kri'eit] *v* create anew. **re—cre·a·tion** *n.* **re—cre·a·tive** *adj.*

re·crim·i·nate [rɪ'krɪmə,neit] *v* accuse (someone) in return: *She said he had lied, and he recriminated by saying she had manipulated him.* **re·crim·i·na·tion** *n.* ⟨Latin *re-* back + *crimen* charge⟩

rec room [rɛk] *Informal* RECREATION ROOM (def. 2).

re·cruit [rɪ'krut] *n* **1** a newly enlisted member of the armed forces. **2** a new member of any group or class.
v **1** persuade (people) to join one of the armed forces. **2** engage in seeking out talented people with a view to hiring or enrolling them: *She recruits for IBM.* **3** engage: *She recruited the support of her mother in her*

appeal for renovations to the basement. **re·cruit·er** *n.* **re·cruit·ment** *n.* ⟨French *recrue* new growth; *re-* + *croître* grow; Latin *crescere*⟩

rec·tal See RECTUM.

rec·tan·gle ['rɛk,tæŋgəl] *n* any quadrilateral with four right angles. ⟨Latin *rectus* right + *angulus* angle⟩
rec·tan·gu·lar *adj* **1** shaped like a rectangle. **2** of a solid, having a base shaped like a rectangle: *a rectangular tower.* **3** placed at right angles. **rec·tan·gu·lar·ly** *adv.* **rec·tan·gu·lar·i·ty** *n.*

rec·ti·fy ['rɛktə,fai] *v* **1** make right; put right: *The storekeeper was willing to rectify his mistake.* **2** *Electricity* change (an alternating current) into a direct current. **rec·ti·fi·a·ble** *adj.* **rec·ti·fi·ca·tion** *n.* **rec·ti·fi·er** *n.* ⟨Latin *rectus* right + *facere* make⟩

rec·ti·lin·e·ar [,rɛktə'lɪniər] *adj* to do with straight lines. Also, **rec·ti·lin·e·al.**
rec·ti·lin·e·ar·ly *adv.* ⟨Latin *rectus* straight + LINEAR⟩

rec·ti·tude ['rɛktə,tjud] *or* ['rɛktə,tud] *n* **1** upright conduct or character; honesty; righteousness. **2** correctness, esp of judgment, procedure, etc. ⟨Latin *rectus* right⟩

rec·tor ['rɛktər] *n* **1** *Anglican Church* a member of the clergy in charge of a parish. **2** *Roman Catholic Church* a priest in charge of a college or a religious house. **3** the head of certain schools, colleges, or universities. **rec·tor·i·al** *adj.* ⟨Latin = ruler; *regere* rule⟩
rec·to·ry ['rɛktəri] *n* the residence of a rector.

rec·tum ['rɛktəm] *n, pl* **-tums** or **-ta** [-tə] the lowest part of the large intestine. **rec·tal** *adj.* **rec·tal·ly** *adv.* ⟨Latin *intestinum rectum* straight intestine⟩

re·cum·bent [rɪ'kʌmbənt] *adj* **1** lying down or leaning. **2** inactive; resting. **re·cum·bent·ly** *adv.* ⟨Latin *re-* back + *cumbere* lie down⟩

re·cu·per·ate [rɪ'kupə,reit] *v* **1** get back to a former state , esp, to recover from sickness: *She is at home, recuperating from surgery.* **2** get back: *to recuperate one's losses after a fire.* **re·cu·per·a·tion** *n.* **re·cu·per·a·tive** *adj.* ⟨Latin *recuperare*⟩

re·cur [rɪ'kɜr] *v* **-curred, -cur·ring** **1** occur again; be repeated: *A leap year recurs every four years.* **2** return in thought or speech: *Old memories constantly recurred to him.* **re·cur·rence** *n.* **re·cur·rent** *adj.* **re·cur·rent·ly** *adv.* ⟨Latin *recurrere*; *re-* back + *currere* run⟩
recurring decimal See REPEATING DECIMAL.

re·cy·cle [ri'saikəl] *v* **1** reprocess waste material so that it can be used again: *Old cars can be recycled and the steel used again.* **2** use over again: *They recycle egg trays on their farm.* **3** adapt to a new use without changing the essential form: *The old factory was recycled as loft apartments.* **re·cy·cling** *n.*

red [rɛd] *n* **1** the colour of blood; the colour of the visible spectrum having the longest light waves, at the end opposite to violet. **2 Red** a radical socialist; a revolutionary; a Communist. **3** ☀ *Informal* a Liberal.

adj **red·der, red·dest 1** to do with the colour of blood, etc.; being like it: *red ink, red hair.* **2** bloodshot: *red eyes.* **3** blushing. **4** Usually, **Red**, radically socialist or communist; revolutionary. **5 ✳** *Informal* to do with Liberals. **red·ly** *adv.* **red·ness** *n.* ⟨Old English *rēad*⟩

in the red in debt: *We'll be in the red soon if we don't cut down our expenses.* **see red** become very angry: *She sees red as soon as you mention the new by-law.*

red alert 1 *Military or Civil Defence* the final stage of alert, when an attack is expected at any moment. **2** a signal of imminent danger. **red blood cell** in the blood of vertebrates, one of the cells that carry oxygen to the tissues of the body. Red blood cells contain hemoglobin and give blood its red colour. **red–blood·ed** *adj* full of life and spirit. **red·cap** ['rɛd,kæp] *n* a porter at a railway station, airport, etc., usually wearing a red cap as part of the uniform. **red carpet** a carpet, traditionally red, laid out at formal receptions for important persons. **red–car·pet** *adj.* **roll out the red carpet (for)** treat (someone) with special consideration. **red cedar 1** a small, cone-shaped juniper. **2** WESTERN RED CEDAR. **red cent** *Informal* the smallest amount of money: *That thing is not worth a red cent.* **Red Chamber ✳** a name sometimes given to the Canadian Senate because of the colour of the rugs, draperies, etc. of the room in which the Senate meets. **red·coat** *n* ✳ a member of the RCMP. **Red Crescent** a society in Muslim countries that parallels the RED CROSS; its emblem is a red crescent on a white background. **Red Cross** a group of societies that work to relieve human suffering in time of war or peace. The badge is a red cross on a white background. **red·den** *v* **1** make or become red: *The sky was just beginning to redden.* **2** blush: *She reddened with shame.* **red·dish** *adj* somewhat red. **Red Ensign ✳ 1** the Canadian flag until 1965, having a red ground with the arms of Canada on the fly and the Union Jack in the upper corner near the staff. **2** the provincial flag of Ontario. **red·eye** *n* ✳ *Slang* **1** a drink made of beer and tomato juice. Also, **Calgary redeye. 2** any cheap liquor, esp whisky. **red–eye** *n* **1** *Informal* a commercial airline flight leaving late at night and arriving early in the morning. **2** a phenomenon of flash photography in which the pupils of a subject's eyes appear red because of reflection by the blood vessels of the retina. **red flag 1** a symbol of rebellion, revolution, etc. **2** a sign of danger. **3** anything that stirs up anger. **red flag** *v.* **red giant** *Astronomy* a star in an intermediate stage of development, characterized by large volume and reddish colouring. Compare WHITE DWARF. **red–hand·ed** *adj* in the very act of crime: *caught red-handed.* **red–hand·ed·ly** *adv.* **red–hand·ed·ness** *n.* **red·head** *n* a person having red hair: *All three of their children are redheads.* **red·head·ed** ['rɛd,hɛdɪd] *adj.* **red herring** something used to draw attention

away from the real issue. **red–hot** *adj* **1** red with heat. **2** excited; violent. **3** fresh from the source. **4** exciting; sexy. **5** performing very well. **red ink** a financial deficit. **red–let·ter** *adj* memorable; especially happy: *a red-letter day*, from the custom of printing important feast days in red ink in the Church calendar. **red light 1** a red light as a traffic signal to stop: *He was fined for running a red light.* **2** *Informal* any warning signal or instruction to stop, exercise caution, etc. **red–light** *adj* **1** to do with a red light. **2** characterized by a concentration of brothels: *a red-light district.* **red·line** *v* **1** designate (an area in a city) as undesirable by outlining the area in red on a map. **2** cancel by drawing a red line through. **3** *rev* (an engine) too quickly so that the needle on the tachometer enters the red zone. *n Hockey* the centre line on a hockey rink, midway between the two bluelines. **red meat** beef or any other meat that is red when raw. **red pepper 1** a seasoning having a strong, burning taste, made from the fruit of a PEPPER (def. 2); cayenne. **2** a mild variety of the capsicum. **Red River cart ✳** formerly much used during pioneer days in the West, a strong, two-wheeled cart pulled by oxen or horses. **Red River Rebellion ✳** the uprising in 1869-1870 of mainly Métis settlers in the Red River region against the takeover of their territory by the government of Canada from the Hudson's Bay Company. **red salmon** SOCKEYE. **red shift** *Physics, astronomy* a displacement of the spectral lines of a celestial body toward the red end of the visual spectrum, caused by the Doppler effect. The existence of a red shift in the light emitted by stars of distant galaxies, which suggests that they are receding from our galaxy, is the main evidence for the theory of the expansion of the universe. **red tape** excessive attention to detail, esp in government business, causing delay and irritation, so named because official documents used to be tied with red tape. **red tide** an area of sea water having a reddish coloration due to micro-organisms that in large numbers are poisonous. **Red Tory ✳** a member of the Progressive Conservative party who favours somewhat liberal social policies. **red·wood** *n* a coniferous tree of the Pacific coast of North America that is considered to be the tallest tree in the world (often more than 90 m tall) and also one of the longest-lived, some being over 2000 years old. See also SEQUOIA.

re·deem [rɪ'dim] *v* **1** buy back: *The property was redeemed when the loan was paid back.* **2** convert (certificates, etc.) into cash or goods. **3** fulfill: *We redeem a promise by doing what we said.* **4** *Christianity* of Christ, set (the human soul) free from the consequences of sin by his atoning sacrificial death. **5** make up for; balance: *A very good feature will sometimes redeem several bad ones.* **6** exonerate (oneself) by making amends. **7** reclaim (land). ⟨Latin *redimere; re-* back + *emere* buy⟩

re·deem·a·ble *adj* that will be redeemed or paid: *bonds redeemable in ten years.* re·deem·er Usually, **Redeemer** *Christianity* Jesus Christ. re·demp·tion [rɪ'dɛmpʃən] *n* the process, or an instance of redeeming: *redemption from sin, the redemption of a loan.* re·demp·tive *adj.*

re·de·ploy [,ridɪ'plɔi] *v* change the position of (troops) from one theatre of war to another. re·de·ploy·ment *n.*

re·de·vel·op [,ridɪ'vɛləp] *v* 1 develop again. 2 improve buildings or land. re·de·vel·op·ment *n.*

re·di·rect [,ridə'rɛkt] *v* 1 direct again: *to redirect a letter.* 2 give a new direction to: *to redirect the activities of an organization.* re·di·rec·tion *n.*

re·dis·trib·ute [,ridɪ'strɪbjut] *v* change the distribution of. re·dis·trib·u·tive *adj.* re·dis·tri·bu·tion [,ridɪstrɪ'bjuʃən] *n* 1 a distribution made again or anew. 2 ✺ the revision, every ten years, of the number of seats in the Canadian House of Commons to which each province is entitled on the basis of its population.

re·do [ri'du] *v* -did, -done, -do·ing do again.

red·o·lent ['rɛdələnt] *adj* smelling strongly: *a kitchen redolent of fresh baking.* red·o·lent·ly *adv.* red·o·lence *n.* ⟨Latin *redolere* emit scent; *re-* back + *olere* to smell⟩

re·dou·ble [ri'dʌbəl] *v* 1 double again. 2 increase greatly: *Near land, the swimmer redoubled his speed.* 3 double back: *The wolf redoubled on its trail to escape the hunters.* 4 *Bridge* double one's opponent's double. **redouble one's efforts** try even harder.

re·doubt·a·ble [rɪ'dʌutəbəl] *adj* worthy of fear or great respect: *a redoubtable opponent.* re·doubt·a·bly *adv.* ⟨Old French *redouter* dread; *re-* + *douter* doubt; Latin *dubitare*⟩

re·draft [ri'dræft] *v* draft again or anew. *n* ['ri,dræft] a second or later draft.

re·dress [rɪ'drɛs] *v* 1 set right; repair; remedy. 2 balance: *The new budget redresses the old one.* re·dress ['ridrɛs] *or* [rɪ'drɛs] *n.* re·dress·a·ble *adj.* ⟨French *re-* again + *dresser* straighten, arrange⟩

re·duce [rɪ'djus] *or* [rɪ'dus] *v* 1 make or become less or lower: *to reduce expenses.* 2 *Chemistry* a combine with hydrogen. b remove oxygen from. 3 *Mathematics* simplify (an expression, formula, etc.). 4 consume less: *Reduce, re-use, recycle.* re·duc·i·ble *adj.* re·duc·tion [rɪ'dʌkʃən] *n.* ⟨Latin *re-* back + *ducere* bring⟩

re·dun·dant [rɪ'dʌndənt] *adj* 1 extra; not needed. 2 that says the same thing again. *Example:* In *We two both had an apple each,* the expression *two both* is redundant. 3 duplicate; present as a backup in case of failure. re·dun·dan·cy *or* re·dun·dance *n.* re·dun·dant·ly *adv.* ⟨Latin *redundare* overflow⟩

re–echo [ri 'ɛkou] *v* -ech·oed, -ech·o·ing echo back.
n, pl re–ech·oes the echo of an echo.

reed [rid] *n* 1 any of various tall water or marsh grasses having hollow stems. 2 *Music* a thin piece of wood, metal, etc. in a musical instrument that produces sound when vibrated by air. Clarinets and saxophones are reed instruments. ⟨Old English *hrēod*⟩
reed·y *adj* reed·i·er, reed·i·est 1 full of reeds. 2 made of reeds. 3 sounding like a reed instrument: *a thin, reedy voice.* reed·i·ness *n.*

re–ed·u·cate [ri 'ɛdʒə,keit] *v* educate again with the purpose of: a rehabilitating. b inculcating new attitudes. c indoctrinating with political theories. d preparing for a changed labour market. re–ed·u·ca·tion *n.*

reef¹ [rif] *n* 1 a narrow ridge of rock, sand, or coral at or near the surface of the water: *The ship was wrecked on a hidden reef.* 2 a vein or lode in mining. ⟨Middle Dutch *riffe*; Old Norse *rif* rib⟩

reef² [rif] *Nautical n* the part of a sail that can be rolled or folded up to reduce its size. *v* reduce the size of (a sail) by rolling or folding up a part of it. ⟨Middle English *riff*; Old Norse *rif* rib, reef⟩
reef knot SQUARE KNOT.

reef·er¹ *n* a short coat of thick cloth, worn esp by sailors and fishers. ⟨*reef²*⟩

reef·er² *n Slang* a cigarette containing marijuana. ⟨perhaps *reef²*; for their being rolled by hand⟩

reek [rik] *n* 1 a strong, unpleasant smell. 2 *Archaic* smoke; steam; vapour. *v* 1 send out vapour or a strong, unpleasant smell. 2 be filled with something offensive: *a government reeking with corruption.* 3 give out (an offensive quality) strongly: *His manner reeks of arrogance.* ⟨Old English *rēc*⟩

reel¹ [ril] *n* 1 a frame turning on an axis, for winding thread, a fish line, etc. 2 something wound on a reel: *two reels of movie film.* *v* draw by winding: *to reel in a fish.* ⟨Old English *hrēol*⟩
reel off say, write, or make in a quick, easy way: *She can reel off stories by the hour.*

reel² [ril] *v* 1 sway, fall back, or rock under a blow, shock, etc.: *The sight of the crash site made them reel back in horror.* 2 be dizzy. 3 stand or walk with staggering movements: *The drunk reeled across the room.* *n* a reeling or staggering movement. ⟨special use of *reel¹*⟩

reel³ [ril] *n* 1 a lively dance, orig Scottish. 2 the music for a reel. ⟨special use of *reel²*⟩

re–en·try [ri 'ɛntri] *n* an entering again of a spacecraft into the earth's atmosphere after flight in outer space.

reeve [riv] *n* ✺ in Ontario and some western provinces, the elected head of a rural municipal council; in Ontario, also the elected head of a village or township council. reeve·ship *n.* ⟨Old English *gerēfa*⟩

re·fec·to·ry [rɪ'fɛktəri] *n* a room for meals, esp in a monastery, convent, or school. ⟨Latin *refectorium*; *re-* again + *facere* make⟩

re·fer [rɪ'fɜr] *v* -ferred, -fer·ring 1 make mention (with *to*): *The article refers to the cultural differences between East and West.*

2 apply: *The rule refers only to special cases.* **3** send or direct for information, help, or action: *We referred her to the boss.* **4** turn for information: *Writers often refer to a dictionary.* **5** submit: *Let's refer the dispute to the umpire.* **re·fer·ral** *n.* ⟨Latin *re-* back + *ferre* take⟩

ref·er·ee [ˌrɛfə'ri] *n* **1** a judge of play in certain games and sports. **2** a person to whom something is referred for decision. *Abbrev Informal* **ref. ref·er·ee, -eed, -ee·ing** *v.*
ref·er·ence *n* **1** a word, statement, etc. directing attention: *This history contains many references to larger works.* **2** something used for information: *a book of reference.* **3** a person who can give information about another person's character or ability. **4** the information given: *The boy had excellent references from people for whom he had worked.* **5** regard: *This test is to be taken by all pupils without reference to age or grade.* *v* **1** provide with references. **2** refer to. **in** (or **with**) **reference to** concerning. **make reference to** mention. **reference library** a library whose resources may be used only on the premises.
ref·er·en·dum [ˌrɛfə'rɛndəm] *n, pl* **-dums** or **-da** [-də] **1** the process of submitting a law already passed to a direct vote of the citizens for approval or rejection. Compare PLEBISCITE. **2** the submitting of any matter to a direct vote: *In the 1992 referendum, the Charlottetown Accord was defeated.* **ref·er·ent** ['rɛfərənt] *n* **1** an idea, person, or thing referred to. **2** *Linguistics* the idea, thing, act, etc. that a term stands for. *adj* containing a reference. **ref·er·en·tial** [ˌrɛfə'rɛnʃəl] *adj.*

> **SYNONYMS**
> **Refer** = make direct and specific mention.
> **Allude** = mention incidentally or indirectly:
> *She never referred to the incident in her writing, but often alluded to it in conversation.*

re·fill [ri'fɪl] *v* fill again.
n ['ri,fɪl] a material, supply, etc. to replace something that has been used up: *a coffee refill.* **re·fill·a·ble** *adj.*

re·fine [rɪ'faɪn] *v* **1** make or become free from impurities. **2** make or become finer, or more elegant; improve. **re·fined** *adj.* **re·fine·ment** *n.* **re·fin·er** *n.* ⟨*re-* (intensive) + *fine* make fine **refine on** (or **upon**) **a** improve. **b** excel. **re·fin·er·y** *n* a building and machinery for purifying metal, sugar, petroleum, etc.

re·fin·ish [ri'fɪnɪʃ] *v* give a new surface to (furniture, etc.).

re·fit [ri'fɪt] *v* **-fit·ted, -fit·ting** equip for use again: *to refit an old ship.* **re·fit** ['rifɪt] *n.*

re·flect [rɪ'flɛkt] *v* **1** throw back (light, heat, sound, etc.): *The sidewalks reflect heat on a hot day.* **2** give back an image: *A mirror reflects.* **3** reproduce like a mirror: *The newspaper reflected the owner's opinions.* **4** think: *Take time to reflect.* **5** serve to cast or bring: *Her brave act reflects credit on her.* **re·flec·tion** *n.* **re·flec·tive** *adj.* **re·flec·tive·ly** *adv.* ⟨Latin *re-* back + *flectere* bend⟩
reflecting telescope a type of optical telescope in which the light rays entering it

are brought to a focus by means of a concave mirror. Compare REFRACTING TELESCOPE.
re·flec·tor *n Physics* any thing, surface, or device that reflects light, heat, sound, etc.

re·flex ['riflɛks] *adj* **1** *Physiology* coming as a response to a stimulation; not voluntary. **2** occurring in reaction. **3** bent back. **4** of an angle, more than 180° and less than 360°.
n Physiology an automatic reaction to a stimulation of certain nerve cells. Sneezing and shivering are reflexes. ⟨Latin *reflexus* pp of *reflectere*. See REFLECT.⟩
re·flex·ive *Grammar adj* to do with an action that turns back on the subject, so that the subject and object have the same referent. A **reflexive pronoun** refers back to the subject of the sentence: *Example: I cut myself. n* a reflexive verb or pronoun. A **reflexive verb** is a verb whose subject and object refer to the same person or thing. *Example: The boy hurt himself.* **re·flex·ive·ly** *adv.* **re·flex·iv·i·ty** *n.*

re·for·est [ri'fɔrɪst] *v* replant (a previously logged or burnt over area) with trees. **re·for·est·a·tion** *n.*

re·form [rɪ'fɔrm] *v* **1** improve behaviour, attitudes, etc.: *Prisons try to reform criminals.* **2** improve by removing faults: *to reform an administration.* **re·form** *n.* **re·form·a·ble** *adj.* ⟨Latin *reformare*; *re-* again + *forma* form⟩
Re·form *adj* to do with the liberal branch of Judaism, as contrasted with the Orthodox and Conservative branches. **ref·or·ma·tion** [ˌrɛfər'meɪʃən] *n* **1** a change for the better; improvement. **2 Reformation** the 16c religious movement in Europe that ended with the establishment of certain Protestant churches. **ref·or·ma·tion·al** *adj.* **re·form·a·to·ry** [rɪ'fɔrmə,tɔri] *adj* intended to reform. *n* an institution for reforming young offenders against the law. **re·formed** *adj* **1** improved, esp as regards behaviour. **2 Reformed** of or designating the Protestant churches, esp the Calvinist as distinct from the Lutheran. Compare EVANGELICAL. **re·form·er** *n* **1** a person who tries to reform some state of affairs, custom, etc.; a supporter of reform. **2 Reformer ✹** formerly, in Upper and Lower Canada, a member of a political group advocating a greater measure of responsible government. See REFORM PARTY (def. 1). **Reform Party ✹ 1** formerly, the party that opposed Tory rule in Upper Canada and the Maritimes in the 19th century. **2** formerly, a conservative national political party, later merging with the federal Progressive Conservative Party to form the Conservative Party of Canada. **reform school** reformatory.

re·fract [rɪ'frækt] *v* bend (a ray) from a straight course. ⟨Latin *refractus* pp of *refringere*; *re-* + *frangere* break⟩
refracting telescope a type of optical telescope in which the light rays entering it are brought to a focus by a lens or set of lenses. Compare REFLECTING TELESCOPE.
re·frac·tion *n Physics* **a** the bending of a ray of light when it travels from one medium to

another at an oblique angle. **b** the bending of any other wave, such as sound, when it passes from one medium into another of different density. **refractive index** *Optics* the ratio of the velocities of light in two given media. The **absolute refractive index** which is the ratio of the speed of light in a vacuum to that in a given medium, is always greater than 1. **re·fran·gi·ble** [rɪˈfrændʒəbəl] *adj* capable of being refracted: *Rays of light are refrangible.* **re·fran·gi·ble·ness** *n.*

re·frac·to·ry [rɪˈfræktəri] *adj* **1** hard to manage; stubborn: *Mules are refractory.* **2** not yielding readily to treatment: *She had a refractory cough.* **3** hard to melt, reduce, or work: *Some ores are more refractory than others.* **re·frac·to·ri·ly** *adv.* **re·frac·to·ri·ness** *n.* ⟨Latin *refractarius* obstinate. See REFRACT.⟩

re·frain[1] [rɪˈfrein] *v* hold oneself back: *Refrain from crime.* ⟨Latin *re-* back + *frenum* bridle⟩

re·frain[2] [rɪˈfrein] *n* **1** a phrase or verse repeated regularly in a song or poem; chorus. **2** the music for a refrain. ⟨Latin *refrangere, refringere* break off. See REFRACT.⟩

re·fran·gi·ble See REFRACT.

re·fresh [rɪˈfreʃ] *v* make vigorous again: *He refreshed his memory by a glance at the book. She refreshed herself with a cup of tea.* **re·fresh·er** *n.* **re·fresh·er course** a course taken to bring one's knowledge up to date. **re·fresh·ing** *adj* **1** that makes fresh or vigorous again: *a refreshing drink.* **2** welcome as a pleasing change: *Your change in attitude is most refreshing.* **re·fresh·ing·ly** *adv.* **re·fresh·ment** *n* **1** a refreshing or being refreshed. **2** anything that refreshes. **3** Usually, **refreshments** *pl* food or drink: *to serve refreshments at a party.*

re·frig·er·ate [rɪˈfrɪdʒəˌreit] *v* **-at·ed -at·ing.** **1** make or keep cold or cool. **2** preserve by keeping cold or cool. **re·frig·er·a·tion** *n.* ⟨Latin *re-* again + *frigus* cold⟩ **re·frig·er·ant** *adj* cooling. *n* something that cools. Ice is a refrigerant. **re·frig·er·a·tor** *n* an appliance equipped for keeping things, esp food and drink, cold.

re·fu·el [rɪˈfjuəl] *v* **-elled** or **-eled, -el·ling** or **-el·ing** take on a fresh supply of fuel.

ref·uge [ˈrɛfjudʒ] *n* **1** shelter or protection from danger, trouble, etc.: *The cat took refuge from the angry dog in a tree.* **2** any person, thing, or action regarded as a source of safety: *A deserted farmhouse was their refuge from the storm.* ⟨Latin *re-* back + *fugere* flee⟩ **ref·u·gee** [ˌrɛfjəˈdʒi] or [ˈrɛfjəˌdʒi] *n* a person who flees for refuge or safety, esp to a foreign country, in time of persecution, war, etc.

re·ful·gent [rɪˈfʌldʒənt] *adj* shining brightly; radiant; splendid: *a refulgent sunrise.* **re·ful·gence** *n.* **re·ful·gent·ly** *adv.* ⟨Latin *re-* back + *fulgere* shine⟩

re·fund [rɪˈfʌnd] *v* pay back: *The shop will refund your money if you are not satisfied.* *n* [ˈrifʌnd] the return of money paid. **re·fund·a·ble** *adj.* ⟨Latin *re-* back + *fundere* pour⟩

re·fur·bish [riˈfɜrbɪʃ] *v* polish up again; renovate or restore. **re·fur·bish·ment** *n.*

re·fus·al *n* **1** the act of refusing: *Their refusal to play the game provoked the others.* **2** the right to refuse or take a thing before it is offered to others: *Give me the refusal of the car till tomorrow.*

re·fuse[1] [rɪˈfjuz] *v* **1** decline to accept: *to refuse an offer.* **2** deny (a request, demand, invitation): *to refuse admittance.* **3** decline (to do something): *to refuse to discuss the question.* ⟨Old French *refuser*; Latin *refusus* pp of *refundere.* See REFUND[1].⟩

SYNONYMS
Refuse is the blunt term, implying a direct denial: *He refused to go with me. Decline* is more polite, implying a reluctant denial: *She declined my invitation. Reject* is more emphatic than refuse, implying a very positive denial: *He rejected my friendly advice.*

ref·use[2] [ˈrɛfjus] or [ˈrɛfjuz] *n* waste; rubbish. **ref·use** *adj.* ⟨Old French *refuser.* See REFUSE[1].⟩

re·fute [rɪˈfjut] *v* prove (a claim or argument) to be false. **re·fut·er** *n.* **re·fut·a·ble** *adj.* **re·fut·a·bly** *adv.* **ref·u·ta·tion** [ˌrɛfjəˈteiʃən] *n.* ⟨Latin *re-* back + *futare* make fall⟩

re·gain [rɪˈgein] *v* **1** recover: *to regain health.* **2** get back to; reach again: *to regain the shore.*

re·gal [ˈrigəl] *adj* **1** belonging to a monarch; royal: *Opening Parliament is a regal prerogative.* **2** like a king or queen; splendid; magnificent. **re·gal·ly** *adv.* ⟨Latin *rex, regis* king⟩ **re·ga·li·a** [rɪˈgeiliə] *n pl* **1** the emblems of royalty. Crowns, sceptres, etc. are regalia. **2** the emblems or decorations of any society, order, etc. **3** fine clothes: *in party regalia.*

re·gale [rɪˈgeil] *v* **1** entertain agreeably: *She regaled the children with silly stories.* **2** entertain with a feast. **re·gale·ment** *n.* **re·gal·er** *n.* ⟨French *régaler; gale* merriment⟩

re·gard [rɪˈgɑrd] *v* **1** consider: *She is regarded as the best doctor in town.* **2** respect: *They always regard their parents' wishes.* **3** look at: *The teacher regarded me sternly.* *n* **1** consideration: *Have regard for the feelings of others.* **2** a steady look. **3** good opinion. **4 regards** *pl* good wishes: *My regards to your mother.* **5** a point; particular matter: *in this regard.* ⟨French *re-* back + *garder* guard⟩ **as regards** concerning: *As regards money, I have enough.* **in** (or **with**) **regard to** relating to. **without regard to** not considering. **re·gard·ful** *adj* **1** heedful; observant. **2** considerate; respectful. **re·gard·ful·ly** *adv.* **re·gard·ing** *prep* with regard to. **re·gard·less** *adj* taking no heed; careless. *adv Informal* in spite of what happens: *We plan to leave on Monday, and we will leave then, regardless.* **regardless of** despite; without regard for. **re·gard·less·ly** *adv.* **re·gard·less·ness** *n.*

USAGE
The form **irregardless** is not logical since it literally means 'not regardless'. As a result, it should be avoided.

re·gat·ta [rɪˈgætə] or [rɪˈgatə] *n* a series of boat races: *the annual regatta of the yacht club.* ⟨dialect Italian⟩

re·gen·cy See REGENT.

re·gen·er·ate [rɪ'dʒɛnə,reit] *v* **1** give a new and better spiritual life to. **2** grow again: *The mother's liver regenerated the lobe she had donated to her young child.*
re·gen·er·ate [rɪ'dʒɛnərɪt] *adj.* **re·gen·er·a·ble** *adj.*
re·gen·er·a·tion *n.* **re·gen·er·a·tive** *adj.*
re·gen·er·a·tive·ly *adv.* **re·gen·er·a·tor** *n.* ⟨Latin *re-* again + *generis* birth⟩

re·gent ['ridʒənt] *n* **1** a person who rules in the name of a sick, absent, or underage sovereign. **2** a member of a governing board. Many universities have boards of regents.
adj acting as a regent (after a noun): *a princess regent.* ⟨Latin *regere* rule⟩
re·gen·cy ['ridʒənsi] *n* **1** the position, office, or function of a regent. **2** a state or territory controlled by a regent or regents.

reg·gae ['rɛgei] *n* a style of music that developed in Jamaica in the mid 1970s, a blend of calypso and rock rhythms. ⟨Jamaican English; perhaps *rege* ragged⟩

reg·i·cide ['rɛdʒə,saɪd] *n* **1** the crime of killing a monarch. **2** a person who commits regicide. **reg·i·cid·al** *adj.* ⟨Latin *rex, regis* king + -CIDE[1]⟩

re·gime or **ré·gime** [rɪ'ʒim] *n* **1** a system of government: *a communist regime.* **2** a period of time in which a person or administration is in power: *the Trudeau regime.* **3** a regular system of living; regimen: *Monastic orders follow a strict regime.* ⟨French; Latin *regimen*. See REGIMEN.⟩

reg·i·men ['rɛdʒəmən] *n* **1** *Medicine* a set of rules or habits intended to improve health, reduce weight, etc. **2** the act of governing; government; rule. ⟨Latin; *regere* rule⟩

reg·i·ment ['rɛdʒəmənt] *n* **1** in the army, a unit consisting of several companies or troops etc., organized into one large group commanded by a colonel. **2** a large number: *a whole regiment of school children.*
v ['rɛdʒə,mɛnt] treat in a strict or uniform manner: *A totalitarian state regiments its citizens.* **reg·i·men·tal** *adj.* **reg·i·men·tal·ly** *adv.* ⟨Latin *regimentum* rule; *regere* to rule⟩
reg·i·men·ta·tion *n* **1** a formation into organized groups. **2** a making uniform by rigid discipline. **3** a subjection to control.

re·gion ['ridʒən] *n* **1** any large part of the earth's surface, esp one characterized by certain flora and fauna: *the tundra region.* **2** a place; area: *an unhealthful region.* **3** a sphere; domain: *the region of art, the region of the imagination.* **4** ✹ in Ontario, a geographical division for purposes of government, having wider powers than those of a county. ⟨Latin *regio* direction; *regere* direct⟩
re·gion·al *adj* of or in a particular region, as opposed to a smaller area: *a regional storm.*
re·gion·al·ly *adv.* **re·gion·al·ism** *n* **1** regional patriotism. **2** in art and literature, emphasis on the characteristics of a particular region. **3** a linguistic feature or custom, etc. that is characteristic of a particular geographical region. **4** the division of a country, etc. into partially autonomous administrative areas called regions. **regional municipality** ✹ a unit of local government that takes in all the small municipalities and rural communities in a given region.

reg·is·ter ['rɛdʒɪstər] *n* **1** a list; record: *A register of attendance is kept in schools.* **2** anything that records: *At the end of the day, the cash register tape should tally with the money taken in.* **3** *Computers* a high-speed storage area in the central processing unit. **4** an opening in a wall or floor with a grid to regulate the amount of cooled or heated air that passes through. **5** *Music* part of the range of a voice or musical instrument: *Her upper register sounds a little forced.*
v **1** write in a record: *to register the names of the new members.* **2** enrol: *You must register if you want to attend the conference.* **3** indicate or be indicated: *The thermometer registers 28°.* **4** show (surprise, joy, anger, etc.) by the expression on one's face or by actions. **5** absorb; take in: *She seemed unable to register the fact that her home had been destroyed.*
reg·is·tra·tion *n.* ⟨Latin *regestrum* pp of *regerere* record; *re-* back + *gerere* carry⟩
reg·is·tered *adj* **1** legally certified: *a registered patent, a registered trademark.* **2** of cattle, dogs, cats, etc., recorded with the official breeding association: *registered Holsteins.* **3** *Commerce* of bonds, etc., having the owner's name officially listed with the issuing corporation and inscribed on the face of the bond, stock certificate, etc. **registered mail** a postal service that provides proof that a letter or parcel has been delivered. **Registered Retirement Savings Plan** a personal investment fund for retirement, registered with the government so that no tax is paid on money deposited until it is withdrawn. *Abbrev* **RRSP.** **reg·is·tra·ble** *adj* that can be registered. **reg·is·trant** *n* a person who registers or has registered: *registrants for a conference.* **reg·is·trar** *n* **1** an official recorder. **2** in some universities, colleges, etc., the officer in charge of admissions, examinations, etc. **3** an official of a bank or trust company who registers securities for a corporation and ensures that the shares issued do not exceed the number authorized. **reg·is·try** *n* **1** an office of registration. **2** a book in which a record is kept. **3** a customs document declaring a ship's nationality.

re·gress [rɪ'grɛs] *v* **1** move in a backward direction. **2** return or cause to return to an earlier state: *The hypnotist regressed me to childhood.* **re·gress** ['rigrɛs] *n.* **re·gres·sor** *n.* ⟨Latin *regressus* pp of *regredi; re-* back + *gradi* go⟩
re·gres·sion *n* **1** backward movement. **2** *Psychology* a way of trying to escape problems by assuming characteristics of childhood. **3** *Biology* the reversion of offspring toward a more general condition. **4** *Statistics* a technique for determining the relationship between a dependent variable and an independent variable.

re·gret [rɪ'grɛt] *v* **-gret·ted, -gret·ting** feel sorrow or remorse about.

n 1 sorrow or remorse. 2 **regrets** *pl* a polite reply declining an invitation. **re·gret·ful** *adj*. **re·gret·ful·ly** *adv*. **re·gret·ta·ble** *adj*. **re·gret·ta·bly** *adv*. ⟨Old French *regreter*⟩

re·group [ri'grup] *v* 1 form into a new arrangement: *You can regroup two bags of six oranges each to make three bags of four oranges each.* 2 *Mathematics* in subtraction, decrease the digit in a column of the minuend by 1 in order to increase the value in the column on the right by 10: *To subtract 8 from 64, regroup 64 as 5 tens and 14 ones.* 3 *Informal* reorganize in order to make a fresh start.

reg·u·lar ['rɛgjələr] *adj* 1 fixed by habit or custom: *Six o'clock was her regular hour of rising.* 2 according to rule: *A period is the regular ending for a sentence.* 3 coming or done again and again at the same time: *Saturday is a regular holiday.* 4 habitual: *a regular customer.* 5 even in size, spacing, etc.: *regular features.* 6 symmetrical. 7 *Mathematics* having all its angles equal and all its sides equal: *a regular triangle.* 8 *Botany* having all the same parts of a flower alike in shape and size. 9 orderly: *to lead a regular life.* 10 properly fitted or trained: *I cooked while the regular chef was sick.* 11 *Grammar* of a noun, verb, etc., changing according to the usual pattern to show tense, number, etc.: *a regular verb.* 12 *Informal* complete: *a regular bore.* 13 having bowel movements at consistent intervals *n* 1 a full-time member of a group: *The fire department was made up of regulars and volunteers.* 2 a regular customer, contributor, etc.: *He is a regular on this bus.* 3 a person who makes the armed forces a full-time career. **reg·u·lar·i·ty** *n*. **reg·u·lar·ize** *v*. **reg·u·lar·ly** *adv*. ⟨Latin *regula*. See RULE.⟩

reg·u·late *v* 1 control by rule: *Good schools regulate student's behaviour.* 2 keep at some standard: *This instrument regulates the speed.* **reg·u·la·tor** *n*. **reg·u·la·to·ry** ['rɛgjələ,tɔri] *adj*. **reg·u·la·tion** *n* 1 control by rule. 2 a rule; law: *traffic regulations.* *adj* according to a regulation: *regulation uniform.*

re·gur·gi·tate [ri'gɜrdʒə,teit] *v* bring (partly digested food) back from the stomach to the mouth: *Some birds regurgitate food to feed their young.* **re·gur·gi·ta·tion** *n*. ⟨Latin *re-* back + *gurgitis* whirlpool⟩

re·ha·bil·i·tate [,rihə'bɪlə,teit] *or* [,riə-] *v* 1 restore to former standing, reputation, etc.: *The former criminal completely rehabilitated himself and was respected by all.* 2 restore to a normal state of health by treatment, therapy, etc. **re·ha·bil·i·ta·tion** *n*. **re·ha·bil·i·ta·tive** *adj*. ⟨Latin *re-* again + *habilis* fit⟩

re·hash [ri'hæʃ] *v* work up (old material) into a new form: *The question had been rehashed again and again.* **re·hash** ['rihæʃ] *n*.

re·hearse [rɪ'hɜrs] *v* 1 practise (a play, part, etc.) for a public performance. 2 drill or train (a person, etc.) by repetition. 3 tell in detail; repeat: *The child rehearsed all the happenings of the day from beginning to end.* **re·hears·al** *n*. ⟨Old French *rehercier*; *re-* again + *hercier* harrow; Latin *hirpicis* rake⟩

in rehearsal in the process of being prepared for performance.

reign [rein] *n* the period of power of a ruler: *Queen Victoria's reign lasted sixty-four years.* *v* 1 be a ruler. 2 exist everywhere: *Silence reigned on the lake, except for the sound of our paddles.* ⟨Latin *regnum; regere* rule⟩

re·im·burse [,riɪm'bɜrs] *v* pay back: *His employer reimbursed him for his travelling expenses.* **re·im·burse·ment** *n*. ⟨re- + Latin *imbursare; in-* into + *bursa* purse⟩

rein [rein] *n* 1 a long, narrow strap fastened to the bit of a bridle, used to control an animal, esp a horse. 2 **reins** *pl* a means of control: *to seize the reins of government.* *v* guide and control: *Rein your tongue.* ⟨Latin *retinere* hold back. See RETAIN.⟩

draw rein a tighten the reins: *She drew rein as she approached the gate.* b slow down; stop. **give rein to** let act freely, without control: *to give rein to one's feelings.* **keep on a short** (or **tight**) **rein** keep under close supervision: *Some people work better when kept on a short rein.* **rein in** (or **up**) stop or cause to stop or go slower: *Rein in before your horse tramples the flowers!* **take the reins** take control.

re·in·car·nate [,riɪn'kɑrneit] *v* give a new body to (a soul). *adj* [,riɪn'kɑrnɪt] appearing to be a new incarnation of someone else (after the noun): *She is her grandmother reincarnate.* **re·in·car·na·tion** *n*.

rein·deer ['rein,dir] *n*, *pl* -**deer** a large deer of arctic and subarctic regions, both sexes of which have large, branching antlers. ⟨Old Norse *hreindýri*⟩

re·in·force [,riɪn'fɔrs] *v* 1 strengthen with new force or materials: *to reinforce a wall.* 2 strengthen: *to reinforce an argument, a plea, an effect, etc.* 3 *Psychology* strengthen the probability of (a response to a stimulus) by giving a reward or removing a painful stimulus. Also, **re·en·force** or **re–en·force**. **re·in·force·ment,** **re·en·force·ment,** or **re–en·force·ment** *n*.
reinforced concrete concrete with steel embedded in it to make it stronger.

re·in·state [,riɪn'steit] *v* restore to a former position or condition. **re·in·state·ment** *n*.

re·in·te·grate [ri'ɪntə,greit] *v* 1 make whole again; restore to a perfect state. 2 become whole again; be renewed. **re·in·te·gra·tion** *n*.

re·in·ter·pret [,riɪn'tɜrprɪt] *v* interpret again, esp in a new and different way.

re·is·sue [ri'ɪʃu] *v* 1 issue again: *Snow White has been reissued several times.* 2 come forth again: *The groundhog reissued from its burrow.* *n* 1 something issued again, as a recording or book. 2 an official reprint after the original issue has been stopped: *a reissue of a commemorative stamp.*

re·it·er·ate [ri'ɪtə,reit] *v* repeat (an action, demand, etc.) again and again: *The boy did not move, though the teacher reiterated her command.* **re·it·er·a·tion** *n*. ⟨Latin *reiterare; re-* again + *iterum* again⟩

re·ject [rɪ'dʒɛkt] *v* **1** refuse to take, use, believe, consider, etc.: *He rejected our help.* **2** throw away as useless: *Reject all apples with soft spots.* **3** deny affection to: *He rejected her children.* **4** *Medicine* fail to accept (a transplanted organ or a graft) because of an immunological reaction: *The percentage of transplants that are rejected is lower than it used to be.* **re·ject** ['rɪdʒɛkt] *n.* **re·jec·tion** *n.* ⟨Latin *rejectus* pp of *rejicere*; *re-* back + *jacere* throw⟩

re·joice [rɪ'dʒɔɪs] *v* **1** be glad. **2** make glad. **re·joic·er** *n.* **re·joic·ing** *n.* ⟨Old French *rejoïss-*; Latin *re-* again + *gaudere* be glad⟩

re·join¹ [ri'dʒɔɪn] *v* **1** unite (people or things) again: *The doctor rejoined the severed nerve.* **2** enter the company of (somebody) again: *After conferring briefly in private, the executive rejoined the members.* ⟨*re-* + *join*⟩

re·join² [rɪ'dʒɔɪn] *v* reply: *"No way,"* he *rejoined.* ⟨French *re-* back + *joindre* join⟩ **re·join·der** *n* an answer to a reply; response.

re·ju·ve·nate [rɪ'dʒuvə,neit] *v* **1** make young or vigorous again: *Your holiday seems to have rejuvenated you.* **2** restore a youthful appearance. **re·ju·ve·na·tion** *n.* **re·ju·ve·na·tor** *n.* ⟨*re-* + Latin *juvenis* young⟩

re·lapse [rɪ'læps] *v* fall back into a former state, way of acting, etc.: *After one cry of surprise, she relapsed into silence. After struggling to speak, the patient relapsed into unconsciousness.* **re·lapse** ['rilæps] *n.* ⟨Latin *relapsus* pp of *relabi*; *re-* back + *labi* slip⟩

re·late [rɪ'leit] *v* **1** give an account of: *The traveller related her adventures.* **2** connect: *Better and best are related to good.* **3** be connected in any way: *We are interested in what relates to ourselves.* **4** establish sympathetic feeling toward a person or thing: *I find it hard to relate to punk rock.* **5** interact with others: *unhealthy patterns of relating.* **re·lat·ed** *adj.* **re·lat·ed·ness** *n.* ⟨Latin *relatus* pp of *referre*; *re-* back + *ferre* bring⟩
re·la·tion *n* **1** a connection: *Your answer has no relation to the question.* **2 relations** *pl* dealings: *Our firm has business relations with her firm.* **3** a person who belongs to the same family as another; relative. **4** an account: *She gave us a straightforward relation of the day's events.* **5** *Mathematics* a property, as of equality or inequality, by which an ordered pair of quantities, expressions, etc. is associated.
in (or **with**) **relation to a** in connection with: *Viewed in relation to current trends, her offhand remarks were unacceptable.* **b** in comparison to: *Spending has gone up incredibly in relation to per capita income.* **re·la·tion·ship** *n* **1** a connection; often, specifically, dealings between two persons. **2** the condition of being related. **rel·a·tive** ['rɛlətɪv] *n* a person who belongs to the same family as another. *adj* **1** compared to each other: *We considered the relative merits of fried chicken and roast beef.* **2** depending for meaning on a relation to something else: *West can be a relative term; for example, Fredericton is west of Charlottetown but east of Yellowknife.* **rel·a·tive·ly** *adv.*

relative to in proportion to: *He is strong relative to his size.* **relative clause** an adjective clause introduced by a relative pronoun (**that, which, who**) or a relative adverb (**where, when, why**). *Examples: The ball* that had been lost *was found by the caddie. That is the place* where she lived. See also RESTRICTIVE CLAUSE. **relative humidity** the ratio between the amount of water vapour in the air and the amount it would take to saturate the air at the same temperature, expressed as a percentage. **relative pronoun** the relative pronouns are **that, which** (**of which, whose**) and **who** (**whose, whom**). They introduce relative clauses and refer to an antecedent in the main clause. *Examples: A man* who *was there gave us the details of the accident. Our team,* which *scored first, had the advantage.* **Who** refers to people; **which** to animals or things; and **that** to animals or things, and, less often, to people. **rel·a·tiv·ism** *n Philosophy* any theory which holds that all judgments or criteria of value are relative, varying with individuals, circumstances, cultures, etc. **rel·a·tiv·ist** *n.* **rel·a·tiv·ist·ic** *adj.* **rel·a·tiv·i·ty** *n* **1** the state or quality of being relative. **2** *Physics* the character of being relative rather than absolute, as ascribed to motion or velocity. **3** *Physics* a theory formulated by Albert Einstein in the equation $E = mc^2$ (energy = mass × the square of the speed of light). The **general theory of relativity** states, essentially, there can be no speed greater than that of light in a vacuum; there is no observable absolute motion, only relative motion; matter and energy are equivalent; time is relative.

re·lax [rɪ'læks] *v* **1** loosen up: *Relax your muscles to rest them.* **2** make or become less severe: *Discipline is relaxed on the last day of school.* **3** give or take recreation: *Take a vacation and relax.* **4** weaken: *Don't relax your efforts because the examinations are over.* **re·lax·a·tion** *n.* **re·lax·ed·ly** [-'læksɪdli] *adv.* ⟨Latin *re-* back + *laxus* loose⟩
re·lax·ant *n* a substance that relaxes, esp a drug used to relax muscles.

re·lay ['rilei] *n* **1** a fresh supply: *New relays of men were sent to the battle front.* **2** *Sports* the act of passing on a ball, puck, etc. **3** *Electricity* a device used in transmitting telephone messages over long distances. **4** a system of working, sending messages, etc. by the use of people or groups acting in turn.
v [rɪ'lei] *or* ['rilei] **1** take and carry farther: *Couriers will relay your message.* **2** receive and then pass to another: *to relay a phone message, to relay a thrown ball.* ⟨Old French *re-* back + *laier* leave⟩

re·lease [rɪ'lis] *v* **1** set free: *The nurse is released from duty at seven o'clock. The prisoners were released early in the morning.* **2** permit to be published, shown, sold, etc. *n* **1** a setting free. **2** relief from emotional stress. **3** a device for releasing part of a mechanism. **4** *Law* the legal surrender of right, estate, etc. to another. **5** an authorization for publication, exhibition, sale, etc. **6** an article, statement, film, recording, etc. made available for distribution. ⟨Old French *relaissier*, Latin *relaxare*. See RELAX.⟩

SYNONYMS
Release emphasizes relaxing the hold on the person or thing: *to release the brakes of a car.* **Free** emphasizes giving freedom by unfastening whatever is holding: *to free a bird from a cage.*

rel·e·gate ['rɛlə,geit] *v* **1** send away, usually to a lower position or condition. **2** hand over (a matter, task, etc.). **3** assign or refer to a particular class, kind, order, etc. **rel·e·ga·tion** *n*. ⟨Latin *re-* back + *legare* despatch, commission; *legis* law⟩

re·lent [rɪ'lɛnt] *v* become less harsh, strict, or stubborn: *Mother relented and allowed us to go after all.* ⟨Latin *re-* again + *lentus* slow⟩ **re·lent·less** *adj* **1** without pity; harsh: *The storm raged with relentless fury.* **2** persistent; determined: *Her relentless work finally paid off.* **re·lent·less·ly** *adv*.

rel·e·vant ['rɛləvənt] *adj* bearing upon the matter in hand: *relevant questions.* **rel·e·vance** *adj*. **rel·e·vant·ly** *adv*. ⟨Latin *relevans* refreshing; *re-* back + *levis* light⟩

re·li·a·ble, re·li·ance, re·li·ant See RELY.

rel·ic ['rɛlɪk] *n* **1** a thing, custom, etc. that remains from the past: *This fence is a relic of pioneer days.* **2** something belonging to a holy person, kept as a sacred memorial: *That church is said to house a relic of the True Cross.* **3** relics *pl* remains; ruins. ⟨Latin *reliquiae*, pl, remains. See RELINQUISH.⟩ **rel·i·quar·y** ['rɛlə,kwɛri] *n* a small box or other receptacle for a relic (def. 2).

re·lief See RELIEVE.

re·lieve [rɪ'liv] *v* **1** make less; make easier: *pills to relieve a headache.* **2** set free: *Your phone call relieved me of the bother of writing a long explanation.* **3** rid: *May I relieve you of that used paper cup?* **4** bring aid to: *Soldiers were sent to relieve the fort.* **5** give variety to: *The plain black sweater was relieved by a white collar.* **6** free (a person on duty) by taking his or her place. **re·liev·er** *n*. ⟨Old French *relever*, Latin *relevare* lighten. See RELEVANT.⟩ **re·lief** [rɪ'lif] *n* **1** the lessening of a pain, burden, difficulty, etc. **2** aid; help. **3** something that makes a pleasing change: *light relief.* **4** a change of persons on duty. **5** a *Sculpture, painting, etc.* the projection of figures from a flat surface. **6** differences in height between the summits and lowlands of a region. **in relief** standing out from a surface. **on relief** receiving money to live on from public funds. **relief map** a map that shows the different heights of a surface by using colours, etc., or materials such as clay.

re·li·gion [rɪ'lɪdʒən] *n* **1** belief in or worship of God or gods. **2** a particular system of religious belief: *the Islamic religion.* **3** a matter of zeal and conscience: *She makes a religion of keeping her house neat.* ⟨Latin *religio* respect for sacred traditions; *relegere* go through again; *re-* again + *legere* read⟩

get religion *Informal* undergo a change of lifestyle from non-belief to the acquisition of a system of beliefs. **re·li·gi·os·i·ty** [rɪ,lɪdʒi'ɒsəti] *n* an affectation of religious feelings. **re·li·gious** *adj* **1** to do with religion. **2** devoted to the worship of God or gods. **3** strict; very careful: *Pay religious attention to the doctor's orders. n, pl* **re·li·gious** a member of a religious order. **re·li·gious·ly** *adv*. **re·li·gious·ness** *n*.

re·lin·quish [rɪ'lɪŋkwɪʃ] *v* give up; let go: *She has relinquished all hope of going to Europe.* ⟨Latin *relinquere*; *re-* behind + *linquere* leave⟩ **re·lin·quish·er** *n*. **re·lin·quish·ment** *n*.

rel·i·quar·y See RELIC.

rel·ish ['rɛlɪʃ] *n* **1** a pleasant taste: *Hunger gives relish to simple food.* **2** a pickle made of chopped cucumbers, etc. **3** a liking; appetite: *The hungry boy ate with great relish.* *v* like; enjoy: *She did not relish the prospect of staying after school.* ⟨Old French *reles* remainder; *relesser, relaissier.* See RELEASE.⟩

re·live [ri'lɪv] *v* **-lived, -living** experience (an event, etc.) again, esp in one's imagination.

re·luc·tant [rɪ'lʌktənt] *adj* **1** unwilling: *reluctant approval.* **2** slow to act because unwilling: *He was very reluctant to give his money away.* **re·luc·tance** *n*. **re·luc·tant·ly** *adv*. ⟨Latin *reluctari*; *re-* back + *lucta* wrestling⟩

re·ly [rɪ'laɪ] *v* depend; trust (usually with *on* or *upon*): *Rely on your own efforts.* ⟨Old French *relier*, Latin *religare* bind fast; *re-* + *ligare* bind⟩ **re·li·a·ble** *adj* worthy of trust: *reliable sources.* **re·li·a·bil·i·ty** or **re·li·a·ble·ness** *n*. **re·li·a·bly** *adv*. **re·li·ance** *n* **1** trust: *the reliance of a child on his parents.* **2** confidence: *I have every reliance on their judgment.* **re·li·ant** *adj* depending.

rem [rɛm] *n* the unit for measuring the harm caused by radiation on human tissue. It is equal to the effect of one roentgen of X rays. ⟨roentgen + equivalent + man⟩

REM [rɛm] RAPID EYE MOVEMENT.

re·main [rɪ'mein] *v* **1** stay: *We remained at the lake till September.* **2** continue to be: *The town remains the same year after year.* **3** be left: *A few apples remain on the trees.* *n* **remains** *pl* **a** what is left. **b** a dead body. ⟨Latin *re-* back + *manere* stay⟩ **remain to be seen** be unknowable till later. **re·main·der** *n* **1** the part left over: *After studying for an hour, she spent the remainder of the afternoon in play.* **2** *Arithmetic* **a** a number left over after subtracting one number from another. *Example: In 9 – 2, the remainder is 7.* **b** a number left over after dividing one number by another. *Example: In 14 ÷ 3, the quotient is 4 with a remainder of 2.* **3** copies of a book for which sales have dropped considerably, that the publisher sells at greatly reduced prices. **re·main·dered** *adj*.

re·make [ri'meik] *v* **-made, -making** make (something) again or anew. *n* ['ri,meik] **1** the act of making again: *I had to do a remake of the pattern.* **2** the thing remade, such as a film: *We watched the remake of* Stagecoach *last night.*

re·mand [rɪ'mænd] v **1** send back. **2** *Law*
a send back (a prisoner or an accused person)
into custody. **b** send back (a case) to the
court it came from for further action there.
re·mand n. ⟨Latin *re-* back + *mandare* order⟩

re·mark [rɪ'mɑrk] v **1** say; speak. **2** notice.
n a short statement. ⟨French *remarquer; re-*
(intensive) + *marquer* mark⟩
re·mark·a·ble adj worthy of notice; unusual.
re·mark·a·ble·ness n. **re·mark·a·bly** adv.

re·mas·ter [rɪ'mæstər] v produce a new and
superior master (of a recording), esp digitally.
re·mas·ter·ing n.

re·match ['ri,mætʃ] n a second match between
the same contestants. **re·match** [rɪ'mætʃ] v.

rem·e·dy ['rɛmədi] n **1** anything used to cure
or relieve illness: *Aspirin and chicken soup are
two cold remedies.* **2** anything intended to put
right something bad or wrong: *The free movie
was a remedy for the children's low spirits.*
3 *Law* legal redress; the legal means by which
a right is enforced or a wrong redressed.
v **-died, -dy·ing** put right; make right; cure.
⟨Latin *remederi; re-* again + *mederi* heal⟩
re·me·di·a·ble [rɪ'midiəbəl] adj that can be
remedied or cured. **re·me·di·a·bly** adv.
re·me·dial [rɪ'midiəl] adj **1** intended as a cure.
2 *Education* to do with a special course of
study designed to improve a student's skills
or knowledge in a given area: *remedial math,
remedial English.* **re·me·di·al·ly** adv.
re·me·di·a·tion n.

re·mem·ber [rɪ'mɛmbər] v **1** call to mind.
2 keep in mind. **3** have memory: *Dogs
remember.* **4** make a gift to: *Grandfather
remembered us all in his will.* **5** mention (a
person) as sending friendly greetings:
Remember me to your mother when you see her.
6 honour the memory of: *Let us remember
those who gave their lives for our freedom.* ⟨Old
French *remembrer;* Latin *rememorari; re-* again
+ *memor* mindful⟩
re·mem·brance n **1** memory. **2** a keepsake;
souvenir. **3 remembrances** pl greetings.
Remembrance Day ✻ November 11, the day
set aside to honour the memory of those in
Canada killed in World Wars I and II, and in
subsequent wars in which Canada has been
involved. **re·mind** [rɪ'maɪnd] v make (one)
think (of something). **re·mind·er** n a thing or
person that helps one remember: *I use string
around my finger as a reminder.*

re·mind, re·mind·er See REMEMBER.

rem·i·nisce [,rɛmə'nɪs] v talk or think about
past experiences or events. **rem·i·nis·cence** n.
⟨Latin *re-* again + *men-* mind⟩
rem·i·nis·cent [,rɛmə'nɪsənt] adj **1** recalling
past events, etc.: *reminiscent talk.*
2 awakening memories of something else: *a
manner reminiscent of a statelier age.*
rem·i·nis·cent·ly adv.

re·miss [rɪ'mɪs] adj careless; negligent: *A
police officer who fails to report a crime is remiss
in her duty.* **re·miss·ness** n. ⟨Latin *remissus*
pp of *remittere; re-* back + *mittere* let go⟩

re·mis·sion See REMIT.

re·mit [rɪ'mɪt] v **-mit·ted, -mit·ting 1** send
money to a person or place: *Enclosed is our
bill; please remit.* **2** cancel; pardon: *power to
remit sins.* **3** become less or stop. **re·mit·ta·ble**
adj. **re·mit·ter** n. ⟨Latin *remittere* send back, let
go. See REMISS.⟩
re·mis·sion n **1** a letting off (from debt,
punishment, etc.): *The bankrupt sought
remission of his debts.* **2** pardon; forgiveness:
*Remission of sins is promised to those who
repent.* **3** a lessening (of pain, force, labour,
etc.). **4** a cessation, temporary or permanent,
of a disease: *Her cancer is in remission.*
re·mis·sive adj. **re·mit·tance** n money sent to
someone at a distance. **remittance man**
formerly, a man who lived abroad on money
sent from his relatives at home, often to
ensure that he did not return to the Old
Country to become an embarrassment.

rem·nant ['rɛmnənt] n **1** a leftover part. **2** a
piece of cloth, ribbon, etc., left after the rest
has been used or sold: *She bought a silk
remnant at the sale.* ⟨Old French *remenant* ppr
of *remenoir* remain; Latin. See REMAIN.⟩

re·mod·el [ri'mɒdəl] v **-elled** or **-eled, -el·ling**
or **-el·ing** make over; change or alter: *The old
barn was remodelled into a house.*

re·mon·strate [rɪ'mɒnstreit] or ['rɛmən,streit]
v **1** speak in complaint or protest: *The
supervisor remonstrated with the worker about
his slackness.* **2** present arguments in protest.
re·mon·strance n. **re·mon·stra·tive** adj.
re·mon·stra·tive·ly adv. **re·mon·stra·tor** n.
⟨Latin *remonstrare* point out⟩

re·morse [rɪ'mɔrs] n deep, painful regret for
having done wrong: *Because he felt remorse for
his crime, the thief confessed.* **re·morse·ful** adj.
re·morse·ful·ly adv. ⟨Latin *remorsus* pp of
remordere, re- back + *mordere* bite⟩
re·morse·less adj without remorse; pitiless;
cruel. **re·morse·less·ly** adv. **re·morse·less·ness** n.

re·mote [rɪ'mout] adj **1** far away from a
given place or time: *Dinosaurs lived in remote
ages.* **2** out of the way: *a remote village.*
3 distantly related: *a remote relative.* **4** slight: *I
haven't the remotest idea what you mean.*
5 aloof: *Her attitude toward the visitor was
somewhat remote.* **6** not immediate or direct.
7 *Computers* to do with a terminal located at
a distance from the computer and requiring
a communication line: *All of us who use the
university computers have to do so in remote
mode.* **8** operated by or used for REMOTE
CONTROL: *a remote switch.* **re·mote·ly** adv.
re·mote·ness n. ⟨Latin *remotus* pp of *removere.*
See REMOVE.⟩
remote control 1 control from a distance, by
electrical impulses or radio signals. **2** the
device used to control the operation of a
television set, VCR, garage door opener, etc.
Also called **re·mote. re·mote–con·trol** adj.

re·move [rɪ'muv] v **1** move from a place or
position: *Remove your hat.* **2** get rid of: *to
remove all doubt.* **3** kill. **4** dismiss from a
position: *to remove an official for taking bribes.*
5 go away; move oneself to another place.
n **1** a step or degree of distance: *His cruelty*

was only one remove from crime. **2** the distance by which one thing is separated from another: *at a far remove from the centre of business.* **re·mov·a·ble** *adj.* **re·mov·er** *n.* ⟨Latin *removere*; re- back + *movere* move⟩

re·mov·al *n* **1** a taking away: *We paid ninety dollars for garbage removal.* **2** a change of place: *The store announces its removal to larger quarters.* **3** a dismissal from a position. **re·moved** *adj* **1** emotionally distant. **2** separated by one or more steps or degrees of relationship: *a first cousin once removed.*

re·mu·ner·ate [rɪ'mjunə,reit] *v* pay for work, services, trouble, etc. **re·mu·ner·a·tion** *n.* ⟨Latin *re-* back + *munus* gift⟩ **re·mu·ner·a·tive** *adj* paying; profitable. **re·mu·ner·a·tive·ly** *adv.*

ren·ais·sance ['rɛnə,sɑns] *n* **1** a revival or renewal of interest in (something). **2 the Renaissance** the great revival of classical art and learning in Europe during the 14th, 15th, and 16th centuries. ⟨French = rebirth; Latin *re-* again + *nasci* be born⟩ **Renaissance man** or **woman** someone who has acquired extensive knowledge of or proficiency in a wide range of fields.

> **USAGE**
> The word **renaissance** is capitalized when it refers to the period of history: *art of the Renaissance.* It is not when it refers to a revival: *a renaissance of interest in Westerns.*

re·nal ['rinəl] *adj* to do with the kidneys. ⟨Latin *ren* kidney⟩

re·nas·cent [rɪ'næsənt] *or* [rɪ'neisənt] *adj* being born again; reviving. **re·nas·cence** *n.* ⟨Latin *renasci.* See RENAISSANCE.⟩

rend [rɛnd] *v* **rent, rend·ing** *Archaic, poetic* **1** pull apart violently: *Wolves can rend a lamb.* **2** split: *Lightning rent the tree.* **3** disturb violently: *rent by doubt.* ⟨Old English *rendan*⟩ **rent** *n* a torn place; tear; split. *adj* torn; split.

ren·der ['rɛndər] *v* **1** cause to become: *An accident has rendered her helpless.* **2** give: *He rendered us a great service by his help.* **3** offer for consideration: *to render an account of money spent.* **4** make a statement of: *The jury will render their verdict soon.* **5** give in return: *Render thanks for kindness.* **6** perform or act; play or sing (music): *The actor rendered the part of Hamlet well.* **7** translate: *to render a sentence from Latin into English.* **8** melt (fat, etc.). ⟨Latin *rendere* give as due, pay; *re-* + *dare* give⟩ **ren·der·a·ble** *adj.* **ren·der·er** *n.* ⟨Latin *rendere* give as due, pay; *re-* + *dare* give⟩ **ren·der·ing** *n* **1** an interpretation in music or painting: *Her rendering of Beethoven is quite remarkable.* **2** a translation. **3** a representation of a building, etc., giving the architect's or planner's vision of the furnished product. **ren·di·tion** *n* a performance of a dramatic part, musical composition, etc.

ren·dez·vous ['rɒndei,vu] *French* [Rɑ̃de'vu] *n, pl* **-vous** [-,vuz] *n* **1** an appointment to meet. **2** a usual or habitual meeting place: *Our favourite rendezvous was the library.* *v* **-voused** [-,vud], **-vous·ing** [-,vuɪŋ] meet or

bring together at a rendezvous. ⟨French; *rendez-vous* present yourself⟩

ren·di·tion See RENDER.

ren·e·gade ['rɛnə,geid] *n* **1** a deserter from a religious faith, a political party, etc.; traitor. **2** an outlaw. **ren·e·gade** *adj.* ⟨Latin *renegare* deny. See RENEGE.⟩

re·nege [rɪ'nɛg] *or* [rɪ'neig] *v* **1** *Card games* fail to play a card of the suit that is led, although you have one. **2** *Informal* back out; fail to keep a promise. **re·neg·er** *n.* ⟨Latin *renegare*; *re-* back + *negare* deny⟩

re·new [rɪ'nju] *or* [rɪ'nu] *v* **1** make like new. **2** begin again: *to renew one's efforts.* **3** give or get for a new period: *We renewed the lease for another year.* **re·new·a·ble** *adj.* **re·new·al** *n.* **re·new·er** *n.*

re·nounce [rɪ'naʊns] *v* **1** give up entirely, esp by making a formal declaration: *She renounced her claim to the money.* **2** cast off: *He renounced his wicked son.* **re·nun·ci·a·tion** [rɪ,nʌnsi'eifən] *n.* ⟨Old French *renoncer*, Latin *re-* back + *nuntius* message⟩

ren·o·vate ['rɛnə,veit] *v* make like new; restore to good condition: *to renovate a house.* **ren·o·va·tor** *n.* ⟨Latin *re-* again + *novus* new⟩ **ren·o·va·tion** *n* **1** a restoration to good condition. **2 renovations** *pl* things done, or changes made, to accomplish this.

re·nown [rɪ'naʊn] *n* the condition of being widely known; fame. **re·nowned** *adj.* ⟨Anglo-French *renoun*; Latin *re-* repeatedly + *nomen* name⟩

rent[1] [rɛnt] *n* a payment for the right to occupy or use another's land, buildings, goods, etc. *v* **1** pay at regular times for the use of (property): *We rent our house from her.* **2** receive regular pay for the use of (property) (often with *out*): *She rents several other houses.* **3** be leased for rent: *This house rents for $1550 a month.* **rent·a·ble** *adj.* **rent·er** *n.* ⟨Old French *rente*, Latin *rendere.* See RENDER.⟩ **for rent** available in return for rent paid: *That vacant apartment is for rent.* **rent·al** *n* **1** an amount received or paid as rent: *The monthly rental of her house is $1500.* **2** something rented or able to be rented. **3** the act of renting. *adj* **1** of or in rent. **2** that rents or is rented: *a rental car.*

rent[2] See REND.

re·nun·ci·a·tion See RENOUNCE.

re·o·pen [ri'oupən] *v* **1** open again. **2** bring up again for discussion: *The matter is settled and cannot be reopened.*

re·or·der [ri'ɔrdər] *v* **1** put in order again. **2** give a second or repeated order for goods. *n* a second or repeated order for goods.

re·or·gan·ize [ri'ɔrgə,naɪz] *v* arrange in a new way: *Classes will be reorganized after the first four weeks.* **re·or·gan·i·za·tion** *n.* **re·or·gan·iz·er** *n.*

rep[1] [rɛp] *n* representative: *The company has hired several new sales reps.* ⟨clipped form⟩

rep[2] [rɛp] *n* *Informal* repertory (theatre): *She's playing in rep these days.* ⟨clipped form⟩

re·pack·age [riˈpækɪdʒ] *v* **1** package again in a better or more attractive form. **2** package (a bulk commodity) for sale under one's own label: *Many stores repackage products like detergents, candies,* etc.

re·paid [rɪˈpeid] *v* pt and pp of REPAY.

re·pair¹ [rɪˈpɛr] *v* **1** mend; restore. **2** make up for: *How can I repair the harm done?*
n **1** the act or work of repairing: *the repair of the building.* **2** a piece of repairing: *The repair to the roof was badly done; it still leaks.* **3** a condition with regard to the need for repairs: *The house was in bad repair.* **re·pair·a·ble** *adj.* **re·pair·er** *n.* ⟨Latin *reparare; re-* again + *parare* prepare⟩

re·pair·man *n, pl* **-men** a man whose work is repairing machines, etc. **rep·a·ra·ble** [ˈrɛpərəbəl] *adj* that can be repaired or remedied. **rep·a·ra·bly** *adv.* **rep·a·ra·tion** *n* **1** compensation for wrong or injury: *to make reparation for the damage done.* **2** Usually, **reparations** *pl* compensation demanded from a defeated enemy for the devastation of territory during war.

SYNONYMS

Repairable is more often used with physical objects like shoes, furniture, etc. *These shoes are not repairable; I'll have to buy a new pair.*
Reparable refers more to things like relations between people, etc.: *The partners do not believe the rift between them is reparable.*

---

re·pair² [rɪˈpɛr] *v Formal* go (to a place): *After dinner they repaired to the balcony.* ⟨Old French *repairer*; Latin *repatriare* return to one's own country⟩

rep·a·ra·tion See REPAIR¹.

rep·ar·tee [ˌrɛpərˈti] *or* [ˌrɛpɑrˈti] *n* **1** a witty reply. **2** talk characterized by clever and witty replies. ⟨French *repartie; repartir* reply⟩

re·past [rɪˈpæst] *n* a meal; food. ⟨Latin *re-* again + *pastus* pp of *pascere* feed⟩

re·pa·tri·ate [riˈpeitriˌeit] *v* send back or restore to one's own country: *After peace was declared, prisoners of war were repatriated.*
n [riˈpeitriɪt] a person who is sent back to his or her own country. ⟨Latin *re-* back + *patria* homeland⟩
re·pa·tri·a·tion *n* **1** the act of repatriating. **2 Repatriation** ✱ the return of the Statute of Westminster from the UK to Canada as the Canadian Constitution in 1982.

re·pay [rɪˈpei] *v* **-paid, -pay·ing 1** pay back: *He repaid the money he had borrowed.* **2** make return for: *No thanks can repay such kindness.* **3** act similarly in return for: *to repay a visit.* **re·pay·a·ble** *adj.* **re·pay·ment** *n.*

re·peal [rɪˈpil] *v* withdraw; do away with: *A law may be repealed by act of Parliament.* **re·peal** *n.* ⟨Anglo-French *repeler, rapeler; re-* back + *apeler* call. See APPEAL.⟩

re·peat [rɪˈpit] *v* **1** do or make again: *to repeat an error.* **2** say again. **3** say after another says: *Repeat the oath after me.* **4** tell to another: *I promised not to repeat the secret.* **5** recur (usually reflexive): *History repeats itself.*
n **1** the act of repeating. **2** a thing repeated: *We saw the repeat on television.* **3** *Music* **a** a passage to be repeated, or a sign indicating this. ⟨Latin *repetere* attack again; *re-* again + *petere* aim at⟩

repeat oneself say what one has already said. **re·peat·a·ble** *adj* **1** that can be repeated. **2** fit enough to be repeated: *His jokes were not repeatable in public.* **re·peat·a·bil·i·ty** *n.* **re·peat·ed** *adj* said, done, etc. a number of times: *repeated calls for help.* **re·peat·ed·ly** *adv.* **repeating decimal** *Mathematics* a decimal in which there is an indefinite repetition of the same figure or figures. *Examples:* 0.3333+, 0.2323+, 1.43666+. **repeating rifle** a rifle that fires several shots without being reloaded. **rep·e·ti·tion** [ˌrɛpəˈtɪʃən] *n* **1** the act of repeating. **2** the thing repeated. **rep·e·ti·tious** *adj* full of repetitions; repeating in a tiresome way. **rep·e·ti·tious·ly** *adv.* **rep·e·ti·tious·ness** *n.* **re·pet·i·tive** [rɪˈpɛtətɪv] *adj* characterized by repetition. **re·pet·i·tive·ly** *adv.* **re·pet·i·tive·ness** *n.* **repetitive strain injury** injury caused by doing the same motor task over and over.

re·pel [rɪˈpɛl] *v* **-pelled, -pel·ling 1** force back: *They repelled the enemy.* **2** keep off or out: *This tent repels moisture.* **3** ward off, as with a chemical substance or sound: *Mosquitoes are said to be repelled by very high-pitched tones.* **4** *Physics* force apart by some inherent force. Particles with similar electric charges repel each other. **5** be displeasing (*to*); cause disgust (*in*). ⟨Latin *re-* back + *pellere* drive⟩

re·pel·lent *adj* **1** unattractive. **2** driving back. **3** proof to a certain extent against some substance, etc.: *a water-repellent fabric.*
n something that repels, esp a substance or device used to keep away insects, such as mosquitoes or black flies.

re·pent [rɪˈpɛnt] *v* **1** feel remorse for one's sins or errors, to the extent of changing one's ways. **2** regret: *to repent one's choice.* **re·pent·ance** *n.* **re·pent·ant** *adj.* **re·pent·er** *n.* **re·pent·ant·ly** *adv.* ⟨Old French *repentir*; Latin *re-* + *paenitere* cause to regret⟩

re·per·cus·sion [ˌripərˈkʌʃən] *n* **1** an indirect reaction from an event. **2** a rebound; recoil.

rep·er·toire [ˈrɛpərˌtwɑr] *n* **1** the list of plays, pieces, etc. that a company, an actor, a musician, or a singer is prepared to perform. **2** the entire set of skills or techniques that an individual has: *For a two-year-old, his repertoire of cute tricks is quite amazing.* ⟨French; Latin *repertorium.* See REPERTORY.⟩

rep·er·to·ry [ˈrɛpərˌtɔri] *n* **1** a list of things; repertoire. **2** a store of things ready for use. **3** the production system of a REPERTORY THEATRE: *The company is performing three plays in repertory.* ⟨Latin *repertorium* inventory; *reperire* find; *re-* again + *parere* get⟩
repertory theatre a theatre in which one company presents a different production at regular intervals.

rep·e·ti·tion, rep·e·ti·tious, re·pet·i·tive See REPEAT.

re·phrase [riˈfreiz] *v* phrase in a different way: *to rephrase a speech, to rephrase a melody.*

re·pine [rɪ'paɪn] v be discontented; fret; complain. ⟨re- + pine²⟩

re·place [rɪ'pleɪs] v 1 take the place of. 2 get another in place of. 3 put back; restore. **re·place·a·ble** adj. **re·place·ment** n, adj.

> **SYNONYMS**
>
> **Replace** means fill the place formerly held by another: *When one of the players on the team was hurt, another replaced her.* **Supersede** (chiefly used of things) suggests causing what is replaced to be put aside as out-of-date: *Computers have superseded typewriters.* **Supplant**, when used of a person, suggests taking over his or her place by scheming: *The dictator supplanted the president.*

re·play [ri'pleɪ] v play (a game, a film or tape sequence, etc.) again.
n ['ri,pleɪ] 1 a game thus played. 2 a repeated, often slow-motion, showing of part of a television sportscast.

re·plen·ish [rɪ'plenɪʃ] v fill again; provide a new supply for: *Her wardrobe needs replenishing.* **re·plen·ish·ment** n. ⟨Old French *replenir*; Latin *re-* again + *plenus* full⟩

re·plete [rɪ'plit] adj 1 abundantly supplied; filled. 2 gorged with food and drink. ⟨Latin *repletus* pp of *replere*; *plere* fill⟩

rep·li·ca ['rɛpləkə] n a copy; reproduction: *The artist made a replica of her portrait.* ⟨Latin *replicare* reproduce. See REPLY.⟩
rep·li·cate v duplicate as exactly as possible: *to replicate an experiment.* adj *Botany* folded back on itself: *a replicate leaf.* n ['rɛpləkɪt] any of several identical experiments, procedures, etc. **rep·li·ca·ble** adj. **rep·li·ca·tive** adj. **rep·li·ca·tion** n 1 the act of duplicating: *the replication of an experiment.* 2 a copy.

re·ply [rɪ'plaɪ] v 1 answer by words or action: *The rebels replied with a burst of gunfire.* 2 give as an answer: *She replied, "I have no intention of going."* **re·ply** n. ⟨Old French *replier*, Latin *replicare*; *re-* back + *plicare* fold⟩

re·po ['ripou] n repossession. ⟨clipped form⟩

re·port [rɪ'pɔrt] n 1 a statement of facts: *a news report.* 2 an official account officially expressed: *an annual report.* 3 the sound of a shot or an explosion. 4 common talk; rumour: *Report has it that our neighbours are leaving town.* 5 reputation.
v 1 make a report of. 2 give a formal account of. 3 be answerable to: *The supervisor reports directly to the manager.* 4 present oneself: *Report for duty at 9 a.m.* 5 denounce: *to report someone to the police.* ⟨Latin *re-* back + *portare* carry⟩
re·port·a·ble adj worth reporting: *a reportable news story.* **re·port·age** n the act of reporting factual information, esp in a journalistic style. **report card** a report sent at regular intervals by a school to parents or guardians, showing the quality of a student's work. **re·port·ed·ly** adv according to rumours: *Several firms are reportedly interested in the new design.* **re·port·er** n a person who gathers news for a newspaper, TV station, etc.

re·pose¹ [rɪ'pouz] n 1 rest or sleep: *Do not disturb her repose.* 2 quietness; ease: *He has repose of manner.* 3 peace; calmness.
v 1 lie at rest: *The cat reposed upon the cushion.* 2 lie dead: *His body reposed in the funeral home for two days.* 3 take a rest. 4 be supported. 5 depend; rely (on). **re·pose·ful** adj. ⟨French *reposer*, Latin *repausare*; *re-* + *pausare* pause⟩

re·pose² [rɪ'pouz] v put; place (confidence, trust, faith, etc.) in a person or thing: *We repose complete confidence in him.* ⟨Latin *repositus* pp of *reponere*; *re-* + *ponere* place⟩

re·pos·i·to·ry [rɪ'pɒzɪ,tɔri] n 1 a place where things are stored or kept: *The box was the repository for old magazines.* 2 a person to whom something is confided or entrusted.

re·po·si·tion [,ripə'zɪʃən] v position again or differently: *People reposition themselves for personal advantage.*

re·pos·i·to·ry See REPOSE².

re·pos·sess [,ripə'zɛs] v get possession of again, esp from a purchaser who has defaulted on payments: *His car was repossessed.* **re·pos·ses·sion** n.

rep·re·hen·si·ble [,rɛprɪ'hɛnsəbəl] adj worthy of criticism or blame. **rep·re·hen·si·bly** adv. **rep·re·hen·si·bil·i·ty** n. ⟨Latin *reprehendere* pull back; *re-* back + *prehendere* grasp⟩

rep·re·sent [,rɛprɪ'zɛnt] v 1 stand for: *The stars on this map represent the cities.* 2 act in place of: *People are elected to represent us in the government.* 3 act the part of: *Each child will represent an animal.* 4 give a likeness of; portray: *This painting represents the Fathers of Confederation.* 5 be an example of: *A log represents a simple boat.* 6 describe: *She represented the plan as safe.* **rep·re·sen·ta·tion** n. **rep·re·sen·ta·tion·al** adj *Fine Arts* to do with a style that attempts to portray people, things, etc. as they are. **rep·re·sen·ta·tion·al·ly** adv. **rep·re·sen·ta·tion·al·ism** n. **rep·re·sen·ta·tive** n 1 a person appointed or elected to act for others. 2 **Representative** in the US, a member of the House of Representatives. 3 a typical example. 4 salesperson. adj having its citizens represented by chosen, usually elected, persons: *a representative government.* **rep·re·sent·a·tive·ly** adv. **representative of** typical of: *Oak and maple are representative of North American hardwoods.*

re·press [rɪ'prɛs] v 1 check: *She repressed her desire to laugh.* 2 put down: *The dictator repressed the revolt.* 3 *Psychoanalysis* reject (an undesirable impulse) from the conscious mind. **re·press·i·ble** adj. **re·pres·sion** n. **re·pres·sive** adj. **re·pres·sive·ly** adv. **re·pres·sive·ness** n. ⟨Latin *repressus* pp of *reprimere*; *re-* back + *premere* press⟩

re·prieve [rɪ'priv] v 1 delay the execution of (a person condemned to death). 2 give relief from any hardship or trouble. **re·prieve** n. ⟨earlier *repry*; French *repris* pp of *reprendre* take back⟩

rep·ri·mand ['rɛprə,mænd] n a severe or formal reproof. **rep·ri·mand** v. ⟨French *réprimande*, Latin *reprimere*. See REPRESS.⟩

re·print [rɪ'prɪnt] v print a new impression of. **re·print** n.

re·pris·al [rɪ'praɪzəl] n **1** any measure taken in retaliation by one nation against another. **2** any act of retaliation by one person against another. ⟨Old French reprisaille⟩

re·prise [rə'priz] Music n a repetition or return to a previous theme or subject.
v present a reprise of (a song, theme, etc.) ⟨Old French, pp of reprendre take back.⟩

re·proach [rɪ'proutʃ] n **1** blame. **2** disgrace. **3** any object or source of blame or disapproval. **4** an expression of blame or disapproval: Her reproaches were hard to take, especially when she was not blameless. **re·proach** v. **re·proach·ful** adj. **re·proach·ful·ly** adj. ⟨French reprocher, Latin repropriare lay at the door of; re- again + prope near⟩

rep·ro·bate ['rɛprə,beit] or [-bɪt] n an unprincipled scoundrel. **rep·ro·bate** adj. ⟨Latin reprobare reprove; probus good⟩

re·pro·duce [,riprə'djus] or [,riprə'dus] v **1** produce again: A recording reproduces sound. **2** make a copy of: to reproduce a memo on a photocopier. **3** produce offspring: Most plants reproduce by seeds. **re·pro·duc·er** n. **re·pro·duc·i·ble** adj. **re·pro·duc·tive** adj. **re·pro·duc·tive·ly** adv. **re·pro·duc·tive·ness** n.
re·pro·duc·tion n **1** a copy. **2** the process by which offspring are produced. **reproductive technologies** procedures such as in vitro fertilization, embryo transfer, and surrogate motherhood, used to increase the probability of reproduction.

re·prog·ra·phy [rɪ'prɒgrəfi] n the practice of reproducing copyright material.
⟨reproduction + photography⟩

re·prove [rɪ'pruv] v find fault with; express disapproval to (an offender): Reprove the boy for teasing the cat. **re·proof** n. **re·prov·er** n. **re·prov·ing·ly** adv. ⟨Old French reprover, Latin reprobare. See REPROBATE.⟩

rep·tile ['rɛptaɪl] n any of a class of cold-blooded animals that breathe through lungs, have a body covered by horny scales, and, unlike amphibians, do not undergo metamorphosis. ⟨Latin; from repere crawl⟩
rep·til·i·an [-'tɪliən] adj **1** to do with reptiles. **2** mean, contemptible, or grovelling.

re·pub·lic [rɪ'pʌblɪk] n a state in which the citizens elect representatives to manage the government, the head of which is usually a president. ⟨Latin res publica public interest⟩
re·pub·li·can adj **1** to do with a republic. **2** favouring a republic. **3** Republican US to do with the US Republican Party. n a person who favours a republic. **re·pub·li·can·ism** n.

re·pu·di·ate [rɪ'pjudi,eit] v **1** reject. **2** refuse to acknowledge or pay: to repudiate a debt. **3** disown: to repudiate a son. **re·pu·di·a·tion** n. **re·pu·di·a·tor** n. ⟨Latin repudium a spurning⟩

re·pug·nant [rɪ'pʌgnənt] adj **1** distasteful; disagreeable: Work is repugnant to lazy people. **2** opposed: Segregation is repugnant to our idea of equality. **re·pug·nance** n. **re·pug·nant·ly** adv. ⟨Latin re- back + pugnare fight⟩

re·pulse [rɪ'pʌls] v **1** drive back. **2** reject: She coldly repulsed his offer. **3** disgust; repel: The sight of the garbage repulsed him. **re·pulse** n. ⟨Latin repulsus pp of repellere. See REPEL.⟩
re·pul·sion n **1** a strong dislike. **2** a repelling or being repelled. **3** Physics the force by which bodies of like electrical charge or magnetic polarity are repelled from each other. **re·pul·sive** adj **1** causing strong dislike or aversion: Snakes are repulsive to some people. **2** tending to drive back. **re·pul·sive·ly** adv. **re·pul·sive·ness** n.

rep·u·ta·tion [,rɛpjə'teiʃən] n **1** character in the opinion of others: She had the reputation of being bright. **2** high standing in the opinion of others: The scandal ruined his reputation. **3** fame: She has an international reputation. ⟨Latin re- over + putare think⟩
rep·u·ta·ble ['rɛpjətəbəl] adj having a good reputation. **rep·u·ta·bly** adv. **re·pute** [rɪ'pjut] v (passive only) consider generally (to be, have, do, etc.): I am reputed to be a good cook. n **1** reputation. **2** a good reputation. **re·put·ed** adj generally supposed to be such: the reputed author of a book. **re·put·ed·ly** adv.

re·quest [rɪ'kwɛst] v **1** ask for: He requested a loan from the bank. **2** ask: He requested her to go with him. **re·quest** n. **re·quest·er** or **re·quest·or** n. ⟨Old French requeste; Latin requaesita pp of requaerere. See REQUIRE.⟩
by request in response to a request.

Req·ui·em or **req·ui·em** ['rɛkwiəm] n **1** Roman Catholic Church **a** a Mass or similar religious service sung for the dead. **b** the music for such a service. **2** any composition for the dead. ⟨Latin requiem rest; first word in Mass for the dead⟩

re·quire [rɪ'kwaɪr] v **1** need; want: The government requires more money. **2** command; demand: The rules require us all to be present. **re·quire·ment** n. ⟨Latin requirere, requaerere; re- again + quaerere ask⟩

req·ui·site ['rɛkwəzɪt] adj necessary: the qualities requisite for a leader.
n the thing needed: Food and air are requisites for life. **req·ui·site·ly** adv. **req·ui·site·ness** n. ⟨Latin requisitus pp of requirere. See REQUIRE.⟩
req·ui·si·tion [,rɛkwə'zɪʃən] n a demand made, esp a formal written demand: the requisition of supplies for troops. v demand or take by authority: to requisition supplies.

re·quite [rɪ'kwait] v **1** pay back: People of high morals will requite evil with good. **2** reward: The knight requited the boy for his warning. **re·quit·al** n. ⟨re- + quite variant of quit⟩

rere·dos ['rɪrdɒs], ['rɪrɪdɒs], or ['rɛrɪdɒs] n a screen or a decorated part of the wall behind the altar of a church. ⟨Anglo-French rere rear¹ + dos back, Latin dossus, dorsum⟩

re·route [ri'rut] or [ri'rʌut] v send by a new or different route.

re·run [ri'rʌn] v -ran, -run, -run·ning run again.
n ['ri,rʌn] **1** a running again. **2** a television program or a film that is shown again.

re·sale ['ri,seil] or [ri'seil] n **1** the act of

selling again or to a third party. 2 a selling at retail: *The store has a 20 percent markup over the wholesale price for resale.* **re·sale·a·ble** *adj.*

re·scind [rɪ'sɪnd] *v* deprive of force; cancel: *to rescind a law.* **re·scis·sion** [rɪ'sɪʒən] *n.* ⟨Latin *re-* back + *scindere* cut⟩

res·cue ['rɛskju] *v* save from danger, capture, etc. **res·cue** *n.* **res·cu·er** *n.* ⟨Old French *rescoure*; Latin *re-* back + *ex* out + *quatere* shake⟩

re·search ['risɜrtʃ] *or* [rɪ'sɜrtʃ] *n* a careful hunting for facts or truth; investigation: *Medical research has done much to lessen disease.* **re·search** *v.* **re·search·er** *n.*

re·seat [ri'sit] *v* 1 seat again: *The audience was reseated after the singing of the national anthem.* 2 provide with a new seat or seats.

re·sem·ble [rɪ'zɛmbəl] *v* have likeness to in form, figure, or qualities. **re·sem·blance** *n.* ⟨Old French *resembler*; Latin *re-* again + *similis* similar⟩

re·sent [rɪ'zɛnt] *v* feel injured and angry at: *Our cat seems to resent anyone sitting in its chair.* **re·sent·ful** *adj.* **re·sent·ful·ly** *adv.* **re·sent·ment** *n.* ⟨French *ressentir*; Latin *re-* back + *sentire* feel⟩

re·serve [rɪ'zɜrv] *v* 1 keep back; retain: *to reserve the right to withdraw an offer.* 2 save for future use. 3 set aside or have set aside for the use of a particular person or persons: *to reserve a table for two.*
n 1 something kept for future use: *a reserve of strength, a small cash reserve.* 2 *Finance* assets that can be turned into cash quickly to meet liabilities, etc. 3 Often, **reserves** *pl* a a part of a military force kept ready to help the main force. b a part of the armed forces that in peace time is not on full-time duty. 4 ✹ land set aside by the Federal Government for the exclusive use of a First Nations band, usually by treaty. 5 land set apart by the government for a purpose, esp for the preservation of wild animals and plants; preserve. 6 a person kept available to act as a substitute: *a reserve for the basketball team.* 7 restraint or formality of manner. ⟨Latin *re-* back + *servare* keep⟩
res·er·va·tion [,rɛzər'veɪʃən] *n* 1 a limiting condition: *She outwardly approved of the plan with the mental reservation that she would change it to suit herself.* 2 securing of accommodations, seats, etc. 3 *US* land set apart for the exclusive use of Native American peoples. **re·served** *adj* 1 kept by special arrangement: *reserved seats.* 2 disposed to keep to oneself. **re·serv·ed·ly** *adj.* **re·serv·ed·ness** *n.* **re·serv·ist** *n* a member of the reserve army.

res·er·voir ['rɛzər,vwɑr] *or* ['rɜzər,vɔr] *n* 1 a place where water is collected and stored for use. 2 anything to hold a liquid: *A fountain pen has an ink reservoir.* 3 a place where anything is collected and stored: *Her mind is a reservoir of facts.* 4 a great supply. ⟨French *réservoir*; *réserver* reserve⟩

re·set [ri'sɛt] *v* **-set, -set·ting** set again: *Her broken arm had to be reset.*
n ['ri,sɛt] a device by which something is reset: *Where's the reset on this machine?*

re·shape [ri'ʃeɪp] *v* shape anew; form into a new or different shape.

re·side [rɪ'zaɪd] *v* 1 live *(in* or *at)* for a time. 2 be *(in)*: *Her charm resides in her smile.* ⟨Latin *residere*; *re-* back + *sedere* sit, settle⟩

res·i·dence ['rɛzɪdəns] *n* 1 a place where a person lives; house; home. 2 the fact of living or doing business in a place for the performance of certain duties, to qualify for certain rights, etc.: *a writer in residence.* 3 a building in which students, nurses, etc. live. **in residence** a living in a place: *The owner is not in residence.* b living in an institution while on duty: *a doctor in residence.* **res·i·den·cy** *n* 1 a period of advanced training as a specialist after graduation with a medical degree. 2 the official residence of a governor general, ambassador, or any diplomatic officer. **res·i·dent** *n* 1 a person living in a place, not a visitor. 2 a physician during residency (def. 1). 3 an official sent to live in a foreign land to represent his or her country. 4 a bird or animal that is not migratory. **res·i·dent** *adj.* **res·i·den·tial** *adj* to do with homes or residences: *a good residential district.* **residential school** ✹ esp formerly, a boarding school operated or subsidized by the federal government to accommodate students, particularly First Nations and Inuit students, attending classes at a considerable distance from their homes.

res·i·due ['rɛzə,dju] *or* ['rɛzə,du] *n* 1 what remains after a part is taken: *The syrup had dried up, leaving a sticky residue.* 2 *Law* the part of a testator's estate that is left after all debts, charges, etc. have been satisfied: *the residue of the property went to the daughter.* ⟨Latin *residuum* left over; *residere* stay behind⟩ **re·sid·u·al** [rɪ'zɪdʒuəl] *adj* 1 remaining; left over. 2 *Geology* resulting from the weathering of rock: *residual clay soil, a residual deposit.* *n* 1 remainder. 2 a fee paid to a performer or writer for each rerun of a radio or television broadcast, etc.

re·sign [rɪ'zaɪn] *v* 1 take oneself out of a job, position, etc.: *He resigned in a fit of rage.* 2 give in, often unwillingly, but without complaint (with a reflexive pronoun): *He resigned himself to a week in bed when he hurt his back.* **res·ig·na·tion** [,rɛzɪg'neɪʃən] *n.* ⟨Latin *resignare* unseal; *re-* back + *signum* seal⟩ **re·signed** *adj* accepting, often unwillingly; submissive: *resigned to an unhappy fate.* **re·sign·ed·ly** [rɪ'zaɪnɪdli] *adv.*

USAGE
Resign is often followed by **from**, though sometimes the object follows without the **from**: *She resigned from the editorship of the magazine* or *She resigned the editorship of the magazine.*

re·sil·i·ent [rɪ'zɪljənt] *adj* 1 returning to the original after being bent, compressed, or stretched: *resilient turf.* 2 recovering quickly from trouble: *a resilient child.* **re·sil·i·ence** or

resiliency *n.* **re·sil·i·ent·ly** *adv.* ⟨Latin *resilire; re-* back + *salire* jump⟩

res·in ['rɛzən] *n* a sticky substance that flows from certain plants and trees, esp the pine and fir. The harder portion of resin remaining after heating is called **rosin**. **res·in·ous** *adj.* ⟨Latin *resina*⟩

re·sist [rɪ'zɪst] *v* 1 strive against; oppose: *The Celts resisted the Anglo-Saxons for a long time.* 2 strive successfully against: *I could not resist laughing.* 3 withstand the effect of: *The door resisted her efforts to open it.* **re·sist·ant** *adj.* **re·sist·i·ble** *adj.* ⟨Latin *re-* back + *sistere* make a stand⟩

re·sist·ance *n* 1 the act of resisting: *The bank clerk made no resistance to the robbers.* 2 the power to resist: *She has little resistance to germs.* 3 an opposing force. 4 *Electricity* the property of a conductor that opposes the passage of a current and changes electric energy into heat. 5 Usually, **Resistance** people in a country controlled by another country who secretly organize and fight for their freedom: *the French Resistance in World War II.* **re·sist·or** *n Electricity* a conducting body or device used in an electric circuit, etc. because of its resistance.

res·o·lute ['rɛzə,lut] *adj* 1 determined; firm: *He was resolute in his attempt to climb to the top of the cliff.* 2 indicating firmness, boldness, etc: *a resolute manner.* **res·o·lute·ly** *adv.* ⟨Latin *resolutus* pp of *resolvere.* See RESOLVE.⟩

res·o·lu·tion [,rɛzə'luʃən] *n* 1 something decided on: *a resolution to get up early.* 2 determination. 3 a formal expression of opinion, esp as agreed upon by a group: *The club passed a resolution thanking the consultant for her help.* 4 the act of solving: *the resolution of a problem.* 5 the act of breaking or separating into parts. 6 that section of a novel or play in which the plot is explained or resolved. 7 *Computers* a measure of the clarity of the pictures or characters that a computer monitor or printer is able to produce from a matrix of dots: *The resolution of the monitor is 640 by 480 pixels.*

re·solve [rɪ'zɒlv] *v* 1 make up one's mind firmly: *He resolved to do better.* 2 express (a decision) formally, esp by vote: *It was resolved by the committee that the project be dropped.* 3 separate into parts: *to resolve a chemical compound.* 4 explain so as to remove (doubt, etc.): *Her letter resolved all our fears.* *n* 1 something determined: *a resolve to do better in future.* 2 determination. **re·solv·a·ble** *adj.* ⟨Latin *resolvere; re-* un- + *solvere* loosen⟩ **re·solved** *adj* determined; resolute.

res·o·nance ['rɛzənəns] *n* 1 a resounding quality: *the resonance of an organ.* 2 *Physics* a prolonging of sound by reflection or by vibration. 3 *Chemistry* the molecular property of having more than one structure. ⟨Latin *resonare; re-* back + *sonus* sound⟩ **res·o·nant** *adj* 1 continuing to sound: *a resonant tone.* 2 tending to increase or prolong sound: *a guitar has a resonant body.* 3 of or in resonance. **res·o·nant·ly** *adv.*

res·o·nate *v* 1 exhibit resonance. 2 communicate (something) in a powerful way (with *with*): *Her poems resonate with longing.* **res·o·na·tor** *n* 1 an appliance for increasing sound by resonance. 2 *Electronics* a system that can be put into oscillation by oscillations in another system.

re·sort [rɪ'zɔrt] *v* 1 go: *Many people resort to the beaches in hot weather.* 2 turn for help or use as a means: *to resort to violence.* *n* 1 a place people go to, usually for recreation: *a summer resort in the mountains.* 2 the act of turning for help or using as a means: *The resort to force is a poor substitute for persuasion.* 3 a person or thing turned to for help or used as a means. ⟨Old French *resortir; re-* back + *sortir* go out⟩ **as a last resort** in desperation.

re·sound [rɪ'zaʊnd] *v* 1 echo: *The hills resounded when he shouted.* 2 be filled (with sound): *The room resounded with the children's shouts.* ⟨Middle English *resounen,* Middle French *resoner;* Latin *resonare.* See RESONANCE.⟩ **re·sound·ing** *adj* 1 echoing: *a resounding crash.* 2 loud or high-sounding: *a resounding speech.* 3 impressively thorough or complete: *a resounding victory.* **re·sound·ing·ly** *adv.*

re·source [rɪ'zɔrs] *or* [rɪ'zors] *n* 1 any supply that will meet a need: *We have resources of money, of quick wit, and of strength.* 2 **resources** *pl* the actual and potential wealth of a person, business, or country. 3 NATURAL RESOURCES. 4 mental capability or strength: *inner resources.* ⟨Old French *resourse* pp of *resourdre;* Latin *re-* again + *surgere* rise⟩ **re·source·ful** [rɪ'zɔrsfəl] *adj* good at thinking of ways to do things. **re·source·ful·ly** *adv.* **re·source·ful·ness** *n.*

re·spect [rɪ'spɛkt] *n* 1 honour; esteem: *Show respect to people you admire.* 2 consideration: *Show respect for other people's property.* 3 **respects** *pl* expressions of respect. 4 a point; detail: *The plan is unwise in many respects.* 5 relation; reference. **re·spect** *v.* ⟨Latin *respectus* pp of *respicere* look back, have regard for; *re-* back + *specere* look⟩ **with respect to** with reference to (something): *We must plan with respect to the future of this organization.* **re·spect·a·ble** *adj* 1 worthy of respect: *Respectable citizens obey the law.* 2 conforming to social norms: *We were poor but respectable.* 3 moderate in size or quality: *His career was respectable but not brilliant.* 4 good enough to use; fit to be seen. **re·spect·a·bil·i·ty** *n.* **re·spect·a·bly** *adv.* **re·spect·ful** *adj* showing respect. **re·spect·ful·ly** *adv.* **re·spect·ful·ness** *n.* **re·spect·ing** *prep* about: *A discussion arose respecting the merits of different cars.* **re·spec·tive** *adj* belonging to each: *The wrestlers returned to their respective corners.* **re·spec·tive·ly** *adv* as regards each one in turn or in the order mentioned: *My sister and brother are 27 and 25 years old respectively.*

res·pi·ra·tion [,rɛspə'reiʃən] *n* 1 breathing. 2 *Biology* the processes by which an animal, or plant secures oxygen from the air or water, distributes it, and gives off carbon dioxide. ⟨Latin *re-* regularly + *spirare* breathe⟩

res·pi·ra·tor *n* **1** a device worn to prevent inhaling harmful substances. **2** a device to help a person breathe. **res·pi·ra·to·ry** ['rɛspərə,tɔri] *or* [rɪ'spaɪrə,tɔri] *adj* to do with breathing: *Lungs are respiratory organs.*

res·pite ['rɛspɪt] *or* ['rɛspaɪt] *n* **1** a time of relief and rest: *A thick cloud brought a respite from the glare of the sun.* **2** a putting off; delay. **res·pite** *v.* ⟨Old French; Latin *respectus* pp of *respectare* wait for. See RESPECT.⟩

re·splend·ent [rɪ'splɛndənt] *adj* very bright; shining; splendid: *resplendent with jewels.* **re·splend·ence** *n.* **re·splend·ent·ly** *adv.* ⟨Latin *re-* (intensive) + *splendere* shine⟩

re·spond [rɪ'spɒnd] *v* **1** answer. **2** react: *Our dog responds to speech by wagging its tail.* **3** react positively. ⟨Latin *respondere; re-* in return + *spondere* promise⟩

re·spond·ent *adj* answering. *n* **1** a person who responds. **2** *Law* a defendant, esp in a divorce case. **re·sponse** [rɪ'spɒns] *n* **1** an answer. **2** a set of words said or sung by the congregation or choir in a religious service, in answer to the minister or priest. **3** any activity or behaviour resulting from stimulation; a reaction. **response time** *Computers* the time between a user's entering a command to a computer system, and the computer's providing the result: *The mainframe computer's response time worsened as more users logged on.* **re·spon·sive** *adj* **1** making answer: *a responsive glance.* **2** responding readily: *having a responsive nature.* **re·spon·sive·ly** *adv.* **re·spon·sive·ness** *n.*

re·spon·si·ble [rɪ'spɒnsəbəl] *adj* **1** obliged or expected to account *(for)*: *The government is responsible to the people for its proper conduct of the country's affairs.* **2** deserving credit or blame: *The bad weather is responsible for the small attendance.* **3** trustworthy; reliable: *A responsible person should take care of this money.* **4** involving obligation or duties: *The Prime Minister holds a very responsible position.* **5** able to think and act reasonably: *Babies are not responsible.* **re·spon·si·bly** *adv.* **re·spon·si·bil·i·ty** *n* **1** a being responsible: *A small child does not feel much responsibility.* **2** something for which one is responsible: *Keeping house and caring for the children are his responsibilities.* **responsible government 1** a form of government in which a cabinet, selected from an elected legislature, acts as the executive. **2 Responsible Government** this system of government as it existed in Canada from 1848-1867.

rest¹ [rɛst] *n* **1** sleep; repose: *a good night's rest.* **2** ease after work or effort: *Allow an hour for rest.* **3** freedom from anything that tires, troubles, or pains: *The medicine gave the sick man a short rest from pain.* **4** the absence of motion: *The driver brought the car to a rest.* **5** a support: *a rest for a billiard cue.* **6** *Music* a measured period of silence.
v **1** be still; sleep: *Lie down and rest.* **2** be free

from work, trouble, pain, etc.: *He was able to rest during his holidays.* **3** stop moving; cause to stop moving: *The ball rested at the bottom of the hill.* **4** give rest to: *Rest your horse.* **5** lie, sit, etc., for rest: *She spent the day resting in a chair.* **6** be supported: *The ladder rests against the wall.* **7** fix or be fixed: *Our eyes rested on the open book.* **8** be at ease: *Don't let her rest until she promises to visit us.* **9** become inactive; let remain inactive: *Let the matter rest.* **10** place for support; lay; lean: *to rest one's head in one's hands.* **11** rely or cause to rely *(on)*: *Our hope rests on you.* **12** lie in the grave or at a funeral home. **13** *Law* end the introduction of evidence in (a case): *The lawyer rested his case.* **rest·ful** *adj.* **rest·ful·ly** *adv.* **rest·ful·ness** *n.* ⟨Old English *restan*⟩

at rest a asleep. **b** not moving: *The lake was at rest.* **c** free from pain, trouble, etc.: *The injured woman is now at rest.* **d** dead. **lay to rest a** bury: *Lay his bones to rest.* **b** deal with finally. **rest one's case** stop arguing because the point has been made, often by circumstances.

rest·less *adj* **1** unable to rest: *The dog seemed restless, as if it sensed some danger.* **2** without rest or sleep: *The sick child passed a restless night.* **3** rarely or never still or quiet: *You're very restless today.* **rest·less·ly** *adv.* **rest·less·ness** *n.* **restroom** a public washroom, or toilet, as in a theatre or service station.

rest² [rɛst] *n* what is left; those that are left: *Eat the rest of the sandwiches.*
v continue to be: *You may rest assured that I will keep my promise.* ⟨French *reste;* Latin *restare* be left, *re-* back + *stare* stand⟩

USAGE

Rest in the sense of 'what is left' or 'those that are left' is always used with **the**, and although always singular in form, uses the plural verb when it refers to more than one: *I ate half the stew; the rest is in the freezer. We are leaving early, but the rest are staying for the reception.*

re·state [ri'steit] *v* **1** state again or anew. **2** state in a new way. **re·state·ment** *n.*

res·tau·rant ['rɛstə,rɒnt] *n* a place to buy and eat a meal. ⟨French; *restaurer* restore⟩
res·tau·ra·teur [,rɛstərə'tɜr] *n* the owner or manager of a restaurant.

res·ti·tu·tion [,rɛstə'tjuʃən] *or* [,rɛstə'tuʃən] *n* **1** the act of making good any loss, damage, or injury: *Those who do damage should make restitution.* **2** what is given in compensation for loss, damage, or injury. ⟨Latin *restitutio; re-* again + *statuere* set up⟩

res·tive ['rɛstɪv] *adj* **1** restless; uneasy. **2** hard to manage. **res·tive·ly** *adv.* **res·tive·ness** *n.* ⟨Old French *restif* motionless⟩

re·stock [ri'stɒk] *v* supply with new stock.

re·store [rɪ'stɔr] *v* **-stored, -stor·ing 1** bring back: *to restore order.* **2** bring back to a former condition: *The old house has been restored.* **3** put back: *The thief was forced to restore the money he stole.* **res·to·ra·tion** [,rɛstə'reiʃən] *n.* **re·stor·er** *n.* ⟨Latin *restaurare*⟩

re·stor·a·tive [rɪ'stɔrətɪv] *adj* tending to restore health or strength. **re·stor·a·tive** *n.*

re·strain [rɪ'streɪn] *v* **1** hold back; keep in check: *She could not restrain her curiosity.* **2** keep in prison; confine. **re·strain·a·ble** *adj.* **re·strain·er** *n.* ⟨Old French *restreindre*; Latin *restringere* restrict. See RESTRICT.⟩

re·straint [rɪ'streɪnt] *n* **1** a restraining or being restrained. **2** a means of restraining: *A child's car seat is a restraint.* **3** reserve; discipline: *We must show more fiscal restraint.*

re·strict [rɪ'strɪkt] *v* **1** keep within limits: *Our club membership is restricted to twelve.* **2** put limitations on: *to restrict the meaning of a word.* **re·stric·tion** *n.* ⟨Latin *re-* back + *stringere* draw tight⟩

re·strict·ed *adj* **1** limited: *a restricted diet.* **2** having limiting rules: *a restricted residential section.* **3** limited to members of a specified group: *This club is restricted to lawyers.* **4** of movies, limited to viewers over a specified age. **re·stric·tive** *adj* limiting: *Some laws are prohibitive; some are only restrictive.* **re·stric·tive·ly** *adv.*

> **GRAMMAR**
> A **restrictive** clause is an adjectival clause that is an essential part of the sentence in which it appears: *The man who came to dinner stayed for a month.* In comparison, a **non-restrictive** clause is merely inserted into the main construction, set off by commas: *The principal of the high school, who is a most interesting man, came to our house for dinner last evening.*

re·string [rɪ'strɪŋ] *v* **-strung, -string·ing** put new strings on: *to restring a tennis racket.*

re·struct·ure [rɪ'strʌktʃər] *v* **1** alter or restore the structure of: *His broken jaw was successfully restructured.* **2** change the organization of: *The new government will restructure several ministries.*

re·sult [rɪ'zʌlt] *n* **1** that which happens as the outcome of something: *The result of the fall was a broken leg.* **2 results** *pl* a good outcome: *We want results, not talk.* **3** a score or grade: *The exam results will be posted tomorrow.* **re·sult** *v.* ⟨Latin *resultare* rebound; *re-* back + *salire* spring⟩

re·sult·ant *adj* **1** resulting. **2** being an effect of two or more agents acting together. *n* **1** a result. **2** *Physics, mathematics* any force or vector that has the same effect as two or more forces or vectors acting together. **re·sult·ant·ly** *adv.*

re·sume [rɪ'zum] *or* [rɪ'zjum] *v* **1** go on: *Resume reading where we left off.* **2** get or take again: *Those standing may resume their seats.* **re·sum·a·ble** *adj.* **re·sump·tion** [rɪ'zʌmpʃən] *n.* ⟨Latin *re-* again + *sumere* take up⟩

rés·u·mé ['rɛzə,meɪ] *French* [ʀezy'me] *n* **1** a short account of a person's education, employment history, etc., prepared for submission with a job application. **2** any summary, as of events, etc. ⟨French *résumé*, originally pp of *résumer* resume⟩

re·sur·face [ri'sɜrfɪs] *v* **1** provide with a new or different surface. **2** reappear: *She resurfaced*

in Iqaluit under another name. **3** reappear at the surface: *She resurfaced 30 seconds later, gasping for breath.*

re·surge [rɪ'sɜrdʒ] *v* rise again. **re·sur·gence** *n.* **re·sur·gent** *adj.*

res·ur·rect [,rɛzə'rɛkt] *v* **1** bring back to life. **2** bring back into use or view: *resurrect an old idea.* ⟨Latin *re-* again + *surgere* rise⟩

res·ur·rec·tion *n* **1** a coming to life again. **2 Resurrection** *Christianity* **a** the rising of Christ after His death and burial. **b** the rising of all the dead on Judgment Day. **res·ur·rec·tion·ism** *n* the exhumation and stealing of dead bodies, esp for dissection. **res·ur·rec·tion·ist** *n* **1** a person who practises resurrectionism. **2** a person who brings something back to life again. **3** a believer in the Resurrection.

re·sus·ci·tate [rɪ'sʌsə,teɪt] *v* bring or come back to life or consciousness; revive. **re·sus·ci·ta·tion** *n.* **re·sus·ci·ta·tive** *adj.* ⟨Latin *resuscitare*; *re-* again + *sub-* up + *citare* rouse⟩ **re·sus·ci·ta·tor** *n* an apparatus for forcing air into the lungs of a person who has stopped breathing, in order to revive him or her.

re·tail ['riteɪl] *n* the sale of goods in small quantities directly to the final consumer: *Most stores sell at retail.* Compare WHOLESALE. *adj* to do with selling goods in small quantities: *the retail trade, a retail merchant.* *v* **1** sell in small quantities. **2** be sold in small quantities: *a dress retailing at $150.00.* **3** [rɪ'teɪl] tell over again: *She retails everything she hears about her acquaintances.* *adv* from a retail dealer: *He buys his supplies retail.* **re·tail·er** *n.* ⟨Old French *retail* scrap; *re-* back + *taillier* cut; Latin *talea* rod⟩

re·tain [rɪ'teɪn] *v* **1** keep: *She retained control of the business until she died.* **2** hold or keep in a fixed condition: *"Retain that pose as long as you can," she told the model.* **3** remember. **4** employ by payment of a fee: *He retained a lawyer.* ⟨Latin *re-* back + *tenere* hold⟩

re·tain·er *n* **1** a person or attendant, esp one who is a long-time family servant. **2** a device that keeps teeth in place after orthodontic treatment. **3** a fee paid to secure services: *This lawyer receives a retainer before she begins work on a case.* **on retainer** retained for a fee. **retaining wall** a wall built to hold back or confine a bank of earth, loose stones, etc. **re·ten·tion** [rɪ'tɛnʃən] *n* **1** the fact of retaining or being retained. **2** the ability to remember: *I admired her retention; she remembered all our names.* **re·ten·tive** *adj* **1** able to hold or keep. **2** able to remember. **re·ten·tive·ly** *adv.* **re·ten·tive·ness** *n.*

re·take [ri'teɪk] *v* **-took, -tak·en, -tak·ing** take again: *The director wants to retake the last scene.* *n* ['ri,teɪk] **1** the act of rephotographing: *a retake of a scene in a motion picture.* **2** the film scene, etc. rephotographed.

re·tal·i·ate [rɪ'tæli,eɪt] *v* repay one injury, etc. with another: *If we insult them, they will retaliate.* **re·tal·i·a·tion** *n.* **re·tal·i·a·tive** *or* **re·tal·i·a·to·ry** *adj.* ⟨Latin *re-* in return + *talio* payment in kind⟩

re·tard [rɪ'tɑrd] v **1** make slow; hinder: *Bad nutrition retarded her growth.* **2** be delayed or held back. ⟨Latin *re-* back + *tardus* slow⟩
re·tard·ant n something, often a chemical, that slows up or delays an effect or an action. adj tending to delay or make slower. **re·tar·da·tion** [,rɪtɑr'deɪʃən] n **1** the act of retarding. **2** the extent to which something is retarded. **3** a noticeable limitation of intellectual and social development. **re·tard·ed** adj **1** held back. **2** noticeably limited or slow in development.

retch [rɛtʃ] v make efforts to vomit. ⟨Old English *hrǣcan* clear the throat⟩

re·ten·tion, re·ten·tive See RETAIN.

re·think [ri'θɪŋk] v -**thought**, -**think·ing** think over again, esp with a view to changing one's ideas, tactics, etc.: *to rethink our energy strategy.*

ret·i·cent ['rɛtəsənt] adj disposed to keep silent or say little; not speaking freely. **ret·i·cence** n. **ret·i·cent·ly** adv. ⟨Latin *reticere* keep silent; *re-* back + *tacere* be silent⟩

ret·i·na ['rɛtənə] n, pl -**nas** or -**nae** [-,ni] or [-,naɪ] a membrane at the back of the eyeball that receives images and passes them on to the optic nerve. **ret·i·nal** adj. ⟨Latin⟩

ret·i·nue ['rɛtə,nju] n a group of attendants or retainers; a following: *The king's retinue accompanied him on the journey.* ⟨Old French *retenue* pp of *retenir* retain; Latin. See RETAIN.⟩

re·tire [rɪ'taɪr] v **1** give up an office, occupation, etc.: *She will retire at 65.* **2** go away, esp to be quiet or alone: *She retired to her room to read her book.* **3** withdraw: *The government retires worn bills from use.* **4** retreat: *The enemy retired before the advance of our troops.* **5** go to bed: *We retire early.* **6** *Baseball* put out (a batter, side, etc.). **re·tire·ment** n. ⟨French *re-* back + *tirer* draw⟩ **re·tir·ee** [rətaɪ'ri] or [rə'taɪri] n a person who has retired from his or her occupation. **re·tir·ing** adj shrinking from society or publicity; shy. **re·tir·ing·ly** adv.

re·tool [ri'tul] v **1** adapt the tools of (a factory), usually in order to make a different product. **2** reorganize for updating.

re·tort[1] [rɪ'tɔrt] v reply quickly or sharply. **re·tort** n. ⟨Latin *retortus* pp of *retorquere*; *re-* back + *torquere* twist⟩

re·tort[2] [rɪ'tɔrt] n a long-necked container in a laboratory used for distilling or decomposing by means of heat. ⟨Latin *retorta* fem pp of *retorquere*. See RETORT[1].⟩

re·touch [ri'tʌtʃ] v **1** improve (a painting, photograph, etc.) by making slight changes. **2** tint or bleach (new growth of hair) to match previously dyed growth: *He had his roots retouched.* **re·touch** ['ri,tʌtʃ] n.

re·trace [rɪ'treɪs] v go back over: *We retraced our steps to where we started.* **re·trace·a·ble** adj.

re·tract [rɪ'trækt] v **1** draw back or in: *Cats retract their claws.* **2** withdraw; take back: *to retract an offer.* **re·tract·a·ble** adj. **re·trac·tion** n. ⟨Latin *retractus* pp of *retrahere*; *re-* back + *trahere* draw⟩

re·trac·tile [-taɪl] or [-təl] adj capable of retracting or being retracted.

re·tread [ri'trɛd] v put a new tread on. n ['ri,trɛd] a retreaded tire.

re·treat [rɪ'trit] v move back: *Seeing the big dog, the burglar retreated rapidly.*
n **1** the act of going back: *The army's retreat was orderly.* **2** a signal on a bugle or drum, given in the army for retreat and at sunset. **3** a place of rest or refuge. **4 a** a period of withdrawal from regular life, devoted to prayer and other religious exercises. **b** a period of withdrawal from the regular workplace, usually as a group, devoted to intensive discussion. ⟨Old French *retraite* pp of *retraire*; Latin *retrahere*. See RETRACT.⟩
beat a retreat run away: *We beat a hasty retreat when the dog growled at us.*

re·trench [rɪ'trɛntʃ] v reduce expenses: *In hard times, we must retrench.* **re·trench·ment** n. ⟨Middle French *re-* back + *trencher* cut⟩

ret·ri·bu·tion [,rɛtrə'bjuʃən] n **1** a deserved punishment. **2** the act of punishing. **re·trib·u·tive** [rɪ'trɪbjətɪv] adj. **re·trib·u·tive·ly** adv. ⟨Latin *re-* back + *tribuere* assign⟩

re·trieve [rɪ'triv] v **1** recover: *to retrieve a lost wallet.* **2** make good; repair: *to retrieve a mistake.* **3** find and bring back (killed or wounded game): *Some dogs can never be trained to retrieve.* **4** *Computers* access (data) from storage for display, as on a monitor. **re·triev·a·ble** adj. **re·triev·al** n. ⟨Old French *retrouver*; *re-* + *trouver* find⟩
re·triev·er n any of several breeds of dog often trained to retrieve game.

ret·ro ['rɛtrou] adj **1** returning to something of an earlier time, as clothing, literature, etc. **2** retroactive: *retro pay.* ⟨See RETRO-.⟩

retro– prefix back; backward; behind. ⟨Latin⟩ **ret·ro·ac·tive** [,rɛtrou'æktɪv] adj having an effect on what is past. A retroactive law applies to events that occurred before the law was passed. **ret·ro·ac·tive·ly** adv. **ret·ro·fire** ['rɛtrou,faɪr] v of a retro-rocket, ignite or become ignited. **ret·ro·fit** ['rɛtrou,fɪt] v -**fit·ted**, -**fit·ting** make adaptations to (a building, an airplane, etc.) using new equipment, in order to improve it: *to retrofit a house with insulation.* **ret·ro·fit** n. **ret·ro·flex** ['rɛtrə,flɛks]adj bent backward. **ret·ro·flex·ion** n. **ret·ro·grade** ['rɛtrə,greid] adj **1** retreating. **2** becoming worse: *Eliminating that staff position was definitely a retrograde move.* **3** *Music* proceeding from the last note to the first. **ret·ro·gress** [,rɛtrə'grɛs] or ['rɛtrə,grɛs] v **1** move backward. **2** become worse. **3** go back to an earlier, simpler state. **ret·ro·gres·sion** n. **ret·ro·gres·sive** adj. **ret·ro·gres·sive·ly** adv. **ret·ro·rock·et** ['rɛtrou ,rɒkɪt] n a rocket that fires in a direction opposite to the motion of a spacecraft, thus acting as a brake. Also, **ret·ro·rock·et** or **ret·ro·**. **ret·ro·spect** ['rɛtrə,spɛkt] n a survey of past time, events, etc. **in retrospect** when looking back. **ret·ro·spec·tion** n a looking back on things past. **ret·ro·spec·tive** adj to do with

the past. *n* an exhibition of the work of an artist or artists over a number of years.
ret·ro·spec·tive·ly *adv.* **ret·ro·vi·rus** ['rɛtrə,vaɪrəs] *n* any of a family of single-stranded RNA viruses including those that cause AIDS or are implicated in certain cancers.

re·trous·sé [rətru'sei] *or* [rə'trusei] *adj* turned up: *a retroussé nose.* ⟨French⟩

ret·si·na [ret'sinə] *or* ['rɛtsɪnə] *n* a resin-flavoured Greek wine. ⟨Modern Greek *resina,* Latin = resin⟩

re·turn [rɪ'tɜrn] *v* 1 go back; come back: *My brother will return this summer.* 2 bring, give, send, hit, put, or pay back: *Return that book to the library.* 3 produce: *The concert returned about $150 over expenses.* 4 announce officially: *The jury returned a verdict of guilty.* 5 elect to a lawmaking body: *All of the incumbents were returned to office.*
n 1 a going or coming back; a happening again. 2 something returned. 3 a bringing, giving, sending, or putting back: *a poor return for kindness.* 4 Often, **returns** *pl* a profit. 5 a report: *election returns, income tax return.* 6 *Sports* **a** the act of sending a ball back. **b** *Football* the runback of a ball received on a kick or an interception. 7 *Computers* a computer operation to start a new line. A **hard return** starts a new paragraph.
adj 1 to do with a return: *a return ticket.* 2 sent, done, etc. in return: *a return game.* 3 repeated: *a return engagement.* ⟨Old French *re-* back + *tourner* turn⟩
in return as a return: *They let us borrow their mower, and in return we cut their lawn.*
returning officer in Canada, the official who is responsible for the entire election procedure in a particular constituency.
return trip 1 a trip to a place and back again. 2 the trip back from a place.

re·u·ni·fy [ri'junə,faɪ] *v* restore unity to; bring back together again. **re·u·ni·fi·ca·tion** *n.*

re·u·nite [,riju'naɪt] *v* 1 bring together again: *Mother and child were reunited years later.* 2 come together again. **re·un·ion** [ri'junjən] *n.*

rev [rɛv] *Informal v* revved, rev·ving increase the speed of (an engine or motor). **rev** *n.* ⟨clipped form of *revolution*⟩
rev up *Informal* **a** get ready, mentally, for something demanding: *all revved up for the new school year.* **b** make something more exciting: *How can we rev up this party?*

Rev. Reverend.

re·vamp [ri'væmp] *v* redesign; make over; overhaul completely. **re·vamp** ['rivæmp] *n.*

re·veal [rɪ'vil] *v* 1 make known something secret: *Never reveal my secret.* 2 display; show: *Her smile revealed her even teeth.* **re·veal·er** *n.* ⟨Latin *revelare; re-* back + *velum* veil⟩
rev·e·la·tion [,rɛvə'leiʃən] *n* 1 the act of making known. 2 the thing made known: *Her true nature was a revelation to me.* 3 *Theology* God's disclosure of himself and of his will to his creatures. **rev·e·la·tor·y** ['rɛvələ,tɔri] *adj.*

rev·eil·le ['rɛvəli], [rə'væli], *or* [rə'vɛli] *n* a signal on a bugle or drum to waken military personnel in the morning. ⟨French *réveillez (-vous)* wake up!⟩

rev·el ['rɛvəl] *v* -elled *or* -eled, -el·ling *or* -el·ing 1 take great pleasure *(in): The children revel in country life.* 2 make merry: *The party-goers revelled till the small hours of the morning.* *n* a noisy good time. **rev·el·ler** *or* **rev·el·er** *n.* ⟨Old French *reveler;* Latin *rebellare* rebel⟩
rev·el·ry *n* wild merrymaking.

rev·e·la·tion See REVEAL.

re·venge [rɪ'vɛndʒ] *n* 1 harm done in return for a wrong: *a blow struck in revenge.* 2 a desire for vengeance: *She said nothing but there was revenge in her heart.* 3 a chance to win in a return game after losing a game.
v 1 do harm in return for: *His family vowed to revenge his death.* 2 take vengeance on behalf of (someone or oneself): *He vowed to revenge himself on this enemies.* **re·venge·ful** *adj.* **re·venge·ful·ly** *adv.* **re·venge·ful·ness** *n.* ⟨Latin *re-* back + *vindicare* avenge⟩
be revenged get revenge: *He swore to be revenged on his father's murderers.*

rev·e·nue ['rɛvə,nju] *n* income: *The government gets revenue from taxes.* ⟨French, pp of *revenir;* Latin *re-* back + *venire* come⟩
Revenue Canada the tax-collecting agency of the federal government.

re·ver·ber·ate [rɪ'vɜrbə,reit] *v* 1 echo back: *Her voice reverberates from the high ceiling.* 2 cast or be cast back; reflect (light or heat). **re·ver·ber·a·tion** *n.* ⟨Latin *reverberare* beat back; *re-* back + *verber* a blow⟩

re·vere [rɪ'vir] *v* love and respect deeply; honour; show reverence for. **rev·er·ed** *adj.* **rev·er·ent** *adj.* **rev·er·ent·ly** *adv.* ⟨Latin *re-* (intensive) + *vereri* stand in awe of, fear⟩
rev·er·ence ['rɛvrəns] *n* 1 a feeling of deep respect. 2 a deep bow. 3 **Reverence** usually with *Your* or *His,* a title used in speaking of or to a Roman Catholic priest. *v* regard with reverence. **rev·er·end** ['rɛvrənd] *n* **Reverend** a title for a member of the clergy. **rev·er·en·tial** *adj* reverent. **rev·er·en·tial·ly** *adv.*

rev·er·ie ['rɛvəri] *n* 1 the act of thinking dreamy thoughts; dreamy thinking of pleasant things: *He loved to indulge in reveries about the future.* 2 the condition of being lost in dreamy thoughts. 3 a fantastic idea; ridiculous fancy. 4 *Music* a composition suggesting a dreamy or musing mood. Also, **rev·er·y.** ⟨French *rêverie; rêver* to dream⟩

re·verse [rɪ'vɜrs] *n* 1 the opposite: *She did the reverse of what I ordered.* 2 the gear or gears that reverse the movement of machinery. 3 a backward or contrary movement. 4 a change to bad fortune: *He used to be rich, but he met with reverses.* 5 the back of anything. 6 the side of the coin, medal, etc. that does not have the main design (opposed to OBVERSE).
adj 1 opposite in position or direction: *the reverse side of a piece of cloth.* 2 causing an opposite or backward movement.
v 1 turn the other way; turn inside out; turn upside down. 2 change to the opposite.

3 shift into reverse gear. **re·ver·sal** n. **re·vers·i·ble** adj. **re·vers·i·bly** adv. ⟨Latin reversus pp of revertere. See REVERT.⟩

reverse the charges make a collect phone call.

SYNONYMS

Reverse is a general verb, meaning 'to turn to an opposite position, direction, order' etc.: In wet climates one gets good use of a coat that can be reversed when it begins to rain. **Invert** means to turn upside down, or turn back to front, as in word order: Invert the subject and the auxiliary verb to ask a question.

re·vert [rɪ'vɜrt] v **1** go back: **a** to a previous owner or the heirs: If a man dies without heirs, his property reverts to the government. **b** to a previous practice, state, or belief: After many years as a Buddhist, she reverted to Islam. **2** Biology return to characteristics that have been absent for two or more generations. **re·ver·sion** [rɪ'vɜrʒən] n. ⟨Latin revertere; re- back + vertere turn⟩

re·view [rɪ'vju] v **1** look back on: Before falling asleep, she reviewed the day's happenings. **2** present a survey in speech or writing. **3** examine or re-examine with a view to evaluating: A superior court may review decisions of a lower court. **4** inspect formally: The Admiral reviewed the fleet. **5** examine to give a critique of: He reviews books for a living. **re·view** n. ⟨French revue from revoir see again; Latin re- again + videre see⟩

re·vile [rɪ'vaɪl] v abuse with words: The two drivers began to revile each other. **re·vil·er** n. **re·vile·ment** n. ⟨Old French reviler despise; vil vile; Latin vilis cheap⟩

re·vise [rɪ'vaɪz] v **1** look over and change: She has revised the poem she wrote. **2** change; alter: to revise one's opinion. **re·vis·er** n. **re·vi·sion** n. ⟨Latin re- again + vis- stem of videre see⟩

re·vi·sion·ist n one who reinterprets history in order to provide an account that fits with a change in ideology, **re·vi·sion·ism** n.

re·vive [rɪ'vaɪv] v **1** bring back or come back to consciousness: to revive a half-drowned person. **2** bring or come back to a fresh, lively condition: Flowers revive in water. **3** give energy and strength to: Hot coffee revived me. **4** bring back or come back to notice, use, fashion, etc.: An old play is sometimes revived on the stage. **5** return (someone) to a state of spiritual fervour. **re·viv·al** n. **re·viv·er** n. ⟨Latin re- again + vivere live⟩

re·viv·al·ism n the form of religious activity characteristic of revivals. **re·viv·al·ist** n a person who holds special services to awaken religious faith. **re·viv·i·fy** [rɪ'vɪvə,faɪ] v **1** restore to life; give new life to. **2** revive. **re·viv·i·fi·ca·tion** n. **re·viv·i·fi·er** n.

rev·o·ca·ble See REVOKE.

re·voke [rɪ'vouk] v **1** take back; repeal; cancel; withdraw: The government revoked the bill before it was voted on. **2** Card games fail to follow suit when one can and should. ⟨Latin re- back + vocare call⟩

rev·o·ca·ble ['rɛvəkəbəl] adj that can be

repealed, cancelled, etc. **rev·o·ca·bil·i·ty** n. **rev·o·ca·bly** adv. **rev·o·ca·tion** [,rɛvə'keiʃən] n.

re·volt [rɪ'voult] v **1** rise against authority: The people revolted against the dictator. **2** cause to feel disgust. **re·volt** n. ⟨Latin revolutare frequentative of revolvere. See REVOLVE.⟩ **re·volt·ing** adj disgusting; repulsive. **re·volt·ing·ly** adv.

rev·o·lu·tion [,rɛvə'luʃən] n **1** a complete, often violent, overthrow of a government or political system: The 1917 revolution ended the monarchy in Russia. **2** a complete change: Plastics have brought about a revolution in industry. **3** a movement of an object in a circle or curve around another object: The revolution of the earth around the sun causes the seasons. **4** a single complete turn around a centre: The wheel of the motor turns at a rate of more than one thousand revolutions a minute. ⟨Latin revolutio; revolvere. See REVOLVE.⟩ **rev·o·lu·tion·ar·y** adj **1** of or involving a REVOLUTION (defs. 1, 2). **2** bringing or causing great changes. **3** rotating; revolving. n a person who supports a revolution (def. 1). **rev·o·lu·tion·ize** v change completely: Mechanization revolutionized farm life.

re·volve [rɪ'vɒlv] v **1** move in a circle or curve around another object: The moon revolves around the earth. **2** turn or cause to turn around a centre or axis: The wheels of a moving car revolve. **3** focus on something regarded as a centre: My concerns revolve around cost. **re·volv·a·ble** adj. ⟨Latin re- back + volvere roll⟩

re·volv·er n a pistol with a revolving cylinder for the cartridges, enabling it to be fired several times without reloading. **revolving door** a door made of panels attached to a central axis around which it revolves.

re·vue [rɪ'vju] n a theatrical entertainment including singing, dancing, etc., and usually having humorous treatments of happenings and fads of the past or current year, etc. ⟨French, pp of revoir see again⟩

re·vul·sion [rɪ'vʌlʃən] n **1** a strong feeling of disgust: The stench of rotting vegetables filled us with revulsion. **2** a sudden, violent change of feeling: He suddenly felt a revulsion from the long solitude. ⟨Latin revulsio; re- back + vellere tear away⟩

re·ward [rɪ'wɔrd] n **1** a return made for something good that has been done. **2** a money payment given or offered for capture of criminals, the return of lost property, etc. **re·ward** v. ⟨Old Norman French rewarder, variant of regarder. See REGARD.⟩ **re·ward·ing** adj **1** worthwhile; giving a sense of satisfaction: Helping others can be most rewarding. **2** offering material gain: You will find this a rewarding investment.

re·wire [ri'waɪr] v put new wires on or in.

re·word [ri'wɜrd] v change the wording of; express differently.

re·work [ri'wɜrk] v revise or reprocess.

re·write [ri'rəit] v **-wrote, -writ·ten, -writ·ing** v **1** write in a different form; revise. **2** write (a news story) from material supplied in a form that cannot be used as copy. **re·write** ['riɹəit] *n.*

r.h. right hand.

Rh 1 RH FACTOR. **2** rhodium.
Rh factor a group of antigens often found in the blood of human beings and the higher mammals. Blood containing this substance (**Rh positive**) does not combine favourably with blood lacking it (**Rh negative**). Also formerly called **Rhesus factor**, as it was first discovered in the blood of the rhesus monkey.

rhap·so·dy ['ræpsədi] *n* **1** an utterance marked by extravagant enthusiasm: *She went into rhapsodies over the garden.* **2** *Music* an instrumental composition following no regular form: *Liszt's Hungarian rhapsodies.* **rhap·sod·ic** [-'sɒdɪk] or **rhap·sod·i·cal** *adj.* **rhap·sod·i·cal·ly** *adv.* **rhap·so·dist** *n.* **rhap·so·dize** *v.* ⟨Greek *rhapsōidia* verse composition; *rhaptein* to stitch⟩

rhe·a ['riə] *n* either of two species of large, flightless birds of South America, resembling ostriches. ⟨Greek goddess *Rhea*⟩

rhe·ni·um ['riniəm] *n* a rare metallic element that has properties similar to those of manganese. *Symbol* **Re** ⟨Latin *Rhenus* Rhine⟩

rhe·o·stat ['riə,stæt] *n* *Electricity* an instrument for regulating the strength of an electric current by introducing different amounts of resistance into the circuit. **rhe·o·stat·ic** *adj.* ⟨Greek *rheos* current + *statos* standing still⟩

Rhesus factor See RH.

rhet·o·ric ['rɛtərɪk] *n* **1** the art of using words effectively. **2** language used to influence others: *The crowd was impressed by the speaker's rhetoric.* **3** mere display in language. **rhe·tor·i·cal** [rɪ'tɔrɪkəl] *adj.* **rhe·tor·i·cal·ly** *adv.* **rhet·o·ri·cian** [,rɛtə'rɪʃən] *n.* ⟨Greek *rhētōr* orator⟩
rhetorical question a question asked only for effect, not for information, and not meant to be answered.

rheu·ma·tism ['rumə,tɪzəm] *n* any of various painful conditions of the joints, muscles, or connective tissue, characterized by inflammation, stiffness, etc. **rheu·mat·ic** [ru'mætɪk] *adj.* ⟨Greek *rheuma* a flowing; *rheein* flow⟩
rheumatic fever an acute disease occurring usually in children, characterized by fever, swelling, pain in the joints, and inflammation of the heart. **rheu·mat·ic·ky** *adj* having rheumatism. **rheu·ma·toid arthritis** ['rumə,tɔɪd] a persistent disease that produces painful inflammation of the joints and is often progressively crippling.

rhine·stone ['raɪn,stoun] *n* an imitation diamond, made of glass or paste. ⟨translation of French *caillou du Rhin*⟩

rhi·ni·tis [raɪ'nəitɪs] *n* inflammation in the nose. ⟨Greek *rhinos* nose⟩

rhi·no ['raɪnou] *n, pl* **-nos** rhinoceros.

rhi·noc·er·os [raɪ'nɒsərəs] *n, pl* **-os·es** or (esp collectively) **-os** any of a family of large, plant-eating mammals having a massive body and one or two large horns growing upright on the snout. ⟨Greek *rhinos* nose + *keras* horn⟩

rhi·no·plas·ty ['raɪnə,plæsti] *n* plastic surgery involving the nose. ⟨Greek *rhino*s nose + *plastia*; *plassein* form⟩

rhi·zome ['raɪzoum] *n Botany* a rootlike stem that usually produces roots from below and shoots from above. **rhi·zom·a·tous** [-'zɒmətəs] or [-'zoumətəs] *adj.* ⟨Greek *rhiza* root⟩

rho·di·um ['roudiəm] *n* a greyish white metallic element, forming salts that give rose-coloured solutions. It is similar to aluminum. *Symbol* **Rh** ⟨Greek *rhodon* rose⟩

rho·do·den·dron [,roudə'dɛndrən] *n* any of a very large genus of shrubs of the heath family, found in cooler regions, having showy flowers and evergreen or deciduous leaves. ⟨Greek *rhodon* rose + *dendron* tree⟩

rhom·bus ['rɒmbəs] *n, pl* **-bus·es** or **-bi** [-baɪ] or [-bi] a parallelogram with four equal sides that is not necessarily a square. ⟨Greek *rhombos*⟩
rhom·bic *adj* **1** having the form of a rhombus. **2** having a rhombus as base. **3** *Chemistry* having to do with a system of crystallization characterized by three unequal axes intersecting at right angles. **rhom·boid** *n* a parallelogram with only the opposite sides equal. **rhom·boid** or **rhom·boid·al** *adj.*

rhu·barb ['rubɑrb] *n* any of several plants of the buckwheat family, esp a plant having large, heart-shaped leaves and red-and-green juicy leafstalks that are used for pies, preserves, etc. The leaves are poisonous. ⟨Greek *rhēon barbaron* foreign rhubarb⟩

rhyme [raɪm] *v* **1** sound alike in the last part. *Examples:* Long *rhymes with* song. **2** make rhymes: *She enjoys rhyming.* **3** use (a word) with another that rhymes with it.
n an agreement in the final sounds of words or lines: Cat *is a rhyme for* mat. **rhym·er** *n.* ⟨Old French *rime*; Greek *rhythmos* rhythm⟩
without rhyme or reason having no system or sense.
rhyme scheme the pattern of end rhymes used in a poem, and usually indicated by letters; for example, *abba abba cde cde* and *abab cdcd efef gg* are both rhyme schemes for the sonnet. **rhyme·ster** *n* a maker of rather poor rhymes or verse. **rhyming slang** a form of slang in which a rhyming word is substituted for the intended word, as in *apples and pears* for *stairs.*

rhythm ['rɪðəm] *n* **1** a feature of movement involving a regular repetition of a beat, accent, etc.: *the rhythm of dancing, the rhythm of one's heartbeat.* **2** the arrangement of beats in a line of poetry: *The rhythms of "Twinkle, twinkle, little star" and "O Canada" are different.* **3** *Music* the pattern of movement produced by the combination of accent, metre, and tempo. **4** any sequence of

regularly recurring events: *visual rhythm.*
rhyth·mic *adj.* **rhyth·mi·cal·ly** *adv.* ⟨Greek
rhythmos; rheein flow⟩

rhythm and blues a style of music that
developed in the US in the 1930s that was
blues sung to the accompaniment of large
bands with saxophones, guitars, etc. and
strong rhythm sections. **rhythm method** a
form of birth control involving abstention
from sexual intercourse during the estimated
period of ovulation.

rib¹ [rɪb] *n* **1** one of the curved bones
enclosing the upper part of the body. **2** one
of a number of similar pieces forming a
frame. An umbrella has ribs. **3** a thick vein of
a leaf. **4** a ridge in a knitted or woven fabric.
5 ribs *pl* spareribs. **6** *Architecture* one of the
arches forming the supports for a vault.
v **ribbed, rib·bing** mark with riblike ridges.
⟨Old English⟩

tickle the ribs cause laughter, as a joke.
rib·bing *n Knitting* an effect produced by
knitting alternately plain and purl stitches.
rib cage the cagelike structure formed by the
ribs, enclosing the lungs, heart, etc.

rib² [rɪb] *Informal n* **1** a joke. **2** a satire on or a
parody of something.
v **ribbed, rib·bing** tease. ⟨clipping of *rib-
tickler*⟩
ribbed *adj* having ribs or ridges. **rib–tick·ler**
n a joke or funny story. **rib–tick·ling** *adj.*

rib·ald [ˈrɪbəld] *or* [ˈraɪbəld] *adj* offensive in
speech; irreverent; obscene. **rib·ald·ly** *adv.*
⟨Old French *ribauld; riber* to be wanton⟩
rib·ald·ry *n* ribald language.

rib·bon [ˈrɪbən] *n* **1** material in strips.
2 ribbons *pl* torn pieces; shreds: *Her dress was
torn to ribbons by the thorns.* **3** a small badge
of cloth worn as a sign of membership in an
order, a decoration for bravery, etc.: *the
ribbon of the Victoria Cross.* **rib·bon·like** *adj.*
⟨Old French *riban*⟩
ribbon development the building of houses,
shops, and industrial buildings along a road.
ribbon farm ✱ a long, narrow holding of
land fronting on a river, such as the farms in
the Red River Settlement.

ri·bo·fla·vin [ˈraɪbouˌfleɪvən] *n* a constituent
of the vitamin B complex, present in liver,
eggs, milk, spinach, etc.; lactoflavin. It is
sometimes called vitamin B_2 or G. ⟨*ribose* a
sugar + Latin *flavus* yellow⟩

ri·bo·nu·cle·ic acid [ˌraɪbounjuˈkliɪk] *or*
[-nuˈkliɪk] *Biochemistry* a single-stranded
molecule, transcribed from DNA. One form
carries genetic information from the nuclear
DNA. *Abbrev* **RNA**

rice [raɪs] *n* an annual cereal grass
cultivated for its starchy, edible seeds.
v reduce (cooked potatoes, etc.) to a form
resembling rice, as by forcing through a
sieve. ⟨Ital. *riso;* Greek *oryza;* Iranian⟩
rice paper 1 a thin paper made from the
straw of rice. **2** an edible paper made from a
tree of the ginseng family.

rich [rɪtʃ] *adj* **1** having much money or
property: *a rich man.* **2** well supplied: *Canada
is rich in nickel.* **3** abundant: *a rich supply.*
4 producing abundantly: *rich soil.* **5** having
great worth: *a rich harvest.* **6** costly; elegant;
elaborate: *rich clothes.* **7** of foods, made with
much fat, egg, etc. **8** of colours, smells, etc.,
deep; vivid: *a rich red.* **9** of wine, etc.,
full-flavoured. **10** *Informal* very amusing.
n **the rich** *pl* rich people. **rich·ly** *adv.* **rich·ness** *n.*
⟨Old English *rice*⟩
rich·es [ˈrɪtʃɪz] *n pl* wealth.

SYNONYMS
Rich = having more than enough money,
possessions, etc. for all normal needs: *They
own the mill in our town and are considered
rich.* **Wealthy** = very rich, having a great
store of money, property, etc.: *Wealthy
people are often patrons of the arts.*

Rich·ter scale [ˈrɪktər] a scale, ranging from
1 to 10, for measuring the intensity of an
earthquake. Each whole number on the
scale, beginning with 1, represents a
magnitude 10 times greater than the
preceding one: *The most powerful earthquakes
so far recorded registered 8.9 on the Richter scale.*
⟨Charles F. *Richter,* 20c US seismologist⟩

rick [rɪk] *n* a stack of hay, straw, etc., esp one
covered or thatched so that the rain will run
off it.
v form into a rick. ⟨Old English *hrēac*⟩

rick·ets [ˈrɪkɪts] *n* a disease of childhood
caused by lack of vitamin D or calcium,
resulting in softening and, sometimes,
bending of the bones. ⟨alteration of *rachitis,*
influenced by *wrick* wrench, strain⟩
rick·et·y *adj* **1** liable to fall or break down;
shaky: *a rickety old chair.* **2** having rickets.
3 feeble in the joints. **rick·et·i·ness** *n.*

rick·shaw or **rick·sha** [ˈrɪkʃɒ] *n* a small, two-
wheeled hooded carriage pulled by a cyclist,
the carriage taking the place of the bicycle's
rear wheel. Rickshaws were originally used in
Japan and pulled by one or two men on foot.
⟨short for *jinrikishaw;* Japanese *jin* person +
riki power + *sha* vehicle⟩

ric·o·chet [ˈrɪkəʃeɪ] *n* the rebounding of a
projectile, such as a bullet, after striking a
surface at an angle: *the ricochet of a flat stone
on the water.* **ric·o·chet, -cheted** [-ʃeɪd],
-chet·ing [-ʃeɪɪŋ] *v.* ⟨French⟩

ri·cot·ta [rɪˈkɒtə] *Italian* [riˈkɔtta] *n* a soft,
mild Italian cheese.

ric·tus [ˈrɪktəs] *n, pl* **-tus** or **-tuses** a fixed,
gaping grimace or grin. **ric·tal** *adj.* ⟨Latin
rictus pp of *ringi* open the mouth, gape⟩

rid [rɪd] *v* **rid** or **rid·ded, rid·ding** make free
(from some troublesome thing): *What will rid
a house of rats?* ⟨Old English *ryddan* clear
land⟩
be rid of be freed from. **get rid of a** get free
from: *I can't get rid of this cold.* **b** do away
with: *Poison will get rid of the rats in the barn.*
rid·dance *n* **1** a clearing away. **2** deliverance
from something. **good riddance** an
expression of relief that something or
somebody has been removed.

rid·dle¹ ['rɪdəl] *n* **1** a puzzling problem, usually amusing and often involving a play on words. *Example: Q: When is a door not a door? A: When it is ajar.* **2** a person or thing that is hard to understand, explain, etc.: *Her disappearance remains a riddle.*
v **1** speak in riddles. **2** solve or explain (a riddle or question). ⟨Old English *rǣdels; rǣdan* guess, explain, read⟩

rid·dle² ['rɪdəl] *v* **1** make many holes in: *The door was riddled with bullets.* **2** sift: *to riddle gravel.* **3** permeate (*with* something undesirable): *a government riddled with corruption.*
n a coarse sieve. ⟨Old English *hriddel* sieve⟩

ride [raɪd] *v* **rode, rid·den, rid·ing** *v* **1** sit on (a horse or other animal) and make use of it for transport. **2** be a passenger or driver of (a bicycle, roller coaster, etc.). **3** be carried along by anything: *to ride on a train.* **4** ride over, along, etc.: *to ride a mountain trail.* **5** move along (on), as on water or air currents: *The ship rode the waves.* **6** *Informal* tease. **7** control or tyrannize over: *to be ridden by foolish fears.* **8** be dependent (*on*): *There's a lot riding on the committee's decision.*
n **1** a trip on a horse, in a carriage, car, boat, etc.: *Let's go for a ride.* **2** a path made for riding: *They built a ride through the middle of the park.* **3** a mechanical amusement, such as a merry-go-round, Ferris wheel, etc. **4** a chance for transportation: *Do you need a ride to Saskatoon?* **rid·a·ble** *adj.* **–rid·den** *combining form* obsessed or overwhelmed by; full of: *guilt-ridden, fear-ridden.* ⟨Old English *rīdan*⟩
let ride leave undisturbed: *Let the matter ride until the next meeting.* **ride down a** knock down. **b** overcome. **ride high** enjoy success. **ride out a** withstand (a gale, etc.) without damage. **b** endure successfully. **ride up** slide up out of place: *That coat rides up at the back.* **take for a ride** *Slang* a cheat; trick. **b** murder.
rid·er *n* **1** a person who rides: *The Calgary Stampede is famous for its riders.* **2** anything added to a record, document, or statement after it was considered to be completed. **3** any object mounted so that it straddles another piece.
rid·er·less *adj.* **rid·er·ship** *n* the number of passengers using a system of transportation: *What is the ridership of the Skytrain?* **rid·ing** *adj* **1** used for or in the act of riding: *riding boots, a riding crop.* **2** made to be operated by a rider: *a riding mower.* **riding crop** a short whip with a loop on one end instead of a lash. **riding habit** a suit of clothes worn by horseback riders.

Ri·deau Hall ['rɪdou] *or* [rɪ'dou] ✵ the official residence of the Governor General of Canada, situated in Ottawa.

ridge [rɪdʒ] *n* **1** any raised, narrow strip: *the ridges on corduroy cloth.* **2** the line where two sloping surfaces meet: *the ridge of a roof.* **3** a long, narrow chain of hills or mountains. **4** the long and narrow upper part of something: *the ridge of an animal's back.* **5** a long, narrow area of high barometric

pressure. **ridg·y** *adj.* ⟨Old English *hrycg*⟩
ridge·pole *n* the horizontal timber or pole along the top of a roof or tent.

rid·i·cule ['rɪdə,kjul] *v* laugh at; make fun of. *n* words or actions that make fun of somebody or something. ⟨Latin *ridiculus* ridiculous; *ridere* laugh⟩
ri·dic·u·lous [rɪ'dɪkjələs] *adj* deserving ridicule; absurd; laughable. **ri·dic·u·lous·ly** *adv.* **ri·dic·u·lous·ness** *n.*

> **SYNONYMS**
> **Ridicule** emphasizes making fun of people or things, with the intention of making them seem unimportant: *This boy ridicules his sisters' friends.* **Deride** emphasizes laughing in contempt: *Some people deride patriotic rallies and parades.* **Mock** = ridicule by imitating scornfully: *The cheeky girl mocked the teacher.*

rid·ing¹ ['raɪdɪŋ] *n* ✵ a political division represented by a Member of Parliament or a Member of the Legislative Assembly; constituency. ⟨Middle English *thriding* a third, referring to an administrative division of a British county⟩

rid·ing² ['raɪdɪŋ] See RIDE.

rife [raɪf] *adj* **1** happening often; common; widespread. **2** full: *The land was rife with rumours of war.* ⟨Old English *rīfe*⟩

riff [rɪf] *Jazz music n* a continuously repeated instrumental phrase, supporting a solo improvisation or forming the basis of a tune. **riff** *v.* ⟨probably shortened from *refrain*⟩

rif·fle ['rɪfəl] *v* **1** flip through (a stack of paper, the pages of a book, etc.) quickly by sliding the thumb along the edges. **2** shuffle cards, holding half the deck in each hand, by bending the edges slightly so that the two divisions slide into each other. ⟨perhaps variant of *ripple* or *ruffle*⟩

riff·raff ['rɪf,ræf] *n* **1** worthless people. **2** trash. **riff·raff** *adj.* ⟨Old French *rif et raf* every scrap; *rifler* rifle² + *raffler* carry off⟩

ri·fle¹ ['raɪfəl] *n* a gun having spiral grooves in its barrel to spin the bullet as it is fired, and usually fired from the shoulder.
v cut spiral grooves in (a gun). ⟨French *rifler* scratch, groove⟩
rifle range a place for practice in shooting with a rifle. **ri·fling** *n* the system of spiral grooves in a rifle.

ri·fle² ['raɪfəl] *v* **1** search and rob. **2** strip bare: *The boys rifled the apple tree.* **ri·fler** *n.* ⟨Middle English; Old French *rifler*⟩

rift [rɪft] *n* **1** a gap: *a rift in the clouds.* **2** a breach in relations between individuals, groups, or nations. **3** *Geology* a fault, usually one along which movement was lateral.
v break or cause to break open or split. ⟨Scandinavian⟩

rig¹ [rɪg] *v* **rigged, rig·ging 1** *Nautical* equip (a ship) with masts, sails, ropes, etc. **2** equip (with *out*): *to rig out a football team.* **3** *Informal* clothe; dress (usually with *out* or *up*): *On Halloween the children rig themselves up in funny clothes.* **4** put together in a hurry or by using odds and ends (often with *up*): *The girls rigged up a tent, using a rope and a blanket.* *n* **1** *Nautical* the arrangement of masts, sails, ropes, etc. on a ship. **2** *Informal* clothing, esp when unusual, showy, etc.: *Her rig consisted of a silk hat and overalls.* **3** an outfit; equipment. **4** the machinery used for locating and extracting petroleum or natural gas from the earth: *an oil rig.* **5** *Informal* **a** any combination trucking unit, as a tractor trailer. **b** a wagon, with its horse or horses. ⟨Middle English; Scandinavian⟩ **rig·ging** *n* the ropes, chains, etc. on a ship, used to support and work the masts, sails, etc.

rig² [rɪg] *v* **rigged, rig·ging** manipulate dishonestly for one's own advantage: *to rig a race.* ⟨origin uncertain; perhaps RIG¹⟩

right [raɪt] *adj* **1** good; just; lawful: *He did the right thing when he told the truth.* **2** correct: *the right answer.* **3** proper; fitting: *She always managed to say the right thing at the right time.* **4** favourable: *If the weather is right, we'll go.* **5** normal: *My head doesn't feel right.* **6** meant to be seen: *the right side of cloth.* **7** of the side that is toward the east when the main side faces north: *The right bank of a river is the one to the right as one faces downstream.* **8** Often, **Right** *Politics* to do with the Right. **9** to do with a 90° angle: *a right angle.*
adv **1** in a way that is good, just, or lawful. **2** correctly: *She guessed right.* **3** properly: *It's faster to do a job right the first time.* **4** favourably: *turn out right.* **5** into a good condition: *Put things right.* **6** on or to the right side: *Turn right.* **7** precisely: *Put it right here.* **8** very (used in some titles): *Right Honourable.* **9** toward the political right: *I see her politics are shifting further right all the time.* **10** directly: *Look me right in the eye.* **11** completely: *His hat was knocked right off.* **12** yes; very well: *"Come at once," his mother called. "Right," he replied.*
n **1** that which is right: *Do right, not wrong.* **2** a just claim or privilege: *the right to vote.* **3** the right side or hand: *Turn to your right.* **4** the **Right** or **the right a** a group generally supporting capitalism, opposing socialism, and favouring conservative social policies. **b** esp in some legislatures, the members sitting on the right of the presiding officer by virtue of their conservative views.
v **1** make correct: *to right errors.* **2** get or put into proper position: *The ship righted as the wave passed.* **right·ly** *adv.* **right·ness** *n.* ⟨Old English *riht*⟩
by rights or **by right** rightly; correctly. **in the right** on the lawful side of a conflict. **right away** at once. **right now** immediately: *Stop that right now!* **right off** at once: *I recognized her right off.* **to rights** in or into proper condition, order, etc.: *It took us three hours to set the house to rights after the children's party.* **right angle** an angle of 90°. **right–an·gled** *adj.* **right·eous** ['raɪtʃəs] *adj* **1** behaving justly. **2** morally right: *righteous indignation.* **right·eous·ly** *adv.* **right·eous·ness** *n.* **right face** a turn to the right. **right·ful** *adj* **1** according to law; by rights: *the rightful owner.* **2** just and

right; proper. **right·ful·ly** *adv.* **right·ful·ness** *n.* **right–hand** *adj* **1** on or to the right. **2** to do with the right hand. **3** most helpful or useful: *one's right-hand man.* **right–hand·ed** *adj* **1** using the right hand more easily and readily than the left. **2** turning from left to right: *a right-handed screw.* **right–hand·ed·ly** *adv.* **right–hand·ed·ness** *n.* **right–hand·er** *n.* **Right Honourable** a title given to the prime minister of Canada. *Abbrev* **Rt. Hon.** **right·ist** *Politics n* a person who favours the RIGHT. *adj* to do with the Right. **right·ism** *n.* **right–mind·ed** *adj* having proper opinions. **right–mind·ed·ly** *adv.* **right–mind·ed·ness** *n.* **right of way** the right to pass over property belonging to someone else. **right–siz·ing** *n* the reduction of a company to its optimum size for profitability. **right stuff** *Informal* certain qualities of character that lead to success, such as confidence, dependability, and courage. **right–to–life** *adj* opposing abortion and euthanasia. **right whale** a baleen whale, so named for being large and slow and therefore 'right' for hunting. **right wing 1** *Politics* the more conservative faction of a group. **2** *Hockey, lacrosse, etc.* the position to the right of centre of a forward line. **right–wing** *adj.* **right–wing·er** *n.* **right·y** *n* *Informal* a right-handed person.

rig·id ['rɪdʒɪd] *adj* **1** stiff; not bending: *a rigid support.* **2** strict: *Our club has few rigid rules.* **3** severely exact; rigorous: *a rigid examination.* **rig·id·ly** *adv.* **ri·gid·i·ty** or **rig·id·ness** *n.* ⟨Latin *rigidus; rigere* be stiff⟩

rig·ma·role ['rɪgmə,roul] *n* **1** a fussy or complicated procedure. **2** meaningless or incoherent talk. ⟨earlier *ragman roll; ragman* list, catalogue (origin uncertain) + *roll*⟩

rig·or mor·tis ['rɪgər 'mɔrtɪs] the stiffening of the muscles after death. ⟨Latin = stiffness of death⟩

rig·our or **rig·or** ['rɪgər] *n* **1** strictness; severity. **2** harshness: *the rigour of a long, cold winter.* **3** logical exactness: *the rigour of scientific method.* **4** stiffness, esp in body tissues or organs. ⟨Latin *rigor; rigere* be stiff⟩ **rig·or·ous** *adj* **1** strict: *rigorous discipline.* **2** harsh: *a rigorous climate.* **3** thoroughly logical and scientific; exact. **rig·or·ous·ly** *adv.*

Rig–Ve·da [,rɪg 'veɪdə] *n* the oldest and most important of the ancient sacred writings of Hinduism, consisting of approximately 1000 hymns dating from about 1500 B.C.

rile [raɪl] *v* make angry or irritated. ⟨variant of ROIL⟩

rill [rɪl] *n* a tiny stream; little brook. ⟨Dutch *ril* groove, furrow⟩

rim [rɪm] *n* an edge or border: *a wheel rim.* *v* **rimmed, rim·ming 1** form a rim around: *The well was rimmed with grass.* **2** roll around the rim of: *The roulette ball rimmed the wheel.* **rim·less** *adj.* ⟨Old English *rima*⟩

rime [raɪm] *n* white frost. **rime** *v.* **rim·y** *adj.* ⟨Old English *hrim*⟩

rind [raɪnd] *n* the hard outer covering (of oranges, melons, cheeses, etc.). ⟨Old English⟩

ring¹ [rɪŋ] *n* **1** a circle. **2** a thin circle of metal or other material: *rings on her fingers.* **3** an enclosed space for races, games, showing livestock, etc. **4** prize fighting: *His ambition was success in the ring.* (The ring for a prize fight is square.) **5** a group of people combined for a selfish or bad purpose: *A smuggling ring.* **6** a cut all the way round a branch or the trunk of a tree.
v **ringed, ring·ing 1** put a ring around: *willows ringing a pond.* **2** toss a horseshoe, ring, etc. around a mark or post. **3** form into a ring. **4** cut away the bark in a ring around (a tree or branch): *If you ring a birch tree, it will probably die.* **5** surround so as to prevent escape: *The wolves ringed the injured moose.* **ring·less** *adj.* ⟨Old English *hring*⟩
ringed *adj* **1** wearing rings: *heavily ringed fingers.* **2** surrounded by a ring or rings: *The lake was ringed with evergreens.* **3** ringlike: *a ringed design.* **ringed seal** a small, earless seal found in arctic and subarctic waters, having a coat marked with cream-coloured rings. **ring·er** ['rɪŋər] *n* a quoit, horseshoe, etc., thrown so as to fall over a peg. **ring·ette** *n* an ice game similar to hockey, played by two teams using straight sticks to try to shoot a rubber ring into the opposing team's goal. **ring finger** the finger next to the little finger of either hand, where an engagement and/or wedding ring is customarily worn. **ring·lead·er** *n* a person who leads others, esp in opposition to authority or law. **ring·let** *n* a long curl: *She wears her hair in ringlets.* **ring·let·ed** *adj.* **ring·mas·ter** *n* a person in charge of the performances in the ring of a circus. **ring·side** *n* the area just outside the ring at a circus, prize fight, etc. **ring·side** *adj.* **ring·worm** *n* a contagious skin disease characterized by ring-shaped patches.

ring² [rɪŋ] *v* **rang, rung, ring·ing 1** give forth a clear resounding sound, as a bell does: *Their laughter rang out.* **2** cause to give forth such a sound: *Ring the bell.* **3** cause (a bell or buzzer) to sound: *I had to ring twice before anyone came.* **4** give back sound; echo or resound: *The mountains rang with the roll of thunder.* **5** be filled with report or talk: *The town rang with the news of the Canadian team's victory.* **6** sound: *Her words rang true.* **7** have a sensation as of sounds of bells: *My ears are ringing.* **8** summon by means of a bell or buzzer (with *for*): *to ring for the steward.* **9** record (a specified amount) on a cash register (with *up*): *The cashier rang up $15.50 instead of $155.00.*
n **1** the act of ringing. **2** the sound of a bell or buzzer. **3** a sound like that of a bell: *the ring of steel on steel.* **4** a characteristic sound or quality: *the ring of truth.* ⟨Old English *hringan*⟩ **ring·er** ['rɪŋər] *n* **1** a device for ringing a bell. **2** *Slang* a horse, athlete, etc., entered in a competition under false identification as a substitute for one of lesser ability. **3** *Slang* a person or thing very much like another. **ring·ing·ly** *adv.* ⟨Old English *hringan*⟩
be a (dead) ringer for be almost exactly like. **ring a bell** be familiar: *That name rings a bell.*

ring up (down) the curtain a a signal for a theatre curtain to be raised (lowered). **b** indicate the beginning or end of an action, etc. **run rings around** do much better than.
ring·er¹ ['rɪŋər] See RING¹.
ring·er² ['rɪŋər] See RING².

rink [rɪŋk] *n* **1** a sheet of ice or a smooth floor for skating, playing hockey, roller skating, curling. **2** a curling team of four players. **3** a building in which there is a rink. ⟨Scottish; Old French *renc* course, rank¹⟩
rink house ✱ a small heated cabin near an outdoor rink, used by persons putting on or taking off ice skates. **rink rat ✱** *Informal* a young person who helps with the chores around a hockey rink, often in return for free skating, free admission to hockey games, etc.

rinse [rɪns] *v* **1** cleanse by washing lightly, esp by allowing water, etc. to run through, over, etc. (often used with *out*): *He rinsed his coffee cup under the tap.* **2** give (laundry, etc.) a final washing in clear water to remove soap or detergent. **3** treat (hair) with a rinse: *She rinsed her hair with beer to give it body.*
n **1** the act of rinsing: *Give your sweater a good rinse in soft water.* **2** the liquid used in rinsing: *A lemon rinse is good for blond hair.* ⟨Old French *reincier*; Latin *recens* fresh⟩

ri·ot ['raɪət] *n* **1** a violent public disturbance. **2** a loud outburst: *a riot of laughter.* **3** loose living; wild revelling: *His whole life is one long riot.* **4** a bright display: *The garden was a riot of colour.* **5** *Informal* a very amusing person: *She was a riot at the party.*
v take part in a violent public disturbance. **ri·ot·er** *n.* **ri·ot·ous** *adj.* **ri·ot·ous·ly** *adv.*
ri·ot·ous·ness *n.* ⟨Old French *riote* dispute⟩
read the riot act a give orders for disturbance to cease. **b** reprimand. **run riot a** act without restraint. **b** of plants, grow luxuriantly.

rip¹ [rɪp] *v* **ripped, rip·ping 1** tear apart: *Rip the cover off this box.* **2** become torn apart. **3** saw (wood) along the grain. **4** *Informal* move fast or violently. **5** *Informal* utter violently (with *out*): *He ripped out an angry oath.*
n **1** a torn place. **2** an act of tearing. ⟨Middle English *rippen*⟩
let her (or it) rip *Informal* allow something to proceed unchecked. **let rip** launch into something with extreme energy. **rip into** *Informal* attack violently. **rip off** *Slang* **a** take advantage of; cheat. **b** steal. **rip-off** *n.*
rip cord a cord that, when pulled, opens a parachute. **rip·per** *n* a tool for ripping. **rip·roar·ing** *adj Slang* hilarious. **rip·snort·ing** *adj Slang* exciting, intense, or wild: *a ripsnorting party.* **rip·snort·er** *n.*

rip² [rɪp] *n* **1** a stretch of rough water made by cross currents meeting. **2** a swift current made by the tide. ⟨perhaps special use of *rip¹* or clipping of *ripple*⟩
rip·tide *n* a current of churning water caused by one strong current meeting another.

R.I.P. rest in peace (for Latin *requiescat in pace*).

ripe [raɪp] *adj* **1** full-grown and ready to be

eaten: *ripe fruit*. **2** fully developed; mature: *a ripe cheese*. **3** ready: *ripe for mischief*. **ripe·ly** *adv*. **rip·en** *v*. **ripe·ness** *n*.⟨Old English *ripe*⟩

ri·poste [rə'poust] *n* **1** a quick, sharp reply or return. **2** *Fencing* a quick thrust given after parrying a lunge. **ri·poste** *v*. ⟨French; Italian *risposta*; Latin *respondere* respond⟩

rip·ple ['rɪpəl] *n* **1** a very little wave: *Watch the ripples spread in rings*. **2** anything that seems like a little wave: *ripples in cardboard*. **3** a sound that reminds one of little waves: *a ripple of laughter in the crowd*.
v **1** make a sound like rippling water. **2** form little waves. **3** make little waves on: *A breeze rippled the lake*. **rip·ply** *adj*. ⟨origin uncertain⟩
ripple effect the spreading, with gradually diminishing force, of the results of an event.

rise [raɪz] *v* **rose**, **ris·en** ['rɪzən], **ris·ing** *v* **1** get up: *to rise from a chair*. **2** go up: *The kite rises in the air*. **3** of fish, swim up to the surface to get bait, etc.: *The trout are rising*. **4** slope upward: *Hills rise in the distance*. **5** increase: *Prices are rising*. **6** advance to a higher level of action, position, etc.: *He rose from errand boy to president*. **7** become louder or of higher pitch: *Their angry voices rose*. **8** appear above the horizon: *The sun rises in the morning*. **9** start (with *from*): *The river rises from a spring*. **10** come into being or action: *The wind rose rapidly*. **11** be constructed: *Houses are rising on the edge of the town*. **12** become more cheerful: *Her spirits rose*. **13** rebel: *The slaves rose against their masters*. **14** adjourn: *The House rose for the summer*. **15** be able to deal with (with *to*): *They rose to the occasion*.
n **1** an upward movement. **2** an upward slope: *The rise of that hill is gradual*. **3** a hill. **4** the vertical height of a step, slope, etc. **5** an increase. **6** an advance in rank, power, etc. **7** a start: *the rise of a storm,*.
get a rise out of (someone), get an expected reaction, as of anger, from (someone) by means of a question, comment, etc. **give rise to** start; cause: *The circumstances of his disappearance gave rise to fears for his safety*. ⟨Old English *risan*⟩
ris·er *n* **1** a person or thing that rises: *an early riser*. **2** the vertical part of a step. **ris·ing** *n* **1** the act of a person or thing that rises. **2** a rebellion; revolt. **ris·ing** *adj*.

CONFUSABLES
The verb **raise** is transitive (it takes an object): *Raise your head off the pillow*. The verb **rise** is intransitive (it does not take an object): *Are you early to rise in the morning?*.

ris·i·ble ['rɪzəbəl] *adj* **1** able or inclined to laugh. **2** causing laughter; amusing; funny. ⟨Latin *risus* pp of *ridere* laugh⟩

risk [rɪsk] *n* **1** a chance of harm or loss. **2** *Insurance* a person or thing described with reference to the chance of loss from insuring him, her, or it. **3** a person or thing that cannot be relied on.
v **1** expose to the chance of harm: *A soldier risks his life*. **2** take the risk of: *They risked getting wet*. **risk·y** *adj*. **risk·i·ly** *adv*. **risk·i·ness** *n*. ⟨French *risque*; Italian *risco* from *risciare* dare⟩
at risk a in danger. **b** held financially responsible. **run a risk** or **take a risk** expose oneself to the chance of harm or loss.

ri·sot·to [rɪ'zɒtou] *Italian* [ri'sɔtto] *n* an Italian dish consisting of rice slowly cooked in broth, often with other ingredients added. ⟨Italian⟩

ris·qué [rɪ'skei] *adj* suggestive of indecency; somewhat improper: *a risqué scene in a play*. ⟨French, pp of *risquer* to risk⟩

rite [raɪt] *n* **1** a solemn ceremony: *Secret societies have their special rites*. **2** a particular ceremony performed according to rules. ⟨Latin *ritus*⟩
rite of passage *Anthropology* a ceremony marking the transition of an individual from one status or stage of life to another, such as the onset of puberty.

rit·u·al ['rɪtʃuəl] *n* a form or system of rites. **rit·u·al** *adj*. ⟨Latin *ritualis*; *ritus* rite⟩ **rit·u·al·ism** *n* a fondness for ritual. **rit·u·al·is·tic** *adj*. **rit·u·al·is·ti·cal·ly** *adv*. **rit·u·al·ize** *v* make a ritual of. **rit·u·al·ly** *adv* according to a ritual or as part of a ritual.

ritz·y ['rɪtsi] *adj Slang* elegant or luxurious: *a ritzy nightclub*. ⟨Ritz hotels; 19c Swiss hotelier César Ritz⟩

ri·val ['raɪvəl] *n* **1** a competitor. **2** an equal; match: *Her beauty has no rival*.
v **-valled** or **-valed**, **-val·ling** or **-val·ing 1** try to equal or outdo: *The stores rival each other in beautiful window displays*. **2** equal; match: *The sunset rivalled the sunrise in beauty*. **ri·val** *adj*. **ri·val·ry** *n*. ⟨Latin *rivalis* using the same stream; *rivus* stream⟩

riv·er ['rɪvər] *n* **1** a large natural stream of water that flows into a lake, ocean, etc. **2** any abundant stream or flow: *rivers of blood*. ⟨Old French *rivere*; Latin *ripa* bank⟩
sell down the river betray. **up the river** *Slang* **a** to prison: *He was sent up the river for 30 years*. **b** in prison.
river basin land that is drained by a river and its tributaries. **riv·er·bed** *n* the channel along which a river flows or used to flow. **river·boat** *n* a boat suitable for use on rivers. **river drive** ✳ *Logging* the process of floating logs downstream. **river–driv·er**. **riv·er·side** *n* the bank of a river. **riv·er·side** *adj*.

riv·et ['rɪvɪt] *n* a metal bolt having a head at one end, the other end made to be hammered flat once it is in position.
v **1** fasten with rivets. **2** fasten or fix firmly: *Their eyes were riveted on the speaker*. **riv·et·er** *n*. ⟨Old French, from *river* fix; Latin *ripare* bring ashore; *ripa* bank⟩

riv·u·let ['rɪvjəlɪt] *n* a very small stream. ⟨Italian *rivoletto*; Latin *rivus* stream⟩

rm. 1 room. **2** ream.

RN or **R.N. 1** registered nurse. **2** Royal Navy.

RNA RIBONUCLEIC ACID.

roach [routʃ] *n* **1** cockroach. **2** *Slang* the butt of a marijuana cigarette.

road [roud] *n* **1** a highway between places: *The road from here to the city is being paved.* **2** a way or route: *a road through the woods.* **3** Also, **roads** *Nautical* a place near the shore where ships can ride at anchor.
hold the road travel on a road safely. **on the road a** travelling, esp as a sales rep. **b** of a theatre company, etc., on tour. ⟨Old English *rād* a riding, journey; *rīdan* ride⟩
road allowance ✷ land reserved by the government to be used for roads. **road·bed** *n* the foundation of a road or of a railway. **road·block** *n* **1** a road barricade set up by police, to prevent persons from escaping, or to check vehicles and drivers for infractions of the highway code. **2** any obstacle to progress. **road hockey** a form of hockey played without skates and with a ball instead of a puck, on a hard surface such as a road. **road hog** *Informal* a driver who obstructs traffic by driving in the middle of the road. **road·house** *n* a restaurant near a highway where people can stop for refreshments and, often, entertainment. **road·kill** *n* the body of an animal killed by a vehicle and left on the road or highway. **road·run·ner** *n* a bird related to the cuckoo, that usually runs instead of flying. **road show** or **road·show** a play, opera, ballet, etc. that travels from city to city. **road·side** *n* the side of a road. **road·side** *adj.* **road test 1** a test of the roadworthiness of a vehicle. **2** the practical part of a test for a driver's licence. **road–test** *v.* **road·way** *n* the part of a road used by vehicles. **road·wor·thy** *adj* of vehicles, fit for use on the road. **road·wor·thi·ness** *n.*

roam [roum] *v* **1** go about with no special aim: *to roam through the fields.* **2** wander over: *They roamed the world in search of adventure.* **roam·er** *n.* ⟨Middle English *romen*⟩

roan [roun] *adj* of an animal, brownish sprinkled with grey or white. ⟨French; Spanish *roano*⟩

roar [rɔr] *v* **1** make a loud, deep sound: *The lion roared.* **2** laugh loudly. **roar** *n.* **roar·er** *n.* ⟨Old English *rārian*⟩
roar·ing *adj* booming: *a roaring business.*
adv so much that one seems to roar: *roaring mad.* **roar·ing·ly** *adv.* **roaring forties** the stormy region in the North Atlantic Ocean, between 40° and 50° latitude. **roaring twenties** the decade of the 1920s.

roast [roust] *v* **1** cook (meat, etc.) by dry heat. **2** dry by heating: *to roast coffee beans.* **3** make or become very hot. **4** *Informal* **a** ridicule in public. **b** criticize severely.
n **1** a piece of meat to be roasted. **2** an informal outdoor meal, at which food is cooked over an open fire: *a wiener roast.* **3** a special dinner for a well-known figure who is to be good-humouredly ridiculed by other guests. **roast·ed** *adj.* **roast·ing** *adj.* ⟨Old French *rostir*⟩
roast·er *n* **1** a pan used in roasting. **2** a chicken, young pig, etc. fit to be roasted.

rob [rɒb] *v* **robbed, rob·bing 1** steal from: *He was robbed of all his money.* **2** keep from

having or doing: *The disease has robbed him of his strength.* **rob·ber** *n.* **rob·ber·y** *n.* ⟨Old French *rober;* Germanic⟩
rob Peter to pay Paul take something away from one to pay or satisfy another.

robe [roub] *n* **1** a loose outer garment. **2** a garment that shows rank, office, etc.: *a judge's robe.* **3 ✷** formerly, the dressed skin of a buffalo or other animal, used esp for protection against moisture and cold. **4** a bathrobe or dressing gown.
v put a robe on; dress. ⟨Old French *robe* orig, booty. See ROB.⟩

rob·in [ˈrɒbən] *n* a large thrush having a brick-red breast and abdomen. ⟨Old French, diminutive of Robert⟩
Robin Hood 1 *English legend* the leader of an outlaw band, who robbed the rich to help the poor. **2** a person who helps the poor by acting illegally against wealthy people or institutions. **robin run** the first run of maple syrup. Compare FROG RUN.

ro·bot [ˈroubɒt] *n* **1** a machine in the shape of a human. **2** a person who acts in a dull, mechanical way. **ro·bot·ic** [rouˈbɒtɪk] *adj.* **ro·bot·i·cal·ly** *adv.* ⟨coined by Karel Capek, 20c Czech playwright; Czech *robotnik* serf⟩
ro·bot·ics [rouˈbɒtɪks] or [rə-] *n* the use of robots for tasks normally done by people.

ro·bust [rouˈbʌst] *adj* **1** sturdy: *a robust person.* **2** durable. **3** having a full flavour, as coffee or wine. **4** of software, versatile, flexible, and not likely to cause crashes. **ro·bust·ly** *adv.* **ro·bust·ness** *n.* ⟨Latin *robustus* orig, oaken; *robur* oak⟩

roc [rɒk] *n Legend* a bird of enormous size and strength. ⟨Arabic *rokh, rukhkh*; Persian⟩

rock[1] [rɒk] *n* **1** a large mass of stone. **2** any piece of stone. **3** *Geology* **a** the mass of mineral matter of which the earth's crust is made up. **b** a particular type of such matter. **4** something firm like a rock; support. **5** a curling stone. **6** *Slang* a precious stone, esp a diamond. **7 the Rock ✷** the island of Newfoundland. **rock·like** *n.* ⟨Old French *roque;* Latin *rocca*⟩
on the rocks a wrecked; ruined. **b** *Informal* bankrupt. **c** of alcoholic drinks, with ice but without water or mixes: *whisky on the rocks.*
rock bottom the lowest level. **rock–bot·tom** *adj.* **hit rock bottom** reach the lowest level of one's life. **rock candy** sugar in the form of large, hard crystals. **rock garden** or **rock·er·y** *n* an ornamental garden consisting of an arrangement of rocks and earth for growing plants and flowers. **rock·hound** *n Informal* a person who collects rocks as a hobby. **Rock·ies** *n pl* ROCKY MOUNTAINS. **rock salt** common salt as it occurs in the earth in large crystals. **rock tripe** any of various lichens that grow attached to rocks; they are edible when cooked and can be used as emergency food by northern travellers, etc. **rock·y** *adj* full of rocks: *a rocky shore.* **Rocky Mountains** a range of mountains in Alberta and British Columbia, and the western US.

rock[2] [ˈrɒk] *v* **1** sway. **2** move violently: *The*

earthquake rocked the houses. **3** upset or be upset: *The family was rocked by the news.* **4** put to sleep with swaying movements.
n lively popular music with a heavy, regular beat, usually played with electronically amplified instruments. ⟨Old English *roccian*⟩ **rock the boat** *Informal* make trouble; esp, disturb or upset a stable situation. **rock–and–roll** or **rock'n'roll** *n* a style of popular music with a heavy beat, an early form of rock music. **rock·er** *n* **1** one of the curved pieces on which a cradle, rocking chair, etc. rocks. **2** ROCKING CHAIR. **3** a rock music singer or musician. **4** a fan of rock music. **off one's rocker** *Slang* crazy. **rocking chair** a chair mounted on rockers, or on springs, so that it can rock back and forth. **rocking horse** a toy horse on rockers, for children to ride. **rock·y** *adj* **1** likely to rock; unsteady: *That table is a bit rocky; put a piece of wood under the short leg.* **2** filled with hazards: *New businesses face a rocky future this year.* **3** *Informal* sickish; dizzy. **rock·i·ly** *adv.* **rock·i·ness** *n.*

rock·et¹ [ˈrɒkɪt] *n* **1** a projectile consisting of a tube filled with some substance that burns rapidly, creating expanding gases that propel the tube at great speed. **2** a spacecraft, missile, etc. propelled by such a projectile.
v move extremely fast. ⟨Italian *rochetta* diminutive of *rocca* distaff; for the shape⟩ **rock·et·ry** *n* the designing and firing of rockets, missiles, etc.

rock·et² [ˈrɒkɪt] *n* any of various plants of the mustard family esp one grown as a salad green. ⟨Italian *ruchetta* diminutive of *ruca*; Latin *eruca* a herb⟩

rock·y¹ See ROCK¹.

rock·y² See ROCK².

ro·co·co [rəˈkoukou] *n* **1** *Design* a style marked by elaborate ornamentation. **2** *Literature* a style of florid, ornamental writing. **3** *Music* a style characterized by graceful ornamentation. **ro·co·co** *adj.* ⟨French *rococo*; perhaps *rocaille* shellwork⟩

rod [rɒd] *n* **1** a cylindrical bar of any hard substance such as metal. **2** anything resembling a rod in shape. **3** a springy, tapered piece of wood, metal, etc., used for fishing. **4** *Slang* pistol. **5** one of the sense organs in the retina of the eye that are sensitive to dim light. ⟨Old English *rodd*⟩

rode [roud] *v* pt of RIDE.

ro·dent [ˈroudənt] *n* any of an order of gnawing mammals having a single pair of continually growing incisors in both the upper and lower jaws. ⟨Latin *rodere* gnaw⟩

ro·de·o [ˈroudiou] or [rouˈdeiou] *n, pl* -de·os **1** a contest of skill in roping cattle, riding horses, etc. **2** *esp US* the driving together of cattle; roundup. ⟨Spanish; *rodear* go around⟩

rod·o·mon·tade [ˌrɒdəmənˈteid] or [-ˈtɑd] *n* vain boasting; bragging. **rod·o·mon·tade** *adj, v.* ⟨French; *Rodomonte*, braggart in a work of 16c Italian poet L. Ariosto⟩

roe¹ [rou] *n* **1** fish eggs. **2** the spawn of certain crustaceans. ⟨Middle English *rowe*⟩

roe² [rou] *n* in full, **roe deer** a small Eurasian deer with forked antlers. ⟨Old English *rā*⟩

roent·gen [ˈrɛntgən] or [ˈrɛntjən]; [ˈrʌnt-], [ˈrɒnt-] *n* the unit for measuring the effect of X rays or gamma rays. ⟨W. K. *Roentgen*, 20c German physicist⟩

rog·er [ˈrɒdʒər] *interj Informal* message received and understood; O.K. ⟨signaller's code for the letter *r*, for 'received'⟩

rogue [roug] *n* **1** a dishonest person. **2** a mischievous person. **3** an animal with a savage nature that lives apart from the herd: *rogue elephant.* **4** *Biology* an individual, usually a plant, that varies from the standard. **ro·guish** *adj.* **ro·guish·ly** *adv.* **ro·guish·ness** *n.* ⟨perhaps from *roger* beggar⟩ **ro·guer·y** *n* **1** trickery. **2** mischief. **rogues' gallery** a collection of photographs of known criminals and suspects, kept by the police for identification purposes.

roil [rɔɪl] *v* **1** make (a liquid) cloudy or muddy by stirring up sediment. **2** agitate or disturb. ⟨French *rouiller* rust, earlier, to muddy; Old French *rouil* mud, rust⟩

rois·ter [ˈrɔɪstər] *v* be boisterous; swagger. **rois·ter·er** *n.* **rois·ter·ous** *adj.* ⟨Middle French *ruistre* rude; Latin *rus* the country⟩

role or **rôle** [roul] *n* **1** a performer's part in a play, opera, etc.: *the leading role.* **2** a part played in real life: *He played an important role in the development of art in Canada.* ⟨French *rôle* roll (of paper) on which a part is written⟩ **role model** someone regarded as an inspiration for younger or less experienced people to imitate. **role–play** *v* act in an imaginary situation for therapeutic or other purposes: *to role-play an interview.*

roll [roul] *v* **1** move or cause to move by turning over: *A ball rolls.* **2** wrap or become wrapped around some thing: *Roll the string into a ball.* **3** move or be moved on wheels: *The car rolled along.* **4** move smoothly: *Waves roll in on the beach.* **5** revolve on an axis: *to roll an airplane.* **6** move from side to side: *The ship rolled in the waves.* **7** rise and fall again: *rolling country.* **8** make flat or smooth with a roller. **9** beat (a drum) with rapid continuous strokes. **10** *Informal* have more than enough (only in progressive tenses): *be rolling in money.* **11** of eyes, move or turn from side to side and up and down.
n **1** something rolled up: *rolls of paper.* **2** a rounded mass. **3** motion up and down, or side to side. **4** a rapid, continuous beat on a drum. **5** a deep sound: *the roll of thunder.* **6** a list: *Call the roll.* **7 a** a piece of dough often rolled over and then baked: *a dinner roll.* **b** a cake rolled up after being spread with something: *jelly roll.* ⟨Old French *roller*; Latin *rotula* diminutive of *rota* wheel⟩
roll around occur at regular intervals, esp as part of a cycle: *Exams have rolled around again.* **roll back** cause (prices, wages, etc.) to return to a lower level. **roll in** *Informal.* **a** luxuriate

in large amounts of: *They appear to be rolling in money.* **b** arrive in large numbers: *The pledges rolled in, to the delight of the fundraisers.* **a roll in the hay** *Slang* an occasion of sexual intercourse. **on a roll** *Informal* in a period of good luck: *She's really on a roll; all her deals have paid off lately.* **strike someone off the rolls** expel from membership.

roll·a·way *adj* referring to anything on rollers or wheels designed for easy moving and storage when not in use: *a rollaway cot.* **roll bar** a strong steel bar in the shape of an inverted U that sits over a vehicle, to prevent crushing if the vehicle rolls over. **roll call** the calling of a list of names, as of soldiers, pupils, etc., to find out who are present. **rolled oats** oats that have been pressed flat between rollers. **roll·er** *n* **1** a cylinder of metal, wood, etc., used for pressing, crushing, etc. **2** a covered cylinder used for applying paint, ink, etc. **3** a long, swelling wave. **4 ✴** *Logging* a logger who piles logs on a skidway. **Rollerblade** *n Trademark* a type of roller skate with four wheels in a single row. Also called **inline skate**. **roller coaster** a railway built for amusement, on which small cars roll up and down steep inclines, round corners, etc., at high speed. **roller skate** one of a pair of skates with small wheels, two at the front and two at the back, used on floors, roads, sidewalks, etc. **roll·er–skate** *v.* **roller skater. roll·ing** *n* the action, motion, or sound of anything that rolls or is being rolled: *the rolling of a ball.* *adj* that rolls: *Rolling land rises and falls in gentle slopes.* **rolling pin** a cylinder of solid wood, marble, etc., for rolling out dough. **rolling stock** the locomotives and cars of a railway. **roll·mop** *n* a fillet of herring rolled and marinated in brine, and served as an appetizer. **roll–top** *adj* having a top that rolls back: *a roll-top desk.* **ro·ly–po·ly** ['rouli 'pouli] *adj* short and plump: *a roly-poly puppy.*

rol·lick ['rɒlɪk] *v* frolic; be merry. **rol·lick·ing** *adj.* **rol·lick·ing·ly** *adv.* **rol·lick·some** *adj.* ⟨origin uncertain⟩

ROM Read-Only Memory.

ro·maine [rou'mein] *n* a variety of lettuce having long green leaves with crinkly edges, joined loosely at the base. ⟨French = Roman⟩

Ro·man ['roumən] *n* **1** a native or inhabitant of ancient or modern Rome. **2 roman** roman print. **3** the characters of the Roman alphabet: *The same Mandarin name may have several different spellings in Roman.* *adj* **1** to do with ancient or modern Rome or its people. **2** to do with the Roman Catholic Church. **3** *Architecture* to do with a style developed by the ancient Romans, characterized by rounded arches. **4 roman** of or designating an upright style of type. Compare ITALIC. ⟨Latin *Roma* Rome⟩ **Roman alphabet** or **Latin alphabet** the alphabet used to write Latin; our present alphabet derived from this. **Roman Catholic** a member of the Catholic Church that acknowledges the Pope as its head. **Roman**

Catholicism. **Roman numerals** the system of numerals used by the ancient Romans. The values of the numerals are added together, except when a numeral is followed by another of greater value, in which case the smaller one is subtracted from the larger one. *Examples:* XI = 10 + 1 = 11; IX = 10 − 1 = 9; XIX = 10 + (10 − 1) = 19.

roman à clef [ʀɒmãna'kle] *pl* **ro·mans à clef** [ʀɒmãza'kle] *French* a novel featuring real people or events slightly disguised, as with fictitious names. ⟨French = novel with key⟩

ro·mance ['roumæns] *or* [rou'mæns] *n* **1** a love story. **2 a** a medieval story or poem telling of heroes and adventures. **b** any story of adventure. **3** the literary genre comprising any of these types of story. **4** a quality of real events that suggests such stories: *the romance of an explorer's life.* **5** a love affair. **6** *Music* a short, lyrical composition. *v* [rou'mæns] **1** make up extravagant or romantic stories. **2** think or talk in a romantic way. **3** exaggerate or lie. **4** court romantically. **ro·manc·er** [rou'mænsər] *n.* ⟨Old French *romanz*; Latin *romanice* in a Romance language⟩

Romance languages languages descended from Latin, as Italian, Spanish, Portuguese, Romanian, Catalan, French, and Provençal. **ro·man·tic** [rou'mæntɪk] *adj* **1** characteristic of romances or romance: *romantic tales of love and war.* **2** having feelings suited to romance: *a romantic teenager.* **3** Often, **Romantic** to do with art, music, and literature appealing to the emotions; not classical: *Chopin's music is romantic.* *n* **1** a romantic person. **2 Romantic** an artist of the Romantic period. **ro·man·ti·cal·ly** *adv.* **ro·man·ti·cism** *n* **1** a movement in literature and art characterized by an emotional treatment of life, nature, and the supernatural. **2** *Music* a style characterized by melodic inventiveness and rich harmonies. **ro·man·ti·cist** *n.* **ro·man·ti·cize** *v* **1** give a romantic character to. **2** be romantic; act, talk, or write in a romantic manner. **ro·man·ti·ci·za·tion** *n.*

Rom·a·ny ['rɒməni] *n* **1** Gypsy. **2** the Indic language of the Gypsies. **Rom·a·ny** *adj.*

Ro·me·o ['roumi,ou] *n* any romantic male lover. ⟨hero of Shakespeare's *Romeo and Juliet*⟩

romp [rɒmp] *v* **1** play in a lively, boisterous way. **2** run, go, or win easily. **romp** *n.* ⟨variant of *ramp*. See RAMPANT.⟩

romp·ers *n pl* a loose one-piece garment, worn by young children and consisting of a blouselike top and short, elasticized legs.

ron·deau ['rɒndou] *or* [rɒn'dou] *n, pl* **ron·deaux** [-z] a short poem with thirteen (or ten) lines on two rhymes. The opening words are used in two places as an unrhymed refrain. The poem "In Flanders Fields" is a rondeau. ⟨Middle French variant of *rondel* diminutive of *rond* round; Latin *rotundus*⟩

ron·del ['rɒndəl] *or* [rɒn'dɛl] *n* a short poem, usually with fourteen lines and two rhymes. The initial couplet is repeated in the middle and at the end.

ron·do ['rɒndou] *n, pl* **-dos** *Music* a composition or movement having one principal theme to which return is made after the introduction of each subordinate theme. ⟨Italian; French *rondeau* rondeau⟩

roof [ruf] *n, pl* **roofs** or **rooves** **1** the outermost top covering of a building. **2** something that resembles the roof of a building: *the roof of the mouth.* **3** a home. *v* cover with or as if with a roof. ⟨Old English *hrōf*⟩
go through the roof or **hit the roof** lose one's temper violently. **raise the roof** *Informal* create an uproar.
roof·er *n* a person who makes or repairs roofs. **roof·ing** *n* material used for roofs. **roof·less** *adj* **1** having no roof. **2** having no home or shelter. **roof·top** *n* the roof of a building, esp the outer surface.

rook¹ [rʊk] *n, v n* **1** a common European bird closely related to the North American crow. **2** *Slang* a person who cheats at cards, etc. *v Slang* cheat. ⟨Old English *hrōc*⟩

rook² [rʊk] *n Chess* one of the pieces, also called a castle because its top is the shape of a battlement. ⟨Old French *roc*; Persian *rukh*⟩

rook·ie ['rʊki] *n Informal* a beginner, such as a recruit or a new player on a team. ⟨perhaps alteration of *recruit*⟩

room [rum] *n* **1** a part of a building, with walls separating it from the rest. **2** **rooms** *pl* lodgings. **3** the people in a room: *This room is awfully quiet all of a sudden.* **4** space: *There is little room to move in a crowd.* **5** opportunity: *room for improvement, room for advancement.* *v* rent a room; lodge: *The two women roomed together.*⟨Old English *rūm*⟩
room·er *n* a person who lives in a rented room. **room·ette** *n* a small, single bedroom on some railway cars. **room·ful** *n* **1** enough to fill a room. **2** the people or things in a room. **room·ie** *n Informal* room-mate. **rooming house** a house with rooms to rent. **room–mate** *n* a person who shares a room or apartment with another or others. **room service** in a hotel, lodge, etc., a special service by which one may order food or drink to be brought to one's room. **room·y** *adj* having plenty of space. **room·i·ly** *adv*. **room·i·ness** *n*.

roost [rust] *n* **1** a bar on which birds rest or sleep. **2** a place for birds to roost in. **3** a place to rest or stay: *a robber's roost.* *v* **1** sit or sleep on a roost. **2** settle down, as for the night. ⟨Old English *hrōst*⟩
come home to roost have unforeseen and unfavourable consequences for the originator: *His wild stories came home to roost when everyone thought they were about him.* **rule the roost** *Informal* be in charge. **roost·er** *n* a male domesticated fowl; cock.

root¹ [rut] *n* **1** the part of a plant that grows downward to hold the plant in place, absorb water and food from the soil, and often to store food material. **2** something like a root in shape, use, etc.: *the roots of the hair.* **3** a thing from which other things grow: *What is the root of her success?* **4** the essential part: *to get to the root of a matter.* **5 roots** *pl* one's heritage: *searching for one's roots.* **6** *Mathematics* **a** the quantity that produces another quantity when multiplied by itself a certain number of times. 2 is the cube root of 8 ($2 \times 2 \times 2 = 8$). **b** the quantity that satisfies an equation when substituted for an unknown quantity. **7** *Grammar* a word element from which other words are derived. *Example: Room is the root of* roominess.
v **1** send out roots and begin to grow: *Some plants root more quickly than others.* **2** fix firmly: *She was rooted to the spot by surprise.*
root·like *adj*. ⟨Old English *rōt*; Old Norse *rót*⟩ **root out** get rid of completely: *to root out corruption in government.* **take root** become firmly established.
root beer a soft drink flavoured with the juice of the roots of certain plants such as sarsaparilla. **root canal 1** the central passage in the root of a tooth, containing blood vessels and nerves. **2** treatment for an infected or damaged root canal. **root cellar** part of a house or barn below ground level, used for storing root vegetables. **root crop** a crop grown for its large, edible, underground parts: *Beets, turnips, and parsnips are examples of root crops grown in Canada.* **root·less** *adj* having no roots: *a rootless transient.* **root·less·ness** *n*. **root·less·ly** *adv*. **root·stock** *n* **1** rhizome. **2** a plant with another plant grafted on top.

root² [rut] *v* **1** dig with the snout: *Pigs like to root in gardens.* **2** poke; pry; search. ⟨Old English *wrōtan*⟩

root³ [rut] *v Informal* enthusiastically cheer a contestant, etc. **root·er** *n*. ⟨probably earlier *rout* shout, roar; Old Norse *rauta*⟩

rooves [ruvz] *n* a pl of ROOF.

rope [roup] *n* **1** a thick cord made of smaller cords twisted together. **2** a number of things twisted or strung together: *a rope of pearls.* *v* **1** enclose or mark off with a rope. **2** catch (a horse, etc.) with a lasso. **rop·y** *adj* ⟨Old English *rāp*⟩
give someone rope let a person act freely. **know the ropes** know the procedures involved in an activity. **rope in** (or **into**) *Slang* get or lead (someone) into some activity by trickery or persuasion: *We were roped into hosting this dinner.* **the end of one's rope** the end of one's resources, endurance, etc. **rope ladder** a ladder made of rope. When secured at the top, it hangs down for climbing.

Roque·fort ['roukfərt] *n* a strongly flavoured cheese made of goats' milk and veined with mould. ⟨*Roquefort*, S France⟩

ror·qual ['rɔrkwəl] *n* any of a genus of baleen whales of the same family as the humpback, having grooves running along the throat to the belly. See also BLUE WHALE. ⟨French; Norwegian *röyrkval*, literally, red whale⟩

Ror·schach test ['rɔrʃɑk] a test that reveals personality traits, based on the subject's interpretation of ten different ink-blot designs. ⟨H. *Rorschach*, 20c Swiss psychiatrist⟩

ro·sa·cea [rou'zeiʃə] n a skin disease affecting the face, with redness and pimples. ⟨Latin *rosa* rose[1]⟩

ro·sa·ceous [rou'zeiʃəs] *adj* **1** belonging to the rose family. **2** rose-coloured.

ro·sa·ry ['rouzəri] n **1** a string of beads for keeping count in saying a series of prayers. **2** a series of prayers said with this. ⟨Latin *rosarium* rose garden; *rosa* rose[1]⟩

rose[1] [rouz] n **1** any of a genus of shrubs having compound leaves, showy flowers, and, usually, prickly stems. **2** something suggesting a rose, such as a rosette, compass card, the sprinkling nozzle of a watering can. **rose·like** *adj*. ⟨Latin *rosa*⟩
come up roses go or turn out extremely well. **smell the roses** enjoy life. **under the rose** (**sub rosa** in Latin; the rose is the emblem of silence) in secret; privately.

ro·sé [rou'zei] n a light, pink wine. **ro·se·ate** ['rouziit] *or* [-,eit] *adj* **1** rose-coloured; rosy. **2** cheerful; optimistic. **rose·bud** n the bud of a rose. **rose·bush** n a shrub that bears roses. **rose–col·oured** or **rose–col·ored** *adj* **1** pinkish red. **2** bright; cheerful; optimistic. **rose–coloured glasses** an optimistic, but usually unfounded, view of a situation. **rose·mar·y** n a shrub widely cultivated for its fragrant leaves that are used as a flavouring. **ro·se·o·la** [rou'ziələ] *or* [,rouzi'oulə] n **1** rubella. **2** any rose-coloured rash. **ro·sette** n **1** a rose-shaped ribbon given as a prize at a livestock show, etc. **2** a circular cluster of leaves, petals, etc. **rose water** water containing oil of roses, used as a perfume, cosmetic, and in cooking. **rose window** a circular window, usually of stained glass. **rose·wood** n the reddish wood of any of various tropical trees of the pea family, valued for fine furniture. **ros·y** *adj* **1** like a rose; pinkish red. **2** bright; cheerful: *a rosy future*. **ros·i·ness** n. **ros·i·ly** *adv*.

rose[2] [rouz] *v* pt of RISE.

Rosh Ha·sha·nah or **Ha·sha·na** ['rɒʃ hə'ʃanə] *or* [rouʃ-] *Hebrew* ['ʀɒʃ haʃa'na] the Jewish New Year, falling usually in September or October. ⟨Hebrew = beginning of the year⟩

ro·shi ['rouʃi] n in Zen Buddhism, a term of respect for a wise teacher, the head of a monastery, or the chief priest of a temple.

ros·in ['rɒzən] n a hard, yellow substance made from pine resin that can be rubbed on violin bows and on the shoes of acrobats, etc. to keep them from slipping. **ros·in** *v*. ⟨Middle English variant of *resin*⟩

ros·ter ['rɒstər] n **1** a list of people's names and their duties. **2** any list. ⟨Dutch *rooster*, orig grid, gridiron; *roosten* roast⟩

ros·trum ['rɒstrəm] *n*, *pl* -trums or -tra [-trə] a platform or stage for public speaking. ⟨Latin = beak; for speakers' platform in Roman forum, decorated with the beaks of captured war galleys⟩

rot [rɒt] *v* rot·ted, rot·ting **1** decay; spoil. **2** cause to decay. **3** disintegrate because of

decay. **4** lose or cause to lose vigour.
n **1 a** decay. **b** the state of being decayed. **2** any of various diseases of plants marked by decay. **3** *Slang* nonsense; rubbish.
interj an exclamation expressing annoyance, contempt, disagreement, or disgust. ⟨Old English *rotian*⟩

rot·ten *adj* **1** spoiled: *a rotten egg*. **2** not in good condition: *rotten wood*. **3** corrupt; dishonest. **4** *Slang* bad; nasty. **rot·ten·ly** *adv*. **rot·ten·ness** *n*. **rotten ice** ✹ ice that has become honeycombed in the course of melting and almost decomposed.

ro·ta ['routə] *n* a roster. ⟨Latin *rota* wheel⟩
ro·ta·ry *adj* turning on an axis like a wheel.
rotary system ✹ *Education* a method under which students move to different rooms (and specialist teachers) for different subjects.

ro·tate ['routeit] *or* [rou'teit] *v* **1** move or cause to move around a centre or axis. **2** take turns or cause to take turns: *Farmers rotate crops to keep the soil from losing its fertility.* ⟨Latin *rotare*; *rota* wheel⟩
ro·ta·tion *n* **1** the act of moving around a centre or axis: *The earth's rotation causes night and day.* **2** a regular ordered change. **3** one complete turn of a body around its axis.
ro·ta·tion·al *adj*. **ro·ta·tor** ['routeitər] *or* [rou'teitər] *n* a muscle that turns a part of the body.

rote [rout] *n* a set way of doing things. ⟨Middle English⟩
by rote by memory.

ro·ti·fer ['routəfər] *n* any of a phylum of minute aquatic invertebrates having at one end of the body a disk with one or more rings of cilia. ⟨Latin *rota* wheel + *ferre* carry⟩

ro·ti·ni [rou'tini] *n pl* pasta in the shape of spirals. ⟨Italian⟩

ro·tis·se·rie [rou'tɪsəri] *n* a rotating spit for roasting meat or fowl. ⟨French; *rôtir* to roast⟩

ro·tor ['routər] *n* **1** the rotating part of a machine or apparatus. **2** a system of rotating blades by which a helicopter is enabled to fly. ⟨shortened from *rotator*⟩

ro·to·till·er ['routou,tilər] *n* a tool with motorized rotary blades for breaking up the soil. **ro·to·till** *v*.

rot·ten, rotter See ROT.

Rott·weil·er ['rɒtwailər] *n* any of a breed of large, powerful dogs having a coat of black hair with tan markings. ⟨*Rottweil*, SW Germany where bred for herding⟩

ro·tund [rou'tʌnd] *adj* **1** round; plump. **2** full-toned: *a rotund voice*. **ro·tund·ly** *adv*. **ro·tun·di·ty** *n*. ⟨Latin *rotundus* round; *rota* wheel⟩
ro·tun·da *n* **1** a circular building or part of a building, esp one with a dome. **2** a large room with a high ceiling, such as a hotel lobby or the concourse of a railway station.

rou·é [ru'ei] *or* ['ruei] *n* a dissipated man; rake. ⟨French; *rouer* break on the wheel; *roue* wheel, Latin *rota*⟩

rouge [ruʒ] *n* **1** a red powder or cream for colouring the cheeks or lips. **2** a red powder, chiefly ferric oxide, used for polishing metal, jewels, etc. **3** ✱ _Football_ a play in which the team receiving a punt behind its own goal line does not carry the ball back into play, thus conceding a point to the opposition. _v_ **1** colour with rouge. **2** ✱ _Football_ **a** score a rouge. **b** tackle (a defender) in the end zone so as to score a rouge: ⟨French = red⟩

rough [rʌf] _adj_ **1** not smooth; not level: _a rough road._ **2** without fine finish: _rough diamonds._ **3** without luxury: _a rough life in camp._ **4** without culture: _a rough person._ **5** not perfected: _a rough idea._ **6** harsh; rude: _rough manners._ **7** disorderly: _a rough crowd._ **8** _Informal_ unpleasant; severe: _She was in for a rough time._ **9** requiring strength rather than skill: _rough work._ **10** stormy: _rough weather._ **11** harsh to the ear: _a rough voice._ _n_ **1** a violent person. **2** _Golf_ a part of a golf course where there is long grass, etc. _v_ **1** treat roughly (usually with _up_): _to rough someone up._ **2** _Sports_ illegally check, tackle, etc. (an opponent) with unnecessary roughness. **3** shape roughly: _to rough out a plan, to rough in the outlines for a drawing._ _adv_ in a rough manner: _They play rough._ **rough·ness** _n._ **rough·en** _v._ ⟨Old English _rūh_⟩ **in the rough** coarse; crude. **rough diamond** a good person with a gruff manner. **rough it** live without conveniences: _She spent last summer roughing it in a remote camp._ **rough·age** _n_ the parts of food with a high fibre content which stimulate the intestines. **rough–and–read·y** _adj_ crude, but effective. **rough–and–tum·ble** _adj_ showing confusion and violence; with little regard for rules. **rough·cast** _n_ a coarse plaster for outside surfaces. **rough·cast** _v._ **rough fish** a fish that has no commercial value and is also not valued as a sport fish. **rough–hewn** _v_ crude: _rough-hewn manners._ **rough·house** [-ˌhʌus] _Slang n_ rowdy conduct. **rough·house** [-ˌhaʊz] _v._ **rough·ing** _n Sports_ the illegal act of checking, tackling, etc. an opponent with unnecessary roughness. **rough·ly** _adv_ **1** in a rough manner. **2** approximately. **rough·neck** _n_ **1** _Informal_ a coarse, bad-mannered person; a rowdy. **2** _Slang_ a member of an oil-drilling crew. **rough·rid·er** _n_ **1** a person used to tough riding. **2** a person who breaks and rides wild horses. **rough·shod** _adj_ having horseshoes equipped with sharp caulks to prevent slipping. **ride roughshod over** show no consideration for; treat roughly; domineer.

rou·lette [ruˈlɛt] _n_ a gambling game in which a wheel is spun and players bet on where it will stop. ⟨French; literally = little wheel⟩

round [raʊnd] _adj_ **1** having a circular or curved outline or surface. **2** large: _a good round sum of money._ **3** _Mathematics_ being an integer, not a fraction: _25 is a round number._ **4** to the nearest unit, ten, hundred, etc.: _The cost of the trip should be $500 in round figures._ **5** frank: _We scolded him in good round terms._ **6** with a full tone: _a mellow, round voice._ _n_ **1** anything shaped like a ball, circle, cylinder, etc. **2** a fixed course ending where it begins: _The watchman makes his rounds of the_ building every hour. **3** a series (of events, etc.): _a round of duties._ **4** a section of a game or sport: _a round in a boxing match._ **5** the firing of a single discharge from a number or group of rifles, guns, etc. at the same time. **6** a single bullet, artillery shell, etc. **7** a single serving of something, usually a drink, to each member of the group: _It's my round._ **8** an act that a number of people do together: _a round of applause._ **9** _Music_ a short song, sung by several persons or groups beginning one after the other: _"Three Blind Mice" is a round._ _v_ **1** make or become round: _The carpenter rounded the corners of the table._ **2** go around: _They rounded the corner._ **3** turn around: _The bear rounded and faced the hunters._ _adv, prep_ around: _We stood round her._ **round·ness** _n._ ⟨Old French _roonde_; Latin _rotundus_ round⟩ **in the round** _Theatre_ with the audience sitting all the way around a central area. **make** (or **go**) **the rounds** (or **round**) **a** go about from place to place in a certain course. **b** be passed, told, etc. by people from one to another. **round and about** in various places. **round off a** finish; complete: _round off a meal with dessert._ **b** express (a number) in the nearest unit, ten, hundred, etc.. **round on** turn on to attack, or as if to attack. **round out a** give or acquire a rounder contour. **b** complete: _to round out a paragraph._ **round up a** draw or drive together. **b** collect; muster: _Round up the usual suspects._ **round·a·bout** _adj_ indirect: _a roundabout route._ **round·ed** _adj_ well-balanced in regard to tastes, abilities, etc. (often compounded with **well**-): _a well-rounded person._ **round·house** _n_ **1** a circular building for storing or repairing locomotives, built about a turntable. **2** _Nautical_ a cabin on the after part of a ship's quarterdeck. **3** _Informal_ a punch delivered with a wide swing. **4** _Baseball_ a widely curved pitch. **round·ish** _adj_ somewhat round. **round·ly** _adv_ severely, or fully: _He was roundly scolded for getting in so late._ **round robin 1** a petition, etc., with the signatures written in a circle so that it is impossible to tell who signed first. **2** _Sports_ a system of scheduling a number of games, in which every competing player or team is matched with every other one. **round–shoul·dered** _adj_ having the shoulders bent forward. **round table** a group of persons assembled for an informal discussion, etc. **round–the–clock** _adj_ taking place through all 24 hours of the day: _This retirement home provides round-the-clock care._ **round trip** a journey to a specific destination and back. **round·up** _n_ **1** the act of driving or bringing cattle or horses together from long distances. **2** a gathering together of people or things: _a roundup of criminals._

USAGE

In Canadian usage there is a definite preference for **around**, especially in speech, written dialogue, and technical writing. **Round** has a slightly more literary flavour.

rouse [raʊz] *v* **1** wake up: *I was roused by the telephone.* **2** excite: *She was roused to anger by the insult.* **rous·er** *n*. ⟨origin uncertain⟩
rous·ing *adj* able to rouse: *a rousing speech.* **rous·ing·ly** *adv.*

roust·a·bout ['raʊstə,baʊt] *n Informal* an unskilled labourer on docks, ships, ranches, circuses, etc. ⟨*roust* move, stir + *about*⟩

rout[1] [raʊt] *n* **1** a complete defeat. **2** a group of followers. **3** a mob; rabble. **4** a riot; disturbance.
v **1** put to flight: *Our soldiers routed the enemy.* **2** defeat completely. ⟨Old French *route* breakup; Latin *rupta* pp of *rumpere* break⟩

rout[2] [raʊt] *v* **1** dig (*out*). **2** put (*out*): *The farmer routed his sons out of bed at five o'clock.* **3** dig with the snout, as pigs do. **4** poke; search; rummage. **5** hollow out or gouge with or as with a ROUTER. ⟨variant of *root*[2]⟩
rout·er *n* a tool or machine for cutting grooves in or hollowing out wood or metal.

route [rut] *or* [raʊt] *n* **1** a way to go; road. **2** a fixed, regular course or area assigned to a person making deliveries, sales, etc.: *a newspaper route, a milk route.*
v send by a certain route. ⟨Old French; Latin *rupta (via)* (a way) opened up; *rumpere* break⟩

rou·tine [ru'tin] *n* **1** a fixed, regular method of doing things: *Getting up and going to bed are parts of your daily routine.* **2** an act or skit that is part of some entertainment. **3** a choreographed series of movements in dance, gymnastics, etc. **4** *Computers* a set of instructions for a specific operation. *adj* **1** using routine: *a routine operation.* **2** average or ordinary: *a routine performance.* **rou·tine·ly** *adv.* ⟨French; *route* route⟩

rove [rouv] *v* wander; wander about; roam. ⟨origin uncertain⟩
rov·er *n* **1** a wanderer or roamer. **2** *Lacrosse* a player who holds no special position but who may rove over the entire field.

rov·er[1] See ROVE.

rov·er[2] ['rouvər] *n* **1** a pirate. **2** a pirate ship. ⟨Middle Dutch *rover; roven* rob⟩

row[1] [rou] *n* a line of people or things: *a row of houses.* ⟨Old English *rāw*⟩
hard row to hoe a difficult thing to do.

row[2] [rou] *v* move a boat by means of oars. **row** *n.* **row·er** *n.* ⟨Old English *rōwan*⟩
row·boat *n* a small boat moved by oars. **rowing machine** an exercise machine in which one can perform the movements of rowing. **row·lock** *n* oarlock.

row[3] [raʊ] *n* **1** a noisy disturbance. **2** *Informal* a squabble. **row** *v.* ⟨origin uncertain⟩
row·dy *n* a rough, disorderly, quarrelsome person. **row·dy** *adj.* **row·di·ly** *adv.* **row·di·ness** *n.* **row·dy·ism** *n.*

roy·al ['rɔɪəl] *adj* **1** to do with kings and queens: *the royal family.* **2** like a king or queen; noble; majestic: *royal dignity.* **3** fine; excellent; supreme. **roy·al·ly** *adv.* ⟨Old French *roial,* Latin *regalis; regis* king⟩
royal assent the signature of the Queen or her representative giving approval to a bill, which can then become law. **Royal Canadian Legion** a Canadian organization of former military personnel, esp war veterans. **Royal Canadian Mounted Police** the federal police force of Canada. *Abbrev* **RCMP** or **R.C.M.P.** **royal commission** in Canada and the UK, any investigation commissioned by the Crown to inquire into some matter on behalf of a government. **royal flush** *Poker* a straight flush consisting of the Ace, King, Queen, Jack, and ten of one suit. **roy·al·ist** *n* a supporter of a royal government. **royal jelly** a highly nutritious substance secreted by worker honey bees, fed to all larvae during their first few days, and afterward only to those larvae selected to be queens. **Royal North West Mounted Police** the earlier (1905-1920) name for the ROYAL CANADIAN MOUNTED POLICE. **roy·al·ty** *n* **1** a royal person; royal persons. **2** a share of the profits paid to an owner of a patent or copyright.

rpm or **r.p.m.** revolutions per minute.

rps or **r.p.s.** revolutions per second.

R.R. **1** RURAL ROUTE. **2** railroad.

RRSP Registered Retirement Savings Plan.

R.S.V.P. or **r.s.v.p.** please reply (for French *répondez s'il vous plaît*).

Rt.Hon. RIGHT HONOURABLE.

rub [rʌb] *v* **rubbed, rub·bing** **1** move (one thing) back and forth (against another): *Rub your cold hands to warm them.* **2** apply (polish, a mixture, etc.), using pressure or friction. **3** remove or be removed by rubbing (usually with *off* or *out*): *The spot won't rub off.*
n **1** the act of rubbing. **2** a difficulty: *The rub came when both girls wanted to sit with the driver.* ⟨Middle English *rubben*⟩
rub down massage. **rub·down** *n.* **rub it in** *Informal* keep on mentioning something humiliating. **rub off on** **a** cling to; become part of; take hold of. **b** *Informal* of abstract qualities, become part of someone's behaviour: *Some of her charitable nature has rubbed off on her children.* **rub out a** erase; be erased. **b** *Slang* kill. **rub the right (wrong) way** please (annoy).
rub·bing *n* an image of an engraved surface, made by rubbing charcoal, graphite, etc. over a piece of paper placed on top of the surface. **rub·by** *n* ✷ *Slang* a person who drinks any substance containing rubbing alcohol, hence, an alcoholic, esp a derelict.

rub·a·boo or **rub·ba·boo** ['rʌbə,bu] *n* ✷ a soup made by boiling pemmican in water with flour and other ingredients. ⟨Cdn. French *rababou;* Algonquian⟩

rub·ber[1] ['rʌbər] *n* **1** an elastic substance obtained from various tropical plants. **2** a waterproof overshoe. **3** any of various things made of rubber or a similar substance, such as a condom or an eraser. **4** *Slang* a hockey puck. **rub·ber·like** *adj.* ⟨*rub*⟩
rubber cheque *Slang* a cheque that bounces, i.e. has insufficient funds to cover it. **rub·ber–chick·en circuit** the tour made by an

after-dinner speaker, the dinners being noted for tough chicken as the main course. **rubber ice** ✹ esp in the North, thin, flexible ice on the surface of seas, lakes, etc. Also, **rubbery ice. rub·ber·ize** v cover or treat with rubber. **rub·ber·neck** Slang n a person who stares and gapes, esp a tourist. v stare; gape. **rubber stamp** 1 a stamp for printing dates, signatures, etc. 2 Informal a person or group that approves something without thought or without power to refuse. **rub·ber–stamp** v. **rub·ber·y** adj like rubber; elastic; tough.

rub·ber² ['rʌbər] n Card games, esp bridge or whist 1 a series of three or five games to be won by a majority. 2 the deciding game in such a series. ⟨origin uncertain⟩

rub·bish ['rʌbɪʃ] n 1 useless stuff; trash. 2 nonsense. ⟨Middle English robys⟩

rub·ble ['rʌbəl] n rough, broken stones, bricks, etc. ⟨Middle English robel⟩

ru·bel·la [ru'bɛlə] n a contagious viral infection characterized by a fine red rash; German measles. ⟨Latin, diminutive of rubeus red⟩

ru·be·o·la [ru'biələ] or [,rubi'oulə] n measles. It is commonly called **red measles** to differentiate it from German measles (rubella). ⟨Latin, diminutive of rubeus red⟩

ru·bid·i·um [ru'bɪdiəm] n a metallic element resembling potassium. Symbol **Rb** ⟨Latin rubidus red; for two red lines in its spectrum⟩

ru·bric ['rubrɪk] n 1 any rule or guide. 2 a title of a chapter, a law, etc., written or printed in red or in special lettering. ⟨Latin rubrica red colouring matter; ruber red⟩

ru·by ['rubi] n a red precious stone. adj deep, glowing red: ruby lips. **ru·by·like** adj. ⟨Old French rubi; Latin rubeus red⟩

ruck·sack ['rʌk,sæk] or ['rʊk,sæk] n knapsack. ⟨German = back sack⟩

ruck·us ['rʌkəs] n Slang a noisy disturbance or uproar; row. ⟨possibly ruc(tion) + (rump)us⟩

rud·der ['rʌdər] n 1 a hinged, flat piece of wood or metal that projects into the water at the rear end of a boat, by which the vessel is steered. 2 a similar piece on an aircraft hinged to the rear of the fin. **rud·der·less** adj. **rud·der·like** adj. ⟨Old English rōthor⟩

rud·dy ['rʌdi] adj reddish: a ruddy glow. **rud·di·ly** adv. **rud·di·ness** n. ⟨Old English rudig⟩

rude [rud] adj 1 impolite. 2 coarse; crude: a rude cabin. 3 violent; harsh: Rude hands seized me and threw me into the car. 4 robust: rude health. **rude·ly** adv. **rude·ness** n. ⟨Latin rudis⟩

ru·di·ment ['rudəmənt] n 1 Usually, **rudiments** pl a part to be learned first: the rudiments of grammar. 2 something in an early stage of development. ⟨Latin rudimentum; rudis rude⟩ **ru·di·men·ta·ry** [,rudə'mɛntəri] adj. **ru·di·men·ta·ri·ly** adv.

rue¹ [ru] v be sorry for; regret (something). **rue·ful** adj. **rue·ful·ly** adv. ⟨Old English hrēowan⟩

rue² [ru] n any of a genus of aromatic plants that yield a bitter oil formerly used in medicine. ⟨Latin ruta, Greek rhytē⟩

ruff [rʌf] n a deep frill worn around the neck by people in the 16c. ⟨possibly ruffle⟩

ruf·fian ['rʌfjən] n a brutal, or cruel person. **ruf·fian·ism** n. **ruf·fian·ly** adj. ⟨Middle French⟩

ruf·fle ['rʌfəl] v 1 make rough or uneven: A breeze ruffled the lake. 2 of a bird, make (feathers) stand erect. 3 disturb: Nothing can ruffle her calm temper. 4 become ruffled. n 1 a roughness in a surface. 2 a strip of cloth gathered along one edge and attached to a garment, etc. for decoration. ⟨Middle English⟩

rug [rʌg] n 1 a heavy fabric floor covering. 2 a thick, warm cloth used as covering. 3 Slang artificial turf. 4 Slang a toupee. **rug·like** adj. ⟨Scandinavian⟩

rug·by ['rʌgbi] n a game played by teams who carry, pass, or kick an oval ball toward the opposing team's goal. Also, **rug·ger**. ⟨Rugby, famous school for boys in England⟩

rug·ged ['rʌgɪd] adj 1 uneven: rugged ground. 2 vigorous: The pioneers were rugged people. 3 strong and irregular: rugged features. 4 rude; unrefined: rugged manners. **rug·ged·ly** adv. **rug·ged·ness** n. ⟨Scandinavian⟩

ru·in ['ruən] n 1 a building, wall, etc. that has fallen to pieces. 2 **ruins** pl that which is left, esp of a building, wall, etc. that has fallen to pieces: the ruins of an ancient city. 3 destruction; overthrow: The duke's enemies planned his ruin. 4 the cause of destruction or downfall: Drink was his ruin. 5 bankruptcy. v 1 destroy. 2 make bankrupt. ⟨Latin ruina; ruere collapse⟩ **ru·in·a·tion** n ruin; destruction; downfall. **ru·in·ous** adj 1 bringing ruin. 2 fallen into ruins. **ru·in·ous·ly** adv.

rule [rul] n 1 a principle governing conduct: the rules of the game. 2 what usually happens or is done: Fair weather is the rule in June. v 1 make a formal decision: The judge ruled against them. 2 control; govern; direct. 3 prevail: Prices of wheat ruled high all year. 4 mark with straight lines. ⟨Old French riule; Latin regula straight stick, regere guide⟩ **as a rule** usually. **rule out** eliminate or exclude: The police ruled out foul play in the woman's death. **work to rule** See WORK. **rule of thumb** 1 a rule based on experience rather than on scientific knowledge. 2 a rough, practical method of procedure. **rul·er** n 1 a person who rules; monarch; dictator. 2 a straight strip of wood, metal, etc., marked in units, used in drawing lines or in measuring. **rul·ing** n a decision of a judge or court or a government body. adj 1 that rules; controlling. 2 predominating; prevalent.

rum [rʌm] n a distilled alcoholic drink made from molasses, etc. ⟨origin uncertain⟩ **rum·run·ner** n a person who or ship that smuggles alcoholic liquor into a country.

rum·ba ['rʌmbə] n a dance having a complex, syncopated rhythm. **rum·ba, -baed, -ba·ing** v. Also, **rhum·ba**. ⟨Spanish; probably of African origin⟩

rum·ble ['rʌmbəl] v make a deep, heavy, continuous sound.

n **1** a deep, heavy, continuous sound: *the rumble of thunder.* **2** *Slang* a teenage gang fight. ⟨Middle English *romblen*⟩

ru·mi·nate ['rumə,neit] *v* **1** ponder. **2** chew (food) for a second time; chew the cud. **ru·mi·nat·ing·ly** *adv.* **ru·mi·na·tion** *n.* **ru·mi·na·tor** *n.* ⟨Latin *rumen* gullet⟩ **ru·mi·nant** *n* an animal that chews the cud. Cows, sheep, and camels are ruminants. *adj* **1** belonging to the group of ruminants. **2** meditative; reflective. **ru·mi·na·tive** *adj* meditative. **ru·mi·na·tive·ly** *adv.*

rum·mage ['rʌmɪdʒ] *v* search thoroughly by moving things about: *I rummaged in my drawer for a pair of gloves.* *n* **1** a rummaging search. **2** odds and ends. **rum·mag·er** *n.* ⟨Middle French *arrumage; arrumer* stow cargo; *run* ship's hold⟩ **rummage sale** a sale of odds and ends, usually to raise money for charity.

rum·my ['rʌmi] *n* a card game in which points are scored by assembling sets of three or four cards of the same rank or sequences of the same suit. ⟨origin uncertain⟩

ru·mour or **ru·mor** ['rumər] *n* **1** a story talked of as news without any proof. **2** vague talk: *Rumour has it that she will marry him.* *v* tell or spread by rumour. ⟨Latin *rumor*⟩

rump [rʌmp] *n* **1** the hind part of the body of an animal. **2** the corresponding part of the human body; buttocks. ⟨Scandinavian⟩

rum·ple ['rʌmpəl] *v* crumple; crush; wrinkle: *This dress rumples easily.* *n* a wrinkle; crease. ⟨Middle Dutch *rumpelen*⟩

rum·pus ['rʌmpəs] *n* *Informal* a noisy disturbance or uproar. ⟨origin uncertain⟩ **rumpus room** RECREATION ROOM.

run [rʌn] *v* **ran, run, run·ning** *v* **1** go faster than walking: *I prefer running to jogging.* **2** go hurriedly: *Run for help.* **3 a** perform by, or as by, running: *to run errands.* **b** carry or take by, or as by, running: *Can you run this book over to the library for me?* **4** creep; trail; climb: *Vines run along the sides of the road.* **5** pass or cause to pass quickly: *A thought ran through my mind.* **6** stretch; extend: *Shelves run along the walls.* **7** range: *Her courses this term run from art history to applied chemistry.* **8** force; thrust: *He ran a splinter into his hand.* **9** flow or cause to flow: *Don't run the water needlessly.* **10** discharge fluid: *My nose is running.* **11** get; become: *Never run into debt.* **12** have a typical specified quality, size, price, etc.: *These jeans run $50 a pair.* **13** of colour, spread: *The colour ran when the dress was washed.* **14** continue: *a lease to run two years.* **15 a** be a candidate for election: *She ran in the last election.* **b** put up as a candidate: *All the parties are running more women this time.* **16** enter (a horse, etc.) in a race. **17** expose oneself to: *to run a risk.* **18** keep operating or cause to keep operating: *to run a machine.* **19** be published or publish: *The newspapers didn't run the story about the moose.* **20** conduct; manage: *to run a business.* **21** get through: *to run a blockade.* **22** smuggle: *to run*

rum. **23** have (an advertisement, etc.) published in a newspaper. **24** soften; melt: *The wax ran when the candles were lit.* **25** pass to or from the sea; migrate, as for spawning: *The salmon are running.* **26** return often to the mind: *That tune has been running in my head.* **27** *Computers* execute (a program): *She ran the accounts receivable program.*

n **1** the act of running: *a run to the corner and back.* **2** a running pace: *to set out at a run.* **3** a spell or period of causing (a machine, etc.) to operate. *During a run of eight hours the factory produced a run of 100 cars.* **4** a trip, esp a journey over a certain route: *The ship reached port after a six-week run.* **5** *Baseball, cricket* the unit of score: *Our team scored four runs in the last inning.* **6** a period: *a run of bad luck.* **7** a succession of performances: *This play has had a two-year run.* **8** an unbroken sequence of scoring plays in snooker, etc. **9** a succession of demands: *a run on the bank to draw out money.* **10** *Music* a rapid succession of tones. **11** freedom to use: *The guests were given the run of the house.* **12** a movement of fish to spawning grounds: *a run of salmon.* **13** any large number of animals moving together. **14** a track: *a ski run.* **15** an enclosed space for animals: *a dog run.* **16** a place where stitches have become undone: *a run in a stocking.* **17** an act of smuggling: *a rum run.* **18 the runs** *pl* *Slang* diarrhea. ⟨Old English *rinnan* run, pp *runnen*⟩

a run for one's money a strong competition. **b** satisfaction for one's efforts. **in the long** (or **short**) **run** over the long (or short) term. **on the run** a hurrying: *The butcher had so many orders that he was on the run all day.* **b** in retreat or rout: *Victory is ours; the enemy is on the run.* **c** the state of being a fugitive. **run across** meet by chance. **run a fever** have a body temperature higher than normal. **run after** seek the attention or company of (someone), esp aggressively. **run away a** escape; flee. **b** desert one's home, family, etc. permanently. **run away with a** elope with. **b** steal. **c** win by doing far better than others. **d** cause to go out of control: *Her imagination ran away with her.* **run down a** stop working. **b** hunt down. **c** knock down by running against or by riding or driving. **d** speak disparagingly against. **e** decline or reduce in vigour or health; deteriorate. **f** *Baseball* put (a base runner) out after trapping him or her between bases. **run down** (or **over**) **to** make a quick visit to. **run for it** run for safety. **run in a** pay a short visit: *We'll just run in for a minute.* **b** *Informal* arrest: *He was run in for drunken driving.* **run into a** meet by chance. **b** crash into; collide with. **run off a** drain or flow away. **b** drive away or off. **c** print; duplicate: *I ran off 100 copies.* **d** run away; flee: *He ran off when he heard the police sirens.*

run off at the mouth talk too much, esp about confidential information. **run on** continue indefinitely, esp in speech. **run out** come to an end; become exhausted. **run out** (*of*) use up; have no more: *I've run out of* *sugar.* **run over a** ride or drive over: *The car ran over some glass.* **b** overflow: *Coffee ran over into the saucer.* **c** exceed a limit. **d** go through quickly: *Please run over these figures to check my addition.* **run through a** consume or spend rapidly: *The spendthrift ran through his inheritance in a year.* **b** pierce. **c** review; rehearse. **run up** *Informal* **a** make quickly: *Do you like this dress? I just ran it up.* **b** collect; accumulate: *Don't run up a big bill.*

run·a·round *n Slang* a series of excuses, evasions, etc.: *They gave him the runaround.* **run·a·way** *n* a person or animal that runs away, or that runs out of control. *adj* **1** to do with being a runaway: *a runaway horse.* **2** easily accomplished: *a runaway victory.* **3** of prices or inflation, rising uncontrollably. **run·down** *n* **1** a brief summary. **2** *Baseball* the act of putting a base runner out after trapping him or her between bases. **run–down** *adj* **1** tired; sick. **2** falling to pieces: *a run-down building.* **run–in** *n Informal* a sharp disagreement: *I had a run-in with the director this morning.* **run·ner** *n* **1** a person who or animal that runs. **2** messenger: *a runner for a bank.* **3** either of the narrow pieces on which a sleigh or sled slides. **4** the blade of a skate. **5** RUNNING SHOE. **6** a long, narrow strip: *a carpet runner.* **7** a stem that grows along the ground and takes root, thus producing new plants. **run·ner–up** *n* the person, player, or team that takes second place in a contest. **run·ning** *n* management or care: *the running of a business. adj* **1** flowing: *running water.* **2** carried on continuously and concurrently: *a running commentary.* **3** following in succession: *for three nights running.* **4** of the normal run of a train, bus, etc.: *the running time between towns.* **5** performed with or during a run: *a running leap.* **be in (out) of the running** have a chance (no chance) to win. **running board** a metal step beneath the doors of some vehicles, to make it easier for passengers to get in and out. **running foot** a one-foot length of some continuous material whose width is constant, as carpet on a roll. **running lights 1** lights required by law to be displayed on an aircraft or vessel between the times of sunset and sunrise. **2** lights on a vehicle that go on automatically if the vehicle is running. **running mate** *esp US* a candidate running jointly with another, but for a less important office. **running shoe** a light casual shoe used for sports or for general casual wear. **run·ny** *adj* **1** having a tendency to flow: *The pie filling is a bit runny.* **2** of the nose, continuously discharging mucus. **run·off** *n* **1** the running off of water during a spring thaw or after a heavy rain. **2** a final, deciding race or contest. **run–of–the–mill** *adj* ordinary, average, or commonplace: *a run-of-the-mill design.* **run–on** *adj* **1** *Poetry* continuing to the next line without punctuation. **2** *Grammar* of a sentence, having too many clauses put loosely together, without proper punctuation or transitional material. **run–on entry** in a

dictionary, a derived word that is not defined. *Rurally* may be found as a run-on entry under *rural.* **run·way** *n* **1** a level surface on which aircraft land and take off. **2** a ramp, such as that at a boat launching site. **3 ✹** the channel or bed of a watercourse. **4** a long tongue of stage extending into the audience, commonly used for fashion shows.

rune [run] *n* **1** any letter of an ancient Germanic or Turkic alphabet. **2** a poem or other composition with magic meaning. **ru·nic** *adj.* ⟨Old Norse *rún*⟩
runic alphabet an alphabet used by the ancient Germanic peoples, loosely based on the Greco-Roman alphabet, for carving on wood or stone.

rung[1] [rʌŋ] pp of RING[2].

rung[2] [rʌŋ] *n* **1** a rod or bar used as a step of a ladder. **2** a crosspiece set between the legs of a chair. ⟨Old English *hrung*⟩

run·nel [ˈrʌnəl] *n* a small stream or brook. ⟨Old English *rynel; rinnan* run⟩

runt [rʌnt] *n* an animal, person, or plant that is smaller than the usual size. **runt·y** *adj.* ⟨origin uncertain⟩

rup·ture [ˈrʌptʃər] *n* **1** the tearing apart of body tissue: *the rupture of a muscle.* **2** any breaking apart or break of relations: *the rupture of a marriage.* **rup·ture** *v.* ⟨Latin *ruptura; ruptus* pp of *rumpere* burst⟩

ru·ral [ˈrʊrəl] *adj* **1** to do with the country or the people who live in the country: *a rural upbringing.* **2** to do with agriculture: *the rural economy.* **ru·ral·ly** *adv.* **ru·ral·ism** *n.* **ru·ral·ist** *n.* ⟨Latin *rus, ruris* the country⟩
rural municipality ✹ in certain provinces, a municipal district in a rural area, administered by an elected reeve and council. *Abbrev* **R.M. rural route** a postal service by which mail is delivered to the mailboxes of individual farms or country businesses from a local post office. *Abbrev* **R.R.**

ruse [ruz] *or* [rus] *n* a trick; stratagem. ⟨French; *ruser* dodge⟩

rush[1] [rʌʃ] *v* **1** move with speed or force: *We rushed along.* **2** come, go, act, etc. with speed or haste: *He rushes into things without thinking.* **3** *Informal* lavish much attention on: *He rushed the girl all summer.* **4** *Informal* attempt to persuade to join a fraternity or sorority. **5** advance (a football) by running. *n* **1** the act of rushing: *the rush of the flood.* **2** busy haste: *the rush of city life.* **3** a great or sudden effort of many people to go somewhere or get something: *Few people got rich in the Klondike gold rush.* **4** an eager demand: *A sudden rush of business kept everyone working hard.* **5** *Football* an attempt to carry the ball through the opposing line. **6** *Informal* the lavishing of much attention, as in courting. **7 rushes** *pl* the first prints of film shot for a movie. **8** *Informal* the onset of euphoria, with or without drugs; high. *adj* **1** requiring haste: *a rush order.* **2** done in a rush: *a rush job.* **rush·er** *n.* ⟨Anglo-French *russher,* Old French *ruser.* See RUSE.⟩

with a rush suddenly; quickly.
rush hour the time of day when traffic is heaviest or when trains, buses, etc. are most crowded. **rush–hour** *adj.*

rush² [rʌʃ] *n* any of a genus of marsh plants having round, pithy stems, widely used for mats, baskets, etc. **rush·like** *adj.* ⟨Old English *rysc*⟩

rusk [rʌsk] *n* a light, crisp, sweet biscuit. ⟨Spanish, Portuguese *rosca* roll⟩

rus·set ['rʌsɪt] *adj* reddish brown. *n* a coarse, russet-coloured cloth. ⟨Old French *rousset*; Latin *russus* red⟩

Russian roulette ['rʌʃən] **1** a deadly game in which each player in turn spins the cylinder of a revolver that has been loaded with only one bullet, points the muzzle at his or her head, and pulls the trigger. **2** any potentially deadly or destructive activity.

rust [rʌst] *n* **1** the reddish brown coating that forms on iron or steel when exposed to air or moisture. **2** any oxidization resembling rust. **3** a plant disease that spots leaves and stems. **4** a reddish brown or orange.
v **1** become covered with rust. **2** cause to rust: *Rain rusted the old shovel kept outside.* **3** allow to degenerate by not using. **4** degenerate by not being used: *Don't let your mind rust during vacation.* ⟨Old English *rust, rūst*⟩
rust·buc·ket *n Slang* **1** a leaky boat or ship. **2** a rusting car or one that is prone to rust.
rust·less *adj* **1** free from rust. **2** rustproof.
rust·proof *adj* resisting rust. *v* treat with a preparation that resists rust. **rust·y** *adj* **1** covered with rust; rusted: *a rusty knife.* **2** coloured like rust. **3** faded: *a rusty black.* **4** weakened from lack of use: *My mother says her biology is rusty.* **rust·i·ly** *adv.* **rust·i·ness** *n.*

rus·tic ['rʌstɪk] *adj* **1** to do with the country; rural: *rustic furnishings.* **2** plain: *His rustic speech and ways made him uncomfortable in the city school.* **3** rough; awkward.
n a country person or one regarded as being from the country because he or she is awkward, boorish, etc. **rus·ti·cal·ly** *adv.* ⟨Latin *rus* the country⟩
rus·ti·cate *v* **1** go to or live in the country. **2** send to the country. **rus·ti·ca·tion** *n.*
rus·tic·i·ty *n* **1** a rustic quality, characteristic, or peculiarity. **2** rural life.

rus·tle ['rʌsəl] *v* **1** make a succession of light, soft sounds, as of things gently rubbing together: *leaves rustling in the breeze.* **2** move (something) so that it makes such a sound: *We could hear her rustling papers.* **3** *Informal* steal (cattle, etc.).
n a light, soft sound. ⟨Old English *hrūxlian* make noise⟩
rustle up *Informal* **a** gather; find. **b** get ready; prepare: *I rustled up some food.* **rus·tler** *n Informal* a cattle thief.

rut¹ [rʌt] *n* **1** a track made in the ground, esp by a wheel. **2** a fixed way of acting, esp a dull routine: *She decided to change jobs because she felt she was getting into a rut.* *v* **rut·ted, rut·ting** make a rut or ruts in. ⟨possible variant of *route*⟩

rut² [rʌt] *n* the sexual excitement of deer, goats, etc., occurring at regular intervals.
v **rut·ted, rut·ting** be in rut. ⟨Old French *ruit;* Latin *rugitus* bellowing; *rugire* bellow⟩

ru·ta·ba·ga ['rutə,beigə] *or* [,rutə'beigə] *n* a turnip with a very large yellowish root. ⟨dialect Swedish *rotabagge* literally, root bag⟩

ru·the·ni·um [ru'θiniəm] *n* a brittle, metallic element of the platinum group. *Symbol* **Ru** ⟨*Ruthenia,* Russia, where found⟩

ruth·less ['ruθlɪs] *adj* having no pity; showing no mercy; cruel. **ruth·less·ly** *adv.* **ruth·less·ness** *n.* ⟨Middle English *reuthe* pity⟩

RV RECREATIONAL VEHICLE.

–ry *noun-forming suffix* **1** the occupation or work of a——: *dentistry.* **2** the act of a——: *mimicry.* **3** the quality, state, or condition of a——: *rivalry.* **4** a group of——s, considered collectively: *peasantry.* ⟨short form of *-ery*⟩

rye [raɪ] *n* **1** a cereal grass widely grown for grain and straw. **2** bread made from rye flour: *a corned beef on rye.* **3** whisky made from rye. **4** ✳ a blended whisky made from rye and other grains; Canadian whisky. ⟨Old English *ryge*⟩

Ss

s or S [ɛs] *n, pl* **s's** or **S's 1** the nineteenth letter of the English alphabet, or any speech sound represented by it. **2** the nineteenth person or thing in a series. **3** something shaped like the letter S.

's¹ an abbreviation of *is, has*, or *does*, added to the preceding pronoun or noun. *Examples: He's here. She's put it away. What's that mean?*

's² an abbreviation of *us*, used with *let* to make the first person plural imperative: *Let's go.*

S 1 south; southern. **2** sulphur.

S. 1 south; southern. **2** School. **3** Saturday or Sunday. **4** September. **5** Section. **6** Senate. **7** Sea. **8** Society.

Sab·bath ['sæbəθ] *n* **1** a day of the week observed as a day of rest and worship. The Sabbath is Friday evening to Saturday evening for Jews, and Sunday for most Christians. **2** sabbath any day or period of rest. (Hebrew *shabbāth; shābath* to rest)
sab·bat·i·cal [sə'bætɪkəl] *n* in full, **sabbatical leave** a leave of absence given to academics, esp once in seven years, for study and travel.

sa·ble ['seibəl] *n* a small carnivorous mammal, related to the martens, with glossy dark fur. (Old French; Slavic)

sab·o·tage ['sæbə,taʒ] *n* **1** the destruction of machinery, tools, etc., by workers as a threat or protest. **2** damage by civilians or enemy agents to interfere with a military operation or war effort. **3** any attempt to hinder. **sab·o·tage** *v.* **sab·o·teur** [,sæbə'tɜr] *n.* (French; *saboter* bungle, walk noisily; *sabot* clog)

sa·bre ['seibər] *n* **1** a heavy, curved sword. **2** a light, tapered, flexible sword for fencing. Also, **sa·ber.** (French; alteration of *sable*, Hungarian *száblya; szabni* cut)
sa·bre–rat·tling *n* a show of military strength in order to intimidate.

sac [sæk] *n* a baglike part in an animal or plant, often containing liquid. **sac·like** *adj.* (French; Greek *sakkos* sack¹. See SACK¹.)

sac·cha·rin ['sækərɪn] *n* a sweet substance obtained from coal tar, used as a calorie-free substitute for sugar. (Greek *sakcharon;* Sanskrit *çarkarā* orig gravel, grit)
sac·cha·rine ['sækərɪn] *adj* **1** too sweet. **2** so exaggeratedly friendly or agreeable as to be unpleasant; ingratiating: *a saccharine smile.*

sa·chem ['seitʃəm] *n* **1** among Algonquian First Nation peoples or Native Americans, a hereditary chief, esp of a confederacy. **2** any Aboriginal leader. (Algonquian)

sa·chet [sæ'ʃei] *n* **1** a small bag or pad containing perfumed powder, dried flowers, etc., used for scenting linens and clothes. **2** a small packet of shampoo, lotion, etc. (French, diminutive of *sac* sack¹)

sack¹ [sæk] *n* **1** a large bag, usually made of coarse cloth, for grain, potatoes, coal, etc. **2** *Slang* bed: *He was still in the sack at 10 a.m.*

3 the sack *Informal* dismissal from a job: *He got the sack for always coming in late.*
v **1** *Informal* discharge from a job; fire. **2** put in a sack or sacks. **sack·ful** *n.* (Hebrew *saq*)
hit the sack *Slang* go to bed.
sack·cloth *n* **1** Also, **sacking** coarse cloth for making sacks. **2** a garment of such cloth, worn as a sign of mourning or penance.

sack² [sæk] *v* plunder or pillage: *The invaders sacked the town.* **sack** *n.* **sack·er** *n.* (Latin *saccare* take by force)

sac·ra·ment ['sækrəmənt] *n* **1** in some Christian churches, any of certain sacred ceremonies, such as baptism. **2 Sacrament** the Eucharist. (Latin *sacramentum; sacer* holy)
sac·ra·men·tal *adj* to do with a sacrament.
sac·ra·men·tal·ly *adv.* **sac·ra·men·tal·i·ty** *n.*
sa·cred ['seikrɪd] *adj* **1** dedicated to or coming from God or a god; holy: *a sacred altar.* **2** religious: *sacred music.* **3** worthy of highest respect: *sacred oaths.* **4** dedicated (*to* a revered person or thing): *This tomb is sacred to the memory of the Unknown Soldier.* **sa·cred·ness** *n.*
sacred cow a person or thing so highly regarded as to be beyond criticism. **sac·ri·fice** ['sækrə,fais] *n* **1** the act of offering to a god. **2** the thing offered: *an animal sacrifice.* **3** the act of giving up one valued thing for the sake of a more valued thing: *the sacrifice of one's life for an ideal.* **4** *Baseball* a bunt or fly that lets a runner advance although the batter is put out. **sac·ri·fice** *v.* **sac·ri·fi·cial** [-'fɪʃəl] *adj.*
sac·ri·fi·cial·ly *adv.* **sac·ri·lege** ['sækrəlɪdʒ] *n* disrespectful treatment of anyone or anything sacred: *Robbing a church is a sacrilege.*
sac·ri·le·gious [-'lɪdʒəs] *adj.* **sac·ro·sanct** [-,sæŋkt] *adj* most sacred or revered; not to be violated or mocked.

sad [sæd] *adj* **sad·der, sad·dest 1** feeling, expressing, or bringing sorrow or regret: *a sad day.* **2** drab or dull: *sad browns and greys.* **3** pitiable: *a sad mess.* **sad·den** *v.* **sad·ly** *adv.* **sad·ness** *n.* (Old English *sæd* sated)

sad·dle ['sædəl] *n* **1** a seat for a rider on a horse or other animal. **2** the seat on a bicycle, etc. **3** anything shaped or used like a saddle. **4** a ridge between two mountain peaks.
v **1** put a saddle on. **2** burden: *She is saddled with that big house.* (Old English *sadol*)
in the saddle in a position of control.
sad·dle·bag *n* **1** one of a pair of bags laid over an animal's back behind the saddle. **2** a similar bag hanging over the rear wheel of a bicycle or motorcycle. **sad·dle·cloth** *n* a cloth put between an animal's back and the saddle. **sad·dler** *n* a person who makes or sells saddles and harness. **sad·dler·y** *n.* **saddle soap** a special soap containing oil, used for cleaning and preserving leather articles.

sa·dhu ['sɑdu] *n* a Hindu holy man. (Sanskrit = straight)

sad·ism ['sædɪzəm] *or* ['seidɪzəm] *n* **1** delight in inflicting pain. **2** gratification, esp sexual, obtained by inflicting pain or humiliation on one's partner. Compare MASOCHISM. **sad·ist** *n.* **sa·dis·tic** *adj.* **sa·dis·ti·cal·ly** *adv.* (Marquis de Sade (1740-1814), who described it)

sad·o·mas·o·chism [,seidou'mæsə,kızəm] *or* [,sædou-] *n* the combination of sadism and masochism in a personality or relationship. **sad·o·mas·o·chist** *n*. **sad·o·mas·o·chis·tic** *adj*.

sa·fa·ri [sə'fɑri] *n* a journey or hunting expedition, esp in E Africa.
adj to do with a style of clothing like that worn on safari; esp, designating a belted jacket with pairs of large pockets. ⟨Arabic⟩

safe [seif] *adj* **1** free or giving freedom from harm or danger: *a safe place*. **2** unharmed: *safe and sound*. **3** beyond power of doing harm: *a criminal safe in prison*. **4** free of risk: *a safe move*. **5** reliable: *a safe guide*. **6** *Baseball* (of a player) reaching a base or home plate without being out.
n **1** a strong, lockable container for keeping valuables. **2** *Slang* a condom. **safe·ly** *adv*. ⟨Old French *sauf*; Latin *salvus*⟩
safe–con·duct *n* **1** the privilege of passing safely through a region, esp in time of war. **2** a paper granting this privilege. **safe·crack·ing** *n* the act of breaking into safes and stealing the contents. **safe·crack·er** *n*. **safe·guard** *v* guard against harm: *Food laws safeguard our health*. **safe·guard** *n*. **safe·keep·ing** *n* protection. **safe sex** sexual intercourse using a condom and other precautions to guard against pregnancy and STDs such as AIDS. **safe·ty** *n* **1** the fact or state of being safe; freedom from harm or danger: *to reach safety. I doubt the safety of that procedure*. **2** a device on a firearm, machine, etc., designed to prevent accidental injury. **3** *Football* SAFETY TOUCH. **safety belt** SEAT BELT. **safety deposit box** a box in the vault of a bank, etc., for storing valuables. **safety glass** glass that resists shattering. **safety island** a marked area in the middle of a thoroughfare for pedestrians boarding and getting off streetcars. **safety match** a match that ignites only when struck on a specially prepared surface. **safety pin** a pin bent back on itself to form a spring, with a guard covering the point. **safety touch** ✻ *Football* the act of failing to move the ball from one's end zone, thus conceding two points to the opposing team. **safety valve 1** a valve in a boiler, etc., that opens to let steam or fluid escape when the pressure becomes too great. **2** something that lets one vent anger, etc. harmlessly: *to use aerobics as a safety valve to relieve stress*.

SYNONYMS
Safe emphasizes being not exposed to harm: *The children are safe in their own yard*. **Secure** emphasizes being free from risk and protected against loss, attack, injury, or other perceived danger: *Children feel secure with their parents*.

saf·flow·er [ˈsæ,flaʊər] *n* a herb of the composite family with seeds that are rich in oil. ⟨*saf(fron)* + *flower*⟩

saf·fron [ˈsæfrən] *n* the dried orangey yellow stigmas of a variety of crocus, used to flavour and colour food. **saf·fron** *adj*. ⟨French *safran*; Arabic *za'faran*⟩

sag [sæg] *v* **sagged, sag·ging 1** bend down in the middle under a weight. **2** hang down unevenly or baggily: *Your dress sags in the back*. **3** grow weary or weak; sink: *Her spirits sagged*. **4** of sales, prices, etc., decline. **sag** *n*. ⟨possibly Scandinavian⟩

sa·ga [ˈsɑgə] *or* [ˈsægə] *n* **1** any medieval Norse prose story of heroic deeds. **2** any long or complex story filled with drama (often facetious): *She told us the ongoing saga of her cousin's marital problems*. ⟨Old Norse⟩

sa·ga·cious [sə'geiʃəs] *adj* wise in a practical, far-sighted way; shrewd. **sa·ga·cious·ly** *adv*. **sa·gac·i·ty** [sə'gæsiti] *n*. ⟨Latin *sagacis*⟩

sag·a·more [ˈsægə,mɔr] *n* **1** among some Algonquian First Nations or Native Americans, an elected ruler or chief. **2** sachem. ⟨earlier *sagamo*; Algonquian⟩

sage¹ [seidʒ] *adj* wise.
n a very wise person. **sage·ly** *adv*. **sage·ness** *n*. ⟨Old French; Latin *sapere* be wise⟩

sage² [seidʒ] *n* **1** any of a genus of plants of the mint family used as seasoning. **2** sagebrush. **sage** *adj*. ⟨Old French *sauge*; Latin *salvia*⟩
sage·brush *n* any of several shrubs of the composite family, smelling like sage.

sa·go [ˈseigou] *n*, *pl* **-goes** a starch from the pith of the **sago palm**, used as a thickener and as a fabric stiffener. ⟨Malay *sagu*⟩

sa·hib [ˈsɑb] *or* [ˈsɑhɪb] *n* sir; master; a title of respect used to or of a white man by Indians in colonial India. ⟨Hindi; Arabic *çāḥib* lord⟩

said [sɛd] *v* pt and pp of SAY.
adj mentioned before: *the said witness*.

sail [seil] *n* **1** a piece of cloth spread to the wind to make a boat or raft move over water. **2** anything like a sail, such as the part of an arm of a windmill that catches the wind. **3** a trip on a sailboat: *Let's go for a sail*.
v **1** travel on (water) by the action of wind on sails: *to sail down a river*. **2** travel on any ship: *She is sailing to Europe on a cargo vessel*. **3** manage or navigate (a ship or boat): *learning to sail*. **4** begin a trip by water: *We sail at 2*. **5** move smoothly, effortlessly, etc.: *He sailed through his exams*. ⟨Old English *segl*⟩
sail into a attack; beat. **b** criticize; scold. **set sail** begin a trip by water. **under sail** moving with sails spread out.
sail·board *n* a long, narrow board with a sail, for moving across water. The rider stands and holds onto a horizontal bar attached to the mast. **sail·board·ing** *n*. **sail·boat** *n* a boat moved by a sail or sails. **sail·cloth** *n* canvas or other fabric used for sails. **sail·er** *n* a ship with reference to sailing power: *a fast sailer*. **sail·or** [ˈseilər] *n* **1** a relatively low-ranking member of the navy or of the crew of a ship or boat. **2** a person who travels by water, with reference to skill, or to liability to seasickness: *She's a keen sailor. I'm a bad sailor*. **sail·plane** *n* a light glider that can stay aloft for a long time. *v* fly such a glider.

saint [seint] *n* **1** *Roman Catholic Church* a person formally declared to be in heaven, on the evidence of his or her holy and divinely empowered life on earth. **2** a humble, patient, kind person. **3 Saint** a title before the name of a canonized person or archangel: *Saint Hilda, St. Michael.* **Abbrev St.** or **S.**; *pl* **Sts.** or **SS.** *v* declare or consider a saint. **saint·ed** *adj.* **saint·hood** *n.* **saint·ly** *adj.* ⟨Latin *sanctus*⟩

St. Jean Baptiste Day [sɛ̃ ʒɑ̃ bap'tist] ✹ the former name of June 24, the Québec holiday celebrating French-Canadian culture, now officially called **Fête nationale.** It is the feast day of St. John the Baptist, patron saint of Québec. **St.–John's–wort** ['dʒɒnz ,wɜrt] *n* any of various shrubs or herbs, some cultivated as flowers and one having a mild antidepressant effect. **Saint Nicholas** ['nɪkələs] SANTA CLAUS. **St. Pat·rick's Day** ['pætrɪks] March 17th, the feast of St. Patrick, patron saint of Ireland.

saith [sɛθ] *v Archaic* 3rd person singular, present tense, of SAY. *She saith* means *she says.*

sake¹ [seik] *n* ⟨Old English *sacu* cause at law⟩ **for goodness'** (or **Pete's, heaven's, gosh,** etc.) **sake(s)** *Informal* an exclamation of surprise, impatience, annoyance, etc. **for its own sake** just because it is what it is: *He likes exercise for its own sake.* **for old times' sake** in memory of former days. **for the sake of a** for the benefit of: *Don't trouble for my sake.* **b** for the purpose of: *He let her win for the sake of peace and quiet.*

sa·ke² ['sɑki] *or* ['sæki] *n* a fermented drink made from rice. Also, **sa·ki.** ⟨Japanese⟩

sa·la·cious [sə'leiʃəs] *adj* **1** lecherous. **2** of writing, images, etc., erotic. ⟨Latin *salacis*⟩

sal·ad ['sæləd] *n* **1** raw, leafy green vegetables, such as lettuce, spinach, endive, etc., often mixed with tomatoes or other vegetables, and served with a dressing. **2** any dish with a dressing, usually served cold: *egg salad, bean salad.* ⟨Latin *salata* pp of *salare* to salt⟩ **salad bar** a selection of salad items arranged as a buffet from which customers can choose. **salad days** days of youthful inexperience. **salad dressing** sauce for use in or on a salad.

sa·lal [sə'læl] *n* ✹ a small evergreen shrub of the Pacific coast, with edible purplish berries. ⟨Chinook Jargon *(klkwu)-shala*⟩

sal·a·man·der ['sælə,mændər] *n* any of an order of tailed amphibians similar to lizards, having an aquatic larval stage during which they breathe by gills. ⟨Greek *salamandra*⟩

sa·la·mi [sə'lɑmi] *n* a spicy sausage of pork and beef or beef alone, eaten dried or fresh. ⟨Italian; pl of *salame*; Latin *salare* to salt⟩

sal·a·ry ['sæləri] *n* fixed pay for long-term work, paid at regular intervals. **sal·a·ried** *adj.* ⟨Latin *salarium* salt allowance; *sal* salt⟩

SYNONYMS

Salary is used more for professional and office work, and for pay spoken of as covering a longer period of time: *The young engineer was paid a salary of $40 000.* Wage is used more for manual and physical work, and for pay spoken of as covering an hour, day, or week: *The minimum wage was fixed at $9.50 an hour.*

sa·lat [sə'lɑt] *n Islam* ritual prayer offered five times daily to Allah. ⟨Arabic⟩

sale [seil] *n* **1** the exchange of goods or services for money: *income from the sale of crops.* **2 sales** *pl* the amount sold: *Today's sales were low.* **3** demand; market. **4** an event where goods are sold at reduced prices: *a summer sale.* **5 sales** selling as a field of work (with sg verb): *a job in sales.* ⟨Old English *sala*⟩ **for sale** available for buying: *The house is for sale.* **on sale a** offered at a reduced price: *All the boots are on sale now.* **b** for sale: *Concert tickets will be on sale here Monday.* **sale·a·ble** *adj* easily sold; fit to be sold. **sales·clerk** [-,klɜrk] *n* a person whose work is selling goods in a store. **sales·man·ship** *n* the skill or technique of selling. **sales·per·son** *n,* *pl* **-peo·ple** *pl* a person whose work is selling, either in a store or by visiting customers. Also, **sales·man** *n, pl* **-men** and **sales·wom·an** *n, pl* **-wom·en. sales pitch 1** an argument intended to persuade someone to buy. **2** any argument intended to persuade. **sales representative** a salesperson who represents a company, often one who travels to visit customers. **sales·room** *n* a room where things are sold or shown for sale. **sales tax** a tax on the amount charged for articles sold, collected from the consumer at the time of purchase.

sa·li·ent ['seiliənt] *adj* **1** most striking or easily noticed: *the salient points in a speech.* **2** pointing outward; projecting: *a salient angle.* **sa·li·ence** *n.* **sa·li·ent·ly** *adv.* ⟨Latin *salire* leap⟩

sa·line ['seilin] *or* ['seilaɪn]*adj* **1** of or like salt; salty. **2** containing a salt of any kind. *n* a solution containing salt. **sa·lin·i·ty** [sə'lɪnəti] *n.* ⟨Latin *sal* salt⟩

Sa·lish ['seilɪʃ] *n* **1** a member of a large group of related First Nations or Native American peoples of British Columbia and the NW United States. A division is sometimes made between the **Coast Salish** and the **Interior Salish,** and in the US, the **Straits Salish. 2** any of the group of related languages spoken by the Salish. **Sa·lish** *adj.* **Sa·lish·an** ['seilɪʃən] *n* the group of languages spoken by the Salish. **Sa·lish·an** *adj.*

sa·li·va [sə'laɪvə] *n* spit; the liquid secreted by the **salivary glands** into the mouth to keep it moist, aid in chewing, and start digestion. **sal·i·var·y** ['sælə,veri] *adj.* ⟨Latin⟩ **sal·i·vate** ['sælə,veit] *v* **1** secrete a great or excessive amount of saliva. **2** show eager anticipation. **sal·i·va·tion** *n.*

sal·low ['sælou] *adj* of the complexion, pale and yellowish. **sal·low** *v.* **sal·low·ness** *n.* ⟨Old English *salo*⟩

sal·ly ['sæli] *n* **1** a sudden attack launched from a defensive position. **2** an excursion. **3** a burst of activity or speech. **4** a witty remark. *v* (with *out* or *forth*) make a sally. ⟨French *saillie*; Latin *salire* leap⟩

salm·on ['sæmən] *n, pl* **-on** or **-ons** any of a family of various fishes highly prized as food and game fish and having pinkish flesh. **sal·mon** *adj.* ⟨Latin *salmonis* probably 'leaper'; *salire* leap⟩ **sal·mon·ber·ry** *n* a shrub of the Pacific coast with edible, raspberrylike fruit.

sal·mo·nel·la [ˌsælmə'nɛlə] *or* [ˌsæmə-] *n, pl* **-lae** [-laɪ] *or* [-li] or **las** any of various bacteria causing food poisoning, typhoid, and other diseases. ⟨D. E. *Salmon*, 20c US pathologist⟩

sa·lon [sə'lɒn] *n* **1** a shop providing services such as hairdressing and manicuring. **2** a gathering of artists, writers, and interested people in the home of a prominent person. **3** an elegant room in which to receive guests. ⟨French; Italian *salone*; *sala* hall; Germanic⟩

sa·loon [sə'lun] *n* esp in frontier days in the West, a tavern; bar. ⟨See SALON.⟩

salt [sɒlt] *n* **1** a white crystalline compound found in the earth and in sea water, used as a seasoning, preservative, etc.; sodium chloride. **2** a chemical compound derived from an acid by replacing the hydrogen with a metal or an electropositive radical. **3** liveliness or piquancy. **4** *Informal* sailor. **5** **salts** *pl* **a** a salt prepared for use as a laxative: *Epsom salts.* **b** SMELLING SALTS. **c** scented salt to soften water. *adj* **1** containing salt: *salt water.* **2** growing in or covered with salty water: *salt marshes, salt grasses.* **3** preserved with salt: *salt pork.* *v* **1** add salt to. **2** cure or preserve with salt. **3** make interesting; season: *conversation salted with wit.* ⟨Old English *sealt*⟩ **salt away** (or **down**) **a** pack with salt to preserve: *The fish were salted down in a barrel.* **b** *Informal* store away: *The miser salted a lot of money away.* **salt of the earth** anyone thought to be especially fine, noble, etc. **with a grain** (or **pinch**) **of salt** with some scepticism: *to take a story with a grain of salt.* **worth one's salt** respectable: *Any cook worth her salt knows that.* **salt·cel·lar** *n* saltshaker. **salt chuck** ✹ *W coast, Northwest* the sea and all waters affected by tide. **salt·er** *n* ✹ a vehicle that spreads salt on snowy or icy roads. **salt grass** any of a genus of grasses that grow in saline or alkaline soil. **salt lick 1** a place where common salt occurs naturally on the surface of the ground and animals go to lick it up. **2** a block of salt placed in a pasture for cattle, etc. to lick. **salt pork** fatty pork cured in salt. **salt·shak·er** *n* a container for table salt, with a perforated top for sprinkling. **salt·wa·ter** *adj* **1** to do with salty water or the sea: *saltwater fish.* **saltwater taffy** a chewy candy made with salt water. **salt·y** *adj* containing or tasting of salt or salt water: *a salty breeze, salty soup.* **2** witty and a bit risqué: *a salty remark.* **salt·i·ly** *adv.* **salt·i·ness** *n.*

SALT Strategic Arms Limitation Talks.

Sal·teaux See SAULTEAUX.

salt·pe·tre [ˌsɒlt'pitər] *n* **1** a mineral used in making explosives; potassium nitrate; nitre. **2** sodium nitrate, a fertilizer. Also, **salt·pe·ter**. ⟨Latin *sal petrae* salt of rock; Greek *petra* rock⟩

sal·u·tar·y ['sæljə,tɛri] *adj* beneficial. ⟨Latin *salutaris; salus* good health⟩

sa·lute [sə'lut] *v* **1** show respect formally by raising the hand to the head, dipping flags, etc.: *The soldier saluted the officer.* **2** greet or meet (with kind words, cheers, a kiss, etc.)

3 commend: *I salute your courage.* **sa·lute** *n.* ⟨Latin *salutare* greet; *salus* good health⟩

sal·u·ta·tion [ˌsæljə'teiʃən] *n* **1** a greeting; act of recognition: *He raised his hat in salutation.* **2** words opening a letter and addressing the reader, such as "Dear Sir" or "My Dear Gran."

sal·vage ['sælvɪdʒ] *v* save or reclaim from destruction or loss: *to salvage photos from a burning house, to salvage one's dignity.* *n* **1** the act of salvaging. **2** salvaged scrap metal, wood, etc.: *They used mostly salvage to build their cabin.* ⟨Latin *salvus* safe⟩

sal·va·tion [sæl'veiʃən] *n* **1** a saving or being saved. **2** specifically, the saving of the soul. **3** a person or thing that saves. ⟨Latin *salvatio; salvus* safe⟩ **Salvation Army** an international organization to spread the Christian faith and help the poor, founded in 1865 by William Booth.

salve [sæv] *n* **1** a medicated ointment to put on sores to heal them. **2** something soothing; balm: *The kind words were a salve to her hurt feelings.* **salve** *v.* ⟨Old English *sealf*⟩

sal·vo ['sælvou] *n, pl* **-vos** or **-voes 1** the discharge of several guns, or the release of a load of bombs or missiles, at one time. **2** a round of cheers or applause. ⟨Italian *salva* a cheer; Latin *salve* be in good health!⟩

sa·maj [sə'mɑdʒ] *n Hinduism* a religious society or assembly (often forming part of the name of a place of worship). ⟨Hindi⟩

sam·a·ra ['sæmərə] *or* [sə'mɛrə] *n* any dry fruit that has a winglike extension and does not split open when ripe. The maple bears a double samara. ⟨Latin *samara* elm seed⟩

sa·mar·i·um [sə'mɛriəm] *n* a rare, metallic element used especially in alloys that form permanent magnets. *Symbol* **Sm** ⟨Col. *Samarski*, a Russian⟩

sam·ba ['sɑmbə] *or* ['sæmbə] *n* a Brazilian dance of African origin, with a syncopated rhythm. **samba** *v.* ⟨Portuguese⟩

same [seim] *adj* **1** identical: *We came back the same way we went.* **2** unchanged: *He is the same; he's no better.* **3** just spoken of. *adv* in the same way: Sea *and* see *are* pronounced the same. *n* the same person or thing: *As soon as I sat down he did the same.* ⟨Old English⟩ **all the same** notwithstanding; nevertheless. **just the same a** nevertheless: *It poured, but I went just the same.* **b** exactly alike. **same·ness** *n* **1** the state or fact of being the same. **2** lack of variety; tiresome monotony.

USAGE
Same must always be preceded by a definite determiner (*the, this, that*, etc.).

sa·mo·sa [sə'mousə] *n* a deep-fried pastry containing spicy meat or vegetables. ⟨Hindi⟩

sam·pan ['sæmpæn] *n* a small boat used in SE Asia, sculled by one or more oars at the stern. ⟨Mandarin; Portuguese⟩

sam·ple ['sæmpəl] *n* a part used to represent

a larger whole, for testing or to show what the rest is like: *a soil sample.*
v take or try a sample of: *I sampled the cake and found it very good.* ⟨variant of *example*⟩
sam·pler *n* **1** a piece of cloth embroidered in various stitches to show skill in needlework. **2** a piece of electronic equipment that digitalizes music. **sam·pling** *n* **1** a portion or number selected for testing. **2** the act or process of selecting it.

sam·u·rai [ˈsæməˌraɪ] *n, pl* -**rai** in feudal Japan, the military class, consisting of the retainers of the nobility. ⟨Japanese⟩

san·a·to·ri·um [ˌsænəˈtɔriəm] *n, pl* -**ri·ums** or -**ri·a** a hospital for those with long-term or chronic diseases, such as tuberculosis or mental illness. ⟨Latin *sanus* healthy⟩

sanc·ti·fy [ˈsæŋktəˌfaɪ] *v* **1** make holy or pure: **2** bless. **sanc·ti·fi·ca·tion** *n.* **sanc·ti·fi·er** *n.* ⟨Latin *sanctus* holy⟩
sanc·ti·fied *adj* **1** made holy. **2** sanctimonious. **sanc·ti·mo·ni·ous** [ˌ-ˈmouniəs] *adj* making a great show of piety. **sanc·ti·mo·ni·ous·ly** *adv.* **sanc·ti·mo·ni·ous·ness** *n.*

sanc·tion [ˈsæŋkʃən] *n* **1** official approval: *We have the sanction of the law to play here.* **2** an action by several nations toward another, such as economic restrictions, etc., intended to force it to obey international law. *v* authorize; approve; allow. ⟨Latin *sanctio; sancire* ordain⟩

sanc·ti·ty [ˈsæŋktəti] *n* **1** the fact of being inviolable: *the sanctity of the home.* **2** saintliness. ⟨Latin *sanctitas; sanctus* holy⟩

sanc·tu·ar·y [ˈsæŋktʃuˌɛri] *n* **1** any sacred place or house of worship. **2** a refuge for birds or wildlife. **3** any refuge or protection: *The lost travellers found sanctuary in a deserted hut.* ⟨Latin *sanctuarium; sanctus* holy⟩

sanc·tum [ˈsæŋktəm] *n* **1** a sacred place, esp a shrine inside a church or temple. **2** a private room or office where a person can be undisturbed. ⟨Latin *sanctum* holy⟩

sand [sænd] *n* **1** tiny grains of worn-down or disintegrated rock. **2 sands** *pl* an expanse of sand: *the desert sands.* **3 sands** *pl* the sand in an hourglass thought of as particles of time. *v* **1** sprinkle with sand: *to sand an icy walk.* **2** clean, smooth, or polish by rubbing with sandpaper. **sand** *adj.* ⟨Old English⟩
sand·bank *n* a ridge of sand. **sand bar** a ridge of sand in a river or along a shore, formed by the action of tides or currents. **sand·blast** *v* clean, grind, cut, or decorate (a hard surface such as stone, glass, or metal) by means of a blast of air containing sand. **sand·box** *n* a large box or enclosed area holding sand for children to play in. **sand dollar** any of various disk-shaped marine invertebrates. **sand·er** *n* **1** a truck that spreads sand on icy roads. **2** a machine or tool for cleaning, smoothing, or polishing with sandpaper. **sand flea** any of various tiny hopping crustaceans found in the sand of seashores. **sand fly** any of various small two-winged flies, the females of which suck blood. **Sand**

Hills ✱ a region in SE Alberta, long sacred to the First Nations peoples of the plains as a burial ground; often a euphemism for death. **sand·man** *n* an imaginary man who makes children sleepy by sprinkling sand in their eyes. **sand·pa·per** *n* strong paper with a layer of sand or some other rough material glued to it, used for smoothing, cleaning, or polishing. **sand·stone** *n* a sedimentary rock consisting of sand bound by natural cementing material. **sand·storm** *n* a storm of wind that carries clouds of sand. **sand trap** *Golf* a depression filled with sand, serving as a hazard on the course. **sand·y** *adj* **1** to do with sand: *sandy beaches.* **2** like sand, esp in colour: *sandy hair.* **sand·i·ness** *n.*

san·dal [ˈsændəl] *n* an open shoe consisting of a sole kept on the foot by a set of straps. **san·dalled** or **san·daled** *adj.* ⟨Greek *sandalion*⟩

san·dal·wood *n* the fragrant wood of any of a genus of S Asian evergreen trees, used in cabinetwork, and also burned as incense. ⟨Latin *sandalum*; Sanskrit *çandana*⟩

sand·wich [ˈsænwɪtʃ] or [ˈsænwɪdʒ] *n* **1** two or more slices of bread with a filling between. **2** anything with a layered arrangement: *an ice-cream sandwich.* *v* put or squeeze (*between*): *He found his car sandwiched between two trucks.* ⟨John Montagu, fourth Earl of *Sandwich*, 18c⟩

sane [sein] *adj* **1** mentally healthy. **2** sensible: *a sane foreign policy.* **sane·ly** *adv.* **sane·ness** *n.* **san·i·ty** [ˈsænəti] *n.* ⟨Latin *sanus* healthy⟩

sang [sæŋ] *v* pt of SING.

sang–froid [sɑ̃ˈfRwa] *French n* calmness of mind; composure. ⟨literally, cold blood⟩

san·guine [ˈsæŋgwɪn] *adj* **1** cheerful and optimistic; confident: *a sanguine disposition.* **2** of the complexion, healthy and pink. **san·guine·ly** *adv.* **san·guine·ness** *n.* ⟨Latin *sanguinis* blood⟩

san·i·tar·y [ˈsænəˌtɛri] *adj* **1** free from dirt or anything bad for health: *The top of the picnic table was not very sanitary.* **2** to do with conditions that promote health: *Strict sanitary measures must be taken to ensure that the equipment is germ-free.* **san·i·tar·i·ness** *n.* ⟨French *sanitaire*; Latin *sanus* healthy⟩
san·i·tar·i·um [ˌsænəˈtɛriəm] *n, pl* -**i·ums** or -**i·a** [-iə] sanatorium. **sanitary napkin** or **pad** a disposable absorbent pad worn outside the body to absorb menstrual discharge. **san·i·ta·tion** *n* implementation of sanitary measures such as garbage disposal. **san·i·tize** *v* **1** make clean or sterile. **2** make free of anything objectionable or offensive: *sanitized fairy tales.* **san·i·ti·za·tion** *n.*

san·i·ty [ˈsænəti] *n* See SANE.

sank [sæŋk] *v* pt of SINK.

San·sei [ˈsænˌsei] or [ˈsænˈsei] *n, pl* -**sei** or -**seis** a grandchild of Japanese immigrants. ⟨Japanese *san* third + *sei* generation⟩

San·skrit [ˈsænskrɪt] *n* the ancient literary language of India and of Hindu scripture. ⟨Sanskrit *samskrta* prepared, cultivated⟩

Santa Claus ['sæntə ,klɒz] Saint Nicholas, a symbol of Christmas, represented as a jolly old man in a white beard and fur-trimmed red suit. Often shortened to **Santa**. ⟨Dutch dialect *Sante Klaas* Saint Nicholas⟩

sap¹ [sæp] *n* **1** the liquid circulating through a plant, carrying nutrients. **2** vital spirit; vigour. **3** *Slang* fool. ⟨Old English *sæp*⟩
sap·ling *n* **1** a young tree. **2** a young person.
sap pail (or **bucket**) a pail hung on a sugar maple in spring to collect the sap. **sap·py** *adj* **1** full of sap. **2** *Slang* foolishly sentimental.
sap·suck·er *n* either of two North American woodpeckers that drill holes in trees to feed on sap and insects. **sap weather ✱** spring weather with cold nights and mild days, during which the sap of sugar maples runs and can be collected.

sap² [sæp] *v* **sapped, sap·ping 1** weaken or use up: *The extreme heat sapped their strength.* **2** dig or tunnel under, or wear away the foundation of: *The boathouse walls had been sapped by the waves.* **3** dig protected trenches. *n* a trench protected by earth and used to approach an enemy's position. ⟨Middle French *sapper*; Italian *zappare; zappa* spade⟩
sap·per *n* a soldier in a regiment that digs trenches and builds fortifications.

sap·phire ['sæfaɪr] *n* a precious stone, a (usually blue) variety of corundum. ⟨Greek *sappheiros;* Semitic⟩

sar·casm ['sɑrkæzəm] *n* sneering or cutting remarks; irony meant to hurt. **sar·cas·tic** *adj.* **sar·cas·ti·cal·ly** *adv.* ⟨Greek *sarkazein* strip off flesh; *sarkos* flesh⟩

Sar·cee or **Sar·si** ['sɑrsi] *n, pl* **-cee** or **-cees; -si** or **-sis 1** a member of a First Nations people formerly of the upper Athabasca River region in Alberta, now mainly near Calgary. **2** their Athapascan language. **Sar·cee** or **Sar·si** *adj.*

sar·co·ma [sɑr'koumə] *n, pl* **-mas** or **-ma·ta** [-mətə] a cancerous tumour elsewhere than in an organ. ⟨Greek *sarkōma; sarkos* flesh⟩

sar·coph·a·gus [sɑr'kɒfəgəs] *n, pl* **-gi** [-dʒaɪ] *or* [-dʒi] *or* **-gus·es** a stone coffin, esp one with sculpture or an inscription. ⟨Greek *sarkos* flesh + *phagein* eat⟩

sar·dine [sɑr'din] *n, pl* **-dines** or (collectively) **-dine** any of various food fishes of the herring family, often canned. ⟨Latin *sardina; sarda* sardine; Greek⟩
packed like sardines very crowded.

sar·don·ic [sɑr'dɒnɪk] *adj* bitterly mocking; cynical; disdainful: *a sardonic smile.* **sar·don·i·cal·ly** *adv.* ⟨Greek *sardonios* Sardinian plant supposed to cause convulsions⟩

sa·ri ['sɑri] *n* a garment worn by women esp in India, consisting of a long piece of fabric folded and draped around the body. ⟨Hindi⟩

sa·rong [sə'rɒŋ] *n* **1** a rectangular piece of cloth, usually a brightly coloured print, worn as a skirt by men and women in the Malay Archipelago, Sri Lanka, and some parts of India. **2** a fabric used for it. ⟨Malay *sārung*⟩

sar·sa·pa·ril·la [,sæspə'rɪlə] *n* any of several tropical American prickly vines whose dried roots are used to flavour root beer and other drinks. ⟨Spanish *zarza* bramble + *parrilla,* diminutive of *parra* vine⟩

sar·to·ri·al [sɑr'tɔriəl] *adj* of tailors or tailored clothes. ⟨Latin *sartor* mender; *sarcire* patch⟩

sash¹ [sæʃ] *n* a long, broad strip of cloth or ribbon, worn ornamentally around the waist or over one shoulder. ⟨Arabic *shāsh* turban⟩

sash² [sæʃ] *n* **1** the frame holding the glass in a window or door. **2** a window frame with glass in it, usually movable: *Raise the sash to let in some air.* ⟨altered from *chassis* taken as pl⟩

sa·shay [sæ'ʃeɪ] *Informal v* move or walk casually and boldly: *He sashayed up to the front door as if he owned the place.* ⟨altered from *chassé* gliding dance step; French⟩

Sas·katch·e·wan [sə'skætʃə,wɒn] *or* [sə'skætʃəwən] *n* a central province of Canada. *Abbrev* **SK.** **Sas·katch·e·wan·i·an** [sə,skætʃə'wɒniən] *n, adj.* Also ⟨*n*⟩, **Sas·katch·e·wan·er.** ⟨< Cree⟩

sas·ka·toon [,sæskə'tun] *n* ✱ a shrub of the rose family found in temperate W North America, with edible purple berries. ⟨Cree *misaskwatomin; misaskwat* tree of many branches + *min* fruit⟩

Sas·quatch ['sɑskwɒtʃ] *or* ['sæskwɒtʃ] *n* ✱ according to legend, a large, hairy, humanlike creature that is supposed to live wild in the mountains of the Pacific Coast. Also, **Big·foot.** ⟨Salish *seśxac*⟩

sass [sæs] *Informal n* back talk; cheekiness. *v* talk back or be cheeky to. **sass·y** *adj.* ⟨*sauce*⟩

sas·sa·fras ['sæsə,fræs] *n* an aromatic tree of the laurel family. Its root bark is used in medicine and as flavouring. ⟨Spanish *sasafras*⟩

sat [sæt] *v* pt and pp of sɪт.

SAT Scholastic Aptitude Test, a standardized university entrance examination.

Sa·tan ['seitən] *n* in some religions, the chief evil spirit and the enemy of God; the Devil. ⟨Hebrew = enemy, plotter⟩
sa·tan·ic [sə'tænɪk] *or* [sei-] *adj* **1** of or from Satan. **2** extremely vicious, cruel, or wicked: *satanic crimes.* **sa·tan·i·cal·ly** *adv.* **Sa·tan·ism** ['seitə,nɪzəm] *n* devil worship, often involving blasphemous perversions of Christian rites. **Sa·tan·ist** *adj, n.* **Sa·tan·is·tic** *adj.*

sate [seit] *v* **1** satisfy fully (an appetite or desire). **2** disgust or weary by giving too much. ⟨Old English *sade* (see sᴀᴅ) influenced by Latin *satiare* satiate⟩

sat·el·lite ['sætə,laɪt] *n* **1** a small planet that orbits around a larger one. **2** an artificial object sent into orbit around the earth or other heavenly body, to collect data, receive and transmit communications signals, etc. **3** a nominally independent country controlled by a more powerful one. **4** a community adjacent to and dependent on a large city. ⟨Latin *satellitis* attendant⟩
satellite dish an antenna with a dish-shaped reflector, designed to receive communication signals broadcast by satellites.

sa·ti·ate ['seiʃi,eit] v 1 satisfy fully. 2 weary or disgust with too much. **sa·tia·ble** adj. **sa·ti·a·tion** n. ⟨Latin satiare; satis enough⟩
sa·ti·e·ty [sə'taɪəti] n a satiated condition.

sat·in ['sætən] n 1 a soft fabric with a smooth, lustrous face. 2 a glossiness like that of satin: the satin of a silver bowl. **sat·in·y** adj. ⟨Old French; Arabic zaitūnī⟩

sat·ire ['sætaɪr] n 1 literature characterized by use of exaggeration and irony to expose or attack evil or foolishness. 2 a literary work in this genre. 3 any similar use of irony. **sa·tir·i·cal** [sə'tɪrɪkəl] adj. **sa·tir·i·cal·ly** adv. **sat·i·rist** ['sætərɪst] n. **sat·i·rize** v. ⟨Latin satira; (lanx) satura mixed (dish); satur full⟩

sat·is·fy ['sætɪs,faɪ] v 1 fulfil (hopes, demands, etc.): He satisfied his hunger with a sandwich. 2 fully answer (an objection, doubt, etc.). 3 content: Are you satisfied? 4 convince: I am satisfied that it was a mistake. **sat·is·fi·a·ble** adj. **sat·is·fy·ing** adv. **sat·is·fac·tion** n. **sat·is·fac·to·ri·ly** adv. **sat·is·fac·to·ry** adj. ⟨Latin satis enough + facere do⟩

sat·u·rate ['sætʃə,reit] v 1 soak: to saturate a towel with water. 2 fill; imbue: saturated with tradition. 3 cause (a substance) to unite with the greatest possible amount of another substance: air saturated with water vapour. 4 fully supply the demand of (a market). ⟨Latin saturare glut; satur full⟩
sat·u·rat·ed adj 1 thoroughly wet. 2 a of a solution, containing as much of a dissolved substance as possible. b of fat or any organic compound, not able to unite with other compounds or elements. **sat·u·ra·tion** n.
saturation point the point at which no more can be absorbed, accepted, endured, etc.

Sat·ur·day ['sætər,dei] n the seventh day of the week, following Friday. ⟨Old English Sæterdæg day of Saturn; Latin Saturni dies⟩

Sat·urn ['sætərn] n 1 Roman myth the god of agriculture. 2 the second largest planet in the solar system, sixth from the sun. ⟨Latin; related to satum pp of serere to sow⟩

sat·yr ['sætər] or ['seitər] n 1 Greek myth any of a class of woodland gods who indulged in merrymaking and lechery, variously pictured as men with the horns and legs of a goat. 2 a lecherous man. ⟨Greek satyros⟩

sauce [sɒs] n 1 a liquid served with food to enhance the flavour. 2 fruit stewed to a smooth, thick consistency: cranberry sauce, applesauce. 3 Informal sass. 4 the sauce Slang alcohol. ⟨Old French; Latin salsa; sal salt⟩
sauce·pan [-,pæn] n an ordinary cooking pot. **sau·cer** n 1 a shallow dish to set a cup on. 2 something round or shallow like a saucer. **sau·cy** adj 1 disrespectful. 2 smartly stylish: a saucy hat. **sau·ci·ly** adv. **sau·ci·ness** n.

sauer·kraut ['saʊr,krʌut] n cabbage cut fine, salted, and pickled in the resulting brine. ⟨German sauer sour + Kraut cabbage⟩

sault [su] n ✱ a waterfall or rapids (now only in place names): Sault Ste. Marie. ⟨earlier form of French saut leap, falls⟩

Saul·teaux ['sɒltou] n 1 a member of a First Nations people who are a western branch of the Anishinabe. 2 their Anishinabe dialect. **Saulteaux** adj. Also, **Salteaux**.

sau·na ['sɒnə] n 1 a type of bath using dry heat or steam to cause perspiration. 2 a structure used for such baths. ⟨Finnish⟩

saun·ter ['sɒntər] v walk along in a relaxed, casual way; stroll: to saunter through the park. n 1 a leisurely or careless gait. 2 a stroll. **saun·ter·er** n. ⟨origin uncertain⟩

–saurus combining form dinosaur: brontosaurus. ⟨Greek sauros lizard⟩

sau·sage ['sɒsɪdʒ] n chopped meat, seasoned and stuffed into a thin casing or skin. ⟨Old French saussiche; Latin salsicia; sal salt⟩

sau·té [sou'tei] v fry quickly in a little fat. **sau·té** adj. ⟨French, pp of sauter jump⟩

sav·age ['sævɪdʒ] adj 1 of animals, untamed; wild and fierce: savage jungle beasts. 2 brutal; ferocious: a savage temper, a savage attack. 3 wild and rugged: savage mountain scenery. n a brutal or crude person. v attack brutally: She was savaged by a dog. **sav·age·ly** adv. **sav·age·ness** n. **sav·age·ry** n. ⟨Old French sauvage forest⟩

sa·van·na or **sa·van·nah** [sə'vænə] n a grassy plain with few or no trees, esp in a tropical or subtropical region. ⟨earlier Spanish zavana; Arawakan⟩

sa·vant [sə'vɒnt] n a person of great learning. ⟨French; savoir know, Latin sapere be wise⟩

save¹ [seiv] v 1 rescue: to save a drowning woman. 2 lay aside for future use: She saves string. 3 keep from wasting (money, time, etc.): Save your strength. 4 prevent or avoid (work, expense, etc.); make less. 5 set free from sin and its penalty. 6 Computers copy (data) onto a disk: to save a file. n an act of saving, esp by thwarting an attempt to score: The goalie made a great save. **sav·er** n. ⟨Latin salvare; salvus safe⟩
save one's breath See BREATH.
save up set aside money a little at a time for a future purchase: to save up for a snowboard.
sav·ing ['seivɪŋ] adj 1 that saves. 2 avoiding waste; economical. 3 stating a reservation: a saving clause. n 1 Often, **savings** (sg in use) the amount saved: a savings of 10%. 2 **savings** pl money set aside for the future.
savings account a deposit account in a bank, credit union, etc. on which interest is paid. **sav·iour** or **sav·ior** ['seivjər] n 1 one who saves or rescues. 2 the Saviour Christianity Jesus.

save² [seiv] prep except; but: She works every day of the week save Sunday. ⟨variant of safe, in sense of 'not involved'⟩

sa·vor·y ['seivəri] n any of a genus of fragrant herbs of the mint family, used for seasoning. ⟨Middle English saverey; Latin satureia⟩

sa·vour or **sa·vor** ['seivər] n pleasing flavour. v 1 appreciate the taste or smell of: He savoured each swallow of soup. 2 enjoy fully: to *savour time spent with friends.* **sa·vour·less** or **sa·vor·less** *adj.* ⟨Latin *sapor*⟩

sa·vour·y or **sa·vor·y** *adj* **1** pleasing in taste or smell: *the savoury smell of roasting turkey.* **2** salty or spicy as opposed to sweet: *sweet and savoury relishes.*

sav·vy ['sævi] *Slang adj* shrewd; knowing. *n* shrewd intelligence; sense. ⟨Portuguese or Spanish *sabe* (you) know; Latin *sapere* be wise⟩

saw[1] [sɒ] *n* **1** a tool for cutting material such as wood or metal, consisting of a toothed blade set in a handle. **2** a device or machine with such a blade. **saw, sawed, sawed** or **sawn, saw·ing** *v.* **saw·er** *n.* ⟨Old English *sagu*⟩ **saw·dust** ['sɒ,dʌst] *n* the particles of wood produced in sawing. **sawed–off** *adj* of a shotgun, with the end of the barrel cut off. **saw·horse** *n* a frame on which wood is laid for sawing. **saw·mill** *n* a place where timber is sawed into planks, etc. by machine. **saw–off** *n* ✷ *Slang* **1** any agreement involving a trade-off. **2** *Sports and games* a tie. **saw·yer** ['sɔɪjər] *n* one who saws timber.

saw[2] [sɒ] *v* pt of SEE[1].

saw[3] [sɒ] *n* a saying; proverb. ⟨Old English *sagu;* related to SAY⟩

sax·o·phone ['sæksə,foun] *n* any of a group of single-reed wind instruments with a curved metal body and keys for the fingers. **sax·o·phon·ist** *n.* ⟨Adolphe *Sax,* 19c inventor⟩

say [sei] *v* **said, say·ing;** 3rd sg pres **says** [sez] **1** utter; pronounce: *What did you say?* **2** put into words; declare: *This author says the opposite.* **3** recite: *Say your prayers.* **4** take as an example or estimate: *You'd need, say, ten bucks.* **5** judge: *It is hard to say which dress is nicer.* **6** read: *It says on the bottle, 'Shake well'.* *n* **1** what a person says or has to say. **2** the chance to say something: *I have had my say.* **3** the authority to decide: *Who has the say in this matter?* **say·er** *n.* ⟨Old English *secgan*⟩ **go without saying** be obvious. **that is to say** that is; in other words. **to say nothing of** without even mentioning: *The hotel itself cost a lot, to say nothing of the meals.* **say·ing** *n* something said, esp a set statement that is often repeated. **say–so** *n Informal* **1** an unsupported statement: *Don't do it just on his say-so.* **2** authority to decide; say.

scab [skæb] *n* **1** the crust that forms over a healing sore. **2** *Slang* a worker who will not join a union or who takes a striker's place. **3** *Slang* scoundrel. *v* **scabbed, scab·bing 1** become covered with a scab (usually with over). **2** *Slang* act or work as a scab. **scab·by** *adj.* ⟨Scandinavian⟩

scab·bard ['skæbərd] *n* a sheath or case for the blade of a sword, dagger, etc. ⟨Anglo-French *escaubers,* pl; Germanic⟩

sca·bies ['skeibiz] *n* a contagious skin disease characterized by a very itchy rash and caused by a mite that burrows under the skin and lays its eggs there. **sca·bi·ous** *adj.* ⟨Latin *scabies* itch; *scabere* scratch⟩

scads [skædz] *n pl Slang* a large quantity. ⟨origin uncertain⟩

scaf·fold ['skæfəld] *n* **1** a temporary structure to hold workers working high up. **2** a raised platform for a guillotine or gallows. **3** any raised framework. ⟨Old French *eschaffault*⟩ **scaf·fold·ing** *n* **1** a scaffold or system of scaffolds. **2** materials for building scaffolds.

scal·ar See SCALE[3].

scal·a·wag ['skælə,wæg] *n Informal* a scamp; rascal. Also, **scal·ly·wag.** ⟨origin uncertain⟩

scald [skɒld] *v* **1** burn with or as if with hot liquid or steam. **2** rinse with boiling liquid: *to scald dishes.* **3** heat almost to boiling. *n* a burn caused by hot liquid or steam. ⟨Old French *escalder;* Latin *ex-* very + *calidus* hot⟩

scale[1] [skeil] *n* **1 a** one of the thin, flat, plates covering the body of some fishes reptiles, etc. **b** a similar thin plate on the legs of birds or the wings of certain insects. **2** a thin, hard piece of anything; flake: *scales of peeling paint.* **3** tartar on teeth. **4** the coating that forms on the inside of a kettle, etc. *v* **1** remove scale or scales from. **2** come off in scales: *The paint is scaling.* **3** coat or become coated with scale. **scale·like** *adj.* **scal·y** *adj.* ⟨Old French *escale*⟩ **scale leaf** a tough, modified plant leaf that covers a dormant bud in winter.

scale[2] [skeil] *n* Sometimes, **scales** *pl* **1** an instrument for weighing. **2** specifically, a BALANCE (def. 1). ⟨Old Norse *skál* bowl⟩ **tip the scale(s)** be the deciding factor: *That fact tipped the scales in his favour.* **tip the scales at** weigh: *She tips the scales at 65 kg.*

scale[3] [skeil] *n* **1** a series of graded amounts: *a wage scale.* **2** a measuring instrument marked off at regular intervals. **3** the size of a map, model, etc. compared with the real thing: *a map with a scale of 1 cm to 10 km.* **4** relative size or extent: *the scale of a project.* **5** *Music* a series of tones ascending or descending in pitch according to a fixed system of intervals. *v* **1** climb; get over: *to scale a wall.* **2** reduce or increase by a certain proportion (with *down* or *up*): *All prices were scaled down 10%.* **3** make according to a scale. **scal·a·ble** *adj.* ⟨Latin *scala* ladder⟩ **to scale** consistently using a set of small measurements to represent larger ones: *This map is not to scale.* **scal·ar** ['skeilər] *adj* able to be represented on a scale or line; having magnitude but no direction, such as temperature. *n Physics, mathematics* a scalar quantity. Compare VECTOR. **scale model** a model built TO SCALE.

sca·lene [skei'lin] or ['skeilin] *adj* **1** of a triangle, having all sides unequal. **2** of a cone or cylinder, having its axis not perpendicular to the base. ⟨Greek *skalēnos* limping, uneven⟩

scal·lion ['skæljən] *n* a type of onion that does not form a large bulb; green onion. ⟨Anglo-French *scalon*⟩

scal·lop ['skæləp] *n* **1** any of a family of bivalve molluscs whose fan-shaped shell has ridges giving it a wavy edge. **2** one of a series of curves forming an edge.

v **1** bake with cream sauce, bread crumbs, etc., in a casserole dish: *scalloped potatoes.* **2** decorate (an edge) with a series of scallops: *a scalloped hem.* ⟨Old French *escalope* shell⟩

scalp [skælp] *n* **1** the skin on the top and back of the head. **2** a part of this skin from the crown of the head with the hair attached, among some peoples formerly taken from a conquered enemy as a token of victory.
v **1** cut or tear the scalp from. **2** *Informal* **a** buy and sell (stocks, etc.) for small, quick profits. **b** buy (tickets to an event) and resell at greatly increased prices just before the event. **scalp·er** *n.* ⟨Old Norse *skálpr* sheath⟩
scalp lock a long lock of hair formerly left on the top of the shorn head of a First Nations or Native American man.

scal·pel ['skælpəl] *n* a small, sharp, straight knife used in surgery and dissection. ⟨Latin *scalpellum* diminutive of *scalprum* knife⟩

scal·y See SCALE[1].

scam [skæm] *n* a fraud or swindle. **scam, scammed, scam·ming** *v.*

scamp [skæmp] *n* a mischievous person, esp a child. ⟨dialect = roam, probably from *scamper*⟩

scam·per ['skæmpər] *v* run or move lightly and quickly. **scam·per** *n.* ⟨Old French *escamper* run away; Latin *ex-* out of + *campus* field⟩

scan [skæn] *v* **scanned, scan·ning** **1** look over the whole of: *She scanned his face to see if he was lying.* **2** *Informal* look over hastily: *to scan newspaper headlines.* **3** find (the metre of poetry) by marking the lines off into feet. **4** fit a metrical pattern: *Your poem is good, but this line does not scan.* **5** *Electronics* pass a beam of light over (a text, picture, etc.) in order to transmit or reproduce an image of it. **6** read or interpret (data such as bar codes, magnetic strips on credit cards, etc.) with an electronic device. **7** *Medicine* examine (active tissue) using some form of imaging such as ultrasound. **scan** *n.* **scan·na·ble** *adj.* ⟨Latin *scandere* scan verses, climb⟩
scan·ner *n* a device that scans, such as a bar code reader. **scan·sion** ['skænʃən] *n* the analysis of the metre of poetry.

scan·dal ['skændəl] *n* **1** an event, or state of affairs that brings disgrace or offends public opinion: *the scandal of corruption in the government.* **2** gossip or public outrage caused by this. **scan·dal·ous** *adj.* **scan·dal·ous·ly** *adv.* ⟨Greek *skandalon* trap⟩
scan·dal·ize *v* shock or offend by wrong or disgraceful behaviour. **scan·dal·mon·ger** [-,mɒŋgər] *or* [-,mʌŋgər] *n* one who spreads scandal or malicious gossip. **scandal sheet** a newspaper featuring malicious gossip.

Scan·di·na·via [,skændə'neivjə] *n* a region of N Europe that includes Denmark, Sweden, Norway, and often Iceland and Faeroe Islands. **Scan·di·na·vi·an** *n, adj.*

scan·di·um ['skændiəm] *n* a rare, metallic element. *Symbol* **Sc** ⟨Latin *Scandia* Scandinavia⟩

scan·ner, scan·sion See SCAN.

scant [skænt] *adj* **1** barely enough: *making do with scant provisions.* **2** of a measure, barely complete: *a scant teaspoon of sugar.* ⟨Old Norse *skamt* short⟩
scant·y *adj* not enough or barely enough: *a scanty harvest. His scanty clothing did not keep him warm.* **scant·i·ly** *adv.* **scant·i·ness** *n.*

SYNONYMS
Scanty emphasizes falling short of a required amount: *The scanty rainfall caused a water shortage.* **Sparse** suggests a thin scattering of what there is: *He carefully combs his sparse hair.* **Meagre** suggests a lack of fullness, richness, body, strength, etc.: *His meagre soil produces meagre crops.*

–scape *combining form* a scenic view of a given thing: *cityscape, seascape* ⟨(land)scape; Dutch *landschap, land* land + *schap* -ship⟩

scape·goat ['skeip,gout] *n* **1** a person or thing made to bear the blame for the sins or mistakes of others. **2** in ancient Judaism, a goat on which collective sin was symbolically laid on the Day of Atonement. ⟨(e)scape + goat⟩

scar [skɑr] *n* **1** the mark left by a healed cut, wound, or sore. **2** any disfiguring mark: *That quarry is a scar on the landscape.* **3** a lasting effect from trouble, grief, etc.: *the scars left by war.* **scar, scarred, scar·ring** *v.* ⟨Old French *escare*; Greek *eschara* scab, hearth⟩

scar·ab ['skerəb] *or* ['skærəb] *n* **1** a large black beetle held sacred by the ancient Egyptians. **2** any beetle of the same family, including June bugs and dung beetles. ⟨Latin *scarabaeus*; Greek *kārabos*⟩

scarce [skers] *adj* hard to get; rare: *Good cooks are scarce.* **scarce·ness** *n.* **scar·ci·ty** *n.* ⟨Old Norman French *escars*; Latin *excarpsus*; *ex-* out + *carpere* pluck⟩
make oneself scarce *Informal* leave or stay away. **scarce as hen's teeth** *Informal* very rare. **scarce·ly** *adv* **1** only just; barely: *scarcely old enough for school.* **2** emphatically not: *She can scarcely have said that!*

scare [sker] *v* **1** make or become startled: *The loud bang scared me.* **2** drive (*off* or *away*) by frightening: *She scared off the cat by yelling.* *n* **1** a fright: *a real scare.* **2** a state of general panic about something: *a meningitis scare.* ⟨Old Norse *skirra*; *skjarr* timid⟩
scare up *Informal* get or gather quickly: *We made camp and then tried to scare up some food.* **scare·crow** [-,krou] *n* **1** an object, usually a human figure made of old clothes stuffed with straw, set in a field to frighten birds away from crops. **2** a person who is thin and gaunt or dresses like a scarecrow. **3** anything that fools people into being frightened. **scared** *adj* afraid (*of*): *to be scared of snakes.* **scare·dy·cat** ['skerdi-] *n* *Informal* a person who is easily frightened. **scar·y** ['skeri] *adj* *Informal* causing fear or alarm: *a scary movie.*

scarf[1] [skɑrf] *n, pl* **scarves** **1** a rectangular, square, or triangular piece of cloth worn around the neck, shoulders, or head. **2** a strip of cloth decorating the top of a dresser, table, etc.; runner. ⟨Old French *escarpe*; Germanic⟩

scarf² [skɑrf] v *Slang* eat in large quantities. ⟨origin uncertain⟩

scar·i·fy ['skɛrə,faɪ] or ['skærə,faɪ] v 1 make scratches or cuts in the surface of. 2 loosen (soil) without turning it. 3 break up (a road surface) prior to repaving. **scar·i·fi·ca·tion** n. **scar·i·fi·er** n. ⟨Greek *skariphos* stylus⟩

scar·let ['skɑrlɪt] n bright red with a slight orange tinge. **scar·let** adj. ⟨Old French *escarlate*; perhaps Persian *saqirlat* rich cloth⟩ **scarlet fever** an acute contagious disease characterized by a scarlet rash, sore throat, and fever.

scarves [skɑrvz] n pl of SCARF.

scar·y See SCARE.

scat¹ [skæt] *Informal interj* an exclamation usually used to drive away an animal.
v **scat·ted, scat·ting** get away quickly: *She told the boys to scat.* ⟨scatter⟩

scat² [skæt] n a wild animal's feces. ⟨Greek *skor, skatos*⟩ **sca·tol·o·gy** n 1 the study of excrement, used in paleontology, biological research, etc. 2 an abnormal fascination with excrement or excretion. **scat·o·log·i·cal** adj.

scath·ing ['skeiðɪŋ] adj of criticism, satire, etc., very severe or cutting. **scath·ing·ly** adv. ⟨Old Norse *skathi* injury⟩

sca·tol·o·gy See SCAT².

scat·ter ['skætər] v 1 throw here and there: *to scatter ashes on an icy path.* 2 cover by scattering: *The path was scattered with leaves.* 3 go or send off in all directions: *The hens scattered.* 4 *Physics* irregularly reflect or refract (a beam) in all directions. **scat·ter** or **scat·ter·ing** n. ⟨Middle English; probably variant of SHATTER⟩ **scat·ter·brain** n an absent-minded, frivolous, easily distracted person. **scat·ter·brained** adj. **scat·tered** adj few, unevenly distributed, and far apart: *scattered instances of violence.*

scav·enge ['skævəndʒ] v 1 salvage from discarded materials: *to scavenge usable wood scraps.* 2 pick over (discarded materials) for usable items. 3 of animals, feed on garbage or carrion. **scav·en·ger** n. ⟨Old French *scawager* inspect⟩

sce·nar·i·o [sɪ'nɛriou] n 1 a an outline of a film, play, etc. b a movie script. 2 an outline of a proposed course of action or possible situation: *In our revolution scenario, the rebels are bound to be defeated within a week.* ⟨Italian; Latin *scena*. See SCENE.⟩

scene [sin] n 1 the setting of a play or story: *The scene of the novel is Québec City in the year 1759.* 2 the place where anything happens: *the scene of an accident.* 3 the painted screens, sets, etc., used on a stage to represent places. 4 a formal division of an act of a play: *The king enters in Act I, Scene 2.* 5 an incident or situation, either real or portrayed: *the witch scene in Macbeth. Last night's party was a bad scene.* 6 a view; sight: *The ice on the trees made a pretty scene.* 7 a show of strong feeling in front of others: *The child made such a scene that his father was humiliated.* 8 sphere of activity: *the music scene.* ⟨Latin *scena*; Greek *skēnē* orig tent where actors changed⟩ **behind the scenes a** out of sight of the audience. **b** not seen or noticed by most people: *Much work for the Festival was done behind the scenes.* **behind–the–scenes** adj. **change of scene** a move, usually refreshing, to a different environment. **come on the scene** join an activity or group.

scen·er·y n 1 the appearance of the natural features of a place: *mountain scenery.* 2 *Theatre* the painted screens, etc. used to represent places. **sce·nic** adj 1 full of beautiful views of nature: *a scenic route along the river.* 2 to do with stage scenery or effects: *The play was a scenic triumph.* 3 *Art* representing a scene.

scent [sɛnt] n 1 a smell, esp a pleasant one: *the scent of roses.* 2 a smell left in passing, by which an animal or person can be tracked: *The dogs followed the fox's scent.* 3 perfume.
v 1 fill with a scent: *Lilacs scented the air.* 2 become aware of by smell: *The dog scented the rabbit and dashed off.* 3 get or have a suspicion of: *I scented danger and left at once.* **scent·ed** adj. **scent·less** adj. ⟨Old French *sentir* smell; Latin *sentire* feel⟩

scep·tic See SKEPTIC.

scep·tre ['sɛptər] n the rod carried by a ruler as a symbol of royal authority. Also, **scep·ter.** **scep·tred** adj. ⟨Greek *skēptron* staff⟩

sched·ule ['skɛdʒəl] or ['ʃɛdʒəl] n 1 the times fixed for events, activities, arrivals, etc.: *The bus was an hour ahead of schedule.* 2 a written statement of this, or of any list of items in a series: *to draw up a conference schedule.*
v 1 plan (something) for a definite time: *The move is scheduled for early fall.* 2 make up a schedule of. ⟨Latin *schedula* diminutive of *scheda* papyrus sheet; Greek *schidē*⟩

sche·ma ['skimə] n, pl **sche·ma·ta** ['skimətə] or [skɪ'mætə] 1 an outline, synopsis, diagram, or plan. 2 *Psychology* a systematic view of reality organizing experience and knowledge. ⟨Greek *schēma* figure, appearance⟩ **sche·mat·ic** [skɪ'mætɪk] adj in the nature of a schema. n a schematic diagram. **sche·mat·i·cal·ly** adv. **sche·ma·tize** ['skimə,taɪz] v reduce to a schema.

scheme [skim] n 1 a plot. 2 a system of connected parts; design: *the colour scheme of a room.* 3 a plan of action for achieving some goal: *a scheme for extracting gold from sea water.* 4 SCHEMA (def. 1).
v plot: *They were scheming to assassinate the king.* **schem·er** n. **schem·ing** adj. ⟨See SCHEMA⟩

schism ['skɪzəm] n 1 the division of a group into opposing factions. 2 a faction formed by schism. **schis·mat·ic** adj. ⟨Greek *schisma; schizein* split⟩

schist [ʃɪst] *n* a crystalline metamorphic rock that splits easily into layers. ⟨Greek *schistos* cleft; *schizein* split⟩

schiz·o·phre·ni·a [ˌskɪtsəˈfriniə] *or* [-ˈfrɛniə] *n* a severe mental disorder characterized by dissociation from reality, delusions, and social isolation. **schiz·o·phren·ic** [-ˈfrɛnɪk] *adj*, *n*. ⟨Greek *schizein* split + *phrēn* mind⟩ **schiz·oid** [ˈskɪtsɔɪd] *adj* characterized or caused by, or tending toward, schizophrenia.

schlep *or* **schlepp** [ʃlɛp] *v* **schlepped**, **schlep·ping 1** haul: *I don't want to schlep this suitcase upstairs.* **2** drag oneself: *I schlepped all over town in search of a decent bookstore.* *n* a hard or tiresome trip, etc. ⟨Yiddish⟩

schlock [ʃlɒk] *Slang n* shoddy or inferior stuff: *His writing is pure schlock.* **schlock** or **schlocky** *adj*. ⟨Yiddish⟩

schmaltz *or* **schmalz** [ʃmɒlts] *Slang n* extreme sentimentalism. **schmaltz·y** *adj*. ⟨German *Schmaltz* melted fat⟩

schmo *or* **schmoe** [ʃmou] *Slang n* a fool or unsophisticated person. ⟨Yiddish⟩

schmooze [ʃmuz] *Slang n* idle chat, esp as an ingratiating overture. **schmooze** *v*. ⟨Yiddish *shmues* chat, gossip⟩

schmoz·zle [ˈʃmɒzəl] *Slang n* a messy or complicated business. ⟨Yiddish⟩

schmuck [ʃmʌk] *n Slang* an obnoxious or contemptible person. ⟨Yiddish *shmok* penis⟩

schnapps *or* **schnaps** [ʃnɑps] *or* [ʃnʌps] *n* any of various distilled liquors. ⟨German⟩

schnau·zer [ˈʃnʌutsər] *or* [ˈʃnautzər] *n* a breed of terrier with a short, wiry coat, and a beard. ⟨German; *Schnauze* snout⟩

schnit·zel [ˈʃnɪtsəl] *n* a breaded and seasoned cutlet, usually veal or pork. ⟨German⟩

schol·ar [ˈskɒlər] *n* **1** one who has studied much or enjoys studying; a learned person. **2** pupil; student. **3** a holder of a scholarship: *a Rhodes scholar.* ⟨Latin *schola*. See SCHOOL¹.⟩ **schol·ar·ly** *adj* thorough in studying a topic. **schol·ar·li·ness** *n*. **schol·ar·ship** *n* **1** learning from study; the quality of this: *His analysis shows good scholarship.* **2** a grant of money or other assistance to a student with high academic performance.

scho·las·tic [skəˈlæstɪk] *adj* of schools or scholars; academic: *scholastic achievements.* **scho·las·ti·cal·ly** *adv*. ⟨Greek *scholastikos*; *scholē* school¹⟩

school¹ [skul] *n* **1** a place for teaching and learning. **2** the activity that goes on in school: *She likes school.* **3** the teachers and students: *Half the school is sick.* **4** any place, situation, etc., as a source of instruction: *the school of adversity.* **5** a group of people sharing a set of beliefs, methods, etc.: *the Dutch school of painting.* **6** a department or faculty in a university: *a school of dentistry.* *v* **1** educate in a school. **2** train: *School yourself to control your temper.* ⟨Latin *schola*; Greek *scholē*, orig leisure⟩

school board a group of people, usually elected, who manage the public schools in a given area; board of education. **school·book** *n* a book for study in schools. **school·child** *n*, *pl* **-child·ren** a child who attends school. **school·boy** *n*. **school·girl** *n*. **school district** *esp West* an area designated as a unit for the local administration of public schools. **school·house** *n* a small building used by a rural school. **school·ing** *n* **1** education received at school. **2** the cost of this. **school·marm** [-ˌmɑrm] *n Informal* **1** formerly, a female schoolteacher, esp in a rural school. **2** a very strict, conservative, proper person. **3** ✸ *Logging slang* forked tree. **school·mas·ter** *n* **1** formerly, a male teacher or principal, esp in a rural school. **2** any person or thing that teaches or disciplines. **school·mis·tress** *n*. **school·mate** *or* **school·fel·low** *n* a companion at school. **school patrol** an organized group of older pupils who help younger ones across busy streets. **school·room** *n* a room in which pupils are taught. **school·teach·er** *n* a person who teaches in a school. **school trustee** an elected member of a school board. **school·work** *n* material or lessons worked on in class or at home. **school·yard** *n* a piece of ground around a school, used for play, games, etc. **school year** that part of the year during which school is in session.

school² [skul] *n* a large group of fish or water animals swimming together. *v* form schools. ⟨Middle Dutch *schole* crowd⟩

schoon·er [ˈskunər] *n* **1** a ship with two or more masts and fore-and-aft sails. **2** *Informal* a large beer glass. **3** PRAIRIE SCHOONER. ⟨*scoon* skim, probably from Scandinavian⟩

schwa [ʃwɑ] *n* **1** an unstressed neutral vowel sound such as that of the *a* in *about*, the *u* in *circus*, or the *o* in *lemon*. **2** the symbol (ə) for this sound. ⟨German; Hebrew *sh'wa*⟩

sci·at·ic [saɪˈætɪk] *adj* **1** to do with the region of the hip. **2** to do with sciatica. ⟨Latin *sciaticus, ischiadicus*; Greek *ischion* hip joint⟩ **sci·at·i·ca** *n* pain along the path of the sciatic nerve. **sciatic nerve** the largest nerve in the human body, beginning in the pelvis and running down along the back of the thigh.

sci·ence [ˈsaɪəns] *n* **1** knowledge of facts, laws, and relationships, obtained by observation and experiment, esp as applied to physical phenomena. **2** a branch of such knowledge, such as botany or chemistry. **3** any branch of knowledge as an object of systematic study: *Economics is a social science.* **4** a technique, method, etc. to be studied systematically: *Photography is both art and science.* ⟨Latin *scientia* knowledge; *scire* know⟩ **science fiction** fiction, usually futuristic, based on actual or fanciful elements of science or technology. **sci·en·tif·ic** [ˌsaɪənˈtɪfɪk] *adj* **1** using the facts and principles of science: *a scientific farmer.* **2** used in science: *scientific instruments.* **3** systematic or exact. **sci·en·tif·i·cal·ly** *adv*. **scientific method** the principles and procedures of scientific investigation, including: (1) recognition and description of a specific problem, (2) data collection by observation and experiment,

(3) interpretation of data and formulation of a hypothesis, and (4) testing the hypothesis by further observation and experimentation. **sci·en·tist** *n* a person trained in science, whose work is scientific investigation.

sci–fi ['saɪ 'faɪ] *Informal* SCIENCE FICTION.

scim·i·tar ['sɪmə,tɑr] *n* a short, curved sword with the cutting edge on the convex side. ⟨Italian *scimitarra*⟩

scin·til·la [sɪn'tɪlə] *n* a spark or trace: *not a scintilla of evidence.* ⟨Latin = spark⟩ **scin·til·late** ['sɪntə,leɪt] *v* **1** sparkle. **2** be brilliant (in conversation, etc.). **scin·til·lat·ing** *adj.* **scin·til·la·tion** *n.*

sci·on ['saɪən] *n* **1** a bud or branch cut for grafting or planting. **2** descendant. ⟨Old French *cion*; probably Latin *secare* to cut⟩

scis·sor ['sɪzər] *v* **1** cut with scissors. **2** move (arms or legs) with a scissorlike motion. *n* **scis·sors** **1** a cutting tool with two blades whose edges slide against each other (*usually with pl verb*). **2** *Gymnastics* a movement of the legs separately back and forth, suggesting the action of scissors (*with sg or pl verb*). **3** *Wrestling* a hold in which the opponent's body or head is held with the legs (*with sg verb*). **scis·sor·like** *adj.* ⟨Latin *cisorium; -cisus* pp of *-cidere* cut; influenced by *scindere* split⟩

scle·ro·sis [sklə'rousɪs] *n, pl* -ses [-siz] the abnormal hardening of tissue in humans, animals or plants. **scle·rot·ic** [sklə'rɒtɪk] *adj.* ⟨Greek *skleros* hard⟩

scoff [skɒf] *v* make fun of; mock (with *at*). *n* a mocking insult. **scoff·er** *n.* ⟨Scandinavian⟩

scold [skould] *v* **1** rebuke angrily: *His mother scolded him for tearing his jacket.* **2** find fault; talk angrily: *He's always scolding.* *n* one who habitually scolds. ⟨Middle English; probably Old Norse *skáld* poet, lampooner⟩

sconce [skɒns] *n* a bracket on a wall, designed to hold a candle or other light. ⟨Latin *sconsa; absconsa* pp of *abscondere* hide⟩

scone [skɒn] *n* a TEA BISCUIT. ⟨probably Middle Dutch *schoonbrot* fine bread⟩

scoop [skup] *n* **1** a tool like a small shovel for dipping out or taking up things. **2** a deep spoon for serving ice cream, etc. **3** the part of a dredge, backhoe, etc. that holds earth. **4** a hollowed-out place. **5** the act or process of scooping. **6** *Slang* publication or broadcast of news before a competing media outlet **7** *Informal* the latest news: *So, what's the scoop on those two?* **scoop** *v.* **scoop·ful** *n.* ⟨Middle Dutch *schoepe* bucket and *schoppe* shovel⟩ **scoop up** take or pick up swiftly or eagerly.

scoot [skut] *v* **1** move quickly; dart: *Scoot out the side door.* **2** go away: *Scoot! Get lost!* **scoot** *n.* ⟨probably Scandinavian⟩ **scoot·er** *n* **1** a child's vehicle consisting of a long footboard with a wheel at the front and back, steered by raised handlebars and moved by pushing against the ground with one foot. **2** MOTOR SCOOTER.

scope [skoup] *n* **1** the range over which an activity, one's understanding, etc. extends: *This subject is beyond the scope of our inquiry.* **2** opportunity; room: *The project gives scope for creative thinking.* *v Slang* investigate for possible future action (with *out*): *to scope out potential building sites.* ⟨Greek *skopos* aim, object⟩

–scope *combining form* an instrument for viewing or observing: *stethoscope, telescope.* ⟨Greek *-skopion; skopeein* look at⟩

scorch [skɔrtʃ] *v* **1** burn slightly: *to scorch a shirt in ironing it.* **2** parch with intense heat; wither: *grass scorched by the sun.* **3** *Informal* drive or ride very fast: *She scorched along the empty road.* **scorch** *n.* **scorch·ing** *adj.* ⟨Middle English; Old Norse *skorpna* dry up⟩ **scorched–earth policy** a military policy of destroying everything useful in the course of a retreat, so as to leave the enemy nothing. **scorch·er** *Informal n* **1** a very hot day. **2** anything hot or fast.

score [skɔr] *n* **1** the points earned in a game, contest, test, etc. **2** an amount owed; debt: *to pay one's score.* **3** (*pl* score) a group of twenty. **4 scores** *pl* many, but fewer than hundreds: *Scores died in the epidemic.* **5** a written or printed piece of music. **6** a long scratch, line, or welt: *a score left by a whip.* **7** the act of winning a point. **8** account; reason; ground: *Don't worry on that score.* **9 the score** *Informal* the true state of affairs; the facts. *v* **1** earn (a point) in a game, contest, etc.; make (a run, hit, etc.). **2** succeed. **3 a** *Music* arrange (a composition) for instruments or voices. **b** compose the music for (a film, etc.) **4** mark with a line; scratch: *Score the cardboard along the fold line first.* **5** *Slang* succeed in seducing someone. **score·less** *adj.* **scor·er** *n.* ⟨Old Norse *skor* notch⟩ **pay off** or **settle a score** get revenge. **score·board** *n* a large board displaying the score and, sometimes, other details at a game or sporting event. **score·card** *n* **1** a card with the names of players and other information relevant to a game. **2** a card for recording the score of a game. **score·keep·er** *n* the one who keeps official record of the score in a game.

scorn [skɔrn] *v* **1** think of as unworthy or foolish: *He scorns his critics as know-nothings.* **2** reject or refuse as unworthy: *The judge scorned to take a bribe.* *n* contempt. **scorn·ful** *adj.* **scorn·ful·ly** *adv.* ⟨Old French *escarnir*⟩

scor·pi·on ['skɔrpjən] *n* any of an order of arachnids having a tail with a poisonous stinger at the tip. ⟨Latin *scorpio*; Greek *skorpios*⟩

Scot [skɒt] *n* **1** a native or inhabitant of Scotland. **2** a person of Scottish descent. ⟨Old English *Scottas*; Latin *Scottus* Irishman⟩ **Scotch** [skɒtʃ] *n* a whisky made in Scotland. *adj* (only in compound names) Scottish. **Scotch broth** a thick soup containing mutton, vegetables, and barley. **Scotch tape** *Trademark* a transparent plastic adhesive tape. **Scots** *adj* to do with the people of Scotland or their culture or language. *n* a language spoken in Scotland, closely related to English. **Scots·man** *n, pl* **-men** a man who is a native or inhabitant of Scotland. **Scots·wom·an** *n, pl* **-wom·en**. **Scot·tish** *adj* to do with Scotland or its people. *n* **1 the Scottish** *pl* the people of Scotland or of Scottish descent. **2** Scots.

USAGE

The preferred term for a person from Scotland or having ancestors from Scotland is **Scot**; the corresponding adjective is **Scots**. **Scottish** is used primarily to refer to the country itself (*Scottish climate*), while **Scotch** is potentially offensive and occurs only in fixed compounds.

---

scot–free [ˈskɒt ˈfriː] *adj, adv* completely free from penalty or other negative consequence: *She was convicted of fraud; he got off scot-free.* ⟨Middle English *scot* a tax or levy⟩

scoun·drel [ˈskaʊndrəl] *n* a person without principles; villain. **scoun·drel·ly** *adj.* ⟨Old French *escondre*; Latin *ex-* from + *condere* hide⟩

scour¹ [skaʊr] *v* **1** clean by vigorous rubbing: *Scour the frying pan with cleanser.* **2** dig by the action of running water: *The stream had scoured a channel.* *n* **1** the act or result of scouring. **2 scours** diarrhea in cattle. ⟨probably Old French *escurer*; Latin *ex-* completely + *cura* care⟩ **scour·ings** *n pl* dirt, etc. removed by scouring.

scour² [skaʊr] *v* search by looking into every part of: *to scour the countryside for a lost child, to scour one's memory for a forgotten date.* ⟨probably Old French *escourre* run forth; Latin *ex-* out + *currere* run⟩

scourge [skɜrdʒ] *n* **1** a whip. **2** any severe punishment or affliction. *v* **1** whip; flog. **2** punish severely, afflict or oppress. ⟨Anglo-French *escorge*; Latin *ex-* out + *corrigia* whip⟩

scout [skaʊt] *n* **1** a soldier sent to find out what the enemy is doing. **2** a warship, aircraft, etc. used for this. **3** a person sent to get information about one's competitors, promising opportunities, etc. or find talented recruits. **4** the act of scouting. **5** *Slang* a person: *She's a good scout.* *v* **1** act as a scout. **2** hunt around: *Go scout for firewood.* **3** (often with *out*) observe or examine for information. ⟨Old French *escouter* listen; Latin *auscultare*⟩

scowl [skaʊl] *v* draw the eyebrows down and tighten the mouth in anger or sullenness. **scowl** *n.* ⟨Middle English *skoul*; Scandinavian⟩

scrab·ble [ˈskræbəl] *v* **1** scratch or scrape around with hands, claws, etc. **2** struggle desperately: *to scrabble for a living.* ⟨Dutch *schrabbelen* frequentative of *schrabben* scratch⟩

scrag·gly [ˈskrægli] *adj* rough, irregular, and untidy: *a scraggly garden, scraggly hair.*

scram [skræm] *v* **scrammed, scram·ming** *Slang* go away: *Scram!* ⟨short for *scramble*⟩

scram·ble [ˈskræmbəl] *v* **1** climb, crawl, or run awkwardly: *We scrambled up the slippery bank.* **2** struggle with others for something: *They scrambled for the football.* **3** mix up; put out of order. **4** cook (eggs) with whites and yolks stirred together. **5** *Telecommunications* break up (a signal) so that it cannot be received without special equipment. **6** move or work in a hurried or disorganized way: *We'll have to scramble to get out of here on time.* **scram·ble** *n.* **scram·bler** *n.* ⟨variant of *scrabble*⟩

scrap¹ [skræp] *n* **1** a small discarded or leftover piece of food: *Our dog eats scraps.* **2** a small fragment of anything: *scraps of paper. She read out scraps of the letter.* **3** discarded recyclable material: *a yard full of iron scrap.* *v* **scrapped, scrap·ping 1** throw out: *We should scrap this old sofa.* **2** abandon (a project, idea, etc.). ⟨Old Norse *scrap; scrapa* scrape⟩ **scrap·book** *n* a book in which pictures or clippings are pasted and kept. **scrap iron** or **metal** recyclable iron or other metal waste.

scrap² [skræp] *v* **scrapped, scrap·ping** *Informal* fight; quarrel. ⟨*scrape*⟩ **scrap·per** *n* a spirited fighter, esp a small one. **scrap·py** *adj* fond of fighting.

scrape [skreip] *v* **1** rub with something sharp or rough. **2** remove or clean off in this way: *to scrape old paint off a wall.* **3** scratch by rubbing against something rough: *She fell and scraped her knee on the sidewalk.* **4** dig crudely: *He scraped a hole in the sand.* **5** collect gradually or with difficulty: *to scrape together enough money for a trip.* *n* **1** the act, sound, or result of scraping. **2** a bad position resulting from rash behaviour, that may lead to disgrace or punishment. ⟨Old Norse *skrapa*⟩ **bow and scrape.** See BOW¹. **scrape the bottom of the barrel** take the least desirable solution, candidate, etc. as a last resort. **scrape by** (or **through** or **along**) manage with difficulty: *They can just scrape by but won't accept help.* **scrap·er** *n* a tool for removing something by scraping: *a paint scraper, an ice scraper.* **scrap·ings** *n pl* bits scraped off or up.

scratch [skrætʃ] *v* **1** mark or cut the surface of with something sharp or rough: *Your shoes scratched the chair.* **2** wound with the nails or claws: *Careful; that cat scratches.* **3** rub or scrape to relieve itching: *He scratched his leg.* **4** scrape with a harsh noise: *He scratched his fingernail along the chalkboard.* **5** strike out; delete. **6** withdraw or cancel: *The event has been scratched.* *n* **1** the act, sound, or result of scratching. **2** the starting line of a race. **3** *Slang* money. **4** scribble. **5** *Slang* nothing. *adj* made up from whatever is on hand: *a scratch meal, a scratch football team.* ⟨Middle English *scratten* and *crachen*⟩ **from scratch a** from the beginning: *He lost his notes and had to start over from scratch.* **b** in cooking, without a mix: *to bake a cake from scratch.* **scratch the surface** do something in a superficial way. **up to scratch** up to standard; good enough. **scratch pad** a pad of paper (**scratch paper**) for rough work or casual writing. **scratch test** an allergy test in which the skin is scratched and an allergen applied; redness indicates allergy. **scratch·y** *adj* **1** that scratches or

makes a scratching noise: *a scratchy pen.*
2 giving a prickly or itchy feeling: *a scratchy wool dress.* **3** consisting of scratches: *scratchy drawings.* **scratch·i·ly** *adv.* **scratch·i·ness** *n.*

scrawl [skrɒl] *v* write or draw poorly, hastily, or carelessly. **scrawl** *n.* **scrawled** *adj.* **scrawl·er** *n.* ⟨possible blend of *scratch* and *sprawl*⟩

scraw·ny ['skrɒni] *adj* **1** too thin or lean; skinny: *a scrawny chicken.* **2** of plants, stunted. **scraw·ni·ness** *n.* ⟨Scandinavian⟩

scream [skrim] *v* **1** make a loud, piercing cry of fear, anger, or pain. **2** make a loud, shrill, harsh noise: *The siren screamed.* **3** speak or laugh very shrilly or loudly: *I had to scream to be heard.* **4** produce a very startling effect: *"War declared!" the headlines screamed.*
n **1** a loud, piercing cry or noise. **2** *Informal* a very funny person or thing. ⟨probably Old Norse *skræma* scare⟩

> **SYNONYMS**
>
> **Scream** means to give out suddenly a loud, piercing cry of fear, anger, or pain: *She screamed when she saw the child fall.*
> **Shriek** suggests a more high-pitched, wild, spine-tingling cry, expressing extreme terror, horror, agony, or uncontrollable laughter or rage: *The prisoner shrieked as he was tortured.*
> **Screech** emphasizes the unpleasant effect on the hearer, suggesting a very penetrating, sharp, shrill cry: *the screech of an owl.*

screech[1] [skritʃ] *v, n* scream; shriek. **screech·er** *n.* **screech·y** *adj.* ⟨Middle English *scritch*; imitative⟩ .

screech[2] [skritʃ] *n* ✺ *esp Newfoundland and Labrador Slang* **1** a potent dark rum. **2** any cheap, potent liquor or wine. ⟨Scots *screigh* whisky, influenced by *screech*[1]⟩

screen [skrin] *n* **1** a device consisting of wire mesh or a synthetic substitute, fastened in a frame: *Screens on our windows keep out flies.* **2** a covered frame that protects or hides. **3** a partition, often ornamental. **4** anything that hides or protects like a screen: *A screen of trees hides our house from the road.* **5** a flat, white, specially prepared surface on which a slide or film is projected. **6** films collectively or the film industry: *a star of stage and screen.* **7** the backlit surface of an electronic display device, on which the image appears: *a computer screen.* **8** the data displayed on a computer monitor at one time: *to print out a screen.* **9** a sieve for sifting sand, etc.
v **1** shelter, protect, or hide with or as if with a screen: *to screen one's face from a fire, to screen a guilty person.* **2** test or examine and sort by certain criteria: *to screen job applicants, to screen people for TB.* **3** show or look at on a screen. **4** sift with a screen. **screen·a·ble** *adj.* **screen·ing** *n.* ⟨Old French *escren*; Germanic⟩
screen·play *n* a story or play written for production as a film. **screen saver** *Computers* a pattern appearing on the screen whenever there is a pause in input, to save wear on the screen. **screen test** a trial filming of a prospective actor or scene. **screen–test** *v.*

screw [skru] *n* **1** a fastening device like a nail but with a ridge spiralling around its length, and a slot in the head to fit a screwdriver. **2** a simple machine consisting of a spiral ridge around a cylinder, used to exert pressure or lift things. **3** anything resembling a screw. **4** a spiral motion. **5** *Slang* a prison guard.
v **1** fasten or tighten with a screw or screws. **2** turn as one turns a screw; fasten or remove in this way: *Screw the lid on.* **3** twist or contort (often with *up*): *to screw up one's eyes.* **4** *Informal* force: *They screwed the truth out of him.* **5** *Slang* take unfair advantage of. ⟨Old French *escroue* nut, screw; Latin *scroba*⟩
have a screw loose *Slang* be slightly crazy. **put the screws on** *Informal* use pressure or force to get something from. **screw around** *Slang* **a** waste time. **b** engage in promiscuous sexual intercourse. **screw up a** *Slang* bungle. **b** *Slang* damage psychologically. **screwed–up** *adj.* **c** *Informal* summon (courage, etc.).
screw·ball *n* **1** *Slang* an eccentric or crazy person. **2** *Baseball* a pitch thrown with a spin opposite to that of a curve. *adj Slang* eccentric or crazy. **screw·driv·er** *n* **1** a tool for putting in or taking out screws by turning them. **2** a cocktail made of vodka and orange juice. **screw propeller** a propeller with slightly twisted blades. **screw·y** *adj Slang* **1** crazy or eccentric. **2** out of order; not right.

scrib·ble ['skrɪbəl] *v* **1** write carelessly or hastily. **2** make meaningless marks; doodle. **scrib·ble** *n.* ⟨Latin *scribillare*; *scribere* write⟩ **scrib·bler** *n* **1** ✺ a notebook. **2** a mediocre author. **3** a person who scribbles.

scribe [skraib] *n* **1** formerly, a person whose work was copying manuscript. **2** a member of a class of professional interpreters of Jewish law. **3** a public clerk or secretary. **4** a writer. **5** Usually, **scrib·er** a tool for marking on wood or metal. ⟨Latin *scriba*; *scribere* write⟩

scrim·mage ['skrɪmɪdʒ] *n* **1** a rough struggle. **2** *Football* play that takes place after the two teams line up and the ball is snapped back. **scrim·mage** *v.* ⟨variant of *skirmish*⟩

scrimp [skrɪmp] *v* skimp: *They had to scrimp for years to save for a down payment on a house.* ⟨probably Old Norse *skrimpa* shrivel⟩

scrip [skrɪp] *n* **1** a certificate, voucher, etc. establishing the bearer's right to something. **2** ✺ a certificate issued to the Métis after the Riel Rebellions, as compensation for lands at the rate of one dollar per acre, in amounts of 160 or 240. ⟨variant of *script*⟩

script [skrɪpt] *n* **1** handwriting. **2** a system of symbols for writing: *phonetic script.* **3** the text of a play, film, etc.
v **1** write a script for. **2** constrain as if by a script: *scripted conversation.* ⟨Latin *scriptum* pp of *scribere* write⟩

Scrip·ture ['skrɪptʃər] *n* **1** Sometimes, **the Scriptures** *pl* the Bible. **2 scripture** any sacred or authoritative writing. **scrip·tur·al** or **Scrip·tur·al** *adj.* ⟨Latin *scriptura*; *scriptum* pp of *scribere* write⟩

scrod [skrɒd] *n* a young cod or haddock for cooking. ⟨Middle Dutch *schrode* piece cut off⟩

scroll [skroul] *n* **1** a roll of parchment or paper, esp one with writing on it. **2** an ornamental design resembling a partly rolled sheet of paper in cross-section.
v Computers **1** move images or lines of text up or down on the screen to display what is above or below. **2** view (records, a document, etc.) successively in this way (with *through*). **scroll–like** *adj.* ⟨alteration of *scrow*; Old French *escroe* scrap; influenced by *roll*⟩
scroll bar *Computers* a narrow horizontal or vertical strip on the screen, whose contents indicate the direction of scrolling and one's location in a document. **scroll saw** a very narrow saw for cutting thin wood in ornamental patterns. **scroll·work** *n* decorative work featuring scrolls, esp when done in wood with a scroll saw.

Scrooge [skrudʒ] *n* a mean, stingy person. ⟨miser in *A Christmas Carol* by Dickens⟩

scro·tum ['skroutəm] *n, pl* **-ta** [-tə] or **-tums** in most male mammals, the pouch of skin containing the testicles. **scro·tal** *adj.* ⟨Latin⟩

scrounge [skraundʒ] *v Informal* **1** search or forage for something: *She scrounged around in the drawer for a pen.* **2** get by begging; mooch: *He's always scrounging bus fare.* **3** take without asking: *to scrounge bricks from a building site.* **scroung·er** *n.* ⟨dialect *scrunge* steal⟩
scrounge up get or find by scrounging.

scrub[1] [skrʌb] *v* **scrubbed, scrub·bing 1** wash or clean with hard rubbing. **2** remove or try to remove (dirt, a spot, etc.) in this way. **3** wash the hands and arms before performing surgery (usually with *up*). **4** *Informal* **a** get rid of. **b** cancel (an event): *The launching was scrubbed.* **5** remove pollutants from (gas or vapour): *to scrub factory emissions.* **scrub** *n.* **scrub·ba·ble** *adj.* **scrub·ber** *n.* ⟨perhaps Middle Dutch *schrubben*⟩

scrub[2] [skrʌb] *n* **1** an area of low, stunted trees or shrubs. **2** any undersized or inferior person or thing. **3** *Sports* a player not on the regular team. **scrub** *adj.* **scrub·by** *adj.* ⟨Old English *scrybb* brushwood⟩
scrub pine *Informal* any of various small pines such as the **jack pine** or **whitebark pine**.

scruff [skrʌf] *n* the skin at the back of the neck: *She picked up the kitten by the scruff of the neck.* ⟨possibly Old Norse *skrufr* tuft of hair; *skurfr, skufr* (by metathesis)⟩
scruf·fy *adj* unkempt, slovenly, or shabby.

scrum [skrʌm] *n* **1** mobbing of a politician by reporters for rapid questioning as he or she emerges from a building, vehicle, etc. **2** the group of reporters. **3** *Rugby* a struggle for the ball as it is thrown into play between teams.

scrump·tious ['skrʌmpʃəs] *adj Informal* very delicious: *a scrumptious meal.* ⟨perhaps alteration of *sumptuous*⟩

scrunch [skrʌntʃ] *v* **1** crush or crumple: *He scrunched the paper into a tiny ball.* **2** hunch or crouch: *We scrunched down behind the fence and waited.* ⟨imitative⟩

scru·ple ['skrupəl] *n* **1** a feeling of uneasiness about doing something that might be wrong:

He had scruples about taking the free tickets. **2** moral integrity: *a man of scruple.*
v hesitate or be unwilling (to do what may be wrong): *She does not scruple to lie.* ⟨Latin *scrupulus* diminutive of *scrupus* sharp stone⟩
scru·pu·lous ['skrupjələs] *adj* **1** showing strict regard for what is right: *He was scrupulous in his dealings with customers.* **2** very careful or exact: *scrupulous attention to detail.* **scru·pu·lous·ly** *adv.* **scru·pu·lous·ness** *n.*

SYNONYMS

Scrupulous emphasizes care taken to follow strictly what one knows is right: *She takes scrupulous care of the children's health.*
Punctilious, more formal, suggests excessive attention to fine points of rules, duty, and requirements for conduct: *He is punctilious about paying back every tiny debt.*

scru·ti·ny ['skrutəni] *n* **1** a close inspection; careful examination: *Her work will not stand up under scrutiny.* **2** a searching gaze. **3** an official examination of ballots cast at an election. ⟨Latin *scrutinium; scrutari* ransack⟩
scru·ti·neer *n* a person who ensures that voting procedure and subsequent counting of ballots are properly carried out. **scru·ti·nize** *v* examine closely; inspect carefully: *The jeweller scrutinized the diamond for flaws.*

scu·ba ['skubə] *n* a portable apparatus used for breathing underwater. **scu·ba–dive, –dived** or **–dove, –div·ing** *v.* **scuba diver.** ⟨self-contained underwater breathing apparatus⟩

scud [skʌd] *v* **scud·ded, scud·ding** esp of clouds, move along swiftly and lightly. ⟨possibly Old English *scudan* hurry⟩

scuff [skʌf] *v* **1** injure the surface of by hard use: *to scuff one's shoes, to scuff the carpet.* **2** walk without lifting (the feet); SHUFFLE (def. 1).
n the act, sound or result of scuffing. ⟨*scuffle*⟩

scuf·fle ['skʌfəl] *v* **1** struggle in a rough, manner, but not violently: *The children scuffled for first place in the lineup.* **2** SHUFFLE (def. 1). **scuf·fle** *n.* ⟨Scandinavian; compare Swedish *skuffa* push⟩

scull [skʌl] *n* **1** an oar worked from side to side over the stern of a boat to propel it forward. **2** one of a pair of oars used by a single rower. **3** Also, a light racing boat for one or more rowers using sculls. **scull** *v.* **scull·er** *n.* ⟨origin unknown⟩

scul·ler·y ['skʌləri] *n* a small room where dishes are washed. ⟨Old French *escuelerie*; Latin *scutella* diminutive of *scutra* platter⟩

sculpt [skʌlpt] *v* **1** make (a figure, esp a work of art) by carving, casting, etc. **2** shape in an artistic or interesting way: *snowdrifts sculpted by the wind.* **sculp·tor** *n.* ⟨back-formed from *sculptor*, Latin; *scalpere* carve⟩
sculp·ture ['skʌlptʃər] *n* **1** the art of sculpting. **2** a piece of work made by sculpting, or such works collectively. *v* **1** sculpt. **2** decorate with sculpture. **sculp·tur·al** *adj.* **sculp·tured** *adj.*

scum [skʌm] *n* **1** a surface layer of impurities formed on heated liquids: *to remove the scum*

from the top of boiling maple syrup. **2** the layer of algae or other matter that forms on standing water. **3** the lowest sort of people. **4** a worthless person.
v form scum or become covered with scum. **scum·my** *adj.* ⟨Middle Dutch *schuum*⟩

scup·per ['skʌpər] *n* an opening in the side of a ship to drain water from the deck.
v **1** *Informal* spoil; bring to nothing: *The rain scuppered our plans for a picnic supper.* **2** sink (a ship). ⟨origin uncertain⟩

scurf [skɜrf] *n* **1** small scales of dead skin; dandruff. **2** any scaly matter on a surface. **scurf·y** *adj.* **scurf·i·ness** *n.* ⟨Scandinavian⟩

scur·ri·lous ['skɜrələs] *adj* using abusive or obscene language; foul-mouthed: *a scurrilous rabblerouser, a scurrilous attack.* **scur·ril·i·ty** *n.* **scur·ri·lous·ly** *adv.* **scur·ri·lous·ness** *n.* ⟨Latin *scurrilis; scurra* buffoon⟩

scur·ry ['skɜri] *v* run quickly and lightly; hurry: *A mouse scurried past us.* **scur·ry** *n.* ⟨perhaps *hurry-scurry*, reduplication of *hurry*⟩

scur·vy ['skɜrvi] *n* a disease caused by lack of vitamin C, characterized by swollen and bleeding gums and prostration. It was common among sailors on long voyages with poor food to eat.
adj low; mean; contemptible: *a scurvy fellow, a scurvy trick.* **scur·vi·ness** *n.* ⟨*scurf*⟩

scut·tle¹ ['skʌtəl] *n* a bucket for coal. ⟨Latin *scutella* platter⟩

scut·tle² ['skʌtəl] *v* scamper; scurry. ⟨variant of *scuddle* frequentative of *scud*⟩

scut·tle³ ['skʌtəl] *n* an opening with a trap door, esp in a ship's deck or a floor.
v **1** cut a hole or holes through the hull of (a ship) to sink it. **2** ruin or destroy (a hope, undertaking, etc.): *Their statement to the press scuttled the conference.* **3** SCRAP¹ (*v* 2). ⟨perhaps Spanish *escotilla* hatchway⟩
scut·tle·butt ['skʌtəl,bʌt] *n* **1** a drinking fountain or a cask containing drinking water on a ship. **2** *Slang* rumours; gossip.

scuz·zy ['skʌzi] *adj Slang* grungy or sleazy. ⟨origin uncertain⟩

scythe [saɪð] *n* a tool to cut grass or grain, consisting of a long, slightly curved blade at right angles to the end of a long handle.
v cut with a scythe. ⟨Old English *sīthe*; spelling influenced by Latin *scindere* cut⟩

SE or **S.E.** southeast(ern); southeasterly.

sea [si] *n* **1** the great body of salt water that covers almost three-fourths of the earth's surface; ocean. **2** any large body of salt water partly or wholly enclosed by land: *the North Sea, the Mediterranean Sea.* **3** a large, heavy wave: *A high sea swept away the mast.* **4** a huge amount or vast expanse: *a sea of faces.* **5** *Astronomy* MARE². ⟨Old English *sǣ*⟩
at sea a out on the sea. **b** *Informal* confused. **go to sea a** become a sailor. **b** begin a sea voyage; also, **put to sea.**
sea anemone any of various flowerlike, often colourful polyps found in warm seas. **sea·bed** *n* the bed or bottom of the sea. **sea·board** *n*

the land near the sea; coast: *the Atlantic seaboard.* **sea change** a radical change. **sea·coast** *n* land along the sea. **sea cow** a manatee, dugong, or similar marine mammal. **sea cucumber** any of a class of marine invertebrates with a long, flexible, cylindrical body. **sea dog** a sailor with long experience at sea. **sea·far·er** [-,fɛrər] *n* a traveller on the sea; sailor. **sea·far·ing** *adj, n.* **sea·food** *n* **1** edible saltwater fish or shellfish. **2** loosely, food consisting of any fish, including freshwater fish. **sea·go·ing** *adj* of a vessel, going by sea or fit to go by sea. **sea·gull** *n* any of various large gulls, esp the **herring gull**. **sea·horse** *n* any of a number of small, upright-swimming marine fishes of warm seas with a forward-curled, prehensile tail and a horselike head. **sea ice** masses of ice in the sea. **sea legs** *Informal* the ability to balance on a rolling or pitching ship. **get one's sea legs a** get used to the motion of a ship. **b** get used to anything difficult. **sea level** the level of the surface of the sea, esp when halfway between mean high and low water. Land is measured in metres above or below sea level. **sea lion** any of several large seals of the Pacific, with small external ears and a coat of short, coarse hair that lacks an undercoat. **sea·man** *n, pl* **-men 1** a sailor on the sea. **2** a sailor who is not an officer. **sea·man·like** *adj.* **sea·man·ship** *n* skill in navigating and handling a ship. **sea mile** a nautical mile (about 1.85 km). **sea monster** an imaginary or mythical marine animal of terrifying proportions and shape. **sea otter** a large, rare otter of N Pacific coastal waters with large, flipperlike hind feet and a thick brown coat. It is now a protected species. **sea·plane** *n* an airplane that can take off and come down on water. **sea·port** *n* **1** a port or harbour on the coast. **2** a city or town with a harbour for seagoing ships. **sea power 1** the naval strength of a nation. **2** a nation having great naval strength: *Canada is not a major sea power.* **sea salt** salt obtained from seawater. **sea·scape** *n* a picture or view of the sea. **sea serpent** a snakelike sea monster. **sea·shell** *n* the empty shell of a sea mollusc, such as an oyster, conch, etc. **sea·shore** *n* **1** the land right next to the sea; beach. **2** *Law* that part of the shore between the high-water and low-water marks. **sea·sick** *adj* nauseous and dizzy from the movement of a ship at sea, or from any similar motion. **sea·sick·ness** *n.* **sea·side** *n* the land along the sea; beach; seashore. **sea slug** any of various colourful marine gastropods with fringelike projections. Also, **nu·di·branch. sea urchin** any of a class of marine invertebrates with a spherical body and a rigid outer shell with rows of movable spines. **sea wall** a wall or embankment made to keep waves from wearing away the shore; breakwater. **sea·ward** *adv, adj* **1** toward the sea: *Our house faces seaward.* **2** of a wind, from the sea: *a seaward breeze.* Also (*adv*), **seawards. to seaward** toward the sea. **sea·wa·ter** *n* the salt water in the ocean. **sea·way** *n* **1** a route over the ocean. **2** an inland waterway connected to the open sea, deep enough for seagoing ships: *the St. Lawrence Seaway.* **sea·weed** *n* any plant growing in the sea, esp an alga. **sea·wor·thy** *adj* fit for sailing on the sea. **sea·wor·thi·ness** *n.*

seal¹ [sil] *n* **1** a piece of wax, paper, etc. with a design stamped on it, fixed to a document to show authenticity. **2** any mark of genuineness or authority. **3** a state of being closed tightly so as to keep out air, water, etc.: *Weatherstripping around the door gives a good seal.*
v **1** close tightly: *to seal an envelope.* **2** fill the cracks or pores of. **3** settle finally: *The judge's word sealed the prisoner's fate.* **4** give a sign that (something) is true: *to seal a promise with a kiss.* **seal·a·ble** *adj.* ⟨Anglo-French; Latin *sigillum* diminutive of *signum* sign⟩
set one's seal to approve.
seal·ant ['silənt] *n* a substance for sealing or waterproofing wood, joints in a pipe, etc. **seal·er** *n* **1** sealant. **2** something, such as a rubber ring, etc., that ensures a tight closure. **sealing wax** a waxlike mixture used to make seals or seal things.

seal² [sil] *n, pl* **seals** or **seal** any of various marine mammals having limbs modified into flippers.
v hunt seals. ⟨Old English *seolh*⟩
seal·er *n* **1** a seal hunter. **2** a ship used to hunt seals. **seal·skin** *n* **1** the pelt or fur of a fur seal. **2** a garment made of this.

seal·er¹ See SEAL¹.

seal·er² See SEAL².

seam [sim] *n* **1** the joint where two pieces of cloth, leather, etc. are sewn together. **2** any place where edges come together: *seams in a boat's hull.* **3** any mark or line like a seam. **4** *Geology* a layer; stratum: *a seam of coal.*
v **1** join by or as if by sewing. **2** mark with lines, wrinkles, etc.: *Years of hardship had seamed her face.* ⟨Old English *sēam*⟩
seam·less *adj* **1** without seams. **2** of any transition, smooth and unnoticeable. **seam·stress** ['simstrɪs] *n* a woman who sews professionally. **seam·y** *adj* least attractive; sordid or squalid: *the seamy side of life.* **seam·i·ness** *n.*

sé·ance ['seiɑns] *n* a meeting of people to contact the spirits of the dead. ⟨French *séance*; *seoir* sit; Latin *sedere*⟩

sear [sir] *v* **1** burn or char the surface of: *The hot iron seared his flesh.* **2** make hard or unfeeling: *Years of cruelty had seared her heart.* **3** dry up; wither. ⟨Old English *sēarian*⟩

search [sɜrtʃ] *v* **1** look (*for*): *to search for lost keys.* **2** examine thoroughly in order to find something: *to search a prisoner, to search one's heart.* **3** *Computers* go through (data) to find items meeting certain criteria. **search** *n.* ⟨Old French *cerchier*; Latin *circus* circle⟩
in search of looking for: *kids in search of adventure.* **search out** find by searching.
search and replace *Computers* a text-editing function that finds all character strings

meeting given criteria and replaces them with something specified. **search engine** a piece of software used to find and access files, Web sites, etc. **search·ing** *adj* **1** that examines carefully: *a searching gaze.* **2** penetrating: *a searching wind.* **search·ing·ly** *adv.* **search·light** *n* a device that can throw a powerful beam of light in any direction. **search party** a group of people searching for a lost person. **search warrant** a document authorizing the search of a house or building for stolen goods, evidence, suspects, etc.

sea·son [si'zən] *n* **1** one of the four periods of a year, identified by characteristic weather; spring, summer, fall, or winter. **2** a period of the year with reference to typical weather conditions: *dry season.* **3** any period marked by something special: *the hockey season.* **4** *Poetic* any stage or period: *seasons of life.*
v **1** add salt, herbs, or spices to. **2** add interest or character to: *season conversation with wit.* **3** moderate; temper: *Season justice with mercy.* **4** make fit for use by aging or treating: *to season wood for building.* **5** accustom or train by experience: *seasoned soldiers.* ⟨Old French *seson;* Latin *sationis* sowing⟩
in season a in the right time for hunting: *Deer are in season now.* **b** of produce, available according to the time of year. **c** at the right time. **d** of a female mammal, ready to mate. **out of season** not in season.
sea·son·a·ble *adj* typical for the season: *Hot weather is seasonable in July.* **sea·son·a·bly** *adv.* **sea·son·al** *adj* to do with the seasons: *seasonal work.* **sea·son·al·ly** *adv.* **seasonal affective disorder** depression in winter due to lack of light. *Abbrev* **SAD. sea·son·ing** *n* **1** anything added to food to give extra flavour, such as a spice or herb. **2** anything that adds character or interest. **season ticket** a ticket admitting one to an entire series of games, concerts, etc.

CONFUSABLES

Seasonable indicates appropriateness to a given time of year: *Snow is seasonable during the winter in Canada.* **Seasonal** refers to things dependent on the changing seasons: *Driving a snowplow is a seasonal job.*

---

seat¹ [sit] *n* **1** something to sit on. **2** that part of a chair, bench, etc. on which one sits. **3** the part of the body on which one sits, or the part of a garment covering it. **4** the right to sit as a spectator at an event: *Seats for tonight's performance cost $20.* **5** the right to sit as a member of a legislature, board, etc.: *The Liberals lost 27 seats in the election.* **6** that on which anything rests; base.
v **1 a** cause to sit: *to seat a child on a chair.* **b** usher to a seat. **2** have seats for (a given number of people): *a hall seating 200.* ⟨Old Norse *sǽti*⟩
be seated a sit down. **b** be sitting. **by the seat of one's pants** in an intuitive way. **seat–of–the–pants** *adj.* **take a seat** sit down. **seat belt** a belt or strap in a car, aircraft, etc. designed to hold an occupant in the seat in case of a crash, jolt, bump, etc. **seat·ing** *n*

the arrangement or number of seats for a dinner party, in a theatre, etc.

seat² [sit] *n* the established centre of a given activity, power, group, etc.: *A university is a seat of learning. In this culture, the heart is the seat of the emotions.* **seat** *v.* ⟨Old English *sǣte*⟩

se·cant ['sikənt] *or* ['sikænt] *n* **1** *Geometry* a line that intersects a curve at two or more points. **2** *Trigonometry* the ratio of the length of the hypotenuse of a right triangle to the length of the side adjacent to an acute angle. *Abbrev* **sec.** ⟨Latin *secare* cut⟩

se·cede [sɪ'sid] *v* withdraw from a federation. **se·ced·er** *n.* **se·ces·sion** *n.* **se·ces·sion·ism** *n.* ⟨Latin *se-* apart + *cedere* go⟩

se·clude [sɪ'klud] *v* shut off from other people; isolate. **se·clud·ed** *adj.* **se·clu·sion** *n.* ⟨Latin *se-* apart + *claudere* shut⟩

sec·ond¹ ['sɛkənd] *adj* **1** next after the first; 2nd: *the second seat from the back, the second mate on a ship, second soprano.* **2** other: *Napoleon was a second Caesar.*
n **1** the next after the first. **2 seconds** *pl* goods with some slight defect. **3** one who supports or relieves: *The boxer had a second.* **4** *Music* **a** a tone one degree up from a given tone, the interval between the two, or the combination of both tones. **b** the second note in a scale. **5 seconds** *pl* a second helping of food: *Anyone for seconds?*
v **1** back up or support; especially, express support of (a motion) in parliamentary procedure. **2** [sə'kɒnd] temporarily assign (a person) to some office outside his or her own organization. **second** *adv.* **sec·ond·er** *n.* ⟨Latin *secundus; sequi* follow⟩
at second hand See HAND.
sec·ond·ar·y ['sɛkən,dɛri] *adj* **1** next after the first in order or importance; not main or chief. **2** not original; derived. **3** *Electricity* of a coil or circuit, in which a current is produced by induction. **sec·ond·ar·i·ly** *adv.* **secondary colour** a colour made by mixing primary colours. **secondary school** a school attended after elementary school; high school. **secondary sex characteristic** any of the physical manifestations distinguishing male from female but not needed for reproduction, such as distribution of body fat, female breasts, change of voice in adolescent males, etc. **second base** *Baseball* the base behind the pitcher's mound, opposite home plate. **second childhood** senility. **second class** a class ranking below the first in quality, luxury, level of service, etc. **sec·ond–class** *adj.* **second cousin** the child of one's parent's first cousin. **second–degree** *adj* of a burn, sufficient to cause blistering but not scarring. **second estate** the clergy. **second fiddle** *Informal* a person in a less important role. **play second fiddle** be in such a role. **sec·ond–guess** *v* solve a problem, criticize, etc., using hindsight. **second hand** a hand on a timepiece, showing the passage of seconds. **sec·ond–hand** *adj* **1** not original; obtained from another: *second-hand information.* **2** not new; used: *second-hand clothes.* **3** dealing in

used goods: *a second-hand store.* **sec·ond·ly** *adv* in the second place. **second mortgage** an additional loan on the security of property such as a house. **second nature** an acquired quality, skill, habit, etc. that one has had for so long that it seems to be a part of one's nature. **second person** *Grammar* the category of forms used to indicate the person spoken to. *You* and *your* are pronouns of the second person. **sec·ond–rate** *adj* of inferior quality or value. **second sight** power to see future events; clairvoyance. **second thoughts** doubt about a previous decision or course of action. **second wind 1** a renewal of energy following an initial feeling of exhaustion during a race or other effort. **2** any recovery after a decline.

sec·ond² ['sɛkənd] *n* **1** an SI unit of time, one-sixtieth of a minute. *Symbol* **s 2** a very short period of time: *I'll be there in a second.* **3** an SI unit for measuring plane angles, one-sixtieth of a minute. *Symbol* ″ ⟨Latin *secunda minuta* second minute, i.e., the result of the second division of the hour into sixty parts⟩

se·cret ['sikrɪt] *adj* **1** kept from the knowledge of others: *a secret plan.* **2** keeping information to oneself: *He's as secret as the grave.* **3** acting in secret: *secret police.*
n **1** a secret thing. **2** an explanation; key: *The secret to her delicious sauce is lemon juice.* **se·cre·cy** *n.* **se·cret·ly** *adv.* ⟨Latin *secretus* pp of *secernere* set apart; *se-* apart + *cernere* separate⟩
in secret not openly; without others knowing. **secret agent** a worker for the intelligence service of a government. **se·crete** [sɪ'krit] *v* **1** produce and release (a substance): *Glands in the mouth secrete saliva.* **2** keep secret; hide. **se·cre·tion** *n.* **se·cre·tive** ['sikrətɪv] *adj* **1** not frank and open; having the habit of secrecy. **2** [sɪ'kritɪv] causing or aiding secretion. **se·cre·tive·ly** *adv.* **se·cre·tive·ness** *n.* **secret police** in a totalitarian regime, a special police force that operates covertly to control and suppress activities considered subversive. **secret service** the branch of a government that makes secret investigations.

SYNONYMS
Secret is the general word describing something hidden: *They have secret plans.* **Covert**, more formal, suggests the use of a cover, disguise, pretext, etc.: *A hint is a covert suggestion.* **Clandestine** describes something underhand or with a questionable purpose: *clandestine trips to the liquor store.*

sec·re·tar·y ['sɛkrə,tɛri] *n* **1** someone who writes letters, keeps records, etc. for a person, company, club, etc. **2** in some countries, the head of a government department: *Secretary of State.* **3** a writing desk with drawers. **sec·re·tar·i·al** *adj.* ⟨Latin *secretarius* confidential officer; *secretum.* See SECRET.⟩
sec·re·tar·i·at *n* **1** the office of secretary or secretary-general, usually as administrative head of an organization. **2** the unit headed by a secretary or secretary-general: *the United Nations Secretariat.* **sec·re·tar·y–gen·er·al** *n, pl* **sec·re·tar·ies–gen·er·al** the chief secretary or administrator.

sect [sɛkt] *n* a group forming part of a broader religious community but distinguished by certain beliefs or practices. ⟨Latin *secta* a pp of *sectari, sequi* follow⟩
sec·tar·i·an [sɛk'tɛriən] *adj* to do with or promoting a particular sect or its beliefs, often bigotedly. **sec·tar·i·an·ism** *n*.

sec·tion ['sɛkʃən] *n* **1** a clearly defined part or division of anything. **2** *Military* a formation smaller than a platoon. **3** the act of cutting, esp surgically: *Caesarian section.* **4** a view of a thing as it would appear if cut straight through at a given point; CROSS SECTION. **5** a tract of land one mile square; 260 ha: *She farms two sections near Regina.* **6** one of a set of similar units assembled into a larger one: *sections of a wall unit.*
v divide into sections: *to section an orange.* ⟨Latin *sectio; secare* cut⟩
section off set off by a partition: *Part of the classroom has been sectioned off as a lab.*
sec·tion·al *adj* **1** to do with a certain section. **2** made up of sections (def. 6): *a sectional bookcase.* **sec·tion·al·ly** *adv.* **section line** *esp West* **1** the survey line setting off a section (def. 5). **2** a road running along this line.

sec·tor ['sɛktər] *n* **1** *Geometry* the part of a circle between two radii and the included arc. **2** a part of society, esp with regard to economic role: *private sector.* **3** *Computers* a segment of a track on a disk, accommodating a fixed amount of data. ⟨Latin *sector* cutter; *secare* cut⟩

sec·u·lar ['sɛkjələr] *adj* **1** worldly; not sacred or religious: *secular music, a secular education.* **2** rejecting or excluding religious values. **sec·u·lar·ism** *n.* **sec·u·lar·ize** *v.* **sec·u·lar·ly** *adv.* ⟨Latin *saeculum* age, world⟩

se·cure [sɪ'kjʊr] *adj* **1** safe against loss, attack, escape, etc.: *a secure hiding place, a secure investment.* **2** certain: *We know in advance that our victory is secure.* **3** free from anxiety or fear: *a secure old age. A secure child can take risks.* **4** firmly fixed: *This board is not secure.*
v **1** make secure. **2** get; obtain: *to secure tickets.* **se·cure·ly** *adv.* ⟨Latin *se-* free of + *cura* care⟩
se·cu·ri·ty *n* **1** the fact or state of being secure. **2** anything that makes secure: *My watchdog is a security against burglars.* **3** the taking of measures to prevent illegal entry, sabotage, escape, leak of information, etc.: *Security on this project is tight.* **4** personnel responsible for this: *Visitors must check in with security.* **5 securities** *pl* bonds, stocks, etc.; certified investments. **6** something given to guarantee ability to pay back a loan or fulfil a promise. **Security Council** a United Nations body whose function is to maintain world peace. It has five permanent members (France, China, Russia, the UK, and the US) and ten non-permanent members.

Sec·wep·emc ['ʃəwhɛpmək] *n* **1** a member of a First Nations people living in the Thompson River area in British Columbia. **2** their Salishan language. **Secwepemc** *adj.* Also called **Shuswap**.

se·dan [sɪ'dæn] *n* a closed car seating four or more people. ⟨origin uncertain⟩
sedan chair a closed-in chair carried on poles.

se·date [sɪ'deit] *adj* **1** quiet; calm; serious. **2** very decorous or dignified.
v make calm by giving a drug. **se·date·ly** *adv.* **se·date·ness** *n.* **se·da·tion** *n.* ⟨Latin *sedatus* pp of *sedare* calm⟩
sed·a·tive ['sɛdətɪv] *n* a drug that lessens pain or excitement. **sed·a·tive** *adj.*

sed·en·tar·y ['sɛdən,teri] *adj* **1** used to sitting much of the time: *Sedentary people get little physical exercise.* **2** that keeps one sitting much of the time: *Writing is a sedentary occupation.* ⟨Latin *sedentarius; sedere* sit⟩

Se·der ['seidər] *n, pl* **Se·ders** or **Se·dar·im** [sə'dɑrɪm] *Judaism* the rites and meal held on the first night or two nights of Passover. ⟨Hebrew⟩

sedge [sɛdʒ] *n* any of a family of grasslike bog plants with solid, often triangular stems and long, narrow leaves. ⟨Old English *secg*⟩

sed·i·ment ['sɛdəmənt] *n* **1** matter that settles to the bottom of a liquid; dregs. **2** *Geology* earth, stones, etc. deposited by water, wind, or ice: *Each year the Nile overflows and deposits sediment on the land.* ⟨Latin *settle*⟩
sed·i·men·ta·ry [,sɛdə'mɛntəri] *adj* **1** to do with sediment. **2** *Geology* of rock, made up of sediment, usually layered. **sed·i·men·ta·tion** *n* a depositing of sediment.

se·di·tion [sɪ'dɪʃən] *n* speech or activity that sows rebellion. **se·di·tion·ist** *n.* **se·di·tious** *adj.* ⟨Latin *seditio; sedire; se-* apart + *ire* go⟩

se·duce [sɪ'djus] or [sɪ'dus] *v* **1** persuade or entice (a person other than one's spouse) to engage in sexual activity. **2** lead away from right action or thought. **3** win over; beguile. **se·duc·er** *n.* **se·duc·i·ble** *adj.* **se·duc·tion** *n.* **se·duc·tive** *adj.* ⟨Latin *se-* aside + *ducere* lead⟩

see[1] [si] *v* **saw, seen, see·ing** **1** be aware of (things) through the eyes: *Can you see underwater?* **2** look at: *See that black cloud.* **3** have the power of sight: *Rocks do not see.* **4** understand: *I see your point.* **5** find out: *Go see what happened.* **6** make sure: *See that you lock up.* **7** think of; consider: *I see her as a natural leader.* **8** experience: *to see hard times.* **9** escort: *to see someone home.* **10** meet and talk or visit with: *to see a doctor, to see friends.* **11** watch: *to see a movie.* **12** imagine: *I can see myself winning the lottery.* **13** accept: *I can't see spending $100 for that.* **14** date on a regular basis: *Is he seeing anyone?* **15** reflect: *Let's see now, what's next?* **16** *Poker, etc.* meet (a bet) by staking an equal sum. ⟨Old English *sēon*⟩
see fit consider (it) right: *Do as you see fit.* **see off** go with to the starting place of a journey. **see one's way (clear) to** consider it possible to. **see out** go through with; finish. **see red** become angry. **see through a** understand the real character or purpose of. **b** go through with; finish. **c** watch over or help through a difficulty: *She saw me through hard times.* **see to** look after; take care of.
see·ing *n* vision; the sense of sight. *adj* not blind. *conj* in view of the fact (with *that* or,

informally, *as*): *Seeing that coaxing won't work, let's try force*. **Seeing Eye dog** *Trademark* a dog trained to guide a blind person. **seer** [sir] *n* a person who foretells future events; prophet. **see–through** *adj* transparent; sheer.

see² [si] *n* the position or jurisdiction of a bishop. ⟨Old French *sie;* Latin *sedes* abode⟩

seed [sid] *n* **1** the small, grainlike fruit from which a new plant grows. **2** a bulb, sprout, or any part of a plant used to generate a new plant. **3** seeds collectively. **4** the source of anything: *seeds of trouble*. **5** *Archaic or poetic* **a** descendants: *The Jews are the seed of Isaac*. **b** semen; sperm. **6** a player of high rank in a tournament.
v **1** plant or scatter seeds in: *to seed a field with corn*. **2** produce or shed seeds: *The grass has seeded*. **3** remove seeds from: *to seed grapes*. **4** provide money or anything else to get (something) started. **5** *Sports* **a** schedule (tournament players or teams) so that the best will not meet each other in the early matches. **b** rank (a contestant): *the top-seeded contestant*. **5** scatter chemicals into (clouds) in order to make rain. **seed·less** *adj*. **seed·like** *adj*. ⟨Old English *sǣd*⟩
go to seed a produce and shed seeds: *Dandelions turn white when they go to seed*. **b** decline in vigour, prosperity, etc.: *After the mine closed, the town went to seed*.
seed·bed *n* **1** soil prepared for growing plants from seed. **2** any place conducive to growth; breeding ground. **seed·case** *n* a pod, capsule, or other dry, hollow fruit containing seeds. **seed·ling** *n* **1** a young plant grown from seed. **2** a young tree less than 1 m high. *adj* **1** raised from seed. **2** in the earliest stage: *a seedling company*. **seed money** money provided to start up a new business, research project, etc., often with a view to attracting further funding. **seed pearl** a very small pearl. **seed·y** *adj* **1** full of seeds. **2** *Informal* shabby and not very clean: *seedy clothes, a seedy apartment*. **3** *Informal* being or looking unwell or run down. **seed·i·ness** *n*.

seek [sik] *v* **sought, seek·ing 1** look for: *We are seeking a new home*. **2** search: *to seek for something lost*. **3** try to get: *Friends sought her advice*. **4** aim (to do): *He seeks to be at peace with everyone*. **seek·er** *n*. ⟨Old English *sēcan*⟩

seem [sim] *v* **1** give an impression of being or doing something: *She seems sad. They seem to understand*. **2** appear to oneself: *I still seem to hear the music*. **3** appear to be true (that): *It seems winter has come early*. ⟨Old Norse *sœma; sœmr* seemly⟩
seem·ing *adj* that appears to be: *a seeming advantage*. **seem·ing·ly** *adv*.

seem·ly ['simli] *adj* proper; fitting: *He thought the young couple's behaviour was not seemly*. **seem·li·ness** *n*. ⟨Old Norse *sœmiligr*⟩

seen [sin] *v* pp of SEE¹.

seep [sip] *v* ooze; leak slowly: *Water seeps through fabric*.
n a place where underground liquid, such as water or oil, has oozed through the surface to form a small pool or spring. **seep·age** *n*. ⟨apparently Middle Dutch *sipen*⟩

seer See SEE¹.

seer·suck·er ['sir,sʌkər] *n* thin, crinkly fabric of cotton, linen, etc. ⟨Hindi; Persian *shir o shakkar* literally, milk and sugar⟩

see·saw ['si,sɒ] *n* **1** teeter-totter. **2** continuous motion up and down or back and forth: *the seesaw of a ship*. **see·saw** *v*. **see·saw** *adj*. ⟨varied reduplication of *saw¹*⟩

seethe [sið] *v* **1** bubble and foam: *Water seethed under the falls*. **2** be very excited or angry. ⟨Old English *sēothan* boil⟩

seg·ment ['sɛgmənt] *n* a part cut, marked, or broken off; section: *segments of an orange*. **2** *Geometry* **a** a part of a circle, sphere, etc. cut off by a line or plane. **b** any of the finite sections of a divided line. **3** *Biology* one of a series of linear parts with similar structure: *a segment of a worm*. **4** *Computers* **a** a portion of data. **b** an independent section of a program. ⟨Latin *segmentum; secare* cut⟩

seg·re·gate ['sɛgrə,geit] *v* separate from others; keep apart: *to segregate patients with an infectious disease, to segregate people by race*. **seg·re·ga·tion** *n*. **seg·re·ga·tion·ist** *n, adj*. ⟨Latin *se-* apart + *gregis* herd⟩

se·gue ['sɛgwei] *v* **1** *Music* **a** go immediately into the next part or section without a break. **b** perform as the preceding section. **2** make a smooth and uninterrupted transition from one thing to another. **se·gue** *n*. ⟨Italian = follows; *seguire* follow, Latin *sequī*⟩

sei·gneur [sɪ'njɜr]; *French* [sɛ'njœʀ] *n* formerly: **1 ✱** in French Canada, a person granted a seigneury; landowner. **2** a feudal lord or landowner. **sei·gneu·ri·al** *adj*. ⟨French = lord; Latin *senior*. See SENIOR.⟩
sei·gneur·y ['sɛnjəri] *n* **1 ✱** formerly, in French Canada, a tract of land granted by the King of France. **2** a feudal lord's domain.

seine [sein] *n* a fishing net that hangs straight down in the water, with floats at the upper edge and sinkers at the lower.
v fish or catch with a seine: *to seine for herring*. ⟨Old English *segne;* Greek *sagēnē*⟩
sein·er *n* **1** a fishing boat equipped with a seine. **2** a person who fishes with a seine.

seis·mic ['saɪzmɪk] *adj* **1** to do with or subject to earthquakes or tremors: *a seismic survey*. **2** of great significance: *seismic changes*. ⟨Greek *seismos* earthquake; *seiein* shake⟩
seis·mo·gram *n* the record produced by a seismograph. **seis·mo·graph** *n* an instrument recording direction, intensity, and duration of earthquakes. **seis·mol·o·gy** *n* the study of earthquakes or movements of the earth's crust. **seis·mo·log·i·cal** *adj*. **seis·mol·o·gist** *n*.

seize [siz] *v* **1** take hold of suddenly; grasp: *When she lost her balance, she seized his arm*. **2** grasp with the mind: *to seize an idea*. **3** take by force or legal authority: *Police seized the videos as evidence*. **4** come upon suddenly: *A fever seized her*. **5** of moving parts of an engine, etc., jam; get stuck (often with *up*): *The valve has seized up*. ⟨Old French *seisir*⟩

seize on or **upon** adopt or make use of (an idea, etc.) eagerly. **seize the day** make full use of the present and the opportunities it offers. **sei·zure** ['siʒər] *n* **1** an act of seizing. **2** a sudden short period of unconsciousness with general muscle contraction.

> **SYNONYMS**
> **Seize** emphasizes taking hold suddenly and with force: *The dog seized the bone.* **Grasp** emphasizes taking and holding firmly with the fingers, claws, or talons closed around the object so as not to lose it: *The eagle grasped the rat.* **Clutch** suggests grasping eagerly, sometimes desperately, and very tightly: *The child clutched her toy.*

Se·ka·ni [se'kɑni] *n, pl* **Se·ka·ni** **1** a member of a First Nations people living in N British Columbia. **2** their Athapascan language. **Se·ka·ni** *adj.*

sel·dom ['sɛldəm] *adv* rarely; not often: *She is seldom ill.* ⟨Old English *seldum*⟩

se·lect [sɪ'lɛkt] *v* choose; pick out: *Select the book you want.*
adj **1** carefully chosen as the best: *A few select people were invited to the conference.* **2** careful in choosing or admitting: *He belongs to a very select club.* ⟨Latin *selectus* pp of *seligere*; *se-* apart + *legere* choose⟩
se·lec·tion *n* **1** the act of selecting. **2** the thing selected. **3** a range from which one may select: *The shop offers a good selection of kids' books.* **4** *Biology* the process by which certain organisms survive and are perpetuated while others are not. **se·lec·tive** *adj* **1** that selects, often arbitrarily: *selective memory.* **2** affecting or applying to specific items or categories only. **se·lec·tive·ly** *adv.* **se·lec·tiv·i·ty** or **se·lec·tive·ness** *n.* **se·lec·tor** *n* a person or device that selects.

se·le·ni·um [sɪ'liniəm] *n* an element whose electrical resistance varies with the amount of light. It is used in photo-electric cells. *Symbol* **Se** ⟨Greek *selēnē* moon⟩

self [sɛlf] *n, pron, pl* **selves** **1** one's own person: *his inner self.* **2** one's own welfare, interests, etc.: *to put self first.* **3** the nature, character, etc. of a person or thing: *She does not seem like her former self.*
pron myself; himself; herself; yourself (in business contexts): *a cheque payable to self.* ⟨Old English⟩
self·hood [-,hʊd] *n* the state or fact of being an individual or of having a personality. **self·ish** *adj* **1** caring too much for oneself and too little for others. **2** based only on one's own interests: *selfish motives.* **self·ish·ly** *adv.* **self·ish·ness** *n.* **self·less** *adj* putting others and their needs ahead of oneself and one's own needs; unselfish. **self·less·ly** *adv.* **self·less·ness** *n.* **self·same** *adj* the very same.

self– *prefix* **1** of, by, to, for, etc. oneself or itself: *self-control, self-evident.* **2** automatic; automatically: *self-starter, self-closing.* ⟨*self*⟩
self–ab·sorbed *adj* interested in oneself to the exclusion of other people and things. **self–ab·use** [-ə'bjus] *n* **1** undue reproach of oneself. **2** the practice of injuring oneself. **3** masturbation. **self–ad·dressed** [-ə'drɛst] *adj* addressed to oneself: *a self-addressed envelope.* **self–as·sur·ance** *n* self-confidence; poise. **self–as·sured** *adj.* **self–cen·tred** *adj* thinking only of one's own interests and affairs; selfish. **self–con·cept** *n* one's idea of one's own basic character or nature. **self–con·fessed** *adj* being so by one's own admission: *a self-confessed glutton.* **self–con·fi·dence** *n* trust in one's own ability, judgment, etc. **self–con·fi·dent** *adj.* **self–con·scious** *adj* preoccupied with how one appears to others. **self–con·scious·ly** *adv.* **self–con·scious·ness** *n.* **self–con·tained** *adj* **1** containing in oneself or itself all that is necessary. **2** specifically, of an apartment, etc., having all facilities (bathroom, kitchen, etc.) within itself, and having a private entrance. **self–con·trol** *n* the ability to control one's own speech and actions. **self–con·trolled** *adj.* **self–de·feat·ing** *adj* thwarting its or one's own purposes because of built-in inconsistencies. **self–de·fence** or **self–defense** *n* **1** defence of one's own person, property, reputation, etc. **2** any physical skill, such as a martial art, by which one can defend oneself. **self–de·ni·al** [-dɪ'naɪəl] *n* the act of going without what one wants. **self–de·ny·ing** *adj.* **self–de·struct** *v* of a machine, automatically destroy itself: *The tape-player will self-destruct if it is tampered with.* **self–de·struct·ing** *adj.* **self–de·struc·tion** *n* **1** destruction or ruin of oneself or itself. **2** suicide. **self–de·struct·ive** *adj.* **self–de·ter·mi·na·tion** *n* **1** freedom to make decisions independently. **2** freedom of a people to choose their own government. **self–de·ter·mined** *adj.* **self–de·ter·min·ing** *adj.* **self–dis·ci·pline** *n* the ability to do what one should whether one feels like it or not; the act of doing so. **self–dis·ci·plined** *adj.* **self–ed·u·cat·ed** *adj* educated by one's own reading, observation, etc. **self–ed·u·ca·tion** *n.* **self–ef·fac·ing** *adj* modest; keeping oneself in the background. **self–em·ployed** *adj* working for oneself rather than another employer: *Farmers are usually self-employed.* **self–em·ploy·ment** *n.* **self–es·teem** *n* **1** one's opinion of oneself. **2** a good opinion of oneself. **self–ev·i·dent** *adj* needing no proof or explanation. **self–ev·i·dent·ly** *adv.* **self–ex·am·i·na·tion** *n* **1** examination of one's own inner state, motives, etc. **2** examination of one's own body for signs of disease. **self–ex·ist·ent** *adj* existing independently of any outside cause. **self–ex·plan·a·to·ry** *adj* fully clear in itself; needing no explanation. **self–ex·pres·sion** *n* expression of one's own personality, ideas, feelings, etc., esp through art. **self–fer·til·i·za·tion** *n* **1** *Botany* fertilization of an ovum by pollen from the same flower. **2** *Zoology* in hermaphroditic animals, fertilization of the ovum by sperm from the same individual. **self–fer·til·iz·ing** *adj.* **self–ful·fil·ling** *adj* coming true because it is expected or predicted. **self–gov·ern·ing** *adj* that governs itself. **self–gov·ern·ment** *n* **1** government of a group by its own members. **2** self-control. **self–help** *n* the use of one's

own resources to solve one's problems. **self–help book** a book intended to equip its readers to solve their own problems. **self–help group** a group of people sharing a similar problem, giving one another support of various kinds. **self–im·age** n one's opinion or general idea of oneself. **self–im·por·tant** adj conceited; egotistical. **self–im·posed** adj of a condition, imposed on oneself by oneself. **self–in·duced** adj induced by itself or oneself. **self–in·dul·gent** adj gratifying one's own desires without restraint. **self–in·dul·gence** n. **self–in·flict·ed** adj inflicted on oneself by oneself. **self–in·ter·est** n **1** the prospect of personal gain. **2** an interest in one's own welfare with too little care for that of others; selfishness. **self–knowl·edge** n knowledge of one's own character, ability, etc. **self–love** n **1** love of oneself; selfishness; vanity. **2** proper regard for oneself. **self–made** adj successful through one's own efforts, without the advantage of formal education and without help from others. **self–per·pet·u·at·ing** adj that is renewed or kept in existence indefinitely by its own activity or character: *a self-perpetuating cycle of violence.* **self–pit·y** n pity for oneself. **self–pol·li·na·tion** n the transfer of pollen from a stamen to a pistil of the same flower or of another flower on the same plant. **self–pos·sessed** adj calm and in control of oneself. **self–pres·er·va·tion** n the protection of oneself from harm, esp as an instinct. **self–pro·pelled** adj propelled by an engine, etc., within itself. **self–reg·u·lat·ing** adj regulating oneself or itself. **self–reg·u·la·tion** n. **self–re·li·ance** [-rɪ'laɪəns] n reliance on one's own abilities, resources, etc. **self–re·li·ant** adj. **self–re·proach** n blame directed at oneself by one's own conscience. **self–re·spect** n healthy respect for oneself. **self–re·spect·ing** adj. **self–right·eous** adj thinking that one is more virtuous than others. **self–right·eous·ly** adv. **self–right·eous·ness** n. **self–rule** n SELF-GOVERNMENT. **self–sac·ri·fice** n the act of setting aside one's own interests and desires for another's welfare, one's duty, etc. **self–sac·ri·fic·ing** adj. **self–sat·is·fied** adj quite pleased with oneself and not aware of any need to improve. **self–seek·ing** adj selfish; motivated by self-interest. **self–serve** adj designed for use by the customer without the aid of an operator, attendant, etc. **self–serv·ice** n the serving of oneself in a restaurant, store, gas station, etc. adj self-serve. **self–serv·ing** adj **1** preoccupied with one's own gain; self-seeking. **2** serving to further one's own interests. **self–start·er** n **1** *Informal* a person who has initiative. **2** an electric motor or other device used to start an engine automatically. **self–styled** adj so called by oneself: *a self-styled leader whom no one follows.* **self–suf·fi·cient** adj not asking or needing any help from others; independent. **self–suf·fi·cien·cy** n. **self–sup·port·ing** adj able to pay one's own expenses; getting along without help. **self–sus·tain·ing** adj capable of going on once started; self-perpetuating. **self–taught** adj taught by one's own reading,

observation, etc. **self–will** n insistence on one's own way. **self–willed** adj. **self–wind·ing** [-'waɪndɪŋ] adj that is wound automatically.

sell [sɛl] v sold, sell·ing **1** exchange for money or other payment: *to sell a house, to sell one's services.* **2** deal in; keep for sale: *We don't sell that toy.* **3** do the work of a salesperson. **4** be sold: *This model sells for $95.* **5** betray: *The traitor sold his country for money.* **6** be or cause to be accepted or approved: *to sell an idea to the public. That plan will never sell.* n the act or a method of selling: *a soft sell.* ⟨Old English *sellan*⟩

sell down the river betray; betray the cause of. **sell off** dispose of by sale. **sell out a** sell all that one has of. **b** *Informal* betray, often by a secret bargain. **c** compromise one's integrity: *to sell out to political pressure.* **sell short a** sell (securities) that one does not yet own. **b** undervalue; underestimate. **c** cheat. **sell someone on** convince someone of the good sense, value, truth, etc. of: *She has sold me on the idea of home schooling.*

sell·er n **1** a person who sells. **2** a thing with reference to its sale: *This game is a good seller.* **seller's market** an economic situation in which the seller has the advantage because goods are scarce and prices high. **sell–out** n **1** a selling out of something or someone. **2** an event for which all seats are sold.

selt·zer ['sɛltsər] n **1** a bubbling mineral water containing salt, sodium, calcium, and magnesium carbonates. **2** a flavoured drink of similar composition. ⟨German *Selterser*; *Selters*, Germany, where it is found⟩

sel·vage or **sel·vedge** ['sɛlvɪdʒ] n the edge of fabric finished so as not to fray. ⟨*self* + *edge*⟩

selves [sɛlvz] n pl of SELF.

se·man·tics [sə'mæntɪks] n (with sg verb) **1** the scientific study of the meanings of words. **2 a** the relation between words and their connotations. **b** exploitation of this to mislead. **se·man·tic** adj. **se·man·ti·cal·ly** adv. **se·man·ti·cist** n. ⟨Greek *sēmantikos*; *sēma* sign⟩

sem·a·phore ['sɛmə,fɔr] n a system of signals for sending messages using flags, lights, etc. **sem·a·phore** v. ⟨Greek *sēma* signal + *-phoros* carrying; *pherein* carry⟩

sem·blance ['sɛmbləns] n **1** the outward appearance: *a lie with the semblance of truth.* **2** likeness: *These clouds have the semblance of a huge head.* ⟨Old French; *sembler* seem; Latin *similis* similar⟩

se·men ['simən] n the thick, whitish fluid produced by the reproductive organs of male mammals, containing sperm. ⟨Latin = seed⟩

se·mes·ter [sə'mɛstər] n **1** a half of a school year. **2** loosely, one of any number of school terms. ⟨Latin *semestris*; *sex* six + *mensis* month⟩

se·mi ['sɛmi] n **1** Also ['sɛmaɪ], semitrailer. **2** Usually, **semis** pl the semifinal round of a competition.

semi– prefix **1** half: *semicircle.* **2** incompletely; partly: *semiliterate.* **3** twice in the specified time period: *semi-annually.* ⟨Latin⟩

sem·i–an·nu·al adj occurring every half year.

sem·i·an·nu·al·ly *adv.* **sem·i·ar·id** *adj* having very little rainfall. **sem·i–au·to·mat·ic** *adj* 1 of a firearm, using the ejective power of the shell to reload the gun automatically, but requiring a trigger pull to fire. 2 of machinery, partly automatic and partly run by hand. **sem·i·cir·cle** *n* half a circle: *to place chairs in a semicircle.* **sem·i·cir·cu·lar** *adj.* **sem·i·co·lon** [-ˌkoulən] *n* a punctuation mark (;) that shows a separation not as strong as shown by a period but stronger than by a comma. **sem·i·con·duct·or** *n* any of a group of solids, such as silicon, that are poor conductors of electricity at low temperatures, but good conductors at high temperatures. **sem·i·con·scious** *adj* partly awake. **sem·i·dark·ness** *n* gloom. **sem·i–de·tached** *adj* designating either of two houses joined by a common wall but separate from other buildings. **sem·i·fi·nal** *n* one of two rounds, matches, etc. that settles who will play in the final one. **sem·i·fi·nal** *adj.* **semi·fi·nal·ist** *n.* **sem·i·for·mal** *adj* being or suited to a somewhat formal social occasion: *a semiformal gown, a semiformal dinner party. n* a semiformal gown. **sem·i·pre·cious** *adj* of gemstones, having less commercial value than precious stones. **sem·i–pri·vate** *adj* of a hospital room, designed to accommodate two patients. **sem·i·skilled** *adj* to do with manual work requiring some, but relatively little, training. **sem·i·sol·id** *adj* partly solid. **sem·i·sweet** *adj* containing a small amount of sugar or sweetener: *semisweet chocolate.* **sem·i·tone** *n Music* the smallest interval of the modern scale; a half tone; half step. **sem·i·trail·er** *n* a large trailer used for carrying cargo, with wheels at the back but supported in front by the truck tractor to which it is hitched. **sem·i·trop·i·cal** *adj* halfway between tropical and temperate. **sem·i·vow·el** *n Phonetics* a sound pronounced like a vowel but which cannot by itself form a syllable. *W* and *y* are semivowels in *win* and *yet.* **sem·i·week·ly** *adj, adv* (occurring or appearing) twice a week.

> **USAGE**
> Semi- is usually hyphenated before root words beginning with a vowel and before proper nouns and proper adjectives: *semi-annual, semi-invalid, semi-Christian.* In other cases a hyphen is optional.

sem·i·nal [ˈsɛmənəl] *adj* 1 important because of the development stimulated or suggested by it: *seminal ideas.* 2 of or containing semen or seed. ⟨Latin *seminalis; semen* seed⟩

sem·i·nar [ˈsɛmɑˌnɑr] *n* 1 a conference, workshop, or short, intensive course of study. 2 a group of students doing independent research under direction. 3 a meeting of such a group. ⟨German; Latin *seminarium* plant nursery; *semen* seed⟩

sem·i·nar·y [ˈsɛməˌnɛri] *n* a school or college training students to be priests, ministers, rabbis, etc. ⟨Latin *seminarium.* See SEMINAR.⟩ **sem·i·nar·i·an** *n* a student at a seminary.

se·mi·ot·ics [ˌsimiˈɒtɪks] *or* [ˌsɛmiˈɒtɪks] *n* (with

sg verb) the study of signs and symbols as part of human behaviour. ⟨Greek *semeion* sign⟩

Sem·ite [ˈsɛmait] *or* [ˈsimait] *n* a member of any people speaking a Semitic language: *Jews and Arabs are Semites.* **Se·mit·ic** [səˈmɪtɪk] *adj* 1 to do with a group of languages including Hebrew, Arabic, and others. 2 being a Semite; to do with Semites.

sem·o·li·na [ˌsɛməˈlinə] *n* coarse, hard bits of wheat remaining after grinding into flour. ⟨Italian *semolino*; Latin *simila* fine flour⟩

sen·ate [ˈsɛnɪt] *n* 1 a governing or lawmaking assembly: *the senate of a university.* 2 Often, **Senate** the upper branch of a lawmaking assembly. The Canadian Senate consists of appointed representatives from each province. ⟨Latin *senatus; senex* old man⟩ **Senate Chamber** the room in the Parliament buildings where the Senate of Canada meets. Also called **Red Chamber. sen·a·tor** *n* a member of a senate. **sen·a·tor·ship** *n.*

send [sɛnd] *v* sent, send·ing 1 cause, tell, or enable to go somewhere: *to send a ball through a window. They sent all their children to university.* 2 cause to be carried or delivered: *to send a letter.* 3 cause to come, go, happen, be, etc.: *to send someone mad.* **send·er** *n.* ⟨Old English *sendan*⟩

send around circulate from person to person: *to send a memo around.* **send (away) for** mail a request for. **send for** call or ask to come; have someone fetch: *to send for a doctor.* **send packing** send away quickly: *When I caught the employee stealing, I sent him packing.* **send up** parody; lampoon. **send·up** *n.* **send–off** *n* 1 a friendly gathering in honour of a person starting a journey. 2 *Informal* a start given to a person or thing.

Sen·e·ca [ˈsɛnɛkə] *n, pl* –**ca** or –**cas** 1 a member of a Native American people living in New York State. 2 their Iroquoian language. **Seneca** *adj.*

se·nile [ˈsinail] *or* [ˈsɛnail] *adj* to do with the mental confusion, memory loss, etc. often associated with old age. **se·nil·i·ty** [səˈnɪləti] *n.* ⟨Latin *senilis; senex* old⟩

sen·ior [ˈsinjər] *adj* 1 older or elderly: *a senior citizen.* 2 the older; being one whose child has the same name: *Chris Carra, Senior.* 3 higher in rank or longer in service: *a senior partner.* 4 *esp US* to do with a graduating class. *n* 1 an older person. 2 SENIOR CITIZEN: *Tickets are $8, seniors $5.* 3 a person of higher rank or longer service. 4 *esp US* a member of a graduating class of a high school or college. **sen·ior·i·ty** [sɪˈnjɔrəti] *n.* ⟨Latin, comparative of *senex* old⟩ **be someone's senior** be older than someone. **senior citizen** a person aged 65 or over, or beyond normal retirement age. **senior public school** in some areas, a school for grades 6 to 8.

sen·sa·tion [sɛnˈseiʃən] *n* 1 the action of the senses: *A dead body is without sensation.* 2 a perception through the senses: *Ice gives a sensation of cold.* 3 a strong emotional reaction: *The news caused a sensation.* 4 the cause of this: *The first moonwalk was a sensation.* **5** a vague feeling not attributable to a specific cause. ⟨Latin *sensatio; sensus.* See SENSE.⟩

sen·sa·tion·al *adj* **1** arousing strong or excited feeling: *The Canada-Russia hockey series was a sensational event.* **2** calculated to arouse strong feeling: *sensational reporting.* **3** extremely good: *a sensational performance.* **4** to do with sensation or the senses. **sen·sa·tion·al·ly** *adv.* **sen·sa·tion·al·ism** *n* sensational style in writing, reporting, etc. **sen·sa·tion·al·ist** *n, adj.*

sense [sɛns] *n* **1** one of the special functions of the body by which humans and animals perceive the world around them and changes within themselves. Sight, hearing, touch, taste, and smell are the five senses. **2** anything felt through one of these senses: *a sense of pain.* **3** the ability to perceive. **4** an emotion or mental impression: *a sense of security.* **5** ability to appreciate or understand: *moral sense, a sense of humour.* **6** Usually, **senses** *pl* sound condition of mind: *Have you lost your senses?* **7** good judgment: *He has the sense to keep out of foolish quarrels.* **8** a meaning: *a gentleman in the best sense of the word.* **9** reasonable discourse: *to speak or write sense.* **10** general opinion: *The sense of the assembly was clear even before the vote.* **11** usefulness: *What's the sense of talking if he doesn't listen?* *v* be or become aware, sometimes by subtle clues: *She sensed that he was tired.* ⟨Latin *sensus; sentire* perceive⟩

in a sense in some respect. **make sense** be understandable or reasonable.

sense·less *adj* **1** unconscious: *The fall knocked her senseless.* **2** foolish; stupid. **3** meaningless. **sense·less·ly** *adv.* **sense·less·ness** *n.* **sense organ** the eye, ear, or other body part by which sensations of colours, sounds, smells, etc. are received. **sen·si·bil·i·ty** *n* **1** the ability to feel or perceive; consciousness. **2** fineness of feeling: *an unusual sensibility for colour.* **3** Usually, **sensibilities** *pl* sensitive feelings. **4** a tendency to be offended. **sen·si·ble** *adj* **1** showing good judgment. **2** practical: *sensible shoes.* **3** aware; conscious: *sensible of the risk involved.* **4** that can be noticed: *a sensible reduction in expenses.* **5** that can be perceived by the senses. **sen·si·bly** *adv.* **sen·si·tive** *adj* **1** receiving impressions easily: *The eye is sensitive to light.* **2** easily affected by something: *Many plants are sensitive to cold.* **3 a** easily offended or hurt emotionally. **b** appreciating the feelings of others. **c** very perceptive intellectually, aesthetically, etc. **4** having an unusually adverse physical reaction: *sensitive to lactose.* **5** needing careful handling, for reasons of security, tact, etc. **sen·si·tive·ly** *adv.* **sen·si·tiv·i·ty** *n.* **sen·si·tize** *v* make sensitive. **sen·si·ti·za·tion** *n.* **sen·sor** *n* a device receiving and transmitting a physical stimulus such as heat, light, or pressure: *Sensors applied to the astronaut's body recorded her pulse, temperature, etc.* **sen·so·ry** *adj* to do with sensation: *sensory organs, sensory nerves.* **sen·su·al** [ˈsɛnʃuəl] *adj* **1** to do with the senses as opposed to the mind or soul; exciting the senses. **2** caring too much for the pleasures of

the senses; lustful; decadent. **sen·su·al·i·ty** *n.* **sen·su·al·ly** *adv.* **sen·su·al·ism** *n* too great indulgence in the pleasures of the senses. **sen·su·al·ist** *n.* **sen·su·ous** *adj* **1** of, derived from, or perceived by the senses: *the sensuous thrill of a warm bath, a sensuous love of colour.* **2** appreciating the pleasures of the senses. **sen·su·ous·ly** *adv.* **sen·su·ous·ness** *n.*

CONFUSABLES

Sensual describes things that gratify the bodily appetites and applies to people who indulge their desires for physical pleasure: *A glutton derives sensual pleasure from eating.* **Sensuous** describes people highly sensitive to beauty and the pleasure of the senses, and applies to things that give such pleasure: *She derives sensuous delight from music.*

sent [sɛnt] *v* pt and pp of SEND.

sen·tence [ˈsɛntəns] *n* **1** *Grammar* a group of words making a grammatically complete statement, question, command, or exclamation. A sentence usually consists of a subject plus a predicate with a finite verb. **2** *Mathematics, logic* a group of words or symbols expressing a complete idea (**closed sentence,** *Example:* $4 + 2 = 6$) or a requirement (**open sentence,** *Example:* $x + 2 = 6$). **3 a** a decision by a judge on the punishment of a criminal. **b** the punishment. *v* pronounce punishment on: *The judge sentenced the thief to five years in prison.* ⟨Latin *sententia* orig opinion; *sentire* feel⟩

sen·tient [ˈsɛnʃənt] *adj* that can feel; having feeling: *a sentient being.* **sen·tience** *n.* ⟨Latin *sentiens* ppr of *sentire* feel⟩

sen·ti·ment [ˈsɛntəmənt] *n* **1** a mixture of thought and feeling, such as admiration or patriotism. **2** tender emotion. **3** an opinion. **4** SENTIMENTALISM. ⟨Latin *sentire* feel⟩ **sen·ti·men·tal** *adj* **1** showing much tender feeling, often too much: *sentimental poetry.* **2** directed by sentiment rather than logical thinking. **3** to do with sentiment; dependent on sentiment: *She values the necklace for sentimental reasons.* **sen·ti·men·tal·ly** *adv.* **sen·ti·men·tal·ism** or **sen·ti·men·tal·i·ty** *n* **1** a tendency to be led by sentiment rather than reason. **2** excessive indulgence in sentiment.

sen·ti·nel [ˈsɛntənəl] *n* a person or animal stationed to keep watch. ⟨Italian *sentinella;* Latin *sentinare* avoid danger wisely⟩

sen·try [ˈsɛntri] *n* a person or group posted as a guard. ⟨*sentrinel* variant of *sentinel*⟩

se·pal [ˈsipəl] *n Botany* one of the leaflike parts of a calyx, or outer covering of a flower. ⟨coined by H.J. de Necker in 1790⟩

sep·a·rate [ˈsɛpəˌreit] *v* **1** take apart; divide: *to separate the segments of an orange.* **2** divide (a mass, compound, whole) into parts: *to separate the class into teams.* **3** keep apart: *Those boys must be separated.* **4** come or go apart; break up: *The rope separated under the strain.* **5** of spouses, live apart. **6** put out (a joint): *a separated shoulder.* *adj* [ˈsɛprɪt] apart from others; distinct: *separate rooms, a separate issue.*

sep·a·ble ['sɛprəbəl] *adj.* **sep·a·rate·ly** *adv.* **sep·a·ra·tion** *n.* ⟨Latin *se-* apart + *parare* get⟩
separate school ✱ a publicly funded school for children belonging to the Catholic or other religious minority in a given district.
sep·a·ra·tism ['sɛprə,tɪzəm] *n.* **1** a policy advocating separation. **2** ✱ support for withdrawing a province from Confederation. **sep·a·ra·tist** *n, adj.* **sep·a·ra·tor** *n* a machine for separating cream from milk, wheat from chaff, etc.

Se·phar·dim [sɪ'fɑrdɪm] *n pl, sg* **-di** [-di] Jews of Spain or Portugal, or their descendants, as distinct from the Ashkenazim of central and E Europe. **Se·phar·dic** *adj.* ⟨Hebrew⟩

se·pi·a ['sipiə] *n* **1** a brown paint or ink made from the fluid of cuttlefish. **2** a drawing, photograph, etc. in brown tones. **se·pi·a** *adj.* ⟨Latin; Greek⟩

sep·sis ['sɛpsɪs] *n* a toxic condition caused by the absorption of pus-forming bacteria into the blood or tissues from a wound, etc. ⟨Greek = putrefaction; *sēpein* rot⟩
sep·tic *adj* to do with infection or putrefaction. **sep·ti·ce·mi·a** or **sep·ti·cae·mi·a** [-'simiə] *n* BLOOD POISONING. **sep·ti·ce·mic** or **sep·ti·cae·mic** *adj.* **septic tank** a tank in which sewage is collected and acted on by bacteria.

sep·ta·gon ['sɛptə,gɒn] *n* a closed plane figure with seven interior angles and seven sides. **sep·ta·gon·al** *adj.*

Sep·tem·ber [sɛp'tɛmbər] *n* the ninth month of the year. It has 30 days. ⟨Latin; *septem* seven, for original calendar⟩

sep·tet or **sep·tette** [sɛp'tɛt] *n* **1** *Music* a a group of seven voices or instruments. **b** a piece performed by seven singers or players. **2** any group of seven. ⟨Latin *septem* + (DU)ET⟩

sep·tic, sep·ti·ce·mi·a See SEPSIS.

sep·til·lion [sɛp'tɪljən] *n, adj* **1** followed by 24 zeros; 10^{24}. ⟨Latin *septem* seven + (M)ILLION⟩

sep·tu·a·ge·nar·i·an [,sɛptuədʒə'nɛriən] *n* a person seventy years old, or in his or her seventies. **sep·tu·a·ge·nar·i·an** *adj.* ⟨Latin *septuagenarius; septuaginta* seventy⟩

sep·tum ['sɛptəm] *n, pl* **-ta** [-tə] a dividing wall of tissue, bone, etc., such as that between the nostrils. ⟨Latin *saeptum* fence⟩

sep·tu·ple [sɛp'tʌpəl], [-'tjupəl], *or* [-'tupəl] *adj* **1** seven times as much or many. **2** having seven parts. ⟨Latin *septuplus; septem* seven + (QUADR)UPLE⟩

sep·ul·chre ['sɛpəlkər] *n* a cavelike tomb.
v bury (a dead body) in a sepulchre. Also, **sep·ul·cher.** ⟨Latin *sepulcrum; sepelire* bury⟩ **se·pul·chral** [sə'pʌlkrəl] *adj* suggesting a tomb; deep and hollow; gloomy or dismal.

se·quel ['sikwəl] *n* **1** a story that continues on from an earlier one. **2** any continuation or result. ⟨Latin *sequela; sequi* follow⟩

se·quence ['sikwəns] *n* **1** a number of things coming one after another; series: *a sequence of lessons on one subject.* **2** succession or order based on some principle: *dates arranged in historical sequence.*

v arrange in order. **se·quen·tial** [sɪ'kwɛnʃəl] *adj.* **se·quen·tial·ly** *adv.* ⟨Latin *sequi* follow⟩

se·ques·ter [sɪ'kwɛstər] *v* **1** withdraw from interaction with the public: *The shy old lady sequestered herself in her home. The jury was sequestered during the trial.* **2** Also, **se·ques·trate** a *Law* take away (property) until a claim is satisfied. **b** seize by authority: *The soldiers sequestered food from the people they conquered.* **se·ques·tra·tion** [,sikwɛ'streiʃən] *or* [,səkwɛ'streiʃən] *n.* ⟨Latin *sequester* trustee, mediator; *sequi* follow⟩

se·quin ['sikwɪn] *n* a small, shiny disk used to ornament clothes. **se·quinned** or **se·quined** *adj.* ⟨French; Italian *zecchino; zecca* mint; Arabic *sikka* a stamp⟩

se·quoi·a [sɪ'kwɔɪə] *n* a very long-lived, coniferous evergreen tree of the coastal regions of the SW United States. ⟨latinization of *Sikwayi,* name of a 19c Cherokee⟩

se·ra ['sirə] *n* a pl of SERUM.

ser·aph ['sɛrəf] *n, pl* **-aphs** or **-a·phim** one of the highest of the nine orders of angels. **se·raph·ic** [sə'ræfɪk] *adj.* ⟨Hebrew⟩

sere [sir] *adj* very dry; arid. ⟨variant of *sear*⟩

ser·e·nade [,sɛrə'neid] *n* **1** music played or sung outdoors at night, esp by a lover under his lady's window. **2** an instrumental piece with several movements. **3** *Informal* any piece of music sung or played for others.
v sing or play a serenade to. **ser·e·nad·er** *n.* ⟨French; Italian *serenata;* Latin *serenus sereno*⟩

ser·en·dip·i·ty [,sɛrən'dɪpəti] *n* the fact of accidentally making fortunate discoveries. **ser·en·dip·i·tous** *adj.* ⟨*Three Princes of Serendip,* Turkish story whose heroes make many lucky discoveries; coined 1754 by H. Walpole⟩

se·rene [sə'rin] *adj* **1** calm, esp in the midst of trouble. **2** **Serene** part of some royal titles: *Her Serene Highness.* **se·rene·ly** *adv.* **se·ren·i·ty** [sə'rɛnəti] *n.* ⟨Latin *serenus*⟩

serf [sɜrf] *n* **1** in medieval Europe, a person who worked on a feudal estate and passed with the land from one owner to another. **2** a person treated like a slave. **serf·dom** *n.* **serf·like** *adj.* ⟨French; Latin *servus* slave⟩

serge [sɜrdʒ] *n* woollen or silk cloth with a diagonal surface rib.
v finish (a seam or edge) to prevent fraying. ⟨Old French; Latin *serica* silken, Greek *sērikē.* See SILK.⟩

ser·geant ['sɑrdʒənt] *n* **1** a non-commissioned officer ranking above a master corporal and below a warrant officer. **2** a police officer above a constable and below an inspector. *Abbrev* **Sgt.** or **Sgt** ⟨Old French *sergent;* Latin *servientis; servire* serve⟩
ser·geant–ma·jor *n* a non-commissioned officer above a staff sergeant and below a warrant officer. *Abbrev* **S.M.**

se·ries ['siriz] *n, pl* **-ries 1** a number of similar things, one after the other: *a series of rooms opening off a hall, a series of rainy days.* **2** a set of television programs with the same actors but forming independent episodes. **3** a set of similar things issued together, such as coins, stamps, collectable items, etc. **4** *Electricity* a set of components connected end-to-end such that the same current flows through them all. **5** *Mathematics* the indicated sum of a sequence of numbers. ⟨Latin; *serere* join⟩

se·ri·al *n* a story presented in instalments on television, in a magazine, etc. *adj* **1** published or broadcast in instalments. **2** of or concerning a serial: *serial rights to a book.* **3** doing a thing repeatedly: *a serial killer.* **se·ri·al·ly** *adv.* **se·ri·al·ize** *v* present in the form of a serial: *a novel serialized in a magazine.*

serial number a unique number given to a person, article, etc., as a means of easy identification. **serial port** *Computers* a PORT² (def. 6) which delivers the bits of a data byte one after the other, rather than synchronously as in a **parallel port.**

ser·if ['sɛrɪf] *n Printing* a small, thin line used to finish off a main stroke of a letter, as at the top and bottom of M in this font. ⟨perhaps Dutch *schreef* stroke, line; *schrijven* write; Latin *scribere*⟩

se·ri·ous ['siriəs] *adj* **1** solemn: *a serious face.* **2** not joking: *His remarks were dead serious, though she took them lightly.* **3** deserving careful thought; important: *Career choice is a serious matter.* **4** treating important or weighty subjects: *a serious film.* **5** dangerous: *in serious condition in hospital.* **6** *Informal* large, sophisticated, impressive, etc.: *serious camping gear.* **se·ri·ous·ly** *adv.* **se·ri·ous·ness** *n.* ⟨Latin *serius*⟩

ser·mon ['sɜrmən] *n* **1** a public talk on a religious topic, usually in a service of worship. **2** a long, serious, tiresome talk about morals, conduct, duty, etc.: *After the guests left, we got a sermon on manners from Mom.* ⟨Latin *sermonis* a talk; *serere* join (i.e., words)⟩ **ser·mon·ize** *v* lecture tiresomely.

ser·o·to·nin [,sɛrə'toʊnɪn] *n Biochemistry* a neurotransmitter associated with regulation of emotion, sleep, memory, etc. ⟨*serum* + *ton(ic)*⟩

se·rous See SERUM.

ser·pent ['sɜrpənt] *n* **1** *Poetic* a snake. **2** a sly, treacherous person. **3 the Serpent** the Devil; Satan. ⟨Latin *serpere* creep⟩ **ser·pen·tine** [-,taɪn] *or* [-,tin] *adj* **1** of or like a serpent; twisting. **2** treacherous.

ser·rate [sə'reit] *or* ['sɛreit] *v* notch like a saw. *adj* ['sɛrɪt] *or* ['sɛreit] having a notched edge. **ser·rat·ed** [sə'reitɪd] *adj.* **ser·ra·tion** *n.* ⟨Latin *serra* a saw⟩

se·rum ['sirəm] *n, pl* **se·rums** or **se·ra** ['sirə] **1** the clear, pale yellow, watery part of blood that separates from the clot as the blood coagulates. **2** a liquid antidote or vaccine for a disease. **3** any watery body fluid, such as lymph. **se·rous** ['sirəs] *adj.* ⟨Latin = whey⟩

serv·ant See SERVE.

serve [sɜrv] *v* **1** work or perform duties (for): *She served three years in the armed forces.* **2** wait on at table or in a store: *Are you being served?* **3** present (food) in a given way (sometimes with *up*): *Dinner is served.* **4** help: *I am happy to serve you in any way.* **5** be or do what is needed (for): *Boxes served as seats.* **6** pass (a prison term). **7** *Law* present (someone) with a court order, etc.: *She was served with a summons.* **8** *Tennis, volleyball, etc.* put (the ball or shuttlecock) in play by hitting.

n Tennis, volleyball, etc. **1** the act or way of serving a ball or shuttlecock. **2** a player's turn to serve. ⟨Old French *servir*; Latin *servire*; *servus* slave⟩

serve someone right be just what someone deserves: *The punishment served her right.*

serv·ant *n* **1** a person employed to do household work. **2** a government employee: *public servant, civil servant.* **3** a person devoted to any service: *Priests are the servants of God.* **serv·er** *n* **1** a person who serves. **2** a tray for dishes. **3** any of various utensils for serving food: *a cake or pie server.* **4** *Computers* a computer that provides services (data storage, printing, etc.) to other computers in a network. **serv·ing** *n* the portion of food served to a person at one time. *adj* used for the service of food at table: *a serving spoon.*

serv·ice ['sɜrvɪs] *n* **1** the act of serving. **2** a helpful act: *He performed many services for his hosts.* **3** the arrangements for supplying something useful such as utilities or transportation: *The bus service was good.* **4** employment as a servant. **5 services** *pl* skilled work done for others for pay: *She needs the services of a doctor.* **6** repair or maintenance of merchandise, provided by a retailer or manufacturer. **7** use: *Every available truck was pressed into service.* **8** employment by a government, or the people so employed: *the civil service.* **9 a** duty in the armed forces: *active service.* **b the service(s)** the navy, army, or air force. **10** a religious meeting or ceremony: *to attend church services.* **11** a set of dishes, etc.: *a silver tea service.*

adj **1** for use by tradespeople, servants, etc.: *a service elevator.* **2** belonging to a branch of the armed forces: *a service uniform.* **3** providing maintenance or repairs: *a service department of a store.* **4** supplying a service as opposed to goods: *service industries.*

v **1** do repairs or maintenance on: *to service a car.* **2** provide with a service or services: *a serviced lot. Two trains serviced the city.* ⟨Old French; Latin *servitium*; *servus* slave⟩

at someone's service ready to do, or be used for, whatever someone wants. **in** (**out of**) **service** in (not in) working order: *This ATM is not in service.* **of service** helpful; useful.

serv·ice·a·ble *adj* useful. **serv·ice·ber·ry** *n* any of several shrubs or small trees of the rose family with sweet, purplish, edible berries. Also called **shad·bush** or **sas·ka·toon**. **service centre 1** a stopping area beside an expressway, consisting of a gas station, restaurant, toilet facilities, etc. **2** a place where merchandise can be brought for repairs. **3 ✱** a town or city serving as a shopping and distribution centre for the surrounding region: *In summer our town is the service centre for a large resort area.* **serv·ice·man** *n, pl* **-men 1** a male member of the armed forces. **2** a man who maintains

and repairs machines, appliances, etc.
serv·ice·wom·an *n,* *pl* -wom·en. **service
provider** *Computers* a company that provides
access to the Internet, usually for a montly
charge. **service road 1** a road parallel to an
expressway, to carry local traffic. **2** ACCESS
ROAD. **service station** a place supplying
vehicles with fuel, oil, water, and often
repairs.

ser·vi·ette [ˌsɜrvi'ɛt] *n* a paper NAPKIN.
⟨French *serviette; servir* serve⟩

ser·vile ['sɜrvaɪl] *adj* **1** fawning or overly
submissive; obsequious: *servile flattery.* **2** of or
fit for slaves. **ser·vile·ly** *adv.* **ser·vil·i·ty**
[sər'vɪləti] *n.* ⟨Latin *servilis; servus* slave⟩

ser·vi·tude ['sɜrvɪˌtjud] *or* ['sɜrvɪˌtud] *n*
1 slavery. **2** forced labour as punishment: *The
criminal was sentenced to ten years' servitude.*
⟨Latin *servitudo; servus* slave⟩

ses·a·me ['sɛsəmi] *n* **1** a tropical plant widely
cultivated for its seeds, which are used to
flavour bread, etc. and also as a source of oil.
2 See OPEN SESAME. ⟨Greek ; Semitic⟩

ses·qui·cen·ten·ni·al [ˌsɛskwɪsɛn'tɛnjəl] *n* a
150th anniversary or its celebration.
ses·qui·cen·ten·ni·al *adj.* ⟨Latin *sesqui-* one
and a half + CENTENNIAL⟩

ses·qui·pe·da·li·an [ˌsɛskwɪpə'deiliən] *adj* of
a word, very long. ⟨Latin *sesqui* one and a
half + *pedis* foot⟩

ses·sile ['sɛsaɪl] *adj* **1** *Botany* of a leaf or flower,
attached without a stem. **2** *Zoology* fixed to
one spot, as barnacles and sponges; not
mobile. ⟨Latin *sessum* pp of *sedere* sit⟩

ses·sion ['sɛʃən] *n* **1** a sitting or meeting of a
court, legislature, class, or any other group: *a
session of Parliament, a heated session with the
department head.* **2** a series of such sittings:
the spring session of university. **3** a stretch of
any activity: *a crying session.* **ses·sion·al** *adj.*
⟨Latin *sessio; sessum* pp of *sedere* sit⟩
in session meeting: *The teachers were in
session all Saturday morning.*
sessional indemnity ✹ in certain provinces,
the remuneration paid each session to a
member of a legislative body.

ses·tet [sɛs'tɛt] *n Prosody* a unit of six lines of
poetry. ⟨Italian *sestetto;* Latin *sex* six⟩

set [sɛt] *v* **set, set·ting 1** put; place: *Set the
box over there.* **2 a** put in the right place or
condition: *to set a broken bone.* **b** arrange
(hair) into a given style. **3** adjust to a
standard: *to set a clock.* **4** put in some
condition, activity, etc.: *to set wood on fire, to
set oneself to work.* **5** fix (a price, time, etc.): *to
set a date for a wedding.* **6** appoint for some
duty: *to set a detective on a case.* **7** put or get
into a fixed, firm, or rigid state: *to set one's
mind against something. Jam sets as it cools.*
8 put in a suitable framework, base, etc.;
mount: *to set a gem.* **9** provide a context for
(a story): *The novel is set in pre-Confederation
Montréal.* **10** of the sun or moon, go down.
11 of a dog, indicate the position of game by
standing stiffly and pointing with the nose.
adj **1** that has set or been set; fixed: *a set time.*

2 ready: *set to go. All set? Then let's get going.*
n **1** a number of things or persons belonging
together: *a set of dishes.* **2** *Mathematics* a
specified collection of elements: *the set of all
right triangles, the set of even integers.* **3** a
device for receiving or sending by radio,
television, telephone, etc. **4 a** the complete
scenery for a play, act, scene, etc. **b** the
physical setting for a scene in a movie,
television show, etc. **5** the act or manner of
setting: *He could tell by the set of her jaw she
was angry.* **6** *Tennis* a group of six or more
games. **7** a fishing net, floats, weights, etc., in
place for towing. ⟨Old English *settan*⟩
all set all ready to start, go, etc. **(dead) set on**
(or **against**) **something** (utterly) determined
(not) to do something. **get set** poise oneself
to begin a race. **set about** begin: *He set about
making dinner.* **set against a** make hostile
toward. **b** compare or contrast with. **set an
example** act in a way that others may
imitate. **set apart** keep or devote for a special
purpose. **set aside a** put to one side. **b** keep
for later use. **c** discard or dismiss. **d** repeal;
annul. **set back a** hinder; delay: *The job was
set back by the accident.* **b** *Informal* cost (a
person) a given amount: *The car set her back
$20 000.* **set·back** *n.* **set down** put down in
writing. **set forth a** articulate systematically.
b start out: *We set forth on our trip.* **set (great)
store by** value highly. **set in a** begin (usually
of something undesirable): *Winter has set in.*
b incorporate (a part) into a whole, as a
sleeve into a garment, a paragraph into a text,
etc. **set in one's ways** having stubbornly
fixed habits. **set off a** activate: *to set off a
bomb, to set off an alarm.* **b** start on one's way:
set off for home. **c** enhance by contrast: *The
green shirt sets off your red hair.* **d** balance;
compensate: *Her losses were set off by some
gains.* **e** mark off; separate visually: *The title
should be set off from the main text.* **set on** (or
upon) **a** attack. **b** urge to attack: *He set his
dogs on us.* **set one's heart on** be very eager to
have or do. **set out a** start a trip or other
undertaking. **b** plant. **c** begin with a given
aim: *I set out to help and ended up doing it all
by myself.* **set straight** correct a wrong
impression, opinion, etc. of. **set to a** begin:
Set to work. **b** begin fighting or arguing: *The
two boys set to.* **set** (or **put**) **to music** compose
or select music to fit (words). **set up a** start;
establish. **b** fund, fit out, etc. for some
endeavour: *They set him up in the textile
business.* **c** arrange a situation so as to
incriminate: *They set him up as the thief.*
set piece 1 a work of literature, music, etc.
which is an impressive example of a
conventional form. **2** *Theatre* a piece of a
stage set. **set point** *Tennis* the point that, if
won, enables one to win the set. **set square** a
flat, right-angled piece of wood or metal used
for drawing lines and right angles. **set·ter** *n*
any of several breeds of hunting dog often
trained to locate game and show its presence
by pointing. **set theory** the branch of
mathematics dealing with the relations
between SETS (*n* 2). **set·ting** *n* **1** a frame or

mounting in which something is set. **2** the place, time, etc. of a story. **3** surroundings; background: *a scenic mountain setting.* **4** social context: *This works well in a classroom setting.* **5** the dishes or cutlery required to set one place at a table. **6** the position of a dial or selector that has been set: *I left the radio at the right setting for our favourite station.* **set-to** *n Informal* a fight; dispute. **set-up** or **set·up** *n* **1** the act, fact, or manner of setting up: *He was the victim of a set-up. Set-up for each concert takes about an hour.* **2** *Informal* an organization. **3** the things needed for some task or undertaking.

CONFUSABLES

Set (past, set) takes an object: *Set the post into the ground. The waiter set the soup down with a flourish.*
Sit (past, sat) usually does not take an object: *I like to sit in a hotel lobby. That book has sat on the shelf for a long time.*

set·tee [sɛˈti] *n* a sofa with a back and, usually, arms. ⟨*set*⟩

set·tle [ˈsɛtəl] *v* **1 a** decide; agree (on): *Have you settled on a time for leaving?* **b** resolve (a dispute). **2** put or be put in order: *I must settle my affairs before going away.* **3** pay: *to settle a bill.* **4** take up residence (in a place): *to settle in Regina.* **5** establish communities or colonies in: *The French settled Québec.* **6** make comfortable in a position, way of life, etc.: *She is settled in her new job. The cat settled itself in the chair.* **7** come to rest in a particular place: *His cold settled in his lungs.* **8** calm: *A holiday will settle your nerves.* **9** sink or cause to sink: *The wall has settled 5 cm.* ⟨Old English *setlan; setl* settle⟩
settle down a live a more regular life. **b** direct steady effort or attention: *to settle down to studying.* **c** become calm or quiet. **settle for** accept (something other than what one really wants). **settle up** pay a bill. **settle with a** pay a debt to. **b** come to an agreement with. **c** get revenge on.
set·tle·ment *n* **1** the act of settling. **2** a region settled by people moving in. **3** a small community: *They spent the night in a First Nations settlement.* **4** the amount paid or received in settling a debt, suit, etc. **set·tler** *n* a person who settles in a new region.

sev·en [ˈsɛvən] *n* **1** one more than six; 7. **2** any set of seven persons or things: *Stack the counters in sevens.* **3** a playing card with seven spots. **sev·en** *adj.* ⟨Old English *seofon*⟩
sev·en·fold *adj* **1** seven times as much or as many. **2** having seven parts. *adv* seven times as much or as many. **seven seas** all the seas or oceans of the world; traditionally, the Arctic, Antarctic, North and South Atlantic, North and South Pacific, and Indian Oceans. **sev·enth** *n* **1** the next after the sixth. **2** one of seven equal parts. **3** *Music* **a** the seventh tone in a diatonic scale. **b** the interval between two tones that are six degrees apart. **c** the combination of two such tones. **d** the chord consisting of the tonic, third, fifth, and seventh tones of a diatonic scale.

adj **1** next after the sixth; 7th. **2** being one of seven equal parts. **Seventh Day Adventist** a member of a Christian group that believes the second coming of Christ is near at hand, and that observes the sabbath on Saturday. **seventh heaven 1** *esp Islam* the outermost or highest of seven heavens surrounding the earth; dwelling place of Allah and his angels. **2** the highest state of joy and happiness.

sev·en·teen [ˈsɛvənˈtin] *n* **1** seven more than ten; 17. **2** any set of 17 persons or things. **sev·en·teen** *adj.* ⟨Old English *seofontēne*⟩ **sev·en·teenth** *adj, n* **1** next after the 16th; 17th. **2** one, or being one, of 17 equal parts.

sev·en·ty [ˈsɛvənti] *n* **1** seven times ten; 70. **2 seventies** *pl* the years from 70 to 79 esp of a century or of a person's life: *He was still skiing regularly well into his seventies.* **sev·en·ty** *adj.* ⟨Old English *seofontēne*⟩
sev·en·ti·eth *adj, n* **1** next after the 69th; 70th. **2** one, or being one, of 70 equal parts.

sev·er [ˈsɛvər] *v* **1** remove or separate by cutting or breaking: *The axe severed the branch from the trunk. The rope severed and the swing fell down.* **2** break off; end: *to sever relations.* **3** *Law* divide (land) into separately owned parts for building. ⟨Old French *sevrer*; Latin *separare.* See SEPARATE.⟩
sev·er·ance *n* **1** a severing or being severed. **2** an arrangement to compensate an employee being laid off. **severance pay** extra pay given under such an arrangement.

sev·er·al [ˈsɛvrəl] *adj* **1** more than two but not many; some; a few: *to gain several kilos.* **2** individual; different; respective: *We went our several ways.* **sev·er·al** *pron.* **sev·er·al·ly** *adv.* ⟨Anglo-French; Latin *separ* distinct; *separare.* See SEPARATE.⟩

se·vere [səˈvir] *adj* **1** very strict or stern: *a severe expression, severe measures.* **2** serious; grave: *a severe illness.* **3** very hard to endure: *a severe test, severe criticism.* **4** very plain: *a severe style of dress.* **se·vere·ly** *adv.* **se·ver·i·ty** [səˈvɛrɪti] *n.* ⟨Latin *severus*⟩

sew [sou] *v* **sewed, sewn** or **sewed, sew·ing** **1** make (things) with needle and thread: *Can you sew?* **2** fasten with stitches: *to sew a patch onto a coat.* **sew·er** *n.* **sew·ing** *n.* ⟨Old English *seowian*⟩
sew up a close with stitches: *The doctor sewed up the wound.* **b** *Informal* assure the outcome of. **c** *Informal* gain sole control of. **d** complete or conclude successfully.
sewing machine a machine for sewing.

sew·er¹ [ˈsuər] *n* a pipe or channel, usually underground, to carry off waste water and human waste. ⟨Old French *sewiere* sluice from a pond; Latin *ex* out + *aquaria; aqua* water⟩
sew·age *n* the waste carried through sewers.

sew·er² See SEW.

sex [sɛks] *n* **1 a** either of the two categories, male and female, into which human beings, animals, and plants are divided according to their function in the reproductive process. **b** all members of either category, collectively. **2** the fact or condition of being male or

female: *Sex should not be a barrier to progress.*
3 sexual attraction, or behaviour motivated by such attraction: *Sex sells.* **4** SEXUAL INTERCOURSE, or other sexual activity. *v* determine the sex of. ⟨Latin *sexus*⟩

sex appeal sexual attractiveness. **sex chromosome** *Genetics* in most animals and some plants, a chromosome (X or Y) different in shape and function from the others, that determines an individual's sex. **sexed** *adj* **1** having sexual characteristics. **2** having (a given) appetite for sex: *over-sexed.* **sex·ism** *n* attention paid to a person's sex when it is not relevant. **sex·ist** *adj*, *n*. **sex·less** *adj* **1** lacking sexual characteristics; neuter. **2** lacking interest in sex. **sex·ol·o·gy** *n* the systematic study of human sexual behaviour. **sex·ol·o·gist** *n*. **sex symbol** a person who is famous for his or her sex appeal. **sex·u·al** [ˈsɛkʃuəl] *adj* to do with sex or the sexes: *sexual function, sexual reproduction, sexual conflict.* **sex·u·al·ly** *adv*. **sexual harassment** unwelcome sexual advances, sexual comments, etc. from a colleague or superior in any institutional setting. **sexual intercourse 1** a joining of the sexual organs of a male and a female human being, usually with transfer of semen from the male to the female. **2** any act involving the sex organs. **sex·u·al·i·ty** *n* **1** sexual character; the fact of being a member of either sex. **2** sexual aspects of human nature and behaviour and their social significance, etc. **3** attention to sexual matters; sex drive. **sex·y** *adj Informal* **1** sexually provocative or stimulating: *a sexy dress, a sexy voice.* **2** to do with sex: *a sexy novel.* **sex·i·ly** *adv*. **sex·i·ness** *n*.

sex·a·ge·nar·i·an [ˌsɛksədʒəˈnɛriən] *n* a person who is 60 years old, or between 60 and 70. **sex·a·ge·nar·i·an** *adj*. ⟨Latin *sexagenarius*; *sexaginta* sixty⟩

sex·tant [ˈsɛkstənt] *n* **1** an astronomical instrument for measuring angular distance between objects. It is used at sea to measure the altitude of the sun, a star, etc. in order to determine latitude and longitude. **2** a sixth of a circle. ⟨Latin *sextantis* a sixth; *sex* six⟩

sex·tet or **sex·tette** [sɛksˈtɛt] *n* **1** *Music* **a** a group of six singers or players. **b** a piece of music for six voices or instruments. **2** any group of six. ⟨Latin *sex* six⟩

sex·til·lion [sɛksˈtɪljən] *n* **1** followed by 21 zeros; 10^{21}. ⟨Latin *sextus* sixth + (M)ILLION⟩

sex·ton [ˈsɛkstən] *n* **1** a person employed as caretaker to a church and its grounds. **2** an administrative official in a synagogue. ⟨Old French *secrestein*; Latin *sacristanus*⟩

sex·tu·ple [sɛksˈtʌpəl], [-ˈtjupəl], *or* [-ˈtupəl] *adj* **1** consisting of six parts; sixfold. **2** six times as great. ⟨Latin *sextus* sixth + (QUADR)UPLE⟩ **sex·tu·plet** [sɛksˈtʌplɪt] *n* one of six babies born of the same mother at the same time.

sf or **SF** SCIENCE FICTION.

sh [ʃ] *interj* used to urge silence.

Shab·bat [ʃaˈbat] *n Judaism* Sabbath. Also, **Shab·bos** [ˈʃabəs].

shab·by [ˈʃæbi] *adj* **1** much worn: *His old suit looks shabby.* **2** wearing old or worn clothes. **3** poor or neglected; run-down: *a shabby old house.* **4** mean; not generous: *shabby treatment.* **shab·bi·ly** *adv*. **shab·bi·ness** *n*. ⟨dialect *shab* scab, Old English *sceabb*⟩ **not too shabby** *Informal* an expression of approval.

shack [ʃæk] *n* a roughly built hut. ⟨perhaps Spanish *jacal* wooden hut; Nahuatl *xacalli*⟩ **shack up** *Slang* enter into a common-law union.

shack·le [ˈʃækəl] *n* **1** Usually, **shackles** *pl* metal bands fastened around the ankles or wrists of a prisoner, slave, etc. **2** anything that prevents freedom of action, thought, etc. **3** a device for fastening or coupling. **shack·le** *v*. ⟨Old English *sceacel*⟩

shad [ʃæd] *n*, *pl* **shad** or **shads** any of several edible saltwater fishes of the herring family. ⟨Old English *sceadd*⟩ **shad·ber·ry** *n* ✻ *esp Maritimes* serviceberry. **shad·bush** *n*.

shade [ʃeɪd] *n* **1** a slight darkness or coolness afforded by something that cuts off light: *the shade of a tree.* **2** a covering for a window, lamp, etc. to screen the light. **3** lightness or darkness of colour. **4** a tiny degree: *a shade too long.* **5** **shades** *pl Slang* sunglasses. **6** a ghost; spirit. *v* **1 a** screen the light of: *Shade that lamp.* **b** screen from light: *to shade one's eyes.* **2** show a gradual progression: *shading from deep rose to pale pink.* **3** darken (part of a drawn or painted image) for an effect of light and depth. **shade·less** *adj*. **shad·ing** *n*. ⟨Old English *sceadu*⟩ **shades of —!** how reminiscent of (another from the past): *shades of the Depression!* **shad·y** *adj* **1** shaded. **2** giving shade. **3** *Informal* of questionable honesty: *a shady deal.*

shad·ow [ˈʃædoʊ] *n* **1** the dark image cast by a person or thing cutting off light. **2** shade (*n* 1). **3 the shadows** obscurity. **4** a slight suggestion: *not a shadow of a doubt.* **5** a faint image: *She is only a shadow of her former self.* **6** a prophetic image, foretaste, etc.: *shadows of things to come.* **7** a person who follows another closely and secretly. **8** a constant companion; sidekick. **9** sadness or doubt, or the evidence of it: *A shadow crossed her face.* **10** something insubstantial. *v* **1** cast a shadow on. **2** represent faintly or prophetically. **3** follow closely and secretly. **shad·ow·y** *adj*. ⟨from case form of Old English *sceadu* shade⟩ **under** (or **in**) **the shadow of a** very near to. **b** protected by. **c** obscured by. **shadow cabinet** the senior members of an opposition party in a legislature, each of whom is assigned as critic to the corresponding member of the real cabinet.

shaft [ʃæft] *n* **1** in a machine, a bar that turns or on which other parts turn. **2** a well-like or tunnel-like passage: *an elevator shaft, a mine*

shaft. **3** any long, slender part or object, as the stem of an arrow, midsection of a bone, etc. **4** a ray or beam of light. **5 the shaft** *Slang* unfair treatment: *to get the shaft.*
v Slang cheat; exploit; deal unfairly with. **shaft·like** *adj.* ⟨Old English *sceaft*⟩

shag [ʃæg] *n* **1** a growth of long, rough hair, fur, etc. **2** a long, rough pile on fabric or carpet. **3** a cormorant. **shag·gy** *adj.* ⟨Old English *sceacga*⟩

shake [ʃeik] *v* **shook, shak·en, shak·ing** **1** move quickly back and forth or up and down: *to shake a rug.* **2** tremble, shiver, or cause to do so: *shaking with cold.* **3** make or become less firm: *to shake someone's faith.* **4** agitate or upset: *badly shaken by the news.* **5** *Informal* get rid of (often with *off*): *I can't shake this cough.*
n **1** the act or fact of shaking: *a shake of the head.* **2** a drink made by shaking ingredients together: *a milk shake.* **3** *Slang* a moment: *I'll be there in two shakes.* **4 the shakes** *pl* a fit of trembling. **5** a shingle or board, usually split by hand, used for roofing and siding: *cedar shakes.* **shak·a·ble** or **shake·a·ble** *adj.* ⟨Old English *sceacan*⟩
a fair shake *Informal* fair treatment. **no great shakes** *Informal* not particularly impressive. **shake down a** bring down or settle by shaking. **b** restructure for greater efficiency, etc. **c** *Slang* get money from by blackmail or extortion. **shake-down** *n.* **shake hands** clasp hands (*with* someone) in greeting, agreement, congratulation, etc. **shake up a** shake hard. **b** stir up. **c** unsettle the nerves of. **d** subject to radical changes. **shake–up** *n.*

shak·er *n* **1** a person or thing that shakes something. **2** a container with a perforated top, for dispensing pepper, salt, etc. **3 Shaker** a member of an American religious sect advocating communalism and simplicity.
shak·y *adj* **1** trembling; nervous or unsteady: *a shaky voice.* **2** unstable: *a shaky porch, a shaky business firm.* **3** not reliable: *a shaky knowledge of art.* **shak·i·ly** *adv.* **shak·i·ness** *n.*

SYNONYMS
Shake, the general word, suggests a rapid, irregular, more or less violent motion: *She shook with laughter.* **Tremble** suggests uncontrollable, continued shaking with quick, small movements, caused by fear, strong feeling, cold, etc.: *In his excitement his hands trembled.* **Quiver** suggests a slight trembling: *The dog's nostrils quivered at the scent.*

Shake·spear·e·an [ʃeik'spiriən] *adj* to do with the English dramatist and poet William Shakespeare (1564-1616), or his works.
Shakespearean (or **English**) **sonnet** a sonnet with three quatrains of alternating rhyme (abab cdcd efef) and a hyming couplet (gg).

Shak·ti ['ʃʌkti] *n Hinduism* **1** the mother goddess who stands for nature. **2** the wife of a god, esp Shiva.

shale [ʃeil] *n* a fine-grained sedimentary rock formed from clay. Shale splits easily into thin layers. **shal·y** *adj.* ⟨Old English *scealu* shell⟩

shall [ʃæl] 3rd pres sg **shall** a somewhat formal auxiliary verb used: **1** in questions, to make a polite suggestion: *Shall I wait? Shall we begin?* **2** in statements in the second or third person to show obligation: *Notice shall be given not less than two weeks in advance.* **3** to indicate simple future time: *I shall go tomorrow.* ⟨Old English *sceal*⟩

shal·lot [ʃə'lɒt] *n* a small herb resembling an onion, but with a bulb made up of sections or cloves. ⟨French *eschalotte*⟩

shal·low ['ʃælou] *adj* not deep: *a shallow bowl, shallow breathing, a shallow mind.*
n Usually, **shallows** *pl* a shallow part: *The children splashed in the shallows of the pond.* **shal·low·ly** *adv.* **shal·low·ness** *n.* ⟨Middle English *shalowe*; Old English *sceald*⟩

shalt [ʃælt] *v Archaic* 2nd pres sg of SHALL. *Thou shalt* means *You shall.*

sham [ʃæm] *n* **1** a pretence, counterfeit, or imitation. **2** a fancy cover for a pillow, going over the ordinary pillow case. **sham** *adj.* **sham, shammed, sham·ming** *v.* ⟨orig dialect variant of *shame*⟩

sha·man ['ʃeimən] *or* ['ʃɑmən] *n* a medicine man or woman; a person believed to have power to influence spirits for good or evil. ⟨Russian *shaman*; Sanskrit *sramana* monk⟩
sha·man·ism *n* **1** a religion of the Ural-Altaic peoples of N Asia and Europe, characterized by belief in powerful spirits that can be influenced only by the shamans. **2** any of various similar religions, as among some First Nations or Inuit peoples. **sha·man·is·tic** *adj.*

sham·ble ['ʃæmbəl] *v* walk unsteadily, lazily, or awkwardly: *The tired, sick man shambled to his bed.* **sham·ble** *n.* ⟨probably *shamble* sg of *shambles*; for the straddling legs of a bench⟩

sham·bles ['ʃæmbəlz] *n pl or sg* **1** *Informal* a scene of chaos and disorder: *The room was a shambles.* **2** abbatoir. ⟨Old English *scamel*⟩

shame [ʃeim] *n* **1** a painful feeling of having done something wrong, improper, or silly: *to blush with shame.* **2** disgrace or dishonour, or its cause: *to bring shame on the family.* **3** a fact to be sorry about: *It is a shame to be wasteful.*
v **1** cause to feel shame. **2** use shame to coerce. **3** disgrace. ⟨Old English *sceamu*⟩
for shame! you (or someone else) should be ashamed! **have no shame** be utterly brazen. **put to shame a** disgrace; make ashamed. **b** make dim by comparison: *Her careful work put the rest of us to shame.* **shame on —!** (someone) should be ashamed: *Shame on him for being so hard on that poor child!*
shame·faced *adj* showing shame; sheepish; embarrassed. **shame·fac·ed·ly** [-ˌfeisɪdli] *adv.* **shame·fac·ed·ness** *n.* **shame·ful** *adj* causing or deserving shame. **shame·ful·ly** *adv.* **shame·ful·ness** *n.* **shame·less** *adj* brazen. **shame·less·ly** *adv.* **shame·less·ness** *n.*

sham·my ['ʃæmi] *n* CHAMOIS (def. 2).
v polish with a chamois.

sham·poo [ʃæm'pu] *n* **1** a preparation for washing the hair, fur, a rug, etc. **2** a washing with such a preparation. **sham·poo** v. **sham·poo·er** n. ⟨Hindi *chhāmpo* literally, press⟩

sham·rock [ˈʃæmˌrɒk] n any of various plants with leaves composed of three round leaflets. The shamrock is the national emblem of Ireland. ⟨Irish *seamróg* diminutive of *seamair* clover⟩

shan·dy [ˈʃændi] n a drink made by mixing beer and a soft drink, usually ginger ale or ginger beer. ⟨origin uncertain⟩

shang·hai [ʃæŋˈhaɪ] or [ˈʃæŋhaɪ] v bring by trickery or force. ⟨for the practice of securing sailors for long voyages, such as to *Shanghai*, China, by kidnapping or other illegal means⟩

shank [ʃæŋk] n 1 in humans, the part of the leg between the knee and the ankle. 2 the corresponding part in animals, or a cut of meat from it. 3 the whole leg. 4 any shaftlike part, such as the straight part of a fish-hook. v Golf strike (the ball) with the heel of a club. ⟨Old English *sceanca*⟩
go by (or **ride on**) **shank's mare** walk.

shan·ty[1] [ˈʃænti] n ✱ 1 a roughly built hut or cabin. 2 the log-built living quarters of a gang of loggers. ⟨Cdn. French *chantier*, French = timber yard; perhaps also Irish *sean tig* hut⟩ **shan·ty·town** n a community of people living in small, dilapidated houses or shacks.

shan·ty[2] [ˈʃænti] n a song sung by sailors in rhythm with the motions made during their work. Also, **chan·tey, chan·ty**. ⟨variant of *chantey*; French *chanter* sing⟩

shape [ʃeip] n 1 the outer contour or outline: *We saw the shape of the mountain against the sky.* 2 an assumed appearance: *The witch took the shape of a cat.* 3 something seen but having no definite form: *A white shape stood at her bedside.* 4 condition, esp good condition: *He exercises to keep in shape.* 5 a definite form: *Get your thoughts into shape.* 6 a kind; sort: *dangers of every shape.*
v 1 form into a shape: *to shape clay into balls.* 2 adapt to fit a certain shape: *That hat is shaped to his head.* 3 define the character of: *events that shape people's lives.* **shap·er** n. ⟨Old English *sceapen* pp of *scieppan* create⟩
shape up a take on a certain form; develop. **b** behave as required: *You'd better shape up or you'll be fired.* **take shape** take on a definite form. **whip into shape** bring up to standard by means of stern measures.
shape·less adj 1 without a definite shape. 2 unattractively shaped. **shape·less·ly** adv. **shape·less·ness** n. **shape·ly** adj esp of the female figure, well-formed. **shape·li·ness** n.

shard [ʃɑrd] n a fragment of broken glass, earthenware, etc. ⟨Old English *sceard*⟩

share[1] [ʃer] v 1 a have in common: *to share a bedroom.* b let another join in using: *I shared my book with her.* 2 divide into parts, giving each a part: *We shared the pie among the six of us.* 3 take part: *Everyone shared in making the picnic a success.* 4 tell to others: *He shared his impressions of Japan.*
n 1 a part allotted or belonging to one individual: *Do your share of the work.* 2 a stake in something owned jointly: *She offered to sell her share in the boat.* 3 each of the parts into which the ownership of a company is divided. ⟨Old English *scearu* division⟩
go shares share something.
share·crop·per n a person who farms land owned by another in return for part of the crops. **share·crop, -cropped, -crop·ping** v. **share·hold·er** n a person who owns shares in a company. **share·ware** n Computers software that is copyright but is available free, usually with a request that a user fee be remitted.

share[2] [ʃer] n ploughshare. ⟨Old English *scear*⟩

shark[1] [ʃɑrk] n any of an order of mostly marine, carnivorous, cartilaginous fishes. ⟨origin uncertain⟩

shark[2] [ʃɑrk] n a dishonest person who preys on others: *a loan shark.* ⟨German *Schork* variant of *Schurke* scoundrel⟩

sharp [ʃɑrp] adj 1 having a thin cutting edge or a fine point: *a sharp knife.* 2 relatively pointed: *a sharp nose.* 3 of a turn, slope, etc., abrupt. 4 cold: *a sharp morning.* 5 harsh: *sharp words.* 6 affecting the senses or emotions keenly: *a sharp pain.* 7 distinct: *a sharp contrast.* 8 quick: *a sharp pace.* 9 quick to understand or perceive: *sharp ears. He's pretty sharp, he'll learn fast.* 10 alert: *to keep a sharp watch.* 11 shrewd; almost dishonest: *sharp business practice.* 12 Music a above the true pitch. b raised a half step in pitch: *F sharp.* 13 Slang stylish; smart.
adv 1 exactly: *at one o'clock sharp.* 2 abruptly: *to pull up sharp at the door.* 3 above true pitch: *to sing sharp.*
n 1 Music a a tone raised one half step above a given tone. b the sign (♯) that stands for this. 2 a swindler; cheater. **sharp·en** v. **sharp·en·er** n. **sharp·ly** adv. **sharp·ness** n. ⟨Old English *scearp*⟩
look sharp be quick; act promptly.
sharp·er n 1 a swindler. 2 a gambler who cheats routinely. **sharp·shoot·er** n a person who shoots with good aim. **sharp–tongued** adj harsh or sarcastic in speech.

SYNONYMS
Sharp suggests quickness to see and take an advantage, often dishonestly: *a sharp lawyer.* **Keen** suggests rigour, and quickness of perception and thinking: *a keen mind.* **Acute** suggests penetrating insight: *an acute interpreter of current events.*

shat·ter [ˈʃætər] v 1 break into many pieces: *to shatter a window.* 2 disturb greatly: *shattered nerves.* 3 destroy: *Her hopes were shattered.*
n **shatters** pl fragments. **shat·ter·ing** adj. ⟨Middle English *schateren*⟩
shat·ter·proof adj that can break without shattering.

shave [ʃeiv] v **shaved, shaved** or (as adj) **shav·en, shav·ing** 1 remove (facial hair) with a razor. 2 remove hair (from) with a razor. 3 cut (off) in thin slices; cut thin slices from. 4 cut very close. 5 come very close to. 6 reduce (a price, etc.) slightly; deduct (a small amount). **shave** n. ⟨Old English *sceafan*⟩

a close shave a narrow miss or escape: *The shot missed her, but it was a close shave.*
shav·er *n* **1** an instrument for shaving. **2** *Informal* a small boy. **3** a person who shaves. **shav·ing** *n* a very thin piece shaved off.

Sha·vu·ot [ʃə'vuout] *or* [ˌʃavu'out] *n Judaism* a holiday celebrating the giving of the law at Mount Sinai. Also called **Feast of Weeks.** ⟨Hebrew; *shavua* week; *sheva* seven⟩

shawl [ʃɒl] *n* a large piece of cloth worn around the shoulders or head. ⟨Persian⟩

she [ʃi] *pron, subj* **she** *obj* **her** *poss* **hers** *pl subj* **they** *pl obj* **them,** *pl poss* **theirs** **1** a girl, woman, or female animal that has just been referred to: *My mother is home, but she is asleep.* **2** anything personified as feminine and already referred to and identified.
n pl **she's** a female human being or animal, or a thing personified as female: *The pup is a she.* ⟨Old English *sīo, sēo, sīe*⟩

sheaf [ʃif] *n, pl* **sheaves** **1** a bundle of grain bound in the middle. **2** a bundle of things laid lengthwise: *a sheaf of arrows, a sheaf of papers.* ⟨Old English *scēaf*⟩

shear [ʃir] *v* **sheared, sheared** or **shorn, shear·ing** **1** cut wool or fleece from (sheep). **2** (in passive) strip or deprive: *We have been shorn of our rights.* **3** break by a force causing two parts to slide on each other in opposite directions: *Too much pressure on the handles of the scissors sheared off the centre rivet.*
n **1** the act of shearing (often used to define a sheep's age): *a ewe of two shears.* **2 a** a force causing two parts to slide on each other in opposite directions. **b** strain or damage so caused. **shear·er** *n.* ⟨Old English *sceran*⟩
shear·ling *n* **1** a sheep that has been shorn only once. **2** the hide of a newly-shorn sheep, tanned with the wool on. **shears** *n pl or sg* a cutting tool like a large scissors.

sheath [ʃiθ] *n, pl* **sheaths** [ʃiðz] **1** a cover for the blade of a sword, knife, etc. **2** any similar covering for something long and narrow. ⟨Old English *scēath*⟩
sheathe [ʃið] *v* **1** put into a sheath. **2** encase or cover: *a mummy sheathed in linen, doors sheathed in metal.* **3** retract (claws). **sheath·ing** ['ʃiðɪŋ] *n* a casing; a layer of something that covers, as boards on the frame of a house.

sheaves pl of SHEAF.

she·bang [ʃə'bæŋ] *n Slang* ⟨origin uncertain⟩ **the whole shebang** everything.

shed¹ [ʃɛd] *n* **1** a small building used for shelter or storage: *a tool shed.* **2** a large, sturdy structure with a roof and three sides, for storing and repairing machinery, shearing sheep, etc. ⟨Old English *sced* shelter⟩

shed² [ʃɛd] *v* **shed, shed·ding** **1** cause or allow (tears, blood, etc.) to flow: *He shed his enemy's blood.* **2** throw off or lose (antlers, dead skin, etc.) by a natural process. **3** lose hair in such a way: *Our cat sheds a lot.* **4** repel: *Oilcloth sheds water.* **5** scatter abroad: *The sun sheds light.* **6** get rid of (something unwanted): *to shed some weight.* ⟨Old English *scēadan*⟩
shed blood kill.

sheen [ʃin] *n* soft brightness; lustre, as of satin. **sheen·y** *adj.* ⟨Old English *scēne* bright⟩

sheep [ʃip] *n, pl* **sheep** **1** any of a genus of hoofed, cud-chewing mammals related to goats and cattle, esp one species raised in many breeds for its wool, meat, and hide. **2** a timid, weak, foolish, or gullible person. **sheep·like** *adj.* ⟨Old English *scēap*⟩
make sheep's eyes at look at in a yearning, loving way. **separate the sheep from the goats** sort better people from the rest.
sheep·dip *n* a liquid disinfectant and insecticide in which sheep are immersed to destroy parasites, etc. in their fleece. **sheep·dog** *n* **1** a dog trained to watch or herd sheep. **2** any of various breeds of shaggy work dog. **sheep·fold** *n* a pen or enclosure for sheep. **sheep·ish** *adj* embarrassed, esp when one has been proved wrong: *a sheepish smile.* **sheep·ish·ly** *adv.* **sheep·ish·ness** *n.* **sheep·shear·ing** *n* **1** the act of shearing sheep. **2** a season or festival when this is done. **sheep·skin** *n* **1** the skin of a sheep, esp with the wool on it. **2** a garment or rug, or leather or parchment, made from the skin of a sheep. **3** *Informal* diploma.

sheer¹ [ʃir] *adj* **1** so thin as to be almost transparent: *a sheer white dress.* **2** unmixed with anything else; pure: *sheer bliss.* **3** very steep: *a sheer drop of 50 m to the sea.*
n **sheers** *pl* curtains of nearly transparent fabric. **sheer·ness** *n.* ⟨Old English *scīr* bright⟩

sheer² [ʃir] *v* turn or cause to turn sharply from a course; swerve or cause to swerve. **sheer** *n.* ⟨variant of *shear* in sense of 'cut off'⟩

sheet¹ [ʃit] *n* **1** a large piece of cloth used to sleep on or under. **2** a broad, thin piece of anything: *a sheet of glass.* **3** a piece of paper. **4** a broad, flat pan for baking: *a cookie sheet.* **5** any broad, flat surface: *a sheet of ice.* **6** a sail. ⟨Old English *scēte*⟩
sheet·ing *n* **1** cloth suitable for bed sheets. **2** a protective layer of timber or metal sheets. **sheet lightning** lightning in broad flashes. **sheet metal** metal in broad, thin plates. **sheet music** music printed on unbound pages.

sheet² [ʃit] *n Nautical* **1** a rope that controls the angle at which a sail is set. **2 sheets** *pl* the space at the bow or stern of an open boat. ⟨Old English *scēata*⟩
three sheets to the wind *Slang* drunk.

sheik or **sheikh** [ʃik] *or* [ʃeik] *n* **1** an Arab chief; head of a clan, village, etc. **2** a Muslim religious leader. **3** a Muslim title of respect. **sheik·dom** or **sheikh·dom** *n.* ⟨Arabic *shaikh*⟩

shek·el ['ʃɛkəl] *n* **1** a unit of mass used by the ancient Hebrews, equal to about 14 g. **2** a coin of the ancient Hebrews. **3** the basic unit of money in modern Israel; also, **shequ·el.** **4 shekels** *pl Slang* money. ⟨Hebrew⟩

shelf [ʃɛlf] *n* **1** a thin, flat piece of wood or other material fastened to a wall or frame to hold things, such as books, dishes, etc. **2** anything like a shelf, such as a rock ledge. **shelf·like** *adj.* ⟨probably Low German *schelf*⟩
on the shelf put aside indefinitely.

shelf life the length of time a product can stay on a store shelf before it is considered unfit for sale or consumption. **shelve** *v* 1 place on a shelf: *to shelve books.* 2 set aside indefinitely: *to shelve an issue.* 3 of ground, etc., slope gradually. **shelv·ing** *n* 1 material for making shelves. 2 shelves collectively. **shelving unit** a large storage unit with shelves, built into or attached to the wall.

shell [ʃɛl] *n* 1 a hard outside covering of an animal, nut, egg, etc. 2 the outer part; mere appearance. 3 any outer framework or covering. 4 a long, narrow, light racing boat rowed by a crew. 5 a hollow case of pastry or the lower crust of a pie. 6 a cartridge used in a rifle or shotgun. 7 a metal projectile fired by artillery and exploding on impact. 8 a light waterproof windbreaker. 9 *Computers* a program acting as an interface between the user and the operating system.
v 1 remove a shell from: *to shell peas.* 2 take (kernels) off a cob or ear: *to shell corn.* 3 bombard with artillery fire. 4 collect seashells: *to go shelling.* ⟨Old English *sciell*⟩
come out of one's shell stop being shy or reserved; join in conversation, etc. **retire into one's shell** become shy and reserved. **shell out** *a Informal* pay: *He shelled out $15 for the roses.* **b** give out candy at Halloween.
shell·fish *n, pl* **-fish** or **-fish·es** any aquatic invertebrate animal with a shell, esp edible molluscs or crustaceans such as clams, crabs, etc. **shell game** 1 the game of betting which, if any, of three rapidly manipulated cups or nutshells conceals a small object. 2 *Informal* a swindle. **shell shock** 1 *Psychiatry* any of the nervous or mental disorders due to the accumulated strain of warfare. 2 *Informal* extreme surprise or shock. **shell·shocked** *adj.*

shel·lac [ʃəˈlæk] *n* 1 a purified resin (**lac**) used for making varnishes, leather polishes, etc. 2 a varnish for wood or metal, consisting of shellac dissolved in alcohol.
v **-lacked, -lack·ing** 1 coat or treat with shellac. 2 *Informal* defeat soundly. ⟨shell + *lac*, translation of French *laque en écailles*⟩

shel·ter [ˈʃɛltər] *n* 1 something that covers or protects: *Trees serve as a shelter from the sun.* 2 protection; refuge: *We took shelter from the storm in a barn.* **shel·ter** *v.* ⟨perhaps Middle English *sheltrum*; Old English *scildtruma* guard; *scild* shield + *truma* squad⟩

shelve, shelves, shelv·ing See SHELF.

she·nan·i·gans [ʃəˈnænəgənz] *n pl Informal* mischief. ⟨origin uncertain⟩

shep·herd [ˈʃɛpərd] *n* 1 a person who takes care of sheep. 2 a person who leads and protects. 3 a spiritual guide; pastor.
v 1 be a shepherd to. 2 guide: *She shepherded them safely onto the train.* ⟨Old English *scēap* sheep + *hierde* herder; *heord* herd⟩
shep·herd·ess [ˈʃɛpərdɪs] *n Poetic* a woman or girl who tends sheep. **shepherd's pie** a dish of meat topped with mashed potatoes.

sher·bet [ˈʃɜrbət] *n* a frozen dessert made of fruit juice, sugar, gelatin, and sometimes milk or egg white. ⟨Arabic *sharibah* to drink⟩

sher·iff [ˈʃɛrɪf] *n* 1 in Canada, an official who enforces certain court orders, such as evicting people who fail to pay rent. 2 *US* the chief law officer of a county. ⟨Old English *scīrgerēfa*; *scīr* shire + *gerēfa* reeve⟩

Sher·pa [ˈʃɜrpə] *n* 1 a member of a mountain people living on both sides of the Tibet-Nepal border, famous as mountaineers and guides. 2 their Sino-Tibetan language.

sher·ry [ˈʃɛri] *n* a strong, dry or sweet wine fortified with brandy. ⟨earlier *sherris* (taken as pl) wine from *Jeres*, a Spanish town⟩

Shi·a [ˈʃiə] *n* 1 one of the two major branches of Islam. 2 Shiite. Compare SUNNI. Sometimes, **Shi'·a**.
Shi·ite [ˈʃiait] *n* a member of the Shiah branch of Islam. **Shi·ite** *adj.* ⟨Arabic⟩

shi·at·su [ʃiˈɑtsu] *n* massage therapy making use of acupressure. ⟨Japanese⟩

shib·bo·leth [ˈʃɪbəlɪθ] *n* 1 any peculiarity of speech or custom distinguishing a group. 2 a watchword or pet phrase of a political party, social class, etc. ⟨Hebrew = stream; used to detect Ephraimites, who could not say [ʃ]⟩

shield [ʃild] *n* 1 a piece of armour carried on the arm to protect the body. 2 any of various items that serve to protect or insulate. 3 a badge or coat of arms. 4 anything shaped or used like a shield: *She held up a newspaper as a shield against the sun.* 5 a *Geology* a slightly convex formation of Precambrian rock that covers a large area. **b the Shield ≈** CANADIAN SHIELD. **shield** *v.* ⟨Old English *sceld*⟩

shift [ʃɪft] *v* 1 change from one position, person, etc. to another: *The wind has shifted to the east.* 2 change the position of (gears of a car). 3 switch between lower and upper case using the **shift key** on a typewriter or computer keyboard. 4 make do.
n 1 a change of direction, position, attitude, etc.: *a shift in policy.* 2 a group of workers who work during a certain period: *The night shift comes on at 10 o'clock.* 3 the time during which they work: *I work the day shift.* 4 a scheme; trick: *She tried every shift to avoid work.* 5 gearshift. 6 a woman's loose, casual dress or dresslike undergarment. 7 *Geology* a slight fault or dislocation in a stratum. ⟨Old English *sciftan* arrange⟩
make shift manage, often by improvising. **shift for oneself** manage on one's own.
shift·less *adj* lazy; inefficient. **shift·y** *adj* sly; not straightforward. **shift·i·ly** *adv.* **shift·i·ness** *n.*

Shi·ite See SHIA.

shill [ʃɪl] *Slang n* a person who acts as a decoy to attract customers or supporters. **shill** *v.* ⟨origin unknown⟩

shil·ling [ˈʃɪlɪŋ] *n* 1 a former unit of money in the UK, equal to 1/20 of a pound. 2 the basic unit of money in certain other countries. ⟨Old English *scilling*⟩

shim [ʃɪm] *n* a thin strip of metal or wood used to fill space, make a thing level, etc. ⟨origin uncertain⟩

shim·mer [ˈʃɪmər] *v* 1 shine faintly or with

varying intensity. **2** appear as a wavering image reflected in heat waves or on rippling water. **shim·mer** *n*. **shim·mer·ing** or **shim·mer·y** *adj*. ⟨Old English *scimrian*⟩

shim·my ['ʃɪmi] *n* **1** a ragtime dance characterized by shaking of the hips and shoulders. **2** an unusual shaking or vibration, esp of the wheels of a vehicle. **shim·my** *v*. ⟨variant of *chemise* (taken as pl)⟩

shin [ʃɪn] *n* **1** the front part of the leg from the knee to the ankle. **2** in beef cattle, the lower part of the foreleg.
v **shinned, shin·ning** climb up or down a rope, pole, etc. by gripping alternately with hands and feet or knees: *to shin up a tree.* ⟨Old English *scinu*⟩
shin·bone *n* the front bone of the leg below the knee; tibia. **shin·guard** *n* a protective pad worn on the shins in various sports. **shin splints** or **shinsplints** pain felt in the lower leg muscles, often after prolonged running. **shin·ny** *v Informal* shin: *to shinny up a tree.*

shin·dig ['ʃɪnˌdɪg] *n Informal* a merry or noisy dance, party, etc. ⟨origin uncertain⟩

shine [ʃaɪn] *v* **shone** or (for def. 3) **shined, shin·ing 1** send out or reflect light: *The sun shines.* **2** excel: *She shines in math.* **3** polish: *shine shoes.* **4** cause to shine: *shine a light.*
n **1** radiance or lustre. **2** fair weather: *rain or shine.* **3** the act of polishing shoes. **shin·y** *adj*. **shin·i·ness** *n*. ⟨Old English *scīnan*⟩
shine up to *Slang* ingratiate oneself with. **take a shine to** *Informal* become fond of.
shin·er *n Slang* BLACK EYE. **shin·ing** *adj* outstanding: *a shining example.*

shin·gle¹ ['ʃɪŋgəl] *n* **1** one of many thin pieces of wood, asphalt, etc. used to cover a roof or outer wall and laid in overlapping rows. **2** *Informal* a small signboard, esp for the office of a professional. **shingle** *v*. ⟨Latin *scindulal; scindere* split⟩
hang out one's shingle *Informal* establish a professional practice; open an office.

shin·gle² ['ʃɪŋgəl] *n* loose stones or pebbles such as lie on some beaches. **shin·gly** *adj*. ⟨origin uncertain⟩

shin·gles ['ʃɪŋgəlz] *n sg or pl* a viral disease that causes painful irritation of a group of nerves and an outbreak of itching spots or blisters. ⟨Latin *cingulus; cingere* gird⟩

shin·ny¹ ['ʃɪni] ✳ *n* **1** a simple type of hockey, played on ice or elsewhere. **2** *Slang* ICE HOCKEY. ⟨Scottish dialect *shinny* or *shinty*⟩

shin·ny² See SHIN.

Shin·to ['ʃɪntou] *n* **1** the main religion of Japan, primarily a system of ancestor and nature worship. **2** an adherent of this religion. **Shin·to** *adj*. **Shin·to·ism** *n*. ⟨Japanese; Mandarin *shin tao* way of the gods⟩

ship [ʃɪp] *n* **1** any large vessel for travel on water. **2** an aircraft or spacecraft.
v **shipped, ship·ping 1** send or carry from one place to another: *Did he ship it express?* **2** board or take a job on a ship: *He shipped as cook.* **3** of a ship, take in (water) over the side. **ship·pa·ble** *adj*. ⟨Old English *scip*⟩

jump ship a desert one's ship. **b** leave an organization, etc. to avoid a difficult situation. **run a tight ship** be a very efficient or strict administrator. **ship out** (or **off**) **a** go to sea. **b** send out by ship. **c** dismiss; send away. **d** leave. **when one's ship comes in** when one gets lucky or makes one's fortune.
ship·board *adj* occurring, found, etc. on a ship: *a shipboard romance.* **on shipboard** on or inside a ship. **ship·build·er** *n* a designer or maker of ships. **ship·build·ing** *n*. **ship·load** *n* a full load for a ship. **ship·mate** *n* a fellow traveller on a ship. **ship·ment** *n* **1** the act of shipping goods. **2** the goods sent at one time to a given destination. **ship of the desert** camel. **ship·per** *n* a person or company that ships goods. **ship·ping** *n* **1** the act, business, or cost of sending goods by water or land. **2** ships collectively (of a nation, business, etc.). **ship·shape** *adj* in good order; neat. **ship·wreck** *n* **1** the destruction or loss of a ship at sea. **2** a wrecked ship. **3** ruin: *the shipwreck of one's plans.* *v* cause to suffer shipwreck. **ship·wright** *n* a person who builds or repairs ships. **ship·yard** *n* a place near water where ships are built or repaired.

–ship *suffix* **1** the fact of being or doing: *friendship.* **2** office or position: *to hold a professorship.* **3** art or skill: *workmanship, leadership.* **4** one with the rank or status of (with a possessive, as a term of address): *your ladyship.* **5** the members, collectively, of a class: *readership.* ⟨Old English *-scipe*⟩

shirk [ʃɜrk] *v* avoid (work, duty, etc.).
n a person who does this. **shirk·er** *n*. ⟨German *Schurke* rascal⟩

shirr [ʃɜr] *v* **1** draw up or gather (cloth) on parallel threads. **2** bake (eggs) in a shallow dish with butter. **shirring** *n*. ⟨origin unknown⟩

shirt [ʃɜrt] *n* **1** a garment for the upper body, typically with a collar, sleeves, a front opening with buttons. **2** an upper garment in any of various other styles. **shirt·less** *adj*. ⟨Middle English *schirte*, Old English *scyrte*. See SKIRT.⟩
in one's shirt sleeves with no coat or jacket on. **keep one's shirt on** *Informal* keep one's temper. **lose one's shirt** *Informal* lose all that one owns.
shirt·ing *n* fabric for shirts. **shirt–sleeve** *adj* **1** suitable for wearing no jacket: *shirt-sleeve weather.* **2** carried on in an informal style: *shirt-sleeve diplomacy.* **shirt–tail** *n* the part of a shirt below the waist, usually tucked into the pants or skirt.

shish ke·bab ['ʃɪʃ kəˌbab] cubes of meat cooked with tomatoes, onions, mushrooms, etc. on a skewer or spit. Also, **shish kabob.** ⟨Armenian *shish kabab*⟩

shiv·a or **shi·vah** ['ʃɪvə] *n Judaism* a period of seven days' mourning for a dead relative. ⟨Hebrew *shib'ah* seven⟩

Shi·va ['ʃɪvə] *n Hinduism* the creator and destroyer, worshipped as the highest god by many Hindus. Also, **Si·va.**

shiv·er¹ ['ʃɪvər] *v* shake with cold, excitement, fear, etc.

n **1** a shaking of this kind. **2 the shivers** a fit of shivering. **shiv·er·y** *adj.* ⟨Middle English *schiveren*⟩

SYNONYMS
Shiver, used chiefly of people and animals, suggests a continuous quivering of the flesh: *The child crept shivering into bed.* **Shudder** especially suggests a single sudden sharp shaking of the whole body in horror or disgust: *She shuddered at the ghastly sight.*

shiv·er² [ˈʃɪvər] *v, n* (of glass) splinter. ⟨origin uncertain⟩

shoal¹ [ʃoul] *n* **1** a shallow place in a sea, lake, or stream. **2** a sandbank or sand bar that makes the water shallow and is a hazard to ships: *The ship was wrecked on the shoals.*
v of water, become shallow. **shoal·y** *adj.* ⟨Old English *sceald* shallow⟩

shoal² [ʃoul] *n, v* SCHOOL². ⟨Old English *scolu*⟩

shock¹ [ʃɒk] *n* **1 a** extreme surprise. **b** sudden overwhelming dismay or outrage: *She reeled with shock at the news.* **2** a cause of either of these: *His death was a great shock to his family.* **3** a condition of physical collapse, due to severe injury, blood loss, or emotional trauma. **4** a sudden stimulation of the nerves and muscles due to an electric current passing through the body. **5** the impact or effect of colliding objects. **6** SHOCK ABSORBER.
v **1** surprise, outrage, or dismay greatly: *Her bad language shocked me.* **2** be shocked: *I shock easily.* **3** give an electric shock to. **shock·a·ble** *adj.* **shock·er** *n.* **shock·ing** *adj.* ⟨probably French *choc* n, *choquer* v⟩
shock absorber any device that absorbs or lessens impacts or bumps, esp on a vehicle. **shock·proof** *adj* **1** able to endure or resist shock. **2** protected against electric shock. **shock therapy** ELECTRO-CONVULSIVE THERAPY. **shock treatment 1** any act intended to shock. **2** ELECTRO-CONVULSIVE THERAPY. **shock troops** troops chosen and specially trained for making attacks. **shock wave 1** the disturbance of the atmosphere created by the movement of a craft at supersonic speed. **2** a similar effect caused by an explosion.

shock² [ʃɒk] *n* a thick, bushy mass: *She has a shock of red hair.* ⟨perhaps Middle Dutch *schok* stook of hay⟩

shod [ʃɒd] *v* pt and pp of SHOE.

shod·dy [ˈʃɒdi] *adj* **1** of poor quality: *shoddy construction.* **2** mean; dishonourable: *shoddy treatment.* ⟨origin uncertain⟩

shoe [ʃu] *n* **1** an outer covering for a person's foot, usually consisting of a firm sole and a flexible upper part. **2** anything shaped or used like a shoe, such as a cover that fits on the end of something. **3** a horseshoe.
v **shod** or **shoed, shoe·ing 1** furnish with a shoe or shoes: *A blacksmith shoes horses.* **2** protect or arm at the tip: *a stick shod with steel.* **shoe·less** *adj.* ⟨Old English *scōh*⟩
fill someone's shoes take someone's place. **(if) the shoe fits (wear it)** (if or since) a given statement applies to the case in question (take it to heart). **in someone's shoes** in someone's

circumstances: *I wouldn't like to be in your shoes right now.* **the shoe is on the other foot** the roles are reversed. **wait for the other shoe to drop** See DROP. **where the shoe pinches** where the real difficulty lies.
shoe·box *n* a cardboard box with a lid, in which shoes are packed to be sold. **shoe·horn** *n* a curved piece of metal, horn, etc. inserted at the heel of a shoe to make it slip on easily. *v Informal* force into a tight space. **shoe·lace** *n* a cord for fastening a shoe. **shoe·mak·er** *n* a person who makes or repairs shoes. **shoe·mak·ing** *n.* **shoe·shine** *n* **1** an act of polishing shoes. **2** a person who polishes shoes for others. **shoe·string** *n* **1** a shoelace. **2** a very small amount of money used frugally to run a business, go on a trip, etc.: *"See Europe on a shoestring!" adj* **1** long and thin like a shoestring: *shoestring fries.* **2** using a small amount of money: *a shoestring budget.*

sho·gun [ˈʃou‚ɡʌn] *n* formerly in Japan, the hereditary chief of the army and ruler of the nation. ⟨Japanese; Mandarin *chiang chun*⟩

shone [ʃɒn] *v* a pt and pp of SHINE.

shoo [ʃu] *interj* (to birds, flies, etc.) go away. *v* scare or drive away: *to shoo flies away.* **shoo·fly pie** [ˈʃu‚flaɪ] a one-crust pie with a filling of molasses and sugar. **shoo–in** *n Informal* a candidate, team, election, etc. regarded as certain to win or be won.

shook [ʃʊk] *v* pt of SHAKE.

shoot [ʃut] *v* **shot, shoot·ing 1** hit, wound, or kill with a bullet, arrow, etc.: *to shoot a rabbit.* **2** send with force or speed (*at*): *She shot questions at us.* **3** fire; use (a gun, bow, catapult, etc.). **4** of a gun, etc., send a projectile: *This gun shoots straight.* **5** move suddenly and swiftly: *Pain shot up her arm.* **6** pass quickly over (rapids or a waterfall). **7** a take (a picture) with a camera. **b** photograph or film: *to shoot a movie scene.* **8** *Games, sports* **a** send (a puck, ball, etc.) toward an objective. **b** cast (the dice) in craps. **9** play (craps, pool, casual basketball, etc.). **10** take (a narcotic) by injection: *to shoot heroin.*
n **1** a new, young bud or stem. **2** a session of shooting: *a photo shoot.*
interj Informal **1** an exclamation of mild disappointment, annoyance, etc. **2** go ahead and speak: *"Can I make a comment?" "Shoot!"* **shoot·er** *n.* ⟨Old English *scēotan*⟩
shoot down a kill or bring down by shooting: *shot down in cold blood.* **b** reject or criticize harshly. **shoot for** *Informal* aim for; aspire to. **shoot (straight) from the hip** *Informal* speak frankly or with little forethought. **shoot off one's mouth** *Slang* speak thoughtlessly or insolently. **shoot up a** *Slang* inject oneself with a narcotic. **b** grow taller very quickly.
shooting gallery 1 a long room fitted with targets for shooting practice. **2** *Slang* a place where addicts can inject themselves with narcotics. **shooting star** meteor. **shoot·out** or **shoot–out** *n* **1** a decisive gun battle: *a shootout between rebels and militia.* **2** any desperate, decisive contest or quarrel.

shop [ʃɒp] *n* **1** a small, specialized store or a walk-in business offering certain services: *gift shop, barber shop.* **2** a place where things are made or repaired: *a carpenter's shop. The car is in the shop again.*
v **shopped, shop·ping 1** visit stores to look at or buy things. **2** frequent (sales, a given store, etc.) as a customer: *to shop at the local supermarket.* ⟨Old English *sceoppa*⟩
set up shop start a business. **shop around a** go to stores to compare prices, quality, etc. **b** look for the best option in anything. **shut up shop** stop business temporarily or permanently. **talk shop** talk about one's work.
shop·keep·er *n* a person who owns or runs a shop. **shop·lift·ing** *n* the act of stealing from a store while pretending to be a customer. **shop·lift** *v.* **shop·lift·er** *n.* **shop·per** *n* a person who visits stores to look at or buy things. **shop·ping** *n* **1** the buying of groceries, clothes, etc.: *He does his shopping on the weekends.* **2** the things bought: *Help me carry in the shopping.* **go shopping** go to a store or stores in order to shop. **shopping centre 1** Also, **shopping mall** a large complex of stores, restaurants, etc. offering various services, all under one roof. **2** the main retail area in a town. **shopping plaza** a SHOPPING CENTRE (def. 1), esp a small one; strip mall. **shop steward** a union member elected by co-workers to represent their interests to management and maintain union rules. **shop·talk** *n* **1** the specialized vocabulary of a specific field of work; JARGON (def. 2). **2** discussion of business or work, esp outside office hours. **shop·worn** [-ˌwɔrn] *adj* **1** soiled as a result of being handled in a store. **2** no longer new or interesting: *shopworn ideas.*

shore¹ [ʃɔr] *n* **1** the land at the edge of a sea, lake, etc. **2 shores** *pl Poetic* lands: *foreign shores.* ⟨Middle English *schore*, Old English *scora*⟩
shore·hand *n* a person who loads or unloads ships. **shore ice** *esp North* sea ice anchored to the shore. **shore leave** permission given to a ship's crew to go ashore. **shore·line** *n* the line where shore and water meet. **shore·ward** [-wərd] *adv, adj* toward the shore.

shore² [ʃɔr] *v* prop; support (with *up*).
shore *n.* ⟨perhaps Middle Dutch *schore*⟩

shorn [ʃɔrn] *v* a pp of SHEAR.

short [ʃɔrt] *adj* **1** of little extent from end to end: *a short distance, a short time.* **2** not tall: *short grass.* **3** below the right amount, standard, etc.: *When we counted the copies, we found we were short.* **4** using so few words as to be rude: *She was so short with me that I felt hurt.* **5** of pastry, crumbling easily because of high fat content. **6** of memory, forgetting quickly. **7** of one's temper, easily lost.
adv abruptly; suddenly: *to stop short.*
n **1** SHORT CIRCUIT. **2** a short film. **3 shorts** *pl* **a** short pants ending at or above the knee. **b** loose underpants for men or boys.
v Electricity short-circuit (often with *out*). **short·en** *v.* **short·ness** *n.* ⟨Old English *sceort*⟩
bring up short a halt suddenly. **b** rebuke

sharply. **cut short** bring to an end suddenly. **fall short (of)** fail to reach. **for short** as an abbreviation. **in short a** briefly. **b** in summary. **in short order** promptly; quickly. **just short of** very close to: *just short of midnight.* **make short work of** deal with quickly. **run short** end up having or being less than enough. **sell short a** sell without yet owning the stocks, etc. one sells. **b** fail to give what is due: *By overworking she is selling her family short.* **c** underestimate or understate the strengths of. **short and sweet** pleasantly brief. **short for** as an abbreviation of. **short of a** less than: *Nothing short of your best will do.* **b** not having enough of: *I'm short of money.* **c** away from reaching, doing, etc: *I was a kilometre short of home.* **d** apart from (some extreme measure): *Short of expelling her, there's little we can do.* **the short end of the stick** less than one's due.
short·age *n* **1** too small an amount; a lack: *a shortage of grain due to poor crops.* **2** the amount lacking. **short·bread** *n* a crumbly, rich cookie. **short·cake** *n* a light, sweet cake usually with fruit topping. **short–change** *v Informal* **1** give less than the right change to. **2** give less than is due. **short circuit** *Electricity* **1** an electrical circuit, formed intentionally or accidentally by contact between worn or faulty wires, that bypasses the main circuit. **2** the resulting disruption of the main circuit. **short–cir·cuit** *v* **1** develop or bring about a short circuit (in). **2** get around or avoid; bypass: *to short-circuit the official procedure.* **3** frustrate or hinder: *to short-circuit a plan.* **short·com·ing** *n* a fault; weakness. **short·cut** *n* **1** a quicker or more direct route: *a shortcut through the field.* **2** a method, procedure, etc. simpler or quicker than the standard one, often compromising quality: *to take shortcuts in cooking.* *v* **-cut, -cut·ting** use or take a shortcut. **short·en·ing** *n* fat, sometimes specifically vegetable fat. **short·fall** *n* **1** failure to meet a required amount or level. **2** the degree of such a failure. **short fuse** *Informal* a quick temper. **short·hair** *n* any domestic cat of a breed having short hair. **short–hand·ed** *adj* having too few workers, players, or helpers. **short·horn** *n* a breed of cattle with short horns. **short list** a list of the best candidates, taken from a longer list by some screening process. **short–list** *v.* **short–lived** [-ˈlɪvd] *adj* living or lasting only a short time: *The truce was short-lived and war broke out again.* **short·ly** *adv* **1** soon. **2** a short time: *shortly after midnight.* **3** curtly and rudely. **short–or·der** *adj* to do with restaurant foods that take little time to prepare: *a short-order cook.* **short–range** *adj* **1** of a gun, missile, etc., effective over a limited distance. **2** for the immediate future: *short-range plans.* **short shrift** too little care or attention: *He had so many extra activities that his schoolwork got short shrift.* **short–shrift** *v.* **short–sight·ed** *adj* **1** not able to see far. **2** showing lack of foresight: *a short-sighted strategy.* **short–staffed** *adj* having too few workers. **short·stop** *n Baseball* a player

stationed between second and third base. **short story** a prose story much shorter and less complex than a novel. **short–tem·pered** *adj* controlling one's anger poorly. **short–term** *adj* lasting or covering a short period of time: *a short-term loan*. **short–term memory** memory for recent events. **short wave** *Electricity* a high-frequency radio wave with a length of 60 m or less. **short·wave** *adj* to do with short waves: *a shortwave radio*. *v* transmit by short waves: *The queen's speech was shortwaved overseas*. **short·y** or **short·ie** *n Informal* a relatively short thing or person: *This visit is a real shortie*.

> **SYNONYMS**
>
> **Shorten** is the general word, meaning 'reduce the extent of something': *The new highway shortens the trip*. **Curtail**, more formal, means 'shorten by cutting off a part', and suggests incompleteness: *Bad news made him curtail his trip*. **Abbreviate** implies leaving out inessential parts: *an abbreviated version of a speech*.

shot¹ [ʃɒt] *n* 1 the act or sound of shooting a gun or cannon: *She heard two shots*. 2 small metal pellets inside a shotgun cartridge. 3 a single ball of lead for a gun or cannon. 4 a person who shoots, with reference to skill, etc.: *She is a good shot*. 5 *Sports* a stroke or an attempt to score. 6 the distance a gun, etc. can shoot; range: *within rifle shot of the fort*. 7 injection: *a flu shot*. 8 a sharp remark. 9 an attempt; try. 10 *Track and field* a heavy metal ball thrust from the shoulder. 11 a photo or an uninterrupted sequence of a movie. 12 a single drink of spirits. ⟨Old English *sceot*⟩ **call the shots** *Informal* make the decisions. **like a shot** very quickly. **long shot** an attempt at something difficult. **not by a long shot** not at all. **put the shot** *Track and field* cast the ball in the shot-put event. **shot in the arm** *Informal* anything that stimulates or revives. **shot in the dark** a wild guess. **the (whole) shot** the full amount.

shot·gun *n* a firearm with a long barrel, firing cartridges filled with shot. *adj* covering a broad field; haphazard or indiscriminate: *shotgun criticism*. **shotgun marriage** or **wedding** *Informal* a marriage or wedding enforced or arranged on account of pregnancy. **shot–put** *n Track and field* an event in which a heavy metal ball (the shot) is sent as far as possible with one thrust from the shoulder. **shot–put·ter** *n*. **shot rock** *Curling* the stone nearest the centre of the target.

shot² [ʃɒt] *v* pt and pp of SHOOT. *adj* 1 of fabric, woven so as to show changing colours; iridescent: *shot silk*. 2 streaked: *black hair shot with grey*. 3 permeated; infused (often with *through*): *a clever speech shot through with humour*. 4 *Informal* worn out or used up: *The whole day is shot. His nerves are shot*.

should [ʃʊd] *v* 1 a word used to express: **a** an obligation or duty: *I really should do my work first*. **b** a recommended or desirable state of affairs: *I should be so lucky*. **c** an attitude of the person speaking: *It's strange that they should be so late*. **d** a condition in the future (either with *if* or inverted with the subject): *Should I have any trouble, I'll call you*. **e** a probability or expectation: *She should be there by now*. 2 pt of SHALL (def. 3): *I hoped I should see you*. ⟨Old English *sceolde*⟩

shoul·der [ˈʃoʊldər] *n* 1 the part of the body to which an arm of a human being, a foreleg of an animal, or a wing of a bird is attached. 2 a shoulderlike projection. 3 the edge of a road, often unpaved. *v* 1 carry on the shoulder or shoulders: *to shoulder a tray*. 2 bear (a burden, blame, etc.). 3 push with the shoulders: *He shouldered his way past*. ⟨Old English *sculdor*⟩ **cry on someone's shoulder** tell someone one's problems, hoping for sympathy. **give someone the cold shoulder** ignore socially. **on someone's shoulders** borne by someone, as a responsibility. **put one's shoulder to the wheel** make a great effort. **shoulder to shoulder a** side by side. **b** with united effort. **straight from the shoulder** frankly. **shoulder belt** a safety belt, as in a car, that passes diagonally over the chest and one shoulder. **shoulder blade** the flat triangular bone in the upper back behind each shoulder.

shout [ʃaʊt] *v* call, speak, or laugh loudly. **shout** *n*. ⟨Middle English *schoute*⟩ **give someone a shout** call or telephone someone: *Give me a shout when you're ready*. **shout down** silence by very loud talk.

shove [ʃʌv] *v* push, esp roughly or rudely; jostle. **shove** *n*. ⟨Old English *scūfan*⟩ **shove off a** push away from the shore; row away. **b** *Slang* leave.

shov·el [ˈʃʌvəl] *n* 1 a tool with a long handle and broad, concave blade, used to lift and throw loose matter: *a snow shovel*. 2 a part of a machine with a similar function. *v* **-elled** or **-eled**, **-el·ling** or **-el·ing** 1 lift and throw (dirt, snow, etc.) with a shovel. 2 make with a shovel: *to shovel a path through snow*. 3 scoop up crudely or in large quantities: *to shovel food into one's mouth*. **shov·el·ful** *n*. ⟨Old English *scofl*⟩

show [ʃoʊ] *v* **showed**, **shown** or **showed**, **show·ing** 1 give (someone) the chance to see or look at (something): *She showed us her new coat*. 2 be evidence of: *His gift shows how kind he is*. 3 point out: *Show them the way home*. 4 escort: *Show her out*. 5 make understand by demonstration: *Show them how to use it*. 6 be noticeable or visible: *Joy showed in her face*. 7 grant; give: *to show mercy*. 8 have a given effect on viewers when displayed: *A newly painted house shows better*. 9 *Informal* be present as arranged or expected: *Her date didn't show, so she went alone*. 10 *Sports* **a** finish among the first three in a race. **b** finish third, esp in a horse race. Compare WIN, PLACE. 11 of a movie or performance, be playing: *What's showing at the cinema?* *n* 1 a display, or the effect made by it: *The jewels made a fine show*. 2 a public event at which things are displayed: *a boat show*. 3 an entertainment, such as a movie, television show, etc. 4 a showing: *to vote by a show of*

hands. **5** an appearance, often false: *a show of friendship.* **6** *Sports* third place, esp in a horse race. ⟨Old English *scēawian* look at⟩
for show to impress or to attract attention.
get the show on the road *Slang* get started.
good show! well done! **run the show** be in charge. **show off** make a boastful or proud display (of): *He's just showing off.* **show–off** *n.*
show up a *Informal* arrive or be present: *Who showed up at the party?* **b** *Informal* surpass so greatly as to shame by comparison. **steal the show** take attention away from the main participant, esp by superior performance.
show and tell in primary school, a time for students to pass around and talk about a thing they have brought. **show·biz** [-,bɪz] *n Slang* SHOW BUSINESS. **show·boat** *n* **1** a boat with a theatre, carrying its own actors and stopping frequently for performances. **2** *Informal* showoff. *v Informal* show off. **show business** all the occupations and businesses making up the entertainment industry. **show–bus·i·ness** *adj.* **show·case** *n* **1** a glass case to display articles in stores, museums, etc. **2** anything that displays: *Québec City is a showcase of Canadian history.* *v* display to advantage. **show·down** *n* a confrontation that brings things to a head. **show·girl** *n* CHORUS GIRL. **show·jump·ing** *n* a public display of competitive skill in riding a horse and making it leap over obstacles. **show·jump·er** *n.* **show·man** *n, pl* **-men 1** a manager of a show. **2** a person skilled at presenting things in a dramatic and exciting way. **show·man·ship** *n.* **show·piece** *n* **1** an item in an exhibition. **2** anything displayed as an outstanding example of its kind. **show·room** *n* a room used to display merchandise, esp large items. **show·y** *adj* **1** striking; conspicuous. **2** too bright, gaudy, etc. to be in good taste.

show·er ['ʃaʊər] *n* **1 a** a bath in which water is sprayed over the body in small jets. **b** the apparatus or enclosure for this. **2** a brief fall of rain. **3** anything like a fall of rain: *a shower of sparks.* **4** a giving in abundance: *a shower of good wishes.* **5** a party for giving gifts to someone about to be married, have a baby, etc. *v* **1** rain briefly. **2** spray; sprinkle. **3** take a shower bath. **4** come, fall, send, etc. in or as if in a shower: *to shower a person with compliments. The tree showered blossoms on the lawn.* **show·er·y** *adj.* ⟨Old English *scur*⟩

shrank [ʃræŋk] *v* pt of SHRINK.

shrap·nel ['ʃræpnəl] *n* metal fragments from a shell set to explode in the air. ⟨H. *Shrapnel* 19c British officer, its inventor⟩

shred [ʃred] *n* **1** a small piece torn or cut off; scrap: *The wind tore the sail to shreds.* **2** a particle; fragment; bit: *not a shred of evidence.* **shred** *v.* ⟨Old English *scrēade*⟩
shred·der *n* **1** a machine for tearing sensitive documents into shreds. **2** a machine or blade that shreds vegetables, etc.

shrew [ʃru] *n* **1** any of a family of mouselike mammals having a long, pointed snout, beady eyes, and a reputation for ferocity. **2** a

bad-tempered and quarrelsome person. **shrew·ish** *adj.* ⟨Old English *scrēawa*⟩

shrewd [ʃrud] *adj* having or showing keen, practical intelligence: *a shrewd observer, a shrewd comment.* **shrewd·ly** *adv.* **shrewd·ness** *n.* ⟨earlier *shrewed* from *shrew* meaning 'scold'⟩

SYNONYMS
Shrewd emphasizes cleverness in practical affairs or, sometimes, craftiness: *a shrewd businessperson.* **Astute** adds the idea of having unusual insight and of being hard to fool: *an astute diplomat.* **Sagacious** emphasizes good judgment: *a sagacious decision-maker.*

shriek [ʃrik] *n* **1** a loud, shrill laugh or cry. **2** a loud, sharp, high-pitched sound: *the shriek of a siren.* **shriek** *v.* ⟨Old Norse *skrœkja*⟩

shrike [ʃraɪk] *n* any of a family of songbirds with a hooked bill. ⟨Old English *scrīc*⟩

shrill [ʃrɪl] *adj* **1** high-pitched and piercing: *Crickets make a shrill noise.* **2** offensively insistent: *shrill protests.* **shrill** *v.* **shrill·ly** *adv.* **shrill·ness** *n.* ⟨Middle English *shrille*⟩

shrimp [ʃrɪmp] *n, pl* **shrimp** or **shrimps 1** any of a suborder of edible, mostly marine decapod crustaceans with a slender body in a thin, translucent shell, long antennae, and swimmerets on the abdomen; esp, any of the smaller ones, usually 4 to 8 cm long. **2** any of various other similar crustaceans. **3** a small, weak, or insignificant person.
v fish for shrimp. **shrimp·like** *adj.* ⟨Middle English *shrimpe*⟩

shrine [ʃraɪn] *n* **1** a place of worship: *a wayside shrine.* **2** a saint's tomb, a container holding a holy object, etc. **3** a place with sacred memories, etc. attached to it. ⟨Old English *scrīn*; Latin *scrinium* case⟩

shrink [ʃrɪŋk] *v* **shrank, shrunk, shrink·ing 1** make or become smaller: *Hot water shrinks wool.* **2** draw back; try to avoid (with *from*): *I shrank from contact with the cold water.*
n **1** an act of shrinking. **2** *Slang* a psychiatrist. **shrink·a·ble** *adj.* ⟨Old English *scrincan*⟩
shrink·age *n* **1** the fact, process, or amount of shrinking. **2** inventory lost and not accounted for. **shrinking violet** a very shy person. **shrink–wrap** *v* **-wrapped, -wrap·ping** wrap (merchandise) in thin, clear plastic film that shrinks to the contours of the article as it is sealed. *n* the plastic film.

shriv·el ['ʃrɪvəl] *v* **-elled** or **-eled, -el·ling** or **-el·ing 1** dry up; shrink and wrinkle: *The grass shrivelled under the hot sun.* **2** waste away; become useless. ⟨origin unknown⟩

shroud [ʃraʊd] *n* **1** a cloth to wrap a dead person in for burial. **2** anything that covers, conceals, or veils: *a shroud of fog.* **3** *Nautical* any of the supporting ropes that run from a masthead to the ship's side. **4** on a parachute, any of the lines attaching the canopy to the harness. **shroud** *v.* ⟨Old English *scrūd*⟩

shrub [ʃrʌb] *n* a woody plant smaller than a tree, with many stems starting from or near the ground; bush. ⟨Old English *scrybb* brush⟩
shrub·ber·y *n* shrubs collectively.

shrug [ʃrʌg] v **shrugged, shrug·ging** raise (the shoulders) as an expression of doubt, indifference, resignation, etc. **shrug** n. ⟨Middle English *schruggen* shiver⟩
shrug off dismiss lightly; minimize.

shrunk [ʃrʌŋk] v pp of SHRINK.
shrunk·en adj grown smaller: *a shrunken face.*

shru·ti [ˈʃruti] n the collective term for all sacred Hindu scriptures. ⟨Sanskrit⟩

shtick [ʃtɪk] n **1** a comic routine or scene on stage. **2** any act or gimmick to get attention. **3** a person's characteristic role or ability. ⟨Yiddish *shtik* prank, piece; German *Stück*⟩

shuck [ʃʌk] n **1** a husk; pod, esp of a cob of corn. **2** an oyster or clam shell.
v **1** remove the shucks from. **2** *Informal* take or throw off (clothing, etc.): *He shucked his coat at the door.* **shuck·er** n. ⟨origin uncertain⟩

shud·der [ˈʃʌdər] v shiver with horror, fear, etc. **shud·der** n. ⟨Middle English *shodderen* frequentative of Old English *scūdan* shake⟩

shuf·fle [ˈʃʌfəl] v **1** walk without lifting the feet: *The sick man shuffled feebly along.* **2** drag or scrape (the feet). **3** mix up (cards, etc.) thoroughly. **4** move this way and that: *to shuffle papers.* **5** be evasive.
n **1** an act of shuffling; a shuffling walk. **2** a trick; evasion: *Through some legal shuffle he secured a new trial.* **shuf·fler** n. ⟨perhaps Low German *schuffeln*⟩
lose in the shuffle overlook or lose in the confusion of the moment. **shuffle off** get rid of, esp by evasion: *to shuffle off responsibility.*
shuf·fle·board n a game played by pushing large disks along a surface to certain spots.

shul [ʃul] n, pl **shuln** [ʃuln] synagogue. ⟨Yiddish = school⟩

shun [ʃʌn] v **shunned, shun·ning** avoid; keep away from. **shun·ner** n. ⟨Old English *scunian*⟩

shunt [ʃʌnt] v **1** divert or put aside. **2** switch (a train) from one track to another. **3** carry (part of an electric current) by means of a shunt. **4** furnish or divert with a shunt.
n **1** an act of shunting. **2** a railway switch. **3** *Electricity* a conductor forming a path through which a part of the current will pass. **4** *Medicine* a channel, synthetic or surgically reconstructed, through which bodily fluids may be drained or diverted. ⟨Middle English *schunt* shy¹; perhaps from *shun*⟩

shush [ʃʌʃ] v tell or cause to become silent; silence (someone); hush (often with *up*).
interj quiet! hush!

Shu·swap See SECWEPEMC.

shut [ʃʌt] v **shut, shut·ting 1** close (an opening or container) by bringing parts together or by bringing a lid, etc. into place: *to shut a box, to shut a window, to shut a book.* **2** close or lock the doors and windows of (often with *up*): *We shut our cottage up for the winter.* **3** become shut: *The door doesn't shut properly.* **4** keep out or in (used with *in, out*, etc.): *to shut someone in prison, to shut the cat out.* **5** cease operation (of), permanently or temporarily: *They shut the store early today.*

shut down a stop or cause to stop functioning. **b** *Computers* exit an operating system so that the computer can be turned off. **shut·down** n. **shut off a** prevent the flow or passage of or through: *to shut off the electricity for repairs.* **b** isolate from others: *We were shut off from the world in our cozy cottage.* **shut out** *Sports* defeat (a team) without letting it score. **shut up a** confine (in a place). **b** *Informal* stop or cause to stop talking. **shut–eye** n *Slang* sleep. **shut–in** n a person kept at home by sickness, weakness, etc. **shut–in** adj. **shut–off** n a valve, switch, etc., that shuts something off. **shutout** n **1** *Sports* the defeat of a team without letting it score. **b** *Hockey* the credit a goalie earns for achieving this. **2** a lockout.

shut·ter [ˈʃʌtər] n **1** a movable cover for a window. **2** the device that opens and closes in front of the film or plate in a camera. **shut·ter** v. ⟨shut⟩
shut·ter·bug n a photography enthusiast.

shut·tle [ˈʃʌtəl] n **1** a bus, train, aircraft, etc. going back and forth regularly over a short distance. **2** SPACE SHUTTLE. **3** a device used in weaving to carry the thread from one side of the loom to the other. **4** a device on a sewing machine that carries the lower thread back and forth to loop with the upper thread in making a stitch. **5** any of various other things that go back and forth.
v **1** move quickly to and fro. **2** of buses, aircraft, etc., carry (passengers) between two points: *This bus shuttles between Toronto and Guelph.* ⟨Old English *scutel* dart; *scēotan* shoot⟩
shut·tle·cock n a cone-shaped ring of mesh or feathers, hit back and forth in the game of badminton; also called a **bird** or **birdie.**

shy¹ [ʃaɪ] adj **shy·er, shy·est 1** uncomfortable in company; lacking confidence socially: *He is shy and dislikes parties.* **2** easily frightened away; timid: *A deer is a shy animal.* **3** wary.
v start back or aside suddenly: *The horse shied at the paper blowing along the ground.*
n a sudden start to one side. **shy·ly** adv. **shy·ness** n. ⟨Old English *scēoh*⟩
fight shy of avoid out of fear. **shy away from** hesitate to do, take, etc. out of fear. **shy of a** lacking: *The team is shy of a goalkeeper.* **b** less than: *The arrow fell just shy of the mark.*

shy² [ʃaɪ] v throw: *The girl shied a stone at the tree.* **shy** n. ⟨origin uncertain⟩

shy·ster [ˈʃaɪstər] n *Informal* one who uses shady business methods. ⟨origin uncertain⟩

SI Système international d'unités (International System of Units), the official system of measurement in Canada. See METRIC SYSTEM.

Si·a·mese [ˌsaɪəˈmiz] n, pl **-mese 1** Thai. **2** a breed of cat dark at the ears, feet, and tail. **3** a Y-shaped pipe coupling joining two pipes or hoses to a single pipe. **Si·a·mese** adj. ⟨*Siam* old name of Thailand⟩
Siamese twins twins born joined together, now usually called **conjoined twins.**

sib·i·lant ['sɪbələnt] *adj* 1 hissing. 2 *Phonetics* articulated with a hissing sound.
n Phonetics a hissing sound or its symbol, such as [s], [z], [ʃ], and [ʒ]. **sib·i·lance** *n*. ⟨Latin *sibilans, -antis,* ppr of *sibilare* hiss⟩

sib·ling ['sɪblɪŋ] *n* a brother or sister. ⟨*sib* (Old English *sibb* related by blood) + *-ling*⟩

sic¹ [sɪk] *adv Latin* so; thus.

USAGE
Sic is used, usually in brackets, to indicate that a strange or incorrect word in a quoted passage is recorded just as it is in the original: *The picture caption read "Victoria, capitol [sic] of British Columbia."*

sic² [sɪk] *v* **sicked, sick·ing** 1 set upon or attack. 2 incite to set upon or attack (with *on*). Also, **sick**. ⟨variant of *seek*⟩

sick [sɪk] *adj* 1 in poor health. 2 to do with sickness. 3 feeling nausea; inclined to vomit: *sick to the stomach*. 4 weary (often with *of*): *I'm sick of hearing that same excuse*. 5 deeply affected with regret or longing: *sick at heart*. 6 morbid; sadistic: *sick humour*.
n vomit. **sick·en** *v*. **sick·en·ing** *adj*. **sick·ish** *adj*. ⟨Old English *sēoc*⟩
be sick *Informal* vomit.
sick bay a room for the care of the sick or injured on a ship, in a place of work, etc. **sick·bed** *n* the bed of a sick person. **sick building syndrome** illness due to bad environmental conditions, such as poor ventilation, in a building, esp a large building. **sick day** one day of SICK LEAVE. **sick leave** time off from work, usually with pay, for illness or injury. **sick·ly** *adj* 1 often sick; not strong. 2 suggesting sickness: *a sickly yellow*. 3 causing sickness: *a sickly climate*. 4 weak; mawkish: *sickly sentimentality*. *adv* in a sick manner. **sick·li·ness** *n*. **sick·ness** *n* 1 the condition of being sick. 2 a particular illness. **sick pay** wages paid to an employee on SICK LEAVE. **sick·room** *n* a room set aside for a person or persons who are ill.

sick·le ['sɪkəl] *n* a tool consisting of a short, crescent-shaped blade on a short handle. ⟨Old English *sicol;* Latin *secula; secare* cut⟩

side [saɪd] *n* 1 a surface or line bounding a thing: *sides of a square*. 2 one of the surfaces of an object other than the front, back, top, or bottom: *a door at the side of the house*. 3 either surface of paper, cloth, etc.: *Write only on one side*. 4 either half of a thing: *the east side of a city*. 5 the right or left part of the body: *a pain in one's side*. 6 the slope of a hill or mountain. 7 the shore of a body of water. 8 an aspect of someone or something: *the better side of one's nature*. 9 a group of people opposed to another: *on the winning side of a dispute*. 10 *Informal* an order of food to go with a main dish: *a side of fries*.
adj 1 at, from, or toward one side: *a side view*. 2 less important: *a side issue*. 3 intended to go with a main dish: *a side salad*.
v 1 support one party in a dispute (used with *with*): *She sides with her sister*. 2 put siding on (a house, etc.). ⟨Old English *sīde*⟩

by someone's side near someone: *He wanted his family by his side*. **on the side** *Informal* **a** in addition to one's ordinary duties, etc. **b** as a side dish: *a hamburger with fries on the side*. **on the —— side** tending to be ——: *He's a little on the strict side*. **side by side a** beside each other. **b** equally: *Her work ranks side by side with the best*. **c** co-operatively: *We'll be working side by side with you in your new role*. **split one's sides** laugh very hard. **take sides** align oneself with one party in a dispute.
side·bar *n* 1 a very brief article printed next to a main one, enlarging on some aspect of the main article. 2 a secondary, related issue or fact. **side·board** *n* a piece of dining-room furniture with drawers and shelves and, often, a hutch on top. **side·car** *n* a small, one-wheeled car for a passenger or cargo, attached to the side of a motorcycle. **side dish** a dish served with a main dish. **side effect** an incidental consequence of a course of action, treatment, etc., esp an undesirable reaction to a drug. **side·kick** *n Slang* a close or constant companion. **side·light** *n* 1 a window next to a door or other window. 2 a piece of incidental information about a subject. **side·line** *n* 1 a line marking the limit of play on the side of a playing field. 2 **sidelines** *pl* the space just outside these lines: *They watched the game from the sidelines*. 3 **a** a line of goods, trade, etc. that is not the primary one. **b** any enterprise carried on apart from one's official work. *v* put on the sidelines; make inactive: *to sideline a player for fighting*. **on the sidelines a** in the space along the sidelines of a playing field. **b** not taking an active part in a game, enterprise, etc. **c** involved but not in a central role. **side·long** *adj, adv* indirect(ly) or oblique(ly): *a sidelong glance*. **side road** 1 a secondary road, often unpaved, leading to a main road or highway. 2 ✸ in Ontario, a road running east-west along the side of a concession, between concession roads. Also, **side·road**. **side·sad·dle** *n* a woman's saddle made so that both of the rider's legs are on the same side of the horse. **side·show** *n* 1 a small show in connection with a main one: *the sideshows of a circus*. 2 any proceeding connected with a more important one. **side·split** *n* a SPLIT-LEVEL house in which one end is split into two levels, one of which is partly below ground. Compare BACKSPLIT. **side·split·ting** *adj* extremely funny. **side·step** *v* -**stepped,** -**step·ping** 1 step aside. 2 evade: *She never sidesteps responsibility*. *n* a step to one side. **side street** a street leading off a main road. **side·stroke** *n Swimming* a stroke executed while lying on one's side in the water, the arms moving in a fashion similar to the breast stroke and the legs in a scissor kick. **side·swipe** *v* hit with a sweeping stroke along the side: *to sideswipe a parked car*. **side·swipe** *n*. **side·track** *n* a turning aside: *Stick to the business at hand and avoid sidetracks*. **side·track** *v*. **side trip** a short, extra trip not included in one's main itinerary. **side·walk** *n* a place to walk at the side of a

street, usually paved. **side·ways** *adv, adj* **1** toward one side: *to step sideways.* **2** from one side: *a sideways glimpse.* **3** with one side toward the observer: *to stand sideways.* **side·wind·er** *n* a snake of desert regions, which moves over loose sand by forming sideways loops. **sid·ing** *n* **1** facing on a building, usually overlapping lengths of wood, vinyl, aluminum etc. **2** a railway track to which cars can be switched from a main track. **3** ✹ a rural stop on a railway line for pickup and deposit of freight.

side·burns [ˈsaɪdˌbɜrnz] *n pl* hair growing in front of the ears, esp when the chin is shaved. ⟨alteration of *burnsides*; A. *Burnside*, 19c US general⟩

si·de·re·al [saɪˈdiriəl] *adj* **1** to do with the stars. **2** measured by movement relative to the stars; *a sidereal year.* **si·de·re·al·ly** *adv.* ⟨Latin *sidereus* astral; *sidus, sideris* star⟩

si·dle [ˈsaɪdəl] *v* move sideways, esp shyly or stealthily: *to sidle up to someone. She sidled her chair closer to his.* ⟨*sideling* sidelong⟩

SIDS SUDDEN INFANT DEATH SYNDROME.

siege [sidʒ] *n* **1** the surrounding of a fort, town, etc. by an army trying to capture it. **2** any long or persistent attack: *a siege of illness.* ⟨Old French; Latin *sedere* sit⟩
lay siege to a besiege. **b** attempt to win or get by long and persistent effort.

si·en·na [siˈɛnə] *n* **1** a yellowish brown colouring matter made from earth rich in iron. **2** a reddish brown colouring matter (**burnt sienna**) made by roasting such earth. ⟨*Siena*, city in Italy⟩

si·er·ra [siˈɛrə] *n* a chain of mountains with jagged peaks. ⟨Spanish – a saw; Latin *serra*⟩

si·es·ta [siˈɛstə] *n* a nap or rest taken at noon or in the afternoon. ⟨Spanish; Latin *sexta (hora)* sixth (hour), noon⟩

sieve [sɪv] *n* a utensil with mesh or holes so as to let liquids and fine particles through, but not large pieces. *v* put through a sieve. **sieve-like** *adj.* ⟨Old English *sife*⟩

sift [sɪft] *v* **1** separate larger particles from smaller particles by shaking in a sieve. **2** sprinkle through a sieve: *Sift sugar onto the top of the cake.* **3** fall through, or as if through, a sieve: *The snow sifted softly down.* **4** examine very carefully: *to sift evidence.* **5** distinguish; tell apart and separate: *to sift truth from falsehood.* **sift·er** *n.* ⟨Old English *siftan; sife* sieve⟩

sigh [saɪ] *v* **1** let out a loud breath because one is sad, tired, relieved, etc. **2** say with a sigh. **3** make a sound like a sigh: *The wind sighed in the treetops.* **sigh** *n.* ⟨Middle English *sighen*; Old English *sīcan*⟩

sight [saɪt] *n* **1** the act or power of seeing: *Birds have better sight than dogs.* **2** the range of vision: *Land was in sight.* **3** something seen or worth seeing: *a pretty sight, the sights of the city.* **4** *Informal* something that looks odd: *Her clothes were a sight.* **5** a device on a gun, instrument, etc. for taking aim or observing.

6 *Informal* a great deal: *a sight more money than I can afford.*
adj interpreted, performed, etc. at sight: *Our test included a sight passage to be translated.*
v **1** see: *We sighted land.* **2** take aim (at) or observe by means of sights. **3** aim (a weapon) by using sights ⟨Old English *(ge)siht*⟩
a sight for sore eyes a welcome sight. **at** (or **on**) **sight** as soon as seen or presented: *She reads music at sight.* **catch sight of** see. **in sight of** where one can see or be seen by: *We live in sight of the school.* **know by sight** know sufficiently to recognize when seen: *I know him by sight.* **lower one's sights** reduce one's ambition. **out of sight a** out of the field of vision. **b** *Slang* excellent. **out of sight of** where one cannot see or be seen by: *out of sight of the neighbours.* **set one's sights on** try to attain. **sight unseen** without seeing beforehand: *I bought the car sight unseen.*
sight·ed *adj* **1** not blind. **2** (in compounds) having sight of a given kind: *shortsighted.* **sight·less** *adj* blind. **sight·read** *v* -**read** [-rɛd], -**read·ing** play an instrument or sing by reading (music not previously seen). **sight·see** *v* go around to see objects or places of interest. **sight·se·er** *n.* **sight·see·ing** *n, adj.*

sig·ma [ˈsɪɡmə] *n Mathematics* the summation sign, preceding a set of terms to be added. ⟨eighteenth letter of the Greek alphabet; Σ⟩

sign [saɪn] *n* **1** any mark used to mean something: *a plus sign.* **2** a gesture used to mean something: *A nod is a sign of agreement.* **3** one of the gestures of SIGN LANGUAGE. **4** a board, etc., for advertisement, information, etc.: *The sign reads, "Keep off the grass."* **5** an indication: *signs of spring.* **6** an omen; a supernatural manifestation. **7** *Astrology* any of the divisions of the zodiac: *Her sign is Leo.*
v **1** write or stamp one's name (on): *Sign on the dotted line.* **2** give or accept employment by a written agreement (often with *on*): *to sign a new player.* **3** signal. **4** communicate in SIGN LANGUAGE. ⟨Latin *signum*⟩
sign away give (something) up or away by signing. **sign in** indicate by signing a list, etc., that one is present. **sign off (on)** log off (onto) a computer. **sign out a** indicate by signing a list, etc., that one will not be present. **b** borrow (a book, etc.) by signing a record. **sign over** transfer by signing one's name. **sign up a** enlist in the armed services. **b** indicate an intention to participate by writing one's name.
sign·board *n* a board with an advertisement, sign, etc. on it. **sign language 1** a system for communication esp by and with the deaf, as Signed English, American Sign Language, or the sign language of the First Nations people of the Plains. **2** any communication in which gestures stand for words or ideas. **sign of the cross** *Christianity* a hand gesture indicating the shape of a cross. **sign·post** *n* anything that marks or guides, or from which bearings may be taken.

sig·nal [ˈsɪɡnəl] *n* **1** an object, event, word, gesture, etc. understood to give information: *A flashing red light is a warning signal.*

2 anything that produces a response: *The defeat of the government was the signal for a mass uprising.* **3** *Radio, television, etc.* **a** a wave, current, etc. serving to convey sounds and images. **b** a sound or image so conveyed. *adj* remarkable; notable: *a signal success.* *v* **-nalled** or **-naled, -nal·ling** or **-nal·ing** **1** make a signal or signals (to). **2** make known by a signal or signals: *A bell signals the end of class.* **sig·nal·ler** or **sig·nal·er** *n.* **sig·nal·ly** *adv.* ⟨French *signal;* Latin *signum* sign⟩

sig·na·ture ['sɪgnətʃər] *n* **1** a person's name written by that person. **2** *Music* the sign to show the key and time of a piece of music. **3** a tune or slogan used to identify a radio or television program. **4** any distinctive characteristic: *Garotting with a telephone cord was the serial killer's signature.* ⟨Latin *signatura; signum* sign⟩
sig·na·to·ry ['sɪgnə,tɔri] *n* a person who signs a document, or the nation, corporation, etc. on whose behalf this is done: *The signatories to the agreement were the UK, France, and Russia.* **sig·na·to·ry** *adj.*

sig·net ['sɪgnɪt] *n* **1** a small seal: *a decree sealed with the king's signet.* **2** the impression made by it. ⟨Old French; Latin *signum* seal⟩
signet ring a finger ring engraved with a design so it can be used as a seal.

sig·ni·fy ['sɪgnə,faɪ] *v* **1** be a sign of: *"Oh!" signifies surprise.* **2** make known by signs: *He signified his consent with a nod.* **3** have importance: *What that fool says does not signify.* **sig·ni·fi·a·ble** *adj.* ⟨Latin *significare; signum* sign + *facere* make⟩
sig·nif·i·cance [sɪg'nɪfəkəns] *n* **1** importance: *a matter of some significance.* **2** meaning: *Do you understand the significance of this picture?* **sig·nif·i·cant** *adj* **1** important: *July 1, 1867, is a significant date for Canadians.* **2** expressing a hidden meaning: *a significant smile.* **3** *Statistics* to do with a deviation (from the predicted result) that is too great to be attributed to chance. **sig·nif·i·cant·ly** *adv.*

Sikh [sik] *n* a member of a religious sect founded as an offshoot of Hinduism. It is monotheistic. **Sikh** *adj.* **Sikh·ism** *n.* ⟨Hindi = disciple⟩

Sik·sik·a ['sɪksɪkə] *n* **1** a member of a First Nations people living in Alberta. **2** their Algonquian language. **Siksika** *adj.* Also called **Blackfoot.**

si·lage See SILO.

si·lence ['saɪləns] *n* **1** the absence of sound. **2** secrecy: *Silence in matters of public interest is intolerable in a free society.* *v* **1** stop the speech or noise of: *He tried to silence the noisy children.* **2** make silent on a certain topic by persuasion, force, etc.: *Her strong arguments soon silenced the opposition.* *interj* be silent! ⟨Latin *silere* be silent⟩
in silence without speaking.
si·lenc·er *n* a device deadening the sound of a firearm. **si·lent** *adj* **1** quiet; still; noiseless: *a silent house.* **2** saying little or nothing: *You're*

very silent today. **3** not spoken out loud: *silent disapproval.* **4** of a letter in a word, not pronounced. The *b* in *lamb* is silent. **5** taking no active part. A **silent partner** shares in financing but not in managing a business. **6** not mentioning something: *The book is silent on the question of motive.* **7** without spoken dialogue: *silent movies.* **si·lent·ly** *adv.*

sil·hou·ette [,sɪlu'ɛt] *or* ['sɪlu,ɛt] *n* **1** an outline portrait filled in with black. **2** a dark image outlined against a lighter background. *v* show as a silhouette: *The mountain was silhouetted against the sky.* ⟨Etienne de *Silhouette* 18c French minister of finance⟩
in silhouette shown in outline, or in black against a white background.

sil·i·ca ['sɪləkə] *n* a compound that forms the main ingredient of sand. Also called **silicon dioxide.** ⟨Latin *silicis* flint⟩
silica gel a form of silica resembling sand, but highly absorbent. Silica gel is used as a drying and deodorizing agent. **sil·i·cate** [-kɪt] *n* any of many insoluble compounds of silicon, oxygen, and metal that make up the largest class of minerals, and are found widely in rocks. **sil·i·con** [-,kɒn] *or* [-kən] *n* a non-metallic element found naturally only in compounds. It combines with oxygen to form silica. *Symbol* **Si. silicon chip** a microchip made of silicon. **Silicon Valley** an area near San Francisco where many leading companies in the micro-electronics field are located. **sil·i·cone** [-,koun] *n* any of a large group of organic silicon compounds that are water-resistant and insensitive to temperature change. **sil·i·co·sis** *n* a lung disease caused by continually breathing air filled with dust from quartz or silicates.

silk [sɪlk] *n* **1** a protein fibre produced by silkworms for their cocoons and used to make cloth. **2** thread, cloth, etc. made from this fibre. **3** anything like silk in softness, lustre, etc.: *corn silk.* **4 silks** *pl* the blouse and cap worn by a jockey or harness race driver, the colours of which identify the horse's owner. **silk** *adj.* **silk·like** *adj.* ⟨Old English *sioloc;* Greek *sērikos; Sēres* the Chinese⟩
silk·en ['sɪlkən] *adj* **1** like silk; soft and glossy: *silken hair.* **2** of a voice, manner, etc., smooth, esp when suggesting insincerity: *He spoke in silken tones.* **silk·y** *adj.* **silk·i·ly** *adv.* **silk·i·ness** *n.* **silk–screen** *n* a method of colour printing in which a screen of silk is prepared as a stencil and the colouring matter is forced through the mesh. **silk–screen** *v.* **silk·worm** *n* the larva of an Asiatic moth that produces the silk used for textiles.

sill [sɪl] *n* a horizontal piece of wood, stone, etc. forming the bottom of a window or door frame. ⟨Old English *syll*⟩

sil·ly ['sɪli] *adj* **1** without sense or reason. **2** *Informal* stunned: *to knock someone silly.* **3** trivial: *silly little disagreements.* **sil·li·ness** *n.* ⟨Old English *sælig* happy; *sæl* happiness⟩

si·lo ['saɪlou] *n* **1** a tall, airtight building in

which green fodder for farm animals is stored. **2** a vertical underground shaft in which missiles are kept ready for launching. ⟨Spanish; Greek *siros* grain cellar⟩

si·lage *n* green fodder for farm animals, preserved and stored in a silo; ensilage.

silt [sɪlt] *n* very fine earth, sand, etc. carried by moving water and deposited as sediment: *The river mouth is choked with silt.* *v* clog or become clogged (*up*) with silt or mud. **sil·ta·tion** *n*. **silt·y** *adj*. ⟨Middle Dutch *silte, sulte* salt marsh⟩

sil·van [ˈsɪlvən] *adj* See SYLVAN.

sil·ver [ˈsɪlvər] *n* **1** a white, metallic element that is a precious metal. *Symbol* **Ag 2** coins, esp those of a silver colour. **3** cutlery, dishes, etc. made of or plated with silver; silverware: *I spent half an hour polishing the silver.* *adj* **1** to do with silver: *a silver spoon.* **2** of the colour of silver: *silver slippers.* **3** eloquent: *a silver tongue.* **4** being the 25th anniversary of an event: *a silver jubilee.* *v* cover or coat with silver or something like silver: *to silver a mirror.* ⟨Old English *siolfor*⟩

sil·ver·fish *n, pl* -**fish** or -**fish·es** a wingless insect covered with silver scales, often found in buildings, where it feeds on food scraps fabrics, etc. **silver fox** a colour phase of the red fox of North America, in which the fur is black but tipped with white. **silver lining** the positive aspect of an unfortunate situation. **silver maple** a maple having leaves that are light green above and silvery underneath. **silver plate** dishes, cutlery, etc. made of silver or of copper, etc. coated or plated with silver. **sil·ver–plate** *v*. **silver screen** movies collectively. **sil·ver·smith** *n* an artisan who makes and repairs articles of silver. **silver thaw ✻ 1** a storm of quick-freezing rain. **2** the glitter ice it forms on trees, rocks, and other surfaces. **sil·ver–tongued** *adj* eloquent; persuasive. **sil·ver·ware** *n* **1** articles, such as cutlery or dishes, made of or plated with silver. **2** loosely, cutlery of any metal. **silver wedding** the 25th anniversary of a wedding. **sil·ver·y** *adj* **1** having a sheen like that of silver: *silvery moonbeams.* **2** melodious: *silvery laughter.* **sil·ver·i·ness** *n*.

sil·vi·cul·ture [ˈsɪlvəˌkʌltʃər] *n* the cultivation and care of forests. **sil·vi·cul·tur·al** *adj*. **sil·vi·cul·tur·ist** *n*. ⟨Latin *silva* forest + CULTURE⟩

sim·i·an [ˈsɪmiən] *n* an ape or monkey. **sim·i·an** *adj*. ⟨Latin *simia* ape⟩

sim·i·lar [ˈsɪmələr] *adj* **1** having many features in common: *Their stories are similar.* **2** *Geometry* of figures, having the same shape but not necessarily the same size: *similar triangles.* **sim·i·lar·i·ty** *n*. **sim·i·lar·ly** *adv*. **si·mil·i·tude** *n*. ⟨Latin *similis*⟩

sim·i·le [ˈsɪməli] *n* a figure of speech that expresses a comparison between two unlike things, usually introduced by *like* or *as.* *Examples: a face like marble, a mind as sharp as a razor.* Compare METAPHOR. ⟨Latin = like⟩

sim·mer [ˈsɪmər] *v* **1** keep or stay at or just below the boiling point: *A stew simmered on*

the stove. **2** be on the point of bursting or breaking out: *simmering with anger.* **simmer** *n*. ⟨earlier *simper*; perhaps imitative⟩ **simmer down** calm down.

sim·pa·ti·co [sɪmˈpætɪˌkou] or [sɪmˈpɑtɪˌkou] *adj* congenial; agreeable. ⟨Italian⟩

sim·per [ˈsɪmpər] *v* **1** smile in a silly, affected way. **2** express or say with a simper. *n* a silly, affected smile. **sim·per·ing** *adj*. ⟨compare German *zimper(lich)* affected, coy⟩

sim·ple [ˈsɪmpəl] *adj* **1** easy to understand or do: *a simple problem.* **2** not divided into parts; not compound: *a simple leaf.* **3** not complex or involved: *a simple one-celled animal.* **4** bare; plain: *the simple truth.* **5** not ornate or rich: *simple clothes.* **6** natural and sincere: *a pleasant, simple manner.* **7** not sophisticated or subtle: *a simple child.* **8** common; ordinary. *Her parents were simple people.* **9** weak in mind. **10** insignificant: *Don't fuss, it's just a simple scratch.* **sim·plic·i·ty** [sɪmˈplɪsəti] or **sim·ple·ness** *n*. ⟨Old French; Latin *simplex*⟩

simple fracture a clean fracture in which the broken bone does not pierce the skin. Compare COMPOUND FRACTURE. **simple interest** interest paid only on the principal of a loan. Compare COMPOUND INTEREST. **simple machine** any of several elementary devices for lessening work. Usually considered as the six basic types are the **lever, pulley, wheel and axle, inclined plane, screw,** and **wedge. sim·ple–mind·ed** *adj* **1** feeble-minded or foolish. **2** unsophisticated: *a simple-minded approach to a complex problem.* **simple sentence** *Grammar* a sentence consisting of one main clause. *Examples: The whistle blew.* **sim·ple·ton** *n* a fool. **sim·plex** [ˈsɪmplɛks] *adj* **1** chiefly of concrete objects, not compound or complex. **2** of a computer circuit, etc., permitting transmission of signals in one direction only. Compare DUPLEX (def. 2). *n Geometry* the simplest figure possible in Euclidean space of a specified dimension; in one dimension, a line, in two dimensions, a triangle, etc. **sim·pli·fy** *v* make simpler. **sim·pli·fi·ca·tion** *n*. **sim·plis·tic** *adj* simplified or simplifying to a misleading extent by ignoring important aspects: *a simplistic view of the issue of disarmament.* **sim·plism** *n*. **sim·plist** *n*. **sim·plis·ti·cal·ly** *adv*. **sim·ply** *adv* **1** in a simple manner. **2** merely; only: *He thinks of his car simply as a means of transport.* **3** really; absolutely: *simply perfect.*

sim·u·late [ˈsɪmjəˌleit] *v* **1** pretend: *She simulated interest to please her friend.* **2** imitate: *Certain insects simulate leaves.* **3** make or be an artificial imitation of: *simulated pearls.* **sim·u·la·tion** *n*. **sim·u·la·tor** *n*. ⟨Latin *simulare*; *similis* like⟩

si·mul·cast [ˈsaɪməlˌkæst] or [ˈsɪməlˌkæst] *v* broadcast over radio and television, or over more than one station, at the same time: *CBC FM Radio and Television will simulcast the concert live.* **si·mul·cast** *n*. ⟨*simul(taneous)* + *(broad)cast*⟩

si·mul·ta·ne·ous [ˌsaɪməlˈteiniəs] or [ˌsɪməl-]

adj done or happening at the same time: *The two simultaneous gunshots sounded like one.* **si·mul·ta·ne·ous·ly** *adv.* **si·mul·ta·ne·ous·ness** or **si·mul·ta·ne·i·ty** [-təˈniəti] *or* [-təˈneiəti] *n.* ⟨Latin *simultaneus* simulated; confused with *simul* at the same time⟩

sin [sɪn] *v* **sinned, sin·ning** break a divine law; do wrong; do something immoral.
n **1** an act that is immoral or against a divine law. **2** sins in general or the tendency to sin. **3** *Informal* anything deplorable: *It is a sin to let that pie go to waste.* **sin·less** *adj.* **sin·ner** *n.* ⟨Old English *synn*⟩
sin bin ✱ *Slang Hockey* PENALTY BOX. **sin·ful** *adj.* **1** immoral or violating a divine law. **2** doing or inclined to do wrong. **3** *Informal* so delicious, luxurious, etc. as to suggest overindulgence of fleshly desire: *a sinful love of chocolate.* **sin·ful·ly** *adv.* **sin·ful·ness** *n.*

SIN [sɪn] ✱ SOCIAL INSURANCE NUMBER.

since [sɪns] *prep* **1** from (a given time) till now: *I've been ready since noon.* **2** at any time between (a past time) and the present: *We have not seen her since Saturday.*
conj **1** in the period after: *He has written home only once since he left us.* **2** continuously: *It is six years since we moved.* **3** because: *Since you feel tired, you should rest.*
adv **1** from then till now: *She got sick last Saturday and has been in bed ever since.* **2** at some time between a particular past time and the present: *At first she refused but she has since accepted.* **3** before now; ago: *I heard that old joke long since.* ⟨Middle English *sinnes, sithenes*; Old English *siththan* later; *sith* late⟩

sin·cere [sɪnˈsɪr] *adj* free from pretence; genuine: *sincere sorrow.* **sin·cer·i·ty** [-ˈsɛrəti] *n.* ⟨Latin *sincerus*⟩
sin·cere·ly *adv* **1** in a sincere way. **2** a formula for closing a letter: *Sincerely, Tammi.*

sine [saɪn] *n Trigonometry* in a right triangle, the ratio of the length of the side opposite an acute angle to the length of the hypotenuse. *Abbrev* **sin**. ⟨Latin *sinus* bend; Arabic *jaib* sine, bosom⟩
sine curve a curve whose equation is $y = \sin x$. **sine wave** *Physics* a periodic oscillation having a SINE CURVE as its wave form.

si·ne·cure [ˈsɪnəˌkjʊr] *n* a position that requires little or no work but pays well or is prestigious. ⟨Latin *sine cura* (church position) without care (of souls)⟩

si·ne qua non [ˈsɪni kwɑ ˈnoun] something essential or indispensable: *It was a sine qua non that all three parties should be included in the negotiations.* ⟨Latin = without which not⟩

sin·ew [ˈsɪnju] *n* a tough, strong band that joins muscle to bone; tendon. **sin·ew·y** *adj.* ⟨Old English *sionu*⟩

sing [sɪŋ] *v* **sang, sung, sing·ing 1** make music with the voice. **2** chant: *The priest sings Mass.* **3** make pleasant musical sounds: *Birds sing.* **4** enthusiastically proclaim: *to sing a person's praises.* **5** be full of joy: *His heart sang at the sound of her step.* **6** *Slang* inform; tell all. **sing·a·ble** *adj.* **sing·er** *n.* ⟨Old English *singan*⟩

singing house ✱ in Inuit culture, a special building for communal singing and dancing.
sing·song *n* **1** monotonous, rhythmic speech. **2** a gathering for singing. **sing·song** *adj, v.*

singe [sɪndʒ] *v* burn a little; scorch: *He got too close to the fire and singed his eyebrows.* **singe** *n.* ⟨Old English *sengan*⟩
singe one's wings be slightly harmed, esp by some risky venture.

sin·gle [ˈsɪŋɡəl] *adj* **1** being only one: *a single piece of paper.* **2** for only one: *a room with two single beds.* **3** not married: *a single man.* **4** with only one on each side: *single combat.*
n **1** a single thing or person; specifically, an unmarried person. **2** *Baseball* a hit that allows a runner to advance by one base only. **3** *Football* a single point scored by kicking into or beyond the end zone; rouge. **4 singles** *pl* a game with only one person on each side.
v **1** pick (one) from among others (with *out*): *The teacher singled me out for praise.* **2** *Baseball* make a hit that allows a runner to advance by one base only. **sin·gle·ness** *n.* **sin·gly** *adv.* ⟨Latin *singulus*⟩
single bed a bed designed for one person. **sin·gle–breast·ed** *adj* of a coat, jacket, etc., overlapping just enough to fasten with only one row of buttons. **single file** a line of persons or things arranged one behind another. **sin·gle–hand·ed** *adj, adv* **1** without help from others: *She built all the cupboards single-handed.* **2** using or requiring only one hand: *It's hard to tie a knot single-handed.* **sin·gle–hand·ed·ly** *adv.* **sin·gle–mind·ed** *adj* having devotion to one aim. **singles bar** a bar frequented by single people, often in hopes of finding companions. **sin·gle–space** *v* key or write with no blank lines between lines of print: *Quotations set off within an essay should be single-spaced. adv* with no blank lines between lines of print.

sin·gu·lar [ˈsɪŋɡjələr] *adj* **1** *Grammar* of a form, referring to only one person, thing, etc. *Dog* is singular; *dogs* is plural. **2** strange: *The detectives were puzzled by the singular nature of the crime.* **3** exceptional: *a matter of singular interest to you all.* **4** being the only one of its kind: *an event singular in history.*
n Grammar a singular form, word, etc. **sin·gu·lar·i·ty** *n.* **sin·gu·lar·ize** *v.* **sin·gu·lar·ly** *adv.* ⟨Latin *singulus* single⟩

sin·is·ter [ˈsɪnɪstər] *adj* **1** suggesting ill will; evil: *a sinister motive.* **2** giving signs of trouble: *a sinister sky.* **3** disastrous: *She met a sinister fate.* **sin·is·ter·ly** *adv.* **sin·is·ter·ness** *n.* ⟨Latin = on the left; in foretelling the future, the left side was considered unlucky⟩

sink [sɪŋk] *v* **sank** or **sunk, sunk, sink·ing 1** go lower and lower: *The sun is sinking.* **2** go or cause to go beneath the surface (of water, quicksand, etc.): *The ship is sinking.* **3** reduce: *The wind has sunk.* **4** pass gradually (into a state of sleep, silence, etc.). **5** make by digging or drilling: *to sink a well.* **6** set into a hollow space: *a stone sunk into a wall.* **7** grow discouraged: *Her heart sank.* **8** approach death: *The patient is sinking.* **9** demoralize or defeat. **10** invest (money), esp unprofitably. **11** *Basketball* put (the ball) through the hoop. **12** *Golf* hit (the ball) into a hole.
n **1** a basin with a drainpipe. **2** a drain; sewer. **3** a place where dirty water or any filth collects. **sink·a·ble** *adj.* **sink·age** *n.* ⟨Old English *sincan*⟩
sink in be fully understood or absorbed: *I keep telling him, but it doesn't seem to sink in.*
sink·er *n* **1** a lead weight on a fishing line or net. **2** *Baseball* a ball pitched so as to curve down sharply just in front of the plate.
sink·hole *n* **1** a hollow in limestone, etc. through which surface water drains into an underground passage or cavern. **2 ✹ a** a bog. **b** a depression in the prairie, usually with alkaline springs beneath it and hence having no herbage. **3** a place of vice or corruption. **4** a depression in land caused by the collapse of the structures or materials beneath it.

Sino– ['saɪnou] *combining form* Chinese.

sin·u·ous ['sɪnjuəs] *adj* **1** having many curves or turns; winding. **2** devious or morally crooked. **sin·u·os·i·ty** *n.* **sin·u·ous·ly** *adv.* ⟨Latin *sinuosus; sinus* curve⟩

si·nus ['saɪnəs] *n* one of the cavities in the bones of the skull that connect with the nose. ⟨Latin = curve⟩
si·nus·i·tis [ˌsaɪnəˈsaɪtɪs] *n* inflammation of a sinus of the skull.

Sioux [su] *n, pl* **Sioux** [su] or [suz]; *adj* **1** Dakota. **2** Siouan.
Siou·an ['suən] *n* **1** a family of languages spoken by First Nations or Native American peoples of central and eastern North America. **2** a member of any of the peoples speaking one of these languages. **Siou·an** *adj.*

sip [sɪp] *v* **sipped, sip·ping** drink little by little: *She sipped her tea.* **sip** *n.* ⟨Old English *sypian* take in moisture⟩

si·phon ['saɪfən] *n* a tube through which liquid can be drawn over the edge of one container into another at a lower level by air pressure. **si·phon** *v.* ⟨Greek *siphōn* pipe⟩

sir [sɜr] *n* **1** sometimes, esp in letter saluations, **Sir** a respectful or formal term of address used to a man (never with a name): *Excuse me, sir.* **2 Sir** the title used before the name of a knight or baronet: *Sir Wilfrid Laurier.* ⟨variant of *sire*⟩
sir·rah ['sɜrə] *n Archaic* fellow; angry term of address to men and boys. **sir·ree** [sɜr'ri] *interj Informal* a word used after *yes* or *no* to add emphasis: *Yes, sirree, that was one awful storm!*

sire [saɪr] *n* **1** *Poetic, archaic* a father or male

ancestor. **2** the male parent of an animal: *The sire of Danger, a great racehorse, was Lightning.* **3 Sire** *Archaic* a respectful term of address for a king or great noble: *"I'm killed, Sire!" said the messenger to the king.*
v be the father of; beget (of animals): *Lightning sired Danger.* ⟨Old French; Latin *seior*, earlier *senior* older⟩

si·ren ['saɪrən] *n* **1** a device that produces a loud, penetrating sound, used as a warning of the approach of an ambulance, police vehicle, etc. or as a warning of an air raid. **2** *Greek myth* any of a group of female creatures living on rocks, who by their sweet, enchanting song lured sailors to destruction. **3** a dangerously seductive woman. **si·ren** *adj.* ⟨Greek *seirēn*⟩

sir·loin ['sɜrlɔɪn] *n* a choice cut of beef from the part of the loin in front of the rump. ⟨earlier *surloin*, Old French *surlonge; sur* over + *longe* loin; Latin *lumbus*⟩

si·roc·co [səˈrɒkou] *n* a hot wind of N Africa that picks up moisture as it crosses the Mediterranean, reaching S Italy as a hot, oppressively humid wind. Also, **sci·roc·co.** ⟨Italian; Arabic *shărūq; shărq* east⟩

sis·al ['sɪsəl] or ['saɪsəl] *n* a strong plant fibre used for making rope, twine, etc. ⟨*Sisal*, town in Mexico⟩

sis·ka·wet ['sɪskəˌwɛt] *n* ✹ a variety of lake trout found mainly in Lake Superior. Also, **sis·co·wet.** ⟨Cdn. French *sisquoetle*; Algonkian Ojibwa *pemitewiskawet* one with oily flesh⟩

sis·sy ['sɪsi] *Informal n* a cowardly or weak person. **sis·sy** *adj.* **sis·sy·ish** *adj.* ⟨*sis(ter)* + -*y²*⟩
sis·si·fied *adj Informal* effeminate; cowardly.

sis·ter ['sɪstər] *n* **1** a daughter of the same parents; sometimes, only of the same mother or father (**half sister**). **2** a nun or female member of a faith community. **3** *Informal* a term of address for any woman or girl. **sis·ter·like** *adj.* **sis·ter·ly** *adj.* ⟨Old Norse *systir*⟩
sis·ter·hood *n* **1** the relationship between sisters. **2** an association of women with some common bond: *the sisterhood of midwives.*
sis·ter–in–law *n, pl* **sis·ters–in–law 1** one's spouse's sister. **2** the wife of one's own or of one's spouse's brother.

sit [sɪt] *v* **sat, sit·ting 1 a** rest on the buttocks: *to sit in a chair.* **b** of a four-legged animal, rest on the haunches with the front legs unbent. **2** cause to sit: *She sat the little boy down hard.* **3** be in a certain place: *a clock sitting on a shelf.* **4** have a seat in an assembly, etc.: *to sit in Parliament.* **5** hold a session: *The court sits next month.* **6** baby-sit. **7** write (an examination). ⟨Old English *sittan*⟩
sit back be complacently inactive when action is required. **sit down** take a seat. **sit in** take part in a protest in which people occupy a public place and remain seated there for a long time. **sit–in** *n.* **sit in (on)** attend as an observer: *to sit in on a session at the legislature.* **sit on** *Informal* **a** check or rebuke. **b** delay action on or use of. **sit on one's hands** do nothing when action is required. **sit out**

a remain seated during (a dance). **b** stay or wait through: *to sit out a storm.* **sit up a** raise the body to a sitting position. **b** cause to take such a position. **c** stay up instead of going to bed. **sit up and take notice** be suddenly interested. **sit well with** be acceptable to: *The whole idea does not sit very well with her.*
sit–down *adj* **1** of a labour strike, held in the workplace. **2** of a meal, eaten at a table.
sit·ter *n* babysitter. **sit·ting** *n* **1** a single uninterrupted period of sitting: *The portrait took five sittings.* **2** a meeting or session of a legislature, court, etc. **3** one of two or more times for serving a meal, when all cannot be served at once, as on a train, ship, etc.: *the second sitting for dinner.* **sitting duck** *Informal* an easy target. **sitting room** a room furnished with comfortable chairs, sofas, etc. **sit–up** *n* an exercise that consists of raising the body from a lying to a sitting position, unsupported by the hands.

si·tar [sɪˈtɑr] *n* a lutelike instrument developed in India, having a long neck and a varying number of strings. ⟨Hindi = three-stringed; Persian *Si* three + *tār* string⟩

sit·com [ˈsɪtˌkɒm] *n* SITUATION COMEDY.

site [səit] *n* **1** the actual or potential location of something: *the site of the new civic centre.* **2** *Computers* linked files that can be accessed at an address on the INTERNET.
v choose a position for: *They sited the new building on a hill.* ⟨Latin *situs*⟩

sit·u·ate [ˈsɪtʃuˌeit] *v* put in a certain place; locate. ⟨Latin *situare; situs* location⟩
sit·u·at·ed *adj* having a location of a given kind or in a given place: *a cottage situated by a lake.* **sit·u·a·tion** *n* **1** a set of circumstances: *Act reasonably in all situations.* **2** site; location: *Our house has a beautiful situation on a hill.* **3** a place to work; job. **4** a critical state of affairs. **sit·u·a·tion·al** *adj* to do with situations: *situational ethics.* **situation comedy** a radio or television comedy series consisting of regular unconnected episodes, featuring the same cast in each. Also, **sit·com.**

six [sɪks] *n* **1** one more than five; 6. **2** any set of six persons or things. **3** a playing card or side of a die having six spots: *I threw a six, and got another turn.* **six** *adj.* ⟨Old English *siex*⟩ **at sixes and sevens a** in disorder or confusion. **b** in disagreement. **six of one and half a dozen of the other** the same either way.
six·fold *adj* **1** six times as much or as many. **2** having six parts. *adv* six times as much or as many. **Six Nations** a federation of Iroquois First Nations peoples (Mohawk, Oneida, Onondaga, Seneca, and Cayuga) called the **Five Nations** until the Tuscarora tribe joined in about 1722. **six–pack** *n* six bottles or cans of a soft drink or beer, packaged as a unit. **six–shoot·er** *n* a revolver that can fire six shots without being reloaded. **sixth** *n* **1** the next after the fifth; 6th. **2** one, or being one, of six equal parts. **3** *Music* the interval between one tone and another five tones higher. *adj* being the sixth or a sixth. **sixth·ly**

adv. **sixth sense** a power of perception beyond the five senses.
six·teen [sɪksˈtin] *n* **1** six more than ten; 16. **2** any set of 16 persons or things. **six·teen** *adj.* ⟨Old English *sixtig*⟩
six·teenth *adj, n* **1** next after the 15th; 16th. **2** one, or being one, of 16 equal parts. **sixteenth note** *Music* a note lasting one sixteenth as long as a whole note.

six·ty [sɪksˈti] *n* **1** six times ten; 60. **2 sixties** *pl* the years from 60 through 69, esp of a century or a person's life: *Rock became popular in the sixties.* **six·ty** *adj.* ⟨Old English *sixtēne*⟩
six·ti·eth *adj, n* **1** next after the 59th; 60th. **2** one, or being one, of 60 equal parts.

size¹ [saiz] *n* **1** how big a thing is; dimensions. **2** extent; scale: *the size of an industry.* **3** one of a series of measures: *Her shoes are size 10.*
v **1** sort by size. **2** make of certain size. ⟨*assize,* in sense of 'set a standard measure'⟩ **size up** form an opinion of; estimate. **the size of it** the true state of affairs.
siz·a·ble or **sizeable** *adj* fairly large. **–sized** *adj* having specified size or bulk: *giant-sized.*

size² [saiz] *n* a sticky preparation made from materials like glue, starch, etc, and used as a glaze or filler for cloth, paper, plaster, leather, etc. Also called **siz·ing. size** *v.* ⟨French *assise* a sitting, fixing, layer⟩

siz·zle [ˈsɪzəl] *v* **1** make a hissing sound, as fat does when frying. **2** be very hot: *The asphalt sizzled in the heat.* **3** show or evoke barely restrained emotion: *This thriller absolutely sizzles with suspense.* **siz·zle** *n.* **siz·zler** *n.* ⟨imitative⟩

skate¹ [skeit] *n* **1** a boot with a metal blade fixed to the sole, for gliding over ice. **2** ROLLER SKATE. **3** INLINE SKATES. **skate** *v.* **skat·er** *n.* **skat·ing** *n.* ⟨Dutch *schaats;* Old French *escache* stilt⟩
skate·board *n* a narrow wooden or plastic board with turned-up ends, with a pair of small wheels under each end, for coasting along paths, etc. **skate·board** *v.* **skate·board·er** *n.* **skate·board·ing** *n.* **skate–guard** *n* a piece of plastic with a groove in it, used as a cover for the blade of an ice skate. **skating rink 1** a smooth ice surface for skating. **2** a smooth floor for roller skating or inline skating.

skate² [skeit] *n, pl* **skate** or **skates** any of a family of large, bottom-dwelling rays having very broad fins, and, in some species, weak electric organs in the tail. ⟨Old Norse *skata*⟩

ske·dad·dle [skɪˈdædəl] *Informal v* run away; scatter in flight. ⟨origin uncertain⟩

skeet [skit] *n* a method of target practice using clay disks that are released into the air so as to imitate the flight of birds. Also, **skeet shooting.** ⟨Old Norse *skjóta* to shoot⟩

skein [skein] *n* **1** a loosely coiled bundle of yarn, thread, etc. **2** a confused tangle. **3** a flock of geese in flight. ⟨Old French *escaigne*⟩

skel·e·ton [ˈskɛlətən] *n* **1** the framework of bones and cartilage of a vertebrate animal. **2** a very thin person or animal: *He was just a skeleton after his long illness.* **3** the basic

framework or structure of anything: *the steel skeleton of an office tower.*
adj basic; essential; constituting a minimum: *A skeleton crew stayed on board while the ship was in port.* **skel·e·tal** *adj.* ⟨Greek = dried up⟩ **skeleton at the feast** a person or thing casting gloom on a joyful occasion. **skeleton in the closet** a shameful secret.
skeleton key a key made to open many locks.

skep·tic or **scep·tic** ['skɛptɪk] *n* **1 a** a person who doubts a particular theory, alleged fact, etc. **b** one who habitually doubts what he or she has not experienced first-hand. **2** *Philosophy* a person who doubts the possibility of certain human knowledge of anything. **skep·ti·cal** *adj.* **skep·ti·cal·ly** *adv.* **skep·ti·cism** *n.* ⟨Greek *skeptikos* reflective⟩

sketch [skɛtʃ] *n* **1** a rough, quickly done drawing, painting, etc. **2** an outline; plan. **3** a short, light description, story, play, etc. **sketch** *v.* **sketch·er** *n.* ⟨Dutch *schets*; Greek *schedios* impromptu⟩
sketch·book *n* a book for rough, quick drawings. **sketch·y** *adj* **1** giving only outlines or main features. **2** incomplete; slight: *a sketchy meal.* **sketch·i·ly** *adv.* **sketch·i·ness** *n.*

skew [skju] *adj* **1** twisted to one side. **2** unbalanced; distorted. **3** *Mathematics* lying in different planes, not intersecting and not parallel. **skew** *n, v.* ⟨Old Norman French *eskiuer* shy away from, eschew⟩

skew·er ['skjuər] *n* **1** a long wooden or metal pin on which to thread pieces of meat, vegetable, etc. in order to broil them. **2** anything shaped or used like this. **skew·er** *v.* ⟨earlier *skiver*; origin uncertain⟩

ski [ski] *n* **1** one of a pair of pieces of wood, metal, etc. fastened to boots for gliding over snow. **2** WATER SKI. **ski** *v.* **ski·er** *n.* ⟨Norwegian⟩
ski jump a place for making a jump on skis. **ski lift** a mechanism for taking skiers to the top of a slope, usually by means of a chair running on a suspended cable. **ski pole** either of a pair of light poles used for balance and forward propulsion. **ski tow** a mechanism for towing skiers up a slope, consisting of an endless moving rope or cable which the skiers hang onto.

skid [skɪd] *v* **skid·ded, skid·ding** slide out of control while moving.
n **1** a slip or slide sideways out of control: *His car went into a skid.* **2** a frame on which heavy articles may be piled for moving, often by a forklift. ⟨Compare Old Frisian *skīd* stick of wood⟩
hit the skids *Slang* suffer a serious decline or failure. **on the skids** *Slang* headed for failure. **skid road** or **trail** *Logging* a road or trail for hauling logs. **skid row** a run-down district of cheap hotels and bars, frequented by vagrants, petty criminals, etc.

Ski–Doo [ski'du] or ['skidu] *n Trademark* a type of snowmobile.

skiff [skɪf] *n* a small, light rowboat or sailboat. ⟨Italian *schifo*; Germanic⟩

skill [skɪl] *n* **1** ability gained by practice or knowledge; expertness: *It takes skill to tune a piano.* **2** a specific ability or technique that can be learned: *basic language skills.* **skil·ful** or **skill·ful** *adj.* **skil·ful·ly** or **skill·ful·ly** *adv.* ⟨Old Norse *skil* distinction⟩
skilled *adj* **1** having or showing skill: *a skilled worker.* **2** requiring skill: *the skilled trades.*

skil·let ['skɪlɪt] *n* frying pan. ⟨Middle English *skelet*⟩

skim [skɪm] *v* **skimmed, skim·ming 1** remove (something) from the surface of (a liquid): *to She skimmed the fat off the soup.* **2** move or send moving lightly over: *to skim a flat stone across the water.* **3** glide along: *The skaters went skimming by.* **4** read rapidly or superficially in order to get the general sense: *I skimmed the first page.* **5** *Slang* avoid paying tax on (income) by concealing it.
n **1** that which is skimmed off. **2** the act of skimming. ⟨Old French *escume* scum⟩
skim milk milk with the cream removed.

skimp [skɪmp] *v* **1** supply or use too little of: *Don't skimp the butter in making a cake.* **2** be very thrifty: *She had to skimp to send her son to university.* ⟨perhaps alteration of *scrimp*⟩
skimp·y *adj* barely enough. **skimp·i·ly** *adv.* **skimp·i·ness** *n.*

skin [skɪn] *n* **1** the outer layer of tissue of a body, esp when relatively soft and flexible. **2** the skin of a fur-bearing or hairy animal. **3 a** any outer layer, as the rind of a fruit, a sausage casing, etc. **b** a thin film on the surface of a liquid. **4** the outer covering of a structure such as an aircraft or ship. **5 skins** *pl Slang* drums. **6** *Informal* nudity, esp if portrayed pornographically.
v **skinned, skin·ning 1** take the skin off: *He fell and skinned his knees.* **2** scrape or peel off like skin: *The fall skinned the paint on her new bicycle.* **3** of liquid, develop a filmy coating (with *over*). ⟨Middle English; Old Norse *skinn*⟩ **by the skin of one's teeth** *Informal* barely. **get under someone's skin** annoy someone. **have a thick** (or **thin**) **skin** be very insensitive (or sensitive) to criticism. **in** (or **with**) **a whole skin** safe and sound. **no skin off one's nose** of no interest or concern to one. **save one's skin** *Informal* escape safely. **skin alive** *Slang* **a** torture. **b** scold severely.
skin–deep *adj* **1** of a wound, etc., no deeper than the skin. **2** of an emotion, quality, etc., superficial: *Beauty is only skin-deep.* **skin diving** swimming under water, using a face mask and flippers, usually with scuba gear. **skin–dive** *v.* **skin diver** or **skindiver.** **skin flick** *Slang* a pornographic film. **skin·flint** *n* a stingy person. **skin·head** *n* **1** a member of a group of youths characterized by shaven heads, some of whom engage in rowdyism or support neo-Nazi principles. **2** a neo-Nazi. **skin·ny** *adj* unattractively thin: *She was always skinny as a child, but she was perfectly healthy.* *n Slang* news; current information. **skin·ni·ness** *n.* **skin·ny–dip** *v* **-dipped, -dip·ping** *Informal* go swimming in the nude. **skin·ny–dip** *n.* **skinny dipper. skinny dipping.**

skin test a test in which a substance is introduced under the skin to detect a disease or allergy. **skin–tight** *adj* of clothes, fitting very closely.

SYNONYMS

Skin is the general word applying to the natural covering of a person or animal: *The skin of a calf makes soft leather.* **Hide** applies to the tough skin of a large animal, raw or tanned: *The hide of cows is tough.* **Pelt** applies to the skin of a fur-bearing animal before dressing or tanning: *Trappers sell fox pelts; stores sell dressed skins.*

skink [skɪŋk] *n* any of a family of lizards having a long body with smooth scales, and short limbs or no limbs at all. ⟨Latin; Greek *skinkos*⟩

skin·ny See SKIN.

skip¹ [skɪp] *v* **skipped, skip·ping 1** move along by stepping and hopping first with one foot, then the other. **2** jump over (a moving rope) as a game or exercise. **3** go or send bounding along a surface: *to skip stones.* **4** fail to do, read, attend, etc.: *Don't skip class.* **5** change quickly from one activity, subject, etc. to another. **6** *Informal* leave secretly and hastily: *He skipped town.* **7** be promoted past (the next grade) in school. **skip** *n.* **skip·per** *n.* ⟨perhaps Scandinavian⟩
skip·jack *n* a small tuna of Pacific waters.
skipping rope a rope with a handle at each end, swung over and under a person who leaps over it when it reaches his or her feet.

skip² [skɪp] *n* **1** *Informal* the captain of a boat or ship; skipper. **2** *Sports* the captain of a curling team or a lawn bowling team.
v **skipped, skip·ping** serve as skip of (a team). ⟨clipped form of *skipper*⟩

skip·per¹ ['skɪpər] *n* **1** the captain of a ship. **2** any captain or leader. **skip·per** *v.* ⟨Middle Dutch *schipper; schip* ship⟩

skip·per² See SKIP¹.

skir·mish ['skɜrmɪʃ] *n* a minor conflict, battle, argument, etc. **skir·mish** *v.* **skir·mish·er** *n.* ⟨Old French *eskirmir* orig ward off⟩

skirt [skɜrt] *n* **1** a women's and girls' garment for the lower body that hangs freely from the waist. **2** the part of a dress, jumper, etc. that extends from the waist down. **3** a cloth hanging that resembles a skirt: *a dressing table with a skirt.*
v **1** extend along the border or edge of: *The road skirts the lake.* **2** go around: *The girls skirted the forest because they did not want to go through it.* **3** avoid or evade: *to skirt an issue.* ⟨Middle English *skirte;* Old Norse *skyrta* shirt⟩

skit [skɪt] *n* a short, humorous or satirical play, often improvised. ⟨Scandinavian⟩

skit·ter ['skɪtər] *v* move lightly or quickly; skim or skip along a surface. ⟨frequentative of earlier *skite* dart⟩
skit·tish *adj* **1** easily startled: *a skittish horse.* **2** fickle; changeable.

skiv·vies ['skɪviz] *n pl Slang* underwear: *Don't come in, I'm in my skivvies.*

skoo·kum ['skukəm] *or* ['skʊkəm] ✹ *W Coast, Northwest adj* powerful, big, or brave: *a skookum bacon-and-egg breakfast.*
n an evil genius or spirit. ⟨Chinook Jargon⟩
skookum chuck ✹ *W Coast, Northwest* **1** a swift current; white water. **2** tidal rapids.

skul·dug·ger·y or **skull·dug·ger·y** [skʌl'dʌgəri] *n Informal* trickery; deceit. ⟨origin uncertain⟩

skulk [skʌlk] *v* **1** move in a stealthy manner: *The burglar skulked around the house, looking for an easy way in.* **2** keep out of sight to avoid danger, work, etc.: *He skulked at home to avoid the bully.* **skulk·er** *n.* ⟨Scandinavian⟩

skull [skʌl] *n* **1** the bones of the head. **2** the head as the seat of intelligence: *It's impossible to get anything into his thick skull.* ⟨Middle English *scolle*⟩
out of one's skull *Informal* **a** crazy. **b** (as a complement to **bored**) utterly.
skull and crossbones a picture of a human skull above two crossed bones, a symbol of death often used on pirates' flags and now on the labels of poisonous substances, etc.
skull·cap *n* a close-fitting cap with no brim.

skunk [skʌŋk] *n* **1** any of various small, black-and-white mammals of the weasel family which defend themselves by ejecting a very bad-smelling liquid from a pair of anal glands. **2** *Informal* a despicable person.
v Slang defeat utterly. ⟨Algonquian⟩

sky [skaɪ] *n* **1** the space high above the earth, appearing as a great dome. **2** heaven. **3** climate: *warm tropical skies.* ⟨Old Norse *sky*⟩
out of a clear (blue) sky very unexpectedly.
praise to the skies praise extravagantly.
sky·div·ing *n* the sport of jumping out of a plane and making certain manoeuvres while falling free before opening one's parachute. **sky·dive** *v.* **sky·div·er** *n.* **sky–high** *adv, adj* very high: *sky-high prices.* **sky·jack** *v* take over (an aircraft) by force. **sky·jack·er** *n.* **sky·jack·ing** *n.* **sky·light** *n* a window in a roof. **sky·line** *n* the outline of buildings, mountains, trees, etc. as seen against the sky from a distance: *The skyline of Vancouver is spectacular.* **sky pilot** *Slang* a chaplain. **sky·rock·et** *n* a firework that shoots high into the air, where it bursts in a shower of sparks. *v* rise suddenly and quickly: *Prices skyrocketed.* **sky·scrap·er** *n* a very tall building. **sky·ward** *adv, adj* toward the sky. Also (*adv*), **sky·wards. sky·way** *n* **1** a stretch of elevated highway. **2** a high, covered walkway between upper storeys of two buildings. **sky·writ·ing** *n* the tracing of words, etc. against the sky from an airplane by means of smoke. **sky·write** *v.* **sky·writ·er** *n.*

slab [slæb] *n* a broad, flat, thick piece (of stone, wood, meat, etc.): *a slab of cheese.* ⟨Middle English *slabbe*⟩

slack [slæk] *adj* **1** not tight or firm: *The rope hung slack.* **2** slow; not brisk: *Business is slack at this season.* **3** careless: *a slack housekeeper.*
n **1** the part that hangs loose: *Pull in the slack of the rope.* **2** a dull season; quiet period.
slack·en *v.* **slack·er** *n.* **slack·ly** *adv.* **slack·ness** *n.* ⟨Old English *slæc*⟩
cut someone some slack See CUT. **pick (or**

take) **up the slack** bear the extra load caused by loss of workers, lost time, etc. **slack off** neglect work. **slack up** slow down.

slack–jawed *adj* with the mouth partly open, often in surprise or confusion. **slacks** *n pl* casual, comfortable pants.

slag [slæg] *n* **1** the rough, hard waste left after ore is smelted. **2** a light, spongy lava. ⟨Middle Low German *slagge*⟩

slain [slein] *v* pp of SLAY.

slake [sleik] *v* **1** satisfy (thirst, desire for revenge, etc.). **2 a** treat (lime) with water so it disintegrates. **b** of lime, be so changed. ⟨Old English *slacian; slæc* slack⟩

slaked lime a soft, white crystalline powder, obtained by treating lime with water, used in mortars and cements; calcium hydroxide.

sla·lom ['slɑləm] *n* **1** *Skiing* a zigzag downhill race on a course set between a series of posts. **2** any similar zigzag race around obstacles, with cars, canoes, etc. **sla·lom** *v*. ⟨Norwegian⟩

slam¹ [slæm] *v* **slammed, slam·ming 1** shut, hit, thrust, etc. with force and a loud noise: *to slam a door.* **2** *Informal* criticize severely. **slam** *n*. ⟨Scandinavian⟩
(the) slam·mer *n Slang* jail or prison.

slam² [slæm] *n* **1** *Bridge* the winning of 12 (a **little slam**) or all 13 (a **grand slam**) tricks. **2** in some other card games, the winning of all tricks in a hand. ⟨origin uncertain⟩

slan·der ['slændər] *n* **1** the crime of making false oral statements meant to harm the reputation of another. Compare LIBEL. **2** such a statement. **slan·der** *v*. **slan·der·ous** *adj*. ⟨Old French *esclandre* scandal; Latin *scandalum*⟩

slang [slæŋ] *n* vocabulary and usage that differ from the standard, consisting mainly of innovative, colourful expressions.
v attack with abusive language; rail at; scold. **slang·y** *adj*. ⟨origin uncertain⟩

USAGE
Slang is not usually considered acceptable in formal speech or writing, and should be avoided even in informal situations with people outside one's own group.

slant [slænt] *v* **1** slope: *My handwriting slants to the right.* **2** present so as to appeal to a particular group: *slanted toward the teenage audience.* **3** distort; bias: *to slant a news story.*
n **1** a slope: *The roof has a sharp slant.* **2** a particular viewpoint: *Her stories give an interesting slant on the politics of the sixties.* **3** bias. **slant·ing** *adj*. ⟨Middle English *slent*⟩

slap [slæp] *n* **1** a blow with the open hand or with something flat. **2** the sharp sound of a slap. **3** sharp words of blame; a rebuke.
adv Informal **1** straight; directly: *The thief ran slap into a police officer.* **2** suddenly. **slap, slapped, slap·ping** *v*. ⟨Low German *slappe*⟩
slap·dash *Informal adj* hasty and careless. **slap·hap·py** *adj Informal* **1** in a giggly, or silly mood. **2** punch-drunk. **slap·shot** *n Hockey* a

fast shot made with a powerful swinging stroke. **slap·stick** *n* **1** comedy full of rough play. **2** two boards fastened so as to slap together loudly when a clown, actor, etc. hits somebody with them. **slap·stick** *adj*. **slap–up** *adj Informal* first-rate: *a slap-up job.*

slash [slæʃ] *v* **1** cut with a sweeping stroke; gash: *He slashed the bark off the tree with his knife.* **2** make a violent, sweeping stroke. **3** reduce drastically: *The budget was slashed.* **4** clear (land) of trees and brush. **5** *Hockey* swing one's stick at (an opponent).
n **1** the oblique sign (/). **2** the act or result of slashing: *a slash with a sword, a slash in prices.* **3** a clearing in a forest, littered with chips, broken branches, etc. **4** such debris left by a storm or loggers. **slash·er** *n*. **slash·ing** *adj, n*. ⟨Middle English *slaschen*⟩
slash fire ✱ a fire in SLASH (*n* 4); usually, one deliberately set and carefully controlled to tidy up the area and encourage new growth.

slat [slæt] *n* a thin, narrow piece of wood, metal, etc. **slat·ted** *adj*. ⟨Old French *esclat* split piece⟩

slate [sleit] *n* **1** a fine-grained, bluish grey rock that splits easily into thin layers. **2** a list, as of candidates, activities, agenda items, etc.: *What's on your slate for tonight?*
v **1** cover with slate. **2** list as a candidate, activity, etc.: *The party is slated for Friday at 4 p.m.* **slate** *adj*. **slate·like** *adj*. **slat·y** *adj*. ⟨Old French *esclate* variant of *esclat* slat⟩
a clean slate a record unmarked by dishonour.

slath·er ['slæðər] *Informal v* spread thickly or lavishly. ⟨origin unknown⟩

slaugh·ter ['slɒtər] *v* **1** butcher (an animal). **2** massacre. **3** *Informal* defeat utterly. **slaugh·ter** *n*. ⟨Old Norse *slátr* butcher-meat⟩
slaugh·ter·house *n* a place where animals are killed for food; abattoir.

Slav [slæv] *or* [slɑv] *n* a member of any of a group of E European peoples speaking Slavic languages, such as Russians, Poles, Czechs, etc. **Slav** *adj*. ⟨Latin *Sclavus*. See SLAVE.⟩
Slav·ic *n* the group of languages that includes Czech, Polish, etc. **Slav·ic** *adj*.

slave [sleiv] *n* **1** a person owned by another. **2** a person controlled by some habit, influence, etc.: *a slave to drink.* **3** a very hard worker. **4** an electronic device that receives and relays radio signals from a master control, as in loran navigation.
v **1** work like a slave. **2** deal in slaves. **slav·er** *n*. **slav·er·y** *n*. **slav·ish** *adj*. ⟨Latin *Sclavus* Slav (captive)⟩
slave driver an excessively demanding employer, supervisor, etc. **slave trade** the buying and selling of slaves. **slave trader.**

slav·er¹ See SLAVE.

slav·er² ['slævər] *v* let saliva run from the mouth; drool. **slav·er** *n*. ⟨Scandinavian⟩

Slav·ey or **Slave** See DENE-THAH.

slay [slei] *v* **slew** or **slayed** (for 2), **slain,**

slay·ing 1 kill with violence: *Many soldiers were slain on that hill.* 2 *Slang* amuse greatly: *That line just slays me.* 3 *Slang* be the death of; do in. **slay·er** *n.* ⟨Old English *slēan*⟩

slea·zy ['slizi] *Informal adj* disreputable, dirty, etc.: *a sleazy hotel.* ⟨origin uncertain⟩ **sleaze** *n* a sleazy person, thing, or quality.

sled [slɛd] *n* 1 a small, low vehicle on runners, pulled by dogs and used for carrying loads over ice and snow. 2 a child's plaything consisting of a platform on runners, for sliding down hills on snow. **sled, sled·ded, sled·ding** *v.* **sled·der** *n.* ⟨Middle Dutch *sledde*⟩ **be tough sled·ding** be hard work because of adverse conditions.

sledge·ham·mer ['slɛdʒˌhæmər] *n* a large, heavy hammer swung with two hands.
adj powerful or crushing: *sledgehammer sarcasm.* **sledge·ham·mer** *v.* ⟨Old English *slecg* + HAMMER⟩

sleek [slik] *adj* 1 smooth and glossy: *sleek hair.* 2 having a well-groomed, well-fed appearance: *a sleek cat.* 3 trim and elegant: *a sleek ship.* **sleek** *v.* **sleek·ly** *adv.* **sleek·ness** *n.* ⟨variant of *slick*⟩

sleep [slip] *v* **slept, sleep·ing** 1 rest in such a way as to be without ordinary consciousness. 2 be inactive or dormant: *Seeds sleep in the ground all winter.* 3 provide sleeping accommodation for: *The cabin sleeps six.* 4 fail to be alert.
n 1 the condition of a person, animal, or plant that sleeps, or a state like this. 2 a period spent in sleeping. 3 mucus secreted during sleep by the eyes, that hardens, esp in their inner corners. **sleep·less** *adj.* ⟨Old English *slǣpan*⟩
in one's sleep a while sleeping. **b** effortlessly. **last sleep** death. **put to sleep a** kill (an animal) humanely. **b** cause to fall asleep. **sleep around** *Slang* have sexual intercourse with a number of people. **sleep in a** stay in bed later than usual: *We always sleep in on Sunday mornings.* **b** sleep too long: *He was late because he slept in.* **sleep like a log** sleep soundly. **sleep off** get rid of by sleeping: *to sleep off a headache.* **sleep on** consider further before deciding: *I'll sleep on the idea.* **sleep over** stay overnight at someone's home. **sleep·o·ver** *n.* **sleep with** have sexual intercourse with.
sleep·er *n* 1 one that sleeps (in a given way): *She's a sound sleeper.* 2 a railway sleeping car. 3 a horizontal supporting beam. 4 a book, movie, etc. that is an unexpected hit: *Her first play was the sleeper of the season.* 5 a one-piece garment for infants. **sleeping bag** a zippered, lined bag for sleeping in, esp when camping. **sleeping car** a railway car with berths or small rooms for passengers to sleep in. **sleeping partner** a partner with no active part in managing the business. **sleeping pill** a pill containing a drug that causes sleep. **sleeping sickness** an infectious and generally fatal disease, caused by the bite of the tsetse fly and characterized by fever and lethargy. **sleep·walk** *v* walk around while asleep.

sleep·walk·er *n.* **sleep·walk·ing** *n.* **sleep·y** *adj* 1 ready to fall asleep. 2 showing sleepiness: *a sleepy smile.* 3 inducing sleep: *sleepy music.* 4 not active. **sleep·i·ly** *adv.* **sleep·i·ness** *n.*

sleet [slit] *n* 1 partly frozen rain often mixed with snow. 2 a fall or shower of sleet. **sleet** *v.* **sleet·y** *adj.* ⟨Middle English *slete*⟩

sleeve [sliv] *n* the part of a garment that covers the arm or part of the arm. **sleeve·less** *adj.* ⟨Old English *slīefe*⟩
laugh up (or **in**) **one's sleeve** See LAUGH. **up one's sleeve** hidden but ready for use when needed: *She had a trick up her sleeve.*

sleigh [slei] *n* a light, horse-drawn carriage mounted on runners for carrying passengers over snow or ice. **sleigh** *v.* ⟨Dutch *slee* variant of *slede* sled⟩

sleight of hand skill and quickness in moving the hands to produce an illusion.

slen·der ['slɛndər] *adj* 1 gracefully slim: *a slender hand.* 2 scanty; not adequate: *a slender income.* **slen·der·ness** *n.* ⟨Middle English *slendre*⟩ **slen·der·ize** *v* 1 make slender. 2 cause to look slender or less stout: *a slenderizing dress.*

slept [slɛpt] *v* pt and pp of SLEEP.

sleuth [sluθ] *n Informal* detective.
v be a detective. ⟨Old Norse *slōth* track⟩

slew[1] [slu] *v* pt of SLAY.

slew[2] [slu] *v* turn or swing on a pivot or as if on a pivot: *He slewed around in his seat to get a better look.* **slew** *n.* ⟨origin uncertain⟩

slew[3] [slu] *n Informal* a lot: *A whole slew of people got on the bus.* ⟨Irish Gaelic *sluagh* crowd⟩

slice [slʌis] *n* 1 a thin, flat, broad piece cut from something, esp food: *a slice of bread.* 2 a part; share: *She wanted a slice of the profits.*
v 1 cut into slices: *He sliced the loaf of bread.* 2 cut off as a slice: *I sliced a piece from the loaf.* 3 cut through like a knife: *A bullet sliced the air.* **slic·er** *n.* ⟨Old French *esclice* thin chip⟩
any way (or **no matter how**) **you slice it** no matter how you look at it. **slice of life** a realistic portrayal or view of everyday life.

slick [slɪk] *adj* 1 sleek; smooth: *slick hair.* 2 slippery; greasy: *a road slick with ice.* 3 clever. 4 smooth in manners, etc., esp so as to trick or deceive. 5 showing technical skill but lacking true artistry. 6 *Slang* fine, stylish, etc.: *a slick sports car.*
v make sleek or smooth.
n a smooth patch, esp a patch of oil, etc. on water or a paved road. **slick·ly** *adv.* **slick·ness** *n.* ⟨Old English *slician* make smooth⟩
slick·er *n* a long waterproof coat of oilskin.

slide [slʌid] *v* **slid, slid·ing** 1 move smoothly over a surface: *Drawers slide in and out.* 2 pass or put easily, or secretly: *She slid behind the curtains.* 3 pass by degrees; slip: *She has slid into bad habits.* 4 slip in an uncontrolled way: *The car slid into the ditch.* 5 *Baseball* throw the body along the ground to reach a base.
n 1 the act of sliding. 2 a piece of playground equipment consisting of a smooth inclined surface for sliding down. 3 something that works by sliding. 4 a mass of earth, snow, etc.

sliding down. **5** a small, thin sheet of glass on which objects are placed for examination under a microscope. **6** a small transparent photograph, viewed by projecting onto a screen. **slid·ing** *adj.* ⟨Old English *slīdan*⟩

let slide neglect; not bother about: *He has been letting his schoolwork slide lately.*

slide projector a device for projecting the image on a slide onto a screen or wall. **slide show** the presentation of photographic slides or computer-generated material. **slid·ing** *adj* adjusted relative to some variable: *a sliding fee that depends on income.*

slight [slǝit] *adj* **1** not much: *a slight ache.* **2** light and slender: *a girl of slight build.*
v treat as of little value; neglect: *He felt slighted because he was not asked to the party.*
n an act showing lack of respect or attention toward a person. **slight·ly** *adv.* **slight·ness** *n.* ⟨Old English *sliht* level; in compounds⟩

slight·ing *adj* contemptuous or disrespectful; belittling: *slighting remarks.* **slight·ing·ly** *adv.*

SYNONYMS

Slight emphasizes lack of consideration because one looks down on a person: *He slights his cousins because they are poor.*
Neglect emphasizes failing to give deserved attention or care to a person, duty, etc.: *He neglects his family.*

slim [slɪm] *adj* **slim·mer, slim·mest** **1** slender: *a slim waist.* **2** small; slight: *Her chances of escape are slim.* **slim, slimmed, slim·ming** *v.* **slim·ness** *n.* ⟨Dutch *slim* bad⟩

slime [slaɪm] *n* any soft, slippery, sticky substance, such as muck, the substance given off by snails and slugs, or semiliquid filth.
v **1** smear with, or as if with, slime. **2** *Slang* defame. ⟨Old English *slīm*⟩

slim·y *adj* **1** covered with slime; to do with slime. **2** treacherous; dishonourable; using flattery, insinuation, etc. **slim·i·ness** *n.*

sling [slɪŋ] *n* **1** a strip of leather with a string fastened to each end, for throwing stones by first whirling them around in the air. **2** a hanging loop of cloth fastened around the neck to support an injured arm or hand.
v **slung, sling·ing** **1** throw; fling. **2** hang so as to swing loosely: *The soldier's gun was slung over her shoulder.* **3** *Slang* mix; serve: *to sling hash.* ⟨perhaps Old Norse *slyngva*⟩

sling·shot *n* a Y-shaped stick with a band of rubber between its prongs, used to shoot pebbles, etc.; catapult.

slink [slɪŋk] *v* **slunk, slink·ing** move in a stealthy, guilty way. ⟨Old English *slincan*⟩

slink·y *adj* **1** furtive; sneaking. **2** of clothing, tight-fitting in an alluring, graceful way: *a slinky gown.* **slink·i·ly** *adv.* **slink·i·ness** *n.*

slip¹ [slɪp] *v* **slipped, slip·ping** **1** pass or move smoothly or quietly: *to slip one's coat off.* **2** slide suddenly by accident: *She slipped on the icy path.* **3** get loose or escape from: *His name has slipped my mind.* **4** make a mistake. **5** fall off; decline: *Car sales have slipped.*
n **1** the act or fact of slipping. **2** a cover that can be slipped on or off: *a pillow slip.* **3** a

dresslike or skirtlike undergarment worn by women and girls. **4** a mistake; error: *a slip in grammar.* **slip·page** *n.* ⟨probably Middle Low German *slippen*⟩

give someone the slip escape from someone. **let slip** tell without meaning to: *He let slip that she was pregnant.* **slip of the tongue** something said by mistake. **slip up** *Informal* make a mistake. **slip–up** *n.*

slip·cov·er *n* a removable, fitted cloth cover for a chair, chesterfield, etc. **slip–knot** *n* **1** a knot made to slip along the rope around which it is tied. **2** a knot that can be undone by a pull. Also, **slip·knot. slip–on** *adj* that can be put on or taken off easily without any fastenings. *n* a slip-on shoe or garment. **slip·per** *n* a light, soft, indoor shoe, easily slipped on and off. **slip·pered** *adj.* **slip·per·y** *adj* **1** so smooth, greasy, etc. as to cause slipping: *Wet streets are slippery.* **2** slipping away easily: *slippery, wet soap.* **3** difficult to handle, understand, etc.: *a slippery situation,* **slip·per·i·ness** *n.* **slip·shod** *adj* careless: *slipshod work.* **slip·stream** *n* **1** a backward-moving stream of air created beside a rapidly moving object, such as an aircraft. **2** the area of lower air pressure behind such an object.

slip² [slɪp] *n* **1** a small stem or shoot cut from a plant, used to grow a new plant. **2** a small strip of paper, cloth, etc.: *a sales slip.* **3** a young, slender person: *a slip of a boy.* ⟨probably Middle Dutch *slippen* cut⟩

slit [slɪt] *v* **slit, slit·ting** make a long, straight, narrow cut in: *She slit the envelope open.*
n a straight, narrow cut or opening: *a slit for a buttonhole.* **slit·ter** *n.* ⟨Middle English *slitten*⟩

slith·er [ˈslɪðər] *v* move or go with a gliding, zigzag, or winding motion: *The snake slithered away into the grass.* **slith·er** *n.* **slith·er·y** *adj.* ⟨Old English *slidrian*⟩

sliv·er [ˈslɪvər] *n* **1** a long, thin, sharp piece broken or cut off; splinter: *a sliver of wood.* **2** a very narrow slice: *a sliver of pie.*
v break into slivers. ⟨Old English *slīfan* split⟩

slob [slɒb] *n* **1** *Slang* a very untidy or boorish person. **2** ✱ Usually, **slob ice** densely packed chunks of sludgy ice, esp sea ice, often in a mass. ⟨probably Irish *slab, slaba* mud⟩

slob·ber [ˈslɒbər] *v* **1** let liquid run out from the mouth; drool: *The dog slobbered all over my skirt.* **2** speak in a silly, sentimental way. **slob·ber** *n.* **slob·ber·y** *adj.* ⟨Dutch *slobberen*⟩

slog [slɒg] *Informal v* **slogged, slog·ging** **1** plod heavily: *We slogged through the muskeg to the cabin.* **2** work steadily: *She slogged away at the assignment.* **slog** *n.* ⟨variant of *slug²*⟩

slo·gan [ˈslougən] *n* a word or phrase used by a business, club, political party, etc. to advertise its purpose; motto: *'Service with a smile' was the store's slogan.* ⟨Scots Gaelic *sluagh-ghairm; sluagh* army + *gairm* cry⟩

sloop [slup] *n* a sailboat having one mast, a mainsail, a jib, and sometimes other sails. ⟨Dutch *sloep* earlier *sloepe*⟩

slop [slɒp] *v* **slopped, slop·ping** **1** spill liquid on. **2** splash through mud, slush, or water.

n **1** liquid spilled around. **2** *Slang* food that is mushy and unappetizing. **3** *Slang* mawkish talk or writing: *How can you listen to that slop?* **4** Often, **slops** *pl* partly liquid waste, esp kitchen waste. **5** *Slang* a sloppy person. ⟨Middle English *sloppe* mud hole⟩
slop over overflow; spill over the edge of a container when it is tilted or bumped. **slop through** *Slang* do carelessly.
slop·py *adj* **1** very wet; slushy: *sloppy ground.* **2** careless: *sloppy writing.* **3** *Informal* mawkish: *sloppy sentiment.* **slop·pi·ly** *adv.* **slop·pi·ness** *n.*

slope [sloup] *v* lie or cause to lie at an angle: *a sloping roof.*
n **1** any line, surface, land, etc. that goes up or down at an angle: *a steep slope.* **2** the amount of slope. **slop·ing** *adj.* ⟨Old English *-slopen* pp of *-slūpan* slip⟩

slosh [slɒʃ] *v* **1** splash in slush, mud, or water: *We sloshed through the deep puddle.* **2** of liquid, splash around: *The soapy water sloshed on the floor when he shoved the pail.* ⟨perhaps blend of *slop* + *slush*⟩
sloshed *adj Slang* drunk.

slot [slɒt] *n* **1** a narrow opening or groove: *a coin slot.* **2** a place in a series or scheme: *a good time slot for a new TV show.* **3** *Hockey* **the slot** the area two or three paces in front of the goal crease. **4** *Informal* SLOT MACHINE.
v **slot·ted, slot·ting** place in a series or scheme: *Your interview has been slotted after the evening news.* ⟨Old French *esclot* cleavage⟩
slot machine a coin-operated gambling machine.

sloth [slɒθ] *or* [slouθ] *n* **1** laziness. **2** any of several slow-moving, tree-dwelling mammals that hang by all four feet from tree branches and feed on leaves and fruits. **sloth·ful** *adj.* ⟨*slow* + *-th* noun suffix⟩

slouch [slaʊtʃ] *v* stand, sit, walk, etc. in a lazy, drooping way: *Sit up straight; don't slouch.*
n **1** a slouching position. **2** a slovenly or inefficient person. ⟨origin uncertain⟩
be no slouch be surprisingly good at something.

slough¹ [slu] *or* [slaʊ] *n* **1** ✳ *West* a body of fresh water formed by rain or melted snow. **2** a soft, deep, muddy place; a mud hole, bog, backwater, etc. ⟨Old English *slōh*⟩

slough² [slʌf] *v* **1** cast off; shed: *The snake sloughed its skin.* **2** be shed or cast off: *A scab sloughs off when new skin takes its place.* **slough** *n.* ⟨Middle English *slugh(e), slouh*⟩

slov·en·ly ['slʌvənli] *adj* messy; careless; sloppy. **slov·en·li·ness** *n.* ⟨perhaps Flemish *sloef* dirty, Dutch *slof* careless⟩

slow [slou] *adj* **1 a** taking a relatively long time: *slow progress.* **b** moving at a low speed: *a slow current.* **2** behind schedule: *Mail delivery is slow today.* **3** of low mental ability. **4** indicating time earlier than the right time: *The clock is slow.* **5** not brisk or lively: *Business is slow.* .
v make or become slow or slower (often with *down*, sometimes *up*): *The car slowed to a stop. Slow down the pace a little.*

adv slowly. **slow·ly** *adv.* **slow·ness** *n.* ⟨Old English *slāw*⟩
slow–cook·er *n* an electric pot used for cooking food for hours at low temperature.
slow·down *n* a slowing down: *a slowdown in housing construction.* **slow motion** action at less than normal speed, esp as seen on film or videotape played more slowly than the speed at which it was recorded. **slow–mo·tion** *adj.* **slow·poke** *n Informal* a person who moves, or acts very slowly. **slow–wit·ted** *adj* not intelligent; dull; stupid.

USAGE
Slow and slowly are both used as adverbs. In most written English, **slowly** is preferred, except in road signs (*go slow*). Also, note the distinction between *This bus is going slow* (speed) and *The buses are running slow* (late).

sludge [slʌdʒ] *n* **1** soft mud; mire. **2** a soft, thick, muddy mixture, sediment, etc. **3** treated sewage. **4** small pieces of newly formed sea ice. **sludg·y** *adj.* ⟨origin uncertain⟩

slug¹ [slʌg] *n* **1** any of various gastropod molluscs resembling snails but having no shell. **2** a bullet. **3** a roundish lump of metal. **4** a small disk, such as one used illegally instead of a coin in a coin-operated machine. ⟨Middle English *slugg* sluggard⟩
slug·gard ['slʌgərd] *n* a lazy, idle person. **slug·gard** *adj.* **slug·gish** *adj* slow, esp due to a lack of energy: *a sluggish mind, a sluggish economy.* **slug·gish·ly** *adv.* **slug·gish·ness** *n.*

slug² [slʌg] *Informal v* **slugged, slug·ging** hit hard with the fist, a bat, or a blunt weapon.
n Informal a hard blow. ⟨origin uncertain⟩
slug·ger *n* a person who hits hard or well, as a boxer, a batter in baseball, etc.

sluice [slus] *n* **1** a gate for controlling a flow of water. **2** the channel controlled by such a gate. **3** something that controls the flow of anything: *War opens the sluices of bloodshed.* **4** a sloping trough through which water flows, used to wash gold from sand, dirt, etc. *v* **1** flow in a stream; rush: *Water sluiced down the channel.* **2** flush, wash out (gold), or propel (logs) with water. ⟨Old French *escluse*, Latin *exclusa* pp of *excludere*. See EXCLUDE.⟩

slum [slʌm] *n* Often, **slums** *pl* an area in a city, characterized by poor housing and sanitation, and social problems. **slum·my** *adj.* ⟨origin uncertain⟩
slum·lord *n Informal* an absentee owner of slum property, esp one who charges exorbitant rent.

slum·ber ['slʌmbər] *v* **1** sleep, esp peacefully. **2** be inactive or dormant: *The volcano had slumbered for years.*
n Sometimes, **slumbers** *pl* sleep: *deep in slumber. His slumbers were broken by the sound of a siren.* ⟨Old English *slūma*⟩

slump [slʌmp] *v* **1** drop suddenly and heavily: *He slumped to the floor in a faint.* **2** have a drooping posture: *They slumped in their seats.* **3** go into a decline in activity, performance, etc. **slump** *n.* ⟨perhaps imitative⟩

slung [slʌŋ] [slʌŋ] *v* pt and pp of SLING.

slunk [slʌŋk] *v* pt and pp of SLINK.

slur [slɜr] *v* **slurred, slur·ring** 1 utter (sounds, words, etc.) indistinctly. 2 *Music* sing or play (two or more tones) so they are connected smoothly. 3 insult; slight.
n 1 a slurred pronunciation. 2 an insulting or slighting remark. ⟨Middle English *slor* mud⟩
slur ice ✸ *Maritimes* a thin mixture of mushy ice and water, found especially near shore.

slurp [slɜrp] *Informal v* eat or drink with a sucking sound. **slurp** *n*. ⟨Dutch *slurpen* lap⟩

slush [slʌʃ] *n* 1 partly melted snow. 2 finely ground ice, flavoured and sweetened. **slush·y** *adj*. ⟨origin uncertain⟩
slush fund 1 money set aside for special projects. 2 money set aside for dishonest purposes such as bribery.

slut [slʌt] *n* a woman of loose morals. **slut·tish** *adj*. ⟨Middle English *slutte, slotte*⟩

sly [slaɪ] *adj* **sly·er** or **sli·er, sly·est** or **sli·est** 1 clever in deceiving: *The sly cat stole the meat while her back was turned.* 2 underhanded; not straightforward: *sly questions.* 3 playfully mischievous: *a sly wink.*
n **on the sly** in a way meant to avoid notice; secretly: *They got their information on the sly.* **sly·ly** *adv*. ⟨Middle English *slēgh* skilful⟩

smack¹ [smæk] *n* 1 a slight taste, trace, or suggestion: *a smack of nutmeg.* 2 *Slang* heroin.
v have a smack: *The Irishman's speech smacked of the Old Country.* ⟨Old English *smæcc*⟩

smack² [smæk] *v* 1 slap. 2 open (the lips) quickly so as to make a sharp sound. 3 kiss loudly. 4 make a sharp, slapping sound.
adv 1 *Informal* suddenly and sharply; with or as if with a smack. 2 exactly: *smack in the middle.* **smack** *n*. ⟨imitative⟩

smack³ [smæk] *n* a small sailboat with one mast. ⟨probably Dutch *smak*⟩

small [smɒl] *adj* 1 not large in size, degree, importance, etc.: *a small house, small bills.* 2 young: *small children.* 3 of low social position: *people great and small.* 4 with little land, capital, etc.: *a small businessman.* 5 quiet; low: *a small voice.* 6 mean: *That was small of you.* 7 of letters, lower-case.
n a part that is small or narrow, esp the lower back: *the small of the back.* **small·ish** *adj*. **small·ness** *n*. ⟨Old English *smæl*⟩
feel small be ashamed or humiliated.
small change 1 coins of small value, such as nickels. 2 anything small and unimportant.
small claims court a court with limited jurisdiction, handling civil cases involving small claims for breach of contract or debt.
small fry 1 children. 2 unimportant people or things. **small game** relatively small wild animals and birds such as rabbits, grouse, etc., hunted as game. Compare BIG GAME.
small hours the early hours of the morning, from midnight to 3 or 4 a.m. **small letter** a lower-case letter. **small–mind·ed** *adj* petty.
small potatoes *Informal* an unimportant person or thing: *The last deal was just small potatoes compared with this one.* **small·pox** *n* an acute, contagious viral disease, now

thought to be eradicated, characterized by blisters that leave permanent pitlike scars called pocks. **small–scale** *adj* 1 small in operation or scope: *a small-scale import business.* 2 of a map, etc., drawn to a small scale, not permitting much detail. **small screen** television. **small–screen** *adj*. **small talk** light, informal conversation. **small–time** *adj Slang* minor: *a small-time crook.*

smarm·y ['smɑrmi] *Informal adj* ingratiating; obsequiously flattering. **smarm·i·ness** *n*. ⟨dialect *smalm* plaster down⟩

smart [smɑrt] *adj* 1 clever: *a smart child.* 2 neat: *He looked smart in his uniform.* 3 stylish. 4 sharp; severe: *a smart slap.* 5 brisk: *a smart pace.* 6 witty in a disrespectful or annoying way: *Don't get smart!* 7 to do with some degree of artificial intelligence.
v feel or cause to feel sharp pain or irritation: *The cut smarts. She smarted from the rebuke.*
n 1 a sharp pain or feeling of resentment: *He still felt the smart of her rejection.* 2 **smarts** *pl Informal* astuteness; sense. **smart·ly** *adv*. **smart·ness** *n*. ⟨Old English *smeorten*⟩
smart al·eck or **al·ec** ['ælɪk] an obnoxious person who tries to show, esp by flippant retorts, that he or she is very clever. **smart–a·leck·y, smart–a·leck** or **smart–a·lec** *adj*. **smart·ass** *Slang n, adj* smart aleck. **smart·en** *v* 1 improve in appearance. 2 make or become brisker or more alert. **smarten up** come or bring to one's senses.

smash [smæʃ] *v* 1 break into pieces with violence and noise: *to smash a window.* 2 destroy utterly (often with *up*). 3 crash or hit hard: *The car smashed into a tree.*
n 1 the act or sound of smashing: *The two cars collided with a terrific smash.* 2 *Informal* an instant popular success.
adj instantly popular; very successful. ⟨blend of *smack²* and *mash*⟩
smashed *adj Slang* very drunk. **smash hit** a very successful pop song, film, etc. **smash–up** *n* 1 a bad motor vehicle accident. 2 *Informal* complete ruin or destruction.

smat·ter·ing ['smætərɪŋ] *n* 1 a slight knowledge of a language or a subject: *I've picked up a smattering of Italian.* 2 a small quantity. ⟨Middle English *smateren* talk idly⟩

smear [smɪr] *v* 1 cover or mark with anything sticky, greasy, or dirty: *Her face was smeared with jam.* 2 spread (oil, paint, etc.): *to smear ointment on a sore.* 3 blur: *Don't smear the ink.* 4 deliberately harm the reputation of: *She tried to smear her opponent by suggesting he had accepted bribes while in office.*
n 1 the act or result of smearing. 2 a small amount of blood, etc. spread on a slide to be examined under a microscope. **smear·y** *adj*. ⟨Old English *smerian; smeoru* grease⟩
smear campaign a planned series of efforts to damage someone's reputation.

smell [smɛl] *v* **smelled** or **smelt, smell·ing** 1 detect the odour of: *I smell smoke.* 2 sniff (at) in order to detect an odour: *Smell the meat to see if it's off.* 3 give out a certain smell (with *of* or *like*): *to smell of curry.* 4 give out a

bad smell: *Damp socks smell.* **5** detect or have a suggestion (of): *I smelled trouble. The plan smells of trickery.*
n **1** the sense of smelling: *Smell is keener in dogs than in people.* **2** the peculiar odour of a thing: *the smell of burning cloth.* **3** a trace. **smell·er** *n.* ⟨Middle English *smellen*⟩
smell out track down by or as if by smelling: *to smell out a thief.* **smell up** *Informal* cause to have a bad smell: *That dog is smelling up the whole house.*
smelling salts a form of ammonia that, when inhaled, helps to relieve faintness, headache, etc. **smell·y** *adj* giving off a strong and unpleasant odour. **smell·i·ness** *n.*

SYNONYMS

Smell is the general word, but often suggests that the effect is unpleasant: *She never got used to the farmyard smells.* **Odour** is often interchanged with smell, but is more neutral: *I find the odour of hay especially pleasing.* **Scent** is usually used when the effect is pleasant: *He loves the scent of roses.*

smelt¹ [smɛlt] *v* **1** melt (ore) in order to get metal out of it. **2** obtain or refine (metal) by melting. **smelt·er** *n.* ⟨Middle Dutch *smelten*⟩
smelt² [smɛlt] *n, pl* **smelt** or **smelts** any of various small, edible fishes having a long, slender, silvery body. ⟨Old English⟩
smelt³ [smɛlt] *v* a pt and a pp of SMELL.
smid·gen ['smɪdʒən] *n Informal* a tiny piece or amount: *toast with just a smidgen of butter.* ⟨origin uncertain⟩
smile [smaɪl] *v* **1** show pleasure, amusement, favour, etc., or sometimes scorn, by an upward curve of the mouth. **2** look pleasantly or agreeably; look with favour: *The gods have smiled on us.* **smile** *n.* **smil·er** *n.* **smil·ing·ly** *adv.* ⟨Middle English *smilen*⟩
smirk [smɜrk] *v* smile in a self-satisfied way. **smirk** *n.* ⟨Old English *smearcian* smile⟩
smite [smaɪt] *v* **smote**, **smit·ten** or **smote**, **smit·ing** **1** *Archaic, poetic* strike with force: *The waves smote upon the shore.* **2** have a sudden, strong effect on: *His conscience smote him.* ⟨Old English *smītan*⟩
smit·ten ['smɪtən] *adj* **1** suddenly and strongly affected: *smitten with terror.* **2** *Informal* very much in love. **3** *Informal* very favourably impressed: *We were quite smitten with her idea.*
smith [smɪθ] *n* **1** a craftsperson who makes things out of metal (mainly in compounds): *a goldsmith.* **2** a blacksmith. ⟨Old English⟩
smith·y ['smɪθi] *or* ['smɪði] *n* the workshop of a smith, esp a blacksmith.
smith·er·eens [ˌsmɪðəˈrinz] *n pl Informal* small broken bits: *smashed to smithereens.* ⟨apparently Irish *smidirín* fragments⟩
smit·ten See SMITE.
smock [smɒk] *n* a loose, coatlike garment worn to protect clothing.
v ornament with smocking: *a dress with a smocked bodice.* ⟨Old English *smocc*⟩
smock·ing *n* decorative stitching made by

gathering material closely with rows of stitches in a honeycomb pattern.
smog [smɒg] *n* polluted air hanging low in the atmosphere and perceptible to the eye or nose. **smog·gy** *adj.* ⟨blend of *smoke* + *fog*⟩
smoke [smouk] *n* **1** the mixture of gases and particles of carbon that rises from anything burning. **2** something resembling this. **3** *Physics, chemistry* gas containing solid particles. **4** the act of smoking tobacco.
v **1** give off smoke, esp undesirably: *The fireplace smokes.* **2 a** inhale the smoke from (a pipe, cigarette, etc.). **b** smoke tobacco as a habit. **3** preserve or flavour (meat, fish, etc.) by exposing to smoke. **4** drive (out or away) by or as if by smoke. **5** stupefy (bees, etc.) with smoke. **6** darken or stain with smoke. **smoke·less** *adj.* **smok·er** *n.* **smok·y** *adj.* ⟨Old English *smoca*⟩
go up in smoke be unsuccessful; fail to materialize, as a plan or dream.
smoke and mirrors manoeuvres meant to create a false impression. **smoke detector** a device that emits a piercing noise to indicate the presence of excessive smoke or heat in the area. **smoke·house** *n* an outbuilding where meat or fish is smoked. **smoke screen** **1** a mass of thick smoke used to hide a ship, aircraft, etc. from the enemy. **2** anything used to hide or disguise: *a smoke screen of misinformation.* **smoke·stack** *n* a tall chimney, as on a factory or ship. **smoking gun** *Informal* proof of wrongdoing.
smooch [smutʃ] *v, n Slang* kiss. **smooch·y** *adj.*
smooth [smuð] *adj* **1** having an even, flat surface, like glass or still water: *smooth stones.* **2** characterized by easy movement: *smooth sailing.* **3** without lumps: *smooth sauce.* **4** without hair: *a smooth face.* **5** without trouble: *a smooth course of affairs.* **6** polite, usually insincerely: *smooth talk.* **7** not harsh in taste, sound, etc.: *smooth wine.* **smooth** *v.* **smooth·ly** *adv.* **smooth·ness** *n.* ⟨Old English *smōth*⟩
smooth out (or **away**) get rid of (troubles, difficulties, etc.). **smooth over** make seem less wrong or noticeable: *The teacher tried to smooth over the argument between the two girls.*
smor·gas·bord ['smɔrgəsˌbɔrd] *n* **1** a buffet meal, featuring a large variety of meats, salads, etc. **2** any wide variety to choose from. ⟨Swedish *smörgås* sandwich + *bord* table⟩
smote [smout] *v* a pt of SMITE.
smoth·er ['smʌðər] *v* **1** make unable to get air; kill in this way: *The murderer smothered his victim with a pillow.* **2** be unable to breathe freely: *I almost smothered in that stuffy room.* **3** cover thickly: *In the fall the grass is smothered with leaves.* **4** deaden or put out by covering thickly: *to smother a fire.* **5** suppress: *She smothered a laugh.* **6** hamper or oppress by too much affection, protection, etc. **smoth·er·ing** *n, adj.* ⟨Middle English *smorther* suffocate⟩
smoul·der or **smol·der** ['smouldər] *v* **1** burn and smoke without flame. **2** exist in a

suppressed state: *Their discontent smouldered for years before breaking into open rebellion.* **3** show suppressed feeling: *His eyes smouldered with anger.* ⟨Middle English *smolderen*⟩

smudge [smʌdʒ] *n* **1** a smear. **2** a smoky fire made to drive away insects or to protect plants from frost. **smudge** *v.* **smudg·y** *adj.* ⟨origin uncertain⟩

smug [smʌg] *adj* **smug·ger, smug·gest** too pleased with one's own goodness, cleverness, respectability, etc. **smug·ly** *adv.* **smug·ness** *n.* ⟨orig neat, spruce; probably Dutch *smuk*⟩

smug·gle ['smʌgəl] *v* **1** secretly take (things) into or out of a country which are banned by law or on which duty has not been paid: *to smuggle heroin, to smuggle watches.* **2** bring, take, etc. secretly: *He smuggled the puppy into his room.* **smug·gler** *n.* **smug·gling** *n, adj.* ⟨Low German *smuggeln*⟩

smut [smʌt] *n* **1** soot, dirt, etc. **2** obscene talk, writing, or pictures. **3** any of various plant diseases characterized by formation of sooty masses of spores on the affected plant parts. **smut·ty** *adj.* ⟨Old English *smitte*; influenced by *smudge*⟩

snack [snæk] *n* a light meal: *She eats a snack before going to bed.*
v eat a snack. ⟨Middle Low German *snakken*⟩
snack on eat as a snack.
snack bar a counter where light meals, coffee, etc. are served.

snag [snæg] *n* **1** a sharp or rough projecting point, such as the broken end of a branch. **2** a hidden or unexpected obstacle: *He had to drop his plans because of a snag.* **3** a pulled or broken thread in fabric.
v **snagged, snag·ging 1** run or catch on a point. **2** acquire; get hold of: *How did he snag that job?* ⟨Scandinavian⟩

snail [sneil] *n* **1** any gastropod mollusc with a spirally coiled shell, esp those species that live on land or in fresh water. **2** a lazy or slow-moving person or animal. **snail–like** *adj.* ⟨Old English *snegel*⟩
snail's pace a very slow pace. **snail–paced** *adj.*

snake [sneik] *n* **1** any of a suborder of reptiles with an elongated, scaly-skinned body, and no legs, moving by means of undulations of the body. **2** a crafty, treacherous person. **3** a long, flexible metal rod for clearing drains.
v move, wind, or curve like a snake. **snake-like** *adj.* ⟨Old English *snaca*⟩
snake in the grass a sly, treacherous person. **snake-bite** *n* the bite of a poisonous snake, or the resulting condition. **snake charmer** a person with an apparent power to hypnotize snakes. **snake dance 1** a procession of people who join hands or hold the waist of the person in front, and dance in a weaving path. **2** a ceremonial dance among certain peoples in which snakes are handled, invoked, etc. **snake oil** any liquid presented as a cure-all or tonic but having no true medicinal properties. **snake·skin** *n* leather made from the skin of a snake. **snak·y** *adj* **1** of or like a snake. **2** curving, or twisting: *a*

snaky path up the hill. **3** sly; treacherous. **snak·i·ly** *adv.* **snak·i·ness** *n.*

snap [snæp] *v* **snapped, snap·ping 1** make or cause to make a sudden, sharp sound: *She snapped her fingers to the music.* **2** move, shut, etc. with a snap: *The latch snapped into place.* **3** break suddenly with a sharp sound: *The violin string snapped.* **4** become suddenly unable to bear a strain: *Her nerves snapped.* **5** bite or snatch; seize (often with *at* or *up*): *The dog snapped at my hand.* **6** speak sharply: *"Silence!" snapped the captain.* **7** move quickly and sharply: *to snap to attention.* **8** of the eyes, seem to flash or spark: *Her eyes snapped with anger.* **9** take a snapshot of. **10** *Football* pass (the ball) between the legs to start play.
n **1** the act or sound of snapping: *The box shut with a snap.* **2** *Informal* energy: *Put some snap into it.* **3** DOME FASTENER. **4** a thin, crisp cookie: *a gingersnap.* **5** *Informal* snapshot. **6** *Slang* a very easy job, piece of work, etc.: *The exam was a snap.* **7** *Football* the act of snapping the ball.
adj done quickly or unexpectedly: *a snap election.* ⟨Middle Dutch *snappen*⟩
cold snap a short spell of cold weather. **snap out of it** *Informal* change one's attitude suddenly. **snap up** accept or buy eagerly.
snap·per *n* **1** any of a family of marine fishes of warm waters. **2** SNAPPING TURTLE. **snapping turtle** any of a family of edible, freshwater turtles with powerful, hooked jaws. **snap·pish** *adj* **1** curt and irritable. **2** apt to bite or snap. **snap·py** *adj* **1** *Informal* brisk: *a snappy pace.* **2** *Informal* chilly: *a snappy fall day.* **3** *Informal* stylish: *a snappy dresser.* **4** snappish. **make it snappy** *Informal* hurry. **snap·pi·ly** *adv.* **snap·pi·ness** *n.* **snap·shot** *n* a photograph taken hastily with a simple camera.

snare¹ [snɛr] *n* **1** a noose or other simple trap to catch small animals and birds. **2** anything regarded as a trap: *caught in the snare of popularity.* **snare** *v.* ⟨Old Norse *snara*⟩

snare² [snɛr] *n* one of the strings or wires stretched across the bottom of a drum (**snare drum**), causing it to make a rattling sound when struck. ⟨probably Middle Dutch⟩

snark·y ['snɑrki] *adj Slang* sarcastic: *No snarky comments, please!* **snark·i·ly** *adv.* **snark·i·ness** *n.* ⟨Dutch *snorken* to snore⟩

snarl¹ [snɑrl] *v* **1** of a dog, etc., growl and bare the teeth: *The dog snarled at the stranger.* **2** speak in an angry, menacing tone. **snarl** *n.* **snarl·y** *adj.* ⟨earlier *snar*; compare Middle Dutch *snarren* rattle⟩

snarl² [snɑrl] *n* a tangle; confused mess: *She combed the snarls out of her hair. His affairs were all in a snarl.* **snarl** *v.* **snarl·y** *adj.* ⟨*snarl¹*⟩

snatch [snætʃ] *v* **1** seize suddenly: *I snatched my jacket and ran.* **2** take suddenly (with *off, away,* etc.): *He snatched off his hat.* **3** attain narrowly or by quick action: *to snatch victory from defeat.* **4** *Slang* steal: *to snatch a purse.*
n **1** the act of snatching: *She made a snatch at the ball.* **2** a bit: *snatches of conversation.* **snatch·er** *n.* ⟨compare Middle Dutch *snakken*⟩
snatch at try to seize or grasp.

snaz·zy ['snæzi] *adj Slang* attractive in a showy and stylish way: *a snazzy new car.* **snaz·zi·ly** *adv.* **snaz·zi·ness** *n.* ⟨perhaps blend of *snappy* and *jazzy*⟩

sneak [snik] *v* **sneaked** or **snuck** (esp def. 1), **sneak·ing** **1** move in a stealthy way: *He snuck into the kitchen to get a cookie.* **2** take, put, etc. in a stealthy way: *to sneak a cookie.* **3** act in a cowardly way (usually with *around*).
n a dishonest, cowardly person.
adj stealthy; underhand: *a sneak thief, a sneak attack.* ⟨Old English *snican*⟩
sneak out of avoid by slyness.
sneak·er *n* **1** RUNNING SHOE. **2** one who sneaks.
sneak·ing *adj* **1** that one cannot justify or does not like to confess: *a sneaking suspicion.* **2** mean and cowardly. **sneak preview** a special showing of a film prior to regular distribution, as a test of audience reaction. **sneak thief** a person who takes advantage of open doors, windows, etc. to steal. **sneak·y** *adj* sly, mean, or underhand. **sneak·i·ly** *adv.* **sneak·i·ness** *n.*

sneer [snir] *v* smile, laugh, speak, etc. so as to show contempt or scorn: *She sneered at his attempts to curry favour with the boss.* **sneer** *n.* **sneer·ing** *adj.* ⟨Middle English *sneren*⟩

sneeze [sniz] *v* expel air suddenly and violently through the nose and mouth by an involuntary spasm. **sneeze** *n.* ⟨Middle English *snesen, fnesen,* Old English *fnēosan*⟩
not to be sneezed at *Informal* not to be made light of or despised: *A savings of ten dollars is not to be sneezed at.*

snick·er ['snɪkər] *n* a half-suppressed, usually disrespectful laugh. **snick·er** *v.* ⟨imitative⟩

snide [snaɪd] *adj* spitefully or slyly sarcastic: *snide remarks.* **snide·ly** *adv.* **snide·ness** *n.* ⟨perhaps Dutch; compare *snijdend* cutting⟩

sniff [snɪf] *v* **1** draw air through the nose in short breaths that can be heard. **2** smell with sniffs (often with *at*): *to sniff a new perfume.* **3** inhale (the fumes of): *to sniff glue.* **4** show contempt by or as if by sniffing: *to sniff at an inexpensive gift.* **5** suspect; detect: *The police sniffed a plot and broke up the meeting.* **sniff** *n.* ⟨Middle English *sniffen*⟩
sniff out smell out.
snif·fle *v* **1** sniff again and again: *The child stopped crying, but kept on sniffling.* **2** breathe audibly through a partly clogged nose. *n* **1** the act or sound of sniffling. **2 the sniffles** a head cold marked by a runny nose and sniffling. **snif·fler** *n.* **snif·fly** *adj.*

snig·ger ['snɪgər] *n, v* snicker.

snip [snɪp] *v* **snipped, snip·ping** cut with a small, quick stroke: *He snipped the thread.* *n* **1** the act or sound of snipping: *With a few snips she cut out a paper doll.* **2** a small piece cut off: *Pick up the snips of cloth from the floor.* **3** *Informal* **a** a small or unimportant person. **b** a cheeky, impertinent person. **4 snips** *pl* hand shears for cutting metal. **snip·per** *n.* ⟨Dutch *snippen*⟩
snip·pet ['snɪpɪt] *n* a scrap; fragment: *snippets of information.* **snip·py** *adj Informal* **1** sharp; curt. **2** haughty; disdainful.

snipe [snaɪp] *n, pl* **snipe** or **snipes** any of several shore birds of the sandpiper family, . *v* shoot from a hidden place at one enemy or target at a time. **snip·er** *n.* ⟨Old Norse *-snípe* orig snapping bird⟩
snipe at attack unexpectedly, esp in words.

snip·pet, snip·py See SNIP.

snit [snɪt] *n Informal* a state of agitation, esp of peevish annoyance.

snitch¹ [snɪtʃ] *v Slang* pilfer. **snitch·er** *n.* ⟨origin unknown⟩

snitch² [snɪtʃ] *Slang v* tell (*on* someone). *n* an informer. ⟨orig nose; origin uncertain⟩

sniv·el ['snɪvəl] *v* **-elled** or **-eled, -el·ling** or **-el·ing** **1** cry with sniffling. **2** whine. **sniv·el** *n.* **sniv·el·ler** or **sniv·el·er** *n.* ⟨Old English *snyflan; snofl* mucus⟩

snob [snɒb] *n* **1** a person who cares too much for social position, is too anxious to imitate people above him or her and too ready to ignore those below. **2** a person who has contempt for the popular taste, and is attracted to esoteric things for their own sake: *a wine snob.* **snob·ber·y** *n.* **snob·bish** *adj.* **snob·by** *adj.* ⟨origin uncertain⟩

snook·er ['snʊkər] *n* a type of pool played with 15 red balls, a white cue ball, and 6 other balls of different colours. Compare POOL² (def. 1).
v **1** leave (one's opponent) in the position of being unable to aim directly at the object ball and having to reach it off the cushion. **2** place (someone) in a difficult or frustrating situation; thwart. **3** outwit. ⟨origin unknown⟩

snoop [snup] *Informal v* sneak around trying to find or find out things; pry.
n a person who snoops. **snoop·y** *adj.* ⟨Dutch *snoepen* eat in secret⟩

snoot·y ['snuti] *adj Informal* snobbish; conceited. **snoot·i·ly** *adv.* **snoot·i·ness** *n.* ⟨slang *snoot* nose; orig Scots variant of *snout*⟩

snooze [snuz] *Informal v, n* nap; sleep; doze. ⟨origin uncertain⟩

snore [snɔr] *v* breathe with a harsh, rough sound while asleep. **snore** *n.* **snor·er** *n.* ⟨Middle English *snoren;* perhaps imitative⟩

snor·kel ['snɔrkəl] *n* a curved tube held in the mouth to enable a swimmer to breathe just below the surface of water.
v **-kelled** or **-keled, -kel·ling** or **-kel·ing** swim and explore underwater, using a snorkel to breathe. ⟨Low German slang *snorkel* nose⟩

snort [snɔrt] *v* **1** force the breath violently through the nose with a loud, harsh sound: *The horse snorted.* **2** make a sound like this: *The engine snorted.* **3** *Slang* ingest (a powdered narcotic, esp cocaine) by inhaling it. *n* **1** the act or sound of snorting. **2** *Slang* a small, quick drink, esp of liquor taken neat. **snort·er** *n.* ⟨*snore*⟩

snot [snɒt] *n* **1** *Vulgar* mucus from the nose. **2** *Slang* an insolent, disrespectful person. **snot·ty** *adj.* ⟨Old English *gesnot*⟩

snout [snʌut] *n* the projecting part of the head of an animal, containing the nose, mouth, and jaws. ⟨Middle English *snoute*⟩

snow [snou] *n* **1** water vapour frozen in the upper atmosphere and falling to earth in crystal form. **2** *Slang* cocaine or heroin. **3** a pattern of dots on a television screen caused by interference with the signals.
v **1** be the case that snow or something like it is falling (with the subject *it*): *It has been snowing all night.* **2** cover, block, shut in, etc. with snow or as if with snow (with *in, up, under,* etc., and usually in the passive): *The town was snowed in for a week after the blizzard. She is snowed under with work.* **3** *Slang* deceive by glib talk. ⟨Old English *snāw*⟩

snow angel a shaped depression in the snow resembling a traditional angel figure, made by lying down and moving the arms and legs over the surface of the snow. **snow·ball** *n* a rounded mass of pressed snow, thrown in play. *v* increase or accumulate ever more quickly: *Demands for a public inquiry are snowballing.* **snow·bank** *n* a large mass or drift of snow, esp one thrown up by a snowplow. **snow·bird** *n* a tourist who travels to the warm south to escape the winter in Canada or the northern US and returns home in late spring. **snow blindness** inflammation of the eyes, caused by overexposure to the glare of sunlight on snow or ice, resulting in temporary blindness. **snow–blind** *adj.* **snow·blow·er** *n* a machine that clears snow by drawing it in by means of a large fan and blowing it out in another direction. **snow·board** *n* a short board with upturned ends, for standing on while sliding down a snowy slope. **snow·board·er** *n.* **snow·board·ing** *n.* **snow·bound** *adj* snowed in. **snow–capped** *adj* topped with snow: *snow-capped peaks.* **snow·drift** *n* a mass of snow piled up by the wind. **snow·drop** *n* any of a genus of spring-blooming, bulbous herbs of the amaryllis family with drooping, white, bell-shaped flowers. **snow·fall** *n* **1** a fall of snow. **2** the amount of snow falling within a certain time and area: *The snowfall at Banff in that one storm was 30 cm.* **snow fence** a lath and wire fence erected in winter alongside roads, etc. to prevent snow from drifting. **snow·field** *n* a large expanse of snow. **snow·flake** *n* a feathery crystal or mass of crystals of snow. **snow goose** a wild goose that breeds in the Arctic, the adult typically white with black wing tips. See also BLUE GOOSE. **snow·house** *n* **1** an igloo. **2** formerly, among the Inuit, a large building of snow blocks intended for communal gatherings. **3** a crude hut, cave, or fort made out of snow as a form of play. **snow job** *Slang* an effort to persuade or deceive by flattering or glib talk. **snow leopard** a leopard of the central Asian mountains, whose coat is grey marked with dark spots. **snow line** a height on mountains, etc. above which there is snow all year round. **snow·man** *n, pl* **-men** a mass of snow made into a figure shaped somewhat like a man. **snow·melt** *n* liquid resulting from the melting of snow. **snow·mo·bile** *n* **1** a small, open vehicle for travelling over snow and ice, with skis at the front and a caterpillar track. **2** a large, closed-in vehicle similar to this, designed to carry persons, goods, etc.; bombardier. *v* travel by snowmobile. **snow·mo·bil·er** *n.* **snow·mo·bil·ing** *n, adj.* **snow·pack** *n* the snow accumulating over an area during the winter and melting in the spring. **snow·pants** *n* warm pants, often waterproof worn in cold or snowy weather over regular pants. **snow pea** a variety of pea whose pods, eaten whole, are flat, sweet, and crisp. **snow·plow** or **snow·plough** *n* **1** a large machine for clearing snow from streets, etc. by means of a large blade. **2** a skiing manoeuvre used for stopping, in which the tips of the skis are pointed toward each other. *v* to stop, using this manoeuvre. **snow·shoe** *n* either of a pair of light frames with a network of strips stretched across them, worn on the feet to keep from sinking in deep, soft snow. *v* walk or travel on snowshoes. **snow·sho·er** *n.* **snowshoe hare** a hare with very large, broad hind feet which in winter are heavily furred. **snow·slide** *n* the sliding down of a mass of snow on a steep slope. **snow·storm** *n* a storm with falling snow. **snow·suit** *n* a warm, heavily padded outer garment, worn esp by children in cold or snowy weather. **snow tire** a tire with deep tread for extra traction when driving in snow. **snow–white** *adj* white as snow. **snow·y** *adj* **1** with falling snow: *a snowy day.* **2** covered with snow or like snow. **3** white: *snowy hair.* **snowy owl** a large owl having mainly white plumage.

snub [snʌb] *v* **snubbed, snub·bing** treat coldly or with contempt.
n **1** a rebuff or slight. **2** a sudden stop. ⟨Old Norse *snubba* reprove⟩
snub nose a short, turned-up nose.
snub–nosed *adj.*

snuck [snʌk] *v* a pt and a pp of SNEAK.

snuff¹ [snʌf] *v* **1** draw up into the nose. **2** sniff; smell (*at*): *The dog snuffed at my hand.* *n* **1** powdered tobacco. **2** an act or the sound of snuffing. ⟨Middle Dutch *snuffen* sniff⟩
up to snuff *Informal* in perfect order or condition; as good as expected.
snuff·box *n* a small, often ornamented box for holding snuff.

snuff² [snʌf] *v* **1** put out (a flame, esp on a candle). **2** *Slang* murder.
adj of a pornographic film, showing sexual activity ending in murder of one partner by the other. ⟨Middle English⟩
snuff out a extinguish. **b** put an end to completely: *to snuff out all hope of freedom.*
snuf·fer *n* a device for extinguishing a candle.

snuf·fle [ˈsnʌfəl] *v* **1** breathe noisily through a partly clogged nose. **2** smell; sniff.
n **1** the act or sound of snuffling. **2 the snuffles** *Informal* a stuffed-up condition of the nose, caused by a cold, hay fever, etc. **snuf·fly** *adj.* ⟨*snuff²* or its source⟩

snug [snʌg] *adj* **snug·ger, snug·gest 1** warm and comfortable: *The cat found a snug corner behind the stove.* **2** neat and compact: *snug cabins on a boat.* **3** fitting closely: *That coat is a little too snug.* **4** hidden: *He lay snug until the searchers passed by.* **snug·ly** *adv.* **snug·ness** *n.* ⟨compare Swedish *snygg* neat, trim⟩
snug·gle *v* **1** lie closely together for warmth or comfort or from affection; nestle; cuddle. **2** hold or draw close. **snug·gly** *adj.*

> **SYNONYMS**
> **Snug** emphasizes the comfort and security of a small space: *The children were snug in their beds.* **Cosy** emphasizes warmth and contentment: *a cosy corner by the fire.*

snye [snaɪ] *n* ✹ *Ontario* a side channel of a stream, esp one that bypasses a falls or rapids. ⟨Cdn. French *chenail*; compare French *chenal* channel⟩

so [sou] *adv* **1** in this or that way; as shown: *Hold your pen so.* **2** as described: *She was always active and is still very much so.* **3** to this or that degree: *Don't walk so fast.* **4** to a certain unspecified maximum degree: *I can only do so much.* **5** to the same degree (*as*): *He was not so old as she was.* **6** very: *You are so kind.* **7** likewise; also: *She likes dogs; so does he.* **8** indeed (used emphatically to contradict a negative): *I did so clean my room!*
adj true (only predicatively): *Is that really so, or are you making it up?*
conj **1** with the effect that: *The snow had drifted so it resembled a giant lying on its back.* **2** in order that: *Go away so I can rest.* **3** and therefore: *The dog was hungry, so we fed it.*
interj **1** well! I see! **2** (interrogatively) what does it matter?
pron **1** approximately that: *an hour or so.* **2** the same; whatever has just been said: *He was lazy and I told him so.* ⟨Old English *swā*⟩
and so forth or **and so on** et cetera; and other things of the same sort. **just so** *Informal* exactly correct(ly) and in order: *She insists on everything being just so.* **or so** more or less: *It cost a dollar or so.* **so much for a** that is enough said or done about: *So much for my opinion; now let's hear yours.* **b** it is clear that (something) has completely failed to live up to expectations: *So much for their 'sale to end all sales!'* **so that a** with the result that. **b** with the purpose that. **c** provided that; as long as: *I don't care how much it costs, just so that I know it's done right.* **so what?** why should anyone care about that?
so–and–so *n* **1** a person or thing not named. **2** *Informal* an unpleasant person. **so–called** *adj* called thus improperly: *Her so-called friend gossips about her.*

soak [souk] *v* **1** make very wet. **2** stay or leave in liquid until wet through. **3** remain in a bath, etc. for relaxation or therapy. **4** be absorbed (often with *in* or *into*): *Just let that idea soak in for a while.* **5** absorb or suck (*up*): *A sponge soaks up water.* **6** *Slang* make pay (too much): *He soaked me $80 for a tow!*
n **1** the process of soaking. **2** *Slang* a heavy drinker. ⟨Old English *socian*⟩

soap [soup] *n* **1** a lathering substance used with water for washing. **2** *Slang* money, esp a bribe. **3** *Informal* SOAP OPERA.
v rub with soap. **soap·y** *adj.* ⟨Old English *sāpe*⟩
no soap *Slang* **a** no; that is an unacceptable proposal. **b** no results; no success.
soap·box *n* **1** a box used as a platform by open-air speakers or agitators. **2** a position, forum, etc. exploited to make opinionated or impassioned addresses to the public: *The Letters page is not a soapbox for fanatics.* **soap opera** a radio or television drama presented in serial form, usually featuring emotional situations involving human relationships. **soap·stone** *n* a heavy, soft stone that feels somewhat like soap and is much used for carving; steatite. **soap·suds** *n pl* bubbles and foam made with soap and water.

soar [sɔr] *v* **1** fly upward or at a great height: *The eagle soared without flapping its wings.* **2** move through the air on rising air currents: *A glider can soar for a great distance.* **3** of sales, prices, etc., rise rapidly and to an extreme level: *During the tourist season, hotel rates soared.* **4** rise above the common and ordinary; aspire: *soaring ambition.* ⟨Old French *essorer*; Latin *ex-* out + *aura* breeze⟩

sob [sɒb] *v* **sobbed, sob·bing 1** cry with short breaths. **2** make a sound like a sob: *The wind sobbed.* **sob** *n.* ⟨Middle English *sobben*⟩
sob story *Informal* a story calculated to arouse pity for the teller.

so·ber ['soubər] *adj* **1** not drunk. **2** serious: *a sober expression.* **3** sensible: *sober judgment.* **4** dark in colour: *sober greys.*
v make or become sober: *The experience of being lost in the bush sobered her.* **so·ber·ly** *adv.* **so·ber·ness** *n.* ⟨Old French; Latin *sobrius*⟩
sober up (or **down** or **off**) **a** recover or cause to recover from drunkenness. **b** make or become serious, quiet, or solemn.
so·bri·e·ty [sə'braɪəti] *n* soberness; esp temperance, moderation, or seriousness.

so·bri·quet [ˌsoubrə'kei], ['soubrəˌkei], *or* [-ˌkɛt] *n* nickname. Also, **sou·bri·quet.** ⟨French⟩

soc·cer ['sɒkər] *n* a game played between two teams of eleven players each, using a round ball. In soccer, only the goalie may touch the ball with hands and arms. ⟨*assoc.*, for *association (football); -er* as in *rugger*⟩

so·cia·ble ['souʃəbəl] *adj* **1** liking company: *They are a sociable family and love company.* **2** marked by conversation, for: *a sociable afternoon.* **so·cia·bil·i·ty** *n.* **so·cia·bly** *adv.* ⟨Latin *sociare* associate; *socius.* See SOCIAL.⟩

> **CONFUSABLES**
> **Sociable** describes one's disposition, and means being inclined to seek and enjoy company: *He is a sociable child and says hello to everyone.* **Social** suggests being in the habit of mingling with others at events intended for this purpose: *They are a very social couple and entertain often.*

so·cial ['souʃəl] *adj* **1** to do with the life of humans in communities: *social problems.*

2 naturally living in organized communities: *Ants are social insects.* **3** for friendly group activity: *a social club.* **4** taking part in group events: *She is a social person.*
n an informal gathering for fun, of people who usually meet for other purposes. **so·cial·ly** *adv.* ⟨Latin *socius* companion⟩
social assistance ✹ benefits paid through SOCIAL INSURANCE programs. See also WELFARE. **social climber** a person who actively tries to gain admission to a group with higher social standing. **social contract** the agreement on which all government depends, namely the consent of the governed to give up certain personal liberties in exchange for protection. **social credit** an economic theory and political movement that aimed to increase consumer purchasing power. **Social Credit Party** ✹ a Canadian political party founded in Alberta in the 1930s. **social insurance** benefits, such as old-age pension, welfare, family allowance, unemployment insurance, etc., provided by a government. **Social Insurance Number** ✹ a nine-digit number by which the federal government identifies an individual for purposes of income tax, pension, etc. *Abbrev* **SIN**. **so·cial·ism** *n* a political and economic system in which the means of production and distribution are owned or managed by a democratically elected authority. Compare CAPITALISM, COMMUNISM. **so·cial·ist** *n, adj.* **so·cial·ite** *n* a person who is prominent in fashionable society. **so·cial·ize** *v* **1** make social; make fit for living with others. **2** engage in social activity: *She liked to socialize after class.* **3** regulate in accordance with socialism, esp by bringing under control of a government. **so·cial·i·za·tion** *n.* **social science** the study of people's activities, and their customs in relationship to others. Sociology, economics, anthropology, and political science are social sciences. **social scientist. social security** *esp US* SOCIAL INSURANCE. **social studies** a subject in elementary schools that includes elements of history, geography, sociology, civics, economics, etc. **social work** work intended to improve social conditions in a community, with such services as clinics, counselling, recreational activities, etc. **social worker.**
so·ci·e·ty [sə'saɪəti] *n* **1 a** all the people of a particular place and time who have developed organized cultural and social institutions: *Laws are for the good of society.* **b** a particular form of such organization: *Urban society is a recent phenomenon.* **2** people thought of as a group because of their common economic position, attitudes, etc.: *in cultivated society.* **3** the fashionable or privileged people in a community: *a society ball.* **4 a** club, association, etc. **5** company: *I enjoy the society of my friends.* **6** *Ecology* an interdependent community of organisms. **so·ci·e·tal** *adj.* ⟨Latin *societas; socius.* See SOCIAL.⟩
(Religious)Society of Friends a Christian sect, also called the QUAKERS. **Society of Jesus** the Jesuits, a Roman Catholic religious order for men.

so·ci·o– ['souʃou] *or* ['sousiou] *combining form* to do with the social behaviour of humans: *sociopolitical.*
so·ci·o–e·co·nom·ic [-ˌɛkə'nɒmɪk] *or* [-ˌikə-] *adj* to do with social and economic matters: *a socio-economic study on poverty in big cities.*
so·ci·ol·o·gy *n* the study of the structure and development of human society, dealing with such issues as power, poverty, or crime, and with institutions such as marriage or the church. **so·ci·o·log·i·cal** *adj.* **so·ci·ol·o·gist** *n.*
so·ci·o·path [-ˌpæθ] *n* a person in whom psychopathic personality leads to a complete lack of responsibility. **so·ci·o·path·ic** *adj.*
sock¹ [sɒk] *n* **1** a cloth foot covering extending above the ankle, sometimes to the knee. **2** windsock. ⟨Latin *soccus*⟩
sock away *Informal* save up (money).
sock² [sɒk] *Slang v* punch hard. **sock** *n.* ⟨origin uncertain⟩
sock·et ['sɒkɪt] *n* **1** a hollow part or piece for receiving and holding something: *the eye socket.* **2** an electrical outlet. ⟨Anglo-French *soket; soc* ploughshare; Celtic⟩
sock·eye ['sɒk,aɪ] *n, pl* **sock·eye** or **sock·eyes** a Pacific salmon whose red, oily flesh is highly valued for its flavour. ⟨Salish *suk-kegh* red fish, altered by folk etymology⟩
So·crat·ic [sə'krætɪk] *adj* to do with Socrates (5c B.C.), a famous Athenian philosopher.
Socratic method the use of a series of questions to lead students to think, to make opponents contradict themselves, etc.
So·cred ['sou,krɛd] *n* ✹ *Informal* a member of the SOCIAL CREDIT PARTY.
sod [sɒd] *n* **1** ground covered with grass. **2** a layer of ground including grass and its roots. *v* **sod·ded, sod·ding** cover with sods. ⟨Middle Dutch *sode*⟩
under the sod dead and buried.
sod·bust·er *n Slang* a prairie farmer, esp an early homesteader or one raising crops instead of livestock. **sod·dy** *n Western North America* a simple dwelling with roof and sometimes walls made of sods. Also, **sod house, hut,** or **shack. sod–turning** *n* the first breaking of ground for digging the foundations of a building, often celebrated with a ceremony.
so·da ['soudə] *n* **1** any of several substances containing sodium, such as sodium bicarbonate. **2** SODA WATER. **3** flavoured soda water, often containing ice cream. **4** *US* SOFT DRINK; POP¹ (def. 2). ⟨Latin⟩
soda cracker a simple cracker made with little or no sugar or shortening, often sprinkled with salt before baking. **soda fountain** in a restaurant, etc., an apparatus dispensing pop or, formerly, soda water and flavoured syrups, by means of taps. **soda water** water charged with carbon dioxide to make it fizz.
sod·den ['sɒdən] *adj* **1** soaked through: *His clothing was sodden with rain.* **2** dull-witted, esp from drunkenness. **sod·den·ly** *adv.* **sod·den·ness** *n.* ⟨old pp of *seethe*⟩

so·di·um ['soudiəm] *n* a soft metallic element which reacts violently with water and occurs naturally in compounds. *Symbol* Na ⟨*soda*⟩
sodium bi·car·bo·nate [baɪ'kɑrbənɪt] *or* [-,neɪt] baking soda, a powdery white salt used in cooking, medicine, etc.; bicarbonate of soda. **sodium chlo·ride** ['klɔraɪd] common salt.

sod·o·my ['sɒdəmi] *n* anal sexual intercourse. **sod·om·ite** *n*. **sod·om·ize** *v*. ⟨*Sodom* a city in the Bible destroyed for its wickedness⟩

–soever *suffix* no matter——; ——ever: *whosoever, whatsoever, whensoever, wheresoever, howsoever.*

so·fa ['soufə] *n* a long, upholstered seat with a back and arms; couch; chesterfield. ⟨French; Arabic *ṣuffah*⟩
sofa bed a sofa that opens out into a bed.

sof·fit ['sɒfɪt] *n* the under surface of an arch, eave, cornice, etc. ⟨Italian *soffitto*; Latin *sub*-under + *figere* fix⟩

soft [sɒft] *adj* 1 not hard; yielding readily to pressure: *a soft pillow.* 2 more easily cut, bent, etc., than other things of the same kind: *Pine wood is soft.* 3 not sharp or contrasting: *soft shadows.* 4 fine in texture; not rough or coarse: *soft fur.* 5 not harsh, loud, intense, etc.: *a soft voice.* 6 gentle; tender: *a soft heart.* 7 lacking in endurance, self-discipline, etc.: *grown soft from lack of exercise.* 8 *Phonetics* of the consonants *c* and *g*, pronounced as [s] *city* and [dʒ] *gem*, not as in *corn* and *get.* 9 *Informal* easy; easy-going, esp excessively so: *a soft job.* 10 of water, relatively free of mineral salts that prevent soap from lathering. 11 of a drug, not seriously addictive or harmful to health. 12 of currency or the stock market, unstable; tending to decline. 13 Also, **soft–core** of pornography, not very explicit. **soft·en** ['sɒfən] *v*. **soft·en·er** *n*. **soft·ly** *adv*. **soft·ness** *n*. ⟨Old English *sōfte*⟩
soft in the head foolish. **soft on a** lenient toward. **b** fond of or infatuated with.
soft·ball *n* a modified baseball game using a larger, softer ball. **soft–boiled** *adj* of eggs, boiled only briefly so that the yolk is still liquid. **soft·bound** *adj* of a book, having covers of paper or a similar flexible material; paperback. **soft·cov·er** *adj, n* softbound. **soft drink** a non-alcoholic carbonated drink. **soft–heart·ed** *adj* gentle; kind; tender. **soft·ie** or **soft·y** *n Informal* 1 a soft-hearted person. 2 one who is easily imposed upon. **soft palate** the fleshy back part of the roof of the mouth; velum. **soft pedal** on a piano or other instrument, a pedal used to reduce volume or resonance. **soft–ped·al** *v* **-alled** or **-aled**, **-al·ling** or **-al·ing** 1 use a pedal to soften (tones on a piano, organ, etc.). 2 *Informal* de-emphasize: *They soft-pedalled some of the party's less popular policies.* **soft return** *Computers* a RETURN (def. 7) that starts a new line, but not a new paragraph. **soft sell** *Informal* a sales approach that uses indirect persuasion rather than aggressive tactics. **soft–sell** *adj*. **soft soap** *Informal* flattery. **soft–soap** *v*. **soft–spo·ken** *adj* speaking gently

or with a soft voice. **soft spot 1** affection: *She still had a soft spot for her first boyfriend.* **2** a vulnerable point. **soft touch** *Informal* one who lends or gives money easily. **soft·ware** *n* computer programs. **soft·wood** *n* a tree with needles and soft wood, such as pine or fir.

sog·gy ['sɒgi] *adj* thoroughly wet; soaked: *a soggy washcloth.* **sog·gi·ly** *adv*. **sog·gi·ness** *n*. ⟨dialect *sog* bog, swamp; Scandinavian⟩

soh [sou] *n Music* SOL.

soil¹ [sɔɪl] *n* 1 earth; dirt; esp the top layer in which plants grow. 2 **the soil** farming as a way of life or livelihood: *people of the soil.* ⟨Latin *solium* seat, influenced by *solum* soil⟩

soil² [sɔɪl] *v* 1 make or become dirty; stain: *He soiled his clothes. White shirts soil easily.* 2 disgrace: *to soil the family name.*
n 1 dirt; stains. 2 sewage or manure. ⟨Old French *soillier*; Latin *suile* pigsty; *sus* pig⟩

soi·rée or **soi·ree** [swɑ'reɪ] *n* an evening party or social gathering. ⟨French; *soir* evening⟩

so·journ ['soudʒɜrn] *or* [sou'dʒɜrn] *v* stay for a time: *to sojourn in a foreign land.* **so·journ** ['soudʒɜrn] *n*. **so·journ·er** *n*. ⟨Old French *sojorner*; Latin *sub* under + *diurnus* of the day⟩

sol [soul] *n Music* 1 the fifth tone of an eight-tone major scale. 2 the tone G. ⟨Latin *Solve*, word sung on this note in a medieval song set to the scale⟩
sol–fa ['soul ,fɑ] *Music n* the syllables used to represent the tones of any scale: do, re, mi, fa, so(l), la, ti, do.

sol·ace ['sɒlɪs] *n* comfort or relief, or a source of this: *She found solace from her troubles in music.* **sol·ace** *v*. ⟨Latin *solacium*; *solari* console⟩

so·lar ['soulər] *adj* to do with the sun: *a solar eclipse, a solar year.* ⟨Latin *sol* sun⟩
solar cell a small device for converting sunlight into electrical energy. **solar flare** a brief eruption of gases on the sun. **so·lar·i·um** [sə'lɛriəm] *n, pl* **-lar·i·ums** or **-lar·i·a** [-'lɛriə] a sunroom or sunporch. **solar panel** a panel on a roof, etc., that collects solar radiation so the energy can be converted to electricity or heat. **solar plexus 1** *Anatomy* the network of nerves behind the stomach. **2** *Informal* the pit of the stomach. **solar system** the sun and all the planets, satellites, etc. within its gravitational field. **solar wind** the flow of charged particles from the sun into space. **solar year** the time taken for one revolution of the earth around the sun; about 365 days.

sold [sould] *v* pt and pp of SELL.

sol·der ['sɒdər] *n* a metal that can be melted and used for joining metal surfaces. **sol·der** *v*. ⟨Old French *soldure*; Latin *solidus* solid⟩
sol·der·ing iron an electric tool that is heated in order to melt and apply solder.

sol·dier ['souldʒər] *n* 1 a person who serves in an army, esp a private. 2 a person who serves in any cause. 3 of certain ants or termites, an individual adapted for defence. *v* act or serve as a soldier. **sol·dier·ly** *adj*. ⟨Old French; *solde* pay; Latin *solidus* Roman coin⟩
soldier on carry on despite difficulty.

soldier of fortune 1 a person ready to serve in any army for money or adventure. **2** any person in pursuit of adventure.

sole¹ [soul] *adj* **1** only: *the sole heir, the sole survivors.* **2** restricted to one person or group; exclusive: *the sole right of use.* **sole·ly** *adv.* ⟨Latin *solus*⟩

sole² [soul] *n* **1** the bottom of the foot. **2** the bottom of a shoe, slipper, boot, etc. *v* put a sole on. ⟨Old French *sole*; Latin *solea; solum* bottom, ground⟩

sole³ [soul] *n, pl* **sole** or **soles** any of various flatfishes. ⟨Latin *solea* orig sole²⟩

sol·e·cism ['sɒlə,sɪzəm] *n* **1** a violation of grammar or usage. **2** a breach of etiquette. ⟨Greek *soloikismos* supposedly from *Soloi* colony in Cilicia⟩

sol·emn ['sɒləm] *adj* **1** serious; earnest; grave: *a solemn face.* **2** evoking serious thoughts: *solemn music.* **3** strictly observed in accord with ritual and tradition. **sol·emn·ly** *adv.* **sol·em·ness** *n.* ⟨Latin *sollemnis*⟩ **so·lem·ni·ty** *n* **1** a solemn quality. **2** Often, **solemnities** *pl* a solemn, formal ceremony: *The solemnities were concluded with a prayer by the college chaplain.* **sol·em·nize** *v* perform (a rite): *The marriage was solemnized in the cathedral.* **sol·em·ni·za·tion** *n.*

so·le·noid ['soulə,nɔɪd] *or* ['sɒlə,nɔɪd] *n Electricity* a spiral or cylindrical coil of wire that acts like a magnet when a current passes through it. ⟨Greek *sōlēn* pipe⟩

so·lic·it [sə'lɪsət] *v* **1** ask (for) or try to get· *to solicit for donations.* **2** influence to do wrong, as by bribing: *to solicit a judge.* **3** accost (a person) to offer sex for money. **so·lic·i·ta·tion** *n.* ⟨Latin *sollicitare; sollus* all + *citus* stirred up⟩ **so·lic·it·ing** *n.* **so·lic·i·tor** *n* **1** one who solicits something. **2** a lawyer. **solicitor general** *pl* **solicitors general 1** in Canada: **a** the federal cabinet minister in charge of law enforcement and correctional services. **b** *Alberta* the minister in charge of correctional services. **c** *Ontario* the minister in charge of the police. Compare ATTORNEY GENERAL. **2** a law officer ranking just below an attorney general. **so·lic·i·tous** *adj.* showing care or concern for others. **so·lic·i·tous·ly** *adv.* **so·lic·i·tude** *n.*

sol·id ['sɒlɪd] *adj* **1** not liquid or gas: *Water becomes solid when it freezes.* **2** not hollow: *a solid chocolate egg.* **3** hard; firm: *solid ground.* **4** sound, reliable, etc.: *solid construction.* **5** of a single substance, colour, etc. throughout: *a solid gold brooch.* **6** unbroken: *It rained for three solid days.* **7** *Mathematics* having length, breadth, and thickness: *A cone is a solid figure.* **8** good, but not creative: *a solid performance.* *n* **1** a substance that is not a liquid or a gas. **2** a body with length, width, and thickness. **so·lid·i·fy** *v.* **so·lid·i·ty** *n.* **sol·id·ly** *adv.* ⟨Latin *solidus*⟩ **in solid with** *Informal* on a favourable footing: *to get in solid with one's employer.*

sol·i·dar·i·ty *n* fellowship or unity, esp against opposition, arising from common interests.

sol·id–state *adj Electronics* using the properties of solid materials, esp semiconductors: *a solid-state radio receiver.*

so·lil·o·quy [sə'lɪləkwi] *n* **1** a speech made by an actor to himself or herself when alone on the stage. **2** the act of talking to oneself. **so·lil·o·quist** *n.* **so·lil·o·quize** *v.* ⟨Latin *solus* alone + *loqui* speak⟩

sol·ip·sism ['sɒlɪp,sɪzəm] *n Philosophy* the theory that the only real or knowable thing is the self. **sol·ip·sist** *n.* **sol·ip·sis·tic** *adj.* ⟨Latin *solus* alone + *ipse* self⟩

sol·i·taire ['sɒlə,tɛr] *or* [,sɒlə'tɛr] *n* **1** any of various card games played by one person. **2** a diamond or other gem set by itself. ⟨French; Latin *solitarius*⟩

sol·i·tar·y ['sɒlə,tɛri] *adj* **1** single; only: *a solitary rider.* **2** away from people: *a solitary life. n* **1** *Informal* SOLITARY CONFINEMENT. **2** recluse. **sol·i·tar·i·ness** *n.* ⟨Latin *solitarius; solus* alone⟩

solitary confinement total isolation of one prisoner from others, often as a penalty for misbehaviour in prison.

sol·i·tude ['sɒlə,tjud] *or* ['sɒlə,tud] *n* **1** the condition of being alone: *He hates solitude.* **2** a lonely place. **3** loneliness. ⟨Latin *solitudo; solus* alone⟩

so·lo ['soulou] *n* a piece of music arranged for or performed by one voice or instrument. *adj* **1** arranged for or performed by one voice or instrument: *a solo part.* **2** done or acting alone: *a solo violin, a solo flight.* **so·lo** *adv, v.* **so·lo·ist** *n.* ⟨Italian = alone; Latin *solus*⟩

so long *Informal* goodbye; farewell. ⟨by folk etymology from Arabic *salaam*⟩

sol·stice ['sɒlstɪs] *or* ['soulstɪs] *n* either of the two times in the year when the sun is furthest from the celestial equator. In the Northern Hemisphere, June 21 or 22, the **summer solstice**, is the longest day of the year and December 21 or 22, the **winter solstice**, is the shortest. **sol·sti·tial** [sɒl'stɪʃəl] *or* [soul-] *adj.* ⟨Latin *solstitium; sol* sun + *sistere* stand still⟩

sol·u·ble ['sɒljəbəl] *adj* **1** that can be dissolved: *Salt is soluble in water.* **2** able to be solved. ⟨Latin *solubilis; solvere* dissolve⟩ **sol·ute** ['sɒljut] *n* a solid, gas, etc. dissolved in a liquid. **so·lu·tion** *n* **1** the act or process of solving. **2** an explanation or answer: *The police are seeking a solution to the crime.* **3** *Mathematics* the set of values that satisfy a given equation. **4** the process of dissolving or condition of being dissolved: *Sugar and salt can be held in solution in water.* **5** a liquid or mixture formed by dissolving.

solve [sɒlv] *v* find the answer to; figure out;

explain: *The puzzle was never solved.* **solv·er** *n.*
solv·a·ble *adj.* ⟨Latin *solvere* loosen⟩
sol·ven·cy ['sɒlvənsi] *n* the ability to pay all one owes. **sol·vent** ['sɒlvənt] *adj* **1** able to pay all one owes. **2** able to dissolve another substance. *n* a substance, usually a liquid, that can dissolve other substances.
so·mat·ic [sə'mætɪk] *adj* to do with the body as opposed to the mind. ⟨Greek *sōma* body⟩
somatic cell any of the cells of an organism other than the reproductive or germ cells.
som·bre ['sɒmbər] *adj* **1** dark: *a sombre, cloudy day.* **2** serious; sober, grave, or solemn. Also, **som·ber**. **som·bre·ly** *adv.* **som·bre·ness** *n.*
⟨French; Latin *sub-* under + *umbra* shade⟩
som·brer·o [sɒm'brɛrou] *n* a broad-brimmed hat with a high crown, worn esp in Mexico. ⟨Spanish; Latin *sub-* under + *umbra* shade⟩
some [sʌm] *adj* **1** certain, but not known or not named: *Some people own cars.* **2** a number or quantity of: *some years ago.* **3** a; any: *Ask some passerby for help.* **4** *Informal* remarkably big, good, poor, etc.: *That was some storm!*
pron **1** certain unnamed persons or things: *Some say so.* **2** a certain number or quantity: *She ate some and threw the rest away.*
adv **1** *Informal* to some degree or extent; somewhat: *He's some better today.* **2** *Informal* to a great degree or extent: *That's going some!* **3** approximately (a given number of): *Some twenty people saw it.* ⟨Old English *sum*⟩
and then some *Informal* and a good deal more than that, too.
some·bod·y ['sʌm,bʌdi] *or* [-,bɒdi]; ['sʌmbədi] *pron* a person not known or not named. *n* an important person: *She acts as if she were somebody.* **some·day** *adv* at some unknown future time. **some·how** *adv* in a way not known or not stated: *I'll finish this work somehow.* **somehow or other** in one way or another. **some·one** *pron* a person not known or not named. **some·place** *adv* in or to some place; somewhere. **some·thing** *n* **1** a particular thing not named or not known: *I've got something to tell you.* **2** a thing or person of some value or importance: *At least you tried; that's something.* **3** a remarkable person or thing: *Isn't he something!* **something like** to some extent like: *He is something like his father.* **some·time** *adv* at an indefinite past or future time: *Come over sometime.* *adj* **1** former: *a sometime pupil of the school.* **2** being so only at times: *a sometime supporter.* **some·times** *adv* now and then; at times. **some·what** *adv* to some degree: *somewhat tired.* **somewhat** (or **something**) **of** to some extent: *She is something of a traditionalist.* **some·where** *adv* **1** in, at, or to some place: *He lives somewhere in the neighbourhood.* **2** at some point along a continuum or in a series: *a colour somewhere between blue and green.* *n* some indefinite place: *a ticket to somewhere.* **get somewhere** *Informal* make progress.
–some[1] *suffix* **1** tending to be or do: *meddlesome.* **2** causing: *awesome, troublesome.* ⟨Old English *-sum*⟩

–some[2] *suffix* a group of (a given quantity): *a twosome, a foursome.* ⟨*some*⟩
som·er·sault ['sʌmər,sɒlt] *n* a complete roll of the body, forward or backward, bringing the feet over the head. **som·er·sault** *v.* ⟨Middle English *sombresault;* Provençal *sobresaut;* Latin *supra* over + *saltus* jump⟩
som·nam·bu·late [sɒm'næmbjə,leit] *v* walk around while asleep. **som·nam·bu·lant** *adj.* **som·nam·bu·la·tion** *n.* **som·nam·bu·la·tor** *n.* ⟨Latin *somnus* sleep + *ambulare* walk⟩
som·no·lent ['sɒmnələnt] *adj* **1** sleepy; drowsy. **2** causing sleepiness. **som·no·lence** *n.* ⟨Latin *somnolentus; somnus* sleep⟩
son [sʌn] *n* **1** someone's male child or descendant. **2** a male thought of as being produced or formed by something: *a son of the revolution.* **3** the **Son** *Christianity* Jesus Christ as the second person of the Trinity. ⟨Old English *sunu*⟩
son–in–law *n, pl* **sons–in–law** the husband of one's daughter. **son·ny** ['sʌni] *n Informal* a term of address for a young boy. **Son of God** *Christianity* Jesus Christ. **Son of Man** *Christianity* Jesus Christ, esp as the promised Messiah.
so·nar ['sounɑr] *n* a device using reflected underwater sound waves for navigation, range finding, detecting submerged objects, etc. ⟨*so*und *na*vigation *a*nd *r*anging⟩
so·na·ta [sə'nɑtə] *n Music* a composition for one or two instruments, traditionally having three or four movements. ⟨Italian *sonata* sounded (on an instrument); Latin *sonus* sound⟩
song [sɒŋ] *n* **1** a short poem set to music. **2** a poetry: *fame celebrated in song.* **b** a poem with a lyrical quality. **3** a a piece of music suitable for voice. **b** any piece of music. **4** the act of singing: *to burst into song.* ⟨Old English *sang*⟩
for a song for very little money. **song and dance** **a** a complicated account, often intended to impress or deceive. **b** fuss: *She made a great song and dance about being late.* **song·bird** *n* a bird with vocal organs specialized for producing melodic calls. **song·writ·er** *n* a composer of music, lyrics, or both, esp a composer of pop songs.
son·ic ['sɒnɪk] *adj* to do with or using sound waves. ⟨Latin *sonus* sound⟩
sonic boom the sound, like an explosion, of the shock wave formed in front of an aircraft travelling above the speed of sound.
son·net ['sɒnɪt] *n* a poem having 14 lines, usually in iambic pentameter, and a certain arrangement of rhymes. ⟨Provençal *sonet;* Latin *sonus* sound⟩
so·no·gram ['sounə,græm] *or* ['sɒnə,græm] *n* **1** *Medicine* the visual image produced by reflected sound waves using ultrasound equipment. **2** *Physics* a graphic representation of sound patterns. ⟨Latin *sonus* sound + *-GRAM*⟩ **so·no·graph** *n* a machine that produces sonograms. **so·nog·ra·phy** [sə'nɒgrəfi] *n.*
son·o·rous ['sɒnərəs] *or* ['sounərəs] *adj* **1** of sound, full, rich, or deep. **2** of words, having an impressive sound: *sonorous phrases, a*

sonorous style. **so·nor·i·ty** [sə'nɔrəti] *n.*
son·o·rous·ly *adv.* ⟨Latin *sonor* sound⟩

soon [sun] *adv* **1** in a short time: *I'll see you soon.* **2** early: *I must go soon.* **3** promptly: *As soon as I hear, I'll call you.* **4** willingly: *I would as soon die as yield.* ⟨Old English *sōna* at once⟩
sooner or later ultimately; eventually.

soot [sʊt] *n* a black powder, mostly carbon, in the smoke from burning coal, wood, oil, etc. **soot·y** *adj.* ⟨Old English *sōt*⟩

sooth·say·er ['suθ,seiər] *n* a fortuneteller or prophet. ⟨Old English *sōth* truth⟩

soothe [suð] *v* **1** comfort; make calm: *to soothe a crying child.* **2** ease (pain, grief, etc.). **sooth·ing** *adj.* ⟨Old English *sōthian*⟩
sooth·er *n* a baby's pacifier.

sop [sɒp] *n* **1** a piece of food dipped or soaked in milk, broth, etc. **2** something given to appease or quiet; bribe.
v **sopped, sop·ping 1** dip or soak. **2** wipe or mop (*up*): *Sop up the water with a cloth.* **3** of liquid, soak in or through: *The water sopped through the rug.* ⟨Old English *sopp*⟩
sop·ping *adj* extremely wet; dripping; soaked.

soph·ism ['sɒfɪzəm] *n* a clever but misleading or specious argument. **soph·ist** *n.* **so·phis·tic** [sə'fɪstɪk] *adj.* **soph·ist·ry** *n.* ⟨Greek *sophisma*; *sophos* clever⟩

so·phis·ti·cate [sə'fɪstə,keit] *v* **1** cause to lose one's natural simplicity and innocence and take on worldly ways. **2** make more informed, polished, and cultured. **3** refine (technology, methods, etc.) and make more complex. *n* [-kɪt] a worldly-wise, cultured person. **so·phis·ti·cat·ed** *adj.* **so·phis·ti·ca·tion** *n.* ⟨Greek *sophistikos* sophistic; *sophos* clever⟩

soph·ist·ry See SOPHISM.

soph·o·more ['sɒfə,mɔr] *US n* a student in the second year of college or high school. **soph·o·more** *adj.* ⟨earlier *sophomer* orig doing dialectic exercises; *sophom* variant of *sophism*⟩
soph·o·mor·ic *adj* conceited and pretentious but crude and ignorant.

sop·o·rif·ic [,sɒpə'rɪfɪk] *adj* tending to cause sleep. **sop·o·rif·ic** *n.* ⟨Latin *sopor* deep sleep⟩

so·pran·o [sə'prænou] *n Music* **1** the highest singing voice for women, girls, or boys. **2** an instrument having the highest range in a family of instruments. ⟨Italian; *sopra* above; Latin *supra*⟩

sor·cer·y ['sɔrsəri] *n* magic performed with the aid of evil spirits; witchcraft; black magic. **sor·cer·er** *n.* **sor·cer·ess** *n.* **sor·cer·ous** *adj.* ⟨Old French *sorcerie*; Latin *sors* lot⟩

sor·did ['sɔrdɪd] *adj* **1** dirty; filthy: *living in a sordid hut.* **2** morally disgusting. **3** motivated by greed. **sor·did·ly** *adv.* **sor·did·ness** *n.* ⟨Latin *sordidus* dirty; *sordes* dirt⟩

sore [sɔr] *adj* **1** feeling or causing physical pain or emotional distress: *a sore throat, a sore*

subject. **2** *Informal* angry: *He is sore at missing the game.* **3** severe: *in sore need of improvement.*
n a painful place on the body where the skin or flesh is broken or bruised.
adv Archaic very: *sore afraid.* **sore·ly** *adv.* **sore·ness** *n.* ⟨Old English *sār*⟩
sore·head ['sɔr,hɛd] *n Slang* a touchy person.

sor·ghum ['sɔrgəm] *n* a cornlike grass widely grown as a cereal crop. ⟨Latin *syricum* Syrian⟩

so·ror·i·ty [sə'rɔrəti] *n* a club or society of women or girls, esp at a university. Compare FRATERNITY. ⟨Latin *soror* sister⟩

sor·rel[1] ['sɔrəl] *n* a reddish brown horse. **sor·rel** *adj.* ⟨Old French *sorel*; *sor* brown⟩

sor·rel[2] ['sɔrəl] *n* **1** any of several plants of the buckwheat family, with bitter leaves used in salads and as flavouring. **2** a Caribbean hibiscus with red flowers. **3** a sweet, red drink made from this plant. ⟨Old French *surele*; *sur* sour⟩

sor·row ['sɔrou] *n* **1** grief; sadness; regret. **2** a cause of this; trouble; misfortune: *Her sorrows have aged her.* **3** mourning; outward expression of grief or regret. **sor·row** *v.* **sor·row·ful** *adj.* **sor·row·ing** *adj.* ⟨Old English *sorg*⟩

sor·ry ['sɔri] *adj* **1** feeling pity, regret, sympathy, etc.; sad: *I'm sorry that you're sick.* **2** wretched; poor; pitiful: *The shack they lived in was a sorry sight.* **3** worthless: *a sorry excuse.* *interj* **a** I am sorry. **b** (with rising intonation) Pardon? ⟨Old English *sārig*; *sār* sore⟩
be sorry suffer the ill consequences of one's actions: *If you don't behave, you'll be sorry!*

sort [sɔrt] *n* **1** a kind; class; character: *What sort of work does he do?* **2** a person or thing of a certain kind: *She's a good sort.* **3** the act of sorting: *to do an alphabetical sort on a list.*
v arrange by kinds or classes: *Sort these cards by colour.* ⟨Old French *sorte*; Latin *sors* lot⟩
of a sort or **of sorts a** of some kind. **b** of a poor or mediocre quality. **out of sorts** ill or cross. **sort of** *Informal* **a** somewhat: *I'm sort of scared.* **b** in a way: *I didn't work at this poem, it just sort of came to me.* **sort out a** find and separate from others. **b** *Informal* resolve; make sense of: *to sort out one's problems.*

sor·tie ['sɔrti] *n* **1** a sudden attack by troops from a defensive position. **2** a single round trip of a military aircraft against an enemy. ⟨French *sortie*; *sortir* go out⟩

S O S **1** a signal of distress consisting of the letters *s o s* in Morse code (. . .– – –. . .), used in wireless telegraphy. **2** *Informal* any urgent call for help.

so–so ['sou ,sou] *or* ['sou 'sou] *adj, adv* only moderately good or well.

sot [sɒt] *n* drunkard. ⟨Latin *sottus*⟩

sot·to vo·ce ['sɒtou 'voutʃi] *Italian* ['sɔtto 'vɔtʃe] **1** in a low tone. **2** aside; privately. ⟨Italian = below (normal) voice⟩

souf·flé [su'flei] *or* ['suflei] *n* a frothy baked dish, made light by adding stiffly beaten egg whites: *cheese soufflé.* **soufflé** or **souffléed** *adj.* **soufflé** *v.* ⟨French, orig pp of *souffler* puff up⟩

sought [sɒt] *v* pt and pp of SEEK. **sought–after** *adj* desirable; much in demand.

soul [soul] *n* **1 a** the spiritual part of a person, considered as distinct from the body. **b** the moral or emotional nature of human beings as opposed to the physical nature. **2** a quality showing energy or spirit: *Her music is technically sophisticated but has no soul.* **3** a source of inspiration: *He was the soul of the labour movement.* **4** the essential part: *Brevity is the soul of wit.* **5** a person: *Don't tell a soul.* **6** an embodiment: *She is the soul of honour.* **7** among North American blacks, pride in their African heritage. **8** SOUL MUSIC. *adj* to do with the cultural heritage of American blacks: *soul food.* ⟨Old English *sāwol*⟩ **upon my soul!** an exclamation of surprise. **soul·ful** *adj* expressing or suggesting deep feeling. **soul·less** *adj* having no soul; without spirit or noble feelings. **soul·mate** *n* a person emotionally or spiritually bonded to another by shared longings, loves, etc. **soul music** a style of rhythm and blues developed by black Americans, with elements of gospel music and emotionally intense vocals. **soul–search·ing** *n* an honest effort, esp in a crisis, to evaluate one's motives, beliefs, etc.

sound¹ [saʊnd] *n* **1** what is or can be heard. **2** a noise, tone, etc. whose quality indicates its source or nature: *the sound of fighting.* **3** the range of hearing: *within sound.* **4** *Phonetics* any of the simplest segments of speech: *a vowel sound.* **5** sounds as transmitted by television, radio, or film, or their quality or volume: *She turns off the sound during commercials. The movie had poor sound.* *v* **1** make or cause to make a sound: *The doorbell sounded.* **2** seem to the hearer: *His excuse sounds odd.* **3** pronounce or be pronounced: *'Rough' and 'ruff' sound alike.* **sound·less** *adj.* ⟨Middle English *sounen;* Old French *son,* Latin *sonus*⟩ **sound off** *Informal* speak arrogantly. **sound out** read (an unfamiliar or hard word) one letter or syllable at a time. **sound barrier** the sudden increase in air resistance experienced by an aircraft as it approaches the speed of sound. **sound bite** a short clip on a news program, featuring a brief statement by a reporter, celebrity, etc. **sound·board** *n* **1** a thin piece of wood forming part of a musical instrument, as in a violin or piano, to increase resonance. **2** SOUNDING BOARD (def. 2). **sound effects** noises, as of rain, traffic, etc., called for in the script of a play or movie. **sounding board 1** SOUNDBOARD (def. 1). **2** a structure used to direct sound toward an audience. **3** a means of bringing opinions, etc. out into the open. **4** a person or group with whom one can test ideas. **sound·proof** *adj* letting no sound through. **sound·proof** *v.* **sound track 1** a recording of the sounds of words, music, etc., made along one edge of a movie film. **2** a separate recording of it, or of its musical parts only, on a cassette, CD, etc.: *I bought the sound track.* Also, **sound·track. sound waves** the vibrations by which sound travels.

sound² [saʊnd] *adj* **1** free from injury, decay, disease, or defect: *sound fruit, a sound mind.* **2** strong; secure: *a sound business firm.* **3** reasonable: *sound argument.* **4** orthodox: *politically sound.* **5** thorough: *a sound sleep.* *adv* deeply; thoroughly: *sound asleep.* **sound·ly** *adv.* **sound·ness** *n.* ⟨Middle English *sund,* Old English *(ge)sund*⟩

sound³ [saʊnd] *v* **1** measure (the depth of water) by letting down a weight fastened to a line. **2** inquire into the feelings, inclination, etc. of (a person) (often with *out*): *to sound someone on his or her political views.* **3** of a whale, etc., dive. **sound·a·ble** *adj.* ⟨Old French *sonder*⟩

sound⁴ [saʊnd] *n* a narrow passage of water or arm of the sea. ⟨Old English *sund* water, sea, power of swimming⟩

soup [sup] *n* **1** a liquid food made by simmering meat, vegetables, etc. **2** *Informal* anything dense or opaque like soup, such as heavy fog. *v* **soup up** *Slang* **a** increase the power or capacity of: *to soup up an engine.* **b** jazz up; make more interesting or exciting. ⟨French *soupe;* Germanic⟩ **in the soup** *Informal* in difficulties; in trouble. **soup kitchen** a place that serves food free or at a very low charge to poor or unemployed people or to disaster victims. **soup·y** *adj* **1** dense and opaque: *soupy fog.* **2** maudlin; overly sentimental. **3** resembling soup: *soupy stew.*

soup·çon [sup'sɔ̃] *n French* a slight trace; very small amount. ⟨French = suspicion⟩

sour [saʊr] *adj* **1** having a sharp, acid taste: *Lemon juice is sour.* **2** fermented; spoiled: *sour milk.* **3** grumpy: *a sour face.* **4** unpleasant: *sour weather, a sour experience.* *v* **1** make or become sour. **2** fall below usual standards of excellence or interest. **sour·ly** *adv.* **sour·ness** *n.* ⟨Old English *sūr*⟩ **go sour** sour (*v*). **sour on** (make or become) resentful toward or disillusioned with. **sour cream** a sour-tasting dairy product with a thick, smooth consistency. **sour·dough** *n* **1** dough containing active yeast, saved from one baking for the next. **2** bread made with sourdough. **3** a prospector or pioneer in NW Canada or Alaska. **4** any old resident, experienced hand, etc. **5** a native or resident of Yukon Territory. **sour grapes** contempt for a thing because one cannot have it or do it oneself. **sour·puss** [-ˌpʊs] *n Informal* a person who is habitually gloomy or grumpy.

source [sɔrs] *n* a thing, person, or place from which anything comes or is obtained.

v **1** obtain (parts, materials, services, etc.) from a supplier, professional, etc. under contract. **2** find or determine the source of (information, etc.) ⟨Old French *sourse* pp of *sourdre* spring up; Latin *surgere*⟩

source·book *n* an anthology of writings used as basic resource material on a subject: *a sourcebook in medieval history.* **source code** *Computers* programming that has not been compiled or put into machine language.

souse [saʊs] *v* **1** plunge into liquid; drench. **2** soak in vinegar, brine, etc.; pickle. *n* **1** a drenching. **2** brine for pickling. **3** food soaked in brine, esp parts of a pig. **4** *Slang* drunkard. ⟨Old French *sous* pickled pork⟩ **soused** *Slang adj* drunk.

south [saʊθ] *n* **1** the direction to the right as one faces the rising sun. **2 the South** the southern part of any country, esp the US. **south** or **South** *adj*. **south** *adv*. ⟨Old English *sūth*⟩

south of farther south than.

south·bound *adj* going toward the south. **south·east** *n* halfway between south and east. **south·east** *adj, adv.* **south·east·er** *n* a wind or storm from the southeast. **south·east·er·ly** *adj, adv.* **south·east·ern** *adj* to do with the southeast. **south·east·ward** *adv, adj* toward the southeast. Also *(adv)*, **south·east·wards. south·east·ward·ly** *adj, adv.* **south·er·ly** ['sʌðərli] *adj, adv* to do with the south. **south·ern** ['sʌðərn] **1** toward the south. **2** from the south. **3** of or in the south. **South·ern·er** *n* a native of the southern part of a country. **southern lights** AURORA AUSTRALIS. **south·ern·most** *adj* farthest south. **south·ing** ['saʊθɪŋ] *or* ['saʊðɪŋ] *n* the distance measured in a southerly direction. **south·land** [-lənd] *or* [-,lænd] *n* a southern region. **south·paw** *Slang n* a left-handed person, esp a baseball pitcher. **south·paw** *adj.* **South Pole** the southern end of the earth's axis. **south–south·east** *n* a direction halfway between south and southeast. **south–south·west** *n* a direction halfway between south and southwest. **south·ward** *adj, adv* toward the south. Also *(adv)*, **south·wards. south·ward·ly** *adj, adv.* **south·west** *n* halfway between south and west. **south·west** *adj, adv.* **south·west·er** [,sʌθ'wɛstər] *or* [,saʊ'wɛstər] *n* **1** a wind or storm from the southwest. **2** SOU'WESTER (defs. 1, 2). **south·west·er·ly** *adj, adv.* **south·west·ern** *adj* to do with the southwest. **south·west·ward** *adv, adj* toward the southwest. Also *(adv)*, **south·west·wards. south·west·ward·ly** *adj, adv.*

sou·ve·nir [,suvə'nir] *or* ['suvə,nir] *n* a thing kept as a pleasant reminder of a place, person, or occasion. ⟨French; Latin *subvenire* come to mind; *sub-* up + *venire* come⟩

souv·la·ki [suv'lɑki] *or* [suf'lɑki] *n* a Greek dish of meat cooked on a skewer over an open flame. ⟨Greek *soubla* skewer⟩

sou'west·er [,saʊ'wɛstər] *n* **1** a waterproof hat with a broad brim at the back to protect

the neck, worn esp at sea. **2** an oilskin coat worn at sea. **3** SOUTHWESTER (def. 1).

sov·er·eign ['sɒvrən] *or* ['sʌvrən] *n* a king or queen; monarch. *adj* **1** supreme in rank or power: *an issue of sovereign importance.* **2** not under the control of other governments. **sov·er·eign·ly** *adv.* ⟨Old French *soverain*; Latin *super* over⟩ **sov·er·eign·ty** *n* **1 a** political independence of a nation. **b** ❋ independence from the federation of Canada, advocated for a province. **2** an independent state. **sov·er·eign·tist** or **sov·er·eign·ist** *n, adj.* **sovereignty association** or **sovereignty–association** ❋ a proposed policy under which Québec would become an independent state but remain associated with Canada.

so·vi·et ['souviɪt] *n* Often, **Soviet** in the former Soviet Union, an elected local or national council. **so·vi·et** or **So·vi·et** *adj.* **so·vi·et·ism** *n.* ⟨Russian *soviet* council⟩

sow¹ [soʊ] *v* **sowed, sown** or **sowed, sow·ing 1** plant (seed or a crop): *It was time to begin sowing.* **2** introduce or spread: *to sow discontent.* **sow·er** *n.* ⟨Old English *sāwan*⟩

sow² [saʊ] *n* **1** a fully grown female pig. **2** the adult female of certain other mammals, esp the bear. ⟨Old English *sugu* or *sū*⟩

sown [soʊn] *v* a pp of SOW¹.

soy [sɔɪ] *n* **1** SOY SAUCE. **2** soybean. Also, **soy·a.** ⟨Japanese *shoyu*⟩ **soy·bean** *n* a bean widely cultivated for its protein-rich seeds. **soy sauce** a thin, dark brown sauce used as a flavouring, made from soybeans fermented in brine.

spa [spɑ] *n* **1** a mineral spring. **2** a health resort. **3** a fitness centre. **4** a whirlpool bath seating several people on a ledge around the inside. ⟨*Spa*, resort city in Belgium⟩

space [speɪs] *n* **1** the unlimited expanse stretching in all directions and in which all material things exist: *The earth moves through space.* **2** total available area or volume: *We have plenty of space in this house.* **3** a limited place for a given purpose: *a parking space.* **4** a blank between words, etc.: *Fill in the spaces as directed.* **5** *Music* one of the intervals between lines of a staff. **6** *Informal* freedom to pursue one's own interests without interference. *v* separate by spaces: *Space your words evenly when you write.* ⟨Middle English; Old French *espace*; Latin *spatium*⟩

space out arrange (items, or elements of a whole) with more space or time in between: *If you space the interviews out a little, you won't feel so rushed. Space your letters out more.*

space age the current period of history, thought of as being marked by the first efforts to explore outer space. **space bar** a horizontal bar at the bottom of a keyboard, used to leave a blank space. **space capsule** an unmanned spacecraft. **space·craft** *n, pl* **space·craft** any manned or unmanned vehicle designed for flight in outer space. **spaced–out** *adj Slang* **1** dazed or stupefied, as if or because of being under the influence of

a drug. **2** out of touch with the real world.
space heater a small electric or gas-powered unit used to heat an enclosed area, as a room. **space·man** *n, pl* **–men 1** a male astronaut. **2** a humanlike extraterrestrial being. **space·ship** *n* spacecraft, esp manned. **space shuttle** a manned spacecraft used more than once to go from earth to a space station. **space station** an artificial earth satellite used as an observatory or launching site. **space·suit** *n* an airtight suit designed to protect astronauts from radiation, heat, etc. **space–time continuum** the four-dimensional continuum, having three spatial co-ordinates and one temporal, in which all physical entities and events may be located. **space·walk** *n* action performed by an astronaut in outer space while outside the craft. **space·walk** *v*. **spa·cious** ['speiʃəs] *adj* **1** having much space; large; roomy: *a spacious house*. **2** extensive; vast. **spa·tial** ['speiʃəl] *adj* to do with space. **spa·tial·ly** *adv*.

spade¹ [speid] *n* a tool for digging, having a blade which can be pressed into the ground with the foot, and a handle with a grip.
v dig (up), cut, etc. with a spade. **spade·ful** *n*. ⟨Old English *spadu*; akin to Latin *spatha*. See SPADE².⟩
call a spade a spade call a thing by its real name; speak plainly and frankly.

spade² [speid] *n* a black figure (♠) used on playing cards. ⟨Italian *spada*; Latin *spatha*; Greek *spathē* sword, broad blade⟩
in spades *Informal* to an extreme degree.

spa·dix ['speidɪks] *n, pl* **spa·dix·es** or **spa·di·ces** ['speidə,siz] *Botany* a spike composed of tiny flowers on a fleshy stem, usually enclosed in a petal-like leaf called a spathe, as in the jack-in-the-pulpit. ⟨Greek *spadix* palm branch⟩

spa·ghet·ti [spə'gɛti] *n* **1** slender sticks of pasta. **2** anything that resembles this, such as a bundle or tangle of wires, etc. ⟨Italian, pl diminutive of *spago* cord⟩
spa·ghet·ti·ni [,spægɛ'tini] *n* pasta thinner than spaghetti.

spam [spæm] *n* unsolicited e-mail, esp advertising sent to large numbers of people.
v **spammed, spam·ming** send such e-mail (to). ⟨*Spam* a brand of canned meat; from its repetitive use in a skit by Monty Python⟩

span [spæn] *n* **1** a distance between two supports: *The arch had a span of 15 m*. **2** the maximum or average extent (often in compounds): *lifespan, attention span*.
v **spanned, span·ning 1** extend over: *A bridge spans the river*. **2** encircle with one's spread hand(s): *This post can be spanned by one's two hands*. ⟨Old English *spann*⟩

span·dex ['spændɛks] *n* a light, synthetic, very elastic fibre. ⟨anagram of *expands*⟩

span·gle ['spæŋgəl] *n* a bit of glittering material used for decoration.
v decorate with or as if with spangles: *The dark sky is spangled with stars*. **span·gly** *adj*. ⟨probably Middle Dutch *spange* brooch⟩

span·iel ['spænjəl] *n* any of several breeds of dog with long, silky hair and droopy ears. ⟨Old French *espagneul* orig Spanish⟩

spank [spæŋk] *v* strike (a child), usually on the buttocks, with the open hand as a punishment. **spank** *n*. **spank·ing** *n*. ⟨imitative⟩

spank·ing¹ ['spæŋkɪŋ] *n* See SPANK.

spank·ing² ['spæŋkɪŋ] *adv Informal* **(brand) spanking new** completely new. ⟨compare Danish *spanke* strut⟩

spar¹ [spɑr] *n* a long horizontal pole or beam supporting a ship's sail or forming part of a crane or derrick. ⟨Middle English *sparre*, akin to Old English *spere* spear⟩

spar² [spɑr] *v* **sparred, spar·ring** box with feinting movements or light blows, as when training. **spar** *n*. ⟨Italian *sparare* fling; *s-* intensive (Latin *ex-*) + *parare* parry⟩
sparring partner 1 one who spars with a professional boxer for practice or training. **2** a person with whom one habitually engages in friendly debate.

spare [spɛr] *v* **1** refrain from harming or destroying: *He spared his enemy*. **2** save from (labour, pain, etc.): *I'll go, to spare you the trip*. **3** get along without: *Mom couldn't spare the car, so I walked*. **4** be saving of: *to spare no expense*. **5** have free or available: *Can you spare the time?*
adj **1** free for other use: *spare time*. **2** in reserve: *a spare tire*. **3** thin; lean: *a tall, spare man*. **4** not lavish: *a spare diet*.
n **1** an extra or duplicate person or thing. **2** *Bowling* the knocking down of all the pins with two rolls of a ball. **spare·ly** *adv*. **spare·ness** *n*. ⟨Old English *sparian*⟩
(enough and) to spare more than enough.
not spare oneself do one's utmost.
spare·rib *n* a rib, esp of pork, having less meat than the ribs near the loins. **spar·ing** *adj* avoiding waste: *a sparing use of sugar*. **spar·ing·ly** *adv*.

spark [spɑrk] *n* **1** a tiny particle of flame or burning material. **2** a flash; flicker: *a spark of light*. **3** the smallest bit: *not a spark of interest*. **4** energy; vitality.
v **1** produce a spark. **2** flash. **3** stimulate: *to spark a revolt*. ⟨Old English *spearca*⟩
spar·kle *v* **1** glitter; flash: *sparkling diamonds*. **2** be brilliant and lively: *sparkling wit*. **3** fizz: *sparkling wine*. **spar·kle** *n*. **spar·kler** *n* **1** a handheld firework that sends out showers of little sparks. **2** *Informal* diamond. **spark plug** a device in a gasoline engine, producing an electric spark that explodes the mixture of gasoline and air.

spar·row ['spɛrou] *or* ['spærou] *n* any of a genus of small, dull-coloured finches or similar related birds. ⟨Old English *spearwa*⟩

sparse [spɑrs] *adj* **1** thinly scattered: *a sparse population*. **2** scanty; meagre: *sparse provisions*. **sparse·ly** *adv*. **sparse·ness** or **spar·si·ty** *n*. ⟨Latin *sparsus* pp of *spargere* scatter⟩

Spar·tan ['spɑrtən] *adj* stern, frugal, simple, austere, disciplined, etc.: *a Spartan upbringing*. **Spar·tan** *n*. **Spar·tan·ism** *n*. ⟨*Sparta* city in ancient Greece⟩

spasm ['spæzəm] *n* **1** a sudden, involuntary muscle contraction. **2** any sudden, brief spell of activity: *a spasm of industry.* **spas·mod·ic** [spæz'mɒdɪk] *adj.* ⟨Greek *spasmos; spaein* draw up, tear away⟩

spat[1] [spæt] *n* a slight quarrel. **spat, spat·ted, spat·ting** *v.* ⟨perhaps imitative⟩

spat[2] [spæt] *v* a pt and a pp of SPIT[1].

spate [speit] *n* a flood or sudden outburst: *a spate of words.* ⟨Old English *spātan* spit⟩

spathe [speið] *n Botany* a large bract or pair of bracts enclosing a flower cluster. **spathed** *adj.* ⟨Greek *spathē* palm branch, oar blade⟩

spa·tial See SPACE.

spat·ter ['spætər] *v* **1** fall in drops: *Rain spattered on the car.* **2** splash with drops: *Her pants were spattered with paint.* **3** strike in many places: *Bullets spattered the wall.* **spat·ter** *n.* ⟨Dutch *spatten*⟩

spat·u·la ['spætʃələ] *n* any of various small tools with a wide, flat, flexible blade. ⟨Latin, diminutive of *spatha* flat blade; Greek *spathē*⟩ **spat·u·late** *adj* **1** shaped like a spatula. **2** *Botany* having a broad, rounded end and a narrow base: *a spatulate leaf.* **3** wide at the tips: *spatulate fingers.*

spawn [spɒn] *n* **1** the eggs of fish, frogs, etc. **2** (undesirable) offspring or product. *v* **1** of fish, etc., produce or deposit (eggs): *Salmon spawn in the rivers of British Columbia.* **2** bring forth (usually something undesirable) in great quantity. ⟨Old French *espandre;* Latin *expandere* spread out⟩

spay [spei] *v* remove the ovaries, and in some cases the uterus, of (a female animal). ⟨Anglo-French *espeir*, Old French *espee* sword; Latin *spatha*. See SPADE[2].⟩

speak [spik] *v* **spoke, spok·en, speak·ing** **1** talk: *We spoke on the phone.* **2** consult (with *to*): *Speak to your doctor.* **3** mention (with *of, about,* etc.): *He spoke of renovating their house.* **4** give a speech: *Who is going to speak at the conference?* **5** use or know how to use (a language) in speaking: *Do you speak French?* **6** be evidence: *Her clothing speaks of wealth.* ⟨Old English *specan*⟩
speak for **a** reserve: *to speak for seats ahead of time.* **b** speak on behalf of: *She spoke for us all.* **speak for itself** be obvious. **speak out** (or **up**) **a** speak loudly and clearly. **b** speak freely: *to speak out against injustice.* **speak volumes** See VOLUME. **speak well for** be evidence in favour of. **to speak of** of any significance (with interrogatives and negatives): *no complaints to speak of.*
speak·eas·y *n esp US Slang* during the era of Prohibition, a place where alcohol was sold illegally. **speak·er** *n* **1** a person who speaks, esp before an audience or on behalf of others. **2** **Speaker (of the House)** a person who presides over a legislative assembly. **3** loudspeaker. **speak·er·phone** *n* a phone equipped with a microphone and loudspeaker, so that it does not need to be held in the hand.

spear [spir] *n* **1** a weapon with a long shaft and a pointed head. **2** a similar instrument forked at one end, for catching fish. **3** anything shaped like a spear.
v **1** stab with anything sharp. **2** *Hockey* check (an opponent) illegally by jabbing with the stick blade. ⟨Old English *spere*⟩
spear·head *n* **1** the pointed striking end of a spear. **2** the leader or initiator of an attack, undertaking, etc.: *She was the spearhead of the environmental movement here.* *v* go first in (an attack, undertaking, etc.): *Tanks spearheaded the army's advance.* **spear·mint** *n* a European mint cultivated for its aromatic leaves.

spec [spɛk] speculation.
on spec in the hope of making a profit.

spe·cial [spɛʃəl] *adj* **1** of a specific kind, with a specific purpose, etc., different from others: *This desk has a special lock.* **2** not general; of or for an individual. **3** greater than average: *a topic of special interest.* **4** held in exceptionally high regard: *a special favourite.*
n a special thing, as a featured bargain in a restaurant or store, a one-time television show.
spe·cial·ly *adv.* **spe·cial·ness** *n.* ⟨Latin *specialis; species* appearance⟩
on special for sale at a special low price.
special delivery mail delivery by messenger rather than by regular mail. **special effects** *Film, television* illusions generated by computer or by editing, etc. **spe·cial·ist** *n* a person who concentrates on one particular branch of study, business, etc. **spe·cial·ize** *v* **1** pursue a particular branch of study, work, etc.: *She specialized in engineering.* **2** adapt to special conditions by a special form, use, etc. **spe·cial·i·za·tion** *n.* **spe·cial·ty** *n* a field of study, line of work, product, etc. to which attention is devoted or in which one is expert: *Repairing watches is his specialty.* *adj* of stores or their goods, specialized; catering to a specialized clientele.

> **SYNONYMS**
> **Special** suggests qualities making a thing different from others of its kind or other kinds: *Babies need special food.* **Particular** emphasizes individuality, a thing being considered separately from all others of the same kind: *You asked for a sci-fi novel; were you thinking of a particular author?*

spe·cie ['spiʃi] *n* money in the form of coins. ⟨Latin *(in) specie* form of *species* kind⟩

spe·cies ['spiʃiz] or ['spisiz] *n, pl* **-cies** **1** *Biology* the narrowest major category in the classification of plants and animals; the major subdivision of a genus or subgenus. **2** kind or sort. **3** **the species** the human race. ⟨Latin *species* appearance, sort, form⟩
spe·ci·a·tion [,spiʃi'eiʃən] or [,spisi-] *n Biology* the emergence of new species in the course of evolution. **spe·ci·ate** *v.*

spe·cif·ic [spə'sɪfɪk] *adj* **1** that is or can be identified definitely: *There was no specific reason for the quarrel.* **2** characteristic: *Scaly skin is a specific feature of snakes.* **3** *Biology* to do with a species. **4** (often in compounds) determined by: *gender-specific, culture-specific*. *n* **1** a particular fact, detail, etc. **2** *Medicine* a cure for a certain disease: *Quinine is a specific for malaria.* **spe·cif·i·cal·ly** *adv.* **spec·i·fic·i·ty** *n.* 〈Latin *specificus; species* sort + *facere* make〉 **specific gravity** the ratio of the density of any substance to the density of some standard substance. *Abbrev* **s.g.**

spec·i·fy [ˈspɛsə,faɪ] *v* **1** state or describe in detail: *Did she specify any time for us to call?* **2** state as a requirement: *The contractor would have used cement block, but brick was specified.* **spec·i·fi·a·ble** *adj.* 〈See SPECIFIC.〉
spec·i·fi·ca·tion [,spɛsəfə'keɪʃən] *n* **1** the act of specifying, or something specified. **2** Usually, **specifications** *pl* a detailed written list of the dimensions, parts, performance standards, etc. for a building, computer, boat, etc.

spec·i·men [ˈspɛsəmən] *n* **1** one of a group taken to show what the others are like: *The statue was a fine specimen of Greek sculpture.* **2** *Informal* human being: *The professor was an odd specimen.* **3** *Medicine* a sample of a bodily excretion or tissue for laboratory analysis. 〈Latin; *specere* view〉

spe·cious [ˈspiʃəs] *adj* seeming or trying to seem reasonable or good, but not really being so: *a specious argument, a specious hypocrite.* **spe·cious·ly** *adv.* **spe·cious·ness** *n.* 〈Latin *speciosus; species* appearance〉

speck [spɛk] *n* **1** a small spot: *specks of paint on the floor* **2** a tiny bit; particle: *I have a speck in my eye.* **speck** *v.* 〈Old English *specca*〉
speck·le *n* one of many small spots or marks: *This hen is grey with white speckles.* **speck·le** *v.*

specs¹ [spɛks]*n pl* spectacles.

specs² [spɛk] *n pl Informal* specifications.

spec·ta·cle [ˈspɛktəkəl] *n* **1** something to look at; sight: *The rainbow was a beautiful spectacle.* **2** an object of public curiosity, contempt, wonder, etc. **3** **spectacles** *pl* a pair of glasses to correct vision. **spec·ta·cled** *adj.* 〈Latin *spectaculum; specere* view〉
make a spectacle of oneself behave foolishly or crudely in public.
spec·tac·u·lar [spek'tækjələr] *adj* **1** making a great display: *a spectacular storm.* **2** excellent; outstanding: *a spectacular performance. n* a spectacular event or show: *a TV spectacular.* **spec·tac·u·lar·ly** *adv.*

spec·ta·tor [ˈspɛkteitər] *n* one who watches without taking part; onlooker. 〈Latin; *spectare* watch; *specere* view〉
spectator sport a sport that attracts many spectators who do not themselves play: *Hockey and football are spectator sports.*

spec·tra [ˈspɛktrə] *n* a pl of SPECTRUM.

spec·tre [ˈspɛktər] *n* **1** ghost. **2** a prospect causing terror or dread: *the spectre of war.* Also, **spec·ter. spec·tral** *adj.* 〈See SPECTRUM.〉

spec·trum [ˈspɛktrəm] *n*, *pl* **-tra** [-trə] or **-trums 1** the band of colours formed when light is broken up by being passed through a prism or by some other means. **2** *Radio* the frequency range between 10 kilohertz and 300 000 megahertz. **3** range; continuum: *the spectrum of political thought.* **spec·tral** *adj.* 〈Latin *spectrum* appearance; *specere* view〉

spec·u·late [ˈspɛkjə,leit] *v* **1** reflect; theorize: *to speculate on the nature of time.* **2** guess: *to speculate about the likely winner.* **3** buy or sell stocks, land, etc. in the hope of profit. **spec·u·la·tion** *n.* **spec·u·la·tor** *n.* 〈Latin *specula* watchtower; *specere* look〉
spec·u·la·tive *adj* **1** reflective. **2** theoretical or hypothetical. **3** involving speculation in land, stocks, etc. **spec·u·la·tive·ly** *adv.* **spec·u·la·tive·ness** *n.*

sped [spɛd] *v* a pt and a pp of SPEED.

speech [spitʃ] *n* **1** the act or manner of speaking: *Animals lack speech.* **2** something said: *a little speech of apology.* **3** a public address. **4** a language or dialect: *her native speech.* 〈Old English *spǣc*〉
Speech from the Throne in Commonwealth countries whose head of state is the British monarch, a statement of government policy for the coming year, read in the opening session of Parliament by the monarch or his or her representative. **speech·i·fy** *v Humorous or contemptuous* make a speech; talk as if making a speech. **speech·less** *adj* **1** unable to speak temporarily because of strong emotion: *speechless with terror.* **2** silent; unspoken.

speed [spid] *n* **1** the quality of being fast. **2** a rate of movement: *a speed of 100 km/h.* **3** a gear giving a certain rate of movement: *a ten-speed bike.* **4** *Photography* a measure of the sensitivity (of a film or paper) to light. **5** *Informal* one's level of ability or interest, etc.: *Using the computer for word-processing is about my speed.* **6** *Slang* any of various mood-elevating amphetamines.
v **sped** or **speed·ed, speed·ing 1** go or cause to go quickly: *The boat sped over the water.* **2** drive faster than is safe or lawful: *She was speeding in a school zone.* **3** help forward; promote: *to speed an undertaking.* **speed·er** *n.* **speed·ing** *n.* 〈Old English *spēd*〉
speed up go or cause to go more quickly. **up to speed a** performing at the normal or expected rate or level: *The new manager is not quite up to speed yet.* **b** up to date.
speed·boat *n* a fast motorboat. **speed bump** a ridge across the pavement to deter drivers from going too fast. **speed limit** the top legal driving speed on a given road. **speed·om·e·ter** [spə'dɒmətər] *n* an instrument to indicate the speed of a vehicle. **speed·read·ing** *n* the technique of reading much faster than normal, but with normal comprehension and memory. **speed·read** *v.* **speed skating** the sport of racing on ice skates. **speed skater. speed trap** a section of road where police set up a means, usually hidden, of catching speeders. **speed–up** *n* an increase in speed or production rate. **speed·y** *adj* fast: *a speedy decision.* **speed·i·ly** *adv.* **speed·i·ness** *n.*

spell¹ [spɛl] *v* **spelled** or **spelt, spell·ing 1** write or say the letters of (a word) in order: *He cannot spell well.* **2** of letters, make up or form (a word): *C-a-t spells cat.* **3** mean: *Delay spells danger.* 〈Old French *espeller*〉

spell out a write out in full: *Spell out numerals under 100.* **b** explain very clearly: *You have to spell everything out for her.*
spell check the process of checking spelling using a SPELL CHECKER: *Run a spell check on this before printing it.* **spell checker** *Computers* a function or program that attempts to verify whether words entered by the user are spelled correctly. **spell·er** *n* **1** a person with regard to skill in spelling: *I'm a poor speller.* **2** a textbook in spelling. **spell·ing** *n* **1** the writing or saying of the letters of words in order. **2** the way a word is spelled: *There are two spellings for this word.* **3 a** the way words in general (in a given language) are spelled. **b** the study of this. **spelling bee** a spelling contest in which players drop out if they make errors, until only the winner is left.

spell² [spεl] *n* **1** a word or set of words with magic power. **2** fascination; charm: *the spell of the sea.* ⟨Old English *spell* story⟩
cast a spell on put under or as if under the influence of magic power. **under a spell** controlled by or as if by a spell: *The story held the children under a spell.*
spell·bound *adj* fascinated; enchanted.

spell³ [spεl] *n* **1** a period of work or duty: *a spell at the wheel.* **2** a period during which some condition lasts: *a spell of coughing.* **3** *Informal* an attack of illness or fainting.
v Informal relieve for a while (often with *off*): *to spell another person at rowing a boat.* ⟨Old English *spelian*, v.⟩

spelt [spεlt] *v* a pt and a pp of SPELL¹.

spe·lunk·ing [spɪ'lʌŋkɪŋ] *n* the hobby of exploring caves. **spe·lunk·er** *n.* ⟨Latin *spelunca* cave; Greek *spēlaion*⟩

spend [spεnd] *v* **spent, spend·ing 1** pay out (money): *I spent ten dollars today.* **2** use; put forth (effort, thought, etc.): *Don't spend any more energy on that job.* **3** pass (time, etc.): *to spend a day at the beach.* **4** wear out; exhaust: *The storm has spent its force.* **spend·er** *n.* ⟨Old English -*spendan*; Latin *expendere*; *ex-* out + *pendere* weigh⟩
spend·thrift *n* a person who wastes money.

SYNONYMS
Spend is the common word, meaning 'pay out for some thing or purpose': *He spends all he earns.* **Expend**, more formal, suggests using up by spending large amounts that reduce or exhaust a fund: *She expends her energy on parties.* **Disburse**, formal and exclusively financial, means 'pay out from a fund for expenses': *The treasurer reports what he disburses.*

spent [spεnt] *v* pt and pp of SPEND.
adj used up or worn out: *a spent swimmer, a spent horse. Her energy was soon spent.*

sperm [spɜrm] *n, pl* **sperm 1** the male reproductive cell of almost all animals and plants that reproduce sexually. **2** semen. ⟨Greek *sperma* seed⟩
sper·ma·to·zo·on [ˌspɜrmətə'zouən] *n, pl* **-zo·a** [-'zouə] sperm (def. 1). **sperm bank** a collection of frozen sperm for use in artificial

insemination. **sperm·i·cide** *n* a contraceptive substance that kills sperm. **sperm·i·cid·al** *adj.*

spew [spju] *v* **1** throw or be thrown out with force: *a volcano spewing lava, to spew out insults.* **2** vomit. ⟨Old English *spiwan*⟩

sphag·num ['sfægnəm] *n* any of a genus of mosses found growing in bogs and used as a soil conditioner, etc.; peat moss. ⟨Greek *sphagnos*⟩

sphere [sfir] **1** *Geometry* a round solid figure bounded by a surface that is at all points equally distant from the centre. **2** an object approximately like this in form. **3** a place or field of activity or existence: *His sphere is advertising.* **4** range; extent: *a sphere of influence.* ⟨Greek *sphaira*⟩
spher·i·cal ['sfɛrɪkəl] *or* ['sfɪrɪkəl] *adj* **1** to do with a sphere. **2** *Geometry* **a** formed on the surface of a sphere: *spherical angles.* **b** dealing with spheres: *spherical trigonometry.* **sphe·roid** ['sfirɔɪd] *n* a body shaped somewhat like a sphere. **sphe·roi·dal** *adj.*

sphinc·ter ['sfɪŋktər] *n* a ringlike muscle that controls an opening or passage of the body. ⟨Greek *sphinktēr*; *sphingein* squeeze⟩

sphinx [sfɪŋks] *n* **1** a statue of a lion's body with the head of a man, ram, or hawk. **2 Sphinx** a *Greek myth* a monster with the head and breasts of a woman, the body of a lion, and wings. **b** the immense sphinx by the Pyramids at Giza in Egypt. **3** a puzzling or mysterious person. **sphinx·like** *adj.* ⟨Latin. The Sphinx at Thebes told a riddle to passersby and killed those unable to answer it.⟩

spice [spəis] *n* **1** a seasoning, such as ginger, obtained from a plant and used to flavour food. **2** character or interest: *A few good metaphors add spice to a narrative.*
v **1** put spice in; season. **2** add character or interest to (often with *up*). **spic·y** *adj.* ⟨Old French *espice*; Latin *species* sort⟩

spick–and–span ['spɪk ən 'spæn] *adj* neat and very clean. ⟨*spick* variant of *spike* + *span-new*; Old Norse *spánn* chip + *nyr* new⟩

spi·der ['spaidər] *n* **1** any of an order of arachnids, having eight legs, and spinning nests and webs to catch prey, or cocoons for their eggs. **2** any object with many radiating legs, spokes, etc. **spi·der·like** *adj.* ⟨Old English *spīthra*; *spinnan* spin⟩
spi·der·y *adj* **1** long and thin like a spider's legs. **2** full of or infested with spiders.

spiel [spil] *or* [ʃpil] *Slang n* a set speech, esp a glib, repetitive one; harangue.
v **spiel off** recite rapidly: *The waiter spieled off the entire menu by heart.* ⟨German *spielen* play⟩

spiff·y ['spɪfi] *adj Slang* smart; neat; snazzy. **spiff·i·ly** *adv.* **spiff·i·ness** *n.* ⟨dialect *spiff* dandified (person)⟩
spiff up make spiffy or spiffier.

spig·ot ['spɪgət] *n* **1** a valve controlling the flow of liquid from a pipe, tank, barrel, etc. **2** a tap or faucet. ⟨Middle English⟩

spike [spəik] *n* **1** a large, strong nail. **2** a long, pointed object or part: *He gelled his hair*

and formed it into spikes. **3** Also, **spike heel** a high, thin heel on a woman's dress shoe. **4** one of a set of projections on a shoe sole to improve traction. **5 spikes** *pl* shoes having these. **6** *Volleyball* the act of spiking the ball. **7** a rapid increase in voltage, followed by a rapid decrease.
v **1** fasten with spikes. **2** provide or equip with spikes. **3** *Slang* add liquor to (a drink, etc.). **4** *Slang* make more exciting by adding special elements. **5** *Volleyball* hit (the ball) sharply straight down into the opposing team's court. **6** illegally drive spikes into (trees) as a form of protest against their being cut down. **7** thwart; block: *to spike an attempt.* **8** increase then decrease rapidly. **spik·er** *n.* **spik·y** *adj.* ⟨Scandinavian⟩
spike someone's guns thwart someone.

spile [spaɪl] *n* **1** a plug used to stop the hole of a barrel. **2** a spout for drawing off sap from maple trees. **3** a post driven into the ground as a support. ⟨Middle Dutch *spile* peg⟩

spill [spɪl] *v* **spilled** or **spilt, spill·ing 1** let (liquid or matter in loose pieces) fall or flow out, esp accidentally: *to spill salt.* **2** fall or flow out: *Water spilled from the pail.* **3** *Informal* cause to fall from a horse, boat, etc. **spill** *n.* **spill·age** *n.* ⟨Old English *spillan*⟩
spill over a overflow. **b** spread beyond the intended bounds. **spill·o·ver** *n, adj.* **spill the beans.** See BEAN.
spill·way *n* a channel for surplus water.

spin [spɪn] *v* **spun, spin·ning 1** turn or make turn rapidly: *The wheel spins round.* **2** of the wheels of a vehicle, turn rapidly without traction, as on ice. **3** feel dizzy: *My head is spinning.* **4** draw out and twist (cotton, wool, etc.) into thread. **5** of a spider or insect, make (a thread, web, cocoon, etc.) by producing sticky material that hardens. **6** ride, drive, etc. fast. **7** invent and tell (stories). **8** drain (wet clothes) in the drum of a washing machine by rapid rotation.
n **1** the act of spinning. **2** a short ride or drive: *Get your bike and come for a spin.* **3** a rapid spiralling of an aircraft as it falls. **4** *Informal* a slanted interpretation. **5** *Physics* rotation of an elementary particle about its axis. **spin·ner** *n.* **spin·ing** *adj, n.* ⟨Old English *spinnan*⟩
spin out prolong (a story, speech, etc.).
spin doctor *Informal* one whose function is to provide a suitable SPIN (def. 4) on events, statements, etc. on behalf of a government, politician, etc. **spinning wheel** an apparatus for spinning cotton, wool, etc. into thread or yarn, consisting of a manually operated wheel and a spindle. **spin-off** or **spin–off** *n* a by-product or fringe benefit.

spi·na bi·fi·da [ˈspaɪnə ˈbɪfədə] a congenital defect in which the spinal column is imperfectly closed, exposing the spinal cord.

spin·ach [ˈspɪnɪtʃ] *n* a plant of the goosefoot family cultivated for its large, dark green, edible leaves. ⟨Spanish *espinaca;* Arabic⟩

spin·dle [ˈspɪndəl] *n* **1** a rod used in spinning to twist, wind, and hold thread. **2** any rod or

pin that turns, or on which something turns. **3** one of the more or less cylindrical supports of a railing, or in the back of some chairs. **4** *Biology* a rod-shaped bundle of fibres formed during cell division. ⟨Old English *spinel;* related to *spinnan* spin⟩
spin·dly *adj* very long and thin.

spine [spaɪn] *n* **1** SPINAL COLUMN; backbone. **2** something that looks like a backbone, such as a ridge of land, or that functions as a main support. **3** one of the stiff growths on a cactus, porcupine, etc. **4** the part of a book where the pages are held together. **5** courage, resolve, etc.: *Threats merely stiffened his spine.* **spine·less** *adj.* ⟨Latin *spina* orig thorn⟩
spi·nal *adj* to do with the spine. *n Medicine* an anesthetic for the lower part of the body. **spinal column** in vertebrates, the series of small bones (vertebrae) along the middle of the back, enclosing and protecting the spinal cord. **spinal cord** the thick cord of nerve tissue that extends from the brain down through the backbone. **spin·y** *adj* **1** having many spines; thorny: *a spiny cactus, a spiny porcupine.* **2** difficult; troublesome: *a spiny problem.* **spin·i·ness** *n.*

spin·ster [ˈspɪnstər] *n* a woman who has never married, esp a middle-aged or elderly one. **spin·ster·hood** *n.* **spin·ster·ish** *adj.* **spin·ster·ly** *adj.* ⟨Middle English; *spin*⟩

spi·ral [ˈspaɪrəl] *n* **1** *Geometry* **a** a plane curve formed by a point moving around a fixed central point in a continuously increasing or decreasing arc. **b** helix. **2** an object or course in the shape of a spiral, such as a watch spring. **3** a continuous increase or decrease, esp of two or more interdependent quantities: *an inflationary spiral.* **spi·ral** *adj.* **spi·ral·ly** *adv.* **spi·ral, -ralled** or **-raled, -rall·ing** or **-ral·ing** *v.* ⟨Latin *spira* a coil; Greek *speira*⟩

spire [spaɪr] *n* **1** the top part of a tower or steeple that narrows to a point. **2** anything tapered and pointed: *the rocky spires of the mountains.* ⟨Old English *spīr*⟩

spir·it [ˈspɪrɪt] *n* **1** the immaterial part of a human being; the soul, believed by some to live on after the body dies. **2** the moral or emotional aspect of human nature. **3** consciousness in general, as distinct from matter. **4** a supernatural being, such as a god, ghost, or fairy. **5 the Spirit** *Christianity* the Holy Spirit, third Person of the Trinity. **6** Often, **spirits** *pl* a state of mind; mood: *in good spirits.* **7** a characteristic attitude or quality: *the spirit of the age.* **8** courage; vigour: *That racehorse has spirit.* **9** loyalty and enthusiasm: *school spirit.* **10** the real intent: *the spirit of the law.* **11** Often, **spirits** *pl* **a** a solution in alcohol: *spirits of camphor.* **b** an alcoholic drink made by distilling, such as brandy, whisky, etc. **c** *Chemistry* any liquid distillate, such as turpentine.
v carry (*away* or *off*) secretly. ⟨Latin *spiritus* orig breath; *spirare* breathe⟩
spir·it·ed *adj* full of energy; lively: *a spirited racehorse.* **spir·it·less** *adj* without courage; depressed. **spirit level** an instrument laid on

a surface to detect, by the position of a bubble of air in a tube, whether the surface is level. **spir·i·tu·al** ['spɪrɪtʃuəl] *or* ['spɪrɪtʃəl] *adj* **1** to do with a spirit, or with the human spirit: *our spiritual nature.* **2** religious: *spiritual songs, spiritual authority.* **3** devoted to or very interested in spiritual things. *n* a deeply emotional religious song with a jazz rhythm, developed from the folk music of Southern US blacks. **spir·i·tu·al·ly** *adv.* **spir·i·tu·al·ism** *n* the belief that spirits of the dead communicate with the living. **spir·i·tu·al·ist** *n.* **spir·i·tu·al·i·ty** *n* **1** a devotion to spiritual things. **2** the spiritual aspect of human existence.

spit¹ [spɪt] *v* **spat** or **spit, spit·ting** **1** eject saliva from the mouth. **2** eject from the mouth (often with *out*): *Spit the seeds into this dish.* **3** throw out with force: *The gun spits fire.* **4** of a cat, make an angry hissing noise. **5** rain or snow slightly. **6** utter viciously. *n* **1** the liquid produced in the mouth; saliva. **2** the noise or act of spitting. **3** a frothy secretion given off by some insects. **spit·ter** *n.* ⟨Old English *spittan*⟩
be the spit of *Informal* look just like. **spit up** esp of a baby, regurgitate.
spit and polish *Informal* a high standard of cleanliness or neatness. **spit·ball** *n* **1** a small ball of chewed-up paper, used as a missile. **2** *Baseball* an illegal curve resulting from the pitcher's moistening one side of the ball with saliva. **spit·fire** *n* **1** a very hot-tempered person. **2** a cannon or firework that sends forth fire. **spitting image** or **spit and image** *Informal* exact or perfect likeness: *In that dress she was the spitting image of her grandmother.* **spit·tle** *n* saliva. **spit·toon** [spɪ'tun] *n* a receptacle for spitting into.

spit² [spɪt] *n* **1** a rotating rod on which meat is roasted. **2** a narrow point of land running into the water. ⟨Old English *spitu*⟩

spite [spaɪt] *n* ill will; a grudge. *v* show ill will toward; anger on purpose: *He left his yard dirty to spite the neighbours.* **spite·ful** *adj.* ⟨Middle English *despit* despite⟩
in spite of unprevented by the existence or occurrence of: *We went in spite of the rain.*

splake [spleik] *n, pl* **splake** or **splakes** ⚹ a fertile hybrid game fish, produced from lake trout eggs fertilized with sperm from brook (speckled) trout. ⟨*sp(eckled)* + *lake* trout⟩

splash [splæʃ] *v* **1** cause (liquid) to fly about: *to splash mud on a car.* **2** fall in scattered masses or drops: *The waves splashed on the beach.* **3** dash liquid on. **4** move with splashes: *She splashed across the brook.* **5** mark with colour: *forests splashed with red and gold.* **6** display prominently in print: *The scandal was splashed all over the front page.* **splash** *n.* ⟨earlier *plash*; Old English *plæsc* puddle⟩
make a splash *Informal* attract attention.
splash·down *n* the landing of a capsule or other spacecraft in the ocean after re-entry. **splash·y** *adj* **1** tending to splash. **2** *Informal* attracting attention; causing excitement.

splat [splæt] *v* **splat·ted, splat·ting** make a

sharp slapping or splashing sound: *The heavy rain splatted against the window.* *adv* with such a sound: *He threw the tomato splat against the wall.* **splat** *n.* ⟨imitative⟩

splat·ter ['splætər] *v, n* splash; spatter. ⟨blend of *spatter* and *splash*⟩

splay [splei] *v* spread out wide and flat. **splay** *adj.* ⟨*display*⟩

spleen [splin] *n* **1** an organ in mammals and other vertebrates, serving to store blood, destroy worn-out red blood cells, filter bacteria, etc. **2** ill humour, esp when mingled with spite: *to vent one's spleen.* ⟨Greek *splēn*⟩

splen·did ['splɛndɪd] *adj* **1** brilliant; glorious; magnificent: *a splendid victory.* **2** excellent: *a splendid opportunity.* **splen·did·ly** *adv.* **splen·dour** or **splen·dor** *n.* ⟨Latin *splendidus; splendere* be bright⟩
splen·dif·er·ous [splɛn'dɪfərəs] *adj Informal* splendid; magnificent.

splice [splais] *v* **1** join (ropes, cables, etc.) by weaving together the untwisted ends. **2** join (two beams or planks) by overlapping. **3** join (segments of film, tape, etc.) by means of a third piece overlapping the two ends. **4** *Slang* marry. **splice** *n.* ⟨Middle Dutch *splissen*⟩

splint [splɪnt] *n* a rigid arrangement of wood, metal, plaster, etc. to hold a broken or dislocated bone in place. *v* secure or support with or as if with a splint. ⟨Middle Dutch *splinte*⟩

splin·ter [splin'tər] *n* a thin, sharp piece of wood, glass, etc.: *He got a splinter in his hand.* *v* break into splinters. **splin·ter·y** *adj.* ⟨Middle Dutch⟩
splinter group a small dissenting faction that splits from a larger group.

split [splɪt] *v* **split, split·ting** **1** break or cut lengthwise, or in layers. **2** share: *We split the cost between us.* **3** divide into different groups. **4** *Chemistry* **a** divide (a molecule) into two or more atoms. **b** divide (an atomic nucleus) into two parts. **5** *Slang* leave: *Let's split.* *n* **1** the act, process, or result of splitting. **2** *Slang* a portion or share, esp of loot. **3** a piece of fruit, usually a banana, split lengthwise and topped with ice cream, nuts, etc. **4** Often, **splits** *pl* an exercise in which one lowers oneself to the floor with the legs stretched in opposite directions. **split** *adj.* **split·ter** *n.* ⟨Middle Dutch *splitten*⟩
split hairs See HAIR. **split off** remove or separate by splitting. **split up a** divide into parts or shares. **b** end a relationship: *They split up after five years together.* **c** go off in different directions.
split infinitive *Grammar* an infinitive having an adverb between *to* and the verb. *Example: She plans to eventually move to Europe.* **split–lev·el** *adj* of a house, divided so that each floor is half a storey higher or lower than the one beside it, with a short flight of stairs between levels. **split–lev·el** *n.* **split personality** a personality characterized by two seemingly independent, contradictory patterns of behaviour. **split second** an

imperceptible length of time: *I'll be finished in a split second*. **split–sec·ond** *adj*. **split·ting** *adj* of the head or a headache, very painful.

Although **split infinitives** are not necessarily wrong, awkward ones should be avoided.
Awkward: *After a while I was able to, with increasing accuracy, distinguish the good customers from the sulky ones.*
Improved: *After a while I was able to distinguish, with increasing accuracy, the good customers from the sulky ones.*

splotch [splɒtʃ] *n* a large, irregular spot. **splotch** *v*. **splotch·y** *adj*. ⟨blend of *spot* and *blotch*⟩

splurge [splɜrdʒ] *Informal v* spend money or indulge oneself extravagantly: *He splurged and had two pieces of pie*. **splurge** *n*. ⟨possible blend of *splash* and *surge*⟩

splut·ter ['splʌtər] *v* talk or utter in a hasty, confused way, esp when excited: *She spluttered an explanation*. **splut·ter** *n*. ⟨perhaps variant of *sputter*⟩

spoil [spɔɪl] *v* **spoiled** or **spoilt, spoil·ing** **1** mar; ruin: *She spoiled the dress by ripping it*. **2** of perishable food, go sour or start to rot; become unfit for use: *Fruit spoils if kept too long*. **3** weaken the character of by being too indulgent: *to spoil a child*.
n Often, **spoils** *pl* **a** plunder taken in war: *The soldiers carried the spoils back to camp*. **b** anything won by a struggle with a rival. **spoil·age** *n*. ⟨Latin *spolium* booty, spoil⟩
be spoiling for *Informal* be longing for (a fight, revenge, etc.).
spoil·er *n* **1** a device intended to interrupt airflow around an aerodynamic surface such as that of a car or airplane wing, so as to reduce lift. **2** a person or thing that spoils something. **3** a competitor who does not win but does well enough to affect another participant's success. **spoil·sport** *n* a person who spoils or prevents the fun of others.

Spoil emphasizes damage that reduces the value, strength, beauty, usefulness, etc. of something: *Her friend's unkind comments spoiled her pleasure in her new dress.*
Ruin emphasizes irretrievably or completely destroying the value, soundness, beauty, usefulness, etc. of someone or something: *He ruined his health by a lifetime of bad habits.*

spoke[1] [spouk] *n* **1** one of the bars running from the centre of a wheel to the rim. **2** one of the grips protruding from the outer edge of a ship's wheel. ⟨Old English *spāca*⟩

spoke[2] [spouk] *v* a pt of SPEAK.
spo·ken *v* pp of SPEAK. *adj* **1** expressed orally: *spoken promises, the spoken word*. **2** (in compounds) speaking in a certain way: *a soft-spoken man*. **spokes·per·son** *n* a person who speaks on behalf of another or others. **spokes·man** *n, pl* -men. **spokes·wom·an** *n, pl* -wom·en.

spon·dee ['spɒndi] *n Prosody* a foot or measure consisting of two long or accented syllables. *Example:* Só stróde | hé báck | slów to | the wóund | ed Kíng. **spon·da·ic** *adj*. ⟨Greek *spondeios; spondē* libation; orig used in songs accompanying libations⟩

sponge [spʌndʒ] *n* **1** any of a phylum of invertebrate marine animals usually living attached to rocks, certain species having a porous internal skeleton. **2** a piece of such a skeleton, used to absorb liquids. **3** a product resembling this, made of rubber, cellulose, etc. **4** the act of wiping or rubbing with a sponge: *Just give that floor a sponge, will you?* **5** *Informal* SPONGER. **6** *Informal* a heavy drinker. **7** a person who absorbs much: *Children are sponges for knowledge.*
v **1** clean, dampen, apply, or soak up with a sponge. **2** *Informal* live at another's expense (with *on* or *off*): *That lazy man won't work; he just sponges on his family*. **sponge·like** *adj*. **spon·gy** *adj*. ⟨Greek *spongia*⟩
throw or **toss in the sponge** give up.
sponge bath a washing of the body with a wet sponge or cloth without getting into water. **sponge cake** a light, porous cake made with eggs, sugar, flour, etc. but no shortening. **spong·er** *n Informal* a person who lives at the expense of others.

spon·sor ['spɒnsər] *n* **1** a person or group that takes responsibility for a person or thing: *the sponsor of an immigrant applying for admission, the sponsor of a community program*. **2** a person who takes vows for a baby at baptism. **3** an organization paying the cost of a radio or television show for purposes of public relations, advertising, etc. **spon·sor** *v*. **spon·sor·ship** *n*. ⟨Latin; *spondere* bind oneself⟩

spon·ta·ne·ous [spɒn'teiniəs] *adj* **1** caused by natural impulse or desire; not planned: *spontaneous cheers*. **2** inclined to such action: *She's so spontaneous*. **3** happening without any external cause: *the spontaneous eruption of a volcano*. **spon·ta·ne·i·ty** [ˌspɒntə'niəti] *or* [-'neiəti] *or* **spon·ta·ne·ous·ness** *n*. **spon·ta·ne·ous·ly** *adv*. ⟨Latin *sponte* of one's own accord⟩
spontaneous abortion MISCARRIAGE (def. 2). **spontaneous combustion** the bursting into flame of a substance as a result of the heat produced by chemical action within it.

spoof [spuf] *Informal n* a light satirical parody; takeoff; sendup. **spoof** *v*. ⟨coined by Arthur Roberts, 20c British comedian⟩

spook [spuk] *n Informal* **1** a ghost. **2** a spy. *v* startle or scare; become startled or scared: *I was spooked by the strange tone in her voice. Our cat spooks at whistling noises*. ⟨Dutch⟩ **spook·y** *adj* **1** ghostly; eerie. **2** scary. **3** easily spooked; jumpy; skittish.

spool [spul] *n* **1** a cylinder, often with a flange at each end, on which thread, wire, etc. is wound. **2** anything shaped or used like a spool, as a reel on a fishing rod. *v* **1** wind on a spool. **2** *Computers* transfer (a print job, etc.) to a peripheral via a spooler. ⟨Middle Dutch *spoele*⟩
spool·er *n Computers* a piece of system

hardware or software transferring output to a peripheral, such as a printer, so as to free the main application to do other tasks.

spoon [spun] *n* **1** a utensil with a shallow bowl, to take up or stir food or drink. **2 spoons** *pl* a rhythm instrument consisting of two metal spoons struck together against a surface. **3** anything shaped like a spoon, esp a fishing lure.
v **1** take up or dispense with a spoon. **2** *Slang* kiss and caress amorously. **3** fish with a spoon. **spoon·ful** *n*. ⟨Old English *spōn* chip, shaving⟩ **born with a silver spoon in one's mouth,** born lucky or rich.
spoon–feed *v* **–fed, –feed·ing 1** feed with a spoon. **2** coddle; overprotect: *to spoon-feed industry with government grants.* **3** teach in such a way as to stifle independent thought.

spoon·er·ism ['spunə,rɪzəm] *n* an accidental, often humorous, transposition of initial sounds of words, as in *boil your icicle* for *oil your bicycle.* ⟨Rev. W. A. *Spooner* of Oxford, famous for this⟩

spoor [spur] *n* the trail of a wild animal; track. ⟨Afrikaans; Middle Dutch⟩

spo·rad·ic [spə'rædɪk] *adj* **1** happening at irregular intervals in time: *sporadic outbursts of violence.* **2** isolated; scattered: *sporadic cases of scarlet fever.* **spo·rad·i·cal·ly** *adv.* ⟨Greek *sporadikos* scattered; *spora* a sowing⟩

spore [spɔr] *n* **1** a single cell capable of developing into a new plant or animal. Ferns produce spores. **2** a germ or seed.
v produce spores. ⟨Greek *spora* seed⟩

sport [spɔrt] *n* **1** a game, contest, or other pastime requiring skill and physical exertion. Baseball and fishing are outdoor sports; bowling and basketball are indoor sports. **2** amusement or recreation. **3** teasing; ridicule **4** *Informal* **a** a co-operative, cheerful, generous-spirited person. **b** a person with regard to how he or she takes losing or other setbacks: *a poor sport.* **5** *Biology* an animal or plant varying markedly from the norm.
v **1** amuse oneself; play: *Lambs sport in the fields.* **2** *Informal* display or wear proudly: *to sport a new hat.* ⟨Old French *desporter* divert; *des-* away + *porter* carry, Latin *portare*⟩ **make sport of** make fun of; laugh at.
sport·ing *adj* **1** of, interested in, or engaging in sports. **2** sportsmanlike: *Letting the little boy throw first was a sporting gesture.* **3** willing to take a chance. **sport·ing·ly** *adv.* **sporting chance** a reasonably good chance of success. **sports** *adj* **1** of sports; suitable for sports: *a sports outfit.* **2** esp of a man's garment, not intended for wear with or as part of a suit; casual: *a sports jacket, sports shirt.* **sports car 1** any low, fast, two-seater car, usually with an open top. **2** any small car designed for speed and manoeuvrability. **sports·cast** *n* a broadcast of a sports event or news or discussion of sports events. **sports·cast·er** *n*. **sports·man** *n, pl* **-men 1** a man who engages in sports, esp fishing or hunting. **2** a person who plays fair and is generous to opponents. **3** a person who is willing to take a chance.

sports·man·like or **sports·man·ly** *adj.* **sports·man·ship** *n*. **sports·plex** *n* a site with facilities for a number of indoor and outdoor sports. **sports·wear** *n* clothing designed for casual wear or sports. **sports·wom·an** *n, pl* **-wom·en** a woman who engages in sports. **sports·writ·er** *n* a reporter who covers sporting events. **sport·y** *adj Informal* flashy.

spot [spɒt] *n* **1** a small, round or irregular patch of a different colour: *Her shirt is blue with white spots.* **2** a patch or part that differs in character from the rest of something: *There are a few rough spots in the road.* **3** a stain; speck: *a spot on a sweater.* **4** a place: *From this spot I can see the ocean.* **5** *Informal* a position with reference to: **a** employment. **b** scheduling for television or radio. **6** *Informal* spotlight.
adj **1** on hand; ready: *a spot answer.* **2** done at random: *a spot check.*
v **spot·ted, spot·ting 1** make spots (on): *to spot a dress.* **2** become spotted. **3** stain; sully (one's reputation, etc.). **4** see; find: *to spot a mistake.* **5** stay near (a performing gymnast) to guard against injury. **6** *Informal* loan: *I'll spot you a fiver.* **spot·ted** *adj.* **spot·ter** *n*. ⟨Middle English⟩
hit the spot *Informal* esp of food or drink, be just right; be satisfying. **in a spot** in a difficult situation. **in spots a** in various parts: *Their argument was weak in spots.* **b** at times. **on the spot a** at the very place. **b** at once. **c** in an awkward or difficult situation.
spot check 1 a brief, rough sampling. **2** a check made without warning. **spot–check** *v*. **spot·less** *adj* perfectly clean. **spot·light** *n* **1** a strong light directed on a person, thing, or small area. **2** public notice: *in the spotlight.* **spot·light, -light·ed** or **-lit, -light·ing** *v.* **spot·ty** *adj* **1** having spots; spotted. **2** not of uniform quality; irregular: *Her work was spotty.*

spouse [spʌus] *n, pl* **spous·es** ['spʌusɪz] or ['spʌuzɪz] a husband or wife. **spous·al** ['spʌuzəl] *adj.* ⟨Old French; Latin *sponsus, sponsa,* pp of *spondere* bind oneself⟩

spout [spʌut] *n* **1** a tube or lip on a teapot, jug, tap, etc. by which liquid is poured out. **2** a gushing stream or jet. **3** a column of spray blown by a whale in breathing.
v **1** flow out with force: *Water spouted from a break in the pipe.* **2** throw out (a liquid) in a stream or spray: *A whale spouts water when it breathes.* **3** *Informal* utter loudly, affectedly, or glibly: *The actor spouted his lines.* **spout·like** *adj.* ⟨compare Middle Dutch *spouten*⟩ **up the spout** *Slang* ruined; done for.

sprain [sprein] *v* injure (a joint or muscle) by a sudden twist or wrench: *He sprained his ankle.* **sprain** *n*. ⟨origin uncertain⟩

sprang [spræŋ] *v* pt of SPRING.

sprawl [sprɒl] *v* **1** lie or sit with limbs spread out ungracefully: *People sprawled on the beach.* **2** spread out in an irregular or straggling way: *Her handwriting sprawls across the page.*
n a sprawling position or development: *urban sprawl.* ⟨Old English *sprēawlian*⟩

spray¹ [sprei] *n* **1** liquid moving or sent

through the air in small drops: *We were wet with the sea spray.* **2** something like this: *A spray of bullets hit the target.*
v **1 a** apply (a liquid) in a mist or small drops: *Spray this paint on the far wall.* **b** be so dispensed. **2** scatter spray on or over: *We spray apple trees to protect them from disease.* **3** direct numerous small missiles, etc. at: *to spray the enemy with bullets.* **4** direct (anything that dispenses spray): *Spray the hose over here.* **spray·er** *n.* ⟨perhaps Middle Dutch *sprayen*⟩
spray gun a device used to spray paint, insecticide, or other liquids.

spray² [sprei] *n* **1** a small branch of some plant, with its leaves, flowers, or fruit: *a spray of lilacs, a spray of berries.* **2** a floral arrangement. ⟨Middle English⟩

spread [spred] *v* **spread, spread·ing 1** stretch out; unfold: *to spread blankets on the bed.* **2** cause to be continued over time: *He spread his assignment over several days.* **3** move further apart: *The rails of the track have spread.* **4** make or become more widely experienced, known, etc.: *Disease spread rapidly.* **5** put or be put as a thin layer: *to spread jam on bread. This paint spreads evenly.*
n **1** the act or amount of spreading: *the spread of disease.* **2** the width of something spread out: *the spread of a bird's wings.* **3** a stretch; expanse. **4** the difference between the highest and lowest numbers of a set, as scores, prices, etc. **5** a cloth covering for a bed or table. **6** food set out for a feast. **7** something to spread on bread, crackers, etc., such as butter or jam. **8** an area of land owned by a rancher. **9** an advertisement, article, etc. filling multiple columns: *a three-column spread on the election.* **spread·er** *n.* ⟨Old English *sprǣdan*⟩
spread oneself thin take on too many projects at once, so that either the work or one's health suffers. **spread one's wings a** exercise one's independence. **b** develop one's abilities.
spread·sheet *n* **1** *Computers* an application making calculations in rows and columns, allowing for easy manipulation and retrieval of numerical data. **2** *Accounting* a worksheet arranged in columns.

spree [spri] *n* **1** a lively frolic; a jolly time. **2** a period of indulging in anything: *drinking spree, shopping spree.* ⟨origin uncertain⟩

sprig [sprɪg] *n* a twig or small branch: *He wore a sprig of holly in his buttonhole.* ⟨Middle English *sprigge*⟩

spright·ly ['sprəitli] *adj* lively and quick. **spright·li·ness** *n.* ⟨*spright* variant of *sprite*⟩

spring [sprɪŋ] *v* **sprang** or **sprung, sprung, spring·ing 1** move or rise rapidly or suddenly: *She sprang to her feet.* **2** cause to move or operate suddenly: *to spring a trap.* **3** come spontaneously: *When I say 'sea', what springs to mind?* **4** originate; arise; grow (often with *up*): *Towns sprang up where oil was discovered.* **5** produce, reveal, etc. suddenly: *to spring a surprise.* **6** *Informal* pay (for): *Who'll spring for*

pizza? **7** crack or warp: *Frost had sprung the rock wall.* **8** *Slang* secure the release of (a person) from prison by bail or otherwise.
n **1** the act or result of springing: *a spring over the fence.* **2** an elastic device to regulate motion or cushion impact, that returns to its original shape after being stretched or pressed: *springs in a mattress.* **3** elastic quality: *a spring in her step.* **4** Also, **spring·time a** the season after winter, when plants begin to grow. **b** the first and freshest period: *in the spring of life.* **5** a stream of water flowing naturally from the earth. **6** source; origin: *springs of knowledge.* **spring·like** *adj.* **spring·y** *adj.* ⟨Old English *springan*⟩
spring a leak crack and begin to leak.
spring·board *n* **1** a flexible board for diving, jumping, or vaulting from. **2** anything that gives one a good start toward a goal: *Hard work was her springboard to success.* **spring chicken** *Slang* a young person: *She's no spring chicken.* **spring fever** a listless, lazy feeling that comes over some people in early spring. **spring roll** an appetizer like an EGG ROLL, but with crisper pastry. **spring salmon ✴** the largest Pacific salmon, with red, white, or, sometimes, pink flesh.

sprin·kle ['sprɪŋkəl] *v* **1** fall (on) in drops or tiny bits: *The rain sprinkled the earth.* **2** scatter (something) in drops or tiny bits: *I sprinkled sand on the icy sidewalk.* **3** dot or vary with something scattered here and there. **4** rain a little. **sprin·kle** *n.* **sprin·kling** *n.* ⟨Middle English *sprenklen* or *sprinklen*⟩
sprin·kler *n* **1** a device used to water lawns. **2** a device fixed to the ceiling of a building and spraying water in the event of a fire.

sprint [sprɪnt] *v* run at top speed, esp for a short distance. **sprint** *n.* **sprint·er** *n.* ⟨Middle English *sprenten*⟩

sprite [sprəit] *n* an elf; fairy; goblin. **sprite·like** *adj.* ⟨Old French *esprit* spirit; Latin *spiritus*⟩

spritz [sprɪts] *or* [ʃprɪts] *v* squirt or spray (something) in sudden bursts: *She spritzed herself with fragranced body mist.*
n any of various hair-care products applied by spritzing. ⟨German *spritzen* squirt⟩
sprit·zer *n* a drink made of chilled white wine and club soda.

sprock·et ['sprɒkɪt] *n* **1** one of a set of teeth on the rim of a wheel, arranged to fit into the links of a chain to keep the chain from slipping. **2** such a wheel. ⟨origin uncertain⟩

sprout [sprʌut] *v* **1** begin to grow: *Seeds sprout.* **2** cause to grow: *The rain sprouted the corn.* **3** develop rapidly: *She sprouted like a weed.*
n **1** a small shoot or bud. **2** a small child. **3 sprouts** *pl* BRUSSELS SPROUTS. **4 sprouts** *pl* the first stalks of germinating seeds, eaten as a vegetable: *bean sprouts, alfalfa sprouts.* ⟨Old English *āsprūtan*⟩

spruce¹ [sprus] *n* any of a genus of trees of the pine family, with short, evergreen needles growing singly along the stems. ⟨Middle English, variant of *Pruce* Prussia, possible origin of the tree⟩

spruce² [sprus] *adj* neat; fresh; trim: *You looked very spruce in your new suit.*
v **spruce up** make spruce or make oneself spruce: *The new rugs spruce up the living room. I spruced up for the interview.* ⟨perhaps *Spruce leather* superior Prussian leather. See SPRUCE¹.⟩

sprung [sprʌŋ] *v* a pt and pp of SPRING.

spry [spraɪ] *adj* **spry·er, spry·est** of an elderly or convalescent person, active; nimble: *The spry old lady travelled all over.* **spry·ly** *adv.* **spry·ness** *n.* ⟨perhaps Scandinavian⟩

spud [spʌd] *n Informal* potato. ⟨perhaps Scandinavian⟩
Spud Island ✳ *Slang* Prince Edward Island.

spu·mo·ne [spə'mouni] *n* Italian ice cream, often containing fruit, nuts, etc. ⟨Italian⟩

spun [spʌn] *v* a pt and pp of SPIN.
spun glass glass fibre.

spunk [spʌŋk] *n Informal* courage; pluck; spirit; mettle, esp as shown by a small person or animal. **spunk·y** *adj.* ⟨Irish or Scots Gaelic *sponnc*; Latin *spongia* sponge; Greek⟩

spur [spɜr] *n* **1** a pricking device worn on a rider's heel for urging a horse on. **2** anything that urges on: *Love was the spur that made her work.* **3** something shaped like a spur, such as the clawlike growth on the back of a cock's leg. **4** an abnormal bony outgrowth, usually on a joint. **5** a section projecting from a main mountain range, railway, etc.
v **spurred, spur·ring 1** prick with spurs. **2** urge on: *Pride spurred him to fight.* ⟨Old English *spura*⟩
on the spur of the moment on a sudden impulse. **spur–of–the–moment** *adj.* **spur on** encourage. **win one's spurs** earn distinction.

spu·ri·ous ['spjʊriəs] *adj* illegitimate or invalid; not genuine; false. **spu·ri·ous·ly** *adv.* **spu·ri·ous·ness** *n.* ⟨Latin *spurius*⟩

spurn [spɜrn] *v* refuse or resist with scorn: *to spurn a bribe.* ⟨Old English *spurnan*⟩

spurt [spɜrt] *v* **1** gush; squirt: *Blood spurted from the wound.* **2** show a sudden, brief, and intense increase in energy or activity: *The runners spurted at the end of the race.* **spurt** *n.* ⟨variant of *sprit*, Old English *spryttan*⟩

sput·ter ['spʌtər] *v* **1** make spitting or popping noises: *fat sputtering in the frying pan.* **2** throw out drops of saliva, bits of food, etc. in excitement or in talking fast. **3** say in haste and confusion. **4** falter just before failing. **sput·ter** *n.* ⟨probably imitative⟩

spu·tum ['spjutəm] *n* **1** spit¹. **2** fluid coughed up from the lungs and spat out. ⟨Latin⟩

spy [spaɪ] *n* **1** a person who keeps secret watch on the actions of others, esp of an enemy or a competitor. **2** a person paid by a government to gather secret information about another country.
v **1** keep secret watch, esp for a hostile purpose (with *on*): *A man was spying on the house.* **2** work as a spy. **3** catch sight of: *We spied a car in the lane.* **4** try to find out by observation (with *out*): *to spy out all the happenings in the area.* ⟨Old French *espier*⟩

spy·glass *n* a small handheld telescope.
spy·ware *n Computers* software that tracks an Internet user's surfing habits without the user's knowledge.

sq. square (in non-SI square measure): *sq. ft.*

squab·ble ['skwɒbəl] *n* a petty, noisy quarrel. **squab·ble** *v.* **squab·bler** *n.* ⟨perhaps imitative⟩

squad [skwɒd] *n* a small group of soldiers, police officers, or other people working as a unit. ⟨Italian *squadra* square⟩
squad·ron ['skwɒdrən] *n* **1** any of various units of an armed force. **2** any group.

squal·id ['skwɒlɪd] *adj* **1** filthy and wretched. **2** sordid; degraded. **squal·or** *n.* ⟨Latin *squalere* be filthy⟩

squall¹ [skwɒl] *n* a sudden, violent gust of wind, often with precipitation. **squall·y** *adj.* ⟨Swedish *skval-regn* sudden downpour of rain⟩
squall jacket windbreaker.

squall² [skwɒl] *v* cry loudly in a high voice: *The baby squalled.* **squall** *n.* **squall·y** *adj.* ⟨Old Norse *skvala* cry out⟩

Squa·mish ['skwɒmɪʃ] *n* **1** a First Nations people of the SW coast of British Columbia. **2** their Salishan language. **Squa·mish** *adj.*

squan·der ['skwɒndər] *v* spend foolishly; waste: *He squandered his money in gambling.* **squan·der·er** *n.* ⟨origin uncertain⟩

square [skwɛr] *n* **1** a plane figure with four equal sides and four right angles. **2** anything of or near this shape. **3** an open space in a town bounded by streets on four sides. **4** an instrument with two straight edges that form a right angle, used for drawing and testing right angles. **5** *Mathematics* the product of a number multiplied by itself: *The square of 4 is 16.* **6** *Slang* an old-fashioned person. **7** (often *pl*) *Slang* SQUARE MEAL: *three squares a day.*
adj **1** having four equal sides and four right angles. **2** cubical or nearly so. **3** having a square face in cross section. **4** of a specified length on each side of a square: *a room five metres square.* **5** angular: *square jaw.* **6** making a right angle: *a square corner.* **7** straight; level. **8** leaving no balance; even: *to make accounts square.* **9** just; fair: *a square deal.* **10** direct: *a square refusal.* **11** *Slang* old-fashioned.
v **1** make square or even: *to square a picture on the wall, to square accounts.* **2** agree or cause to agree: *I can't square his story with hers.* **3** *Mathematics* **a** find the equivalent of (a figure) in square measure. **b** multiply (a number) by itself. **4** secure the consent of, esp by a bribe. **squar·ish** *adj.* ⟨Old French *esquarre*; Latin *ex* out + *quadrus* square⟩
on the square a at right angles. **b** *Informal* just(ly); fair(ly); honest(ly). **out of square a** not at right angles. **b** out of order; incorrect(ly). **c** not in agreement. **square away a** tidy. **b** take care of (a matter). **square off** *Informal* take up a position of defence or attack. **square one** the starting point. **square the circle a** find a square equal in area to a circle. **b** attempt the impossible. **square up a** settle accounts. **b** take up a fighting stance. **c** make square.

square dance a dance performed by four or more couples arranged in a set form, usually a square. **square–dance** v. **square–danc·er** n. **square deal** Informal fair treatment. **square knot** a knot joining two loose ends of rope or cord. Each end is formed into a loop which both encloses and passes through the other. **square·ly** adv **1** exactly: to land squarely in the centre. **2** in a square way or form. **square meal** a substantial meal. **square measure** a unit or system of units for measuring area. **square–rig·ger** n a ship with sails set at right angles across the masts. **square–rigged** adj. **square root** Mathematics a number that yields a given number when multiplied by itself: The square root of 25 is 5.

squash¹ [skwɒʃ] v **1** press until soft or flat: Don't squash the cream puffs. **2** suppress: to squash a protest, to squash a riot. **3** crowd; squeeze: We all squashed into the back seat. **4** move with a splashing or sucking sound. n **1** a squashing sound. **2** a game played in a walled court with racquets and a rubber ball. **squash·y** adj. ⟨Old French esquasser; Latin ex out + quassare, intensive of quatere shake⟩

squash² [skwɒʃ] n, pl **squash** or **squash·es** the edible fruit of various trailing vines or bushy plants of the gourd family, having a tough rind and yellowish pulp with many seeds in the middle. ⟨Algonquian⟩

squat [skwɒt] v **squat·ted**, **squat·ting** v **1** crouch on the heels or haunches. **2** settle in or on another's property without title or right. **3** settle on public land to acquire ownership of it. adj **1** crouching. **2** short and thick. n a squatting posture. **squat·ter** n. ⟨Old French esquatir crush⟩

squawk [skwɒk] v **1** make a loud, harsh sound like a parrot. **2** utter harshly and loudly. **3** Slang complain loudly. **squawk** n. **squawk·er** n. ⟨imitative⟩

squeak [skwik] v make or speak with a short, sharp, high-pitched sound: A mouse squeaks. n **1** a squeaking sound. **2** Informal an instance of getting by or through with difficulty: a narrow squeak. **squeak·y** adj. ⟨imitative⟩ **squeak through** or **by** Informal get through (something) with difficulty and by a narrow margin. **squeak·y–clean** adj Informal **1** very clean. **2** morally pure, wholesome, etc. (often ironic).

squeal [skwil] v **1** make a long, shrill cry: A pig squeals when it is hurt. **2** utter sharply and shrilly. **3** Slang inform (on): He squealed on the other gang members. **squeal** n. **squeal·er** n. ⟨imitative⟩

squeam·ish ['skwimɪʃ] adj **1** too scrupulous, proper, etc.; easily shocked. **2** nauseated. **3** easily nauseated. ⟨earlier squeamous; Anglo-French escoymous⟩

squee·gee ['skwidʒi] n a sponge with a rubber blade on one side and set at right angles to a handle, for washing windows and then scraping the water off. **squee·gee** v. ⟨perhaps squeege variant of squeeze⟩

squeegee kid Informal a homeless youth who makes money by cleaning the windows of cars stopped in traffic.

squeeze [skwiz] v **1** press hard, esp from both sides: Don't squeeze the kitten; you'll hurt it. **2** hug. **3** force (something) into or out of by pressing: to squeeze juice out of lemons. **4** fit (into a schedule, etc.) with difficulty. **5 a** get (from someone) by force: The dictator squeezed money from the people. **b** Informal put pressure on (someone) to do something, esp pay money. **6** force a way: He squeezed through the crowd. n **1** the act or an instance of squeezing. **2** a hug. **3** an amount squeezed out at one time. **4** Informal a difficult situation. **5** Informal pressure used to extort a favour, money, etc. **6** SQUEEZE PLAY. **7** Business pressure resulting from shortages. **8** Slang girlfriend or lover: my main squeeze. ⟨Old English cwȳsan⟩ **squeeze play** Baseball a play in which a runner on third base starts for home as soon as the pitcher begins to pitch.

squelch [skwɛltʃ] v **1** silence; put down: She squelched him with a cold look. **2** walk in mud, wet shoes, etc., with a sucking sound. **3** make such a sound. **squelch** n. ⟨earlier quelch blend of quell and crush⟩

squib [skwɪb] n **1** a short, witty attack in speech or writing. **2** a short piece of writing. **3** a small firework that burns with a hiss and then explodes. ⟨origin uncertain⟩

squid [skwɪd] n, pl **squid** or **squids** any of various marine cephalopod molluscs having a mouth surrounded by ten sucker-bearing arms. ⟨squit variant of squirt⟩ **squid·jig·ger** n ✱ esp Newfoundland and Labrador **1** a device for catching squid, made of several hooks joined so that their points form a compact circle which is pulled or jerked through the water. **2** one who so fishes for squid. **squid·jig·ging** n.

squig·gle ['skwɪgəl] n a twisting or crooked scribble; curlicue. ⟨blend of squirm + wiggle⟩

squint [skwɪnt] v **1** look or peer with eyes partly closed: He squinted at the sun. **2** be cross-eyed. **3** look sideways. **4** cause (an eye) to squint. n **1** an act of squinting. **2** cross-eye. **3** Informal a brief, casual look: Take a squint. adj squinting. ⟨asquint, of uncertain origin⟩

squire [skwaɪr] n **1** in England, a country gentleman. **2** formerly, a young nobleman who attended a knight till he himself was made a knight. v attend as squire (often with for). ⟨variant of esquire⟩

squirm [skwɜrm] v **1** wriggle; writhe; twist: The little boy squirmed in his seat. **2** show great embarrassment, confusion, etc. **squirm** n. **squirm·y** adj. ⟨perhaps imitative⟩

squir·rel [skwɜrl] n **1** any of numerous small arboreal rodents having a long, bushy tail and feeding mainly on nuts and seeds. **2** any other rodent of the same family, esp a **flying squirrel** or a **ground squirrel**.

v -relled or -reled, -rel·ling or -rel·ing store or hide for future use (with *away*): *He had vast supplies of paper squirrelled away in the closet.* ⟨Anglo-French *esquirel;* Latin *sciurus;* Greek *skiouros; skia* shadow + *oura* tail⟩ squir·rel·ly *adj Slang* crazy.

squirt [skwɜrt] *v* 1 force out (liquid) through a narrow opening: *squirt water through a tube.* 2 come out in a jet or stream: *Water squirted from the hose.* 3 wet with a jet of liquid: *The elephant squirted me with its trunk.* *n* 1 the act of squirting. 2 a jet of liquid. 3 *Informal* an insignificant and impudent person. 4 a young child. ⟨Middle English⟩ **squirt gun** WATER PISTOL.

squish [skwɪʃ] *v* 1 *Informal* squash; squeeze. 2 make a soft splashing sound when walking in mud, water, etc. **squish** *n.* **squish·y** *adj.* ⟨imitative alteration of *squash*⟩

Sr. 1 Senior. 2 Sister.

SSE or **S.S.E.** south-southeast.

SSW or **S.S.W.** south-southwest.

St. 1 Street. 2 Saint. 3 Strait.

stab [stæb] *v* **stabbed, stab·bing** 1 pierce or wound with a pointed weapon. 2 thrust (a pointed weapon). 3 of pain, be felt sharply and suddenly. 4 wound sharply or deeply in the feelings: *The mother was stabbed to the heart by her son's thoughtlessness.* *n* 1 an act of stabbing or the resulting wound. 2 *Informal* an attempt. 3 a sudden, sharp pain. ⟨related to *stub*⟩ **have** or **make a stab at** try; attempt. **stab in the back** harm treacherously.

sta·ble¹ [ˈsteibəl] *n* 1 a building with stalls to house horses or, sometimes, other farm animals. 2 a group of animals housed in such a building or belonging to one owner. 3 a group of artists, writers, etc. working under one management. *v* put or keep (horses or other livestock) in a stable. ⟨Old French; Latin *stabulum*⟩

sta·ble² [ˈsteibəl] *adj* 1 unlikely to move, fall apart, change, etc.; firm; steady. 2 permanent; lasting. 3 reliable, mentally and emotionally balanced, etc. 4 of a chemical compound, not easily decomposed. **sta·bil·i·ty** [stəˈbɪləti] *n.* **sta·bi·lize** *v.* **sta·bly** *adv.* ⟨Latin *stabilis*⟩ **sta·bi·liz·er** *n* 1 a device for keeping a ship, aircraft, spacecraft, etc. steady. 2 a substance added to foods, chemical compounds, etc., to prevent deterioration. 3 a person or thing that makes something stable.

stac·ca·to [stəˈkɑtou] *adj* 1 *Music* played so that each note is short and detached from others. 2 full of disconnected, abrupt sounds. **stac·ca·to** *adv, n.* ⟨Italian = detached⟩

stack [stæk] *n* 1 an orderly pile of anything: *a stack of wood, a stack of coins.* 2 a heap of straw, hay, etc. 3 anything made up of parts set one on top of another. 4 Often, **stacks** *pl Informal* a large quantity: *stacks of work.* 5 a smokestack. 6 Usually, **stacks** *pl* the shelves holding the main collection in a library. 7 a number of aircraft circling an airport at different altitudes.

v 1 pile or arrange in a stack: *We stacked the books on the floor.* 2 load with something in a stack or stacks: *The table is stacked with boxes.* 3 arrange (a deck of playing cards) secretly in order to cheat. 4 assign (aircraft) to circling patterns at different altitudes to wait for clearance to land. 5 arrange (anything) so as to unfairly influence the outcome. **blow one's stack** *Slang* lose one's temper. **stack the deck** unfairly arrange circumstances beforehand. **stack up** a *Informal* measure up; compare: *How does this software stack up against the competition?* b seem plausible: *His story doesn't stack up.* ⟨Old Norse *stakkr*⟩

sta·di·um [ˈsteidiəm] *n, pl* **-di·ums** or **-di·a** an oval or U-shaped structure with rows of seats around a large, open space, used for games, concerts, etc. ⟨Greek *stadion,* ancient Greek measure of length, about 185 m⟩

staff [stæf] *n, pl* **staves** or **staffs** 1 a pole or rod used as a support, emblem of office, weapon, etc.: *The flag hangs on a staff.* 2 *pl* **staffs** a group of office workers, military officers, etc. functioning under a leader: *a school staff, the premier's staff.* 3 the five lines and four spaces between them on which music is written. *v* provide with workers. ⟨Old English *stæf*⟩ **staf·fer** *n* a member of a staff.

stag [stæg] *n* 1 an adult male deer, esp the European red deer. 2 *Informal* a a man who goes to a dance, party, etc. without a female partner. b Also, **stag party** a party for men only, held especially to honour a groom before his wedding. **stag** *adj, adv.* ⟨Old English *stagga*⟩

stage [steidʒ] *n* 1 one step or degree in a process: *an insect in the pupa stage.* 2 the raised platform in a theatre or any area where actors perform. 3 the theatre; an actor's profession: *to write for the stage.* 4 a section of a rocket that has its own motor and fuel and drops off after serving its purpose. 5 *Archaic* a a stagecoach. b a regular stopping place on a journey, or the part of a journey between stops. 6 any platform, such as one for drying meat or fish. *v* 1 a produce (a play) on a stage. b be suited for this: *That scene will not stage well.* 2 plan and carry out: *The angry workers staged a protest.* 3 fake; do for effect only: *The fight wasn't real, it was staged.* 4 do or carry out by stages: *stage disarmament.* **stage·like** *adj.* ⟨Old French *estage;* Latin *stare* stand⟩ **by** (or **in**) **easy stages** gradually; a little at a time. **on the stage** as an actor. **stage·coach** *n* formerly, a large, four-wheeled, horse-drawn coach carrying mail and passengers over a regular route. **stage·craft** *n* skill in, or the art of, producing plays. **stage direction** 1 an instruction in the script of a play or added by the director, indicating the arrangement of the stage and how the actors are to move, speak, etc. 2 the technique and skill practised by a stage director. **stage director** STAGE MANAGER. **stage fright** extreme nervousness felt when appearing before an audience. **stage·hand** *n* a person whose work is moving scenery, arranging lights, etc. in a theatre. **stage–man·age** *v* **1** be STAGE MANAGER for (a theatrical production). **2** arrange for a particular effect, esp from behind the scenes: *A few revolutionaries had stage-managed the whole crisis.* **stage manager** the person who plans the placing and changing of scenery, props, etc. for a play and ensures the proper running of each performance. **stage–struck** *adj* fascinated with acting. **stage whisper** a loud whisper meant to be overheard.

stag·fla·tion [stæg'fleiʃən] *n* inflation with rising unemployment and lack of economic growth. ⟨blend of *stagnation + inflation*⟩

stag·ger ['stægər] *v* **1** sway or cause to sway (from weakness, drunkenness, or a heavy load): *She staggered and fell.* **2** waver; become unsteady. **3** astonish greatly: *We were staggered by the news.* **4** arrange (things or sets of things) in a zigzag or steplike fashion: *The rows of theatre seats are staggered so that no person is directly behind another.* **5** schedule at intervals to avoid congestion or confusion: *Vacations were staggered so that only one person was away at a time.* **stag·ger** *n.* **stag·ger·er** *n.* ⟨Old Norse *stakra*⟩

stag·nant ['stægnənt] *adj* **1** not moving or flowing: *stagnant air, stagnant water.* **2** foul from standing still: *a stagnant pool.* **3** not active or developing; sluggish: *a stagnant economy.* **stag·nan·cy** *n.* ⟨Latin *stagnare* be stagnant; *stagnum* standing water⟩ **stag·nate** *v* make, be, or become stagnant. **stag·na·tion** *n.*

staid [steid] *adj* **1** very conservative or set in one's ways. **2** sedate; sober; dull. ⟨orig pp of *stay*¹ in sense of 'restrain'⟩

stain [stein] *n* **1** an unwanted mark left by something. **2** a cause of disgrace: *a stain on one's character.* **3** liquid dye used on wood, fabric, etc. **stain** *v.* ⟨earlier *distain;* Latin *dis*- off *+ tingere* dye⟩ **stained glass** pieces of glass coloured by metallic oxides, joined by strips of lead, in a window or ornament, usually arranged so as to form a picture or design lit up by the sun shining through. **stain·less** *adj* **1** without stain; spotless. **2** that will not stain or rust. **3** made of STAINLESS STEEL. *n* stainless steel cutlery. **stainless steel** steel containing chromium, nickel, or some other metal that makes it resistant to rust.

stair [stɛr] *n* **1** one of a series of steps for going from one level or floor to another. **2 stairs** *pl* a set of such steps; stairway: *the top of the stairs.* ⟨Old English *stǣger*⟩ **stair·case** *n* a flight of steps in its framework. **stair·way** *n* a flight of steps. **stair·well** *n* the vertical space containing a staircase.

stake [steik] *n* **1** a stick with a pointed end for driving into the ground to secure, support, or to serve as a marker. **2** formerly, a post to which one was tied for execution by burning: *Joan of Arc was burned at the stake.* **3** Often, **stakes** *pl* **a** something risked for gain or loss: *They played for high stakes.* **b** the prize in a contest. **4** an interest or share, esp in a business venture. *v* **1** fasten to or with a stake. **2** *Mining, Lumbering* mark the boundaries of (territory) with stakes. **3** risk (money or any valuable thing) on the result of a game or on any chance. **4** *Informal* help (a person) with money or other resources (with *to*): *I'll stake you to a dinner.* ⟨Old English *staca*⟩ **at stake** to be won or lost; risked: *My honour is at stake.* **pull up stakes** move away: *They finally pulled up stakes and left the farm.* **stake out a** put or keep under police surveillance. **b** claim (a territory, area of activity, etc.): *The kids have staked out part of the basement as a play area.* **stake a claim** See CLAIM. **stake·hold·er** *n* **1** the person who takes care of what is bet and pays it to the winner. **2** a person or group with an interest, or stake, in some undertaking or decision. **stake·out** or **stake–out** *n* **1** police surveillance of a building or area in anticipation of an arrest. **2** the place from which this is carried out.

sta·lac·tite [stə'læktait] *or* ['stælək,tait] *n* an icicle-shaped mass of calcium carbonate hanging from the roof of a limestone cave, formed by dripping water. ⟨Greek *stalaktos* dripping; *stalassein* trickle⟩

CONFUSABLES
For a way of distinguishing **stalactites** and **stalagmites**, remember stala**C**tites hang from a **C**eiling; stala**G**mites rise from the **G**round.

sta·lag·mite [stə'lægmait] *or* ['stæləg,mait] *n* a cone-shaped mass of calcium carbonate built up from the floor of a limestone cave by water dripping from the roof. ⟨Greek *stalagmos* a drop; *stalassein* trickle⟩

stale [steil] *adj* **1** not fresh: *stale bread.* **2** of a fizzy drink, flat. **3** old; no longer interesting: *a stale joke.* **4** out of condition as a result of overtraining or excessive exertion over time: *The horse has gone stale.* **stale** *v.* **stale·ness** *n.* ⟨Middle English⟩

stale·mate ['steil,meit] *n* **1** *Chess* the position of a player who cannot move without putting his or her king in check. **2** any situation in which no action can be taken. *v* bring to a stalemate. ⟨Middle English *stale* standstill + *mate* as in *checkmate*⟩

stalk¹ [stɔk] *n* **1** the main stem of a plant. **2** a slender part supporting a flower or leaf. **3** any similar part of an animal. The eyes of a crayfish are on stalks. ⟨Middle English *stalke*⟩

stalk² [stɔk] *v* **1** approach or pursue stealthily and with hostile intent: *The hunter stalked the lion.* **2** spread silently and steadily (through): *Disease stalked the land.* **3** walk haughtily or angrily: *She stalked from the room in a huff.* **4** harass or terrorize by persistent following, telephoning, loitering near the home or workplace of, etc. **stalk·er** *n.* ⟨Old English -*stealcian,* as in *bestealcian* steal along⟩

stall¹ [stɔl] *n* **1** a place in a stable for one animal. **2** an enclosed compartment for some purpose; cubicle: *a shower stall.* **3** an enclosed seat in a church choir or chancel.

4 an act or instance of stalling (*v* 2, 3).
v **1** put, keep, or stay in a stall. **2** come or bring to a standstill, usually against one's wish: *She stalled the engine.* **3** of an aircraft, lose so much speed that it cannot be controlled. ⟨Old English *steall*⟩

stall² [stɒl] *Informal v* be evasive; use pretexts to avoid commitment or delay action. **stall** *n.* ⟨Anglo-French *estal* decoy⟩

stal·lion ['stæljən] *n* a male horse, esp one kept for breeding. ⟨Old French *estalon*⟩

stal·wart ['stɒlwərt] *adj* **1** strongly built; sturdy. **2** firm; steadfast: *stalwart supporters.* *n* a stalwart person; faithful supporter. ⟨Old English *stathol* position + *wierthe* worthy⟩

sta·men ['steimən] *n* the male reproductive organ of a flower, consisting of a threadlike stem (filament) and a pollen-producing head (anther). ⟨Latin *stamen* warp, thread⟩

stam·i·na ['stæmənə] *n* endurance; strength or energy sustained over time: *A long-distance runner needs stamina.* ⟨Latin = threads (of life), spun by the Fates)⟩

stam·mer ['stæmər] *v* stumble or hesitate repeatedly in speaking: *She stammers when she is nervous.* **stam·mer** *n.* **stam·mer·er** *n.* **stam·mer·ing** *adj.* ⟨Old English *stamerian*⟩

Stammer usually suggests a painful effort to form sounds and words, with breaks or silences in or between words. **Stutter** more often suggests a habit of rapidly repeating the same sound, especially initial consonants.

stamp [stæmp] *v* **1** step or walk, bringing down (one's foot or feet) with force: *to stamp on a cockroach.* **2** press with an instrument that cuts or imprints a design, official mark, etc.: *to stamp coins, to stamp a deed.* **3** impress, mark, or cut out (a design, words, etc.) on something: *to stamp the date on a letter.* **4** fix firmly or deeply: *His words were stamped on my mind.* **5** consign to a certain category, outlook, etc., as if by stamping: *Certain events stamp you for life.* **6** stick a stamp on.
n **1 a** a small piece of paper with a sticky back, put on mail to show that the postage has been paid. **b** a similar piece of paper used for any of various purposes: *a trading stamp.* **2** an act of stamping. **3** an instrument that shapes or marks by stamping. **4** the mark it makes. **5** lasting effect(s): *Her face bore the stamp of suffering.* **6** identifying feature: *the stamp of good breeding.* **7** kind; type: *Men of his stamp are rare.* **stamp·er** *n.* ⟨Middle English *stampen*⟩
stamp out a extinguish by stamping. **b** put an end to by force.
stamp pad a pad soaked with ink for use with a rubber or metal stamp.

stam·pede [stæm'pid] *n* **1** a sudden headlong flight of a herd of animals or group of people: *the stampede of a panic-stricken crowd.* **2** a general rush: *a stampede to newly discovered gold fields.* **3** a rodeo, often with attractions like those at a fair: *the Calgary Stampede.* **stam·pede** *v.* ⟨Spanish *estampida*⟩

stance [stæns] *n* **1** way of standing; posture. **2** an attitude or mental position taken with respect to something: *a political stance.* ⟨Old French *estance*; Latin *stare* stand⟩

stand [stænd] *v* **stood, stand·ing 1** take or have an upright position on one's feet: *We stood there for an hour.* **2** have specified height when upright: *He stands 180 cm in his socks.* **3** set or be upright or in a given location: *cups standing in the sink.* **4** take or keep a given position: *"Stand back!" the officer called to the crowd.* **5** maintain a way of thinking or acting: *to stand for fair play.* **6** be in a given condition: *to stand in need of help.* **7** remain unchanged or in force: *The rule against lateness will stand.* **8** bear; tolerate: *I can't stand that song!* **9** be submitted to: *to stand trial.* **10** *Informal* bear the expense of: *I'll stand you a trip to Hawaii for your birthday.* **11** be or stay still: *"Stand!" cried the sentry.* **12** be a candidate: *to stand for election.*
n **1** the act or state of standing. **2** a stop for defence, resistance, etc.: *a last stand against the enemy.* **3** a halt on a theatrical tour, for a performance: *a one-night stand.* **4** stands *pl* tiered seats for spectators or an audience. **5** a position or attitude with regard to an issue, etc.: *to take a moral stand.* **6** a place for waiting taxis: *a taxi stand.* **7** the place where a witness testifies in court. **8** a thing to put things on or in: *an umbrella stand.* **9** a stall, booth, table, etc. for a small business: *a newspaper stand.* **10** a standing growth of plants: *a fine stand of timber, a stand of wheat.* ⟨Old English *standan*⟩
stand a chance have a chance. **stand behind** support; guarantee. **stand by a** be near. **b** help; support: *to stand by a friend.* **c** keep (a promise, etc.). **d** be ready for action: *The radio operator was ordered to stand by.* **e** be a passive onlooker. **stand down** retire from an office. **stand for a** mean; represent. **b** be on the side of: *Our school stands for fair play.* **c** *Informal* put up with: *I won't stand for any nonsense.* **stand in** be a substitute (*for*). **stand off** remain at a distance. **stand on a** be founded on. **b** insist on; claim: *to stand on one's rights.* **stand on ceremony** care much for formalities. **stand out a** be noticeable or prominent: *Certain facts stand out.* **b** contrast with a background: *The trees stand out against the sunset.* **c** refuse to yield: *to stand out against popular opinion.* **stand over** supervise closely. **stand pat** refuse to give in to change. **stand to serve at one's post. stand up a** get to one's feet: *She stood up.* **b** endure: *That fabric won't stand up under hard wear.* **c** *Informal* fail to meet as planned: *She apologized for standing him up.* **stand up for** take the part of; defend: *to stand up for a friend.* **stand up to** defy: *She stood up to the bully.* **stand up with** *Informal* act as best man, bridesmaid, etc. to. **take a stand** commit oneself to a position on an issue. **take the stand** testify in court.
stand–a·lone *Computers adj* independent of other hardware or software. *n* a stand-alone unit, program, etc. **stand·by** *n, pl* **-bys 1** a person or thing that can be relied on. **2** an

order to stand by. **3** any person or thing held in reserve. **4** a person waiting to board an aircraft if space becomes available. *adv* on standby: *to fly standby.* **on standby a** waiting to be called as needed. **b** waiting for a chance to board a plane. **stand–in** *n* substitute. **stand·ing** *n* **1** position or rank; reputation: *citizens of high standing, members in good standing.* **2** duration: *a feud of long standing. adj* **1** that stands: *standing water.* **2** done from or in an erect position: *a standing ovation.* **3** always ready or in effect: *a standing order.* **standing room** space to stand in, esp after all seats are taken. **stand–off** *n* **1** a confrontation. **2** a draw in a conflict. **stand–off·ish** *adj* reserved; aloof. **stand–out** *n Informal* an outstanding person or thing. *adj* outstanding. **stand·point** *n* point of view; aspect. **stand·still** *n* a full stop. **stand–up** *adj* **1** that stands up: *a stand-up collar.* **2** done or used in a standing position: *a stand-up meal.* **3** of a comedian, performing alone, standing and talking to the audience. **4** *Informal* reliable; honest: *A stand-up kind of person can be trusted. n* stand-up comedy.

stand·ard [ˈstændərd] *n* **1** anything against which other things are judged or compared; model; norm: *Your work is not up to standard.* **2** a rule, test, or requirement. **3** a commodity serving as the basis of a monetary system: *the gold standard.* **4** the lowest grade of excellence of a product, etc. **5** a flag or emblem. **6** the largest size of car. Compare SUBCOMPACT and COMPACT. **7** a car with a manual transmission. **8** a piece of music, literature, etc. routinely studied, played, etc. because of its enduring quality. **standard** *adj.* ⟨Old French *estandart*⟩
stand·ard·bear·er *n* **1** one who carries a flag or standard in a procession or into battle. **2** a conspicuous leader of a movement, party, etc. **stand·ard·ize** *v* cause to conform to a standard. **stand·ard·i·za·tion** *n.* **standard of living** the kind and quantity of material possessions, conveniences, etc. considered necessary. **standard time** the time officially adopted for a region or country, based on distance from Greenwich, England. The world is divided into 24 standard time zones. Compare DAYLIGHT-SAVING TIME.

Standard applies to a rule, principle, etc. generally accepted as a basis of comparison in evaluating the quality, value, etc. of something: *high standards of teaching.*
A **criterion** is a single feature used as a test in judging whether a person or thing fits in a certain category: *Popularity is not everybody's criterion of a good movie.*

stank [stæŋk] *v* pt of STINK.

Stan·ley Cup [ˈstænli] the cup presented annually to the winning team in the final playoff in a National Hockey League season. ⟨Sir Frederick *Stanley*, Governor General of Canada, 1888-1893⟩

stan·za [ˈstænzə] *n* **1** a group of lines of poetry set off as a unit, often following a

fixed rhyme scheme, etc. **2** a verse of a song. ⟨Italian, orig place to stop; Latin *stare* stand⟩

staph·y·lo·coc·cus [ˌstæfələˈkɒkəs] *n, pl* **-coc·ci** [-ˈkɒkaɪ] *or* [-ˈkɒksaɪ] any of a genus of bacteria often occurring in irregular clusters, including many disease-causing species. ⟨Greek *staphylē* bunch of grapes + *kokkos* grain⟩

sta·ple¹ [ˈsteipəl] *n* a fastener consisting of wire in the form of a square U, whose ends are driven into wood or through sheets of paper. **sta·ple** *v.* ⟨Old English *stapol* post⟩
sta·pler *n* a device that drives a staple through paper and clinches it on the other side. A **staple gun** drives staples into wood.

sta·ple² [ˈsteipəl] *n* **1** a food item forming a basic part of the diet: *to stock up on staples.* **2** the main raw material or commodity produced: *Wheat is the staple in Saskatchewan.* **3** any major element of something. **4** a fibre of cotton, wool, etc.
adj important; principal: *a staple topic of conversation.* ⟨Old French *estaple* mart⟩

star [stɑr] *n* **1** a heavenly body made of gases and giving off light, such as the sun. **2** a conventional figure having five points, or sometimes six, like this: ☆ **3** anything of this shape, used as a mark of excellence, sign of rank, etc. **4** an asterisk (*). **5** a person of brilliant qualities, or one who is famous in some field: *an athletic star.* **6** a person who plays the lead in a performance.
v **starred, star·ring 1** ornament with stars: *Her card was starred for perfect attendance.* **2** mark with an asterisk. **3** feature as a star: *to star in a film.* **star·dom** *n.* **star·less** *adj.* **star·ry** *adj.* ⟨Old English *steorra*⟩
see stars see flashes of light as a result of a hard blow on the head. **thank one's lucky stars** be thankful for one's good luck.
star–crossed *adj* ill-fated: *Romeo and Juliet are star-crossed lovers.* **star·dust** *n* glamour; enchanting mystique. **star·fish** *n, pl* **-fish** or **-fish·es** any of a class of marine invertebrates having a flat, spiny body with five or more arms radiating from a central disk. **star·gaze** *v* **1** gaze at the stars. **2** daydream. **star·gaz·er** *n.* **star·let** *n* a talented young female actor or singer being groomed for stardom. **star·light** *n* light from the stars. **star·lit** *adj* lit by the stars. **Star of David** a six-pointed star formed by two superimposed equilateral triangles, a symbol of Judaism. Also called **Magen David.** **star·ry–eyed** *adj* idealistic; romantically naive. **star–stud·ded** *adj* filled or covered with stars: *a star-studded sky, a movie with a star-studded cast.*

star·board [ˈstɑrbərd] *n* the right side of a ship or aircraft, facing forward.
star·board *adj.* ⟨Old English *stēorbord; stēor* steering paddle + *bord* side (of a ship)⟩

starch [stɑrtʃ] *n* **1** a tasteless carbohydrate found in many vegetables and cereal crops. **2** a preparation of this, used as a stiffener or thickener. **3 starches** *pl* foods high in starch. *v* stiffen (fabric) with starch. **starch·y** *adj.* ⟨Old English *stercan* stiffen; *stearc* stiff, strong⟩

take the starch out of *Informal* cause to lose courage, confidence, energy, or vigour.

stare [stɛr] *v* **1** look long and directly with the eyes wide open, out of wonder, surprise, stupidity, curiosity, or rudeness. **2** of the eyes, be very wide, bulging, or penetrating. **stare** *n*. ⟨Old English *starian*⟩
stare down confuse or embarrass by staring.
stare someone in the face be very evident: *His mistake was staring him in the face.*

stark [stɑrk] *adj* **1** desolate: *a stark landscape.* **2** grim: *stark reality.* **3** complete: *stark nonsense.* *adv* entirely: *stark naked.* **stark·ly** *adv*. **stark·ness** *n*. ⟨Old English *stearc* stiff, strong⟩

star·ling [ˈstɑrlɪŋ] *n* any of a family of songbirds, esp a common, brown or black bird, often considered a pest. ⟨Old English *stærling*⟩

start [stɑrt] *v* **1** begin: *to start a book, to start working.* **2** get or cause to get happening, moving, etc.: *to start a fire. My car won't start.* **3** establish: *to start a business.* **4** jerk or jump, as in surprise or alarm: *She started at the loud noise.* **5** rise up suddenly: *Tears started from his eyes.* **6** stick out: *eyes starting from their sockets.* **7** cause to begin: *You have started me thinking.* **start** *n*. ⟨variant of Old English *styrtan* leap up⟩
by fits and starts in spurts. **start in (on) a** begin vigorously. **b** begin scolding. **start out a** begin a journey. **b** begin with a given intention: *I didn't start out to get him fired!* **start off** begin a journey or race. **start up a** rise suddenly. **b** come suddenly into being or notice. **c** of an engine, begin or cause to begin operating. **d** set up: *to start up a new operation.* **to start with** in the first place: *To start with, you can clear up this huge mess.*

start·er *n* **1** a person or thing that starts. **2** a person who gives the signal for starting. **3** an electric motor used to start an internal-combustion engine. **4** a chemical agent or bacterial culture used to start a reaction, esp in the formation of acid to make cheese, sourdough, etc. **for starters** *Informal* **a** first of all. **b** as a first course: *Shall we have soup for starters?* **starting blocks** blocks against which a runner places the feet for a start in a race.

star·tle [ˈstɑrtəl] *v* **1** frighten suddenly. **2** surprise; shock. **3** move or cause to move suddenly in surprise or fear: *The horse startled when the gun went off.* **star·tle** *n*. **star·tling** *adj*. ⟨Old English *steartlian* struggle⟩

starve [stɑrv] *v* **1** die or kill through hunger. **2** suffer or cause to suffer because of hunger. **3** bring to a certain state by depriving of food: *to starve someone into surrendering.* **star·va·tion** *n*. ⟨Old English *steorfan* die⟩
starving *adj Informal* hungry; having a good appetite. **be starving for** suffer from lack of: *That child is starving for affection.*

stash [stæʃ] *Informal v* hide or put away for safekeeping or future use.
n **1** something hidden away or stored: *a small stash of money.* **2** the place where it is hidden away or stored. ⟨origin uncertain⟩

sta·sis [ˈsteɪsɪs] *or* [ˈstæsɪs] *n, pl* **-ses** [-siz] a state of balance or motionlessness. ⟨Greek = a standing; *sta-* a root of *histanai* stand⟩

state [steɪt] *n* **1** the condition of a person or thing: *in a state of poor health. Ice is water in a solid state.* **2** a person's position in life; rank: *a humble state.* **3** dignified and luxurious style: *living in state.* **4** *Informal* a condition of upset or confusion: *She was in quite a state when we got there.* **5** NATION (def. 1). **6** one of the political units that together form a nation: *the state of Alaska.* **7** the government: *The state provides citizens with legal protection.* *adj* to do with very formal and ceremonious occasions: *state robes.*
v tell in speech or writing: *to state one's views.* **stat·a·ble** *adj*. **state·hood** *n*. ⟨Latin *status* condition, position; *stare* stand⟩
lie in state of the body of a monarch, political leader, etc., lie in a coffin for public view before burial.
state·craft *n* the art of governing a nation. **state·less** *adj* **1** without citizenship in any country. **2** without political boundaries: *a stateless world.* **state·ly** *adj* dignified; grand. **state·li·ness** *n*. **state·ment** *n* **1** the act of stating something. **2** a report; something stated. **3** a summary of an account, showing credits, debits, and balance. **4** a declarative sentence. **state of the art** the current, most sophisticated stage of a technology or art. **state–of–the–art** *adj*. **state·room** *n* a private room on a ship or, formerly, on a passenger train. **states·man** *n, pl* **-men** a man skilled in the management of public affairs. **states·wom·an** *n, pl* **-wom·en**. **states·man·like** or **states·man·ly** *adj*. **states·man·ship** *n*. **the States** *n pl* the United States of America.

stat·ic [ˈstætɪk] *adj* **1** not moving or changing: *Civilization does not remain static, but changes constantly.* **2** to do with bodies at rest or with forces in balance. **3** acting by weight without motion: *static pressure.* **4** *Electricity* to do with stationary charges in balance. **5** to do with atmospheric electricity that interferes with radio reception.
n **1** atmospheric electricity. **2** interference, esp with radio signals, due to such electricity. **3** *Slang* a negative reaction; FLAK (def. 2): *She got a lot of static for what she said on TV.* **stat·i·cal·ly** *adv*. ⟨Greek *statikos* causing to stand. See STASIS.⟩
static cling the clinging of things to each other, esp clothing, due to STATIC ELECTRICITY. **static electricity** the electricity contained in or produced by charged bodies, rather than flowing as a current. **stat·ics** *n* (*with sg verb*) the study of bodies at rest and the action of forces in balance; a branch of mechanics.

sta·tion [ˈsteɪʃən] *n* **1** a place to which a person is assigned for duty: *The police officer took her station at the corner.* **2** a building used for a usually public purpose: *a weather station.* **3 a** the place for sending signals by radio or television. **b** the organization that owns it. **c** the frequency reserved for its use; channel. **4** a stopping place on a train or bus route. **5** social position. **6** *Australian* a ranch or large farm. **7** ⚓ *Newfoundland and Labrador* temporary quarters established on shore during fishing season.

v **1** place: *He stationed himself just outside the hotel.* **2** assign to a place or position: *soldiers stationed in Italy.* ⟨Latin *statio*; *stare* stand⟩

sta·tion·ar·y ['steiʃə,nɛri] *adj* **1** not movable; fixed. **2** not moving. **3** not changing in size, number, activity, etc.: *The population there has been stationary for ten years.* **sta·tion·er** *n* a person who sells writing supplies. **sta·tion·er·y** ['steiʃə,nɛri] *n* paper, cards, envelopes, etc. and, sometimes, other writing supplies. **Stations of the Cross** *Roman Catholic Church* **1** fourteen scenes from the Passion of Christ, usually ranged around the walls of a church. **2** the prayers, devotions, etc. performed in sequence at these stations.

> **CONFUSABLES**
> **Stationary** is an adjective meaning 'not moving'. **Stationery** is a noun meaning 'writing materials'.

sta·tis·tic [stə'tɪstɪk] *n* an item in a set of STATISTICS (def. 1). ⟨Latin *statisticus* political; *status* state. See STATE.⟩

sta·tis·tics [stə'tɪstɪks] *n pl* **1** numerical data about people, the weather, etc., tabulated systematically. **2** the science of collecting, tabulating, and analyzing such data. (*with sg verb*). **sta·tis·ti·cal** *adj.* **sta·tis·ti·cal·ly** *adv.* **stat·is·ti·cian** [,stætə'stɪʃən] *n.* **stats** *n pl Informal* statistics. **Stats·Can** ['stæts'kæn] *n Informal* **Statistics Canada**, the federal agency that issues statistics on many subjects.

stat·ue ['stætʃu] *n* an image of a person or animal, or an abstract form, made by carving, casting, or modelling. ⟨French; Latin *statua*; *stare* stand⟩

stat·u·ar·y *n* statues collectively; statues as an artistic genre. *adj* of or for statues: *statuary marble.* **stat·u·esque** [-'ɛsk] *adj* like a statue in dignity, grace, or classic beauty. **stat·u·ette** [-'ɛt] *n* a small statue.

stat·ure ['stætʃər] *n* **1** a person's height. **2** reputation: *a woman of great stature in her profession.* ⟨Latin *statura*; *stare* stand⟩

sta·tus ['stætəs] *or* ['steitəs] *n* **1** condition; state: *the status of world affairs.* **2** social or professional standing: *Serfs had low status.* **3** high rank; prestige. **4** legal position or category. ⟨Latin; pp of *stare* stand⟩ **status Indian ✶** a First Nations person registered with the federal government as a member of a band, with certain rights under the Indian Act. **status quo** [kwou] the existing state of affairs. **status symbol** a thing indicating high social position, as a certain car, membership in a certain club, etc.

stat·ute ['stætʃut] *n* a law formally enacted and documented by a legislative body of any kind. ⟨Old French *estatut*, ult.; Latin *statuere* establish, ult.; *stare* stand⟩ **statute law** written law; statutes collectively. **statute mile** a unit of distance on land, equal to 1.61 km. **statute of limitations** *Law* any statute that specifies a certain period of time after which legal action cannot be brought or

offences punished. **Statute of Westminster** an act of the British Parliament, passed in 1931, by which Canada and other dominions were granted full authority to make their own laws. **stat·u·to·ry** *adj* **1** to do with statutes. **2** fixed, defined, or punishable by statute. **statutory holiday** a legal public holiday on which courts, government offices, schools, etc. are closed. **statutory rape** the crime of a male having sexual intercourse with a girl below the age of consent.

staunch[1] [stɒntʃ] *v* stop (a flow of blood), etc. Also, **stanch**. ⟨Old French *estanchier*; Latin *extanicare* press together⟩

staunch[2] [stɒntʃ] *adj* loyal and steadfast. **staunch·ly** *adv.* **staunch·ness** *n.* ⟨Old French *estanchier* cause to stop flowing. See STAUNCH[1].⟩

stave [steiv] *n* **1** one of the curved pieces of wood forming the sides of a barrel, tub, etc. **2** STAFF (defs. 1, 3).
v **staved** or **stove**, **stav·ing** **1** smash a hole in (a barrel, boat, etc.) (often with *in*). **2** furnish with staves. ⟨*staves*, pl of *staff*⟩ **stave off** hold off; delay or prevent: *The lost campers ate birds' eggs to stave off starvation.*

staves [steivz] *n* **1** a pl of STAFF. **2** pl of STAVE.

stay[1] [stei] *v* **1** continue to be as or where indicated: *to stay clean. Stay here.* **2** live (somewhere) for a while: *She is staying with her aunt.* **3** stop, esp to visit: *Sorry, we can't stay.* **4** wait: *Time and tide stay for no man.* **5** satisfy temporarily (hunger, appetite, etc.). **6** delay; restrain: *to stay someone's anger.* **7** keep up or keep moving (*with*) as in a contest or race, discussion, etc.: *Stay with me while I explain each part.*
n **1** time spent in one place: *a pleasant stay in the country.* **2** a suspension (of judgment, etc.). ⟨Old French *ester* stand; Latin *stare*⟩ **stay put** remain in the same place: *Stay put till I get there. This label won't stay put.* **stay–at–home** *n* a person who prefers to stay home rather than go out or travel. *adj* **1** being a stay-at-home. **2** not working at a job outside the home: *a stay-at-home mom.* **staying power** ability to endure: *She doesn't work very fast, but she has great staying power.*

stay[2] [stei] *n* **1** a support; prop; brace. **2** a spiritual or moral support.
v **1** support; prop; hold up. **2** secure mentally or spiritually. ⟨probably Old French *estayer*⟩

stay[3] [stei] *n* a strong rope, etc., attached to something to steady it: *The mast of a ship is held in place by stays.*
v support or secure with or as if with stays. ⟨Old English *stæg*⟩

St. Saint.

STD sexually transmitted disease.

Ste. Sainte.

stead [stɛd] *n* the place of a person or thing, filled by a substitute: *She could not come, but sent me in her stead.* ⟨Old English *stede*⟩ **stand someone in good stead** be of advantage or service to someone.
stead·fast [-,fæst] *adj* **1** loyal; firm. **2** fixed; not moving or changing. **stead·fast·ly** *adv.*

stead·fast·ness *n.* **stead·y** *adj* **1** continuing regularly: *steady progress.* **2** fixed; firm: *to hold a ladder steady.* **3** calm: *steady nerves.* **4** having good habits; reliable: *a steady young man.* *v* make, keep, or become steady. *n Informal* a regular girlfriend or boyfriend. *interj* **1** stay calm! **2** *Nautical* keep on course! **go steady** *Informal* date one person or each other only. **stead·i·ly** *adv.* **stead·i·ness** *n.* **stead·y–state** *adj* unchanging in quality, structure, behaviour, etc. **steady–state theory** the theory that the universe has now the same basic form as always, amtter being continuously created to replace that which is naturally destroyed. Compare BIG BANG THEORY.

steak [steik] *n* a thick slice of meat, usually broiled, grilled, or fried. ⟨Old Norse *steik*⟩ **steak tartare** [tɑr'tɑr] raw beefsteak ground up and mixed with seasoning and raw egg.

steal [stil] *v* **stole, sto·len, steal·ing 1** take (something) that does not belong to one: *to steal money.* **2** take, get, or do secretly or without permission: *to steal a look at someone.* **3** move secretly or quietly: *She stole out of the house.* **4** *Baseball* of a runner, advance a base without the help of a hit or error. *n* **1** *Informal* an excellent bargain: *At that price the car is a steal.* **2** *Baseball* an act of stealing. **steal·er** *n.* ⟨Old English *stelan*⟩ **steal someone's heart** win someone's love by art, charm, etc. **steal the scene** (or **show**) dominate a performance.

stealth [stelθ] *n* secret or sly action: *He obtained the letter by stealth, taking it while his sister's back was turned.* **stealth bomber** a bomber plane designed to be hard to detect. **stealth·y** *adj* done or acting in a secret manner: *a stealthy intruder.* **stealth·i·ly** *adv.*

steam [stim] *n* **1** the invisible vapour into which water is changed when it is heated to the boiling point. **2** the white mist formed when the invisible vapour from boiling water cools and condenses. **3 a** the vapour from boiling water, kept under pressure to generate mechanical power. **b** power so generated. **4** *Informal* power; energy. *v* **1** give off steam: *steaming soup.* **2** become covered with steam (usually with *up*): *The windshield steamed up inside the car.* **3** prepare, treat, etc. with steam: *to steam a pudding.* **4** move by or as if by the power of steam: *The ship steamed away.* ⟨Old English *stēam*⟩ **full steam ahead** with all possible power or energy. **let** (or **blow**) **off steam** *Informal* **a** get rid of excess energy. **b** relieve one's feelings of anger, etc. **run out of steam** *Informal* lose energy or enthusiasm. **steamed** (**up**) *Informal* angry, fuming: *all steamed up about nothing.* **steam bath** a kind of bath taken by sitting or standing in a steam-filled room. **steam·boat** *n* a boat propelled by a STEAM ENGINE (def. 1). **steamed** *adj* **1** *Informal* angry. **2** cooked, etc. by steam. **steam engine 1** an engine operated by steam, typically one with a sliding piston moved inside a cylinder by the action of steam. **2** a locomotive powered by such an engine. **steam·er** *n* **1** steamboat; steamship. **2** a container in which something may be

steamed. **3** a soft-shelled clam. **steam·ing** *adj Informal* very angry. **steamroll·er** *n* **1** a road roller, esp one powered by steam. **2** an overpowering force used to crush opposition. *v* **1** make (pavement) level, smooth, etc. with a steam-roller. **2** override by crushing power: *to steam-roller all opposition.* **3** force by this means: *to steam-roller a bill through Parliament.* **steam·ship** *n* a ship propelled by a STEAM ENGINE (def. 1). **steam·y** *adj* **1** to do with steam. **2** *Slang* **a** with sexual content: *a steamy romance.* **b** passionate. **3** sultry; hot and humid. **steam·i·ly** *adv.* **steam·i·ness** *n.*

steed [stid] *n Poetic* a horse, esp a spirited riding horse. ⟨Old English *stēda*⟩

steel [stil] *n* **1** an alloy of iron and carbon. **2** great hardness or strength: *nerves of steel.* **3 ⚒** railway track: *to lay steel.* *v* make hard or strong like steel: *He steeled himself for the coming ordeal.* **steel–like** *adj.* ⟨Old English *stēle*⟩ **steel band** a band composed of steel drums, common in the West Indies. **steel drum** a tuned percussion instrument originating in Trinidad, made from an oil drum. **steel guitar** an electric guitar held on the lap, played by picking with one hand while sliding a shaped piece of metal along the strings with the other. **steel·head** (**trout**) *n, pl* **-head** or **-heads** a fish of the Pacific coast. **steel wool** fine steel threads in a pad, used for cleaning or polishing. **steel·works** *n* a factory where steel is made. **steel·work·er** *n.* **steel·y** *adj* like steel in colour, strength, or hardness. **steel·i·ness** *n.*

steep¹ [stip] *adj* **1** having a sharp slope: *The hill is steep.* **2** *Informal* of a price, very high. **3** unreasonable; exaggerated. **steep·ly** *adv.* **steep·ness** *n.* ⟨Old English *stēap*⟩

steep² [stip] *v* **1** soak (something), esp so as to soften, cleanse, or extract an essence. **2** undergo such soaking: *Let the tea steep.* ⟨probably Old English *stēap* bowl⟩ **steeped in** saturated or permeated with: *ruins steeped in gloom, a mind steeped in hatred.*

stee·ple ['stipəl] *n* a high tower on the roof of a church. ⟨Old English *stēpel*; *stēap* steep⟩ **stee·ple·chase** *n* **1** a horse race over a course having hedges and other obstacles. **2** a foot race over a similar course. **stee·ple·chas·er** *n.*

steer¹ [stir] *v* **1** guide; control the course of (a moving object): *to steer a car.* **2** be so guided: *This car steers easily.* **3** guide: *to steer a person toward the exit.* **4** direct one's way: *to steer for home.* **steer·er** *n.* ⟨Old English *stēoran*⟩ **steer clear of** keep away from; avoid. **steer·age** *n* the part of a passenger ship occupied by passengers paying the lowest fare. **steering committee** a committee struck to consider order of business, priorities, etc. **steering wheel** the wheel that is turned to steer a car, ship, etc.

steer² [stir] *n* a full-grown, castrated male of cattle, less than four years old, raised for meat.

steg·o·sau·rus [ˌstegə'sɔrəs] *n, pl* **-ri** [-raɪ] *or* [-ri] a large, plant-eating dinosaur of the late

Jurassic period, with bony plates along the back. ⟨Greek *stegos* roof + *sauros* lizard⟩

stel·lar ['stɛlər] *adj* **1** to do with stars; of or like a star. **2** outstanding: *a stellar performance.* **3** chief: *a stellar role.* ⟨Latin *stella* star⟩

stem¹ [stɛm] *n* **1** the main supporting part of a plant, usually above ground. **2** the small part joining a flower, fruit, or leaf to the plant; petiole or pedicel. **3** anything like or suggesting the stem of a plant: *the stem of a goblet.* **4** *Grammar* the part of a word to which endings are added and inside which changes are made. *Run* is the stem of *runs, runner, ran,* etc.
v **stemmed, stem·ming 1** remove the stem from (a fruit, leaf, etc.). **2** arise: *The difficulty stems from a lack of proper planning.* **stem·less** *adj.* **stem·like** *adj.* ⟨Old English *stemn*⟩
from stem to stern a from one end of the ship to the other. **b** along the full length of anything.
stem cell *Genetics* an unspecialized cell that can differentiate into any of several types. **stem·ware** *n* wine glasses and other glasses with stems.

stem² [stɛm] *v* **stemmed, stem·ming 1** stop; check; dam up. **2** make progress against: *to stem the swift current.* ⟨Old Norse *stemma*⟩

stench [stɛntʃ] *n* a very bad smell; stink. ⟨Old English *stenc*; related to *stincan* smell⟩

sten·cil ['stɛnsəl] *n* **1** a sheet of metal, stiff paper, etc. with letters or designs cut out of it. **2** the letters or designs made by tracing or filling in the cutouts. **sten·cil, -cilled** or **-ciled, -cil·ling** or **-cil·ing** *v.* ⟨Old French *estanceler* ornament with colours; Latin *scintilla* spark⟩

sten·to·ri·an [stɛn'tɔriən] *adj* very loud or powerful in sound. ⟨*Stentor* in Greek legend a herald whose voice was as loud as fifty men⟩

step [stɛp] *n* **1** an act of lifting the foot and putting it down again in a new position, as in walking, etc. **2** the distance so covered: *two steps away.* **3** a short distance: *The school is only a step away.* **4** a way of walking, dancing, etc.: *a slow step.* **5** a place for the foot on a stairway, ladder, etc. **6** the sound or print made by putting the foot down: *I heard steps.* **7** an action toward a goal: *taking steps to reduce absenteeism.* **8** a degree in a series or stage in a process.
v **stepped, step·ping 1** move the legs as in walking, running, dancing, etc.: *Step lively!* **2** put the foot down (*on*): *to step on a worm.* ⟨Old English *steppan*⟩
in step a keeping pace with another or keeping in time with music. **b** in agreement (*with*). **keep step** move, think, or act in step. **out of step a** not keeping pace with others or in time to music. **b** not in harmony or accord. **step by step** little by little. **step down a** resign from a position: *She stepped down from the presidency.* **b** decrease: *to step down the rate of flow.* **step in** intervene. **step into** assume or take on (a role, job, etc.). **step off** measure by taking steps: *Step off the distance from the door to the window.* **step on it** *Informal* go fast. **step out** *Informal* leave a

room or building very briefly: *He's just stepped out for a minute.* **step up a** approach. **b** increase: *to step up production.* **take steps** carry out actions considered to be necessary, desirable, etc. **watch one's step a** step carefully. **b** be careful.
step–down *adj* **1** causing a gradual decrease. **2** *Electricity* of a transformer, lowering the voltage of a current. **step·lad·der** *n* a short ladder with a support hinged to the top so as to be free-standing. **step·ping–stone** *n* **1** a stone in shallow water, wet earth, etc., used in crossing. **2** any means of advancing. **step–up** *adj* **1** causing a gradual increase. **2** *Electricity* of a transformer, increasing the voltage of a current. *n* an increase.

step– *prefix* related by the remarriage of a parent, not by blood: *stepmother, stepsister, stepson.* ⟨Old English *stēop-*⟩

steppe [stɛp] *n* a treeless plain, esp in SE Europe and Asia. ⟨Russian *step*⟩

–ster *suffix Often facetious* **1** one that is, does, or makes: *youngster, rhymester.* **2** other special meanings: *gangster, roadster, teamster.* ⟨Old English *-estre, -istre*⟩

ster·e·o ['stɛri,ou] *n* **1** a radio, cassette or CD player, television set, etc. equipped with a stereophonic sound system. **2** stereophonic reproduction. **ster·e·o** *adj.* ⟨*stereophonic*⟩

ster·e·o·phon·ic [,stɛriə'fɒnɪk] *adj* in sound reproduction, of or produced by the use of multiple loudspeakers, etc. to give a three-dimensional effect. **ster·e·o·phon·i·cal·ly** *adv.* ⟨Greek *stereos* solid + PHONIC⟩

ster·e·o·type ['stɛriə,təip] *n* **1** a conventional mental image applied to all members of a category: *He fits the stereotype of the insecure bully.* **2** a person or thing that matches such an image: *The novel's hero is a stereotype of the romantic artist.*
v view or treat according to a stereotype. **ster·e·o·typed** *adj.* **ster·e·o·typ·i·cal** [-'tɪpɪkəl] *adj* conforming to a stereotype.

ster·ile ['stɛraɪl] *or* ['stɛrəl] *adj* **1** free from living micro-organisms, esp harmful ones: *sterile surgical instruments.* **2** of animals or plants, failing to reproduce. **3** not producing vegetation: *sterile land.* **4** not producing results: *sterile hopes.* **5** evoking no feeling, warmth, etc.; lifeless. **ste·ril·i·ty** [stə'rɪləti] *n.* **ster·i·lize** *v.* **ster·i·li·za·tion** *n.* ⟨Latin *sterilis*⟩

ster·ling ['stɜrlɪŋ] *adj* **1** to do with a silver alloy of a standard quality, not less than 92.5 percent pure silver, the other 7.5 percent usually being copper. **2** of dependable excellence: *a sterling character.* **3** of or payable in British money.
n **1** sterling silver or things made of it. **2** British money. ⟨probably Old English *steorra* star (as on certain early Norman coins)⟩

stern¹ [stɜrn] *adj* **1** severe; strict; harsh: *a stern master, stern punishment.* **2** hard; not yielding; firm: *stern necessity.* **stern·ly** *adv.* **stern·ness** *n.* ⟨Old English *stirne*⟩

stern² [stɜrn] *n* the rear of a ship or boat. **stern·most** *adj.* ⟨Old Norse *stjórn* steering⟩

ster·num ['stɜrnəm] *n, pl* **-na** [-nə] or **-nums** breastbone. ⟨Greek *sternon* chest⟩

ster·oid ['stɛrɔid] *n* any of a group of organic compounds, including hormones, found in living plant and animal cells. Some enhance muscular strength. ⟨*(chole)ster(ol)* + *-oid*⟩

stet [stɛt] *n* a proofreading direction to retain cancelled material, often accompanied by a row of dots under the material in question. **stet, stet·ted, stet·ting** *v.* ⟨Latin = let it stand⟩

steth·o·scope ['stɛθə,skoup] *n* an instrument used by doctors for listening to sounds in the lungs, heart, etc. ⟨Greek *stēthos* chest + SCOPE⟩

stew [stju] *or* [stu] *v* **1** cook by slow boiling or simmering. **2** *Informal* worry; fret. *n* **1** a dish consisting of meat, vegetables, etc., cooked by slow boiling or simmering: *chicken stew.* **2** *Informal* a state of fretful worry. ⟨Old French *estuver;* Latin *extufare; ex-* out + Greek *typhos* vapour⟩
stew in one's own juice suffer the results of one's actions.
stewed *adj* **1** prepared by stewing. **2** *Slang* drunk.

stew·ard ['stjuərd] *or* ['stuərd] *n* **1** a person who serves passengers on a ship, aircraft, etc. **2** a person responsible for the management of any kind of resources or property. **3** SHOP STEWARD. **stew·ard·ship** *n.* ⟨Old English *stigweard; stig* hall + *weard* ward⟩

stick¹ [stɪk] *n* **1** a long, thin piece of wood, esp a small branch. **2** such a piece of wood shaped for a special use: *a hockey stick.* **3** a long, slender piece of anything: *celery sticks.* **4** a lever used to operate a car's manual transmission, a video game, etc. **5 the sticks** *pl Informal* back country. ⟨Old English *sticca*⟩
on the stick *Informal* alert and efficient. **shake a stick at** *Informal* notice (with negatives): *not enough snow to shake a stick at.*
stick figure 1 a simple figure of a person drawn using lines with a circle for the head. **2** a poorly developed character in a novel, play, etc. **stick·han·dle** *v* **1** *Hockey* manoeuvre (the puck) by deft handling of the stick. **2** manoeuvre (anything) skilfully: *to stickhandle a proposal through committees.* **stick·han·dler** *n.* **stick·han·dling** *n.* **stick·shift** *n* a manual transmission. **stick·work** *n* skilful use of a stick in hockey.

stick² [stɪk] *v* **stuck, stick·ing 1** thrust (a sharp point) into: *to stick a pin in a notice board.* **2** fasten by thrusting a point into something: *He stuck a flower in his buttonhole.* **3** *Informal* put: *Stick it in a drawer.* **4** thrust or be thrust: *Your hair is sticking up.* **5** fasten or be fastened by an adhesive: *Stick a stamp on the letter.* **6** keep close: *The boy stuck to his mother's heels.* **7** come or bring to a standstill: *Our car got stuck in the mud.* **8** *Informal* tolerate: *I won't stick her insults much longer.*
n a jab or stab. ⟨Old English *stician*⟩
stick around *Informal* stay nearby. **stick at a** hesitate: *She sticks at nothing to get her own way.* **b** keep doing: *Stick at your work.* **stick by** remain faithful to: *to stick by one's friends.*

stick in one's craw (or **throat**) be very hard for one to do or accept. **stick (it) out** *Informal* endure (something): *Try to stick it out for a few more days.* **stick it to someone** *Slang* make someone suffer. **stick out like a sore thumb** be conspicuous. **stick someone with** *Informal* make someone take responsibility for. **stick to a** remain faithful to: *Stick to your principles.* **b** keep doing, talking about, etc.: *Stick to the main issue.* **stick together** support one another. **stick to one's ribs** of food, be filling. **stick up** *Slang* mug; rob. **stick–up** *n.* **stick up for** *Informal* defend.

stick·er *n* a label or small picture for sticking to something. **sticker price** the price displayed on an article, esp if subject to negotiation, rebates, etc. **sticking point** a factor that prevents the solution of a problem: *When the contract was being reviewed, the sticking point was shorter hours.* **stick–in–the–mud** *n Informal* a person who resists change or is slow to agree to things. **stick·pin** *n* a decorative straight pin worn for ornament or to hold a necktie in place. **stick–up** *n Slang* a holdup. **stick·y** *adj* **1** that sticks or makes things stick: *sticky jam, sticky tape.* **2** *Informal* unpleasantly humid: *sticky weather.* **3** *Informal* puzzling; difficult: *a sticky problem.* **4** *Slang* unpleasant: *a sticky situation.* **sticky end** a painful death. **stick·i·ness** *n.*

SYNONYMS
Stick, the general word, suggests being fastened by or as if by something gluey: *Flies stick to flypaper.* **Adhere,** more formal, can be used of something that remains attached by itself or through some force: *Static electricity will make a balloon adhere to the wall.*

stick·ler ['stɪklər] *n* a stubborn or very picky person (with *for*): *a stickler for detail.* ⟨Middle English *stightlen* control⟩

stiff [stɪf] *adj* **1** not easily bent: *a stiff collar.* **2** aching and not able to move easily: *She was stiff after running.* **3** firm or holding its shape: *stiff egg whites.* **4** not easy in manner; formal: *a stiff style of writing.* **5** strong and steady: *stiff resistance.* **6** severe: *a stiff penalty.* **7** of a drink, strong. **8** high; severe: *a stiff price.*
n Slang **1** a corpse. **2** any person: *lucky stiff.* **3** a stingy person, esp one who does not tip enough or at all. **4** a priggish or dull person.
v cheat, esp by not paying or tipping as due: *He stiffed me.* **stiff·en** *v.* **stiff·ly** *adv.* **stiff·ness** *n.* ⟨Old English *stíf*⟩
stiff–necked *adj* stubborn; obstinate.

sti·fle ['staifəl] *v* **1** smother: *The smoke stifled us.* **2** be unable to breathe freely: *I am stifling.* **3** suppress: *to stifle a cry, to stifle the imagination.* **4** hamper by overprotection, etc. **5** be stifled. **sti·fling** *adj.* ⟨Middle English *stufflen, stifflen; stuffen* stuff, stifle⟩

stig·ma ['stɪgmə] *n, pl* **stig·mas** or **stig·ma·ta** ['stɪgmətə], [stɪg'mætə], *or* [-'matə] **1** a mark of disgrace. **2** a distinguishing mark. **3** a small spot on the skin, on a butterfly's wing, etc. **4** *Pathology* a visible mark symptomatic of a disease. **5** the part of the pistil of a plant that receives the pollen. **6 stigmata** *pl* marks or wounds like the five wounds on the crucified body of Christ, said to appear supernaturally on the bodies of certain devout persons. **stig·mat·ic** [stɪɡ'mætɪk] *adj*. ⟨Greek = scar, brand; *stizein* prick, tattoo⟩ **stig·ma·tize** *v* cause to bear a mark of disgrace; view or treat negatively. **stig·ma·ti·za·tion** *n*.

sti·let·to [stɪ'lɛtou] *n, pl* **-tos** or **-toes** 1 a dagger with a narrow, tapered blade. 2 In full, **stiletto heel** SPIKE HEEL. ⟨Italian; Latin *stilus* pointed instrument⟩

still¹ [stɪl] *adj* 1 motionless: *still water.* 2 silent. 3 not bubbling: *still wine.* 4 of a photograph, consisting of a single frame, as of a movie. *v* make or become calm: *to still a crying child. n* 1 *Poetic* silence: *the still of the night.* 2 a still photograph. *adv* 1 at or up to some time, later than might be expected: *She came yesterday and is still here.* 2 even: *still more.* 3 nevertheless: *He is slow; still, he tries hard.* 4 motionlessly. **still·ness** *n.* ⟨Old English *stille*⟩ **still·born** *adj* 1 dead when born. 2 a destined never to be realized or to succeed: *stillborn hopes.* **still·birth** *n.* **still life** *pl* **still lifes** a picture of inanimate objects, such as flowers, fruit, etc. **still–life** *adj.*

still² [stɪl] *n* an apparatus for distilling liquids, esp alcoholic liquors. ⟨(di)stil⟩

stilt [stɪlt] *n* 1 one of a pair of poles to stand on and hold while walking, each with a footrest at a distance above the ground. 2 a post or pole supporting a building above the water. 3 any of various shore birds with long, thin legs. **stilt·like** *adj.* ⟨Middle English *stilte*⟩ **stilt·ed** *adj* stiffly formal: *stilted conversation.* **stilt·ed·ly** *adv.* **stilt·ed·ness** *n.*

stim·u·late ['stɪmjə,leit] *v* 1 spur on: *Praise stimulates her to work hard.* 2 temporarily increase the activity of (a nerve, bodily function, etc.). 3 excite intellectually. **stim·u·la·tor** *n.* **stim·u·la·tion** *n.* ⟨Latin *stimulare; stimulus* goad⟩ **stim·u·lant** *n* 1 a food, medicine, etc. that temporarily increases the activity of some body part or function. 2 anything that stimulates: *Hope can be an effective stimulant. adj* stimulating. **stim·u·lus** *n, pl* **-li** [-,laɪ] or [-,li] 1 anything that stirs to action. 2 that which excites some body part to activity.

sting [stɪŋ] *v* **stung, sting·ing** 1 prick with a sharp-pointed organ: *Bees sting.* 2 feel or cause to feel sharp emotional pain: *She was stung by the jeers of the other children.* 3 cause a tingling pain (in): *Salt in a wound stings.* 4 spur as if by a sting: *His words stung me into a rage.* 5 *Slang* swindle. 6 cause to suffer in any way. *n* 1 an act of stinging. 2 a wound or pain so caused: *the sting of defeat.* 3 something that stings. 4 *Slang* a means used by authorities to catch criminals by pretending to be their customers, etc. **sting·ing** *adj.* **sting·less** *adj.* ⟨Old English *stingan*⟩ **sting·er** *n* the part of an insect or animal that pricks. **sting·ray** *n* any of a family of rays having poisonous spines on the tail that inflict a painful, even fatal, wound.

stin·gy ['stɪndʒi] *adj* 1 unwilling to spend, lend, or give; not generous: *He tried to save money without being stingy.* 2 cheap; meagre. **stin·gi·ly** *adv.* **stin·gi·ness** *n.* ⟨Related to STING⟩

stink [stɪŋk] *v* **stank** or **stunk, stunk, stink·ing** 1 have a bad smell. 2 fill with a bad smell (with *up*): *That fish is stinking up the whole house.* 3 *Informal* be of very poor quality or very disagreeable: *That idea stinks. n* 1 a bad smell. 2 *Slang* a fuss; outrage: *There was a big stink about the new ruling.* **stin·ky** *adj.* ⟨Old English *stincan* to smell⟩ **stink out** drive out with stinking smoke or fumes. **stink·bug** *n* any of various plant-eating bugs with a foul odour. **stink·er** *n* 1 a foul-smelling person or thing. 2 *Slang* an unpleasant or contemptible person or thing. **stink·ing** *adj* 1 foul-smelling. 2 extremely objectionable. *adv* excessively; objectionably: *stinking rich.* **stink·weed** *n* any of various plants, esp a certain plant of the mustard family, whose leaves exude a foul smell when crushed.

stint [stɪnt] *v* be very sparing (toward) in using or spending: *Don't stint the cream! n* 1 a task: *Making lunch is his daily stint.* 2 a period spent in some way: *a stint of writing.* **stint·ing·ly** *adv.* ⟨Old English *styntan* blunt⟩

sti·pend ['staɪpɛnd] *n* 1 in some professions, fixed pay; salary: *A magistrate receives a stipend.* 2 a regular allowance paid under the terms of a scholarship or other arrangement. ⟨Latin *stipendium; stips* wages + *pendere* weigh out⟩

stip·ple ['stɪpəl] *v* paint, draw, plaster, etc. with many tiny dots or points. **stip·ple** *n.* **stip·pled** *adj.* ⟨Du. *stippelen*⟩

stip·u·late ['stɪpjə,leit] *v* specify or demand as a condition: *The contract stipulates weekly payments.* **stip·u·la·tion** *n.* ⟨Latin *stipulari*⟩

stir [stɜr] *v* **stirred, stir·ring** 1 move or cause to move around: *The wind stirred the leaves.* 2 mix by moving around with a spoon, fork, stick, etc. 3 incite: *Rage stirred him to action.* 4 strongly affect the feelings of: *We were stirred by her impassioned plea.* 5 be aroused: *The countryside was stirring with new life. n* 1 an act of stirring. 2 a state of activity, excitement, etc. 3 a commotion. **stir·rer** *n.* **stir·ring** *adj, n.* ⟨Old English *styrian*⟩ **stir up a** excite. **b** provoke: *to stir up trouble.* **stir–cra·zy** *adj Slang* psychologically affected by long confinement or regimentation. **stir–fry** *v* cook (small pieces of vegetables, meat, etc.) by frying them briefly in oil while stirring constantly. *n* a dish made in this way.

SYNONYMS

Stir particularly suggests a disturbance, especially where there has been quiet: *His answer produced a stir in the courtroom.* **Bustle** suggests noisy, energetic activity: *The day before the class picnic, studying gave way to the bustle of preparations.*

stir·rup ['stɜrəp] *n* one of a pair of foot supports that hang from a saddle. ⟨Old English *stigrāp; stige* climbing + *rāp* rope⟩

stitch [stɪtʃ] *n* 1 a in sewing, one movement

of a threaded needle through cloth, skin, etc. and back again. **b** in crocheting, knitting, etc., a single twist of yarn around the needle or hook. **2** the loop so made: *The doctor took the stitches out.* **3** the smallest bit of clothing: *without a stitch on.* **4** *Informal* the smallest bit: *He wouldn't do a stitch of work.* **5** a sudden, sharp pain (in one's side).
v make, fasten, or decorate with stitches. **stitch·er** *n.* ⟨Old English *stice* puncture⟩
in stitches laughing uncontrollably.

sto·chas·tic [stə'kæstɪk] *adj* at random but capable of being analyzed statistically. **sto·chas·ti·cal·ly** *adv.*

stock [stɒk] *n* **1** a supply or store of goods: *a large stock of information, a stock of canned food at the cottage.* **2** livestock: *purebred Jersey stock.* **3** *Botany* rhizome. **4** *Finance* **a** the capital of a company, divided into equal shares. **5** family; descent: *She is of Spanish stock.* **6** a part forming a handle to which other parts are attached: *the wooden stock of a rifle.* **7 stocks** *pl* a wooden frame with holes for the feet and, sometimes, for the hands and head, into which people were formerly locked in public as punishment for minor offences. **8** raw material for manufacturing something: *All the cabinetmaker's wood was kiln-dried stock.* **9** a particular kind of paper: *The advertisement was printed on heavy stock.* **10** liquid in which meat or fish has been cooked, used as a base for soup, etc.: *chicken stock.* **11** *Theatre* **a** the repertoire of plays produced by a company at one theatre. **b** such companies and their work as a category of theatrical production: *She is playing in summer stock.* **12 a** a tree or plant that furnishes cuttings for grafting **b** the stem into which a graft is inserted.
adj **1** of or for livestock: *a stock farm.* **2** trite; commonplace: *a stock response.*
v **1** supply (*with*): *to stock a lake with fish.* **2** fill (shelves) with merchandise. **3** keep for sale: *Do you stock stationery?* ⟨Old English *stocc*⟩
in stock available for sale or use. **out of stock** sold out or used up. **stock up** supply oneself (with *on*): *to stock up on cereal.* **take stock a** find out how much stock is on hand. **b** make an assessment: *Let's take stock of our situation before continuing.* **stock·tak·ing** *n.*
stock·bro·ker [-ˌbroukər] *n* an agent who buys and sells stocks and bonds for customers. **stock·bro·ker·age** *n.* **stock car 1** a railway car for livestock. **2** an ordinary car that has been altered for use in racing. **stock exchange** a place where stocks and bonds are bought and sold. **stock·hold·er** *n* an owner of stocks or shares in a company. **stock in trade** or **stock–in–trade 1** the goods regularly stocked by a dealer. **2** tools or other materials needed to carry on a trade or business. **3** resources, practices, etc. characteristic of a particular person or group: *The singer's stock in trade is a slightly rumpled look and a big smile.* **stock market 1** STOCK EXCHANGE. **2** the trade going on in such a place. **3** the prices of stocks and bonds across a country: *The stock market is falling.* **stock·pile** *n* a supply built up and held

in reserve: *a stockpile of weapons. v* collect or bring together such a supply. **stock·pot** *n* a pot in which soup stock is prepared. **stock·room** *n* a room where stock is kept. **stock–still** *adj* motionless. **stock·y** *adj* solid, sturdy: *a stocky young man.* **stock·i·ly** *adv.* **stock·i·ness** *n.* **stock·yard** *n* a place housing livestock to be slaughtered or sent to market.

stock·ade [stɒ'keid] *n* **1** a fortification made of upright posts placed closely together in the ground. **2** an enclosure for military prisoners. **stock·ade** *v.* ⟨French *estacade*; Provençal *estaca* stake⟩

stock·ing ['stɒkɪŋ] *n* **1** a woman's close-fitting covering of nylon, etc. for the foot and leg. **2** a man's sock. **stock·inged** *adj.* ⟨*stock* stocking, Old English *stocc*⟩
in one's stocking feet wearing stockings or socks but no shoes.
stocking cap TUQUE (def. 1).

stodg·y ['stɒdʒi] *adj* very old-fashioned; conservative. **stodg·i·ly** *adv.* **stodg·i·ness** *n.* ⟨*stodge* stuff; origin unknown⟩

sto·gie or **sto·gy** ['stougi] *n* a long, slender, cheap cigar. ⟨*Conestoga*, Pennsylvania⟩

Sto·ic ['stouɪk] *n* **1** an adherent of an ancient Greek philosophy which taught that people should be free from passion and unmoved by life's events. **2 stoic** a person who remains calm and is indifferent to pain or pleasure. **Sto·ic**, **sto·ic** *adj.* **sto·i·cal·ly** *adv.* **Sto·i·cism**, **sto·i·cism** *n.* ⟨Greek *stoïkós*; *stoa* portico (for teaching site)⟩

stoke [stouk] *v* **1** stir up and feed (a fire, furnace, etc.) (often with *up*). **2** stir up or feed (anything). **stok·er** *n.* ⟨Dutch *stoken*⟩

stole[1] [stoul] *v* pt of STEAL.

stole[2] [stoul] *n* **1** a woman's long, wide scarf worn around the shoulders: *a knitted stole.* **2** a narrow strip of cloth worn around the neck by a minister or priest. ⟨Greek *stolē* robe⟩

sto·len ['stoulən] *v* pp of STEAL.

stol·id ['stɒlɪd] *adj* showing no emotion; not excitable. **sto·lid·i·ty** or **stol·id·ness** *n.* **stol·id·ly** *adv.* ⟨Latin *stolidus* immovable⟩

sto·lon ['stoulən] *n* **1** *Botany* a branch that takes root at the tip to produce a new plant; runner. **2** *Zoology* a stemlike growth, as in certain polyps, producing buds from which new individuals grow. ⟨Latin *stolonis* a shoot⟩

sto·ma ['stoumə] *n, pl* **sto·ma·ta** ['stoumətə] *or* ['stɒm-] or **sto·mas 1** *Botany* one of many pores in the surface of a leaf, etc. **2** *Zoology* a small, mouthlike opening in lower animals. **3** a permanent artificial opening made on the surface of the body, leading to a cavity or canal inside. ⟨Greek = mouth⟩

stom·ach ['stʌmək] *n* **1** a large internal organ joining the esophagus and the intestines. **2** *Zoology* in ruminant animals, a similar section of the alimentary canal, or all such sections taken as a whole. **3** the lower abdomen: *He was hit in the stomach.* **4** appetite: *no stomach for dinner.* **5** tolerance or desire: *I had no stomach for a fight.*

v **1** eat: *She can't stomach spinach.* **2** put up with: *He won't stomach arrogance.* ⟨Greek *stomachos*; *stoma* mouth⟩

stomach ache a steady pain in the abdomen.

stomp [stɒmp] *v* step heavily or stamp with the feet: *to stomp on a bug. He stomped angrily out of the room.* **stomp** *n.* ⟨variant of *stamp*⟩

–stomy *combining form* a surgical procedure in which an artificial opening is made in some part: *colostomy.* ⟨Greek *-stomia*; *stoma* mouth⟩

stone [stoun] *n* **1** hard mineral matter; rock. **2** a piece of rock of definite size, shape, etc. used for a particular purpose: *a curling stone.* **3** a gem; jewel. **4** *Medicine* a stonelike mass that may form in the kidneys or gall bladder, causing sickness and pain. **5** the single seed found in such fruits as peaches; pit.
v **1** throw stones at; drive out or kill by throwing stones. **2** take stones out of (fruit).
adv completely: *stone cold, stone broke.* **stone·like** *adj.* ⟨Old English *stān*⟩
cast the first stone be the first to criticize.
leave no stone unturned do everything that can be done.
Stone Age 1 the earliest known period of human culture, characterized by the use of tools and weapons made of stone. **2** a very primitive stage in the development of anything. **Stone–Age** or **stone–age** *adj.* **stone·boat** *n* a low kind of sled, often with runners made of logs, used for heavy hauling in the field or forest. **stone·cut·ter** *n* a person or machine that cuts or carves stone. **stoned** *adj* **1** of fruit, with stones removed. **2** *Slang* intoxicated by drugs or alcohol. **stone–ground** *adj* of flour, made by grinding whole kernels of grain. **stone·ma·son** *n* a person who cuts stone or builds walls, etc. of stone. **stone·ma·son·ry** *n.* **stone's throw** a short distance. **stone·wall** *v* meet (questions, etc.) with complete lack of co-operation or response: *to stonewall an official inquiry.* **stone·wal·ler** *n.* **stone·wal·ling** *n, adj.* **stone·ware** *n* a hard pottery fired at high temperature. **stone·work** *n* work done in stone. **stone·work·er** *n.* **ston·y** *adj* **1** having many stones: *a stony beach.* **2** hard, cold, or unmoving like stone: *a stony stare, a stony heart.* **ston·i·ly** *adv.* **ston·i·ness** *n.*

Ston·ey ['stouni] *n, pl* **Ston·ey, Ston·eys,** or **Ston·ies** ASSINIBOINE. Also, **Ston·y.**

stood [stʊd] *v* pt and pp of STAND.

stook [stuk] *or* [stʊk] *n* a usually tepeelike arrangement of sheaves on end, intended to speed up drying. **stook** *v.* **stook·er** *n.* ⟨Middle English *stouke*⟩

stool [stul] *n* **1** a seat for one person, with no back or arms. **2** a low bench: *I stand on a stool to reach the top shelf.* **3** feces. ⟨Old English *stōl*⟩
stool pigeon 1 *Slang* a spy or informer for the police or other intelligence-gathering agency. **2** any decoy.

stoop¹ [stup] *v* **1** bend forward and down: *to stoop over a desk.* **2** condescend: *She would never stoop to speak to us.* **3** lower oneself morally: *to stoop to cheating.*
n a habitual forward and downward bend of the head and shoulders: *She walks with a noticeable stoop.* ⟨Old English *stūpian*⟩

stoop² [stup] *n* a small porch or platform at the entrance of a house. ⟨Dutch *stoep*⟩

stop [stɒp] *v* **stopped, stop·ping 1** keep from moving, functioning, etc.: *to stop a clock. We couldn't stop her making a fool of herself.* **2** cease: *Stop making so much fuss!* **3** withhold: *to stop supplies.* **4** close by filling or plugging (often with *up*): *to stop a leak.* **5** instruct a bank not to honour (a cheque, bill, etc.).
n **1** an act of stopping: *We made a stop for lunch.* **2** a being stopped: *to come to a stop.* **3** the place where someone or something stops. **4** a cork, plug, etc. that closes an opening. **5** *Music* **a** on an instrument, a key or other device that closes an opening to alter pitch. **b** in organs, a graduated set of pipes of the same kind, or the handle controlling them. **6** *Photography* the aperture of a lens, or the f number indicating this. **stop·page** *n.* ⟨Old English *stoppian*; Latin *stuppa* tow; Greek *styppē*⟩
pull out all the stops exert maximum effort.
put a stop to stop; end: *We put a stop to his tricks.* **stop at nothing** have no moral scruples. **stop in** (**or by,** or **off**) stop for a short stay on the way to somewhere else. **stop·off** *n.* **stop over a** make a short stay. **b** interrupt a journey by air, train, etc., proceeding later on the same ticket. **stop·o·ver** *n.*
stop·cock *n* a valve regulating flow of a gas or liquid. **stop·gap** *n* a temporary solution or substitute. **stop·light** *n* **1** a traffic signal. **2** a light at the rear of a vehicle that comes on whenever the brakes are applied. **stop·per** *n* **1** a plug or cork to close a bottle, tube, etc. **2** one that stops. *v* close with a stopper: *to stopper a flask.* **stop·watch** *n* a watch that can be stopped or started at any instant, for use in timing races, etc. exactly.

store [stɔr] *n* **1** a place where goods are offered for retail sale. **2 a** a supply laid up for use; stock. **b stores** *pl* supplies; provisions: *You'll find bandages among the camp's stores.*
v **1** stock: *Her cupboards are stored with useless knick-knacks.* **2** put away for future use. **3** remain usable when stored: *Cooked rice stores well in the fridge.* **4** *Computers* retain (data) in memory. ⟨Old French *estorer* store⟩
in store a on hand; in reserve. **b** to be faced in the near future: *Had she known what lay in store, she wouldn't have gone.* **mind the store** *Informal* look after or keep a check on things. **set** (or **put,** or **lay**) **store by** value; esteem: *She sets great store by her mother's opinion.*
stor·age *n* **1** the act of storing or condition of being stored. **2** space for storing: *This house has very little storage.* **3** the cost of storing. **store–bought** *adj Informal* bought at a store; not homemade: *store-bought cookies.* **store·front** *adj* of a business office, social service, etc., located at street level in storelike accommodations: *a storefront legal office.* **store·house** *n* **1** a building where

things are stored; warehouse. **2** an abundant source: *A library is a storehouse of information.* **store·keep·er** *n* a person who runs a store. **store meat ✹** *North* the meat obtainable in a store rather than by hunting. **store·room** *n* a room where things are stored. **store·wide** *adj* to do with all or most of the departments in a STORE (def. 1): *storewide sales.*

sto·rey ['stɔri] *n, pl* **-reys** or **-ries 1** a level or floor of a house or other building. **2** any other horizontal division. ⟨perhaps *story* in sense of 'row of historical statues across a building'⟩

sto·ried See STORY.

stork [stɔrk] *n* any of a family of long-legged wading birds with a long, heavy bill. **stork·like** *adj.* ⟨Old English *storc*⟩

storm [stɔrm] *n* **1 a** strong wind with heavy rain, snow, hail, etc. and, often, thunder and lightning. **b** a strong wind carrying sand or dust. **2** a violent outburst: *a storm of angry words.* **3** a violent attack.
v **1** be stormy: *It stormed for days.* **2** speak loudly and angrily. **3** rush violently: *to storm out of the room.* **4** attack violently: *The troops stormed the city.* **storm·y** *adj.* ⟨Old English⟩ **storm in a teacup** great excitement or fuss over something unimportant. **take by storm** conquer or win swiftly and decisively.
storm·bound *adj* cut off or confined by a storm. **storm cellar** a cellar for shelter during cyclones, tornadoes, etc. **storm centre** or **center 1** the moving centre of a cyclone. **2** any centre of trouble, tumult, etc. **storm door** an extra door fixed outside a regular door as protection against cold, wind, etc. **storm·proof** *adj* not liable to storm damage. **storm·proof** *v.* **storm window** an extra window fixed on the outside of a regular one as protection against cold, wind, etc.

sto·ry ['stɔri] *n* **1** an account of an event or group of events: *Tell me the story of your life.* **2** such an account, either true or made up. **3** a rumour or falsehood. **4** the plot of a play, novel, etc. **5** a news article or report, or material for it. ⟨Latin, Greek *historia*⟩
another (or **a different**) **story** a completely different matter. **cut** (or **make**) **a long story short** get to the point. **the same old story** the same tedious routine or excuse.
sto·ried *adj* celebrated in stories or history: *the storied Klondike.* **sto·ry·board** *n* a large board or series of panels carrying the outline of all the action for a film, video, etc. **sto·ry·book** *n* a children's book containing stories. *adj* like that of a storybook; romantic: *a storybook hero.* **sto·ry·tell·ing** *n* the art of telling stories. **sto·ry·tell·er** *n.*

SYNONYMS
Story applies to any account, true or made up, long or short, in prose or verse, intended to interest another: *I like stories about science.* **Tale** applies to an account told as if true but usually made up or exaggerated: *She reads adventure tales of frontier days.*

stout [staut] *adj* **1** somewhat fat. **2** solid; strong: *a stout walking stick.* **3** brave and resolute: *a stout heart, stout resistance.*
n a strong, dark beer brewed with roasted malt. **stout·ly** *adv.* **stout·ness** *n.* ⟨Old French *estout* strong; Latin *stultus* foolish⟩

stove¹ [stouv] *n* an apparatus for cooking and heating, using electricity, wood, gas, etc. ⟨Old English *stofa* warm bathing room⟩
stove·pipe *n* **1** a pipe connected to a fuel-burning stove, carrying smoke and gases to a chimney. **2** *Informal* a tall silk hat.

stove² [stouv] *v* a pt and a pp of STAVE.

stow [stou] *v* **1** pack; store: *to stow things in a cupboard, to stow a boat with supplies.* **2** *Slang* stop: *Stow the jokes!* ⟨Old English *stōw* place⟩
stow away hide on a ship, etc. to avoid paying the fare or to escape. **stow·a·way** *n.*
stow·age *n* **1** a stowing or being stowed. **2** space for stowing: *The boat has stowage fore and aft.* **3** what is stowed. **4** a fee for stowing.

stra·bis·mus [strə'bɪzməs] *n Ophthalmology* a disorder in which one or both eyes are turned in or out; squint. ⟨Greek *strabos* squint-eyed⟩

strad·dle ['strædəl] *v* **1** sit, stand, or lie with legs or end parts on either side of: *to straddle a chair.* **2** favour or appear to favour both sides of (an issue). **strad·dle** *n.* **strad·dler** *n.* ⟨variant of dialect *striddle; stride*⟩

strafe [streif] *v* bomb or shell heavily, esp from low-flying aircraft. **straf·er** *n.* ⟨German *strafen* punish⟩

strag·gle ['strægəl] *v* **1** wander in a scattered fashion: *Cows straggled along the lane.* **2** lag behind the rest. **3** spread in an irregular, rambling way: *Vines straggled over the wall.* **strag·gler** *n.* ⟨blend of *stray* and *draggle*⟩
strag·gly *adj* **1** straggling. **2** of hair, a beard, etc., long, limp, and messy.

straight [streit] *adj* **1** without curves or bends. **2 a** honest; frank: *straight talk.* **b** right; correct: *straight thinking.* **3** in proper order: *to keep accounts straight.* **4** continuous: *six straight days.* **5** unmodified; undiluted: *straight whisky.* **6** *Poker* being a sequence of five cards: *a straight flush.* **7** serious rather than comic: *a straight part in a play.* **8** *Slang* **a** conventional in dress, views, etc. **b** free of drugs and alcohol. **c** not engaging in criminal behaviour. **9** *Informal* heterosexual.
n **1** a straight part, as of a racecourse. **2** *Poker* a five-card sequence. **3** *Slang* heterosexual. **straight** *adv.* **straight·ness** *n.* ⟨Old English *streht* pp of *streccan* stretch⟩
set straight See SET. **straight away** (or **off**) at once. **straight out** *Informal* frankly. **straight up** (of alcoholic drinks) without ice. **the straight and narrow** an honest, upright lifestyle: *following the straight and narrow.*
straight–arm *v* **1** force or push one's way as if with a stiff arm. **2** *Football* hold off (an opponent) with one's arm held straight out. **straight arrow** *Informal* a person of integrity. **straight·edge** *n* anything with an edge that is accurately straight, for making or testing straight lines and level surfaces. **straight·en** *v* **1** make or become straight: *Straighten your*

shoulders. **2** (with *up* or *out*) **a** put in order: *to straighten up a room.* **b** reform in behaviour, etc. **c** correct the misunderstanding of (someone). **straight face** an expressionless face, esp one showing no amusement. **straight–faced** *adj.* **straight·for·ward** *adj* **1** frank: *a straightforward reply.* **2** simple: *straightforward instructions.* **straight man** an actor who feeds lines to a comic. **straight–out** *adj, adv Informal* thorough(ly).

strain¹ [strein] *v* **1** draw tight; stretch: *The weight strained the rope.* **2** pull hard: *The dog strained at its leash.* **3** make a great effort (with): *He strained his eyes to see.* **4** injure or damage by too much effort or by stretching, twisting, etc.: *to strain one's heart.* **5** press through something that lets only liquid through: *to strain lumps out of gravy.* *n* the act, cause, or effect of straining: *muscle strain.* ⟨Old French; Latin *stringere* draw tight⟩ **strained** *adj* **1** forced; not natural: *a strained laugh.* **2** tense; near open conflict: *strained relations between nations.* **strain·er** *n* a utensil or device for straining, filtering, or sifting.

strain² [strein] *n* **1** a line of descent; stock: *the Scottish strain in her.* **2** a group of animals or plants forming part of a breed or variety. **3** an inherited quality: *There is a strain of musical talent in her family.* **4** Often, **strains** *pl* melody. **5** a style or manner, esp of writing or speaking: *She wrote in a playful strain.* ⟨variant of Old English *strēon* gain, begetting⟩

strait [streit] *n* **1** a narrow channel between two larger bodies of water. **2 straits** *pl* difficulty; need; distress. ⟨Old French *estreit* narrow; Latin *strictus* drawn tight⟩ **strait·en** *v* restrict in range, scope, etc. **in straitened circumstances** very short of money. **strait·jack·et** *n* a strong garment used to bind the arms so as to keep a violent person from harming himself or herself or others. **strait·jack·et** *v.* **strait–laced** *adj* very strict in matters of conduct; prudish.

strand¹ [strænd] *v* (usually passive) **1** leave helpless: *I was stranded far from home.* **2** run aground: *The ship was stranded on the rocks.* *n Poetic* a shore. ⟨Old English⟩

strand² [strænd] *n* **1** one of the threads, strings, or wires twisted together to make yarn, rope, etc. **2** a fibre, hair, etc. **3** a string of beads, pearls, etc. ⟨Old French *estran*⟩

strange [streindʒ] *adj* **1** very unusual; odd: *She had the strangest laugh.* **2** unfamiliar: *strange faces.* **strange·ly** *adv.* **strange·ness** *n.* ⟨Old French *estrange;* Latin *extraneus* foreign⟩ **feel strange** feel awkward or out of place. **make strange** of a baby, show distress at the presence of someone unfamiliar. **stran·ger** *n* **1** a person not known, seen, or heard of before. **2** a person who is new to some place or thing: *He is a stranger in this area. She is no stranger to hard work.*

stran·gle ['stræŋgəl] *v* **1** kill by squeezing the throat so as to stop the breath. **2** suffocate; choke: *She almost strangled on a cherry caught in her throat.* **3** suppress; stifle: *to strangle an impulse to laugh.* **stran·gler** *n.*

stran·gu·la·tion *n.* ⟨Latin *strangulare;* Greek *strangalaein; strangos* twisted⟩ **stran·gle·hold** *n* **1** *Wrestling* an illegal hold by which an opponent is choked. **2** a position of control that chokes opposition, freedom of action, etc.: *a stranglehold on the market.*

strap [stræp] *n* a strip of material that bends, used to hold or secure something: *a dress with shoulder straps, luggage straps.* *v* **strapped, strap·ping** fasten or bind with a strap. ⟨variant of *strop*⟩ **strap·less** *adj* of a dress, bra, etc., having no shoulder straps. **strapped** *adj* **1** without cash: *I'm strapped; I won't be able to go to the movies.* **2** suffering from a shortage of anything (with *for*): *strapped for time.* **strap·ping** *adj Informal* tall, strong, and healthy: *a fine, strapping girl.*

stra·ta ['strætə] *or* ['streitə] *n* a pl of STRATUM.

strat·a·gem ['strætədʒəm] *n* a clever trick or scheme. ⟨Greek *stratēgēma; stratēgos* general. See STRATEGY.⟩

SYNONYMS

Stratagem applies to a careful plan to gain one's own ends: *The general planned a stratagem to trap the enemy.* **Ruse** applies to a trick that conceals one's real purpose: *His so-called appointment was simply a ruse to leave early.*

strat·e·gy ['strætədʒi] *n* **1** the art of careful management to achieve any goal: *military strategy. Strategy is important in an election campaign.* **2** a plan based on this: *a strategy to gain time.* **strat·e·gist** *n.* ⟨Greek *stratēgia; stratēgos* general; *stratos* army + *agein* lead⟩ **stra·te·gic** [strə'tidʒik] *adj* **1** to do with strategy: *strategic skill, a strategic location.* **2** to do with materials essential for warfare. **3** serving to destroy enemy bases, industry, etc. behind the lines of battle: *a strategic bomber.* **stra·te·gi·cal·ly** *adv.* **stra·te·gize** *v* develop strategy.

stra·tum ['strætəm] *or* ['streitəm] *n, pl* **-ta** [-tə] *or* **-tums 1** a horizontal layer, esp one of many. **2** *Geology* such a layer of rock in the earth's crust. **3** a distinct horizontal region of the sea or atmosphere. **4** *Biology* a single layer of tissue or cells. **5** *Sociology* a socio-economic level: *Professional people represent one stratum of society.* ⟨Latin; pp of *sternere* spread out⟩ **strat·i·fy** ['strætə,fai] *v* arrange or deposit in layers or strata; form strata. **strat·i·fi·ca·tion** *n.* **stra·to–cu·mu·lus** [-'kjumjələs] *n* a low cloud layer consisting of rounded masses. **strat·o·sphere** ['strætə,sfir] *n* the region of the atmosphere above the troposphere, extending from about 20 km above the earth to about 50 km. **strat·o·spher·ic** [-'sferik] *adj.* **stra·tus** ['streitəs] *or* ['strætəs] *n, pl* **-ti** [-tai] *or* [-ti] a very low layer of grey cloud like fog, from which rain may fall as drizzle.

straw [strɒ] *n* **1** the stalks or stems of grain after drying and threshing. **2** a pale yellow colour. **3** a single stem or stalk, esp of a grass. **4** a slender tube for sucking up drinks. **straw·y** *adj.* ⟨Old English *strēaw*⟩

grasp at a straw (or **at straws**) try anything in desperation. **straw in the wind** something taken as an indication of a trend.

straw·ber·ry *n* the small, juicy, edible, red fruit of any of several plants of the rose family. **strawberry blond** or **blonde** reddish blond. **strawberry mark** a small, reddish birthmark. **straw boss** a member of a work crew who acts as a supervisor. **straw man** 1 scarecrow. 2 a weak opposing argument put forward for the purpose of attacking and easily defeating it. 3 a token candidate or opponent entered for appearances only, not expecting to win.

stray [strei] *v* 1 go off the right course. 2 wander aimlessly: *Her gaze strayed around the room as she listened.* 3 digress or be distracted: *to stray from the topic.*
n a person or thing that has strayed, such as a domestic animal wandering at large.
adj 1 wandering; lost: *a stray cat.* 2 isolated or scattered: *a few stray huts on the beach.* 3 out of place: *a stray hair.* ⟨Old French *estraier*; Latin *stratarius* roaming the street. See STREET.⟩

streak [strik] *n* 1 a long, thin part with a different colour or texture, or of different material: *green streaks in her hair.* 2 an element in a character: *a mean streak.* 3 a brief period: *a streak of luck, a losing streak.*
v 1 make streaks in or on: *hair streaked by the sun.* 2 become streaked. 3 go at speed. 4 *Informal* run naked through a public place. **streak·er** *n*. **streak·y** *adj.* ⟨Old English *strica*⟩ **like a streak** *Informal* at top speed: *The dog heard the whistle and was off like a streak.* **talk a blue streak** See BLUE STREAK.

stream [strim] *n* 1 a body of flowing water, esp a narrow river. 2 a flow of liquid. 3 a steady flow like that of a liquid: *a stream of traffic.* 4 a prevailing trend: *against the stream.*
v 1 flow or cause to flow in a stream: *Light streamed in the window.* 2 extend or float at full length: *Her hair streamed out behind her as she ran.* 3 *Computers* send a continuous flow of data through the Internet, so that users have access without a long download time. **stream·ing** *n*. **stream·like** *adj.* ⟨Old English *strēam*⟩ **on stream** in or into production.

stream·er *n* 1 any long, narrow, flowing or floating thing: *paper streamers.* 2 a newspaper headline running all the way across a page. **stream·line** *v* 1 make with a contour that minimizes resistance to motion through air or water: *to streamline an aircraft.* 2 organize (a procedure, etc.) to make more efficient. **stream·lined** *adj.* **stream–of–con·scious·ness** *adj* to do with a narrative style that purports to record a narrator's or character's thoughts and perceptions as they occur.

street [strit] *n* 1 a public road in an urban area. 2 the people who live in the buildings on a street: *The whole street celebrated.* 3 **the street** an environment characterized by crime, homelessness, poverty, and prostitution, where one survives by toughness, shrewdness, etc. ⟨Old English *strǣt*; Latin *strata* paved, pp of *sternere* lay out⟩

on (or **in**) **the street a** homeless. **b** jobless. **the man in the street** the average person. **street·car** *n* a large, electrically powered public vehicle that runs on rails on city streets. **street clothes** clothes suitable for everyday wear in public. **street·light** *n* one of a series of powerful lights mounted on poles to light a street. **street people** homeless people or those who frequent city streets. **street·proof** *v* teach (children) the caution, procedures, etc. that will ensure safety in a city. **street smarts** the ability to survive in an environment of poverty, danger, or neglect. **street urchin** (or **kid**) a homeless child. **street·walk·er** *n* a prostitute who solicits on the streets. **street·wise** *adj Informal* having STREET SMARTS.

strength [strɛŋθ] *n* 1 capacity to exert force: *a man of great strength.* 2 capacity to resist force, strain, etc.: *the strength of a rope, the strength of an argument.* 3 effectiveness measured by the number of players, etc.: *Our team was not at full strength for the game.* 4 intensity: *the strength of a drink, strength of feeling.* 5 a source of power or endurance: *His wife was his strength in hard times.* 6 a desirable trait or skill, area of proficiency, etc. of a person: *Math is your strength.* **strength·en** *v*. **strong** [strɒŋ], **strong·er** ['strɒŋər], **strong·est** ['strɒŋɪst] *adj.* **strong·ly** *adv.* ⟨Old English *strengthu*; *strang* strong⟩ **going strong a** in good health: *Eighty years old and still going strong.* **b** continuing (an activity) vigorously. **on the strength of** relying on: *We hired the woman on the strength of your recommendation.*

strong–arm *Informal v* use force or violence on: *to strong-arm someone into submission.* **strong–arm** *adj.* **strong·box** *n* a small safe. **strong drink** alcohol; liquor. **strong·hold** *n* 1 a fort or fortress. 2 a secure place or centre: *This city is a Liberal stronghold.*

stren·u·ous ['strɛnjuəs] *adj* requiring or marked by much energy or effort: *a strenuous game, strenuous opposition.* **stren·u·ous·ly** *adv.* **stren·u·ous·ness** *n.* ⟨Latin *strenuus*⟩

strep [strɛp] *n Informal* 1 streptococcus. 2 in full, **strep throat** a streptococcal infection characterized by a sore throat.

strep·to·coc·cus [ˌstrɛptəˈkɒkəs] *n, pl* **-coc·ci** [-ˈkɒksaɪ] any of a group of disease-causing bacteria that multiply by forming chains. **strep·to·coc·cal** *adj.* ⟨Greek *streptos* curved + *kokkos* grain⟩

stress [strɛs] *n* 1 physical, mental, or emotional strain: *the stresses of urban living.* 2 *Physics* **a** force exerted when one body or part pushes against, pulls, or twists another: *Stresses must be carefully balanced in building a bridge.* **b** the intensity of such force per unit area, usually measured in pascals. **c** weakness caused by such force. 3 emphasis: *The course lays stress on basic computer skills.* 4 emphasis placed on a syllable or word in speech, making it louder than the ones surrounding it. 5 a mark indicating which syllable of a word receives stress. 6 *Music* accent.

v **1** give emphasis or importance to: *to stress job safety.* **2** pronounce with stress: *'Ado' is stressed on the second syllable.* **3** place under stress. ⟨partly *distress*, partly Old French *estrece* oppression; Latin *strictus*. See STRICT.⟩

stretch [stretʃ] *v* **1** draw out or be drawn out: *Rubber stretches.* **2** extend through space or time: *The forest stretches for miles.* **3** extend one's body or limbs. **4** reach (out): *He stretched out his hand.* **5** draw out of the original shape or proportion: *Stretch the shoe a bit.* **6** make or cause to make more effort: *The challenge stretched us.* **7** distort or exaggerate: *to stretch the truth.*
n **1** the act of stretching. **2** an unbroken extent of space or time: *a stretch of rainy weather.* **3** one of the two straight sides of a race course, esp the part between the last turn and the finish line. Also, **home stretch.** **4** *Informal* a demanding or difficult task: *Finishing on time was a stretch.* **stretch·y** *adj.* ⟨Old English *streccan*⟩

stretch·er *n* **1** a frame covered with material, on which to move a sick, injured, or dead person. **2** a frame or other device for stretching something. **3** *Masonry* a brick or stone laid horizontally with its length along the length of a wall. Compare HEADER (def. 3).

strewn [strun] *v, pp of* **strew** scattered; sprinkled: *The pages were strewn all over the floor.* ⟨Old English *strēowian*⟩

strick·en ['strɪkən] *adj* overwhelmed by trouble, sorrow, etc.: *a stricken conscience, a disease-stricken city.* ⟨pp of *strike*⟩

strict [strɪkt] *adj* **1** enforcing or following a standard, rules, etc. with great care: *a strict Muslim.* **2** requiring complete obedience: *strict orders.* **3** exact: *a strict translation.* **4** complete: *in strict confidence.* **strict·ness** *n.* ⟨Latin *strictus* pp of *stringere* bind tight⟩
strict·ly *adv* **1** in a strict manner. **2** exclusively: *Parking places are strictly for residents.*

SYNONYMS
Strict suggests care and consistency in following or enforcing rules: *Our supervisor is strict and insists on proper safety procedures.*
Rigid emphasizes refusal to change regardless of circumstances: *He maintains a rigid work schedule.* **Rigorous** emphasizes the severity of the demands made, conditions imposed, etc.: *We believe in rigorous discipline.*

stric·ture ['strɪktʃər] *n* **1** an unfavourable criticism. **2** an abnormal narrowing of a duct or tube of the body. **3** a restriction or constraint. ⟨Latin *strictura; stringere* bind tight⟩

stride [straɪd] *v* **strode, strid·den, strid·ing** walk with long steps (along or through): *striding through the mall. He strode the streets all morning.*
n a long step or the distance covered by it. ⟨Old English *strīdan*⟩
hit one's stride reach one's normal speed or level of efficiency: *Once she hit her stride she was translating a page an hour.* **take in stride** (or **in one's stride**) handle without difficulty or hesitation: *She took the defeat in stride.*

stri·dent ['straɪdənt] *adj* **1** making or having a harsh, shrill sound: *a strident voice.* **2** commanding attention in an irritating way: *strident colours.* **stri·den·cy** *adj.* **stri·dent·ly** *adv.* ⟨Latin *stridens, -entis*, ppr of *stridere* sound harshly⟩

strife [straɪf] *n* bitter or violent conflict. ⟨Old French *estrif;* Germanic⟩

strike [straɪk] *v* **struck, struck** or **strick·en, strik·ing** **1** hit: *The sled struck a fence.* **2** affect the mind or feelings of: *The plan strikes me as silly.* **3** set (a match) on fire by rubbing. **4** overcome, as by death, disease, fear, etc.: *They were struck with terror.* **5** attack: *The enemy will strike at dawn.* **6** occur to: *A funny thought struck her.* **7** find or come upon (ore, oil, water, etc.). **8** refuse to work in order to get better pay or achieve other demands. **9** delete (with *out* or *off*): *Strike my name off the list.* **10** assume (a pose, attitude, etc.). **11** arrive at: *to strike an agreement.* **12** lower or take down (a sail, flag, tent, etc.).
n **1** the act or fact of finding ore, oil, etc. **2** a refusal to work in order to force an employer to agree to demands. **3** *Baseball* **a** the failure of the batter to make a proper hit. **b** a pitched ball that passes through the STRIKE ZONE. **4** *Bowling* an upsetting of all the pins with the first ball. **5** an attack. ⟨Old English *strican* rub, stroke⟩
on strike having stopped work to get more pay, shorter hours, etc. **strike a balance** adopt a moderate course between two extremes. **strike home a** make an effective thrust with a weapon or tool. **b** make a strong impression: *The words of warning struck home.* **strike it rich** *Informal* **a** find rich ore, oil, etc. **b** achieve sudden wealth. **strike out a** cross out. **b** *Baseball* fail or cause to fail to hit three times. **c** fail. **d** aim a blow (*at*). **e** start a journey or enterprise: *We struck out for home.* **strike up** begin or cause to begin: *The two boys struck up a friendship.*
strike–bound *adj* immobilized by a labour strike. **strike·break·er** *n* a person hired to replace a striking employee. **strike·break·ing** *n.* **strike-out** *n Baseball* **1** an out made by a pitcher throwing three strikes against the batter. **2** the act of striking out. **strik·er** *n* **1** a person or thing that strikes. **2** a worker on strike. **3** *Soccer* the main attacking forward of a team. **strike zone** *Baseball* the area above home plate, from the level of the batter's knees to that of his or her shoulders. **strik·ing** *adj* attracting attention: *a striking use of colour.* **strik·ing·ly** *adv.*

string [strɪŋ] *n* **1** twine or heavy thread consisting of twisted fibres. **2** a series of objects threaded or hung on a string: *a string of pearls.* **3** a length of wire, etc. for a musical instrument or sports racquet. **4 strings** *pl* stringed instruments collectively. **5** anything used for tying: *apron strings.* **6** a line or series: *a string of victories.* **7** *Informal* a condition: *no strings attached.* **8** a squad of players grouped by ability, as **first string** (best), **second string**, etc. **9** *Computers* any sequence of characters, words, etc. treated as a unit.

v **strung, strung, string·ing 1** thread or hang on a string: *to string beads.* **2** furnish with strings: *to string a violin.* **3** cause to extend from one point to another: *to string a cable.* ⟨Old English *streng*⟩
have (or **keep**) **on a string** control completely. **have two strings to one's bow** have more than one way of doing or getting something. **pull strings** use one's influence, esp secretly. **pull the strings** control events or actions, often indirectly: *She's ostensibly retired, but she still pulls the strings around here.* **string along** *Informal* deceive; cause to have false hopes. **string out** prolong. **string someone a line** *Informal* lie to someone. **string together** join (words, sentences, etc.) in a series, often with poor cohesion. **string up** *Informal* kill by hanging.
string bean 1 a variety of green bean or wax bean with tough fibres connecting the halves of the pod. **2** *Informal* a tall, very thin person. **stringed instrument** a musical instrument with strings. **string·er** *n* **1** a person or thing that strings. **2** a horizontal supporting timber, girder, etc. **3** a part-time or local correspondent for a newspaper or magazine. **4** a player or other person ranked by ability: *a first-stringer.* **string quartet** a quartet of stringed instruments, usually two violins, a viola, and a cello. **string·y** *adj* **1** fibrous: *stringy meat.* **2** straggly: *stringy hair.* **3** forming strings: *stringy syrup.* **4** lean and sinewy; wiry.
strin·gent ['strɪndʒənt] *adj* strict; severe: *stringent laws, stringent demands.* **strin·gen·cy** *n.* **strin·gent·ly** *adv.* ⟨Latin *stringere* bind tight⟩

strip¹ [strɪp] *v* **stripped, strip·ping 1** remove (the covering or outer layer) from: *to strip bark from a tree.* **2** undress: *He stripped down to his shorts.* **3** perform a striptease. **4** empty: *to strip a house of its furniture.* **5** deprive or rob: *stripped of one's pride.* **6** damage the thread or teeth of (a gear, screw, etc.). ⟨Old English *-striepan*, as in *bestriepan* plunder⟩
strip down reduce to essentials. **stripped–down** *adj.*
strip mine a mine operated by digging out layers of earth on the surface to expose the ore. **strip mining. strip·per** *n* **1** a striptease dancer. **2** a person, device, substance, etc. that strips a surface. **strip poker** poker in which the loser must take off a piece of clothing. **strip·tease** *n* a show in which a performer slowly undresses to music.
strip² [strɪp] *n* **1** a long, narrow, flat piece of some material: *a strip of paper.* **2** a long, narrow tract of land. **3** an airstrip. **4** a COMIC STRIP. ⟨probably Low German *strippe* strap⟩
tear a strip off *Slang* criticize severely.
strip mall a mall in which the stores open only to the outside.
stripe [straɪp] *n* **1** a long, narrow band of different colour or texture: *A tiger is orange with black stripes.* **2 stripes** *pl* strips of braid on the sleeve of a uniform, showing rank. **3** sort; type: *people of every stripe.*
v mark with stripes. **striped** *adj.* ⟨Middle Dutch⟩

strive [straɪv] *v* **strove** or **strived, striv·en** ['strɪvən], **striv·ing 1** try hard. **2** *Poetic* fight or contend: *The swimmer strove against the tide.* ⟨Old French *estriver*⟩
strobe [stroub] *n* in full, **strobe light** an apparatus for producing brief, brilliant flashes of light, used in photography, theatre, etc. *v* shine in brilliant, often rhythmic flashes. ⟨Greek *strobos* a whirling⟩
strode [stroud] *v* pt of STRIDE.
stroke¹ [strouk] *n* **1 a** a sudden injury to the brain caused by the rupture or blockage of a blood vessel, often with loss of consciousness. **b** an attack of any of various conditions (in compounds): *sunstroke.* **2** an act of striking: *a stroke of lightning.* **3** a sound made by striking, as of a clock: *We arrived on the stroke of three.* **4** a piece of luck, fortune, etc.: *a stroke of bad luck.* **5** one complete movement to be made many times: *one stroke of a paddle.* **6** a movement or mark made by a pen, brush, etc. **7** a feat or achievement: *a stroke of genius.* **8** a sudden action like a blow in its effect, as in causing pain, injury, or death: *a stroke of fate.* **9** *Swimming* a style or method of swimming: *the butterfly stroke.*
v mark with a stroke, esp so as to cancel (with *out* or *off*). ⟨related to STRIKE⟩
stroke² [strouk] *v* **1** move the hand gently over; caress: *She stroked the kitten.* **2** flatter; praise, compliment, etc.
n **1** a stroking movement. **2 strokes** *pl* praise; recognition; flattery. ⟨Old English *strācian*⟩
stroll [stroul] *v* walk in a leisurely way. **stroll** *n.* ⟨origin uncertain⟩
stroll·er *n* a light carriage for wheeling a young child. **stroll·ing** *adj* travelling; roving: *strolling minstrels.*
strong See STRENGTH.
stron·tium ['strɒnʃəm] *or* ['strɒntiəm] *n* a soft, metallic element which occurs only in combination. *Symbol* **Sr** ⟨*Strontian* in Scotland, site of lead mines where first discovered⟩
strontium 90 a radioactive isotope of strontium, occurring in fallout from nuclear explosions.
strove [strouv] *v* a pt of STRIVE.
struck [strʌk] *v* pt and a pp of STRIKE.
struc·ture ['strʌktʃər] *n* **1** something built; a building. **2** anything composed of parts in orderly arrangement: *The human body is an amazing structure.* **3** the arrangement of parts, esp as it determines the special character of the whole: *the structure of a sentence.*
v **1** build. **2** put together in a systematic arrangement. **3** make structured. ⟨Latin *structura; struere* arrange⟩
struc·tur·al *adj* **1** of or for building: *structural steel.* **2** to do with structure. **struc·tur·al·ly** *adv.* **struc·tur·al·ism** *n* any theory emphasizing conceptual structure over function, esp in the social sciences. **struc·tur·al·ist** *n, adj.* **struc·tured** *adj* regimented; formal: *a highly structured classroom environment.*
stru·del ['strudəl] *German* ['ʃtruːdəl] *n* a

pastry made of thin dough rolled up around a filling, usually fruit, and baked. ⟨German⟩

strug·gle ['strʌgəl] *v* **1** move around violently in an effort to get free: *The child struggled in my arms.* **2** try hard against opposition, natural inclination, etc.: *to struggle to control one's anger.* **3** move with great effort: *The sick man struggled to his feet.* **strug·gle** *n.* **strug·gler** *n.* ⟨Middle English *struglen*⟩

strum [strʌm] *v* **strummed, strum·ming 1** play by brushing the fingers across the strings (of): *to strum a guitar.* **2** produce (music) in this way: *strum a tune.* **strum** *n.* **strum·mer** *n.* ⟨perhaps imitative⟩

strung [strʌŋ] *v* pt and a pp of STRING. **strung out** *Slang* **1** weakened, etc. in body or mind by addiction to a drug. **2** suffering the effects of severe mental strain.

strut¹ [strʌt] *v* **strut·ted, strut·ting** walk in a stiff, erect manner, suggesting vanity: *He strutted about the room in his new suit.* **strut** *n.* ⟨Old English *strūtian* stand out stiffly⟩ **strut one's stuff** *Informal* show off one's capabilities or skills.

Strut emphasizes putting on an air of dignity and importance by holding oneself stiffly and proudly: *The little boy put on his new boots and strutted around the room.* **Swagger** suggests boasting, defiance, or contempt for others: *After being put on probation again, the girls swaggered out of the courtroom.*

strut² [strʌt] *n* a supporting bar in a frame, designed to resist longitudinal pressure; brace. ⟨perhaps Low German *strutt* stiff⟩

strych·nine ['strɪknɪn], [-nɪn], *or* [-naɪn] *n* a bitter, poisonous compound obtained from plants, and used in small doses as a stimulant for the central nervous system. ⟨Greek *strychnos* nightshade⟩

stub [stʌb] *n* **1** a short piece that is left: *the stub of a pencil.* **2** the torn-off end of a ticket, cheque, etc. kept as a record. **3** something cut off or stunted: *a stub of a tail.* *v* **stubbed, stub·bing 1** strike (one's toe) on something. **2** put out (a cigarette or cigar) by crushing the burning end in an ashtray, etc. (with *out*). ⟨Old English⟩ **stub·by** ['stʌbi] *adj* short and thick or blunt: *stubby fingers, a stubby crayon.*

stub·ble ['stʌbəl] *n* **1** the lower ends of stalks left in the ground after grain is cut. **2** a short growth of beard. **stub·bly** *adj.* ⟨Old French *stuble;* Latin *stupula, stipula* stem⟩ **stub·ble–jump·er** *n* ✹ *Slang* a prairie farmer.

stub·born ['stʌbərn] *adj* **1** obstinate: *too stubborn to admit he is wrong.* **2** determined: *a stubborn fight for freedom.* **3** hard to control or manage: *a stubborn cough.* **stub·born·ly** *adv.* **stub·born·ness** *n.* ⟨probably *stub*⟩

stub·by See STUB.

stuc·co ['stʌkou] *n* **-coes** *or* **-cos 1** a rough mixture of cement, sand, and lime, used to cover walls and ceilings. **2** fine plaster used for moulding into architectural decorations.

v decorate with stucco. ⟨Italian; Germanic; compare Old High German *stukki* crust⟩

stuck [stʌk] *v* pt and pp of STICK². **stuck–up** *adj Informal* snobbish; conceited.

stud¹ [stʌd] *n* **1** a small knob: *The belt was ornamented with metal studs.* **2** a small button. **3** one of a row of upright posts to which drywall or plywood are nailed in making a wall of a building. **4** a small, buttonlike, ornament for a pierced ear, tongue, etc. *v* **stud·ded, stud·ding 1** set with studs or something like studs: *studded winter tires.* **2** set or be set here and there (over): *Little islands stud the lake.* ⟨Old English *studu*⟩

stud² [stʌd] *n* **1** a male animal, esp a stallion, kept for breeding. **2** a group of such animals. **3** a place where such animals are kept. **4** *Slang* a virile, sexy man. ⟨Old English *stōd*⟩ **at stud** of a male animal, available to be bred. **stud poker** a type of poker in which cards are dealt face down on the first round and then face up for successive rounds.

stu·dent ['stjudənt] *or* ['studənt] *n* **1** a person studying at a school, university, etc. **2** a person who studies systematically: *a student of human nature.* ⟨Latin *studere* orig be eager⟩ **student body** all the students at a school, etc. collectively.

stu·di·o ['stjudiou] *or* ['studiou] *n* **1** the workroom of an artist or musician. **2** a place where films or recordings are made. **3** a place from which a radio or television program is broadcast. **4** in full, **studio apartment** a small apartment consisting of one main room and a bathroom. ⟨Italian; Latin *studium* study⟩

stud·y ['stʌdi] *v* **1** try to learn (about) by means of books, observation, etc: *to study history.* **2** examine carefully: *to study a map.* **3** consider with care: *The prisoner studied ways to escape.* **4** try to memorize by going over repeatedly: *to study one's notes for a test.* **5** be a student: *She's studying to be a doctor.* *n* **1** the act of studying. **2** a particular body of research on a topic: *According to this study, flu shots do reduce the incidence of flu.* **3** a room for study, reading, etc. **4** a literary or artistic work dealing with one subject in careful detail. **5** *Music* a composition designed mainly for practice in a technical problem. **6 studies** a person's work as a student: *to go back to one's studies after a break.* ⟨Latin *studium*⟩ **a quick study** someone who learns material quickly. **stud·ied** *adj* produced by deliberate effort: *studied politeness.* **stud·ied·ly** *adv.* **stu·di·ous** ['stjudiəs] *or* ['studiəs] *adj* **1** fond of or disciplined about studying. **2** thoughtful and painstaking: *a studious effort to please.* **stu·di·ous·ly** *adv.* **stu·di·ous·ness** *n.*

stuff [stʌf] *n* **1** a substance: *What's this green stuff in the bottle?* **2** things: *Get your stuff off the table.* **3** inward qualities: *He's got the right stuff to succeed.* **4** one's area of expertise: *She really knows her stuff.* *v* **1** pack full. **2** block (often with *up*): *My nose is stuffed up by a cold.* **3** fill the skin of (a dead animal) to make it look as it did when alive.

4 fill (a turkey, etc.) with a seasoned mixture before cooking. **5** force; thrust: *to stuff clothes into a bag.* **6** eat or cause to eat too much. ⟨Old French *estoffe;* origin uncertain⟩ **strut one's stuff** See STRUT¹. **that's the stuff!** *Informal* an expression of encouragement.
stuffed shirt *Informal* a pompous, conceited, conservative person. **stuff·ing** *n* **1** any soft material used to fill cushions, toys, etc. **2** seasoned bread crumbs, etc. cooked inside a turkey, etc. **knock the stuffing out of** defeat or tire out. **stuff·y** *adj* **1** lacking fresh air: *a stuffy room.* **2** dull: *a stuffy conversation.* **3** stopped up: *a stuffy nose.* **4** narrow-minded: *Don't be so stuffy; it was only a harmless joke.* **stuff·i·ly** *adv.* **stuff·i·ness** *n.*

stul·ti·fy ['stʌltə,faɪ] *v* **1** make passive or weak by lack of stimulation, etc.: *the stultifying atmosphere of a prison.* **2** make foolish or absurd. **stul·ti·fi·ca·tion** *n.* **stul·ti·fy·ing** *adj.* ⟨Latin *stultus* foolish + *facere* make⟩

stum·ble ['stʌmbəl] *v* **1** lose one's balance or fall. **2** walk unsteadily: *The hikers stumbled along.* **3** speak, act, etc. in a hesitating way: *He stumbled through his speech.* **4** come (*on, upon, across*, etc.) by chance: *I stumbled upon some fine antiques.* **stum·ble** *n.* **stum·bler** *n.* **stum·bling** *adj.* ⟨Middle English; related to Norwegian *stumla*⟩
stum·bling–block *n* an obstacle; hindrance.

stump [stʌmp] *n* **1** the bottom of a tree trunk left after the tree has fallen or been cut down. **2** anything left after the main part has gone. *the stump of a tail.* **3** a heavy step. **4** the place from which a political speech is made. **5** Usually, **stumps** *pl Informal* legs.
v **1** remove stumps from (land). **2** travel through (an area), making speeches: *All the candidates are out stumping the riding this week.* **3** walk in a heavy, clumsy way. **4** *Informal* baffle; be too hard for: *The second question stumped him.* ⟨Middle English *stompe*⟩
on the stump making a political speech. **up a stump** *Informal* in a predicament.
stump·age *n* **1** a price paid for the right to cut standing timber. **2** a tax or royalty paid to the government on each tree cut. **3** standing timber viewed as an asset. **stump·y** *adj* **1** short and thick. **2** full of stumps.

stun [stʌn] *v* **stunned, stun·ning 1** knock unconscious. **2** daze: *She was stunned by the news.* ⟨Old English *stunen;* Old French *estoner*⟩
stun·ning *adj* **1** that stuns: *a stunning blow.* **2** very attractive. **3** excellent: *a stunning performance.* **stun·ning·ly** *adv.*

stung [stʌŋ] *v* pt and pp of STING.

stunk [stʌŋk] *v* a pt and pp of STINK.

stunt¹ [stʌnt] *v* check or hinder in growth or development: *Lack of proper food stunts a plant.* ⟨Old English *stunt* stupid, foolish⟩

stunt² [stʌnt] *n* **1** a feat showing boldness and skill: *Circus riders perform stunts on horseback.* **2** an act meant to attract attention; gimmick. ⟨probably variant of *stint* task⟩
stunt·man *n, pl* **-men** a man who substitutes

for an actor in scenes involving dangerous manoeuvres. **stunt·wom·an** *n, pl* **-wom·en.**

stu·pa ['stupə] *n* a Buddhist shrine in the shape of a large dome. ⟨Sanskrit *stupa* heap⟩

stu·pe·fy ['stjupə,faɪ] *or* ['stupə,faɪ] *v* **1** make dazed, dull, or senseless: *stupefied by drugs.* **2** overwhelm with shock, fear, etc.: *stupefied by terror.* **stu·pe·fac·tion** *n.* ⟨Latin *stupere* be amazed + *facere* make⟩

stu·pen·dous [stju'pɛndəs] *or* [stu'pɛndəs] *adj* amazing; awesome: *Niagara Falls is a stupendous sight.* ⟨Latin *stupere* be amazed⟩

stu·pid ['stjupɪd] *or* ['stupɪd] *adj* **1** showing little intelligence: *a stupid remark.* **2** dazed: *still stupid from the sedative.* **3** *Slang* a general term of contempt or annoyance: *This stupid pen won't write.* **stu·pid·i·ty** *n.* **stu·pid·ly** *adv.* ⟨Latin *stupidus; stupere* be dazed⟩

stu·por ['stjupər] *or* ['stupər] *n* a state of being without power to feel or think. ⟨Latin; *stupere* be dazed⟩

stur·dy ['stɜrdi] *adj* **1** strong; solidly built: *sturdy legs, a sturdy table.* **2** unyielding; firm: *sturdy resistance.* **stur·di·ly** *adv.* **stur·di·ness** *n.* ⟨Old French *esturdi* violent, orig dazed⟩

stur·geon ['stɜrdʒən] *n, pl* **-geon** or **-geons** any of a family of sharklike fishes, valued as a source of caviar. ⟨Anglo-French *esturgeon*⟩

stut·ter ['stʌtər] *v* **1** repeat the same sound in an effort to speak. **2** say with a stutter: *to stutter a reply.* **stut·ter** *n.* **stut·ter·er** *n.* See also STAMMER. ⟨Middle English *stutten*⟩

sty¹ [staɪ] *n* **1** a pen for pigs. **2** any filthy place. ⟨Old English *stig*⟩

sty² *or* **stye** [staɪ] *n, pl* **sties** or **styes** a small boil on the edge of the eyelid. ⟨Middle English *styanye;* Old English *stigend* rising + *ēage* eye⟩

style [staɪl] *n* **1** fashion: *dressed in the latest styles.* **2** a manner, esp of expression in the arts: *the Gothic style of architecture.* **3** an elegant manner: *to travel in style.* **4** *Botany* the stemlike part of the pistil of a flower.
v **1** design or arrange: *to style one's hair.* **2** name; call: *Joan of Arc was styled the Maid of Orléans.* ⟨Latin *stilus* orig writing instrument⟩
styl·ish *adj* fashionable: *a stylish new coat.* **styl·ish·ly** *adv.* **styl·ist** *n* **1** a writer whose work shows good or unique style. **2 a** hairstylist. **b** a designer or fashion consultant. **sty·lis·tic** *adj* to do with style in writing. **sty·lis·ti·cal·ly** *adv.* **styl·ize** *v* design according to a conventional style rather than realistically: *wallpaper with tiny stylized tulips on it.* **styl·i·za·tion** *n.*

sty·lus ['staɪləs] *n* any of various pointed marking instruments. ⟨Latin *stilus*. See STYLE.⟩

sty·mie ['staɪmi] *v* block or hinder completely. ⟨perhaps Scots *stymie* person with poor eyesight⟩

Sty·ro·foam ['staɪrə,foum] *n Trademark* a lightweight plastic used for insulation, packaging, etc.

suave [swɑv] *adj* smoothly agreeable or polite. **suave·ly** *adv.* **sua·vi·ty** or **suave·ness** *n.* ⟨French; Latin *suavis* agreeable⟩

sub [sʌb] *Informal n, adj* **1** substitute. **2** submarine. **3** subordinate.
v **subbed, sub·bing** act as a substitute.

sub– *prefix* **1** under: *subway.* **2** again: *subdivide.* **3** near or nearly: *subarctic.* **4** secondary: *substation.* ⟨Latin⟩

sub·arc·tic [sʌb'arktɪk] *or* [sʌb'artɪk] *n* the region just south of the Arctic Circle. **sub·arc·tic** *adj.*

sub·ar·id [sʌb'ɛrɪd] *or* [sʌb'ærɪd] *adj* somewhat arid.

sub·a·tom·ic [ˌsʌbə'tɒmɪk] *adj* to do with the particles smaller than atoms.

sub–base·ment ['sʌb ˌbeɪsmənt] *n* a storey below the main basement of a building.

subcategory ['sʌb,kætə,gɔri] *n* a division of a category.

sub·class ['sʌb,klæs] *n* **1** *Biology* a secondary category in the classification of plants and animals, within a class and including one or more orders. **2** a division within a class.

sub·com·mit·tee ['sʌbkə,mɪti] *n* a small committee chosen from a larger one for some special duty.

sub·com·pact [sʌb'kɒmpækt] *or* ['sʌb,kɒm-] *n* the smallest of the basic sizes of car. Compare COMPACT, STANDARD.

sub·con·scious [sʌb'kɒnʃəs] *adj* affecting behaviour but not consciously recognized: *subconscious fears, a subconscious motive.*
n **the subconscious** thoughts, feelings, etc. not consciously recognized but affecting attitudes and behaviour. **sub·con·scious·ly** *adv.*

sub·con·tract ['sʌb,kɒntrækt] *n* a contract under a previous contract: *The contractor for the new arena gave my father the subcontract to install the roof.* **sub·con·tract** [sʌb'kɒntrækt] *v.* **sub·con·trac·tor** [sʌb'kɒntræktər] *n.*

sub·cul·ture ['sʌb,kʌltʃər] *n* group within a culture, distinguished from it by features of custom, conduct, etc.: *The academic community is a subculture.*

sub·cu·ta·ne·ous [ˌsʌbkju'teɪniəs] *adj* under the skin. **sub·cu·ta·ne·ous·ly** *adv.* ⟨sub- + Latin *cutaneus; cutis* skin⟩

sub·di·vide ['sʌbdə,vaɪd] *v* divide the parts of into still smaller parts.
sub·di·vi·sion *n* **1** a subdivided tract of land. **2** a housing development on it.

sub·due [səb'dju] *or* [səb'du] *v* **1** conquer: *to subdue the wilderness.* **2** suppress: *to subdue a desire to laugh.* **3** tone down; soften. ⟨Latin *sub-* under + *ducere* lead⟩
sub·dued *adj* **1** low in intensity: *subdued colours.* **2** less lively or spirited than usual: *He was quiet and subdued all afternoon.*

sub·en·try ['sʌb,ɛntri] *n* an entry listed under a main entry: *In this dictionary, idioms are subentries.* **sub·en·ter** *v.*

sub·freez·ing ['sʌb'frizɪŋ] *adj* below the freezing point of water (0° Celsius).

sub·group ['sʌb,grup] *n* a division of a group; group within a group.

sub·head ['sʌb,hɛd] *n* a subtitle, subordinate headline, etc. Also, **sub·head·ing.**

sub·hu·man [sʌb'hjumən] *adj* **1** less than human. **2** almost human: *subhuman primates.*

subj 1 subject; subjective(ly). **2** subjunctive.

sub·ject ['sʌbdʒɪkt] *n* **1** anything thought about, discussed, etc. **2** a course of study, field of learning, etc.: *Art is a required subject in this school.* **3** a person under the authority of another, esp a monarch. **4** a person or thing that undergoes something, such as an experiment. **5** *Grammar* the part of a sentence about which something is said in the predicate, as *His little brother* in *His little brother went to find him.* **6 a** the theme of a literary work. **b** that which is represented in a piece of art.
adj under some power or influence.
v [səb'dʒɛkt] **1** bring under some power or influence: *Rome subjected all Italy to its rule.* **2** cause to undergo something: *The terrorists subjected their captives to torture.* **3** make liable or vulnerable *(to):* *His kindness subjects him to impositions.* **sub·jec·tion** *n.* ⟨Latin *subjectus* pp of *subjicere; sub-* under + *jacere* throw⟩
subject to a under the power or authority of: *We are subject to the law.* **b** liable to have: *He is subject to seizures.* **c** on condition of: *I bought the car subject to your approval.*
sub·jec·tive *adj* **1** influenced by a person's state of mind, bias, etc.: *a subjective judgment.* **2** dealing with a writer's or artist's own thoughts or feelings; personal: *a subjective poem.* **3** *Grammar* to do with the form of an English pronoun, such as *we* (as opposed to *us*) used as the subject of a sentence. **sub·jec·tive·ly** *adv.* **sub·jec·tiv·i·ty** *n.* **subject matter** the thing or things dealt with in a book, speech, debate, etc.

┌─────────────────────┐
│ SYNONYMS │
Subject is the general word for something talked or thought about: *She tried to change the subject.* **Topic** suggests a definitely stated subject for a lecture, essay, discussion, etc.: *"Debt management" is today's topic.*

sub·ju·gate ['sʌbdʒə,geɪt] *v* conquer; make subservient or submissive. **sub·ju·ga·tion** *n.* ⟨Latin *subjugare; sub-* under + *jugum* yoke⟩

sub·junc·tive [səb'dʒʌŋktɪv] *adj* *Grammar* expressing a state as conditional, desirable, etc. rather than as fact. In *If I were you,* the verb *were* is in the **subjunctive mood.** Compare INDICATIVE, IMPERATIVE. ⟨Latin *subjunctivus; sub-* under + *jungere* join⟩

sub·lease [sʌb'lis] *v* of a person leasing property from an owner, lease (it or part of it) in turn to another. **sub·lease** ['sʌb,lis] *n.* **sub·les·see** [-lɛ'si] *n.* **sub·les·sor** [-lɛ'sɔr] *n.*

sub·let [sʌb'lɛt] *v* **-let, -let·ting 1** rent to another (property rented to oneself): *to sublet one's apartment while on an extended vacation.* **2** rent from another tenant.
n ['sʌb,lɛt] an apartment, etc. so rented.

sub·lime [sə'blaɪm] *adj* **1** noble; lofty; exalted: *the sublime beauty of the mountains.* **2** perfect; complete: *sublime indifference.*

v Chemistry change or be changed from a solid to a vapour, or vice versa, without being liquid. **sub·lime·ly** *adv.* ⟨Latin *sublimis* orig sloping up; *sub-* up + *limen* lintel⟩

sub·li·mate ['sʌblə,meit] *v* **1** *Psychology* change the natural expression of (an impulse or desire) into a more acceptable one: *sublimate one's aggressiveness.* **2** *Chemistry* sublime; extract or purify by subliming. **3** make purer or nobler. *n* [-mɪt] *or* [-,meit] a substance, such as frost, produced by subliming. **sub·li·mate** *adj.* **sub·li·ma·tion** *n.*

sub·lim·i·nal [sə'blɪmənəl] *adj Psychology* existing or acting below the threshhold of conscious awareness: *the subliminal self, subliminal advertising.* **sub·lim·i·nal·ly** *adv.* ⟨*sub-* + Latin *limen, liminis* threshold⟩

sub·ma·chine gun [,sʌbmə'ʃin] a light automatic or semi-automatic gun designed to be fired from the shoulder or hip.

sub·ma·rine ['sʌbmə,rin] *or* [,sʌbmə'rin] *n* **1** a craft that operates under water. **2** a large sandwich made with a long bun.
adj **1** to do with or carried out by submarines: *submarine tactics.* **2** used, growing, etc. below the surface of the sea: *submarine plant life.* **sub·mar·i·ner** [sʌb'mɛrənər] *or* [-'mærənər] *n.*

sub·merge [səb'mɜrdʒ] *v* **1** put or go under water or other liquid: *At high tide this path is submerged.* **2** cover; bury: *talent submerged by shyness.* **sub·mer·gence** *n.* ⟨Latin *sub-* under + *mergere* plunge⟩
sub·merse [səb'mɜrs] *v* submerge.
sub·mersed *adj.* **sub·mer·sion** *n.*
sub·mers·i·ble *adj* that can be submerged: *a submersible pump. n* a craft that can operate under water for research, exploration, etc.

sub·mit [səb'mɪt] *v* **-mit·ted, -mit·ting 1** yield to the authority of another: *The thief submitted to arrest by the police.* **2** give to others for consideration: *to submit a report to a manager.* **3** offer as an opinion: *We submit that the proposed expansion is unnecessary.* ⟨Latin *submittere; sub-* under + *mittere* let go⟩
sub·mis·sion *n* **1** the act of submitting or the state or attitude of one who has submitted. **2** something submitted for consideration, as a petition, contest entry, etc. **sub·mis·sive** *adj* ready to submit. **sub·mis·sive·ly** *adv.* **sub·mis·sive·ness** *n.*

sub·nor·mal [sʌb'nɔrməl] *adj* lower or less than normal: *subnormal temperatures.*

sub·or·di·nate [sə'bɔrdənɪt] *adj* **1** inferior in rank. **2** less important: *a subordinate point.* **3** dependent on or controlled by something else. **4** *Grammar* of a clause, functioning as an adjective, adverb, or noun in a complex sentence and unable to stand on its own.
n a subordinate person or thing.
v [-,neit] make subordinate: *He subordinated his wishes to mine.* **sub·or·di·nate·ly** *adv.* **sub·or·di·na·tion** *n.* ⟨Latin *subordinare; sub-* under + *ordinis* order⟩

sub·orn [sə'bɔrn] *v* **1** *Law* persuade to give false testimony: *to suborn a witness.* **2** obtain

in this way: *to suborn perjury.* **sub·or·na·tion** *n.* ⟨Latin *sub-* secretly + *ornare* equip⟩

sub·plot ['sʌb,plɒt] *n* a subordinate plot within the main plot of a novel, film, etc.

sub·poe·na [sə'pinə] *or* [səb'pinə] *Law n* a written order requiring one to appear in court for a stated purpose at a stated time.
v summon with a subpoena. ⟨Latin *sub poena* under penalty⟩

sub·po·lar [sʌb'poulər] *adj* of the regions near the South or North Pole.

sub·rout·ine ['sʌbru,tin] *n Computers* an instruction sequence in a program that forms a unit and can be used as often as needed.

sub·scribe [səb'skraib] *v* **1** pay to receive a periodical regularly (with *to*): *He subscribes to several magazines.* **2** agree: *I will not subscribe to that.* **sub·scrib·er** *n.* **sub·scrip·tion** [-'skrɪpʃən] *n.* ⟨Latin *sub-* under + *scribere* write⟩
sub·script ['sʌb,skrɪpt] *n* a small number, letter, etc. written below the line, as the *2* in H_2O. **sub·script** *adj.*

sub·sec·tion ['sʌb,sɛkʃən] *n* part of a section.

sub·se·quent ['sʌbsəkwənt] *adj* later; coming after: *subsequent events.* **sub·se·quent·ly** *adv.* ⟨Latin *sub-* up + *sequi* follow⟩

sub·ser·vi·ent [səb'sɜrviənt] *adj* **1** submissive. **2** useful (*to* a purpose). **3** subordinate. **sub·ser·vi·ence** *n.* **sub·ser·vi·ent·ly** *adv.*

sub·set ['sʌb,sɛt] *n Mathematics, logic* a set whose members also belong to a larger set: *The set of poodles is a subset of the set of dogs.*

sub·side [səb'said] *v* **1** sink to a lower level: *After the rain stopped, the flood waters subsided.* **2** become less intense: *Her rage subsided.* ⟨Latin *subsidere; sub-* down + *sidere* settle⟩

sub·sid·i·ar·y [səb'sɪdiəri], [-'sɪdʒəri], *or* [-'sɪdi,ɛri] *adj* **1** in a supporting role; supplementary. **2** subordinate; secondary.
n a company with over half its stock owned or controlled by another. ⟨Latin *subsidium* reserve troops⟩

sub·si·dy ['sʌbsədi] *n* a grant of money, esp from a government. **sub·si·dize** *v.*
sub·si·di·za·tion *n.* ⟨Latin *subsidium* aid⟩

sub·sist [səb'sɪst] *v* stay alive, esp barely: *The stranded hikers subsisted on berries.* ⟨Latin *sub-* up to + *sistere* stand⟩
sub·sist·ence *n* a marginal livelihood: *The sea provides a subsistence for fishers. adj* yielding no surplus for trade: *subsistence farming.*

sub·soil ['sʌb,sɔil] *n* the layer of earth just under the surface soil.

sub·spe·cies ['sʌb,spiʃiz] *or* ['sʌb,spisɪz] *n, pl* **-cies** a grouping within a species, based on inherited biological differences.

sub·stance ['sʌbstəns] *n* **1** matter; material. **2** the essential part of anything: *the substance of a speech.* **3** solid quality: *Pea soup has more substance than milk.* **4** significant content: *Her writing is superficial and lacks substance.* **5** wealth. **6** a particular kind of matter: *a sticky substance.* ⟨Latin *substantia; substare* stand firm; *sub-* up to + *stare* stand⟩

substance abuse use of a substance, such as alcohol or drugs, in a way that damages health and interferes with one's ability to function. **sub·stan·tial** [səb'stænʃəl] *adj* **1** real: *Dreams are not substantial.* **2** significant: *a substantial improvement.* **3** solid: *substantial construction.* **4** of real value: *something substantial to eat.* **sub·stan·tial·ly** *adv.* **sub·stan·ti·ate** [-'stænʃi‚eit] *v* establish by evidence: *to substantiate a rumour.* **sub·stan·ti·a·tion** *n.* **sub·stan·tive** *adj* **1** *Grammar* **a** used as a noun. **b** showing or expressing existence. *Be* is the substantive verb. **2** substantial. **sub·stan·tive·ly** *adv.*

SYNONYMS
Substance suggests 'what a particular thing consists of', and applies to concrete and to abstract things: *Spider webs consist of a sticky substance. The substance of the plan is good.* **Matter** applies to all substances that physical objects consist of: *Matter may be gaseous, liquid, or solid.* **Material** applies particularly to matter that is made into something: *wood and other building material.*

sub·stan·dard [sʌb'stændərd] *adj* falling short of a standard: *substandard work.*

sub·sti·tute ['sʌbstɪ‚tjut] or ['sʌbstɪ‚tut] *n* a person or thing taking the place of another: *Margarine is a common substitute for butter.* *v* **1** put in the place of another: *We substituted brown sugar for molasses in this cake.* **2** take the place of another (with *for*): *She substituted for me at the meeting.* **sub·sti·tu·tion** *n.* ⟨Latin *substituere; sub-* instead + *statuere* establish⟩

sub·stra·tum ['sʌb‚strætəm] or [-‚streitəm] *n*, *pl* **-ta** [-tə] or **-tums** **1** a layer lying under another. **2** a basis; foundation: *The story has a substratum of truth.*

sub·sume [səb'sum] or [səb'sjum] *v* bring under a broader category: *Your suggestion has been subsumed under Part A of the report.* ⟨Latin *sub-* under + *sumere* assume⟩

sub·ten·ant ['sʌb‚tɛnənt] *n* a tenant renting from a tenant. **sub·ten·an·cy** *n.*

sub·tend [səb'tɛnd] *v* **1** *Geometry* **a** define by marking off the endpoints of: *A chord subtends an arc of a circle.* **b** of a line, arc, etc., be opposite to (an angle): *The hypotenuse subtends the right angle of a right triangle.* **2** *Botany* underlie, usually so as to enclose or surround: *a flower subtended by a leafy bract.* ⟨Latin *sub-* under + *tendere* stretch⟩

sub·ter·fuge ['sʌbtər‚fjudʒ] *n* a trick, excuse, or other deception used to avoid something. ⟨Latin *subter-* from under + *fugere* flee⟩

sub·ter·ra·ne·an [‚sʌbtə'reiniən] *adj* **1** underground: *a subterranean cave.* **2** secret; hidden. ⟨Latin *sub-* under + *terra* earth⟩

sub·text ['sʌb‚tɛkst] *n* an underlying meaning, esp in literature and drama.

sub·ti·tle ['sʌb‚taitəl] *n* **1** an additional or subordinate title. **2** a written piece of dialogue, esp translated, displayed at the bottom of a movie screen. **sub·ti·tle** *v.*

sub·tle ['sʌtəl] *adj* **1** hard to detect: *a subtle distinction.* **2** discerning: *a subtle thinker.* **3** sly; crafty; tricky: *a subtle scheme.* **4** skilful; clever; expert. **sub·tle·ty** *n.* **sub·tly** *adv.* ⟨Latin *subtilis* orig woven under; *sub-* + *tela* web⟩

sub·to·tal ['sʌb‚toutəl] *n* the total of a group of figures forming part of a larger series. **sub·to·tal, -talled** or **-taled, -tal·ling** or **-tal·ing** *v.*

sub·tract [səb'trækt] *v* **1** *Mathematics* take away (a quantity) from another quantity. **2** take away (a part) from a whole. **sub·trac·tion** *n.* ⟨Latin *subtractus* pp of *subtrahere; sub-* from under + *trahere* draw⟩ **sub·tra·hend** ['sʌbtrə‚hɛnd] *n Mathematics* a quantity to be subtracted. In 10 − 8, the subtrahend is 8.

sub·trop·ics [sʌb'trɒpɪks] *n pl* the regions bordering on the tropics. **sub·trop·i·cal** *adj.*

sub·urb ['sʌbərb] *n* **1** a community near or just outside a city or town. **2** **the suburbs** residential areas on the outskirts of a city or town. ⟨Latin *sub-* below + *urbs* city⟩ **sub·ur·ban** [sə'bɜrbən] *adj* **1** to do with or in a suburb: *suburban transit.* **2** supposedly typical of a suburb or its residents; esp, boring, middle-class, etc. **sub·ur·ban·ite** *n* a resident of a suburb. **sub·ur·bi·a** *n* the suburbs, esp with reference to supposedly typical values, attitudes, etc. of residents.

sub·vert [səb'vɜrt] *v* overthrow, esp from within: *to subvert democracy.* **sub·ver·sion** *n.* ⟨Latin *sub-* from under + *vertere* turn⟩ **sub·ver·sive** *adj* tending to subvert a regime, etc.: *a subversive scheme. n* a person who seeks to do this. **sub·ver·sive·ly** *adv.*

sub·way ['sʌb‚wei] *n* **1** an electric railway running mostly underground in a city. **2** an underground passage for pipes, etc.

suc·ceed [sək'sid] *v* **1** achieve what is attempted: *The plan succeeded.* **2** prosper in life. **3** come next after: *Who succeeded Trudeau as Prime Minister?* **4** come into possession of a title, property, etc. by right of birth. (with *to*): *The Prince of Wales succeeds to the throne of England.* ⟨Latin *succedere; sub-* up (to) + *cedere* go⟩

suc·cess [sək'sɛs] *n* **1** a favourable result. **2** the gaining of wealth, position, etc.: *He has had no success in life.* **3** a person or thing that succeeds. **4** result; fortune: *What success did you have in finding a new car?* **suc·cess·ful** *adj.* **suc·cess·ful·ly** *adv.* **suc·ces·sion** *n* **1** a series of people or things following one after another: *a succession of misfortunes.* **2** the right of succeeding to an office, property, or rank: *a dispute about succession.* **3** the order of people having such a right: *The monarch's eldest child is next in succession to the throne.* **in succession** one after another: *several sunny days in succession.* **suc·ces·sive** *adj* coming one after another: *three successive occasions.* **suc·ces·sive·ly** *adv.* **suc·ces·sor** *n* a person or thing coming next after another and taking the other's place.

suc·cinct [sək'sɪŋkt] *adj* clear, precise, and brief: *a succinct definition.* **suc·cinct·ly** *adv.*

suc·cinct·ness *n.* ⟨Latin *succinctus* pp of *succingere*; *sub-* up + *cingere* gird⟩

suc·cour or **suc·cor** ['sʌkər] *n* help; aid; relief: *to give succour in time of need.* **suc·cour** *v.* ⟨Latin *succurrere* run to help⟩

suc·cu·bus ['sʌkjəbəs] *n*, *pl* **-bi** [-baɪ] an evil spirit in female form supposed, in medieval times, to have sexual intercourse with men while they sleep. Compare INCUBUS. ⟨Latin, from *succubare* to lie beneath⟩

suc·cu·lent ['sʌkjələnt] *adj* **1** juicy: *succulent fruit.* **2** of a plant, having thick, fleshy tissues adapted for storing water. **suc·cu·lent** *n.* **suc·cu·lence** *n.* ⟨Latin *succulentus*; *succus* juice⟩

suc·cumb [sə'kʌm] *v* **1** give way; yield: *to succumb to temptation.* **2** die or die of (with *to*): *She succumbed to her injuries two days later.* ⟨Latin *sub-* down + *-cumbere* lie⟩

such [sʌtʃ] *adj* **1** of this or that kind: *I have never seen such a sight.* **2** being as described to so great an extent: *such a liar.* **3** whatever; whichever: *Make such repairs as are needed.*
pron one or more people or things of a given kind: *Bring chips and such for snacks.* ⟨Old English *swylc*, *swelc*; *swa* so + *līc* like⟩
as such a as what is indicated: *A leader, as such, deserves respect.* **b** in or by itself: *Mere good looks, as such, will not get you far.* **such and such** referring to people or things not identified: *He lives in such and such a town.*
such as a of the kind that: *behaviour such as might be expected of a toddler.* **b** of the same kind as: *stories such as this one.* **c** for example: *members of the dog family, such as the wolf.*
such as it is (or **was**) although barely adequate: *The food, such as it was, was cheap.*
such·like *adj* of such a kind. *pron* such people or things: *costumes, masks, and suchlike.*

suck [sʌk] *v* **1** draw into the mouth by using the lips and tongue to create a partial vacuum: *to suck lemonade through a straw.* **2** make a sucking action or noise: *He sucked his thumb.* **3** absorb: *A sponge sucks up water.* **4** draw in; swallow up: *The whirlpool sucked the boat down.* **5** hold in the mouth to dissolve: *to suck a lollipop.* **6** *Slang* be very unsatisfactory: *This movie sucks.* **suck** *n.* ⟨Old English *sūcan*⟩
suck in a absorb. **b** pull in (one's stomach, etc.) **c** *Slang* dupe. **d** force to participate. **suck up to** *Slang* ingratiate oneself with.
suck·er *n* **1** a lump of candy on a stick. **2** a thing that sucks, such as a part or organ for holding fast by a sucking force. **3** any of a family of North American freshwater fishes having a soft, thick-lipped, toothless mouth. **4** *Botany* a shoot growing from the trunk, a branch, or an underground stem or root. **5** *Slang* a person easily exploited. *v Slang* dupe. **be a sucker for** *Slang* have a weakness or predilection for. **suck·le** *v* **1** feed with milk from the breast, udder, etc.: *to suckle a baby.* **2** suck at the breast, teat, etc. **suck·ling** *n* an unweaned young animal or child.

su·crose ['sukrous] *n* the sugar found in sugar cane, sugar beets, etc. ⟨French *sucre* sugar⟩

suc·tion ['sʌkʃən] *n* **1** the production of a vacuum so that pressure forces fluid into the space or causes surfaces to stick together: *Lemonade is drawn through a straw by suction.* **2** the force so caused. **3** the process of sucking. ⟨Latin *suctus* pp of *sugere* suck⟩

sud·den ['sʌdən] *adj* **1** unexpected: *a sudden attack.* **2** swift; instant: *a sudden rise in value.* **sud·den·ly** *adv.* **sud·den·ness** *n.* ⟨Anglo-French *sodein*; Latin *subitaneus*; *subitus* sudden⟩
all of a sudden in a sudden manner.
sudden death 1 instant or unexpected death. **2** *Sports* an extra game or period played to break a tie, ending as soon as anyone scores. **sud·den–death** *adj.* **sudden infant death syndrome** death due to cessation of breathing in a seemingly healthy sleeping infant, from unknown causes; **crib death**. *Abbrev* SIDS.

suds [sʌdz] *n pl* **1** froth or foam, esp on soapy water. **2** soapy water. **3** *Slang* beer. **sud·sy** *adj.* ⟨origin unknown⟩

sue [su] *v* **1** *Law* take legal action (against): *to sue for damages.* **2** beg or ask (*for*): *to sue for peace.* ⟨Anglo-French *suer*; Latin *sequi* follow⟩

suede or **suède** [sweɪd] *n* soft leather with a velvety nap. ⟨French *(de) Suède* (from) Sweden⟩

su·et ['suɪt] *n* hard fat around the kidneys and loins of cattle or sheep, used in cooking and to make tallow. **su·et·y** *adj.* ⟨Anglo-French; Old French *sieu* tallow; Latin *sebum*⟩

suf·fer ['sʌfər] *v* **1** experience (pain, grief, loss, etc.): *Sick people suffer.* **2** permit: *He suffered his great-aunt to kiss him on the cheek.* **suf·fer·er** *n.* **suf·fer·ing** ['sʌfrɪŋ] *n*, *adj.* ⟨Latin *sufferre*; *sub-* up + *ferre* bear⟩
suf·fer·ance ['sʌfrəns] *n* consent implied by a failure to object: *They managed to get through with the sufferance of the neutral country.*
on sufferance tolerated, but not wanted.

suf·fice [sə'faɪs] *v* be enough (for): *That will suffice, thank you. A small sum sufficed her.* ⟨Latin *sufficere*; *sub-* up (to) + *facere* make⟩
suffice it to say it is enough to say only (*that*): *Suffice it to say that she is upset.*
suf·fi·cient [sə'fɪʃənt] *adj* enough or good enough: *sufficient proof.* **suf·fi·cien·cy** *n.* **suf·fi·cient·ly** *adv.*

suf·fix ['sʌfɪks] *n Grammar* an ending added to a word to change its meaning or function, as in bad*ly*, bad*ness*, or to indicate tense, number, etc., as in talk*ed*. ⟨Latin *suffixum* pp of *suffigere*; *sub-* upon + *figere* fasten⟩

suf·fo·cate ['sʌfə,keɪt] *v* **1** kill by stopping the air supply. **2** die for lack of air. **3** have or cause to have trouble breathing: *I'm suffocating in this hot room.* **4** be or cause to be unable to develop; stifle. **suf·fo·cat·ing** *adj.* **suf·fo·ca·tion** *n.* ⟨Latin *suffocare* orig narrow up; *sub-* up + *foces* variant of *fauces* throat⟩

suf·frage ['sʌfrɪdʒ] *n* the right to vote; franchise: *Alberta granted suffrage to women in 1916.* ⟨Latin *suffragium* supporting vote; *sub-* nearby + *fragor* applause⟩
suf·fra·gette [,sʌfrə'dʒɛt] *n* formerly, a female advocate of suffrage for women. **suf·fra·gist** *n* one who favours extending the franchise.

suf·fuse [sə'fjuz] *v* flood from within or below with colour, fluid, etc.: *At twilight the sky was suffused with colour.* **suf·fu·sion** *n.* ⟨Latin *suffusus* pp of *suffundere; sub-* from under + *fundere* pour⟩

Su·fi ['sufi] *n* **1** any of various sects of Islam which tend toward mysticism and asceticism. **2** a member of any of these sects. **Su·fism** *n.* ⟨Arabic = ascetic, man of wool; *suf* wool⟩

sug·ar ['ʃʊgər] *n* **1** a sweet, edible, crystalline substance consisting of sucrose. **2** *Chemistry* any of the class of carbohydrates to which this substance belongs. **3** *Informal* darling. *v* **1** put sugar in or on. **2** form sugar: *Honey sugars if kept too long.* **3** make more palatable: *to sugar a deal.* **su·gar·less** *adj.* **sug·ar·y** *adj.* ⟨Old French *sucre;* Sanskrit *sarkara,* orig grit⟩ **sugar off** make maple sugar by boiling sap until it crystallizes. **sugaring off.** **sugar beet** a variety of beet having a root high in sugar. **sugar bush** a grove of SUGAR MAPLES. **sugar cane** a very tall, coarse, grass, widely cultivated as a source of sugar. **sug·ar–coat** *v* **1** cover with sugar. **2** make more palatable. **sug·ar–coat·ing** *n.* **sugar cube** a small cake of sugar in cube form. **sugar daddy** *Slang* a wealthy, elderly or middle-aged man who lavishes gifts and money on a younger lover. **sugar maple** a large maple yielding a sweet sap that is the source of maple syrup and maple sugar. **sugar shack ✹** an outbuilding in which maple sap is boiled to make syrup or sugar.

sug·gest [sə'dʒɛst] *or* [səg'dʒɛst] *v* **1** propose: *She suggested a swim, and we agreed.* **2** bring to mind: *The word 'summer' suggests holidays.* **3** show indirectly: *His yawns suggest that he would like to go to bed.* ⟨Latin *suggestus* pp of *suggerere; sub-* up + *gerere* bring⟩ **sug·gest·i·ble** *adj* easily influenced. **sug·ges·tion** *n* **1** the act or fact of suggesting. **2** the thing suggested: *an excellent suggestion.* **3** a slight trace: *just a suggestion of ginger.* **4** the insinuation of an idea or impulse into the mind, esp under hypnosis. **sug·ges·tive** *adj* **1** tending to suggest (with *of*): *a mildness suggestive of spring.* **2** tending to suggest something sexual; risqué. **sug·ges·tive·ly** *adv.*

su·i·cide ['sua,saɪd] *n* **1** the intentional killing of oneself. **2** a person who does this. ⟨Latin *sui* of oneself + *-cidium* killing⟩ **su·i·cid·al** *adj* **1** of suicide: *suicidal tendencies.* **2** considering suicide: *He had been suicidal for some time.* **3** ruinous to one's own interests: *To quit now would be suicidal.* **su·i·cid·al·ly** *adv.*

su·i ge·ne·ris ['sui 'dʒɛnərɪs] *or* ['suaɪ] *Latin* of his, her, its, or their peculiar kind; unique.

suit [sut] *n* **1** a matched set of clothes: *a business suit, a sweatsuit.* **2** an application to a court for justice: *to file a suit.* **3** *Cards* any of the four sets of cards (clubs, diamonds, hearts, spades) in a deck. **4** a courting: *His suit was successful; she married him.* **5** *Slang* a business executive. **6** a petition. *v* **1** fit: *to suit the punishment to the crime.* **2** be suitable for: *Canada's climate suits apples.* **3** be agreeable (to): *A snack would suit me fine.*

4 look good on: *That hat suits you.* ⟨Anglo-French *siute;* Latin *sequita; sequi* follow⟩ **bring a suit (against)** sue. **follow suit a** *Cards* play a card of the same suit as that first played. **b** follow the example of another. **suit oneself** do as one pleases. **suit up** put on the gear required for some activity. **suit·a·ble** *adj* right for the occasion, purpose, etc. **suit·a·bil·i·ty** *n.* **suit·a·bly** *adv.* **suit·case** *n* a more or less rigid travelling case. **suit·or** *n* **1** a man who is courting a woman. **2** *Law* a person bringing a suit in court. **3** anyone seeking or asking for something.

suite [swit] *n* **1** a set of connected rooms forming a unit: *a hotel suite.* **2** a set of matching furniture. **3** any set of like things. **4** *Music* a series of related compositions. ⟨Old French; Latin *sequita.* See SUIT.⟩

Suk·koth or **Suk·kot** ['sʊkəs], [sə'kous], *or* [su'kout] *Hebrew* [su'kɔt] *n Judaism* an eight-day fall festival celebrating the harvest and commemorating the wandering of the Jews in the wilderness after the Exodus. Also, **Succoth, Feast of Booths,** or **Feast of Tabernacles.** ⟨Hebrew = booths⟩

sulk [sʌlk] *v* be silent and aloof because of resentment: *He sulks if proven wrong. n* **1** a sulky mood: *in a sulk.* **2 the sulks** *pl* ill humour shown by sulking. **sulk·y** *adj.* **sulk·i·ly** *adv.* ⟨Compare Old English *āsolcen* lazy⟩

sul·len ['sʌlən] *adj* **1** angry and silent. **2** gloomy; dismal: *sullen skies.* **sul·len·ly** *adv.* **sul·len·ness** *n.* ⟨Old French *solain*⟩

sul·ly ['sʌli] *v* soil; stain; tarnish. ⟨Old English *sōlian; sōl* dirty⟩

sul·phur or **sul·fur** ['sʌlfər] *n* a yellow, non-metallic element that burns with a blue flame and a stifling odour. *Symbol* **S** ⟨Latin = brimstone⟩ **sul·phate** or **sul·fate** *n* a salt or ester of SULPHURIC ACID. **sul·phide** or **sul·fide** *n* any compound of sulphur. **sulphur dioxide** or **sulfur dioxide** a heavy gas with a sharp odour, used as a disinfectant, preservative, etc. **sulphuric acid** or **sulfuric acid** a heavy, oily, very strong acid used in making explosives, refining petroleum, etc.; oil of vitriol. **sul·phur·ous** or **sul·fur·ous** ['sʌlfərəs] *or* ['sʌlfjərəs]; *in chemistry also* [sʌl'fjʊrəs] *adj* to do with sulphur.

sul·tan ['sʌltən] *n* the ruler of a Muslim country. **sul·tan·ate** *n.* ⟨Arabic = ruler⟩ **sul·tan·a** [sʌl'tɑnə] *or* [-'tænə] *n* **1** the wife, mother, sister, or daughter of a sultan. **2** a small, seedless raisin.

sul·try ['sʌltri] *adj* **1** uncomfortably hot and humid. **2** full of or arousing passion or sensuality: *a sultry glance, a sultry movie scene.* ⟨obsolete *sulter,* v; akin to *swelter*⟩

sum [sʌm] *n* **1** an amount of money: *to pay a huge sum.* **2** the quantity obtained by adding two or more quantities together. **3** net effect; general purport: *the sum of his argument. v* **summed, sum·ming** find the total of. ⟨Latin *summa,* orig highest⟩ **in sum** to summarize. **sum up a** summarize:

sumac   859   sun

to sum up the main points of a lesson. **b** review
the chief points of evidence for a jury. **c** form
an idea of the qualities or character of.
sum·ma·tion *n* **1** the process of finding the
sum; addition. **2** sum. **3** a judge's final charge
to a jury before they consider the verdict.
sum total 1 the total amount. **2** the net effect.

su·mac ['ʃumæk] *or* ['sumæk] *n* any of a
genus of trees, shrubs, and vines whose
compound leaves turn bright red in the fall.
The leaves of the **poison sumac** are poisonous
to the touch. ⟨Old French; Arabic *summāq*⟩

su·mi ['sumi] *n* **1** a Japanese form of art and
calligraphy using sticks made of soot held
together with glue and dipped in water.
2 this writing material. ⟨Japanese⟩

sum·ma cum lau·de ['sumə ˌkʊm 'laʊdei]
Latin with the highest honour.

sum·ma·ry ['sʌməri] *n* a brief statement
giving the main points.
adj **1** brief but comprehensive. **2** prompt and
without regard for formalities; often, hasty.
3 *Law* without the usual formal process.
⟨Latin *summarium; summa* sum⟩
sum·ma·ri·ly [sə'mɛrəli] *or* ['sʌmərəli] *adv* in a
summary manner. **sum·ma·rize** *v* make or be
a summary (of): *to summarize the plot.*
sum·ma·ri·za·tion *n.* **summary offence** *Law* a
criminal offence less serious than an
INDICTABLE OFFENCE.

SYNONYMS
Summary applies to a brief statement giving
only the main points: *Give a summary of the
play in one or two sentences.* **Digest** applies
to a shortened form of a book, article, etc.,
leaving out minor details but keeping the
original order, emphasis, and style: *a digest
of current research in botany.*

sum·ma·tion See SUM.

sum·mer ['sʌmər] *n* **1** the warmest season of
the year, between spring and fall. **2** a period
of fulfilment: *in the summer of life.*
v spend or cause to spend the summer: *to
summer up north.* **sum·mer·y** *adj.* ⟨Old English
sumor⟩
sum·mer·house *n* a small structure in a park
or garden in which to sit in warm weather,
often with no walls. **summer house** a house
lived in during the summer. **summer sausage**
a spicy smoked sausage that keeps
unrefrigerated. **summer school** a school or
university session held in summer, offering
courses compressed into daily classes of
several hours. **sum·mer·time** *n* summer.

sum·mit ['sʌmɪt] *n* **1** the highest point; peak:
the summit of her career. **2** *Informal* a
conference at the highest political level. ⟨Old
French *somete;* Latin *summus* highest⟩

sum·mon ['sʌmən] *v* **1** call with authority or
urgency: *to summon citizens to defend their
country.* **2** order formally to appear in court.
3 gather: *He summoned his courage and spoke.*
sum·mon·er *n.* ⟨Latin *summonere* hint to; *sub-*
secretly + *monere* warn⟩
sum·mons *n, pl* **-mons·es 1** an urgent or
authoritative call. **2** *Law* **a** an order to appear

before a court or judge. **b** the writ (**writ of
summons**) by which such an order is made.
v serve with a summons.

sum·mum bo·num ['sʊməm 'bounəm]
Latin the highest or chief good.

su·mo ['sumou] *n* a stylized form of Japanese
wrestling, the contestants being tall and
unusually heavy. ⟨Japanese = compete⟩

sump [sʌmp] *n* a pit or reservoir collecting
water, oil, sewage, etc. and emptied by a
sump pump. ⟨Middle Low German = swamp⟩

sump·tu·ous ['sʌmptʃuəs] *adj* rich; lavish: *a
sumptuous banquet.* **sump·tu·ous·ly** *adv.* ⟨Latin
sumptuosus; sumptus expense; *sumere* spend⟩

sun [sʌn] *n* **1** the star around which the
earth and planets revolve. **2** the light and
warmth of the sun: *to sit in the sun.* **3** any
heavenly body made up of burning gas and
having satellites. **4** anything like the sun in
brightness, splendour, or centrality.
v **sunned, sun·ning** expose (oneself) to the
sun's rays; tan, warm, etc. in the sunshine.
sun·less *adj.* ⟨Old English *sunne*⟩
a place in the sun a position in the public
eye. **under the sun** on earth; in the world.
sun·baked *adj* **1** baked by exposure to the
sun: *sunbaked bricks.* **2** dried out by too much
sunlight: *sunbaked soil.* **sun·bathe** *v* bask in
the sun. **sun·bath·er** *n.* **sun·beam** *n* a ray of
sunlight. **sun·block** *n* a substance that blocks
out some of the sun's harmful ultraviolet
rays. **sun·burn** *n* inflammation of the skin
caused by too much exposure to the rays of
the sun or of a sunlamp. *v* **-burned** or **-burnt,
-burn·ing** get or cause to get a sunburn.
sun·burst *n* a design that looks like the sun
with rays radiating out from it. **sun·deck** or
sun deck 1 a passenger ship's upper deck. **2** a
balcony, terrace, etc. for lounging,
sunbathing, etc. **sun·dew** *n* any of a genus
of insect-eating bog plants. **sun·di·al** *n* an
instrument for telling the time of day by the
shadow of a pointer, cast by the sun on a
disk marked off in hours. **sun·dog** *n* a small
halo or incomplete rainbow near the
horizon, due to refraction by ice crystals in
the atmosphere. **sun·down** *n* sunset (def. 2).
sun–dried *adj* dried by exposure to the sun:
sun-dried tomatoes. **sun·fish** *n, pl* **-fish** or **-
fish·es 1** any of a family of small, freshwater
fishes with a deep, brightly coloured body
and a long dorsal fin. **2** any of a family of
large ocean fishes, esp one species whose
body is about as deep as it is long. **sun·flow·er**
n **1** a very tall plant of the composite family
with a large, flat flower head surrounded by
rays of yellow petals. **2** any of a number of
other plants of the same genus, such as the
prairie sunflower. **sun·glass·es** *n pl* eyeglasses
with tinted lenses to protect the eyes from
sunlight. **sun·lamp** *n* an electric lamp
emitting ultraviolet rays, used for therapy or
for giving an artificial suntan. **sun·light** *n* the
light of the sun. **sun·lit** *adj.* **sun·ny** *adj* **1** with
much sunshine: *a sunny day.* **2** lighted by the
rays of the sun: *a sunny room.* **3** bright;
cheerful: *a sunny smile.* **sunny side** the

cheerful or optimistic aspect of something: *She usually looks at the sunny side of things.* **sunny side up** of an egg, fried on one side only and with the yolk unbroken. **sun porch** a porch enclosed by glass or screen, designed to admit plenty of sunlight. **sun·proof** *adj* unaffected by the rays of the sun: *Sunproof drapes don't fade.* **sun·rise** *n* **1** the appearance of the sun above the horizon in the morning. **2** the time of day when the sun rises. **sun·roof** *n* a car roof with a panel that can be opened. **sun·room** *n* a room with many windows to let in sunlight. **sun·screen** *n* a substance put on the skin to filter out ultraviolet rays and prevent sunburn. **sun·set** *n* **1** the last appearance of the sun in the evening. **2** the time of day when the sun sets. **sun·shade** *n* an umbrella, awning, blind, etc. giving protection from the sun. **sun·shine** *n* **1** the light or warmth of the sun. **2** sunny weather. **3** brightness; cheerfulness: *to bring sunshine into someone's life.* **sun·shin·y** *adj.* **sun·spot** *n* one of the dark spots, caused by temporary cooling. **sun·stroke** *n* a heatstroke caused by overexposure to sunlight, causing the body's sweat system to stop functioning so it can no longer cool the body. **sun·tan** *n* a darker colouring of a person's skin due to exposure to the sun. *v* sunbathe in order to get a tan. **sun·tanned** *adj.* **sun·up** *n* sunrise (def. 2). **sun·ward** *adv, adj* toward the sun. Also (*adv*), **sun·wards.**

sun·dae ['sʌndei] *n* a serving of ice cream with syrup, crushed fruits, nuts, etc. poured over it. ⟨probably *Sunday*, orig the only day on which it was served⟩

Sun·day ['sʌndei] *n* **1** the first day of the week, the day before Monday. **2** this day as a day of recreation: *Sunday drivers.* ⟨Old English *sunnandæg*; Latin *dies solis* day of the sun⟩ **a month of Sundays** an indefinitely long time: *not in a month of Sundays.* **Sunday best** *Informal* best clothes. **Sunday school** a school held by a church on Sundays for teaching religion, esp to children.

sun·dry ['sʌndri] *adj* several; various; miscellaneous: *sundry bits of news.* *pron* **all and sundry** everybody; one and all: *He has invited all and sundry.* *n* **sundries** *pl* miscellaneous items. ⟨Old English *syndrig* separate; *sundor* apart⟩

sung [sʌŋ] *v* pp of SING.

sunk [sʌŋk] *v* pp of SINK. *adj Informal* doomed; ruined; done for: *If anyone finds out I told you this, I'm sunk.* **sunk·en** *adj* **1** that has been sunk: *a sunken ship.* **2** submerged: *a sunken rock.* **3** set below the level of the surrounding area: *a sunken garden.* **4** fallen in; hollow: *sunken cheeks.*

Sun·na ['sʊnə] *n* the traditional part of Muslim law, attributed to Muhammad and preserved alongside the Qur'an. ⟨Arabic⟩ **Sun·ni** ['sʊni] *n, pl* **Sun·ni** a member of one of the two great sects of Islam. The Sunni observe the Sunna. Compare SHIA. **Sun·ni** *adj.* **Sun·nite** *n, adj.*

sup [sʌp] *v* **supped, sup·ping** eat the evening

meal; have supper: *He supped alone on bread and milk.* ⟨Old French *soper*. See SUPPER.⟩

su·per ['supər] *adj Slang* excellent. *adv Informal* extremely: *super polite.* *n Informal* a superintendent.

super– *prefix* **1** over; above: *superimpose.* **2** extra: *supertax.* **3** to a greater than normal degree: *supersensitive.* **4** beyond: *supernatural.* **5** having a superior rank: *superintendent.* **6** larger, stronger, better, etc. than others: *supermall, superglue.* ⟨Latin *super* over, above⟩ **su·per·a·bun·dant** *adj* more than is needed. **su·per·a·bun·dance** *n.* **su·per·a·bun·dant·ly** *adv.* **su·per·charge** *v* **1** charge with high emotion, energy, etc.: *an atmosphere supercharged with tension.* **2** fit (an engine) with a supercharger. **su·per·charg·er** *n* in an internal-combustion engine, a device to boost power and efficiency by forcing more of the mixture of air and gasoline vapour into the cylinders. **su·per·con·duc·tiv·i·ty** *n Physics* the ability to conduct electricity with no resistance, found in some metals at temperatures near absolute zero (–273.16°C). **su·per·con·duc·tive** *adj.* **su·per·con·duc·tor** *n.* **su·per·cool** *v* cool (a liquid) below its freezing point without causing it to solidify. **su·per·e·go** [-'igou] *n Psychoanalysis* the part of the psyche that enforces learned moral standards; conscience. **su·per·fine** *adj* **1** very fine in texture: *superfine cotton.* **2** of very high quality: *superfine china.* **3** too refined or subtle: *superfine distinctions.* **su·per·gi·ant** ['supər,dʒaɪənt] *n Astronomy* a very large and brilliant star with a diameter greater than our sun's. **su·per·heat** *v* **1** heat (a liquid) above its boiling point without causing vaporization. **2** heat (steam apart from water) above the saturation point so that cooling will not result in condensation. **3** overheat. **su·per·high·way** *n* a high-speed expressway divided by a median and having two or more lanes in each direction. **su·per·hu·man** *adj* **1** beyond ordinary human experience or power: *By a superhuman effort, he hoisted himself up onto the ledge.* **2** above what is human: *Angels are superhuman beings.* **su·per·hu·man·ly** *adv.* **su·per·hu·man·ness** *n.* **su·per·im·pose** *v* lay on top of something else. **su·per·im·po·si·tion** *n.* **su·per·mar·ket** *n* a large self-service store selling groceries and household articles. **su·per·nat·u·ral** *adj* to do with some force outside the known laws of nature; esp, to do with or caused by God or a god or other spirit: *supernatural powers.* *n* **the supernatural** supernatural influences, phenomena, etc. **su·per·nat·u·ral·ly** *adv.* **su·per·no·va** *n, pl* **-vae** [-vi] *or* [-vaɪ] *or* **-vas** a star that has exploded, becoming much brighter than our sun, and leaving an expanding shell of gases and debris that radiate light, radio waves, etc. **su·per·pow·er** *n* a nation with great power and influence in the world. **su·per·sat·u·rate** *v* add a substance to (a solvent) beyond the ordinary saturation point. **su·per·sat·u·ra·tion** *n.* **su·per·sen·si·tive** *adj* extremely sensitive. **su·per·sen·si·tiv·i·ty** *n.* **su·per·star** *n* a person who is outstanding in

his or her field, esp sports or entertainment.
su·per·stra·tum *n, pl* **-ta** [-tə] or **-tums** a layer
or stratum lying over, often concealing,
another. **su·per·struc·ture** *n* **1** the part of a
building above the foundation. **2** the parts of
a ship above the main deck.

su·per·an·nu·ate [ˌsupərˈænjuˌeit] *v* **1** cause
to retire on a pension. **2** make out-of-date.
su·per·an·nu·at·ed *adj.* **su·per·an·nu·at·ion** *n.*
⟨Latin *super annum* beyond a year⟩

su·perb [suˈpɜrb] *adj* **1** grand; magnificent:
superb scenery. **2** first-rate: *a superb novel.*
su·perb·ly *adv.* ⟨Latin *superbus; super-* above⟩

su·per·cil·i·ous [ˌsupərˈsɪliəs] *adj* indifferent
because of feeling superior. **su·per·cil·i·ous·ly**
adv. ⟨Latin *supercilium* eyebrow⟩

su·per·fi·cial [ˌsupərˈfɪʃəl] *adj* **1** of or on the
surface: *superficial burns.* **2** shallow; casual: *a
superficial study.* **su·per·fi·ci·al·i·ty** *n.*
su·per·fi·cial·ly *adv.* ⟨Latin *superficies* surface;
super- above + *facies* form⟩

su·per·flu·ous [suˈpɜrfluəs] *adj* **1** more than
needed; excess: *superfluous detail.* **2** uncalled
for; irrelevant; gratuitous: *a superfluous remark.*
su·per·flu·i·ty [ˌsupərˈfluəti] *n.* **su·per·flu·ous·ly**
adv. **su·per·flu·ous·ness** *n.* ⟨Latin *super-* over +
fluere flow⟩

su·per·in·tend [ˌsupərɪnˈtɛnd] *v* oversee and
direct (work or workers). **su·per·in·tend·ence** *n.*
⟨Latin *super-* above + *intendere* direct⟩

su·per·in·tend·ent *n* **1** a person who oversees,
directs, or manages: *a superintendent of schools.*
2 a police officer of high rank, above an
inspector. **3** a person in charge of the
maintenance of an apartment building.
Abbrev **Supt.** **su·per·in·tend·en·cy** *n.*

su·pe·ri·or [səˈpiriər] *adj* **1** better than most:
superior work in school. **2** better or greater
than some other: *Your cooking is superior to
mine.* **3** higher in importance, rank, etc.: *a
superior officer.* **4** patronizing or proud.
5 higher in physical position.
n **1** a superior person or thing: *A captain is a
lieutenant's superior.* **2** the head of a convent
or monastery. **su·pe·ri·or·i·ty** [səˌpiriˈɔrɪti] *n.*
⟨Latin, comparative of *superus* above⟩
superiority complex an exaggerated feeling
of self-importance.

su·per·la·tive [suˈpɜrlətɪv] *adj* **1** of the highest
or best kind: *a person of superlative courage.*
2 exaggerated: *Such superlative praise could not
be sincere.* **3** *Grammar* to do with the highest
degree of comparison of an adjective or
adverb. *Fairest*, *best*, and *most slowly* are the
superlative forms of *fair*, *good*, and *slowly.*
n a person, thing, or degree above all others.
su·per·la·tive·ly *adv.* **su·per·la·tive·ness** *n.*
⟨Latin; *super-* beyond + *latus* pp of *ferre* carry⟩

su·per·nu·mer·ar·y [ˌsupərˈnjuməˌrɛri] *or*
[-ˈnuməˌrɛri] *adj* in excess of the usual or
necessary number; extra.
n an extra person or thing. ⟨Latin *super
numerum* beyond the number⟩

su·per·script [ˈsupərˌskrɪpt] *adj* written above
the line, as the 2 in *x²*. **su·per·script** *n.*

su·per·sede [ˌsupərˈsid] *v* **1** cause to be set

aside as obsolete or inferior: *Electric lighting
has superseded gas lighting.* **2** fill the place of;
succeed: *She superseded him as principal.*
⟨Latin *super-* above + *sedere* sit⟩

su·per·son·ic [ˌsupərˈsɒnɪk] *adj* **1** to do with
a speed greater than the speed of sound in air
(about 1200 km/h at sea level). **2** having a
frequency above the human ear's audibility
limit (about 20 kHz). **su·per·son·i·cal·ly** *adv.*

su·per·sti·tion [ˌsupərˈstɪʃən] *n* **1** a belief or
practice based on ignorant fear or mistaken
reverence: *It is a common superstition that the
number 13 is unlucky.* **2** a system of such
beliefs. **su·per·sti·tious** *adj.* ⟨Latin *superstitio;
super-* above + *stare* stand⟩

su·per·vene [ˌsupərˈvin] *v* come as something
additional, esp if unusual. **su·per·ven·ient** *adj.*
su·per·ven·tion [-ˈvɛnʃən] *n.* ⟨Latin *super-
upon* + *venire* come⟩

su·per·vise [ˈsupərˌvaɪz] *v* **1** oversee and
direct (work, workers, a process, etc.). **2** keep
watch over (someone) to ensure safety, good
behaviour, etc. **su·per·vi·sion** *n.* **su·per·vi·sor** *n.*
su·per·vi·so·ry *adj.* ⟨Latin *super-* over + *visum*
pp of *videre* see⟩

su·pine [ˈsupaɪn] *adj* lying on the back with
the face upward. ⟨Latin *supinus*⟩

sup·per [ˈsʌpər] *n* **1** the evening meal: *We
usually have supper at 6 o'clock.* **2** an informal
social event in the evening, featuring a meal:
a church supper. **sup·per·less** *adj.* ⟨Old French
soper, orig infinitive, to sup⟩
sup·per·time *n* the time when supper is eaten.

sup·plant [səˈplænt] *v* displace or set aside,
often unjustly: *Machinery has supplanted skilled
labour in many industries.* ⟨Latin *supplantare*
trip up; *sub-* under + *planta* sole of the foot⟩

sup·ple [ˈsʌpəl] *adj* **1** capable of bending or
folding without cracking: *supple leather.* **2** able
to move easily and gracefully: *a supple dancer.*
3 readily adapting to circumstances, etc.: *a
supple mind.* **sup·ple·ly** *adv.* **sup·ple·ness** *n.*
⟨Old French; Latin *supplex* submissive;
supplicare. See SUPPLICATE.⟩

sup·ple·ment [ˈsʌpləmənt] *n* **1** something
added to complete a thing or make it larger
or better: *a diet supplement.* **2** a section added
to a printed work to improve or complete it:
The newspaper has a weekend supplement.
v [ˈsʌpləˌmɛnt] supply what is lacking in; add
to and complete: *to supplement one's income.*
sup·ple·men·ta·ry [ˌsʌpləˈmɛntəri] *adj, n.*
sup·ple·men·ta·tion *n.* ⟨Latin *supplementum;
sub-* up + *-plere* fill⟩
supplementary angle *Geometry* either of two
angles which together equal 180°.

SYNONYMS

A **supplement** is a section added later or
printed separately to give completeness by
updating information, correcting errors, or
presenting special features: *This world history
has a supplement covering recent events.* An
appendix is added at the end of a book to
give extra information that is useful for
reference but not necessary for completeness:
The appendix contains a list of currencies.

sup·pli·ant ['sʌpliənt] *adj* making a humble, earnest entreaty: *raising suppliant hands.*
n a person who asks humbly and earnestly. Also, **sup·pli·cant**. ⟨French *supplier;* Latin. See SUPPLICATE.⟩

sup·pli·cate ['sʌplə,keit] *v* **1** beg (a person) humbly and earnestly: *The mother supplicated the judge to spare her son.* **2** beg humbly for (something): *to supplicate a blessing.* **3** pray humbly. **sup·pli·cant** *adj, n.* **sup·pli·ca·tion** *n.* ⟨Latin *supplicare;* sub- down + *plicare* bend⟩

sup·ply [sə'plaɪ] *v* **1** provide: *This filtration plant supplies the whole city with water.* **2** satisfy (a loss, need, etc.): *to supply a deficiency.* **3** fill (a position) as a substitute.
n **1** a quantity of something, ready for use: *a supply of paper.* **2** specifically, the quantity of an item available: *The coffee supply exceeds demand.* **3 supplies** *pl* equipment and food required for an army, expedition, etc. **4** a person who fills a vacancy as a substitute. **5** the act of supplying. **sup·pli·er** *n.* ⟨Latin *supplere;* sub- up + *-plere* fill⟩
in (**short, good,** etc.) **supply** available to a given extent: *Rice is in short supply this year.*

sup·port [sə'pɔrt] *v* **1** hold up: *Walls support the roof.* **2** give strength or help to: *Hope supports us in trouble.* **3** provide for: *She supports him while he is at university.* **4** maintain: *Water is needed to support life.* **5** be in favour of: *Do you support two-tier health care?* **6** help prove; bear out: *The facts support his claim.*
n **1** the act of supporting or the condition of being supported: *to have the support of friends during a crisis.* **2** a person or thing that supports: *a back support.* **sup·port·a·ble** *adj.* **sup·port·er** *n.* **sup·port·ive** *adj.* ⟨Latin *sub- up + portare* carry⟩
support group a group of people affected by some disease, traumatic experience, etc. who meet regularly to encourage one another, exchange useful information, etc.

sup·pose [sə'pouz] *v* **1** assume for the sake of argument: *Suppose it doesn't work; what will I do then?* **2** think probable: *I suppose I'll be left with the dishes again.* **3** imply as necessary: *An invention supposes an inventor.* **sup·po·si·tion** [,sʌpə'zɪʃən] *n.* **sup·po·si·tion·al** *adj.* ⟨Old French *supposer⟩*
sup·posed [sə'pouzd] *or* [sə'pouzɪd] *for 1;* [-'poust] *for 2-4 adj* **1** believed without proof: *a supposed insult.* **2** intended: *What is that supposed to mean?* **3** obliged or expected (*to*): *I was supposed to bring the disk, but I forgot.* **4** permitted (*to*) (in negative only): *I'm not supposed to eat fried foods.* **sup·pos·ed·ly** [sə'pouzɪdli] *adv* according to what is or was supposed: *He's supposedly asleep but I think he's faking.* **sup·pos·ing** *conj* in the event that: *Supposing it rains; shall we still go?*

sup·pos·i·to·ry [sə'pɒzə,tɔri] *n* a cylindrical or cone-shaped mass of medication to be put into the rectum or other opening of the body, where it is released by melting. ⟨Latin *suppositorium;* sub- under + *ponere* place⟩

sup·press [sə'prɛs] *v* **1** stop by force: *The*

military suppressed the rebellion. **2** hold back: *to suppress a yawn.* **3** keep from being made known, published, etc.: *to suppress information.* **4** *Psychiatry* consciously keep from thinking or expressing (an undesirable idea, impulse, etc.). **sup·pres·sion** *n.* ⟨Latin *suppressus* pp of *supprimere;* sub- down + *premere* press⟩
sup·pres·sant *n* a substance that suppresses: *a cough suppressant.*

sup·pu·rate ['sʌpjə,reit] *v* form or discharge pus; fester. **sup·pu·ra·tion** *n.* ⟨Latin *suppurare;* sub- under + *pus* pus⟩

su·preme [sə'prim] *adj* **1** highest in rank or authority: *a supreme ruler.* **2** highest in degree or quality: *the supreme sacrifice.* **su·preme·ly** *adv.* ⟨Latin *supremus; super* above⟩
su·prem·a·cy [sə'prɛməsi] *n* **1** the state of being supreme. **2** the supposed or wished-for superiority of a certain group, esp a race: *propaganda advocating white supremacy.* **su·prem·a·cist** *n, adj.* **Supreme Being** God. **Supreme Court** the highest criminal and civil court of appeal of a nation, province, etc. Canada's Supreme Court has nine judges.

Supt. *or* **supt.** superintendent.

sur·charge ['sɜr,tʃɑrdʒ] *n* an extra charge: *a surcharge for deliveries outside city limits.*
sur·charge [sər'tʃɑrdʒ] *or* ['sɜr,tʃɑrdʒ] *v.* ⟨French *sur-* over + *charger.* See CHARGE.⟩

surd [sɜrd] *n Mathematics* a quantity that cannot be expressed as a rational number. *Example:* √2 **surd** *adj.* ⟨Latin *surdus* unheard⟩

sure [ʃʊr] *or* [ʃɜr] *adj* **1** free of doubt; certain: *I am sure of her guilt.* **2** never failing, missing, etc.: *a sure remedy.* **3** certain to be or to happen: *She is sure to win.*
adv Informal surely; certainly: *I sure will!*
interj certainly; yes indeed (sometimes ironic). **sure·ness** *n.* ⟨Old French *sur;* Latin *securus⟩*
be sure do not fail: *Be sure to lock the door.* **for sure** *Informal* **a** definitely: *He'll be here for sure.* **b** certainly true: *That's for sure.* **make sure a** act so as to make something certain: *Make sure you don't lose this.* **b** get sure knowledge: *Make sure of your facts.* **sure enough** *Informal* certainly: *She'll be a winner, sure enough.* **to be sure a** surely; certainly. **b** it must be acknowledged; admittedly.
sure–fire *adj Informal* that cannot fail: *a sure-fire formula.* **sure–foot·ed** *adj* not liable to slip or fall. **sure·ly** *adv* **1** certainly: *Half a loaf is surely better than none.* **2** really (to emphasize): *Surely you're not serious!* **3** steadily: *slowly but surely.* **sure thing** *Informal* **1** something sure to happen, succeed, etc. **2** yes! certainly!: *Can you open this for me? Sure thing!* **sur·e·ty** ['ʃʊrəti] *n* security against loss, damage, failure to repay, etc.: *The car is surety for the loan.*

surf [sɜrf] *n* the waves of the sea breaking on the shore or on reefs, etc.
v **1** ride on the crest of the waves, esp with a surfboard. **2** *Computers* search for material of interest on the INTERNET or WORLD WIDE WEB. **surf·er** *n.* **surf·ing** *n.* ⟨earlier *suff;* possible variant of *sough⟩*
surf·board ['sɜrf,bɔrd] *n* a long board with

rounded ends, on which one stands or lies in order to ride the waves as they come in.

sur·face ['sɜrfɪs] *n* **1** the outer side of a thing: *the surface of a ball.* **2** the top of the ground, or of a body of liquid: *The stone sank below the surface.* **3** any of the faces of an object: *A cube has six surfaces.* **4** outward appearance: *She's stern, but kind below the surface.*
v **1** put a top layer on: *to surface a road.* **2** bring or come to the surface: *The submarine surfaced.* **3** be noticed, become known, etc. after being hidden: *The truth has surfaced at last.* ⟨French; *sur-* above (Latin *super-*) + *face*; see FACE.⟩
surface mail mail carried by land and sea rather than by air. **surface tension** *Physics* a property of the surface of a liquid that makes it tend to contract, due to forces of attraction between molecules of the liquid.

sur·feit ['sɜrfɪt] *n* an excessive indulgence in something; so much as to disgust: *A surfeit of candy made her sick.*
v cause to have too much, esp to the point of nausea or disgust. ⟨Old French *surfait* overdone; *sur-* over + *faire* do; Latin *facere*⟩

surge [sɜrdʒ] *v* **1** rise and fall in great waves: *the surging sea.* **2** move as a wave: *Joy surged through him. The crowd surged out of the arena.* **3** of electric voltage, increase abruptly. **surge** *n.* ⟨Latin *surgere* rise; *sub-* up + *regere* reach⟩

sur·ger·y ['sɜrdʒəri] *n* **1** the treatment of disease, injury, etc. by using instruments to mend, move, or remove an organ, tissue, etc. **2** the branch of medicine dealing with this. ⟨Old French *surgerie, cirurgie*; Greek *cheirourgia; cheir* hand + *ergon* work⟩
sur·geon ['sɜrdʒən] *n* a doctor specializing in surgery. **sur·gi·cal** *adj* to do with surgeons or surgery: *surgical precision.* **sur·gi·cal·ly** *adv.*

sur·ly ['sɜrli] *adj* bad-tempered and rude. **sur·li·ly** *adv.* **sur·li·ness** *n.* ⟨*sir* in sense of 'lord'⟩

sur·mise [sər'maɪz] *n* **1** formation of an idea with little or no evidence; guesswork: *It was all a matter of surmise; there was no proof.* **2** a guess. **sur·mise** *v.* ⟨Old French *surmise* accusation; *sur-* on + *mise* pp of *mettre* put⟩

sur·mount [sər'maʊnt] *v* **1** overcome: *to surmount a difficulty.* **2** be or put something on the top of: *a scoop of ice cream surmounted by a cherry.* **3** get up and over: *to surmount a hill.* **sur·mount·a·ble** *adj.* ⟨Old French *sur-* over (Latin *super-*) + *monter* mount⟩

sur·name ['sɜr,neim] *n* **1** family name; last name: *Kahn is the surname of Nate Kahn.* **2** a name added to one's real name: *William I of England had the surname "the Conqueror."* ⟨French *sur-* over + *nom* name⟩

sur·pass [sər'pæs] *v* **1** do or be better: *She surpasses all the others in scoring ability.* **2** be too much or too great for: *a beauty that surpasses description.* **sur·pass·ing·ly** *adv.* ⟨French *sur-* beyond + *passer* pass⟩

sur·plice ['sɜrplɪs] *n* a loose white gown worn by some Christian clergy and choir members during a service. **sur·pliced** *adj.* ⟨Old French *surpelice; sur-* over + *pelice* fur⟩

sur·plus ['sɜrpləs] *or* ['sɜrplʌs] *n* **1** an amount over and above what is needed. **2** *Accounting* an excess of assets over liabilities.
adj forming a surplus: *surplus stock.* ⟨Old French *sur-* over + *plus* more; Latin⟩

sur·prise [sər'praɪz] *or* [sə'praɪz] *n* **1** something unexpected. **2** the feeling caused by this.
adj unexpected: *a surprise visit.*
v **1** cause to feel surprise; be a surprise to. **2** catch unprepared; come upon suddenly: *I surprised her looking through my papers.* **3** present unexpectedly (*with*): *They surprised her with a gift.* **sur·prised** *adj.* **sur·pris·ing** *adj.* **sur·pris·ing·ly** *adv.* ⟨Old French *surprise* pp of *surprendre; sur-* over + *prendre* take⟩
take by surprise a catch unprepared. **b** be surprising or unexpected to.

sur·real·ism [sə'rɪlɪzəm] *n* a style in art and literature attempting to portray the workings of the subconscious, esp as in dreams. **sur·real·ist** *n, adj.* **sur·real·is·tic** *adj.* ⟨French *sur-* beyond + *réalisme* realism⟩
sur·real *adj* bizarre in a dreamlike way that suggests a surrealist work of art.

sur·ren·der [sə'rɛndər] *v* **1** give up (control or possession of), esp after a struggle: *to surrender to an invader.* **2** abandon (oneself) to an emotion, etc. **3** cancel (an insurance policy) in return for a cash sum. **sur·ren·der** *n.* ⟨Old French *sur-* over + *rendre* render, give⟩

sur·rep·ti·tious [,sɜrəp'tɪʃəs] *adj* secret or stealthy; furtive; sly: *a surreptitious wink.* **sur·rep·ti·tious·ly** *adv.* **sur·rep·ti·tious·ness** *n.* ⟨Latin *surrepticius; sub-* secretly + *rapere* snatch⟩

sur·ro·gate ['sɜrəgɪt] *n* a person who acts for or takes the place of another. **sur·ro·gate** *adj.* **sur·ro·gate·ship** *n.* ⟨Latin *sub-* instead + *rogare* ask for⟩
surrogate court a court dealing with wills and other matters relating to the estates of deceased persons. **surrogate mother** a woman who undergoes artificial insemination and bears a child for another who cannot.

sur·round [sə'raʊnd] *v* **1** shut in on all sides: *The little girl was surrounded by her toys.* **2** form part of the environment of: *Love surrounds him.* **3** cause to be surrounded by: *to surround oneself with comfort.* ⟨Anglo-French *surounder* surpass⟩
sur·round·ings *n pl* environment.

sur·tax ['sɜr,tæks] *n* an additional or extra tax. **sur·tax** *v.* ⟨French *sur-* over + *taxe* tax⟩

sur·veil·lance [sər'veiləns] *n* a close watch kept over a person, place, thing, activity, etc.: *under police surveillance.* ⟨French; *sur-* over + *veiller* watch; Latin *vigilare*⟩

sur·vey ['sɜrvei] *n* **1** a general but careful study of something: *a survey of Canadian poetry.* **2** a questionnaire, interview, etc. administered to a number of people as part of an investigation of a social, political, etc. nature: *A recent survey shows that public opinion on the issue has changed.* **3 a** the act determining the exact boundaries and contours of (land) by measuring distances, angles, etc. **b** the resulting map. **4 ✳ a** a tract of land divided into building lots; subdivision. **b** the housing development built on it. **sur·vey** [sər'vei] *v*. **sur·vey·ing** *n*. **sur·vey·or** *n*. ⟨Anglo-French *surveier*; Latin *super-* over + *videre* see⟩

sur·vive [sər'vaɪv] *v* **1** endure (attack, disaster, etc.) without dying or being destroyed: *The roses did not survive the winter.* **2** continue to exist: *Some of the old books still survive.* **3** live longer than: *He survived his son.* **sur·viv·al** *n*. ⟨Anglo-French *sur-* over + *vivre* live⟩

sur·viv·al·ist *n* a person determined to survive at all costs, esp one who stores food, weapons, etc. against the prospect of natural disaster, nuclear war, etc. **sur·viv·al·ism** *n*. **survival of the fittest** the process or result of NATURAL SELECTION. **sur·vi·vor** *n* **1** a person or animal that survives. **2** a person likely to survive almost anything by virtue of his or her determination, adaptability, wits, etc.

sus·cep·ti·ble [sə'sɛptəbəl] *adj* **1** vulnerable to an influence, disease, etc. (with *to*): *He is susceptible to colds.* **2** easily influenced: *Tales of adventure appealed to her susceptible nature.* **sus·cep·ti·bil·i·ty** *n*. ⟨Latin *susceptibilis; sub-* up + *capere* take⟩

su·shi ['suʃi] *n* a Japanese dish consisting of cakes of cold cooked rice with raw fish or other garnish in the centre. ⟨Japanese⟩

sus·pect [sə'spɛkt] *v* **1** have an impression of the existence of: *He suspected a trap and did not answer.* **2** consider guilty, false, bad, etc. without proof: *The police suspected him.* **3** be suspicious: *I'm sure she suspects.* **4** be inclined to think: *I suspect she meant to arrive on time.* *n* ['sʌspɛkt] a person suspected. *adj* ['sʌspɛkt] open to or deserving suspicion: *That excuse is suspect.* ⟨Latin *suspectus* pp of *suspicere; sub-* under + *specere* look⟩

sus·pend [sə'spɛnd] *v* **1** hang from a support above: *a lamp was suspended from the ceiling.* **2** cause to stay somewhere between the top and bottom, as solid particles in a fluid: *smoke suspended in the still air.* **3** stop for a while: *to suspend work on a project.* **4** defer (a convicted person's sentence). **5** punish by excluding for a while from some privilege or place: *to suspend a student from school.* **6** defer; put off: *to suspend judgment.* **7** Music hold (a note) while the chord changes. ⟨Latin *suspendere; sub-* up + *pendere* hang⟩

sus·pend·ed animation a state induced by freezing, etc. in which vital bodily functions cease temporarily. **sus·pend·ers** *n* straps worn over the shoulders to hold up pants. **sus·pen·sion** [sə'spɛnʃən] *n* **1** the act of suspending or the state of being suspended. **2** an arrangement of springs, etc. for supporting the body of a car, rail car, etc. **3** *Chemistry* a mixture in which tiny particles of a solid remain suspended in a fluid without dissolving. **suspension bridge** a bridge hung on cables between towers. **suspension of disbelief** the convention of pretending to oneself that the events in a fictional story may be true.

sus·pense [sə'spɛns] *n* a feeling of tension or excitement arising from uncertainty about an outcome: *We were full of suspense waiting for the announcement.* **sus·pense·ful** *adj.* ⟨Old French *(en) suspens* (in) abeyance. See SUSPEND.⟩

sus·pen·sion See SUSPEND.

sus·pi·cion [sə'spɪʃən] *n* **1** the act of suspecting or state of being suspected: *to allay suspicion.* **2** the theory of a person who suspects: *He had a suspicion that the will was forged.* **3** a slight trace: *She speaks with just a suspicion of an accent.* ⟨Latin *suspicio; suspicere.* See SUSPECT.⟩

above suspicion so honest, honourable, etc. as not to be suspected. **on suspicion** because of being suspected: *arrested on suspicion of robbery.* **under suspicion** suspected.

sus·pi·cious *adj* **1** arousing suspicion: *suspicious circumstances.* **2** feeling suspicion: *Her tone of voice made me suspicious.* **3** habitually mistrustful. **sus·pi·cious·ly** *adv.*

SYNONYMS

Suspicion suggests fearing that someone or something is guilty, wrong, false, etc. in a particular case: *His extreme nervousness filled me with suspicion.* **Distrust** emphasizes general lack of trust in a person: *Even her mother feels distrust toward her.* **Doubt** emphasizes lack of certainty, and suggests inability to commit oneself: *In spite of his many recommendations, she had some doubt about the candidate.*

suss [səs] *Informal*
suss out find out by investigation or clever deduction. ⟨*suspect*⟩

sus·tain [sə'stein] *v* **1** keep going: *I can't sustain creativity for long.* **2** supply with food, etc.: *to sustain an army.* **3** support: *Hope sustains him in his misery.* **4** withstand: *The sea wall sustains the shock of the waves.* **5** suffer: *to sustain a loss.* **6** allow: *Objection sustained.* **sus·tain·a·ble** *adj.* **sus·tain·er** *n.* ⟨Latin *sustinere; sub-* up + *tenere* hold⟩

sus·te·nance *n* that which sustains a person; especially, food.

sut·ra *n* ['sutrə] **1** *Hinduism* **a** a Sanskrit saying based on any of the Vedic writings. **b** a collection of such sayings. **2** *Buddhism* a narrative or dialogue from scripture. ⟨Sanskrit = thread⟩

su·ture ['sutʃər] *n Surgery* **1** the process of closing a cut by stitching. **2** the closure, or one of the stitches. **3** a length of material used in stitching wounds. **su·ture** *v.* ⟨Latin *sutura; suere* sew⟩

svelte [svɛlt] *adj* slender or lithe. ⟨French; Italian *svelto*; Latin *ex-* out + *vellere* pluck⟩

SW, S.W. or **s.w.** southwest; southwestern.

swab [swɒb] *n* **1** a mop for cleaning decks, floors, etc. **2** a bit of absorbent material attached to a small stick, for cleaning, taking a specimen from, or appling medicine to some part of the body. **swab, swabbed, swab·bing** *v.* ⟨Dutch *zwabben*⟩

swad·dle ['swɒdəl] *v* wrap (a baby) securely in a blanket. ⟨Old English *swæthel* band⟩

swag [swæg] *n* **1** *Slang* things stolen; booty. **2** an ornamental festoon of ribbons, drapery, etc. ⟨related to *sway*; probably Scandinavian⟩

swag·ger ['swægər] *v* **1** walk with a bold, defiant, or superior air: *The bully swaggered into the schoolyard.* **2** brag or show off noisily. **swag·ger** *n*. **swag·ger·er** *n*. ⟨*swag*⟩

swal·low[1] ['swɒlou] *v* **1** pass (food, drink, etc.) from the mouth to the stomach. **2** move the throat muscles in this way: *It hurts when I swallow.* **3** *Informal* believe: *They'll never swallow that story.* **4** accept without protest: *to swallow an insult.* **5** engulf or absorb (usually with *up*): *The waves swallowed her up.* **swal·low** *n*. ⟨Old English *swelgan*⟩

swal·low[2] ['swɒlou] *n* any of a family of birds with long, narrow, pointed wings and a long forked tail. ⟨Old English *swealwe*⟩

swal·low·tail *n* **1** anything shaped like the deeply forked tail of a swallow, esp the back of a tailcoat. **2** any of various butterflies with a tail-like extension at the end of each hind wing. **swal·low–tailed** *adj*.

swam [swæm] *v* pt of SWIM.

swa·mi ['swɑmi] *n* guru. ⟨Hindi; Sanskrit *svāmin* master, lord, owner⟩

swamp [swɒmp] *n* **1** an area of wet land, usually with trees and shrubs as well as grasses and reeds. **2** anything suggesting this. *v* **1** cover or fill with water: *A wave swamped the boat.* **2** overwhelm as by a flood: *swamped with work.* **3 a** make (a road) through bush, esp for hauling lumber (sometimes with *out*). **b** haul (lumber) along such a road. **swamp·y** *adj*. ⟨perhaps Middle Dutch *somp*⟩

swamp buggy ✱ *North* a tracked vehicle capable of pulling a heavy trailer over boggy terrain. **swamp·land** *n* a tract of land with swamps. **Swampy Cree** one of the three main divisions of the Cree, living in the lowlands around Hudson and James Bays.

swan [swɒn] *n* any of a subfamily of large, aquatic birds with a long, slender neck that is curved back in swimming but stretched out straight in flight. **swan·like** *adj*. ⟨Old English⟩ **swan dive** a dive in which the legs are held straight from toes to hips, the back is arched, and the arms spread like the wings of a gliding bird. **swan song 1** the song that a swan is said to sing just before dying. **2** a person's final performance or statement, composition, painting, etc.

swank [swæŋk] *Slang v* show off; swagger: *swanking around in her new outfit.* *n* **1** style; smartness. **2** swaggering behaviour. *adj* swanky: *a swank apartment.* **swank·y** *adj*. ⟨Compare Old English *swancor* lithe⟩

swap [swɒp] *Informal v* **swapped, swap·ping,** *n* trade: *to swap seats, a fair swap.* **swap·per** *n*. ⟨Middle English *swappe* strike; for practice of 'striking hands' in concluding a bargain⟩

sward [swɔrd] *n* a grassy surface; turf. ⟨Old English *sweard* skin⟩

swarm[1] [swɔrm] *n* **1** a group of bees, led by a queen, leaving a hive to start a new colony elsewhere. **2** a large number of insects, birds, people, etc., moving around: *a swarm of children.* **3** such a group, specifically, of youth, who surround, attack, and rob a victim.
v **1** of bees, fly off to start a new colony. **2** fly or move around in great numbers: *Flies swarmed around us.* **3** crowd or be crowded: *Tourists swarmed all over the town.* **4** of a group of youth, surround, attack, and rob (a victim). ⟨Old English *swearm*⟩

swarm[2] [swɔrm] *v* climb by shinning. ⟨origin uncertain⟩

swarth·y ['swɔrði] *or* ['swɔrθi] *adj* dark-complexioned. ⟨earlier *swarty; swart* dark⟩

swash·buck·ler ['swɒʃ,bʌklər] *n* a pirate or a swaggering adventurer. **swash·buck·ling** *adj*. ⟨*swash* earlier, strike+ *buckler* shield⟩

swas·ti·ka ['swɒstıkə] *or* [swɒ'stikə] *n* an ancient symbol found in various cultures, consisting of a cross whose ends are bent at right angles, all in the same direction. The Nazis adopted the swastika with the arms bent clockwise. ⟨Sanskrit *svastika; svasti* luck⟩

swat [swɒt] *Informal v* **swat·ted, swat·ting** hit with a smart or quick blow: *to swat a fly.* **swat** *n*. **swat·ter** *n*. ⟨orig variant of *squat*⟩

swatch [swɒtʃ] *n* a sample of cloth or other similar material. ⟨origin uncertain⟩

swath [swɒθ] *n* **1** the space covered by one pass of a mowing machine. **2** a long, wide strip or belt. ⟨Old English *swæth* track, trace⟩ **cut a wide swath** make a destructive sweep.

swathe [swɒð] *or* [sweıð] *v* **1** wrap up closely or completely: *swathed in a blanket.* **2** envelop or wrap: *mountains swathed in fog.* *n* wrapping; bandage. ⟨Old English *swathian*⟩

sway [sweı] *v* **1** swing or cause to swing slowly to and fro: *The trees swayed in the wind.* **2** move slowly down or to one side, as if from pressure: *She felt dizzy and swayed against the wall.* **3** influence in opinion.
n **1** a swaying: *the sway of a branch in the wind.* **2** a controlling influence: *The rebel leader held sway over a large territory.* ⟨Scandinavian; akin to Old Norse *sveigja*⟩
sway·back *n* **1** a sagging back in horses, etc., esp as a result of strain or overwork. **2** an abnormal forward curve of the middle of the spine in humans. **sway·backed** *adj*.

swear [swɛr] *v* **swore, sworn, swear·ing 1** use profane or obscene language. **2** state firmly: *I swear it was the strangest thing I ever saw.* **3** promise solemnly to observe or do something: *A trial witness has to swear to tell the truth.* **4** bind by an oath: *Club members are sworn to secrecy.* ⟨Old English *swerian*⟩
swear by have great confidence in. **swear in** admit to office by causing to take an oath: *to swear in a jury.* **swear off** promise to give up. **swear out** get (a warrant) by taking an oath that a charge is true.
swear·word *n* a profane or obscene word.

sweat [swɛt] *v* **1** release moisture through the pores of the skin. **2** give out or gather drops of moisture: *A pitcher of ice water sweats on a hot day.* **3** get rid of by sweating or as if by sweating: *to sweat out a fever.* **4** work or

cause to work very hard. **5** be very uncomfortable, anxious, etc.: *to sweat under severe questioning.* **6** *Slang* worry about; take great pains over: *Don't sweat it.*
n **1** moisture coming through the pores of the skin. **2** a fit of sweating from anxiety, impatience, etc.: *in a cold sweat from fear.* **3** moisture from condensation, oozing, etc.: *a water pipe covered with sweat.* **4** hard work. **5 sweats** *pl Informal* sweatpants; sweatsuit. **sweat·y** *adj.* ⟨Old English *swǣtan*⟩
by the sweat of one's brow by one's own efforts and hard work. **no sweat** *Slang* easily. **sweat blood** *Informal* be subjected to great strain, as by overwork, extreme anxiety, etc. **sweat it out** *Informal* wait anxiously for something to happen. **sweat out** *Informal* struggle, wait, or suffer through (something): *She sweated out the long, anxious night.*
sweat·band *n* **1** a band lining the inside edge of a hat or cap to protect it from sweat. **2** an elastic cloth band worn around the head or wrist to absorb sweat. **sweat·er** *n* an outer garment for the upper body, made of knit material. **sweat lodge** a building used by some First Nations for ceremonies meant to cleanse the body, mind, and soul using steam. **sweat·pants** *n pl* long pants made of fleece-lined fabric, worn for athletics or as all-purpose casual dress. **sweat·shirt** *n* a long-sleeved pullover made of fleece-lined fabric. **sweat·shop** *n* a place where workers are employed at low pay for long hours under adverse conditions. **sweat·suit** *n* a suit consisting of a sweatshirt and sweatpants.

SYNONYMS

Sweat is used especially when the moisture is flowing freely or is mixed with grime: *Sweat streamed down the horse's flanks.* **Perspiration** is applicable only to human beings: *Drops of perspiration formed on his forehead.*

sweep [swip] *v* **swept, sweep·ing 1** clean or clear with a broom, brush, etc. **2** remove with a sweeping motion: *A flood swept away the bridge.* **3** pass or cause to pass over with a steady movement: *She swept the flashlight beam to and fro over the yard.* **4** move swiftly, forcefully, etc. (over): *Enthusiasm for the candidate swept the country.* **5** move with purpose and grace: *She swept out of the room.* **6** win (a contest or series of contests) overwhelmingly or in its entirety.
n **1** the act of sweeping. **2** a continuous extent; stretch: *a wide sweep of grassland.* **3** a person who sweeps chimneys, streets, etc. **4** a wide-ranging search or survey. ⟨Middle English *swepen*; Old English *swāpan*.⟩
make a clean sweep of get rid of completely in one decisive act. **sweep under the carpet** try to hide or ignore (a problem).
sweep·er *n* **1** a person or thing that sweeps: *a carpet sweeper.* **2** ✾ a tree undermined by the current of a river so that some of its leaves and branches hang in the water. **3** *Curling* either of the lead and second members of a rink. **sweep·ing** *adj* **1** passing over a wide space: *a sweeping glance.* **2** extensive: *sweeping reforms, sweeping generalizations.* **3** extending

in a long, curved line. *n* **1** the act of one that sweeps: *The porch needs a good sweeping.* **2 sweepings** *pl* bits swept up: *Put the sweepings in that box.* **sweep·stakes** *n sg or pl* a lottery or contest in which each entrant pays a specified sum for a ticket, and the money paid in goes to the winner.

sweet [swit] *adj* **1** having a taste like sugar. **2** pleasing to the sense of smell, to the ear, mind, etc.: *sweet music, sweet revenge.* **3** charming, kind, etc.: *a sweet smile.* **4** sentimental: *those sweet verses on greeting cards.* **5** fresh; not sour, salty, or fermented: *sweet cider, sweet butter.* **6** *Slang* a general intensifier: *I accomplished sweet diddly today.*
n **1** sweetheart. **2 sweets** *pl* candy, cake, etc. **3 sweets** *pl* gratifying features: *the sweets of success.* **sweet·ish** *adj.* **sweet·ly** *adv.* **sweet·ness** *n.* ⟨Old English *swēte*⟩
sweet on *Informal* in love with.
sweet–and–sour *adj* of food, prepared with a sauce containing sugar and vinegar or lemon juice: *sweet-and-sour pork.* **sweet·bread** *n* the pancreas or thymus of a calf, lamb, etc., used as meat. **sweet corn** corn having kernels with a high sugar content, eaten when young and tender. **sweet·en** *v* **1** make or become sweet. **2** make more attractive. **sweet·en·er** *n.* **sweeten the pot** make an offer more attractive, usually with more money. **sweet·grass** *n* a herb that smells sweet when dried. Many First Nations people burn it to create fragrant smoke during ceremonies. **sweet·heart** *n* **1** darling. **2** *Informal* a very charming, pleasant, or obliging person. **sweetheart deal** or **contract** an agreement arranged by union leaders and management, setting terms that are detrimental to the interests of workers but advantageous to management. **sweet·ie** *n Informal* sweetheart. **sweet·meat** *n* an article of food made with much sugar or honey; esp, candied or crystallized fruit or preserves. **sweet nothings** endearments exchanged by lovers. **sweet potato** a vine of the morning-glory family whose large tuberous root is used for food. **sweet talk** flattery; cajoling talk. **sweet–talk** *v.* **sweet–tem·pered** *adj* good-natured; gentle. **sweet tooth** a fondness for sweet foods.

swell [swɛl] *v* **swelled, swelled** or **swol·len, swell·ing 1** grow or make larger in size, force, etc.: *a river swollen by rain.* **2** be larger or in a particular place: *A barrel swells in the middle.* **3** rise or cause to rise: *Hills swell from the plain.*
n **1** an increase in amount, degree, force, etc. **2** a part that swells out or up. **3** a long, unbroken wave or series of waves. **4** *Music* a crescendo followed by a diminuendo.
adj **1** *Informal* stylish; grand. **2** *Slang* first-rate; excellent. **swell·ing** *n.* ⟨Old English *swellan*⟩
swelled head an exaggerated view of one's own importance.

swel·ter [ˈswɛltər] *v* **1** suffer from heat, as by sweating freely, feeling faint, etc. **2** oppress with heat. **swel·ter** *n.* **swel·ter·ing** *adj.* ⟨Old English *sweltan* die⟩

swept [swept] *v* pt and pp of SWEEP.

swept–back *adj* of the wings of an aircraft, slanting backward from the base to the tip.

swerve [swɜrv] *v* turn aside sharply from a straight course: *The driver swerved to avoid the child.* **swerve** *n.* ⟨Old English *sweorfan* rub⟩

swift [swɪft] *adj* 1 able to move very fast: *a swift horse.* 2 prompt; quick: *a swift response.* *n* 1 any of a family of small birds noted for their speed in flight. 2 a small fox, formerly common on the prairies. Also called **kit fox. swift·ly** *adv.* **swift·ness** *n.* ⟨Old English⟩

swig [swɪg] *Informal n* a big or hearty drink or swallow. **swig, swigged, swig·ging** *v.* ⟨origin uncertain⟩

swill [swɪl] *n* 1 kitchen scraps, esp when partly liquid, fed to pigs. 2 a swig. *v* 1 drink greedily. 2 wash by flooding with water. ⟨Old English *swilian*⟩

swim [swɪm] *v* **swam, swum, swim·ming** 1 propel oneself in water by movements of the arms and legs, tail, or fins. 2 float in a liquid: *beans swimming in the soup.* 3 be flooded: *We are swimming in magazines; cancel a few subscriptions.* 4 of the head, feel dizzy. 5 seem to spin or whirl: *Faces swam before me. n* an act or period of swimming: *to go for a swim.* **swim·mer** *n.* ⟨Old English *swimman*⟩

in the swim in the main current of activity in fashion, business, politics, etc.

swim·ming·ly *adv* easily; smoothly. **swimming pool** a large tank or container of concrete, plastic, etc., on or built into the ground for swimming in. **swim·suit** *n* a close-fitting garment worn for swimming; bathing suit. **swim·wear** *n* swimsuits collectively.

swin·dle [ˈswɪndəl] *v* get (money, etc.) from (someone) by deceit or fraud; cheat: *She swindled them out of their savings. He swindled $200 from us.* **swin·dle** *n.* **swin·dler** *n.* ⟨German *schwindeln* be dizzy, act thoughtlessly, cheat⟩

swine [swaɪn] *n, pl* **swine** 1 a pig. 2 a coarse or beastly person. **swin·ish** *adj.* ⟨Old English *swīn*⟩

swing [swɪŋ] *v* **swung, swing·ing** 1 move freely in an arc from a support. *The screen door was swinging in the wind.* 2 move swiftly and as if on a pivot: *He swung around and faced them.* 3 cause to swing: *to swing a golf club.* 4 move with a rhythmic motion: *swinging to the music.* 5 move or cause to move to and fro on a swing, in a hammock, etc. 6 *Slang* be put to death by hanging. 7 *Informal* manage successfully: *I think we can swing this deal. n* 1 the act of swinging; stroke, or blow: *One swing of the axe split the log in two.* 2 *Golf, etc.* the manner of swinging. 3 a seat hung on ropes or chains, on which one may swing for fun. 4 the normal rhythm of activity: *to get into the swing of a new job.* 5 *Music* a style of jazz that evolved in the 1930s, played by big bands; lively, syncopated rhythm. 6 a quick trip or tour: *a swing through the Maritimes.* ⟨Old English *swingan* beat⟩

in full swing going on in a lively way: *The party was in full swing.* **take a swing at** aim a blow at.

swing·er *n* a person or thing that swings. **swing riding** ✹ a riding in which the majority vote could go any way. **swing shift** working hours between the day and night shifts, usually from 4 p.m. to midnight.

SYNONYMS

Swing applies to something attached at a side or end, and suggests regular movement: *The lantern swung in the wind.* **Sway** suggests the motion of something that bends: *Branches sway in the breeze.* **Rock** is used of something on a surface, and may suggest gentle rhythm or violent shaking: *The boat rocked lightly on the waves. The house rocked in the storm.*

swipe [swaɪp] *v* **swiped, swip·ing** 1 strike (*at*) with a swift, sweeping blow. 2 *Informal* steal. 3 pass a card with a magnetic strip through an electronic device that reads it. **swipe** *n.* ⟨Compare Old French *swipu* scourge⟩

take a swipe at try to hit; aim a blow at.

swirl [swɜrl] *v* 1 move with a fast, twisting motion; whirl: *dust swirling in the air.* 2 have a twisting or spiral shape. **swirl** *n.* ⟨perhaps Scandinavian; compare Norwegian *svirla*⟩

swish [swɪʃ] *v* move with a light brushing sound: *The horse swished its tail.* **swish** *n.* ⟨perhaps imitative⟩

switch [swɪtʃ] *n* 1 a device for making or breaking a connection in an electric circuit. 2 a pair of movable rails by which a train can shift tracks. 3 a change: *Canada made the switch to metric in the 70s.* 4 an exchange. 5 a slender, flexible stick. 6 a roke: *The dog knocked over a vase with a switch of its tail.* *v* 1 start or stop the electric current to (an appliance, lamp, etc.) by operating a switch: *Don't forget to switch the light off.* 2 move from one railway track to another by means of a switch. 3 change or shift: *He was driving in the left lane but suddenly switched.* 4 exchange or reverse: *We switched lunches.* 5 lash back and forth: *The cat switched its tail.* ⟨probably variant of Low German *swutsche*⟩

switch·blade *n* a pocketknife whose blade springs open at the press of a button. **switch·board** *n* a panel of switches for connecting electric circuits or telephone lines.

swiv·el [ˈswɪvəl] *n* a fastening joining two parts so that one may turn without moving the other. *v* **-elled** or **-eled, -el·ling** or **-el·ing** turn on a swivel or as if on a swivel: *She swivelled the chair around.* ⟨Old English *swīfan* move⟩

swivel chair a chair that turns on a swivel in its base.

swol·len [ˈswoʊlən] *or* [ˈswʊlən] *adj* swelled: *swollen feet. v* a pp of SWELL.

swoon [swun] *v* 1 faint. 2 become ecstatic. **swoon** *n.* ⟨Old English *geswōgen* in a swoon⟩

swoop [swup] *v* 1 move with a lunge or rush; esp, make a sudden, swift attack (usually with *down*): *The eagle swooped down on the mouse.* 2 scoop; snatch (with *up*): *She swooped the puppy up in her arms.* **swoop** *n.* ⟨Old English *swāpan* sweep⟩

at (or **in**) **one fell swoop** all at once.

swoosh [swuʃ] *v* move with or make a sound like a rush of liquid or air: *A car swooshed by.* **swoosh** *n.* ⟨imitative⟩

sword [sɔrd] *n* **1** a hand weapon with a long blade fixed in a handle or hilt. **2** a symbol of power, authority, or honour: *the sword of justice.* **3 the sword** war or violence: *to die by the sword.* **sword·like** *adj.* ⟨Old English *sweord*⟩ **cross swords** fight or quarrel. **put to the sword** kill, esp in war.
sword·fish *n, pl* -**fish** or -**fish·es** a very large food and game fish, having a swordlike upper jawbone with which it slashes its prey. **sword·play** *n* the art of skilfully wielding a sword. **swords·man** *n, pl* -**men** a man skilled in using a sword. **swords·man·ship** *n.*

swore [swɔr] *v* pt of SWEAR.

sworn [swɔrn] *v* pp of SWEAR. *adj* bound or declared with an oath: *sworn enemies, a sworn statement.*

swum [swʌm] *v* pp of SWIM.

swung [swʌŋ] *v* a pt and pp of SWING.

syb·a·rite ['sɪbə,rɑit] *n* a lover of luxury and pleasure. **syb·a·rit·ic** [-'rɪtɪk] *adj.* ⟨*Sybaris*, ancient Greek city known for its luxury⟩

syc·a·more ['sɪkə,mɔr] *n* a large North American hardwood with brownish outer bark that flakes off, revealing the whitish inner bark. ⟨Greek *sykomoros*⟩

syc·o·phant ['sɪkə'fænt] *n* a servile, self-seeking flatterer or toady. **syc·o·phan·tic** *adj.* ⟨Greek *sykophantēs* informer, slanderer⟩

syl·la·ble ['sɪləbəl] *n* **1** a word or part of a word spoken as a unit, usually consisting of a vowel alone or a vowel with one or more consonants. **2** a corresponding part of a word in writing, regarded as a unit for purposes of hyphenation. ⟨Greek *syllabē* orig a taking together; *syn-* together + *lambanein* take⟩ **syl·lab·ic** [sɪ'læbɪk] *adj* **1** to do with syllables. **2** constituting a syllable. *n* **syllabics** *pl* any writing system that uses one character per syllable, esp such a system orig designed for Cree and adapted for other Aboriginal languages. Inuktitut is also written in syllabics. **syl·lab·i·cate** *v* syllabify. **syl·lab·i·ca·tion** *n.* **syl·lab·i·fy** *v* divide into or form syllables. **syl·lab·i·fi·ca·tion** *n.*

syl·la·bus ['sɪləbəs] *n, pl* -**bus·es** or -**bi** [-,bɑɪ] *or* [-,bi] an outline of a course of study. ⟨Latin, erroneous reading of Greek *sittyba* label⟩

syl·lo·gism ['sɪlə,dʒɪzəm] *n* **1** *Logic* a form of argument consisting of two statements, a general (**major premise**) and a particular (**minor premise**), and a conclusion drawn from them. *Example: All trees have roots; an oak is a tree; therefore, an oak has roots.* **2** a deduction made in this way. **3** a specious or subtle argument. **syl·lo·gis·tic** *adj.* **syl·lo·gize** *v.* ⟨Greek *syllogismos*; *syn-* together + *logos* a reckoning⟩

sylph [sɪlf] *n* **1** a slender, graceful girl or woman. **2** in the ancient Greek theory of the four elements, the spirit inhabiting the air.

sylph·like *adj.* ⟨Latin *sylphes*; a coinage of Paracelsus, 16c Swiss alchemist⟩

syl·van ['sɪlvən] *adj* to do with the woods: *a sylvan retreat.* ⟨Latin *silva* forest⟩

sym·bi·o·sis [,sɪmbɑɪ'ousɪs] *n* **1** *Biology* the association or living together of two unlike organisms in a relationship that benefits both. **2** any relationship of interdependence between unlike things or people. **sym·bi·ot·ic** [-'ɒtɪk] *adj.* ⟨Greek; *syn-* together + *bios* life⟩

sym·bol ['sɪmbəl] *n* **1** a thing or person that represents, or recalls something else: *The dove is a symbol of peace.* **2** a letter, figure, or sign used in writing or printing to stand for a sound, quantity, relation, etc. **sym·bol·ic** [sɪm'bɒlɪk] *adj.* **sym·bol·i·cal·ly** *adv.* ⟨Greek *symbolon* token; *syn-* together + *ballein* throw⟩ **sym·bol·ism** *n* **1** the use of symbols to represent or evoke things. **2** a traditional system of symbols: *The cross is part of Christian symbolism.* **3** a movement in art and literature seeking to express ideas, feelings, or states of mind indirectly through symbols. **sym·bol·ize** *v* **1** be a symbol of; represent: *A dove symbolizes peace.* **2** express by a symbol: *We symbolize the chemical composition of water by the formula H_2O.* **sym·bol·o·gy** *n* **1** the study of symbols. **2** symbolism (def. 2).

sym·me·try ['sɪmətri] *n* **1** a regular, balanced arrangement of equal parts on opposite sides of a line or plane, or around a centre or axis. **2** balance in an arrangement. **sym·met·ri·cal** [sɪ'metrɪkəl] *adj.* **sym·met·ri·cal·ly** *adv.* ⟨Greek *syn-* together + *metron* measure⟩

sym·pa·thy ['sɪmpəθi] *n* **1** a sharing or ability to share in another's feelings: *to feel sympathy for a bereaved person.* **2** a harmony of feeling or opinion: *He is in sympathy with my plan.* ⟨Greek *syn-* together + *pathos* feeling⟩ **sym·pa·thet·ic** *adj* **1** sharing in the feelings of another; sympathizing. **2** generally kind and understanding toward others. **3** favourably inclined: *They are sympathetic to our idea.* **4** likable: *a sympathetic character.* **5** *Anatomy, physiology* of the autonomic nervous system other than the cerebro-spinal part. **6** *Physics* of vibrations, caused by vibrations of exactly the same period in an adjacent body. **7** being a response to some influence or disorder in another part of the body or in another person: *sympathetic weight gain by husbands of pregnant women.* **sym·pa·thet·i·cal·ly** *adv.* **sym·pa·thize** *v* **1** feel or show sympathy: *to sympathize with a child who is hurt.* **2** regard with favour; agree (with *with*): *He sympathizes with our cause.* **3** enjoy the same things and get along well together. **sym·pa·thiz·er** *n.*

sym·pho·ny ['sɪmfəni] *n* **1** a long, elaborate musical composition for a full orchestra. **2** in full, **symphony orchestra** a large orchestra made up of brass, woodwind, percussion, and stringed instruments. **3** a beautiful, harmonious blend, etc., as of sounds or colours: *In fall the woods are a symphony in red, brown, and gold.* **sym·phon·ic** [sɪm'fɒnɪk] *adj.* ⟨Greek *syn-* together + *phōnē* voice, sound⟩

sym·po·si·um [sɪm'pouziəm] *or* [-'pouʒəm] *n, pl* **-si·ums** *or* **-si·a** [-ziə] *or* [-ʒə] **1** a book or article which is a collection of the opinions of several people on a subject. **2** a formal conference at which several specialists give their views on a subject. ⟨Greek *syn-* together + *posis* drinking⟩

symp·tom ['sɪmptəm] *n* **1** a sign of the existence of some condition: *symptoms of unrest.* **2** *Pathology* a noticeable change in the normal working of the body, giving evidence of disease or injury. **symp·to·mat·ic** *adj.* ⟨Greek *symptōma; syn-* together + *piptein* fall⟩ **symp·to·ma·tol·o·gy** *n* **1** the branch of medicine dealing with symptoms and diagnosis. **2** the collective symptoms of a patient or disease.

syn·a·gogue ['sɪnə,gɒg] *n* **1** a Jewish house of worship and religious instruction. **2** a Jewish congregation or assembly. ⟨Greek *synagōgē* assembly; *syn-* together + *agein* bring⟩

syn·apse ['sɪnæps] *n Physiology* a place where a nerve impulse passes from one nerve cell to another. ⟨Greek *synapsis* conjunction; *syn-* together + *haptein* fasten⟩

sync [sɪŋk] *Informal n* synchronization, as of sound and action or of speech and lip movement in television or films. *v* synchronize.
in sync synchronized; in harmony. **out of sync** not synchronized or in harmony: *Her ideas are out of sync with mine.*

syn·chron·ic [sɪŋ'krɒnɪk] *adj* **1** regarding a subject from a single point in time, without reference to historical change: *synchronic linguistics.* **2** synchronous. **syn·chron·i·cal·ly** *adv.* ⟨Greek *syn-* together + *chronos* time⟩ **syn·chro·nic·i·ty** *n* **1** the fact of being concurrent. **2** the occurrence at the same time of two apparently unrelated events that later are seen to be somehow connected, often symbolically. **syn·chro·nize** *v* **1** make occur or operate at the same time or speed: *to synchronize the sound with the action in a movie.* **2** establish or show the correspondence of the dates of (events). **syn·chro·ni·za·tion** *n.* **synchronized swimming** a competitive sport in which pairs or groups of swimmers perform identical dancelike movements in the water. **syn·chro·nous** *adj* **1** occurring or existing at exactly the same time. **2** moving or taking place at the same rate and exactly together. **3** *Physics* having coincident periods, as an alternating electric current. **syn·chro·nous·ly** *adv.*

syn·co·pate ['sɪŋkə,peit] *v Music* change (a regular rhythm) by beginning a note on an unaccented beat and holding it into an accented one or beginning it midway through a beat and continuing it midway into the next one. **syn·co·pa·tion** *n.* ⟨Greek *syncopē; syn-* together + *koptein* cut⟩

syn·cre·tism ['sɪŋkrə,tɪzəm] *n* a tendency or effort to reconcile different belief systems, or to absorb some of the tenets of one into the system of the other. **syn·cret·ic** [sɪn'krɛtɪk] *or* **syn·cre·tis·tic** *adj.* **syn·cre·tize** *v.* ⟨Greek

synkrētizein ally, orig as in a union of Cretan communities; *Krēs, Krētos* Crete⟩

syn·di·cate ['sɪndəkɪt] *n* **1** a group of individuals or organizations joining to carry out some undertaking, esp one that requires a large capital investment. **2** an agency that sells articles, photographs, etc. to many newspapers or magazines for simultaneous publication. **3** an association of criminals controlling organized crime.
v ['sɪndə,keit] **1** combine into a syndicate. **2** publish or broadcast through a syndicate. **syn·di·ca·tion** *n.* ⟨French *syndicat;* Greek *syndikos; syn-* with + *dikē* justice⟩

syn·drome ['sɪndrəm] *or* ['sɪndroum] *n* **1** a number of symptoms that together indicate the presence of a specific condition or disease. **2** the condition or disease. **3** any set of ideas, attitudes, or behaviours regarded as typical of a certain group, phase of life, etc.: *the yuppie syndrome.* ⟨Greek *syn-* with + *dromos* course; *dramein* run⟩

syn·ec·do·che [sɪ'nɛkdəki] *n* a figure of speech by which a part is put for the whole, the special for the general, the material for the thing made from it, or vice versa. *Examples: a factory employing 500 hands* (= *persons*). ⟨Greek *synekdochē; syn-* with + *ek-* out + *dechesthai* receive⟩

syn·er·gy ['sɪnərdʒi] *n* the co-operative action of two or more agents, parts, groups, etc. that increase each other's effectiveness. **syn·er·get·ic** *adj.* ⟨Greek *syn-* together + *ergon* work⟩ **syn·er·gism** *n* synergy. **syn·er·gist·ic** *adj.*

syn·od ['sɪnəd] *n* an assembly called together under authority to discuss and decide church affairs. ⟨Greek *synodos* assembly; *syn-* together + *hodos* a going⟩

syn·o·nym ['sɪnənɪm] *n* **1** one of two or more words of a language having the same or nearly the same meaning. **2** a word, name, etc. strongly associated with something: *Our name has become a synonym for high quality.* **syn·on·y·mous** [sɪ'nɒnəməs] *adj.* **syn·on·y·my** *n.* ⟨Greek *syn-* together + *dial. onyma* name⟩

syn·op·sis [sɪ'nɒpsɪs] *n, pl* **-ses** [-siz] a brief overview or summary of a plot, book, film, etc. **syn·op·size** *v.* **syn·op·tic** *adj.* ⟨Greek *syn-* together + *opsis* a view⟩

syn·tax ['sɪntæks] *n* **1** the arrangement of words to form sentences, clauses, or phrases; sentence structure. **2** the patterns of such arrangement in a given language. **3** *Computers* the structure of a computer language and its rules. **syn·tac·tic** *adj.* ⟨Greek *syntaxis; syn-* together + *tassein* arrange⟩

syn·the·sis ['sɪnθəsɪs] *n, pl* **-ses** [-,siz] **1** a combination of parts or elements into a whole. Compare ANALYSIS. **2** the resulting whole. **3** *Chemistry* formation of a compound by the chemical union of elements, combination of simpler compounds, etc. **4** the manufacture of a substance in this way. **syn·the·size** *v.* ⟨Greek *synthesis; syn-* together + *tithenai* put⟩

syn·the·siz·er *n* an electronic device that simulates and blends conventional and ultrasonic musical sounds. **syn·thet·ic** [sɪn'θɛtɪk] *adj* **1** manufactured by chemical synthesis: *synthetic silk*. **2** artificial: *synthetic affection*. **3** to do with synthesis: *synthetic chemistry*. *n* a fabric or other substance made by chemical synthesis: *I can't wear synthetics*.

syph·i·lis ['sɪfəlɪs] *n* a sexually transmitted disease characterized by a long progress, and if untreated, in the degeneration of bones, muscles, and nerve tissue. **syph·i·lit·ic** [ˌsɪfə'lɪtɪk] *adj, n*. ⟨*Syphilus* infected hero of a poem by 16c Italian Fracastoro⟩

sy·ringe [sə'rɪndʒ] *n* **1** a device consisting of a narrow tube with a nozzle at one end and a compressible rubber bulb at the other, for drawing in a quantity of fluid and then forcing it out in a stream. **2** a similar device consisting of a hollow needle attached to a hollow barrel with a plunger, used for injecting medicine, withdrawing body fluids, etc; hypodermic syringe.
v clean, wash, inject, etc. by means of a syringe. ⟨Greek *syringos* pipe⟩

syr·up ['sɪrəp] *or* ['sɜrəp] *n* **1** the condensed juice of a plant or fruit. **2** a thick solution of sugar and water, usually combined with flavouring or medicine: *cough syrup*. **3** *Informal* excessive sweetness of style or manner. **syr·up·y** *adj*. ⟨Old French *sirop*; Arabic *sharāb* drink⟩

sys·op ['sɪsˌɒp] *n* *Computers Informal* SYSTEMS OPERATOR. ⟨ *sys(tems) op(erator)*⟩

sys·tem ['sɪstəm] *n* **1** a set of things or parts forming an integrated whole: *a railway system, a computer system*. **2** an ordered group of principles, beliefs, practices, etc.: *a system of government*. **3** a theory or hypothesis of the relationship of parts and the laws that govern them: *the Copernican system*. **4** a method: *a system for betting*. **5** orderliness or organization. **6** *Biology* **a** a set of organs or parts in a body serving the same function: *the respiratory system*. **b** the body as an organized whole: *to take food into the system*. **7** *Geology* a major division of rocks including two or more series, formed during a geological period. **8** *Chemistry* an assemblage of substances which are in, or approach, equilibrium. **sys·tem·a·tize** or **sys·tem·ize** *v*. **sys·tem·less** *adj*. ⟨Greek *systēma*; *syn-* together + *stēsai* cause to stand⟩

sys·tem·at·ic *adj* **1** involving or forming a system. **2** orderly and methodical; organized. **sys·tem·at·i·cal·ly** *adv*. **sys·tem·ic** [sɪ'stɛmɪk] *adj* **1** to do with or affecting the body as a whole. **2** of an insecticide, fungicide, etc., entering the tissues of a plant and making the plant itself poisonous to pests. **3** to do with a system: *The causes of poverty in our society are largely systemic*. *n* a systemic pesticide. **systems analysis** the process or profession of using various techniques to break down a system, such as a business organization or an information system, into its basic elements in order to understand it and discover ways to improve it. **systems analyst. systems operator** a person in charge of an information or computer system.

sys·to·le ['sɪstəli] *n* *Physiology* the normal rhythmic contraction of the heart. Compare DIASTOLE. **sys·tol·ic** [sɪ'stɒlɪk] *adj*. ⟨Greek = contraction; *syn-* together + *stellein* wrap⟩ **systolic pressure** the blood pressure when the heart is fully contracted. It is higher than DIASTOLIC PRESSURE.

Sze·chu·an ['sɛtʃwɒn] *adj* to do with the spicy cuisine of S China. ⟨province in SW China⟩

Tt

t or **T** [ti] *n, pl* **t's** or **T's** **1** the twentieth letter of the English alphabet, or any speech sound represented by it. **2** the twentieth person or thing in a series.
to a T exactly; perfectly: *That suits me to a T.*
t tonne(s).
TA or **T.A.** teaching assistant.
tab [tæb] *n* **1** a small flap or projecting piece: *a cap with tabs over the ears.* **2** *Informal* a check: *to pay the tab.* **3** short form of TABULATOR (def. 2).
v **tabbed,** **tab·bing** **1** put a tab on (something): *to tab index cards.* **2** fix paragraph or column indentions. **3** use the tab key: *Tab to the next column.* **4** identify: *She was tabbed as a show-off.* ⟨origin uncertain⟩
keep tabs (or **tab,** or **a tab**) **on** keep watch on: *Keep tabs on your brother.* **pick up the tab** pay.
tab·by ['tæbi] *n* **1** a domestic cat having a brownish coat with dark stripes. **2** any cat, esp a female. ⟨Arabic *'attābiy,* striped silk⟩
tab·er·nac·le ['tæbər,nækəl] *n* **1** **Tabernacle** the wooden framework carried by the Israelites for use as a place of worship during their journey from Egypt to Palestine. **2** a Jewish temple. **3** a building used as a place of worship. **tab·er·nac·u·lar** [-'nækjələr] *adj.* ⟨Latin *tabernaculum* tent⟩
tab·la ['tʌblə] *n* a pair of small, tuned hand drums. ⟨Hindi or Urdu; Arabic *ṭabla* drum⟩
ta·ble ['teibəl] *n* **1** a piece of furniture having a flat top on legs. **2** the food put on a table to be eaten: *She sets a good table.* **3** a flat land surface. **4** a list: *the table of contents.*
v **1** present (a motion, report, etc.) for consideration. **2** *esp US* put off discussion of (a bill, motion, etc.). ⟨Latin *tabula* plank⟩
at table at a meal. **on the table** of a bill, motion, etc., before a committee, etc. for discussion. **set** (or **lay**) **the table** arrange dishes, etc. on the table for a meal. **turn the tables** reverse circumstances completely: *The enemy troops had advanced, but our sudden attack turned the tables on them.* **under the table a** secretly. **b** drunk and insensible.
ta·ble·cloth *n* a cloth for covering a table.
ta·ble d'hôte ['tɑbəl 'dout] or ['tæbəl 'dout] *French* [tabl'dot] *or* ['tæbəlz-] *French* [tabl-] in a restaurant, a complete meal with specified courses, offered at a fixed price. Compare À LA CARTE.
ta·ble·land *n* a plateau that rises sharply from a lowland area or the sea. **table linen** tablecloths, napkins, etc. **table salt** refined salt, such as that used to season food.
ta·ble·spoon *n* **1** a large spoon, used to serve vegetables, etc. **2** a standard unit of measurement in cookery, equal to three teaspoons, or about 15 mL. *Abbrev* **tbs.**
ta·ble·spoon·ful *n.* **table talk** conversation at or as at meals. **table tennis** an indoor game resembling tennis, played on a table with small wooden paddles and a very light,

plastic ball. Also called **ping–pong. ta·ble·top** *n* the top of a table: *The tabletop was scarred with cigarette burns.* **ta·ble·ware** *n* the dishes, cutlery, etc. used at meals. **table wine** an ordinary wine for drinking with meals.
tab·u·lar ['tæbjələr] *adj* **1** to do with tables or lists; esp, written or printed in columns and rows. **2** flat like a table: *a tabular rock.*
tab·u·lar·ly *adv.* **tab·u·la ra·sa** ['tæbjələ 'rɑsə] *or* ['rɑzə] *pl* **tab·u·lae ra·sae** ['tæbjə,li 'rɑsi] *or* ['tæbjə,lai 'rɑsaɪ] *Latin* the human mind viewed as blank (literally, erased slate) as at birth, before any outside impressions are received. **tab·u·late** *v* arrange (facts, figures, etc.) in tables or lists. **tab·u·la·tion** *n.* **tab·u·la·tor** *n* **1** a person, piece of software, etc. that tabulates. **2** a device or function key on a typewriter or computer for fixing paragraph or column indentions.
tab·leau [tæ'blou] *or* ['tæblou] *n, pl* **-leaux** or **-leaus** a striking scene; picture. ⟨French = picture⟩
tab·let ['tæblɪt] *n* **1** a small slab of stone, wood, etc. used in ancient times to write or draw on. **2** a small, flat surface with an inscription. **3** a small, flat piece of medicine, candy, etc.: *vitamin tablets.* ⟨French *tablette;* diminutive of *table* table⟩
tab·loid ['tæblɔɪd] *n* **1** a newspaper, usually having a page that is half the ordinary size. **2** a newspaper of this size that exploits sensationalism. ⟨*tablet* + *-oid*⟩
ta·boo [tə'bu] *adj* **1** banned or prohibited by custom: *Eating human flesh is taboo in most cultures.* **2** set apart as sacred, unclean, or cursed, and forbidden to general use.
v **-booed, -boo·ing** *v* forbid; prohibit; ban.
n **1** a ban or customary prohibition. **2** the system of setting things apart as sacred or cursed. Also, **ta·bu.** ⟨Tongan (of Tonga Islands in S Pacific) *tabu*⟩
tab·u·lar, tab·u·late, tab·u·la·tor See TABLE.
ta·chom·e·ter [tə'kɒmətər] *n* an instrument for measuring engine rpm (revolutions per minute). ⟨Greek *tachos* speed + METER⟩
ta·chy·car·dia [,tækə'kardiə] *n* an excessively rapid heartbeat.
tach·y·on ['tæki,ɒn] *n Physics* a hypothetical elementary particle that moves faster than light. ⟨Greek *tachys* swift⟩
tac·it ['tæsɪt] *adj* **1** silent: *a tacit prayer.* **2** implied or understood without being openly expressed: *Eating the food was a tacit admission that I liked it.* **tac·it·ly** *adv.* **tac·it·ness** *n.* ⟨Latin *tacitus* pp of *tacere* be silent⟩
tac·i·turn ['tæsə,tɜrn] *adj* speaking very little. **tac·i·turn·ly** *adv.* **tac·i·tur·ni·ty** *n.*
tack¹ [tæk] *n* **1** any of various types of short nail with a flat head, used for fastening carpets, etc. in place, pinning notices on a bulletin board, etc. **2** a sewing stitch used as a temporary fastening. **3** *Nautical* a zigzag course against the wind. **4** a course of action: *Whining is the wrong tack to take with me.*
v **1** fasten with tacks. **2** sew with temporary stitches. **3** add, esp as an afterthought: *She*

tacked the postscript to the end of the letter. **4** Nautical sail (a vessel) in a zigzag course against the wind. ⟨Old French taque nail⟩ **tack·y** adj sticky. **tack·i·ness** n.

tack² [tæk] n equipment for saddle horses, such as bridles and saddles. ⟨tackle⟩

tack³ See TACKY².

tack·le ['tækəl] n **1** equipment: fishing tackle. **2** a set of ropes and pulleys for moving heavy things. **3** the act of tackling. **4** Football a player between the guard and the end on either side of the line.
v **1** try to deal with: We have problems to tackle. **2** seize: She tackled the runner and pulled him to the ground. **3** Football seize and stop (an opponent having the ball) by bringing to the ground. **4** Soccer obstruct (an opponent) in order to get the ball away from him or her. **tack·ler** n. ⟨Middle Dutch takel⟩

tack·y¹ See TACK¹.

tack·y² ['tæki] adj Informal **1** of poor quality or appearance: a row of tacky little houses. **2** vulgar; in bad taste: a tacky necklace. **tack** n. **tack·i·ly** adv. **tack·i·ness** n. ⟨origin uncertain⟩

ta·co ['tɑkou] n, pl tacos a Mexican food consisting of a tortilla folded around a filling of meat, cheese, beans, etc. ⟨Spanish⟩

tact [tækt] n sensitivity in dealing with people. **tact·ful** adj. **tact·ful·ly** adv. **tact·less** adj. **tact·less·ly** adv. **tact·less·ness** n. ⟨Latin tactus sense of feeling; pp of tangere touch⟩
tac·tile ['tæktaɪl] or [-təl] adj **1** to do with the sense of touch: The tongue is a tactile organ. **2** that can be perceived by touch: Heat is a tactile quality.

tac·tic ['tæktɪk] n a method for accomplishing a goal. ⟨Greek taktikos; tassein arrange⟩
tac·ti·cal adj **1** to do with tactics; esp, having to do with the disposal of armed forces in action. **2** having skill in manoeuvring: a tactical statesman. **tac·ti·cal·ly** adv. **tac·ti·cian** [tæk'tɪʃən] n. **tac·tics** n pl **1** the art of managing armed forces in active combat (with a sg verb). **2** the operations themselves. **3** any devices to gain advantage or success: When his coaxing failed, the little boy changed his tactics and began to cry.

tac·tile See TACT.

tad [tæd] n Informal a small amount; bit: Move the picture to the right just a tad. ⟨origin uncertain; perhaps tadpole⟩

tad·pole ['tæd,poul] n the aquatic larva of a frog or toad. ⟨Middle English tad toad + pol poll (head); thus 'toad that is all head'⟩

tae kwon do ['taɪ 'kwɒn 'dou] a Korean martial art similar to karate but more aggressive, esp in its use of powerful, leaping kicks. ⟨Korean tae kick + kwon fist + do way⟩

taf·fe·ta ['tæfətə] n a stiff, glossy cloth of silk, rayon, nylon, etc. ⟨Persian taftah silk, linen⟩

taf·fy ['tæfi] n **1** a kind of hard but chewy candy made of brown sugar or molasses. **2** ✳ maple-syrup candy, often made by pouring the syrup over snow so that it hardens in brittle sheets. Also, **tof·fee**. ⟨variant of toffee⟩

taffy apple an apple stuck on a stick and dipped in hot taffy. **taffy pull** ✳ a social affair at which taffy is made.

tag¹ [tæg] n **1** a piece of paper, cloth, etc. to be fastened to something as a label: Each coat has a tag with the price marked on it. **2** a loose end. **3** a quotation, moral, etc. added at the end of a speech, story, etc., for ornament or effect. **4** the last line or lines of a song, play, actor's speech, etc. Also, **tag line**.
v **tagged**, **tag·ging** **1** add for ornament or effect. **2** label: Tag your suitcase. **3** trail behind (usually with along): She didn't want her brother to tag along. **4** put a parking ticket on (a vehicle). ⟨Middle English tagge⟩
tag question a question formed by the addition of a short interrogative structure to a statement and usually expecting agreement. Example: You can go, can't you?

tag² [tæg] n **1** a children's game in which the player who is 'it' chases the others until he or she touches one. The one touched is then 'it'. **2** Baseball the act of touching a base runner with the ball, or of touching a base with the foot or with the ball while holding the ball. **tag, tagged, tag·ging** v. ⟨probably extended meaning or special use of tag¹⟩

Tag·ish ['tægɪʃ] n, pl **-ish 1** a member of a First Nations people living in the southern Yukon and northern British Columbia. **2** their Athapascan language. **Tag·ish** adj.

ta·hi·ni [tə'hini] n sesame seed paste, much used in Middle Eastern cuisine. ⟨Arabic tahin flour; tahana grind⟩

Tahl·tan ['tɑltæn] n, pl **-tan** or **-tans 1** a member of a First Nations people of British Columbia. **2** their language. **Tahltan** adj.

tai chi ['taɪ 'tʃi] or ['taɪ 'dʒi] a Chinese martial art also used as slow exercise movements. Also, **tai chi chuan, t'ai chi,** or **tai ji**. ⟨Mandarin tai ji quan fist of the Great Ultimate⟩

tai·ga ['taɪgə] n BOREAL FOREST. ⟨Russian⟩

tail [teil] n **1** rearmost part of an animal's body, esp if it extends from the back in a thin, flexible piece. **2** something like an animal's tail: the tail of a comet. **3** the hind part of anything: the tail of a cart. **4** Informal a person who follows another to watch and report on his or her movements. **5** tails pl **a** the reverse side of a coin. **b** Informal a tailcoat.
adj **1** at the tail, back, or rear. **2** coming from behind: a strong tail wind.
v **1** Informal follow closely and secretly, esp in order to watch or to prevent escaping. **2** occur less and less (with off or away). **tail·less** adj. **tail·like** adj. ⟨Old English tægel⟩
at the tail of following. **on one's tail** Informal following one, esp very closely. **turn tail** run away from danger, trouble, etc. **with one's tail between one's legs** afraid; humiliated.
tail·coat n a man's formal coat extending at the back in two tapering pieces, or tails. **tail end 1** the rear: the tail end of the parade. **2** the last part: the tail end of the school year. **tail·gate** n a tailboard, esp on a truck. v of a

driver or a motor vehicle, follow (another vehicle) too closely. **tail·ing** *n* **1** the part of a projecting stone or brick put in a wall. **2** tailings *pl* waste matter left over after the mining or milling of ore. **tail–light** *n* a light, usually red, at the back end of a vehicle. Also, tail–lamp. **tail·piece** *n* a piece forming the end or added at the end. **tail·pipe** or **tail pipe** a pipe leading from the muffler to the rear of a motor vehicle, through which exhaust gases are discharged. **tail·spin** *n* **1** a downward spin of an aircraft with the nose down. **2** a state of panic: *The news threw the whole house into a tailspin.* **tail wind** a wind coming from behind.

tai·lor ['teilər] *n* a person whose business is making or repairing clothes.
v **1** make clothes, esp clothes that are cut and shaped to fit the body. **2** make or adjust to suit a particular need. **3** render (something) neat and trim: *a suburb full of neatly-tailored lawns.* ⟨Anglo-French *taillour*; *tailler* cut, Latin *taliare*⟩
tai·lored *adj* **1** having simple, fitted lines: *a tailored bedspread.* **2** very neat. **tai·lor·ing** *n* the skill of a tailor: *expert tailoring.* **tai·lor–made** *adj* **1** made by a tailor: *a tailor-made suit.* **2** made esp to suit a particular person or purpose: *a tailor-made course of study.*

taint [teint] *n* **1** a trace of infection or decay. **2** a trace of discredit: *a taint of vice.*
v **1** infect, spoil, or contaminate: *Her reputation had been tainted by a questionable business deal.* **2** become infected, spoiled, or corrupted: *Meat taints quickly if not kept cold.* **taint·ed** *adj* ⟨Middle English; variant of *attaint* disgrace, and Old French *teint* dyed⟩

take [teik] *v* **took, tak·en, tak·ing 1** grasp: *He took her by the hand.* **2** accept: *Take my advice.* **3** assume possession of: *She took the gifts and opened them.* **4** steal: *What did the thieves take?* **5** a win: *He took first prize.* **b** receive: *to take a degree in science.* **6** receive in an indicated manner: *Take it seriously.* **7** receive into the body: *to take medicine.* **8** indulge in: *to take a rest.* **9** withstand: *I can only take so much pressure.* **10** need: *It takes time to learn how to drive.* **11** choose: *I'd take the green over the blue.* **12** remove; remove by death or killing: *She took her own life.* **13** travel by means of: *to take the train.* **14** escort; carry: *Take her home.* **15** obtain by some method: *Please take my photograph.* **16** form and hold in mind: *to take pride in your work.* **17** occupy (time): *This could take all day.* **18** understand: *How did you take his remark?* **19** suppose: *He took her to be a tourist.* **20** assume: *She took responsibility for the household.* **21** record: *to take a message on the phone.* **22** resort: *The deer took to the woods.* **23** become: *He took sick.* **24** *Baseball* of a batter, let (a pitched ball) pass without swinging at it. **25** *Slang* swindle; cheat.
n **1** the amount or number taken: *a great take of fish.* **2** *Slang* receipts; profits: *the box-office take.* **3** in films, a scene photographed at one time. **4** the process of making a recording for a record, tape, etc. **tak·er** *n*. ⟨Old Norse *taka*⟩
on the take *Slang* taking or seeking bribes.

taken aback See ABACK. **take after** resemble: *She takes after her mother.* **take against** oppose. **take amiss** be offended at. **take back a** retract. **b** remind of the past: *The letter took me back ten years.* **take down a** write down (something said). **b** lower. **c** abase; humiliate. **take five** (or **ten**, etc.), take a break. **take for** suppose (esp erroneously) to be. **take in a** receive; admit: *to take in boarders.* **b** make smaller. **c** register mentally. **d** deceive; trick: *I was taken in by his friendly manner.* **e** include: *The Golden Horseshoe takes in all the cities around the western end of Lake Ontario.* **f** attend: *to take in a movie.* **take it** assume: *Do I take it you agree?* **take it on the chin** *Informal* undergo verbal or physical assault: *He's really been taking it on the chin lately—first he lost his job and then his wife died.* **take it or leave it** accept or reject it without modification. **take it out of a** *Informal* exhaust. **b** take something in compensation. **take (it) out on** *Informal* relieve (one's anger) by scolding or hurting (someone). **take it upon oneself** assume the responsibility: *They took it upon themselves to pay the debt.* **take kindly to** look favourably upon. **take lying down** *Informal* endure without a protest. **taken with** favourably impressed by: *I was quite taken with the new furniture.* **take off a** leave the ground or water: *Three airplanes took off at the same time.* **b** *Informal* give an amusing imitation of. **c** *Informal* rush away: *He took off at the first sign of trouble.* **d** spend (time) away from work, school, etc.: *She took a day off.* **e** deduct: *We'll take 20 percent off.* **f** be successful: *His new song has really taken off.* **take on a** hire. **b** undertake to deal with: *to take on an opponent.* **c** *Informal* show great excitement, grief, etc. **d** acquire: *to take on the appearance of health.* **take one's time** not hurry. **take out a** borrow (a book, etc.) from a library. **b** apply for and obtain (a licence, patent, etc.). **c** go on a date with. **d** destroy: *The bomb took out two munitions factories.* **take over** take control of. **take someone up on** accept: *She took him up on his invitation.* **take to a** become fond of: *She has taken to skiing.* **b** develop a habit of: *She's taken to throwing tantrums.* **take to one's heels** run away. **take up a** absorb: *A sponge takes up liquid.* **b** begin to do, study, etc.: *He's taken up the piano.* **c** fill: *The description took up a whole page.* **take up the slack** fill the gap left by someone. **take up with** begin to associate with. **well taken** of a point in a discussion, worth considering.
take–charge *adj Informal* forceful; assertive. **take–home pay** the balance remaining after taxes, etc. have been deducted from one's wages or salary. **take·off** or **take–off** *n* **1** *Informal* a mocking but good-humoured imitation: *a clever takeoff on the prime minister.* **2** the act of leaving the ground or other surface, as in jumping or flying: *The plane was ready for takeoff.* **take·out** or **take–out** *adj* to do with food packaged in disposable containers and sold by a restaurant, etc. to be eaten away from the premises: *a takeout dinner.* *n* **1** *Curling* a shot that hits an

opposing stone so as to remove it from the house. **2** food prepared in a restaurant to be eaten elsewhere: *Let's eat takeout tonight.* **take·o·ver** or **take–over** *n* **a** a seizure of control: *a takeover of a country by the army.* **b** buy-out: *the takeover of one business enterprise by a larger one.* **take–up** *n* the action of taking up, as by absorbing, reeling in, etc. **take–up** *adj.* **tak·ing** *adj* attractive or winning: *a taking smile. n* **takings** *pl* money taken in; receipts. **tak·ing·ly** *adv.*

talc [tælk] *n* a soft mineral used in making talcum or face powder, lubricants, etc.; hydrated magnesium silicate. Also, **tal·cum**. ⟨Latin *talcum;* Arabic *talq,* Persian *talk*⟩ **tal·cum powder** a powder made of talc, often perfumed, for use on the body.

tale [teil] *n* **1** a recital or account: *They listened in silence to his tale of the day's events.* **2** a story of events, esp when imaginatively treated: *tales of dragons.* **3** a malicious piece of gossip, either true or false: *She's always telling tales.* **4** a lie: *Children, don't tell tales.* **tell tales** spread gossip. **tell tales out of school** reveal confidential matters. **tell the tale a** show the true state of affairs **b** be effective; work. ⟨Old English *talu*⟩ **tale·bear·er** *n* a person who spreads gossip or scandal; telltale. **tale·bear·ing** *n, adj.*

tal·ent ['tælənt] *n* **1** a special natural ability: *a talent for music.* **2** general intelligence or ability: *a person of talent.* **3** a person or persons having talent: *They were looking for local talent.* ⟨Greek *talanton*⟩ **tal·ent·ed** *adj* gifted: *a talented musician.* **talent scout** a person who looks for and recruits people having talent in a particular field of activity, esp in the public entertainment field or professional sports. **talent show** a show made up of separate performances of singing, dancing, etc. by amateurs looking for recognition.

tal·is·man ['tælɪsmən] *or* ['tælɪz-] *n, pl* **-mans** **1** a stone, ring, etc. engraved with figures or characters supposed to have magic power; charm. **2** anything that acts as a charm. ⟨Greek *telesma* initiation into the mysteries⟩

talk [tɒk] *v* **1** express oneself in words. **2** converse: *The two friends talked for an hour.* **3** bring, put, help, etc. by talk: *If you don't know how to load the program, I'll talk you through it over the phone.* **4** communicate: *to talk in sign language.* **5** *Informal* speak of: *I'm talking billions of dollars!* **6** gossip: *You were talking behind my back.* *n* **1** speech; conversation. **2** an informal speech. **3** a conference: *peace talks.* **4** gossip or rumour. **5** *Informal* empty words: *Their threat was just talk.* ⟨Middle English *talken*⟩ **big talk** boastful talk; bragging. **have a talk with** admonish; advise. **look who's talking** *Slang* the person talking critically has no right to do so, as he or she is himself or herself guilty. **now you're talking** *Informal* now you are saying what I want to hear. **talk around** discuss without coming to the point. **talk at** preach to. **talk away a** spend (time) in

talking. **b** remove by talking: *I talked away my fears.* **talk back** *Informal* answer disrespectfully. **talk big** *Slang* brag. **talk down a** silence by talking louder or longer. **b** speak condescendingly *(to).* **c** belittle: *He talks down his competitor's products.* **d** give (a pilot) radio instructions for landing. **talk into** persuade (someone) into (doing something). **talk of** or **about a** deal with in talk or writing: *In her article she talks about the national debt.* **b** consider with a view to doing: *They're talking of selling everything and moving away.* **talk off** (or **out of**) **the top of one's head** *Informal* utter one's thoughts without consideration. **talk out a** try to resolve (a problem, etc.) by means of discussion. **b** in Parliament, discuss (a bill) until the time for adjournment and so prevent its being put to a vote. **talk out of** dissuade (someone) from (doing something): *We talked him out of trying to drive home.* **talk over a** discuss. **b** persuade or convince by arguing: **talk someone's ear** (or **leg**, etc.) **off** *Informal* talk to (someone) at seemingly interminable length. **talk the hind leg off a donkey** talk constantly. **talk the talk** say the expected thing. **talk up** talk in favour of. **you should talk** *Informal* you are guilty of the very thing you are criticizing. **talk·a·thon** *n* an extra-long public discussion. **talk·a·tive** *adj* having the habit of talking a great deal. **talk·a·tive·ly** *adv.* **talk·a·tive·ness** *n.* **talk·er** *n* a talkative person. **talk·ie** *n Informal* TALKING PICTURE. **talking book** the text of a book recorded on audiotape. **talking head** a person shown close up on television, engaged only in speaking, esp pompously or tiresomely. **talking picture** an early name for a film with synchronized sound. **talking point** a point to be emphasized or that serves as a basis for discussion: *These facts may not prove our case but at least they are a talking point.* **talk·ing–to** *n Informal* a scolding. **talk show** a radio or television show featuring interviews with well-known people or people who have some special interest, in which a studio audience may be encouraged to participate, or listeners invited to phone in. **talk–show** *adj.* **talk·y** *adj* **1** talkative. **2** having too much talk or dialogue: *a talky novel.* **talk·i·ness** *n.*

SYNONYMS
Talkative, the common word, emphasizes a tendency to talk a great deal: *He is a talkative person who knows everybody in town.* **Loquacious**, a formal word, adds the idea of talking smoothly and easily: *The president of the club is a loquacious person.*

tall [tɒl] *adj* **1** high: *Mountains are tall.* **2** higher than the average or than surrounding things: *a tall woman.* **3** of a particular height: *He is 185 cm tall.* **4** *Informal* **a** unreasonable: *That's a tall order.* **b** exaggerated: *a tall tale.* **tall·ish** *adj.* **tall·ness** *n.* ⟨Old English *getæl* prompt, active⟩ **tall ship** a large sailing ship of traditional design. **tall story** (or **tale**) an unlikely or exaggerated story.

tal·low ['tælou] *n* the rendered fat of cattle and sheep, used mainly for making candles, soap, lubricants, etc. ⟨Middle English *talgh*⟩ **tal·low·y** *adj* 1 fat; greasy. 2 pale.

tal·ly ['tæli] *n* 1 an account or score: *the tally of a game.* 2 a specific number, or a mark representing such a number, used as a unit in counting: *The ballots were counted in tallies of 20.* 3 a mark used for identification: *Check the tallies on the crates.* 4 agreement. *v* 1 count or add (often with *up*): *to tally a score.* 2 agree: *Your account tallies with mine.* 3 provide with an identifying mark. ⟨Anglo-French *tallie*; Latin *talea* rod⟩ **tally sheet** a sheet on which a record or score is kept, esp a record of votes.

Tal·mud ['tælməd] *or* ['talmud] *n* the body of traditional Jewish civil and canonical law. **Tal·mud·ic** [tæl'mʌdɪk] *or* [-'mudɪk] *adj.* ⟨Hebrew = instruction⟩

tal·on ['tælən] *n* 1 a claw, esp of a bird of prey. 2 the part of the bolt of a lock against which the key presses. **tal·oned** *adj.* ⟨Old French *talon* heel; Latin *talus* ankle⟩

tam·a·rack ['tæmə,ræk] *n* a larch tree found mainly in muskeg and swamp areas throughout most of Canada. ⟨Algonquian⟩ **tamarack swamp** (or **muskeg**) a low-lying, wet tract of land where tamarack flourish.

tam·bour ['tæmbur] *or* [tæm'bur] *n* 1 a drum. 2 a circular frame for holding in place cloth to be embroidered. ⟨French = drum⟩ **tam·bou·rine** [,tæmbə'rin] *n* a drum with one head and with jingling metal disks around the side, played by shaking, striking with the knuckles, etc. **tam·bou·rin·ist** *n.*

tame [teim] *adj* 1 of an animal, changed by humans from a wild state to a state of being able to serve as a beast of burden, source of food or clothing, pet, etc. 2 gentle and easy to control. 3 dull and lifeless: *a tame story.* *v* 1 make or become tame, or domesticated. 2 make submissive or docile. 3 tone down or mitigate: *He was told to tame his language.* 4 take away the ruggedness, challenging quality, etc. of: *to tame the wilderness.* **tame·a·ble** or **tam·a·ble** *adj.* **tame·ly** *adv.* **tame·ness** *n.* **tam·er** *n.* ⟨Old English *tam*⟩

tamp [tæmp] *v* 1 pack down firmly by a series of taps. 2 in blasting, fill (the hole containing explosive) with dirt, etc. ⟨perhaps *tampion* plug for gun muzzle⟩

tam·per ['tæmpər] *v* interfere with so as to damage or weaken (with *with*): *Someone had tampered with the evidence.* **tam·per·er** *n.* ⟨variant of *temper*⟩

tam·pon ['tæmpɒn] *n* a plug of cotton or other absorbent material inserted into a wound or body cavity to stop bleeding or to absorb blood, etc. ⟨French = plug; Old French *tapon*; *taper* to plug⟩

tan [tæn] *v* **tanned, tan·ning** 1 make (hide) into leather by treating it with a solution containing tannin. 2 make (light skin) brown by exposure to the sun or a sunlamp: *He was deeply tanned after a summer spent out of doors.* 3 become tanned: *My sister tans more quickly than I do.* 4 *Informal* spank or thrash in punishment (esp in **tan someone's hide**). *n* 1 a medium or light, slightly reddish brown. 2 the brown colour acquired by light skin from exposure to the sun or a sunlamp. **tan·ning** *n.* ⟨Latin *tannare; tannum* crushed oak bark used in tanning hides⟩ **tan·ner** *n* a person whose work is tanning hides. **tan·ner·y** *n* a place where hides are tanned. **tan·nic** *adj* 1 of or obtained from tannin. 2 of red wine, tasting of tannin absorbed from the oak barrels in which the wine is aged. **tannic acid** a form of tannin. **tan·nin** *n* an acid obtained from the bark of oaks, etc. and from certain plants, used in tanning, dyeing, etc. **tanning parlour** an establishment where clients may tan themselves, esp under sun lamps.

tan·dem ['tændəm] *adv* one behind the other: *to drive horses tandem.* *adj* having animals, seats, parts, etc. arranged one behind the other. *n* a bicycle with two seats and two sets of pedals, one behind the other. ⟨Latin *tandem* at length; *tam* so⟩ **in tandem a** in tandem formation: *mounted in tandem.* **b** in partnership or co-operation: *working in tandem.*

tan·doo·ri [tan'duri] *adj* of any of various East Indian dishes, cooked in a clay oven or **tan·door.** ⟨Hindi *tandur* portable oven⟩

tang [tæŋ] *n* 1 a pleasantly strong and distinctive taste or flavour or smell: *the tang of sea air.* 2 a stimulating quality: *a slogan with tang.* **tang·y** *adj.* ⟨Old Norse *tangi* point⟩

Tang or **T'ang** [tæŋ] *n* a Chinese dynasty, A.D. 618-906, a period during which China expanded and its art and science flourished.

tan·gent ['tændʒənt] *adj* 1 touching. 2 *Geometry* touching at one point only and not intersecting. *n* 1 a line, curve, or surface that is tangent to a curve or curved surface. 2 *Trigonometry* in a right triangle, the ratio of the length of the side opposite an acute angle to the length of the side (not the hypotenuse) adjacent to the angle. *Abbrev* **tan.** ⟨Latin *tangere* touch⟩ **fly (or go) off on** (or **at**) **a tangent** change suddenly from one course of action or thought to another. **tan·gen·tial** *adj* 1 to do with a tangent. 2 only slightly connected. **tan·gen·tial·ly** *adv.*

tan·ge·rine [,tændʒə'rin] *or* ['tændʒə,rin] *n* any of several varieties of mandarin orange having a thin skin. ⟨French *Tanger* Tangiers, seaport in Morocco⟩

tan·gi·ble ['tændʒəbəl] *adj* 1 capable of being touched or felt by touch: *A chair is a tangible object.* 2 real: *tangible evidence.* 3 whose value can be accurately appraised: *Real estate is tangible property.* *n* **tangibles** *pl* material assets. **tan·gi·bly** *adv.* **tan·gi·bil·i·ty** *n.* ⟨Latin *tangere* touch⟩

tan·gle ['tæŋgəl] *v* 1 twist together in a confused mass. 2 involve in something that

hampers (often with *up*): *to become tangled in a complicated business deal.* **3** get into a fight or argument (*with*): *Don't tangle with her.*
n **1** a twisted or confused mass: *a tangle of contradictory statements.* **2** a complicated or confused condition: *Her business affairs are in a tangle.* **3** a matted bit of hair. **tan·gled** *adj.* ⟨Middle English *tanglen, taglen* entangle⟩
tan·gly *adj* full of tangles; tangled.

tan·go ['tæŋgou] *n* a Latin American ballroom dance characterized by dips and slow glides. **tan·go, -goed, -go·ing.** ⟨Spanish⟩

tan·gram ['tæŋ,græm] *or* ['tæn,græm] *n* a Chinese puzzle consisting of a square cut into seven pieces (five triangles, a square, and a rhomboid) that can be combined so as to form a great variety of figures. ⟨perhaps Mandarin *t'ang* Chinese + -GRAM⟩

tank [tæŋk] *n* **1** a large container for liquid or gas: *an oil tank.* **2** an armoured combat vehicle moving on tracks. ⟨perhaps Portuguese *tanque;* Latin *stagnum* pool⟩
tank up a *Informal* fill the tank of one's vehicle with fuel. **b** *Slang* drink a lot of alcoholic liquor.
tanked *adj Slang* drunk. **tank·er** *n* a ship, aircraft, or truck having a tank for carrying oil, etc. **tank·ful** *n* as much as will fill a tank. **tank top** a sleeveless knit shirt with low neck and back, worn in very hot weather, for athletics, etc.

tank·ard ['tæŋkərd] *n* a large, usually silver or pewter drinking mug with a handle and, often, a hinged cover. ⟨Middle English⟩

tan·nic, tan·nin See TAN.

tan·ta·lize ['tæntə,laɪz] *v* torment or tease by keeping something desired in sight but out of reach, or by holding out hopes that are repeatedly disappointed. **tan·ta·li·za·tion** *n.* **tan·ta·liz·er** *n.* **tan·ta·liz·ing** *adj.* **tan·ta·liz·ing·ly** *adv.* ⟨*Tantalus,* in Greek myth punished by having water and fruit kept just out of reach⟩

tan·ta·lum ['tæntələm] *n* a rare metallic element that is resistant to acids. *Symbol* Ta ⟨*Tantalus.* See TANTALIZE.⟩

tan·ta·mount ['tæntə,maʊnt] *adj* equivalent (*to*): *Silence can be tantamount to an admission of guilt.* ⟨Anglo-French *tant amunter* amount to as much⟩

tan·tra *or* **Tan·tra** ['tɑntrə] *or* ['tʌntrə] *n* any of a number of ancient writings underlying Hindu and Buddhist mysticism. **tan·tric** *adj.* **tan·trism** *n.* ⟨Sanskrit⟩

tan·trum ['tæntrəm] *n* a violent, childish outburst of bad temper. ⟨origin uncertain⟩

Tao [daʊ] *n* in Taoism, 'the way', the supreme principle of harmony underlying the universe. ⟨Mandarin = the way⟩
Tao·ism *n* a Chinese philosophy and religion based on the teachings of Laotse (c. 500 B.C.) that conceives a balance between positive and negative forces underlying the existence of all things.
Tao·ist *n, adj.* **Tao·is·tic** *adj.* **Tao Te Ching** [,də 'dʒɪŋ] *n* an ancient text ascribed to Laotse

that establishes the philosophical basis of Taoism.

tap¹ [tæp] *v* **tapped, tap·ping 1** strike lightly: *to tap on a window.* **2** select or designate, esp for membership in a society. **3** tap-dance.
n **1** a light, audible blow: *a tap at the door.* **2** tap-dancing. ⟨Old French *taper;* imitative⟩
tap dance a dance in which the steps are accented by loud taps of the toe or heel, performed wearing shoes having metal plates. **tap–dance** *v.* **tap–danc·er** *n.*

tap² [tæp] *n* **1** a device for turning on and off the flow of fluid in a pipe. **2** a stopper to close a hole in a cask containing liquid. **3** a tool for cutting threads of internal screws, etc. **4** a wiretapping. **5** surgery to let out liquid: *spinal tap.*
v **tapped, tap·ping 1** make a hole in to let out liquid: *They tapped the sugar maples when the sap began to flow.* **2** draw the plug from: *to tap a cask.* **3** let out (liquid) by piercing or by drawing a plug. **4** make (resources, reserves, etc.) accessible (often with *into*): *This TV program taps into a large audience.* **5** make a connection with (a telephone line) in order to eavesdrop. **6** make an internal screw thread in. **7** *Slang* ask (a person) for money, help, etc. **tap·per** *n.* ⟨Old English *tæppa*⟩
on tap a ready to be let out of a keg or barrel and served. **b** ready for use; on hand.
tap·room *n* a room where alcoholic liquor is sold; barroom. **tap·root** *n* the main root of certain plants, such as the carrot, that grows straight downward with root hairs or rootlets branching out from it.

tape [teip] *n* **1** a long strip of cotton, linen, paper, metal, plastic, etc. **2** such a strip coated with a sticky substance: *adhesive tape.* **3 a** audio recording tape. **b** videotape.
v **1** fasten with tape; wrap with tape. **2** record on tape. **tape·like** *adj.* ⟨Old English *tæppe* strip of cloth⟩
get (something or someone) **taped** *Slang* understand (something or someone): *I had problems with this, but I think I've got it taped.*
tape deck an apparatus for making and playing tape recordings. **tape measure** a strip of flexible steel, cloth, paper, etc., marked off in centimetres, etc., for measuring length. **tape–re·cord** *v* record on magnetic tape. **tape recorder** *n* a device for recording and playing back sound on magnetic tape. **tape recording** *n.* **tape·worm** *n* any of numerous flatworms that live as parasites in the intestines of vertebrates.

tap·er ['teipər] *v* **1** make or become gradually smaller toward one end: *The church spire tapers to a point.* **2** diminish: *Their business tapered to nothing as people moved away.*
n **1** a gradual lessening in width toward one end: *pant legs with a slight taper.* **2** a slender candle. **ta·per·ing** *adj.* ⟨Old English *tapor* (the candle)⟩
taper off a gradually reduce: *She has been a heavy drinker but is trying to taper off.* **b** become less and less: *When he stood his ground, opposition eventually tapered off.*

tap·es·try ['tæpəstri] *n* heavy fabric having designs or pictures woven into it, used to hang on walls, cover furniture, etc. **tap·es·tried** *adj*. ⟨Old French *tapisserie* from *tapis;* Greek *tapēs* carpet⟩

tap·i·o·ca [ˌtæpi'oukə] *n* a starchy food in the form of white grains prepared from the root of the cassava plant. ⟨Tupi-Guarani *tipioca*⟩

taps [tæps] *n* (usually with a sg verb) the last bugle call at night, signalling that all lights in soldiers' quarters are to be put out. Taps is also played at military funerals and memorial services, esp in the US. Compare LAST POST. ⟨probably *taptoo,* form of *tattoo²*⟩

tar¹ [tɑr] *n* **1** a thick, black, sticky substance obtained by the distillation of wood or coal. **2** a similar substance found in the smoke from burning tobacco.
v **tarred, tar·ring 1** cover with tar: *a tarred roof.* **2** smear as if with tar: *tarred by his own bad reputation.* **tar·ry** *adj.* ⟨Old English *teoru*⟩ **tar and feather** smear heated tar on and then cover with feathers as a punishment. **tarred with the same brush** having similar faults. **tar paper** heavy paper coated with tar to make it waterproof, for use on roofs, etc. **tar sands** a deposit (esp the **Alberta tar sands**) of bitumen mixed with sand, clay, etc.

tar² [tɑr] *n Informal* sailor. ⟨special use of *tar¹* or short for *tarpaulin*⟩

tar·an·tel·la [ˌterən'telə] *or* [ˌtærən-] *n* a rapid, whirling, southern Italian dance. ⟨Italian; *Taranto,* city in S Italy; influenced by *tarantola* tarantula⟩

ta·ran·tu·la [tə'ræntʃʊlə] *n, pl* **-las** *or* **-lae** [-ˌli] *or* [-ˌlaɪ] **1** a large, hairy, European wolf spider whose bite is painful, but not serious. Its bite was formerly believed to cause an uncontrollable desire to dance. **2** any of a family of spiders found in tropical America, Mexico, and the southern United States, whose bite can be dangerous. ⟨Latin *tarantula; Tarentum* Taranto. See TARANTELLA.⟩

tar·boosh [tɑr'buʃ] *n* a close-fitting, brimless cap like a fez, worn by Muslim men either alone or as the inner part of a turban. ⟨Arabic *tarbūsh*⟩

tar·dy ['tɑrdi] *adj* **1** late: *a tardy attempt at reform.* **2** slow or sluggish: *a tardy pace.* **tar·di·ly** *adv.* **tar·di·ness** *n.* ⟨Latin *tardus*⟩

tar·get ['tɑrgɪt] *n* **1** something aimed at: *The bomber's target was a bridge.* **2** a flat, round object, usually marked with concentric circles, the centre of which is to be aimed at in shooting practice or a contest. **3** a goal: *The target for the fund-raising drive was $10 000.* **4** an object of scorn or abuse: *Her forgetfulness made her a target for their jokes.* *v* **1** make into a target. **2** direct at a target. ⟨Middle English *targete* diminutive of *targe* round shield, Old French⟩ **on target** to the purpose; appropriate or valid: *Her criticism was right on target.*

tar·iff ['terɪf] *or* ['tærɪf] *n* **1** a list of taxes imposed by a government on imports and, sometimes, exports. **2** a schedule of prices of

a business, etc.: *This hotel has a high tariff.* ⟨Arabic *tar'īf* information⟩

Tar·mac ['tɑrmæk] *n Trademark* a paving material consisting of crushed stone bound with coal tar. ⟨*tar¹* + *mac(adam)*⟩

tarn [tɑrn] *n* a small mountain lake or pool. ⟨Old Norse *tjörn*⟩

tar·nish ['tɑrnɪʃ] *v* **1** dull the brightness of: *The salt tarnished the silver saltshaker.* **2** lose brightness, esp through exposure to the air or certain chemicals: *This metal does not tarnish.* **3** spoil: *His involvement in that deal has tarnished his reputation.* **tar·nish** *n.* ⟨French *ternir; terne* dark⟩

ta·ro ['tɑrou] *n* a tropical plant of the same family as the jack-in-the-pulpit, grown for its edible starchy roots. ⟨Polynesian⟩

tar·ot ['terou] *or* ['tærou]; [-rət] *n* **1** a pack of 14c Italian playing cards, consisting of 78 cards including 22 trumps. **2** the 22 trump cards, often used by fortunetellers. ⟨French; Italian *tarocchi*⟩

tarp [tɑrp] *n Informal* tarpaulin.

tar·pau·lin [tɑr'pɒlən] *n* a sheet of waterproofed canvas or other cloth, used for protection against the weather. ⟨*tar¹* + *pall* in sense of 'covering'⟩

tar·ra·gon ['terəgən] *or* ['tærəgən] *n* a herb widely cultivated for its aromatic leaves, which are used as seasoning in salads, sauces, etc. ⟨Old French *targon;* Arabic *tarkhūn*⟩

tar·ry¹ ['teri] *or* ['tæri] *v Poetic, archaic* **1** stay for a time: *He tarried at the inn till he felt well again.* **2** be tardy: *Why do you tarry so long?* ⟨Old English *tergan* vex; sense influenced by Old French *targer* delay, Latin *tardare*⟩

tar·ry² See TAR¹.

tar·sal See TARSUS.

tar·sus ['tɑrsəs] *n, pl* **-si** [-ˌsaɪ] *or* [-si] **1** the bones forming the ankle and the back half of the foot. **2** the corresponding part in a four-footed animal, a bird's leg, or an insect's leg. **tar·sal** *adj.* ⟨Greek *tarsos* sole of the foot⟩

tart¹ [tɑrt] *adj* **1** having a pleasantly sharp taste: *a tart apple.* **2** having a sharp or caustic quality: *a tart reply.* **tart·ly** *adv.* **tart·ness** *n.* ⟨Old English *teart*⟩

tart² [tɑrt] *n* **1** a shell of pastry filled with fruit, chocolate, etc. **2** *Slang* prostitute. *v Informal* dress or decorate, esp in a gaudy way (with *up*): *The resort was all tarted up for the tourist season.* ⟨Old French *tarte*⟩ **tart·y** *Slang* like that of a prostitute: *That's a really tarty outfit.*

tar·tan ['tɑrtən] *n* a plaid pattern originating in Scotland. ⟨perhaps Middle French *tiretaine* fabric of linen and wool⟩

tar·tar¹ ['tɑrtər] *n* **1** an acid substance that collects as a crustlike deposit on the inside of wine casks. Purified tartar is called cream of tartar. **2** a hard deposit on the teeth, consisting of proteins from saliva, salts, and, usually, food particles. **tar·tar·ic** [tɑr'terɪk] *or* [-'tærɪk] *adj.* ⟨Greek *tartaron*⟩

tartaric acid an acid found in many plants, esp grapes, used in food and medicines.

tar·tar² ['tɑrtər] *n* a violent-tempered or savage person. ⟨Persian *Tātār*, influenced by Latin *Tartarus* Hades⟩

tartar sauce sauce made of mayonnaise with chopped pickles, olives, etc., typically eaten with seafood.

task [tæsk] *n* **1** work to be done: *One of his tasks was to take the garbage out.* **2** something unpleasant that has to be done: *She was left with the task of breaking the news to her mother.* ⟨Old Norman French *tasque, tasche;* Latin *tasca, taxa; taxare.* See TAX.⟩

take to task reprove: *The teacher took him to task for not studying harder.*

task force a group specially organized for a particular task: *The mayor set up a task force to study the effects of the proposed expressway.*

task·mas·ter *n* a person who sets tasks for others, esp one who is very demanding.

tas·sel ['tæsəl] *n, v* **-selled** or **-seled, -sell·ing** or **-sel·ing** *n* **1** a hanging bunch of lengths of yarn, strung beads, etc. fastened together at the top and used to ornament curtains, etc. **2** something resembling a tassel, such as the group of flowers at the top of a corn plant.

v remove the tassels from (growing corn) to improve the crop. ⟨Old French; Latin *taxillus* small die⟩

taste [teist] *n* **1** flavour: *the taste of olives.* **2** the sensation produced in taste organs: *Sweet, sour, salt, and bitter are four important tastes.* **3** a sample: *to take a taste of a cake.* **4** a liking: *Suit your own taste.* **5** the ability to perceive what is beautiful and excellent. **6** a manner or style that shows such ability: *Their house is furnished in excellent taste.*

v **1** try the flavour of (something) by taking a little into the mouth. **2** perceive by the sense of taste: *She tasted almond in the cake.* **3** have a particular flavour: *The soup tastes of onion.* **4** eat or drink a little bit (*of*): *I was too sick to even taste dinner.* **5** experience: *to taste freedom* **tast·a·ble** *adj.* ⟨Old French *taster*, orig feel⟩

a bad (or **nasty**) **taste in the mouth** an unpleasant feeling or memory left by a negative experience. **in bad** (or **good**, or **poor**, etc.) **taste** of a remark, action, etc., showing an inadequate (or good, etc.) sense of propriety: *Her joke was in poor taste.* **to one's taste** to one's liking: *That style of furniture is not to his taste.* **to taste** in the amount that suits one's palate: *Add salt and pepper to taste.*

taste bud any of certain small groups of cells, most of which are in the outer layer of the tongue, that are sense organs of taste. **taste·ful** *adj* having good taste: *tasteful furnishings.* **taste·ful·ly** *adv.* **taste·ful·ness** *n.* **taste·less** *adj* **1** without flavour: *The meat was dry and tasteless.* **2** having a lack of sensitivity to artistic worth: *a tasteless choice of accessories.* **3** showing a lack of sensitivity to what is proper: *She made a tasteless remark about his having gained weight.* **taste·less·ly** *adv.* **taste·less·ness** *n.* **tast·er** *n* **1** a person

whose work is testing the quality of tea, wine, etc. by tasting it. **2** formerly, a person who took a bit of food or drink before it was touched by an employer as a precaution against poison. **tast·y** *adj* appetizing; flavourful. **tast·i·ly** *adv.* **tast·i·ness** *n.*

SYNONYMS

Taste is the general and neutral word: *Mineral oil has no taste.* **Flavour** refers to a specially noticeable quality in the taste: *These berries have no flavour, but merely a sweet taste.*

tat·ter ['tætər] *n* **1** a shred: *After the storm the flag hung in tatters on the mast.* **2 tatters** *pl* torn or ragged clothing.

v make or become ragged. **tat·ter·ed** *adj.* ⟨Scandinavian⟩

tat·tle ['tætəl] *v* **1** betray (with *on*): *He tattled on his sister.* **2** talk idly or foolishly.

n idle talk or gossip. **tat·tler** *n.* ⟨Middle Dutch *tatelen, tateren* stutter, babble⟩

tat·tle·tale *n* a person who tells secrets, esp to get other people into trouble.

tat·too¹ [tæ'tu] *or* [tə'tu] *v* **-tooed, -too·ing** mark (the skin), often permanently, with designs or patterns by pricking it and putting in colours. **tat·too** *n.* **tat·too·er** *n.* **tat·too·ist** *n.* ⟨Polynesian *tatau*⟩

tat·too² [tæ'tu] *or* [tə'tu] *n* **1** a signal on a bugle or drum calling soldiers to their quarters at night. **2** a series of raps, taps, etc.: *The hail beat a loud tattoo on the roof.* **3** a military display, esp with music and parades. *v* tap continuously; drum: *tattooing with one's fingers on the table.* ⟨Dutch *taptoe; tap* tap of a barrel + *toe* shut⟩

tat·ty ['tæti] *n* shabby or tacky: *a row of tatty little houses.* ⟨Scottish dialect⟩

taught [tɔt] *v* pt and pp of TEACH.

taunt [tɔnt] *v* **1** jeer at; mock: *They taunted him with cowardice.* **2** get or urge by taunts: *They taunted him into taking the dare.*

n a scornful or insulting remark. **taunt·ing·ly** *adv.* ⟨obsolete *taunt pour taunt*, French *tant pour tant* tit for tat⟩

taupe [toup] *adj* medium brownish grey. ⟨French, orig mole; Latin *talpa*⟩

taut [tɔt] *adj* **1** tightly drawn: *a taut rope.* **2** strained; tense: *a taut smile.* **taut·ly** *adv.* **taut·ness** *n.* ⟨earlier *taught*⟩

tau·tol·o·gy [tɔ'tɒlədʒi] *n* **1** the saying of a thing over again in other words without making it clearer or more forceful. *Example: the modern student of today.* **2** *Logic* a statement that is true by virtue of its form. *Example: She is either present or not.* ⟨Greek *tautologia; to auto* the same + *legein* say⟩ **tau·to·log·i·cal** or **tau·tol·o·gous** *adj* redundant. **tau·to·log·i·cal·ly** *adv.*

tav·ern ['tævərn] *n* a place where alcoholic drinks are sold and drunk. ⟨Latin *taberna*, orig, rude dwelling⟩

taw·dry ['tɔdri] *adj* showy and cheap. **taw·dri·ly** *adv.* **taw·dri·ness** *n.* ⟨alteration of *St. Audrey*, for cheap lace sold at St. Audrey's fair in Ely, England⟩

taw·ny ['tɒni] *adj* brownish yellow: *the tawny coat of a lion.* **taw·ni·ness** *n.* ⟨Old French *tanné* pp of *tanner* tan⟩

tax [tæks] *n* **1** money paid by people for the support of the government, public works, etc. **2** a strain: *Climbing is a tax on a weak heart.* *v* **1** put a tax on. **2** cause to pay taxes. **3** be hard on: *Reading in poor light taxes the eyes.* **4** accuse (with *with*): *The manager taxed me with having neglected my work.* **tax·a·tion** *n.* ⟨Latin *taxare* assess; Greek *tassein* assign⟩ **tax·a·ble** *adj* subject to taxation: *Children's clothes are not taxable in some provinces.* **tax–de·duct·i·ble** *adj* allowed as a deduction from the gross when calculating income tax. **tax–ex·empt** *adj* free from taxes. **tax–free** *adj* **1** not taxable. **2** of an economy, jurisdiction, etc., in which there are no taxes. **tax haven** a foreign country or corporation where taxes are not imposed, used by residents or investors from another country to escape taxation: *Switzerland is used as a tax haven by many wealthy people.* **tax·pay·er** *n* a person who pays a tax or taxes or is required by law to do so. **tax·pay·ing** *adj.* **tax return** the report of one's income to a government for purposes of taxation. **tax shelter** any financial arrangement that results in a reduction of taxes.

tax·i ['tæksi] *n* a car driven for hire, with a meter for recording the fare. Also, **tax·i·cab.** *v* **tax·ied, tax·i·ing** or **tax·y·ing** of an aircraft, move across the ground or water under its own power. ⟨*taximeter cab;* French *luxe* fare + *mètre* meter⟩

tax·i·der·my ['tæksə,dɜrmi] *n* the art of stuffing dead animals in lifelike form. **tax·i·der·mal** or **tax·i·der·mic** *adj.* **tax·i·der·mist** *n.* ⟨Greek *taxis* arrangement + *derma* skin⟩

tax·on·o·my [tæk'sɒnəmi] *n* **1** the study of the principles of scientific classification. **2** *Biology* the classification of animals and plants. The basic categories, from general to specific, are *kingdom, phylum* (or for plants, *division*), *class, order, family, genus,* and *species.* **tax·o·nom·ic** [,tæksə'nɒmɪk] *adj.* **tax·o·nom·i·cal·ly** *adv.* **tax·on·o·mist** *n.* ⟨Greek *taxis* arrangement + *-nomos* assigning⟩ **tax·on** *n, pl* **tax·a** a taxonomic unit, such as a family or a genus.

TB *Informal* tuberculosis.

TBA, t.b.a., or **tba** to be announced.

T–bar ['ti ,bɑr] *n* a horizontal bar attached by a vertical bar to a cable which tows skiers up a hill as they hold onto the bar.

T–bill TREASURY BILL.

T–bone ['ti ,boun] *n* a beefsteak taken from the middle part of the loin, containing a T-shaped bone. Also, **T–bone steak.**

tbs or **tbsp** tablespoon; tablespoons.

T cell the type of lymphocyte that recognizes foreign proteins and triggers mechanisms for their destruction.

TD or **td** *Football* touchdown.

tea [ti] *n* **1** a dark brown or greenish drink made by pouring boiling water over the crushed, dried leaves of a tropical Asian shrub. **2** the dried and prepared leaves from which this drink is made. **3** an afternoon reception at which tea is served. **4** a hot drink made from herbs, meat broth, etc.: *chamomile tea, beef tea.* ⟨dialect Cantonese *t'e*⟩ **another cup of tea** *Informal* a very different sort of thing. **one's cup of tea** *Informal* just what one likes.

tea bag a small porous packet containing enough tea leaves for one or two cups of tea. **tea biscuit** a small, cakelike baked good made with baking powder; scone. **tea·cup** *n* a cup used with a saucer for drinking tea, coffee, etc. **tea·cup·ful** *n.* **storm in a teacup** See STORM. **tea·ket·tle** *n* a covered kettle with a spout and handle, used for boiling water to make tea, etc. **tea·pot** *n* a container with a handle and a spout, for making tea. **tempest in a teapot** See TEMPEST. **tea·room** *n* a shop where tea, coffee, and light meals are served. **tea rose** any of several varieties of hybrid rose typically having a scent resembling that of dried tea leaves. **tea service** a set that includes a teapot, hot water pot/coffee pot, cream jug, and sugar bowl. **tea set** a set of china dishes for serving tea, etc., usually consisting of a teapot, sugar bowl, cream jug, teacups, saucers, and small plates. **tea·spoon** *n* **1** a small spoon commonly used to stir tea or coffee. **2** a standard unit of measurement in cooking, equal to one third of a tablespoon, or about 5 mL. *Abbrev* **tsp.** **tea·spoon·ful** *n* the amount that a teaspoon can hold. **tea·time** *n* the time tea is served. **tea towel** a towel for drying dishes.

teach [titʃ] *v* **taught, teach·ing 1** show or explain how to do: *We taught our dog a new trick.* **2 a** help (someone) acquire (a skill, habit, etc.) by instruction, example, or both: *She taught us honesty.* **b** cause (someone) to learn, realize, etc.: *That experience taught me not to believe everything I hear.* **3** give lessons in: *She teaches mathematics.* **4** be a teacher by profession: *He taught for 40 years.* **teach·a·ble** *adj.* **teach·a·bil·i·ty** *n.* **teach·er** *n.* **teach·ing** *n.* ⟨Old English *tæcan* show⟩

teaching assistant a graduate student in a university or college, who teaches classes on behalf of a professor. *Abbrev* **TA** or **T.A.**

CONFUSABLES

Teach emphasizes giving information, explanation, and training, by guiding the studies of the person who wants to **learn**: *Some children learn to read by themselves, but most need to be taught.*

teak [tik] *n* a tall tree of the verbena family; one of the most valuable timber trees in the world, for its hardness and durability. ⟨Portuguese; Malayalam *tēkka*⟩

teal [til] *n, pl* **teal** or **teals** any of several small freshwater ducks of America, Europe, and Asia. ⟨Middle English *tele*⟩

team [tim] *n* **1** a group of people forming one of the sides in a competition: *a football team.* **2** a group of people working or acting

together: *the clean-up team*. **3 a** two or more horses or other animals harnessed together to work. **b** the animals and vehicle together. *adj* to do with a team: *a team effort*. *v* join together in a team (usually with *up*): *She teamed stronger students with weaker ones*. ⟨Old English *tēam*⟩
team·mate *n* a fellow member of a team. **team·ster** *n* a truck driver. **team·work** *n* the acting together of a number of people to make the work of the group successful.

tear[1] [tir] *n* **1 tears** *pl* **a** salty liquid secreted by a gland in the eyelid that overflows the eyelids, esp in weeping. **b** the act of weeping: *She broke into tears*. **2** a drop of the liquid secreted by the eyes. **3** something suggesting a tear: *a tear of dew*. *v* of an eye or the eyes, fill with tears: *The wind made her eyes tear*. ⟨Old English *tēar*⟩ **tear·drop** *n* a single tear. *adj* shaped like a tear: *teardrop earrings*. **tear·ful** *adj* accompanied by tears: *a tearful face, a tearful goodbye*. **tear·ful·ly** *adv*. **tear·ful·ness** *n*. **tear gas** a gas that irritates the eyes, used esp in breaking up riots. **tear–gas, -gassed, -gas·sing** *v*. **tear·jerk·er** *n Informal* a story, film, etc. calculated to play on the emotions (usually sadness) of the audience or reader. **tear·less** *adj* **1** without tears. **2** incapable of weeping. **tear·less·ly** *adv*. **tear·less·ness** *n*. **tear·y** *adj* tearful; crying. **tear·i·ly** *adv*. **tear·i·ness** *n*.

tear[2] [tɛr] *v* **tore, torn, tear·ing** *v* **1** pull apart by force: *to tear a box open*. **2** make a hole, rip, or injury in by a pull: *She tore a ligament while running*. **3** pull hard: *He tore down the enemy's flag*. **4** cut badly: *The jagged stone tore his skin*. **5** rend by conflict: *Her affections were torn between her family and her lover*. **6** remove by effort: *He could not tear himself from that spot*. **7** distress greatly: *She was torn by grief*. **8** become torn: *Lace tears easily*. **9** hurry; rush; dash: *Stop tearing through the house!* *n* **1** a torn place. **2** a hurry. **3** *Slang* a spree. **4** a fit of violent anger. ⟨Old English *teran*⟩
tear at make violent attempts to tear or remove with the hands: *He tore at the straps holding the box closed*. **tear down** pull down; destroy: *The city tore down a whole block of houses*. **tear into a** criticize severely. **b** begin (an activity) with speed and gusto.
tear sheet a page that can be removed from a magazine or newspaper for a special purpose, such as giving an advertiser proof of publication.

tease [tiz] *v* **1** bother (someone) by means of jokes, ridicule, etc.: *The other boys teased me about my curly hair*. **2** say something playfully without meaning it: *I don't know when to believe you—you're always teasing*. **3** tantalize. **4** comb (hair) by holding it up and working the hairs back toward the scalp, giving it a frizzy or fluffy appearance. **5** gently pull apart (plant roots, etc.). *n* **1** a person or thing that teases. **2** the act of teasing. **teas·ing·ly** *adv*. ⟨Old English *tǣsan*⟩ **teas·er** *n* **1** a person or thing that teases. **2** *Informal* a puzzle.

tea·sel ['tizəl] *n* any of several plants having prickly leaves and heads of small flowers with sharp, stiff, hooked bracts. Also, **tea·zel** or **tea·zle**. ⟨Old English *tǣsel*⟩

teat [tit] *n* **1** of female mammals, the nipple from which the young suck milk. **2** any similar small projection. ⟨Old French *tete*⟩

tech·ne·ti·um [tɛk'niʃəm] or [tɛk'niʃiəm] *n* an artificial, radioactive, metallic element. *Symbol* **Tc** ⟨Greek *technētos* artificial⟩

tech·ni·cal ['tɛknəkəl] *adj* **1** to do with a mechanical or industrial art or with applied science: *a technical school*. **2** specialized: *Electrolysis is a technical word*. **3** strictly according to the principles of a certain science, art, game, etc.: *a technical distinction*. **4** *Informal* making unduly fine distinctions: *OK, I was 90 seconds late; let's not get technical*. **5** to do with technique: *Her singing shows technical skill but her voice is weak*. **tech·ni·cal·ly** *adv*. ⟨Greek *technikos; technē* art⟩ **te·chie** *n Informal* **1** a student in a technical course. **2** a skilled technician or an avid user of high tech. **tech·ni·cal·i·ty** *n* **1** a technical detail, esp one that only a specialist is likely to appreciate: *She was acquitted on a legal technicality*. **2** the quality or state of being technical: *The technicality of the article soon discouraged him*. **technical knockout** *Boxing* a knockout called by the referee when a fighter is too injured to continue. *Abbrev* **TKO**. **tech·ni·cian** *n* **1** a person skilled in the technical details of a subject: *a laboratory technician*. **2** a person skilled in the technique of an art: *a superb technician at the keyboard*. **Tech·ni·col·or** *n Trademark* a process for making films in colour, in which three single-colour films are combined into one full-colour print. **tech·ni·col·our** or **tech·ni·col·or** *adj* highly colourful; vivid. **tech·ni·col·oured** or **tech·ni·col·ored** *adj*. **tech·nique** [tɛk'nik] *n* **1** technical skill: *The pianist's technique was brilliant, but his interpretation lacked warmth*. **2** a special method used to accomplish something: *a new technique for removing cataracts*. **tech·nol·o·gy** *n* **1** applied science: *Engineering is a branch of technology*. **2** a process, etc., arising from applied science and designed esp for dealing with a given task: *We have the technology for that kind of scanning*. **tech·no·log·i·cal** or **tech·no·log·ic** *adj*. **tech·no·log·i·cal·ly** *adv*. **tech·nol·o·gist** *n*. ⟨Greek *technē* craft⟩

tec·ton·ic [tɛk'tɒnɪk] *adj Geology* to do with changes in the earth's crust. **tec·ton·i·cal·ly** *adv.* ⟨Greek *tektōn* carpenter⟩
tec·ton·ics *n* the study of the earth's crust.

ted·dy ['tɛdi] *n* **1** a woman's one-piece undergarment combining a chemise top with short underpants. **2** TEDDY BEAR.

teddy bear a stuffed toy made to look like a bear cub. ⟨*Teddy*, nickname of US President Theodore Roosevelt, fond of hunting⟩

te·di·um ['tidiəm] *n* **1** tiresomeness. **2** boredom. **te·di·ous** *adj.* **te·di·ous·ly** *adv.* **te·di·ous·ness** *n.* ⟨Latin *taedere* be wearisome⟩

tee¹ [ti] *n* **1** *Curling* the centre circle of the target toward which the stones are aimed; button. **2** *Golf* **a** an area from which a player makes the first stroke in playing a hole. **b** a peg on which the ball is placed.
v **teed**, **tee·ing** *Golf* place (the ball) in position for hitting it, on, or as if on, a tee (often with *up*). ⟨Scots *teaz*⟩
tee off a drive a golf ball from a tee. **b** begin. **c** *Slang* make angry: *That really teed me off.*
tee line *Curling* the line that runs through the centre of the house, parallel to the HOG LINE.

tee² [ti] *n* **1** the letter T. **2** a T-shirt.

teem¹ [tim] *v* **1** abound: *The swamp teemed with mosquitoes.* **2** be fertile, fruitful, or prolific. ⟨Old English *tēman; tēam* progeny⟩

teem² [tim] *v* pour; come down in torrents. ⟨Old Norse *tœma* empty out⟩

teen [tin] *n* **1** **teens** *pl* of a person's age, the years from thirteen to nineteen: *He married in his teens.* **2** a teenager. *adj Informal* teenage. ⟨*-teen* in the numbers *thirteen* to *nineteen*⟩
teen·age ['tin,eidʒ] *adj* to do with teenagers: *a teenage club.* **teen·ag·er** *n.* **tee·ny–bop·per** or **teenybopper** *n* a pre-adolescent, esp a girl, who follows the latest fads in music, etc.

teen·sy ['tinsi] *adj Informal* tiny. Also, **teen·y**, **teen·sy–ween·sy**, or **teen·y–ween·y**.

tee·pee ['tipi] *n* a cone-shaped tent used mainly by First Nations peoples, consisting of a frame of poles spread out at the ground and joined at the top, covered with animal skins (orig buffalo hide), canvas, etc. Compare WIGWAM. Also, **te·pee** or **ti·pi**. ⟨Dakota *tipi*⟩

tee·ter ['titər] *n* a swaying movement. *v* rock unsteadily; sway: *to teeter on stilts.* ⟨probably Old Norse *titra* shake⟩
tee·ter–tot·ter *n* a plank balanced on a central support, used esp by children in a game in which they sit at opposite ends and move alternately up and down; seesaw. **tee·ter–tot·ter** *v.*

teeth [tiθ] *n* pl of TOOTH.
by the skin of one's teeth barely: *He escaped by the skin of his teeth.* **cut one's teeth on** See CUT. **grit** (or **set**) **one's teeth** prepare to endure something without complaining. **in someone's teeth** to someone's face; openly. **in the teeth of a** in the face of: *She advanced in the teeth of the wind.* **b** in defiance of. **lie through one's teeth** tell an outright

falsehood. **put teeth in** (or **into**) put force into. **show one's teeth** show anger; threaten. **sink** (or **get**) **one's teeth into** have one's abilities fully occupied by. **throw in someone's teeth** a blame someone for: *He threw the lie in her teeth.* **b** utter (an insult, etc.) at someone viciously. **to the teeth** to the utmost: *armed to the teeth.*
teethe [tið] *v* grow primary teeth: *The baby is teething.* **teeth·er** *n* an object of hard plastic, etc. for babies to bite on when they are teething. **teeth·ing** *n.*

tee·to·tal·ler or **tee·to·tal·er** ['ti'toutələr] *n* a person who never drinks alcoholic liquor. ⟨*total*, with initial T repeated⟩

Tef·lon ['tɛflɒn] *n Trademark* a synthetic resin used as a coating to prevent sticking. *adj* seemingly unaffected by criticism.

tele– or **tel–** *combining form* **1** over, from, or to a long distance: *telegraph, telephone.* **2** of, in, or by television: *telecast.* ⟨Greek *tēle* far⟩

tel·e·cast ['tɛlə,kæst] *v* **-cast** or **-cast·ed**, **-cast·ing** broadcast by television.
n a television program or broadcast.
tel·e·cast·er *n.* ⟨*tele*(*vision*) + (*broad*)*cast*⟩

tel·e·com ['tɛlə,kɒm] *n* telecommunication.

tel·e·com·mu·ni·ca·tion [,tɛləkə,mjunə'keifən] *n* **1** communication at a distance, esp by means of electromagnetic impulses, as in telegraph, telephone, radio, television, or computer. **2** Usually, **telecommunications** the science that deals with such communication (with sg or pl verb).

tel·e·com·mut·ing [,tɛləkə'mjutɪŋ] *n* the practice of working outside one's place of employment, by means of a computer link. **tel·e·com·mut·er** *n.*

tel·e·con·fer·ence ['tɛlə,kɒnfrəns] *n* a meeting, workshop, etc., with participants in various locations using closed-circuit television, speakerphones, etc. **tel·e·con·fer·enc·ing** *n.*

tel·e·gram See TELEGRAPH.

tel·e·graph ['tɛlə,græf] *n* an outdated system for sending or receiving coded messages by electricity, esp over a wire.
v **1** send (a message) by telegraph: *They telegraphed the news of the escape.* **2** send a telegram to (someone): *She telegraphed us yesterday.* **3** send by means of an order made by telegraph: *to telegraph flowers.* **4** *Informal* **a** in boxing, indicate unintentionally that one is about to punch. **b** give away (an intention) in advance.
tel·e·gram ['tɛlə,græm] *n* a message sent by telegraph. **tel·e·graph·ic** *adj* **1** to do with transmission by telegraph: *a telegraphic message.* **2** of prose style, clipped, concise, or elliptical. **tel·e·graph·i·cal·ly** *adv.*

tel·e·ki·ne·sis [,tɛləkə'nisɪs] *n* the moving of an object by means of the power of thought alone, without physical contact. **tel·e·ki·net·ic** [-'nɛtɪk] *adj.* ⟨*tele-* + Greek *kinēsis; kineein* move⟩

tel·e·mar·ket·ing [,tɛlə'mɑrkətɪŋ] *n* selling, advertising, or promoting goods or services over the telephone. **tel·e·mar·ket·er** *n.*

te·le·ol·o·gy [ˌtili'ɒlədʒi] *or* [ˌtɛli-] *n Philosophy* **1** the study of final causes or of ultimate purposes. **2 a** purpose as shown in nature, or the study of this. **b** the doctrine that all things in nature were made to fulfil a plan or design. **te·le·o·log·i·cal** *adj.* **te·le·ol·o·gist** *n.* ⟨Greek *telos* end⟩

te·lep·a·thy [tə'lɛpəθi] *n* the communication of one mind with another without speech or any sense used normally to communicate. **tel·e·path·ic** *adj.* **tel·e·path·i·cal·ly** *adv.* ⟨*tele-* + Greek *pathēs* feeling⟩ **tel·e·path** ['tɛlə,pæθ] *n* a person who is capable of telepathy.

tel·e·phone ['tɛlə,foun] *n* an apparatus for transmitting and receiving sound over distances by converting it into electrical impulses sent through a wire or via satellite. *v* communicate by telephone. ⟨*tele-* + Greek *phōnē* sound⟩
telephone book TELEPHONE DIRECTORY. **telephone booth** a small enclosure in a public place, containing a telephone that is operated by coins or by a card similar to a credit card. **telephone directory** a book containing an alphabetical list of names of individuals or companies subscribing to the telephone system in a particular area, together with their telephone numbers and, often, their addresses. **telephone number** a number assigned to a particular telephone and used in making connection to it.

tel·e·pho·to ['tɛlə,foutou] *adj* to do with a system of lenses for a camera, designed to produce a large image of a distant object. **telephoto lens** a lens for a camera that produces a large image of a distant object.

tel·e·port ['tɛlə,pɔrt] *v* move (something) without touching it, by telekinesis. **tel·e·port·a·tion** *n.* ⟨*tele-* + Latin *portare* carry⟩

tel·e·scope ['tɛlə,skoup] *n* **1** an instrument for directly viewing distant objects, using lenses or mirrors or both to make the object appear nearer and larger. **2** RADIO TELESCOPE. *v* **1** slide one part within the other like the sections of a hand telescope: *Built-in radio aerials are made so that they can be telescoped.* **2** force or be forced one into the other as in a collision: *When the two trains collided, the force of the crash telescoped the first few cars.* **3** shorten; condense. **tel·e·scop·ic** [-'skɒpɪk] *adj.* **tel·e·scop·i·cal·ly** *adv.* ⟨*tele-* + Greek *skopeein* look at, watch⟩

tel·es·the·sia [ˌtɛləs'θiʒə] *n* extrasensory perception of remote objects or happenings. **tel·es·thet·ic** [-'θetɪk], *adj.* ⟨*tele-* + Greek *aisthēsis* sensation, perception⟩

tel·e·thon ['tɛlə,θɒn] *n* a television program or series of programs lasting a very long time and, usually, serving to solicit funds for a charitable cause. ⟨*tele-* + (mara)*thon*⟩

tel·e·vi·sion ['tɛlə,vɪʒən] *n* **1** the process of transmitting the image of a scene by radio or wire so that a person in some other place can see it at once. **2** the apparatus on which these images may be seen. **3** the television

industry. **tel·e·vised** *adj.* **tel·e·vi·sion** *adj. Abbrev* **TV** *or* **T.V.**
tel·e·vise ['tɛlə,vaɪz] *v* pick up and transmit by television: *All the games are being televised.*

tell [tɛl] *v* **told, tell·ing 1** say or write: *Tell the truth.* **2** inform: *Tell us about it.* **3** reveal something secret or private: *Promise not to tell.* **4** know or distinguish: *He couldn't tell which house it was.* **5** order: *Tell him to stop!* **6** be an indication (*of*): *Her clenched hands told of her anger, though she said nothing.* **7** count (votes, etc.). **8** have effect or force: *Every blow told.* ⟨Old English *tellan* count, reckon, tell⟩
all told altogether: *We'll be 15 people all told.* **do tell!** *Informal* Oh, really? Is that a fact? (often sarcastic). **I tell you** I emphasize: *I tell you, he knows.* **let me tell you** I emphasize. **tell apart** distinguish one from the other: *Nobody could tell the sisters apart.* **tell me about it** *Slang* I have experienced exactly what you mean: *"This machine is such a pain to use." "Tell me about it!* **tell me another one** *Slang* that's hard to believe. **tell off a** count off. **b** *Informal* rebuke strongly: *His father told him off for staying out late.* **tell on a** tell tales about. **b** have a harmful effect on: *The strain told on the man's health.* **tell one's beads** See BEAD. **tell time** know what time it is by the clock: *a child learning to tell time.* **you're telling me** *Slang* I agree with you!
tell·a·ble *adj* capable or worthy of being told. **tell·er** *n* **1** a person who tells a story. **2** a cashier in a bank. **3** a person appointed to count votes, etc. **tell·ing** *adj* **1** impressive or effective: *a telling blow.* **2** significant: *a telling glance.* **tell·ing·ly** *adv.* **tell·tale** *n* a person who tells tales on others. *adj* revealing thoughts, actions, etc. that are supposed to be secret: *a telltale blush.*

tell·er See TELL.

tel·lu·ri·an [tɛ'lʊriən] *n* an inhabitant of the earth. **tel·lu·ri·an** *adj.* ⟨Latin *telluris* earth⟩

tel·lu·ri·um [tɛ'lʊriəm] *n* a rare element usually found combined with gold or other metals. *Symbol* **Te** ⟨Latin *telluris* earth⟩

te·mer·i·ty [tə'mɛrəti] *n* reckless boldness; rashness. **tem·er·ar·i·ous** [ˌtɛmə'rɛriəs] *adj* reckless; rash; bold. ⟨Latin *temere* heedlessly⟩

temp [tɛmp] *n Informal* temporary employee.

tem·per ['tɛmpər] *n* **1** a state of mind: *in a good temper.* **2** an angry state of mind: *In her temper she broke a vase.* **3** a calm state of mind: *He became angry and lost his temper.* **4** a tendency to anger quickly: *That young lady has quite a temper—watch out!* **5** the degree of hardness, toughness, etc. of a substance: *The temper of the clay was right for shaping.* *v* **1** moderate: *Temper justice with mercy.* **2** bring to a desired condition of hardness, toughness, etc.: *A painter tempers colours by mixing them with oil.* ⟨Latin *temperare*, orig observe due measure; *temporis* time, interval⟩
tem·pered *adj* **1** moderated. **2** having a particular disposition (in compounds): *an even-tempered person.* **3** treated by tempering: *a sword of tempered steel.*

tem·per·a ['tempərə] *n Painting* **1** a method in which colours are mixed with white of egg or some similar substance instead of oil. **2** a powdered colouring matter with gum or glue binder, used dissolved in water for painting posters, for children's artwork, etc. Also called **poster colour** or **poster paint.** ⟨Italian; *temperare* temper. See TEMPER.⟩

tem·per·a·ment ['temprəmənt] *n* **1** an individual's natural disposition: *a person of shy temperament.* **2** great sensitivity, esp when characterized by irritability: *Temperament is often attributed to actors and artists.* ⟨Latin *temperamentum; temperare.* See TEMPER.⟩ **tem·per·a·men·tal** *adj* **1** to do with temperament. **2** *of a machine, erratic; unpredictable.* **tem·per·a·men·tal·ly** *adv.*

tem·per·ance ['temprəns] *n* **1** moderation in action, habits, etc. **2** moderation in the use of alcoholic drinks. **3** the principle and practice of not using alcoholic drinks at all. ⟨Latin *temperare.* See TEMPER.⟩ **tem·per·ate** ['temprɪt] *adj* **1** not very hot and not very cold: *a temperate climate.* **2** to do with regions with a moderate climate: *temperate plants.* **3** moderate: *They spoke in a calm, temperate manner.* **4** moderate in using alcoholic drinks. **tem·per·ate·ly** *adv.*

tem·per·a·ture ['temprətʃər] *n* **1** the degree of heat or cold measured on a scale. **2** the degree of heat contained in a living body (normal about 37°C). **3** a level of body heat that is above normal: *He stayed home with a temperature.* ⟨Latin *temperatura; temporis* time⟩

tem·pest ['tempɪst] *n* **1** a violent windstorm. **2** a violent disturbance: *a tempest of cheers.* **tem·pes·tu·ous** *adj.* **tem·pes·tu·ous·ly** *adv.* **tem·pes·tu·ous·ness** *n.* ⟨Latin *tempestas; tempus* time, season⟩ **tempest in a teapot** great excitement or commotion over something unimportant.

tem·plate ['templɪt] *or* ['templeit] *n* **1** a thin piece of wood, plastic, etc., used as a pattern in cutting a shape out of metal, cloth, etc. **2** any pattern, model, or mould determining the form of a series of similar things. **3** *Computers* something used as a guide (for creating a spreadsheet, for drawing flowchart symbols, etc.): *She built her own income-tax spreadsheet from the templates provided.* ⟨French *templet,* diminutive of *temple,* device regulating width of cloth on a loom⟩

tem·ple[1] ['tempəl] *n* **1** a building used for religious services or worship. **2** specifically, **a** a synagogue. **b** a Mormon church. **3** any large building having a particular function: *a Masonic temple.* ⟨Latin *templum*⟩

tem·ple[2] ['tempəl] *n* the flat part of the head on either side of the forehead. ⟨Old French; Latin *tempora* pl of *tempus* side of the forehead, span⟩

tem·po ['tempou] *n, pl* **-pos** *or* **-pi** [-pi]. **1** *Music* the rate of speed of a composition: *The tempo of this piece is very fast.* **2** pace: *the fast tempo of modern life.* ⟨Italian = time; Latin *tempus*⟩

tem·po·ral ['tempərəl] *adj* **1** to do with time as opposed to eternity or as opposed to space. **2** to do with secular things: *temporal concerns.* **tem·po·ral·ly** *adv.* **tem·po·rary** *adj* lasting or used for a short time only; not permanent: *a temporary shelter. n* a person employed for a short time: *They hired several temporaries last summer.* **tem·po·rar·i·ly** *adv.* **tem·po·rar·i·ness** *n.*

tem·po·rize ['tempə,raɪz] *v* **1** evade action or decision in order to gain time, avoid trouble, etc. **2** negotiate, often only to gain time. **tem·po·ri·za·tion** *n.* **tem·po·riz·er** *n.* ⟨Latin *tempus, temporis* time⟩

tempt [tempt] *v* **1** try to make (a person) do something wrong by promising some advantage: *They tempted him to steal.* **2** appeal to strongly: *sweets that tempt one's appetite.* **3** cause to feel strongly inclined (usually in the passive): *I'm tempted to quit.* **4** provoke or defy: *It would be tempting fate to take that old car on the road.* **temp·ta·tion** *n.* **tempt·ing** *adj.* ⟨Latin *temptare* try⟩ **tempt·er** *n* **1** a person who tempts. **2 the Tempter** the Devil; Satan. **tempt·ress** *n* a woman who tempts, esp for sexual purposes.

tem·pu·ra [tem'purə] *n* a dish of shrimp, vegetables, etc. coated in a light batter and deep-fried. ⟨Japanese⟩

ten [tɛn] *n* **1** one more than nine; 10. **2** any set of ten persons or things: *Bundle the ticket books into tens.* **3** a playing card having ten spots: *a ten of clubs.* **4** a ten-dollar bill. **ten** *adj.* ⟨Old English *tien, tēn*⟩ **Ten Commandments** in the Bible, the ten rules for living and for worship that God gave to Moses on Mount Sinai. **ten·fold** *adj* **1** ten times as much or as many. **2** having ten parts. *adv* ten times as much or as many. **ten–gal·lon hat** a wide-brimmed hat, often worn by cowboys. **ten·pin** *n* **tenpins** (with a sg verb), a bowling game similar to fivepins, but using a larger and heavier ball. **tenth** *adj, n* **1** next after the 9th; 10th. **2** one, or being one, of 10 equal parts. **tenth·ly** *adv.*

ten·a·ble ['tenəbəl] *adj* capable of being held or defended: *a tenable position.* **ten·a·bly** *adv.* **ten·a·bil·i·ty** *or* **ten·a·ble·ness** *n.* ⟨French *tenir* hold; Latin *tenere*⟩

te·na·cious [tə'neiʃəs] *adj* **1** holding fast: *a tenacious grip.* **2** stubborn or persistent: *tenacious courage.* **3** esp good at remembering: *a tenacious memory.* **4** tending to cling: *tenacious burrs.* **5** not easily pulled apart: *a tenacious metal.* **te·na·cious·ly** *adv.* **te·nac·i·ty** [tə'næsəti] *n.* ⟨Latin *tenacis; tenere* hold⟩

ten·an·cy See TENANT.

ten·ant ['tenənt] *n* **1** a person paying rent for the use of the land or buildings of another person. **2** a person or thing that occupies: *Birds are tenants of the trees.* *v* hold or occupy as a tenant; inhabit. **ten·ant·less** *adj.* **ten·ant·a·ble** *adj.* ⟨See TENABLE.⟩ **ten·an·cy** *n* **1** the state of being a tenant. **2** the length of time a tenant occupies a property. **3** the period of holding an office or position: *a long tenancy as mayor*. **tenant elector** ❋ *British Columbia* a rent-paying resident (as opposed to a property owner) having the right to vote in municipal elections. **tenant farmer** a person who farms someone else's land, paying rent.

tend¹ [tend] *v* **1** have an inclination: *She tends to use large canvases for her paintings*. **2** lead as a general rule: *Authoritarianism tends toward oppression*. ⟨Latin *tendere* stretch, aim⟩ **tend·en·cy** *n* **1** an inclination toward a particular kind of behaviour, etc.: *a tendency to reject new ideas without considering them*. **2** trend: *The tendency in industry is toward more and more automation*.

tend² [tend] *v* **1** take care of: *She tends shop for her father*. **2** *Informal* pay attention (*to*): *Just tend to your work and never mind what everyone else is doing*. ⟨*attend*⟩

ten·den·tious [tɛn'dɛnʃəs] *adj* promoting a particular aim or point of view, esp in an aggressive or distorted manner; biassed: *tendentious writings*. **ten·den·tious·ly** *adv.* **ten·den·tious·ness** *n.* ⟨Latin *tendentia*. See TEND¹.⟩

ten·der¹ ['tɛndər] *adj* **1** soft: *tender meat*. **2** delicate: *tender young grass*. **3** kind; affectionate: *tender words*. **4** gentle: *tender, loving hands*. **5** young: *at the tender age of two*. **6** feeling pain or grief easily: *a tender heart*. **ten·der·ly** *adv.* **ten·der·ness** *n.* ⟨Old French *tendre*; Latin *tener*⟩
ten·der·foot *n, pl* **-foots** or **-feet** *Informal* **1** a newcomer to the pioneer life of the West. **2** a person not used to rough living and hardships. **3** an inexperienced person.
ten·der–heart·ed *adj* kindly; sympathetic.
ten·der–heart·ed·ly *adv.* **ten·der–heart·ed·ness** *n.*
ten·der·ize *v* make (meat) tender; soften by applying a tenderizer, pounding with a wooden mallet, etc. **ten·der·i·za·tion** *n.*
ten·der·iz·er *n* a substance containing enzymes or other softening ingredients, rubbed into meat to tenderize it.

ten·der² ['tɛndər] *v* **1** offer formally: *We tendered our thanks*. **2** *Business* make (an offer to buy, supply, etc.): *to tender for a contract*.
n **1** a formal offer: *She refused his tender of marriage*. **2** the thing offered. Money that may be offered as payment is called **legal tender**. **3** *Business* an offer to buy, supply, etc. **ten·der·er** *n.* ⟨Latin *tendere* extend⟩

tend·er³ ['tɛndər] *n* a small boat carried or towed by a big one and used for landing passengers. ⟨*tend²*⟩

ten·di·ni·tis *n* inflammation of a tendon.

ten·don ['tɛndən] *n* a tough band of tissue that joins a muscle to a bone or some other part; sinew. ⟨Latin *tendonis* influenced by *tendere* stretch; Greek *tenōn*⟩

ten·dril ['tɛndrəl] *n* **1** a threadlike part of a climbing plant that attaches itself to something and helps support the plant. **2** something resembling such a part of a plant: *tendrils of hair*. ⟨French *tendrillon; tendre*. See TENDER¹.⟩

ten·e·ment ['tɛnəmənt] *n* a building, esp in

a poor section of a city, divided into sets of rooms for separate families. ⟨Latin *tenere* hold⟩

ten·et ['tɛnɪt] *n* a doctrine, principle, belief, or opinion held as true. ⟨Latin = he holds⟩

ten·nis ['tɛnɪs] *n* a game played on an outdoor court or on grass by two or four players who hit a ball back and forth over a net with a **tennis racquet**. ⟨perhaps Old French *tenez* hold!; *tenir*, Latin *tenere*⟩
tennis court a place prepared and marked out to play tennis on.

ten·on ['tɛnən] *n* the end of a piece of wood cut so as to fit into a hole (the mortise) in another piece and so form a joint. ⟨Old French; *tenir* hold, Latin *tenere*⟩

ten·or ['tɛnər] *n* **1** the general tendency or direction: *The calm tenor of her life has never been disturbed by trouble*. **2** the general meaning: *I understand French well enough to get the tenor of her conversation*. **3** the second highest adult male singing voice. Compare COUNTERTENOR. **4** an instrument having a range next above that of the bass in a family of musical instruments.
adj to do with a tenor voice or instrument. ⟨Latin = a holding on; *tenere* hold⟩

tense¹ [tɛns] *adj* **1** stretched tight: *a tense rope*. **2** strained; unable to relax: *tense nerves*. **3** full of mental tension: *a tense moment*.
v stiffen. **tense·ly** *adv.* **tense·ness** *n.* ⟨Latin *tensus* pp of *tendere* stretch⟩
ten·sile ['tɛnsaɪl] *or* ['tɛnsəl] *adj* **1** to do with tension. **2** capable of being stretched; ductile.
tensile strength a measure of resistance to stress in the direction of length: *Steel has great tensile strength*. **ten·sil·i·ty** [tɛn'sɪləti] *n.*
ten·sion ['tɛnʃən] *n* **1** a stretched condition: *The tension of the spring is caused by the weight*. **2** mental stress or strain: *family tensions*. **3 a** a stress caused by the action of a pulling force. **b** the force exerting such a pull. **4** voltage: *high-tension wires*. **ten·sor** ['tɛnsər] *or* ['tɛnsɔr] *n* **1** *Physiology* a muscle that stretches or tightens some part of the body. **2** *Mathematics* a vector quantity that transforms linearly.

tense² [tɛns] *n* a form of a verb indicating a particular time, duration, etc. of an action or state. **tense·less** *adj.* ⟨Old French *tens* time⟩

tent [tɛnt] *n* a movable shelter, usually made of canvas or nylon and often supported by one or more poles and ropes. **tent·like** *adj.* ⟨Old French *tente*; Latin *tenta; tendere* stretch⟩
tent caterpillar the larva of any of various moths that lives in tentlike webs in trees.
tent ring a ring of stones used to hold down a tent such as a teepee or tupik.

ten·ta·cle ['tɛntəkəl] *n* **1** a flexible growth on the head or around the mouth of an animal, used to touch, hold, or move; feeler. **2** a sensitive, hairlike growth on a plant. **3** something that resembles a tentacle in its reach and grasp: *the tentacles of a dictator's power reach everywhere*. **ten·ta·cled** *adj.* ⟨Latin *tentaculum; tentare* try. See TENTATIVE.⟩

ten·ta·tive ['tɛntətɪv] *adj* **1** experimental: *a*

tentative plan. **2** not final; provisional: *a tentative schedule.* **3** hesitant; timid: *a tentative smile.* ⟨Latin *tentare* try, intensive of *tendere* stretch, aim; associated with *temptare* test⟩ **ten·ta·tive·ly** *adv.* **ten·ta·tive·ness** *n.*

ten·ter·hooks ['tɛntər,hʊks] *n* **on tenterhooks** in painful suspense; anxious. ⟨hooks securing cloth on a *tenter,* frame for drying; Latin *tentus* a pp of *tendere* stretch⟩

ten·u·ous ['tɛnjuəs] *adj* **1** slender. **2** not dense: *tenuous air.* **3** not firm or substantial: *a tenuous agreement.* **ten·u·ous·ly** *adv.* **ten·u·ous·ness** *n.* ⟨Latin *tenuis* thin⟩

ten·ure ['tɛnjər] *n* **1 a** a holding. **b** the right to hold. **2** the length of time of holding: *The tenure of office of the president of our club is one year.* **3** the manner of holding land, buildings, etc. from a feudal lord or superior. **4** permanent status in one's job, granted esp to a university professor, after certain conditions have been met. **ten·ured** *adj.* **ten·u·ri·al** [tə'njuriəl] *adj.* ⟨Old French; Latin *tenere* hold⟩

tep·id ['tɛpɪd] *adj* **1** slightly warm. **2** having little enthusiasm: *a tepid welcome.* **tep·id·ly** *adv.* **te·pid·i·ty** or **tep·id·ness** *n.* ⟨Latin *tepidus*⟩

te·qui·la [tə'kilə] *n* **1** a Mexican agave from which mescal is made. **2** a strong alcoholic liquor made by redistilling mescal. ⟨*Tequila,* a town in Mexico⟩

ter·bi·um ['tɜrbiəm] *n* a rare metallic element of the yttrium group. *Symbol* **Tb** ⟨*Ytterby,* a town in Sweden⟩

ter·cen·ten·ar·y [,tɜrsɛn'tɛnəri] or [-'tinəri] *adj, n* tricentennial. Also, **ter·cen·ten·ni·al.** ⟨Latin *ter* three times + CENTENARY⟩

ter·cet ['tɜrsɪt] or [tər'sɛt] *n* **1** a group of three lines rhyming together, or connected by rhyme with the adjacent group or groups of three lines. **2** *Music* triplet. ⟨Italian *terzetto* diminutive of *terzo* third, Latin *tertius*⟩

ter·gi·ver·sate ['tɜrdʒəvər,seit] *v* **1** change one's attitude with respect to a cause; turn renegade. **2** be evasive. **ter·gi·ver·sa·tor** *n.* **ter·gi·ver·sa·tion** *n.* ⟨Latin *tergum* back + *versare* spin; *vertere* turn⟩

ter·i·ya·ki [,tɛri'jɑki] or [,tɛri'jæki] *n* meat, fish, vegetables, etc. broiled or grilled after being marinated in specially seasoned soy sauce. ⟨Japanese *teri* shine + *yaki* broil⟩

term [tɜrm] *n* **1** a word or phrase used in a recognized sense in some particular subject, science, art, business, etc.: *medical terms.* **2** a word or expression: *an abstract term.* **3** the length of time that a thing lasts: *a president's term of office.* **4** one of the long periods into which the school year may be divided: *the fall term.* **5** *Mathematics* **a** one of the members in a proportion or ratio. **b** one or more numerals or symbols constituting a unit in an expression. Terms in an algebraic expression are always separated by + or –. **6 terms** *pl* **a** conditions: *the terms of a treaty.* **b** a way of speaking: *flattering terms.* **c** personal relations: *on good terms.* *v* name; describe as: *He might be termed*

handsome. **term·less** *adj.* ⟨Old French *terme;* Latin *terminus* end, limit, that which defines⟩ **bring to terms** force to reach an agreement. **come to terms** reach an agreement; become reconciled: *She finally came to terms with her own mortality.* **in terms of a** with regard to: *How's he doing in terms of financial stability?* **b** in the conceptual framework of: *It can't be understood in terms of pure science.*

ter·mi·nol·o·gy [,tɜrmə'nɒlədʒi] *n* the set of special terms used in a science, art, business, etc.: *medical terminology.* **ter·mi·no·log·i·cal** *adj.* **ter·mi·no·log·i·cal·ly** *adv.* **term insurance** life insurance that expires at the end of a specified period of time. **term paper** a major essay or report assigned for a term at an academic institution. **terms of reference** instructions indicating the scope of an inquiry.

ter·ma·gant ['tɜrməgənt] *n* a quarrelling, violent, scolding woman. **ter·ma·gant** *adj.* **ter·ma·gant·ly** *adv.* ⟨Old French *Tervagan,* fictitious Muslim deity⟩

ter·mi·na·ble, ter·mi·nal See TERMINATE.

ter·mi·nate ['tɜrmə,neit] *v* **1** bring to an end: *to terminate a partnership.* **2** come to an end or terminus: *His contract terminates soon.* **3** fire or dismiss (a worker). **4** *Slang* kill. **ter·mi·na·tion** *n.* **ter·mi·na·tor** *n.* ⟨Latin *terminare; terminus* end⟩

ter·mi·na·ble *adj* **1** able to be ended. **2** to end after a certain time: *a loan terminable in ten years.* **ter·mi·nal** *adj* **1** at the end. A terminal bud is one growing at the end of a stem, branch, etc. **2** coming at the end: *a terminal examination.* **3** at the end of a railway, bus, or aircraft line: *a terminal station.* **4** marking a boundary, limit, or end. **5 a** of a disease, incurable and fatal. **b** of a patient, fatally ill. *n* **1** the end part. **2** either end of a railway line, airline, shipping route, etc. where sheds, offices, etc., are located. **3** a station for the transfer of passengers and cargo, or any of the buildings located there: *We picked her up at the bus terminal.* **4** a device for making an electrical connection: *the terminals of a battery.* **5** an apparatus, such as a visual display unit, by which a user can give information to or receive information from a computer, communications system, etc. **ter·mi·nal·ly** *adv.* **ter·mi·nus** ['tɜrmənəs] *n, pl* **-nus·es** or **-ni** [-,naɪ] or [-,ni] **1** either end of a railway line, bus line, etc. **2** an ending place; final point; goal; end.

ter·mi·no·lo·gy See TERM.

ter·mite ['tɜrmaɪt] *n* any of an order of antlike insects that eat cellulose, the main constituent of wood, and can be very destructive if they invade buildings. ⟨Latin *termes* woodworm⟩

tern [tɜrn] *n* any of a subfamily of aquatic birds, related to gulls but usually smaller. ⟨Scandinavian⟩

ter·na·ry ['tɜrnəri] *adj* **1** consisting of three; based on three; triple. **2** third in order or rank. ⟨Latin *ternarius; ter* thrice⟩

terp·si·cho·re·an [ˌtɜrpsəkə'riən] *or* [-'kɔriən] *adj* to do with dancing. ⟨*Terpsichore*, in Greek myth the muse of dancing⟩

ter·race ['tɛrɪs] *n* **1** a flat level of land like a step, made by humans for cultivation. **2** a geological formation like this. **3** a paved outdoor space for lounging, dining, etc. *v* form into a terrace or terraces. ⟨Old French; Latin *terra* earth⟩

ter·ra cot·ta ['tɛrə 'kɒtə] a brownish red earthenware, used for tiles, decorations, etc. **ter·ra–cot·ta** *adj*. ⟨Italian = baked earth⟩
ter·ra fir·ma ['tɛrə 'fɜrmə] *Latin* dry land; solid earth. **ter·ra in·cog·ni·ta** ['tɛrə ˌɪnkɒg'nitə] *or* [ɪn'kɒgnətə] *Latin* unknown territory: *Anything other than English cuisine seemed to be terra incognita to the new chef.*

ter·rain [tə'rein] *n* a tract of land, esp considered as to its extent and natural features in relation to its use for some purpose. ⟨French; Latin *terra* land⟩

ter·ra·pin ['tɛrəpɪn] *n* any of various small, edible turtles living in fresh or brackish water. ⟨Algonquian⟩

ter·rar·i·um [tə'rɛriəm] *n*, *pl* **-i·ums** *or* **-i·a** [-iə] a glass or plastic enclosure in which plants or small animals are kept. ⟨Latin; *terra* land⟩

ter·raz·zo [tɛ'rɑtsou] *n* a floor made of small pieces of marble embedded in cement. ⟨Italian = terrace, balcony; *terra* earth⟩

ter·res·tri·al [tə'rɛstriəl] *adj* **1** to do with the earth. **2** of land, not water or air: *Islands and continents make up the terrestrial parts of the earth.* **3** living on the ground, not in the air or water or in trees: *terrestrial animals.* **4** growing on land: *terrestrial plants.* ⟨Latin *terrestris; terra* earth⟩

ter·ri·ble See TERRIFY.

ter·ri·er ['tɛriər] *n* any of several breeds of dog formerly used to pursue burrowing animals. ⟨French; Latin *terra* earth⟩

ter·rif·ic See TERRIFY.

ter·ri·fy ['tɛrəˌfaɪ] *v* fill with great fear; frighten very much. **ter·ri·fied** *adj*. **ter·ri·fy·ing** *adj*. **ter·ri·fy·ing·ly** *adv*. ⟨Latin *terrificare; terrere* terrify + *facere* make⟩
ter·ri·ble *adj* **1** causing great fear: *a terrible roar.* **2** severe: *the terrible suffering in wartime.* **3** *Informal* extremely bad, unpleasant, etc.: *She has a terrible temper.* **ter·ri·ble·ness** *n*. **ter·ri·bly** *adv*. **ter·rif·ic** [tə'rɪfɪk] *adj* **1** causing great fear; terrifying. **2** *Informal* extraordinary: *A terrific hot spell ruined many of the crops.* **3** *Slang* very good: *She is a terrific goalie.* **ter·rif·i·cal·ly** *adv*.

ter·rine [tɛ'rin] *or* [tə'rin] *n* **1** a dish for baking a pâté or similar combination of game, meat, vegetables, etc. **2** food cooked in such a dish. ⟨French. See TUREEN.⟩

ter·ri·to·ry ['tɛrəˌtɔri] *n* **1** land: *Much territory in Africa is desert.* **2** an area of land: *The company leased a large territory for oil explorations.* **3** land under the rule of a government or nation: *Most of Canadian territory is north of the 49th parallel.* **4 Territory** in Canada, a region which has its own elected legislature headed by a premier and which is administered by a commissioner appointed by the federal government: *the Northwest Territories, Yukon Territory.* **5** a region assigned to a sales representative or agent. **6** a domain of knowledge or activity: *Baby care used to be strictly female territory.* **7** *Ethology* the area defended by an animal or animals, esp against intruders of the same species. ⟨Latin *territorium; terra* land⟩

ter·ri·to·ri·al *adj* **1** to do with territory: *Many wars have been fought for territorial gain.* **2 Territorial** to do with a Territory: *the Territorial Council.* **3** *Ethology* characterized by territoriality. **ter·ri·to·ri·al·ly** *adv*. **Territorial Council ✱** formerly, the governing body of a Territory, now superseded by a Legislative Assembly. **ter·ri·to·ri·al·i·ty** *n* *Ethology* the behaviour shown by an animal in defining and defending its territory.

ter·ror ['tɛrər] *n* **1** great fear. **2** *Informal* a person or thing that causes much trouble and unpleasantness. **3** violence or threats of violence as a means of organized coercion; ⟨Latin; *terrere* terrify⟩
ter·ror·ism *n* **1** the act of terrorizing. **2** a method of opposing a government through the use of violence against civilians, taking of hostages, etc., to gain specific demands. **ter·ror·ist** *n*, *adj*. **ter·ror·ize** *v* **1** fill with terror. **2** subdue by causing terror. **ter·ror·i·za·tion** *n*. **ter·ror·iz·er** *n*. **ter·ror–strick·en** *adj* terrified.

ter·ry ['tɛri] *n* a rough cloth made of uncut looped yarn, usually cotton. Also, **terry cloth**. ⟨perhaps French *tiré* drawn⟩

terse [tɜrs] *adj* **1** brief and to the point: *a terse account.* **2** abrupt or curt. **terse·ly** *adv*. **terse·ness** *n*. ⟨Latin *tersus* pp of *tergere* polish⟩

ter·ti·ar·y ['tɜrʃəri] *or* ['tɜrʃiˌɛri] *n* **1** third in order of importance. **2 Tertiary** *Geology* the third chief period of time in the formation of the earth's surface, beginning approximately 66 million years ago. ⟨Latin *tertius* third⟩

ter·za ri·ma ['tɛrtsə 'rimə] an Italian form of iambic verse consisting of ten-syllable or eleven-syllable lines arranged in tercets, the middle line of each tercet rhyming with the first and third lines of the following tercet. Shelley's *Ode to the West Wind* is in terza rima. ⟨Italian = third rhyme⟩

TESL ['tɛsəl] teaching English as a second language.

tes·sel·late ['tɛsəˌleit] *v* **1** of blocks or tiles, be of such a shape that they fit together without leaving spaces. **2** make of such blocks or tiles. **tes·sel·la·tion** *n*. ⟨Latin *tessella*, diminutive of *tessera*. See TESSERA.⟩

tes·ser·a ['tɛsərə] *n*, *pl* **tes·ser·ae** [-ˌi] *or* [-ˌaɪ] **1** a small piece of marble, glass, etc. used in mosaic work. **2** a small square of bone, wood, etc. used in ancient times as a token, tally, ticket, die, etc. ⟨Latin, Greek = square or cubic piece; Greek dialect *tesseres* four⟩

tes·ser·act ['tɛsəˌrækt] *n* the generalization

of a cube to four dimensions. ⟨Greek dialect *tesseres* four + *actis* ray⟩

test [tɛst] *n* **1** a trial of knowledge or skill: *a test in arithmetic*. **2** any means of trial: *Trouble is a test of character*. **3** *Chemistry* an examination of a substance to see what it is or what it contains. **test** *v*. **test·a·ble** *adj*. **test·er** *n*. ⟨Old French *test* vessel used in assaying; Latin *testum*⟩

test case *Law* a case whose outcome may set a precedent. **test–drive** *v* **–drove, –driv·en, –driv·ing** drive (a vehicle) to try it out.

test–driv·er *n*. **test–mar·ket** *v* advertise and sell (a new product, etc.) experimentally and evaluate its success so as to make necessary changes. **test tube** a thin glass tube closed at one end, used in doing chemical tests. **test–tube baby** or **test tube baby** a baby conceived by IN VITRO FERTILIZATION.

Test applies to a trial to end uncertainty about quality or the presence of some substance, as by thorough examination: *The new plane passed all tests*. **Trial** applies to the process of discovering the qualities of something and establishing its worth, genuineness, strength, effect, etc.: *He gave the new toothpaste a trial*. **Experiment** applies to a process to find out something still unknown or to test conclusions, a hypothesis, etc.: *Experiments indicate the new drug will cure infections*.

tes·ta·ment ['tɛstəmənt] *n* **1** written instructions telling what to do with a person's property after his or her death; a will. **2** a solemn agreement, esp between God and human beings. **3** **Testament** a main division of the Christian Bible; the Old Testament or the New Testament. ⟨Latin *testamentum*; *testis* witness⟩

tes·tate ['tɛsteɪt] *adj* having made and left a valid will. **tes·ta·tor** ['tɛsteɪtər] *or* [tɛ'steɪtər] *n* a person who makes or has left a valid will.

test·er[1] See TEST.

tes·ter[2] ['tɛstər] *n* a canopy over a four-poster bed or an altar. ⟨Old French *testre*; Latin *testa* earthen pot⟩

tes·ti·cle ['tɛstəkəl] *n* the male reproductive organ of most animals, producing sperm. **tes·ti·cu·lar** [tɛ'stɪkjələr] *adj*. ⟨Latin *testiculus* diminutive of *testis*. See TESTIS.⟩

tes·ti·fy ['tɛstə,faɪ] *v* **1** give evidence (of); (usually with *to*): *The excellence of Shakespeare's plays testifies to his genius*. **2** declare solemnly. **3** *Law* give evidence under oath before a judge, coroner, etc. **tes·ti·fi·er** *n*. ⟨Latin *testis* witness⟩

tes·ti·mo·ny ['tɛstə,mouni] *n* **1** a statement, esp one used for evidence: *A witness gave testimony that the accused was at home at 9 p.m*. **2** evidence: *The students presented their teacher with a watch in testimony of their respect and affection*. **3** an open declaration or profession of one's faith. ⟨Latin *testimonium*; *testis* witness⟩

tes·ti·mo·ni·al *n* **1** a certificate of character, conduct, etc.; recommendation: *Ads for patent medicines often contain testimonials from people who have used them*. **2** something done to show esteem, gratitude, etc.: *We collected money for a testimonial to our retiring pastor*. **tes·ti·mo·ni·al** *adj*.

Testimony = something said or done to prove something true or false: *His speech was clear testimony of his good intentions*. **Evidence** applies to any facts that point toward, but do not prove, the truth or falsehood of something: *Running away was evidence of their guilt*. **Proof** = evidence that leaves no doubt: *Her actions were proof that she was telling the truth*.

tes·tis ['tɛstɪs] *n, pl* **-tes** testicle. ⟨Latin *testis* witness (of virility)⟩

tes·tos·ter·one [tɛ'stɒstə,roun] *n* a male steroid hormone produced mainly by the testicles. ⟨*testes* + *steroid*⟩

tes·ty ['tɛsti] *adj* easily irritated; impatient. **tes·ti·ly** *adv*. **tes·ti·ness** *n*. ⟨Anglo-French *testif* headstrong; Latin *testa* pot⟩

Tet [tɛt] the Vietnamese festival of the lunar New Year. ⟨Vietnamese⟩

tet·a·nus ['tɛtənəs] *n* a disease caused by bacilli usually entering the body through wounds, characterized by violent spasms, stiffness, and even death. Tetanus of the lower jaw is called lockjaw. **te·tan·ic** [tɛ'tænɪk] *adj*. ⟨Greek *tetanos*; *teinein* stretch⟩

tête–à–tête [tɛt ə 'tɛt] *adv* of two people, together in private: *They dined tête-à-tête*. *n* a private conversation between two people. **tête–à–tête** *adj*. ⟨French = head to head⟩

teth·er ['tɛðər] *n* a rope or chain for fastening an animal so that it can graze only within certain limits.
v fasten with a tether. ⟨Old Norse *tjóthr*⟩
at the end of one's tether at the end of one's resources or endurance

tet·ra ['tɛtrə] *n* any of various colourful freshwater fishes of tropical America, often kept in aquariums. ⟨Latin *tetragonopterus* former genus name⟩

tetra– [,tɛtrə] *or* [,tɛtræ] *combining form* four. Also, before vowels, **tetr-**. ⟨Greek *tetra-*, combining form of *tessares* four⟩

tet·rad ['tɛtræd] *n* **1** a group or collection of four. **2** *Chemistry* an atom, element, or radical with a valence of four. **3** *Biology* a group of four cells formed within a diploid cell by meiosis. **4** *Genetics* a group of four chromatids formed when a pair of chromosomes splits during meiosis. **tet·ra·he·dron** [,tɛtrə'hidrən] *n, pl* **-drons** or **-dra** [-drə] a solid with four faces. The most common tetrahedron is a pyramid whose base and three sides are equilateral triangles. **tet·ra·he·dral** *adj*. **te·tram·e·ter** [tɛ'træmətər] *n* a line of poetry having four metrical feet. **tet·rarch** ['tɛtrɑrk] *n* **1** in ancient Rome, the ruler of a part (orig a fourth part) of a province. **2** any subordinate ruler.

text [tɛkst] *n* **1** the main body of reading matter in a book, as distinct from appendices, illustrations, etc.: *This history contains 300 pages of text and about 50 pages of notes*. **2** the original words of a writer or public speaker: *Always quote the exact words of a text*. **3** a short Biblical passage used as the subject of a sermon: *The minister preached on the text "Love thy neighbour."* **4** textbook. *v Informal* communicate by TEXT MESSAGING. **text·less** *adj*. **tex·tu·al** ['tɛkstʃuəl] *adj*. ⟨Latin *textus* orig texture; *texere* weave⟩

text·book *n* a book used as a basis of instruction or as a standard reference in a particular course of study. *adj* typical; classic: *Her behaviour was a textbook example of how not to impress people*. **text editor** *Computers* a program for manipulating text files. **text messaging** the sending of messages on the Internet, usually using abbreviations, to appear on the screen of a cellphone or pager.

tex·tile ['tɛkstaɪl] *n* a woven or knit fabric. *adj* **1** to do with weaving. **2** to do with the making, selling, etc. of textiles: *the textile business*. ⟨Latin *textilis; texere* weave⟩

tex·ture ['tɛkstʃər] *n* the arrangement, thickness, etc. in a woven fabric: *Burlap has a coarser texture than linen*. *v* give a particular texture to. **tex·tur·al** *adj*. **tex·tur·al·ly** *adv*. ⟨Latin *textura; texere* weave⟩ **tex·tured** *adj* **1** having a certain texture. **2** bulky; looped: *textured wool*.

TGIF *Informal* Thank God it's Friday.

–th *suffix* used in the formation of ordinal numbers from the cardinal numbers four and up (*fourth, thirteenth, seventy-fifth*) except those compounds ending in -one, -two, or -three (*forty-first, eighty-second, thirty-third*). ⟨Old English -(o)*the*, (o)*tha*⟩

tha·lid·o·mide [θə'lɪdə,maɪd] *n* a drug formerly used as a tranquillizer. Its use by pregnant women was found to cause malformation of their babies.

thal·li·um ['θæliəm] *n* a rare metallic element that is soft and malleable. *Symbol* **Tl** ⟨Greek *thallos* green shoot⟩

than [ðæn] *conj, prep* **1** in comparison with: *This train is faster than that one*. **2** except: *How else can we come than on foot?* ⟨Old English⟩

Than acts usually as a conjunction joining comparative adjectives and adverbs with the second part of the comparison: *nicer than usual; more quickly than yesterday*. The part of speech, case, tense, etc. of the word following **than** depends on its function in the clause containing it, whether the clause itself is completely expressed or not: For example, *She likes him better than (she likes) me*. (comparing objects)
She likes him better than I (do). (comparing subjects)
In informal speech, however, the objective case is often used, making **than** into a preposition: *I am taller than him*.

than·a·tol·o·gy [,θænə'tɒlədʒi] *n* the scientific study of death and dying, esp from

a social perspective. **than·a·tol·o·gist** *n*. ⟨Greek *thanatos* death⟩

thank [θæŋk] *v* **1** express gratitude to: *Thank you for your hospitality*. **2** hold responsible: *You have only yourself to thank if you're late*. *n* **thanks** *pl* **a** the act of thanking: *to give thanks for a favour*. **b** a feeling of kindness and gratitude: *You have our heartful thanks*. *interj* **thanks** *Informal* thank you. ⟨Old English *thanc*, orig thought⟩ **thank goodness** (or **heavens,** or **God,** etc.), an expression of relief or satisfaction: *Thank goodness, they arrived safely*. **thank you** the standard courteous expression of appreciation: *"It's a lovely present. Thank you."* **thank·ful** *adj* feeling or expressing thanks; grateful. **thank·ful·ly** *adv* **1** gratefully. **2** (as a sentence modifier) fortunately: *She had an accident; thankfully, she was not hurt*. **thank·ful·ness** *n*. **thank·less** *adj* **1** not appreciated: *Giving advice is a thankless act*. **2** not feeling or expressing thanks: *The thankless woman did nothing for the neighbour who had helped her*. **thank·less·ly** *adv*. **thank·less·ness** *n*. **thanks·giv·ing** ['θæŋks,gɪvɪŋ] or [,θæŋks'gɪvɪŋ] *n* a giving of thanks. **Thanksgiving Day 1** in Canada, the second Monday in October, a statutory holiday on which to give thanks for the harvest. **2** in the US, the fourth Thursday in November, a holiday observed for similar reasons. **thanks to** owing to; because of: *Thanks to his efforts, we won the game*. **thank–you** *n* an expression of thanks: *She left without so much as a goodbye or a thank-you*. *adj* expressing thanks: *a thank-you letter*.

that [ðæt] *pl* **those** [ðouz] *adj* indicating some person, thing, idea, etc., esp one some distance away in place or time: *Do you know that boy over there?* When used with *this, that* refers to something farther away: *That book is better than this one*. *pron* **1** some person, thing, idea, etc., esp one that is to be emphasized or contrasted with another nearer in place or time: *That is a better drawing than this*. **2** (*relative pron*) which, who, or whom: *Is he the man that trains dogs?* **3** the one; the thing or person to be identified: *Those calling in will win a prize*. **4 a** at or in which: *The year that we went to England, they had a drought*. **b** *Informal* at or in which: *For our holiday we went to the place that we first met*. *conj* **that** is used: **1** to introduce a noun clause and connect it with the preceding verb as its object: *I know that 6 and 4 are 10*. **2** to show purpose: *He ran fast that he might not be late*. **3** to show result: *He ran so fast that he was five minutes early*. *adv* **1** to that extent or degree; so. *He cannot stay up that late*. **2** very (with negatives and often preceded by *all*): *He's handsome, but not that bright*. ⟨Old English *thæt*⟩ **at that** *Informal* **a** with no more talk, work, etc.: *Let's leave it at that*. **b** in fact; moreover: *She made it all by herself, and without a recipe at that*. **in that** in the sense that: *His plan is superior in that it is more practical*. **that is**

a namely: *Only one person, that is, the principal herself, opposed the idea.* **b** in other words: *If you have other plans, that is, if you can't go, just say so.* **that's that** *Informal* that is finished: *We're not going, and that's that.*

That introduces only clauses that are restrictive: *The book that she selected for her report was the longest in the list.* **Which** may also introduce clauses that are non-restrictive. Note that the non-restrictive clause is set off by commas: *The privilege of free speech, which we hold so dear, is now endangered.*

thatch [θætʃ] *n* **1** straw, rushes, etc., bound or woven together and used as a roof or covering. **2** the layer of decaying bits of grass, leaves, etc., at the base of growing vegetation: *Rake your lawn to clear the thatch.* *v* roof or cover with thatch. **thatch·y** *adj.* **thatch·er** *n.* ⟨Old English *thæc*⟩

thaw [θɒ] *v* **1** melt (ice, snow, or anything frozen): *Thaw these chicken legs before frying them.* **2** become free of frost, ice, etc.: *The ground has begun to thaw.* **3** make or become less formal in manner; soften: *Our shyness thawed under her kindness.*
n **1** a thawing. **2** a period of weather above the freezing point (0°C). ⟨Old English *thawian*⟩

the¹ [ðə]; *stressed, and before vowels* [ði] *definite article* The word *the* shows that a certain one (or ones) is meant, already identified, or about to be identified. Various special uses are: **1** to mark a noun as indicating something well-known or unique: *the Rockies, the hour of victory.* **2** to mark a noun as indicating the best known or most important of its kind (usually stressed): *the* [ði] *place to dine.* **3** to mark a noun as being used generically: *The dog is a mammal.* **4** before adjectives used as nouns: *to visit the sick.* ⟨Old English *sē* (masculine, subject form) that⟩

Repetition of the article before various nouns of a series emphasizes their distinctness: *The colour, the fragrance, and the size of these flowers make them universal favourites.* Compare: *The colour, fragrance, and size of these flowers make them universal favourites.*

the² [ðə] *or* [ði] *adv* The word *the* is used to modify an adjective or adverb in the comparative degree: **1** signifying 'on that account': *If you start now, you will be back the sooner.* **2** used correlatively, and signifying 'by how much, by so much': *the more the merrier, the sooner the better.* ⟨Old English *thŷ*⟩

the·a·tre ['θiətər] *n* **1** a place where stage performances are acted or where films are shown. **2** a scene of action: *France has often been a theatre of war.* **3 a** drama. **b** a situation, dialogue, etc. considered as to its effectiveness on the stage: *This scene is bad theatre.* **4** the community of people engaged in theatrical work: *She's been in the theatre for years.* **5** the study of acting, directing, stagecraft, etc., as an academic subject: *She*

took her degree in theatre. Sometimes, **the·a·ter.** ⟨Greek *theatron; thea* view⟩
the·a·tre·go·er [-ˌgouər] *n* one who goes to the theatre, esp one who goes frequently. **the·a·tre–in–the–round** *n* a theatre having the stage situated in the centre, surrounded with seats on all sides. **theatre of the absurd** drama that represents absurd situations and rejects the usual dramatic conventions in order to express the meaninglessness and alienation of human existence. **the·at·ri·cal** [θi'ætrɪkəl] *adj* **1** to do with the theatre or actors: *a theatrical company.* **2** for display or effect; artificial; melodramatic; exaggerated. **the·at·ri·cal·i·ty** *n.* **the·at·ri·cal·ly** *adj.* **theatricals** *pl* theatrics. **the·at·rics** *n, pl* **1** dramatic performances, esp as given by amateurs. **2** actions of a theatrical character.

thee See THOU.

theft See THIEF.

their [ðɛr] *adj* **1** a possessive form of THEY: *That's their house.* **2** **Their** a word used in certain formal titles: *Their Majesties are resting.* ⟨Old Norse *theirra*⟩
theirs *pron* a possessive form of THEY: *The painting isn't theirs, it's just rented.* **of theirs** associated with them: *We're friends of theirs.*

Their is a determiner and is always followed by a noun: *This is their farm.* **Theirs** is a pronoun and stands alone: *This farm is theirs.*

the·ism ['θiɪzəm] *n* **1** belief in one god as the creator of the universe, and who has a personal connection to its creatures. Opposed to DEISM. See DEITY. **2** religious faith. **the·ist** *n.* **the·is·tic** *adj.* **the·is·ti·cal·ly** *adv.* ⟨Greek *theos* god⟩

them See THEY.

theme [θim] *n* **1** a topic; subject: *Patriotism was the speaker's theme.* **2** a short written composition. **3** a dominant, recurring and unifying idea or motif. **4** *Music* the principal melody in a composition. **5 a** a melody used to identify a particular radio or television program; signature tune. **b** the main piece of music recurring throughout a film: *Can you play the theme from Dr. Zhivago?* **the·mat·ic** [θə'mætɪk] *adj.* ⟨Greek *thema* literally, something set down⟩
theme park an amusement centre in which the buildings, landscaping, rides, etc., are designed around a central theme, such as outer space, cartoon characters, etc. **theme song** THEME (def. 5).

them·selves See THEY.

then [ðɛn] *adv* **1** at that time: *Prices were lower then.* **2** soon afterwards: *The noise stopped, and then began again.* **3** next in time or place: *First comes spring, then summer.* **4** in that case: *If you broke the window, then you should pay for it.*
n that time: *By then we shall know the result.* *adj* being at that time in the past: *the then prime minister.* ⟨Old English *thænne*⟩
but then but at the same time. **then and there** at that time and place.

thence [θɛns] or [ðɛns] adv Literary, archaic **1** from there: A few kilometres thence was a river. **2** from that time: a year thence. ⟨Middle English thennes; Old English thanane⟩
thence·forth adv from then on.

the·oc·ra·cy [θi'ɒkrəsi] n, pl **1** a system of government in which a god is recognized as the supreme civil ruler. **2** a system of government by priests. **the·o·crat·ic** [ˌθiə'krætɪk] adj. **the·o·crat·i·cal·ly** adv. ⟨Greek theos god + kratos rule⟩

the·od·o·lite [θi'ɒdə,ləɪt] n a surveying instrument for measuring horizontal and vertical angles. **the·od·o·lit·ic** [-'lɪtɪk] adj. ⟨origin unknown⟩

the·ol·o·gy [θi'ɒlədʒi] n **1** the study of the nature of God. **2** the study of religious beliefs. **3** a system of religious beliefs. **the·o·lo·gian** [-'loudʒən] n. **the·o·log·i·cal** adj. **the·o·log·i·cal·ly** adv. ⟨Greek theos god⟩
the·ol·o·gize v engage in theological speculation.

the·o·rem ['θirəm] n **1** Mathematics **a** a statement to be proved. **b** a statement of relations that can be expressed by an equation or formula. **2** any statement that can be proved to be true. ⟨Greek theōreein consider; thea a sight + horaein see⟩

the·o·ry n **1** an explanation based on speculation. **2** an explanation based on observation and reasoning: the theory of relativity. **3** the principles of a science or art rather than its practice: the theory of music. **4** an idea about something. **5** speculative thought as opposed to fact. **6** Mathematics a set of theorems that constitute a systematic view of some branch of mathematics: the theory of probabilities. ⟨Greek theōria; theōreein. See THEOREM.⟩ **the·o·ret·i·cal** [ˌθiə'rɛtəkəl] or **the·o·ret·ic** adj. **the·o·ret·i·cal·ly** adv. **the·o·re·ti·cian** n a person who knows much about the theory of an art, science, etc. **the·o·rist** n a person who forms theories. **the·o·rize** v form a theory; speculate. **the·o·ri·za·tion** n. **the·o·riz·er** n.

the·os·o·phy [θi'ɒsəfi] n a philosophy or religion that claims to have insight through spiritual self-development. Modern theosophy includes many of the teachings of Buddhism. New Age is a form of theosophy. **the·o·soph·i·cal** adj. **the·os·o·phist** n. ⟨Greek theos god + sophos wise⟩

ther·a·peu·tic [ˌθɛrə'pjutɪk] adj to do with the treatment of disease or the preservation of good health. **ther·a·peu·ti·cal·ly** adv. ⟨Greek therapeuein treat; theraps attendant⟩

ther·a·py ['θɛrəpi] n the treatment of diseases or disorders after or instead of surgery (often in compounds): physiotherapy. **ther·a·pist** n.

there [ðɛr] adv **1** in, at, or to that place: Sit there. **2** at that point in an action, speech, etc.: You have done enough; you may stop there. **3** in that matter, particular, or respect: You are mistaken there. **4** A meaningless there is used as a dummy subject in sentences in which the real subject has been moved out of the usual slot: There are three new houses on our street. **5** There is used with inversion of the verb and real subject to call attention to some person or thing: There goes the bell.
n that place: From there go on to Hamilton. interj There is used to express satisfaction, defiance, dismay, etc.: There, there, don't cry. ⟨Old English thǣr⟩
all there Informal **a** alert. **b** not crazy; sane. **there·a·bouts** ['ðɛrə,baʊts] or [ˌðɛrə'baʊts] adv **1** near that place: She's from Halifax, or thereabouts. **2** near that time. **3** near that number, amount, etc. **there·af·ter** adv after that. **there·at** adv **1** when that happened. **2** because of that. **3** at that place. **there·by** adv **1** in that way: He wished to travel and thereby study the customs of other countries. **2** in connection with that: We won the game, and thereby hangs a tale. **3** near there. **there·in** adv in that place, matter, respect, etc. **there·of** adv **1** of that. **2** from that source. **there·on** adv **1** on that. **2** immediately after that. **there·to** adv Formal **1** to that; to it: The castle stands on a hill, and the road thereto is steep. **2** also. **there·un·der** adv **1** under that; under it. **2** according to that. **there·up·on** adv **1** immediately after that. **2** therefore. **3** on that; on it. **there·with** adv Formal **1** with that; with it. **2** immediately after that.

there·fore ['ðɛr,fɔr] adv for that reason; as a result of that; consequently. ⟨Middle English ther there + fore, for for⟩

ther·mal ['θɜrməl] adj **1** to do with heat or warmth: thermal springs. **2** designed to conserve heat or warmth: thermal underwear. n a column of rising air that is warmer than the surrounding air. Thermals are used by gliders and by certain migratory birds to gain altitude. **ther·mal·ly** adv. ⟨Greek thermē heat⟩
thermal spring a natural hot spring.

thermo– combining form heat. ⟨Greek thermē⟩
ther·mo·dy·nam·ics n the branch of physics that deals with relations between heat and mechanical energy. **ther·mo·dy·nam·ic** adj. **ther·mo·dy·nam·i·cal·ly** adv. **thermodynamic temperature** temperature considered as a physical quantity that measures the thermal energy possessed by a body, expressed in kelvins. Symbol T See also ABSOLUTE ZERO. **ther·mo–e·lec·tric** or **ther·mo–e·lec·tri·cal** adj to do with the relation between heat and

electricity. **ther·mo–e·lec·tri·cal·ly** *adv.*
ther·mom·e·ter [θər'mɒmətər] *n* an instrument
for measuring temperature. **ther·mo·nu·cle·ar**
adj **1** to do with the fusion of atoms (as in
the hydrogen bomb) through very high
temperature: *a thermonuclear reaction.* **2** to do
with the heat energy released in a nuclear
reactor. **ther·mo·sphere** *n* the layer of the
atmosphere lying above the mesosphere,
extending from about 85 km to about
450 km above the earth's surface, where the
exosphere begins, and characterized by an
increase in temperature with increasing
altitude. Air is very thin in the
thermosphere, where it is very hot.
ther·mo·stat *n* an automatic device for
regulating temperature. **ther·mo·stat·ic** *adj.*
ther·mo·stat·i·cal·ly *adv.* **ther·mot·ro·pism**
[θər'mɒtrə,pɪzəm] *n Botany* the oriented
growth of a plant in response to a source of
heat, either toward it or away from it.
ther·mo·trop·ic [-mə'trɒpɪk] *adj.*

the·sau·rus [θɪ'sɔrəs] *n, pl* **-ruses** or **-ri** [-raɪ]
or [-ri] **1** a book of synonyms and antonyms.
2 a computer program serving a similar
purpose. ⟨Greek *thesauros* treasury⟩

these See THIS.

the·sis ['θisɪs] *n, pl* **-ses** [-siz] **1** a statement to
be proved or to be maintained against
objections. **2** a long essay, esp one based on
original research and presented by a
candidate for a postgraduate degree. ⟨Greek
= a setting down; *tithenai* set, put⟩

they [ðeɪ] *pron pl, subj* **they** *obj* **them** *poss*
theirs **1** plural of HE, SHE, or IT. **2** *Informal*
people in general: *They say she's really a very
serious person.* ⟨Old Norse *their*⟩
them·selves *pron* **1** a reflexive pronoun, the
form of **they** used as an object: *They hurt
themselves in climbing down.* **2** a form of **they**
or **them** added for emphasis: *They did it
themselves.* **3** their usual selves: *They were ill
and were not themselves.*

USAGE

They in all its inflected forms is increasingly
used in informal English, as a gender-neutral
singular pronoun: *Someone left their coat
behind. If anyone calls, tell them I'm out.*
This conveniently avoids the more circuitous
"he or she" ("his or her," etc.), especially
where it would occur several times in the
same passage. Many people strongly object to
this usage, and it can be avoided in formal
English by rewriting.

thick [θɪk] *adj* **1** of an object, filling much
space from one surface to the other: *thick
stone walls.* **2** large in diameter relative to
length: *a thick cable.* **3** measuring between
two opposite surfaces of an object: *3 cm
thick.* **4** dense, abundant, or heavy: *thick hair,
thick fumes.* **5** like syrup, not like water: *Thick
liquids pour more slowly than thin liquids.*
6 stupid; dull: *too thick to come in out of the
rain.* **7** *Informal* very friendly: *She's very thick
with the boss these days.* **8** *Informal* too much
to be endured: *That's a bit thick!*

adv thickly: *Spread the jam thick.*
n the part that is thickest, most crowded,
most active, etc.: *in the thick of the fight.*
thick·ly *adv.* ⟨Old English *thicce*⟩
lay it on thick *Informal* praise or blame too
much. **thick skin** the ability to take criticism,
etc. without being affected by it. **thick–skinned**
adj. **through thick and thin** in good times
and bad.
thick·en *v* **1** make or become thick or
thicker. **2** of the plot of a play, novel, etc.,
become more complex. **thick·en·er** *n.*
thick·en·ing *n* **1** a material used to thicken
something. **2** a thickened part. **3** the process
of making or becoming thick or thicker.
thick·et *n* a dense growth of shrubs.
thick–head·ed *adj* dull. **thick·ish** *adj*
somewhat thick. **thick·ness** *n* **1** the distance
between opposite surfaces; depth, not length
or breadth. **2** the thick part. **3** a layer: *three
thicknesses of paper.* **thick·set** *adj* **1** closely
planted, etc.: *a thickset hedge.* **2** thick in form
or build: *a thickset man.*

thief [θif] *n, pl* **thieves** [θivz] a person who
steals, esp one who steals secretly and
without using force. ⟨Old English *thēof*⟩
theft [θeft] *n* **1** the act of stealing: *She was
put in prison for theft.* **2** an instance of
stealing: *The theft of the jewels caused much
excitement.* **thieve** [θiv] *v.* **thiev·er·y** *n.* ⟨Old
English *thēoft; thēof* thief⟩
thiev·ish *adj* **1** likely to steal. **2** like a thief;
stealthy; sly. **thiev·ish·ly** *adv.* **thiev·ish·ness** *n.*

SYNONYMS

Thief applies to someone who takes
something in a secret or stealthy way: *A thief
stole my bicycle from the yard.* **Robber** applies
to one who takes another's property by force
or threats of violence: *The robbers bound and
gagged the security guard.*

thigh [θaɪ] *n* **1** in humans, the part of the leg
between the hip and the knee. **2** the femoral
region of certain other creatures, esp poultry.
⟨Old English *thēoh*⟩

thim·ble ['θɪmbəl] *n* a small cap of metal,
plastic, etc. worn on the finger to protect it
when pushing the needle in sewing. ⟨Old
English *thȳmel; thūma* thumb⟩
thim·ble·ful *n* as much as a thimble will
hold; a very small quantity.

thin [θɪn] *adj* **thin·ner, thin·nest** *adj* **1** of an
object, filling little space from one surface to
the other: *thin paper.* **2** having little flesh or
fat: *a long, thin face.* **3** scanty; sparse; not
dense: *thin hair, thin air.* **4** not like syrup, like
water: *thin milk.* **5** having little depth,
fullness, or intensity: *a thin colour.* **6** easily
seen through; sheer: *a thin shirt.* **7** of
something abstract, weak: *a thin excuse.*
v **thinned, thin·ning** **1** make or become thin:
to thin paint. **2** make or become less crowded
(often with *out*): *to thin a row of beets.*
thin·ly *adv.* **thin·ness** *n.* ⟨Old English *thynne*⟩
thin skin the condition of being easily
affected by criticism, etc. **thin–skinned** *adj.*
thin·ner *n* a substance added to another to
give it a more fluid consistency, as

turpentine to paint. *adj* comparative of THIN.

thin·nish *adj* somewhat thin.

thine See THOU.

thing [θɪŋ] *n* **1** any object: *Put these things away.* **2** any act, deed, fact, situation, idea, or concern: *A strange thing happened.* **3 a** a person or creature (referred to with pity, scorn, condescension, etc.): *a mean thing.* **b** any object whose name is forgotten, unknown, or which is regarded with contempt: *Are you still driving around in that thing?* **4 the thing** anything considered desirable, suitable, important, etc.: *the latest thing in swimsuits.* **5 things** *pl* **a** belongings: *Take your things and go.* **b** clothes: *Put on your things.* **c** equipment for a given purpose: *I'll need some painting things for that course.* **d** circumstances: *How are things?* **6** *Informal* **a** a person's special interest or strong point: *Gardening is not my thing.* **b** an irrational attitude to someone or something: *I have a thing about driving in the city.* ⟨Old English⟩ **do one's (own) thing** do what one enjoys most. **know a thing or two (about)** be experienced (in). **make a (big) thing (out) of** blow out of proportion. **make a good thing of** profit from. **see** (or **hear**) **things** have hallucinations.

thing·a·ma·bob, thing·a·ma·jig, or **thing·um·my** [ˈθɪŋəmi] *n Informal* something whose name one forgets or does not bother to mention.

think [θɪŋk] *v* **thought, think·ing** **1** generate ideas, link concepts, etc.: *I can't think clearly right now.* **2** have one's thoughts full of: *She thinks of nothing but sports.* **3** have a mental image (with *of*): *He had thought of her as still a child.* **4** have as an opinion; believe: *What do you think about the new budget?* **5** consider: *Think before answering.* **6** remember (often with *of*): *I can't think of her name.* **7** consider the needs or happiness (*of*): *She thinks of no one but herself.* **8** entertain the possibility of (usually with a negative): *I wouldn't think of parking in your spot!* *n Informal* a period of pondering: *to sit down for a long think on something.* See also THOUGHT. *adj* to do with contemplation: *a think session.* **think·a·ble** *adj.* **think·er** *n.* ⟨Old English *thencan*⟩ **think aloud** say what one is thinking. **think better of a** change one's mind about: *She was going to stay, but then thought better of it and went home.* **b** have a more favourable opinion of (a person, idea, etc.): *She thought better of him for his apology.* **think fit** regard as a suitable course of action: *We thought fit to stay away for a few days.* **think little** (or **nothing**) **of** have no scruples about: *They think nothing of taking supplies home from the office.* **think nothing of it** you're welcome (in response to an expression of thanks). **think out** plan or understand by thinking. **think out loud** say what one is thinking. **think over** consider carefully. **think the world** (or **much,** etc.) **of** regard very highly. **think through** think about until one reaches an understanding. **think twice** think again before acting: *I'd think twice about jogging*

after dark if I were you. **think up** plan or discover by thinking: *We will have to think up a better strategy.*

think·ing *adj* **1** reasoning. **2** thoughtful. *n* THOUGHT. **put on one's thinking cap** take time for thinking over something. **think piece** *Slang* a piece of analytic journalistic writing. **think–tank** *n Informal* a centre for technological research, often engaged in government and defence projects: *The Fraser Institute is a well-known Canadian think-tank.*

third [θɜrd] *adj* **1** next after the second; 3rd. **2** being one of three equal parts. *n* **1** the next after the second. **2** one of three equal parts: *The pizza was divided into thirds.* **3** *Music* **a** a tone three degrees from another tone. **b** the interval between such tones. **c** the combination of such tones. **4** in cars and similar machines, the forward gear next above second. **5** *Curling* the team member next in importance to the skip, and next after the second player in throwing the rock. ⟨Old English *thirda, thridda; thrēo* three⟩ **third base** *Baseball* the base across from first base. **third–class** in some railway, ship, etc., systems, the least expensive accommodation. **third–class** *adj.* **third degree** the use of severe treatment by the police to force a person to give information or to make a confession. **third–de·gree** *adj* of a burn, the most severe, damaging the lower layers of tissue. **third estate** persons not in the nobility or clergy; common people. **third·ly** *adv* in the third place. **third party** **1** a person or group affected by the actions of two major parties in a contract, arrangement, etc. **2** a person or group unaffected by the actions or arrangements of two others, and therefore impartial. **third person** **1** the form of a pronoun or verb used to refer to a person who is neither the person speaking nor the one spoken to. **2** a style of narration that makes use primarily of such forms: *The story is told in the third person.* **third rail** a rail parallelling the ordinary rails of a railway, with a powerful electric current. **third–rate** *adj* distinctly inferior. **third–rat·er** *n.* **Third World** the developing countries of the world. **third–world** *adj.*

thirst [θɜrst] *n* **1** desire or need for something to drink. **2** a strong desire: *a thirst for adventure.* **thirst** *v.* ⟨Old English *thurst*⟩ **thirst·y** *adj* **1** feeling thirst. **2** without moisture. **3** *Informal* arousing thirst: *Mowing the lawn is thirsty work.* **4** eager. **thirst·i·ly** *adv.*

thir·teen [ˈθɜrtˈtin] *n* **1** three more than ten; 13. **2** any set of 13 persons or things. **thir·teen** *adj.* ⟨Old English *thrēotēne*⟩ **thir·teenth** *adj, n* **1** next after the 12th; 13th. **2** one, or being one, of 13 equal parts.

thir·ty [ˈθɜrti] *n* **1** three times ten; 30. **2 thirties** *pl* the years from 30 through 39, esp of a century or of a person's life: *His grandfather still vividly remembered the drought of the thirties.* **thir·ty** *adj.* ⟨Old English *thrītig*⟩ **thir·ti·eth** [ˈθɜrtiɪθ] *adj, n* **1** next after the 29th; 30th. **2** one, or being one, of 30 equal parts.

this [ðɪs] *pl* **these** [ðiz] *adj* **1** indicating some person, thing, etc. esp one near in place or time: *I liked this book a lot.* When used with *that, this* refers to something closer: *This route is shorter than that one.* **2** *Informal* designating a certain unidentified person or thing: *I saw this really tall guy in the coffee shop today.* *pron* some person, thing, idea, etc., esp one that is to be emphasized or contrasted with another farther away in place or time: *This is a better drawing than that.* *adv* to this extent or degree. ⟨Old English⟩

this·tle ['θɪsəl] *n* any plants of the composite family having prickly leaves and stem and showy flowers. ⟨Old English *thistel*⟩ **this·tle·down** *n* the down or fluff from the ripe flower head of a thistle. **this·tly** *adj* **1** prickly. **2** having many thistles.

thith·er ['θɪðər] *Archaic, poetic, or formal adv* toward that place. ⟨Old English *thider*⟩

thong [θɒŋ] *n* **1** a narrow strip of leather, etc., esp one used as a fastening. **2** the lash of a whip. **3** a kind of sandal held on the foot by a narrow piece that passes between the first and second toes. ⟨Old English *thwang*⟩

tho·rax ['θɔræks] *n, pl* **-rax·es** or **-ra·ces** [-rə,siz] **1** the part of the body between the neck and the abdomen. **2** the second division of an insect's body, between head and abdomen. **tho·rac·ic** [θə'ræsɪk] *adj.* ⟨Greek⟩

tho·ri·um ['θɔriəm] *n* a radioactive metallic element present in certain rare minerals. *Symbol* **Th** ⟨Thor, Norse god⟩

thorn [θɔrn] *n* a sharp-pointed growth on a plant, esp a tree or shrub. ⟨Old English⟩ **thorn in the flesh** (or **side**) a cause of discomfort or irritation. **thorn·y** *adj* **1** having thorns or spines. **2** full of difficulties or complexities.

thor·ough ['θɜrou] *or* ['θɜrə] *adj* **1** complete: *a thorough search.* **2** doing all that should be done: *The doctor was very thorough with the patient.* **3** absolute: *I've made a thorough fool of myself.* **thor·ough·ly** *adv.* **thor·ough·ness** *n.* ⟨Old English *thuruh* variant of *thurh* through⟩ **thor·ough·bred** *adj* of pure stock. *n* **1** Thoroughbred a breed of horse, used esp in racing, orig bred from European mares and Arabian stallions. **2** a pedigreed animal. **thor·ough·fare** *n* a main road; highway. **no thoroughfare** do not go through. **thor·ough·go·ing** *adj* thorough; complete.

those See THAT.

thou[1] [ðaʊ] *pron Archaic, poetic* you (sg). ⟨Old English *thū*⟩ **thee** [ði] the objective form of THOU. **thine** [ðaɪn] the possessive form of THOU. *adj* the form of THY used before a vowel or mute *h*: *thine honour.* **thy** [ðaɪ] *adj* the possessive form of THOU used before a consonant: *Thy will be done.* **thy·self** the reflexive or intensive form of THOU: *Thou shalt love thy neighbour as thyself.*

thou[2] [ðaʊ] *n Informal* thousand: *The contract is worth forty thou.*

though [ðou] *conj* **1** in spite of the fact that: *Though it was pouring, the girls went to school.* **2** nevertheless: *He is better, though not yet cured.* **3** even if: *Though I fail, I shall try again.* *adv* however: *I'm sorry about our quarrel; you started it, though.* ⟨Old Norse *thó*⟩ **as though** as if.

thought [θɒt] *n* **1** what one thinks; an idea. **2** mental activity: *Plants are incapable of thought.* **3** consideration; care: *Show some thought for others.* **4** intention: *His thought was to avoid controversy.* *v* pt and pp of THINK. ⟨Old English *thōht*⟩ **thought·ful** *adj* **1 a** deep in thought. **b** in the habit of thinking critically and seriously: *Thoughtful educators will see the difference.* **2** careful of others; considerate: *She is always thoughtful of her mother.* **thought·ful·ly** *adv.* **thought·ful·ness** *n.* **thought·less** *adj* **1** done, or doing things, without thinking. **2** not considerate. **3** stupid. **thought·less·ly** *adv.* **thought·less·ness** *n.*

thou·sand ['θaʊzənd] *n* **1** ten hundred; 1000. **2 thousands** *pl* a very large but unstated number: *There were thousands of tourists in town today.* **thou·sand** *adj.* ⟨Old English *thūsend*⟩ **thou·sandth** *adj, n* **1** the last in a series of a thousand. **2** one, or being one, of a thousand equal parts.

thrall [θrɒl] *n* the state of being in another's power or having power over someone (with *in*): *He was in thrall to his former girlfriend.* ⟨Old Norse *thrǽll*⟩

thrash [θræʃ] *v* **1** beat severely: *The man thrashed the boy for stealing the apples.* **2** move violently; toss: *Unable to sleep, the patient thrashed about in her bed.* **3** defeat thoroughly. **thrash·ing** *n.* ⟨variant of *thresh*⟩ **thrash out** settle by thorough discussion: *to thrash out a problem.* **thrash over** go over again and again.

thread [θred] *n* **1 a** a cotton, silk, nylon, etc., spun out into a fine cord: *Thread is for sewing.* **b** a similar filament of glass, metal, or plastic. **2** something long and slender like a thread: *Threads of gold could be seen in the ore.* **3** a connecting element: *I've lost the thread of our conversation.* **4** the sloping ridge that winds around a bolt, screw, etc.: *The thread of a nut interlocks with the thread of a bolt.* **5 threads** *pl Slang* clothes, esp an outfit or suit. *v* **1** pass a thread through: *to thread a needle.* **2** pass (a tape, film, etc.) through (a projector, recorder, etc.) as though threading a needle. **3** make (one's way) carefully: *She threaded her way through the crowd.* **4** cut threads into (a bolt, screw, pipe, joint, etc.) **thread·like** *adj.* ⟨Old English *thrǽd*⟩ **hang by** (or **on**) **a thread** be in a precarious position. **thread·bare** *adj* **1** worn so much that the threads show: *a threadbare coat.* **2** old and worn; stale. **thread·y** *adj* **1** fibrous; stringy. **2** of the pulse, thin and feeble. **3** of the voice, etc., lacking in fullness. **thread·i·ness** *n.*

threat [θrɛt] *n* **1** a statement of what will be done to hurt or punish someone. **2** a sign of possible harm: *Those black clouds are a threat of rain.* **threat·en** *v.* **threat·en·ing** *adj.* ⟨Old English *thrēat* troop, throng; coercion⟩ **threatened species** a species that is not yet considered endangered, but whose rarity indicates it may well be so in the near future.

three [θri] *n* **1** one more than two; 3. **2** any set of three persons or things. **3** a playing card or side of a die having three spots. **three** *adj.* ⟨Old English *thrēo*⟩

three–base hit *Baseball* a hit which advances the batter to third base. **three–D** or **3–D** *adj* three-dimensional. **three–di·men·sion·al** *adj* **1** to do with the three dimensions of width, depth, and height. **2** appearing to have depth, esp of flat images which have the illusion of depth. **3** of a character in a novel, play, etc., true to life. **three·fold** *adj* **1** three times as much or as many. **2** having three parts. *adv* three times as much or as many. **three–point turn** a standard method of turning a motor vehicle 180°, using forward and reverse gears and involving three steps, each moving the vehicle through an arc. **three R's** reading, writing, and arithmetic. **three–ring circus 1** a circus in which there are simultaneous acts being performed in each of three rings. **2** a situation in which there is a confusing or dazzling array of activities. **three·score** *adj* three times twenty; 60. **three·some** *n* a group of three people.

thresh [θreʃ] *v* **1** separate the grain or seeds from (wheat, etc.). **2** move violently; toss. ⟨Old English *threscan*⟩ **thresh out** settle by thorough discussion. **thresh over** go over again and again. **thresh·er** or **threshing machine** *n* a machine used for separating the grain or seeds from the stalks and other parts of wheat, oats, etc.

thresh·old ['θreʃould] *or* ['θreʃhould] *n* **1** a piece of wood or stone under a door. **2** doorway. **3** the point of entering; a beginning point: *The scientist was on the threshold of an important discovery.* **4** *Physics* the limit below which no reaction occurs. ⟨Old English *therscold, threscold*⟩

threw [θru] *v* pt of THROW.

thrice [θrais] *adv Archaic, poetic* **1** three times. **2** three times as many; three times as much. ⟨Middle English *thries*⟩

thrift [θrift] *n* **1** economical management; the habit of saving: *By thrift she managed to get along on her small salary.* **2** any of several plants native to mountainous, marshy, and sandy coastal regions. **thrift·y** *adj.* **thrift·i·ly** *adv.* **thrift·i·ness** *n.* ⟨*thrive*⟩ **thrift·less** *adj* wasteful. **thrift·less·ly** *adv.* **thrift·less·ness** *n.* **thrift shop** a second-hand store, usually managed and staffed by a charitable organization.

thrill [θril] *n* **1** a shivering, exciting feeling. **2** a throbbing; tremor. **3** something causing great pleasure, emotion, or excitement: *Being here is a real thrill for me.* **4** thrilling quality: *the thrill of freedom after long imprisonment.* *v* **1** give an exciting feeling to: *Stories of adventure thrilled him.* **2** have a shivering,

exciting feeling. **3** quiver; tremble: *Her voice thrilled with terror.* **thrill·ing** *adj.* **thrill·ing·ly** *adv.* ⟨Old English *thyrlian* pierce⟩ **thrill·er** *n Informal* a very suspenseful story, play, or film, esp one involving a murder.

thrive [θraiv] *v* **throve** or **thrived**, **thrived** or **thriv·en** ['θrivən], **thriv·ing 1** grow vigorously: *thriving crops.* **2** be successful: *Her business is thriving.* **thriv·ing** *adj.* **thriv·ing·ly** *adv.* ⟨Old Norse *thrífa(sk)*⟩

throat [θrout] *n* **1** the front of the neck. **2** the passage from the mouth to the stomach or lungs. ⟨Old English *throte*⟩ **cut one's own throat** *Informal* cause one's own downfall. **jump down someone's throat** *Informal* attack or criticize a person with sudden violence. **lump in one's throat a** a feeling of inability to swallow. **b** a feeling of being about to cry: *The story brought a lump to his throat.* **ram something down someone's throat** force acceptance of (something). **throat·y** *adj* produced from far back in the throat; low-pitched and resonant: *a throaty voice.* **throat·i·ly** *adv.* **throat·i·ness** *n.*

throb [θrɒb] *v* **throbbed**, **throb·bing 1** beat more rapidly or strongly than normally: *Our hearts were throbbing from the long climb up the hill.* **2** beat steadily. **3** tremble: *They were throbbing with excitement.* **throb** *n.* **throb·bing** *adj.* ⟨Middle English *throbben*⟩

throe [θrou] *n* Usually, **throes** *pl* **1** a violent pang or pangs; great pain: *the throes of childbirth.* **2** a hard or agonizing struggle: *the throes of revolution.* ⟨fusion of Old English *thrōwian* suffer, *thrāwan* twist, throw⟩

throm·bo·sis [θrɒm'bousɪs] *n* the formation of a blood clot in a blood vessel or in the heart. **throm·bot·ic** [-'bɒtɪk] *adj.* ⟨Greek *thrombos* clot⟩

throne [θroun] *n* **1** the chair on which a king, queen, or other person of high rank sits during ceremonies. **2** the power or authority of a king, queen, etc. ⟨Greek *thronos*⟩ **Throne Speech** SPEECH FROM THE THRONE.

throng [θrɒŋ] *n* a crowd; multitude. *v* **1** crowd; fill with a crowd. **2** come together in a crowd. ⟨Old English *gethrang*⟩

throt·tle ['θrɒtəl] *n* **1** a valve regulating the flow of steam, gasoline vapour, etc. to (an engine). **2** a lever or pedal working such a valve. The throttle of a car is called an accelerator. **3** throat or windpipe. *v* **1** lessen the speed of (an engine) or the flow of (fuel, steam, etc.) by closing a throttle (often with *down* or *back*): *to throttle down a steam engine.* **2** choke; strangle: *The thief throttled the dog to keep it from barking.* **3** suppress: *Increased tariffs soon throttled trade between the two countries.* ⟨Middle English; perhaps diminutive of *throat*⟩

through [θru] *prep* **1** from end to end of: *The soldiers marched through the town.* **2** here and there in or among: *We travelled through Québec, visiting many old towns.* **3** because of: *The woman refused help through pride.* **4** by means of: *He became rich through hard work*

and ability. **5 a** during the whole of: *to work from dawn through the day and into the night.* **b** during and until the finish of: *to help a person through hard times.* **6** up to and including: *The store is open Monday through Saturday.* **7** past without stopping: *She drove right through a stop sign.*
adv **1** from end to end. **2** completely: *He walked home in the rain and was wet through.* **3** from beginning to end: *She read the book through.* **4** all the way: *The train goes through to Vancouver.*
adj **1 a** going all the way without change: *a through train from Montréal to Vancouver.* **b** for the whole distance: *a through ticket.* **2** at the end; done: *I am almost through.* ⟨earlier *thourgh,* Old English *thurh*⟩
through and through completely. See also idioms with **through** at COME, GET, PULL, PUT, and SEE.
through·out *prep* all the way through: *Canada Day is celebrated throughout Canada.* *adv* in or to every part: *The house is well built throughout.* **through street** a street on which traffic is given the right of way at intersections. **through·way** *n* a thoroughfare, esp an expressway.

throve [θrouv] *v* a pt of THRIVE.

throw [θrou] *v* **threw, thrown, throw·ing** **1 a** toss: *to throw a ball.* **b** propel through the air with the aid of a catapult, hose, etc.: *The fire hose threw water on the fire.* **2** bring to the ground: *His horse threw him.* **3** put carelessly or in haste: *Throw some clothes on and run.* **4** put or move quickly or by force: *to throw oneself onto a bed.* **5** deliver, esp quickly: *She threw a glance at each car that passed us.* **6** move (a lever, switch, etc.) that connects or disconnects parts of a mechanism. **7** *Informal* let an opponent win (a race, etc.), often for money. **8** *Informal* **a** give (a party, etc.). **b** have (a fit, tantrum. etc.). **9** *Informal* confuse (often with *off*): *Her remark really threw me for a minute.*
n **1** the act of throwing: *a good throw.* **2** the distance a thing is or may be thrown: *a record throw.* **3** a light cover for the body, such as a blanket or shawl, or for a piece of furniture to protect or decorate it. **throw·er** *n.* ⟨Old English *thrāwan* twist⟩
throw a monkey wrench into complicate: *The rail strike threw a monkey wrench into our plans.* **throw away a** get rid of. **b** waste: *to throw away a chance.* **c** *Theatre* speak (a line or speech) in a deliberately casual way. **throw·a·way** *n, adj.* **throw back** revert to an ancestral type. **throw·back** *n.* **throw cold water on** discourage by being indifferent or unwilling. **throw in** add as a gift: *The store owner often throws in an extra apple.* **throw off a** get rid of. **b** cause to lose: *to throw a hound off the scent.* **c** *Informal* produce (a poem, etc.) in an offhand manner. **d** put out of sync. **e** get free from (a pursuer). **throw oneself at** try hard to get the love or favour of. **throw oneself into** engage in wholeheartedly. **throw oneself on** (or **upon**) appeal to as one's only hope. **throw one's voice** practise

ventriloquism. **throw open** a open suddenly or widely. **b** remove all obstacles from. **throw out a** get rid of. **b** reject. **c** expel. **d** *Baseball* put out (a base runner) by throwing the ball to a base. **e** utter offhandedly: *to throw out a suggestion.* **throw over** abandon. **throw together a** make (something) quickly and carelessly. **b** cause to become acquainted by chance: *They were thrown together by the war.* **throw up a** *Informal* vomit. **b** give up: *He threw up his plan to go to Europe.* **throw up one's hands** express helpless dismay.
SYNONYMS
Throw is the general word: *The children threw pillows at each other.* **Toss** means throw lightly or carelessly: *Please toss me the matches.*

thrush[1] [θrʌʃ] *n* any of a subfamily of songbirds found throughout the world, esp those species having brownish plumage with a spotted breast. ⟨Old English *thrȳsce*⟩

thrush[2] [θrʌʃ] *n* **1 a** an infection in which white blisters form on the mouth and throat. **b** a similar vaginal infection. **2** a diseased condition of a horse's foot. ⟨perhaps Old Norse *thruskr*⟩

thrust [θrʌst] *v* **thrust, thrust·ing** **1** push with force: *He thrust his hands into his pockets.* **2** force one's way: *She thrust into the crowd.*
n **1** a sudden or forceful push. **2** a push with a weapon or instrument, esp a pointed one. **3 a** the endwise push exerted by the rotation of a propeller, producing forward motion. **b** the force exerted by a high-speed jet of gas, etc., producing forward motion. **4** main purpose or direction: *the thrust of an argument.* ⟨Middle English; Old Norse *thrȳsta*⟩
thrust something on someone force or impose something on someone.
thrust·er *n* a small manoeuvring rocket engine on a spacecraft, as on re-entry.

thud [θʌd] *n* **1** a dull sound caused by a blow or fall: *The book hit the floor with a thud.* **2** a blow or thump. **thud, thud·ded, thud·ding** *v.* ⟨Old English *thyddan* strike⟩

thug [θʌg] *n* a cutthroat; gangster. **thug·gish** *adj.* ⟨Hindi *thag;* Sanskrit *sthaga* rogue⟩
thug·ger·y *n* violent or brutal behaviour.

Thu·le ['θuli] *n* **1** the part of the world that the ancient Greeks and Romans regarded as farthest north, that is, some island or region north of Britain. Also, **Ultima Thule. 2** ['tuli] an Inuit culture of N Greenland, lasting from about A.D. 500 to 1400. See ULTIMA THULE. ⟨Greek *Thoulē*⟩

thu·li·um ['θuliəm] *or* ['θuliəm] *n* a metallic element of the rare-earth group. *Symbol* **Tm** ⟨*Thule*⟩

thumb [θʌm] *n* the short finger that can be opposed to each of the other fingers.
v **1** turn (the pages of a book, magazine, etc.) rapidly. **2** soil by or as if by repeated leafing through: *The books were badly thumbed.*
thumb·like *adj.* **thumb·less** *adj.* ⟨OE *thūma*⟩
all thumbs very clumsy, awkward, etc.: *I'm all thumbs when it comes to tying bows.* **thumb one's nose** express scorn or defiance by or as

if by placing one's thumb on the end of one's nose and extending the fingers: *He thumbed his nose at the promise of success and went on his way.* **thumbs down a** a gesture of disapproval, made by closing the hand and pointing the thumb downward. **b** any expression of disapproval: *The principal gave them thumbs down on the proposal for another field trip.* **thumbs up a** a gesture of acceptance or satisfaction, made by closing the hand and pointing the thumb up. **b** an expression of satisfaction. **under someone's thumb** under someone's control or influence. **thumb index** a series of labelled, usually semi-circular cuts down the side of a reference book, Bible, etc., making it easier to find the desired section. **thumb·nail** *n* **1** the nail of the thumb. **2** something very small. **thumbnail sketch 1** a small or quickly drawn picture. **2** a short description. **thumb·screw** *n* formerly, an instrument of torture for squeezing the thumbs. **thumb·tack** *n* a tack with a flat head, to be pressed into a surface with the thumb.

thump [θʌmp] *v* **1** strike with something heavy: *He thumped the table with his fist.* **2** strike against (something) heavily and noisily: *The shutters thumped the wall in the wind.* **3** make a dull sound: *The hammer thumped against the wood.* **4** beat violently or heavily: *His heart always thumped as he walked past the cemetery at night.* **5** beat severely. **thump** *n*. ⟨imitative⟩
thump·ing *adj Informal* huge; whopping.

thun·der [ˈθʌndər] *n* **1** the loud rumbling or crashing that often follows lightning. **2** any noise like thunder: *a thunder of applause.* *v* **1** give forth thunder: *We heard it thunder in the distance.* **2** utter very loudly: *to thunder a reply.* **3** utter a denunciation violently: *The article thundered against the injustices of the system.* **thun·der·er** *n*. ⟨Old English *thunor*⟩
steal someone's thunder make someone's idea, method, etc. less effective by using it first or doing something more startling: *The Liberals stole the Tories' thunder by announcing their election platform first.*
thun·der·bird *n* in the mythology of several First Nations peoples, a huge bird that creates thunder with its beating wings and lightning with its flashing eyes. Carved representations are often found on totem poles of the Pacific Coast. **thun·der·bolt** *n* **1** a flash of lightning and the thunder that follows it. **2** something sudden and terrible: *The news of his death came as a thunderbolt.* **thun·der·clap** *n* **1** a loud crash of thunder. **2** something sudden, startling, and terrible. **thun·der·cloud** *n* a dark cloud that brings thunder and lightning. **thun·der·head** *n* one of the masses of cumulus clouds often seen before thunderstorms. **thun·der·ing** *adj* **1** extremely loud. **2** *Informal* extremely great. **thun·der·ing·ly** *adv.* **thun·der·ous** *adj* **1** producing thunder. **2** making a noise like thunder. **thun·der·ous·ly** *adv.* **thun·der·storm** *n* a storm with thunder and lightning and, usually, heavy rain. **thun·der·struck** *adj*

overcome, as if hit by a thunderbolt; amazed. **thun·de·ry** *adj* thunderous.

Thurs·day [ˈθɜrzdei] *n* the fifth day of the week, following Wednesday. ⟨Old Norse *Thórsdagr* day of Thor⟩

thus [ðʌs] *adv* **1** in this way: *He spoke thus.* **2** therefore. **3** to this extent: *thus far.* ⟨Old English⟩
thus·ly *adv Informal* THUS (def. 1).

thwart [θwɔrt] *v* keep from doing something: *Lack of money thwarted his plans for a trip.*
n **1** a seat across a boat, on which a rower sits. **2** a brace in a canoe. ⟨Old Norse *thvert*, across⟩

thy See THOU.

thyme [taɪm] *n* any of several herbs of the mint family. ⟨Greek *thymon*⟩

thy·roid [ˈθaɪrɔɪd] *n* **1** THYROID GLAND. **2** a medicine made from the thyroid glands of certain animals, used in the treatment of goitre, obesity, etc. ⟨Greek *thyra* door⟩
thyroid gland an important gland in the neck of vertebrates producing a hormone that regulates growth and metabolism.

thy·self See THOU.

ti [ti] *n Music* **1** the seventh tone of an eight-tone major scale. **2** the tone B. Sometimes, **te**. ⟨altered from si, for *Sancte Iohannes*, words sung on this note in a song sung to the scale⟩

ti·ar·a [tiˈɛrə] or [tiˈɑrə] *n* **1** a band of gold, jewels, flowers, etc., worn around the head by women as an ornament. **2** *Roman Catholic Church* the triple crown of the Pope. ⟨Greek⟩

tib·i·a [ˈtɪbiə] *n*, *pl* -i·ae [-i,i] or [-i,aɪ] or -i·as **1** *Anatomy* the thicker of the two bones of the leg from the knee to the ankle; shinbone. **2** in animals or birds, a corresponding bone. **3** the fourth joint of the leg of an insect. **tib·i·al** *adj.* ⟨Latin⟩

tic [tɪk] *n* an involuntary twitching of the muscles, esp those of the face. ⟨French⟩

tick¹ [tɪk] *n* **1** a sound made by a clock or watch. **2** a sound like it. **3** *Informal* a moment: *I'll be ready in two ticks.* **4** a small mark used in checking, usually √
v **1** mark off by a ticking sound: *The clock ticked away the minutes.* **2** mark an item in a list, etc. with a tick (usually with *off*): *I ticked off things I had bought.* **3** *Informal* function: *What makes it tick?* ⟨probably imitative⟩
tick along proceed smoothly: *The renovations are ticking along just fine.* **ticked off** *Informal* fed up; annoyed. **tick off** *Informal* annoy.
tick·er *n* something that ticks, esp a clock or watch. **tick–tock** *n* the sound made by a clock with a pendulum. *v* make this sound; tick: *A tall clock tick-tocked on the stair.*

tick² [tɪk] *n* **1** any of a large group of small arachnids having sucking mouthparts with which they feed on the blood of dogs, cattle, human beings, etc. **2** any of various species of insect that live as parasites on cattle, sheep, birds, etc. ⟨Old English *ticia*⟩

tick³ [tɪk] *n* **1** the cloth cover for a mattress or pillow. **2** *Informal* ticking. ⟨probably Latin *theca* case; Greek *thēkē*⟩

tick·ing *n* a strong cotton or linen cloth, used for mattress covers, tents, and awnings.

tick·et ['tɪkɪt] *n* **1** a card or other piece of paper showing that a fee has been paid: *a theatre ticket.* **2** an official notification that a person is charged with a traffic violation: *a parking ticket.* **3** a label or tag attached to an article for sale, showing its size, price, etc. **4** *US* the list of candidates to be voted on that belong to one political party. **5** *Informal* a certificate: *a chief engineer's ticket.*
v **1** mark with a ticket: *All articles in the store are ticketed with the price.* **2** give a ticket to, indicating a traffic violation: *She was ticketed for speeding.* ⟨French *étiquette* ticket, label⟩

tick·le¹ ['tɪkəl] *v* **1** touch lightly causing wriggles and, often, laughter. **2** have a feeling like this; cause such a feeling: *My nose tickles.* **3** excite pleasantly; amuse; delight or gratify: *The story tickled her.* **4** play, get, etc. with light strokes. **tick·le** *n.* ⟨Middle English *tikelen*⟩
be tickled pink *Informal* be very pleased. **tickle someone's fancy** appeal to someone. **tickle the ivories** *Informal* play the piano.
tick·lish *adj* **1** sensitive to tickling. **2** requiring careful handling: *a ticklish situation.* **3** easily annoyed or offended. **tick·lish·ly** *adv.* **tick·lish·ness** *n.*

tick·le² ['tɪkəl] *n* ✹ *esp Newfoundland and Labrador* **1** a narrow channel between an island and the mainland, or between islands. **2** a narrow entrance to a harbour. ⟨perhaps British dialect *stickle* rapids, riffle⟩

tic–tac–toe [,tɪk tæk 'tou] *n* a game in which two players alternately put circles or crosses in a figure of nine squares, each player trying to be the first to fill three spaces in a row. Also, **tick–tack–toe, Xs and Os.**

tid·al See TIDE.

tid·bit ['tɪd,bɪt] *n* a very pleasing bit of food, news, etc. ⟨*tid* nice + *bit* morsel⟩

tide [taɪd] *n* **1** the rise and fall of the ocean, usually every twelve hours, caused by the pull of the moon and the sun. **2** anything that rises and falls like the tide: *the tide of popular opinion.* **tid·al** *adj.* **tid·al·ly** *adv.* **tide·less** *adj.* ⟨Old English *tīd*, orig time⟩
tide over help to overcome a difficulty, etc.: *He said twenty dollars would tide him over until payday.* **turn the tide** change a condition to the opposite.
tidal wave 1 a large wave caused by strong winds. **2** a destructive ocean wave which is caused by an earthquake. **3** any great manifestation of feeling, etc.: *a tidal wave of popular indignation.* **tide line** ✹ a line etched near the top of a glass for use in a beer parlour or pub, intended to show the level to which the glass must legally be filled. **tide·mark** *n* a mark left by the tide at its highest point, or, sometimes, at its lowest point. **tide·wa·ter** *n* **1** water affected by tides. **2** an area whose waters are so affected. **3** water flooding land at high tide.

ti·dings ['taɪdɪŋz] *n pl* news; information. ⟨Old English *tīdung; tīdan* happen⟩

ti·dy ['taɪdi] *adj* **1** in order: *a tidy room.* **2** inclined to keep things in order: *a tidy person.* **3** *Informal* fairly large: *a tidy sum.*
v make (a place) tidy (often with *up*).
n a small container to hold little items or scraps: *a sink tidy.* **ti·di·ly** *adv.* **ti·di·ness** *n.* ⟨Old English *tīd* time⟩

tie [taɪ] *v* **1** fasten, attach, or close with cord or the like: *Tie your shoes.* **2** make by tying: *to tie a knot.* **3** be capable of being tied: *This paper ribbon doesn't tie well.* **4** restrain: *She did not want to be tied to a steady job.* **5** make the same score (as): *The two teams tied.*
n **1** a cord, ribbon, etc. used for fastening parts: *An apron has ties.* **2** a shaped length of cloth worn under a shirt collar and knotted in front: *He always wears a shirt and tie to work.* **3** anything that unites or binds: *family ties.* **4** one of the wooden beams on a railway bed that supports the rails. **5** a connecting beam as in a framework supporting a roof, etc. **6** equality in points, votes, etc. ⟨Old English *tīgan; tēag* rope⟩
tie down a confine: *She's tied down with a job and night school.* **b** fasten by tying: *Tie down the tarp to stop it flapping.* **tie in a** connect: *Where does this line tie in with the main circuit?* **b** relate: *The illustrations tie in well with the story.* **tie–in** *n.* **tie one on** *Slang* get drunk. **tie up a** bind with cord, etc.: *The thieves tied him up.* **b** hinder the progress of: *The stalled truck tied up traffic for half an hour.* **c** engage, occupy, or commit (money, a person, equipment, etc.) so as to make unavailable for other purposes: *Don't tie up the phone.*
tie breaker an extra period of play, etc., often with special rules, held to choose a winner from among contestants with equal scores.
tie–dye *n* a method of hand-dyeing cloth in patterns by tying parts together so that they will not absorb the dye. **tie–dye** *v.* **tie–up** *n* **1** a connection. **2** a place to moor a boat.

tier [tir] *n* one of a series of rows arranged one above another: *tiers of seats in a football stadium.* ⟨French *tire*, orig order; *tirer* draw⟩

tiff [tɪf] *n* **1** a slight quarrel. **2** a slight fit of ill humour or peevishness. ⟨origin uncertain⟩

ti·ger ['taɪgər] *n* **1** a large feline having yellow fur striped with black. **2** a fierce and wild person: *He becomes a tiger if you criticize his work.* **3** an energetic person: *a tiger for work.* **ti·ger·like** *adj.* **ti·gress** *n.* ⟨Greek *tigris*⟩
have a tiger by the tail be in a situation in which remaining may be preferable to flight. **ti·ger·ish** *adj* like a tiger; wild and fierce.

tight [taɪt] *adj* **1** firm; put together firmly: *a tight knot.* **2 a** stretched: *a tight canvas.* **b** showing strain: *a tight smile.* **3** not allowing much room: *a tight fit.* **4** closely spaced: *a tight schedule.* **5** not letting water, air, or gas in or out (often in compounds): *airtight.* **6** difficult: *His lies got him in a tight place.* **7** *Informal* almost even: *a tight race.* **8** scarce: *Money is tight just now.* **9** *Informal* stingy. **10** *Informal* drunk. **11** strict; severe: *to rule with a tight hand.* **12** of a group, having close ties to each other.

adv closely; securely; firmly: *The rope was tied too tight.* **tight·en** *v.* **tight·en·er** *n.* **tight·ly** *adv.* **tight·ness** *n.* ⟨Old English *getyht* pp of *tyhtan* stretch⟩

(run) a tight ship (operate) a highly efficient organization. **sit tight** keep the same position, opinion, etc. and see what develops. **sleep tight** sleep soundly.

tight–fist·ed *adj* stingy. **tight·knit** *adj* **1** of prose, etc., tight. **2** closely united: *a tightknit community.* **tight–lipped** *adj* **1** keeping the lips firmly together, as in determination or when controlling emotion: *tight-lipped fury.* **2** reluctant to speak: *He's very tight-lipped; you won't get any information out of him.* **tight·rope** *n* a rope or wire stretched tight some distance above the ground, for acrobats to perform on. **on a tightrope** in a dangerous or extremely delicate situation. **tights** *n pl* a close-fitting garment covering the lower body and each leg and foot separately, worn by acrobats, dancers, etc. or as stockings. **tight squeeze** a difficult situation; narrow escape. **tight·wad** *n Slang* a stingy person.

SYNONYMS
Tight, the general word, emphasizes the idea of drawing or being drawn around so firmly that there is no looseness: *You need a tight string around that package.* **Taut** emphasizes stretching until the thing described would break if pulled more tightly: *The covering on a drum must be taut.*

ti·gress See TIGER.

ti·ka ['tikə] *n Hinduism* the dot of colour or other marking on the forehead. ⟨Hindi⟩

ti·ki·na·gan [ˌtɪkəˈnɑgən] *n* ✹ cradle-board. Also, **tic·ca·na·gon.**

til·de ['tɪldə] *n* a diacritical mark (~) over a letter, used mainly to indicate nasalization. ⟨Latin *titulus* title⟩

tile [taɪl] *n* **1** a thin piece of baked clay, stone, etc. used for surfacing floors, walls, or ceilings. **2** a porous pipe or trough, usually earthenware, used for draining land. **3** a piece of plastic, wood, etc., used in games such as Scrabble or mah-jongg.
v cover with tiles. ⟨Latin *tegula*⟩

till¹ [tɪl] *prep, conj* up to the time when; until. ⟨Old English *til*⟩

till² [tɪl] *v* plough; harrow, etc.: *Farmers till the land.* **till·a·ble** *adj.* ⟨Old English *tilian*⟩ **till·er** *n* a machine for tilling.

till³ [tɪl] *n* a drawer or box for money, esp in a store, etc.: *The till is under the counter.* ⟨Old English *-tyllan* draw, as in *betyllan* lure⟩

till⁴ [tɪl] *n* glacial drift composed of clay, stones, gravel, boulders, etc. mixed together. ⟨origin unknown⟩

till·er¹ ['tɪlər] *n* a bar or handle used to turn the rudder in steering a boat. ⟨Old French *telier* weaver's beam; Latin *tela* web, loom⟩

till·er² See TILL².

til·li·cum ['tɪləkəm] *n Pacific Coast* **1** friend; pal. **2** person. **3** orig, among coastal First Nations, one's own people. ⟨Chinook Jargon *tillikum*; Chinookan *tilikum*⟩

tilt¹ [tɪlt] *v* **1** incline: *She tilted the board to let the water run off.* **2** bias (a policy, treatment of an issue, etc.) **3** take part in a jousting match. **tilt** *n.* ⟨Old English *tealt* shaky⟩
(at) full tilt at full speed or with full force: *The car ran full tilt against the tree.* **tilt at windmills** See WINDMILL.

tilt² [tɪlt] *n* ✹ **1 a** (*esp Labrador*) a temporary shelter of canvas, sealskins, etc.; tent. **b** (*West*) formerly, the canvas covering of a PRAIRIE SCHOONER. **2** (*esp Labrador*) **a** a log hut or cabin used by fishers or trappers. **b** any simple dwelling, esp one made of wood. ⟨Middle English *telte*, Old English *teld*; compare German *Zelt* tent⟩

tim·ber ['tɪmbər] *n* **1** wood suitable for building. **2** a curved piece forming a rib of a ship. **3** mature growing trees: *Half of their land is covered with timber.* **4** logs, green or cured, cut from such trees. **5** figuratively, quality: *a woman of her timber.*
interj a warning shout that a tree is about to fall. ⟨Old English⟩
tim·bered *adj* **1** made or furnished with timber. **2** covered with growing trees. **tim·ber·land** *n* land with trees, esp trees that may be used for timber. **timber limit** ✹ **1** timberline. **2** *Logging* a tract of land in which a person or company has the right to fell trees and remove timber. **tim·ber·line** *n* a line on mountains and in high latitudes beyond which trees will not grow because of climatic conditions. **timber wolf** a large grey wolf esp any found in wooded northern regions of Canada and in Alaska.

tim·bre ['tɪmbər] *or* ['tæmbər] *French* [tɛ̃bʀ] *n* the quality in sounds that distinguishes a certain voice, instrument, etc. from other voices, instruments, etc. ⟨Middle French *timbre*; Greek *tympanon* drum⟩

time [taɪm] *n* **1** the past, present, and future: *We measure time in years, months, days, etc.* **2** a part of time: *A minute is a short time.* **3 a** a period of history: *the time of the Renaissance.* **b** a particular season: *haying time.* **4** a term of imprisonment, apprenticeship, etc.: *to complete one's time.* **5** a long time: *What a time it took you!* **6** some point in time: *What time is it?* **7** one's turn (to do something, succeed, etc.): *a leader whose time has come.* **8 times** *pl* **a** multiplied by (prepositional use): *Four times three is twelve.* **b** period of history: *modern times.* **9** period for some activity: *With every race, she improved her time.* **10** an experience during a certain time: *She had a good time at the party.* **11** *Music* **a** the length of a note or rest. **b** the tempo of a composition. **c** the rhythm of a composition: *waltz time.* **12** lifetime: *That was before my time.*
v **1** measure the duration of: *to time a race.* **2** fix, set, or regulate the length of in time: *to time an exposure correctly.* **3** set, regulate, or adjust (a timepiece): *to time an alarm clock.* **4** do in rhythm with; set the rhythm of: *The dancers timed their steps to the music.* **5** choose

the moment or occasion for: *The demonstrators timed their march through the business section so that most shoppers would see them.* ⟨Old English *tīma*⟩
about time near the proper time: *It's about time to go home.* **against time** trying to finish before a certain time. **ahead of time** early. **at a time** together: *He took the steps two at a time.* **at one time** formerly: *At one time he was famous.* **at the same time a** simultaneously. **b** nevertheless. **at times** now and then. **behind the times** old-fashioned. **do** (or **serve**) **time** *Informal* spend time in prison as a criminal: *do time for bank robbery.* **for the time being** for now. **from time to time** now and then. **in good time a** at the right time: *We arrived in good time for the first act.* **b** soon; quickly. **in no time (flat)** *Informal* instantly. **in time a** after a while. **b** soon enough: *We got there just in time, before he left.* **c** *Music* in the right rate. **it's about time** *Informal* it's past due: *You're cleaning your room? It's about time!* **keep time** sound or move at the right rate. **make (good, excellent,** etc.**) time** go with speed. **make time (for)** set aside time (for). **mark time a** beat out the proper rhythm. **b** pass time doing nothing. **on one's own time** outside of one's paid working hours. **on time a** not late. **b** on credit: *She bought a car on time.* **pass the time (away)** occupy oneself: *I passed the time away by knitting.* **tell time** read the clock. **time after time** or **time and again** again and again. **time of life** age: *a foolish thing to do at his time of life.* **time out of mind** TIME IMMEMORIAL.
time–and–a–half *n* a rate of pay one and a half times the usual, for working overtime or on holidays. **time and motion study** a study of the methods used and the time taken to do a certain job, conducted to establish the most effective way of doing that job. **time bomb 1** a bomb with a timing device, set to explode at a certain moment. **2** *Informal* a situation leading to inevitable disaster, unless action can be taken to avert it. **time capsule** a container with items representative of the current age, that is buried, to be discovered in a future generation. **time-card** *n* a card used with a time clock for recording the arrival and departure times of an employee. **time clock** a clock with a device to stamp an employee's timecard. **time–con·sum·ing** *adj* requiring a great deal of time: *The calculations weren't hard, but they were time-consuming.* **time frame** the period of time allotted for some activity. **time–hon·oured** or **time–hon·ored** *adj* honoured because old and established: *a time-honoured custom.* **time immemorial** a period in time so distant that it is before the beginning of records. **time·keep·er** *n* a person who or thing that keeps time: *My watch is an excellent timekeeper.* **time–lag** *n* an interval between the cause of an event and its happening. **time–lapse photography** motion photography in which separate pictures are taken at intervals and then projected at normal speed to give the illusion

of speeded-up action. **time·less** *adj* **1 a** never ending. **b** eternal. **2** confined to no special time; always suitable: *timeless classics of literature.* **time·less·ly** *adv.* **time·less·ness** *n.* **time·line a** a line, marked with dates and events at approximate intervals, that shows which events were concurrent, which people were contemporaries, etc. **b** a similar device used to show the sequence or concurrence of events in a detailed plan. **time·ly** *adj* happening at the right time: *The timely arrival of the police stopped the robbery.* **time·li·ness** *n.* **time of day** the time as shown by the clock. **give the time of day to** notice or acknowledge. **pass the time of day** exchange greetings. **time–out** *n* **1** *Sports* an interval during which play is stopped and time not counted, for players to make substitutions, confer, etc. **2 a** time during which a child is excluded from the company of others as an opportunity to reflect on his or her misbehaviour. **time·piece** *n* a clock or watch. **tim·er** *n* a device similar to a clock that can be set to indicate when a period of time has elapsed, or to start or stop another device or mechanism: *a timer on a stove.* **time·sav·ing** *adj* that saves time: *timesaving household appliances.* **time·sav·er** *n.* **time·serv·er** *n* a person who for selfish purposes conforms with the opinions of persons in power. **time·serv·ing** *adj.* **time·shar·ing** or **time–sharing** *n* **1** *Computers* a system whereby different users can have access to a single computer at virtually the same time, due to the high speed at which the computer operates. **2** a system whereby several owners occupy a vacation home, each for a specified period with certain dates. **time sheet** a sheet on which an employee's hours of work, time off, etc., are recorded. **time signature** *Music* a symbol, usually in the form of a fraction, put at the beginning of a composition or where the time changes. The numerator of the fraction indicates the number of beats in a bar or measure; the denominator gives the length of the note that receives one beat. **time·ta·ble** *n* any schedule showing a planned sequence of events, such as arrival and departure times for trains, times for classes in a school or university, etc. **time–test·ed** *adj* having a value that has been proven over a long period of time: *a time-tested recipe for bread.* **time warp** a theoretical change in the nature of time, according to certain conditions in the universe. **time·worn** *adj* **1** worn by long use: *the timeworn steps of the old house.* **2** trite: *a timeworn excuse.* **time zone** a geographical region within which the same standard of time is used. The world is divided into 24 time zones, beginning and ending at the International Date Line, an imaginary line running mostly through the Pacific Ocean at the 180th meridian of longitude. **tim·ing** *n* the choice of the speed or occurrence of a thing to produce the best effect: *The timing of the engine is off. The actor's timing was perfect.*

tim·id ['tɪmɪd] *adj* lacking self-confidence;

easily frightened. **tim·id·ly** *adv.* **ti·mid·i·ty** *n.*
⟨Latin *timidus; timere* to fear⟩
tim·or·ous ['tımərəs] *adj* timid. **tim·or·ous·ly**
adv. **tim·or·ous·ness** *n.*

tim·pa·ni ['tımpəni] *n pl* a set of kettledrums
played by one person. (sometimes with a sg
verb). **tim·pa·nist** *n.* ⟨Italian, pl of *timpano*
kettledrum; Latin *tympanum*⟩

tin [tın] *n* a soft metallic element *Symbol* **Sn**
⟨Old English⟩
tin ear a lack of sensitivity to sounds or
musical tones. **tin–eared** *adj.* **tin foil** very
thin sheeting of tin, aluminum, etc, used for
wrapping food products, for insulation, etc.
tin god a person who gets respect out of all
proportion to his or her actual merit: *The
new CEO, so highly extolled in a recent business
journal, was autocratic and distant—a real tin
god.* **tin·ny** *adj* **1** shrill or thin in sound: *the
tinny music of an old juke box.* **2** of poor
quality: *tinny jewellery.* **tin·ni·ly** *adv.* **tin·ni·ness**
n. **tin plate** thin sheets of iron or steel coated
with tin. **tin–plate** *v.* **tin·pot** or **tin–pot** *adj
Informal* inferior; petty; *a tin-pot dictator.*

tinc·ture ['tıŋktʃər] *n* **1** a 10 to 20 percent
solution in alcohol: *tincture of iodine.*
Compare SPIRIT. **2** a slight colour or flavour.
v affect slightly with a certain quality (with
with): *Everything he says is tinctured with
conceit.* ⟨Latin *tinctura; tingere* tinge⟩

tin·der ['tındər] *n* anything that catches fire
easily. ⟨Old English *tynder*⟩
tin·der·box *n* **1** a box formerly used for
holding tinder, flint, and steel for making a
fire. **2** an object, structure, etc. that is highly
flammable. **3** a situation likely to burst into
conflict or violence of some kind.

tine [taın] *n* a sharp point or prong: *the tines
of a fork.* **tined** *adj.* ⟨Old English *tind*⟩

tinge [tındʒ] *v* **tinged, tinge·ing** or **ting·ing**
1 colour slightly: *A drop of ink will tinge a
glass of water.* **2** add a trace of some quality
to: *Sad memories tinged their joy.* **tinge** *n.*
⟨Latin *tingere*⟩

tin·gle ['tıŋgəl] *v* **1** have a stinging feeling,
esp from excitement, cold, etc.: *The cold
made his fingers tingle.* **2** cause this feeling
(in): *The fine rain tingled her cheeks.* **3** be
thrilling: *Her account of their misadventures
tingled with excitement.* **tin·gle** *n.* **tin·gly** *adj.*
⟨probably variant of *tinkle*⟩

tink·er ['tıŋkər] *n* a person who mends pots,
pans, etc., usually one who travels from
place to place to practise his or her trade.
v adjust in an unskilled or experimental way
(with *with*): *She likes to tinker with TV sets.*
tink·er·er *n.* ⟨perhaps from *tin*⟩

tin·kle ['tıŋkəl] *v* **1** make short, light, ringing
sounds: *Little bells tinkle.* **2** cause to tinkle.
3 *Informal* urinate. **tin·kle** *n.* **tin·kly** *adj.*
⟨probably imitative⟩

tin·ni·tus [tı'naıtəs] an abnormal ringing or
buzzing in the ears. ⟨Latin, pp of *tinnire* ring⟩

tin·sel ['tınsəl] *or* ['tınzəl] *n* **1** extremely thin
strips of a metallic substance, used to add
glitter to decorations, etc. **2** something

showy and attractive, but not worth much.
tin·sel *adj.* **tin·sel–like** *adj.* **tin·sel·ly** *adj.*
⟨French *étincelle* spark; Latin *scintilla*⟩

tint [tınt] *n* **1** a variety of a colour, esp one
mixed with white. **2** a tendency toward a
different colour: *white with a bluish tint.* **3** a
preparation for colouring hair; dye.
v put a tint on or in; colour: *to tint a black-
and-white photograph, to tint one's hair.*
⟨earlier *tinct;* Latin *tinctus* pp of *tingere* dye⟩

tin·tin·nab·u·la·tion [ˌtıntəˌnæbjə'leıʃən] *n*
the ringing of bells. ⟨Latin *tintinnabulum* bell⟩

ti·ny ['taıni] *adj* very small. **ti·ni·ly** *adv.*
ti·ni·ness *n.* ⟨Middle English *tine*⟩

–tion *suffix* **1** the result or process of ——ing:
addition. **2** the condition of being——ed:
exhaustion. ⟨Latin *-tio(nis)*⟩

tip¹ [tıp] *n* **1** the end; point: *the tips of the
fingers.* **2** a small piece put on the end of
something: *a rubber tip for a cane.*
v **tipped, tip·ping** put a tip on: *spears tipped
with steel.* ⟨Middle English *tippe*⟩
tip of the iceberg a few instances of some
bigger problem: *They've caught 200 tax
evaders and that's just the tip of the iceberg!*
tip·toe *n* the tips of the toes. *v* walk with the
heels raised off the ground. **on tiptoe**
a (walking) on the balls and toes of the feet.
b eager. **c** furtively, stealthily, or quietly.
tip·top *n* the highest point or degree. **tip·top**
adj **1** situated at the very top. **2** *Informal*
first-rate; excellent.

tip² [tıp] *v* **tipped, tip·ping** **1** slope: *She tipped
the table toward her.* **2** upset; overturn: *He
tipped over the milk jug.* **3** empty out; dump.
n a slope; slant. ⟨Middle English *tipen*⟩
tip the scales at See SCALE².
tip·py *adj* liable to tip: *Kayaks are tippy craft.*
tip·sy *adj* **1** slightly intoxicated. **2** unsteady.
tip·si·ly *adv.* **tip·si·ness** *n.*

tip³ [tıp] *n* **1** a small present of money in
return for service: *He gave the waiter a tip.* **2** a
piece of secret information: *She had a tip that
the black horse would win.* **3** a useful hint: *a
book of tips on caring for your pet.* **tip, tipped,
tip·ping** *v.* **tip·per** *n.* ⟨origin uncertain⟩
tip off give secret information or a warning
to. **tip-off** *n.* **tip one's hand** disclose one's
secret plans, esp by accident.

ti·pi ['tipi] See TEEPEE.

tip·ple ['tıpəl] *v* drink (alcoholic liquor) often.
n alcoholic liquor. **tip·pler** *n.* ⟨origin
uncertain⟩

ti·rade ['taıreid] *n* a long, vehement, usually
scolding, speech. ⟨French; *tirer* shoot⟩

tire¹ [taır] *v* **1** make or become weary: *The
work tired him.* **2** become impatient or bored:
I tired of his games. ⟨Old English *tȳrian*⟩
tire out make very weary.
tired *adj* **1** exhausted. **2** trite: *the same tired
old arguments.* **tired of** bored with: *I'm tired of
hearing about it.* **tired·ly** *adv.* **tired·ness** *n.*
tire·less *adj* **1** requiring little rest: *a tireless
worker.* **2** never stopping: *tireless efforts.*
tire·less·ly *adv.* **tire·less·ness** *n.* **tire·some** *adj*
1 tiring, because boring: *a tiresome speech.*

2 *Informal* vexing; annoying or irritating. **tire·some·ly** *adv.* **tire·some·ness** *n.*

SYNONYMS

Tired is the general and least precise word: *I am tired, but I must get back to work.* **Weary** suggests feeling worn out and unable or unwilling to go on: *Weary shoppers waited for buses.* **Exhausted** emphasizes being without enough energy left to be able to go on: *Exhausted by play, the child could not eat.*

tire² [tair] *n* a circular tube or ring fitted around the rim of a wheel to provide a smooth ride and to increase traction. ⟨*attire*, in sense of 'covering'⟩
tire iron an iron bar for prying a tire off a wheel rim. **tire·less** having no tires.

tire·less¹ See TIRE¹.

tire·less² See TIRE².

ti·sane [tɪ'zæn]; *French* [ti'zan] *n* herbal tea. ⟨Greek *ptisane* peeled barley; *ptissein* peel⟩

tis·sue ['tɪʃu] *n* **1** *Biology* **a** cell material that distinguishes organic structure as opposed to inorganic. **b** a mass of similar cells that form some part of an animal or a plant: *muscle tissue.* **2** a web; network: *Her whole story was a tissue of lies.* **3** a thin, soft paper that absorbs moisture easily: *toilet tissue.* ⟨Old French *tissu; tistre* weave, Latin *texere*⟩
tissue paper a very thin, crisp paper, used mainly for wrapping.

ti·tan ['taitən] *n* a person or thing of great size, power, or strength. **ti·tan·ic** [tai'tænɪk] *adj.* **ti·tan·i·cal·ly** *adv.* ⟨Greek myth *Titan*, a family of giants⟩

ti·ta·ni·um [tə'teiniəm] *n* a light, strong, silvery or grey metallic element, used esp in steel alloys for aircraft parts. *Symbol* **Ti** ⟨*Titan*⟩

tithe [taɪð] *n* **1** one-tenth. **2** Often, **tithes** *pl* one-tenth of the yearly produce of land, personal work, etc., paid as a tax, a donation, or an offering to God. **3** a very small part.
v put a tax or a levy of a tenth on. ⟨Old English *teogotha* tenth⟩

ti·tian ['tɪʃən] *n, adj* light auburn; golden red. ⟨*Titian*, 16c Italian painter, who used it a lot⟩

tit·il·late ['tɪtə,leit] *v* **1** excite pleasantly, often sexually. **2** tickle. **tit·il·la·tion** *n.* ⟨Latin *titillare*⟩

tit·i·vate or **tit·ti·vate** ['tɪtə,veit] *v Informal* dress or spruce up; make smart. **tit·i·va·tion** or **tit·ti·va·tion** *n.* ⟨perhaps *tidy*⟩

ti·tle ['taitəl] *n* **1 a** the name of a book, poem, picture, song, etc. **b** a descriptive heading, as of a chapter of a book, etc. **2** a book: *There are 5000 titles in our library.* **3** a name showing a person's rank, occupation, or condition in life. *Examples: doctor, Ms., queen, captain.* **4** a descriptive name or nickname. *Example:* Robin Hood, *Prince of Thieves.* **5** a first place position: *the tennis title.* **6** *Law* the legal right to the possession of property. **7** a legitimate claim. **8** a caption, esp dialogue or a credit, displayed on the screen in a television program or film.
v call by a title; name. ⟨Latin *titulus*⟩
ti·tled *adj* having a title such as that of a

duke, countess, lord, dame, etc.: *a titled lady.*
title deed a document showing that a person owns certain property. **title page** the page at the beginning of a book that carries the title, the author's name, etc. **title role** or **rôle** the character for which a play is named. Hamlet is a title role. **tit·u·lar** ['tɪtʃələr] *adj* **1** in name only: *He is a titular prince, without any power.* **2** to do with a title: *the titular heroine of Tolstoy's* Anna Karenina. **tit·u·lar·ly** *adv.*

ti·tre ['təitər] *or* ['titər] *n Chemistry* **1** a standard strength of a solution. **2** the minimum quantity of a standard solution needed to produce a given result in titration. Also, **ti·ter.** ⟨Old French *titre* proportion of gold/silver in an alloy⟩

ti·tra·tion [təi'treiʃən] *n* the process of determining the amount of some substance present in a solution by measuring the amount of a different substance that must be added to cause a chemical change. **ti·trate** *v.*

tit·ter ['tɪtər] *v* laugh or giggle nervously or affectedly: *Some of the audience tittered nervously when the actor forgot his lines.* **tit·ter** *n.* **tit·ter·er** *n.* ⟨imitative⟩

tit·u·lar See TITLE.

TKO or **t.k.o.** *Boxing* TECHNICAL KNOCKOUT.

TLC *Informal* tender loving care.

Tlin·git ['tlɪŋgɪt] *n, pl* **Tlin·git** or **Tlin·gits** *n* **1** a member of a group of First Nations peoples of the northern Pacific coast. **2** the languages spoken by these peoples. **Tlin·git** *adj.*

TM trademark.

TM or **T.M.** TRANSCENDENTAL MEDITATION.

TNT or **T.N.T.** trinitrotoluene.

to¹ [tu] *prep* **1** in the direction of: *Go to the right.* **2** as far as: *rotten to the core.* **3** in telling time, before (the hour): *ten to four.* **4** for the purpose of: *to the rescue.* **5** toward the position, state, etc of: *She tore it to pieces.* **6** by: *a fact known to few.* **7** with: *We danced to the music.* **8** as a response stimulated by: *What did she say to that?* **9** compared with: *The score was 9 to 5.* **10** as perceived by: *a symptom alarming to the doctor.* **11** of: *the key to my car.* **12** on or onto; against; at: *Fasten it to the wall.* **13** included in: *four beats to the bar.* **14** *To* is used to show action directed toward: *Speak to her.* ⟨Old English *tō*⟩
to and fro first one way and then back again. **to–and–fro** *adj.* **to–do** [tə 'du] *n Informal* a fuss; excitement: *There was a great to-do when the new puppy arrived.*

to² [tu] a grammatical function word marking the infinitive of verbs: *He likes to read.* ⟨Middle English; see TO¹.⟩

toad [toud] *n* any of numerous amphibians resembling frogs, but living mostly on land and having rough, dry, often warty skin. ⟨Old English *tāde*⟩
toad·stool *n* an umbrella-shaped fungus, esp a poisonous one. Compare MUSHROOM.

toast¹ [toust] *n* a slice or slices of bread browned by heat.
v **1** brown or be browned by heat. **2** heat or

become heated thoroughly. ⟨Old French *toster*; Latin *tostus* pp of *torrere* parch, roast⟩
be toast *Slang* be ruined or done for: *Try that once more and you're toast!*

toast² [toust] *n* **1** a tribute to a person or thing, in which people raise their glasses, express a wish for the health or success of the person or thing, and take a drink together: *a toast to the bride.* **2** a person having many admirers: *She was the toast of the town.* **toast** *v.* ⟨for the custom of flavouring drinks with spiced toast⟩
toast·er *n* an electrical appliance for toasting bread, etc. **toast·mas·ter** *n* **1** a person who presides at a dinner and introduces the speakers. **2** a person who proposes toasts. **toast·mis·tress** *n.* **toas·ty** *adj* cosily warm.

to·bac·co [tə'bækou] *n, pl* **-cos** or **-coes** a plant of the nightshade family, cultivated for its leaves, from which cigars, cigarettes, etc. are made. ⟨Spanish *tabaco*; Carib⟩
Tobacco Nation the Petun First Nations people, an Iroquoian people once inhabiting SW Ontario.

to·bog·gan [tə'bɒgən] ✶ *n* a narrow sleigh with a flat bottom and no runners, having the front end curved up and back.
v **1** ride or carry on a toboggan: *The supplies were tobogganed to camp.* **2** decline sharply and rapidly in value: *House prices tobogganed.* ⟨Cdn. French *tabagane*; Algonquian⟩

toc·ca·ta [tə'kɑtə] *n Music* a composition for a keyboard instrument, often intended to exhibit the player's technique. ⟨Italian, orig pp of *toccare* touch⟩

toc·sin [ˈtɒksən] *n* an alarm sounded on a bell. ⟨French; Provençal *tocasenh; tocar* strike, touch + *senh* bell⟩

to·day [tə'dei] *n* the present day, time, or period: *The photographer of today has many types of film to choose from.*
adv **1** on or during this day: *I have to go to the dentist today.* **2** at the present time or period; these days: *Most Canadian homes today have a refrigerator.* ⟨Old English *tō dæge* on (the) day⟩

tod·dle [ˈtɒdəl] *v* walk with short, unsteady steps, as a baby does. **tod·dle** *n.* ⟨origin unknown⟩
tod·dler *n* a young child, esp one between the ages of one and two or three.

tod·dy [ˈtɒdi] *n* a usually hot drink made of an alcoholic liquor mixed with water, sugar, and spices. ⟨Hindi *tārī* palm sap; *tār* palm⟩

toe [tou] *n* **1** one of the five end parts of the foot. **2** anything resembling a toe: *the toe and heel of a golf club.*
v **1** touch or reach with the toes: *to toe a line.* **2** turn the toes or have toes that turn in walking, dancing, etc.: *to toe in, to toe out.* **toe·less** *adj.* **toe·like** *adj.* ⟨Old English *tā*⟩
on one's toes alert. **step on someone's toes** offend someone, esp by encroaching on his or her domain of responsibility. **toe the line** obey rules, conform to a doctrine, etc.
toe·cap *n* the outer covering, often reinforced, of the toe of a boot or shoe.

toe·hold *n* **1** a small place of support for the toes when climbing: *The climber cut toeholds in the glacier as he went.* **2** any means of support in progressing, esp at the start of a venture, etc.: *She bought a neighbourhood store to get a toehold in the business.* **toe·nail** *n* **1** the nail growing on a toe. **2** *Carpentry* a nail driven obliquely. **toe·shoe** *n* either of a pair of ballet shoes with stiffening material in the toe, on which to balance.

tof·fee [ˈtɒfi] *n* taffy. ⟨origin uncertain⟩

to·fu [ˈtoufu] *n* a protein-rich food of a cheeselike consistency, made from soybeans. ⟨Japanese; Mandarin *to* bean + *fu* rot⟩

tog [tɒg] *n* Usually, **togs** *pl Informal* clothes. *v* **togged, tog·ging** clothe; dress (usually with *out* or *up*). ⟨earlier *togman* cloak; influenced by Latin *toga*⟩
tog·ger·y *n Informal* **1** clothes. **2** a clothing store.

to·geth·er [tə'gɛðər] *adv* **1** with each other: *They walked away together.* **2** in or into one unit, mass, etc.: *Mix the two colours together.* **3** in or into contact: *Bang the cymbals together.* **4** considered as a whole: *All together, there were 25 people at the party.* **5** in or into one gathering: *They get together to play cards.* **6** without a break: *He worked for days together.* *adj Slang* having a well-adjusted personality: *She is so together, she makes me nervous!* ⟨Old English *tō* to + *gædere* together⟩
get it (all) together *Slang* get affairs under control. **together with** along with.
to·geth·er·ness *n* the condition of being closely associated or united, esp in family or social activities.

USAGE
A singular subject followed by 'together with—' still takes a singular verb: *My uncle, together with my two cousins, was there to meet me.* Compare this with: *My uncle and my two cousins were there to meet me.*

tog·gle [ˈtɒgəl] *n* **1** a pin, bolt, etc. put through a loop to keep it in place, to act as a fastening for a coat, etc. **2** *Computers* a function that is activated and deactivated by the same command. **tog·gle** *v.* ⟨perhaps earlier *tog* tug⟩
toggle switch an electric switch having a projecting lever that is pushed up or down to open or close the circuit.

toil [tɔɪl] *n* hard work: *to succeed after years of toil.* **toil** *v.* **toil·er** *n.* ⟨Old French *toeillier* drag around; Latin *tudiculare* stir up⟩
toil·some *adj* requiring hard work; laborious. **toil·some·ly** *adv.* **toil·some·ness** *n.* **toil·worn** *adj* showing the effects of toil: *toilworn hands.*

toi·let [ˈtɔɪlɪt] *n* **1** a fixture, usually flushed by water, into which waste from the body is passed. **2** a room containing a toilet. **3** the process of washing, dressing, and grooming oneself: *She took an hour to complete her toilet.* *adj* **1** for a toilet: *a toilet brush.* **2** for use in the process of dressing and grooming: *toilet articles.* ⟨French *toilette* cloth bag for clothes⟩
go to the toilet *Informal* urinate or defecate.

toi·let·ing *n* independent use of a toilet (by a small child). **toilet paper** thin, soft, absorbent paper for use in cleaning the body after passing waste. **toi·let·ry** *n* Usually, **toiletries** *pl* soap, perfume, shaving cream, etc. used in washing and grooming oneself. **toi·lette** [twɑ'lɛt] *n* **1** the process of washing, dressing, and grooming. **2** fashionable attire. **toilet training** *n* the process of training a child to control bladder and bowel movements and to use a toilet. **toi·let–train** *v.* **toilet water** weak perfume.

to·ken ['toukən] *n* **1 a** a symbol: *Black is a token of mourning.* **b** an evidence: *His actions are a token of his sincerity.* **2** a keepsake: *She received many birthday tokens.* **3** a piece of metal, plastic, etc. stamped for a higher value than of the material, often for use as a single bus or train fare, etc. **4** a piece of metal, plastic, etc. indicating a right or privilege: *This token will admit you to the swimming pool. adj* **a** serving only as a symbol: *token resistance.* **b** included merely as a show of non-discrimination: *the token Asian on the committee.*⟨Old English *tācen*⟩ **by the same token** for the same reason; similarly. **in token of** as a token of; to show. **to·ken·ism** *n* the practice of making only a partial effort, esp in providing equal opportunity to disadvantaged or minority groups: *Putting a few women on boards of directors is just tokenism.*

told [tould] *v* pt and pp of TELL. **all told** including all.

tol·er·ate ['tɒlə,reit] *v* **1** permit: *He would never tolerate insolence.* **2** put up with: *They tolerated his manners because he was their employer.* **3** recognize the validity of (the beliefs, practices, etc. of others) although one may not share them. **4** endure or resist the effect of: *to tolerate pain.* **tol·er·ance** *n.* **tol·er·ant** *adj.* **tol·er·a·tion** *n.* ⟨Latin *tolerare*⟩ **tol·er·a·ble** *adj* **1** that can be endured: *The pain was tolerable.* **2** fairly good: *in tolerable health.* **tol·er·a·bil·i·ty** *n.* **tol·er·a·bly** *adv.*

> **CONFUSABLES**
> **Toleration** = the act of putting up with things, often because of indifference or a desire to avoid conflict: *Toleration of dishonest officials encourages corruption.* **Tolerance** = the state of being willing to let others live or worship according to their own beliefs: *Canadians value tolerance and understanding.*

toll[1] [toul] *v* **1** sound (a bell, etc.) with single strokes slowly: *Bells were tolled at the king's death.* **2** announce, etc. by tolling: *The bells tolled the death of the king.* **toll** *n.* ⟨related to Old English *-tyllan* draw. See TILL[3].⟩

toll[2] [toul] *n* **1** a fee paid for some service or privilege: *We pay a toll when we use the bridge.* **2** something paid, lost, suffered, etc.: *Automobile accidents take a heavy toll of human lives.* ⟨Old English *toll;* Latin *tolonium,* Greek *telōnion* toll house; *telos* tax⟩ **toll·booth** *n* a booth, as at the entry to a toll bridge, where drivers must stop and pay a

toll. **toll·free** *adj, adv* done, or that can be done, without charge.

tom [tɒm] *n* the male of some animals: *This turkey is a tom.* **tom** *adj.* ⟨*Tom,* commonly used as a male name⟩ **tom·boy** ['tɒm,bɔi] *n* a girl who has boyish mannerisms, tries to look like a boy, etc. **tom·cat** *n* a male cat. **tom·fool** *n* a silly fool; stupid person. **tom·fool** *adj.* **tom·fool·er·y** *n.* **tommy cod** ✱ any of several small saltwater fishes, esp of the St. Lawrence and adjacent waters, related to the cod.

tom·a·hawk ['tɒmə,hɒk] *n* a light axe formerly used by many First Nations peoples as a weapon and as a tool. *v* strike or kill with a tomahawk. **bury the tomahawk** stop fighting; make peace. ⟨Algonquian⟩

to·ma·to [tə'meitou], [tə'mɑtou], *or* [tə'mætou] *n, pl* **-toes** a juicy, red or yellow fruit commonly eaten as a vegetable, either raw or cooked. ⟨Spanish; Nahuatl *tomatl*⟩

tomb [tum] *n* **1** a vault or chamber for the dead, often built above ground. **2** a grave. **3** a monument to commemorate the dead. **tomb·like** *adj.* ⟨Greek *tymbos* mound⟩ **tomb·stone** *n* a stone that marks a grave.

tome [toum] *n* a book, esp a large, scholarly book. ⟨Greek *tomos,* orig piece cut off⟩

to·mor·row [tə'mɔrou] *n* **1** the day after today. **2** the future: *the world of tomorrow. adv* **1** on the day after today. **2** at some indefinite time in the future: *Tomorrow these same youth will be leaders of the nation.* ⟨Old English *to morgne; morgen* morning⟩

tom–tom ['tɒm ,tɒm] *n* a tall or long drum; esp, any of various such drums of India or Africa or of the First Nations. ⟨Hindi *tam-tam;* imitative⟩

ton [tʌn] *n* **1** formerly, a standard unit for measuring mass. A **short ton** equalled 2000 pounds (about 907 kg) and a **long ton** equalled 2240 pounds (about 1016 kg). **2** any of several units for measuring the capacity of a ship. **3** *Informal* a large number or amount: *These books weigh a ton.* ⟨variant of *tun,* cask⟩ **ton·nage** *n* **1** the capacity of a ship. **2** total mass in tons.

ton·al, to·nal·i·ty See TONE.

tone [toun] *n* **1** any sound considered with reference to its quality, pitch, etc.: *shrill tones.* **2** *Music* **a** the basic frequency of a musical note. **b** a pitch difference of one step between two notes. **3** a manner of speaking or writing: *the haughty tone of her letter.* **4 a** a style: *a tone of elegance.* **b** mental or emotional state: *a healthful tone of mind.* **5** *Physiology* normal firmness of healthy muscle at rest. **6** a shade of colour: *tones of brown.* **7** elegance; distinction. *v* harmonize (often with *in*): *This rug tones in well with the chair.* ⟨Greek *tonos* orig a stretching, taut string⟩ **tone down** soften; make or become less intense. **tone up** make or become louder, brighter, stronger, more intense, etc.

ton·al *adj* **1** to do with tones or tone. **2** characterized by TONALITY (def. 1): *tonal music.* **ton·al·ly** *adv.* **to·nal·i·ty** *n* **1** *Music* adherence to a particular arrangement of tones in a scale or musical system. **2** in painting, etc., the overall colour scheme: *The colours in the painting are dark, but the tonality is good.* **tone–deaf** *adj* not able to distinguish differences in musical pitch accurately. **tone deafness. tone language** or **tonal language** a language, such as Yoruba or Mandarin, in which homophones are distinguished in meaning by pitch or intonation. **tone·less** *adj* lacking variation of tone: *a toneless voice.* **tone·less·ly** *adv.* **tone·less·ness** *n.* **ton·er** *n* **1** the powdered ink used in xerography, usually in a cartridge. **2** an astringent cleanser for the face. **to·ny** *adj Informal* stylish; high-toned; fashionably elegant.

tongs [tɒŋz] *n pl* a tool for seizing, holding, or lifting, usually consisting of two long arms joined like a pair of scissors or by a spring piece. ⟨Old English *tonge, pl*⟩

tongue [tʌŋ] *n* **1 a** the movable organ in the mouth of most vertebrates. **b** an analogous part in invertebrates, as the proboscis of an insect. **2** the power of speech: *You are silent— have you lost your tongue?* **3** a way of speaking; speech; talk: *a flattering tongue.* **4** the language of a people: *the English tongue.* **5** the strip of material under the laces of a shoe. **6** a narrow strip of land running out into water. **7** anything shaped or used like a tongue. *v* touch with the tongue. **tongue·less** *adj.* **tongue·like** *adj.* ⟨Old English *tunge*⟩ **give tongue a** of hounds, etc., bark or bay. **b** of humans, speak, cry, etc. vociferously (*facetiously*): *The infant opened her mouth and gave tongue.* **hold one's tongue** keep silent. **on the tip of one's tongue a** almost spoken. **b** ready to be spoken. **speak in tongues** practise glossolalia. (**with one's**) **tongue in** (**one's**) **cheek** ironically; facetiously. **tongue–in–cheek** *adj* **tongue–and–groove joint** *Carpentry* a joint made by fitting a projecting strip, or tongue, along one edge of a board into a groove in another board. **tongue–lash·ing** *n* a severe scolding. **tongue-lash** *v.* **tongue–tied** *adj* unable to speak because of shyness. **tongue twister** a phrase or sentence having a sequence of sounds that are difficult to say quickly. *Example: She sells sea shells on the seashore.* **tongu·ing** *n* use of the tongue in playing a wind instrument.

ton·ic ['tɒnɪk] *n* **1** anything that gives strength, vigour, or refreshment: *Conversation with children was a tonic for the old man.* **2** *Music* the first note of a scale; keynote. *adj* **1** restoring to health and vigour; giving strength; bracing: *The mountain air is tonic.* **2** *Music* **a** to do with a tone. **b** to do with a keynote. **to·nic·i·ty** [tə'nɪsəti] *n.* ⟨See TONE.⟩ **tonic water** quinine-flavoured carbonated water. **tonic sol-fa** See SOL.

to·night [tə'naɪt] *adv* on or during the present or the coming night or evening.

n the present or the coming night or evening: *I wish tonight would come!* ⟨Old English *tō niht*⟩

tonne [tʌn] *n* a unit used with the SI for measuring mass, equal to 1000 kg. Also called **metric ton.** *Symbol* **t** ⟨French⟩

ton·sil ['tɒnsəl] *n* either of the two oval masses of tissue on the inner sides of the throat. **ton·sil·lar** or **ton·sil·ar** *adj.* ⟨Latin *tonsillae* pl, diminutive of *toles* pl, goiter⟩ **ton·sil·lec·to·my** [-'lɛktəmi] *n* a removal of the tonsils by surgery. **ton·sil·li·tis** [-'laɪtɪs] *n* inflammation of the tonsils.

ton·sure ['tɒnʃər] *n* the shaved part of the head of a priest or monk. **ton·sure** *v.* ⟨Latin *tonsura; tonsus* pp of *tondere* shave⟩

too [tu] *adv* **1** also: *The dog is hungry, and thirsty too.* **2** more than enough: *Time passed too quickly.* **3** very: *I didn't do too well on the exam.* **4** most definitely (to contradict a negative): *I didn't. You did too!* ⟨variant of *to*⟩

took [tʊk] *v* pt of TAKE.

tool [tul] *n* **1** a knife, hammer, saw, or any instrument used in doing manual work. **2** anything used in one's profession or occupation: *Books are a scholar's tools.* **3** a person used by another like a tool: *He is a tool of the department head.* *v* **1** work, shape, or cut with a tool: *He tooled beautiful designs in leather with a knife.* **2** *Slang* drive, esp fast: *tooling along the highway in a beat-up old car.* ⟨Old English *tōl*⟩ **tool up** install equipment (in) for a certain task: *The factory is tooling up for the production of new cars.* **tool·box** *n* a box with compartments and a handle, for storing and carrying hand tools. **tool chest** a toolbox large enough for big items such as power saws, drills, etc., and having a lid. **tool·ing** *n* ornamentation made with a hand tool; esp, lettering or designs made on leather. **tool·mak·er** *n* a person who makes tools, or who makes or maintains machine tools. **tool·mak·ing** *n.*

SYNONYMS
Tool indicates an instrument designed to be held in doing manual work: *Plumbers, mechanics, and carpenters need tools.* **Implement** is a general word meaning a tool, instrument, utensil, or machine: *Hoes and tractors are agricultural implements.*

toon [tun] *n Slang* cartoon; cartoon character. ⟨shortened from *cartoon*⟩

toon·ie or **toon·y** ['tuni] *n* ✳ the Canadian two-dollar coin. Also, **twon·ie** or **twoon·ie.** ⟨alteration of *two* + *-nie* on the analogy of *loonie*⟩

toot [tut] *n* the short sound of a horn, whistle, etc. **toot** *v.* ⟨probably imitative⟩ **too·tle** *v* toot softly and continuously, as on a whistle. **too·tle** *n.* **too·tler** *n.*

tooth [tuθ] *n, pl* **teeth 1** one of the bony projections in the mouth, used for biting and chewing. **2** something like a tooth. Each one of the projecting parts of a comb is a tooth. **tooth·like** *adj.* ⟨Old English *tōth*⟩

fight tooth and nail fight fiercely, with all one's force. **long in the tooth** ageing or old. For idioms with **teeth**, see TEETH.
tooth·ache [-ˌeik] *n* a pain in a tooth.
tooth·brush *n* a small, long-handled brush for cleaning the teeth. **toothed** [tuθt] *or* [tuðd] *adj* 1 having teeth, esp of a certain kind or number (often in compounds): *yellow-toothed.* 2 indented: *a toothed blade.*
tooth·less *adj* 1 without teeth. 2 without force. **tooth·paste** *n* an abrasive paste for cleaning the teeth. **tooth·pick** *n* a small piece of wood, plastic, etc., for removing food from between the teeth. **tooth·some** *adj* 1 tasting good. 2 attractive; voluptuous. **tooth·some·ly** *adv.* **tooth·some·ness** *n.* **too·thy** *adj* having prominent teeth: *a toothy grin.*

top¹ [tɒp] *n* 1 the highest part: *the top of a mountain.* 2 the upper surface: *the top of a table.* 3 the highest rank, etc.: *the top of his class.* 4 the highest degree: *yelling at the top of her voice.* 5 a lid or cap: *Put the top back on the bottle.* 6 a piece of clothing for the upper part of the body: *She wore white shorts and a pink top.* 7 *Baseball* the first half of an inning. 8 the first or opening part (of a song, scene, etc. to be performed): *Let's take it from the top.*
adj 1 to do with the top: *the top shelf.* 2 greatest: *at top speed.* 3 chief: *top honours.*
v **topped, top·ping** 1 be on or at the top of: *A church tops the hill.* 2 reach the top of: *They topped the mountain.* 3 rise above: *The sun topped the horizon.* 4 do better than. *His story topped all the rest.* 5 remove the top of (a plant, etc.). ⟨Old English *topp*⟩
blow one's top *Slang* lose one's temper. **from top to toe a** from head to foot. **b** completely. **off the top** *Informal* deducted from the gross amount (of income, etc.) before other deductions. **off the top of one's head** without reflection or preparation. **on top** with victory: *to come out on top.* **on top (of) a** in addition (to). **b** right after: *The accident came right on top of the death of his mother.* **c** in control (of): *on top of the situation.* **top off** put the finishing touches to: *We topped off the evening with an excellent dinner.* **top up** replenish or refill (something).
top banana *Slang* 1 in show business, the star performer, esp the leading comedian. 2 the leader of any group. **top boot** a high boot. **top brass** *Slang* 1 high-ranking officers of the armed forces. 2 high-ranking officials of any organization. **top·coat** *n* 1 an overcoat. 2 a finishing coating of paint, etc. **top dog** *Informal* the best, most successful or most important individual or group. **top dollar** a great amount of money (paid or earned for something). **top drawer** *Informal* the highest level of excellence, importance, good breeding, etc.: *a family in the top drawer of society.* **top–draw·er** *adj.* **top dressing** 1 a layer of compost or rich soil spread on arable land. 2 a top layer of gravel, crushed rock, etc. on a roadway. **top–dress** *v.* **top–flight** *adj* of the highest excellence; the best in its (or his or her) class or field. **top hat** a tall, black silk hat worn with formal clothes by men.

top–heav·y *adj* 1 too heavy at the top, so as to be likely to fall over. 2 having too many officials of high rank: *a school board top-heavy with administrators.* **top–heav·i·ly** *adv.*
top–heav·i·ness *n.* **top·knot** [-ˌnɒt] *n* 1 a tuft of hair on the top of the head. 2 a plume or crest of feathers on the head of a bird. 3 a cluster of feathers, a bow, or other decoration worn on the top of the head. **top·less** *adj* 1 having no top: *a topless table.* 2 wearing no clothes on the upper part of the body: *a topless waitress.* 3 so high that the top cannot be seen. **top·most** *adj* highest. **top–notch** *adj Informal* first-rate. **top·per** *n Informal* TOP HAT. **top·ping** *n* something that forms a top, such as a garnish placed on food: *a topping of whipped cream.* **tops** *Slang adj* of the highest degree in quality, popularity, etc. (never before a noun): *She's tops in her field. n.* **the tops** an excellent person or thing of its kind. **top–se·cret** *adj* of utmost secrecy. **top·soil** *n* surface soil suitable for growing plants in. **top·spin** *n* a fast spinning motion applied to a ball, esp in tennis. **top·stitch·ing** *n* a decorative line of stitching on the outside of a garment near an edge or seam. **top·stitch** *v.*

top² [tɒp] *n* a toy having a point at one end on which it can spin. ⟨Old English *topp*⟩
sleep like a top sleep soundly.

to·paz ['toupæz] *or* [tou'pæz] *n* a mineral occurring in crystals in various colours. ⟨Greek *topazos*⟩

tope [toup] *v* drink alcohol excessively or habitually; tipple. **top·er** *n.* ⟨origin uncertain⟩

to·pi ['toupi] *n* in the Indian subcontinent, the brimless cap worn by men. ⟨Hindi⟩

to·pi·ar·y ['toupiˌɛri] *Gardening adj* trimmed into figures or designs: *topiary shrubs.*
n the art of such trimming. ⟨Latin *topia* fancy gardening; Greek *topos* place⟩

top·ic ['tɒpɪk] *n* 1 a subject that people think, write, or talk about: *The main topic at lunch was the weather.* 2 a short phrase or sentence used in an outline to give the main point of part of a speech, writing, etc. ⟨Greek *(ta) topika* study of logical and rhetorical commonplaces by Aristotle; *topos* place⟩
top·i·cal *adj* 1 to do with topics of current interest. 2 to do with the topics of a speech, writing, etc.; arranged according to topic: *a topical index.* 3 of or designed for a particular part of the body: *a topical medicine.*
top·i·cal·i·ty *n.* **top·i·cal·ly** *adv.*

to·pog·ra·phy [tə'pɒɡrəfi] *n* 1 the art of detailed description of the natural and artificial features of a place. 2 a detailed description of the surface features of a place. 3 the features themselves: *The topography of a region includes hills, valleys, streams, lakes, bridges, tunnels, roads, etc.* 4 a description of an area of the body, of a galaxy, or of any other system, giving the different parts, their features and interrelationships, etc.: *a topography of the human brain.* **to·pog·ra·pher** *n.*
top·o·graph·i·cal *or* **top·o·graph·ic** *adj.*
top·o·graph·i·cal·ly *adv.* ⟨Greek *topos* place + *graphein* write⟩

to·pol·o·gy [tə'pɒlədʒi] *n Mathematics* the study of the properties of geometric forms and spatial relations that remain unchanged under continuous change of shape or size. **top·o·log·i·cal** *adj.* **top·o·log·i·cal·ly** *adv.* **to·pol·o·gist** *n.* ⟨Greek *topos* place⟩

top·ple ['tɒpəl] *v* **1** tumble down: *The tree toppled over onto the roof.* **2** cause the fall of: *The rebel army toppled the government.* ⟨related to *top, v*⟩

top·sy–tur·vy ['tɒpsi 'tɜrvi] *adj* **1** upside down. **2** in confusion or disorder. ⟨probably related to Old English *tearflian* roll over⟩ **top·sy–tur·vi·ly** *adv.* **top·sy–tur·vi·ness** *n.*

toque [touk] *n* **1** a hat with no brim or with very little brim. **2** tuque. ⟨French⟩

tor [tɔr] *n* a high, bare, rocky hill or small mountain. ⟨Old English *torr* tower, crag⟩

to·rah or **to·ra** ['tɔrə] *n* in Jewish usage: **1** a doctrine, teaching, or law. **2** Usually, **Torah**, the totality of sacred writings, including actual Scripture, the Talmud, etc. **3 the Torah** the law of Moses; Pentateuch. ⟨Hebrew⟩

torch [tɔrtʃ] *n* **1** a makeshift light consisting of a piece of wood dipped in pitch, grease, etc., and ignited. **2** a device for producing a very hot flame; blowtorch. *v Slang* set on fire or burn down, esp maliciously. **torch·like** *adj.* ⟨Old French *torche*, probably Latin *torquere* twist⟩ **carry a** (or **the**) **torch** (**for**) *Slang* suffer unrequited love (for): *He has been carrying the torch for her for months.* **torch·bear·er** *n* **1** one who carries a torch. **2** *Informal* one who is prominent in support of a cause. **tor·chiere** or **tor·chère** [tɔr'ʃir] or [tɔr'ʃɛr] *n* a floor lamp with a reflector facing upward. **torch·light** *n* the light of a torch. *adj* performed by torchlight: *a torchlight procession.* **torch song** a popular song having unrequited love as its theme. **torch singer.**

tore [tɔr] *v* pt of TEAR².

to·re·ro [tə'rɛrou] *Spanish* [tɔ'rero] *n* bullfighter. Also called **to·re·a·dor** ['tɔriə,dɔr]. ⟨Spanish; *toro* bull, Latin *taurus*⟩

to·ri·i ['tɔri,i] *n, pl* **-ri·i** in Japan, a gateway at the entrance to a Shinto temple, built of two uprights and two crosspieces. ⟨Japanese⟩

tor·ment *v* [tɔr'mɛnt] **1** cause great pain or mental anguish to. **2** annoy very much: *He torments everyone with silly questions.* *n* ['tɔrmɛnt] **1** great pain or mental anguish, or its cause. **2** a cause of annoyance. **tor·men·tor** or **tor·ment·er** *n.* ⟨Latin *tormentum* orig twisted sling; *torquere* twist⟩

[SYNONYMS]
Torment emphasizes hurting again and again: *She is tormented by a racking cough.* **Torture** emphasizes severity, and suggests a deliberate cruelty: *We do not torture prisoners.*

torn [tɔrn] *v* pp of TEAR².

tor·na·do [tɔr'neidou] *n, pl* **-does** or **-dos 1** a violent cyclone, seen as a funnel-shaped, whirling cloud that moves across the land.

2 any whirlwind. **tor·nad·ic** [-'nædɪk] *adj.* ⟨Spanish *tronada; tronar* thunder⟩

tor·pe·do [tɔr'pidou] *n, pl* **-does** a large shell that contains explosives and travels by its own power. Torpedoes are launched under water from a vessel, to blow up enemy ships. *v* **1** attack or destroy with a torpedo. **2** bring completely to an end: *to torpedo a peace conference.* ⟨Latin *torpere* be numb⟩

tor·pid ['tɔrpɪd] *adj* dull or sluggish: *a torpid mind.* **tor·pid·i·ty** *n.* **tor·pid·ly** *adv.* ⟨Latin *torpere* be numb⟩ **tor·por** ['tɔrpər] *n* **1** a state of being dormant or inactive. **2** sluggishness or dullness.

torque [tɔrk] *n* **1** a force that produces rotation. **2** a measure of rotatory tendency. ⟨Latin *torquere* twist⟩

tor·rent ['tɔrənt] *n* **1** a violent, rushing stream of liquid, esp water or lava. **2** any violent stream or flood: *a torrent of abuse.* **3** a downpour of rain. **tor·ren·tial** [tə'rɛnʃəl] *adj.* **tor·ren·tial·ly** *adv.* ⟨Latin *torrere* boil, parch⟩

tor·rid ['tɔrɪd] *adj* **1** very hot: *a torrid climate.* **2** exposed to great heat: *the torrid wastes of the Sahara.* **3** passionate: *torrid love letters.* **tor·rid·ly** *adv.* **tor·rid·ness** or **tor·rid·i·ty** *n.* ⟨Latin *torrere* parch⟩

tor·sion ['tɔrʃən] *n* **1** the process of twisting. **2** stress, strain, or distortion resulting from such a process. **3** the torque exerted by a body being twisted. ⟨Latin *torsio, tortio; tortus* pp of *torquere* twist⟩

tor·so ['tɔrsou] *n* the body without any head, arms, or legs. ⟨Italian, orig stalk; Greek *thyrsos* wand⟩

tort [tɔrt] *n Law* a civil, as opposed to criminal, wrong for which the law requires damages: *If your car breaks a fence, you may have committed a tort against the owner.* ⟨Latin *tortum* injustice⟩

tor·te ['tɔrtə] or [tɔrt] *n, pl* **tor·tes** or **tor·ten** ['tɔrtən] a rich cake with a filling or topping of cream, fruit, nuts, etc. ⟨German; Italian *torta;* Latin, round or twisted (loaf)⟩

tor·tel·li·ni [,tɔrtə'lini] *n* pasta in the form of small pouches filled with meat, etc. ⟨Italian, double diminutive of *torta.* See TORTE.⟩

tor·til·la [tɔr'tijə] *n* esp in Spanish America, a thin, flat, round corn cake. ⟨Spanish, diminutive of *torta.* See TORTE.⟩

tor·toise ['tɔrtəs] *n, pl* **-toise** or **-tois·es** a turtle, esp any land-dwelling turtle. ⟨Middle English *tortuce;* Latin *tortuca*⟩ **tor·toise·shell** *n* **1** the mottled shell of some species of turtle, used for ornaments, combs, etc. **2** a breed of domestic cat, having a coat of mottled black, tan, and cream. **3** any of various butterflies having orange-and-black wings. **tor·toise·shell** *adj.*

tor·tu·ous ['tɔrtʃuəs] *adj* **1** full of twists, turns, or bends. **2** not straightforward; devious: *tortuous reasoning.* **tor·tu·os·i·ty** *n.* **tor·tu·ous·ly** *adv.* **tor·tu·ous·ness** *n.* ⟨Latin *tortuosus; tortus* pp of *torquere* twist⟩

tor·ture ['tɔrtʃər] *n* **1** the act or fact of

inflicting extreme pain, esp to make people confess. **2** extreme pain. **3** something that causes extreme pain.
v **1** cause extreme pain to, esp in order to obtain evidence, a confession, etc. **2** twist the meaning of. **3** distort: *Winds tortured the trees.* **tor·tur·er** *n.* **tor·tur·ous** *adj.* **tor·tur·ous·ly** *adv.* ⟨Latin *tortura; tortus* pp of *torquere* twist⟩

CONFUSABLES

Torturous and **tortuous** are sometimes confused because of their similar sound. Anything that causes torture can be called **torturous. Tortuous** has a much narrower meaning; it means simply 'twisted'.

To·ry ['tɔri] *n* **1** in Canada, a member or supporter of a Conservative Party. **2** Often, **tory** a person who has conservative political principles. **To·ry** *adj.* **To·ry·ism** *n.* ⟨Irish *tóraí* persecuted person, outlaw; *toír* pursuit⟩

toss [tɒs] *v* **tossed** or *Poetic* **tost, tos·sing** *v* **1** throw lightly: *toss a ball.* **2** throw about: *The ship was tossed by the heavy waves.* **3** lift quickly: *She tossed her head.* **4** throw (a coin) up in the air to decide something by the side that falls upward. **5** roll restlessly. **toss** *n.* ⟨perhaps Scandinavian⟩
toss and turn sleep poorly. **toss off a** do or make quickly and easily. **b** drink all at once: *He tossed off a whole glass of whisky.* **toss up** toss a coin as a way of deciding something.
toss–up *n* an even chance: *It was a toss-up whether he or she would get the nomination.*

tot [tɒt] *n* a little child.

to·tal ['toutəl] *adj* **1** whole, esp having all parts included: *The total cost of the furnishings will be $10 000.* **2** complete: *total darkness. n* the whole amount; sum.
v **-talled** or **-taled, -tal·ling** or **-tal·ing** *v* **1** add: *Total those figures.* **2** amount (sometimes with *to*): *The money spent yearly on chewing gum totals millions of dollars.* **3** *Slang* wreck completely: *Her car was totalled in the accident.* ⟨Latin *totalis; totus* all, the whole⟩
to·tal·i·tar·i·an [tou,tælə'tɛriən] *adj* to do with a form of government in which a centralized authority permits no competing political group and exercises strict control. *n* a person who supports totalitarianism. **to·tal·i·tar·i·an·ism** *n.* **to·tal·i·ty** *n* **1** whole; sum. **2** entirety. **3** a total eclipse. **to·tal·ly** *adv* completely. **total recall** the ability to remember clearly every detail about an experience in the past. **total war** a war in which all the resources of a nation are used, and in which offensive action includes that against people and property.

tote [tout] *v Informal* carry; haul.
n **1** a carrying. **2** the distance of this: *a long tote.* **3** a TOTE BAG.⟨origin uncertain⟩
tote bag a large handbag used for carrying small packages, clothing, etc.

to·tem ['toutəm] *n* **1** among First Nations peoples of the northern Pacific coast, an animal or plant taken as the emblem of a people, clan, or family. **2** among many peoples, a creature or object associated with their ancestral traditions and looked on with reverence. **3** a representation of a totem. **4** anything used as an emblem or symbol. **to·tem·ic** [tou'tɛmɪk] *adj.* ⟨Algonquian⟩
to·tem·ism *n* **1** belief in a mystical kinship between humans and animals and plants. **2** the use of totems to distinguish tribes, clans, or families. **to·tem·ist** *n.* **to·tem·is·tic** *adj.*
totem pole 1 a large upright log carved and painted with representations of clan emblems, or totems. Traditionally erected by the First Nations peoples of the northern Pacific coast, totem poles serve as a record of the ancestry of a family and sometimes also of historical or mythological happenings. **2** *Informal* hierarchy; pecking order: *He's low on the totem pole at work.*

tot·ter ['tɒtər] *v* **1** walk with unsteady steps. **2** tremble as if about to fall: *The old wall tottered and fell.* **3** be about to collapse: *The old regime was already tottering before the revolution broke out.* **tot·ter** *n.* **tot·ter·er** *n.* **tot·ter·ing** *adj.* ⟨perhaps Scandinavian; compare Swedish *tuttra* shake⟩
tot·ter·y *adj* tottering; shaky.

touch [tʌtʃ] *v* **1** put some part of the body on or against: *She touched the pan to see whether it was still hot.* **2** put something against: *He touched the post with his umbrella.* **3** injure slightly: *The flowers were touched by the frost.* **4** affect with some feeling: *The sad story touched us.* **5** (in the negative) **a** use at all: *He won't touch liquor.* **b** eat or drink the slightest amount of: *You haven't touched your dinner.* **6** take, use, or handle without right: *Who touched the file on my desk?* **7** rival: *No one can touch her in music.* **8** mark slightly, as with some colour: *a sky touched with pink.*
n **1** a touching or being touched. **2** the sense by which a person perceives things by feeling them: *People who are blind have keen touch.* **3** communication: *A newspaper keeps one in touch with the world.* **4** a bit: *It needs a touch more salt.* **5** of a keyboard, the resistance that the keys offer: *A piano should not have too light a touch.* **6** a distinctive manner: *an expert's touch.* **7** special ability or skill: *The magician seemed to have lost his touch.* **8** *Slang* **a** the act of getting money from a person. **b** a person from whom one has got money in this way: *He's a soft touch.* **9** *Football, soccer, etc.* the part of the field, including the sidelines, lying outside the field of play. **touch·a·ble** *adj.* **touch·er** *n.* ⟨Old French *tuchier;* Latin *toccare* strike (as a bell)⟩
not touch with a bargepole (or **ten-foot pole**) See BARGEPOLE. **touch down a** land. **b** *Football* touch the ground with (the ball) behind the opposing team's goal line. **touch·down** *n.* **touch off** cause to start: *The new tax touched off a rebellion.* **touch on** (or **upon**) **a** speak of: *Our conversation touched on many subjects.* **touch up** improve: *to touch up a photograph.* **touch wood** expression used facetiously as a charm after mentioning one's good fortune, as if to prevent its reversal.
touch–and–go *adj* uncertain: *So far it's been*

touch-and-go, but we're still hoping for the best.
tou·ché [tu'ʃei] *n* a touch by an opponent's weapon in fencing. *interj* **1** an exclamation at this touch. **2** an exclamation acknowledging a clever reply or a point well made in discussion. **touched** *adj* **1** stirred emotionally, esp by gratitude or sympathy: *I was touched by their offer to help.* **2** *Informal* slightly unbalanced mentally. **touch football** football in which the person carrying the ball is touched rather than tackled. **touch·ing** *adj* arousing tender feeling. *prep* concerning. **touch·ing·ly** *adv.* **touch·pad** *Computers* a soft pad used esp on laptops, as an alternative to a mouse. Also, **track·pad. touch·screen** *n Computers* a specially adapted screen covered with a membrane sensitive to touch, as an alternative to a mouse. **touch·stone** *n* **1** a stone containing silica, formerly used to test the purity of gold or silver. **2** any test or standard for determining the genuineness or value of something: *Her work is the touchstone of excellence in art.* **touch–tone** *adj* designating a phone with buttons instead of a dial. **touch·y** *adj* **1** apt to take offence at trifles. **2** requiring skill in handling: *a touchy situation.* **touch·i·ly** *adv.* **touch·i·ness** *n.* **touch·y–feel·y** *adj Informal* to do with an approach that emphasizes emotional sensitivity and physical contact.

tough [tʌf] *adj* **1** hard to cut, tear, etc: *Leather is tough.* **2** stiff; sticky: *tough clay.* **3** strong: *a tough plant.* **4** showing great mental or moral strength. **5** not easily affected emotionally: *He never cries because he thinks he must be tough.* **6** hard; difficult: *tough work.* **7** bad; unpleasant: *tough luck.* **8** stubborn: *a tough customer.* **9** violent; strenuous: *Football is a tough game.* **10** rough; disorderly: *a tough neighbourhood.* *n* a rough person; rowdy. **tough·en** *v.* **tough·en·er** *n.* **tough·ly** *adv.* **tough·ness** *n.* ⟨Old English *tōh*⟩
tough it out *Slang* endure a difficulty to the end in a bold or stoic manner.
tough·ie *n Informal* something or someone that is tough. **tough–mind·ed** *adj* practical, realistic, and unemotional.

tou·pee [tu'pei] *n* a wig worn to cover a bald spot. ⟨Old French *toupe* tuft⟩

tour [tur] *n* **1** a long journey through a country or countries: *a European tour.* **2** a regular spell of work or duty: *Her last tour of duty was in France.* **3** a short trip or walk around, as for inspection: *a tour of the boat.*
on tour of a theatre company, entertainer, etc., travelling from place to place.
v **1** travel through: *Last year they toured Europe.* **2** *Theatre* take (a play, show, etc.) on tour. **3** go through (a building) to see its exhibits, etc.: *to tour a museum.* ⟨French; Greek *tornos* turner's wheel, lathe⟩
tour·ism *n* **1** travelling as a pastime or recreation. **2** the business of providing services for tourists. **tour·is·tic** *adj.* **tour·ist** *n* a person travelling for pleasure. **tourist class**

the lowest class of accommodation for passengers on a ship, train, etc. **tourist trap** a place that exploits tourists. **tour·ist·y** *adj Informal, often pejorative* **1** like a tourist: *a touristy outfit.* **2** catering to tourists: *They tried to avoid the touristy places on their trip.*

tour de force ['tur də 'fɔrs] *pl* **tours de force** ['tur də 'fɔrs] **1** a notable feat of strength, skill, or ingenuity. **2** something done that is merely clever or ingenious: *His later brilliance showed that his first novel was little more than a tour de force.* ⟨French = feat of strength⟩

tour·na·ment ['tɜrnəmənt] *n* **1** a series of contests testing the skill of many persons: *a golf tournament.* **2** in the Middle Ages: a jousting contest between two groups of knights on horseback. ⟨Old French *torneiement; torneier;* Latin *tornus.* See TURN.⟩
tour·ney ['tɜrni] *n, pl* **-neys** tournament. *v* take part in a tournament.

tour·ni·quet ['tɜrnəkɪt] *or* ['tɜrnə,kei] *n* any device to stop bleeding by compressing a blood vessel. ⟨French; *tourner* to turn⟩

tour·tière [tur'tjɛr] *French* [tuʀ'tjɛʀ] *n* ✹ a pie made with ground pork, often mixed with some veal or chicken. ⟨Cdn. French⟩

tou·sle ['tauzəl] *v* put into disorder: *She tousled her brother's hair to tease him.*
n a disordered or tangled mass of hair, etc. ⟨Middle English *tousen*⟩

tout [taut] *Informal v* **1** praise highly and insistently. **2** try to get (customers, jobs, votes, etc.). **3** urge betting on (a horse) by claiming to have special information. **tout** *n.* ⟨variant of Old English *tȳtan* peep out⟩

tow [tou] *v* pull along by a rope, chain, etc. *n* **1** the act or an instance of towing: *He charges a lot for a tow.* **2** something used for towing: *a ski tow.* ⟨Old English *togian* drag⟩
in tow a in the state of being towed: *The launch had a sailboat in tow.* **b** under guidance: *He was taken in tow by his aunt.* **c** in the position of follower: *The movie producer arrived with several admirers in tow.*
tow·age *n* **1** towing or being towed. **2** a charge for towing. **tow·line** *n* a chain, etc. for towing. **tow truck** a truck equipped for towing disabled or illegally parked vehicles.

to·ward [tʊ'wɔrd], [twɔrd], *or* [tɔrd] *prep* **1** in the direction of. **2** concerning: *What is your attitude toward war?* **3** as a help to: *Will you give something toward our new hospital?* Also, **to·wards**. ⟨Old English *tōweard*⟩

tow·el ['tauəl] *v* **-elled** *or* **-eled, -el·ling** *or* **-el·ing** *n* an absorbent piece of cloth or paper for wiping and drying something wet.
v dry with a towel. ⟨Old French *toaille*⟩
throw in the towel *Informal* admit defeat. **tow·el·ette** [-'lɛt] *n* a small paper towel, usually moistened and in a foil package, for wiping the hands, etc. when travelling or eating out. **tow·el·ling** *or* **tow·el·ing** *n* material used for towels, esp cotton terry.

tow·er ['tauər] *n* **1** a high structure that may be walled, or consist only of a framework: *a lookout tower.* **2** a highrise: *an office tower.*

v rise or reach to a great height: *He was a giant of a man, towering over all his friends.* ⟨Old French *tor, tur*; Latin *turris*⟩

tower of strength a person or thing that acts as a support in a difficult situation: *She's a tower of strength in an emergency.*

tow·er·ing *adj* **1** very high. **2** very tall: *a towering basketball player.* **3** very great: *Making electricity from atomic power is a towering achievement.* **4** very violent: *a towering rage.*

tow·head *n* a person having light, pale yellow hair. **tow·head·ed** *adj.* ⟨Old English *tōw-* spinning + HEAD⟩

tow·hee ['tauhi] *or* ['touhi] *n* a North American finch having a call that sounds somewhat like its name. ⟨imitative of its call⟩

town [taun] *n* **1** a large group of houses, stores, schools, churches, etc. that forms a community with its own local government. A town is usually smaller than a city but larger than a village. **2** any large place with many people living in it: *Toronto is an exciting town.* **3** the people of a town: *The whole town was having a holiday.* **4** the part of a town or city where the stores and office buildings are: *Let's go into town.* **5** TOWNSHIP (def. 1). *adj* to do with a town. ⟨Old English *tūn*⟩

go to town *Informal* do something thoroughly: *The hungry girls really went to town on that pie.* **in town** in a specified town or city: *He is not in town today.* **out of town** happening, located, etc. outside a specified town or city: *The restaurant is a short distance out of town.* (**out**) **on the town** out for entertainment and pleasure as available in a city or town. **paint the town red** *Slang* celebrate in a noisy manner.

town council the elected government of a municipality smaller than a city. **town hall 1** the headquarters of a town's government. **2** a local public meeting to discuss a political issue. **town·house** *n* a house in a row of attached houses two or more storeys high, with its own street entrance and yard. **town·ie** *n Informal* **1** a permanent resident of a town, esp as contrasted with residents of the surrounding rural area, tourists, etc. **2** ✱ *Newfoundland and Labrador* a resident of St. John's as opposed to one who lives in an outport. **town meeting** a general meeting of the inhabitants of the town. **towns·folk** *n pl* townspeople. **town·ship** *n* **1** in Canada and the US, a division of a county having certain powers of government; municipality. **2** a land-survey area on which later subdivisions may be based. In the Prairie Provinces, a township is an area of about 93 km². *Abbrev* **Tp.**, **tp.**, **twp.**, or **Twp.** **towns·people** *n pl* the people of a town or city.

tox·ic ['tɒksɪk] *adj* **1** to do with a poison or toxin: *a toxic reaction.* **2** poisonous: *Car exhaust fumes are toxic.* **tox·i·cal·ly** *adv.* ⟨Latin *toxicum* poison; Greek *toxon* bow; from use of poison on arrows⟩

tox·ic·i·ty [tɒk'sɪsəti] *n* the quality or state of being toxic. **tox·i·co·gen·ic** *adj* that produces toxic substances. **tox·i·col·o·gy** *n* the science

that deals with poisons, antidotes, etc. **tox·i·co·log·i·cal** *adj.* **tox·i·col·o·gist** *n.* **tox·in** *n* any poisonous product of animal or vegetable metabolism, esp one of those produced by bacteria.

toy [tɔi] *n* **1** something to play with, esp for a child: *Put that carving down; it is not a toy.* **2** something small and pleasing like a toy, but having little real value: *That little calculator is nothing but a toy.* **3** a small breed or variety of dog: *Chihuahuas are toys.* *adj* as a model of a real thing: *a toy truck.* *v* handle in a light, careless, or trifling way (with *with*): *She toyed with her beads as she talked.* **toy·like** *adj.* ⟨perhaps Dutch *tuig* tools, stuff as in *speeltuig* plaything⟩

toy·shop *n* a store whose chief line is toys.

trace¹ [treis] *n* **1** a sign of the existence of something in the past: *The explorer found traces of an ancient city.* **2** a track; trail: *We saw traces of rabbits in the snow.* **3** a very small amount: *There wasn't a trace of grey in her hair.* **4** the record made by the moving pen or stylus of a recording instrument. *v* **1** follow the development of: *He traced the river to its source.* **2** track down: *They have been unable to trace the suspect.* **3** copy by following the lines of: *He put thin paper over the map and traced it.* **trace·a·ble** *adj.* **trace·a·bly** *adv.* **trace·a·bil·i·ty** *n.*⟨Old French *tracier*, Latin *tractiare*; *trahere* drag⟩

trace element any element occurring in very small amounts, esp one necessary to the physiological and biological processes of an organism. **trac·er** *n* **1** an inquiry sent from place to place to trace a missing person, letter, parcel, etc. **2** a bullet containing a substance that marks its course with a trail of smoke or fire. **trac·er·y** *n* **1** ornamental openwork in stone, consisting of interlacing lines. **2** any decorative pattern suggesting this: *the tracery in a butterfly's wing.* **trac·er·ied** *adj.* **trac·ing** *n* **1** a copy of a map, drawing, etc. made by following its lines on thin paper that has been placed over it. **2** a line made by a recording instrument that registers movement: *An electrocardiograph makes tracings of the contractions of the heart.*

Trace applies to any mark left by something that has happened or been present: *The campers removed all traces of their fire.* **Vestige** applies particularly to an actual remnant of something that existed in the past: *Some of our social manners are vestiges of very old customs.*

trace² [treis] *n* either of the two straps, ropes, or chains by which an animal pulls a wagon, carriage, etc.⟨Old French *traiz* pl of *trait*; Latin *tractus* pp of *trahere* drag⟩

kick over the traces throw off control; become unruly.

tra·che·a ['treikiə] *or* [trə'kiə] *n, pl* **tra·che·ae** ['treiki,i] *or* ['treiki,ai], [trə'kii] *or* [trə'kiai] the tube extending from the larynx to the bronchi; windpipe. **tra·che·al** *adj.* ⟨Greek *tracheia artēria* rough artery⟩

tra·che·ot·o·my [-'ɒtəmi] *n* an operation that involves cutting an opening into the trachea, esp to relieve an obstruction to breathing. Also, **tra·che·ost·o·my** [-'ɒstəmi].

tra·cho·ma [trə'koumə] *n* a contagious disease of the eye characterized by inflamed granulations on the inner surface of the eyelids. **tra·cho·ma·tous** *adj*. ⟨Greek *trachōma* roughness; *trachys* rough⟩

track [træk] *n* **1** Often, **tracks** *pl* the pair of parallel steel rails on which a locomotive, etc. runs. **2** marks left by something that has passed by: *The tires left tracks in the snow.* **3** a path. **4** a course for running or racing: *The school has an oval track.* **5** the sport made up of contests in running. See TRACK AND FIELD. **6 a** a path on a tape, disc, diskette, etc. or along one side of a film, on which sound or information is recorded. **b** *Computers* the part of a storage device (disk, tape, etc.) passing under a particular position of the reading head. **7** an endless belt of linked steel treads by which a bulldozer, tank, etc. moves. *v* **1** follow by means of marks, smell, etc.: *The hunter tracked the bear and killed it.* **2** trace in any way until found (usually with *down*): *to track down a criminal.* **3** bring (snow, mud, etc.) into a place on one's feet: *to track mud into the house.* **4** follow and plot the course of, as by radar. **5** *Film* follow (the subject) with a moving camera. **6 ⚹** draw or lead (a canoe, etc.) through difficult stretches of water by means of lines running from the craft to people on the bank or shore. **7** of moving parts (e.g., gears, videotape in a VCR, etc.), be in proper alignment. **track·er** *n*. ⟨Old French *trac*⟩

in one's tracks *Informal* right where one is: *He saw the bear and stopped in his tracks.* **keep track of** keep within one's sight, knowledge, or attention: *The noise of the crowd made it difficult to keep track of what was going on.* **lose track of** fail to keep track of. **make tracks** *Informal* go very fast; run away. **off (the) track** a off the subject. **b** wrong. **on (the) track** a on the subject. **b** right. **the beaten track** the ordinary or usual way. **the wrong (or other) side of the tracks** the part of town regarded as inferior.

track and field the group of athletic events performed on a running track and a field next to it, including running, jumping, pole-vaulting, etc. **track–and–field** *adj.* **track·ball** *n Computers* a rotatable sphere that controls the location of an object or a cursor on a screen. **track·less** *adj* **1** without tracks: *a trackless streetcar.* **2** not leaving any tracks: *the trackless passage of a rabbit over hard ground.* **3** without paths: *the trackless desert.* **track lighting** directional, swivelling lights set in a track attached to the wall or ceiling. **track meet** a series of contests in track-and-field events. **track record** a record of the performance of a person or institution, esp with regard to a specific issue: *Their track record in dealing with environmental issues is poor.* **track suit** a casual, loose, two-piece suit

(**track pants** and a **track top**) worn for jogging, warming-up exercises, etc.

tract[1] [trækt] *n* **1** a stretch of land, water, etc.: *A tract of desert land is of little value to farmers.* **2** a system of related parts in the body: *the digestive tract.* **3** a housing development. ⟨Latin *tractus* pp of *trahere* drag⟩

tract[2] [trækt] *n* a pamphlet on a religious or political subject. ⟨Latin *tractare* handle, treat⟩

trac·ta·ble ['træktəbəl] *adj* easily managed or controlled: *Dogs are more tractable than mules.* **trac·ta·bly** *adv.* **trac·ta·bil·i·ty** *n.* ⟨Latin *tractare* handle, treat⟩

trac·tion ['trækʃən] *n* **1** the friction between a body and the surface on which it moves: *Wheels slip on ice because there is too little traction.* **2** the process of pulling a load over a surface. **3** the pulling of neck, leg, or arm muscles to relieve pressure, bring a fractured bone into place, etc., or the state of tension produced by such a device: *She spent months in traction after the accident.* **trac·tion·al** *adj.* ⟨Latin *tractio; tractus* pp of *trahere* drag⟩

trac·tor ['træktər] *n* **1** a vehicle with a powerful engine, used for pulling farm implements, wagons, etc. **2** a powerful truck used to pull a large trailer. ⟨Latin *tractor; tractus* pp of *trahere* drag⟩

trac·tor–trail·er *n* a very large truck consisting of a TRACTOR (def. 2) together with a trailer.

trade [treid] *n* **1** the process of buying and selling: *Canada has trade with many foreign countries.* **2** an even trade. **3** *Informal* a bargain: *He made a good trade.* **4** the market related to a specific group, commodity, etc.: *the tourist trade.* **5** a kind of work: *the carpenter's trade.* **6** *Informal* customers: *That store has a lot of trade.*
adj to do with trade or a particular trade: *a trade secret, trade journals.*
v **1** buy and sell. **2** have dealings (with *in*): *This organization trades in lies and terror.* **3** swap: *to trade seats.* **4** be a customer: *We've been trading at that grocery store for years.* ⟨Middle Dutch *trade* track⟩

trade in give (a car, radio, etc.) as part payment for a new item of the same kind. **trade–in** *n.* **trade off** get rid of by trading. **trade–off** *n.* **trade on** take advantage of: *He traded on his father's good name.*

trade balance the difference between the value of a country's imports and its exports; BALANCE OF TRADE. **trade barrier** anything that restricts international trade: *Tariffs and embargoes are trade barriers.* **trade edition** an edition of a book designed for sale to the general public through retail stores, as opposed to a school text edition, etc. **trade gap** the difference in value between the total imports and total exports of a country, taking the form of either a **trade surplus** or a **trade deficit**. **trade·mark** *n* **1** a mark, symbol, or name that identifies a product or service as coming from a particular company, and that is protected by law. **2** a characteristic feature, utterance, etc. **trade name** **1** a distinctive name that identifies a product or service as coming from a particular company; brand name. **2** the name under which a company conducts its business. **trad·er** *n* **1** a merchant. **2** a person who buys and sells stocks and securities for himself or herself rather than for customers. **trades·man** *n, pl* **-men** **1** a storekeeper. **2** one who practises a skilled trade, as a carpenter, baker, etc. **trades·wo·man** *n, pl* **-wo·men** **trades·peo·ple** *n pl.* **trade union** an association of workers formed to protect and promote their interests; labour union. **trade unionism** the system of having trade unions. **trade unionist** *n.* **trade winds** tropical winds blowing steadily toward the equator from about 30° north latitude to about 30° south latitude. North of the equator, they blow from the northeast; south of the equator, from the southeast. **trading post** a store or station of a trader or trading company, esp in a remote place: *The Hudson's Bay Company operated many trading posts in the North.*

tra·di·tion [trə'dɪʃən] *n* **1** the body of customs, stories, etc. handed down from one generation to another. **2** an established custom: *Eating turkey at Thanksgiving is a tradition.* **tra·di·tion·ist** *n.* **tra·di·tion·less** *adj.* ⟨Latin *tradere* hand down⟩
tra·di·tion·al *adj* **1** to do with tradition. **2** to do with a style of jazz originating in New Orleans. **tra·di·tion·al·ly** *adv.* **tra·di·tion·al·ism** *n* strict adherence to tradition. **tra·di·tion·al·ist** *n.* **tra·di·tion·al·is·tic** *adj.*

traf·fic ['træfɪk] *n* **1** the people, cars, wagons, ships, etc. coming and going along a way of travel. **2** trade in a specific commodity, esp illegal or illicit: *drug traffic.* **3 a** the volume or rate of movement of vehicles, ships, pedestrians, etc.: *Traffic is slow today.* **b** the total amount of business done by any company or industry within a certain time. **c** the volume of calls, etc. transmitted by a communications company in a given period, the amount of electronic mail carried by a computer, etc. **4** dealings.
v **-ficked, -fick·ing** **1** carry on trade: *They were arrested for trafficking in ivory.* **2** have social dealings (*with*): *He won't traffic with strangers.* **traf·fic** *adj.* ⟨Italian *tra-* across (Latin *trans-*) + *ficcare* poke; Latin *figere* fix⟩
traf·fick·er *n* a person who deals illicitly in drugs or other goods. **traffic light** or **traffic signal** a device for controlling traffic at intersections. A green light means go ahead, amber means caution, and red means stop.

trag·e·dy ['trædʒədi] *n* **1** a serious play having, usually, an unhappy ending. **2** a novel, long poem, etc. similar to a tragic play. **3** a sad or terrible situation. **4** the tragic quality or element of such a happening or piece or writing. ⟨Greek *tragōidia; tragos* goat (connection obscure) + *ōidē* song⟩
tra·ge·di·an [trə'dʒidiən] *n* **1** a writer of tragedies. **2** an actor who specializes in tragic roles. **trag·ic** *adj* **1** to do with tragedy: *a tragic actor.* **2** sad or dreadful: *a tragic event.* **trag·i·cal·ly** *adv.* **tragic flaw** a flaw in the character of a tragic hero or heroine that

brings about his or her downfall. **trag·i·com·e·dy** *n* **1** a play having both tragic and comic elements. **2** a real-life situation in which serious and comic elements are mixed. **trag·i·com·ic** *adj.* **trag·i·com·i·cal·ly** *adv.*

trail [treil] *n* **1** an unpaved path, often in a wild region. **2** a track or smell: *The dogs found the trail of a rabbit.* **3** anything that follows along behind, including consequences: *The car left a trail of dust behind it.*
v **1** drag or be dragged along behind: *The child trailed a toy horse after her.* **2** hang down or float loosely from something: *a trailing scarf.* **3** follow the track of: *to trail a bear.* **4** bring after itself: *a car trailing dust.* **5** follow: *The dog trailed him constantly.* **6** *Sports* be behind (an opponent): *trailing by seven points.* **7** move in a long, uneven line: *refugees trailing from their ruined village.* **8** become gradually less (with *off* or *away*): *Her voice trailed off into silence.* ⟨Old French *trailler* tow; Latin *tragula* dragnet⟩
trail bike a small motorcycle for riding on rough terrain. **trail·bla·zer** *n* **1** a person who marks a trail by chipping bark off trees along the way. **2** a person who prepares the way to something new. **trail·er** *n* **1** a vehicle designed to be pulled along by a truck, car, etc., used for transporting goods, animals, a boat, etc. **2** a closed-in vehicle designed to be pulled by a car or truck and equipped for use as a dwelling or place of business; a camper: *Large trailers are often called mobile homes.* **3** a short film made up of selected scenes from a feature film, shown as an advertisement: *We saw the trailer on TV.* **trailer camp** or **park** an area to accommodate TRAILERS (def. 2), often having electricity, running water, etc. **trailer hitch** a projection for attaching a trailer, fixed to the rear of a vehicle. **trailing arbutus** a plant of the heath family, having evergreen leaves and fragrant flowers very early in spring; MAYFLOWER. The trailing arbutus is the provincial flower of Nova Scotia.

train¹ [trein] *n* **1** a connected line of railway cars pulled by an engine. **2** a line of people, animals, wagons, etc. moving along together. **3** a part of a dress, cloak, etc. that trails behind the wearer: *the bride's train.* **4** a group of followers. **5 a** a series; succession: *a train of misfortunes.* **b** a succession of results following some event: *The flood brought starvation and disease in its train.*
v **1** teach: *to train a child.* **2 a** instruct (an animal) to be obedient, race, find drugs, etc. **b** sometimes, specifically, to make (an animal) housebroken. **3** make or become fit for some athletic activity by exercise and diet: *Runners train for races.* **4** point; aim: *to train cannon upon a fort.* **5** bring (plants, etc.) into a position so as to direct future growth: *Train the vine around this post.* ⟨Old French *trainer;* Latin *trahere* drag⟩
in train a in proper order. **b** in process. **train of thought** connected thoughts passing through one's mind at a particular time: *From the way the speaker paused, it was obvious that he had lost his train of thought.*

train·ee *n* one who is receiving training.
train·ee·ship *n*. **train·er** *n* **1** a person who trains athletes. **2** a person who trains animals. **train·ing** *n* **1** practical education in some art, profession, etc.: *training for teachers.* **2** the development of strength and endurance. **in training** in the process of being trained. **training pants** absorbent underpants for young children being trained to use the toilet. **training wheels** small wheels attached on either side of the rear wheel of a bicycle to steady the vehicle for a child learning to ride. **train·load** *n* as much as a train can hold or carry.

train² [trein] *n* ✹ **1** dog-team. **2** a dog-team and dog-sled together. ⟨Cdn. French⟩

traipse [treips] *Informal v* walk or wander: *We traipsed all over town looking for a gift. n* a walk, esp a long or tiring one. ⟨probably Old French *trespasser*. See TRESPASS.⟩

trait [treit] *n* a quality of mind, character, etc.: *Courage is a desirable trait.* ⟨French; Latin *tractus* pp of *trahere* drag⟩

> **SYNONYMS**
> **Trait** applies to a distinguishing feature of a person's character: *Cheerfulness is her most outstanding trait.* **Characteristic** applies to a feature that shows the nature of a person or thing, distinguishing it from others: *Lack of moisture is a characteristic of desert regions.*

trai·tor ['treitər] *n* **1** a person who betrays his or her country, or commits TREASON. **2** a person who betrays a trust, friend, duty, etc., or commits TREACHERY. **trai·tor·ous** *adj.* **trai·tor·ous·ly** *adv.* ⟨Old French; Latin *traditor*; *trans-* over + *dare* give⟩

tra·jec·to·ry [trə'dʒɛktəri] *n* the curved path of something moving through space, such as a bullet from a gun or a planet in its orbit. ⟨Latin *trans-* across + *Jacere* throw⟩

tram [træm] *n* **1** a truck on which loads are carried in mines. **2** the basket on an overhead conveyor cable. ⟨Middle Dutch *trame* beam⟩
tram·way *n* **1** a track for carrying ore from mines. **2** a cable on which suspended cars carry ore, etc.

tram·mel ['træməl] *n* **1** Usually, **trammels** *pl* anything that hinders: *A large bequest freed the artist from the trammels of poverty.* **2** a fine net to catch fish, birds, etc.
v -**melled** or -**meled**, -**mel·ling** or -**mel·ing** **1** hinder; restrain. **2** entangle. **tram·mel·ler** or **tram·mel·er** *n.* ⟨Old French *tramail* net; Latin *trimaculum*, *tri-* three + *macula* mesh⟩

tramp [træmp] *v* **1** walk heavily. **2** go on foot, esp wearily or for a long way: *We tramped through the fields.*
n **1** the sound of heavy footsteps: *the tramp of booted feet.* **2** a long, steady walk. **3** a person who goes about on foot, living by begging, doing odd jobs, etc. **4** a freighter that takes a cargo when and where it can. **5** *Slang* a sexually promiscuous woman. **tramp·er** *n.* ⟨perhaps Middle Low German *trampen*⟩
tram·ple ['træmpəl] *v* **1** crush or destroy by treading heavily (on): *The cattle broke through*

the fence and trampled the farmer's crops. **2** hurt or violate, as if by treading on (often with *on*): *to trample on someone's rights. n* the act or sound of trampling: *We heard the trample of many feet.* **tram·pler** *n.*

tram·po·line [ˌtræmpə'lin] or ['træmpəˌlin] *n* an apparatus for tumbling, acrobatics, etc. consisting of a taut piece of fabric attached by springs to a metal frame. **tram·po·lin·ist** *n.* ⟨Italian *trampolino* springboard⟩

trance [træns] *n* **1** a state of unconsciousness resembling sleep. **2 a** a dreamy, absorbed condition that is like a trance: *She sat before the fire in a trance, thinking of her past life.* **b** stupor; daze. **3** rapture; ecstasy, as from a mystical experience. **trance·like** *adj.* ⟨Old French *transe*; Latin *trans-* across + *ire* go⟩

tran·quil ['træŋkwəl] *adj* calm; peaceful: *a tranquil mood.* **tran·quil·li·ty** or **tran·quil·i·ty** *n.* **tran·quil·ly** *adv.* ⟨Latin *tranquillus*⟩
tran·quil·lize or **tran·quil·ize** *v* -**lized** or -**ized**, -**liz·ing** or -**iz·ing** make peaceful or quiet; esp, reduce tension or anxiety in (someone) by the use of drugs. **tran·quil·li·za·tion** *n.* **tran·quil·liz·er** or **tran·quil·iz·er** *n* any of several drugs used to reduce mental tension and anxiety, control certain psychoses, etc.

trans— *prefix* **1** across, over, or through: *transcontinental, trans-Canada.* **2** beyond; on the other side of: *transcend.* **3** across, etc., and also beyond: *transatlantic, transcontinental.* **4** into a different place, condition, etc.: *transform.* Also, **tran-** before *s*, and **tra-** before *d, j, l, m, n,* or *v* in words of Latin origin. ⟨Latin⟩

trans·act [træn'zækt] *v* manage, carry on (business, etc.): *She transacts business with many stores.* ⟨Latin *transactus* pp of *transigere* accomplish; *trans-* through + *agere* drive⟩
trans·ac·tion *n* **1** the act or an instance of transacting **2** a piece of business: *A record is kept of all transactions.* **3 transactions** *pl* a record of what is done at the meetings of a society, club, etc. **trans·ac·tion·al** *adj.* **trans·ac·tor** *n.*

tran·scend [træn'sɛnd] *v* **1** go beyond the limits or powers of: *The grandeur of Niagara Falls transcends description.* **2** surpass; excel. **3** of God, be above (the physical universe). **tran·scend·ence** *n.*   **tran·scend·ent** *adj.* **tran·scend·ent·ly** *adv.* ⟨*trans-* beyond + Latin *scandere* climb⟩
tran·scen·den·tal *adj* **1** transcendent. **2** supernatural. **3** fantastic; incomprehensible. **4** abstract or metaphysical. **5** *Philosophy* to do with those elements of human experience stemming from the mind's organizing processes. **6** *Mathematics* **a** incapable of being the root of any algebraic equation having coefficients that are rational numbers. **b** of a function, incapable of algebraic expression. **tran·scen·den·tal·ly** *adv.* **tran·scen·den·tal·ism** *n* any philosophy based upon the doctrine that reality is to be discovered by a study of processes of thought. **tran·scen·den·tal·ist** *n.* **transcendental meditation** Sometimes, **Transcendental Meditation** a technique for

detaching oneself from problems, stress, etc. through meditation and the recitation of a mantra. *Abbrev* **TM**

tran·scribe [træn'skraɪb] *v* **1** copy in print: *The speech was transcribed in the newspaper.* **2** arrange (a musical composition) for a different instrument or voice. **tran·scrib·er** *n*. **tran·scrip·tion** *n*. **tran·scrip·tive** *adj.* ⟨*trans-* + Latin *scribere* write⟩

tran·script *n* a printed copy: *The university requires a transcript of your high-school grades.*

trans·duce [trænz'djus] *or* [trænz'dus] *v* convert (one form of energy) into another. ⟨*trans-* + Latin *ducere* lead⟩ **trans·duc·tion** *n* **1** *Biology* the transfer of genetic material from one cell to another by means of a bacterial virus. **2** *Physics* the transfer of one form of energy to another. **trans·du·cer** *n* an electrical device that converts one form of energy into another: *Microphones and loudspeakers are transducers.*

trans·fer ['trænsfər] *or* [træns'fɜr] *v* **-ferred, -fer·ring 1** go, or cause to go, from one person, place, etc. to another: *The company transferred her from Saskatoon to Fredericton.* **2** convey (a drawing, design, pattern) from one surface to another. **3** make over (a title, right, or property) by legal process: *to transfer a bond by endorsement.* **4** change from one streetcar, bus, train, etc. to another without having to pay another fare: *I transferred at Islington station.* **trans·fer** ['trænsfər] *n*. **trans·fer·a·ble** [træns'fɜrəbəl] *or* ['trænsfərəbəl] *adj.* **trans·fer·a·bil·i·ty** *n*. **trans·fer·ral** *n*. ⟨Latin *trans-* across + *ferre* bear⟩ **trans·fer·ee** *n* **1** a person who has been or is being transferred. **2** a person to whom something, esp property, is transferred. **trans·fer·ence** ['trænsfərəns] *or* [træns'fɜrəns] *n* **1** the act of transferring or the state of being transferred. **2** *Psychoanalysis* a revival of emotions previously experienced and repressed, as toward a parent, with a new person as the object, often the analyst. **trans·fer·en·tial** *adj.* **transfer payment ✱** a payment made by a government to an individual, in the form of benefits, or to a lower level of government.

trans·fig·ure [træns'fɪgjər] *or* [træns'fɪgər] *v* **1** change in appearance, esp for the better: *New paint had transfigured the old house.* **2** change so as to glorify. **trans·fig·u·ra·tion** *n* **1** a change in appearance. **2 the Transfiguration** *Christianity* in the Bible, the radiant appearance of Christ before his disciples on a mountain.

trans·fix [træns'fɪks] *v* **1** pierce through: *The hunter transfixed the wild boar with a spear.* **2** make motionless (with terror, amazement, etc.). **trans·fix·ion** *n*. ⟨Latin *transfixus* pp of *transfigere; trans-* through + *figere* fix⟩

trans·form [træns'fɔrm] *v* **1** change in form, function, etc: *Her face was transformed by a sudden smile.* **2** *Physics* change (one form of energy) into another. **3** *Mathematics* change (a figure, term, etc.) to another differing in form but having the same value or quantity.

trans·for·ma·tion *n*. **trans·form·a·tive** *adj.* ⟨Latin *trans-* across + *forma* form⟩ **trans·form·er** *n* a device for changing the voltage of an electric current.

SYNONYMS

Transform suggests a fundamental change in the appearance or nature of a thing or person: *Responsibility transformed him from a carefree youth into a capable leader.* **Convert** suggests turning from one state to another, especially for a new use: *to convert boxes into furniture.*

trans·fuse [træns'fjuz] *v* **1** transfer (blood) from one person or animal to another intravenously. **2** instil: *The speaker transfused his anger into the audience.* **trans·fu·sion** *n*. ⟨Latin *trans-* + *fusus* pp of *fundere* pour⟩

trans·gress [trænz'grɛs] *v* **1** break a law; sin. **2** go beyond (a limit): *The interviewer's questions transgressed the bounds of good taste.* **trans·gres·sion** *n*. **trans·gres·sive** *adj.* **trans·gres·sor** *n*. ⟨Latin *trans-* + *gressus* pp of *gradi* to step⟩

tran·si·ent ['trænziənt]*adj* **1** fleeting; not lasting; transitory. **2** passing through and not staying long: *a transient guest in a hotel.* *n* **1** a boarder who stays for a short time. **2** *Electricity* a sudden surge of voltage or current. **tran·si·ence** *or* **tran·si·en·cy** *n*. **tran·si·ent·ly** *adv.* ⟨Latin *trans-* through + *ire* go⟩ **tran·si·to·ry** *adj* passing soon or quickly; lasting only a short time. **tran·si·to·ri·ly** *adv.* **tran·si·to·ri·ness** *n*.

tran·sis·tor [træn'zɪstər] *n* a small electronic device that amplifies electricity by controlling the flow of electrons. ⟨Latin *trans-* + *sistere* send, convey⟩ **tran·sis·tor·ize** *v* equip with transistors.

tran·sit ['trænzɪt] *n* **1** the process of passing across or through. **2** the process of carrying or being carried across or through: *The goods were damaged in transit.* **3** transportation by trains, buses, etc. **4** *Surveying* in full, **transit theodolite** an instrument used for measuring angles. **5** *Astronomy* the passage of a small heavenly body across the disk of a larger one. *v* pass through, over, or across (something or some place). ⟨Latin *transitus* pp of *transire.* See TRANSIENT.⟩

tran·si·tion *n* **1** a change from one condition, place, etc. to another: *a period of transition in history.* **2** *Music* **a** a change of key. **b** a passage linking one section, subject, etc. of a composition with another. **3** in writing, a word, phrase, etc. serving to link ideas or to lead smoothly from one topic to the next. **tran·si·tion·ar·y** *adj.* **tran·si·tion·al** *adj.* **tran·si·tion·al·ly** *adv.* **tran·si·tive** *adj Grammar* of a verb, taking a direct object. *Bring* and *raise* are transitive verbs. Compare INTRANSITIVE. **tran·si·tive·ly** *adv.* **tran·si·tive·ness** or **tran·si·tiv·i·ty** *n*.

tran·si·to·ry See TRANSIENT.

trans·late ['trænzleɪt] *or* [trænz'leɪt] *v* **1** change from one language into another. **2** change into other words, esp in order to explain the meaning of: *to translate a*

scientific treatise for the average person.
3 *Theology* take to heaven, esp without death.
4 *Physics, mathematics* cause (a body) to move so that all its points move in the same direction at the same speed and at the same time. **trans·lat·a·ble** *adj.* **trans·la·tion** *n.* **trans·la·tion·al** *adj.* ⟨Latin *trans-* + *latus* pp of *ferre* bear⟩
trans·la·tor *n* a person who translates from one language into another.

trans·lit·er·ate [trænz'lɪtə,reit] *v* change (letters, words, etc.) into the corresponding characters of another alphabet or language: *We transliterate the Greek* ξ *as ch and* φ *as ph.* **trans·lit·er·a·tion** *n.* ⟨*trans-* + Latin *litera* letter⟩

trans·lu·cent [trænz'lusənt] *adj* letting diffused light through: *Frosted glass is translucent.* **trans·lu·cence** *n.* **trans·lu·cent·ly** *adv.* ⟨Latin *trans-* through + *lucere* shine⟩

trans·mi·grate [trænz'maɪgreit] *v* of the soul, pass at death into another body. **trans·mi·gra·tion** *n.*

trans·mis·sion See TRANSMIT.

trans·mit [trænz'mɪt] *v* **-mit·ted, -mit·ting 1** pass along: *Rats transmit disease.* **2** send (signals, broadcasts, etc.) through space via radio waves: *The prime minister's message will be transmitted at 6 p.m.* **trans·mit·ta·ble** *adj.* ⟨Latin *trans-* across + *mittere* send⟩
trans·mis·sion *n* **1** a passing along: *Mosquitoes are the only means of transmission of malaria.* **2** something transmitted. **3** of a motor vehicle, the part that transmits power from the engine to the driving axle. **4** the passage through space of radio waves from a transmitting station: *When radio transmission is good, distant stations can be received.* **trans·mis·si·ble** *adj.* **trans·mis·si·bil·i·ty** *n.*
trans·mis·sive *adj.* **trans·mit·ter** *n* **1** the part of a telephone into which one speaks. **2** in radio and TV, the apparatus that generates and sends waves. **3** any person or thing that transmits.

trans·mute [trænz'mjut] *v* change from one substance or form into another: *We can transmute water power into electrical power.* **trans·mut·er** *n.* ⟨Latin *trans-* thoroughly + *mutare* change⟩
trans·mu·ta·tion *n* **1** a change into another substance or form. **2** *Physics, chemistry* the conversion of atoms of one element into atoms of a different element or a different isotope, either naturally, as by radioactive disintegration, or artificially, as by bombardment with neutrons, etc. **3** *Alchemy* the (attempted) conversion of a baser metal into gold or silver. **trans·mu·ta·tion·al** *adj.* **trans·mu·ta·tive** *adj.*

tran·som ['trænsəm] *n* a window over a door or window. ⟨Latin *transtrum* orig crossbeam⟩

trans·par·ent [træn'spɛrənt] *or* [-'spærənt] *adj* **1** transmitting light so that something behind or beyond can be distinctly seen: *Window glass is transparent.* **2** easily seen through or detected: *The excuse she gave was transparent.* **3** easily understood; lucid; clear.

trans·par·ent·ly *adv.* ⟨Latin *trans-* through + *parere* appear⟩
trans·par·en·cy *n* **1** the quality or state of being transparent. **2** something transparent, esp, a photograph. Also (def. 1) **trans·par·ence.**

tran·spire [træn'spaɪr] *v* **1** take place. **2** send off (moisture) in the form of vapour through a surface, as from leaves. **tran·spi·ra·tion** *n.* ⟨Latin *trans-* through + *spirare* breathe⟩

trans·plant [trans'plænt] *v* **1** plant again in a different place. **2** remove from one place to another: *The colony was transplanted to a more healthful location.* **3** transfer (skin, an organ, etc.) from one person or animal to another, or from one part of the body to another: *transplant a kidney.*
n ['trænsplænt] **1** the transfer of an organ: *a heart transplant.* **2** something transplanted. **trans·plant·a·ble** *adj.* **trans·plant·er** *n.* **trans·plan·ta·tion** *n.*

tran·spon·der [træn'spɒndər] *n* a system for radio or radar signals that automatically transmits when it receives a predetermined signal. ⟨*trans(mitter)* + *(res)ponder*⟩

trans·port [trans'pɔrt] *v* **1** carry from one place to another, esp a relatively distant one. **2** carry away by strong feeling: *She was transported with joy by the good news.* **3** send away to another country as a punishment.
n ['trænspɔrt] **1** a carrying from one place to another by vehicle. **2** a large truck used to carry freight long distances by road. **3** a strong feeling: *a transport of rage.* **trans·port·a·ble** *adj.* **trans·port·a·bil·i·ty** *n.* **trans·port·er** *n.* ⟨Latin *trans-* across + *portare* carry⟩
trans·por·ta·tion *n* **1** a transporting or being transported: *free transportation.* **2** a means of transport. **3** a sending away or being sent to another country as a punishment.

trans·pose [træns'pouz] *v* **1** change the position or order of. **2** change the usual order of (letters, words, or numbers); invert. *Example: Up came the wind, and off went her hat.* **3** *Music* **a** rewrite in another key. **b** play in another key. **4** *Algebra* transfer (a term) to the other side of an equation, changing plus to minus or minus to plus. **trans·pos·a·ble** *adj.* **trans·pos·al** or **trans·po·si·tion** *n.* **trans·pos·er** *n.* **trans·po·si·tion·al** *adj.* **trans·pos·i·tive** *adj.* ⟨French *trans-* + *poser* put. See POSE.⟩

trans·sex·u·al [træn'sɛkʃuəl] *n* **1** a person who identifies so strongly with the opposite sex as to assume its usual roles, clothing, mannerisms, etc. **2** a person of this sort who has undergone surgery and hormone treatment in order to effect a change of sex. **trans·sex·u·al** *adj.* **trans·sex·u·al·ism** *n.*

tran·sub·stan·ti·a·tion [,trænsəb,stænʃi'eiʃən] *n* **1** a changing of one substance into another. **2** *Theology* in some Christian belief systems, the miraculous changing of the substance of the bread and wine of the Eucharist into the substance of the body and blood of Christ.
tran·sub·stan·ti·ate *v.* ⟨Latin *trans-* over + *substantia* substance⟩

trans·verse [trænz'vɜrs] *or* ['trænzvɜrs] *adj*
1 lying across: *The transverse beams in the
barn were fir.* **2** *Geometry* designating the axis
that passes through the foci of a hyperbola.
n **1** a transverse part or piece. **2** *Geometry* the
transverse axis. 〈Latin *trans-* across + *versus*
pp of *vertere* turn〉
trans·ver·sal *n* *Geometry* a line intersecting
two or more other lines. **trans·ver·sal·ly** *adv.*
trans·verse·ly *adv* across; from side to side.

trans·vest·ite [trænz'vɛstaɪt] *n* a person who
derives sexual pleasure from wearing
clothing usually associated with the opposite
sex. **trans·vest·ism** *n.* 〈Latin *trans-* + *vestire* dress〉

trap [træp] *n* **1** a device for catching animals,
lobsters, birds, etc. **2** a trick for catching
someone off guard: *He knew that the question
was a trap.* **3** a bend in a pipe for holding a
small amount of water to prevent the escape
of air, gas, etc. **4** a light two-wheeled carriage.
5 *Golf* bunker. **6** *Slang* mouth: *Shut your trap!*
7 traps *pl* drums, cymbals, bells, gongs, etc.
v **trapped, trap·ping 1** catch in a trap.
2 engage in trapping animals for their fur.
3 stop with a trap: *a gutter to trap rainwater.*
4 *Football, baseball* catch (a ball) on the first
rebound. 〈Old English *træppe*〉
trap·boat *n* ✹ *Newfoundland and Labrador* a
low-sided boat capable of carrying a cod trap.
trap·door *n* a hinged or sliding door in a
floor, ceiling, or roof, to provide access to an
attic or cellar or to the space below a stage.
trap·line *n* a series of traps set and
maintained by a trapper. **trap·per** *n* a person
who traps wild animals for their fur.
trap·shoot·ing *n* the sport of shooting at clay
pigeons thrown into the air. **trap·shoot·er** *n.*

SYNONYMS

Trap suggests a situation deliberately set to
catch someone by surprise: *Suspecting a trap,
the detachment of soldiers withdrew.* **Snare**
applies to a device to lure a person into
getting caught: *The detectives placed marked
money in the safe as a snare for the thief.*

tra·peze [trə'piz] *n* a short horizontal bar
hung by ropes like a swing, used in
gymnastics and acrobatics. 〈Greek *trapezion*
diminutive of *trapeza* table〉

tra·pe·zi·um [trə'piziəm] *n, pl* **-zi·ums** or **-zi·a**
[-ziə] a four-sided plane figure having no
sides parallel. **trap·e·zoid** ['træpə,zɔɪd] *n* **1** a
four-sided plane figure having only two sides
parallel. **trap·e·zoid** or **trap·e·zoid·al** *adj.*

trap·pings *n pl* **1** ornamental coverings for a
horse. **2** ornamental dress: *the trappings of a
king.* **3** outward appearances: *all the trappings
of a cowboy.* 〈obsolete *trap* deck out; Old
French *drap* cloth〉

trash [træʃ] *n* **1** discarded or worthless stuff;
garbage. **2** a person of worthless character or
such persons as a group; riffraff.
v *Slang* **1** destroy; vandalize: *Last winter our
summer cottage was trashed by vandals.*
2 criticize harshly: *The reviewer trashed the
movie.* **3** reject: *Let's just trash the whole idea.*
〈probably Scandinavian〉

trash·y *adj* of inferior quality: *a trashy
magazine.* **trash·i·ly** *adv.* **trash·i·ness** *n.*

trat·to·ria [trɑ'tɔriə] *n, pl* **-ri·e** [-rie] *Italian* a
small, casual Italian restaurant. 〈Italian〉

trau·ma ['trɒmə] *or* ['traʊmə] *n, pl* **-ma·ta**
[-mətə] or **-mas 1** *Medicine* **a** an injury to
living tissue. **b** the resulting physical
condition. **2** *Psychiatry* **a** an emotional shock
that has lasting effects on the victim. **b** a
state of emotional disturbance resulting from
an injury or shock. **trau·mat·ic** [trɒ'mætɪk],
[trə-], *or* [traʊ-] *adj.* **trau·mat·i·cal·ly** *adv.*
〈Greek = wound〉
trau·ma·tize *v* subject to physical, mental, or
emotional trauma. **trau·ma·tism** *n.*

trav·ail ['træveil] *or, esp v* [trə'veil] *n* **1** hard
work. **2** trouble or pain. **3** the pains of
childbirth. **trav·ail** *v.* 〈Old French *travail;*
Latin *tripalium* torture device〉

trav·el ['trævəl] *v* **-elled** or **-eled, -el·ling** or
-el·ing 1 go on a trip from one place to
another: *to travel across the country.* **2** move:
Sound travels in waves. **3** go from place to
place selling things: *She travels for a large firm.*
4 pass through or over: *to travel a road.*
5 *Informal* move rapidly: *That car was really
travelling when it hit the abutment!* **6** *Basketball*
commit the fault of moving more than two
steps while holding the ball.
n **1 a** the act of going in aircraft, cars, etc.
from one place to another. **b** the industry
that facilitates this: *a career in travel.*
2 movement in general. **3 travels** *pl* journeys.
trav·el·ler or **trav·el·er** *n.* 〈variant of *travail*〉
travel agency a business that makes
arrangements for travellers by booking
reservations, drawing up itineraries, etc.
travel agent. trav·elled or **trav·eled** *adj*
1 that has done much travelling. **2** used by
travellers: *It was a well-travelled road.*
traveller's cheque or **traveler's cheque** a
cheque issued by a financial institution, in
any of various fixed denominations, that is
signed by the buyer and countersigned by
him or her at the time of cashing.
trav·e·logue [-,lɒg] *n* **1** a lecture describing
travel, usually accompanied by pictures. **2** a
film depicting travel or a place worth
travelling to. Also (*esp US*), **trav·e·log.**

trav·erse [trə'vɜrs] *or* ['trævərs] *v* **1** pass across
or through: *The caravan traversed the desert.*
2 stretch across; intersect. **3** move back and
forth or from side to side: *That horse traverses.*
4 ski in a zigzag manner, or climb sideways,
across. **5** turn (big guns) to right or left.
n ['trævərs] **1** the act of crossing.
2 something put or lying across.
adj ['trævərs] lying across.
adv [trə'vɜrs] *or* ['trævərs] across; crosswise.
tra·vers·a·ble *adj.* **tra·vers·al** *n.* **tra·vers·er** *n.*
〈Old French *traverser;* Latin. See TRANSVERSE.〉

trav·es·ty ['trævɪsti] *n* **1** an imitation of a
serious literary work done in such a way as to
make it seem ridiculous. **2** any treatment
that makes a serious thing seem ridiculous:
Her acquittal was a travesty of justice. 〈French
travesti disguised; Latin *trans-* + *vestire* dress〉

tra·vois [trə'vwɑ] *or* [trə'vɔɪ], ['træv-] *French* [tRɑ'vwɑ] *n, pl* **-vois** [-vwɑ] ✱ formerly: **1** a wheelless vehicle used by First Nations peoples of the plains, made of two shafts to which was attached a platform or net for holding the load, and dragged by a dog hitched to the shafts. **2** a larger conveyance drawn by a horse or pony. **3** any of a number of similar conveyances. ⟨Cdn. French; French *travail* frame for a horse being shod⟩

trawl [trɒl] *n* **1** a net dragged along the bottom of the sea. Also called **trawl net**. **2** a line having attached to it many short lines with baited hooks. Also called **trawl line**. **trawl** *v.* ⟨Middle Dutch *traghel;* Latin *tragula* dragnet⟩
trawl·er *n* **1** a boat used in trawling. **2** a person who fishes by trawling.

tray [treɪ] *n* a flat holder with a low rim around it: *We carried the dishes on a tray.* ⟨Old English *trēg*⟩

treach·er·y ['trɛtʃəri] *n* **1** a breaking of faith; deceit. **2** treason. ⟨Old French *trecherie; trechier* cheat⟩ See also TRAITOR, TREASON.
treach·er·ous *adj* **1** not faithful; disloyal. **2** having a false appearance of strength, security, etc.: *Thin ice is treacherous.*
treach·er·ous·ly *adv.* **treach·er·ous·ness** *n.*

tread [trɛd] *v* **trod**, **trod·den** *or* **trod**, **tread·ing 1** walk: *Don't tread on the flower beds.* **2** trample on; crush: *to tread grapes.* **3** make, form, or do by walking: *Cattle had trodden a path to the pond.* **4** follow; pursue: *to tread the path of virtue.*
n **1** the act or sound of treading: *the tread of marching feet.* **2** a way of walking: *He walks with a heavy tread.* **3** the horizontal part of a step. **4** the raised pattern on the surface of a tire or the sole of a shoe or boot: *The tread on the back tires is almost gone.* **5** either of the tracks of a caterpillar tractor or similar vehicle. **tread·er** *n.* ⟨Old English *tredan*⟩
tread on someone's toes offend or annoy someone. **tread the boards** play a part in a play. **tread water** keep afloat in water, with the body upright, by slowly moving the legs as if bicycling.

trea·dle *n* a rocking pedal worked by the foot to drive a machine, such as a sewing machine. *v* work a treadle. **tread·mill** *n* **1** an apparatus for producing motion by having a person or animal walk on the moving steps of a wheel or of a sloping, endless belt. **2** any monotonous round of work or life that seems to go nowhere.

trea·son ['trizən] *n* the act of betraying one's country. **trea·son·ous** *adj.* **trea·son·a·ble** *adj.* ⟨Anglo-French *treson;* Latin *traditio*⟩

treas·ure ['trɛʒər] *n* **1** wealth or riches stored up; valuable things. **2** any thing or person much loved or valued. **treas·ure** *v.* ⟨Old French *tresor;* Greek *thēsauros* treasury⟩
treasure house a storehouse of anything valuable. **treasure hunt** a game in which players are directed from place to place by a series of clues, ending at the spot where some object is concealed. **treas·ur·er** *n* a

person in charge of the finances of a club, government body, etc. **treas·ur·er·ship** *n.*
treas·ure–trove [-,trouv] *n* money, jewels, or other treasure that a person finds, esp if the owner of it is not known. **treas·ur·y** *n* **1** the place where public revenues are kept. **2** money belonging to a society, club, etc.: *We paid for the party out of the club treasury.* **3** a government department that has charge of the collection and expenditure of public revenues. **4** a book, person, etc. thought of as a valued source: *a treasury of adventure stories. She is a treasury of information on rocks.*
treasury bill an obligation issued by the treasury of Canada, bearing no interest but sold at a discount and maturing in less than a year. **Treasury Board** ✱ a committee of the federal Cabinet, responsible for overseeing the management of public funds.

treat [trit] *v* **1** handle: *My father treats our new car with care.* **2** regard: *She treated her mistake as a joke.* **3** deal with to relieve or cure: *The dentist is treating my tooth.* **4** express in literature, music, or art: *to treat a theme realistically.* **5** entertain by giving food, drink, or amusement: *He treated us to lunch.*
n **1** a gift of food, drink, or amusement: *"This is my treat," she said, as she paid for the tickets.* **2** anything that gives pleasure. **treat·er** *n.* ⟨Old French *traitier;* Latin *tractare,* handle, frequentative of *trahere* drag⟩
treat·a·ble *adj* that will respond to treatment: *a treatable disease.* **treat·a·bil·i·ty** *n.*
trea·tise ['tritis] *n* writing dealing formally and systematically with some subject. **treat·ment** *n* **1** a way of treating. **2** something done or used to treat something else, esp a disease: *a treatment for colds.*

trea·ty ['triti] *n* **1** an agreement, esp one between nations, signed and approved by each nation. **2** ✱ one of a number of official agreements between the federal government and certain bands of First Nations peoples whereby the latter gave up their land rights, except for reserves, and accepted treaty money and other kinds of government assistance. ⟨Old French *traitie;* Latin *tractare* handle, discuss⟩
take treaty *or* **take the treaty** ✱ of a First Nations band or people, accept the terms of treaty with the federal government.
Treaty Day ✱ **1** the day on which treaty was orig taken by a First Nations group. **2** an anniversary of this day, celebrated with festivities. **3 treaty day** any day on which treaty money is paid. **treaty Indian** ✱ a STATUS INDIAN belonging to a First Nations band that signed a treaty with the Federal Government. **treaty money** ✱ an annual payment made by the federal government to TREATY INDIANS. **treaty rights** ✱ the rights guaranteed to First Nations people in their treaties with the federal government.

tre·ble ['trɛbəl] *adj* **1** three times as much or as many. **2** *Music* to do with the treble.
v make or become three times as much: *She trebled her income by going into advertising.*
n **1** *Music* **a** the highest voice part in choral

music, esp for a boys' choir; soprano. **b** the upper half of the whole musical range of a voice or instrument. Compare BASS¹ (def. 4). **2** a shrill, high-pitched voice or sound. ⟨Old French; Latin *triplus* triple⟩
treble clef *Music* a symbol (𝄞) indicating that the pitch of the notes on a staff is above middle C. **tre·bly** *adv* three times.

tree [tri] *n* **1** a large plant having a woody trunk, branches, and leaves. **2** less accurately, any of certain other plants that resemble trees in form or size. **3** a piece of wood, etc., for some special purpose: *a shoe tree.*
v **1** chase up a tree: *The cat was treed by a dog.* **2** *Informal* put into a difficult position. **tree·less** *adj.* **tree·like** *adj.* ⟨Old English *trēo*⟩
bark up the wrong tree See BARK². **up a tree** *Informal* in a difficult position.
treed 1 *adj* planted or covered with trees: *treed lands.* **2** driven up a tree: *a treed raccoon.* **tree house** a structure, such as a playhouse, built in the branches of a tree. **tree line** or **tree·line** a limit on mountains and in high latitudes beyond which trees will not grow because of the cold, etc.; timberline. **tree surgery** the treatment of diseased trees. **tree surgeon. tree·top** *n* the top part of a tree.

tre·foil ['trifɔil] *n* **1** any of various herbs having leaves made up of three leaflets, esp clover. **2** an ornamental figure shaped like such a leaf. ⟨Latin *tri-* three + *folium* leaf⟩

trek [trek] *v* **trekked, trek·king 1** travel, esp slowly and for a long distance or under difficult conditions. **2** *Informal* go; traipse: *to trek down to the office.* **3** go on a long, arduous hike, on foot or horseback and esp through wild country, for recreation or sightseeing: *You need a permit to trek in Nepal.* **trek** *n.* **trek·ker** *n.* ⟨Dutch *trekken*, orig draw, pull⟩

trel·lis ['trelɪs] *n* a frame of light strips of wood or metal crossing one another with open spaces in between; lattice. ⟨Old French *trelis*; Latin *trilix* triple-twilled⟩
trel·lis·work *n* trelliswork; latticework.

trem·ble ['trembəl] *v* **1** shake because of fear, cold, etc. **2** of a sound, voice, etc., quaver: *His voice trembled on high notes.* **3** feel fear, anxiety, etc: *She trembled for their safety.*
trem·ble *n.* **trem·bling** *adj.* **trem·bling·ly** *adv.* **trem·bly** *adj.* ⟨Latin *tremulus; tremere* tremble⟩
trem·o·lo ['tremə,lou] *n* **1** *Music* a trembling or vibrating quality. **2** in an organ, a device used to produce this. **trem·or** ['tremər] *n* **1** an involuntary trembling as from disease, weakness, etc.: *a nervous tremor in the voice.* **2** a thrill of excitement. **3** a shaking movement. An earthquake is an earth tremor. **trem·or·ous** *adj.* **trem·u·lous** ['tremjələs] *adj* **1** trembling: *a tremulous voice.* **2** marked by tremors: *tremulous handwriting.* **3** timid; fearful. **trem·u·lous·ly** *adv.* **trem·u·lous·ness** *n.*

tre·men·dous [trə'mendəs] *adj* **1** dreadful. **2** *Informal* very great: *a tremendous house.* **3** *Informal* especially good: *a tremendous movie.* **tre·men·dous·ly** *adv.* **tre·men·dous·ness** *n.* ⟨Latin *tremendus* to be trembled at; *tremere* tremble⟩

trem·or See TREMBLE.

trench [trentʃ] *n* **1** a long, narrow cut in the ground, to be used as a defence for soldiers in battle. **2** a long furrow in the ocean floor. *v* **1** surround or fortify with a trench or trenches. **2** dig ditches. ⟨Old French *trenchier* to cut; Latin *truncare* lop off⟩
trench coat a loose-fitting raincoat worn with a belt, usually having epaulettes. **trench mouth** a contagious disease of the gums characterized by ulceration of the mucous membranes and foul-smelling breath.

trench·ant ['trentʃənt] *adj* **1** sharp; keen: *trenchant wit.* **2** vigorous; effective: *a trenchant policy.* **3** clear-cut: *in trenchant outline against the sky.* **trench·an·cy** *n.* **trench·ant·ly** *adv.* ⟨Old French; *trenchier* cut. See TRENCH.⟩

trench·er ['trentʃər] *n* a wooden platter formerly used for serving food, esp meat. ⟨Old French *trencheoir* knife; *trenchier* cut. See TRENCH.⟩

trend [trend] *n* **1** a course or tendency: *the trend of modern living.* **2** a current style in fashion, etc. ⟨Old English *trendan*⟩
trend·setter *n* a person, design firm, etc. that promotes new fashions in clothing or other products, ideas, etc. **trend·y** *adj Informal* following the latest fashions or trends: *a trendy boutique.* **trend·i·ly** *adv.* **trend·i·ness** *n.*

trep·i·da·tion [,trepə'deiʃən] *n* nervous dread; apprehension. ⟨Latin *trepidus* alarmed⟩

tres·pass ['trespæs] *or* ['trespəs] *v* **1** go on somebody's property without any right. **2** go beyond the limits of what is right or polite: *We won't trespass on your time.* **3** sin. *n* **1** the act of trespassing. **2** a wrong; a sin. **tres·pass·er** *n.* ⟨Old French *tres-* (trans-) + *passer.* See PASS.⟩

tress [tres] *n* **1** a lock, curl, or braid of hair. **2 tresses** *pl* a woman's or girl's hair, esp when long. ⟨Old French *tresce*⟩

tres·tle ['tresəl] *n* **1** a structure, such as a sawhorse, used to support a table top, platform, etc. **2** a framework used as a bridge to support a road, railway, etc. ⟨Old French *trestel* crossbeam; Latin *transtrum*⟩

trey [trei] *n* a card, die, etc. having three spots. ⟨Old French *trei*; Latin *tres* three⟩

tri– *prefix* **1** three; having three; having three parts: *triangle.* **2** three times; triply; into three parts or in three ways: *trisect, trilingual.* **3** containing three atoms, etc. of the substance specified: *trioxide.* **4** once in three; every third: *trimonthly.* ⟨Latin or Greek⟩

tri·ad ['traɪæd] *n* **1** a group of three, esp of three closely related persons or things. **2** *Music* a chord of three tones. **3** *Chemistry* an element, atom, or radical with a valence of three. **tri·ad·ic** *adj.* ⟨Greek *triados; treis* three⟩

tri·age [tri'ɑʒ] *n* the sorting of a number of casualties by a system of priorities which ensures that those with the best chance of benefiting from treatment are looked after first. ⟨French; *trier* to sort, sift⟩

tri·al ['traɪəl] *n* **1** the process of examining and deciding a case in court. **2** the process of testing: *She gave the machine another trial.* **3** the condition of being tried or tested: *He is employed on trial.* **4** a trouble or hardship. **5** a cause of trouble or hardship: *She is a trial to her big sister.* **6** an attempt. **7** a preliminary competition in field or track events .
adj **1** to do with a trial in a law court: *trial testimony.* **2** being a try or test: *a trial run.* **3** *adj* that is on trial: *a trial employee.* ⟨Anglo-French *trier.* See TRY⟩
on trial a being tried in court. **b** being tested or tried out. **trial and error** the process of arriving at a solution of a problem by trying several ways and learning from the errors so made. **tri·al–and–er·ror** *adj.*

SYNONYMS
Trial applies to the process of establishing the worth, effect, etc. of something: *He gave the new toothpaste a trial.* **Test** applies to a trial to end uncertainty about quality: *The new plane passed all tests.* **Experiment** applies to a process to find out something still unknown or to test a hypothesis, etc.: *Experiments indicate the new drug will cure infections.*

tri·an·gle ['traɪˌæŋgəl] *n* **1** a plane figure having three sides and three angles. **2** any object having three sides or three angles: *Our backyard is a triangle.* **3** a musical instrument consisting of a steel rod bent in a triangle, that produces a light ringing sound when struck with a steel rod. **4** a measuring instrument consisting of a flat right-angled triangle of wood, plastic, etc. **5** a situation involving three persons or points of view, esp an emotional relationship: *the eternal triangle.* **tri·an·gu·lar** [-ˈæŋgjələr] *adj.*
tri·an·gu·lar·i·ty *n.* **tri·an·gu·lar·ly** *adv.*
tri·an·gu·late [-ˌleɪt] *v* **1** survey or map out (a region) by dividing it into triangles and measuring their angles. **2** find by trigonometry: *to triangulate the height of a mountain.* **tri·an·gu·la·tion** *n.*

Tri·as·sic [traɪˈæsɪk] *Geology n* the earliest period of the Mesozoic era, beginning about 245 million years ago. **Tri·as·sic** *adj.* ⟨German *Trias* a certain series of strata with three types of deposit⟩

tri·ath·lon [traɪˈæθlɒn] *n* an Olympic sport in which athletes compete in swimming, bicycling, and running. **tri·ath·lete** *n.* ⟨tri- + Greek *athlon* contest⟩

tribe [traɪb] *n* **1** a group of families, clans, etc. united under one leader or ruling group. **2** a group of people, esp a large one, having a common interest, profession, etc.: *the whole tribe of gossips.* **3** a minor category in the classification of animals and plants ranking between a genus and a subfamily or family. **trib·al** *adj.* **tribes·man** *n,* *pl* **-men.** **tribes·peo·ple** *n pl.* ⟨Latin *tribus*⟩
trib·al·ism *n* **1** social organization according to tribes. **2** strong identification with a tribe or tribelike group. **trib·al·ist** *n.* **trib·al·is·tic** *adj.*
trib·u·la·tion [ˌtrɪbjəˈleɪʃən] *n* great trouble or affliction, esp as a result of persecution or oppression. ⟨Latin *tribulare* afflict; *tribulum* threshing board⟩

tri·bu·nal [traɪˈbjunəl] *or* [trɪˈbjunəl] *n* a court of justice: *She was brought before the tribunal for trial.*

trib·une ['trɪbjun] *n* **1** in ancient Rome: an official chosen by the plebeians to protect their rights and interests. **2** a military officer, one of six who rotated command of a legion in the course of a year. ⟨Latin *tribus* tribe⟩

trib·u·tar·y ['trɪbjəˌteri] *n* a stream that flows into a larger stream or body of water: *The Ottawa River is a tributary of the St. Lawrence.* **trib·u·tar·y** *adj.* ⟨Middle English; Latin *tributarius* ⟩

trib·ute ['trɪbjut] *n* **1** money paid by one nation to another for peace or protection or because of some agreement. **2** any forced payment: *The pirates demanded tribute from passing ships.* **3** an acknowledgment of thanks or respect: *to pay tribute to a brave soldier.* **4** testimony; a fact that proves how good something is. ⟨Latin *tributum* pp of *tribuere* allot; *tribus* tribe⟩

tri·cen·ten·ni·al [ˌtraɪsenˈtenjəl] *n* **1** a period of 300 years. **2** a 300th anniversary. **tri·cen·ten·ni·al** *adj.* Also, **tri·cen·te·nar·y** [ˌtraɪsenˈtɛnəri] *or* [-ˈtinəri].

tri·ceps ['traɪseps] *n, pl* **-ceps** or **-ceps·es** the large muscle at the back of the upper arm. It extends, or straightens, the arm. ⟨Latin; *tri-* three + *caput* head⟩

tri·chot·o·my [trəɪˈkɒtəmi] *or* [trəˈkɒtəmi] *n* **1** division into three mutually exclusive groups, classes, parts, etc. **2** specifically, the division of human nature into body, soul, and spirit. **tri·chot·o·mous** *adj.*
tri·chot·o·mous·ly *adv.* **tri·chot·o·mize** *v.* ⟨Greek *tricha* in three parts + *tomē* a cutting⟩

trick [trɪk] *n* **1** something done to deceive or cheat: *to play a trick on someone.* **2** a feat of skill: *Their dog does tricks.* **3** the best way of doing something: *the trick of making pies.* **4** a peculiar habit: *He has a trick of pulling at his collar.* **5** a single round of certain card games. **6** *Slang* a single transaction of a prostitute. *adj* involving tricks or illusions: *trick photography, a trick question.*
v **1** deceive: *We were tricked into buying that car.* **2** play pranks. **3** dress, esp in an ornate way (with *out*): *She was tricked out in her mother's clothes.* **trick·ish** *adj.* ⟨Old French *trique*⟩
do the trick do what one wants done. **how's tricks?** *Informal* how are things? **not miss a trick** *Informal* be very alert or quick. **trick of the trade** an effective technique in a particular line of work. **turn tricks** *Slang* engage in sexual acts for money.
trick·er·y *n* the act of deceiving or cheating. **trick or treat** a call used by children at Halloween, while begging for candy under the threat of playing tricks if refused. **trick·ster** *n* a cheat; deceiver. **trick·sy** *adj* **1** mischievous. **2** tricky. **trick·si·ness** *n.* **trick·y** *adj* **1** deceiving; cheating. **2** difficult to

handle, because unreliable or delicate: *a tricky situation.* trick·i·ly *adv.* trick·i·ness *n.*

trick·le ['trɪkəl] *v* 1 flow or cause to flow in a small stream: *Tears trickled down her cheeks.* 2 move slowly and unevenly: *People began to trickle into the theatre.* trick·le *n.* ⟨Middle English *strikle; strike* flow, move⟩

trick·le–down *adj* of or referring to an economic theory that government aid to big business will eventually result in benefits to ordinary consumers.

tri·col·our or **tri·col·or** ['traɪkʌlər] *adj* having three colours.
n a flag having three colours, esp the flag of France.

tri·cy·cle ['traɪsəkəl] *n* a three-wheeled vehicle usually worked by pedals attached to the large single wheel in front, now used esp by small children. ⟨*tri-* + Greek *kyklos* wheel⟩

tri·dent ['traɪdənt] *n* a three-pronged spear, esp as the attribute of Poseidon (Neptune), the ancient Greek (Roman) god of the sea. ⟨Latin *tri-* three + *dentis* tooth⟩

tried See TRY.

tri·en·ni·al [traɪ'ɛniəl] *n* 1 an event occurring every three years. 2 the third anniversary of an event. tri·en·ni·al *adj.* tri·en·ni·al·ly *adv.* ⟨Latin *tri-* three + *annus* year⟩
tri·en·ni·um *n* a three-year period.

tri·fle ['traɪfəl] *n* 1 something having little value or importance. 2 a small amount. 3 a rich dessert made of sponge cake, whipped cream, custard, fruit, wine, etc.
v 1 talk or act lightly, not seriously: *Don't trifle with serious matters.* 2 play *(with):* *He trifled with his pencil while he was talking.* ⟨Old French *trufle*⟩
tri·fler *n* a frivolous or shallow person.
tri·fling *adj* not important; small.

tri·fo·cal [traɪ'foukəl] *adj* of a lens, etc., adjusted to three focal lengths.
n [traɪ'foukəls] *or* ['traɪ-] **trifocals** *pl* a pair of glasses with trifocal lenses.

tri·fo·li·ate [traɪ'foulɪt] *adj* of a plant, having leaves in groups of three. Poison ivy is trifoliate. ⟨*tri-* + Latin *folium* leaf⟩
tri·fo·li·o·late [traɪ'fouliəlɪt] *adj* of a leaf, divided into three leaflets, as a clover leaf.

trig [trɪg] *n Informal* trigonometry: *We have a test in trig tomorrow.*

trig·ger ['trɪgər] *n* 1 the small lever pulled back by the finger in firing a gun. 2 any lever that releases a spring, catch, etc. 3 anything that sets off something else.
v 1 activate: *The explosion was triggered by a spark.* 2 cause to start: *Her speech triggered an outburst of violence.* ⟨Dutch *trekken* pull⟩
quick on the trigger a quick to shoot. **b** *Informal* quick to act or speak; alert.
trig·ger–hap·py *adj Informal* 1 inclined to use armed force at the slightest provocation. 2 too readily inclined to overreact, esp with violent action or adverse criticism.

tri·glyc·er·ide [traɪ'glɪsə,raɪd] *n* fats and oils

occurring in animal and vegetable tissues. ⟨*tri-* + Greek *glykeros* sweet⟩

trig·o·nom·e·try [,trɪgə'nɒmətri] *n* the branch of mathematics that deals with the relations between the sides and angles of triangles and the calculations based on these. **trig·o·no·met·ric** [,trɪgənə'mɛtrɪk] or **trig·o·no·met·ri·cal** *adj.* **trig·o·no·met·ri·cal·ly** *adv.* ⟨Greek *tri-* + *gōnia* angle + *metron* measure⟩
trigonometric function any one of the functions of an angle, such as sine, cosine, tangent, cotangent, secant, or cosecant, that can be expressed as a ratio of two sides of a right triangle.

tri·he·dron [traɪ'hidrən] *n, pl* -drons or -dra [-drə] a figure formed by three planes meeting at a point. **tri·he·dral** *adj.* ⟨*tri-* + Greek *hedra* base⟩

trike [traɪk] *n Informal* tricycle.

tri·lat·er·al [traɪ'lætərəl] *adj* having three sides or involving three parties. **tri·lat·er·al·ly** *adv.* ⟨Latin *tri-* three + *lateris* side⟩

tri·lin·gual [traɪ'lɪŋgwəl] *or* [-'lɪŋgjəwəl] *adj* 1 able to speak three languages: *a trilingual person.* 2 using or involving three languages. **tri·lin·gual·ly** *adv.* ⟨Latin *tri-* + *lingua* language⟩

trill [trɪl] *v* 1 sing, play, or speak with a quivering sound. 2 *Phonetics* pronounce with rapid vibration of the tongue. Many Scots trill the sound of *r.* **trill** *n.* ⟨Italian *trillare*⟩

tril·lion ['trɪljən] *n, adj* 1 in Canada and the US, 1 followed by 12 zeros; 1 000 000 000 000; a million million. 2 in some countries, 1 followed by 18 zeros. ⟨*tri-* + (M)ILLION⟩
tril·lionth *adj, n* one, or being one, of a trillion equal parts.

tril·li·um ['trɪljəm] *n* any of a genus of small plants of the lily family having a whorl of three leaves. The white trillium is the provincial flower of Ontario. ⟨*tri-*⟩

tri·lo·bite ['traɪlə,baɪt] *n* any of a large group of extinct marine arthropods that flourished in the Paleozoic era, having a segmented outside skeleton divided into three lobes. **tri·lo·bit·ic** [-'bɪtɪk] *adj.* ⟨*tri-* + Greek *lobos* lobe⟩

tril·o·gy ['trɪlədʒi] *n* three plays, novels, etc. that make a related series. Any of the three is itself a complete work. ⟨*tri-* three + Greek *logos* story⟩

trim [trɪm] *v* **trimmed, trim·ming** 1 make neat by cutting away parts: *The gardener trimmed the hedge.* 2 remove (unwanted parts or amounts): *I have to trim 8 kg from my baggage or pay extra.* 3 reduce (something) to the required size by cutting out parts: *This year's budget has been trimmed drastically.* 4 decorate: *to trim a Christmas tree.* 5 balance (a boat, airplane, etc.) by arranging the load carried, adjusting the stabilizers, etc. 6 change (opinions, views, etc.) to suit circumstances or to avoid conflict.
adj 1 neat in appearance: *A trim maid answered the door.* 2 well designed and maintained: *a trim little boat.*
n 1 condition; order: *to get in good trim for a*

race. **2** an act of trimming: *My hair needs a trim.* **3** trimming: *the trim on a dress.* **4** woodwork used as a finish or ornament on or in a building. **5** the upholstery, accessories, etc. inside a car or the chrome, colour scheme, etc. on the outside. **6** the position of a ship or aircraft relative to the horizontal, esp the fore-and-aft axis. **7** the position or angle of sails, yards, etc. in relation to the wind direction. **trim·ly** *adv.* **trim·ness** *n.* ⟨Old English *trymman* strengthen, make ready⟩

trim·mer *n* **1** a person or thing that trims: *a window trimmer.* **2** a person who changes his or her actions, etc. to suit circumstances. **3** a beam that supports the ends of headers, as around a stairwell, chimney, etc. **trim·ming** *n* **1** something added as a decoration: *black trimming on a blue suit.* **2 trimmings** *pl* **a** parts cut away in trimming. **b** *Informal* accompaniments to a main dish: *turkey with all the trimmings.* **3** the act of adjusting one's behaviour, etc. to suit circumstances.

tri·ma·ran ['traɪmə,ræn] *n* a boat with three hulls side by side. Compare CATAMARAN. ⟨*tri-* + (*cata*)*maran*⟩

tri·mes·ter [traɪ'mɛstər] *or* ['traɪmɛstər] *n* **1** a third part of a school year. **2** a three-month period. ⟨Latin *trimestris; tri-* + *mensis* month⟩

trim·e·ter ['trɪmətər] *Prosody n* a line of verse having three metrical feet. **trim·e·ter** *adj.*
tri·met·ric [traɪ'mɛtrɪk] *or* **tri·met·ri·cal** *adj* **1** to do with trimeters. **2** to do with a system in which three unequal axes intersect one another at right angles.

tri·month·ly [traɪ'mʌnθli] *adj* occurring every three months.

tri·mor·phism [traɪ'mɔrfɪzəm] *n Biology* the occurrence in one species of three types distinct in size, colour, etc. **tri·morph·ic** *adj.* **tri·morph·ous** *adj.* ⟨*tri-* + Greek *morphē* form⟩ **tri·morph** ['traɪmɔrf] *n* a substance, species, etc. that exhibits trimorphism.

Tri·mur·ti [trɪ'mʊrti] the Hindu trinity, Brahma, Vishnu, and Siva. ⟨Sanskrit *tri* three + *murti* form, body⟩

tri·ni·tro·tol·u·ene [traɪ,nəitrou'tɒlju,in] *n* a powerful explosive, usually known as TNT. Also, **tri·ni·tro·tol·u·ol.** ⟨*tri-* + *nitro*(gen) + *toluene*⟩

Trin·i·ty ['trɪnəti] *n* **1** *Christianity* the union of Father, Son, and Holy Spirit in one divine nature. **2 trinity** a group of three closely related persons or things. ⟨Latin *trinitas; trinus* triple⟩

trin·ket ['trɪŋkɪt] *n* **1** any small, fancy article, bit of jewellery, etc. **2** a trifle. ⟨Middle English *trenket* little knife⟩

tri·no·mi·al [traɪ'noumiəl] *n* **1** *Mathematics* an expression consisting of three terms connected by plus or minus signs. *Example:* $a + bx^2 - 2$. **2** *Biology* the Latin name of an animal or plant consisting of genus, species, and subspecies. **tri·no·mi·al** *adj.* **tri·no·mi·al·ly** *adv.* ⟨*tri-* + (BI)NOMIAL⟩

tri·o ['triou] *n* **1** a musical composition for three voices or instruments. **2** a group of

three singers or players. **3** any group of three persons or things. ⟨Italian; Latin *tres* three⟩

trip [trɪp] *n* **1** a journey: *a trip to Europe.* **2** any act of going and returning: *It took three trips to unload the car.* **3** a stumble; slip. **4** a mistake. **5** a projecting part on a mechanism for starting or checking some movement. **6** *Slang* **a** the mental state induced by hallucinogenic drugs, such as LSD. **b** a period of activity, mode of thinking, etc., that is intense, or in some other way analogous to a drug trip: *an ego trip, a guilt trip.*
v **tripped, trip·ping 1** stumble, or cause to stumble and fall: *The loose board tripped her.* **2** make a mistake or cause to make a mistake (sometimes with *up*): *The difficult question tripped me.* **3** take light, quick steps: *She tripped across the floor.* **4** release the catch of (a wheel, clutch, etc.): *Trip the switch.* **5** *Slang* experience a trip (*n* 6) (often with *out*): *to trip out on LSD.* ⟨Old French *tripper*⟩
trip·wire *n* a wire that activates a hidden explosive, camera, trap, etc. when tripped on, stepped on, or driven over.

tri·par·tite [traɪ'partəit] *adj* **1** divided into or composed of three parts. **2** made or shared by three parties: *a tripartite treaty.*

tripe [trəip] *n* **1** the walls of the stomachs of a beef animal, sheep, etc. used as food. **2** *Slang* something foolish or worthless. ⟨Old French *tripe* entrails; Arabic *tharb*⟩

Tri·pit·a·ka [trɪ'pɪtəkə] *n* the corpus of sacred texts containing the teachings of Buddha, orig written in the Pali language.

tri·ple ['trɪpəl] *adj* **1** having three parts: *the triple petals of the trillium.* **2** three times as much: *She got triple points for that question.* **3** *Music* having three (or a multiple thereof) beats per measure: *triple time.*
n **1** a number, amount, etc. that is three times as much or as many. **2** *Baseball* a hit that allows a batter to run three bases. **3** any group of three or threefold thing.
v **1** make or become three times as much or as many. **2** *Baseball* **a** hit a triple. **b** advance (another runner) by hitting a triple. **tri·ply** *adv.* ⟨Latin *triplus; tri-* + *-plus* fold⟩
triple crown 1 *Horse racing* a championship won by a horse that in a single season wins the three classic races for its category. **2** a similar championship in football, tennis, etc. **triple jump** a track-and-field event consisting of three successive jumps preceded by a running start. **triple play** *Baseball* a play that puts three players out. **tri·plet** ['trɪplɪt] *n* **1** one of three children born at the same time from the same mother. **2** *Music* a group of three notes to be performed in the time of two notes having the same time value. **3** three successive lines of poetry, usually rhyming and equal in length. **4** any group of three similar or equal things. **tri·plex** ['traɪplɛks] *n* ✷ a three-storey building having a separate apartment on each floor. **trip·li·cate** ['trɪpləkɪt] *adj* existing in three identical copies. **in triplicate** in three copies exactly alike.

tri·pod ['traipɒd] *n* a stand having three legs, as for a telescope, etc. **trip·o·dal** ['trɪpədəl] *adj.* ⟨*tri-* + Greek *podos* foot⟩

trip·tych ['trɪptɪk] *n* a set of three panels side by side, having pictures, carvings, etc. on them. ⟨Greek *tri-* + *ptyx* fold⟩

tri·sect [traɪ'sɛkt] *v* divide into three equal parts. **tri·sec·tion** *n.* **tri·sect·or** *n.* ⟨*tri-* + Latin *sectus* pp of *secare* cut⟩

tri·ser·vice or **tri–ser·vice** [traɪ'sɜrvɪs] *adj* ✹ of, for, or involving the land, maritime, and air forces or elements of the Canadian Forces.

tris·kai·dek·a·pho·bia [ˌtrɪskaɪˌdɛkə'foubiə] or [ˌtrɪskə-] *n* fear of the number thirteen. ⟨Greek *triskaideka* thirteen + PHOBIA⟩

trite [traɪt] *adj* commonplace; stale; no longer interesting: *The movie turned out to be very trite, so we left.* **trite·ly** *adv.* **trite·ness** *n.* ⟨Latin *tritus* pp of *terere* rub away⟩

trit·i·ca·le [ˌtrɪtə'keili] or [ˌtrɪtə'kɑli] *n* a fertile hybrid cereal, a cross between wheat and rye, that has high protein and a high yield. ⟨*Tritic(um)* wheat genus + (*Sec)ale* rye genus⟩

trit·i·um ['trɪtiəm] or ['trɪʃiəm] *n* a radioactive isotope of hydrogen that occurs in minute amounts in natural water, having a mass three times that of hydrogen. Tritium is used with deuterium in a hydrogen bomb. *Symbol* T or ^{3}H ⟨Greek *tritos* third⟩

tri·umph ['traɪʌmf] *n* **1** the state of being victorious: *They returned in triumph.* **2** a great victory or achievement: *a triumph of modern science.* **3** joy because of victory or success.
v **1** gain victory: *Our team triumphed over theirs.* **2** rejoice because of victory or success. ⟨Latin *triumphus*⟩ **tri·um·phal** *adj* to do with a triumph: *a triumphal parade.* **tri·um·phant** *adj* **1** victorious. **2** rejoicing because of victory: *triumphant soldiers.* **tri·um·phant·ly** *adv.*

tri·um·vi·rate *n* **1** government by three persons together. **2** any group of three. ⟨Latin; *trium virorum* 'of three men'⟩

triv·et ['trɪvɪt] *n* a stand usually having three feet, used under hot platters, etc. ⟨Old English *tri-* (Latin) + *-fēte* footed⟩

triv·i·a ['trɪviə] *n pl* (sometimes with sg verb) **1** unimportant matters. **2** obscure bits of information: *a storehouse of baseball trivia.* **triv·i·al** *adj.* **triv·i·al·ly** *adv.* ⟨Latin pl of *trivium* crossroads (where vulgar conversation occurred); *tri-* + *via* way⟩ **triv·i·al·i·ty** *n* **1** the quality or state of being trivial. **2** something trivial; trifle. **triv·i·al·ize** *v* downplay; minimize. **triv·i·al·i·za·tion** *n.*

tro·chee ['trouki] *n Prosody* a foot of two syllables, the first accented and the second unaccented or the first long and the second short. *Example:* Síng a | sóng of | síxpence. **tro·cha·ic** [trou'keiɪk] *adj.* ⟨Greek *trochaios*, orig running; *trochos* a course, *trechein* run⟩

trod, trod·den See TREAD.

trog·lo·dyte ['trɒgləˌdəit] *n* **1** a member of a prehistoric people who lived in caves. **2** a person who is antisocial. **3** an anthropoid ape. **trog·lo·dyt·ic** [-'dɪtɪk] *adj.* ⟨Greek *trōglē* cave + *dyein* go in⟩

troi·ka ['trɔɪkə] *n* **1** a Russian vehicle, esp a sleigh, drawn by three horses abreast. **2** any group of three. ⟨Russian; *troie* three together⟩

Tro·jan ['troudʒən] *n* **1** a native or inhabitant of Troy, an ancient city in NW Asia Minor. **2** a person who shows courage or energy: *They all worked like Trojans.* **Tro·jan** *adj.* **Trojan horse 1** *Greek myth* a huge wooden horse in which the Greeks concealed soldiers and had them brought into Troy during the Trojan War. **2** any person or group stationed inside a country, institution, etc. to sabotage its activities. **3** *Computers* an apparently normal program that contains hidden instructions for performing unexpected, and often destructive, processes.

troll¹ [troul] *v* fish with a moving line, usually by trailing the line behind the boat: *She trolled for bass.*
n a lure or a lure and line used in trolling. ⟨Old French *troller* wander; Germanic⟩ **troll·er** *n* a fishing boat equipped with poles for trolling lines behind the boat.

troll² [troul] *n Scandinavian folklore* any of a race of malevolent supernatural beings, thought of as giants or, more recently, as dwarfs. ⟨Old Norse⟩

trol·ley ['trɒli] *n, pl* **-leys 1** a pulley moving against a wire to carry electricity to a streetcar, etc. **2 a** a wheeled table, for serving food. **b** a wheeled frame for carrying luggage, etc. ⟨probably from *troll¹* in sense of 'roll'⟩ **off one's trolley** *Slang* crazy. **trolley bus** an electrically powered bus having two overhead trolleys and running on tires like a motor bus. **trolley car** streetcar.

trol·lop ['trɒləp] *n* **1** an untidy or slovenly woman. **2** a morally loose woman; slut. **3** prostitute. ⟨probably from *troll¹*⟩

trom·bone [trɒm'boun] *n* a wind instrument resembling a trumpet and having a sliding piece for varying the pitch. **trom·bon·ist** *n.* ⟨Italian *trombone; tromba* trumpet; Germanic⟩

tromp [trɒmp] *v Informal* tramp; stamp; stomp. ⟨variant of *tramp*⟩

trompe l'oeil [tʀɔp løj] *French* a life-size still-life painting, mural, etc. painted to create an illusion of reality, temporarily deceiving the viewer. ⟨French = fools the eye⟩

troop [trup] *n* **1** a large group or collection of people or animals: *a troop of deer.* **2** a formation of armed forces smaller than a squadron. **3 troops** *pl* armed forces. **4** a group of Scouts or Guides made up of several patrols.
v **1** gather or move in a troop or band: *We all trooped into the living room.* **2** carry (the colours) before troops as part of a ceremony. ⟨French *troupe;* Latin *troppus* herd⟩ **troop·er** *n* **1** a soldier in a cavalry or an armoured regiment. **2** *Informal* a courageous, hard-working, dependable person: *a real trooper.* **3** a mounted police officer. **4** *US* a state police officer. **troop·ship** *n* a ship used to carry soldiers; transport.

trope *n* [troup] the use of a word or phrase in a sense different from its ordinary meaning. *Example:* The *bloody* sun at noon. ⟨Greek *tropos* turn⟩

tro·phy ['troufi] *n* **1** something taken or won in war, hunting, etc., esp if displayed as a memorial or souvenir: *The hunter kept the moose's head as a trophy.* **2** a prize, often a silver cup or statue, awarded in sports or other competitions: *a tennis trophy.* ⟨Latin *trophaeum;* Greek *tropaion; tropē* rout, turn⟩

trop·ic ['trɒpɪk] *n* **1** either of two parallels of latitude, one 23°27′ north and the other 23°27′ south of the equator. The northern parallel is the **Tropic of Cancer** and the southern is the **Tropic of Capricorn. 2 the tropics** or **Tropics** *pl* the region between these parallels. **trop·ic** *adj.* ⟨Greek *tropikos; tropē* a turn, a change⟩
trop·i·cal *adj* **1** to do with the tropics: *tropical diseases.* **2** like the tropics, very hot or sultry. **trop·i·cal·ly** *adv.*

trop·o·sphere ['trɒpə,sfir] *n* the lowest layer of the atmosphere, from about 10 km above the earth up to the stratosphere (at about 20 km). **trop·o·spher·ic** [-'sferɪk] *adj.* ⟨Greek *tropē* a turn, change + SPHERE⟩

trot [trɒt] *v* **trot·ted, trot·ting 1** of horses, etc., go at a gait between a walk and a run. **2** of a person, run at a moderate pace. *n* **1** the gait of a trotting animal or person: *We started off at a trot.* **2 the trots** *pl Slang* diarrhea. ⟨Old French *trotter;* Germanic⟩
trot·ter *n* **1** an animal that trots, esp a horse trained for harness racing. **2** a pig's foot used for food.

troth [trɒθ] *or* [trouθ] *Archaic, poetic n* **1** loyalty. **2** a promise to marry. ⟨Old English *trēowth; trēow* faith⟩
by my troth *or* **in troth** truly. **plight one's troth** pledge to marry.

trou·ba·dour ['trubə,dɔr] *n* **1** one of a class of medieval lyric poets who wrote poems of chivalry and courtly love. **2** any minstrel or poet. ⟨Provençal *trobador;* Latin *tropus* song, mode (in music), Greek *tropos* orig a turn⟩

trou·ble ['trʌbəl] *n* **1** distress; difficulty: *We're having trouble with the furnace.* **2** a distressing fact or event: *a life full of troubles.* **3** a cause of distress, vexation, etc.: *Is she a trouble to you?* **4** public disturbance: *trouble on the picket line.* **5** extra work; effort: *She took the trouble to make extra copies.* **6** illness or disease: *stomach trouble.* **7** faulty operation: *engine trouble.* **8** the trouble the cause of annoyance, worry, etc.: *She's too easygoing, that's the trouble.* **trou·ble** *v.* ⟨Old French *trubler;* Latin *turbulare; turba* turmoil⟩
in (or **into**) **trouble** in or into a situation in which one is caught in wrongdoing and is liable to be blamed, punished, etc.: *in trouble with the police.* **make trouble** cause problems: *Mind your own business and don't make trouble.* **trouble someone for** ask (someone) to give: *May I trouble you for the salt?*
trou·ble·mak·er *n* a person who deliberately causes disagreement between people.

trou·ble·mak·ing *n, adj.* **trou·ble·shoot·er** *n* **1** a person employed to eliminate causes of trouble in equipment, machinery, etc. **2** a person who is skilled in mediating disputes. **trou·ble·shoot, -shot, -shoot·ing. trou·ble·some** *adj* causing trouble; annoying. **trou·ble·some·ly** *adv.* **trou·ble·some·ness** *n.*

trough [trɒf] *n* **1** a container for holding food or water for animals. **2** a channel for carrying water; gutter. **3** a long hollow between two ridges, etc.: *the trough between two waves.* **4** *Meteorology* a narrow area of low barometric pressure. **5** a low point in a cycle. **trough·like** *adj.* ⟨Old English *trōh*⟩

trounce [trauns] *v* **1** beat; thrash. **2** *Informal* defeat severely in a contest, game, etc. ⟨origin uncertain⟩

troupe [trup] *n* a troop, or band, , esp a group of actors, singers, or acrobats. ⟨French⟩

trous·seau ['trusou] *or* [tru'sou] *n, pl* **-seaux** or **-seaus** [-ouz] a bride's outfit of clothes, linen, etc. ⟨French, orig bundle⟩

trout [traut] *n, pl* **trout** or **trouts** any of several freshwater food fishes of the salmon family. ⟨Old English *trūht;* Greek *trōktēs* literally, gnawer; *trōgein* gnaw⟩

trow·el ['trauəl] *n* **1** a hand tool with a thin blade, used for spreading plaster, mortar, etc. **2** a garden tool similar to a scoop, used for taking up plants, etc. *v* **-elled** or **-eled, -el·ling** or **-el·ing** apply (plaster) with a trowel. ⟨Old French *truele;* Latin *truella* diminutive of *trua* skimmer⟩

tru·ant ['truənt] *n* a student who stays away from school without permission. **tru·an·cy** *n.* **tru·ant** *adj.* ⟨Old French; probably Celtic⟩
play truant neglect one's work or duty; esp, stay away from school without permission. **truant officer** a school official employed to investigate and deal with cases of truancy.

truce [trus] *n* **1** a stop in fighting by agreement between opposing armed forces. **2** a rest from quarrelling, turmoil, trouble, etc. ⟨Middle English *trewes* pl of *trewe;* Old English *trēow.* See TROTH.⟩

truck[1] [trʌk] *n* a motor vehicle designed primarily for carrying heavy things or animals rather than people. *v* transport goods by truck, esp as a business; **truck·er** *n.* ⟨perhaps Greek *trochos* wheel⟩
truck·ing *n* the business of transporting goods by truck. **truck·load** *n* a load that fills a truck. **truck stop** a restaurant and service station together on a highway, that is frequented by truckers.

truck[2] [trʌk] *n* **1** vegetables raised for market. **2** small articles of little value. **3** *Informal* rubbish. **4** *Informal* dealings: *I want no truck with you.* ⟨Old French *troquer* barter, trade⟩
truck farm a farm where vegetables are raised for market; market garden. **truck farmer. truck farming. truck system ✱** *Atlantic Provinces* a credit system under which a fisher, logger, trapper, etc. gets his or her supplies for the season as an advance, and is

committed to deal only with the merchant extending the credit.

truck·le ['trʌkəl] *v* give up or submit tamely (*to*): *to truckle to one's superiors.* **truck·ler** *n.* **truck·ling·ly** *adv.* ⟨*truckle* low bed rolled under a high one when not in use; for its low position⟩

truc·u·lent ['trʌkjələnt] *adj* **1** showing a readiness to fight or quarrel: *a truculent attitude.* **2** fierce and cruel. **3** of speech or writing, scathing; harsh. **truc·u·lence** *n.* **truc·u·lent·ly** *adv.* ⟨Latin *trucis* fierce⟩

trudge [trʌdz] *v* walk, esp wearily or with effort: *The tired hikers trudged home.* **trudge** *n.* ⟨origin uncertain⟩

true [tru] *adj* **1** agreeing with fact; not false. **2** real: *true gold, a true friend.* **3** exact; accurate: *a true copy.* **4** representative of the class named: *A sweet potato is not a true potato.* **5** rightful; lawful: *the true heir.* *adv* **1** in a true manner: *Her words ring true.* **2** in agreement with the ancestral type: *breed true.* ⟨Old English *trīewe, trēowe*⟩

come true become real. **true north** etc. north, etc., according to the earth's axis, not the magnetic north. **true to form** behaving according to expectation.

true–blue *adj* staunch and unchanging: *a true-blue conservative.* **true–bred** *adj* purebred. **true–heart·ed** *adj* **1** faithful. **2** honest, sincere. **true–heart·ed·ly** *adv.* **true–heart·ed·ness** *n.* **tru·ism** *n* a statement that is obviously true, esp one that is too obvious to mention, such as "You're only young once." **tru·ist·ic** *adj.* **true–life** *adj* that corresponds to, or actually occurred in, real life: *a true-life romance.* **true love** **1** genuine, faithful love. **2** a sweetheart or lover. **tru·ly** *adv* **1** in a true manner. **2** in the formal closing of a letter, sincerely (often preceded by "Yours (very)"). **truth** [truθ] *n, pl* **truths** [truðz] *or* [truθs] **1** the quality of being in accord with fact: *She doubted the truth of the story.* **2** an accepted or proven fact: *a basic scientific truth.* **3** the true answer(s) to the ultimate questions of existence: *He is studying philosophy in search of truth.* **in truth** truly. **truth·ful** *adj.* **truth·ful·ly** *adv.* **truth·ful·ness** *n.* **truth serum** *Informal* any drug thought to make a person speak freely when questioned.

truf·fle ['trʌfəl] *n* **1** any of several European underground fungi valued as food. **2** a soft, rich chocolate candy. ⟨probably French *truffe*⟩

trump¹ [trʌmp] *n* **1** *Card games* **a** any card of a suit that for the duration of a deal or game ranks higher than the other suits. **b** Often, **trumps** *pl* the suit itself. **2** any resource or advantage held back until needed. **3** *Informal* a fine, dependable person. *v* **1** *Card games* play a trump when another suit was led: *We didn't expect her to trump.* **2** surpass; beat. ⟨alteration of *triumph*⟩ **trump up** think up or invent falsely: *He trumped up an excuse.* **trumped–up** *adj.* **trump card** **1** any playing card of a suit that for a particular hand ranks higher than the other suits. **2** a decisive fact, argument, etc., esp one that is held in reserve until needed.

trump² [trʌmp] *Archaic, poetic n* **1** a trumpet. **2** the sound of a trumpet. **trump** *v.* ⟨See TRUMPET.⟩

trump·er·y ['trʌmpəri] *n* something showy but without value. **trump·er·y** *adj.* ⟨French *tromperie; tromper* deceive⟩

trump·et ['trʌmpɪt] *n* **1** a wind instrument having a looped tube that is bell-shaped. **2** anything shaped like a trumpet. *v* **1** blow a trumpet. **2** make a sound like a trumpet: *The elephant trumpeted.* **3** proclaim: *He'll trumpet that story all over town.* **trum·pet·er** *n.* ⟨Old French *trompette* diminutive of *trompe*⟩ **blow one's own trumpet** boast about oneself.

trun·cate ['trʌŋkeit] *v* shorten (something) by cutting off the top or end. *adj Botany* having a blunt or square end: *the truncate leaf of the tulip tree.* **trun·cat·ed** *adj.* **trun·ca·tion** *n.* ⟨Latin *truncus* maimed⟩

trun·dle ['trʌndəl]   *v* roll   or   push (something) along: *He trundled a wheelbarrow full of cement.* ⟨Middle English variant of *trendle* wheel; Old English *trendel* ring, disk⟩

trunk [trʌŋk] *n* **1** the main stem of a tree, as distinct from the branches and the roots. **2** the main or central part of something. **3** a compartment in a car for storing luggage etc. **4** a large box with a hinged lid, used for transporting or storing clothes, etc. **5** the body apart from the head, arms, and legs; torso. **6** the snout of an elephant. **7 trunks** *pl* very short pants worn by male athletes, swimmers, etc. ⟨Latin *truncus* orig mutilated⟩

truss [trʌs] *v* **1** tie; bind (often with *up*): *We trussed the burglar up and called the police.* **2** fasten the wings or legs of (a fowl) in preparation for cooking. *n* a framework of beams for supporting a roof, bridge, etc. ⟨Old French *trusser*⟩

trust [trʌst] *n* **1** a firm belief; faith: *He put no trust in the strangers.* **2** a confident expectation: *Our trust is that she will soon be well.* **3** either of two arrangements which are illegal in Canada if the intent is to frustrate the free market: **a** a group controlling much of a certain business: *a steel trust.* **b** a group having a committee that controls stock of constituent companies, thus defeating competition. **4** something managed for the benefit of another. **5** the condition of one in whom trust has been placed: *A guardian is in a position of trust.* **6** business credit. **trust** *v.* ⟨Old Norse *traust*⟩

in trust for the benefit of another: *The money was held in trust for her.* **on trust a** on business credit. **b** without evidence: *We took his assurances on trust.* **trust to** rely on; depend on: *Trust to luck.*

trust company a business concern formed primarily to act as a trustee but also often engaged in financial activities performed by banks. **trus·tee** *n* **1** a person responsible for the affairs of another person, of a company, or of an institution. **2** a person elected to a board responsible for the schools in a district. **trus·tee·ship** *n.* **trust·ful** *adj* ready to

confide; believing. **trust·ful·ly** *adv.*
trust·ful·ness *n.* **trust fund** money, property, or other valuables held in trust. **trust·ing** *adj* that trusts. **trust·ing·ly** *adv.* **trust·wor·thy** *adj* that can be trusted; honest: *We chose a trustworthy person for treasurer.* **trust·wor·thi·ly** *adv.* **trust·wor·thi·ness** *n.* **trust·y** *adj* reliable: *a trusty servant. n* a prisoner who is given special privileges because of his or her good behaviour. **trust·i·ly** *adv.* **trust·i·ness** *n.*

truth See TRUE.

try [traɪ] *v* **1** make an attempt. **2** find out the qualities of by testing: *I tried the candy but didn't like it.* **3** find out the effectiveness of (an action, process, or thing): *Did you try the hardware store?* **4** attempt to open (a door, window, etc.): *Try the door.* **5** *Law* examine (a case) in a court: *tried and found guilty.* **6** put to a severe test: *His complaining tried her patience.* **7** subject to trials: *She was greatly tried by family tragedies.*
n **1** an attempt. **2** a test. **3** *Rugger* the act of touching the ball to the ground behind the opponent's goal line. ⟨Old French *trier* sift⟩
try on put on (clothing, etc.) to test the fit, looks, etc. **try one's hand at** attempt. **try out a** a test by using: *She drove the car to try it out.* **b** take a test to show fitness for a role: *to try out for the hockey team.* **try·out** *n.*
tried [traɪd] *adj* tested; proved. **tried and true** that has proved effective on previous occasions. **try·ing** *adj* annoying: *It's been a trying day.* **try·ing·ly** *adj.* **try square** an instrument for drawing right angles and testing the squareness of anything.

GRAMMAR
Although the formal idiom is **try to**, informal English has long used **try and**.
Formal: *Let us try to get permission to go.*
Informal: *Let's try and get permission to go.*

tryst [trɪst] *n* **1** an agreement by lovers for a secret meeting. **2** a meeting held by appointment. **3** a place of meeting. ⟨Old French *triste* in hunting, a place to which game was driven⟩

tsar, tsa·ri·na, etc. See CZAR.

TSE or **T.S.E.** Toronto Stock Exchange.

tsetse fly ['tsitsi] *or* ['tsetsi] any of several bloodsucking flies that transmit diseases, including sleeping sickness in human beings. ⟨Bantu⟩

Tsilh·qot'·in ['tsɪlkʊtɪn] *n* **1** a member of a First Nations people living in British Columbia. **2** their language. **Tsilhqot'in** *adj.* Also called **Chilcotin.**

T–shirt ['ti ˌʃɜrt] *n* a sport shirt or undershirt having no collar and, usually, short sleeves.

Tsim·shi·an ['tsɪmʃiən] *or* ['tʃɪmʃiən] *n, pl* **-an** or **-ans** **1** a First Nations people who originally lived in the lower Skeena and Nass Valleys in British Columbia. **2** the language of this people. **Tsim·shi·an** *adj.*

tsp teaspoon(s).

tsu·na·mi [tsʊ'nɑmi] *n* a gigantic sea wave caused by an earthquake on the ocean floor,

occurring esp in the Pacific Ocean. **tsu·nam·ic** *adj.* ⟨Japanese *tsu* port + *nami* wave⟩

Tsu·nuk·wa *n* the female version of BUKWUS.

tub [tʌb] *n* **1** bathtub. **2** washtub. **3** a usually round, flat-bottomed, open container. **tub·ba·ble** *adj.* ⟨Middle Dutch *tubbe*⟩ **tub·by** *adj* **1** like a tub in shape. **2** short and fat or pudgy. **tub·bi·ness** *n.*

tu·ba ['tjubə] *or* ['tubə] *n* a large, brass wind instrument. **tub·ist** *n.* ⟨Latin = war trumpet⟩

tube [tjub] *or* [tub] *n* **1** a hollow cylinder, esp one used to carry liquids or gases. **2** a small cylinder with a screw cap, used for holding paste substances: *a tube of toothpaste.* **3** an inflatable casing of rubber that fits inside a tire. **tub·al** *adj.* **tube·less** *adj.* **tube·like** *adj.* ⟨Latin *tubus*⟩
(go) down the tube(s) *Informal* (be) destroyed, vanished, failed, or defeated.
tub·ing *n* **1** material in the form of a tube: *rubber tubing.* **2** a system of tubes. **tu·bu·lar** ['tjubjələr] *or* ['tu-] *adj* cylindrical and hollow. **tu·bu·lar·i·ty** *n.* **tu·bu·lar·ly** *adv.*

tu·ber ['tjubər] *or* ['tubər] *n* a fleshy underground stem, as of the potato, for food storage and from which new plants grow. **tu·ber·ous** *adj.* ⟨Latin = lump⟩

tu·ber·cle ['tjubərkəl] *or* ['tubərkəl] *n* **1** a small, rounded swelling or knob on an animal or plant. **2** a small lump in the lungs that is characteristic of tuberculosis. ⟨Latin *tuberculum* diminutive of *tuber* lump⟩
tu·ber·cu·lo·sis *n* an infectious disease affecting humans and some other mammals. **tu·ber·cu·lous** *adj.*

tuck [tʌk] *v* **1** put (something) into a place where it is held tightly or concealed: *He tucked the newspaper under his arm.* **2** cover by tucking in the bedclothes (with *in*): *He always came up to tuck the children in.* **3** fold or make shorter by folding (with *up*): *She tucked up her long skirt and waded into the lake.* **4** fold (the legs) back when sitting or lying: *She sat with her legs tucked under her.* **5** eat heartily (with *into* or *away*): *He tucked away a big meal.* **6** pull in or back (with *in*): *to tuck in one's stomach.*
n **1** a fold sewn into a garment, etc. for decoration, to shorten, etc. **2** *Diving, etc.* a position in which the knees are drawn up to the body. ⟨Middle English *tuken* stretch; Old English *tūcian* torment⟩
tuck in eat with gusto. **tuck–in** *n.*

Tues·day ['tjuz,dei] *or* ['tuz,dei] *n* the third day of the week, following Monday. ⟨Old English *tiwesdæg* day of Tiw, god of war⟩

tuft [tʌft] *n* **1** a bunch of feathers, grass, etc. growing from one place: *A goat has a tuft of hair on its chin.* **2** a bunch of threads sewn through a comforter, cushion, etc. to keep the padding in place.
v provide or decorate with a tuft or tufts. **tuft·ed** *adj.* **tuft·y** *adj.* ⟨perhaps Old French *touffe;* Latin *tufa* helmet crest⟩

tuf·fet ['tʌfɪt] *n* **1** a tuft of grass. **2** a low stool.

tug [tʌg] *v* **tugged, tug·ging** pull hard: *She tugged the rope and it came loose.*
n **1** a hard pull. **2** a tugboat. ⟨See TOW¹.⟩
tug·boat *n* a small, powerful boat used to tow or push ships or boats. **tug–of–war** *n* **1** a contest between two teams pulling at the ends of a rope, each trying to drag the other over a line marked between them. **2** any hard struggle for power.

tu·i·tion [tju'ɪʃən] *or* [tu'ɪʃən] *n* **1** the money paid for instruction: *Her yearly tuition is $5000.* **2** instruction: *The child made excellent progress under the teacher's capable tuition.* ⟨Latin *tuitio; tueri* watch over⟩

tuk·tu ['tʌktu] *n* **1** caribou. **2** caribou or reindeer furs. Also, **tuk·too**. ⟨Inuktitut⟩

tu·la·di See TOULADI.

tu·le ['tuli] *n* either of two large bulrushes found in marshy areas in SW Canada. ⟨Spanish; Nahuatl *tolin*⟩
out in the tules ✱ *esp Western Slang* in the country, away from the urban centres.

tu·lip ['tjulɪp] *or* ['tulɪp] *n* any of a genus of plants belonging to the lily family that have cup-shaped flowers. ⟨obsolete Dutch *tulipa;* Turkish *tülbend* turban; for shape of bloom⟩
tulip tree a large tree of the magnolia family having cup-shaped flowers that appear before the leaves.

tulle [tul] *n* a fine, stiff, machine-made net, used esp for bridal veils and ballet costumes. ⟨*Tulle* city in SW France⟩

tul·li·bee ['tulə,bi] *n, pl* **-bee** *or* **-bees ✱** any of several ciscoes valued as a food fish. ⟨Cdn. French *toulibi;* Algonquian⟩

tum·ble ['tʌmbəl] *v* **1** fall headlong, or end over end. **2** fall or cause to fall: *The quake tumbled buildings.* **3** toss about: *clothes tumbling in the dryer.* **4** move in a headlong way: *The children tumbled through the door.* **5** perform leaps, springs, etc. **6** decline rapidly: *The stock market tumbled.* **7** *Informal* understand (with *to*): *She tumbled to the trick right away.*
n **1** a fall. **2** a state of confusion or disorder. ⟨Old English *tumbian* dance about⟩
tum·ble·down *adj* ready to fall down; dilapidated **tum·bler** *n* **1** an acrobat. **2** a drinking glass. Tumblers orig had rounded or pointed bottoms so that they could not be set down until empty. **3** the part in a lock that must be moved to release the bolt. **tum·ble·weed** *n* any of various plants that after drying up in the fall break off from their roots and are blown about by the wind. **tum·bling** *n* the sport of performing gymnastic feats without the use of apparatus.

tu·mes·cent [tju'mɛsənt] *or* [tu'mɛsənt] *adj* **1** becoming swollen. **2** somewhat swollen. **tu·mes·cence** *n.* ⟨Latin *tumescere* begin to swell; *tumere* swell⟩

tum·my ['tʌmi] *n Informal* stomach (*a child's word*).

tu·mour *or* **tu·mor** ['tjumər] *or* ['tumər] *n* **1** an abnormal mass of tissue in any part of the body, that develops from existing tissue, but has no function. Tumours can be either benign (doing little harm) or malignant (cancerous). **2** any abnormal swelling. **tu·mor·ous** *adj.* ⟨Latin *tumor; tumere* swell⟩

tump·line ['tʌmp,laɪn] *n* a harness for carrying heavy loads, consisting of a long strap placed around the forehead or chest, the two ends being attached to the pack or load. Also, **tump**. ⟨Algonquian *tump* + LINE⟩

tu·mult ['tjumʌlt] *or* ['tumʌlt] *n* **1** a violent disturbance or disorder: *the tumult of the storm.* **2** a great disturbance of mind or feeling: *Her mind was in a tumult.* **tu·mul·tu·ous** [tju'mʌltʃuəs] *or* [tu-] *adj.* **tu·mul·tu·ous·ly** *adv.* **tu·mul·tu·ous·ness** *n.* ⟨Latin *tumultus*⟩

tun [tʌn] *n* a large cask for holding liquids, esp wine, beer, or ale. ⟨Old English *tunne;* perhaps Celtic⟩

tu·na ['tunə] *or* ['tjunə] *n* any of various spiny-finned fishes having a rounded body and a crescent-shaped tail. Also, **tuna fish**. **tuna–fish** *adj.* ⟨Spanish *tuna;* Latin *thunnus*⟩

tun·dra ['tʌndrə] *n* a vast, treeless plain in the arctic regions. ⟨Russian⟩

tune [tjun] *or* [tun] *n* **1** a succession of musical tones forming a unit. **2** the proper pitch: *She can't sing in tune.* **3** harmonious relation: *in tune with one's surroundings.*
v **1** adjust to the proper pitch: *to tune a piano.* **2** of an orchestra, adjust instruments to the proper pitch (with *up*). **3** adjust (a motor, etc.) for precise performance (often with *up*). **4** adjust (a radio or television set) to receive a particular frequency of signals (often with *in*): *Tune in tomorrow for another episode.* **tun·a·ble** *or* **tune·a·ble** *adj.* **tun·a·bly** *or* **tune·a·bly** *adj.* ⟨variant of *tone*⟩
call the tune have control: *He talks big, but his partner calls the tune.* **change one's tune** change one's mood or manner: *He was very cheeky at first, but soon changed his tune.* **sing a different tune** behave differently: *She's singing a different tune since she lost her job.* **to the tune of** *Informal* to the amount of: *He received a bill to the tune of $800 for car repairs.* **tune in** *Informal* become or make aware: *The experience quickly tuned her in to her family's needs.* **tune out** *Slang* turn one's mind away from; ignore: *She tunes out complaints she doesn't want to hear.*
tune·ful *adj* musical; melodious: *a tuneful song.* **tune·ful·ly** *adv.* **tune·ful·ness** *n.* **tune·less** *adj* **1** not tuneful: *tuneless humming.* **2** silent: *Her guitar, now tuneless, gathered dust in a corner.* **tune·less·ly** *adv.* **tune·less·ness** *n.* **tun·er** *n* **1** a person whose work is tuning musical instruments, esp pianos. **2** the part of a radio or television receiver that detects signals and feeds them to other circuits. **tune·smith** *n Informal* a songwriter of popular music. **tune–up** *n* adjustment of a motor, etc. to the proper running condition. **tuning fork** a two-pronged steel instrument that sounds a fixed tone when struck.

tung·sten ['tʌŋstən] *n* a hard metallic element with a very high melting point. *Symbol* **W** ⟨Swedish *tung* heavy + *sten* stone⟩

tu·nic ['tjunɪk] *or* ['tunɪk] *n* **1** a loose garment with or without sleeves, usually reaching to the knees. **2** a jacket worn as part of the uniform by soldiers, police officers, etc. ⟨Latin *tunica*; Semitic⟩

tun·nel ['tʌnəl] *n* an artificial underground passage: *The railway passes through several tunnels on its way through the Rockies.* **tun·nel, -nelled** or **-neled, -nel·ling** or **-nel·ing** *v.* **tun·nel·ler** or **tun·nel·er** *n.* ⟨Old French *tonel* cask; *tonne* tun; Celtic⟩
tunnel vision 1 a very narrow field of vision. **2** narrow-mindedness.

tun·ny ['tʌni] *n, pl* **-nies** or **-ny** TUNA¹. ⟨French *thon*; Latin *thunnus*; Greek *thynnos*⟩

tu·pik ['tupək] *n* ✹ a compact, portable tent of skins, traditionally used by Inuit as a summer dwelling. ⟨Inuktitut *tupiq*⟩

tuque [tuk] *or* [tjuk] *n* ✹ **1** a knitted cap resembling a long stocking, usually knotted at the end. **2** a tight-fitting, short knitted cap, often having a round tassel on top. ⟨Cdn. French variant of French *toque* cap⟩

tur·ban ['tɜrbən] *n* **1** a headdress for men worn esp by Muslims and Sikhs, consisting of a scarf wound around the head. **2** any similar headdress. **tur·baned** *adj.* ⟨Turkish; Persian *dulband*⟩

tur·bid ['tɜrbɪd] *adj* **1** thick, dark, or cloudy with or as if with mud: *a turbid river.* **2** confused: *a turbid mind.* **tur·bid·i·ty** *n.* **tur·bid·ly** *adv.* ⟨Latin *turbidus*; *turba* turmoil⟩

tur·bine ['tɜrbaɪn] *or* ['tɜrbɪn] *n* a rotary engine driven by a current of water, steam, or air. ⟨Latin *turbo, turbinis* whirling object or motion⟩
tur·bo ['tɜrbou] *n* **1** turbine. **2** turbocharger. **turbo–** *combining form* consisting of or driven by a turbine: *turbojet.* **tur·bo·charg·er** *n* a supercharger driven by a turbine that in turn is powered by the engine's exhaust gases. **tur·bo·charge** *v.* **tur·bo·jet** *n* an aircraft powered by turbojet engines. **turbojet engine** a jet engine using a turbine to supply compressed air to the combustion chamber.

tur·bot ['tɜrbət] *n, pl* **-bot** or **-bots** a large flatfish valued as food. ⟨Old Swedish *törnbut; törn* thorn; for the fish's prickles⟩

tur·bu·lent ['tɜrbjələnt] *adj* greatly agitated: *the turbulent sea, a turbulent state of mind.* ⟨Latin *turbulentus; turba* turmoil⟩
tur·bu·lence *n* **1** commotion. **2** *Meteorology* an unstable condition of the atmosphere, characterized by strong, irregular air currents. **tur·bu·lent·ly** *adv.*

turd [tɜrd] *n* a piece of excrement. ⟨Old English *tord*⟩

tu·reen [tjə'rin] *or* [tə'rin] *n* a deep, covered dish for serving soup, etc. ⟨French *terrine* earthen vessel; Latin *terra* earth⟩

turf [tɜrf] *n, pl* **turfs** or (sometimes) **turves 1** grass, roots, and soil in a thick layer. **2** an artificial surface made to resemble grass. **3** Usually, **the turf** the business of horse racing. **4** *Informal* a particular territory: *Relax now that you are back on your own turf.*
v **1** cover with turf. **2** *Slang* evict forcefully (usually with *out*): *The manager turfed us out when we got rowdy.* **turf·y** *adj.* ⟨Old English⟩

tur·gid ['tɜrdʒɪd] *adj* **1** bloated. **2** using big words and elaborate comparisons. **tur·gid·i·ty** *n.* **tur·gid·ly** *adv.* ⟨Latin *turgere* swell⟩

tur·key ['tɜrki] *n, pl* **1** a large bird having a bare head and neck with wattles. **2** ✹ *esp Prairie Provinces* sandhill crane. **3** *Slang* a flop, esp a play or movie that has failed. **4** *Slang* an unattractive, stupid, or silly person: *I don't want that turkey as a partner.* ⟨*turkey-cock, turkey-hen*, names for guinea fowl imported from Turkey, and confused with this bird⟩
talk turkey *Informal* talk frankly and bluntly.

Turkish bath ['tɜrkɪʃ] **1** a bath in which the bather stays in a hot room until he or she sweats freely, and then is washed and massaged. **2** Often, **Turkish baths** *pl* a place used for such baths.

tur·moil ['tɜrmɔɪl] *n* a commotion; disturbance; confusion. ⟨origin uncertain⟩

turn [tɜrn] *v* **1** spin as a wheel does. **2** change in direction or position: *to turn a page.* **3** move or cause to move around in order to open, close, raise, etc.: *Turn the key.* **4** change or cause to change so as to become: *She turned pale. The rain turned to snow.* **5** depend: *The success of the picnic turns on the weather.* **6** send: *to turn a person away.* **7** aim: *He turned his flashlight on us.* **8** revolve in the mind (often with *over*): *to turn a problem in one's mind.* **9** direct one's attention: *Let us turn to more global concerns.* **10** put (to use): *to turn money to good use.* **11** go around or beyond (a corner). **12** shape or be shaped on a lathe. **13** make or become curved, rounded, bent, or twisted. **14** make or become sick: *The smell turned my stomach.* **15** reach or pass (a particular age, amount, etc.): *a man turning sixty.* **16** of leaves, cause to change, or change colour. **17** recoil or cause to recoil: *Her remarks were turned against her.* **18** change in attitude: *She turned against her sister.* **19** exchange for something else: *to turn stock into cash.* **20** make; earn (a profit).
n **1** a single revolution. **2** a change of direction: *a turn to the left.* **3** a change in affairs or circumstances: *a turn for the better.* **4** a chance to do something, in an ordered rotation: *My turn next.* **5** an act: *One good turn deserves another.* **6** a stage act. **7** a short walk, drive, or ride: *a turn in the park.* **8** a spell of dizziness: *This morning I had one of my turns.* **9** a version (with *on*): *a new turn on an old idea.* ⟨Old English *turnian*; Latin *tornare; tornus* lathe, Greek *tornos*⟩
at every turn a every time. **b** all the time. **by turns** one after the other: *She was by turns amused and angered by their prank.* **in turn a** in proper order. **b** in reaction: *He overspent; she, in turn, became paranoid about money.* **out of turn a** not in proper order. **b** at the wrong stage, etc.: *Your comments are out of turn.* **take it in turns** (to do something) act alternately. **take turns** play, act, etc. one after another in

proper order. **to a turn** to just the right degree. **turn about** (or **turn and turn about**) one after another in order. **turn·a·bout** *n*. **turn down a** fold downward. **b** place face downward. **c** *Informal* refuse: *to turn down a proposal*. **d** lower. *Turn the sound down*. **turn in a** of toes, point inward. **b** go to bed. **c** deliver. **d** exchange: *to turn a car in for a new one*. **e** hand over to the police: *He turned himself in*. **turn loose** free (someone): *to turn a prisoner loose*. **turn off a** shut off. **b** *Slang* make or become bored, disgusted, etc. (by): *I just turn off when people start talking like that*. **turn·off** *n*. **turn on a** start the operation of. **b** *Slang* take a narcotic; esp, smoke marijuana. **c** *Slang* make or become stimulated by, or as if by, the use of a psychedelic drug. **d** *Slang* make or become enthusiastic (with *to*): *He turned me on to jazz*. **e** arouse sexually; be so aroused. **turn–on** *n*. **turn out a** shut off (a light, etc.). **b** drive out: *They were turned out of their home*. **c** go out to some event (with *for*): *to turn out for hockey practice*. **d** produce: *That factory turns out 500 chairs a day*. **e** result: *It turned out that we couldn't go*. **f** end up: *It turned out all lopsided*. **g** have the hoped-for outcome: *We planned it carefully, but it just didn't turn out*. **h** be found out or known: *They turned out to be a couple of frauds*. **turn·out** *n*. **turn over a** hand over: *He turned the job over to his assistant*. **b** of an engine, start: *It makes a noise but it won't turn over*. **turn someone's head** make someone too proud. **turn tail** turn one's back to flee. **turn to a** refer to. **b** go to for help. **c** resort to: *They turned to violence*. **turn up a** fold up or over, esp so as to shorten. **b** be directed upward: *Her nose turns up at the end*. **c** make more intense. **d** appear: *My lost book turned up the other day*. **e** bring to light; unearth: *Her research turned up several interesting facts*.

turn·a·round *n* **1** a reversal. **2** the time it takes a ship, airplane, etc. to unload, load, etc., before being ready to depart. **3** the time taken for any process involving the sending and return of anything: *The turnaround for your application should be about a week*. **turn·coat** *n* a person who changes his or her political party or principles. **turning circle** the minimum circular space needed by a vehicle to turn. **turning point** a point in time or space at which a significant change takes place: *the turning point of her life*. **turn·key** *adj* ready to be put into immediate use: *a turnkey computer system with hardware*. **turn·o·ver** *n* **1** a small, filled, folded-over pastry. **2** the rate at which people leave a job or company and have to be replaced: *a high turnover*. **3** the amount of business done in a given time: *There was a large turnover on the stock exchange this week*. **4** the paying out and getting back of the money involved in a business transaction: *The store reduced prices to make a quick turnover*. **5** *Football, basketball* the act of losing possession of the ball to the opposing team through a fumble, pass interception, etc. **turn·o·ver** *adj*. **turn·stile** *n* a barrier set into a revolving central post, allowing people to pass through only on foot, one at a time, and only in one direction.

SYNONYMS

Turn is the general word, meaning 'spin as a wheel does': *That wheel turns freely now*. **Rotate** means especially to go around and around on its own axis: *The earth rotates once every 24 hours*. **Revolve** means especially to go in a circular path around some centre: *The earth revolves around the sun once each year*.

tur·nip [ˈtɜrnɪp] *n* **1** a plant of the mustard family, having a thick, round root. **2** the rutabaga, closely related to this plant. ⟨probably Middle English *turn* (for rounded shape) + *nepe* turnip; Latin *napus*⟩

tur·pen·tine [ˈtɜrpən,taɪn] *n* a volatile oil obtained from conifers, used esp as a solvent for paints, etc. **tur·pen·tin·ic** [-ˈtɪnɪk] *adj* ⟨Greek *terebinthos* terebinth, turpentine source⟩

tur·pi·tude [ˈtɜrpə,tjud] *or* [ˈtɜrpə,tud] *n* a shameful wickedness. ⟨Latin *turpis* vile⟩

tur·quoise [ˈtɜrkɔɪz] *or* [ˈtɜrkwɔɪz] *n* a blue or greenish blue precious stone. ⟨French *turquoise*, orig Turkish⟩

tur·ret [ˈtɜrɪt] *n* **1** a small tower. **2** a rotating structure in which guns are mounted. ⟨Old French *torete* diminutive of *tor*. See TOWER.⟩ **tur·ret·ed** *adj* **1** having a turret or turrets. **2** of a shell, forming a long spiral.

tur·tle [ˈtɜrtəl] *n* any of an order of toothless, slow-moving reptiles having the body encased in a bony shell into which it can withdraw its head, tail, and feet. ⟨French *tortue* tortoise; influenced by *turtle(dove)*⟩ **turn turtle** turn bottom side up **tur·tle·neck** *n* a sweater with a high, snugly fitting collar.

tur·tle·dove [ˈtɜrtəl,dʌv] *n* any of a genus of wild doves noted for its sad-sounding cooing and the affection that it appears to have for its mate. ⟨Old English *turtle*; Latin *turtur*; imitative of its cooing⟩

Tus·ca·ro·ra [,tʌskəˈrɔrə] *n*, *pl* **-ra** or **-ras** **1** a member of an Iroquois people who occupied what is now North Carolina, but later migrated to New York and Ontario. The Tuscarora were the sixth nation to join the Iroquois Confederacy. **2** the Iroquoian language of the Tuscarora. **Tus·ca·ro·ra** *adj*.

tush [tʊʃ] *n Slang* buttocks. ⟨Yiddish⟩

tusk [tʌsk] *n* a long, pointed tooth, usually one of a pair, in animals like the elephant. **tusked** *adj*. ⟨Old English *tusc* tooth of a horse⟩

tus·sle [ˈtʌsəl] *n* a scuffle or struggle. **tus·sle** *v*. ⟨variant of *tousle*⟩

tus·sock [ˈtʌsək] *n* a tuft of growing grass, etc. **tus·sock·y** *adj*. ⟨origin uncertain⟩

Tut·cho·ne [tuˈtʃouni] *n* **1** a member of a First Nations people of the southern Yukon. **2** either dialect of their Athapascan language. **Tut·cho·ne** *adj*.

tu·te·lage, tu·te·lar·y See TUTOR.

tu·tor [ˈtjutər] *or* [ˈtutər] *n* **1** a private teacher. **2** in certain colleges and universities,

an assistant teacher; TUTORIAL ASSISTANT.
v teach individually or privately. **tu·tor·ship** *n*.
⟨Latin *tutor* guardian; *tueri* watch over⟩

tu·te·lage ['tjutəlɪdʒ] *or* ['tutəlɪdʒ] *n*
1 instruction: *expert tutelage*. **2** guardianship;
tu·te·lar·y *adj* guardian: *a tutelary saint*.
tu·to·ri·al [tju'tɔriəl] *or* [tu-] *adj* to do with a
tutor: *tutorial authority. n* a class given by a
tutor. **tutorial assistant** a graduate student
who takes some tutorials.

tut·ti·frut·ti ['tuti 'fruti] *n* ice cream
containing a variety of fruits or fruit
flavouring. ⟨Italian *tutti frutti* all fruits⟩

tut–tut ['tʌt 'tʌt] (also pronounced as a
reduplicated click) *n*, *interj* an expression of
mild rebuke or disapproval.
v **–tut·ted, –tut·ting** make such a sound.

tu·tu ['tutu] *n* a ballet dancer's very short,
frilly skirt. ⟨French, alteration of *cucu*, child's
reduplication of *cul* buttocks; Latin *culus*⟩

tux [tʌks] *n Informal* tuxedo.

tux·e·do [tʌk'sidou] *n*, *pl* **-dos** or **-does** a
man's semiformal jacket for evening wear.
⟨*Tuxedo* Park, NY, where supposedly first worn⟩

TV or **T.V.** *n* **1** television. **2** a television set.
adj to do with television or television sets.
TV dinner a frozen, precooked dinner, ready
to serve after being heated in its container.

twad·dle ['twɒdəl] *n* sill talk; drivel.
⟨alteration of earlier *twattle*; perhaps *tattle*⟩

twain [twein] *n*, *adj Archaic, poetic* two. ⟨Old
English *twēgen*⟩

twang [twæŋ] *n* **1** a ringing sound like that
of an elastic band when plucked. **2** a nasal
tone: *Some Nova Scotians speak with a twang.*
3 a dialect with such a tone: *the Prairie twang*.
v play, pluck, shoot, etc. with a twang: *to
twang a guitar.* **twang·y** *adj*. ⟨imitative⟩

tweak [twik] *v* **1** pull sharply and twist with
the fingers: *She tweaked her little brother's ear
and made him cry.* **2** make minor revisions to.
tweak *n*. ⟨Old English *twiccian* pluck⟩

tweed [twid] *n* **1** a woollen cloth with a
rough surface. **2** a garment made of tweed:
He wears tweeds. **tweed·y** *adj*. ⟨said to be a
misreading of *tweel* variant of *twill*⟩

tween [twin] *n* person aged between 9 and
14. Also **tween·ag·er**. ⟨(be)*tween age* (on the
analogy of *teenage*), i.e., between childhood
and the teen years⟩

tweet [twit] *n*, *interj* the sound made by a
small or young bird.
v utter a tweet or tweets. ⟨imitative⟩

tweet·er *n* a small high-fidelity loudspeaker
used to reproduce sounds in the higher
frequency range. Compare WOOFER.

tweez·ers ['twizərz] *n pl or sg* small pincers
or tongs for pulling out hairs or slivers,
picking up small objects, etc. **tweeze** *v*.
⟨*tweeze* instrument case, French *étui*⟩

twelve [twɛlv] *n* **1** two more than 10; 12.
2 any set of 12 persons or things. **twelve** *adj*.
⟨Old English *twelf*⟩

twelfth *adj*, *n* **1** next after the 11th; 12th.
2 one, or being one, of 12 equal parts.

Twelfth Night *n* the evening before January 6,
which is the twelfth day after Christmas,
often celebrated as the end of Christmas
festivities. **Twelfth–night** *adj*.

twen·ty ['twɛnti] *n* **1** two times ten; 20.
2 twenties *pl* the years from 20 through 29,
esp of a century or of a person's life. **3** a
20-dollar bill. **4** any set of 20 persons or
things. **twen·ty** *adj*. ⟨Old English *twēntig*⟩
twen·ti·eth *adj*, *n* **1** next after the 19th; 20th.
2 one, or being one, of 20 equal parts. **24/7**
Slang (read `twenty-four seven') at all times;
twenty-four hours a day, seven days a week.
twenty–one *n* blackjack, a card game. **20/20**
or **twen·ty–twen·ty** or *adj* of vision, normal,
as indicated by the ability to distinguish at a
distance of 20 feet (6 m) a character 1/3 inch
(8 mm) high.

twice [twəis] *adv* **1** two times: *twice a day.*
2 doubly: *twice as much.* ⟨Middle English
twies; Old English *twiga*⟩
twice–told *adj* trite or very familiar: *twice-
told tales.* **twice–trav·elled** or **–trav·eled** *adj* ✻
Newfoundland and Labrador referring to a very
strong variety of port wine that has twice
been transported across the Atlantic by ship.

twid·dle ['twɪdəl] *v* **1** twirl: *to twiddle one's
pencil.* **2** play with (something) idly. **twid·dle**
n. ⟨origin uncertain⟩
twiddle one's thumbs a keep turning one's
thumbs idly about each other. **b** do nothing.

twig[1] [twɪg] *n* a slender branch of a tree or
other woody plant. ⟨Old English *twigge*⟩
twig·gy *adj* **1** thin like a twig. **2** full of twigs.

twig[2] [twɪg] *v* **twigged, twig·ging** *Informal*
catch on (*to*): *I didn't twig that he wanted a
lift.* ⟨Irish *tuigim* I understand⟩

twi·light ['twaɪ,ləit] *n* **1** the faint light from
the sky before the sun rises and after it sets.
2 any faint light. **3** a period of decline in
fame, vigour, etc.: *the twilight of one's life.*
4 any intermediate state: *an uneasy twilight
between sickness and health.* **twi·light** *adj*.
⟨Middle English *twi-* two + *light*[1]⟩
twilight zone 1 an area or condition not
clearly defined, as that between day and
night, good and evil, etc. **2** a realm of strange
goings-on: *What a weirdo! Our conversation
was like something out of the twilight zone!*
twi·lit *adj* lighted by twilight or as if by
twilight: *the twilit forest.*

twill [twɪl] *n* a textile weave with raised
diagonal lines. Denim is a twill. **twilled** *adj*.
⟨Old English *twi-* two + Latin *licium* thread⟩

twin [twɪn] *n* **1** one of two offspring born at
the same time from the same mother. See
also FRATERNAL and IDENTICAL, MONOZYGOTIC
and DIZYGOTIC. **2** one of two persons or things
very much alike in structure, appearance, etc.
v **twinned, twin·ning** join or associate
closely: *Our town is twinned with one in
Denmark.* ⟨Old English *twinn*⟩
twin bed a single bed about one metre wide.
twin–en·gined *adj* of an aircraft, with two
identical engines. **twin–en·gine** *n*. **twin–size**

or **twin-sized** *adj* designed for a twin bed. Compare KING-SIZE, QUEEN-SIZE.

twine [twaɪn] *n* a strong thread made of strands twisted together.
v **1** twist together: *She twined holly into wreaths.* **2** wind (*around*): *The vine is twining around the post.* ⟨Old English *twīn*⟩

twinge [twɪndʒ] *n* a sudden, sharp pain that lasts only a moment: *a twinge of remorse.* ⟨Old English *twengan* pinch⟩

twin·kle ['twɪŋkəl] *v* **1** shine with quick little gleams: *The stars twinkle.* **2** of a person's eyes, shine with fun. **3** of the feet, move quickly: *The dancer's feet twinkled.* **twin·kle** *n.* **twin·kling** *n, adj.* ⟨Old English *twinclian*⟩
in a twinkling or **in the twinkling of an eye** in an instant.

twirl [twɜrl] *v* **1** revolve rapidly; spin. **2** turn or twist round and round: *She twirled her hair with the curling iron.* **3** *Baseball* pitch. **twirl** *n.* **twirl·er** *n.* ⟨origin uncertain; perhaps *twist* + *whirl*, but compare German *zwirlen* twirl⟩

twist [twɪst] *v* **1** wind together or around. **2** give a spiral form to by turning one end while the other remains stationary. *The belt is twisted at the back.* **3** move part way around: *He twisted around in his chair.* **4** spin: *She twisted the ring on her finger.* **5** pull off by turning one end (with *off*): *to twist off the stem of an apple.* **6** force out of the natural shape or position: *I twisted my ankle.* **7** distort: *Don't twist my words; I didn't mean that at all.* **8** have a winding shape: *The path twists in and out among the rocks.* **9** pervert: *Years of bitterness had twisted his mind.* **10** force (something) out of someone's possession: *They twisted the story out of him.*
n **1** a twisting or being twisted. **2** something made by twisting, such as a roll made of twisted pieces of dough. **3** a curve or bend. **4** an unexpected change: *an old story with a new twist.* **5** a dance in which the hips are vigorously turned back and forth while the dancer stands in one place. **6** a small slice of lemon or lime, twisted and added to a drink: *gin and tonic with a twist.* **7** ✱ formerly, tobacco prepared in twisted ropes, prominent among trade goods of the fur companies. **8** a doughnut made by folding a 15 cm roll of dough in half and twining the two parts around each other. **twist·a·ble** *adj.* ⟨Old English -*twist*, as in *mæsttwist* mast rope⟩
twist someone's arm force or coerce, either physically or verbally.
twist·er *n* a tornado, whirlwind, etc.
twist–tie *n* a bit of wire in a narrow strip of paper or soft plastic, used for closing plastic bags, tying up plants, etc.

twit [twɪt] *v* **twit·ted, twit·ting** tease.
n **1** a taunt; jibe. **2** *Informal* a fool. ⟨Old English *ætwītan; æt* at + *wītan* blame⟩

twitch [twɪtʃ] *v* **1** move with slight jerks: *The child's mouth twitched as if she were about to cry.* **2** jerk: *He twitched the curtain aside.* **3** ache with sudden, sharp pain. **twitch** *n.* ⟨related to Old English *twiccian* pluck⟩
twitch·y *adj* **1** nervous; irritable. **2** twitching.

twit·ter ['twɪtər] *v* **1** chirp: *Birds began to twitter just before sunrise.* **2** chatter or titter. **3** tremble with excitement.
n **1** chirping. **2** an excited condition: *My nerves are in a twitter when I have to sing in public.* **twit·te·ry** *adj.* ⟨imitative⟩

two [tu] *n* **1** one more than one; 2. **2** any set two persons or things. **3** a playing card or side of a die having two spots. **two** *adj.* ⟨Old English *twā*⟩
in two in two parts or pieces: *Break the cookie in two.* **put two and two together** form an obvious conclusion from the facts.
two–bag·ger *n Baseball Informal* TWO-BASE HIT.
two–base hit *Baseball* a hit that allows the batter to reach second base. **two–bit** *adj Slang* cheap; small-time: *a two-bit gangster.*
two bits *Slang* twenty-five cents.
two–by–four *adj* **1** of lumber, measuring two inches thick by four inches wide, untrimmed (about 5 cm by 10 cm). **2** *Informal* small; limited: *a two-by-four apartment.* **two cents' worth** *Slang* an opinion: *We wanted a chance to put in our two cents' worth.* **two–di·men·sion·al** *adj* **1** having two dimensions: *Drawing is a two-dimensional art form.* **2** of a character in a novel, etc., lacking depth or individuality. **two–edged** *adj* **1** of a sword, etc., having two cutting edges. **2** of a comment, etc., able to be taken in two ways; ambiguous: *a two-edged compliment.* **3** able to be used or to be effective in two ways: *a two-edged policy.* **two–faced** *adj* deceitful; hypocritical.
two–fac·ed·ly *adv.* **two–fac·ed·ness** *n.* **two·fer** ['tufər] *n Informal* a special offer allowing the purchase of two items for the price of one: *Our local theatre has a twofer on Tuesdays.* **two·fold** *adj* **1** two times as much or as many. **2** made up of two parts. *adv* two times as much or as many. **two nations** ✱ English and French Canada. **two·nie** or **twoo·nie** ✱ See TOONIE. **two–piece** *adj* of a dress, swimsuit, etc., consisting of matching top and bottom parts. **two–seater** *n* a vehicle with seats to accommodate the driver and one passenger, as a sportscar. **two–sided** *adj* **1** having two sides. **2** having two sides the same: *two-sided fabric.* **3** having two aspects: *a two-sided proposition.* **two·some** *n* a group of two people. **two–step** *n* a dance in 2/4 time. **two–step, –stepped –step·ping** *v.* **two–stroke** *adj* to do with an engine in which the piston makes two strokes with every explosion. Compare FOUR-STROKE. **two–tone** *adj* having two colours or two shades of one colour: *two-tone shoes.* **two–way** *adj* **1** of a street, bridge, etc., allowing traffic to move in either direction. **2** designed for both sending and receiving messages: *a two-way radio.* **3** of or designating a valve, pipe, wire, etc. that connects with two outlets or operates in two directions. **4** involving reciprocal action between two people or groups: *a two-way cultural exchange.* **two–way street** any activity, relationship, etc. that is reciprocal: *Communication is a two-way street.*

twp. or **Twp.** township.

ty·coon [tǝi'kun] *n Informal* a person who holds an important position in business, industry, etc. ⟨Japanese *taikun;* Mandarin *tai* great + *kiun* lord⟩

ty·ee ['taɪi] *n, pl* **ty·ees ✻ 1** a spring salmon, esp one weighing more than 13 kg. Also, **tyee salmon**. **2** *esp British Columbia pl* **ty·ee a** the chief of a First Nations band. **b** any important person; boss. ⟨Chinook Jargon⟩

ty·ing ['taɪɪŋ] *v* ppr of TIE.

tyke [tǝik] *n* **1** *Informal* a small child. **2** a dog, esp an inferior one. ⟨Old Norse *tík* bitch⟩

tym·pa·ni ['tɪmpǝni] See TIMPANI.

type [tǝip] *n* **1** a group having characteristics in common: *a new type of engine.* **2** a person or thing having the characteristics of a particular group: *She is a perfect type of the conscientious student.* **3** *Printing* **a** a block, having a raised letter, sign, etc. in reverse, from which an inked impression can be made. **b** a collection of letters, numerals, or signs that are reproduced photographically for printing. **c** a particular kind or size of letters, numerals, or signs: *The poem was set in italic type.* **4** *Biology* **a type species** (**genus**, etc.) a species (genus, etc.) for which the group is usually named. **b type specimen** the specimen on which the description of a species is based.
v **1** classify according to type: *to type a blood sample.* **2** write with a typewriter. **3** cause (letters, etc.) to be displayed on the screen by entering them on a computer keyboard. **typ·al** *adj.* ⟨Greek *typos* dent, impression⟩
type·cast *v* **1** cast (an actor) in a role to fit his or her personality, etc. **2** cast (an actor) repeatedly in the same kind of role. **type·face** *n* the design or style of type; face: *an ornate typeface.* **type·script** *n* typewritten matter. **typeset, -set, -set·ting** *v* set (text) in type. **type·set·ter** *n.* **type·set·ting** *n, adj.* **type·write** *v* -**wrote, -writ·ten, -writ·ing** write with a typewriter; type. **type·writ·er** *n* a machine for producing letters, numerals, etc., operated by a keyboard. **type·writ·ing** *n.* **type·writ·ten** *adj.* **typ·i·cal** ['tɪpǝkǝl] *adj* representative; characteristic: *a typical Thanksgiving dinner of roast turkey.* **typ·i·cal·i·ty** *n.* **typ·i·cal·ly** *adv.* **typ·i·fy** ['tɪpǝ,faɪ] *v* be an example of; represent: *The dove typifies peace.* **typ·i·fi·ca·tion** *n.* **typ·i·fi·er** *n.* **ty·po** *n Informal* a mistake made in keying or setting type. **ty·pog·ra·phy** [tǝi'pɒgrǝfi] *n* the work of setting and arranging type and of printing from it. **ty·pog·ra·pher** *n.* **ty·po·graph·i·cal** [,tǝipǝ'græfǝkǝl] *or* [,tɪpǝ-] *adj.* **ty·po·graph·i·cal·ly** *adv.* **ty·pol·o·gy** [tǝi'pɒlǝdʒi] *n* the study of types, as of specimens in archaeology or grammatical features in languages. **ty·po·log·i·cal** [,tǝipǝ'lɒdʒǝkǝl] *or* [,tɪpǝ-] *adj.*

typhoid fever ['tǝifɔɪd] a severe infectious disease caused by a bacterium that enters the body in contaminated food or drink.

ty·phoon [tǝi'fun] *n* a violent tropical cyclone that forms over the Pacific Ocean. **ty·phon·ic** [-'fɒnɪk] *adj.* ⟨Mandarin *tai fung* big wind⟩

ty·phus ['tǝifǝs] *n* any of a group of very serious infectious diseases carried esp by lice or fleas. **ty·phous** *adj.* ⟨Greek *typhos* stupor⟩

typ·i·cal, typ·i·fy See TYPE.

ty·po, ty·pog·ra·phy, ty·pol·o·gy See TYPE.

ty·ran·no·sau·rus [tǝ,rænǝ'sɔrǝs] *n* a huge carnivorous dinosaur (*Tyrannosaurus rex*) of the Cretaceous. Also, **ty·ran·no·saur** [tǝ'rænǝ,sɔr]. ⟨Greek *tyrannos* tyrant + *sauros* lizard⟩

ty·rant ['taɪrǝnt] *n* **1** a person who uses power cruelly or unjustly or who exercises complete control over others: *That spoiled child is a regular tyrant in their household.* **2** a cruel or unjust ruler. **3** a ruler with absolute power. **tyr·an·ny** ['tirǝni] *n.* **tyr·an·nous** *adj.* ⟨Greek *tyrannos* (def. 3)⟩
ty·ran·ni·cal [tǝ'rænǝkǝl] *adj* wielding power in an arbitrary, cruel, or unjust way: *a tyrannical king.* **ty·ran·ni·cal·ly** *adv.* **ty·ran·ni·cide** *n* **1** the act of killing a tyrant. **2** a person who kills a tyrant. **ty·ran·ni·cid·al** *adj.* **tyr·an·nize** ['tirǝ,naɪz] *v* use power cruelly or unjustly (sometimes with *over*): *Those who are strong should not tyrannize over the weak.*

ty·ro ['taɪrou] *n* a beginner in learning anything; novice; greenhorn. Also, **tiro**. ⟨Latin *tiro* recruit⟩

tzar, tza·ri·na, etc. See CZAR.

tze·tze See TSETSE.

Uu

u or **U** [ju] *n, pl* **u's** or **U's 1** the twenty-first letter of the English alphabet, or any speech sound represented by it. **2** the twenty-first person or thing in a series.

u·biq·ui·tous [ju'bɪkwətəs] *adj* being or seeming to be everywhere at the same time: *He wanted quiet, but found it impossible to escape from his ubiquitous little sister.* **u·biq·ui·tous·ly** *adv.* **u·biq·ui·ty** *n.* ⟨Latin *ubique* everywhere⟩

U–boat ['ju ˌbout] *n* a German submarine. ⟨German *U-boot*, short for *Unterseeboot* undersea boat⟩

u.c. upper case; one or more capital letters.

ud·der ['ʌdər] *n* in a cow or female sheep or goat, etc., a large baglike organ containing milk-producing glands. ⟨Old English *ūder*⟩

u·dom·e·ter [ju'dɒmətər] *n* a rain gauge. ⟨Latin *udus* wet + -METER⟩

U.E.L. UNITED EMPIRE LOYALIST.

UFO *n, pl* **UFOs** or **UFO's** an unidentified flying object, esp one regarded as possibly being a spacecraft from another planet. **u·fol·o·gy** [ju'fɒlədʒi] *n* the study of UFOs. **u·fol·o·gist** *n.*

ugh [ʌx], [ʌ], [ʊx], or [ʌg] *interj* an exclamation expressing disgust or horror.

ug·ly ['ʌgli] *adj* **1** very unpleasant to look at, hear, smell, etc.: *an ugly house, an ugly sound.* **2** morally bad; objectionable: *ugly rumours.* **3** threatening; dangerous: *an ugly wound.* **4** *Informal* ill-natured; quarrelsome: *He's ugly when he's drunk.* **ug·li·ness** *n.* ⟨Old Norse *uggligr* dreadful⟩ **ug·li·fy** *v* make ugly or more ugly: *uglifying the parkway with a lot of billboards.* **ug·li·fi·ca·tion** *n.* **ugly duckling** a person or thing thought to be ugly, unpromising, etc. but that turns out to have unusual beauty, talent, value, etc., from a folk tale recorded by Hans Christian Andersen.

> **SYNONYMS**
> **Ugly**, when restricted to the visual, means 'unpleasant or offensive in appearance': *There are five ugly lamps in that room.* **Unsightly** emphasizes sometimes causing one to turn away to avoid seeing what is described: *Trains approach the city through an unsightly section.* **Homely** emphasizes lack of physical beauty, but does not suggest unpleasant or disagreeable moral qualities: *a homely child.*

uh [ʌ] *or* [ʌ̃] *interj* a sound made by a speaker hesitating while he or she thinks of the right word or words to say next.

UHF or **U.H.F.** ULTRAHIGH FREQUENCY.

uh–huh [ɜ'hʌ̃] *interj* an expression of agreement or affirmation; yes.

uh–uh ['ʌ̃'ʌ̃] *or* ['ʌ̃ˌʌ̃] *interj* an expression of disagreement, refusal, etc.; no.

UK or **U.K.** United Kingdom.

u·ku·le·le [ˌjukə'leili] *n* a small, guitar-shaped instrument having four strings. Also, **u·ke·le·le**. ⟨Hawaiian *uku* flea + *lele* jump, leap⟩

ul·cer ['ʌlsər] *n* **1** an open sore on the skin or on a mucous membrane such as the lining of the stomach or the inside of the mouth. **2** a visual blight: *Those huge open-pit mines are ulcers on the landscape.* ⟨Latin *ulceris*⟩ **ul·cer·ate** *v* **1** affect or be affected with an ulcer: *An ulcerated tooth may be very painful.* **2** form or be formed into an ulcer. **ul·cer·a·tive** *adj.* **ul·cer·a·tion** *n.* **ul·cer·ous** *adj.*

–ule *suffix* small: *globule.* ⟨Latin *-ulus, -ula, -ulum*, diminutive suffix⟩

u·le·ma [ˌulə'ma] *or* ['ulə,ma] *n pl Islam* **1** religious scholars or leaders. **2** (with sg verb) a group of these; council. ⟨Arabic *ulama* pl of *ulim* learned; *alima* know⟩

ul·na ['ʌlnə] *n, pl* **-nae** [-ni] *or* [-nai] or **-nas 1** the bone of the forearm on the side opposite the thumb. **2** the corresponding bone in the foreleg of an animal. **ul·nar** *adj.* ⟨Latin = elbow⟩

ul·ster ['ʌlstər] *n* a long, loose, heavy overcoat, often belted at the waist. ⟨*Ulster* province of Ireland⟩

ul·te·ri·or [ʌl'tiriər] *adj* **1** beyond what is seen or expressed: *an ulterior motive.* **2** more distant. **3** later. **ul·te·ri·or·ly** *adv.* ⟨Latin, comparative of *ultra* beyond⟩

ul·ti·mate ['ʌltəmɪt] *adj* **1** coming at the end; final: *She never stopped to consider the ultimate result of her actions.* **2** beyond which nothing further may be discovered by investigation or analysis; basic: *the ultimate source.* **3** greatest possible. **ul·ti·ma·cy** or **ul·ti·mate·ness** *n.* **ul·ti·mate·ly** *adv.* ⟨Latin *ultimatus* pp of *ultimare* to end; *ultimus* last⟩ **ul·ti·ma·tum** [-'meitəm] *n, pl* **-tums, -ta** [-tə] a final proposal or demand, esp one whose rejection may result in a breaking off of relations between negotiating parties.

ul·tra ['ʌltrə] *adj, adv* beyond what is usual; excessive(ly); extreme(ly). ⟨Latin = beyond⟩

ultra– *prefix* **1** beyond a specified limit, range, or place: *ultraviolet.* **2** very; unusually: *ultra-ambitious, ultramodest.* **3** of instruments, machines, etc., useful or operating at an extreme range of speed, size, temperature, etc.: *ultracentrifuge.* ⟨Latin *ultra* beyond⟩ **ul·tra·high frequency** the range of radio frequencies between 300 and 3000 MHz. *Abbrev* **UHF** or **U.H.F.** **ul·tra·light** *n* microlight. **ul·tra·ma·rine** *n* a deep blue. **ul·tra·mi·cro·scope** *n* a powerful instrument for making visible any particles that are invisible to the common microscope. **ul·tra·mi·cro·scop·ic** *adj* too small to be seen with an ordinary microscope. **ul·tra·mi·cros·co·py** [-mai'krɒskəpi] *n.* **ul·tra·mod·ern** *adj* extremely advanced in design, ideas, or technology. **ul·tra·mon·tane** [-'mɒntein] *or* [-mɒn'tein] *adj* **1** beyond the mountains. **2** south of the Alps; Italian. **3** *Roman Catholic Church* supporting a policy advocating extreme centralization of papal power. **ul·tra·mon·tan·ism** [-'mɒntə,nɪzəm] *n* **ul·tra·mon·ta·nist** *n, adj.* **ul·tra·short** *adj* **1** very short. **2** to do with a radio wavelength of less than ten metres in length and above 30 MHz in frequency. **ul·tra·son·ic** *adj* to do with sound waves having a pitch above the upper limit of human hearing, that is, above 20 000 Hz. **ul·tra·son·ic·al·ly** *adv.* **ul·tra·sound** *n* **1** a single ultrasonographic examination: *I had an ultrasound yesterday.* **2** ultrasonic waves. **ul·tra·so·nog·ra·phy** [-sə'nɒgrəfɪ] *n Medicine* a technique used to visualize structures in the body by recording pulses of ultrasonic waves directed into the tissues. **ul·tra·son·o·graph·ic** [-,sɒnə'græfɪk] *adj.* **ul·tra·vi·o·let** *adj* to do with the invisible rays, or waves, of the electromagnetic spectrum that are shorter than light rays but longer than X rays.

u·lu ['ulu] *n* ✴ a knife traditionally used by Inuit women, with a crescent-shaped blade and a handle of bone, ivory, wood, etc. Also, **oo·loo.** ⟨Inuktitut⟩

ul·u·late ['juljə,leit] *or* ['ʌljə,leit] *v* **1** of a dog, wolf, etc., howl. **2** lament loudly. **3** make a yodelling, hooting sound. **ul·u·lant** *adj.* **ul·u·la·tion** *n.* ⟨Latin *ululare* howl⟩

um [ʌm] *interj* a sound made by a speaker pausing or hesitating.

um·bel ['ʌmbəl] *n* a type of flower cluster in which stalks spring from a common centre and form a flat or slightly curved surface, as in parsley. **um·bel·late** [-lɪt] *or* [-,leit] *adj.* **um·bel·lif·er·ous** *adj.* ⟨Latin *umbella* parasol⟩

um·ber ['ʌmbər] *n* a brown earth consisting mainly of ferric oxide and used in its natural state **(raw umber)** as a brown pigment, or after heating **(burnt umber)** as a reddish brown pigment. ⟨Italian *terra di ombra* earth of shadow; or *Umbria* district in central Italy⟩

um·bil·i·cus [ʌm'bɪləkəs] *or* [,ʌmbə'laikəs] *n*, *pl* **-ci** [-sai] *or* [-si] the navel. ⟨Latin = navel⟩ **umbilical cord 1** in mammals, a cordlike structure through which a fetus in the womb receives food and discharges waste. The cord runs from the navel of the fetus to the placenta. **2** a flexible line or cable that carries essential supplies or services.

um·bra ['ʌmbrə] *n, pl* **-brae** [-bri] *or* [-brai] *Astronomy* **1** a shadow of the earth or moon that completely hides the sun. **2** of any heavenly body, the region on the side turned away from the sun and receiving none of its light. **3** the dark central part of a sunspot. ⟨Latin⟩

um·brage ['ʌmbrɪdʒ] *n* a feeling that one has been insulted; resentment (now used mainly in the phrases **take umbrage** and **give umbrage**): *She took umbrage at any criticism.* ⟨French *ombrage*; Latin *umbra* shade⟩

um·brel·la [ʌm'brelə] *n* **1** a collapsible device used for protection against rain or sun. **2** anything that protects or provides shelter. **3** an official organization, department, etc. uniting a broad range of activities, agencies,

or spheres of interest: *The Community Chest is an umbrella for many local charities.* **4** the gelatinous body of a jellyfish. ⟨Italian *ombrella*; Latin *umbra* shade⟩

u·mi·ak ['umi,æk] *n* ✴ a large, flat-bottomed boat made of skins stretched over a wooden frame and propelled by paddles. Umiaks are used by Inuit for carrying freight and are usually worked by women. Also, **oo·mi·ak.** ⟨Inuktitut *umiaq*⟩

ump [ʌmp] *n, v Informal* umpire.

um·pire ['ʌmpair] *n* **1** a person who rules on the plays in certain games: *The umpire called the ball a foul.* **2** a person chosen to settle a dispute. **um·pire** *v.* ⟨earlier *a numpire*; Old French *nonper* odd; *non* + *per* equal; Latin *par*⟩

ump·teen ['ʌmp'tin] *adj Informal* a great many: *I've heard umpteen different suggestions, but not one of them is practical.* ⟨*umpty,* slang, 'dash' in Morse + *-teen*⟩

ump·teenth *adj Informal* the last in an extremely long series: *I've just redialled for the umpteenth time, but there's still no answer.*

un-[1] *prefix* not; the opposite of: *unequal, unjust, unobtrusive.* ⟨Old English⟩

un-[2] *prefix* do the opposite of or do what will reverse the act: *undress, unlock, untie.* ⟨Old English *un-, on-*⟩

UN or **U.N. 1** UNITED NATIONS. **2** UNION NATIONALE.

un·a·bashed [,ʌnə'bæʃt] *adj* not embarrassed, ashamed, or awed. **un·a·bash·ed·ly** *adv.*

un·a·ble [ʌn'eibəl] *adj* **1** lacking ability or power (*to*): *A newborn baby is unable to walk.* **2** incompetent: *He is a most unable leader.*

un·a·bridged [,ʌnə'brɪdʒd] *adj* not shortened; complete: *an unabridged book.*

un·ac·com·pa·nied [,ʌnə'kʌmpənid] *adj* **1** not accompanied. **2** *Music* without an accompaniment.

un·ac·count·a·ble [,ʌnə'kauntəbəl] *adj* **1** that cannot be accounted for or explained; strange or puzzling: *She flew into one of her unaccountable rages.* **2** not responsible: *The accused was judged insane and thus unaccountable for his actions.* **un·ac·count·a·bly** *adv.* **un·ac·count·a·bil·i·ty** or **un·ac·count·a·ble·ness** *n.*

un·ac·count·ed-for [,ʌnə'kauntid ,fɔr] *adj* unexplained: *unaccounted-for noises.*

un·ac·cus·tomed [,ʌnə'kʌstəmd] *adj* **1** not used (to). **2** not familiar; unusual; strange: *unaccustomed heat.*

un·af·fect·ed[1] [,ʌnə'fɛktɪd] *adj* not influenced: *unaffected by criticism.* ⟨*un-*[1] + *affected*[1]⟩ **un·af·fect·ed·ly** *adv.* **un·af·fect·ed·ness** *n.*

un·af·fect·ed[2] [,ʌnə'fɛktɪd] *adj* natural; without airs or pretense. ⟨*un-*[1] + *affected*[2]⟩ **un·af·fect·ed·ly** *adv.* **un·af·fect·ed·ness** *n.*

un·al·ter·a·ble [ʌn'ɒltərəbəl] *adj* that cannot be altered; not changeable. **un·al·ter·a·bly** *adv.*

u·nan·i·mous [ju'nænəməs] *adj* **1** in complete accord; agreed: *The delegates were unanimous that the issue needed to be discussed further.* **2** having the consent of everyone:

unanimous consent. The vote was unanimous.
u·na·nim·i·ty [ˌjunəˈnɪməti] *n.* **u·nan·i·mous·ly** *adv.* **u·nan·i·mous·ness** *n.* ⟨Latin *unanimus; unus* one + *animus* mind⟩

un·an·swer·a·ble [ʌnˈænsərəbəl] *adj* **1** that cannot be answered or has no answer: *unanswerable questions about life and death.* **2** that cannot be refuted: *an unanswerable argument.* **un·an·swer·a·bly** *adv.*

un·ap·proach·a·ble [ˌʌnəˈproutʃəbəl] *adj* **1** very hard to approach; aloof. **2** unrivalled; without an equal. **un·ap·proach·a·bil·i·ty** *n.* **un·ap·proach·a·bly** *adv.*

un·apt [ʌnˈæpt] *adj* **1** not suitable. **2** not likely. **3** not skilful; not well qualified. **4** not quick to learn. **un·apt·ly** *adv.* **un·apt·ness** *n.*

un·armed [ʌnˈɑrmd] *adj* **1** without weapons or armour. **2** of plants and animals, without horns, teeth, spines, thorns, etc.

u·na·ry [ˈjunəri] **1** to do with one; single. **2** *Mathematics* to do with a function whose domain is a given set and whose range is confined to that set. ⟨Latin *unus* one⟩

un·as·sum·ing [ˌʌnəˈsumɪŋ] *or* [-ˈsjumɪŋ] *adj* not putting on airs; modest. **un·as·sum·ing·ly** *adv.* **un·as·sum·ing·ness** *n.*

un·at·tached [ˌʌnəˈtætʃt] *adj* **1** not attached. **2** not connected with a particular body, group, organization, etc; independent. **3** not married or engaged to be married.

un·at·tend·ed [ˌʌnəˈtɛndɪd] *adj* **1** without attendants or companions; alone. **2** not taken care of; not attended to.

un·a·vail·ing [ˌʌnəˈveilɪŋ] *adj* not successful; useless. **un·a·vail·ing·ly** *adv.*

un·a·void·a·ble [ˌʌnəˈvɔɪdəbəl] *adj* that cannot be avoided or prevented; inevitable: *an unavoidable delay.* **un·a·void·a·ble·ness** *n.* **un·a·void·a·bly** *adv.*

un·a·ware [ˌʌnəˈwɛr] *adj* ignorant: *They were unaware of her change in plans.* *adv* **unawares 1** by surprise: *The police caught the burglar unawares.* **2** without knowing: *We made the error unawares.* **un·a·ware·ness** *n.*

un·bal·ance [ʌnˈbæləns] *n* lack of balance; condition of being out of balance. *v* throw out of balance; disorder or derange. **un·bal·anced** *adj* **1** not balanced; improperly balanced. **2** mentally disordered; deranged.

un·bear·a·ble [ʌnˈbɛrəbəl] *adj* that cannot be endured: *unbearable pain.* **un·bear·a·ble·ness** *n.* **un·bear·ab·ly** *adv.*

un·beat·en [ʌnˈbitən] *adj* **1** not defeated or surpassed. **2** not travelled: *unbeaten paths.* **3** not beaten or pounded: *unbeaten eggs.*

un·be·com·ing [ˌʌnbɪˈkʌmɪŋ] *adj* **1** not suited to the wearer: *an unbecoming dress.* **2** not fitting or proper: *unbecoming behaviour.* **un·be·com·ing·ly** *adv.* **un·be·com·ing·ness** *n.*

un·be·knownst [ˌʌnbɪˈnounst] *adj Informal* **1** not known: *Her present whereabouts are unbeknownst to me.* **2** without the knowledge of (used with *to*): *Unbeknownst to me, they had pulled up all the roses.* Also, **un·be·known.**

un·be·lief [ˌʌnbɪˈlif] *n* a lack of belief, esp in God or in a particular religion or doctrine. **un·be·liev·a·ble** [ˌʌnbɪˈlivəbəl] *adj* beyond belief; incredible: *an unbelievable story.* **un·be·liev·a·bly** *adv.* **un·be·liev·er** *n* **1** a person who does not believe. **2** a person who does not believe in a particular religion. **un·be·liev·ing** *adj* not believing; doubting. **un·be·liev·ing·ly** *adv.*

CONFUSABLES

Unbelief suggests only lack of belief in something held as true, with no positive feelings one way or the other: *The Inquisition punished people for their unbelief.* **Disbelief** suggests a refusal to believe, or an inability to believe in something too surprising to be true: *I stared in disbelief at the damage to my car.*

un·bend [ʌnˈbɛnd] *v* **-bent, -bend·ing 1** become straight or straighten. **2** release from strain. **3** relax: *The judge unbent and smiled at her.* **un·bend·ing** *adj* **1** not bending or curving; rigid: *the unbending boughs of an old oak.* **2** not yielding; inflexible: *an unbending attitude.* **3** of someone's manner, distant; stern. **un·bend·ing·ly** *adv.*

un·bi·assed *or* **un·bi·ased** [ʌnˈbaɪəst] *adj* impartial; fair: *an unbiassed account.*

un·bid·den [ʌnˈbɪdən] *adj* not invited or not commanded.

un·blem·ished [ʌnˈblɛmɪʃt] *adj* without blemishes; flawless: *unblemished skin, an unblemished reputation.*

un·blush·ing [ʌnˈblʌʃɪŋ] *adj* shameless or unabashed: *unblushing impudence.* **un·blush·ing·ly** *adv.*

un·bolt [ʌnˈboult] *v* open or unlock (a door, etc.) by drawing back the bolt or bolts.

un·born [ʌnˈbɔrn] *adj* **1** not yet born: *an unborn child.* **2** not brought into being: *That joke should have stayed unborn.* **3** still to come; future: *unborn generations.*

un·bos·om [ʌnˈbuzəm] *or* [ʌnˈbuzəm] *v Archaic* relieve (oneself) of feelings, secrets, etc. by revealing them: *I unbosomed myself to my understanding sister.*

un·bound·ed [ʌnˈbaundɪd] *adj* without bounds or limits; very great: *His unbounded good spirits cheered all of us up.*

un·break·a·ble [ʌnˈbreikəbəl] *adj* that cannot be easily broken: *an unbreakable cup.*

un·brid·led [ʌnˈbraɪdəld] *adj* not restrained.

un·bro·ken [ʌnˈброukən] *adj* **1** not broken; whole: *There was only one unbroken plate left in the set.* **2** not interrupted; continuous: *He had eight hours of unbroken sleep.* **3** not tamed: *an unbroken colt.* **4** of a record, not surpassed.

un·bur·den [ʌnˈbɜrdən] *v* **1** free from a burden. **2** relieve (oneself or one's mind) by confessing or revealing something: *She unburdened her mind to her friend.*

un·busi·ness·like [ʌnˈbɪznɪsˌləik] *adj* without system and method; not efficient.

un·but·ton [ʌnˈbʌtən] *v* unfasten the button or buttons of (a garment).

un·but·toned *adj* **1** not buttoned: *Her coat was unbuttoned.* **2** unrestricted in expression or action; casual: *He was in an unbuttoned mood, talking freely of his past.*

un·cage [ʌnˈkeidʒ] *v* release.

un·called–for [ʌnˈkɒld ˌfɔr] *adj* unjustified; impertinent or rude: *an uncalled-for remark.*

un·can·ny [ʌnˈkæni] *adj* **1** strange and mysterious; eerie: *The trees had uncanny shapes in the dim light.* **2** seeming to have or show powers beyond what is natural or normal: *an uncanny sense of timing.* **un·can·ni·ly** *adv.* **un·can·ni·ness** *n.*

un·cer·e·mo·ni·ous [ˌʌnsɛrəˈmouniəs] *adj* **1** informal. **2** abrupt or rude: *an unceremonious dismissal.* **un·cer·e·mo·ni·ous·ly** *adv.* **un·cer·e·mo·ni·ous·ness** *n.*

un·cer·tain [ʌnˈsɜrtən] *adj* **1** not known with certainty; indefinite: *The election results are still uncertain.* **2** not assured or secured; problematic: *an uncertain future.* **3** likely to change; unreliable: *The weather remains uncertain.* **4** dubious; hesitating: *an uncertain smile.* **5** indistinct: *an uncertain shape in the mist.* **6** wavering: *an uncertain flicker of light.* **un·cer·tain·ly** *adv.* **un·cer·tain·ty** *n.*

SYNONYMS

Uncertain emphasizes not knowing definitely or surely, or not having complete confidence, and thus suggests the presence of doubt: *Their plans for the summer are uncertain.* Insecure emphasizes not being protected from or guarded against danger or loss, and suggests the presence of fear or anxiety: *Her position at the trust company is insecure.*

un·char·i·ta·ble [ʌnˈtʃɛrətəbəl] *or* [-ˈtʃærətəbəl] *adj* not generous; not compassionate; severe. **un·char·i·ta·ble·ness** *n.* **un·char·i·ta·bly** *adv.*

un·chart·ed [ʌnˈtʃɑrtɪd] *adj* not yet mapped; not recorded on a chart: *uncharted seas.*

un·checked [ʌnˈtʃɛkt] *adj* not restrained.

un·ci·al [ˈʌnʃiəl] *or* [ˈʌnʃəl] *n* a letter or writing having heavy, rounded strokes, used especially in manuscripts from the 4th to the 8th century. **un·ci·al** *adj.* ⟨Latin *uncialis* inch-high; *uncia* inch⟩

un·civ·il [ʌnˈsɪvəl] *adj* **1** rude; impolite. **2** not civilized. **un·civ·il·ly** *adv.*

un·civ·i·lized *adj* **1** not civilized; barbarous or unenlightened. **2** *Informal* badly behaved; rude: *It was quite uncivilized of her not to tell us she was leaving.*

un·clasp [ʌnˈklæsp] *v* **1** unfasten the clasp or clasps of. **2** release or be released from a clasp or grasp. **3** loosen one's grip.

un·cle [ˈʌŋkəl] *n* **1** the brother of one's father or mother. **2** the husband of one's aunt. **say** (or **cry**) **uncle** *Informal* give in; surrender: *They wouldn't let him up until he said uncle.* ⟨Latin *avunculus* one's mother's brother⟩

un·clean [ʌnˈklin] *adj* **1** dirty; filthy. **2** not pure morally; evil. **3** ceremonially unclean; defiled or defiling. **un·clean·ness** *n.*

un·clench [ʌnˈklɛntʃ] *v* open or become opened from a clenched state: *unclench one's fists.*

Uncle Sam [sæm] *Informal* the government of the United States. ⟨the initials *US*⟩

un·clog [ʌnˈklɒg] *v* make free from an obstruction: *to unclog a drain.*

un·clothe [ʌnˈklouð] *v* **-clothed** or **-clad**, **-cloth·ing** strip (oneself or another) of clothes; undress.

un·com·fort·a·ble [ʌnˈkʌmfərtəbəl] *adj* **1** not comfortable: *I am uncomfortable in this chair.* **2** uneasy: *She feels uncomfortable at formal dinners.* **3** disagreeable; causing discomfort: *an uncomfortable chair.* **un·com·fort·a·bly** *adv.* **un·com·fort·a·ble·ness** *n.*

un·com·mit·ted [ˌʌnkəˈmɪtɪd] *adj* **1** not bound to a certain viewpoint, relationship, etc.: *an uncommitted candidate.* **2** neutral or undecided: *uncommitted voters.*

un·com·mon [ʌnˈkɒmən] *adj* **1** rare; unusual: *Serious injuries were uncommon in the factory.* **2** remarkable: *uncommon strength, an uncommon grasp of the subject.* **un·com·mon·ly** *adv.* **un·com·mon·ness** *n.*

un·com·mu·ni·ca·tive [ˌʌnkəˈmjunəkətɪv] *or* [ˌʌnkəˈmjunəˌkeitɪv] *adj* not giving out any opinions, etc.; silent and reserved; taciturn. **un·com·mu·ni·ca·tive·ly** *adv.* **un·com·mu·ni·ca·tive·ness** *n.*

un·com·pro·mis·ing [ʌnˈkɒmprəˌmaizɪŋ] *adj* unyielding; firm; unwilling to compromise. **un·com·pro·mis·ing·ly** *adv.*

un·con·cern [ˌʌnkənˈsɜrn] *n* lack of care, interest, or anxiety; indifference: *The children looked with unconcern at the odd surroundings.* **un·con·cerned** *adj* **1** indifferent or nonchalant: *unconcerned about the results of the exam.* **2** not involved: *They need an unconcerned party to settle the dispute.* **un·con·cern·ed·ly** [-ˈsɜrnɪdli] *adv.* **un·con·cern·ed·ness** [-ˈsɜrnɪdnɪs] *n.*

un·con·di·tion·al [ˌʌnkənˈdɪʃənəl] *adj* without conditions; absolute: *unconditional surrender, unconditional love.* **un·con·di·tion·al·ly** *adv.*

un·con·di·tioned [ˌʌnkənˈdɪʃənd] *adj* **1** unconditional. **2** *Psychology* not learned; not dependent on conditioning; natural or instinctive: *Withdrawing one's hand on contact with fire is an unconditioned reflex.*

un·con·quer·a·ble [ʌnˈkɒŋkərəbəl] *adj* that cannot be conquered. **un·con·quer·a·bly** *adv.*

un·con·scion·a·ble [ʌnˈkɒnʃənəbəl] *adj* **1** not sanctioned or guided by conscience; unscrupulous: *an unconscionable liar.* **2** unreasonable; excessive: *to wait an unconscionable time.* **un·con·scion·a·bly** *adv.*

un·con·scious [ʌnˈkɒnʃəs] *adj* **1** not able to feel or think: *to be knocked unconscious.* **2** not aware: *The general was unconscious of being followed by a spy.* **3** not deliberate: *unconscious neglect.* **4** relating to that part of a person's mind of which he or she is not normally aware, but that can affect behaviour: *unconscious bigotry.* **un·con·scious·ly** *adv.* **un·con·scious·ness** *n.*

the **unconscious** a person's unconscious thoughts, desires, fears, etc.

un·con·ven·tion·al [ˌʌkən'vɛnʃənəl] *adj* being out of the ordinary: *an unconventional way of dressing.* **un·con·ven·tion·al·ly** *adv.* **un·con·ven·tion·al·i·ty** *n.*

un·cork [ʌn'kɔrk] *v* **1** pull the cork from. **2** release: *to uncork one's pent-up feelings.*

un·cou·ple [ʌn'kʌpəl] *v* disconnect; separate.

un·couth [ʌn'kuθ] *adj* awkward or crude in appearance, conduct, etc.: *uncouth manners.* **un·couth·ly** *adv.* **un·couth·ness** *n.* ⟨Old English *uncūth; un-*¹ + *cūth* pp of *cunnan* know⟩

un·cov·er [ʌn'kʌvər] *v* **1** remove the cover from. **2** make known; reveal. **3** remove the hat or cap from (one's head) in respect.

unc·tion ['ʌŋkʃən] *n* **1** the act of anointing with oil, ointment, etc. for medical purposes or as a religious rite: *The priest gave the dying man extreme unction.* **2** something soothing or comforting: *the unction of flattery.* **3** a fervent quality in behaviour. **4** affected fervour. ⟨Latin *unctio; unguere* anoint⟩

unc·tu·ous ['ʌŋktʃuəs] *adj* **1** like an oil or ointment; greasy. **2** of a person's manner, very smooth, or earnest, esp in an affected way when trying to please: *The stranger's unctuous manner made us suspicious.* **unc·tu·ous·ly** *adv.* **unc·tu·ous·ness** *n.*

un·cut [ʌn'kʌt] *adj* **1** not cut into: *The cake was on the table, still uncut.* **2** of a gem, not shaped: *uncut diamonds.* **3** of a book, having the folded edges of the leaves not cut open, or having untrimmed margins. **4** of a book, film, etc., not shortened: *the uncut version.*

un·daunt·ed [ʌn'dɒntɪd] *adj* not daunted; not discouraged or dismayed. **un·daunt·ed·ly** *adv.* **un·daunt·ed·ness** *n.*

un·de·ceive [ˌʌndɪ'siv] *v* make free from error, illusion, or deception.

un·de·cid·ed [ˌʌndɪ'saɪdɪd] *adj* **1** not decided or settled. **2** not having one's mind made up. **un·de·cid·ed·ly** *adv.* **un·de·cid·ed·ness** *n.*

un·de·fined [ˌʌndɪ'faɪnd] *adj* **1** not defined. **2** indefinite; imprecise or vague.

un·de·ni·a·ble [ˌʌndɪ'naɪəbəl] *adj* **1** that cannot be denied; indisputable: *undeniable guilt.* **2** unquestionably genuine or excellent: *Her references are undeniable.* **un·de·ni·a·bly** *adv.*

un·der ['ʌndər] *prep* **1** in or to a position directly below: *It rolled under the table.* **2** below and through to the other side of: *The road goes under a bridge.* **3** below the surface of: *under the ground.* **4** on the inside of; covered by: *a soft heart under his gruff exterior.* **5** lower or less than in degree, amount, etc.: *under ten dollars.* **6** subject to the influence or authority, of: *under orders from the general.* **7 a** in the position of being affected by: *under these conditions.* **b** undergoing: *under discussion.* **8** in a given category: *Books on golf are classified under Sports.* **9** using: *under a new name.* **10** planted with: *two hectares under corn.* *adv* **1** in or to a position below something or below the surface: *The swimmer went under.*

2 rendered unconscious, esp by an anesthetic: *He was put under for surgery.* *adj* facing downward or located below: *The under surface was rough.* ⟨Old English⟩

under way or **underway 1** in progress: *Plans are under way for a new city hall.* **2** moving; travelling: *The ship got under way at noon.*

un·der·age ['ʌndərɪdʒ] *n* a shortage; the amount by which something is short.

un·der·ling *n* a person of lower rank; inferior.

un·der·most *adj, adv, n* lowest. **un·der·neath** [-'niθ] *prep* **1** directly below; beneath; under: *a basement underneath a house.* **2** on the inside of; covered by: *to wear a T-shirt underneath a shirt.* **3** under the control or authority of: *Clerical staff are underneath the administrative assistants.* *adv* **1** below something: *He crawled underneath.* **2** on or at the lower part or surface: *The box is wet underneath.* **un·der–the–count·er** *adj* made, done, or sold dishonestly or illegally: *an under-the-counter transaction.*

SYNONYMS

Under suggests being directly lower: *The basement is under the kitchen.* **Below** suggests being on a lower level, but not necessarily straight below nor without anything between: *His picture hangs below and to the right of mine.* **Beneath** can be used in place of either *under* or *below*, but is usually more formal or literary: *She lies buried beneath an oak.*

under– *prefix* **1** in, from, or to a lower place: *undercurrent, underlie.* **2** below the surface of: *underground.* **3** on or for the inside; covered: *underwear.* **4** lower in rank: *undersecretary.* **5** below some standard: *underfed, underripe.* **6** less or for less than: *underbid, undersell.*

un·der·a·chieve *v* work or perform to a lower standard than expected, esp in school. **un·der·a·chieve·ment** *n.* **un·der·a·chiev·er** *n.* **un·der·age** [-'eidʒ] *adj* younger than the legal or minimum age for voting, marrying, drinking liquor in bars, etc. **un·der·arm** *adj* **1** of or for the armpit: *underarm deodorant.* **2** underhand: *an underarm throw.* *n* armpit. *adv* underhand: *She threw the ball underarm.* **un·der·brush** *n* bushes, small trees, etc. growing under the large trees in a forest. **un·der·car·riage** *n* **1** the framework of a car, etc. **2** landing gear of an aircraft. **un·der·class** *n* the lowest social class; the poor. **un·der·clothes** [-ˌklouz] *or* [-ˌklouðz] *n pl* underwear. **un·der·cloth·ing** *n* underwear. **un·der·coat** *n* **1** a coat or layer of paint, etc. applied before the finishing coat. **2** the soft, thick fur of certain animals, hidden by the longer hair of the outer coat. **un·der·coat** *v.* **un·der·coat·ing** *n* a coating sprayed on the underside of a motor vehicle to protect it against rust, etc. **un·der·cov·er** *adj* working or carried out in secret: *an undercover attack.* *adv* secretly: *working undercover.* **un·der·cur·rent** *n* **1** a current flowing below other currents in a body of water, air, etc. **2** an underlying tone, often contrary to what is expressed or shown: *There was an undercurrent of sadness beneath her joking manner.* **un·der·cut**

[ˌʌndər'kʌt] v -cut, -cut·ting 1 cut material from underneath so as to leave an overhang. 2 undermine; weaken: *He is undercutting my authority.* 3 sell or work for less than (a competitor). 4 *Golf, tennis, etc.* hit (a ball) with a downward slant to give it a backward spin. **un·der·cut** [ˈʌndər,kʌt] *n.* **un·der·de·vel·oped** *adj* 1 less fully developed at a given stage than others: *an underveloped child.* 2 of a region, country, etc., poorly developed in industry and commerce and having a low standard of living. 3 of film, a print, etc., showing an indistinct image because of poor processing. **un·der·de·vel·op·ment** *n.* **un·der·dog** *n* 1 a person or group that is or seems to be losing any contest. 2 a victim of persecution or social or political injustice. **un·der·done** *adj* not cooked enough. **un·der·dress** *v* dress too casually for the occasion. **un·der·dressed** *adj.* **un·der·em·ployed** *adj* of a person in the work force, employed in a way that does not allow use of his or her full abilities. **un·der·es·ti·mate** [-ˌmeit] *v* estimate at too low a value, amount, etc. **un·der·es·ti·mate** [-mɪt] *n.* **un·der·es·ti·ma·tion** *n.* **un·der·ex·pose** *v* expose (film) for too short a time, or to too little light. **un·der·ex·po·sure** *n.* **un·der·foot** *adv, adj* 1 underneath one's feet: *enjoying the grass underfoot.* 2 in the way: *The dog is always underfoot.* **un·der·fund·ed** *adj* poorly supported financially. **un·der·gar·ment** *n* an article of underwear. **un·der·go** *v* -went, -gone, -go·ing experience: *to undergo much pain.* **un·der·grad** *n, adj* undergraduate. **un·der·grad·u·ate** *n* a university student in a course of study leading to a bachelor's degree. **un·der·grad·u·ate** *adj.* **un·der·ground** [ˈʌndər'graʊnd] *or* [-ˌgraʊnd] *adv, adj* 1 beneath the surface of the ground: *underground cables.* 2 in or into hiding or secret operation: *The thieves went underground after the robbery.* 3 to do with a group outside the establishment, esp radical groups: *an underground theatre, an underground newspaper.* *n* [ˈʌndər,graʊnd] 1 a place or space beneath the surface of the ground. 2 a secret organization working to overthrow foreign domination or an autocratic regime. 3 any avant-garde or revolutionary movement. **Underground Railroad** formerly, a secret system set up by opponents of slavery in Canada and the US before the Civil War, to help slaves escape to freedom from the US to Canada. **un·der·growth** *n* underbrush. **un·der·hand** [ˈʌndər,hænd] *adj* 1 underhanded. 2 made with an upward movement of the hand from below the shoulder: *an underhand pitch.* **un·der·hand** *adv.* **un·der·hand·ed** [ˈʌndər'hændɪd] *adj* not open or honest; sly: *an underhanded trick.* **un·der·hand·ed·ly** *adv.* **un·der·hand·ed·ness** *n.* **un·der·lay¹** [ˌʌndər'lei] *v* -laid, -lay·ing 1 lay (something) under something else. 2 raise, support, cushion, etc. with something laid underneath. *n* [ˈʌndər,lei] anything laid beneath to raise, support, cushion, etc.: *The carpet has a rubber underlay.* **un·der·lay²** [ˌʌndər'lei] *v* pt of UNDERLIE. **un·der·lie** *v* -lay, -lain, -ly·ing 1 lie

under; be beneath. 2 form the basis of; be a reason for: *Strong resentment underlay his outburst.* **un·der·line** *v* 1 draw a line or lines under. 2 emphasize: *Her speech underlined the importance of co-operation.* **un·der·ly·ing** *adj* 1 foundational; supporting. 2 not explicit; partly hidden by other words or actions: *a compliment with an underlying tone of sarcasm.* **un·der·mine** *v* 1 wear away the foundations of: *The wave had undermined the cliff.* 2 weaken or destroy gradually or covertly: *to undermine someone's authority, to undermine someone's health.* **un·der·nour·ish** *v* provide with too little food for proper growth, health, etc. **un·der·nour·ish·ment** *n.* **un·der·pants** *n pl* long or short pants worn as an undergarment. **un·der·pass** *n* a way to go underneath, esp a road going under railway tracks or under another road. **un·der·pay** *v* -paid, -pay·ing 1 pay too little to or for: *to underpay employees. This work is underpaid.* 2 pay less than (what is due): *Not knowing about the increase, we underpaid our rent.* **un·der·pay·ment** *n.* **un·der·pin** *v* -pinned, -pin·ning 1 support or strengthen from below with props, stones, masonry, etc. 2 provide a foundation for (a theory, etc.); substantiate. **un·der·pin·ning** *n* 1 the material or structure used to support a building or wall from beneath. 2 Sometimes, **underpinnings** *pl* foundation or support: *the underpinnings of society.* **un·der·play** *v* 1 **a** act (a role or scene) in a restrained way. **b** play (a role) in too subtle a way. 2 avoid or reduce emphasis on. **un·der·priv·i·leged** *adj* having fewer advantages than most people, esp because of poor economic status. **un·der·pro·duce** *v* produce less of (a thing) than is normal or needed. **un·der·pro·duc·tion** *n.* **un·der·rate** *v* set too low a value on. **un·der·re·port** *v* report fewer instances of, or a lower amount of, than actually exists: *Date rape is underreported.* **un·der·ripe** *adj* not fully ripe. **un·der·score** [ˌʌndər'skɔr] *v,* [ˈʌndər,skɔr] *n* underline. **un·der·sea** *adj, adv* beneath the surface of the sea: *undersea explorations.* Also (*adv*), **un·der·seas.** **un·der·sec·re·tar·y** *n* an assistant secretary, esp of a government department. **un·der·sell** *v* -sold, -sell·ing 1 sell things at a lower price than: *to undersell a competitor.* 2 sell at a loss. 3 promote or advertise (merchandise, etc.) in a restrained manner. **un·der·sexed** *adj* having a weaker sex drive than is considered normal. **un·der·shirt** *n* a collarless, often sleeveless, knit undergarment for the upper body. **un·der·shorts** *n pl* underpants for men or boys. **un·der·side** *n* the surface underneath; the bottom or hidden side. **un·der·signed** *n* **the undersigned** the person or persons signing a document: *The undersigned accepts the agreement.* **un·der·sized** *adj* smaller than the usual, desired, or required size: *undersized trout.* **un·der·staffed** *adj* having not enough personnel. **un·der·stand** *v* -stood, -stand·ing 1 get the meaning (of); comprehend: *Now I understand the message.* 2 be in rapport (with); be sympathetic (to): *He understands* today's youth. **3** infer from information received: *I understand you've been hired.* **4** know how to deal with; know well: *A good teacher should understand child psychology.* **5** realize: *You understand, don't you, that I will be away for three weeks?* **6** take for granted: *It is understood that you will come.* **7** supply in the mind. In *He hit the tree harder than I,* the word *did* is understood after *I.* **understand each other** know each other's meaning and wishes; agree. **un·der·stand·a·ble** *adj* **1** able to be understood. **2** reasonable; not surprising; only natural: *It's understandable that he was offended by that remark.* **un·der·stand·a·bly** *adv.* **un·der·stand·ing** *n* **1** comprehension: *a clear understanding of the problem.* **2** insight and intelligence: *a woman of great understanding.* **3** knowledge of each other's meaning and wishes: *True friendship is based on understanding.* **4** agreement: *They have come to an understanding.* **5** a perception or interpretation: *That was her understanding of the event. adj* intelligent and sympathetic: *an understanding reply.* **un·der·stand·ing·ly** *adv.* **un·der·state** *v* **1** state too weakly; minimize. **2** show or express in a subtle way: *understated elegance.* **un·der·state·ment** *n.* **un·der·stood** *adj* **1** taken for granted; implied. **2** agreed upon in advance. **3** comprehended; known. **un·der·stud·y** *n* a person who is ready to substitute in an emergency for a regular performer. *v* learn (a part) in order to replace the regular performer if necessary. **un·der·take** *v* **-took, -tak·en, -tak·ing** **1** try. **2** agree to do. **3** promise. **4** *Formal* act on behalf of (used with *for*). **un·der·tak·er** *n* ['ʌndər,teikər] a person whose business is preparing the dead for burial or cremation and taking charge of funerals; funeral director. **un·der·tak·ing** ['ʌndər,teikɪŋ] *or* [,ʌndər'teikɪŋ] *n* **1** task; enterprise; something undertaken. **2** ['ʌndər,teikɪŋ] the business of an undertaker. **un·der·things** *n pl* women's underwear. **un·der·tone** *n* **1** a low or quiet tone: *to talk in undertones.* **2** a subdued colour; a colour seen through other colours: *There was an undertone of brown beneath all the gold and crimson of fall.* **3** a quality or feeling beneath the surface: *an undertone of sadness in her gaiety.* **un·der·tow** *n* **1** a strong current below the surface, moving in a direction different from that of the surface current. **2** the backward flow from waves breaking on a beach. **un·der·val·ue** *v* put too low a value on. **un·der·wa·ter** *adj* growing, done, or used below the surface of the water: *underwater plants, underwater work. adv* below the surface of the water: *He stayed underwater for two minutes.* **un·der·way** See UNDER. **un·der·wear** *n* clothing worn next to the skin under outer clothing. Compare OUTERWEAR (OUT). **un·der·weight** *adj* **1** of a person or animal, having a mass that is too small in proportion to height and build. **2** weighing less than required for something: *He was put in a lower class for boxing because he was underweight.* **un·der·whelm** [-'wɛlm] *v* fail to impress or excite: *The response was*

underwhelming. **un·der·world** *n* **1** the criminal part of society. **2** *Myth* the world of the dead. **un·der·write** *v* **-wrote, -writ·ten, -writ·ing** **1** insure (property) against loss. **2** sign (an insurance policy), thus accepting the risk of insuring something against loss. **3** agree to buy (all the stocks or bonds of a certain issue that are not bought by the public): *The bankers underwrote the steel company's bonds.* **4** sponsor: *Local businesses underwrote the concert series.* **un·der·writ·er** *n* **1** a person who underwrites an insurance policy or carries on an insurance business; insurer. **2** an official of an insurance company who determines risks to be accepted, premiums to be paid, etc. **3** a person who underwrites (usually with others) issues of bonds, stocks, etc.

un·de·sir·a·ble [,ʌndɪ'zaɪrəbəl] *adj* objectionable; disagreeable.
n a person who is not wanted.
un·de·sir·a·bly *adv.* **un·de·sir·a·bil·i·ty** *n.*

un·de·vel·oped [,ʌndɪ'vɛləpt] *adj* **1** not fully grown. **2** not put to full use. **3** having resources not yet exploited; having little modern technology: *undeveloped countries.*

un·did [ʌn'dɪd] *v* pt of UNDO.

un·dies ['ʌndiz] *n pl Informal* underthings.

un·dis·ci·plined [ʌn'dɪsəplɪnd] *adj* without proper control; untrained.

un·dis·guised [,ʌndɪs'gaɪzd] *adj* open; plain; unconcealed. **un·dis·guis·ed·ly** [-'gaɪzɪdli] *adv.*

un·dis·put·ed [,ʌndɪ'spjutɪd] *adj* not doubted. **un·dis·put·ed·ly** *adv.*

un·dis·turbed [,ʌndɪ'stɜrbd] *adj* not troubled; calm.

un·do [ʌn'du] *v* **-did, -done, -do·ing** **1** untie, unwrap, etc.: *I can't undo my shoelace.* **2** do away with; cancel or reverse: *We mended the roof, but a heavy storm undid our work.* **3** bring to ruin; spoil; destroy. **un·do·er** *n.*
un·do·ing *n* **1** a spoiling; destroying. **2** a cause of ruin: *Drink was his undoing.* **un·done** *adj* **1** not done; not finished: *to leave a job undone.* **2** unfastened or not done up: *The top button was undone.* **3** ruined.

un·doubt·ed [ʌn'dautɪd] *adj* not doubted; accepted as true. **un·doubt·ed·ly** *adv.*

un·dress [ʌn'drɛs] *v* **1** take the clothes off (someone); strip: *She undressed the doll and gave it a bath.* **2** take off one's own clothes.
n lack of clothing; partial nakedness.

un·due [ʌn'dju] *or* [ʌn'du] *adj* **1** not fitting; not right; improper. **2** too great; too much.
un·du·ly *adv* **1** too much: *unduly harsh, unduly optimistic.* **2** unjustly or improperly.

un·du·late ['ʌndʒə,leit] *or* ['ʌndjə,leit] *v* **-lat·ed, -lat·ing** **1** move in waves: *undulating water.* **2** have a wavy form or surface: *undulating hair.* **un·du·late** *adj.* **un·du·la·tion** *n.* ⟨Latin *undula* diminutive of *unda* wave⟩
un·du·lant *adj* waving; wavy.

un·du·ly See UNDUE.

un·dy·ing [ʌn'daɪŋ] *adj* **1** deathless; immortal. **2** enduring: *Her courageous action earned his undying gratitude.* **un·dy·ing·ly** *adv.*

un·earned [ʌn'ɜrnd] *adj* **1** not earned; not gained by labour or service: *unearned income.* **2** not deserved. **3** *Baseball* scored because of a defensive error or errors.
unearned income income from investments, rents, etc. and not from wages, royalties, etc.

un·earth [ʌn'ɜrθ] *v* **1** dig up: *to unearth a buried city.* **2** discover: *to unearth a plot.*

un·earth·ly *adj* **1** not of this world; supernatural. **2** strange; weird; ghostly. **3** *Informal* unnatural; extraordinary; preposterous. **un·earth·li·ness** *n.*

un·ease [ʌn'iz] *n* a state of restlessness, perturbation, or anxiety.
un·eas·y *adj* **1** restless. **2** not comfortable. **3** that makes uncomfortable: *an uneasy silence.* **4** not easy in manner; awkward. **un·eas·i·ly** *adv.* **un·eas·i·ness** *n.*

un·em·ploy·ment [ˌʌnɛm'plɔɪmənt] *n* **1** being out of work. **2** the number of persons unemployed at a particular time: *a period of high unemployment.* **3** UNEMPLOYMENT INSURANCE (def. 2).
un·em·ploy·a·ble *adj* that cannot be employed. *n* a person who cannot be given work. **un·em·ployed** *adj* **1** not having a job; having no work: *an unemployed person.* **2** not employed; not in use: *an unemployed skill.* **the unemployed** people out of work. **unemployment insurance 1** a program providing regular payments to people in the regular labour force who are temporarily unemployed. Now officially called **employment insurance**. **2** benefits paid through such a program: *She collected unemployment insurance for two months.*

un·e·qual [ʌn'ikwəl] *adj* **1** not the same in amount, size, value, etc. **2** not balanced; not well matched. **3** not fair; one-sided: *an unequal contest.* **4** not enough; not adequate: *Her strength was unequal to the task.* **5** not regular; not even; variable or inconsistent. **un·e·qual·ly** *adv.* **un·e·qual·ness** *n.*
un·e·qualled or **un·e·qualed** *adj* matchless.

un·e·quiv·o·cal [ˌʌnɪ'kwɪvəkəl] *adj* **1** clear; plain. **2** speaking straightforwardly. **un·e·quiv·o·cal·ly** *adv.* **un·e·quiv·o·cal·ness** *n.*

un·err·ing [ʌn'ɛrɪŋ] or [ʌn'ɜrɪŋ] *adj* making no mistakes; exactly right; never missing: *unerring aim.* **un·err·ing·ly** *adv.* **un·err·ing·ness** *n.*

UNESCO [ju'nɛskou] *n* the United Nations Educational, Scientific, and Cultural Organization.

un·es·sen·tial [ˌʌnɪ'sɛnʃəl] *adj* not of prime importance. **un·es·sen·tial** *n.*

un·e·ven [ʌn'ivən] *adj* **1** not level: *uneven ground.* **2** not equal; one-sided: *an uneven contest.* **3** of a number, leaving a remainder of 1 when divided by 2; odd. *Example: 9.* **4** not uniform; variable: *of uneven thickness. It was an uneven performance, but quite enjoyable.* **5** of lines, crooked; not parallel; not straight. **un·e·ven·ly** *adv.* **un·e·ven·ness** *n.*

un·e·vent·ful [ˌʌnɪ'vɛntfəl] *adj* without important or striking occurrences. **un·e·vent·ful·ly** *adv.* **un·e·vent·ful·ness** *n.*

un·ex·cep·tion·a·ble [ˌʌnɛk'sɛpʃənəbəl] *adj* beyond criticism (sometimes mildly pejorative, as having perfect correctness as its only virtue). **un·ex·cep·tion·a·bly** *adv.*

un·ex·cep·tion·al [ˌʌnɛk'sɛpʃənəl] *adj* ordinary. **un·ex·cep·tion·al·ly** *adv.*

un·fail·ing [ʌn'feilɪŋ] *adj* **1** tireless; dependable. **2** endless. **3** sure; certain. **un·fail·ing·ly** *adv.*

un·fair [ʌn'fɛr] *adj* not fair; unjust. ⟨Old English *unfæger*⟩ **un·fair·ly** *adv.* **un·fair·ness** *n.*

un·faith·ful [ʌn'feiθfəl] *adj* **1** not true to duty or one's promises; faithless. **2** not accurate; not true to the original: *an unfaithful translation.* **3** having committed adultery. **un·faith·ful·ly** *adv.* **un·faith·ful·ness** *n.*

un·fa·mil·iar [ˌʌnfə'mɪljər] *adj* **1** not well-known; strange: *That face is unfamiliar to me.* **2** not acquainted: *She is unfamiliar with the Greek language.* **un·fa·mil·i·ar·i·ty** *n.*

un·fas·ten [ʌn'fæsən] *v* **1** undo; open. **2** become undone: *Your zipper has unfastened.*

un·fath·om·a·ble [ʌn'fæðəməbəl] *adj* **1** so deep that the bottom cannot be reached. **2** too mysterious or profound to be understood.

un·fa·vour·a·ble or **un·fa·vor·a·ble** [ʌn'feivərəbəl] *adj* **1** opposed or adverse: *Most of the reviews were unfavourable.* **2** not advantageous: *an unfavourable aspect.* **un·fa·vour·a·ble·ness** or **un·fa·vor·a·ble·ness** *n.* **un·fa·vour·a·bly** or **un·fa·vor·a·bly** *adv.*

un·feel·ing [ʌn'filɪŋ] *adj* **1** hard-hearted; insensitive: *a cold, unfeeling person.* **2** not able to feel: *numb, unfeeling hands.* **un·feel·ing·ly** *adv.* **un·feel·ing·ness** *n.*

un·feigned [ʌn'feind] *adj* sincere; real. **un·feign·ed·ly** [-'feinɪdli] *adv.*

un·fin·ished [ʌn'fɪnɪʃt] *adj* **1** not finished; not complete. **2** without some special finish or final stage of processing; not polished; rough; not painted: *unfinished furniture.*

un·fit [ʌn'fɪt] *adj* **1** not suitable. **2** not good enough; unqualified. **3** physically or mentally unsound. **4** not adapted. **un·fit·ly** *adv.* **un·fit·ness** *n.*

un·fit·ted *adj* **1** inappropriate; not suitable. **2** not tailored or fitted: *an unfitted coat.*

un·flag·ging [ʌn'flægɪŋ] *adj* not drooping or failing: *unflagging efforts.* **un·flag·ging·ly** *adv.*

un·flap·pa·ble [ʌn'flæpəbəl] *adj* *Informal* having or showing self-control or coolness: *an unflappable pilot.* **un·flap·pa·bil·i·ty** *n.*

un·flinch·ing [ʌn'flɪntʃɪŋ] *adj* not drawing back from difficulty, danger, or pain; firm; resolute. **un·flinch·ing·ly** *adv.*

un·fold [ʌn'fould] *v* **1** open the folds of; spread out: *to unfold a newspaper.* **2** unbend and straighten out: *to unfold your arms.* **3** reveal or explain stage by stage: *to unfold the plot of a story.* **4** open out; develop, literally or figuratively: *Buds unfold into flowers. History is unfolding as it should.*

un·forced [ʌn'fɔrst] *adj* **1** not compelled; willing. **2** natural; spontaneous.

un·fore·seen [ˌʌnfɔr'sin] *adj* not known or thought of beforehand; unexpected.

un·for·get·ta·ble [ˌʌnfər'gɛtəbəl] *adj* that can never be forgotten. **un·for·get·ta·bly** *adv.*

un·formed [ʌn'fɔrmd] *adj* **1** shapeless. **2** undeveloped. **3** *Biology* unorganized.

un·for·tu·nate [ʌn'fɔrtʃənɪt] *adj* **1** not lucky. **2** bringing bad luck; inauspicious. **3** not suitable; not fitting: *Dr. Ow is an unfortunate name for a dentist.* **4** undesirable; deplorable: *The unfortunate consequence was that most of the original manuscript was lost.* *n* an unfortunate person. **un·for·tu·nate·ly** *adv.* **un·for·tu·nate·ness** *n.*

un·found·ed [ʌn'faundɪd] *adj* without foundation; baseless: *an unfounded complaint.* **un·found·ed·ly** *adv.* **un·found·ed·ness** *n.*

un·freeze [ʌn'friz] *v* **-froze, -fro·zen 1** melt or cause to melt or thaw: *That roast you took out this morning hasn't unfrozen yet.* **2** remove financial controls or restrictions from.

un·friend·ly [ʌn'frɛndli] *adj* **1** hostile: *an unfriendly dog.* **2** not favourable: *unfriendly weather.* **un·friend·li·ness** *n.*

un·furl [ʌn'fɜrl] *v* spread out; shake out; unfold: *to unfurl a sail.*

un·gain·ly [ʌn'geinli] *adj* awkward; clumsy. **un·gain·li·ness** *n.* ⟨Middle English *un-* not + *gaynly* agile⟩

un·glued [ʌn'glud] *adj* **1** no longer stuck together by glue. **2** with no glue on it. **come unglued** *Informal* lose one's self-possession; become disquieted.

un·god·ly [ʌn'gɒdli] *adj* **1** wicked; sinful. **2** *Informal* outrageous; dreadful; shocking: *to pay an ungodly price, at an ungodly hour in the morning.* **un·god·li·ness** *n.*

un·gov·ern·a·ble [ʌn'gʌvərnəbəl] *adj* hard or impossible to control: *an ungovernable temper.* **un·gov·ern·a·ble·ness** *n.* **un·gov·ern·a·bly** *adv.*

un·gra·cious [ʌn'greiʃəs] *adj* **1** not polite; rude. **2** unpleasant; disagreeable. **un·gra·cious·ly** *adv.* **un·gra·cious·ness** *n.*

un·grate·ful [ʌn'greitfəl] *adj* **1** characterized by or displaying lack of gratitude: *an ungrateful wretch, an ungrateful silence.* **2** thankless; not appreciated or rewarded: *an ungrateful task.* **3** unpleasant; disagreeable. **un·grate·ful·ly** *adv.* **un·grate·ful·ness** *n.*

un·grudg·ing [ʌn'grʌdʒɪŋ] *adj* willing; hearty; liberal. **un·grudg·ing·ly** *adv.*

un·guard·ed [ʌn'gɑrdɪd] *adj* **1** not protected. **2** careless: *In an unguarded moment, she gave away the secret.* **3** open and free in manner; not hedging, defensive, or sly. **un·guard·ed·ly** *adv.* **un·guard·ed·ness** *n.*

un·gu·late ['ʌŋgjəlɪt] *or* ['ʌŋgjə,leit] *n* any of a large group of four-footed, plant-eating mammals having hoofed feet. *adj* **1** having hoofs. **2** resembling a hoof. **3** to do with ungulates. ⟨Latin *ungula* diminutive of *unguis* nail, claw, hoof⟩

un·hal·lowed [ʌn'hæloud] *adj* **1** not made holy; not sacred. **2** wicked.

un·hand [ʌn'hænd] *v Poetic* let go of; take the hands from (*often facetious*).

un·hand·y [ʌn'hændi] *adj* **1** not easy to handle or manage: *an unhandy tool.* **2** not skilful in using the hands: *an unhandy man.* **un·hand·i·ly** *adv.* **un·hand·i·ness** *n.*

un·hap·py [ʌn'hæpi] *adj* **1** sad; sorrowful. **2** dissatisfied: *She is unhappy with the recent changes at work.* **3** unlucky. **4** not suitable. **un·hap·pi·ly** *adv.* **un·hap·pi·ness** *n.*

un·health·y [ʌn'hɛlθi] *adj* **1** not possessing good health. **2** characteristic of or resulting from poor health: *an unhealthy paleness.* **3** hurtful to health: *an unhealthy climate.* **4** morally unsound or harmful: *an unhealthy preoccupation with gambling.* **5** *Informal* filled with danger or risk. **un·health·i·ly** *adv.* **un·health·i·ness** *n.*

un·heard [ʌn'hɜrd] *adj* **1** not perceived by the ear: *unheard melodies.* **2** not given a hearing: *the unheard minority.* **un·heard of 1** unknown: *The electric light was unheard of 200 years ago.* **2** outrageous; preposterous: *A price of $6 a dozen for eggs is unheard of.* Either meaning is spelled **un·heard-of** if before a noun: *unheard-of prices.*

un·hes·i·tat·ing [ʌn'hɛzə,teitɪŋ] *adj* prompt; ready; immediate: *unhesitating acceptance.* **un·hes·i·tat·ing·ly** *adv.*

un·hinge [ʌn'hɪndʒ] *v* **1** take (a door, etc.) off its hinges. **2** separate from something; detach. **3** unsettle; disorganize; upset: *Sorrow has unhinged this poor man's mind.*

un·his·tor·ic [ˌʌnhɪ'stɔrɪk] *adj* **1 a** not famous in history; unimportant: *an unhistoric event.* **b** not having a celebrated heritage: *an unhistoric town.* **2** *Linguistics* arising accidentally or arbitrarily rather than by regular development from earlier forms, as the *s* in *island* or the *b* in *thumb.* **un·his·tor·i·cal** *adj* **1** not in accordance with the facts of history. **2** not recorded in history; mythological. **un·his·tor·i·cal·ly** *adv.* **un·his·tor·i·cal·ness** *n.*

un·hitch [ʌn'hɪtʃ] *v* free from being hitched; unfasten.

un·ho·ly [ʌn'houli] *adj* **1** not hallowed or consecrated. **2** wicked; sinful. **3** *Informal* outrageous or dreadful: *They were raising an unholy row.* **un·ho·li·ness** *n.*

un·hook [ʌn'huk] *v* **1** remove from a hook or come off a hook. **2** undo or open by unfastening a hook.

un·hoped for [ʌn'houpt ,fɔr] *adj* unexpected; unanticipated: *The win was unhoped for.* This is spelled **un·hoped-for** if before a noun: *an unhoped-for benefit.*

un·horse [ʌn'hɔrs] *v* **1** cause to fall from a horse: *The knight was unhorsed by his opponent.* **2** dislodge; overthrow: *The prime minister was unhorsed by rebels in her own party.*

uni– *prefix* one: *unicellular, unilateral.* ⟨Latin⟩

U·ni·at ['juni,æt] *n* a member of any Eastern

Christian church that is in communion with the Roman Catholic Church and acknowledges the supremacy of the Pope. **U·ni·at** *adj.* Also, **U·ni·ate** ['juni,It] *or* ['juni,eit]. ⟨Russian; *uniya* union⟩

u·ni·cam·er·al [ˌjunəˈkæmərəl] *adj* having only one house in a lawmaking body. All Canadian provinces except Québec have unicameral legislatures. ⟨*uni-* + Latin *camera* chamber⟩

UNICEF ['junə,sɛf] *n* United Nations Children's Fund (orig United Nations International Children's Emergency Fund).

u·ni·cel·lu·lar [ˌjunəˈsɛljələr] *adj* of an organism, consisting of a single cell. The amoeba is a unicellular animal.

u·ni·corn ['junə,kɔrn] *n* a legendary animal resembling a horse, and having a single long horn growing from its forehead, often a symbol of virtue or chastity. ⟨Latin *unicornis; unus* one + *cornu* horn⟩

u·ni·cy·cle ['junə,saɪkəl] *n* a vehicle with a single wheel and a saddle, propelled by pedals: *Unicycles are ridden mostly by acrobats and entertainers.* **u·ni·cy·clist** *n.*

un·i·den·ti·fied flying object [ˌʌnaɪˈdɛntə,faɪd] an object in the sky that cannot be identified as a known aircraft from earth or explained as any natural phenomenon. *Abbrev* **UFO.**

u·ni·di·men·sion·al [ˌjunədəˈmɛnʃənəl] *or* [ˌjunədaɪ-] *adj* having only one dimension.

u·ni·di·rec·tion·al [ˌjunədəˈrɛkʃənəl] *or* [ˌjunədaɪ-] *adj* functioning or moving in only one direction.

u·ni·form [ˌjunə,fɔrm] *adj* **1** always the same; regular: *The earth turns at a uniform rate.* **2** all alike: *All the bricks are of a uniform size.* *n* the distinctive clothes worn by the members of a group when on duty, by which they may be recognized as belonging to that group: *Soldiers wear uniforms.* *v* clothe or furnish with a uniform. ⟨Latin *uniformis; unus* one + *forma* form⟩ **u·ni·form·i·ty** *n.* **u·ni·form·ly** *adv.*

u·ni·fy ['junə,faɪ] *v* make or form into one; unite. **u·ni·fi·a·ble** *adj.* **u·ni·fi·er** *n.* ⟨Latin *unificare; unus* one + *facere* make⟩ **u·ni·fi·ca·tion** *n* **1** a union: *the unification of many states into one nation.* **2** a making or being made more alike: *The traffic laws of the different provinces need unification.* **3 ✹** the policy of completely merging the traditional navy, army, and air force into one combined force having a unified command.

u·ni·lat·er·al [ˌjunəˈlætərəl] *adj* **1** of, on, or affecting one side only. **2** of a contract, etc., done by or affecting one party or person only: *unilateral disarmament.* **3** to do with only one side of a matter. **u·ni·lat·er·al·ly** *adv.* **u·ni·lat·er·al·ism** *n* advocacy of a unilateral disarmament policy. **u·ni·lat·er·al·ist** *adj, n.*

u·ni·lin·gual [ˌjunəˈlɪŋgwəl] *adj* having knowledge or use of only one language.

un·im·peach·a·ble [ˌʌnɪmˈpitʃəbəl] *adj* free from fault; blameless; above suspicion; impeccable. **un·im·peach·a·bly** *adv.*

un·im·pressed [ˌʌnɪmˈprɛst] *adj* **1** not impressed one way or the other. **2** unfavourably impressed.

un·in·spired [ˌʌnɪnˈspaɪrd] *adj* dull.

un·in·tel·li·gi·ble [ˌʌnɪnˈtɛlədʒəbəl] *adj* that cannot be understood. **un·in·tel·li·gi·bly** *adv.*

un·in·ter·est·ed [ʌnˈɪntrɪstɪd] *adj* not interested; showing no interest. **un·in·ter·est·ed·ly** *adv.*

Uninterested implies having no feelings about something: *She was uninterested in watching the game.* **Disinterested** means having no selfish interest: *A referee must be disinterested in the outcome of the game.*

un·in·ter·rupt·ed [ˌʌnɪntəˈrʌptɪd] *adj* without interruption; continuous. **un·in·ter·rupt·ed·ly** *adv.*

un·ion ['junjən] *n* **1** the act of uniting or the state of being united: *The US was formed by the union of thirteen colonies.* **2** something formed by combining members, sets, or parts. **3** a group of workers joined together to protect and promote their interests; LABOUR UNION; TRADE UNION. **4** marriage. **5 the Union a ✹** formerly, the uniting of Upper and Lower Canada, effected by the Union Act of 1840. **b ✹** Confederation. **c** the 'North' in the American Civil War, as opposed to the Confederacy of Southern States. ⟨Latin *unionis; unus* one⟩ **un·ion·ist** *n* **1** a person who promotes or advocates union or unionism. **2** a member of a labour union. **3 Unionist** formerly: **a ✹** a person who was in favour of union among the provinces of British North America, esp of Upper and Lower Canada. **b** a supporter of the federal government of the United States during the Civil War. **4 Unionist,** since 1920, a person who favours keeping Northern Ireland as part of the UK. **un·ion·ism** *n* **1** the principle of union. **2** a loyalty to a union. **3** the system, principles, or methods of labour unions. **un·ion·ize** *v* **1** form into a labour union: *The teaching assistants want to unionize themselves.* **2** organize under a labour union: *Many professions are not unionized.* **un·ion·i·za·tion** *n.* **un·i·on·ized** *adj.* **Union Jack** the flag of the UK. **Union Na·tion·ale** [ˌnæʃəˈnæl] *French* [ynjɔnasjɔˈnal] a political party in Québec, formed in the early 1930s. **union shop** a business establishment that hires only members of a labour union. **union suit** long johns and long-sleeved undershirt combined in a one-piece garment for men.

Union emphasizes the joining together of things to form a whole, or the state of being joined together as a unit: *A combat team is formed by the union of infantry and other forces.* **Unity** emphasizes a quality, and applies to the oneness of the whole that is formed: *The strength of any group is in its unity.*

u·ni·par·ous [ju'nɪpərəs]   *adj*   **1** *Botany* producing only one axis at each branching. **2** *Zoology* producing only one ovum or offspring at a time. ⟨*uni-* + Latin *-parus* bearing⟩

u·nique [ju'nik] *adj* **1** having no like or equal. **2** being the only one. **3** *Informal* interestingly original. ⟨French; Latin *unicus; unus* one⟩ **u·nique·ly** *adv.* **u·nique·ness** *n.*

USAGE

In formal English, **unique** means 'being one of a kind', and so it cannot be compared or qualified; something is either unique or not. In informal English, **unique** also has the sense 'interesting', and so is sometimes used with a qualifier like quite, rather, or really: *Her clothes are rather unique.* This usage should be avoided in careful speech and writing.

u·ni·sex ['junə,sɛks] *adj* to do with clothing, hairstyles, etc. that are the same for members of both sexes.

u·ni·son ['junəsən] *or* ['junəzən] *n Music* **a** identity of pitch of two or more tones. **b** a performing together by voices, instruments, etc. of the same melody, etc., at the same pitch or an octave apart. ⟨Latin *unisonus; unus* one + *sonus* sound⟩ **in unison** together as one, at the same time; united(ly): *They moved and spoke in unison.*

u·nit ['junɪt] *n* **1** a single thing or person. **2** any group considered as one. **3** one of the individual parts of which a whole is composed: *the storage unit of a computer.* **4** a standard amount, used as a basis for measuring: *A metre is a unit of length.* ⟨probably from *unity*⟩ **U·ni·tar·i·an** *n* a member of a religious denomination based on the belief that God exists as one, rejecting the doctrine of the Trinity. **U·ni·tar·i·an** *adj* **U·ni·tar·i·an·ism** *n.* **u·ni·tar·y** *adj* **1** to do with a unit or units. **2** to do with unity. **unit pricing** a system of pricing commodities based on a unit of measure, such as a millilitre, rather than on the container such as a can.

u·nite [ju'nəit] *v* **1** join together; make one: *Several firms were united to form one company.* **2** join by formal bond: *to unite two people in marriage.* **3** become one; join in action, etc. **u·nit·er** *n.* ⟨Latin *unire* unite; *unus* one⟩ **u·nit·ed** *adj* **1** joined together to make one. **2 a** having or showing cohesion, harmony, or accord: *a united effort.* **b** acting together or resulting from joint action. **u·nit·ed·ly** *adv.* **United Empire Loyalist ✹** any of the Loyalists in the American Revolution who emigrated to what are now Ontario and the Maritimes, or their descendants. **United Nations** a worldwide organization devoted to establishing world peace and promoting economic and social welfare. The United Nations charter was put into effect on October 24, 1945. *Abbrev* **UN** or **U.N.**

u·ni·ty ['junəti] *n* **1** oneness; being united: *A circle has unity; a row of dots doesn't.* **2** a union of parts forming a complex whole. **3** a single,

distinct thing. **4 a** harmony: *to live together in unity.* **b** singleness: *unity of purpose.* **5** the number one (1). **6** an arrangement and choice of material to give a single effect, main idea, etc.: *A pleasing picture has unity; so has a well-written essay.* **7 the unities** *pl* the rules of dramatic structure derived from Aristotle, according to which a play should have one main action occurring on one day in one place. ⟨Latin *unitas; unus* one⟩

u·ni·va·lent [,junə'veilənt] *or* [ju'nɪvələnt] *adj* **1** *Chemistry* having a valence of one. **2** *Biology* of a chromosome, unpaired. **u·ni·va·lence** *n.* ⟨*uni-* + Latin *valere* be worth⟩

u·ni·valve ['junə,vælv] *Biology n* a mollusc having a shell consisting of a single piece, called a valve. **u·ni·valve** *adj.*

u·ni·verse ['junə,vɜrs] *n* **1** everything that exists, including all space and matter. **2** a field of thought considered as being complete and independent: *the universe of chemistry.* **3** *Sociology* the total population from which a sample population is drawn. ⟨Latin *universum* turned into one; *uni-* one + *versus* pp of *vertere* turn⟩

u·ni·ver·sal *adj* **1** concerning all: *Food, fire, and shelter are universal needs.* **2** existing everywhere: *The law of gravity is universal.* **3** covering a whole class of persons, things, etc.; general. **4** adaptable to different sizes, angles, kinds of work, etc. **5** constituting a complete whole: *the universal cosmos.* **6** wideranging: *universal knowledge.* **7** allowing or providing for movement in any direction: *a universal joint.* **u·ni·ver·sal·ly** *adv.* **u·ni·ver·sal·ism** *n* **1** universality of interest, application, etc. **2 U·ni·ver·sal·ism** the beliefs of Universalists. **u·ni·ver·sal·ist** *n* **1** a person whose interests, knowledge, etc. cover a very wide range. **2 U·ni·ver·sal·ist** a member of a Christian church holding the belief that all people will eventually be saved. **u·ni·ver·sal·ist** *adj.* **u·ni·ver·sal·i·ty** [,junəvər'sæləti] *n* **1** the fact of being universal. **2** something universal. **universal joint** a joint that moves in any direction. **Universal Product Code** *Computers* a barcode printed on consumer products, indicating product classification, price, etc., that can be read by an electronic scanner. *Abbrev* **UPS**

u·ni·ver·si·ty [,junə'vɜrsəti] *n* a postsecondary educational institution, for studies leading to a degree. ⟨Latin *universitas* aggregate, whole; *universus.* See UNIVERSE.⟩

un·just [ʌn'dʒʌst] *adj* not fair: *It is unjust to punish lawbreakers who are insane.* **un·just·ly** *adv.* **un·just·ness** *n.*

un·kempt [ʌn'kɛmpt] *adj* **1** not combed. **2** neglected in appearance; untidy. ⟨*un-¹* + Old English *cembed* pp of *cemban* to comb⟩

un·kind [ʌn'kaɪnd] *adj* harsh; cruel; mean. **un·kind·ness** *n.* **un·kind·ly** *adj* harsh; unfavourable. *adv* in an unkind way; harshly. **un·kind·li·ness** *n.*

un·known [ʌn'noun] *adj* not familiar; unexplored, etc.: *an unknown country.*

n **1** a person who or thing that is unknown: *The main actor in this movie is an unknown.* **2** *Mathematics* a symbol, as in an equation, for a quantity whose value is to be found. **Unknown Soldier** an unidentified soldier killed in battle, who is buried in a national monument and honoured as the representative of all unidentified war dead.

un·lace [ʌn'leis] *v* undo the laces of.

un·lash [ʌn'læʃ] *v* untie or detach (something fastened by a cord or rope).

un·latch [ʌn'lætʃ] *v* unfasten or open by lifting a latch.

un·law·ful [ʌn'lɒfəl] *adj* contrary to law; against a law; forbidden; illegal. **un·law·ful·ly** *adv.* **un·law·ful·ness** *n.*

un·lead·ed [ʌn'lɛdɪd] *adj* not containing compounds of lead; lead-free.

un·learn [ʌn'lɜrn] *v* get rid of (learned ideas, habits, or tendencies); forget.

un·leash [ʌn'liʃ] *v* **1** release from a leash: *to unleash a dog.* **2** let loose: *to unleash one's anger.*

un·leav·ened [ʌn'lɛvənd] *adj* made without yeast or any other rising agent.

un·less [ən'lɛs] *or* [ʌn'lɛs] *conj* if not (that); in any or every case except if: *We'll go unless it rains.* ⟨Middle English *on lesse* (*that*) on a less condition (than)⟩

un·let·tered [ʌn'lɛtərd] *adj* **1** not educated. **2** not able to read or write.

un·like [ʌn'ləik] *adj* **1** different: *The two problems are quite unlike.* **2** different in size or number; unequal: *unlike weights.*
prep **1** different from: *Act unlike others.* **2** uncharacteristic of: *It's unlike you to be so quiet.* **un·like·ness** *n.*

un·like·ly [ʌn'ləikli] *adj* **1** not probable: *an unlikely story. He is unlikely to win the race.* **2** not likely to succeed: *an unlikely undertaking.* **un·like·li·ness** *n.* **un·like·li·hood** *n.*

un·lim·it·ed [ʌn'lɪmətɪd] *adj* **1** without limits; boundless: *unlimited energy.* **2** not restrained; not restricted: *a government of unlimited power.* **3** vast. **un·lim·it·ed·ness** *n.*

un·list·ed [ʌn'lɪstɪd] *adj* not included in a list or reference book: *an unlisted phone number.*

un·load [ʌn'loud] *v* **1** remove (a load): *She unloaded the bales of hay.* **2** take the load from: *Help me unload the wagon.* **3** get rid of. **4** remove powder, shot, bullets, or shells from (a gun). **5** be unloaded: *The ship is unloading.* **6** *Informal* relieve oneself by expressing (one's bad feelings): *Can I unload on you for a minute?* **un·load·er** *n.*

un·lock [ʌn'lɒk] *v* **1** open the lock of; open (anything firmly closed). **2** release; let loose. **3** disclose; reveal. **4** become unlocked.

un·looked for [ʌn'lʊkt ˌfɔr] *adj* unexpected; unforeseen. This is spelled **un·looked-for** if before a noun: *unlooked-for compliments.*

un·love·ly [ʌn'lʌvli] *adj* without beauty or charm; unpleasant; disagreeable. **un·love·li·ness** *n.*

un·luck·y [ʌn'lʌki] *adj* **1** unfortunate.

2 bringing or thought to bring bad luck: *Superstitious people think that the number 13 is unlucky.* **un·luck·i·ly** *adv.* **un·luck·i·ness** *n.*

un·make [ʌn'meik] *v* **-made, -mak·ing** **1** undo; destroy; ruin. **2** deprive of rank or station. **3** reduce to an original condition.

un·man [ʌn'mæn] *v* **-manned, -man·ning** **1** deprive of the qualities of a man. **2** weaken or break down the spirit of. **3** deprive of virility or manhood; castrate.
un·man·ly *adj* **1** weak; cowardly. **2** not befitting a man; effeminate. **un·man·li·ness** *n.* **un·manned** *adj* not operated by people: *an unmanned spacecraft.*

un·man·ner·ly [ʌn'mænərli] *adj* having bad manners; discourteous. **un·man·ner·li·ness** *n.* **un·man·ner·ly** *adv.*

un·mar·ried [ʌn'mɛrid] *or* [ʌn'mærid] *adj* not married; single.

un·mask [ʌn'mæsk] *v* **1** remove a mask or disguise: *The guests unmasked at midnight.* **2** take off a mask or disguise from. **3** expose the true character of: *to unmask a hypocrite.*

un·mean·ing [ʌn'minɪŋ] *adj* without sense; without expression: *an unmeaning stare.* **un·mean·ing·ly** *adv.*

un·men·tion·a·ble [ʌn'mɛnʃənəbəl] *adj* not fit to be spoken about. **un·men·tion·a·ble·ness** *n.* **un·men·tion·a·bly** *adv.*

un·mer·ci·ful [ʌn'mɜrsəfəl] *adj* **1** cruel. **2** excessive: *I waited an unmerciful length of time.* **un·mer·ci·ful·ly** *adv.* **un·mer·ci·ful·ness** *n.*

un·mis·tak·a·ble [ˌʌnmɪ'steikəbəl] *adj* clear; plain; evident. **un·mis·tak·a·ble·ness** *n.* **un·mis·tak·a·bly** *adv.*

un·mit·i·gat·ed [ʌn'mɪtəˌgeitɪd] *adj* **1** not softened or lessened: *unmitigated harshness.* **2** absolute: *an unmitigated fraud.* **un·mit·i·gat·ed·ly** *adv.*

un·moved [ʌn'muvd] *adj* **1** firm. **2** not disturbed; emotionally unaffected.

un·muz·zle [ʌn'mʌzəl] *v* **1** take off a muzzle from (a dog, etc.). **2** make free from restraint; allow to speak or write freely.

un·nat·u·ral [ʌn'nætʃərəl] *adj* **1** not in accordance with the usual course of nature. **2** totally at variance with natural feeling or normal decency, morality, etc.; depraved; showing perversion: *unnatural cruelty.* **3** artificial or affected: *an unnatural laugh.* **un·nat·u·ral·ly** *adv.* **un·nat·u·ral·ness** *n.*

un·nec·es·sar·y [ʌn'nɛsəˌsɛri] *adj* not necessary; needless. **un·nec·es·sar·i·ly** *adv.* **un·nec·es·sar·i·ness** *n.*

un·nerve [ʌn'nɜrv] *v* deprive of firmness, courage, or composure: *The thought of having surgery unnerved me.* **un·nerv·ing** *adj.*

un·num·bered [ʌn'nʌmbərd] *adj* **1** not numbered; not counted: *The pages of the book were left unnumbered.* **2** too many to count: *There are unnumbered fish in the ocean.*

un·ob·tru·sive [ˌʌnəb'trusɪv] *adj* not noticeable or intrusive; inconspicuous. **un·ob·tru·sive·ly** *adv.* **un·ob·tru·sive·ness** *n.*

un·oc·cu·pied [ʌn'ɒkjə,paɪd] *adj* **1** not occupied; vacant: *an unoccupied parking space.* **2** not in action or use: *an unoccupied mind.*

un·or·gan·ized [ʌn'ɔrgə,naɪzd] *adj* **1** not formed into an organized or systematized whole. **2** not organized into labour unions. **3** disorganized.

un·pack [ʌn'pæk] *v* **1** take out (things packed in a box, trunk, etc.). **2** *Computers* convert compressed data into a usable form.

un·paid [ʌn'peɪd] *adj* **1** not paid: *unpaid bills.* **2** without pay: *Volunteers are unpaid workers.*

un·pal·at·a·ble [ʌn'pælətəbəl] *adj* not agreeable to the taste; distasteful; unpleasant. **un·pal·at·a·ble·ness** *n.* **un·pal·at·a·bly** *adv.*

un·par·al·leled [ʌn'pɛrə,lɛld] or [ʌn'pærə,lɛld] *adj* unequalled; matchless.

un·peo·pled [ʌn'pipəld] *adj* **1** not (yet) inhabited. **2** deprived of people.

un·pleas·ant [ʌn'plɛzənt] *adj* not pleasant; disagreeable. **un·pleas·ant·ly** *adv.* **un·pleas·ant·ness** *n* **1** the quality of being unpleasant. **2** something unpleasant. **3** a quarrel.

un·plug [ʌn'plʌg] *v* **-plugged, -plug·ging 1** open or set free (something) by removing a plug or stopper. **2** unclog. **3** disconnect (an electric light, appliance, etc.) by removing the plug from an outlet.
un·plugged *adj* **1** open; not plugged, or not plugged in. **2** of rock music, not amplified.

un·plumbed [ʌn'plʌmd] *adj* **1** not not measured; of unknown depth. **2** not fully explored: *an unplumbed area of physics.*

un·prac·tised [ʌn'præktɪst] *adj* **1** not skilled; not expert. **2** not put into practice; not used. **3** unrehearsed. Also, **un·prac·ticed.**

un·prec·e·dent·ed [ʌn'prɛsə,dɛntɪd] or [ʌn'prisə,dɛntɪd] *adj* having no precedent; never done before; never known before.

un·pre·pared [,ʌnprɪ'pɛrd] *adj* **1** not worked out ahead: *an unprepared speech.* **2** not ready: *a person unprepared to answer.*

un·pre·ten·tious [,ʌnprɪ'tɛnʃəs] *adj* modest; simple. **un·pre·ten·tious·ly** *adv.* **un·pre·ten·tious·ness** *n.*

un·prin·ci·pled [ʌn'prɪnsəpəld] *adj* lacking or resulting from a lack of good moral principles; bad.

un·print·a·ble [ʌn'prɪntəbəl] *adj* not fit to be printed.

un·pro·fes·sion·al [,ʌnprə'fɛʃənəl] *adj* **1** contrary to professional etiquette. **2** not up to professional standards; amateurish. **un·pro·fes·sion·al·ly** *adv.*

un·prof·it·a·ble [ʌn'prɒfətəbəl] *adj* producing no gain or advantage. **un·prof·it·a·ble·ness** *n.* **un·prof·it·a·bly** *adv.*

un·pro·voked [,ʌnprə'voukt] *adj* not provoked: *an unprovoked attack.*

un·qual·i·fied [ʌn'kwɒlə,faɪd] *adj* **1** not fitted. **2** not modified or restricted in any way: *unqualified praise.* **3** complete; absolute: *an unqualified failure.* **un·qual·i·fied·ly** *adv.*

un·ques·tion·a·ble [ʌn'kwɛstʃənəbəl] *adj* **1** beyond doubt; certain: *an unquestionable advantage.* **2** impeccable in quality or nature. **un·ques·tion·a·ble·ness** *n.* **un·ques·tion·a·bly** *adv.* **un·ques·tioned** *adj* not disputed.

un·qui·et [ʌn'kwaɪət] *adj* restless; uneasy. **un·qui·et** *n.* **un·qui·et·ly** *adv.* **un·qui·et·ness** *n.*

un·quote [ʌn'kwout] *v* mark the end of (a quotation) either in speech or writing, or by a gesture: *He quoted but he didn't unquote, so we couldn't tell where the quotation ended.*

un·rav·el [ʌn'rævəl] *v* **-elled** or **-eled, -el·ling** or **-el·ing 1** separate the threads of; undo: *The kitten unravelled my knitting.* **2** come apart; ravel: *My knitted gloves are unravelling at the wrist.* **3** bring or come out of a tangled state: *to unravel a mystery.* **4** make or become confused, distracted, etc.: *I've got to get out of here before my mind completely unravels.*

un·read [ʌn'rɛd] *adj* **1** not read: *an unread book.* **2 a** not having read much: *an unread person.* **b** not familiar with (used with *in*): *I'm afraid I'm unread in European politics.*

un·re·al [ʌn'ril] *adj* **1** imaginary; not real; not substantial. **2** *Slang* incredible. **un·re·al·ly** *adv.* **un·re·al·i·ty** [,ʌnri'æləti] *n* **1** lack of substance; a fanciful quality. **2** impracticality. **3** something unreal: *Unrealities, such as elves and goblins, are fun to imagine.*

un·rea·son [ʌn'rizən] *n* irrationality; action or thought that is not reasonable. **un·rea·son·a·ble** *adj* **1** not sensible; irrational: *an unreasonable fear of the dark.* **2** not moderate: *I think $190 is an unreasonable price for those shoes.* **un·rea·son·a·ble·ness** *n.* **un·rea·son·a·bly** *adv.* **un·rea·son·ing** *adj* not using reason. **un·rea·son·ing·ly** *adv.*

un·re·gen·er·ate [,ʌnrɪ'dʒɛnərɪt] *adj* stubbornly bad or wicked. **un·re·gen·er·a·cy** *n.* **un·re·gen·er·ate·ly** *adv.* **un·re·gen·er·ate·ness** *n.*

un·re·lent·ing [,ʌnrɪ'lɛntɪŋ] *adj* **1** merciless. **2** not slackening in force, effort, etc.; constant. **un·re·lent·ing·ly** *adv.* **un·re·lent·ing·ness** *n.*

un·re·mit·ting [,ʌnrɪ'mɪtɪŋ] *adj* never stopping; not slackening: *unremitting vigilance.* **un·re·mit·ting·ly** *adv.*

un·re·serve [,ʌnrɪ'zɜrv] *n* frankness; candour. **un·re·served** *adj* **1** frank; open: *an unreserved manner.* **2** not restricted or qualified: *unreserved praise.* **3** not kept for a special person or purpose: *unreserved seats.* **un·re·serv·ed·ly** [,ʌnrɪ'zɜrvɪdli] *adv.*

un·rest [ʌn'rɛst] *n* **1** lack of ease and quiet; restlessness. **2** social or political agitation or disturbance amounting almost to rebellion.

un·re·strained [,ʌnrɪ'streɪnd] *adj* **1** not constrained; spontaneous; free: *unrestrained joy.* **2** uncontrolled: *unrestrained urban sprawl.*

un·ripe [ʌn'raɪp] *adj* **1** not ripe; green. **2** of persons, plans, etc., not fully developed or grown; immature. **un·ripe·ness** *n.*

un·ri·valled or **un·ri·valed** [ʌn'raɪvəld] *adj* having no rival; without an equal.

un·roll [ʌn'roul] v **1** open or spread out (something rolled). **2** become opened or spread out. **3** unfold, esp gradually: *Our interest increased as the story unrolled.*

un·ruled [ʌn'ruld] adj **1** not under control. **2** not marked with lines: *unruled paper.*

un·ru·ly [ʌn'ruli] adj hard to rule or control: *an unruly crowd.* **un·ru·li·ness** n.

> **SYNONYMS**
> **Unruly** = not inclined to accept discipline, and suggests getting out of hand: The angry mob become unruly. **Ungovernable** = incapable of being controlled, either because never subjected to rule or because of escape from it: One of the dogs became ungovernable.

un·sad·dle [ʌn'sædəl] v take the saddle off (a horse).

un·safe [ʌn'seif] adj dangerous. **un·safe·ly** adv. **un·safe·ness** n.

un·said [ʌn'sɛd] adj not said or spoken.

un·sat·u·rat·ed [ʌn'sætʃə,reitid] adj of a solution, able to dissolve or absorb more of a substance. **un·sat·u·ra·tion** n.

un·sa·vour·y or **un·sa·vor·y** [ʌn'seivəri] adj **1** unpleasant in taste or smell. **2** morally unpleasant; offensive: *an unsavoury reputation.* **un·sa·vour·i·ly** or **un·sa·vor·i·ly** adv. **un·sa·vour·i·ness** or **un·sa·vor·i·ness** n.

un·say [ʌn'sei] v -said, -say·ing. take back something said: *What is said cannot be unsaid.*

un·scathed [ʌn'skeiðd] adj not harmed; uninjured. ⟨un- + Old Norse *skathi* injury⟩

un·schooled [ʌn'skuld] adj not learned or taught.

un·sci·en·tif·ic [,ʌnsaiən'tifik] adj **1** not in accordance with the facts or principles of science: *an unscientific notion.* **2** not acting in accordance with such facts or principles: *an unscientific farmer.* **un·sci·en·tif·i·cal·ly** adv.

un·scram·ble [ʌn'skræmbəl] v **1** reduce from confusion to order. **2** restore (a transmitted signal, etc.) to the original condition; make intelligible: *unscramble a coded message.* **un·scram·bler** n.

un·screw [ʌn'skru] v **1** take out the screw or screws from. **2** untwist. **3** become unscrewed: *This light bulb doesn't want to unscrew.*

un·scru·pu·lous [ʌn'skrupjələs] adj showing a lack of principles or conscience: *unscrupulous business practices.* **un·scru·pu·lous·ly** adv. **un·scru·pu·lous·ness** n.

> **SYNONYMS**
> **Unscrupulous** means not held back by conscience or by a sense of honour: She would stoop to any unscrupulous trick to avoid paying her bills. **Unprincipled** means being without good moral principles: Only an unprincipled person would defend that man's conduct.

un·sealed [ʌn'sild] adj not sealed; left open.

un·search·a·ble [ʌn'sɜrtʃəbəl] adj not to be searched into; that cannot be understood by searching; mysterious or profound. **un·search·a·bly** adv.

un·sea·son·a·ble [ʌn'sizənəbəl] adj **1** not suitable to the season. **2** coming at the wrong time. **un·sea·son·a·ble·ness** n. **un·sea·son·a·bly** adv.

un·seat [ʌn'sit] v **1** displace from a seat or saddle; unhorse: *The bronco unseated everyone who tried to ride it.* **2** remove from office: *Our previous MP was unseated in the last election.*

un·seem·ly [ʌn'simli] adj not suitable; improper: *unseemly laughter.* adv improperly; unsuitably. **un·seem·li·ness** n.

un·seen [ʌn'sin] adj **1** not seen: *an unseen error.* **2** not visible: *an unseen spirit.*

un·self·ish [ʌn'sɛlfɪʃ] adj considerate of others; generous: *an unselfish act.* **un·self·ish·ly** adv. **un·self·ish·ness** n.

un·set·tle [ʌn'sɛtəl] v make or become unstable; disturb or be disturbed. **un·set·tle·ment** n. **un·set·tled** adj **1** disordered. **2** not fixed or stable. **3** liable to change; uncertain: *The weather is unsettled.* **4** not adjusted or disposed of: *an unsettled bill.* **5** not decided. **6** not inhabited. **7** not having found a permanent residence. **un·set·tled·ness** n.

un·sex [ʌn'sɛks] v deprive of sexual capacity or of the attributes of one's sex.

un·shak·en [ʌn'ʃeikən] adj firm: *an unshaken belief in the faithfulness of a friend.*

un·sheathe [ʌn'ʃið] v draw (a sword, knife, etc.) from a sheath.

un·shod [ʌn'ʃɒd] adj without shoes.

un·sight·ly [ʌn'saitli] adj ugly or unpleasant to look at. **un·sight·li·ness** n.

un·skil·ful or **un·skill·ful** [ʌn'skilfəl] adj awkward; clumsy; inexpert: *This artist's unskilful work needs the tempering of time.* **un·skil·ful·ly** or **un·skill·ful·ly** adv. **un·skil·ful·ness** or **un·skill·ful·ness** n.

un·skilled adj **1** not skilled or trained: *For a person unskilled in carpentry, you certainly helped a lot.* **2** not requiring special skills or training: *unskilled labour.* **3** employed at an unskilled job: *Though they may work hard, unskilled workers usually earn less than skilled workers.*

un·snarl [ʌn'snɑrl] v untangle: *My long hair is difficult to unsnarl when it is wet after I have been simming.*

un·so·cia·ble [ʌn'souʃəbəl] adj **1** not associating easily with others: *an unsociable hermit.* **2** not conducive to, or preventing, sociability: *an unsociable atmosphere.* **un·so·cia·bil·i·ty** n. **un·so·cia·ble·ness** n. **un·so·cia·bly** adv.

un·so·phis·ti·cat·ed [,ʌnsə'fistə,keitid] adj **1** simple; natural. **2** not advanced or developed: *unsophisticated technology.* **un·so·phis·ti·cat·ed·ly** adv. **un·so·phis·ti·ca·tion** n.

un·sound [ʌn'saund] adj **1** not in good condition: *an unsound business.* **2** not based on truth or fact: *an unsound doctrine, theory, etc.* **3** not restful; disturbed: *an unsound sleep.* **un·sound·ly** adv. **un·sound·ness** n.

un·speak·a·ble [ʌn'spikəbəl] *adj* **1** that cannot be expressed in words: *unspeakable joy.* **2** so bad that it can hardly be spoken of: *That was an unspeakable thing to do!* **un·speak·a·bly** *adv.*

un·spot·ted [ʌn'spɒtɪd] *adj* without spot or stain; pure.

un·sta·ble [ʌn'steibəl] *adj* **1** not firmly fixed. **2** variable. **3** *Chemistry* **a** easily decomposed. **b** radioactive. **4** emotionally unsound. **un·sta·ble·ness** *n.* **un·sta·bly** *adv.*
unstable element a radioactive element that eventually changes into a radioactive isotope.

un·stead·y [ʌn'stedi] *adj* **1** shaky: *an unsteady voice.* **2** likely to change: *unsteady winds.* **3** not regular in habits.
v make unsteady. **un·stead·i·ly** *adv.* **un·stead·i·ness** *n.*

un·stick [ʌn'stɪk] *v* **-stuck, -stick·ing** make or become free from being stuck.
un·stuck [ʌn'stʌk] *adj* loosened or freed from being stuck. **come unstuck** become disordered: *The timetable came unstuck when she wanted to change her time slot.*

un·struc·tured [ʌn'strʌktʃərd] *adj* having no formal or rigid structure or organization: *unstructured classes.*

un·strung [ʌn'strʌŋ] *adj* upset; emotionally disturbed.

un·suc·cess·ful [ˌʌnsək'sɛsfəl] *adj* not successful. **un·suc·cess·ful·ly** *adv.*

un·suit·a·ble [ʌn'sutəbəl] *adj* not suitable; unfit. **un·suit·a·bil·i·ty** *n.* **un·suit·a·bly** *adv.*

un·sung [ʌn'sʌŋ] *adj* **1** not sung. **2** not honoured in song or poetry; unpraised.

un·sus·pect·ed [ˌʌnsə'spɛktɪd] *adj* **1** not under suspicion: *He had already committed several burglaries but was still unsuspected.* **2** not thought of or known about: *an unsuspected danger.* **un·sus·pec·ted·ly** *adv.*

un·tan·gle [ʌn'tæŋgəl] *v* **1** take the tangles out of; disentangle. **2** straighten out or clear up (anything confused or perplexing).

un·taught [ʌn'tɒt] *adj* **1** not instructed. **2** known without being taught; learned naturally. **3** of a lesson, etc., not delivered or presented: *Owing to time pressures, two units of the course remained untaught.*

un·think·a·ble [ʌn'θɪŋkəbəl] *adj* **1** that cannot be imagined: *the unthinkable vastness of the universe.* **2** out of the question: *It is unthinkable that she could be a thief.* **un·think·a·bly** *adv.*
un·think·ing *adj* **1** thoughtless; careless: *An unthinking comment can sometimes cause a lot of trouble.* **2** characterized by absence of thought: *blind, unthinking anger.* **3** not having the faculty of thought. **un·think·ing·ly** *adv.*

un·thought of [ʌn'θɒt ˌʌv] *adj* not imagined or considered. This is spelled **un·thought-of** if before a noun: *an unthought-of problem.*

un·ti·dy [ʌn'taɪdi] *adj* **1** not in order; not neat. **2** not given to neatness; slovenly:

Unlike her mother, she is a rather untidy person. **un·ti·di·ly** *adv.* **un·ti·di·ness** *n.*

un·tie [ʌn'taɪ] *v* **-tied, -ty·ing** **1** loosen; unfasten; undo: *to untie a horse.* **2** become untied: *A properly tied knot should untie easily.* **3** release: *He untied his horse.* **4** make clear; resolve.

un·til [ən'tɪl] *prep* **1** up to the time of: *It was cold until April.* **2** before (only with a negative): *She did not leave until morning.*
conj **1** up to the time when: *She waited until morning.* **2** before (only with a negative): *He did not come until the meeting was half over.* **3** to the point or stage that: *He worked until he was too tired to do more.* ⟨Middle English *untill*; Old Norse *und* up to + *till* till'⟩

un·time·ly [ʌn'taɪmli] *adj* **1** happening at a wrong time: *an untimely snowstorm.* **2** happening too soon: *an untimely death.* **un·time·li·ness** *n.*

un·tir·ing [ʌn'taɪrɪŋ] *adj* tireless; unwearied. **un·tir·ing·ly** *adv.*

un·ti·tled [ʌn'taɪtəld] *adj* **1** having no title. **2** not of titled rank.

un·to ['ʌntu] *prep* *Archaic, poetic.* **1** to: *I say unto you.* **2** till; until: *The soldier was faithful unto death.* ⟨Middle English *unto*; *un-* (see UNTIL) + *to*⟩

un·told [ʌn'tould] *adj* **1** not revealed. **2** too many to be counted; countless; immense: *untold wealth, untold stars in the sky.* **3** not permitting of being told; indescribable: *He experienced untold horrors in wartime.*

un·touch·a·ble [ʌn'tʌtʃəbəl] *adj* **1** out of reach. **2** that must not be touched. **3** beyond suspicion. **4** too disgusting to touch. **5** of or being an untouchable or untouchables.
n **1** in India, a person outside the caste system whose touch supposedly defiles others. It is now illegal in India to discriminate on the basis of caste. **2** any person rejected by his or her social group. **un·touch·a·bil·i·ty** *n.*
un·touched *adj* **1** not used, consumed, handled, etc.: *The cat left the milk untouched.* **2** not affected or moved: *The miser was untouched by the poor family's story.* **3** not dealt with: *The last topic was left untouched.*

un·tow·ard [ˌʌntə'wɔrd] *or* [ʌn'tɔrd] *adj* **1** unfavourable; unfortunate: *an untoward accident.* **2** improper: *untoward behaviour.* **un·to·ward·ly** *adv.* **un·to·ward·ness** *n.*

un·tram·melled *or* **un·tram·meled** [ʌn'træməld] *adj* not hindered; not restrained; free: *untrammelled passions.*

un·tried [ʌn'traɪd] *adj* **1** not tried; not tested. **2** not tried in a court of law.

un·true [ʌn'tru] *adj* **1** false. **2** not faithful. **3** not true to a standard or rule. **un·tru·ly** *adv.* **un·truth** *n* **1** lack of truth. **2** a lie; falsehood. **un·truth·ful** *adj* **1** contrary to the truth. **2** given to lying. **un·truth·ful·ly** *adv.* **un·truth·ful·ness** *n.*

un·tu·tored [ʌn'tjutərd] *or* [ʌn'tutərd] *adj* **1** untaught. **2** simple; natural.

un·twist [ʌn'twɪst] *v* **1** undo or loosen (something twisted). **2** become untwisted.

un·used [ʌn'juzd] *adj* **1** not being used: *an unused room.* **2** never having been used: *We'll keep the unused paper cups for our next picnic.* **unused** [ʌn'just] **to** unaccustomed to: *The actor's hands were unused to manual labour.*

un·u·su·al [ʌn'juʒʊəl] *adj* not usual; not common; not ordinary; rare. **un·u·su·al·ly** *adv.* **un·u·su·al·ness** *n.*

un·ut·ter·a·ble [ʌn'ʌtərəbəl] *adj* that cannot be expressed; unspeakable. **un·ut·ter·a·bly** *adv.*

un·veil [ʌn'veɪl] *v* **1** remove a veil or cover from: *The statue was unveiled in the town square yesterday.* **2** disclose; reveal: *to unveil a secret.* **3** take off one's veil; reveal oneself.

un·voiced [ʌn'vɔɪst] *adj* not spoken; not expressed in words.

un·war·y [ʌn'wɛri] *adj* not cautious; unguarded. **un·war·i·ly** *adv.* **un·war·i·ness** *n.*

un·whole·some [ʌn'hoʊlsəm] *adj* **1** bad for the body or the mind. **2** unhealthy. **un·whole·some·ly** *adv.* **un·whole·some·ness** *n.*

un·wieldy [ʌn'wildi] *adj* not easily managed, because of size, shape, or weight: *the unwieldy armour of knights.* **un·wield·i·ness** *n.*

un·will·ing [ʌn'wɪlɪŋ] *adj* **1** not consenting: *I begged her to go, but she was unwilling.* **2** done, said, etc. against one's will: *an unwilling smile.* **un·will·ing·ly** *adv.* **un·will·ing·ness** *n.*

un·wind [ʌn'waɪnd] *v* **-wound**, **-wind·ing** **1** take from a spool, etc. **2 a** uncoil. **b** make (something coiled) less tight. **3** become unwound. **4** *Informal* relax: *I need to unwind when I come home.* ⟨Old English *unwindan*⟩

un·wit·ting [ʌn'wɪtɪŋ] *adj* not knowing; unaware; unintentional. **un·wit·ting·ly** *adv.*

un·won·ted [ʌn'woʊntɪd] *adj* not customary; not usual. **un·wont·ed·ly** *adv.* **un·wont·ed·ness** *n.*

un·wor·thy [ʌn'wɜrði] *adj* **1** not deserving: *Such a silly story is unworthy of belief.* **2** not befitting: *a gift not unworthy of a king.* **3** base; shameful: *unworthy conduct.* **4** worthless. **un·wor·thi·ness** *n.* **un·wor·thi·ly** *adv.*

un·wound [ʌn'waʊnd] *v* pt and pp of UNWIND.

un·wrap [ʌn'ræp] *v* **-wrapped**, **-wrap·ping** **1** open. **2** become opened.

un·writ·ten [ʌn'rɪtən] *adj* **1** not written. **2** understood, but not actually expressed in writing: *unwritten laws, an unwritten contract.* **unwritten law 1** COMMON LAW. **2** a practice established by general usage.

un·yield·ing [ʌn'jildɪŋ] *adj* **1** hard; resistant to the touch: *an unyielding mattress.* **2** firm; not giving in: *an unyielding determination.*

up [ʌp] *adv* **1** in or to a higher place, rank, etc.: *to climb up.* **2** at or to a greater amount or degree: *Prices have gone up.* **3** to or at a place or condition thought of as higher: *He lives up north.* **4** in or into an erect position: *Stand up.* **5** out of bed: *I get up before dawn.* **6** at an end; over: *Time's up.* **7** *Baseball* to or at bat. **8** *Computers* into an operational state: *The system is up again.* **9 up** is also used with many verbs as an intensive, or in various idiomatic senses: *to dress up, to phone up a friend, to catch up, to put up with.*
adj **1** moving or directed upward: *an up trend.* **2** in or producing a good mood.
prep **1** upward, along, or through: *to walk up the street.* **2** at or to the higher part of: *They live further up the river.*
n Informal a period of good luck, prosperity, or happiness: *Her life is full of ups and downs.*
v **upped**, **up·ping** *Informal* raise; put, lift, or get up: *to up the price.* ⟨Old English *upp(e)*⟩
it's all up with there's no further hope for. **on the up and up** *Informal* **a** honest; legitimate. **up against** *Informal* facing (something) as a thing to be dealt with. **up against it** *Informal* in difficulties. **up and** (sometimes inflected as a verb) suddenly and inexplicably: *He up and left. She upped and hit me.* **up and around** active as usual, esp after an illness, injury, etc. **up and doing** active. **up and down** in many or different places throughout (an area): *She travelled up and down without finding a place to settle.* **up for a** in contention as a candidate or applicant for: *She is up for election to the committee.* **b** before the court on trial for (some charge). **c** in the mood for; expecting to take part in: *Are you up for a game of euchre?* **up on** well informed about: *up on the latest methods.* **up to a** busy with: *What are you up to these days?* **b** doing (something bad or secret): *She is up to some mischief.* **c** capable of: *Do you feel up to such a long hike?* **d** incumbent on as a duty or task: *It's up to the judge to decide.* **e** as many as: *You can reuse it up to five times.* **f** as far as: *up to now.* **g** dependent on the free choice or will of: *The topic of the presentation is up to you.* **up to the ears** (or **eyes**, or **neck**) **in** *Informal* thoroughly embroiled in (trouble, work, etc.). **what's up?** *Informal* **a** what's going on? **b** what's wrong?

up-and-com·ing *adj Informal* promising; : *an up-and-coming young actor.* **up-and-down** *adj* **1** fluctuating: *up-and-down sales activity.* **2** vertical. **up·beat** *n* **1** *Music* unaccented beat. **2** revival; upswing. *adj* **1** *Informal* rising; hopeful: *an upbeat market opening.* **2** *Informal* cheerful; optimistic: *an upbeat atmosphere.* **up·braid** See main entry. **up·bring·ing** *n* the care and training given to a child while growing up: *a Catholic upbringing.* **up·chuck** *v Informal* vomit. **up·com·ing** *adj* forthcoming; approaching. **up·coun·try** ['ʌp,kʌntri] *n* the interior of a country. *adv, adj* ['ʌp'kʌntri] toward or in the interior of a country. **up·date** [ʌp'deɪt] *v* bring up to date: *The files are updated once a month.* *n* ['ʌp,deɪt] **1** the act of updating: *a monthly update.* **2** an updated version: *a news update.* **up·draft** *n* an upward movement of gas, air, etc. **up·end** *v* **1** set on end; stand on end. **2** topple. **up front 1** in or to the front. **2** in or into a prominent position. **3** forthright(ly); candid(ly). **4** of payment, immediately. **up-front** *adj.* **up·grade** ['ʌp,greɪd] *n* **1** an upward slope. **2** something upgraded. **3** *Computers* an additional or replacement component that can upgrade a system. *v* [ʌp'greid] **1** improve the grade, quality, or level of. **2** *Computers* bring to a more advanced state of technology. **on the upgrade** rising. **up·grad·ing** ['ʌp,greidɪŋ] *n* a program for improvement in qualifications: *He took high school upgrading before entering university.* **up·heav·al** *n* **1** the action of lifting up part of the earth's crust: *Geologists say that the Rockies were formed by an upheaval of the earth's crust.* **2** turmoil: *The sale of the cottage caused a great upheaval.* **up·hill** *adj* **1** sloping up: *an uphill road.* **2** difficult: *an uphill fight.* *adv* up the slope of a hill: *to walk uphill.* **up·hold** *v* **-held, -hold·ing** approve; confirm; endorse: *The manager upheld my decision.* **up·hol·ster** See main entry. **up·keep** *n* **1** the act of maintaining in (a given) condition. **2** the cost of maintaining in good condition: *What's the upkeep on your car?* **up·land** *n* high land. **up·lift** [ʌp'lɪft] *v* **1** raise. **2** improve: *He had been greatly uplifted by his friends' cheerful optimism.* **up·lift** ['ʌp,lɪft] *n.* **up·lift·ing** *adj.* **up·link** *n* **1** the sending of communication from an earth station to a space station or satellite. **2** the earth station used to send such communication. **up·load** *v, n Computers* transfer (files, programs, etc.) from a smaller or remote computer to a larger or central computer via a telecommunications link. *n* the act or an instance of uploading: *The upload was successful.* Compare DOWNLOAD. **up·pi·ty** *adj Informal* arrogant. **up·pi·ti·ness** *n.* **up·raised** *adj* lifted up; stretched upward: *upraised hands.* **up·right** ['ʌpɹəit] *adj* **1** erect. **2** good; honest; righteous. *adv* straight up. *n* a vertical part or piece: *The boards for the fence were nailed across the uprights.* **on the upright** in a vertical position. **up·right·ly** *adv.* **up·right·ness** *n.* **upright piano** a piano with a vertical frame and strings. Compare GRAND PIANO. **up·ris·ing** *n* a rebellion: *The revolution began with small uprisings in several towns.* **up·riv·er** *adj, adv* to do with the upper end of a river. **up·roar** See main entry. **up·root** *v* **1** tear up by the roots: *The storm uprooted two trees.* **2** force away (from a settled position): *Famine uprooted many families from their homes* **3** eradicate or destroy completely: *By these acts, the dictator uprooted the democratic process.* **up·root·er** *n.* **ups–a–dai·sy** *interj* an expression of encouragement used especially to a small child when the child is being lifted or helped up after a fall. Also, **up·sy–dai·sy.** **up·scale** ['ʌp,skeil] *adj* of or for affluent people: *an upscale neighbourhood.* **up·set** [ʌp'sɛt] *v* **-set, -set·ting 1** tip over: *to upset a boat.* **2** disturb greatly: *Rain upset our plans. The shock upset her nerves.* **3** overthrow: *to upset a regime.* **up·set** *n, adj.* **upset price** the lowest price at which a thing will be sold. **up·shot** *n* **1** the end result: *The upshot will be that we'll have to cancel the program.* **2** the main drift or effect (of a message). **up·side** ['ʌp,said] *n* **1** the upper side. **2** a positive aspect: *There is an upside to this nasty business.* **upside down 1** having at the bottom what should be on top. **2** in or into complete

disorder: *The room was turned upside down.* **up·side–down** *adj.* **up·stage** *adv* toward or at the back of the stage of a theatre. *adj* **1** to do with the back part of the stage. **2** haughty; snobbish: *an upstage manner. v* **1** force (another actor) to turn away from the audience by moving or staying upstage of him or her. **2** steal the show from: *She upstaged the hostess by welcoming everyone herself.* **upstage** of farther back on the stage than. **up·stairs** *adv* **1** up the stairs: *I ran upstairs.* **2** on or onto an upper floor: *She lives upstairs. adj* on or of an upper floor: *an upstairs hall. n* the upper storey or storeys (with a sg verb): *The upstairs of the house is very small.* **kick someone upstairs** get rid of a person by promotion to a higher but ineffectual position. **up·stand·ing** *adj* **1** honourable: *a fine, upstanding young person.* **2** standing up; erect. **up·start** *n* a person who has suddenly risen to wealth or importance, esp one who is arrogant. **up·start** *adj.* **up·stream** *adv, adj* in the direction opposite to the current of a stream. **up·stretched** *adj* esp of the arms, stretched upward. **up·stroke** *n* a movement upward, esp of something that goes up and down repeatedly, as a pen, paintbrush, piston, etc. **up·surge** ['ʌp,sɜrdʒ] *n* sudden or rapid rise: *an upsurge in prices, an upsurge of feeling.* **up·swing** ['ʌp,swɪŋ] *n* **1** a swing upward. **2** a marked improvement. **up·take** *n* **1** the act or process of taking or drawing up. **2** a flue or ventilating shaft. **quick (or slow) on the uptake** quick (or slow) to understand: *He's a little slow on the uptake.* **up–tem·po** *Music adj, adv* in or at a fast tempo. **up·thrust** *n* an upward push. **up·tight** *adj Informal* **1** angry and defensive. **2** tense or worried: *His mother gets uptight if he's late getting home.* **3** rigid and conformist in attitude: *an uptight approach to new ideas.* **up·tight·ness** *n.* **up·time** *n* the time during which a machine, esp a computer, is available for use. Compare DOWNTIME. **up–to–date** *adj* **1** including the latest information: *an up-to-date map of the city.* **2** modern: *He's very up-to-date in his selling methods.* Adverbially, the phrase **up to date** is used: *Let me bring you up to date.* **up–to–the–min·ute** *adj* modern; latest. **up·town** *adv* **1** to or in a main part of a town or city that is away from the main business area: *to go uptown, an uptown store.* **2** in rural areas and small towns, of, to, or in the business district or central area of town. *n* **1** the better-class neighbourhoods, away from the main business area. **2** the central business area of a small town. **up·turn** *n* **1** an upward turn. **2** improvement. **up·turned** *adj* **1** turned upside down. **2** turned upward: *a mustache with upturned ends.* **up·ward** *adv* **1** to or toward a higher place. **2** uppermost: *to store glasses with the bottoms upward.* **3** toward a higher or greater rank, amount, age, etc.: *From public school upward, she studied French.* **4** above; more: *Children of five and upward must pay bus fare. adj* directed or situated in a higher place: *an upward glance.*

Also (adv), **up·wards. upward mobility** movement to a higher socioeconomic status, or opportunity for such movement. **upwardly mobile. upwards of** more than: *Repairs to the car will cost upwards of $800.* **up·well·ing** n 1 an instance of welling up, as of joy, public opinion, etc. 2 a current of warm water that rises from the depths of the sea. **up·wind** adv, adj on or toward the side from which the wind is blowing.

up·braid [ʌpˈbreɪd] v blame; reprove: *The captain upbraided his crew for falling asleep.* **up·braid·ing** n. ⟨Old English *upp* up + *bregdan* weave, snatch, move suddenly⟩

UPC UNIVERSAL PRODUCT CODE.

up·hol·ster [ʌpˈhoʊlstər] v provide (furniture) with padding, etc. and a covering of cloth, leather, vinyl, etc. **up·hol·ster·er** n. ⟨obsolete *uphold* keep in repair⟩
up·hol·ster·y n the padding, covering, etc. of an upholstered piece of furniture.

up·on [əˈpɒn] prep *Formal* on: *Her view was based upon her experience.*

up·per [ˈʌpər] adj 1 higher in position, rank, degree, etc., esp of a set of two: *the upper lip, the upper house of a parliament.* 2 farther upstream or inland: *the upper St. Lawrence.*
n 1 the part of a shoe or boot above the sole. 2 an upper berth or bunk. 3 *Slang* any drug that acts as a stimulant.
on one's uppers in financial difficulty.
Upper Canada ✲ 1 *esp Maritimes* the province of Ontario. 2 until 1841, the official name of the region west of the Ottawa River and north of Lakes Ontario and Erie, now included in the province of Ontario. **upper case** capital letters. *Abbrev* **u.c. up·per–case** adj. **Upper Chamber** or **upper chamber** UPPER HOUSE. **upper class** the social class that has the greatest power in a society, usually because of wealth or birth. **up·per–class** adj. **upper crust** *Informal* the upper classes. **up·per·cut** n *Boxing* a short swinging blow directed upward and toward the chin. **upper hand** a position of control: *During the first two periods, the visiting team had the upper hand.* **Upper House** or **upper house** in a legislature having two branches, the branch that is less representative. In some countries, the members of the Upper House are elected, as in the US; in others they are appointed, as the Senate is in Canada. **Upper Lakes** the most northerly of the Great Lakes; Lakes Superior and Huron and, sometimes, Lake Michigan. **up·per·most** adj 1 highest: *the uppermost branches of a tree.* 2 most prominent. **up·per·most** adv.

up·roar [ˈʌpˌrɔr] n 1 a noisy or violent disturbance: *There was a great uproar when the theft was discovered.* 2 a loud or confused noise; din. ⟨Dutch *oproer* insurrection⟩
up·roar·i·ous adj 1 noisy and confused. 2 loud and boisterous: *in uproarious good spirits.* 3 very funny: *an uproarious comedy.*
up·roar·i·ous·ly adv. **up·roar·i·ous·ness** n.

u·ra·ni·um [jʊˈreɪniəm] n a heavy, radioactive metallic element. *Symbol* **U** ⟨*Uranus*, the planet⟩

U·ra·nus [ˈjʊrənəs] or [juˈreɪnəs] n 1 *Greek myth* the first god of the heavens, original ruler of the world. 2 the planet seventh in order from the sun.

ur·ban [ˈɜrbən] adj to do with cities or towns: *an urban district, urban planning.* ⟨Latin *urbs* city⟩
ur·bane [ərˈbeɪn] adj courteous and refined: *an urbane manner.*
ur·bane·ly adv. **ur·ban·i·ty** [ərˈbænəti] n.
ur·ban·ite n someone who lives in a city.
ur·ban·ize v render or become urban: *to urbanize a district.* **ur·ban·i·za·tion** n. **urban renewal** the process of rehabilitating or replacing rundown buildings in a city, as well as upgrading roads, facilities, etc., esp in the downtown core. **urban sprawl** the uncontrolled spreading of new subdivisions, shopping centres, etc., into rural areas.

ur·chin [ˈɜrtʃən] n 1 a small child, esp a mischievous one. 2 a poor, ragged child. ⟨Old French *irechon*; Latin *er* hedgehog⟩

u·re·a [jʊˈriə] or [ˈjʊriə] n a soluble crystalline compound present especially in the urine of mammals. Urea is made synthetically for use in making fertilizers, adhesives, and plastics. **u·re·al** adj. ⟨Latin; Greek *ouron* urine⟩
u·re·ter [jʊˈritər] or [ˈjʊrətər] n a duct that carries urine from a kidney to the bladder or the cloaca. **u·re·thane** [ˈjʊrə,θeɪn] n a compound and ethyl derivative used especially to make polyurethane. **u·re·thra** [jʊˈriθrə] n, pl -thrae [-θri] or [-θraɪ] or -thras in most mammals, the duct by which urine is discharged and also, in males, through which semen is discharged. **u·re·thral** adj.

urge [ɜrdʒ] v 1 cause to go faster: *The rider urged his horse on with spurs.* 2 try to persuade with arguments: *They urged her to stay.*
n a driving force; impulse. ⟨Latin *urgere*⟩
ur·gent adj 1 demanding immediate action: *an urgent need.* 2 insistent: *an urgent appeal.*
ur·gen·cy n. **ur·gent·ly** adv.

u·ric See URINE.

u·rine [ˈjʊrɪn] n waste material produced by the kidneys of vertebrates. **u·ric** adj. **u·ri·nate** v. **uri·na·tion** n. ⟨Latin *urina*⟩
uric acid a crystalline compound found in small quantities in the urine of mammals and in large quantities in the urine of birds and reptiles. **u·ri·nal** n 1 an upright plumbing fixture into which to urinate, for use by men and boys. 2 a container for urine, such as for use by bedridden persons. **u·ri·nar·y** adj 1 to do with urine. 2 to do with the organs that secrete and discharge urine: *the urinary tract.* **u·ro·gen·i·tal** [,jʊroʊˈdʒɛnətəl] adj to do with the urinary and genital organs. **u·rol·o·gy** n the branch of medicine concerned with the study of the urinary tract in the female or of the urogenital tract in the male. **u·ro·log·i·cal** adj. **u·rol·o·gist** n.

URL *Computers* the address of a site on the Web. ⟨Universal Resource Locator⟩

urn [ɜrn] *n* **1** a vase having a pedestal. **2** such a vase used for holding the cremated ashes of the dead. **3** a large coffee percolator or teapot with a tap. **4** *Botany* the spore-bearing capsule of a moss. ⟨Latin *urna*⟩

u·ro·gen·i·tal, u·rol·o·gy See URINE.

ur·sine [ˈɜrsaɪn] *or* [ˈɜrsən] *adj* to do with a bear or the bear family. ⟨Latin *ursus* bear⟩

us [ʌs] *pron* **1** the objective form of **we:** *Mom went with us.* **2** *Informal* we: *It's us against them.* ⟨Old English *ūs*⟩

US or **U.S.** United States (of America).

USA or **U.S.A.** United States of America.

USB port a socket for connecting devices such as printers, scanners, and digital cameras to a computer via a cable. ⟨*Universal Serial Bus*⟩ **USB drive** or **USB key** FLASH DRIVE.

use [juz] *v* **1** put into action or service: *May I use your phone?* **2** employ or practise actively: *to use one's judgment, to use bad language.* **3** partake of, esp habitually: *to use drugs or alcohol.* **4** expend by using: *The car uses too much gas.* **5** treat: *They use their furniture very hard.* **6** exploit: *She uses people.*
n [jus] *n* **1** the act of using: *the use of tools.* **2** the state of being used: *Our phone is in constant use.* **3** benefit: *a thing of no practical use.* **4** the purpose that a thing is used for: *to find a use for something.* **5** a way of using: *a poor use of materials.* **6** the quality of serving the needs (of people): *a park for the use of all.* **7** a need or occasion to use: *She had no further use for it.* **8** the power or privilege of using: *to have the use of a boat for the summer.* **us·a·ble** or **useable** [ˈjuzəbəl] *adj.* **us·a·bil·i·ty** *n.* **us·a·bly** *adv.* **use·ful** [ˈjusfəl] *adj.* **use·ful·ly** *adv.* **use·ful·ness** *n.* ⟨Latin *usus*, pp of *uti* to use⟩
have no use for *Informal* be impatient with: *I have no use for people who expect you to guess their thoughts.* **make use of** use. **put to use** use. **used** [just] *or* [jus] **to a** accustomed to: *She is used to hardships.* **b** had as one's custom in the past: *We used to talk for hours.* **use up a** expend entirely. **b** *Informal* exhaust.
us·age [ˈjusɪdʒ] *or* [ˈjuzɪdʒ] *n* **1** a manner of using: *The car has had rough usage.* **2** a habit; custom. **3** the customary way of using words: *In Shakespeare's time "most unkindest" was accepted usage.* **used** [juzd] *adj* **1** that has belonged to another: *a used car.* **2** of a single-use item, spent or soiled by use: *Throw the used paper cups in this bag.* **use·less** [ˈjuslɪs] *adj* **1** having no use or being of no use: *She is useless in the kitchen.* **2** futile: *It was useless to complain.* **use·less·ly** *adv.* **use·less·ness** *n.* **us·er** *n* a person or thing that uses, often specifically a consumer: *a drug user.* **u·ser–friend·ly** *adj Computers* of a computer or a program, easy to understand and use.

ush·er [ˈʌʃər] *n* **1** a person who shows people to their seats in a church, theatre, etc. **2** a groom's attendant in a wedding party.
v **1** conduct; escort: *The patrons were ushered to their seats.* **2** introduce or inaugurate (used with *in*): *to usher in a new age.* ⟨Old French *uissier;* Latin *ustiarius* doorkeeper⟩

USSR or **U.S.S.R.** Union of Soviet Socialist Republics, the name of the former country that consisted of a union of fifteen republics, including Russia.

u·su·al [ˈjuʒuəl] *adj* ordinary or customary: *She didn't take her usual route home last night.* *n* **the usual** something that is customarily done, used, etc.: *She ordered the usual.* **u·su·al·ly** *adv.* **u·su·al·ness** *n.* ⟨Latin *usualis; usus* use, n; *uti* use, v⟩
as usual in the usual manner.

u·surp [juˈsɜrp] *or* [juˈzɜrp] *v* **1** seize and hold (power) by force or without right: *The king's brother tried to usurp the throne.* **2** infringe or encroach (*on*). **u·surp·er** *n.* **u·sur·pa·tion** *n.* ⟨Latin *usurpare; usu* through use + *rapere* seize⟩

u·su·ry [ˈjuʒəri] *n* the lending of money at an extremely high or unlawful rate of interest. **u·su·rer** *n.* **u·su·ri·ous** [juˈʒuriəs] *adj.* ⟨Latin *usuria; usus* use, n; *uti* use, v⟩

u·ten·sil [juˈtɛnsəl] *n* **1** a container or implement used for practical household purposes, esp in the kitchen. **2** a tool used for a special purpose. Pens are writing utensils. ⟨Latin *utensilis* that may be used; *uti* use, v⟩

u·ter·us [ˈjutərəs] *n, pl* **-ter·i** [-təˌraɪ] *or* [-təˌri] in female mammals, a muscular organ lying within the pelvic cavity, that holds and nourishes the young till birth; womb. ⟨Latin⟩
u·ter·ine [ˈjutərɪn], [-ˌraɪn], *or* [-ˌrɪn] *adj* **1** to do with the uterus. **2** having the same mother, but a different father. Uterine brothers are stepbrothers born of the same mother.

u·til·i·dor [juˈtɪləˌdɔr] *n* ❋ *North* a large insulated tube mounted above ground and housing water, steam, and sewage pipes that supply services to a settlement built on permafrost. ⟨*utili(ty)* + *(corri)dor*⟩

u·til·i·ty [juˈtɪləti] *n* **1** usefulness: *The cottage was designed more for utility than beauty.* **2** PUBLIC UTILITY. **3** the supplying of gas, water, electricity, etc. by a public utility: *They pay a lot more for utilities than we do.* **4** *Computers* a piece of system software for manipulating applications, rearranging stored data, detecting and removing viruses, etc.
adj **1** designed for usefulness rather than appearance: *utility furnishings.* **2** capable of being used in different ways: *a utility knife.* **3** designating the lowest and cheapest government grade of meat: *utility grade turkey.* ⟨Latin *utilitas; uti* use, v⟩
u·til·i·tar·i·an [juˌtɪləˈtɛriən] *adj* **1** to do with usefulness rather than beauty: *a utilitarian furniture design.* **2** to do with utilitarianism. *n* a person who believes in utilitarianism. **u·til·i·tar·i·an·ism** *n Philosophy* **1** the doctrine

that the greatest good of the greatest number should be the purpose of human conduct. **2** the belief that things are good if and only if they are useful. **3** attention to utility rather than beauty. **utility room** a room in a house or apartment where such appliances as the furnace, washing equipment, hot water tank, etc. are located. **u·ti·lize** ['juta,laɪz] *v* put to a practical use: *to utilize leftovers in cooking.* **u·ti·liz·a·ble** *adj.* **u·ti·li·za·tion** *n.* **u·ti·liz·er** *n.*

ut·most ['ʌt,moust] *adj* **1** of the greatest or highest degree, amount, or quantity: *Sleep is of the utmost importance to health.* **2** farthest or most distant: *the utmost ends of the earth.*
n **1** the most that is possible: *I enjoyed myself to the utmost.* **2** all that one can do: *She did her utmost to help him find a good job.* ⟨Old English *ūtemest; ūte* outside + *-mest* -most⟩

u·to·pi·a [ju'toupiə] *n* **1** an ideal place or state, such as the ideal commonwealth described in *Utopia* (1516) by Sir Thomas More. **2** a visionary, impractical system of political or social perfection. Compare DYSTOPIA. **u·to·pi·an** *adj, n.* ⟨Greek *ou* not + *topos* place⟩
u·to·pi·an·ism *n* **1** for the creation of a utopia.

ut·ter[1] ['ʌtər] *adj* complete; total; absolute: *utter surprise, utter darkness, an utter failure.* **ut·ter·ly** *adv.* **ut·ter·most** *adj, n* utmost. ⟨Old English *ūtera* outer⟩

ut·ter[2] ['ʌtər] *v* **1** speak; express: *the last words she uttered, to utter one's thoughts.* **2** give out as sound: *He uttered a cry of pain.* **3** *Law* pass off (forged documents, counterfeit money, etc.) as genuine. **ut·ter·a·ble** *adj.* ⟨Middle English *uttren* literally, put forth; Old English *ūtor* comparative of *ūt* out⟩
ut·ter·ance *n* **1** expression in words or sounds: *The child gave utterance to her grief.* **2** the power or a way of speaking: *defective utterance.* **3** something uttered: *Some of her famous political utterances are included in the book.* **4** *Law* the passing off of counterfeit money, forged cheques, etc.: *He was arrested for the utterance of forged cheques worth $75 000.*

U–turn ['ju ,tɜrn] *n* **1** a complete reversal of direction on a road, as, from the northbound to the southbound lane: *U-turns are illegal on some roads.* **2** *Informal* a complete reversal of tactics or policy.

UV ultraviolet.
UV index ultraviolet index, an indication of the strength of ultraviolet radiation on a given date in a given place, intended as a guide to the amount of sunshine one can absorb safely.

u·vu·la ['juvjələ] *n, pl* **-las** or **-lae** [-,li] or [-,laɪ] the small lobe of flesh hanging down from the soft palate in the back of the mouth. ⟨Latin *uvula* diminutive of *uva* orig grape⟩
u·vu·lar *adj* **1** to do with the uvula. **2** of a speech sound, produced with the uvula and the back of the tongue. The standard French pronunciation of *r* is uvular.

ux·o·ri·ous [ʌk'sɔriəs] *or* [ʌg'zɔriəs] *adj* excessively or foolishly devoted or subservient to one's wife. **ux·o·ri·ous·ly** *adv.* **ux·o·ri·ous·ness** *n.* ⟨Latin *uxor* wife⟩

Vv

v or **V** [vi] *n, pl* **v's** or **V's 1** the twenty-second letter of the English alphabet, or any speech sound represented by it. **2** the twenty-second person or thing in a series. **3** the Roman numeral for 5.

v or **v. 1** verb. **2** verse. **3** versus. **4** see (for Latin *vide*). **5** voice. **6** vector. **7** volume. **8** von (*used in names*). **9** version. **10** velocity. **11** very.

V 1 vanadium. **2** volt.

va·cant ['veikənt] *adj* **1** empty; not occupied or filled: *a vacant post, a vacant chair.* **2** having no thought or intelligence: *a vacant smile.* **3** having no expression: *a vacant face.* **4** free from work, business, etc.: *vacant time.* **5** *Law* having no tenant or claimant, nor any furniture or fixtures. **va·can·cy** *n.* **va·cant·ly** *adv.* ⟨Latin *vacare* be empty⟩

va·cate [vei'keit] *or* ['veikeit] *v* make vacant: *They will vacate the house next month.* **va·ca·tion** [vei'keiʃən] *or* [və'keiʃən] *n* a scheduled time of freedom from work or activity; holidays: *Is he taking a vacation this year? v* take or spend a vacation: *They are vacationing in the North.* **va·ca·tion·er** *n.* **va·ca·tion·less** *adj.*

vac·cine [væk'sin] *or* ['væksɪn] *n* **1** a preparation used to inoculate a person to protect him or her from a disease by causing the formation of antibodies against it: *Salk vaccine is used against polio.* **2** *Computers* a program whose purpose is to protect a computer from viruses. **vac·cin·al** *adj.* **vac·ci·nate** ['væksə,neit] *v.* **vac·ci·na·tion** *n.* ⟨Latin *virus vaccinus* virus of cowpox (*vacca* cow), the first vaccine⟩

vac·il·late ['væsə,leit] *v* **1** alternate; fluctuate; waver. **2** waver in mind: *She keeps vacillating and finds it hard to decide.* **vac·il·la·tion** *n.* ⟨Latin *vacillare*⟩

vac·u·um ['vækjum] *or* ['vækjəm] *n, pl* **vac·u·ums** or (defs 1-3) **vac·u·a** ['vækjuə] **1** an empty space utterly devoid of matter, even air. **2** an enclosed space from which almost all air, gas, etc. has been removed. **3** a void; emptiness: *His wife's death left a vacuum in his life.* **4** VACUUM CLEANER. *v* clean with a vacuum cleaner: *to vacuum a rug.* ⟨Latin *vacuum* empty⟩ **vac·u·ole** ['vækju,oul] *n* a tiny cavity in the cytoplasm of a living cell, containing fluid. **vac·u·ous** *adj* showing no thought or intelligence: *a vacuous statement.* **va·cu·i·ty** [və'kjuəti] *n.* **vac·u·ous·ly** *adv.* **vac·u·ous·ness** *n.* **vacuum bottle** (or **flask**) bottle or flask made with a vacuum between its inner and outer walls so that its contents will stay hot or cold for a long time. **vacuum cleaner** an electrical appliance for cleaning carpets, curtains, floors, etc. by suction. **vac·u·um–packed** *adj* of a container, having most of the air removed before being sealed to preserve the freshness, etc. of the contents: *Coffee is often sold in vacuum-packed cans.* **vacuum pump** a pump in which a partial vacuum is used to raise water. **vacuum tube** an electron tube with an almost perfect vacuum through which an electric current can pass freely.

va·de me·cum ['vɑdi 'meikəm] anything, esp a book a person carries about with him or her because of its usefulness. ⟨Latin = go with me⟩

vag·a·bond ['vægə,bɒnd] *n* **1** a wanderer, esp a tramp. **2** an idle person; rascal. *adj* **1** wandering; moving from place to place: *The Gypsies are traditionally a vagabond people.* **2** irresponsible. **vag·a·bond·ish** *adj.* ⟨Old French; Latin *vagabundus; vagus* rambling⟩

va·gar·y ['veigəri] *n* **1** an odd fancy; extravagant notion: *the vagaries of a dream.* **2** an odd action; caprice: *the vagaries of fashion.* ⟨probably Latin *vagari* wander⟩

va·gi·na [və'dʒainə] *n, pl* **-nas** or **-nae** [-ni] *or* [-nai] in female mammals, the passage from the uterus to the vulva or external opening. **vag·i·nal** ['vædʒənəl] *adj.* ⟨Latin = sheath⟩

va·grant ['veigrənt] *n* **1** a wanderer, often living by begging, etc. **2** *Law* a beggar, prostitute, drunkard, etc. living without lawful or visible means of support. *adj* **1** to do with a vagrant. **2** migrant. **va·gran·cy** *n.* **va·grant·ly** *adv.* ⟨perhaps Anglo-French *wacrant*⟩

vague [veig] *adj* **1** not clearly expressed or defined: *a vague statement.* **2** having no definite meaning or character: *'Nice' is a vague term.* **3** not thinking or expressing oneself clearly: *He was very vague about his plans.* **4** having no definite outline: *a vague shape in the mist.* **5** uncertain: *a vague destination, a vague rumour.* **vague·ly** *adv.* **vague·ness** *n.* ⟨Latin *vagus* wandering⟩

va·gus ['veigəs] *n, pl* **va·gi** ['veidʒai] *or* ['veidʒi] either of a pair of nerves extending from the brain to the heart, lungs, and other organs. Also, **vagus nerve.** ⟨Latin *vagus* wandering⟩

vain [vein] *adj* **1** having too much pride in one's looks, ability, etc. **2** without effect or success: *a vain attempt to pull herself out of the icy water.* **3** worthless; empty: *a vain boast.* **in vain a** without effect or success: *My shout for help was in vain.* **b** in an irreverent way (also used facetiously): *to take the Lord's name in vain. Did I hear you take my name in vain?* **vain·ly** *adv.* ⟨Old French; Latin *vanus* empty⟩ **vain·glo·ry** ['vein,glɔri] *or* [,vein'glɔri] *n* **1** boastful vanity. **2** worthless pomp or show. **vain·glo·ri·ous** *adj.* **van·i·ty** ['vænəti] *n* **1** too much pride in one's looks, ability, etc. **2** a lack of real value: *the vanity of wealth.* **3** a worthless thing or action. **4** worthless pleasure or display. **5** lack of success. **6** DRESSING TABLE. **7** a bathroom counter with a built-in sink and storage space. **vanity plate** a custom-made licence plate for a motor vehicle, sometimes bearing the owner's name or other personal code: *I saw an old rusty car that had the licence plate "Ruff."*

vanity press or **vanity publisher** a press or publisher specializing in printing and publishing books at the author's own cost.

SYNONYMS

Vain describes thinking, action, effort, etc. that fails to produce any valuable result: *The principal made another vain appeal for better equipment in the high-school laboratories.* **Futile** adds the idea of being inherently incapable of producing any result, and often suggests being useless to attempt: *Without modern antibiotics, early attempts to treat many diseases were futile.*

val·ance ['væləns] *n* **1** a decorative frame or short curtain around the top of a window, used to hide curtain fixtures, etc. **2** a short curtain hanging around the edge of a bed, dressing table, etc. ⟨probably from *Valence* town in SE France⟩

vale [veil] *n Poetic* valley. ⟨Old French *val;* Latin *vallis*⟩

val·e·dic·to·ri·an [,vælədɪk'tɔriən] *n* a student who gives the farewell address at the graduation of his or her class. ⟨Latin *valedicere* bid farewell; *vale* be well! + *dicere* say⟩

val·e·dic·to·ry [,vælə'dɪktəri] *n* a farewell address, esp at the graduation exercises of a school or college. **val·e·dic·to·ry** *adj.*

va·lence ['veiləns] *n Chemistry* the quality of an atom or radical that determines the number of other atoms or radicals with which it can combine, indicated by the number of hydrogen atoms with which it can combine or which it can displace. ⟨Latin *valere* be strong⟩

valence electron any of the orbital electrons of an atom that can be shared with or transferred to another atom. **–va·lent** *combining form* **1** having a valence of: *monovalent.* **2** having (a given number of) different valences: *monovalent, trivalent.*

val·en·tine ['vælən,taɪn] *n* **1** a greeting card or small gift sent or given on the feast day of Saint Valentine, February 14. **2** a sweetheart, esp one chosen on this day. **Valentine's Day** in full, **Saint Valentine's Day** February 14.

va·le·ri·an [və'lɛriən] *or* [və'liriən] *n* any of a genus of herbs, esp the common valerian having clusters of small, very fragrant flowers and a strong-smelling root. ⟨Latin *Valerius* a Roman gens name⟩

val·et [væ'lei] *or* ['vælei] *n* **1** a male servant who takes care of a man's clothes, helps him dress, etc. **2** an employee of a hotel, etc. who cleans or presses clothes. *adj* designating any of various services, as in a hotel for cleaning or pressing clothes, or for parking, etc., at restaurants. *v* serve as a valet. ⟨French; Old French *vaslet* orig young man⟩

val·iant ['væljənt] *adj* courageous and determined: *a valiant soldier, a valiant deed.* **val·iance** or **val·iant·ness** *n.* **val·iant·ly** *adv.* ⟨Old French *vaillant* ppr of *valoir* be strong, Latin *valere*⟩

val·id ['vælɪd] *adj* **1** supported by facts; true: *a valid argument.* **2** legally binding: *A contract made by a minor is not valid.* **3** effective: *a valid approach to a problem.* **va·lid·i·ty** *n.* **val·id·ly** *adv.* ⟨Latin *validus* strong⟩

val·i·date *v* **1** declare legally binding: *to validate election results.* **2** support by facts or authority: *The results of the experiments validated their hypothesis.* **val·i·da·tion** *n.*

va·lise [və'lis] *or* [və'liz] *n* a travelling bag to hold clothes, etc. ⟨French⟩

Va·lium ['væliəm] *n Trademark* a tranquilizer and relaxant drug. **take a valium** calm down (disparaging).

val·ley ['væli] *n, pl* **-leys** **1** an area of low land between hills or mountains. **2** a wide region drained by a great river system: *the Ottawa valley.* **3** any hollow or structure like a valley. ⟨Old French *valee; val* vale; Latin *vallis*⟩

val·our or **val·or** ['vælər] *n* great bravery, esp in battle: *The Victoria Cross, the highest decoration given for bravery, is inscribed simply 'For Valour'.* **val·or·ous** *adj.* ⟨Latin *valor* strength; *valere* be strong⟩

val·ue ['vælju] *n* **1** worth; importance: *the value of education.* **2** the proper price: *The antique plate was insured for much less than its value.* **3** a proper equivalent in return for payment: *Shop here for value.* **4** the current market price: *The value of a house varies greatly over the years.* **5** the power to buy things: *The value of the dollar dropped.* **6** the meaning; effect; force: *the value of a symbol.* **7** a number represented by a symbol: *If x is 3, find the value of y.* **8 values,** *pl* the established ideals of life. **9** *Music* the relative length of a tone or silence indicated by a note or rest. **10** bargain: *Snap up these values!* *v* **1** estimate the value of. **2** think highly of: *to value someone's judgment.* **3** ascribe a certain relative worth to (something): *When it comes to footwear, she values comfort over style.* **val·ue·less** *adj.* ⟨Old French *valu* pp of *valoir* be worth; Latin *valere*⟩

val·u·a·ble ['væljəbəl] *adj* **1** being worth something. **2** having great value; costly. **3** of great use or benefit; very worthwhile. *n* Usually, **valuables** *pl* articles of value: *She keeps her jewellery and other valuables in a safe.* **val·u·a·bly** *adv.* **val·u·a·tion** [,vælju'eiʃən] *n* **1** the process of estimating the value of something. **2** the value assigned: *The valuation of the necklace was $10 000.* **val·u·a·tion·al** *adj.* **val·u·a·tion·al·ly** *adv.*

value judgment or **judgement** a subjective judgment of the excellence, desirability, etc. of an action, person, program, etc.

valve [vælv] *n* **1** a movable part that controls the flow of a liquid, gas, etc. by opening and closing a passage. **2** *Anatomy* a flaplike structure that works as in def. 1. **3** *Zoology* one of the two halves of the shell of an oyster, clam, etc. **4** *Botany* one of the sections formed when a seed vessel bursts open. **5** *Music* a device in certain wind instruments for changing the pitch by changing the direction and length of the column of air.

valve·less *adj.* **valve·like** *adj.* ⟨Latin *valva* one of a pair of folding doors⟩

val·vu·lar *adj* to do with a valve, esp of the heart: *a valvular disorder.*

va·moose [væ'mus] *v Slang* go away quickly. ⟨Spanish *vamos* let us go⟩

vamp[1] [væmp] *n* **1** the upper front part of a shoe or boot **2** a piece added to an old thing to make it look new. **3** *Music* an improvised musical accompaniment, introduction, etc.
v **1** furnish or repair with a new vamp. **2** patch up; make (an old thing) look new (usually with *up*). **3** invent, esp in order to deceive (often with *up*): *He vamped up a story about needing the money to help out a friend.* **4** *Music* improvise (an accompaniment, introduction, etc.): *'Vamp till ready' is an instruction often given to accompanists.* **vamp·er** *n* ⟨Old French *avanpie* forepart of the foot; *avant* before + *pie* foot⟩

vamp[2] [væmp] *Slang n* a woman who seduces and exploits men.
v act as a vamp; use wiles and charm on: *to vamp an unsuspecting man.* ⟨*vampire*⟩

vam·pire ['væmpaɪr] *n* **1** an imaginary creature believed to be a corpse that comes back to life at night and sucks the blood of people while they sleep. **2** a person who ruthlessly takes advantage of others. **3** any of various bats that live by sucking the blood of vertebrates. ⟨Hungarian *vampir*⟩
vam·pir·ism ['væmpə,rɪzəm] *n* belief in the existence of VAMPIRES (def. 1).

van[1] [væn] *n* the front part of an army, fleet, or other advancing group, social or political movement, etc.; vanguard: *The magazine tries to be in the van of current fashion.* ⟨*vanguard*⟩

van[2] [væn] *n* **1** a large, enclosed motor truck or trailer used for moving furniture, etc. **2** a small, buslike vehicle which can be used as a camper, for delivering goods to customers, etc. ⟨*caravan*⟩

va·na·di·um [və'neɪdiəm] *n* a rare metallic element used in making certain kinds of steel. *Symbol* **V**. **van·a·dous** ['vænədəs] *adj.* ⟨Old Norse *Vanadis* name for Freya, goddess of love and beauty⟩

van·dal ['vændəl] *n* a person who willfully destroys or damages things, esp beautiful or valuable ones. **van·dal·ism** *n*. **van·dal·ize** *v*. ⟨Latin *Vandalus*, a member of a Germanic people who sacked Rome.⟩

vane [veɪn] *n* **1** WEATHER VANE. **2** a blade or similar part on an axis, wheel, etc., so as to be turned by a current of air or liquid or to produce a current when turned. **3** any projecting plane on the outside of a rocket. **4** the flat, soft part of a feather. ⟨Old English *fana* banner⟩

van·guard ['væn,gɑrd] *or* ['væŋ,gɑrd] *n* **1** a body of soldiers marching ahead of the main part of an army. **2** the leading position; VAN[1]. **3** the leaders of a movement, esp persons who work with new ideas. ⟨Old French *avantgarde*; *avant* before + *garde* guard⟩

va·nil·la [və'nɪlə] *n* a food flavouring made from vanilla beans. **va·nil·la** *adj.* ⟨Spanish *vainilla* literally, little pod⟩
vanilla bean the long, beanlike fruit of a genus of tropical American orchids.

van·ish ['vænɪʃ] *v* **1** disappear: *The sun vanished behind a cloud.* **2** cease to be: *Dinosaurs have vanished from the earth.* **van·ish·er** *n*. ⟨Old French *esvanir*; Latin *evanescere*. See EVANESCE.⟩
vanishing point the point toward which receding parallel lines seem to converge.

van·i·ty See VAIN.

van·quish ['væŋkwɪʃ] *v* conquer; defeat. **van·quish·a·ble** *adj*. **van·quish·er** *n*. ⟨Old French *vainquir*; Latin *vincere* conquer⟩

van·tage ['væntɪdʒ] *n* advantage. ⟨*advantage*⟩
vantage point **1** a superior position from which a person can see. **2** a favourable condition that gives a person an advantage.

vap·id ['væpɪd] *adj* without much life or flavour; flat; dull. **vap·id·ly** *adv*. **va·pid·i·ty** *n*. ⟨Latin *vapidus*⟩

va·pour *or* **va·por** ['veɪpər] *n* **1** moisture in the air that can be seen; fog; mist. **2** *Physics* **a** a gas formed by heating a substance that is usually a liquid or a solid. **b** a gas below its critical point or below its boiling point. **3** something without substance; empty fancy. **4 the vapours** *Archaic* low spirits. **va·por·iz·a·ble** *adj*. **va·por·i·za·tion** *n*. **va·por·ize** *v*. **va·por·ous** *adj*. ⟨Latin *vapor*⟩
va·por·iz·er *n* a device for converting liquid to vapour, as a perfume atomizer. **vapour trail** *or* **vapor trail** a white trail of water droplets or ice crystals, sometimes seen in the wake of an aircraft flying at high altitudes, caused by the condensation of moisture in the atmosphere or of exhaust gases from the aircraft.

variable, variation, various, etc. See VARY.

var·i·cose ['vɛrə,kous] *or* ['værə,kous] *adj* swollen or enlarged: *varicose veins.* ⟨Latin *varicosus; varix* dilated vein⟩

var·let ['vɑrlɪt] *n* **1** *Archaic* a low fellow; rascal. **2** formerly, an attendant, specifically the page serving a knight. ⟨Old French variant of *vaslet* orig young man; Celtic⟩

var·mint ['vɑrmənt] *n Informal, dialect* **1** vermin. **2** an objectionable animal or person. ⟨*vermin*⟩

var·nish ['vɑrnɪʃ] *n* a liquid that gives a smooth, glossy appearance to wood, metal, etc., made from resin dissolved in oil or turpentine. **var·nish** *v*. **var·nish·er** *n*. ⟨Old French *vernis*; perhaps Greek *Berenikē* ancient city in Libya⟩

var·si·ty ['vɑrsəti] *n Informal* university. ⟨clipping from *university*⟩

var·y ['vɛri] *v* **1** change: *The driver can vary the speed of an automobile.* **2** be or make different from each other: *The stars vary in brightness.* **3** give variety to: *to vary one's TV viewing.* **4** deviate; depart (*from*): *The report varies from the first draft only in minor details.* **5** *Mathematics, physics* undergo a change in value according to some law: *Pressure varies inversely with volume.* **6** *Biology* exhibit or be subject to variation, as by natural or artificial selection. **var·y·ing** *adj.* ⟨Latin *variare; varius* various⟩

var·i·a·ble *adj* **1** changeable: *variable winds.* **2** adjustable: *This curtain rod is of variable length.* **3** *Biology* deviating from the normal species, type, etc. **4** likely to increase or decrease in size, degree, etc.: *a variable ratio.* *n* **1** a thing, quality, or quantity that varies: *Temperature and rainfall are variables.* **2** *Mathematics, statistics, computers* a quantity or function that may assume any value in a set of related values. **var·i·a·bil·i·ty** *n.*

var·i·a·bly *adv.* **var·i·ance** *n* **1** disagreement; dispute: *She had had a slight variance with her brother over the matter.* **2** *Law* a discrepancy between two legal documents. **3** a varying or a tendency to vary. **4** *Statistics* the square of the standard deviation. **5** official permission to do something forbidden by regulations, esp zoning bylaws. **at variance a** in disagreement: *Her actions are at variance with her promises.* **b** in a state of discord: *at variance with the neighbours.* **var·i·ant** *adj* showing disagreement or variety: *a variant pronunciation of a word.* *n* **1** something that is different from a standard or norm: *She showed us two variants of the original design.* **2** one of different versions of the same thing, esp forms, pronunciations, or spellings of one word: *The spellings* colour *and* color *are variants.* **var·i·a·tion** *n* **1** a change in condition, degree, etc. **2** the amount of change. **3** a changed form. **4** *Music* a changing of a tune or theme. **5** *Biology* an animal or plant showing deviation from type. **var·i·col·oured** or **var·i·col·ored** *adj* having various colours. **var·ied** *adj* **1** having variety: *a varied assortment.* **2** changed. **var·ied·ly** *adj.* **var·i·e·gat·ed** ['vɛrɪˌgeɪtɪd] *or* ['vɛriə-] *adj* **1** marked with different colours: *variegated pansies.* **2** having variety. **var·i·e·ga·tion** *n.* **va·ri·e·ty** [vəˈraɪəti] *n* **1** lack of sameness; variation. **2** a number of different kinds: *The store has a great variety of toys.* **3** a kind; sort: *Which variety do you prefer?* **variety show** an entertainment in a theatre, on television, etc., made up of acts such as songs, dances, and comic skits. **variety store** a store selling a large variety of different things, esp small, inexpensive items, and often basic groceries and non-prescription drugs. **var·i·ous** ['vɛriəs] *adj* **1** differing from one another: *various opinions.* **2** several different (members of some category): *We have looked at various houses and have decided to buy this one.* **3** varied; many-sided: *lives made various by learning.* **var·i·ous·ly** *adv* in various ways or at various times: *She has been variously involved in editing, proofreading, and research.*

vas [væs] *n, pl* **va·sa** ['veisə] *Anatomy* a vessel or duct. **va·sal** ['veisəl] *adj.* ⟨Latin = vessel⟩ **vas·cu·lar** *adj* to do with vessels that carry blood, sap, etc.: *vascular tissue.* **vas def·er·ens** ['dɛfərənz] *or* ['dɛfəˌrɛnz] *pl* **va·sa def·er·en·ti·a**

[ˌdɛfəˈrɛnʃiə] especially in higher vertebrates, the duct that carries sperm from the testicles to the penis. **vas·ec·to·my** [vəˈsɛktəmi] *n* the surgical removal of part or all of the VAS DEFERENS, esp as a method of contraception. **vas·o·con·strict·or** [ˌvæsou-] *or* [ˌveizou-] *adj* that causes constriction of the blood vessels. **vas·o·con·stric·tion** *n.* **vas·o·di·lat·or** *adj* that causes dilation of the blood vessels. **vas·o·di·la·tion** *n.*

vase [veiz] *n* an open container used for ornament or for holding flowers. **vase·like** *adj.* ⟨French; Latin *vas* vessel⟩

Vas·e·line [ˌvæsəˈlin] *or* ['væsəˌlin] *n Trademark* a brand of petroleum jelly. ⟨German *Wasser* water + Greek *elaion* oil⟩

vas·sal ['væsəl] *n* **1** in feudal times, a person who held land from a lord or superior, to whom in return he gave help in war or some other service. **2** a person in a subordinate position; a servant, etc. ⟨Latin *vassallus*⟩

vast [væst] *adj* extremely great; immense: *a vast amount of money, a vast desert.* **vast·ly** *adv.* **vast·ness** *n.* ⟨Latin *vastus*⟩

vat [væt] *n* a large container for liquids; tank: *a vat of dye.* ⟨Old English *fæt*⟩

vat·ic ['vætɪk] *adj* to do with a prophet; prophetic. ⟨Latin *vates* prophet⟩ **Vat·i·can** *n* **1** in Vatican City, the buildings of the Roman Catholic Church and the palace of the Pope. **2** the office or authority of the Pope. **Vatican City** an independent papal state within the city of Rome.

vaude·ville ['vɒdˌvɪl] *or* ['vɒdəˌvɪl] *n* **1** a type of entertainment consisting of a variety of acts, such as singing, dancing, juggling, and short plays. **2** a light, comic stage play with songs interspersed. **vaude·vil·li·an** [-ˈvɪliən] *n.* ⟨French; *Vau de Vire* valley in Normandy; for songs composed there by O. Basselin, 15c poet⟩

vault¹ [vɒlt] *n* **1** an arched roof or ceiling. **2** something like an arched roof. **The vault of heaven** means the sky. **3** an underground cellar. **4** a place, esp in a bank, for storing valuable things and keeping them safe. **5** a burial chamber.

v make in the form of a vault: *a vaulted roof.* **vault·ed** *adj.* **vault·like** *adj.* ⟨Old French *voute;* Latin *voluta* pp of *volvere* roll⟩

vault² [vɒlt] *v* **1** jump by resting on one or both hands or by using a pole: *He vaulted the fence.* **2** *Gymnastics* leap or spring over a pommel or vaulting horse, usually using the hands to push off. **3** advance as if by a leap: *She vaulted to the top of her profession before she was 25.* **vault** *n.* **vault·er** *n.* ⟨Old French *volter;* Latin *volvitare* frequentative of *volvere* roll⟩

vaunt [vɒnt] *n* boast (about). **vaunt·ing** *adj.* ⟨French *vanter;* Latin *vanitare; vanus* vain⟩

VCR VIDEO CASSETTE RECORDER.

VDU *Computers* VISUAL DISPLAY UNIT.

veal [vil] *n* the flesh of a calf, used for food. ⟨Old French *veel;* Latin *vitulus* calf⟩

vec·tor ['vɛktər] *n* **1** *Mathematics* **a** a quantity involving direction as well as magnitude.

Compare SCALAR. **b** a line representing both the direction and magnitude of some force, etc. **2** an agent, esp an insect, that transmits a disease-producing micro-organism from one host to another. **3** *Molecular biology* a micro-organism used to carry a cloned DNA segment. **4** a direction to be followed by an aircraft; compass heading. **vec·to·ri·al** *adj.* **vec·to·ri·al·ly** *adv.* ⟨Latin = carrier; *vectum* pp of *vehere* carry⟩
vector analysis the branch of calculus dealing with vectors.

Ve·da ['veidə] *or* ['vidə] *n* any or all of the four collections of Hindu sacred writings. **Ve·da·ic** [vɪ'deiɪk] *adj.* ⟨Sanskrit = knowledge⟩ **Ve·dic** *adj* to do with the Vedas. *n* the form of Sanskrit in which the Vedas are written.

vee·jay ['viˌjei] *Informal* VIDEO JOCKEY. ⟨the initials *VJ*⟩

veer [vɪr] *v* change in direction, esp abruptly: *The wind veered to the south. The talk veered to ghosts.* **veer** *n.* ⟨French *virer*⟩

veg [vɛdʒ] *v Informal* VEGETATE (often with *out*).

veg·an ['vɛdʒən] *or* ['vigən] *n* a vegetarian who eats no flesh foods or animal products, such as eggs or milk.

veg·e·ta·ble ['vɛdʒtəbəl] *or* ['vɛdʒətəbəl] *n* **1** a part of a plant used for food usually as part of a main dish. **2** *Offensive* a person who cannot physically and mentally function due to an illness or injury. **veg·e·ta·ble** *adj.* ⟨Old French *vegetable*; Latin *vegetus* vigorous⟩
vegetable marrow any of several varieties of summer squash. **veg·e·tar·i·an** [ˌvɛdʒɜ-] *n* a person who eats no meat or fish and, sometimes, no animal products. See also VEGAN. **veg·e·tar·i·an** *adj.* **veg·e·tar·i·an·ism** *n.* **veg·e·tate** *v* **1** lead a dull, passive existence. **2** be temporarily passive, esp as a rest from too much activity or concentration. **veg·e·ta·tion** *n* **1** plant life; growing plants: *There is not much vegetation in deserts.* **2** the process of vegetating. **veg·e·ta·tion·al** *adj.* **veg·e·ta·tive** *adj* **1** of plants or plant life. **2** *Botany* concerned with growth and development rather than reproduction: *vegetative root cells.* **3** to do with vegetablelike involuntary functions of the body: *the vegetative processes of the body, such as growth and repair.* **4** having very little action, thought, or feeling. **veg·e·ta·tive·ly** *adv.* **veg·e·ta·tive·ness** *n.* **veg·gie** ['vɛdʒi] *n Informal* a vegetable (often in pl).

ve·he·ment ['viəmənt] *adj* intense or passionate: *a vehement denial, vehement patriotism.* **ve·he·mence** *n.* **ve·he·ment·ly** *adv.* ⟨Latin *vehere* carry⟩

ve·hi·cle ['viəkəl] *n* **1** a carriage, cart, bicycle, automobile, sled, or any other conveyance used on land. **2** any form of conveyance or transportation: *a space vehicle.* **3** a means by which something is communicated, done, etc.: *Language is the vehicle of thought.* **ve·hic·u·lar** [vɪ'hɪkjələr] *adj.* ⟨Latin *vehiculum*; *vehere* carry⟩

veil [veil] *n* **1** a piece of cloth worn by women so as to fall over the head, shoulders and, sometimes, the face. **2** anything that covers or hides: *A veil of clouds hid the sun.* *v* **1** cover with a veil: *In some places, Muslim women still veil their faces before going out in public.* **2** cover, screen, or hide: *Fog veiled the shore. Their plans were veiled in secrecy.* **veil·like** *adj.* ⟨Latin *velum* covering⟩
take the veil become a nun.
veiled *adj* **1** covered with a veil. **2** indirectly expressed: *veiled threats.* **3** concealed.

vein [vein] *n* **1** one of the tubes that carry blood to the heart from all parts of the body. **2** a rib of an insect's wing. **3** one of the bundles of tissue forming the principal framework of a leaf. **4** a distinct mass of mineral or ore occurring in rock: *a vein of copper.* **5** any streak of a different colour in wood, marble, etc. **6** a strain of some quality in character, conduct, writing, etc.: *He has a vein of cruelty.* **7** a course of thought, feeling, or action: *If you continue to think in this vein you will just discourage yourself.* *v* cover or mark with veins or veinlike lines. **vein·less** *adj.* **vein·like** *adj.* **vein·y** *adj.* ⟨Latin *vena*⟩
veined *adj* having veinlike markings: *veined marble.* **vein·let** or **veinule** [-jul] *n* a small vein. **ve·na·tion** [vi'neiʃən] *or* [və'neiʃən] *n* the arrangement of veins in a leaf or in an insect's wing.

Vel·cro ['vɛlkrou] *n Trademark* a type of fastener used for clothing, etc., consisting of two strips, one covered with tiny hooklike filaments and the other with loops. ⟨French *vel(ours)* velvet + *cro(ché)* hooked⟩

veld or **veldt** [vɛlt] *or* [fɛlt] *n* in South Africa, open country having grass or bushes but few trees. ⟨Afrikaans *veld* field; Dutch *veld*⟩

vel·lum ['vɛləm] *n* **1** the finest kind of parchment, orig made from calfskin. **2** writing paper made to imitate vellum. **vel·lum** *adj.* ⟨Old French *velin*; *veel* calf. See VEAL.⟩

ve·loc·i·ty [və'lɒsəti] *n* **1** speed: *to fly with the velocity of a bird.* **2** the rate of motion in a particular direction: *The velocity of light is about 300 000 km/s.* ⟨Latin *velocis* swift⟩
ve·loc·i·pede [və'lɒsəˌpid] *n* an early bicycle or tricycle. **ve·lo·drome** ['vɛləˌdroum] *or* ['vilaˌdroum] *n* a building having a track for bicycle racing.

ve·lour or **ve·lours** [və'lur] *n, pl* **velours** any of various fabrics resembling velvet. ⟨French *velours* velvet; Latin *villus* shaggy hair⟩

ve·lou·té [vəlu'tei] *n* a rich white sauce made from stock thickened with flour and, often, egg yolk and butter. ⟨French = velvety⟩

vel·vet ['vɛlvət] *n* **1** cloth having a thick, short, cut pile that makes it smooth and soft to the touch. **2** something suggesting velvet, esp in softness or smoothness. **3** the soft, furry skin that covers the growing antlers of a deer. **4** *Slang* clear profit or gain. **vel·vet** *adj.* ⟨Latin *velvetum*; *villus* tuft of hair⟩

vel·vet·een [ˌvɛlvə'tin] *or* ['vɛlvə,tin] *n* cloth having a pile similar to velvet. **vel·vet·y** *adj* **1** smooth and soft like velvet. **2** of liquor, mellow; smooth in flavour.

ve·nal ['vinəl] *adj* **1** open to bribes; corrupt: *venal judges.* **2** influenced or obtained by bribery: *venal conduct.* **ve·nal·i·ty** *n.* **ve·nal·ly** *adv.* ⟨Latin *venum* sale⟩

vend [vɛnd] *v* sell (goods). ⟨Latin *vendere; venum dare* offer for sale⟩
vend·ee [vɛn'di] *n* a person to whom a thing is sold. **vending machine** a coin-operated machine from which one may obtain coffee, candy, etc. **ven·dor** or **ven·der** *n* a person who sells something.

ven·det·ta [vɛn'dɛtə] *n* **1** a feud in which the relatives of a person who has been wronged try to take vengeance on the wrongdoer or on his or her relatives. **2** any bitter, prolonged quarrel or rivalry: *There has been a vendetta between the two newspapers for years.* **ven·det·tist** *n.* ⟨Italian; Latin *vindicta* revenge; *vindex* protector, avenger⟩

ve·neer [və'nir] *n* **1** a thin layer of wood or other material covering a cheaper grade of wood, fibreboard, etc.: *a desk made of pine with a walnut veneer, a brick veneer.* **2** surface appearance: *a veneer of honesty.* **ve·neer** *v.* ⟨German *furnieren;* French *fournir* furnish⟩

ven·er·ate ['vɛnə,reit] *v* regard with deep respect: *He venerates his mother's memory.* **ven·er·a·tion** *n.* ⟨Latin *venerari; Venus* orig love⟩
ven·er·a·ble *adj* **1** deserving respect because of age, character, or associations: *a venerable matriarch.* **2** *Roman Catholic Church* a title given to a deceased person who has not yet become beatified or canonized. **ven·er·a·bil·i·ty** *n.* **ven·er·a·bly** *adv.*

ve·ne·re·al [və'niriəl] *adj* **1** to do with sexual intercourse. **2** arousing sexual desire. **3** to do with diseases communicated by sexual intercourse. ⟨Latin *venereus; Venus* orig love⟩
venereal disease a disease transmitted only or mainly by sexual intercourse.

Venetian blind a window blind consisting of horizontal slats that can be set at different angles to vary the amount of light let in. Also, **venetian blind.** ⟨Latin *Venetia* Venice⟩

venge·ance ['vɛndʒəns] *n* the inflicting of injury in retaliation for a wrong or injury: *to take vengeance on an enemy.* ⟨Old French *vengier* take revenge, Latin *vindex* avenger⟩
with a vengeance with great intensity: *It was raining with a vengeance.*
venge·ful *adj* **1** inflicting vengeance; serving as an instrument of vengeance. **2** seeking vengeance; vindictive: *vengeful enemies.* **3** feeling a strong desire for vengeance. **venge·ful·ly** *adv.* **venge·ful·ness** *n.*

ve·ni·al ['viniəl] *adj* of shortcomings or misdeeds, that can be excused or overlooked; minor: *venial faults.* **ve·ni·al·ly** *adv.* **ve·ni·al·i·ty** *n.* ⟨Latin *venia* forgiveness⟩
venial sin *Theology* a minor offence, or any offence committed without knowledge and consent and so does not deprive the soul of divine grace. Compare MORTAL SIN.

ven·i·son ['vɛnəsən] *or* ['vɛnəzən] *n* the flesh of a deer, used for food; deer meat. ⟨Old French; Latin *venatio* hunting; *venari* hunt⟩
venison bird ✱ CANADA JAY.

ven·om ['vɛnəm] *n* **1** the poison produced by some snakes, spiders, etc. and introduced mainly by a bite or sting. **2** spite; malice: *There was venom in her voice.* **ven·om·less** *adj.* **ven·om·ous** *adj.* **ven·om·ous·ly** *adv.* **ven·om·ous·ness** *n.* ⟨Old French *venin;* Latin *venenum* poison⟩

vent¹ [vɛnt] *n* **1** an opening, esp one serving as an outlet. **2** an outlet; way out: *His great energy found vent in hard work.*
v **1** let out; express freely: *Don't vent your anger on the dog.* **2** make a vent in or for. ⟨Middle French *vent* wind, Latin *ventus*⟩
ven·ti·late ['vɛntə,leit] *v* **1** change or freshen the air in: *to ventilate a room by opening windows.* **2** purify by introducing oxygen: *The lungs ventilate the blood.* **3** make known publicly: *to ventilate a grievance.* **4** furnish with a vent or opening for the escape of air, gas, etc. **ven·ti·la·tion** *n.* **ven·ti·la·tor** *n* any apparatus or means for changing or improving the air in an enclosed space.

vent² [vɛnt] *n* a slit made in a garment for ease of fit, esp in a coat or jacket. ⟨Middle French *fente* slit; Latin *findere* split⟩

ven·tral ['vɛntrəl] *adj* **1** *Anatomy* to do with the belly. **2** *Zoology* to do with the part opposite the back: *a ventral fin.* **3** *Botany* to do with the inner or lower surface of a structure. **ven·tral·ly** *adv.* ⟨Latin *venter* belly⟩

ven·tri·cle ['vɛntrəkəl] *n* **1** either of the two lower chambers of the heart which force blood into the arteries. **2** any of the series of four communicating cavities in the brain, which connect with the spinal cord. **ven·tric·u·lar** *adj.* ⟨Latin *ventriculus* diminutive of *venter* belly⟩

ven·tril·o·quism [vɛn'trɪlə,kwɪzəm] *n* the art of speaking without moving the lips so that the voice may seems to come from some source other than the speaker. Also, **ven·tril·o·quy. ven·tril·o·quist** *n.* ⟨Latin *venter* belly + *loqui* speak⟩

ven·ture ['vɛntʃər] *n* **1** a risky or daring undertaking: *Her courage was equal to any venture.* **2** a speculation to make money: *A lucky venture in oil stock made his fortune.*
v **1** expose to risk of danger or loss: *People venture their lives in war.* **2** dare (*to*): *No one ventured to interrupt.* **3** dare to go: *He ventured out on the thin ice.* **4** utter or offer at the risk of a negative reaction: *She ventured a critique of the newly drafted policy.* ⟨*aventure* earlier form of *adventure*⟩
nothing ventured, nothing gained profit is forfeited by overcautiousness.
venture capital funds invested in an unproven, but potentially highly profitable, business undertaking. **ven·ture·some** *adj* **1** inclined to take risks: *a venturesome explorer.*

2 hazardous; risky: *A trip to the moon is a venturesome journey.* **ven·ture·some·ly** *adv.* **ven·ture·some·ness** *n.*

ven·ue ['vɛnju] *n* **1** *Law* **a** the place or neighbourhood of a crime or cause of action. **b** the place where the jury is gathered and the case tried. **2** the scene or setting of a real or fictional action or event. ⟨Old French *venue* coming; *venir* come, Latin *venire*⟩

Ve·nus ['vinəs] *n* **1** *Roman myth* goddess of love and beauty, corresponding to the Greek goddess Aphrodite. **2** any beautiful woman. **3** the planet second in order from the sun. **Ve·nu·sian** [və'nuʒən] *or* [-'nuʃən] *adj, n.*

ve·ra·cious [və'reɪʃəs] *adj* **1** of a person, truthful. **2** accurate: *a veracious account.* **ve·ra·cious·ly** *adv.* **ve·rac·i·ty** [və'ræsəti] *n.* ⟨Latin *veracis; verus* true⟩

ve·ran·da or **ve·ran·dah** [və'rændə] *n* a large covered porch along one or more sides of a house. ⟨Hindi; Portuguese *varanda* railing⟩

verb [vɜrb] *n* a word that expresses an action, event, or state. The verb is the main part of the predicate of a sentence. ⟨Latin *verbum* orig word⟩
ver·bal *adj* **1** in or of words: *A description is a verbal picture.* **2** oral as opposed to written: *a verbal promise.* **3** word for word; literal: *a verbal translation from the French.* **4** *Grammar* to do with a verb: *a verbal noun.* **5** having to do only with words rather than facts, action, thought, or belief: *Her religion is purely verbal.* *n* **1** *Grammar* a verb form that functions as a noun, adjective, or adverb. Participles, gerunds, and infinitives are verbals. **2** *Linguistics* a word or group of words that functions like a verb. **ver·bal·ly** *adv.* **ver·bal·ize** *v* **1** use language; speak: *Humans can verbalize.* **2** express in words: *He finds it difficult to verbalize his feelings.* **3** use too many words; be wordy: *The tendency of inexperienced writers is to verbalize.* **4** change (a noun, etc.) into a verb. **ver·bal·i·za·tion** *n.* **ver·ba·tim** [vɜr'beɪtɪm] *adv, adj* word for word; in exactly the same words: *Her speech was printed verbatim in the paper.* **ver·bi·age** ['vɜrbiɪdʒ] *n* abundance of useless words: *Cut out the verbiage and make your point.* **ver·bose** [vɜr'bous] *adj* using too many words; wordy. **ver·bose·ly** *adv.* **ver·bos·i·ty** [vər'bɒsəti] *n.*

USAGE
Verbs are classified on the basis of what complements them as a necessary part of the sentence structure. A verb taking a noun or noun substitute as an object is called **transitive**: *She broke the mirror.* A verb not taking an object is called **intransitive**: *They succeeded.* Many verbs in English can be transitive or intransitive: *I broke the mirror. The mirror broke.* A verb taking a noun or adjective as a complement referring back to the subject is called a **linking verb**: *She became a lawyer.*

ver·be·na [vər'binə] *n* any of a genus of plants having flowers of various colours growing in clusters. ⟨Latin = leafy branch⟩

ver·dant ['vɜrdənt] *adj* **1** green in colour: *verdant grass.* **2** covered with growing green plants: *verdant fields.* **3** inexperienced, unsophisticated, or immature; green. **ver·dan·cy** *n.* **ver·dant·ly** *adv.* ⟨*verdure;* Old French; Latin *viridis* green⟩
ver·dure ['vɜrdʒər] *n* **1** the fresh greenness of growing vegetation. **2** a flourishing growth of vegetation. **3** a condition of vigour.

ver·dict ['vɜrdɪkt] *n* **1** the decision of a jury: *The jury returned a verdict of not guilty.* **2** any decision: *the verdict of history.* ⟨Anglo-French *verdit; ver* true + *dit* pp of *dire* speak⟩

ver·di·gris ['vɜrdə,gris] *or* ['vɜrdəgrɪs] *n* a green or bluish coating that forms on brass, copper, or bronze when exposed to the air for long periods of time. ⟨Old French *vert de grece* green of Greece⟩

ver·dure See VERDANT.

verge¹ [vɜrdʒ] *n* **1** the point at which something begins: *His business is on the verge of ruin.* **2** a limiting border of something, as the strip of grass along a sidewalk. *v* border: *Their silly talk verged on nonsense.* ⟨Old French; Latin *virga* staff⟩

verge² [vɜrdʒ] *v* tend or incline (*toward*); pass gradually (*into*): *Her sadness is verging toward depression.* ⟨Latin *vergere* turn, bend⟩

ver·i·est See VERY.

ver·i·fy ['vɛrə,faɪ] *v* **1** confirm: *verified by eyewitnesses.* **2** check for accuracy: *Verify the spelling of a word by looking in a dictionary.* **ver·i·fi·a·ble** *adj.* **ver·i·fi·a·bly** *adv.* **ver·i·fi·ca·tion** *n.* **ver·i·fi·er** *n.* ⟨Latin *verificare;* Latin *verus* true + *facere* make⟩

ver·i·ly ['vɛrəli] *adv Archaic, poetic* in truth; truly; really. ⟨*very* + *-ly¹*⟩

ver·i·si·mil·i·tude [,vɛrəsə'mɪlə,tjud] *or* [-,tud] *n* **1** appearance of truth; probability; credibility: *A story must have verisimilitude to interest most people.* **2** something having merely the appearance of truth or reality. ⟨Latin *verus* true + *similis* like⟩

ver·i·ty ['vɛrəti] *n* **1** the quality of being true or real. **2** a basic principle or belief: *eternal verities.* ⟨Latin *veritas; verus* true⟩
ver·i·ta·ble ['vɛrətəbəl] *adj* real or genuine; true. **ver·i·ta·bly** *adv.*

ver·meil ['vɜrmeil] *or* ['vɜrməl] *n* silver, bronze, or copper coated or plated with gold. **ver·meil** *adj.* ⟨Old French; Latin *vermiculus* diminutive of *vermis* worm⟩

ver·mi·cel·li [,vɜrmə'tʃɛli] *or* [-'sɛli] *Italian* [,vɛrmi'tʃɛlli] *n* a pasta similar to spaghetti, but thinner. ⟨Italian, literally, little worms; Latin *vermis* worm⟩

ver·mi·cide ['vɜrmə,saɪd] *n* any agent that kills worms. ⟨Latin *vermis* worm + -CIDE⟩

ver·mic·u·lite [vər'mɪkjə,ləɪt] *n* any of various silicate minerals in the form of small, lightweight granules that readily absorb water. ⟨Latin *vermiculus.* See VERMEIL.⟩

ver·mil·ion [vər'mɪljən] *n* bright, orangy red. ⟨Old French *vermillon; vermeil.* See VERMEIL.⟩

ver·min ['vɜrmən] *n* (usually used as pl) **1** small animals that are troublesome or destructive, esp insects such as lice, fleas, and bedbugs, or rodents such as rats and mice. **2** a vile, offensive, or dangerous person or persons. ⟨Old French; Latin *vermis* worm⟩ **ver·min·ous** *adj* **1** infested with vermin. **2** caused by vermin. **3** like vermin; vile.

ver·mouth [vər'muθ] *or* ['vɜrməθ] *n* a fortified white wine flavoured with herbs. ⟨French; German *Wermut(h)* wormwood, for its orig flavouring⟩

ver·nac·u·lar [vər'nækjələr] *n* **1** a language used by the people of a certain country or place. **2** informal speech. **3** the language of a trade, profession, etc.: *the vernacular of lawyers.* *adj* **1** used, practised, etc. by the people of a certain country, place, etc.: *vernacular customs.* **2** to do with everyday language, rather than literary language. ⟨Latin *vernaculus* domestic; *verna* home-born slave⟩

ver·nal ['vɜrnəl] *adj* **1** to do with spring: *the vernal equinox.* **2** like spring; fresh, new, mild, etc. **3** youthful: *a young girl's vernal freshness.* **ver·nal·ly** *adv.* ⟨Latin *vernalis*; *ver* spring⟩

ver·ru·ca [və'rukə] *n, pl* **-cas** or **-cae** [-si] *or* [-saɪ] a wart, esp one on the hand or foot. **ver·ru·cose** ['vɛrə,kous] *adj.* **ver·ru·cous** *adj.* ⟨Latin = wart⟩

ver·sa·tile ['vɜrsə,taɪl] *or* ['vɜrsətəl] *adj* **1** able to do many things well: *He is very versatile; he is an actor, a poet, and a singer.* **2** having many uses: *A pocketknife is a versatile tool.* **3** *Zoology* **a** capable of turning forward or backward: *the versatile toe of an owl.* **b** moving freely up and down and from side to side: *versatile antennae.* **4** *Botany* attached at or near the middle so as to swing freely: *a versatile anther.* **ver·sa·tile·ly** *adv.* **ver·sa·til·i·ty** *n.* ⟨Latin *versatilis* turning; *vertere* turn⟩

verse [vɜrs] *n* **1** a form of literary expression using lines of words, the lines often having rhyme; poetry. **2** sometimes, poetry of poor quality. **3** stanza: *Sing the first verse of "O Canada."* **4** a type of verse; METRE¹ (def. 1): *blank verse.* **5** one of the short sections into which the chapters of the books of the Bible are traditionally divided. ⟨Old English *vers*; Latin *versus* orig row; *vertere* turn around⟩ **versed** *adj* experienced; practised: *A doctor should be versed in medical theory.* **ver·si·fy** *v* **1** write verses, esp mediocre ones. **2** tell in verse. **3** turn (prose) into poetry. **ver·si·fi·ca·tion** *n.* **ver·si·fi·er** *n.*

ver·sion ['vɜrʒən] *n* **1** a translation from one language to another, esp a translation of the Bible: *the King James Version.* **2** a statement from a particular point of view: *Each of the three boys gave his own version of the quarrel.* **3** a special form of something: *The tent trailer is a modern version of the travois.* ⟨Latin *versio* orig a turning; *vertere* turn⟩

ver·sus ['vɜrsəs] *prep* **1** against. **2** in contrast to: *strength versus agility. Abbrev* **v.**, **vs.** ⟨Latin *versus* turned toward; pp of *vertere* turn⟩

ver·te·bra ['vɜrtəbrə] *n, pl* **-brae** [-,breɪ] *or* [-,brɪ] *or* **-bras** one of the bones of the spinal column. ⟨Latin; *vertere* turn⟩ **ver·te·brate** [-brɪt] *or* [-,breɪt] *n* any animal that has a backbone. *adj* to do with vertebrates.

ver·tex ['vɜrtɛks] *n, pl* **-tex·es** or **-ti·ces** [-tə,siz] **1** the highest point. **2** *Mathematics* **a** the point opposite to and farthest away from the base of a triangle, pyramid, etc. **b** the point of meeting of lines that form an angle. **c** a point where the axis of a hyperbola, parabola, or ellipse intersects it. **3** *Astronomy* a point in the heavens directly overhead. **4** *Anatomy, zoology* the top of the head. ⟨Latin *vertex* orig whirl, n; *vertere* turn⟩

ver·ti·cal ['vɜrtəkəl] *adj* **1** straight up and down. **2** of or at the highest point. **3** directly overhead. **ver·ti·cal·ly** *adv.* **ver·ti·cal·i·ty** *n.* ⟨Latin *vertex, verticis* highest point. See VERTEX.⟩
vertical file a file, as in a library, bringing together various different media, such as photographs, articles, drawings, recordings, etc., organized by subject.

ver·ti·ces ['vɜrtə,siz] *n* a pl of VERTEX.

ver·ti·go ['vɜrtə,gou] *n* a sensation of dizziness or of giddiness. ⟨Latin; *vertere* turn⟩ **ver·tig·i·nous** [vər'tɪdʒənəs] *adj* **1** whirling; rotary. **2** affected with vertigo; dizzy. **3** likely to cause vertigo. **ver·tig·i·nous·ly** *adv.* **ver·tig·i·nous·ness** *n.*

ver·vain ['vɜrvein] *n* verbena. ⟨Old French; Latin *verbena* leafy bough⟩

verve [vɜrv] *n* enthusiasm; energy; vigour; spirit; liveliness. ⟨French⟩

ver·y ['vɛri] *adv* **1** much; extremely: *The sun is very hot.* **2** exactly: *in the very same place.* *adj* **1** same: *The very people who used to love her hate her now.* **2** mere: *The very thought of blood makes him sick.* **3** complete: *He did the very opposite.* **4** actual: *He was caught in the very act of stealing.* **5** exactly right: *That picture is the very thing for our living room wall.* ⟨Old French *verai*; Latin *verus* true⟩ **ver·i·est** *adj* utmost: *the veriest nonsense.* **very high frequency** the band of radio frequencies between 30 and 300 kHz. *Abbrev* **VHF.**

ves·i·cle ['vɛsəkəl] *n* **1** a small bladder, pouch, etc. in a plant or animal. **2** an abnormal, raised part in the outer layer of skin, containing a watery fluid; blister. **3** *Geology* a small cavity, the result of trapped gas, in a rock or mineral, esp in volcanic rock. ⟨Latin *vesicula* diminutive of *vesica* bladder, blister⟩

ves·per ['vɛspər] *n* **vespers** or **Vespers** *pl* **1** a Christian church service held in the late afternoon or in the evening. **2** the sixth of the canonical hours. ⟨Latin *vespera* evening⟩

ves·sel ['vɛsəl] *n* **1** a ship. **2** an airship. **3** a hollow container. **4 a** a tube carrying blood or other body fluid. Veins are blood vessels. **b** a tube or duct in the xylem of plants, carrying fluids. ⟨Old French; Latin *vascellum* diminutive of *vas* vessel⟩

vest [vɛst] *n* **1** a sleeveless, waist-length

garment. **2** a piece of equipment of this general form: *a life vest.* **3** an undershirt, esp for women or children.
v **1 a** dress in vestments: *The vested priest.* **b** put on garments or vestments. **2** furnish with authority, rights, etc.: *Parliament is vested with power to declare war.* **3** put in the control of a person or persons: *The management of the hospital is vested in a board of trustees.* ⟨Old French *veste*; Latin *vestis* garment⟩

vest·ed *adj* **1** *Law* placed in the permanent control of a person or persons; fixed: *vested rights.* **2** clothed or robed, esp in church garments: *a vested choir.* **vested interest 1** a legally established right to the possession of property. **2** a self-interested concern for something (used with *in*): *Manufacturers have a vested interest in low freight rates.* **3** a person, group, or institution having such a concern.
vest·ment *n* any of the official garments worn by some members of the Christian clergy during church services. **ves·try** *n* a room in a Christian church, where vestments, etc. are kept.

ves·ti·bule [ˈvɛstəˌbjul] *n* **1** a hall between the outer door and the inside of a building. **2** the enclosed space at the end of a railway passenger car, for entering and exiting. ⟨Latin *vestibulum*⟩

ves·tige [ˈvɛstɪdʒ] *n* **1** a slight remnant; trace: *Ghost stories are vestiges of a former widespread belief in ghosts.* **2** *Biology* a part, organ, etc. that is no longer fully developed or useful. **ves·tig·i·al** [vɛˈstɪdʒiəl] *adj.* ⟨Latin *vestigium* footprint⟩

vest·ment, ves·try See VEST.

vet[1] [vɛt] *Informal n* veterinarian. *v* **vet·ted, vet·ting** examine carefully; check: *to vet a report.*

vet[2] [vɛt] *n Informal* VETERAN (def. 1).

vetch [vɛtʃ] *n* any of a genus of trailing or climbing plants of the pea family. ⟨dialect Old French; Latin *vicia*⟩

vet·er·an [ˈvɛtərən] *n* **1** a person who has served in the armed forces, esp during wartime. **2** a person who has had (much) experience in war. **3** a person who has had much experience in some position, occupation, etc.: *veterans on a teaching staff.* **vet·er·an** *adj.* ⟨Latin *veteris* old⟩

vet·er·i·nar·y [ˈvɛtrəˌnɛri] *or* [ˈvɛtərəˌnɛri] *adj* to do with the medical treatment of animals. *n* veterinarian. ⟨Latin *veterinus* of beasts of burden and draft⟩
vet·er·i·nar·i·an *n* a person trained in veterinary medicine.

ve·to [ˈvitou] *n, pl* **-toes** the right to forbid or reject: *The Senate has the power of veto over most bills passed in the Commons.* **ve·to** *adj.* *v* **-toed, -to·ing** **1** reject formally by a veto. **2** refuse to consent to: *We vetoed her plan to buy a motorcycle.* **ve·to·er** *n.* ⟨Latin = I forbid⟩

vex [vɛks] *v* **1** anger by trifles; annoy; provoke. **2** disturb; trouble. **vex·a·tion** *n.* ⟨Latin *vexare*⟩

vex·a·tious *adj* **1** vexing; annoying. **2** *Law* of legal action, brought merely in order to annoy the defendant. **vex·a·tious·ly** *adv.*
vex·a·tious·ness *n.* **vexed question** a question causing much difficulty and debate.

VHF or **V.H.F.** VERY HIGH FREQUENCY.

VHS *Trademark* an electronic audio and video recording system. ⟨*video home system*⟩

vi·a [ˈviə] *or* [ˈvaɪə] *prep* **1** by way of: *They travelled from Winnipeg to Saskatoon via Regina.* **2** by means of: *We sent the package via airmail.* ⟨Latin way, by way of⟩

vi·a·ble [ˈvaɪəbəl] *adj* **1** able to stay alive. **2** able to keep functioning: *a viable economy.* **3** workable; practicable: *That is not a viable solution to our problem.* **4** of a fetus or newborn infant, sufficiently developed to maintain life outside the uterus. **5** *Botany* capable of living, as a spore or seed. **vi·a·bil·i·ty** *n.* **vi·a·bly** *adv.* ⟨Latin *vita*⟩

vi·a·duct [ˈvaɪəˌdʌkt] *n* a bridge, esp one consisting of a series of arches resting on towers, for carrying a road or railway over a valley, a part of a city, etc. ⟨Latin *via* road + *-duct* as in *aqueduct*⟩

vi·al [ˈvaɪəl] *n* a small bottle, esp a glass bottle, for holding medicines, perfumes, etc. ⟨variant of *phial*⟩

vibes [vaɪbz] *n pl Informal* **1** vibraphone. **2** a distinctive emotional atmosphere: *He left because the vibes were bad.*
vib·ist [ˈvaɪbɪst] *n Informal* vibraphonist.

vi·brate [ˈvaɪbreɪt] *v* **1** move or cause to move rapidly to and fro: *A piano string vibrates when a key is struck.* **2** swing or cause to swing to and fro. **3** resound: *The clanging vibrated in our ears.* **vi·bra·tion** *n.* **vi·bra·tion·al** *adj.* **vi·bra·tion·less** *adj.* ⟨Latin *vibrare* shake⟩
vi·brant *adj* **1** throbbing with vitality, enthusiasm, etc.: *a vibrant personality.* **2 a** of sounds, resounding or resonant: *a vibrant voice.* **b** of colours, bright and rich: *vibrant reds.* **vi·bran·cy** *n.* **vi·brant·ly** *adv.* **vi·bra·phone** *n* a musical instrument similar to a xylophone, but motor-driven. **vi·bra·phon·ist** *n.* **vi·bra·to** [vɪˈbrɑtou] *n Music* a vibrating effect, produced by slight variations of pitch. **vi·bra·tor** *n* **1** an electrical appliance or device that vibrates, used in massage or sexual stimulation. **2** a vibrating device in an electric bell or buzzer.

vic·ar [ˈvɪkər] *n* **1** *Anglican Church* a member of the clergy who carries out the duties of a parish but is not officially the rector. **2** *Roman Catholic Church* **a** a deputy or representative of the pope or a bishop. **b Vicar of Christ** the pope thought of as Christ's representative on earth. **3** a substitute or representative. ⟨Latin *vicarius* substitute (orig adj); *vicis* of change⟩
vic·ar·age *n* the residence of a vicar. **vi·car·i·ous** [vaɪˈkɛriəs] *or* [vɪ-] *adj* **1** felt by sharing in one's imagination the actual experience of another person: *She obtains a vicarious delight in foreign countries from reading travel books.* **2** done or suffered for

others: *a vicarious sacrifice.* **3** taking the place of or doing the work of another: *As a ghost writer, he is a vicarious autobiographer.* **vi·car·i·ous·ly** *adv.* **vi·car·i·ous·ness** *n.*

vice¹ [vəis] *n* **1** moral corruption. **2** an evil or immoral habit, character trait, practice, etc.: *the vice of gluttony.* **3** a fault; a bad habit: *You said that this horse had no vices.* **4** prostitution. ⟨Old French; Latin *vitium*⟩ **vice squad** a division of a police force, concerned especially with the enforcement of prostitution and gambling laws. **vi·cious** ['vɪʃəs] *adj* **1** depraved or wicked: *He had led a vicious life.* **2** dangerously aggressive: *a vicious dog.* **3** fierce or violent: *a vicious brawl.* **4** spiteful; malicious: *a vicious rumour.* **5** *Informal* severe: *a vicious headache.* **6** of reasoning, etc., unsound or invalid; fallacious. **vi·cious·ly** *adv.* **vi·cious·ness** *n.* **vicious circle** or **cycle** **1** two or more undesirable things, each of which keeps causing the other. **2** a situation where the resolution of one problem creates another whose resolution in turn leads back to the first, often in a still worse form than before. **3** in logic, false reasoning that uses one statement to prove a second statement when the first statement really depends upon the second for proof.

vice² [vəis] *n Informal* a vice-principal, vice-president, vice-chairman, etc. ⟨Latin *vice* for change⟩ **vice–** *prefix* substitute; deputy: *vice-president.* **vice–pres·i·dent** *n* the officer next in rank to a president, who takes the president's place when necessary. *Abbrev* **VP** or **V.P.** **2** one of several officers next in rank to a president, each of whom oversees a particular department or has a special function: *She is vice-president, Human Resource Systems.* **vice–pres·i·den·cy** *n.* **vice–pres·i·den·tial** *adj.*

vice·roy ['vəis,rɔɪ] *n* a person governing a province or colony as the representative of the sovereign. **vice·roy·ship** *n.* **vice·re·gal** *adj.* **vice–re·gal·ly** *adv.* ⟨French *vice-roi; vice* vice- + *roi* king; Latin *rex*⟩ **vice·reine** ['vəis,rein] *n* **1** the wife of a viceroy. **2** a woman holding the rank or office of viceroy.

vice ver·sa ['vəis 'vɜrsə] *or* ['vəisə 'vɜrsə] the other way round; conversely: *I blamed her, and vice versa (She blamed me).* ⟨Latin; see ⟩

vi·cin·i·ty [və'sɪnəti] *n* **1** a region near or about a place; surrounding district: *He knew many people in the city and its vicinity.* **2** a nearness in place: *The vicinity of the school to the house was an advantage on rainy days.* ⟨Latin *vicinus* neighbouring; *vicus* village⟩ **in the vicinity of** **a** near: *a farm in the vicinity of Erin.* **b** approximately: *Costs were in the vicinity of $2000.*

vi·cious See VICE¹.

vi·cis·si·tude [və'sɪsə,tjud] *or* [və'sɪsə,tud] *n* **1** a change in circumstances, fortune, etc. that occurs by chance: *The vicissitudes of life may suddenly make a rich man poor.* **2** constant

change or variation. **vi·cis·si·tu·di·nous** *adj.* ⟨Latin *vicissitudo; vicis.* See VICAR.⟩

vic·tim ['vɪktəm] *n* **1** a person or animal injured, killed, or mistreated: *victims of war, the victim of several harsh attacks in the press.* **2** a person tricked by another: *the victim of a swindler.* **3** a person or animal sacrificed in a religious rite. **vic·tim·ize** *v.* **vic·tim·i·za·tion** *n.* **vic·tim·less** *adj.* ⟨Latin *victima*⟩

vic·tor ['vɪktər] *n* a winner; conqueror. ⟨Latin *victor; victum* pp of *vincere* conquer⟩ **vic·to·ry** *n* **1** the defeat of an opponent. **2** the achievement of success in a struggle. **vic·to·ri·ous** *adj.* **vic·to·ri·ous·ly** *adv.* ⟨Latin *victoria*, ult.; *vincere* conquer⟩

SYNONYMS

Victory emphasizes winning a fight of any kind, and implies defeating the opponent: *We celebrated our victory.* **Conquest** adds and emphasizes bringing the defeated under complete control: *Some day we may complete the conquest of disease.* **Triumph** applies to a glorious victory: *The granting of the vote to women was a triumph for the suffragettes.*

Victoria Day ✱ a national holiday established in 1845 to celebrate the birthday of Queen Victoria (May 24); since 1952, celebrated on the Monday immediately preceding May 25.

Vic·to·ri·an [vɪk'tɔriən] *adj* **1** to do with the reign of Victoria (1819-1901), Queen of Great Britain and Ireland and Empress of India from 1837 to 1901. **2** possessing characteristics attributed to Victorians, such as prudishness, smugness, bigotry, etc. **3** to do with the style of architecture, decor, etc., usually ornate and massive, of the latter half of Queen Victoria's reign. *n* **1** a person, esp an author, who lived during the reign of Queen Victoria. **2** a native or inhabitant of any place called Victoria, such as Victoria, BC.

vic·to·ri·ous, victory See VICTOR.

vict·ual ['vɪtəl] *n* **victuals** *pl* provisions or food, esp when prepared for use. *v* **-ualled** or **-ualed, -ual·ling** or **-ual·ing** supply with food or provisions: *He victualled the ship for the voyage.* **vict·ual·ler** or **vict·ual·er** *n.* ⟨Latin *victualia* pl; *victus* food *vivere* live⟩

vid·e·o ['vɪdi,ou] *adj* **1** of or used in the transmission or reception of television images. **2** making use of a computer screen. *n* **1** television. **2** the visual part, as opposed to the sound, of a film or television program. **3** a presentation, etc., designed to be videotaped and shown on a TV or VCR: *The group is working on a video to accompany their new hit.* **4** a videotape, esp one on which a movie or other entertainment has been recorded. ⟨Latin = I see⟩ **video camera** a camera for recording sounds and moving images simultaneously. **video cassette** a videotape mounted in a cassette, for recording and playing back video programs. **video cassette recorder** a device for recording and playing back video cassettes. *Abbrev* **VCR. vid·e·o·disc** *n* a disc on which video and, usually, audio signals have been recorded for playback on a television or computer screen. **video game** an electronic game in which the player manipulates the action on a screen. **vid·e·og·ra·phy** [ˌvɪdiˈɒɡrəfi] *n* videos collectively and the making of videos. **vid·e·og·ra·pher** *n.* **vid·e·o·graph·i·cal** *adj.* **video jockey** a person who chooses, introduces, and plays videos, esp music videos, for a TV program. *Abbrev* **VJ. video lottery terminal** a coin-operated gambling machine with a screen displaying the player's actions in any of various games. *Abbrev* **VLT. vid·e·o·phone** *n* a telephone equipped to send and receive both audio and video signals. **vid·e·o·tape** *n* a magnetic tape for recording video and audio signals.

vie [vaɪ] *v* **vied, vy·ing** strive for superiority; contend in rivalry; compete. ⟨French *envier* challenge; Latin *invitare* invite⟩

view [vju] *n* **1** an act of seeing: *It was our first view of the ocean.* **2** the range of the eye: *A ship came into view.* **3** a scene: *The view from our house is beautiful.* **4** a mental picture; idea: *This book will give you a general view of the way the pioneers lived.* **5** opinion: *A child's view of school is different from a teacher's.*
v **1** look at: *They viewed the scene with pleasure.* **2** consider: *The plan was viewed favourably.* **3** watch (esp something televised or filmed). **view·less** *adj.* ⟨Anglo-French *vewe*; Old French *veoir* see; Latin *videre*⟩
in view a in sight: *As long as the cliffs were in view, she could find her way.* **b** under consideration: *Keep this advice in view as you try to improve your work.* **c** as a purpose: *He has a definite aim in view.* **in view of** because of. **on view** to be seen: *The exhibit is on view from 9 a.m. to 5 p.m.* **take a dim view of** look upon with disapproval, doubt, etc. **with a view to** with the purpose of: *He worked hard with a view to earning money for a new bicycle.* **view·er** *n* **1** a person who views: *a television viewer.* **2** a device for viewing, esp a small instrument for viewing photographic transparencies. **view·find·er** *n Photography* a device on a camera that shows the scene or area within view of the lens. Also, **view finder. view·ing** *n* **1** an occasion for inspecting, as of articles to be sold at auction, etc. **2** a time for people to see a dead person's remains laid out at a funeral parlour for the paying of last respects, etc. **view·point** *n* **1** the place from which one looks at something. **2** mental point of view: *Rain may be good from the viewpoint of farmers but bad from the viewpoint of tourists.*

SYNONYMS
View emphasizes the idea of someone looking from a certain point or position: *That new building spoils the view from our windows.*
Scene applies to a setting that is spread out before the eyes: *We stopped to gaze at the mountain scene.*

vig·il [ˈvɪdʒəl] *n* **1** a staying awake for some purpose: *All night the mother kept vigil over the child.* **2** a night spent in prayer. **3** Often, **vigils** *pl* prayers, etc. on the night before a religious festival. ⟨Latin *vigilia; vigil* watchful⟩

vig·i·lance *n* watchfulness. **vigilance committee** *US* a self-appointed committee of citizens organized to maintain order in places or situations where official law enforcement appears inadequate. **vig·i·lant** *adj* watchful; alert: *a vigilant guard.* **vig·i·lant·ly** *adv.* **vig·i·lan·te** [ˌvɪdʒəˈlænti] *n* a member of a VIGILANCE COMMITTEE. **vig·i·lan·tism** [-ˈlæntɪzəm] *n.* **vig·i·lan·tist** *adj.*

vi·gnette [vɪnˈjɛt] *n* **1** a decorative design on a page of a book, esp on the title page. **2** a short verbal description. **3** a short and memorable or striking incident or scene, as in a movie or play. **vi·gnet·tist** *n.* ⟨French; diminutive of *vigne* vine⟩

vig·our or **vig·or** [ˈvɪɡər] *n* **1** active physical strength. **2** mental energy. **3** intensity of action: *The vigour of her refusal surprised me.* **4** legal or binding force; validity: *a law in full vigour.* **vig·or·ous** *adj.* **vig·or·ous·ly** *adv.* ⟨Old French, Latin *vigor; vigere* thrive⟩

Vi·king or **vi·king** [ˈvaɪkɪŋ] *n* one of the bands of Norsemen who raided the coasts of Europe during the 8th, 9th, and 10th centuries A.D. ⟨Old Norse *vikingr*⟩

vile [vaɪl] *adj* **1** despicable: *a vile attempt to defraud an old man of his savings.* **2** physically repulsive: *the vile smell of rotting garbage.* **3** very bad or unpleasant: *The weather has turned really vile.* **4** mean; low: *vile servitude.* **vile·ly** *adv.* **vile·ness** *n.* ⟨Latin *vilis* cheap⟩

vil·i·fy [ˈvɪləˌfaɪ] *v* speak evil of; slander. **vil·i·fi·ca·tion** *n.* **vil·i·fi·er** *n.* ⟨Latin *vilis* vile + *facere* make⟩

vil·la [ˈvɪlə] *n* a country house as opposed to a town house. A villa is usually a large or elegant dwelling, used as a summer or holiday residence. ⟨Italian; Latin⟩

vil·lage [ˈvɪlɪdʒ] *n* **1** a group of houses, stores, schools, etc. that form a community. In Canada, a village is the smallest community that can have its own local government. **2** the people of a village: *The whole village was out to see the fire.* **3** an informal section of a large urban centre, regarded as a neighbourhood: *We do our shopping in Cook Street village.* **vil·lag·er** *n.* ⟨Old French *village*; Latin *villa* country house⟩

vil·lain [ˈvɪlən] *n* **1** a scoundrel; wicked person. **2** the main, unsympathetic character in a play, novel, etc. whose evil actions form an important element in the plot. **3** a person or thing blamed for a particular problem: *City health experts studying the epidemic decided the chief villain was overcrowding.* **4** *Informal* rascal or rogue. **vil·lain·ous** *adj.* **vil·lain·ous·ly** *adv.* ⟨Latin *villanus* farmhand; *villa* country house⟩
vil·lain·y *n* **1** great wickedness. **2** a very wicked act; crime.

vim [vɪm] *n* vitality and enthusiasm; energy: *Now that your cold has gone, you seem very lively and full of vim!* ⟨Latin *vim* form of *vis* force⟩

vin·ai·grette [ˌvɪnəˈgrɛt] *n* a salad dressing made of seasoned oil and vinegar. ⟨French; *vinaigre*. See VINEGAR.⟩

vin·di·cate [ˈvɪndəˌkeit] *v* **1** clear from suspicion, dishonour, etc.: *The verdict of "Not guilty" vindicated the accused.* **2** defend successfully against opposition: *He vindicated his claim to his uncle's fortune.* **3** justify: *Now that the facts are known, my faith in her has been vindicated.* **vin·di·ca·ble** *adj.* **vin·di·ca·tor** *n.* **vin·di·ca·to·ry** *adj.* **vin·di·ca·tion** *n.* ⟨Latin *vindicare; vindicis* defender⟩

vin·dic·tive [vɪnˈdɪktɪv] *adj* **1** feeling a strong tendency toward revenge: *He is so vindictive that he never forgives anybody.* **2** involving revenge: *vindictive punishment.* **3** spiteful; malicious: *He has a vindictive nature, and will never forgive anyone who upsets him.* **vin·dic·tive·ly** *adv.* **vin·dic·tive·ness** *n.* ⟨Latin *vindicta* revenge. See VENDETTA.⟩

vine [vaɪn] *n* **1** any plant that creeps along the ground or climbs by twining or by putting out tendrils. **2** grapevine: *the fruit of the vine.* **vine·like** *adj.* ⟨Latin *vinum* wine⟩
vine·yard [ˈvɪnjərd] *n* a place planted with grapevines. **vin·i·cul·ture** [ˈvɪnɪˌkʌltʃər] *n* the art or science of making wines. **vi·ni·fer·ous** [vɪˈnɪfərəs] *adj* yielding wine: *viniferous grapes.*

vin·e·gar [ˈvɪnəgər] *n* a sour liquid produced by the fermentation of cider, wine, etc. and consisting largely of dilute, impure acetic acid. **vin·e·gar·y** *adj.* ⟨Middle French *vinaigre; vin* wine + *aigre* sour⟩

vin·i·cul·ture, vi·ni·fer·ous See VINE.

vin·tage [ˈvɪntɪdʒ] *n* **1** the wine or grapes of one season or from a particular vineyard or region: *Wines of Niagara vintage are popular nowadays.* **2** the year of the harvest from which a particular wine was produced: *The vintage of this wine is 1978.* **3** the season of gathering grapes and making wine. **4** a kind typical of a particular period or year of origin: *songs of prewar vintage.*
adj **1** of a good vintage: *vintage wines.* **2** being the best example or model; classic: *Sunshine Sketches of a Little Town is vintage Stephen Leacock.* **3** to do with an earlier time: *vintage comic books.* ⟨Anglo-French; Old French *vendange;* Latin *vindemia; vinum* wine + *demere* take off⟩
vintage year **1** a year in which a vintage wine is produced. **2** an outstandingly successful year: *a vintage year in hockey.* **vint·ner** [ˈvɪntnər] *n* **1** a dealer in wine. **2** a person who makes wine.

vi·nyl [ˈvaɪnəl] *n* a polymer of any of several organic compounds, used for the manufacture of furniture coverings, toys, etc. ⟨Latin *vinum* wine + *-yl* chemical suffix⟩

vi·ol [ˈvaɪəl] *n* one of a family of usually six-stringed musical instruments similar to the violin. **vi·ol·ist** [ˈvaɪəlɪst] *n.* ⟨Old French *viole;* Latin *vitula* fiddle⟩
vi·o·la [viˈoulə] *n* a musical instrument of the violin family that is larger and tuned a fifth lower than the violin. **vi·ol·ist** [viˈoulɪst] *n.*

vi·o·lin [ˌvaɪəˈlɪn] *n* a musical instrument with four strings tuned at intervals of a fifth, played by drawing a bow across the strings. **vi·o·lin·ist** *n.*

vi·o·late [ˈvaɪəˌleit] *v* **1** break (a law, promise, etc.): *Speeding violates traffic regulations.* **2** treat with disrespect: *The soldiers violated the church by using it as a stable.* **3** offend: *Such treatment violates all sense of decency.* **4** disturb: *The sound of the explosion violated the calm of Sunday morning.* **5** trespass on: *to violate the right of free speech.* **6** commit rape on. **vi·o·lence** *n.* **vi·o·la·tor** *n.* **vi·o·la·tive** *adj.* **vi·o·la·tion** *n.* ⟨Latin *violare; vis* violence⟩
do violence to violate: *It would do violence to her principles to work on Sunday.*

vi·o·lent *adj* **1** characterized by the use of, rough, harmful force: *a violent blow.* **2** caused by strong, rough force: *a violent death.* **3** caused by very strong feeling, action, etc.: *violent language, a violent disagreement.* **4** promoting or based on violence: *violent films.* **5** severe: *a violent pain.* **vi·o·lent·ly** *adv.*

vi·o·let [ˈvaɪələt] *n* any of numerous plants having small, usually yellow, white, or purple flowers. The purple violet is the provincial flower of New Brunswick. ⟨Old French *violette;* Latin *viola*⟩
violet rays the shortest rays of the visible spectrum, with wavelengths just above that of the invisible ultraviolet rays

vi·o·lin See VIOL.

VIP *Informal* very important person.

vi·per [ˌvaɪpər] *n* any of a family of poisonous snakes having hollow fangs in the upper jaw, through which poison is injected. ⟨Latin *vipera; vivus* alive + *parere* bring forth⟩
vi·per·ous or **viperish** *adj* like a viper; treacherous and malicious. **vi·per·ous·ly** *adv.*

vi·ra·go [vəˈrɑgou] or [vəˈreigou] *n, pl* **-goes** or **-gos** a violent, bad-tempered, or scolding woman. ⟨Latin; *vir* man⟩

vi·ral See VIRUS.

vir·gin [ˈvɜrdʒən] *n* **1** a person, esp a woman, who has never had sexual intercourse. **2** an unmarried girl. **3** a member of any religious order of women who have vowed to remain virgins. **4 the Virgin,** the VIRGIN MARY. **5** *Zoology* **a** a female animal that has not mated. **b** a female insect that lays eggs without impregnation by a male.
adj **1** having to do with or suitable for a virgin: *virgin modesty.* **2** being a virgin. **3** untouched: *virgin snow; virgin forest.* **4** of olive oil, obtained from the first pressing, without the use of heat. **vir·gin·i·ty** *n.* ⟨Latin *virgo, virginis*⟩
virgin birth *Biology* parthenogenesis. **Virgin Birth** *Christianity* the doctrine that Jesus had no human father, but was miraculously conceived by the Virgin Mary through the power of the Holy Spirit. **Virgin Mary** the mother of Jesus Christ

vir·gin·al¹ [ˈvɜrdʒənəl] *adj* **1** of or suitable for a virgin. **2** pure; untouched. **3** remaining in a state of virginity. **vir·gin·al·ly** *adv.*

vir·gin·al² ['vɜrdʒənəl] *n* a musical instrument like a small harpsichord. ⟨apparently from *virginal¹*⟩

vir·gule ['vɜrgjul] *n* a slanting stroke (/) between two words, indicating that either word applies, as in *and/or*, also used sometimes in fractions (1/2), in dates (26/04/96), and to express 'per' as in *km/h* (kilometres per hour). ⟨Latin *virgula* little rod⟩

vir·ile ['vɪraɪl] *or* ['vɪrəl] *adj* **1** belonging to or characteristic of a man; masculine; manly. **2** having masculine vigour or forcefulness: *a virile writing style.* **3** of a male, sexually potent. **vi·ril·i·ty** [və'rɪləti] *n.* ⟨Latin *vir* man⟩

vi·rol·o·gy See VIRUS.

vir·tu [vər'tu] *or* ['vɜrtu] *n* **1** merit in an object of art because of its quality, rarity, etc. **2** objects of art collectively. **3** knowledge of objects of art. Also, **ver·tu.** ⟨Italian *virtù* excellence; Latin *virtus* virtue⟩

vir·tu·al ['vɜrtʃuəl] *adj* **1** being something in effect, though not according to strict definition: *The battle was won with so great a loss of soldiers that it was a virtual defeat.* **2** *Computers* **a** of a data storage that is temporary, consisting in the use of disk space to store information while a large program, occupying all or most of the regular memory, is being run. **b** to do with VIRTUAL REALITY. **3** *Physics* to do with a virtual IMAGE. **vir·tu·al·i·ty** [,vɜrtʃu'æləti] *n.* ⟨*virtue*⟩ **vir·tu·al·ly** *adv* almost entirely: *The two houses are virtually identical.* **virtual office** any place, such as one's home, that is computerized and equipped to handle office business. **virtual reality** *Computers* a simulation of reality achieved through programming, in which the user or viewer experiences physical sensations associated with the events, etc. represented on the computer system, and can interact with them as though they were real.

vir·tue ['vɜrtʃu] *n* **1** moral excellence. **2 a** merit or value: *There is virtue in making a detailed plan.* **b** a specific feature that has merit or value: *He praised the virtues of his car.* **3** chastity, esp in a woman. **vir·tu·ous** *adj.* **vir·tu·ous·ly** *adv.* **vir·tu·ous·ness** *n.* ⟨Latin *virtus* virtue, manliness; *vir* man⟩ **by** (or **in**) **virtue of** because of: *By virtue of getting to the theatre early, they got the best seats.* **make a virtue (out) of necessity,** do willingly what must be done anyway.

vir·tu·o·so [,vɜrtʃu'ousou] *n, pl* **-sos** or **-si** [-si] a person highly skilled in the methods of an art, esp in playing a musical instrument. *adj* showing the skills of a virtuoso: *a virtuoso performance.* **vir·tu·o·sa** *n fem, pl* **-se.** **vir·tu·os·i·ty** [-'ɒsəti] *n.* ⟨Italian = learned⟩

vir·u·lent ['vɪrələnt] *or* ['vɪrjələnt] *adj* **1** very poisonous or harmful: *a virulent poison.* **2** of disease, characterized by a rapid and severe malignant or infectious condition. **3** intensely bitter or spiteful. **vir·u·lence** *n.* **vir·u·lent·ly** *adv.* ⟨Latin *virulentus; virus* poison⟩

vi·rus ['vaɪrəs] *n* **1** any of a large group of submicroscopic entities that are capable of reproduction and growth only in living cells. **2** a disease caused by a virus: *She's been off work for two weeks with a bad virus.* **3** a corrupting influence: *the virus of prejudice.* **4** *Computers* a piece of code inserted in a computer program so as to be very hard to detect, having a destructive or corrupting effect on the system and any data stored in it. **vi·ral** *adj.* ⟨Latin = poison⟩.

vi·rol·o·gy [vaɪ'rɒlədʒi] *n* the study of viruses and virus diseases. **vi·ro·log·i·cal** *adj.* **vi·rol·o·gist** *n.*

vi·sa ['vizə] *n* an official document or endorsement on a passport allowing the person or persons identified in the passport to visit a particular country or region. ⟨Latin, pp of *videre* see⟩

vis·age ['vɪzɪdʒ] *n* **1** the face, esp with reference to its form or expression: *a grim visage.* **2** appearance; aspect: *the sad visage of late autumn.* ⟨Old French; *vis* face; Latin *visus* a look; *videre* see⟩

vis–à–vis [,vi zə 'vi] *adv, adj* face to face; opposite: *We sat vis-à-vis.* *prep* **1** face to face with: *She sat vis-à-vis the guest of honour.* **2** in comparison with or in relation to: *Vis-à-vis their competitors, they were doing very well.* *n* **1** a person or thing that is face to face with another. **2** a person who corresponds to one in another group, etc.; counterpart. ⟨French⟩

vis·cer·a ['vɪsərə] *n pl* the internal organs of the body, esp those in the cavity of the trunk, such as the stomach, intestines, etc. ⟨Latin, pl of *viscus* internal body part⟩ **vis·cer·al** *adj* **1** to do with the viscera. **2** of or springing from emotion, rather than reason: *a visceral reaction.* **vis·cer·al·ly** *adv.*

vis·cid See VISCOUS.

vis·cose ['vɪskous] *n* rayon fibres, yarn, or fabric. ⟨Latin *viscosus.* See VISCOUS.⟩

vis·cos·i·ty See VISCOUS.

vis·count ['vaɪ,kaʊnt] *n* a nobleman ranking below an earl or count and above a baron. **vis·count·cy** *n.* ⟨Old French *visconte; vis-* vice- + *comte* count²⟩ **vis·count·ess** *n* **1** the wife or widow of a viscount. **2** a woman who holds in her own right a rank equivalent to that of a viscount.

vis·cous ['vɪskəs] *adj* of a liquid, sticky; thick like syrup; viscid. **vis·cous·ly** *adj.* ⟨Latin *viscosus; viscum* birdlime⟩ **vis·cid** ['vɪsɪd] *adj* **1** thick and sticky like heavy syrup. **2** *Botany* covered with a sticky substance. **vis·cid·i·ty** *n.* **vis·cid·ly** *adv.* **vis·cos·i·ty** [vɪ'skɒsəti] *n Physics* the property of a fluid that tends to prevent it from flowing; the frictional resistance of a fluid to the motion of its molecules.

vise or **vice** [vaɪs] *n* a tool having two jaws moved by a screw or lever, etc., used to hold an object firmly while work is being done on it. ⟨Old French *vis* screw⟩

Vish·nu ['vɪʃnu] *n Hinduism* one of the three great divinities of classical Hinduism, regarded as the highest god, and usually worshipped in one of his human forms, esp Krishna or Rama. **vish·nu·ism** *n.* ⟨Sanskrit⟩

vis·i·ble ['vɪzəbəl] *adj* **1** that can be seen. **2** apparent; obvious: *There was no visible improvement in her condition.* **3** available; existing: *visible assets.* **vis·i·bly** *adv.* ⟨Latin *visibilis; visum* pp of *videre* see⟩
vis·i·bil·i·ty *n* **1 a** the quality or state of being visible. **b** the relative probability of being noticed under specific conditions: *White clothing gives pedestrians higher visibility at night.* **2** the condition of light, etc. with reference to the distance at which things can be clearly seen: *poor visibility.* **3** the ability to provide a wide range of unobstructed vision: *The windshield in this car has better visibility than my old car had.*

vi·sion ['vɪʒən] *n* **1** the sense of sight: *He wears glasses because of poor vision.* **2** the power of perceiving by the imagination or by clear thinking: *a prophet of great vision.* **3 a** something seen in the imagination, in a dream, etc.: *visions of great wealth.* **b** such an image adopted as a goal: *As the new president, what is your vision for the company?* **4** a phantom. **5** a very beautiful person, scene, etc. **vi·sion·al** *adj.* ⟨Latin *visio; visum* pp of *videre* see⟩
vi·sion·ar·y *adj* **1** not practical; utopian: *a visionary scheme for a just society.* **2** to do with ideas that are far more advanced than others of the time. **3** imaginary. **vi·sion·ar·y** *n.*

vis·it ['vɪzɪt] *v* **1** make a call on or stay with for social reasons: *They're visiting friends in Halifax this month.* **2** *Informal* converse; chat amicably: *We sat visiting for an hour after the gifts were opened.* **3** punish (a sin, etc.): *to visit the sins of the fathers upon the children.* **vis·it** *n.* ⟨Latin *visitare* visit; *visum* pp of *videre* see⟩
vis·it·ant *n Zoology* a migrating bird in any of the places it stays temporarily. **vis·it·a·tion** *n* **1** the rights accorded a divorced parent to visit his or her child. **2 a** punishment, reward, vision, etc. sent by a deity. **3** any severe affliction, blow, or trial. **vis·i·tor** *n* a person who visits or is visiting.

SYNONYMS

Visitor is the general word, applying to anyone who comes to see a person or place, for any reason: *Our visitors from the East Coast arrived last night.* Guest applies especially to someone invited: *We usually entertain our guests at the curling club.*

vi·sor ['vaɪzər] *n* **1** formerly, the movable front part of a knight's helmet. **2** a movable section attached to a safety helmet to protect the eyes of welders, motorcyclists, etc. **3** a projecting part, such as the peak of a cap, intended to protect the eyes from strong light. **4** a movable shade attached inside a car at the top of the windshield. **vi·sored** *adj.* ⟨Anglo-French *viser; vis* face. See VISAGE.⟩

vis·ta ['vɪstə] *n* **1** a view seen through a narrow opening or passage: *The opening between two rows of trees afforded a vista of the*

lake. **2** a mental view, esp over a period of time or series of events: *The book had opened up a new vista for her future.* ⟨Italian, pp of *vedere* see; Latin *videre*⟩

vis·u·al ['vɪʒuəl] *adj* **1** to do with sight or vision: *Near-sightedness is a visual defect.* **2** that can be seen; visible: *the visual arts.* **3** of the nature of a mental vision: *to form a visual image from an author's description.*
n Usually, **visuals** *pl* the graphic elements of a movie, etc. as distinct from the sound, etc.: *The plot is poor, but the visuals are great.* **vis·u·al·ly** *adv.* ⟨Latin *visus* sight; *videre* see⟩
visual aid a device such as a chart, movie, etc. for aiding communication through the sense of sight. **visual display unit** *Computers* a monitor, often incorporating a keyboard for user interaction. **vis·u·al·ize** *v* form a mental picture of: *I can visualize his reaction when he hears the news.* **vis·u·al·i·za·tion** *n.*

vi·tal ['vaɪtəl] *adj* **1** to do with life: *Eating is a vital function.* **2** of the greatest importance: *Perfect timing was vital to the success of the plan.* **3** causing death, failure, or ruin: *a vital blow to an industry.* **4** full of life and spirit. *n* **vitals** *pl* the vital organs, such as the heart, brain, lungs, etc. **vi·tal·ly** *adv.* ⟨Latin *vita* life⟩
vi·tal·i·ty [vaɪ'tæləti] *n* mental or physical vigour: *She has great vitality.* **vi·tal·ize** *v* put vitality into. **vi·tal·i·za·tion** *n.* **vital signs** physical signs of life, such as pulse. **vital statistics 1** data about births, deaths, marriages, etc. **2** *Slang* a woman's bust, waist, and hip measurements.

vi·ta·min ['vaɪtəmɪn] *n* any of certain complex organic substances required for the normal growth of the body. **vi·ta·min·ic** *adj.* ⟨Latin *vita* life + AMINE⟩
vi·ta·min·ize *v* add vitamins to: *This breakfast cereal has been vitaminized.*

vi·ti·ate ['vɪʃiˌeit] *v* **1** impair the quality of; spoil: *His illness vitiated his chances of success.* **2** destroy the legal authority of: *The contract was vitiated because one person signed under compulsion.* **vi·ti·a·tion** *n.* **vi·ti·a·ble** *adj.* ⟨Latin *vitiare; vitium* fault⟩

vit·i·cul·ture ['vɪtəˌkʌltʃər] *n* the cultivation of grapes. **vi·ti·cul·tur·al** *adj.* **vi·tl·cul·tur·lst** *n.* ⟨Latin *vitis* vine + CULTURE⟩

vit·re·ous ['vɪtriəs] *adj* **1** to do with glass. **2** like glass in texture, brittleness, etc.: *vitreous rocks.* ⟨Latin *vitrum* glass⟩
vitreous humour or **humor** the jellylike substance that fills the interior of the eyeball. **vit·ric** *adj* to do with glass; like glass. *n* **1** vitrics (with a sg verb), the study of glass and glassmaking. **2** vitrics *pl* glassware. **vit·ri·fy** *v* change into glass by heat. **vit·ri·fi·a·ble** *adj.* **vit·ri·fi·ca·tion** *n.*

vit·ri·ol ['vɪtriˌɒl] or ['vɪtriəl] *n* **1** any of certain sulphates. **2** SULPHURIC ACID. **3** very sharp speech or severe criticism. ⟨Latin *vitriolum; vitrum* glass⟩
vit·ri·ol·ic *adj* bitterly severe: *vitriolic criticism.*

vi·tu·per·ate [vɪ'tjupəˌreit] or [vɪ'tupəˌreit] *v* find fault with in abusive words; revile.

vi·tu·per·a·tion *n.* vi·tu·per·a·tive *adj.* ⟨Latin *vituperare; vitium* fault + *parare* prepare⟩

vi·va ['vivə] *Italian interj* a word used in exclamation of praise or as a salute. *Viva Italia!* means *Long live Italy!* ⟨Italian = live⟩

vi·va·cious [vɪ'veɪʃəs] *or* [vaɪ'veɪʃəs] *adj* lively; animated: *a vivacious personality, a vivacious smile.* vi·vac·i·ty [-'væsəti] *n.* vi·va·cious·ly *adv.* vi·va·cious·ness *n.* ⟨Latin *vivax, vivacis*⟩

vi·va vo·ce ['vivə 'voutʃeɪ] *or* ['vaɪvə 'vousɪ] spoken; oral: *a viva voce examination.* ⟨Latin, literally, by living voice⟩

vive [viv] *French interj* a word used in exclamation of praise or as a salute. *Vive la France!* means *Long live France!* ⟨French = live⟩

viv·id ['vɪvɪd] *adj* 1 brilliant; strikingly bright: *Dandelions are a vivid yellow.* 2 full of life: *a vivid personality.* 3 a clearly and strikingly perceived: *a vivid impression.* b very evocative: *vivid imagery.* 4 very active: *a vivid imagination.* viv·id·ly *adv.* viv·id·ness *n.* ⟨Latin *vividus; vivus* alive⟩

viv·i·fy *v* give life or vigour to; make vivid. viv·i·fi·ca·tion *n.*

vi·vip·a·rous [vɪ'vɪpərəs] *or* [vaɪ'vɪpərəs] *adj* Zoology bringing forth living young rather than eggs. Compare OVIPAROUS. ⟨Latin *vivus* alive + *parere* bring forth⟩

viv·i·sec·tion [,vɪvə'sekʃən] *n* the practice of cutting into or experimenting on living animals for scientific study. viv·i·sec·tion·al *adj.* ⟨Latin *vivus* alive + SECTION⟩

viv·i·sec·tion·ist *n* a person who engages in vivisection, or who defends it.

vix·en ['vɪksən] *n* a female fox. ⟨Old English *fyxen; fox* fox⟩

viz. to wit; namely: *Two members have been asked to attend the conference, viz., Ms. Sanchez and Mr. Faber.* ⟨Latin *videlicet* as *vi + z,* medieval symbol for *-et*⟩

USAGE

Viz. is used mainly in formal documents or reference works. It is a written form that is not pronounced [vɪz], except humorously, but is usually spoken or read as 'namely'.

vi·zier [vɪ'zɪr] *or* ['vɪzjər] *n* in Muslim countries, a high official or minister of state. vi·zier·al *adj.* vi·zier·ate *or* vi·zier·ship *n.* ⟨Turkish; Arabic *wazīr,* orig porter⟩

VJ VIDEO JOCKEY.

VLT VIDEO LOTTERY TERMINAL.

V neck a neckline that is V-shaped at the front. Also, V–neck. V–neck or V–necked *adj.*

vo·cab·u·lar·y [və'kæbjə,lɛri] *n* 1 the stock of words known to or used by a person: *Reading will increase your vocabulary.* 2 a list of words with their translations or meanings: *There is a vocabulary in the back of our French book.* ⟨Latin *vocabulum; vocare* call, *vox* voice⟩

vo·cal ['voukəl] *adj* 1 to do with the voice: *vocal music.* 2 inclined to talk freely: *He became vocal with indignation.*
n Music the part of a composition that is sung: *She did the background vocals for this*

song. vo·cal·ly *adv.* ⟨Latin *vocalis; vox* voice⟩

vocal cords either of two pairs of folds of membrane in the larynx. vo·cal·ic [vou'kælɪk] *adj Phonetics* 1 to do with a vowel: I *is a vocalic word.* 2 functioning as a vowel: *The word* pyre *has a vocalic* y. vo·cal·i·cal·ly *adv.* vo·cal·ise [,voukə'liz] *n Music* a piece of music sung on one vowel sound or on sol fa syllables as a voice exercise. vo·cal·ist *n* singer. vo·cal·ize *v* make vocal; articulate; express with the voice: *The dog vocalized its pain in a series of long howls.* vo·cal·i·za·tion *n.*

vo·ca·tion [vou'keɪʃən] *n* 1 an occupation, business, profession, or trade: *He chose teaching as his vocation.* 2 a an inclination to a particular activity, esp to religious work: *She had a vocation for nursing.* b the work to which one is so called. ⟨Latin *vocare* call⟩
vo·ca·tion·al *adj* to do with some occupation, trade, etc. vo·ca·tion·al·ly *adv.*

CONFUSABLES

Vocation applies to the way a person earns his or her living. Avocation applies to a kind of work a person does in his or her spare time, a hobby: *Teaching is her vocation, and photography is her avocation.*

vo·cif·er·ate [və'sɪfə,reɪt] *v* cry out loudly. vo·cif·er·a·tion *n.* ⟨Latin *vociferari; vox, vocis* voice + *ferre* bear⟩
vo·cif·er·ous *adj* loud and noisy: *a vociferous person, vociferous cheers.* vo·cif·er·ous·ly *adv.* vo·cif·er·ous·ness *n.*

vod·ka ['vɒdkə] *n* a colourless alcoholic liquor distilled from rye, wheat, potatoes, etc. ⟨Russian, diminutive of *voda* water⟩

vogue [voug] *n* 1 something that is in fashion: *Hoopskirts were the vogue many years ago.* 2 a period of popularity: *a short vogue. adj* popular or fashionable: *vogue colours.* vogu·ish *adj.* ⟨French = a rowing, course, success; *voguer* float, row⟩

voice [vɔɪs] *n* 1 the sound human beings make in speaking, singing, shouting, etc.: *The voices of the children could be heard coming from the playground.* 2 such sound regarded as having a particular quality: *to recognize someone's voice, a low voice.* 3 anything thought of as being like speech or song: *the voice of the wind.* 4 *Music* ability as a singer: *a good voice.* 5 an instrument of expression: *That newspaper claims to be the voice of the people.* 6 the right to express an opinion: *We have no voice in the matter.* 7 *Grammar* a form of a verb showing the relation of the subject to the action expressed. The **active voice**, as *sees* in *he sees,* shows that the subject is performing the action. The **passive voice**, as *is seen* in *he is seen,* shows that the subject is receiving the action.
v 1 express: *They voiced their approval of the plan.* 2 *Phonetics* utter with vibration of the vocal cords, not with breath alone. The consonants *z, v,* and *d* are voiced; *s, f,* and *t* are not. ⟨Old French *vois, voiz;* Latin *vox*⟩
in voice in condition to sing or speak well.
with one voice unanimously.

voice box larynx. **voiced** *adj* **1** having a voice of a particular kind (usually in compounds): *deep-voiced*. **2** *Phonetics* produced with vibration of the vocal cords. All vowel sounds are voiced; many consonants, such as *b* are also voiced. Compare VOICELESS. **voice·less** *adj* **1** mute; speechless. **2** not expressed. **3** *Phonetics* produced or uttered without vibration of the vocal cords. The consonants *p*, *t*, and *k* are voiceless. Compare VOICED. **voice·less·ly** *adv*. **voice·less·ness** *n*. **voice mail 1** an automated answering system using a series of prerecorded prompts to which callers may respond by pressing the appropriate button. **2** messages recorded on such a system. **voice–o·ver** *n* the voice of an unseen commentator in a film or on television. *adj* made with an unseen narrator: *voice-over commercials*. **voice·print** *n* a graphic representation of an individual's voice.

void [vɔɪd] *adj* **1** *Law* without legal force: *A contract made by a person under legal age is void*. **2** empty; vacant: *a void space*. *v* **1** cancel: *to void a transaction on a cash register*. **2** excrete (urine or feces). **3** empty. *n* **1** an empty space. **2** a feeling of loss or emptiness: *The death of his wife left an aching void in his heart*. **3** *Card games* complete lack of cards (*in* a given suit) in one's hand as dealt: *a void in hearts*. **void·a·ble** *adj*. **void·ance** *n*. **void·er** *n*. ⟨Old French *voide*; Latin *vocitus*, variant of *vacuus* empty⟩ **void of** devoid of; without; lacking.

voi·là [vwɑ'lɑ] *interj French* there it is; behold.

voile [vɔɪl] *or* [vwal] *n* a sheer cloth, used for blouses, curtains, etc. ⟨French, orig veil⟩

voir dire ['vwɑr 'dir] *Law* a preliminary examination by a judge to determine the competence, interest, etc. of a trial witness or the voluntary nature of a confession. ⟨Old French; *voire* truly + *dire* to speak⟩

vol·a·tile ['vɒlə,taɪl] *or* ['vɒlətəl] *adj* **1** evaporating rapidly: *Gasoline is volatile*. **2** changing rapidly from one mood or interest to another: *a volatile disposition*. **3** of an unstable situation, likely to break into open revolt. **4** short-lived. **5** *Computers* of memory, not retaining data when the power is cut off. **vol·a·til·i·ty** *n*. ⟨Latin *volatilis* flying⟩ **vol·a·til·ize** ['vɒlətə,laɪz] *v* evaporate or cause to evaporate. **vol·a·til·i·za·tion** *n*.

vol·ca·no [vɒl'keɪnou] *n*, *pl* **-noes** or **-nos** **1** an opening in the earth's crust through which steam, ashes, and lava are expelled. **2** a hill around this opening, built up of the material that has been forced out. ⟨Italian; Latin *Vulcanus* Vulcan⟩ **vol·can·ic** [vɒl'kænɪk] *adj* **1** to do with a volcano: *a volcanic eruption*. **2** made of materials from volcanoes: *volcanic rock*. **3** like a volcano in breaking forth violently: *a volcanic temper*. **vol·can·i·cal·ly** *adv*.

vole [voul] *n* any of numerous rodents resembling mice, but having a blunt nose, short ears, and a short tail. ⟨*volemouse*; *voll* field (Scandinavian) + *mouse*⟩

vo·li·tion [və'lɪʃən] *n* **1** the act of using one's will to make a choice or decision: *He gave himself up to the police of his own volition*. **2** the power of making a choice or decision; will: *By a tremendous exercise of volition, she made one last effort*. **vo·li·tion·al** *adj*. **vo·li·tion·al·ly** *adv*. ⟨Latin *volitio*; *volo* I wish⟩

vol·ley ['vɒli] *n*, *pl* **-leys** *n* **1** the discharge of a number of weapons at once. **2** a burst of words, oaths, shouts, cheers, etc.: *a volley of questions*. **3** *Tennis, volleyball, etc.* **a** the return of the ball before it touches the ground. **b** an uninterrupted series of such returns. **vol·ley** *v*. ⟨French *volée* flight; Latin *volare*⟩ **vol·ley·ball** *n* a game played with a large ball and a high net. Two teams of players hit the ball with their hands back and forth across the net without letting it touch the ground.

volt [voult] *n* an SI unit for measuring the pressure of an electric current. One volt of pressure drives a current of one ampere through a resistance of one ohm. *Symbol* **V** ⟨Count A. *Volta*, 19c Italian physicist⟩ **volt·age** *n* the strength of electric pressure measured in volts. **vol·ta·ic** [vɒl'teɪɪk] *adj* to do with direct electric current: *a voltaic cell*. **vol·tam·e·ter** [vɒl'tæmətər] *n* a device for measuring the quantity of electricity passing through a conductor by indicating the amount of gas produced or of metal deposited on an electrode. **vol·ta·met·ric** *adj*. **vol·tam·me·ter** ['voult,æm,mitər] *n* a device for measuring voltage or amperage. **volt–am·pere** *n* the product of one volt and one ampere, i.e., one watt. **volt·me·ter** *n* an instrument for measuring electromotive force.

volte face [,voult 'fɑs] *French* [vɔlt 'fɑs] *n* an about-face; reversal in attitude. ⟨French; Italian *volta* a turn + *faccia* face; Latin *facies*⟩

vol·u·ble ['vɒljəbəl] *adj* talkative; characterized by a rapid flow of words: *a voluble protest*. **vol·u·bil·i·ty** *n*. **vol·u·bly** *adv*. ⟨Latin *volubilis* orig rolling; *volvere* roll⟩

vol·ume ['vɒljum] *n* **1** a collection of printed sheets bound together to form a book; book: *We own a library of five hundred volumes*. **2** a book forming part of a set: *His memoirs were published in three volumes*. **3** space measured in cubic units: *The storeroom has a volume of 20 m³*. **4** a large quantity: *Volumes of smoke poured from the chimneys of the factory*. **5** degree of loudness or fullness of tone: *A pipe organ gives much more volume than a violin or flute*. ⟨Latin *volumen* scroll; *volvere* roll⟩ **speak volumes** be full of meaning: *His loving glance spoke volumes*. **vo·lu·mi·nous** [və'lumənəs] *adj* **1** of great size or volume: *A voluminous cloak covered her from head to foot*. **2** filling a large book or several books: *a voluminous report*. **3** writing or speaking much: *a voluminous author*. **vo·lu·mi·nous·ly** *adv*. **vo·lu·mi·nous·ness** *n*.

vol·un·tar·y ['vɒlən,teri] *adj* **1** done, given, etc. of one's free will: *Churches are supported by voluntary contributions*. **2** supported entirely by voluntary gifts: *She works for a voluntary organization*. **3** acting or able to act of one's own free will: *Voluntary workers built this road.* **4** *Physiology* controlled by the will: *Talking is voluntary; breathing is only partly so.* **5** *Music* an organ solo played before, during, or after a church service. **vol·un·tar·i·ly** *adv.* ⟨Latin *voluntas* will; *volo* I wish⟩

vol·un·teer [ˌvɒlən'tir] *n* **1** a person who performs a voluntary service, esp a public service. **2** a person who enters military service of his or her own free will. **3** a person who serves without pay: *In some towns, the firefighters are volunteers.* *v* **1** offer one's services as a volunteer: *As soon as war was declared, many citizens volunteered.* **2** offer of one's own free will: *He volunteered to do the job.* **3** tell or say voluntarily: *She volunteered the information.* **vol·un·teer** *adj.*

SYNONYMS

Voluntary emphasizes the idea of something done of one's own choice, not in obedience to the will of another: *The state is supported by taxes, the church by voluntary contributions.* **Spontaneous** emphasizes the idea of something neither compelled by another nor directed by one's own will, but done from natural impulse: *The laughter at her jokes is never forced, but always spontaneous.*

vo·lup·tu·ar·y [və'lʌptʃu‚ɛri] *n* a person who cares much for luxury and sensual pleasures. **vo·lup·tu·ar·y** *adj.* ⟨Latin *voluptas* pleasure⟩

vo·lup·tu·ous *adj* **1** full of or giving pleasure to the senses: *a voluptuous dance.* **2** of a woman, shapely. **vo·lup·tu·ous·ly** *adv.* **vo·lup·tu·ous·ness** *n.*

vom·it ['vɒmɪt] *v* **1** expel stomach contents through the mouth. **2** throw up or out with force: *The chimneys vomited forth smoke.* *n* the substance thrown up from the stomach. ⟨Latin *vomitus* pp of *vomere* spew forth⟩

voo·doo ['vudu] *n* **1** a polytheistic religion that involves belief in the existence of spirits which act as guides, and belief in the magical power of charms and spells. **2** a charm, curse, or fetish of voodoo origin. *v* affect by voodoo sorcery. **voo·doo** *adj.* **voo·doo·ism** *n.* **voo·doo·ist** *n.* **voo·doo·is·tic** *adj.* ⟨of African origin⟩

vo·ra·cious [və'reiʃəs] *adj* **1** having an enormous appetite: *voracious sharks.* **2** very eager: *a voracious reader.* **vo·ra·cious·ly** *adv.* **vo·rac·i·ty** [və'ræsəti] *n.* ⟨Latin *voracis* greedy⟩

vor·tex ['vɔrtɛks] *n, pl* **-tex·es** or **-ti·ces** **1** a whirling mass of water, air, etc. that sucks everything near it into its centre. **2** a whirl of activity from which it is hard to escape: *The two nations were drawn into the vortex of war.* ⟨Latin variant of *vertex*. See VERTEX.⟩

vo·ta·ry ['voutəri] *n* **1** an adherent of a particular religion, cause, ideal, etc. **2** a person, such as a monk or nun, bound by vows to a religious life. *adj* of, like, or consecrated by a vow. ⟨Latin *votum* vow⟩

vo·tive *adj* **1** done, given, etc. to express or fulfill a vow or promise. **2** *Roman Catholic*

Church voluntarily done or given, esp for a special intention or occasion: *a votive candle.*

vote [vout] *n* **1** a formal expression of a person's decision in response to a specific question, a choice between candidates, etc.: *She won by twenty votes.* **2** the total number of votes cast: *The vote was higher than in the last election.* **3** the act or process of voting: *We decided by vote.* **4** a choice of an individual or group: *My vote is for peace.* **vote** *v.* **vot·a·ble** *adj.* **vote·less** *adj.* ⟨Latin *votum* vow⟩
put to a vote decide (a matter) by voting. **take a vote** vote. **vote down** defeat (esp a motion or proposal) by voting against. **vote in** elect. **vote out** defeat (an incumbent) by voting against.
vote of confidence **1** in parliament, a majority vote of support for the government, esp in a crisis. **2** any show of support or approval. **vot·er** *n* **1** a person who votes. **2** a person who has the right to vote. **voters' list** at an election, a list giving the names and addresses of all those entitled to vote in a given riding, ward, etc.

vo·tive See VOTARY.

vouch [vautʃ] *v* be responsible; give a guarantee (*for*): *I can vouch for the truth of the story.* ⟨Anglo-French *voucher;* Latin *vocare* call⟩
vouch·er *n* **1** a person or thing that vouches for something. **2** a written evidence of payment in advance, as a bonus coupon, gift certificate, etc. **3** receipt. **vouch·safe** *v* grant or give: *The man vouchsafed no reply.*

vow [vau] *n* **1** a solemn promise: *a vow of secrecy.* **2** a promise made to God: *a nun's vows.* **3** any solemn declaration, pledge, etc.: *a vow of revenge, a vow of eternal friendship.* *v* **1** make a vow. **2** declare emphatically: *She vowed she would never shop there again.* ⟨Old French *vou;* Latin *votum*⟩
take vows become a member of a religious order.

vow·el ['vauəl] *n* **1** a speech sound in which the vocal cords are vibrating and the breath is not blocked by the tongue, teeth, or lips. When you say *awe*, you are uttering a vowel. **2** a letter or symbol representing such a sound. The vowels used in writing English are *a, e, i, o, u,* and sometimes *y*. ⟨Old French *vouel;* Latin *vocalis* sounding; *vox* voice⟩

vox po·pu·li [vɒks 'pɒpjə‚lai] or [-‚li] *Latin* the voice or opinion of the people.

voy·age ['vɔɪdʒ] *n* **1** a journey by water, esp a long journey: *a voyage to Japan.* **2** a journey through the air or through space. **voy·age** *v.* ⟨French; Latin *viaticum; via* road⟩
voy·ag·er *n* **1** a person who makes a voyage; traveller. **2** ✱ voyageur.

voy·a·geur [‚vɔɪə'ʒɜr] *French* [vwaja'ʒœR] *n, pl* **-geurs** [-'ʒɜrz] *French* [-'ʒœR] ✱ **1** formerly, a boatman, esp a French Canadian, in the service of the fur-trading companies. **2** a person who travels the northern wilderness, esp by canoe. ⟨French; *voyage* voyage⟩

voy·eur [vwa'ʒɜr] or [vɔɪ'ʒɜr] *n* a person who finds sexual gratification in observing the nude bodies or sexual acts of others. **voy·eur·ism** *n.* **voy·eur·ist·ic** *adj.* ⟨French; *voir* to see; Latin *videre*⟩

VP or **V.P.** vice-president.

VRML interface ['vɜrməl] *Computers* Short for Virtual Reality Modelling Language, allowing the creation of virtual images.

vroom [vrum] *interj* an exclamation imitating the sound of a motor vehicle revving or accelerating. ⟨imitative⟩

vs. versus.

vul·can·ite ['vʌlkə,naɪt] *n* a hard black rubber made by treating crude rubber with sulphur and heating it to high temperatures. **vul·can·i·za·tion** *n.* **vul·can·ize** *v.* **vul·can·iz·er** *n.* ⟨*Vulcan,* Roman god of fire and metalworking⟩

vul·gar ['vʌlgər] *adj* **1** utterly lacking in good manners, taste, sensitivity, etc.; coarse: *vulgar ambition, a vulgar show of wealth.* **2** indecent; lewd; obscene: *vulgar language.* **3** in common use; ordinary. **4** of the common people: *Modern French developed from a vulgar variety of Latin.*
n **the vulgar** *Archaic* the common people. **vul·gar·ly** *adv.* ⟨Latin *vulgus* common people⟩
vul·gar·ism *n* **1** a word, phrase, or expression that is regarded as coarse, or obscene. **2** vulgarity. **vul·gar·i·ty** [vʌl'gɛrəti] *n* **1** the quality or state of being vulgar. **2** an action, habit, remark, etc. that is vulgar. **vul·gar·ize** *v* **1** make vulgar; make cheap, coarse, or indecent. **2** make widely known; popularize. **vul·gar·i·za·tion** *n.* **vul·gar·iz·er** *n.*

vul·ner·a·ble ['vʌlnərəbəl] *adj* **1** capable of being wounded or injured; open to attack: *The head is a vulnerable part of the body.* **2** open to criticism, moral attack, or temptation. **3** sensitive to or affected by certain influences (with *to*): *Most people are vulnerable to ridicule.* **4** *Contract bridge* in the position where penalties and premiums are increased. **vul·ner·a·bly** *adv.* ⟨Latin *vulneris* wound⟩
vul·ner·a·bil·i·ty *n* **1** the fact of being open to attack or injury. **2** a specific respect in which one is vulnerable; weak point.

vul·pine ['vʌlpaɪn] *or* ['vʌlpɪn] *adj* **1** to do with a fox. **2** clever; crafty; cunning. ⟨Latin *vulpes* fox⟩

vul·ture ['vʌltʃər] *n* **1** any of a family of large, carrion-eating birds having a naked head and neck and relatively weak feet and claws. **2** a greedy, ruthless person who preys on others. ⟨Latin *vultur*⟩

vul·va ['vʌlvə] *n, pl* **-vae** [-vi] *or* [-vaɪ] or **-vas** the external parts of the genital organs of female mammals. **vul·var** *adj.* **vul·vate** *adj.* **vul·vi·form** *adj.* ⟨Latin = womb⟩

vv 1 verses. **2** volumes.

vy·ing ['vaɪɪŋ] *adj* competing. *v* ppr of VIE.

Ww

w or **W** ['dʌbəl,ju] *n, pl* **w's** or **W's 1** the twenty-third letter of the English alphabet, or any speech sound represented by it. **2** the twenty-third person or thing in a series.

W 1 watt. **2** west; western. **3** *Chemistry* tungsten (for *wolfram*). **4** *Physics* work; energy or force.

wack·y ['wæki] *adj Slang* unconventional in behaviour; eccentric; crazy.

wad [wɒd] *n* **1** a small, soft mass of material: *He plugged his ears with wads of cotton to keep out the noise.* **2** a small compact lump of something: *a wad of chewing gum.* **3** *Informal* a roll of paper money. **4** *Slang* a large amount of money: *She made her wad in real estate.*
v **wad·ded, wad·ding** crush, press, or roll into a wad: *He wadded up the paper and threw it into the wastebasket.* ⟨origin uncertain⟩

wad·dle ['wɒdəl] *v* walk with short steps and an awkward, swaying motion, like a duck. **wad·dle** *n*. **wad·dler** *n*. ⟨*wade*⟩

wade [weid] *v* **1** walk through water, snow, mud, or anything that hinders free motion. **2** walk about in shallow water for amusement: *We loved to go wading in the spring.* **3** make one's way with difficulty (with *through*): *to wade through an uninteresting book.* **4** *Informal* go to work vigorously (with *in* or *into*): *He waded right in and got the job done.*
n the act or an instance of wading. ⟨Old English *wadan* proceed⟩
wad·er *n* **1** Usually, **waders** *pl* high waterproof boots used for wading, esp by fishers, etc. **2** WADING BIRD. **wading bird** any long-legged bird that wades in water to look for food, as herons, and flamingos. **wading pool 1** a shallow pool provided, as in a public park, for small children to play in. **2** a small, shallow, portable pool of plastic, fibreglass, etc. for small children to play in.

wa·di ['wɑdi] *n* **1** in parts of the Arabian peninsula, N Africa, etc., a valley through which a stream flows during the rainy season. **2** an oasis. ⟨Arabic⟩

wa·fer ['weifər] *n* **1** a very thin, crisp biscuit, cookie, or piece of candy. **2** in some Christian churches, a thin, round piece of unleavened bread used in the Eucharist. **wa·fer·like** *adj*. ⟨Anglo-French *wafre*⟩
wa·fer–thin *adj* exceedingly thin.

waf·fle[1] ['wɒfəl] *n* a light, thin, crisp, moulded cake made from a batter and baked in a WAFFLE IRON. ⟨Dutch *wafel*⟩
waffle iron a device for cooking waffles, consisting of two hinged metal plates with a gridlike pattern of surface projections.

waf·fle[2] ['wɒfəl] *v* **1** avoid making a decision or commitment by speaking ambiguously or evasively: *The ratepayers' association accused their MP of waffling on the airport issue.* **2** talk nonsense; prattle; talk on and on. **waf·fle** *n*. **waf·fler** *n*. ⟨dialect *waff* yelp + *-le*⟩

waft [wɒft] *or* [wæft] *v* **1** carry over water or through air: *The waves wafted the boat to shore.* **2** float: *A feather wafted to the ground.*
n **1** the act of wafting. **2** a breath or puff of air, wind, etc. ⟨earlier *wafter* convoy ship; Dutch *wachter* guard⟩

wag [wæg] *v* **wagged, wag·ging 1** move or cause to move from side to side or up and down, esp rapidly and repeatedly: *The dog's tail started wagging.* **2** of a person's tongue, move in speaking, esp to chatter or gossip: *Tongues began to wag after the police left.*
n **1** the act of wagging. **2** a person who is fond of making jokes. ⟨Middle English *waggen*, Old English *wagian* shake⟩
wag·gish *adj* **1** fond of making jokes. **2** done or made in fun; playful or funny; characteristic of a wag: *a waggish look.*
wag·gish·ly *adv*. **wag·gish·ness** *n*. **wag·gle** *v* **1** move quickly and repeatedly from side to side; wag. **2** wobble or waver while moving along: *The ball waggled into the hole.* *n* a waggling motion. **wag·gly** *adj*.

wage [weidʒ] *n* **1** Often, **wages** *pl* an amount paid for work, esp work on a weekly, hourly, daily, or piecework basis: *the minimum wage.* **2** Usually, **wages** something given in return (with *a sg* or *pl verb*): *Her illness taught her the wages of poor eating.*
v carry on: *to wage war.* **wage·less** *adj*. ⟨Anglo-French⟩
wage scale a schedule of wages paid to workers, taking into account skill, responsibility, seniority, etc.

wa·ger ['weidʒər] *n* **1** an agreement between two persons that the one who is proved wrong about the outcome of an event will give a particular thing or sum of money to the person who is proved right; bet: *They made a wager on the result of the election.* **2** the thing or sum risked: *What's your wager?*
v **1** make a wager; bet; gamble: *She wagered two dollars on the first race.* **2** be fairly certain; say with some certainty: *I wager he'll come if you stop coaxing him.* ⟨Anglo-French *wageure*; related to WAGE⟩

wag·gle See WAG.

wag·on ['wægən] *n* **1** a four-wheeled vehicle, usually drawn by a horse or tractor: *a hay wagon.* **2** a child's four-wheeled cart, usually low and steered by a handle. ⟨Dutch *wagen*⟩
fix someone's wagon *Informal* hurt someone to avenge real or imagined wrong. **hitch one's wagon to a star** have high ambitions. **off the wagon** drinking alcoholic liquors after a period of abstaining from them. **on the wagon** no longer drinking alcohol.
wag·on·load *n* the load carried by a wagon.
wagon train a group of wagons moving along in a line one after another; esp such a group carrying a company of settlers.

waif [weif] *n* **1** a person without home or friends, esp a homeless or neglected child. **2** a stray animal found and not claimed. **waif·ish** *adj*. **waif·like** *adj*. ⟨Anglo-French *waif*; probably Scandinavian⟩

wail [weil] *v* **1** cry loud and long because of

grief or pain. **2** make a mournful sound: *The wind wailed around the old house.* **wail** *n.* **wail·er** *n.* ⟨perhaps Old Norse *vǽla* woe⟩

wain·scot ['wein,skɒt] *or* ['weinskət] *n* a facing of wood panels on the walls of a room. ⟨Middle German *wagen* wagon + *schot* partition⟩ **wain·scot·ting** or **wain·scot·ing** *n* **1** material used for wainscots. **2** wainscots collectively.

waist [weist] *n* **1** the part of the human body between the ribs and the hips. **2** a narrow middle part: *the waist of a violin.* **3** *Nautical* the part of a ship amidships. ⟨Middle English *wast*; probably Old English *wæst* growth⟩ **waist·band** *n* a band of cloth attached to the top of a skirt or pants to fit around the waist. **waist·line** *n* an imaginary line around the body at the smallest part of the waist. .

wait [weit]*v* **1** stay until someone comes or something happens: *Let's wait in the shade.* **2** *Informal* put off serving (a meal): *Can you wait dinner for me?* **3** look forward: *They were waiting impatiently for the holidays.* **4** wait for: *Wait your turn.* **5** be ready and available: *The car was waiting for us when we got there.* **6** be left undone: *That can wait till tomorrow.* **7** be about to be encountered: *A surprise is waiting for you at home.* **8** be a waiter or waitress (usually in the phrase **wait** (**on** or **at**) **table**): *He waits tables in a hotel dining room.*
n the act or an instance of waiting: *I had a long wait at the doctor's office.* ⟨Old North French *waitier* watch; Germanic⟩
lie in wait stay hidden ready to surprise or attack: *An assassin lay in wait for the dictator.* **wait on** supply the wants of, as a clerk in a store, a waiter in a restaurant, etc. **wait on** (or **upon**) *Formal* **a** be a servant to: *He waits on the prince.* **b** pay a respectful visit to (a superior): *Tomorrow the prime minister will wait on the queen.* **wait out a** do nothing until (something) is finished: *to wait out a storm.* **b** *Baseball* refrain from swinging at the pitches, in the hope of being walked. **wait up a** delay going to bed until something happens: *Don't wait up for me.* **b** *Informal* stop and wait for someone to catch up: *Wait up! He's fallen behind again.*
wait·er *n* a person who waits on table in a hotel, restaurant, etc. **wait·ing** *n* the act of a person who waits. *adj* **1** that waits: *a waiting crowd.* **2** used to wait in: *a waiting room.* **in waiting** in attendance on royalty: *in waiting to the queen.* **waiting list** a list of people who have applied for something that may become available in the future. **wait–list** *v* enter on a list of persons waiting, esp for a seat on an airliner: *I'm wait-listed for tonight's flight.* **waitperson** *n* a waiter or waitress. **wait·ress** *n* a woman who waits on table in a hotel, restaurant, etc. *v* work as a waitress. **wait staff** the waiters and waitresses of an establishment collectively. **wait state** *Computers* the state of a system processing a task and unable to receive other instructions.

waive [weiv] *v* give up or forgo: *The lawyer waived her right to cross-examine the witness.* ⟨Anglo-French *weyver* abandon⟩

waiv·er *n* **1** *Law* **a** a giving up of a right, claim, etc. **b** a written statement of this: *For $5000 the man signed a waiver of all claims against the railway.* **2** *Professional sports* (usually in the phrase **on waivers**) provisions which a club must follow to dispose of the services of any player in which it has a proprietary interest.

Wa·kash·an [wɑ'kæʃən] *or* ['wɒkə,ʃæn] *n* a family of First Nations languages of the Pacific region. **Wa·kash·an** *adj.*

wake[1] [weik] *v* **woke** or **waked**, **wo·ken** or **waked**, **wak·ing 1** stop sleeping (often with *up*): *to wake up early.* **2** rouse from sleep (often with *up*): *The noise will wake the baby.* **3** become alive or active (often with *up*): *Flowers wake in the spring.* **4** make alive or active (often with *up*): *He needs some interest to wake him up.*
n a watch held around a dead person before burial, sometimes accompanied by eating and drinking. ⟨Old English *wacian, wæcnan*⟩
wake (**up**) **to** become aware of: *She finally woke up to the fact that her money was gone.*
wake·ful *adj* **1** not able to sleep: *She was still wakeful long after midnight.* **2** without sleep: *They spent a wakeful night.* **3** watchful; alert. **wake·ful·ly** *adv.* **wake·ful·ness** *n.* **wak·en** *v* WAKE. **wak·en·er** *n.* **wak·ing** *adj* **1** that is awake or becoming awake. **2** spent awake: *60 percent of our waking hours.*

wake[2] [weik] *n* **1** the track left behind a moving ship. **2** the track left by anything. ⟨Middle Dutch⟩
in the wake of a close behind; very soon after: *Floods came in the wake of the hurricane.* **b** as a consequence or result of.

wale [weil] *n* a long, narrow, raised surface, esp one of a series of parallel ribs or ridges in cloth such as corduroy. ⟨Old English *walu*⟩

walk [wɒk] *v* **1** go on foot. **2** stroll for pleasure, exercise, etc. **3** cause to walk: *The rider walked his horse.* **4** accompany or escort in walking: *to walk a guest to the door.* **5** *Baseball* **a** of a batter, go to first base after the pitcher has thrown four balls. See BALL[1] (def. 3). **b** of a pitcher, allow (a batter) to do this. **c** cause (a run) to be scored in this way. (with *in*). **6** take part in a formal walking event for some cause: *I'm walking for cancer; will you sponsor me?* **7** leave or cause to leave negotiations, a position, opportunity, etc. in dissatisfaction: *If you don't pay your people enough, they'll walk.* **8** be released or acquitted or fined instead of sentenced to prison after committing an offence: *If they don't present better evidence than this, he'll walk.*
n **1** the act of walking: *a walk in the country.* **2** a manner or way of walking: *We knew the man was a sailor from his rolling walk.* **3** the relatively slow pace of a person who or animal that walks: *As she neared the house, she slowed to a walk.* **4** a sidewalk or path for walking: *I shovelled the snow off the walk.* **5** occupation or social position: *An electrician and a farmer are in different walks of life.*

6 *Baseball* the advance of a batter to first base by walking. ⟨Old English *wealcan* roll⟩ **in a walk** easily: *Our team will win in a walk.* **take a walk** *Informal* get out of here. **walk (all) over** a defeat easily. **b** *Informal* exploit or victimize: *Don't let them walk all over you.* **walk away from** a reject. **b** survive (an accident or other ordeal) unhurt. **walk off** a walk away (from), esp in an abrupt manner: *She walked off without saying anything.* **b** get rid of by walking: *He walked off his anger.* **walk off** (or **away**) **with** a take; get; win. **b** steal. **walk out a** *Informal* go on strike. **b** leave suddenly. **walk out on** *Informal* desert. **walk tall** have self-respect. **walk through** do a walk-through of (a play, etc.) **walk·a·bout** *n* **1** a relatively informal stroll taken by royalty or a politician to greet the public. **2** *Australian* a temporary return to the outback by an Aborigine to wander the bush and renew traditional skills and practices. **walk·a·thon** [-ə,θɒn] *n* a walk to raise money for a cause, with sponsors pledging a certain amount for every kilometre walked. **walk·er** *n* **1** a person who walks, esp one who walks in a particular way: *She's a fast walker.* **2 a** a framework on wheels designed to support a child learning to walk. **b** a framework designed to help an elderly person, or a person with a disability, to walk. **walk–in** *adj* **1** large enough to be walked into: *a walk-in closet.* **2** of a clinic or other professional or service agency, taking clients without an appointment. **walk–in** *n.* **walk·ing** *n* **1** the action of a person or thing that walks: *Walking is good exercise.* **2** the condition of a road, sidewalk, etc. for walking: *The walking was treacherous after the ice storm. adj* **1** to do with walking: *walking shoes.* **2** personified: *She's a walking encyclopedia.* **walking papers** *Informal* dismissal from a position, etc. **walking shorts** shorts ending just above the knee and cut very full for ease of movement. **walking wounded 1** those whose battle wounds do not force them to be bedridden. **2** those having emotional or mental problems. **walk–on** *n* a small role in which an actor appears on stage but usually has no lines to speak. **walk·out** *n* **1** a work stoppage; strike. **2** the departure of a group of people from a meeting, etc. as a protest. **walk·o·ver** *n Informal* an easy victory. **walk–through** *n* a rehearsal of a play when the lines are read, accompanied only by rough stage action. **walk·way** *n* **1** a walk specially constructed for the use of pedestrians, for their safety. **2** a raised framework on which to walk, often sheltered, as between buildings over a street.

SYNONYMS

Walk is the general word: *He walked downstairs.* **Stride** means 'walk with long, regular steps': *When walking for exercise, we stride briskly.* **Plod** means 'walk heavily, slowly, and with effort': *The old horse plodded along.*

Walk·man ['wɒkmən] *n Trademark* a small cassette or CD player with headphones, often including a radio.

wall [wɒl] *n* **1** the side of a building or room. **2** a structure of stone, etc., built to enclose, divide, etc. **3** something like a wall in looks or function: *a wall of water 4 m high.* **4** the side of any hollow thing: *the wall of a cylinder.* *v* **1** enclose, divide, etc. with a wall, or as if with a wall: *The garden is walled.* **2** close or fill with a wall (often with *up*): *Workers walled up the doorway.* **wall–less** *adj.* **wall–like** *adj.* ⟨Old English *weall;* Latin *vallum*⟩ **come** (or **be**, etc.) **up against a blank wall** be completely unsuccessful: *She tried several departments, but always ran up against a blank wall.* **drive** (or **push**) **to the wall** make desperate or helpless: *driven to the wall by debts.* **go to the wall a** give way; be defeated. **b** fight or insist on something to the end. **off the wall** *Slang* eccentric; bizarre; unreasonable. **up the wall** *Informal* frantic with frustration or anger: *His constant whining drives me up the wall!* **with one's back to** (or **against**) **the wall** in an extreme or desperate situation.

wall·board *n* any of various types of board such as particleboard, used in place of plaster to finish interior walls and ceilings. **walled** *adj* surrounded by walls: *a walled garden.* **wall·flow·er** *n Informal* a person, esp a girl or woman, who remains on the sidelines of an activity, either from shyness or because of not being asked to participate. **wall hanging** a large woven, appliquéd, etc. decoration hung on a wall. **wall·pa·per** *n* paper, usually having a design, used for covering the walls of rooms. *v* paste wallpaper (on a wall): *They spent all weekend wallpapering.* **wall–to–wall** *adj* **1** covering a floor from one wall to the other. **2** so abundant as to seem to be everywhere in a place: *In the den of the tennis star's home there were wall-to-wall trophies.*

wal·la·by ['wɒləbi] *n, pl* **-bies** or (esp collectively) **-by** any of various small marsupials of the same family as the kangaroo. ⟨native Australian *wolabā*⟩

wal·let ['wɒlɪt] *n* a small, flat, folding case, having compartments for carrying money, credit cards, etc. ⟨Middle English *walet*⟩

wall·eye ['wɒl,aɪ] *n* **1** esp in a horse, an eye with a white iris. **2** an eye having a white cornea. **3** a condition of the eyes in which one or both eyes are turned outward because of an imbalance of the muscles; strabismus. **4** a freshwater fish of the perch family that is one of the most important food and game fishes of Canada's inland waters. Also called **yellow walleye, pickerel, yellow pickerel, pikeperch, walleyed pike, doré,** and **dory.** ⟨Old Norse *vagl-eygr; vagl* speck + *auga*⟩

wal·lop ['wɒləp] *Informal v* **1** hit very hard. **2** defeat thoroughly, as in a game. **3** move along rapidly and awkwardly: *The puppy walloped across the lawn to meet us.* *n* **1** a very hard blow. **2** the power to deal very hard blows: *He's got a real wallop!* ⟨Old North French *waloper* gallop⟩ **pack a wallop** *Informal* deliver, or be capable of delivering, a very forceful effect or

impression: *That punch she made for the party certainly packed a wallop!*
wal·lop·ing *Informal n* **1** a beating. **2** a thorough defeat. *adj* very big or impressive: *That's a walloping serving of ice cream! adv* extremely: *a walloping big baby.*

wal·low ['wɒlou] *v* **1** roll about lazily or pleasurably, as animals in dust or mud: *The pigs wallowed in the cool mud.* **2** roll about clumsily: *The boat wallowed helplessly in the stormy sea.* **3** indulge oneself excessively in some pleasure, state of mind, way of living, etc.: *to wallow in luxury, to wallow in self-pity.* *n* **1** the act of wallowing. **2** a place where an animal wallows. 〈Old English *wealwian* roll〉

Wall Street the money market or the financiers of the United States. 〈*Wall Street*, street in financial district of New York City〉

wal·nut ['wɒl,nʌt] *or* ['wɒlnət] *n* any of a genus of hardwood trees, having a large wrinkled nut enclosed in a thick husk. 〈Old English *wealh* foreign + *hnutu* nut〉

wal·rus ['wɒlrəs] *n, pl* **-rus·es** *or* **-rus** a large sea mammal of the Arctic regions, like a seal but larger and having long tusks. 〈Dutch *walros; wal(vis)* whale + *ros* horse〉
walrus mustache a heavy mustache, hanging down over the upper lip, like the hairs on the face of a walrus.

waltz [wɒlts] *n* **1** a smooth, even, gliding ballroom dance in 3/4 time. **2** *Informal* something achieved effortlessly, such as an easy victory: *We won in a waltz, 15 to 0. adj* to do with the waltz: *waltz time.*
v **1** dance a waltz. **2** move nimbly, quickly, or showily: *She waltzed through the room, cheerfully greeting all the guests.* **3** *Informal* advance easily and successfully: *She waltzed through the exam in half the time.* **4** *Informal* move or lead briskly: *His mother waltzed him into the living room to apologize to his brother.* 〈German *walzen* roll〉
waltz up to *Informal* approach boldly or abruptly; accost: *He just waltzed up to the supervisor and said he was quitting.*

wam·pum ['wɒmpəm] *n* **1** beads made from polished shells strung in belts and sashes, formerly used by eastern First Nations and Native Americans as money, as a treaty reminder, or as ornament. **2** *Slang* money. 〈Narraganset (Algonquian) *wampompeag* strings of white (things); *wampan* white + *api* string + *-ag* pl suffix〉

wan [wɒn] *adj* **wan·ner, wan·nest 1** pale and sickly: *Her face looked wan after her illness.* **2** faint or weak: *a wan smile.* **wan·ly** *adv.* **wan·ness** *n.* 〈Old English *wann* dark〉

wand [wɒnd] *n* **1** a slender stick that is used as if it had magic power: *The magician waved his wand.* **2** a hand-held electronic device that reads bar codes by being passed over them. **3** any slender stick or rod, including a stem or shoot of a young tree. **wand·like** *adj.* 〈Old Norse *vöndr*〉

wan·der ['wɒndər] *v* **1** move about without any special purpose: *I wandered through the mall.* **2** depart from the right way: *The dog wandered off and we had to call it back.* **3** talk or think in a rambling or incoherent way: *The fever made his mind wander.* **wan·der·er** *n.* 〈Old English *wandrian*〉

wan·der·lust *n* a strong desire to travel: *His wanderlust led him all over the world.*

wane [wein] *v* **1** of the moon, go through the regular decrease in the size of its visible portion: *The moon wanes after it has become full.* **2** become less intense: *The light of day wanes in the evening.* **3** lose strength or importance: *Her influence over me has waned.* **4** of a period of time, draw to a close: *Summer wanes as autumn nears.* 〈Old English *wanian*〉
on the wane waning: *His popularity was on the wane.*

wan·gle ['wæŋgəl] *v Informal* manage to get by schemes, manipulation, persuasion, etc. 〈origin uncertain〉

wan·i·gan ['wɒnəgən] *n* ✻ **1** a logger's chest or trunk. **2** a sled equipped as living quarters and pulled by tracked vehicles as part of a train for carrying supplies in the North. **3** a boat used by loggers for carrying supplies, tools, etc. and as a houseboat. 〈Algonquian *waniigan* trap, place for stray objects〉

want [wɒnt] *v* **1** wish (for): *He wants to become a singer.* **2** need; ought to have: *Plants want water.* **3** *Informal* ought (to): *You want to eat a balanced diet.* **4** *Informal* wish to come or go: *The dog wants in. He was keen at first, but now he wants out of the project.* **5** wish to speak to, or use the help of (a person): *Call me if you want me.* **6** seek in order to question or arrest: *She is wanted for theft.* **7** suffer from a lack, esp the necessities of life: *In spite of the new aid program, many people are still wanting.* **8** be short or lacking by (a given amount): *It wants an hour until train time.*
n **1** a desire or need: *The new park supplied a long-felt want.* **2** shortage or lack: *The plant died for want of water.* **3** extreme poverty: *Many families were in want this past winter.* 〈Old Norse *vant; vanr* lacking〉
want for have a lack or shortage of: *She has never wanted for friends.*
want ad *Informal* a notice in a newspaper that an employee, job, apartment, car, etc. is wanted or that an apartment, car, etc. is for sale or rent. **want·ing** *adj* **1** not coming up to a standard: *The stranger was wanting in courtesy.* **2** lacking; missing: *One volume of the set is wanting.* *prep* **1** without: *an old chair wanting a back.* **2** minus; less: *a month, wanting three days.*

wan·ton ['wɒntən] *adj* **1** without excuse or reason: *a wanton disregard of others' rights.* **2** sexually immoral. **3** *Archaic, poetic* **a** playful: *a wanton mood, a wanton breeze.* **b** of vegetation, luxuriant; rank. **3** extravagant; lavish: *a wanton display of wealth.*
n an immoral person. **wan·ton·ly** *adv.* **wan·ton·ness** *n.* 〈Old English *wan-* poorly + *togen* pp of *tēon* train〉

wap·i·ti ['wɒpɪti] *n, pl* **-ti** *or* **-tis** the North American elk. 〈Algonquian〉

war [wɔr] n **1** open fighting carried on by armed forces between nations or groups. **2** any active struggle: *a price war*. **3** military science: *Soldiers are trained in war*.
v **warred**, **war·ring** make war: *warring against poverty*. **war·less** adj. **war·ring** adj. ⟨Anglo-French *werre* variant of Old French *guerre*⟩
at war taking part in a war; warring: *Her emotions were at war with one another*. **go to war** a start or enter a war. **b** go as a soldier. **on the warpath** looking for a fight; angry.
war bonnet a ceremonial headdress traditionally worn as a mark of honour among First Nations and Native American peoples of the North American plains, consisting of a row or rows of feathers attached to a headband and trailing down the back. **war bride 1** a woman who marries a soldier during wartime, esp a soldier about to go overseas. **2** a woman who marries a soldier met during wartime, esp a foreign soldier, and then returns with him to his country: *After World War II many war brides came to Canada from the Netherlands*. **war correspondent** a journalist assigned to send back reports directly from a war zone. **war crime** any violation of the rules of warfare, esp atrocities against civilians, prisoners of war, etc. **war criminal**. **war cry 1** a word or phrase shouted in fighting. **2** a slogan in any contest. **war·fare** ['wɔr,fɛr] n **1** war. **2** any struggle or contest. **war game** a training exercise that simulates war. **war·head** n the forward part of a rocket, missile, etc.: *The warhead holds the explosive charge*. **war·horse 1** *Informal* a person, esp a veteran soldier or a person in public life, who has survived many battles or struggles. **2** *Informal* a piece of music, a play, etc. so often performed as to become overly familiar and uninteresting. **war·like** adj **1** fond of and ready for war: *a warlike nature*. **2** threatening war: *a warlike speech*. **war·lord** n a military commander, esp one who has supreme civil authority in a particular region. **war·mon·ger** [-,mɒŋɡər] or [-,mʌŋɡər] n a person who is in favour of war or attempts to bring about war. **War of 1812** a war between the United States and Great Britain, 1812-1815, fought on the Atlantic Ocean and in North America. **war paint** paint put on the face or body by certain peoples before going to war. **war·ri·or** ['wɔriər] n a person who engages in armed combat; an experienced soldier. **war·ri·or·like** adj. **war·ship** n a ship used in war. **war·time** n a time of active hostilities. **war·time** adj.

war·ble ['wɔrbəl] v **1** sing in a melodious way, with trills, etc.: *Birds warbled in the trees*. **2** make a sound like that of a bird warbling: *The brook warbled over its rocky bed*. **war·ble** n. ⟨Old North French *werbler*; Germanic⟩
war·bler n any of a subfamily of small songbirds.

ward [wɔrd] n **1** a division of a hospital, consisting of a group of rooms: *a maternity ward*. **2** a division of a prison, such as a block of cells. **3** a political subdivision of a city, esp one represented by a municipal councillor.
4 a person under the care of a guardian or of a court: *a ward of the Children's Aid Society*. **5** the act of keeping guard: *The soldiers kept ward over the castle*. **6** the large open space within the walls of a castle or fortress.
v turn aside or keep away (usually with *off*): *He warded off the blow with his arm*. ⟨Old English *weardian* guard; Germanic⟩
ward·ship n **1** guardianship or custody, esp over a minor. **2** the condition of being a ward, or under a legal or feudal guardian.

–ward *suffix* in or to a particular direction or point in time: *backward, seaward, upward*. ⟨Old English *-weard*⟩

Of variants such as **downward/downwards**, only the **-ward** form is used as adjective or noun: *a forward movement, looking to the westward*. Either variant may be used as adverb or preposition: *He fell backward* or *He fell backwards*.

ward·en ['wɔrdən] n **1** an official who enforces certain rules: *a fire warden*. **2** a person in charge of the operation of a prison. **3** in certain institutions, an official with administrative duties. **4** ✷ in provinces having county governments, the head of the county council. **ward·en·ship** n. ⟨Old North French *wardein, g(u)arden* guardian⟩

ward·robe ['wɔr,droub] n **1** a stock of clothes: *She is shopping for her spring wardrobe*. **2** a closet for holding clothes. **3** all the costumes of a theatrical show or film. ⟨Old North French *warderobe, garderobe; garder* keep + *robe* gown⟩

ware [wɛr] n **1** Usually, **wares** pl goods for sale (as by merchants, etc.): *He peddled his wares from door to door*. **2** goods of a particular kind (mainly in compounds): *hardware, kitchenware*. **3** pottery: *Biscuit ware is unglazed porcelain*. ⟨Old English *waru*⟩
ware·house n **1** a building or large room where goods are stored. **2** a wholesale or large, reasonably-priced retail outlet. v ['wɛr,hauz] put or keep in a warehouse.

war·fa·rin ['wɔrfərɪn] n *Chemistry* an anticoagulant, chiefly used to kill rodents. It causes internal bleeding. ⟨*Wisconsin Alumni Research Foundation* (original patent holders) + (*coum*)*arin* toxic substance⟩

war·lock ['wɔr,lɒk] n a man who practises black magic; sorcerer. Compare WITCH. ⟨Old English *wǣr* covenant + *-loga* denying one⟩

warm [wɔrm] adj **1** more hot than cold: **2** having a feeling of greater than usual body heat: *She was warm from running*. **3** that makes or keeps warm: *a warm coat*. **4** having or showing affection, enthusiasm, etc.: *a warm welcome*. **5** of a trail, scent, etc., recent and strong. **6** *Informal* in treasure hunts, etc., near what one is searching for. **7** of a colour, suggesting warmth. **8** uncomfortable; unpleasant: *to make things warm for a person*. v **1** make or become warm: *to warm a room*. **2** make or become cheered, friendly, or sympathetic: *Their kindness warmed our hearts*.

warm·ly *adv.* **warm·ness** *n.* **warmth** *n.* ⟨Old English *wearm*⟩

warm over reheat (leftover food, etc.). **b** rehash; rework with tiresome effect. **warmed–o·ver** *adj.* **warm to** become more enthusiastic about or sympathetic toward: *The speaker warmed to his subject.* **warm up a** heat or cook again. **b** make or become more interested, friendly, etc. **c** practise or exercise for a few minutes before entering a game, contest, etc. **d** of an engine, etc., operate in order to reach a proper working temperature: *It takes the car a long time to warm up.*

warm–blood·ed *adj* having warm blood that stays about the same temperature (between 36°C and 44°C) regardless of the surrounding air or water. **warm front** *Meteorology* the front edge of a warm air mass. **warm fuzzy** *Informal* (sometimes disparaging) **1** an encouraging remark. **2** the warm, positive feeling it causes. **warm–heart·ed** *adj* having a kind, affectionate, or friendly nature. **warm·ish** *adj* somewhat warm. **warm–up** *n* exercises or a routine used for warming up, as before a game, contest, etc.

warn [wɔrn] *v* **1** give notice (to) in advance about a possible unpleasantness or danger: *The clouds warned of the coming storm.* **2** give notice of something that requires attention: *His mother warned us that we would have to leave by 8 o'clock.* **3** give notice to keep out, etc. (with *off* or *away*): *There was a sign warning off trespassers.* **4** caution (with an infinitive): *She warned us to keep away from the dog.* **warn·ing** *n, adj.* **warn·ing·ly** *adv* ⟨Old English *warnian*⟩

SYNONYMS

Warn emphasizes giving information that lets a person avoid or prepare for what is likely to come: *Her mother warned her not to speak to strangers.* **Caution** emphasizes giving advice to guard against something (or someone): *Drivers are cautioned against driving too long without a break.*

warp [wɔrp] *v* **1** bend out of shape: *The heat from the radiator has warped the shelf.* **2** make or become perverted or distorted: *Prejudice warps our judgment.*
n **1** a bend in something that should be straight: *This board has a warp.* **2** a distortion of the mind, judgment, etc. **3** the threads stretched lengthwise in a loom, through which the crosswise threads are woven. See WOOF, WEFT. **4** See TIME WARP. ⟨Old English *weorpan* throw⟩
warp·age *n* the amount or degree of warping.

war·rant ['wɔrənt] *n* **1** a written order giving legal authority for something, esp one authorizing a search, arrest, etc.: *a warrant for your arrest.* **2** authorization: *Their vote of confidence was his warrant to continue his investigation.* **3** a promise; guarantee.
v **1** justify: *The situation warranted fast action.* **2** guarantee (something) to (someone): *to warrant the genuineness of goods purchased.* **3** *Informal* declare confidently: *I warrant I'll

get there before you.* **4** authorize: *The law warrants his arrest.* **war·rant·a·ble** *adj.* **war·rant·a·bly** *adv.* ⟨Old North French *warant*⟩ **war·ran·ty** *n* a written promise that a manufacturer will take the responsibility for repairing or replacing a product if it proves to be defective.

war·ren ['wɔrən] *n* **1** an area of ground having many interconnected burrows where rabbits live. **2** a crowded district or building. ⟨Anglo-French *warenne*; Celtic⟩

war·ri·or See WAR.

wart [wɔrt] *n* **1** a small growth on the skin, caused by a virus. **2** a defect or imperfection. **wart·y** *adj.* ⟨Old English *wearte*⟩
wart·hog or **wart hog** a wild pig having large tusks and large wartlike growths on its face.

war·y ['weri] *adj* **1** cautious and watchful (*of*): *They were wary of the stranger.* **2** done with caution: *She gave wary answers to all of my questions.* **war·i·ly** *adv.* **war·i·ness** *n.* ⟨Archaic *ware* beware; Old English *wær*⟩

was [wʌz] *v* the first and third person singular, past indicative, of BE: *I was late. Was he late, too?* ⟨Old English *wæs*⟩

wash [wɒʃ] *v* **1** clean (anything) with water or other liquid: *to wash clothes.* **2** make clean; purify: *This one act of heroism washed him of all his guilty past.* **3** of a stain, etc., be removed by washing (with *out*): *That ink won't wash out.* **4** carry or be carried by the action of water or other liquid (often with *away, out,* etc.): *Wood is often washed ashore by the waves.* **5** cover with a thin coating of colour: *to wash walls with blue.* **6** *Mining* sift (earth, ore, etc.) by action of water to separate valuable material. *You won't wash any gold out of this heap of gravel!* **7** *Informal* of an excuse, account, etc., stand up under examination: *That story just won't wash; what's the truth?*
n **1** a washing or being washed. **2** a quantity of clothes washed or to be washed. **3** *Geology* the material carried along by water and then deposited as sediment: *A delta is formed by the wash of a river.* **4** the sound of water: *We listened to the wash of the waves against the boat.* **5** a liquid for a special use: *a mouthwash.* **6** a thin coating of colour, as in painting. **7 a** the broken water left behind a ship. **b** the disturbed air left behind a plane or propeller. ⟨Old English *wascan*⟩
come out in the wash *Informal* resolve itself with the passage of time. **wash down a** wash from top to bottom or from end to end. **b** swallow liquid along with or after (solid food, pills, etc.) to help in swallowing. **wash out a** *Slang* fail or cause to fail a course, test, etc. **b** cause to lose colour or vigour. **c** *Informal* cancel: *The whole program was washed out.* **wash up a** wash the hands and face, as before meals. **b** wash the dishes after meals: *We washed up right after supper.*
wash·a·ble *adj* that can be washed without damage: *washable silk.* **wash–and–wear** *adj* of a garment, easily washed and needing little or no ironing. **wash·ba·sin** *n* a basin for

holding water to wash one's face and hands, do laundry by hand, etc. **wash·board** *n* **1** a rectangular sheet of heavy glass, metal, etc. with a ridged surface, used for rubbing the dirt out of clothes, etc. **2** a road having a surface with many crosswise ridges. **wash·bowl** *n* a bowl for holding water to wash one's face and hands. **wash·cloth** *n* a small cloth for washing oneself. **washed–out** *adj* **1** pale or faded, as if from much washing: *washed-out photos*. **2** *Informal* exhausted: *She was feeling washed-out after a day of meetings*. **washed–up** *adj Informal* no longer able to function; failed: *After three unsuccessful films, he is probably washed-up as a director*. **wash·er** *n* **1** an automatic washing machine. **2** a flat ring of metal, rubber, etc. used to protect surfaces held by bolts or nuts, to seal joints, etc. **wash·ing** *n* **1** clothes or linens that have been washed or are to be washed. **2** sometimes, **washings** *pl* material obtained in washing something: *washings of gold obtained from earth*. **washing machine** a machine for washing clothes, etc. **washing soda** a crystalline form of sodium carbonate, used dissolved in water for washing clothes, etc. **wash·out** *n* **1** a washing away of earth, a road, etc. by rainfall or other sudden rush of water. **2** *Slang* an utter failure: *The party was a complete washout*. **wash·rag** *n* a washcloth. **wash·room** *n* a room equipped with a toilet and sink, esp such a room in a public building. **wash·stand** *n* a stand for holding a washbowl, pitcher, etc. for washing. **wash·tub** *n* a tub or large, deep sink, used to wash or soak laundry in. **wash·y** *adj* **1** too watery: *washy tea*. **2** not having enough colour, force, etc.: *washy colours, washy poetry*.

wasp [wɒsp] *n* any of numerous winged insects having biting mouthparts, and, in the females and workers, a powerful sting. **wasp·like** *adj*. ⟨Old English *wæsp*⟩ **wasp·ish** *adj* **1** of or like a wasp. **2** irritable or snappish: *a waspish temper*. **wasp·ish·ly** *adv*. **wasp·ish·ness** *n*. **wasp waist** a very slender waist. **wasp–waist·ed** *adj*. **wasp·y** *adj* **1** like a wasp. **2** waspish.

waste [weist] *v* **1** make poor use of; spend uselessly: *Don't waste time or money*. **2** wear or be worn down little by little: *The sick man was wasted by disease*. **3** damage greatly; destroy: *The soldiers wasted the enemy's fields*. *n* **1** poor use; useless spending. **2** useless or worthless material; stuff to be thrown away: *Garbage is waste*. **3** desert; wilderness. **4** gradual destruction or loss. **5** that which is excreted from the body. **6** destruction or devastation caused by war, floods, fires, etc. **7** a vast, dreary, desolate expanse, as of water or snow-covered land. *adj* **1** thrown away as useless or worthless. **2** left over; not used. **3** not cultivated. **4** in a state of desolation or ruin. **5** carrying off or holding refuse: *a waste pipe*. **6** unused by or unusable to, and therefore excreted. ⟨Old North French *waster;* Latin *vastare* lay waste⟩ **go to waste** be wasted. **lay waste** damage greatly; destroy; ravage: *The invading army laid waste the countryside*.

waste·bas·ket *n* a basket or other open container for waste paper, etc. **waste·ful** *adj* using or spending too much. **waste·ful·ly** *adv*. **waste·ful·ness** *n*. **waste·land** *n* **1** barren, uncultivated land. **2** a devastated, ruined region: *The advancing troops left a wasteland behind them*. **3** anything that has been improperly managed or is unproductive or barren: *Television has been described as a cultural wasteland*. **waste management** the business of reducing and disposing of a community's waste. **waste paper** *n* paper thrown away or to be thrown away as useless or worthless. **waste·pa·per basket** See WASTEBASKET. **wast·ing** *adj* **1** gradually destructive to the body: *Tuberculosis is a wasting disease*. **2** laying waste; devastating. **was·trel** [ˈweistrəl] *n* a good-for-nothing.

watch [wɒtʃ] *v* **1** observe closely: *The medical students watched while the surgeon operated*. **2** look at: *to watch a play*. **3** be on the alert (for): *The boy watched for a chance to cross the busy street*. **4** maintain an interest in: *to watch one's children growing up*. *n* **1** a careful looking: *Be on the watch for cars when you cross the street*. **2** a guarding: *A security guard keeps watch over the bank at night*. **3** a staying awake for some purpose. **4** a device for indicating time, small enough to be carried in a pocket or worn on the wrist. **5** *Nautical* **a** the time of duty of one part of a ship's crew. A watch usually lasts four hours. **b** the part of a crew on duty at one time. **watch·er** *n*. ⟨Old English *wæccan*⟩ **watch oneself** be careful. **watch out** be on guard. **watch over** guard or supervise; protect or preserve from danger, harm, error, etc. **watch·band** *n* a strap of leather, metal, etc. for holding a wristwatch on the wrist. **watch chain** a chain attached to a watch and fastened to one's clothing or worn around one's neck. **watch·dog** *n* **1** a dog kept to guard property. **2** a person or organization whose mandate is to keep guard against immoral or unethical behaviour, practices, etc.: *a consumer watchdog*. **watch·ful** *adj* alert and vigilant: *a watchful guard. He is watchful of his health*. **watch·ful·ly** *adv*. **watch·ful·ness** *n*. **watch·ma·ker** *n* a person who makes and repairs watches and clocks. **watch·making** *n*. **watch·man** *n, pl* -men a person who keeps watch; guard. **watch·tow·er** *n* a tower from which watch is kept for enemies, fires, etc. **watch·word** *n* **1** a password: *We gave the watchword, and the sentinel let us pass*. **2** a motto; slogan: *"Truth" is our watchword*.

wa·ter [ˈwɒtər] *n* **1** the liquid that falls as rain and makes up the seas, lakes, and rivers, and that is also the main constituent of all living matter. **2** a body of water; a sea, river, lake, etc.: *He lived across the water from them*. **3 waters** *pl* **a** a particular part of the ocean, a lake, etc.: *fishing in Canadian waters*. **b** mineral water, as at a spa: *to take the waters*. **4** the water of a river, etc. with reference to the tide: *high water*. **5** the surface of a body of water: *to swim under water*. **6 a** a liquid containing water: *soda water.* **b** a liquid resembling water: *When you cry, water runs from your eyes.*

adj **1** found in or near water: *water lilies, waterfowl.* **2** using or operated by water: *water sports, water power.*

v **1** wet with water: *to water the grass.* **2** provide with water to drink: *to water the horses.* **3** supply water to (a region, etc.): *British Columbia is well watered by rivers and streams.* **4** fill with or discharge water: *Her mouth watered when she saw the cake.* **5** weaken by adding water. **6** get or take in a supply of water: *A ship waters before sailing.* **7** of animals, drink water: *The cattle usually watered at the creek.* ⟨Old English *wæter*⟩

by water by means of a ship or boat: *She would rather travel by water than by air.* **hold water** be shown to be consistent, effective, etc.: *That argument won't hold water.* **keep one's head above water** keep out of trouble or difficulty, esp financial difficulty: *Business is so bad that he is finding it hard to keep his head above water.* **like water** very freely or recklessly: *to spend money like water.* **make someone's mouth water** arouse a desire (for something): *a sports car to make your mouth water.* **of the first water** of the highest quality or most extreme degree: *He is a bungler of the first water.* **throw** (or **pour**) **cold water on** actively discourage or belittle: *She didn't tell her friends her scheme because she knew they'd throw cold water on it.* **tread water a** keep afloat in the water, with the body upright and the head above the surface, by moving the legs as if bicycling. **b** maintain one's position in the face of adversity. **water down a** reduce in strength by diluting with water: *We watered down the punch because it was too strong.* **b** reduce the force of by altering: *The original hill had to be watered down before being presented to Parliament.* **water under the bridge** (or **over the dam**) something done and finished with. **wa·ter·bed** *n* a bed having a mattress that is a water-filled plastic bag. **water bomber** an aircraft equipped with tanks filled with water, used for fighting forest fires. **wa·ter–borne** *adj* supported, carried, or transmitted by water; floating. **water buffalo** the common buffalo of S Asia and the Philippines, having large, spreading horns. **water chestnut** a button-shaped tuber, used esp in Chinese cooking. **wa·ter·col·our** or **wa·ter·col·or** **1** paint mixed with water instead of oil. **2** a picture painted with water colours. **wa·ter·col·our** or **wa·ter·col·or** *adj.* **water cooler** a device for cooling and dispensing drinking water. **wa·ter·course** *n* **1** a stream of water. **2** a channel for water; a stream bed, canal, etc. **wa·ter·craft** *n* **1** skill in handling boats or in water sports. **2** any ship or boat. **3** boats and ships collectively. **wa·ter·cress** *n* a plant of the mustard family that grows in running water and has crisp leaves often used in salads, sandwiches, etc. **wa·ter·fall** *n* a stream or river falling over a cliff or down a very steep hill. **wa·ter·fowl** *n, pl* -**fowls** or (esp

collectively) -**fowl** a water bird, esp one that swims. **wa·ter·front** *n* **1** the part of a city, town, etc. beside a river, lake, or harbour. **2** land at the water's edge. **wa·ter·front** *adj.* **water gun** WATER PISTOL. **water hole 1** a hole in the ground where water collects; small pond or pool. **2** a source of drinking water, as a spring in the desert. **watering can** a container with a handle and a spout, for sprinkling or pouring water on plants, etc. **watering hole 1** *Informal* a bar, nightclub, etc., where alcoholic beverages are served. **2** Also, **watering place** a place where water may be obtained, esp a pool, a part of a stream, etc. where animals go to drink. **water jacket** a casing with water or other liquid in it, surrounding something to keep it at a certain temperature. **wa·ter·less** *adj* not needing or using water: *waterless cookware.* **water lily** any of a family of water plants having floating leaves and showy, fragrant flowers. **wa·ter·line** *n* the line where the surface of the water touches the side of a ship or boat, river bank, container, etc. **wa·ter·logged** *adj* **1** of a boat, etc., so full of water that it will barely float. **2** completely soaked with water. **water main** a main conduit in a system of water pipes. **wa·ter·mark** *n* **1** a faint mark produced on some paper during manufacture, indicating the maker, etc. **2** a mark showing how high water has risen or may rise. **wa·ter·mel·on** *n* a large fruit having sweet, juicy, red, pink, or yellowish pulp with seeds scattered through it and a hard, thick green rind. **water pipe 1** a pipe for conveying water. **2** hookah. **water pistol** a toy gun designed to shoot a jet of water. **water polo** a game played in a swimming pool by two teams of seven players, who try to throw or push a round ball into the opponents' goal. **water power** the power from flowing or falling water, used to drive machinery and make electricity. **wa·ter·proof** *adj* that will not let water through: *a waterproof tarpaulin, a waterproof watch.* **wa·ter·proof** *v.* **wa·ter·proof·ing** *n.* **water rat 1** a large vole found along the banks of streams and lakes in Europe and Asia. **2** ✺ a muskrat. **wa·ter–re·pel·lent** *adj* that repels water but is not waterproof. **wa·ter–re·sis·tant** *adj* **1** water-repellent. **2** not likely to be damaged by water. **water right** the right to use the water of a given stream, lake, or other body of water. **wa·ter·shed** *n* **1** a high ridge of land that divides two areas drained by different river systems; a divide. **2** the region drained by one river system. **3** an important point of division or decision; turning point: *Hitler's decision to invade Poland was one of the watersheds of 20th century history.* **wa·ter·side** *n* land along the sea, a lake, a river, etc. **wa·ter·side** *adj.* **water ski** a broad ski, usually one of a pair, for skimming over the water while being towed by a motorboat. **wa·ter–ski** *v.* **wa·ter–ski·er** *n.* **wa·ter–ski·ing** *n.* **wa·ter·slide** *n* a slide, often with a stream of water running down it, ending in a swimming pool. **water snake** any of various snakes that live in or near water. **water softener 1** a chemical added to hard water to give it more sudsing capability by removing minerals from it. **2** a device using such a chemical and attached to a water supply. **wa·ter–sol·u·ble** *adj* capable of being dissolved in water. **wa·ter·spout** *n* **1** a pipe that spouts water, or that carries it away, as from an eavestrough. **2** a rotating column of spray between a cloud and the surface of the ocean or of a large lake, produced by the action of a whirlwind. **water table** the level below which the ground is saturated with water. **wa·ter·tight** *adj* **1** so tight that no water can get in or out. **2** leaving no opening for misunderstanding, criticism, etc.; perfect: *a watertight argument.* **wa·ter·tight·ness** *n.* **water torture** a form of torture in which water is let fall in a steady, slow drip on the victim's forehead. **water tower 1** an elevated tank for storing water in a water supply system. **2** any of several types of firefighting equipment designed to deliver water under pressure at a great height for fighting fires in tall buildings. **water vapour** or **vapor** water in a gaseous state, esp when below the boiling point and fairly diffused, as in the atmosphere. Compare STEAM. **wa·ter·way** *n* a river, canal, or other body of water that ships can go on. **water wheel 1** a wheel turned by running or falling water, used to supply power. **2** a wheel having buckets around the rim, for drawing water. **3** the paddle wheel of a steamboat. **water wings** a device consisting of two air-filled floats joined together, designed to give support to a swimmer or a person learning to swim. **wa·ter·works** *n pl or sg* **1** a system of pipes, reservoirs, pumps, etc. for supplying a city or town with water. **2** a building containing pumps for pumping water. **3** *Slang* a flow of tears, esp a sudden or violent flow. **turn on the waterworks** *Slang* begin to weep, esp deliberately. **wa·ter·y** *adj* **1** sodden; soggy: *watery soil. The potatoes were overcooked and watery.* **2** of eyes, tending to water. **3** of a liquid, containing too much water: *watery soup.* **4** like water in consistency or appearance: *A blister is filled with a watery fluid.* **5** weak or pale: *watery winter sunlight.*

Wa·ter·loo [ˌwɒtərˈlu] *n* any decisive or crushing defeat: *She has met her Waterloo and will not run for election again.* ⟨Waterloo town in Belgium, site of Napoleon's final defeat⟩

watt [wɒt] *n* an SI unit used to measure the power, or energy available per second, needed to send one ampere of electric current across one volt. One watt is equal to one joule of energy per second. *Symbol* **W** ⟨J. *Watt,* 18c Scots engineer and inventor⟩ **watt·age** *n* electric power expressed in watts: *This heater has a higher wattage than that one.*

wat·tle [ˈwɒtəl] *n* **1** a construction of sticks interwoven with twigs or reeds to form a wall, fence, etc.: *a hut built of wattle.* **2** the skin hanging down from the throat of certain birds. **wat·tled** *adj.* ⟨Old English *watul*⟩

wave [weiv] *v* **1** move or cause to move back and forth or up and down: *A flag waved in the breeze.* **2** make a signal with an up-and-down or back-and-forth movement of the hand or arm: *We waved until the train was out of sight.* **3** shake in the air: *He waved the stick at them.* **4** have a wavelike form: *Her hair waves naturally.* *n* **1** the action of waving. **2** a moving ridge or swell of water, as on the sea. **3** a group or one of a series of groups advancing, swaying, etc. like ocean waves: *A wave of new settlers followed the completion of the railway.* **4** an emotion, activity, etc. passing from one person to the next in a group: *A wave of hysteria passed through the crowd.* **5** a swell of emotion, influence, activity, hot or cold weather, etc.: *a heat wave. A wave of fear swept over him.* **6** *Physics* a periodic disturbance in which energy is carried forward through local displacement of particles. **wave·less** *adj.* **wave·like** *adj.* ⟨Old English *wafian*⟩ **make waves** cause a stir; disturb a peaceful situation or attract attention. **wave·length** *n Physics* the distance between any point in a wave and the next point that is in the same phase, as from one peak to the next. **on the same wavelength** *Informal* sharing a line of thought: *He and I were just never on the same wavelength.* **wave·let** *n* a little wave. **wave pool** a swimming pool equipped with a mechanism that produces large waves in the water. **wav·y** *adj* **1** having undulations or curves: *wavy hair, a wavy line.* **2** moving or proceeding in waves, or undulating curves. **wav·i·ly** *adv.* **wav·i·ness** *n.*

wa·ver [ˈweivər] *v* **1** move unsteadily to and fro. **2** vary in intensity: *a wavering light.* **3** be undecided in opinion, direction, etc. **4** tremble or pulsate. **5** become unsteady; falter: *The battle line wavered and then broke.* *n* the act of wavering. **wa·ver·er** *n.* **wa·ver·ing** *adj.* ⟨compare Old English *wæfre* restless; related to WAVE⟩

wa·vey [ˈweivi] *n* ❇ a wild goose, esp the snow goose. Also called **wa·wa** [ˈwɑwɑ] or [ˈwɑwə]. ⟨Cdn. French; Cree⟩

wax¹ [wæks] *n* **1** a substance akin to fats and oils, secreted by bees for constructing their honeycomb cells; beeswax. **2** any of various substances resembling this. Paraffin, used for candles, etc., is often called wax. *v* rub or treat with wax or something like wax to polish, stiffen, condition, etc.: *We wax that floor once a month.* **wax·like** *adj.* ⟨Old English *weax*⟩ **be wax in someone's hands** be totally under the influence of someone. **whole ball of wax** See BALL. **wax bean** a variety of garden bean having yellow pods. **wax·en** *adj* like wax in being smooth, pale, and lustrous: *a waxen skin.* **wax museum** a museum containing effigies in wax of famous persons, historical tableaux, etc. **wax paper** or **waxed paper** paper made water-repellent by being coated with a waxy substance such as paraffin, used mostly for wrapping food. **wax·work** *n* **1** a figure made of wax. **2 waxworks** *pl* an exhibition of such figures, esp one showing figures of famous or notorious people; WAX MUSEUM. **wax·y** *adj* **1** made of, containing, or covered with wax: *The candles left a waxy mess on the tablecloth.* **2** like wax; smooth, glossy, pale, etc.: *Bayberries are waxy.* **wax·i·ness** *n*.

wax² [wæks] *v* **1** of the moon, go through the regular increase in the size of its visible portion: *The moon waxes till it becomes full and then it wanes.* **2** increase in size, strength, importance, etc.: *During this period her wealth waxed steadily.* **3** grow or become: *to wax indignant.* ⟨Old English *weaxan*⟩

way [wei] *n* **1** a manner or style: *a funny way of talking.* **2** a method or means: *Doctors are using new ways of curing illness.* **3** a feature; detail: *This plan is bad in several ways.* **4** a direction: *Look this way.* **5** movement along a course: *The guide led the way.* **6** a distance: *The sun is a long way off.* **7** a road; path; street; course. **8** Often, **ways** *pl* habit; custom. **9** one's wish; will: *Spoiled children want their own way all the time.* **10** *Informal* a condition; state: *That patient is in a bad way.* **11** a course of life, action, or experience: *Let us choose the way of non-violence.* **12** *Informal* district; area; region: *She lives out our way.*
adv Informal far: *His first novel was way better than this one.* ⟨Old English *weg*⟩
by the way a along the side of the road, path, etc. **b** incidentally. **by way of** **a** through. **b** as; for: *By way of an answer he just nodded.* **c** making a reputation for (being or doing something): *She is by way of being a clever cartoonist.* **come one's way** meet or happen to one. **give way** **a** retreat; yield. **b** break down or fall: *Several people were hurt when the platform gave way.* **c** abandon oneself (to emotion): *to give way to tears.* **go one's way** **a** depart. **b** turn out as desired. **go out of one's** (or **the**) **way** make a special effort. **have a way with one** be persuasive. **in a way** to some extent. **in the** (or **one's**) **way** being an obstacle, hindrance, etc. **in the way of** **a** in a favourable position for doing or getting: *He put me in the way of a good investment.* **b** in the category of: *Would you have anything in the way of hedge clippers?* **in the worst way** *Informal* to an extraordinary degree: *I need a new skirt in the worst way.* **lead the way** act as a guide or example. **look the other way** pretend not to notice wrongdoing. **lose one's way** not know any longer where one is or how to get to where one is going. **make one's way** **a** go: *They made their way to the road.* **b** get ahead; succeed: *He's sure to make his way in the world.* **make way** give space for passing or going ahead. **no way** *Informal* absolutely not. **on the** (or **one's**) **way** in the process of going. **out of the way** **a** so as not to be an obstacle, hindrance, etc.: *Move the chair out of the way.* **b** far from where most people live or go. **c** unusual; strange. **d** finished; taken care of: *I'd like to get this job

out of the way first. **pay one's way** contribute one's share. **put out of the way** kill or murder. **see one's way** (**clear**) be willing or able: *Can you see your way clear to help with the party?* **way·bill** *n* a paper describing a shipment, its destination, its route, and the cost involved. **way·far·er** *n* a traveller, esp one who travels on foot. **way·far·ing** *adj*. **way·lay** [wei'lei] *or* ['wei,lei] *v* **-laid**, **-lay·ing** **1** lie in wait for and attack: *The bandit waylaid and robbed rich travellers.* **2** stop (a person) on his or her way. **way·lay·er** *n*. **ways and means** **1** the resources, methods, etc. available to accomplish a purpose, esp of some administrative body: *The plan seemed good but the committee had to consider ways and means.* **2** methods, including legislation, used by a government to generate revenue. **way·side** *n* the edge of a road or path. *adj* along the edge of a road or path. **fall** (or **go**) **by the wayside** fail to continue or to be completed: *The rally weekend fell by the wayside for lack of interest.* **way station** **1** a station between main stations on a railway, etc. **2** any stopping place along a route. **way·ward** *adj* **1** tending to go against the advice, wishes, or orders of others; willful. **2** irregular; unpredictable. **way·ward·ly** *adv*. **way·ward·ness** *n*.

SYNONYMS
Way is the common and general word: *The way in which she spoke hurt me.* **Method** applies to an orderly way of doing something: *Follow her method of cooking.* **Manner** applies to a particular way of acting or happening: *He rides in the western manner.*

we [wi] *pron pl, subj* **we** *obj* **us** *poss* **ours** **1** the speaker or writer plus the person or persons spoken or written to or about: *Bring your swimsuit so we can go to the pool.* **2** the speaker or writer, thinking of himself or herself as in a formal or official role. Authors, sovereigns, judges, and newspaper editors sometimes use *we* when others would say *I.* **3** people in general, including the speaker; ONE (def. 2); YOU (def. 2): *We need some fibre in our diet.* **4** you (slightly patronizing, as to a child): *Shall we take our bath now?* ⟨Old English *we*⟩

weak [wik] *adj* **1** lacking strength or health: *She is still weak from her illness.* **2** that can too easily be broken, overcome, etc.: *a weak link in a chain.* **3** lacking authority or power: *a weak argument.* **4** lacking moral strength: *a weak character.* **5** less strong or potent than is usual: *a weak solution of boric acid, a weak strain of a virus.* **6** lacking skill or aptitude: *The weaker students were given extra help in the subject.* **7** poor in a particular thing: *This novel is weak on character development, but it has an exciting plot.* **weak·en** *v*. **weak·ly** *adv*. ⟨Old Norse *veikr*⟩
weak–kneed *adj* giving in easily to opposition, intimidation, etc. **weak·ling** *n* a weak person or animal. **weak·ness** *n* **1** the condition of being weak. **2** a weak point. **3** something one finds difficult to resist: *Chocolate is my weakness.*

weal [wil] *n* a streak or ridge on the skin made by a stick or whip. ⟨variant of *wale*⟩

wealth [wɛlθ] *n* **1** much money or property. **2** *Economics* all things that have money value or that add to the capacity for production. **3** a large quantity; abundance: *a wealth of hair.* **wealth·y** *adj.* **wealth·i·ly** *adv.* **wealth·i·ness** *n.* ⟨*well*'⟩

wean [win] *v* **1** accustom (a child or young animal) to food other than milk. **2** accustom (a person) to do without something: *The delinquent was sent away to wean him from his bad companions.* ⟨Old English *wenian*⟩

weap·on ['wɛpən] *n* **1** any instrument or device designed or used to injure or kill: *The murder weapon was a rock.* **2** a part of an animal or plant used for fighting or protection, such as claws, horns, or stings. **3** a means used to get the better of an opponent: *Drugs are used as weapons against disease.* **weap·on·less** *adj.* **weap·oned** *adj.* ⟨Old English *wǣpen*⟩

weap·on·ry *n* weapons collectively.

wear [wɛr] *v* **wore, worn, wear·ing 1** have or carry on the body as clothing, adornment, etc.: *She was wearing a ring.* **2** show as part of one's appearance: *The old house wore an air of sadness.* **3** have as a quality or attribute: *to wear one's honours modestly.* **4** change, make less, or damage by constant handling, etc.: *Water had worn the stones smooth.* **5** suffer deterioration from constant handling, etc. (often with *away* or *down*): *The cuffs of the shirt are starting to wear at the edges.* **6** tire; exhaust (often with *out*): *A visit with him always wears me out.* **7** last under use: *This coat has worn well.* **8** of time, pass or go gradually: *It grew hotter as the day wore on.* *n* **1** the act of wearing or the state of being worn: *clothing for summer wear.* **2** clothing: *children's wear.* **3** deterioration due to use: *The rug showed signs of wear.* **4** capacity for resisting deterioration: *The shoes still have lots of wear in them.* **wear·a·ble** *adj.* **wear·er** *n.* ⟨Old English *werian*⟩

wear down a overcome by persistent effort: *She tried to wear her parents down by asking again and again why she couldn't go.* **b** make less, smaller, etc. by wearing: *shoes worn down at the heel.* **c** weary (someone): *She was worn down by the constant struggle of surviving poor crops and low prices.* **wear off** gradually disappear: *As the freezing wore off, my tooth started to ache.* **wear out a** wear until no longer fit for use: *She wore the shoes out in six months.* **b** make very tired or weary. **wear thin a** become weak from being used too much: *My patience was wearing thin.* **b** become tiresome and unconvincing because of repetition: *That excuse of his is wearing thin.* **wear and tear** damage or deterioration as a result of ordinary use over a period of time.

wea·ry ['wiri] *adj* **1** tired: *weary feet.* **2** tiring: *a weary wait.* **3** having one's tolerance exhausted (with *of*): *I'm weary of his stupid jokes.* **4** showing weariness: *a weary smile.* *v* make or become weary. **wea·ri·ly** *adv.* **wea·ri·ness** *n.* ⟨Old English *wērig*⟩

wea·ri·some *adj* wearying; tiring; tiresome. **wea·ri·some·ly** *adv.* **wea·ri·some·ness** *n.*

wea·sel ['wizəl] *n* **1** any of several small, carnivorous mammals having a long, slender body, short legs, and short, thick fur that is mainly reddish brown above and creamy below. Northern weasels turn white in winter. **2** a sly and sneaky person. *v* **-seled** or **-selled, -sel·ing** or **-sel·ling 1** use misleading words to avoid committing oneself: *Stop weaselling and give me a straight answer.* **2** escape from or evade some responsibility in a crafty way (with *out*): *She had promised to help but weaselled out at the last minute.* **wea·sel·ly** *adj.* ⟨Old English *weosule*⟩

weasel word Often, **weasel words** *pl* a word intended to soften what one says, making the message vague or confusing.

weath·er ['wɛðər] *n* **1** the condition of the atmosphere at a particular time and place: *windy weather.* **2** bad weather: *a shelter for protection against the weather.* *adj* of or designating the side of a ship toward the wind; windward. *v* **1** become discoloured or worn by air, rain, sun, frost, etc. **2** pass safely through (bad weather or a difficult time): *to weather a storm.* **3** resist the effects of the weather: *This paint weathers very well, so we will not have to repaint next year.* ⟨Old English *weder*⟩

under the weather *Informal* **a** somewhat sick: *He's been feeling under the weather for several days.* **b** slightly drunk.

weath·er–beat·en *adj* hardened by the wind, rain, sun, etc.: *a weatherbeaten face.* **weath·er–bound** *adj* delayed or immobilized by bad weather: *a weather-bound ship.* **weath·er·cock** *n* **1** a weather vane, esp one in the shape of a rooster. **2** someone who easily changes opinions or loyalties. **weather eye** a close watch for expected change of any kind: *The news media were keeping a weather eye on the labour situation.* **weath·er·man** *n, pl* **-men** *Informal* a person who forecasts the weather, esp a meteorologist. **weath·er·proof** *adj* able to stand exposure to all kinds of weather. **weath·er·proof** *v.* **weath·er·proof·ing** *n.* **weath·er·strip** or **weath·er·strip·ping** *n* a narrow strip, of metal, felt, etc., to fill the space between a door or window and the casing, so as to keep out rain, snow, and wind. **weather vane** a revolving device, mounted on a roof, steeple, etc. so that it will turn with the wind and point to its direction.

weave [wiv] *v* **wove, wo·ven** or **wove, weav·ing 1** form (threads or strips) into a fabric. **2** construct mentally by skilfully combining various elements: *to weave a tale.* **3** include so as to make seem a natural part: *The author wove regionalisms into the dialogue.* *n* a method or pattern of weaving: *Homespun is a cloth of coarse weave.* **weav·er** *n.* ⟨Old English *wefan*⟩

weave one's way make one's way by twisting and turning.

> USAGE
> **Woven** is the usual past participle. **Wove** is now chiefly used in certain technical terms, such as wire-wove and wove paper.

web [wɛb] *n* **1** a cobweb or something similar produced by any of various insects. **2** any complicated network, esp one that entangles like a cobweb: *a web of lies*. **3** the skin joining the toes of swimming birds and animals. **4** *Computers* **the Web** *Informal* WORLD WIDE WEB. **web·like** *adj*. ⟨Old English *webb*⟩

webbed *adj* of digits or toes, joined by a web: *Ducks have webbed feet*. **web·bing** *n* **1** cloth woven into strong strips, used in upholstery and for belts. **2** any netlike structure of interlaced cords. **web–foot·ed** *adj* having the toes joined by a web. Also, **web–toed**. **web·log** BLOG. **web·mas·ter** *n* a person whose job it is to oversee an organization's website. **web page** a document on the WORLD WIDE WEB. **web server** the computer system from which web browsers download files, or the application that enables them to do this. **web·site** a site on the WORLD WIDE WEB consisting of a HOME PAGE and, often, other related files.

wed [wed] *v* **wed·ded, wed·ded** or **wed, wed·ding** **1** marry (another) in a formal ceremony. **2** unite; bind by close ties. ⟨Old English *weddian*⟩

wed·ded *adj* **1** of marriage or married persons: *wedded bliss*. **2** united. **wed·ding** *n* **1** a marriage ceremony and the subsequent celebration. **2** a uniting: *His writing shows a remarkable wedding of thought and language.* **wedding band** a finger ring exchanged by bride and groom. **wedding party** the group of people (bridesmaids, best man, etc.) who formally attend the bride and groom at a wedding. **wed·lock** *n* married life; marriage.

wedge [wɛdʒ] *n* **1** a piece of wood or metal with a tapering thin edge:*Put that wedge under the door to keep it open.* **2** something tapered from a wide edge to a point: *He cut the big pie into ten wedges.* **3** *Golf* a club used for high, short shots, so called because of the shape of the club head. **4** anything that divides in some way: *Their disagreement about politics drove a wedge between the friends.* *v* **1** brace or tighten with a wedge or something squeezed in. **2** squeeze in or through: *She wedged herself through the narrow window.* ⟨Old English *wecg*⟩

wed·gie *n* **1** *Informal* a shoe with a wedge-shaped heel and sole all in one piece. **2** *Slang* the practical joke of grabbing the back waistband of someone's pants or underpants and yanking them sharply upward. **thin end of the wedge** an act that seems harmless but could lead to worse developments

Wednes·day ['wɛnzdeɪ] *n* the fourth day of the week, following Tuesday. ⟨Old English *Wōdnes dæg* day of Woden (a god)⟩

wee [wi] *adj* **we·er, we·est** very small; tiny. ⟨*little wee* little bit, Old English *wǣg* weight⟩ **wee hours** the early morning hours.

weed [wid] *n* **1** a wild plant growing where it is not wanted, as in gardens, etc. **2 the weed** *Informal* tobacco or marijuana. *v* **1** take weeds out of: *to weed a garden.* **2** remove or discard as not wanted (usually with *out*): *Weak players are weeded out before the regular season begins.* **weed·like** *adj*. ⟨Old English *wēod*⟩ **weed·er** *n* a tool or machine for digging up weeds. **weedkiller** *n* a chemical used to kill weeds. **weed·y** *adj* **1** full of weeds: *a weedy garden.* **2** thin and lanky: *a tall and weedy youth.* **weed·i·ly** *adv*. **weed·i·ness** *n*.

week [wik] *n* **1** seven days, one after another. **2** the time from one Sunday through the following Saturday. **3** the working days or hours of a seven-day period: *The typical full-time work week is 40 hours.* ⟨Old English *wice*⟩ **a week Monday** (or **Tuesday**, etc.) the Monday one week from this Monday (or Tuesday, etc.). **a week today** one week from today. **week in, week out** week after week. **week·day** *n* **1** any day except Sunday or other weekly holy day in various religions. **2** any day except Saturday or Sunday. **week·day** *adj*. **week·end** *n* Saturday and Sunday as a time for recreation, visiting, etc. *v* spend a weekend: *They are weekending at their cottage.* **week·end** *adj*. **week·end·er** *n* a small suitcase capable of holding enough clothes, etc. for a weekend. **week·ly** *adj* done, happening, coming, etc. every week: *a weekly letter home.* *adv* every week; week by week. *n* a newspaper or magazine published once a week.

weep [wip] *v* **wept, weep·ing** **1** shed tears. **2** give off (moisture) in drops: *That basement wall sometimes weeps.* **weep·er** *n*. **weep·y** *adj*. ⟨Old English *wēpan*⟩

wee·vil ['wivəl] *n* any of a family of beetles having an elongated snout called a rostrum. Many weevils are serious agricultural pests. **wee·vil·ly** or **wee·vil·y** *adj*. ⟨Old English *wifel*⟩

weft [wɛft] *n* the threads running from side to side across a woven fabric; woof. See WARP. ⟨Old English *weft; wefan* weave⟩

weigh [wei] *v* **1** determine the mass of: *She weighed herself.* **2** have as a measure of mass: *She weighs 50 kg.* **3** measure by mass (with *out*): *The grocer weighed out 2 kg of potatoes.* **4** balance in the mind; consider carefully: *She weighed her words before speaking.* **5** have an oppressive effect: *The mistake weighed heavily upon her mind.* **6** *Nautical* lift up (an anchor). ⟨Old English *wegan*⟩ **weigh down a** bend by weight: *The boughs of the tree are weighed down with fruit.* **b** burden: *She is weighed down with many troubles.* **weigh in** find out one's weight before a contest. **weigh in at** weigh (a given amount). **weigh on** be a burden to.

weight *n* **1** MASS (def. 5); *The dog's weight is 20 kg.* **2** the quality of anything that makes it tend toward a centre of attraction: *Your *weight would be less on the moon than on earth; your mass would be the same.* **3** something heavy used to hold down light things or maintain balance: *A weight keeps the papers in place.* **4** influence or importance: *What he says carries a lot of weight around here.* **5** the relative heaviness of an article of clothing appropriate to the season's weather: *summer weight.* **6** *Statistics* **a** a number assigned to an item, as in a cost-of-living index, to make its effect reflect its importance. **b** the frequency of an item in a statistical compilation. **7** *Sports* a metal ball, barbell, etc. thrown, pushed, or lifted in contests of strength. **8** a class in which contestants are placed according to their mass, esp in boxing, wrestling, etc. **by weight** as measured by weighing. **pull one's weight** do one's share. **throw one's weight around** *Informal* make too much use of one's rank or position. *v* **1** add weight to: *The drapes were weighted to hold them straight.* **2** *Statistics* give a weight to: *to weight an average.* **3** *Skiing* direct a downward thrust onto: *to weight the left ski.*

weight·less *adj* **1** appearing to have no weight: *The snow felt weightless on my shoulders.* **2** being free from the pull of gravity: *In space, all things are weightless.* **weight·less·ly** *adv.* **weight·less·ness** *n.* **weight·y** *adj* **1** heavy. **2** oppressively heavy: *weighty cares of state.* **3** important; influential: *a weighty speaker.* **4** convincing: *weighty arguments.* **weight·i·ly** *adv.* **weight·i·ness** *n.*

weir [wir] *n* **1** a dam in a river to raise the level of the water or to divert its flow. **2** a fence of stakes or branches put in a stream or channel to catch fish. ⟨Old English *wer*⟩

weird [wird] *adj* **1** unearthly; mysterious: *a weird shriek.* **2** *Informal* odd; eccentric; queer: *She's been acting pretty weird lately, and nobody knows why.* **weird·ly** *adv.* **weird·ness** *n.* ⟨Old English *wyrd* fate⟩
weird·o *n Slang* a very odd person.

wel·come ['wɛlkəm] *v* **1** greet in a friendly way: *to welcome a guest.* **2** receive gladly: *We welcome new ideas.*
n **1** a friendly reception. *You will always have a welcome here.* **2** an expression of greeting.
adj **1** gladly received: *a welcome rest.* **2** freely permitted: *You are welcome to pick the flowers.*
interj an exclamation of friendly greeting: *Welcome!* **wel·com·er** *n.* ⟨Old English *wilagreeable + cuma* comer⟩
wear out one's welcome visit a person too much. **you're welcome** a reply to thanks.
welcome mat doormat. **put out the welcome mat** *Informal* offer an enthusiastic reception.

weld [wɛld] *v* **1** join together (metal) by pressing while hot. **2** unite closely: *Working together welded them into a strong team.* *n* a welded joint. **weld·er** *n.* ⟨*weld²*, v⟩

wel·fare ['wɛl,fɛr] *n* health, happiness, and prosperity: *She asked about my welfare.* ⟨Middle English *wel* well; *fare* go⟩
on welfare receiving benefits from the government or from some organization to provide a basic standard of living: *There was no harvest and many families were on welfare.*
welfare state a state whose government provides for citizens through such social measures as old-age pensions, unemployment insurance, Medicare, etc.

well¹ [wɛl] *adv* **1** in a satisfactory, favourable, or advantageous manner: *Is everything going well at school?* **2** thoroughly: *Shake well before using.* **3** much: *The fair brought in well over a hundred dollars.* **4** in a friendly or kind manner: *to treat them well.* **5** in an excellent manner: *She draws well.* **6** without doubt: *You know very well what I meant.*
adj **bet·ter, best 1** satisfactory. *All is not well at home.* **2** in good health: *I am very well.*
interj an expression used to show surprise, agreement, etc. or to fill in: *Well! Well! Here you are. Well, I'm not sure.* ⟨Old English *wel*⟩
all very well an expression used concessively: *It's all very well for you to criticize, but can you do better?* **as well a** also. **b** equally. **as well as a** in addition to. **b** and also: *He is witty as well as handsome.* **well and good** I am content (though not particularly excited) about that. **well–ad·just·ed** *adj* of persons, emotionally balanced. **well–ad·vised** *adj* **1** proceeding with wisdom. **2** based on prudence. **well–ap·point·ed** *adj* with good furnishings or equipment. **well–bal·anced** *adj* **1** rightly regulated. **2** sensible. **well–be·haved** *adj* having good manners or conduct. **well·be·ing** *n* health and happiness. **well·born** *adj* from a respected family. **well–bred** *adj* well brought up. **well–de·fined** *adj* clearly indicated. **well–dis·posed** *adj* having sympathetic or friendly feelings. **well–done** *adj* **1** performed with skill. **2** of meat, thoroughly cooked. **well–fed** *adj* plump. **well–fixed** *adj Informal* WELL-TO-DO. **well–groomed** *adj* well cared for: *a well-groomed appearance.* **well–ground·ed** *adj* **1** based on good reasons. **2** fully instructed in the fundamental principles of a subject. **well–heeled** *adj* *Slang* well-to-do. **well–in·formed** *adj* **1** with reliable information on a subject. **2** having information on a wide variety of subjects. **well–kept** *adj* carefully tended. **well–knit** *adj* of a person's body, of strong, supple build. **well–known** *adj* fully or widely known. **well–man·nered** *adj* polite. **well–mean·ing** or **well–meant** *adj* proceeding from good intentions. **well·ness** *n* the state of being maximally healthy. **well–nigh** *adv* almost. **well–off** *adj* **1** in a good condition: *Your family is healthy, so think yourself well-off.* **2** fairly rich. **well–pre·served** *adj* showing few signs of age or use. **well–pro·por·tioned** *adj* having a pleasing shape. **well–read** *adj* knowing a lot about books and literature. **well–round·ed** *adj* **1** properly balanced, as a program or education. **2** having a variety of interests or attainments. **3** fully developed. **well–thought–of** *adj* of good reputation. **well–to–do** *adj* prosperous. **well–turned** *adj* **1** rounded expertly. **2** elegantly expressed: *a well-turned phrase.* **well–turned–out** *adj* elegantly dressed. **well–wish·er** *n* a person

who wishes well to a person, cause, etc. **well–wish·ing** *adj, n.*

well² [wɛl] *n* **1** a hole dug in the ground to find water, oil, gas, etc. **2** a natural source of water from the earth. **3** fountain or source: *He's a well of ideas.* **4** something like a well in shape or use: *the well of a fountain pen.* **5** a shaft for light, or for stairs, etc., extending vertically through the floors of a building. **6** a storage compartment for fish in the hold of a fishing boat.
v spring; rise: *Joy welled up inside her at the sight of her baby.* ⟨Old English *wella*⟩
well·head *n* **1** the source of a spring or stream. **2** the top of a well or a structure built around it. **well·spring** *n* **1** fountainhead. **2** a source, esp of a supply that never fails.

welsh [wɛlʃ] *v Slang* **1** cheat by failing to pay a bet. **2** evade the fulfilment of an obligation. Also, **welch. welsh·er** *n.* ⟨origin uncertain⟩
welsh on fail to keep an agreement with.

welt [wɛlt] *n* **1** a strip of leather between the upper part and the sole of a shoe. **2** the trim on the edge of a garment or upholstery. **3** a ridge made on the skin by a blow, esp from a stick or whip. ⟨Middle English *welte*⟩

wel·ter ['wɛltər] *v* **1** roll about. **2** lie soaked in some liquid.
n a confused mass of things or people: *The fighting children were a welter of arms and legs.* ⟨Middle Low German *welteren*⟩

wel·ter·weight ['wɛltər,weit] *n* a boxer weighing between 63.5 kg and 67 kg. ⟨earlier *welter* literally, beater (from *welt*) + *weight*⟩

Welt·schmerz ['vɛltʃmɛʀts] *n German* sadness arising from life in an imperfect world. ⟨German, literally 'world pain'⟩

wench [wɛntʃ] *n* **1** *Facetious* a girl or young woman. **2** *Archaic* a female servant. ⟨*wenchel* child; Old English *wencel*⟩

wend [wɛnd] *v* direct (one's way): *We wended our way home.* ⟨Old English *wendan*⟩

wen·di·go ['wɛndɪ,gou] *n* ✻ *Algonquian myth* an evil spirit of a cannibalistic nature. Also, **win·di·go.** ⟨Ojibwa *weendigo* cannibal⟩

went [wɛnt] *v* pt of GO.

wept [wɛpt] *v* pt and pp of WEEP.

were [wɜr] *v* **1** plural and second person singular, past indicative, of BE: *The officers were obeyed by the men.* **2** past subjunctive of BE: *If I were rich, I would travel.* ⟨Old English *wǣron*⟩
as it were as if it were; so to speak.

were·wolf ['wɛr,wʊlf] *or* ['wɜr,wʊlf] *n, pl*

-wolves [-,wʊlvz] *Folklore* a person, esp male, who can change into a wolf, while retaining human intelligence. ⟨Old English *wer* man + *wulf* wolf⟩

Wes·ak ['wesæk] *n Buddhism* the New Year festival, celebrated at the full moon in the month of May and commemorating the birth, enlightenment, and death of Buddha.

west [wɛst] *n* **1** the direction of the sunset. **2 the West a** ✻ the part of any country toward the west, esp the western part of Canada or the US. **b** the countries in Europe and the Americas as distinguished from those in Asia. **west** or **West** *adj.* **west** *adv.* ⟨Old English⟩
out West ✻ any point to the west of about Winnipeg. **west of** farther west than. **west·bound** *adj* going toward the west. **West Coast** ✻ the western coast of Canada, esp southwestern British Columbia, including Vancouver Island, the Gulf Islands, and the Queen Charlotte Islands. **west·er·ly** *adj, adv* **1** toward the west: *walking in a westerly direction.* **2** from the west: *a westerly wind.* **west·ern** *adj* **1** toward the west. **2** from the west. **3** of or in the west. **4** of or in the West. **Western** *n Informal* **1** a story or film dealing with life in the western part of North America, esp cowboy life in the United States in the late 19th century. **2** an omelette made with the addition of chopped green peppers, chopped onions, and ham, or a sandwich filled with that. **West·ern·er** *n* a native of the western part of the country. **western flowering dogwood** a tree of the dogwood family, having blossoms with white petal-like bracts. The blossom of the western flowering dogwood is the floral emblem of British Columbia. **west·ern·ize** *v* cause to adopt western ideas, customs, culture, etc. **west·ern·most** *adj* farthest west. **western red cedar** a very large arborvitae found along the Pacific coast and in interior British Columbia. The western red cedar is used by the people of the First Nations of the Pacific Northwest for carving totem poles. **Western saddle** a saddle with a horn on the pommel, orig intended to tie a rope to when lassoing cattle. **West Indian** *n* **1** a native or inhabitant of the WEST INDIES. **2** a person whose recent ancestors came from the West Indies. **West Indies** ['ɪndiz] a large group of islands and island countries between Florida and South America. **west–north·west** *n* a direction midway between west and northwest. *adj, adv* in, toward, or from this direction. **west–south·west** *n* a direction midway between west and southwest. **west·ward** *adj, adv* toward the west: *He walked westward. We live on the westward slope of the hill.* Also (*adv.*), **westwards. west·ward·ly** *adj, adv.*

wet [wɛt] *adj* **wet·ter, wet·test** **1** covered, with water or other liquid: *wet hands.* **2** not dry: *Don't touch wet paint.* **3** rainy: *wet weather.* **4** permitting the sale of alcoholic drinks: *a wet town.*
v **wet** or **wet·ted, wet·ting** **1** make or become wet. **2** pass urine; make wet by passing urine.

n **1** water or other liquid: *I dropped my scarf in the wet.* **2** wet weather: *We enjoy walking in the wet.* **wet·ly** *adv.* **wet·ness** *n.* ⟨Middle English *wett, weten*; Old English *wǣtan*⟩ **all wet** *Informal* completely mistaken. **wet behind the ears** *Informal* too young to know very much.

wet blanket *Informal* a person who has a discouraging effect. **wet dream** an erotic dream with ejaculation of semen. **wet·land** *n* **1** a marsh. **2** Usually, **wetlands** *pl* a marshy area set aside for the preservation of wildlife. **wet nurse** a woman employed to suckle the infant of another. **wet–nurse** *v* **1** act as a wet nurse to. **2** treat with special care; pamper. **wet suit** a skin-tight suit of rubber or a similar material that will retain body heat, worn esp by skindivers in cold water. **wet·tish** *adj* somewhat wet.

Wet'·su·wet'·en [wət'suwət,en] *n* **1** a member of a First Nations people living along the Skeena River in British Columbia. **2** their Tsimshian language. **Wet'·su·wet'·en** *adj.* Also called **Carrier.**

whack [wæk] *n* **1** *Informal* a sharp blow or the sound of it. **2** *Slang* portion; share: *Each of the thieves took his whack and left town.* *v* **1** *Informal* strike with a sharp blow: *The batter whacked the ball out of the park.* **2** *Slang* chop or take (*off*): *She whacked off branches with her axe.* ⟨perhaps imitative⟩ **have** (or **take**) **a whack at** *Slang* make an attempt at; try: *I'd like to take a whack at flying a glider.* **out of whack** *Slang* not in proper condition: *The timing of the engine is out of whack.* **whacked** *adj Slang* **1** exhausted; worn out. **2** heavily intoxicated. **whack·ing** *adj Informal* large or tremendous: *a whacking success.* *adv Informal* very: *a whacking good story.*

whale [weil] *n, pl* **whales** or **whale** any of an order of aquatic mammals that are shaped like fish; esp, any of the larger members. *v* hunt and catch whales. **whal·ing** *n.* ⟨Old English *hwæl*⟩ **a whale of a** *Informal* a big or impressive example of: *a whale of a good time.* **whale·bone** *n* **1** the horny substance growing in the mouth of baleen whales. **2** a thin strip of this, esp as formerly used for stays in corsets, dresses, etc. **whal·er** *n* **1** a person who hunts whales. **2** a ship used for hunting and catching whales.

wham [wæm] *Informal n* a loud bang. *interj* an exclamation representing the sound of a hard impact. Also, **wham·mo.** *v* **whammed, wham·ming** smash; beat. ⟨imitative⟩ **wham·my** *n Slang* **1** a supposedly magical spell bringing bad luck: *The magician put the whammy on him.* **2** a catastrophe: *Over-fishing and the increase in the seal population were a double whammy for the fishing industry.*

wharf [wɔrf] *n, pl* **wharves** [wɔrvz] or **wharfs** *n* a platform built on the shore or out from the shore, beside which ships can load and unload. ⟨Old English *hwearf*⟩

what [wʌt] *pron* **1** as an interrogative pronoun, a word used in asking the identity of a thing: *What is your name? She asked the child what was wrong.* **2** as a relative pronoun: **a** that which: *I know what you mean.* **b** anything that: *Do what you please.* **3** what it is; what to do, etc.: *I'll tell you what: you can go see and I'll save your spot.* *adj* **1** as an interrogative adjective, a word used in asking the identity of persons or things: *What time is it? She asked me what I was doing.* **2** as a relative adjective: **a** which: *Put back what money is left.* **b** whatever: *Take what supplies you will need.* **3** as a generalized exclamatory adjective, how great, wonderful, bad, etc.: *What a fool!* *adv* **1** how much; how: *What does it matter?* **2** a word used to intensify an adjective in an exclamation: *What a good time we had!* *interj* a word used to show surprise, doubt, anger, liking, etc. or to add emphasis: *What? Are you late again?* ⟨Old English *hwæt*⟩ **and what not** and all kinds of other things. **give someone what for** *Informal* punish. **what about a** what is to be done about (a given thing): *But what about the other people?* **b** what does (a thing) matter: *And if I do go, what about it?* **c** a formula introducing a suggestion: *What about some Chinese food?* **what for** why; for what purpose. **what have you** *Informal* anything else like this; and so on. **what if a** what would happen if. **b** what difference does it make if: *And what if he did tell her? I don't care!* **what's what** *Informal* the true state of affairs: *I'm still trying to find out what's what.* **what's with** *Informal* **a** what's wrong with: *What's with him?* **b** what is the significance of: *What's with the balloons?* **what with** on account of (an accumulation of things): *What with our long walk and all the excitement, we were exhausted.*

what·ev·er *pron* **1** anything or everything that: *Do whatever you like.* **2** no matter what: *Whatever happens, he is safe.* **3** *Informal* a word used for emphasis instead of *what* (emphatic): *Whatever do you mean?* **4** any of a number of things that will qualify (also dismissively or concessively as a sentence substitute): *Cake and jelly and whatever.* "*It's a spade, not a shovel.*" "*Whatever.*" *adj* **1** any that: *Ask whatever girls you like to the party.* **2** no matter what: *Whatever excuse he makes, it will not be believed.* **3** (after the noun) at all: *Any person whatever can tell you.* **what·not** *n* **1** a stand with several shelves for books, ornaments, etc. **2** a thing that or person who may be variously described; nondescript. **what·so·ev·er** *pron, adj* whatever.

wheat [wit] *n* any of a genus of cereal grasses bearing grain in dense spikes. ⟨Old English *hwǣte*⟩ **wheat·en** *adj* **1** made of wheat or wheat flour. **2** being the colour of wheat, a pale yellow. **wheat germ** the embryo of the wheat kernel, used as a cereal and as a vitamin supplement. **wheat pool** ✱ a co-operative founded by western farmers to store and sell the wheat they produce.

whee·dle ['widəl] *v* persuade by flattery: *The children wheedled their mother into letting them go out.* **whee·dler** *n.* **whee·dling** *adj.* ⟨Old English wǣdlian beg⟩

wheel [wil] *n* **1** a round frame or disk that can turn on a pin or shaft in its centre. **2** any instrument, machine, etc. shaped or moving like a wheel. **3** any force thought of as moving or propelling: *the wheels of government.* **4** a pivoting movement by which dancers, ships in line, etc. change direction while maintaining a straight line. **5** *Informal* BIG WHEEL. **6 wheels** *pl Informal* a motor vehicle, esp a car: *Do you have wheels?*
v **1** *Informal* go by bicycle: *She wheeled along happily.* **2** turn or cause to turn: *The rider wheeled his horse about.* **3** move on wheels; push a wheeled object: *The worker was wheeling a load of bricks on a wheelbarrow.* **4** travel along smoothly. ⟨Old English hwēol⟩ **at** (or **behind**) **the wheel a** at the steering wheel. **b** in control: *The variety night is bound to be a success with you at the wheel.* **wheel and deal** *Slang* do business rapidly, esp in an aggressive way. **wheel·er–deal·er** *n.* **wheels within wheels** complicated circumstances, motives, etc.
wheel·bar·row *n* a small vehicle for carrying loads, having one wheel at the front and two legs at the back, and handles for pushing it. **wheel·base** *n* in motor vehicles, the distance from the centre of the front axle to the centre of the rear axle. **wheel·chair** *n* a chair mounted on wheels so that it can be pushed from behind or moved by the person sitting in it. Wheelchairs are used by people who are unable to walk or who have difficulty walking. **wheeled** *adj* **1** having a wheel or wheels. **2** having wheels of a specified number: *a three-wheeled bicycle.* **wheel·house** *n* a small, enclosed place on a ship to shelter the steering wheel and those who steer the ship. **wheel·ie** *n Informal* a stunt done on a cycle, by pulling up the front wheel so that only the rear wheel is on the ground. **pop a wheelie** do this stunt. **wheel·wright** *n* a person whose work is making or repairing wheels, carriages, and wagons.

wheeze [wiz] *v* **1** breathe with difficulty and with a whistling sound. **2** make a sound like this: *The old engine wheezed, but it didn't stop.* *n* **1** a breath taken with difficulty and with a whistling sound. **2** *Slang* a funny saying or story, esp one that has been told many times. ⟨probably Old Norse hvæsa hiss⟩
wheez·y *adj* habitually wheezing: *a fat, wheezy old dog.* **wheez·i·ly** *adv.* **wheez·i·ness** *n.*

whelk [wɛlk]*n* any of a family of marine gastropod molluscs typically having a strong, spiral shell. ⟨Old English weoloc⟩

whelp [wɛlp] *n* a young animal, esp a puppy or wolf cub.
v give birth to one or more puppies or cubs. ⟨Old English hwelp⟩

when [wɛn] *adv* at what time or stage: *When does school close?*
conj **1** at the time that: *Rise when your name is called.* **2** at any time that: *He is impatient when he is kept waiting.* **3** at which time: *The dog growled till its owner spoke, when it gave a joyful bark.* **4** whereas: *We have only three books when we need five.* **5** considering that: *How can I help you when I can't help myself?* *pron* **1** which time: *Since when have they had a car?* **2** at which: *That was a time when every penny counted.*
n the time: *the when and where of an act.* ⟨Old English hwænne⟩

whence *Archaic, formal adv* from what place, source, or cause: *Whence do you come?* *pron* from which or from where: *Let them return whence they came.* **when·ev·er** *conj, adv* at whatever time; when (emphatic).

where [wɛr] *adv* **1** in, at, or to what place: *Where are you going?* **2** from what source: *Where did you hear that?* **3** in, at, or to which: *the house where he was born.* **4** in what way, position, or state: *Where would I be without her?* *pron* what place: *Where does he come from?* *n* the place: *the when and the where of it.* *conj* **1** to the place to, or at which: *I will go where you go.* **2** in or at the place in which: *The book is where you left it.* **3** in or at which place: *They came to the town, where they stayed for the night.* **4** *Informal* that: *Did you read where he is suing the Liberal Party?* ⟨Old English hwǣr⟩
where·a·bouts *adv* where: *Whereabouts can I find him?* *n pl or sg* the place where a person or thing is: *Do you know the whereabouts of the cottage?* **where·as** ['wɛrəz] *or* [wɛr'æz] *conj* **1** on the contrary: *Some people like opera whereas others do not.* **2** since (often used at the beginning of a formal proclamation): *Whereas all people are human, so all people should show humanity.* **where·at** *adv, conj Archaic* at what; at which. **where·by** *adv, conj* by what; by which: *There is no other way whereby she can be saved.* **where·fore** *adv Archaic* why: *Wherefore do you weep?* *n* Usually, **wherefores** *pl* an explanation: *I don't want to hear all the whys and wherefores.* **where·in** *Archaic, formal adv* in what place or respect: *Wherein had he erred? conj* in which place or respect: *the place wherein they lived.* **where·of** *adv, conj Archaic, formal* of what, which, or whom: *I know whereof I speak.* **where·up·on** *adv* upon what; upon which: *The foundation whereupon we build our children's future must be a secure one. conj* at which point: *She read him the letter, whereupon he flew into a rage.* **wher·ev·er** *conj, adv* **1** where: *Sit wherever you like.* **2** no matter where: *Wherever I go, her face appears before me.* **where·with·al** [-wɪð,ɒl] *or* [-wɪθ,ɒl] *n* supplies or money needed: *Does she have the wherewithal to pay for the trip?*

whet [wɛt] *v* **whet·ted, whet·ting 1** sharpen by rubbing on a stone: *to whet a knife.* **2** stir up: *The smell of food whetted my appetite.* ⟨Old English hwettan⟩
whet·stone *n* a stone for sharpening knives.

wheth·er ['wɛðər] *conj* **1** *Whether* is a conjunction expressing a choice: *He does not know whether to work or play.* **2** if (in indirect

questions): *He asked whether he should finish the work.* ⟨Old English *hwether*⟩
whether or no no matter what happens.

whew [hwju] *interj, n* an exclamation of surprise, relief, dismay, exhaustion, etc.: *Whew! it's hot!*

whey [wei] *n* the watery part of milk that separates from the curd when milk sours and becomes coagulated. ⟨Old English *hwǣg*⟩

which [wɪtʃ] *pron* **1** an interrogative pronoun used to introduce direct or indirect questions that single out one or more members of a group: *Which seems the best plan? Tell me which you like best.* **2** as a relative pronoun, a word used to introduce a clause telling about a place or thing just mentioned: *The book, which we like very much, is on sale. The boat in which you are sitting leaks.*
adj **1** an interrogative adjective used to introduce direct or indirect questions that single out one or more members of a group: *Which boy won the prize? I don't know which shoes to wear.* **2** a word used to raise the possibility of alternatives: *No matter which camera he uses, his pictures never turn out.* ⟨Old English *hwilc*⟩
which is which which is one and which is the other: *It's hard to tell which is which.*
which·ev·er *pron, adj* **1** any that: *Take whichever you want.* **2** no matter which: *Whichever side wins, I shall be satisfied.*

whiff [wɪf] *n* **1** a slight gust: *A whiff of fresh air cleared his head.* **2** a slight smell: *Take a whiff of this perfume.* **3** *Informal* **a** *Baseball, golf, etc.* a swing at a ball without hitting it. **b** *Baseball* a strikeout. ⟨Middle English *weffe* vapour, whiff; partly imitative⟩

while [waɪl] *n* a time: *We waited a long while.*
conj **1** during the time that: *While I was speaking, she said nothing.* **2** although: *While I like the colour of the hat, I don't like the style.* **3** and: *The second act was an acrobat, while the third was a trapeze artist.*
v spend in an easy, pleasant manner (usually with *away*): *We whiled away the day playing at the beach.* ⟨Old English *hwil*⟩
(all) the while at or during the same time.
worth one's while worth effort: *The business trip was hardly worth their while, as all their contacts were on vacation.*

whim [wɪm] *n* a sudden fancy or notion: *Her whim for gardening won't last long.* ⟨compare Icelandic *hvim* unsteady look⟩
on a whim without planning or purpose: *She went to India on a whim.*
whim·si·cal [-zɪkəl] *adj* **1** having many playfully odd fancies. **2** full of whimsy.
whim·si·cal·ly *adv.* **whim·sy** *n* odd or fanciful humour: *The story Alice's Adventures in Wonderland is full of whimsy.*

whim·per ['wɪmpər] *v* **1** cry with soft, broken sounds: *The sick child whimpered.* **2** complain in a weak way; whine. **whim·per** *n.* ⟨probably imitative⟩

whine [waɪn] *v* **1** make a high-pitched, complaining cry: *The dog whined to go out.*

2 complain in a peevish way: *He's just whining about trifles.* **whine** *n.* **whin·y** *adj.* **whin·er** *n.* **whin·ing·ly** *adv.* ⟨Old English *hwīnan*⟩

whin·ny ['wɪni] *n* a soft neighing sound. **whin·ny** *v.* ⟨related to WHINE⟩

whip [wɪp] *n* **1** a stick with a cord or thong at the end. **2** a whipping motion. **3** a dessert made by beating cream, fruit, etc. into a froth: *Prune whip is not my favourite dessert.* **4** WHISK (def. 3). **5** a member of a political party who controls and directs the other members in a lawmaking body.
v **whipped** or **whipt, whip·ping 1** strike with or as with a whip: *He whipped the horse to make it go faster.* **2** move or pull suddenly: *He whipped off his coat.* **3** flap about in a whiplike manner, as flags in a high wind. **4** incite: *The speaker whipped her audience into a fervour.* **5** *Informal* defeat: *The mayor whipped her opponent in the election.* **6** beat (cream, eggs, etc.) to a froth. **7** wind (cord, etc.) around something. **whip·like** *adj.* ⟨Middle English *wippen* swing⟩
whip up a make quickly: *She whipped up some masks for us to wear on Halloween.* **b** stir up: *We are trying to whip up interest in skating.*
whip·cord *n* **1** a strong, twisted cord. **2** a strong cloth with ridges on it. **whip hand 1** the hand that holds the whip while driving a horse-drawn vehicle. **2** a position of control: *A clever person often gets the whip hand over others.* **whip·lash** *n* **1** the lash of a whip. **2** anything considered as similar to this: *the whiplash of fear.* **3** an injury to the neck caused by a sudden jolt that snaps the head backward and then forward, or forward and then backward. **whip·per–snap·per** *n* a young person who thinks he or she is important. **whipping boy 1** formerly, a boy who was educated with a young prince and made to take punishment due to the prince. **2** any person who takes the blame for the wrongdoings of others. **whipping cream** heavy cream with a high butterfat content.

whip·pet ['wɪpɪt] *n* a breed of swift, lean racing and hunting dog that looks like a small greyhound.

whip·poor·will ['wɪpər,wɪl] *n* a goatsucker of central and E North America having an enormous mouth. Also, **whip–poor–will.** ⟨imitative of the bird's cry⟩

whir or **whirr** [wɜr] *n* a soft buzzing noise: *the whir of a hummingbird's wings.*
v **whirred, whir·ring** operate with this noise: *The motor whirred.* ⟨probably imitative⟩

whirl [wɜrl] *v* **1** cause to turn or swing round or move round and round: *The dancers whirled about the room.* **2** move or carry quickly: *We were whirled away in an airplane.* **3** become dizzy: *My mind was whirling.*
n **1** a whirling movement. **2** a dizzy or confused condition: *His thoughts were in a whirl.* **3** a rapid round of happenings, parties, etc.: *the whirl of the holidays.* **4** *Informal* a try: *She had never been in a canoe before, but decided to give it a whirl.* **whirl·er** *n.* ⟨probably Old Norse *hvirfla*; *hverfla* turn⟩

whirl·i·gig ['wɜrli,gɪg] *n* **1** a toy that whirls. **2** a merry-go-round. **3** something that whirls or seems to whirl round and round. **whirl·pool** *n* water whirling round and round, creating a current that sucks things downward. **whirl·wind** *n* **1** a whirling windstorm. **2** an overwhelming, inexorable or rapid series of events. *adj* fast: *a whirlwind romance.* **whirl·y·bird** *n Informal* a helicopter.

whisk [wɪsk] *v* **1** remove with a quick sweeping motion: *to whisk crumbs from a table.* **2** move or carry quickly: *The mouse whisked into its hole.* **3** beat (eggs, etc.) to a froth. *n* **1** a quick sweeping movement: *a whisk of the horse's tail.* **2** WHISK BROOM. **3** a small wire utensil for beating eggs, cream, etc. by hand. ⟨Middle English *visk*; probably Scandinavian⟩ **whisk broom** a small, short-handled broom for brushing away crumbs, dirt, etc.

whisk·er ['wɪskər] *n* **1** Usually, **whiskers** *pl* the hair growing on a man's cheeks and chin. **2** any of the stiff sensory hairs growing near the mouth of a cat, rat, etc. **3** a very small amount: *Could you move just a whisker, please?* **whisk·ered** *adj.* **whisk·er·y** *adj.* ⟨*whisk*⟩

whisk·y or **whiskey** ['wɪski] *n* a strong alcoholic drink made from grain. ⟨short for *whiskybae;* Gaelic *uisge beatha* water of life⟩

whis·ky–jack ['wɪski ,dʒæk] *n* ✸ CANADA JAY. Also, **whis·key–jack.** ⟨earlier *whisky-john*, alteration of Cree *weskuchanis*⟩

whis·per ['wɪspər] *v* **1** speak very softly. **2** tell secretly: *It is whispered that his health is failing.* **3** make a soft, rustling sound: *The wind whispered in the pines.* **whis·per** *n.* **whis·per·er** *n.* **whis·per·y** *adj.* ⟨Old English *hwisprian*⟩ **whispering campaign** a campaign of discreditation, defamation, etc., using gossip.

whist [wɪst] *n* a card game, resembling bridge, for two pairs of players. ⟨alteration of *whisk*⟩

whis·tle ['wɪsəl] *v* **1** make a shrill, often musical sound by forcing breath through one's teeth or pursed lips. **2** make a shrill sound resembling this: *The old steam engine whistled.* **3** blow a whistle. *n* **1** the sound made by whistling. **2** a device for making shrill sounds by means of forced air or steam. ⟨Old English *hwistlian*⟩ **blow the whistle (on)** inform (on). **wet one's whistle** *Informal* take a drink. **whistle for** *Informal* go without; fail to get. **whistle in the dark** try to be courageous in a fearful or trying situation. **whis·tler** *n* **1** a person who or thing that whistles. **2 a** HOARY MARMOT. **b** pika. **whist·le–stop** *Informal n* a small town along a railway line at which a train stops only when signalled. *v* **-stopped, -stop·ping** make a series of electioneering appearances at various small towns along a route.

whit [wɪt] *n* a very small bit: *The sick woman is not a whit better.* ⟨variant of Old English *wiht* thing⟩

white [wəit] *n* **1** the colour of fresh snow; the opposite of black. **2** Often, **whites** *pl* white cloth or clothing. **3** something white: *the white of an egg.* **4** a member of a light-skinned race. *adj* **1** having the colour of snow. **2** pale: *She turned white with fear.* **3** light-coloured: *white wines.* **4** having a light-coloured skin. **5** snowy: *a white winter.* *v* **1** make or become white. **2** remove (an error) by covering it with white (usually with *out*). **white·ness** *n.* ⟨Old English *hwīt*⟩ **bleed someone white** gradually take away all of (someone's) money, strength, etc. **white birch** a large birch common throughout most of Canada, noted esp for its papery white bark, that can be readily peeled off in layers and was traditionally used by North American First Nations peoples of the eastern woodlands for making canoes, etc. **white blood cell** any of the white or colourless blood cells found in the blood and lymph of vertebrates; leucocyte. White blood cells help the body to fight infection. **white·board** *n* **1** a framed white surface specially designed for writing on with dry erasable markers. **2** *Computers* software that simulates such a surface, and allows users to write or draw as though with a pen. **white·cap** *n* a wave with a foaming white crest. **white·coat** *n* a young harp seal. **white–col·lar** *adj* to do with clerical, professional, or business work or workers. Compare BLUE-COLLAR, PINK-COLLAR. **white dwarf** *Astronomy* a small star of little brightness. Compare RED GIANT. **white elephant 1** something rare or valuable that is expensive and troublesome to take care of. **2** something very costly or elaborate that turns out to be useless: *The new airport is just a white elephant.* **white feather** a symbol of cowardice. **show the white feather** act like a coward. **white·fish** *n, pl* **-fish** or **-fish·es** any of a subfamily of freshwater fishes of northern regions that are important food fishes. **white flag** a plain white flag or piece of cloth, used as a sign of truce or surrender. **white gold** an alloy of gold, nickel, or platinum that looks much like platinum. **white heat 1** an intense heat at which things give off a dazzling, white light. **2** a state of intense activity or excitement. **white–hot** *adj.* **White House 1** the official residence of the President of the US, in Washington, D.C. **2** *Informal* the office, authority, opinion, etc. of the President of the United States: *What is the opinion of the White House on this matter?* **whit·ish** almost white. **white lie** a lie about some small matter, esp one told to avoid hurting someone's feelings. **white light** *Physics* light that is a mixture of wavelengths but is perceived by the eye as having the quality of noontime sunlight. **white magic** good magic. Compare BLACK MAGIC. **white meat** any light-coloured meat or poultry as opposed to beef. **whit·en** *v* **1** make or become white: *to whiten sheets with bleach.* **2** make or become pale or paler: *He whitened when he heard the bad news.*

whit·en·er *n.* whit·en·ing *n.* white noise the sound produced by using the whole range of audible frequencies at once. Also, white sound. white·out *n* 1 an arctic weather condition in which the snow-covered ground, the cloudy sky, and the horizon become a continuous, shadowless mass of dazzling white. 2 a winter weather condition in which blowing snow completely fills the range of vision: *Many highway accidents are caused by whiteouts.* 3 an opaque liquid used to erase errors in print or writing. white paper a government report concerning matters of lesser importance than those appearing in BLUE BOOKS. white pepper a hot-tasting seasoning made by grinding the dried, husked berries of the black pepper vine. Compare BLACK PEPPER. white pine any of various pines having soft, light wood. white sale a sale of household linens such as sheets, towels, etc. white sauce a sauce made of milk, butter, flour, and seasonings cooked together. white shark a large, ferocious shark having a greyish back and white underside. white supremacy the belief that the white race is superior to other races. white supremacist. white tie men's formal evening dress with tailcoat and white tie. Compare BLACK TIE. white·wash *n* 1 a liquid for whitening walls, woodwork, etc., usually made of lime and water. 2 a covering up of faults or mistakes. 3 *Sports* a defeat in which the loser fails to score. white·wash *v.* white water rapids. white·wa·ter *adj* to do with movement through rapids, esp as recreation: *white-water rafting.* whit·ish *adj* almost white.

whith·er ['wɪðər] *adv, conj, Archaic, poetic* where. ⟨Old English *hwiðer*⟩

whit·tle ['wɪtəl] *v* 1 cut (shavings) from (wood, etc.) with a knife. 2 shape or make by whittling: *to whittle a boat.* whit·tler *n.* ⟨earlier *thwittle*; Old English *thwītan* cut⟩

whittle down (or away) cut down little by little: *We tried to whittle down our expenses.*

whiz[1] [wɪz] *n, pl* whiz·zes *Informal* a person who is very good in a particular activity: *a computer whiz.* ⟨alteration of *wiz*; *wizard*⟩ whiz–kid or whiz kid *n* a young person who is unusually talented, expert, or influential for his or her age in a given field.

whiz[2] or whizz [wɪz] *n, pl* whiz·zes a hissing sound, esp such a sound made by very rapid movement.

v whizzed, whiz·zing make a hissing sound: *An arrow whizzed past his head.* ⟨imitative⟩

who [hu] *pron poss* whose [huz] *obj* whom [hum] 1 an interrogative pronoun used in direct or indirect questions about the identity of a person or persons: *Who is she?* 2 a relative pronoun used to introduce a clause giving extra information about someone just mentioned: *The girl who spoke has left.* ⟨Old English *hwā*⟩

who's who a which is one person and which is another. b which people are important.

who·ev·er [hu'ɛvər] *pron* 1 any person that: *Whoever wants the book may have it.* 2 no matter who: *Whoever else goes hungry, he won't.* 3 an emphatic version of the interrogative *who: Whoever thought that up?*

whom [hum] *pron* the objective form of WHO: *No one knows for whom that house is being built.* whom·ev·er *pron* 1 any person whom. 2 no matter whom. 3 used interrogatively, whom (emphatic): *Whomever could he have meant?* whose [huz] *pron, adj* the possessive form of WHO and of WHICH: *Whose car is that? I found this pen, but I don't know whose it is.*

In informal English who is commonly used in both subject and object positions, though whom is obligatory immediately after a preposition: *Who did you speak to?* but *I saw the man to whom you spoke yesterday.* Formal and written English require whom in object position.

WHO WORLD HEALTH ORGANIZATION.

whoa [wou] *interj* (esp to horses) stop!

who·dun·it [hu'dʌnɪt] *n Slang* a story, film, or play dealing with crime, esp murder, and its detection. ⟨*who* + *done* + *it*⟩

whole [houl] *adj* 1 having all its parts; complete: *a whole set of dishes.* 2 comprising the full quantity, extent, etc.; entire: *a whole page.* 3 not injured, broken, or defective: *to get out of a fight with a whole skin.* 4 in one piece: *to swallow a piece of meat whole.* 5 *Mathematics* not fractional: *a whole number.* 6 well; healthy.

n 1 the total: *Four quarters make a whole.* 2 a system. whole·ness *n.* ⟨variant of Middle English *hole*, Old English *hāl*⟩

as a whole altogether. made out of whole cloth *Informal* entirely false. on the whole a considering everything. b for the most part. whole blood blood used for transfusions that is exactly as taken from the donor. whole–hearted *adj* earnest; sincere. whole–heart·ed·ly *adv.* whole–heart·ed·ness *n.* whole–hog *adv Slang* completely: *She gives herself whole-hog to any project she takes up.* whole language *Education* the teaching of reading and writing in context, i.e., by its use in learning other things, rather than in isolation. whole milk milk with none of the butterfat removed. whole note *Music* a note used as the basis for determining the time value of all other notes, equal to two half notes, four quarter notes, etc. whole number a number denoting zero or one or more whole units. whole·sale *n* the sale of goods in large quantities at a time, usually to retailers: *He buys at wholesale and sells at retail.* Compare RETAIL. *adj* 1 to do with sale in large quantities: *a wholesale fruit business.* 2 broad and general: *Avoid wholesale condemnation. adv* 1 in large quantities. 2 at a wholesale price: *I can get it for you wholesale.* 3 indiscriminately or on a large scale. *v* sell or be sold in large quantities: *They wholesale these jackets at $10 each.* whole·sal·er *n.* whole·some *adj* 1 good for the health: *wholesome food.* 2 healthy-looking: *a* *wholesome face.* **3** good for the mind or morals: *wholesome books.* **whole·some·ly** *adv.* **whole·some·ness** *n.* **whole step** *Music* an interval consisting of two adjoining semitones and equal to one-sixth of an octave. **whole tone** WHOLE STEP. **whole–wheat** *adj* made of the entire wheat kernel or from the flour derived from this. **whol·ly** ['houlli] *or* ['houli] *adv* completely; totally.

whom See WHO.

whoop [hup] *or* [wup] *n* **1** a loud cry: *The player let out a whoop of joy.* **2** the cry of an owl, crane, etc.; hoot. **3** the loud, gasping noise a person with whooping cough makes after a fit of coughing. **whoop** *v.* ⟨imitative⟩ **whoop it up** *Slang* make a noisy disturbance, as in celebrating.

whoop–de–do ['wup di 'du] *or* ['hup] *n Informal* **1** loud commotion or display. **2** *Ironic* big deal; so what. Also, **whoop–de–doo. whoop·ee** ['wupi] *or* ['wʊ'pi] *interj* an exclamation of unrestrained joy or pleasure. **make whoopee a** have a noisy, hilarious good time. **b** make love. **whoop·ing cough** ['hupɪŋ] *or* ['wupɪŋ] an infectious disease of children, characterized by fits of coughing ending with a loud, gasping sound. **whoops** [wʊps] *interj* oops. **whoop–up** ['hup ˌʌp] *or* ['wup ˌʌp] *n* ✹ *esp West Slang* a noisy party or other celebration.

whop·per *n Informal* **1** something very large. **2** a big lie. ⟨origin unknown⟩ **whop·ping** *adj Informal* very large of its kind.

whore [hɔr] *or* [hur] *n* a promiscuous person or one who is a prostitute.
v **1** have intercourse with whores. **2** be or act as a whore. **3** pursue (something unworthy) (with *after*). ⟨Old English *hōre*⟩ **whore·house** *n* brothel.

whorl [wɔrl] *or* [wɜrl] *n* **1** a circle of leaves or flowers around the stem of a plant. **2** one of the turns of a spiral shell. **3** any coil or curl. **4** a type of fingerprint in which the ridges in the centre turn through at least one complete circle. **whorled** *adj.* ⟨probably variant of *whirl*⟩

whose See WHO.

USAGE

Whose is always used when referring to people, but it can also be used for things, in order to make a long sentence smoother. For instance, it is easier to read the second of the following sentences than the first:
1. *The plant has three new generators, the combined capacity of which is greater than that of the five we had before.*
2. *The plant has three new generators whose combined capacity is greater than that of the five we had before.*

why [waɪ] *conj* **1** for what reason: *Why did you do it?* **2** for which; because of which: *That is the reason why he failed.*
n, pl **whys** the reason: *I can't understand the whys and wherefores of her behaviour.*
interj an expression used to show surprise, doubt, etc. or to fill in: *Why! The car is gone.*

Why, yes, if you wish. ⟨Old English *hwȳ* instrumental case of *hwā* who, *hwæt* what⟩ **why not** *Informal* formula for introducing or agreeing with a suggestion: *Why not give her a call? "How about some coffee?" "OK, why not?"*

Wic·ca ['wɪkə] *n* the belief in the old pagan religion of northern Europe. Its followers are organized in groups called covens. **Wic·can** *n, adj.* ⟨Old English = wizard⟩

wick [wɪk] *n* the part of an oil lamp or candle that is lighted, usually a cord through which oil or melted wax is drawn up and burned. ⟨Old English *wēoce*⟩

wick·ed ['wɪkɪd] *adj* **1** bad; evil: *a wicked person.* **2** mischievous: *a wicked smile.* **3** *Informal* unpleasant; severe: *a wicked storm.* **4** *Slang* skilful: *a wicked golfer.* **wick·ed·ly** *adv.* **wick·ed·ness** *n.* ⟨*wick* wicked; probably Old English *wicca* wizard⟩

wick·er ['wɪkər] *n* easily bent branches that can be woven together. ⟨compare dialect Swedish *vikker* willow⟩ **wick·er·work** *n* **1** branches woven together; wicker. **2** anything made of wicker.

wick·et ['wɪkɪt] *n* **1** a small door or gate: *The big door has a wicket in it.* **2** a small window or opening at a counter, etc., often protected by a screen: *Buy your tickets at this wicket.* **3** *Croquet* a wire arch stuck in the ground to knock the ball through. **4** *Cricket* **a** either of the two sets of sticks that one side tries to hit with the ball. **b** the level space between these. ⟨Anglo-French *wiket*; Germanic⟩

wick·i·up ['wɪkiˌʌp] *n* ✹ **1** a brush- or mat-covered shelter among certain Algonquian First Nations people. **2** a crude shelter; a lean-to. ⟨Algonquian; compare Fox *wikiyap* dwelling⟩

wide [waɪd] *adj* **1** filling much space from side to side: *a wide street,* **2** extending a certain distance from side to side: *The door is 90 cm wide.* **3** full; ample; roomy: *a wide room.* **4** of great range: *wide reading.* **5** far or fully open: *to stare with wide eyes.* **6** far from a named target, etc.: *a wide shot.*
adv **1** to a relatively great extent from side to side: *wide apart.* **2** over an extensive region: *They travel far and wide.* **3** fully: *Open your mouth wide.* **4** astray: *Her shot went wide.* **wid·en** *v.* **wide·ness** *n.* ⟨Old English *wīd*⟩

wide–a·wake *adj* **1** fully awake. **2** alert. **wide–eyed** *adj* as if with the eyes wide open, as with innocence, sleeplessness, or surprise. **wide·ly** *adv* **1** to a great extent: *a widely distributed plant.* **2** very: *The boys gave two widely different accounts of the quarrel.* **wide–o·pen** *adj* (only before the noun; two words elsewhere) **1** opened as much as possible. **2** lax in the enforcement of laws to do with liquor, gambling, and prostitution. **3** quite undecided: *a wide-open question.* **wide·spread** *adj* **1** spread widely: *widespread wings.* **2** spread over a wide space: *a widespread flood.* **3** occurring in many places: *a widespread belief.* **width** [wɪdθ] *or* [wɪtθ] *n* **1** distance across. **2** a piece of a certain width: *curtains taking two widths of cloth.*

widg·eon ['wɪdʒən] *n, pl* **-eons** or **-eon** any of several freshwater ducks. ⟨Compare Middle French *vigeon* wild duck⟩

wid·get ['wɪdʒɪt] *n* a small, unspecified tool or gadget, esp a hypothetical one. ⟨origin unknown⟩

wid·ow ['wɪdou] *n* **1** a woman whose husband is dead and who has not married again. **2** a woman whose husband is often away or preoccupied because of some pastime: *a computer game widow.*
v make a widow or widower of: *She was widowed when she was only thirty years old.* **wid·ow·hood** *n.* ⟨Old English *widewe*⟩
wid·ow·er *n* a man whose wife is dead and who has not married again. **widow's peak** a V-shaped point formed by the hairline in the middle of the forehead.

width See WIDE.

wield [wild] *v* hold and use: *He wielded his sword well.* **wield·er** *n.* ⟨Old English *wieldan*⟩

wie·ner ['winər] *n* a bland sausage. ⟨German *Wienerwurst* Vienna sausage⟩
wiener roast an outdoor social function at which wieners are cooked over an open fire.

wife [wəɪf] *n, pl* **wives** a married woman, esp when considered with reference to her husband. **wife·hood** *n.* **wife·ly** *adj.* ⟨Old English *wīf*⟩

wig [wɪg] *n* an artificial covering of hair for the head: *The bald man wore a wig.* ⟨*periwig*, earlier *perewyke*; French *perruque*⟩

wig·gle ['wɪgəl] *v* move with quick, twisting movements: *This key doesn't work unless you wiggle it in the lock.*
n a wiggling movement. ⟨Middle English *wiglen* frequentative of dialect *wig* wag⟩
wig·gly *adj* **1** wiggling: *a wiggly caterpillar.* **2** wavy: *Draw a wiggly line under the heading.*

wig·wam ['wɪg,wɒm] *n* **1** a dwelling traditionally used by First Nations peoples from Manitoba to the Atlantic Provinces, consisting of an arched or cone-shaped framework of poles covered with hide, bark, mats made from rushes, etc. Compare TEEPEE. **2** teepee. ⟨Ojibwa⟩

wild [waɪld] *adj* **1** not tamed or cultivated: *The tiger is a wild animal.* **2** not civilized. **3** not in proper control or order: *wild hair.* **4** violently excited. **5** violent: *a wild storm.* **6** rash; crazy: *wild schemes.* **7** *Informal* very eager. **8** *Card games* of a card, able to be used to represent any number or suit.
n Often, **wilds** *pl* an uncultivated region.
adv in a wild manner or to a wild degree. **wild·ly** *adv.* **wild·ness** *n.* ⟨Old English *wilde*⟩
run wild live or grow without restraint. **wild about** extremely fond of or impressed by: *I'm not wild about working late.*
wild card 1 *Cards* a card substitutable for any other card. **2** *Sports* a team or player who, although not qualifying, is admitted to a tournament at the discretion of the organizers: *In tennis, wild cards sometimes get to the final rounds.* **3** a completely unpredictable or uncontrollable variable.

wild·cat *n* **1** any of various wild members of the cat family, such as the lynx. **2** a well drilled for oil or gas in a region where none has been found before. *adj* of a strike, etc., illegal or without union approval. **wild–eyed** *adj* **1** staring wildly or angrily. **2** irrational; impractical: *a wild-eyed scheme.* **wild·fire** *n* a substance that burns fiercely and is hard to put out, formerly used in warfare. **like wildfire** very rapidly: *The news spread like wildfire.* **wild·flower** *n* any flowering plant that grows in the woods, fields, etc. **wild–goose chase** a useless search or pursuit. **wild·life** *n* wild animals and birds as a group, esp those native to a particular area: *the northern wildlife.* **wild rice** a tall North American grass that grows in wet places, having edible, ricelike grain. **wild rose** any uncultivated rose. The wild rose is the floral emblem of Alberta. **wild West** or **Wild West** the western US during pioneer days, when it was uncultivated and unpoliced.

wil·der·ness ['wɪldərnɪs] *n* **1** a desolate region. **2** a bewildering collection: *a wilderness of streets.* ⟨Old English *wildēorn*; *wilde* wild + *dēor* animal⟩
wilderness area an area of crown land set aside as an ecological preserve.

wile [waɪl] *n* **1** a trick to deceive. **2** craftiness.
v entice: *The sunshine wiled me from my work.* **wil·y** *adj.* **wil·i·ly** *adv.* **wil·i·ness** *n.* ⟨Old English *wīgle* magic⟩
wile away while away; spend (time, a vacation, etc.) easily or pleasantly.

will¹ [wɪl] *v pt* **would** *pres sg* or *pl* **will** a modal auxiliary verb used: **1** to refer to future happenings: *The train will be late.* **2** to express a promise: *I will come at 4 o'clock.* **3** to introduce a polite request or offer: *Will you please hand me that book?* **4** to express a capacity or power that something has: *This pail will hold 8 L.* **5** to express inevitability or habit: *She will read for hours at a time.* **6** as an imperative with the subject *you*: *Don't argue; you will do it at once!* ⟨Old English *willan*⟩

> **USAGE**
> Will is the usual auxiliary for forming the future tense: *Tomorrow will come.* In formal English, however, some people still prefer to use **shall** when the subject is *I* or *we*: *We shall arrive before lunch.*

will² [wɪl] *n* **1** the power of the mind to decide and do: *a strong will.* **2** the act of choosing to do something: *He did it of his own will.* **3** determination: *the will to live.* **4** what is chosen to be done. **5** *Law* a legal statement of a person's wishes about what is to be done with his or her property after he or she is dead. **6** feeling toward another: *good will, ill will.*
v **willed, will·ing 1** use the will: *She willed herself to keep awake.* **2** to influence by control over thought and action: *She willed the person in front of her to turn around.* **3** wish; desire: *All right, as you will.* ⟨Old English⟩
at will whenever one wishes. **do the will of** obey. **with a will** with energy

will·ful or **wil·ful** *adj* **1** stubborn. **2** done on purpose: *willful destruction.* **will·ful·ness** or **wil·ful·ness** *n.* **will·ful·ly** or **wil·ful·ly** *adv.* **will·ing** *adj* **1** ready: *He is willing to wait.* **2** cheerfully ready: *a willing worker.* **will·ing·ly** *adv.* **will·ing·ness** *n.* **will·pow·er** *n* self-control or determination.

wil·lies ['wɪliz] *n* **the willies** *Informal* a feeling of uneasiness; jitters: *Being alone in the house at night gives me the willies.* ⟨origin unknown⟩

will–o'–the–wisp ['wɪl ə ðə 'wɪsp] *n* **1** a moving light appearing at night over marshy places, caused by the combustion of marsh gas. **2** something that misleads by luring on.

wil·low ['wɪloʊ] *n* any of a genus of trees and shrubs, usually having narrow, pointed leaves arranged alternately on the twigs. ⟨Old English *welig*⟩ **wil·low·y** *adj* like a willow; slender; supple.

wil·ly–nil·ly ['wɪli 'nɪli] *adv* willingly or not: *He found himself involved willy-nilly in the promotion campaign.* **wil·ly–nil·ly** *adj.* ⟨*will I, nill I;* Old English *nyllan; ne* not + *willan* will⟩

wilt [wɪlt] *v* **1** become limp. **2** lose strength, vigour, assurance, etc. **3** cause to wilt. ⟨variant of *welt* wither, alteration of *welk*⟩

wil·y See WILE.

wimp [wɪmp] *n Slang* a timid and weak-willed individual. ⟨probably from *whimper*⟩

wim·ple ['wɪmpəl] *n* a cloth draped closely about the face and covering the head, forming part of the habit of some nuns. ⟨Old English *wimpel*⟩

win [wɪn] *v* **won, win·ning** **1** finish first in (a competition): *to win a race.* Compare PLACE and SHOW. **2** get victory or success (in): *You won't win if the chairperson is against the idea.* **3** gain the support of (often with *over*): *We won most of the voters over to our side.* **win** *n.* **win·na·ble** *adj.* ⟨Old English *winnan*⟩ **win out** *Informal* prevail: *Reason won out over stubbornness in the end.*

win·ner *n* **1** a person who or thing that wins. **2** someone or something that seems sure to succeed. **win·ning** *adj* **1** that wins: *a winning team.* **2** charming; attractive: *a winning smile.* *n* **winnings** *pl* what is won. **win·ning·ly** *adv.*

wince [wɪns] *v* flinch slightly, often with a grimace: *The boy winced at the sight of the dentist's drill.* *n* the act of wincing. ⟨Anglo-French *wencir,* Old French *guencir*⟩

winch [wɪntʃ] *n* a machine for lifting or pulling, having a roller around which a cable is wound. **winch** *v.* ⟨Old English *wince*⟩

wind¹ [wɪnd] *n* **1** air in motion. **2** gas in the stomach or bowels. **3** the power of breathing: *A runner needs good wind.* *v* put out of breath: *I was winded by walking up the steep hill.* **wind·y** *adj.* **wind·i·ly** *adv.* **wind·i·ness** *n.* ⟨Old English⟩ **before the wind** in the direction toward which the wind is blowing. **break wind** pass gas. **get** (or **have**) **the wind up** become

worried. **get wind of** find out about: *Don't let them get wind of our plans.* **in the eye** (or **teeth**) **of the wind** directly against the wind. **in the wind** impending: *There's an election in the wind.* **into the wind** pointing toward the direction from which the wind is blowing. **sail close to the wind** **a** manage with the utmost economy. **b** come very near to dishonesty, indecency, etc. **take the wind out of someone's sails** suddenly take away someone's advantage, pride, etc.

wind·bag *n Slang* a person who talks a lot but says little that is significant. **wind–blown** *adj* blown by the wind. **wind·break** *n* a row or clump of trees or bushes planted to provide protection from the wind and, often, to prevent soil erosion. **wind·break·er** *n* a short outdoor jacket that has close-fitting cuffs and waist. **wind·burn** *n* inflammation of the skin due to exposure to wind. **wind chill** the chilling effect of wind in combination with low temperature. **wind chill factor** a measure of the combined chilling effect of wind and low temperature. **wind·ed** *adj* out of breath. **wind·fall** *n* **1** fruit blown down by the wind. **2** an unexpected piece of good luck. **wind·flow·er** *n* in the West, any of several anemones, esp the prairie crocus. **wind instrument** a musical instrument sounded by blowing air into it by mouth. **wind·jam·mer** *n Informal* formerly, a sailing ship as opposed to a steamship. **wind·mill** *n* a machine operated by the action of the wind upon a wheel of vanes. **tilt at** (or **fight**) **windmills** expend one's energy in futile attacks on what cannot be overcome (from the story of Don Quixote tilting at windmills under the illusion that they were giants). **wind·pipe** *n* the passage by which air is carried from the throat to the lungs; trachea. **wind·shield** *n* the sheet of glass or plastic that forms the front window of a motor vehicle, or the screen at the front of a motorcycle, motorboat, etc. **wind·storm** *n* a storm with much wind but little or no rain. **wind·surf·ing** *n* the sport of gliding over water on a sailboard that is like a surfboard equipped with a sail. **wind·surf·er** *n.* **wind tunnel** a chamber in which the effect of air pressures on aircraft, missiles, etc. can be calculated by means of artificially made winds. **wind·ward** *adv* in the direction from which the wind is blowing. *adj* on the side toward the wind.

wind² [waɪnd] *v* **wound, wind·ing** **1** move in a crooked way: *A brook winds through the woods.* **2** proceed in a roundabout manner: *His speech wound slowly toward its conclusion.* **3** wrap about something: *The mother wound her arms about the child.* **4** make (a machine) go by turning some part of it: *to wind a clock.* *n* a bend; turn; twist. **wind·ing** *n, adj.* **wind·ing·ly** *adv.* ⟨Old English *windan*⟩ **wind down** **a** bring or come gradually to a conclusion. **b** relax. **wind up** **a** end; conclude: *Wind up this project today.* **b** *Baseball* make swinging and twisting movements just before pitching the ball.

c excite. **d** involve. **e** end up: *If you keep spending like that, you'll wind up destitute.* **wind–up** or **wind·up** *n.*

win·dow ['wɪndou] *n* **1** an opening in the wall of a building, car, etc. to let in light or air. **2** anything suggesting a window in giving access: *This play opens a new window on human nature.* **3** *Computers* **a** means of interrupting a computer program to perform some other function without disturbing the existing file. **b** the boxlike screen compartment displaying activity in such a function. **4** a period of time favourable for launching a spacecraft, or for any other undertaking. **win·dow·less** *adj.* ⟨Old Norse *vindauga; vindr* wind + *auga* eye⟩

window box a box placed outside a window, for growing plants and flowers. **window dressing 1** the art of attractively displaying merchandise in shop windows. **2** any display or statement made, often misleadingly, to create a favourable impression: *Much of the president's report was window dressing.* **win·dow·pane** *n* a piece of glass in a window. **window seat** a bench built into the wall of a room, under a window. **win·dow-shop** *v* **-shopped, -shop·ping** look at articles in store windows without going in to buy anything. **win·dow–shop·per** *n.* **windowsill** *n* a piece of wood, etc. across the bottom of a window.

wine [waɪn] *n* the juice of grapes or other fruits that has been fermented and contains alcohol. **win·y** *adj.* ⟨Old English *wīn;* Latin *vinum*⟩ **wine and dine** entertain or be entertained by food and drink. **wine cellar** a cellar where wine is stored. **wine·glass** *n* a stemmed drinking glass for wine. **wine·grow·er** *n* a person who cultivates grapes and makes wine. **wine·grow·ing** *n, adj.* **wine·mak·er** *n* an expert in the production of wines. **win·er·y** *n* a place where wine is made. **wi·no** *n Slang* an alcoholic who is addicted to cheap wine.

wing [wɪŋ] *n* **1** the part of a bird, insect, or bat used in flying. **2** anything like a wing in shape or use. **3** a part that sticks out from the main part, such as an extension at the side of a building. **4** a part of an organization whose views contrast with those of the mainstream: *the left wing.* **5** *Hockey, lacrosse, etc.* a player whose position is on either side of the centre. **6** *Theatre* **wings** *pl* the area at either side of the stage.
v **1** fly or fly through: *The birds are winging south.* **2** wound in the wing or arm: *The bullet winged the bird but did not kill it.* **wing·less** *adj.* **wing·like** *adj.* ⟨Old Norse *vængr*⟩
clip someone's wings restrict or confine someone. **get one's wings** be awarded one's pilot's licence. **lend** (or **give**) **wings to** cause to fly or to seem to fly. **on a wing and a prayer** with slim chances of success. **on the wing a** flying. **b** active; busy. **c** while flying, moving, etc. **take wing a** fly away. **b** depart in haste. **under someone's wing** under someone's protection or sponsorship. (**waiting**) **in the wings** ready to intervene or be used if necessary. **wing it** *Informal* speak or

act with little preparation or planning.
winged [wɪŋd] *Poetic* ['wɪŋɪd] *adj* **1** having wings. **2** swift; rapid. **wing·er** *n Hockey, lacrosse, etc.* WING (def. 5). **wing nut 1** a NUT (def. 2) having a projecting piece so that it can be turned with the thumb and forefinger. **2** *Slang* NUT (def. 4). **wing·span** *n* the distance between the tips of the wings of a bird or insect when they are spread out, or between the tips of the wings of an airplane. **wing·spread** *n* wingspan.

wing·ding or **wing–ding** ['wɪŋˌdɪŋ] *n Slang* **1** a lively, lavish party or celebration. **2** something remarkable or memorable of its kind: *a wingding of a fight.* ⟨origin uncertain⟩

wink [wɪŋk] *v* **1** close the eyes and open them again quickly. **2** close one eye and open it again as a hint or signal.
n **1** the act or an instance of winking. **2** the very shortest bit of sleep: *I didn't sleep a wink.* ⟨Old English *wincian*⟩
wink at pretend not to see.
forty winks a short sleep; nap.

Win·ni·peg couch ['wɪnəˌpɛg] ✱ a couch having no arms or back and opening out into a double bed.

win·now ['wɪnou] *v* **1** blow off the chaff from (grain). **2** sort out: *to winnow truth from falsehood.* **win·now·er** *n.* ⟨Old English *windwian; wind* wind[1]⟩

wi·no See WINE.

win·some ['wɪnsəm] *adj* charming; attractive; pleasing: *a winsome child.* **win·some·ly** *adv.* **win·some·ness** *n.* ⟨Old English *wynn* joy⟩

win·ter ['wɪntər] *n* **1** the coldest season of the year, between fall and spring. **2** a period of decline, dreariness, or adversity.
v **1** spend or cause to spend the winter: *Many Canadians winter in Florida.* ⟨Old English⟩
win·ter·green *n* **1** any of several evergreen shrubs of the heath family, having shiny, aromatic leaves and edible red berries. **2 oil of wintergreen** an aromatic oil used for flavouring and in medicine. **win·ter·ize** *v* **1** make (a car, a building, etc.) ready for use during the winter. **2** prepare (a building, such as a cottage) for use in winter. **win·ter·time** *n* winter. **winter wheat** wheat planted in the fall to ripen in the following year. **win·try** *adj* **1** to do with winter. **2** chilling: *a wintry smile.* **win·tri·ly** *adv.* **win·tri·ness** *n.*

wipe [waɪp] *v* rub with paper, cloth, etc. in order to clean or dry: *to wipe the table.*
n **1** the act of wiping: *She gave his face a hasty wipe.* **2** a piece of absorbent material, usually disposable, for wiping any of various surfaces: *baby wipes.* ⟨Old English *wīpian*⟩
wipe out a destroy completely. **b** cancel. **c** erase. **d** *Slang* lose control: *When the wind caught her sails, she wiped out.* **e** *Slang* fail miserably: *I wiped out on that exam!* **wipe-out** *n.* **wipe the floor with** defeat overwhelmingly.
wip·er *n* a rubber blade that moves across the windshield of a vehicle to clear it.

wire [waɪr] *n* **1** metal drawn out into a thread: *copper wire.* **2** a wire above the finish line of a racecourse, that is broken as the winner runs through it.

v 1 furnish with wiring: *to wire a house for electricity.* 2 fasten with wire: *He wired the two pieces together.* 3 *Informal* attach concealed electronic recording equipment in (a place) or on (a person): *The police often wire an informant, to get information.* **wire·like** *adj.* ⟨Old English *wīr*⟩

down to the wire *Informal* up to or at the last moment. **get (in) under the wire** *Informal* arrive or finish just before it is too late. **get one's wires crossed** miscommunicate.

wired *adj Slang* extremely excited, disoriented, etc. **wire–haired** *adj* having coarse, stiff hair: *a wire-haired terrier.* **wire·less** *adj* to do with devices or systems that use no wires, such as cellphones. **wire service** a business that collects news stories, photos, etc. and distributes them to newspapers and radio and television stations that subscribe to their service. **wire·tap·ping** *n* the act of making a secret connection with telephone wires to find out the messages sent over them. **wire·tap** *n, v* -**tapped** -**tap·ping.** **wire·tap·per** *n.* **wir·ing** *n Electricity* a system of wires to carry an electric current. **wir·y** *adj* 1 like wire. 2 lean and tough. **wir·i·ly** *adv.* **wir·i·ness** *n.*

wise¹ [waɪz] *adj* 1 having knowledge and good judgment: *a wise counsellor.* 2 showing wisdom: *wise advice.* **wise·ly** *adv.* **wis·dom** ['wɪzdəm] *n.* ⟨Old English *wīs*⟩

get wise *Slang* find out; understand; realize (often with *to*). **put someone wise to** *Slang* enlighten (someone) about. **wise up** *Slang* inform, or become informed.

wisdom tooth the back tooth on either side of the upper and lower jaw, ordinarily appearing between the ages of 17 and 25. **wise·crack** *Informal n* a smart remark. *v* make wisecracks. **wise·crack·er** *n.* **wise guy** *Slang* a know-it-all. **wise–guy** *adj.*

wise² [waɪz] *n Formal* way: *He is in no wise a scholar; he prefers machinery.* ⟨Old English *wīse*⟩

–wise *suffix* 1 in——manner: *likewise.* 2 in a——ing manner: *slantwise.* 3 in the characteristic way of a——: *clockwise.* 4 in the——respect: *otherwise.* 5 in the direction of——: *lengthwise.* 6 with regard to——: *businesswise.* ⟨*wise²*⟩

USAGE

In Old and Middle English -wise was freely added to nouns to form adverbs of manner. This usage has recently been revived and is popularly used to form words as needed: *He is doing well salarywise.* However, many people regard the usage as appropriate only to informal speech and professional jargon. It should, therefore, be used with discretion, especially in writing.

wise·a·cre ['waɪz,eikər] *n* a person who thinks that he or she knows everything. ⟨Middle Dutch *wijssegger* soothsayer⟩

wish [wɪʃ] *v* 1 desire; want: *Do you wish to go home?* 2 express a desire or hope: *I wish you a*

Happy New Year. 3 request or command: *Do you wish me to send her in now?* 4 impose (something undesirable) (with *on*): *They wished the hardest job on him.* 5 cause to be, etc., by sheer force of wishing: *We can't just wish this war away.*

n 1 an instance of wishing. 2 Usually, **wishes** *pl* the expressed desire for someone's happiness, fortune, etc.: *best wishes.* 3 the thing wished for: *They got their wishes.* ⟨Old English *wȳscan*⟩

make a wish have or express a wish.

wish·bone *n* in birds, the forked bone in the front of the breast. **wish·ful** *adj* longing. **wish·ful·ly** *adv.* **wish·ful·ness** *n.* **wish fulfilment** *Psychology* the satisfaction of a subconscious desire through fantasy. **wishful thinking** a believing something to be true that one wants to be true. **wish list** a hypothetical list of things wished for, and usually unlikely to be received.

wish·y–wash·y ['wɪʃi ,wɒʃi] *adj* 1 weak; insipid. 2 indecisive. **wish·y–wash·i·ly** *adv.* **wish·y–wash·i·ness** *n.* ⟨varied reduplication of *washy* watery, weak⟩

wisp [wɪsp] *n* 1 a small bunch: *a wisp of hay.* 2 a fine bit of something insubstantial: *a wisp of smoke.* 3 a small and delicate person: *a wisp of a girl.* **wisp·y** *adj.* ⟨Middle English⟩

wist·ful ['wɪstfəl] *adj* 1 yearning: *wistful eyes.* 2 melancholy. **wist·ful·ly** *adv.* **wist·ful·ness** *n.* ⟨obsolete *wist* attentive + *-ful*⟩

wit [wɪt] *n* 1 the power to perceive quickly, and express cleverly, ideas that are unusual and amusing. 2 a person with such power. 3 Often, **wits** *pl* the power of understanding: *She has quick wits.* ⟨Old English *witt*⟩

at one's wits' end not knowing what to do or say. **have** (or **keep**) **one's wits about one** remain calm and in control of one's thoughts. **live by one's wits** make one's living by clever or crafty devices rather than by any settled occupation.

wit·less *adj* lacking intelligence; foolish. **wit·less·ly** *adv.* **wit·less·ness** *n.* **wit·ti·cism** *n* a witty remark. **wit·ty** *adj* clever and amusing: *a witty remark.* **wit·ti·ly** *adv.* **wit·ti·ness** *n.*

witch [wɪtʃ] *n* 1 a person, esp a woman, who practises usually black magic. Compare WARLOCK. 2 a a Wiccan priest or priestess. b a devotee of Wicca. 3 *Informal* a fascinating girl or woman. 4 *Informal* a woman who is malicious. **witch·like** *adj.* **witch·y** *adv.* ⟨Old English *wicce*⟩

witch·craft *n* 1 the practices and the cult of witches. 2 a fascination suggesting supernatural power. **witch doctor** a professional practitioner of magic and healing among certain preliterate peoples. **witch hunt** a campaign to seek out and purge all those who may be accused of disloyalty, subversion, etc. **witching hour** midnight.

with [wɪθ] *or* [wɪð] *prep* 1 in the company of: *Come with me.* 2 into or among: *Mix the butter with the sugar.* 3 having, wearing, carrying, etc.: *a man with brains.* 4 by means of: *to cut meat with a knife.* 5 using: *Work with care.* 6 as

an addition to: *Do you want sugar with your tea?* **7** in relation to: *They are friendly with us.* **8** because of: *to shake with cold.* **9** in the experience or opinion of: *High taxes are unpopular with people.* **10** after: *With this warning, she left.* **11** on the side of: *They are with us in our plan.* **12** against: *We fought with them.* **13** in spite of: *With all his size he was not strong.* ⟨Old English *with* against⟩
with it *Slang* **a** up to date. **b** alert. **with that** when that occurred: *The train reached the station, and, with that, our long trip ended.*
with·draw *v* **-drew, -drawn, -draw·ing 1** draw back; draw away. **2** remove: *to withdraw money from an account.* **3** go away: *She withdrew from the room.* **4** retract (a statement, etc.). **with·draw·al** [-'drɔəl] *n* **1** the act of drawing back or taking back, taking away or going away. **2** the amount or thing withdrawn. **3** *Psychology* a mental condition during which a person ceases to communicate with others. **4** the effects experienced by a person trying to overcome an addiction. **with·hold** *v* **-held, -hold·ing** refrain from giving: *to withhold consent.*
with·er ['wɪðər] *v* **1** dry up or fade: *a face withered with age.* **2** cause to feel ashamed: *She blushed under her aunt's withering look.* **with·er·ing·ly** *adv.* ⟨Middle English *wideren, wederen* weather⟩
with·in [wɪ'ðɪn] *or* [wɪ'θɪn] *prep* **1** inside the limits of: *The task was within my powers.* **2** in or into the inside of: *to see within the body by means of X rays.*
adv **1** inside: *The house has been painted within and without.* **2** in the inner being: *to keep one's grief within.* ⟨Old English *withinnan*⟩
with·out [wɪ'ðaʊt] *or* [wɪ'θaʊt] *prep* **1** with no: *A cat walks without noise.* **2** so as to omit: *She walked past without looking at us.*
adv externally: *The house is clean within and without.* ⟨Old English *withūtan*⟩
do (or **go**) **without** remain in want of something: *Cook your own food or go without.*
with·stand [wɪθ'stænd] *v* **-stood, -stand·ing** oppose, esp successfully: *The pioneers withstood many hardships.* ⟨Old English *with-* against + *standan* stand⟩
wit·ness ['wɪtnɪs] *n* **1** one who has direct knowledge of an event. **2** a person who gives evidence or testifies under oath. **3** testimony. **4** a person who signs a document to show that another signature on it is genuine. **wit·ness** *v.* ⟨Old English *witnes* knowledge⟩
bear witness testify:*The man's fingerprints bore witness to his guilt.*
wit·ti·cism See WIT.
wives [waɪvz] *n* pl of WIFE.
wiz·ard ['wɪzərd] *n* **1** a man supposed to have magic power. **2** *Informal* a person of amazing skill. **3** *Computers* an interactive utility that guides a user through a program or application. **wiz·ard·ly** *adj.* **wiz·ar·dry** *n.* ⟨*wise*[1]⟩
wiz·en ['wɪzən] *v* dry up. **wiz·ened** *adj.* ⟨Old English *wisnian* become dry⟩

WNW or **W.N.W.** west-northwest.
w/o without.
wob·ble ['wɒbəl] *v* **1** shake; tremble. **2** move from side to side when rotating, as an unevenly balanced wheel. **3** cause to wobble. **4** waver. **wob·ble** *n.* **wob·bly** *adj.* **wob·bli·ness** *n.* ⟨Compare Low German *wabbeln*⟩
woe [woʊ] *n* **1** great grief. **2** a cause of this. ⟨Old English *wā,* interj⟩
woe·be·gone [-bɪ,gɒn] *adj* looking sorrowful, or wretched. **woe·ful** *adj.* **woe·ful·ly** *adv.* **woe·ful·ness** *n.*
wok [wɒk] *n* a wide metal cooking utensil used esp in Chinese cooking, having sides that curve in. ⟨Guangdong dialect *wohk* pan⟩
woke [woʊk] *v* a pt of WAKE[1].
wo·ken *v* a pp of WAKE[1].
wolf [wʊlf] *n, pl* **wolves 1** a wild member of the dog family. **2** *Slang* a man who makes a habit of aggressively flirting with women.
v Informal eat greedily (often with *down*). **wolf·like** *adj.* **wolf·ish** *adj.* **wolf·ish·ly** *adv.* **wolf·ish·ness** *n.* ⟨Old English *wulf*⟩
cry wolf give a false alarm. **keep the wolf from the door** keep safe from poverty. **wolf in sheep's clothing** a person who pretends to be friendly, but intends to do harm.
wolf call *Slang* a characteristic whistle made by a male expressing appreciation of an attractive female. **wolf·hound** *n* any of several breeds of very large dog formerly used in hunting wolves.
wol·ver·ine ['wʊlvə,rin] *or* [,wʊlvə'rin] *n* a powerful, carnivorous mammal of the weasel family. ⟨earlier *wolvering; wolf*⟩
wolves [wʊlvz] *n* pl of WOLF.
wom·an ['wʊmən] *n, pl* **wom·en** ['wɪmən] **1** an adult female person. **2** women as a group: *the modern woman.* **3** a female servant. **4** *Informal* a wife or mistress. **wom·an·hood** *n.* ⟨Old English *wīfman; wīf* woman + *man* human being⟩
be one's own woman. See MAN.
wom·an·ish *adj* effeminate: *He had a womanish way about him.* **wom·an·ish·ly** *adv.* **wom·an·ish·ness** *n.* **wom·an·ize** *v* of a man, indulge frequently in casual sexual relationships with women. **wom·an·iz·er** *n.* **wom·an·kind** *n* women collectively. **wom·an·like** *adj* **1** like or characteristic of women. **2** suitable for a woman; feminine. **wom·an·ly** *adj* **1** as a woman should be: *a womanly nature.* **2** suitable for a woman; feminine: *Hockey, sewing, and business are all equally womanly pursuits.* **wom·an·li·ness** *n.* **wo·men·folk** *n* **1** women collectively. **2** a group of women, such as the female members of a family. **women's lib** *Informal* WOMEN'S LIBERATION. **Women's Liberation** a movement beginning in the late 1960s, committed to combatting sexual discrimination and to obtaining full rights equal to those granted to men.
womb [wum] *n* **1** the uterus of the human female and of the female of certain higher

mammals. **2** a place where something is conceived or developed. ⟨Old English *wamb*⟩

wom·bat ['wɒmbæt] *n* either of two Australian marsupials that resemble small bears. ⟨a native Australian language⟩

wom·en ['wɪmən] *n* pl of WOMAN.

won [wʌn] *v* pt and pp of WIN.

won·der ['wʌndər] *n* **1** a strange, surprising, awesome, etc. event: *the wonders of the city.* **2** the feeling caused by what is strange, surprising, etc.
adj amazingly effective, brilliant, etc.: *a wonder drug.*
v **1** feel wonder. **2** feel some doubt or curiosity: *I wonder what happened.* **3** be surprised: *I shouldn't wonder if she wins.* **4** ask oneself: *"Where could she have gone?" he wondered.* **won·der·er** *n.* **won·der·ing** *adj.* **won·der·ing·ly** *adv.* ⟨Old English *wundor*⟩
do (or **work**) **wonders** achieve extraordinary results. **for a wonder** for once. **no** (or **small** or **little**) **wonder a** it is nothing surprising: *No wonder he left.* **b** that explains it. **wonders** (**will**) **never cease** what a pleasant surprise.

won·der·ful *adj* **1** marvellous; remarkable: *The explorer had wonderful adventures.* **2** *Informal* excellent: *a wonderful time.* **won·der·ful·ly** *adv.* **won·der·land** *n* a land, etc. full of wonders. **won·der·ment** *n* **1** wonder. **2** something that causes wonder. **won·drous** *adj* wonderful. *adv Poetic* wonderfully: *wondrous strange.* **won·drous·ly** *adv.* **won·drous·ness** *n.*

won·ky ['wɒŋki] *adj Slang* shaky; appearing not to function normally: *He must have a fever; his eyes look wonky.* ⟨perhaps dialect *wankle*; Old English *wancol* shaky⟩

wont [wount] *or* [wɒnt] *adj* accustomed: *She was wont to read the paper at breakfast.*
n a custom or habit: *He rose early, as was his wont.* ⟨orig pp of Old English *wunian* be accustomed⟩
wont·ed *adj* usual: *My wonted route to work was blocked off, so I had to go the long way around.* **wont·ed·ness** *n.*

won't ['wount] will not.

won ton ['wɒn ˌtɒn] a Chinese dumpling consisting of chopped meat, etc. in a very thin casing of dough, served either fried or in broth. ⟨Cantonese *wan t'an* dumpling⟩

woo [wu] *v* **1** seek to marry. **2** seek to win: *Some people woo fame; some woo riches.* ⟨Old English *wōgian*⟩
woo·er *n* a person who woos; suitor.

wood [wʊd] *n* **1** the hard substance beneath the bark of trees and shrubs. **2** trees cut up for use. **3** Usually, **woods** *pl* a large number of growing trees; forest. **4** a golf club, orig with a wooden head. ⟨Old English *wudu*⟩
out of the woods out of danger or difficulty. **saw wood** *Informal* **a** work steadily at one's task. **b** snore.
wood alcohol METHANOL. **wood·bine** [-ˌbaɪn] *n* honeysuckle. **wood buffalo** or **woods buffalo ✿** a variety of bison found in northern Alberta and the Mackenzie District.

wood·carv·ing *n* **1** the art of carving wood. **2** an object carved out of wood. **wood·carv·er** *n.* **wood·craft** *n* **1** knowledge about how to get food and shelter in the woods. **2** skill in making things out of wood. **wood·cut** *n* a block of wood with a design cut into the surface, from which prints are made. **wood·cut·ter** *n* a person who fells trees or chops wood. **wood·cut·ting** *n.* **wood·ed** *adj* filled with trees: *The park is well wooded.* **wood·en** *adj* **1** made of wood. **2** stiff; awkward: *The boy gave a wooden bow and left the stage.* **3** dull; insensitive. **4** lacking in animation. **wood·en·ly** *adv.* **wood·en·ness** *n.* **wood engraving** a woodcut. The distinction is often made that a **wood engraving** is cut on the end grain of the wood, while a **woodcut** is made with the grain. **wood·land** *n* land covered with trees. **wood·land·er** *n.* **woodland caribou ✿** a species of caribou of the forested areas of northern Canada. **Woodland Cree 1** a member of one of the three main branches of the Cree people, living mainly in northern Saskatchewan and Manitoba. **2** their dialect of Cree. **wood·lot** *n* a piece of land on which trees are grown and cut. **wood louse** *pl* **wood lice** any of various terrestrial crustaceans having a flattened, segmented body covered with protective plates. **wood·peck·er** *n* any of a family of climbing birds having a straight, strong bill adapted for chiselling through the wood of trees in search of insects. **wood·pile** *n* a pile of wood cut for fuel. **wood pulp** wood made into pulp for making paper. **wood screw** a sharp-pointed screw with a slotted head, used in woodworking. **wood·shed** *n* a shed for storing wood. **woods·man** *n,* *pl* **-men** a man who lives, works, or frequently engages in recreation in the woods, esp one who is skilled in making his way in the woods. **woods·y** *adj* **1** of or like the woods. **2** of people, at home in the woods. **woods·i·ness** *n.* **wood thrush** a large thrush common in eastern North America. **wood·wind** *n* **woodwinds** *pl* certain wind instruments of an orchestra, including clarinets, oboes, etc. **wood·work** *n* **1** things made of wood, esp the doors, mouldings, etc. inside a house. **2** the craft of making things out of wood. **come out of the woodwork** *Informal* make an unexpected and often unwanted appearance. **wood·work·er** *n* a person who makes things out of wood. **wood·work·ing** *n, adj.* **wood·worm** *n* the larva of a beetle that is destructive to furniture and buildings. **wood·y** *adj* **1** having many trees: *a woody hillside.* **2** of a plant, having stems containing lignin, the main element of wood. **3** like wood; tough and stringy: *Turnips become woody when they are left in the ground too long.* **wood·i·ness** *n.*

wood·chuck ['wʊd,tʃʌk] *n* a groundhog. ⟨Ojibwa *wejack*; influenced by *wood*⟩

woof [wuf] *n* the crosswise threads of a fabric; weft. See WARP. ⟨Old English *ōwef; on* on + *wefan* weave⟩

woof·er ['wufər] *n* in a sound system, a speaker producing sounds of low frequency.

wool [wʊl] *n* 1 the soft hair or fur of sheep and some other animals. 2 something like wool, such glass wool, used for insulation. **wool** *adj.* ⟨Old English *wull*⟩ **pull the wool over someone's eyes** *Informal* deceive someone.

wool·gath·er·ing *n* daydreaming: *Pay close attention, please, and stop all that woolgathering.* *adj* absent-minded.

wool·gath·er·er *n.* **wool·len** or **wool·en** *adj* 1 made of wool: *a woollen suit.* 2 to do with wool: *a woollen mill.* *n* Usually, **woollens** or **woolens** *pl* clothing made of wool. **wool·ly** *adj* 1 consisting of wool. 2 like wool. 3 confused: *woolly thinking.* *n Informal* an article of clothing made from wool, as winter underwear. Also, **wool·y**. **wool·li·ness** *n.* **woolly bear** a hairy brown or black caterpillar, esp of the tiger moth.

wooz·y ['wuzi] *adj Informal* 1 somewhat dizzy: *to feel woozy.* 2 confused. 3 slightly drunk. **wooz·i·ly** *adv.* **wooz·i·ness** *n.* ⟨perhaps altered from *boozy*⟩

word [wɜrd] *n* 1 an independent unit of speech, or the writing that stands for it. 2 a short talk: *May I have a word with you?* 3 speech: *honest in word and deed.* 4 a brief comment: *a word of advice.* 5 a command: *Wait till she gives the word.* 6 a promise: *The boy kept his word.* 7 news: *No word has come from the battlefront.* 8 **words** *pl* angry talk: *They had words about whose fault it was.* 9 **the Word** *Christianity* **a** the Bible. **b** the message of the gospel. 10 *Computers* a unit that can be processed by a computer. *v* put into words: *Word your ideas clearly.* ⟨Old English⟩ **a good word** a commendation: *Put in a good word for me, will you?* **a man** (or **woman**) **of his** (or **her**) **word** a person who keeps a promise. **be as good as one's word** keep one's promise. **by word of mouth** orally: *Invitations to the party were by word of mouth.* **eat one's words** take back what one has said. **hang on someone's words** listen attentively to someone. **have the last word** in an argument, have the final say. **in a word** briefly. **in so many words** exactly. **mince words** avoid coming to the point by using evasive words. **my word!** an expression of surprise. **of few words** not talkative. **take someone at his** (or **her**) **word** take someone's words seriously. **take someone's word for it** believe because someone has said so. **take the words out of someone's mouth** say exactly what someone was just going to say. **the last word a** the latest fashion. **b** the final thing, beyond which no improvement is possible. **word for word** in the exact words. **words fail me** I'm speechless.

word·book *n* a list of words, usually with explanations, etc.; dictionary; vocabulary. **word element** a COMBINING FORM, such as a base or root, affix, etc. **word–for–word** *adj* reproduced in exactly the same words. **word·ing** *n* the choice and use of words: *Careful wording made the meaning clear.* **word·less** *adj* unexpressed or inexpressible. **word·less·ly** *adv.* **word of honour** or **honor** a solemn promise. **word–of–mouth** *adj* communicated orally. **word order** the arrangement of words in a sentence, phrase, etc. **word·play** ['wɜrd,plei] *n* verbal wit. **word processing** *Computers* the input, editing, etc. of information in words. **word–pro·ces·sing** *adj.* **word processor** *Computers* a type of computer designed for word processing. **word·y** *adj* using too many words. **word·i·ly** *adv.* **word·i·ness** *n.*

wore [wɔr] *v* pt of WEAR.

work [wɜrk] *n* 1 the effort of doing something: *hard work.* 2 occupation: *He is out of work at the moment, but has several interviews arranged for next week.* 3 something made or done, esp something creative: *That picture is her greatest work.* 4 one's place of employment: *I left my umbrella at work.* 5 **works** *pl* **a** a factory or other place for doing some kind of work. **b** the moving parts of a device: *the works of a watch.* **c** deeds: *good works.* 6 *Physics* that which is accomplished by a force when it acts through a distance. 7 **works** *pl* the business of erecting and maintaining public buildings: *the department of public works.* 8 **the** (**whole**) **works** *Slang* everything involved: *a pizza with the works.* *v* 1 do work. 2 be employed. 3 operate effectively: *The plan worked.* 4 cause to do work: *He works his men hard.* 5 handle in making: *This clay works easily.* 6 gradually become: *The window catch has worked loose.* 7 excite: *Don't work yourself into a temper.* **at work** working. **give someone the works** *Slang* treat harshly. **in the works** *Informal* in the planning stage. **make short** (or **quick**) **work of** do or get rid of quickly. **out of work** unemployed. **work a room** (or **crowd**) move through a room or crowd greeting people, shaking hands, etc. **work off a** get rid of by working. **b** pay (a debt, etc.) with work rather than money. **work on** try to persuade. **work out a** plan. **b** solve. **c** result. **d** add up to a specified total (with *at* or *to*). **e** exercise. **f** succeed: *We hired a nanny but she didn't work out so we fired her.* **work to rule** of employees, work only as much as is demanded by terms of employment, as a form of protest. **work up a** develop. **b** excite; stir up. **c** bring about (a sweat or appetite) by vigorous activity. ⟨Old English *weorc, wyrcean*⟩

work·a·ble *adj* that can work or be worked: *a workable plan.* **work·a·day** *adj* ordinary: *These are my workaday clothes.* **work·a·hol·ic** *n Informal* someone addicted to work. **work·bench** *n* a table at which a mechanic, carpenter, etc. works. **work·book** *n* a book for notes of work planned or done. **work·day** *n*

1 a day for work. **2** the part of a day during which work is done. *adj* workaday. **work·er** *n* **1** a person who does a specified kind of work: *a research worker.* **2** a person who works hard: *She's really a worker.* **3** in a colony of bees, ants, etc., one that cares for the larvae, finds food for the colony, etc. **workers' compensation** compensation for personal injuries suffered at work. **work ethic** the principle that work is honourable and takes priority over leisure. **workfare** *n* a policy whereby recipients of welfare benefits must work a number of hours, ususally at a job co-ordinated by the government. **work force 1** the total number of people employed by a particular company. **2** the total number of people potentially available for employment. **work·horse** *n* **1** a horse used mostly for work, not for racing, etc. **2** a person who is an exceptionally hard worker. **3** a machine that is especially powerful, productive, etc. Also, **work horse. work·ing** *n* **1** Often, **workings** operations: *the workings of one's mind.* **2** Usually, **workings** *pl* the parts of a mine, etc. where work is being done. *adj* **1** that works. **2** used to operate with or by: *a working majority.* **3 a** performing its function: *a working model of a train.* **b** workable: *a working arrangement.* **working capital 1** the amount of capital needed to operate a business. **2** *Accounting* the amount left when current liabilities are subtracted from current assets. **3** *Business* the liquid, or immediately usable, capital of a business, as distinguished from frozen assets, such as property, etc. **working class** a group thought of as including all those people who work for wages, esp manual and industrial workers. **working hypothesis** a theory accepted only to guide investigations. **work·load** *n* the amount of work assigned to a person, position, department, etc. **work·man** *n, pl* **-men** a man who is skilled in a trade or craft; craftsman. **work·man·like** *adj* skilful: *The job was done in a workmanlike manner.* **work·man·ship** *n.* **work of art 1** a product of any of the arts, esp a painting, statue, etc. **2** anything done or made with great artistry or skill: *He makes a sandwich a work of art.* **work·out** *n Informal* a session of vigorous physical or mental exercise. **work·place** *n* **1** the specific location where one does one's job. **2** the environment in which one works at one's job. **work·room** *n* a room set aside for working in. **work·sheet** *n* **1** a sheet of paper on which a record of work, including times, productivity, etc. is kept. **2** a sheet of paper printed with practice exercises, on which students record their answers. **work·shop** *n* **1** a room or building where manual work is done. **2** a meeting for discussion, study, etc. of a particular subject: *The history teachers had a workshop in September.* **3** the group of people so meeting. **work·shy** *adj* lazy. **work·space** *n* a space set aside in which to do regular work. **work station** or **work·sta·tion** a desk, chair and other equipment where a computer system is

set up. **work·ta·ble** *n* a table to work at. **work·week** *n* the standard number of hours or days constituting a week of work.

Work is the general word, applying to the effort or to the activity of a force or machine: *Keeping house is not easy work.* **Labour** applies to hard work: *Put labour into your homework.* **Toil** applies to long and wearying labour: *The farmer's toil was rewarded with good crops.*

world [wɜrld] *n* **1** the earth. **2** all of certain parts or things of the earth: *the insect world.* **3** a sphere of interest, etc.: *the world of music.* **4** human affairs: *She's ready to go out into the world.* **5** a star or planet, esp when considered as inhabited. **6** a great deal: *The rest did him a world of good.* ⟨Old English *weorold*⟩ **bring into the world** give birth to. **come into the world** be born. **for all the world** in every respect. **in the world a** anywhere. **b** at all: *Why in the world not?* **not for worlds** or **not for (all) the world** not for any reason. **on top of the world** in high spirits. **out of this world** great; distinctive: *Our decorations are out of this world.* **think the world of** regard highly. **worlds apart** very different.

World Bank the International Bank for Reconstruction and Development, an agency of the United Nations. **world–class** *adj* **1** capable of competing at the highest levels: *a world-class athlete.* **2** of a very high standard: *a world-class city.* **World Court** the International Court of Justice under the United Nations. **World Health Organization** a United Nations organization, established to improve health conditions worldwide. **world·ly** *adj* absorbed in the interests and pleasures of this world. **world·li·ness** *n.* **world·ly–wise** *adj* sophisticated. **world power** a nation powerful enough to influence worldwide events. **World Series** *Baseball* the series of games played between the winners of the two major league championships to decide the professional championship of the US and Canada. **World's Fair** an international exposition featuring recent developments in a wide variety of technologies, the arts, etc. **world–wea·ry** *adj* weary of this world; tired of living. **world–wea·ri·ness** *n.* **world·wide** *adj, adv* throughout the world. **World Wide Web** *Computers* a network of text files, linked by hypertext and accessible through the Internet using any of various pieces of software. The files, or pages, originate with a wide variety of international private and public users. Also called **the Web.**

worm [wɜrm] *n* **1** any of numerous slender, often segmented invertebrates, usually legless. **2** a person who is the object of contempt or pity. **3 worms** *pl* a disease caused by parasitic worms in the body. **4** *Computers* **write once read many** a program that reproduces and spreads across a network, to harmful effect.
v **1** insinuate: *She wormed herself into my confidence.* **2** get by persistent and devious means: *They tried to worm the secret out of me.*

3 purge worms from (plants or animals): *Puppies should be wormed.* **worm·like** *adj.* ⟨Old English *wyrm*⟩

can of worms *Informal* a complicated, usually unpleasant, problem.

worm–eat·en *adj* **1** eaten into by worms: *worm-eaten timbers.* **2** worn-out; worthless.

worm·hole *n* a hole made by a worm.

worm·y *adj* **1** having worms. **2** damaged by worms. **3** contemptible: *a wormy creature.* **worm·i·ness** *n.*

worn [wɔrn] *v* pp of WEAR.
adj **1** damaged by use: *worn rugs.* **2** tired; wearied: *a worn face.*

worn–out *adj* **1** used until no longer fit for use. **2** exhausted; fatigued.

wor·ry ['wʌri] *v* **1** feel anxious or cause to feel anxious. **2** annoy: *Don't worry me with so many questions.* **3** seize and shake with the teeth: *A dog will worry a rat.* **4** harass, as if by repeated biting, etc.
n **1** anxiety. **2** a cause of trouble: *A mother has many worries.* **wor·ri·er** *n.* ⟨Old English *wyrgan* strangle⟩

not to worry! don't worry! **worry at** keep picking at: *Stop worrying at that scab.*

wor·ri·ment *n Informal* **1** the act of worrying. **2 a** worry; anxiety. **b** a cause of worry.

wor·ri·some *adj* **1** causing worry. **2** inclined to worry. **wor·ri·some·ly** *adv.* **wor·ri·some·ness** *n.*

wor·ry·wart *n* someone who constantly worries, esp over insignificant matters.

worse [wɜrs] *adj comparative of* BAD **1** more harmful, painful, etc.: *It could be worse.* **2** of even lower quality or value: *The soil is worse in the valley.* **3** more ill: *He is worse today.*
adv comparative of BADLY and ILL in a worse manner or to a worse degree: *It is raining worse than ever.*
n that which is worse: *She thought the loss of her property bad enough, but worse followed.* ⟨Old English *wyrsa*⟩

for the worse to a worse state: *The change was for the worse.* **go from bad to worse** worsen. **none** (or **a little, somewhat,** etc.) **the worse for** not (or a little, etc.) suffering or damaged because of: *She was none the worse for her adventure.* **worse off a** in a worse condition. **b** having less money.

wor·sen *v* make or become worse.

wor·ship ['wɜrʃɪp] *n* **1** great honour and respect paid to a deity. **2** great love and admiration: *hero worship.* **3 Worship** a title used in addressing or referring to a mayor. **wor·ship, -shipped** or **-shiped, -ship·ping** or **-ship·ing** *v.* **wor·ship·per** or **·wor·ship·er** *n.* ⟨Old English *weorthscipe; weorth* worth + *-scipe* -ship⟩

wor·ship·ful *adj* expressing worship: *worshipful silence.* **wor·ship·ful·ly** *adv.*

worst [wɜrst] *adj superlative of* BAD **1** most harmful, painful, etc. **2** of the poorest quality or value: *This district has some of the worst soil in the province.*
adv superlative of BADLY and ILL in the worst manner or to the worst degree: *He acts worst when he's tired.*

n that which is worst: *That was bad, but the worst is yet to come.*
v beat, defeat: *The hero worsted his enemies.* ⟨Old English *wyrresta*⟩

at worst under the least favourable circumstances: *At worst, all we can lose is a little money.* **give someone the worst of it** defeat someone. **if (the) worst comes to (the) worst** if the very worst thing happens.

wor·sted ['wɜrstɪd] *or* ['wʊstɪd] *n* smooth, firm yarn or thread. ⟨*Worsted,* a town in England, where it was orig made⟩

wort [wɜrt] *n* a plant, esp any of various herbaceous plants formerly used in medicine (now chiefly in compounds): *liverwort, figwort.* ⟨Old English *wyrt*⟩

worth [wɜrθ] *adj (functioning prepositionally)* **1** good enough for: *Iqaluit is definitely worth visiting.* **2** equal in value to: *That stamp is worth twenty dollars.* **3** having property that amounts to: *He's worth millions.*
n **1** merit; importance: *a book of real worth.* **2** value in money: *He had to sell his car for less than its worth.* **3** a quantity of something of specified value: *a dollar's worth of sugar.* ⟨Old English *weorth*⟩

for all one is worth to the full extent of one's power or ability: *She ran for all she was worth.* **worth·less** *adj* without worth; useless. **worth·less·ly** *adv.* **worth·less·ness** *n.*

worth·while *adj* having real merit: *He ought to do some worthwhile reading.* **wor·thy** *adj* **1** having merit: *a worthy analysis of the situation.* **2** deserving: *I don't mind donating my time to a worthy cause.* **worthy of a** deserving. **b** having enough worth for. **wor·thi·ly** *adv.* **wor·thi·ness** *n.*

–wor·thy *suffix* **1** worthy of: *noteworthy, praiseworthy.* **2** capable of being used in or on a——: *roadworthy, seaworthy.*

would [wʊd] *v* **1** an auxiliary verb used: **a** to introduce a request or command in a polite manner: *Would you please close the window?* **b** to express uncertainty: *I don't know whose that would be.* **c** to express the hypothetical consequence of an unlikely or an impossible condition: *If I asked him, he would say no.* **d** to express habitual action in the past: *When we were small, we would spend hours playing in the sand.* **e** to express desire: *Nutritionists would have us all eat whole grains.* **2** pt of WILL¹. ⟨Old English *wolde*⟩

would–be *adj* wishing or pretending to be.

Would as the past tense of **will** is used most often in reported speech. Compare *He said, "I will come."* with *He said that he would come.*

wound¹ [wund] *n* **1** an injury caused by cutting, shooting, etc. **2** any hurt or injury to feelings, reputation, etc.: *The loss of her job was a wound to her pride.* **wound** *v.* ⟨Old English *wund*⟩

wound² [waʊnd] *v* a pt and a pp of WIND².

wove [woʊv] *v* a pt and a pp of WEAVE.
wo·ven *v* a pp of WEAVE.

wow[1] [waʊ] *n* a variation in the sound pitch of a tape recorder, caused by an irregularity in the driving mechanism. ⟨imitative⟩

wow[2] [waʊ] *Slang n* a complete success. *v* dazzle or impress: *My father really wowed everyone with his new suit.*
interj an exclamation of admiration, etc.

wrack[1] [ræk] *n* seaweed cast ashore. ⟨Middle Dutch *wrak* wreck⟩

wrack[2] [ræk] *v* **1** hurt very much: *wracked by convulsions.* **2** strain. ⟨variant of *rack*[1]⟩

wraith [reiθ] *n* **1** ghost; spectre. **2** anything insubstantial, pale, thin, etc: *wraiths of fog lingering over the fields.* **wraith·like** *adj.* ⟨Scots; perhaps Old Norse *vörthr* guardian spirit⟩

wran·gle[1] ['ræŋgəl] *v* argue in a noisy way. **wran·gle** *n.* ⟨perhaps Low German *wrangeln*⟩

wran·gle[2] ['ræŋgəl] *n West* herd or tend (horses, etc.) on the range. **wran·gler** *n.* ⟨Spanish *caverango* hostler⟩

wrap [ræp] *v* **wrapped, wrap·ping 1** cover by winding something around: *She wrapped herself in a shawl.* **2** cover with paper, etc. and fasten: *to wrap a gift.*
n **1 a** a garment worn draped or wrapped about the shoulders. **b wraps** *pl* overcoat, scarf, etc.: *Just throw your wraps on the bed.* **2** wrapping paper: *gift wrap.* **3** a successful and hence final filming of a scene. **4** a piece of flatbread rolled up around a filling. ⟨Middle English *wrappen*⟩
under wraps secret. **wrapped up in a** devoted to: *He is wrapped up in his children.* **b** involved in. **wrap up a** put on warm clothes. **b** bring to a successful conclusion: *They wrapped up the game with three runs in the ninth.* **c** come to the end (of a presentation, etc.): *I'll just make one more point and then I'll wrap up.* **d** wrap.

wrap·per *n* **1** a person who or thing that wraps. **2** covering; cover. **3** a woman's long, loose-fitting garment for wearing in the house. **4** the outside layer of tobacco in a cigar. **wrap·ping** *n* Often, **wrappings** *pl* the material in which something is wrapped.

wrap–up *Informal adj* summarizing: *She will give the wrap-up presentation at the seminar. n* **1** a summarizing statement. **2** the act of concluding or summarizing.

wrath [ræθ] *n* very great anger. **wrath·ful** *adj.* **wrath·ful·ly** *adv.* **wrath·ful·ness** *n.* ⟨Old English *wræththu*⟩

wreak [rik] *v* **1** work off (negative feelings, etc.): *The bully wreaked his bad temper on his dog.* **2** inflict: *The hurricane wreaked havoc on the city.* ⟨Old English *wrecan*⟩

wreath [riθ] *n, pl* **wreaths** [riðz] *or* [riθs] **1** a ring of flowers, leaves, etc. twisted together. **2** something suggesting a wreath: *a wreath of smoke.* ⟨Old English *wræth*⟩
wreathe *v* **1** twist together in a circle. **2** make a ring around; encircle: *Mist wreathed the hills.* **wreathed in smiles** smiling broadly.

wreck [rek] *n* **1** the destruction of a ship, building, train, etc. **2** any destruction or serious injury: *Heavy rains caused the wreck of* many crops. **3** what is left of anything that has been severely damaged: *the wreck of a ship.* **4** a person or animal that has lost physical or mental health.
v destroy or ruin. ⟨Old Norse *wrek;* Germanic *wrecan* to drive⟩

wreck·age *n* **1** what is left by wreck: *The shore was covered with the wreckage of ships.* **2** a wrecking or being wrecked: *the wreckage of one's hopes.* **wreck·er** *n* **1** a person who or machine that tears down buildings. **2** a person or machine that removes wrecks and salvages and sells parts that are still usable. **3** a person who or ship that recovers wrecked or disabled ships or their cargoes. **4** formerly, a person who caused shipwrecks by false lights on shore so as to plunder the wrecks. **wrecking ball** or **wrecker's ball** a large heavy metal ball swung by a machine against a building in order to demolish it.

wren [ren] *n* any of a family of small songbirds having a short, cocked tail. ⟨Old English *wrenna*⟩

wrench [rentʃ] *n* **1** a violent twist: *She broke the branch off the tree with a sudden wrench.* **2** an injury caused by twisting. **3** a surge of grief or pain. **4** a cause of grief or pain: *It was a wrench to leave our old home.* **5** a tool for holding, turning, or twisting something. **wrench** *v.* ⟨Old English *wrencan* twist⟩

wrest [rest] *v* **1** tear away: *He wrested the knife from his assailant.* **2** take by force: *The usurper wrested the power from the king.* ⟨Old English *wræstan*⟩

wres·tle ['resəl] *v* **1** grapple with (an opponent) without striking with the fist. **2** struggle (with): *wrestling with a problem.* **wres·tle** *n.* **wres·tler** *n.* **wres·tling** *n.* ⟨*wrest*⟩

wretch [retʃ] *n* **1** a very unfortunate person. **2** a scoundrel. ⟨Old English *wrecca* exile⟩
wretch·ed *adj* **1** very unfortunate or unhappy. **2** very unsatisfactory: *a wretched hut.* **3** wicked; contemptible: *a wretched traitor.*
wretch·ed·ly *adv.* **wretch·ed·ness** *n.*

wrig·gle ['rɪgəl] *v* **1** twist and turn; squirm: *Children wriggle when they are restless.* **2** move by twisting and turning: *A snake wriggled across the road.* **3** make one's way by tricks, excuses, etc.: *Some people can wriggle out of any difficulty.* **wrig·gle** *n.* **wrig·gler** *n.* **wrig·gly** *adj.* ⟨Compare Dutch *wriggelen*⟩

–wright [rait] *combining form* a person who creates or fixes something: *wheelwright, playwright.* ⟨Old English *wryhta; weorc* work⟩

wring [rɪŋ] *v* **wrung, wring·ing 1** twist and squeeze hard, esp so as to extract moisture (often with *out*): *to wring clothes.* **2** twist violently: *to wring a chicken's neck.* **3** get by force, effort, or persuasion: *to wring money from someone.* **4** clasp; press: *They wrung their old friend's hand.* **5** cause pain or pity in: *Their poverty wrung my heart.* **wring** *n.* ⟨Old English *wringan*⟩
wring·er *n* a device or machine for squeezing water from clothes. **put someone**

through the wringer *Slang* subject (someone) to an ordeal.

wrin·kle ['rɪŋkəl] *n* **1** an irregular fold: *The dress was full of wrinkles.* **2** a small problem to be overcome: *The plan has a few wrinkles.* *v* make a wrinkle or wrinkles in. **wrin·kled** *adj.* ⟨Compare Old English *gewrinclod* pp, twisted, winding⟩
wrin·kly *adj* wrinkled or prone to wrinkling.

wrist [rɪst] *n* the part of the arm between the hand and the forearm. ⟨Old English⟩
slap on the wrist a punishment that is much lighter than deserved.
wrist·band *n* **1** the band of a sleeve or mitten, etc. fitting around the wrist. **2** a strap worn around the wrist, as of a wristwatch.
wrist·watch *n* a watch worn on a strap around the wrist.

writ [rɪt] *n Law* a formal written order directing a person to do or not to do something: *A writ from the judge ordered the prisoner's release from jail.* ⟨Old English *writ; wrītan* write⟩

write [rəit] *v* **wrote, writ·ten, writ·ing. 1** make (letters or words), esp in cursive style. **2** put down or form the letters, words, etc. of: *Write your name and address.* **3** make up (stories, etc.): *He writes reviews for magazines.* **4** show plainly: *Honesty is written on her face.* **5** *Computers* record (data) in memory.
write down a put into writing: *Many early folk songs were never written down.* **b** put a lower value on. **write home about.** See HOME.
write in a insert (a fact, statement, etc.) in a piece of writing. **b** *US* cast a vote for (an unlisted candidate) by writing his or her name on a ballot. **write off a** cancel (an entry in an account) as uncollectable: *My father agreed to write off my debt to him.* **b** note the deduction of for depreciation. **c** dismiss or treat as if nonexistent. **write out a** put into writing. **b** write in full: *She made quick notes during the interview and wrote out her report later.* **c** eliminate (a character) from a television or radio script by means of story events: *When his contract ended, they wrote him out in a murder episode.* **write up a** write a description or account of. **b** write in detail. **c** put a higher value on. ⟨Old English *wrītan* orig scratch⟩
write–off *n* **1** something recognized as a loss: *We treated the money we had lent him as a write-off.* **2** *Informal* a total wreck, such as might be written off as a loss: *They weren't hurt but their car was a write-off.*
write–pro·tect *v Computers* modify a file so that its data cannot be edited or erased.
writ·er *n* a person whose profession is writing. **write–up** *n Informal* a written description or account. **writ·ing** *n* **1** written form: *Put your ideas in writing.* **2** handwriting. **3** something written. **writ·ten** ['rɪtən] *adj* put down in a form intended to be read; not spoken.

writhe [raɪð] *v* **1** twist and turn: *to writhe in pain.* **2** suffer embarrassment, revulsion, annoyance, etc.: *He writhed when he thought of the blunder he had made.* **writhe** *n.* ⟨Old English *wrīthan*⟩

writ·ten See WRITE.

wrong [rɒŋ] *adj* **1** immoral; unjust; unlawful: *It is wrong to tell lies.* **2** incorrect: *the wrong answer.* **3** unsuitable: *the wrong clothes for the occasion.* **4** in a bad state or condition: *Something is wrong with the car.* **5** not meant to be seen or shown: *the wrong side of the cloth.*
adv so as to be wrong: *to guess wrong.*
n **1** a wrong thing or things: *Two wrongs do not make a right.* **2** an injustice; injury: *to do someone a wrong.*
v treat unjustly; injure: *He forgave those who had wronged him.* **wrong·ly** *adv.* **wrong·ness** *n.* ⟨Old English *wrang;* Old Norse *rangr* crooked⟩
get (someone or something) **wrong** misinterpret; misunderstand (someone or something). **go wrong a** turn out badly. **b** stop being good and become bad. **in the wrong** at fault; in error: *He argues all the more vehemently when he suspects he's in the wrong.*
wrong·do·er *n* a person who does wrong. **wrong·do·ing** *n.* **wrong·ful** *adj* **1** unjust. **2** unlawful. **wrong·ful·ly** *adv.* **wrong·ful·ness** *n.* **wrong–head·ed** *adj* **1** wrong in judgment or opinion. **2** stubborn even when wrong. **wrong–head·ed·ly** *adv.* **wrong–head·ed·ness** *n.*

wrote [rout] *v* a pt of WRITE.

wrought [rɒt] *adj* **1** shaped with skill and care. **2** of metals, **a** shaped by hammering, etc.: *a plate of wrought silver.* **b** made with elaborate decoration.
wrought iron a form of iron that is soft enough to be easily forged, but will not break as easily as cast iron. **wrought–i·ron** *adj.*

wrung [rʌŋ] *v* pt and pp of WRING.

wry [raɪ] *adj* **wry·er** or **wri·er, wry·est** or **wri·est 1** made by distorting the features to show disgust, doubt, irony, etc.: *a wry grin.* **2** marked by grim irony: *wry humour.* **3** turned to one side in an abnormal way: *a wry nose.* **4** perversely wrong: *wry behaviour.* **wry·ly** *adv.* ⟨Old English *wrīgian* turn⟩

WSW or **W.S.W.** west-southwest.

Wy·an·dot ['waɪənˌdɒt] *n, pl* **-dots** or **-dot 1** a member of a First Nations group originating among Huron-speaking peoples of Ontario and formerly living in Ontario and adjacent states of the US. **2** their Iroquoian language. **Wy·an·dot** *adj.*

WYSIWYG ['wɪzɪwɪg] *adj Computers* displaying text, graphics, etc. on the screen exactly as they will appear when printed out. ⟨acronym for *what you see is what you get*⟩

Xx

x or **X** [ɛks] *n, pl* **x's** or **X's 1** the twenty-fourth letter of the English alphabet, or any speech sound represented by it. **2** the twenty-fourth person or thing in a series. **3** the first of a series consisting of x, y, and, sometimes, z. **4 X** the Roman numeral for 10. **5** *x Algebra* an unknown quantity, as in *x* + *y* = 5. **6** *Geometry* an abscissa. **7 X** an unidentified person or thing: *Ms. X.* **8 x** or **X** is also used: **a** to indicate a certain place on a map, etc.: *X marks the spot.* **b** to symbolize a kiss. **c** to represent the signature of a person who cannot write. **9 x** is also used to indicate **a** multiplication: *3* x *2 = 6.* **b** dimensions, as a 3 x 5 rug. **10 X** extra or oversize: *XL;* or children's sizes: *2X.* **11** used to make one's choice or answer on a ballot, questionnaire, survey, etc.

x [ɛks] *v* **x·ed** or **x'd**, **x·ing** or **x'ing** cancel or cross out with an x or a series of x's (often with *out*): *to x out a mistake.*

x–ax·is ['ɛks ,æksɪs] *n, pl* **-es** [-iz] *Geometry* **1** in a plane Cartesian coordinate system, the horizontal axis along which the abscissa is measured. **2** in a three-dimensional Cartesian coordinate system, the axis along which values of *x* are measured. Compare Y-AXIS, Z-AXIS.

X chromosome *Biology* one of the two chromosomes bearing the genes that determine sex. Each female body cell normally contains two X chromosomes and each egg cell contains one X chromosome. Compare Y CHROMOSOME.

xe·non ['zinɒn] *or* ['zɛnɒn] *n* a rare, heavy, gaseous element that is chemically inactive. It occurs in the air in minute quantities. *Symbol* **Xe** ⟨Greek = strange⟩

xen·o·phi·lia [,zɛnə'fɪliə] *n* an attraction to strange or foreign peoples, cultures, or customs. ⟨Greek *xenos* stranger + -PHILIA⟩

xen·o·pho·bi·a [,zɛnə'foubiə] *n* a hatred or fear of foreigners or foreign things.
xen·o·pho·bic *adj.* ⟨Greek *xenos* stranger + -PHOBIA⟩
xen·o·phobe *n* one who has a morbid fear or dislike of foreign persons or things.

xe·ric ['zirɪk] *adj* to do with a dry or desertlike environment. ⟨Greek *xeros* dry⟩

xe·rog·ra·phy [zɪ'rɒgrəfi] *n* a process for making copies of written or printed material, pictures, etc., by the action of magnetic attraction rather than ink and pressure. Tiny, negatively-charged particles are spread on positively-charged paper in an arrangement that exactly copies the printing, etc. on the original paper. **xe·ro·graph·ic** [,zirə'græfɪk] *adj.* ⟨Greek *xeros* dry + -GRAPH⟩
Xe·rox *Trademark* a copy made by this process. **Xe·rox** *v.*

X–linkage ['ɛks ,lɪŋkədʒ] *n Genetics* the pattern of inheritance of genes located on the X chromosome.
X–linked *adj* **1** of a gene, located on the X chromosome. **2** involving traits determined by such genes: *X-linked inheritance.* See DOMINANT, RECESSIVE.

Xmas ['ɛksməs] *or* ['krɪsməs] *n Informal* Christmas.

X ray or **X–ray** ['ɛks ,rei] *n* **1** radiation of the same type as visible radiation (i.e., light) but having an extremely short wavelength. It can go through substances that ordinary light rays cannot penetrate, but will act in the same way as light does on a photographic film to produce a picture. **2** a picture obtained by means of X rays.
adj **X–ray** or **x–ray** made by or using X rays. ⟨*X* in sense of 'unknown'⟩
X–ray or **x–ray** *v* examine, photograph, or treat with X rays.

X's and O's TIC-TAC-TOE.

xy·lem ['zaɪləm] *n Botany* the more rigid tissue in the vascular system of plants and trees that conducts water and mineral salts up from the roots and supports the softer tissue. Compare PHLOEM. ⟨Greek *xylon* wood⟩

xy·lo·phone ['zaɪlə,foun] *n* a musical percussion instrument consisting of two rows of wooden bars that are graduated in length to produce the tones of two octaves of the chromatic scale. It is played by striking the bars with wooden hammers.
xy·lo·phon·ist *n.* ⟨Greek *xylon* wood + PHONE⟩

Yy

y or **Y** [waɪ] *n* **y's** or **Y's 1** the twenty-fifth letter of the English alphabet, or any speech sound represented by it. **2** the twenty-fifth person or thing in a series. **3** the second of a series consisting of x, y, and, sometimes, z. **4** *y Algebra* an unknown quantity, as in 2*x* + 3*y* = 7. **5** *Geometry* an ordinate. **6 the Y** *Informal* YMCA; YWCA; YMHA; YWHA.

–y¹ *suffix* **1** having, or characterized by——: *juicy*. **2** somewhat——: *salty*. **3** inclined to ——: *fidgety*. **4** resembling or suggesting——: *sugary*. ⟨Old English *-ig*⟩

–y² *suffix* used to indicate that someone or something is thought of as small, attractive, loved, etc.: *dolly, Mommy*. ⟨Middle English⟩

Y2K symbol for **Year 2000**, esp with reference to technological problems involving the recording of dates. Technology designed to avoid these difficulties is **Y2K-compliant.**

yacht [jɒt] *n* **1** a light sailing vessel. **2** a similar vessel having sails and/or motor power, used for private pleasure cruising. **yacht·ing** *n*. ⟨Dutch *jaghtschip* chasing ship⟩

Ya·hoo ['yæhu] or ['jɑhu] *n* **1** in Swift's *Gulliver's Travels*, a type of brute in human shape who works for a race of intelligent horses. **2** *yahoo*, any rough, coarse, or uncouth person.
interj [jæ'hu] **yahoo**, a cry of delight.

Yah·weh or **Yah·we** ['jɑweɪ] or ['jɑwɛ] *n* the name of God in the Hebrew Bible (the Old Testament). Also, **Yah·veh, Yah·ve, Jah·ve, Jah·veh.** ⟨Hebrew⟩

yak¹ [jæk] *n* a large, long-haired animal related to buffalo and cattle. ⟨Tibetan *gyag*⟩

yak² [jæk] *Slang v* **yakked, yak·king** chatter; talk idly and constantly. **yak** *n*. Also, **yack, yak–yak, yakety–yak.** ⟨imitative⟩

yam [jæm] *n* the edible, starchy tuber of any of several vines, used as a staple food. ⟨Spanish *iñame*; Senegalese *nyami* eat⟩

yam·mer ['jæmər] *v* **1** whine or whimper in a complaining way. **2** clamour: *dogs yammering for their food.* **3** talk loudly and persistently. **yam·mer** *n*. ⟨Middle English *yameren*; Old English *geomerian*⟩

yang [jæŋ] *n* **1** *Taoism* the positive force in the cosmos; the counterpart to the yin. **2** *Chinese philosophy* the male principle, active and positive, the source of heat and light, complementary to and contrasting with the yin. Compare YIN. ⟨Mandarin⟩

yank [jæŋk] *Informal v* pull with a sudden motion; jerk: *She almost yanked my arm off!* **yank** *n*. ⟨origin uncertain⟩

Yank [jæŋk] *n, adj Slang* Yankee.

Yan·kee ['jæŋki] *n* a native or inhabitant of: **1** the US; an American. **2** one of the six New England states of the US. **3** any of the northern states of the US. **4** a Union, or northern, soldier in the American Civil War.

Yan·kee *adj.* ⟨probably Dutch *Jan Kees* John Cheese (nickname); *-s* taken as pl⟩

yap [jæp] *n* **1** a snappish bark; yelp. **2** *Slang* noisy or foolish talk. **3** *Slang* the mouth. **yap, yapped, yap·ping** *v*. **yap·py** *adj*. ⟨imitative⟩

yard¹ [jɑrd] *n* **1** the piece of ground around a house, school, etc. **2** a piece of ground surrounded by buildings: *a courtyard.* **3** *Railroads* a space with tracks where railway cars are stored, switched, etc. **4** a clearing where moose or deer feed in winter. **5** a place where musk-oxen huddle together for warmth and protection. **6** an assembly point for logs.
v of moose or deer, come together in a yard (often with *up*). ⟨Old English *geard*⟩
yard sale an informal sale of personal possessions, used furniture, etc., usually held in a private yard. See also GARAGE SALE.

yard² [jɑrd] *n* **1** a non-metric unit for measuring length, equal to about 90 cm. *Abbrev* **y.** or **yd. 2** a cubic yard: *It took two yards of gravel to surface the driveway.* **3** *Nautical* a long, slender beam fastened across a mast and used to support a sail. ⟨Old English *gierd* rod⟩
make yards *Football* advance the ball from the line of scrimmage.
yard·age *n* length in yards. **yard·arm** *n Nautical* either end of a yard supporting a sail. **yard goods** cloth, etc. sold by the yard. **yard·stick** *n* **1** a stick one yard long, used for measuring. **2** any standard of comparison.

yar·mul·ke ['jɑrməlkə] *n* a skullcap worn especially by Jewish men and boys for prayer and ceremonial occasions or by Othodox Jews at all times. Also, **yar·mul·ka.** ⟨Yiddish; Ukrainian, Polish *yarmulka* cap⟩

yarn [jɑrn] *n* **1** any spun thread, esp that prepared for weaving or knitting. **2** *Informal* an exaggerated, often humorous, story: *Who told you that yarn?* **yarn** *v*. ⟨Old English *gearn*⟩
spin a yarn *Informal* tell such a story.

yash·mak or **yash·mac** [jaʃ'mak] or ['jæʃmæk] *n* a veil worn in public by Muslim women. ⟨Turkish *yasmak*⟩

yaw [jɔ] *v* **1** of a ship, swing from side to side across a horizontal course. **2** of an aircraft, turn from a straight course by a motion about its vertical axis. **3** of a rocket or guided missile, wobble or swing on the longitudinal axis in the horizontal plane.
n a movement from a straight course. ⟨possibly Old Norse *jaga* sway⟩

yawl [jɔl] *n* a boat having a large mast near the bow and a short mast near the stern. ⟨Dutch *jol*⟩

yawn [jɔn] *v* **1** open the mouth widely and inhale as an involuntary effect of sleepiness, boredom, etc. **2** be wide open: *A deep gorge yawned beneath our feet.* **yawn** *n*. **yawn·er** *n*. **yawn·ing** *adj*. ⟨Old English *geonian*⟩

yaws [jɔz] *npl* contagious disease of the tropics, characterized by skin sores. ⟨Carib⟩

y-ax·is ['waɪ ˌæksɪs] *n pl* **-es** [-iz] *Geometry* **1** in a plane Cartesian coordinate system, the vertical axis along which the ordinate is measured and from which the abscissa is measured. **2** in a three-dimensional Cartesian coordinate system, the axis along which the values of *y* are measured. Compare X-AXIS, Z-AXIS.

Y chromosome *Biology* one of the two chromosomes bearing the genes that determine sex. Each male body cell normally contains one Y and one X chromosome and each sperm contains either a Y or an X chromosome. If an egg cell is fertilized by a sperm with an X chromosome, the resulting embryo will be a female; if the sperm is one with a Y chromosome, the embryo will be a male. Compare X CHROMOSOME.

yd. yard(s).

ye [ði] *definite article. Archaic spelling of* THE[1].

USAGE

In Old and Middle English, **the** was written as þe. The early printers did not have this consonant symbol (called 'thorn') in their fonts. They substituted **y** for it, but this was never intended to be read as a **y**.

yea [jei] *adv* **1** aye; yes (used for assent, as in voting). **2** *Informal* this: *a piece about yea big. n* an affirmative vote. ⟨Old English *gēa*⟩

yeah [jæ] *adv Informal* yes.

year [jir] *n* **1** in the Gregorian calendar, a period of 365 or, in a leap year, 366 days; January 1 to December 31. **2** 12 months reckoned from any point. A **fiscal year** is a period of 12 months at the end of which the accounts of a government, business, etc. are balanced. **3** the part of a year spent in a certain activity: *The school year goes from September to June.* **4** *Astronomy* **a** the exact period of the earth's revolution around the sun. The **solar year** or **astronomical year** is 365 days, 5 hours, 48 minutes, 46 seconds. **b** the time it takes for the apparent travelling of the sun from a given fixed star back to it again. The **sidereal year** is 20 minutes, 23 seconds longer than the solar year. **c** the time in which any planet completes its revolution around the sun. **d** LUNAR YEAR. **5 years** *pl* a very long time: *I hadn't seen her for years.* ⟨Old English *gēar*⟩
a year and a day *Law* a period constituting a term for certain purposes, in order to ensure that a full year is completed. **year by year** as years go by. **year in, year out** always; continuously: *She works hard, year in, year out.* **year-book** *n* **1** a book or report published every year. **2** an annual school publication containing pictures of students, information about school activities, etc. **year–end** *n* the end of a calendar or fiscal year. **year–end** *adj.* **year-ling** *n* an animal one year old. **year-long** *adj* **1** lasting for a year. **2** lasting for years. *adv* all year long: *She works yearlong.* **year-ly** *adj* done, happening, coming, etc. once a year: *a yearly trip to the farm. adv* every year; annually: *A new volume is published yearly.* **year–round** *adj, adv* (used, happening, etc.) throughout the year: *year-round residents.*

yearn [jɜrn] *v* desire earnestly: *After so many years abroad, he yearns for home.* **yearn-ing** *n.* ⟨Old English *giernan*⟩

yeast [jist] *n* **1** a substance consisting of very small fungi which grow on the surface of liquids containing sugar. **2** a fungus that may infest moist, protected areas of the human body. **yeast-y** *adj.* ⟨Old English *gist*⟩

yech [jex], [jʌk], *or* [jʌx] *interj Slang* an exclamation used to express disgust, etc.

yell [jel] *v* cry out loudly.
n **1** a loud cry. **2** a special cheer, esp one used by a school or college to encourage its sports team. ⟨Old English *giellan*⟩

yel·low ['jɛlou] *adj* **1** having the colour of gold, or ripe lemons. **2** *Informal* cowardly. *v* become yellow: *Paper yellows with age.* **yel·lo·wy** *adj.* **yel·low·ness** *n.* ⟨Old English *geolu*⟩ **yel·low–bel·ly** *n* a coward. **yellow cake** uranium oxide concentrate used to produce fuel elements for nuclear reactors. **yellow fever** an infectious disease caused by a virus transmitted by the bite of a mosquito. **yel·low·ish** *adj* somewhat yellow. **yellow jacket** any of a genus of wasps having bright yellow markings. **Yel·low·knife** *n, pl* **-knife** or **-knives 1** a member of a First Nations people, allied to the Chipewyan, orig living in the region between Great Bear Lake and Great Slave Lake to the east. **2** the Athapascan language of these people. **Yel·low·knife** *adj.* **Yellow Pages** *Trademark* a telephone directory printed on yellow paper, that lists firms and professionals classified by the nature of their business.

yelp [jelp] *n* a quick, sharp bark or cry. **yelp** *v.* ⟨Old English *gielpan* boast⟩

yen [jen] *Informal n* **1** a desire or longing: *a yen to see the world.* **2** a desire: *a yen for pizza. v* **yen, yenned, yen·ning.** ⟨Pekinese *yen* opium; literally, smoke⟩

yes [jɛs] *adv* a word used to accept or agree. *n, pl* **yes·es** agreement; acceptance; consent. ⟨Old English *gēse; gēa* yea + *sī* let it be⟩ **yes man** *Slang* a man who always agrees with his employer, superior officer, etc., in order to curry favour.

ye·shi·va [jəˈʃivə] *or* [jəʃiˈva] *n, pl* **ye·shi·vas** or **ye·shi·voth** [jəʃiˈvout] **1** a Jewish school for higher studies. **2** a Jewish day school. ⟨Hebrew *yeshibah* sitting⟩

yes·ter·day ['jɛstər,dei] *n* **1** the day before today. **2** the recent past: *fashions of yesterday. adv* **1** on the day before today. **2** recently. ⟨Old English *geostran* yesterday + *dæg* day⟩

yes·ter·year ['jɛstər,jir] *n, adv Poetic* **1** last year. **2** (in) recent years. ⟨coined by 19c poet D.G. Rossetti to render French *antan*⟩

yet [jet] *adv* **1** (used with a negative or interrogative) thus far: *Are you finished yet?* **2** (used with a negative) as this time, as opposed to later on: *Don't go yet.* **3** besides: *a huge dinner, with two desserts yet!* **4** sometime: *The thief will be caught yet.* **5** even now: *The new legislation may yet be introduced before summer recess.*

conj but; however: *The work is good, yet it could be better.* ⟨Old English *gīeta*⟩
as yet up to now.

ye·ti ['jɛti] *n* ABOMINABLE SNOWMAN. ⟨Tibetan⟩

yew [ju] *n* any of a genus of evergreens having needles that are dark green above and light green below. ⟨Old English *īw*⟩

Yid·dish ['jɪdɪʃ] *n* a language that developed from Middle High German, written in Hebrew characters. Yiddish is used in Jewish communities elsewhere. **Yid·dish** *adj*. ⟨German *jüdisch* Jewish⟩

yield [jild] *v* **1** produce; bear: *This land yields good crops.* **2** give up or in; surrender: *I yielded to temptation and ate all the candy.* **3** give way. *n* the amount yielded; product: *This year's yield from the silver mine was very large.* ⟨Old English *gieldan* pay⟩
yield·ing *adj* **1** submissive: *a yielding nature.* **2** soft; giving way under weight or force: *We lay back in the yielding grass.*

yikes [jaiks] *interj* an exclamation of alarm. Also, **yipe** [jəip] or **yipes.**

yin [jɪn] *n* **1** *Taoism* the negative cosmic force; the counterpart to the yang. **2** *Chinese philosophy* the female principle, passive and negative, the source of dark, complementary to and contrasting with the yang. Compare YANG. ⟨Mandarin⟩

yip [jɪp] *v* **yipped, yip·ping** esp of dogs, bark or yelp briskly. **yip** *n*. ⟨imitative⟩

yo·del ['joudəl] *v* **-delled** or **-deled, -del·ling** or **-del·ing** sing or call with frequent, sudden changes from the ordinary voice pitch to a much higher pitch. **yo·del** *n*. Also, **yo·dle.** **yo·del·ler** or **yo·de·ler** *n*. ⟨German *jodeln*⟩

yo·ga or **Yo·ga** ['jougə] *n* a system of slow, rhythmic body movements, controlled breathing exercises, and complete relaxation of the body and the mind. Yoga originated in India as an ancient Hindu system of religious observance and meditation. **yo·gic** *adj*. ⟨Hindi; Sanskrit = union⟩
yo·gi ['jougi] *n, pl* **-gis** one who practises or follows yoga.

yo·gurt ['jougərt] *n* a semisolid food made from milk fermented by a bacterial culture. Also, **yo·ghurt** or **yo·ghourt**. ⟨Turkish *yōghurt*⟩

yoke [jouk] *n* **1** a wooden frame which fits around the neck of two work animals for pulling a plough or vehicle. **2** any frame connecting two other parts: *The girl carried two buckets on a yoke, one at each end.* **3** a separate upper section of a shirt, blouse, etc. that fits closely over the shoulder area and to which the bodice is attached.
v **1** put a yoke on. **2** join; unite: *to be yoked in marriage.* ⟨Old English *geoc*⟩

yo·kel ['joukəl] *n* a person from a rural area, and perceived as being uncouth, backward, etc. ⟨origin uncertain⟩

yolk [jouk] *n* **1** the yellow substance of an egg, as distinguished from the white. **2** the corresponding part in any animal ovum,

which serves for the nutrition of the embryo. ⟨Old English *geolca; geolu* yellow⟩

Yom Kip·pur [jɒm kɪ'pʊr] *or* [jɒm 'kɪpər] *Judaism* the Day of Atonement, an annual day of fasting and atoning for sin, observed on the tenth day of the first month of the Jewish civil year. ⟨Hebrew *yōm kippūr*⟩

yon·der ['jɒndər] *adv* over there: *Look yonder.* *adj* **1** situated over there: *She lives in yonder cottage.* **2** farther: *There is snow on the yonder side of the mountains.* ⟨Middle English extension of *yond*; compare Gothic *jaindrē*⟩

yore [jɔr] *n Archaic, poetic.*
of yore of long ago: *in days of yore.* ⟨Old English *geāra*, form of *gēar* year⟩

York boat [jɔrk] ✹ formerly, a type of heavy freight vessel developed at York Factory on Hudson Bay, used especially on inland waterways from about 1820 to 1930.

you [ju]; *unstressed,* [jə] *pron sg or pl, subj or obj* **you** *poss* **yours 1** the person or persons spoken to: *Are you ready?* **2** one; anybody: *You press this button to turn it on.* ⟨Old English *ēow*, form of *gē* ye⟩

young [jʌŋ] *adj* **young·er** ['jʌŋgər], **young·est** ['jʌŋgɪst] *adj* **1** in the early part of life or growth. **2** in an early stage: *The night was still young when she left the party.* *n* **1** young offspring: *An animal fights to protect its young.* **2** **the young** *pl* young people. ⟨Old English *geong*⟩
young·ish *adj* rather young. **young·ster** *n* a child: *a lively youngster.*

your [jɔr], [jʊr], *or* [jɜr] *adj* **1** a possessive form of YOU: *Give me your hand.* **2** to do with people in general: *The government guarantees your basic freedoms.* **3** *Informal* that you know of: *your average reader.* **4 Your** a word used in certain formal titles: *Your Highness, Your Worship.* ⟨Old English *ēower*, form of *gē* ye⟩
yours [jɔrz], [jʊrz], *or* [jɜrz] *pron sg and pl* **1** a possessive form of YOU: *This scarf is yours.* **2** at your service: *yours sincerely.* **of yours** associated with you: *Is she a friend of yours?*
your·self [jər'sɛlf] *pron, pl* **-selves 1** a reflexive pronoun, the form of **you** used as an object: *You will hurt yourself if you aren't careful.* **2** a form of **you** added for emphasis: *You yourself know the story is not true.* **3** your usual self: *Come see us when you feel better and are yourself again.* **yours truly 1** a phrase often used at the end of a letter, before the signature. **2** *Informal* I; me.

youth [juθ] *n, pl* **youths** [juðz] *or* [juθs] *or* (collectively) **youth 1** the fact of being young: *He has the vigour of youth.* **2** the time

between childhood and adulthood. **3** a young man. **4** young people collectively (with a sg or pl verb). **5** the first or early stage of anything: *during the youth of this country.* ⟨Old English *geoguth*⟩
youth·ful *adj* **1** young. **2** of youth: *youthful enthusiasm.* **3** having the looks or qualities of youth: *The old man had a youthful spirit.* **4** early; new. **youth·ful·ly** *adv.* **youth·ful·ness** *n.*
youth hostel a supervised, inexpensive lodging place for travelling young people, usually one of a system of such places.

yowl [jaʊl] *n* a long, distressful, or dismal cry; howl. **yowl** *v.* ⟨imitative⟩

yo–yo ['joujou] *n* a small wheel-shaped toy made of two disks joined by a peg around which a string is wound. The toy is spun out and reeled in on the string.
adj Informal fluctuating between extremes: *yo-yo dieting.* ⟨Yoyo, a trademark; origin uncertain⟩

yr. 1 year(s). **2** your; yours.

yrs. 1 years. **2** yours.

yt·ter·bi·um [ɪ'tɜrbiəm] *n* a rare metallic element belonging to the YTTRIUM GROUP. *Symbol* **Yb** ⟨*Ytterby* town in Sweden⟩

yt·tri·um ['ɪtriəm] *n* a rare metallic element. *Symbol* **Y** ⟨See YTTERBIUM.⟩
yttrium group a series of related metallic elements including yttrium, holmium, erbium, thulium, ytterbium, lutetium, terbium, gadolinium, and dysprosium.

yuc·ca ['jʌkə] *n* any of a tropical and subtropical genus of plants of the agave family having long, stiff, sword-shaped leaves and a single erect cluster of large, white, lilylike flowers. ⟨Spanish *yuca*⟩

yuck [jʌk] *Slang interj* an expression of disgust or distaste. **yuck·y** *adj*

yuk [jʌk] *Slang n* **1** a loud and hearty laugh. **2** something evoking such a laugh.
v **yukked, yuk·king** laugh loudly and heartily.

Yu·kon Territory ['jukɒn] a territory of Canada, north of British Columbia.
Yu·kon·er *n* a native or long-term resident of the Yukon Territory. *Abbrev* **YT**

Yule or **yule** [jul] *n Archaic, poetic* Christmas; Christmastime. ⟨Middle English; Old English *geol, iul* winter solstice festival⟩
Yule log 1 a large log burned at Christmas. **2** a Christmas confection made of ice cream, cake, and icing, decorated to resemble a Yule log. **Yule·tide** or **yule·tide** *Archaic, poetic n* Christmastime; the Christmas season. *adj* of Christmastime: *Yuletide cheer.*

yum [jʌm] *interj Informal* an exclamation expressing pleasure or delight at the taste of something. ⟨imitative⟩
yum·my *Informal adj* delighting the senses, esp the taste; delicious. *n* something very tasty or delicious. *interj* an exclamation expressing delight at the taste of something.

Yu·pik ['jupɪk] *n pl* **Yu·pik** or **Yu·piks 1** a member of an Arctic aboriginal people related to the Inuit, living mainly on the southwestern coasts of Alaska. **2** the languages spoken by these people. **Yu·pik** *adj.*

yup·pie or **Yup·pie** ['jʌpi] *Informal n* a young urban professional, regarded as a member of a social class characterized by expensive tastes, middle-class values, and devotion to career.
adj to do with such people. **yup·pie·dom** *n.* ⟨*y*oung *u*rban *p*rofessional⟩
yup·pi·fy *v Informal* adapt to yuppie tastes and values.

Zz

z or **Z** [zɛd] *n, pl* **z's** or **Z's** **1** the twenty-sixth and last letter of the English alphabet, or any speech sound represented by it. **2** the twenty-sixth person or thing in a series. **3** the last in a series consisting of x, y, and z. **4** *z Algebra* an unknown quantity. **5** *Z* the Roman numeral for 2000.

Zam·bo·ni [zæm'bouni] *n Trademark* an apparatus for scraping off the surface of an ice rink and laying down a new surface.

za·ny ['zeini] *adj* comically foolish or absurd. *n* a zany person. **za·ni·ly** *adv.* **za·ni·ness** *n.* ⟨French; dialect Italian *zanni,* orig variant of *Giovanni* John⟩

zap [zæp] *Informal interj* a word used to indicate a sudden, swift happening: *I was just standing there when—zap—something hit me.* *n* the sound of a sudden slap, blow, blast, etc. *v* **zapped, zap·ping 1** hit with a hard blow. **2** kill. **3** beat; defeat. **4** move very fast. **5** delete (commercials) while videotaping a television program. **6** heat quickly in a microwave oven. ⟨imitative⟩

z–ax·is ['zɛd ˌæksɪs] *n pl* **-es** [-iz] *Geometry* in a three-dimensional Cartesian coordinate system, the axis along which values of *z* are measured. Compare X-AXIS, Y-AXIS.

zeal [zil] *n* intense or fervent devotion to or enthusiasm for something or someone, as displayed in action. ⟨Greek *zelos; zeein* boil⟩ **zeal·ot** ['zɛlət] *n* a person who shows too much zeal; a fanatic. **zeal·ot·ry** *n.* **zeal·ous** *adj* eager; earnest: *The children made zealous efforts to clean up the house for the party.* **zeal·ous·ly** *adv.* **zeal·ous·ness** *n.*

ze·bra ['zibrə] *or* ['zɛbrə] *n* any of several wild mammals closely related to the horse but marked with conspicuous black or brown stripes on a light background. **zeb·rine** ['zibraɪn] *or* ['zibrɪn] *adj.* ⟨Portuguese; Bantu⟩

ze·bu ['zibju] *or* ['zibu] *n* any of numerous breeds of domestic cattle characterized by a hump over the shoulders and loose folds of skin hanging from the throat and chest. ⟨French⟩

zed [zɛd] *n* the name of the letter Z. ⟨French *zède;* Greek *zēta*⟩

Zeit·geist ['tsaɪtˌgəist] *n German* a pattern of thought or feeling characteristic of a particular period of time. ⟨German *Zeit* time + *Geist* spirit⟩

Zen **(Buddhism)** [zɛn] *n* a mystical Japanese form of Buddhism that emphasizes contemplation and solitary study to achieve self-discipline and enlightenment. **Zen** *adj.* **Zen Buddhist.** ⟨Japanese *zen* contemplation⟩

Zend–A·ves·ta ['zɛnd ə'vɛstə] *n* the sacred writings of the Zoroastrian religion. ⟨Persian *zend* commentary + *Avesta* the language⟩

ze·nith ['zinɪθ] *or* ['zɛnɪθ] *n* **1** the point in the heavens directly overhead. **2** the highest or greatest point: *At the zenith of its power Rome ruled Europe.* ⟨Old French *senit;* Arabic *samt (ar-rās)* the way (over the head)⟩

zeph·yr ['zɛfər] *n* **1** the west wind. **2** any soft, gentle wind. ⟨Greek *zephyros*⟩

Zep·pe·lin or **zep·pe·lin** ['zɛpələn] *n* an early type of airship shaped like a cigar with pointed ends, having compartments for gas, engines, passengers, etc. ⟨Count Ferdinand von *Zeppelin,* 20c German airship builder⟩

ze·ro ['zirou] *n, pl* **-ros** or **-roes 1** nought; the figure 0. **2** the point marked as 0 on a scale. **3** the complete absence of quantity; nothing. **4** the lowest point: *The team's spirit sank to zero after its third defeat.* *v* **-roed, -ro·ing.** *v* adjust (a device) to a zero point from which readings will be measured. *adj* **1** of or at zero: *a zero score.* **2** not any: *a zero gravity.* ⟨Italian; Arabic *sifr* empty⟩ **zero in** adjust the sights of (a rifle) so a bullet will strike the centre of the target. **zero in on** direct attention toward. **zero gravity** weightlessness. **zero hour 1** the time for beginning an attack, etc. **2** any crucial moment.

zest [zɛst] *n* **1** keen enjoyment: *to eat with zest.* **2** an exciting quality, flavour, etc.: *Wit gives zest to conversation.* **3** the thin, outer peel of a citrus fruit, used as flavouring. *v* give an exciting flavour or quality to (usually with up). **zest·ful** *adj.* **zest·ful·ly** *adv.* **zest·ful·ness** *n.* **zest·y** *adj.* ⟨French *zeste* orange or lemon peel⟩

zeug·ma ['zugmə] *n* a figure of speech in which one word governs or modifies others that are normally related to the first in different ways. *Example: She put out the cat and the light.* ⟨Greek = yoke⟩

zig·gu·rat ['zɪgəˌræt] *n* an ancient Assyrian or Babylonian temple in the form of a pyramid of terraced towers. Also, **zik·ku·rat.** ⟨Akkadian *ziqqurata* pinnacle, tower⟩

zig·zag ['zɪgˌzæg] *adj* with sharp turns, from one side to the other: *a zigzag course.* *adv* turning sharply from one side to the other: *The path ran zigzag up the hill.* **zig·zag, -zagged, -zag·ging** *v.* **zig·zag** *n.* ⟨French; German *Zickzack;* perhaps *Zacke* prong⟩

zilch [zɪltʃ] *n Slang* nothing; zero. ⟨orig a character in the 1930s magazine *Ballyhoo*⟩

zil·li·on ['zɪljən] *n Informal* an extremely large but indefinite number. ⟨by analogy with *million, billion,* etc.⟩

zinc [zɪŋk] *n* a metallic element that, at ordinary temperatures, is little affected by air and moisture. *Symbol* **Zn** ⟨German *Zink;* related to *Zinke* point⟩ **zinc oxide** *Chemistry pharmacy* a powder used in making paint, rubber, glass, cosmetics, ointments, etc.

zing [zɪŋ] *n* **1** a sharp humming sound. **2** spirit; vitality; liveliness; zest. *v* make a sharp humming sound, esp in going fast: *A bullet zinged by her ear.* ⟨imitative⟩ **zing·er** *n* a person, remark, etc. showing spirit or zest.

zip [zɪp] **1** a sudden, brief hissing sound, as of a flying bullet. **2** *Informal* energy or vim. **3** *Informal* nothing; zero; a score of nil. *v* **zipped, zip·ping 1** make a sudden, brief hissing sound. **2** *Informal* act, go, etc. with speed and energy. **3** fasten or close the zipper of (often with *up*). ⟨imitative⟩
zip·py *adj Informal* full of energy; lively.

zip code a system for addressing and sorting mail in the US, in which a five-digit number is assigned to each postal delivery area in the country. ⟨Zone Improvement *P*lan⟩

zip·per [ˈzɪpər] *n* a fastening device of two parallel rows of coils or teeth and a sliding tab that interlocks or opens them. **zip·pered** *adj.* ⟨*Zipper* former trademark⟩

zir·co·ni·um [zərˈkouniəm] *n* a rare, ductile, metallic element. *Symbol* **Zr** ⟨probably French; Arabic *zarqūn*⟩
zir·con [ˈzɜrkɒn] *n* a gem made of zirconium silicate that occurs in various colours.

zith·er [ˈzɪðər] *n* a musical instrument with 30 to 40 strings over a flat sounding board, played with a plectrum and the fingers. ⟨German *Zither;* Latin *cithara,* Greek *kithara*⟩

zo·di·ac [ˈzoudi,æk] *n* an imaginary belt of the heavens covering the apparent yearly path of the sun. The zodiac is divided into 12 equal parts, called signs, named after 12 groups of stars and used in astrology. **zo·di·a·cal** [zouˈdaɪəkəl] *adj.* ⟨Greek *zōdiakos (kyklos)* (circle) of the animals; *zōion* animal⟩

zom·bie [ˈzɒmbi] *n* **1** a corpse supposedly brought back to life by a supernatural power. **2** the snake god of voodoo. **3** *Slang* a dazed, or lethargic person. ⟨Haitian Creole *zôbi;* West African *zumbi* good-luck fetish⟩

zone [zoun] *n* **1** an area set off as distinct from surrounding areas: *a hospital zone.* **2** an area having a particular environment and characterized by certain forms of plant and animal life. **3** an area within which certain rates are charged for such services as public transit, parcel post, etc. **4** *Sports* a designated area of a game surface, as a football field, hockey rink, etc. *v* set (an area or areas) apart for a special purpose: *This area is zoned for apartment buildings.* ⟨Greek *zōnē* orig girdle⟩
zoned *adj* **1** marked with or having zones. **2** divided into zones. **zon·ing** *n* building restrictions in an area. *adj* to do with building restrictions: *zoning bylaws.*

zonked [zɒŋkt] *adj Slang* **1** totally exhausted or tired out: *I was really zonked after climbing those hills all day.* **2** high on drugs; intoxicated; drunk. ⟨imitative⟩

zoo [zu] *n* **1** a place where animals, esp wild animals, are kept and shown. **2** any very busy, overwhelming, chaotic place or situation: *The mall was a real zoo today, with all the tourists.* ⟨short for *zoological garden*⟩

zo·ol·o·gy [zuˈɒlədʒi] *or* [zouˈɒlədʒi] *n* the science that deals with animals and animal life. **zo·ol·o·gist** *n.* ⟨Greek *zōion* animal⟩
zo·o·log·i·cal [ˌzuəˈlɒdʒɪkəl] *or* [ˌzouə-] *adj* **1** of animals and animal life. **2** to do with zoology: *zoological science.* **zo·o·log·i·cal·ly** *adv.*
zoological garden a zoo.

zoom [zum] *v* **1** move or travel rapidly. **2** of an aircraft, fly suddenly upward in a nearly vertical ascent at great speed. **3** increase sharply or rapidly: *Prices zoomed.* **4** move rapidly from one focal length to another, as with a ZOOM LENS.
n **1** a sudden upward flight or increase. **2** a humming or buzzing sound, esp of something moving. ⟨imitative⟩
zoom in on photograph by means of a zoom lens.
zoom lens *Photography* a type of lens that can be adjusted between telephoto close-ups and wide-angle shots without loss of focus.

Zo·ro·as·ter [ˌzɔrouˈæstər] *or* [ˈzɔrou,æstər] *n* the prophet and founder of Zoroastrianism. His birthday is celebrated each year by Zoroastrians on the 26th of March. Also called **Zarathustra.**
Zo·ro·as·tri·an·ism [ˌzɔrouˈæstriə,nɪzəm] *n* an ancient Persian religion founded by the prophet Zoroaster in the 6th century B.C. It is expounded in the Zend-Avesta and teaches that the supreme god Ormazd (or Ahura Mazda) is struggling continuously with Ahriman, the spirit of evil. **Zo·ro·as·tri·an** *adj.*

zuc·chi·ni [zuˈkini] *or* [zəˈkini] *n, pl* **-ni** or **-nis** a small variety of summer squash having a smooth, dark green or bright yellow skin and white flesh with small seeds. ⟨Italian *zucchino* diminutive of *zucco* gourd, squash⟩

zwie·back [ˈzwi,bɑk] *or* [-,bæk], [ˈswi-] German [ˈtsvibak] *n* bread cut into slices and toasted dry in an oven. ⟨German *Zwieback* biscuit; *zwie-* two + *backen* bake⟩

zy·gote [ˈzaɪgout] *n Biology* any cell formed by the union of two gametes (i.e., reproductive cells). A fertilized egg is a zygote. **zy·got·ic** [-ˈgɒtɪk] *adj.* **zy·got·i·cal·ly** *adv.* ⟨Greek *zygotos* yoked; *zygon* yoke⟩

APPENDIX

Provinces and Territories

	Capital	Area (km^2)	Population*
Newfoundland & Labrador (NF) WEBSITE www.gov.nf.ca	St. John's	405 200 km^2	512 900
Prince Edward Island (PE) WEBSITE www.gov.pe.ca	Charlottetown	5 660 km^2	135 300
Nova Scotia (NS) WEBSITE www.gov.ns.ca	Halifax	55 300 km^2	908 000
New Brunswick (NB) WEBSITE www.gov.nb.ca	Fredericton	72 900 km^2	729 500
Québec (QC) WEBSITE www.gov.qc.ca	Québec	1 542 100 km^2	7 237 000
Ontario (ON) WEBSITE www.gov.on.ca	Toronto	1 076 400 km^2	11 410 000
Manitoba (MB) WEBSITE www.gov.mb.ca	Winnipeg	647 800 km^2	1 119 600
Saskatchewan (SK) WEBSITE www.gov.sk.ca	Regina	651 000 km^2	978 900
Alberta (AB) WEBSITE www.gov.ab.ca	Edmonton	661 900 km^2	2 947 800
British Columbia (BC) WEBSITE www.gov.bc.ca	Victoria	944 700 km^2	3 907 700
Yukon Territory (YT) WEBSITE www.gov.yk.ca	Whitehorse	482 400 km^2	28 700
Northwest Territory (NT) WEBSITE www.gov.nt.ca	Yellowknife	1 346 100 km^2	37 300
Nunavut (NU) WEBSITE www.gov.nu.ca	Iqaluit	2 093 200 km^2	26 700
CANADA WEBSITE canada.gc.ca	Ottawa	9 984 700 km^2	30 007 100

*2001, to nearest hundred

Standard Time Zones in Canada

Standard Time Zones were invented by Sir Sandford Fleming in 1878.

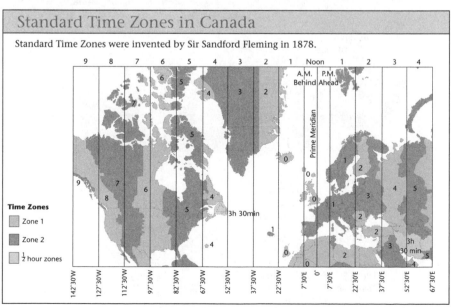

Time Zones
- Zone 1
- Zone 2
- $\frac{1}{2}$ hour zones

Map of Canada — Provinces and Aboriginal Peoples

Bearlake	Hare
Chipewyan (Dene)	Kaska
Dene-thah	Sekani
Dogrib (Dene)	Tagish
Dunne-Za	Tahltan
Gwich'in (Dene)	Tutchone
Han	Yellowknife

•Inuvik

Yukon Territory

•Whitehorse

Northwest Territories

•Yellowknife

Nunavut

British Columbia

Alberta

Edmonton •

Manitoba

Gitksan	
Haida	
Haisla	
Heiltsuk	Chilcotin
Ktunaxa	Cowichan
Kwakwaka'wakw	Kaska
Nisga'a	Okanagan
Nlaka'pamux	Salish
Nuu-chah-nulth	Secwepemc
Nuxalk	Squamish
Tlingit	Tsilhquot'in
Tsimshian	Wet'suwet'en

Victoria • • Vancouver

•Calgary

Saskatchewan

Regina •

Winnipeg •

Dakota
Kainai
Nakoda
Nakota
Piikani
Siksika
Sarcee

Métis

Inuit

Iqaluit

Mi'kmaw

Newfoundland
and Labrador

St. John's

Québec

Maliseet

Prince
Edward
Island

Charlottetown

Ontario

Fredericton

Halifax

New
Brunswick

Nova
Scotia

Québec

Montréal

Ottawa

Toronto

Abenaki	Huron	Onondaga
Algonquin	Innu	Ottawa
Anishinabe	Iroquois	Saulteaux
Attikamek	Kahnawake	Seneca
Cayuga	Kanien'keha	Tuscarora
Cree	Oneida	

Countries of the World

Country	Nationality	Adjective	Official Language	Currency
Afghanistan	Afghan	Afghan	Pushtu	afghani
Albania	Albanian	Albanian	Albanian	lek
Algeria	Algerian	Algerian	Arabic	dinar
Argentina	Argentine	Argentinian	Spanish	peso
Armenia	Armenian	Armenian	Armenian	dram
Australia	Australian	Australian	English	dollar
Austria	Austrian	Austrian	German	euro
Azerbaijan	Azerbaijani	Azerbaijani	Azerbaijani	manat
Bahamas	Bahamian	Bahamian	English	dollar
Bangladesh	Bangladeshi	Bangladeshi	Bangla	taka
Barbados	Barbadian	Barbadian	English	dollar
Belarus	Belarusian	Belarusian	Byelorussian	ruble
Belgium	Belgian	Belgian	Dutch/French	euro
Bolivia	Bolivian	Bolivian	Spanish	Boliviano
Bosnia and Herzegovina	Bosnian and Herzegovinian		Serbo-Croatian	dinar
Brazil	Brazilian	Brazilian	Portuguese	real
Bulgaria	Bulgarian	Bulgarian	Bulgarian	lev
Cambodia	Cambodian	Cambodian	Khmer	new riel
Canada	Canadian	Canadian	English/French	dollar
Chile	Chilean	Chilean	Spanish	peso
China	Chinese	Chinese	Mandarin Chinese	yuan
Colombia	Colombian	Colombian	Spanish	peso
Costa Rica	Costa Rican	Costa Rican	Spanish	colón
Croatia	Croat	Croatian	Serbo-Croatian	kuna
Cuba	Cuban	Cuban	Spanish	peso
Czech Republic	Czech	Czech	Czech/Slovak	koruna
Denmark	Dane	Danish	Danish	krone
Ecuador	Ecuadorian	Ecuadorian	Spanish	sucre
Egypt	Egyptian	Egyptian	Arabic	pound
El Salvador	Salvadoran	Salvadoran	Spanish	colón
Ethiopia	Ethiopian	Ethiopian	Amharic	birr
Finland	Finn	Finnish	Finnish/Swedish	euro
France	French	French	French	euro
Germany	German	German	German	euro
Ghana	Ghanaian	Ghanaian	English	cedi
Greece	Greek	Greek	Greek	euro
Guatemala	Guatemalan	Guatemalan	Spanish	quetzal
Guyana	Guyanese	Guyanese	English	dollar
Haiti	Haitian	Haitian	French	gourde
Honduras	Honduran	Honduran	Spanish	lempira
Hungary	Hungarian	Hungarian	Hungarian	forint
Iceland	Icelander	Icelandic	Icelandic	króna
India	Indian	Indian	Hindi	rupee
Indonesia	Indonesian	Indonesian	Bahasa Indonesia	rupiah
Iran	Iranian	Iranian	Farsi (Persian)	rial
Iraq	Iraqi	Iraqi	Arabic/Kurdish	dinar
Ireland, Republic of	Irish	Irish	Irish/English	euro
Israel	Israeli	Israeli	Hebrew/Arabic	shekel
Italy	Italian	Italian	Italian	euro
Jamaica	Jamaican	Jamaican	English	dollar
Japan	Japanese	Japanese	Japanese	yen
Kazakhstan	Kazakhstani	Kazakhstani	Kazakh	tenge
Kenya	Kenyan	Kenyan	English/Swahili	shilling
Korea, North	Korean	Korean	Korean	won

Country	Nationality	Adjective	Official Language	Currency
Korea, South	Korean	Korean	Korean	won
Kuwait	Kuwaiti	Kuwaiti	Arabic	dinar
Lebanon	Lebanese	Lebanese	Arabic/French	pound
Libya	Libyan	Libyan	Arabic	dinar
Lithuania	Lithuanian	Lithuanian	Lithuanian	litas
Malaysia	Malaysian	Malaysian	Malay	ringgit
Mexico	Mexican	Mexican	Spanish	peso
Morocco	Moroccan	Moroccan	Arabic	dirham
Mozambique	Mozambican	Mozambican	Portuguese	metical
Namibia	Namibian	Namibian	Afrikaans/German/English	dollar
Netherlands	Dutch	Dutch	Dutch/Frisian	euro
New Zealand	New Zealander	New Zealander	English	dollar
Nicaragua	Nicaraguan	Nicaraguan	Spanish	córdoba
Nigeria	Nigerian	Nigerian	English	naira
Norway	Norwegian	Norwegian	Norwegian	krone
Pakistan	Pakistani	Pakistani	Urdu	rupee
Panama	Panamanian	Panamanian	Spanish	balboa
Paraguay	Paraguayan	Paraguayan	Spanish	guaraní
Peru	Peruvian	Peruvian	Spanish/Quechua	nuevo sol
Philippines	Filipino	Filipino	English/Pilipino	peso
Poland	Polish	Polish	Polish	zloty
Portugal	Portuguese	Portuguese	Portuguese	euro
Romania	Romanian	Romanian	Romanian	leu
Russia	Russian	Russian	Russian	ruble
Rwanda	Rwandan	Rwandan	French/Kinyarwanda	franc
Saudi Arabia	Saudi	Saudi	Arabic	riyal
Serbia and Montenegro	Serb, Montenegrin	Serb, Montenegrin	Serbo-Croatian	dinar
Singapore	Singaporean	Singaporean	Chinese/Malay/Tamil	dollar
Slovakia	Slovak	Slovak	Slovak	koruna
Somalia	Somali	Somali	Somali	shilling
South Africa	South African	South African	See below*	rand
Spain	Spanish	Spanish	Spanish	euro
Sri Lanka	Sri Lankan	Sri Lankan	Sinhala/Tamil	rupee
Sweden	Swedish	Swedish	Swedish	króna
Switzerland	Swiss	Swiss	German/French/Italian	franc
Syria	Syrian	Syrian	Arabic	pound
Taiwan	Chinese	Chinese	Chinese	dollar
Tajikistan	Tajik	Tajikistan	Tajik	ruble
Tanzania	Tanzanian	Tanzanian	Swahili/English	shilling
Thailand	Thai	Thai	Thai	baht
Tunisia	Tunisian	Tunisian	Arabic	dinar
Turkey	Turk	Turkish	Turkish	lira
Uganda	Ugandan	Ugandan	English	shilling
Ukraine	Ukrainian	Ukrainian	Ukrainian	hryvna
United Arab Emirates	Emiri	Emirian	Arabic	dirham
United Kingdom	British	British	English/Welsh/Scottish	pound
United States	American	American	English	dollar
Uruguay	Uruguayan	Uruguayan	Spanish	peso
Uzbekistan	Uzbek	Uzbek	Uzbek	som
Venezuela	Venezuelan	Venezuelan	Spanish	bolívar
Vietnam	Vietnamese	Vietnamese	Vietnamese	dong
Zimbabwe	Zimbabwean	Zimbabwean	English	dollar

* Afrikaans, English, isiNdebele, Sepedi, Sesotho, siSwati, Xitsonga, Setswana, Tshivenda, isiXhosa, isiZulu

Prime Ministers of Canada

Sir John A. Macdonald	Conservative	1867–1873, 1878–1891
Alexander Mackenzie	Liberal	1873–1878
Sir John Abbot	Conservative	1891–1892
Sir John Thompson	Conservative	1892–1894
Sir Mackenzie Bowell	Conservative	1894–1896
Sir Charles Tupper	Conservative	1896
Sir Wilfrid Laurier	Liberal	1896–1911
Sir Robert Borden	Conservative/Unionist	1911–1920
Arthur Meighen	Unionist/Conservative	1920–1921, 1926
Mackenzie King	Liberal	1921–1930, 1935–1948
Richard B. Bennett	Conservative	1930–1935
Louis St. Laurent	Liberal	1948–1957
John Diefenbaker	Progressive Conservative	1957–1963
Lester Pearson	Liberal	1963–1968
Pierre Trudeau	Liberal	1968–1979, 1980–1984
Joe Clark	Progressive Conservative	1979–1980
John Turner	Liberal	1984
Brian Mulroney	Progressive Conservative	1984–1993
Kim Campbell	Progressive Conservative	1993
Jean Chrétien	Liberal	1993–2003
Paul Martin	Liberal	2003–2006
Stephen Harper	Conservative	2006–

Titles of Elected Representatives in Canada

MHA	Member of the House of Assembly	in Newfoundland and Labrador
MLA	Member of the Legislative Assembly	in most Canadian provinces and territories
MNA	Member of the National Assembly	in Québec
MP	Member of Parliament	in the Federal Government, Ottawa
MPP	Member of the Provincial Parliament	in Ontario

O Canada

O Canada! Our home and native land!
True patriot love in all thy sons command.
With glowing heart we see thee rise,
The True North strong and free!
From far and wide, O Canada,
We stand on guard for thee.
God keep our land glorious and free!
O Canada, we stand on guard for thee.
O Canada, we stand on guard for thee!

Ô Canada

Ô Canada! Terre de nos aïeux,
Ton front est ceint de fleurons glorieux!
Car ton bras sait porter l'épée,
Il sait porter la croix!
Ton histoire est une épopée
Des plus brillants exploits,
Et ta valeur, de foi trempée,
Protégera nos foyers et nos droits,
Protégera nos foyers et nos droits.

Abbreviations

AD	in the year of our Lord	N.B.	note well
a.m.	midnight to noon		(Latin *nota bene*)
	(Latin *ante meridian*)	NHL	National Hockey League
anon.	anonymous	p. or pp.	page or pages
Ave.	avenue	Ph.D.	Doctor of Philosophy
BC	before Christ	p.m.	noon to midnight
BCE	before the Common Era		(Latin *post meridiem*)
CE	Common Era	Prof.	Professor
Co.	company	P.S.	postscript
C.O.D.	cash on delivery	PTA	parent-teacher association
D.D.S.	Doctor of Dental Surgery	RCMP	Royal Canadian Mounted
Dr.	Doctor		Police
D.S.T.	daylight saving time	Rd.	road
E	east	Rev.	reverend
e.g.	for example/and similar things	rpm	revolutions per minute
	(Latin *exempli gratia*)	R.S.V.P.	please reply
i.e.	that is		(French *répondez s'il*
	(Latin *id est*)		*vous plaît*)
H.M.C.S.	Her (or His) Majesty's	S	south
	Canadian Ship	Sr.	senior
H.M.S.	Her (or His) Majesty's Ship	S.S.	steamship
H.R.H.	Her (or His) Royal Highness	St./Ste.	saint
H.S.	High School	St.	street
Jr.	junior	TD	touchdown
L.	lake	TOC	table of contents
Ltd.	limited	vol.	volume (of a book)
M.D.	doctor of medicine	vs.	against
Mt.	mount (mountain)		(*Latin* versus)
N	north	W	west

Numbers

Cardinal	Ordinal	Roman	Cardinal	Ordinal	Roman
1	first	I	13	thirteenth	XIII
2	second	II	14	fourteenth	XIV
3	third	III	15	fifteenth	XV
4	fourth	IV	16	sixteenth	XVI
5	fifth	V	17	seventeenth	XVII
6	sixth	VI	18	eighteenth	XVIII
7	seventh	VII	19	nineteenth	XIX
8	eighth	VIII	20	twentieth	XX
9	ninth	IX	50	fiftieth	L
10	tenth	X	100	hundredth	C
11	eleventh	XI	1000	thousandth	M
12	twelfth	XII	1 000 000	millionth	$\overline{M}$

SI Units

Name	Symbol	Quantity
metre	m	length
kilogram	kg	mass
second	s	time
ampere	A	electric current
kelvin	K	thermodynamic temperature
mole	mol	amount of substance
candela	cd	luminous intensity
hertz	Hz	frequency
pascal	Pa	pressure, stress
watt	W	power
volt	V	electric potential, electromotive force
newton	N	force
joule	J	energy, work
ohm	Ω	electric resistance
farad	F	electric capacitance
litre	L	volume, capacity (= $1dm^3$)
degree celsius	°C	temperature
hectare	ha	area (= 10 000 m^2)
tonne	t	mass (= 1000 kg)
electronvolt	eV	energy
nautical mile	M	distance (= 1852 m)
knot	kn	speed (=1M/h)
radian	rad	plane angle

SI Prefixes

Name	Symbol	Multiplying Factor	Example
giga-	G	1 000 000 000	a gigabyte (about one billion bytes)
mega-	M	1 000 000	a megavolt (one million volts)
kilo-	k	1 000	a kilometre (one thousand metres)
hecto-	h	100	a hectolitre (one hundred litres)
deca-	da	10	a decagram (ten grams)
deci-	h	0.1	a decigram (one-tenth of a gram)
centi-	c	0.01	a centimetre (one-hundredth of a metre)
milli-	m	0.001	a millilitre (one-thousandth of a litre)
micro-	m	0.000 001	a micrometre (one-millionth of a metre)
nano-	n	0.000 000 001	a nanosecond (one-billionth of a second)

Conversion Factors

to Metric

1 inch	= 2.54 cm
1 yard	= 91.44 cm
1 mile	= 1.61 km
1 pound	= 0.45 g
1 gallon	= 4.55 L (US 3.79 L)

Conversion Factors

from Metric

1 centimetre	= 0.39 inches
1 metre	= 39.4 inches
1 kilometre	= 0.62 miles
1 kilogram	= 2.20 pounds
1 litre	= 1.76 pints

GRAMMAR AND USAGE GUIDE

Abbreviation

An abbreviation is a shortened form of a word or phrase. There is a trend away from using periods in many abbreviations, especially names of companies or organizations. While abbreviations are useful in lists, tables, footnotes, and technical documents, most are inappropriate in formal writing.

A few exceptions are:

- titles, such as Mrs., Mr., Ms., and Dr.
- St. for Saint in place names
- degrees and professional titles, such as Ph.D., B.A., C.A., when placed after a person's name
- indications of time, when used with figures, such as 7:00 p.m., A.D. 500

Active and Passive Voice

A verb is in the active voice if its subject is the doer of the action. A verb is in the passive voice (*be* + past participle) when the subject of the verb receives the action:

Active: *The firefighters extinguished the fire.*

Passive: *The fire was extinguished.*

The passive voice allows the doer of the action to be omitted. Thus the doer may be unknown, unimportant, or obvious. Writers of scientific papers usually prefer the passive voice: *the experiment was conducted.*

Adjective

An adjective is a word that describes a noun or a pronoun: *We heard a loud noise. His icy blue eyes stared at nothing. She looked pale.*

Adverb

An adverb can describe a verb, an adjective, another adverb, or a whole clause or sentence. Adverbs usually tell how, when, where, or in what manner. Adverbs such as *who, when, where, what,* and *how* are also used to indicate a question:

That singer sings beautifully. I have an extremely tight schedule today.

I work too hard! Strangely, the door was unlocked. Where are you going?

Agreement

SEE Pronoun; Subject/Verb Agreement

Apostrophe [']

Use an apostrophe

- to show possession: *Jane's boat*
- to indicate a contraction: *don't, can't*
- to replace missing letters in speech: *"How 'bout you?"*
- to replace missing numbers in a date: *class of '99*
- to show the plural of letters or symbols: *There are three a's in Saskatchewan and two 9's in 1998.*

Bias

SEE Racist Language; Sexist Language

Bibliography

A bibliography is a list of all the works used in an essay or paper. Place it on a separate page at the end of the paper. Although there are variations in style, all bibliographies include the same basic information: the name of the author(s), the title of the work, and the name, date, and place of publication. (NOTE: If the author is unknown, start with the title of the work.) Indent all lines except the first line of each entry. Arrange the sources alphabetically, by author's name. Below are some examples.

- book with one author:
Smucker, Barbara Claasen. *Days of Terror.* Toronto: Clarke, Irwin, 1979.

- book with more than one author:
Nida, Patricia Cooney, and Wendy M. Heller. *The Teenager's Survival Guide to Moving.* New York: Macmillan, 1985.

- work in an anthology:
London, Jack. "The Hunger Cry." *Great Canadian Animal Stories.* Ed. Muriel Whitaker. Edmonton: Hurtig, 1978.

- magazine or newspaper article:
Place the volume number after the title of the magazine. Place the page numbers, preceded by a colon, at the end of the citation.
Jarzen, David. "Pollen Power." *Owl* 22 (Mar. 1997): 12-14.

- video or film:
Perspectives in Science. Dir. Julie Stanfel. National Film Board, 1989.

- CD-ROM:
Canadian Encyclopedia Plus. CD-ROM, videodisc. Toronto: McClelland & Stewart Inc., 1996.

- Internet document:
[Author]. [Year]. [*Title of document*]. Available: [address] [date accessed]

- interview:
Singh, T. Jai. Personal interview. 10 March 1997.

SEE ALSO Citation and Footnote

Capitalization

Capitalize the following.

- the first word in a sentence or a quotation: *The novelist Farley Mowat once said, "Truth I have no trouble with."*
- the name of a particular person, place, or nation: *My English penpal, Sterling Sawyer, will be visiting Canada this fall.*
- the main words in a title: *Roughing It in the Bush, Mathematics 201, Romeo and Juliet*
- titles and family relationships, when used as part of a person's name: *I saw Dad go downstairs.* (BUT *I saw my dad go downstairs.*) *Doctor Namis* (BUT *the doctor*)

Prime Minister Macdonald
(BUT _the prime minister_)

- days of the week, months, and holidays:
Tuesday; September; Ramadan

- organizations, political parties, religions: _the
United Nations; the Liberal Party; Judaism_

- historical events, eras, and documents: _the
Great Depression; the BNA Act_

Citation and Footnote

In essays and papers, use citations or footnotes
to acknowledge the sources of quotations,
charts, tables, diagrams, and all ideas other than
your own. Below are some general guidelines for
writing **citations**.

- Place the author's name and the page
numbers (if appropriate) in parentheses, as
close to the relevant material as possible.
If the citation is at the end of a sentence,
the period follows the citation: _Inventors are
enchanted by ideas, beguiled into following a
trail of investigation to its end (Carpenter 8)._

- If you have already mentioned the author,
you do not need to repeat the name in the
citation: _According to Thomas Carpenter,
"Inventors are enchanted by ideas, beguiled into
following a trail of investigation to its end."(8)._

- If you have referred to more than one work
by the same author, include a shortened
version of the title in the citations. For
example, if you mentioned two of Alice
Munro's short stories in a paper, perhaps
"Miles City, Montana" and "Jesse and
Meribeth," you could refer to _("Miles" 119)_
or _("Jesse" 249)_ in your citations.

For **footnotes**, instead of placing information in
parentheses within the text, put a small raised
number at the end of the relevant material, and
add a corresponding footnote at the bottom of
the page, separated from the text by a short line
(about ten spaces). Indent the first line of the
footnote. Here is an example: _"Inventors are
enchanted by ideas, beguiled into following a trail of
investigation to its end."[1]_

[1]_Thomas Carpenter, Inventors: Profiles in
Canadian Genius (Camden East, Ont.: Camden
House, 1990), p. 8._

The first time you cite a source, give a full
reference. Then cite only the author's last name
and the page number: [2]_Carpenter, p. 23._ Here are
some other sample footnote references:

- book with more than one author:
[3]Patricia Cooney Nida and Wendy M.
Heller, _The Teenager's Survival Guide to
Moving_ (New York: Macmillan, 1985), p. 34.

- work in an anthology:
[4]Jack London, "The Hunger Cry," in _Great
Canadian Animal Stories_, ed. Muriel
Whitaker. (Edmonton: Hurtig, 1978), p. 37.

- magazine or newspaper article:
[5]David Jarzen, "Pollen Power," _Owl_,
Mar. 1997, p. 12.

- video or film:
[6]_Perspectives in Science_, dir. Julie Stanfel.
National Film Board, 1989.

- CD-ROM:
[7]"Film Animation," _Canadian Encyclopedia_
(Edmonton: Hurtig, 1996). CD-ROM.

- Internet document:
[8][Author]. [Year]. [_Title of document_].
Available: [address] [date accessed]

- interview:
[9]Singh, T. Jai. Personal interview.
10 March 1997.

Clause

A clause is a group of words that has a subject
and a verb. Main clauses (also known as
independent or principal clauses) can stand on
their own as full sentences, while subordinate
clauses (also known as dependent clauses) need a
main clause to complete them. A sentence may
have more than one clause within it.

In the following examples, main clauses are
underlined, and subordinate clauses are in italics.

This is the secret place _that I like to visit._ Marta,
who sometimes looks after our dog, is going to
veterinary college. _When Riswan smiles_ the whole
room lights up. _When Riswan smiles the whole
room lights up._

SEE ALSO Sentence

Cliché

Clichés are overworked expressions that no longer
have much impact. They are best avoided. Here
are some examples: _free as a bird; sick as a dog; stay
the course; between a rock and a hard place; last but
not least; in the home stretch; under the weather_

Colon [:]

A colon warns you that something is to follow.
Use colons in the following situations.

- to introduce a list: _Colours have different
meanings in western culture: red for danger,
black for mourning, and white for purity._

- to introduce a quotation in formal writing:
_Back in 1957, Professor Kenneth Boulding said:
"Canada has no cultural unity, no linguistic
unity, no religious unity, no economic unity, no
geographic unity. All it has is unity."_

- to express time: _8:45; 20:00_

- to separate the volume and page numbers
of a magazine: _Food Lovers Digest, 4:17-19_

- after the salutation of a business letter:
Dear Ms. Rosen:

Comma [,]

A comma indicates a slight pause in a sentence.
The common practice, especially in informal
writing, is to use as few commas as possible
without obscuring the meaning. Use commas:

- between compound sentences: _Rula thought
hard, but no solutions came to mind._

- with nouns of address: _David, take the
garbage out._

- with words, phrases, or clauses that interrupt
a sentence: _We will, nevertheless, do our best to
win. Mother was delighted when, for the first
time, the baby smiled. Marcus, who has thick
hair, can never get his bathing cap on._

- with introductory words, phrases, or clauses: _Naturally,_ George was pleased. _In the end,_ I stayed home and read. _When we had finished eating,_ we took the boat out for a spin.
- between items in a series: They took a _long, slow, boring_ flight to Calgary. _Jim, Walter, and Aviva_ work together at the factory. NOTE: some people omit the comma just before the _and_ in a series. This is acceptable, as long as the use is consistent and it does not make the sentence unclear.
- to set off _which_ clauses: The house_, which I own,_ is on a hill. (_which I own_ is not essential to the main idea) BUT The house that I own is on a hill. (_that I own_ identifies which house is being discussed, so it is considered part of the main idea). SEE ALSO That/Which
- in some forms of dates: _January 14, 1997_ BUT _14 January 1997_
- in addresses: _Please send an information kit to Serge Laflamme, 334 Grosvenor Avenue, Montréal, Québec H3H 3C7._ BUT _Serge Laflamme 334 Grosvenor Avenue Montréal, Québec H3H 3C7_ NOTE: there is no comma before the postal code.
- between a city and a country: _Ottawa, Canada_
- in salutations of personal letters: _Dear Sam,_
- to set off degrees and titles: _Peter Mishinski, Ph.D; Lorraine Markotic, M.P._

SEE ALSO Quotation and Quotation Marks

Comma Splice
SEE Run-on Sentence

Comparative/Superlative
When you compare things, you can make changes to the positive form of the modifier. Generally, use _more_ and _most_ to form the comparative and superlative of longer modifiers.

- **positive**, used for regular descriptions: _She is a strong swimmer._
- **comparative**, used to compare two things: _He lives more economically than I do._
- **superlative**, used to compare more than two things: _You are the finest singer in our class._

Avoid doubling comparisons.

Incorrect: _She looks more happier these days._

Correct: _She looks happier these days._ OR _She looks more happy these days._

Conjunction
A conjunction is a word that connects other words, phrases, clauses, or sentences. There are three types of conjunction, as follows.

- co-ordinating conjunctions (_and, or, nor, for, but, so, yet_): _Mico and I are best friends._
- subordinating conjunctions (_whenever, after, if, since, because, before, unless_): _I break out in hives whenever I eat pickles._
- correlative conjunctions (_both...and, either...or, neither...nor, not only...but also_): _My watch is neither on my wrist nor by my bed._

Dangling Modifier
SEE Misplaced or Dangling Modifier

Dash (—)
A dash marks a strong break in a sentence: _It wasn't until Friday—or it may have been Saturday—that I discovered my wallet was missing. Did you ever see the film—but no, it was made before you were born. Three students—Ruby, Amina, and Michael—were named as finalists. Jack works hard—when he has to._

Dashes are useful for emphasis. However, using many dashes can make your writing disjointed and difficult to read. Consider using other punctuation instead.

Double Negative
Using two negative words (such as _not_ and _never_) in the same sentence creates a double negative. Avoid confusion by removing or replacing one of the two words. Double negatives are often created in sentences where the word _not_ is hidden in a contraction, such as _can't, won't,_ or _don't._

Confusing: _I can't barely see!_
Better: _I can barely see!_ OR _I can't see!_

Confusing: _There isn't scarcely enough to go around._
Better: _There is scarcely enough to go around._ OR _There isn't enough to go around._

Euphemism
A euphemism is a word or expression that is meant to blunt the impact of harsh or unpleasant words or phrases. Some common euphemisms are: _pass away; senior citizen; rest room; special needs._
As the military use of terms like _collateral damage_ instead of _deaths_ shows, there can be a fine line between using a euphemism and obscuring the truth. As a general rule, the direct way to say something is usually best.

Exclamation Mark [!]
An exclamation mark gives emphasis, and expresses surprise, delight, or alarm: _Hey! How sweet! Watch out!_ Most writers trust their words to express whatever mood or emotion they wish to convey. When used sparingly, exclamation marks can be helpful, but too many may weaken their effect.

Weak: _The room was a mess! Tables were overturned! The drawers had been pulled out! I understood immediately! The house had been robbed!!!!_

Better: _The room was a mess. Tables were overturned. The drawers had been pulled out. I understood immediately —the house had been robbed!_

SEE ALSO Quotation and Quotation Marks

Footnote

SEE Citation and Footnote

Homonym

Homonyms are words that are pronounced the same but have different meanings, such as *see* and *sea*. The following homonyms are often confused: *complement/compliment; hear/here; its/it's; passed/past; piece/peace; principal/principle; their/they're/there; to/too/two; through/threw; who's/whose; your/you're.*

If you are unsure of the correct spelling, check your dictionary.

Homograph

Homographs are words that are written the same, but have different meanings, such as *bank* (edge of a river) and *bank* (place that lends money).

Hyphen [-]

Use hyphens in the following ways.

- in compound numbers between 21 and 99: *twenty-one*
- in time: *the five-fifteen bus*
- in fractions: *one-half of the pie*
- in some numerical expressions: *a ten-year-old boy; a twenty-dollar bill*
- to divide a word between syllables at the end of a line: *dis-satisfied; dissat-isfied; dissatis-fied* NOTE: Never break proper nouns or words of only one syllable.
- in many expressions formed with prefixes: *all-round; co-operate; de-ice; ex-boyfriend; half-baked; post-mortem; pre-test; pro-Canadian; re-elect; self-centred* Note: As there are many exceptions to these rules, it is safest to check your dictionary for guidance.
- when a compound modifier precedes a noun, unless the first word ends in *-ly*: *rosy-fingered dawn; black-eyed Susan* BUT *carefully woven cloth*
- in some compound words: since compound words are often written as one word (*handbook*), or as two words with or without a hyphen (*hand-held; hand brake*), it is best to consult your dictionary for the proper form.

Italics and Underlining

Use italics in print (or underline when writing by hand) to identify a whole work, such as the title of a play, piece of music, movie, book, newspaper, or magazine: *I read a great article about Margaret Atwood's book, Alias Grace, in Saturday Night the other day.* Italics and underlining can also be used to indicate emphasis (*To avoid charges of bias, the committee listened to arguments both for and against the proposal.*); to indicate a word that is being referred to (*My dictionary defines fatuous as "stupid but self-satisfied."*); or to indicate a foreign phrase: (*ad hoc*).

SEE ALSO Title

Metaphor and Simile

Metaphors and similes are both forms of comparison. A simile compares two things or ideas using *like* or *as*. A metaphor makes the comparison implicitly, without using *like* or *as*.

Simile: *The icicles looked like bony fingers, pointing down at him accusingly.*

Metaphor: *Bony fingers of ice pointed down at him accusingly.*

SEE ALSO Cliché

Misplaced or Dangling Modifier

When a modifier (a word or phrase that limits or describes other words) is too far from what it modifies, the result can be a misplaced modifier. In the following examples, the modifiers are in italics, and the word being modified is underlined.

Misplaced: *Growling,* my hat was being eaten by the <u>dog</u>.

Better: *Growling,* the <u>dog</u> was eating my hat.

Better: My hat was being eaten by a *growling* <u>dog</u>.

Misplaced: <u>She</u> watched the moon rise *from her chair.*

Better: *From her chair,* <u>she</u> watched the moon rise.

A dangling modifier occurs when the word being modified is implied but does not appear in the sentence.

Dangling: *While on holiday,* a thief broke into our house.

Better: *While* <u>we</u> were *on holiday,* a thief broke into our house.

Noun

A noun is a word that refers to people, places, qualities, things, actions, or ideas: *When <u>Joe</u> was at the <u>library</u> in <u>Guelph</u>, <u>curiosity</u> enticed him to read an <u>article</u> that claimed <u>fear</u> could be cured by <u>meditation</u>.*

SEE ALSO Subject/Verb Agreement

Number

The number of a noun, pronoun, or verb indicates whether it is singular or plural.

SEE Pronoun; Subject/Verb Agreement

Object

English has three types of objects. In the following examples, the direct object is in italics, and the indirect object is underlined.

- A direct object is a noun or pronoun that answers the question *what?* or *who?* about the verb: He bought a *kite.*
- An indirect object answers the question *to what?, to whom?, for what?,* or *for whom?* about the verb: He bought <u>me</u> a *kite.*
- The object of a preposition is a noun or pronoun that comes at the end of a phrase that begins with a preposition: He bought a *kite* for <u>me</u>.

Paragraph

A paragraph is a group of sentences that develop one aspect of a topic, or one phase of a narrative. The sentences in a paragraph should be clearly related to each other. Sometimes, especially in essays, the aspect or point being developed is expressed in a topic sentence, and the other sentences in the paragraph expand on this statement.

Parallel Structure

In a sentence, two or more elements that are of equal importance, expressed in similar grammatical terms to emphasize their relationship, are called parallel. Sentences without parallel structure can sound both confusing and awkward. Parallel structure is especially important in lists; with expressions like *both...and, not only...but also, whether...or,* and *either...or;* and in words, phrases, or clauses joined by *and.*

Not Parallel:	*Campers are taught hiking, swimming, and how to paddle a canoe.*
Parallel:	*Campers are taught to hike, swim, and canoe.* OR *Campers are taught hiking, swimming, and canoeing.*
Not Parallel:	*Raoul can't decide whether to work as a lifeguard or if he would prefer to renovate houses.*
Parallel:	*Raoul can't decide whether to work as a lifeguard or to renovate houses.* OR *Raoul can't decide whether to work as a lifeguard or as a renovator.*

Parentheses [()]

Use parentheses to set off comments or asides in a sentence: *They lived happily ever after (and so did the dog).*

When necessary, you can use punctuation marks within the parentheses, even if the parenthetical comment is in the middle of a sentence: *All of us except Peter (Peter is always optimistic!) were sure it was going to rain on our picnic.*

You can place whole sentences in parentheses. If the sentence stands alone and is not grammatically related to the ones before and after it, punctuate the sentence within the parentheses as you would a regular sentence: *The French colony of Upper Volta, now called Burkina Faso, gained its independence in 1960. (Burkina Faso means "land of honest men.")*

Participle

The present participle (or gerund) is the form of the verb that ends in *-ing* (*wanting, eating, burning, hearing, growing*). The past participle usually ends in *-ed, -en, -t, -d,* or *-n* (*wanted, eaten, burnt, heard, grown*). Participles have three main uses.

- as part of certain verb tenses: *I am thinking about what I will eat for lunch. I had been there too long.* NOTE: a participle cannot act as a verb on its own. It must be accompanied by a helping verb, such as *is, have, were.*

- to modify a noun or pronoun, either alone or as part of a phrase: *a broken doll; a spoiled child; The man standing at the back is my father; Exhausted by our long hike, we arrived back at the campsite.*

- to modify a whole sentence, either alone or as part of a phrase: *Talking of food, here comes the lunch truck! All things considered, we did quite well.*

Part of Speech

Parts of speech are nouns, adjectives, verbs, adverbs, conjunctions, pronouns, interjections, and prepositions.

Period [.]

Use a period

- to mark the end of a sentence: *The sky is blue.*

- after abbreviations and initials: *J.J. Cale; Mr.; St.*

SEE ALSO: Quotation and Quotation Marks

Phrase

A phrase is a group of words, used together in a sentence, that does not have a subject and a verb: *Marcel spoke for the first time.* (prepositional phrase) *Thinking fast,* I covered my face. (participial phrase) *Catrina wants to be a scientist.* (infinitive phrase)

COMPARE Clause

Plagiarism

Plagiarism is the presenting of the ideas of others as if they were your own. This is a very serious offence. To avoid unintentional plagiarism, be sure to include a citation or footnote whenever you borrow ideas or quote directly from another source.

SEE Citation and Footnote

Possessive

Use possessive forms of nouns and pronouns to show ownership.

- To form the possessive of most singular nouns, add *'s*: *Jim's idea; the cat's paw; Toronto's night life*

- To form the possessive of plurals that end in *-s*, add only an apostrophe: *the students' project; the Livakos' pet; the cars' lights*

- Plurals that do not end in *-s* form the possessive in the same way as singular nouns: *children's games; people's pets; geese's flying patterns*

- Proper nouns of two or more syllables that end in *-s* sometimes sound awkward when an *'s* is added to form the possessive. In such cases, some writers omit the final *-s*: *Jesus' words; Laertes' death*

Prefix

A prefix is a word or syllable added on to the beginning of a word to make a new word. For example, *dis-* added to *appear* makes *disappear.* Often, knowing what a prefix means can help you to figure out the meaning of a new word.

Here is a list of some common prefixes and their meanings:

a- (not)	*mis-* (wrong)
ante- (before)	*mono-* (one)
anti- (against)	*non-* (not)
multi- (many)	*post-* (after)
bi- (two)	*pseudo-* (false)
circum- (around)	*re-* (again)
co- (together)	*retro-* (back)
dis- (not)	*semi-* (half)
extra- (beyond)	*super-* (over)
fore- (before)	*trans-* (across)
hyper- (excessively)	*tri-* (three)
in- (not)	*un-* (not)
inter- (between; among)	*uni-* (one)
mal- (bad)	

Preposition

A preposition is a word that shows a relationship between a noun (called the object of the preposition; SEE Object) and some other word in the sentence. Some words that sometimes function as prepositions are: *above, at, before, behind, by, down, for, from, in, of, on, past, since, to, under, until, with*.

In this example, the prepositions are underlined, and the objects of the prepositions are in italics:
The hut <u>in</u> *the valley* was swept away <u>by</u> *the flood*.

Pronoun

A pronoun is a word that replaces a noun or another pronoun. There are many different types of pronouns, and most of them cause no problems. However, there are a few pitfalls.

- Antecedent: It should be clear what word the pronoun replaces (its antecedent). Here are some examples of sentences with unclear antecedents.

  Unclear: *Linda loves looking after Sandra, because <u>she</u> is so good.*

  Clear: *Linda loves looking after Sandra, because Sandra is so good.*

  Unclear: *I completed the report, <u>which</u> pleased my boss.*

  Clear: *My boss was pleased with the report that I completed. OR My boss was pleased that I completed the report.*

- Case: Personal pronouns have three forms, or cases:

  the **subject** form (*I, you, he, she, we, they*)

  the **object** form (*me, you, him, her, us, them*)

  the **possessive** form (*mine, yours, his, hers, ours, theirs*)

  Usually you will have no trouble choosing the right form. However, pay attention when the pronoun is joined to another noun or pronoun by *and, or,* or *nor*. Use the form of the pronoun that you would use if the other noun or pronoun were not there:

  Incorrect: *Neither John nor me had done the work.* (*me had done* is wrong)

  Correct: *Neither John nor I had done the work.* (*I had done* is correct)

Incorrect: *He read the book to Saritsa and I.* (*read the book to I* is wrong)

Correct: *He read the book to Saritsa and me.* (*read the book to me* is correct)

When we use a personal pronoun immediately after a form of the verb *be* (*am, is, are, was, were, had been, will be,* etc.), most of us use the object form when we are talking: *It is me.* However, in formal language, it is more correct to use the subject form: *It is I who did all the work.*

SEE ALSO Who/Whom

- Agreement: Personal pronouns (*I, me, you, they, us,* etc.) should agree in number and gender with the noun or pronoun they replace:

  Incorrect: *A clown always looks happy, even if they are crying inside.*

  Better: *Clowns always look happy, even if they are crying inside.*

- Indefinite pronouns: (*any, every, some, each, all,* etc.) do not refer to a specific person or thing. When an indefinite pronoun is the subject of a verb, the verb should agree in number with the pronoun.

  Some are considered singular (*no one, each, another, either, neither,* and words with *any-, every-, no-,* or *some-,* such as *anybody, everything*).

  Some are treated as plural (*many, few,* and *several*).

  Some can be singular or plural, depending on the context (*all, any, enough, more, most, none, one(s), other(s), plenty, some*):

  Singular: *Most of the pie is gone.*
  Plural: *Most of the people are gone.*
  Singular: *Some of the money is lost.*
  Plural: *Some of the tickets are lost.*

  A pronoun that refers to an indefinite pronoun should also agree with the indefinite pronoun in number and gender: *Everyone who is going on the trip should bring his or her own lunch.* (*everyone* is singular, so the pronouns *his or her* must be singular)

  SEE ALSO Sexist Language

- Sometimes the pronouns *we* and *us* are used just before a noun. In sentences like the following examples, check that you are using the right form of the pronoun by reading the sentence without the following noun, to see if it is correct:

  Incorrect: *Us dog lovers love to talk about our pets.* (*Us...love* is wrong)

  Correct: *We dog lovers love to talk about our pets.* (*We...love* is correct)

  Incorrect: *The cast gave we students a preview.* (*The cast gave we* is wrong)

  Correct: *The cast gave us students a preview.* (*The cast gave us* is correct)

  SEE ALSO Who/Whom; That/Which

Proofreading Symbols

The following symbols may be used to mark changes on your writing.

∧	INSERT	The house on fire.
_e_	DELETE	Rattlesnakes are very very dangerous.
∼	TRANSPOSE (SWITCH)	Raisa, Louise, and Karin are 12, 14, and 16 years old, respectively.
≡	CAPITAL	Planet earth may be in danger.
/	LOWER CASE	We Compost all our food scraps.
¶	NEW PARAGRAPH	So that day ended badly. The next day...
⊙	ADD PERIOD	Liu wondered which way to go
∧	ADD COMMA	Bring your tent a sleeping bag, and a flashlight.
∨	APOSTROPHE	"Its Hans!" he cried.
#	ADD SPACE	Daniel and I are leaving tomorrow.
◯	CLOSE SPACE	Chickens can't fly, but duc ks can.
....	LEAVE AS IS	The pictures are not ready.

Proofreading Tips

Proofreading is the final stage in the writing process. Before you reach this stage, you will have already edited your writing to the point where you are satisfied with the content, style, and words used. When proofreading written work, do the following.

- Read slowly, focussing on each word.
- Check for errors in spelling (especially those items that have been troublesome to you in the past), capitalization, and punctuation.
- Check that all place names and proper names are spelled correctly.
- Check that each paragraph is indented, and that each sentence begins with a capital letter.
- Spend extra time checking lists, charts, and tables.
- Ensure that you have acknowledged all your sources correctly and completely. (SEE Citation and Footnote)
- Make sure you have used quotation marks correctly. (SEE Quotation and Quotation Marks)

Question Mark [?]

A question mark indicates a direct question:
Where is the remote? BUT
Sasha asked where the remote was.

SEE ALSO Quotation and Quotation Marks

Quotation and Quotation Marks [" "]

Indicate a direct quotation by enclosing it in quotation marks.

NOTE: Very long quotations (over 100 words, or over 3 lines of your writing) should be indented from the body of the text, and begun on a separate line, without quotation marks.

- Separate the words that introduce the quotation (*Camila asked*) from the quotation itself by commas: *Camila asked, "Where is the notebook that you borrowed from me?"*
- Indicate deleted words within a sentence by three dots (...). If the missing words come after the end of a sentence, add a fourth dot (....). Any added words or explanations that are not part of the original should be placed in square brackets:

Original quotation:
Our concepts of what is attractive or worthwhile are learned, so we can modify our ideas of style and esthetics to include durability and quality. Instead of stressing something as arbitrary and temporary as fashion, we can take pride in clothing that will last for years.

Shortened version:
In 1989, David Suzuki wrote, "...we can modify our ideas [of what is attractive]...to include durability and quality...[and] take pride in clothing that will last for years."

- A question mark or exclamation mark goes inside the quotation marks if it relates to the quoted material, and outside if it applies to the whole sentence: *Theo called out, "Where are you going?" I'm sick of hearing you say, "I'll clean it up tomorrow"!*
- A period or comma at the end of a quotation goes inside the quotation marks: *"The trouble is," he muttered, "I can't get the machine to work."*
- A semicolon at the end of a quotation goes outside the quotation marks: *Kathy announced, "I don't want any more cookies, thank you"; then she sank back down in the bed and stayed asleep until morning.*
- A quotation within a quotation should be marked by single quotation marks: *Camila wailed, "Did I hear you say, 'I lost them both'?"*
- You can use quotation marks in place of italics or underlining to indicate a word that is being defined or explained: *The term "downsizing" is a euphemism that usually means firing a lot of employees.*

Racist Language

Racist language is any language that refers to a particular cultural or ethnic group in insulting terms. But racism also exists in more subtle forms. Be sensitive to the issues.

- Mention a person's race only if that is relevant to the context:

Relevant: *Mr. Wilkes, who is black, says he faced a lot of racism growing up in rural Alberta.*

Unnecessary: *A Chinese man has been charged after four stores were set on fire in the downtown area yesterday.*

Better: *A man has been charged after four stores were set on fire deliberately in the downtown area yesterday.*

- If a person's race or ethnic origin is relevant, be as specific as possible:

  Vague: *Ying Yee emigrated from Asia in 1963.*
  Better: *Ying Yee emigrated from Beijing, China, in 1963.*

- Avoid making generalizations about any racial or cultural group:

  Stereotyped: *The Welsh are great singers.*
  Better: *The Welsh have a long tradition of singing.*

- The word "ethnic" should be used only as an adjective, never as a noun:

  Inappropriate: *Many ethnics live in the area.*
  Better: *Many ethnic groups live in the area.*

Redundancy

Redundancy is the use of unnecessary words in a sentence:

Redundant: *I woke up at 7:30 a.m. in the morning.*
Better: *I woke up at 7:30 a.m.*

Redundant: *The reason I stayed home is because I was sick.*
Better: *I stayed home because I was sick.*

Redundant: *That area is restricted and not everyone is allowed in there.*
Better: *That area is restricted.*

Run-on Sentence

A run-on sentence is formed when two sentences are run into one. To fix a run-on sentence, add the proper punctuation, or change the wording to make it a single sentence:

Run-on: *The sky is clear it is spring at last.*
Better: *The sky is clear; it is spring at last.*
OR
The sky is clear, and it is spring at last.
OR
The sky is clear because it is spring at last.

Two sentences separated only by a comma is called a **comma splice**. Fix a comma splice the same way you would fix a run-on sentence:

Comma Splice: *The doctor said I need rest, I am taking the week off.*
Better: *The doctor said I need rest; I am taking the week off.*
OR
The doctor said I need rest, so I am taking the week off.
OR
Because the doctor said I need rest, I am taking the week off.

Semicolon [;]

Use a semicolon to separate two related sentences: *I love watching television after school; it relaxes me.*

A semicolon may also be used along with a co-ordinating conjunction (*and, or, nor, for, but, so, yet*) to join main clauses, if one or more of the clauses already contains a comma: *I threw on my coat, picked up my jacket, and raced to the bus stop; but the bus had already left.*

Finally, semicolons are used to separate items in a list, when one or more of the items contains a comma: *Walter has lived in Tokyo, Japan; London, England; and Estevan, Saskatchewan.*

SEE ALSO Quotation and Quotation Marks

Sexist Language

Sexist language is language that degrades either women or men. As with racist language, it is best to avoid generalizing about men or women unless you are basing your claims on scientific fact.

Also, whenever possible, replace words such as *fireman, policeman,* and *man-made* with non-sexist alternatives such as *firefighter, police officer,* and *fabricated.*

Finally, avoid using the masculine pronouns *he, him, his* (or the feminine pronouns, *she, her, hers*) to refer to both men and women. Instead, try one or more of the following methods.

- Use the plural.

  Sexist: *A good teacher can always command the respect of his students.*
  Better: *Good teachers can always command the respect of their students.*

- Replace the pronoun with *the, a,* or *an.*

  Sexist: *Whoever holds the winning ticket has not claimed his prize.*
  Better: *Whoever holds the winning ticket has not claimed the prize.*

- Substitute *one* or *you.* Use *one* in more formal writing, and *you* in informal contexts.

  Sexist: *A man never knows when his time will come.*
  Better: *One never knows when one's time will come.*

- Use *her or his, her or him, she or he.*

  Sexist: *Each child will be given his own seat.*
  Better: *Each child will be given her or his own seat.*

  Choose this method only when necessary, as some people object to it.

- Sometimes, the best way to avoid sexism is to change the wording of the sentence.

  Sexist: *I have never met a nurse who was not rushed off her feet.*
  Better: *I have never met a nurse who was not in a great hurry.*

Sentence

A sentence is a group of words that expresses a complete thought. Every sentence needs a subject and an action.

A **simple sentence** has one subject and one verb: *Yukio's house has six bedrooms.*

A **compound sentence** has two or more main clauses (that is, smaller sentences that can stand alone). The sentences are usually joined together either by a semicolon, or by a comma or semicolon followed by *and, or, nor, for, but, so,* or *yet*: *Yukio's house has six bedrooms, and the yard is huge.*